THE GEOGRAPHY OF TOURISM AND RECREATION

Environment, place and space

Fourth edition

C. Michael Hall and Stephen J. Page

Routledge
Taylor & Francis Group

LONDON AND NEW YORK

First published 1999
by Routledge
2 Park Square, Milton Park, Abingdon, Oxon OX14 4RN

And by Routledge
711 Third Avenue, New York, NY 10017

Third Edition 2006
Fourth Edition 2014

Routledge is an imprint of the Taylor & Francis Group, an informa business

British Library Cataloguing in Publication Data
A catalogue record for this book is available from the British Library

Library of Congress Cataloging in Publication Data
Hall, Colin Michael, 1961-
The geography of tourism and recreation : environment, place and space /
C. Michael Hall, Stephen J. Page. – Fourth edition.
    pages cm
    Includes bibliographical references and index.
    1. Tourism. 2. Recreation. 3. Recreation areas. I. Page, Stephen, 1963-
II. Title.
    G155.A1H343 20141
    338.4'791–dc23   2013043778

ISBN: 978-0-415-83398-1 (hbk)
ISBN: 978-0-415-83399-8 (pbk)
ISBN: 978-0-203-79609-2 (ebk)

Typeset in Garamond 3
by Sunrise Setting Ltd, Paignton, UK

THE GEOGRAPHY OF TOURISM AND RECREATION

Fourth edition

This fourth edition of *The Geography of Tourism and Recreation* provides students with a comprehensive introduction to the interrelationship between tourism, leisure and recreation from geographical and social science perspectives. It still remains the only book to systematically compare and contrast, in a spatial context, tourism and recreation in relation to leisure time, offering insight into the demand, supply, planning, destination management and impacts of tourism and recreation.

Whilst retaining its accessible style and approach, this edition has been significantly updated to reflect recent developments and new concepts from geography which are beginning to permeate the tourism and recreational field. New features include:

- content on the most recent developments, climate change, sustainability, mobilities and crisis management in time and space as well as trends such as low cost airlines and the control of land transport by transnational operators in the EU such as Arriva;
- more attention to management issues such as innovation and the spatial consequences for tourism and leisure development;
- new case studies and examples to showcase real life issues, from both developed and developing countries, especially the USA, China and South Africa;
- completely revised and redeveloped to accommodate new, user-friendly features: case studies, insights, summary points and learning objectives.

Written by leading academics, this is essential reading for all tourism, geography, leisure and recreation students.

An eResource including a case study archive and image bank is available for this title: www.routledge.com/9780415833998.

C. Michael Hall is Professor of Marketing in the Department of Management, Marketing and Entrepreneurship, University of Canterbury, New Zealand; Docent in Geography, Oulu University; Visiting Professor, Linneaus University, and Senior Research Fellow, University of Johannesburg. He has published widely on tourism, sustainability, governance and food issues.

Stephen J. Page is Professor of Tourism in the School of Tourism, Bournemouth University, author and editor of 36 books on Tourism, Leisure and Events, and Associate Editor of the journal *Tourism Management*.

Contents

Figures

Tables

Boxes

Acknowledgements

The purpose of this book is to provide an account of the growth, development and changes that are occurring within the geography of tourism and recreation, a purpose made all the more interesting because it is written by two geographers who, at the time this manuscript was completed, did not work in geography departments. While the book covers a lot of material, the authors acknowledge that there are a number of significant areas which have not been fully covered, and could not be unless the book was almost twice its size and more encyclopaedic than some of the reviewers of the previous editions noted!

To a great extent this book concentrates on the developed world. However, it is not a discussion solely of Anglo-North American geography, as this would neglect the substantial contribution of geographers from Australia, New Zealand, Singapore, South Africa and the South Pacific; rather, it deals with the literature on the geography of tourism and recreation in English. This is not to deny the substantial research base that European and other geographers have in tourism and recreation (see Chapter 1). However, arguably, the majority of English-speaking geographers have developed most of their work in tourism and recreation in isolation from the European and Asian experience, although as tertiary education and research becomes increasingly globalised and English the international language of the academy, such isolation is changing rapidly.

This book therefore serves to identify many of the major concerns and interests of geographers in the fields of tourism and recreation. There is clearly a substantial body of work in the sub-discipline. However, as the book also notes, the field is not seen as seriously as perhaps it should be; a conclusion with substantial implications not only for the further development of the sub-discipline but also for the growth of tourism studies as a separate field of academic endeavour. Indeed, the book observes that we are in a time of transformation and change in terms of a better positioning of tourism and recreation issues within the contemporary concerns of social theory and human geography as well as global environmental change, while simultaneously also having increased demands to be more 'applied' with respect to industry and tourism education. The fourth edition has been thoroughly revised, updated and expanded within the very tight constraints of space. At a time of rapid growth in tourism- and recreation-related literature by geographers, this was more than a challenge. For that reason, many of the seminal and leading studies which have been incorporated where space permits are reflected in the bibliography. Indeed, one of the things that this book seeks to do is emphasise the substantial legacy of studies in the geography of tourism and recreation before all students of tourism and recreation needed to do was download articles from the web. And as the book demonstrates, tourism and recreation, and the geography of tourism and recreation in particular, are not new subjects!

Every edition of the book highlights new people to be thanked. In addition to previous acknowledgements, Michael Hall would like to thank Nicole Aignier, Tim Baird, Tim and Vanessa Coles, David and Melissa Duval, Stefan Gössling, Johan Hultman, John Jenkins, Dieter Müller, Paul Peeters, Jarkko Saarinen, Anna-Dora Saetorsdottir, Dan Scott, Dallen Timothy and Maria-Jose Zapata Campos, who have all recently contributed in various ways to some of the ideas contained within, although the interpretation of their thoughts is, of course, my own. Paul Buchanan, Nick Cave, Bruce Cockburn, Elvis Costello, Ebba Forsberg, First Aid Kit, Fountains of Wayne, P.J. Harvey, Laura Marling, Vinnie Reilly, Glen Tilbrook, Loudon Wainwright, BBC Radio 6 and KCRW were also essential to the writing process. Michael also acknowledges the assistance of Academy of Finland grant SA 255424 with respect to the second homes component of the book.

At the personal level Stephen would like to thank Jo, Rosie and Toby, while Michael would like to thank Jody, Cooper and JC. Both of us realise that without the support and incentive that you all give us our work would be considerably more difficult and our recreation not so much fun. Finally, the authors would like to express their appreciation to Emma Travis and all at Routledge for their continued interest in the project.

Introduction
Tourism matters!

Geographical knowledge is more important than ever in an increasingly global and interconnected world. How can a graduate claim to be a learned scholar without any understanding of geography?

(Susan Cutter, President of the Association of American Geographers, 2000: 2)

Who we are is shaped in part by where we are. Human interactions with each other and the environment are rooted in geographical understandings, as well as the opportunities and constraints of geographical circumstance. Geographical approaches and techniques offer critical insights into everything from local land-use decisions to international conflict.

(Alexander Murphy, President of the Association of American Geographers, 2004: 3)

Tourism is widely recognised as one of the world's most significant forms of economic activity. Despite concerns as to the effects of financial crises, climate change and the increasing costs of oil, tourism is forecast to continue to grow in the foreseeable future. In 2012, international tourist arrivals reached one billion for the first time, up from 25 million in 1950, 277 million in 1980 and 528 million in 1995 (United Nations World Tourism Organization [UNWTO] 2012a).

International tourism is projected to nearly double by 2030 (UNWTO 2011a) from its 2012 figure. The UNWTO predicts the number of international tourist arrivals will increase by an average 3.3 per cent per year between 2010 and 2030 (an average increase of 43 million arrivals a year), reaching an estimated 1.8 billion arrivals by 2030 (UNWTO 2011a, 2012a). Upper and lower forecasts for global tourism in 2030 are between approximately two billion arrivals ('real transport costs continue to fall' scenario) and 1.4 billion arrivals ('slower than expected economic

recovery and future growth' scenario), respectively (UNWTO 2011a).

However, tourism, tourists and their impacts are clearly not evenly distributed over space or over time (Tables 1.1–1.4). Substantial differentiation occurs at a variety of international, regional and local scales. Most growth is forecast to come from the emerging economies and the Asia-Pacific, and by 2030 it is estimated that 57 per cent of international arrivals will be in what are currently classified as emerging economies, e.g. China, India, Malaysia (UNWTO 2011a, 2012a) (Figure 1.1). The UNWTO suggests that international tourism in emerging and developing markets is growing at twice the rate of the industrialised countries that have been the mainstay of the global tourism industry for nearly all of the past 50 years. Nevertheless, the international geography of tourism is changing. The UNWTO (2007) estimated that tourism is a primary source of foreign exchange earnings in 46 out of 50 of the world's least developed countries (LDCs) (Figure 1.2). Between 1996 and

Table 1.1 **International tourism arrivals and forecasts 1950–2030 (millions)**

Year	World	Africa	Americas	Asia & Pacific	Europe	Middle East
1950	25.3	0.5	7.5	0.2	16.8	0.2
1960	69.3	0.8	16.7	0.9	50.4	0.6
1965	112.9	1.4	23.2	2.1	83.7	2.4
1970	165.8	2.4	42.3	6.2	113.0	1.9
1975	222.3	4.7	50.0	10.2	153.9	3.5
1980	278.1	7.2	62.3	23.0	178.5	7.1
1985	320.1	9.7	65.1	32.9	204.3	8.1
1990	439.5	15.2	92.8	56.2	265.8	9.6
1995	540.6	20.4	109.0	82.4	315.0	13.7
2000	687.0	28.3	128.1	110.5	395.9	24.2
2005	799.0	34.8	133.3	153.6	440.7	36.3
2010	940.0	50.2	150.7	204.4	474.8	60.3
forecast						
2020	1360	85	199	355	620	101
2030	1809	134	248	535	744	149

Source: WTO 1997; UNWTO 2006a, 2011a, 2012a.

Table 1.2 **Average annual growth in international tourism arrivals and forecasts 1980–2030 (%)**

Year	World	Africa	Americas	Asia & Pacific	Europe	Middle East
1950–2000	6.8	8.3	5.8	13.1	6.5	10.1
1950–2005	6.5	8.1	5.4	12.5	6.1	10.1
1950–1960	10.6	3.7	8.4	14.1	11.6	12.3
1960–1970	9.1	12.4	9.7	21.6	8.4	11.5
1970–1980	5.3	11.6	4.0	13.9	4.7	14.3
1980–1990	4.7	7.8	4.1	9.3	4.1	3.1
1980–1985	2.9	6.1	0.9	7.4	2.7	2.7
1985–1990	6.5	9.5	7.3	11.3	5.4	3.5
1980–1995	4.4	6.7	3.8	8.9	3.7	4.5
1990–2000	4.6	6.4	3.3	7.0	4.1	9.6
1990–1995	4.2	6.1	3.3	8.0	3.5	7.3
1995–2000	4.9	6.7	3.3	6.0	4.7	12.0
2000–2005	3.3	5.7	0.8	7.1	2.2	10.0
1995–2010	3.9	6.7	2.1	6.3	3.0	10.5
forecast						
2010–2030	3.3	5.0	2.6	4.9	2.3	4.6
2010–2020	3.8	5.4	2.9	5.7	2.7	5.2
2020–2030	2.9	4.6	2.2	4.2	1.8	4.0

Source: UNWTO 2006a, 2012a.

2006, international tourism in developing countries expanded by 6 per cent, by 9 per cent for LDCs, and 8 per cent for other low and lower-middle income economies (UNWTO 2008). Growth between 2000 and 2009 was also most marked in emerging economies (58.8 per cent), with their overall global market share growing from 38.1 per cent in 2000 to 46.9 per cent in 2009 (UNEP 2011). Table 1.5 indicates that although travel as an export activity has continued to

grow over 2000–11 its relative proportion of total global export of services has declined, as with the developing countries, although its contribution to export activity in the LDCs has continued to grow over the same period. In addition, it should be noted that tourism's relative importance in service exports varies by region, with it being considerably more significant for Oceania and Africa, a slight decline in Asia and a considerable decline in the Americas.

However, changes in the international tourism market will also be related to domestic holiday travel, as consumers can switch their travel plans not only between international destinations but also between domestic and international destinations. It is extremely important to remember that although international tourism is usually the primary national policy focus because of its trade dimensions and it is where many national tourism organisations (NTOs) focus their marketing attention (Coles and Hall 2008), the vast majority of tourism is domestic in nature and accounted for an estimated 4.7 billion arrivals in 2010 (Cooper and Hall 2013) (Table 1.6).

Tourism, as with other forms of economic activity, therefore reflects the increasing interconnectedness of the international economy. Indeed, by its very nature, in terms of connections between generating areas, destinations and travel routes or paths, tourism is perhaps a phenomenon which depends more than most not only on transport, service and trading networks but also on social, political and environmental relationships between the consumers and producers of the tourist experience. Such issues have clearly long been

Table 1.3 International tourist arrivals by region per 100 population 1995–2030

(Sub)Region	1995	2010	2030
Western Europe	62	81	114
Southern/Mediterranean Europe	47	71	103
Northern Europe	42	63	80
Caribbean	38	48	65
Central/eastern Europe	15	25	47
Middle East	9	27	47
Southern Africa	9	22	46
Oceania	28	32	40
Central America	8	19	38
North Africa	6	15	28
South-East Asia	6	12	27
North America	21	21	26
North-East Asia	3	7	18
South America	4	6	13
East Africa	2	4	7
West and Central Africa	1	2	3
South Asia	0	1	2

Note: figures are rounded off.
Source: after UNWTO 2011a, 2011b.

Table 1.4 Generation of outbound tourism by region per 100 population 1980–2030

Year	World	Africa	Americas	Asia & Pacific	Europe	Middle East
1980	6	1	12	1	21	6
1995	9	2	14	3	36	6
2010	14	3	17	5	57	17
forecast 2030	22	6	24	12	89	25

Source: after UNWTO 2011a, 2011b.

Table 1.5 **Travel as an export activity 2000–11**

Country grouping	Billions of dollars				As % of total services			
	2000	2005	2010	2011	2000	2005	2010	2011
World	479.4	694.6	950.5	1,067.4	31.5	27.1	24.8	25.2
Least developed countries	2.5	4.8	9.8	11.3	35.9	41.3	44.1	44.0
Developing economies	130.3	213.6	362.4	411.4	37.1	33.9	31.9	32.5
Developing economies excluding China	114.1	184.3	316.6	362.9	35.6	33.2	32.8	33.5
Developing economies: Africa	14.5	28.8	42.2	40.5	43.7	48.2	46.6	44.1
Developing economies: America	31.6	42.9	55.8	58.8	51.2	48.7	41.9	39.6
Developing economies: Asia	83.9	140.5	262.9	310.4	32.9	29.4	28.9	30.4
Developing economies: Oceania	0.3	1.4	1.5	1.7	33.4	45.9	45.6	46.1
Transition economies	8.4	20.5	29.5	35.8	34.8	35.6	28.6	29.6
Developed economies	340.7	460.5	558.5	620.2	29.7	24.5	21.5	21.7
Developed economies: America	111.5	119.9	151.9	166.8	33.9	27.7	24.3	24.6
Developed economies: Asia	8.6	9.5	18.0	15.9	10.0	7.8	10.9	9.2
Developed economies: Europe	209.0	309.0	354.9	400.6	29.6	24.1	20.3	20.6
Developed economies: Oceania	11.6	22.1	34.7	36.9	47.6	55.6	61.1	59.7

Source: adapted from UNCTAD 2008, 2012.

of interest to geographers. For example, according to Mitchell:

> The geographer's point-of-view is a trilogy of biases pertaining to place, environment and relationships. . . . In a conceptual vein the geographer has traditionally claimed the spatial and chorographic aspects as his realm . . . The geographer, therefore, is concerned about earth space in general and about place and places in particular. The description, appreciation, and understanding of places is paramount to his thinking although two other perspectives (i.e. environment and relationships) modify and extend the primary bias of place.
> (Mitchell 1979: 237)

Yet despite the global significance of tourism and the potential contribution that geography can make to the analysis and understanding of tourism, the position of tourism and recreation studies within geography is perhaps not as strong as it should be (Gibson 2008; Hall and Page 2009; Hall 2013a). However, within the fields of tourism and recreation studies outside mainstream academic geography, geographers have made enormous contributions to the understanding of tourism and recreation phenomena (Butler 2004; Gibson 2008, 2009, 2010; Hall and

Page 2009; Wilson 2012). It is therefore within this somewhat paradoxical situation that this book is written. Although the contribution of geography and geographers is widely acknowledged and represented in tourism and recreation departments and journals, relatively little recognition is given to the significance of tourism and recreation in geography departments, journals, non-tourism and recreation specific geography texts, and within other geography subdisciplines (Hall 2013a). Although, as Lew (2001) noted, not only do we have an issue of how we define leisure, recreation and tourism (see pp. 7–11), but also there is the question of what is geographical literature.

This book takes an inclusive approach and includes material published by geographers who work in both geography and other academic departments; material published in geography journals; and, where appropriate, includes discussion of literature that has a geographical theme and which has influenced research by geographers in tourism and recreation. In part the categorisation of literature into either 'recreation' or 'tourism' is self-selecting in terms of the various works that we cite. If one was to generalise, recreation research tends to focus on more local behaviour, often has an outdoors focus and is less commercial. Tourism research tends to look at leisure mobility over greater

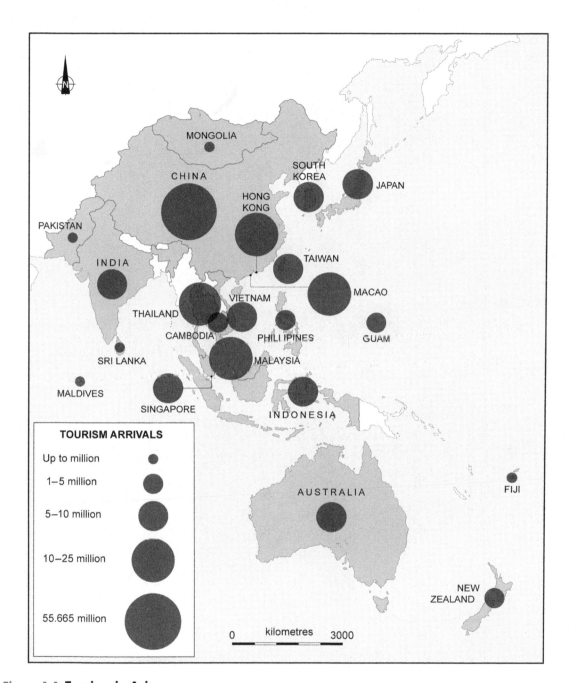

Figure 1.1 Tourism in Asia

Source: Developed from UNWTO data.

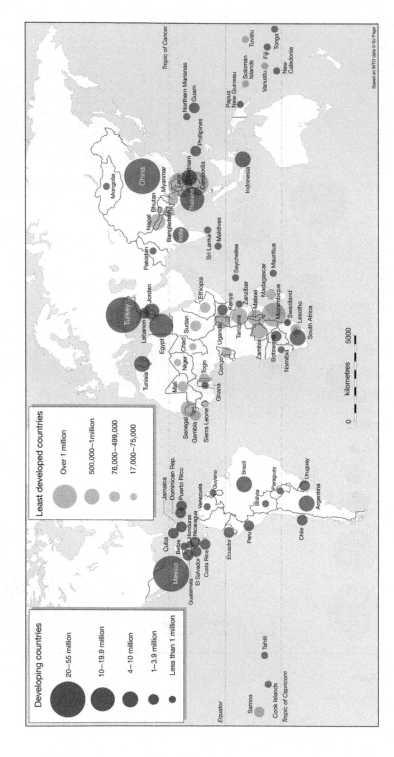

Figure 1.2 Tourism in the developing world

Source: Developed from UNWTO data.

Table 1.6 Global international and domestic tourist arrivals 2005–30

	Year/billions			
	2005	*2010*	*2020*	*2030*
Actual/estimated number of international visitor arrivals	0.80	0.94	1.36	1.81
Approximate/estimated number of domestic tourist arrivals	4.00	4.7	6.8	9.05
Approximate/estimated number of total tourist arrivals	4.80	5.64	8.16	10.86
Approximate/estimated global population	6.48	6.91	7.67	8.31

Note: actual and estimated forecasts of international visitor arrivals based on UNWTO (2012a); 2005 approximate figures based on Scott *et al.* (2008) and used to estimate domestic arrivals; approximate and estimated global population figures are based on United Nations Department of Economic and Social Affairs Population Division 2010 revisions in Cooper and Hall (2013).

distances, often international, usually including overnight stay, and is more commercial. However, such categories are not absolutes and arguably, as the book indicates, are increasingly converging over time. This book therefore seeks to explain how the contemporary situation of the geography of tourism and recreation has developed, indicate the breadth and depth of geographical research on tourism and recreation and its historical legacy, and identify ways in which the overall standing of research and scholarship by geographers on tourism and recreation may be improved, including their contributions to new and emerging themes. We therefore adopt the working definition of Hall:

> Tourism geography is the study of tourism within the concepts, frames, orientations, and venues of the discipline of geography and accompanying fields of geographical knowledge. The notion of tourism geographies describes the multiple, and sometimes contested, theoretical, philosophical and personal orientations of those who undertake tourism research from geographical perspectives.
>
> (Hall 2013a)

This first chapter is divided into several sections. First, it examines the relationship between tourism and recreation. Second, it provides an overview of the development of various approaches to the study of tourism and recreation within geography. Finally, it outlines the approach of this book towards the geography of tourism and recreation.

Tourism, recreation, leisure and mobility

Tourism, recreation and leisure are generally seen as a set of interrelated and overlapping concepts. While there are many important concepts, definitions of leisure, recreation and tourism remain contested in terms of how, where, when and why they are applied (Poria *et al.* 2003; Butler 2004; Coles and Hall 2006; Coles *et al.* 2006). In a review of the meaning of leisure, Stockdale (1985) identified three main ways in which the concept of leisure is used, and that continue to influence contemporary understandings of the concept:

- as a period of time, activity or state of mind in which choice is the dominant feature;
- an objective view in which leisure is perceived as the opposite of work and is defined as non-work or residual time;
- a subjective view which emphasises leisure as a qualitative concept in which leisure activities take on a meaning only within the context of individual perceptions and belief systems and can therefore occur at any time in any setting.

Leisure is therefore best seen as time over which an individual exercises choice and in which that individual undertakes activities in a free, voluntary way. Leisure activities have long been of considerable interest to geographers (e.g. Lavery 1975; Patmore 1977, 1978, 1979, 1980; Coppock 1982; Herbert 1987).

Traditional approaches to the study of leisure by geographers focused on leisure in terms of activities. In contrast, Glyptis (1981a) argued for the adoption of the concept of leisure lifestyles, which emphasised the importance of individual perceptions of leisure.

> This allows the totality of an individual's leisure experiences to be considered and is a subjective approach which shifts the emphasis from activity to people, from aggregate to individual and from expressed activities to the functions which these fulfill for the participant and the social and locational circumstances in which he or she undertakes them.
>
> (Herbert 1988: 243)

Such an experiential approach towards leisure has been extremely influential. For example, Featherstone (1987: 115) argued that the meaning and significance 'of a particular set of leisure choices . . . can only be made intelligible by inscribing them on a map of the class-defined social field of leisure and lifestyle practices in which their meaning and significance is relationally defined with reference to structured oppositions and differences'. Such an experiential definition of leisure was also used by Shaw and Williams (1994) in their critical examination of tourism from a geographical perspective, and has arguably been important in understanding concepts from business studies such as 'the experience economy' (Pine and Gilmore 1999), in which the experiential dimension of leisure has come to be increasingly marketised and commoditised (Çalıskan and Callon 2009).

However, while such a phenomenological approach to defining leisure, and therefore tourism and recreation, is valuable in highlighting the social context in which leisure both is defined and occurs, it is clearly at odds with 'objective', technical approaches towards definitions which can be applied in a variety of situations and circumstances (see Chapter 2). Yet it should be emphasised that such definitions are being used for different purposes. A universally accepted definition of leisure, tourism and recreation is an impossibility. Definitions will change according to their purpose and context. They are setting the 'rules

of the game' or 'engagement' for discussion, argument and research. By defining terms we give meaning to what we are doing.

Even given the subjective nature of leisure, however, at a larger scale it may still be possible to aggregate individual perceptions and activities to provide a collective or commonly held impression of the relationship between leisure, tourism and recreation. In this sense, tourism and recreation were generally regarded as subsets of the wider concept of leisure (Coppock 1982; Herbert 1988). Figure 1.3 illustrates the relationship between leisure, recreation and tourism. As Parker (1999: 21) eloquently explained, 'It is through studying leisure as a whole that the most powerful explanations are developed. This is because society is not divided into sports players, television viewers, tourists and so on. It is the same people who do all these things.'

This indicates the value of viewing tourism and recreation as part of a wider concept of leisure. Broken lines are used to illustrate that the boundaries between the concepts are 'soft'. Work is differentiated from leisure, with there being two main realms of overlap: first, business travel, which is seen as a work-oriented form of tourism in order to differentiate it from leisure-based travel; second, serious leisure, which refers to the breakdown between leisure and work pursuits and the development of leisure career paths with respect to their hobbies and interests (Stebbins 1979). As Stebbins observed:

> leisure in postindustrial society is no longer seen as chiefly a means of recuperating from the travail of the job . . . If leisure is to become, for many, an improvement over work as a way of finding personal fulfillment, identity enhancement, self-expression, and the like, then people must be careful to adopt those forms with the greatest payoff. The theme here is that we reach this goal through engaging in serious rather than casual or unserious leisure.
>
> (Stebbins 1982: 253)

An important third dimension that incorporates elements of work (especially with respect to sense of

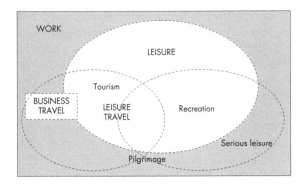

Figure 1.3 Relationships between leisure, recreation and tourism

obligation), leisure travel, tourism and serious leisure is that of pilgrimage, which is a major driver for tourism in countries such as India, Israel, Palestine, Saudi Arabia and the Vatican. Figure 1.3 also indicates the considerable overlap that exists between recreation and tourism which occurs with respect not only to conceptualising the field but also to the actual undertaking of activities. For example, D. Pearce (1987a: 1) observed that 'tourism constitutes one end of a broad leisure spectrum'.

Historically, research in outdoor recreation developed relatively independently of tourism research. As Crompton and Richardson (1986: 38) noted: 'Traditionally, tourism has been regarded as a commercial economic phenomenon rooted in the private domain. In contrast, recreation and parks has been viewed as a social and resource concern rooted in the public domain.' This has been very much influenced by traditional mid-nineteenth and twentieth century perspectives on recreation as a public good, although changes in the role of the state in the late twentieth century led to a more commercial outlook on recreation that has brought it closer to tourism's business foundations (Dredge and Jenkins 2007, 2011). Since the 1960s outdoor recreation studies have focused on public sector (i.e. community and land management agencies) concerns, such as wilderness management, social carrying capacity and non-market valuation of recreation experiences. In contrast, tourism tended to have a more 'applied orientation' which concentrated

on private sector (i.e. tourism industry) concerns, such as the economic impacts of travel expenditures, travel patterns and tourist demands, and advertising and marketing (Harris *et al.* 1987).

Although the division between public and private activities may have held relatively true from the end of the post-war period through to the early 1980s, in more recent years the division between public and private sector activities has been substantially eroded in western countries (Hall and Jenkins 1995; Dredge and Jenkins 2007; Hall 2011a). The distinction between tourism and recreation may therefore be regarded as one of degree. Tourism primarily relates to leisure and business travel activities that centre around visitors to a particular destination, which will typically involve an infusion of new money from the visitor into the regional economy (Hall 1995). From this perspective, tourism is a primary industry which, through visitor spending, increases employment opportunities and tax revenues, and enhances the community's overall economic base. On the other hand, recreation generally refers to leisure activities that are undertaken by the residents of an immediate region, with their spending patterns primarily involving a recycling of money within the community associated with day, overnight and extended-stay recreation trips.

Natural settings and outdoor recreation opportunities are clearly a major component of tourism, perhaps especially so since the development of interest in nature-based and ecotourism activities (e.g. Valentine 1984, 1992; Lindberg and McKercher 1997). Indeed, outdoor recreation and tourist resources should be seen as complementary contexts and resources for leisure experiences. The reality is that as tourism and recreation studies have grown and borrowed concepts from each other (Ryan 1991), and as society has changed, particularly with respect to the role of government, so the demarcation line between recreation and tourism has rapidly become 'fuzzy and overlap is now the norm' (Crompton and Richardson 1986: 38). As Pigram argued:

Little success has been afforded to those attempting to differentiate between recreation and tourism and such distinctions appear founded on the assumption that outdoor recreation appeals to the rugged, self-reliant element in the population, whereas tourism caters more overtly for those seeking diversion without too much discomfort.

(Pigram 1985: 184)

Similarly, in a wider context, Jansen-Verbeke and Dietvorst (1987: 263) argued that, 'in the perception of the individual at least, the distinction between recreation and tourism is becoming irrelevant'. As with Shaw and Williams (1994), we would argue that this is not completely the case, particularly with respect to how individuals define their own activities as well as their economic significance. Aitchison (2006) has also sought to argue that leisure studies has also been a more critical and culturally informed disciplinary approach than tourism. Yet, this is a gross oversimplification of the fields and fails to recognise the potentially critical and counter-institutional value of quantitative and non-'cultural' research in tourism and leisure studies (Ayikoru et al. 2009; Peeters and Landré 2011; Hall 2012a). However, despite some misgivings by a few individuals, it is readily apparent that there is increasing convergence between the two concepts in terms of theory, activities and impacts, particularly as recreation becomes increasingly commercialised and the boundaries between public and private responsibilities in recreation and leisure change substantially. It is interesting to note the inclusion of a same-day travel, 'excursionist' category in official international guidelines for the collection and definition of tourism statistics, thereby making the division between recreation and tourism even more arbitrary (United Nations (UN) 1994). Tourism may therefore be interpreted as only one of a range of choices or styles of recreation expressed through either travel or a temporary short-term change of residence. Technical definitions of tourism are examined in more detail in Chapter 2.

A more recent approach to conceptualising tourism is to regard tourism as simply one, albeit highly significant, form of human mobility (Bell and Ward 2000; Coles et al. 2004; Hall 2005a, 2005b; Sheller and Urry 2006; Hannam 2008; Adey 2010), with Coles et al. (2004) arguing that research on tourism

must be willing to formulate a coherent approach to understanding the meaning behind the range of mobilities undertaken by *individuals*, not tourists. The notion of tourism as a form of mobility has therefore meant the development of an approach that relates tourism to other dimensions of mobility such as migration (King et al. 2000; Williams and Hall 2000; Hall and Williams 2002; Duval 2003), transnationalism and diaspora (Coles and Timothy 2004; Coles et al. 2004), second homes (Hall and Müller 2004; Müller 2006, 2011; Paris 2009) and long distance mobility (Frändberg and Vilhelmson 2003). Such approaches parallel recent developments in sociology (Urry 2000, 2004) but actually have a far longer lineage dating to the work of geographers such as Hägerstrand (1970, 1984) and Pred (1977) on time geography, which itself was a major influence on sociology (Giddens 1984). Indeed, considerations of mobility in tourism are nothing new. For example, Wolfe (1966: 7) observed that 'most students of recreation concentrate on the reasons for travel, but few have much to say about the significance of mobility'. Mobility is 'at the very heart of certain aspects of leisure activity today—outdoor recreation in particular and, by definition, recreational travel'. Similarly, Cosgrove and Jackson, in writing on resort development, noted:

'Fashion' is therefore capable of analysis, and it can be shown to be motivated by social distinction, which is characterised by geographical segregation. Within the confines of such segregated areas individual initiative may then account for variations in development. The geographic mobility of the different social strata results in continuous changes in the location and extent of these segregated areas. The word 'mobility' is used here deliberately rather than accessibility, since access alone did not create the resorts of the nineteenth century. Only when incomes were sufficiently high and when free time was readily available could the facilities of access be fully exploited.

(Cosgrove and Jackson 1972: 34)

Cosgrove and Jackson's (1972) identification of time and income level is highly significant for the study of tourism (Hall 2005a, 2005b), for while time budgets have been a major focus of time geography, their role in tourism has been relatively little explored. Arguably, one of the main reasons for this is that tourism is often portrayed as being an escape from the routine (Hall 2005a, 2005b). Yet space–time compression has led to fundamental changes to individual space–time paths in recent years. The routinised space–time paths of those living in 2014 are not the same as those of people in 1984 when Giddens was writing and even more so in the 1960s and 1970s when Hägerstrand (1970) was examining daily space–time trajectories (Hall 2005a, 2005c). Instead, for those with sufficient income and time, particularly in the developed world, extended voluntary leisure or business travel (what we would usually describe as tourism) is part of their routine on a seasonal or annual basis, and for some highly mobile individuals, on a weekly or even daily basis. Indeed, some have argued that tourism is part of a 'mobility gap' in which the 'hypermobile' or 'kinetic elite' travel ever more frequently while many do not travel far for leisure or business at all (Gössling et al. 2009c). For example, it is estimated that the percentage of the world's population participating in international air travel is in the order of just 2–3 per cent (Peeters et al. 2006). Immobility is therefore just as important to understand as mobility (Adey 2006; Hall 2010a, 2011b). Accessibility and mobility have long been regarded as integral to the development process (e.g. Addo 1995). In the African context, Pirie has also powerfully noted that

> The mobility gap may match the wide differentials of income and life chances on the continent; it is surely rooted in and expresses gaps in privilege and plenty. The condition presupposes what might be termed a 'mobility morality'.
>
> Super-mobile people are at one end of the mobility scale. At the other extreme are Africans stranded in rural villages where mobility deprivation is acute. They are the kinetic underclass.
> (Pirie 2009: 22)

Pirie (2009: 21) also concludes that the 'way we act on, and the way we think, talk and write about,

geographical mobility needs reconceptualising in terms of fairness, equity, environmental justice, and human rights'. Yet issues of who does not travel and why receives only passing interest in most mainstream tourism research, leading Hall (2005b) to argue that one possible interpretation of this is that the study of tourism is intrinsically the study of the wealthy, particularly given the relative lack of research in tourism as to those who do not travel and are relatively immobile – as you have to be relatively wealthy in time and money to be able to travel for leisure. But leaving such sanguine aside, the dominant discourse in tourism focuses on the 'given' of mobility and movement rather than immobility, and issues of social and economic exclusion are more likely to be dealt with in relation to destination communities in the developing world under the umbrella of pro-poor tourism than the exclusion of potential consumers from tourism opportunities per se because of wider economic disparities in society (Hall 2010a).

Despite the expansion of spatial mobility for many people, time constraints still operate; there is always only a finite amount of time in which people can travel in or take part in touristic activities (Hägerstrand 1970; Pred 1977; Hall 2005a). Through increased access to transport resources and the economic capacity to utilise them it may be possible to increase the amount of geographical space available to visit within a given time. Given that a travel money budget represents the fraction of disposable income devoted to travel, a fixed travel money budget establishes a direct relationship between disposable income and distance travelled, provided average user costs of transport remain constant (see Schafer and Victor 2000). If people are on a fixed time budget, then those who are willing to pay the increased costs will shift from one mode of transport to another so as to increase speed and therefore reduce the amount of time engaged in travelling relative to other activities within the constraints of the overall time budget (Schafer 2000; Hall 2005a), thereby challenging both conceptually and technically the commonly used approaches to defining tourism in time (see Chapter 2).

The issue of scale: empiricism, paradigms and transformations

The geographer's preoccupation with place, space and environment, all of which feature in many of the seminal studies of geography (e.g. Haggett 1979), reveals a preoccupation with the fundamental concept of scale (Del Casino and Hanna 2000). For the geographer, it is the scale at which phenomena are studied, analysed and explained which differentiates it from many other areas of social science. The ability to recognise phenomena at different geographical scales ranging from global, national, regional through to local scales and the interactions of processes and change at each scale have traditionally been the hallmark of an empiricist geography (see Johnston 1991 for more detail). The preoccupation with building and 'testing' models and theories in human geography and their application to tourism and recreation has largely mirrored trends in the main discipline, while new developments in behavioural geography, humanistic geography, spatial analysis, environmental studies and cultural geography have also influenced tourism and recreation geographers (Hall and Page 2009; Wilson 2012).

What began to develop during the 1990s and has now gathered momentum in tourism and recreation geography is the evolution of new paradigms (i.e. ways of thinking about and conceptualising research problems). As a result, developments in the 'new cultural geography' have begun to permeate, transform and redefine the way in which geographers approach tourism and recreation. Crouch (1999a) conceptualised leisure and tourism as an encounter, in the anthropological tradition, noting the geographer's contribution to this perspective, where the concern is between people, between people and space and the contexts of leisure/tourism. However, what is a fundamental redefinition of geographers' concern with space is the manner in which space is viewed and contextualised. Crouch (1999a) argued that space may be something material, concrete, metaphorical or imagined questioning the traditional notion of location and space, where activity is located. This new conceptualisation is reflected in that 'The country and the

city, the garden, the beach, the desert island, and the street hold powerful metaphorical attention in significant areas of leisure/tourism' (Crouch 1999a: 4).

This concern with conceptions from cultural geography, where space is something metaphorical, whereby it is something that shapes people's enjoyment of leisure/tourism, derives many of its origins from humanistic geography (Relph 1976, 1981) and cultural studies. For example, Squire (1994) argued that leisure and recreation practices are a reflection of the way in which people make maps of meaning of their everyday world. This concern with the individual or group, the human experience and the symbolic meaning of leisure and tourism in space, has opened a wide range of geographical avenues for research in tourism and recreation. For example, Cloke and Perkins (1999) examined representations of adventure tourism, exploring many of the issues of meaning and symbols.

Williams and Kaltenborn's (1999) analysis of the use and meaning of recreational cottages is significant in this context because it also questioned the traditional notion of geography and tourism, with the focus on tourism as a temporary phenomenon in time and space (see also Williams and Hall 2000). Indeed, they argued that tourism and leisure needs to be viewed as a more dynamic phenomenon, where the circulation and movement of people in space is the rule rather than the exception. The movement to tourism and leisure spaces therefore adds meaning, by allowing people to establish an identity and to connect with place. In other words, tourism and leisure are deeply embedded in everyday lives and the meaning that people attach to their lives, since changing work practices and less separation of work, leisure and pleasure have made tourism and recreation more important to people's lives (Hiltunen *et al.* 2013).

The influence of cultural geography is also to be found in studies of tourism in the urban context. Culture, and cultural tourism in particular, is integral to many urban regeneration strategies (Jayne 2006). Culture in this context can be understood both in a narrow commoditised sense with respect to specific cultural attractions, such as arts, heritage, museums and events, as well as in the wider notion of the ways of life of those who live in particular locations (which, of course, may also be commoditised via advertising, promotion and visitor consumption) (Hall 2013b). Either way, the significant interactions between culture, urban political economy and regeneration have become enmeshed in the development of 'cultural economy' (Scott 2001). The contemporary importance of culture in urban political economy is therefore a result not only of the increasing explicit use of culture as an economic development strategy (e.g. European Capitals of Culture or the use of museums and art galleries as economic flagships), but also of the growth of postmodernism and new conceptualisations of the culture–economy relationship (e.g. gender studies, ethnic networks, postcolonialism, sexual identities, performity, virtual space), what is sometimes referred to as the 'cultural turn' in the social sciences (Ribera-Fumaz 2009).

The development of new cultural geographies of leisure and tourism reflects the broader cultural turn in the wider discipline (Johnston and Sidaway 1997; Smith *et al.* 2012). Yet such 'turns' or paradigms are the norm in human geography and reflect tourism geography's connections with not only geography and the other social sciences but also changes in society. Furthermore, the absorption of such ideas does not necessarily mean that previous notions 'disappear'; rather, new synergies occur – as well as new debates and schisms. Such movements, as we will see, are very much the norm in the history of geography and tourism geography in particular, and the lack of a specific frame of reference or guiding research agenda to incorporate these perspectives into mainstream tourism and recreation geography should not necessarily be seen as a negative. Instead it means that debate is very much alive, although the key issue, of course, for any student of tourism geography, is to be able to understand the range of perspectives that are able to be applied to tourism problems and their relative advantages and disadvantages. With these issues in mind, attention now turns to the historical development of the geography of tourism and recreation and a discussion of many of the formative studies.

Development of the geography of tourism and recreation

Tourism and recreation have been the subject of research and scholarship in Anglo-American geography since the early twentieth century, with an early focus on demographic and economic issues (Cleveland 1910; Wrigley 1919; Whitbeck 1920; Allix 1922; Cornish 1930, 1934; McMurray 1930; Jones 1933; O'Dell 1935; Selke 1936; Carlson 1938), as well as the role of recreation in the national parks and national forest areas of the United States (e.g. Carhart 1920; Graves 1920; Meinecke 1929; Atwood 1931; Chapman 1938). Brown offered what he termed 'an invitation to geographers' in the following terms:

> From the geographical point of view the study of tourism offers inviting possibilities for the development of new and ingenious techniques for research, for the discovery of facts of value in their social implications in what is virtually a virgin field.
>
> (Brown 1935: 471)

However, as Campbell (1966: 85) wryly commented, 'it would appear that this invitation was declined'. As Deasy (1949: 240) observed: 'because of the inadequate attention to the tourist industry by geographers, there exists a concomitant dearth of techniques, adaptable to the collection, analysis, interpretation and cartographic representation of geographical data of the subject'. Yet the period from 1945 to the late 1960s is perhaps not as barren as Campbell would have us believe.

Building on the initial research on tourism and recreation in American economic geography in the 1930s, research was primarily undertaken in the postwar period in the United States on the economic impact of tourism both in a regional destination setting (e.g. Crisler and Hunt 1952; Ullman 1954; Ullman and Volk 1961; Deasy and Griess 1966) and on travel routes (Eiselen 1945). Although Cooper's (1947) discussion of issues of seasonality and travel motivations foreshadowed some of the geographical research of the 1980s and 1990s, interest in this topic lay dormant for many years. Nevertheless, the geography of recreation and tourism was at least of a sufficient profile in the discipline to warrant a chapter in an overview text on the state of geography in the United States in the 1950s (McMurray 1954). (See also Meyer-Arendt's (2000) article on tourism as a subject of North American doctoral dissertations and master's theses from 1951 to 1998.)

In Britain, significant research was undertaken by Gilbert (1939, 1949, 1954) on the development of British seaside resorts, with geographers also contributing to government studies on coastal holiday development (*Observer* 1944). But, little further direct research was undertaken on tourism and recreation in the United Kingdom until the 1960s, although some doctoral work on resorts was undertaken (Butler 2004). There was certainly an interest from the generation of geographers studying patterns of tourism and recreation in postcolonial South Asia, as Robinson (1972) noted the contribution of earlier studies by Spencer and Thomas (1948), Withington (1961) and Sopher (1968). In Canada over the same period substantive geographical research on tourism was primarily focused on one geographer, Roy Wolfe (1964), whose early work on summer cottages in Ontario (Wolfe 1951, 1952), laid the foundation for later research on the geography of second home development (e.g. Coppock 1977a; Hall and Müller 2004) and tourism and migration (Williams and Hall 2000; Hall and Williams 2002).

While significant work was undertaken on tourism and recreation from the 1930s to the 1950s, it was not really until the 1960s that research started to accelerate, with a blossoming of publications on tourism and recreation in the 1970s. During the 1960s several influential reviews were undertaken of the geography of tourism and recreation (Murphy 1963; Wolfe 1964, 1966; Winsberg 1966; Mitchell 1969a, 1969b; Mercer 1970), while a substantive contribution to the development of the area also came from regional sciences (e.g. Guthrie 1961; Christaller 1963; Piperoglou 1966), and the conceptual developments and research undertaken on carrying capacity in a resource and land management context (Lucas 1964; Wagar 1964) still resonate in present-day discussions on sustainability and environmental management

(Coccossis 2004; Hall and Lew 2009). Nevertheless, even as late as 1970, Williams and Zelinsky (1970: 549) were able to comment that 'virtually all the scholarship in the domain of tourism has been confined to intra-national description and analysis'. Indeed, in commenting on the field of tourism research as a whole they observed:

> In view of its great and increasing economic import, the probable significance of tourism in diffusing information and attitudes, and its even greater future potential for modifying patterns of migration, balance of payments, land use, and general socio-economic structure with the introduction of third-generation jet transport and other innovations in travel, it is startling to discover how little attention the circulation of tourists has been accorded by geographers, demographers, and other social scientists.
>
> (Williams and Zelinsky 1970: 549)

Yet, in one sense, the focus of tourism and recreation geographers on domestic tourism should not be surprising given that the vast majority of people could not afford to travel internationally and those that could afford to take holidays did so domestically. It was not until the arrival of the age of mass aviation in the late 1960s that this picture would start to change substantially. Geographers were only reflecting their times. Nevertheless, Mercer's (1970: 261) comment with respect to leisure was definitely apt: 'Until recently geographers have had surprisingly little to say about the implications of growing leisure time in the affluent countries of the world. Even now, leisure still remains a sadly neglected area of study in geography.' Butler (2004: 146) noted that a large body of research on recreation and leisure was undertaken in North America by geographers and non-geographers alike, although 'Until the 1980s it was hard to find much research on tourism conducted in North America by geographers, except for the work of British ex-patriots (Butler, Marsh, Murphy and Wall, for example) and their students'.

During the 1970s and early 1980s, a number of influential texts and monographs appeared in the geography literature (e.g. Lavery 1971c; Cosgrove and Jackson 1972; Coppock and Duffield 1975; Matley 1976; Robinson 1976; Coppock 1977a; Pearce 1981, 1987a; Mathieson and Wall 1982; Patmore 1983; Pigram 1983; Smith 1983a), giving the appearance of a healthy area of research. Indeed, a number of extremely significant concepts in the tourism literature, such as a tourism area life cycle (Butler 1980) and the notion of a tourism system (Board *et al.* 1978), emerged from geographers during this period before being taken on board and popularised in the work of other researchers such as Leiper (Hall and Page 2010). For example, in their 1972 study of leisure behaviour in the Dartmoor National Park, Board *et al.* commented:

> The tourism system then consists of concentrations of visitors (nodes) and road networks (links) set within areas of varying character: the relationships between them are expressed in terms of flows of people. Researchers set out to examine a tourist system in inner Dartmoor . . . by making observations at all major nodes, several minor nodes and three sets of links in the network, here called circuits.
>
> The information collected related to three basic properties of the system—the characteristics of the visitors, the activities they carry out at these various places and between various places within it.
>
> (Board *et al.* 1978: 46)

However, despite the growth in publications by geographers on tourism and recreation, concerns were being expressed about the geography of tourism. In the introduction to a special issue of *Annals of Tourism Research* on the geography of tourism, Mitchell (1979: 235) observed that 'the geography of tourism is limited by a dearth of published research in geographical journals, the relatively few individuals who actively participate in the sub-discipline, and the lack of prestige the subject matter specialty has in geography'. In the same issue, Pearce (1979: 246), in an excellent historical review of the field, commented, 'even after half a century, it is difficult to speak of the geography of tourism as a subject with any coherence within the

wider discipline of geography or in the general field of tourism studies'. Smith, in a discussion of recreation geography, referred to the development of geographies of recreation and leisure in terms of Kuhn's (1969) notion of paradigms:

> One might also argue that recreation geography is in a pre-paradigmatic state—The history of recreation geography is one of growing intellectual diversity with no convergence towards a set of unified theories and methods . . . If there is any special challenge that recreation geography is faced with as a field of intellectual activity it is not the lack of a paradigm.
>
> (Smith 1982: 19)

Nevertheless, in a comment as appropriate now as it was then, he went on to note that there was 'a lack of appreciation and knowledge of past accomplishments and of the complexity of the field' (Smith 1982: 19). Pearce (1995a: 3) also argued that 'the geography of tourism continues to lack a strong conceptual and theoretical base'; even so, models such as Butler's (1980, 2006) cycle of evolution and those reviewed in Pearce (1987a) have assisted to a limited degree in developing a conceptual understanding, while Mitchell (1991: 10) also expressed concern that 'there is no widely accepted paradigm or frame-of-reference that serves as a guide to tourism research'. Indeed, Butler (2000, 2004) has even argued not only that leisure, recreation and tourism (LRT) research may have a negative image in geography, but also that 'geography pales in terms of its influence in LRT compared to economics, sociology and even anthropology' (Butler 2004: 152; see also Meyer-Arendt and Lew 1999). These comments therefore raise questions about the contemporary status of the geography of tourism and recreation, and it is to these concerns that we now turn.

Status of the geography of tourism and recreation

Since 2005 there has been a burst of reflective reviews and collections on tourism geography (e.g. Gibson

2008, 2009, 2010; Nepal 2009a, 2009b; Wilson 2012). Several reasons can be given. Tourism geography is undergoing a significant generational change as those geographers who gained their doctorates in the 1970s or previous decades enter retirement (Hall and Page 2009). Such a change is leading to a 'stock take' of the field before cultural, disciplinary and personal memories fade (Hall and Page 2009, 2010; Smith 2010, 2011; Gill 2012). The generation that is now entering retirement is not the first generation of tourism geographers but, given the expansion of tourism as an academic field, it is the first generation whose work has simultaneously existed in both geography and tourism studies (Hall 2013a). Their work is also significant because they were the first generation whose publications become internationalised as a result of information and communication technology, and of the confirmation of English as the dominant language of the international academy (Hall 2013a). In addition, there has been a clear change in publishing style, with review papers given greater importance in tourism- and geography-related journals. This is perhaps related to the need for greater intellectual stocktaking at a time of rapidly expanding publication rates. The field has also been served with multi-authored edited handbooks and companions on tourism geography (Lew *et al.* 2004, 2014; Wilson 2012), as well as other thematic volumes edited by geographers (Page and Connell 2012; Holden and Fennell 2013; Smith and Richards 2013; Hall *et al.* 2014).

The study of the geography of tourism and recreation does not occur in isolation from wider trends in geography and academic discourse, nor of the society of which we are a part. Tourism and recreation geographers are 'a society within a society', academic life 'is not a closed system but rather is open to the influences and commands of the wider society which encompasses it' (Johnston 1991: 1). The study of the development and history of a discipline 'is not simply a chronology of its successes. It is an investigation of the sociology of a community, of its debates, deliberations and decisions as well as its findings' (Johnston 1991: 11). Yet this also means that there is no 'view from nowhere'; knowledge is always 'local, situated and embedded' (Shapin 1998: 6). Recognition of how knowledge is produced and circulated is therefore fundamental to establishing its credibility, its beneficiaries and how it is read in different places (Hall 2013a). (See Box 1.1.)

BOX 1.1 PRODUCING GEOGRAPHICAL KNOWLEDGE

At a time when there is much emphasis on knowledge management and transfer in tourism geography (Cooper 2006; Coles *et al.* 2008; Shaw and Williams 2009; Williams and Shaw 2011) there is a need to understand how the knowledge of tourism geography travels and is made as it circulates. Agnew (2007) identifies four dominant approaches in considering knowledge production that inform thinking about tourism geographies (Hall 2013a): the market of ideas, conceptions of world geography, temporal periodicity and the categorisation of knowledge.

Knowledge may be regarded as a commodity like any other that competes and is exchanged in the 'marketplace of ideas'. Ideally, success is dependent on the truthfulness of the idea as it competes in the evolutionary competition of ideas in research institutes and universities as well as the users of such knowledge in the public and private sectors. Alternatively, it could be argued that the marketplace of ideas is not a level playing field and how knowledge becomes normalised or dominant – or marginal – has something to do with the proponent and where they are located (Agnew 2007) as well as the receptors and sponsors of knowledge (Truong and Hall 2013; Hall 2014). This perspective is important for not only describing the geography of knowledge transfer and the mobility of tourism and recreation knowledge, but also the marginality of ideas, including perhaps that of tourism geography itself (Hall 2013a).

The manner in which world geography is conceived is significant because it influences perspectives on ease of movement, directional bias and the role of time. The question of where and when 'brings together a wide range of potential ontological and epistemological effects' under the rubric of spatial and temporal difference (Agnew and Livingstone 2011: 7). Many theoretical positions contain within them specific grids of space and periods of time that can 'disturb' commonly held spatial and temporal designations, i.e. reference to a location such as 'Asia' or the 'Mediterranean', or a time period such as 'modern', that influence knowledge formation and reproduction (Deprest 2002; Hall, 2009a; Teo 2009; Winter 2009).

Space may be characterised in terms of progressive temporal periods. This is most closely associated with notions of developed and less developed countries and regions, but is also clearly tied in to intellectual ideas on tourism development processes (Butler 2006; Hall and Lew 2009). Finally, there is the contrast often drawn between space, the general and universal, and place, the local and specific. However, Cloke and Johnston (2005a) highlight the relationality of space and place and the deconstruction of concepts that are often presented as binary categories, including the categorisation of knowledge into 'socially created' academic disciplines. 'In academic life, just as everywhere else, we simplify by creating categories – and then people identifying with those categories come into conflict' (Cloke and Johnston 2005b: 4).

Academic communities argue on both empirical and theoretical grounds, and what constitutes evidence 'becomes a way of challenging the very meaningfulness of a particular concept from those affiliated to . . . some competing concept or theory' (Agnew and Livingstone 2011: 13). Claiming that tourism is atheoretical or poorly theorised (Franklin and Crang 2001) becomes a way of challenging or demeaning the value of research not undertaken within a particular theoretical context (Hall 2005a, 2005b). In addition, criticisms may also be grounded in disputes over method, social-normative qualities and ethics – concerns over the way knowledge is 'made' (Hall 2013a).

One other interesting aspect of the production of geographical knowledge is that it is important to recognise that not only ideas circulate but also tourism geographers. Of the 59 most cited (>5 publications) authors in Hall and Page (2006) and Wilson (2012) 22 had multiple institutional affiliations in different countries, with several having visiting positions in non-English speaking countries simultaneously with their permanent position. Such movement reflects not only the transfer of tourism geographers from geography departments to business schools (Hall and Page 2009; Smith 2010, 2011; Gill 2012), but also the interest of some institutions in non-English speaking countries in embedding the academic and linguistic capacities of Anglophone academics in their own knowledge production and promotion. The creation of such transnational networks is 'less intense and durable than local networks' (Lillis and Curry 2010: 86) but is intensely attractive to institutions and departments seeking to increase their international profile. Of course, individual mobility and linkages reflect academic interests, career development and personal lifestyle reasons as well as, in some cases, financial incentives. Whatever the reasons for the circulation and stickiness of ideas and academics, they will have undoubted effects on the institutional and disciplinary characteristics of tourism geography (Hall 2013a).

The problem in tourism and recreation is that the organisation, management and funding of research is primarily a public and private sector activity. In this sense, it raises moral dilemmas for the geographer since it is increasingly difficult to disengage from the public policy framework or economic/decision-making context in which research is commissioned or undertaken. Indeed, detachment can lead to valid criticisms of academic 'ivory towers' and a fundamental failure to engage in critical public and private sector policy-making.

Tourism geographers are a sub-community of the geographic community within the wider community of academics, scientists and intellectuals, which is itself a subset of wider society; that society has a culture, including a scientific subculture within which the content of geography and tourism is defined. Action is predicated on the structure of society and its knowledge base: research praxis is part of that programme of action, and includes tourism research. The community of tourism academics is therefore an 'institutionalizing social group' (Grano 1981: 26), a context within which individual tourism academics are socialised and which defines the internal goals of their sub-discipline in the context of the external structures within which they operate (after Johnston 1991). The content of the sub-discipline must be linked to its milieu, 'so that disciplinary changes (revolutionary or not) should be associated with significant events in the milieu' (Johnston 1991: 277). Similarly, Stoddart (1981: 1), in his review of the history of geography, stated, 'both the ideas and the structure of the subject have developed in response to complex social, economic, ideological and intellectual stimuli'.

Although the above is recognised, there is relatively little overt discussion from academics within the tourism geography community and the wider tourism studies field as to the reasons why certain topics are studied and approaches developed (Coles and Hall 2006; Coles *et al.* 2006; Hall 2004a, 2010b; Tribe 2009, 2010; Smith 2010, 2011). Reflections on academic debates are often presented as part of a rational discourse in which the role of interests, ideologies and institutions are minimised or not noted at all, and in which the positionality of disciplinary gatekeepers is ignored (Hall 2010c). According to Hall (2013a) this may be because of fears of professional repercussions, especially from gatekeepers such as journal editors, or the receipt of negative manuscript and publication reviews:

> Rational accounts of disciplinary growth stands in stark contrast to the discussions that occur 'backstage' at conferences, on emails and in general conversation between colleagues with respect to who and what is being published and research, where, how and why. You are not told who drank with who, who slept with who, and who is pissed off with who – and why.
>
> (Hall 2013a)

It is also not how science really works (Feyerabend 2010). As Livingstone (1992: 2) observed, 'Social context, metaphysical assumptions, professional aspirations, or ideological allegiances rarely feature in the textbook histories of the growth of geographical knowledge'. Barnes' (2010: 1) comments with respect to economic geography arguably also hold true with tourism geography: 'Its practitioners tend toward the "just do it"' school of scholarship, in which a concern with the present moment in . . . geography subordinates all else.'

'The contents of a discipline at any one time and place reflect the response of the individuals involved to external circumstances and influences, within the context of their intellectual socialization' (Johnston 1983a: 4). See Table 1.7 for categorisations of the main approaches to the geography of tourism and recreation from the later 1970s to the 1990s and note, for example, that sustainable development was not a focal point until later in the period. Grano (1981) developed a model of external influences and internal change in geography that provides a valuable framework within which to examine the geography of tourism and recreation (Figure 1.4). The figure is divided into three interrelated areas:

- *knowledge* of the content of the geography of tourism and recreation studies;
- *action*: tourism and recreation research within the context of research praxis;
- *culture*: academics and students within the context of the research community and the wider society.

Knowledge

The Dictionary of Human Geography (Johnston *et al.* 1986) defines geography as 'The study of the earth's surface as the space within which the human population lives' (Haggett 1986: 175). Such a concise definition is deceptively simple, and conceals the changing and contested nature of academic geography and, consequently, the geography of tourism and recreation. The academic domain of geography cannot easily be summarised in a brief, succinct statement as it spans the natural, biological, social and behavioural sciences as well as the humanities (Hall 2013a). There is as much

Table 1.7 Categorisations of main approaches to the geography of tourism and recreation 1979–98

Pearce (1979)	Smith and Mitchell (1990)	Mitchell and Murphy (1991)	Pearce (1995a)	Hall and Lew (1998)
Spatial patterns of supply	Spatial patterns	Environmental considerations	Tourism models	Environmental considerations
Spatial patterns of demand	Tourism in developing countries	Regional considerations	Demand for tourist travel	Regional considerations
Geography of resorts	Evolution of tourism	Spatial considerations	International tourism patterns	Spatial considerations
Tourist movements and flows	Impacts of tourism	Evolutionary considerations	Intra-national travel patterns	Evolutionary considerations
Impact of tourism	Tourism research methods		Domestic tourist flows	Tourism planning
Models of tourist space	Planning and development		Spatial variations in tourism	Urban tourism
	Coastal tourism		National and regional structures of tourism	Modernisation and development
	Tourism accommodation		Spatial structure of tourism on islands	Gender and identity
	Resort cycles		Coastal resorts	Place-marketing and promotion
	Tourism concepts		Urban areas	Globalisation and economic and cultural change
	Tourism destinations			Sustainable development

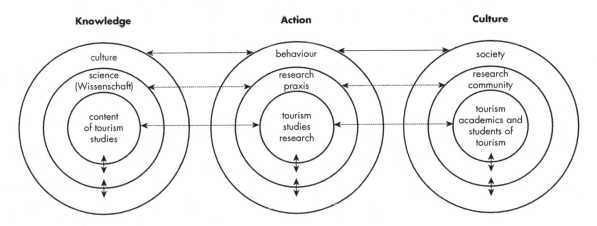

Figure 1.4 The context of tourism studies
Source: after Grano 1981.

contention and debate over what constitutes 'geography' as 'tourism'. Emphasis has changed over time and, appropriately for geography, over space as well. Geographical scholarship is not neatly demarcated. Geography 'is quintessentially an interdisciplinary tradition when its various "parts" (physical and human, cultural and economic, etc.) are considered together' (Agnew and Livingstone 2011: 1).

The development of geography as an academic discipline and its ability to provide specialist educational contributions to knowledge can be dated to the 1870s when geography departments were established in Germany (Taylor 1985). Similar developments were closely followed in the UK and the USA, although the main growth of the discipline came in the twentieth century. James (1972) argued that the establishment of specialised programmes of training marked the evolution of geography from the classical age as it entered the contemporary period. Freeman's (1961) *A Hundred Years of Geography* identified six principal trends within geography. These were:

- The encyclopaedic trend where new information about the world was collated for the rulers, mercantile classes and residents of western Europe and North America.
- The educational trend where an academic discipline began to establish its need to generate knowledge, determine relevance and ensure its own reproduction to derive its future. The development of geographical work in schools, colleges and universities characterised this trend.
- The colonial tradition in the early decades of the twentieth century characterised by a concern with the environment. In the UK, the focus on empire, and its spatial and political organisation from a metropolitan hub, made extensive use of geographical skills.
- The generalising trend describes the use to which data are put, generated through the encyclopaedic and colonial tradition. The methods used to interpret these data formed the basis of the early paradigms of the discipline's development.
- The political trend was indicative of the way in which contemporary uses of geographical expertise were used for political purposes (e.g. the redrawing of the map of Europe after the First World War).
- The specialisation trend was the natural corollary of the expansion of knowledge in geography and the inability of one person to be an expert in every field. The expansion of more rigorous research training required geographers to specialise.

Following on from these trends, Johnston (1991: 38) argued that 'some of these trends represent philosophies, some methodologies, and some ideologies with regard to the purpose of academic geography'. However, Johnston regarded three particular paradigms as being especially important in the development of human geography: exploration, environmental determinism and possibilism, and the region.

Exploration

Exploration refers to the situation where unknown areas of the world (to those who live outside them) are explored to collect and classify information. Many of these activities were financed by geographical societies as well as by philanthropists. The Royal Geographical Society of London (RGS) is one such example, and even nowadays the RGS is a major sponsor of expeditions, a focus only enhanced by the role of high profile television geographers such as Michael Palin, Nick Crane and Benedict Allen within the RGS. However, the theme of exploration remains significant in tourism geography, particularly as the images of places conveyed by explorers and the media to the metropolitan regions have served to create destination images that remain to the present day.

Environmental determinism and possibilism

Environmental determinism and possibilism were two competing approaches which, according to Johnston (1991), were early attempts at generalisation in the modern period. These approaches sought explanations rather than just descriptions of patterns of human occupation on the earth. The underlying assumption was that human activity was controlled by the elements in the physical environment within which it was located. Environmental determinism can be dated to interpretations of the research by Darwin and *On the Origin of Species* (published in 1859), where ideas on evolution were used by an American geographer William Morris Davies to develop the model of landform development. The nineteenth century also saw a number of geographers become protagonists of environmental determinism, especially the German geographer Friedrich Ratzel (1844–1904), and the American geographer Ellen Churchill Semple (1863–1932), whose book *Influences of Geographic Environment* (1891) stated that 'man is the product of the earth's surface'.

The response to determinism was the counterthesis of possibilism. French geographers presented arguments to show that people perceive a range of alternative uses to which the environment could be put.

This was, in part, determined by cultural traditions and predispositions. The debate on possibilism and determinism continued into the 1960s and has had some influence on tourism geography because of the extent to which concepts such as place, cultural landscape and heritage underlie much debate about tourism's impacts. Arguably some elements of environmental determinism are to be found in some of the discussions on the role of climate in tourism behaviour (Paul 1972; Adams 1973; Mieczkowski 1985; de Freitas 1990, 2003; Scott and Lemieux 2010; Gössling *et al.* 2012c) and the potential impact of climate change (Wall *et al.* 1986; Wall and Badke 1994; Hall and Higham 2005; Gössling *et al.* 2010; Scott *et al.* 2012).

The region

Ideas of the region and regional geography dominated British and American geography until the 1950s, based on the principle that generalisations and explanations were best derived from an areal approach. Johnston (1991) points to the role of Herbertson (1905) in dividing the earth into natural regions and the attempt to examine areas at a smaller scale to identify particular characteristics. In North America, the influence of Richard Hartshorne's ongoing research established the focus of geography as a concern for areal differentiation so that the principal purpose of geographical scholarship is synthesis, an integration of relevant characteristics to provide a total description of a place as a powerful focus for the discipline which remained a feature of many school, college and university programmes even in the 1990s. In the new millennium the region has become integrated into what Murphy and Le Heron (1999: 15) describe as the '"new regional geography" which incorporates elements of the earlier regional geography and new elements from political economy, geography, feminist geography and geographic information systems'. The development of regional synthesis required topical specialisms in geography to contribute to the regional paradigm.

Regional concepts continue to play a major role in the geography of tourism and recreation and underlie five main areas of research and scholarship:

- *Regional tourism geographies*: a number of collections of regional material have been developed by geographers since the late 1980s, in part influenced by the development of regional economic and political blocs, which serve as frameworks for the development of baseline studies of contemporary tourism processes as well as primers for college level geographies of travel and tourism (Lew *et al.* 2011). Major regional reviews of tourism have been undertaken by geographers on western Europe (Williams and Shaw 1988); Canada (Wall 1989); eastern Europe (D.R. Hall 1991); Europe (Montanari and Williams 1995); polar regions (Hall and Johnston 1995; Hall and Saarinen 2010; Grenier and Müller 2011); Australia (Hall 1995, 2003a); Asia (Winter *et al.* 2009); China (Lew and Wu 1995); India (Hannam and Diekmann, 2010); Nordic countries (Hall *et al.* 2009); South Africa (Rogerson and Visser 2004; Visser and Rogerson 2004; Hottola 2009; Saarinen *et al.* 2009), Oceania (Cooper and Hall 2005); the South Pacific (Hall and Page 1996); the Pacific Rim (Hall *et al.* 1997); and South and South-East Asia (Hall and Page 2000). However, it is important to note that the constitution of such regions is often not uncontested (Hall 2009a; Winter *et al.* 2009).
- *Destination regions*: given the importance of the destination as an analytical concept in tourism, significant effort has been given to the ways in which destination regions can be conceptualised, identified, managed and marketed (see Smith and Brown 1981; Smith 1983a, 1987b, 1995; Mitchell 1984; Heath and Wall 1992; Dredge 1999; Jenkins *et al.* 2011).
- *Regional planning and development*: the delineation of political and administrative regions provides a focus for administrative and planning research as well as a focus for the encouragement of development efforts through tourism and recreation. There is a longstanding body of research in this area, particularly with reference to Europe and the overall focus by government on tourism as a tool for economic development (see e.g., Pearce 1988a, 1992a, 1995a, 1995b; Williams and Shaw 1988; D.R. Hall 1991; Heath and Wall 1992; Hall *et al.* 1997; Hall 1999, 2008a; Hall and Boyd 2005; Müller and Jansson 2006; Dredge and Jenkins

2007; Grenier and Müller 2011; Jenkins *et al.* 2011).

- *Synthesis and integration*: the importance of synthesis and integration within regions has proven to be an important component in the development of approaches to integrated resource management within a regional context (see, e.g., Lang 1988; Wight 1993, 1995; Pearce 1995b; Hall 1999, 2008a).
- *Regional reviews of progress*: in the development of the sub-discipline (e.g. Pearce 1979; Butler 2004) and specific progress reports for individual countries such as the UK (Duffield 1984), Spain (Bote Gomez 1996), Germany (Kreisel 2004), Australasia (Pearce and Mings 1984; Pearce 1999a), China (Bao 2002, 2009; Bao and Ma 2010), Japan (Takeuchi 1984), France (Barbier and Pearce 1984; Iazzarotti 2002), South Africa (Rogerson and Visser 2004; Visser and Rogerson 2004) and the USA (Mitchell 1969a, 1979, 1984; Smith and Mitchell 1990; Mitchell and Murphy 1991).

Geographical trends and the geography of tourism and recreation

Johnston (1991) also charts the development of geography as a discipline, focusing on a number of other trends which provided a direction for development, including:

- The growth of *systematic studies* and adoption of a scientific method, where methods of investigation are developed.
- The development of a new focus around *spatial variables* and the analysis of spatial systems in the 1960s and 1970s, where spatial analytical techniques were developed and systems theory was introduced.
- The development of *behavioural geography* as a response to the spatial science approaches, recognising that human behaviour cannot easily be explained using logical positivist models. Behavioural geography focuses on the processes which underlie human decision-making and spatial behaviour rather than the outcomes which are the focus of much conventional spatial analysis (J. Gold 1980).

- The rise of *humanistic geography*, with its emphasis on the individual as a decision-maker. The behavioural approach tended to view people as responses to stimuli to show how individuals do not correspond to models built to predict possible human outcomes. In contrast, humanistic geography treats the individual as someone constantly interacting with the environment that changes both self and milieu (Johnston 1991). It does not use any scientifically defined model of behaviour, with each paradigm recognising appropriate contexts where the respective approaches are valid.
- *Applied geography*, which refers to 'the application of geographical knowledge and skills to the solution of economic and social problems' (Johnston 1986: 17).
- *Radical* approaches to geography, often with a neo-Marxist base (Peet 1977a, 1977b), but which broadened in the 1980s and 1990s to consider issues of gender, globalisation, localisation, identity, postcolonialism, postmodernism and the role of space in critical social theory (e.g. Harvey 1987, 1988, 1989a, 1989b, 1990, 1993; Soja 1989; Benko and Strohmmayer 1997; Crouch 1999b; Blom 2000). Arguably the development of poststructural perspectives that arise out of 'radical' geography have, together with more humanistic approaches, also given a strong impetus to the 'cultural turn' in geography (Johnston and Sidaway 1997) and also in tourism (Richards 1996; Richards and Wilson 2006; Smith and Richards 2013), especially in relation to the urban cultural economy (Hall 2013b) and cultural geographies of tourism (Crang 2014).

All of the above approaches to geography have relevance to the study of tourism and recreation. However, their application has been highly variable, with the greatest degree of research being conducted in the areas of spatial analysis and applied geography (Table 1.8). However, it is also important to note that there are some significant emerging approaches, such as those that relate strongly to integrated resource management and sustainable tourism, which has emerged out of applied geography, and the research theme of environmental change. Both of these emerging themes have strong links to physical geography and environmental studies (Hall 2013a).

Table 1.8 Approaches to geography and their relationship to the study of tourism and recreation

Approach	Key concepts	Exemplar publications
Spatial analysis	Positivism, locational analysis, maps, systems, networks, morphology	• spatial structure: Fesenmaier and Lieber 1987 • spatial analysis: Smith 1983b; Wall et al. 1985; Hinch 1990; Ashworth and Dietvorst 1995; Chhetri et al. 2008 • tourist flows and travel patterns: Williams and Zelinsky 1970; Corsi and Harvey 1979; Forer and Pearce 1984; Pearce 1987a, 1990, 1993b, 1995a; Murphy and Keller 1990; Oppermann 1992; McKercher et al. 2008 • gravity models: Mamud 1973; Bell 1977 • morphology: Pigram 1977 • regional analysis: Smith 1987b
Behavioural geography	Behaviouralism, behaviourism, environmental perception, diffusion, mental maps, decision-making, action spaces, spatial preference	• mental maps: Walmsley and Jenkins 1992; Jenkins and Walmsley 1993 • environmental cognition: Aldskogius 1977 • tourist spatial behaviour: Carlson 1978; Cooper 1981; Debbage 1991 • tourist behaviour: Murphy and Rosenblood 1974; Arbel and Pizam 1977; Pearce 1988a; Gössling et al. 2012c; Hibbert et al. 2013 • environmental perception: Wolfe 1970; Kaltenborn et al. 2011 • recreational displacement: Anderson and Brown 1984 • social marketing and behaviour change: Barr et al. 2011; Hall 2013e, 2014; Truong and Hall 2013
Humanistic geography	Human agency, subjectivity of analysis, hermeneutics, place, landscape, existentialism, phenomenology, ethnography, lifeworld	• placelessness of tourism: Relph 1976 • historical geography: Wall and Marsh 1982; Marsh 1985; Towner 1996
Applied geography	Planning, governance, remote sensing, Geographic Information Systems (GIS), public policy, cartography, regional development, carrying capacity	• planning: Murphy 1985; Getz 1986a; Dowling 1993, 1997; Hall et al. 1997; Hall 2000a, 2008a; Dredge and Jenkins 2007, 2011 • regional development: Coppock 1977a, 1977b; Pearce 1988b, 1990, 1992a • tourism and development: Pearce 1981, 1989; Cooke 1982; Lew 1985; Murphy 1985; Cater 1987; Saarinen et al. 2011 • indigenous peoples: Mercer 1994; Butler and Hinch 1996; Lew and van Otten 1997 • rural tourism and recreation: Coppock and Duffield 1975; Getz 1981; Glyptis 1991; Page and Getz 1997; Butler et al. 1998 • urban tourism and recreation: Ashworth 1989, 1992b; 1993, 1996; Page 1995a; Hinch 1996; Murphy 1997; Page and Hall 2003 • food and culinary systems: Hall and Mitchell 2002; Mitchell and Hall 2003; Baird and Hall 2013; Gössling and Hall 2013; Hall 2013f • health: Clift and Page 1996

(Continued)

Table 1.8 (Continued)

Approach	Key concepts	Exemplar publications
		• medical tourism: Connell 2006, 2011; Hall and James 2011; Hall, 2012b
		• destination marketing: Dilley 1986; Heath and Wall 1992
		• place marketing: Ashworth and Voogd 1988; Madsen 1992; Fretter 1993
		• small business and entrepreneurship: Buhalis and Cooper 1998; Page et al. 1999; Ateljevic and Doorne 2000; Getz and Carlsen 2000; Getz et al. 2004
		• innovation and knowledge transfer: Cooper 2006; Hall and Williams 2008; Shaw and Williams 2009; Williams and Shaw 2011; Weidenfeld 2013
		• public policy and administration, governance: Cooper 1987; Pearce 1992b; Jenkins 1993; Hall 1994; Hall and Jenkins 1995; Bramwell and Lane 2000; Hall 2011a, 2011f
		• security: Hall 2002; Hall et al. 2003b
		• tourism life cycle: Butler 1980, 2005; Cooper and Jackson 1989; Debbage 1990; Agarwal 1994
		• attractions: Lew 1987
		• second homes: Aldskogius 1968; Coppock 1977a; Gartner 1987; Hall and Müller 2004; Müller 2006, 2011
		• GIS: Kliskey 1994; Elliott-White and Finn 1998; van der Knapp 1999; Silberman and Rees 2010
		• tracking tourists: Shoval and Isaacson 2007
		• accessibility: Tóth and Lóránt 2010
		• natural hazards/disaster response: Biggs et al. 2012a, 2012b; Mulligan et al. 2012
		• resource evaluation: Sæþórsdóttir and Ólafsson 2010a, b.
Emerging approach: sustainability/ integrated resource management	Integrated resource management, sustainable development, sustainable tourism	• tourism impacts: Pigram 1980; Mathieson and Wall 1982; Edington and Edington 1986; Edwards 1987; Wall and Mathieson 2006; Hall and Lew 2009; Scott 2011
		• outdoor recreation management: Pigram and Jenkins 1999
		• heritage management: Gale and Jacobs 1987; Lew 1989; Ashworth and Tunbridge 1990, 1996; Hall and McArthur 1996, 1998; Graham et al. 2000
		• sustainable tourism: Butler 1990, 1991, 1992, 1998; Pigram 1990; Ashworth 1992b; Bramwell and Lane 1993; Cater 1993; Dearden 1993; McKercher 1993a, 1993b; Cater and Lowman 1994; Murphy 1994; Mowforth and Munt 1998; Hall and Lew 1998; Aronsson 2000; Saarinen 2006; Weaver 2006
		• ecotourism: Weiler 1991; Eagles 1992; Cater 1993; Cater and Lowman 1994; Blamey 1995; Weaver 1998; Fennell 1999; Page and Dowling 2001
		• national parks: Nelson 1973; Olwig and Olwig 1979; Marsh 1983; Calais and Kirkpatrick 1986; Cole et al. 1987; Davies 1987; Hall 1992a; McKercher 1993c
		• weather and climatological information: de Freitas 2003; Scott and Lemieux 2010
		• transition management: Gössling et al. 2012a
		• water use: Gössling et al. 2012b
		• biosecurity: Hall and Baird 2013
		• co-management: Plummer and Fennell 2009

Table 1.8 (Continued)

Approach	Key concepts	Exemplar publications
Emerging approach: environmental change	Global environmental change, ecological footprint	• Global environmental change: Gössling 2002; Gössling and Hall 2006a • Ecological footprint analysis: Gössling et al. 2002 • Climate Change: Smith 1990; Wall and Badke 1994; Hall and Higham 2005; Gössling and Hall 2006b; Scott et al. 2008, 2012; Steiger 2012; Gössling et al. 2013; Tervo-Kankare et al. 2013 • Carbon management: Gössling 2011 • Tourism's contribution to change: Peeters et al. 2007
'Radical' approaches	Neo-Marxist analysis, role of the state, gender, globalisation, localisation, identity, postcolonialism, postmodernism, poststructuralism, role of space	• political economy: Britton 1982; Ley and Olds 1988; Williams 2004; Bramwell 2011 • social theory: Britton 1991; Shaw and Williams 1994, 2002, 2004 • semiotic analysis: Waitt 1997 • place commodification: Ashworth and Voogd 1990a, 1990b, 1994; Kearns and Philo 1993; Waitt and McGuirk 1997; Chang et al. 1996; Tunbridge and Ashworth 1996
Emerging approach: 'cultural turn'		• cultural identity: Byrne et al. 1993; Crouch 1994; Squire 1994 • gender: Adler and Brenner 1992; Kinnaird and Hall 1994; Aitchison 1997, 1999, 2000 • 'new cultural studies': Aitchison 1999, 2000; Crouch 1999b • postcolonialism: Hall and Tucker 2004; Winter 2007, 2009 • the mundane: Edensor 2004, 2007 • performity: Coleman and Crang 2002; Edensor 2007; Molz 2010 • automobility: Edensor 2004 • the body/senses: Obrador 2007; Waitt and Duffy 2010; Barratt 2011 • sexuality: Waitt et al. 2008; Qian et al. 2012 • visual methods: Jenkins 2003; Scarles 2010

It is useful to note that two of the most influential books on the geography of tourism and recreation in the 1980s and early 1990s – Pearce (1987a, 1995a) on tourism and S. Smith (1983a) on recreation – primarily approach their subjects from a spatial perspective, although both give an acknowledgement to the role of behavioural research. In contrast, the text on geographical perspectives on tourism by Shaw and Williams (1994) provides a far more critical approach to the study of tourism, with acknowledgement of the crucial role that political economy, production, consumption, globalisation and commodification plays in the changing nature of tourism. Such a critical perspective is also reflected in Britton's (1983) review of the first edition of Pearce's (1981) *Tourism Development*, where he emphasised that the spatial structures of tourism

> cannot be adequately theorized about without a clear understanding of the organization and structure of the tourism product group, or, for example, the profound impact of the inclusive package tour travel mode on long-distance, especially third world, tourism and its association with multinational companies. Due recognition must be given to the fact that, like other sectors of advanced capitalist enterprise, tourism capital is immersed in competitive pressures and motivated by the maximization of market shares and profits. In turn these forces have led to the progressive centralization, concentration and internationalization of tourism enterprises while non-tourism capital (banks, breweries and multifaceted industrial conglomerates) is increasingly buying into the industry. Tourism is moving towards more monopolistic forms of organization. Similarly, the notion of 'development', tourism or otherwise, is not simply an exercise in technical planning but involves conflict and compromise between classes and subgroups in society which, usually, have unequal capacity to achieve their goals or preserve their interests. Some of these issues Pearce mentions in passing. But they are not considered in depth, fully understood or used as a basis for empirical analysis. If one takes the position that spatial structures realize social structures, then the dynamics of tourism

can only be fully understood with reference to its wider societal contexts.

(Britton 1983: 620)

In one sense, Pearce (1995a) and Shaw and Williams (1994, 2002, 2004) were representative of two of the most significant strands in tourism and recreation geography at the end of the twentieth century. The former, dominant approach represents a more 'traditional' form of spatial analysis and 'applied' geography (in the sense that it may be immediately useful to some public sector and commercial interests). The latter, emerging approach represents more discursive and reflexive forms of analysis with a broader perspective on what the appropriate focus for the study of tourism and recreation should be, although arguably Crouch (1999b) represents another reflexive form of analysis that has taken a different direction through its focus on identities, encounters and people as socialised and embodied subjects, but which may act as a bridge for greater communication between tourism and cultural geography. Undoubtedly, leisure and tourism are 'beginning to be rendered visible, situated and placed within the rapidly evolving discourses of post-positivist or post-structuralist geographies' (Aitchison *et al.* 2000: 1).

The 'cultural turn' in human geography has substantially influenced tourism research (Debbage and Ioannides 2004), particularly with respect to issues of performance, the body, gender, postcolonialism (Hall and Tucker 2004), power (Church and Coles 2007; Hall 2010d) and the study of cultural activities (Richards and Wilson 2006; Hall 2013b). Arguably, the terrain of human geography has shifted so much that it is rather debatable whether the 'radical' geography of Johnston (1991) can really be described as radical any more, at least within a disciplinary context. This is also significant criticism of the applied vs theoretical 'divide' as the notion of there being a simple binary relationship between applied and theoretical geographies is increasingly being questioned (Cloke and Johnston 2005a, 2005b; Hall 2013a). Indeed, it can be argued that in some cases the notion of being 'applied' can be read as being 'thematic' and theoretically grounded rather than being 'atheoretical'. For example, recent research on medical tourism by geographers, while looking at particular issues, is strongly grounded in under-standings of transnationalism and mobility (e.g. Connell 2006, 2011; Hall 2011d; 2012b; Ormond 2011, 2012).

Much of the tourism geographer's interest in applied geography is part of a desire to be 'relevant' and engage with broader public, community and business issues. For example, in many ways Shaw and Williams (1994, 2002, 2004) represent an explicit response to Britton's (1991) call for a theorisation of geography of tourism and leisure that explicitly rec-ognises, and unveils, tourism as a predominantly cap-italistically organised activity driven by the inherent and defining social dynamics of that system, with its attendant production, social and ideological relations. An analysis of how the tourism production system markets and packages people is a lesson in the political economy of the social construction of 'reality' and social construction of place, whether from the point of view of visitors and host communities, tourism cap-ital (and the 'culture industry') or the state – with its diverse involvement in the system (Britton 1991: 475).

The 'applied vs theory' debate

The 'applied vs theory' debate is germane to broader discussions in tourism research and the social sciences (Tribe 2009). It also reflects the emergence of concepts, i.e. creative class, experience economy, service-dominant logic, co-creation, destination com-petitiveness, and 'isms' or 'turns' that are sometimes uncritically adopted (Bianchi 2009; Hall 2010c) as part of the discourses of tourism geography. Many 'turns' have antecedents within geography that are unacknowledged (Hall and Page 2009). It is not clear if this is a product of a loss of collective and individual memory, a failure to teach the history of a discipline, the relatively poor availability of pre-1990 geography books in libraries or on Google Scholar, or just delib-erate ignorance (Hall 2011c, 2013a). But it does highlight the embeddedness of tourism geography in academic fashion cycles, 'which plays out through a particular industrial actor-network of academic knowledge production, circulation and reception' (Gibson and Klocker 2004: 425); within which

'Dedicated followers of fashion hurry to buy the new . . . book, an act of discernment and discrimination that starkly reveals the truism that identity is con-structed in and through the consumption of com-modities' (Barnett 1998: 388).

While it is quite easy to agree with Matley's (1976: 5) observation that 'There is scarcely an aspect of tourism which does not have some geographical implications and there are few branches of geography which do not have some contribution to make to the study of the phenomenon of tourism' (see also Mercer 1970), one must also note that the relative influence of these branches has proven to be highly variable since the late 1920s. One of the great difficulties has been that while tourism and recreation geographers have seen the significance of relationships to other geographical sub-disciplines and, indeed, other disci-plines, such relationships are not reciprocal (Mercer 1970; Debbage and Ioannides 1998; Ioannides 2006; Gibson 2008; Hall 2013a). Perhaps the most signifi-cant indicator of the way the geography of tourism and recreation is seen by the wider discipline can be found in various editions of Johnston's (1991; Johnston and Sidaway 1997, 2014) standard work on post-war Anglo-American geography. Here the terms leisure, recreation and tourism are absent from the index, while the only comment on the subject is three lines in the environmentalism section of the chapter on applied geography: 'A topic of special interest was the study of leisure, of the growing demand for recreation activities on the environment', followed by reference to the work of Patmore (1970, 1983) and Owens (1984). The lack of reference to tourism and recreation is commonplace in many pub-lications on the history of geographical thought. For example, the only mention of tourism by Peet is in relation to its perceived irrelevancy by Marxist geog-raphers in the 1960s:

There was a growing intolerance to the topical coverage of academic geography, a feeling that it was either an irrelevant gentlemanly pastime con-cerned with esoterica like tourism, wine regions, or barn types, or it was an equally irrelevant 'science' using quantitative methods to analyze spatial trivia like shopping patterns or telephone calls, when geography should be a working interest in ghettos, poverty, global capitalism, and imperialism.

(Peet 1998: 109)

It is probably an appropriate comment on the perception of the standing of tourism and recreation geography in Anglo-American geography that the only area where tourism and recreation are considered significant is in rural areas, with its longstanding tradition of recreational analysis (Patmore 1983), where, perhaps, tourists and recreationists are seen as a nuisance! There are no tourism geographers who are *Key Thinkers on Space and Place* (Hubbard *et al.* 2004). If textbooks are regarded as terrains of struggle over power and control (Silverman 1992), tourism geography is excluded from the landscape.

Interestingly, tourism geography is much better received in tourism studies than in geography, with tourism geographies being among the most highly cited tourism authors. For example, 15 of the 58 most cited tourism authors from 1970 to 2007 had PhDs in geography, including four of the ten most cited (McKercher 2008). As Gibson (2008: 418) observes, tourism geography 'still struggles to pervade publishing in "global" [geography] journals, and yet, when eventually appearing elsewhere, tourism geography appears to be on the whole more cosmopolitan. To me this seems an important – even defining – contradiction of tourism in contemporary geography'. The reasons for this paradoxical situation are manifold but perhaps lie in the cultural and action dimensions of geographical research discussed in more detail below.

Action: development of an applied geography of tourism and recreation

One consequence of geography's development in the 1950s and 1960s and the rise of a more 'applied' focus was the increasing move towards narrow specialisation, which appears to have reached its peak in the 1990s. Johnston (1991) outlines an increasing tension within geography in the 1960s and 1970s over the focus of the discipline, which in part transcended

the debate over radical approaches (see Harvey 1974). The basic tension related to how geographers should contribute their skills to the solution of societal problems. This questioned the philosophical basis of geography – who should the geographer benefit with an applied focus?

Both British and American geography conferences in the 1970s saw an increasing debate and awareness of the value of geographers contributing to public policy. Coppock (1974) felt that policy-makers were unaware of the contribution geographers could make to policy-making. But critics questioned the value of advising governments, which were the paymasters and already constrained what geographers could undertake research on. Harvey (1974) raised the vital issue of 'what kind of geography for what kind of public policy?', arguing that individuals involved in policy-making were motivated by

> personal ambition, disciplinary imperialism, social necessity and moral obligation at the level of the whole discipline, on the other hand, geography had been co-opted, through the Universities, by the growing corporate state, and geographers had been given some illusion of power within a decision-making process designed to maintain the status quo.

(Johnston 1991: 198)

Indeed, Pacione's defence of applied geography reiterates many of the inherent conflicts and problems which the 'purists' in human geography raise, in that

> Applied geography is concerned with the application of geographical knowledge and skills to the resolution of real-world social, economic and environmental problems. The underlying philosophy of relevance of usefulness and problem-orientated goals of applied geography have generated critical opposition from other 'non-applied' members of the geographical community. Particular criticism of the applied geography approach has emanated from Marxist and, more recently, postmodern theorists who reflect the potential of applied geography

to address the major problems confronting people and places in the contemporary world.

(Pacione 1999a: 1)

The emergence of the 'new cultural geography' highlights the increasing tensions within the discipline where 'the idea of applied geography or useful research is a chaotic concept which does not fit with the recent "cultural turn" in social geography or the postmodern theorising of recent years' (Pacione 1999a: 3). In fact, Pacione claimed that it was a matter of individual conscience as to what individual geographers study. What is clear is that some research is more 'useful' than other forms, and the application to tourism and recreation phenomenon is certainly a case in point. Although the 'concept of "useful research" poses the basic questions of useful for whom? Who decides what is useful' (Pacione 1999a: 4) is part of the wider relevance debate which continues in human geography as paradigm shifts and new ways of theorising and interpreting information question the central role of the discipline. In P.J. Taylor's (1985) provocative and thoughtful analysis of 'The value of a geographical perspective', a cyclical function emerged in the development of eras of pure and applied research. What Taylor observed was that when external pressures are greatest, problem-solving approaches are pursued within the discipline. Conversely, in times of comparative economic prosperity, more pure academic activity is nurtured. Taylor related these trends to longer-term trends in the world economy, identifying three distinct periods when applied geography was in its ascendance: the late nineteenth century, the inter-war period and the mid-1980s.

Sant (1982) argued that applied geography was not a sub-discipline but had a dependent relationship with academic geography. It has a different *modus operandi*. It is intended to offer prescription, has to engage in dialogue with 'outsiders' not familiar with the discipline, its traditions, problems and internal conservatism, and has an ability to overtly criticise developments which are not central to the prevailing paradigm. While the discipline has published a range of journals with an applied focus (e.g. *Applied Geography*) and offers a number of applied courses in

universities, the term is used loosely. As Sant (1982: 136) argued, 'the crux of applied geography is (at the risk of tautology) fundamentally that it is about geography. That is, it deals with human and physical landscapes.'

In applied geography, theory provides the framework for asking questions, managing the problem, and deriving solutions (Pacione 2004; Stimson and Haynes 2012). As Livingstone (1992: 3) commented, 'Too often the practical outworkings of theory are overlooked'. Much applied spatial analysis appears to be criticised because it is grounded in a different set of scientific theory, usually in a quantitative and empirical vein, than those who criticise it (Hall 2012a). As Forer (1999: 96) argued, 'New geographic information technology is becoming ubiquitous, and is revolutionising what we measure and how we measure it'. In fact, as Tarrant and Cordell (1999) noted in their examination of outdoor recreation in US national forest areas, the use of GIS can be an extremely valuable tool in the analysis of environmental justice and equity, issues that are often not associated with quantitative analysis. Yet Wyly (2009) emphasises that the alignment between positivist epistemology, quantitative methodology and conservative political ideology was contingent and contextual, and was not a necessary outcome of quantitative and applied studies. Post-positivists committed to progressive politics have also suggested ways in which the critical/quantitative binary can be at least partially eclipsed, and emphasise that spatial and quantitative analysis and critical geographies are not mutually exclusive (Kwan and Schwanen 2009; Schwanen and Kwan 2009). Hall (2013c) is more provocative, suggesting that in

focussing on the qualitative [alone] as being critical there is a danger that the potential critical powers of quantitative research ... are undermined or, just as significantly, lead to accusations that those who advocate the qualitative without appreciating the quantitative do so only because they cannot do or understand statistics or mathematical modelling.

(Hall 2013c)

In the case of recreation and tourism, many geographers involved in these areas may also no longer be based in geography departments in universities. However, they maintain and extend the value of geographical analysis and understanding for the wider field of recreation and tourism studies. The discipline of geography, in the UK at least, paid very little attention to the growing role of geographers in the educational and research environment of tourism. Only in the 1990s did organisations such as the Institute of British Geographers acknowledge the significance of recreation and tourism as a serious area of academic study. In contrast, the Association of American Geographers and the Canadian Association of Geographers have been much more active, with their study groups being established since the 1970s. International organisations such as the International Geographical Union (IGU) Study Group on the Geography of Tourism, Leisure and Global Change (formerly the IGU Study Group on the Geography of Sustainable Tourism, and IGU Commission on Tourism and Leisure) provided another forum for research developments and interaction by geographers and non-geographers with similar research interests. Nevertheless, despite such initiatives, the relationship of the geography of tourism and recreation to the broader discipline of geography has suffered three major problems:

- the rise of applied geography within the discipline, and tourism and recreation geography within it, has seen some critics, often from outside of the field altogether, view it as rather ephemeral and lacking in substance and rigour;
- in some countries (e.g. the UK and Australia), national geographical organisations and geography departments have often failed to recognise the significance of recreation and tourism as a legitimate research area capable of strengthening and supporting the discipline;
- national research assessment exercises may primarily define the assessment of tourism research in the narrow context of business studies, rather than in a geographical or wider social scientific framework (Hall 2011e).

One consequence is that many geographers who developed recreational and tourism research interests in the 1980s and 1990s have moved to fresh pastures where autonomous tourism research centres or departments have eventuated. For example, a significant number of geographers are now based in business schools or tourism, recreation or leisure departments, where their research interests are aligned within a multidisciplinary environment that can cross-fertilise their research and support an applied focus. Indeed, in some respects, history is perhaps repeating itself all over again, as where planning emerged as a discipline and split from some of its geographical roots and where the development of environmental studies departments has also led to a departure of geographers to such centres. For example, in New Zealand, with one or two exceptions, all the geographers with a tourism or recreation focus are now located in business schools, departments of tourism and recreation or other non-geographical departments. This situation is not dramatically different from that in Australia, where educational expansion in tourism has made extensive use of professional geographers to develop and lead such developments (Weiler and Hall 1991). As Janiskee and Mitchell concluded:

> This is certainly an interesting and exciting time to be a recreation geographer. After a slow start, the subdiscipline has achieved a critical mass and seems destined to enjoy a bright future . . . There is no question that the application of recreation geography knowledge and expertise to problem solving contexts outside academia offers potential rewards of considerable worth to the sub-discipline: more jobs for recreation geographers, a stimulus to academic research with implications for problem solving, a more clearly defined sense of purpose or social worth, and greater visibility, both within and outside academic circles.
>
> (Janiskee and Mitchell 1989: 159)

It is interesting to note that Janiskee and Mitchell also perceive that

> since there is no clear distinction between 'basic' and 'applied' research, nor any appreciable threat

to quality scholarship, there is no simmering argument on the issue of whether applied research is good for recreation geography. Rather, the real question is whether recreation geographers will have the resources and the zeal to move into the problem solving domain on a much more widespread and consistent basis.

(Janiskee and Mitchell 1989: 159)

While this may be true in a North American context, it is certainly not the case in the UK, and a number of other countries where applied geographical research in recreation and tourism has been viewed as dissipating the value and skills of the geographer for pecuniary reward, or without contributing to the development of the discipline. Ironically, however, the proliferation of 'dabblers' (i.e. people who do not consider themselves recreation geographers, but contribute articles to journals using simplistic notions of tourism and recreation) has grown and still abounds in the geography and, to a lesser extent, in the recreation and tourism journals.

Gibson (2008) used the Social Science Citation Index (SSCI) (now Web of Science) to analyse tourism within selected geography journals and found that very little work was conducted in the 1960s and 1970s:

Growth occurred in the late 1980s and particularly into the 1990s, as human geography itself diversified. About 40 articles have been published annually [in the 1990s and 2000s], across the selected geography journals (not including the specialist *Tourism Geographies*), and their breadth and diversity is striking.

(Gibson 2008: 409)

Gibson's analysis suggested an equivalent of about one paper per Indexed geography journal examined each year. A slightly higher rate was found by Hall (2013d) in an analysis conducted of tourism articles in selected leading geographical journals from 1998 to 2009, with *Geografiska Annaler, Series B: Human Geography* and *Geographical Research* (formerly *Australian Geographical Studies*) having the largest number of papers. Nevertheless, as Gibson (2008: 409) noted, 'many

researchers featuring in the SSCI bibliography would probably not consider themselves tourism geographers or may not even list tourism as a specialist research interest'.

Indeed, tourism and recreation have been 'discovered' by geographers and other social scientists in the late 1980s and 1990s as tourism is utilised by governments to respond to the effects of global economic restructuring and increasing concerns over conserving the environment (Hall and Lew 1998). Such contributions, according to Janiskee and Mitchell (1989: 157), 'although welcome, are not a satisfactory substitute for output of a substantial number of specialists doing scientific-theoretical-nomothetic research which is needed for the area to progress'. Calls for a 'heightened awareness and appreciation of problem solving needs and opportunities outside the traditional bounds of scholarly research' (Janiskee and Mitchell 1989: 159) are vital if academics are to connect with the broad range of stakeholders and interests that impinge upon geography and academia. Geographers with knowledge and skills in the area of tourism and recreation research need to develop a distinctive niche by undertaking basic and applied research to address public and private sector problems, which illustrates the usefulness of a spatial, synthesising and holistic education. Even so,

the list of research undertaken by applied geographers is impressive, but there are no grounds for complacency [as] the influence of applied geography has been mixed, and arguably less than hoped for ... Several reasons may account for this [including] the eclectic and poorly focused nature of the discipline of geography and the fact that 'geographical work' is being undertaken by 'non-geographers' in other disciplines. This undermines the identity of geography as a subject with something particular to offer.

(Pacione 1999a: 10–11)

Culture

The cultural dimensions of the geography of tourism and recreation – the sociology of knowledge of the sub-discipline – as with that of tourism and recreation studies as a whole, have been little studied. This is extremely unfortunate as it means there is a very incomplete comprehension of where the sub-discipline has been, which must also clearly affect our understanding of where it might go. As Barnes commented:

> Social, technical and economic determinants routinely affect the rate and direction of scientific growth . . . It is true that much scientific change occurs despite, rather than because of, external direction or financial control . . . Progress in the disinterested study [of certain] . . . areas has probably occurred just that bit more rapidly because of their relevance to other matters.
>
> (Barnes 1982: 102–3)

Similarly, Johnston observed that

> the study of a discipline must be set in its societal context. It must not necessarily be assumed, however, that members of academic communities fully accept the social context and the directives and impulses that it issues. They may wish to counter it, and use their academic base as a focus for their discontent. But the (potential) limits to that discontent are substantial. Most academic communities are located in universities, many of which are dependent for their existence on public funds disbursed by governments which may use their financial power to influence, if not direct, what is taught and researched. And some universities are dependent on private sources of finance, so they must convince their sponsors that their work is relevant to current societal concerns.
>
> (Johnston 1991: 24–5)

As noted above, research into the geographical dimensions of tourism has received relatively little attention in the wider fields of academic geography. Several related factors can be recognised as accounting for this situation:

- there is only a narrow set of official interest in conducting research into the geography of tourism;

- tourism is not regarded as a serious scholarly subject;
- there is no theoretical and epistemological consensus in conducting geographical studies of tourism and recreation;
- tourism and recreation geographers have had little success in promoting their sub-discipline in the broader geographical context;
- many tourism and recreation geographers are now operating in non-geography departments or in the private sector.

Unlike some areas of tourism research, such as politics and public policy, for example (Hall 1994; Hall and Jenkins 1995), there is some government support for research and consulting on the geography of tourism and recreation. However, such research support tends to be given to the analysis of spatial patterns of tourist flows and issues of infrastructure location rather than areas of applied geographical research in gender and social impacts that may produce unwanted political results. Indeed, even support for research on the environmental impacts on tourism has the potential to produce politically contestable results, particularly if the results are not seen as supportive of industry interests. Despite the apparent lack of interest in studies of the broader dimensions of tourism by government and industry, and the community conflicts that occur in relation to tourism development, it is important to recognise that such research may be of an extremely practical nature. The results of such research may help facilitate and improve tourism planning through an increased understanding of decision-making processes (Dredge and Jenkins 2007, 2011; Hall 2008a), and help maintain the long-term viability of tourist destinations.

Despite the extensive growth of research on tourism and recreation in the 1980s and 1990s, many people still do not regard tourism as a serious subject of study, often equating it with booking a holiday at a travel agency or learning how to pour a beer. Indeed, research on tourism is often seen as frivolous. The observation of Matthews (1983: 304) that 'at a typical American university, a political scientist with a scholarly interest in tourism might be looked upon as dabbling in frivolity – not as a serious scholar but as an opportunist looking for a tax-deductible holiday', holds almost universal applicability. Similar to V.L. Smith's (1977: 1) observations on the anthropology of tourism in the 1970s, it is a topic that still appears to be thought by many in the discipline to be unworthy of consideration by the serious geography scholar. Indeed, L.S. Mitchell, a noted scholar within tourism and recreation geography, in a personal communication following a discussion on RTSnet (the newsgroup of the recreation, tourism and sport speciality group of the Association of American Geographers) regarding the position of recreation and tourism in American geography, argued that

> Recreation geography, has never been a valued member of the establishment, because, it is believed, it is impossible to be serious about individuals and groups having fun. Note the subtitle of the feminist oriented tourism conference being held in California this month ('Tourism is not about having fun'). In spite of the fact that tourism is the number one economic activity in the world, that recreation (especially passive recreation) takes up a large portion of the population's time, and that sport is almost a religion for many in this country, geographers who study these phenomena are not highly regarded.
>
> (Mitchell 1997)

There are also substantial methodological, theoretical and spatial problems in conducting geographical research. Problems have arisen because of the multiplicity of potential frameworks for analysis as well as relatively weak theorisation by some. As Ioannides (1996: 221) notes, 'Although tourism geography has long been an established specialization, the weak theoretical grounding associated with this research area relegates it to the discipline's periphery'.

The lack of a clearly articulated or agreed-upon methodological or philosophical approach to geography per se, let alone the geography of tourism and recreation, may create an intellectual and perceptual minefield for the researcher, particularly as the value position of the author will have an enormous bearing on the results of any research. Burton (1982: 323–4), for example, argued that leisure and tourism

research is plagued by problems of 'lack of intellectual co-ordination and insufficient cross-fertilization of ideas among researchers; an inadequacy of research methodologies and techniques; and a lack of any generally agreed concepts and codes in the field'. However, in contrast, Hall (1994: 7) argued that 'In fact, the debate which marks such concepts should probably be seen as a sign of health and youthful vigour in an emerging area of serious academic study and should be welcomed and encouraged rather than be regarded as a source of embarrassment'. Indeed, it can be argued that the post-disciplinary characteristics of much tourism research by geographers enhance its capacity to engage with a wide range of theoretical approaches and ideas (Coles *et al.* 2006).

Another factor which may have influenced the standing of the geography of tourism and recreation is the extent to which the sub-discipline is being promoted to the discipline as a whole. For example, in the American context, Mitchell argued:

> There is no one individual superstar in the US who has popularized the subject matter through publications and/or personality. From my perspective a lot of good geographic research has been published and the research frontier has been advanced, however, little of this research has appeared in the geographic literature; rather it tends to be found in specialty or multi-disciplinary journals . . . Lots of publications are produced but they do not engender the kind of interest or reputation that leads to widespread recognition.
>
> (Mitchell 1997)

In the British context, the publication of *Critical Issues in Tourism* by Shaw and Williams (1994) as part of the Institute of British Geography Studies in Geography Series helped raise the profile of the area. Nevertheless, the situation remains that the key academic audience of the majority of research and publications by tourism and recreation geographers are people within tourism and recreation departments rather than geography. However, there are some signs that this situation may be changing. First, there is the publication of the journal *Tourism Geographies* in 1999 (edited by Alan Lew and published by Routledge), which seeks to promote the sub-discipline both within its immediate audience and beyond. To some extent the emergence of this specialist journal may be regarded as a sign of maturity of the field akin to other specialist geography journals (e.g. *Applied Geography*, *Journal of Transport Geography*). Second, there are activities of the IGU Study Group on the Geography of Tourism, Leisure and Global Change and its forerunner, the Study Group on the Geography of Sustainable Tourism, which has co-hosted a number of conferences and special sessions with other IGU Commissions, such as Sustainable Rural Systems, and with national associations, such as the Association of American Geographers. Third, the increased significance of tourism and recreation in urban and rural environments in contemporary society as well as being a mechanism for economic development has led to a greater appreciation of the potential significance of the field. In other words, tourism is now such a significant activity in the cultural and economic landscape that it would be difficult for other geographies to ignore it for much longer. Finally, tourism and recreation geographies are now arguing that they have something to contribute to the wider discipline, particularly in such areas as understanding the service economy, industrialisation, innovation and regional development (e.g. Ioannides 1995, 1996; d'Hauteserre 1996; Hall and Williams 2008; Hall 2009b; Shaw and Williams 2009; Shaw *et al.* 2011; Williams and Shaw 2011; Weidenfeld 2013), as well as more traditional resource management concerns and sustainability (e.g. Zurick 1992; Hall and Lew 1998). Indeed, this last element is extremely important as it highlights the growing links of tourism geographers with physical geography and environmental studies.

Tourism, the environment and physical geography

Perceptions of tourism geography are affected more by the intellectual debates of human geography than physical geography (Hall 2013a, 2013d). Nevertheless, a longstanding theme in geography (Johnston 1983b), and in tourism geography, is the relationship between physical and human geography. 'Frequently

physical and human geography are separated out from one another as if they had completely different historical trajectories. Yet, over a fairly long period of time, it is their very co-existence that is one of the things that has helped to constitute the field at large' (Agnew and Livingstone 2011: 1).

A core reason for the sometime unease between physical and human geographers is their different methods, reasons and foci (Valentine *et al.* 2010). The physical/human binary, with the quantitative scientific methods of physical geography at one extreme and the qualitative, poststructuralist, humanistic methods of human geography at the other, revisits many elements of the applied/theoretical binary. Gregory (1978: 75) influentially suggested that the integration of human and physical geography was an ontological problem, in that, even though they are connected by social practices, 'there is nothing in this which requires them to be connected through a formal system of common properties and universal constructs'.

Ontological differences raise fundamental questions about how the environment can actually be understood, the ethical relationships between humans and the environment, as well as criticism of instrumental science (Demeritt 2006). Despite often little ontological common ground, there is a substantial history of multi-method and interdisciplinary approaches in tourism geography, including environmental perception, natural hazards research, tourism impacts and resource evaluation. Tourism geographers have also made substantial contributions to research on sustainable tourism (Weaver 2006), including in developing regions (Saarinen *et al.* 2011). However, its most substantial contemporary contribution is arguably in the complex areas of global environmental change (Gössling and Hall 2006a) and climate change (Scott *et al.* 2010, 2012) that necessitate integrated physical and human geographic approaches (Demeritt 2009).

Inside/outside

The final factor influencing the standing of the sub-discipline is the extent to which geographers in the field are increasingly undertaking employment outside geography departments and in tourism, recreation and leisure studies departments, business schools, and environmental studies and planning departments. Across most of the western world, tourism has become recognised as a major employer, which, in turn, has placed demands on educational institutions to produce graduates with qualifications relevant to the area. Therefore, there has been a substantial growth in the number of universities and colleges that offer undergraduate and graduate qualifications in tourism, recreation and hospitality, which provide potential employment for tourism and recreation geographers. The opportunity to develop a career path in tourism and recreation departments which are undergoing substantial student growth, or in a new department, will clearly be attractive to individuals whose career path may be slower within long-established geography departments and who carry the burden of being interested in a sub-discipline often on the outer edge of mainstream geographic endeavour. As Johnston (1991: 281) recognised, 'this reaction to environmental shifts is undertaken by individual scholars, who are seeking not only to defend and promote their own status and careers within it'.

The massive growth of tourism and recreation studies outside geography also means that increasingly many geographers publish in tourism and recreation journals rather than in geography journals. Such publications may be extremely significant for tourism studies but may carry little weight within geography beyond the sub-discipline (e.g. Butler's (1980) hugely influential article on the destination life cycle). This has therefore meant that geographers who work in non-geography departments may find themselves being drawn into interdisciplinary studies with only weak linkages to geography. The question that of course arises is: does this really matter? Disciplines change over time, areas of specialisation come and go depending on intrinsic and extrinsic factors. As Johnston observes:

> The continuing goal of an academic discipline is the advancement of knowledge. Each discipline pursues that goal with regard to particular areas of study.
>
> Its individual members contribute by conducting research and reporting their findings, by integrating material into the disciplinary corpus, and by pedagogical activities aimed at informing about, promoting and reproducing the discipline: in addition, they may argue the discipline's 'relevance' to society at large. But there is no fixed set of disciplines, nor any one correct division of academic according to subject matter. Those disciplines currently in existence are contained within boundaries established by earlier communities of scholars. The boundaries are porous so that disciplines interact. Occasionally the boundaries are changed, usually through the establishment of a new discipline that occupies an enclave within the preexisting division of academic space.
>
> (Johnston 1991: 9)

However, to borrow the title of a leading geography textbook of the 1980s, *Geography Matters!* (Massey and Allen 1984), it matters because concepts at the heart of geography such as spatiality, place, identity, landscape and region are critical, not only to the geography of tourism and recreation but also to tourism and recreation studies as a whole. Indeed, the growing interest in the concept of mobility among the social sciences (e.g. Bell and Ward 2000; Urry 2000; Adey 2010) is testimony to the long focus that tourism and recreation geographers have had on leisure mobility (Wolfe 1966; Hall 2005a). In commenting on work undertaken by geographers in the tourism field, Britton noted that they have

> been reluctant to recognise explicitly the capitalistic nature of the phenomenon they are researching . . . This problem is of fundamental importance as it has meant an absence of an adequate theoretical foundation for our understanding of the dynamics of the industry and the social activities it involves.
>
> (Britton 1991: 451)

However, such a criticism of tourism and recreation studies by geographers arguably does not hold as

BOX 1.2   THE GEOGRAPHY OF TOURISM AND RECREATION OUTSIDE THE ANGLO-AMERICAN TRADITION: THE 'MARGIN OF THE MARGIN'?

While this book concentrates on the geography of tourism and recreation within the English speaking world, what is sometimes referred to as the Anglo-American tradition (Johnston and Sidaway 1997), it is important to note that the interest of geographers in tourism and recreation is also occurring within other geographical traditions. The internationalisation of the tourism and recreation academic community through such organisations as the IGU Study Group on Tourism, the growth of student and academic exchanges within the European Union and the use of English as the international language of scholarship have also meant a growing interchange between native English speaking and English as a second language scholars. Academic journals in English are now increasingly being produced in countries where English is not the native tongue, for example *Anatolia* in Turkey and *Tourism Today* in Cyprus. Nevertheless, the market of ideas in tourism geography is clearly affected by 'the uneven geographies of international journal publishing spaces' (Paasi 2005: 769) that are shaped by different national and institutional research agendas as well as language, leading to what Hall (2013a) described as the possibilities of non-English geographies of tourism becoming the 'margin of the margin'.

An analysis by Hall (2013d) found that the 25 most cited papers in Scopus under 'tourism and geography/ies' were mainly from authors with institutional affiliations in the UK, New Zealand, Canada and the USA. Even given the inclusion of more non-English journals in Scopus, authors based at institutions in primarily English speaking countries accounted for 57.6 per cent of institutions contributing two or more papers of all publications listed in Scopus under tourism and geography/ies up to the end of 2010. The leading countries (≥5 per cent) being the UK (21.8 per cent), USA (14.1 per cent), China (10.3 per cent), Australia (7.2 per cent), Canada (6.5 per cent), New Zealand (6.5 per cent) and France (5 per cent) (Hall 2013d). However, when the total number of Scopus listed publications was categorised according to language of publication an even higher proportion (68 per cent) were in English (French being the next most used, 8.1 per cent), reflecting concerns not only about the peripheralisation of non-English publications (and hence ideas) in the 'international' discourse of tourism geography (Hall 2013a; Wilson and Anton Clavé 2013), but also about the emerging linguistic and institutional monopolisation of international publishing spaces (Paasi 2005).

The paramount status of English as the international language of ideas reflects not only the unreality of level playing fields in the knowledge market but also the extent to which the local and specific affects the geography of reading (Hall 2013a). It also indicates a problem for some linguistically defined bodies of tourism geography knowledge at a time when there are increasing demands from policy-makers and university administrations to figure in international subject and university rankings – which tend to be in English (Mohrman *et al.* 2008). No matter how important local and national knowledge is within a specific spatial context, unless it is conveyed in English it has little chance to enter the global marketplace and be reproduced and recirculated. Somewhat ironically, given the desire to give voice to local and indigenous perspectives, unless that voice can be spoken in English it is likely not to be heard (Hall 2013a). It is also notable that, in returning to Hall's (2013d) analysis, while China accounts for over 10 per cent of all tourism geography publications in Scopus, only a little over one-quarter of these are actually in Chinese, reflecting the efforts of Chinese institutions to compete internationally (Bao and Ma 2010). Although the hegemony of the centre in the knowledge production process has long been acknowledged (Canagarajah 1996), the

English language has become part of the 'ideological complex' that produces and maintains the increasing hegemony of the English speaking academy (Tietze and Dick 2013), including with respect to the geographies of tourism and recreation.

In examining the tourism and recreation literature of a number of languages and countries, it may be noted that the growth of publishing on tourism and recreation in English is mirrored in these other traditions, along with some of the disciplinary differences and issues noted above (Rubio 1998–9; Kraas and Taubmann 2000; Wayens and Grimmeau 2003; Kreisel 2012).

French speaking geography also has a strong tradition of research on tourism and recreation (Iazzarotti 2002; Coëffé 2007) that was, arguably, much further advanced in the 1960s and 1970s in terms of both theoretical development and extent of publication than the Anglo-American tradition. One reason for this advanced interest possibly lay in the long recognition of tourism as a factor in the economic development of French alpine regions and its impact on the cultural and physical landscape (e.g. Knafou 1978). In addition, the growth of tourism on the Mediterranean coast provided a basis for research on coastal resort development (e.g. Burnet 1963; Barbaza 1966), while the significance of second homes for tourism and leisure also has a strong research tradition. More recently, French speaking geographers have written substantive works regarding the impacts of tourism (e.g. Michaud 1983, 1992; Escourrou 1993; Debarbieux 1995), urban tourism (e.g. Iazzarotti 1995; Potier and Cazes 1996, 1998), as well as the social construction of tourism (e.g. Boyer 1996; Deprest 1997, 2002; Gagnon 2007; Kadri 2008). In a review of the geography of tourism and leisure in France, Knafou (2000) notes the diversity of approaches and topics that exist. Indeed, an examination of several French language texts and readings (e.g. Lozato 1985; Clary 1993; Dewailly and Flument 1993; Deprest 1997; Baron-Yellés 1999; Coëffé 2007) suggests that, as in Anglo-American human geography, traditional spatial approaches to studying tourism geography are increasingly under challenge from perspectives strongly influenced by postmodernism (Knafou et al. 1997; Deprest 2002) and ideas of mobility (Dehoorne 2002) (see also Morisset et al. 2012).

Dutch and Nordic geographies have been much more influenced by Anglo-American tourism and recreation geography than their French and German counterparts to a great extent because of the role of English as a second language and the publication of much of their research in English (Hall et al. 2009). Coastal tourism, rural tourism and regional development are particularly strong themes in Dutch tourism geography (Ashworth and Dietvorst 1995; Dietz and Kwaad 2000), while the work of Greg Ashworth has had a major influence on the fields of urban and heritage tourism (e.g. Ashworth 1989, 1999; Ashworth and Tunbridge 1996; Ashworth and Ennen 1998) (see also Chapter 5). Nordic tourism and recreation geography has had considerable influence in the areas of tourism in peripheral regions and second home development (e.g. Finnveden 1960; Aldskogius 1968; Jaakson 1986; Halseth and Rosenberg 1995; Kaltenborn 1997a, 1997b, 1998; Müller 1999, 2006, 2011; Aronsson 2000; Saarinen 2001, 2003, 2006; Hall and Müller 2004; Saarinen and Hall 2004; Müller and Jansson 2006; Hiltunen et al. 2013) and global environmental change and contemporary mobility (Gössling 2002; Frändberg and Vilhelmson 2003; Gössling and Hall 2006a; Tervo-Kankare et al. 2013). Nevertheless, as with Anglo-American tourism geography, a number of geographers are not based in departments of geography and are instead located in business schools, schools of service management or departments of tourism (e.g. Gössling 2011; Hultman and Hall 2012). Asian tourism geographers have also been substantially influenced by Anglo-American publications and research, although unfortunately there is much Asian research which is yet to be published in English. For example, reviews of Korean human geography (Kim 2000) and applied geography (Lee 2000) indicate a large body of literature in Korean on event tourism, rural tourism, coastal tourism and resort development. There is also evidence of a growing interest in the geography of tourism in China (e.g. Lew and Wu 1995; Guo *et al.* 2000; Bao 2002, 2009; Bao and Ma 2010; Li *et al.* 2012), although, as noted above, much of this is being published in English.

One area which has shown a massive growth in tourism research by geographers is Southern Africa. Although some areas of South African geography were undoubtedly substantially influenced by developments in Anglo-American geography, relationships also existed with Dutch and German geographical traditions, while the apartheid years also contributed to a reduced contact with the international academic community. The removal of apartheid reconnected South African geography with the wider field (perhaps best indicated in the hosting of an IGU regional conference in South Africa in 2002, with tourism being one of the largest stream of papers at the conference) as well as reinforcing the importance that South African tourism and recreation geographers would be able to connect with specific development issues in the new South Africa in a manner that responded to local issues as much as international concerns (Rogerson and Visser 2004; Visser and Rogerson 2004). Significantly, research on sub-Saharan Africa has since expanded dramatically (Saarinen *et al.* 2009; Hottola 2009; Rogerson and Visser 2011).

The above discussion is by no means a comprehensive review of the enormous body of literature of tourism and recreation which exists outside English. Nevertheless, it does indicate that there appears to be almost universal growth in research on tourism and recreation by geographers regardless of language, and that several of the tensions existing in Anglo-American tourism and recreation geography exist elsewhere. Moreover, there is also increasing crossover between the different literatures as English continues to expand its academic influence, as indicated by both the growing literature by non-native English speakers in journals published in English and the continued growth in attendance at IGU and other conferences in which papers are primarily presented in English. However, such growth may be problematic for some non-English geographical traditions, especially as more English tourism texts are translated into other languages than the other way around. The long-term implications of this for tourism and recreation geographies may be substantial and this is an issue that we will return to in the concluding chapter (Chapter 10).

firmly some 20 years later, although the lack of an agreed theoretical foundation does mean that debates over theory will remain with us for a considerable time yet.

Transforming the geography of tourism and recreation

The situation described in this chapter is that of an area of academic endeavour which is at a critical point in its evolution. Tourism and recreation geography is a relatively applied area of study that is at the periphery of its own discipline but with strong connections to academic research and scholarship outside the area.

Dominated by systematic spatial analysis, it has historically had a relatively weak theoretical base that exacerbated its inability to influence wider disciplinary endeavours. Nevertheless, since the late 1980s there has been a gradual transformation in its character and fortunes. First, there has been a major growth in the number and quality of publications by tourism and recreation geographers, which, although not greatly influencing geography outside the subdiscipline, has had a major impact on the direction of tourism and recreation studies, and has also informed broader social scientific debates on mobility, transnationalism, services, heritage and regional studies; and increasingly environmental science debates on conservation and environmental change. Second, there is

clearly a conscious attempt to provide a stronger theoretical base to tourism and recreation geography
which would both be informed by and contribute to
contemporary social theory, particularly with respect
to such issues as globalisation, localisation, commodification, restructuring and sustainability. Third,
tourism and recreation geographers are seeking to
promote their work more actively in academic and
non-academic spheres, especially as international and
domestic temporary mobility continue to expand.
Finally, in a time of increased theoretical, epistemological and policy fluidity the cosmopolitan nature of
tourism and recreation geography (Gibson 2008;
Hall and Page 2009; Hall 2013a) has come to be recognised as a strength rather than a weakness, allowing
greater engagement in a range of intellectual debates
and business, social and environmental issues.

This book reinforces several of the above themes.
At one level it seeks to highlight the scope, nature
and contribution of geography and geographers to the
study of tourism and recreation. However, at another
it also aims to provide some insights into the nature
of the theoretical transformations which are occurring
in the field. Figure 1.5 provides an overall framework
for many of the key issues discussed in the book. The
figure attempts to illustrate the relationships between
some of the foci of the geography of tourism and recreation, including the opportunity spectrum that
exists in relation to home-based leisure, recreation
and tourism, and corresponding factors of demand
and supply. These are themselves influenced and
mediated by regulatory structures and the institutional arrangements that govern tourism. The impacts
that occur through the intersection of supply and

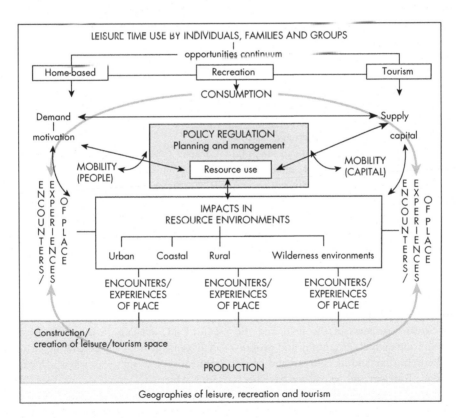

Figure 1.5 Organising framework for the book

demand, consumption and production are located in a range of different environments which each provide separate experiences of place and constructed leisure/tourism spaces.

The following two chapters examine the demand and supply elements of tourism and recreation. Chapter 2 examines how the demand for tourism and recreation is conceptualised and analysed, the concepts developed to derive a focus for research and the implications for a geographical analysis. In Chapter 3, the main techniques and methods of evaluating tourist and recreational resources are discussed as a basis for Chapter 4, and the chapter looks at the interactions of demand and supply variables in relation to the impacts of tourism and recreation. The role of the state and government policy as a determinant of tourist and recreational opportunities is examined, as are issues of access to public and private space for tourists and recreationists.

Chapter 4 examines the differing types of impacts generated by tourist and recreational activities and the way in which different methodologies have been devised to analyse the environmental, socio-cultural and economic impacts. The following four chapters (Chapters 5–8) consider the distinctive nature of tourist and recreational activities in a variety of environmental contexts (urban, rural, wilderness, coastal and ocean areas), emphasising their role in shaping and influencing people's tourist and recreational opportunities, and the effects of such activities on the places in which they occur.

One of the strongest contributions of geography in the tourism and recreation field is in terms of the development of planning and policy analysis. Chapter 9 reviews the need for developing a planning and policy framework at different geographical scales, with particular concern for the different traditions of tourism planning which exist. Chapter 10, the final chapter, examines the future prospects of the field and the potential contributions which geography and geographers may make to understanding tourism and recreation phenomena. Tourism and recreation have been the direct subject of geographical analysis since the late 1920s. In that time methodologies and philosophies have changed, as has the subject matter. Tourism

is now regarded as one of the world's largest industries and is forecast to continue growing in the foreseeable future. Tourism and recreation are complex phenomena with substantial economic, socio-cultural, environmental and political impacts at scales from the global through to the individual. It is now time for geographers not only to develop a deeper understanding of the processes which led to the spatial outcomes of tourism and recreation, but also to convey this understanding to other geographers, students of tourism and recreation, the public and private sectors and the wider communities which are affected by these phenomena.

Further reading

Useful introductions to some of the main approaches to the field of the geography of tourism and recreation include a number of recent reviews of the field, such as:

Bianchi, R. (2009) 'The "critical turn" in tourism studies: a radical critique', *Tourism Geographies*, 11: 484–504.

Gibson, C. (2008) 'Locating geographies of tourism', *Progress in Human Geography*, 32: 407–22.

Gibson, C. (2009) 'Geographies of tourism: critical research on capitalism and local livelihoods', *Progress in Human Geography*, 33: 527–34.

Gibson, C. (2010) 'Geographies of tourism: (un)ethical encounters', *Progress in Human Geography*, 34: 521–7.

Hall, C.M. (2013) 'Framing tourism geography: notes from the underground', *Annals of Tourism Research*, DOI: 10.1016/j.annals.2013.06.007.

Hall, C.M. and Page, S.J. (2009) 'Progress in tourism management: from the geography of tourism to geographies of tourism – a review', *Tourism Management*, 30: 3–16.

There are also a number of edited collections that provide good thematic introductions to various issues and concepts in the geographies of tourism and recreation. See:

Lew, A., Hall, C.M. and Williams, A. (eds) (2014) *The Wiley-Blackwell Companion to Tourism*, Oxford: Wiley-Blackwell Publishers (a large collection of essays on various major research themes and traditions in the geography of tourism as well as the wider tourism literature).

Wilson, J. (ed.) (2012) *The Routledge Handbook of Tourism Geographies*, London: Routledge.

Wilson, J. and Anton Clavé, S. (eds) (2013) *Geographies of Tourism: European Research Perspectives*, London: Emerald.

For recent tourism statistics, see:

United Nations World Tourism Organization (The UN body responsible for tourism): www.unwto.org/

World Travel & Tourism Council (an international organisation of travel industry executives promoting travel and tourism interests worldwide): www.wttc.org/

Questions to discuss

1 **Is geographical knowledge more important than ever? What is its relevance to understanding the contemporary world?**

2 **'This is an interesting time to be a recreational geographer.' Discuss.**

The demand for recreation and tourism

Understanding why human beings engage in recreational and tourism activities is an increasingly important and complex area of research for social scientists. Historically, geographers have played only a limited part in studying the behavioural aspects of recreational and tourists' use of free time (Jackson 1988), tending to have a predisposition towards the analysis of aggregate patterns of demand using quantitative measures and statistical sources as well as novel techniques (e.g. Xiaa *et al*. 2011). In only a few cases have more qualitative approaches been used (e.g. Stokowski 2002) which embody notions of leisure and place, and few studies have developed the behavioural geography advances of the period since the 1970s in human geography and applied them to the subject area.

This almost rigid demarcation of research activity has, with a few exceptions (e.g. Goodall 1990; Mansfeld 1992), meant that behavioural research in recreation and tourism has only since the early 1990s made any impact on the wider research community (see, e.g., Walmsley and Lewis 1993 on the geographer's approach to behavioural research), with notable studies (e.g. Walmsley and Jenkins 1992; Jenkins and Walmsley 1993) applying spatial principles to the analysis of recreational and tourism behaviour. But these remain the exception rather than the norm, given that the 'cultural turn' (see Chapter 1; Wilson 2012) has dominated the production of outputs, with little critical impact on advancing our knowledge of tourism behaviour (Hall and Page 2009). Nevertheless, at least three significant advances can be recognised. First, geographers have begun to identify how the demand for leisure and tourism has resulted in *geographies* of leisure and tourism specific to certain

social, ethnic, gendered and marginalised groups (e.g. disabled people) and the meanings they attach to the spaces they consume in their leisure time, or are unable to consume due to barriers and constraints. As McAvoy's (2002) work demonstrates, there are distinct place meanings attached to the ways that Native American Indians and white Americans value and use leisure resources. The results are a series of leisure and tourism landscapes, socially, culturally and politically constructed for different groups of people (Aitchison *et al*. 2000). Second, work undertaken at the intersection of behavioural and spatial analytical approaches has resulted in new geographies of spatial tracking and geomatics (Shoval and Isaacson 2007; Hall 2012a). Third, studies of the way in which demand for tourism may need to be modified in relation to sustainable consumption strategies and concerns over climate change as they challenge thinking about the logic of sustainability where discretionary travel contributes directly to climate change (Gössling *et al*. 2012c).

Geographers and demand: historical and temporal perspectives

Even historians of tourism and recreation, such as Durie (2003: 1), note: 'There has been in the last few years a major sea change in the literature on tourism'. Quite a number of substantial studies have been published on the history of tourism, many of which have described the evolution of tourism and recreation in different eras, typically as monographs (e.g. Walton 1983, 2009; Gold and Gold 1995; Durie 2003). These types of historical studies have been apparent in the tourism and recreation literature in the English speaking and French literature (e.g. McGibbon 2000; Tissot 2000). Yet geographers are beginning to make a greater contribution to developing the historical analyses of tourism and recreation demand, building on seminal studies such as Towner (1996) which are based upon two important processes of development: continuity in the patterns and nature of demand through time, and contextual changes as the continuity in tourism and leisure phenomena is shaped by evolving social, political, cultural and economic forces within society (Page 2003a). An important transformation in modern societies was observed by Pred (1981) in the way urban industrial society separated the home and production. This led to a spatial and temporal demarcation of leisure and productive activities, as time discipline provided coupling constraints in the nature of leisure consumption, which we will explore in more detail on pp. 65–67. Historical analysis, as Page and Connell (2010) demonstrate, is fundamental to understanding the emergence of tourism and recreation through time, as well as how transformations in different eras of society (e.g. wartime – see Page and Durie 2009) can create distinctive geographies of leisure and tourism.

The interconnection between historical geography and history and the methodologies used to analyse tourism and recreation phenomena remain hugely undervalued in geographical analysis but are frequently referred to, to contextualise the complexity of modern leisure phenomena. This is reinforced by the arguments that the past is the key to the present. Such an approach can also question current assumptions on prevailing interpretations of modern leisure. For example, Bayliss' (2003) study of leisure on two Unwin-designed quasi-rural council estates in outer London in the inter-war period used oral histories and documentary evidence to reconstruct the leisure lives of residents. It illustrates the complexity of generalising about inter-war council estates, which provided over one million homes in the period 1919–39. These estates were often seen by researchers as social failures in the post-war period, being desolate areas devoid of community feelings and spirit. Bayliss (2003) showed the diversity of leisure pursuits in the two contrasting

estates studied, the importance of organisations and social groups in promoting formal and informal leisure, and the ideology and rhetoric of attempts at social control in the physical planning of such estates to create leisure spaces designed to promote the enrichment of life, to educate and promote physical recreation as well as the provision of gardens and allotments. The results were far from indicative of such estates as social failures as oral histories suggest. Bayliss (2003) also illustrated how the inter-war years saw the evolution of home-based forms of leisure demand, as the radio became a commonplace item of mass consumed media, shaping leisure behaviour and social interaction. In contrast, Figure 2.1 depicts community leisure life during the 1920s in an inner city area of the East End of London (not more than five miles from the location described by Bayliss (2003)). In contrast to Bayliss (2003), it is evident time–space compression occurred in leisure and coupling constraints in the East End of London as observed by the anthropological observations by Harris (1927). What Figure 2.1 also identifies is the notion of the home and out-of-home as spatial contexts for leisure, including community-based leisure.

Similarly, Dias and Melo's (2011) analysis of leisure and industrialisation in Brazil illustrates how similar processes of change depicted by Pred (1981) were replicated in a modern setting where later urban industrial development transformed the leisure lives of the urban dwellers. It highlights the importance of understanding the demand for leisure and recreation historically and how changes through time affect the way demand is shaped and conditioned.

The geographers' contribution to demand-based research: an overview

Within the recreational literature, the geographers' contributions have largely been subsumed into social science perspectives, such as sociology, psychology and planning, so that the spatiality and placefulness of their contribution has been implicit rather than explicit. This chapter discusses some of the key behavioural issues associated with recreation and tourism demand and some of the new concepts being

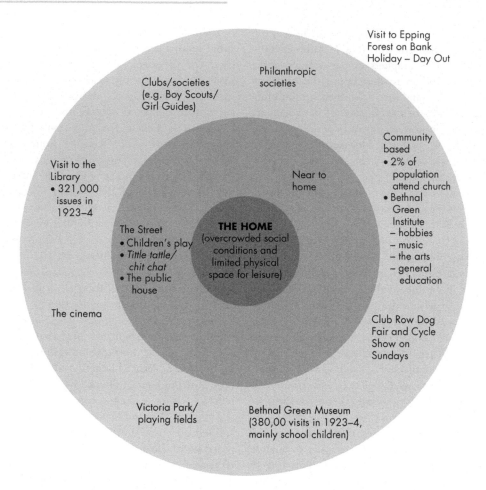

Figure 2.1 Inventory of the supply of leisure in a working class community, Bethnal Green, East London 1925–6

Source: Page and Connell 2010: 203.

used to understand why certain social groups are not able to participate in leisure (i.e. social exclusion) and how this shapes leisure patterns. The spatiality of leisure has been implicit in much of the research on leisure spaces (e.g. Shields 1991; Urry 1995). This discussion is followed by an analysis of the major data sources which researchers use, emphasising how the geographer has used and manipulated them to identify the patterns, processes and implications of such activity. Running parallel to this and perhaps in a supplementary role is the growing volume of qualitative research typically using very small sample sizes,

focusing on highly specialised themes and lacking the generalities of the much larger-scale quantitative research. The challenge for current research is to integrate and blend somewhat polarised views of how to study social science phenomena to understand how human behaviour is conceptualised and analysed. Recent reviews of tourism and leisure within the journal *Progress in Human Geography* have largely accentuated these polarised views and not offered a roadmap or way to develop this agenda more productively.

Within the literature on recreation and tourism, there is a growing unease over the physical separation of the theoretical and conceptual research that isolates behavioural processes and spatial outcomes, and fails to derive generalisations applicable to understanding tourism in totality (see Chapter 1). According to Moore *et al.* (1995: 74) there are common strands in the 'relationships between the various motivating factors applicable to both leisure and tourism'; as Leiper (1990) argued, tourism represents a valued category of leisure, where there is a degree of commonality between the factors motivating both tourist and recreational activities and many of the needs, such as relaxation or being with friends, can equally be fulfilled in a recreational or tourism context (Page and Connell 2010). Although there is some merit in Leiper's (1990) approach, grouping leisure into one amorphous category assumes that there are no undifferentiated attributes which distinguish tourism from leisure. As Pigram and Jenkins (1999: 19) confirm, 'the term recreation demand is generally equated with an individual(s) preferences or desires, whether or not the individual has the economic and other resources necessary for their satisfaction'. In this respect, it is the preference–aspiration–desire level, reflected in behaviour or participation in activities. It is interesting to note that Leiper's (1990) approach has a great deal of validity if one recognises that some tourism motivations may in fact differentiate tourism from leisure experiences, just as the reverse may be true, and that ultimately the particular range of motives associated with a tourism or recreational activity will be unique in each case despite a range of similarities. For this reason, the following examines recreational demand, emphasising many of the explanations commonly advanced in the recreational literature, then discusses the tourism context and the issues raised, bearing in mind the need to compare and contrast each literature base in the light of the seminal arguments advanced by Moore *et al.* (1995) and Leiper (1990).

Recreational demand

Human activity related to recreation and tourism is a function of an individual's or group's willingness or desire to engage in such pursuits. Yet understanding this dimension in recreation and tourism requires a conceptual approach which can rationalise the complex interaction between the desire to undertake leisure activities, however defined, and the opportunities to partake of them. As Coppock and Duffield argued:

> the success of any study of outdoor recreation depends on the synthesis of two contrasting elements: the sociological phenomenon of leisure or . . . that part of leisure time which an individual spends on outdoor recreation [and tourism] and . . . the physical resources that are necessary for the particular recreational activities
>
> (Coppock and Duffield 1975: 2)

Coppock and Duffield acknowledged the need to recognise the interrelationship between human *demand* as participation or a desire to engage in recreation and tourism, and *the supply* of resources, facilities and opportunities which enable such demand to be fulfilled. As Lipscombe (2003) outlined, there are various forms of leisure demand, comprising:

- *effective demand*, sometimes referred to as participation;
- *latent demand*, which is demand that has been constrained for various reasons and could be realised if the variables that restrict participation are removed;
- *future demand*, which may occur if further provision of resources becomes available in future;
- *induced demand*, where latent demand is converted into effective demand where new facilities or resources become available;
- *diverted demand*, which is demand that can be supplanted or displaced by the provision of a new facility whereby the participants move to a new resource or form of provision;
- *substitute demand*, where people may relocate their demand to alternative provision.

(Source: developed from Lipscombe 2003: 106–7; Page and Connell 2010)

The concepts of demand and supply have largely been developed and applied to conventional market economies, where the individual has a choice related to the consumption of recreation and tourism (for a discussion of these issues in non-market economies such as the former Soviet Union, see Vendenin 1978; Shaw 1979; Riordan 1982). As Roberts *et al.* (2001) show, since the 1980s the former Soviet Union (now Russian Federation) has gone from one of the most equal societies to one of the most unequal, but leisure still makes a significant contribution to the Russian quality of life, despite inequalities in leisure provision. In numerous reviews of Soviet geography in the post-war period, the impact and influence of Russian research has been deemed to have had little impact on the development of geography internationally (excluding theoretical debates on Soviet ideology and Marxism). Yet within the field of leisure and recreation there has been a strong tradition of the study of leisure demand and an ongoing interest in leisure phenomena, as various studies attest (Nefedova and Zemlianoi 1997; Tchistiakova and Cabanne 1997; Ioffe and Nefedova 2001; Kruzhalin 2002), as well as wider social science contributions such as Gvozdeva's (1999) study exploring the expansion of women's leisure time in post-communist Russia. Indeed, Koenker (2003) pointed to the transition from a collective tourism experience in Soviet tourism and leisure to a search for more autonomy in the post-reform period. However, Sedova (2011) observed that leisure and free time still command a secondary position in Russian society in juxtaposition to the role of work.

Patmore (1983: 54) acknowledges that 'leisure is far more easily recognised than objectively analysed . . . the difficulties are only in part conceptual: equally important are the nature and limitations of available data', which this section will seek to explain in a recreation context. According to Pigram (1983) there is a general lack of clarity in the use of the term *demand* in the recreational literature. One can distinguish between demand at a generic level, where it refers to an 'individual's preferences or desires, whether or not the individual has the economic or other resources necessary for their satisfaction' (Pigram 1983: 16), reflecting behavioural traits and preference for certain activities. At another level, there are the specific

activities or participation in activities often expressed as visitation rates and measured to reflect the actual observed behaviour. One factor that prevents observed demand equating with participation is the concept of latent demand (the element which is unsatisfied due to a lack of recreational opportunities). Knetsch (1969) identified the mismatch and confusion between participation and demand, arguing that one cannot simply look at what people do and associate it with what people want to do, so ideally any analysis of demand should also consider why people do not participate, and examine ways of overcoming such obstacles by the provision of new resources as well as understanding social and cultural barriers.

Attempting to summarise the factors which influence the decision to participate in recreation led Pigram (1983) to construct Figure 2.2, which highlights the complex range of variables that affect the process. Most research has examined effective demand, which is actual participation, rather than latent demand, and the geographers' contribution has largely been related to the spatial and temporal expression of demand in relation to supply (i.e. demand at specific sites). This is very much resource specific, and dates back to the geographical tradition of resource identification, use and analysis, which can be traced to at least the 1930s. However, Coppock and Duffield (1975) also distinguish between passive recreation and active recreation, thereby beginning to differentiate between different forms of demand. While passive recreation is by far the most important type numerically, it is difficult to study due to its diffuse and often unorganised nature.

As Pigram and Jenkins argued,

In the real world, recreation demand rarely equals participation. The difference between aggregate demand and actual participation (or expressed, effective, observed, revealed demand) is referred to as latent demand or latent participation – the unsatisfied component of demand that would be converted to participation if conditions of supply of recreation opportunities were brought to ideal levels.

(Pigram and Jenkins 2006: 26)

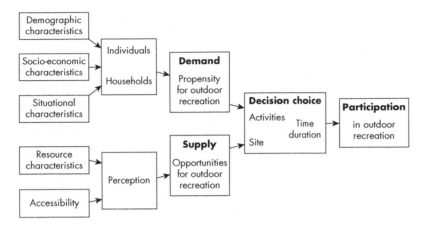

Figure 2.2 The decision-making process in outdoor recreation
Source: Pigram 1983.

But what motivates people to engage in recreational activities?

Argyle (1996) argues that part of the reason why people undertake leisure and recreational activities can be found in the process of socialisation and personality traits, where childhood influences such as parents and peers are forms of social influence and learning that affect future activity choice. In fact, nearly half of adult leisure interests are acquired after childhood, and personality factors influence preferences towards specific forms of recreation. However, understanding the broader psychological factors which motivate individuals to undertake forms of recreation is largely the remit of psychologists, being an intrinsic form of motivation (i.e. something one is not paid to undertake).

A simplistic approach to recreational motivation is to ask recreationalists what actually motivates them. For example, Crandall (1980) outlined 17 factors from leisure motivation research, and among the most frequently cited by other studies of leisure motivation were included enjoying nature and the outdoors, space from everyday routine, exercise, relaxation, contact with other people and spending time with one's family, though Argyle (1996) argues that specific motivations are evident in particular forms of recreation. Torkildsen (1992: 79), however, posits that

homeostasis is a fundamental concept associated with human motivation where people have an underlying desire to maintain a state of internal stability. Human needs, which are 'any lack or deficit within the individual either acquired or physiological' (Morgan and King 1966: 776), disturb the state of homeostasis. At a basic level, human needs have to be met where physiological theory maintained that all human behaviour is motivated. This leads to one of the most commonly cited studies in relation to recreation and tourism motivation – Maslow's hierarchy of human needs.

Maslow's hierarchy model of human needs and recreational and tourist motivation

Within the social psychology literature on recreation and tourism, Maslow's (1954) needs hierarchy remains one of the most frequently cited theories of motivation. It follows the principle of a ranking or hierarchy of individual needs (usually illustrated as in Figure 2.3, although Maslow never used this figure himself), based on the premise that self-actualisation is a level to which people should aspire, although it should be noted that Maslow never actually used such a diagram in his own work. Maslow argued that if the lower

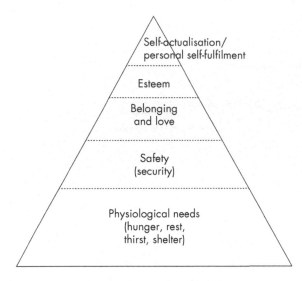

Figure 2.3 Maslow's hierarchy of needs

needs in the hierarchy were not fulfilled they would dominate human behaviour. Once these were satisfied, the individual would be motivated by the needs of the next level of the hierarchy. In the motivation sequence, Maslow identified 'deficiency or tension-reducing motives' and 'inductive or arousal-seeking motives' (Cooper *et al.* 1993: 21), arguing that the model could be applied to work and non-work contexts. Despite Maslow's research shaping much of the recreation and tourism demand work, how and why he selected five basic needs remains unclear, though its universal application in recreation and tourism appears to have a relevance with regard to understanding how human action is related to understandable and predictable aspects of action compared to research which argues that human behaviour is essentially irrational and unpredictable.

While Maslow's model is not necessarily ideal, since needs are not hierarchical in reality because some needs may occur simultaneously, it does emphasise the development needs of humans, with individuals striving towards personal growth. Therefore, Maslow assists in a recreational (and tourism) context in identifying and classifying the types of needs people have. Tillman (1974) summarised some of the broader

leisure needs of individuals within which recreational needs occur, and these may include the pursuit of:

- new experiences (i.e. having an adventure);
- relaxation, escape and fantasy;
- recognition and identity;
- security (being free from thirst, hunger or pain);
- dominance (controlling one's environment);
- response and social interaction (relating and interacting with others);
- mental activity (perceiving and understanding);
- creativity;
- a need to be needed;
- physical activity and fitness.

A different perspective was offered by Bradshaw (1972), who argued that social need is a powerful force, explaining need by classifying it as normative, felt, expressed and comparative need. Mercer (1973), Godbey (1976) and McAvoy (1977) extended Bradshaw's argument within a recreational context, modifying the four categories of need by adding created, changing and false needs. Normative needs are based on value judgements, often made by professionals who establish that what individuals feel is appropriate to the wider population. Felt needs, which individuals may have but not necessarily express, are based on what someone wants to do and are a perceived need. Expressed needs relate to those needs and preferences for existing recreational activities which are often measured but can only be a partial view of demand, since new recreational opportunities may release latent demand. Comparative needs are apparent where existing provision for the general population is compared with special groups (e.g. disabled or elderly people, or ethnic minorities) to establish if existing provision is not fulfilling the needs of the special group. Created needs may result from policy-makers and planners introducing new services or activities which are then taken up by the population. A false need is one that may be created by individuals or society, and which is not essential and may be marginal to wider recreational needs. Changing needs, however, are a recognition of the dynamic nature of human needs, which change through time as individuals develop and their position in the life cycle changes. Thus what is important at one point in the life cycle may change through time as an individual passes through four key stages (Ken and Rapoport 1975):

- youth (school years);
- young adulthood;
- establishment (extended middle age);
- final phase (between the end of work and of life).

Other researchers (e.g. Iso-Ahola 1980; Neulinger 1981) prefer to emphasise the importance of perceived freedom from constraints as a major source of motivation.

Argyle (1996) synthesises such studies to argue that intrinsic motivation in leisure relates to three underlying principles:

- social motivation;
- basic bodily pleasures (e.g. eating, drinking, sex and sport);
- social learning (how past learning explains a predisposition towards certain activities).

One useful concept which Csikszentmihalyi (1975) introduced to the explanation of motivation was that of *flow*. Individuals tend to find a sense of intense absorption in recreational activities, when self-awareness declines, and it is their peak experience – a sense of flow – which is the main internal motivation. The flow is explained as a balance resulting from being challenged and skill which can occur in four combinations:

- where challenge and skill are high, flow results;
- where the challenge is too great, anxiety results;
- if the challenge is too easy, boredom may occur;
- where the challenge and skill level are too low, apathy may result.

But this does not mean that everyone always seeks recreational activities that provide forms of high arousal. Some recreational activities may just fulfil a need to relax, being undemanding and of low arousal.

As Ewert and Hollenhurst (1989) reported, those who engaged in outdoor recreational sports with a high risk factor (e.g. white-water rafting) viewed the sport as providing a flow experience, and the study predicted that as their skill level improved they would increase the level of participation and risk. Yet even though this occurred, the internal motivation of the group remained unchanged, where low and high arousal seem to be juxtaposed. Thus levels of arousal vary from time to time, a factor which can be used by adventure tourism operators to manage the adventure experience and increase the level of satisfaction of participants (Hall and McArthur 1994; Egner 2002; Page *et al.* 2005).

Recreation may also lead to an enhanced self-image, where the identity becomes a basis for motivation because recreational activities can lead to a sense of belonging to a particular and identifiable group. Some activities may also require the development of special skills and enhanced self-esteem. Where recreational activities require a degree of competency, Bandura (1977) proposed that perception of one's ability to perform the skill is a motivator and may result in self-efficacy, a form of self-confidence and judgement of one's ability.

In spite of the significance of motivation, it is apparent that no single theory or even a clear consensus exists in relation to recreation. Instead, 'in theories of motivation need is seen as a force within the individual to gain satisfactions and completeness. There appear to be many levels and types of need, including the important needs of self-actualisation and psychological growth' (Torkildsen 1992: 86). An understanding of needs and intrinsic motivation and some of the ideas implicit in studies of recreational motivation may offer a range of insights into why people engage in recreational activities. However, it is necessary to understand not only why people engage in recreation, but also what factors or barriers may inhibit them from participating. Torkildsen (1992) outlines the influences on leisure participation in terms of three categories: personal, social and circumstantial, and opportunity factors. These influences (Table 2.1) are also of value in understanding some of the constraints on recreation.

Table 2.1 Influences on leisure participation

Personal	Social and circumstantial	Opportunity factors
Age	Occupation	Resources available
Stage in life cycle	Income	Facilities – type and quality
Gender	Disposable income	Awareness
Marital status	Material wealth and goods	Perception of opportunities
Dependants and ages	Car ownership and mobility	Recreation services
Will and purpose in life	Time available	Distribution of facilities
Personal obligations	Duties and obligations	Access and location
Resourcefulness	Home and social environment	Choice of activities
Leisure perceptions	Friends and peer groups	Transport
Attitudes and motivation	Social roles and contacts	Costs: before, during, after
Interests and preoccupations	Environment factors	Management: policy and support
Skill and ability – physical, social and intellectual	Mass leisure factors	Marketing
Personality and confidence	Education and attainment	Programming
Culture born into	Population factors	Organisation and leadership
Upbringing and background	Cultural factors	Social accessibility
	Political factors	Political policies

Source: Torkildsen 1992.

Barriers to recreation

Within the wider literature on recreation and leisure, a specialist research area has developed, focused on constraints, namely those factors, elements or processes which inhibit people from participating in leisure activities. From the diverse range of studies published, two forms of constraint have been identified: intervening constraints, namely those which intervene between a preference and participation, and antecedent constraints, which influence a person's decision not to undertake an activity.

Although the constraints on recreation and leisure literature can be dated to the 1960s, the 1980s saw a range of studies published, a number of which (e.g. Crawford and Godbey 1987; Crawford *et al.* 1991) have set the research agenda in recent years. In the initial formulation, Crawford and Godbey (1987) proposed that constraints were associated with intrapersonal, interpersonal and structural constraints. In the subsequent reformulation of their thinking, Crawford *et al.* (1991) proposed a hierarchical process model, with their three types of constraint integrated. As a consequence of their model, they proposed that:

- participation in leisure is a negotiation process, where a series of factors became aligned in a sequence;

- the order in which constraints occur leads to a 'hierarchy of importance', where intrapersonal constraints are the most powerful in a sequence ending with no structural constraints;
- social class has a strong influence on participation and non-participation, leading to a hierarchy of social privilege, i.e. social stratification is a powerful conditioning factor and may act as a constraint.

This research has provided a framework for further evaluations of constraints (e.g. Samdahl and Jekubovich 1997, and subsequent criticisms by Henderson 1997). In fact, research by Jackson *et al.* (1993) suggested that the real key to understanding leisure constraints was embedded in the negotiation process, namely how an individual will proceed with experiencing an activity even when constraints are apparent. In a fascinating review of poor rural women's leisure experiences in Bangladesh by Khan, it is evident that 'the conventional approach to leisure studies which has a myopic view of leisure as free or non-obligatory time' (Khan 1997: 18) is meaningless due to blurring of boundaries between free or non-work time and obligatory activities which are often cumbersome and all-encompassing in everyday life. At an empirical level, a range of notable studies have highlighted the prevailing constraints to recreation. For example,

Kay and Jackson's (1991) study of 366 British adults' recreational constraints identified:

- 53 per cent who cited money as the main constraint;
- 36 per cent who felt lack of time was the main limitation;
- conflicts with family or work, transportation problems and health concerns as other contributory factors.

Barriers may be negotiable or solvable, as Kay and Jackson (1991) suggest. Patmore (1983) summarises the main physical barriers to recreation in terms of:

- seasonality;
- biological and social constraints;
- money and mobility;
- resources and fashions;

with the availability of time also being a major constraint.

Coppock and Duffield (1975) recognised the principal variations which exist in terms of demand due to variable uses of leisure time budgets by individuals and groups in relation to the day, week and year. Both Coppock and Duffield (1975) and Patmore (1983) used similar data sources, for example the UK's Pilot National Recreation Survey (British Travel Association and University of Keele 1967, 1969) and sociological studies of family behaviour in the pioneering study by Young and Wilmott (1973), to examine time budgets, variations in demand and constraining factors. One of the most important distinctions to make is that 'the weekend thus represents a large increase in the time that can be committed to leisure pursuits, which in turn affects the weekend time budget' (Coppock and Duffield 1975: 14). Yet when one looks beyond the day and week to the individuals and groups concerned, a wider range of influences emerge which are important in explaining recreation patterns.

Argyle (1996: 33) highlights the fact that one of the main reasons for examining constraining and facilitating factors is to understand 'how many people engage in different kinds of leisure, how much time they spend on it, and how this varies between men

and women, young and old, and other groups'. This is because some groups such as

> women, the elderly and unemployed face particular constraints which may affect their ability to engage in leisure and recreational activities which people do because they want to, for their own sake, for fun, entertainment or self-improvement, or for goals of their own choosing, but not for material gain.
>
> (Argyle 1996: 33)

Seasonality

Patmore argued that

> one of the most unyielding of constraints is that imposed by climate, most obviously where outdoor activities are concerned. The rhythms of the seasons affect both the hours of daylight available and the extent to which temperatures are conducive to participant comfort outdoors.
>
> (Patmore 1983: 70)

This is reflected in the seasonality of recreational activity, which inevitably leads to peaks in popular seasons and a lull in less favourable conditions. Patmore (1983) identified a continuum in recreational activities, from those which exhibit a high degree of seasonality to those with a limited degree of variation in participation by season. The first type, which is the most seasonal, includes outdoor activities (often of an informal nature) which are weather dependent. The second, an intermediate group, is transitional in the sense that temperature is not necessarily a deterrent since a degree of discomfort may be experienced by the more hardened participants (e.g. when walking and playing sport). The final group is indoor activities, which can be formal or informal, and have virtually no seasonality. In addition, the physical constraints of season, climate and weather inhibit demand by curtailing the periods of time over which a particular resource can be used for the activity concerned (Patmore 1983: 72), although resource substitution (e.g. using a human-made ski slope instead of a snowclad one) may assist in some contexts, but often the human-made resource cannot offer the same degree of excitement or enjoyment.

Financial resources and access to recreational opportunity

Argyle (1996) observed that while many studies emphasised lack of money as a barrier to engaging in recreational activities, Coalter (1993) found that it had little impact on participation in sports. In fact, Kay and Jackson (1991) also acknowledged that money or disposable income was a barrier to undertaking activities which were major consumers of money (drinking and eating socially) whereas it had little impact on sport, which was comparatively cheap. Bittman (2002) noted in Australia that the results of a time use survey highlighted that time to participate in leisure was determined by hours of employment, family responsibilities and gender. The research found that household income had no significant impact on available leisure time. Income, occupation and access to a car combined have a significant impact on participation (see also Hall 2010a).

As Page (2009a: 1) argues, 'Our desire to travel is underpinned by three distinct methods of human transport: self-propelled modes (e.g. walking); augmented modes (using technology or tools to amplify our bodily effort such as skiing); and fuelled modes (especially motorised transport) as outlined by Stradling and Anable (2008)'. These modes have shaped the spatial occurrence of leisure and recreation (as well as tourism activity). Above all, it is the car which has provided the greatest degree of personal mobility and access to a wider range of recreational opportunities in time and space since the 1960s in many developed countries (and earlier in some cases such as the USA and Canada).

The issue of accessibility and financial resources also raises issues of social inclusion, which are dealt with more fully below. However, as Mather (2003) observed, participation in outdoor recreation (as opposed to leisure per se) is closely correlated with socio-economic status and affluence, which posits that lower socio-economic groups have a lower participation rate, due to constraints such as a lack of

supply and limitations from financial resources. In a rural context, Slee (2002) noted that in a survey of visits to the countryside in 1998, among the 17 per cent of the sample respondents who did not visit, no interest and no appeal were key reasons for not visiting rather than financial reasons. Therefore, arguments that supply should be increased to meet perceived demand due to constraints may not necessarily be valid. Mather (2003) debates the implications of legislation in England and Wales (the Countryside and Rights of Way Act 2000) and Scotland (the Land Reform (Scotland) Act 2003) which extended the legal basis and public access to land more widely. Some of the complex arguments associated with these new approaches to making recreational access to land more widely available relate to health goals, for promoting exercise, reflected in the growth of footpaths and walking. Even so, Mather (2003) suggests that the opening of land for recreation will not lead to massive increase in recreational activity.

Gender and social constraints

The influence of gender on recreation remains a powerful factor influencing participation, a feature consistently emphasised in national surveys of recreational demand. As Argyle argues,

> there is an influential theory about this topic, due to a number of feminist writers, that women have very little or no leisure, because of the demands of domestic work and the barriers due to husbands who want them at home . . . [and] that leisure is a concept which applies to men, if it is regarded as a reaction to or contrast with paid work.
>
> (Argyle 1996: 44; see also Deem 1986)

Thus women with children appear to have less time for recreation, while those in full- and part-time employment have less time available than their male counterparts (Argyle 1996). These general statements find a high degree of support within the recreational literature, with gender differences in part explained by the male free time occurring in larger blocks and in prime time (e.g. evenings and weekends) (Pigram 1983). Even so, studies by Talbot (1979) explore this theme in more detail. Recent analyses informed by cultural geography have suggested that different types of body with gendered, classed, aged and sexed meanings may encourage or discourage an individual's participation in specific forms of leisure. In other words, it illustrates the importance of theorising the setting for leisure as spaces which individuals engage in through both body and mind (Mowl and Towner 1995; Scraton *et al*. 1998). In terms of sexed meanings, Pritchard *et al*. (2002) examined the example of Manchester's gay village as one such setting.

Age also exerts a strong influence on participation in recreation, with Hendry *et al*. (1993) describing adolescence as the peak time of leisure needs. Therein lie two key explanations of participation and constraints. However, there is a growing body of evidence on ageing and leisure that contests these notions and assumptions (Mansvelt 2005). Stages in the life course present a useful concept to explain why women with young children appear to have fewer opportunities for recreation than adolescents. Likewise, physical vigour and social energy are traditionally explained in terms of a decline in the later stages of adulthood resulting in a decline in active recreation throughout later life, but there is also a need to consider the significance of the life cycle in relation to changes or 'triggers' (Patmore 1983), illustrated by recent studies of ageing and leisure such as that by Pereira (2008) and the analysis of the leisure habits of specific age groups. One such trigger is retirement, and while it is sometimes interpreted as a stressful life event, what Argyle (1996: 63) emphasises from studies of retirement is that 'people carry on with the same leisure as before, though they are more passive and more house-bound, and do not take up much new leisure'. Interestingly the growing international interest in the onset of dementia and its rise as a global health issue amongst the aged has seen a rise in leisure research that has started to assess the positive benefits of leisure and recreation (e.g. Schreiner *et al*. 2005) in slowing down onset/progress through active lifestyles. But active interests in leisure participation may be affected by barriers, as the next section illustrates.

The geography of fear in recreation and leisure spaces: gender-based barriers to participation

Since the 1980s, there has been a growing interest in the role of fear, personal safety and the spatial implications in the urban environment (e.g. Fyfe and Banister 1996; Koskela and Pain 2000; England and Simon 2010; Abrahamsson and Simpson 2011). There has also been an accompanying interest in the gender dimensions of personal safety (Smith 1987a; Valentine 1989), which has important implications within an urban environment in relation to the use of public leisure resources such as open space and urban parks (Beebeejaun 2009). For example, in the context of Bolivia, Wright Wendel *et al*. (2012) point to the gender inequalities and use of urban parks and open space. In fact, the concern with such issues may be traced to the changes in the discipline of geography 'and transformative developments both resulting from, and contributing to, a number of new and competing philosophies with the social sciences' (Aitchison 1999: 20), although as noted in Chapter 1 such concerns with relevant social research have been a theme in geography since at least the late 1960s. In relation to leisure and recreation geography, this transformation effect can be related to the concern with gender relations and theoretical perspectives associated with the new cultural geography as a mechanism to conceptualise and theorise leisure space. One of the central tenets of this approach is embodied in Green *et al*.'s (1990: 311) comment where 'A significant aspect of the social control of women's leisure is the regulation of their access to public places, and their behaviour in such places'. These perspectives have only recently begun to emerge in tourism geography (Crouch 2000), where empirical approaches to personal safety have paid little attention to gender and public places.

In conceptual terms, the analysis of the geography of fear, particularly the implications for gender, is a good illustration of the participation issues for particular groups of women. The application of this perspective to recreational and leisure spaces in the city reveals the male domination of public leisure space (Aitchison 1999). The new cultural geographies have seen some leisure and recreational geographers move away, albeit slowly, from a positivist paradigm and the model building era as new perspectives were conceptualised and theorised as well as identifying the implications for new groups where fear is an issue, such as older children (e.g. Bromley and Stacey 2012). The rise of feminist perspectives in leisure studies by geographers is also a notable development (e.g. Talbot 1979; Deem 1986; Green *et al.* 1987).

One of the principal problems with the emergence of a new cultural geography is epitomised in Shurmer-Smith and Hannam's (1994: 13) comments: 'Place is a deceptively simple concept in geographical thought. We want to make it difficult, uneasy.' Criticisms of this perspective by Hamnett dispute the value of such approaches by geographers who

> simply treat theory and concepts as a sort of intellectual game which has become increasingly detached from real world problems and concerns . . . Under the guise of liberation, empowerment and giving voice to those hitherto excluded, [this trend] simply reinforces the privileges of the intellectual elite to play an elaborate language game written by and for a tiny minority of participants
> (Hamnett 2001: 160–1)

Herein lie many of the criticisms of the new cultural geography: one must have a sound grounding in social theory, cultural studies and a knowledge of the new terms underpinning the debates. One consequence is that

> the new cultural geography as it has been referred to since the early 1990s demonstrates that space, place and landscape – including landscapes of leisure and tourism – are not fixed but are in a constant state of transition as a result of continuous, dialectical struggles of power and resistance among and between the diversity of landscape providers, users and mediators.
> (Aitchison 1999: 29)

This means that the focus is on agency rather than structure, criticising earlier geographical studies of leisure and recreation which did not problematise space or recognise the human element in the landscape. This perspective – and one has to recognise it is only one perspective in geographical research – emphasises the diversity, differences and nuances in cultural phenomena, which is the antithesis of logical positivist geographical thought, which searches for certainty, coherence and generalisations in relation to patterns, forms and processes of spatial phenomena. As a consequence the new interest in leisure and tourism as cultural phenomena in the

> post-positivist geography [is such] that the new cultural geography has emerged and become merged with sociological and cultural studies analyses which are now combining to investigate the multiplicity of behaviours, meanings, consumption trends and identities constructed in and through leisure and tourism.
> (Aitchison 1999: 30)

Box 2.1 focuses on the sexuality dimension. Given the growing interest in feminism within the leisure constraints literature (e.g. Henderson 1997) and the concern with constraints to participation (e.g. Jackson 1994), it is timely to focus on the issue of fear.

Social exclusion: conditioning leisure participation

Box 2.1, the constraints on participation derived from fear, highlights societal constraints on leisure participation – social exclusion. Byrne (1999) traces the emergence of this new phrase in political terms, which is used to explain how changes in the whole of society affect particular people and groups. This is indicative of systematic problems in the structure of society, which determines the lives of certain groups. This has superseded earlier arguments and explanations of poverty related to an underclass (see Page 1988), replacing simpler notions of poverty. Poverty has been viewed as an absence of resources, notably income, as a factor conditioning participation in society. Exclusion, in contrast, is a more dynamic

BOX 2.1   THE GEOGRAPHY OF FEAR AND RECREATIONAL PARTICIPATION IMPLICATIONS FOR EXCLUSION

Urban parks are estimated to be used by 40 per cent of the British population (Garner 1996) on a regular basis, but critics argue that urban parks as a recreational resource are being avoided by the general public (Vidal 1994). This is particularly acute for certain groups of the population (e.g. women, children and ethnic groups), where fear acts as a constraint on use. As Ravenscroft and Markwell (2000) point out, the accessibility of parks to ethnic young people is notable, if they are properly maintained and managed. This is reiterated by Gobster (2002) in the USA, while notions of environmental justice and leisure resources emerge from such discussions (Floyd and Johnson 2002), where certain groups are able to use or prohibited from using such resources. In fact Woolley and Ul-Amin's (1999) study of Pakistani teenagers' use of public open space in Sheffield considered the diverse passive and active uses made of these spaces. This adds a new dimension to the recreational constraints literature compounded by a declining investment in measures to make these spaces safe to use.

In the 1990s there was a growing body of evidence urban parks were not perceived as peaceful sanctuaries for recreational and leisure pursuits among the wider population. Burgess et al. (1988a) documented the dimensions of fear which included antisocial behaviour among teenagers and vandalism that reduced local enjoyment and participation. Similar concerns of insecurity, fear and use of parks and open spaces have also been evident in reviews of the park literature (e.g. Byrne and Wolch 2009). Research also shows how women, black people, elderly people and the gay community may be excluded from using urban space as freely as other subgroups of the population (Adler and Brenner 1992; Maitland 1992). As Burgess et al. (1988a: 472) remarked 'many people expressed feelings of insecurity and vulnerability in open spaces, reflecting fears of personal attack and injury. Among the Asian community, these feelings are exacerbated by the growing incidence of racially motivated attacks in public open spaces.' The outcome, as Madge (1997: 238) recognised, was that 'This fear, which reflects structural inequalities in society, is translated into spatial behaviour which usually involves a reluctance to occupy certain public spaces at certain times of the day'. For the geographer, it is the spatial manifestation of that fear and its implications for recreational resource use that are significant (Page et al. 1994).

The geography of fear and urban park use in Leicester

Leicester, located in the English East Midlands, is a medium-sized city of around 270,000 people, which is 73.09 km^2 in spatial extent. What is notable is its diverse ethnic mix: 72 per cent of the population are white, 24 per cent are Asian, 2 per cent African Caribbean, 2 per cent Chinese and other 'ethnic groups'. Despite the city's urban-industrial development (see Pritchard 1976; Page 1988), it is widely acknowledged that the city has an enviable distribution of public open space (i.e. over 1,200 ha of open space, which comprised 20 per cent of the total city area). This is a significant level of provision within an international context, and certainly enhances the city's green and open feel. Madge (1997) identified 10 main constraints which influenced park use. In order of importance they were: fear, weather, lack of time due to work, family constraints, lack of transport, lack of interest, limited awareness of facilities available, housework, distance of parks/too far away, physically unable to get to the parks. Some 43 per cent of respondents said fear was a 'very important' factor constraining their use of parks. The gender difference was striking, with 75 per cent of women compared to 50 per cent of men stating fear was a major constraint on park use. This is in line with Westover's (1985) finding in North America, where 90 per cent of female respondents felt unsafe if alone in parks. Studies of victimisation in Leicester (e.g. Willis 1992) recognise that women have a greater sense of insecurity due to their vulnerability to crime.

When ethnicity was examined, Asian groups expressed higher levels of fear compared with white and African Caribbean groups, reflecting victimisation statistics on racial abuse and attacks in the urban environment. In terms of age, those aged over 45 years of age expressed the greatest levels of fear. As Madge (1997: 241) rightly acknowledged, 'The result of fear of crime is, however, concrete: the elderly are less likely to use public parks for recreation'.

In terms of causes of fear, Madge (1997) observed that the main causes of fear of park use were anxieties related to actual or potential bodily harm (e.g. mugging, sexual attack, loitering people, gangs of youths, dogs and racial attack). Women's fears were greatest in relation to fear of sexual attack by men. These findings reflected the prevailing levels of fear of sexual violence which women in Leicester harbour, particularly the high level of sexual harassment. In fact 77 per cent of female respondents were fearful of sexual attacks in parks, a much higher figure than in similar surveys in Edinburgh (Anderson *et al.* 1990) and Seattle (Warr 1985). Fear of racial attack was also much higher for African Caribbean and Asian groups than for white groups.

The implications of these findings are reflected in behaviour and the use of parks. Women tended to avoid large open spaces, unlit areas and those areas with dense undergrowth and trees. The onset of nightfall also elevated fear of using such places, especially if they were alone. As Madge suggested:

Fear is a significant factor structuring the use of public parks in Leicester. The intensity and cause of fear varied with social traits of gender, ethnicity and age and affected spatial behaviour regarding use of parks. The geography of fear is mediated through a set of overlapping social, ideological and structural power relations which become translated into spatial behaviour.

(Madge 1997: 245)

Although Madge (1997) criticises the existing recreational literature for neglecting this issue, fear is a more profound issue in urban environments. Koskela and Pain (2000) point to the problems and failures of designing out fear from the urban environment, given the extent to which fear of crime pervades city spaces. In a review of surveillance Lyon (2007) recognised the growth in the surveillance of public spaces to improve security, which could lead to a return to private spaces and attempts to modify social behaviour in recreational spaces. This is a feature which Giddens (1990: 20) recognised, whereby 'surveillance is a means of levering the modern social world away from traditional modes of social activity'. In a wider context, Button (2003: 227) noted that 'during the post-war period there has been a growth in what has been termed "mass private property" encompassing large shopping malls, leisure facilities, gated communities, airports . . . These facilities, which are usually private but freely open to the public, have created new debates concerning . . . what is termed "quasi-public" or "hybrid" space. The result is that public access to these spaces is at the discretion of the landowner.' Critiques of such spaces for leisure (e.g. Uzzell 1995) illustrate that even private spaces, such as malls, provide social places and spaces which meet many psychological needs and preferences, particularly in terms of leisure consumption. This space is controlled, replacing a former communal culture and public spaces which met many informal needs for leisure like parks and open spaces. These mall spaces have been seen as leading to a sense of placelessness (Relph 1976), as they do not develop a relationship with the place/space for leisure. Therefore, highly managed and secure areas like malls may reduce the perception of fear, but conversely these privately managed spaces will detract from people developing a positive relationship with the space, that people do with urban open spaces.

Indeed, Koskela and Pain (2000: 279) argued that 'Geographers and planners should take greater account of the complexity of fear . . . Places have some influence on fear, but perhaps of equal or greater significance is the ways in which fear shapes our understanding, perception and use of space and place.' This is certainly a truism in the case of recreational use of urban parks in Madge's (1997) findings, which have a wider application to urban recreational resource use in the developed world. A great deal of progress will need to be made in addressing fear of crime and recreational and leisure spaces in urbanised societies before Koskela and Pain's (2000: 274) analysis that 'Green urban spaces and woodlands are commonly perceived as dangerous places and feelings of insecurity often have a deterrent effect on women's use of them' is no longer a valid assessment. Yet simply providing synthetic and artificially created leisure spaces such as malls as a substitute will not meet such informal leisure needs, since many private leisure spaces within cities are highly designed environments connected with and motivated by consumption, which by their very nature may also exclude some groups who are unable to access the resources to be consumers.

concept which implies that people are shut out (fully or partially) from the systems in society that allow full integration and participation in society. In political terms, exclusion may also be seen as denying the rights of individuals as citizens. In a post-industrial society, theoretical explanations of exclusion are attributed to the changing nature of work in society, increased insecurity in employment, a growing service sector and reconstructed welfare state systems to reduce public expenditure, where ethnic origin may also be a further factor contributing to exclusion and access to goods and services. For example, in the USA the National Poverty Centre points to the changing geography of exclusion arising from a rise in the numbers of people in poverty since 2000, now around 15 per cent of households. An added dimension recognised is the high numbers in poverty segregated from the non-poor in inner city neighbourhoods along with the rise of rural poor among ethnic groups moving to rural localities. In the UK, around 13.5 million of the population are living on low incomes.

Consequently, social exclusion is a multifaceted process, like poverty, but embodies exclusion from participation in decision-making that allows access to the means of being a citizen, employment, and engagement in the social and cultural processes which the majority of citizens have access to. In geographical terms, such exclusion has been characterised by its concentration in particular neighbourhoods (e.g. areas of multiple deprivation). Multiple deprivation has been mapped by geographers to identify the intersection of poverty and other social conditions (e.g. poverty, unemployment, poor housing conditions and education, high levels of crime and poor health), thereby creating a distinct geography of exclusion. As Sletten (2010) observed in a study of Norwegian 13–16 year olds living in poor families, this led to the loss of leisure opportunities and growing social isolation, which is a dimension of exclusion and leisure. Social well-being is, according to Rodgers (1993: 126), 'a strong influence on both the volume and structure of leisure demand and on the relative roles of public and commercial provision in meeting it'.

Using the Department of the Environment (DoE) Social Deprivation Index (for a discussion of deprivation indices, see Page 1988), which derives negative indices based on unemployment, overcrowding, single-parent and pension households, housing quality and ethnic origin, Rodgers (1993) ranked the districts in the North West of England on this composite measure of social stress and also included levels of car ownership. The results were used to identify a range of geographically based leisure markets which were strong or weak in terms of demand, particularly in relation to their capacity to pay for recreational activities in a market-driven local leisure economy.

Not surprisingly, government agencies concerned with leisure (e.g. the Department for Culture, Media and Sport in the UK) have turned to new ideologies such as the government's shift towards communities and third sector bodies to realise ambitions for a Big Society to target groups at risk of social exclusion in terms of tourism, leisure and sport. The *Count Me In* report (Long 2002) identified the contribution which leisure could make to social inclusion through sports, arts, media, heritage and outdoor activities by increased involvement of social groups at risk of exclusion (e.g. unemployed people, older people and women) through personal development (e.g. self-esteem, interpersonal skills and relationship building), social cohesion (civic pride, celebrating one's own culture and relationship building with other cultural and social groups) and in promoting active citizenship, through taking greater responsibility and in exercising one's rights as well as promoting human potential. In fact recent developments in time geography (McQuaid and Dijst 2012) argue for a greater integration of time–space and experiences of poverty to address the understanding of exclusion. But the problem with these debates, as Cameron (2006) argues, is the difficulty of using the term exclusion (and conversely inclusion as the antithesis of exclusion) because of the way it fails to highlight who is affected and what action is needed to remove the often structural constraints that create conditions of exclusion amongst different sections of society. In geographical terms this has led to a preoccupation with localism in the spatial understanding of geographies of exclusion.

Resources and fashions

Traditional models of participation and obstacles to recreation have attempted to predict the probability of people participating in activities, using variables such as age, sex, marital status and social variables (e.g. housing tenure, income and car ownership), but predictions decline in accuracy when attempting to identify individual activities (e.g. golf). What such recreational models often fail to acknowledge is the role of choice and preference given a range of options. In this respect, geographical proximity to recreational resources and access to them is a major determinant. This is demonstrated by Burton (1971), who found that in Britain people were three times as likely to use a recreational resource if they lived between half and three-quarters of a mile away, a feature emphasised by Patmore (1983) and Page et al. (1994) in research on urban parks. Veal (1987) expressed this using classic distance-decay theory, reproduced in Figure 2.4 (see also Baxter 1979; Greer and Wall 1979; Chavas et al. 1989; McKercher and Lew 2003; Hall 2005a, 2006a; Lew and McKercher 2006). This shows that the proximity to a recreational resource increased the propensity for use at a swimming pool, yet for leisure centres where people used cars to visit them, the distance-decay function had a less rapid decline in attendance in relation to distance. Outside urban areas, the occurrence of recreational resources is more varied in its spatial distribution, and recreational opportunities need to be closely examined in relation to demand and supply. More recently, Colwell et al. (2002) examined the influence of recreation demand on residential location. Their research argued that consumers may live in areas according to their preference for recreational activities, and the trade-offs in terms of wages, location to live and recreation. What they also point to is the significance of second home ownership in areas of recreation preference. However, even here distance plays a major factor in recreational decision-making (Hall and Müller 2004).

In the Swedish case Jansson and Müller (2003) demonstrated that 25 per cent of all second home owners have their property within 14 km of their primary residence, 50 per cent less than 37 km from

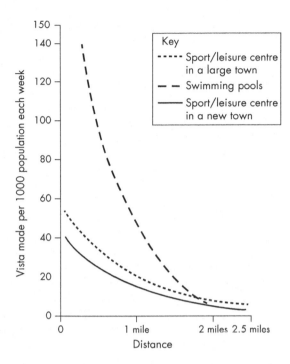

Figure 2.4 The impact of distance and geographical catchment areas on the provision of leisure facilities

Source: based on Veal 1987.

their property, and 75 per cent less than 98 km. The time sensitivity of leisure travel means that the location of overnight stays from a generating region tends to cluster at a location related to time/distance from a point of origin (Hall 2005a, 2005b). This means that second home ownership outside the weekend leisure zone is relatively independent of the location of the primary residence; the second home is visited once or twice annually. However, second home location is not dependent solely on travel times. Instead, second home locations are also influenced by the geography of amenity rich landscapes that concentrates the geographical patterns of at least purpose-built second homes in coastal and mountain areas. Furthermore, fashions and tastes can act as a powerful influence on demand, as the following example of walking suggests.

Walking as a leisure pursuit: a function of resources and fashion

Walking is a human necessity for able-bodied people to achieve mobility, to engage in work, social activities and non-work functions. Although the industrial and post-industrial period has seen a move towards more mechanised forms of transport such as the car, giving people a greater spatial reach and flexibility in travel patterns, walking remains a key activity in everyday life and as a leisure activity. As Short (1991: 4) noted, 'Walking has created roads, trade routes; generated local and cross-continental senses of place; shaped cities; parks; generated maps . . . This history of walking is an amateur history, just as walking is an amateur act.' The desire to walk as a leisure pursuit is the result of history over the last 300 years and according to Short (1991) is based on specific beliefs, tastes and values. Prior to the eighteenth century, walking for pleasure was the pastime of a leisured elite, many of whom resided in mansions, castles and palaces and who walked within the confines of corridors or enclosed garden spaces, many of which were formally designed. The eighteenth and nineteenth centuries saw the rise of Romantic notions of nature through the writing of Wordsworth in the Lake District (such as the 1807 *Poems in Two Volumes*) and of other Romantic poets, where the taste for the natural, long-distance walks, admiring natural features and the associated landscaping of country house estates in the natural style of landscape designers such as Capability Brown, created environments with opportunities for views, solitude, natural surroundings and the removal of traditional designs with geometric layouts (see also Chapter 7 and the implications of this for perceptions of wilderness and the natural environment). De Botton (2003: 138) argues that Wordsworth's poetry led to 'regular travel through nature as a necessary antidote to the evils of the city'. The significance of such surroundings for pleasure walking was also extolled in Jane Austen's novels, where escapism from house-based social groups and gatherings could allow leisurely strolls. Such virtues gradually permeated the evolving middle classes in the urban industrial cities of the western world in the nineteenth century (see Chapter 5) and eventually the working classes, as more leisure time was made available after the 1850s.

The provision of urban parks and other spaces for walking allowed for formal walks or promenading on Sunday afternoons, which was governed by social rules and norms. This also manifests itself in the day trips to the coast, with formal areas provided for promenading for the Victorians and Edwardians at leisure. Gradually, walking clubs and organised groups emerged which saw the spatial extent and dispersion of leisure walking as rambling (British term), bushwalking (Australia) and tramping (New Zealand) evolve into popular culture and an important factor in gaining increased access to the countryside and the creation of parks, reserves and walkways (see Box 2.2 on the New South Wales bushwalking movement and the creation of national parks in Australia).

The pursuit of walking as a leisure activity in the urban environment in the twenty-first century has seen a significant transformation, as Short argues:

Walking is about being outside, in public space, and public space is also being abandoned and eroded in older cities, eclipsed by technologies and services that don't require leaving home, and shadowed by fear in many places . . . In many new places, public space isn't even in the design: what was once public space is designed to accommodate the privacy of automobiles; malls replace main streets, streets have no sidewalks; buildings are entered through their garages . . . Fear has created a whole style of architecture and urban design, notably in Southern California, where to be a pedestrian is to be under suspicion in many of the subdivisions and gated communities.

(Short 1991: 10)

BOX 2.2 MYLES DUNPHY AND THE AUSTRALIAN BUSHWALKING MOVEMENT

Myles Dunphy has been described as the 'father of conservation in New South Wales' (Barnes and Wells 1985: 7). Dunphy was born in Melbourne in 1891, the eldest child of an Irish father and a Tasmanian mother. The family moved to Sydney in 1907 but because of the economic pressures in a large family, Dunphy left school early to join the workforce as a draughtsman, a career that would stand him in good stead to influence the public's appreciation of wilderness through high quality maps and drawings (Thompson 1986). Although not a follower of organised religion, Dunphy did appreciate the spiritual significance of wilderness. Thompson (1985: 26–7), on studying an old notebook of Dunphy, observed that Dunphy had scribbled, 'For a knowledge of God, study nature', lines reminiscent of the Romantic ecological writings of John Muir (Hall 1992a).

Dunphy's central importance in any account of the development of parks in Australia lies in his contribution to the development of the bushwalking movement. Along with friends Herbert Gallop and Roy Rudder, Dunphy formed the Mountain Trails Club in October 1914 (Dunphy 1979b: 55). As revised in 1924, the objects of the club combined an aim 'to reach and enjoy the canyons, ranges and tops of the wildest parts of this country' with an intention to 'establish a definite regard for the welfare and preservation of the wildlife and natural beauties' (Prineas and Gold 1983: 29). According to Dunphy (1979a), the Mountain Trails Club 'had become a kind of bush brotherhood . . . They liked to travel quietly and see wildlife. It was good to boil the billy in the welcome shade of river oaks harping in the breeze to watch wood smoke drift down the reach, and the bars where the stream purled over the lapstones' (Dunphy 1979a: 30).

The 'Trailers', as they were known, eschewed 'the roads of the crowd' and practised 'a kind of religion [of] mateship, self-reliance, endurance, protection of wildlife and bushland . . . a way of life close to the manifestations, beauties and outstanding miracles of nature' (Dunphy 1973, in Bardwell 1979: 16). The fervent espousal of the Australian tradition of mateship was well reflected in the club's refusal to admit women to its ranks and in membership being by invitation only; although this strategy was recognised as being flawed in assisting the club to be open to wider conservation and bushwalking interests (Dunphy 1973: 3). Nevertheless, the Mountain Trails Club played a major regional role in developing an ethic of nature appreciation and walking experiences in New South Wales comparable to that of the Appalachian Mountain Club in the eastern United States (Manning 1985) and the Sierra Club in the west (Duncan and Burns 2009).

The Romantic notion of wilderness and the belief that contact with nature was beneficial were not isolated to the Mountain Trails Club and reflected broader changes in society with respect to mental and physical health and outdoor recreation. In response to letters from Mr J. Debbit in the *Sun* newspaper advocating the formation of a 'hikers' club', a Miss Jess Scott wrote that 'with the approach of spring the beauties of the countryside seem to lift their voices appealingly to the "hiker", calling him to view their unadorned splendour'. However, pressures on the Mountain Trails Club to provide information on walking tours helped lead to the formation of a new bushwalking club (Dunphy 1973: 3), although 'its members would not damage their bush brotherhood' and decided to 'render a public service by forming a new walking club with an easy constitution and easy conditions of membership, with the definite object of being a recreational walkers' club, purely and simply, and open to members of both sexes' (Dunphy 1973: 4).

Initially called the Waratah Walking Club, the new club changed its name to the Sydney Bush Walkers at its second meeting on 8 December 1927 (Dunphy 1973: 5). The new walking club had an important part to play in the evolution of an appreciation of wild country as it enabled many people, both men and women, to become involved in an organisation which consciously supported the idea of nature conservation. The establishment of the Sydney Bush Walkers also served as the catalyst for the creation of several other clubs, notably the Bush Tracks Club and the Coast and Mountain Walkers. In 1932 the walking clubs combined to form the New South Wales Federation of Bushwalking Clubs. However, also of significance was the bushwalkers' contribution to the establishment of the National Parks and Primitive Areas Council (NPPAC) in the same year, with Myles Dunphy as secretary.

Among its objectives the NPPAC was concerned with advocacy of 'the protection of existing tracks, paths and trails in use, particularly those having scenic and historical interests and values' (Dunphy 1973: 7–8, in Bardwell 1979: 17). Although the council viewed wilderness from a recreational perspective (see Chapter 7), the NPPAC was extremely concerned with preserving wilderness in a similar fashion to the United States. Indeed, the NPPAC, along with Myles Dunphy, was strongly influenced by American conservation initiatives (Hall 1992a). In 1932 Dunphy obtained a supply of booklets on American national parks which served to promote the national park idea in Australia and the establishment of parks and natural walking areas.

Upon its creation the NPPAC focused upon the preservation of two primitive areas – the Blue Mountains and the Snowy-Indi area – both regions of major personal concern to Myles Dunphy. Dunphy had first put forward the idea of a national park to protect the Blue Mountains wilderness areas as early as 1922 when a park proposal was discussed and adopted by the Mountain Trails Club (Prineas 1976–7; Dunphy 1979b). However, even at this stage Dunphy (quoted in Colley 1984: 29) recalled it had taken '10 years or so to appreciate all the damaging forces at work in this country and to become aware of the need to protect it'. In 1927 the proposal was adopted by the Sydney Bush Walkers (Dunphy 1979b), yet it was not until the 1930s that a major campaign for a Blue Mountains park got underway.

In 1931 the Mountain Trails Club, the Sydney Bush Walkers and the Wildlife Preservation Society joined forces and bought a 40-acre lease to prevent the ringbarking of a Blue Gum forest on the Grose River. The romantic nature of the bushwalkers who helped save the Blue Gums is indicated in the reflections of the poet Roland Robinson on the Grose River area:

> No Greek temple, no Gothic cathedral could have been so bountiful. Here we set up our tents, and here the possums came down out of the trees with their babies on their backs to be fed by us. Because today the vulgar and ignorant 'Yankee Australians' will destroy anything in order to make a fast buck, this is one place that, thanks to the bushwalkers, is preserved in its primal Aboriginal state.
>
> (Robinson 1973: 163)

The preservation of the Grose River Blue Gums provided a basis for the NPPAC on which to campaign for further reservations in the Blue Mountains. The NPPAC's Greater Blue Mountains National Park Scheme probably represented the first major attempt of an Australian conservation group to mobilise mass support for the preservation of wilderness. On 24 August 1934, the NPPAC paid for a four-page supplement, complete with maps and photographs, to be included in the *Katoomba Daily*. The supplement was highlighted by Myles Dunphy's map of a proposed Blue Mountains National Park with 'primitive areas':

> The Blue Mountains of Australia are justly famous for their grand scenery of stupendous canyons and gorges, mountain parks and plateaux up to 4400 feet altitude, uncounted thousands of ferny, forested dells and gauzy waterfalls, diversified forest and river beauty, much aloof wilderness – and towns and tourist resorts replete with every convenience for the comfort and entertainment of both Australian and overseas visitors.
>
> (*Katoomba Daily*, 24 August 1934)

That the supplement attempted to link the scenic attractions of the area with tourism is hardly surprising. Australia was then in the grips of a depression and linking preservation and walking with positive economic benefits was a logical ploy. However, it is also interesting to note that in 1934 the NPPAC argued that the sandstone country of the Blue Mountains 'is potentially desert land', thereby reinforcing the 'worthless' lands concept of wilderness (see Chapter 7). Dunphy (1979a: 30) himself noted that 'the great Blue Mountains barrier region providentially was rugged and unproductive in general'. Yet the NPPAC also put forward in 1934 some positive values of wilderness, noting the necessity of providing for wilderness within regional planning in order to prevent stream erosion and land degradation. Otherwise, 'a rocky, useless and repulsive region unsuitable for either forestry, water conservation, residential, recreation, stock-raising, or other useful purposes will be created'. Despite the appeal to the values of 'progressive' conservation the main thrust of the supplement undoubtedly relied on the aesthetic, health and spiritual aspects of outdoor recreational experiences. However, no action was taken on the park proposal until 25 September 1959, when the Blue Mountains National Park of 62,000 ha in the central Blue Mountains was gazetted. The area is now part of the Blue Mountains World Heritage area and a major tourist attraction and walking area.

Despite some success for Dunphy and the NPPAC in having areas reserved for wilderness recreation, the outlook of government towards land use was still dominated by utilitarian need. Nevertheless, it was in the inter-war period when walking clubs flourished that the first tentative steps towards nature conservation in Australia were made, especially in the more populous and urbanised states of Victoria and New South Wales. National parks during this period were generally perceived by governments as 'revenue producing tourist resorts in scenic surroundings' (Bardwell 1982: 5) rather than as areas of scientific and ecological importance. For instance, in 1926 a request for the protection of flora as well as fauna within national parks was rejected by the West Australian Department of Lands and Survey, 'for the primary inducement for people to go to the reserves . . . is to gather the wildflowers with the object of adorning their homes and taking part in the wildflower shows' (Under Secretary to Minister of Lands and Surveys, Lands and Surveys Department (Western Australia), File No. 13479/98, 19 October 1926, in Hall 1992a) – a far cry from the motto of the Sydney Bush Walkers: 'The bushland was here before you; leave it after you' (Dunphy 1979b: 60).

Consequently walking in many urban industrial societies has seen a move into rural settings and become embodied as a recreational activity, where the rural environment is encountered both physically and mentally, rather than just as a visual contemplation (Edensor 2000).

Therefore, to understand how specific activities are shaped by fashions, culture, societal changes, economic transformations and the rise of new technology (e.g. the multimedia home-based entertainment systems associated with television, Gershuny 2002), the role of constraining and facilitating factors and the trends associated with leisure, attention now turns to: how demand is measured, the problems it raises for geographers, and the ways it can be analysed at different geographical scales from the national and regional down to the local level or micro scale.

Measuring recreational demand

Most geographers acknowledge the continued lack of suitable data on recreational demand. Although studies, such as the US Outdoor Recreation Resources Review Commission (1962), had a number of limitations – they were 'one-off studies, the methods of

data collection did not allow comparability of the data for each survey, and the results are often dated on publication due to the time required to analyse the results – they were a valuable starting point for analysing demand. Yet since 1972 no major survey specifically focusing on leisure has been undertaken in the UK, although the General Household Survey (GHS), which normally occurs every four years (see Parker 1999), has included a number of questions on leisure.

Problems and methods of measuring recreational demand

When seeking to understand their recreational habits, asking individuals questions about their recreational habits using social survey techniques remains the most widely used approach. A landmark study by Rowntree and Lavers (1951) of *English Life and Leisure* provides a good illustration of the early use of a diverse range of research methods and sources to construct patterns of participation in leisure and recreation in post-war Britain. Even so, researchers recognise that precision is needed to identify participation, non-participation and the frequency of each. For this reason, questions on surveys need to follow the type of format used on the GHS, to provide both a temporal and quantitative measure of demand. Patmore (1983: 57) cites the GHS, which begins by asking respondents: 'What . . . things have you done in your leisure time . . . in the four weeks ending last Sunday?'

Survey data rarely record all the information a researcher seeks (e.g. respondents' recall ability may not accurately record the full pattern), or respondents have a different understanding of a term from that intended by the researcher. As a result, a variety of survey techniques are necessary to derive a range of complementary and yet unique insights into recreation demand. Within the recreation literature, three techniques have primarily been used:

- A continuous record of recreation activities of a sample population for a given time period which involves respondents keeping a diary of activities (the time budget approach). This has a long history of use in social science and leisure research as outlined by Gershuny (2011) which can be dated to nineteenth century Russia and its use in the UK by Pember-Reeves (1913) and Sorokin and Berger (1939) in the USSR, with more recent studies of leisure such as Zuzanek et al.'s (1998) cross-national survey of Dutch and Canadian use of time.
- Questionnaire surveys which require respondents to recall activities either in the form of an individual case study, which is detailed and sometimes contains both qualitative and quantitative questions and which is inevitably small scale due to the time involved in in-depth qualitative interviews.
- Questionnaire surveys which are large scale, enabling subsamples to be drawn which are statistically significant. Such surveys may be derived using simple and unambiguous questions which focus on a specific recreation activity or one that covers the entire spectrum of leisure activities.

To illustrate how these techniques have been used and the way such data have been analysed, the time budget approach and national surveys of recreational activities are now examined.

Time budget survey techniques

Leisure time budgets

Recreation takes place in that portion of people's lives in which they are free (within constraints) to choose their activities, that is, their leisure time, [and] how they spend their time (time-budgets) is of paramount importance in any attempt to establish recreational demand, since it determines where recreational activities are possible.

(Coppock and Duffield 1975: 5)

Time budget analysis is a vital tool in analysing demand (Anderson 1971; Fukaz 1989; Pentland et al. 2002). Time budgets provide a systematic record of a person's use of time. They describe the duration, sequence and timing of a person's activities for a given period, usually of between a day and a week. When combined with the recording of the location at which activities occur, the record is referred to as a space–time budget. Time budget studies provide for the understanding of spatial and temporal behaviour patterns which may not be directly observable by other research techniques because of either their practicality or their intrusion into individual privacy. Such studies are often undertaken through the use of detailed diaries which are filled in by participants (see Jäckal and Wollscheid 2004; Aguiar and Hurst 2009; Gershuny 2011). However, this method has not been widely used in comparison with more traditional survey techniques due to the difficulty for individuals of accurately keeping records. Glyptis (1981a) used a diary technique which examined a sample of 595 visitors to the countryside. Respondents kept a diary record spanning three days and five evenings, recording the dominant pursuit in half-hour periods. While respondents identified up to 129 different leisure activities, each cited an average of 11. The value of the study was that through the use of cluster analysis to statistically analyse the sample and to group the population, it identified the leisure lifestyles of respondents with distinct groupings, where people of different social classes engaged in similar activities.

Tourism time budgets

In tourism studies, this technique has been used to provide a systematic record of a person's use of time over a given period, typically for a short period ranging from a single day to a week (Pearce 1988a; Debbage 1991). One of the fundamental assumptions in using this research method is that tourist behaviour and activities are the result of choices, a point illustrated by Floor (1990). Where questionnaire surveys have addressed such issues, the results have often failed to provide a comprehensive assessment of tourist activities, both formal/informal, and the relative importance of each. Thrift (1977) provides an assessment of three principal constraints on tourists' daily activity patterns, which are:

- *comparability constraints* (e.g. the biologically based need for food and sleep);
- *coupling constraints* (e.g. the need to interact and undertake activities with other people);
- *authority constraints* (e.g. where activities are controlled, not allowed or permitted at a certain point in time).

Thus both Chapin (1974) and Thrift (1977) identify choices and constraints which will influence the specific activities and context of tourist daily activities, which has similarities with the leisure constraints literature discussed earlier. The use of time budgets via diaries to record tourists' activity patterns has been used in a number of contexts (Gaviria 1975; Cooper 1981; P.L. Pearce 1981; D.G. Pearce 1986; Debbage 1991; McInnis and Page 2009). Methodological issues raised by these studies highlight the problem of selecting appropriate temporal measures to record tourists' activities. P.L. Pearce (1981) used three main time periods (morning, afternoon and evening), with Gaviria (1975) selecting quarter-hour periods and Cooper (1981) using five time sequences. While the recording of activities by time is a demanding activity for tourists, the main methodological concerns for such surveys are the type of technique to be used, the period to be covered and the type of sample selected. In addition, Chapin (1974) argues that such studies

can choose to use three main survey techniques as follows:

- *a checklist technique*, where respondents select the list of activities they engage in from a precategorised list;
- *the yesterday technique*, where subjects are asked to list things they did the previous day, and where and when they did them;
- *the tomorrow technique*, where participants keep a diary on what they do, and where and when.

Although time budget studies may still be viewed as experimental in tourism research, they do offer great potential to gain a detailed insight into tourists' use of time and their activity patterns (Woo 1996). In particular, recent advances in technology, particularly mobile tracking technology (see Shoval and Issaacson 2007) and ICT, offer potentially substantial insights into recreational and tourism activities and mobility (Hall 2012a).

The UK 2000 Time Use Survey (ONS 2002), which set out to measure how people spent their time, comprised a representative sample of households and individuals within households, based on a household questionnaire survey and diaries, and a one week work and education time sheet. It was undertaken in 2000–1. What is interesting is the aggregated results which were used to produce time spent on main and secondary activities, by category of time use. The profile of time use based on the main activities over a day is shown in Figure 2.5. Whilst this is now dated and has seen the impact of new technologies, it highlights the general principles of time use and leisure. This shows that almost 44 per cent of male and just over 44 per cent of female time is spent on personal care and sleeping each day, followed by employment as the next major time use. This varied between almost 15 per cent of male and almost 9 per cent of female time being devoted to employment-related activities, while family and household care accounts for almost 17 per cent of female time and less than 10 per cent of male time. In terms of time spent on leisure activities (e.g. sport, hobbies, games, social life, entertainment and mass media), 20 per cent of male and 20.33 per cent

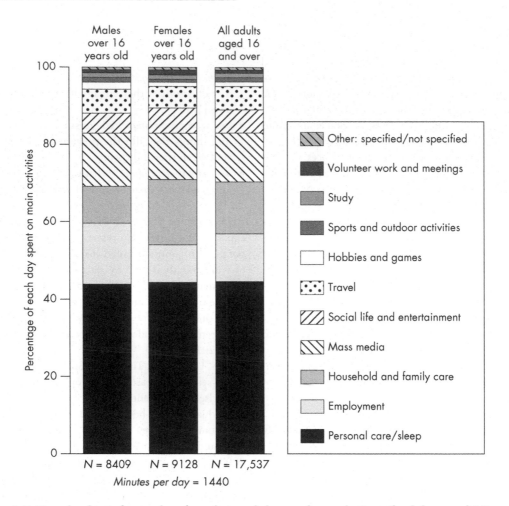

Figure 2.5 Time budgets for males, females and the total population of adults aged 16 and over in 2000

Source: based on ONS 2002 data.

of female time is devoted to such pursuits, with marginally more male time given over to mass media (e.g. watching the television). Almost 65 per cent of male leisure time is devoted to watching television, compared to 55 per cent of female time. What is also notable is the dominance of passive leisure pursuits. In terms of the timing of leisure activities for all adults, at 8 a.m., 7 per cent were engaged in leisure, which increased to 14 per cent at 12 noon; this increased to 23 per cent at 4 p.m. and to 57 per cent at 8 p.m.,

dropping to 13 per cent at midnight, when 79 per cent were sleeping. This, however, varied between weekdays (Monday to Thursday), with 17 per cent of adults in leisure at midnight on a Friday. At weekends, rest and recuperation were principal leisure activities. Weekend evenings were the most popular for leisure activities, with two-thirds of adults engaged in leisure especially socialising on Saturday evenings at 9 p.m.

The value of such research is in the identification of factors beyond simplistic analogies of demand determined by biological, social and economic factors, where the relationships between different time-consuming activities are examined in a holistic manner. Indeed, at EU level, in July 2003 a Time Use at Different Stages of Life survey of time use was undertaken in 13 different EU countries, with a further study in 2007. The 2007 study of 15 countries identifies time use according to daily allocations for personal care, employment study, domestic matters, leisure, travel and other uses. Despite variations by category and country (with male–female differences the data between countries is broadly consistent with the data in Figure 2.5 in terms of the amounts spent on different activities. Likewise the 2011 American Time Use Survey by the Bureau of Labor identifies different categories but a broadly consistent pattern emerges for weekday activities, where around 5 hours a day is spent on work-related activities, 4.73 hours a day on leisure and sports during the week and 6.34 hours a day at the weekend. The survey breaks the categories for leisure and sport into five broad categories (socialising, relaxing and leisure; relaxing and leisure; arts and entertainment; sports, exercise and recreation; and travel related to leisure and sport). The growth of social media and networking is reflected in the average 0.13 hours spent during weekends and holidays and 0.16 hours on weekdays on telephoning, emailing and mail in 2012 [latest figures from the time use survey].

Even so, it is important to recognise the criticisms and concerns with national participation surveys observed by Cushman *et al.* (1996b: 12): 'in light of the growing popularity – and indeed orthodoxy – of qualitative research methods in the field'. As a result, qualitative researchers point to the shortcomings and limitations of quantitative research methods (see Johnston and Sidaway 2014 for a discussion of philosophical perspectives on geography, geographers and research methodologies). However, regional studies have also been undertaken by geographers to understand the dynamics of demand. Millward and Spinney's (2011) study of Nova Scotia, Canada, highlighted the notion of 'active living', in which daily participation rates were analysed from time budgets in a time–space setting where the region was broken down into the inner city, suburbs, inner commuter belt and outer commuter belt to distinguish regional patterns of active living, including sport and leisure across an urban–rural continuum. Studies such as the UK Day Trips Survey have a distinct regional geographic element in their analysis of demand. Activities and their spatial catchments are highly localised and related to the population distribution in major conurbations and adjacent to other urban settlements such as coastal towns. The American Time Use survey has also modelled future changes in urban development to 2050, which illustrates how the future urbanisation of the USA may also impact upon regional patterns of leisure and recreation as settlements expand and rural land is absorbed into urban agglomerations. However, one of the most important contributions has been made through site-specific studies of demand, notably site surveys. For this reason, the remaining focus of this section on recreation examines recreation site surveys.

Spatial analysis of demand at the micro level: site surveys

Within the growing literature on geographical studies of recreation in the 1960s and 1970s (see, e.g., Rodgers 1973), site surveys have become the most documented (a feature reiterated in Chapter 6). As Glyptis (1981b: 277) indicated, numerous site surveys – mostly set in the format devised by Burton (1966) 'established the characteristics of visitors and their trips. Social profiles, trip distances, modes of transport and the duration, purpose and frequency of visits are well documented (Elson 1977)', a feature also observed in early studies by Wolfe (1964) and Lavery (1975). However, research methods that examine the behaviour of recreationalists have remained less common. Glyptis' (1981b) analysis of one 242 ha site – Westwood Common, Beverley, near Hull (UK) – is one such example. By employing participant observation methods to examine an undulating grassland area of common pasture land 13 km from the urban area of Hull, the spatial distribution of site use by recreationalists was observed and analysed. The main recreational activities observed at the site were sitting, sunbathing, walking, picnicking, informal games and staying inside one's car. On a busy Sunday in summer, up to 2,000 visitors came to the site. Using dispersion maps, observational mapping permitted the visitor distributions to be located in time and space, while length of stay (using car registration data) and maps of use for different days and times complemented traditional social survey methods to analyse visitor behaviour. The site features, access points, availability of parking and location of landscape features and facilities permit a more detailed understanding of site use. Glyptis (1981b) used observations on five days in August and September between 11 a.m. and 6 p.m. to collate data. Visitor arrivals at the site during the weekend occurred between 12 noon and 2 p.m., and peak use occurred at 4.30 p.m., with the majority of visitors spending one to two hours on site. The gradual increase in intensity of use by time of day varied by activity, with informal games and picnicking declining after Sunday lunch and walking increasing throughout the afternoon. Local users also displayed a preference to use the site at off-peak times, with increased patterns of dispersion and clumping through time. This reflects access roads, with visitors parking close to (within 15 yards of) the site they visited. Visitors were also recorded going to landmarks and facilities (e.g. viewpoints) as well as buying refreshments (e.g. from mobile vans), with the density of use increasing through the day rather than the distribution.

Glyptis (1981c) devised a simple model to explain the dynamics of visitor dispersion (Figure 2.6). Figure 2.6 shows that initial visitors to a site choose a favoured location linked to parking areas, with further inflows of visitors during the early afternoon marking an 'invasion phase' which extends the initial cluster. Thereafter, as the pace of arrivals slows, a degree of infilling and consolidation occurs. Then as people depart, dispersion occurs, with a more irregular pattern of distribution arising, although it may be affected by new arrivals in the afternoon, who intensify the pattern. What Glyptis (1991: 119) recognised was that even though 'sites clearly experience an increase in visitor density, visitor dispersion in a spatial sense remains fairly constant, even with space to spare and no restrictions on public access'.

Using nearest neighbour analysis, Glyptis (1981c) was able to measure the distances between groups of visitors, and that comfortable levels of tolerance exist for visitors in terms of proximity to other people, although the amount of personal space which recreationalists require may vary between different cultures. In fact, Glyptis (1991: 119) remarked that, 'as levels of use increase on a given day, the percentage occupancy of space actually decreases: visitors only ever use about a fifth of the space available to them, and at times of heaviest use they choose to occupy even less. In other words, site carrying capacity changes continually.' This study also highlighted the significance of recreation sites with multiple uses,

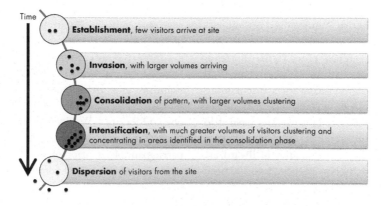

Figure 2.6 Glyptis' model of visitor dispersion at an informal recreation site
Source: redrawn from Glyptis 1981c.

where a variety of recreational needs are capable of being met and, as Burton's (1974) survey of Cannock Chase, Staffordshire (UK), found, individual sites cannot be viewed in isolation: there are relationships between them and understanding them is vital to site management. Glyptis (1981c) highlighted a certain degree of consistency in visitor use of a site, explaining the patterns as a function of the resource base, visitor use and behavioural factors. It may be possible to accommodate or reduce capacity through simple modifications as 'the geographer is well placed to examine fundamental aspects of . . . recreation, to diagnose issues in site management, and to propose solutions' (Glyptis 1981b: 285). For example, see Jones *et al.* (2009) on issues of equity of access to parks.

Recent extensions of the spatial analytic approaches of the period from the 1960s to 1980s are more social-psychologically engaged with the notion of place attachment in repeat recreation and leisure activities (Hailu *et al.* 2005; White *et al.* 2008). Whilst space is still implicit in many analyses of recreational demand at a site level (e.g. Arnberger *et al.*'s 2010 analysis of recreational use of forests in inner and peri-urban locations), issues such as site conflict (e.g. Vaske *et al.* 2007) have marked a change in research emphasis. One notable shift is the displacement of the spatial analytic approach by the rise of environmental economics and demand modelling (e.g. Phaneuf and Smith 2005) with the short-run effects of demand in time and space using economic models and techniques (e.g. revealed preferences and contingent valuation methods) which largely omit the spatial preferences in favour of resource use. Therefore, having outlined many of the factors and dimensions of recreational demand at a variety of spatial scales from the national, regional and local level, the discussion now turns to tourism demand.

Tourism demand

One of the fundamental questions that tourism researchers consistently seek to answer is: why do tourists travel? This seemingly simple proposition remains one of the principal challenges for tourism research. D.G. Pearce (1995a: 18) expands this proposition by asking, 'What induces them to leave their home area to visit other areas? What factors condition their travel behaviour, influencing their choice of destination, itineraries followed and activities undertaken?' Such questions not only underpin issues of spatial interaction, but also lead the geographer to question:

- why tourists seek to travel;
- where they go;
- when they go;
- how they get there;
- what do they do and where do they do it.

These basic issues have spatial implications in terms of the patterns of tourism, where tourism impacts occur and the nature of destination management. In other words, an understanding of tourism demand is a starting point for the analysis of why tourism develops, who patronises specific destinations and what appeals to the client market. As de Botton (2003: 9) argues in *The Art of Travel*, 'we are inundated with advice on *where* to travel to; we hear little of *why* and *how* we should go'. However, geographers are at a comparative disadvantage in answering some of the principal questions associated with work on tourism demand primarily led by psychologists, sociologists, marketers and economists. Interestingly, regional economists are also embracing the notion of space utilising gravity and other spatial models to explain the patterns of origin/destination flows (e.g. Marrocu and Paci 2011, 2013) in much the same way that the quantitative revolution in the 1960s saw these approaches applied to human behaviour with the antecedent criticisms of their value and application by behavioural geography (Johnston and Sidaway 2014). Much of the research by geographers 'has trodden the well worn path of the potential significance of variations in motivation on destination choice' (D.G. Pearce 1995a: 18), which has yielded a massive literature focused on generic and more specialised forms of destination choice such as the decision to travel to film tourism locations (Connell 2012) or for medical tourism (Connell 2011, 2013; Hall 2012b). However, tourist behaviour and the analysis of motivation have not traditionally been the forte of the logical positivist and empirical approach of traditional forms of spatial analysis on tourism, with some exceptions (e.g. Walmsley and Jenkins 1992). The area of tourist behaviour has a more developed literature within the field of social psychology than geography, and the emphasis in this section is on the way such approaches assist in understanding how tourist behaviour may result in the spatial implications for tourism.

What is tourism demand?

The approach one adopts to the analysis of tourism demand is largely dependent upon the disciplinary perspective of the researcher (see Crouch 1994). Geographers view demand in a spatial manner as 'the total number of persons who travel, or wish to travel, to use tourist facilities and services at places away from their places of work and residence' (Mathieson and Wall 1982: 1). In this context demand 'is seen in terms of the relationship between individuals' motivation [to travel] and their ability to do so' (D.G. Pearce 1995a: 18), with an attendant emphasis on the implications for the spatial impact on the development of domestic and international tourism. In comparison, the economist emphasises 'the schedule of the amount of any product or service which people are willing and able to buy at each specific price in a set of possible prices during a specified period of time. Psychologists view demand from the perspective of motivation and behaviour' (Cooper et al. 1993: 15).

In conceptual terms, there are three principal elements to tourism demand:

- *Effective or actual demand* comprises the number of people participating in tourism, usually expressed as the number of travellers. This is most commonly measured by tourism statistics, which means that most official sources of data are measures of effective demand.
- *Suppressed demand* is the population who are unable to travel because of circumstances (e.g. lack of purchasing power or limited holiday entitlement), which is called potential demand. Potential demand can be converted to effective demand if the circumstances change. There is also deferred demand, where constraints (e.g. lack of tourism

supply such as a shortage of bed spaces) can also be converted to effective demand if a destination or locality can accommodate the demand.
- *No demand* is a distinct category for the population who have no desire to travel, which has a considerable degree of overlap with the discussion earlier on leisure demand.

Figure 2.7, based on Uysal's (1998) overview of tourism demand, summarises the main determinants of demand within a multidisciplinary context. There has, however, been comparatively little discussion of the significance of what might be termed 'background' factors which act as geographical constraints on travel, such as the role of travel epidemiology (Steffen et al. 2003; Page 2009b). It can be argued that exposure to pathogens in high risk countries with poor endemic hygiene standards can pose major risk factors to tourist health which are not given sufficient credence in many debates on demand (Wilks and Page 2003). For example, the UK Foreign and Commonwealth Office (FCO) advice to travellers and risk notices do illustrate the scale of risk (see Figure 2.8), which outlines an evolving and ever-changing spatial landscape of potential risk in travelling to high risk areas with a myriad of risk factors, including assault, attacks, robberies, mild stomach bugs from drinking local tap water and lost/stolen passports (Figure 2.9).

However, the factors which shape the tourist decision-making process to select and participate in specific forms of tourism are largely within the field of consumer behaviour and motivation.

Tourist motivation

According to Moutinho (1987: 16), motivation is 'a state of need, a condition that exerts a push on the individual towards certain types of action that are seen as likely to bring satisfaction'. In this respect Cooper et al. (1993: 20) rightly acknowledge that 'demand for tourists at the individual level can be treated as a consumption process which is influenced by a number of factors. These may be a combination of needs and desires, availability of time and money, or images, perceptions and attitudes.' Not surprisingly, this is an

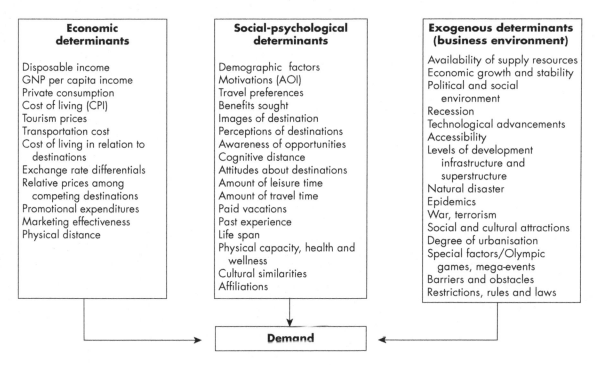

Figure 2.7 Determinants of tourism demand
Source: after Uysal 1998.

incredibly complex area of research and it is impossible within a chapter such as this to overview the area in depth. Nevertheless, P.L. Pearce's (1993) influential work in this field outlined a 'blueprint for tourist motivation', arguing that in an attempt to theorise tourist motivation one must consider the following issues:

- the conceptual place of tourism motivation;
- its task in the specialism of tourism;
- its ownership and users;
- its ease of communication;
- pragmatic measurement concerns;
- adopting a dynamic approach;
- the development of multi-motive perspectives;
- resolving and clarifying intrinsic and extrinsic motivation approaches.

To date no all-embracing theory of tourist motivation has been developed which has been adapted and legitimised by researchers in other contexts. This is largely due to the multidisciplinary nature of the research issues identified above and the problem of simplifying complex psychological factors and behaviour into a set of constructs and ultimately a universally acceptable theory that can be tested and proven in various tourism contexts (Pearce 2011). As a result, Cooper *et al.* (1993: 20) prefer to view the individual as a central component of tourism demand to understand what motivates the tourist to travel. Their research rightly acknowledges that

> No two individuals are alike, and differences in attitudes, perceptions and motivation have an important influence on travel decisions [where] attitudes depend on an individual's perception of the world. Perceptions are mental impressions of . . . a place or travel company and are determined by many factors which include childhood, family and work experiences. However, attitudes and perceptions in themselves do not explain why people

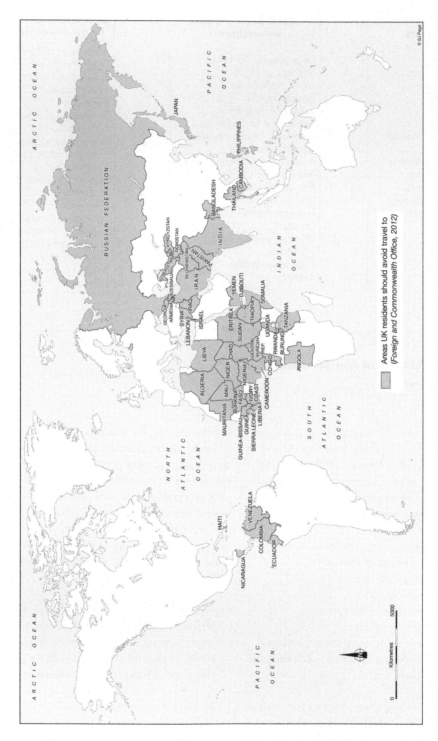

Figure 2.8 The geography of travel risk: Foreign and Commonwealth Office (UK) advice of areas to avoid travel to in 2012

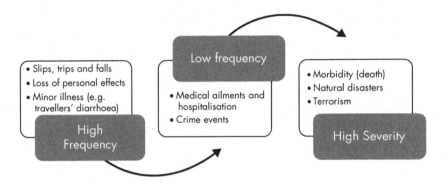

Figure 2.9 The tourist and safety continuum
Source: developed from Wilks and Page 2003.

want to travel. The inner urges that initiate travel demand are called travel motivators.

(Cooper *et al.* 1993: 20)

If one views the tourist as a consumer, then tourism demand is formulated through a consumer decision-making process, and therefore one can discern four elements which initiate demand:

- *energisers of demand*, factors that promote an individual to decide on a holiday;
- *filterers of demand*, which means that even though motivation may prevail, constraints on demand may exist in economic, sociological or psychological terms;
- *affecters*, which are factors that may heighten or suppress the energisers that promote consumer interest or choice in tourism;
- *roles* where the family member involved in the purchase of holiday products is the arbiter of group decision-making on choice of destination, product, and the where, when and how of consumption.

These factors underpin the tourist's process of travel decision-making although they do not explain why people choose to travel.

Maslow's hierarchy model and tourist motivation

Within the social psychology of tourism there is a growing literature which has built upon Maslow's work (discussed earlier in relation to recreation) to identify specific motivations beyond the concept of needing 'to get away from it all' pioneered by Grinstein (1955), while push factors motivating individuals to seek a holiday exist, and pull factors (e.g. promotion by tourist resorts and tour operators) encourage as attractors. Ryan's (1991: 25–9) analysis of tourist travel motivators (excluding business travel) identifies the following reasons commonly cited to explain why people travel to tourist destinations for holidays:

- a desire to escape from a mundane environment;
- the pursuit of relaxation and recuperation functions;
- an opportunity for play;
- the strengthening of family bonds;
- prestige, since different destinations can enable one to gain social enhancement among peers;
- social interaction;
- educational opportunities;
- wish fulfilment;
- shopping.

Within most studies of tourist motivations these factors emerge in one form or another. While researchers such as Crompton (1979) emphasise that sociopsychological motives can be located along a continuum, Iso-Ahola (1980) theorised tourist motivation in terms of an escape element complemented by a search component, where the tourist is seeking something. However, Dann's (1981) conceptualisation is probably one of the most useful attempts to simplify the principal elements of tourist motivation into:

- travel as a response to what is lacking yet desired;
- destination pull in response to motivational push;
- motivation as fantasy;
- motivation as classified purpose;
- motivation typologies;
- motivation and tourist experiences;
- motivation as definition and meaning.

This was simplified a stage further by McIntosh and Goeldner (1990) into:

- physical motivators;
- cultural motivators;
- interpersonal motivators;
- status and prestige motivators.

On the basis of motivation and using the type of experiences tourists seek, Cohen (1972) distinguished between four types of travellers:

- The organised mass tourist, on a package holiday, who is highly organised. Their contact with the host community in a destination is minimal.

- The individual mass tourist, who uses similar facilities to the organised mass tourist but also desires to visit other sights not covered on organised tours in the destination.
- The explorers, who arrange their travel independently and who wish to experience the social and cultural lifestyle of the destination.
- The drifter, who does not seek any contact with other tourists or their accommodation, preferring to live with the host community (see also V.L. Smith 1992).

Clearly, such a classification is fraught with problems, since it does not take into account the increasing diversity of holidays undertaken and inconsistencies in tourist behaviour (P.L. Pearce 1982). Other researchers suggest that one way of overcoming this difficulty is to consider the different destinations that tourists choose to visit, and then establish a sliding scale similar to Cohen's (1972) typology, but which does not have such an absolute classification. In contrast, Plog (1974) devised a classification of the US population into psychographic types, with travellers distributed along a continuum (see Figure 2.10) from psychocentrism to allocentrism. The psychocentrics are the anxious, inhibited and less adventurous

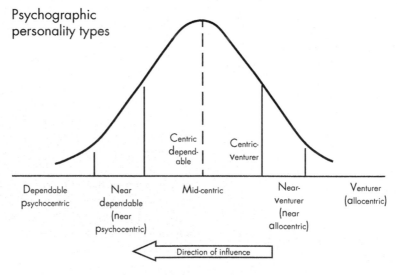

Figure 2.10 Plog's psychographic positions of destinations
Source: Plog (2001) reproduced with permission from Elsevier.

travellers, while at the other extreme the allocentrics are adventurous, outgoing, seeking new experiences due to their inquisitive personalities and interest in travel and adventure (also see Smith 1990a, 1990b; Plog 2001).

D.G. Pearce (1995a) highlights the spatial implications of such conceptualisations, that each tourist type will seek different destinations which will change through time. However, P.L. Pearce (1993) suggests that Plog's model is difficult to use because it fails to distinguish between extrinsic and intrinsic motivations without incorporating a dynamic element to encompass the changing nature of individual tourists. P.L. Pearce discounts such models, suggesting that individuals have a 'career' in their travel behaviour where people 'start at different levels, they are likely to change levels during their life-cycle and they can be prevented from moving by money, health and other people. They may also retire from their travel career or not take holidays at all and therefore not be part of the system' (P.L. Pearce 1993: 125).

Figure 2.11 outlines Pearce's model based on a leisure ladder, which builds on Maslow's hierarchical

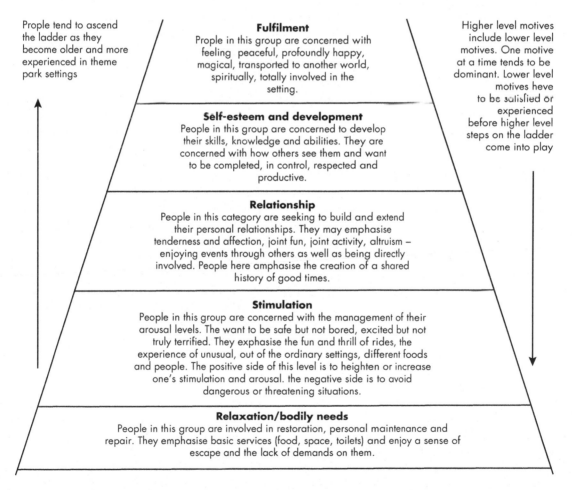

Figure 2.11 The leisure ladder for theme park settings (domestic visitors)
Source: Pearce 1993a.

system, where there are five motivational levels. These are:

1 a concern with biological needs;
2 safety and security needs;
3 relationship development and extension needs;
4 special interest and self-development needs;
5 fulfilment or self-actualisation needs.

From the existing literature on tourist motivation, the problems of determining tourist motivation may be summarised as follows:

- Tourism is not one specific product; it is a combination of products and experiences which meet a diverse range of needs.
- Tourists are not always conscious of their deep psychological needs and ideas. Even when they do know what they are, they may not reveal them.
- Motives may be multiple and contradictory (push and pull factors).
- Motives may change over time and be inextricably linked together (e.g. perception, learning, personality and culture are often separated out but they are all bound up together), and dynamic conceptualisations such as P.L. Pearce's (1993) leisure ladder are crucial to advancing knowledge and understanding in this area.

Having examined some of the issues associated with what motivates tourists to travel, attention now turns to the process of measuring and recording tourist demand using statistical measures.

Measurement of tourism demand: tourism statistics

The measurement of tourists, tourism activity and the effects on the economy and society in different environments is crucial to the development of tourism as an established area of study within the confines of social science (Latham and Edwards 2003; Lennon 2003). While most tourism researchers acknowledge that statistics are a necessary feature to provide data to enable researchers, managers, planners, decision-makers and public and private sector bodies to gauge the significance and impact of tourism on destination areas, Burkart and Medlik (1981: 74) identify four principal reasons for statistical measurement in tourism:

- to evaluate the magnitude and significance of tourism to a destination area or region;
- to quantify the contribution to the economy or society, especially the effect on the balance of payments;
- to assist in the planning and development of tourism infrastructure and the effect of different volumes of tourists with specific needs;
- to assist in the evaluation and implementation of marketing and promotion activities where the tourism marketer requires information on the actual and potential markets and their characteristics.

Consequently, tourism statistics are essential to the measurement of the volume, scale, impact and value of tourism at different geographical scales, from the global to the country level down to the individual destination. A more recent development has been the evolution of Tourism Satellite Accounts (TSAs) for individual countries to establish a set methodology for assessing the tourism economy in each country (see Frechtling 2010 for more detail on this technique). Yet an information gap often still exists between the types of statistics provided by organisations and the needs of users. The compilation of tourism statistics provided by organisations associated with the measurement of tourism has established methods and processes to collect, collate and analyse tourism statistics, yet these have been understood by only a small number of researchers and practitioners. Thus this section attempts to demystify the apparent sophistication and complexity associated with the presentation of statistical indicators of tourism and their value to spatial analysis, since geographers have a strong quantified methods tradition (Johnston and Sidaway 2014), which is reflected in the use of and reliance upon such indicators to understand spatial variations and patterns of tourism activity. All too often, undergraduate and many postgraduate texts assume a prior knowledge of tourism statistics and they are dealt with only in a limited way by most tourism texts; where such issues are raised they are usually discussed in over-technical texts aimed at a limited audience.

A commonly misunderstood feature which is associated with tourism statistics is that they are a complete and authoritative source of information (i.e. they answer all the questions posed by the researcher) (Lennon 2003). Other associated problems are that statistics are recent and relate to the previous year or season, implying that there is no time lag in their generation, analysis, presentation and dissemination to interested parties. In fact, most tourism statistics are 'typically measurements of arrivals, trips, tourist nights and expenditure, and these often appear in total or split into categories such as business or leisure travel' (Latham 1989: 55–6). Furthermore, the majority of published tourism statistics are derived from sample surveys, with the results being weighted or statistically manipulated to derive a measure which is supposedly representative of the real world situation. In reality, this often means that tourism statistics are subject to significant errors depending on the size of the sample, although this is often not readily acknowledged by authorities when they report such data.

The statistical measurement of tourists is far from straightforward. Latham and Edwards (2003) identify a number of distinctive and peculiar problems associated with the tourist population:

- Tourists are a transient and highly mobile population, making statistical sampling procedures difficult when trying to ensure statistical accuracy and rigour in methodological terms.
- Interviewing of mobile populations such as tourists is often undertaken in a strange environment, typically at ports or points of departure or arrival where there is background noise which may influence responses.
- Other variables, such as the weather, may affect the responses.

Even where sampling and survey-related problems can be minimised, one has to treat tourism statistics with a degree of caution because of additional methodological issues that can affect the results. For example, tourism research typically comprises (Hall 2011c):

- pre-travel studies of tourists' intended travel habits and likely choice of destination (intentional studies);
- studies of tourists in transit to provide information on their actual behaviour and plans for the remainder of their holiday or journey (actual and intended studies);
- studies of tourists at the destination or at specific tourist attractions and sites, to provide information on their actual behaviour, levels of satisfaction, impacts and future intentions (actual and intended studies);
- post-travel studies of tourists on their return journey from their destination or on-site experience or once they have returned to their place of residence (post-travel measures).

In an ideal world, where resource and/or political constraints are not a limiting factor on the generation of statistics, each of the aforementioned approaches should be used to provide a broad spectrum of research information on tourism and tourist behaviour. In reality, organisations and government agencies select a form of research which meets their own particular needs. In practice, most tourism statistics are generated with practical uses in mind and they may usually, though not exclusively, be categorised as follows:

- measurement of tourist volume, enumerating arrivals, departures and the number of visits and stays;
- expenditure-based surveys which quantify the value of tourist spending at the destination and during the journey;
- the characteristics and features of tourists to construct a profile of the different markets and segments visiting a destination.

However, before any tourism statistics can be derived, it is important to deal with the complex and thorny issue of defining the population – the tourist. Therefore, how does one define and differentiate between the terms *tourism* and *tourist*?

Defining tourism

The terms *travel* and *tourism* are often interchanged within the published literature on tourism, though they are normally meant to encompass 'the field of research on human and business activities associated with one or more aspects of the temporary movement of persons away from their immediate home communities and daily work environments for business, pleasure and personal reasons' (Chadwick 1994: 65). These two terms tend to be used in differing contexts to mean similar things, although there is a tendency for researchers in the United States to continue to use the term 'travel' when in fact they mean tourism. Despite this inherent problem, which sometimes may be little more than an exercise in semantics, it is widely acknowledged that the two terms are used in isolation or in unison to 'describe' three concepts:

- the movement of people;
- a sector of the economy or an industry;
- a broad system of interacting relationships of people (including their need to travel outside their communities and services that attempt to respond to these needs by supplying products) (Chadwick 1994; Hall and Lew 2009).

From this initial starting point, one can begin to explore some of the complex issues in arriving at a working definition of the terms *tourism* and *tourist*. Burkart and Medlik's (1981) approach to the concept of *tourism* continues to offer a valid assessment of the situation, where five main characteristics are associated with the concept:

- Tourism arises from the movement of people to, and their stay in, various destinations.
- There are two elements in all tourism: the journey to the destination and the stay, including activities at the destination.
- The journey and the stay take place outside the normal place of residence and work, so that tourism gives rise to activities which are distinct from those of the resident and working populations of the places through which tourists travel and in which they stay.

- The movement to tourist destinations is of a temporary, short-term character, with the intention of returning home within a few days, weeks or months.
- Destinations are visited for purposes other than taking up permanent residence or employment remunerated from within the places visited (Burkart and Medlik 1981: 42).

Furthermore, Burkart and Medlik's (1981) conceptual definition of tourism recognises that much tourism is a leisure activity which involves a discretionary use of time and money, and recreation is often the main purpose of participation in tourism. But this is no reason for restricting the total concept in this way and the essential characteristics of tourism can best be interpreted to embrace a wider concept. All tourism includes some travel but not all travel is tourism, while the temporary and short-term nature of most tourist trips distinguishes it from migration. Hall and Lew (2009) also emphasise that tourism is voluntary and does not include the forced movement of people for political or environmental reasons; that is, tourists are not refugees. 'In fact, the more impoverished someone is the less likely it is that they travel for leisure; and if they have to travel across a border, they are less likely to be welcomed. Rich people, by contrast, are usually welcomed and given far more privileges in crossing international borders than are the poor' (Hall and Lew 2009: 6). Therefore, from the broad interpretation of tourism, it is possible to consider the technical definitions of tourism (also see Leiper (1990) for a further discussion, together with Medlik (1993) and Hall and Lew (2009); see also Chapter 1).

Technical and statistical definitions of tourism

Technical definitions of tourism are commonly used by organisations seeking to define the population to be measured, and there are three principal features which normally have to be defined:

- Purpose of travel (e.g. the type of traveller, be it business travel, holidaymakers, visits to friends and relatives or for other reasons).

Classification of tourists

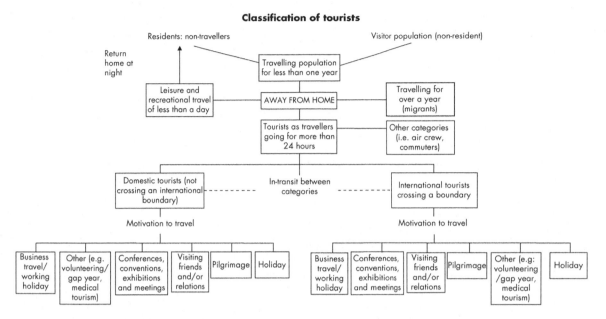

Figure 2.12 A classification of travellers

Source: developed and adapted from Chadwick 1994 and Page and Connell 2014, with additions by the authors.

- The time dimension involved in the tourism visit, which requires a minimum and a maximum period of time spent away from the home area and the time spent at the destination. In most cases, this would involve a minimum stay of more than 24 hours and a maximum of less than a year.
- Those situations where tourists may or may not be included as tourists, such as cruise passengers, those tourists in transit at a particular point of embarkation/departure and excursionists who stay less than 24 hours at a destination (e.g. the European duty-free cross-Channel day trip market).

R. Chadwick (1994) provides a typology of travellers (tourists) which highlights the distinction between tourists (travellers) and non-travellers (non-tourists) and which is summarised in Figure 2.12. Figure 2.12 indicates that all sections of society are involved in travel of some kind, but also looks at the motivation to travel. It is also useful because it illustrates where technical problems may occur in deciding which groups to include in tourism and which to exclude.

From this classification of travellers, the distinction between international and domestic tourism is made, and this is discussed in more detail on pp. 80–81.

The term *trip* is also used extensively in technical approaches to tourism and refers to the movement of an individual outside their home environment until they return. The term, therefore, actually refers to a 'roundtrip'. The trip concept and its implications can be understood through what is referred to as the tourism system, which is usually conceptualised as a geographical or spatial system (see Chapter 1). The tourism system includes the various elements that make up a trip:

- the generation or origin region (or place) of the tourist;
- the transit region that the tourist travels through;
- the destination location where the tourist is going;
- the overall environment in which these exist.

A trip may also be made up of visits to different destinations. To simplify statistical data collection, countries will usually define a multi-destination trip in one of two ways:

- Based on the point of first arrival after departing the home environment, e.g on an international flight this would be the city where you get off the aircraft, even though you may be going on to somewhere else.
- Based on the main destination of the trip, which is defined as either the location outside of the home environment where the most time was spent or as the place that most influenced the decision to take the trip. If the same amount of time was spent in two or more places during the trip, then the main destination is usually defined as the one that is the farthest from the place of usual residence (UN and UNWTO 2007).

Based on generally accepted international agreements for collecting and comparing tourism statistics, the term tourism trip has come to refer to a trip of not more than 12 months and for a main purpose other than being employed at the destination (UN and UNWTO 2007). An international trip is one in which the main destination is outside the country of residence of the traveller. A domestic trip is one in which the main destination is within the country of residence of the traveller (UN and UNWTO 2007). However, despite UN and UNWTO recommendations (WTO 1991a; UN 1994; UN and UNWTO 2007) there are substantial differences between countries with respect to the length of time that they use to define a tourist, as well as how employment is defined (Chadwick 1994; Lennon 2003; Hall and Page 2006).

Three types of tourism are usually recognised (Hall and Lew 2009):

1 *Domestic tourism*, which includes the activities of resident visitors within their home country or economy of reference, as part of either a domestic or an international trip.
2 *Inbound tourism*, which includes the activities of non-resident visitors within the destination country or economy of reference, as part of either a domestic or an international trip (from the perspective of the traveller's country of residence).

3 *Outbound tourism*, which includes the activities of resident visitors outside their home country or economy of reference, as part of either a domestic or an international trip.

The term 'economy of reference' is used for special conditions, such as Hong Kong, which although a Special Autonomous Region (SAR) of China, is a separate economy of reference with respect to statistical and other purposes. Travel between China and Hong Kong is, therefore, considered international travel. However, for statistical purposes the UN and UNWTO (2007: 21–2) have recommended the adoption of the following concepts:

- *Internal tourism*, which comprises both domestic tourism and international inbound tourism, including the activities of resident and non-resident visitors within the economy of reference as part of a domestic or an international trip; this is all of the tourism expenditures in a country or economy.
- *National tourism*, which comprises both domestic tourism and international outbound tourism, including the activities of resident visitors within and outside the economy of reference, as part of either a domestic or an international trip; this is all of the tourism expenditures of domestic tourists both inside and outside their home country or economy.
- *International tourism*, which comprises inbound tourism and outbound tourism, including the activities of resident visitors outside the economy of reference, as part of either a domestic or an international trip, and the activities of non-resident visitors within the economy of reference, as part of a domestic or an international trip (from the perspective of their country of residence); this is all tourist expenditures that are made by tourists outside their home country or economy.

In order to improve statistical collection and improve understanding of tourism, the United Nations (1994) and the WTO (1991a) also recommended differentiating between visitors, tourists and excursionists (day-trippers). The WTO (1991a) recommended that an international tourist be defined as 'a visitor who travels to a country other than that in which he/she has his/her usual residence for at least one night but not more than one year, and whose main purpose of visit is other than the exercise of an activity remunerated from within the country visited', and that an international excursionist (e.g. cruise ship visitors) be defined as 'a visitor residing in a country who travels the same day to a country other than which he/she has his/her usual environment for less than 24 hours without spending the night in the country visited and whose main purpose of visit is other than the exercise of an activity remunerated from within the country visited'. Similar definitions were also developed for domestic tourists, with domestic tourists having a time limit of 'not more than six months' (WTO 1991a; UN 1994).

Interestingly, the inclusion of a same-day travel, 'excursionist' category in UN/WTO technical definitions of tourism (also known as day-trippers) makes the division between recreation and tourism even more arbitrary, and there is increasing international agreement that 'tourism' refers to all activities of visitors, including both overnight and same-day visitors (UN 1994: 5). Given improvements in transport technology, same-day travel is becoming increasingly important to some countries (Hall and Lew 2009).

In order to try to clarify an increasingly complex series of travel categories the UN and UNWTO (2007) have recommended use of the term *visitor* rather than *tourist* per se, with a number of criteria needing to be satisfied for an international traveller to qualify as an international visitor, although the terms international visitor and international tourist tend to be used interchangeably in everyday usage (Hall and Lew 2009):

- The place of destination within the country visited is outside the traveller's usual environment.
- The stay, or intention of stay, in the country visited should last no more than 12 months, beyond which this place in the country visited would become part of his/her usual environment. At which point this would lead to a classification as migrant or permanent resident. The UN and UNWTO recommend that this criterion should be applied to also cover long-term students and patients, even though their stay might be interrupted by short stays in their country of origin or elsewhere.

- The main purpose of the trip is other than being employed by an organisation or person in the country visited.
- The traveller is not engaged in travel for military service or is a member of the diplomatic services.
- The traveller is not a nomad or refugee (UN and UNWTO 2007).

Domestic visitors can be similarly classified. Therefore, for a traveller to be considered a domestic visitor to a place in the country where he or she is resident, the following conditions should be met (Hall and Lew 2009):

- The place (or region) visited should be outside the visitor's usual environment, which would exclude frequent trips, although the UN and UNWTO (2007) recommend that trips to vacation homes should always be considered as tourism trips.
- The stay, or intention of the stay, in the place (or region) visited should last no more than 12 months, beyond which this place would become part of his/her usual environment. As with the international visitor classification the UN and UNWTO recommend that this criterion should be applied to also cover long-term students and patients, even though their stay might be interrupted by short stays in their place of origin or elsewhere.
- The main purpose of the visit should be other than being employed by an organisation or person in the place visited.

Although the term 'tourist' will undoubtedly stay in common usage it is significant to note that the focus on visitors has meant that policy discussions with respect to tourism are increasingly being focused on the visitor economy so as to highlight the significance of different forms of international and domestic tourism (Morgan *et al.* 2009; Middleton 2012).

Domestic tourism statistics

Domestic tourism is often viewed as the poorer partner in the compilation of statistics, even though, as noted in Chapter 1, it accounts for almost 85 per cent of the total number of tourist trips. For example, most domestic tourism statistics tend to underestimate the scale and volume of flows since certain aspects of domestic tourist movements are sometimes ignored in official sources. In contrast to international tourism, domestic tourism statistics also remain generally poor in quantity and quality (Latham and Edwards 2003). This is compounded by the fact that domestic tourism has little direct impact on a government's foreign exchange earnings or balance of payments. The 'visits to friends and relatives, the use of forms of accommodation other than hotels (for example, second homes, camp and caravan sites) and travel by large segments of a population from towns to the countryside are not for the most part included' (Latham and Edwards 2003: 64). Relatively few countries collect domestic travel and tourism statistics, and some rely exclusively on the hotel or accommodation sector for statistical information, thereby excluding the many travellers staying with friends and relatives or at second homes (Hall and Müller 2004). Therefore, the collection of domestic tourism statistics requires the use of different data sources aside from hotel records which identify the origin and duration of a visitor's stay.

Problems in applying WTO definitions may also reflect an individual country's reasons for generating such statistics, which may not necessarily be to contribute to a better understanding of statistics per se. For example, WTO (1981) identified four uses of domestic tourism statistics:

- To calculate the contribution of tourism to the country's economy, whereby estimates of tourism's value to the gross domestic product is estimated due to the complexity of identifying the scope of tourism's contribution.
- To assist in the marketing and promotion of tourism, where government-sponsored tourism organisations seek to encourage the population to take domestic holidays rather than to travel overseas.
- To aid the regional development policies of governments, which harness tourism as a tool for area development where domestic tourists in congested environments are encouraged to travel to less developed areas and to improve the quality of tourism in different environments.

- To achieve social objectives, where socially oriented tourism policies may be developed for the underprivileged, which requires a detailed understanding of the holiday-taking habits of a country's nationals.

Regional and local tourist and economic development organisations also make use of such data to develop and market destinations and different businesses within the tourism sector. Burkart and Medlik (1981) argue that two principal features need to be measured: first, the volume, value and characteristics of tourism among the population of the country; second, the same data relating to individual destinations within the country. The WTO (1981, cited in Latham 1989) considers the minimum data requirements for the collection of domestic tourism statistics in terms of arrivals and tourist nights in accommodation classified by:

- month;
- type or grade of accommodation establishment;
- location of the accommodation establishment and overall expenditure on domestic tourism.

The cost of such data collection means that the statistical basis of domestic tourism in many less developed countries remains poor. The methods used to generate domestic tourism statistics are normally based on the estimates of volume, value and scale derived from sample surveys due to the cost of undertaking large-scale surveys of tourist activities. The immediate problem facing the user of such material is the type of errors and degree of accuracy that can be attached to such data.

International tourism statistics

The two principal organisations which collate data on international tourism are the United Nations World Tourism Organization and the OECD. In addition, international regional tourism organisations such as the Pacific Asia Travel Association also collect international tourism statistics. However, it has long been recognised that there is often an imbalance in statistical collection, as Withyman argued:

Outward visitors seem to attract less attention from the pollsters and the enumerators. Of course, one country's outward visitor is another country's (perhaps several countries') inward visitor, and a much more welcome sort of visitor, too, being both a source of revenue and an emblem of the destination country's appeal in the international market. This has meant that governments have tended to be generally more keen to measure inward than outward tourism, or at any rate, having done so, to publish the results.

(Withyman 1985: 69)

This statement indicates that governments are more concerned with the direct effect of tourism on their balance of payments. But as Seetaram, Page and Song (2012) demonstrate in the case of the UK, outbound tourism has grown significantly, using outbound air travel as a surrogate, which rose from 30 million in 1970 to over 218 million in 2011, with forecasts that it will rise to 500 million by 2030. Yet as Withyman (1985: 61) argued: 'In the jungle of international travel and tourism statistics, it behoves the explorer to step warily; on all sides there is luxuriant growth. Not all data sources are what they appear to be – after close scrutiny some show themselves to be inconsistent and often unsuitable for the industry researcher and planner.'

The key point Withyman (1985) recognises is the lack of comparability in tourism data in relation to what is measured (e.g. is it visitor days or visitor nights?) and the procedures and methodology used to measure international tourism. Latham (1989) suggests that the main types of international tourism statistics collated relate to:

- volume of tourists;
- expenditure by tourists;
- the profile of the tourist and their trip characteristics.

As with domestic tourism, estimates form the basis for most statistics on international tourism since the method of data collection does not generate exact data. For example, volume statistics are often generated from counts of tourists at entry/exit points (i.e. gateways such as airports and ports) or at accommodation. But such data relate to numbers of trips rather than individual tourists since one tourist may make more than one trip a year and each trip is counted separately. In the case of expenditure statistics, tourist expenditure normally refers to tourist spending within a country and excludes payments to operators of tourist transport. Yet deriving such statistics is often an indirect measure based on foreign currency estimates derived from bank records, from data provided by tourism service providers or more commonly from social surveys undertaken directly with tourists, and there may be substantial bias in such studies (Baretje 1982).

According to Edwards (1991: 68–9), 'expenditure and receipts data apart, tourist statistics are usually collected in one of the five following ways':

- Counts of all individuals entering or leaving the country at all recognised frontier crossings, often using arrival/departure cards where high volume arrivals/departures are the norm. Where particularly large volumes of tourist traffic exist, a 10 per cent sampling framework is normally used (i.e. every tenth arrival/departure card). Countries such as New Zealand actually match the arrival/departure cards, or a sample, to examine the length of stay.
- Interviews carried out at frontiers with a sample of arriving and/or departing passengers to obtain a more detailed profile of visitors and their activities within the country. This will often require a careful sample design to gain a sufficiently large sample, with detail required from visitors on a wide range of tourism data, including places visited, expenditure, accommodation usage and related items.
- Selecting a sample of arrivals and providing them with a self-completion questionnaire to be handed in or posted. This method is used in Canada but it fails to incorporate those visitors travelling via the United States by road.
- Sample surveys of the entire population of a country, including travellers and non-travellers, though the cost of obtaining a representative sample is often prohibitive.

- Accommodation arrivals and nights spent are recorded by hoteliers and owners of the accommodation types covered. The difficulty with this type of data collection is that accommodation owners have no incentive to record accurate details, particularly where the tax regime is based on the turnover of bed-nights.

The final area of data collection is profile statistics, which examine the characteristics and travel habits of visitors. For example, the UK's International Passenger Survey (IPS) is one survey that incorporates volume, expenditure and profile data on international tourism. The IPS collects information on behalf of the UK Office for National Statistics about overseas passengers entering and leaving the UK. The survey results are used by a range of bodies, including VisitBritain (the national tourism agency) and the tourism organisations for London, England, Wales and Scotland, for the purposes of assessing the impact of tourists' expenditure and taxation on the economy, estimating migration rates and monitoring changes in international tourism over time. In 2009 the IPS employed a multi-stage random sample of over 311,000 people (representing about 0.2 per cent of all travellers to and from the UK), who were interviewed at all the major airports, sea routes, Eurostar terminals and on Eurotunnel trains.

Methodological issues

Latham and Edwards (2003) review the major types of data collection used for tourism statistics. They report that among state-sponsored tourism research in the United States, conversion studies are a popular method to examine and evaluate advertising campaigns and visitor surveys, to assess a sample of visitors to individual states. Other methods of data collection may include diary questionnaires, participant observation and personal interviews. Yet each approach has different issues of sampling, sample design and the sources of error that users of such data may not be aware of. In fact the lack of research on the reliability of the estimate from a sample survey (the standard error) is rarely discussed in most tourism surveys (for a more technical discussion of this point, see Latham

and Edwards 2003). In many cases, large tourism surveys focus on the logistics of drawing the sample and the bias which may be reflected in the results. Therefore, any tourism survey will need to pay careful attention to the statistical and mathematical accuracy of the survey, especially the survey design and the effect it may have on the results, a feature which is discussed in great detail by Ryan (1995).

Ryan (1995) provides an excellent review of survey design, questionnaire design, sampling and also an insight into the statistical techniques to use for different forms of tourism data. As a result it serves as an important reference point for issues of methodology and the technical issues associated with the statistical analysis of tourism data. Without reiterating the features of Ryan's findings, it is appropriate to consider some of the main accuracy problems associated with the collection of domestic and international tourism statistics.

Ryan (1995) argues that errors in data collection can lead to errors in data analysis. Among the most frequently cited problems associated with domestic and international tourism statistics are:

- the methods by which the data are collected, which are influenced by administrative, bureaucratic and legislative factors in each country
- sample sizes which are too small and lead to unacceptable sampling errors and in some instances where the sample design is flawed;
- the procedures for collecting tourism statistics are not adhered to by the agency collecting the data.

Edwards (1991: 68) argues that a 'fourth potential reason – arithmetic mistakes and data processing errors – only occasionally produce[s] significant errors'. In the case of tourist expenditure and receipts data, organisations such as the International Monetary Fund (IMF) issue guidelines for the compilation of balance of payments statistics. But errors may occur where leakage results from tourist services paid for in overseas bank accounts and, in extreme cases, where a black market exists in currency exchange. Edwards (1991) suggests that a regular programme of interviews with departing tourists and returning residents may assist in estimating levels of expenditure.

Identifying trends in tourism data remains one of the main requirements for travel industry organisations. Edwards (1991: 73) lists some key issues to consider in examining tourism trends:

- Have arrivals or accommodation data been changed in coverage or definition?
- Have provisional data for earlier years been subsequently revised?
- Has the reliability of the data changed and how are changing tastes in travel products affecting the statistics?

Having considered the issues associated with how tourism statistics are generated, attention now turns to the ways in which geographers analyse such statistics, and variations in tourism activity at different scales.

Patterns of global tourism

The UNWTO provides the main source of data for international tourism, collated from a survey of major government agencies responsible for data collection. While most international tourists are expressed as 'frontier arrivals' (i.e. arrivals determined by means of a frontier check), arrival/departure cards (where used) offer additional detail to the profile of international tourists, and where they are not used periodic tourism surveys are often employed. UNWTO statistics are mainly confined to categories of travellers, and in some cases geographical disaggregation of the data may be limited by the collecting agency's use of descriptions and categories for the sake of simplicity (e.g. rest of the world) rather than listing all categories of arrivals.

In terms of the growth of international travel, the expansion of outbound travel saw constant growth in the 1960s in an age of discovery of outbound travel for many developed nations. The late 1960s saw international travel expanded by new technology in air travel (e.g. the introduction of the Boeing 747 jumbo jet and the 737 as well as the DC10), which led to rapid growth until the oil crisis in the early 1970s. Growth rates varied in the 1980s, with 'shock waves' to the upward trend being caused by events such as the Gulf Crisis, but international travel has maintained strong growth rates, often in excess of 5 per cent per annum until the late 1990s, when growth rates slowed down considerably. Since 2000, the rate of growth has slowed, especially with 9/11 and the terrorist threats and other shock events, including the effect of the swine flu virus in 2009 and the credit crunch (Page et al. 2012). Crises in tourism affect the geographical pattern of arrivals by world region (Hall 2010e), although a notable pattern of change since the 1990s has been the major expansion of arrivals in the developing world. As Figure 1.2 shows, in 2012 many of the world's least developed and developing nations as defined by the United Nations have international arrivals in excess of one million, dominated by China and Turkey as international destinations. This is a major shift since the late 1990s, when many of these destinations were fledgling or developing their tourism sector. Yet in terms of volume of international arrivals France has remained in a prominent position despite certain developing nations recording major growth, with the exception of the USA. To date Europe still dominates the pattern of arrivals by country, but China is the notable success story in terms of growth in inbound arrivals. The USA and Spain have retained their prominence in the top rankings as world earners of tourism receipts. Key changes in the last decade have been the rise of four major outbound regions labelled the BRIC Countries (Brazil, Russia, India and China, see UNWTO 2011a) with a rapidly expanding demand for outbound (and domestic) travel which will shape future patterns of tourist travel globally, to which attention now turns.

Future trends in the geography of international tourism to 2030

UNWTO produces future growth scenarios for world tourism, based on existing patterns and past trends in growth, to extrapolate to the future using forecasting methods which economists use from the area known as econometrics (see Song and Li 2008 for more detail). These are interesting to the geographer as they make assumptions and predict where tourist growth is likely to occur in time and space, including modelling tourist flows (origin/destination matrices of data). UNWTO (2011a) reported these findings in its *Towards Tourism 2030* report, which is a long-term forecast assessment using 2010 as the base year and making forecasts for 2030. As the period of growth examined is up to 20 years in length, short-term fluctuations such as rapid growth are often followed by short-term downturns and slower growth rates in arrivals, which has tended to compensate and smooth out growth rates over the forecasting periods in the past. As a result, UNWTO suggests that, globally, international tourism will rise to 1.8 billion in 2030. Global growth in international tourist arrivals is expected to continue at a more moderate pace, from 4.2 per cent per year (1980–2020) to 3.3 per cent (2010–30), as a result of four factors:

- The base volumes are higher, so smaller increases still add substantial numbers;
- Lower GDP growth, as economies mature;
- A lower elasticity of travel to GDP;
- A shift from falling transport costs to increasing ones (UNWTO 2011a).

The greatest growth rates will occur in emerging countries (especially the BRIC Countries), so that whereas 70 per cent of arrivals in 1980 were in the industrialised regions of North America, Europe and Asia-Pacific, this will change to 58 per cent of arrivals in emerging countries by 2030 (e.g. Latin America, Eastern and Central Europe, the Eastern Mediterranean, the Middle East and Africa). South Asia will see growth rates of around 6 per cent per annum, albeit growing from a low base figure, while the Middle East and Africa will see arrivals double over the period. UNWTO also forecast a greater geographical dispersion of tourist arrivals to a wider range of destinations by 2030 as more localities develop tourism, thereby increasing competition, a feature highlighted by OECD (2008) as a key feature of future growth in tourism globally.

Patterns of domestic tourism

The development of Tourism Satellite Accounts has seen a growing research focus on domestic tourism in many countries. What might have been a fair assessment of the situation in the early 1990s by D.G. Pearce (1995a: 67), that 'domestic tourism, which is often more informal and less structured than international tourism, [involves] a consequent tendency by many government agencies, researchers and others to regard it as less significant', has been re-examined in many countries, as slow growth rates in international tourism and crises in arrivals after disasters such as 9/11 and the credit crunch/recession, or slowdown, have led to a major refocusing of attention on domestic travel in the USA and Europe, for example. In the UK this has been respun as a focus on 'staycation' to coincide with the appreciation of the pound Sterling against the Euro making travel to Europe more expensive. The UK has certainly seen tourism agencies realise the significance of domestic tourism, particularly for the UK visitor economy. Similarly, in New Zealand domestic tourism generated NZD 13.8 billion in 2012 whereas international tourism yielded NZD 9.6 billion, illustrating why domestic tourism is a significant sector of the tourism economy. Nevertheless, a paucity of data in some countries is problematic, since it requires an analysis of tourism patterns and flows at different spatial scales to consider spatial interaction of tourists between a multitude of possible origin and destination areas within a country, as well as a detailed understanding of inter-regional flows. In some cases, these flows can be identified from well-known tourist circuits, such as the UK's milk run of coach tourism circuits between the popular key destinations (D.G. Pearce 1995a) and more recent analysis of VisitScotland data at a regional level by Page (2003a) to assess the regional distribution of coach tourist visits in Scotland. At the micro level, studies of specific areas such as small islands may yield contained environments where spatial analysis is much easier and the effects of tourist activity can be monitored.

At a methodological level, it is evident that where government agencies and other public sector organisations undertake data collection on domestic tourism, 'the results are not often directly comparable, limiting the identification of general patterns and trends' (D.G. Pearce 1995a: 67). As Pearce (1995a: 67) rightly acknowledges, 'there are still few examples of comprehensive interregional studies where the analysis is based on a complete matrix of both original and destination regions ... [since] few appropriate and reliable sets of tourism statistics exist which might be used to construct such a matrix'.

Micro studies of tourism demand: innovations in technology

One of the principal developments since the early 1990s which has assisted in the analysis of demand at the micro scale, typically in cities or confined geographical areas, has been the rise of geomatics. This is the technical name to describe the rise of geospatial technology that combines innovations in Geographical Information Systems and mobile technology that uses geo-referenced information such as mobile phone and satellite positioning systems, as two examples. A wide range of geographical and associated disciplinary studies (e.g. from computer science) have sought to combine the notion of time–space paths to analyse what tourists who can be tracked are doing, where and when. Whilst the research has substantially expanded our knowledge of the spatial aspects of demand, such as Xiao-Ting and Bi-Hu's (2012) study of intra-attraction travel systems and McKercher et al.'s (2012) study of first-time and repeat travellers to Hong Kong (which demonstrated that first-time visitors have a broader search and exploratory domain than repeat visitors, who focus on specific places and themes), this still does not address the wider debates on the nature of tourist decision-making as the basis for spatial behaviour (i.e. Smallman and Moore 2010), although Pearce (2011) does highlight the major contributions which the new technological advances can make towards a more spatially contingent awareness of tourist behaviour in a dynamic setting – space and place.

Conclusions

The analysis of behavioural issues in recreational and tourism research indicates that 'in behavioural terms then, there seems little necessity to insist on a major distinction between tourism and leisure phenomena. Therefore, it should follow that a greater commonality between the research efforts in the two areas would be of advantage' (Moore et al. 1995: 75), although different social theoretical approaches exist towards the analysis of recreation and tourism phenomena. As a result, Moore et al. (1995: 79) conclude that 'there is little need, if any, to take a dramatically different approach to the behavioural analysis of tourism and leisure'. Similarly, the UNWTO (2009: 3) argues, 'Travel motivation is increasingly characterised by a search for leisure, emotional recharge, authenticity, fulfilling experience, outdoor activities/adventure, and a general desire to participate and explore, rather than merely relax. In particular, there is a need to "get away from it all", and to use travel and holidays as discovery of place, culture and of self', which spills over into leisure behaviour, as the motivations for tourism and leisure demonstrate.

One needs to view each activity in the context of the everyday life of the people involved to understand how each is conceived. There is a clear distinction within the literature between what motivates recreationalists and tourists and comparative studies of similar groups of people, and the similarities and differences between these motivations has yet to permeate the research literature. While geographers have focused on recreational and tourist behaviour in relation to demand issues, the analysis has largely been quantitative, site specific and has not adapted a comparative methodology to examine the recreation–tourism continuum. One notable study by Connell (2005) questions the tendency to overlook the historical context of much tourism and leisure research, which is particularly pertinent to the spatial analysis of tourism and leisure phenomena. As Page (2003a) argued, the patterns of continuity and change in the analysis of tourism and leisure geographies provide a containing context for research, since cultural, social and spatial interactions shape and form the landscapes and forms of leisure and tourism experience through time that are constantly evolving. This historical imperative is essential, as many of the chapters in this book demonstrate, to understand tourism and leisure beyond the research context as a snapshot in time. This is nowhere more evident than in the analysis of supply issues, which demonstrate their enduring ability to adapt and evolve through time as the demand and markets for their products and services change.

Further reading

For recreational demand the following studies are very useful introductions:

Pigram, J.J. and Jenkins, J. (1999) *Outdoor Recreation Management*, London: Routledge (by far the best book on recreational research published to date by geographers).

In terms of factors constraining demand, see:

Crawford, D., Jackson, E. and Godbey, G. (1991) 'A hierarchical model of leisure constraints', *Leisure Sciences*, 13: 309–20.

A good example of the constraints on demand can be found in:

Madge, C. (1997) 'Public parks and the geography of fear', *Tijdschrift voor Economische en Sociale Geografie*, 88: 237–50.

At a general level, the best overviews of studies of tourism demand are:

Crouch, G. (1994) 'The study of tourism demand: a review of findings', *Journal of Travel Research*, 33(1): 2–21.

Shaw, G., Agarwal, S. and Bull, P. (2000) 'Tourism consumption and tourist behaviour: a British perspective', *Tourism Geographies*, 2: 264–89.

Uysal, M. (1998) 'The determinants of tourism demand: a theoretical perspective', in D. Ioannides and K. Debbage (eds) *The Economic Geography of the Tourist Industry: A Supply-side Analysis*, London: Routledge.

An interesting account of changes in demand is:

Shaw, G. and Williams, A. (eds) (1997) *The Rise and Fall of British Coastal Resorts: Cultural and Economic Perspectives*, London: Mansell.

A useful collection of readings with respect to tourism statistics is:

Lennon, J. (ed.) (2003) *Tourism Statistics: International Perspectives and Current Issues*, London: Continuum.

and the chapter by:

Latham, J. and Edwards, C. (2003) 'The statistical measurement of tourism', in C. Cooper (ed.) *Classic Reviews in Tourism*, Clevedon: Channel View.

Questions to discuss

1   **What is recreational demand and how have geographers attempted to measure it?**

2   **How far does the use of recreational resources conform with models of leisure and recreational demand?**

3   **What is the role of tourism demand in the analysis of tourism patterns in time and space?**

4   **'The use of psychological constructs and models of tourist behaviour does not explain why people go on holiday to specific locations.' Discuss.**

The supply of recreation and tourism

Within the literature on recreation and tourism, there has been a paucity of conceptual and theoretical research on the supply component of these activities, although Song (2012) has provided a recent review of the advances in tourism supply chain management. The geographer has traditionally approached the supply issues informed by concepts and models from economic geography focusing on the location and the spatial distribution of recreational and tourism resources which shape the activity patterns and spectrum of opportunity for leisure pursuits. However, since the mid-1990s more qualitative research challenged the positivist approach to spatial analysis with reference to leisure supply (e.g. Aitchison 1999; Mansvelt 2010). This has resulted in more sophisticated cultural geographies of leisure (as discussed more fully in Chapter 2) that highlight the importance of more theoretically derived explanations of key geographical questions on leisure and tourism provision (i.e. supply). In particular, such research questions the notion of who gets what, where, with more emphasis on why, the classic statement by Lasswell (1936) with respect to the study of politics. More theoretically informed research from a political economy perspective (Hall 2012c) tends to utilise structural explanations to help understand issues of location. This approach focuses on the way society is managed and controlled by those exercising power in examining causes rather than just the effects in time and space. The result is that the geographer needs to consider more challenging perspectives related to the way in which leisure (and tourism) supply is produced by the state and private sector at different scales. Indeed, Schwanen and Kwan (2009) extend the debate, arguing for more critical spatial analysis by geographers that challenges the different forms of oppression and exploitation that reflect the long tradition of radical geography developed by Peet (2009; see also Hall 2012a). This chapter will review some of these new debates together with the evolution of the geographer's contribution to the analysis of supply issues.

What is supply?

Supply is the overarching concept to explain how resources and services are delivered to the source of demand (the consumer) and has developed divergent approaches within the leisure and tourism literature. Although supply and demand are, in one sense, inseparable – as the leisure or tourism experience occurs at the point they coincide – it is often conceptually useful to separate the concepts for ease of analysis. The term 'supply' is also often used interchangeably with the concept of production. Leisure supply has predominantly adopted a localised and regional focus reflected in the distances people could travel to consume resources (as well as the in-home consumption). In contrast, tourism supply has developed a range of perspectives that expands upon the regional and national scale of analysis through to the international scale in view of the distance and scale of consumption in relation to the place of residence which most leisure trips are focused around in terms of origin/destination flows (see Chapter 1). While changing definitions and conceptualisations of the boundaries of tourism and leisure question this artificial distinction between the spatial continuum of what and where tourism and leisure end and begin, scale and distance remain critical factors in the differentiation of different forms of supply for leisure and tourism consumers even though they may sometimes consume the same resource/location.

The supply factor in leisure and recreation

According to Kreutzwiser (1989: 21), 'supply refers to the recreational resources, both natural and man-made, which provide opportunities for recreation. It is a complex concept influenced by numerous factors and subject to changing interpretations.' Recreational supply is also a concept which has prompted much thought in terms of classification and evaluation, particularly among geographers. Although, as Page and Connell (2010) show, studies of leisure back to the 1890s through to the 1950s included descriptive research on supply issues so the geographer cannot claim to have been the main contributor to its analysis and interpretation. Coppock and Duffield (1975: 151) pursue this theme a stage further in a spatial context, claiming that it is the 'spatial interaction between the homes of recreationalists and the resources they use [which] has emerged as a key factor in the demand/supply model', and arguing for an integrated analysis of such interactions to explain how the activity patterns of recreationalists in terms of their origins and destinations affect the supply variable in terms of where they go, what they do there and how this affects the resource base. Even so we need to recognise, as McIntyre (2003) argues, that leisure consumption is about how supply fulfils many of the underlying motivations associated with leisure, particularly in a time–space setting. According to Mihalic (2003), the supply of leisure is rather unusual because:

- It is associated with a variety of goods and services, which may be connected to specific places or environments that determine the characteristics and forms of leisure that may be undertaken.

For example, in coastal environments, the natural environment determines the type of leisure activities and uses which are largely resource dependent.
- The supply of leisure is a complex amalgam of different suppliers (i.e. the commercial sector, public sector and voluntary bodies) who have a variety of objectives in relation to the resources, facilities or opportunities they provide (Page and Connell 2010: 155).

The next section commences with a discussion of the underlying approach used to describe and document the supply of recreational opportunities by geographers, which is followed by an analysis of the spatial interaction of demand and supply to illustrate how the two components are interrelated. This is developed in relation to the three characteristics that geographers have synthesised to analyse recreational activities, namely:

- the locational characteristics associated with the supply of different forms of recreational resource;
- the patterns of demand and usage;
- the spatial interactions which occur between the demand for and supply of the recreational resource, emphasising journey patterns and the patterns of usage of specific resources.

This gives rise to concentrated, dispersed and combinations of each pattern at the site of the resources, which therefore raises questions as to how to evaluate the capacity of such resources to accommodate users and to reconcile conflicts in use and the identification of management and planning issues. For the cultural geographer with an interest in leisure, the interest is less about the resulting spatial patterns of supply, but how the cultural dimension conditions, affects and impacts upon the spatial interactions between supply and demand.

How has the geographer approached the analysis of recreational supply issues?

The geographer's approach is epitomised in many of the classic recreational texts (e.g. Patmore 1970;

Lavery 1971c; I. Simmons 1975; Pigram 1983), where the supply perspective is largely dependent upon the evaluation and assessment of resources for recreation, the highly influential 1962 US Outdoor Recreation Resources Review Commission studies being a template for this approach. The concept of a resource may often be taken to include those tangible objects in nature which are of economic value and used for productive purposes. But when looking at leisure and recreation natural resources have an important bearing, particularly those such as water bodies, countryside and open space. The fact that resources have a physical form (i.e. coal and iron ore) does not actually mean they constitute a resource. Such elements become a resource only when society's subjective evaluation of their potential leads to their recognition as a resource to satisfy human wants and needs (O'Riordan 1971).

Yet a resource is far from just a passive element – it has to be used creatively to meet certain socially valued goals. Thus recreational resources are 'an element of the natural or man-modified environment which provides an opportunity to satisfy recreational wants. Implicit is a continuum ranging from biophysical resources to man-made facilities' (Kreutzwiser 1989: 22). However, according to Glyptis (1989a: 135), to 'couple recreational with resources complicates definitions . . . In a recreational context resources are the natural resources of land, water and landscape, together with manmade resources including sport centres, swimming pools, parks and playing fields', though she also notes that few recreational activities make use of resources solely designed or in existence for recreational purposes.

As Pigram and Jenkins (1999: 59) argued, 'identification and valuation of elements of the environment as recreation resources will depend upon a number of factors (e.g. economics, social attitudes and perceptions, political perspectives and technology)'. As a result, Pigram and Jenkins (1999: 59) recognised that outdoor recreational resources may encompass a wide range of settings associated with space, topography and climatic characteristics. This expands upon Hart's (1966) early notion of the 'recreation resource base', which was the natural values of the countryside or respective landscape. Such a notion was clarified in specific terms by Clawson and Knetsch:

> There is nothing in the physical landscape or features of any particular piece of land or body of water that makes it a recreation resource; it is the combination of the natural qualities and the ability and desire of man to use them that makes a resource out of what might otherwise be a more or less meaningless combination of rocks, soil and trees.
>
> (Clawson and Knetsch 1966: 7)

However, such resources are not static, since new trends, technologies or cultural appraisals can lead to new notions of the environment as a recreational resource.

Recreation in rural contexts (Chapter 6) often occurs alongside agriculture, forestry and water supply functions (Goodall and Whittow 1975; Jennings 2006), especially near large urban centres where there are many resource users. In this respect the identification of recreational resources needs to recognise the management implications of multiple use, a feature discussed on pp. 103–107. While Glyptis (1989a) also outlined the demands of many forms of recreation which have few land needs, this analysis is concerned with recreational forms that have a land use component, given the geographer's interest in how human activities and phenomena are interrelated and occur on the earth's surface. Yet even Glyptis (1989a) pays little explicit attention to the resource base – the supply dimension – beyond highlighting Patmore's (1983) geographical perspective, which concentrates on 'contemporary patterns of recreational activity and the demands they place on the land and water resources, with myriad references to management issues and solutions' (Glyptis 1989a: 137).

But this still does not illuminate the approaches, concepts and specific skills the geographer brings to the analysis of recreational supply issues. To understand supply, Roberts (2004) identified a series of interconnected leisure industries (and organisations within each industry sector) which influence both home-based and non-home-based leisure, which Page and Connell (2010) identified as different *spheres of influence* which these interrelated sectors (i.e. the commercial, not for profit and public sectors) have on leisure. As Page and Connell (2010) suggest, it is the interplay of these three different sectors which then lead to the final supply of leisure in any specific context, as illustrated by Figure 3.1, where the site of consumption was the ultimate spatial context for analysis. This framework needed to pay attention to the economic, social, psychological, political and environmental factors shaping leisure provision as a basis for understanding the resulting patterns of consumption. As organisations are responsible for the provision of certain forms of leisure provision and resulting experiences, space is one interconnected component of a broader setting conditioning leisure and recreation provision.

Although early criticisms of the geography of recreation research by S.J. Smith (1983a) pointed to the lack of analytical and theoretical framework, with exceptions the rise of social and cultural geographies of leisure has addressed these weaknesses. One might even argue that such research is almost spatially devoid of any understanding of leisure, being less able to derive wider generalisations of the applicability of such

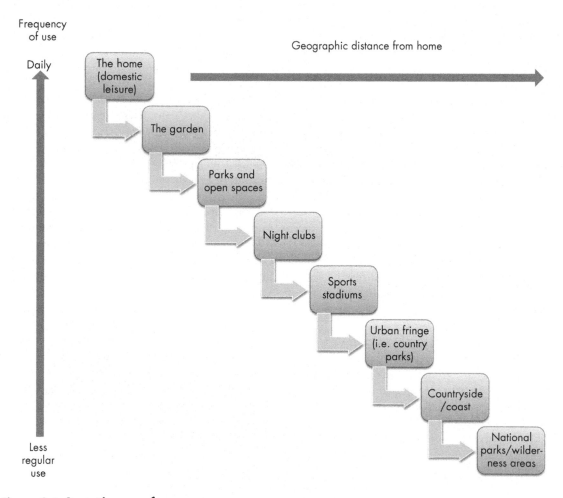

Figure 3.1 **A continuum of resources**

research to knowledge. S.J. Smith (1989: 304) listed the principal research questions geographers pose, which outline the particular concerns for supply issues:

- Where are the resources? What is their quality and capacity? What effect will use of those resources have on the resource base and the local environment? What will the effect be on other people who live in the area and on other users?
- How easy is it for people to travel to the resource or facility? What are their travel costs? Are there other constraints, such as problems of physical accessibility, inconvenient scheduling, excessive admission fees, and racial, linguistic and social barriers?
- What new facilities or resources need to be supplied? What areas have priority for the new supply? Who should pay to support those who play? How many people are expected to use a new facility at a given location?
- What are the regional differences in recreation preferences? Why do these exist? Do they represent differences in tastes, culture or historical inequalities?

It is interesting to note that advice from the UK's Audit Commission (2003: 9) on managing leisure resources in the public sector (i.e. by local authorities), under the heading of 'strategic advice', associated with what type of management models to adopt towards managing their portfolio of leisure resources, asks many similar questions. This illustrates the implicit application of geography as a discipline to ensure not only best value for money in leisure service provision, but also that different groups of people gain access to resources and so are not excluded from participating as Box 2.1 illustrated.

According to S.J. Smith (1983a) geographers have approached the analysis of recreational geography in a number of ways, including descriptive research on location and travel, explanatory research on location and travel, predictive research on location and travel and normative research on location and travel (for more detail on other aspects of the research developed in this context, see Smith (1983a).

Recreational research: descriptive, explanatory, predictive and normative perspectives

S.J. Smith (1983a: 1) argued that the 'description of location is the study of differences' which can be classified in terms of description of facility of recreational resource location, where the distribution of resources pertinent to the specific activity may be enumerated and mapped. Within this context the inventories of recreational resources have attracted a great deal of attention, which arguably underpins much of the

Table 3.1 The land use classes of the Canada land inventory

Class	Description
1 Very high capability	These lands have natural capability to engender very high total annual use of one or more intensive activities. These lands should be able to generate and sustain a level of use comparable to that evident at an outstanding and large bathing beach or a nationally known ski slope
2 High capability	These lands have natural capability to engender and sustain high total annual use based on one or more intensive activity.
3 Moderately high capability	These lands have a natural ability to engender and sustain moderately high total annual use based on moderate to intensive or intensive activities.
4 Moderate capability	These lands have natural capability to engender and sustain moderate total annual use based on dispersed activities.
5 Moderately low capability	These lands have natural capability to engender and sustain moderately low total annual use based on dispersed activities.
6 Low capability	These lands lack the natural quality and significant features to rate higher, but have the natural capability to engender and sustain low total annual use based on dispersed activities.
7 Very low capability	These lands have practically no capability for any popular type of recreation activity, but there may be some opportunity for very specialised activities with recreation aspects, or they may simply provide open space.

preliminary research undertaken to establish recreational supply features in quantity and quality. Resource inventories, such as the Outdoor Recreation Resources Review Commission (1962; see also Chapter 7), typify this approach, whereby, for example, the quantity and number of designated public recreation areas were tabulated and mapped by area along US coastlines. A more complex method is to develop a typology of resource types and uses such as Clawson and Knetsch's (1968) widely cited model of recreational resources which can be classified as urban and rural resource based, intermediate and user oriented. Additional variables which might be added to such classifications include human-modified and natural resources; formal and informal; intensive and extensive; fragile and resistant; while public and private ownership may also be included (Wall 1989).

The Canada Land Inventory (Department of Regional Economic Expansion 1972) is a useful example of one such inventory that set out to provide an overview of the quality, quantity and distribution of natural recreation resources within settled regions of Canada; to indicate comparative levels of recreation capability for non-urban lands based upon preferences; and to indicate the types of recreation and land use (see Table 3.1). While there are criticisms of this approach related to the consistency of data collection and interpretation, it provides a valuable synthesis on the potential of Canadian land resources to support recreational activity. S.J. Smith (1983a) also explored more advanced methods used to classify recreational resources, including deglomerative methods (where resources are subdivided into distinct groups) and agglomerative methods (where resource types are grouped into general categories). Deglomerative studies remain more widely used than the latter. Yet such methods of analysis pay less attention to the importance of human (i.e. subjective) evaluations of resources for recreation (e.g. Coppock and Duffield's 1975 assessment of recreational potential in the countryside). Such approaches remain influential to the present day and often serve as the basis for regional outdoor recreation planning (Pigram and Jenkins 2006).

One of the notable debates in resource studies for recreation in the late 1960s and early 1970s was the evaluation of recreation environments (Duffield and Owen 1970) related to preferential descriptions of recreational resources, namely aesthetic studies which measure human preferences and how they respond to landscape alterations. According to Pigram and Jenkins (1999: 76) the multifaceted nature of landscape, personal preferences and individual perception make evaluation a highly subjective activity. In the assessment of scenic landscape elements, two fundamental elements exist: the character of the landscape (i.e. the components of the landscape which are visual and part of an inventory such as vegetation, water, human occupation) and quality, which is a comparative-evaluative concept, in part determined by landscape characteristics. Unwin (1976) identified landscape quality as a three-stage process:

- *Landscape description*, which is the objective inventory of landscape characteristics to classify the landscape type.
- *Landscape preference*, where visual preference ratings are allocated to specific landscape characteristics. This is largely dependent upon subjective preferences and value judgements.
- *Landscape evaluation*, where the specific qualities of the landscapes being considered are assessed to examine preferences of specific respondents.

Fines' (1968) influential study in East Sussex epitomises this approach, where a group of people with a background in design work were asked to assign a value to a series of landscape photographs compared to a reference photograph with an indifferent landscape. Once the landscapes were assessed by individuals, a consensus score was assigned and then the people were asked to rank landscapes viewed around East Sussex. While Linton (1968) disagreed with both the nomenclature and scale used by Fines (1968), he concluded that two key elements existed in the landscape: land use and landforms. These could be mapped and categories established, where a composite score could be devised to reflect the beauty of the landscape (Table 3.2). Linton (1968) developed his study in Scotland, and again, controversy was associated with the almost arbitrary use of a points system, where urban areas were seen as low scoring.

In the 1980s, landscape assessment became used as a tool to separate classification and description of

Table 3.2 **Linton's landscape evaluation scale**

Landforms	Points	Land uses	Points
Mountains	8	Wild landscapes	6
Bold hills	6	Richly varied farming	5
Hill country	5	Varied forest with moors and farms	4
Plateau uplands	3	Moors	3
Low uplands	2	Treeless farms	1
Lowlands	0	Continuous forest	−2
		Urban and industrial land	−5

Source: Linton (1968).

landscape character, as the Countryside Agency (2003) suggests. This has now been superseded by more holistic approaches to landscape, based on the concept of Landscape Character Assessment, with a clearer link to sustainable development and environmental protection. The characterisation of landscape involves the integration of identification, mapping, classification, description and the associated formulation of a character. The significance is that it has a clearer basis for the spatial management of landscapes for recreation and leisure. The importance of the geographer's contribution to landscape evaluation (see Cornish 1934 for an early contribution) was summarised by Penning-Rowsell (1975), whereby it could assist in landscape management with direct consequences for outdoor recreation. The four areas of significance were as follows:

- *Landscape preservation*, so that landscapes worthy of conservation could be identified.
- *Landscape protection*, where landscapes that are under threat from pressure for development (e.g. economic activity and environmental impacts) can be placed under planning controls.
- *Recreation policy*, where specific policies and forms of outdoor recreation can be facilitated in valued environments within planning constraints.
- *Landscape improvement*, where potential negative landscape features (e.g. brownfield sites) can be remedied to transform the landscape into more attractive recreational purposes. A good example is the transformation of former extractive sites for gravel within urban fringe locations to provide angling and recreational boating opportunities.

Indeed, the application of such techniques in a wider recreational context is noted by Pigram and Jenkins (1999) in relation to New Zealand. The Resource Management Act 1991 (see Page and Thorn 1997, 1998, 2002; Connell *et al.* 2009) has seen planning move away from land use zoning methods to ones where the impacts of specific activities are evaluated so that potential environmental outcomes are also considered. More recent combinations of economic valuation techniques and the linking to spatial analysis using GIS technologies have seen a greater quantification of the landscape elements which constitute the resource base for leisure (e.g. Pastor *et al.* 2007), along with an assessment of public preferences for specific landscape types (e.g. Kienast *et al.* 2012) at a city level. Even so, such research still reiterates that the supply of leisure resources most heavily used is within a 10–15 minute distance of a home and so this is the most important locale for accessibility to supply (Patmore 1983). Even recent research in China (e.g. Jim and Chen 2009) confirms the significance of these underlying principles of time–space relationships in local leisure use. Yet more critical research on more marginalised social groups such as the disabled suggests that places with no financial resource are sought out in the urban environment (typically the city centre) and the urban fringe amongst the less mobile (Taylor and Józefowicz 2012). As the main location of the population in many countries, urban areas remain important for recreation and tourism (Chapter 5) and it seems naive to dismiss certain resources in such a generalised manner as many studies do, especially given the future growth in urbanisation in Latin America and Asia forecast to 2030.

While a great deal of debate exists in relation to such approaches to landscape evaluation, it does illustrate the importance of human perception, and recognition of what is attractive and valued by different people in relation to recreational time. In terms of descriptive research on travel, it has little immediate relevance to supply unless one is concerned with the impact of demand on the resource base. As a result, the geographer's concern with recreational travel using concepts such as nodes, routes, mode of travel and accessibility of resources for recreationalists has little immediate value unless it is linked with more recent agendas such as social inclusion and access (Taylor and Józefowicz 2012).

Moving from purely descriptive to explanatory research illustrates the importance of location as a recreational facility which someone may want to use. S.J. Smith (1983a) outlined two concerns regarding the location of such facilities: those factors affecting public and those affecting private location decisions, although the distinction between such issues has blurred where public–private sector involvement, co-operation and management have complicated traditional locational models developed in economic geography, which has separated public and private goods (Hall and Jenkins 1995; Roberts 2004; Page and Connell 2010). For example, L. Mitchell (1969b) applied central place theory to the location of urban parks as public recreational resources, establishing that a hierarchy existed, but rather simplified a number of real world issues by substituting assumptions, while also ignoring influential variables such as land prices, availability and political influences (see Chapter 5). Other studies (e.g. Mitchell and Lovingwood 1976) adopted empirical measures to examine correlations between variables that might explain locational patterns, where Haley (1979) made the vital, though often missed, observation that present-day patterns often reflect the demands of previous generations. Likewise, where new suburban developments did not require developers to provide park facilities, a dearth of parks exist. Communities in such areas have not sought such provision due to local factors (e.g. private recreation sites and access to the urban fringe). The role of private recreation provision was examined by Mitchell and Lovingwood (1976; Lovingwood and

Mitchell 1978), who mapped 172 public and 112 private recreational facilities, using nearest neighbour analysis to examine the spatial patterns. They concluded that public facilities had a tendency to cluster, while private facilities had a regular pattern of distribution for campsites, country clubs and miscellaneous uses, and water-based facilities and hunting/fishing clubs tended to cluster. The outcome of their analysis was that

- *public facilities* are concentrated in areas of population density to meet the wider good and in accessible locations, having no major resource considerations;
- *private facilities* are located on one of two bases: either in or near open space, as in the case of campsites and country clubs, and are located throughout the region, or, conversely, water-based facilities and hunting clubs are closely tied to a land or water location, clustering around the resource.

In contrast, much of the geographical research on private recreational facility development has been based on the approach developed in retail marketing and location studies, where location is seen as the critical success factor, although Bevins *et al.* (1974) observed that this was not necessarily a critical factor for private campsites in north-east USA. Within most studies of recreational location, principal concepts are related to the threshold population, catchment areas or hinterlands and distance to travel to the facility. As Crompton and Van Doren (1976) observed, tram companies in mid-nineteenth century America built amusement parks at the end of tramlines to attract weekend visitors, illustrating the importance of recreational travel as part of the overall experience.

The geographer's tradition of model building to predict location of characteristics of private enterprise has been applied to recreational geography in terms of the transfer of location theory and site selection methods. Within the research on location theory, transport cost has played a significant role based on Von Thünen's agricultural land use model, and Vickerman (1975) simplistically applied the model to predict urban recreation businesses. Yet the use of concepts such as locational interdependence, where the potential buyers are not uniformly distributed in space, means that businesses may be able to exercise a degree of control over their clients by their location. Such studies based on the early work of economic geographers such as Reilly (1931), Christaller (1933) and Lösch (1944) developed a number of principles which geographers have used to underpin locational modelling recreational research. While subsequent research by Isard (1956) and Greenhut (1956) can be added to the list, S.J. Smith (1983a: 106) summarises the contribution of such studies to the analysis of recreational location choices by business:

- A firm with relatively low transportation costs and a relatively large market area will have a greater chance of success than a firm with high transportation costs and a small market area.
- Some trade-offs are possible between transportation costs, production costs, land rents and market size.
- Transportation costs include both the cost of bringing resources to the site of the firm and the costs of distributing the product to the customer. The relative costs of transporting both resources and products determine, in part, where the firm will locate: high resource transportation costs pull a business close to the resource; high product transportation costs pull a business close to the market.
- Some types of business seek to locate close to each other; some are indifferent to each other; some are repelled by each other.
- Different locations will be attractive to different types of businesses. Attractiveness is based on resources; market location; transportation services; availability of capital, labour and business services; and personal preferences of the decision-maker.
- Firms in any given industry will tend to divide up the available market by selecting different locations to control different spatial segments of the market.
- The size of the market and the number and location of competitors tend to limit the size of the potential development.

These need to be examined in relation to the decision-making of entrepreneurs and individual firms. In terms of site selection methods, feasibility studies have provided a starting point for geographers seeking to assess the most suitable site from a range of alternatives, with the purpose of maximising profit (or wider social benefits in the public sector) though comparatively little research has been published given the scope of such studies (i.e. sources of capital, management issues, design and development issues, market size, population characteristics, economic profile of the potential market and the suitability of the site) and the tendency for such documents to remain commercially sensitive in both the public and private sector. What is evident from the existing research seeking to predict locational characteristics for recreational activities and facilities is the reliance upon economic geography, particularly retail geography, with its concomitant concern for marketing.

In terms of normative research, it is evident that within the public sector, the objectives for locational decision-making are distinctly different (or at least traditionally have been different, despite changing political philosophies towards public recreation provision). The characteristics of public sector provision have traditionally been associated with taxes paid for facility provision and operation, with a collective use that cannot be withheld, so that access is not knowingly prohibited to anyone. In other words, their contribution to the quality of life and wider social well-being of the affected population underpins public provision that cannot easily be accommodated into conventional locational theory, which is market driven. Austin (1974) identifies recreational facilities as 'site preferred' goods, where proximity to their location is often seen as a measure of their use (i.e. its utility function). Thus maximum distances exist as in the case of urban parks (see Chapter 5). The object, therefore, in public facility location for recreation is to balance the 'utility' factor with minimising the distance people have to travel and providing access to as many people as possible; though Cichetti (1971) examined a number of the problems associated with different methods of balancing travel distances, social utility and other approaches to demand maximisation. Smith (1983a) reviews a range of methods of analysis used by geographers to assist in work on public facility site selection, namely models, which emphasise mechanical analogues, comparative needs assessment, demand maximisation, heuristic programming and intuitive modelling (for more detail, see Smith 1983a).

Howell and McNamee (2003) reviewed the literature on how public sector leisure policy allocates scarce resources, particularly how fiscal retrenchment in the public sector, as a response to a greater managerialism, has placed a greater emphasis on private sector provision as well as 'best value' in local authority provision. Erkip's (1997) evaluation of the distribution of urban parks and recreational services in Ankara, Turkey, raised a number of important debates which the geographer, public policy-maker and recreational planner need to address. The normative nature of urban public service provision for recreation as public goods raises distribution issues such as:

- To what extent can the spatial distribution of public goods and services achieve equal versus selective access? Although equal access is a normative concept, in reality goods and services will rarely achieve equality of access, particularly where fixed resources have to be located.
- The extent to which the public versus private sector should be responsible for the provision of services, a feature which is inherently politically determined and has transformed the nature of leisure and recreation provision since 1980 (Coalter 1998).
- The extent to which private sector profit objectives can be balanced with public sector distributional objectives for public goods and services such as leisure and recreation resources.

In the case of Ankara, Erkip (1997) found that the use of the nearest park or recreational facility was a function of users' income and distance from the resource. As a result, for low income groups proximity was more important, with higher income groups enjoying greater distributional justice. This highlights one of the inherent concerns of welfare geographers such as D.M. Smith (1977): concepts of territorial justice obscure the social and economic processes which condition recreational activity, whereby distributional justice by social group is neglected and access to certain public goods is constrained. In fact, Crouch (2000: 72) questions the value of such rational concepts as territorial justice that were used in the early research on welfare geography, since in a leisure context 'People behave subjectively rather than rationally. It is easy to apply explanations of rationality to what people do, but very often that provides categories that do not fit subjective practices' – again questioning the empiricist-positivist tradition of model building and testing to understand critical recreational supply issues. As a result of Crouch's (2000) criticisms of the empiricist-positivist paradigm in human geography, which have been applied to recreational issues, one might add a new category to the geographical analysis of supply – the interaction between supply and demand. While this results in distinct spatial interactions, research informed by the new cultural geography (Aitchison 1999; Mansvelt 2010) departs from a model building tradition, to understand the nuances, unique features and, above all, the individual human experiences of different forms of encounter with recreation and leisure supply. Again, to reiterate some of the comments from Chapter 2, the approach, methodologies used and lines of inquiry pursued in seeking to understand the human geographies of recreation and leisure supply place the people to the fore, affected by agency, structure and the political economy of leisure provision.

This places many of the conventional spatially derived explanations of leisure supply in a different context, seeking more theoretically informed answers to conventional place- and space-specific forms of leisure consumption by focusing at the level of individual experiences. This highlights many of the tensions reviewed in Chapter 10 on the nexus between academic analyses of tourism and recreation which are objective and robust, and the challenge of applied geographical research, often for clients, that does not permit more challenging analyses that are associated with issues of power, control and political economy. This has become a major focal point in the *International Encyclopedia of Human Geography* (Kitchin and Thrift 2009) in many of the chapters that epitomise the wider concerns now pervading human geography (and thereby influencing and cross-fertilising the analysis of leisure), including new philosophical approaches to geography, social and cultural geographies (including key contributions on issues of feminism, the body and sexuality), and interdisciplinary developments. The diversity of research now in vogue within human geography and seeing their application to leisure (and tourism) geographies is embodied in Wilson's (2012) review of the field.

Supply and demand in recreational contexts: spatial interactions

Given the comparative neglect of recreational supply issues by geographers and the overriding emphasis in demand studies and impact assessment (Owens 1984), it is pertinent to acknowledge the geographer's synthesising role in recognising that 'recreationalists and the resources they use are separated in space, [and] the interaction between demand and supply creates patterns of movement, and the distances between origins and destinations influence not only the scale of demand, but also the available supply of resources' (Coppock and Duffield 1975: 150). Few studies, with the exception of Coppock and Duffield's (1975), acknowledge this essential role the geographer has played in contextualising the real world impact of recreational activities in a spatial framework as space has now faded into the background in much of the social and cultural analysis of leisure geographies in pursuit of more meaning and understanding of what creates distinct leisure experiences. One might argue that the division in qualitative and quantitative analysis in leisure and recreation studies undertaken by geographers (and increasingly social scientists with an implicit interest in space) has led to an almost insurmountable disconnect between the two areas. A more positive analysis would argue that the foundations established by key researchers in the period up to the 1990s has created the macro settings in which more in-depth and qualitative research can yield detailed explorations of leisure and recreation practices. While many recreational researchers may view these early seminal contributions as passé, they are notable since no other discipline offers such a holistic and integrative assessment of recreation and tourism phenomena since much of social science is concerned with the micro scale of analysis in leisure and recreation (with the exception of environmental economics).

Coppock and Duffield (1975) acknowledge the resource base as a precondition of assessing the 'space needs' of recreationalists in that the amount of land, the activities to be undertaken, length of journey and nature of the resource help to determine the type of interactions which occur. Clawson et al.'s (1960) typology which comprised an:

- user oriented zone which is located close to the users in close proximity and within an urban setting might include public or private resources such as a park, places for games and activities such as swimming pools
- a resource based area which is located in remoter areas and may be used for sightseeing, outdoor activities such and walking or climbing, camping epitomised by National Parks, the coast or lakes
- an intermediate area in between the two other areas (user and resource-based) which is characterised by many of the routine outdoor activities that are the focus of day trips, activity trips for walking and camping and are in a reasonable travel distance (perhaps up to 3 hours) and are characterised by reservoirs, forest parks and rural area around major city regions (Source: Developed from Clawson et al. (1960: 136))

and its subsequent application to England and Wales (Law 1967) both confirm the importance of distance and the 'zones of influence' of recreational resources according to whether they had a national, regional, sub-regional, intermediate or local zone of influence, using actual distance to classify the resource according to the 'pull' or attraction of each. Law (1967) argued that the majority of day-trippers would be drawn from no more than 48 km away. What Coppock and Duffield (1975) recognised was that it was not individual but groups of resources which attract active recreation.

At a descriptive level, the relationships outlined in the Clawson et al. (1960) model appears to have an application, where:

- in a 0–16 km zone, many resource needs for recreation can be met in terms of golf, urban parks and the urban fringe;

- in a 16–32 km zone, the range of activities is greater, though particular types of resource tend to dominate activity patterns (e.g. horse riding, hiking and field sports);
- in a zone of 32 km or greater, sports and physical pursuits with specific resource requirements (e.g. orienteering, canoeing, skiing and rock climbing) exist.

Yet despite increased mobility of recreationists, the majority of popular activities are undertaken relatively near to the home, as past and current research continues to reiterate. To expand upon these findings, attention now turns to classifying and analysing the supply of recreational resources within the context of the urban fringe.

Classifying recreational resources

In the analysis of recreation patterns, trends and resource use by specific groups, the complexity of the existing recreation stock requires some form of classification to improve our understanding (see Fisher *et al.* 1974; Doren *et al.* 1979; Gilg 1985), thereby simplifying the existing complexity. In other words, the recognition of recreational resources needs to be accompanied by an inventory process to take stock of the quantity, quality and extent of the resource base. For this reason, classification schemes have been derived. In the previous section, the preliminary attempt by Clawson *et al.* (1960) to derive a classification system distinguished between recreation areas according to location, activity type, major uses, size of the area and who was responsible for recreation resource management (Table 3.2). One of the problems with this classification scheme was that it neglected urban and near-urban sites and developed a narrow conception of outdoor recreation resources. Even so, this classification was a critical turning point in recreational thinking, since it spurned numerous adaptations, stimulating new ways of thinking about classifying recreational resources. Although no definitive scheme exists for classifying recreational resources, the need to distinguish between human-made and natural resources, different resource environments and

resource types provides a useful starting point. In this respect, Chubb and Chubb's (1981) classification is valuable since it incorporates much of the thinking in recreational research, building on Clawson *et al.* (1960), where the following classes of recreation resources exist:

- *the undeveloped recreation resources*, where the physical attributes of land, water and vegetation are untouched;
- *private recreation resources*, such as second homes, resources owned by quasi-public organisations (e.g. conservation groups, farm and industrial sites);
- *commercialised private recreation resources*, such as shopping malls, theme parks, museums, gardens, stadiums and resorts;
- *publicly owned recreation resources*, including parks, sports and leisure facilities, national parks, forest and tourist sites;
- *cultural resources*, based in both the public and private sector, such as libraries, the Arts and what are increasingly being termed 'the cultural industries' (see Pratt 1998);
- *professional resources*, which may be divided into the administrative functions for recreational provision (organisation, policy-making and financial support systems) and management (e.g. research, planning, development and conservation/programming functions).

Other attempts to classify recreational resources have also recognised that a continuum exists from the home-oriented space through to the neighbourhood (including the street – see Williams 1995a), with increasing scale through to community and regional space (S. Gold 1980). With these issues in mind, attention now turns to the recreational resources that exist in an urban landscape – the urban fringe.

Recreational resources and the urban fringe

The impact of urbanisation on the development of industrial societies and the effects in terms of recreational resource provision are discussed in detail in

Chapter 6. Yet the growing consumption of rural land for urban uses has led to increased concerns for the loss of non-urban land, as observed by Abercrombie (1938). Pigram (1983: 106) observed that 'every year some 1.2 million ha of rural land are converted to urban and built-up uses across America' and the greatest competition over the retention of land for recreational uses is in the city periphery or what is termed the 'urban fringe'. Elson (1993) recognised the considerable potential of the urban fringe as a resource able to accommodate recreation and sport for four reasons:

- It comprises an area of recreational supply, accessible with good public transport to large populations, though Fitton (1976) and Ferguson and Munton (1978, 1979) recognised the inaccessibility to the most deprived areas of inner London. As the Countryside Commission (1992) noted, one in five informal recreational day trips to the countryside had a return trip of less than 10 miles.
- It may be an overflow location for recreational and sporting activities displaced from urban areas.
- It can function as an 'interceptor area', reducing pressure on more fragile and vulnerable rural resources.
- It may be an area of opportunity as environmental improvements and landscape regeneration (e.g. the reclamation of former quarry sites or gravel extraction), and may generate new forms of recreation including fishing, sailing and informal use.

As Elson (1993) observes, with active recreation the fastest growing sector of countryside recreation in the UK, the urban fringe has the potential to absorb such uses. Thus by altering supply, it is assumed that demand may be directed to new resources. In this sense, the urban fringe is a useful example in which to examine the nature of spatial interactions between demand and supply.

The green belt concept

Within the UK the urban fringe has been a created landscape. In the 1930s the green belt concept was developed in London, along with many other European cities, based on the influential work of Raymond Unwin and the Green Belt Act 1933. Unwin helped establish the principle of creating a band of open space on the city's periphery in order to compensate for the lack of open space in the built urban environment. These principles were embodied in post-war planning during the 1950s (Ministry of Housing and Local Government 1955). While such designations were intended to limit urban sprawl, recreational provision was never their intended purpose and recent syntheses of the idea (e.g. Gant *et al.* 2011) indicate that the concept has been concerned with urban restraint rather than the characteristics of the land itself and its use. Elson (1986) shows that planning authorities in the West Midlands, Manchester and Sheffield identified green belt plans (e.g. green wedges, recreation and amenity areas) in their development plans only to find them downgraded or removed through the ministerial assessment of the plans. In fact, Harrison argued that

> public authorities adopted a standards approach to provision that was a legacy of the inter-war period with its heavy emphasis on organised sport rather than on a wider range of individual and family pursuits. Moreover, while these standards were based on the number of active members of the population who might be expected to participate . . . even the minimum standard of provision of 2.4 hectares per 1000 head of population could not be met in inner cities.
>
> (Harrison 1991: 32)

As a result, the urban fringe and its green belt were seen as the likely location for provision. At a policy level it is interesting to note that in the late 1960s both the Countryside Commission and local authorities used green belts as a mechanism to reduce standards of provision in the inner city (for more discussion of the politics of green belt land and recreational use, see Harrison 1991). Even so, Harrison (1980–1) found that the carrying capacity of many sites could be improved through better resource management, with the Greater London Council (1975) study of London's green belt indicating that

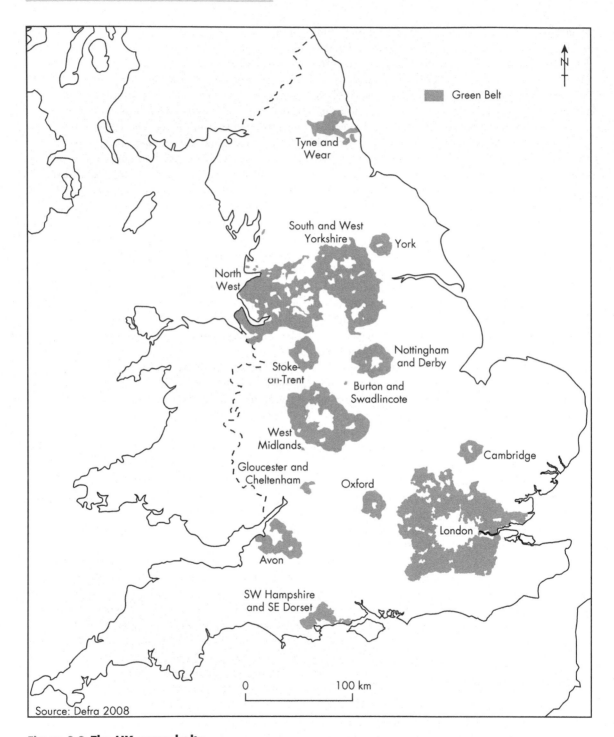

Figure 3.2 The UK green belts

Source: Gant, Robinson and Fazal 2011: 268, reproduced with permission from Elsevier.

organised activities constituted half of the trips to the green belt for recreation. Elson (1993) reports that the designation of 12 community forests in the UK of between 8,000 and 20,000 ha will add environmental improvements and resources for the urban fringe. In 2000, green belt land in England comprised 1.65 million hectares (13 per cent of the land area), with six such designations in Scotland of 156,000 ha and 236,000 ha in Northern Ireland (Figure 3.2). The significance of these landscapes of pressure as described by Gant *et al.* (2011) traces not only the evolution and rise of a chaotic set of conflicting land uses amidst pressure for urban growth, but also the major recreational role key sites play in the locale, although their lack of identity and seemingly anonymous non-place status is juxtaposed, as in the case of London (Figure 3.3), with a rapidly expanding suburban population with affluent tastes and recreational interests, reflected

in the encroachment of commercial leisure use such as golf course development.

The growing consensus of opinion is that these edgelands are important settings globally around major cities despite their underrated status as zones that are neither urban or rural (Hall 2013g). One notable development which predates much of the early research on the urban fringe is the Countryside Commission's (1974) involvement in the establishment of country parks in the urban fringe, following on from a UK government Rural White Paper on *Leisure and the Countryside* in 1966.

Multiple use of recreational resources

The example of the urban fringe highlights the diversities of land uses which may occur in a sometimes contested landscape, where a wide range of resource

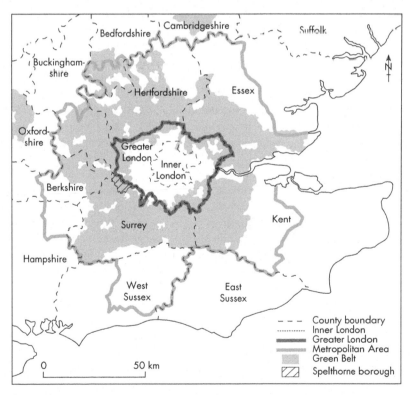

Figure 3.3 The metropolitan green belt in London and SE England
Source: Gant, Robinson and Fazal 2011: 269, reproduced with permission from Elsevier.

BOX 3.1   COUNTRY PARKS AS A SPATIAL RECREATIONAL TOOL: INTERCEPTING URBAN RECREATIONALISTS SEEKING THE COUNTRYSIDE

The Countryside Commission viewed country parks as an area of '25 acres in extent, with basic facilities, for the public to enjoy informal open air recreation' (Harrison 1991: 95). Between 1969 and 1993 the Countryside Commission spent £16 million developing these resources, establishing a network of 206 country parks and 239 picnic sites. After 1993, the Countryside Commission capital works grants were cut and this marked the end of the development of these types of capital-intensive projects in and around urban areas. However, their significance cannot be underestimated as in 2003 it was estimated that they attracted 57 million visits a year. While a number of studies account for the evolution of country park policy (Zetter 1971; Slee 1982; Groome and Tarrant 1984), it is clear that the researchers point to the absence of research which indicates whether park provision provides the experiences recreationalists require. Despite growing provision of country parks in the 1970s, disparities existed in their spatial distribution, with large conurbations having only limited provision (Ferguson and Munton 1979).

Thus spatial inequalities in supply simply reinforced existing patterns of provision, though country parks have assisted in retaining land for recreation at a time of pressure for development. Fitton (1979), for example, found that while country parks comprised 0.13 per cent of the land surface of England and Wales, they accounted for 4.2 per cent of trips, a finding supported by Elson (1979), whose analyses of 31 sites visited in south-east England found that urban fringe sites with a range of facilities were visited more frequently than other recreational destinations, though patterns of use were related to distance-decay functions, distance from individuals' home area, other attractions, individual choice and a range of other factors. As Harrison (1991: 103) suggests, country parks 'had not achieved a separate identity but people's experiences of particular sites within [them] . . . contributed to their own separate evaluations of what particular locations offered'. The continual gap between provision and users was evidenced in the Countryside Commission's (1988) study, which concluded that while 58 per cent of people had heard of a country park, only 26 per cent could name one correctly, reflecting a lack of promotion and general awareness of their existence.

At a national level, country parks appear to have only a minor role to play in diverting demand from the countryside, with some parks having catchments that are extremely localised. This was due to the impact of the car in diverting traffic straight to countryside sites. For example, Harrison (1981, 1983) found that 75 per cent of visitors to south London's green belt were car users. Their study discovered that inner city residents never comprised more than 10 per cent of users. Although sites were also accessible to those not having access to a car over short distances, Groome and Tarrant (1984) found public transport to country parks effective over a 5–8 km distance (i.e. short distance) for a local population. At an aggregate level, it is clear that country parks (and their forerunner, regional parks) in the UK play a vital role in locating recreational resources near to demand. The somewhat dated 1981 National Survey of Countryside Recreation found that 40 per cent of destinations were within the urban area or within 1 km (Sidaway and Duffield 1984), with a further 22 per cent in the countryside around urban areas. Only 16 per cent of destinations were located 10 km from the urban areas. In 2003, the Countryside Agency argued that these sites were still focal points for leisure, acting as honeypots and as gateways to the countryside. The recent interest in redeveloping the resource base of these sites has been apparent in the serious decline that has occurred in open space provision in the UK, especially as many of these country parks rely upon local authorities for over 90 per cent of their funding at a time of cuts in leisure spending and new priorities, such as social inclusion and the problems of inner city deprivation. A report for the UK government in 1999 by consultants PricewaterhouseCoopers found that in the UK there were 60,000 parks, gardens and designed landscapes that were competing for funding, 33,000 of which were owned by the local authority. These sites saw expenditure of around £800 million a year, £325 million of which came from the local authority. Yet using economic techniques of contingent valuation, these sites were deemed to be worth £5,000 million to the people who used them, comprising around 6 per cent of all recreational visits each year.

The example of Havering in Greater London illustrates how the early development of a management plan by a project officer acknowledged the problems of multiple use and the legacy of formerly derelict land. In the case of Havering, the scale of dereliction and the variety of land agencies involved created problems for the development of recreation provision. The land was a former First World War Royal Flying Corps base, defending London from Zeppelin attack, and in the Second World War it had been a frontline 'Battle of Britain' spitfire squadron base. The land was also used for sand and gravel extraction to the point that by the 1970s a legacy of dereliction remained, as housing development surrounded the site. While the Countryside Commission (1983) reviewed Havering's scheme and found a legacy of poor public provision in public housing areas and inadequate recognition of rights of way, landscaping schemes also remained a neglected feature. The expectation that the London Borough of Havering would set a precedent for landowners to follow has taken a long time to reach fruition. Nevertheless, the approach has brought modest success through environmental improvements establishing attractive recreational facilities by effectively tidying up many sites (Harrison 1991). The success of such projects was also followed by a new initiative in 1985 – the Groundwork Trust, based on a scheme in St Helen's urban fringe (Groundwork Foundation 1986). Since the early 1990s, this area has been further developed to comprise 250 acres of fields and trees, with four miles of parks and horse rides, a lake and picnic sites. The nature reserve (Ingrebourne Marshes) which now forms a key component of the site is classified as a Site of Special Scientific Interest (SSSI). It has also been incorporated as part of the Thames Chase Community Forest Initiative since 1990.

Variability in the usage of country parks reflects public knowledge of their existence and the attraction of individual locations. The precise location of recreation sites in the urban fringe appears to directly influence usage, with those located near to residential areas which permit residents to walk to them recording highest usage rates. As Harrison concludes:

> the recreational role played by sites in the urban fringe will differ depending upon their ease of access to local people who walk or cycle to them and not necessarily on the preferences of a wider constituency served by car . . . [and] the recreational role of countryside areas embedded in the urban area or abutting it is likely to be very different from that of more distant countryside sites.
>
> (Harrison 1991: 166)

What is clear is that the supply of recreational resources alone (e.g. country parks) is not sufficient in the urban fringe if the needs and recreational preferences of users are not analysed since these factors directly affect recreational behaviour.

management issues emerge. O'Riordan (1971: 19) described resource management 'as a process of decision-making whereby resources are allocated over space and time according to the needs, aspirations and desires of man'. In this process, it is the ability to accommodate multifunctional resource use in specific recreational spaces that is critical to achieving societal recreation objectives. The key to achieving this lies in the compatibility of specific recreational activities with both the resource base and other users. Progress in research which considers the allocation of resources to different users to achieve compatibility (e.g. Bone and Dragicevic 2009) illustrates how important this issue is, particularly the multi-use of sites, which also poses pressure in terms of the sheer volume of visitors (e.g. Arnberger et al. 2010). Although Chapter 9 discusses the role of planning and management in more detail, it is important to recognise at this point that two fundamental concepts need to be explored in managing the supply of recreational resources: *conflict* and *compatibility*.

Many notions of recreational conflict (avoidance of which is one of the goals of planning) are predicated on the concept of the incompatibility of one activity versus another. Jacob and Schreyer (1980: 369) define conflict thus: 'For an individual, conflict is defined as goal interference attributed to another's behaviour'. This definition assumes that people recreate to achieve certain outcome goals. Yet they argue that goal interference does not necessarily lead to incompatibility. In understanding the nature of recreation user conflict, the interactions which occur need to be understood in relation to a range of factors:

- the nature of the activity and personal meaning attached to it;
- the significance attached to a specific recreation resource;
- the mode of experience, especially how the natural environment is perceived;
- lifestyle tolerance, namely an individual's willingness to accept or reject lifestyles different from their own.

These factors provide an interesting framework in which to evaluate conflict, especially for recreational

resources with a high degree of conflict potential. As Jacob and Schreyer (1980: 378) assert, 'In failing to recognise the basic causes of conflict, inappropriate resolution techniques and management strategies are likely to be adopted'. These findings are reflected in the recreational behaviour observed in Illinois by Bristow et al. (1995), where a wide variety of activities were incompatible and led to increased travel times to seek recreational sites able to accommodate personal preferences. Not only does this raise important planning issues for recreation site planning and design (for more technical detail, see Ravenscroft 1992; Pigram and Jenkins 2006), it also raises the importance of recreation resource management to monitor sites to ensure the resource base can continue to accommodate the compatibility of uses. For example, Bell's (2000) analysis of the public inquiry into attempts to impose a speed restriction on the use of Lake Windermere to curb power boating serves as a notable example of the conflicting demands often faced in recreational settings between passive and active users, both recreational and tourist, together with the arguments levelled by the local community as stakeholders in the process of recreational management (see also Hall and Härkönen 2006).

Conflict has an important influence upon the experience of recreation and leisure in different situations and three specific approaches to evaluating leisure experiences exist:

- the form of the leisure experience, particularly the activity undertaken or where it is undertaken (the setting);
- the immediate experience of leisure at the place of consumption, which is evaluated at the time of experience and during the actual participation of leisure;
- the experience of leisure after the event, to ask people to reflect on the experience (Page and Connell 2010).

In each case place and space is a clear component, particularly the behavioural attachment and meaning attached to the experience, and recent developments in the notion of the leisure experience led Driver (2003: 170) to argue that 'The total experience approach is oriented to what people experience during their entire recreational engagement and is sometimes called the "lived experience". Such research relies upon qualitative methods and the use of storytelling by respondents.' Yet as Wray *et al*.'s (2010) review of visitors to Fiordland National Park indicated, there is also a growing concern over multiple users of such resources, with recreationalists questioning the compatibility of the notion of wilderness with the increasing use of the area by international tourists. This provides an important link between leisure and tourism, to which attention now turns.

The supply of tourism

Shaw and Williams (1994) prefer to view supply in relation to production and consumption and recent studies of tourism supply (Song 2012) review the multidisciplinary perspectives on this theme from geography, economics, logistics, operations management and other areas of social science. Ioannides' (2006) review of progress from economic geography discusses the limited engagement within geography on tourism supply issues and this has largely remained a neglected area in view of the business aspects of tourism and a lack of engagement with the commercial operation and management of tourism enterprises. Shaw and Williams (1994: 16) acknowledge that the production and consumption of tourism are important approaches to the analysis of tourism since 'production is the method by which a complex array of businesses and industries are involved in the supply of tourism services and products, and how these are delivered to consumers, and consumption is how, where, why and when the tourist actually consumes tourism services and products'. These weaknesses are compounded by a lack of data on the operation and performance of individual tourism enterprises. Sessa (1993: 59), however, considers 'tourism supply is the result of all those productive activities that involve the provision of goods and services required to meet tourism demand and which are expressed in tourism consumption', which comprises resources for tourists, infrastructure, receptive facilities, entertainment, sports venues, as well as tourism reception services

(e.g. travel agencies, promotional activities and tourist information offices).

One transformation that has affected the interest of geographers in the supply of tourism is the impact of the digital revolution and the rise of e-tourism (Hays *et al*. 2013). This has removed the physical importance of locational access to sources of information for tourism supply (e.g. travel agencies and tourist information offices). The result is that access to gateways of knowledge and information upon which to base decision-making has changed for the consumer and other businesses, rendering traditional models of location less valid as alternative sources of digital supply that are boundless in spatial terms and accessible 24 hours a day. This challenges some of the conventional notions of what Urry (1990) describes as 'spatial fixity'. In other words, tourists are mobile consumers and able to consume at a global level. This contrasts with most forms of supply for consumption purposes that have a major infrastructure requirement (e.g. accommodation) which are fixed at specific locations. Underlying the concept of spatial fixity is the nature of tourism entrepreneurs, who are largely small scale in their operations and less able to access forms of capital to relocate to new sources of demand compared to the smaller number of larger companies with the resources to adapt to demand. Thus supply is often unable to respond geographically to demand beyond a fixed point, and this means that peaks and troughs in demand at particular locations (i.e. destinations) need to be managed through differential forms of pricing (Seaton and Bennett 1996) and the use of seasonal labour (Ball 1989). Law expands upon these simple notions, arguing that

> in many respects tourism is the geography of consumption outside the home area; it is about how and why people travel to consume . . . [On] the production side it is concerned to understand where tourism activities develop and on what scale. It is concerned with the process or processes whereby some cities are able to create tourism resources and a tourism industry.
>
> (Law 1993: 14)

Law emphasises here the way in which scale is a critical concept in understanding supply issues together with the ways in which the tourism industry is organised and geographically distributed through time and space.

One useful illustration of the effect that a new form of production can have on the landscape of tourism and leisure consumption is the rise of the low cost airline sector. As Page (2011) has shown, this new form of production has revolutionised the supply of air transport not only in Europe and the USA but also in Asia-Pacific, with lower units of production and a no-frills model of delivery. The digital revolution has also made air travel accessible and easy to book,

favouring the promotional activities of low cost carriers. The principal geographical changes initially developed by low cost carriers was their use of regional airports and point-to-point services without the use of expensive hubs. These carriers have not only led to huge growth in volumes of leisure travel but also aided the growth of business travel This has seen entrepreneurial organisations like EasyJet and Ryanair not only outperform existing scheduled carriers, but also generate new markets for low cost air travel and domestic/international travel. As Figure 3.4 shows, growth of international arrivals in Spain has seen a

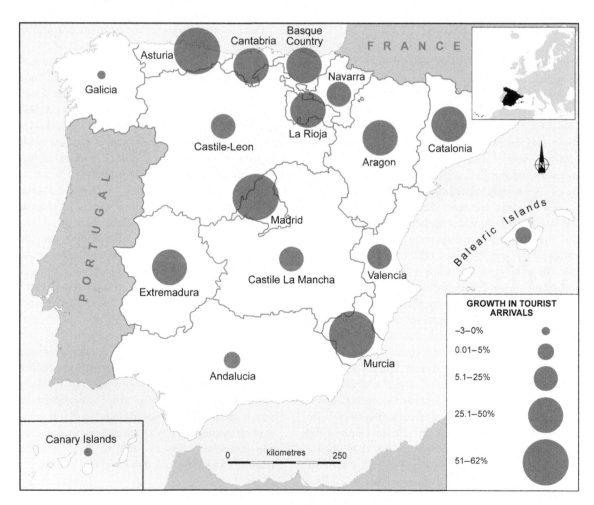

Figure 3.4 International arrivals in Spain by regional airport
Source: developed from UNWTO data.

major boost in coastal areas such as Asturia and Murcia, which is attributable to low cost carriers (Graham 2013), compared to relatively slower rates of growth in other areas of Spain. A direct result of this growth has also been a rise in the number of second homes in these expanding locations as a direct result of new air access. The low cost carriers have stimulated the growth of regional tourism, thereby illustrating how new forms of supply can affect the geographical patterns of demand, away from conventional mass resort tourism in Spain. Similar transformations have also occurred as competition between different modes of

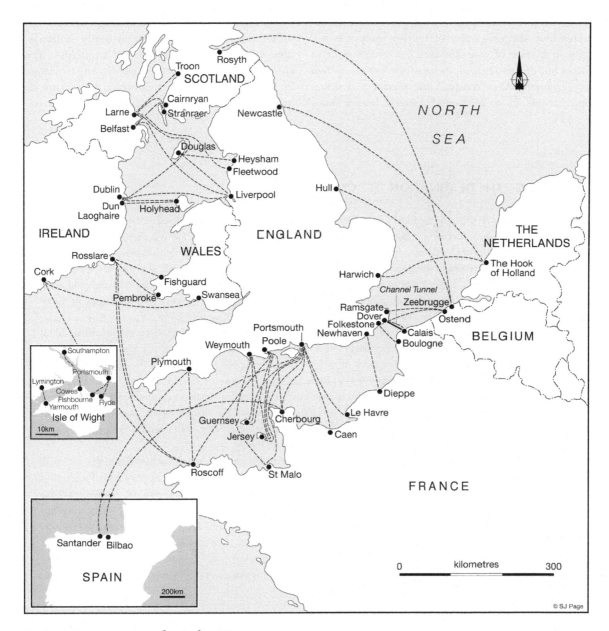

Figure 3.5 Ferry routes from the UK

transport (e.g. the Channel Tunnel, low cost carriers and ferries) has split the demand and market for each form of transport. The competitive result is that the ferry companies with a degree of mobile investment (i.e. their ferries) have relocated capacity in the UK to develop a wider range of routes (Figure 3.5) distributed away from the traditional high capacity short sea crossing (Dover–Calais) to other routes. This illustrates how the geography of tourism supply is not only in a state of constant flux due to competitive forces but can also help shape new patterns of tourism development. As a result, some coastal and urban destinations in western and eastern Europe have enjoyed the expansion of new price-sensitive markets, especially short breaks and VFR travel (visiting friends and relations), together with new niche markets such as stag parties and hen nights in Prague and Dublin.

Low cost airlines have changed the geographical access to leisure consumption by widening the domestic tourist and leisure traveller's search area for new consuming experiences, while radically impacting upon scheduled airline services and standards of provision as competition increases and leading to changes in the development process, which highlights the importance of the destination life cycle.

BOX 3.2   THE DESTINATION LIFE CYCLE

The notion of a destination product life cycle has been extremely influential in tourism research and probably ranks as one of the most substantial contributions by geographers to the wider tourism literature. The tourist area life cycle (TALC) also has a wider significance beyond a focus on tourism destination development because it challenges the notion of tourism studies having a simplistic theoretical base. As Oppermann (1998a: 180) noted: 'Butler's model is a brilliant example of how scientific progress could and should work . . . [having] been scrutinized in many different contexts with modifications suggested to fit specific situations and circumstances'.

Butler's (1980, 2006) concept of a tourist area life cycle of evolution, based on some of the initial observations of Christaller (1963) and Plog (1974, 1977), has been applied in a number of environments and settings representing the development of a destination through time and space (Cooper and Jackson 1989; Cooper 1992, 1994; Ioannides 1992; Butler 2006). Because of its relative simplicity the concept of a tourist area life cycle has emerged as a significant concept for strategic destination marketing and planning, and which underpins much of our understanding of urban tourism development. As Lundgren (1984: 22) commented, 'Butler put into the realistic cyclical context a reality that everyone knew about, and clearly recognised, but had never formulated into an overall theory'.

According to Cooper and Jackson (1989), the two most substantial managerial benefits of the life cycle concept are its use as a descriptive guide for strategic decision-making and its capacity as a forecasting tool. As a descriptive guide the life cycle idea implies that in the early stages of product development the focus will be on building market share, while in the later stages the focus will be on maintaining that share (Rink and Swan 1979). However, the utility of the life cycle concept as a forecasting tool relies heavily on the identification of those forces that influence the flow of tourists to a specific destination. As Haywood (1986) recognised, most models work well in their early stages but then fail in their prediction of the latter stages of the model. Haywood (1986), along with other commentators (e.g. Rink and Swan 1979; Cooper

1992; Ioannides 1992), notes that there are a variety of differently shaped curves, with the shape of the curve depending on both supply- and demand-side factors. Indeed, Haywood (1986: 154) goes so far as to argue that the life cycle approach 'represents the supply side view of the diffusion model', by which consumers adopt new products.

According to Haywood (1986) there are six operational decisions when using the life cycle concept: unit of analysis; relevant market; pattern and stages of the tourist area life cycle; identification of the area's shape in the life cycle; determination of the unit of measurement; determination of the relevant time unit.

Using Haywood's insights as a basis for undertaking research on the life cycle, Graber (1997) undertook an analysis of the destination life cycles of 43 European cities using the variables of growth data for domestic and international tourism, first-time visitor percentage, length of stay, guest-mix distribution and number of competitors. Only a small number of the variables tested proved to be significant correlates of the life cycle. According to Graber (1997: 69), 'A diminishing rate of first-time visitors is obvious for cities passing through later stages of the cycle'. In contrast to many of the more product life cycle interpretations of Butler's life cycle model which have come from a marketing orientation, Hall (2005a, 2005c, 2006a) argued that the life cycle of a destination should be assessed in terms of accessibility and spatial interaction modelling and observed that the model is an analogue of changed accessibility between generating areas and a destination.

Hall (2005a, 2006a) argues that a destination should be primarily conceptualised as a geographical place (e.g. as a point in space which is subject to a range of factors which influence locational advantage and disadvantage). Most significant to these is the movement outward from a tourist generating region and trips as a function of distance. Such travel movement cannot be adequately represented in the classic linear form of a distance-decay model whereby the location of numbers of trips or people travelling at any given time is highest closer to the generating area and diminishes in relation to distance. Instead, factors which influence travel behaviour, such as decisions relating to overnight stays and time to undertake leisure activities, as well as overall amenity values, create a series of peaks and troughs in relation to distance from the generating area (Hall 2005a) (Figure 3.6). However, regardless of what form of transport is used, there will be a different set of distance/time functions at which overnight stays will need to be made because all travellers need to stop at some stage to sleep.

Given the above assumptions then changes in distance (whether time, cost, behavioural, or network) between the tourist generating origin and the surrounding hinterland will then lead to corresponding changes in the number of travellers for any given point in the spatial system. However, locations within the spatial system are spatially fixed, towns and cities do not suddenly get up and move away in order to maximise advantageous distance functions although they do change and adapt over time in relation to new networks and patterns of accessibility . . . if the numbers of tourist bed-nights (or other measures of tourism related density) at a spatially fixed point 'destination' (L) are drawn at t_1, t_2, t_3, . . . in relation to the changed accessibility with respect to a tourist generating region or trip origin then this provides a representation of overnight stay density at a specific location which is analogous to that of the [TALC] when presented in its standard two dimensional form.

(Hall 2005a: 119)

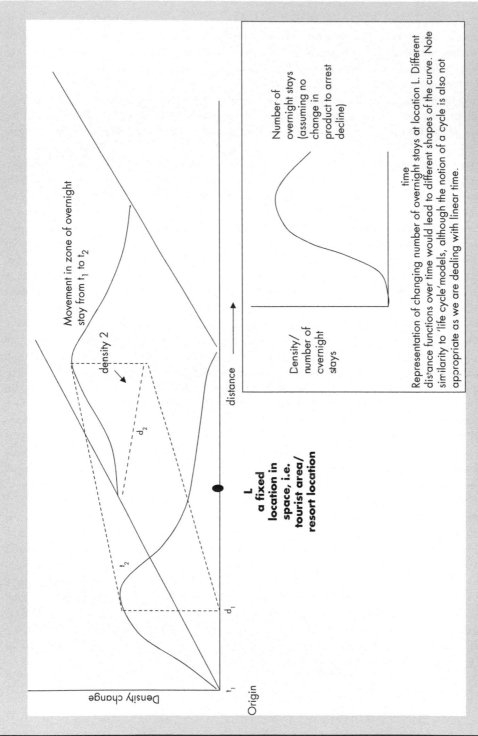

Figure 3.6 A wave analogue model of the implication of changed accessibility for a fixed location in space

Source: Witt et al. (1991); Page (1994).

More theoretically derived explanations of tourism production (e.g. Mullins 1991) illustrate the importance of understanding production in a spatially contingent framework and how this shapes the consumption of tourism, and so the wider theorisation of the interactions between supply and demand are now examined in terms of critical contributions to tourism thinking, which remain a key element of current geographical thought (Schwanen and Kwan 2009), as discussed in Chapter 2.

Towards a critical geography of tourism production?

According to Britton (1991: 451), the geography of tourism has suffered from weakly developed theory since 'geographers working in the field have been reluctant to recognise explicitly the capitalistic nature of the phenomenon they are researching'. This critical geographies focus has developed through a long history dating to radical geography (Peet 1977a, 1977b, 2009) and a more recent concern with the neoliberal project and the growth of inequalities in contemporary society (Harvey 2000). While Shaw and Williams (1994) review the concepts of production and consumption (also see Debbage and Ioannides 2004; Williams 2004; Ioannides 2006), it is pertinent to examine critically Britton's (1991) innovative research in this area since it provides a theoretical framework in which to interpret tourism production, whereby the notion of political economy, inequality and power are key elements in the explanatory framework. Within the tourism production systems are:

- economic activities designed to produce and sell tourism products;
- social groups, cultural and physical elements included in tourism products as attractions;
- agencies associated with the regulation of the production system.

In a theoretical context, Britton (1991: 455) argued that the tourism production system was 'simultaneously a mechanism for the accumulation of capital, the private appropriation of wealth, the extraction of surplus value from labour, and the capturing of (often unearned) rents from cultural and physical phenomena (especially public goods) which are deemed to have both a social and scarcity value'. The production system may therefore be viewed as having a division of labour between its various components (transport, accommodation, tour operators, attractions and ancillary services), markets (the demand and supply of tourist products) and regulatory agencies (e.g. industry associations), as well as industry organisations and structures to assist in the production of the final product. Britton (1991: 456) rightly points out that many tourism texts 'offer little more than a cursory and superficial analysis of how the tourism industry is structured and regulated by the classic imperatives and laws governing capitalist accumulation'.

The tourism industry is made up of a range of separate industry suppliers who offer one or more components of the final product that requires intermediaries to co-ordinate and combine the elements which are sold to the consumer as a discrete package. Both tour operators and travel agents have a vital role to play in this context when one recognises the existence of a supply chain (Figure 3.7). What this emphasises is the variety of linkages which exist and the physical separation of roles and responsibilities to the supply chain (see Page 1994b).

While information technology may assist in improving communication and co-ordination between different components associated with the production of tourism, other developments (notably horizontal and vertical integration) assist in addressing the fragmentation of elements within the supply system. Likewise, tour operators are able to use economies of scale and their sheer buying power over suppliers to derive a competitive advantage in the assembly of tour components into packages. The tour operators also have the power and ability to shift the product to match demand, and to exercise an extraordinary degree of power over both inter-industry transactions and the spatial distribution of tourist flows. As Agarwal *et al*. (2000: 244–5) indicate, 'increasing scale, or market concentration, has been achieved through horizontal and vertical integration as airlines expand into tour

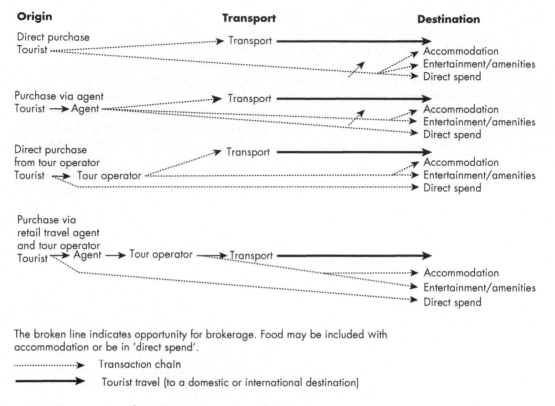

Figure 3.7 Four types of tourism transaction chain
Source: Witt et al. (1991); Page (1994).

operations, tour operators acquire airlines and travel agencies and invest in the accommodation sector', a feature also observed by Ioannides (1995). As a result, the process of market concentration can occur through various strategies (or a combination thereof): strategic alliances, mergers, acquisitions and take-overs, franchising agreements and the use of marketing consortia. Such strategies are used by the highly globalised multinational economies of scale, to reduce competition and to seek greater control of the market. Strategic alliances also assist in this regard, since suppliers in one part of the system are dependent on those either upstream or downstream. Therefore, there is pressure on suppliers to exert control over other suppliers through transaction arrangements (i.e. through long-term contracts, vertical and horizontal integration), as well as through commissions, licensing and

franchising. The two most powerful organisations in this respect are national airlines and tour wholesalers (also known as tour operators). Through the financial resources and industry leverage that these organisations can wield in the tourism business, they are able to exact advantageous business terms and the introduction of computer reservation systems (CRS), now referred to as global distribution systems (GDS), which provide not only integration of the supply chain but also a competitive advantage in revenue generation through bookings made through these systems.

Papatheodorau (2003) examined the oligopolistic behaviour (i.e. bargaining power) of the transnational tour operators in the Mediterranean in relation to their corporate strategies. He observed that in the UK mass package holiday market and it is widely accepted that local producers and specific destinations are heavily dependent upon mass tourism as well as oligop-olistic behaviour in the way contracts in the supply of services are negotiated. These may seek maximum discounts and long settlement terms on payment of goods/services supplied to tour operators, reinforcing Ioannides' (1998) argument that tour operators are gatekeepers to tourism, applying a similar concept to that developed by P. Williams (1978) with an analysis of housing markets and how agencies such as building societies can 'redline' areas. This means that building societies delineate areas they will not lend in. In a similar vein, tour operators can redline destinations, based on previous experience of tourist problems, particularly terrorism. A combination of tour opera-tors and insurers can effectively redline resorts and destinations.

Britton (1991) also indicates that the state has a fundamental role to play in encouraging industry groups to meet and co-ordinate problem-solving such as reducing critical incidents (Bitner *et al.* 1990) in the supply chain. In addition, the state makes a major contribution in terms of funding the marketing of regions and destinations via national and regional tourism organisations so that place promotion takes place (Ashworth and Voogd 1990a, 1990b; Page 1995a; Pike 2008). The state may also offer induce-ments to underwrite major supply inputs where terri-torial competition or development may not otherwise occur. Interventions in the market include the under-writing of national 'flag-carrier' airlines (see Kissling 1989), and public economic and welfare goals are emphasised to justify state intervention.

One of the interesting areas hitherto ignored in geographical research on tourism supply is labour supply and markets. Since in the tourism business many workers simultaneously provide and are part of the consumed product, service quality assumes a vital role. This is broadened in many research studies to include the 'tourist experience' (Ryan 1997, 2002) along with the key role of emotional labour as a source of service provision. While Britton (1991) rightly points to the role of capitalist social relations in the production of tourist experiences, such experiences cannot easily be characterised as tangible elements of tourist supply. This poses major difficulties for capi-tal, where quality of service is easily influenced by

personal factors, the behaviour and attitude of staff, as well as by the perception of the consumer in relation to their expectations, values and belief system. One result is that much of the demand for labour is not necessarily recognised through formal qualifications but through personal qualities, which leads to an undervaluing of labour. Add to this the fact that the labour willing to supply such skills is often casual and female (and often with a local ethnic component), and the tourism labour market is characterised by ethnic and gender divisions, with relatively poor employ-ment conditions existing relative to other sectors (UNWTO 2011d; Zampoukos and Ioannides 2011). For example, in the Australian context, the Industry Commission (1995: 21) characterised the tourism workforce and its working conditions as follows:

- on average, young;
- characterised by female, part-time employment;
- has more casual and part-time work than other industries, but the majority of hours are neverthe-less worked by full-time employees;
- is poorly unionised;
- is relatively low skilled work;
- the hours of work are sometimes considered unsociable;
- the pay is relatively low;
- a mobile workforce with high turnover rates;
- the workforce has low levels of formal educational qualifications.

Tourism employment has particular characteristics stemming from the spatial and temporal fixity of tour-ism consumption and production (Shaw and Williams 1994; Tufts 2009; Zampoukos and Ioannides 2011). Tourism services have to be experienced *in situ*, and (in most senses) they are not spatially transferable and cannot be deferred (Urry 1987). This implies that the tourism labour force has to be assembled *in situ* at the point of consumption and, moreover, that it is availa-ble at particular time periods. The nature of demand is such that a labour force is required with sufficient flex-ibility to meet daily, weekly and seasonal fluctuations (Ladkin 2011). The extent to which these conditions generate migration flows, rather than reliance on local labour, is contingent on a number of factors, intrinsic both to the tourism development and to the locality. Two prime considerations are the scale of demand and the speed of tourism development, the latter affecting the extent to which labour may be transferred from other sectors of the local economy/society. In addition, the degree of enclavism or spatial polarisation is important, with the dependency on migration likely to be positively correlated with this. Over time the spatial form of tourism consumption and production is in constant flux. In addition, local demographic, social and economic structures will condition the availability of local labour and the requirement for in-migration. Comparative wage differentials, levels of education and training, working conditions and job status in tourism and other sectors all influence the availability of workers, as does the overall level of unemployment. For example, the availability of better paid and higher status jobs in other sectors has conditioned the requirement for immigrant labour in the Swiss tourist industry (King 1995). Finally, the degree of temporal polarisation is also significant, for the demands for in-migration are likely to be greatest in large-scale, single-peaked season destinations. All else being equal, the lack of alternative jobs outside the peak time period will mean either seasonal unemployment in the local labour market or reliance on seasonal labour migrants (King 1995).

Tourism labour migration is also highly segmented (Williams and Hall 2002). King (1995) identified a hierarchy of labour migrants in respect of tourism. In the first rank are skilled managerial posts, typically found in the upper enclaves of major international hotels and local branches of leading airlines. It can be hypothesised that there will be greater reliance on immigrants to fill such posts in less developed economies where there are shortages of such human capital. The second rank consists of intermediate posts such as tour guides and agency representatives, where the ability to speak the language of international tourists, and even to share their nationality (if only for the purpose of consumer reassurance), is considered critical. Finally, the third level of the hierarchy comprises unskilled labour, which is relatively common, given low entry thresholds to most tourist jobs. The pay and working conditions of each of these three ranks in the

hierarchy are likely to be varied, as are the national origins of each stream of migrants.

The significance of migration in tourism labour markets therefore stems from three main features (Williams and Hall 2000; Janta et al. 2011). First, it serves to fill absolute shortages of labour, particularly in areas of rapid tourism expansion or where tourism is highly spatially polarised. However, the first two levels of the migration hierarchy may also function to fill particular employment niches, even where there are no generalised labour shortages. Second, the availability of migrant labour will help to reduce labour market pressures, and consequently wage inflation pressures (Janta et al. 2011). Third, labour migration can contribute to labour market segmentation, and especially where the divisions are along racial/ethnic or legal/illegal lines, this can serve to reduce the costs of labour to firms. Labour migration therefore serves to ensure that the process of tourism capital accumulation is not undermined. Nevertheless, labour migration also has two other significant functions with respect to tourism. The first of these is the generation of visits to friends and visitors. Second, labour migration experiences do help to define the search spaces of lifestyle and retirement migrants, as King et al. (1998) have shown with respect to retirement from the UK to southern Europe (Williams and Hall 2002).

Thus to understand some of these components of the tourism production system the geographer is required to appreciate concepts related to capital–labour relations, the interweaving of consumption, the business environment associated with the competitive strategies of enterprises, economic concepts (e.g. transaction analysis), product differentiation, international business as a mode of operation and global markets, along with basic business and marketing concepts. Within a capitalist mode of production this is essential so that one may understand how each component in the tourism production system operates (i.e. how it develops products, generates profits and competes with other businesses) and how social groups and places are incorporated into the production system, so that the production system and the spatial relationships which exist may be fully understood (see Box 3.3). However, critical

BOX 3.3   ECONOMIC GLOBALISATION

Globalisation is a complex, chaotic, multiscalar, multitemporal and multicentric series of processes operating in specific structural and spatial contexts (Jessop 1999; Amin 2002). Globalisation should be seen as an emergent, evolutionary phenomenon which results from economic, political, socio-cultural and technological processes on many scales, rather than a distinctive causal mechanism in its own right. It is both a structural and a structuring phenomenon, the nature of which depends critically on sub-global processes. According to Jessop (1999: 21) 'structurally, globalisation would exist in so far as covariation of relevant activities becomes more global in extent and/or the speed of that covariation on a global scale increases'. Such an observation clearly suggests that globalisation is uneven across space and time. Indeed, 'a key element in contemporary processes of globalisation is not the impact of "global" processes upon another clearly defined scale, but instead the relativisation of scale' (Kelly and Olds 1999: 2). Such relativities occur in relation to both 'space–time distantiation' and 'space–time compression'. The former refers to the stretching of social relations over time and space, e.g. through the utilisation of new technology such as the internet, so that they can be co-ordinated or controlled over longer periods of time, greater distances, larger areas and on more scales of activity. The latter involves the intensification of 'discrete' events in real time and/or increased velocity of material and non-material flows over a given distance; again this is related to technological change, including communication technologies, and social technologies (Harvey 2000), all of which affect tourism (Hall 2005a).

The discourse of globalisation, i.e. the way in which the term is used and applied in various situations, is important because it goes further than the simple description of contemporary social change; it also carries with it the power to shape material reality via policy formulation and implementation (Gibson-Graham 1996; Kelly and Olds 1999). It can also construct a view of geographical space that implies the deferral of political options from the national to the supranational and global scales, and from the local to the national. In effect, globalisation 'itself has become a political force, helping to create the institutional realities it purportedly merely describes' (Piven 1995: 8), as indicated by the growth of structures that encourage yet further 'free trade' and openness to change such as Asia-Pacific Economic Cooperation (APEC). In addition to the 'structural context' of globalisation noted above, authors such as Ohmae (1995) and Jessop (1999) point to a more strategic interpretation of globalisation, which refers to individual and institutional actors' attempts to promote the global co-ordination of activities on a continuing basis within different orders or functional systems, for example interpersonal networking, inter-firm strategic alliances, the creation of international and supranational regimes to govern particular fields of action, and the broader development of modes of international and supranational systems of governance. Therefore, given the multiscale, multitemporal and multicentric nature of globalisation, we can recognise that globalisation 'rarely, if ever, involves the full structural integration and strategic coordination across the globe' (Jessop 1999: 22). Processes usually considered under the rubric of 'economic globalisation' include the following:

- The formation of regional economic and trading blocs that provide for greater economic integration, e.g. North American Free Trade Area (NAFTA), European Union (EU) and APEC, and the development of formal links between those blocs (e.g. the Asia-Europe Meetings). In all of these regions tourism is a major component of economic and social policy (Hall 2001a).
- The growth of 'local internationalisation', 'virtual regions', through the development of economic ties between contiguous (e.g. 'border regions') or non-contiguous local and regional state authorities

(e.g. growth regions and triangles) in different national economies which often bypass the level of the nation state but which still retain support at the national level. For example, the Pacific North West Economic Region (PNWER), consisting of the American states of Alaska, Idaho, Montana, Oregon and Washington plus the Canadian provinces of Alberta, British Columbia and Yukon Territory, as well as private sector members, has a tourism working group to promote greater economic development in the region (Hall 2001a).

- The widening and deepening of international and supranational regimes which cover economic and economically relevant issues and which may also provide for regional institutionalised governance, e.g. the World Trade Organisation and associated agreements with respect to trade (Coles and Hall 2011).
- The internationalisation of national economic spaces through growing penetration (inward flows) and external (outward) flows as with the increasing mobility of tourists and capital (Coles and Hall 2008).
- The extension and deepening of multinationalisation by multinational firms, including hospitality and tourism firms, as illustrated in the next section in relation to international hotel chains.
- The introduction and acceptance of global norms and standards, the development of globally integrated markets together with globally oriented strategies, and firms with no evident national operational base (Jessop 1999).

geographical perspectives (e.g. Schwanen and Kwan 2009) also argue that conventional geography would have viewed space and time relationships in relation to tourism supply as a context in which tourist behaviour and activities occur rather than being conditioned and controlled by the activities of global businesses, with their predominant focus on profit and exploitation of the resource base for their business activities (Page 2011), where policy-makers and planners become powerless to stop the gathering snowball rolling downhill called tourism that takes over society and the local economy, so that vested interests simply accentuate the growth and development trajectories, with little long-term consideration of the consequences. To illustrate these ideas further, Box 3.3, on economic globalisation, is one explanatory approach to understanding the growing control of international tourism by globalised companies.

International hotel chains

The hotel industry is arguably a global industry, since it fulfils some of the criteria which distinguish businesses as truly global, whereby it may be one which can create a competitive advantage from its activities

on a worldwide basis. Alternatively it may be one in which the strategic positions of competitors in major geographic or national markets are fundamentally affected by their overall global positions (Porter 1980: 175). Much of the debate on the influence of international hotel chains may be dated to the research by Dunning and McQueen (1982) on what constitutes a multinational, international and transnational firm. Dunning and McQueen's (1982) use of an international hotel company, which has direct investments and other types of contractual agreements in more than one country, remains a simple but effective definition (see also Shaw and Williams 1994). One concept which economists and sociologists have embraced to analyse the linkages of transnational companies in local and regional tourism economies is embeddedness. This essentially refers to the links between external capital and local firms' relationships, though it has proved problematic to adequately operationalise in tourism, since the concept is also opaque, as researchers seek to define the most appropriate methodologies to use to measure and understand embeddedness.

Britton (1991: 460) analysed the product which hotel chains offered in terms of their competitive strategies as a package of on-premises services which provide a certain experience (ambience, lifestyle) based on different kinds and qualities of accommodation, on-site recreation and shopping facilities, and catering, the offering of off-premises services (airport shuttles, local excursions, booking facilities) and a trademark guarantee which signals to the customer a predictable quality of service. The competitive strategies which follow from these features are based on an understanding of the customer (i.e. needs and preferences), where the brand name is able to command a premium price in the marketplace. Britton (1991: 460) explains the commercial advantage of international chains in terms of

- the firms' location in the customers' home country;
- experience in understanding demand through operating hotels in the domestic markets;
- managerial expertise and staff training to ensure the elements of the tourists' experience related to the brand name are met through appropriate training and operating manuals

The key to successful competition is for the hotel company to internalise its firm-specific intellectual property (i.e. training methods and manuals), while ensuring profit levels for shareholders. Unfortunately this is extremely difficult when staff leave and move to competitors, since the intellectual property is essentially 'know-how'. Yet this is often the basis for horizontal integration into overseas markets, with management contracts a preferred mechanism for operation rather than outright ownership to control design, operation, pricing and staffing, though the same companies (e.g. Holiday Inns) prefer to use franchising as a mechanism to control managerial, organisational and professional input. One notable dimension here is the effect of international hotel and tourism development on less developed countries. For example, in Kenya 60 per cent of hotel beds were accounted for through equity participation schemes with such hotel groups (Rosemary 1987; Sinclair 1991). The implications are that where international involvement occurs there is a concomitant loss of central control and leakage of foreign earnings, and where there is concentrated development of enclaves

remote from local population this inevitably leads to little benefit for the host country. This view is confirmed in more recent studies. Blake (2008), for instance, raises the concern that tourism development leads to the contraction of other export sectors. In a review of the situation in Kenya, Tanzania and Uganda, results indicate that hotels and restaurants, and in particular the transport industry, provide below-average shares of income to poor households compared to other export sectors, leading to the conclusion that 'these results paint a fairly poor picture of the ability of tourism to alleviate poverty' (Blake 2008: 511). Tourism tends to be disproportionately beneficial to the already wealthy (Blake et al. 2008; Schilcher 2007) and can enhance existing inequalities (Scheyvens and Momsen 2008a, 2008b).

International hotel development may therefore lead to dependency relationships, as Britton (1980a) indicated in his innovative study of the distribution of ownership and commercial control by metropolitan tourist markets of less developed world destinations. In the context of the UK, the corporate organisation of tourism production also exhibits a core–periphery relationship, defined by the location of corporate headquarters and the higher level posts in the hotel, airline and tour operator sector, which are largely located in London. While some lower level order jobs have been located in peripheral regions to take advantage of low labour and premises costs (e.g. call centres), decisions involving capital, the form of production and its spatial distribution are firmly embedded in London and south-east England. Indeed, the transnational nature of some international tour operators (e.g. TUI) highlights how investment and production decisions also have a transnational and global dimension. For example, TUI now operates in 180 countries, using 200 brands, and has around 300 million customers. In the case of China, Gu et al. (2012) outlined the rapid growth and the nature of financing for hotel investment and development of hotel projects in China, which has shifted from an initial growth stimulated by joint ventures funded by government agencies and Chinese overseas investors. This has been supplemented by international hotel corporations entering

China's emergent tourism sector in the 1980s. As Gu *et al.* (2012) show, the main mode of entry into the Chinese hotel market was through management contracts and joint ventures. For example, by 1991, 202 hotels were classified as joint ventures and 215 hotels were managed by international hotel companies. Initially, the high quality international hotel brands entered the main cities of Shanghai, Guangzhou and Beijing. This was followed by brands moving into secondary cities and major tourist destinations. Through time, international management expertise has passed into domestic hotel companies and the international hotel companies have established a major presence throughout China's major cities. In 2010, the top five international brands were the Intercontinental Group (IHG), Wyndham, Hilton, Marriot and Accor.

Britton's model of tourism development (Figure 3.8) illustrates the nature of tourism dependency, where international tourism organisations (in the absence of strong government control) develop and perpetuate a hierarchical element to tourism development. While dependency theory is useful in explaining how capitalist production leads to the resulting patterns of tourism demand and supply, it is evident that this is only a simplification of the wider geographical dimensions of capital–labour relations in a global context, where political economy perspectives assist in explaining the processes leading to the spatial patterns of tourism development that occur. The economic dynamics of the tourism production system begin to help to develop a more central perspective of tourism which fits into the broader conceptualisation of capitalist accumulation, and the social construction of reality, though marketing and the construction of place may provide new areas for future geographical research. In fact, what one realises from a critical analysis of tourism using political economy perspectives is that it is a constantly changing phenomenon, with an ever-changing spatial organisation. This was evident from the examples of low cost airline growth and its impact on both destinations (e.g. Spain) and other competing modes of transport (e.g. the UK ferry industry). The processes affecting the political economy of production and consumption require a critical

awareness of the role and activities of entrepreneurs, the flow of capital and its internationalisation, the impact of industrial and regional restructuring, urban development, changes in the service economy and how the production of tourism results in new landscapes of tourism in a contemporary society (Meethan 2004). Aside from theoretical analysis, geographers have developed other concepts and methods of analysis, and we now turn to these approaches.

The leisure product

Within the context of urban tourism, Jansen-Verbeke (1986) viewed the urban area as a 'leisure product' which comprises primary elements including a variety of facilities that may be grouped into:

- an *activity place*, thereby defining the overall supply features within the city, particularly the main tourist attractions;
- a *leisure setting*, which includes both the physical elements in the built environment and the sociocultural characteristics which give a city a distinct image and 'sense of place' for visitors;

and secondary elements which consist of:

- the supporting facilities and services which tourists consume during their visit (e.g. hotel and catering outlets and shopping facilities) and which shape the visitors' experience of the services available in the city;
- additional elements which consist of the tourism infrastructure that conditions the visit, such as the availability of car parking, tourist transport provision and accessibility, and tourist-specific services (e.g. visitor information centres and tourist signposting) (see Table 3.4 for a more detailed description).

The urban tourism system helps in understanding the interrelationships between supply and demand and the interaction between the consumers and the products. In this respect, it is also useful to identify what aspect of the 'leisure product' tourists consume; some may

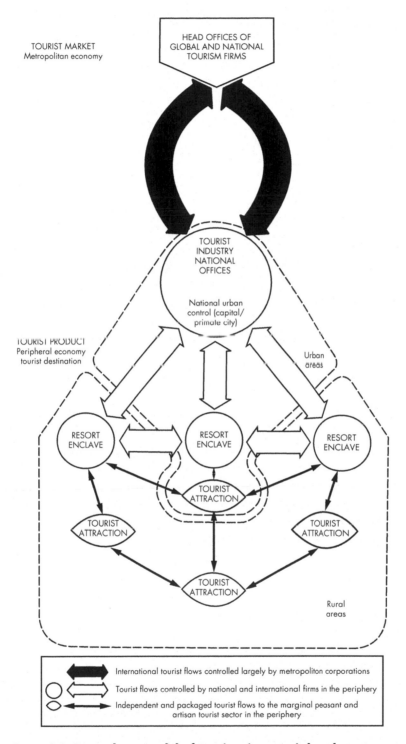

Figure 3.8 An enclave model of tourism in a peripheral economy

Source: redrawn from Britton 1980a. Reproduced with permission from Elsevier.

Table 3.3 Some reasons for government involvement in tourism

Economic reasons

- to improve the balance of payments in a country;
- to attract foreign exchange;
- to aid national, regional and/or local economic development;
- to diversify the economy;
- to increase income levels;
- to increase state revenue from taxes;
- to generate new and/or maintain existing employment opportunities.

Social and cultural reasons

- to achieve social objectives related to 'social tourism' to ensure the well-being and health of families and individuals;
- to protect cultural mores, traditions, resources and heritage;
- to promote a greater cultural awareness of an area and its people;
- to promote international understanding.

Environmental reasons

- to undertake stewardship of the environment and tourism resources to ensure that natural capital, e.g. air, water, biodiversity, is not denuded;
- to create or maintain a natural resource which will serve to attract tourists.

Political reasons

- to further political objectives by promoting the development of tourism in order to broaden the political acceptance of a government among visitors;
- to control the development process associated with tourism;
- to protect the public interest and the interests of minorities;
- to further political ideology.

Sources: Jenkins and Henry 1982; D.G. Pearce 1989; Hall 1994, 2008a; Hall and Jenkins 1995; Dredge and Jenkins 2007, 2011.

consume only one product (e.g. a visit to an art gallery), while others may consume what Jansen-Verbeke (1988) terms a 'bundle of products' (i.e. several products during their stay, such as a visit to a theatre, museum and a meal in a restaurant). One of the important points to note from this observation is the extent to which multiple counting of users of such products may inflate visitor numbers and the viability of tourism attractions and businesses on account of the same tourist being counted several times by different sites they visit.

Jansen-Verbeke (1986) identified the nature of tourists visiting the inner city and the organisations responsible for the promotion of the inner city as an area for tourists to visit. The role of organisations promoting urban areas for tourism is discussed in more detail in Chapter 6, but to explain Jansen-Verbeke's

(1986) analysis it is useful to consider the relationship which she believes exists between the product, the tourist and the promoter. Promoters affect the relationship in two ways:

- they build an image of the inner city and its tourist resources to attract potential tourists, investors and employers;
- the promotion of the inner city may also lead to direct product improvement.

Consequently, the model that Jansen-Verbeke (1986) constructs illustrates how different elements of the inner city tourism system are interrelated and the significance of the inner city as a leisure product. However, the public and private sector have distinct roles to play in this context.

Role of the public and private sector in tourism supply

The public sector is a term used to refer to the range of organisations that are operated and owned by governments in order to implement public policy. The public sector operates at a variety of geographical scales and may become involved in tourism for various economic, political, social and environmental reasons (Table 3.3). The International Union of Tourism Organisations (IUOTO 1974), the forerunner to the UNWTO, in its discussion of the role of the state in tourism, identified five areas of public sector involvement in tourism: co-ordination, planning, legislation, regulation and entrepreneur stimulation. To this may be added two other functions: a social

Table 3.4 The elements of tourism

Primary elements	Secondary elements	Additional elements
Activity place	• Hotels and accommodation	• Accessibility and parking facilities
Cultural facilities	• Markets	• Transport
• Concert halls	• Restaurants, cafés and catering facilities	• Tourist facilities:
• Cinemas	• Retail and shopping facilities	– information offices
• Exhibitions		– signposts
• Museums and art galleries		– guides
• Theatres		– websites, maps and leaflets
Sports facilities		
• Indoor and outdoor		
Convention and exhibition facilities		
Amusement facilities		
• Bingo halls		
• Casinos		
• Festivities		
• Night clubs		
• Organised events		
Leisure setting		
Physical characteristics		
• Ancient monuments and statues		
• Ecclesiastical buildings		
• Harbours		
• Historical street pattern		
• Interesting buildings		
• Parks and green areas		
• Water, canals and river fronts		
Socio-cultural features		
• Folklore		
• Food and cuisine		
• Friendliness		
• Language		
• Liveliness and ambience of the place		
• Local customs and costumes		
• Security		

Source: after Jansen-Verbeke 1986; Page and Hall 2003.

tourism role (Walton 2013), which is very significant in European tourism (McCabe *et al.* 2011), and a broader role of interest protection (Hall 1994). However, it is important to note that the role of government in tourism changes over time and in different jurisdictions. Although some generalisations can be noted (Table 3.3), significant differences with respect to government's role in tourism occur both within and between countries.

Much government intervention in tourism is related to market failure, market imperfection and social need (Dredge and Jenkins 2007; Hall 2008a). However, the market method of deciding who gets what and how is not always adequate, and therefore government often changes the distribution of income and wealth by measures that work within the price system. Across the globe almost every industry has been supported at various times by subsidies, the imposition of tariff regulations, taxation concessions, direct grants and other forms of government intervention, all of which serve to affect the price of goods and services and therefore influence the distribution of income, production and wealth. The size or economic importance of the tourism industry, so commonly emphasised by the public and private sectors, is no justification in itself for government intervention; within market-driven economies justification must lie in some aspect of:

- market failure;
- market imperfection;
- public/social concerns about market outcomes.

Therefore, implicit in each justification for intervention is the view that government offers a corrective alternative to the market (Hall and Jenkins 1998).

The role of the state as entrepreneur in tourist development is closely related to the concept of the 'devalorisation of capital' (Damette 1980), the process by which the state subsidises part of the cost of production, for instance, by assisting in the provision of infrastructure or by investment in a tourism project. In this process what would have been private costs are transformed into public or social costs. The provision of infrastructure, particularly transport networks, is

regarded as crucial to the development of tourist destinations (Page 2009a). There are numerous formal and informal means for government at all levels to assist in minimising the costs of production for tourism developers. Indeed, the offer of government assistance for development is often used to encourage private investment in a particular region or tourist project; for instance through the provision of cheap land or government-backed low interest loans.

As well as acting as entrepreneurs, governments can also stimulate tourism in several ways: first, financial incentives such as low interest loans or a depreciation allowance on tourist accommodation or infrastructure; second, sponsor research for the benefit of the tourism industry; third, marketing and promotion generally aimed at generating tourism demand, although it may also take the form of investment promotion aimed at encouraging capital investment for tourism attractions and facilities (Hall 1995, 2008a; Dredge and Jenkins 2007).

One of the more unusual features of tourism promotion by government tourism organisations is that they have only limited control over the product they are marketing, with very few actually owning the goods, facilities and services that make up the tourism product (Hall 2005a). This lack of control is perhaps testimony to the power of the public good argument used by industry to justify continued maintenance of government funding for destination promotion. However, it may also indicate the political power of the tourism lobby, such as industry organisations, to influence government tourism policies (Hall and Jenkins 1995; Dredge and Jenkins 2007, 2011).

The private sector's involvement in tourism is usually perceived as being primarily motivated by profit, as tourism entrepreneurs (Shaw and Williams 1994) invest in business opportunities. This gives rise to a complex array of large organisations and operators involved in tourism (e.g. multinational chain hotels – Forte and the Holiday Inn) and an array of smaller businesses and operators, often employing fewer than ten people or working on a self-employed basis (Page *et al.* 1999; Getz *et al.* 2004; Hall and Rusher 2004; Ateljevic and Page 2009). However, while many governments seek to encourage the role of the private sector in tourism their actions are often regulated in areas such as health and safety, planning, environmental quality, labour law and taxation (Hall 2009c).

Historically there has been a distinction between the role of the private and public sector in the provision of services and facilities for tourists that existed for much of the twentieth century (Dredge and Jenkins 2007). However, the tendency to privatise and commercialise functions that were once performed by government, what is usually described as neoliberalism, has been almost universal in western nations since the late 1970s and has affected the nature of many national governments' involvement in the tourism industry (Hall 1994, 2009d, 2013e; Schilcher 2007; Ayikoru et al. 2009). According to Hall and Jenkins (1995), three principal reasons for this trend may be identified. Market-oriented governments are interested in:

- reducing the dependency of public enterprises on public budgets;
- reducing public debt by selling state assets;
- raising technical efficiencies by commercialisation.

This has meant that there has been a much greater blurring in the roles of the public and private sectors with the development of enterprise boards, development corporations and similar organisations. In such a political and economic climate the role of government in tourism has undergone a dramatic shift, from a traditional public administration model that sought to implement government policy for a perceived public good, to a corporatist model which emphasises efficiency, investment returns, the role of the market and relations with stakeholders, usually defined as industry. Corporatism, here, is used in the sense of a dominant ideology in western society which claims rationality as its central quality and supports a notion of individualism in terms of self-interest rather than the legitimacy of the individual citizen acting in the democratic interest of the public good. However, in many policy areas, including tourism, the changed role of the state and the individual's relation to the state provides a major policy quandary (Hall 2013e).

On the one hand, there is the demand for less government interference in the market and allowing industries to develop and trade without government subsidy or assistance, while, on the other, industry interest groups seek to have government policy developed in their favour, including the maintenance of government funding for promotion as in the case of the tourism industry (Bramwell 2011). This policy issue has generally been resolved through the restructuring of national and regional tourist organisations, not only to reduce their planning, policy and development roles and increase their marketing and promotion functions, but also to engage in a greater range of partnerships, network and collaborative relationships with stakeholders (Hall 2011a). Such a situation has been described by Milward (1996) as the 'hollowing out' of the state, in which the role of the state has been transformed from one of hierarchical control to one in which governing is dispersed among a number of separate, non-government entities. This has therefore led to increased emphasis on governance in tourism (Hall 2011a), through network structures as a 'new process of governing; or a changed condition of ordered rule; or the new method by which society is governed' (Rhodes 1997: 43).

Awareness of the need of tourist organisations to create links with stakeholders is, of course, not new. For example, the community tourism approach (Murphy 1985, 1988) emphasised the importance of involving the community in destination management because of their role as key stakeholders, although in actuality this often meant collaboratively working with industry and community-based groups in a destination context rather than through wider public participation mechanisms (Zapata et al. 2011). The difficulty in implementing community-based tourism strategies is reflective of wider difficulties with respect to effective destination management and tourism planning (Davidson and Maitland 1997; Dredge and Jenkins 2011). Nevertheless, while collaboration clearly has potential to contribute to the development of more sustainable forms of tourism in that they can create social capital, it has to be stressed that the goal of partnership, as emphasised by a number of western governments which have restructured their involvement in tourism in recent years, need not be the same as an inclusive collaborative approach (Hall 1999). Furthermore, the development of networks as a good in its own right has been criticised by Hall (2011f), who suggests that more focus should be given to what networks actually do.

In the case of the United Kingdom, for example, many of the partnerships established between government and business in the 1980s and early 1990s as part of urban and regional development programmes have been heavily criticised for their narrow stakeholder and institutional base. Goodwin (1993: 161) argued that in order to ensure that urban leisure and tourism development projects were carried out, 'local authorities have had planning and development powers removed and handed to an unelected institution. Effectively, an appointed agency is, in each case, replacing the powers of local government in order to carry out a market-led regeneration of each inner city.' Harvey (1989a: 7) recognised that the 'new entrepreneurialism' of the supposedly smaller central and local state 'has, as its centrepiece, the notion of a 'public–private partnership: in which a traditional local boosterism is integrated with the use of local government powers to try [to] attract external sources of funding, new direct investments, or new employment sources'. In such cases, partnership does not include all members of a community, i.e. those who do not have enough money, are not from the right lifestyle or simply do not have sufficient power are ignored.

Spatial analytical approaches to the supply of tourism facilities

Much of the research on tourism supply in relation to facilities and services is descriptive in content, based on inventories and lists of the facilities and where they are located. In view of the wide range of literature that discusses the distribution of specific facilities or services, it is more useful to consider two specific examples of how such approaches and concepts may be used to derive generalisations of patterns of tourism activity.

The tourism business district

Within the literature on the supply of urban tourism, Ashworth and Page (2011) review the 'facility approach', which offers researchers the opportunity to map the location of specific facilities, undertaking inventories of facilities on a city-wide basis. The difficulty with such an approach is that the users of urban services and facilities are not just tourists, since workers and residents as well as recreationists may use the same facilities. Therefore, any inventory will be only a partial view of the full range of facilities and potential services tourists could use. One useful approach is to identify the areas in which the majority of tourist activities occur and to use it as the focus for the analysis of the supply of tourism services in such a multifunctional city that meets a wide range of uses for a wide range of users (see Chapter 5). This avoids the individual assessments of the location and use of specific aspects of tourism services such as accommodation (Page and Sinclair 1989), entertainment facilities such as restaurants (Smith 1983b, 1989) and night-life entertainment facilities (Ashworth et al. 1988), plus other attractions. This approach embraces the ecological approaches developed in human geography to pinpoint regions within cities as a basis to identify the processes shaping the patterns.

The ecological approach towards the analysis of urban tourism dates back to E.W. Gilbert's (1949) assessment of the development of resorts, which was further refined by Barrett (1958). The outcome is a resort model where accommodation, entertainment and commercial zones exist and the central location of tourism facilities were dominant elements. The significance of such research is that it identifies some of the features and relationships which were subsequently developed in urban geography and applied to tourism and recreation. The most notable study is Stansfield and Rickert's (1970) development of the Recreational Business District (RBD). This study rightly identifies the multifunctional land use of the central areas of cities, including tourism and recreational activities, in relation to the central area for business (Central Business District (CBD)).

Meyer-Arendt (1990) also expands this notion in the context of the Gulf of Mexico coastal resorts, while D.G. Pearce (1989) offers a useful critique of these studies. The essential ideas in the RBD have subsequently been extended to urban and resort tourism to try to explain where the location and distribution of the range of visitor-oriented functions occur in space.

Burtenshaw *et al*.'s (1991) seminal study of tourism and recreation in European cities deals with the concept of the Central Tourist District (CTD), where tourism activities in cities are concentrated in certain areas. This was retitled the Tourism Business District (TBD) by Getz, who argues that it is

> The concentration of visitor-oriented attractions and services located in conjunction with urban central businesses (CBD) functions. In older cities, especially in Europe, the TBD and CBD often coincide with heritage areas. Owing to their high visibility and economic importance, TBDs can be subjected to intense planning by municipal authorities ... The form and evolution of TBDs reveals much about the nature of urban tourism and its impacts, while the analysis of the planning systems influencing TBDs can contribute to concepts and methods for better planning of tourism in urban areas.
>
> (Getz 1993a: 583–4)

Figure 3.9, based on Getz's (1993a) analysis of the TBD, is a schematic model in which the functions rather than geographical patterns of activities are considered. The model illustrates the difficulty of separating visitor-oriented services from the CBD and use of services and facilities by residents and workers. While the TBD may offer a distinctive blend of activities and attractions for tourist and non-tourist alike, it is important to recognise functional and behavioural issues where tourism clusters in areas such as the TBD (Jansen-Verbeke and Ashworth 1990). Even so, the use of street entertainment and special events and festivals (Getz 1997) may also add to the ambience and sense of place for both the city worker and visitor. By having a

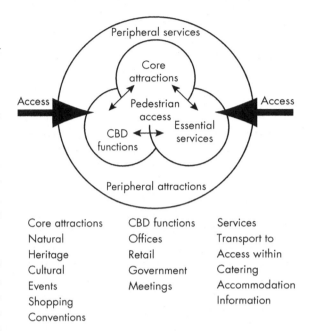

Core attractions	CBD functions	Services
Natural	Offices	Transport to
Heritage	Retail	Access within
Cultural	Government	Catering
Events	Meetings	Accommodation
Shopping		Information
Conventions		

Figure 3.9 The tourism business district
Source: based on Getz 1993a.

concentration of tourism and non-tourism resources and services in one accessible area within a city, it is possible to encourage visitors to stay there, making it a place tourists will want to visit, as is the case in the West End of London (Page and Sinclair 1989; Page and Hall 2003). However, the attractions in urban areas are an important component in the appeal to potential visitors.

Tourism attractions

Attractions are an integral feature of tourism, which offer visitors passive and more active occupations on which to spend their time during a visit (Page and Hall 2003). Lew's (1987) study and Leiper's (1990) synthesis and conceptual framework of 'Tourist Attraction Systems' remain among the most theoretically informed literature published to date. Page and Connell (2014) highlight the nature of the visitor attraction as a complex product with distinct place attributes, although place and space tends to be the neglected element in most studies of attractions, with a number of exceptions (e.g. Ding *et al.* 2011). Lew (1987) identifies three perspectives used to understand the nature of tourist attractions:

- *The ideographic perspective*, where the general characteristics of a place, site, climate, culture and customs are used to develop typologies of tourism attractions, involving inventories or general descriptions. For example, Standard Industrial Classification codes (SICs) are one approach used to group attractions (see Smith 1989).
- *The organisational perspective*, in contrast, tends to emphasise the geographical, capacity and temporal aspects (the time dimension) of attractions rather than the 'managerial notions of organisation' (Leiper 1990: 175). This approach examines scales ranging from the individual attraction to larger areas and their attractions.
- *The cognitive perspective* is based on 'studies of tourist perceptions and experiences of attractions' (Lew 1987: 560). P. Pearce (1982: 98) recognises that any tourist place (or attraction) is one capable of fostering the feeling of being a tourist. Therefore, the cognitive perspective is interested in understanding the tourists' feelings about and views of the place or attraction.

Leiper (1990) pursues the ideas developed by MacCannell (1976: 41), that an attraction incorporates 'an empirical relationship between a tourist, a sight and a marker, a piece of information about a sight'. A 'marker' is an item of information about any phenomenon which could be used to highlight the tourist's awareness of the potential existence of a tourist attraction. This implies that an attraction has a number of components. In this respect, 'the tourist attraction is a system comprising three elements: a tourist, a sight and a marker' (Leiper 1990: 178). Although sightseeing is a common tourist activity, the idea of a sight really refers to the nucleus or central component of the attraction (Gunn 1972). In this context a situation could include a sight where sightseeing occurs, but it may also be an object, person or event. Based on this argument, Leiper (1990: 178)

introduces the following definition of a tourist attraction: 'a system comprising three elements: a tourist or human element, a nucleus or central element, and a marker or informative element. A tourist attraction comes into existence when the three elements are interconnected.' On the basis of this alternative approach to attractions, Leiper (1990) identifies the type of information which is likely to give meaning to the tourist experience of urban destinations in relation to their attractions.

These ideas were developed further in Leiper's model of a tourist attraction system (Figure 3.10), breaking the established view that tourists are not simply 'attracted' or 'pulled' to areas on the basis of their attractions. Instead, visitors are motivated to experience a nucleus and its markers in a situation where the marker reacts positively with their needs and wants. Figure 3.10 identifies the linkages within the model and how tourist motivation is influenced by the information available and the individual's perception of their needs. Thus, an attraction system may develop only when the following have become connected:

- a person with tourist needs;
- a nucleus (a feature or attribute of a place that tourists seek to visit);
- a marker (information about the nucleus).

This theoretical framework has a great deal of value in relation to understanding the supply of urban tourism resources for visitors. First, it views an attraction system as a subsystem of the larger tourism system in an urban area. Second, it acknowledges the integral role of the tourist as consumer: without the tourist (or day-tripper/visitor) the system would not exist. Third, the systems approach offers a convenient social science framework in which to understand how urban destinations attract visitors, with different markers and nuclei to attract specific groups of visitors. Having examined the significance of different approaches towards the analysis of tourism supply in urban areas, attention turns to the significance of different components of Jansen-Verbeke's (1986) leisure product and tourism destinations.

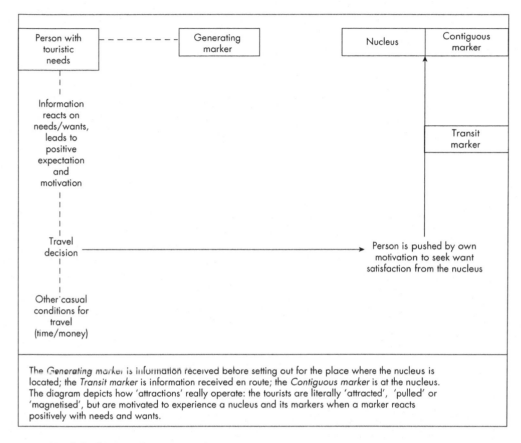

The *Generating marker* is information received before setting out for the place where the nucleus is located; the *Transit marker* is information received en route; the *Contiguous marker* is at the nucleus. The diagram depicts how 'attractions' really operate: the tourists are literally 'attracted', 'pulled' or 'magnetised', but are motivated to experience a nucleus and its markers when a marker reacts positively with needs and wants.

Figure 3.10 Model of a tourism attraction system

Source: based on Leiper 1990. Reproduced with permission from Elsevier.

Tourist facilities

Among the 'secondary elements' of the leisure product in urban areas, four components emerge as central to servicing tourist needs (Jansen-Verbeke 1986). These are:

- accommodation;
- restaurants, cafés and catering facilities;
- tourist shopping;
- conditional elements.

Accommodation

Tourist accommodation performs an important function in cities: it provides the opportunity for visitors to stay for a length of time to enjoy the locality and its attractions, while their spending contributes to the local economy. Accommodation forms a base for the tourists' exploration of the urban (and non-urban) environment. The tendency for establishments to locate in urban areas is illustrated in Figure 3.11, which is based on the typical patterns of urban hotel location in west European cities (Ashworth 1989; see also the seminal article on urban hotel location by Arbel and Pizam 1977). Figure 3.11 highlights the importance of infrastructure and accessibility when hotels are built to serve specific markets, i.e. the exhibition and conference market will need hotels adjacent to a major conference and exhibition centre, as Law (1996) emphasised. The accommodation sector

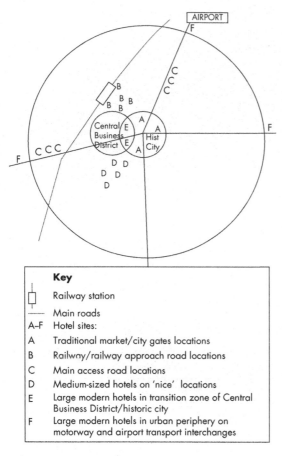

Key

▯	Railway station
-----	Main roads
A–F	Hotel sites:
A	Traditional market/city gates locations
B	Railway/railway approach road locations
C	Main access road locations
D	Medium-sized hotels on 'nice' locations
E	Large modern hotels in transition zone of Central Business District/historic city
F	Large modern hotels in urban periphery on motorway and airport transport interchanges

Figure 3.11 Model of urban hotel location in west European cities

Source: after Ashworth 1989.

within cities can be divided into serviced and non-serviced sectors (Figure 3.12). Each sector has developed in response to the needs of different markets, and a wide variety of organisational structures have emerged among private sector operators to develop this area of economic activity.

In London, the number of bedrooms in hotels and other forms of accommodation has grown from 44,000 bedrooms in 1966 to 80,000 in 1970, 130,000 in 1974, 137,844 in 1989, 150,419 in 1999 and 249,000 in 2011. The patterns of accommodation supply remained geographically concentrated in

Westminster, Kensington, Chelsea and Camden, with one outlier – Hillingdon – with its Heathrow Airport hotel. However, in the mid-1990s a new cluster in Croydon developed to equal and then exceed the number of bedspaces in Hillingdon. Croydon developed to service Gatwick Airport and routes to London by rail and the M25 orbital motorway. Consequently, since 1989 the spatial distribution of bedspaces has expanded from the CTD concentrated on the West End. One immediate beneficiary was the area to the south of the River Thames, as planning constraints in the main CTD area and limited development saw the CTD expand across the river (e.g. in Southwark). Bedspaces have also developed on this overspill principle to the east (i.e. in Tower Hamlets) and to the west (i.e. in Hammersmith), and also at other 'honey-pots' or hubs such as Greenwich. These have also been on the periphery in outer London, where the M25 leisure/business traveller has seen budget hotels developed by many of the hotel chains (e.g. Travelodge).

At a more global scale, Ivy (2001) examined the development of gay tourism and recreation space, particularly accommodation establishments catering for this niche market. Based on the Spartacus International Gay Guide for 1997, Ivy (2001) found that the Top 10 countries for gay-friendly accommodation were, in order of significance, the USA (35.1 per cent of the total), Germany, France, the UK, the Netherlands, Italy, Spain, Brazil, Japan and Belgium. These 10 countries accounted for 74.1 per cent of bedspaces and the location of accommodation within countries was not spatially uniform, with a distinct clustering in certain locations, and even within such locations a further clustering in districts offering gay travel services. The distinctive spatial accommodation patterns of specific markets, such as the gay and lesbian market, are significant as they highlight the importance of cultural and even regulatory factors in the development and attractiveness of particular tourism spaces (Waitt *et al.* 2008).

Restaurant, café and catering facilities

Ashworth and Tunbridge (1990) note that restaurant and catering facilities are among the most frequently

Sector Market segment	Serviced sector		Non-serviced sector (self-catering)	
	Destination	Routes	Destination	Routes
Business and other non-leisure	City/town hotels (Monday–Friday) Resort hotels for conferences, exhibitions Educational establishments Serviced apartments	Motels Inns Airport hotels	Unserviced apartments Urban second homes	Not applicable
Leisure and holiday	Resort hotels Guest house/ pensions Farm houses City/town hotels (Friday–Sunday) Some educational establishments	Motels Bed and breakfast Inns	Hotels Condominia Holiday villages Holiday centres/ camps Caravan/chalet parks Gîtes Cottages Villas Apartments/flats Some motels Second homes (primarily rural)	Touring pitches for caravans, tents, recreation vehicles Backpackers Some hotels

Figure 3.12 Types of tourism accommodation
Source: after Middleton 1988.

used tourism services after accommodation. One initial way of grouping this sector is to use the Standard Industrial Classification which comprises restaurants, eating places, public houses, bars, clubs, canteens and messes, hotels and other forms of tourist accommodation. Using the products which this sector produces, the sector can be further divided into the provision of accommodation and the provision of food for immediate consumption. While there is considerable overlap between the two sectors, there are organisational links between each sector and integration within larger hospitality organisations (e.g. the Compass Group), with their subsidiaries offering various products. One of the immediate difficulties is in identifying specific outlets for tourist use, as many such facilities are also used by residents.

Tourist use of restaurant and catering facilities varies according to the specific service on offer, and to their being located throughout cities, often in association with other facilities (Smith 1983b). Many restaurant and catering establishments in cities reflect local community needs, and tourism complements the existing pattern of use. Nevertheless, Ashworth and Tunbridge (1990: 65) acknowledge that restaurants and establishments combining food and drink with other entertainments, such as night clubs and casinos, have two important locational characteristics that render them useful in this context: they have a distinct

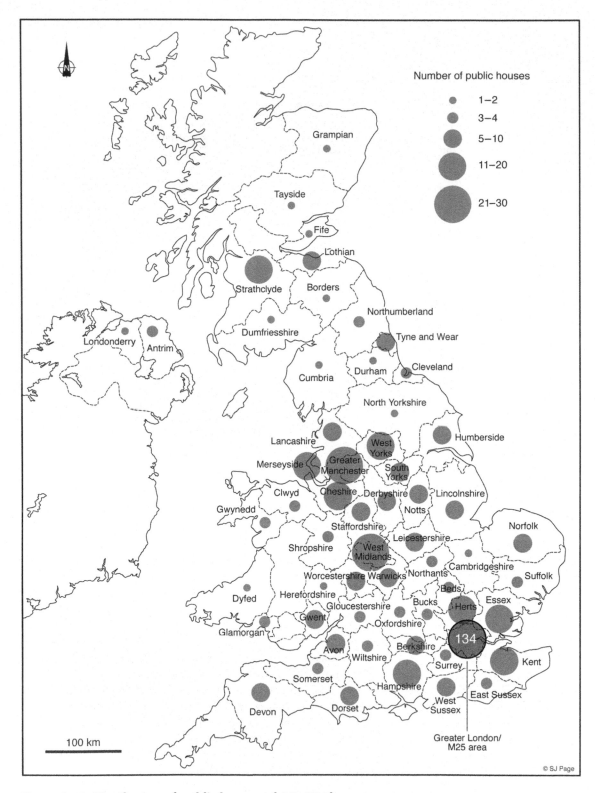

Number of public houses

- 1–2
- 3–4
- 5–10
- 11–20
- 21–30

Grampian

Tayside

Fife

Lothian

Strathclyde

Borders

Londonderry

Antrim

Northumberland

Dumfriesshire

Tyne and Wear

Cumbria

Durham

Cleveland

North Yorkshire

Lancashire

Humberside

West Yorks

Merseyside

Greater Manchester

South Yorks

Clwyd

Cheshire

Derbyshire

Lincolnshire

Gwynedd

Notts

Staffordshire

Leicestershire

Norfolk

Shropshire

West Midlands

Worcestershire

Warwicks

Northants

Cambridgeshire

Suffolk

Beds

Dyfed

Herefordshire

Bucks

Herts

Essex

Gwent

Gloucestershire

Oxfordshire

134

Glamorgan

Avon

Wiltshire

Berkshire

Surrey

Kent

Somerset

Hampshire

West Sussex

East Sussex

Devon

Dorset

Greater London/ M25 area

100 km

© SJ Page

Figure 3.13 Distribution of public houses of J.D. Wetherspoon

tendency to cluster together into particular streets or districts (what might be termed the 'Latin-quarter effect') and they tend to be associated spatially with other tourism elements, including hotels, which probably themselves offer public restaurant facilities. Catering facilities also have a predisposition to cluster within areas where shopping is also a dominant activity, particularly in mall developments, where food courts have become a popular concept in the USA and Australasia, while cosmopolitan cities have also developed a distinctive café culture aimed at residents and the visiting market who seek a café ambience. In the UK, deregulation of the brewery-owned (tied) public houses in the 1990s led to the development of new chains which have moved into this leisure market and continue to expand their UK presence, as Figure 3.13 illustrates for the more dynamic and enterprising chains such as J.D. Wetherspoon.

BOX 3.4 TOWARDS GEOGRAPHICAL ANALYSES OF HOSPITALITY: THE GEOGRAPHY OF HOSPITALITY EMPLOYMENT IN THE UK

While the geographer has primarily focused on the spatial and cultural implications of catering and hospitality, there is a well-developed hospitality literature which has examined the historical evolution of the hospitality trades (Walton 2000, 2012). Critical debates associated with the 'McDonaldization' of society (Ritzer 1993) and linked to globalisation, where the principles of fast food restaurants are dominating society, especially hospitality (e.g. the use of technology in place of people, service standardisation, set rules and procedures and clear division of labour) have introduced predictability into hospitality services globally (Zampoukos and Ioannides 2011). For the tourist experience, a global and spatial homogeneity associated with the McDonaldisation concept raises important cultural questions related to the type of experience being produced and consumed by tourists. In new conceptualisations of hospitality, Lashley (2000: 3) challenges existing concerns with hospitality as a narrowly defined commercial activity, namely the 'provision of food and/or drink and/or accommodation away from home', preferring new approaches. Lashley (2000: 4) introduces a new breadth of definition with the use of the social, private and commercial domains of hospitality. Each domain represents one aspect of hospitality which is both independent and overlapping. From the social domain, the social setting of hospitality shapes the production and consumption of food/drink/accommodation. In the private domain, the issues of hospitableness and the host–guest encounter and cultural context of these relationships became important. In the commercial domain, the focus is on the production of hospitality services and their consumption as an economic activity. For the geographer, much of the research has been conceived in the empiricist tradition and primarily concerned with employment in hospitality, its spatial form and processes shaping the supply of hospitality businesses (Getz et al. 2004; Hall and Rusher 2004). Again, this area of research is particularly underdeveloped and certainly is well situated to utilise a wide range of research approaches (Walle 1997) and agendas, ranging from an empiricist mode to new cultural geographies.

Research on the geography of tourism employment continues to be a rather neglected area of academic endeavour as previous studies in the UK (e.g. Bull and Church 1994) and Italy (Lazaretti and Capone 2008) have highlighted both regional variations and concentrations in employment growth in time and space. Even macro studies of tourism employment do not readily accommodate the agglomerative principles associated with many hospitality businesses that tend to cluster in areas of demand and visitor activity, albeit with a defined seasonal element to the structure of the labour market (Ball 1989) which has persisted as a structural feature of the sector even in cities where the seasonal nature of visitation is less subject to seasonal fluctuations (Ashworth and Page 2011). Despite the seasonal variations within cities, temporal variations within the day have been a characteristic feature of the sector (Hall 2005a). What research demonstrates is that the clustering of employment tends to be associated with business ventures in a wide range of sectors each of which has its own locational characteristics.

In the UK, The People 1st (2010) *State of the Nation* report provides a number of interesting insights on the nature of the hospitality sector in one country as a description of its scale, reviewing five key themes (economic performance, workforce size and characteristics, recruitment and retention, employee engagement, workforce skills and development). The scale of the sector was reported as comprising 2.1 million workers (equivalent to 7.2 per cent of the working population) and representing 1 in 14 jobs in the UK. In terms of economic output, tourism includes travel services (18 per cent). 'Tourist Services' is only 2 per cent of the total, while self-catering accommodation is a further 2 per cent. Output is dominated by restaurants (18 per cent), pubs/bars/night clubs (18 per cent) and gambling (15 per cent). This reflects an often overlooked aspect of employment, that the sector is staff intensive to deliver the experiential aspects of hospitality operations (including tourism and leisure consumers). Much of the sector is dominated by small and medium-sized enterprises (SMEs), with half of all businesses employing fewer than five people and 24 per cent being sole traders. In contrast, almost half of the workforce is employed by large employers with over 100 employees. The sector is dependent upon part-time employees as almost half of the workforce fall into this category (compared to 28 per cent for the national economy, which is also on the increase).

The subsequent report by ONS (2012) illustrates one of the perennial problems of measuring the tourism and hospitality sector as the study used 43 different employment categories to measure tourism employment (which effectively equates to the hospitality sector as it is much broader than just tourism) and concluded that the sector employed 2.7 million people in the UK in 2011. While these issues of measurement and consistency are not uncommon (though partly addressed where countries have implemented a Tourism Satellite Accounting system), the spatial dimension to the ONS (2012) study is illustrative of the geographical patterns of tourism and leisure employment, where food and beverage service activities dominate the sector. Some 30 per cent of employment is concentrated in London and the South East, although this urban London and home counties pattern is complemented as the Top 10 regional concentrations (where tourism employment is greater than 12 per cent of the local employment structure) in more rural and remote locations (i.e. western Scotland, the west of England, North Wales, North West England (i.e. Cumbria and the Lake District), key urban/resort areas such as Torbay, Blackpool and York) and other rural locations, including the Orkney Islands, the Isle of Anglesey and the Perthshire/Stirlingshire region). These statistics at a regional level reflect the notion of hotspots within these regions, where employment concentrates in some cases around the major attractions and destinations. The statistics also mask a wider contribution of tourism to some of these seasonal destinations (e.g. Torbay, Blackpool and rural areas) versus the more year-round tourism trade in major tourism cities (e.g. London and York), as well as an underlying contribution of leisure spending (as well as the night-time economy) to underpinning such employment patterns in the food and beverage employment (as opposed to the accommodation spending by tourists).

Tourist shopping

A number of studies in the tourism and leisure litera-ture have expanded the knowledge base on tourist shopping, providing more detailed insights on this increasingly significant activity (Hobson 2000; Snepenger *et al.* 2003; Wong and Law 2003; Timothy 2005; Henderson *et al.* 2011), with one of the most important aspects being shopping in relation to other tourist pursuits (Guo *et al.* 2009; Al-Saleh and Hannam 2010). An English Historic Town Forum's (1992) study on retailing and tourism highlights many of the relationships between tourism and retail activity that are 'inextricably linked to historic towns with three-quarters of tourists combining shopping with visiting attractions . . . The expenditure is not only on refreshments and souvenirs, as might be expected, but also on clothing and footwear, stationery and books' (English Historic Towns Forum 1992: 3). The study emphasises the overall significance of the environmental quality in towns, which is vital to the success of urban tourism and retailing. In fact the report argues that, for towns wishing to maintain or increase leisure visitor levels, the study reveals a num-ber of guidelines, for example cleanliness, attractive shop fronts and provision of a safe environment. Research by organisations such as VisitEngland views these measures as a key element of destination hygiene factors (i.e. the need to conform to a high standard) where tourists are asked about whether the places they visited had a 'clean and tidy environment' which is underpinned by the work of other organisations such as Keepbritaintidy.org which identifies key causes of visual and physical cleanliness: dog fouling, fly posting, fly tipping, graffiti, chewing gum on the floor, litter and waste. Keep Britain Tidy operates the Blue Flag and Quality Coast Awards as a means to drive up the quality of the environment for tourists (English Historic Towns Forum 1992: 3). Unfortunately, iden-tifying tourist shopping as a concept in the context of urban tourism is difficult, since it is also an activity undertaken by other users, such as residents. The range of motives associated with tourism and leisure shopping are complex: people visit areas due to their appeal, and shopping may be a spontaneous as well as a planned activity. Even so, the quality and range of retail facilities may be a useful determinant of the likely demand for tourism and leisure shopping: the longer the visitor is enticed to stay in a destination, the greater the likely spending in retail outlets (Jansen-Verbeke 1990, 1991; Timothy 2005; Henderson *et al.* 2011).

One important factor which affects the ability of cit-ies to attract tourism and leisure shoppers is the retail mix – namely the variety of goods, shops and presence of specific retailers (Henderson *et al.* 2011; Davies 2012). For example, the English Historic Towns Forum (1992) notes that over 80 per cent of visitors consider the retailing mix and general environment of the town to be the most important attraction of the destination. Although the priorities of different tourist market seg-ments vary slightly, catering, accessibility (e.g. avail-ability of car parking, location of car parks and public transport), tourist attractions and the availability of visitor information shape the decision to engage in tourism and leisure shopping. The constant search for the unique shopping experience, especially in con-junction with day trips in border areas and neigh-bouring countries (e.g. the US–Canada or US–Mexico border) are well-established forms of tourism and lei-sure shopping (Arreola 2010; Sullivan *et al.* 2012).

The global standardisation of many consumer prod-ucts has meant that the search for the unique shopping experience continues to remain important. The growth of the North American shopping malls and tourist-specific projects (Lew 1985, 1989; Getz 1993b) and the development in Europe of out-of-town complexes (e.g. the Metro Centre in Gateshead and Lakeside at Thurrock in the UK, adjacent to the M25 motorway) have extended this trend. Such developments have been of great concern for many cities as out-of-town shopping has reduced the potential in-town urban tourism in view of the competition it poses for estab-lished destinations. The difficulty with most existing studies of leisure shopping is that they fail to disentan-gle the relationships between the actual activity tour-ists undertake and their perception of the environment. For this reason, Jansen-Verbeke (1991) distinguishes between intentional shopping and intentional leisure shopping in a preliminary attempt to explain how and why tourists engage in this activity; and suggests criteria of the behaviour pattern of visitors; the functional characteristics of the environment; environmental quality and hospitableness of the environment in order to distinguish between intentional shopping and intentional leisure and tourism. Such criteria have also been expanded and developed in more recent research, with considerable attention given to behaviours and experiences (Wong and Wan 2013), and the overall role of the servicescape (Park *et al*. 2010; Xu and McGehee 2012).

Many successful cities in western Europe have used tourism and leisure shopping to establish their popularity as destinations as a gradual process of evolution. For example, Page and Hardyman (1996) examine the concept of town centre management (TCM) as one attempt to address the impact of out-of-town shopping malls and complexes as a threat to tourism and leisure spending in town centres. Since that initial research, TCM has become a well-established principle in many cities, especially to identify their users (especially the leisure and tourist shopper) more closely and undertake in-town improvements to attract the user as a means of developing leisure shopping. In particular, improvements to town centres by city authorities have acted as catalysts to this process by:

- establishing pedestrian precincts;
- managing parking problems and implementing park-and-ride schemes to improve access and convenience;
- marketing the destination based around an identifiable theme, often using the historical and cultural attractions of a city;
- investing in new and attractive indoor shopping galleries, improving facades, the layout and design of the built environment and making the environment more attractive.

The English Historic Towns Forum (1992: 12) identifies the following factors which tourism and leisure shoppers deemed important:

- the cleanliness of the town;
- pedestrian areas/pavements which are well maintained;

- natural features such as rivers and parks;
- the architecture and facades/shop fronts;
- street furniture (seating and floral displays);
- town centre activities (e.g. outdoor markets and live entertainment).

One can also add issues of urban safety (Walker and Page 2003), particularly where new shopping environments are now designing out crime in consultation with the police. Indeed, the discussion in Chapter 2 regarding social inclusion and the rise of private spaces as shopping malls also raises many accessibility and environmental issues, where many new retail environments are being developed as synthetic, protective and cosseted environments, lacking in character and a sense of place. Many shopping malls are becoming global in their design, retail mix and focus so that attracting the tourist and leisure shopper is more competitive, given that many areas have similar retail offerings in larger cities and in out-of-town locations.

Changes that alter the character of the town, where it becomes more tourist oriented, are sometimes characterised by the development of speciality and gift/souvenir shops and catering facilities in certain areas. However, as Owen (1990) argues, many traditional urban shopping areas are in need of major refurbishment, and tourism may provide the necessary stimulus for regeneration, especially in downtown areas that are competing with out-of-town centres. Developments such as theme shopping (Liu and Wang 2010) and festival marketplaces (Sawicki 1989) are specialised examples of how this regeneration has proceeded internationally.

Jansen-Verbeke (1991) described the 'total experience' as the future way forward for this activity – retailers will need to attract tourism and leisure spending using newly built, simulated or refurbished retailing environments with a variety of shopping experiences. The opportunity to undertake a diverse range of retail activities in a locality may increase the visitor's propensity to spend. However, the growing saturation of retailing provision in many industrialised countries may pose problems for further growth in tourism and leisure shopping due to the intense competition for such spending. Urban tourism destinations are likely to have to compete more aggressively for such spending in the future, as new investment strategies, constant expansion and value adding to the shopping experience are part of this competitive development, with public–private sector partnerships promoting such development (Albayrak and Caber 2013).

Conditional elements

The fourth feature which Jansen-Verbeke (1986) views as central to the city's 'leisure product' is conditional elements, such as transport, physical infrastructure and the provision of signposting. Unless adequate infrastructure is provided, tourists will be reluctant to divert from established patterns of visitor activity and tourism and leisure shopping will fail to materialise. Transport is a vital element in the facilitation of tourism, as it allows people to move from origin to destination (i.e. it permits mobility), and at the destination it provides the mechanism to enjoy sightseeing, touring and the linking for visitors of their place of accommodation with the attractions they wish to visit and the activities they wish to pursue (Le-Klähn et al. 2014). Good signposting, connectivity in transport systems, inter-modal interchanges and a clear circuit/itinerary are important to link visitors and resources/places. Numerous studies exist which examine the conceptual basis of the transport–tourism interface (Page 1994b, 1999, 2009a), with new perspectives on research agendas questioning the significance of transport (Lumsdon and Page 2004). In fact many geographical analyses of tourism have mapped the routes tourists take by car on holiday within cities and regions (Page 1998), the flows by means of air travel (Graham 1998; Page 2003b) as well as by coach (Page 2003c) and rail (Page 2002), and the importance of transport as an attraction in the 'leisure product' (e.g. Melbourne's refurbished tram restaurant) and as icons in destinations like the London Routemaster bus, which has been withdrawn from all but two tourist routes for supposed health and safety reasons. This last issue of sightseeing also highlights one new area for geographical research on tourism as part of the conditional elements – tourism and visual culture.

There is a growing body of interdisciplinary research, informed by cultural geography, which examines how tourists consume visual culture, which refers to the image-making devices and skills of a particular culture. This has been broadened in context to include fine art, the media, television, video, photography and advertising and the way these forms of media are used to attach meanings to artefacts, objects and places. In a tourism context, Crouch and Lübbren (2003: 5) note that 'visual culture is consumed in spaces. Geographical thought is an important component of understanding the consumption of, or encounter with, visual culture. Tourism has frequently been depicted and theorized, as a journey; a journey to and in places, identities and experiences.' As the physical space and places that tourists visit are consumed, the visual culture is part of the tourist experience of the place, site and way in which it is visually consumed. In other words, tourism is a sensual encounter, based on visual images, and Baudrillard (1981) noted the strategies of desire, whereby tourists' interests and needs are met through consumption. The tourism industry is therefore very adept at using visual culture to develop the tourist offering, as well as using advertising, promotion, signs and symbols which the tourist gazes at, observes and consumes. Therefore, visual culture has important links in the conditional elements of tourism, since the consumption of tourism is part of a cultural process.

Conclusion

This chapter has examined a range of issues and concepts associated with the analysis of recreation and tourism supply issues. One interesting comparison which appears to hold true is S.J. Smith's (1983a) criticisms of recreational research being applicable to tourism due to the simplistic conceptualisation of the subject matter. In fact, Britton's (1980a, 1991) innovative and theoretically derived analyses remain a fresh and welcome attempt to rethink the geography of tourism, particularly the production side, which has been notoriously descriptive and somewhat naive in its borrowing of geographical concepts, while making little contribution to theory (Debbage and Ioannides 2004). This chapter has achieved two purposes: the first is to show how the geographer approaches the spatial complexity of supply issues in both recreation and tourism, while introducing some of the concepts, methods and ways of thinking about supply; second, it has detailed the importance of developing a more meaningful assessment of tourism and the production system by situating the supply of tourism and recreation within the contexts of concepts of core and periphery, consumption and production, and tourism as a capitalist activity. It is apparent that in the more theoretically derived analyses of supply issues there is a need to derive more culturally specific explanations which indicate why certain phenomena exist, have developed and now dominate the tourism and leisure environment (Debbage and Ioannides 2004). Terkenli (2002) offered a number of insights on how space is organised in the postmodern western world based on a number of trends:

- conventional notions of place, particularly our sense of place, transcend geographical barriers of distance (i.e. the media and information technology have created globally aware consumers in the west);
- a de-differentiation occurring between public and private spheres of everyday life;
- a desegregation of leisure from home and work life, making distinctions such as leisure more tentative;
- globalisation processes, where communications media provide images, information and awareness of leisure travel opportunities on a daily basis through television programmes, consumer magazines and a strong dependence upon visual communication.

These trends have led to a cultural economy of space with leisure/tourism interactions shaped by processes that are simultaneously transforming geographical configurations of supply. Such processes, operating at a global scale, also have a local impact, as reflected in the many forms of mass consumption in tourism and leisure as well as changes to place and space (Hall 2013b). The spatial articulation of these forms of consumption is in a constant state of flux, particularly as the blurring of work–home life questions the geographer's conventional supply-side models of

leisure, defined in relation to home and patterns of consumption (Pacione 2001). As a result, the geographer's understanding of how tourism and leisure is integrated into the everyday lives of people is now a more complex process in both a theoretical and spatial context. Consequently, understanding the impacts of tourism and leisure activity poses questions for postmodern society and the 'myriad of ways in which local people have responded to, and sometimes resisted, tourism development' (Scheyvens 2002: 37).

Chapter 4 now turns to the impact of tourism and recreation.

Further reading

In terms of recreational supply, the following are useful introductions to the subject:

Hill, E., Bergstrom, J., Cordell, H.K. and Bowker, J.M. (2009) *Natural Resource Amenity Service Values and Impacts in the US*, Athens: University of Georgia, Department of Agricultural & Applied Economics and the USDA Forest Service, Southern Research Station.

Marcouiller, D.W. and Prey, J. (2005) 'The tourism supply linkage: recreational sites and their related natural amenities', *Journal of Regional Analysis & Policy*, 35: 23–32.

Marcouiller, D.W., Prey, J. and Scott, I. (2009) 'The regional supply of outdoor recreation resources: demonstrating the use of location quotients as a management tool', *Journal of Parks and Recreation Administration*, 27(4): 92–107.

For good reviews of conceptual issues on the supply of tourism services and facilities, see:

Agarwal, S., Ball, R., Shaw, G. and Williams, A. (2000) 'The geography of tourism production: uneven disciplinary development', *Tourism Geographies*, 2(3): 241–63.

Williams, A.M. (2004) 'Toward a political economy of tourism', in A. Lew, C.M. Hall and A.A. Williams (eds) *Companion to Tourism*, Oxford: Blackwell.

For discussions of the role of business in supply, and corresponding issues, see:

Ateljevic, J. and Page, S. (eds) (2009) *Progress in Tourism and Entrepreneurship*, Oxford: Elsevier.

Getz, D., Carlsen, J. and Morrison, A. (2004) *The Family Business in Tourism and Hospitality*, Wallingford: CAB International.

Zampoukos, K. and Ioannides, D. (2011) 'The tourism labour conundrum: agenda for new research in the geography of hospitality workers', *Hospitality & Society*, 1: 25–45.

Useful historical reviews of recreational and tourism/hospitality service provision include:

Maver, I. (1998) 'Glasgow's public parks and the community 1850–1914', *Urban History*, 25(3): 323–47.

Walton, J. (2000) 'The hospitality trades: a social history', in C. Lashley and A. Morrison (eds) *In Search of Hospitality: Theoretical Perspectives and Debates*, Oxford: Butterworth-Heinemann.

Walton, J.K. (2012) '"The tourism labour conundrum" extended: historical perspectives on hospitality workers', *Hospitality & Society*, 2: 49–75.

Questions to discuss

1 **How have geographers conceptualised recreational supply?**

2 **What techniques and tools have geographers used to examine the supply of recreational facilities?**

3 **What is the role of Britton's (1991) geography of production and consumption in the analysis of tourism?**

4 **Are the majority of studies of tourism supply descriptive and based on empirical data rather than theoretical models?**

The impacts of tourism and recreation

The growth of international and domestic tourism has been matched by a corresponding increase in the numbers of those who study tourism and its impacts. Indeed, it has even been suggested that tourism research was one of the academic growth industries of the late twentieth century (Hall 1995)! The literature on tourism has expanded enormously. Mathieson and Wall's (1982: 2) suggestion from over 30 years ago that tourism research has become 'highly fragmented, with researchers following separate and often divergent paths' remains as true today as when it was written. Nevertheless, one of the major areas of interest for geographers, as well as other tourism researchers, is the impacts of tourism and recreation.

Tourism and recreation cannot be studied in isolation from the complex economic, environmental, political and social milieux in which they occur (Mason 2003; Hall and Lew 2009). If geographers are to make a valid contribution to the study of tourism and recreation and their impacts, it is vital that they are aware of the widest possible implications of such effects for host communities and destinations, particularly as concerns over the sustainability of tourism and recreation grow (Butler 1990, 1991, 2000; Hall and Lew 1998; Hughes 2004; Weaver 2004; Gössling and Hall 2006a; Gössling *et al.* 2010; Gössling *et al.* 2013; Hall 2011f). This has therefore meant that there has been substantial interchange of ideas, frameworks and methodologies between geographers and non-geographers in analysing the impacts of tourism and recreation. This chapter will provide a broad overview of the development of frameworks to manage recreation and tourism impacts, the impacts of tourism and recreation, and some of the main issues which arise out of the analysis and management of

impacts. However, before discussing different types of recreational and tourism impacts in more depth it is important that we address the concept of 'impact' and difficulties in its application.

The concept of 'impact'

The way the term 'impact' is used implies that tourism and recreation has an affect on something, be it a place, person, environment, community, destination or economy. The term tourism 'impact' is therefore usually used as a kind of shorthand – and a poor one at that – to describe changes in the state of something related to visitation over time. Hall and Lew (2009) suggest that a term such as tourism-related change would be a much better way of describing what people mean when they say tourism impacts, but unfortunately people tend to be lazy, and apart from discussions between a few tourism and recreation researchers the term impact is the one in common use, and the one we are stuck with! Nevertheless, there is increasing awareness of tourism and recreation and environmental, social, economic and political change, and these are issues that will be addressed in this chapter and as we go through the rest of the book. Indeed, this concept of impact as 'changes in a given state over time' is one of the key concepts contained in this chapter.

Furthermore, the term 'impact' also suggests that this is a unidimensional or 'one-way' affect (Figure 4.1) (Hall and Lew 2009). However, the impacts of tourism and recreation are very rarely, if ever, a one-way relationship. In fact, tourism and recreation affects both people and things and, in turn, is affected by

How tourism impacts are often conceived – as a
one-way affect or unidimensional relationship

Tourism 'impacts' as a two-way relationship. Realisation that tourism not only
affects something but is also affected itself

Recognition of tourism 'impacts' as change over time. A and B are constantly
influencing and affecting each other, with each observation being a different
state of the relationship between them

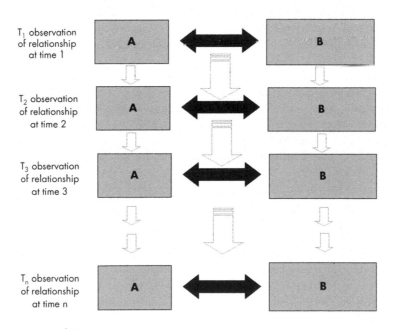

Figure 4.1 The nature of impacts
Source: Hall and Lew 2009.

them. This is something that is extremely important for issues such as climate change where there may be a time lag between the effects of the emissions of the tourism industry and the consequent effects of climate change events on tourism destinations and industry (Scott *et al.* 2012). Impacts are also rarely, if ever, just an issue of isolated environmental, social, economic or political impact. This is because visitation affects the physical environment; it affects people, communities and the broader social environment;

it has economic effects; and it can be very political, especially with respect to how places both attract and manage visitors and how the impacts of tourism may be mitigated or adapted to. Therefore, management of the impacts of tourism and recreation requires an integrated approach that aims to bring these various dimensions of tourism together in a coherent manner.

The publication of George Perkins Marsh's book, *Man and Nature; Or, Physical Geography as Modified by Human Action* (1965) in 1864 provides a starting point for impact studies. The book had an enormous impact when it was first published, as it was the first comprehensive critique of the extent to which inappropriate development had damaged the physical environment and hence human well-being. According to Marsh (1965 [1864]: 52), 'Even now, we are breaking up the floor and wainscoting and doors and window frames of our dwelling, for fuel to warm our bodies and seethe our pottage, and the world cannot afford to wait till the slow and sure progress of exact science has taught it a better economy'. Marsh observed:

> The earth is fast becoming an unfit home for its noblest inhabitant, and another era of equal human crime and human improvidence, and of like duration with that through which traces of that crime and that improvidence extend, would reduce it to such a condition of that impoverished productiveness, of shattered surface, of climatic excess, as to threaten the depravation, barbarism, and perhaps even extinction of the [human] species.
>
> (Marsh 1965 [1864]: 43)

Such words strike a distinct chord when compared to contemporary concern over biodiversity loss, deforestation, declining quality of agricultural lands, desertification and climate change. Marsh's work had an international impact, leading to a growing awareness of the limits of resources, a theme which, again, remains with us to the present day given concerns over water, energy, resource and food security. Marsh's approach, along with the closing of the American frontier in 1890, led to the development of the 'progressive conservation' movement (Hays 1959). The progressive conservation movement represented a 'wise use' approach to the management of natural resources, and its conservation motives were economic rather than aesthetic in intent, and their focus laid the foundations for the notion of sustainable development. In contrast, the 'Romantic ecology' (Worster 1977) of John Muir, the 'grandfather of National Parks', stressed the spiritual values of wilderness and nature and can be broadly categorised as more of a 'preservation' focus. Such points are important as the differing perceptions of the appropriate use of resources exist to the present day, and also underlie many of the arguments surrounding tourism development, especially in natural areas.

According to Hall (2008a: 27) 'Sustainable tourism is a sub-set of both tourism and sustainable development'. Sustainable tourism development is not the same as sustainable development, although the principles of sustainable development do inform sustainable tourism (Figure 4.2). The key difference between the two concepts is one of scale. Sustainable tourism only refers to the application of sustainability concepts at the level of the tourism industry and related social, environmental and economic change. Sustainable development, on the other hand, operates beyond tourism at a broader scale that incorporates all aspects of human interaction with the earth's environment. The implications of this scale difference are important because, for example, a tourism enterprise's operations may meet the criteria of being sustainable at the business level, but in a destination context it may be unsustainable because of its interaction with other resource users (Hall 2008a). The implications of sustainable tourism and sustainable development for planning are discussed in more detail in Chapter 9.

As noted above, an impact is a change in a given state over time as the result of an external stimulus. This is often considered in relation to specific environmental, economic or social impacts. However, increasingly, and prompted by the insights of sustainable development, impacts are being approached in a combined fashion, taking into account the interrelationship of two, or even all three, of the main impact categories of economic, social and physical (environmental) impact. A more detailed typology of the impacts of tourism is provided in Table 4.1, where

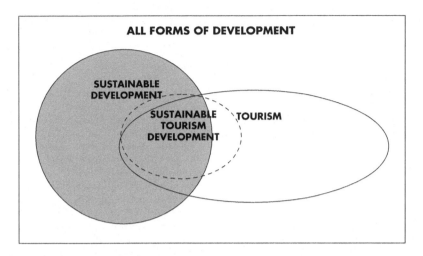

Figure 4.2 Sustainable tourism and sustainable development

they are categorised in terms of their positive or negative nature for a destination community. However, it should be noted that such a division is not absolute, as whether something is seen as positive or negative will often depend on the goals, ideology and value position of an individual and/organisation with respect to different types of tourism development and their broader development perspectives (Hall 2008a).

Understanding change in the tourism system

'Systems' approaches are integral to conceptualising the causality that exists between external factors and the subject of any study of change (Glasson *et al*. 2005). The concept of a 'tourism system' is one that has existed since the late 1960s in various forms (Hall 2008a) (see also Chapters 1 and 3). A system is a group of elements organised such that each element is, in some way, either directly or indirectly interdependent with every other element, and comprises:

1 a set of elements (also called entities);
2 the set of relationships between the elements;
3 the set of relationships between those elements and their larger environment;

4 a definition or identification of the system's boundaries;
5 for some analysts, identification of the system's function, goal or purpose, even if that only means the ongoing maintenance of the system.

Studies of systems have to address four main issues (Hay 2000; Hall and Lew 2009):

• *Whether the system is open or closed.* A closed system has no links to or from any environment that is external to it. Open systems interact with elements or environments outside their system boundary. Tourism constitutes an open system; however, this then raises the issue of difficulties in defining the boundary of a tourism system and therefore their arbitrary nature.
• *Whether the system can be divided into subsystems*, clusters or interdependent elements that are only weakly linked to the remainder of the system. In the case of tourism, depending on the definition of the overall tourism system, it is possible to identify a number of subsystems, although the relative strength of their relationship to the broader system will depend on the structure and dynamics of the system, e.g. particular tourism firm networks

Table 4.1 Positive and negative dimensions of the impacts of tourism on destinations

Type of impact	Positive	Negative
	Economic dimensions	
Economic	• increased expenditures • creation of employment • increase in labour supply • increase in standard of living • increase in investment	• localised inflation • real estate speculation • failure to attract tourists • better alternative investments • capital outflows • inadequate estimation of costs of tourism development • undesirable opportunity costs • lower wage levels
Business	• increased awareness of the region as a travel/tourism destination • increased knowledge concerning the potential for investment and commercial activity in the region • creation of new facilities, attractions and infrastructure • increase in accessibility	• acquisition of a poor reputation as a result of inadequate facilities, improper practices or inflated prices • negative reactions from existing enterprises due to the possibility of new competition for local personnel and government assistance • increased competition for local businesses
	Socio-cultural dimensions	
Social/cultural	• increase in permanent level of local interest and participation in types of activity associated with tourism • strengthening of destination values and traditions	• commercialisation and commodification of activities which may be of a personal or private nature, including culture • modification of nature of event or activity to accommodate tourism • potential increase in crime • changes in community structure • social dislocation
Psychological	• increased local pride and community spirit • increased awareness of non-local perceptions	• tendency toward defensive attitudes concerning host regions • high possibility of misunderstandings leading to varying degrees of host/visitor hostility
Political/ administrative	• enhanced international recognition of region and values • development of skills among planners • improved spatial planning	• economic exploitation to satisfy ambitions of political elite • distortion of true nature of event to reflect values of political system • increase in administrative costs • failure to cope and inability to achieve aims • loss of local planning control • use of tourism to legitimise unpopular decisions and/or ideology of local elite
	Environmental/physical dimensions	
	• development of new facilities • improvement of local infrastructure, e.g. sewerage • conservation of heritage • visitor management strategies	• environmental damage • changes in natural and ecological processes, including wildlife behaviour • architectural pollution and heritage loss • drop in water, air and soil quality • overcrowding • increased pollution and waste

Sources: after Getz 1977; Mathieson and Wall 1982; Ritchie 1984; Hall 1992b, 2008a; Wall and Mathieson 2006.

can be identified as subsystems within a larger innovation system (Weidenfeld and Hall 2014).

- *Whether the links involve flows*, causal relationships or 'black-box' relationships (the latter referring to when the consequences of a linkage is known but the causal factors are not). In a tourism system, the flows of tourists can clearly be identified, along with, in some cases, the flows of capital and energy. However, some of the causal relationships that result from those flows are not so well understood.
- *Whether there is feedback in the system*, such that a change in x may stimulate a change in y, and this in turn will have either a positive or negative impact on x. This is well recognised in the case of the impacts of tourism associated with the interaction between markets in tourism generating regions and in destinations (see Chapters 2 and 3), for example, so that a change in the destination (x) created in part by visitors (y) leads to changes in the behaviour of visitors (y) at a later point in time (see Figure 4.3a and b).

Representations of the relationships between generating regions and destinations have also been influential with respect to research on the life course of destinations (Christaller 1963; Butler 2006; Hall 2006a) (see also Box 3.2). Perhaps appropriately for understanding tourism systems, the interval between a disturbance to the system and the return to an equilibrium state is known in life cycle literature as the 'relaxation time' (Hall and Lew 2009). However, in many instances in life cycle studies of tourism the characteristics and conditions of equilibrium have not been identified, nor has the time scale of analysis been such that a return to an equilibrium state has been observed, or, if it has, it has not been recognised (Butler 2006).

McKercher (1999) argued that tourism essentially functions as a chaotic, non-linear, non-deterministic system. As such, many existing tourism frameworks and models fail to explain fully the complex relationships that occur between and among the various elements that constitute a tourism system. One of the main reasons for this is the difference between using the notion of a system as a metaphor for a kind of explanatory or educational device (e.g. Leiper 1989,

1990; Cornelissen 2005) versus using it as a framework to statistically explain positive and negative relationships between variables and to conduct a formal systems analysis (e.g. Lazanski and Kljajic 2006). In tourism studies the metaphor framework has dominated, which has often meant that terms for systems characteristics such as 'complexity' and 'chaos' have been used, often with little appreciation of the concrete analytical and predictive dimensions that such concepts provide to other fields of systems research (e.g. Faulkner and Russell 2003; Hall and Lew 2009).

A system is regarded as complex 'if its parts interact in a nonlinear manner. Simple cause and effect relationships among the elements rarely exist and instead a very little stimulus may cause unpredictably large effects or no effect at all' (Baggio 2007: 5). A complex system can also only be understood 'by considering it as a whole, almost independently by the number of parts composing it' (Baggio 2007: 5). In contrast, a complicated system is 'a collection of an often high number of elements whose collective action is the cumulative sum of the individual ones' (Baggio 2007: 6). This is a very important difference because it affects how knowledge of a part of the system affects our understanding of the whole. Tourism is usually described as a complex system (Walker *et al.* 1998; Hall and Lew 2009). For ecology, and correspondingly studies of tourism and the environment, a key question is: 'Can an ecological entity be understood through an analysis of its biotic and abiotic components (reductionism), or must any ecological entity be explained by treating it as a unitary entry with unique characteristics (holism)?' (Keller and Golley 2000: 171). Table 4.2 outlines some of these issues and the assumptions on which they rest. The different methodological assumptions pose a very real challenge for extrapolating the results of studies at one scale to other scales and to the tourism system as a whole.

Indeed, issues related to the use of the term 'impacts' has real influence on how we treat them. Head (2008: 374) argues that 'the metaphor of human impacts has come to frame our thinking and circumscribe debate about what constitutes explanation'. The metaphor of impact has several features, many of

(a)

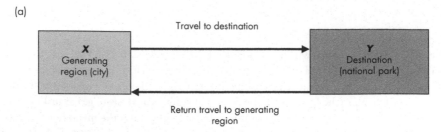

Systems diagram of hypothetical example of the interaction between markets in tourism generating regions X and destination Y. This could be imagined to be the relationship between an urban area that generates visitors (X) and a national park (Y).

(b)

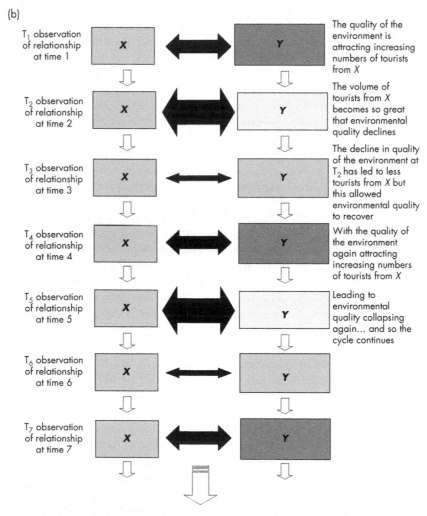

Hypothetical example of the interaction between markets in tourism generating regions X and destination Y so that change in Y is affected by X. Size of arrow illustrates strength of relationship between X and Y in terms of numbers of tourists travelling to and returning from X. Number of tourists is regarded as affecting the quality of the environment in destination Y, with the feedback in the system also indicating that the quality of the environment also influences the number of visitors who come from X to Y in the future, which is observed at the next point of time. Quality of environment in Y also indicated by shading; the darker the shading, the higher the quality of environment.

Figure 4.3 **Feedback in the tourism system**

Table 4.2 Ontologies and epistemologies of ecological systems

Methodological approach	Ontology	Epistemology
Reductionism	Properties of wholes are always found among the properties of their parts	Knowledge of the parts is both necessary and sufficient to understand the whole
Mechanism	Properties of wholes are of the same kind or type of those parts	Knowledge of the kind or type of the cause suffices to understand the type of kind of the effect
Emergentism	There is at least one property of some wholes not possessed by any of their parts. Parts can exist independently of the whole, and novel properties of wholes can be lost via submergence when a system is reduced to its parts	Knowledge of the parts and their relations is a necessary but not a sufficient condition to understand the whole
Organicism	Recognise the existence of emergent properties of wholes. Once a whole has appeared, its parts cannot exist or be understood independently of a whole	Knowledge of the whole is a necessary condition to understand the parts and vice versa
Holism	The emergent novel properties of the whole can be understood without further consideration of the parts and their relationships. The basic unit is the whole – wholes are independent of parts	Knowledge of the parts is neither necessary nor sufficient to understand the whole

Source: after Blitz 1992: 175–8; Keller and Golley 2000.

which are not adequately considered in tourism research (Hall 2013g):

1 The emphasis on *the moment(s) of collision between two separate entities* (e.g. the 'impact' between tourism and the environment) has favoured explanations that depend on correlation in time and space (Weyl 2009), and methodologies that are fully focused on dating and/or particular moments in time, to the detriment of the search for mechanisms of connection and causation rather than simple correlation (Head 2008).

2 The emphasis on the moment(s) of impact also *assumes a stable natural (environmental), social and/or economic baseline* (Mathieson and Wall 1982; Hall and Lew 2009), *and an experimental method in which only one variable is changed* (Head 2008). Such an approach is also inappropriate for understanding complex and dynamic socio-environmental systems (Farrell and Twinning-Ward 2004; Head 2008; Hall and Lew 2009).

3 Third, and perhaps most profoundly influential (Head 2007, 2008), is the way the terms 'tourism impacts' or 'tourist impacts' ontologically *position*

tourism and tourists as 'outside' the system under analysis, as outside nature (or whatever it is that is being impacted) (Hall and Lew 2009; Hall 2013g). This is ironic given that research on global environmental change demonstrates just how deeply entangled tourism is in environmental systems (Gössling and Hall 2006a; Hall 2009e, 2010f; Gössling *et al*. 2010; Hall and Saarinen 2010), yet the metaphor remains in widespread use.

4 Putting a significant explanatory divide between humans and nature requires the *conflation of bundles of variable processes* under such headings as 'human', 'climate', 'environment' and 'nature' (Head 2007, 2008).

5 A further characteristic of dichotomous explanations is their *veneer of simplicity and elegance*. Yet, 'The principle that preference should be given to explanations that require the fewest number of assumptions has been incorrectly conflated with the idea that simpler explanations are more likely to be true than complex ones . . . In fact, the view that causality is simple takes many more assumptions than the view that it is complex' (Head 2008: 374).

Much of the research undertaken in tourism with respect to impacts tends to be at the destination, omitting other elements of the geographical tourism system or trip, such as the transit region and the origin area (Figure 4.3a). However, if impact research is highly localised in one site or place, it clearly limits not only our capacities to generalise about the tourism system as a whole (see also Gössling and Hall 2006a), but also how tourism activities in one location can affect the entire system. For example, greenhouse gas (GHG) emissions at one location contribute to the global balance of GHG and therefore have more than a localised effect. Similarly, because tourism is a globalised industry with extended supply chains (see Chapter 3), resource use in one location can affect resource availability in another. The boundary of the system you are examining therefore determines the identification and measurement of impact.

Issues of scale and the boundary definition of systems are also important for tourism management, planning and policy-making as there is a need to try

and ensure that different levels — or scales — are in sync with one another so as to increase planning effectiveness. Environmental issues are particularly problematic with respect to trying to connect jurisdictional or governance scale (Gössling and Hall 2006a; Hall 2008a), especially because many environmental problems cross international borders. For example, smoke from forest clearance in Indonesia often travels to Malaysia and Singapore, causing health problems and creating negative images for those countries' tourism industries (Quah 2002; Aiken 2004).

Tourism is stretched over time and space, therefore it is extremely important to set appropriate boundaries for the system being examined, particularly as the smaller the size of the subsystem being examined, the more open it is to external forces for change. The selection of the boundary of a destination, or any boundary in analysing impacts, will affect the relative size and degree of system change within that boundary. Figure 4.4 illustrates some of the relativities of scales that affect tourism systems. Yet all scales are

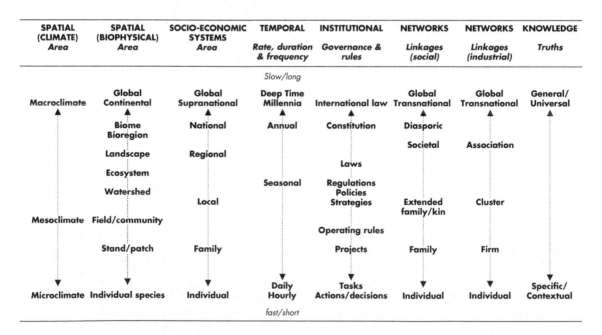

Figure 4.4 Relativities of scale in analysing tourism

Source: after Hall 2004c, in Hall and Lew 2009.

not studied equally, while there may also be a mismatch between the primary focus of tourism research and the effects that tourism brings and is also affected by. For example, the majority of tourism research in relation to ecology is at a species level rather than examining environmental change as a whole. Figure 4.5 contrasts the focus of tourism studies with the types of change that occur over space and time.

This issue has significant implications for understanding the spatial boundaries of destinations because governance jurisdictions may not match with the relative boundaries of a destination as perceived by visitors and tourism firms. To further complicate matters the destination boundary may not match with ecological boundaries, such as a watershed. Figure 4.6 illustrates some of the implications of the relativities of scale by highlighting how tourism policies, actors, climate and weather, and research intersect with the issue of tourism and climate

change. Understanding the issue of scale is therefore fundamental to being able to assess the impacts of tourism and effectively manage them. However, in the long run being able to work across scales will probably be essential for impact management and control.

Impacts: recreation resource management

Resource management for recreation purposes is a useful tool with which to begin understanding the relationships between recreation and tourist impacts, sites and the action needed to address conflicts, namely planning (Seeley 1983), a theme further explored in Chapter 9. In this context, resource management is concerned with the way the geographical approach meshes with the multidisciplinary contributions to understanding how resources need to be

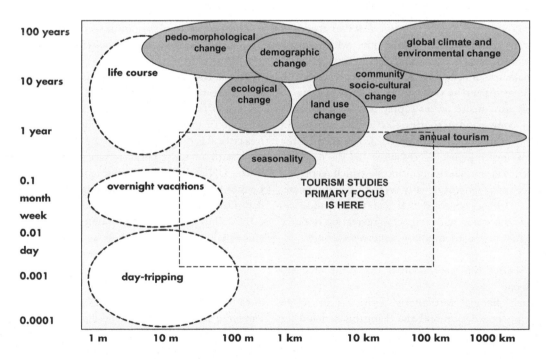

Figure 4.5 The influence of temporal and spatial resolution on assessing tourism-related phenomena

Source: adapted from Hall 2004a.

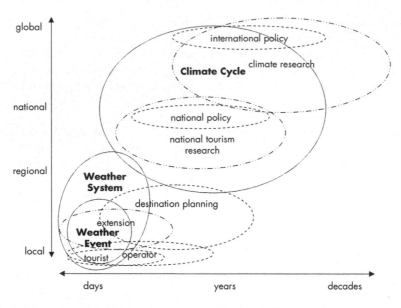

Figure 4.6 Relativities of scale with respect to tourism and climate change

managed (Mercer 2004). Glyptis (1989a) made an important fundamental assumption which many recreational texts overlook: that few recreational activities make use of resources that are solely recreational. Indeed, recreation is often juxtaposed in relation to forestry, agriculture, water supply, conservation and a host of competing activities that each make use of socially constructed leisure spaces. Consequently, the issue of multiple use of resources (as discussed in Chapter 3) is an underlying principle which recreation resource management usually seeks to accommodate. Glyptis (1989a) observed that four major influences could be discerned with respect to recreation resource management in contemporary western society:

- the belief that recreation is the right of every citizen;
- social change, particularly with respect to an ageing population and the changing demand for specific forms of recreation;
- changing economic and political doctrines which have seen debates associated with the demise of notions of full employment and leisure as non-work or of less significance than work;

- strategic planning by public sector recreation agencies in relation to the previous three influences.

Within a UK context, the 1980s under the Thatcher government saw the privatisation of many forms of recreation and leisure provision, a theme discussed later in Chapter 5 in terms of urban parks. What was critical here was the changing public policy framework with respect to public service provision in leisure in the UK and other countries (e.g. Aitchison 1997; Coalter 1998), the effects of which linger in the present day (Dahmann *et al.* 2010; Erickson 2011; Mowbray 2011). Thus political and ideological changes in government can have a major bearing on the nature and approach to recreation resource management.

What emerged from the wide range of geographical contributions to recreational resource analysis during the 1960s, 1970s and 1980s was that the fundamental starting point for any discussion is demand (Masser 1966–7; Chubb and Chubb 1981; Patmore 1983). Reiterating the discussion in Chapter 2, data from site surveys and overall levels of participation in time and space as a dynamic process provide the baseline information for resource management. It is then a question of establishing the impact of specific activities.

Understanding the extent of impacts such as the effect on natural resources, social and psychological impacts arising from overcrowding, traffic congestion, aesthetic intrusions and conflict between recreational activities illustrates how the resource is being impacted upon (Spink 1994). Even at the present time, over four decades since Burton's (1974) innovative study of carrying capacity of Cannock Chase, Staffordshire, UK, its methodological and conceptual value remains high despite innovations in mapping and analysis with GIS. Indeed, the pursuit of critical spatial concepts such as overcrowding, tolerance to visitor numbers and contested notions of rurality has seen only a growing interest by geographers since the 1970s, especially in the context of rural recreation (Robinson 1999; Edwards and Matarrita-Cascante 2011).

Probably one of the greatest challenges facing recreational resource planners in a non-urban context is the impact of the motor car in the post-war period. Many novel studies in the 1960s and 1970s (e.g. J. Hall 1972; Wall 1971, 1972) highlighted both the greater spatial reach and flexibility of access to recreational sites afforded by the car. Even so, the car is not a surrogate for individual mobility and recreational resource use (Glyptis 1989a), although, as Page (1998, 1999) highlighted, the car is one of the major issues facing the recreational planner, especially in national parks (Eaton and Holding 1996). Mobility and access to transport do limit certain socioeconomic groups from enjoying the wider continuum of outdoor recreation opportunities (Millward 1993, 1996, 2000; Hall 2010a), and especially as public transport access becomes more limited, a feature constantly reiterated in peripheral areas and urban recreation and summarised by S. Williams (1995b: 35): 'The net effect of car ownership is that participation rates in sports and outdoor recreations are significantly higher in households with access to a car'.

Population growth and increased affluence have also seen increased pressures on other rural resources such as lakes and waterways (Hall and Härkönen 2006). In the case of Loch Lomond, the pressure has come from another form of transport: recreational boating (see Bisset et al. 2000; Dickinson 2000). This concern has been heightened by the designation of the area as part of Scotland's first national park – the Loch Lomond and Trossachs National Park (Page and Dowling 2001). Recreational boat pressure, as in the case of the East Anglia Broads (Page 1999), has also posed concerns in terms of environmental pollution (Bannan et al. 2000). For resource managers, much of the concern is with the use and management of individual sites, where specific tools such as site closure, rejuvenation, reconfiguring visitor flows on sites and discriminatory measures such as placing obstacles are used. In this respect, vehicles such as the private car have been prohibited or closely controlled to minimise impacts. At a practical level, recreation resource management involves maintaining and enhancing sites, and the geographer has a valid role to play in understanding visitor behaviour, usage patterns, potential conflicts and spatial measures which can harmonise multiple use. This provides fundamental information to feed into the management and planning process.

Carrying capacity

Carrying capacity is one of the most complex and confusing concepts which faces the geographer in seeking to understand recreation sites and their ability to support a certain level of usage (Coccossis 2004; Manning et al. 2010; Zacarias et al. 2011). In many early applications of the concept, it was viewed as a management tool to protect sites and resources from excessive use, while also seeking to balance usage with recreational enjoyment for participants (Wagar 1964; Stankey 1973; Graefe et al. 1984a, 1984b; Shelby and Heberlein 1984, 1986; Stankey and McCool 1984). In many respects, it is a precursor of the much wider concept of 'sustainability' which has now embraced both recreation and tourism (see Hall and Lew 1998; Page et al. 2001). One early definition of carrying capacity by the Countryside Commission (1970: 2), with its central precept of the long-term capacity of resources and human activity, embodied the dual characteristics of protection and use: the level of recreation use an area can sustain without an unacceptable degree of deterioration of the character and quality of the resource or recreation experience. This was followed by an identification of four types of recreational carrying capacity: physical, economic, ecological and social carrying capacity.

The notion of physical carrying is primarily concerned with quantitative measures of the number of people or usage a site can support, primarily being a design concept. This may also act as a constraint on visitor use by deliberately limiting access to sites. The notion of economic carrying capacity is primarily concerned with multiple use of resources (Pigram and Jenkins 1999; Coccossis 2004), particularly its compatibility with the site and wider management objectives for the site. The notion of ecological (or what Lavery (1971a) terms 'environmental capacity') is primarily 'concerned with the maximum level of recreational use, in terms of numbers and activities, that can be accommodated by an area or ecosystem before an unacceptable or irreversible decline in ecological values occur' (Pigram and Jenkins 1999: 91). The chief problem here lies in what individuals and groups construe as acceptable change. In an early study by Dower and McCarthy (1967) of Donegal, Ireland, they estimated the environmental capacity which recreational and tourism resources could support at any point in time. Lavery (1971a) developed these ideas to produce a series of suggested space standards for environmental capacity. Although this table may be criticised for using such absolute values of capacity, it is notable that it provides a starting point for discussing how many visitors can support a site and how many might be too many. While critics have questioned the notion of fixed capacity for individual sites, it should be stressed that carrying capacity will only ever be one element of a management strategy for outdoor recreation. This shows the need to move beyond environmental capacity to recognise the significance of users, visitor satisfaction and the role of perception – embodied in the last notion – of social carrying capacity.

Social carrying capacity, often referred to as perceptual, psychological or behavioural carrying capacity, is 'the maximum level of recreational use, in terms of numbers and activities, above which there is a decline in the quality of the recreation experience, from the point of view of the recreation participant' (Pigram and Jenkins 1999: 93). The basic principles inherent in this approach relate to the ability of individuals and groups to tolerate others, their activities and the level of acceptability (Hallo and Manning 2010). Patmore (1973: 241) summed this up as 'the number of people [a site] can absorb before the latest arrivals perceive the area to be full and seek satisfaction elsewhere'. This has both a spatial and temporal dimension.

Developing a carrying capacity for a site involves at least eight steps (Hall and McArthur 1998):

1   Specify management objectives or standards for the state of the heritage resource to be maintained or attained and the type of experience to be provided.
2   Identify current levels of use for a defined period (e.g. hour, day, week, month, year).
3   Identify indicators for the biophysical, socio-cultural, psychological and managerial components.
4   Measure the current state of each indicator.
5   Identify apparent relationships between the state of the indicator and the level of use.
6   Make value judgements about the acceptability of the various impacts.
7   Determine a carrying capacity that is more, the same as or less than current visitation.
8   Implement management strategies to ensure carrying capacity is not breached.

The most defendable carrying capacity is an estimate representing a compromise between individual capacities for each component (Needham et al. 2011). For example, suppose there was a biophysical carrying capacity set at 50 visits per day, a socio-cultural capacity set at 100 visits per day, a psychological capacity set at 80 visits a day and a managerial capacity set at 90 visits a day. If each component was valued equally, then an overall carrying capacity may be set at 80 visits per day. However, the typical scenario is one where the overall figure is influenced by the most sensitive or threatened factor, so in this example the capacity may be set at 50 visits per day (Hall and McArthur 1998).

Despite the concept of carrying capacity having originated in the early 1960s, it remains in practice. Although it is a challenge to successfully implement it, it remains an extremely significant and influential management concept:

It is commonly recognised that there are no fixed or standard tourism carrying capacity values. Rather, carrying capacity varies, depending upon place, season and time, user behaviour, facility design, patterns and levels of management, and the dynamic character of the environments themselves. Moreover, it is not always possible in practice to separate tourism activity from other human activities.

(Ceballos-Lascuarain 1996: 131)

Indeed, it is relatively easy to argue that there is no such thing as a single carrying capacity for any given site and that any capacity put forward is highly subjective and thus difficult to defend. A good example of the judgemental limitation is Green Island in far north Queensland. Concern over crowding resulted in a carrying capacity being set at 1,900 visitors per day, or no more than 800 at any one time (Queensland Department of Environment and Heritage 1993), a number reset to a maximum number of 2,240 a day arriving mainly by the five reef tour operators several years later (Zeppel 2010). Beaumont (1997) recommended a daily maximum of 1,200 to 1,345 visitors. Green Island currently receives over 300,000 visits per year, with a maximum of 1,200 to 1,500 day visitors (Zeppel 2010). Nevertheless, the notion of carrying capacity has made a methodological and practical contribution to recreational and tourism resource management and has been at the heart of a number of visitor management tools in natural areas (Page and Connell 2006). Yet management ideas are changing as new debates within the recreational literature emerge, particularly regarding recreation opportunity spectrum and the limits of acceptable change framework (Newsome *et al.* 2012).

The Recreation Opportunity Spectrum

The Recreation Opportunity Spectrum (ROS) is a conceptual framework to clarify the relationship between recreational settings, activities and experiences (Clark and Stankey 1979). It is premised on the assumption that quality is best assured through the provision of a diverse array of opportunities. The ROS provided a conceptual framework for thinking about how to create a diversity of recreation experiences, rather than just provide standard recreational facilities (Driver 1989).

A ROS is developed by identifying a spectrum of settings, activities and opportunities that a given region may contain. For example, a national park may contain a spectrum of settings that range from easily accessible, highly developed areas and facilities, to remote, undeveloped areas with no facilities. The information relating to each setting is entered into a tabular format to present the characteristics of the site, the type of activities undertaken and the opportunities available alongside each other. Comparisons can then be made across sites to determine what sort of core opportunities appear to be provided and the under- or oversupply of specific activities and opportunities. The ROS can therefore be very useful at reviewing then repositioning the type of visitor experiences most appropriate to a recreation site (Hall and McArthur 1998; Harshaw and Sheppard 2013; Oishi 2013).

Management factors considered when determining which recreational class a setting should include the following:

- access (e.g. difficulty, access system (roads and trails) and means of conveyance);
- the non-recreational resource;
- on-site management (e.g. extent, apparentness, complexity and facilities);
- social interaction;
- acceptability of visitor impact (e.g. magnitude and prevalence);
- regimentation.

The standard range of recreational classes established by ROS are developed, semi-developed, semi-natural and natural.

Perhaps the key limitation to the use of the ROS is its emphasis on the setting at the expense of the type of visitor. Part of the reason for this is the influence of earlier cultures from the landscape planning and architecture professions that suggested visitor management could be largely addressed through site and facility design. Although the ROS was extensively used in the early 1980s, its adoption by recreation resource managers was starting to wane by the early 1990s (Hall and McArthur 1998) but has had a resurgence in recent years, particularly as the result of the adoption of new technologies that can assist in the setting up of different opportunities (e.g. Joyce and Sutton 2009; Oishi 2013).

The Limits of Acceptable Change

The Limits of Acceptable Change (LAC) system began with the fundamentals of the Recreation Opportunity Spectrum and initial principles of carrying capacity. Its designers then shifted the focus from a relationship between levels of use and impact to identifying desirable conditions for visitor activity to occur in the first place, as well as management actions required to protect or achieve the conditions (Clark and Stankey 1979; Stankey and McCool 1984). The LAC implies an emphasis on establishing how much change is acceptable, then actively managing accordingly. The LAC model avoids the use/impact conundrum by focusing on the management of the impacts of use (Stankey et al. 1985). The model informs management whether the conditions are within acceptable standards; that is, that current levels and patterns of use are within the capacity of the host environment. When conditions reach the limits of acceptable change they have also reached the area's capacity under current management practices. Management is then equipped with a logical and defensible case to implement strategic actions before any more use can be accommodated. One action may be to limit use.

The LAC system is based on a nine-stage process:

1 Identification of area concerns and issues.
2 Definition and description of opportunity classes.
3 Selection of indicators for conditions.
4 Inventory of resource and social conditions.
5 Specification of standards for indicators.
6 Identification of alternative opportunity class allocations.
7 Identification of management actions for each alternative.
8 Evaluation and selection of the preferred option.
9 Implementation of actions and monitoring of conditions.

Prosser (1986a) identified a number of key strengths of the LAC system as being:

- emphasis on explicit, measurable objectives;
- promotion of a diversity of visitor experiences;
- reliance on quantitative field-based standards;
- flexibility and responsiveness to local situations;
- opportunity for public involvement;
- minimisation of regulatory approaches;
- a framework for managing conditions.

The most critical aspect of the development of the LAC system has been establishing stakeholder endorsement and support (Prosser 1986b). Stakeholders from the local recreation and tourism sector and community can provide valuable input into desired conditions and acceptable standards, and are usually essential in providing the economic and political support necessary to maintain monitoring programmes and implement management decisions. The failure to establish sufficient stakeholder support has largely occurred because the LAC was created by natural area managers, for natural area managers (Stankey et al. 1985). According to Hall and McArthur (1998), the culture of the LAC is not attuned to attracting wider stakeholder involvement, and they provide three examples of problems in its implementation: first, the use of the term 'limits' within the title, which the tourism industry has interpreted as being discouraging to growth and thus business, although this may be more attractive to some recreation organisations; second, the conventional narrow focus on the condition of the physical environment and, to some extent, the nature of the visitor experience – other critical dimensions such as characteristics of the visitor market, socio-cultural aspects of the local community and economic activity associated with the tourism industry are not included; third, the lack of co-operative involvement of the tourism and recreation sector in identifying acceptable indicators and standards. Without this involvement the monitoring results become prone to conjecture, particularly if they reveal surprising or controversial implications. However, as the culture of the LAC system has diversified and its components broadened it has become more widely adopted as a recreation resource management tool (McCool and Cole 1997; Diedrich et al. 2011).

The Tourism Optimisation Management Model (TOMM)

The Tourism Optimisation Management Model (TOMM) is one of the more recent models developed to monitor and manage visitors (McArthur 1996, 2000b; Hall and McArthur 1998; Brown 2006; Newsome et al. 2012). The conceptual emphasis of the TOMM is on achieving optimum performance rather than limiting activity. The TOMM positions a range of influences in the heritage–visitor relationship to focus on sustainability of the heritage, viability of the tourism industry and empowerment of stakeholders. The TOMM has borrowed the key strengths of the Visitor Impact Management Model (VIMM) developed by the United States National Parks and Conservation Association (Graefe 1991) and LAC, then broadened their focus into fields linked with the tourism industry and local community. Besides environmental and experiential elements, the TOMM addresses characteristics of the tourist market, economic conditions of the tourism industry and socio-cultural conditions of the local community. The expansion recognises the complex interrelationships between heritage management, the tourism industry and supporting local populations. In this respect the TOMM is arguably more politically sensitive to the forces which shape visitation and subsequent impacts (McArthur 2000a, 2000b). The TOMM contains three main components: context analysis, a monitoring programme and a management response system (Manidis Roberts Consultants 1996; McArthur 2000b).

The context analysis identifies the current nature of community values, tourism product, tourism growth, market trends and opportunities, positioning and branding. This information is collected through literature reviews, face-to-face interviews with relevant expertise and a community workshop. The context analysis also identifies alternative scenarios for the future of tourism, used later to test the validity of the model.

The second stage of the development of a TOMM is the development of a monitoring programme. The basis for the monitoring programme is a set of optimal conditions which tourism and visitor activity should create (rather than impacts they should avoid). In this way the model avoids setting limits, maximum levels or carrying capacities, and can offer the tourism industry opportunities to develop optimal sustainable performance. The monitoring programme is essentially designed to measure how close the current situation is to the optimal conditions. The measurement yardstick is a set of indicators (one for each optimal condition). Table 4.3 provides a list of assessment criteria for selecting the most appropriate indicators for a TOMM. Each indicator has a benchmark and an acceptable range for it to be expected to operate within. The desired outcomes should have supporting indicators and acceptable ranges. The data generated from the monitoring programme is then plotted to determine whether the status is within the acceptable range or not. Annual performance is presented via report charts already displaying benchmarks, and a relatively simple table that is principally designed to quickly reflect whether each indicator is within its acceptable range or not. The presentation of data is therefore designed to provide a 'quick and

Table 4.3 Assessment criteria for selecting indicators for the Tourism Optimisation Management Model

Criterion	Explanation
Degree of relationship	Indicator needs to have a clear relationship with visitor activity
Accuracy	Needs to represent desired conditions
Utility	The indicator is more worthwhile if it generates additional insights
Availability of data	The indicator is more worthwhile if it already exists
Cost to collect and analyse	The indicator is more worthwhile if it requires minimal additional funding to operationalise

dirty look' that all stakeholders can utilise (Hall and McArthur 1998).

The third stage of development is a management response system. This system involves the identification of poor performing indicators, the exploration of cause-and-effect relationships, the identification of results requiring a response and the development of management response options. The first part of the response system is to annually identify which indicators are not performing within their acceptable range. This involves reviewing the report charts to identify and list each indicator whose annual performance data are outside its acceptable range. It also involves identifying the degree of the discrepancy and whether the discrepancy is part of a longer-term trend. The trend is determined by reviewing previous annual data that have been entered onto the report charts. A qualitative statement is then entered under the degree of discrepancy. The second part in the response mechanism is to explore cause-and-effect relationships. The essential question relating to cause and effect is whether the discrepancy was principally induced by tourism activity or other effects such as the actions of local residents, initiatives by other industries, and regional, national or even global influences. The third part in the system simply involves nominating whether a response is required. Specific choices for the response could include a tourism-oriented response, a response from another sector, or identification that the situation is beyond anyone's control.

The fourth and final part involves developing response options, dependent upon whether they:

- require a response from a non-tourism sector (this involves identifying the appropriate body responsible, providing them with the results and suggesting a response on the matter);
- were out of anyone's control (in this instance no response is required);
- require a response from the tourism and recreation sector (this involves generating a series of management options for consideration, such as additional research to understand the issue, modification of existing practices, site-based development, marketing and lobbying).

After the tourism-related options are developed, the preferred option is tested by brainstorming how the option might influence the various indicators. This requires the reuse of the predicted performance and management response sections of the model. The final application of the model is to test potential options or management responses to a range of alternative scenarios. The first form of testing for application is the performance of a sample of individual indicators. The second form of testing the model's performance is against several potential future scenarios that have already been developed and presented in the contextual analysis. The testing helps ensure that the model has some degree of predictive capability.

The first TOMM was produced in late 1996 and implemented during 1997 (Hall and McArthur 1998; McArthur 2000a). It spanned public and private land in South Australia's Kangaroo Island, and was co-funded by the Federal and South Australian Tourism Departments and the South Australian Department of Environment and Natural Resources. The TOMM initially attracted support not only from its three public sector funders, but also from local government, the local tourism association, the tourism industry, conservation groups and members of the local community (Hall and McArthur 1998; McArthur 2000a), although it was not able to reconcile visitation with the environmental goals in the longer term (Higgins-Desbiolles 2011). The approach has also been applied in Western Australia (Hughes and MacBeth 2005), New Zealand (Wiltshier and Cardow 2008) and South Africa (Ngubane and Diab 2005).

Economic analysis

Within tourism and recreation research, 'attention has concentrated on the more obvious economic impacts with comparatively little consideration being given to the environmental and social consequences of tourism' (Mathieson and Wall 1982: 3–4). However, considerable debate has arisen over methodological problems in the economic analysis of tourism, including the hosting of events (see p. 161), particularly in the measurement of tourism as an economic activity, through the use of satellite accounts, economic multipliers and cost–benefit analysis (Archer 1976, 1977a, 1977b, 1984; Smith 1994, 2000; Smith and Wilton 1997; World Tourism Organization 1999; Sinclair *et al.* 2003; Song *et al.* 2012; Li and Jago 2013; O'Malley *et al.* 2013; Robles Teigeiro and Díaz 2014), the evaluation of opportunity cost (Vaughan 1977; Andersson and Lundberg 2013), and the relationship of tourism and recreation to regional development and employment (Royer *et al.* 1974; Doering 1976; Frechtling 1976b; Ellerbrook and Hite 1980; Williams and Shaw 1988; Sinclair 1998; Plaza *et al.* 2011).

Many economic impact studies focus on what is known as the 'multiplier effect'. This effect is concerned with the way in which tourism expenditure filters through the economy, stimulating other sectors as it does so. Several different types of multiplier are in use, each with their own emphasis (Archer 1977a, 1977b, 1982; Song *et al.* 2012). A multiplier is regarded as 'a coefficient which expresses the amount of income generated in an area by an additional unit of tourist spending' (Archer 1982: 236). It is the ratio of direct and secondary changes within an economic region to the direct initial change itself. In this context geographers have surprisingly not played a major role, although multiplier analysis is not devoid of a spatial component with its linkage to regional science and its spatial concerns for quantitative analysis of areas and locations. Although economic geography has overlapped with economics in some cases, tourism and recreation is not an area where this occurred on a wide scale (Ioannides 1995; Ioannides and Debbage 1998). Likewise, collaborative research between geographers and economists did not emerge as a theme in research until the mid-1990s (Martin 1999; G. Clark *et al.* 2000). This is often because each subject area has its own concepts, language, approach and few obvious intersections in the research field because tourism and recreation remained a fringe area for research in the 1960s and 1970s for both geographers and economists. Nevertheless, there has been increased overlap between geographers and economists since the 1990s given increased focus on regional economies and issues such as competitiveness, innovation

and the role of geographical factors in economic development, tourism being an important element in all of these issues (Hall and Williams 2008; Shaw and Williams 2009; Schmallegger *et al.* 2010; Brouder and Eriksson 2013; Weidenfeld and Hall 2014).

The economic impacts of tourism and recreation are usually classified as being either primary or secondary in nature (Archer 1982). Primary or direct impacts are those economic impacts which are a direct consequence of visitor spending (e.g. the purchase of food and beverages by a tourist in a hotel). Secondary impacts may be described as being either indirect or induced. Indirect impacts are those arising from the response of money in the form of local business transactions (e.g. the new investment of hotel owners in equipment and supplies). Induced impacts are those arising from the additional income generated by further consumer spending (e.g. the purchase of goods and services by hotel employees). For each round of spending per unit of initial visitor expenditure leakage will occur from the regional economy until little or no further re-spending is possible. Therefore, the recreation or tourism multiplier is a measure of the total effects (direct plus secondary effects) which result from the additional tourist or recreational expenditure. However, despite their extensive use, it should be noted that 'multipliers are difficult to calculate precisely under the best circumstances. They require substantial amounts of very detailed data. The methods used are also difficult and require a high degree level of statistical and/or macro-economic expertise' (Smith 1995: 16; see also Saeter 1998).

The size of the visitor multiplier will vary from region to region and will depend on a number of factors, including:

- the size of area of analysis;
- the proportion of goods and services imported into the region for consumption by visitors;
- the rate of circulation;
- the nature of visitor spending;
- the availability of suitable local products and services;
- the patterns of economic behaviour for visitor and local alike.

Selection of the size of the economy being examined is extremely important for understanding what is included in any economic analysis and what is excluded. Where boundaries are set can therefore have a substantial impact on the results of any economic analysis of tourism. As a measure of economic benefit from recreation and tourism, the multiplier technique has been increasingly subject to question, particularly as its use has often produced exaggerated results (Archer 1977a, 1982; Cooper and Pigram 1984; Frechtling 1987; Smith 1995; Sinclair *et al.* 2003; Song *et al.* 2012). Nevertheless, despite doubts about the accuracy of the multiplier technique, substantial attention is still paid to the results of economic impact studies by government and the private sector as a measure of the success of tourism development or as a way of estimating the potential contribution of a proposed development in order to justify policy or planning decisions (Hall 2008a). As S. Smith (1995: 16) noted, 'Regrettably, the abuses of multipliers often seem to be as frequent as legitimate uses – thus contributing further to the industry's lack of credibility'.

The size of the tourist multiplier is regarded as a significant measure of the economic benefit of visitor expenditure because it will be a reflection of the circulation of the visitor dollar through an economic system. In general, the larger the size of the tourist multiplier, the greater the self-sufficiency of that economy in the provision of tourist facilities and services. Therefore, a tourist multiplier will generally be larger at a national level than at a regional level, because at a regional level leakage will occur in the form of taxes to the national government and importation of goods and services from regions. Similarly, at the local level, multipliers will reflect the high importation level of small communities and tax payments to regional and national governments (Hall 1995).

According to Murphy (1985: 95), 'for practical purposes it is crucial to appreciate that local multiplier studies are just case studies of local gains and no more', and several questions remain unanswered about the real costs and benefits of tourism for local and regional development. Indeed, a major question should be: 'Who are the winners and losers in tourism development?' As Coppock argued four decades ago

in relation to the use of tourism as a tool for economic development:

> Not only is it inevitable that the residents of an area will gain unequally from tourism (if indeed they gain at all) and probable that the interests of some will actually be harmed, but it may well be that a substantial proportion does not wish to see any development of tourism.
>
> (Coppock 1977b: 1)

One of the primary justifications used by government in the encouragement of tourism development is tourism's potential employment benefits (Pearce 1992a; Hall 1994; Jenkins *et al.* 1998; Hudson 2000). However, as Hudson and Townsend (1992: 64) observed, 'often the actual impacts of tourism on local employment and the economy are imperfectly understood. The direction of causality between growing employment and increasing policy involvement is often obscure and in any case variable'. Similarly, international tourism is increasingly promoted by organisations such as the UNWTO and many government agencies in the international development community as an important element in national poverty reduction strategies and in development financing. According to the UNWTO (2005: 3) 'Tourism development, if properly developed and supported, can indeed be a "quick-win" in overcoming the economic and social conditions that prevail in LDCs and in accelerating their integration into the world economy'. The UNWTO (2006b: 1) has argued that there are several reasons that make tourism an 'especially suitable economic development sector for LDCs':

1   Tourism is consumed at the point of production; the tourist has to go to the destination and spend his/her money there, opening an opportunity for local businesses of all sorts, and allowing local communities to benefit through the informal economy, by selling goods and services directly to visitors.
2   Most LDCs have a comparative advantage in tourism over developed countries. They have assets of enormous value to the tourism industry – culture,

art, music, natural landscapes, wildlife and climate, and World Heritage Sites. Visits by tourists to such sites can generate employment and income for communities as well as helping in the conservation of cultural and natural assets.

3 Tourism is a more diverse industry than many others. It has the potential to support other economic activities, both through providing flexible, part-time jobs that can complement other livelihood options and through creating income throughout a complex supply chain of goods and services.

4 Tourism is labour intensive, which is particularly important in tackling poverty. It also provides a wide range of different employment opportunities, especially for women and young people – from the highly skilled to the unskilled – and generally it requires relatively little training.

5 It creates opportunities for many small and micro entrepreneurs, either in the formal or informal economy; it is an industry in which start-up costs and barriers to entry are generally low or can easily be lowered.

6 Tourism provides not only material benefits for the poor but also cultural pride. It creates greater awareness of the natural environment and its economic value, a sense of ownership and reduced vulnerability through diversification of income sources.

7 The infrastructure required by tourism, such as transport and communications, water supply and sanitation, public security and health services, can also benefit poor communities.

Similar perspectives have been advocated by other international bodies, such as the World Travel and Tourism Council (WTTC) (2004), the World Economic Forum (WEF) (2008), the Asian Development Bank and the World Bank, as well as the international development co-operation sector in many nations (Gössling *et al.* 2009a), often as part of poverty alleviation or pro-poor tourism (PPT) initiatives. Yet, as Chok *et al.* (2007) emphasised in their review of poverty alleviation strategies, tourism is all too often regarded as a panacea – an economic, social and environmental 'cure-all' whose claims for sustainable development, including welfare equity and poverty reduction, need to be seriously evaluated and considered in context (see also Winters *et al.* 2013).

Although the focus of many in the development community is on small-scale, so-called 'alternative' cultural and ecotourism projects in more peripheral regions, the reality is that the majority of leisure tourism is what may best be described as 'mass' tourism which is spatially and temporally concentrated in resort areas. Development community projects are also highly dependent on mass tourism, as: (1) they rely on the mass international transport infrastructure to bring people to a country; and (2) visits to community projects are often a form of secondary activity that people will undertake in addition to, rather than instead of, travel to more conventional mass tourism attractions.

The difficulty faced by many tourism development projects is that their proponents have often not considered their relative inaccessibility to markets, especially in comparison with competing activities and/or destinations. For example, in some short-term situations ecotourism can provide win–win situations for local people and local nature, but there are substantial difficulties in maintaining such results over time, as a result of competition within the tourism sector, loss of project assistance, relative value of tourism in comparison with alternative resource use, and economic and environmental change (Hall 2007a; Zapata *et al.* 2011). Nevertheless, despite potential drawbacks, many governments continue to perceive tourism as a key development strategy (e.g. Harrison 2004). This is understandable given the disparate perspectives that exist, and particularly for island LDCs, where tourism may represent perhaps the only development option with the exception of fishing or offshore energy development.

One of the ironies of the perceived employment benefits of tourism and recreation is that areas which have tourism as a mainstay of the local economy often tend to have high levels of unemployment where there is substantial flexibility in the regulation of the labour market (Hall 2003a). For example, two of Australia's major destination areas, the Gold Coast and the Sunshine Coast in Queensland, have often had unemployment rates significantly above the national average (Mullins 1984, 1990). Such a situation is often regarded by local politicians as an 'imported problem', as a result of temporary domestic migration. Instead, the reason rests on the nature of the two regions' economies. The economies of both areas are founded on two industries that are affected by substantial fluctuations in demand: tourism, which is seasonal, and construction, which is cyclical and is itself related to actual or predicted tourist flows. Therefore, as Mullins (1990: 39) reported, 'high rates of unemployment seem inevitable', although as destination regions diversify their economic base unemployment levels should fall over time as a result of less dependence on tourism demand.

Another major consideration in the potential contribution of tourism to the national economy is the organisation and spatial allocation of capital and, in particular, the penetration of foreign or international capital (Hudson 2000; Shaw and Williams 2004). The distribution and organisation of capital and tourists are also spread unevenly between and within regions; indeed, tourism may be regarded as a mechanism for redistributing wealth between regions (Pearce 1990, 1992a). However, the extent to which this actually occurs once all capital flows are taken into account is highly problematic. Geographers have long noted the manner in which tourism tends to distribute development away from urban areas towards those regions in a country which have not been developed (e.g. Christaller 1963), with the core–periphery nature of tourism being an important component of political-economy approaches towards tourism (Britton 1980a, 1980b, 1982; Shaw and Williams 2004; Hall 2005a), particularly with respect to tourism in island microstates (Connell 1988; Lea 1988; Weaver 1998; Gössling 2003; Duval 2004).

More recently, geographers have begun to critically analyse tourism with reference to issues of economic restructuring, processes of globalisation and the development of post-Fordist modes of production, including recognition of 'the cultural turn' in economic geography (e.g. Britton 1991; Hall 1994; Debbage and Ioannides 1998, 2004; Milne 1998;

Williams and Shaw 1998; Shaw and Williams 2004). Tourism is a significant component of these shifts which may be described as 'post-industrial' or 'post-Fordist', which refers to the shift from an industrial to an information technology/service base. In addition, tourism is part of the globalisation of the international economy, in which economic production is transnational, interdependent and multipolar, with less and less dependence on the nation state as the primary unit of international economic organisation (see Box 3.3). As Williams and Shaw recognise:

> The essence of tourism is the way in which the global interacts with the local. For example, mass tourism emphasises a global scan for destinations for global (or at least macro-regional) markets, while some forms of new tourism seek to exploit the individuality of places. These global–local relationships are not static but are subject to a variety of restructuring processes.
>
> (Williams and Shaw 1998: 59)

The notion of the 'globalisation' of tourism implies its increasing commodification. The tourist production system simultaneously 'sells' places in order to attract tourists, the means to the end (travel and accommodation) and the end itself (the tourist experience). Therefore, tourism finds itself at the forefront of an important recent dynamic within capitalist accumulation in terms of the creation and marketing of experiences. Tourists 'are purchasing the intangible qualities of restoration, status, lifestyle signifier, release from the constraints of everyday life, or conveniently packaged novelty' (Britton 1991: 465). Within this setting, place is therefore commodified and reduced to an experience and images for consumption (see Chapter 5 for a further discussion).

Related to the economic analysis of tourism has been the study of the forecasting of visitor demand (e.g. Blake and Sinclair 2003; Durbarry and Sinclair 2003). Several studies of hallmark events, for example, have attempted to deal with the problem of forecasting visitor demand (see Ritchie and Aitken 1984; Hall 1992b) (see also Box 4.1). Nevertheless,

BOX 4.1 THE ECONOMIC IMPACT OF EVENTS

An area which has long seen attention by geographers (e.g. Shaw 1985; Getz 1991a, 1991b, 2005, 2012; Hall 1992b, 2006b; Hall *et al.* 1995; Hall and Hodges 1996; Macbeth *et al.* 2012) is the impact of hosting staged, short-term attractions, usually referred to as hallmark, special or mega events (Ritchie 1984; Ritchie and Yangzhou 1987; Hall 1989), and particularly the impact of sports teams and events (Hall 2001b; Hinch and Higham 2003; Owen 2003). The hallmark event is different in its appeal from the attractions normally promoted by the tourist industry as it is not a continuous or seasonal phenomenon. Indeed, in many cases the hallmark event is a strategic response to the problems that seasonal variations in demand pose for the tourist industry (Ritchie and Beliveau 1974), although, the ability of an event 'to achieve this objective depends on the uniqueness of the event, the status of the event, and the extent to which it is successfully marketed within tourism generated regions' (Ritchie 1984: 2). As with other areas of research on the economic impacts of tourism, the analysis of hallmark events has been controversial and often characterised by overstated large benefit–cost ratios (Hall 1989, 1992b; Getz 1991b; Li and Jago 2013). Several reasons can be cited for this:

- There has been a failure to account for the economic impact that would have occurred anyway but has switched from one industry to another.
- There has been an 'unfortunately common mistake' of attributing all the benefits received from the event to government expenditure, instead of establishing the marginal impact of that contribution' (Burns and Mules 1986: 8, 10).
- The taxation benefits of expenditure generation have been counted as additional to the multiplier 'flow-ons' when they have already been included.
- 'Output' rather than 'value-added' multipliers, which can result in major overestimates of the economic impact of events, are frequently uncritically used.
- There has been a general failure to delimit the size of the regional economy that is to be studied. The smaller the area to be analysed, the greater will be the number of 'visitors' and hence the greater would be the estimate of economic impact.

substantial methodological problems still remain, and 'although relatively sophisticated statistical measures have been used, forecasts of tourism demand can produce only approximations' (Uysal and Crompton 1985: 13).

Tourism Satellite Accounts

Another significant area of the assessment of the economic impacts of tourism is with respect to the development of Tourism Satellite Accounts (TSAs). The national government statisticians of France were the first to explore ways to analyse aspects of a nation's economy that are not adequately represented within the System of National Accounts (SNA), such as tourism which crosses over existing International Standards Industry Classifications (ISIC) and the Central Product Classification (CPC). To do this they developed a concept called *comptes satellites* (satellite accounts). The TSA approach identifies the tourism percentage of each ISIC/CPC listed industrial sector (account) in a country's overall economy (System of National Accounts (SNA)) and identified the economic contribution of tourism from that calculation (Smith 2004). However, it is impossible to compare TSA results between two places unless they have used exactly the same methodology from data collection through to application (Hall and Lew 2009).

TSAs can be used to determine which industrial classifications have the highest proportion of tourism-related sales in order to try and relate tourism economic activity and behaviour to research on standard industrial classifications (Hall 2009b), as well as potentially compare labour productivity between sectors (Hall and Lew 2009). Its use is also being explored with respect to GHG emissions (Jones 2013). However, one of the most significant problems with the TSA approach is that the selection of sectors to include in the analysis, and the portions of each sector to assign to tourism, is subjective and open to debate. Although the TSA provides a useful basis for understanding the economic effects of visitor-related activity and its inter-industry linkages within an economy, the TSA approach can too easily include items as tourism outputs that are far removed from tourism, at least as it is popularly understood (Productivity Commission 2005). For example, in calculating the global economic size of travel and tourism, the WTTC includes the full budget of the US Federal Railroad Administration, the US National Park Service, and the US Fish and Wildlife Service (Hall and Lew 2009). This situation has led some commentators to argue that the use of TSAs, and the promotion of their results, by tourism interest groups has misled people in many countries because they exaggerate of the size of the industry and the employment it provides (Leiper 1999). The TSA is therefore best used to understand linkages and compare changes within a single economy at one point in time, or over a specific time period for which data is available (Hall and Lew 2009).

Competitiveness

One area in which there are some fundamental differences between geographers and much tourism research is the issue of destination competitiveness (Hall 2007b, 2013h). There is 'no single, all-encompassing economic or economic geographic theory that provides a generally accepted definition and explanation of regional competitiveness. What we have instead is a range of different theoretical accounts of (relative) regional growth' (Martin 2005: 16), from which implications for regional, and potentially destination, competitiveness are inferred. From a regional studies perspective at least, much of what happens in tourism policy with respect to place promotion, subsidised competition to host events, build stadiums and engage in the serial replication of other infrastructure such as convention centres, casinos and leisure/retail complexes is often regarded as a 'low road' route to regional competitiveness (Malecki 2004). This compares to a 'high road' competitiveness strategy founded on high productivity achieved through constant innovation in products, services and processes, investment, a highly skilled labour force, internal and external networking, high connectivity and accessibility and continued scanning for new knowledge (Malecki 2004; Hall 2007b; Hall and Williams 2008).

The price competitiveness of destinations is clearly important (Dwyer and Forsyth 2011). However, much tourism writing on destination competitiveness fails to appreciate the broader debates over the applicability of the concept to places in regional studies and economic geography thinking on place and regions, a field in which the basic question of 'can a nation or a region be treated as a firm?' is much debated (Krugman 1994, 1996, 2005; Bristow 2005, 2010). In contrast this issue appears a virtually unquestioned basic assumption in tourism studies with respect to destinations (Hall 2007b). Yet there are surely some fundamental questions about the way in which the notion of a destination and place competitive discourse in tourism is constructed and reflects some of the ontological issues discussed in the introduction to this chapter between the parts and the whole of the tourism system (Hall 2013h). How and why is it assumed that a destination is a business entity (as opposed to an economic entity) that is somehow 'more' than a region or location to which people travel. If it is more than a place, then what has been 'defined out'? A destination is clearly more than the sum of the tourism firms within it. Furthermore, to what extent can tourism be treated as a zero-sum game; does the success of one destination actually occur at the expense of another over time, as opposed to being part of the 'aware set' of potential destinations of an individual decision-maker at a specific point in time, or are there other factors at play (Hall 2013h)?

Many of the early studies of the effects of tourism were restricted to economic analyses and enumerated the financial and employment benefits which accrued to destination areas as a result of tourism development. However, since the late 1970s a number of studies have emerged that examine the socio-cultural impacts of tourism which cast a more negative light on tourism's development capacities (Mathieson and Wall 1982).

Analysis of tourism's social impacts

The social impact of tourism refers to the manner in which tourism and travel effect changes in collective and individual value systems, behaviour patterns, community structures, lifestyle and the quality of life (Hall 1995; Mason 2003). The major focus of research on the social impacts of tourism is on the population of the tourist destination rather than on the tourist generating area and the tourists themselves, although significant work is also done in this area, particularly with respect to outdoor recreationists. The variables which contribute to resident perceptions of tourism may be categorised as either extrinsic or intrinsic (Faulkner and Tideswell 1996). Extrinsic variables refer to factors which affect a community at a macro level (e.g. stage of tourism development, the ratio between tourists and residents, cultural differences between tourists and residents, and seasonality). Intrinsic variables are those factors which may vary in association with variations in the characteristics of individuals in a given population (e.g. demographic characteristics, involvement in tourism and proximity to tourist activity) (Hall 1998).

Researchers from a number of disciplinary backgrounds have conducted work on the social impacts of tourism. For example, interest in tourism marketing strategies and increased concern for the social consequences of tourism led to the social psychology of tourism becoming a major area of research (e.g. Pearce

1982, 2005; Stringer 1984; Stringer and Pearce 1984). Research in the marketing of the tourist product sees attention being paid to the demand, motivations and preferences of the potential tourist (e.g. Van Raaij and Francken 1984; Kent et al. 1987; Smith 1995; Pearce 2005), the evaluation of the tourist product and potential tourist resources (e.g. Ferrario 1979a, 1979b; Gartner 1986; Smith 1995), the intended and unintended use of tourist brochures (e.g. Dilley 1986), the utility of market segmentation for specific targeting of potential consumers (e.g. Murphy and Staples 1979; Smith 1995) and tourist and recreationist satisfaction. In the latter area, geographers have done a substantial amount of work in the outdoor recreation and backcountry use field, particularly with respect to the effects of crowding on visitor satisfaction (e.g. Shelby et al. 1989; see also Chapter 7).

Marketing research acts as a link between economic and psychological analysis of tourism (Van Raaij 1986; Hall 2014) and gives notice of the need for a wider understanding of the social impact of tourism on visitor and host populations. Research on the social psychology of tourism has run parallel with the research of behavioural geographers in the area, with there being increased interchange between the two fields in recent years (e.g. Jenkins and Walmsley 1993; see also Walmsley and Lewis 1993). Interestingly, the development of a more radical critique of behaviour in geography also has parallels in the social psychology of tourism as well (Pearce 2005). For example, the research of Uzzell (1984) on the psychology of tourism marketing from a structuralist perspective offered a major departure from traditional social psychology. Uzzell's (1984) alternative formulation of the role of social psychology in the study of tourism has been reflected in much of the research conducted in anthropological, geographical (e.g. Britton 1991) and sociological approaches to the social impacts of tourism (e.g. Urry 1990, 1991). Such work has also become increasingly important as geographers seek to find ways to encourage more appropriate environmental behaviours in an attempt to reduce GHG emissions (Gössling 2011; Hall 2011g, 2013e; Hibbert et al. 2013; Peeters 2013; Ram et al. 2013).

The early work of Forster (1964), Cohen (1972, 1974, 1979a, 1979b), Smith and Turner (1973) and MacCannell (1973, 1976), along with the more recent contribution by Urry (1990), have provided the basis for formulating a sociology of tourism, while V. Smith (1977) and Graburn (1983) provided a useful over-view of anthropology's early contributions to tourism studies. The research of geographers such as Young (1973), Butler (1974, 1975, 1980), D. Pearce (1979, 1981), Mathieson and Wall (1982) and Murphy (1985) also yielded significant early insights into tourism's social impacts.

Many studies of the social impacts of tourism ini-tially focused on the impact of tourism on developing countries (UNESCO 1976). This research is no doubt necessary, yet caution must be used in applying research findings from one culture to another. Never-theless, problems of cultural change and anxiety, social stress in the host community and social disloca-tion resulting from changes to the pattern of eco-nomic production may be identified in a wide number of studies undertaken in a variety of cultures and social settings (e.g. Farrell 1978; Mathieson and Wall 1982; Clary 1984b; Meleghy *et al.* 1985; Lea 1988; Getz 1993c; Shaw and Williams 1994; Hall and Page 1996; Nash 1996; Mowforth and Munt 1998, 2003; Weaver 1998; Mason 2003; Reid 2003).

The social costs of tourism to the host community will vary according to the characteristics of both visitor and host (Pizam 1978). However, tourism does undoubtedly cause changes in the social character of the destination (Long 1984; Mason 2003). These changes may be related to the seasonality of tourism (Hartmann 1984), the nature of the tourist (Harmston 1980), the influence of a foreign culture (Mathieson and Wall 1982) and/or the disruption of community leisure and 'private' space (O'Leary 1976). An appre-ciation by planners of the social costs of tourism is essential for both financial and social reasons (Reid 2003; Dredge and Jenkins 2007). Rejection of visitors by segments of the host community may well result in a decline in the attractiveness of the tourist desti-nation, in addition to the creation of disharmony within the host community (Murphy 1985; Getz 1994; Page and Lawton 1997). Nevertheless, it is also important to recognise that it may be difficult at times to distinguish between tourism as a factor in social change and other dimensions of change, such as globalisation of communication technology.

Tourism development may initiate changes in gov-ernment and private organisations (Hall and Jenkins 1995; Mason 2003; Reid 2003) in order to cater for the impact of tourism. For instance, additional law enforcement officers may be required (Rothman *et al.* 1979), while special measures may be needed to restrict dislocation created by increased rents and land values (Cowie 1985) where such regulation is possible. Geographers have long emphasised the importance of meaningful community participation in the decision-making process that surrounds the formulation of tourism policy and development (e.g. Butler 1974, 1975; Brougham and Butler 1981; D.G. Pearce 1981; Getz 1984; Murphy 1985; Mason 2003; Reid 2003; Murphy and Murphy 2004). Fur-thermore, the social impacts of tourism are complex and need to be examined within the context of the various economic, environmental, political and cul-tural factors that contribute to tourism development in a destination (Runyan and Wu 1979; Wu 1982; Keller 1984; Shaw 1985, 1986; Mason 2003; Murphy and Murphy 2004; Hall 2005a, 2008a).

Community attitudes towards tourism invariably simultaneously reveal both positive and negative atti-tudes towards tourism (Butler 1975). For example, various positive and negative attitudes towards tour-ism were indicated in several highly cited studies of resident attitudes towards tourism in northern New South Wales, Australia (Hall 1990). Pigram (1987) utilised Doxey's (1975) 'irridex' scale of euphoria, apathy, annoyance and antagonism to investigate res-ident attitudes in the resort town of Coffs Harbour. According to Pigram (1987: 67), 'the overwhelming majority felt that the economic and otherwise benefits of tourism outweighed the disadvantages'. Despite the overall favourable or apathetic response of resi-dents, several negative reactions towards tourism did emerge from the study. According to Pigram (1987), the greatest impact of tourism on the local commu-nity was the perceived increase in the cost of goods and services because of the presence of tourists. The respondents also indicated that they believed that petty crime was also worse during the tourist season, an observation supported by Walmsley *et al.*'s (1981, 1983) study of crime in the region during the late 1970s. Furthermore, the natural environment of the Coffs Harbour area was perceived as slightly worse as a result of tourism, with the greatest impact being on the beaches. However, opportunities for public recreation were perceived as the attribute of community life registering the most significant improvement as a result of tourism (Pigram 1987).

Resident attitudes are undoubtedly a key component in the identification, measurement and analysis of tourism impacts. However, investigation of community attitudes towards tourism is not just an academic exercise. Such attitudes are also important in terms of the determination of local policy, planning and management responses to tourism development and in establishing the extent to which public support exists for tourism (Page and Lawton 1997). For example, Getz (1994) argued that resident perceptions of tourism may be one factor in shaping the attractiveness of a destination, where negative attitudes may be an indicator of an area's ability to absorb tourism. Although Getz suggests (1994: 247) that 'identification of causal mechanisms is a major theoretical challenge, and residents can provide the local knowledge necessary to link developments with their

consequences', it assumes that residents are sufficiently aware, perceptive and able to articulate such views to decision-makers and planners. Nevertheless, negative resident perceptions may lead to adverse reactions towards tourism and create substantial difficulties for the development of further facilities and infrastructure (Page and Lawton 1997). For example, although communities with a history of exposure to tourism may adapt and change to accommodate its effects (Rothman 1978), active or passive support or opposition may exist at any given time, as interest groups take political action to achieve specific objectives in relation to tourism (Hall and Jenkins 1995; Murphy and Murphy 2004).

In locations where the original community is 'swamped' by large-scale tourism development in a relatively short space of time, disruption to the community values of the original inhabitants is more likely to occur (Hudson 1990a, 1990b). Table 4.4 details the costs and benefits of such tourism development in Broome, Western Australia. However, it must be emphasised that resident attitudes to tourism development will be influenced by where they fit into the existing social and economic order, their personal gains from the development process, and/or their response to the changing environment in light of their pre-existing values and attitudes (Hudson 1990b). Indeed, one of the interesting aspects of

Table 4.4 Costs and benefits of tourism development in Broome, Australia

Costs	Benefits
Marginalisation of the Aboriginal and coloured people	Expansion of new services and businesses
Too much power in vested interests	More infrastructure and community facilities
Destruction of multicultural flavour of the town and the original form of Shinju Matsuri	More sealed roads and kerbing and guttering
Increased racism	Increased variety of restaurants/entertainment
High accommodation costs/shortage	Restoration of Broome architecture
High local prices	Better health system
Less friendly/more local conflicts	Tidier town
Environmental impacts (e.g. dune destruction)	
Loss of historical character of town and imposition of artificially created atmosphere	
More crime/domestic violence	

Source: P. Hudson (1990b: 10).

tourism development in Broome is that, as in many other destinations, even though tourism is recognised as having some negative impacts, it nevertheless continues to be embraced for economic development and employment purposes (Frost 2004; Collins 2008). Such a situation indicated that while individuals may perceive there to be negative tourism impacts, they may still be favourable towards tourism's overall benefits to the community. Faulkner and Tideswell (1996) referred to this phenomenon as the 'altruistic surplus' and suggested that this could be the result of a mature stage of tourism development in a destination region whereby residents have adapted to tourism through experience and migration.

In addition to attitudinal studies, a number of other approaches and issues are of interest to the geographer. For example, historical studies of tourism may indicate the role tourism has in affecting attitudes and values with a destination community (e.g. Wall 1983a; Butler and Wall 1985). Studies of tourism policy may assist in an understanding of the way governments develop strategies to manage the negative impacts of tourism and in the overall manner that tourism is used in regional development (e.g. Papson 1981; Kosters 1984; Hall and Jenkins 1995, 2004; Reid 2003; Dredge and Jenkins 2007).

Another area of tourism's social impact which has received more attention in recent years is that of health (Clift and Page 1996; Wilks and Page 2003). Researchers have examined the spatial misinformation provided by travel agents when advising clients of the potential health risks they may face when travelling to Pacific Island destinations (Lawton and Page 1997a, 1997b). What such research shows is the vital role of understanding place, space and the geography of risk in relation to the epidemiology of disease (Hall and James 2011). While geographers have studied disease for many years, making the link between travel and disease is a comparatively new development (Clift and Page 1996; Hall 2011d). For example, tourism may assist in the spread of disease, while tourists themselves are vulnerable to illness while travelling. Indeed, one of the major focal points for geographers' research on tourist health in recent years has been the spread of AIDS and its association with

sex tourism (Kinnaird and Hall 1994; Ryan and Hall 2001). There is growing evidence that the geographer will continue to develop expertise in this area and a major contribution could be made at a public policy level in the rapid dissemination of disease alerts to medical practitioners and health professionals through the use of GIS technology.

Another area to which geographers have been paying increasing attention is the relationship between tourism and indigenous peoples in both developed and less developed nations. While anthropology has focused considerable attention on the impacts and effects of tourism on indigenous peoples (e.g. V.L. Smith 1977, 1992), geographers have assisted greatly in broadening the research agenda to include greater consideration of the way in which indigenous peoples interact with wildlife, the relationship between indigenous peoples and ecotourism and national parks, tourism and land rights, and indigenous business development (e.g. Nelson 1986; Nickels et al. 1991; Mercer 1994; Butler and Hinch 1996, 2007; Lew and van Otten 1997; Weaver 2010; Blangy et al. 2012).

One of the most important concepts in humanistic geography is that of a 'sense of place'. A sense of place arises where people feel a particular attachment or personal relationship to an area in which local knowledge and human contacts are meaningfully maintained. 'People demonstrate their sense of place when they apply their moral or aesthetic discernment to sites and locations' (Tuan 1974: 235). However, people may only consciously notice the unique qualities of their place when they are away from it or when it is being rapidly altered. The sense of place concept is of significance to tourism development for a number of reasons. The redevelopment and re-imaging of communities for tourism purposes (see Chapter 5) may force long-term residents to leave and may change the character of the community (Ley and Olds 1988). In these instances, the identification of residents with the physical and social structure of the neighbourhood may be deeply disturbed, leading to a condition of 'placelessness' (Relph 1976). Residents of destinations which find themselves faced with rapid tourism development may therefore attempt to preserve components of the townscape, including buildings and parks, in order to retain elements of their identity.

The conservation of heritage is often a reaction to the rate of physical and social change within a community. Generally, when people feel they are in control of their own destiny they have little call for nostalgia. However, the strength of environment and heritage conservation organisations in developed nations is perhaps a reflection of the desire to retain a sense of continuity with the past (Lowenthal 1975, 1985). In addition, the protection of historic buildings and the establishment of heritage precincts can also effect a significant economic return to destinations because of the desire of many visitors to experience what they perceive as authentic forms of tourism (Konrad 1982; Hall and McArthur 1996; Timothy 2011).

Physical environmental impacts

One of the areas of major interest for geographers is the impacts of tourists and recreationists on the physical environment (Butler 2000). The reason for this lies in part in the nature of geography, which has a strong tradition of study of the interactions of humans with their environment (Mitchell and Murphy 1991; Wong 2004). Indeed, the impacts of tourism and recreation on the physical environment and the subsequent resource analysis are one area where human and physical geographers find a degree of common ground in studying visitor issues (Johnston 1983b; Butler 2000; Mason 2003). However, another reason is the sheer significance of the physical environment for the recreation and tourism industry.

The relationship between tourism and the environment is site and culture dependent and will probably change through time and in relation to broader economic, environmental and social concerns. As noted in Chapter 3, the recognition of something as a resource is the result of human perception; so it is also with the recognition that there are undesirable impacts on an environmental resource.

Increasing attention has been given to the impacts that tourism and recreation may have on the environmental and physical characteristics of a host

community since the early 1970s (Walter 1975; Organisation for Economic Co-operation and Development 1980). Interest in this area of applied geography is partly a response to the growth of tourism and the sheer impact that increased numbers of visitors will have on specific sites. However, concern has also developed because of the activities of environmental interest groups, which have often provided an advocacy role for geographers in terms of arguing the results of the research and scholarship in direct involvement in the planning and policy process (Hall 1992a; Mercer 2000, 2004). The rise of the environmental movement has not only led to improvements in conservation practices but also encouraged public interest in natural areas and helped shape how the environment is seen. According to O'Riordan and Turner:

> Although environmentalists are not the only people who object to much of what they interpret as modern day values, aspirations and ways of life, it is probably fair to say that one of the two things which unite their disparate perceptions is a wish to alter many of the unjust and foolhardy features they associate with modern capitalism of both a state and private variety. The other common interest is a commitment to cut waste and reduce profligacy by consuming resources more frugally. Environmentalists do not agree, however, about how the transition should be achieved.
>
> (O'Riordan and Turner 1984: 1)

Nevertheless, despite confusion about what is meant by an environmentally 'responsible' approach to tourism development, it is apparent that the protection of the natural and cultural resources upon which tourism is based is essential for the sustainable development of a location (Hall and Lew 1998).

There is no fundamental difference in conducting research on the effects of tourism on the natural environment and research on the environmental impacts of recreation. The footprints of a recreationalist are the same as those of the tourist. The majority of research has been undertaken on the effects of tourism and recreation on wildlife and the trampling of vegetation, with historically relatively little attention being given to impacts on soils and air and water quality (Wall and Wright 1977; Mathieson and Wall 1982; Edington and Edington 1986; Meyer-Arendt 1993; Parliamentary Commissioner for the Environment 1997). However, the latter is now changing because of growing concerns over climate change (Gössling 2002; Hall and Higham 2005; Scott *et al.* 2012), as well as the pressures of water use by tourism development (Gössling 2001; Gössling *et al.* 2012b).

The majority of studies have examined the impacts of tourism and recreation on a particular environment or component of the environment rather than over a range of environments. According to Mathieson and Wall (1982: 94), 'there has been little attempt to present an integrated approach to the assessment of the impacts of tourism'. However, there is clearly a need to detect the effects of tourism on all aspects of an ecosystem. For example, the ecology of an area may be dramatically changed through the removal of a key species in the food chain or through the introduction of new species, such as trout, for enhanced benefits for recreational fishing or game for hunters (Hall 1995). In addition, it is important to distinguish between perceptions and actual impacts of tourism (Orams 2002). For example, many visitors believe an environment is healthy as long as it looks 'clean and green'. The ecological reality may instead be vastly different; an environment may be full of invasive introduced species, which, although contributing to a positive aesthetic perception, may have extremely negative ecological implications (Newsome *et al.* 2012). For example, while New Zealand promotes its tourism very strongly on the basis of its 'clean, green' image, the reality is quite different with respect to many tourist locations, which may have very few indigenous species present and may have very low biodiversity (Parliamentary Commissioner for the Environment 1997; Hall 2010g).

Research on impacts has focused on particular regions or environments, which has limited the ability to generalise the findings from one area to another. In addition, research on visitor impacts is comparatively recent and is generally a reaction to site-specific problems. We therefore rarely know what conditions were like before tourists and recreationalists arrived. Few longitudinal studies exist by which the long-term impacts of visitation can be assessed. Therefore, there are a number of significant methodological problems which need to be addressed in undertaking research on the environmental effects of tourism (Mathieson and Wall 1982; Hall and Lew 2009):

- the difficulty of distinguishing between changes induced by tourism and those induced by other activities;
- the lack of information concerning conditions prior to the advent of tourism and, hence, the lack of a baseline against which change may be measured;
- the paucity of information on the numbers, types and tolerance levels of different species of flora and fauna;
- the concentration of researchers upon particular resources or locations.

Nevertheless, despite the difficulties that have emerged in studying the relationship between tourism and the natural environment, it is apparent that 'a proper understanding of biological, or more specifically, ecological factors can significantly reduce the scale of environmental damage associated with recreational and tourist development' (Edington and Edington 1986: 2).

Tourism and recreation can have an adverse impact on the physical environment in numerous ways; for example, the construction of facilities that are aesthetically unsympathetic to the landscape in which they are situated, what D. Pearce (1978: 152) described as 'architectural pollution', and through the release of airborne and water-borne pollutants (de Freitas 2003; Hall and Härkönen 2006). Tourist or special-event facilities may change the character of the urban setting. Indeed, the location of a facility or attraction may be deliberately exploited in an attempt to rejuvenate an urban area through the construction of new infrastructure, as with the 1987 America's Cup in Fremantle (Hall 1992b) or other hallmark events such as the Olympic Games or World Fairs (see Chapter 5). The promotion of tourism without the provision of an adequate infrastructure to cope with increased visitor numbers may well cause a decline in urban environmental quality, for instance in the impacts of increased traffic flows (Schaer 1978). However, there is a wide range of tourism and recreation impacts on the urban physical environment (Table 4.5) that may have substantial implications for the longer-term sustainability of a destination which are only now being addressed in the tourism literature (Page 1995a; Hinch 1996).

Many of the ecological effects of tourist facilities may well take a long time to become apparent because of the nature of the environment, as in the case of the siting of marinas or resorts (Hall and Selwood 1987). The impact of outdoor recreation on the natural environment has been well documented (Wall and Wright 1977; Mathieson and Wall 1982; Liddle 1997; Hammitt and Cole 1998; Mason 2003) and is discussed further in Chapter 7. However, research on the physical impacts of tourism and tourism development presents an important area of future research, particularly with respect to sustainable tourism development (Farrell and McLellan 1987; Farrell and Runyan 1991; Hunter and Green 1995; German Federal Agency for Nature Conservation 1997; Hall and Lew 1998; Briassoulis and van der Straaten 1999; Gössling 2003; Mason 2003; Gössling and Hall 2006a).

Where the geographer has employed techniques from environmental science such as Environmental Assessment (EA), the spatial consequences of tourism and recreation activity have not always been fully appreciated. For example, Page (1992) reviewed the impact of the Channel Tunnel project on the natural and built environment and yet the generative effects of new tourist trips had been weakly articulated in the mountains of documents describing the effects to be mitigated, failing to recognise how this might impact

Table 4.5 **The impact of tourism on the urban physical environment**

The urban physical environment
- land lost through tourism development which might have been used for other purposes
- changes to urban hydrology

Visual impact
- development of tourism/leisure/cultural/entertainment districts
- introduction of new architectural styles
- potential reinforcement of vernacular architectural forms
- potential contribution to urban population growth

Infrastructure
- potential overloading of existing urban infrastructure with the following utilities and developments:
  - roads
  - railways
  - car parking
  - energy
  - sewerage and water supply
- provision of new infrastructure
- additional environmental management measures to accommodate tourists and adapt areas for tourist use

Urban form
- changes to land use as residential areas are replaced by accommodation developments
- alterations to the urban fabric from pedestrianisation and traffic management schemes which have been constructed to accommodate visitation
- changes to the streetscape as urban designs are modified

Restoration
- the restoration and conservation of historic sites and buildings
- reuse of the facades of heritage buildings

Source: after Page (1995a); Page and Hall (2003).

on destination areas. Again, planners and researchers had failed to recognise that recreational and tourist behaviour cannot easily be incorporated into spatially specific plans for individual infrastructure projects which will have knock-on effects for other parts of the tourism system. Page (1999) also reviews the role of geographers in developing more meaningful appraisals of environmental impacts resulting from tourist transport and the need to scrutinise private sector claims of minimising environmental impacts. Nevertheless, tourism's impacts on the natural environment have often been exaggerated. This is because the impacts of tourism have often failed to be distinguished from other forms of development impact or even such factors as overpopulation, poor agricultural practices or poor resource management (Mercer 2000). This is not to say that tourism has not affected the environment. Yet, what is often at issue are aesthetic or cumulative impacts rather than effects that can be related solely to tourism development; such an observation may apply with respect to individual species, such as manta rays (O'Malley *et al.* 2013), albatross (Higham 1998) and dolphins and whales (Orams 2005), specific environments, such as caves (Baker and Genty 1998), and locations, for example the Great Barrier Reef (Lawrence *et al.* 2002). Indeed, to focus on tourism as a form of negative impact on the natural environment can lead to a lack of appreciation of environmental problems which arise from other forms of economic development, such as depletion of fisheries and forest resources and the loss of biodiversity, and the overall lack of monitoring and management of many environments (Farrell and Marion 2001).

In the South Pacific, a region threatened by major environmental problems (Hall and Page 1996; Harrison 2004; Hall 2010h), including climate change (Hay 2013; Nunn 2013) and biodiversity loss (Hall 2010i), data and information are highly fragmented (Milne 1990; Sun and Walsh 1998; Warnken and Buckley 2000). Baseline data, i.e. information regarding the condition of the natural environment prior to tourism development, are invariably lacking. The range of tourism-related impacts is similar to that for many other destinations. However, in the case of Pacific islands, tourism impacts may be more problematic because tourism is concentrated on or near the

ecologically and geomorphologically dynamic coastal environment. Due to the highly dynamic nature of the coastal environment and the significance of mangroves and the limited coral sand supply for island beaches in particular, any development which interferes with the natural system may have severe consequences for the long-term stability of the environment. The impact of poorly developed tourism projects on the sand cays (coral sand islands) of the Pacific, for example, has been well documented (Baines 1987; Orams 2002; Wong 2003):

- near-shore vegetation clearing exposes the island to sea storm erosion and decreases plant material decomposition on the beach, thereby reducing nutrient availability for flora and fauna;
- manoeuvring by bulldozer (instead of hand clearing) results in scarring and soil disturbance and makes sand deposits loose and vulnerable to erosion;
- excessive tapping of the fresh groundwater lens induces saltwater intrusion, which then impairs vegetation growth and human water use and renders the cay susceptible to storm damage and further erosion;
- sewage outfall in shallow water and reef flats may lead to an excessive build-up of nutrients, thereby causing algal growth, which may eventually kill coral;
- sea-walls built to trap sand in the short term impair the natural seasonal distribution of sand, resulting, in the long run, in a net beach loss and a reduction of the island's land mass;
- boat channels blasted in the reef act as a sand trap; in time they fill with sand which is no longer circulating around the island; in turn this sand is replaced by other sand eroded from the vegetated edges, changing the size and shape of the island and in time threatening the island's integrity.

Another component of the coastal environment in the Pacific and in other tropical and subtropical areas that are substantially affected by tourism is the clearing and dredging of mangroves and estuaries for resorts. Mangroves and estuarine environments are extremely significant nursery areas for a variety of fish species. The loss of natural habitat due to dredging or infilling may therefore have a dramatic impact on fish catches. In addition, there may be substantial impacts on the whole of the estuarine food chain, with a subsequent loss of ecological diversity. A further consequence of mangrove loss is reduced protection against erosion of the shoreline, thereby increasing vulnerability to storm surge, particularly given the likely increase of high magnitude events and sea-level rise as a result of climate change (Nunn 2013), as well as increased pressures on coral reefs as a result of bleaching and ocean acidification (Scott *et al.* 2012). Therefore, removal of mangroves and loss of coral reefs will not only have an adverse impact on the immediate area of clearance, but also affect other coastal areas through the transport of greater amounts of marine sediment (Clarke 1991; Barnett and Adger 2003). However, despite concerns over environmental change in the South Pacific, tourism development continues to occur in the absence of other development opportunities for rapidly growing urbanised populations.

Such expressions of concern clearly give rise to questions regarding how sustainable tourism can really be and the need to provide limits on the expansion of tourism and corresponding human impact. Indeed, observation of the potential combined pressures of the social and environmental impacts of tourism has long led researchers to speculate as to whether there exists a carrying capacity for tourist destinations (e.g. J.M. Hall 1974; McCool 1978; Getz 1983; Coccossis 2004). Yet regardless of the empirical validity of the notion of carrying capacity (Wall 1983b; Coccossis 2004), attention must clearly be paid to the ability of an area, and especially island environments, to absorb tourism in relation to the possibilities of environmental degradation in both the short and long term (see Chapter 9).

Conclusion

The purpose of this chapter has been to give a brief account of some of the potential economic, social and environmental impacts of tourism and recreation. This provides a framework for the discussion of specific forms of tourism and recreation in Chapters 5–8.

Tourism and recreation needs to be well managed in order to reduce possible adverse impacts (Mason 2003; Reid 2003; Murphy and Murphy 2004; Hall 2008a). In turn, good management is likely to be related to the level of understanding of tourism and recreation phenomena. There is clearly a need to go beyond the image of tourism and recreation, and develop rigorous integrated economic, environmental, social and political analyses.

Geographers have contributed much to the understanding of the impacts of tourism and recreation, particularly with respect to the impacts on the physical environment and the spatial fixity of such effects. What the geographer has contributed is a better understanding of the wider consequences of individual impacts and their cumulative effect on the natural environment. However, there has been considerable exchange of approaches and methodologies through the various social sciences, which means that the demarcation line between geographical and other approaches has become increasingly fuzzy (Goodenough and Page 1994; Hall and Lew 2009). Nevertheless, no one discipline will have all the answers. Given the complex nature of tourism phenomena, particularly with respect to 'solving' environmental problems, the development of multidisciplinary approaches towards recreation and tourism may provide an appropriate starting point for the development of more sustainable forms of tourism.

Further reading

Although now somewhat dated, one of the most influential books on understanding the impacts of tourism is:

Mathieson, A. and Wall, G. (1982) *Tourism: Economic, Physical and Social Impacts*, London: Longman.

Most general textbooks on recreation and tourism will include overview chapters on the impacts of tourism. However, for some specific work on impacts, see:

Gössling, S. (2003) *Tourism and Development in Tropical Islands: Political Ecology Perspectives*, Aldershot: Edward Elgar.

Hall, C.M. and Lew, A. (eds) (2009) *Understanding and Managing Tourism Impacts: An Integrated Approach*, London: Routledge.

Hall, C.M. and Saarinen, J. (eds) (2010) *Polar Tourism and Change: Climate, Environments and Experiences*, London: Routledge.

Wall, G. and Mathieson, A. (2006) *Tourism: Change, Impacts and Opportunities*, Harlow: Pearson.

Useful books which deal with the environmental dimensions of tourism and recreation and their management include:

Gössling, S. and Hall, C.M. (eds) (2006) *Tourism and Global Environmental Change*, Routledge: London.

Newsome, D., Moore, S. and Dowling, R. (2012) *Natural Area Tourism: Ecology, Impacts and Management*, 2nd edn, Clevedon: Channel View.

Scott, D., Gössling, S. and Hall, C.M. (2012) *Tourism and Climate Change: Impacts, Adaptation and Mitigation*, London: Routledge.

Questions to discuss

1 What are the key factors in determining the accuracy of assessment of the economic impacts of tourism?

2 What may determine the acceptability of a recreation resource management model to stakeholders?

3 Why are the impacts of tourism on the natural environment poorly assessed?

4 Is tourism necessarily a negative impact on a destination?

5 What is the difference between 'impact' and 'change'?

Urban recreation and tourism

Towns and cities hold a special fascination for the geographer, since their evolution as places where people live, work, shop and engage in leisure has resulted from the process of urbanisation (Johnston *et al*. 1994; Pacione 2001). Since classical times, towns and cities have performed tourism and leisure functions (Page 2011), and therefore such places have a long history as places where tourism and leisure experiences have been produced and consumed. In recreational terms, town and city dwellers traditionally consumed their leisure time in the areas where they lived, with the exception of the wealthy elites (Borsay 2012) who were able to afford properties in the country, and up to the mid-nineteenth century mass forms of urban leisure and recreation were undertaken in close proximity to the home, local family and kinship networks, and local pastimes and holidays. As Page and Connell (2010: 302) argue, 'urban places are potentially the most significant environments in which to examine . . . leisure given the increasing urbanization of the world'. By 2020 there will be 16 world cities with a population of 20 million, while the regional focus of this growth in Asia and Latin America will create new conditions for urban leisure and tourism.

Page and Connell (2010) outline the growing urbanisation of leisure (and tourism) through history, particularly as processes of change transform the nature of society and the economy (i.e. a shift from pre-industrial to industrial to post-industrialism) and the concomitant changes in the spatial configuration of urban land uses. In the case of nineteenth century Warsaw, Olkusnik (2001) documents the process of change in urban recreation. Therefore, urbanisation is a major force contributing to the development of towns and cities, where people live, work and shop (see Johnston *et al*. 1994 for a definition of the term 'urbanisation'). Towns and cities function as places where the population is concentrated in a defined area, and economic activities locate in the same area or nearby, to provide the opportunity for the production and consumption of goods and services in capitalist societies. Consequently, towns and cities provide the context for a diverse range of social, cultural and economic activities which the population engage in, and where tourism, leisure and entertainment form major service activities in the developed and developing world (Okello *et al*. 2012; Minhat and Amin 2012). These environments also function as meeting places, major tourist gateways, accommodation and transportation hubs, and as central places to service the needs of visitors. Most tourist trips will contain some experience of an urban area, for example when an urban dweller departs from a major gateway in a city, arrives at a gateway in another city-region and stays in accommodation in an urban area. Within cities, however, the line between tourism and recreation blurs to the extent that at times one is indistinguishable from the other, with tourists and recreationalists using the same facilities, resources and environments, although some notable differences exist. Therefore, many tourists and recreationalists will intermingle in many urban contexts.

While most tourists will experience urban tourism in some form during their holiday, visits to friends and relatives, business trips or visits for other reasons (e.g. a pilgrimage to a religious shrine such as Lourdes), recreationalists will not use the accommodation but frequent many similar places as tourists.

This chapter seeks to examine some of the ways geographers conceptualise, analyse and research urban recreation and tourism, emphasising their contribution to understanding the wider context in which such activities take place. One key feature of the chapter is the emphasis on five specific aspects of geographical inquiry: description; classification; analysis; explanation; application of theoretical and conceptual issues to practical problem-solving contexts.

According to Coppock, the geographer's principal interest in the geographical analysis of leisure provides a useful starting point in understanding the areas of research which have also been developed in urban recreation and tourism research in that they examine

> the way in which . . . pursuits are linked to the whole complex of human activities and physical features that determine the distinctive characters of places and region, and the interactions between such pursuits and the natural and man-made environments in which they occur . . . [and] the study of the spatial interactions between participants and resources probably represents the most significant contribution the geographer can make.
>
> (Coppock 1982: 2–3)

The focus on the behavioural aspects of recreational and tourism behaviour together with the planning and, more recently, the management implications of such activities in the urban environment have become fruitful areas for geographical research, particularly the critical and radical perspectives where inequality and access to leisure are politicised and imbued with exclusivity (e.g. Byrne 2012). Issues of race along with ageing and the implications for individuals' and groups' quality of life have clear spatial divisions (Engberg *et al*. 2012).

BOX 5.1   STANLEY PARK, VANCOUVER

In 1886, 1,000 acres (404 hectares) of federal government land on a largely logged peninsula was leased to the Vancouver City Council for park and recreation purposes. The area, which was named Stanley Park, after Lord Stanley, Governor General of Canada in 1888 when the park was officially opened, now lies at the heart of Vancouver's park system and attracts an estimated 8 million visitors a year to North America's third largest urban park. As well as providing a significant secondary growth forest ecosystem and wetland (Kheraj 2007), the park also contains a number of built attractions and recreation opportunities. Although the former zoo in the park has been closed, the park still contains such attractions as the Vancouver Aquarium Marine Science centre, a miniature railway and children's farmyard, summer theatre and Brockton Point Visitor's centre, which features a number of First Nations totem poles. Recreational sites include swimming areas, golf course and putting green, tennis courts and, probably most significantly in terms of use, numerous bicycling, roller blade, jogging and walking paths. Stanley Park therefore continues many of the traditions of a multiple-use large urban park or commons of the Victorian Period (Mawani 2004), comparable with similar large areas of urban green space elsewhere in the world, such as Kings Park in Perth, Western Australia, Centennial Park in Sydney, New South Wales, or the Domain, in Auckland, New Zealand.

Stanley Park also has considerable ecological importance and is an urban ecotourism attraction. The great blue heron, the largest in the heron family, with a wing span of up to 2 metres, and a bird species considered vulnerable because of the loss of its natural habitat, has recently staged a revival in the park, with about 80 adult herons nesting in the park in 2004. The species was first identified in the park in the

1920s, but they had deserted the park by 1998. The return of the birds has turned them into something of a tourist attraction. However, as well as being noisy the colony is also quite smelly during springtime because of the waste of nesting chicks and adults and the regurgitation of crab and fish by parents in the feeding of chicks. Indeed, park officials have received complaints from people living in apartments near the colony (Hutchinson 2004), which illustrates the potential conflicts that may arise between different users of urban space. (See http://vancouver.ca/parks-recreation-culture/stanley-park.aspx.)

Geographical approaches to urban recreation

Despite the growth in geographical research on leisure and recreation (Coppock 1982), the focus on urban issues remained neglected. (Three geographical studies which are exceptions are Seeley (1983); Williams (1995a); and Page and Connell (2010)). As Patmore (1983: 87) noted, 'in the past geographers, with their inherently spatial interest, have tended to concentrate on outdoor recreation in rural areas, where spatial demands, and spatial conflicts have been the greatest'. This is a strange paradox according to Patmore, since

the greatest changes in recreation habits [since the early 1930s] have taken place in two opposing directions. High personal mobility has extended opportunities away from the home and brought a growing complexity to the scale and direction of leisure patterns. Conversely, the home has come to provide for a greater range of leisure opportunities, and home-centred leisure has acquired a greater significance. The family has become socially more self-sufficient, its links with the immediate community and with its own extended kinship network weaker. Social independence has been underpinned by greater physical independence of homes in the expanding suburban communities, by the weakening need for communal space that comes with lower housing densities and the command of greater private space.

(Patmore 1983: 87)

For the geographer, understanding the spatial implications of such processes and the geographical manifestation of the urban recreational demand for and the supply of resources requires the use of concepts and methodologies to understand the complexity and simplify the reality of recreational activities to a more meaningful series of concepts and constructs. However, one area that has been largely neglected in reviews of urban recreational activities is the historical dimension (Borsay 2006). Although Towner (1996) and Page and Connell (2010) provide an all-embracing review of tourism and leisure in an historical context, it is important to acknowledge the significance of social, political, economic and geographical factors which shaped the evolution of modern-day urban recreation.

For this reason, no analysis of urban recreation can commence without an understanding of the historical and geographical processes associated with its development (see Bailey 1989). By focusing on the development of modern-day recreation in cities since their rapid expansion in the early nineteenth century, it is possible to examine many changes to the form, function and format of urban recreation and its spatial occurrence in the nascent urban-industrial cities and conurbations in England and Wales.

Evolution of urban recreation in Britain

Within the context of towns and cities, S. Williams argues that

urban populations engage in most of their leisure activities within the same urban area in which they live. The geographical patterns of residence are translated very readily into a pattern of recreation that is focused upon the urban environment, purely by the fact that most people spend the majority of their leisure time in, or close to the home.

(Williams 1995a: 8)

Patterns of residence and recreation are closely related. Contemporary patterns of recreation and the ways in which they developed in Britain are fundamental to any understanding of the development of recreational opportunities in urban areas. According to Williams (1995a), these passed through three distinct phases: foundation, consolidation and expansion.

Phase 1: foundation

During the nineteenth century, public provision for urban recreational activities emerged through legislative provision (e.g. the number of urban parks in Britain increased from 19 between 1820 and 1850 to 111 between 1850 and 1880 (Conway 1991), while innovations in town planning and urban design led to improved quality of streets and housing areas, expanding the space for recreation. In addition, the nineteenth century saw the social geography of towns and cities in England and Wales (Lawton 1978) develop, with social patterns of segregation and suburbanisation fuelled by urban growth. This also affected the development of recreational opportunities as cities expanded during the late nineteenth and early twentieth centuries. In the case of Liverpool, Marne (2001) examined the class, gender and ethnicity issues associated with the growth of urban park provision in Liverpool, highlighting many of the socio-geographic inequalities which exist at the present time.

Phase 2: consolidation

The period 1918 to 1939 saw a growth in more specialised forms of urban recreational land uses stimulated by legislation such as the rise of the Small Holdings and Allotments Act 1908, which expanded the range and type of amenity space in towns and cities, while other gaps in provision (e.g. the National Playing Fields Association, formed in 1925)

recognised the need for space in urban areas to support the role of sport. Likewise, the Physical Training and Recreational Act 1937 effectively signalled the emergence of public sector aid from central government for local authority provision of playing fields, gymnasia and swimming baths.

Phase 3: expansion

During the post-war period several key trends emerged, including 'greater levels and diversity of provision in which traditional resources established in earlier phases have been augmented by new forms of provision designed to reflect the diversity and flexibility of contemporary recreational tastes' (Williams 1995a: 20). One common theme is the recognition of recreation as an element in statutory planning procedures as the range and consumption of land for recreational purposes increased. However, according to Williams (1995a: 21), in the absence of theoretical approaches to describing and explaining the pattern of recreation resources in urban areas, the approach to the task must inevitably become empirical, outlining the typical patterns of provision where older parks and recreation grounds are concentrated towards the core of the settlement (see Box 5.2 on Leicester), while newer parks and grounds associated with inter-war and post-1945 housing produce further significant zones of provision to the periphery of the city. The outer edges of the built area are important for provision of extensive facilities such as sports grounds and golf courses.

While these conclusions are typical of recreational land use patterns in many towns and cities in England and Wales, one must question the extent to which a purely empirical analysis truly explains the spatial development of recreational resources in Britain's urban areas. For this reason it is valuable to consider the social, economic and political processes which contributed to the spatial organisation and occurrence of urban recreation in such areas in the period after 1800, because traditional empirical analyses are devoid of the diversity of people and users of such resources. For this reason, a series of historical snapshots taken in 1800, the 1840s, 1880s, 1920s, 1960s and post-1960s help to explain how present-day patterns were shaped.

Urban recreation: a socio-geographic perspective

According to Clark and Crichter (1985), during the evolution of British capitalism the analysis of leisure and recreation has traditionally emphasised institutional forms of provision, while each social class has its own history of organised and informal leisure and recreation. The predominant urban histories are those of male leisure, with female leisure and recreation structured around the family, with free-time activities associated with the family, the street and neighbourhood in working class society. Within historical analyses of urban recreation during the evolution of mass urban society in Victorian and Edwardian Britain, the emergence of distinctive forms of urban recreation and leisure and their spatial occurrence within different social areas of cities have been associated with a number of concepts, the most notable being 'popular culture' (see Williams 1976). As Clark and Crichter (1985: 55) argue, 'the early nineteenth century was to bring a dramatic transformation to the form . . . and context of popular culture, imposing very different parameters of time and space, rhythms and routines, behaviour and attitude, control and commerce'. However, the resulting changes cannot simply be conceptualised as a straightforward linear progression since different influences and cross-currents meant that this transformation affected different people and areas at different rates and in varying degrees.

Clark and Crichter (1985) provide an historical analysis of leisure and recreational forms in Britain during the nineteenth and twentieth centuries, with the emphasis on the urban forms and political factors, forms of social control (Donajgrodski 1978), and the underlying development and functioning of an urban capitalist society; leisure and recreational forms emerged as a civilising and diversionary process to maintain the productive capacity of the working classes as central to the continued development of capitalism. Therefore, the geographical patterns and

manifestation of urban recreation and leisure for all social classes in the British city in the nineteenth and twentieth centuries have to be viewed against the background of social, economic and political processes which conditioned the demand for and supply of leisure and recreation for each social class (see Dagenais (2002) for a comparable discussion of Montreal). However, Huggins (2000) questioned conventional stereotypes of the respectable urban middle class in different leisure contexts during the Victorian period. Huggins (2000) highlights the spatial differentiation between highly respectable behaviour in cities where work, home and respectability were interconnected. Yet in more liminal locations away from the home (e.g. the seaside and the racecourse), less respectable and 'sinful' pleasures were consumed by the same middle class, where less respectable behaviour occurred.

According to Billinge (1996: 450), 'Perhaps the single newest element in the townscape after the general regulation of the street, was the park, and more specifically the recreation ground . . . [since] the urban park, as distinct from the garden square, was essentially a nineteenth century phenomenon' and a symbol of civic pride. As Maver (1998: 346) argued, 'the development of Glasgow's public parks . . . sparked municipal interest during the 1850s, given the recognised impact of parks in improving the amenity value of middle-class residential areas'. The acknowledged role of parks as the 'lungs of the city', as a haven from industrialisation, was an attempt to recreate notions of community well-being. Similarly, in the development of San Francisco's city parks between 1850 and 1920, the main proponents of park development were a middle to upper class elite who embodied notions of parks contributing to well-being, reflecting elements of nature which were balanced and inherently good (Young 1996).

Billinge (1996: 444) recognised the way in which the Victorians engineered the term 'recreation' 'to perfection, they gave it a role and a geography. Confined by time, defined by place and regulated by content, recreation and the time it occupied ceased to be possessions freely enjoyed and became instead, obligations dutifully discharged.' The Victorians established a system of approved urban leisure and recreation activities and, as Billinge (1996) recognised, these were allocated to appropriate times and places. In spatial terms, this led to a reconfiguration of the Victorian and Edwardian town and its hinterland to accommodate new, organised and, later, informal recreational and leisure pursuits in specific spaces and at nominated places. In fact, the natural corollary of this in the late nineteenth century was the rise of the English seaside resort (Gilbert 1939, 1949, 1954; Walton 1983; Towner 1996). As Billinge (1996: 447) argued, it was 'the provision of set aside resorts for the masses at the scale of the whole township: the seaside resort where behaviour inappropriate in any other occasion could be loosed to burn itself out'. This can be viewed as a further example of the way in which Victorian society sought to exercise both a degree of social and spatial control of recreational spaces and activities among its populace. This created a social necessity for recreation as freedom from work: a non-work activity to recreate body and soul, to be refreshed for the capitalist economic system, with its regulated time discipline of a place for everything, and everything in its place.

For this reason, it is pertinent to consider the key features of Clark and Crichter's (1985) historical synthesis of urban leisure and recreation in Britain, since it helps to explain how changes in society shaped the modern-day patterns of urban recreation. Clark and Crichter (1985) adopt a cross-section approach to analyse key periods in nineteenth and twentieth century British urban society to emphasise the nature of the changes and type of urban recreation and leisure pursuits. It also helps to explain how the evolution of urban places and recreational activities emerged. This also has many parallels, as Page and Connell (2010) outline, with the increasing urbanisation of leisure in the USA and other countries at different times and with varying results.

The 1800s

As emphasised earlier in this chapter, Britain was in the process of emerging from a pre-industrial state. While cities were not a new phenomenon, the movement of the rural population to nascent cities meant that the traditional boundary between work and non-work among the labouring classes was increasingly dictated by the needs of factory or mechanised production. Therefore, pre-industrial flexibility in the work–non-work relationship associated with cottage industries and labouring on the land changed. This led to a clearer distinction between work and non-work time, as time discipline emerged as a potent force during the Industrial Revolution (Pred 1981). In the pre-industrial, non-urbanised society, leisure and recreational forms were associated with market days, fairs, wakes, holidays, religious and pagan festivals which provided opportunities for sport. While the 1800s are often characterised by brutish behaviour and ribaldry, civilising influences emerged in the form of Puritanism to engender moral sobriety and spatial changes associated with the enclosure movement, which removed many strategic sites of customary activity. In contrast, the geographical patterns of recreation of the ruling classes

> eschewed contact with lower orders. Its forms were as yet disparate. Shooting, hunting and horse racing . . . the major flat race classics date from the 1770s onwards . . . For the increasingly influential urban bourgeoisie, the theatre, literature, seaside holidays and music hall denoted more rational forms of leisure which depended for their decorum on the exclusion of the mass of the population.
> (Clark and Crichter 1985: 55)

The 1840s

In historical analysis, this period is often characterised as a period of deprivation for the urban working classes. Endemic poverty, associated with rapid urbanisation and inadequate housing, poor living standards and limited infrastructure, culminated in high rates of mortality, disease and exploitation of the labouring classes through long hours of work (12 hour, six day weeks) (Page 1988). In terms of urban leisure and recreation, the pre-industrial opportunities for pursuits decreased, as did the legal outlets, with many customary pastimes suppressed so that popular culture was conditioned through legislative changes. For example, the New Poor Law Act 1834 (Rose 1985) aimed to control the movement of 'travelling balladeers', 'entertainers' and 'itinerant salesmen', all of whom were deemed to be vagabonds and returned to their parish of origin. Similarly, the Highways Act 1835 was intended to remove street nuisances such as street entertainers and traders while the Cruelty to Animals Act 1835 sought to suppress working class pastimes involving animals, thereby driving many activities underground and leading to the emergence of a hybrid range of recreational activities, including popular theatre, pantomime and circuses. In the late 1840s, railway excursions marketed by Thomas Cook also developed. In addition, a range of rational recreation pursuits emerged in purpose-built facilities made possible by Parliamentary Acts, including the Museums Act 1845, the Baths and Wash Houses Act 1846 and the Libraries Act 1850. Social theorists argue that such legislation may have acted as a form of social control (Donajgrodski 1978), to tame a new industrial workforce while demarcating recreation and work. Furthermore, the 1840s saw the emergence of the Victorian concept of domesticity and a bourgeois culture, with the use of a gender separation of male and female work.

The 1880s

While the early Victorian period saw the establishment of urban recreational facilities, improved working conditions and living standards in the mid- to late Victorian period were accompanied by greater municipal provision (Briggs 1969). Yet as Clark and Crichter (1985) argue, four processes were at work in the 1850s and 1860s which led to significant changes in the 1880s:

- a rise of middle class urban recreation which excluded the working classes;
- the expansion of local government's role in leisure and recreational provision;
- an increasing commercialisation and greater capitalisation of urban recreation, relying upon mass audiences and licensing (e.g. the rise of football), which also required large areas of land;

- attempts by the working classes to organise urban recreation according to their own aspirations.

By the 1880s, the pattern of urban conurbations had emerged in England, which focused on London, the West Midlands, West Yorkshire, Merseyside and Tyneside (Lawton 1978). In addition to these trends in urban recreation, the rise of urban middle class recreational pursuits centred on religion, reading, music and annual holidays reflected a more rational form of recreational activity.

Nevertheless, the 1870s saw growth in public parks and by 1885 nearly 25 per cent of the urban population had access to public libraries. At the same time, informal urban recreation based on street and neighbourhood activities largely remains invisible in documentary sources and official records, although limited evidence exists in the form of autobiographies and oral history. For example, R. Roberts' (1971, 1976) *The Classic Slum* observed that the pub played a major role in informal recreation in Victorian and Edwardian Salford, where a community of 3,000 people had 15 beer houses. Through sexual segregation it was possible to observe the rise of male-only urban recreational pursuits in the 1880s. Yet the street life and neighbourhood forms of recreation remained unorganised and informal despite the institutionalisation, segmentation and emergence of a customer–provider relationship in Victorian urban recreational pursuits.

The 1920s

In Britain, the 1920s are frequently viewed as the era of mass unemployment, with social class more spatially defined in the urban environment. While the 1900s saw rising patronage of the cinema, with 3,000 cinemas operating in Britain by 1926 and audiences of 20 million, and many people visiting the cinemas once or twice a week, this pursuit increasingly met the recreational needs of women as it displaced the Victorian music-hall, being more heavily capitalised and more accessible in terms of price and social acceptability. The ideological separation of work and home was firmly enshrined in the 1920s, with a greater physical separation and the rise of annual holidays and day trips using charabancs and cars. Spectator sports also retained large audiences, although the social segregation of urban recreation based on social class, mass markets and institutional provision characterised this era (see Page and Connell 2010).

The 1960s and beyond

Clark and Crichter (1985) identified six distinct trends occurring from the 1960s on (see also Pahl 1975; Page and Connell 2010):

- rising standards of domestic consumption;
- family-centred leisure;
- the decline of public forms of urban leisure and recreation;
- emergence of a youth culture;
- the establishment of ethnic leisure and recreation cultures;
- increased state activity in prescribed spheres of urban recreation and a growing commercial domination of leisure institutions and services.

In terms of urban recreation, various debates exist in relation to the changes induced by a post-industrial society and the implications for urban recreation. Social theorists point to the concomitant changes induced by economic, occupational and technological change, associated with the demise of manufacturing and the rise of the service sector in towns and cities, affecting the pattern of life and recreational activities of urban populations associated with a growing polarisation of wealth and opportunity. S. Williams (1995a: 213) outlines the impact of such changes for post-industrial towns and cities, as older central areas of towns decayed as they lost their economic rationale. In some cases this has led to the creation of space for recreation, as high density housing and industry have been removed and urban regeneration results.

Williams (1995a) also points to the effect of the rise of environmentalism since the 1960s, reflected in the concept of the 'green city', where redundant space is 'greened' to enhance the quality of the city environment while adding recreational opportunities (e.g.

greenways, linear parks, green wedges and natural corridors). The greening of cities also has a wider concern with the sustainability of urban life. Williams (1995a) also argues that a range of factors militate against the continued well-being of urban recreation provision, many of which are associated with political change (Page *et al.* 1994). A greater concern with financial costs of publicly provided services, more efficient service delivery and the introduction of compulsory competitive tendering (Benington and White 1988; Page *et al.* 1994) characterised public and private sector recreational provision in urban areas in the 1980s and 1990s. Henry (1988) argued that the outcome will be determined by the political climate and philosophy prevailing in public sector environments, fluctuating between a limited role for the state characterised by right-wing ideology and one based on principles of social equity and significant levels of public intervention influenced by principles of equality (see Page and Connell 2010 for detail post-1990).

In the UK in the new millennium, New Labour sought to critically analyse the quality of the urban environment, given the previous 20 years of changing policies to towns and cities to improve their liveability. A number of notable developments emanating from the Office of the Deputy Prime Minister (ODPM) include the *Cleaner, Safer, Greener Public Space* (ODPM 2002) report, which identified a typology of open space in cities that could be divided into green space, comprising parks, gardens, amenity green space, children's play areas, sports facilities, green corridors, natural/semi-natural green space and other functional green space, and civic space, comprising civic squares, marketplaces, pedestrian streets, promenades and seafronts.

Having briefly examined the evolution of urban recreational opportunities in Britain since the 1880s, it is pertinent to focus on one example which typifies the development processes in time and space, notably the evolution of parks and open space. This is considered in relation to one particular city in Britain – Leicester – although similar patterns of evolution occurred in many other cities in Europe, the USA and antipodes at later points in time.

BOX 5.2   THE EVOLUTION OF PARKS AND OPEN SPACE IN VICTORIAN LEICESTER

The development of open space in towns and cities in Britain traditionally developed through the emergence of commons and walks prior to the nineteenth century, followed by private squares and greens for the wealthy classes. While towns and cities remained small in scale, the populations were able to enjoy recreation in the surrounding rural areas (Clarke 1981). Urban industrial growth in the Industrial Revolution transformed the spatial form of towns and cities, as open land was consumed for economic and residential development. Two specific legislative changes during the Victorian era in Britain contributed to the development of large parks, namely the Select Committee on Public Walks (1833) and the Health of Towns (1840), in a period of concern for the health and social well-being of the labouring classes. As Strachan and Bowler (1976) acknowledged, early park development was prompted by donations from industrialists and landowners, and four pieces of legislation enabled local authorities to purchase land for park development, notably the Towns Improvement Act 1847, the Public Health Act 1848, the Public Parks, Schools and Museums Act 1871 and the Public Improvements Act 1860. While Edwardian and subsequent legislation enhanced park development, including the Housing and Town Planning Act 1909 and Town and Country Planning Acts of 1932 and 1947, the Victorian era was important in terms of the development of large-scale parks and open space as permissive legislation permitted councils to engage in park and open space development.

Park development in Victorian Leicester

Leicester expanded as a Victorian city: its population grew from 18,445 in 1801 to 64,829 in 1851, 174,624 in 1891 and 211,579 in 1901. While Pritchard (1976) and Page (1988) examine the spatial development of the city (Figure 5.1), and constraints and opportunities for urban development, the city retained a medieval pattern of land development up until the 1800s. The poorly drained River Soar constrained development to the west of the river and also by owners of estates who refused to sell land for development. Most early urban growth in the 1800s occurred to the east and north-east. Prior to 1850, two open spaces existed: St Margaret's Pasture, a 13 acre (5.2 ha) meadow to the north of the urban area; and at Southfield race course, established in 1806 (Figure 5.2). In 1838, the city council provided 40 acres (16 ha) of land at Southfield at Welford to form the first public recreation ground, although only 8 acres (3.2 ha) now remain. This was complemented by a series of private gardens and squares laid out from 1785 at the town council's request along New Walk, which forms the sole surviving urban pedestrian way in England (Strachan and Bowler 1976: 279).

With the growth in population by 1851 urban development occurred to the west of the Soar and the city council developed four parks and recreation grounds (Figure 5.2) in the period 1880–1900. Victoria Park (27.6 ha), established in 1882 on city-owned land, was made possible by the relocation of the city's race course from Southfield to Oadby. The purchase of Abbey Meadows (22.8 ha) in 1877, for the purpose of draining a marsh area unsuitable for building, resulted in an ornamental park. The third park, aimed at providing open space access for the fast growing suburb of Highfields, led to the development of 13.6 ha at Spinney Hill with a formal park in 1885. The fourth major park, established in the western suburbs, saw the establishment of the new parks estate (71.2 ha) in 1899. Each park developed in the tradition of

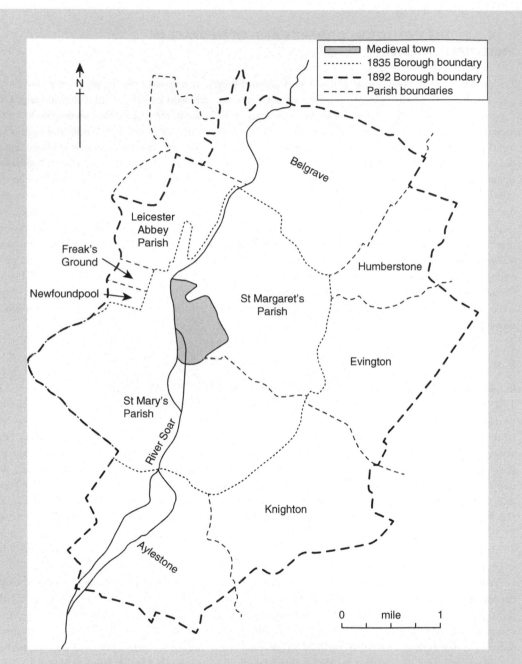

Figure 5.1 The expansion of Leicester in the nineteenth century
Source: S. Page.

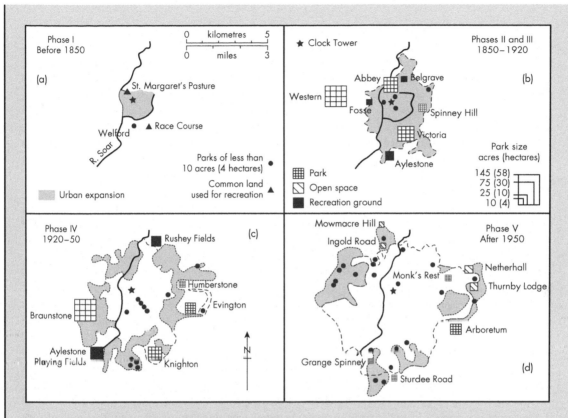

Figure 5.2 Urban park development in Leicester

Source: redrawn from Strachan and Bowler 1976 and with permission from Leicester City Council's Legal Services Department.

Victorian formal use, with fountains, band stands, gardens and open stretches of grass. In the case of Abbey Park boating, river views, greenhouses and formal flower beds attracted users from across the city. To complement formal park provision, recreation grounds were also established in 1892 at Belgrave (4.8 ha) and Fosse Road (4.4 ha) in 1897.

Post-Victorian park development

In 1902, the Aylestone site (8 ha) was purchased as a recreation ground, followed by a lull up until the 1920s. Between 1900 and 1920 small open spaces in the town centre led to the establishment of three ornamental gardens (Castle, Westcotes and St George's Church), two playgrounds and a small park at Westcotes. After 1920, further urban expansion led to the establishment of six multipurpose parks with sports facilities, the largest at Braunstone (66.8 ha) in 1925 on the periphery of the city as a focal point of a large inter-war council estate. In contrast, other parks developed in the inter-war period were located in private housing areas, such as Humberstone (8 ha) in 1928, Knighton (32.9 ha) in 1937, Evington (17.6 ha) in 1949, in eastern and southern suburbs. To balance the geographical distribution of provision, two large recreation grounds were opened at Rusley Fields (11.4 ha) in 1921 and Aylestone Playing Fields (33.2 ha) in 1946; a number of smaller open spaces were also developed on new council estates at Braunstone Park and Humberstone and a number of amenity open spaces amounting to 40.8 ha. In the post-war period, attention in Leicester City Council shifted towards provision of small neighbourhood and local facilities as key features of new council estates. Only a limited number of larger open spaces were created, on land unsuitable for residential development (e.g. Netherhall's 12.8 ha site in 1958 and Ingeld's 5.6 ha site in 1970). Amenity open space was also incorporated into 13 council estates, providing 105.6 ha of open space. A number of small village parks and playgrounds in old villages (e.g. Old Humberstone) contributed to the 27 parks and recreation grounds opened between 1950 and 1975. Since 1975 Leicester City Council has maintained an active role in enhancing open space and park provision, to the point where in 1994 it maintained 1,200 ha of parkland and open space. This represented one-fifth of the total area of the city, an extremely high level of provision by European and North American standards.

By 2000, this had risen to 3,000 ha of public open space, comprising country parks, formal parks, gardens, wetlands, allotments (for a discussion of allotments as a form of recreation, see Thorpe 1970; Crouch 1989a, 1989b) and woodlands. This is complemented by the provision of gardens with houses, which perform an important recreational function (Halkett 1978) in the wider leisure context of the home (Glyptis and Chambers 1982). However, the dominant element is parkland. The City of Leicester Local Plan aim is to have public open space within 500 metres of every home. Within new residential developments, the City Council requires developers to provide 1.6 ha of open space per 1,000 people housed. As a result in Leicester recreation space is an average of only 2.9 km from the city centre for parks/gardens, 3.6 km for recreation grounds, 3.5 km for playing fields, 3.7 km for sports grounds and 4.6 km for golf courses, illustrating the role of low cost land for such facilities. Thus, as S. Williams (1995a) argues, the level of recreational opportunity in modern-day Leicester increases with distance from the city. The result of such patterns of park development and other recreational resources in the case of Leicester is the rationalisation of provision into a geographical planning framework whereby an open space hierarchy results, with different parks fulfilling different functions according to their size, characteristics and resource base.

Methods of analysing urban recreation

Within the limited literature on urban recreation, the geographer has developed a number of concepts used within human geography and applied them in a recreational context to understand how the supply of recreational resources fits within the broader recreational context. For example, the use of the concept of a 'hierarchy of facilities' (Patmore 1983) highlights the catchment relating to the users' willingness, ability and knowledge of the facility or resource (Smith 1983a). What the hierarchy concept does is allow one to ascertain what type of catchment a recreational resource has at different spatial scales, taking into account users' willingness to travel to use them. Constraints of time and distance act as a friction on the potential use of resources. The outcome is an ordered pattern of resources which serve specific catchments depending on their characteristics, whereby the typical levels of provision may include:

- the neighbourhood level (e.g. a community centre);
- local areas (e.g. a recreation ground);
- regions within cities;
- a city-wide level (e.g. an art gallery).

An illustration of such a hierarchy for urban open space is given in Table 5.1. The result is an ordered provision, each with its own set of users and meeting the needs and aspirations of users, which will vary in time and space. Within any urban context the challenge for recreational planning is to match the supply and demand for such resources. One further technique which Patmore (1983) advocated for urban recreation is the resource inventory, whereby the range of existing resources is surveyed and mapped in relation to the catchment population. This population may then be compared to existing recommended levels of provision set by organisations for recreational provision. For example, the National Playing Fields Association in the UK recommended 2.4 ha of space per 1,000 population, 'excluding school playing fields except where available for general use, woodlands and commons, ornamental gardens, full-length golf courses

and open spaces where the playing of games by the general public is either discouraged or not permitted' (Patmore 1983: 118). In the UK, such playing fields were under increased pressure for housing development, to the point that new guidelines were issued to prevent schools and local authorities from selling such leisure assets for short-term development gains.

Patmore (1983) outlined the range of urban recreational resources and facilities and provides a detailed spatial analysis of their occurrence and level of provision within the UK in terms of:

- capital-intensive facilities (those with modest land requirements but a high capital cost – and those with a high capital cost where the land requirement is extensive);
- parks and open spaces;
- golf courses.

Table 5.1 **Hierarchical pattern of public open space**

Type and main function	Approximate size and distance from home	Characteristics
Regional park Weekend and occasional visits by car or public transport	400 ha (3.2–8 km)	Large areas of natural heathland, common woodland and parkland, primarily providing for informal recreation, with some non-intensive active recreations. Car parking at strategic locations.
Metropolitan park Weekend and occasional visits by car or public transport	60 ha (3.2 km but more when park is larger than 60 hectares)	Either natural heath, common, woods or formal parks providing for active and passive recreation. May contain playing fields, provided at least 40 hectares remain for other pursuits. Adequate car parking.
District parks Weekend and occasional visits on foot, by cycle, car or short bus trip	20 ha (1.2 km)	Landscaped settings with a variety of natural features providing for a range of activities, including outdoor sports, children's play and informal pursuits. Some car parking.
Local parks For pedestrian visitors	2 ha (0.4 km)	Providing for court games, children's play, sitting out, etc. in a landscaped environment. Playing fields if the park is large enough.
Small local parks Pedestrian visits, especially by old people and children, particularly valuable in high density areas	2 ha (0.4 km)	Gardens, sitting-out areas and children's playgrounds.
Linear open space Pedestrian visits	Variable Where feasible	Canal towpaths, footpaths, disused rail lines, etc., providing opportunities for informal recreation.

Source: Williams 1995a.

S. Williams (1995a) adds an interesting array of other contexts, including:

- the home;
- the street;
- gardens and allotments;
- playgrounds;
- other sporting contexts.

In the case of the street, there has been a retreat from its focus in Victoria and Edwardian times as a leisure environment, progressively eroded as the car has filled many such spaces (see Box 5.3, on the street as a leisure environment). One interesting example that runs contrary to this trend in the western world was observed by Drummond (2000) in Vietnam. Here the street as a pseudo public leisure space is actually expanding as a phenomenon.

To assist in understanding the spatial analysis of these resources and their interrelationship in an urban context, Williams (1995a) developed a typology of urban recreational resources. To achieve this, and to incorporate the perception and use of the resource by urban users, he used seven variables to construct a simple typology (illustrated in Table 5.2). However, as Patmore (1983: 98) rightly argued, patterns of facility use are not related to location alone: effective access is not synonymous with convenience of location. As a result, barriers to urban recreational use include:

- *physical barriers* based on factors such as age, stage in the family life cycle (e.g. dependent children) and physical access;
- *financial barriers* include direct economic constraints due to costs of participation such as admission

Table 5.2 Summary and explanation of key variables deployed within the recreation resource typology

Variable	Sub-categories	Explanation
Design	Purpose-built	Resource is designed for specific recreational uses
	Adapted	Resource has been converted to a recreational use from a previous function
	Annexed	Resource is not designed or intended for recreational use, but will be used as such by some groups
Organisational	Formal	Resource has a structured design/layout and/or management
	Informal	Resource has no such structure
Function	Single	Resource has one intended recreational function
	Multi	Resource has a diversity of intended recreational functions
	Shared	Resource has a variety of functions of which recreation is one
Space/use characteristics	Extensive	Individual recreational functions range over large areas, with generous use of space
	Intensive	Functions are concentrated, with little or no unused/wasted space
Scale	Large	Over 10 acres in extent
	Medium	Between 2 and 10 acres in extent
	Small	Below 2 acres in extent
Catchment	City-wide	Resource draws use from across the urban area
	District	Resource draws use primarily from its district
	Local	Resource draws use primarily from its neighbourhood
Source of provision	Public	Funded/managed by government at either local or national level
	Private	Funded/managed by private individuals/groups for their own use
	Voluntary	Funded/managed by groups acting as co-operatives, clubs or societies, for the use of members

Source: Williams 1995a.

or membership costs (e.g. golf club fees), which may raise issues related to the public sector's role in provision;

- *social barriers* often reinforce the financial barriers whereby lower socio-economic groups do not participate due to financial barriers – even when such barriers are removed, the image of participation still has cultural and social barriers (e.g. opera-going);
- *transport* can be a deterrent to urban recreational participation where access is limited by car ownership or where a short journey by bus may be difficult and costly in time for public transport users.

Using the key variables, which reflect basic resource attributes, Williams (1995a) devised a further typology of urban recreational resources (Table 5.3).

The challenge for recreational provision in any urban context is the planning and management undertaken to ensure that principles of equity and equal access are permitted where possible, and it is to this that we now turn.

Urban recreational planning

It may be possible to view [urban recreation] provision in a rational, hierarchical frame, to develop models for that precision that equate access and opportunity in a spatial pattern with mathematical precision, but reality rarely gives an empty canvas where such a model can be developed in an unfettered form. Rather, reality is conditioned by the accident of historic legacy, by the fashions of spending from the public purse and by the commercial dictates of the public sector.

(Patmore 1983: 117–18)

In geographical terms, urban recreational provision in town and cities grew in an ad-hoc fashion, and in many western European contexts the task of city planners in the 1960s and 1970s was to tidy up the decades of incremental growth. In the UK, one solution used was to create 'leisure directorates' in city councils to amalgamate public recreation interests into one consolidated department. As Burtenshaw *et al.* (1991) argued, the consolidation of recreation

Table 5.3 Basic typology of outdoor recreation facilities in urban areas

Scale	Public facilities		Private/voluntary facilities		
	Formal	Informal	Formal	Informal	By groups
Large scale City-wide catchment	Major parks Major sports fields/ stadiums Municipal golf courses	Major commons Major urban woodland Major water space Urban country parks	Private golf courses		Major shopping centres Major transport centres, e.g. airports, stations
Medium scale District catchment	Recreation grounds Small parks	Urban greenways Minor urban woodland Minor water space Cycleways	Sports clubs, e.g. bowls or cricket		
Small scale local catchment	Children's play areas			Domestic gardens	Local streets/ pavements Waste ground Grass verges

Source: Williams 1995a.

BOX 5.3   THE STREET

The street (usually 'Main Street' in the USA) has been a central feature of the leisure lives of urban dwellers since the rapid growth of industrial cities, highlighted earlier in the chapter. Historians have examined the street as a site of consumption and leisure activity (e.g. Roberts 2004; Bailey 1999) characterised by retail activity, children's play and as a setting for social gatherings. It is a key element in the 'routine of everyday life' (Moran 2005) as cultural studies have evaluated the nature of such locations for leisure consumption. Moran (2012) illustrates the transition in the way the street has developed since 1945 as a space of spontaneous community. The street has even become a setting for television soap operas in the UK (e.g. *Coronation Street* and *EastEnders*), where leisure time is spent in social interaction.

Previous reviews of the street as a location for modern-day leisure argued that because 'little is known . . . in the realm of public space, it is arguably the street that has been overlooked as the location for popular leisure' (Williams 1995b: 23). Recent developments in urban studies (incorporating cultural studies, cultural geography, architecture, leisure studies and planning) have begun to redress this imbalance in attention. Whilst much of this research is not necessarily undertaken by geographers, the street represents the micro scale of analysis of out-of-home leisure epitomised in London by its colourful street markets (e.g. Brick Lane) and leisure shopping areas (e.g. Carnaby Street, Oxford Street and Regent Street) where tourists, leisure shoppers, workers and residents coalesce. In an event context, streets are also the setting for celebratory carnivals and festivals (e.g. the Notting Hill Carnival in London, Sydney's Mardi Gras (Waitt and Stapel 2011) and the world's largest carnival, Rio's Mardi Gras). The street provides the spatial setting for these transitory and performing events that have a unique identity and sense of place, transformed by these performances. As Duffy (2009: 91) argues 'festivals and spectacles formalize space, time and behavior in ways that distinguish these events from everyday events'. In the tourism and hospitality literature there is also a growing interest in the notion of the street in the 'night-time city' (see the next section, on urban tourism, pp. 198–208) and the performances of night market food vendors in Taiwan (Sun *et al.* 2012) and Singapore (Yeo *et al.* 2012) in its Little India district. The informality of these urban nightscapes focused on the street creates unique cosmopolitan settings for leisure consumption, building upon the notion of public consumption in city spaces and in cafés by Oosterman (1992). Not only does this consumption generate activity for small businesses (Mehta 2011), but the vitality of activity in the street provides sensory stimulation, forms of engagement where urban design can reduce problems and conflict with the car and road traffic.

Social changes since 1945 have also shifted leisure consumption indoors both in a home and commercial setting, to the detriment of the street. Even so, Williams (1995b: 23) argues that people at leisure may use streets in a number of ways. Streets are, of course, a means of access to other recreational resources in the built-up area but they are also recreational resources in themselves. As Page and Connell (2010) argue, Williams (1995b) presents the essential spatial element of the street as a linear structure, where principal users are:

- pedestrians walking from A to B as part of the leisure or to go shopping or to start a commuter journey;
- residents who commence a journey on a bicycle or in a motorised vehicle;

- localised groups as a setting for leisure activity, as in the case of children's play;
- people who use the street for other leisure-related activities such as socialising or as a place to hang out.

At a micro scale, Gehl (1980, cited in Williams 1995b) outlined six distinct activities which occurred within the street based on research undertaken in Canada and Australia, which included (see also Jansen-Verbeke 1989):

- people sitting down or standing around;
- people engaged in domestic chores such as washing the car;
- walking (particularly significant where it can be used as a recreational activity to address the ongoing national epidemic of obesity in many developed countries (Huston *et al.* 2003));
- social interaction;
- children's play;
- movement of traffic within the street.

Many challenges face planners with the street, namely road traffic and the safety/pollution this causes, along with concerns over the design of the environment and personal safety, as outlined in Chapter 2. Planners and town centre managers have sought to re-image the street as a place of vitality despite the rise of out-of-town shopping. Measures to improve the attractiveness of the street as a place to visit and space in which to consume one's leisure time have been aided by improved seating, lighting, better environmental design (i.e. trees and vegetation) and a vibrancy through attractive cafés, shops and increasingly pedestrianisation to add a spatial zone of pedestrian safety. Creating better opportunities for people to dwell, interact, relax and to perform leisure activities through enhancements such as public art have sought to regenerate public leisure spaces such as the street. The geographer has a major contribution to make in understanding how people engage with the street, its central attributes as a leisure space and the social dimensions of consumption in such spaces (Hall 2008b).

activities in the public sector led to debates on the extent to which such activities should be a commercial or municipal enterprise. In fact, no one coherent philosophy has been developed, with individual cities deciding the precise range of activities which should be publicly funded. However, as Veal (1994: 185) poignantly noted, 'urban outdoor recreation takes place primarily in parks, playing fields and playgrounds. The provision of such facilities constitutes the largest single public leisure sector, in terms of expenditure, land allocation and staff and is the longest established.' As a result, the public sector is a key agent in developing urban areas for leisure and recreation. For this reason, it is interesting to focus on

some of the spatial principles used in open space planning in cities.

Open space planning: spatial principles

Within cities, open space can provide a focal point for community interaction (Fleischer and Tsur 2003), a context for conservation, allowing opportunities for meeting recreation needs, provision of visual amenity and a context for enhancing environmental education. To achieve these functions, open space planning needs to be able to integrate such areas into the wider city environment. This is often easier if initially undertaken as part of a master plan. For example, as Tables 5.4 and 5.5 show, for Warsaw this was developed along many of the principles discussed so far in this chapter, with standards for open space provision. At the time the standards were developed Warsaw covered 495 km^2, with a population of over 1.6 million and a population density of 3,258 persons per km^2. Open spaces cover over 50 per cent of the urban area (e.g. agricultural land, open space and open water), with residential areas comprising 27 per cent and open green space at 36.3 per cent of the open space. Warsaw is managed by 11 local authorities and an independent capital city council (Szulczewska and Kaliszuk 2003).

Similarly, in the planning for open space in the Papakura District, Auckland, New Zealand, the planners stated that in the new millennium planning for urban recreation would need to develop a system that could accommodate:

- active leisure areas (e.g. playing fields, sports centres);
- passive leisure areas (e.g. picnic sites, walking/ horse riding trails, cycle routes, grassed areas);
- conservation areas (e.g. nature reserves, nature trails);
- agricultural areas (e.g. allotments and market gardening);
- informal areas (e.g. street reserves and public spaces such as reserves) (after Pentz 2002).

In the development of an open space system Pentz (2002) pointed to the use of three spatial

Table 5.4 The evolution of greenstructure planning in Warsaw

Era	Concepts used in planning at the city level	Key features of Warsaw greenstructure
1916	First spatial development plan	System of existing and planned urban parks
1929	Master plan for Warsaw	Linking of recreational areas of the city centre to the suburbs
1934	Functional Warsaw	Green space to be analysed as a key element of land-use zoning Neighbourhood green spaces established
1950s	Political and social aspects of planning in post-war reconstruction	Cultural entertainment, sport and recreation facilities (i.e. stadiums and parks constructed) Multifunctional centres for leisure and entertainment
1968–1974	System of open spaces in cities	Structural role for open spaces Standards and indicators of green space used 1960s–1980s. (8–15 m^2 greenery per inhabitant) and facilities Hierarchical pattern of recreational provision at neighbourhood, district and city level
1970s onwards	Ecological emphasis and development of the concept of an urban natural system (e.g. 1998 The Study of Preconditions and Directions for Spatial Development of Warsaw and the 2001 Capital City of Warsaw Development Plan)	Environmental protection (e.g. areas for nature)
1990s	Sustainability debate embodied in two competing ideas: the green city and compact city concepts in the wider idea of an ecological city	The green city to protect green structure and the compact city adds to more intensified development in built-up areas, which may lead to the loss of green space The competing demands of developers with the move to a market economy, as green space has been lost to development

Source: developed from Szulczewska and Kaliszuk 2003.

Table 5.5 **Categories of green space in Warsaw in 2001**

Category	%
Parks	17
Forest	36.4
Residential green space	9.8
Allotment garden	8.1
Botanical garden and zoo	0.4
Cemeteries	2.5
Promenades and squares	1.0
Greenery associated with the transport system	6.7
Other greenery	18.2

Source: developed from Szulczewska and Kaliszuk 2003.

concepts around which conservation zones could be incorporated:

* cores;
* corridors, to provide connectivity between elements in the system;
* buffers (e.g. sports fields) between densely developed areas and cores.

In planning for urban leisure facilities, Pentz (2002) identified changing patterns of leisure provision, reflecting many of the issues discussed in Chapter 2. The effect of changing trends has been specific spatial requirements for leisure facility locations, including:

* agglomeration of urban leisure facilities in nodes or centres;
* links between education/social facilities to create shared facilities;
* increased emphasis on capital-intensive facilities such as stadiums;
* rising numbers of spectators at sporting events;
* overcrowding at some sports venues due to common leisure periods (late afternoons and weekends);
* a range of small-scale suburban facilities that no longer meet modern-day needs;
* disparities between small and large urban areas in the funding and development of capital projects;
* gaps in the hierarchy of provision of urban leisure facilities.

In terms of a hierarchy of urban leisure facilities, different standards exist in different countries. Table 5.6 highlights one of two distinct approaches which exist in planning urban leisure and recreation. The first is a more traditional approach, using quantitative measures based on minimum standards regardless of quality, need and locality. In contrast, more innovative approaches are local needs based and less dependent upon the space standards. The latter approach has become a feature of modern recreation planning, with a greater emphasis on 'users', 'market research', 'local culture' and specific target groups with individual needs, including pre-school children, primary school children, teenagers, adults and elderly people. Add to this, gender, ethnicity and the policies towards social inclusion in urban recreation provision, and one begins to understand the complexity of modelling and planning local leisure needs. However, place and

Table 5.6 **Open space standards**

Facility	USA Minimum space (ha)	Total population it should serve
Playlot	0.020	1,000
Playground	1.5	3–5,000
Local park	1	3–10,000
Community park	15	10–50,000
Urban park	45	40,000
Regional park	450	city-wide
Average provision	3–7.5 ha per 1,000 people	

UK: National Playing Fields Association Standards	
Facility	*ha per 1,000 people*
Children's playground	0.68
General park	0.90
Sports ground	1.10
Average provision	4.5

South Africa: Natal	
Facility	*ha per 1,000 people*
Playlots	0.4
Active recreation	1.6
Passive recreation	0.8
Average	2.8

Source: modified from Pentz 2002.

space are vital in the planning of open space and leisure facilities, as individual localities and their populations have divergent needs and wants.

While the use of space standards has the advantage of simplicity, efficiency, equity and uniformity in the planning process, it has many disadvantages, including the lack of fit with the social, economic and resource base of the locality, as well as the lack of spatial specificity in the fit with the local area (e.g. in relation to the catchment, social mix, uses by social groups and need). As a result more innovative

approaches are being proposed, which include a substantial market research element to assess local needs, the use of GIS to match supply with demand and models of provision that are linked to current leisure consumption trends and more sophisticated than simple space standard methods. To illustrate how these issues have been embodied in one large urban area and the implications for the local population, the case study in Box 5.4 highlights many of the basic principles used in urban recreational provision and planning in the London Borough of Newham.

BOX 5.4   THE MANAGEMENT, PLANNING AND PROVISION OF PARKS AND OPEN SPACE IN THE LONDON BOROUGH OF NEWHAM

There has been a comparative neglect of urban parks by leisure and recreation researchers (Veal 2001; Byrne and Wolch 2009; Page and Connell 2010). A number of early notable studies (e.g. Greater London Council 1968; Balmer 1971; Bowler and Strachan 1976) have been expanded in terms of the locations examined and range of themes reviewed. Previous studies of urban park use indicated that their catchments were localised and for informal, fulfilling, short-distance and short-stay recreational needs (Patmore 1983), and this continues to be valid, as subsequent studies confirm.

The largest single area of research on urban parks has focused on accessibility (Harrison 1983) and behavioural-type studies, exemplified by Burgess *et al.* (1988a, 1988b, 1988c). In addition, Gregory (1988) and Grahn (1991) examined the attitudes and psychological constructs of different socio-economic groups using parks and open spaces, while Grocott (1990) considered the role of public participation in the design and creation of community parks. There has also been a growing interest in the management issues associated with urban parks, particularly the state of green space at a national level, as discussed in Chapter 3 and, by Reeves (2000), where budget cuts in green space management have occurred since the early 1970s despite green space comprising 13.5 per cent of the developed land in England and Wales. One major development which has altered the philosophy and delivery of leisure services in local authorities concerns the management of services through a unified 'Leisure Services Department'. These departments have created a new organisational structure for leisure service provision to accommodate the additional administrative functions created by the Local Government Act 1988. However, critics have argued that this organisational structure has contributed to fragmentation and poor integration in service provision, owing to the increased bureaucracy and centralised management of service provision by administrators rather than practitioners, who had daily contact with clients.

Barber (1991) examined the significance of management plans of parks and the role of local accountability, identifying individual park managers as the most effective personnel to ensure that the delivery of park-based services contributed to the quality of life in the local area, moving away from the principle of space standard planning at a regional level, with greater emphasis needed at the community level.

However, being responsive to local needs has an economic cost and this may not always be compatible with the pursuit of efficiency in service provision. G. Morgan (1991) acknowledged the growing importance of consumer orientation in the planning and management process for parks and open spaces, to ensure that community needs and desires were adequately considered. The increased use of attitude surveys and monitoring of urban park planning and management by local authorities is a direct response to the new ethos pervading public service provision. Against this background, attention now turns to London in terms of open space provision and the London Borough of Newham as a context in which to understand the role of spatial analysis.

Urban park and open space provision in London

Research on recreation and leisure in London has hitherto attracted little interest at a city-wide level following the abolition of the Greater London Council (GLC) in 1986 and its various replacement bodies prior to the formation of the Greater London Authority. After 1986 each London borough's Unitary Development Plan was the framework for the formulation of policies to guide the provision of parks and open spaces. Planning advice from the London Planning Advisory Committee (LPAC) has continued with many of the former GLC leisure planning principles, although the draft London Plan (http://www.london.gov.uk/) launched in June 2002 was a spatial development strategy for London and seeks to maintain strategic open spaces in the capital – particularly London's green belt, Metropolitan Open Land and green corridors or chains. These designations were incorporated into most London boroughs' leisure and recreation plans with the Unitary Development Plans (UDPs). Since 2011, the London Plan produced by the Greater London Authority represents the overall regional spatial strategy for London and outlines the broad planning principles it embraces for public open space categories (see Table 5.7). At the local level, London boroughs have been required to prepare Local Development Frameworks, replacing the previous UDPs. Major studies of London's urban geography and expanding service sector (e.g. Hoggart and Green 1991) fail to acknowledge the significance of leisure service provision, although R. Bennett (1991) did examine the London boroughs' statutory responsibility for leisure and recreation provision. The scale and nature of open space provision in London was set out in the Greater London Development Plan (Greater London Council 1969).

Table 5.1 outlined the hierarchy of parks and open space provision envisaged in the late 1980s within the revised Greater London Development Plan (see Nicholls 2001 for a North American illustration of this hierarchy). This is still very much a space standard driven approach. Provision was based on a hierarchical principle, with different parks fulfilling various functions according to their size and distance from the users' home. The concept of variety in park supply was to be achieved by the diversity of functions offered by parks in the capital, emphasising the social principle that parks of equal status were to be accessible to all sections of London's population. According to Burgess et al. (1988a), research in Greenwich questioned the suitability of a hierarchical system of park provision at the local area level, arguing that local communities did not recognise parks in terms of the differing functions that the GLC park hierarchy assigned to them. They claimed that most people in their survey felt that open spaces closest to their home failed to meet their leisure needs. This reinforces why some local authorities, such as Newham in East London, have recognised that improving accessibility and use among all sections of the population is an important objective.

Table 5.7 **Public open space categorisation**

Open space categorisation	Size guideline	Distances from homes
Regional parks Large areas, corridors or networks of open space, the majority of which will be publicly accessible and provide a range of facilities and features offering recreational, ecological, landscape, cultural or green infrastructure benefits; offer a combination of facilities and features that are unique within London, are readily accessible by public transport and are managed to meet best practice quality standards	400 ha	3.2–8 km
Metropolitan parks Large areas of open space that provide a similar range of benefits to regional parks and offer a combination of facilities at a sub-regional level, are readily accessible by public transport and are managed to meet best practice quality standards	60 ha	3.2 km
District parks Large areas of open space that provide a landscape setting with a variety of natural features, providing a wide range of activities, including outdoor sports facilities and playing fields, children's play for different age groups and informal recreation pursuits	20 ha	1.2 km
Local parks and open spaces Providing for court games, children's play, sitting-out areas and nature conservation areas	2 ha	400 m
Small open spaces Gardens, sitting-out areas, children's play spaces or other areas of a specialist nature, including nature conservation areas	Under 2 ha	Less than 400 m
Pocket parks Small areas of open space that provide natural surfaces and shaded areas for informal play and passive recreation and that sometimes have seating and play equipment	Under 0.4 ha	Less than 400 m
Linear open spaces Open spaces and towpaths alongside the Thames, canals and other water-ways, paths, disused railways, nature conservation areas, and other routes that provide opportunities for informal recreation; often characterised by features or attractive areas which are not fully accessible to the public but contribute to the enjoyment of the space	Variable	Wherever feasible

Source: Greater London Authority 2011: 232.

The London Borough of Newham

Newham is an east London borough (http://www.newham.gov.uk/) created in the 1960s from the amalgamation of two former town councils – West Ham and East Ham. The area developed in the Victorian and Edwardian periods, with the extension of the London Underground, the creation of the Royal Docks and other service/utilities (e.g. the Beckton Gas Works, Beckton Sewage Works and Railway Yards at West

Ham and Stratford) and manufacturing activities (e.g. Tate and Lyle in Silvertown). The population reached a peak of 249,000 in 1949, declining in the 1980s due to out-migration with the closure of the docks and other employers. In 1991, the population was 212,170, and it had risen to 236,000 in 2001 and over 300,000 in 2011. Newham is one of London's largest boroughs, with a very diverse ethnic population. Despite gentrification in pockets of London Docklands and around Stratford, the London Borough of Newham's (LBN) Unitary Development Plan (UDP) of 2001 stated that the area is one of the most deprived areas in the UK, using the government's own deprivation indices, a feature apparent in geographies of London (Hoggart and Green 1991). Although Newham is an outer London borough, it has many inner city characteristics, which has led it to consider being classified as part of inner London. In 2012, the borough hosted the Olympic Games, benefiting from the regeneration programme which preceded the Games, although the borough's main open spaces and parks were created in the Victorian and Edwardian periods, with notable additions in the inter-war and post-war period. In 1991, the proportion of the borough deemed to be parks/open space was 180 ha, or 4.9 per cent of the total area of the borough. By 2001, this had increased to 253 ha (6.95 per cent of the borough) and in 2012 it had increased to 479 ha, reflecting the creation of new sites/improvements to existing sites as development has occurred in the south and north of the borough, often as a condition of planning consent for development alongside the Olympic-led regeneration in the Lea Valley.

Newham Council undertakes a number of roles in leisure service provision (e.g. sports centres, libraries, arts and cultural services, parks and open space provision and tourism). Prior to 2011, the UDP was guided by the borough's Leisure Development strategy and London-wide strategies that have to be accommodated at a local level. In planning terms, the LBN established policies in its UDP to guide open space provision which are now embodied in the Local Development Framework – Newham 2027 – Planning Newham – the Core Strategy. Prior to 2011, two of its key objectives for increasing open space provision were to incorporate its needs into larger urban regeneration plans for the Stratford railyards area adjacent to the new Channel Tunnel rail terminal and the redevelopment of the Beckton Gas Works site, the former achieved by the Olympic Park.

The council has a number of open space designations: green belt land to the north of the borough (for example Wanstead Flats and the City of London Cemetery); Metropolitan Open Land; sites of borough-wide importance; sites of local importance and green corridors, complemented by urban parks (Archer and Yarman 1991). Urban parks form one of the most widely available forms of open space either as large multipurpose parks or smaller community-based recreation grounds.

What is notable in the LBN 1993 and 2001 UDP is the lack of open and green space, with Newham among the lowest of London borough's for green space and park provision. The LBN, utilising the National Playing Fields Association Standard of 2.43 ha of playing space per 1,000 population, observed that even with new developments. By 2012, the LBN Core Strategy parks deficiency mapping began to use individual address points to identify populated areas (see concentrations of dots on the map in Figure 5.3), which used coverage from parks in adjacent local authorities to meet local leisure needs. Clearly, while Figures 5.4a–5.4d still remain valid for many areas, changes to planning policy guidelines mean some park types can project an 800 m catchment instead of 400 m (although they have not become any more accessible as a result) by being able to spatially extend access into other boroughs to meet local park demand. In 2012, the LBN was still short of national standards of provision. In 2001 this provision was only 1.1 ha per 1,000 population and in 2012 it was 1.99 ha, illustrating the progress towards the national target. The

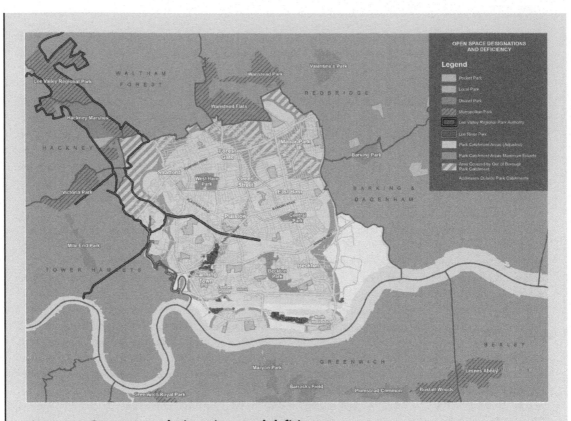

Figure 5.3 Open space designations and deficiency

Source: London Borough of Newham Geospatial Team (2012) Core Strategy, http://www.newham.gov.uk/ Pages/ServiceChild/Planning-policy-documents.aspx, reproduced with kind permission of the London Borough of Newham.

spatial distribution of similar deficiencies in park provision are shown in Figure 5.4c, which shows that in 2001 large areas of the borough fell short of access to local parks (i.e. where the population is more than 400 metres from any park area over 2 ha). Similarly, the extent of area which is more than 200 metres from an equipped children's play space is also notable (Figure 5.4b). But the 2001 UDP did acknowledge that by 2006 a further 12 ha of play space would be provided. This under-provision is reflected in areas needing additional space, but the UDP recognised that the absence of sites may make this difficult. A study by Page *et al.* (1994) examined the user groups within the hierarchy of open spaces in Newham and confirmed many of the assumptions on park use, namely:

- the overwhelming pattern of use was local in relation to the catchment area;
- parks perform an important social role, being an accessible leisure resource regardless of gender, race, age and disability;
- many concerns related to conflicts between dog owners and non-dog owners emerged in the management of park areas;

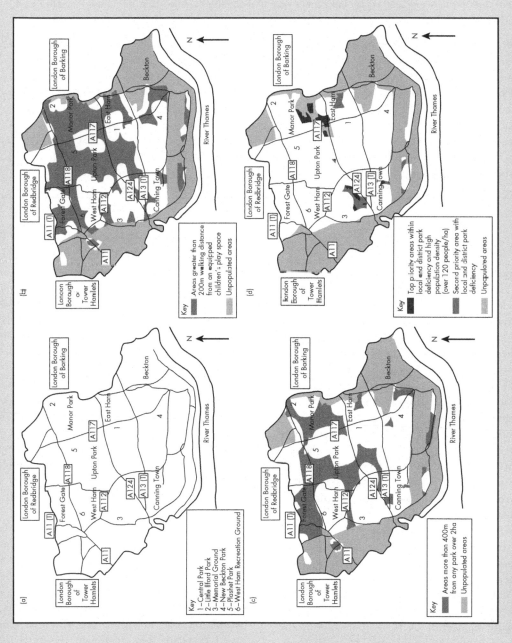

Figure 5.4 London Borough of Newham maps: (a) Location of urban parks in the London Borough of Newham; (b) Children's play space deficiency; (c) Areas of local park deficiency; (d) Priority areas for tackling open space deficiency

- passive leisure pursuits dominated park use;
- local park plans were seen as an innovative way of matching user needs to the management of parks and open spaces.

Therefore while parks and open spaces may not be as fashionable as capital-intensive leisure facilities, they are operated on a non-commercial basis and offer access to the entire population. Their value within the urban environment should be given greater recognition as they contribute to the wider public good of metropolitan populations compared with more specialised and targeted sport and leisure facilities. It is clear that further research is needed to establish how local leisure needs can be met in terms of park provision, so that park management plans focus attention on local areas and communities. Urban parks and open spaces are an important sustainable leisure resource which can accommodate multiple uses, being accessible to local communities who may not have access to countryside areas. They are an integral feature of the urban landscape and assume an important part in the daily lives of local communities.

Urban tourism

The second half of this chapter examines the concept of urban tourism, reviewing the principal contributions towards its recognition as a tourism phenomenon worthy of study, and it also emphasises the scope and range of environments classified as urban destinations, together with some of the approaches towards its analysis. It then considers a framework for the analysis of the tourist's experience of urban tourism, which is followed by a discussion of key aspects of urban tourist behaviour: where do urban tourists go in urban areas, what activities do they undertake, how do they perceive these places and learn about the spatial attributes of the locality, and how is this reflected in their patterns of behaviour? Having reviewed these features, the chapter concludes with a discussion of service quality issues for urban tourism.

Ashworth's (1989) seminal study of urban tourism acknowledges that a double neglect occurred in the 1980s and earlier with respect to urban tourism. Those interested in the study of tourism 'have tended to neglect the urban context in which much of it is set, while those interested in urban studies . . . have been equally neglectful of the importance of the tourist function of cities' (Ashworth 1989: 33). However, since then the field has changed rapidly. Indeed Ashworth and Page (2011) highlighted that there are now over a thousand research articles on urban

tourism. Ashworth and Page (2011: 1–2) shifted the discussion from the neglect thesis, arguing that a series of strange paradoxes characterise urban tourism:

1   Urban tourism is an extremely important, worldwide form of tourism. It has received a disproportionately small amount of attention from scholars of either tourism or the city, particularly in linking theoretical research to Tourism Studies more generally. Consequently, despite its significance urban tourism has remained only imprecisely defined and vaguely demarcated, with little development of a systematic structure of understanding.
2   Tourists visit cities for many purposes. The cities that accommodate most tourists are large multifunctional entities into which tourists can be effortlessly absorbed and thus become to a large extent economically and physically invisible.
3   Tourists make an intensive use of many urban facilities and services but little of the city has been created specifically for tourist use.
4   Tourism can contribute substantial economic benefits to cities but the cities whose economies are the most dependent upon tourism are likely to benefit the least. It is the cities with a large and varied economic base that gain the most from tourism but are the least dependent on it.
5   Thus, ultimately, and from a number of directions, we arrive at the critical asymmetry in the

relationship between the tourist and the city, which has many implications for policy and management. The tourism industry clearly needs the varied, flexible and accessible tourism products that cities provide; it is by no means so clear that cities need tourism.

Ashworth and Page (2011) point to the lack of theoretical engagement by tourism researchers, with debates in urban studies as well as noting that many geographers who engage in urban studies research ignore tourism phenomena in spite of the obvious importance of cities as tourist places. They point to key research themes that assist in a better understanding of urban tourism, including: urbanisation, particularly the wider development of cities in middle and low income countries; and globalisation and world cities, particularly the role of cities as business centres and the world city hierarchy.

Within cities the processes of change arising from globalisation are creating internal micro-geographies within which tourism may feature. In fact Pacione (2004) argues that in a postmodern society the emergence of the cultural industries in world cities may be blurring the distinction of production and consumption, leading to:

- re-globalisation and urban tourism, where globalisation is a continuous process in which capital and political decision-makers are constantly repackaging and re-presenting cities as places to visit (and live and work in);
- rescaling and globalisation, where political processes are challenging the conventional notion of the nation state so localities and regions can take advantage of globalisation benefits;
- internal geographies of tourism in cities predicated on 'why tourists visit cities', 'how they use cities'.
- Ashworth and Page (2011) characterised tourist use of cities around the following themes:
  - *selectivity*, where visitors only make use of a small element of the city's tourist offer;
  - *rapidity*, where urban tourists tend to consume cities rapidly, compounded by short stays (i.e measured in hours in small cities and days in large cities) (also see UNWTO 2012b);

- *repetition*, where urban tourists are unlikely to be repeat visitors;
- *capriciousness*, being very susceptible to shifts in trends and tastes.

Approaches to urban tourism: geographical analysis

To understand how research on urban tourism has developed distinctive approaches and methodologies, one needs to recognise why tourists seek urban tourism experiences. Shaw and Williams (1994) argue that urban areas offer geographical concentration of facilities and attractions that are conveniently located to meet both visitor and resident needs alike. But the diversity and variety among urban tourist destinations have led researchers to examine the extent to which they display unique and similar features. Shaw and Williams (1994) identify three approaches:

- the diversity of urban areas means that their size, function, location and history contribute to their uniqueness;
- towns and cities are multifunctional areas, meaning that they simultaneously provide various functions for different groups of users;
- the tourist functions of towns and cities are rarely produced or consumed solely by tourists, given the variety of user groups in urban areas.

Ashworth (1992a) conceptualises urban tourism by identifying three approaches towards its analysis, where researchers have focused on

- the supply of tourism facilities in urban areas, involving inventories (e.g. the spatial distribution of accommodation, entertainment complexes and tourist-related services), where urban ecological models have been used; the facility approach has also been used to identify the tourism product offered by destinations;
- the demand generated by urban tourists, to examine how many people visit urban areas, why they choose to visit and their patterns of behaviour, perception and expectations in relation to their visit;

- perspectives of urban tourism policy, where the public sector (e.g. planners) and private sector agencies have undertaken or commissioned research to investigate specific issues related to their own interests in urban tourism.

A limited number of attempts to interpret urban tourism theoretically can be traced to Mullins (1991) and Roche (1992), and other studies are reviewed by Ashworth and Page (2011). While these studies do not have a direct bearing on attempts to influence or affect the tourist experience of towns and cities, their importance should not be neglected in wider reviews of urban tourism: they offer explanations of the sudden desire of many towns and cities with a declining industrial base to look towards service sector activities such as tourism. Such studies examine urban tourism in the context of changes in post-industrial society and the relationship with structural changes in the mode of capitalist production. In other words, both studies question the types of process now shaping the operation and development of tourism in post-industrial cities, and the implications for public sector tourism and leisure policy. One outcome of such research is that it highlights the role of the state,

especially local government, in seeking to develop service industries based on tourism and leisure production and consumption in urban areas, as a response to economic restructuring, which has often led to employment loss in the locality. It also illustrates the significance of place-marketing in urban tourism promotion (Ashworth and Voogd 1990a, 1990b; Gold and Ward 1994; Gold and Gold 1995; Hall 1997b) as destinations seek to reinvent and redefine themselves in the market for cultural and heritage tourism (Houinen 1995; Judd 1995; Bramwell and Rawding 1996; Chang *et al*. 1996; Schofield 1996; Dahles 1998; Hall and McArthur 1998; Timothy 2011).

Mullins' (1991) concept of tourism urbanisation is also useful as it assists in developing the following typology of urban tourist destinations:

- capital cities;
- metropolitan centres, walled historic cities and small fortress cities;
- large historic cities;
- inner city areas;
- revitalised waterfront areas;
- industrial cities;
- seaside resorts and winter sport resorts;

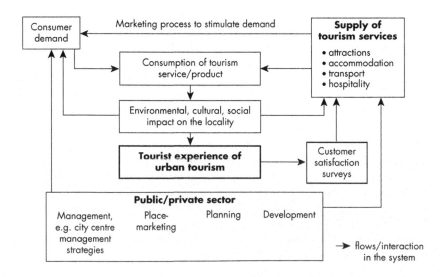

Figure 5.5 A systems approach to urban tourism
Source: Page and Hall (2003).

- purpose-built integrated tourist resorts;
- tourist-entertainment complexes;
- specialised tourist service centres;
- cultural/art cities (after Page 1995b: 17).

This typology illustrates the diversity of destinations which provide an urban context for tourist visits, and highlights the problem of deriving generalisations from individual case studies without a suitable conceptual framework. Page and Hall (2003) provide a framework for understanding the complexity of urban tourism, as shown in Figure 5.5, which identifies many of the interrelationships between the supply, demand and external factors.

Ashworth and Page (2011) posed the question: 'Is there a distinct urban geography of tourism?' They concluded that research in the last 20 years by geographers has begun to advance our understanding, albeit in a partial manner as the wider themes of the urban tourist, the urban tourism industry and planning and management. Even so, few studies have derived wider generalisations and urban services and space is too multifunctional to identify a distinctive urban geography of tourism.

Interpreting urban tourism: from concepts to theoretically informed analysis

Page and Hall (2003) point to the growing geographical research on postmodernism (e.g. Dear 1994, 1999; Dear and Flusty 1999) to identify the defining characteristics of the postmodern city. These characteristics have highlighted the significance of sociological literature in the arising urban places and spaces used to produce and consume urban tourism. The postmodern era has been characterised by cultural transformations which have a spatiality, epitomised by the cultural industries that embody the arts, leisure and tourism. Dear and Flusty (1998) coined a number of buzz words to describe the postmodern urbanscape, including:

- *privatopia*, an edge city residential form and housing development on the periphery;

- *cultures of heteropolis*, where cultural diversity and social polarity arise from the combined processes of racism, structural inequality, homelessness and social unrest;
- *the city as a theme park*, embodied in Hannigan's (1998) *Fantasy City*;
- *the fortified city*, where residents' concerns with safety, fear and crime have created 'fortified cells of affluence' juxtaposed with 'places of terror', where police seek to try and control crime;
- *interdictory space*, where spaces within cities exclude people through their activities and design (i.e. shopping malls as private spaces that have replaced high streets as public spaces).

In the postmodern city, Dear and Flusty (1998: 65) argued that the concentric ring structure of the Chicago School 'was essentially a concept of the city as an organic accretion around a central, organising core. Instead, we have identified a postmodern urban process in which the urban periphery organises the centre within the context of a globalising capitalium.' The urban core is no longer the defining and controlling influence upon development, although ironically strengthening of the urban core is often a justification for encouraging tourism development (Hall 2005a). Instead, Dear and Flusty (1998) argued that a 'Keno' capitalism had developed where a collage of non-contiguous consumption-oriented spaces develop. The process of urbanisation and development is far more complex in shaping tourism and leisure spaces. As a result, Page and Hall (2003) produce a model of tourism in the postmodern city where capital defines the nature, form and extent of consumption experiences. The tourism and leisure landscapes that emerge are part of a mosaic of social and cultural layers that add diversity to the urban fabric. The visitor may not easily recognise the tourist city as a distinct entity, since the patchwork of consumption experiences is often grouped into zones.

Figure 5.6a identifies a series of processes at work, including gentrification, interconnected zones of tourism and leisure where the conventional downtown area is rivalled by more space-extensive out-of-town areas, such as Garreau's (1991) *Edge City* and

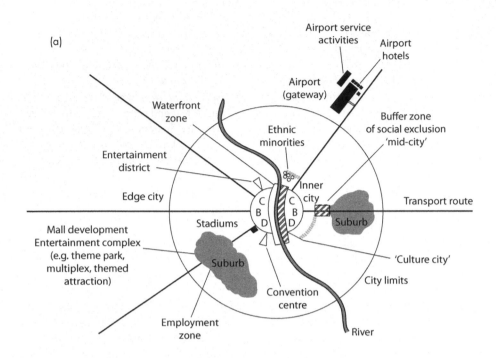

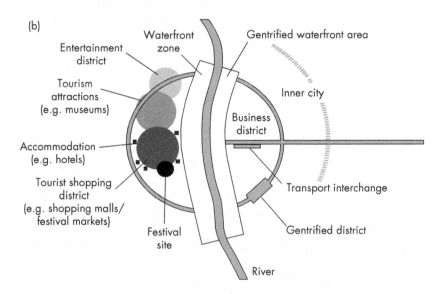

Figure 5.6 (a) Tourism, leisure and the postmodern city (b) Tourism, leisure and the postmodern city: the inner city dimension

Source: Page and Hall (2003).

Hannigan's (1998) *Fantasy City* (e.g. a theme park/ entertainment zone). These developments further accentuate social exclusion and social polarity as Figure 5.6b suggests, as neighbourhoods are cleared by gentrification and marginalised by the emergence of consumption-oriented activities in former housing areas. This contributes to the development of what Roche (2000) called the 'new urban tourism', based on the consumption of places in a post-industrial society, which Meethan points to as involving

> the visual consumption of signs and increasingly, simulacra and staged events in which urban townscapes are transformed into aestheticised spaces of entertainment and pleasure . . . within these places of consumption . . . a variety of activities can be pursued, such as promenading, eating, drinking, watching staged events and street entertainment and visually appreciating heritage and culture of place.
>
> (Meethan 1996: 324)

For this reason, it is pertinent to focus on the concept of the 'tourist experience of urban tourism' as a framework to assess some of the experiential aspects of this phenomenon.

The tourist experience of urban tourism

There is a growing literature on tourist satisfaction (e.g. Ryan 1995) and what constitutes the experiential aspects of a tourist visit to a locality. In the context of urban tourism, the innovative research by Graefe and Vaske (1987) offers a number of important insights as well as a useful framework. Graefe and Vaske (1987) acknowledge that the 'tourist experience' is a useful term to identify the experience of an individual, which may be affected 'by individual, environmental, situational and personality-related factors as well as the degree of communication with other people. It is the outcome which researchers and the tourism industry constantly evaluate to establish

if the actual experience met the tourist's expectations' (Page 1995a: 24). Operationalising such a concept may prove difficult in view of the complex array of factors which may affect the visitor experience (Table 5.8) (Haywood and Muller 1988; Page and Hall 2003; Le-Klähn *et al.* 2014).

For example, where levels of overcrowding occur at major tourist sites (e.g. Canterbury, Venice, St Paul's Cathedral, London and the Tower of London), this can have a negative effect on visitors who have a low tolerance threshold for overcrowding at major tourist sites. Yet conversely, other visitors may be less affected by use levels, thereby illustrating the problem within tourism motivation research – predicting tourists' behaviour and their responses to particular situations. In fact Graefe and Vaske (1987: 394) argue that 'the effects of increasing use levels on the recreation/tourist experience can be explained only partially . . . as a function of use level'. Therefore, the individual

Table 5.8 Factors to consider in evaluating the urban tourism experience

- Weather conditions at the time of visit
- Standard and quality of accommodation available
- The cleanliness and upkeep of the city
- The city's aesthetic value (i.e. its setting and beauty)
- Tourists' personal safety from crime
- Accessibility of attractions and points of interest in the city
- Extent to which local people welcome visitors in a warm manner
- Ability of tourism employees to speak foreign languages
- Availability of signage
- Range of cultural and artistic amenities
- Ambience of the city environment as a place to walk around
- Level of crowding and congestion
- Range of night-life and entertainment available
- Range of restaurants and eating establishments in the city
- Pleasurability of leisure shopping
- Price levels of goods and services in the city
- Level of helpfulness among local people
- Adequacy of emergency medical care
- Quality of public transport

Source: modified from Page and Hall 2003.

BOX 5.5   TOURISM IN CAPITAL CITIES

Capital cities represent a special case of urban tourism (Hall 2002; Maitland and Ritchie 2007; Maitland 2012). As Canada's National Capital Commission (NCC) (2000b: 9) observed, 'The combination of political, cultural, symbolic and administrative functions is unique to national capitals'. The capital functions as 'the political centre and symbolic heart of the country. It is the site of crucial political decision-making, yet it is also a setting for the nation's culture and history, where the past is highlighted, the present displayed and the future imagined.' Although such statements are obviously significant in political and cultural terms the wider significance of capital city status for tourism has been grossly under-researched and, perhaps, under-appreciated (Taylor *et al.* 1993; Hall 2000a, 2002; Pearce 2007; Maitland and Ritchie 2007). Nevertheless, capital status is important. As capitals provide an administrative and political base of government operations there will therefore be spin-off effects for business travel in terms of both those who work in the capital and those who are seeking to lobby government or influence decisions. In addition to business-related travel, capital cities are also significant for tourism because of their cultural, heritage and symbolic roles. They are frequently home to some of the major national cultural institutions while also tending to have a significant wider role in the portrayal, preservation and promotion of national heritage and which showcase national culture (Therborn 1996). Such a concentration of arts and cultural institutions will therefore have implications for the travel and activity behaviour of culturally interested tourists as well as contributing to the image of a city as a whole. If capital status is lost it can have a significant affect on visitor numbers, as in the case of the transfer of the German national capital from Bonn to Berlin after the reunification of Germany, as a result of which Berlin has witnessed a dramatic increase in overnight stays and Bonn a decline.

The use of the notion of a capital in terms of branding and culture is significant for tourism not only regarding place promotion but also for attracting high yielding cultural tourists. Indeed, given the growth of place-marketing in an increasingly competitive global economic environment such a development is logical in terms of branding places and place competition. However, for the purpose of this discussion the notion of a capital is related primarily to political, administrative and symbolic functions which operate at a national or provincial level. Indeed, as Dubé and Gordon (2000: 6) observed, 'Planning for cities that include a seat of government often involves political and symbolic concerns that are different from those of other urban areas'. The historical development of capital cities may also provide them with a significant transport gateway or hub function, e.g. London and Paris.

A good example of the relationship between capital city status and tourism is Ottawa in Canada, which was declared the capital of the new Canadian Confederation in 1867. Tourism now contributes well over CAN$1 billion to the Ottawa region economy and makes a substantial contribution to employment as well as government taxes. Ottawa is an excellent example of Gottmann's (1983) observation that 'capital cities often act as hinges between different regions of a country'. Ottawa lies at the border between French and English speaking Canada, a history of interaction between labour and capital, as well as being at a location where different ecological regions also coincide (NCC 1999). There are a number of primary benefits of visiting Ottawa that are unique to a capital city. In a survey conducted in 1991 85 per cent of respondents agreed that it was a good way for young people to learn about their country, while the opportunity to learn about Canada was cited as important by 57 per cent of respondents (NCC 1991). Indeed, a unique characteristic that is shared among all visitors to Ottawa Hull is 'the desire to visit national cultural institutions and physical landmarks that symbolize and reflect all of Canada' (NCC 1991: v):

> The function of a national cultural institution (e.g., museum) is to display, protect and explain past, present and future national phenomena and human achievements. National cultural institutions are also used to communicate social, cultural, political, scientific, technical, or other knowledge through various media.
>
> (NCC 1999: 63)

The main avenue for Canadian government actions to reinforce the role of Ottawa's capital city status is the National Capital Commission, which has the mission 'To create pride and unity through Canada's Capital Region' (NCC 2000a: 5). Established in 1959, the NCC is a Crown corporation governed by a national board of directors (the Commission) and reports to the Canadian Parliament through the Minister of Canadian Heritage. The NCC is not primarily a tourist organisation, but its actions and policies over the years have created substantial tourism resources for the region in the form of attractions as well as imaging the city through its promotional and marketing campaigns. The significance of the NCC for tourism cannot be overstated. As Tunbridge observed,

> In an unmanaged state Ottawa's tourism resource would be modest: a physical environment recreationally attractive, but unexceptional in Canada; a historic ambience with distinctive elements, but weak by international standards; and an overall cultural environment which was in the 1960s the butt of jests . . . and a non-place to most further afield.
>
> (Tunbridge 1998: 95)

According to the NCC, it 'exists to promote national pride through the creation of a great capital for an increasingly diverse body of Canadians' (2000a: 8). A key focus of achieving its strategic goals since the early 1990s has been the theme of renewal and the development of core area vision for the National Capital Region (NCR). In order to achieve its goals it has fostered the redevelopment of the By Ward Market heritage neighbourhood (see also Tunbridge 2000; Picton 2010) and continues to try and regenerate the Sparks Street mall area one block from Parliament Hill. In addition, the NCC has developed a series of parkways in the Ottawa region that have an historic role as recreational and leisure corridors for motorists and cyclists. The parkways also link into the transitway system and act as 'gateways' to the NCR which remain, 'influencing the perception of visitors and to communicating the image and landscape of the Capital' (NCC 1998: 52) (see also Amati and Taylor 2010).

tourist's ability to tolerate the behaviour of other people, level of use, the social situation and the context of the activity are all important determinants of the actual outcome. Thus, evaluating the quality of the tourist experience is a complex process which may require careful consideration of the factors motivating a visit (i.e. how tourists' perception of urban areas makes them predisposed to visit particular places), their actual patterns of activity and the extent to which the expectations associated with their perceptions are matched in reality (Page 1995a: 25). For this reason, attention now turns to some of the experiential aspects of urban tourists' visits and the significance of behavioural issues influencing visitor satisfaction. In view of the diversity of tourists visiting urban areas, it is useful to define the market for urban tourism.

The urban tourism market: data sources

Identifying the scale, volume and different markets for urban tourism remains a perennial problem for researchers. Urban tourism is a major economic activity in many of the world's capital cities, but identifying the tourism markets in each area is problematic. Page (1995a) provides a detailed assessment of the principal international data sources on urban tourism, reviewing statistics published by the World Tourism Organization and the OECD. Such data sources commonly employ the domestic and international tourist use of accommodation as one measure of the scale of tourism activity. In the context of urban tourism, they require researchers to have an understanding of spatial distribution of tourist accommodation in each country to identify the scale and distribution of tourist visits. In countries where the majority of accommodation is urban based, such statistics may provide preliminary sources of data for research. While this may be relevant for certain categories of tourist (e.g. business travellers and holidaymakers), those visitors staying with friends and relatives within an urban environment would not be included in the statistics. Cockerell (1997) recognised that data on urban-based business travel were notoriously difficult to monitor, since it was often associated with a range of non-tourism functions and more specific activities located in towns and cities due to their central place functions in regions and countries, notably the meetings, incentives, conferences and exhibitions (MICE) market. The specialist facilities and infrastructure required for such business are frequently located in urban areas to make use of complementary facilities such as

accommodation, transport hubs (i.e. airports) and the wider range of tourist attractions to provide the wider context for MICE venues.

Within a European context, Cockerell (1997) indicated that comparative data on urban tourism rarely exists due to the different survey methodologies, sampling techniques and inconsistency in the use of terminology or lack of agreement on what an urban tourist is. For example, many European surveys do not consider the day trip or excursion market as a pure form of urban tourism, and therefore exclude them from surveys. Cockerell (1997) pointed to the only pan-European data source – *The European Travel Monitor* (ETM). The section on city trips refers only to the holiday sector, ignoring business and VFR travel, and including only those international trips involving a minimum stay of one night. A number of other data sources, including academic studies (e.g. Mazanec 1997; Mazanec and Wöber 2010) and research institutes in Paris, namely the Institut National de la Recherche sur les Transports et leur Sécurité (INRETS), and Venice, the Centro Internazionale di Studi sull'Economica Turistica (CISET), have generated research data on urban tourism demand.

Even where statistics can be used, they provide only a preliminary assessment of scale and volume, and more detailed sources are needed to assess specific markets for urban tourism. For example, Page (1995a) reviews the different market segmentation techniques used by marketing researchers to analyse the tourism market for urban areas, which helps one to understand the types of visitors and motives for visiting urban destinations. According to Blank and Petkovich (1980), the motives for visiting urban areas can be classified as:

- visiting friends and relatives;
- outdoor recreation activities business/convention visitation;
- entertainment and sightseeing activities;
- personal reasons;
- shopping;
- other factors.

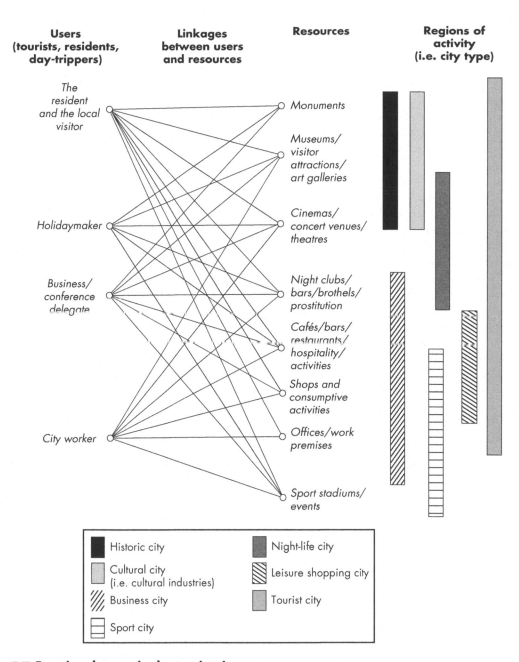

Figure 5.7 Functional areas in the tourist city

Source: modified and developed from Burtenshaw et al. 1991.

In contrast, Page (1995a: 48) identified a broader range of motivations for visiting urban areas:

• visiting friends and relatives;
• business travel;
• conference and exhibition attendance;
• educational reasons;
• cultural and heritage tourism;
• religious travel (e.g. pilgrimages);
• hallmark events attendance;
• leisure shopping.

However, Jansen-Verbeke (1986) does point to the methodological problem of distinguishing between the different users of the tourist city. For example, Burtenshaw *et al.* (1991) discuss the concept of functional areas within the city, where different visitors seek certain attributes for their city visit (e.g. the historic city, the culture city, the night-life city, the shopping city and the tourist city) and no one group has a monopoly over its use (Figure 5.7 shows the idea of such functional areas as extended by Page and Hall 2003). In other words, residents of the city and its hinterland, visitors and workers all use the resources within the tourist city, but some user groups identify with certain areas more than others. Thus, the tourist city is a multifunctional area, which complicates attempts to identify a definitive classification of users and the areas/facilities they visit.

Ashworth and Tunbridge (1990) prefer to approach the market for urban tourism from the perspective of the consumers' motives, focusing on the purchasing intent of users, their attitudes, opinions and interests for specific urban tourism products. The most important distinction they make is between use/non-use of tourism resources, leading them to identify international users (who are motivated by the character of the city) and incidental users (who view the character of the city as irrelevant to their use). This twofold typology is used by Ashworth and Tunbridge (1990) to identify four specific types of users:

• intentional users from outside the city-region (e.g. holidaymakers and heritage tourists);

• intentional users from inside the city-region (e.g. those using recreational and entertainment facilities – recreating residents);
• incidental users from outside the city-region (e.g. business and conference/exhibition tourists and those on family visits – non-recreating visitors);
• incidental users from inside the city-region (e.g. residents going about their daily activities – non-recreating residents).

Such an approach recognises the significance of attitudes and the use made of the city and services rather than the geographical origin of the visitor as the starting point for analysis. Although the practical problem with such an approach is that tourists tend to cite one main motive for visiting a city, any destination is likely to have a variety of user groups. For example, a recent review of urban tourism in China (UNWTO 2012c) focusing on its top tourism cities (Figure 5.8) identified the scale of demand in Beijing, with a 16.3 million population and receiving 140 million domestic tourists whose main purpose for visiting was: sightseeing (48 per cent); vocational reasons (31.2 per cent); VFR (13.8 per cent); business tourism (0.5 per cent); conference tourism (3.2 per cent); pilgrimage (0.8 per cent); as part of an exchange (1 per cent); other reasons (0.9 per cent). This illustrates the uniqueness of the visitor market in different cities and the problem of deriving generalisations. But this does confirm the multi-use hypothesis advanced by Ashworth and Tunbridge (1990), which was subsequently developed in a geographical context by Getz (1993a).

Having outlined some of the methodological issues associated with assessing the market for urban tourism, attention now turns to the behavioural issues associated with the analysis of tourist visits to urban areas.

Urban tourism: behavioural issues

Any assessment of urban tourist activities, patterns and perceptions of urban locations will be influenced by the supply of services, attractions and facilities

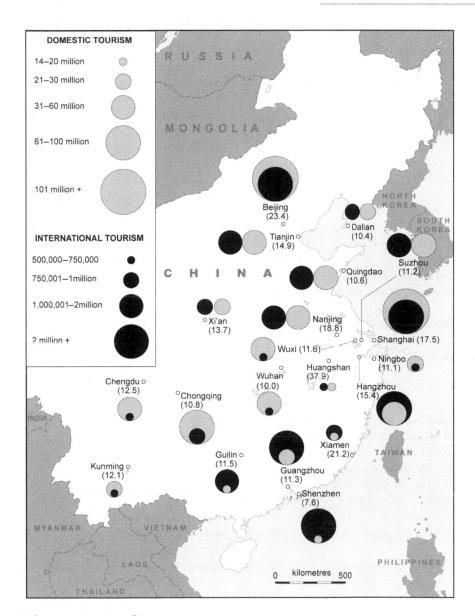

Figure 5.8 Urban tourism in China
Source: developed from UNWTO data.

in each location. It is necessary to understand the operation and organisation of tourism in terms of the production of tourism services and the ways in which tourists consume the products in relation to the locality, their reasons for consumption, what they consume

and possible explanations for the consumption outcome as visitor behaviour. As Law argues:

tourism is the geography of consumption outside the home area; it is about how and why people travel to consume ... on the production side it is concerned to understand where tourism activities develop and on what scale. It is concerned with the process or processes whereby some cities are able to create tourism resources and a tourism industry.

(Law 1993: 14)

One framework developed in the Netherlands by Jansen-Verbeke (1986) to accommodate the analysis of tourism consumption and production in urban areas is that of the 'leisure product'. The facilities in an urban environment may be divided into the 'primary elements', 'secondary elements' and 'additional elements' (see Chapter 3). To distinguish between user groups, Jansen-Verbeke (1986) identified tourists' and recreationalists' first and second reasons for visiting three Dutch towns (Deneter, Kampen and Zwolle). The inner city environment provides a leisure function for various visitors regardless of the prime motivation for visiting. As Jansen-Verbeke (1986) suggests:

On an average day, the proportion of visitors coming from beyond the city-region (tourists) is about one-third of all visitors. A distinction that needs to be made is between week days, market days and Sundays. Weather conditions proved to be important . . . the hypothesis that inner cities have a role to play as a leisure substitute on a rainy day could not be supported.

(Jansen-Verbeke 1986: 88–9)

Among the different user groups, tourists tend to stay longer, with a strong correlation between 'taking a day out', sightseeing and 'visiting a museum' as the main motivations to visit. Nevertheless, leisure shopping was also a major 'pull factor' for recreationalists and tourists, though it is of greater significance for the recreationalists. Using a scaling technique, Jansen-Verbeke (1986) asked visitors to evaluate how important different elements of the leisure product were to their visit. The results indicate that there is not a great degree of difference between tourists' and recreationalists' rating of elements and characteristics of the city's leisure product. While recreationalists attach more importance to shopping facilities than to events and museums, the historical characteristics of the environment and decorative elements combined with other elements, such as markets, restaurants and the compact nature of the inner city, to attract visitors. Thus 'the conceptual approach to the system of inner-city tourism is inspired by common features of the inner-city environment, tourists' behaviour and appreciation and promotion activities' (Jansen-Verbeke 1986: 97). Such findings illustrate the value of relating empirical results to a conceptual framework for the analysis of urban tourism and the necessity of replicating similar studies in other urban environments to test the validity of the hypothesis, framework and interpretation of urban tourists' visitor behaviour, as reflected in Box 5.6.

But how do tourists and other visitors to urban areas learn about, find their way around and perceive the tourism environment?

Tourist perception and cognition of the urban environment

How individual tourists interact and acquire information about the urban environment remains a relatively poorly researched area in tourism studies, particularly in relation to towns and cities. This assumes an even greater significance, as Box 5.6, on modelling tourist movements, illustrates. Modelling mobility is an important element of advancing research knowledge, but we also need to explore beyond this to explain, as the 11 movement styles McKercher and Lau (2008) constructed reflect the degree of tourist engagement with the destination urban environment. This area of research is traditionally seen as the forte of social psychologists with an interest in tourism, though much of the research by social psychologists has focused on motivation (e.g. Guy and Curtis 1986).

Reviews of the social psychology of tourism indicate that there has been a paucity of studies of tourist

BOX 5.6 MODELLING THE MOVEMENT PATTERNS OF TOURISTS IN URBAN DESTINATIONS

According to McKercher and Lau (2008: 355), 'understanding movements within a destination plays a funda-mental role in understanding tourist behavior, which in turn is directly applicable to the entire suite of destination management activities, including planning, tour product development, transport, attraction planning and accommodation development. In short, it is central to the understanding of how tourism works at a destination level'. McKercher and Lau (2008) identified four broad types of itinerary, operating at different geographical scales. These were: the single destination with or without side trips; transit leg and circle tour at a destination; circle tour with or without multiple access; egress points and various itinerary styles and a hub and spoke style. Whilst Connell and Page (2008) reviewed these four types within the context of a national park in Scotland, it is more problematic when seeking to understand the totality of tourist travel in a destination. In other words, tourists have an unlimited number of places to go and McKercher (2014) concluded that tourist itineraries are highly individualistic. Despite these obvious problems of scale and the complexity of visits in an urban setting, Walmsley and Jenkins (1992) observed that two broad types of urban visitor characteristics existed in the same trip: space searchers, who had a wide search area and visited multiple sites; and space sitters, who had a very confined spatial activity space. The decision to adopt either behavioural characteristic was dependent upon the knowledge of the destination (which we explore further on pp. 214–217).

Understanding the factors which condition tourist trips (e.g. spatial relationship between the tourist(s) and the accommodation–attraction–transport nexus) and the pattern of tourist supply will partly explain the resulting patterns of tourist travel and exploration in a destination. McKercher and Lau (2008) use the concept of 'territoriality' to explain the resulting movement patterns, ranging from the very restricted to unrestricted patterns of movement, and examined the daily movement patterns of tourists in Hong Kong: 250 respondents, some 5,274 visit points/places were observed (an average of 3.6 visits to places per

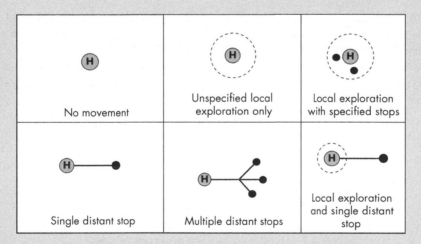

Figure 5.9 **Tourist movement styles**

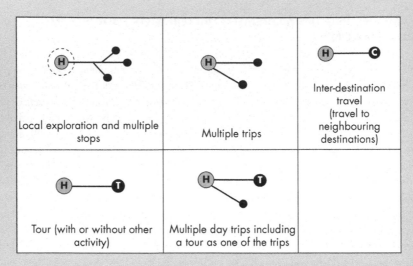

Figure 5.9 (Continued)

Source: McKercher and Lau 2008: 366.

tourist per day). Using GIS technology, the visualisation of the individual itineraries was grouped into 78 discrete patterns of movement. These patterns were categorised with seven key factors in mind (i.e. territoriality; the number of trips taken per day; number of stops per journey; observed pattern of multi-stop journeys; participation in a commercial day tour; participation in cross-border trips to China/Macau; combinations of the previous factors).

These 78 patterns were then summarised into 11 broad movement styles (Figure 5.9). The 11 movement types, while not exhaustive, do begin to address the weaknesses of urban tourism research identified by Ashworth and Page (2011) in relation to the geography of urban tourism. Figure 5.10 is a useful starting point for further research to assess the generalisability of the main findings. McKercher and Lau (2008) found the most common trip type was a single day trip with a local exploration element and visits to additional distant visitor attractions.

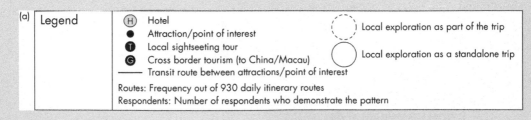

Figure 5.10 Observed tourist movement patterns

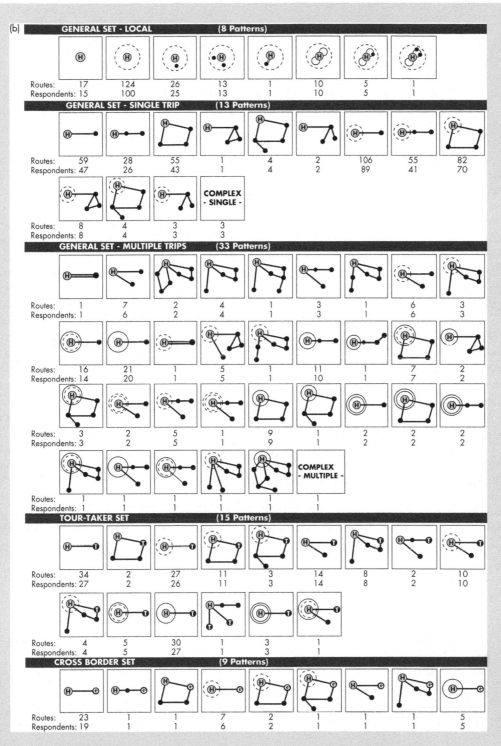

Figure 5.10 (Continued)

Source: McKercher and Lau 2008: 362.

behaviour and adaptation to new environments they visit. This is somewhat surprising since 'tourists are people who temporarily visit areas less familiar to them than their home area' (Walmsley and Jenkins 1992: 269). Therefore, one needs to consider a number of fundamental concerns related to the following questions:

- How will the tourists get to know the areas they visit?
- How do they find their way around unfamiliar environments?
- What features in the urban environment are used to structure their learning experience in unfamiliar environments?
- What type of mental maps and images do they develop?

These issues are important in a tourism planning context since the facilities which tourists use and the opportunities they seek will be conditioned by their environmental awareness. This may also affect the commercial operation of attractions and facilities, since a lack of awareness of the urban environment and the attractions within it may mean tourists fail to visit them. Understanding how tourists interact with the environment to create an image of the real world has been the focus of research into social psychology and behavioural geography (Walmsley and Lewis 1993). Geographers have developed a growing interest in the geographic space perception of all types of individuals (Downs 1970), without explicitly considering tourists

in most instances. Behavioural geographers emphasise the need to examine how people store spatial information and 'their choice of different activities and locations within the environment' (Walmsley and Lewis 1993: 95). The process through which individuals perceive the urban environment is shown in Figure 5.11. While this is a simplification, Haynes (1980) notes that no two individuals will have an identical image of the urban environment because the information they receive is subject to mental processing. This is conditioned by the information signals they receive through their senses (e.g. sight, hearing, smell, taste and touch) and this part of the process is known as *perception*. As our senses may comprehend only a small proportion of the total information received, the human brain sorts the information and relates it to the knowledge, values and attitudes of the individual through the process of *cognition* (Page 1995a: 222).

The final outcome of the perception and cognition process is the formation of a mental image of a place. These images are an individual's own view of reality, but they are important to the individual and group when making decisions about their experience of a destination, whether to visit again, and their feelings in relation to the tourist experience of place. As Downs and Stea (1977: 2) observed, 'a cognitive map is a cross section representing the world at one instant in time', a feature explored by Crang and Travelou (2001) in relation to the historic sites of Athens. In the psychology literature, Curiel and Radvansky (2002) note that one way to examine this issue is to understand how people memorise a map to recognise

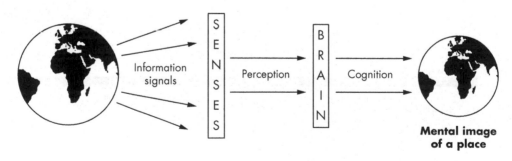

Figure 5.11 Perceptions of place

how their resulting mental representation of that map influences their use of that map.

Nevertheless, as Walmsley and Lewis (1993: 96) suggested, the distinction between cognition and perception is 'a heuristic device rather than a fundamental dichotomy because in many senses, the latter subsumes the former and both are mediated by experience, beliefs, values, attitudes, and personality such that, in interacting with their environment, humans only see what they want to see'. Consequently, an individual tourist's knowledge of the environment is created in their mind as they interact with the unfamiliar environment they are visiting (or a familiar environment on a return visit). Pacione (2001: 353) observed that 'Certain places are regarded as distinctive or memorable through their unique characteristics or imageability and so have a strong *sense of place*'. This may be explained in terms of the attachments people have to a specific place, gained through experience, memory and intention, a condition described by Tuan (1974) as topophilia. Such issues are relevant for tourism as place attachment can be a significant indicator of future visitation and positive word of mouth.

According to Powell (1978: 17–18), an image of the environment comprises 10 key features, which include:

- a spatial component accounting for an individual's location in the world;
- a personal component relating the individual to other people and organisations;
- a temporal component concerned with the flow of time;
- a relational component concerned with the individual's picture of the universe as a system of regularities;
- conscious, subconscious and unconscious elements;
- a blend of certainty and uncertainty;
- a mixture of reality and unreality;
- a public and private component expressing the degree to which an image is shared;
- a value component that orders parts of the image according to whether they are good or bad;
- an affectional component whereby the image is imbued with feeling.

Among geographers, the spatial component of behavioural research has attracted most interest, with much inspiration derived from the pioneering research of Lynch (1960). Lynch asked respondents in North American cities to sketch maps of their individual cities, and, by simplifying the sketches, derived images of the city. Lynch developed a specific technique to measure people's urban images in which respondents drew a map of the centre of the city from memory, marking on it the streets, parks, buildings, districts and features they considered important. Lynch (1960) found five elements in the resulting maps that suggested fundamental ways that people collect spatial information about a city. These were:

- *paths*, which are the channels along which individuals move;
- *edges*, which are barriers (e.g. rivers) or lines separating one region from another;
- *districts*, which are medium to large sections of the city with an identifiable character;
- *nodes*, which are the strategic points in a city which the individual can enter and which serve as foci for travel;
- *landmarks*, which are points of reference used in navigation and way finding, into which an individual cannot enter.

The significance of such research for the tourist and visitor to the urban environment is that the information they collect during a visit will shape their image of the place, influencing their feelings and impressions of that place. Furthermore, this imageability of a place is closely related to its legibility, by which is meant the extent to which parts of the city may be recognised and interpreted by an individual as belonging to a coherent pattern. Thus a legible city would be one where the paths, edges, districts, nodes and landmarks are both clearly identifiable and clearly positioned relative to each other (Walmsley and Lewis 1993: 98). Indeed, Lynch argued that a successful urban landscape would possess two desirable urban qualities of *imageability* (the value of objects in the landscape to provoke a strong emotional response in observers) and *legibility* (the extent to which the elements of a city can be seen as a coherent whole).

Although there may sometimes be confusion among individuals regarding recognition of Lynchean urban landscape elements, it does help researchers to understand how individuals perceive the environment. Although researchers have criticised Lynch for the small sample sizes in his work based on the cities of Boston, Los Angeles and Jersey City, with 60 responses, the real value is the subsequent interest and research activity which his work stimulated. In fact Lynch (1984), in a review of his work, noted the problems of implementing his findings in a public policy context, since many cities are quite idiosyncratic in character and development.

Walmsley and Lewis (1993) review many of the issues associated with the methodology of imagery research and raise a range of concerns about deriving generalisations from such results. Such studies do have a role to play in understanding how people view, understand and synthesise the complexity of urban landscapes into images of the environment. Nevertheless, criticisms of spatial research of individual imagery of the environment are that it uses a 'borrowed methodology, a potpourri of concepts, and liberal doses of borrowed theory' (Downs and Stea 1977: 3, cited in Walmsley and Lewis 1993). In a tourism context, Walmsley and Jenkins (1992) observed that tourism cognitive mapping may offer a number of useful insights into how tourists learn about new environments, and, for this reason, it is pertinent to consider how visitor behaviour may be influenced by the ability to acquire spatial knowledge and synthesise it into meaningful images of the destination to assist them in finding their way around the area or region.

Tourism cognitive mapping

Walmsley and Lewis (1993: 214) review the factors that affect visitor behaviour in terms of five interrelated factors which may initially shape the decision to visit an urban environment. These are:

- antecedent conditions;
- user aspirations;

- intervening variables;
- user satisfaction;
- real benefits.

These factors will, with experience, raise or reduce the individual's desire for recreational (and tourism) activity. The opportunities and constraints on visitors' behaviour are affected by income, disposable time available and a host of other socio-economic factors. Research by Stabler (1990) introduces the concept of 'opportunity sets', where the individual or family's knowledge of tourism opportunities is conditioned by their experience and the constraints on available time to participate in leisure and tourism activities. Thus, once the decision is taken to visit an urban environment, the tourist faces the problem of the familiarity/unfamiliarity of the location. It is the latter which tends to characterise most urban tourist trips, though visitors are often less hesitant about visiting urban destinations if they live in a town or city environment.

P.L. Pearce (1977) produced one of the pioneering studies of cognitive maps of tourists. Using data from sketch maps from first-time visitors to Oxford, England, the role of landmarks, paths and districts was examined. The conclusion drawn indicated that visitors were quick to develop cognitive maps, often by the second day of their visit. The interesting feature of the study is that there is evidence of an environmental learning process at work. Walmsley and Jenkins (1992: 272) critiqued P.L. Pearce's (1977) findings, noting that:

- the number of landmarks, paths and districts increased over time;
- the number of landmarks identified increased over a period of two to six days, while recognition of the number of districts increased from two to three days;
- the resulting sketch maps were complex, with no one element dominating them.

A further study by P.L. Pearce (1981) examined how tourists came to know a route in Northern Queensland (a 340 km strip from Townsville to Cairns). The

URBAN RECREATION AND TOURISM

217

study indicated that experiential variables are a major influence upon cognitive maps. For example, drivers had a better knowledge than passengers, while age and prior use of the route were important conditioning factors. But, as Walmsley and Jenkins (1992: 273) argue, very little concern has been shown for the cognitive maps of tourists except for the work by Aldskogius (1977) in Sweden and Mercer (1971a) in Australia. However, as Pacione (2004: 355) notes: 'Although cognitive mapping can identify sub-areas in a city, it does not capture the sense of place . . . To achieve this goal we need to move from cognitive mapping to the "mapping of meaning" based on a humanistic approach, where the world of experience is used to understand what the places mean to those people.'

This is more phenomenological in approach and has a strong synergy with ethnography (see Jackson 1985; Hall 2011c) and the early work of the Chicago School of urban research (Park *et al.* 1925; Wirth 1938). What is clear for tourists in an urban setting is that human needs should be met, particularly in terms of urban design, including the innate need for security, clarity (such as the need to be able to move easily and freely in what Lynch 1960 called a *legible* city), environments where social interaction can occur (e.g. public spaces and places), conveniently located facilities and districts for visiting the urban leisure product, and an opportunity to gain a sense of place during the visit from a memorable and easily assimilated urban form and structure. In the latter context, not only have urban regeneration strategies for cities (see Page and Hall 2003) pursued physical regeneration but also massive investment has gone into the re-imaging of places that hitherto have not been high in tourists' consciousness as places to visit with a strong imagery and sense of place even when one visits (Hall 2013b). This has become part of what Pacione (2004) describes as the pursuit of the liveable city, so that planning and redesign of the city environment seek to accommodate a better living environment for residents and short-term visitors in pursuit of gaining a better sense of place, rather than becoming part of what have been described in the UK as 'Crap Towns' (Jordison and Kieran 2003), which also have quite limited tourism potential. Many of the government strategies within western countries seek to improve the living environment as a basis for also attracting tourism, a feature noted in post-event reports on hosting the Commonwealth Games in Manchester, which improved the city's image and visitor numbers post-event (Hall and Page 2012). However, in the context of developing countries such as Africa, Hoyle (2001) observed the potential for urban redevelopment of waterfront sites such as Lamu, which may have beneficial effects for tourism and urban conservation, but the juxtaposition of rich visitors with poor local residents could have potential for conflict and crime.

BOX 5.7 THE VALUE OF URBAN HERITAGE RESOURCES IN THE CULTURAL ECONOMY

Heritage does not just refer to old buildings. At its most basic, heritage represents the things we want to keep. Nevertheless, as Glasson *et al.* (1995: 20) described the situation, 'Public definitions of heritage are still largely dominated by highly educated professionals . . . This often places the professional at considerable remove from the visitor's need.' Tunbridge and Ashworth (1996) identified five different aspects of the meaning of heritage:

- a synonym for any relict physical survival of the past;
- the idea of individual and collective memories in terms of non-physical aspects of the past when viewed from the present;

- all accumulated cultural and artistic productivity;
- the natural environment;
- a major commercial activity, e.g. the 'heritage industry'.

Undoubtedly, there is significant overlap between these various conceptions of heritage. However, according to Tunbridge and Ashworth (1996: 3), there are intrinsic dangers in the stretching of the concept to cover so much: 'Inevitably precision is lost, but more important is that this, in turn, conceals issues and magnifies problems intrinsic to the creation and management of heritage.' Ironically, the uncertainty about what constitutes heritage is occurring at a time when heritage has assumed greater importance *because* of its relationship to identity in a constantly changing world as well as its commercial value with respect to image and promotion, including with respect to cultural quarters (Hall 2013b) and the generation of attractive servicescapes (Hall 2008b). Such recognition highlights the implications of the extension of urban entrepreneurialism to the cultural economy in that it has provided a stronger dialectical articulation of the material (urban form, design, and architecture) and the immaterial (place branding, marketing, identity, image) as co-created and produced urban economic practice (Jessop and Sum 2001).

The formulation of what constitutes heritage is therefore intimately related to wider political, social, economic and technological changes which appear to reflect postmodern concerns over the end of certainty and the convergence between cultural forms which were once seen as separate aspects of everyday life, e.g. education and tourism or, in even more of a heritage context, marketing and conservation. Much discussion in heritage studies has focused on the recognition of multiple meanings of heritage, particularly with respect to the recognition of other voices in heritage. In many urban areas, particularly those which have a substantial migrant and/or labour heritage, other histories are also finding their voice and recognition through the work of heritage managers. For example, the comments of Norkunas with reference to the heritage of Monterey, California, apply to many other communities:

Ethnic and class groups have not forgotten the totality of their own pasts. They have certainly preserved a sense of themselves through orally transmitted family stories, and through celebrations and rituals performed inside the group. But their systematic exclusion from official history fragments the community so that feelings of alienation and 'loss of soul' are experienced most deeply by minorities.

(Norkunas 1993: 99)

Nevertheless, commercial use of the symbolic capital of heritage dominates in the cultural economy and highlights three things about the use of heritage and tourism in regeneration projects in the contemporary city (Evans 2005; Hall 2013b): first, the urban morphology of economic restructuring in which regeneration is tied to the cultural-material production of urban space (Evans 2003); second, the development of the 'new' and 'symbolic' economy, in which regeneration projects, including heritage, in conjunction with the leisure and tourism sectors, are integral to postmodern economic and political urban competitiveness strategies (Malecki 2004; Hall 2007b); third, entrepreneurialism and ethnicity, in which cultural discourses of race and ethnic difference become part of entrepreneurial place strategies (Hall and Rath 2007).

Place promotion and the accompanying transformation of urban space require distinct boundaries in order to be effectively commodified, and this may be done via the (re)development and (re)branding of urban heritage spaces and/or distinctive cultural precincts or quarters. However, the cultural economic value of heritage is creating a new challenge for urban planners. Historically, the attention of public sector heritage managers and planners has been focused on environmental and cultural values, and they have only a poorly developed understanding of the significance of economic values. This situation reflects a substantial set of new pressures which has begun to affect the manner in which heritage management and conservation operates:

- demands for smaller government concentrating on 'core' activities;
- the development of a user-pays philosophy;
- recognition of the significance of the visitor economy for business and regional development;
- use of heritage to anchor real estate development and urban regeneration projects;
- the emergence of public–private partnership;
- greater limitations on government expenditure.

From the new context within which heritage conservation occurs several significant principles can be identified, which McMillan (1997) has labelled, somewhat provocatively, as the 'undeniable truths' regarding heritage conservation:

- *That the choice for heritage conservation has both a value and a cost.* While much heritage literature and the activities of heritage groups have focused on the values of heritage, relatively little attention has been given to the costs. As McMillan (1997: 4) recognised, 'there is a financial cost in pursuing heritage conservation. Someone has to pay that cost.'
- *In the longer term viability means commercial rates of return.* If capital cannot be applied to achieve a return on equivalent applications – the opportunity cost of heritage conservation – in the long term, support for conservation of a particular site by the public and/or private sectors will dwindle.
- *Facilitation is productive, while confrontation leads to little real progress in conservation.* Creative outcomes can now be achieved through co-operation and understanding of the mutual needs of stakeholders. Indeed, one of the challenges for many heritage management agencies is to recognise the range of stakeholders that may exist for a particular site, including commercial stakeholders.
- *Reducing uncertainty, reduces time and costs and increases viability.*

This fourth principle is extremely important for heritage conservation from the perspective of the private sector.

Service quality issues in urban tourism

The competitive nature of urban tourism is increasingly being reflected in the growth in marketing and promotion efforts by towns and cities as they compete for a share of international and domestic tourism markets. Such competition has led to tourists demanding higher standards of service provision and improved quality in the tourist experience. As Clewer *et al.* (1992) note, certain urban tourists (e.g. the German market) have higher expectations of service quality than do others. But developing an appropriate definition or concept of urban tourism quality is difficult due to the intangible nature of services as products which are purchased and consumed.

In the context of urban tourism, three key issues need to be addressed. First, place-marketing generates an image of a destination that may not be met in reality due to the problems of promoting places as tourist products. The image promoted through place-marketing may not necessarily be matched in reality through the services and goods which the tourism industry delivers. As a result, the gap between customers' perception of a destination and the bundle of products they consume is reflected in their actual tourist experience, which has important implications for their assessment of quality in their experience. Second, the urban tourism product is largely produced by the private sector either as a package or as a series of elements which are not easily controlled or influenced by the place-marketer. Third, there is a wide range of associated factors which affect a tourist's image of a destination, including less tangible elements like the environment and the ambience of the city, which may shape the outcome of a tourist's experience. As a result, the customer's evaluation of the quality of the services and products provided is a function of the difference (gap) between expected and perceived service. It is in this context that the concept of service quality is important for urban tourism.

New concepts such as service dominant logic (Figure 5.12) have transformed thinking on service quality. In the case of urban tourism, it was traditionally the practical management of the 'gap' between the expected and the perceived service that required

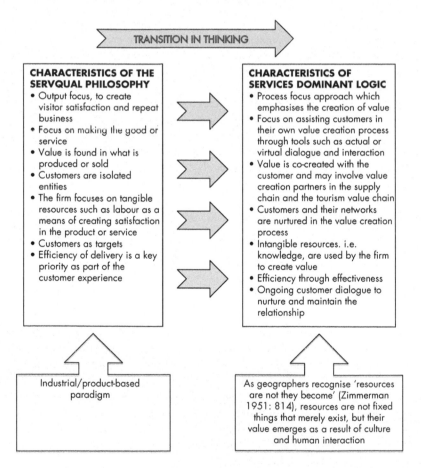

Figure 5.12 Paradigm shift from SERVQUAL to service dominant logic

Source: Page 2011, developed from Vargo and Lusch 2004, 2008.

attention by urban managers and the tourism industry. In reviewing Parasuraman *et al.*'s (1985) service quality model, Gilbert and Joshi (1992: 155) identify five gaps which exist:

- between the expected service and the management's perceptions of the consumer experience (i.e. what they think the tourist wants) (Gap 1);
- between the management's perception of the tourist needs and the translation of those needs into service quality specifications (Gap 2);
- between the quality specifications and the actual delivery of the service (Gap 3);
- between the service delivery stage and the organisation/provider's communication with the consumer (Gap 4);
- between the consumers' perception of the service they received and experienced, and their initial expectations of the service (Gap 5).

Gilbert and Joshi (1992) argue that the effective utilisation of market research techniques could help to bridge some of the gaps:

- Gap 1: by encouraging providers to elicit detailed information from consumers on what they require;
- Gap 2: by the management providing realistic specifications for the services to be provided which are guided by clear quality standards;
- Gap 3: by the employees being able to deliver the service according to the specifications; these need to be closely monitored, and staff training and development is essential – a service is only as good as the staff it employs;
- Gap 4: by the promises made by service providers in their marketing and promotional messages being reflected in the actual quality offered; therefore, if a city's promotional literature promises a warm welcome, human resource managers responsible for employees in frontline establishments need to ensure that this message is conveyed to their customers;
- Gap 5: by the major gap between the perceived service and delivered service being reduced

through progressive improvements in the appropriate image which is marketed to visitors and in the private sector's ability to deliver the expected service in an efficient and professional manner.

Such an approach to service quality can be applied to urban tourism, as it emphasises the importance of the marketing process in communicating and dealing with tourists. To obtain a better understanding of the service quality issues associated with the urban tourist's experience of urban tourism, Haywood and Muller (1988) identify a methodology for evaluating the quality of the urban tourism experience. This involves collecting data on visitors' expectations prior to and after their city visit by examining a range of variables (see Page 1995a for a fuller discussion). Such an approach may be costly to operate, but it does provide a better appreciation of the visiting process, and they argue that cameras may also provide the day-to-day monitoring of city experiences. At a city-wide level, many North American and European cities have responded to the problem of large visitor numbers and the consequences of mass tourism for the tourist experience by introducing Town Centre and Visitor Management Schemes (Page 1994a; Page and Hardyman 1996; Sadd 2009).

While there is insufficient space here to review these new management tools to combat the unwieldy and damaging effect of mass tourism on key tourist centres in developed and developing countries, it is notable that many small historic cities in Europe are taking steps to manage, modify and in some cases deter tourist activities as part of the strategic management and planning of urban destinations and visitor satisfaction. A range of potential visitor management strategies that seek to influence visitor behaviours in urban destinations are outlined in Table 5.9. However, the application of strategies will depend on perceptions of problems arising from visitation as well as management philosophies with respect to service (see Figure 5.12), with the most critical factor being pressure applied by different public and private stakeholders which are seeking to fulfil their own goals with respect to tourism (Hall 2014).

Table 5.9 Applications of visitor management techniques

Visitor management technique	Application
Regulating access – by area	• All visitors are prohibited from visiting highly sensitive sites • Different types and levels of use are regulated through zoning • Access is regulated to pedestrians only
– by transport	• Access is regulated to pedestrians or by bicycle • Public transport is the only allowable form of transport • A location may have a 'car-free day' in which alternative ways to enter and move about the park must be found
Regulating visitation – visitor numbers – group size – type of visitor	• Regulations on total visitation per year, day or at any moment may be generated for a specific site • Group size restrictions have been implemented in some European cathedrals • Some sites and attractions have a limit on visitation and the type of visitor • Some urban attractions target older high and middle income groups and actively discourage other segments using strict controls on all accommodation and services, keeping prices high and scrutinising all marketing to maintain consistency
Regulating behaviour	• Zoning in some cities and towns allocates different types of use to specified areas • Restrictions on length of stay may be imposed • Tour operators may be required to operate under a detailed set of guidelines of conduct for visitors • Visitors must visit with a guide
Regulating equipment	• Vehicular access may be restricted • Loudspeakers may be restricted because of noise disturbance
Implementing entry or user fees	• Highly visited sites now often charge fees to access the site or use facilities at the site in order to pay maintenance costs, influencing some visitors to choose whether to visit or find an alternative destination • Some heritage sites have days during low season when residents are offered free entry • Cities may require tourism operators to pay for a permit or licence to access the heritage site, and operators must also collect entrance fees from each of their clients • A portion of user fees collected is returned to local stakeholders as a means of demonstrating the value of tourism
Modifying the site	• Some urban heritage sites may have specially designed walkways so as to reduce visitor impact • Streetscapes may be designed in certain ways so as to encourage particular visitor flows and behaviours
Undertaking market research	• A study of the domestic and international visitor market may be conducted in order to identify the market segments most likely to visit urban tourism attractions
Undertaking visitor monitoring and research	• Visitors may be asked to complete special 'day diary' forms to identify their motivations for visiting and the activities they undertook • Visitors may be asked for their attitudes towards their experience and the performance of the respective heritage manager as a means of improving visitor management strategies • Visitor impact monitoring and research are widely undertaken in sensitive urban heritage attractions
Undertaking marketing – promotional	• Visitation pressure may be relieved through the development, marketing and promotion of value-added alternative attractions • Different urban tourism organisations may undertake common promotional activities in order to reinforce the profile of the destination
– strategic information	• Tour guides can avoid sensitive areas by using a map and pictorial guide that identifies the best vantage points for attractions

Table 5.9 (Continued)

Visitor management technique	Application
Implementing interpretation programmes and facilities	• A walking 'trail selector' (website, brochure and map) may be developed to provide information on lightly used walking trails in order to redistribute use away from heavily used areas • Some urban tourism destinations may generate greater levels of visitor respect for the local culture through the provision of opportunities such as learning to cook with a local family or spending a night with a local family in a homestay • Visitors may be taken on guided tours by local people who then convey their personal experiences and knowledge of the area to the visitor, and this level of authenticity can greatly enhance the quality of the visitor experience
Implementing education programmes and facilities	• Theme trails may be created to educate visitors about specific aspects of local history and culture • Many urban locations and attractions have interpretation and signage encouraging appropriate behaviour
Modifying the presence of management	• Most museums and heritage attractions strategically position security staff in corners and corridors to create a high profile when visitors are moving between exhibits and a low profile when they are studying an individual exhibit
Encouraging and assisting alternative industry	• Some urban destination management organisations encourage the development of small-scale homestay accommodation and tours by local guides who are highly trained in heritage providers, tourism and interpretation, with profits therefore being reinvested in the local community
Encouraging and assisting alternative providers – volunteers	• Many urban heritage attractions, such as museums and historic sites, have volunteer and friends' associations which assist in various aspects of management as well as providing a source of financial support
Concentrating on accredited organisations bringing visitors to a site	• National and regional accreditation programmes may be used to check on the appropriateness of tourism operator practices and the quality of facilities

Source: after Hall and McArthur 1998, Hall 2014.

Conclusion

Tourism's development in urban areas is not a new phenomenon, but its recognition as a significant activity to study in its own right is only belatedly gaining the recognition it deserves within tourism studies (UNWTO 2012b). The reasons why tourists visit urban environments, to consume a bundle of tourism products, continues to be overlooked by the private sector, which often neglects the fundamental issue – cities are multifunctional places. Despite the growing interest in urban tourism research, the failure of many large and small cities which promote tourism to understand the reasons why people visit, the links between the various motivations, and the deeper reasons why people are attracted to cities, remains a fertile area for theoretically informed and methodologically sound research. Many cities are beginning to recognise the importance of monitoring visitor perceptions and satisfaction and the activity patterns and behaviour of tourists. While such studies may have provided rich pickings for market research companies, all too often the surveys have been superficial, naive and devoid of any real understanding of urban tourism.

For the public and private sector planners and managers with an interest, involvement or stake in urban tourism, the main concern continues to be the potential for harnessing the all-year-round appeal of urban tourism activity, despite the often short-stay nature of such visitors. Ensuring that such stays are part of a high quality experience, where visitor expectations are realistically met through well-researched, targeted and innovative products, continues to stimulate interest among tour operators and other stakeholders in urban tourism provision. Yet the urban tourism industry, which is so often fragmented and poorly co-ordinated, rarely understands many of the complex issues of visitor behaviour, the spatial learning process which tourists experience and the implications for making their visit as stress free as possible.

These concerns should force cities seeking to develop an urban tourism economy to reconsider the feasibility of pursuing a strategy to revitalise the city-region through tourism-led regeneration. All too often both the private and public sectors have moved headlong into economic regeneration strategies for urban areas, seeking a tourism component as a likely back-up for property and commercial redevelopment (Evans 2005). The implications here are that tourism issues are not given the serious treatment they deserve. Where the visitors' needs and spatial behaviour are poorly understood and neglected in the decision-making process, this affects the planning, development and eventual outcome of the urban tourism environment. Therefore, tourist behaviour, the tourism system and its constituent components need to be evaluated in the context of future growth in urban tourism to understand the visitor as a central component in the visitor experience as well as the goals that are sought from tourism development.

One way many cities have sought to embellish the tourist experience is through the use of events and festivals. This critical transformation of the everyday into places and spaces of spectacle and consumption can re-energise and reconfigure places as part of a new international economic geography of competitiveness (Hall and Page 2012). In some cities, the competition for conferences and trade fairs (Bathelt and Spigel 2012) due to the impact on the economy has also led to some cities pursuing events as a route to urban development (Gladstone 2012). Bluetooth technology has also recently been employed to track the spatio-temporal dynamics of visitors at a mass event (Versichele et al. 2012), examining 80,000 visitors over 10 days to assess crowding and visitor behaviour at an event in Ghent, Belgium. The study found a dwell time of 3.5 hours, typically with a wide variation in visitation, with up to 11 per cent staying 7 hours. Such evidence helps in planning and crowd control and safety, including the intricacies of visitor flows in festival zones.

Research has a vital role to play in understanding the increasingly complex reasons why tourists continue to visit urban environments and the factors which influence their behaviour and spatial activity patterns, along with the role of place-marketing. This chapter has reviewed the role of recreation and tourism within the context of an urban environment, where recreationalists and tourists inevitably use some of the same resources, a feature recognised in Toronto's launch of a Green Tourism Map which also includes many recreational sites. This feature of multiple use is best summarised by Burtenshaw et al.'s (1991) conceptualisation of different users and functional areas of the city, where no one group has a monopoly over its use, a feature now being recognised in more integrated recreational planning that begins to recognise that residents and visitors use similar resources. The urban environment is still a growing field of academic endeavour in relation to the geographer's analysis of tourism and recreation, as Ashworth and Page (2011) observe. It is ironic, therefore, that many of the methodologies, techniques and skills which the geographer can harness and utilise with new technology, such as the use of GIS, can help both the public and private sector to understand how a range of research issues affect the functioning of the recreational and tourism system. For the more applied geographical researcher, this is a straightforward process in many instances of utilising a synthesising role to adopt the holistic view of the city, to provide what Lynch (1960) described as *legibility*. It is this absence of legibility that seems to affect the management of urban tourism and recreation even in the new millennium. For example, in recreational planning, issues of access, equality, need and social justice can easily be integrated into spatial analysis using secondary data, but the spatially informed planning framework is often only portrayed as a static one point in time analysis produced for structure plans and development plans, as this chapter has shown. Few attempts have been made to build and maintain urban models of recreation and tourism that accommodate the dynamic and changing needs of the users of such services. Where data do not exist, spatially oriented social surveys have proved to be extremely valuable in understanding the processes shaping and under-pinning existing patterns of use and activity, provision and future development. However, applied geographical research (Sant 1982) can be used to pose questions and address problem-solving tasks for managerial solutions as well as providing a basis for raising more fundamental questions about the nature of tourism and recreation in contemporary capitalist society.

Further reading

Useful texts on urban tourism include:

Judd, D. and Fainstein, S. (1999) *The Tourist City*, New Haven, CT: Yale University Press.

Page, S.J. and Hall, C.M. (2003) *Managing Urban Tourism*, Harlow: Pearson Education.

Helpful reviews of the state of urban tourism research since the 1980s can be found in:

Ashworth, G. (2003) 'Urban tourism: still an imbalance in attention', in C. Cooper (ed.) *Classic Reviews in Tourism*, Clevedon: Channel View.

Ashworth, G.J. and Page, S.J. (2011) 'Progress in tourism management: urban tourism research: recent progress and current paradoxes', *Tourism Management*, 32: 1–15.

A useful case study to complement the London Borough of Newham example on equality of access is:

Nicholls, S. (2001) 'Measuring the accessibility and equity of public parks: a case study using GIS', *Managing Leisure*, 6(4): 201–19.

For a useful study of urban tourism in a developing country context, see:

Rogerson, C.M. (2013) 'Urban tourism, economic regeneration and inclusion: evidence from South Africa', *Local Economy*, 28: 188–202.

An interesting in-depth case study of the impact of urban events and relationships on processes of gentrification and restructuring is:

Olds, K. (1998) 'Urban mega-events, evictions and housing rights: the Canadian case', *Current Issues in Tourism*, 1(1): 2–46.

The above study can be usefully compared with more recent analyses of Vancouver and of the hosting of large urban events:

Hall, C.M. (2006) 'Urban entrepreneurship, corporate interests and sports mega-events: the thin policies of competitiveness within the hard outcomes of neoliberalism', *Sociological Review Monograph, Sports Mega-events: Social Scientific Analyses of a Global Phenomenon*, 54(s2): 59–70.

Porter, L., Jaconelli, M., Cheyne, J., Eby, D. and Wagenaar, H. (2009) 'Planning displacement: the real legacy of major sporting events; "just a person in a wee flat": being displaced by the Commonwealth Games in Glasgow's East End; Olympian masterplanning in London; Closing ceremonies: how law, policy and the Winter Olympics are displacing an inconveniently located low-income community in Vancouver; Commentary: recovering public ethos: critical analysis for policy and planning', *Planning Theory & Practice*, 10(3): 395–418.

Questions to discuss

1 What are the key geographical approaches to the geography of urban recreation?

2 What difficulties might exist in measuring the significance of urban tourism?

3 Is it possible to reconcile social and economic values in conserving urban heritage?

4 To what extent might urban recreation resources also act as resources for tourism?

Rural recreation and tourism

Geographical research on the recreational and tourism potential of rural areas has a long tradition (Clout 1972; Owens 1984; Page and Getz 1997; Sharpley and Sharpley 1997; Butler *et al.* 1998; Hall and O'Hanlon 1998). However, much early research failed to adopt a holistic view of the rural resource base as a multifaceted environment capable of accommodating a wide range of uses (e.g. agriculture, industrialisation, recreation and tourism) and values. As Patmore (1983: 124) recognised, 'recreation use must compete with agriculture, forestry, water abstraction, mineral extraction and military training' within the rural environment, which has spatial implications both for competing and complementary land uses as well as for the identification of the ways in which recreation and tourism may be accommodated in an ever-changing rural environment. According to Coppock,

> the contribution to research that geographers have made has been focused primarily on outdoor recreation in the countryside. No clear distinction has been made between tourism and recreation which is not surprising in a small, densely settled country [Britain] where there is considerable overlap between the two; in any case, geographical studies in tourism have been much less numerous than those in outdoor recreation.
>
> (Coppock 1982: 8)

This is an assertion that, to a certain extent, still holds true for present-day rural areas in developed countries. Butler *et al.* argued:

> In many cases, however, the specific activities which are engaged in during leisure, recreation

and tourism are identical, the key differences being the setting or location of the activities, the duration of time involved, and, in some cases, the attitudes, motivations and perceptions of the participants. In recent years the differences between recreation and tourism in particular, except at a philosophical level, have become of decreasing significance and distinctions increasingly blurred.

> (Butler *et al.* 1998: 2)

In fact, as Pigram (1983: 15) observed, where such 'space consumption and spatial competition and conflict are most likely to occur', 'spatial organisation and spatial concerns become paramount', along with the 'imbalance or discordance between population related demand and environmentally related supply of recreation [and tourism] opportunities and facilities'. This point is reiterated by Hall and Lew (2009) in the examination of visitor impacts. In contrast, Patmore (1983: 123) argues that 'outdoor recreation in rural areas rapidly achieves a distinctive character of its own and needs separate consideration for more than convention'. Either way, recreation and tourism are increasingly important activities in rural areas. For example, in the UK different surveys by the Department of Environment, Food and Rural Affairs (DEFRA) have highlighted how people value the natural rural environment. DEFRA undertook surveys in 2007 and 2009 in which, respectively, 79 per cent and 80 per cent of respondents agreed that they worry about the changes to the countryside in the UK and the loss of native plants and animals. Significantly, with respect to recreation in 2007, the importance of accessible green space was also highlighted, with

Table 6.1 **Visitors and spend in English National Parks (2011 or most recent available)**

National park	Year designated	Estimated permanent population (000s)	Estimated number of visitors per year (millions)	Estimated number of visitor days per year (millions)	Estimated visitor spend per year (£ millions)
Broads*	1989	6	7.2	11.3	419
Dartmoor	1951	34	2.4	3.1	111
Exmoor	1954	11	1.4	2.0	85
Lake District	1951	42	15.8	23.1	952
New Forest^	2005	34	12.3	13.5	123
Northumberland	1956	2	1.5	1.7	190
North York Moors	1952	25	7.0	10.7	411
Peak District	1951	38	8.3	10.6	410
South Downs^	2010	110	44.7	46.3	464
Yorkshire Dales	1954	20	9.5	12.6	400

Note: * The Broads have equivalent status to a national park
^ 2005 figures
Source: Association of National Park Authorities 2010 in Commission for Rural Communities 2010; New Forest National Park Authority 2007; Peak District National Park Authority 2013; TSE Research 2013.

two-thirds stating that it was 'very important' to have green spaces (including public gardens, parks and commons) nearby. Respondents also clearly placed a high value on the natural environment where it related to their day-to-day activities and contributed to their quality of life (Commission for Rural Communities 2010).

The significance of such demand for access to the rural environment can also be seen in the economic importance of visitation to the countryside. For example, tourism and recreation are extremely significant for the English national parks, which, unlike 'New World' national park systems, often have substantial permanent populations living within them. The Commission for Rural Communities (2010) estimates that more than 45 million visits are made per year to eight of the ten English national parks and more than £2.2 billion is spent each year (Table 6.1) (also see Box 6.1).

This chapter examines the growing interest from geographers in the way in which the rural environment is examined as a recreational and tourism resource, together with some of the ways in which it has been conceptualised and researched. The chapter commences with a review of the concept of 'rural' and the ways in which geographers have debated its meaning and definition. This is followed by a discussion of the geographer's contribution to theoretical debate in relation to rural recreation and tourism. The contribution made by historical geography to the analysis of continuity and change in the rural environment and its consumption for leisure and tourism are also briefly examined. The other contributions made by geographers to the analysis of recreation and tourism in rural environments are examined, and new developments such as the focus on food and wine tourism are highlighted with respect to the policy interest that they have created in light of the ongoing economic and social restructuring of rural areas.

In pursuit of the 'rural'

G.M. Robinson's (1990) synthesis of rural change illustrates that the term 'rural' has remained an elusive one to define in academic research, even though popular conceptions of rural areas are often based on images of rusticity and the idyllic village life that are reinforced by the media (Walmsley 2003; Cadieux 2005). However, Robinson argued that:

> defining rural . . . in the past has tended to ignore common economic, social and political structures

in both urban and rural areas . . . In simple terms . . . 'rural' areas define themselves with respect to the presence of particular types of problems. A selective list of examples could include depopulation and deprivation in areas remote from major metropolitan centres; a reliance upon primary activity; conflicts between presentation of certain landscapes and development of a variety of economic activities; and conflicts between local needs and legislation emanating from urban-based legislators. Key characteristics of 'rural' are taken to be extensive land uses, including large open spaces of underdeveloped land, and small settlements at the base of the settlement hierarchy, but including settlements thought of as rural.

(Robinson 1990: xxi–xxii)

Therefore, research on rural recreation and tourism needs to recognise the essential qualities of what is 'rural'. While national governments use specific criteria to define 'rural', often based on the population density of settlements, there is no universal agreement on the critical population threshold which distinguishes between urban and rural populations. For the developed world, Robinson (1990) summarises the principal approaches used by sociologists, economists and other groups in establishing the basis of what is rural and this need not be reiterated here. What is important is the diversity of approaches used by many researchers who emphasise the concept of an urban–rural continuum as a means of establishing differing degrees of rurality and the essential characteristics of ruralness. Shaw and Williams (1994: 224) advocate the use of the concept of a rural opportunity spectrum, where the countryside is viewed as the location of a 'wide range of outdoor leisure and tourist activities, although over time the composition of these has changed'. In contrast, Hoggart's provocative article 'Let's do away with rural' argues that 'there is too much laxity in the treatment of areas in empirical analysis . . . [and] that the undifferentiated use of "rural" in a research context is detrimental to the advancement of social theory' (Hoggart 1990: 245), since the term 'rural' is unsatisfactory due to inter-rural differences and urban–rural similarities.

Hoggart (1990) argued that general classifications of urban and rural areas are of limited value, although the fact that many governments throughout the developed world identify rural areas and rural problems as significant policy issues (e.g. Commission for Rural Communities 2010) means that use of the term cannot be easily defined away given the significance of its social construction (McCarthy 2007). For this reason, development in social theory may offer a number of important insights into conceptualising the rural environment and tourism-related activities.

According to Cloke (1992), rural places have been traditionally associated with specific rural functions – agriculture, sparsely populated areas, geographically dispersed settlement patterns – and rurality has been conceptualised in terms of peripherality and remoteness (Page 1994c; Hall and Boyd 2005; Müller and Jansson 2006), even though such places remain linked to the national and international political economy. Changes in the way society and non-urban places are organised and function have rendered traditional definitions of rurality less meaningful for the following reasons (Mormont 1987; McCarthy 2007; López-i-Gelats et al. 2009):

- increased mobility of people, goods and information and communication technology have eroded the autonomy of local communities;
- delocalisation of economic activity makes it difficult to define homogeneous economic regions;
- new specialised uses of rural spaces (as tourist sites, parks and development zones) have created new specialised networks of relationships in the areas concerned, many of which are no longer localised;
- people who 'inhabit' a given rural area include a diversity of temporary visitors as well as residents;
- rural spaces perform functions for non-rural users that may exist independently of the action of permanent rural populations.

Mormont (1987) therefore conceptualises rural areas as a set of overlapping social spaces, each with their own logic, institutions and network of actors (e.g. users and administrators). This reiterates many of the early ideas from behavioural scientists – that a rural space needs to be defined as a social construct where the occupiers of rural spaces interact and participate in activities such as recreation and tourism. This implies that the nature and use of rural areas for activities such as recreation and tourism are best explained by examining the processes by which their meaning of 'rural' is 'constructed, negotiated and experienced' (Cloke 1992: 55). Cloke focuses on the commodification of the countryside which has occurred, leading to the rise of (new) markets for (new) rural products where:

the countryside . . . [is] an exclusive place to be lived in; rural communities [are considered] as a context to be bought and sold; rural lifestyle [is something] which can be colonized; icons of rural culture [are commodities which] can be crafted, packed and marketed; rural landscapes [are imbued] with a new range of potential from 'pay as-you-enter' national parks, to sites for the theme park explosion; rural production [ranges] from newly commodified food to the output of industrial plants whose potential or actual pollutive externalities have driven them from more urban localities.

(Cloke 1992: 55)

In this respect, rural areas are places to be consumed and where production is based on establishing new commodities or in re-imaging and rediscovering places for recreation and tourism. The new political economy influencing agriculture, tourism and governance in the EU has also facilitated farm diversification into new forms of tourism accommodation (e.g. farm-stays) and attractions (Williams and Balaz 2000; Wilson and Anton Clavé 2013). Yet the critical processes stimulating the demand for the mass consumption of rural products have been essential in effecting such changes. Urry (1988) points to changes in taste following the emergence of a new service class which have led to greater emphasis on consumption in rural environments. These tastes have also influenced other

social groups, who have adopted similar values in the consumption of rural areas, including:

- the pursuit of a pastoral idyll;
- acceptance of cultural symbols related to the rural idyll;
- a greater emphasis on outdoor pursuits in such environments.

Influentially, Poon (1989) interpreted these changes in terms of a 'shift from an "old tourism" (e.g. the regimented and standardized holiday package) to a "new tourism" which is segmented, customized and flexible in both time and space' (see also Hummelbrunner and Miglbauer (1994) on 'new rural tourism'). This reflects changes in society from a 'Fordist' to 'post-Fordist' stage, which have involved a shift in the form of demand for tourist services from a former pattern of mass consumption 'to more individual patterns, with greater differentiation and volatility of consumer preferences and a heightened need for producers to be consumer-driven and to segment markets more systematically' (Urry 1991: 52), although this has not meant the end of mass tourism (Deprest 1997). Butler *et al.* (1998) also point to the increasing use of rural areas for purposes, e.g. mountain biking, which are juxtaposed with more traditional recreational and tourist uses, e.g. hunting. From a supply perspective, this has manifested itself in terms of 'an increasing interest in rural tourism among a better-off clientele, and also among some holidaymakers as a growing environmental awareness and a desire to be integrated with the residents in the areas they visit' (Bramwell 1994: 3). This not only questions the need to move beyond existing concepts such as core and periphery, with rural tourism as a simplistic consumption of the countryside, but also raises the question of how rural areas are being used to provide tourism and recreational experiences and how businesses are pursuing market-oriented approaches to commodification in rural environments. If the 1990s was the start of a 'new era of commodifying rural space, characterised by a speed and scale of development which far outstrip farm-based tourism and recreation of previous eras' (Cloke 1992: 59), then a critical review of this process remains significant.

Yet in reflecting on the above it is important to emphasise that change in rural areas is nothing new. Arguably the countryside in developed countries has been undergoing ongoing and, at times, rapid change since the European discovery of the Americas (Hall and Mitchell 2000). It is therefore somewhat ironic that the image of the rural as somehow more simple and unchanging is so at odds with the fundamental realities of rural change. For example, Towner (1996) documents many of the historical changes and factors which have shaped tourism and leisure in the rural environment in Europe since 1540, observing how the rural landscape has become fashionable and been developed for the use of social elites at certain times in history (e.g. the landed estates of the seventeenth and eighteenth centuries). The growth of towns and cities during the industrialisation of Europe led to an urbanised countryside around those nascent industrial centres (i.e. the construction of an urban fringe). Such patterns of recreational and tourism activity all combine to produce a wide variety of leisure and, more belatedly, tourism environments which exhibit elements of continuity in use as well as influencing our present frames of reference, but also have been in a constant state of change. For example, Towner characterises the pre-industrial period:

> where popular recreation in the countryside throughout much of Europe was rooted in the daily and seasonal rhythms of agricultural life . . . and took place in the setting of home, street, village green or surrounding fields and woods and throughout the year, a distinction can be made between ordinary everyday leisure and the major annual holiday events, and between activities that were centred around home and immediate locality and those which caused people to move.
>
> (Towner 1996: 45–6)

Changes in taste were also important. In the late eighteenth and early nineteenth century the 'Grand Tour' in Europe allowed for the circulation of new ideas of Romanticism and scenery that favoured rural environments in contrast to the industrialising cities (Towner 1985; see also Chapter 6), while innovations in transport technology facilitated a move away from a focus on urban centres to rural environments (Walton 1983). The gradual transition towards more 'private rural landscapes for the more affluent and higher social classes' began a process of restricting access to the countryside which has remained a source of contention ever since. At the same time, the rise of rural retreats and landed estates, a feature of earlier leisure history, is complemented by the 'movement of the upper and middle classes into the countryside . . . During the nineteenth century, however, the scale of movement in Britain, Europe and North America increased considerably' (Towner 1996: 232–3).

In England, not only did the urban middle classes begin to visit the countryside in growing numbers in the nineteenth and early twentieth centuries as recreationists and tourists, visiting scenic areas (e.g. the Lake District) and more remote areas (e.g. the Highlands of Scotland: see Butler and Wall 1985), but also such visits raised spatial issues of access for increasing numbers of urbanites that were celebrated by the mass trespass of Kinder Scout in the Derbyshire Peak District in 1932, which anticipated the controversy over access to the countryside that continues in Britain to the present day. Such pressures certainly contributed to the establishment of the principle of access in the National Parks and Access to the Countryside Act 1949 in the UK. As of 2010 England had about 190,000 km (118,000 miles) of public rights of way, legal rights that were modernised in the Countryside and Rights of Way (CROW) Act of 2000; 78 per cent of those trails are footpaths but others are bridleways or byways open to cyclists or even to motor vehicles. According to the Commission for Rural Communities (CRC) (2010), if England is divided into 133,676 1 km squares, 81.5 per cent of those have public rights of way, and 55.4 per cent have public rights of way with a length of 1 km or more. Following the UK precedent, similar legislative changes in other countries led to further measures to improve access to such resources (Jenkins and Prin 1998; McIntyre et al. 2001; Doody and Booth 2006). What is significant here is to emphasise that, despite imaging to the contrary, change is the norm in rural areas, and that historical factors weigh heavily not

BOX 6.1 USE OF THE NEW FOREST NATIONAL PARK

The New Forest National Park in southern England is one of the most used national parks in the country and highlights the difficulties not only in managing such spaces but also in differentiating between recreationalists and tourists. The New Forest has more visitors per square kilometre than any other national park (7.5 visits/km^2), with 15 million people living within a 90 minute drive of the Forest (New Forest National Park Authority (NFNPA) 2007). The results of a 2005 survey indicated that local day visitors from home had made an average of 257 recreational visits to the New Forest during the previous 12 months. Other day visitors from home had made an average of 45 recreational visits to the New Forest in the previous year, with overnight visitors making an average of three visits (NFNPA 2007). Forty-six per cent of visitors are over the age of 55. Walking the dog (24 per cent), relaxing, enjoying views and picnicking (13 per cent) and short walks of less than one hour were the most frequently mentioned main purposes to visit.

Although walking is a major reason for using the park, 96 per cent of visitors staying within the park used a car or private vehicle as the main mode of transport to travel to their accommodation base. Furthermore, the 2005 survey found that 88 per cent of local residents and 94 per cent of non-local day visitors used a car or private vehicle to travel to the site where they were interviewed, compared to 67 per cent of staying visitors.

The results of such research are important as they highlight the central role of the private motor car as a means of recreational access, with subsequent implications for those without car access. Furthermore, the importance of dog-walking may also seem at odds with many people's understanding of a national park, but it is important on several counts. First, it illustrates that the way that recreational space is actually used may differ from how it is often portrayed in the media. Second, it identifies an important recreational activity with respect to its size that is relatively ignored in the academic literature. Third, it highlights the importance of empirical research in identifying what actually *does* happen in recreation and tourism spaces.

---

only on how rurality is constructed but also on the institutions and structures that influence rural locales and the recreation and tourism-related issues and conflicts that occur in them.

Conceptualising the rural recreation–tourism dichotomy

One of the problems within the literature on recreation and tourism is that the absence of a holistic perspective has continued to encourage researchers to draw a distinction between recreation and tourism as complementary and yet semantically different activities, without providing a conceptual framework within which to view such issues. Cloke (1992)

suggested that the relationship between rural areas and tourism and leisure activities has changed, with the activities being the dominant elements in many rural landscapes which control and affect local communities to a much greater degree than in the past. Therefore, while a critical debate has occurred in the tourism and recreational literature in terms of the similarities and differences between tourists and recreationists, it is the social, economic and spatial outcomes that are arguably the most significant features to focus on in the rural environment. However, there is still a need to recognise the magnitude and effect of recreational and tourist use because of their timing, scale, resource impact and implications. But ultimately each use is a consumption of resources and space in relation to the user's discretionary leisure time and income. There are a range of issues to consider in relation to this debate. For example, in many countries in which rates of urbanisation are increasing, use of the countryside is a popular and growing pastime (Reeder and Brown 2005), and there is a need to avoid simplistic classifications of what constitutes tourist and recreationalist use.

Shaw and Williams (1994) prefer to use a more culturally determined definition to show that the use of rural landscapes for tourist and recreational purposes is conditioned by a wide range of social, economic and cultural meanings which affect the host area. Cultural definitions of urban and rural areas highlight not only the intrinsic qualities of the countryside which are significantly different from urban areas, but also the interpretation that 'there is nothing that is inherent in any part of the countryside that makes it a recreational resource' (Shaw and Williams 1994: 223). As Patmore (1983: 122) argued, 'there is no sharp discontinuity between urban and rural resources for recreation but rather a complete continuum from local park to remote mountain park'. If one maintains such an argument, to a certain extent it makes the geographer's role in classifying tourism and recreational environments and their uses for specific reasons and purposes rather meaningless if they are part of no more than a simple continuum of recreational and tourism resources, thereby denying new attempts to understand what motivates users to seek and consume such resources in a cultural context. Therefore, Shaw and Williams (1994: 224) prefer to view 'rural areas as highly esteemed as locales for leisure and tourism', and their use is heavily contingent upon particular factors, especially social access, and the politics of countryside ownership (see also Adey (2006) on the politics of mobility and immobility). Yet these contingencies may only really be fully understood in the context of the developed world, according to Shaw and Williams (1994), by considering three critical concepts used by geographers: the rural opportunity spectrum, accessibility and time–space budgets. However, prior to any discussion of such key concepts, it is pertinent to consider the historical dimension to tourism and recreational pursuits in rural environments, since historical

geographers emphasise continuity, change and the role of spatial separation of social classes in past periods as factors which affected the past use of rural locales.

The geographer's contribution to theoretical debate in rural contexts

'During the mid-1970s there was a hiatus in leisure and recreation research which marked a profound change from the enthusiastic promotion of agency dependent ad hoc applied research to an evaluative phase characterised by introspection and self-criticism' (Owens 1984: 174), since, prior to 1975, empirical case studies dominated the literature. After 1975 there were numerous calls for a greater consideration of leisure behaviour, and its contribution to theory was advocated (e.g. Patmore 1977, 1978, 1979, 1980; Coppock 1980; Mercer 1979a; Patmore and Collins 1981). A series of new texts in the 1980s (e.g. Kelly 1982; Smith 1983a; Torkildsen 1983) and the appearance of two journals, *Leisure Studies* and *Leisure Sciences*, raised the need for more theoretically determined research, but only a limited range of studies by geographers focused on theoretical and conceptual issues (e.g. Owens 1984), while other disciplines contributed to the debate in a more vigorous and central manner (e.g. Graefe *et al*. 1984a). Despite large-scale research funding by government research agencies (e.g. the Social Science Research Council in the UK) in the 1970s and 1980s, a lack of concern for theory has meant that geographers have made little impact on the problem that

> the large body of rural outdoor recreation research has not been consolidated in more theoretical work but one wonders whether researchers have set themselves an intellectual challenge which they are unable to meet. Certainly, there is now a steady flow of publication, albeit mainly directed to traditional ends, and because of this the argument that lack of progress towards a theory of leisure and recreation simply reflects poor funding is now much less plausible.
>
> (Owens 1984: 176)

As a consequence, Perkins (1993: 116–17) suggested four reasons for the neglect of theoretical geographical leisure research. First, within the discipline, leisure research is considered to be unimportant when compared to the central concerns of economic, social and urban geography. The second reason is that very little research funding has been made available to geographers to pursue theoretical leisure research. Third, much research has been British or North American in origin, 'where pressures between recreational uses of particular sites are very great . . . geographers have worked closely with recreational site managers to develop short to medium term management strategies for these areas'. Finally, recreation geographers 'have hardly participated in the theoretical debates which have thrived in their discipline since the 1970s' (Perkins 1993: 117).

In fact, Perkins (1993) offered one of the few attempts by geographers to rise to this challenge, using social theory, particularly structuration theory (Giddens 1984), and his research is valuable in relation to the understanding of locales for the analysis of human and spatial interaction. Locales comprise a range of settings which are different and yet connected through interactions. The interactions result from

> the life path of individuals . . . in ways that reflect patterns of production and consumption. These interactions result in a particular pattern of locales which have social and physical forms. Each life path is essentially an allocation of time between these different locales. A particular mode of production will emphasise dominant locales to which time must be allocated.
>
> (Perkins 1993: 126)

Within the literature on structuration, in a capitalist society, structure and human interaction are brought together through the concept of the locale. The dominant locales are home, work and school, and they are settings in which consumption occurs. Thus a leisure locale is a setting for interaction whereby 'people pursue leisure within the context of their life commitments and access to resources. Leisure interactions, of course, occur in and are influenced by places, and to

this extent the leisure locale includes a spatial component' (Perkins 1993: 126). Perkins (1993) argues for consideration of the position and internal organisation of the leisure locale in a rural setting, in relation to the dominant locales (i.e. home, work and school) and other institutional locales such as religion and the arts.

Structuration theory and the new regional geography emphasised producers of the interpenetration of structure and agency. Structure 'both constrains and enables people to take particular life paths, the collective effect of which is to produce and enable new members of society in their life paths . . . [where] geographical behaviour' (Perkins 1993: 117) affects people's specific situations (see also Hall (2005a), Adey (2010) for related discussions of mobilities in time and space). Therefore, the geographer in a rural setting needs to consider both structure and human interaction and how they are brought together in the context of the locale. In the context of rural tourism, the theoretical analysis advocated by Perkins (1993) for rural recreation connects closely to the debate engendered by Bramwell (1994: 2): 'does the physical existence of tourism in rural areas create a rural tourism that has a significance beyond the self-evident combination of particular activities in a specific place? In other words, do the special characteristics of rural areas help shape the pattern of tourism so that there is a particular rural tourism?' – issues that remain relevant to the present day.

Towards a concept of rural tourism

Keane et al.'s (1992) innovative but little known study on rural tourism offers a number of insights into the definition of rural tourism acknowledging that there are a variety of terms used to describe tourism activity in rural areas: agritourism, farm tourism, rural tourism, soft tourism, alternative tourism and many others which have different meanings from one country to another. Keane also points out that it is difficult to avoid some of this confusion in relation to labels and definitions because the term 'rural tourism' has been adopted by the European Union to refer to the entire tourism activity in a rural area (Keane *et al*. 1992) (a situation that arguably remains to the present day). One way of addressing this seemingly tautological proposition, that tourism in rural areas is not necessarily rural tourism when so many typologies exist for types of tourism that may or may not be deemed rural tourism, is to examine what makes rural tourism distinctive.

What makes rural tourism distinctive?

Lane (1994) discusses the historical continuity in the development of rural tourism and examines some of the key issues which combine to make rural tourism distinctive. Bramwell (1994: 3) suggests that, despite the problems of defining the concept of 'rural', 'it may be a mistake to deny our commonsense thoughts that rural areas can have distinctive characteristics or that these can have consequences for social and economic interactions in the countryside'. The views and perceptions that people hold of the countryside are different from those of urban areas, which is an important starting point for establishing the distinctiveness of rural tourism. Lane (1994) lists the subtle differences between urban and rural tourism, in which individual social representations of the countryside are a critical component of how people interact with rural areas. In fact, Squire (1994) acknowledges that both the social representations and personal images of the countryside condition whether people wish to visit rural areas for tourism, and what they see and do during their visit.

Lane (1994) also highlights the impact of changes in rural tourism since the 1970s, with far greater numbers of recreationalists and tourists now visiting rural areas. As Patmore's (1983) seminal study on recreation and leisure acknowledges, the impact of car ownership has led to a geographical dispersion of recreationalists and tourists beyond existing fixed modes of transport (e.g. railways). Consequently, tourism has moved away from a traditional emphasis on resorts, small towns and villages to become truly rural, with all but the most inaccessible wilderness areas awaiting the impact of the more mobile tourist. Despite this strong growth in the demand for rural tourism,

Lane (1994) acknowledges the absence of any systematic sources of data on rural tourism, since neither the UNWTO nor OECD has appropriate measures. In addition, there is no agreement on how to measure this phenomenon. One way of establishing the distinctive characteristics of rural tourism is to derive a working definition of rural tourism. Here the work by Lane (1994) is invaluable since it dismisses simplistic notions of rural tourism as tourism which occurs in the countryside. Lane (1994) cites seven reasons why it is difficult to produce a complex definition of rural tourism to apply in all contexts:

- Urban or resort-based tourism is not confined to urban areas, but spills out into rural areas.
- Rural areas are difficult to define, and the criteria used by different nations vary considerably.
- Not all tourism which takes place in rural areas is strictly 'rural' – it can be 'urban' in form, and merely be located in a rural area, e.g. 'theme parks', time shares or leisure hotel developments. Their degree of rurality can be both an emotive and a technical question.
- Historically, tourism has been an urban concept; the great majority of tourists live in urban areas. Tourism can be an urbanising influence on rural areas, encouraging cultural and economic change, and new construction.
- Different forms of rural tourism have developed in different regions.
- Rural areas are in a complex process of change. The impact of global markets, communications and telecommunication has changed market conditions and orientations for traditional products. The rise of environmentalism has led to increasing control by 'outsiders' over land use and resource development. Although some rural areas still experience depopulation, others are experiencing an inflow of people to retire or to develop new 'non-traditional' businesses. The once clear distinction between urban and rural is now blurred by exurbanisation, long-distance commuting and second home development.
- Rural tourism is a complex multifaceted activity: it is not just farm-based tourism. There is also a

large general-interest market for less specialised forms of rural tourism, where a major requirement of the main holiday is simply the ability to provide peace, quiet and relaxation in rural surroundings.

Consequently, rural tourism in its purest form should be:

- located in rural areas;
- functionally rural – built upon the rural world's special features of small-scale enterprise, open space, contact with nature and the natural world, heritage, 'traditional' societies and 'traditional' practices;
- rural in scale – both in terms of buildings and settlements – and, therefore, usually small scale;
- traditional in character, growing slowly and organically, and connected with local families. It will often be very largely controlled locally and developed for the long-term good of the area; and of many different kinds, representing the complex pattern of rural environment, economy, history and location (after Lane 1994).

Lane (1994: 16) argues that the following factors also have to be considered in defining rural tourism:

- holiday type;
- intensity of use;
- location;
- style of management;
- degree of integration with the community.

Using the continuum concept allows for the distinction to be made between those tourist visits which are specifically rural, those which are urban and those which fall into an intermediate category. Figure 6.1 illustrates one interpretation of this in light of the continuum notion of wilderness (see Chapter 7 for a further discussion) and the discussion above (Hall and Lew 2009). Thus, any workable definition of rural tourism needs to establish the parameters of the demand for, and supply of, the tourism experience and the extent to which it is undertaken in the continuum of rural to urban environments.

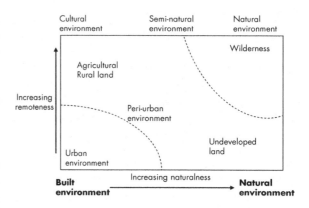

Figure 6.1 The urban, rural, wilderness continuum
Source: after Hall and Lew 2009.

The geographer's approach to rural recreation and tourism

Coppock (1982: 2) argues that 'much of the literature in the leisure field has been produced by multidisciplinary teams', of which geographers have been a part. According to Owens (1984),

> until very recently at least, leisure and recreation have been overwhelmingly viewed as synonymous with the rural outdoors. Participation in rural leisure and recreation grew rapidly during the 1950s and 1960s and was accompanied by a surge of interest in applied research . . . In the 1950s and 1960s two types of study became particularly important, national and regional demand surveys, and site studies which tackled a wide range of applied problems.
>
> (Owens 1984: 157)

There was a tendency towards such studies being published quite rapidly in Europe and North America, though, as Coppock (1982: 9) observed, 'little attention has been paid to geographical aspects of leisure in developing countries', an area which still remains poorly researched in the English language literature (Pronovost 1991; Tsai 2010).

In documenting the development of geographical research on rural recreation, Coppock (1980) points to the legacy of books on leisure and recreation which appeared in five years from 1970, which were those by Patmore (1970, later updated in 1983), Lavery (1971c), Cosgrove and Jackson (1972), I.G. Simmons (1974), Coppock and Duffield (1975), H. Robinson (1976) and Appleton (1974). These books highlight the early breadth of focus in recreation and policy management, with the spatial dimension being discussed within each text. Yet, according to Owens (1984), in the period 1975 to 1984 few major contributions were published by geographers in the UK due to the reduction in government research funds for this area. At the same time overlapping areas of research emerged in terms of a behavioural focus and perception studies, e.g. R. Lucas (1964) on wilderness perception. Yet, such research was perhaps dominated by the focus on management-oriented and site-based empirical studies often funded as consultancy reports, at the expense of conceptual and theoretical studies.

Studies of demand

Demand for rural recreation grew at 10 per cent per annum in the period 1945 to 1958 in the USA (Clawson 1958) and in the UK at a compound rate of 10–15 per cent per annum up to 1973 (Coppock 1980), and for researchers this heralded an era of rapid growth. As G.M. Robinson (1990) observes, the demand for rural recreation is strongly affected by social class, and participation rates consistently show that the more affluent, better educated and more mobile people visit the countryside, while women have much lower visiting rates. As long ago as the mid-1960s, Dower (1965) recognised leisure as the 'fourth wave' and compared the leisure phenomenon with three previous events in history that changed human activity and behaviour, the advent of industrialisation, the railway age and urban sprawl, with leisure being the fourth wave, with a 'consequent pressure on fragile environments … By any measure, the phenomenon is of immense significance' (Patmore 1983: 124). Patmore (1983) outlined the geographer's principal concerns with the demand for rural recreation in

terms of research on the increasing participation among different socio-economic groups using rural areas for recreational activities coupled with the impact of car ownership, and the resulting development of, and impact on, destinations. As a means of assessing the patterns and processes shaping recreational use in rural areas, Patmore examined the routes and range and impact of trips by users within the countryside and, at the micro level, the assessment of site patterns and activities yielded detailed insights into rural recreational behaviour. The interest in second homes was also developed, though arguably this is one clear area of overlap between rural tourism and recreation as it attracted extensive research in the 1970s (e.g. Coppock 1977a, 1982). In fact G.M. Robinson summarises the main concerns for rural areas and how the geographer's interest in spatial concerns have largely remained unchanged since the 1960s and 1970s:

> various studies have shown that, increasingly, people's leisure time is being used in a space-extensive way: a move from passive recreation to participation. Growth has been fastest in informal pursuits taking the form of day or half-day trips to the countryside with the rise in the ownership of private cars, the urban population has discovered the recreational potential of both the countryside on its doorstep and also more remote and less occupied areas.
>
> (Robinson 1990: 260)

For managers, the challenge is in equating demand with supply. As Owens (1984: 159) rightly observed, 'research in terms of people's leisure behaviour [saw] … a need to emphasise social science perspectives as a means to providing a more explicit task of managing use with supply'. The development of participation studies (e.g. the US Outdoor Recreation Resources Review Commission and the General Household Survey in Britain) provided a new direction. Here the argument developed was that specific factors such as socio-demographic variables like age, sex, income and education shaped the spatial patterns of participation. Yet many early surveys proved to be only snapshots of recreational use and were not replicated on a regular basis, making comparisons difficult, while demand changed at such a rapid rate that forecasting exercises from such results was difficult to sustain. This situation has only been complicated by changes in the institutional arrangements that surround rural tourism and recreation research. For example, Table 6.2 shows the transformation of the main agency responsible for rural recreation and tourism research, the National Parks Commission, to the Commission for Rural Communities, itself abolished in 2013, with each successor agency having different foci and funding.

Site studies

Studies of demand for rural recreation appear to have been the most numerous among geographers, with the site a spatial entity and the source of supply and ultimate object of demand. Such micro scale studies of demand and supply proliferated due to the tendency for research agencies to fund individual site studies, and the subsequent publication of results in research articles. Such studies may be classified in terms of studies of demand, in relation to economic evaluation, carrying capacity and user perception. In terms of demand such studies used a range of innovative techniques, including participant observation (e.g. Glyptis and Chambers 1982), while the geographer's preoccupation with patterns of usage together with a concern for methodological issues such as sampling and respondent bias (e.g. Mercer 1979a) also dominated the literature. The studies of economic evaluation have seen some geographers move into the

cost–benefit analysis (e.g. Mansfield 1969), where demand is often conceptualised in terms of sensitivity to distance travelled, cost of travel and entrance fees to derive a simulated demand curve. Yet research has questioned the rationality of recreational users in spatial patterns of behaviour and activity in models which assume distance minimisation is the sole pursuit for satisfaction (see Smith 1983a, 1995).

Two of the most significant themes in site studies in the 1970s and 1980s were carrying capacity and user perception studies (Owens 1984). In trying to put the concept into practice, a range of studies were developed to measure capacity (e.g. Dower and McCarthy 1967; Stankey 1973), with the attempt to differentiate between ecological, physical, social and psychological (or perceptual) capacity (see Chapter 4). The other area of study noted by Owens (1984) was user perception studies, especially in relation to the use of public lands in the United States (Stankey and McCool, 1984; Kil et al. 2012) and elsewhere (Williamson et al. 2012). The key perception studies undertaken have focused on the following range of themes, although in practice a number of the studies have often been dealt with under more than one theme:

- perception of scenery and evaluation of landscape quality;
- perception of wilderness, wilderness management, and the psychology of wilderness experience;
- social and psychological carrying capacity;
- comparison of managers' and users' perceptions;
- social benefits of recreation, socialisation into leisure, quality of life elements in leisure experience;

Table 6.2 **Changing institutional arrangements surrounding rural tourism and recreation research in England**

Organisation	Date successor organisation established
National Parks Commission	1949
Countryside Commission for England and Wales	1968
Countryside Commission for England	1991
Countryside Agency	1999
Commission for Rural Communities	2006

- behaviour at sites and social meaning of recreation in relation to particular activities;
- perceived similarities between recreation activities and substitutability;
- psychological structure of leisure, leisure activity types, typology of recreation activity preferences.

It is also important to note that the majority of such studies were conducted from the 1960s to the 1990s, with recreation perception studies not as popular a research focus at present compared to tourism perceptions or shifts into related areas such as environmental justice (Floyd and Johnson 2002), and the role of culture in influencing outdoor recreation (Johnson et al. 2004; Buijs et al. 2009).

Supply of rural recreation

The types of studies developed and published reflect the geographer's interest in rural land use and the geographer's concern with the spatial distribution of resources, which led to a range of studies of resource inventories and rural recreation. According to Pigram (1983), for many people the concept of resources is commonly taken to refer only to tangible objects in nature. An alternative way is to see resources not so much as material substances but as functions. In this sense resource functions are created by humans through the selection and manipulation of certain attributes of the environment. Resources are therefore constituted by society's subjective evaluation of their value and potential so that they satisfy recreational needs and wants.

Clawson et al. (1960) identified one of the standard approaches to recreational resources, which has been developed and modified by geographers since the early 1960s: what constitutes a recreational resource and how can you classify them so that effective planning and management can be developed? Clawson et al. (1960) distinguished between recreation areas and opportunity using a range of factors: location, size, characteristics, degree of use and extent of artificial development of the recreation resource. The result was the development of a continuum of recreational opportunities from user-oriented to resource-based, with rural areas falling into resource-based and intermediate areas (i.e. the urban fringe). While geographers have reworked and refined such ideas, resource use remains one of the underlying tenets of the analysis of recreational resources (Williamson et al. 2012). For example, Hockin et al. (1978), perhaps rather unusually from a present-day perspective, classified land-based recreational activities into:

- overnight activities (e.g. camping and caravanning);
- activities involving shooting;
- activities involving a significant element of organised competition (e.g. golf);
- activities involving little or no organised competition (e.g. angling, cycling, rambling, picnicking and wildlife observation).

Coppock and Duffield (1975) outlined their principal contribution in terms of understanding what resources were used and consumed by recreationalists, the levels and volume of use, the capacity of resources to absorb recreationalists, the range of potential resources available, the role of resource evaluation and the techniques of resource evaluation developed by geographers, though their own experience was largely confined to major studies undertaken in Lanarkshire and Greater Edinburgh. By comparing Coppock and Duffield's (1975) synthesis with Patmore (1983), assessment of the geographer's principal concern with recreational resources may be seen to concentrate around three themes. First, there is the visual character of the resource itself, the very quality that gives stimulus and satisfaction (Penning-Rowsell 1973; Appleton 1974; Dakin 2003). The second theme is recreational opportunity, the direct use of the rural environment for recreational pursuits, both on sites with a uniquely recreational purpose and on those where recreation must compete directly and indirectly with other uses (Ribe 1994). The third theme is recreational variety, the variety of rural landscapes and the variety of recreational opportunity that each affords (Nassauer et al. 2007).

It is evident that the range of issues which have guided research exhibit a large degree of commonality. Patmore (1983) outlined the main themes associated with the spatial analysis of rural recreational resources in terms of lost resources (to development and progress), preservation of resources, the active use and enjoyment of resources, the role of balancing conservation and use, and preservation and profit-recreation attractions. In addition, Patmore (1983) outlined the range of resources designed for rural recreation (e.g. forests, parks and the urban fringe), the use of linear resources (e.g. roads and footpaths), water resources and the coastal fringe, each of which has a significant rural dimension. However, as noted in Chapter 3, an important element in the supply of resources is not only their identification but also their accessibility. The latter is an issue of growing significance in many countries given concern over loss of rights to access recreational resources, such as forests, at a time when the regulatory spaces of recreation are being changed in light of neoliberal ideology.

BOX 6.2 FOREST AND WOODLAND ACCESS

In the European historical context the capacity to access forests for recreational purposes, especially foraging, has often been integral to the rights of commoners to access forest. The freedom to roam, or 'everyman's right' (*allemansrätten* in Swedish; *jokamiehenoikeus* in Finnish) is the general public's right to access certain public or privately owned, usually uncultivated, land for recreational and foraging purposes. In the Nordic countries that has become extremely important for non-commercial access to berries, herbs and mushrooms, with the public rights upheld in law (Pouta *et al.* 2006). In England and Scotland the right to roam has been much contested, with farmers and landowners often seeking to restrict public access from certain lands and walkways even if there were ancient rights to use. Nevertheless, urban population growth and the desire for countryside access, the activities of ramblers clubs, as well as the growing interest in foraging (Hall 2013i), have seen changes to law in both Scotland (Land Reform (Scotland) Act 2003) and England and Wales (Countryside and Rights of Way Act 2000) that guarantee rights of access (see p. 242).

The historic significance of forests, here used in its original meaning of uncultivated woodlands but also areas of grassland, heath and wetland, any areas that held Royal game and were outside fenced land, with respect to rights of access is often not realised by many people in Anglo-American societies. For example, King John's *Magna Carta* of 1215 contained five clauses relating to royal forests, while the arguably even more important 1217 *Charter of the Forest* of King Henry III re-established rights of access to the Royal Forest for free men, including for food foraging, which had been lost under the Norman monarchy. Elements of the Charter remained in place in British law until superseded in 1971 (Linebaugh 2008). This historical dimension is significant as it is part of the cultural and legal context of the rights to access forests, including those on private land, for recreation in present-day Anglo-American societies, as well as colonial societies such as New Zealand, even if people are unaware of them.

According to a 2009 UK Forestry Commission survey, when asked about what was important to the public generally (not specifically linked to public money) at least 90 per cent of respondents agreed with the statements that woodlands 'are important places for wildlife', 'are places where people can relax and de-stress', 'are places where people can have fun and enjoy themselves', 'make areas nicer places to live' and 'are places where people can learn about the environment'. In the UK, according to the Woodland Trust and Forestry Commission (in CRC 2010), in 2003 46 per cent of all woodlands were accessible to the public. The most extensive areas of accessible woodland are in Thetford Forest, the Forest of Dean, and within the National Parks of the New Forest, the North York Moors, Northumberland National Park and the

Lake District. However, being accessible in terms of being open to the public is not the same as accessibility in the sense of people being able to reach woodland by walking or public transport. In 2010 only 14.5 per cent of the English population had access to a wood of at least 2 ha within 500 m, although 63 per cent have access to a wood of at least 20 ha within 4 km. According to the CRC (2010), even if all existing woods were available to the public, 62 per cent of the population would still need woodland creation within 500 m to reach the minimum of a 2 ha wood and 16 per cent of the population would still require woodland creation to reach the standard of a 20 ha wood accessible within 4 km. Such a situation reflects the challenge in ensuring that existing woodland resources are maintained at a time when green belts are under pressure and there are insufficient incentives to plant new ones.

Impact of rural recreation

G.M. Robinson (1990: 270) observed that 'awareness and concern has grown over the environmental impact of recreational activity (see also Chapter 4). In fact the growing severity of this impact reflects the concentrated form of rural recreation with distinctive foci upon a few "honey-pot" sites' where concentrated use may lead to adverse environmental impacts. However, there is substantial debate with respect to the control of environmental impacts as to whether it is better to have visitors concentrated in a specific location rather than dispersed throughout the countryside. It may well be the case that dispersal is better in terms of economic objectives while concentration is best for environmental goals (Hall and Lew 2009). In addition to direct impacts, the issue of conflict remains a consistent problem associated with recreational resources in the countryside (Wray *et al.* 2010; Shilling *et al.* 2012). Recreational conflict is the condition that exists when people experience an interference of goals or the likelihood of incompatible goals as the result of another person's or group's actions, threat of action or personal/group attributes (Ångman *et al.* 2011).

Many conflicts occur between recreation and agriculture (Di Minin *et al.* 2013), which Shoard (1976) attributed to the ad-hoc manner in which recreational use of agricultural land has developed. For example, farmers are frequently dissatisfied with recreationalists' use of rights of way across their land due to the damage and problems caused by a minority of recreationalists (e.g. litter, harassment of stock and pollution). One problem which has emerged in New Zealand as well as many other countries is a rise in the prevalence of giardia, a water-borne disease spread by recreationalists and tourists defecating and urinating in streams and water sources (Boehm and Soller 2013). However, as Owens summarised:

> In general, research has been problem-orientated to meet specific managerial requirements, with the consequence that ad hoc site studies proliferated without there being any particular intention of making a contribution to the development of testable theory. Interest has tended to focus on concepts (e.g. social carrying capacity) and the intricacies of methodology (e.g. attitude scales and factor analysis). Of course conceptual and methodological development is a vital part of research, but the main criticism here relates to the degree to which there has been introspection.
>
> (Owens 1984: 173)

In view of these comments, attention is now turned to the geographer's contribution to the analysis of rural tourism.

Rural tourism: spatial analytical approaches

In the literature on rural tourism (e.g. Sharpley 1993; Page and Getz 1997; Sharpley and Sharpley 1997;

Butler *et al.* 1998), there are few comparatively explicit spatial analytical approaches which make the geographer's perspective stand out above other social science contributions. The following section discusses the impact of rural tourism followed by a consideration of understanding some aspects of rural tourism, such as second home tourism, from a mobilities and multiple dwelling perspective.

Impact of rural tourism

The literature on tourism impacts has long since assumed a central position within the emergence of tourism research, as early reviews by geographers confirm (e.g. Mathieson and Wall 1982). However, in a rural context, impact research has not been at the forefront of methodological and theoretical developments. Within the social and cultural dimensions of rural tourism influential early works include Bracey's (1970) work on the countryside and Bouquet and Winter's (1987a, 1987b) diverse anthology of studies that consider the relationship between tourism, politics and the issue of policies to control and direct tourism (and recreation) in the countryside in the post-war period. Up until the mid-1990s geographers had largely remained absent from this area of study as Hall and Jenkins (1998) and Jenkins *et al.* (1998) indicate, although since then the policy dimensions of access, the role of the state in peripheral regions, as well as second home ownership have all become very significant research areas (Curry 2000; Hall and Müller 2004; Doody and Booth 2006; Müller and Jansson 2006).

A number of researchers have sought to diversify the focus of social and cultural impact research to include concerns about the way in which tourism development may change rural cultures (e.g. Byrne *et al.* 1993) and the consumption of rural environments and cultures in relation to late modernity or the postmodern society, which has a specific relevance for studies in geography. The role of women in rural tourism has also belatedly attracted interest as a highly seasonal and unstable economic activity, although the gendered nature of such service work may contribute to the marginal status of women in the rural workforce or, at the very least, reinforcement of traditional gender roles (Bensemann and Hall 2010). Other studies also indicate the importance of community participation in tourism planning so that the local population, and women in particular, is not excluded from the benefits of rural tourism development (Edwards 1991; Keane *et al.* 1992; Timothy 2002; Ngubane and Diab 2005), as well as indigenous people and traditional cultures, including with respect to land and resource rights (Butler and Hinch 1996, 2007; Hall 1996a).

Considerable attention has been paid in the literature to residents' perceptions and attitudes towards tourism (in common with recreation research), including studies of small towns and rural areas (e.g. Long *et al.* 1990; Johnson *et al.* 1994; Lipkina and Hall 2014), but few geographers have undertaken longitudinal studies of rural tourism's impact on the way communities view, interact, accept or deny tourism (Page 1997a). However, as Butler and Clark (1992: 180) conclude, 'More research is needed on the relationship between the uneven social composition of the countryside, the spatially variable development of tourism, and the problematic relationship between the two'. This is especially important because of the role of tourism consumption and production in exurbanisation processes.

Within the developed world, exurbanisation, the migration of urban residents to rural environments, has increased greatly since the 1970s. Often characterised as an 'escape to the country' or 'rural dilution' (Smailes 2002), exurban processes are usually associated with a post-productivist countryside in which 'landscapes of production' are transformed into 'landscapes of leisure and consumption' (Butler *et al.* 1998; Williams and Hall 2000, 2002; Hall and Müller 2004). Primary residences there mingle with second homes and country acreages. These are situated in natural or countryside settings that have usually until recently been worked for agriculture, but which, through their exurbanisation, are increasingly entering the land logic of the metropolis (Cadieux 2005). Such moves are often motivated by perceptions of an improved quality of life in rural or peri-urban locations, with such ideas seemingly reinforced by lifestyle shows on commercial television, films and novels. In Australia and New Zealand, this has often been witnessed in the processes of 'sea change' or 'tree change', in reference to permanent and temporary (second home) lifestyle migration to high amenity rural areas (Walmsley 2003; Burnley and Murphy 2004).

Tourism is deeply embedded in exurban processes for at least three main reasons (Hall 2009d). First, tourism and hospitality have assisted in the promotion of particular images of rurality and rural idylls. Second, for many families and individuals that make the move to rural areas and the peri-urban fringe, hospitality and tourism become an important source of income. Tourism and hospitality are therefore simultaneously involved in the consumption and (re)production of idealised exurban spaces by both temporary and more permanent migrants, with the development of so-called 'lifestyle' businesses by exurbanites being widely recognised (Ateljevic and Doorne 2000; Hall and Rusher 2004; Hall 2009d). Third, the majority of tourism businesses in peri-urban areas are geared towards day-trippers and short-stay visitors who are seeking easy access to the countryside, with their desire to visit itself being geared towards certain idealised notions of rurality which are also shared by many of the owners of such businesses (Hall 2005a). Here, visitor and producer motivations for mobility are almost identical, with tourism arguably serving to produce and reinforce certain idealised images of nature and rurality, thereby only further enhancing the amenity values of such locations within exurban processes (Cadieux 2005) – an observation borne out in Halfacree's (1994) research into exurban migrant decision-making in Lancaster and mid-Devon, United Kingdom, and Crump's (2003) exploration of exurban migrants' identification of key 'pull' factors in their move to Sonoma County, California, USA. In both cases it was the perceived 'quality' of the rural environment that was the largest explanatory factor in explaining the decision to migrate. However, there is surprisingly little research on the home spaces of exurban migrants and the ways in which the commercial utilisation of private space may affect perceptions and understandings of the exurban experience and the manner in which notions of home are managed (Hall 2009d). It is therefore somewhat ironic that, with rural geographers making such a major contribution to rural studies, only a limited number have examined the implications in terms of social theory as well as the empirical dimensions of tourism development.

Economic impact

The economic impact of rural tourism has been a fruitful area for social science research, often emphasising or challenging the role of tourism as a panacea for all the economic and social ills of the countryside, although the major contribution of geographers has largely been in relation to the study of farm tourism and alternative food networks (although see Getz (1981, 1986b, 1993c, 1994) for a longitudinal study of the Spey Valley, Scotland). As Butler and Clark rightly acknowledge, tourism in rural areas is not necessarily the magical solution to rural development, given its

> income leakages, volatility, declining multipliers, low pay, imported labour and the conservatism of investors. The least favoured circumstance in which to promote tourism is when the rural economy is already weak, since tourism will create highly unbalanced income and employment distributions. It is a better supplement for a thriving and diverse economy than as a mainstay of rural development.
> (Butler and Clark 1992: 175)

In this respect, Butler and Clark's (1992) research is useful in that it identifies the principal concerns in rural economic research and the role of tourism in development in relation to:

- income leakage;
- multipliers;
- labour issues (local versus imported and low pay);
- the limited number of entrepreneurs in rural areas;
- the proposition that tourism should be a supplement rather than the mainstay of rural economies.

Farm tourism

Farm tourism has long been portrayed as offering one way of facilitating agricultural diversification (Vogeler 1977; Wrathall 1980; Dernoi 1983; Frater 1983; Oppermann 1995, 1998b; Hall and Kearsley 2001). According to N.J. Evans (1992a: 140), research on farm tourism can be divided into two categories. The first is an expanding literature concerned with 'differing types of farm diversification as a major option adapted by farm families to aid business restructuring, necessitated by falling farm incomes'. The second is 'one devoted specifically to farm tourism' (Evans 1992a: 140). However, the second group of studies often lack definitional clarity, and fail to distinguish between the accommodation, recreational and agricultural components of farm tourism (Evans and Ilbery 1989). Furthermore, a major impediment to developing a more sophisticated understanding of farm tourism remains the absence of accurate national studies of the growth and development of farm tourism, although some national studies are available of specific areas of the tourism and agriculture relationship, such as those on wine tourism in New Zealand (Baird and Hall 2013, 2014; Hall and Baird 2014).

A survey of England and Wales undertaken in the early 1990s identified almost 6,000 farm businesses with accommodation (Evans 1992b). It also undertook a geographical analysis of the distribution of such accommodation, with the upland areas and South West England being the dominant locations, with a diversity of modes of operation (bed and breakfast, self-catering, camping and caravanning) and niche marketing used to satisfy particular forms of tourism demand (e.g. weekend breaks, week-long breaks and traditional two-week holidays). At the time Evans (1992b) acknowledged the absence of national studies of why farm businesses have pursued this activity and the range of factors influencing their decision to undertake it. In an Australian study Ollenburg and Buckley (2007) noted that farm tourism enterprises combine the commercial constraints of regional tourism, the non-financial features of family businesses and the inheritance issues of family farms.

In contrast to Europe and the United States, social motivations were found to be marginally more important overall than economic motivations in Ollenburg and Buckley's (2007) research. For most operators, however, both are important. Similar findings were also reported in Hall and Rusher's (2004) research in New Zealand, which found that such businesses often had multiple income streams as well as both economic and social motivations, the latter being especially important for more peripheral operations. As with earlier UK research (Ilbery 1991), Hall and Rusher (2004) found that larger farm businesses had also diversified into farm tourism and reflected the capital requirements of many farm tourism ventures. More recent New Zealand research (Bensemann and Hall 2010) raised the important issue that many rural tourism businesses that were often described as family businesses were in fact examples of co-preneurship in which there was no intention to pass such businesses on to other members of the family. They further highlighted that because many such households had multiple income streams rural tourism operations were often highly gendered.

A longstanding issue with farm tourism is the extent to which tourism can effectively offer farms alternative income streams. In the UK Maude and van Rest (1985) argued that due to the limited returns for small farmers and the constraints of existing planning legislation it is not a significant means of tackling the serious problem of low farm incomes in upland areas (see also Jenkins *et al.* 1998). However, such a perspective potentially provides only a limited understanding of the various financial and economic mechanisms that households may use to hold on to family farms. Therefore, the use of farm tourism as a supplementary form of income needs to be understood in the wider set of social relations that individuals and households may have with the land and the place that they live (Hall and Rusher 2004). Nevertheless, the continued debate and focus on farm tourism need to be understood in the context of a more critical debate on the wider socio-economic significance of rural tourism and the way it may be integrated into other contemporary theoretically informed analyses.

Food and tourism

One area of growing relationship between tourism and agriculture is the development of food tourism, including the associated areas of wine tourism. Food, wine (and many other alcoholic beverages such as whisky), and tourism are all products that are differentiated on the basis of regional identity (Hall *et al.* 2003a). For example, wine is often identified by its geographical origin (e.g. Burgundy, Champagne, Rioja), which, in many cases, has been formalised through a series of appellation controls in turn founded on certain geographical characteristics of a place (Moran 1993, 2001; Hall and Mitchell 2008; Overton 2010). Foods (e.g. cheese) are also identified by their place of origin. Similarly, tourism is promoted by the attraction of regional or local destinations. It should therefore be of little surprise that the relationship between food and tourism is extremely significant at a regional level through the contribution that regionality provides for product branding, place promotion and, through these mechanisms, economic development (Ilbery and Kneafsey 2000a, 2000b; Bruwer and Johnson 2010; Blichfeldt and Halkier 2013). Ilbery and Kneafsey (2000b) appropriately described this process within the context of globalisation as 'cultural relocalization'.

The wine, food and tourism industries all rely on regional branding for market leverage and promotion (Hall and Mitchell 2008). Indeed, the geographic origins of food are increasingly being protected under intellectual property regulation (Hall *et al.* 2003a; Coombe and Aylwin 2011). Hall (1996b: 114) describes the importance of tourism place and wine appellation or region thus: 'there is a direct impact on tourism in the identification of wine regions because of the inter-relationships that may exist in the overlap of wine and destination region promotion and the accompanying set of economic and social linkages'. In addition, relationships between food and tourism are also created through the purchasing patterns of tourists, which may have a significant impact on local production and the maintenance or expansion of the local farming economy (Telfer and Wall 1996; Mitchell and Hall 2001, 2003; Smith and Hall 2003).

Tourism has long been regarded as having the potential to contribute to regional development. However, ongoing economic restructuring and change in rural areas have increased the focus on tourism and how agricultural production may be enhanced through tourism demand. Moreover, these changes have been accompanied by the perceived need to retain or attract people in rural areas, maintain aspects of 'traditional' rural lifestyles and agricultural production, and conserve aspects of the rural landscape. Many wine regions around the world have been affected by changed patterns of demand for wine and levels of tariff protection, which have led to the planting of new grape varieties or, in some cases, loss of vineyards to other forms of production. Yet demand has also meant that some areas, particularly in Australia, Canada, China, New Zealand and the United States, have now been planted which had previously not been seriously considered for commercial wine production (Hall and Mitchell 2008). Within this context food and wine tourism is therefore emerging as an increasingly important component of rural diversification and development (Hall *et al.* 2000a, 2000b; OECD 2012).

Strategies to integrate tourism and cuisine in order to promote economic development and the creation of sustainable food systems occur at national, regional and local levels (Hall and Mitchell 2002; Hall 2012c). Ideally, these levels should be integrated in order to maximise the likelihood of policy success (Thorsen and Hall 2001). However, often the reality is that different levels of government and industry will undertake their own initiatives without consulting or co-operating with other levels. As Figure 6.2 indicates, there are a number of mechanisms for promoting sustainable food systems utilising the relationship between wine and food, each of which operates most effectively at particular levels. Although intervention by the national and local state will occur at all levels it is very common for the policy activities at the higher level to be implemented at the lower level in order to achieve targeted regional and local development goals (Hall *et al.* 2000a; Telfer 2000a, 2000b; OECD 2012).

At the national and regional level promotion and branding are extremely common strategies to link

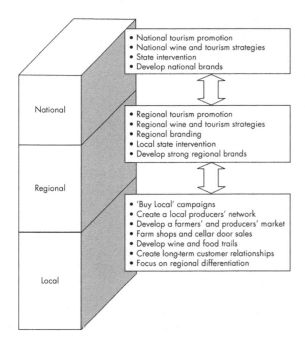

Figure 6.2 Relationship between national, regional and local strategies

food with tourism. For example, in an effort to capitalise on and maximise the tourism potential of the wine industry, several Australian states and regions created specific wine and food tourism bodies to facilitate and co-ordinate promotion and development (Hall and Macionis 1998). However, despite the ability of regions to brand themselves in terms of wine and food tourism, the establishment of other forms of network relationships between food and wine producers and the tourism industry may be more problematic (Smith and Hall 2003; Hall 2004a, 2004b, 2012c). Hall *et al.* (1997–8) noted several barriers to creating effective links between wine producers and the tourism industry that remain pertinent to the present:

- the often secondary or tertiary nature of tourism as an activity in the wine industry;
- a dominant product focus of wine-makers and wine marketers;

- a general lack of experience and understanding within the wine industry of tourism, and a subsequent lack of entrepreneurial skills and abilities with respect to marketing and product development;
- the absence of effective intersectoral linkages, which leads to a lack of inter- and intra-organisational cohesion within the wine industry, and between the wine industry and the tourism industry.

In the case of wine and food tourism in Australia, the federal government intervened to create relevant networks in the development of specific organisations and/or the provision of funding for research, education, co-operative strategies and mechanisms, and information provision. Information gaps are a major factor in the impairment of network formation (N. Scott *et al.* 2008). Indeed, there are often substantial negative attitudes towards tourism by wineries and some food producers, whereas tourism organisations tend to be far more positive towards the wine and food industry. This situation reflects Leiper's (1989, 1990) concept of tourism's partial industrialisation, which suggests that businesses need to perceive that they are part of the tourism industry before they will formally interact with tourism suppliers. Empirical research in New Zealand has also demonstrated that partial industrialisation and network relations appear to affect innovation practices in wine tourism as well (Hall and Baird 2014).

Several models of local network development are utilised in food systems (Figure 6.3). The classic industrial model of the food supply chain of producer–wholesaler–retailer–consumer all linked through transport networks has provided for a relatively efficient means of distributing food but it has substantially affected the returns producers get, as well as placing numerous intermediaries between consumers and producers. The industrial model has allowed for the development of larger farm properties, reduced labour costs and supported export industry, but it has done little to promote sustainable economic development and food systems, especially in relation to hospitality and tourism (Gössling and Hall 2013). In tourism terms this relationship has been utilised in

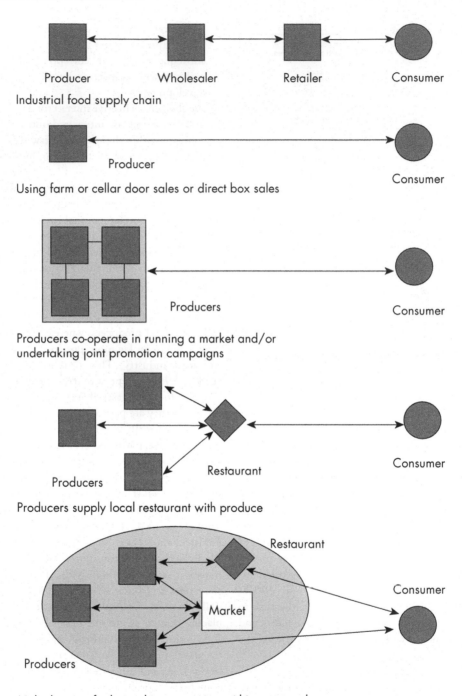

Industrial food supply chain

Using farm or cellar door sales or direct box sales

Producers co-operate in running a market and/or
undertaking joint promotion campaigns

Producers supply local restaurant with produce

Multiple sets of relationships operating within a network
providing a co-operative basis for branding and promotion

Figure 6.3 Creating different supply chains and local food systems

national branding and promotion when multiple supply chains are bundled together to attract the foreign customer. One alternative is to create a direct relationship between producers and consumers. This may be done by direct marketing and 'box deliveries' (e.g. the delivery of a box of seasonal produce direct to the consumer). In relation to tourism an important direct relationship is the opportunity for the consumer to purchase at the farm or cellar door, allowing the consumer to experience where the produce is from and the people who grow or make it, thereby creating the potential for the development of long-term relationship marketing. Such direct sales are extremely popular with small wineries and horticultural producers and are often utilised by peri-urban and rural producers who are located close to urban centres where they can take advantage of the day-trip market. Nevertheless, such individual developments, while useful at the business level and adding to the overall attractiveness and diversity of a location, do not necessarily promote a region more effectively.

Co-operative relationships between producers provide the basis for the creation of producer networks that can pool resources to engage in local promotion and branding and undertake research (Hall *et al.* 1997–8; N. Scott *et al.* 2008). The pooling of resources can also lead to the development of produce and farmers' markets, which have experienced massive growth since the 1990s (Hall and Sharples 2008; Hall 2013f). In the United States there were 1,755 farmers markets operating nationwide by 1994, 2,863 by 2000, just under 4,500 by 2006 and 7,175 in 2012 (Hall 2013f). In the UK the first of the modern farmers' markets was (re-)established in 1997 as a pilot project in Bath, which followed many of the elements of the most successful US markets (Holloway and Kneafsey 2000). In 2002 there were 240, and by 2006 the number had risen to more than 550 markets, with approximately half being certified, and there were estimates that up to 800 markets would be sustainable throughout the UK (Hall 2013f). The positive impacts of farmers' markets on the regional economy and in generating employment may be substantial, including the enlivening of public space (Hall and Sharples 2008; Hall 2013f).

Another model of generating local food production is the use of a restaurant to act as the conduit by which local produce is presented to tourists. The development of local purchasing relationships by restaurants can have a substantial impact on local produce as it can assist in developing quality produce, allow producers to gain a clearer understanding of how their produce is being used, as well as providing a guaranteed sales outlet for their produce (Smith and Hall 2003). In the case of the latter the knowledge of a guaranteed minimum income may allow producers the opportunity to expand production and find other markets for their produce. Finally, we arrive at the ideal model of multiple sets of producer and consumer relationships operating within a formal network structure which provides for branding and promotion as well as economic networking and resource sharing. A good example of this type of development is Tastes of Niagara in Ontario, which is a Quality Food Alliance of Niagara food producers, wine-makers, chefs, restaurateurs and retailers that was established in 1993 (Telfer 2000a, 2000b, 2001), or the more recently created Ontario Culinary Tourism Alliance (http://ontarioculinary.com/). However, as with farm tourism, it is important to recognise that tourism may not be a viable sales avenue for all producers and that diversification goals may be better achieved through other means. Table 6.3 therefore provides a summary of advantages and disadvantages of food tourism at the business level, while at the regional/ destination level the advantages to developing food-related tourism include the following (Hall and Sharples 2008; Hall 2012c):

- The high profile of some foods and cuisines attract tourists and can provide other regional business opportunities.
- A positive image of the region is promoted through association with a quality product.
- Food tourism can help differentiate a region's position in the tourism marketplace if connected with local foods.
- Food tourism is an attraction in its own right that can help extend the range of reasons for visiting a destination. Food tourism may therefore help

Table 6.3 Summary of advantages and disadvantages of food tourism at the food business level

Advantages	Disadvantages
Consumer exposure	Increased costs and management time
Brand awareness and potential loyalty	Inability to significantly increase sales
Customer relationships	May not be the right market from the
Better margins	perspective of broader business products
Additional sales outlet	Capital required
Market intelligence on products and consumers	Issues associated with seasonality
Customer education	Potential risks from biosecurity breaches
New sales opportunities via direct sales and/or new B2B	Additional health and safety requirements
relationships, i.e. growers to restaurants and food vendors	Opportunity costs
Greater control of supply chain and value chain with potentially	
positive implications for income, branding and sustainability	

Sources: Hall 2004b, 2012c; Hall and Mitchell 2008; Hall and Baird 2014.

extend length of stay and increase visitor expenditure on local product. For example, in Walla Walla, the most prominent wine county in Washington, USA, slightly less than 17 per cent of all restaurant and approximately 40 per cent of all hotel revenue is tied to the wine industry (Storchmann 2010).

Recreation, tourism and sustainability

Ideas of sustainable development have been as influential in the area of rural policy as they have elsewhere (Murdoch 1993; Whatmore 1993). However, much of the discussion on applications of sustainability has been about individual components of rurality (e.g. attempts at developing sustainable agriculture), rather than a comprehensive approach to integrate the socio-cultural, economic and environmental components of both sustainability and rurality. For example, the Rural White Paper entitled *Rural England: A Nation Committed to a Living Countryside* (Department of the Environment and Ministry of Agriculture, Fisheries and Food (DoE/MAFF) 1995) was the first specifically rural policy from a British government for 50 years (Blake 1996).

According to Butler and Hall (1998), in many western regions and countries the structure of the relatively homogeneous and distinct rural systems of the post-Second World War period has been either destroyed or weakened. They argue that such weakness is a result of at least three types of restructuring, namely: the collapse of peripheral areas unable to shift to a more capital-intensive economy; the selective and reductionist process of industrialisation of the remaining agricultural sector; and the pressures of urban and exurban development. Butler and Hall concluded that the result is a rural system

> suffering absolute decline along its extensive margins and the rural–urban interface, with the intervening core area weakened by decoupling of farm and non-farm sectors and the shift of decision making to urban based corporations and governments. Restructuring has created a fragmented and reduced rural system which seems to lack most of the criteria for sustainability in either economic or community terms.
>
> (Butler and Hall 1998: 252)

Despite images to the contrary, rurality is no longer dominated by concepts of food production, and new uses of the countryside, particularly related to recreational and tourism activities, are redefining the idea of what constitutes the rural landscape. In Britain, as in many other industrialised countries, these uses are exerting extreme pressures and creating new conflicts not only in terms of rural policy-making and their relationship to agriculture but also between different user groups and perceptions of a desired countryside (Curry 1992; Mercer 2000; Ångman *et al.* 2011). For example, at the same time as there are large numbers of people visiting the English countryside, which inevitably leads to the transformation of villages, and the creation of tourist facilities and infrastructure, the majority of the population also believe that the countryside should be protected at all costs (Blake 1996; Countryside Agency 2000; Commission for Rural Communities 2010) (presumably as long as this cost would not result in the exclusion of those who wanted it saved). In the case of the United Kingdom the outbreak of foot and mouth disease in February 2001 probably focused more attention on what is really happening in the countryside than ever before. As the story unfolded in the media, it quickly became apparent that tourism was a far greater economic contributor to rural areas than was farming. Nevertheless, policy measures were still being primarily developed in relation to the agricultural sector rather than the needs of the tourism sector to recover from the impacts of the measures to control the disease on tourist and recreational mobility and access to the countryside (Coles 2003; Miller and Ritchie 2003). However, the management, policy and planning responses that have been put in place by the central and local governments in Britain in response to the economic and social crisis that the disease revealed to the wider public has only been one of less government involvement, and more stress on the market and the role of volunteers and non-government organisations. The vital role of appropriate regulatory structures has not been addressed. Indeed, issues of biosecurity remain integral to tourism development in agricultural areas because of the possibilities of diseases and pests being spread through human mobility (Hall 2003c, 2005a, 2005e), a point perhaps borne out by the massive decline of the ash tree population in the UK as a result of the introduction of a pathogen from the European continent (Hall and Baird 2013).

Indeed, one of the major errors which policy-makers and some academics have often made with respect to tourism and recreation in rural areas is to treat them in isolation from other factors that contribute to the social, environmental and economic fabric of rural regions. Tourism needs to be appropriately embedded within the particular set of linkages and relationships which comprise the essence of rurality, with tourism being recognised as but one component of the policy mix which government and the private sector formulate with respect to rural development (Curry and Owen 2009; Curry 2010; Kizos *et al.* 2010). Butler and Hall (1998) argue that many regional authorities fail to recognise that it is the visual complexity of the rural landscape which generates amenity values for locals and visitors alike. In the attempt to generate economic development, a wider tax base and employment, inappropriate policies and strategies may be followed. As Hall and Butler (1998: 255) observed, 'Policy measures in one sector, such as the attraction of agribusinesses or large foreign investments to a region, may lead to a decline of the industrial value of the region to other industries, such as tourism and businesses which are based on adding-value to local primary production'.

A genuinely integrated approach to rural resource development is therefore essential for sustainable rural development. As Jenkins (1997) observed with respect to rural Australia, government can best assist rural areas to meet the challenges of economic restructuring and change by supporting the development of 'soft infrastructure', such as education and entrepreneurial skills, and by attaching greater importance to the provision of relevant research to improve decision-making, rather than specifically supporting programmes which encourage the production of brochures, walking trails and other small-scale local tourism initiatives, such as visitor centres. Such an integrated approach to rural policy is also essential given the extent to which tourism and recreation are embedded in broader processes of counter- and exurbanisation (Buller and Hoggart 1994; Swaffield and Fairweather 1998; Mitchell 2004; Marcoullier *et al.* 2011), multiple dwelling (Hall and Müller 2004; McIntyre *et al.* 2006; Paris 2009), and amenity and lifestyle migration (Hall 2005a; Janoschka and Haas 2014) that serve to promote rather than divide the connections between rural and urban spaces and centres. According to Champion (1998),

> A key theme in the debate is the extent to which those moving into rural areas are motivated by a desire for 'rurality' in terms of rural living environment and lifestyle – in essence making a 'new start' that represents a 'clean break' from their past – as opposed to choosing (or even being forced) to move because of a geographical redistribution of elements that have always been important to their quality of life such as jobs, housing, services and safety.
>
> (Champion 1998: 22)

Nevertheless, such movements are not new and are part of processes that have been occurring in the developed world since the late 1960s and which tie rural tourism back to some of the issues raised in Chapter 1 with respect to the growth in temporary mobility and the need to see tourism and recreation within the broader context of human movement. As Law and Warnes (1973: 377) observed in the early 1970s, 'evidence from both North America and north-west Europe is that rural areas, preferably in either waterside or hilly areas are the preferred setting for vacation and retirement homes'.

Mobilities and multiple dwelling: second homes in the countryside

A growing number of people in the western world have not only one fixed home, but share their lives between various places of dwelling (Hiltunen et al. 2013). The decision to own leisure-oriented multiple dwellings is often related to a desire to spend time at a second home in a high amenity environment and pursue recreational interests and quality-of-life goals (Müller 2007, Marcouiller et al. 2011). The utilisation of second homes therefore represents a significant portion of the leisure activities of many tourists and day-trippers in a number of countries around the world, and as such they are an integral, though often ignored, component of both domestic

and international tourism, and rural economic development (Jaakson 1986; Hall and Müller 2004). However, more than that they also illustrate the way in which tourism, recreation and leisure serve to connect various locations, as well as the growing difficulties for some in separating tourism from the mundane (Edensor 2007) and home from away (Hall 2005a).

Second homes are defined as:

> a permanent building which is the occasional residence of a household that usually lives elsewhere and which is primarily used for recreation purposes. This definition excludes caravans, boats, holiday cottages (rented for a holiday) and properties in major cities and industrial towns.
>
> (Shucksmith 1983: 174)

Shucksmith's definition is comparable to a number of approaches to second home research such as in Scandinavia and Canada, where the primary focus is the summer cottage. However, it should be noted that mobile second homes, such as caravans and camper trailers, which are also a very significant form of holidaying as well as housing in some instances, have had very little research undertaken on them.

The size of the second home market can be substantial. For example, in Finland at the end of 2011 there were nearly 0.5 million registered second homes and approximately 3,600 new ones being built annually. In addition, there are around 170,000 rural vacant detached houses, of which over 70 per cent are used as second homes. The result is that every other family had access to a second home through friends or extended family relations (Hiltunen et al. 2013). In Denmark second homes are the most important category of recreational accommodation, with approximately 220,000 second homes available to the 5.2 million people living in Denmark (Tress 2002). In Sweden there are between 500,000 and 700,000 second homes, with second homes accounting for 23 per cent of all overnight stays (Lundmark and Marjavaara 2004). In the case of New Zealand approximately 8 per cent of domestic overnight stays occur in second homes; while for holiday and leisure purposes holiday homes account for 13.9 per cent of accommodation used (Keen and Hall 2004).

Historically, the research into second homes has focused on motivational, planning, regional development and impact-related issues. Second homes development has emerged as a major issue in a number of countries, including Canada, Denmark, Sweden and Wales, where, in some cases, local communities have perceived second home purchase by 'outsiders' as being socially and economically invasive (Selwood and May 2001; Janoschka and Haas 2014; Lipkina and Hall 2014). However, despite their economic, social and cultural significance, geographical research on second homes has been highly variable in terms of regions studied and the maintenance of continued interest in second homes as a research issue. Two reasons may be put forward for this. First, the degree of research interest they generate may vary in relation to their value or impact, whether it be economic, social or environmental. Second, second home research may well have fallen out of fashion due to the development of other research interests, for example the rise of interest in ecotourism. Regardless of these points, there exists a large body of international research focusing specifically on, or around, second homes (Hall and Müller 2004).

The first major period for research on second homes was in the 1970s. Prior to this time research was undertaken primarily in North America (especially Canada), France and Scandinavia, where there is a strong tradition of second home ownership (Coppock 1977a). During the 1970s an increase in the research undertaken from the United Kingdom culminated in Coppock's (1977a) benchmark publication *Second Homes: Curse or Blessing?* Since the mid-1990s, there has been renewed interest in second home development, as indicated by work in Australia (e.g. Selwood and May 2001) Canada (e.g. Halseth 1998), China (e.g. Huang and Yi 2011), Denmark (e.g. Tress 2002), Finland (e.g. Hiltunen 2007; Pitkänen 2011; Hiltunen *et al.* 2013), Ireland (Norris and Winston 2010), New Zealand (e.g. Fountain and Hall 2002), Norway (e.g. Kaltenborn 1997a, 1997b, 1998; Flognfeldt 2002; Vittersø 2007; Farstad 2011), South Africa (e.g. Visser 2006; Hoogendoorn and Visser 2011), Sweden

(Müller 1999, 2002a, 2002b, 2002c; Gustafson 2002b; Müller and Hall 2003), the United Kingdom (Gallent 1997; Gallent and Tewdwr-Jones 2000; Paris 2009, 2010) and the United States (Marcouiller *et al.* 2011), as well as the development of international overviews of the topic (Hall and Müller 2004; Müller 2004; Roca *et al.* 2013).

Regional economic development is often advocated by local governments as one of the major benefits of second homes. Second homes provide a means for regional development through:

- increasing direct visitor expenditure to the region from second home owners and their visitors;
- the provision of infrastructure used for both home owners and other tourists;
- the support of service and construction industries via the construction of new and maintenance of existing homes;
- the opportunity for further regional development via population gain through owners retiring to their second home.

However, despite the opportunities second homes may provide for regional development, the actual contribution varies from location to location, with no consistent benchmark available from which to judge the effect that they will have, particularly in the long term. Though the benefits to a region of second home development are potentially high, they may not always exceed the costs created for government in relation to increases in waste, health care and other services, as well as the social and environmental impacts that may also occur (Hall and Müller 2004; Hoogendoorn and Visser 2011; Müller 2011). For example, Deller *et al.* (1997) estimated that for the United States second homes generate revenues that just cover the increased expenses for public services. However, in other locations second home tourism is considered an important cornerstone of many rural economies. Second home owners tend to favour small rural shops and therefore contribute to the maintenance of service levels in the countryside (Marcouiller *et al.* 1998; Müller 1999: Hall and Müller 2004). For example, Müller (1999) established that four

German second home owners in Sweden spent as much as a permanent Swedish household. In a study of recreational homes in Wisconsin and Minnesota in the United States, Marcouiller *et al.* (1998) found that at the county level the expenditure patterns of the residents and recreational home owners were generally similar with respect to how much money was spent outside the county.

As with all tourism development, second homes invariably bring a range of impacts to an area. Undesirable physical impacts may occur due to a lack of adequate infrastructure and planning; this includes lack of sewerage systems, inappropriate site choice, excessive development and a failure to consider the excessive burden upon areas at peak holiday times (Gartner 1987). It has long been recognised that the responsibility for the management of these impacts usually lies with regional and local government, which must put effective regulatory controls into place (Dower 1977; Shucksmith 1983). Local government may also have a significant role in relation to social impacts, as it can regulate development so as not to incur conflict between second home owners and various groups over levels of development (Jordan 1980; Gartner 1986; Green *et al.* 1996; Visser 2004), perceived social inequality (Paris 2010) and competition for the use of land (Gallent 1997; Hoogendoorn and Visser 2011). Second homes, and the related issues of 'homes for locals', development controls and the cost of maintaining services, are therefore the focus of contested physical and social space issues (Girard and Gartner 1993; Fountain and Hall 2002; Hall and Müller 2004; Müller 2011; Lipkina and Hall 2014), especially given growing economic inequalities in many developed countries.

To understand the impacts of second homes, one must discover the motivations behind the decisions to have a second home. Second home owners are motivated by a number of reasons, many of which have to do with the specific amenity characteristics of a location, including distance from primary residence, physical and social characteristics of the area and availability of recreational opportunities. However, one of the most significant aspects of second home ownership is the extent to which it is related to broader travel and lifestyle behaviour and the overall personal, spatial and temporal mobilities of individuals and families. The identification of a desirable second home environment tends to be related to an environmental search process of which travel is a key component. Holidaymaking provides opportunities to identify potential second home locations, while second homes may also be part of a wider lifestyle strategy that utilises second home purchase as a precursor to more permanent retirement or lifestyle migration. Indeed, recent renewed interest by geographers in second homes and their relationship to domestic and international migration suggests that second home tourism needs to be increasingly seen within a broader framework that examines the interrelationships between different mobilities over the lifecourse (Warnes 1992; King *et al.* 2000; Williams and Hall 2000; Hall and Williams 2002; Hall and Müller 2004; Coles *et al.* 2004, 2006; Hall 2005a; Paris 2010; Halfacree 2011; Dufty-Jones 2012).

Conclusion

This chapter has emphasised the development of geographical research in rural recreation and tourism and its changing emphases. The geographer has sometimes found it hard to distinguish between the context of recreation and tourism, as users consume the same resources in the rural environment (Jenkins and Pigram 1994). The 1960s and 1970s saw the development of a strong recreational geography of the rural environment emerge from the UK and North America, followed by the influential work of S.L.J. Smith (1983a). However, there is a lack of continuity and theoretical development for much of the period after the 1970s. One possible explanation may be derived from Chapter 1 with the denial of mainstream geography and its reluctance to embrace such research as critical to the conceptual and theoretical development of the discipline in spite of the establishment of journals such as *Rural Studies* within which recreation and tourism are occasionally featured. As Müller (2011: 137) noted with respect to research on second homes in rural areas, 'despite the fact that most second homes are located in rural areas, they have seldom been addressed within rural studies . . . second homes should be brought back into rural studies, but also that the rural has to be integrated more clearly into second home research'. Second homes are almost accepted as a by-product of tourism and a spatial outcome of urban consumption in the main, and so this highlights the interconnectedness of urban and rural areas in the production, consumption and impacts associated with tourism, recreation and leisure. Even so, one would expect that research assessment exercises in countries such as the UK would do little to foster a spirit of mainstream incorporation of tourism and recreation into the discipline as it may be assessed under business and management rather than as a subgroup of geography (Hall 2011e), particularly with the concerns for 'impact', reach and significance in the ways academic research in the field influences policy and contributes to the wider public good. The nearest inroad is through the study groups of professional bodies such as the Institute of British Geographers (IBG), the Canadian Association of Geographers (CAG), the Association of American Geographers (AAG) and the International Geographical Union (IGU).

The scope of the studies reviewed and discussed in this chapter have a common theme associated with some of the problems connected to rural areas in general, namely peripherality. Yet, ironically, this can also be a major feature associated with place-marketing of rural areas, where the peaceful rural idyll is marketed and commodified around the concepts of space and peripherality at different scales and the associated 'distance' from modernity and urbanisation. The rural geographer has made some forays into this area of research but, more often than not, the texts on rural geography pay only limited attention to tourism and recreation despite its growing significance in economic, social and political terms. Indeed, the outbreak of foot and mouth disease in the United Kingdom in February 2001 served only to highlight both the critical importance of tourism for the countryside and the absence of appropriate policy and intellectual frameworks that understand how tourism is embedded in the production and consumption of rural areas.

Further reading

Useful collections of readings on rural tourism include:

Mitchell, M. and Hall, D. (eds) (2005) *Rural Tourism and Sustainable Business*, Clevedon: Channel View.

On exurbanisation, amenity migration and second homes, see:

Burnley, I. and Murphy, P. (2004) *Sea Change: Movement from Metropolitan to Arcadian Australia*, Sydney: University of New South Wales.

Hall, C.M. and Müller, D. (2004) *Tourism, Mobility or Second Homes: Elite Landscapes or Common Ground*, Clevedon: Channel View.

McIntyre, N., Williams, D.R. and McHugh, K.E. (2006) *Multiple Dwelling and Tourism: Negotiating Place, Home and Identity*, Wallingford: CAB International.

Marcouiller, D., Lapping, M. and Furuseth, O. (eds) (2011) *Rural Housing, Exurbanization, and Amenity-Driven Development: Contrasting the Haves and the Have Nots*, Aldershot: Ashgate.

Janoschka, M. and Haas, H. (eds) (2014) *Contested Spatialities of Lifestyle Migration*, London: Routledge.

On tourism in more peripheral rural areas, see:

Hall, C.M. and Boyd, S. (eds) (2005) *Nature-based Tourism in Peripheral Areas: Development or Disaster?*, Clevedon: Channel View.

Müller, D.K. and Jansson, B. (eds) (2006) *Tourism in Peripheries: Perspectives from the Far North and South*, Wallingford: CAB International.

For an overview of rural recreation issues, see:

Pigram, J.J. and Jenkins, J. (2006) *Outdoor Recreation Management*, 2nd edn, London: Routledge.

On food tourism and alternative food networks, see:

Hall, C.M. and Gössling, S. (eds) (2013) *Sustainable Culinary Systems: Local Foods, Innovation, and Tourism & Hospitality*, London: Routledge.

Hall, C.M. and Sharples, L. (eds) (2008) *Food and Wine Festivals and Events around the World: Development, Management and Markets*, Oxford: Butterworth Heinemann.

Kneafsey, M., Holloway, L., Venn, L., Dowler, E., Cox, R. and Tuomainen, H. (2008), *Reconnecting Consumers, Food and Producers: Exploring Alternatives*, Oxford: Berg.

Questions to discuss

1 How did the outbreak of foot and mouth disease in the United Kingdom in 2001 affect tourism?

2 Is rural tourism distinctive?

3 To what extent should second homes be regarded as part of the geography of tourism and recreation in rural areas?

4 To what extent are rural recreation and tourism dependent on amenity values?

Tourism and recreation in wilderness and protected areas

There are few really wild areas left in Britain today, and yet the lure of a 'wilderness' experience acts as a strong attraction to outdoor purists. The danger of overuse and degradation by outdoor recreationalists creates an urgent need to comprehensively identify, map and manage these wilder areas. It is possible to map both wild land quality and recreational use, and use the resulting overlays to identify spatial patterns and possible conflict areas. This is essential to developing an understanding of the conflicting needs of different stakeholders in landscape character and/in wilder areas. Only from such an understanding can we then hope to develop appropriate and well-founded policies on protected areas and wild land that are required to protect these unique parts of our natural heritage for future generations.

(Carver 2000)

Historically, wilderness has been one of the main sources of 'the other' in western society. Wilderness was what lay beyond the boundaries of a 'civilised', ordered landscape. Since the beginning of the nineteenth century, however, wilderness and wild areas began to assume a more favourable impression under the influence of the Romantic and transcendentalist movements, which favoured wild nature as an antidote to an increasingly industrialised and technocratic society. More recently, the conservation and commodification of wilderness have become entwined with the growth of recreation and tourism and wider interest in ecology and the conservation of biodiversity, which has seen protected areas, including national parks, established not only for outdoor and adventure recreation enthusiasts but also as one of the main sites in which ecotourism occurs. The establishment of protected areas and their use is therefore significant not only in terms of recreation, tourism and conservation but also as part of the wider story of changing attitudes towards nature.

Geographers have long played a significant role in understanding and contributing to the conservation of natural resources and natural areas and their relationship with recreation and tourist activities (e.g. Graves 1920; Marsh and Wall 1982; Sewell and Dearden 1989). Indeed, recreation and tourism have long been used as an economic and political justification for the conservation and legal protection of such areas. This chapter therefore examines a number of the ways in which geographers have contributed to an understanding of wilderness and protected area concepts as well as their management.

The changing meaning of wild nature in western society

Definition presents a major problem in the identification of wilderness. Definition is important 'because it is the basis for common understanding and communication' and it 'provides a basis for putting a concept into action through creating and preserving a referent' (Gardner 1978: 7). However, wilderness is an elusive concept with many layers of meaning (Gardner 1978; Graber 1978). Tuan (1974: 112) has gone so far as to claim that 'wilderness cannot be defined objectively: it is as much a state of mind as a description of nature'. Wilderness has now become 'a symbol of the orderly progress of nature. As a state of mind, true wilderness exists only in the great sprawling cities.'

The problem of defining wilderness was well summarised by R. Nash, who emphasised that the notion of wilderness was loaded with personal symbolic meaning:

> 'Wilderness' has a deceptive concreteness at first glance. The difficulty is that while the word is a noun it acts like an adjective. There is no specific material object that is wilderness. The term designates a quality (as the '-ness' suggests) that produces a certain mood or feeling in a given individual and, as a consequence, may be assigned by that person to a specific place. Because of this subjectivity a universally acceptable definition of wilderness is elusive.
>
> (Nash 1967: 1)

The notion of wilderness is substantially culturally determined and is derived in the main from the northern European experience of nature (Oelschlaeger 1991). Although the meaning of wilderness has changed over time, several themes may be distinguished. The word 'wilderness' is derived from the old English word *wild-deoren*, meaning 'of wild beasts', which in turn is derived from the Teutonic languages of northern Europe. In German, for example, *Wildnis* is a cognate verb, and *Wildor* signifies wild game (Nash 1967: 2).

The Romance languages have no single word which expresses the idea of wilderness but rely instead on its attributes. In French equivalent terms are *lieu desert* (deserted place) and *solitude inculte*, while in Spanish wilderness is *la naturaleza*, *immensidad* or *falls da cultura* (lack of cultivation). 'Italian uses the vivid *scene di disordine o confusione*' (Nash 1967: 2). The Latin root of desert, *de* and *serere* (to break apart, becoming solitary), connotes not only the loneliness and fear

associated with separation but also an arid, barren tract lacking cultivation. Both the northern European and the Mediterranean traditions define and portray wilderness as a landscape of fear which is outside the bounds of human settlement (Tuan 1971, 1979).

The landscape of fear that dominated early European attitudes towards wilderness is found in the eighth century classic *Beowulf* (Wright 1957), 'where *wildeor* appeared in reference to savage and fantastic beasts inhabiting a dismal region of forests, crags, and cliffs' (Nash 1967: 1). The translation of the Scriptures into English from Greek and Hebrew also led to the use of wilderness as a description of uninhabited, arid land (Nash 1967). It was at this point that wilderness came to be associated with spiritual values. Wilderness was seen as both a testing ground for humans and an area in which humans could draw closer to God.

The attitudes towards nature in the Abrahamic religions was an essential ingredient of western attitudes towards wilderness (Glacken 1967; Passmore 1974; Graber 1978; Attfield 1983; Pepper 1984; Short 1991). The dominant tradition within Judaeo-Christianity concerning humankind's relationship with nature was that it was 'God's intention that mankind multiply itself, spread out over the earth, make its domain over the creation secure' (Glacken 1967: 151). This relationship is best indicated in Genesis 1:28: 'Be fruitful and multiply, and fill the earth and subdue it; and have dominion over the fish of the sea and over the birds of the air and over every living thing that moves upon the earth.'

To the authors of the Old Testament, wilderness had a central position as a descriptive and symbolic concept. To the ancient Hebrews, wilderness was 'the environment of evil, a kind of hell' in which the wasteland was identified with God's curse (Nash 1967: 14–15). Paradise, or Eden, was the antithesis of wilderness. The story of Adam and Eve's dismissal from the Garden of Eden, from a watered, lush paradise to a 'cursed' land of 'thorns and thistles' (Genesis 2:4), reinforced in western thought the notion that wilderness and paradise were both physical and spiritual opposites (Williams 1962). Isaiah (51:3), for instance, contains the promise that God will comfort

Zion and 'make her wilderness like Eden, her desert like the garden of the Lord', while Joel (2:3) stated that 'the land is like the garden of Eden before them, but after them a desolate wilderness'.

The experience of the Israelites during the Exodus added another dimension to the Judaeo-Christian attitude towards wilderness. For 40 years the Jews, led by Moses, wandered in the 'howling waste of the wilderness' (Deuteronomy 32:10) that was the Sinai peninsula (Funk 1959). The wilderness, in this instance, was not only a place where they were punished by God for their sins but also a place where they could prove themselves and make ready for the Promised Land. Indeed, it was precisely because it was unoccupied that it 'could be a refuge as well as a disciplinary force' (Nash 1967: 16).

The Exodus story helped to establish a tradition of going to the wilderness 'for freedom and purification of faith' (Nash 1967: 16). Elijah spent 40 days in the wilderness in order to draw guidance and inspiration from God (1 Kings 19:4–18). John the Baptist was the voice crying in the wilderness to prepare for the coming of the Messiah (Matthew 4:1), while Christ himself 'was led by the spirit into the wilderness to be tempted by the devil' (Matthew 4:1; Mark 1:12ff.). It was through contact with a difficult environment that spiritual catharsis could occur, a sentiment that exists to the present (Graber 1978).

The example of the prophets venturing into the wilderness was followed by early Christian ascetics and Jewish sects (Williams 1962). Hermits and monks established themselves in wilderness surroundings in order to avoid the temptations of earthly wealth and pleasure and to find a solitude conducive to spiritual ideals: 'The monastic community in the wilderness was a model of paradise set in an unredeemed world. Wilderness was often perceived as the haunt of demons but in the neighbourhood of the monastery it could acquire some of the harmony of redeemed nature' (Tuan 1974: 148).

The desert ascetics drew on an appreciation of nature that sprang from the Bible itself. As Glacken (1967: 151) observed, 'The intense otherworldliness and rejection of the beauties of nature because they turn men away from the contemplation of God are elaborated upon far more in theological writings than in the Bible itself'. The desert monks lived in the solitude of the wilderness to remove themselves from other humans, not from nature. Psalm 104 provides one of the clearest statements of the existence of a sympathetic attitude towards nature, noting that everything in nature has its place in a divine order: 'the high mountains are for the wild goats; the rocks are a refuge for the badgers' (Psalm 104:18). 'O Lord, how manifold are thy works! In wisdom hast thou made them all' (Psalm 104:24). As Glacken noted:

> It is not to be wondered at that Psalm 104 has been quoted so often by thinkers sympathetic to the design argument and the physico-theological proof for the existence of God. The life, beauty, activity, order, and reasonableness in nature are described without mysteries, joyously – even triumphantly. God is separate from nature but he may be understood in part from it.
>
> (Glacken 1967: 157)

The theme of the wisdom of the Lord being shown in the order of nature was similarly indicated elsewhere in the Bible. The notion that 'The heavens are telling the glory of God; and the firmament proclaims his handiwork' (Psalm 19:1) proved to be influential throughout Christendom in the Dark and Middle Ages, although by no means enabling a universally sympathetic attitude towards nature. Nature came to be regarded as a book which could reveal the works of the Lord in a manner similar to the Scriptures. In the early exegetical writings, God was regarded as being made manifest in his works:

> There is a book of nature which when read along with the book of God, allows men to know and understand Him and his creation; not only man but nature suffered from the curse after the Fall; one may admire and love the beauty of the earth if this love and admiration is associated with the love of God.
>
> (Glacken 1967: 203)

This view of nature played an important role in establishing a favourable attitude towards wild country.

St Augustine (in Glacken 1967: 204) wrote, 'Some people in order to discover God, read books. But there is a great book: the very appearance of created things.'

Reading the book of nature for the word of God was eventually to lead to the reading of nature itself, but the notion of nature as a book was also to prepare the way for the development of a natural theology in the writings of St Francis of Assisi, St Bonaventura and Ramon Sibiude. To St Francis, living creatures were not only symbols, but also 'placed on earth for God's own purposes (not for man's), and they, like man, praise God' (Glacken 1967: 216). St Francis' theology represented a revolutionary change in Christian attitudes towards nature because of the distinct break they make with the anthropocentric nature of earlier theology (White 1967). Upon the foundation built by the natural theologians and their intellectual heirs, such as John Ray and Gilbert White, came to be built the framework for the discovery of nature by the Romantic movement.

Despite a continuing appreciation of nature as part of God's divine presence by some theologians, the dominant attitude in the Judaeo-Christian tradition until the seventeenth century was that true appreciation of God could be gained only by looking inwards, not out at nature. Nature was provided for humans to utilise. Wilderness and wild lands were to be tamed and cultivated to display the divine order as interpreted by humankind. Nevertheless, while in the minority within Christian attitudes towards nature, the environmental theology of St Francis remains a significant theme within Christian thought because of not only attitudes towards wild nature but also responsibilities for environmental stewardship.

The dominant Abrahamic view of wilderness may be contrasted with that of eastern religions. In eastern thought, wilderness 'did not have an unholy or evil connotation but was venerated as the symbol and even the very essence of the deity' (Nash 1967: 20). The aesthetic appreciation of wild land began to change far earlier in the Orient than in the West. By the fourth century AD, for instance, large numbers of people in China had begun to find an aesthetic appeal in mountains, whereas they were still seen as objects of fear in Europe (Nicholson 1962; Tuan 1974).

Eastern faiths such as Shinto and Taoism 'fostered love of wilderness rather than hatred' (Nash 1982: 21). Shinto deified nature in favour of pastoral scenes. The polarity that existed between city and wilderness in the Judaeo-Christian experience did not exist outside European cultural traditions (Callicott 1982). In contrast, western civilisation has tended to dominate, rather than adapt to, its surrounding landscape. As Tuan (1974: 148) noted, 'In the traditions of Taoist China and pre-Dorian Greece, nature imparted virtue or power. In the Christian tradition sanctifying power is invested in man, God's vice regent, rather than nature.' However, it should be emphasised that Oriental civilisations, such as those of China, India and Japan, have also had highly destructive impacts on the environment despite arguably a more sympathetic cultural attitude towards nature, and will continue to do so as long as production and consumption imperatives prevail in contemporary policy settings.

The attitude of different cultures to nature and, hence, wilderness is important (Tuan 1971, 1979; Saarinen 1998). As Eidsvik (1980) recognised, wilderness has only recently taken on global meaning with the increasing dominance of western culture throughout the world and with respect to the governance and regulation of the environment and natural heritage. The perception of wilderness as an alien landscape of fear is derived from the northern European set of attitudes towards nature, where the Judaeo-Christian perception of nature became combined with the Teutonic fear of the vast northern forests. It is perhaps of no coincidence, therefore, that the creation of designated wilderness areas began in lands occupied by peoples who have inherited European cultural attitudes that frame the 'otherness' of wild nature. However, despite retaining something of its original attributes the meaning of wilderness has changed substantially over time and now incorporates wider scientific and conservation values, while there are now attempts to rewild some European landscapes for the ecological and recreational values it would create (Brown *et al.* 2011).

Table 7.1 portrays the development of the wilderness concept in the United States, Canada, New Zealand and Australia: those countries within which

Table 7.1 The development of the wilderness concept in the United States, Canada, New Zealand and Australia

Date	United States	Canada	New Zealand	Australia
Pre-1860	Major romantic influence on American art and literature 1832 Joseph Catlin calls for the creation of a 'nation's Park'; Arkansas Hot Springs reserved 1851 Transcendentalism – Thoreau's 'Walking' proclaims that 'in Wildness is the preservation of the World'	Development of a Romantic perception of the Canadian landscape		A 'New Britannia' Aesthetic and utilitarian visions of the Australian landscape Rapid clearfelling of land for agriculture and mining
1860s	Romantic Monumentalism 1864 George Perkins Marsh's *Man and Nature* is published, heralds the start of 'economic conservation'; Yosemite State Park established			Marsh's book well received in Australia 1866 Jenolan Caves reserved
1870s	Wilderness perceived as 'worthless land' 1872 Yellowstone National Park established; John Muir begins writing and campaigning for wilderness preservation			The need to conserve forests argued by Clarke, Goyder and von Mueller 'Scientific Vision'
1880s	Rise of 'Progressive Conservation' led by Gifford Pinchot	1885 Banff Hot Springs Reserve declared	1878 T. Potts publishes 'National Domains' 1881 Thermal Springs Districts Act 1887 Tongariro deeded to the New Zealand Government	1879 Royal National Park established in New South Wales Rise of the "Bush Idyll" – "Sydney or the Bush" National Parks associated with recreation and tourism
1890s	F.J. Turner declares the end of the American frontier; Yosemite National Park created with the help of railroads Forests Reserves Act 1891	Strengthening of a Romantic vision of nature in Canada and rise of progressive conservation 1894 Algonquin Park established	1892 J. Matson calls for Australasian Indigenous Parks	1891 National Park Act (S.A.) 1892 Tower Hill National Park Act (Vic.)
1900s	Cult of the Wilderness			

(Continued)

Table 7.1 (Continued)

Date	United States	Canada	New Zealand	Australia
	Tourism a major motive for the establishment of parks in all four countries 1905 US Forest Service created			1905 State Forests and National Parks Act (Queensland)
1910s	1913 Preservationists lose battle to prevent Hetch Hetchy being dammed 1916 US National Park Service created	1911 Dominion Forest Reserves and Parks Act		1915 Scenery Preservation Act (Tas.)
1920s	Rise of Ecological Perspectives; Forest Service areas retained as 'primitive lands' 1926 Forest Service Wilderness Inventory 1928 Forest Service Regulation L-20		Negative reaction to introduced animals in National Parks begins	Growth of the Bushwalking Movement under Myles Dunphy 1927 Formation of the National Parks and Primitive Areas Council
1930s	1934 Everglades National Park established 1937 Formation of the Wilderness Society 1939 Forest Service 'U' Regulations	1930 National Parks Act		1934 Greater Blue Mountains National Scheme Development of Snowy-Indi Park Scheme Proposal (NSW)
1940s	1949 Keyser Report			1944 Kosciusko State Park Act
1950s	Dinosaur National Monument Campaign 1956 First Wilderness Bill	1955 Wilderness Areas Act (Ontario)	1952 National Parks Act 1955 Reserves and Domains Act	1957 Victorian National Park Authority created
1960s	1962 ORCC Report 1964 Wilderness Act becomes law; RARE I commences		1969 Study tour of National Parks Director to North America	1963 Kosciusko Primitive Area established (NSW) 1967 NSW National Parks and Wildlife Service created
1970s	Mounting pressure from tourists and commercial interests in national parks in all countries 1974 Eastern Wilderness Act RARE II commences		1977 Reserves Act	Wilderness a major policy issue: Little Desert, Great Barrier Reef, Fraser Island and Lake Pedder 1975 National Parks and Wildlife Service (Commonwealth) created

Table 7.1 (Continued)

Date	United States	Canada	New Zealand	Australia
1980s	'Sagebrush Rebellion' Provision for wilderness in Alaska	Major conflicts over wilderness preservation 1984 South Moresby Island campaign	1980 National Parks Act 1981 Wilderness Advisory Group established 1984 New wilderness areas established 1986 World Heritage listing for South Westland Park 1987 Creation of Department of Conservation	1982 National Conservation Strategy 1983 Franklin Dam Case 1984 Calls for establishment of National Wilderness System 1985 CONCOM discussion paper 1987 Federal government acts to preserve the Wet Tropics, Kakadu, and the Lemonthyme and Southern Forests 1987 NSW Wilderness Act
1990s	Increased attention given to the concept of ecotourism and sustainable tourism by governments and industry bodies			
2000s	Renewed threats to explore for oil in the Alaskan wildlife reserve during Bush presidency	Continued debate over timber cutting in British Columbia, Ontario and Newfoundland	Labour government restricts cutting of native forest on government land 2004 renewed focus on public access rights to crown land and reserves	Continuing concern over vegetation clearance and soil and river salination
2010s	Growing concern as to effects of climate change on Alaskan wilderness	Effects of climate change on Arctic wilderness		

the idea of wilderness has historically been most influential in outdoor recreation and tourism as well as in promoting the idea of protected areas. However, it should be noted that changing attitudes towards wilderness were common in much of northern European society in the mid-nineteenth to early twentieth centuries and played a part in the Romantic nationalism of Finland, Norway and Sweden that promoted the idea of wild national landscapes (Wall Reinius 2009, 2012), many examples of which are now protected areas and significant tourist attractions. In addition, changing attitudes towards wild country and rural areas led to areas such as Scotland, the Lake District in the UK, and Switzerland becoming favoured as tourism destinations (see Chapter 6). Furthermore, shifts in cultural taste even led to the changes in garden design, with 'wild gardens' becoming popular from the 1870s on (see Robinson 2009; the original was published in 1870 and went to seven editions).

The classic example of changing popular attitudes towards wilderness in western culture is witnessed in the history of the evolution of the wilderness concept in the United States (Table 7.1). The founding fathers of the American colonies saw the wild lands before them in classical biblical terms as a 'howling wilderness', and although attitudes towards wilderness did change gradually through the seventeenth and eighteenth centuries it was not until the late eighteenth century that positive appreciation of American nature began to emerge. The political independence of the American nation found cultural expression in the extolment of the virtues of American natural scenery. However, a similar cultural expression was not to be found in colonial Canada, where untamed nature still assumed the guise of a landscape of fear (Kline 1970). Nevertheless, America's cultural independence from the Old World produced a desire to laud the moral purity of the wild forests and mountains of the New World, untainted as they were by the domination of things European, a cultural movement which, perhaps somewhat ironically, sprang from the Romantic movement then sweeping Europe.

The American Romantic movement laid the groundwork upon which a popular appreciation of the value of wild land would come to be based.

Artistic, literary and political perceptions of the importance of contact with wild nature provided the stimulus for the creation of positive cultural attitudes towards the American wilderness. Once positive attitudes towards primitive, unordered nature had developed, the emergence of individuals and societies dedicated to the preservation of wilderness values was only a short step away. However, an appreciation of the aesthetic values of wild land was countered by the utilitarian ethic that dominated American society.

As with many European colonial societies, the majority of North American settlers saw the land as an object to be conquered and made productive. The first reservations for the preservation of scenery therefore tended to be established in areas that were judged to be wastelands that had no economic value in terms of agriculture, grazing, lumbering or mining. The aesthetic value of wilderness was upheld by national parks and reserves which were intended to protect national scenic monuments that expressed the cultural independence of America, in addition to providing for the development of the area through the tourist dollar. Monumentalism was characterised by the belief that natural sites, such as Niagara Falls or the Rockies, were grand, noble and elevated in idea and had something of the enduring, stable and timeless nature of the great architecture of Europe, and proved a significant theme in the establishment of American parks (Runte 2010).

Although the national parks in Australia, Canada and New Zealand did not assume the same importance as national monuments, their development nevertheless parallels that of the American park system. The themes of aesthetic romanticism, recreation and the development of 'worthless' or 'waste' lands through tourism characterised the creation of the first national parks in Australia, Canada and New Zealand. Banff National Park in Canada was developed by the Canadian Pacific Railroad as a tourist spa (Marsh 1985). New Zealand's first parks had lodges and hostels established within them that matched the tourist developments in the US and Canadian parks. Australia's first parks, particularly those of Queensland and Tasmania, were also marked by the influence of the desire of government to boost tourism. However, the Australian parks were also noted for their establishment, in unison with railway development, as areas where city dwellers could find mental restoration in recreation and communion with nature (Hall 1985, 1992a).

With the closing of the American frontier at the end of the nineteenth century the preservation of America's remaining wilderness received new impetus. A massive but unsuccessful public campaign by wilderness preservationists led by John Muir to protect Hetch Hetchy Valley in Yosemite National Park from a dam scheme, a conservation minded President (Theodore Roosevelt) in the White House, and the emergence of economically oriented 'progressive conservation', a precursor of present-day sustainable development (Hall 1998), under the leadership of Gifford Pinchot all led to wilderness preservation becoming a matter of public importance in the United States.

The United States Forest Service and National Park Service responded to pressure from recreationalists for the creation of designated wilderness areas. Contemporaneously, the development of the science of ecology led to a recognition of the scientific importance of preserving wilderness (Leopold 1921, 1925). The various elements of wilderness preservation blended together in the inter-war years to lay a framework for the establishment of legally protected wilderness areas.

Economic conservation and the development of a scientific perception of wilderness were also influential in Australia, Canada and New Zealand. In Australia, the publication of George Perkins Marsh's (1965 [1864]) book *Man and Nature* stimulated the colonial governments to establish forest reserves. In addition, significant scientists such as Baron von Mueller and bodies such as the Australasian Association for the Advancement of Science argued for the preservation of native flora and fauna in both Australia and New Zealand. However, the first national parks in Australia were created for reasons of aesthetics, tourism and recreation, with science gaining little recognition (Hall 1992a). In Canada, progressive conservation proved influential in the creation of forest reserves, and it is significant to note that many of the

early Canadian parks were established under forestry legislation, although wilderness preservation lagged behind the USA (Nicol 1969).

The declaration of the Wilderness Act in 1964 marked the beginning of the legislative era of wilderness preservation in the United States. Under the Wilderness Act wilderness is defined as 'an area where the earth and its community of life are untrammelled by man, where man himself is the visitor that does not remain'. The four defining qualities of wilderness areas protected under the Act are that such areas:

- generally appear to be affected by the forces of nature, with the imprint of man substantially unnoticeable;
- have outstanding opportunities for solitude or a primitive and unconfined type of recreation;
- have at least 5,000 acres or are of sufficient size as to make practical its preservation and use in an unimpaired condition;
- may also contain ecological, geological or features of scientific, educational, scenic or historical value.

The protection of wilderness through legal means gave new impetus to the task of improving the process of defining and compiling a wilderness inventory as well as providing for its management, a process that is still continuing in many parts of the world. There is no specific legislation for the preservation of wilderness in New Zealand (Hall and Higham 2000). Similarly, until late 1987, with the passing of the New South Wales Wilderness Act, no wilderness legislation had been enacted in Australia (Hall 1992a). In Canada, wilderness areas have received a degree of protection under provincial legislation. However, as in Australia and New Zealand, there is no national wilderness Act. Yet, in recent years increasing attention has been given to the implications of international conservation and heritage agreements, such as the World Heritage and Biodiversity Conventions, as mechanisms for the preservation of wilderness and other natural areas of international significance (Hall 1992a, 2010j).

Table 7.2 provides an overview of the number and area of protected areas around the world as of 2003. Strict nature reserves and protected wilderness areas

Table 7.2 Number and area of protected areas under IUCN Protected Area Management Categories 2003

Category	Description	Global no. of categories (2003)	Global no. of categories (2003) (%)	Global area of categories (2003) (km^2)	Global area of categories (2003) (%)
Ia) Strict Nature Reserve: protected area managed mainly for science	Area of land and/or sea possessing some outstanding or representative ecosystems, geological or physiological features and/or species, available primarily for scientific research and/or environmental monitoring	4,731	4.6	1,033,888	5.5
Ib) Wilderness Area: protected area managed mainly for wilderness protection	Large area of unmodified or slightly modified land and/or sea, retaining its natural character and influence, without permanent or significant habitation, which is protected and managed so as to preserve its natural condition	1,302	1.3	1,015,512	5.4
II) National Park: protected area managed mainly for ecosystem protection and recreation	Natural area of land and/or sea, designated to (a) protect the ecological integrity of one or more ecosystems for present and future generations, (b) exclude exploitation or occupation inimical to the purposes of designation of the area and (c) provide a foundation for spiritual, scientific, educational, recreational and visitor opportunities, all of which must be environmentally and culturally compatible	3,881	3.8	4,413,142	23.5
III) Natural Monument: protected area managed mainly for conservation of specific natural features	Area containing one, or more, specific natural or natural/cultural feature which is of outstanding or unique value because of its inherent rarity, representative or aesthetic qualities or cultural significance	19,833	19.4	275,432	1.5
IV) Habitat/Species Management Area: protected area managed mainly for conservation through management intervention	Area of land and/or sea subject to active intervention for management purposes so as to ensure the maintenance of habitats and/or to meet the requirements of specific species	27,641	27.1	3,022,515	16.1

Table 7.2 (Continued)

Category	Description	Global no. of categories (2003)	Global no. of categories (2003) (%)	Global area of categories (2003) (km²)	Global area of categories (2003) (%)
V) *Protected Landscape/ Seascape:* protected area managed mainly for landscape/seascape conservation and recreation	Area of land, with coast and sea as appropriate, where the interaction of people and nature over time has produced an area of distinct character with significant aesthetic, ecological and/or cultural value, and often with high biological diversity; safeguarding the integrity of this traditional interaction is vital to the protection, maintenance and evolution of such an area	6,555	6.4	1,056,088	5.6
VI) *Managed Resource Protected Area:* protected area managed mainly for the sustainable use of natural ecosystems	Area containing predominantly unmodified natural systems, managed to ensure long-term protection and maintenance of biological diversity, while providing at the same time a sustainable flow of natural products and services to meet community needs	4,123	4.0	4,377,091	23.3
No category Total		34,036 102,102	33.4 100	3,569,820 18,763,407	19.0 100.0

Source: categories identified in IUCN 1994; Figures derived from Chape *et al.* 2003.

BOX 7.1   WHAT IS THE EFFECT OF WORLD HERITAGE LISTING?

World Heritage properties are areas or sites of outstanding universal value recognised under the Convention for the Protection of the World's Cultural and Natural Heritage (the World Heritage Convention (WHC)), adopted by a UNESCO Conference on 16 November 1972. The Convention is usually regarded as one of the pinnacles of international conservation.

> The philosophy behind the Convention is straightforward: there are some parts of the world's natural and cultural heritage which are so unique and scientifically important to the world as a whole that their conservation and protection for present and future generations is not only a matter of concern for individual nations but for the international community as a whole.
>
> (Slatyer 1983: 138)

Such is the significance of World Heritage Status (WHS) that World Heritage sites have been described as 'magnets for visitors' and World Heritage designation 'virtually a guarantee that visitor numbers will increase' (Shackley 1998: preface). Indeed, it is often suggested that WHS increases the popularity of a location or destination with visitors (e.g. Drost 1996; Pocock 1997; Thorsell and Sigaty 2001). However, many of the assertions regarding the tourist attractiveness of World Heritage sites and, similarly, the attractiveness of newly designated national parks are often based on extremely weak empirical evidence that does not consider locations within the context of historical visitation trends; other factors influencing visitation may have very little to do with designation (see also Buckley 2004). This does not mean that locations may be unattractive to visitation, rather that the attraction is primarily derived from other attributes. For example, Hall and Piggin (2001) reported on a survey of 44 World Heritage managers in OECD countries. Over two-thirds of sites reported an increase in visitor numbers since gaining WHS, the majority of them natural sites. Most of the sites reported an average increase of 1–5 per cent per annum since designation. However, significantly, the rate of increase or decline in visitation since designation was little different from overall trends with respect to tourism visitation. Indeed, less than half of respondents reported that the sites they managed had specific areas for the explanation of the World Heritage Convention and why the sites were granted WHS, even though almost two-thirds of sites used such status in order to attract international and domestic visitors. Over half of the sites considered the effect of WHS on tourism at the sites to have been either 'positive' or 'extremely positive', 18 site managers were neutral about the relationship between tourism and WHS, and only one site manager reported that WHS had been 'extremely negative' for tourism.

An interesting study of the effects of World Heritage designation was that of Wall Reinius (2004, 2012), who examined the Laponian World Heritage site in north-western Sweden, which was declared a World Heritage site in 1996. The site includes four national parks established under the provisions of the Nature Protection Act 1909: Sarek National Park and Stora Sjöfallet National Park (1909), Muddus National Park (1941) and Padjelanta National Park (1962), and two nature reserves established under the provisions of the Nature Conservation Act 1964: Sjaunja (1986) and Stubba (1988). In total, 95 per cent of the site is protected as national park or nature reserve. The World Heritage site has a total area of approximately 9,400 km^2. According to Wall Reinius (2004), only 3.7 per cent of her respondents (primarily Swedish and German tourists) stated that the visit would never have occurred or that they would have had different travel plans if it had not been a World Heritage site. Nevertheless, 64 per cent of her respondents agreed either completely or in part that World Heritage designation had value for the surroundings, while 51 per cent agreed either completely or in part that WHS also had value for visitors. As Wall Reinius (2004) noted, redesignation from national park to World Heritage may have long-term effects on perceptions of a location as a destination; however, such influences required longitudinal analysis in order to be better understood. Indeed, acquisition of WHS may have more impact in a developing country context rather than in the industrialised nations because of the development of infrastructure and improved accessibility that designation may make possible.

only account for about 11 per cent of categories by area, with national parks being the most significant category by area. However, it should be noted that managed resource areas are not far behind, highlighting the challenge of enabling both use, including via tourism and recreation, as well as conservation.

Environmental histories of protected and wilderness areas

Environmental history is a field concerned with the role and place of nature in human life (Worster 1977, 1988). Research and scholarship on the environmental history of national parks and wilderness lie at the intersection of a number of fields of human and physical geography. Within geography, as with history, the increased awareness of the environment as a social, economic and political issue has led geographers and historians to attempt to chart the history of land use of a given region or site in order to increase understanding of its significance, values and present-day use (Simmons 1993; Dovers 1994, 2000a, 2000b; Crosby 1995; Pawson and Brooking 2002). Such research is not just an academic exercise. At a macro-level it can assist in understanding how natural resource management problems and user conflicts have developed and policies may be improved (e.g. Sæþórsdóttir et al. (2011) in Iceland; see also Sæþórsdóttir and Ólafsson 2010a, 2010b). At a micro-level such research can help develop interpretive material for visitors as part of heritage

management strategies, an area in which geographers are becoming increasingly involved (e.g. Ashworth and Tunbridge 1990; Tunbridge and Ashworth 1996; Hall and McArthur 1996, 1998). Cronan (1990) asserts that good work in environmental history incorporates three levels of analysis. These are the dynamics of natural ecosystems in time (ecology), the political economies that people erect within these systems (economy) and the cognitive lenses through which people perceive those systems (the history of ideas). Geographers, with their integrative approach to environment, cultural landscapes and land use, would therefore seem to be ideally poised to work in this area. As Mark (1996: 153) observed, 'Widening the scope of historical narrative has frequently resulted in more complex interpretation of the past and should point the way toward greater understanding of the past in heritage management'.

National parks are a major focus of heritage management but have been a relatively quiet backwater in traditional historical narrative, including historical and cultural geography (Parker 2010). Environmental history, however, can place them within the larger context of interaction between nature and culture (Mark 1996). For example, a number of extremely valuable park histories which highlight the role of tourism and outdoor recreation in park development have been written on the Yellowstone (Haines 1977), Grand Canyon (Hughes 1978), Rocky Mountain (Buchholtz 1983), Olympic (Twight 1983), Sequoia and Kings Canyon (Dilsaver and Tweed 1990) and Yosemite (Runte 1990) national parks in the United

States; the Albertan (Bella 1987) and the Ontario (Killan 1993) national park systems in Canada, and with useful national overviews being provided by Nelson (1970), Hall (1992a), Dearden and Rollins (1993) and Runte (2010).

Environmental and park histories can provide substantial methodological challenges. In North America and the Antipodes, travel accounts written during the period of initial European settlement have been utilised by scholars interested in historic environments (Powell 1978). They often hope to establish a pre-European settlement landscape as a baseline from which to assess subsequent environmental change. One difficulty with using travel accounts, however, is that they are often written in places where the journalist is not actually travelling; instead, the diarist is summarising past events at a convenient place (Mark 1996). Another problem is how to tie the usually limited detail (little of which could be utilised quantitatively) to specific localities. The paucity of locality information is often present in even the best accounts, such as those left by collectors of natural history specimens.

The only site-specific records available in many areas on pre-colonial settlement landscapes are land survey notes. These have been helpful in establishing an historic condition of some forests, riparian habitats and grasslands. Their reliability varies, however, because there can be limitations associated with insufficient description, bias in recording data, contract fraud and land use prior to survey (Galatowitsch 1990). Another technique for developing an historical record of land use change or for reconstructing past environments or heritage sites is repeat photography (Rogers et al. 1984). However, while such techniques may be useful for specific sites or attractions, the photographic record of 'ordinary' landscapes, i.e. those which were not subject to the interest of visitors as a view or panorama, is more difficult to construct because of incomplete records. Indeed, the overall lack of longitudinal data on visitors to national parks and particular environments is a major problem in determining impacts of visitation and changing perceptions of the environment (Frost and Hall 2009a).

Cultural landscape documentation is somewhat narrower in scope than environmental history because the question of nature's character is not so central (Mark 1996). Nevertheless, it emphasises change over time and represents a way of integrating nature with culture (Muller 2003). In a protected area setting, its emphasis becomes one of design, material, change, function and use, with one of its main effects on heritage management being the broadening of the focus of historic preservation beyond buildings to the associated landscape and environmental context (Mark 1991; Antrop 2005).

The value of natural areas and wilderness

Decisions affecting environmental policies grow out of a political process (Henning 1971, 1974), in which 'value choice, implicit and explicit . . . orders the priorities of government and determines the commitment of resources within the public jurisdiction' (Simmons et al. 1974: 457). Therefore, in order to consider the means by which natural areas are utilised, it is essential to understand what the values of wilderness are. As Henning (1987: 293) observed, 'In the end, the survival of the wilderness will depend upon values being a respected factor in the political and governmental process'.

The value of wilderness is not static. As we have seen at the start of this chapter and throughout the book, the value of a resource alters over time in accordance with changes in the needs and attitudes of society. As noted above, ideas of the values of wild land have shifted in relation to changing cultural perceptions. Nevertheless, the dynamic nature of the wilderness resource does not prevent an assessment of its values as they are seen in present-day society. Indeed, such an evaluation is essential to arguments as to why natural areas should be conserved.

Broadly defined, the values of wilderness may be classified as being either anthropocentric or biocentric in nature. The principal emphasis of the anthropocentric approach is that the value of wilderness emerges in its potential for direct human use. In contrast, 'the biocentric perspective places primary emphasis on the preservation of the natural order'. The former approach places societal above ecological values and emphasises recreational and aesthetic rather than environmental qualities. Both perspectives focus on human benefits. However, 'the important distinction between them is the extent to which these benefits are viewed as being independent of the naturalness of wilderness ecosystems' (Hendee *et al.* 1978: 18).

A more radical, and increasingly popular, interpretation of the notion of the value of wilderness has been provided by what is often termed a deep ecology perspective (Godfrey-Smith 1979; Nash 1990; Oelschlaeger 1991). Deep ecologists argue that wilderness should be held as valuable not just because it satisfies a human need (instrumental value) but as an end in itself (intrinsically valuable). Instrumental anthropocentric values, derived from a Cartesian conception of nature, are regarded as being opposed to a holistic or systematic view that emphasises the symbiotic interdependencies of the natural world (Hall 2013g). The holistic view broadly corresponds with the ecological conception of wilderness (Worster 1977; Nash 1990; Oelschlaeger 1991). However, it goes further by arguing that 'the philosophical task is to try and provide adequate justification . . . for a scheme of values according to which concern and sympathy for our environment is immediate and natural, and the

desirability of protecting and preserving wilderness self-evident' (Godfrey-Smith 1979: 316), rather than justified purely according to human needs and the services it provides. Indeed, from a genuinely ecocentric point of view the question 'What is the use of wilderness?' would be as absurd as the question 'What is the use of happiness?' (Godfrey-Smith 1979: 319).

Hendee *et al.* (1978) identified three consistent themes in the values associated with wilderness: experiential, mental and moral restorational, and scientific. Experiential values highlight the importance of the 'wilderness experience' for recreationists and tourists (Scott 1974). Several themes emerge in an examination of the wilderness experience, including the aesthetic, the spiritual and the escapist (Table 7.3). Given its essentially personal nature, the wilderness experience is extremely difficult to define (Scott 1974). Nevertheless, the values recorded from writings on wilderness listed in Table 7.3 do point to the various aspects of the wilderness experience that are realised in human contact with wild and primitive lands.

Associated with the values of the wilderness experience is the idea that wilderness can provide mental and moral restoration for the individual in the face of modern civilisation (Carhart 1920; Boyden and Harris 1978). This values wilderness as a 'reservoir for renewal of mind and spirit' and in some cases

Table 7.3 Components of the wilderness experience

Component	Nature of experience
Aesthetic appreciation	Finding beauty in nature
Religious	The experience of God in the wilderness
Escapist	Finding freedom away from the constraints of city living
Challenge	The satisfaction that occurs in overcoming dangerous situations and fully utilising physical skills
Historic/romantic	The opportunity to relive or imagine the experiences of pioneers of the 'frontier' that formed national culture
Solitude	The pleasure of being alone in a wild setting
Companionship	Paradoxically, in relation to the previous category, the desire to share the setting with companions
Discovery/learning	The thrill of discovering or learning about nature in a natural setting
Vicarious appreciation	The pleasure of knowing that wilderness exists without actually ever having experienced it directly
Technology	Influence of technological change on outdoor activities

Sources: Marshall 1930; McKenry 1972; Smith 1977; Hendee *et al.* 1978; Nash 1990.

offers 'an important sanctuary into which one can withdraw, either temporarily or permanently, to find respite' (Hendee *et al*. 1978: 12). This also harks back to the biblical role of wilderness as a place of spiritual renewal (Funk 1959) and the simple life of Thoreau's Walden Pond (Thoreau 1968 [1854]). The encounter with wilderness is regarded as forcing the individual to rise to physical challenge, with corresponding improvements in feelings of self-reliance and self-worth. As Ovington and Fox wrote, 'In the extreme', wilderness

> generates a feeling of absolute aloneness, a feeling of sole dependence on one's own capacities as new sights, smells and tastes are encountered . . . The challenge and the refreshing and recreating power of the unknown are provided by unadulterated natural wilderness large enough in space for us to get 'lost' in. Here it is possible once again to depend upon our own personal faculties and to hone our bodies and spirits.
>
> (Ovington and Fox 1980: 3)

The third major theme in the values associated with wilderness is that of the scientific values of wilderness

(Table 7.4) The preservation of wilderness is regarded as an essential component in the scientific study of the environment and human impact on the environment. Furthermore, wilderness has increasingly come to assume tremendous economic importance because of the value of the genetic material that it contains. However, the multidimensional nature of the wilderness resource may lead to value conflicts over the use of wilderness areas.

A fourth theme which is inherent in the values of wilderness is that of economic worth. In addition to the economic significance of genetic and other extractable resources, wilderness has importance as a tourist and recreation attraction. Indeed, the economic valuation of wilderness and natural areas has now become a critical factor in their designation (Hall 1992a), although it should be noted that the economic value of tourism has long been used to justify national park creation in areas that would otherwise be deemed worthless (Runte 1972, 1973, 1977, 2002, 2010; Hall and Frost 2009). As discussed on pp. 266–267, such a value may also be enhanced through international recognition such as that achieved through World Heritage listing.

McKenry (1977) has provided an analysis of the degree to which the values of wilderness are disrupted

Table 7.4 **The scientific values of wilderness**

Value	*Description*
Genetic resources/biodiversity	Large natural communities such as those provided for in wilderness areas can serve as sources of genetic materials which are potentially useful to humans. As more of the world's natural ecosystems are removed or simplified, the remaining natural areas will assume even greater importance as storehouses of genetic material.
Ecological research and biological monitoring	Wilderness areas provide protection for large natural ecosystems. Within these areas a variety of research on ecological processes can occur. Research may consist of ecosystem dynamics, comparative ecology, ethology, surveys of fauna and flora, and the relationship of base ecological data to environmental change.
Environmental baselines	Wilderness areas, representative of particular biomes, can be used as reference areas in the monitoring of environmental change both within the biome and on a global scale.
The evolutionary continuum	Wilderness areas provide the conditions in which the evolutionary continuum of adaptation, extinction and speciation can occur without the direct interference of humans.
Long term	Wilderness areas provide conditions in which flora and fauna conservation can occur, particularly for those species which require large territories to reproduce and be preserved.

Sources: P.E. Smith 1977; Frankel 1978; Hendee *et al*. 1978; Hall 1992a.

Table 7.5 Interactions between values associated with wilderness and common disruptive activities

Common disruptive activities	Water resources	Traditional aboriginal habitat	Wildlife resources and habitat	Plant resources and habitat	Research and education	Wilderness recreation resources	Vicarious appreciation of wilderness	Reserve resource pool
Hydro	1–2	5	3–4	3–4	4–5	4–5	4–5	4–5
Forestry	3–4	5	3–4	3–4	3–4	4–5	4–5	2–3
Mining	3–4	5	3–4	3–4	3–4	4–5	5	4–5
Agriculture	5	3–4	4–5	3–4	5	5	4–5	3–4
Grazing	3–4	4–5	2–3	3–4	2–3	3–4	3–4	2–3
Road	2–3	4–5	2–3	2–3	2–3	4–5	4–5	2–3
Tourism	3–4	5	3–4	2–3	2–3	4–5	4–5	2–3
Off-road	2–3	4–5	2–3	2–3	2–3	4–5	2–3	1–2

Scale of disruption to wilderness values:

1 No incompatible interaction (i.e. mutually compatible).
2 Slightly incompatible.
3 Substantial incompatibility.
4 Slight compatibility only.
5 Totally incompatible (i.e. mutually exclusive).

Source: adapted from McKenry 1977.

by activities such as forestry, mining, grazing and road construction. Table 7.5, based on McKenry's research, records the level of compatibility between wilderness values and common disruptive activities. The significant factor which emerges from Table 7.5 is that because of the intrinsic characteristics of wilderness as primitive and remote land, the range of uses that can occur within wilderness areas without diminishing the value of wilderness is extremely limited and will require careful management. As soon as the characteristics of the wilderness resource are infringed through the activities of western humans, wilderness values are reduced. Emphasis is placed upon the impacts of western society, rather than those of technologically underdeveloped peoples, because, as the following discussion will illustrate, the present-day concept of wilderness is a product of western thought. Indeed, geographers such as Nelson (1982, 1986) have argued for the adoption of a human-ecological approach to wilderness and park management which sees the incorporation of the attitudes and practices of indigenous peoples as being an essential part of a contemporary perspective on the notion of wilderness.

BOX 7.2 NATIONAL PARKS AND INDIGENOUS PEOPLES

National parks are a western concept (Nash 1967, 1982). National parks have their origins in the New World desire to conserve nature and appropriately aesthetic landscapes for economic development through tourism (Hall 1992a, 2000b). Until recently, the creation of national parks was marked by the exclusion of aboriginal populations as undesirable elements in the 'natural' landscape. In the Americas, Australia and New Zealand historically this has meant that national park and other forms of government land ownership have often been used to exclude indigenous peoples from their own land. The drawing of boundaries between the natural parks and the rural human landscape available for agriculture, forestry, mining and/ or grazing reflecting the Cartesian divide of western society has long sought to separate 'civilisation' and 'wilderness'. However, since the late 1960s, the separation between natural and cultural heritage has come to be seen as increasingly artificial (Mels 1999). In part, this has been due to the renaissance of aboriginal and indigenous cultures in the New Worlds of North America and Australasia, as well as greater assertion of native cultural values in postcolonial societies (Butler and Hinch 1996; Ryan and Huyton 2002; Hall and Tucker 2004). In addition, there has been an increased realisation by ecologists and natural resource managers that many ecological relationships in so-called natural landscapes are actually the result of a complex set of interrelations between the use of the land by native peoples and the creation of habitat, for example through burning regimes (e.g. Aagesen 2004) or through grazing in relation to transhumance (e.g. Bunce et al. 2004), as in the case of the Sami in the Nordic countries. Such developments have had enormous influence not only on the ways in which parks are managed but also on how they are established and re-created for tourist consumption (Cohen 1993; Pedersen and Viken 1996; Hinch 1998; Waitt 1999; Muller 2003; Pettersson 2004). Importantly, this has also meant that indigenous populations have been brought back into the management and even ownership of national parks and protected areas, although the reconciliation of different management goals as well as ownership and the right to control decision-making processes is clearly a difficult one with many competing interests. The role of indigenous peoples has therefore changed considerably over time.

The influence of the Romantic movement on the establishment of national parks was extremely significant (Hall 1992a). The first call for the establishment of national parks in the United States came in 1832 from an artist, George Catlin, who on seeing the slaughter of buffalo on the Great Plains described the waste of animals and humankind to be a ' "melancholy contemplation", but he found it "splendid" when he imagined that there might be in the future [by some great protecting policy of government] . . . a magnificent park', which preserved animals and the North American Indian 'in their pristine beauty and wildness'. 'What a beautiful and thrilling specimen for America to preserve and hold up to the view of her refined citizens and the world, in future ages! A nation's Park, containing man and beast, in all the wild and freshness of their nature's beauty!' Catlin's seminal call for 'a nation's park' highlighted the new mood in America towards wilderness. Almost exactly 40 years after Catlin's journal entry, President Ulysses S. Grant signed an Act establishing Yellowstone Park, creating the institution of which Catlin desired 'the reputation of having been the founder' (Catlin 1968: 8, 9).

Similarly, John Matson (1892) compared the efforts made in New Zealand to protect wildlife with the absence of such attempts in the Australian colonies and appealed for the creation of 'indigenous parks' in order to preserve the animal and bird life of Australasia. Significantly, Matson quoted New Zealand 'poet' George Phipps Williams to conclude his case for the preservation of Maori, wildlife and their habitat, in a manner which is reminiscent of Catlin:

> Out in the wilderness is there no desolate space,
> Which you may spare to the brutes of indigenous race?
> Grant us the shelter we need from the pitiless chase. . . .
> Gone are the stateliest forms of the apteryx kind,
> Short is the space that the kiwi is lagging behind;
> Soon you shall painfully seek what you never shall find.
> (George Phipps Williams, *A Plea of Despair*,
> in Matson 1892: 359)

Williams' comments, along with those of Catlin, may seem ill at ease with twenty-first century political and cultural sensibilities. However, in the late nineteenth century such sentiments were commonplace. Maori, along with other aboriginal peoples, were seen as the remnant of a dying race, and placing them in protected areas, so long as the land was not required for other economic purposes, was often seen as the most appropriate course of action. Despite the initial Romantic sentiments which helped create the momentum for the establishment of national parks, humans, including the aboriginal peoples who had often created the park landscapes through their food-gathering practices, were excluded from the parks through loss of ownership and access rights, management and regulatory actions and policing strategies. Such measures were the result of ecological and cultural blindness at best, and outright racism and cultural imperialism at worst, with park boundaries serving as the demarcation between the natural and the cultural in European eyes.

Although the political status of aboriginal peoples is still a highly contested issue in many societies, substantial shifts have occurred in management practices with respect to aboriginal peoples and their role in national parks and protected areas since the 1890s. A number of broad social and political factors in relation to the overall rights of aboriginal peoples have contributed to these changes, including:

- a renaissance of aboriginal culture in a number of western countries, which has led to renewed pride in traditional cultural practices;
- the withdrawal of colonial powers and the development of new modes of administration and management;
- the assertion of ownership of and/or access to natural resources through treaty settlements, protests and other legal and political channels;
- changed government policies with respect to native peoples, which have led to greater economic and political self-determination;
- greater political influence.

The management of protected areas has been substantially affected and a number of changes have occurred at the micro-level in parallel to the shifts which have occurred at the macro-political level. This has occurred in a number of different locations and jurisdictions, but aboriginal peoples have gradually had a greater involvement in national park management in Australia, Canada, New Zealand, northern Europe, South Africa and the United States (Muller 2003). Hall (2000c) identified several factors in influencing these processes:

- A recognition that many supposedly 'natural' landscapes are the product of a long period of aboriginal occupancy which has created a series of ecological conditions and relationships which are dependent on certain types of human behaviour. This means that the traditional knowledge of native peoples becomes a vital ingredient in effective ecosystem management at times of environmental change.
- Growth of the tourist appeal of some indigenous cultural attractions.
- Greater emphasis by park management authorities on the role of various stakeholder groups, including native peoples, in park management and the development of appropriate co-operative management strategies.
- Changed park management practices and strategies which are aimed at specifically satisfying the concerns and needs of native peoples, including, in some cases, the management of national park lands owned by native peoples, which are then leased to park management agencies.

One of the challenges in managing wilderness and protected areas is to be able to identify them. This is especially so given that, as discussed at the start of this chapter, it is clear that our relationship to nature is socially constructed. How, then, may this relationship be understood? Figure 7.1 illustrates the relationship between perceptions of nature and the physical constitution of the areas and sites under investigation. It is also noted that different research approaches are connected to different ways of understanding nature and wilderness, but that these approaches are brought together under the rubric of resource management, which typically seeks to integrate human and physical geographies in a relatively applied framework.

Since the early 1980s, there has been growing academic attention in the field of wilderness perception imagery (e.g. Kliskey 1994; Higham 1997). Stankey and Schreyer (1987), for example, demonstrate that wilderness perceptions may be shaped by a wide range of influences. These include social attitudes, cultural influences, recreational experiences, expectation and personal cognition. However, wilderness perceptions can also be mapped so as to gain a better understanding of visitor perceptions of different locations and environments and the values placed upon them (Flanagan and Anderson 2008). Understanding the spatial distribution of recreationists based upon an appreciation of wilderness perceptions could contribute to the attainment of two fundamental goals: the maximisation of visitor satisfaction and the mitigation of environmental impact at tourist sites (Kliskey 1998, 2000; Alessa *et al*. 2008). Yet the management of protected areas requires the management not only of the visitor but also of the underlying resource upon which the visitor experience is based and which is, in many cases, the primary motivation for conserving an area. Therefore an extremely important area to which geographers have made a contribution is the identification and inventory of natural resources. This is illustrated in the next section with respect to the identification and inventory of wilderness.

Identifying wilderness

Although the values of wilderness are well recognised, for management and legislative purposes such values need to be translated by a method by which

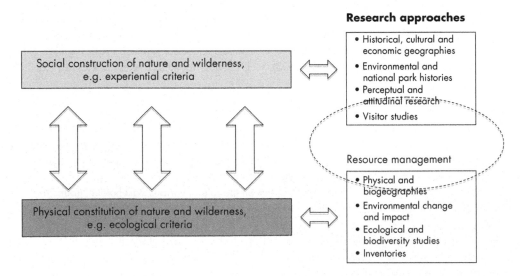

Figure 7.1 **The relationship between the social construction and physical constitution of nature and wilderness**

wilderness can be mapped in space and over time. In addition, such a process can assist in the provision of conservation, scientific and tourism information, technical advice, recognition of management issues and objectives, the integration of conservation and development, and the design of national and regional conservation systems.

According to Dasmann's (1973: 12) classification of national parks and equivalent reserves, wilderness areas have two principal purposes: 'that of protecting nature (defined as primary) and that of providing recreation for those capable of enduring the vicissitudes of wilderness travel by primitive means'. These purposes reflect the values of wilderness identified in the previous section. 'The area is maintained in a state in which its wilderness or primitive appearance is not impaired by any form of development, and in which the continued existence of indigenous animal and plant species is assured' (Dasmann 1973: 12). However, unlike some of the use limitations of strict natural areas, wilderness is available to recreationists (see also Table 7.2).

In 1984 the IUCN General Assembly recommended 'that all nations identify, designate and protect their wilderness areas on both public and private lands' (Resolution 16/34, in Eidsvik 1987: 19). Yet such measures need to have a basis by which wilderness can be identified if they are to succeed. Although wilderness inventory has been undertaken in the United States as part of the obligations under the Wilderness Act, probably the series of inventories that have been undertaken in Australia since the 1970s have been the most influential, especially with respect to the undertaking of inventories in Europe (Carver et al. 2002, 2012; McMorran et al. 2008; Comber et al. 2010; Ólafsdóttir and Runnström 2011; Orsi et al. 2013), where institutions are supporting the mapping of wild areas (European Parliament 2009). Therefore, it is to the Australian experience that we will now turn to illustrate some of the challenges of the inventory process. This is important because it is not just wilderness, but the entire set of wildness conditions of a given area that matter, because they reflect all the available functions, services and recreational opportunities offered by that area (Joyce and Sutton 2009; Sæþórsdóttir and Ólafsson 2010b). Arguably two major issues become critical in such an exercise. The first is the need for consistency, i.e. the adoption of an approach that can detect the particular conditions of a location, e.g. morphology, extent of human presence, adapt to them and eventually supply results that are replicable between areas. The second problem is the need for inventory outputs that not only estimate the gradient of wildness across an area but also identify and cluster land parcels characterised by similar wildness conditions because these can then eventually be assigned a common management strategy (Lesslie et al. 1988a; Orsi et al. 2013). However, as will be seen, these elements have often been difficult in the Australian context.

Wilderness inventory in Australia

> an inventory of potential wilderness areas should be compiled by all states and Territories, where possible in consultation with user groups. The inventory would assess areas within existing parks and extend to other land if appropriate. It would be desirable for a consistent approach to be adopted for the surveys.
>
> (Council of Nature Conservation Ministers (CONCOM) 1985: 7)

Definition is the major problem in the inventory of wilderness. The definition, and its accompanying criteria, provide the source from which all else flows. Two different conceptions of wilderness are generally recognised, one anthropocentric, the other biocentric or ecocentric. From the anthropocentric view, wilderness is seen from a perspective in which human needs are considered paramount. Adherents of this approach tend to ascribe a recreational role to wilderness. In contrast, the biocentric approach defines 'wilderness in ecological terms and [equates] wilderness quality with a relative lack of human disturbance' (Lesslie and Taylor 1983: 10).

The recreational values of wilderness have tended to be dominant in wilderness literature (Hendee et al. 1978). This is partly the result of the 'Americanisation' of the national park and wilderness concepts, where the recreational perspective of United States research has predominated, but it is also probably related to the way in which the wilderness idea has developed (Nash 1963, 1990; P.E. Smith 1977; Stankey 1989; Oelschlaeger 1991; Frost and Hall 2009b). Nevertheless, over recent years the biocentric concept of wilderness has become increasingly important in research given the growth of the importance of ecological research relative to recreational research in national park and reserve management, as well as the growing importance of biodiversity conservation overall (Mittermeier *et al.* 2003; Hall 2010f).

Table 7.6 demonstrates the major features of the wilderness inventories that had been carried out in Australia until the methodology for the National Wilderness Inventory supported by the then Australian Heritage Commission had become well developed, as well as its continuation in the form of the national-level Vegetation Assets, States and Transitions (VAST) dataset for Australia (Thackway and Lesslie 2006, 2008; Lesslie *et al.* 2010). For each inventory the study area, wilderness definition, dimensional criteria, status of coastal areas, database and status of roadworks are recorded. The status of roadworks criterion is included because it provides a basis for comparison with the 'roadless area' concept that permeates American notions of wilderness (e.g. Stritthold and Dellasala 2001), and also illustrates one of the major problems in standardising wilderness criteria (Bureau of Land Management 1978). As Lesslie and Taylor (1983: 23) observed, 'road definition is a major point of contention in the general wilderness literature. Controversy centres on the qualities which make a high grade road an unacceptable intrusion into wilderness and a low grade road a detrimental but nevertheless acceptable intrusion.'

The first Australian study of wilderness of any consequence, the wilderness study of eastern New South Wales and south-east Queensland by Helman *et al.* (1976) was designed as a model for future Australian wilderness inventories and it was applied in Victoria (Feller *et al.* 1979) and Tasmania (Russell *et al.* 1979). However, the inventory procedures may not be valid for arid and semi-arid environments because they were undertaken in relatively humid, forested and mountainous environments (Lesslie and Taylor 1983); also, they failed to recognise the remoteness and primitiveness which constitute the key qualities of wilderness (Mark 1985). Stanton and Morgan's (1977) study of Queensland identified four key areas as fitting rigid conservation-based criteria, while 24 other areas were identified as being 'equivalent to the wilderness areas delineated by Helman *et al.* (1976) in their study of eastern Australia' (Morgan 1980).

Kirkpatrick's (1980) study of south-west Tasmania identified wilderness as a recreational resource, 'as land remote from access by mechanised vehicles, and from within which there is little or no consciousness of the environmental disturbance of western man' (Kirkpatrick and Haney 1980: 331). Kirkpatrick assigned absolute wilderness quality scores, which had not been attempted in Australian wilderness inventories, although it was characteristic of American ones. However, unlike the United States inventories, Kirkpatrick focused on the more readily quantifiable characteristics of wilderness: remoteness and primitiveness.

Remoteness and primitiveness are the two essential attributes of wilderness (Helburn 1977; Hall 1987). Remoteness is measured 'as the walking time from the nearest access point for mechanised vehicles', while primitiveness, which 'has visual, aural and mental components', is 'determined from measures of the arc of visibility of any disturbance . . . and the distance to the nearest disturbance' (Kirkpatrick and Haney 1980: 331). The identification of remoteness and primitiveness as the essential attributes of a wilderness area helped create the methodological basis for the wilderness inventory of South Australia by Lesslie and Taylor (1983, 1985) and provides the basis for a national survey of wilderness.

Lesslie and Taylor (1983) saw previous wilderness inventory procedures as unsatisfactory because they sought to express a relative concept in absolute terms. They identified four indicators of wilderness quality: remoteness from settlement, remoteness from access, aesthetic primitiveness (or naturalness) and biophysical primitiveness (or naturalness). These indicators were used to provide an inventory of relatively high quality wilderness areas in South Australia. The

Table 7.6 Australian wilderness inventories

Study and area	Definitions of wilderness	Dimensional criteria	Status of coastal areas	Status of roadworks	Database
Helman et al. 1976: Eastern New South Wales and south-east Queensland	Large area of land perceived to be natural, where genetic diversity and natural cycles remain essentially unaltered	• a minimum core area of 25,000 ha; • a core area free of major indentations; • a core area of at least 10 km in width; • a management (buffer) zone surrounding the core of about 25,000 ha or more	Coastal areas were not required to meet the dimensional criteria as rigidly as inland areas, due to the r linear characteristics and the type of ecosystems and recreation they support	If roads do not seriously impair the user's perception of the wilderness or the natural functioning of the ecosystem and use can be controlled by management, their presence to a limited degree should not preclude wilderness status	Landsat images in conjunction with DNM 1:250,000 maps. Aerial reconnaissance to check results
Stanton and Morgan 1977: Queensland	An extensive pristine area with extremely limited access	Size based on a core area defined as a day's walk from any access point. A minimum wilderness area (with no core) of about 40,000 ha	No specific criteria	Roadworks are incompatible with the strict definition of wilderness	Aerial photographs at approximately 1:84,000. 1:1,000,000 maps.
Feller et al. 1979: Victoria	As for Helman et al. 1976	As for Helman et al. 1976, with special criteria for semi-arid and mountain wilderness, a minimum area of about 150,000 ha for semi-arid wilderness and 50,000 ha for mountain wilderness	Minimum area as close as possible to 50,000 ha; it may be smaller if: • the core area is free of major indentations; • there is a buffer on the landward side of the core; • there is a reasonable length of coast included in the core	• All two-wheel drive roads and substantial four-wheel drive tracks were excluded from the core. Substantial tracks were included only if they were dead-end and not often used; • sealed and gravel roads were excluded from the core and buffer; • an acceptable density of tracks was determined for each wilderness	DNM 1:100,00 maps, aerial photographs at 1:20,000 to 1:50,000. Additional information from Forests Commission, National Parks Service and Land Conservation Council maps. Some field checking was carried out

(Continued)

Table 7.6 (Continued)

Study and area	Definitions of wilderness	Dimensional criteria	Status of coastal areas	Status of roadworks	Database
Russell et al. 1979: Tasmania	As for Helman et al. 1976	As for Helman et al. 1976, with special attention to exclusion of intrusions and the use of natural topographic boundaries to determine core area boundaries. Minimum areas of approximately 10,000 ha were also identified and delineated	The core of a wilderness area with a coastal boundary may extend to the coastline with an as yet undefined buffer zone extending into the surrounding coastal waters	The buffer zone boundary excluded all formed access roads and high-density or high-impact vehicular tracks. Vehicular roads and tracks were excluded from the inner core wilderness areas	Lands Department 1:500,000, 1:250,000 geographic and 1:100,000 topographic maps. Land tenure maps at 1:100,000 and 1:250,000. Aerial photographs at 1:50,000. Some field checking
Kirkpatrick 1980: south-west Tasmania	An area of land remote from access by mechanised vehicles and within which there is little or no consciousness of the environmental disturbances of western man	Wilderness was assumed to exist in relatively undisturbed environments at places greater than 5 km or more from access point or human disturbance. Wilderness quality scores were derived from mathematical functions which represent the relationship between the intensity of the wilderness experience, the time/distance from the access point or nearest sign of human disturbance, and the proportion of the area of visibility occupied by signs of human disturbance	No special consideration	No roadworks are included in wilderness areas	Lands Department 1:100,000 and 1:250,000 map series. Additional information from the National Parks and Wildlife Service and the South West Tasmanian Resource Survey

Table 7.6 (Continued)

Study and area	Definitions of wilderness	Dimensional criteria	Status of coastal areas	Status of roadworks	Database
Lesslie and Taylor 1983: South Australia	Land which is remote from and undisturbed by the presence and influences of settled people	Wilderness quality was scaled according to four indicators: remoteness from settlement, remoteness from access, aesthetic primitiveness and biophysical primitiveness. Wilderness quality was then expressed as classes: very high, high or moderately high. Additive and weighted additive procedures ranked sites according to their wilderness value. High quality wilderness could then be distinguished	No special consideration	High grade roads were regarded as access points while low grade roads were treated as aesthetic disturbances. Wilderness quality relates to the density of linear structures (such as roadworks) per unit area. Four-wheel drive transport was seen as an appropriate wilderness travel mode in arid and semi-arid areas	DNM 1:250,000 and 1:100,000 topographic series, Department of Lands 1:50,000 topographic series and South Australian Royal Automobile Association Touring maps
Hawes and Heatley 1985: Tasmania	• largely free of evidence of human artefacts, activity and disturbance; • remote from substantial human artefacts and areas where there is substantial human activity or disturbance; and • remote of access	Land whose direct remoteness (the map distance between that point and the nearest intrusion) and access remoteness (the minimum time separation between that point and any access point) are d and t respectively, for a suitable choice of values d (km) and t (hours and days)	• regular use of mechanised vehicles is regarded as a major intrusion; and • no special provision was made for the use of coastal areas by mechanised vehicles as it was assumed that use was still low due to the relative inaccessibility	The following were regarded as major intrusions: • all roads, and all vehicular tracks accessible to and frequently used by off-road vehicles; • all areas where mechanised transport is intensively used or where the use of such transport has led or is likely to lead to the formation of permanent tracks or cause long-term environmental disturbance	1:100,000 maps of Tasmania and 1:500,000 vegetation map of Tasmania; primitive country and wilderness were identified manually on 1:500,000 maps

(Continued)

Table 7.6 (Continued)

Study and area	Definitions of wilderness	Dimensional criteria	Status of coastal areas	Status of roadworks	Database
Lesslie et al. 1987; Preece and Lesslie 1987: Victoria	As for Lesslie and Taylor 1983	Modification of Lesslie and Taylor methodology for ease of digitising, storing and spatially organising wilderness quality indicators through a grid cell framework. (NWI Stage I)	No special consideration	Three grades of road and track access were distinguished according to the level of access and the degree of use: major two-wheel drive roads; minor two-wheel drive roads; and four-wheel drive tracks	DNM 1:100,000 topographic maps, Department of Conservation Forests and Lands regional maps, RAC Victoria Guide maps, governmental reports, land tenure information and personal knowledge
Lesslie et al. 1988a: Tasmania	As for Lesslie et al. 1987	NWI Stage II, as for Lesslie et al. 1987	No special consideration	As for Lesslie et al. 1987	National 1:250,000 topographic mapping grid, of Tasmania, 1:100,000 topographic maps, 1:25,000 1:500,000 vegetation map topographic series, RAC Tasmania touring information, Forestry Commission 1:100,000 maps, large-scale aerial photography, Forestry Commission Tasmania GIS Forest type database
Lesslie et al. 1991a: Cape York Peninsula, Queensland	As for Lesslie et al. 1987	NWI Stage III	No special consideration	As for Lesslie et al. 1987	National 1:250,000 topographical mapping grid
Lesslie et al. 1991b: Kangaroo Island, South Australia	As for Lesslie et al. 1987	NWI: South Australia	Lakes, rivers and oceans included as natural bodies	In addition to the three grades utilised in previous National Wilderness Inventory stages a fourth grade of access was distinguished: very low – established but unconstructed vehicle access routes (e.g. beach access) and cleared lines; established walking tracks; cleared land	National 1:250,000 topographical mapping grid, 1:100,000 map series, Department of Lands 1:50,000 map series

Table 7.6 (Continued)

Study and area	Definitions of wilderness	Dimensional criteria	Status of coastal areas	Status of roadworks	Database
Manidis Roberts Consultants 1991: Western New South Wales	A wilderness area is a large tract of land remote at its core from access and settlement, substantially unmodified by modern technological society or capable of being restored to that state, and of sufficient size to make practical the long-term protection of its natural system	Combination of Helman *et al.* 1976 and NWI methodology in order to indicate prospective wilderness areas	Not applicable	A paved road excludes the surrounding land from a wilderness area classification. Tracks and loose surface roads are acceptable in small quantities, because it is possible to reduce the impact and restore the wilderness value. Walking track and maintenance track impacts are not considered to reduce wilderness value substantially	Literature review, contacts within the network of conservation groups, 1:100,000 scale maps, by NATMAP and the Central Mapping Authority
Lesslie *et al.* 2010: Australia	As for Lesslie *et al.* 1987	A minimum size criterion was imposed (8,000 ha for temperate environments in eastern and southern Australia and 50,000 ha for remote and pastoral areas). A minimum size of 20,000 ha applied in Victoria. For Western Australia a high Total Wilderness Quality value and an area of greater than 100,000 ha were used	No special consideration	As for NWI	Combines data derived from the Australian Land Disturbance Database, satellite imagery, land use and vegetation datasets

DNM: Division of National Mapping
NWI: National Wilderness Inventory
RAC: Royal Automobile Club

Source: adapted from Hall 1992a: 12–17.

attributes of remoteness and primitiveness may be expressed as part of a continuum which indicates the relative wilderness quality of a region (Figure 7.2). Such a continuum or gradient approach can accommodate the ecological and recreational characteristics of a far wider range of environments than can the inventories formulated for the higher rainfall areas of Australia (Lesslie and Taylor 1983; Hall and Mark 1985; Hall 1987; Lesslie *et al.* 1987; Lesslie 1991; Manidis Roberts Consultants 1991; Thackway and Lesslie 2006, 2008).

The variation in approaches to wilderness inventory in Australia is 'systematic of confusion concerning the definition of wilderness, since areas which satisfy biocentric considerations need not be consistent with areas which satisfy anthropocentric considerations' (Lesslie and Taylor 1983: 11). Indeed, given the nature of the wilderness experience it has long been recognised that the area required to satisfy recreational criteria for wilderness may be much smaller than the area required for maintaining the ecological balance of a region (Valentine 1980). Therefore, the experiential criterion for wilderness remains substantially different from the ecological criterion and the concept of 'wilderness experience' must be separated from that of 'wilderness area'. As Lesslie and Taylor (1983: 14) observed, there has been an 'almost universal tendency to confuse the benefits derived from wilderness with the nature of wilderness itself, a point of crucial importance in the delineation, inventory and management of wilderness. Hence, the two attributes which are definitive of wilderness, remoteness from the presence and influences of settled people, and primitiveness, the absence of environmental disturbance by settled people, need to be based at the high quality end of the wilderness continuum in order to accommodate the anthropocentric and biocentric dimensions of wilderness (Taylor 1990; Lesslie 1991). In Australia, the methodology of Lesslie and Taylor (1983), modified in the 1987 Victorian inventory (Lesslie *et al.* 1987; Preece and Lesslie 1987), comes closest to achieving this goal and served as the model for other studies within the National Wilderness Inventory (NWI), discussed below. Lesslie *et al.*'s (1987) methodology is able to indicate low quality wilderness areas which are not indicated in an inventory along the lines of Helman *et al.* (1976), but which may nevertheless be of significant conservation and recreation value (Hall 1987).

National wilderness inventory and beyond

In 1987 the Australian government, through the then Australian Heritage Commission, initiated the NWI to provide information in order to improve decisions about wilderness conservation (Lesslie *et al.* 1991b). This action arose from 'the rapid decline in area and quality of relatively remote and natural lands in Australia and in recognition that an inventory of the remaining resource was the necessary first step in formulating appropriate measures for conservation and management' (Lesslie *et al.* 1991a: 1).

The NWI had three main emphases (Lesslie *et al.* 1988a): to compile a national wilderness database; to refine database maintenance procedures and analytical techniques; and to produce information relevant to policy and management issues. Several inventories were conducted under the auspices of the National Wilderness Inventory, including surveys of Victoria (Lesslie *et al.* 1987; Preece and Lesslie 1987), Tasmania (Lesslie *et al.* 1988a), South Australia (Lesslie *et al.* 1991b) and Queensland (Lesslie *et al.* 1991a). In 1990 the NWI was accelerated to provide a comprehensive coverage for the whole of Australia. The NWI was later renamed the Australian Land Disturbance Database, comprising databases of total wilderness quality and biophysical naturalness (Lesslie and Maslen 1995) as well as wilderness of potential national significance

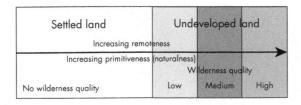

Figure 7.2 The wilderness continuum
Source: Hall 1992a.

identified from existing databases in 2000. These datasets were then used in the Vegetation Assets, States and Transitions (VAST) dataset for Australia (Lesslie *et al.* 2010), together with satellite imagery, land use and vegetation datasets, to give a national picture of vegetation condition which further identified areas of high wilderness quality. The VAST classification orders native vegetation condition in a spectrum from *naturally bare* (VAST 0), *residual* (VAST I), through *modified* (VAST II), *transformed* (VAST III), *replaced* (*adventive* (VAST IV) or *managed* (VAST V)), to *removed* (VAST VI) (non-vegetated) (Lesslie *et al.* 2010). Wilderness of potential national significance was therefore assigned to the VAST residual class. (See Table 7.7.)

The evaluation of wilderness in the NWI and subsequent datasets is based upon the notion of wilderness quality as a continuum of remote and natural conditions from pristine to urban. A spatial framework utilising the techniques of Geographic Information Systems (GIS) is used to sample variation in values of the four wilderness quality indicators. There are two major advantages in using a GIS to formulate wilderness evaluation databases. First, the approach is open-ended: new data may be added and current data modified as has been the case with VAST (Lesslie *et al.* 2010), which also offers the potential to see the impact of future developments, land use change and other forms of environmental change on wilderness quality and levels of biophysical naturalness. Second,

the process is spatially flexible, enabling scale to be matched to purpose. Furthermore, maps showing the distribution of wilderness identified in the inventory can be generated rapidly and efficiently in order to assist decision-making (Lesslie and Maslen 1995; Lesslie *et al.* 1993, 2010; Thackway and Lesslie 2006).

Inventories provide a systematic means of ensuring the designation areas of high environmental quality: 'Recognition of wilderness is the necessary first step towards protecting, appreciating and managing wilderness areas' (Manidis Roberts Consultants 1991: 2). However, identifying an area as wilderness does not, by itself, ensure that its wilderness qualities can be maintained; this may only be done through the appropriate legislation and management. 'Decisions of this kind are inevitably judgemental, requiring comparative assessments of the social worth of alternative and often conflicting landuse opportunities' (Lesslie *et al.* 2008b: v).

The Australian Council of Nature Conservation Ministers (CONCOM) (1986: 8) proposed that the following key criteria be used to identify and evaluate land which has potential as a wilderness area:

- *remoteness and size*: a large area, preferably in excess of 25,000 ha, where visitors may experience remoteness from roads and other facilities;
- *evidence of people*: an area with minimal evidence of alteration by modern technology.

However, CONCOM (1985) criteria may be contrasted with the United States wilderness legislation, which suggests as a guideline for minimum wilderness size an area of 5,000 acres (2,023 ha), and where impacted ecosystems may be included if they contribute to the viability and integrity of the wilderness area. One of the ironies of the criteria for wilderness identification chosen by CONCOM is that they exclude many of the wilderness areas that have already been established under state legislation! According to CONCOM (1986: 4), 'Wilderness areas are established to provide opportunities for the visitor to enjoy solitude, inspiration and empathy with his or her natural surroundings'. The CONCOM position is to preserve the 'wilderness experience', not necessarily the

Table 7.7 Area of the VAST condition class 1 (residual) for Australian states and territories

Territory	area (hectares)	% of total area
Australian Capital Territory	103,900	44.08
New South Wales	8,945,000	11.18
Northern Territory	93,732,200	69.67
Queensland	57,555,000	33.34
South Australia	46,610,600	47.45
Tasmania	3,532,600	53.05
Victoria	3,074,300	13.56
Western Australia	171,949,200	68.19
Total	*385,502,800*	*50.25*

Source: Lesslie *et al.* 2010.

intrinsic qualities of wilderness. However, to preserve wilderness mainly for recreational values is to ignore the significant range of other values of a wilderness area (see pp. 268–274) (Watson *et al.* 2009).

Unlike the United States government, the Australian government does not have vast areas of federal land upon which wilderness legislation would be readily enforceable. State governments, which under the Australian constitution have primary control over land use, regard the reservation of wilderness areas under appropriate legislation as being a state responsibility, and several states have enacted specific legislation for wilderness (e.g. New South Wales, South Australia) or have developed wilderness policies under existing state national parks laws (e.g. Western Australia). This situation therefore means that unless the federal government exercises its constitutional powers in relation to the environment, any Australian national wilderness system may be achieved only through consensus between the Commonwealth and the various state and territory governments. However, the political controversy surrounding wilderness conservation in Australia means that this is not very likely. Indeed, the renaming by the Australian federal government of the NWI as a disturbance database, with disturbance referring to that resulting from post-European technological and population impacts, perhaps reflects the politically charged nature of wilderness (Dovers 2000a). Nevertheless, the NWI and its successors still serve as valuable management tools by which to evaluate the potential loss of wilderness quality which new developments might bring and the potential corresponding loss of visitor satisfaction.

Managing tourist and recreational demand for wilderness and protected areas

Tourism and recreation have increasingly become significant as one of the main values attached to wilderness and its conservation, with substantial increases in demand for access to wilderness in recent years. Demand for tourist or recreational experience of

wild country or wilderness may be related to two major factors: (1) changing attitudes towards the environment; (2) access to natural areas.

The increase in demand for contact with nature has gone hand in hand with the production of natural areas for tourist consumption. While the setting of a boundary for a national park may be appropriate for assisting conservation management, it can also serve as a marker for tourist space. In the same way that notions of rurality are complex spaces of production and consumption (see Chapter 6), so it is that the ideas of wilderness and naturalness are bound up in the commodification of landscapes for tourist and recreational enjoyment (Olwig and Olwig 1979; Short 1991; Evernden 1992; Mels 1999, 2002; Saarinen 2001, 2005). For some, such a perspective is at odds with the mythology that national parks are ecological rather than cultural landscapes but, as R. Nash (1982: 1) noted, wilderness is 'heavily freighted with meaning of a personal, symbolic and changing kind'. Although the personal meaning of wilderness may not be of great value when it comes to the designation of wilderness areas from a biocentric perspective which concentrates on actual rather than perceived naturalness (see p. 269), it is of value in terms of the recreation and tourism values of wilderness. For example, Higham's (1997) examination of the dimensions of wilderness imagery by international tourists in the South Island of New Zealand found that the desire for remoteness is reinforced in the similar high regard for the scale of the location ('big enough to take at least two days to walk across'). However, there is also a desire for the provision of safeguard mechanisms to reduce risk, with the provision of search and rescue operations receiving the highest mean score of all listed variables. The desire for swing bridges and walkwires over watercourses, signposting and well-marked and maintained tracks confirms the widely held desire for wilderness recreation in a natural but relatively safe and humanised environment. Furthermore, the placing of restrictions upon access and group size was widely considered acceptable by international visitors.

Higham's (1997) research raises important questions about the role of accessibility to wilderness areas and the cultural context from which visitors approach wilderness areas. Indeed, issues of access are now presenting major management problems in wilderness and national parks. For many years access to wilderness was restricted by both the nature of the terrain and the capacity of individuals to travel there. Up until the Second World War the main means of access to most national parks was by train, with many of the national parks in the New World actually being developed in association with the railroads (Hall 1992a; Runte 2010). However, in the post-war period there was a substantial increase in the proportion of personal car ownership, thereby increasing accessibility of parks. National park management agencies also promoted themselves to the public through 'parks for the people campaigns'. Herein, though, lies the critical situation in which many parks and wilderness managers now find themselves. National parks were originally established to provide both recreational enjoyment and conservation (Hall 1992a). The founders of the park movement, though, such as John Muir, could never have imagined the almost continuous growth in demand for park access from tourists and recreationists seeking to escape the urban environment. The situation now sees traffic jams occurring in some parks, congestion on walking tracks, displacement of local users by tourists, increased pollution and other adverse environmental impacts, and reduced visitor satisfaction. Within this context, therefore, park and wilderness managers are now seeking both a better understanding of their visitors and how they may be satisfied, and strategies to find a better match between visitor needs and the capacities of the resource to be used, yet to retain the values that attract people in the first place (Hall and McArthur 1998; Taff *et al.* 2013). Historically, tourist profiles have been generated to assist in the planning and management of visitor demand at a particular destination, attraction or site. Analysing tourist demand has traditionally been based on one of two main approaches: a socioeconomic approach and a psychological or psychographic approach that also includes lifestyle analysis (Roberts and Hall 2004; see Chapter 2).

Another major issue in terms of tourism and recreation in national parks and wilderness areas is the extent to which tourism economically benefits such peripheral areas (Rudkin and Hall 1996; Weaver 1998; Walpole and Goodwin 2000; Hall and Boyd 2005). As an influential World Wildlife Fund publication on ecotourism states:

> One alternative proposed as a means to link economic incentives with natural resources preservation is the promotion of nature tourism. With increased tourism to parks and reserves, which are often located in rural areas, the populations surrounding the protected areas can find employment through small-scale tourism enterprises. Greater levels of nature tourism can also have a substantial economic multiplier effect for the rest of the country. Therefore, tourism to protected areas demonstrates the value of natural resources to tourists, rural populations, park managers, government officials and tour operators.
>
> (Boo 1990: 3)

Tourism and recreation in natural environments can undoubtedly bring economic benefits in some cases both to communities on the periphery and to the wholesalers and suppliers of such experience if managed appropriately, and it is for this reason that increasing attention is being given to the supply of the experience of wild nature (Fennell 1999). However, a number of issues are starting to emerge with the potential impact of visitors not just on the landscape but also on individual species (MacLellan 1999; Woods 2000; Orams 2002; Hall and Boyd 2005), as well as the distribution of where money is spent and how long expenditure stays within local economies (see Chapter 4).

Supplying the wilderness and outdoor recreation experience

In many ways the idea that one can 'supply' a wilderness or outdoor recreation experience seems at odds with the implied freedom of wilderness. However, the tourism industry is in the business of producing such experiences, while national parks and wilderness areas, by virtue of their formal designation, are places which have been defined as places where such experiences may be found (Arnould *et al.* 1998; Zegre *et al.* 2012). One of the most important transformations in the production of leisure on the periphery has been the way in which the initial construction of national parks as places of spectacular scenery and national monuments for the few were transformed into places of mass recreation in the 1950s and 1960s and to places of tourist commodification in the 1980s and 1990s, particularly through the notion of ecotourism.

A number of different meanings were applied to the concept of 'ecotourism' (Valentine 1992; Weaver 1998, 2001; Fennell 2001; Higham and Lück 2002) which range from 'shallow' to 'deeper' statements of the tourism environment relationship:

- ecotourism as any form of tourism development which is regarded as environmentally friendly and has the capacity to act as a branding mechanism for some forms of tourist products;
- ecotourism as 'green' or 'nature-based' tourism, which is essentially a form of special interest tourism and refers to a specific market segment and the products generated for that segment;
- ecotourism as a form of nature-based tourism that involves education and interpretation of the natural environment and is managed to be ecologically and culturally sustainable.

Many destinations around the world are now focusing on the supply of an ecotourism product as a means of tourism development (Fennell 1999; Garrod and Wilson 2003). Unfortunately, much of the ecotourism promotion best fits into the shallow end of the ecotourism spectrum, in that much of it revolves around the branding of a product or destination rather than seeking to ensure sustainability. Indeed, one of the greatest problems of ecotourism is the extent to which such experiences can be supplied without a limit on the number of people who visit natural areas, as visitation may lead not only to environmental damage, but also to perceptions of crowding, thereby reducing the quality of the experience (Boller *et al.*

2010; Needham *et al.* 2011). As Kearsley *et al.* (1997: 71) noted, 'From the viewpoint of tourism . . . it is the impact of tourists upon tourists that has increasingly led to concern. Issues of crowding, displacement and host community dissatisfaction have risen to prominence.'

Crowding is a logical consequence of rising participation in outdoor recreation and nature-based tourism activities (Gramann 1982; Needham 2013). It should therefore be no great surprise that crowding is one of the most frequently studied aspect of wilderness recreation (Shelby *et al.* 1989). Indeed, many issues in wilderness management and outdoor recreation, such as satisfaction, desired experiences, carrying capacity and displacement, are all related to the primary issue of crowding. Furthermore, social carrying capacity is increasingly being recognised as the most critical of all types of carrying capacity, since ecological impacts can often be controlled by management actions other than limiting use levels; for example, facilities may be extended and made more effective, and physical capacities are usually high (Shelby and Heberlein 1984; Needham *et al.* 2011).

Importantly, crowding should not be confused with density. Density refers to the number of individuals in a given area, while crowding refers to the evaluation of a certain density (Graefe *et al.* 1984a, 1984b). Shelby *et al.* (1989) identified four sources of variation in perceptions of crowding:

- *temporal variation*: variation either in terms of the time or season within which outdoor recreation activities are taking place – for example, weekends and public holidays are likely to experience higher than average use densities thereby resulting in inflated perceptions of crowding;
- *resource availability*: variation of resource availability (e.g. the opening and closing of tracks in alpine areas) may act to alter the presence of people at recreational sites;
- *accessibility*: distance (expressed in terms of time, cost, spatial or perceived distance) will affect crowding and densities, particularly if there is little or no recreation resource substitution;

- *management strategies*: management can intervene directly (e.g. use restrictions) or indirectly (e.g. de-marketing) to reduce visitor numbers at recreation sites.

Shelby *et al.* (1989) also investigated the hypothesis that crowding perceptions would vary according to the type of recreational use, although they were not able to resolve this hypothesis. However, recreational use history is a substantial factor in influencing perceptions of crowding. Concerns over crowding are also closely related to issues of social carrying capacity in wilderness and outdoor recreation areas. Social carrying capacity in recreation areas 'has typically been defined as a use level beyond which some measure of experiential quality becomes impaired' (Graefe *et al.* 1984b: 500). However, there is no 'absolute value' of social carrying capacity and there is no single response to specific levels of use in a particular area. Instead, indicators of social or behavioural capacity will be dependent on the management objectives for a given recreation site. Shelby and Heberlein (1986: 21) therefore refined this definition to read: 'Social carrying capacity is the level of use beyond which social impacts exceed acceptable levels specified by evaluative standards.'

Several factors have been identified as influencing crowding norms, with a number of variables contributing to the interpretation of increasing recreational use density as perceived crowding:

- *visitor characteristics*: motivations, preferences and expectations, previous use experiences, visitors' attitudes towards wilderness;
- *characteristics of those encountered*: type and size of groups encountered, behaviour of those encountered, perceptions of alikeness;
- *situational variables*: type of area and location within an area.

Manning (1985) concluded that crowding norms are extremely diverse, yet the significance of visitor characteristics as a factor and the psychographic variables which comprise this factor indicate the possibility of a high degree of agreement being reached on crowding norms within particular subsets of the recreational population. This latter possibility highlights the importance of managers having a good understanding of the psychographic and demographic profiles of their visitor base in order to optimise levels of visitor satisfaction and attainment of management objectives (Manning *et al.* 2010).

Density alone therefore provides no measure of visitor satisfaction. Satisfaction will be determined by expectations, prior experiences and commitment to the recreational activity. Perceptions of crowding are therefore influenced by use densities, but this relationship is mediated by a range of other factors and variables (Graefe *et al.* 1984a). Indeed, a range of reactions or coping strategies are possible in recreationalist response to decreased recreational satisfaction, which may result not only from crowding, but also from such factors as littering, noise and worn-out campsites (e.g. Anderson and Brown 1984; Hardiman and Burgin 2011). Such reactions include:

- modifying behavioural patterns (e.g. by camping rather than using developed facilities);
- changing time of visit or use (e.g. visiting in shoulder or off-peak periods in order to avoid conflicts with other users);
- changing perceptions, expectations and recreation priorities, e.g. developing a new set of expectations about a recreational setting in order to maintain satisfaction;
- recreational displacement, where those who are most sensitive to recreational conflicts seek alternative sites to achieve desired outcomes.

Of the above strategies, recreational displacement is probably the most serious from the manager's perspective as displacement appears to be a reality of wilderness use regardless of the level of recreational experience (Becker 1981; Anderson and Brown 1984). Therefore, increases in numbers of visitors to wilderness and other natural areas, particularly at a time when such areas have to cope with their promotion as places for ecotourism experiences as well as the pressures of traditional recreation users, may lead to a

BOX 7.3 WILDERNESS AND GLOBAL ENVIRONMENTAL CHANGE: THE ARCTIC

Although human impacts have long been recognised as a threat to the integrity of wilderness area they have usually been seen in terms of immediate or relatively short-term impacts in the form of erosion, changed species behaviour or reduction of naturalness. Arguably, a far more serious long-term impact that is also wider in scale is that of global and regional environmental change (Hall and Higham 2005; Gössling and Hall 2006a; Scott *et al.* 2012). One of the most affected areas is the Arctic (Arctic Climate Impact Assessment (ACIA) 2004), which is warming at nearly twice the rate of the rest of the globe, and increasing greenhouse gases from human activities are projected to make it even warmer, with the region projected to warm an additional 7–13°F (4–7°C) by 2100.

Such rapid climatic change is affecting both terrestrial and marine polar ecosystems. More than any other species, the polar bear (*Ursus maritimus*) has become a symbol of global climate change, evidenced by images in the popular media of polar bears 'struggling' to survive in a warming Arctic climate. Although some of these images may be misleading, across the Arctic many polar bear populations are under threat due to significant decreases in the extent, thickness and increased variability of sea-ice (Dawson *et al.* 2010). The polar bear tourism industry that has developed in Churchill, Canada, is threatened by declining sea-ice conditions on Hudson Bay. Projections are that over the next 30 years sea-ice conditions may deteriorate to the point that the polar bear population may collapse in this region (Dawson *et al.* 2010). However, the polar bear is not the only polar species threatened by climate change. Other terrestrial iconic species such as musk ox, caribou and reindeer may also experience a decline in numbers as a result of climate change (Tyler 2010), while seal populations are also affected by the changing abundance and dynamics of sea-ice (Scott *et al.* 2012).

Polar ecosystems are also particularly vulnerable to environmental change as their species richness prior to the current period of anthropogenic-induced change is low, with correspondingly low levels of redundancy making it relatively easier for new species to outcompete existing species in the same ecological niche. The general vulnerability of Arctic ecosystems to warming and the lack of adaptive capacity of Arctic species and ecosystems are therefore likely to lead, where possible, to relocation rather than rapid adaptation to new climates (Hall 2010k; Hall *et al.* 2010). Overall in such a situation tourism may only add another level of stress on Arctic species and ecosystems at the very time that the Arctic will potentially become more accessible for nature-based tourism activities.

decline in wilderness qualities as users are displaced from site to site. The case of crowding and other variables which influence visitor satisfaction and behaviour, including displacement, highlights the significance of understanding the factors of supply and demand of the recreation and tourist experience (see Chapters 2 and 3). Just as importantly, they indicate the need for sound planning and management practice in trying to achieve a balance between the production and consumption of tourism and recreation, particularly in environmentally sensitive areas.

Conclusion

This chapter has highlighted a number of areas in which geographers have contributed to research and scholarship in the tourism and recreation periphery. From the topophilia of Tuan (1974), the sacred space of Graber (1978) and the breathtaking historical analysis of Glacken (1967), geographers have been at the forefront of understanding the human relationship not only to the natural environment, and wild lands in particular, but also to the behaviours of tourists and recreationists in the wilderness. In addition, geographers have assisted in developing techniques to identify wilderness areas, undertake environmental histories and cast light on their values. More recently, geographies have been at the forefront of understanding the development and management of nature-based tourism (Valentine 1992; Fennell 1999, 2001; Weaver 2001), including the impact of human visitation on wildlife (Orams 2002, 2005; Higham and Shelton 2011).

As a resource analyst, the geographer therefore 'seeks to understand the fundamental characteristics of natural resources and the processes through which they are allocated and utilised' (Mitchell 1979: 3). The geographer's task is also relayed by Coppock (1970: 25), who has made remarks of direct relevance to a better understanding of the relationship between tourism, recreation and wilderness conservation: 'A concern with problem solving and with the processes of human interaction with resources, particularly in respect of decision making, will powerfully assist a more effective geographical contribution to conservation.'

Further reading

On the development of wilderness and national park ideas, see:

Nash, R. (1982) *Wilderness and the American Mind*, 3rd edn, New Haven, CT: Yale University Press.

Oelschlaeger, M. (1991) *The Idea of Wilderness: From Prehistory to the Age of Ecology*, New Haven, CT: Yale University Press.

Runte, A. (2010) *National Parks: The American Experience*, 4th edn, Lanham, MD: Taylor Trade Publishing.

On wilderness inventories in Europe, see:

Carver, S., Evans, A. and Fritz, S. (2002) 'Wilderness attribute mapping in the United Kingdom', *International Journal of Wilderness*, 8(1): 24–9.

Orsi, F., Geneletti, D. and Borsdorf, A. (2013) 'Mapping wildness for protected area management: a methodological approach and application to the Dolomites UNESCO World Heritage Site (Italy)', *Landscape and Urban Planning*, 120: 1–15.

For an international overview on national parks and tourism, see:

Frost, W. and Hall, C.M. (eds) (2009a) *Tourism and National Parks: International Perspectives on Development, Histories and Change*, London: Routledge.

For an excellent introduction to some of the problems encountered in the management of natural areas, see:

Newsome, D., Moore, S. and Dowling, R. (2002) *Natural Area Tourism: Ecology, Impacts and Management*, Clevedon: Channel View.

Questions to discuss

1 Is wilderness only a concept of the New World or does the concept also have relevance to western Europe?

2 Is the methodology of Australia's national wilderness inventory easily transferable to other countries?

3 What are the main factors which influence crowding norms?

Coastal and marine recreation and tourism

The coast is a magnet for tourists and recreationists, although its role in leisure activities has changed in time and space, as coastal destinations have developed, waned, been re-imaged and redeveloped through time. The coastal environment is a complex system which is utilised by the recreationist for day trips, while juxtaposed to these visits are those made by the domestic and international tourist. However, the understanding and focus of this system have shifted over time. Pearce and Kirk (1986) identified three elements to the coastal environment: the *hinterland* (where accommodation and services are provided); the *transit* zone (i.e. dunes); and the *recreational activity* zone (beach and sea). This model typifies much of the research by geographers prior to the 1990s: to observe, describe, record, synthesise and model recreational and tourism phenomena in pursuit of an explanation of the spatial relationships and nature of the coast. In Lavery's (1971b) analysis of resorts, the distinction between recreation and tourism is blurred but the coastal resort was a dominant element of the observed patterns and models of tourism activity. The pursuit of explanations of the spatial structure of coastal tourism and preoccupation with the resort morphology have led to the replication of a multiplicity of studies that look at the similarities and differences between resorts in different parts of the world.

This assessment may equally be applied to the recreational activities of visitors to the coastal environment since this neglect is not germane to tourism alone. This was confirmed by Patmore (1983: 209) since, 'For such extensive resource, it has been little studied in any comprehensive fashion'. As Page and Connell (2010) observed, the coast has attracted a great deal of interest from social scientists (e.g. anthropologists, sociologists, historians, cultural studies, transport studies and coastal and environmental science) but this has not yielded a body of knowledge that adequately explains why the coast continues to be a magnet for leisure use. Indeed, ocean and coastal tourism is widely regarded as one of the fastest growing areas of contemporary tourism (Pollard 1995; Kim and Kim 1996; Orams 1999), especially the rise of cruising (Rodrigue and Notteboom 2013), with its distinct itineraries that are concentrated in North American, European, Caribbean and Asian waters, with distinct relationships with the coastal areas and ports and their perceived safety for visitors (Bowen *et al.* 2012). While tourism development has been spatially focused on the beach for much of the postwar years, as witnessed, for example, in the slogan of the four 'S's of tourism – sun, sand, surf and sex – the coastal and the marine environment as a whole has become one of the new frontiers and fastest growing areas of the world's tourism industry (Miller and Auyong 1991). The exact numbers of marine tourists remain unknown, although Zacarias *et al.* (2011) indicated that in Spain 0.001 per cent of the beach area generated 10 per cent of GDP; Miami Beach had a tourism economy worth US$2.4 billion and Florida US$65 billion. As many studies of the environmental impact of tourism acknowledge, the selling of 'sun, sand and surf experiences', the development of beach resorts and the increasing popularity of marine tourism (e.g. fishing, scuba diving, windsurfing and yachting) have all placed increased pressure on the coast, an area for which use may already be highly concentrated in terms of agriculture, human settlements, fishing and industrial location (Miller 1993). However, because of the highly dynamic nature of the coastal environment any development which interferes with the natural coastal system may have severe consequences for the long-term stability of the environment (Cicin-Sain and Knecht 1998). Indeed, in the United States, the National Oceanic and Atmospheric Administration (NOAA) recognised that,

> Of all the activities that take place in coastal zones and the near-shore coastal ocean, none is increasing in both volume and diversity more than coastal tourism and recreation. Both the dynamic nature of this sector and its magnitude demand that it be actively taken into account in government plans, policies, and programs related to the coasts and ocean. Indeed, virtually all coastal and ocean issue areas affect coastal tourism and recreation either directly or indirectly. Clean water, healthy coastal habitats, and a safe, secure, and enjoyable environment are clearly fundamental to successful coastal tourism. Similarly, bountiful living marine resources (fish, shellfish, wetlands, coral reefs, etc.) are of critical importance to most recreational experiences. Security from risks associated with natural coastal hazards such as storms, hurricanes, tsunamis, and the like is a requisite for coastal tourism to be sustainable over the long term.
>
> (NOAA 1997)

The concept of coastal tourism embraces the full range of tourism, leisure and recreationally oriented activities that take place in the coastal zone and the offshore coastal waters. These include coastal tourism development (accommodation, restaurants, food industry and second homes) and the infrastructure supporting coastal development (e.g. retail businesses, marinas and activity suppliers). Also included are tourism activities such as recreational boating, coast- and marine-based ecotourism, cruises, swimming, recreational fishing, snorkelling and diving (Miller and Auyong 1991; Miller 1993; Wiener *et al.*

2009). Marine tourism is closely related to the concept of coastal tourism but also includes ocean-based tourism such as deep-sea fishing and yacht cruising. Orams (1999: 9) defines marine tourism as including 'those recreational activities that involve travel away from one's place of residence and which have as their host or focus the marine environment (where the marine environment is defined as those waters which are saline and tide-affected)'. Such a definition is significant, for as well as having a biological and recreational base it also emphasises that consideration of the elements of marine and coastal tourism must include shore-based activities, such as land-based whale watching, reef walking, cruise ship supply and yachting events, within the overall ambit of marine tourism.

This chapter seeks to review the principal ways in which the geographer has approached the coastal and marine environment. In particular, it highlights the reluctance of geographers to adopt a holistic understanding, whereby recreation and tourism are analysed as competing and yet complementary activities using the same resource base. The chapter commences with a discussion of the way in which the coast, and the beach in particular, was created by recreationalists and tourists. Like wilderness areas, the discovery of the coast as a potential resource for leisure use illustrates that leisure resources are *created*: they exist in a latent form until their discovery, recognition and their development lead to their use. In most geographical analyses of the coastline as such a resource, the value of an historical approach is acknowledged in virtually every textbook on resorts. And yet the geographer has been largely remiss in addressing this vital theme – how the resource was discovered and developed in time and space, with a number of exceptions of individual resorts and classic studies (e.g. Gilbert 1939). It developed in the human consciousness, supplanting perceptions of the coastal zone as a repulsive environment once the lure of the seaside marked a changing sensibility in society. For this reason, historical reconstructions of the coastal environment need to recognise the way in which the resource was discovered, popularised and developed, and assumed a cultural significance in society.

Coastline as a recreation and tourist resource: its discovery and recognition as a leisure resource

The beach as we know it is, historically speaking, a recent phenomenon. In fact, it took hundreds of years for the seashore to be colonised as the pre-eminent site for human recreation . . . A proscenium for history, the beach has become a conspicuous signpost against which Western culture has registered its economic, aesthetic, sexual, religious, and even technological milestones.

(Lenček and Bosker 1999: xx)

The perception of the beach as a natural resource for leisure has changed throughout history. For example, the European acceptance of the beach embodied notions of utility which replaced a reverence for the sea and images of nature dominating human existence in the littoral zone. In the Romantic period the beach represented a site for pleasure, spiritual exercise and a positive experience. The symbolic value of the beach was also incorporated in poetry and landscape painting, and created a new sensibility and practices. This brought new social, psychological, economic and spatial prestige to a landscape as a place of leisure and pleasure (see Lenček and Bosker 1999). In Corbin's (1995) *The Lure of the Sea: The Discovery of the Seaside 1750–1840*, the dramatic changes in western attitudes towards the sea, the seaside and the landscape are reviewed in a European context. As a French translation of the European literature, it provides a fascinating reconstruction of those elements in western society which contributed to the discovery of the coast as a leisure resource (i.e. Romanticism) and the impact on perceptions of the seaside. The publication of Jane Austen's *Sanditon* in 1817, heralded as the first 'seaside' novel, was a parody of coastal tourism as a fashion-driven experience with health and recuperative benefits. Yet the discovery of the pleasure qualities of the coast and the transformation from the classical period 'knew nothing of the attraction of seaside beaches, the emotion of a bather plunging into the waves, or the pleasures of a stay at the seaside. A veil of repulsive images prevented the seaside from

exercising its appeal' (Corbin 1995: 1). What the period 1750 to 1840 witnessed was a fundamental reassessment of the ways in which leisure time and places were used with the evolution of the seaside holiday. Within that evolutionary process the beach was invented as part of a resort complex. As Figure 8.1 identifies, the coast as a resource has gone through a process of invention, rejection and rediscovery, and this has occurred at different times and in various spatial contexts since no two countries have identical patterns of development in coastal tourism and recreation (Page and Connell 2010).

The beach developed as the activity space for recreation and tourism, with distinct cultural and social forms emerging in relation to fashions, tastes and innovations in resort form. The development of piers, jetties and promenades as formal spaces for organised recreational and tourism activities led to new ways of experiencing the sea. The coastal environment, resort and the beach have been an enduring resource for tourism and recreation since the 1750s in western consciousness, with their meaning, value to society and role in leisure time remaining a significant activity space. The coastal environment has distinct spatial characteristics, as Figure 8.2 illustrates, which ranges from the highly developed resort towns that have pre-occupied the analysis of the tourism area life cycle (TALC) through to more, isolated and remoter locations (Butler 2006; Page and Connell 2010).

Indeed, the beach 'invites watchers to unearth not only the dominant, culturally elite themes of a period, but its popular sensibilities: a blank piece of real estate on which each wave of colonizers puts up its own idea of paradise' (Lenček and Bosker 1999: xx): in short, the coast represents a liminal landscape in which the juncture of pleasure, recreation and tourism is epitomised in the postmodern consumption of leisure places (Preston-Whyte 2002). However, as Preston-Whyte (2004) acknowledged, the discussion on beaches as liminal spaces needs to be deepened, particularly the dominance of a western perspective that assumes liminality to be associated with heightened sensibilities associated with the temporary suspension of normal states, and a paucity of empirical exploration of the nature of the symbolism of these

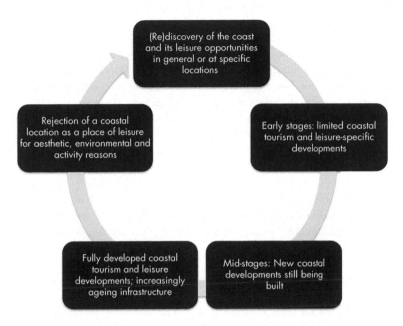

Figure 8.1 The cyclical life course of society's approach to coastal leisure
Source: adapted from Page and Connell 2010.

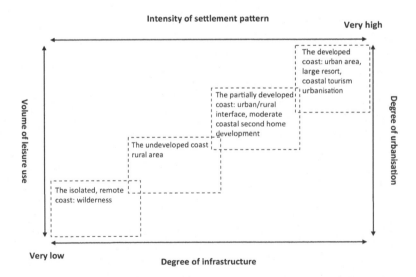

Figure 8.2 The scope of the coastal environment
Source: Page and Connell 2010.

spaces. Preston-Whyte (2004) argued that two main issues need to be addressed. First, the human actors, with their cultural discourse and symbols to conceptualise and tame the beach, and the non-human actors that constitute the material conditions of the beach itself with its attractions and dangers, must be dealt with on equal terms. Second, dualisms such as nature/culture, that feature so strongly in socio-spatial analysis (Murdock 1997; Watmore 1998, 2000; Cloke and Johnston 2005a), need to be addressed. In doing so, Preston-Whyte (2004) believed that researchers would then be in a better position to understand the cryptic comment made by Richard in Alex Garland's influential novel (and subsequent film) *The Beach*: 'It doesn't matter why I found it so easy to assimilate myself into beach life. The question is why the beach life found it so easy to assimilate me' (Garland 1997: 116, quoted in Preston-Whyte 2004: 357).

As Edgerton (1979) observed, for some Californian beaches in the 1970s, 400,000 visitors a day was not uncommon. Given the spatial distribution of beaches in California (Figure 8.3 indicates the distribution of state beaches), this is a dominant cultural element of the region's leisure culture. In fact, in 2001 the visits to California's top three state beaches were: Santa Monica (7.8 million visits), Lighthouse Field (7.3 million visits) and Dockweiler (3.8 million visits). Beach visits generated US$75.4 million in travel and tourism expenditure for the Californian economy, supporting up to one million jobs and generating a further US$4.8 million in tax revenue. The scale of such visits also illustrates the evolution of California's beaches as a leisure playground (Löfgren 2002; Dwight *et al.* 2007), popularised in popular culture in the 1950s by the diffusion of surfing from Waikiki beach in Hawaii. In the 1960s, the evolution of a Californian beach music culture (e.g. the Beach Boys) generated a new stimulus to beach use, especially with the rise of the beach party. The 1970s and 1980s saw additional stimuli which have continued the beach culture, particularly the television series *Baywatch* (Löfgren 2002).

As Braun and Soskin (2002) show in relation to Daytona Beach, Florida, day-trippers to coastal areas can help stabilise seasonal fluctuations in visitor demand. Yet, conversely, they can also increase resource degradation due to volume of use, generate image problems and additional policing and maintenance costs. This has led researchers such as Zacarias *et al.* (2011) to assess the recreation carrying capacity for beaches. Their study of Faro beach in Portugal concluded that 1,328–2,628 beach users a day was the optimum threshold for its recreational carrying capacity, while the socio-cultural capacity was much lower at 305–608 visitors a day. In fact economists utilising Willingness to Pay methodologies (see Birdir *et al.* 2013) highlighted that in a study of Turkey beach users were prepared to pay €1.90–2.30 for a visit to the beach if the fee was used to improve the environment (including the cleanliness and maintenance of the resource). Rolfe and Gregg's (2012) valuation study of Australian beaches placed the value of beach visits at $587.3 million.

The beach is therefore an environment where, sometimes, hordes of people are prepared to tolerate overcrowding to experience the human–nature environmental landscape – being at one with nature so that the sun, sea and sand can be experienced in the tourist and recreationalist consciousness and pursuit of the liminal existence.

The geographer's contribution to the analysis of coastal recreation and tourism

The coast has emerged as one of the popular, yet hidden and underplayed elements in the geographer's application of the hallmark traits of spatial analysis, observation and explanation. From the early context for economics, such as Hötelling's (1929) model of ice-cream sellers on the beach, to Weaver's (2000) model of resort scenarios, the coast has assumed a significance as a context for research, but not as a veritable resource for the legitimate analysis of tourism and recreation. This dependence on the coast as a laboratory for the analysis of spatial concepts, interdependencies and the application of geographical methodologies does not adequately reflect the

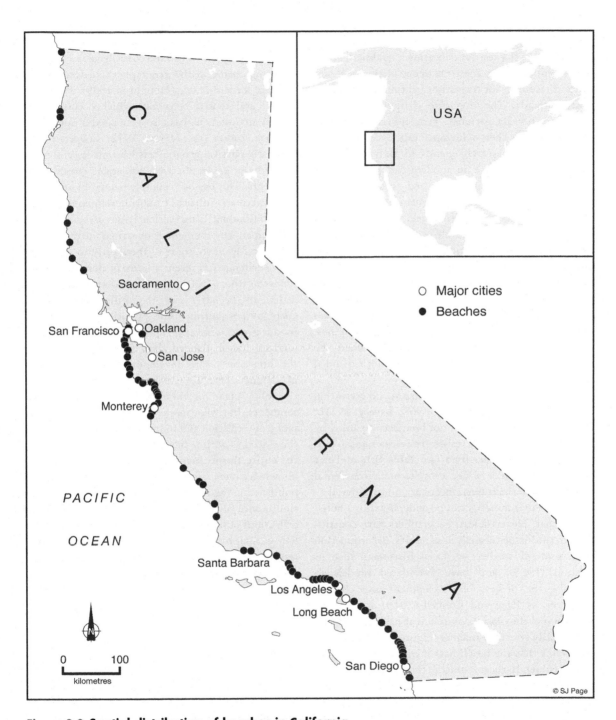

Figure 8.3 **Spatial distribution of beaches in California**

cultural and leisure significance of the beach and coastline in recreational and tourism activity in time and space. To the contrary, locating a landmark study which embodies the coastline as one of the most significant resources for recreation and tourism is notoriously difficult. The literature is fragmented, with tourism and recreational geographers seemingly obdurate given their reluctance to move this theme higher up the research agenda to fully appreciate its wider significance in modern-day patterns and consumption of day trips and holidaymaking. Despite the fact that the coast remains one of the most obvious contexts for tourism and recreation, it is poorly understood. Research is reliant on a host of very dated and highly disjointed studies of the coastal environment. Despite the publication of two important works in the 1990s (Fabbri 1990; Wong 1993b), the area has barely moved forward in the mainstream tourism literature. This is extremely problematic for both tourism and recreation studies and geographers, as observed by Page and Connell (2010), where the wider social science contributions have not expanded the spatial dimensions.

The early interest in coastal tourism and recreation (e.g. Gilbert 1939; Patmore 1968; Lavery 1971b; Pearce and Kirk 1986) has not been accompanied by a sustained interest; as a result, the research published has been highly specialised (see Table 8.1) and not been situated in a wider ecosystem/environmental context where the interconnections and sustainability of coastal environments can be understood in a holistic context. Nevertheless, geographers have contributed to the historical analysis of resorts, in conjunction with seminal studies by social historians such as Walton (1983), and have formulated models to describe the process of development and change. However, as Page and Connell (2010) argued, the evolution of the coastal environment has also emerged as a socially stratified manner (Figure 8.4). Figure 8.4 illustrates that the beach has emerged in a democratised manner, in those countries that do not allow privatisation of the beach, as the use of the coast has gradually permeated down the social scale and gradually appealed to a mass audience, as beach spaces have been consumed by larger audiences.

The main dynamics of change, combined with temporal and spatial seasonality embodied in tourist and recreational travel to the coast, have remained an enduring theme in the geographer's analysis of this resource for leisure (e.g. Houghton 1989). The recreational and tourist behaviour which occurs in the coastal environment has also generated a number of seminal studies (i.e. Mercer 1972; Cooper 1981), while the physical geographers have made valid studies of the processes affecting vulnerable coastal environments. This has been complemented by studies of the pattern and impact of resort development, which raises important conservation issues associated with the human–environment interactions in these environments. Even so, some of these early models have been challenged in recent studies of Boracay, Philippines (Smith *et al.* 2011), and Benidorm (Baidal *et al.* 2013). In the latter case, the ability of a resort to adapt by reinventing itself, providing differentiated products and innovating in terms of providing new services, has challenged the conventional notion of the direction resort development follows. Finally, geographers have also made useful contributions to the policy, planning and management of coastal environments. But what marks this area out in the geography of recreation and tourism is the sparse nature of these studies within the mainstream literature, with the entire theme seeming almost unfashionable and knowledge often being based on findings from studies published in the 1960s, 1970s and 1980s, despite the significance of Fabbri's (1990) and Wong's (1993b) collections of papers on the topic by geographers and non-geographers (e.g. Phillips and House 2009). As a result, the following section examines the different contributions geographers have made and the significance to increasing our knowledge of the coast in the formation of distinct leisure and tourism geographies.

Historical analysis of recreation and tourism in the coastal zone

In many Anglo-American geographical analyses of recreation and tourism the English seaside resort is a popular topic for discussion and it is often portrayed as a salutory lesson with respect to the rise and fall of

Table 8.1 Illustrations of the geographer's contribution to the analysis of coastal recreation and tourism

Theme	Examples
Historical analysis of recreation and tourism in the coastal zone	Gilbert (1939) The development of coastal resorts Naylon (1967) The development of tourism in Spain Patmore (1968) Spa resorts in Britain Robinson (1976) Geography of tourism and resort development Barke and Towner (1996) The evolution of tourism in Spanish resorts Towner (1996) Synthesis of the process of development of resorts and patterns of tourism
Models of recreation and tourism	Stansfield and Rickert (1970) The recreational business district Miossec (1977) The process of resort development Pigram (1977) Analysis of beach resort morphology Britton (1982) Model of postcolonialist resort development Jeans (1990) Analysis of beach resort morphology in England and Australia Weaver (2000) Destination development scenarios
Tourist and recreationalist travel to the coast	Patmore (1971) Routeways and tourist/recreational travel Wall (1971, 1972) Patterns of travel by Hull car owners Mercer (1972) Recreational use of Melbourne beaches
Tourist and recreationalist behaviour	Coppock (1977a) Second home ownership Cooper (1981) The behaviour and activities of tourists in Jersey Wong (1990) Recreational activities in coastal areas of Singapore Walmsley and Jenkins (1994) Perception of coastal areas Pearce (1998) Tourist time budget study in Vanuatu Tunstall and Penning-Rowsell (1998) Beach user perceptions in England
Geomorphology of coasts and interrelationship with tourism/recreation	May (1993) Survey of South England Morris (1996) Environmental management in coastal Spain Burns et al. (1990) Analysis of coastal processes affecting the SW Cape coastline in South Africa
Resort development	Pearce (1978) The form and function of French resorts Wong (1986, 1993a) The development of island tourism in Peninsular Malaysia Morrison and Dickinson (1987) Costa Brava in Spain Kent et al. (2002) Water supply and coastal resorts in Mallorca McEwen et al. (2002) Flood warning and caravan parks
Conservation of coastal environment	Kirkby (1996) Recreation and the quality of coastal water in Spain White et al. (1997) Special Area Management and coastal tourism resources in Sri Lanka Leafe et al. (1998) Shoreline management Turner et al. (1998) Sustainable management of the coastline Barke and Towner (2003) Sustainable tourism in Andalucia Wong (2003) Coastal erosion in South-East Asia
Human–environment interactions within coastal environments	Edwards (1987) Ecological impacts of tourism on heritage coasts in the UK Carter et al. (1990) Impacts on the Irish coastline McDowell et al. (1990) Impacts on the Costa del Sol Catto (2002) Anthropogenic pressure on coastal dunes
Management and planning of coastal areas for recreation and tourism	Pearce and Kirk (1986) Carrying capacity for coastal tourism Carter (1988) The coastline as an area to manage for recreation and tourism Ghelardoni (1990) Planning the Aquitaine coastline in France for tourism Nielsen (1990) Constructing a recreational beach in Denmark Nichols (1999) Integrated coastal management
Business and economic dimensions of coastal development	Dumas (1982) The commercial structure of Benidorm Penning-Rowsell et al. (1992) Economics of coastal management

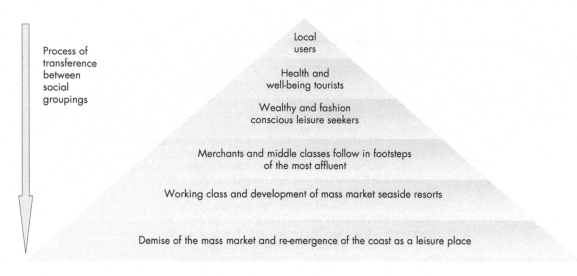

Process of transference between social groupings

Local users

Health and well-being tourists

Wealthy and fashion conscious leisure seekers

Merchants and middle classes follow in footsteps of the most affluent

Working class and development of mass market seaside resorts

Demise of the mass market and re-emergence of the coast as a leisure place

Figure 8.4 Evolution of the coast as a leisure environment

tourism destinations. Indeed, A.M. Williams and Shaw's (1998) interesting analysis of the rise and fall of the English seaside or coastal resort examined two principal concerns of the historical geographer and contemporary tourism geographer: continuity and change in the development, organisation and prospects for the resort. Most analyses of the English seaside resort by geographers (e.g. Patmore 1968) refer to the seminal studies by E.W. Gilbert (1939, 1949) and the doctoral thesis by Barrett (1958). Despite these influential studies, the most notable contributions to the analysis of English resorts came from the social and economic historians, such as Walton (1983), and the geographical analysis by Towner (1996). What these studies emphasise are the role of historical sources, such as the census, development plans, advertising, photographic archives and other documentary sources, in reconstructing the recreational and tourism environments in coastal areas in the Victorian, Edwardian and subsequent periods. Specific phenomena, such as the English holiday camp, examined by Ward and Hardy (1986), are also charted using similar sources. An illustration of the importance of examining the historical issues in the development of the coast as a tourism and leisure resource is seen in Box 8.1.

In each of the studies of the English seaside resort, geographers have sought to map and analyse the changing dynamics of resort development. A number of useful historical analyses of Spanish coastal tourism exist (e.g. Barke and Towner 1996; Walton and Smith 1996), which review the emergence of coastal areas in the era during and after the Grand Tour. The late nineteenth and early twentieth century patterns of coastal tourism in Spain, and the dynamics of tourist circuits, were reconstructed from historical guidebooks. The relationship of tourist circuits, the evolution of the Spanish railway system and the development of tourist accommodation highlighted the consumption of leisure resources, particularly the evolution of seaside resorts. Walton and Smith (1996: 57) concluded that 'The importance of the quality of local government to resort success has been strongly apparent in studies of English resorts, but its role in San Sebastian was even more impressive'. Evaluations of coastal resources, such as the development of the England and Wales Heritage Coastline (Romeril 1984, 1988), have emerged as an historical resource. In other countries (e.g. the USA and Australia), historical studies of coastal tourism and recreation (see Pigram 1977; Miller 1987; Jeans 1990; Pigram and Jenkins 2006) have considered resorts, their life cycles

BOX 8.1 PROMOTION OF THE SEASIDE RESORT: PLACE-PROMOTION STRATEGIES

Following the promotion of spa resorts in the UK, with the royal patronage of individual sites such as by Queen Anne in 1702, the link with the coast was harnessed where spa resorts were located in seaside locations as spa visitors began to bathe in the sea and use the beach. 'By the 1730s Brighton and Margate, along with Scarborough, had distinct seabathing seasons' (Ward 2001: 31). But the rise of the coastal resorts did not simply mirror those of earlier spa resorts. The seaside, with its beach and sea, were not in private ownership, providing opportunities for different social classes to partake of the pleasures of the coast. As Walton (1983: 190–1) argued, 'At the seaside rich and poor, respectable and ungodly, staid and rowdy, quiet and noisy not only rubbed shoulders . . . they also had to compete for access to, and use of, recreational space'. This reflects the improved access. For example, in the 1820s London Steamers to Thanet in Kent improved access, as did the railway in the period after the 1840s, initially as day excursionists then as holidaymakers.

To encourage visitors, resorts in the nineteenth century engaged in place-promotion strategies, building on the more crude methods which predate this period, such as guidebooks, limited newspaper advertising and editorials in popular national journals such as the *Gentleman's Magazine* (Brown 1988). One of the prime movers in place-promotion was the railway companies. While some resorts produced guidebooks to promote their wares, the railway companies used newspapers, posters and handbills to promote day excursions. This in turn also helped shape place-images and stereotypes of individual resorts, where hedonism and cheap excursions were popular (e.g. Blackpool). In contrast, private promoters of railway tours such as Thomas Cook adopted a more educative approach to tours, aiming the products at specific niches rather than the mass market.

Blackpool, among the UK resorts, entered the place-promotion role after the Lancashire and Yorkshire Railway's fare policy threatened its excursion and holiday business from working class areas. By an Act of 1879, the town council levied a local tax on the rates to undertake advertising at railway stations, attractions and amusements in the town. Not only did the town's Advertising Committee start with illustrated brochures aimed at the middle class market, but after 1881 Blackpool posters began to appear to publicise attractions, the Blackpool Tower, constructed in 1894, and the illuminations, introduced after 1912. In France, railway advertising on the Compagnie de l'Ouest after 1886 saw colour posters introduced to advertise coastal destinations. Soon, individual resorts also used this method of place advertising, despite the expense and print runs of up to 6,000. Due to the cost many posters in France were displayed for up to three years and brochures would also have a similar life expectancy.

In the UK, the railway companies approached this method of promotion more cautiously (Ward 2001). Although some companies produced posters for individual resorts, such as 'Skegness is so bracing' by the Great Northern Railway in 1908, this was not the norm. Indeed, the Local Government Board in 1914 deemed municipal advertising on tourism inappropriate despite Blackpool's highly developed publicity programme on the rates. Even so, a 'highly competitive resort selling game' (Ward 2001: 37) existed in the UK, and only limited powers were granted prior to 1914. After 1914, the UK saw a greater resort and railway company partnership in place-promotion, with the Health Resorts and Watering Places Act 1921 allowing resort municipalities the right to spend up to a 1d rate on certain forms of advertising. After this point, co-operative railway-resort marketing emerged, although the 1930s saw greater pressure for local authorities to increase their marketing and place-promotion activities as the car and charabancs opened up new day trip markets. In the case of the most prolific railway advertiser, the Great Western Railway (GWR), A. Bennett acknowledged that

> The GWR's literary and visual representations drew heavily upon the concept of departure, that is, the qualitative distinction between daily or accepted routine and that of a special experience. Departure could assume an historical form, a particular location, an aesthetic appreciation or the sheer, exuberant pleasures of the seaside . . . GWR marketing also stressed the experience of the journey itself in its various forms, as a spectacle, an adventure and often as a unique and glamorous event . . . These were brought together in prestige advertising, a dimension of place marketing.
>
> (Bennett 2002: 3)

The iconography of railway poster advertising provides not only an expression of place-marketing, but also a distinct style and mode of representing the imagery of the coast for potential visitors (Hewitt 1995). As Bennett (2002) observed, the GWR view of the seaside had two key elements: that of a fashionable and exclusive 'watering place' for certain locations (e.g. Torquay) and that of family-based resorts (e.g. Paignton and Porthcawl). GWR also took a lead role in the overseas marketing of Britain, with its influential role in developing the Travel Association of Great Britain and Ireland, to promote the country overseas due to the economic benefits of inbound tourism.

Ward (2001) acknowledged that the 1920s were the heyday of railway company place-promotion and the 1930s saw municipalities increase their role. By 1939, Blackpool was producing 150 holiday guides to send to potential visitors, while resorts began a greater market segmentation, attracting conferences off-season. Therefore what this Box shows is that a number of agents and actors in coastal resorts (e.g. the railway companies and municipalities) devised a wide range of promotional tools to sell and advertise their localities. This was highly controversial in the Victorian, Edwardian and inter-war periods and remains so even to the present day. It is also interesting to note that entrepreneurial companies like GWR created images and marketing strategies which saw a massive investment in tourism advertising. This was very influential in developing new and repeat business among the domestic and overseas markets, with carefully targeted market positioning of specific resorts to meet the expectations, desires and perception of prospective visitors.

and development in a longitudinal context. The historical geography of specific resorts has provided a focal point for research, where a range of factors explain why resorts developed where they did, why they developed and the pace and scale of change. This often remains a starting point for most analyses of the coast as an evolving resource for leisure use.

Models of coastal recreation and tourism

In the early studies of coastal recreation and tourism (e.g. Gilbert 1939), the major contribution to spatial knowledge was predicated on developing models which had a universal or more general application. D.G. Pearce (1995a) reviewed models of resort development, acknowledging the role of historical antecedents (e.g. the role of developers in developing resorts for different social classes). Using the resort life cycle developed by Butler (1980), various factors were used to explain similarities and differences in development paths and the resulting morphological structure of the resort. D.G. Pearce (1995a) identified the problem of tourism functions being added to existing urban centres in coastal locations where a day trip market may also exist. What Pearce concluded was that 'a spectrum of coastal resorts exists, ranging from those with a wholly tourist function, notably the new planned resorts, to those where a significant amount of tourist activity occurs alongside a variety of other functions' (Pearce 1995a: 137). Interestingly, this reiterates the earlier typology developed by Lavery (1971c) in a recreational context, where a similar notion of a continuum was implicit but not explicitly developed. What Pearce (1995a) could have added is that the local recreational market in many resorts will numerically outnumber the tourist market, though the behaviour of the former is very much more climatically conditioned and opportunistic as they have more alternative leisure opportunities.

Among the most widely cited models of the resort is Stansfield and Rickert's (1970) discussion of the impact of consumption on resort morphology. Their resulting model, identified as the Recreational Business District (RBD), utilised earlier concepts from urban morphology models where central place functions of urban centres exist. The RBD, as distinct from the CBD, was viewed as the locale for recreational services and activities. Stansfield and Rickert (1970: 215) defined the RBD as 'the seasonally oriented linear aggregation of restaurants, various specialty food stands, candy stores and a varied array of novelty and souvenir shops which cater to visitors' leisurely shopping needs'. Although the model was based only on two New Jersey seaside resorts, the important distinction for current cultural interest in coastal recreation and tourism was that the RBD was not only an economic manifestation but also a social phenomenon. Similar relationships between the CBD, which is spatially detached from the RBD in resorts, was an important focus for research in the 1970s and 1980s. Had such models been developed in the 1990s, the research agenda and formulation of the model framework would have been very different. A greater emphasis would potentially have been placed upon the supply dynamics which created the RBD (i.e. the role of capital) (Judd and Fainstein 1999), the cultural and social meaning attached to the tourist, and recreationalists' experience of the RBD as a place in time and space (Britton 1991). It would arguably not be viewed in a static context, since the processes of change and evolution of the

RBD to accommodate consumer tastes would be more emphasised.

In the emerging tourist destinations of the Asia-Pacific (Hall and Page 2000), the RBD is a more complex phenomenon where the addition of hawker stalls, souvenir sellers and the informal economy combine to create a distinct entertainment district. D.G. Pearce (1995a) identified the addition of a night-life function in Patong, Phuket (Thailand), where the commodification of sex tourism is an additional function evident in the RBD (Ryan and Hall 2001). In integrated resort development in the Asia-Pacific, the RBD function is typically incorporated as a key function, e.g. Densarau Island in Fiji (Smith 1991, 1992a, 1992b; Xie *et al.* 2013). Land use zoning and the spatial separation of accommodation from the RBD to increase resort carrying capacity in locations such as Cancun (Gormsen 1982) highlighted the use of spatial concepts to manage tourist development. Pigram's (1977) influential study of morphological changes in Surfers Paradise (Queensland, Australia) between 1958 and 1975 recognised the spatial separation of the RBD and CBD. Yet relatively little interest has been shown in models of beach use, with a notable exception (Jeans 1990) where a semiotic model was developed. This model distinguished between the resort, which represented culture, and the sea, which represented nature. What emerged was a transitional zone between culture and nature, a zone of 'ambiguity' – the beach. A second axis of meaning was also recognised, where the beach zone had a social periphery, where nonconformists (i.e. semi-nude and nude bathers and surfers) inhabited the area.

Tourist and recreational travel to the coast

Within the tourism literature, the role of transport as a facilitating mechanism to explain tourist travel, patterns of tourism and development has only belatedly been acknowledged (Page 1994b, 1998, 1999, 2005, 2009a). There are a number of seminal studies (e.g. Patmore 1968) in explaining the development of spas. Similarly, Pearson's (1968) study of the evolution of coastal resorts in East Lincolnshire illustrated the geographers' interest in the transport dimension.

Patmore's (1971: 70) recognition that 'Deep-rooted in the very concept of outdoor recreation is the "journey to play", the fundamental movement linking residence or workplace to recreation resource. Such movement varies in scale, in duration and frequency.' A similar analogy may also be applied to tourism, and geographers have utilised a wide range of concepts from transport geography to analyse the patterns of travel for coastal activity by recreationalists and tourists. As Patmore (1971) recognised, it is the identification of the routeways (the lines of movement) and the link to nodes of intensive leisure activity which have preoccupied geographers' analysis of tourism and recreational travel, seeking to model and understand this phenomenon (Mansfield 1969). As Patmore argued:

> The crux of recreational planning is therefore the location, design and management of a relatively limited number of sites devoted wholly or partially to recreation, together with a concern for the routes which link them both to each other and to the residences of the users.
>
> (Patmore 1971: 72)

For the coastal environment, it has been the mobility afforded by the car (Wall 1971, 1972) that has posed many of the resulting pressures, planning problems and conflicts in environments that are constrained in the number of visitors they can absorb. Wall (1971) recognised that holidaymakers generate a considerable proportion of the road traffic in resorts. As Wall (1971: 101) poignantly and ironically commented, 'One of the major advantages of automobile travel is that it appears to be quite cheap. The capital expenditure involved in the purchase of an automobile is likely to be large, but having incurred this outlay, the cost of additional increments of travel is comparatively small.'

The car remains convenient and flexible, and adds a degree of readily available mobility which is not constrained by public transport timetables. Probably the greatest constraint for the car is in accommodating the space demand in relation to recreational and tourist routeways in coastal environments (i.e. parking space) (Davenport and Davenport 2006). There is also growing evidence from the public sector of pressure in some coastal environments to exclude the car from certain areas. The car can reduce 'the friction of distance', making coastal environments attractive and accessible to urban dwellers. However, one has to place the coastal environment in the wider recreational and tourist context of participation levels. Patmore (1971: 76–7) aptly summarised this issue: 'The nearest seaside or open moorland may lure people from conurbations six times a year, while the local park is used every day to exercise the dog.' This hierarchy of tourism and leisure resources can often be overlooked.

Access to the coastal environment is a key concept, though, as Patmore (1971) argued, it was a relative term, since improvements in transport routes and technology may directly change the nature of the access. The historical geographer's emphasis on the role of railway companies in Victorian Britain has identified their function in developing major visitor hinterlands for specific coastal resorts. Even some 150 years later, coastal resorts in many countries still have a limited reliance upon the rail network as a source of visitors, although the car is by far the most important mode of travel for recreational trips. The coastal environment and the routeways developed along coastlines, with viewing areas and a network of attractions, may also be a major recreational resource. For example, on the upper North Island of New Zealand, the collaboration between regional tourism organisations (see Page *et al*. 1999) created the Pacific Coastal Highway scenic drive. Not only did this utilise coastal routeways that receive comparatively limited traffic outside the main summer season, but it also reduced congestion on other routeways between Auckland and the Bay of Islands.

Coastal recreational footpaths are also a major routeway resource, a linear recreational resource that often transects a variety of other leisure resources, from the coastline to the built environment through to the countryside (Huxley 1970). Many countries contain dense networks of footpaths, with Patmore (1971) referring to an estimated 120,000 miles in England and Wales. The issue is contentious, especially in coastal environments where the coastline is adjacent to privately owned land, and access is carefully guarded. In England and Wales, the designation of Heritage Coasts (Romeril 1988) has improved access issues and provided an opportunity for management agreements to be developed between private landowners and planners. As Keirle (2002) has shown in relation to Wales, coastal land should be considered as open countryside so that the public have right of access, while some forms of personal leisure transport may also contribute to environmental pollution and management issues (Davenport and Davenport 2006).

Tourist and recreational behaviour: use and activity patterns in coastal environments

Among the influential studies by geographers from the 1970s were the development of a behavioural geography and its application to recreation and tourism, especially in relation to coastal environments. Mercer (1971a: 51) summarised the significance of the behavioural perspective, where 'The values and attributes of any outdoor recreation site, whether a local neighbourhood park or major wilderness area are perceived somewhat differently by numerous subgroups within society'. Mercer (1971a) outlined the recreationalists' decision-making process (subsequently modified by Pigram 1983) and the meaning attached to tourism and recreational experiences. Mercer's (1970) analysis of recreational trips to beaches in Melbourne highlighted the urban resident's vague notion of the outdoor recreational opportunities open to them. The role of image in choosing beach environments is an important factor, and may override concerns of overcrowding and even pollution (Roca and Villares 2008). Perceived distance and accessibility are also important factors affecting recreational search behaviour, and may account for why certain coastal environments attract large crowds and others do not. In England and Wales, the coast is no more than 120 km away for the most inland population, and, building on the model by Pearce and Kirk (1986), it is evident that the coast contains a variety

of recreational environments: the shore, beach and the marine environment (Orams 1999). Each resource is perceived in a variety of ways by different individuals and groups, and the potential for resource conflict is high unless research can harmonise the needs and wishes of multiple resource users (Concu and Atzeni 2012).

There is also a need to understand fundamental differences in the user's perception of the developed coastal resort and the nature of the natural environment, such as the beach, sea and coastline, because, as Patmore (1983: 209) remarked, 'the coast is the epitome of the wider problems of recreational use' of resources. The behaviour and activities of coastal tourists and recreationalists are therefore vital to understanding the nature of the problems and impacts which occur. The use of coastal environments is very much contingent on the availability of leisure time as holidays and free time at weekends. This led Patmore (1983: 158) to argue that, 'on a day-to-day basis, holidaymakers' patterns of activities within the holiday area differ, but little from the use of day visitors ... Little attention, however, has been given to the sequence of those activities as the holiday progresses.' One of the seminal studies which addressed this topic was Cooper's (1981) analysis of holidaymaker patterns of behaviour in Jersey. As a laboratory for tourism research, Jersey offers many attractions, for it is almost a closed system with a limited number of resorts, attractions and defined tourist itineraries.

What Cooper (1981) observed was a spatial and temporal pattern of tourist use of the coastal environment and non-coastal resources. For example, the holiday begins at the tourist's accommodation to maximise uncertainty in visiting unknown places. As a result, at St Heliers (the location of two-thirds of the island's accommodation stock) 75 per cent of tourists surveyed spent their first day in the town. After that point, a growing spatial awareness of coastal resources developed, and the two most popular beaches (St Brelade's Bay and Gorey) were visited on days two and three. The touring of the island to derive spatial familiarity with the tourist resources also occurred on days two and three. As spatial knowledge of the island developed, smaller and lesser known recreational sites were visited. What Cooper's (1981) research high-lighted was a wave pattern in visitation, as visitors' use of resources (especially the use of the coastal environment) moved down the hierarchy, spreading to a wider distribution of sites. This indicates a classic geographical diffusion process and offers a great deal of advice for planners and coastal management (see also Pearce 1988a; Tudor and Williams 2006).

Probably one of the most interesting studies published by geographers was Tunstall and Penning-Rowsell's (1998) review of the English beach. As they observed,

> England's beaches and coasts have a special place in the nation's consciousness. A day at the English beach is a particularly notable experience, full of rituals, symbolism, nostalgia and myths. The holiday at the coast, or the day visit, brings special activities, enjoyment and memories that virtually no other recreational experience provides. The English beach, with its particular characteristics and contexts, holds special meanings for those it attracts, and creates experiences which have life-long echoes.
>
> (Tunstall and Penning-Rowsell 1998: 319)

In their analysis of the beach, they precisely identify it as the inter-tidal zone, the area which occurs above the high-water mark where beach material exists (i.e. sand, shingle and mud). The significance of the coast is epitomised in the UK Day Visits Survey, with over 137 million visits a year in England to rural areas, seaside resorts and the coastline. A similar study in Australia by Maguire et al. (2011) also highlighted the role of beaches as national icons, as well as their place in popular culture (see also Booth 2001). Maguire et al. (2011) confirmed the finding by Oh, Draper and Dixon (2010) that beach use was polarised in its use between local users and non-local users: local beaches are used frequently, typically daily, and non-local beaches infrequently, typically for walking and swimming.

Cultural geographies of the beach and coastal environment (e.g. Shields 1991) mark the change, continuity and endurance of the beach as a social construction. In the post-war period, the English coastline has attracted a growing retirement migration (for an early analysis of this trend in the UK, see Cosgrove and Jackson 1972), increasing the recreational appeal of these environments. This is complemented by the rise of second home ownership in coastal locations (Coppock 1977a; Hall and Müller 2004; Roca et al. 2013), a feature that Page and Connell (2010) observed alongside the repopularisation of the beach as a postmodern construct, contributing to its rebirth and regeneration in some locations. Some coastal resorts have also sought to diversify their appeal, with the development of conference and convention business (Shaw and Williams 1997). What Tunstall and Penning-Rowsell (1998) recognised was that the coastal resort, and particularly the beach/sea-wall/promenade which protects the RBD from nature, is a costly infrastructure that needs ongoing investment.

Tunstall and Penning-Rowsell used a longitudinal research technique, focused on 15 beaches in England over a decade, examining preferences towards beaches and protection methods to consider the values attached to beaches. A model of beach users' attitudes and values was developed to explain the factors which contribute to the values attached to beaches. The role of recreational constraints (i.e. time and income), frequency of visitation, cost of visit, tastes and values (i.e. subjective enjoyment value), and the values assigned to specific resorts and beaches were incorporated into the model. A range of popular and less popular beaches were examined, with commercial resort towns and smaller towns. Each location had the potential to experience beach erosion problems. Among the main factors motivating beach visits to popular recreational sites were the cleanliness of the site, type of beach material available, the natural setting and familiarity with the site. In the case of undeveloped coasts such as Spurn Head (Humberside), the quietness and natural setting were important attractions. The convenience of access and a number of other factors were important (albeit in varying degrees according to the place visited) as pull factors, including:

- the town and its facilities;
- quality of the seafront promenade;

- characteristics of the beach;
- the coastal scenery;
- scenery and places to visit in the hinterland;
- suitability of the sea for swimming and paddling;
- convenience of the journey;
- cost of the trip (modified from Tunstall and Penning-Rowsell 1998).

What Tunstall and Penning-Rowsell's (1998) study confirmed is Patmore's (1983) earlier assertion on the diversity of coastal resources and reasons for visiting them. The coast, the sea, the seashore and landscape are all integral elements associated with the social, aesthetic and cultural meaning attached to the coast. However, 'There is considerable diversity in what attracted visitors to particular places but it is clear that seafront elements were more important at almost all locations than other aspects of the resort' (Tunstall and Penning-Rowsell 1998: 323). What detracted from visitation at specific sites was sewage, cleanliness, litter and the water bathing quality, though, as R. Morgan (1999) found, it was complex to deconstruct and explain even the visitors' perception of these issues, since perception and behaviour were not necessarily rational and predictable.

In temporal and spatial terms, Tunstall and Penning-Rowsell (1998) found that beach visits not only are experienced differently but also have different meanings. This varied according to whether the visits were made by residents, day visitors or tourists. For residents, the beach was a local leisure resource, a regular and routine element of their everyday lives (similar to parks for urban dwellers). For the day visitor, the beach was construed as a special event, an occurrence perhaps experienced only a couple of times a year. For holidaymakers, it is a special experience, but one often repeated, with tourists who return to the same location year on year. What is culturally significant with a beach visit is the way in which it can enable the visitor to recollect childhood memories and a process repeated through time by families. It also marks a social occasion, with large proportions arriving by car as groups of two to four. In the summer season, beach visits are interconnected with families and young children. Even so, the beach readily

accommodates solitary visitors, and in some locations up to one-third of users were unaccompanied. In this respect, the beach can function like a park with its ability to accommodate a multitude of users (see also Maguire et al. 2011).

The amount of time spent at the beach varied by resort, with the majority of people spending less than four hours on the beach. It was typically between two and four hours in duration. Beach activities included a diversity of marine activities (sailboarding, jetskiing for a minority) and a common range of activities, including:

- sitting/sunbathing/picnicking on the beach;
- sitting/sunbathing/picnicking on the promenade;
- swimming/paddling;
- walking/strolling on the promenade/cliffs;
- long walks (3 km or more);
- informal games or sports;
- walking the dog;
- playing with sand, stones and shells (modified from Tunstall and Penning-Rowsell 1998).

This shows that, while activities are important, so are relaxing and passive pastimes in different countries (Maguire et al. 2011). This seminal study by Tunstall and Penning-Rowsell (1998: 330) recognised not only that 'English beaches are important to the English' but also that environmental concerns for pollution and the quality of the resource are important to recreationalists, tourists and residents alike. The following assessment by Tunstall and Penning-Rowsell really encapsulates the wider meaning, significance and value of the beach and could certainly also be applied to other countries such as Australia, as illustrated in Maguire et al.'s (2011) study:

> The seaside and its beaches are special because they are special places to play, to relax, to exercise or to enjoy. They bring back memories — mainly of families and childhood. They are places of discovery and adventure, and contact with nature. Their meanings come from these imaginings and these activities, and from the repeated visits to the same familiar and reassuring locales. Their beaches have

a coherence that derives from their enduring physical character – waves, tides, sand and noise and
from the assemblage of features that keeps them
there: the sea-wall, the promenade and the groynes.
Each is understood and valued, for its timelessness
and familiarity.

(Tunstall and Penning-Rowsell 1998: 331)

Carr (1999) explored the youth market and their
behaviour within resorts, particularly the meaning
and significance of the beach and liminality. What
Carr (1999) emphasised was that there were comparatively few gendered differences in leisure and tourism
activities among visitors aged 18 to 24 years of age. In
fact, these results appear to confirm the findings of
Tunstall and Penning-Rowsell (1998), in that the
resort and beach are major attractions for coastal tourism. Other studies published in non-geographical
journals (e.g. Morgan *et al.* 1993) have also examined
issues of perception among beach users, but the literature is increasingly scattered across a wide range of
coastal-related journals which are not necessarily
tourism- or recreation-related. However, R. Morgan's
(1999) examination of beach rating systems for tourist
beaches highlighted the contribution which coastal
researchers can make to understanding the perception
of beach users. By using beach awards, such as the
European Blue Flag (UNEP/WTO 1996; Mihalic
2002), there are indications of a growing interest in
the promotion of beach tourism in relation to quality
measures (Williams and Morgan 1995). Even so, poor
public knowledge of these rating schemes and their
significance, even though in the EU the number of
Blue Flag beaches increased from 1,454 in 1994 to
1,927 in 19 countries in 1998, and this figure grew in
2013 to 3,850 Blue Flag beaches internationally as the
ecolabel has been extended. Morgan (1999) assessed
70 beaches in Wales and concluded that beaches are
different, with users having different preferences in
line with Tunstall and Penning-Rowsell's (1998)
study. Many of these issues have also been examined in
the context of Ireland and Portugal, where beaches
were valued in different ways, with cultural and climatic factors influential in attitudes to beach use
(MacLeod *et al.* 2002).

Environmental perspectives on coastal recreation and tourism

The environment for coastal leisure pursuits has seen
the geographer make a number of influential contributions from a range of perspectives. In the early analysis of the coastline for tourism and recreation,
Cosgrove and Jackson (1972) identified the vital characteristic which makes the coast a major focal point
for geographical analysis: it is a zonal resource, with
activities concentrated at specific places, making
management a key issue in time and space (Jennings
2006). Although the coast may have a number of different resource designations (e.g. Heritage Coastline
and Area of Outstanding Natural Beauty in England
and Wales), the impacts of tourism and recreation are
multifaceted. In the wide-ranging study by the German
Federal Agency for Nature Conservation (1997), the
dominant coastline regions globally were the Mediterranean, the Caribbean, the Gulf of Mexico, the
Indian Ocean islands, Australasia and the Pacific
islands. In this context, the coastal resource is a global
environmental issue which is complex, diverse and
not simply reduced to beach resorts, as the discussion
has alluded to so far. (See Visser and Njunga's (1992)
examination of the Kenyan coastline, where the ecological diversity in the coastal environment comprises
coral reefs, sea grass and seaweed beds, mangrove forests, sand dunes and inland tropical forests.)

According to the German Federal Agency for Nature
Conservation (1997), coastal tourism environments
may be categorised as follows:

- oceanic islands;
- coral reefs;
- offshore waters;
- mangroves;
- near-coastal wetlands;
- sandy beaches;
- coastal dunes.

The environments under the greatest recreational and
tourism pressure are sandy beaches, followed by
coastal dunes (see Nordstom *et al.* 2000 for a review of
management practices to restore dunes). Within a

European context, the principal erosion and sedimentation processes affecting coastal environments are related to natural processes, including:

- wave and tidal action;
- geomorphological factors (e.g. rivers which impact upon the river mouth and deltas);
- meteorological factors (e.g. wind and storms);
- changes in sea level;
- geological processes (e.g. seismic and volcanic activity).

In addition, the European coastline is also subjected to a great number of environmental stresses, to the point where some researchers consider it to be under the greatest pressure of any coastal environment globally (German Federal Agency for Nature Conservation 1997; Hall 2006c). For example, Jiménez et al. (2011) found that 72 per cent of Catalan beaches in Spain were experiencing an average rate of erosion of 1 m a year, a feature also observed in other studies of beach erosion (e.g. Phillips and House 2009). Indeed, El Mrini et al.'s (2012) analysis of beaches in northwest Morocco highlighted the dependence upon the beach of tourism but also the pressure it places upon the resource base under conditions of annual erosion. As a consequence, the pressures on the natural environment are being compounded by (Gössling 2001; Hall 2006c):

- large-scale pollution by oil spills;
- harbour and marina development;
- increasing shore erosion caused by interruption of sediment processes as a result of building on the coastline;
- high levels of freshwater removal which is causing salt water to encroach upon the water table;
- increasing levels of nutrient run-off;
- clearance and filling of wetlands for resort and golf course development as well as 'aesthetic improvements';
- increasing impacts from tourism and recreational activities: approximately 100 million tourists visit the European coastline annually, a figure which could rise to 230 million by 2030.

Some of the visible signs of environmental deterioration include water pollution and the increase in frequency of algal blooms. This problem is exacerbated by nutrient enrichment from sewage pollutants (Daby et al. 2002). In the Mediterranean between 1900 and 1990 there was a 75 per cent loss of sand dunes in France and Spain due to sand loss. As A.T. Williams et al. (2001) suggest, visitor pressure increases dune degradation and vulnerability, highlighting the need for close monitoring of impacts and changes in dune morphology. In fact Kindermann and Gormally (2013) pointed to the destabilising effect of recreational trampling and use of dunes. This is a clear indication of the scale of the problem in relation to tourism which is sand and beach dependent. How has the geographer contributed to the wider understanding, analysis and debates associated with coastal environments for recreation and tourism?

Physical geographers have examined the geomorphological characteristics which underlie the creation of existing coastal environments (May 1993; Wong 2003; El Mrini et al. 2012). In the case of the Cape coastline in South Africa, Burns et al. (1990) indicated the need to develop tourism according to sound environmental principles. They argued that the physical characteristics of soft shorelines need to be recognised, and near-shore and aeolian sediment transport regimes must be understood and quantified. This highlighted the active nature of the littoral zone of coastlines, so that long-term shore erosion can be reduced to create recreational environments. What emerges from much of the literature on beach erosion, particularly dune erosion, is that intervention is a costly strategy. In the case of Florida, 'there has been a tendency to build so close to the shoreline as possible: Florida is no exception. Such actions have destroyed dunes, wetlands and beaches which formed protective barriers against storms and floods' (Carter 1990: 8). In an historical analysis of coastline destruction in Florida, Carter examined the speed of environmental degradation:

The first shoreline buildings were beach houses in the dunes. Very often the seawardmost dunes were lowered or removed altogether to give a view of the sea. Very soon, house owners became aware of shore-line changes, especially natural erosion, and began to protect against it. Much of this protection was unapproved, unsightly and ineffective. Along the east coast, bulkheads and groynes were common after 1925, yet by the mid 1930s, much of the duneline was destroyed ... It quickly became clear that such an approach was exacerbating erosion, and there was mounting pressure for official assistance ... Florida became a natural laboratory for shore protection devices, including inlet bypassing and back-passing, beach nourishment and diverse species of revetments, breakwaters and groynes ... Not all were successful.

(Carter 1990: 8–9)

What emerged from Carter's (1990) study was that by the 1980s, of the 870 km of Florida's coastline, 40 per cent of the coastline with sand dunes was under threat, which also affected roads, houses and other development. This figure had increased further by 2010 (Paterson et al. 2010). Much of the impact is recreation- and tourism-related, since in areas where no recreation occurs no erosion exists. In the case of Denmark, Nielsen (1990) examined the positive enhancement of the environment with the creation of Koege Bay Beach Park in 1980 to meet the recreational needs of the Greater Copenhagen area. Using land reclamation methods, including extensive beach nourishment, a new beach environment was created. Some 5 million m^3 of sand were used, dredged from lagoon areas, and a 20 m wide dyke was built of sand to a height of 3 m above sea level. Various environmental management measures were needed, including sluices for the lagoon environment to prevent stagnant water. A programme of planting on the dunes was also implemented to stabilise the resource. By developing the beach park to fit the underlying geomorphology, the creation of the beach park represents a good example of an attempt to develop a sustainable leisure resource, although it is not without environmental effects. However, the time frame is too short at this stage to observe long-term consequences and impacts or to assess the extent to which it is a truly sustainable resource. What is clear is that where significant demand exists in close proximity to an urban population, the creation of a local resource may act as a honeypot and attract a significant number of visitors, taking pressure off other sites.

What Nielsen (1990) identified was the close involvement in physical geographers' monitoring and evaluation of coastal processes to understand how the coastal geomorphology will respond to such a radical change – the creation of a new recreational environment. In a detailed coastal geomorphological study of the German coastline, Kelletat (1993) documented the major beach nourishment needed for islands along the German North Sea coast. This was due to tourism, recreation and storms. However, in a study of Sylt Island, the growth of tourism has also provided the impetus and funding for nourishment on islands of the German North Sea coast (Kelletat 1993).

A range of other studies (e.g. Carter et al. 1990; McDowell et al. 1990; Hall 2009f) have also documented the production of coastal recreation strategies and coastal management plans to co-ordinate decision-making in the coastal zone. The diverse range of interest groups associated with coastal environments highlights the complexity of developing management plans where collaboration, communication and management solutions are introduced to control tourist and recreational use (Goodhead and Johnson 1996).

One related aspect of the geographers' interest in the coastal environment has been the development of resorts and planning measures to manage these physical impacts. In a conceptual context, the dynamics of resort development and change have hinged on the Butler (1980, 2006) model, and subsequent criticisms (e.g. Cooper and Jackson 1989; Cooper 1990) and concerns with the post-stagnation phase (Agarwal 1994; Priestley and Mundet 1998). This distinguishes between the land use and physical planning and management measures needed for the coastal environment and strategic planning measures needed to ensure the long-term prosperity, viability and development of the resort (Inskeep 1994), with specific examples of planning measures implemented in resort development documented by Meyer-Arendt (1990), P.P. Wong (1986, 1990) and Hao et al. (2013). However, it is important to recognise that an over-focus on tourism-specific planning measures may ignore the need to manage tourism within the demands of the wider coastal system (Peel and Lloyd 2010; Lloyd *et al.* 2013).

A major criticism which may be levelled at coastal planning and research is the omission of major environmental problems associated with water that are now assuming a greater role in geographical research on tourism and coastal destinations, especially in water-stressed areas (e.g. Gössling *et al.* 2012b). Many coastal environments, particularly in semi-arid zones, have seen coastal tourism development occur unabated, while the inequity of water availability has fallen upon local residents, who have forfeited the right to access to clean water as hotel groups have usurped their power and access rights to ensure luxury tourism is retained for high spending overseas tourists. One might argue that systematic planning for coastal tourism in such environments should pay particular attention to the sustainability issues and equity issues before luxury tourism that is highly water consumptive is permitted, at huge cost to the local environment and local population. Such a situation highlights the need for integrated coastal zone management (ICZM) approaches to the management of coastal areas (Johnson 2002).

Integrated coastal zone management

As the DoE (1996: n.p.) explained, ICZM is 'the process which brings together all those involved in the development, management and use of the coast within a framework which facilitates the integration of their interests and responsibilities to achieve common objectives' (see also European Commission 1997). This reflects the increased demands placed on coastal resources for recreation and tourism use. ICZM is underpinned by the need for beach management, where a well-planned beach layout with effective spatial zoning and development can accommodate increased opportunities for recreation (Micallel and Williams 2002). This can also lead to reduced maintenance costs, and more clearly articulated strategies for coastal defence and conservation and improved bathing water quality.

In a more strategic context, ICZM is based upon the need to integrate environmental considerations with coastal tourism policies and plans. This can assist in integrating key decisions on the carrying capacity of specific beach sites, the necessary management plans for specific sites and zones as a means of integrating a diverse range of planning policies and stakeholder needs. It may also assist in achieving a sustainable balance between recreational use and nature conservation, so that conflicts associated with achieving a consensus on appropriate recreational uses can be progressed. Here, core or activity centre locations for active water sports are one option in zoning informal and formal/active recreational activities. As Roe and Benson argue:

> zoning in time and space is a well-established method of recreational management. It has been recommended for coastal zone management . . . as has the reduction of the levels of activity in particular areas through the provision of alternative sites. It is, however, understood that by itself, zoning is unlikely to prevent the emergence of problems. Time zoning allows a particular activity access to a stretch of water between specified time limits on a voluntary basis.
>
> (Roe and Benson 2001: 32)

Yet such a system is often ineffective due to irregular loss of waterspace in tidal areas and ineffective sanctions for non-compliance. In some instances the use of by-laws may help in the enforcement of zoning strategies. This requires education strategies and co-operation with formal clubs (e.g. sport clubs), and reflects the importance of the need to involve the local community in ICZM (see Caffyn and Jobbins 2003). One development in Maine, USA, was the introduction of a volunteer programme to help monitor the shoreline change with scientists from the University of Maine, to understand the changes induced by anthropogenic effects, sea-level changes and changing mechanism of erosion (Hill *et al.* 2002).

One immediate problem facing policy-makers and planners in relation to the implementation of ICZM is the challenge posed by climate change (Gössling

2002; WTO 2003; Gössling and Hall 2006a; Hall and Higham 2005; Scott *et al.* 2012), particularly for small island states which have a dependence upon coastal locations for inbound tourism (Gössling *et al.* 2009a). However, the impacts of climate change are not necessarily negative for tourism in all coastal regions. For example, in a report on the implications of a warming Arctic, it was noted that because of the decline of sea-ice, tourism-related shipping through key marine routes, including the Northern Sea Route and the Northwest Passage, is increasing (Arctic Climate Impact Assessment 2004).

As Johnson has shown in the UK, there are a number of instances of urban coastal resorts pursuing regeneration projects, reflecting the fact that 'the UK coastline is an example of a natural resource that has been used and abused for many years' (Johnson 2002: 177). Much of the leadership is from the local government sector, but sustainability is the antithesis of the resort development models by which many mass tourism destinations in the UK and Europe are promoted, often driven by private sector interests. Although not developed by geographers, ICZM offers a useful range of perspectives on the planning process for marine and coastal areas in relation to land use and the different needs of stakeholders. Yet one also has to be cognisant of the fact that the coast, the beach and the resort are major cultural icons in contemporary society, retaining much of their value, meaning and significance from previous eras. In this context, the experience of the coast, the beach, the resort and of the place is socially and culturally conditioned. There is a continuity in the transmission and formation of values of the beach and coast, which may help to explain the ongoing love affair the recreationalist and tourist have with such special 'places'. In historical terms, the resort morphology, rules, meanings and behaviour embodied in the coastal environment have changed in line with what society will tolerate, condone and legitimate. But these special, highly valued, natural and human-made environments remain central to the recreational and tourist experience of leisure places and space.

Probably one of the greatest challenges facing many coastal environments relates to the potential effects of climate change as such environments are amongst the most vulnerable to sea-level rises and the effects of increasing temperature rises, making summer coastal visits less desirable and comfortable, as observed by Moreno and Becken (2009). As Hadley (2009: 198) noted, 'The major effect of climate change on the coastal zone will be due to increasing sea level which, in combination with possible increases in the frequency and intensity of storms, will bring about:

- change in patterns of erosion and sedimentation;
- increased risk of flooding;
- change in the distribution and types of coastal habitats'.

BOX 8.2   CRUISE TOURISM

Cruise tourism accounts for about 2 per cent of total world tourism (Gui and Russo 2011). It is a high yield growing segment of the market that is of increasing importance to many coastal destinations, including the Caribbean and the Pacific Islands. The global cruise sector has grown rapidly since the 1970s, from an estimated 600,000 to 10.4 million in 2000 and an estimated 16.4 million passengers in 2011. Annual passenger growth averaged 7.5 per cent per year between 1980 and 2011, with almost 73 per cent of all passengers in 2010 being sourced from North America (Gui and Russo 2011). This share is constantly declining, however, as cruises become increasingly popular around the world (Rodrigue and Notteboom 2013). The Cruise Line Industry Association reports an average length of cruises of seven plus days. There has also been growth in the capacity of cruise ships, and in 2012 a total of 14 ships with 17,984 beds were introduced. By 2015, another 25 ships are anticipated to join the global cruise fleet, representing an investment of U$10 billion.

Cruise tourism has become significant for a number of ports because cruise tourists are higher yield tourists, spending, on average, much higher amounts per day than other categories of international tourists (Kester 2003). There is substantial competition for the cruise ship market in various parts of the world, particularly because it tends to be highly seasonal in nature. In a study of cruise tourism in Australia, Dwyer and Forsyth (1996) reported that home-porting cruise ships in Australia, with a marketing emphasis on fly–cruise packages for inbound tourists, had the greatest potential for generating large expenditure inflows to Australia. In addition, they reported that because of leakages due to foreign ownership and foreign sourcing of inputs, the average expenditure per passenger per cruise injected into the Australian economy is twice as great for the coastal as opposed to the international cruise.

Because of the overall growth in the cruise ship market, partly allied to ageing populations in developed countries, greater numbers of retirees and security concerns, a number of coastal destinations are aggressively competing for cruise ship visitation. For example, in the case of Newfoundland, 'Cruise was seen as having long-term growth potential, and is appealing since cruise visitors return for conventional vacations' (Environmental Planning Group of Canada (EPGC) 2002: 49). However, in an evaluation of potential activity markets, 'The cruise potential rated lowest as it is the cruise lines, not the destination, that develops the market, although the cruise lines like to see marketing support for their efforts, particularly destination awareness marketing support' (EPGC 2002: 60). The provincial capital, the City of St John's, has placed substantial emphasis on developing the cruise market and has developed a public–private partnership in order to attract more cruise ships. Traditionally, cruise lines utilised St John's as a stopover port of call for their small to mid-sized vessels. However, since the late 1990s the economic value of the cruise industry has been fuelled by both the increased efforts placed on home-porting vessels out of St John's and the widening of the navigation channel to St John's Harbour to accommodate the newer and larger vessels in the marketplace.

Nevertheless, there is significant concern over the impacts of cruise ships. Wood (2000) argued that the global nature of the cruise market has meant that cruise ships have become examples of 'globalisation at sea', with corresponding deterritorialisation, cultural theming and simulation. Once the realm of exploration, the polar seas have now become incorporated into the global cruising industry. Hall *et al.* (2010) highlight the extent to which cruise tourism may be a threat to polar destinations because of the extent to which ships and their passengers can carry biota and disease as well as the particular characteristics of such tourism:

- tourists are disproportionately attracted to sites of relative high/medium diversity;
- the intensity of visitor use is increasing both in absolute terms and, in general, over time and space;
- sites of high popularity are not consistent over time, meaning that the potential for human impact is not contained in a number of specific sites but varies as a result of tourist trends and changing fashions;
- the range of tourist activities is expanding: in addition to being able to land on beaches and observe immediately accessible wildlife, options now include extensive walks and kayaking trips.

In much of the Arctic region the growth in shipping, including cruise ships, is expected to play a major role in introducing marine and terrestrial invasives, especially given the substantial growth in Arctic tourism (Hall and Saarinen 2010). For example, the number of cruise ships operating in Greenland waters grew from 13 in 2003 to 39 in 2008, with the number of port arrivals increasing from 164 to 375 in the same period, and growth in cruise ship visits also occurring in Alaska, Iceland, Nunavut and Svalbard (Hall *et al.* 2010). Areas that were once impossible to reach for cruise ships are now becoming accessible. Hull fouling and ballast water are identified as major sources of alien maritime species, while other biota may come ashore via tourists. As a result of climate change new Arctic locations are also opening up to tourist visitation, creating opportunities for the introduction of alien species (Hall 2010k).

In fact the potential effect on some Small Island States (SIDS) (Jones and Phillips 2011) may lead to some coastal destinations being eradicated by sea-level rises. A further challenge will be the overall impact of climate change on the relative attractiveness of some coastal destinations to tourists (Scott *et al.* 2012; Bujosa and Rosselló 2013). Therefore, while the coast may be a social leveller, a free resource to be enjoyed and consumed according to the vagaries of the season and weather, this assumption may well be challenged in terms of the effect of climate change in different regions of the world.

Conclusion

The coastal environment has been neglected in one sense by the geographer, where recreational and tourism activity have not been understood in the wide context of the resource, its use, impacts and planning needs. Given the growing concerns over sea-level rise, coastal urbanisation and environmental change, the coastline needs to be moved higher up the geographer's research agenda in tourism and recreation, reiterating Patmore's (1983) criticism of the comparative neglect of this issue. Given the value and significance attached to the beach and coast, observed by Tunstall and Penning-Rowsell (1998), it is evident that the coast is a major recreational environment. The association with resorts and the geographer's preoccupation with resort models and development should arguably be directed to a fuller understanding of the impact of human beings on the coastal environment, particularly interference with coastal processes and the resulting measures needed to redress the consequences for the coastal environment.

There is no doubt that the coastal environment is facing a wide range of environmental pressures, not least of which is the growing intensity of use. This, combined with environmental impacts from human activity, poses many severe planning problems for one simple reason: the scale and rate of change associated with coastal processes (e.g. erosion) may be extremely rapid. This requires costly remedial action, particularly in the case of beach nourishment and in coastal protection schemes where the natural environment is directly altered by tourist and recreational development.

Given the potential impacts of tourism on the coastal environment, it is therefore not surprising that government agencies have been trying to encourage more sustainable forms of coastal development in Asia and the Pacific. Sustainable development of coastal tourism is recognised as being dependent on:

- good coastal management practices (particularly regarding proper siting of tourism infrastructure and the provision of public access);
- clean water and air, and healthy coastal ecosystems;

- maintaining a safe and secure recreational environment through the management of coastal hazards (such as erosion, storms, floods) and the provision of adequate levels of safety for boaters, swimmers and other water users;
- beach restoration efforts that maintain the recreational and amenity values of beaches;
- sound policies for wildlife and habitat protection (NOAA 1997).

However, such a statement, while laudable, fails to reflect the complexities and difficulties of the management and regulation of tourism with respect to the physical environment. Unfortunately, there is usually little or no co-ordination between programmes that promote and market tourism and those that aim to manage coastal and marine areas. Environmental or planning agencies often fail to understand tourism, while tourism promotion authorities tend not to be involved with the evaluation of its effects or its planning and management. This particularly appears to be the case with some species of charismatic marine fauna, although significant advances have been made with respect to whale watching management in some countries. Nevertheless, for many peripheral coastal destinations marine ecotourism (Garrod and Wilson 2003, 2004) and commercial recreational fishing would appear to be an appropriate development mechanism if they can be managed appropriately. Implementation strategies often fail to recognise the interconnections that exist between agencies in trying to manage environmental issues, particularly when, as in the case of the relationship between tourism and the environment, responsibilities may cut across more traditional lines of authority. Therefore, one of the greatest challenges facing coastal managers is how to integrate tourism development within the ambit of coastal management, and thus increase the likelihood of long-term sustainability of the coast as a whole. Nevertheless, solving such dilemmas will clearly be of importance to many countries in the region, which has a substantial emphasis on marine and coastal tourism, particularly when environmental quality becomes another means to achieve a competitive edge in the tourism marketplace.

The coastal environment has a great deal of potential for cultural and social geographers to explore the value and role of tourism and recreation in these leisure places. There is also a role for applied geographers to combine their skills with those of planners, to understand, explain and develop planning measures to safeguard these threatened environments. The coastal environment is one of the best examples of how geographers can harness their ability to construct a holistic understanding of the human and physical environment in a coastal context, where the interactions, impacts and measures needed to ameliorate negative effects can be addressed. The period since 1970 has not, with a few notable exceptions, seen the geographical fraternity rise to this challenge and lead the coastal research agenda in a tourism and recreational context. One would hope, indeed expect, geographers to engage their skills, building on a long tradition of the geographer's involvement with the recreational and tourism use of the coast.

Further reading

For general overviews of marine and ocean tourism, see:

Garrod, B. and Wilson, J.C. (eds) (2003) *Marine Ecotourism: Issues and Experiences*, Clevedon: Channel View.

Orams, M. (1999) *Marine Tourism*, London: Routledge.

In terms of the environmental impact of tourism and recreational activities in coastal environments, see:

Baldwin, J. (2000) 'Tourism development, wetland degradation and beach erosion in Antigua, West Indies', *Tourism Geographies*, 2(2): 193–218.

Davenport, J. and Davenport, J. (2006) 'The impact of tourism and personal leisure transport on coastal environments: a review', *Estuarine, Coastal and Shelf Science*, 67: 280–92.

Defeo, O., McLachlan, A., Schoeman, D.S., Schlacher, T.A., Dugan, J., Jones, A., Lastra, M. and Scapini, F. (2009) 'Threats to sandy beach ecosystems: a review,' *Estuarine, Coastal and Shelf Science*, 81(1): 1–12.

German Federal Agency for Nature Conservation (ed.) (1997) *Biodiversity and Tourism: Conflicts on the World's Seacoasts and Strategies for Their Solution*, Berlin: Springer.

Rutin, J. (2010) Coastal tourism: a comparative study between Croatia and Tunisia. *Tourism Geographies*, 12(2): 264–77.

With respect to cruise tourism, see:

Rodrigue, J.P. and Notteboom, T. (2013) 'The geography of cruises: itineraries, not destinations,' *Applied Geography*, 38: 31–42.

Questions to discuss

1 Why is the coastline such a popular area for recreationalists and tourists in some locations and not others?

2 What techniques have geographers used to examine tourist use of the coastline, and how effective are they in explaining the motivation for such activities?

3 What are the environmental problems associated with the coastal environment as a recreational and tourist resource?

4 What are the planning and management measures which have been successful in reconciling the use of coastal environments with the need for preservation and recuperation of the resource base?

Tourism and recreation planning, policy and governance

Geographers have long been interested in planning and the cognate areas of planning and governance. Indeed, a number of academic departments combine geography and planning, while many geography students have gone on to specialise in planning as a professional career. Planning and the associated area of policy analysis are therefore substantive areas of applied geographical research, particularly as geographers have sought to make their work more relevant to the society in which they work (Dredge and Jenkins 2007).

It should therefore come as no surprise that tourism and recreation planning and policy have long been major areas of interest for geographers (Hall and Jenkins 1995, 2004; Church *et al.* 2000; Jenkins 2001; Bramwell 2004; Church 2004; Gill 2004; Dredge and Jenkins 2007, 2011). This chapter examines the nature of recreation and tourism planning, policy and governance, and then goes on to discuss the contributions that geographers have made in these fields, particularly with respect to the role of planning and policy at a regional or destination level. More specific applications in recreational and tourism planning have been introduced in earlier chapters and so this chapter discusses many of the principles, concepts and geographical contributions to the field as a whole.

Recreation planning and policy

According to Henry and Spink (1990: 33), prior to the 1990s the 'treatment of leisure planning in the literature can be described as unsystematic and fragmented'. In part this criticism remains, as the

planning for commercial and public leisure and recreation organisations and spatial planning, where the public good is normally the underlying rationale (Jenkins 2000), are often conflated. Geographers have tended to focus on the latter (Pigram and Jenkins 2006).

In many industrialising nations, the nineteenth century saw the intervention by philanthropists and reformers to address the squalor and living conditions of the working population, embodied in government legislation. Environmental improvement was predicated on the notion that it had a positive effect on the human condition. This shaped government legislation where a wide range of Utopian, humanitarian and determinist attitudes (see Taylor 1999) were reflected in the debates on improvement. In the UK, the Housing and Town Planning Act 1909 highlighted the need for government intervention to generate more socially appropriate forms of land use which market forces would not address (i.e. public open space). In the period after 1800, and the UK planning acts of 1909, 1919, 1932, 1947, 1968, 1980 and 1986 shaped the subsequent role of the state in town and planning in relation to leisure, where political ideology shaped the nature of state intervention in the UK (Veal 2010). In a rural context, the Countryside Act 1968 established a network of country parks, picnic sites, nature trails and bird sanctuaries. This was accompanied by the state's division of planning powers into two levels of local government: structure plans came under county and regional authorities, with a view to a 10 to 20 year time frame and framework for local plans which were the responsibility of district authorities. Despite subsequent modifications in the 1980s and 1990s in the 'retreat from state planning', these two levels of planning remain. They can also be discerned in many other countries. Much of their concern has been with land use planning and site-specific planning for recreation, since this has been the public sector concern: the ordering of leisure space and provision through time.

Recreation planning: the concern with space and place

According to Pigram and Jenkins (1999: 270), 'In the planning of recreation space, the aim should be to provide a range of functional and aesthetically pleasing environments for outdoor recreation, which avoid the friction of unplanned development, without lapsing into uniformity and predictability'. Since people decide on recreation participation as a discretionary use of time and on a voluntary basis, planning is beset by a wide range of factors that need to be considered. One of the most persuasive issues is the trends and tastes in leisure and outdoor recreation. Here the problem is in matching potential demand to the supply of recreation space, while a growing sophistication among recreation users means issues such as quality and satisfaction are also important in public sector provision (Veal 2011).

There is also a temporal and cyclical factor which is often overlooked in leisure planning, namely that in times of economic downturn, recreation assumes a new dimension in the amelioration of hardship (Glyptis 1989b). At the same time, such economic stringencies may also put the public sector under increased pressure in terms of its priorities for resource allocation (i.e. what is the opportunity cost of additional expenditure on leisure provision). At the local planning level, different local authorities will have varying levels of commitment to recreation provision, which will also vary according to the political persuasion of the elected politicians, which varies in time and space. However, it is also important to note that the economic capacity of local leisure planning is often greatly dictated by policies of national governments with respect to local government funding as well as priorities.

Against this background, planners need to understand societal changes, namely demographic trends, lifestyle changes (Havighurst and Feigenbaum 1959), social attitudes to recreation and the increasing demands of ethnic groups (Floyd 1998; Johnson et al. 1998; Veal 2010), people with disabilities and other minority groups to achieve equity goals in local planning for leisure (Shinew and Arnold 1998; Stumbo et al. 2011). In many countries, notably the USA, Canada, New Zealand, Britain and Australia, issues of cultural pluralism and a multicultural population pose new challenges to conventional notions of recreation planning, while in countries such as Indonesia recreation has been used to try and develop national identity (Moser 2010).

Probably one of the greatest technological innovations that now exist to assist planners in integrating these new perspectives into social and land use planning is GIS. It enables planners to spatially integrate the demand and supply of recreation and to evaluate possible locational issues and outcomes. This is also invaluable in modelling resource degradation. In essence, GIS operates on spatial data, which have a standard geographical frame of reference. It also utilises attribute data, which are statistical and non-locational. GIS allows planners to link planning goals to basic geographical issues such as location, trends through time, patterns at specific points in time and an ability to model issues such as recreational demand, supply and impacts (Nahuelhual et al. 2013; Kienast et al. 2012) (see also the discussion on wilderness inventories in Australia in Chapter 7).

Pigram and Jenkins (2006) argued that a more strategic approach to recreation planning is needed but much of the existing practice of planning is concerned with geographical issues of the availability of recreational opportunities, the location of services and facilities. Although recreation planning should be a complex process, its application in the public sector often remains a simplistic activity, focused on the provision of specific facilities rather than the wider context of recreation opportunity, desire and provision. Several approaches to planning for leisure can be identified and a number of them utilise spatial principles (Table 9.1). However, it is important to note that

Table 9.1 Approaches to leisure planning

Approach	Content
Standards	Planning based on per capita specifications of levels of provision laid down by some authoritative body. Usually based on demand and demographic estimates.
Gross demand	Estimation of broad demand levels based on existing national or regional participation surveys. This is the most basic of demand estimation approaches but can be varied to consider local socio-demographic conditions.
Spatial approaches	Localised demand estimation, incorporating consideration of facility catchment areas. This extends the gross demand approach when considering the question of facility location. Increasingly similar to retail catchment studies as a result of the marketisation of many leisure services.
Hierarchies of facilities	Recognises that different types and scales of facility have different catchment areas. Especially relevant for planning new communities and for facilities involving spectator audiences.
Grid or matrix approach	Examines impacts of all of an authority's leisure services on all social groups via impact evaluation. Focused on outcomes.
Service quality	Examines perceptions of the consumers of leisure services as to the quality of the services they use or which are available in their area. Focused on perceptions.
Organic approach	Strategy development based on assessment of existing service provision and spatial gaps in demand. It is incremental rather than comprehensive and is common within the private sector.
Community development approach	Planning and policy development based on community consultation. Increasingly being undertaken via online mechanisms.
Issues approach	Plans based on initial identification of 'key issues' rather than comprehensive needs/demand assessment. Most common for ad-hoc, one-off projects.
Strategic approach	An integrative approach that combines a number of other approaches in seeking to identify to match current and future supply capacities with estimates of current and future demand. The approach also serves to identify what authorities can, may and cannot do in the future, and enables them to prioritise services and approaches to their provision.

Sources: after Veal 1994, 2010; Robinson 1999; Pigram and Jenkins 2006.

these approaches have changed over time, with the emphasis depending on the national and regional political and economic context as well as changes in leisure behaviours and demands (Veal 2011) (see Figure 9.1, which outlines shifts in UK focus). The selection and use of a planning approach therefore depend on the definition of the planning problem and the political context. Significantly, some of the main features in such planning shift that appear common to the developed countries are:

- growing marketisation of state leisure and recreation services and the growth of commercial approaches and public–private partnerships in their provision;

- increased use of strategic business planning methods as focus shifts from leisure outcomes (effectiveness and equity) to cost and efficiencies of provision;
- increasing integration of planning for leisure, recreation, tourism, sports, arts and events as authorities seek to gain efficiencies in provision, respond to multiple markets and increase income levels.

The national and local state and its agencies have a wide remit for the management and planning of leisure and outdoor recreation resources given the diversity and extent of recreational environments (Veal 2010). However, the relative priorities of public providers and the role of leisure and outdoor recreation in spatial planning need to be understood within the

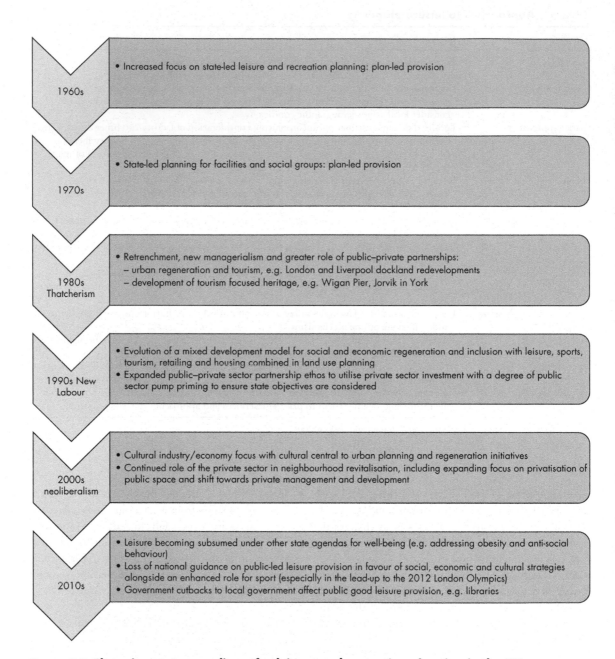

1960s
- Increased focus on state-led leisure and recreation planning: plan-led provision

1970s
- State-led planning for facilities and social groups: plan-led provision

1980s Thatcherism
- Retrenchment, new managerialism and greater role of public–private partnerships:
  – urban regeneration and tourism, e.g. London and Liverpool dockland redevelopments
  – development of tourism focused heritage, e.g. Wigan Pier, Jorvik in York

1990s New Labour
- Evolution of a mixed development model for social and economic regeneration and inclusion with leisure, sports, tourism, retailing and housing combined in land use planning
- Expanded public–private sector partnership ethos to utilise private sector investment with a degree of public sector pump priming to ensure state objectives are considered

2000s neoliberalism
- Cultural industry/economy focus with cultural central to urban planning and regeneration initiatives
- Continued role of the private sector in neighbourhood revitalisation, including expanding focus on privatisation of public space and shift towards private management and development

2010s
- Leisure becoming subsumed under other state agendas for well-being (e.g. addressing obesity and anti-social behaviour)
- Loss of national guidance on public-led leisure provision in favour of social, economic and cultural strategies alongside an enhanced role for sport (especially in the lead-up to the 2012 London Olympics)
- Government cutbacks to local government affect public good leisure provision, e.g. libraries

Figure 9.1 Changing state paradigms for leisure and recreation planning in the UK
Source: adapted from Page and Connell 2010.

broader statutory planning framework, which tends to be based on the twin goals of development plans and development control, even if they are part of broader state entrepreneurial objectives (Bounds and Morris 2006; Davidson and McNeill 2012). Over 20 years ago, Ravenscroft (1992) concluded that the whole framework upon which state planning has been predicated has, for the most part, tended to neglect recreation. By largely basing development plans on land use zoning, it has tended to subjugate multiple uses in favour of primary ones. Moreover, this is often done against the backdrop of increased priority being given to private and commercial interests as opposed to public goods and environmental services. This means that in locations where leisure and recreation provision 'is seen as important, such as National Parks, primary uses such as agriculture and forestry still dominate . . . [and] the reactive nature of the planning process means that opportunities to secure recreation provision are not taken up' (Ravenscroft 1992: 135). To a great extent such concerns exist in the present where recreational access has been difficult to achieve in the absence of supportive regulatory and spatial frameworks, for example in countries such as Australia, Canada and New Zealand (McIntyre *et al.* 2001). Indeed, in urban areas the political processes associated with local authority recreation planning and issues such as planning gain are increasingly being used by developers as betterment payments for the right to develop, making recreation and community benefit a tool to exercise leverage on planning applications, while in rural areas provision and access issues remain problematic (Pigram and Jenkins 2006).

Tourism planning and policy

The partially industrialised nature of tourism means that tourism, like the environment, should be regarded as a meta-problem which represents highly interconnected planning and policy 'messes' (Ackoff 1974) which cut across fields of expertise and administrative boundaries and, seemingly, become connected with almost everything else. Tourism, therefore, 'is merely an acute instance of the central problem of society' (P. Hall 1992: 249), of creating a sense of the whole which can then be effectively planned and managed. Nevertheless, planning for tourism is still regarded as important because its effects are so substantial and potentially longstanding. Indeed, concern with making tourism, along with all development, sustainable has provided an even greater imperative for developing relevant tourism planning frameworks (Hall 2000a, 2008a; Dredge and Jenkins 2007; Hall and Lew 2009). Yet despite increased use by tourism researchers of the evolving network paradigm and governance literature (e.g. Selin 1993; Jamal and Getz 1995; Hall 2008a, 2011a; N. Scott *et al.* 2008) there has been, given the central role of government in tourism promotion and development, surprisingly little reference to the wider planning and public policy literature.

Planning for tourism has traditionally focused on land use zoning, site development, accommodation and building regulations, the density of tourist development, the presentation of cultural, historical and natural tourist features, and the provision of infrastructure, including roads and sewerage (Getz 1987). However, in recent years tourism planning has adapted and expanded to include broader environmental and socio-cultural concerns, and the need to develop and promote economic development strategies at local, regional and national scales, particularly within an increasingly globalised tourism environment (Dredge and Jenkins 2007; Hall 2008a).

The diverse nature of recreation and tourism has meant that the industry is difficult for policy-makers and planners to define and grasp conceptually. This has meant that there have been substantial difficulties for policy-makers in developing appropriate policies, while the co-ordination of the various elements of the recreation and tourism product has been extremely difficult (Hall 1994; Hall and Jenkins 1995). Yet, somewhat paradoxically, it is the very nature of the industry, particularly the way in which local communities, their culture and lifestyles, and the environment are part of the broad leisure tourism product, which makes planning so important (Murphy 1985) and, perhaps, academically appealing (Hall *et al.* 1997; Dredge and Jenkins 2011).

Planning and policy-making are 'filtered through a complex institutional framework' (Brooks 1993: 79). However, the institutional arrangements for tourism have received little attention in the tourism literature (Pearce 1992b; Hall and Jenkins 1995; Hall 2008a, 2011h). Institutions may be thought of as a set of rules, which may be explicit and formalised (e.g. constitutions, statutes and regulations) or implicit and informal (e.g. organisational culture, rules governing personal networks and family relationships). Thus institutions order interrelationships between individuals or groups of individuals by influencing their behaviour. The role of institutional structures has also been increasingly seen as significant in affecting the directions that policy can take as they can serve to exclude some policy alternatives that may be regarded as not fitting into policy norms. This may be extremely important when it comes to the process of policy learning and the development of post-carbon tourism strategies to respond to climate and environmental change (Hall 2011f, 2013e; Gössling et al. 2012a).

As a concept and as an aspect of tourism policy-making, institutions cast a wide net; they are extensive and pervasive forces in the tourism policy system (Jenkins 2000; Beaumont and Dredge 2010). In a broad context, O'Riordan observed that

> One of the least touched upon, but possibly one of the most fundamental, research needs in resource management [and indeed, tourism management] is the analysis of how institutional arrangements are formed, and how they evolve in response to changing needs and the existence of internal and external stress. There is growing evidence to suggest that the form, structure and operational guidelines by which resource management institutions are formed and evolve clearly affect the implementation of resource policy, both as to the range of choice adopted and the decision attitudes of the personnel involved.
>
> (O'Riordan 1971: 135)

Institutions therefore 'place constraints on decision-makers and help shape outcomes . . . by making some solutions harder, rather than by suggesting positive alternatives' (Simeon 1976: 574). As the number of checkpoints for policy increase, so too does the potential for bargaining and negotiation. In the longer term, 'institutional arrangements may themselves be seen as policies which, by building in to the decision process the need to consult particular groups and follow particular procedures, increase the likelihood of some kinds of decisions and reduce that of others' (Simeon 1976: 575). For example, new government departments may be established as part of the growth in the activity and influence of government, particularly as new demands, such as concerns over sustainability and environmental change, reach a high priority on the political agenda:

> The setting up of entirely new government departments, advisory bodies or sections within the existing administration is a well established strategy on the part of governments for demonstrating loudly and clearly that 'something positive is being done' with respect to a given problem. Moreover, because public service bureaucracies are inherently conservative in terms of their approach to problem delineation and favoured mode of functioning . . . administrative restructuring, together with the associated legislation, is almost always a significant indicator of public pressure for action and change.
>
> (Mercer 1979b: 107)

The implications of the structure and nature of the tourist industry are not merely academic, as it is difficult for government to develop policies and design institutions for a policy area that is hard to determine (Jenkins 1993; Williams and Balaz 2000). Indeed, quality information concerning the tourist industry is relatively limited when compared to the collection of information on other industries and sectors of the economy. Hall and Jenkins (1995) even hypothesise that there is an element of inexperience in tourism policy formulation and implementation, as much government activity in the tourist industry is relatively recent when compared with other traditional concerns of government, such as economics, manufacturing and social welfare, and suggests that tourism public policies are therefore likely to be ad hoc and incremental. Indeed, Hall (2000a), in a review of the role of government in New Zealand tourism, identified three government agencies with primary responsibilities with respect to tourism policy and over 30 agencies with secondary responsibilities, with there typically being very little formal tourism policy co-ordination between the various agencies. Such a situation, though, should not be surprising, since the nature of tourism means that it cuts across a range of government responsibilities which make policy and planning co-ordination inherently difficult unless a lead agency is clearly identified.

What is tourism planning?

What is planning? 'Planning is a process, a process of human thought and action based upon that thought – in point of fact, forethought, thought for the future – nothing more or less than this is planning, which is a very general human activity' (Chadwick 1971: 24). Similarly, according to P. Hall (1982a: 303), planning 'should aim to provide a resource for democratic and informed decision-making. This is all planning can legitimately do, and all it can pretend to do. Properly understood, this is the real message of the systems revolution in planning and its aftermath'. P. Hall's (1982a) observation reflects Johnston's (1991: 209) comment that underlying the geographer's involvement in planning and policy is 'the basic thesis that geographers should be much more involved in the creation and monitoring of policies', yet, as he went on to note, 'what sort of involvement?,' a point discussed in Chapter 1.

As a general field of research, geographically informed tourism planning has mirrored broader trends within the urban and regional planning traditions (e.g. Getz 1986a, 1987; Hall 2008a) primarily because, as a field of study, it has primarily been focused on destination planning rather than individual tourism business planning. Moreover, planning for tourism tends to reflect the economic, environmental and social goals of government and, increasingly, industry interests, at whichever level the planning

process is being carried out (Hall *et al.* 1997; Dredge and Jenkins 2011). However, it is worth noting that as part of research on tourism entrepreneurship and innovation, as well as networks in a regional and destination context, tourism geographers have also been paying increasing attention to the strategies of individual businesses (Hall and Williams 2008; Ateljevic and Page 2009), including in relation to public policy (Hall 2009c; Weidenfeld and Hall 2014).

Planning for tourism occurs in a number of forms (development, infrastructure, promotion and marketing), structures (different government and non-government organisations), scales (international, national, regional, local and sectoral) and times (different time scales for development, implementation and evaluation) (Hall 2008a). However, public planning is rarely exclusively devoted to tourism per se. Instead, it has long been recognised that planning for tourism tends to be an amalgam of more generic economic, social and environmental considerations which reflect the diversity of the factors which influence tourism development (Heeley 1981). In contrast, as noted on p. 319, recreational planning has historically assumed a more integrated form, being an integral part of most local public sector planning schemes alongside other fundamental themes such as housing (Lavery 1971c; Patmore 1973, 1983). As Chapter 5 demonstrates, this was very evident in urban areas. In this respect, recreation is often a local need-based activity or a regional planning function to deal with the impacts, needs and effects of visitors on the host community (also see Chapters 4 and 7, which note the contribution of geographers to natural area and wilderness planning activities). However, as noted on pp. 317–318, the distinction between public leisure and tourism planning that once existed has been substantially eroded by shifts in government policy and the marketisation of what was formerly state leisure and outdoor recreation policies focused on the public good. Furthermore, much of what is considered as tourism outside urban areas also subsumes recreational activity in natural and wilderness areas (see Chapter 7).

Tourism planning does not just refer specifically to tourism development and promotion, although these are certainly important. The focus and methods of tourism planning have evolved to meet the demands which have been placed on government with respect to tourism. For example, international tourism policies among the developed nations may be divided into four distinct phases (Table 9.2). Of particular importance has been the increased direct involvement of government in regional development, environmental regulation and the marketing of tourism, although more recently there has been reduced direct government involvement in the supply of tourism infrastructure, greater emphasis on the development of public–private partnerships and industry self-regulation.

The attention of government to the potential economic benefits of tourism and recreation has long provided the main proactive driving force for tourism planning (Richards 1995; Charlton and Essex 1996; Dredge and Jenkins 2007), while the environmental dimensions of tourism planning have tended to be more reactive. The result has often been 'top-down planning and promotion that leaves destination communities with little input or control over their own destinies' (Murphy 1985: 153). However, attention is gradually becoming focused on the need to integrate social and environmental concerns into the economic thrust of much tourism development (Timothy 2002). Tourism must be integrated within the wider planning processes in order to promote certain goals of economic, social and environmental enhancement or maximisation that may be achieved through appropriate tourism development and governance (Hall 2008a). As Murphy (1985: 156) observed, 'planning is concerned with anticipating and regulating change in a system, to promote orderly development so as to increase the social, economic, and environmental benefits of the development process'. Therefore, tourism planning must be 'a process, based on research and evaluation, which seeks to optimize the potential contribution of tourism to human welfare and environmental quality' (Getz 1987: 3).

Approaches to tourism planning

Getz (1987) identified four broad traditions or approaches to tourism planning: 'boosterism', an economic, industry-oriented approach, a physical/spatial approach, and a community-oriented approach which emphasises the role the destination community plays in the tourism experience. The four traditions are neither 'mutually exclusive, nor are they necessarily sequential' (Getz 1987: 5). Nevertheless, it is a

Table 9.2 International tourism policies, 1945 to the present

Phase	Characteristics
1945–55	Dismantling and streamlining of the police, customs, currency and health regulations that had been put in place following the Second World War.
1955–70	Greater government involvement in destination marketing in order to increase tourism earning potential.
1970–85	Government involvement in the supply of tourism infrastructure and in the use of tourism as a tool of regional economic development. Continued government funding of destination marketing.
1985–2000	Continued use of tourism as a tool for regional development, increased focus on environmental issues, reduced direct government involvement in the supply of tourism infrastructure, greater emphasis on the development of public–private partnerships and industry self-regulation, and the development of tourism business networks to meet policy goals.
2000 to present	Same as 1985–2000 but increasing growth of tourism as an intermistic political issue with a focus by many sub-national governments on place-marketing and the creation of networks. Increased integration of cultural, event, regeneration and tourism policies. Emergence of global environmental change, including climate change and biodiversity conservation as policy issues. Security policy developments also affect tourism.

Source: after Hall 1994, 2000a, 2005a, 2008a.

convenient categorisation for examining the different approaches to tourism planning, and the research and planning methods primarily associated with each. To these four approaches, Hall (1995) added a fifth approach, that of sustainable tourism planning, and an extension of that approach via the notion of steady-state tourism grounded in ecological economics and degrowth (Hall 2009e, 2010l), and which is also related to concepts of sustainable consumption. Table 9.3 provides a detailed overview of the components of each tourism planning approach. Different planning approaches, while not mutually exclusive, conceptualise tourism planning in distinct ways. Each perspective differs in its underlying assumptions about planning, problem definition, the appropriate level of analysis and research methods. Researchers therefore choose their perspective(s) according to their profession, education, values, the organisational context within which they work and the nature of the planning problem.

Boosterism is the simplistic attitude that tourism development is inherently good and of automatic benefit to the hosts (Woods 2011). Residents of tourist destinations are not involved in the decision-making, planning and policy processes surrounding tourism development. According to Getz,

> Boosterism is still practised, and always will be, by two groups of people: politicians who philosophically or pragmatically believe that economic growth is always to be promoted, and by others who will gain financially by tourism. They will go on promoting it until the evidence mounts that they have run out of resources to exploit, that the real or opportunity costs are too high, or that political opposition to growth can no longer be countered. By then the real damage has usually been done.
>
> (Getz 1987: 10)

In contrast, an economic planning approach towards tourism aims to promote growth and development in specific areas. The planning emphasis is on the economic impacts of tourism and its most efficient use to create income and employment benefits for regions or communities. Since 2000 the economic approach has also focused more on notions of destination competitiveness (Hall 2007b).

One of the main areas to which geographers have contributed is the physical/spatial approach, under which tourism is regarded as having an ecological base with a resultant need for development to be based upon certain spatial patterns, capacities or thresholds that would minimise the negative impacts of tourism on the physical environment (Getz 1983, 1987). Indeed, much of the concern with the physical and behavioural carrying capacities of specific locations discussed in Chapter 8 falls into this particular approach. Research by Page and Thorn (1997) in New Zealand reviewed the impact of a market-led approach to tourism planning at the national level, where a lack of rational national policy or planning advice has significant implications for national conservation estate management (Kane 2013) as well as local areas that are required to deal with the microscale issues (Hall and Wilson 2011). Similarly, as Blowers (1997: 36) noted in the case of the United Kingdom, 'the long period of privatisation, deregulation, cuts in public expenditure and attacks on local government have resulted in a "democratic deficit" – a dispersal of power to unelected quangos and business interests – and have led to unsustainable developments'. An arguably more preferable focus for local areas is the contribution which a community approach can make (Timothy 2002).

A community approach emphasises the social and political context within which tourism occurs and advocates greater local control over the development process. Geographers have also been active in this area, as it builds upon a strong urban and regional planning tradition that is concerned with being relevant to community needs. The best-known exemplar of this approach is the work of Murphy (1985, 1988; Murphy and Murphy 2004), although a community development approach is also influential in developing country destinations as well as in the developed world (Singh et al. 2003).

A community approach to tourism planning is an attempt to formulate a 'bottom-up' form of planning, which emphasises development in the community

Table 9.3 Tourism planning approaches: assumptions, problem definition, methods and models

Planning tradition	Underlying assumptions and related attitudes	Definition of the tourism planning problem	Examples of related methods	Examples of related models
Boosterism	• tourism is inherently good • tourism should be developed • cultural and natural resources should be exploited • industry as expert • development defined in business/corporate terms	• how many tourists can be attracted and accommodated? • how can obstacles be overcome? • convincing hosts to be good to tourists	• promotion • public relations • advertising • growth targets	• demand forecasting models
Economic	• tourism equal to other industries as a form of economic development • use tourism to create employment, earn foreign revenue and improve terms of trade, encourage regional development, overcome regional economic disparities • development defined in economic terms • superiority of economic analysis in planning process to other forms of planning arguments	• improving destination/product competitiveness • can tourism be used as a growth pole? • maximisation of income and employment multipliers • influencing consumer choice • providing economic values for externalities and environmental services	• supply–demand analysis • benefit–cost analysis • product–market matching • development incentives • market segmentation	• management processes • tourism master plans • nudging • economic impact • economic multipliers • hedonistic pricing
Physical/ spatial	• tourism as a resource user • ecological basis to development • tourism as a spatial and regional phenomenon • environmental conservation • development defined in environmental terms • conservation of biological diversity • designation of environmentally sensitive areas • conservation of heritage and management of built environment	• physical carrying capacity • manipulating travel patterns and visitor flows • visitor management • concentration or dispersal of visitors • environmental perception • wilderness and national park management	• ecological studies • environmental impact assessment • regional and urban planning • perceptual studies	• spatial patterns and processes • physical impacts • resort morphology • LAC (limits of acceptable change) • ROS (recreational opportunity spectrum) • destination life cycles
Community	• need for local control • search for balanced development strategies between different community stakeholders • search for alternatives to mass tourism development • planner as facilitator rather than expert • development defined in socio-cultural terms • retaining cultural authenticity and integrity	• how to foster community control? • understanding community attitudes towards tourism • understanding the impacts of tourism on a community • moderating social impact	• community development • awareness and education • attitudinal surveys • social impact assessment	• ecological view of community • social/perceptual carrying capacity • attitudinal change • social multiplier

Table 9.3 (Continued)

Planning tradition	Underlying assumptions and related attitudes	Definition of the tourism planning problem	Examples of related methods	Examples of related models
Sustainable	• finding a balance between economic, environmental and social dimensions of development • integration of economic, environmental and socio-cultural values • tourism planning integrated with other planning processes • holistic planning • preserving inter- and intra-generational equity • creating and maintaining networks • planning and implementation as two sides of the same coin	• understanding the tourism system • setting goals, objectives and priorities • policy co-ordination • co-operative and integrated control systems	• strategic planning to supersede conventional • raising producer awareness • raising consumer awareness • stakeholder input • aspirations analysis • environmental analysis and audit	• systems models • integrated models • resources as culturally determined • learning organisations • social marketing • sustainable culinary systems
Steady-state	• development must be understood in relation to the limits of natural capital • development as a qualitative measure • relation of the marginal benefit of economic growth to costs • the implications of tourism's embeddedness in contemporary capitalism • growth does not equal development • conservation of natural capital, biodiversity and ecological processes • tourism needs to be more localised • use of all four modes of tourism governance	• tourism must reduce its emissions and environmental impacts in absolute terms • implementing the 4Rs: reduce, reuse, recycle and regulate • encouraging sustainable consumption via efficiency- and sufficiency-based approaches • polluter pays • reducing hypermobility	• transition management • post-carbon tourism • degrowth • cradle-to-cradle design • life cycle analysis	• ecological economics • behaviour change • voluntary simplicity • slow tourism • ethical and sustainable consumption • staycations and local tourism

Sources: after Getz 1987; Hall *et al.* 1997; Hall 2008a, 2009e, 2010l.

rather than development *of* the community. Under this approach, residents, not tourists, are regarded as the focal point of tourism planning and decision-making, and the community, which is often equated with a region of local government, is usually used as the basic planning unit. Nevertheless, substantial difficulties will arise in attempting to implement the concept of community planning in tourist destinations. Research into community attitudes towards tourists and tourism development is well developed, although effective incorporation of such views into the planning process so that it influences future patterns of tourism development is less common. J. Jenkins' (1993) list of seven impediments to incorporating public participation in tourism planning still holds to the present:

- the public generally has difficulty in comprehending complex and technical planning issues;
- the public is not always aware of or understands the decision-making process;
- the difficulty in attaining and maintaining representativeness in the decision-making process;
- the apathy of citizens;
- the increased costs in terms of staff and money;
- the prolonging of the decision-making process;
- adverse effects on the efficiency of decision-making.

As the above discussion indicates, one of the major difficulties in implementing a community approach to tourism planning is the political nature of the planning process. Community planning implies a high degree of public participation in the planning process. However, public participation implies that the local community will have a degree of control over the planning and decision-making process. Therefore, a community approach to tourism planning implies that there will be a need for partnership in, or community control of, the tourism development process.

Yet power is not evenly distributed within a community, and some groups and individuals will therefore have the ability to exert greater influence over the planning process than others (Hall and Jenkins 1995).

Therefore, in some circumstances, the level of public involvement in tourism planning may be more accurately described as a form of tokenism in which decisions or the direction of decisions have already been prescribed by government. Communities rarely have the opportunity to say 'no' (Hall 2008a). Nevertheless, as Murphy (1985: 153) argued, 'If tourism is to become the successful and self-perpetuating industry many have advocated, it needs to be planned and managed as a renewable resource industry, based on local capacities and community decision making', with an increased emphasis being given to the interrelated and evolutionary nature of tourist development. Yet despite such a clear statement of planning goals, since then tourism, while growing, has only further run down natural and social capital in many destinations, raising further questions about how sustainable it is in the long term.

Since the late 1990s, geographers have become concerned with the development of sustainable approaches towards tourism (Hall and Lew 1998, 2009; Bianchi 2002; Mercer 2004; Weaver 2004; Gössling *et al.* 2009b; Lew *et al.* 2011). Sustainable tourism planning is an integrative form of tourism planning, which bears much similarity to the many traditionally applied concerns of the geographer as resource manager (Mitchell 1979). Sustainable tourism planning seeks to provide lasting and secure livelihoods with minimal resource depletion, environmental degradation, cultural disruption and social instability. The approach therefore tends to integrate features of the economic, physical/spatial and community traditions.

The concern for equity, in terms of both intra- and intergenerational equity, in sustainable development means that there is concern for the maintenance and enhancement of 'environmental capital' (Jacobs 1991) and social capital (Healey 1997), as well as economic capital. The focus on equity also suggests the use of appropriate policies and programmes of social equality and political participation (Blowers 1997). Such an approach has considerable implications for the structure of tourism planning and policy-making, as decision-making processes should be more inclusive of the full range of values, opinions and interests that surround tourism developments and tourism's overall contribution to development, and provide a clearer space for public argument and debate (Smyth 1994; Dredge and Jenkins 2007, 2011). As B. Evans (1997: 8) argued, 'if environmental planning for sustainability . . . is to be anywhere near effective, the political processes of public debate and controversy, both formal and informal, will need to play a much more significant role than has hitherto been the case'. However, Hall (2011f) has suggested that this has not occurred because policy learning in tourism has tended to be incremental rather than accommodating substantial policy shifts that would incorporate the values of sustainability into the tourism policy process.

Dutton and Hall (1989; see also Page and Thorn 1997; Ruhanen 2004; Pigram and Jenkins 2006) identified five key elements of sustainable tourism planning: co-operative and integrated control systems, development of industry co-ordination mechanisms, raising consumer awareness, raising producer awareness and strategic planning to supersede conventional approaches.

Co-operative and integrated control systems

In a typical planning process, stakeholders are consulted minimally, near the end of the process, and often via formal public meetings. An integrative planning approach to tourism planning and management at all levels (from the regional plan to individual resort projects) would assist in the more equitable distribution of the benefits and costs of tourism development, while focusing on improved relationships and understanding between stakeholders may also assist in agreement on planning directions and goals. However, co-operation alone will not foster commitment to sustainable development without the incentive of increased mutual benefits (Hall 2008a).

One of the most important aspects of co-operative and integrated control systems is the selection of indicators of sustainability. The role of an indicator is to make complex systems understandable. An effective indicator or set of indicators helps a destination,

community or organisation determine where it is, where it is going and how far it is from chosen goals. Sustainability indicators provide a measure of the long-term viability of a destination or community based on the degree to which its economic, environmental and social systems are efficient and integrated (Gill and Williams 1994; Hall and Lew 2009). However, indicators are useful only in the context of appropriately framed questions (Hall and McArthur 1998). In choosing indicators, one must have a clear understanding of planning goals and objectives. For example, a typology of indicators might include:

- economic, environmental and social indicators (measuring changes in the state of the economy, environment and society);
- sustainability indicators (measuring the distance between that change and a sustainable state of the environment);
- sustainable development indicators (measuring progress to the broader goal of sustainable development in a national context).

There has been a tendency to pick indicators that are easiest to measure and reflect most visible change; therefore important concerns from a holistic perspective of tourism development, such as the social and cultural impacts of tourism, may be dropped. In addition, appropriate indicators may not be selected because organisations might not want to be held accountable for the results of evaluations (Hall and McArthur 1998; Dredge and Jenkins 2011). Indicators to reflect desired conditions and use should (Wight 1998; Choi and Sirakaya 2006):

- be directly observable;
- be relatively easy to measure;
- reflect understanding that some change is normal, particularly in ecological systems, and be sensitive to changing use conditions;
- reflect appropriate scales (spatial and temporal);
- have ecological, not just institutional or administrative boundaries;
- encompass relevant structural, functional and compositional attributes of the ecosystem;

- include social, cultural, economic and ecological components;
- reflect understanding of indicator function/type (e.g. baseline/reference, stress, impact, management, system diagnostic);
- relate to the vision, goals and objectives for the destination region;
- be amenable to management.

Development of industry co-ordination mechanisms

While a range of formal and informal tourism industry bodies exist in almost every country in the world, few of these address such complex issues as sustainable development. The support by industry groups for environmental codes is perhaps indicative of possible

---

BOX 9.1 TOURISM INTEREST GROUPS AND THE PUBLIC INTEREST

One of the great problems in examining the role of interest groups in the tourism policy-making process is deciding what the appropriate relationship between an interest group and government should be (Hall and Jenkins 1995; Bramwell 2004; Bramwell and Meyer 2007; Anastasiadou 2008; Thomas 2011), given that governments are meant to be governing in the public interest (Hall 2008a). At what point does tourism industry membership of government advisory committees or of a national, regional or local tourism agency represent a 'closing up' of the policy process to other interest groups rather than an exercise in consultation, co-ordination, partnership or collaboration? This question has long been an issue in political science. As Deutsch recognised:

> this co-operation between groups and bureaucrats can sometimes be a good thing. But it may sometimes be a very bad thing. These groups, used to each other's needs, may become increasingly preoccupied with each other, insensitive to the needs of outsiders, and impervious to new recruitment and to new ideas. Or the members of the various interest group elites may identify more and more with each other and less and less with the interests of the groups they represent.
>
> (Deutsch 1970: 56)

The relationship between the tourism industry and government tourism agencies clearly raises questions about the extent to which established policy processes lead to outcomes which are in the 'public interest' and which contribute to sustainability rather than meeting just narrow sectoral interests. Mucciaroni (1991: 474) noted that 'client politics is typical of policies with diffuse costs and concentrated benefits. An identifiable group benefits from a policy, but the costs are paid by everybody or at least a large part of society.' Several authors (e.g. Hall and Jenkins 1995; Dredge and Jenkins 2007; Hall 2008a) have stressed that tourism policy is one such area, particularly in terms of the direct and indirect costs of tourism promotion and marketing. However, the implications of this situation also affect the overall sustainability of tourism and of communities and who pays, for example, for the environmental and social costs of tourism (Hall 2011f). In reviewing the tourism and collaboration literature Hall (1999) concluded that the present focus by government tourism agencies on partnership and collaboration is laudable:

> But the linguistic niceties of partnership and collaboration need to be challenged by focusing on who is involved in tourism planning and policy processes and who is left out . . . Unless there are attempts to

provide equity of access to all stakeholders then collaboration will be one more approach consigned to the lexicon of tourism planning clichés.

(Hall 1999: 285–6)

Indeed, more than a decade later, when seeking to explain why sustainability thinking had not led to real policy change, he suggested, 'Far too much attention has been given to the assumption that a well-designed institution is "good" because it facilitates cooperation and network development rather than a focus on norms and institutionalisation as first and necessary steps in the assessment of what kind of changes institutional arrangements are promoting and their potential outcomes' (Hall 2011f: 665). Therefore, the policy arguments surrounding networks and collaboration need to be examined within broader ideas of the appropriate role of government and changing relationships and expectations between government and communities.

directions if common needs can be agreed upon. However, for such guidelines to be effective, it must be ensured that they do not constitute a 'lowest common denominator' approach to development and implementation (Hall 1999). Therefore, government and public interest groups tend to use their influence to encourage greater industry co-ordination on planning issues by creating structures and processes which enable stakeholders to talk to each other and create effective relationships and partnerships. In many ways such measures are easier to achieve at a local level because the range of stakeholders which need to be incorporated into co-ordinating bodies will be narrower. In addition, contact at the local level provides a greater capacity for face-to-face contact to occur and therefore trust-building to develop (Hall 2000a; Bramwell 2004).

Co-ordination refers to formal institutionalised relationships among existing networks of organisations, interests and/or individuals, while co-operation is 'characterized by informal trade-offs and by attempts to establish reciprocity in the absence of rules' (Mulford and Rogers 1982: 13). Often, the problem of developing co-ordinated approaches towards tourism planning and policy problems, such as the meta-problem of sustainability, is identified in organisational terms (e.g. the creation of new organisations or the allocation of new responsibilities

to existing ones). However, such a response does not by itself solve the problem of bringing various stakeholders and interests together, which is an issue of establishing collaborative processes. Instead, by recognising the level of interdependence that exists within the tourism system (Dredge and Jenkins 2007; Hall 2008a), it may be possible for 'separate, partisan interests to discover a common or public interest' (Friedmann 1973: 350). Notions of collaboration, co-ordination and partnership are separate, though closely related, ideas within the emerging network paradigm. Networks refer to the development of linkages between actors (organisations and individuals) where linkages become more formalised towards maintaining mutual interests. The nature of such linkages exists on a continuum ranging from 'loose' linkages to coalitions and more lasting structural arrangements and relationships. Mandell (1999) identifies a continuum of such collaborative efforts, as follows:

- linkages or interactive contacts between two or more actors;
- intermittent co-ordination or mutual adjustment of the policies and procedures of two or more actors to accomplish some objective;
- ad-hoc or temporary task force activity among actors to accomplish a purpose or purposes;

- permanent and/or regular co-ordination between two or more actors through a formal arrangement (e.g. a council or partnership) to engage in limited activity to achieve a purpose or purposes;
- a coalition where interdependent and strategic actions are taken, but where purposes are narrow in scope and all actions occur within the participant actors themselves or involve the mutually sequential or simultaneous activity of the participant actors;
- a collective or network structure where there is a broad mission and joint and strategically interdependent action; such structural arrangements take on broad tasks that reach beyond the simultaneous actions of independently operating actors.

However, the caution of Mandell has perhaps not been given sufficient heed in the enthusiasm for network development in tourism:

> we often look for prescriptions or answers as to how to solve ongoing dilemmas . . . it is tempting for both academics and practitioners to try to develop a model of success that will fit this complex world. In this regard, the concepts of networks and network structures can easily become the next in line for those in the field to 'latch onto' and use wholesale. Although it may be tempting to do so, this 'one size fits all' type of modelling does not take into consideration the myriad of factors and events that must be understood before these concepts can be of much use in the 'real world'.
>
> (Mandell 1999: 8)

Raising consumer awareness

One of the hallmarks of tourism, and other industries, in recent years has been a perceived increase in consumer demand for 'green' or 'environmentally friendly' products (Hjalager 2000; Budeanu 2007); such demand is often related to increased consumer awareness of environmental and social issues associated with trade and tourism. However, in many cases, the difference between a sustainable and non-sustainable tourism operation may be difficult for consumers to detect, particularly if the greening of tourism is regarded more as a branding device than as a fundamental change in product development.

One development which is usually regarded as an indicator of increased consumer awareness is the development of tourist codes of behaviour in order to minimise the negative impacts of tourists on the social and physical environment (Valentine 1992; Techera and Klein 2013). However, as Hall (2014) highlighted, awareness of the environmental implications of tourism does not necessarily lead to changes in behaviour, particularly as individual tourists may not believe that their individual consumption is sufficient cause for concern. Although consumer awareness is important and may result in marginal shifts in tourism product, particularly if one believes the old adage that the consumer is king, fundamental changes are also required on the supply side of the tourism equation.

Raising producer awareness

As with the raising of consumer awareness, much attention has been given to the production of environmental codes of conduct or practice for tourism associations (Hall and McArthur 1998). For example, extensive guidelines have been developed for tourism operators in the polar regions (Hall and Johnston 1995; Hall and Saarinen 2010; Lück et al. 2010). However, such guidelines, while undoubtedly influencing the actions of some tourism operators, may need to be backed up by government regulation and environmental planning legislation if they are to have any overall effect on development practices. For example, where such codes of conduct are voluntary, what practical measures exist to punish operators who do not subscribe to them?

Strategic planning to supersede conventional approaches

Strategic tourism planning aims to be proactive, responsive to community needs, to incorporate implementation within a single planning process, and be

BOX 9.2   CRUISE CODES OF CONDUCT AND ARCTIC BIOSECURITY

The introduction of alien species into polar regions affected by climate change has become a major issue in the management of polar tourism. This is because tourism transport, especially cruise ships, and tourists are potential vectors for macro and micro fauna and flora that may establish themselves in locations where ice is no longer permanent, or may outcompete existing species or introduce new diseases to animal and plant populations. In the case of the Arctic, cruise ships, as well as other forms of tourist transport, pose a significant biosecurity threat not only because they are starting to visit previously little or unvisited areas but also because the frequency of visits is increasing. Biosecurity and environmental management strategies that may have been suitable even a decade previously may therefore become significantly challenged, as – in contrast to the Antarctic – the Arctic biosecurity regime is extremely piecemeal, with regulations or guidelines primarily concentrated on national parks and reserves.

The Association of Arctic Expedition Cruise Operators (AECO), which has developed guidelines for expedition and cruise operations in the Arctic, was founded in 2003. As of June 2010, the AECO had 14 member companies operating within AECO's geographical range of Svalbard, Jan Mayen and Greenland, with craft sizes ranging from small sailing yachts to expedition cruise ships with up to 320 passengers. AECO has produced guidelines both for members (AECO 2007) and for visitors (AECO n.d.), the guidelines for visitors being 'a few basic rules' selected from the more comprehensive guidelines for members. Although the visitor guidelines do not specifically focus on biosecurity, they do note the importance of 'leaving no lasting signs of your visit', no souveniring of natural material, including flowers, and no disturbance of animals and birds (AECO n.d.).

The AECO members' guidelines do not have a specific biosecurity section. However, they do provide a clear set of guidelines with respect to the environment. Particularly relevant is the statement that 'Even if different parts of the area in question have different legal protection status through national and local legislation, it is the policy of AECO to regard all land and marine areas as protected and act according to the highest protection status, which includes':

- Do not remove anything. The regulations are relatively complex on what can be removed and where (plants, bones, driftwood, dead animals/skeletons, fossils, stones, bones, etc.). The expedition staff must know the regulation. Visitors or staff from AECO ships should, however, not move or remove any objects that are not clearly garbage, and thus avoid degradation of the landing sites and their wilderness value.
- Do not allow cairn-building, graffiti creation of any kind or other such disturbances to the physical environment.
- Ensure that visitors, staff or crew do not leave anything behind onshore (or in the water).
- Make every effort to remove garbage found on the shores (and support the 'Clean up Svalbard' project).
- Be considerate to other people or activities: avoid landings near camps, trappers or others unless contact is established and the landing is agreed to (AECO 2007: 8).

Furthermore, visitors are informed about environmental impacts as part of the pre-landing information. Such guidelines 'are in addition to company policy and internal routines. The guidelines are directed to operational staff and to some extent the ship's crew' (AECO 2007: 7). In addition, 'Preparation for cruise operations must include the following steps . . . Communicate relevant AECO policy and guidelines to visitors, agents and the market place, as well as to authorities, Arctic research communities and the interested general public' (AECO 2007: 6). However, the problem with such voluntary measures is that AECO members are not the only cruise ship operators in high latitude waters. In fact more than half of the expedition and cruise ship operators identified by Hall *et al.* (2010) operating in the high Arctic in 2009–10 were non-AECO.

ongoing (Ruhanen 2004, 2010; Soteriou and Coccossis 2010). A 'strategy' is a means to achieve a desired end. Strategic planning is the process by which an organisation effectively adapts to its management environment over time by integrating planning and management in a single process. The strategic plan is the document which is the output of a strategic planning process; it is the template by which progress is measured and which serves to guide future directions, activities, programmes and actions. The outcome of the strategic planning process is the impact the process has on the organisation and its activities. Such impacts are then monitored and evaluated through the selection of appropriate indicators as part of the ongoing revision and readjustment of the organisation to its environment. Strategic planning therefore emphasises the process of continuous improvement as a cornerstone of organisational activity in which strategic planning is linked to management and operational decision-making. According to Hall and McArthur (1998) there are three key mechanisms to achieving strategic planning which differentiate it from conventional planning approaches:

- a planning framework which extends beyond organisational boundaries and focuses on strategic decisions concerning stakeholders and resources;
- a planning process that stimulates entrepreneurial and innovative thinking;
- an organisational values system that reinforces managers and staff commitment to the organisational strategy.

Effective strategic planning for sustainable tourism recognises the importance of factors that affect the broad framework within which strategies are generated, such as institutional arrangements, institutional culture and stakeholder values and attitudes. These factors are significant because it is important to recognise that strategic plans must be in line with the legislative powers and organisational structures of the implementing organisation(s) and the political goals of government (Soteriou and Coccossis 2010). However, it may also be the case that once the strategic planning process is underway, goals and objectives formulated and the process evaluated, the institutional arrangements may be recognised as being inadequate for the successful achievement of sustainable goals and objectives. In addition, it must be recognised that in order to be effective the strategic planning process needs to be integrated with the development of appropriate organisational values (Hall and Jenkins 1995; Dredge and Jenkins 2007). Indeed, with respect to the significance of values it may be noted that the strategic planning process is as important as its output, i.e. a plan. By having an inclusive planning process by which those responsible for implementing the plan are also those who helped formulate it, the likelihood of 'ownership' of the plan and, hence, effective implementation will be dramatically increased (Heath and Wall 1992; Hall and McArthur 1996).

A strategic planning process may be initiated for a number of reasons (Hall and McArthur 1998):

- *stakeholder demands*: demand for the undertaking of a strategic plan may come from the pressure of stakeholders (e.g. environmental conservation groups or government);
- *perceived need*: the lack of appropriate information by which to make decisions or an appropriate

framework with which to implement legislative requirements may give rise to a perception that new management and planning approaches are required;

- *response to crisis*: the undertaking of strategic planning exercises is often the result of a crisis in the sense that the management and planning system has failed to adapt to aspects of the management environment (e.g. failure to conserve the values of an environmentally significant site from visitor pressures);
- *best practice*: visitor managers can be proactive with respect to the adoption of new ideas and techniques. Therefore, a strategic planning process can become a way of doing things better;
- *adaptation, innovation and the diffusion of ideas*: individuals within an organisation can encourage strategic planning processes as part of the diffusion of ideas within and between responsible management agencies.

Strategic planning is rarely initiated for a single reason. However, it is important to understand as much as possible why a particular planning process is being initiated, as this helps the participants understand the expectations which have been created (Ruhanen 2004). Once underway, strategic planning is designed to be iterative. In other words, planning systems are meant to be able to adapt and change; they learn how to be effective in terms of the most appropriate set of goals, objectives, actions, indicators, institutional arrangements and practices. Through such measures they may therefore become potentially more resilient to change within and external to the destination (Milman and Short 2008).

Tourism policy

As with planning, geographers have long held interests in policy-making, although it is only since the early 1990s that such concerns have found substantial expression in the tourism sphere (e.g. Fagence 1990, 1991; Pearce 1992a, 1992b; Hall and Jenkins 1995). Public policy is the focal point of government activity. In its simplest form public policy 'is whatever governments choose to do or not to do' (Dye 1992: 2). This definition covers government action, inaction, decisions and non-decisions as it implies a deliberate choice between alternatives. For a policy to be regarded as public policy, at the very least it must have been processed, even if only authorised or ratified, by public agencies. Public policy-making, including tourism policy-making, is first and foremost a political activity. Public policy is influenced by the economic, social and cultural characteristics of society, as well as by the formal structures of government and other features of the political system. Policy is therefore a consequence of the political environment, values and ideologies, the distribution of power, institutional frameworks and of decision-making processes (Hall and Jenkins 1995; Hall *et al.* 1997; Dredge and Jenkins 2007).

Tourism public policy is therefore whatever governments choose to do or not to do with respect to tourism (Hall and Jenkins 1995). However, as a number of studies by geographers have indicated (e.g. McKercher 1993c, 1997; Jenkins 1997; Dredge and Jenkins 2011), pressure groups (e.g. tourism industry associations, conservation groups, community groups), community leaders and significant individuals (e.g. local government councillors), members of the bureaucracy (e.g. employees within tourism commissions or regional development agencies) and others (e.g. academics and consultants) influence and perceive public policies in significant and often markedly different ways (Anastasiadou 2008).

Research on tourism policy can be broadly divided into two main theoretical approaches: that which adopts prescriptive models and that which adopts descriptive models (Hall 1994; Hall and Jenkins 1995). 'Prescriptive or normative models seek to demonstrate how [planning and] policy making should occur relative to pre-established standards', whereas 'descriptive models document the way in which the policy process actually occurs' (B. Mitchell 1989: 264). Prescriptive (normative) models suggest how tourism policy- and decision-making should occur relative to pre-established standards. The prescriptive-rational approach assumes that a dichotomy exists between the policy-making process and administration and the existence of 'Economic Man [sic]', whereby individuals can 'identify and rank goals, values and objectives', and 'can choose consistently among them after having collected all the necessary data and systematically evaluated them' (L.S. Mitchell 1979: 236). However, such models do not provide detailed insights into the real world of planning and its associated set of values, power and interests. Instead, approaches, methods and techniques need to be evaluated within the context of the goals, objectives and outcomes of tourism planning and development (Hall and Jenkins 1995; Dredge and Jenkins 2007; Hall 2008a).

Descriptive approaches give rise to explanations about what happened during the decision-making, planning and policy-making processes. Case studies are an important component of descriptive tourism research as they help understand the effects that such factors as choice, power, perception, values and process have on tourism planning and policy-making in particular contexts. The main criticism of the case study method is its historical-descriptive chronology; the potential lack of consistency in scope, context and conceptual cohesiveness; and its representativeness (Beeton 2005). However, although a single case study is rarely sufficient for a full inquiry, the duplication of studies may well suggest fundamental relationships and generalisations (L.S. Mitchell 1979; Beeton 2005). This attitude is reflected in the recreation research of La Page (cited in Mercer 1973: 42): 'For sound research planning, I would gladly swap all the "highly significant" correlation coefficients of the past 10 years for a couple of good case studies that yielded some solid conceptual insight to build on.'

Under a descriptive approach, emphasis is therefore placed on understanding the various elements of the policy process and how it arrives at certain outputs and outcomes. Therefore, an understanding of the way in which government utilises tourism as a policy mechanism may be extremely valuable not only in terms of improving the policy-making and planning process, but also in terms of improving the conditions of the people who are affected by such policies.

For example, tourism as a policy response to the economic problems of rural and peripheral areas in developed countries has changed over time (Jenkins et al. 1998; Müller and Jansson 2006). Until the mid-1980s rural tourism was primarily concerned with commercial opportunities, multiplier effects and employment creation (e.g. Canadian Council on Rural Development 1975). In the late 1980s policy guidance shifted to the message that the environment is a key component of the tourism industry. Under this notion, 'tourism is an additive rather than extractive force for rural communities' (Curry 1994: 146). From the late 1980s and early 1990s to the present day, an additional layer to the policy responses of government to tourism and regional development has been added which returns to the earlier economic concerns. This is the perception of rural tourism as a major mechanism for arresting the decline of agricultural employment and therefore as a mechanism for agricultural diversification (Rural Development Commission 1991; Butler et al. 1998). Yet despite government enthusiasm for tourism as a mechanism to counter problems arising out of rural restructuring and depopulation, the these policies have been only marginally successful, with the greatest growth from tourism- and recreation-related industries occurring in the larger rural service centres and the rural–urban fringe, arguably those areas which least need the benefits that tourism can bring (Butler et al. 1998; Jenkins et al. 1998). Why has this occurred?

To a great extent it relates to a failure by government to understand the nature of tourism and its relationship with other sectors of the economy and the policy and planning process itself. First, all the dimensions of development need to be considered. Second, it highlights the need for awareness of the various linkages that exist between the elements of development. Third, it also implies that 'successful' regional development will require co-ordination and, at times, intervention, in order to achieve desired outcomes. Fourth, it also means that tourism should not be seen as the be-all and end-all of regional development, but instead should be utilised as an appropriate response to the real needs of regions (Cater 2000). Furthermore, the role of growth coalitions and the distribution of power in a community have enormous implications for the tourism policy and planning process and its outcomes (Morgan and Pritchard 1999; Church and Reid 2000; Schollmann *et al*. 2001; Bianchi 2002; Church and Coles 2007).

Depending on the parameters used, government involvement in utilising tourism for regional development purposes is therefore often quite unsuccessful (Hall and Jenkins 1998; Dredge and Jenkins 2007). The reason for such failures lies in a lack of understanding of policy processes (Hall and Jenkins 1995; Jenkins 2001; Michael 2001; Dredge and Jenkins 2011). Furthermore, while tourism development goals may be fairly clear at the regional level, little research has been conducted on the most appropriate policy mix to achieve such objectives and there is often minimal monitoring and evaluation of policy measures (Hall and Jenkins 1998; Hall 2008a). As a result of such issues there has been a shift of focus in tourism policy studies to contextualise tourism studies within broader issues of governance.

Governance

Governance is the act of governing. However, there is no single accepted definition of governance. This is reflected in Kooiman's (2003: 4) concept of governance as 'the totality of theoretical conceptions on governing'. Definitions tend to suggest a recognition of a change in political practices, involving, amongst other things, increasing globalisation, the rise of networks that cross the public–private divide, the marketisation of the state, and increasing institutional fragmentation. Nevertheless, two broad meanings of governance can be recognised. First, it describes contemporary state adaptation to its economic and political environment. This is often referred to as 'new governance'. Yee (2004: 487) provided a very basic definition of this approach by describing new modes of governance as 'new governing activities that do not occur solely through governments'. Some of these elements are outlined in Table 9.4. Although, as Treib *et al*. (2007: 16) observe, it is not really 'appropriate to use the labels of "old" and "new" modes of governance for classificatory purposes. What is new in one area could be rather old in another field of study, which makes these labels inadequate as analytical categories.'

The second broad meaning of governance is that it is used to denote a conceptual and theoretical representation of the role of the state in the co-ordination of socio-economic systems. However, it should be noted that the two approaches are not mutually

Table 9.4 The characteristics of 'new' modes of governance

Elements	Characteristics
Participation and power sharing	Policy-making is not regarded as the sole domain of regulators, but private and public stakeholders from different levels are meant to participate in the policy process as part of public–private partnership
Multi-level integration	Co-ordination between different levels of government needs to occur both horizontally and vertically and should involve private actors
Diversity and decentralisation	Rather than a standard legislative or regulatory approach, a diverse range of co-ordinated approaches is instead encouraged
Deliberation	Greater deliberation is encouraged between public and private stakeholders so as to improve the democratic legitimation of policy-making processes
Flexibility and revisability	Soft law measures are often applied that rely on flexible guidelines and open-ended standards that are implemented voluntarily and may be revised as policy circumstances change
Experimentation and knowledge creation	Greater encouragement of local experimentation in governance measures as well as knowledge creation and sharing in connection with multilateral surveillance, benchmarking and the exchange of results and best practice

Source: Hall 2011a: 441.

exclusive, as the use of the term 'governance' as a form of shorthand for new forms of governance in western societies is itself predicated on particular conceptions of what the role of the state should be in contemporary society and the desirability and nature of state intervention. This second meaning can, in turn, be divided into two further categories (Pierre and Peters 2000). The first focuses on state capacity to 'steer' the socio-economic system and therefore the relationships between the state and other policy actors. The second focuses on co-ordination and self-government, especially with respect to network relationships and public–private partnerships (Hall 2011a).

Understanding how the institutional arrangements of governance are conceptualised is important as it affects the way in which the state acts in the tourism policy arena and therefore selects instruments and indicators that are used to achieve policy goals (Beaumont and Dredge 2010). The focus of most discussions on policy instruments in tourism is on their utilisation or their effects rather than on the understandings of governance that led such instruments to be selected. However, Hall (2011a, 2013e) emphasises that the application of instruments must be seen within the broader understanding of governance, and

its associated assumptions, ideologies and values, that governments have.

Hall (2011a) identifies four conceptualisations of governance structures that are related to the use of particular sets of policy instruments (Figure 9.2 and Table 9.5). Given the artificiality of any policy–action divide (Barrett and Fudge 1981), these instruments and modes of governance can also be connected to different conceptual approaches to implementation (Hall 2009g). Critical to the value of the different modes of governance are the relationships that exist between public and private policy actors and the steering modes, ranging from hierarchical top-down steering to non-hierarchical approaches.

Although much contemporary governance literature in tourism stresses public–private relationships (Bramwell 2005; Dredge and Jenkins 2007), hierarchical governance remains significant because of the continued role of the state in international relations, the development of institutions that enforce international and supranational law, and the ongoing importance of legislation and regulation as part of the exercise of state control. Although the use of markets as a governance mechanism has been very much in

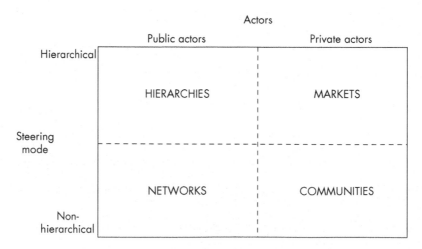

Figure 9.2 Frameworks of governance typology
Source: Hall 2011a: 443.

Table 9.5 Frameworks of governance and their characteristics

	Hierarchies	Communities	Networks	Markets
Classificatory type characteristics	– idealised model of democratic government and public administration as the enabler of public good – distinguishes between public and private policy space – focus on public or common good – command and control (i.e. 'top-down' decision-making) – hierarchical relations between different levels of the state	– notion that communities should resolve their common problems with minimum of state involvement – builds on a consensual image of community and the positive involvement of its members in collective concerns – governance without government – fostering of civic spirit	– facilitate co-ordination of public and private interests and resource allocation and therefore enhance efficiency of policy implementation – range from coherent policy communities/policy triangles through to single-issue coalitions – regulate and co-ordinate policy areas according to the preferences of network actors rather than public policy considerations – mutual dependence between network and state	– belief in the market as the most efficient and just resource allocative mechanism – belief in the empowerment of citizens via their role as consumers – employment of monetary and economic criteria to measure efficiency – policy arena for economic actors where they co-operate to resolve common problems
Governance/policy themes	hierarchy, control, compliance	complexity, local autonomy devolved power, decentralised problem-solving	networks, multi-level governance, steering, bargaining, exchange and negotiation	markets, bargaining, exchange and negotiation
Policy standpoint	top: policy-makers; legislators; central government	bottom: implementers, 'street-level bureaucrats', and local officials	where negotiation and bargaining take place	where bargaining takes place between consumers and producers
Underlying model of democracy Primary focus	meritocracy effectiveness: to what extent are policy goals actually met?	participatory what influences action in an issue area?	hybrid/stakeholder; significant role given to interest groups bargained interplay between goals set centrally and actor (often local) innovations and constraints	consumer determined; citizen empowerment efficiency: markets will provide the most efficient outcome
View of non-central (initiating) actors	passive agents or potential impediments	potentially policy innovators or problem shooters	tries to account for the behaviour of all those who interact in the development and implementation of policy	market participants are best suited to 'solve' policy problems
Distinction between policy formulation and implementation	actually and conceptually distinct; policy is made by the top and implemented by the bottom	blurred distinction: policy is often made and then re-made by individual and institutional policy actors	policy–action continuum: policy-making and implementation seen as a series of intentions around which bargaining takes place	policy–action continuum
Criterion of success	when outputs/outcomes are consistent with a priori objectives	achievement of actor (often local) goals	difficult to assess objectively, success depends on actor perspectives	market efficiency

(Continued)

Table 9.5 (Continued)

	Hierarchies	Communities	Networks	Markets
Implementation gaps/deficits	occur when outputs/outcomes fall short of a priori objectives	'deficits' are a sign of policy change, not failure; they are inevitable	all policies are modified as a result of negotiation (there is no benchmark)	occur when markets are not able to function
Reason for implementation gaps/deficits	good ideas poorly executed	bad ideas faithfully executed	'deficits' are inevitable as abstract policy ideas are made more concrete	market failure; inappropriate indicator selection
Solution to implementation gaps/deficits	simplify the implementation structure; apply inducements and sanctions	'deficits' are inevitable	'deficits' are inevitable	increase the capacity of the market
Primary policy instruments	– law – regulation – clear allocation and transfers of power between different levels of the state – development of a clear set of institutional arrangements – licensing, permits, consents and standards – removal of property rights – development guidelines and strategies that reinforce planning law	– self-regulation – public meetings/town hall meetings – public participation – non-intervention – voluntary instruments – information and education – volunteer associations – direct democracy (citizen-initiated referenda) – community opinion polling – capacity building of social capital	– self-regulation and co-ordination – accreditation schemes – codes of practice – industry associations – non-government organisations	– corporatisation and/or privatisation of state bodies – use of pricing, subsidies and tax incentives to encourage desired behaviours – use of regulatory and legal instruments to encourage market efficiencies – voluntary instruments – non-intervention – education and training to influence behaviour

Source: after Hall 2011a.

political vogue since the mid-1980s (see also Chapters 3 and 5), including with respect to the corporatisation and privatisation of tourism functions that had previously been the domain of the state, the contemporary focus on the role of the market is very much associated with neoliberal political considerations of the appropriate level of state intervention in socio-economic systems (Harvey 2005). The decision by the state to allow the market to act as a form of governance also does not mean that government ceases to influence the market. Rather, instead of using imposed regulatory mechanisms, government may seek to use other forms of intervention, such as financial incentives, education and even the potential for future intervention, to encourage the tourism industry to move in particular directions, often via 'nudging', social marketing and self-regulation (Dredge and Jenkins 2007; Hall 2013e, 2014).

The concept of networks, and public–private partnerships in particular, has received considerable attention in tourism policy and planning because of the way in which they may facilitate co-ordination of public and private interests and resources (N. Scott et al. 2008; Beaumont and Dredge 2010) and act as a 'middle way' between hierarchical and market approaches (Hall 2011a). The communities approach is very much influenced by communitarianism and demands for more direct citizen involvement in governance (Etzioni 1998). However, in addition to the communitarian focus on the development of more appropriate scales of governance, the communities framework also builds on traditions of deliberative and direct democracy (Hall 2011a). As noted on pp. 326–327, community governance in tourism planning has been a significant theme in the tourism literature since the early 1980s and is also a part of the sustainable and evolving steady-state approaches. Although the framework has been criticised as being overly idealistic and exaggerating the benefits of perceived consensus (Hall 2008a), community participation and even control over planning and decision-making remain an important issue in tourism planning and policy-making (Dredge and Jenkins 2007), and has become fundamental to much thinking about local governance with respect to, for example, the management of conservation and pro-poor tourism initiatives in less developed countries (Zapata et al. 2011).

Nevertheless, the selection of the most appropriate measure – or, more likely, a range of measures – is dependent on the particular circumstances of each region as well as the philosophical perspectives of different governments. There is no universal 'best way'; each region or locale needs to select the appropriate policy mix for its own development requirements (Sharpley and Telfer 2002; Dredge and Jenkins 2007; Hall 2008a). However, this does not mean that the policy and planning process occurs in a vacuum. Rather, the attention to policy and planning processes has the intention of making such processes as overt as possible, so that the values, influence and interests of various stakeholders are relatively transparent. There is no perfect planning or policy process, yet we can, through the geographer's contribution, help make it more relevant to the people who are affected by tourism development and continually strive for improvement.

Conclusion

This chapter has provided a broad overview of the tourism and recreation planning and policy process. It has noted the various strands of tourism planning and governance, and emphasised the particular contribution of geographers to the physical/spatial, community and sustainable approaches to tourism planning.

The reasons for focusing on tourism which is not as well developed or articulated in local, regional and national development plans beyond statements and broad objectives contrasts with recreational planning, which has a much longer history of development and application. In fact if the experience of urban areas is considered, one can see the emergence of recreational planning in the nineteenth century in the UK with the role of the public sector in park development, the provision of libraries and other items to meet the wider public good (see also Chapter 5). What geographers have contributed to recreational planning is the synthesis and analysis of good practice, rather than being actively involved as academics, beyond a research role, to assist public and private sector bodies in locational analysis and land use planning. This chapter has therefore placed a great deal of emphasis on the importance of policy analysis, especially from a descriptive approach. This does not mean that prescription is without value; rather, it argues that prescription must be seen in context, with particular reference to those who are in any way affected by policy statements.

In looking at the application of policy analysis to tourism issues we have therefore almost come full circle. The interests which have long concerned tourism and recreation geographers that are applied and relevant to the needs of the subjects of our research remain, and it is to these issues that we will return in the final chapter (Chapter 10).

Further reading

There are several classic works that relate to tourism and recreation planning. In particular, see Gunn (2002), Ravenscroft (1992) and Murphy (1985). Dredge and Jenkins (2007) and Hall (2008a) are theoretically informed comprehensive tourism planning works which attempt to integrate planning and policy concerns at different scales of analysis, while planning is discussed more specifically in relation to impacts in Hall and Lew (2009). See also the planning and policy chapters in more general texts such as Page and Connell (2014) and Cooper and Hall (2013). An example of strategic planning principles applied to tourism destinations is:

Murphy, P.E. and Murphy, A.E. (2004) *Strategic Management for Tourism Communities: Bridging the Gaps*, Clevedon: Channel View.

On community development, see:

Singh, S., Timothy, D. and Dowling, R. (eds) (2003) *Tourism in Destination Communities*, Wallingford: CAB International.

On leisure and recreation planning, see:

Page, S.J. and Connell, J. (2010) *Leisure: An Introduction*, Harlow: Prentice Hall.

Pigram, J.J. and Jenkins, J. (2006) *Outdoor Recreation Management*, 2nd edn, London: Routledge.

On implementation and policy processes, see:

Anastasiadou, C. (2008) 'Tourism interest groups in the EU policy arena: characteristics, relationships and challenges', *Current Issues in Tourism*, 11: 24–62.

Beaumont, N. and Dredge, D. (2010) 'Local tourism governance: a comparison of three network approaches', *Journal of Sustainable Tourism*, 18: 7–28.

Hall, C.M. (2009) 'Archetypal approaches to implementation and their implications for tourism policy', *Tourism Recreation Research*, 34: 235–45.

There is surprisingly little useful work on international dimension of tourism policy, although the aftermath of 9/11 has meant a focus on issues of security in particular, while climate change has also become a significant issue. See:

Coles, T.E. and Hall, C.M. (2011) 'Rights and regulation of travel and tourism mobility', *Journal of Policy Research in Tourism, Leisure and Events*, 3(3): 209–23.

Gössling, S., Scott, D. and Hall, C.M. (2013) 'Challenges of tourism in a low-carbon economy', *WIRES Climate Change*, DOI: 10.1002/wcc.243.

Hall, C.M. (2002) 'Travel safety, terrorism and the media: the significance of the issue-attention cycle', *Current Issues in Tourism*, 5(5): 458–66.

Hall, C.M. (2010) 'Tourism and the implementation of the Convention on Biological Diversity', *Journal of Heritage Tourism*, 5: 267–84.

Hall, C.M., Timothy, D. and Duval, D. (2003) 'Security and tourism: towards a new understanding?', *Journal of Travel and Tourism Marketing*, 15(2–3): 1–18.

Hall, C.M., Timothy, D. and Duval, D. (eds) (2004) *Safety and Security in Tourism: Relationships, Management and Marketing*, New York: Haworth Press.

Timothy, D.J. (2001) *Tourism and Political Boundaries*, London: Routledge.

Timothy, D.J. (2004) 'Political boundaries and regional cooperation in tourism', in A. Lew, C.M. Hall and A. Williams (eds) *Companion to Tourism*, Oxford: Blackwell.

On power in tourism, see:

Church, A. and Coles, T.E. (eds) (2007) *Tourism, Power and Space*, London: Routledge.

Hall, C.M. (2010) 'Power in tourism: tourism in power', in D. Macleod and J. Carrier (eds) *Tourism, Power and Culture: Anthropological Insights*, Bristol: Channel View.

Questions to discuss

1 Is there anything that makes planning for tourism distinct from other forms of planning?

2 Why is recreation planning such an integral component of resource management?

3 What are the institutional arrangements for tourism and recreation in your country? Describe them and their interrelationships between the national, regional and local level.

4 What is the appropriate relationship between government and the tourism industry in the formulation of tourism policy?

The future

If geographical research is to maintain its own distinctiveness, which it surely has to do for the sake of its own survival and respect, it needs to make explicit its sense of what is important. The sheer number of people, the economic value and the significance to people's lives of leisure, recreation and tourism will eventually make even the most doubting sceptic accept that these topics are worthy of study and that [the] battle for acceptance of [leisure, recreation and tourism] as valid areas of research will be won. It would be depressing if geography was not there to claim its unique place and interests.

(Butler 2004: 156)

As the various chapters in this book have indicated, geographers have made substantial contributions to the understanding of tourism and recreation. However, as noted in Chapter 1, the geographers who are working in the field are, increasingly, not based in geography departments but instead are located in departments of tourism and recreation or leisure, environmental studies or business. Such a situation is a reflection of several things: the growth of tourism and recreation as a separate, legitimate area of academic endeavour; the relatively poor standing in which studies of tourism and recreation have generally been held within academic geography; and the applied nature of much work in tourism and recreation geography, which has meant a professional career in the public and private sectors for many geography graduates (Perkins and Thorns 2001).

Such a situation clearly raises substantial questions about what the future of the sub-discipline will be. As Johnston (1991: 2) recognised, 'It is the advancement of knowledge – through the conduct of fundamental research and the publication of its original findings – which identifies an academic discipline; the nature of

its teaching follows from the nature of its research'. As long ago as 1890, Keltie's (1890) *Applied Geography: A Preliminary Sketch* suggested: 'In short one great task of geography in its advanced stages is to investigate the interaction between humanity and its geographical environment' and this remains extremely germane to the study of tourism and recreation by geographers over a 100 years later, particularly at a time of extensive environmental change. The application of geography to the study of what was termed 'commerce' and 'Empire' highlighted the early business application of spatial analysis, whilst almost 80 year later House (1978: preface) noted that 'applied geography has grown as a result, to serve the needs of society, economy and polity', especially in terms of planning. However, Patmore's (1989) discussion of leisure and tourism as important strands of the society and economy made the clear case for a spatially informed analysis of these phenomena within an applied context. But geography has also undergone many profound transformations in the period since Keltie's (1890) treatise and, as discussed in Chapter 1, since 1900 a number of different schools of geographical thought have evolved from the regional geographies in the late nineteenth century, through to the 1960s, to quantitative geography in the 1960s and 1970s, critical, Marxist, behavioural and humanistic geographies in the 1970s and 1980s, to GIS, political economic geographies, feminist geographies, new regional geographies, postmodern geographies and cultural turns since the 1980s. This plurality is reflected in many of the approaches towards tourism and recreation embodied in this book. These new approaches have spawned new research agendas, critical debate, and often opposing philosophical and methodological positions as each perspective has been informed by the multiplicity of knowledge from each platform of research. Yet critics of this growing diversity of research agendas in human geography have also become alarmed at the lack of coherence and focus in geography as a discipline as geographies have been (re)discovered, (re)invented and (re)imaged. If one of the core strengths of geography is its ability to offer synthesis and a conceptual underpinning based on notions of space, place, people and environment, the geographer faces a growing challenge in synthesising a seemingly exponential growth in 'geographies of leisure, recreation and tourism' within the broader growth in human knowledge (Hall and Page 2009; Wilson 2012; Hall 2013d). As a result of such a situation there are conflicting interpretations of where geography is heading.

Bailey *et al.* (2008) cite the very influential arguments of Martin (2001) that some of the principal problems associated with human geography and its lack of relevancy to modern society relate to:

- a lack of relevancy in much social and cultural geographical research;
- the effect of the postmodern cultural turn on research and teaching;
- the emphasis on sexy theoretical issues;
- a retreat from rigorous and detailed empirical research;
- a reversion of policy studies, mainly because of the perceived unfashionable association with, and loss of independence with, governments that compromises the geographers' impartiality.

This is in direct contrast to the analysis by Warf and Arias (2009) that argued that geography had now become a net exporter of ideas to other fields in science and social science, thereby spatialising their thinking. This may have a more profound effect in the social science so that space becomes every bit as important as the construction of human affairs. It may be a useful perspective, reflecting some of the concerns of Chapter 1, that 'geography matters, not for the simplistic and overly used reason that everything happens in space, but because where things happen is critical to knowing how and why they happen' (Warf and Arias 2009: 1). But it is difficult to see how this revelation is anything different from the 'who gets what, where and how' of classic studies such as Smith's (1974). Moreover, the spatialisation of the social sciences raises the broader issue that if space or geography is everything, then maybe it is nothing.

It is therefore apposite that the final chapter of this new edition will briefly revisit the place of tourism and recreation geography in the applied geography tradition, particularly in the context of declining perceived influence of human geography and internal schisms within the spatial approach to leisure-related phenomenon in spite of recent attempts to refresh thinking on this area (e.g. Stimson and Haynes 2012). It will then discuss the contributions that geography can bring to the study of tourism and recreation and highlight possible futures for the field.

Geography – the discipline: direction and progress

According to R.J. Johnston (1985: 326), 'geographers, especially but not only human geographers, have become parochial and myopic in recent decades' and have been accompanied by a disengagement from close field contact and a global concern with human phenomena. The disengagement from the region has been seen as a mechanism to synthesise systematic investigations. In seeking to advance the discipline, Johnston (1985) argued that geographers need both a theoretical appreciation of the general processes of the capitalist mode of production and an empirical appreciation of the social formations that result. The discipline versus detachment from the skills of field-work, observation and description debate continues to remain a fundamental weakness, and in many respects the 'core' elements of a geographical education at university level now reflect the often fragmented specialisation that characterises many geography curricula. In fact, geography is a subject in retreat in many contexts, particularly in Australia and New Zealand, where the specialisation function has now led to the dissipation of geography departments and affiliation with more multidisciplinary groupings, such as environmental science. In the UK, the declining enrolments being experienced by many geography departments have been attributed to the rapid growth in tourism and recreation studies with a focus on business, management and vocationalism and a declining interest at the post-16 level in schools and colleges. Geography is perceived as having failed to move with the times to integrate a greater vocationalism and applied focus. Even though the rise of GIS and its application to planning and problem-solving have assisted in real world problem-solving, the main body of the discipline has often not engaged students in fundamental elements of the real world through fieldwork and practical knowledge.

In the United States the position of geography may be slightly more positive thanks in great part to the growth of government and industry awareness of the value of GIS; nevertheless, as the President of the Association of American Geographers noted, there is only a very limited presence of geography in the elite universities and institutions (Cutter 2000). While the authors may agree with Cutter's (2000: 3) remarks that 'The lack of formal geography (courses, an undergraduate minor, major, or graduate study) in many of the most prestigious universities in the nation is a missed opportunity for these elite institutions of higher education', such a situation makes geography and geographers beholden to more effectively communicate their interests and contributions in a wide range of contemporary issues and subjects, including tourism and recreation, as well as the vagaries of academic conflict for resources.

Although the new synthesis of applied geography (Pacione 1999b) outlines the way in which

some geographers perceive themselves and their contribution to research, this is not being adequately communicated to students, particularly in the marginalisation of applied geography as a hybrid according to concerns purists and qualitative researchers have about social and cultural theory as their analytical framework. Nevertheless, it is important to revisit applied geography and to provide some illustrations of how tourism and recreational geographers make contributions to 'problem-solving', 'policy analysis' and the wider public good. Pacione (1999b), in his protocol for applied geographical analysis (Figure 10.1), outlines the DEEP process – description, explanation, evaluation and prescription – which may be followed by implementation and monitoring.

Revisiting applied geography

Within the literature on the geography of recreation and tourism there have been comparatively few studies which have emphasised how the tourism and recreation geographer has made a valuable contribution to the wider development of 'applied geography'. According to Sant (1982), the scope of applied geography comprises a concern with 'policy-making and the monitoring of problems'. More specifically, it focuses on 'the sense of the problem, the contribution to decision making and policy, the monitoring of actions and the evaluation of plans. But these are common to all applied social sciences' (Sant 1982: 3) and so the geographer must ensure that he or she can make a distinctive contribution through the use of approaches, tools, techniques or skills which other social scientists, consultants and policy-makers do not possess, if it is regarded as important that a geographical approach survives.

Pacione (1999b: 1) argued that 'Applied geography is concerned with the application of geographical knowledge and skills to the resolution of real-world social, economic and environmental problems' such as those associated with recreation and tourism. Pacione also developed the argument of 'useful knowledge', which also raises the inevitable criticisms of what might be non-useful geographical knowledge and useful for whom? As Frazier (1982: 17) observed, 'applied geography uses the principles and methods

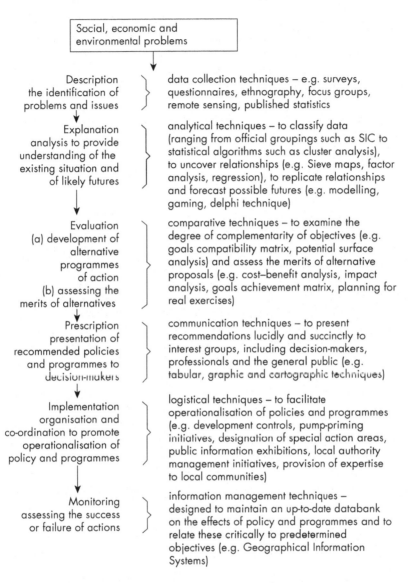

Figure 10.1 The DEEP process for applied geographical analysis

Source: Pacione 1999b.

of pure geography but is different in that it analyses and evaluates real-world action and planning and seeks to implement and manipulate environmental and spatial realities'. Indeed Sant (1982) viewed theory as crucial to applied geography in providing a framework for analysis and a context by which moral goals could be judged. These arguments were developed by Palm and Brazel (1992: 342) as 'applied research in any discipline is best understood in contrast with basic or pure research'.

In geography, basic research aims to develop new theory and methods that help explain the processes through which the spatial organisation of physical or human environments evolves. In contrast, applied research uses existing geographic theory or techniques to understand and solve specific empirical problems. In practice, a dichotomy between pure and applied knowledge has been laboured, particularly to question the academic value of applied research, even though it has often had policy or decision-making outcomes that esoteric and seemingly inward-looking pure research can rarely contribute. To the contrary, as Harvey (1984: 7) commented, 'geography is far too important to be left to generals, politicians and corporate chiefs. Notions of applied and relevant geography pose questions of objectives and interests served . . . there is more to geography than the production of knowledge.' By engaging outside the university, applied geography makes a broad contribution to society, even if there are questions about the values and objectives of applied research and its potential uses. Critics of publicly commissioned research may point to the role of studies in validating perspectives on the agenda of the commissioning agency, not seeking critical debate in extreme cases. But any applied geographical researcher with the skills and experience to engage with agencies must also need to recognise the constraints and limits imposed by the private and public may be outweighed by the wider benefits to society. Moreover, applied research need not be research undertaken for development agencies, government or industry and also includes community-based research or research undertaken for public interest and non-government organisations (Hall 2010c). For example, Croy and Hall (2003) described how student research undertaken as part of their degree programme could be used to transfer intellectual capital to rural communities that otherwise did not have the resources to either afford or undertake such research. Such an activity directly connects with the issue of the relevance of research, and, as Hall commented in writing on the issue of reflexivity in qualitative tourism research:

> I have great frustration with much of the research and scholarship undertaken in tourism. Often competently done, but without reflexion and thought as to whose interests are being served – which is normally those from business and government with access to power. For all the talk of sustainable and alternative tourism, few alternatives have really shown up which explore the potential for other spaces and places which reflexivity may provide. In my more sanguine moments I believe that this is because researchers often take the easier path in tourism research because within current academic structures that is what provides the rewards.
>
> (Hall 2004a: 151)

Given the growing marketisation of university and society, in which academic research is driven by evaluations of academic outputs (see Page 2003b; Hall 2010c, 2011e), applied research has, until relatively recently, been downgraded or dismissed. Yet this in itself is self-defeating and inward-looking, missing the wider community service and benefits of the knowledge economy associated with universities and its main clients – the population. In the UK a recent development in the assessment of University Research Outputs (the Research Excellence Framework – REF) has now completely come full circle for applied geography. Now the mantra is all about the 'impact' of the research and its ability to have a wider benefit to society, especially in policy-making and in addressing societal and economic and environmental problems. However, assessing and attributing impact in a simple cause and effect relationship has become extremely problematic as the effects of academic research are often indirect and long term (aside from consultancy projects designed to shape policy). But this does have an additional spin in a UK context: any impact research which universities wish to have considered as case study exemplars of best practice have to be underpinned by high quality academic outputs, which actually places applied geography centre stage in areas such as tourism and leisure, where relevancy and academic quality assume a greater importance than more theoretically oriented research. In other words, the research focus in tourism and leisure research has a greater role to play if underpinned by sound applied geographical training and quality outputs.

These debates have also been aired in a different vein in the Spanish geographical community (e.g. Segrelles-Serrano 2002) and the lack of social awareness in the training and education of geography graduates for professional careers (Naranjo 2001). Indeed, while there is much discussion about knowledge management in tourism, it often tends to be seen just in terms of transferring knowledge to industry rather than all those for whom knowledge, in its various forms, may be relevant.

All too often the application of geographical skills outside the academy in commercial and non-commercial contexts has been poorly expedited. In the post-war period some aspects of geography clearly dissipated to new disciplines such as town planning, while the greater social science involvement and expansion of geographical subject matter saw geographers lose some of their competitive edge which had been gained in the pre-war and inter-war years. In recent times, some geographers have made transitions into the public and private sector, where their skills have been in high demand (e.g. GIS and spatial tracking), and some have made major contributions to public policy formulation and analysis in recreation and tourism (e.g. Patmore 1983). There has been the development of new specialisms which have emerged from a geographical tradition with an explicit public and commercial dimension. Recreation and tourism are two areas which have furnished many opportunities for geographers to apply their skills in a wider context than academia, although this has not always meant that they have been particularly successful in capitalising on such opportunities.

While geographers still make a substantial contribution to planning, this contribution is perhaps not widely acknowledged by society at large. Similarly, GIS and spatial tracking are increasingly being usurped by marketers, while the contribution of geographers to tourism and recreation is now adding far more of an academic base for tourism and recreation studies than it is for geography. Should we care? The answer, we believe, is: 'Yes'. As Harvey commented:

In facing up to a world of uncertainty and risk, the possibility of being quite undone by the consequences of our own actions weighs heavily upon us, often making us prefer 'those ills we have than flying to others that we know not of'. But Hamlet, beset by angst and doubt and unable to act, brought disaster upon himself and upon his land by the mere fact of his inaction.

(Harvey 2000: 254)

As the book stated at the outset by imitating the title of Massey and Allen's (1984) work *Geography Matters!*, the geography of tourism and recreation also matters. Given increasing demands for the development of sustainable forms of tourism on the one hand and a relevant academic geography on the other, geography and geographers have an important role to play. In some senses many of those geographers who have moved to business schools to pursue their interest in tourism and recreation have at least managed to retain a spatial component to such curricula.

Contributions

According to Stamp (1960: 9), 'the unique contribution of the geographer is the holistic approach in which he sees the relationship between man and his [sic] environment'. This statement is just as relevant to the application of geography to problem-solving today as it was when originally written; indeed, perhaps more so given the size of the environmental, social and economic problems we face. Doornkamp (1982) posed a range of questions related to the role of applied geography, and two of these are of significance to tourism and recreation:

- Is the geographical contribution sufficiently unique to make it worth pursuing?
- How, in the commercial world, can the work of the applied geographer be promoted?

These two questions highlight the need for geographers to assess what inherent skills they have which may be of value in an applied context. While accepting that the nature of geographical training today may be somewhat different from that in the 1970s and 1980s, Table 10.1 does still provide a useful assessment of how the geographer can contribute to problem-solving. Doornkamp (1982) highlights the need to separate knowledge from the ability to use skills. During a geographical education, exposure to the systematic elements of the discipline in human and physical geography combines with practical and fieldwork in spatial techniques, which, together with regional studies, is where many of the former elements can be synthesised. This continues to provide the core of knowledge for the geographer and more advanced training then focuses on a specialised study in a particular sub-discipline of geography. It is often at this point that the crossover between geography and other social science disciplines occurs when the knowledge base becomes shared. The problem within business schools is that the spatial component is often watered down to an extremely basic conceptualisation of place, space and environment. Indeed, many business schools in the Anglo-American tradition have seemingly so come to believe that the economy is virtual or placeless that they have lost traditional courses in business

location, although this is generally not the case in the Nordic countries.

At the same time, the inquisitive nature of geographical research, particularly the interest in human–environment relationships at a variety of spatial scales, often means that the geographer pursues a holistic perspective not often found in other disciplines. Yet conveying this to the new generation of students interested in the business applications of recreation and tourism requires the geographer not only to sell the value of a synthesising holistic approach. Equally, the geographer also has a formidable challenge in convincing colleagues and researchers in mainstream geography of the validity and intellectual rigour associated with research in recreation and tourism.

But harnessing this training and the range of skills acquired in order to apply them in a problem-solving context requires one important prerequisite. According to Doornkamp (1982: 9), this is an ability to see the problem from the point of view of the person who needs a solution. Having convinced this person of their ability to conceptualise the problem in their

Table 10.1 The skills of a geographer

- To think in spatial terms
- To be able to assess the implications of the distribution of any one landscape characteristic
- To be able to think about more than one distribution at a time – and to perceive from this any likely generic links between the items under study
- To be able to change the scale of thinking according to the needs of the phenomena or problems being analysed
- To be able to add the dimension of time as appropriate
- To be able to place phenomena within a 'model' or 'systems' framework
- To be able to comprehend and initiate thinking that links the human and physical systems operating in the landscape
- To 'read' and 'understand' landscape
- To be able to use certain techniques, for example:
  – to acquire information through fieldwork, map analysis or from remote sensing sources – with an emphasis on spatial distributions and relationships
  – to be able to handle and analyse large datasets, incomplete datasets, spatial data or time-based data, through quantitative methods using computer technology
  – to be equally at home in a literary search among archives and historical records
  – to be able to monitor landscape components, and to be able to submit them to further analyses as appropriate
  – to present information with clarity, and especially in map form
  – to utilise technological developments such as GIS to assist in gaining a holistic view of the problem in hand
- To be able to provide a statement of one's findings which integrates one's own knowledge with that of allied disciplines

Source: after Doornkamp 1982: 7.

terms, in order to provide a solution three principal factors need to be considered:

- The research must be framed and reported in a manner which the client requires: it needs to be as concise and as thorough as possible. It is not to be a thesis or academic research paper, otherwise the client will simply not recommend or use the organisation again. This is a principal failing for many academics who are unable to bridge the industry–academic interface.

- Personal relationships of trust and respect need to be built up in a commercial environment, often framed around numerous meetings and regular interfacing, and the work must be professionally presented, being easy to read, targeted at the audience intending to read it, and precise and unambiguous.

- Even where the client is a non-paying customer (i.e. if the research is undertaken as a contribution to the local community or a public interest group), such criteria are equally important. Otherwise, the outside world's image of the geographer will remain one of the ivory tower academic perceived as being distant from the real world and problem-solving contributions they can make. Likewise, academics need to be willing to incorporate changes on drafts and to recognise that in this environment their view is not necessarily without reproach. This is nowhere more the case than in recreation and tourism, where an explicit business dimension is incorporated into such research.

It is fair to agree with Doornkamp's (1982: 26) analogy that practising geographers left the discipline in the immediate post-war period and joined the commercial world, calling themselves planners. A similar move may be occurring in recreation and tourism, with the movement of staff to business schools and specialist tourism and/or recreation departments, either from academic positions in departments of geography or after completion of their graduate studies. The 'professional practice' side of the discipline of geography has continued to lose out to other disciplines even when its skills are more relevant and analytical. Interfacing with the real world has meant that a small proportion of recreation and tourism geographers have made a steady transition to professional practice without compromising their academic integrity and reputation. In summary, it is clear that applied geography problem-solving in recreation and tourism contexts can enhance the geographer's skills and relationship with society. In the longer term, it may help address the public image of the discipline as being of major value to research in applied fields such as tourism. But ultimately the main barrier to geographers using their skills for an applied purpose is their own willingness and ability to interface in commercial and public contexts where they can be heard, listened to, taken seriously and their skills harnessed. In many cases, there is often a belated recognition of the value of such skills when a client uses such a person. Therefore, the public face of geography can be enhanced only if it embraces recreation and tourism as legitimate sub-disciplines of a post-industrial society/geography in both theoretical and various applied contexts.

BOX 10.1 GIS AND TOURISM: A TOOL FOR APPLIED GEOGRAPHIC RESEARCH

GIS, developed by advances in computer hardware and software (such as ArcInfo), incorporates more sophisticated systems to search, query, present and analyse data in a spatial context. It has long been recognised that the functional capabilities of GIS (i.e. data entry, map generation and spatial analysis) and the posing of spatial questions (i.e. related to location, pattern and modelling) enable the examination of who, where, what, why and when related to tourism and leisure (Bahaire and Elliott-White 1999). However, GIS is important not only because of its capacity to integrate data (Hultman 2007), but also because of its potential to represent data to users (Forer 1999) and the supply of tourism resources (Connell and Page 2008), including the mobility of tourists (Chen 2007), as well as their impact on the business development (Page *et al.* 1999).

The capacities of GIS as an accessible business and public planning tool have also been greatly advanced by developments in personal computing as well as the availability of GIS platforms on mobile phones and computing devices, which allow members of the public to access maps which may include a variety of different information sources embedded in them to enable improved visitor decision-making (Dye and Shaw 2007). The inclusion of visitor monitoring and survey data into GIS can also allow a thorough analysis of visitor use patterns, perceptions, activities and product usage, which can be extremely important in the management of public use pressures at tourist sites and destinations (Chhetri 2006; Connell and Page 2008), as well as identifying tourism and leisure opportunities (Chhetri and Arrowsmith 2008). Indeed, a significant contemporary development in GIS modelling and mapping is the growth of neogeography (Turner 2006), also referred to as volunteered or user-generated geographic information (Goodchild 2007), and how this can be incorporated into spatial analysis and understandings of tourism behaviour (Elwood 2008). In addition, user-generated content also has potential for inclusion in dynamic maps for mobile tourism applications developed by private and public providers (Schilling *et al.* 2005).

GIS has proven to be valuable for studying the effects of changing land use by virtue of being able not only to record resources within a given region but also to illustrate the effects of developments, such as the construction of new transport networks or resorts, on other elements in the system. For example, Chapter 7 noted the use of GIS in wilderness inventories and management. The dynamic element of GIS also allows future scenarios and forecasts to be spatially visualised. For example, Marshall and Simpson (2009) combined GIS with forecasting methods to explore issues of population sustainability in the Cairngorms and Peak District National Parks.

Simulation has become an increasingly important planning tool for studying the spatial behaviour of tourists and their impacts that has become increasingly integrated with GIS environments (Hunt *et al.* 2010). Information provided by simulations can allow planners to assess the effects of different management strategies. Both probabilistic simulation and agent-based models (ABM) are used in the development of spatial simulation models (Gimblett and Skov-Peterson 2008). Probabilistic models are developed via the collection of data from tourists while undertaking their trips and/or from data gained from observation (Sacchi *et al.* 2001). This approach has been used, for example, with respect to national park and wilderness camping and recreational behaviour (Lawson *et al.* 2003). In contrast, ABM are a collection of autonomous decision-making entities (agents) in which each agent individually assesses its situation and makes decisions on the basis of a set of rules that have been developed from 'real world' data, and which is also used to calibrate and validate spatio-temporal simulation models (O'Connor *et al.* 2005). The repetitive competitive interactions between agents within the system then provide information on behaviour, some of which may have been unanticipated, at different points in time. The benefits of ABM over other modelling techniques are: (1) ABM captures emergent phenomena; (2) ABM provides a natural description of a system; and (3) ABM is flexible. However, it is the ability of ABM to deal with emergent phenomena which drives the other benefits. ABMs are particularly useful for simulating tourism environments in which visitors are restricted to movement on a network such as roads, trails or rivers, and have therefore come to be used in a national park and protected area context (Hunt *et al.* 2010).

In the same way that the advent of the personal computer revolutionised use of GIS from a user perspective, so further revolutions in informational and communication technology provide new opportunities for spatial analysis (Hall 2012a). Paramount among the new developments is the use of GPS devices and cellular phones, which both allow for the tracking of tourists in space–time (Shoval and Isaacson 2007, 2010; Shoval 2008; Chhetri et al. 2010; Ahas 2011). The method has a range of applications, including not only improved collection of data over traditional methods such as diaries, but also management, planning and marketing applications. For example, Shoval and Isaacson (2010) highlighted the possibility of using aggregative data obtained from GPS receivers in order to better understand the impact of visitors on destinations, and provided examples from Port Aventura amusement park and the Mini Israel theme park (two enclosed outdoor environments), the Old City of Akko in Israel (a small historic city) and Hong Kong.

Mobile phone technological developments also provide significant opportunities for analysing tourist behaviour over various scales (Asakura and Iryob 2007). Tiru et al. (2010) discuss the operation of a mobile-positioning-based online tourism monitoring tool that uses as source data mobile operators' log files, in which the starting locations of foreign roaming clients' call activities have been stored. (The database is anonymous and the identity of phones, phone owners and phone numbers are strictly protected pursuant to EU directives.) Although such approaches have often been incorrectly criticised for being uncritical and untheoretical, it is important to recognise that GIS and other forms of quantitative analysis are increasingly being used in a counter-institutional fashion (Barnes 2009), as Schwanen and Kwan (2009) eloquently put it, 'doing critical geography with numbers'. As Hall concluded,

> critical geographies, and critical tourisms, are all the poorer without an understanding of spatial analysis. In the end the problem of being academically critical is not so much an issue of method per se but rather a conscious reflection on the questions, craft, methods, results and arguments of research, and a decision about the interests that are served.
>
> (Hall 2012a: 173)

The role of the geographer in the new millennium: whither tourism and recreation?

The perceived domain of the geographer – the quest for investigations associated with environment, humans, place and space – is not necessarily viewed by other social scientists and non-academics in the same way. Indeed, a multidisciplinary approach to problems underpinned and informed by a spatial analytical approach often provides an understanding beyond that achieved by the geographer working in isolation. One consequence of building multidisciplinary research teams peopled by non-geographers is a potential disciplinary marginalisation by other geographers and the stated 'gatekeepers' within the sub-discipline. This can impair the wider assimilation of the research area within the sub-discipline and within the wider context of geography as a discipline. This is somewhat ironic at a time when tourism and recreation have experienced rapid growth as activities within global, national and local space economies. There are also growing signs of non-geographical research adopting spatially contingent modes of analysis, as in the example of analysis of the Love Parade disaster in event studies (Helbing and Mukeriji 2012), where micro-scale site-level analysis was used to reconstruct the disaster to model and analyse the critical accident sequence in time and space. Consequently, geography does not have a monopoly on spatial analysis, although the purist might point to the need to understand specific rules and conventions in spatial analysis.

Further, with tourism and recreation comprising major components of the service economies of many countries and regions, it is somewhat surprising that the contribution of geographers to understanding this phenomenon is still constrained by perceptions within the discipline of what it is appropriate to study and research as serious topics of geographical investigation. This is part of a wider poor image of geography as a school-level subject associated with places and maps and not as a useful discipline to assess and problem-solve for organisations with its ability to offer a holistic understanding of issues.

Ironically, both authors of this book are probably viewed as 'outsiders' in the wider geographical domain of consciousness that now besets the discipline, even though there is a growing strength of interest in tourism and recreation. (If some of Butler's (2004) comments regarding the relatively peripheral role of geography in tourism studies generally hold true, then they may also be seen as outsiders in that disciplinary context as well!) The major 'internal' problem facing the discipline of geography is related to the old (false) tension between positivism and humanism/the new cultural geography and social theory. This fragmentation or internal realignment to develop careers related to the latest academic fashion has certainly made a geographical education a less unified and structured process (Barnett 1998). Disciplinary fragmentation within the wider domain of geography creates barriers and constraints to the wider integration of this exciting, dynamic and fast changing area of research. One of the central messages implicit in this book is that it is inappropriate to simply decry previous paradigms as redundant and analytically bankrupt: within tourism and recreation geography, the early studies established many of the central tenets and building blocks of the sub-discipline and, in fact, laid much of the intellectual foundation for current interests in themes such as mobility, the body, performity and place (Hall 2005a). Indeed, as Livingstone commented,

> Fragmentation of knowledge, social differentiation, and the questioning of scientific rationality have all coalesced to reaffirm the importance of the particular, the specific, the local. And in this social and cognitive environment a geography stressing the salience of place is seen as having great potential.
>
> (Livingstone 1992: 358)

The importance of place and the application of geographical knowledge is reflected in the richness of the literature reviewed throughout the book, and the value it has added to spatial analysis of tourism. The discontinuities between positivism, humanism, critical social theory and Marxism may enrich a geographical awareness of how to interpret the real world, but they need to be fashioned into an integrated whole together with accompanying skill sets.

These constant revolutions in geographical knowledge and thinking pose central questions for the student of tourism and recreation. What is the role of the geographer? Is there a role? How is that role mediated, nurtured and negotiated within the discipline, outside the discipline, and how does the geographer engage political influence to ensure the profile, relevance and continued survival of the subject? One way of engaging in this debate is through introspection and reflexivity – or through a refocusing of attention on the possible contribution which specific approaches to geography may make to problem-solving (i.e. the applied perspective).

These questions and issues are a useful starting point to assess the role of the geographer beyond the synthesising role and integrating ability to harmonise a wide range of social science perspectives. R. Bennett (1985) warned of the dangers of such an approach since it may contribute to a loss of identity among geographical contributions, as other disciplines and their methodologies overtake the spatial focus. What is clear is that the quest for relevance, understanding and explanation cannot solely be achieved from the logical positivist approach to research. It can be as blind as it is revealing: it can obscure understanding and explanation – it is only a partial focus on a problem and its solution. Thus, the non-positivist or humanist perspective needs to be used as a counterweight to expand, develop, question and reinterpret the positivist paradigm. In this context, Powell (1985) re-examined the four main concerns of the geographer, which remain as relevant three decades later. These are:

- *Space*: what is the human meaning and experience of space?
- *Place*: as a centre of action and intention in relation to human activity, where perception, human activity and changes in the life course of individuals and groups occur.
- *Time*: how it is fundamental to human activity, action and the interaction with humans and their environment, in terms of resource conflict in outdoor recreation and their use of leisure time.
- *People*: as the fundamental focus in a relevant 'human geography'.

These four central themes characterise the geographer's focus and, even though they are grounded in humanist views of the world, place, space and time, they are also key elements in establishing research questions throughout tourism and recreation geography. At a personal level, the authors recognise the criticisms of applied geography as critiqued and debated by Pacione (1999a, 1999b) and would proffer the following role for the geographer in a wider leisure context: to utilise an applied analytical science with its focus on space, place, time and people with a view to problem-solving, understanding and explanation. Furthermore, to actually improve the human condition (and we remain such unreconstructed children of the Enlightenment that we still see this as a goal of geography and ourselves as academics), one needs to engage and communicate effectively with stakeholders/people/communities, most especially the wider public and those who are affected by our work. This applies regardless of whether one is inspired by older (e.g. Peet 1977a, 1977b; Britton 1991), or more recent (e.g. Debbage and Ioannides 2004; Aitchison 2006; Barnes 2009), critical geographies or engaged in applied tourism and recreation geography.

This means we need to argue and communicate in a manner which can be understood in the public sphere. As one of the authors' experience of working on the education–industry interface, being funded by an enterprise company, suggests, geographers and other academics who engage with the wider world need to be able to 'talk the talk' of industry and other groups when required to engage them effectively, rather than remain marginalised on the periphery looking in. It is that marginalisation that has continued to dominate the discipline's relationships with the outside world. Being able to engage effectively requires not only a specific skill set to understand the needs and values of such bodies, but also a direct, focused and concise manner of communication. In very simple terms, government, industry and communities pose problems to solve and want a credible, robust and methodologically sound solution, although people may not want to engage with all the complexities of how you arrived at such a solution. They just need to know it has integrity and will stand up to scrutiny. What industry does not want is the ephemeral and somewhat indulgent rhetoric that surrounds many academics when they engage with outside bodies on what they have published recently and how influential it is. External agencies and companies frequently return to a set series of questions:

- Do you have the right skill set for the job?
- Do you have relevant experience and expertise supported by a track record in similar activities (i.e. commercial reports and consultancies rather than academic publications on the topic)?
- Can you deliver a solution on time?
- Is the solution cost-effective and value for money?
- Will the outcomes be capable of being used and solutions implemented in a direct and effective manner?

If the answer to these questions is yes, then it is apparent that individual geographers or groups of geographers rather than geography per se can be relevant to society, to the needs of policy-makers, planners, communities, individuals and to the future of the planet. In the tourism–recreation context, the skills of the geographers are increasingly being harnessed, recognised and utilised within academia, frequently in the field of market surveys, position papers and data analysis rather than in the more skilled area of feasibility studies, though examples of the latter do exist. Ironically, it is often when geographers drop the label of 'geography' and move to an applied academic environment such as a business school or planning department that their skills gain a greater acceptance, legitimacy and validity with political decision-makers.

To the discipline's gatekeepers of knowledge, tourism and recreation will likely continue to remain fringe activities – amorphous and seemingly didactic in their conception of space, place and environment. Yet in a changing postmodern society where consumption is integral to the growth of tourism, leisure and recreation, a discipline which does not embrace this new domain of study is relegating itself to a 'non-relevant', esoteric and increasingly distant position. Recreational activity and tourism per se are now culturally embedded in the lifestyles of much of the world's population. This may be a function of globalisation, westernisation, consumerism, marketisation or other socially contingent processes; if they wish to pursue them, it is a reality. It exists – and poses new research agendas and opportunities for a generation of geographers. Indeed, joining up these interests with other growing agendas on issues such as urbanisation (Burdett and Sudjic 2011) highlights that the evolving city environments of the twenty-first century will lead to major changes in the scale of urban growth, connectivity and spatial form as the dominant mode of living. This will inevitably lead to changes in the nature of tourism and leisure activity, as the scale of the world's urban population is expected to grow by 2 per cent per annum, so that by 2030 the world's urban population will surpass 5 billion (Katz and Wagner 2011) out of a population of between 8 and 9 billion. Consequently, Katz and Wagner (2011) suggest that the speed and velocity of change will

continue to be huge, fuelled by migration and increased mobility of diverse populations, urban expansion creating conurbations of increased complexity with greater social and spatial divisions. In mega-cities, the multi-polar region will dramatically change the spatial nature of leisure and tourism activity in the future. In particular, Katz and Wagner (2011) argue that places will be bound to each other more closely by economic globalisation. From a tourism perspective, this means that flows of professionals, tourists and migrants will be brought about by air travel and other transports in circuits of intercity geographies (Katz and Wagner 2011), with mega-cities becoming the gateways and control points for tourist space, as well as the sites for mega-events and new forms of tourism activity such as medical tourism. This also raises, as Chapter 5, on urban leisure and tourism, highlighted, issues for the balance of public and private space in these new multi-polar regions, and for access to public and privatised leisure and tourism resources, again raising the issue of who gets what, where and why.

The area of leisure and tourism is exciting, ever changing, and socially, economically, politically and environmentally challenging. Understanding the dynamics, processes, elements of change (e.g. see Box 10.2) and wider meaning and value of recreation and tourism in society has opened so many avenues for spatial and multidisciplinary research. For the wider discipline, these opportunities should be fostered, nurtured and encouraged since the area has the potential to engage not only students, but the wider public, decision-makers and politicians. Geographers can make a difference, even if it is in a neoliberal market-driven economy.

BOX 10.2   THE FUTURE: RESPONDING TO CLIMATE CHANGE

In September 2013 the IPCC concluded 'Warming of the climate system is unequivocal, and since the 1950s, many of the observed changes are unprecedented over decades to millennia. The atmosphere and ocean have warmed, the amounts of snow and ice have diminished, sea level has risen, and the concentrations of greenhouse gases have increased' (IPCC 2013: SP3). Such a situation creates a major challenge for the world's tourism industry, which both contributes to and is affected by climate change.

Tourism and travel contribute to climate change through emissions of greenhouse gases (GHGs), including in particular CO_2, as well as methane (CH_4), nitrous oxides (NO_x), hydrofluorocarbons (HFCs), perfluorocarbons (PFCs) and sulphur hexafluoride (SF_6). There are also various short-lived GHGs that are important in the context of aviation. Tourism transport, accommodation and activities are estimated to have contributed approximately 5 per cent to global anthropogenic emissions of CO_2 in the year 2005 (United Nations World Tourism Organization, United Nations Environment Programme, and World Meterological Organization (UNWTO–UNEP–WMO) 2008) (Table 10.2). Most CO_2 emissions are associated with transport, with aviation accounting for 40 per cent of tourism's overall carbon footprint, followed by car transport (32 per cent) and accommodation (21 per cent) (UNWTO–UNEP–WMO 2008). Cruise ships are included in 'other transport' and, with an estimated 19.2 Mt CO_2, account for around 1.5 per cent of global tourism emissions (Eijgelaar *et al.* 2010). These independent assessments of the tourism sector's contribution to climate change do not include the impact of non-CO_2 short-lived GHGs. A more accurate assessment of tourism's contribution to global warming can be made on the basis of radiative forcing (RF). With RF considered, it was estimated that tourism contributed 5.2–12.5 per cent of all anthropogenic forcing in 2005, with a best estimate of approximately 8 per cent (Scott *et al.* 2010).

The implications of climate change are substantial, ranging from increased atmospheric and ocean warming, loss of 'permanent' ice cover in high latitudes and alpine areas, sea-level rise, to changes in climate extremes. These also have flow-on effects with respect to ocean acidification and biological processes. A summary of some of the impacts of different levels of climate change are indicated in Table 10.3. However, at the same time that worsening impacts of climate change are forecast, so too is further growth in tourism (see Chapter 1). Yet forecasts suggest a substantial increase in tourism growth well above any forecast or suggested increases in per passenger/tourist efficiency, which are estimated at around 1.5–2 per cent per year. How, then, may the effects of tourism's contributions to climate change be limited. Gössling *et al.* (2013) suggest that no credible plan has yet been offered as to how combinations of technological investment,

Table 10.2 Tourism sector emissions and mitigation targets

Year	Emission estimates and BAU* projections (CO_2)		Mitigation targets	
	UNWTO–UNEP–WMO (2008)	*WEF (2009)*	*WTTC (2009)***	*5% allocation of CO_2 emissions from a 'below +2°C scenario' to tourism sector****
2005	1.304 Gt	1.476 Gt	–	
2020	2.181 Gt	2.319 Gt	0.978 Gt	1.254 Gt
2035	3.059 Gt	3.164 Gt	0.652 Gt	0.940 Gt

* Business as usual

** WTTC (2009) aspirational emission reduction targets are –25 per cent in 2020 and –50 per cent in 2035 (both from 2005 levels specified in UNWTO–UNEP–WMO 2008)

*** Pathway that limits global average temperature increase to below 2°C; assuming CO_2 continues to representing approximately 57 per cent (IPCC 2007a,b) of the median estimate of 44 Gt CO_2-e total GHG emissions in 2020 and 2035 (Rogelj *et al.* 2011) and the tourism sector continues to represent approximately 5 per cent of global CO_2 emissions (UNWTO–UNEP–WMO 2008; WTTC 2009) over the same time frame (D. Scott *et al.* 2012).

Table 10.3 Likely consequences of climate change

Scenario	Global warming (over pre-industrial average temperature)					Examples of likely consequences for tourism			
	+0.8°C "Already happened"	+1.5°C "Inevitable"	+2°C "Safe limit"	+3–4°C "Tipping point"	+5–6°C "Nightmare"	Environmental	Economic	Social	Political
Sea-level rise by 2100 (relative to 1990 sea level)		0.85 m	1.04 m (Amsterdam flooded)	1.24 m (New York flooded)	1.43 m (Bangkok flooded)	Coastal areas inundated; some coastal ecosystems such as mangroves and tidal marsh will adapt	High adaptation costs for many destinations	Loss of some coastal destination and heritage	Political instability
Ocean acidification	30% more acidic	Coral stops growing	Coral dissolves	Coral dies	150% more acidic	Serious decline in coral reefs; some coastal areas more vulnerable to erosion and impacts of storms	Negative impacts on reef and dive tourism	Decline in reef tourism dependent communities	Increased competition for marine resources between tourism and other users
Arctic sea-ice annual reduction		15%	30%	45–60%	75%	Extinction of some Arctic species	Increased access to shipping and tourism	Arctic cultural change	Increased competition for Arctic resources

Table 10.3 (Continued)

Scenario	Global warming (over pre-industrial average temperature)					Examples of likely consequences for tourism			
	+0.8°C "Already happened"	+1.5°C "Inevitable"	+2°C "Safe limit"	+3–4°C "Tipping point"	+5–6°C "Nightmare"	Environmental	Economic	Social	Political
Increased heatwaves	Increasing global heat waves		Every European summer a heatwave	Mediterranean region drier	Unknown	Extinction or decline of some species and ecosystems; increased water scarcity in some destinations	Changes to destination attractiveness and tourism seasonality	Changes in outdoor leisure activities	Difficulty in responding to scale of event
% more heavy rain over land		7%	13%	20–26%	35–42%	Increased flooding	Increased infrastructure and insurance costs	Increased flood threats affect communities	Watershed management conflicts
Hurricane destructiveness		+7.5%	+15%	+22.5–30%	+37.5–45%	Increased damage to coastal environments	Increased damage to tourism infrastructure and resort communities	Increased destination vulnerability	Difficulty in responding to scale of event
Species at risk of extinction			30%	40%	Unknown	Ecosystem change and extinction of some charismatic species	Significant effects for ecotourism dependent communities	Indigenous cultural change	Renewable resource security concerns

(Continued)

Table 10.3 (Continued)

Scenario	Global warming (over pre-industrial average temperature)					Examples of likely consequences for tourism			
	+0.8°C "Already happened"	+1.5°C "Inevitable"	+2°C "Safe limit"	+3–4°C "Tipping point"	+5–6°C "Nightmare"	Environmental	Economic	Social	Political
'Really scary things'		Last time CO_2 levels were this high was 15 million years ago	Greenland icesheet starts to disintegrate	Huge amounts of CO_2 and methane released by melting permafrost in the Arctic and Siberia	Ocean floor methane released, causing runaway climate change; minimum time needed to reabsorb all this CO_2 from the atmosphere: 300,000 years	Likelihood of mass extinction event	Major economic instability	Massive rapid cultural change	High levels of political instability and increasing conflict over scarce resources: 'resource wars'

Source: Adapted from Gössling and Hall 2006a; IPCC 2007a, 2007b, 2013; UN Framework Convention on Climate Change (UNFCCC) 2007; Hall and Saarinen 2010; National Intelligence Council 2012; *Guardian* 2012; Scott et al. 2012.

management strategies, marketing and consumer behavioural change could achieve the declared tourism sector emission reductions targets of the UNWTO or World Travel and Tourism Council (WTTC). For example, the International Energy Agency (IEA) (2009) suggests that the technical capacity to reduce the energy intensity of new aircraft is equivalent to 0.6–1.0 per cent per year on average, and that the annual historical rate of improvement in load factors (approximately 0.2 per cent per year) could reach close to its upper limit by 2025. The reliance on biofuel as a technological solution remains problematic because of uncertainties over full life cycle emission benefits and land use requirements that put energy and food crops in conflict. As Gössling *et al.* observe, the lack of a credible transformative strategy to achieve emission reduction goals and become a part of the low carbon economy by mid-century raises fundamental questions about the future of global tourism growth projections and whether long-haul SIDS and LDCs should rely on tourism as an economic mainstay for future development (Gössling *et al.* 2013).

Transformations?

As this book has indicated, the geography of tourism and recreation, as with the discipline as a whole, has undergone considerable change since it began in the 1920s. This is to be expected, since geography, as with any discipline, adapts and reacts in relation to the society and culture within which it operates (see Chapter 1). The case for understanding the changing nature of tourism and recreation 'contextually closely parallels the case made by realists for appreciating all human activity; the operation of human agency must be analysed within the constraining and enabling conditions provided by its environment' (Johnston 1991: 280). In this sense the environment for the study of tourism and recreation must be positive given the growth of international tourism and the role it now plays within government policy-making. Given the significance of globalisation, mobility, postmodernism, post-Fordism and localisation to contemporary social theory, it should also be no surprise that many human geographers and other social scientists are now discovering tourism and recreation as having some significance for social change. Indeed, the emerging paradigm of mobility which is acting to link research in tourism geography with that of migration, and is also connecting geographers, sociologists and demographers, appears to be a research direction potentially rich in possibilities (see, e.g., Urry 2000; Hall and Williams 2002; Coles *et al.*

2004; Hannam 2008). However, previous work in the area is often ignored, while many authors discussing contemporary tourism phenomena, particularly in an urban or rural setting, seem to think that all tourists and tourism are the same and fail to perceive the complexity of the phenomena they are investigating.

It would also be true to note that many tourism and recreation geographers find the discovery of 'their' field by social theory and cultural studies somewhat amusing given that they have been ignored for so long. Others will also find it threatening given that their own work bears all the hallmarks of traditional spatial science, excellent maps, flows and patterns but a limited role for more critical examination of tourism phenomena.

The geography of tourism and recreation therefore bears the hallmarks of much Anglo-North American geography in terms of the tensions that exist between the different approaches within the discipline. Such tensions, if well managed, can be extremely healthy in terms of the debate they generate and the 'freshness' of the subject matter (Hall 2013a). However, if they are not well managed and if external influences become too attractive, splits will occur. Research and scholarship in the geography of tourism and recreation are now at this stage. Unless greater links are built between the sub-discipline and the discipline as a whole, potentially much of the field will be swallowed up by the rapidly expanding field of tourism studies, which bears many of the hallmarks of being a discipline in its own right (Hall 2005a). Even if only in terms of student numbers, such a shift would have substantial implications for geography, as already mentioned above.

The geography of tourism and recreation remains at a crossroads. It is to be hoped that a situation will not develop where those concerned with social theory will stay in geography and those who do not will go to the business and tourism schools. An understanding of social theory by itself will not provide geography graduates or tourism graduates with a career. Of course it should never be just about jobs; we hope it is also about the joy of gaining knowledge for its own sake. However, the integration of some of the central concerns of social theory and the central concerns of the geographer – sites, places, landscapes, regions and national configurations, and the spatial arrangements and relationships that interconnect them – with the subject of tourism and recreation will lead to the development of a more relevant area of geography that can better contribute to all its stakeholders, including its students, who are then exposed to the right range of traditions that have contributed to geographical knowledge and its application. To this end we can only reiterate the words of Gilbert White as a guiding light for a relevant tourism and recreation geography:

> Speaking only as one individual, I feel strongly that I should not go into research unless it promises results that would advance the aims of the people affected and unless I am prepared to take all practicable steps to help translate the results into action.
> (White 1972: 102)

Further reading

There are a number of edited collections that provide good thematic overviews to various issues and concepts in the geographies of tourism and recreation. See:

Hall, C.M. (ed.) (2011) *Fieldwork in Tourism: Methods, Issues and Reflections*, Abingdon: Routledge (a collection of reflections, essays and reviews on the important fieldwork dimension in tourism and geography).

Lew, A., Hall, C.M. and Williams, A. (eds) (2014) *The Wiley-Blackwell Companion to Tourism*, Oxford: Wiley-Blackwell Publishers (a large collection of essays on various major research themes and traditions in the geography of tourism as well as the wider tourism literature).

Smith, S. (ed.) (2010) *The Discovery of Tourism*, Bingley: Emerald (autobiographical accounts of tourism geographers with a useful overview by the editor).

Wilson, J. (ed.) (2012) *The Routledge Handbook of Tourism Geographies*, London: Routledge.

Wilson, J. and Anton Clavé, S. (eds) (2013) *Geographies of Tourism: European Research Perspectives*, London: Emerald.

An interesting exercise in the examination of change in tourism studies and tourism geographies would be to compare Lew *et al.* (2014) with the 2004 version: Lew, A.A., Hall, C.M. and Williams, A. (eds) (2004) *A Companion to Tourism*, Oxford: Blackwell. Similarly, the series of papers by Gibson on geographies of tourism (Gibson, 2008, 2009, 2010) could be usefully compared with the reviews of leisure and recreation by Patmore (1977, 1978, 1979, 1980).

Questions to discuss

1 Is geography a relevant subject to study in the twenty-first century as a basis for understanding tourism and recreational phenomena?

2 What is applied geography and how does it relate to tourism and recreation?

3 How has the geographer contributed to the wider public policy and problem-solving approach to tourism and recreation research? Has this been at the expense of academic credibility within the discipline?

4 What is the role of GIS in tourism and recreational research?

Bibliography

Aagesen, D. (2004) 'Burning monkey-puzzle: native fire ecology and forest management in northern Patagonia', *Agriculture and Human Values*, 21: 233–42.

Abercrombie, P. (1938) 'Geography, the basis of planning', *Geography*, 20(3): 196–200.

Abrahamsson, S. and Simpson, P. (2011) 'The limits of the body: boundaries, capacities, thresholds', *Social & Cultural Geography*, 12: 331–8.

Ackoff, R.L. (1974) *Redesigning the Future*, New York: Wiley.

Adams, D.L. (1973) 'Uncertainty in nature: weather forecasts and New England beach trip decision', *Economic Geographer*, 49: 287–97.

Addo, S.T. (1995) 'Accessibility, mobility and the development process', *Institute of African Studies: Research Review*, 11(1&2): 1–15.

Adey, P. (2006) 'If mobility is everything then it is nothing: towards a relational politics of (im)mobilities', *Mobilities*, 1: 75–94.

— (2010) *Mobility*, London: Routledge.

Adler, S. and Brenner, J. (1992) 'Gender and space: lesbians and gay men in the city', *International Journal of Urban and Regional Research*, 16: 24–34.

Agarwal, S. (1994) 'The resort cycle revisited: implications for resorts', in C. Cooper and A. Lockwood (eds) *Progress in Tourism, Recreation and Hospitality Management*, vol. 5, London: Belhaven Press.

Agarwal, S., Ball, R., Shaw, G. and Williams, A. (2000) 'The geography of tourism production: uneven disciplinary development', *Tourism Geographies*, 2: 241–63.

Agnew, J. (2007) 'Know-where: geographies of knowledge of world politics', *International Political Sociology*, 1: 138–48.

Agnew, J. and Livingstone, D.N. (2011) 'Introduction', in J. Agnew and D. Livingstone (eds) *The SAGE Handbook of Geographical Knowledge*, London: Sage.

Aguiar, M. and Hurst, E. (2009) 'A summary of trends in American time allocation: 1965–2005', *Social Indicators Research*, 93(1): 57–64.

Ahas, R. (2011) 'Mobile positioning', in M. Büscher, J. Urry and K. Witchger (eds) *Mobile Methods*, London: Routledge.

Aiken, S.R. (2004) 'Runaway fires, smoke-haze pollution, and unnatural disasters in Indonesia', *Geographical Review*, 94(1): 55–79.

Aitchison, C. (1997) 'A decade of compulsory competitive tendering in the UK sport and leisure services: some feminist perspectives', *Leisure Studies*, 16: 85–105.

— (1999) 'New cultural geographies: the spatiality of leisure, gender and sexuality', *Leisure Studies*, 18: 19–39.

— (2006) 'The critical and the cultural: explaining the divergent paths of leisure studies and tourism studies', *Leisure Studies*, 25: 417–22.

Aitchison, C., Macleod, N. and Shaw, S. (2000) *Leisure and Tourism Landscapes: Social and Cultural Geographies*, London: Routledge.

Al-Saleh, S. and Hannam, K. (2010) 'Tourism shopping in Jeddah', in N. Scott and J. Jafari (eds) *Tourism in the Muslim World*, London: Emerald Group Publishing.

Albayrak, T. and Caber, M. (2013) 'The symmetric and asymmetric influences of destination attributes on overall visitor satisfaction', *Current Issues in Tourism*, 16: 149–66.

Aldskogius, H. (1968) 'Modeling the evolution of settlement patterns: two case studies of vacation house settlement', *Geografiska regionstudie*, 6, Uppsala: Geografiske institutionen.

— (1977) 'A conceptual framework and a Swedish case study of recreational behaviour and environmental cognition', *Economic Geography*, 53: 163–83.

Alessa, L.N., Kliskey, A.A. and Brown, G. (2008) 'Social–ecological hotspots mapping: a spatial approach for identifying coupled social–ecological space', *Landscape and Urban Planning*, 85: 27–39.

Allix, A. (1922) 'The geography of fairs: illustrated by old-world examples', *Geographical Review*, 12: 532–69.

Amati, M. and Taylor, L. (2010) 'From green belts to green infrastructure', *Planning, Practice & Research*, 25(2): 143–55.

Amin, A. (2002) 'Spatialities of globalisation', *Environment and Planning A*, 34: 385–99.

Anastasiadou, C. (2008) 'Tourism interest groups in the EU policy arena: characteristics, relationships and challenges', *Current Issues in Tourism*, 11: 24–62.

Anderson, D.H. and Brown, P.J. (1984) 'The displacement process in recreation', *Journal of Leisure Research*, 16(1): 61–73.

Anderson, J. (1971) 'Space–time budgets and activity studies in urban geography and planning', *Environment and Planning*, 3: 353–68.

Anderson, S., Smith, C., Kinsey, R. and Wood, J. (1990) *The Edinburgh Crime Survey: First Report*, Edinburgh: Scottish Office.

Andersson, T.D. and Lundberg, E. (2013) 'Commensurability and sustainability: triple impact assessments of a tourism event', *Tourism Management*, 37: 99–109.

Ångman, E., Hallgren, L. and Nordström, E.M. (2011) 'Managing impressions and forests: the importance of role confusion in co-creation of a natural resource conflict', *Society & Natural Resources*, 24: 1335–44.

Antrop, M. (2005) 'Why landscapes of the past are important for the future', *Landscape and Urban Planning*, 70: 21–34.

Appleton, I. (1974) *Leisure Research and Policy*, Edinburgh: Scottish Academic Press.

Arbel, A. and Pizam, A. (1977) 'Some determinants of hotel location: the tourists' inclination', *Journal of Travel Research*, 15 (winter): 18–22.

Archer, B.H. (1973) *The Impact of Domestic Tourism*, Cardiff: University of Wales Press.

— (1976) 'Uses and abuses of multipliers', in W.W. Swart and T. Var (eds) *Planning for Tourism Development: Quantitative Approaches*, New York: Praeger.

— (1977a) 'The economic costs and benefits of tourism', in B.S. Duffield (ed.) *Tourism a Tool for Regional Development*, Edinburgh: Tourism and Recreation Research Unit, University of Edinburgh.

— (1977b) *Tourism Multipliers: The State of the Art*, Occasional Papers in Economics No. 11, Bangor: University of Wales Press.

— (1978) 'Tourism as a development factor', *Annals of Tourism Research*, 5: 126–41.

— (1982) 'The value of multipliers and their policy implications', *Tourism Management*, 3: 236–41.

— (1984) 'Economic impact: misleading multiplier', *Annals of Tourism Research*, 11: 517–18.

Archer, J. and Yarman, I. (1991) *Nature Conservation in Newham*, Ecology Handbook 17, London: Ecology Unit.

Arctic Climate Impact Assessment (ACIA) (2004) *Impacts of a Warming Arctic*, Cambridge: Cambridge University Press.

Argyle, M. (1996) *The Social Psychology of Leisure*, London: Penguin.

Arnberger, A., Aikoh, T., Eder, R., Shoji, Y. and Mieno, T. (2010) 'How many people should be in the urban forest? A comparison of trail preferences of Vienna and Sapporo forest visitor segments', *Urban Forestry & Urban Greening*, 9: 215–25.

Arnould, E.J., Price, L.L. and Tierney, P. (1998) 'Communicative staging of the wilderness service-scape', *Service Industries Journal*, 18(3): 90–115.

Aronsson, L. (2000) *The Development of Sustainable Tourism*, London: Continuum.

Arreola, D.D. (2010) 'The Mexico–US borderlands through two decades', *Journal of Cultural Geography*, 27: 331–51.

Asakura, Y. and Iryob, T. (2007) 'Analysis of tourist behaviour based on the tracking data collected using a mobile communication instrument', *Transportation Research Part A: Policy and Practice*, 41: 684–90.

Ashworth, G.J. (1989) 'Urban tourism: an imbalance in attention', in C.P. Cooper (ed.) *Progress in Tourism, Recreation and Hospitality Management*, vol. 1, London: Belhaven Press.

— (1992a) 'Is there an urban tourism?', *Tourism Recreation Research*, 17(2): 3–8.

— (1992b) 'Planning for sustainable tourism: A review article', *Town and Planning Review*, 63: 325–9.

— (1999) 'Heritage tourism: a review', *Tourism Recreation Research*, 25(1): 19–29.

Ashworth, G.J. and Dietvorst, A. (eds) (1995) *Tourism and Spatial Transformations*, Wallingford: CAB International.

Ashworth, G.J. and Ennen, E. (1998) 'City centre management: Dutch and British experiences', *European Spatial Research and Policy*, 5(1): 1–15.

Ashworth, G.J. and Page, S.J. (2011) 'Progress in tourism management: urban tourism research: recent progress and current paradoxes', *Tourism Management*, 32: 1–15.

Ashworth, G.J. and Tunbridge, J.E. (1990) *The Tourist–Historic City*, London: Belhaven Press.

— (1996) *Dissonant Heritage*, Chichester: Wiley.

Ashworth, G.J. and Voogd, H. (1988) 'Marketing the city: concepts, processes and Dutch applications', *Town Planning Review*, 59(1): 65–80.

— (1990a) *Selling the City*, London: Belhaven Press.

— (1990b) 'Can places be sold for tourism?', in G.J. Ashworth and B. Goodall (eds) *Marketing Tourism Places*, London: Routledge.

— (1994) 'Marketing of tourism places: what are we doing?', in M. Uysal (ed.) *Global Tourist Behaviour*, New York: International Press.

Ashworth, G.J., White, P.E. and Winchester, H.P. (1988) 'The red light district in the West-European city: a neglected aspect of the urban landscape', *Geoforum*, 19: 201–12.

Association of Arctic Expedition Cruise Operators (AECO) (2007) *AECO's Guidelines for Expedition Cruise Operations in the Arctic*, Longyearbyen: AECO.

— (n.d.) *Guidelines for Visitors to the Arctic*, Longyearbyen: AECO.

Ateljevic, I. and Doorne, S. (2000) '"Staying within the fence": lifestyle entrepreneurship in tourism', *Journal of Sustainable Tourism*, 8: 378–92.

Ateljevic, J. and Page, S. (eds) (2009) *Progress in Tourism and Entrepreneurship*, Oxford: Elsevier.

Attfield, R. (1983) *The Ethics of Environmental Concern*, Oxford: Blackwell.

Atwood, W.W. (1931) 'What are National Parks?', *American Forests*, 37 (September): 540–3.

Audit Commission (1993) *Realising the Benefits of Competition: The Client for Contracted Services*, London: HMSO.

— (2003) *Leisure Services: Walsall Metropolitan Borough Council Inspection Report*, October, Leicester: Audit Commission.

Austin, M. (1974) 'The evaluation of urban public facility location: an alternative to cost–benefit analysis', *Geographical Analysis*, 6: 135–46.

Ayikoru, M., Tribe, J. and Airey, D. (2009) 'Reading tourism education: neoliberalism unveiled', *Annals of Tourism Research*, 36: 191–221.

Baggio, R. (2007) 'Symptoms of complexity in a tourism system', arXiv:physics/0701063v2[physics.soc-ph].

Bahaire, T. and Elliott-White, M. (1999) 'The application of geographical information systems (GIS) in sustainable tourism planning', *Journal of Sustainable Tourism*, 7: 159–74.

Baidal, J.A.I., Sánchez, I.R. and Rebollo, J.F.V. (2013) 'The evolution of mass tourism destinations: new approaches beyond deterministic models in Benidorm (Spain)', *Tourism Management*, 34: 184–95.

Bailey, A., Gibson, L. and Haynes, K. (eds) (2008) *Applied Geography for the Entrepreneurial University*, Paris: Economica.

Bailey, M. (1989) 'Leisure, culture and the historian: reviewing the first generation of leisure historiography in Britain', *Leisure Studies*, 8: 107–27.

Bailey, P. (1999) 'The politics and poetics of modern British leisure: a late twentieth century review', *Rethinking History*, 3(2): 131–75.

Baines, G.B.K. (1987) 'Manipulation of islands and men: sand-cay tourism in the South Pacific', in

S. Britton and W.C. Clarke (eds) *Ambiguous Alternative: Tourism in Small Developing Countries*, Suva: University of the South Pacific.

Baird, T. and Hall, C.M. (2013) 'Sustainable winegrowing in New Zealand', in C.M. Hall and S. Gössling (eds) *Sustainable Culinary Systems: Local Foods, Innovation, and Tourism & Hospitality*, London: Routledge.

— (2014) 'Between the vines: wine tourism in New Zealand', in P. Howland (ed.) *Social, Cultural and Economic Impacts of Wine in New Zealand*, London: Routledge.

Baker, A. and Genty, A. (1998) 'Environmental pressures on conserving cave speleothems: effects of changing surface land use and increased cave tourism', *Journal of Environmental Management*, 53: 165–75.

Ball, R.M. (1989) 'Some aspects of tourism, seasonality and local labour markets', *Area*, 21: 35–45.

Balmer, K. (1971) 'Urban open space and outdoor recreation', in P. Lavery (ed.) *Recreation Geography*, Newton Abbot: David and Charles.

Balram, S., Dragicevic, S. and Feick, R. (2009) 'Collaborative GIS for spatial decision support and visualization', *Journal of Environmental Management*, 90: 1963–5.

Bandura, A. (1977) 'Self-efficacy: toward a unifying theory of behavioural change', *Psychological Review*, 84: 191–215.

Bannan, M., Adams, C. and Pirie, D. (2000) 'Hydrocarbon emissions from boat engines: evidence of recreational boating impact on Loch Lomond', *Scottish Geographical Journal*, 116: 245–56.

Bao, J. (2002) 'Tourism geography as the subject of doctoral dissertations in China 1989–2000', *Tourism Geographies*, 4: 148–52.

— (2009) 'From idealism to realism to rational idealism: reflection on 30 years of development in tourism geography in China', *Acta Geographica Sinica*, 64: 1184–92.

Bao, J. and Ma, L.J.C. (2010) 'Tourism geography in China, 1978–2008: whence, what and whither?', *Progress in Human Geography*, 35: 3–20.

Barbaza, Y. (1966) *Le Paysage humain de la Costa Brava*, Paris: A. Colin.

Barber, A. (1991) *Guide to Management Plans for Parks and Open Spaces*, Reading: Institute of Leisure and Amenity Management.

Barbier, B. and Pearce, D.G. (1984) 'The geography of tourism in France: definition, scope and themes', *GeoJournal*, 9(1): 47–53.

Bardwell, S. (1974) 'The National Park movement in Victoria', unpublished PhD thesis, Melbourne: Department of Geography, Monash University.

— (1979) 'National parks for all – a New South Wales interlude', *Parkwatch*, 118: 16–20.

— (1982) '100 years of national parks in Victoria: themes and trends', *Parkwatch*, 129 (winter): 4–11.

Baretje, R. (1982) 'Tourism's external account and the balance of payments', *Annals of Tourism Research*, 9: 57–67.

Barke, M. and Towner, J. (1996) 'Exploring the history of leisure and tourism in Spain', in M. Barke, J. Towner and M. Newton (eds) *Tourism in Spain: Critical Issues*, Wallingford: CAB International.

— (2003) 'Learning from experience? Progress towards a sustainable future for tourism in the Central and Eastern Andalucian littoral', *Journal of Sustainable Tourism*, 11(2/3): 162–80.

Barke, M., Towner, J. and Newton, M. (eds) (1996) *Tourism in Spain: Critical Issues*, Wallingford: CAB International.

Barnes, B. (1982) *T.S. Kuhn and Social Science*, London: Macmillan.

Barnes, M. and Wells, G. (1985) 'Myles Dunphy father of conservation dies', *National Parks Journal*, 29(1): 7.

Barnes, T.J. (2009) '"Not only . . . but also": quantitative and critical geography', *Professional Geographer*, 61: 292–300.

— (2010) 'Roepke Lecture in economic geography: notes from the underground: why the history of economic geography matters: the case of central place theory', *Economic Geography*, 88: 1–26.

Barnett, C. (1998) 'The cultural turn: fashion or progress in human geography?', *Antipode*, 30: 379–94.

Barnett, J. and Adger, W.N. (2003) 'Climate dangers and atoll countries', *Climatic Change*, 61: 321–37.

Baron-Yellés, N. (1999) *Le Tourisme en France: territoires et stratégies*, Paris: A. Colin.

Barr, S., Gilg, A. and Shaw, G. (2011) '"Helping people make better choices": exploring the behaviour change agenda for environmental sustainability', *Applied Geography*, 31: 712–20.

Barratt, P. (2011) 'Vertical worlds: technology, hybridity and the climbing body', *Social & Cultural Geography*, 12: 397–412.

Barrett, J. (1958) 'The seaside resort towns of England and Wales', unpublished PhD thesis, London: University of London.

Barrett, S. and Fudge, C. (1981) *Policy and Action*, London: Methuen.

Bastakis, C., Buhalis, D. and Butler, R. (2004) 'The perception of small and medium sized tourism accommodation providers on the impacts of the tour operators' power in Eastern Mediterranean', *Tourism Management*, 25: 151–70.

Bathelt, H. and Spigel, B. (2012) 'The spatial economy of North American trade fairs', *Canadian Geographer*, 56(1): 18–38.

Baudrillard, J. (1981) *For a Critique of the Economy of the Sign*, St Louis, MO: Telos Press.

Baxter M.J. (1979) 'The interpretation of the distance and attractiveness components in models of recreational trips', *Geographical Analysis*, 11: 311–15.

Bayliss, D. (2003) 'Building better communities: social life on London's cottage council estates, 1919–1939', *Journal of Historical Geography*, 29: 376–95.

Beaumont, N. (1997) 'Perceived crowding as an evaluative standard for determining social carrying capacity in tourist recreation areas: the case of Green Island, North Queensland', in C.M. Hall, J. Jenkins and G. Kearsley (eds) *Tourism Planning and Policy in Australia and New Zealand: Cases, Issues and Practice*, Sydney: Irwin Publishers.

Beaumont, N. and Dredge, D. (2010) 'Local tourism governance: a comparison of three network approaches', *Journal of Sustainable Tourism*, 18: 7–28.

Becker, R.H. (1981) 'Displacement of recreational users between the Lower St. Croix and Upper Mississippi Rivers', *Journal of Environmental Management*, 13: 259–67.

Beebeejaun, Y. (2009) 'Making safer places: gender and the right to the city', *Security Journal*, 22(3): 219–29.

Beeton, S. (2005) 'The case study in tourism research: a multi-method case study approach', in B. Ritchie, P. Burns and C. Palmer (eds) *Tourism Research Methods: Integrating Theory with Practice*, Wallingford: CAB International.

Belford, S. (1983) 'Rural tourism', *Architects Journal*, 178: 59–71.

Bell, M. (1977) 'The spatial distribution of second homes: a modified gravity model', *Journal of Leisure Research*, 9: 225–32.

Bell, M. and Ward, G. (2000) 'Comparing temporary mobility with permanent migration', *Tourism Geographies*, 2: 87–107.

Bell, P.J.P. (2000) 'Contesting rural recreation: the battle over access to Windermere', *Land Use Policy*, 17(4): 295–303.

Bella, L. (1987) *Parks for Profit*, Montreal: Harvest House.

Benington, J. and White, J. (eds) (1988) *The Future of Leisure Services*, Harlow: Longman.

Benko, G. and Strohmmayer, U. (1997) *Space and Social Theory: Interpreting Modernity and Postmodernity*, Oxford: Blackwell.

Bennett, A. (2002) *Great Western Lines and Landscapes*, Cheltenham: Runpast Publishing.

Bennett, R. (1985) 'Quantification and relevance?', in R. Johnston (ed.) *The Future of Geography*, London: Methuen.

— (1991) 'Rethinking London government', in K. Hoggart and D. Green (eds) *London: A New Metropolitan Geography*, London: Edward Arnold.

Bensemann, J. and Hall, C.M. (2010) 'Copreneurship in rural tourism: exploring women's experiences', *International Journal of Gender and Entrepreneurship*, 2: 228–44.

Bentley, T. and Page, S.J. (2001) 'Scoping the extent of tourist accidents in New Zealand', *Annals of Tourism Research*, 28: 705–26.

Bentley, T., Page, S.J. and Laird, I. (2000) 'Safety in New Zealand's adventure tourism industry: The client accident experience of adventure tourism operators', *Journal of Travel Medicine*, 7(5): 239–45.

Bentley, T., Page, S.J., Meyer, D. and Chalmers, D. (2001) 'The role of adventure tourism recreation injuries among visitors to New Zealand: an exploratory analysis using hospital discharge data', *Tourism Management*, 22: 373–81.

Bevins, M., Brown, T., Cole, G., Hock, K. and LaPage, W. (1974) *Analysis of the Campground Market in the Northeast*, USDA, Forest Service Bulletin 679, Burlington, VT: University of Vermont Agricultural Experimental Station.

Bianchi, R. (2002) 'Towards a new political economy of global tourism', in R. Sharpley and D.J. Telfer (eds) *Tourism and Development: Concepts and Issues*, Clevedon: Channel View.

— (2009) 'The "critical turn" in tourism studies: a radical critique', *Tourism Geographies*, 11: 484–504.

Biggs, D., Ban, N. and Hall, C.M. (2012a) 'Lifestyle values, resilience, and nature-based tourism's contribution to conservation on Australia's Great Barrier Reef', *Environmental Conservation*, 39: 370–9.

Biggs, D., Hall, C.M. and Stoeckl, N. (2012b) 'The resilience of formal and informal tourism enterprises to disasters – reef tourism in Phuket', *Journal of Sustainable Tourism*, 20: 645–65.

Billinge, M. (1996) 'A time and place for everything: an essay on recreation, re-creation and the Victorians', *Journal of Historical Geography*, 22: 443–59.

Birdir, S., Ünal, Ö., Birdir, K. and Williams, A.T. (2013) 'Willingness to pay as an economic instrument for coastal tourism management: cases from Mersin, Turkey', *Tourism Management*, 36: 279–83.

Bisset, N., Grant, A. and Adams, C. (2000) 'Long term changes in recreational craft utilisation on Loch Lomond', *Scottish Geographical Journal*, 116: 257–66.

Bitner, M.J., Booms, B.H. and Tetreault, M.S. (1990) 'The service encounter: diagnosing favourable and unfavourable incidents', *Journal of Marketing*, 54(2): 71–84.

Bittman, M. (2002) 'Social participation and family welfare: the money and time costs of leisure in Australia', *Social Policy and Administration*, 36(4): 408–25.

Blackwell, J. (1970) 'Tourist traffic and the demand for accommodation: some projections', *Economic and Social Review*, 1: 323–43.

Blake, A. (2008) 'Tourism and income distribution in East Africa', *International Journal of Tourism Research*, 10: 511–24.

Blake, A. and Sinclair, M.T. (2003) 'Quantifying the effects of foot and mouth disease on tourism and UK economy', *Tourism Economics*, 9: 449–65.

Blake, A., Arbache, J.S., Sinclair, M.T. and Teles, V. (2008) 'Tourism and poverty relief', *Annals of Tourism Research*, 35: 107–26.

Blake, J. (1996) 'Resolving conflict? The rural white paper, sustainability and countryside policy', *Local Environment*, 1: 211–18.

Blamey, R.K. (1995) *The Nature of Ecotourism*, Occasional Paper No. 21, Canberra: Bureau of Tourism Research.

Blangy, S., Donohoe, H.M. and Mitchell, S. (2012) 'Developing a geocollaboratory for Indigenous tourism research', *Current Issues in Tourism*, 15: 693–706.

Blank, U. and Petkovich, M. (1980) 'The metropolitan area: a multifaceted travel destination complex', in D. Hawkins, E. Shafer and J. Ravelstad (eds) *Tourism Planning and Development*, Washington, DC: George Washington University Press.

Blichfeldt, B.S. and Halkier, H. (2013) 'Mussels, tourism and community development: a case study of place branding through food festivals in rural North Jutland, Denmark', *European Planning Studies*, DOI: 10.1080/09654313.2013.784594.

Blitz, D. (1992) *Emergent Evolution: Qualitative Novelty and the Levels of Reality*, Boston: Kluwer.

Blom, T. (2000) 'Morbid tourism – a postmodern market niche with an example from Althrop', *Norsk Geografisk Tidsskrift*, 54(1): 29–36.

Blowers, A. (1997) 'Environmental planning for sustainable development: the international context', in A. Blowers and B. Evans (eds) *Town Planning into the 21st Century*, London: Routledge.

Board, C., Brunsden, D., Gerrard, J., Morgan, B.S., Morley, C.D. and Thornes, J.B. (1978) 'Leisure and the countryside: the example of the Dartmoor National Park', in J. Blunden, P. Haggett, C. Hamnett and P. Sarre (eds) *Fundamentals of Human Geography: A Reader*, London: Harper & Row.

Boehm, A.B. and Soller, J.A. (2013) 'Recreational water risk: pathogens and fecal indicators', in E.A. Laws (ed.) *Environmental Toxicology*, New York: Springer.

Boller, F., Hunziker, M., Conedera, M., Elsasser, H. and Krebs, P. (2010) 'Fascinating remoteness: the dilemma of hiking tourism development in peripheral mountain areas: results of a case study in southern Switzerland', *Mountain Research and Development*, 30: 320–31.

Bone, C. and Dragićević, S. (2009) 'Evaluating spatio-temporal complexities of forest management: an integrated agent-based modeling and GIS approach', *Environmental Modeling and Assessment*, 14(4): 481–96.

Boo, E. (1990) *Ecotourism: The Potentials and Pitfalls*, 2 vols, Washington, DC: World Wildlife Fund.

Booth, D. (2001) *Australian Beach Cultures: The History of Sun, Sand and Surf*, London: Frank Cass.

Borsay, P. (2006) *A History of Leisure: The British Experience since 1500*, Basingstoke: Palgrave.

— (2012) 'Town or country? British spas and the urban–rural interface', *Journal of Tourism History*, 4: 155–69.

Bote Gomez, V. (1996) 'La investigacion turistica española en economia y geografia', *Estudios Turisticos*, special issue.

Bounds, M. and Morris, A. (2006) 'Second wave gentrification in inner-city Sydney', *Cities*, 23: 99–108.

Bouquet, M. (1987) 'Bed, breakfast and an evening meal: commensality in the nineteenth and twentieth century farm household in Hartland', in M. Bouquet and M. Winter (eds) *Who from Their Labours Rests? Conflict and Practice in Rural Tourism*, Aldershot: Avebury.

Bouquet, M. and Winter, M. (eds) (1987a) *Who from Their Labours Rests? Conflict and Practice in Rural Tourism*, Aldershot: Avebury.

— (1987b) 'Introduction: tourism, politics and practice', in M. Bouquet and M. Winter (eds) *Who from Their Labours Rests? Conflict and Practice in Rural Tourism*, Aldershot: Avebury.

Bowen, C., Fidgeon, P. and Page, S.J. (2012) 'Maritime tourism and terrorism: customer perceptions of the potential terrorist threat to cruise shipping', *Current Issues in Tourism*, DOI: 10.1080/13683500.2012.743973.

Bowler, I. and Strachan, A. (1976) *Parks and Gardens in Leicester*, Leicester: Recreation and Cultural Services Department, Leicester City Council.

Boyden, S.V. and Harris, J.A. (1978) 'Contribution of the wilderness to health and wellbeing', in G. Mosley (ed.) *Australia's Wilderness: Conservation Progress and Plans, Proceedings of the First National Wilderness Conference*, Australian Academy of Science, Canberra, 21–23 October 1977, Hawthorn, Vic.: Australian Conservation Foundation.

Boyer, M. (1996) *L'Invention du tourisme*, Paris: Le Seuil.

Bracey, H. (1970) *People and the Countryside*, London: Routledge & Kegan Paul.

Bradshaw, J. (1972) 'The concept of social need', *New Society*, 30(3): 640–3.

Bramham, P. and Henry, I. (1985) 'Political ideology and leisure policy in the United Kingdom', *Leisure Studies*, 4: 1–19.

Bramwell, B. (1991) 'Sustainability and rural tourism policy in Britain', *Tourism Recreation Research*, 16(2): 49–51.

— (1993) *Tourism Strategies and Rural Development*, Paris: OECD.

— (1994) 'Rural tourism and sustainable rural tourism', *Journal of Sustainable Tourism*, 2: 1–6.

— (2004) 'Partnerships, participation, and social science research in tourism planning', in A. Lew, C.M. Hall and A. Williams (eds) *A Companion to Tourism*, Oxford: Blackwell.

— (2005) 'Interventions and policy instruments for sustainable tourism', in W. Theobold (ed.) *Global Tourism*, 3rd edn, Oxford: Elsevier.

— (2011) 'Governance, the state and sustainable tourism: A political economy approach', *Journal of Sustainable Tourism*, 19: 459–77.

Bramwell, B. and Lane, B. (1993) 'Sustainable tourism: an evolving global approach', *Journal of Sustainable Tourism*, 1(1): 6–16.

— (eds) (2000) *Tourism Collaboration and Partnerships: Politics, Practice and Sustainability*, Clevedon: Channel View.

Bramwell, B. and Meyer, D. (2007) 'Power and tourism policy relations in transition', *Annals of Tourism Research*, 34: 766–88.

Bramwell, B. and Rawding, L. (1996) 'Tourism marketing images of industrial cities', *Annals of Tourism Research*, 23(2): 201–21.

Braun, B. and Soskin, M. (2002) 'The impact of day trips to Daytona Beach', *Tourism Economics*, 8: 289–301.

Briassoulis, H. and van der Straaten, J. (1999) 'Tourism and the environment: an overview', in H. Briassoulis and J. van der Straaten (eds) *Tourism and the Environment*, 2nd edn, Dordrecht: Kluwer Academic.

Briggs, A. (1969) *Victorian Cities*, Middlesex: Pelham.

Bristow, G. (2005) 'Everyone's a "winner": problematising the discourse of regional competitiveness', *Journal of Economic Geography*, 5: 285–304.

— (2010) *Critical Reflections on Regional Competitiveness: Theory, Policy, Practice*, Abingdon: Taylor & Francis.

Bristow, R., Leiber, S. and Fesenmaier, D. (1995) 'The compatibility of recreation activities in Illinois', *Geografiska Annaler B*, 77(1): 3–15.

British Travel Association and University of Keele (1967 and 1969) *Pilot National Recreation Survey*, Keele: University of Keele.

Britton, S.G. (1980a) 'A conceptual model of tourism in a peripheral economy', in *South Pacific: The Contribution of Research to Development and Planning*, NZ MAB Report No. 6, Christchurch: NZ National Commission for UNESCO/Department of Geography.

— (1980b) 'The spatial organisation of tourism in a neo-colonial economy: a Fiji case study', *Pacific Viewpoint*, 21: 144–65.

— (1982) 'The political economy of tourism in the Third World', *Annals of Tourism Research*, 9: 331–58.

— (1983) 'Book review: Pearce, D.G. 1981: Tourist development. Topics in applied geography', *Progress in Human Geography*, 7, 618–21.

— (1991) 'Tourism, capital and place: towards a critical geography of tourism', *Environment and Planning D: Society and Space*, 9: 451–78.

Brocx, M. (1994) *Visitor Perceptions and Satisfaction Study Winter 1993*, Auckland: Tourism Auckland.

Bromley, R.D. and Stacey, R.J. (2012) 'Feeling unsafe in urban areas: exploring older children's geographies of fear', *Environment and Planning A*, 44: 428–44.

Brooks, S. (1993) *Public Policy in Canada*, Toronto: McClelland and Stewart.

Brouder, P. and Eriksson, R.H. (2013) 'Tourism evolution: on the synergies of tourism studies and evolutionary economic geography', *Annals of Tourism Research*, DOI: 10.1016/j.annals.2013.07.001.

Brougham, J.E. and Butler, R.W. (1981) 'A segmentation analysis of resident attitudes to the social impacts of tourism', *Annals of Tourism Research*, 8: 569–90.

Brown, B. (1988) 'Developments in the promotion of major seaside resorts: how to effect a transition by really making an effort', in B. Goodall and G. Ashworth (eds) *Marketing in the Tourism Industry*, London: Routledge.

Brown, C., McMorran, R. and Price, M.F. (2011) 'Rewilding – a new paradigm for nature conservation in Scotland?', *Scottish Geographical Journal*, 127(4): 288–314.

Brown, G. (2006) 'Mapping landscape values and development preferences: a method for tourism and residential development planning', *International Journal of Tourism Research*, 8: 101–13.

Brown, R.M. (1935) 'The business of recreation', *Geographical Review*, 25: 467–75.

Bruwer, J. and Johnson, R. (2010) 'Place-based marketing and regional branding strategy perspectives in the California wine industry', *Journal of Consumer Marketing*, 27: 5–16.

Bryant, C. (1989) 'Entrepreneurs in the rural environment', *Journal of Rural Studies*, 5: 337–48.

Buchholtz, C.W. (1983) *Rocky Mountain National Park: A History*, Boulder, CO: Colorado Associated University Press.

Buckley, R. (2004) 'The effects of World Heritage listing on tourism to Australian national parks', *Journal of Sustainable Tourism*, 12: 70–84.

Budeanu, A. (2007) 'Sustainable tourist behaviour – a discussion of opportunities for change', *International Journal of Consumer Studies*, 31: 499–508.

Buhalis, D. and Cooper, C. (1998) 'Competition or Co-operation? small and medium sized tourism enterprises at the destination', in E. Laws, B. Faulkner and G. Moscardo (eds) Embracing and Managing Change in Tourism: International Case Studies, London: Routledge.

Buijs, A.E., Elands, B.H. and Langers, F. (2009) 'No wilderness for immigrants: cultural differences in images of nature and landscape preferences', *Landscape and Urban Planning*, 91(3): 113–23.

Bujosa, A. and Rosselló, J. (2013) 'Climate change and summer mass tourism: the case of Spanish domestic tourism', *Climatic Change*, 117(1–2): 363–75.

Bull, A. (1991) *The Economics of Travel and Tourism*, London: Pitman.

Bull, P. and Church, A. (1994) 'The hotel and catering industry of Great Britain during the 1980s: sub-regional employment change, specialisation and dominance', in C.P. Cooper and A. Lockwood (eds) *Progress in Tourism, Recreation and Hospitality Management*, vol. 5, Chichester: Wiley.

Buller, H. and Hoggart, K. (1994) *International Counterurbanization: British Migrants in Rural France*, Aldershot: Avebury.

Bunce, R.G.H., Pérez Soba, M., Jongman, R.H.G., Gómez Sal, A., Herzog, F. and Austad, I. (eds) (2004) *Transhumance and Biodiversity in European Mountains*, IALE Publication No. 1.

Burdett, R. and Sudjic, D. (eds) (2011) *The Endless City*, London: Phaidon.

Bureau of Land Management (1978) *Wilderness Inventory Handbook: Policy, Direction, Procedures, and Evidence for Conducting Wilderness Inventory on the Public Lands*, Washington, DC: US Department of the Interior, Bureau of Land Management.

Burgess, J., Harrison, C. and Limb, M. (1988a) 'People, parks and the urban green: a study of popular meanings and values for open spaces in the city', *Urban Studies*, 26: 455–73.

— (1988b) 'Exploring environmental values through the medium of small groups. Part one: Theory and practice', *Environmental and Planning A*, 20: 309–26.

— (1988c) 'Exploring environmental values through the medium of small groups. Part two: Illustrations of a group at work', *Environment and Planning A*, 20: 457–76.

Burkart, A. and Medlik, S. (1974) *Tourism, Past, Present and Future*, Oxford: Heinemann.

— (1981) *Tourism, Past Present and Future*, 2nd edn, London: Heinemann.

Burnet, L. (1963) *Villégiature et tourisme sue les côtes de France*, Paris: Hachette.

Burnley, I. and Murphy, P. (2004) *Sea Change: Movement from Metropolitan to Arcadian Australia*, Sydney: University of New South Wales.

Burns, J.P.A. and Mules, T.L. (1986) 'A framework for the analysis of major special events', in J.P.A. Burns, J.H. Hatch and T.L. Mules (eds) *The Adelaide Grand Prix: The Impact of a Special Event*, Adelaide: Centre for South Australian Economic Studies.

Burns, M., Barwell, L. and Heinecken, T. (1990) 'Analysis of critical coastal processes affecting recreation and tourism development opportunities along South-Western Cape coastline', in P. Wong (ed.) *Tourism vs Environment: The Case for Coastal Areas*, Dordrecht: Kluwer.

Burtenshaw, D., Bateman, M. and Ashworth, G.J. (1991) *The City in West Europe*, 2nd edn, Chichester: Wiley.

Burton, R. (1974) *The Recreational Carrying Capacity of the Countryside*, Occasional Publication No. 11, Keele: Keele University Library.

Burton, T. (1966) 'A day in the country – a survey of leisure activity at Box Hill in Surrey', *Chartered Surveyor*, 98(7): 378–80.

— (1971) *Experiments in Recreation Research*, London: Allen & Unwin.

— (1982) 'A framework for leisure policy research', *Leisure Studies*, 1: 323–35.

Butler, R.W. (1974) 'The social implications of tourist developments', *Annals of Tourism Research*, 2: 100–11.

— (1975) 'Tourism as an agent of social change', in F. Helleiner (ed.) *Tourism as a Factor in National and Regional Development*, Occasional Papers in Geography No. 4, Peterborough: Trent University.

— (1980) 'The concept of a tourist area cycle of evolution: implications for management of resources', *Canadian Geographer*, 24(1): 5–12.

— (1990) 'Alternative tourism: pious hope or Trojan horse', *Journal of Travel Research*, 28(3): 40–5.

— (1991) 'Tourism, environment, and sustainable development', *Environmental Conservation*, 18(3): 201–9.

— (1992) 'Alternative tourism: the thin edge of the wedge', in V.L. Smith and W.R. Eadington (eds) *Tourism Alternatives: Potentials and Problems in the Development of Tourism*, Philadelphia: University of Pennsylvania Press.

— (1998) 'Sustainable tourism – looking backwards in order to progress?', in C.M. Hall and A. Lew (eds) *Sustainable Tourism Development: A Geographical Perspective*, London: Addison Wesley Longman.

— (2000) 'Tourism and the environment: a geographical perspective', *Tourism Geographies*, 2: 337–58.

— (2004) 'Geographical research on tourism, recreation and leisure: origins, eras and directions', *Tourism Geographies*, 6: 143–62.

— (ed.) (2006) *The Tourism Life Cycle: Conceptual and Theoretical Issues*, 2 vols, Clevedon: Channel View.

Butler, R.W. and Clark, G. (1992) 'Tourism in rural areas: Canada and the UK', in I. Bowler, C. Bryant and M. Nellis (eds) *Contemporary Rural Systems in Transition*, vol. 2: *Economy and Society*, Wallingford: CAB International.

Butler, R.W. and Hall, C.M. (1998) 'Conclusion: the sustainability of tourism and recreation in rural areas', in R. Butler, C.M. Hall and J. Jenkins (eds) *Tourism and Recreation in Rural Areas*, Chichester: Wiley.

Butler, R.W. and Hinch, T. (eds) (1996) *Tourism and Indigenous Peoples*, London: International Thomson Publishing.

— (eds) (2007) *Tourism and Indigenous Peoples*, 2nd edn, Oxford: Elsevier.

Butler, R.W. and Wall, G. (1985) 'Themes in research on the evolution of tourism', *Annals of Tourism Research*, 12: 287–96.

Butler, R.W., Hall, C.M. and Jenkins, J. (eds) (1998) *Tourism and Recreation in Rural Areas*, Chichester: Wiley.

Button, M. (2003) 'Private security and the policing of quasi-public space', *International Journal of the Sociology of Law*, 31: 227–37.

Byrne, A., Edmondson, R. and Fahy, K. (1993) 'Rural tourism and cultural identity in the West of Ireland', in B. O'Connor and M. Cronin (eds) *Tourism in Ireland: A Critical Analysis*, Cork: Cork University Press.

Byrne, D. (1999) *Social Exclusion*, Buckingham: Open University Press.

Byrne, J. (2012) 'When green is White: The cultural politics of race, nature and social exclusion in a Los Angeles urban national park', *Geoforum*, 43: 595–611.

Byrne, J. and Wolch, J. (2009) 'Nature, race, and parks: past research and future directions for geographic research', *Progress in Human Geography*, 33: 743–65.

Cadieux, K.V. (2005) 'Engagement with the land: redemption of the rural residence fantasy?', in S. Essex, A. Gilg and R. Yarwood (eds) *Rural Change and Sustainability: Agriculture, the Environment and Communities*, Wallingford: CAB International.

Caffyn, A. and Jobbins, G. (2003) 'Governance capacity and stakeholder interactions in the development and management of coastal tourism: examples from Morocco and Tunisia', *Journal of Sustainable Tourism*, 11: 224–45.

Caffyn, A. and Lutz, J. (1999) 'Developing the heritage tourism product in multi-ethnic cities', *Tourism Management*, 20: 213–21.

Calais, S.S. and Kirkpatrick, J.B. (1986) 'The impact of trampling on the natural ecosystems of the Cradle Mt. Lake St. Claire National Park', *Australian Geographer*, 17: 6–15.

Çalıskan, K. and Callon, M. (2009) 'Economization, part 1: Shifting attention from the economy towards processes of economization', *Economy and Society*, 38: 369–98.

Callicott, J.B. (1982) 'Traditional American Indian and Western European attitudes toward nature: an overview', *Environmental Ethics*, 4: 293–318.

Cameron, A. (2006) Geographies of welfare and exclusion: social inclusion and exception. *Progress in Human Geography*, 30(3), 396–404.

Campbell, C.K. (1966) *An Approach to Recreational Geography*, B.C. Occasional Papers No. 7.

Canadian Council on Rural Development (1975) *Economic Significance of Tourism and Outdoor Recreation for Rural Development*, Working Paper, Ottawa: Canadian Council on Rural Development.

Canagarajah, A.S. (1996) '"Nondiscursive" requirements in academic publishing, material resources of periphery scholars, and the politics of knowledge production', *Written Communication*, 13: 435–72.

Carhart, A.H. (1920) 'Recreation in the forests', *American Forests*, 26: 268–72.

Carlson, A.S. (1938) 'Recreation industry of New Hampshire', *Economic Geography*, 14: 255–70.

Carlson, A.W. (1978) 'The spatial behaviour involved in honeymoons: the case of two areas in Wisconsin and North Dakota', *Journal of Popular Culture*, 11: 977–88.

Carr, N. (1999) 'A study of gender differences: young tourist behaviour in a UK coastal resort', *Tourism Management*, 20: 223–8.

Carter, R. (1988) *Coastal Environments*, London: Academic Press.

— (1990) 'Recreational use and abuse of the coastline of Florida', in P. Fabbri (ed.) *Recreational Uses of Coastal Areas*, Dordrecht: Kluwer.

Carter, R., Eastwood, D. and Pollard, J. (1990) 'Man's impact on the coast of Ireland', in P. Wong (ed.) *Tourism vs Environment: The Case for Coastal Areas*, Dordrecht: Kluwer.

Carver, S. (2000) 'Wilderness and landscape', Wilderness Britain? Social and Environmental Perspectives on Recreation and Conservation, Newsletter No. 4, *Mapping the Wild: Spatial Patterns and Landscape Character*.

Carver, S., Evans, A. and Fritz, S. (2002) 'Wilderness attribute mapping in the United Kingdom', *International Journal of Wilderness*, 8(1): 24–9.

Carver, S., Comber, A., McMorran, R. and Nutter, S. (2012) 'A GIS model for mapping spatial patterns and distribution of wild land in Scotland', *Landscape and Urban Planning*, 104: 395–409.

Cater, E.A. (1987) 'Tourism in the least developed countries', *Annals of Tourism Research*, 14: 202–26.

— (1993) 'Ecotourism in the third world: problems for sustainable development', *Tourism Management*, 14: 85–90.

— (2000) 'Tourism in the Yunnan Great Rivers National Parks System Project: prospects for sustainability', *Tourism Geographies*, 2: 472–89.

Cater, E.A. and Lowman, G. (eds) (1994) *Ecotourism: A Sustainable Option?*, Chichester: Wiley.

Catlin, G. (1968) 'An artist proposes a National Park', in R. Nash (ed.) *The American Environment: Readings in the History of Conservation*, Reading: Addison-Wesley.

Catto, N. (2002) 'Anthropogenic pressures on coastal dunes, Southwestern Newfoundland', *Canadian Geographer*, 46(1): 17–32.

Ceballos-Lascuarain, H. (1996) *Tourism, Ecotourism and Protected Areas: The State of Nature Based Tourism around the World and Guidelines for Its Development*, Gland: IUCN.

Chadwick, G. (1971) *A Systems View of Planning*, Oxford: Pergamon Press.

Chadwick, R. (1994) 'Concepts, definitions and measures used in travel and tourism research', in J.R. Brent Ritchie and C. Goeldner (eds) *Travel, Tourism and Hospitality Research: A Handbook for Managers and Researchers*, 2nd edn, New York: Wiley.

Champeaux, J.P. (1987) 'Le marché du tourisme social en Europe', *Espaces*, 86: 17–20.

Champion, A.G. (1998) 'Studying counter-urbanisation and the rural population turnaround', in P. Boyle and K. Halfacree (eds) *Migration Into Rural Areas: Theories and Issues*, Chichester: John Wiley & Sons.

Chang, T.C. (2000) 'Singapore's Little India: a tourist attraction in a contested landscape', *Urban Studies*, 37: 343–66.

Chang, T.C. and Yeoh, B. (1999) 'New Asia-Singapore: communicating local cultures through global tourism', *Geoforum*, 30(2): 101–15.

Chang, T.C., Milne, S., Fallon, D. and Pohlmann, C. (1996) 'Urban heritage tourism: the global–local nexus', *Annals of Tourism Research*, 23: 1–19.

Chape, S., Blyth, S., Fish, L., Fox, P. and Spalding, M. (compilers) (2003) *2003 United Nations List of Protected Areas*, Gland and Cambridge: IUCN and UNEP-WCMC.

Chapin, F. (1974) *Human Activity Patterns in the City*, New York: Wiley.

Chapman, H.H. (1938) 'National parks, national forests and wilderness areas', *Journal of Forestry*, 36(5): 469–74.

Charlton, C. and Essex, S. (1996) 'The involvement of District Councils in tourism in England and Wales', *Geoforum*, 27: 175–92.

Chavas, J.P., Stoll, J. and Sellar, C. (1989) 'On the commodity value of travel time in recreational activities', *Applied Economics*, 21: 711–22.

Chen, R.J.C. (2007) 'Geographic information systems (GIS) applications in retail tourism and teaching curriculum', *Journal of Retailing and Consumer Services*, 14: 289–95.

Chhetri, P. (2006) 'Modelling attractiveness of scenic views: a case study of the Grampians National Park', *Tourism Recreation Research*, 31(3): 101–8.

Chhetri, P. and Arrowsmith, C. (2008) 'GIS-based modelling of recreational potential in nature-based tourist destinations', *Tourism Geographies*, 10: 235–59.

Chhetri, P., Corcoran, J. and Arrowsmith C. (2010) 'Investigating the temporal dynamics of tourist movements: an application of circular statistics', *Tourism Analysis*, 15: 71–88.

Chhetri, P., Corcoran, R. and Hall, C.M. (2008) 'Modelling the patterns and drivers of tourism related employment for South East Queensland, Australia – a spatial econometric approach', *Tourism Recreation Research*, 33(2): 25–38.

Choi, H.C. and Sirakaya, E. (2006) 'Sustainability indicators for managing community tourism', *Tourism Management*, 27: 1274–89.

Chok, S., Macbeth, J. and Warren, C. (2007) 'Tourism as a tool for poverty alleviation: a critical analysis of "pro-poor tourism" and implications for sustainability', *Current Issues in Tourism* 10: 144–65.

Christaller, W. (1933) *Die zentralen Orte in Süddeutschland*, Jena: Gustav Fischer.

—— (1963) 'Some considerations of tourism location in Europe: the peripheral regions – underdeveloped countries – recreation areas', *Regional Science Association Papers*, 12: 95–105.

Chubb, M. and Chubb, H. (1981) *One Third of Our Time? An Introduction to Recreation Behaviour and Resources*, New York: Wiley.

Church, A. (1988) 'Urban regeneration in London's Docklands: a five year policy review', *Environment and Planning C: Government and Policy*, 6: 187–208.

—— (1990) 'Transport and urban regeneration in London Docklands', *Cities: The International Journal of Urban Policy and Planning*, 7(4): 289–303.

—— (2004) 'Local and regional tourism policy and power', in A. Lew, C.M. Hall and A. Williams (eds) *A Companion to Tourism*, Oxford: Blackwell.

Church, A. and Coles, T.E. (eds) (2007) *Tourism, Power and Space*, London: Routledge.

Church, A. and Reid, P. (2000) 'Urban power, international networks, and competition: the example of cross-border co-operation', *Urban Studies*, 33: 1297–318.

Church, A., Ball, R., Bull, C. and Tyler, D. (2000) 'Public policy engagement with British tourism: the national, local and the European Union', *Tourism Geographies*, 2: 312–36.

Cichetti, C. (1971) 'Some economic issues in planning urban recreation facilities', *Land Economics*, 47: 14–23.

Cicin-Sain, B. and Knecht, R.W. (1998) *Integrated Coastal and Ocean Management: Concepts and Experiences*, Washington, DC: Island Press.

Clark, G., Gertler, M. and Feldman, M. (eds) (2000) *Handbook of Economic Geography*, Oxford: Oxford University Press.

Clark, J. and Crichter, C. (1985) *The Devil Makes Work: Leisure in Capitalist Britain*, Basingstoke: Macmillan.

Clark, P. (ed.) (1981) *Country Towns in Pre-industrial England*, Leicester: Leicester University Press.

Clark, R.N. and Stankey, G.H. (1979) *The Recreation Opportunity Spectrum: A Framework for Planning, Management and Research*, USDA Forest Service, General Technical Report PNW-98.

Clarke, P. (ed.) (1981) *Country Towns in Pre-industrial England*, Leicester: Leicester University Press.

Clarke, W.C. (1991) 'Time and tourism: an ecological perspective', in M.L. Miller and J. Auyong (eds) *Proceedings of the 1990 Congress on Coastal and Marine Tourism*, Honolulu: National Coastal Research and Development Institute.

Clary, D. (1984a) 'Coastal tourism: research methods', *Revue de géographie de Lyon*, 59(1/2): 63–72.

—— (1984b) 'The impact of social change on a leisure region, 1960–1982: A study of Nord Pays d'Auge', in J. Long and R. Hecock (eds) *Leisure, Tourism and Social Change*, Dunfermline: Centre for Leisure Research, Dunfermline College of Physical Education.

—— (1993) *Le Tourisme dans l'espace français*, Paris: Editions du CRNS.

Clawson, M. (1958) *Statistics on Outdoor Recreation*, Washington, DC: Resources for the Future.

Clawson, M. and Knetsch, J. (1966) *The Economics of Outdoor Recreation*, Baltimore, MD: Johns Hopkins University Press.

— (1968) *The Economics of Outdoor Recreation*, Baltimore, MD: Johns Hopkins University Press.

Clawson, M., Held, R. and Stoddart, C. (1960) *Land for the Future*, Baltimore, MD: Johns Hopkins University Press.

Cleveland, T., Jr. (1910) 'National forests as recreation grounds', *Annals, American Academy of Political and Social Science*, 35 (March): 25–31.

Clewer, A., Pack, A. and Sinclair, M.T. (1992) 'Price competitiveness and inclusive tour holidays', in P. Johnson and B. Thomas (eds) *Choice and Demand in Tourism*, London: Mansell.

Clift, S. and Page, S.J. (eds) (1996) *Health and the International Tourist*, London: Routledge.

Cloke, P. (1992) 'The countryside', in P. Cloke (ed.) *Policy and Change in Thatcher's Britain*, Oxford: Pergamon Press.

Cloke, P.J. and Johnston, R. (eds) (2005a) *Spaces of Geographical Thought: Deconstructing Human Geography's Binaries*, London: Sage.

— (2005b) 'Deconstructing human geography's binaries', in P.J. Cloke and R. Johnston (eds) *Spaces of Geographical Thought: Deconstructing Human Geography's Binaries*, London: Sage.

Cloke, P. and Perkins, H. (1999) 'Cracking the canyon with the awesome foursome: representation of adventure tourism in New Zealand', *Environment and Planning D: Society and Space*, 16: 185–218.

Clout, H.D. (1972) *Rural Geography: An Introductory Survey*, Oxford: Pergamon Press.

— (1987) 'Western Europe in context', in H.D. Clout (ed.) *Regional Development in Western Europe*, 3rd edn, London: David Fulton.

Coalter, F. (1993) 'Sports participation: price or priorities?', *Leisure Studies*, 12: 171–82.

— (1998) 'Leisure studies, leisure policy and social citizenship: the failure of welfare or the limits of welfare?', *Leisure Studies*, 17: 21–36.

Coccossis, H. (2004) *Tourism and Carrying Capacity*, London: Continuum.

Cockerell, N. (1997) 'Urban tourism in Europe', *Travel and Tourism Analyst*, 6: 44–67.

Coëffé, V. (2007) 'Mondialisations et mondes touristiques', *L'Information géographique*, 71(2): 83–96.

Cohen, E. (1972) 'Towards a sociology of international tourism', *Social Research*, 39: 164–82.

— (1974) 'Who is a tourist? A conceptual clarification', *Sociological Review*, 22: 527–55.

— (1979a) 'Rethinking the sociology of tourism', *Annals of Tourism Research*, 6: 18–35.

— (1979b) 'A phenomenology of tourist experiences', *Sociology*, 13: 179–201.

— (1983) 'Thai girls and farang men', *Annals of Tourism Research*, 9: 403–8.

— (1993) 'The study of touristic images of native people: mitigating the stereotype of a stereotype', in D.G. Pearce and R.W. Butler (eds) *Tourism Research: Critiques and Challenges*, London: Routledge.

Cole, D.N., Petersen, M.E. and Lucas, R.C. (1987) *Managing Wilderness Recreation Use: Common Problems and Potential Solutions*, USDA Forest Service General Technical Report INT–230, Utah: Intermountain Forest and Range Experiment Station.

Coleman, S. and Crang, M. (eds) (2002) *Tourism: Between Place and Performance*, Oxford: Berghahn.

Coles, T.E. (2003) 'A local reading of a global disaster: some lessons on tourism management from an annus horribilis in Southwest England', *Journal of Travel and Tourism Marketing*, 15: 143–62.

Coles, T.E. and Hall, C.M. (2006) 'Editorial: The geography of tourism is dead. Long live geographies of tourism and mobility', *Current Issues in Tourism*, 9: 289–92.

— (ed.) (2008) *Tourism and International Business*, London: Routledge.

— (2011) 'Rights and regulation of travel and tourism mobility', *Journal of Policy Research in Tourism, Leisure and Events*, 3(3): 209–23.

Coles, T.E. and Timothy, D.J. (eds) (2004) *Tourism, Diasporas and Space*, London: Routledge.

Coles, T.E., Duval, D. and Hall, C.M. (2004) 'Tourism, mobility and global communities: new approaches to theorising tourism and tourist spaces', in

W. Theobold (ed.) *Global Tourism*, 3rd edn, Oxford: Heinemann.

Coles, T., Hall, C.M. and Duval, D.T. (2006) 'Tourism and post-disciplinary enquiry', *Current Issues in Tourism*, 9: 293–319.

Coles, T.E., Liasidou, S. and Shaw, G. (2008) 'Tourism and new economic geography: issues and challenges in moving from advocacy to adoption', *Journal of Travel & Tourism Marketing*, 25: 312–24.

Colley, A. (1984) 'The Greater Blue Mountains National Park', *National Parks Journal*, 28(4): 29–31.

Collins, J.H. (2008) 'Marine tourism in the Kimberley region of Western Australia', *Geographical Research*, 46: 111–23.

Colwell, P., Dehring, C. and Turnbull, G. (2002) 'Recreation demand and residential location', *Journal of Urban Economics*, 51: 418–28.

Comber, A., Carver, S., Fritz, S., McMorran, R., Washtell, J. and Fisher, P. (2010) 'Different methods, different wilds: evaluating alternative mappings of wildness using fuzzy MCE and Dempster-Shafer MCE', *Computers, Environment and Urban Systems*, 34: 142–52.

Commission for Rural Communities (CRC) (2010) *State of the Countryside 2010*, London: CRC.

Commission of the European Community (1991) *Fourth Periodic Report on the Social and Economic Situation and Development of the Regions of the Community*, Luxembourg: Commission of the European Community.

Concu, N. and Atzeni, G. (2012) 'Conflicting preferences among tourists and residents', *Tourism Management*, 33: 1293–300.

Conforti, J. (1996) 'Ghettos as tourism attractions', *Annals of Tourism Research*, 23: 830–42.

Connell, Jo (2005) 'Managing gardens for visitors: a story of continuity and change', *Tourism Management*, 26: 185–201.

— (2012) 'Film tourism – evolution, progress and prospects', *Tourism Management*, 33: 1007–29.

Connell, Jo and Page, S.J. (2008) 'Exploring the spatial patterns of car-based tourism in Loch Lomond and Trossachs National Park', *Tourism Management*, 29: 561–80.

Connell, J., Page, S.J. and Bentley, T. (2009) 'Towards sustainable tourism planning in New Zealand: monitoring local government planning under the Resource Management Act', *Tourism Management*, 30(6): 867–77.

Connell, John (1988) *Sovereignty and Survival: Island Microstates in the Third World*, Research Monograph No. 3, Sydney: Department of Geography, University of Sydney.

— (2006) 'Medical tourism: sea, sun, sand and . . . surgery', *Tourism Management*, 27: 1093–100.

— (2011) *Medical Tourism*, Wallingford: CAB International.

— (2013) 'Contemporary medical tourism: conceptualisation, culture and commodification', *Tourism Management*, 34: 1–13.

Conway, H. (1991) *People's Parks: The Design and Development of Victorian Parks in Britain*, Cambridge: Cambridge University Press.

Cooke, K. (1982) 'Guidelines for socially appropriate tourism development in British Columbia', *Journal of Travel Research*, 21(1): 22–8.

Cooke, P. (ed.) (1986) *Global Restructuring, Local Responses*, London: Economic and Social Research Council.

— (1989) *Localities: The Changing Face of Urban Britain*, London: Unwin Hyman.

Coombe, R.J. and Aylwin, N. (2011) 'Bordering diversity and desire: using intellectual property to mark place-based products', *Environment and Planning A*, 43: 2027–42.

Cooper, C.E. (1947) 'Tourism', *Journal of Geography*, 46: 115–20.

Cooper, C.P. (1981) 'Spatial and temporal patterns of tourist behaviour', *Regional Studies*, 15: 359–71.

— (1987) 'The changing administration of tourism in Britain', *Area*, 19: 249–53.

— (1990) 'Resorts in decline: the management response', *Tourism Management*, 11: 63–7.

— (1992) 'The life cycle concept and tourism', in P. Johnson and B. Thomas (eds) *Choice and Demand in Tourism*, London: Mansell.

— (1994) 'Product lifecycle', in S.F. Witt and L. Moutinho (eds) *Tourism Marketing and Management Handbook*, Englewood Cliffs, NJ: Prentice Hall.

— (2006) 'Knowledge management and tourism', *Annals of Tourism Research*, 33: 47–64.

Cooper, C.P. and Hall, C.M. (eds) (2005) *Oceania: A Tourism Handbook*, Clevedon: Channel View.

— (2013) *Contemporary Tourism: An International Approach*, 2nd edn, Oxford: Goodfellow.

Cooper, C.P. and Jackson, S. (1989) 'Destination life cycle: the Isle of Man case study', *Annals of Tourism Research*, 16(3): 377–98.

Cooper, C.P., Fletcher, J., Gilbert, D.G. and Wanhill, S. (1993) *Tourism: Principles and Practice*, London: Pitman.

Cooper, M.J. and Pigram, J.J. (1984) 'Tourism and the Australian economy', *Tourism Management*, 5(1): 2–12.

Cope, A., Doxford, D. and Probert, C. (2000) 'Monitoring visitors to UK countryside resources: the approaches of land and recreation resource management organisations to visitor monitoring', *Land Use Policy*, 17: 59–66.

Coppock, J.T. (1966) 'The recreational use of land and water in rural Britain', *Tidschrift voor Economische en Sociale Geografie*, 57: 81–96.

— (1970) 'Geographers and conservation', *Area*, 2: 24–6.

— (1974) 'Geography and public policy: challenges, opportunities and implications', *Transactions of the Institute of British Geographers*, 63: 1–16.

— (1976) 'Geography and public policy: challenge, opportunities and implications', in J.T. Coppock and W. Sewell (eds) *Spatial Dimensions of Public Policy*, Oxford: Pergamon Press.

— (ed.) (1977a) *Second Homes: Curse or Blessing?*, Oxford: Pergamon Press.

— (1977b) 'Tourism as a tool for regional development', in B.S. Duffield (ed.) *Tourism: A Tool for Regional Development*, Edinburgh: Tourism and Recreation Research Unit, University of Edinburgh.

— (1980) 'The geography of leisure and recreation', in E.H. Brown (ed.) *Geography Yesterday and Tomorrow*, London: Royal Geographical Society.

— (1982) 'Geographical contributions to the study of leisure', *Leisure Studies*, 1: 1–27.

Coppock, J.T. and Duffield, B. (1975) *Outdoor Recreation in the Countryside: A Spatial Analysis*, London: Macmillan.

Coppock, J.T. and Sewell, W. (1976) *Spatial Dimensions of Public Policy*, Oxford: Pergamon Press.

Corbin, A. (1995) *The Lure of the Sea: The Discovery of the Seaside 1750–1840*, London: Penguin.

Cordell, H., Betz, C. and Green, G. (2002) 'Recreation and the environment as cultural dimensions in contemporary American society', *Leisure Sciences*, 24: 13–41.

Cornelissen, S. (2005) *The Global Tourism System: Governance, Development and Lessons from South Africa*, Aldershot: Ashgate.

Cornish, V. (1930) 'The claim of the coast', *Geography*, 15(5): 384–7.

— (1934) 'A national park at the Lands End', *Geography*, 19(4): 288–91.

Cornwall, G.W. and Holcomb, C.J. (eds) (1966) *Guidelines to the Planning, Developing, and Managing of Rural Recreation Enterprises*, Bulletin 301, Blacksburg: Cooperative Extension Service, Virginia Polytechnic Institute.

Corsi, T.M and Harvey, M.E. (1979) 'Changes in vacation travel in response to motor fuel shortages and higher prices', *Journal of Travel Research*, 17(4): 6–11.

Cosgrove, I. and Jackson, R. (1972) *The Geography of Recreation and Leisure*, London: Hutchinson.

Council of Nature Conservation Ministers (CONCOM) Working Group on Management of National Parks (1985) *Identification and Management of Wilderness Areas in Australia*, Discussion Paper, Canberra: CONCOM.

— (1986) *Guidelines for Reservation and Management of Wilderness Areas in Australia*, Canberra: CONCOM.

Countryside Agency (1999) *The State of the Countryside 1999*, Cheltenham: The Countryside Agency.

— (2000) *The State of the Countryside 1999*, Cheltenham: Countryside Agency.

— (2003) *Living Landscapes*, Cheltenham: Countryside Agency,

Countryside Commission (1970) *Countryside Recreation Glossary*, London: Countryside Commission.

— (1974) *Advice Note on Country Parks*, Cheltenham: Countryside Commission.

— (1983) *A Management Plan for the Green Belt Area in Barnet and South Havering*, Cheltenham: Countryside Commission.

— (1988) *Countryside Management in the Urban Fringe*, Cheltenham: Countryside Commission.

— (1992) *Enjoying the Countryside – Policies for People*, Cheltenham: Countryside Commission.

Coventry, N. (1998) 'December dive', *Inside Tourism*, March: 1.

Cowie, I. (1985) 'Housing policy options in relation to the America's Cup', *Urban Policy and Research*, 3: 40–1.

Crandall, R. (1980) 'Motivations for leisure', *Journal of Leisure Research*, 12: 45–54.

Crang, M. (2014) 'Cultural geographies of tourism', in A. Lew, C.M. Hall and A. Williams (eds) *The Wiley-Blackwell Companion to Tourism*, Oxford: Wiley-Blackwell.

Crang, M. and Travelou, S. (2001) 'The city and topology of memory', *Environment and Planning D*, 19(2): 161–77.

Crawford, D. and Godbey, G. (1987) 'Reconceptualising barriers to family leisure', *Leisure Sciences*, 9: 119–27.

Crawford, D., Jackson, E. and Godbey, G. (1991) 'A hierarchical model of leisure constraints', *Leisure Sciences*, 13: 309–20.

Crisler, R.M. and Hunt, M.S. (1952) 'Recreation regions in Missouri', *Journal of Geography*, 51(1): 30–9.

Crompton, J.L. (1979) 'An assessment of the image of Mexico as a vacation destination', *Journal of Travel Research*, 17 (fall): 18–23.

Crompton, J.L. and Richardson, S.L. (1986) 'The tourism connection where public and private leisure services merge', *Parks and Recreation*, October: 38–44, 67.

Crompton, J.L. and Van Doren, C. (1976) 'Amusement parks, theme parks, and municipal leisure services: contrasts in adaptation to cultural change', *Journal of Physical Education and Recreation*, 47: 18–22.

Cronan, W. (1990) 'Modes of prophecy and production: placing nature in history', *Journal of American History*, 76(4): 1122–31.

Crosby, A.W. (1995) 'The past and present of environmental history', *American Historical Review*, 100(4): 1177–90.

Crotty, R. (1979) 'Capitalist colonialism and peripheralisation: the Irish case', in D. Seers, B. Schaffer and M.L. Kiljunen (eds) *Under-developed Europe: Studies in Core–Periphery Relations*, Totowa, NJ: Humanities Press.

Crouch, D. (1989a) 'Patterns of cooperation in the cultures of outdoor leisure – the case of allotments', *Leisure Studies*, 8(2): 189–99.

— (1989b) 'The allotment, landscape and locality', *Area*, 21(3): 261–7.

— (1994) 'Home, escape and identity: rural identities and sustainable tourism', *Journal of Sustainable Tourism*, 2(1/2): 93–101.

— (1999a) 'Introduction: encounters in leisure/tourism', in D. Crouch (ed.) *Leisure/Tourism Geographies: Practices and Geographical Knowledge*, London: Routledge.

— (ed.) (1999b) *Leisure/Tourism Geographies: Practices and Geographical Knowledge*, London: Routledge.

— (2000) 'Places around us: embodied lay geographies in leisure and tourism', *Leisure Studies*, 19(2): 63–76.

Crouch, D. and Lübbren, N. (eds) (2003) *Visual Culture and Tourism*, Berg: Oxford.

Crouch, G. (1994) 'The study of tourism demand: a review of findings', *Journal of Travel Research*, 33(1): 2–21.

Croy, G. and Hall, C.M. (2003) 'Developing a tourism knowledge: educating the student, developing the rural area', *Journal of Teaching in Travel and Tourism*, 3(1): 3–24.

Crump, J. (2003) 'Finding a place in the country: exurban and suburban development in Sonoma County, California', *Environment and Behavior*, 35: 187–202.

Csikszentmihalyi, M. (1975) *Beyond Boredom and Anxiety*, San Francisco, CA: Jossey Bass.

Curiel, J. and Radvansky, G. (2002) 'Mental maps in memory retrieval and comprehension', *Memory*, 10(2): 113–26.

Curry, N. (1992) 'Recreation, access, amenity and conservation in the United Kingdom: the failure of integration', in I.R. Bowler, C.R. Bryant and M.D. Nellis (eds) *Contemporary Rural Systems in Transition*, vol. 2, Wallingford: CAB International.

— (1994) *Countryside Recreation: Access and Land Use Planning*, London: E&FN Spon.

— (2000) 'Community participation in outdoor recreation and the development of Millennium Greens in England', *Leisure Studies*, 19(1): 17–35.

— (2010) 'The incompatibility of economic development policies for rural areas in England', *Local Economy*, 25: 108–19.

Curry, N. and Owen, S. (2009) 'Rural planning in England: a critique of current policy', *Town Planning Review*, 80: 575–96.

Cushman, G., Veal, A. and Zuzanek, J. (eds) (1996a) *World Leisure Participation: Free Time in the Global Village*, Wallingford: CAB International.

— (eds) (1996b) 'National participation surveys: an overview', in G. Cushman, A. Veal and J. Zuzanek (eds) *World Leisure Participation: Free Time in the Global Village*, Wallingford: CAB International.

Cutter, S. (2000) 'President's column: bring geography back to Harvard and Yale and . . . ', *AAG Newsletter*, 35(10): 2–3.

Cybriwsky, R. (1999) 'Changing patterns of urban public space: observations and assessments from the Tokyo and New York metropolitan areas', *Cities: The International Journal of Urban Policy and Planning*, 4: 223–31.

d'Hauteserre, A. (1996) 'A response to Dimitri Ioannides, "Strengthening the ties between tourism and economic geography: a theoretical agenda"', *Professional Geographer*, 48: 218–19.

Daby, D., Turner, J. and Jago, C. (2002) 'Microbial and nutrient pollution of coastal bathing waters in Mauritius', *Environmental International*, 27(7): 555–66.

Dagenais, M. (2002) 'Inscribing municipal power in urban space: the formation of a network of parks at Montreal and Toronto, 1880–1940', *Canadian Geographer*, 46(4): 347–64.

Dahles, H. (1998) 'Redefining Amsterdam as a tourism destination', *Annals of Tourism Research*, 25: 55–69.

Dahmann, N., Wolch, J., Joassart-Marcelli, P., Reynolds, K. and Jerrett, M. (2010) 'The active city? Disparities in provision of urban public recreation resources', *Health & Place*, 16: 431–45.

Dakin, S. (2003) 'There's more to landscape than meets the eye: towards inclusive landscape assessment in resource and environmental management', *Canadian Geographer*, 47: 185–200.

Damette, F. (1980) 'The regional framework of monopoly exploitation: new problems and trends', in J. Carney, R. Hudson and J.R. Lewis (eds) *Regions in Crisis*, London: Croom Helm.

Dann, G. (1981) 'Tourist motivation: an appraisal', *Annals of Tourism Research*, 8: 187–219.

— (1993) 'Limitations in the use of nationality and country of residence variable', in D. Pearce and R. Butler (eds) *Tourism Research: Critique and Challenges*, London: Routledge.

Dasmann, R.F. (1973) *Classification and Use of Protected Natural and Cultural Areas*, IUCN Occasional Paper No. 4, Morges: International Union for Conservation of Nature and Natural Resources.

Davenport, J. and Davenport, J. (2006) 'The impact of tourism and personal leisure transport on coastal environments: a review', *Estuarine, Coastal and Shelf Science*, 67: 280–92.

Davidson, M. and McNeill, D. (2012) 'The redevelopment of Olympic sites: examining the legacy of Sydney Olympic Park', *Urban Studies*, 49: 1625–41.

Davidson, R. and Maitland, R. (1997) *Tourism Destinations*, London: Hodder & Stoughton.

Davies, E. (1987) 'Planning in the New Zealand National Parks', *New Zealand Geographer*, 43(2): 73–8.

Davies, K. (2012) 'The composition of Singaporean shopping centres', *International Review of Retail, Distribution and Consumer Research*, 22: 261–75.

Dawson, J. and Doornkamp, J. (eds) (1973) *Evaluating the Human Environment: Essays in Applied Geography*, London: Edward Arnold.

Dawson, J., Stewart, E.J., Lemelin, H. and Scott, D. (2010) 'The carbon cost of polar bear viewing in Churchill, Canada', *Journal of Sustainable Tourism*, 18: 319–36.

de Botton, A. (2003) *The Art of Travel*, London: Penguin.

de Freitas, C.R. (1990) 'Recreation climate assessment', *International Journal of Climatology*, 10: 89–103.

— (2003) 'Tourism climatology: evaluating environmental information for decision making and business planning in the recreation and tourism sector', *International Journal of Biometeorology*, 47(4): 190–208.

De Kadt, E. (ed.) (1979) *Tourism – Passport to Development?*, Oxford: Oxford University Press.

Dear, M. (1994) 'Postmodern human geography: a preliminary assessment', *Erdkunde*, 48(1): 2–13.

— (1999) 'The relevance of post modernism', *Scottish Geographical Magazine*, 115(2): 143–50.

Dear, M. and Flusty, S. (1998) 'Postmodern urbanism', *Annals of the Association of American Geographers*, 88(1): 50–72.

— (1999) 'Engaging postmodern urbanism', *Urban Geography*, 20(5): 412–16.

Dearden, P. (1993) 'Cultural aspects of tourism and sustainable development: tourism and the hilltribes of Northern Thailand', in J.G. Nelson, R. Butler and G. Wall (eds) *Tourism and Sustainable Development: Monitoring, Planning and Managing*, Waterloo: Department of Geography, University of Waterloo.

Dearden, P. and Rollins, R. (eds) (1993) *Parks and Protected Areas in Canada: Planning and Management*, Toronto: Oxford University Press.

Deasy, G.F. (1949) 'The tourist industry in a north woods county', *Economic Geography*, 25(2): 240–59.

Deasy, G.F. and Griess, P.R. (1966) 'Impact of a tourist facility on its hinterland', *Annals of the Association of American Geographers*, 56(2): 290–306.

Debarbieux, B. (1995) *Tourisme et montagne*, Paris: Economica.

Debbage, K.G. (1990) 'Oligopoly and the resort cycle in the Bahamas', *Annals of Tourism Research*, 17: 513–27.

— (1991) 'Spatial behaviour in a Bahamian resort', *Annals of Tourism Research*, 18: 251–68.

Debbage, K.G. and Ioannides, D. (eds) (1998) *The Economic Geography of the Tourism Industry*, London: Routledge.

— (2004) 'The cultural turn? Towards a more critical economic geography of tourism', in A. Lew, C.M. Hall and A. Williams (eds) *A Companion to Tourism*, Oxford: Blackwell.

Deblock, A. (1986) 'Tourisme et pêche', *Espaces*, 82: 22–5.

Deem, R. (1986) *All Work and No Play? The Sociology of Women and Leisure*, Milton Keynes: Open University Press.

Defeo, O., McLachlan, A., Schoeman, D.S., Schlacher, T.A., Dugan, J., Jones, A., Lastra, M. and Scapini, F. (2009) 'Threats to sandy beach ecosystems: a review', *Estuarine, Coastal and Shelf Science*, 81(1): 1–12.

Dehoorne, O. (2002) 'Tourisme, travail, migration: interrelations et logiques mobilitaires', *Revue européenne des migrations internationales*, 18(1): 7–36.

Del Casino, V. and Hanna, S. (2000) 'Representations and identities in tourism map spaces', *Progress in Human Geography*, 24: 23–46.

Deller, S.C., Marcouiller, D.W and Green, G.P. (1997) 'Recreational housing and local government finance', *Annals of Tourism Research*, 24: 687–705.

Demeritt, D. (2006) 'Science studies, climate change and the prospects for constructivist critique', *Economy and Society*, 35: 453–79.

— (2009) 'Geography and the promise of integrative environmental research', *Geoforum*, 40: 127–9.

Department for Culture, Media and Sport (1999) *Policy Action Team 10: Report on Social Exclusion*, London: Department for Culture, Media and Sport.

Department of Environment, Food and Rural Affairs (DEFRA) (2007) *Survey of Public Attitudes and Behaviours Towards the Environment*, London: DEFRA.

— (2009) *Survey of Public Attitudes and Behaviours Towards the Environment*, London: DEFRA.

Department of Regional Economic Expansion (1972) *The Canada Land Inventory: Land Capability Classification for Outdoor Recreation*, Report No. 6, Ottawa: Queens Printer for Canada.

Department of the Environment (DoE) (1990) *Tourism and the Inner City*, London: HMSO.

— (1996) *Coastal Zone Management – Towards Best Practice*, London: Department of the Environment.

Department of the Environment and Ministry of Agriculture, Fisheries and Food (DoE/MAFF) (1995) *Rural England: A Nation Committed to a Living Countryside*, London: HMSO.

Deprest, F. (1997) *Enquête sur le tourisme de masse: l'écologie face au territoire*, Paris: Belin.

— (2002) 'L'Invention géographique de la Méditerranée: éléments de reflexion', *L'Espace géographique*, 31: 73–92.

Dernoi, L.A. (1983) 'Farm tourism in Europe', *Tourism Management*, 4: 155–66.

Deutsch, K. (1970) *Politics and Government: How People Decide Their Fate*, Boston, MA: Houghton Mifflin.

Dewailly, J. and Flament, E. (eds) (1993) *Géographie du tourisme et des loisirs*, Paris: SEDES.

Dias, C. and Melo, V. (2011) 'Leisure and urbanisation in Brazil from the 1950s to the 1970s', *Leisure Studies*, 30: 333–43.

Dickinson, G. (2000) 'The use of the Loch Lomond area for recreation', *Scottish Geographical Journal*, 116(3): 231–44.

Diedrich, A., Balaguer Huguet, P. and Tintoré Subirana, J. (2011) 'Methodology for applying the limits of acceptable change process to the management of recreational boating in the Balearic Islands, Spain (Western Mediterranean)', *Ocean & Coastal Management*, 54: 341–51.

Di Minin, E., Macmillan, D., Goodman, P., Escott, B., Slotow, R. and Moilanen, A. (2013) 'Conservation businesses and conservation planning in a biological diversity hotspot', *Conservation Biology*, 27: 808–20.

Dietz, T. and Kwaad, F. (2000) *Dutch Geography 1996–2000*, Utrecht: International Geographical Union.

Dilley, R.S. (1986) 'Tourist brochures and tourist images', *Canadian Geographer*, 30(1): 59–65.

Dilsaver, L.M. and Tweed, W.C. (1990) *Challenge of the Big Trees: A Resource History of Sequoia and Kings Canyon National Parks*, Three Rivers: Sequoia Natural History Association.

Ding, L., Wang, Y., Zhang, F., Wu, X. and Tang, S. (2011) 'Spatial structure of tourist attractions in Nanjing, China—Based on statistical analysis of 317 tourist attractions', in *19th International Conference on Geoinformatics, 2011*, Shanghai: IEEE.

Ding, P. and Pigram, J. (1995) 'Environmental audits: an emerging concept for sustainable tourism development', *Journal of Tourism Studies*, 2: 2–10.

Dingsdale, A. (1986) 'Ideology and leisure under socialism: the geography of second homes in Hungary', *Leisure Studies*, 5: 35–55.

Doering, T.R. (1976) 'A reexamination of the relative importance of tourism to state economies', *Journal of Travel Research*, 15(1): 13–17.

Donajgrodski, A. (ed.) (1978) *Social Control in Nineteenth Century Britain*, London: Croom Helm.

Doody, B. and Booth, K. (2006) 'Rights of public access in New Zealand: public opinion about foreshore access and proposals to improve land access', *Annals of Leisure Research*, 9(1–2): 62–85.

Doornkamp, J. (1982) *Applied Geography*, Nottingham Monographs in Applied Geography No. 1, Department of Geography, University of Nottingham.

Doren, C., Priddle, G. and Lewis, J. (1979) *Land and Leisure: Concepts and Methods in Outdoor Recreation*, London: Methuen.

Dovers, S. (ed.) (1994) *Australian Environmental History: Essays and Cases*, Melbourne: Oxford University Press.

—— (ed.) (2000a) *Environmental History and Policy: Still Settling Australia*, Melbourne: Oxford University Press.

—— (2000b) 'On the contribution of environmental history to current debate and policy', *Environment and History*, 6: 131–50.

Dower, M. (1965) *The Challenge of Leisure*, London: Civic Trust.

—— (1977) 'Planning aspects of second homes', in Coppock, J.T. (ed.) *Second Homes: Curse or Blessing*, Oxford: Pergamon Press.

Dower, M. and McCarthy, P. (1967) 'Planning for conservation and development', *Journal of the Royal Town Planning Institute*, 53(1): 99–105.

Dowling, R.K. (1993) 'Tourism planning, people and the environment in Western Australia', *Journal of Travel Research*, 31(4): 52–8.

—— (1993) 'Plans for the development of regional ecotourism: theory and practice', in C.M. Hall, J. Jenkins and G. Kearsley (eds) *Tourism Planning and Policy in Australia and New Zealand: Cases, Issues and Practice*, Sydney: Irwin Publishers.

Downs, R.M. (1970) 'Geographic space perception: past approaches and future prospects', *Progress in Geography*, 2: 65–108.

Downs, R.M. and Stea, D. (1973) *Image and Environment*, New York: Aldine.

—— (1977) *Maps in Minds: Reflections on Cognitive Mapping*, New York: Harper & Row.

Doxey, G.V. (1975) 'A causation theory of visitor–resident irritants: methodology and research inferences', in *Proceedings of the Travel Research Association 6th Annual Conference*, San Diego: Travel Research Association.

Dredge, D. (1999) 'Destination place planning and design', *Annals of Tourism Research*, 26: 772–91.

Dredge, D. and Jenkins, J. (eds) (2007) *Tourism Policy and Planning*, Milton: Wiley & Sons.

— (eds) (2011) *Stories of Practice: Tourism Policy and Planning*, Farnham: Ashgate.

Driver, B.L. (1989) 'Recreation Opportunity Spectrum: a framework for planning, management and research', in *Proceedings of a North American Workshop on Visitor Management in Parks and Protected Areas*, Waterloo: Tourism Research and Education Centre, University of Waterloo and Environment, Canada Park Service.

— (2003) 'Experiences', in J. Jenkins and J. Pigram (eds) *Encyclopedia of Leisure and Outdoor Recreation*, London: Routledge.

Drost, A. (1996) 'Developing sustainable tourism for World Heritage sites', *Annals of Tourism Research*, 23: 479–92.

Drummond, L. (2000) 'Street scenes: practices of public and private space in urban Vietnam', *Urban Studies*, 37(12): 2377–91.

Dubaniewicz, H. (1976) 'An appraisal of the natural environment of the Ködz Region for the needs of economic development and recreation', *Geographica Polonica*, 34: 265–71.

Dubé, P. and Gordon, G. (2000) 'Capital cities: perspectives and convergence', *Plan Canada*, 40(3): 6–7.

Duffield, B. (1984) 'The study of tourism in Britain – a geographical perspective', *GeoJournal*, 9(1): 27–35.

Duffield, B. and Coppock, J. (1975) 'The delineation of recreational landscapes: the role of computer-based information systems', *Transactions of the Institute of British Geographers*, 66: 141–8.

Duffield, B. and Long, J. (1981) 'Tourism in the Highlands and Islands of Scotland: rewards and conflicts', *Annals of Tourism Research*, 8: 403–31.

Duffield, B. and Owen, M. (1970) *Leisure + Countryside =: A Geographical Appraisal of Countryside Recreation in Lanarkshire*, Edinburgh: University of Edinburgh.

Duffield, B. and Walker, S. (1983) *Urban Parks and Open Spaces: A Review*, Edinburgh: Tourism and Recreation Research Unit.

Duffy, M. (2009) 'Festivals and spectacle', in R. Kitchin and N. Thrift (eds) *International Encyclopedia of Human Geography*, Oxford: Elsevier.

Dufty-Jones, R. (2012) 'Moving home: theorizing housing within a politics of mobility', *Housing, Theory and Society*, 29: 207–22.

Dumas, D. (1982) 'Le Commerce de détail dans une grande station touristique balnéaire espagnole: Benidorm', *Annales de géographie*, 506: 486–9.

Duncan, D. and Burns, K. (2009) *The National Parks: America's Best Idea*, New York: Knopf.

Dunning, J. and McQueen, M. (1982) *Transnational Corporations in International Tourism*, New York: United Nations.

Dunphy, M.J. (1973) 'How the Sydney Bushwalkers began' (compiled from the Minutes Book of the Mountain Trails Club, September, 1948), *The Sydney Bushwalker*, October: 3–5, 7.

— (1979a) 'The incidence of major parklands in New South Wales, Book 1', unpublished manuscript held by the New South Wales National Park and Wildlife Service Library, Sydney.

— (1979b) 'The bushwalking conservation movement, 1914–1965', *Parks and Wildlife*, 2(3–4): 54–64.

Durbarry, R. and Sinclair, M.T. (2003) 'Market shares analysis: the case of French tourism demand', *Annals of Tourism Research*, 30(4): 927–41.

Durie, A (2003) *Scotland for the Holidays: Tourism in Scotland 1780–1939*, East Linton: Tuckwell Press.

Dutton, I. and Hall, C.M. (1989) 'Making tourism sustainable: the policy/practice conundrum', in *Proceedings of the Environment Institute of Australia Second National Conference*, Melbourne: Environment Institute of Australia.

Duval, D.T. (2003) 'When hosts become guests: return visits and diasporic identities in a Commonwealth Eastern Caribbean community', *Current Issues in Tourism*, 6: 267–308.

— (ed.) (2004) *Tourism in the Caribbean*, London: Routledge.

Dwight, R.H., Brinks, M.V., SharavanaKumar, G. and Semenza, J.C. (2007) 'Beach attendance and bathing rates for Southern Californian beaches', *Ocean and Coastal Management*, 50: 847–58.

Dwyer, L. and Forsyth, P. (1996) 'Economic impacts of cruise tourism in Australia', *Journal of Tourism Studies*, 7(2): 36–43.

— (2011) 'Methods of estimating destination price competitiveness: a case of horses for courses?', *Current Issues in Tourism*, 14: 751–77.

Dye, A.S. and Shaw, S. (2007) 'A GIS-based spatial decision support system for tourists of Great Smoky Mountains National Park', *Journal of Retailing and Consumer Services*, 14: 269–78.

Dye, T. (1992) *Understanding Public Policy*, 7th edn, Englewood Cliffs, NJ: Prentice Hall.

Eagles, P. (1992) 'The travel motivations of Canadian ecotourists', *Journal of Travel Research*, 31(2): 3–7.

Eaton, B. and Holding, D. (1996) 'The evaluation of public transport alternatives to the car in British National Parks', *Journal of Transport Geography*, 4(1): 55–65.

Edensor, T. (2000) 'Staging tourism: tourists as performers', *Annals of Tourism Research*, 27: 322–4.

— (2003) 'Defamiliarizing the mundane roadscape', *Space and Culture*, 6: 151–68.

— (2004) 'Automobility and national identity representation, geography and driving practice', *Theory, Culture & Society*, 21(4–5): 101–20.

— (2007) 'Mundane mobilities, performances and spaces of tourism', *Social & Cultural Geography*, 8: 199–215.

Edgerton, R. (1979) *Alone Together: Social Order on an Urban Beach*, Berkeley: University of California Press.

Edington, J.M. and Edington, M.A. (1986) *Ecology, Recreation and Tourism*, Cambridge: Cambridge University Press.

Edwards, J. (1987) 'The UK heritage coasts: an assessment of the ecological impacts', *Annals of Tourism Research*, 14: 71–87.

— (1991) 'Guest–host perceptions of rural tourism in England and Portugal', in M.T. Sinclair and M.J. Stabler (eds) *The Tourism Industry: An International Analysis*, Wallingford: CAB International.

Edwards, M.B. and Matarrita-Cascante, D. (2011) 'Rurality in leisure research: a review of four major journals', *Journal of Leisure Research*, 43: 447–74.

Egner, H. (2002) 'Freizeit als "Individualisierungsplattform". Entwicklung und Ausdifferenzierung sportorientierter Freizeitaktivitäten aus systemtheoretischer Perspektive' (Leisure as a platform for individualization: a systems theory approach to the evolution and diversification of sports oriented leisure activities), *Geographische-Zeitschrift*, 90(2): 89–102.

Eidsvik, H.K. (1980) 'National parks and other protected areas: some reflections on the past and prescriptions for the future', *Environmental Conservation*, 7(3): 185–90.

— (1987) *Categories Revision – A Review and a Proposal, Commission on National Parks and Protected Areas*, Morges: International Union for the Conservation of Nature and Natural Resources.

Eijgelaar, E., Thaper, C. and Peeters, P. (2010) 'Antarctic cruise tourism: the paradoxes of ambassadorship, "last chance tourism" and greenhouse gas emissions', *Journal of Sustainable Tourism*, 18: 337–54.

Eiselen, E. (1945) 'The tourist industry of a modern highway, US16 in South Dakota', *Economic Geography*, 21: 221–30.

El Mrini, A., Maanan, M., Anthony, E.J. and Taaouati, M. (2012) 'An integrated approach to characterize the interaction between coastal morphodynamics, geomorphological setting and human interventions on the Mediterranean beaches of northwestern Morocco', *Applied Geography*, 35: 334–44.

Ellerbrook, M.J. and Hite, J.C. (1980) 'Factors affecting regional employment in tourism in the United States', *Journal of Travel Research*, 18(3): 26–32.

Elliott-White, M. and Finn, M. (1998) 'Growing in sophistication: the application of GIS in postmodern marketing', *Journal of Travel and Tourism Marketing*, 7: 65–84.

Elson, M. (1977) *A Review and Evaluation of Countryside Recreation Site Surveys*, Cheltenham: Countryside Commission.

— (1979) *The Leisure Use of Green Belts and Urban Fringes*, London: Sports Council and Social Science Research Council.

— (1986) *Green Belts: Conflict Mediation in the Urban Fringe*, London: Heinemann.

— (1993) 'Sport and recreation in the green belt countryside', in S. Glyptis (ed.) *Leisure and the Environment: Essays in Honour of Professor J.A. Patmore*, London: Belhaven Press.

Elwood, S. (2008) 'Volunteered geographic information: key questions, concepts and methods to guide emerging research and practice', *GeoJournal*, 72: 133–5.

Engberg, E., Alen, M., Kukkonen-Harjula, K., Peltonen, J., Tikannen. H. and Pekkarinen, H. (2012) 'Life events and change in leisure time physical activity', *Sports Medicine*, 42: 433–47.

England, M.R. and Simon, S. (2010) 'Scary cities: urban geographies of fear, difference and belonging', *Social & Cultural Geography*, 11: 201–7.

English Historic Towns Forum (1992) *Retailing in Historic Towns: Research Study 1992*, London: Donaldsons.

English Tourist Board/Employment Department (1991) *Tourism and the Environment: Maintaining the Balance*, London: English Tourist Board.

Environmental Planning Group of Canada (EPGC) (2002) *Newfoundland and Labrador Tourism Marketing Strategy Review. Final Report*, Halifax: EPGC.

Erickson, B. (2011) 'Recreational activism: politics, nature, and the rise of neoliberalism', *Leisure Studies*, 30: 477–94.

Erkip, F. (1997) 'The distribution of urban public services: the case of parks and recreational services in Ankara', *Cities: The International Journal of Urban Policy and Planning*, 14(6): 353–61.

Escourrou, P. (1993) *Tourisme et environnement*, Paris: SEDES.

Esser, J. and Hirsch, J. (1989) 'The crisis of Fordism and the dimensions of a "post-Fordist" regional and urban structure', *International Journal of Urban and Regional Research*, 13: 417–37.

Etzioni, A. (ed.) (1998) *The Essential Communitarian Reader*, Lanham, MD: Rowman & Littlefield.

European Commission (1997) *Better Management of Coastal Resources – A European Programme for Integrated Coastal Zone Management*, Luxembourg: Official Publication of the European Communities.

European Parliament (2009) European Parliament resolution of 3 February 2009 on wilderness in Europe (2008/2210(INI)).

Evans, B. (1997) 'From town planning to environmental planning', in A. Blowers and B. Evans (eds) *Town Planning into the 21st Century*, London: Routledge.

Evans, G. (1998) 'Urban leisure: edge city and the new leisure periphery', in M. Collins and I. Cooper (eds) *Leisure Management: Issues and Applications*, Wallingford: CAB International.

— (2003) 'Hard-branding the cultural city – from Prado to Prada', *International Journal of Urban and Regional Research*, 27: 417–40.

— (2005) 'Measure for measure: evaluating the evidence of culture's contribution to regeneration', *Urban Studies*, 42: 959–83.

Evans, N.J. (1992a) 'Advertising and farm-based accommodation: a British case study', *Tourism Management*, 13(4): 415–22.

— (1992b) 'The distribution of farm-based accommodation in England and Wales', *Journal of the Royal Agricultural Society of England*, 153: 67–80.

— (1992c) 'Towards an understanding of farm-based tourism in Britain', in A.W. Gilg (ed.) *Progress in Rural Policy and Planning*, vol. 2, London: Belhaven Press.

Evans, N.J. and Ilbery, B.W. (1989) 'A conceptual framework for investigating farm-based accommodation and tourism in Britain', *Journal of Rural Studies*, 5(3): 257–66.

Evernden, N. (1992) *The Social Creation of Nature*, Baltimore, MD: Johns Hopkins University Press.

Ewert, A. and Hollenhurst, S. (1989) 'Testing the adventure model: empirical support for a model of risk recreational participation', *Journal of Leisure Research*, 21: 124–9.

Fabbri, P. (ed.) (1990) *Recreational Use of Coastal Areas: A Research Project of the Commission on the Coastal Environment*, International Geographical Union, Dordrecht: Kluwer.

Fagence, M. (1990) 'Geographically-referenced planning strategies', *Journal of Environmental Management*, 3(1): 1–18.

— (1991) 'Geographic referencing of public policies in tourism', *Revue de tourisme*, 3(3): 8–19.

Farrell, B.H. (ed.) (1978) *The Social and Economic Impact of Tourism on Pacific Communities*, Santa Cruz: Centre for South Pacific Studies, University of California.

Farrell, B.H. and McLellan, R.W. (1987) 'Tourism and physical environment research', *Annals of Tourism Research*, 14: 1–16.

Farrell, B.H. and Runyan, D. (1991) 'Ecology and tourism', *Annals of Tourism Research*, 18: 26–40.

Farrell, B.H. and Twinning-Ward, L. (2004) 'Reconceptualizing tourism', *Annals of Tourism Research*, 31: 274–95.

Farrell, T.A. and Marion, J.L. (2001) 'Identifying and assessing ecotourism visitor impacts in eight protected areas in Costa Rica and Belize', *Environmental Conservation*, 28: 215–25.

Farsari, Y. and Prastacos, P. (2004) 'GIS applications in the planning and management of tourism', in A. Lew, C.M. Hall and A. Williams (eds) *A Companion to Tourism Communities*, Clevedon: Channel View.

Farstad, M. (2011) 'Rural residents' opinions about second home owners' pursuit of own interests in the host community', *Norsk Geografisk Tidsskrift–Norwegian Journal of Geography*, 65(3): 165–74.

Faulkner, B. and Russell, R. (2003) 'Chaos and complexity in tourism: in search of a new perspective', in H.W. Faulkner, L. Fredline, L. Jago and C.P. Cooper (eds) *Progressing Tourism Research – Bill Faulkner*, Clevedon: Channel View.

Faulkner, B. and Tideswell, C. (1996) 'Gold Coast resident attitudes toward tourism: the influence of involvement in tourism, residential proximity, and period of residence', in G. Prosser (ed.) *Tourism and Hospitality Research: Australian and International Perspectives*, Canberra: Bureau of Tourism Research.

Featherstone, M. (1987) 'Leisure, symbolic power and the life course', in J. Horne, D. Jary and A. Tomlinson (eds) *Sport, Leisure and Social Relations*, London: Routledge & Kegan Paul.

Feller, M., Hooley, D., Dreher, T., East, I. and Jung, R. (1979) *Wilderness in Victoria: An Inventory*, Monash Publications in Geography No. 21, Clayton: Department of Geography, Monash University.

Fennell, D. (1999) *Ecotourism: An Introduction*, London: Routledge.

— (2001) 'A content analysis of ecotourism definitions', *Current Issues in Tourism*, 4: 403–21.

Ferguson, M. and Munton, R. (1978) *Informal Recreation in the Urban Fringe: Provision and Management of Sites in London's Green Belt*, Working Paper No. 2, Land for Informal Recreation, London: Department of Geography, University College.

— (1979) 'Informal recreation sites in London's green belt', *Area*, 11: 196–205.

Ferrario, F.F. (1979a) 'The evaluation of tourist resources: an applied methodology part I', *Journal of Travel Research*, 17(3): 18–22.

— (1979b) 'The evaluation of tourist resources: an applied methodology part II', *Journal of Travel Research*, 17(4): 24–9.

Fesenmaier, D.R. and Lieber, S.R. (1987) 'Outdoor recreation expenditure and the effects of spatial structure', *Leisure Sciences*, 9(1): 27–40.

Feyerabend, P. (2010) *Against Method*, 4th edn, London: Verso.

Filoppovich, L. (1979) 'Mapping of recreational development around a large city', *Soviet Geography*, 20: 361–9.

Fines, K. (1968) 'Landscape evaluation: a research project in East Sussex', *Regional Studies*, 2(1): 41–5.

Finn, A. and Erden, T. (1995) 'The economic impact of a mega-multi mall: estimation issues in the case of West Edmonton Mall', *Tourism Management*, 16(5): 367–73.

Finnveden, B. (1960) 'Den dubbla bosättningen och sommermigrationen: exempel från Hallandskustens fritidsbebyggelse', *Svensk Geografisk årsbok*, 36: 58–84.

Fisher, D., Lewis, J. and Priddle, G. (eds) (1974) *Land and Leisure: Concepts and Methods in Outdoor Recreation*, Chicago: Maaroufa Press.

Fitton, M. (1976) 'The urban fringe and the less privileged', *Countryside Recreation Review*, 1: 25–34.

— (1979) 'Countryside recreation – the problems of opportunity', *Local Government Studies*, 5: 57–90.

Flanagan, T.S. and Anderson, S. (2008) 'Mapping perceived wilderness to support protected areas management in the San Juan National Forest, Colorado', *Forest Ecology and Management*, 256: 1039–48.

Fleischer, A. and Tsur, Y. (2003) 'Measuring the recreational value of open space', *Journal of Agricultural Economics*, 54: 269–83.

Fletcher, J. and Snee, H.R. (1989) 'Tourism multiplier efforts', in S.F. Witt and L. Moutinho (eds) *Tourism Marketing and Management Handbook*, Hemel Hempstead: Prentice Hall.

Flognfeldt, T. (2002) 'Second home ownership. A sustainable semi-migration', in C.M. Hall and A.M. Williams (eds) *Tourism and Migration: New Relationships between Production and Consumption*, Dordrecht: Kluwer Academic.

Floor, H. (1990) *Aktiviteten Systemen en Bereikbaaheid*, Amsterdam: Siswo.

Floyd, M. (1998) 'Getting beyond marginality and ethnicity: the challenge for race and ethnic studies in leisure research', *Journal of Leisure Research*, 30(1): 3–22.

Floyd, M. and Johnson, C. (2002) 'Coming to terms with environmental justice in outdoor recreation: a conceptual discussion with research implications', *Leisure Sciences*, 24(1): 59–77.

Forestry Commission (2009) *Public Opinions of Forestry*, London: HMSO.

Forer, P. (1999) 'Fabricating space', in R. Le Heron, L. Murphy, P. Forer and M. Goldstone (eds) *Explorations in Human Geography: Encountering Place*, Auckland: Oxford University Press.

Forer, P. and Pearce, D.G. (1984) 'Spatial patterns of package tourism in New Zealand', *New Zealand Geographer*, 40: 34–42.

Forster, J. (1964) 'The sociological consequences of tourism', *International Journal of Comparative Sociology*, 5: 217–27.

Fountain, J. and Hall, C.M. (2002) 'The impact of lifestyle migration on rural communities: a case study of Akaroa, New Zealand', in C.M. Hall and A.M. Williams (eds) *Tourism and Migration: New Relationships between Production and Consumption*, Dordrecht: Kluwer Academic.

Frändberg, L. and Vilhelmson, B. (2003) 'Personal mobility – a corporeal dimension of transnationalisation: the case of long-distance travel from Sweden', *Environment and Planning A*, 35: 1751–68.

Frankel, O.H. (1978) 'The value of wilderness to science', in G. Mosley (ed.) *Australia's Wilderness: Conservation Progress and Plans, Proceedings of the First National Wilderness Conference, Australian Academy of Science, Canberra, 21–23 October, 1977*, Hawthorn: Australian Conservation Foundation.

Franklin, A. and Crang, M. (2001) 'The trouble with tourism and travel theory?', *Tourist Studies*, 1: 5–22.

Frater, J. (1983) 'Farm tourism in England', *Tourism Management*, 4: 167–79.

Frazier, J. (1982) *Applied Geography: Selected Perspectives*, Englewood Cliffs, NJ: Prentice Hall.

Freathy, P. (2004) 'The changing airport environment: past, present and future imperfect?', in L. Lumsdon and S.J. Page (eds) *Tourism and Transport: Issues and Agendas for the New Millennium*, Oxford: Elsevier.

Frechtling, D. (1976a) 'Proposed standard definitions and classifications for travel research', *Marketing Travel and Tourism, Seventh Annual Conference Proceedings*, Boca Raton: Travel Research Association.

—— (1976b) 'Travel as an employer in the state economy', *Journal of Travel Research*, 15(4): 8–12.

—— (1987) 'Assessing the impacts of travel and tourism – introduction to travel impact estimation', in J.R.B. Ritchie and C.R. Goeldner (eds) *Travel, Tourism and Hospitality Research: A Handbook for Managers and Researchers*, New York: Wiley.

—— (2010) 'The tourism satellite account: a primer', *Annals of Tourism Research*, 37: 136–53.

Freeman, T.W. (1961) *A Hundred Years of Geography*, London: Gerald Duckworth.

Fretter, A.D. (1993) 'Place marketing: a local authority perspective', in G. Kearns and C. Philo (eds) *Selling Places: The City as Cultural Capital, Past and Present*, Oxford: Pergamon Press.

Friedmann, J. (1973) 'A conceptual model for the analysis of planning behaviour', in A. Faludi (ed.)

A Reader in Planning Theory, Oxford: Pergamon Press.

Frost, W. (2004) 'Heritage tourism on Australia's Asian shore: a case study of Pearl Luggers, Broome', *Asia Pacific Journal of Tourism Research*, 9: 281–91.

Frost, W. and Hall, C.M. (eds) (2009a) *Tourism and National Parks: International Perspectives on Development, Histories and Change*, London: Routledge.

— (2009b) 'American invention to international concept: the spread and evolution of national parks', in W. Frost and C.M. Hall (eds) *Tourism and National Parks: International Perspectives on Development, Histories and Change*, London: Routledge.

Fukaz, G. (1989) 'Hungary: More work, less leisure', in A. Olszewska and K. Roberts (eds) *Leisure and Lifestyle: A Comparative Analysis of Free Time*, London: Sage.

Funk, R.W. (1959) 'The wilderness', *Journal of Biblical Literature*, 78: 205–14.

Fyfe, N. and Banister, J. (1996) 'City watching: closed circuit television surveillance in public spaces', *Area*, 28(1): 37–46.

Gagnon, S. (2007) 'Attractivité touristique et «sens» géo-anthropologique des territoires', *Téoros. Revue de recherche en tourisme*, 26(2): 5–11.

Galatowitsch, S.M. (1990) 'Using the original land survey notes to reconstruct presettlement landscapes of the American West', *Great Basin Naturalist*, 50(2): 181–91.

Gale, F. and Jacobs, J.M. (1987) *Tourists and the National Estate Procedures to Protect Australia's Heritage*, Australian Heritage Commission Special Australian Heritage Publication Series No. 6, Canberra: Australian Government Publishing Service.

Gallent, N. (1997) 'Improvement grants, second homes and planning control in England and Wales: a policy review', *Planning Practice and Research*, 12: 401–10.

Gallent, N. and Tewdwr-Jones, M. (2000) *Rural Second Homes in Europe: Examining Housing Supply and Planning Control*, Aldershot: Ashgate.

Gannon, J. and Johnston, K. (1995) 'The global hotel industry: the emergence of continental hotel companies', *Progress in Tourism and Hospitality Research*, 1: 31–42.

Gant, R.L., Robinson, G.M. and Fazal, S. (2011) 'Land-use change in the "edgelands": policies and pressures in London's rural–urban fringe', *Land Use Policy*, 28: 266–79.

Gardner, J.S. (1978) 'The meaning of wilderness: a problem of definition', *Contact – Journal of Urban and Environmental Affairs*, 10(1): 7–33.

Garland, A. (1997) *The Beach*, London: Penguin.

Garner, C. (1996) 'Park life is given £50 million injection', *Independent*, 29 January.

Garreau, J. (1991) *Edge City: Life on the New Frontier*, New York: Doubleday.

Garrod, B. and Wilson, J.C. (eds) (2003) *Marine Ecotourism: Issues and Experiences*, Clevedon: Channel View.

— (2004) 'Nature on the edge? Marine ecotourism in peripheral coastal areas', *Journal of Sustainable Tourism*, 12(2): 95–120.

Gartner, W.C. (1986) 'Temporal influences on image change', *Annals of Tourism Research*, 13: 635–44.

— (1987) 'Environmental impacts of recreational home developments', *Annals of Tourism Research*, 14: 38–57.

Gaviria, M. (1975) *Turismo de Playa en Espana*, Madrid: Edicione S. Turner.

Gehl, J. (1980) 'The residential street environment', *Built Environment*, 6(1): 51–61.

German Federal Agency for Nature Conservation (ed.) (1997) *Biodiversity and Tourism: Conflicts on the World's Seacoasts and Strategies for Their Solution*, Berlin: Springer.

Gershuny, J. (2002) 'Social leisure and home IT: a panel time-diary approach', *IT & Society*, 1(1): 54–72.

— (2011) *Time-Use Surveys and the Measurement of Well-Being*, Oxford: University of Oxford Press.

Getz, D. (1977) 'The impact of tourism on host communities: a research approach', in B.S. Duffield (ed.) *Tourism: A Tool for Regional Development*, Edinburgh: Tourism and Recreation Research Unit, University of Edinburgh.

— (1981) 'Tourism and rural settlement policy', *Scottish Geographical Magazine*, 97 (December): 158–68.

— (1983) 'Capacity to absorb tourism: concepts and implications for strategic planning', *Annals of Tourism Research*, 10: 239–63.

— (1984) 'Tourism, community organisation and the social multiplier', in J. Long and R. Hecock (eds) *Leisure, Tourism and Social Change*, Dunfermline: Centre for Leisure Research, Dunfermline College of Physical Education.

— (1986a) 'Models in tourism planning towards integration of theory and practice', *Tourism Management*, 7(1): 21–32.

— (1986b) 'Tourism and population change: long term impacts of tourism in the Badenoch–Strathspey District of the Scottish Highlands', *Scottish Geographical Magazine*, 102(2): 113–26.

— (1987) 'Tourism planning and research: traditions, models and futures', paper presented at the *Australian Travel Research Workshop*, Bunbury, Western Australia, 5–6 November.

— (1991a) *Festivals, Special Events, and Tourism*, New York: Van Nostrand Reinhold.

— (1991b) 'Assessing the economic impacts of festivals and events: research issues', *Journal of Applied Recreation Research*, 16(1): 61–77.

— (1992) 'Tourism planning and destination life cycle', *Annals of Tourism Research*, 19: 752–70.

— (1993a) 'Planning for tourism business districts', *Annals of Tourism Research*, 20: 583–600.

— (1993b) 'Tourist shopping villages: development and planning strategies', *Tourism Management*, 14: 15–26.

— (1993c) 'Impacts of tourism on residents' leisure: concepts, and a longitudinal case study of Spey Valley, Scotland', *Journal of Tourism Studies*, 4(2): 33–44.

— (1994) 'Residents' attitudes towards tourism: a longitudinal study in Spey Valley, Scotland', *Tourism Management*, 15: 247–58.

— (1997) *Event Management and Tourism*, New York: Cognizant Communication Corporation.

— (2005) *Event Management and Event Tourism*, 2nd edn, Elmsford, NY: Cognizant Communication Corporation.

— (2012) *Event Studies: Theory, Research and Policy for Planned Events*, 2nd edn, Abingdon: Routledge.

Getz, D. and Carlsen, J. (2000) 'Characteristics and goals of family and owner-operated businesses in the rural tourism and hospitality sectors', *Tourism Management*, 21: 547–60.

Getz, D., Carlsen, J. and Morrison, A. (2004) *The Family Business in Tourism and Hospitality*, Wallingford: CAB International.

Ghelardoni, P. (1990) 'Tourist planning along the coast of Aquitane, France', in P. Fabbri (ed.) *Recreational Use of Coastal Areas*, Dordrecht: Kluwer.

Gibson, C. (2008) 'Locating geographies of tourism', *Progress in Human Geography*, 32: 407–22.

— (2009) 'Geographies of tourism: critical research on capitalism and local livelihoods', *Progress in Human Geography*, 33: 527–34.

— (2010) 'Geographies of tourism: (un)ethical encounters', *Progress in Human Geography*, 34: 521–7.

Gibson, C. and Klocker, N. (2004) 'Academic publishing as "creative" industry, and recent discourse of "creative economies": Some critical reflections', *Area*, 36: 423–34.

Gibson-Graham, J.K. (1996) *The End of Capitalism (as We Knew It): A Feminist Critique of Political Economy*, Oxford: Blackwell.

Giddens, A. (1984) *The Constitution of Society: Outline of the Theory of Structuration*, Cambridge: Polity Press.

— (1990) 'Modernity and utopia', *New Statesmen and Society*, 2 November: 20–2.

Gilbert, D. and Clark, M. (1997) 'An exploratory examination of urban tourism impact with reference to residents' attitudes in the cities of Canterbury and Guildford', *Cities: The International Journal of Urban Policy and Planning*, 14(6): 343–52.

Gilbert, D. and Joshi, I. (1992) 'Quality management and the tourism and hospitality industry', in C. Cooper and A. Lockwood (eds) *Progress in Tourism, Recreation and Hospitality Management*, vol. 4, London: Belhaven Press.

Gilbert, E.W. (1939) 'The growth of inland and seaside health resorts in England', *Scottish Geographical Magazine*, 55: 16–35.

— (1949) 'The growth of Brighton', *Geographical Journal*, 114: 30–52.

— (1954) *Brighton: Old Ocean's Bauble*, London: Methuen.

Gilg, A. (1985) *An Introduction to Rural Geography*, London: Edward Arnold.

Gill, A. (2004) 'Tourism communities and growth management', in A. Lew, C.M. Hall and A. Williams (eds) *A Companion to Tourism*, Oxford: Blackwell.

— (2012) 'Travelling down the road to postdisciplinarity? Reflections of a tourism geographer', *Canadian Geographer*, 56: 3–17.

Gill, A. and Williams, P.W. (1994) 'Managing growth in mountain tourism communities', *Tourism Management*, 15(3): 212–20.

Gimblett, R. and Skov-Peterson, H. (eds) (2008) *Monitoring, Simulation, and Management of Visitor Landscapes*, Tucson: University of Arizona Press.

Girard, T.C. and Gartner, W.C. (1993) 'Second home second view: host community perceptions', *Annals of Tourism Research*, 20: 685–700.

Glacken, C. (1967) *Traces on the Rhodian Shore, Nature and Culture in Western Thought from Ancient Times to the End of the Eighteenth Century*, Berkeley: University of California Press.

Gladstone, D. (2012) 'Event-based urbanization and the New Orleans tourist regime: a conceptual framework for understanding structural change in US tourist cities', *Journal of Policy Research in Tourism, Leisure and Events*, 4(3): 221–48.

Glasson, J., Therivel, R. and Chadwick, A. (2005) *Introduction to Environmental Impact Assessment: Principles and Procedures, Process, Practice and Prospects*, 3rd edn, London: Routledge.

Glasson, J., Godfrey, K. and Goodey, B. with Absalom, H. and Van Der Borg, J. (1995) *Towards Visitor Impact Management: Visitor Impacts, Carrying Capacity and Management Responses in Europe's Historic Towns and Cities*, Aldershot: Avebury.

Glyptis, S. (1981a) 'Leisure life-styles', *Regional Studies*, 15: 311–26.

— (1981b) 'People at play in the countryside', *Geography*, 66(4): 277–85.

— (1981c) Room to relax in the countryside', *The Planner*, 67(5): 120–2.

— (1989a) 'Recreational resource management', in C. Cooper (ed.) *Progress in Tourism, Recreation and Hospitality Management*, vol. 1, London: Belhaven Press.

— (1989b) *Leisure and Unemployment*, Milton Keynes: Open University Press.

— (1991) *Countryside Recreation*, Harlow: Longman.

— (1993) 'Leisure and the environment', in S. Glyptis (ed.) *Essays in Honour of Professor J.A. Patmore*, London: Belhaven Press.

Glyptis, S. and Chambers, D. (1982) 'No place like home', *Leisure Studies*, 1(3): 247–62.

Go, F. (1991) *Competitive Strategies for the International Hotel Industry*, London: Economist Intelligence Unit.

Go, F. and Pine, R. (1995) *Globalization Strategy in the Hotel Industry*, London: Routledge.

Gobster, P. (2002) 'Managing urban parks for a racially and ethnically diverse clientele', *Leisure Sciences*, 24(2): 143–59.

Godbey, G. (1976) *Recreation and Park Planning: The Exercise of Values*, Ontario: University of Waterloo.

Godfrey-Smith, W. (1979) 'The value of wilderness', *Environmental Ethics*, 1: 309–19.

Gold, J. (1980) *An Introduction to Behavioural Geography*, Oxford: Oxford University Press.

Gold, J. and Gold, M. (1995) *Imaging Scotland: Tradition, Representation and Promotion in Scottish Tourism since 1750*, Aldershot: Ashgate.

Gold, J. and Ward, S. (eds) (1994) *Place Promotion: The Use of Publicity and Public Relations to Sell Places*, London: Belhaven Press.

Gold, S. (1973) *Urban Recreation Planning*, Philadelphia: Lea & Febiger.

— (1980) *Recreation Planning and Design*, New York: McGraw Hill.

Goodall, B. (ed.) (1989) 'Tourism accommodation: special issue', *Built Environment*, 15(2).

— (1990) 'The dynamics of tourism place marketing', in G.J. Ashworth and B. Goodall (eds) *Marketing Tourism Places*, London: Routledge.

Goodall, B. and Whittow, J. (1975) *Recreation Requirements and Forest Opportunities*, Geographical Paper No. 378, Reading: Department of Geography, University of Reading.

Goodchild, M.F. (2007) 'Citizens as sensors: the world of volunteered geography', *GeoJournal*, 69: 211–21.

Goodenough, R. and Page, S.J. (1994) 'Evaluating the environmental impact of a major transport infrastructure project: the Channel Tunnel high speed rail link', *Applied Geography*, 14(1): 26–50.

Goodhead, T. and Johnson, D. (eds) (1996) *Coastal Recreation Management: The Sustainable Development of Maritime Leisure*, London: E&FN Spon.

Goodwin, M. (1993) 'The city as commodity: the contested spaces of urban development', in G. Kearns and C. Philo (eds) *Selling Places: The City as Cultural Capital, Past and Present*, Oxford: Pergamon Press.

Gormsen, E. (1982) 'Tourism as a development factor in tropical countries – a case study of Cancun, Mexico', *Applied Geography and Development*, 19: 46–63.

Gössling, S. (2001) 'The consequences of tourism for sustainable water use on a tropical island: Zanzibar, Tanzania', *Journal of Environmental Management*, 61: 179–91.

— (2002) 'Global environmental consequences of tourism', *Global Environmental Change* 12(4): 283–302.

— (ed.) (2003) *Tourism and Development in Tropical Islands: Political Ecology Perspectives*, Aldershot: Edward Elgar.

— (2011) *Carbon Management in Tourism: Mitigating the Impacts on Climate Change*, Abingdon: Routledge.

Gössling, S. and Hall, C.M. (eds) (2006a) *Tourism and Global Environmental Change*, Routledge: London.

— (2006b) 'Uncertainties in predicting tourist flows under scenarios of climate change', *Climatic Change*, 79: 163–73.

— (2013) 'Sustainable culinary systems: an introduction', in C.M. Hall and S. Gössling (eds) *Sustainable Culinary Systems: Local Foods, Innovation, and Tourism & Hospitality*, London: Routledge.

Gössling, S., Hall, C.M. and Scott, D. (2009a) 'The challenges of tourism as a development strategy in an era of global climate change', in E. Palosou (ed.) *Rethinking Development in a Carbon-Constrained World*, Helsinki: Ministry of Foreign Affairs.

Gössling, S., Hall, C.M. and Weaver, D. (eds) (2009b) *Sustainable Tourism Futures: Perspectives on Systems, Restructuring and Innovations*, London: Routledge.

Gössling, S., Scott, D. and Hall, C.M. (2013) 'Challenges of tourism in a low-carbon economy', *WIRES Climate Change*, DOI: 10.1002/wcc.243.

Gössling, S., Borgström-Hansson, C., Hörstmeier, O. and Saggel, S. (2002) 'Ecological footprint analysis as a tool to assess tourism sustainability', *Ecological Economics*, 43: 199–211.

Gössling, S., Ceron, J.-P., Dubios, G. and Hall, C.M. (2009c) 'Hypermobile travelers', in S. Gössling and P. Upham (eds) *Climate Change and Aviation*, London: Earthscan.

Gössling, S., Hall, C.M., Ekström, F., Brudvik Engeset, A. and Aall, C. (2012a) 'Transition management: a tool for implementing sustainable tourism scenarios?', *Journal of Sustainable Tourism*, 20: 899–916.

Gössling, S., Hall, C.M., Peeters, P. and Scott, D. (2010) 'The future of tourism: a climate change mitigation perspective', *Tourism Recreation Research*, 35: 119–30.

Gössling, S., Peeters, P., Hall, C.M., Ceron, J., Dubois, G., Lehmann, L.V. and Scott, D. (2012b) 'Tourism and water use: supply, demand, and security. An international review', *Tourism Management*, 33: 1–15.

Gössling, S., Scott, D., Hall, C.M., Ceron, J. and Dubois, G. (2012c) 'Consumer behaviour and demand response of tourists to climate change', *Annals of Tourism Research*, 39: 36–58.

Gottmann, J. (1983) 'Capital cities', *Ekistics*, 50: 88–93.

Graber, K. (1997) 'Cities and the destination life cycle', in J.A. Mazanec (ed.) *International City Tourism: Analysis and Strategy*, London: Pinter.

Graber, L.H. (1978) *Wilderness as Sacred Space*, Monograph No. 8, Washington, DC: Association of American Geographers.

Graburn, N.H.H. (1983) 'The anthropology of tourism', *Annals of Tourism Research*, 10: 9–33.

Graefe, A.R. (1991) 'Visitor impact management: an integrated approach to assessing the impacts of tourism in national parks and protected areas', in A.J. Veal, P. Jonson and G. Cushman (eds) *Leisure and Tourism: Social and Environmental Change, Papers from the World Leisure and Recreation Association Congress, Sydney*, Sydney: University of Technology.

Graefe, A.R. and Vaske, J.J. (1987) 'A framework for managing quality in the tourist experience', *Annals of Tourism Research*, 14: 389–404.

Graefe, A.R., Vaske, J.J. and Kuss, F.R. (1984a) 'Social carrying capacity: an integration and synthesis of twenty years of research', *Leisure Sciences*, 6: 395–431.

— (1984b) 'Resolving issues and remaining questions about social carrying capacity', *Leisure Sciences*, 6: 497–507.

Graham, A. (2013) 'Progress in tourism management: understanding the low cost carrier and airport relationship: a critical analysis of the salient issues', *Tourism Management*, 36: 66–76.

Graham, B. (1995) *Geography and Air Transport*, Chichester: John Wiley & Sons.

— (1998) 'Liberalisation, regional economic development and the geography of demand for air transport in the European Union', *Journal of Transport Geography*, 6(2): 87–104.

Graham, B., Ashworth, G.J. and Tunbridge, J.E. (2000) *A Geography of Heritage*, London: Arnold.

Grahn, P. (1991) 'Landscaped in our minds: people's choice of recreative places in towns', *Landscape Research*, 16: 11–19.

Gramann, J.H. (1982) 'Toward a behavioural theory of crowding in outdoor recreation: an evaluation and synthesis of research', *Leisure Sciences*, 5: 109–26.

Grano, O. (1981) 'External influence and internal change in the development of geography', in D.R. Stoddart (ed.) *Geography, Ideology and Social Concern*, Oxford: Blackwell.

Gratton, C. and Richards, G. (1997) 'Structural change in the European package tour industry – UK and German comparisons', *Tourism Economics*, 3(3): 213–26.

Graves, H.S. (1920) 'A crisis in national recreation', *American Forestry*, 26 (July): 391–400.

Greater London Authority (GLA) (2011) *The London Plan*, London: GLA.

Greater London Council (GLC) (1968) *Surveys of the Use of Open Space*, vol. 1, Greater London Council Research Paper 3, London: GLC.

— (1969) *Greater London Development Plan*, London: GLC.

— (1975) *Greater London Recreation Study*, London: GLC.

— (1976) *Greater London Recreation Study: Part 1, Demand*, London: GLC.

Green, E., Hebron, S. and Woodward, D. (1987) *Leisure and Gender: A Study of Sheffield Women's Leisure Experiences*, Sheffield: Sports Council and Economic and Social Research Council.

— (1990) *Women's Leisure, What Leisure?*, London: Macmillan.

Green, G., Marcouiller, D., Deller, S., Erkkil, D. and Sumathi, N. (1996) 'Local dependency, land use attitudes, and economic development: comparisons between seasonal and permanent residents', *Rural Sociology*, 61: 427–45.

Greenhut, M. (1956) *Plant Location in Theory and Practice*, Chapel Hill: University of North Carolina Press.

Greer, T. and Wall, G. (1979) 'Recreational hinterlands: a theoretical and empirical analysis', in G. Wall (ed.) *Recreational Land Use in Southern Ontario*, Department of Geography Publication Series No. 14, Waterloo: University of Waterloo.

Gregory, D. (1978) *Ideology, Science and Human Geography*, New York: St Martin's Press.

Gregory, J. (1988) *Perceptions of Open Space: A Report on Research Undertaken by the Urban Wildlife Group*, Birmingham: Urban Wildlife Trust.

Grenier, A. and Müller, D.K. (eds) (2011) *Polar Tourism: A Tool for Regional Development*. Montreal: PUQ.

Griffin, K. (1999) 'The inter-organisational relationships in Irish tourism', *Irish Geography*, 32(1): 57–72.

Griffith, D. and Elliot, D. (1988) *Sampling Errors on the IPS*, OPCS New Methodology Series, London: OPCS.

Griffiths, T. and Libby R. (eds) (1997) *Ecology and Empire: Environmental History of Settler Societies*, Edinburgh: Keele University Press.

Grinstein, A. (1955) 'Vacations: A psycho-analytic study', *International Journal of Psycho-Analysis*, 36: 177–86.

Grocott, A. (1990) 'Parks for people', *Leisure Management*, 8: 31–2.

Groome, D. and Tarrant, C. (1984) 'Countryside recreation: achieving access for all?', *Countryside Planning Yearbook 1984*: 77–98.

Groundwork Foundation (1986) *Putting Wasteland to Good Use*, Birmingham: Groundwork Foundation.

Gu, H., Ryan, C. and Yu, L. (2012) 'The changing structure of the Chinese hotel industry: 1980–2012', *Tourism Management Perspectives*, 4: 56–63.

Guardian (2012) 'How many gigatons of carbon dioxide? The Information is Beautiful guide to Doha', Guardian.co.uk, 7 December, http://www.guardian.co.uk/news/datablog/2012/dec/07/carbon-dioxide-doha-information-beautiful (accessed 8 December 2012).

Gui, L. and Russo, A.P. (2011) 'Cruise ports: a strategic nexus between regions and global lines—evidence from the Mediterranean', *Maritime Policy & Management*, 38(2): 129–50.

Gunn, A. (2002) *Tourism Planning: Basics, Concepts, Cases*, 4th edn, London: Routledge.

Gunn, C. (1972) *Vacationscape: Designing Tourist Regions*, Austin: University of Texas.

— (1988) *Tourism Planning*, 2nd edn, London: Taylor & Francis.

Guo, L., Wu, B., Liu, F. and Fau, Y. (2000) 'Study on the tourist resources classification system and types evaluation in China', *Acta Geographica Sinica*, 55(3): 294–301.

Guo, Y., Pei, Y., Ye, Y., Chen, Y., Wang, K.C. and Chan, H.C. (2009) 'Tourist shopping behavior: a case of Shanghai outbound tourists', *Journal of Tourism, Hospitality & Culinary Arts*, 1(2): 49–66.

Gustafson, P. (2002a) *Place, Place Attachment and Mobility: Three Sociological Studies*, Göteborg Studies in Sociology No. 6, Göteborg: Department of Sociology, Göteborg University.

— (2002b) 'Tourism and seasonal retirement migration', *Annals of Tourism Research*, 29: 899–918.

Guthrie, H.W. (1961) 'Demand for goods and services in a world market', *Regional Science Association Papers*, 7: 159–75.

Guy, B.S. and Curtis, W.W. (1986) 'Consumer learning or retail environment: a tourism and travel approach', paper presented at the American Academy of Marketing Conference, Tourism Services Marketing: Advances in Theory and Practice, Cleveland, OH: American Academy of Marketing Conference, Cleveland University.

Gvozdeva, G. (1999) 'Time balance changes and women's use of their right to rest', *Loisir et société*, 22(1): 127–44.

Hadley, D. (2009) 'Land use and the coastal zone', *Land Use Policy*, 26: S198–S203.

Hägerstrand, T. (1970) 'What about people in Regional Science?', *Papers of the Regional Science Association*, 24: 7–21.

— (1984) 'Escapes from the cage of routines: observations of human paths, projects and personal scripts', in J. Long and R. Hecock (eds) *Leisure, Tourism and Social Change*, Dunfermline: Dunfermline College of Physical Education.

Haggett, P. (1979) *Geography: A Modern Synthesis*, New York: Harper & Row.

— (1986) 'Geography', in R.J. Johnston, D. Gregory and D.M. Smith (eds) *The Dictionary of Human Geography*, Oxford: Blackwell.

Hailu, G., Boxall, P.C. and McFarlane, B.L. (2005) 'The influence of place attachment on recreation demand', *Journal of Economic Psychology*, 26: 581–98.

Haines, A.L. (1977) *The Yellowstone Story*, 2 vols, Yellowstone National Park: Yellowstone Library and Museum Association/Colorado Associated University Press.

Haley, A. (1979) 'Municipal recreation and park standards in the United States: central cities and suburbs', *Leisure Sciences*, 2: 277–91.

Halfacree, K. (1994) 'The importance of "the rural" in the constitution of counterurbanization: evidence from England in the 1980s', *Sociologia Ruralis*, 34: 164–89.

— (2011) '"A solid partner in a fluid world" and/or "line of flight"? Interpreting second homes in the era of mobilities', *Norsk Geografisk Tidsskrift–Norwegian Journal of Geography*, 65(3): 144–53.

Halkett, I. (1978) 'The recreational use of private gardens', *Journal of Leisure Research*, 10(1): 13–20.

Hall, C.M. (1985) 'Outdoor recreation and national identity: a comparative study of Australia and Canada', *Journal of Canadian Culture*, 2(2): 25–39.

— (1987) 'Wilderness inventories in Australia', in A. Conacher (ed.) *Readings in Australian Geography, Proceedings of the 21st Institute of Australian Geographers' Conference*, Nedlands: Department of Geography, University of Western Australia.

— (1988) *The Geography of Hope*, PhD thesis, Nedlands: Department of Geography, University of Western Australia.

— (1989) 'The definition and analysis of hallmark tourist events', *GeoJournal*, 19: 263–8.

— (1990) 'From cottage to condominium: recreation, tourism and regional development in northern New South Wales', in D.J. Walmsley (ed.) *Change and Adjustment in Northern New South Wales*, Armidale: Department of Geography and Planning, University of New England.

— (1992a) *Wasteland to World Heritage: Preserving Australia's Wilderness*, Carlton: Melbourne University Press.

— (1992b) *Hallmark Events: Impacts, Management and Planning*, London: Belhaven Press.

— (1994) *Tourism and Politics: Policy, Power and Place*, London: John Wiley.

— (1995) *Introduction to Tourism in Australia*, 2nd edn, South Melbourne: Longman Australia.

— (1996a) 'Tourism and the Maori of Aotearoa/New Zealand', in R.W. Butler and T. Hinch (eds) *Tourism and Indigenous Peoples*, London: International Thomson Business Publishing.

— (1996b) 'Wine tourism in New Zealand', in *Proceedings of Tourism Down Under II: A Tourism Research Conference*, Dunedin: University of Otago.

— (1997a) *Tourism in the Pacific: Development, Impacts and Markets*, 2nd ed., South Melbourne: Addison Wesley Longman.

— (1997b) 'Geography, marketing and the selling of places', *Journal of Travel and Tourism Marketing*, 6: 61–84.

— (1998) 'Historical antecedents of sustainable development and ecotourism: new labels on old bottles?', in C.M. Hall and A. Lew (eds) *Sustainable Tourism Development: Geographical Perspectives*, London: Addison-Wesley Longman.

— (1999) 'Rethinking collaboration and partnership: a public policy perspective', *Journal of Sustainable Tourism*, 7: 274–89.

— (2000a) *Tourism Planning: Policies, Processes and Relationships*, Harlow: Prentice Hall.

— (2000b) 'Tourism and the establishment of national parks in Australia', in R. Butler and S. Boyd (eds) *Tourism and National Parks*, Chichester: John Wiley.

— (2000c) 'Tourism, national parks and aboriginal populations', in R. Butler and S. Boyd (eds) *Tourism and National Parks*, Chichester: John Wiley.

— (2001a) 'Territorial economic integration and globalisation', in C. Cooper and S. Wahab (eds) *Tourism in the Age of Globalisation*, London: Routledge.

— (2001b) 'Imaging, tourism and sports event fever: the Sydney Olympics and the need for a social charter for mega-events', in C. Gratton and I.P. Henry (eds) *Sport in the City: The Role of Sport in Economic and Social Regeneration*, London: Routledge.

— (2002) 'Travel safety, terrorism and the media: the significance of the issue-attention cycle', *Current Issues in Tourism*, 5: 458–66.

— (2003a) *Introduction to Tourism in Australia*, 4th edn, Melbourne: Hospitality Press.

— (2003b) 'Wine and food tourism networks: a comparative study', in K. Pavlovich and M. Akoorie (eds) *Strategic Alliances and Collaborative Partnerships: A Case Book*, Palmerston North: Dunmore Press.

— (2003c) 'Biosecurity and wine tourism: is a vineyard a farm?', *Journal of Wine Research*, 14(2–3): 121–6.

— (2003d) 'Tourism and temporary mobility: circulation, diaspora, migration, nomadism, sojourning, travel, transport and home', paper presented at International Academy for the Study of Tourism (IAST) Conference, 30 June–5 July 2003, Savonlinna, Finland.

— (2004a) 'Reflexivity and tourism research: situating myself and/with others', in J. Phillimore and L. Goodson (eds) *Qualitative Research in Tourism: Ontologies, Epistemologies and Methodologies*, London: Routledge.

— (2004b) 'Small firms and wine and food tourism in New Zealand: issues of collaboration, clusters and lifestyles', in R. Thomas (ed.) *Small Firms in Tourism: International Perspectives*, Oxford: Elsevier.

— (2004c) 'Scale and the problems of assessing mobility in time and space', paper presented at the Swedish National Doctoral Student Course on Tourism, Mobility and Migration, Department of Social and Economic Geography, University of Umeå, Umeå, Sweden, October.

— (2005a) *Tourism: Rethinking the Social Science of Mobility*, Harlow: Prentice Hall.

— (2005b) 'Reconsidering the geography of tourism and contemporary mobility', *Australian Geographical Studies*, 43: 125–39.

— (2005c) 'Time, space, tourism and social physics', *Tourism Recreation Research*, 30(1): 93–8.

— (2005d) 'Demography', in D. Buhalis and C. Costa (eds) *Tourism Dynamics: Present and Future Issues*, Oxford: Butterworth Heinemann.

— (2005e) 'Biosecurity and wine tourism', *Tourism Management*, 26: 931–8.

— (2006a) 'Space–time accessibility and the tourist area cycle of evolution: the role of geographies of spatial interaction and mobility in contributing to an improved understanding of tourism', in R. Butler (ed.) *The Tourism Life Cycle: Conceptual and Theoretical Issues*, vol. 2, Clevedon: Channel View.

— (2006b) 'Urban entrepreneurship, corporate interests and sports mega-events: the thin policies of competitiveness within the hard outcomes of neoliberalism', *Sociological Review Monograph, Sports Mega-events: Social Scientific Analyses of a Global Phenomenon*, 54(s2): 59–70.

— (2006c) 'Tourism urbanization and global environmental change', in C.M. Hall and S. Gössling (eds) *Tourism and Global Environmental Change: Ecological, Economic, Social and Political Interrelationships*, London: Routledge.

— (2007a) 'Pro-poor tourism: do "tourism exchanges benefit primarily the countries of the South"?', *Current Issues in Tourism*, 10: 111–18.

— (2007b) 'Tourism and regional competitiveness', in J. Tribe and D. Airey (eds) *Advances in Tourism Research, Tourism Research, New Directions, Challenges and Applications*, Oxford: Elsevier.

— (2008a) *Tourism Planning: Policies, Processes and Relationships*, 2nd edn, Harlow: Prentice Hall/Pearson.

— (2008b) 'Servicescapes, designscapes, branding and the creation of place-identity: south of Litchfield, Christchurch', *Journal of Travel and Tourism Marketing*, 25: 233–50.

— (2009a) '"A long and still-unfinished story": constructing and defining Asian regionalisms', in T. Winter, P. Teo and T.C. Chang (eds) *Asia on Tour: Exploring the Rise of Asian Tourism*, London: Routledge.

— (2009b) 'Innovation and tourism policy in Australia and New Zealand: never the twain shall meet?', *Journal of Policy Research in Tourism, Leisure and Events*, 1: 2–18.

— (2009c) 'The public policy context of tourism entrepreneurship', in J. Ateljevic and S. Page (eds) *Progress in Tourism and Entrepreneurship*, Oxford: Elsevier.

— (2009d) 'Sharing space with visitors: the servicescape of the commercial exurban home', in P. Lynch, A. McIntosh and H. Tucker (eds) *The Commercial Home*, London: Routledge.

— (2009e) 'Degrowing tourism: décroissance, sustainable consumption and steady-state tourism', *Anatolia*, 20: 46–61.

— (2009f) 'Coastal tourism planning and policy in New Zealand', in R. Dowling and C. Pforr (eds) *Coastal Tourism Development*, New York: Cognizant Communication Corporation.

— (2009g) 'Archetypal approaches to implementation and their implications for tourism policy', *Tourism Recreation Research*, 34: 235–45.

— (2010a) 'Equal access for all? Regulative mechanisms, inequality and tourism mobility', in S. Cole and N. Morgan (eds) *Tourism and Inequality: Problems and Prospects*, Wallingford: CAB International.

— (2010b) 'The life and opinions of C. Michael Hall, gent: a shandy or full beer? Volume the first', in S. Smith (ed.) *The Discovery of Tourism*, Bingley: Emerald Publishing.

— (2010c) 'Academic capitalism, academic responsibility and tourism academics: Or, the silence of the lambs?', *Tourism Recreation Research*, 35: 298–301.

— (2010d) 'Power in tourism: tourism in power', in D. Macleod and J. Carrier (eds) *Tourism, Power and Culture: Anthropological Insights*, Bristol: Channel View.

— (2010e) 'Crisis events in tourism: subjects of crisis in tourism', *Current Issues in Tourism*, 13: 401–17.

— (2010f) 'Tourism and biodiversity: more significant than climate change?', *Journal of Heritage Tourism*, 5: 253–66.

— (2010g) 'Tourism destination branding and its affects on national branding strategies: brand New Zealand, clean and green but is it smart?', *European Journal of Tourism and Hospitality Research*, 1(1): 68–89.

— (2010h) 'Island destinations: a natural laboratory for tourism. Introduction', *Asia Pacific Journal of Tourism Research*, 15: 245–9.

— (2010i) 'An island biogeographical approach to island tourism and biodiversity: an exploratory study of the Caribbean and Pacific Islands', *Asia Pacific Journal of Tourism Research*, 15: 383–99.

— (2010j) 'Tourism and the implementation of the Convention on Biological Diversity', *Journal of Heritage Tourism*, 5: 267–84.

— (2010k) 'Tourism and environmental change in polar regions: impacts, climate change and biological invasion', in C.M. Hall and J. Saarinen (eds) *Tourism and Change in Polar Regions: Climate, Environments and Experiences*, London: Routledge.

— (2010l) 'Changing paradigms and global change: from sustainable to steady-state tourism', *Tourism Recreation Research*, 35(2): 131–45.

— (2011a) 'A typology of governance and its implications for tourism policy analysis', *Journal of Sustainable Tourism*, 19: 437–57.

— (2011b) 'Yes, Virginia, there is a tourism class. Why class still matters in tourism analysis', in J. Mosedale (ed.) *Political Economy and Tourism: A Critical Perspective*, London: Routledge.

— (ed.) (2011c) *Fieldwork in Tourism: Methods, Issues and Reflections*, Abingdon: Routledge.

— (2011d) 'Health and medical tourism: kill or cure for global public health?', *Tourism Review*, 66(1/2): 4–15.

— (2011e) 'Publish and perish? Bibliometric analysis, journal ranking and the assessment of research quality in tourism', *Tourism Management*, 32: 16–27.

— (2011f) 'Policy learning and policy failure in sustainable tourism governance: from first- and second-order to third-order change?', *Journal of Sustainable Tourism*, 19: 649–71.

— (2011g) 'Consumerism, tourism and voluntary simplicity: we all have to consume, but do we really have to travel so much to be happy?', *Tourism Recreation Research*, 36: 298–303.

— (2011h) 'Biosecurity, tourism and mobility: institutional arrangements for managing tourism-related biological invasions', *Journal of Policy Research in Tourism, Leisure and Events*, 3: 256–80.

— (2012a) 'Spatial analysis: a critical tool for tourism geographies', in J. Wilson (ed.) *The Routledge Handbook of Tourism Geographies*, London: Routledge.

— (ed.) (2012b) *Medical Tourism: The Ethics, Regulation, and Marketing of Health Mobility*, Abingdon: Routledge.

— (2012c) 'Boosting food and tourism-related regional economic development', in OECD *Food and the Tourism Experience*, Paris: OECD.

— (2013a) 'Framing tourism geography: notes from the underground', *Annals of Tourism Research*, DOI: 10.1016/j.annals.2013.06.007.

— (2013b) 'Regeneration and cultural quarters: changing urban cultural space', in M. Smith and G. Richards (eds) *The Routledge Handbook of Cultural Tourism*, London: Routledge.

— (2013c) 'Book review. Understanding tourism: a critical introduction', *Annals of Tourism Research*, 41: 244–6.

— (2013d) 'Development(s) in the geographies of tourism: knowledge(s), actions and cultures', in J. Wilson and S. Anton Clavé (eds) *Geographies of Tourism: European Research Perspectives*, London: Emerald.

— (2013e) 'Framing behavioural approaches to understanding and governing sustainable tourism consumption: beyond neoliberalism, "nudging" and "green growth"?', *Journal of Sustainable Tourism*, DOI: 10.1080/09669582.2013.815764.

— (2013f) 'The local in farmers markets in New Zealand', in C.M. Hall and S. Gössling (eds) *Sustainable Culinary Systems: Local Foods, Innovation, and Tourism & Hospitality*, London: Routledge.

— (2013g) 'The natural science ontology of environment', in A. Holden and D. Fennell (eds) *The Routledge Handbook of Tourism and the Environment*, Abingdon: Routledge.

— (2013h) 'Review: competititveness and tourism', *Journal of Sustainable Tourism*, DOI: 10.1080/09669582.2013.820886.

— (2013i) 'Why forage when you don't have to? Personal and cultural meaning in recreational foraging: a New Zealand study', *Journal of Heritage Tourism*, 8: 224–33.

— (2014) *Tourism and Social Marketing*, Abingdon: Routledge.

Hall, C.M. and Baird, T. (2013) 'Ecotourism, biological invasions and biosecurity', in R. Ballantyne and J. Packer (eds) *The International Handbook of Ecotourism*, Aldershot: Ashgate.

— (2014) 'Innovation in New Zealand wine tourism businesses', in G.A. Alsos, D. Eide and E.L. Madsen (eds) *Handbook of Research on Innovation in Tourism Industries*, Cheltenham: Edward Elgar.

Hall, C.M. and Boyd, S. (eds) (2005) *Nature-based Tourism in Peripheral Areas: Development or Disaster?*, Clevedon: Channel View.

Hall, C.M. and Frost, W. (2009) National parks and the "worthless lands hypothesis" revisited', in W. Frost and C.M. Hall (eds) *Tourism and National Parks: International Perspectives on Development, Histories and Change*, London: Routledge.

Hall, C.M. and Härkönen, T. (eds) (2006) *Lake Tourism: An Integrated Approach to Lacustrine Tourism Systems*, Clevedon: Channel View.

Hall, C.M. and Higham, J.E.S. (2000) 'Wilderness management in the forests of New Zealand: historical development and contemporary issues in environmental management', in X. Font and J. Tribe (eds) *Forest Tourism and Recreation: Case Studies in Environmental Management*, Wallingford: CAB International.

— (eds) (2005) *Tourism, Recreation and Climate Change*, Clevedon: Channel View.

Hall, C.M. and Hodges, J. (1996) 'The party's great, but what about the hangover? The housing and social impacts of mega-events with special reference to the Sydney 2000 Olympics', *Festival Management and Event Tourism*, 4(1/2): 13–20.

Hall, C.M. and James, M. (2011) 'Medical tourism: emerging biosecurity and nosocomial issues', *Tourism Review*, 66(1/2): 118–26.

Hall, C.M. and Jenkins, J. (1995) *Tourism and Public Policy*, London: Routledge.

— (1998) 'The policy dimensions of rural tourism and recreation', in R. Butler, C.M. Hall and J. Jenkins (eds) *Tourism and Recreation in Rural Areas*, Chichester: Wiley.

— (2004) 'Tourism and public policy', in A. Lew, C.M. Hall and A. Williams (eds) *A Companion to Tourism*, Oxford: Blackwell.

Hall, C.M. and Johnston, M. (eds) (1995) *Polar Tourism: Tourism in the Arctic and Antarctic Regions*, Chichester: Wiley.

Hall, C.M. and Kearsley, G.W. (2001) *Tourism in New Zealand: An Introduction*, Melbourne: Oxford University Press.

Hall, C.M. and Lew, A.A. (eds) (1998) *Sustainable Tourism Development: Geographical Perspectives*, Harlow: Addison Wesley Longman.

— (2009) *Understanding and Managing Tourism Impacts: An Integrated Approach*, London: Routledge.

Hall, C.M. and McArthur, S. (1994) 'Commercial whitewater rafting in Australia', in D. Mercer (ed.) *New Viewpoints in Australian Outdoor Recreation Research and Planning*, Williamstown: Hepper Marriot & Associates.

— (eds) (1996) *Heritage Management in Australia and New Zealand: The Human Dimension*, Sydney: Oxford University Press.

— (1998) *Integrated Heritage Management*, London: The Stationery Office.

Hall, C.M. and Macionis, N. (1998) 'Wine tourism in Australia and New Zealand', in R.W. Butler, C.M. Hall and J.M. Jenkins (eds) *Tourism and Recreation in Rural Areas*, Chichester: John Wiley & Sons.

Hall, C.M. and Mark, S.R. (1985) *Saving All the Pieces: Wilderness and Inventory and Prospect in Western Australia, a Working Paper*, Nedlands: Department of Geography, University of Western Australia.

Hall, C.M. and Mitchell, R. (2000) 'We are, what we eat: food, tourism and globalization', *Tourism, Culture and Communication*, 2(1): 29–37.

— (2002) 'The changing nature of the relationship between cuisine and tourism in Australia and New Zealand: from fusion cuisine to food networks', in A.-M. Hjalager and G. Richards (eds) *Tourism and Gastronomy*, London: Routledge.

— (2008) *Wine Marketing*, Oxford: Elsevier.

Hall, C.M. and Müller, D. (eds) (2004) *Tourism, Mobility and Second Homes: Elite Landscapes or Common Ground*, Clevedon: Channel View.

Hall, C.M. and Page, S.J. (eds) (1996) *Tourism in the Pacific: Cases and Issues*, London: International Thomson Business Publishing.

— (eds) (2000) *Tourism in South and South-East Asia: Cases and Issues*, Oxford: Butterworth Heinemann.

— (2006) *The Geography of Tourism and Recreation*, 3rd edn, London: Routledge.

— (2009) 'Progress in tourism management: from the geography of tourism to geographies of tourism – a review', *Tourism Management*, 30: 3–16.

— (2010) 'The contribution of Neil Leiper to Tourism Studies', *Current Issues in Tourism*, 13: 299–309.

— (2012) 'Geography and the study of events', in S.J. Page and J. Connell (eds) *The Routledge Handbook of Events*, London: Routledge.

Hall, C.M. and Piggin, R. (2001) 'Tourism and World Heritage in OECD countries', *Tourism Recreation Research*, 26(1): 103–5.

Hall, C.M. and Rath, J. (2007) 'Tourism, migration and place advantage in the global economy', in J. Rath (ed.) *Tourism, Ethnic Diversity and the City*, New York: Routledge.

Hall, C.M. and Rusher, K. (2004) 'Risky lifestyles? Entrepreneurial characteristics of the New Zealand bed and breakfast sector', in R. Thomas (ed.) *Small Firms in Tourism: International Perspectives*, Oxford: Elsevier.

Hall, C.M. and Saarinen, J. (eds) (2010) *Polar Tourism and Change: Climate, Environments and Experiences*, London: Routledge.

Hall, C.M. and Selwood, H.J. (1987) 'Cup gained, paradise lost? A case study of the 1987 America's Cup as a hallmark event', in *Proceedings of the New Zealand Geography Society Conference*, Palmerston North: Department of Geography, Massey University.

Hall, C.M. and Sharples, L. (eds) (2008) *Food and Wine Festivals and Events around the World: Development, Management and Markets*, Oxford: Butterworth Heinemann.

Hall, C.M. and Tucker, H. (eds) (2004) *Tourism and Postcolonialism*, London: Routledge.

Hall, C.M. and Williams, A.M. (eds) (2002) *Tourism and Migration*, Dordrecht: Kluwer.

— (2008) *Tourism and Innovation*, London: Routledge.

Hall, C.M. and Wilson, S. (2010) 'Tourism, conservation and visitor management in the sub-Antarctic Islands', in C.M. Hall and J. Saarinen (eds) *Tourism and Change in Polar Regions: Climate, Environments and Experiences*, London: Routledge.

— (2011) 'Neoliberal urban entrepreneurial agendas, Dunedin Stadium and the Rugby World Cup: or "If you don't have a stadium, you don't have a future"', in D. Dredge and J. Jenkins (eds) *Stories of Practice: Tourism Policy and Planning*, Farnham: Ashgate.

Hall, C.M., Gössling, S. and Scott, D. (eds) (2014) *The Routledge Handbook of Tourism and Sustainability*, Abingdon: Routledge.

Hall, C.M., James, M. and Wilson, S. (2010) 'Biodiversity, biosecurity, and cruising in the Arctic and sub-Arctic', *Journal of Heritage Tourism*, 5: 351–64.

Hall, C.M., Jenkins, J.M. and Kearsley, G. (eds) (1997) *Tourism Planning and Policy in Australia and New Zealand: Cases and Issues*, Sydney: Irwin Publishers.

Hall, C.M., Johnson, G. and Mitchell, R. (2000a) 'Wine tourism and regional development', in C.M. Hall, E. Sharples, B. Cambourne and N. Macionis (eds) *Wine Tourism around the World: Development, Management and Markets*, Oxford: Butterworth Heinemann.

Hall, C.M., Mitchell, R. and Sharples, E. (2003a) 'Consuming places: the role of food, wine and tourism in regional development', in C.M. Hall, E. Sharples, R. Mitchell, B. Cambourne and N. Macionis (eds) *Food Tourism around the World: Development, Management and Markets*, Oxford: Butterworth Heinemann.

Hall, C.M., Müller, D. and Saarinen, J. (2009) *Nordic Tourism*, Clevedon: Channel View.

Hall, C.M., Selwood, H.J. and McKewon, E. (1995) 'Hedonists, ladies and larrikins: crime, prostitution and the 1987 America's Cup', *Visions in Leisure and Business*, 14(3): 28–51.

Hall, C.M., Timothy, D. and Duval, D. (2003b) 'Security and tourism: towards a new understanding?', *Journal of Travel and Tourism Marketing*, 15(2–3): 1–18.

Hall, C.M., Timothy, D. and Duval, D. (eds) (2004a) *Safety and Security in Tourism: Relationships, Management and Marketing*, New York: Haworth Press.

Hall, C.M., Williams, A.M. and Lew, A. (2004b) 'Tourism: conceptualisations, institutions and issues', in A. Lew, C.M. Hall, C.M. and A.M. Williams (eds) *A Companion to Tourism*, Oxford: Blackwell.

Hall, C.M., Cambourne, B., Macionis, N. and Johnson, G. (1997–8) 'Wine tourism and network development in Australia and New Zealand: review, establishment and prospects', *International Journal of Wine Marketing*, 9(2/3): 5–31.

Hall, C.M., Sharples, E., Cambourne, C. and Macionis, N. (eds) (2000b) *Wine Tourism around the World: Development, Management and Markets*, Oxford: Butterworth Heinemann.

Hall, D.R. (ed.) (1991) *Tourism and Economic Development in Eastern Europe and the Soviet Union*, London: Belhaven Press.

Hall, D.R. and O'Hanlon, L. (eds) (1998) *Rural Tourism Management: Sustainable Options, Proceedings of an International Conference*, 9–12 September, Ayr: Scottish Agricultural College Auchincruive.

Hall, J.M. (1972) 'Leisure motoring in Great Britain: patterns and policies', *Geographica Polonica*, 24: 211–25.

Hall, J.M. (1974) 'The capacity to absorb tourists', *Built Environment*, 3: 392–7.

Hall, P. (1982a) *Urban and Regional Planning*, 2nd edn, Harmondsworth: Penguin.

— (1982b) *Great Planning Disasters*, Harmondsworth: Penguin.

— (1992) *Urban and Regional Planning*, 3rd edn, London: Routledge.

— (2000) 'The changing role of capital cities', *Plan Canada*, 40(3): 8–12.

Hallo, J.C. and Manning, R.E. (2010) 'Analysis of the social carrying capacity of a national park scenic road', *International Journal of Sustainable Transportation*, 4(2): 75–94.

Halseth, G. (1998) *Cottage Country in Transition: A Social Geography of Change and Contention in the Rural-Recreational Countryside*, Montreal: McGill-Queen's University Press.

Halseth, G. and Rosenberg, M.W. (1995) 'Cottagers in the urban field', *Professional Geographer*, 47: 148–59.

Hammitt, W.E. and Cole, D.N. (1998) *Wildland Recreation*, 2nd edn, Chichester: John Wiley.

Hamnett, C. (2001) 'The emporer's new clothes or geography without origami', in G. Philo and D. Miller (eds) *Market Killing: What the Free Market Does and What Social Scientists Can Do about It*, London: Longman.

Hannam, K. (2008) 'Tourist geographies, tourist studies and the turn towards mobilities', *Geography Compass*, 2: 127–39.

Hannam, K. and Diekmann, A. (2010) *Tourism and India: A Critical Introduction*, London: Taylor & Francis.

Hannigan, J. (1998) *Fantasy City: Pleasure and Profit in the Postmodern Metropolis*, London: Routledge.

Hao, H., Long, P. and Hoggard, W. (2013) 'Comparing property owners' perceptions of sustainable tourism in a coastal resort county', *Journal of Policy Research in Tourism, Leisure and Events*, DOI: 10.1080/19407963.2013.823975.

Hardiman, N. and Burgin, S. (2011) 'Canyoning adventure recreation in the Blue Mountains World Heritage Area (Australia): the canyoners and canyoning trends over the last decade', *Tourism Management*, 32: 1324–31.

Harmston, F.K. (1980) 'A case study of secondary impacts comparing through and vacationing travelers', *Journal of Travel Research*, 18(3): 33–6.

Harris, C. (1927) *The Use of Leisure in Bethnal Green: A Survey of Social Conditions in the Borough 1925 to 1926*, London: The Lindsey Press.

Harris, C.C., McLaughlin, W.J. and Ham, S.H. (1987) 'Integration of recreation and tourism in Idaho', *Annals of Tourism Research*, 14: 405–19.

Harrison, C. (1980–81) 'Recovery of lowland grassland and heathland in Southern England from disturbance by trampling', *Biological Conservation*, 19: 119–30.

— (1981) *Preliminary Results of a Survey of Site Use in the South London Green Belt*, Working Paper No. 9, Land for Informal Recreation, London: Department of Geography, University College.

— (1983) 'Countryside recreation and London's urban fringe', *Transactions of the Institute of British Geographers*, 8: 295–313.

— (1991) *Countryside Recreation in a Changing Society*, London: TML Partnership.

Harrison, D. (2004) 'Tourism in the Pacific Islands', *Journal of Pacific Studies*, 26(1/2): 1–28.

Harrop, A. and Palmer, G. (2002) *Indicators of Poverty and Social Exclusion in Rural England: 2002*, London: New Policy Institute.

Harshaw, H.W. and Sheppard, S.R.J. (2013) 'Using the recreation opportunity spectrum to evaluate the temporal impacts of timber harvesting on outdoor recreation settings', *Journal of Outdoor Recreation and Tourism*, 1: 40–50.

Hart, W. (1966) *A Systems Approach to Park Planning*, Morges: International Union for the Conservation of Nature.

Hartmann, R. (1984) 'Tourism, seasonality and social change', in J. Long and R. Hecock (eds) *Leisure, Tourism and Social Change*, Dunfermline: Centre for Leisure Research, Dunfermline College of Physical Education.

Harvey, D. (1974) 'What kind of geography, for what kind of public policy', *Transactions of the Institute of British Geographers*, 63: 18–24.

—— (1984) 'On the historical and present condition of geography: an historical materialist manifesto', *Professional Geographer*, 36: 1–11.

—— (1987) 'Flexible accumulation through urbanisation', *Antipode*, 19: 260–86.

—— (1988) 'Voodoo cities', *New Statesman and Society*, 30 September: 33–5.

—— (1989a) 'From managerialism to entrepreneurialism: the transformation in urban governance in late capitalism', *Geografiska Annaler*, 71B: 3–17.

—— (1989b) *The Condition of Postmodernity: An Enquiry into the Origins of Cultural Change*, Oxford: Blackwell.

—— (1990) 'Between space and time: reflection on the geographic information', *Annals of the Association of American Geographers*, 80: 418–34.

—— (1993) 'From space to place and back again: reflections on the condition of postmodernity', in J. Bird, B. Curtis, T. Putnam, G. Robertson and L. Tickner (eds) *Mapping the Futures: Local Cultures, Global Change*, London: Routledge.

—— (2000) *Spaces of Hope*, Berkeley: University of California Press.

—— (2005) *A Brief History of Neoliberalism*, Oxford: Oxford University Press.

Harwood, C. and Kirkpatrick, J.B. (1980) *Forestry and Wilderness in the South West*, rev. edn, Hobart: Tasmanian Conservation Trust.

Havighurst, R. and Feigenbaum, K. (1959) 'Leisure and lifestyle', *American Journal of Sociology*, 64: 396–405.

Hawes, M. and Heatley, D. (1985) *Wilderness Assessment and Management, a Discussion Paper*, Hobart: The Wilderness Society.

Hawkins, J.P. and Roberts, C.M. (1994) 'The growth of coastal tourism in the Red Sea: present and future effects on coral reefs', *Ambio*, 23(8): 503–8.

Hay, A.M. (2000) 'System', in R.J. Johnston, D. Gregory, G. Pratt and M. Watts (eds) *The Dictionary of Human Geography*, Oxford: Blackwell.

Hay, J.E. (2013) 'Small island developing states: coastal systems, global change and sustainability', *Sustainability Science*, 8: 309–26.

Haynes, R. (1980) *Geographical Images and Mental Maps*, London: Macmillan.

Hays, S. (1959) *Conservation and the Gospel of Efficiency: The Progressive Conservation Movement 1890–1920*. Cambridge, MA: Harvard University Press.

Hays, S., Page S. and Buhalis, D. (2013) 'Social media as a destination marketing tool: its use by national tourism organisations', *Current Issues in Tourism*, 16: 211–39.

Haywood, K.M. (1986) 'Can the resort–area life cycle be made operational?', *Tourism Management*, 7: 154–67.

Haywood, K.M. and Muller, T.E. (1988) 'The urban tourist experience: evaluating satisfaction', *Hospitality Education and Research Journal* 12(2): 453–9.

Head, L. (2007) 'Cultural ecology: the problematic human and the terms of engagement', *Progress in Human Geography*, 31: 837–46.

—— (2008) 'Is the concept of human impacts past its use-by date?', *The Holocene*, 18: 373–7.

Healey, P. (1997) *Collaborative Planning: Shaping Places in Fragmented Societies*, Basingstoke: Macmillan.

Heath, E. and Wall, G. (1992) *Marketing Tourism Destinations: A Strategic Planning Approach*, Chichester: Wiley.

Heeley, J. (1981) 'Planning for tourism in Britain', *Town Planning Review*, 52: 61–79.

Helbing, D. and Mukeriji, P. (2012) 'Crowd disaster as systemic failure: an analysis of the Love Parade disaster', *EPT Data Science*, 1(7): 1–40.

Helburn, N. (1977) 'The wilderness continuum', *Professional Geographer*, 29: 337–47.

Helman, P.H. (1979) *Wild and Scenic Rivers: A Preliminary Study of New South Wales*, Occasional Paper No. 2, Sydney: New South Wales National Parks and Wildlife Service.

Helman, P.H., Jones, A.D., Pigram, J.J.J. and Smith, J.M.B. (1976) *Wilderness in Australia: Eastern New South Wales and South-East Queensland*, Armidale: Department of Geography, University of New England.

Hendee, J.C., Stankey, G.H. and Lucas, R.C. (1978) *Wilderness Management*, Miscellaneous Publication No. 1365, Washington, DC: US Department of Agriculture, Forest Service.

Henderson, J.C., Chee, L., Mun, C.N. and Lee, C. (2011) 'Shopping, tourism and retailing in Singapore', *Managing Leisure*, 16: 36–48.

Henderson, K. (1997) 'A critique of constraints theory: a response', *Journal of Leisure Research*, 29(4): 453–7.

Hendry, L., Shucksmith, J., Love, J. and Glendinning, A. (1993) *Young People's Leisure and Lifestyles*, London: Routledge.

Heneghan, P. (1976) 'The changing role of Bord Fáilte 1960–1975', *Administration*, 24: 394–406.

Henning, D.H. (1971) 'The ecology of the political/administrative process for wilderness classification', *Natural Resources Journal*, 11: 69–75.

— (1974) *Environmental Policy and Administration*, New York: American Elsevier Publishing Company.

— (1987) 'Wilderness politics: public participation and values', *Environmental Management*, 11: 283–93.

Henry, I. (1988) 'Alternative futures for the public leisure service', in J. Benington and J. White (eds) *The Future of Leisure Services*, Harlow: Longman.

— (ed.) (1990) *Management and Planning in the Leisure Industries*, Basingstoke: Macmillan.

Henry, I. and Spink, J. (1990) 'Planning for leisure: the commercial and public sectors', in I. Henry (ed.) *Management and Planning in the Leisure Industries*, Basingstoke: Macmillan.

Herbert, D.T. (1987) 'Exploring the work–leisure relationship: an empirical study of south Wales', *Leisure Studies*, 6: 147–65.

— (1988) 'Work and leisure: exploring a relationship', *Area*, 20: 241–52.

Herbertson, A.J. (1905) 'The major natural regions', *Geographical Journal*, 25: 300–10.

Hewitt, J. (1995) 'East Coast joys: Tom Purvis and the LNER', *Journal of Design History*, 8: 291–311.

Hibbert, J.F., Dickinson, J.E., Gössling, S. and Curtin, S. (2013) 'Identity and tourism mobility: an exploration of the attitude–behaviour gap', *Journal of Sustainable Tourism*, DOI: 10.1080/09669582.2013.826232.

Higgins-Desbiolles, F. (2011) 'Death by a thousand cuts: governance and environmental trade-offs in ecotourism development at Kangaroo Island, South Australia', *Journal of Sustainable Tourism*, 19: 553–70.

Higham, J.E.S. (1997) 'Visitors to New Zealand's backcountry conservation estate', in C.M. Hall, J. Jenkins and G. Kearsley (eds) *Tourism Planning and Policy in Australia and New Zealand*, Sydney: Irwin Publishers.

— (1998) 'Tourists and albatrosses: the dynamics of tourism at the Northern Royal Albatross Colony, Taiaroa Head, New Zealand', *Tourism Management*, 19: 521–31.

Higham, J.E.S. and Lück, M. (2002) 'Urban ecotourism: a contradiction in terms?', *Journal of Ecotourism*, 1: 36–51.

Higham, J.E.S. and Shelton, E.J. (2011) 'Tourism and wildlife habituation: reduced population fitness or cessation of impact?', *Tourism Management*, 32: 1290–8.

Hill, E., Bergstrom, J., Cordell, H.K. and Bowker, J.M. (2009) *Natural Resource Amenity Service Values and Impacts in the US*, Athens: University of Georgia, Department of Agricultural & Applied Economics and the USDA Forest Service, Southern Research Station.

Hill, H., Kelley, J., Belknap, D. and Dickson, S. (2002) 'Co-measurement of beaches in Maine, USA: volunteer profiling of beaches and annual meetings', *Journal of Coastal Research*, 36: 374–80.

Hiltunen, M.J. (2007) 'Environmental impacts of rural second home tourism: Case Lake District in Finland', *Scandinavian Journal of Hospitality and Tourism*, 7: 243–65.

Hiltunen, M.J., Pitkänen, K., Vepsäläinen, M. and Hall, C.M. (2013) 'Second home tourism in Finland – current trends and ecosocial impacts', in Z. Roca, M. Nazaré Roca and J. Oliveira (eds) *Second Homes in Europe: Lifestyle Issues to Policy Issues*, Aldershot: Ashgate.

Hinch, T. (1990) 'A spatial analysis of tourist accommodation in Ontario: 1974–1988', *Journal of Applied Recreation Research*, 15(4): 239–64.

— (1996) 'Urban tourism: perspectives on sustainability', *Journal of Sustainable Tourism*, 4(2): 95–110.

— (1998) 'Ecotourists and indigenous hosts: diverging views on their relationship with nature', *Current Issues in Tourism*, 1: 120–4.

Hinch, T. and Higham, J. (2003) *Sport Tourism Development*, Clevedon: Channel View.

Hjalager, A.M. (2000) 'Consumerism and sustainable tourism', *Journal of Travel & Tourism Marketing*, 8(3): 1–20.

Hobson, J.P. (2000) 'Tourist shopping in transit: the case of BAA plc', *Journal of Vacation Marketing*, 6(2): 170–83.

Hockin, R., Goodall, B. and Whitlow, J. (1978) *The Site Requirements and Planning of Outdoor Recreation Activities*, Geographical Paper No. 54, Reading: University of Reading.

Hoggart, K. (1988) 'Not a definition of rural', *Area*, 20: 35–40.

— (1990) 'Let's do away with rural', *Journal of Rural Studies*, 6: 245–57.

Hoggart, K. and Green D. (eds) (1991) *London: A New Metropolitan Geography*, London: Edward Arnold.

Holden, A. (2000) *Environment and Tourism*, London: Routledge.

Holden, A. and Fennell, D. (eds) (2013) *The Routledge Handbook of Tourism and the Environment*, Abingdon: Routledge.

Holloway, L. and Kneafsey, M. (2000) 'Reading the space of the farmers' market: a preliminary investigation from the UK', *Sociologia Ruralis*, 40: 285–99.

Hoogendoorn, G. and Visser, G. (2011) 'Economic development through second home development: evidence from South Africa', *Tijdschrift voor economische en sociale geografie*, 102: 275–89.

Horne, J. (1998) 'Understanding leisure time and leisure space in contemporary Japanese society', *Leisure Studies*, 17: 37–52.

Hötelling, H. (1929) 'Stability in competition', *Economic Journal*, 39: 41–57.

Hottola, P. (ed.) (2009) *Tourism Strategies and Local Responses in Southern Africa*, Wallingford: CAB International.

Houghton, D.S. (1989) 'Some aspects of beach use in the Perth metropolitan area', *Australian Geographer*, 20: 173–84.

Houinen, G. (1995) 'Heritage issues in urban tourism: an assessment of new trends in Lancaster County', *Tourism Management*, 16: 381–8.

House, J.W. (1978) *France: An Applied Geography*, London: Methuen.

Howell, S. and McNamee, M. (2003) 'Local justice and public sector leisure policy', *Leisure Studies*, 22(1): 17–35.

Hoyle, B. (2001) 'Lamu: waterfront revitalization in an East African port-city', *Cities*, 18(5): 297–313.

Hoyle, B.S. and Pinder, D. (eds) (1992) *European Port Cities in Transition*, London: Belhaven Press.

Hoyles, M. (1994) *Lost Connections and New Directions*, Working Paper No. 6, London: Comedia & Demos.

Huang, Y. and Yi, C. (2011) 'Second home ownership in transitional urban China', *Housing Studies*, 26: 423–47.

Hubbard, P., Kitchin, R. and Valentine, G. (eds) (2004) *Key Thinkers on Space and Place*, London: Sage.

Hudman, L. (1978) 'Tourist impacts: the need for regional planning', *Annals of Tourism Research*, 9: 563–83.

Hudson, B. (1996) 'Paradise lost: a planner's view of Jamaican tourist development', *Caribbean Quarterly*, 42(4): 22–31.

Hudson, P. (1990a) 'Stresses in small towns in north-western Australia: the impact of tourism and development', paper presented at the 24th Institute of Australian Geographers Conference, University of New England, Armidale, September.

— (1990b) 'Structural changes in three small north-western Australian communities: the relationship between development and local quality of life', paper presented at the Annual Conference of Regional Science Association, Australian and New Zealand section, Perth, December.

Hudson, R. (2000) *Production, Places and the Environment: Changing Perspectives in Economic Geography*, Harlow: Prentice Hall/Pearson.

Hudson, R. and Townsend, A. (1992) 'Tourism employment and policy choices for local government', in P. Johnson and B. Thomas (eds) *Perspectives on Tourism Policy*, London: Mansell.

Huggins, M. (2000) 'More sinful pleasures? Leisure, respectability and the male middle classes in Victorian England', *Journal of Social History*, 33(3): 585–600.

Hughes, G. (2004) 'Tourism, sustainability and social theory', in A. Lew, C.M. Hall and A. Williams (eds) *A Companion to Tourism*, Oxford: Blackwell.

Hughes, J.D. (1978) *In the House of Stone and Light: A Human History of the Grand Canyon*, Grand Canyon: Grand Canyon Natural History Association.

Hughes, M. and Macbeth, J. (2005) 'Can a niche-market captive-wildlife facility place a low-profile region on the tourism map? An example from Western Australia', *Tourism Geographies*, 7: 424–43.

Hultman, J. (2007) 'Through the protocol: culture, magic and GIS in the creation of regional attractiveness', *Tourism Geographies*, 9: 318–36.

Hultman, J. and Hall, C.M. (2012) 'Tourism place-making: governance of locality in Sweden', *Annals of Tourism Research*, 39: 547–70.

Hummelbrunner, R. and Miglbauer, E. (1994) 'Tourism promotion and potential in peripheral areas: the Austrian case', *Journal of Sustainable Tourism*, 2: 41–50.

Hunt, L.M., Robson, M., Lemelin, R.H. and McIntyre, N. (2010) 'Exploring the acceptability of spatial simulation models of outdoor recreation for use by participants in public participation processes', *Leisure Sciences*, 32: 222–39.

Hunter, C. and Green, H. (1995) *Tourism and the Environment*, London: Routledge.

Hurst, F. (1987) 'Enroute surveys', in J.B. Ritchie and C. Goeldner (eds) *Travel Tourism and Hospitality Research: A Handbook for Managers and Researchers*, New York: John Wiley & Sons.

Huston, S., Evenson, K., Bors, P. and Gizlice, K. (2003) 'Neighbourhood environment, access to places for activity, and leisure-time physical activity in a diverse North Carolina population', *American Journal of Health Promotion*, 18(1): 58–69.

Hutchinson, B. (2004) 'Vancouver adores its stinking herons', *National Post*, 12 May: A1, A6.

Huxley, T. (1970) *Footpaths in the Countryside*, Edinburgh: Countryside Commission for Scotland.

Iazzarotti, O. (1995) *Les Loisirs à la conquête des espaces périurbains*, Paris: L'Harmattan.

— (2002) 'French tourism geographies: a review', *Tourism Geographies*, 4: 135–47.

Ilbery, B. (1991) 'Farm diversification as an adjustment strategy on the urban fringe of the West Midlands', *Journal of Rural Studies*, 7(3): 2–18.

Ilbery, B. and Kneafsey, M. (2000a) 'Registering regional specialty food and drink products in the United Kingdom: the case of PDOs and PGIs', *Area*, 32: 317–25.

— (2000b) 'Producer constructions of quality in regional speciality food production: a case study from South West England', *Journal of Rural Studies*, 16: 217–30.

Ilbery, B., Bowler, I., Clark, G., Crockett, A. and Shaw, A. (1998) 'Farm-based tourism as an alternative farm enterprise. A case study from the Northern Pennines, England', *Regional Studies*, 32: 355–64.

Industry Commission (1995) *Tourism Accommodation and Training*, Melbourne: Industry Commission.

Inskeep, E. (1991) *Tourism Planning: An Integrated and Sustainable Development Approach*, New York: Van Nostrand Reinhold.

— (1994) *National and Regional Tourism Planning*, London: Routledge.

Intergovernmental Panel on Climate Change (IPCC) (2007a) *Climate Change 2007: The Physical Science Basis. Contribution of Working Group I to the Fourth Assessment Report*, Cambridge: Cambridge University Press.

— (2007b) *Climate Change 2007: Impacts, Adaptation and Vulnerability. Contribution of Working Group II to the Fourth Assessment Report of the Intergovernmental*

Panel on Climate Change, Cambridge: Cambridge University Press.

— (2013) *Working Group I Contribution to the IPCC Fifth Assessment Report, Climate Change 2013: The Physical Science Basis, Summary for Policymakers*, 27 September.

International Energy Agency (IEA) (2009) *Transport, Energy and CO₂: Moving towards Sustainability*, Paris: IEA.

International Union of Tourism Organisations (IUOTO) (1974) 'The role of the state in tourism', *Annals of Tourism Research*, 1: 66–72.

Ioannides, D. (1992) 'Tourism development agents: the Cypriot resort cycle', *Annals of Tourism Research*, 19: 711–31.

— (1995) 'Strengthening the ties between tourism and economic geography: a theoretical agenda', *Professional Geographer*, 47: 49–60.

— (1996) 'Tourism and economic geography nexus: a response to Anne-Marie d'Hauteserre', *Professional Geographer*, 48: 219–21.

— (1998) 'Tour operators: the gatekeepers of tourism', in D. Ioannides and K. Debbage (eds) *The Economic Geography of the Tourist Industry: A Supply-side Analysis*, London: Routledge.

— (2006) 'Commentary: the economic geography of the tourist industry: ten years of progress in research and an agenda for the future', *Tourism Geographies*, 8: 76–86.

Ioannides, D. and Debbage, K. (eds) (1998) *The Economic Geography of the Tourist Industry: A Supply-side Analysis*, London: Routledge.

Ioffe, G. and Nefedova, T. (2001) 'Land use changes in the environs of Moscow', *Area*, 33: 273–86.

Isard, W. (1956) *Location and Space Economy*, Cambridge, MA: MIT Press.

Iso-Ahola, S. (1980) *The Social Psychology of Leisure and Recreation*, Springfield, IL: C. Thomas.

IUCN (1994) *Guidelines for Protected Area Management Categories*, Gland: IUCN.

Ivy, R. (2001) 'Geographical variations in alternative tourism and recreation establishments', *Tourism Geographies*, 3(3): 338–55.

Jaakson, R. (1986) 'Second-home domestic tourism', *Annals of Tourism Research*, 13: 367–91.

Jäckel, M. and Wollscheid, D.K.S. (2004) 'Time is money and money needs time: a secondary analysis

of time-budget data', paper presented at the International Association for Research in Income and Wealth (IARIW) Conference Cork, Ireland, 22–27 August.

Jackson, E. (1988) 'Leisure constraints: a survey of past research', *Leisure Sciences*, 10: 203–15.

— (1990) 'Variations in the desire to begin a leisure activity: evidence of antecedent constraints', *Journal of Leisure Research*, 22: 55–70.

— (1994) 'Geographical aspects of constraints on leisure', *Canadian Geographer*, 38: 110–21.

Jackson, E., Crawford, D. and Godbey, G. (1993) 'Negotiation of leisure constraints', *Leisure Sciences*, 15(1): 1–11.

Jackson, P. (1985) 'Urban ethnography', *Progress in Human Geography*, 9: 157–76.

Jacob, G. and Schreyer, R. (1980) 'Conflict in outdoor recreation: a theoretical perspective', *Journal of Leisure Research*, 12: 368–80.

Jacobs, M. (1991) *The Green Economy*, London: Pluto Press.

Jamal, T.B. and Getz, D. (1995) 'Collaboration theory and community tourism planning', *Annals of Tourism Reseach*, 22: 186–204.

James, P.E. (1972) *All Possible Worlds: A History of Geographical Ideas*, Indianapolis: The Odyssey Press.

Janiskee, R. and Mitchell, L. (1989), 'Applied recreation geography', in M. Kenzer (ed.) *Applied Geography Issues, Questions and Concerns*, Dordrecht: Kluwer.

Janoschka, M. and Haas, H. (eds) (2014) *Contested Spatialities of Lifestyle Migration*, London: Routledge.

Jansen-Verbeke, M. (1986) 'Inner-city tourism: resources, tourists and promoters', *Annals of Tourism Research*, 13: 79–100.

— (1988) *Leisure, Recreation and Tourism in Inner Cities: Explorative Case Studies*, Netherlands Geographical Studies 58, Amsterdam/Nijmegen: Instituut voor Sociale Geographie, University of Amsterdam.

— (1989) 'Inner cities and urban tourism in the Netherlands: new challenges for local authorities', in P. Bramham, I. Henry, H. Mommass and H. van der Poel (eds) *Leisure and Urban Processes: Critical Studies of Leisure Policy in Western European Cities*, London: Routledge.

— (1990) 'Leisure and shopping – tourism product mix', in G.J. Ashworth and B. Goodall (eds) *Marketing Tourism Places*, London: Routledge.

— (1991) 'Leisure shopping: a magic concept for the tourism industry', *Tourism Management*, 12: 9–14.

— (1992) 'Urban recreation and tourism: physical planning issues', *Tourism Recreation Research*, 17(2): 33–45.

— (1995) 'Urban tourism and city trips', *Annals of Tourism Research*, 22: 699–700.

Jansen-Verbeke, M. and Ashworth, G.J. (1990) 'Environmental integration of recreation and tourism', *Annals of Tourism Research*, 17: 618–22.

Jansen-Verbeke, M. and Dietvorst, A. (1987) 'Leisure, recreation and tourism: a geographic view on integration', *Annals of Tourism Research*, 14: 361–75.

Jansen-Verbeke, M. and Rekom, J. (1996) 'Scanning museum visitors: urban tourism marketing', *Annals of Tourism Research*, 23: 364–75.

Jansson, B. and Müller, D.K. (2003) *Fritidsboende i Kvarken*. Umeå: Kvarkenrådet.

Janta, H., Brown, L., Lugosi, P. and Ladkin, A. (2011) 'Migrant relationships and tourism employment', *Annals of Tourism Research*, 38: 1322–43.

Jayne, M. (2006) *Cities and Consumption*, Abingdon: Routledge.

Jeans, D. (1990) 'Beach resort morphology in England and Australia: a review and extension', in P. Fabbri (ed.) *Recreational Use of Coastal Areas*, Dordrecht: Kluwer.

Jenkins, C. and Henry, B. (1982) 'Government involvement in tourism in developing countries', *Annals of Tourism Research*, 9: 499–521.

Jenkins, J. (1993) 'Tourism policy in rural New South Wales – policy and research priorities', *GeoJournal*, 29: 281–90.

— (1997) 'The role of the Commonwealth Government in rural tourism and regional development in Australia', in C.M. Hall, J. Jenkins and G. Kearsley (eds) *Tourism Planning and Policy in Australia and New Zealand: Cases, Issues and Practice*, Sydney: Irwin Publishers.

— (2000) 'The dynamics of regional tourism organisations in New South Wales, Australia: history, structures and operations', *Current Issues in Tourism*, 3: 175–203.

— (2001) 'Editorial: Special issue tourism policy', *Current Issues in Tourism*, 4: 69–77.

Jenkins, J. and Pigram, J. (1994) 'Rural recreation and tourism: policy and planning', in D. Mercer (ed.) *New Viewpoints in Australian Outdoor Recreation Research and Planning*, Williamstown: Hepper Marriott & Associates.

Jenkins, J. and Prin, E. (1998) 'Rural landholder attitudes: the case of public recreational access to "private" lands', in R. Butler, C.M. Hall and J. Jenkins (eds) *Tourism and Recreation in Rural Areas*, Chichester: Wiley.

Jenkins, J. and Walmsley, D.J. (1993) 'Mental maps of tourists: a study of Coffs Harbour, New South Wales', *GeoJournal*, 29: 233–41.

Jenkins, J., Dredge, D. and Taplin, J. (2011) 'Destination planning and policy: process and practice', in Y. Wang and A. Pizam (eds) *Destination Marketing and Management: Theories and Applications*, Wallingford: CAB International.

Jenkins, J., Hall, C.M. and Troughton, M. (1998) 'The restructuring of rural economies: rural tourism and recreation as a government response', in R. Butler, C.M. Hall and J. Jenkins (eds) *Tourism and Recreation in Rural Areas*, Chichester: Wiley.

Jenkins, O. (2003) 'Photography and travel brochures: the circle of representation', *Tourism Geographies*, 5: 305–28.

Jennings, G. (ed.) (2006) *Water-Based Tourism, Sport, Leisure, and Recreation Experiences*, Oxford: Elsevier.

Jessop, B. (1999) 'Reflections on globalisation and its (il)logic(s)', in K. Olds, P. Dicken, P.F. Kelly, L. Kong and H.W. Yeung (eds) *Globalisation and the Asia-Pacific: Contested Territories*, London: Routledge.

Jessop, B. and Sum, N.L. (2001) 'Pre-disciplinary and post-disciplinary perspectives', *New Political Economy*, 6: 89–101.

Jim, C.Y. and Chen, W.Y. (2009) 'Leisure participation pattern of residents in a New Chinese City', *Annals of the Association of American Geographers*, 99(4): 657–73.

Jiménez, J.A., Gracia, V., Valdemoro, H.I., Mendoza, E.T. and Sánchez-Arcilla, A. (2011) 'Managing erosion-induced problems in NW Mediterranean urban beaches', *Ocean & Coastal Management*, 54: 907–18.

Johnson, C.Y., Bowker, J.M., Bergstrom, J. and Cordell, K. (2004) 'Wilderness values in America: does immigrant status or ethnicity matter?', *Society and Natural Resources*, 17: 611–28.

Johnson, C.Y., Bowker, J., English, D. and Worthen, D. (1998) 'Wildland recreation in the rural South: an examination of marginality and ethnic theory', *Journal of Leisure Research*, 30(1): 101–20.

Johnson, D. (2002) 'Towards sustainability: examples from the UK coast', in R. Harris, T. Griffin and P. Williams (eds) *Sustainable Tourism: A Global Perspective*, Oxford: Butterworth Heinemann.

Johnson, D., Snepenger, J. and Akis, S. (1994) 'Residents' perceptions of tourism development', *Annals of Tourism Research*, 21: 629–42.

Johnston, R.J. (1983a) 'On geography and the history of geography', *History of Geography Newsletter*, 3: 1–7.

— (1983b) 'Resource analysis, resource management and the integration of human and physical geography', *Progress in Physical Geography*, 7. 127–46.

— (1985) 'To the ends of the earth', in R. Johnston (ed.) *The Future of Geography*, London: Methuen.

— (1986) 'Applied geography', in R.J. Johnston, D. Gregory and D.M. Smith (eds) *The Dictionary of Human Geography*, Oxford: Blackwell.

— (1991) *Geography and Geographers: Anglo-American Human Geography since 1945*, 4th edn, London: Edward Arnold.

Johnston, R.J. and Sidaway, J.D. (1997) *Geography and Geographers: Anglo-American geography since 1945*, 5th edn, John Wiley & Sons.

— (2014) *Geography and Geographers: Anglo-American geography since 1945*, 7th edn, John Wiley & Sons.

Johnston, R.J., Gregory, D. and Smith, D.M. (eds) (1986) *The Dictionary of Human Geography*, 2nd edn, Oxford: Blackwell.

— (eds) (1994) *The Dictionary of Human Geography*, 4th edn, Oxford: Blackwell.

Jones, A.L. and Phillips, M.R. (eds) (2011) *Disappearing Destinations: Climate Change and the Future Challenges for Coastal Tourism*, Wallingford: CAB International.

Jones, A.P., Brainard, J., Bateman, I.J. and Lovett, A.A. (2009) 'Equity of access to public parks in Birmingham, England', *Environmental Research Journal*, 3: 237–56.

Jones, C. (2013) 'Scenarios for greenhouse gas emissions reduction from tourism: an extended tourism satellite account approach in a regional setting', *Journal of Sustainable Tourism*, 21: 458–72.

Jones, S.B. (1933) 'Mining tourist towns in the Canadian Rockies', *Economic Geography*, 9: 368–78.

Jones, T. (1994) 'Theme park development in Japan', in C. Cooper and A. Lockwood (eds) *Progress in Tourism, Recreation and Hospitality Management*, vol. 6, Chichester: Wiley.

Jordan, J.W. (1980) 'The summer people and the natives: some effects of tourism in a Vermont vacation village', *Annals of Tourism Research*, 7: 34–55.

Jordison, S. and Kieran, D. (2003) *Crap Towns: The 50 Worst Places to Live in the UK*, London: Boxtree.

Joyce, K. and Sutton, S. (2009) 'A method for automatic generation of the Recreation Opportunity Spectrum in New Zealand', *Applied Geography*, 29: 409–18.

Judd, D. (1995) 'Promoting tourism in US cities', *Tourism Management*, 16: 175–87.

Judd, D. and Fainstein S. (1999) *The Tourist City*, New Haven, CT: Yale University Press.

Jung, B. (1994) 'For what leisure? The role of culture and recreation in post-communist Poland', *Leisure Studies*, 13: 262–76.

— (1996) 'Poland', in G. Cushman, A. Veal and J. Zuzanek (eds) *World Leisure Participation Free Time in the Global Village*, Wallingford: CAB International.

Kabanoff, B. (1982) 'Occupational and sex differences in leisure needs and leisure satisfaction', *Journal of Occupational Behaviour*, 3: 233–45.

Kadri, B. (2008) 'L'Identité scientifique du tourisme: un mythe ou une réalité en construction?', *Téoros. Revue de recherche en tourisme*, 27(1): 51–8.

Kaltenborn, B.P. (1997a) 'Recreation homes in natural settings: factors affecting place attachment', *Norsk Geografisk Tidsskrift*, 51: 187–98.

— (1997b) 'Nature of place attachment: a study among recreation homeowners in southern Norway', *Leisure Sciences*, 19: 175–89.

— (1998) 'The alternate home: models of recreation home use', *Norsk Geografisk Tidsskrift*, 52: 121–34.

Kaltenborn, B.P., Qvenild, M. and Nellemann, C. (2011) 'Local governance of national parks: the perception of tourism operators in Dovre-Sunndalsfjella National Park, Norway', *Norsk Geografisk Tidsskrift*, 65: 83–92.

Kane, M.J. (2013) 'New Zealand's transformed adventure: from hero myth to accessible tourism experience', *Leisure Studies*, 32: 133–51.

Katz, B. and Wagner, J. (2011) 'An agenda for the urban age', in R. Burdett and D. Sudjic (eds) *The Endless City*, London: Phaidon.

Kay, R. and Alder, J. (1999) *Coastal Planning and Management*, London: E&FN Spon.

Kay, T. and Jackson, G. (1991) 'Leisure despite constraint: the impact of leisure constraints on leisure participation', *Journal of Leisure Research*, 23: 301–13.

Keane, M.J., Briassoulis, H. and van der Stratten, J. (1992) 'Rural tourism and rural development', in H. Briassoulis and J. van der Stratten (eds) *Tourism and the Environment: Regional, Economic and Policy Issues, Environment and Assessment*, vol. 2, Dordrecht: Kluwer Academic.

Kearns, G. and Philo, C. (eds) (1993) *Selling Places: The City as Cultural Capital, Past and Present*, Oxford: Pergamon Press.

Kearsley, G.W. (1990) 'Tourism development and the user's perceptions of wilderness in Southern New Zealand', *Australian Geographer*, 21: 127–40.

Kearsley, G.W., Hall, C.M. and Jenkins, J. (1997) 'Tourism planning and policy in natural areas: introductory comments', in C.M. Hall, J. Jenkins and G. Kearsley (eds) *Tourism Planning and Policy in Australia and New Zealand*, Sydney: Irwin Publishers.

Keeble, D., Owens, P. and Thompson, C. (1982) 'Regional accessibility and economic potential in the European Community', *Regional Studies*, 16: 419–32.

Keen, D. and Hall, C.M. (2004) 'Second homes in New Zealand', in C.M. Hall and D. Müller (eds) *Tourism, Mobility and Second Homes: Elite Landscapes or Common Ground*, Clevedon: Channel View.

Keirle, I. (2002) 'Should access to the coastal lands of Wales be developed through a voluntary or statutory approach? A discussion', *Land Use Policy*, 19(2): 177–85.

Keller, C.P. (1984) 'Centre–periphery tourism development and control', in J. Long and R. Hecock (eds) *Leisure, Tourism and Social Change*, Dunfermline: Centre for Leisure Research, Dunfermline College of Physical Education.

Keller, D.R. and Golley, F.B. (eds) (2000) *The Philosophy of Ecology: From Science to Synthesis*, Athens: University of Georgia Press.

Kelletat, D. (1993) 'Coastal geomorphology and tourism on the German North Sea coast', in P. Wong (ed.) *Tourism vs Environment: The Case for Coastal Areas*, Dordrecht: Kluwer Academic.

Kelly, J. (1982) *Leisure*, Englewood Cliffs, NJ: Prentice Hall.

Kelly, P.F. and Olds, K. (1999) 'Questions in a crisis: the contested meanings of globalisation in the Asia-Pacific', in K. Olds, P. Dicken, P.F. Kelly, L. Kong and H.W. Yeung (eds) *Globalisation and the Asia-Pacific: Contested Territories*, Warwickshire Studies in Globalisation Series, London: Routledge.

Keltie, J.S. (1890) *Applied Geography: A Preliminary Sketch*, London: George Philip and Sons.

Ken, S. and Rapoport, R. (1975) *Beyond Palpable Mass Demand – Leisure Provision and Human Demands: The Life Cycle Approach*, paper presented to Planning and Transport Research and Computation (International) Company Ltd, Summer Annual Meeting.

Kent, M., Newham, R. and Essex, S. (2002) 'Tourism and sustainable water supply in Mallorca: a geographical analysis', *Applied Geography*, 22(3): 351–74.

Kent, W.E., Meyer, R.A. and Reddam, T.M. (1987) 'Reassessing wholesaler marketing strategies: the role of travel research', *Journal of Travel Research*, 25(3): 31–3.

Keogh, B. (1984) 'The measurement of spatial variations in tourist activity', *Annals of Tourism Research*,
11: 267–82.

Kerr, W. (2003) *Tourism Public Policy in Scotland: The
Strategic Management of Failure*, Oxford: Pergamon
Press.

Kester, J.G.C. (2003) 'Cruise tourism', *Tourism Economics*, 9: 337–50.

Khan, N. (1997) 'Leisure and recreation among
women of selected hill-farming families in Bangladesh', *Journal of Leisure Research*, 29(1): 5–20.

Kheraj, S. (2007) 'Restoring nature: ecology, memory,
and the storm history of Vancouver's Stanley Park',
Canadian Historical Review, 88: 577–612.

Kienast, F., Degenhardt, B., Weilenmann, B., Wäger,
Y. and Buchecker, M. (2012) 'GIS-assisted map-
ping of landscape suitability for nearby recreation',
Landscape and Urban Planning, 105: 385–99.

Kil, N., Stein, T.V., Holland, S.M. and Anderson,
D.H. (2012) 'Understanding place meanings in
planning and managing the wildland urban inter
face: the case of Florida trail hikers', *Landscape and
Urban Planning*, 107(4): 370–9.

Killan, G. (1993) *Protected Places: A History of
Ontario's Provincial Parks System*, Toronto: Dundurn
Press.

Kim, K. (2000) 'Topics of human geography', in
W. Yu and I. Son (eds) *Korean Geography and
Geographers*, Seoul: Hanul Publishing.

Kim, S. and Kim, J. (1996) 'Overview of coastal and
marine tourism in Korea', *Journal of Tourism
Studies*, 7(2): 46–53.

Kindermann, G. and Gormally, M.J. (2013) 'Stakeholder perceptions of recreational and management impacts on protected coastal dune systems: a
comparison of three European countries', *Land Use
Policy*, 31: 472–85.

King, R. (1995) 'Tourism, labour and international
migration', in A. Montanari and A.M. Williams
(eds) *European Tourism: Regions, Spaces and Restructuring*, Chichester: Wiley.

King, R., Warnes, A.M. and Williams A.M. (1998)
'International retirement migration in Europe',
International Journal of Population Geography, 4(2):
91–112.

— (2000) *Sunset Lives: British Retirement to the Mediterranean*, London: Berg.

Kinnaird, V. and Hall, D. (eds) (1994) *Tourism:
A Gender Analysis*, Chichester: Wiley.

Kirkby, S. (1996) 'Recreation and the quality of Span-
ish coastal waters', in M. Barke, J. Towner and
M. Newton (eds) *Tourism in Spain: Critical Issues*,
Wallingford: CAB International.

Kirkpatrick, J.B. (1980) 'Hydro-Electric development and wilderness: report to the Department of
the Environment', attachment to *Department of the
Environment (Tas.), Assessment of the HEC Report on
the Lower Gordon River Development Stage Two*,
Hobart: Department of the Environment.

Kirkpatrick, J.B. and Haney, R.A. (1980) 'The quantification of developmental wilderness loss: the case
of forestry in Tasmania', *Search*, 11(10): 331–5.

Kissling, C. (1989) 'International tourism and civil
aviation in the South Pacific: issues and innovations', *GeoJournal*, 19: 309–16.

Kitchin, R. and Thrift, N. (eds) (2009) *International
Encyclopedia of Human Geography*, Oxford: Elsevier.

Kizos, T., Primdahl, J., Kristensen, L.S. and Busck,
A.G. (2010) 'Introduction: landscape change and
rural development', *Landscape Research*, 35: 571–6.

Kline, M.B. (1970) *Beyond the Land Itself: Views of
Nature in Canada and the United States*, Cambridge,
MA: Harvard University Press.

Kliskey, A.D. (1994) 'A comparative analysis of
approaches to wilderness perception mapping',
Journal of Environmental Management, 41: 199–236.

— (1998) 'Linking the wilderness perception mapping concept to the recreation opportunity spectrum', *Environmental Management*, 22: 79–88.

— (2000) 'Recreation terrain suitability mapping: a
spatially explicit methodology for determining
recreation potential for resource use assessment',
Landscape and Urban Planning, 52: 33–43.

Knafou, R. (1978) *Les Stations intégrées de sports d'hiver
des Alpes françaises. L'Aménagement de la montagne à
la 'française'*, Paris: Masson.

— (2000) Tourismes en France: vivre de la diversité', in Union Géographique Internationale
Comité National Français de Géographie, *Histo-
riens & Geographes: Vivre en France dans la diversité*,

Paris: Union Géographique Internationale Comité National Français de Géographie.

Knafou, R., Bruston, M., Deprest, F., Duhamel, P., Gay, J. and Sacareau, I. (1997) 'Une Approche géographique du tourisme', *L'Espace géographique*, 3: 193–204.

Kneafsey, M., Holloway, L., Venn, L., Dowler, E., Cox, R. and Tuomainen, H. (2008) *Reconnecting Consumers, Food and Producers: Exploring Alternatives*, Oxford: Berg.

Knetsch, J. (1969) 'Assessing the demand for outdoor recreation', *Journal of Leisure Research*, 1(2): 85–7.

Koenker, D.P. (2003) 'Travel to work, travel to play: on Russian tourism, travel, and leisure', *Slavic Review*, 62(4): 657–65.

Konrad, V.A. (1982) 'Historical artifacts as recreational resources', in G. Wall and J. Marsh (eds) *Recreational Land Use*, Ottawa: Carleton University Press.

Kooiman, J. (2003) *Governing as Governance*, Los Angeles: Sage.

Koskela, H. and Pain, R. (2000) 'Revisiting fear and place: women's fear of attack and the built environment', *Geoforum*, 31: 269–80.

Kosters, M.J. (1984) 'The deficiencies of tourism social science without political science: comment on Richter', *Annals of Tourism Research*, 11: 609–13.

Kraas, F. and Taubmann, W. (eds) (2000) *German Geographical Research on East and Southeast Asia*, Sankt Augustin: Asgard-Verlag.

Kreisel, W. (2004) 'Geography of leisure and tourism research in the German-speaking world: three pillars of progress', *Tourism Geographies*, 6(2): 163–85.

—— (2012) 'Some thoughts on the future research on leisure and tourism geography', *Current Issues in Tourism*, 15: 397–403.

Kreutzwiser, R. (1989) 'Supply', in G. Wall (ed.) *Outdoor Recreation in Canada*, Toronto: Wiley.

Krugman, P. (1994) 'Competitiveness: a dangerous obsession', *Foreign Affairs*, 73(2): 28–44.

—— (1996) 'Making sense of the competitiveness debate', *Oxford Review of Economic Policy*, 12: 17–35.

—— (2005) 'Second winds for industrial regions?', in D. Coyle, W. Alexander and B. Ashcroft (eds) *New Wealth for Old Nations: Scotland's Economic Prospects*, Princeton: Princeton University Press.

Kruzhalin, K. (2002) 'Economic geographical trends in the formation of the tourism market in Russia', *Vestnik-Moskovskogo-Universiteta-Seriya-Geografiya*, 5: 72–7.

Kuhn, T. (1969) *The Structure of Scientific Revolutions*, 2nd edn, Chicago: University of Chicago Press.

Kuji, T. (1991) 'The political economy of golf', *AMPO, Japan-Asia Quarterly Review*, 22(4): 47–54.

Kwan, M. and Schwanen, T. (2009) 'Quantitative revolution 2: the critical (re)turn', *Professional Geographer*, 61: 283–91.

Kwiatkowska, A. (1999) 'Nomadic-symbolic and settler-consumer leisure practices in Poland', in D. Crouch (ed.) *Leisure/Tourism Geographies: Practices and Geographical Knowledge*, London: Routledge.

Ladkin, A. (2011) 'Exploring tourism labor', *Annals of Tourism Research*, 38: 1135–55.

Lane, B. (1994) 'What is rural tourism?', *Journal of Sustainable Tourism*, 2: 7–21.

Lang, R. (1988) 'Planning for integrated development', in F.W. Dykeman (ed.) *Integrated Rural Planning and Development*, Sackville, NB: Mount Allison University.

Lashley, C. (2000) 'Towards theoretical understanding', in C. Lashley and A. Morrison (eds) *In Search of Hospitality: Theoretical Perspectives and Debates*, Oxford: Butterworth Heinemann.

Lasswell, Harold D. (1936) *Politics: Who Gets What, When, How*, New York: McGraw-Hill.

Latham, J. (1989) 'The statistical measurement of tourism', in C.P. Cooper (ed.) *Progress in Tourism, Recreation and Hospitality Management*, vol. 1, London: Belhaven Press.

Latham, J. and Edwards, C. (2003) 'The statistical measurement of tourism', in C. Cooper (ed.) *Classic Reviews in Tourism*, Clevedon: Channel View.

Lavery, P. (1971a) 'The demand for recreation', in P. Lavery (ed.) *Recreational Geography*, Newton Abbot: David and Charles.

—— (1971b) 'Resorts and recreation', in P. Lavery (ed.) *Recreational Geography*, Newton Abbot: David and Charles.

— (ed.) (1971c) *Recreational Geography*, Newton Abbott: David and Charles.

— (1975) 'The demand for leisure: a review of studies', *Town Planning Review*: 185–200.

Law, C. (1988) 'Conference and exhibition tourism', *Built Environment*, 13(2): 85–92.

— (1992) 'Urban tourism and its contribution to economic regeneration', *Urban Studies*, 29(3/4): 599–618.

— (1993) *Urban Tourism: Attracting Visitors to Large Cities*, London: Mansell.

— (ed.) (1996) *Tourism in Major Cities*, London: International Thomson Business Publishing.

Law, C. and Warnes, A. (1973) 'The movement of retired people to seaside resorts', *Town Planning Review*, 44: 373–90.

Law, S. (1967) 'Planning for outdoor recreation', *Journal of the Town Planning Institute*, 53: 383–6.

Lawrence, D., Kenchington, R. and Woodley, S. (2002) *The Great Barrier Reef: Finding the Right Balance*, Melbourne: Melbourne University Press.

Lawson, S.R., Manning, R., Valliere, W. and Wang, B. (2003) 'Proactive monitoring and adaptive management of social carrying capacity in Arches National Park: an application of computer simulation modeling', *Journal of Environmental Management*, 68: 305–13.

Lawton, G. and Page, S.J. (1997a) 'Evaluating travel agents' provision of health advice to tourists', *Tourism Management*, 18: 89–104.

— (1997b) 'Health advice to the travellers to the Pacific Islands: whose responsibility?', in M. Oppermann (ed.) *Pacific Rim Tourism*, Wallingford: CAB International.

Lawton, R. (1978) 'Population and society 1730–1900', in R. Dodgson and R. Butlin (eds) *An Historical Geography of England and Wales*, London: Academic Press.

Lazanski, T.J. and Kljajic, M. (2006) 'Systems approach to complex systems modeling with special regards to tourism', *Kybernetes: The International Journal of Systems and Cybernetics*, 35(7/8): 1048–58.

Lazzeretti, L. and Capone, F. (2008) 'Mapping and analysing local tourism systems in Italy, 1991–2001', *Tourism Geographies*, 10(2): 214–32.

Le-Klähn, D.-T., Hall, C.M. and Gerike, R. (2014) 'Analysis of visitors' satisfaction with public transport in Munich', *Journal of Public Transportation*, 17.

Lea, J. (1988) *Tourism and Development in the Third World*, London: Routledge.

Leafe, R., Pethich, J. and Townsend, I. (1998) 'Realising the benefits of shoreline management', *Geographical Journal*, 164: 282–90.

Lee, H. (2000) 'Applied geography', in W. Yu and I. Son (eds) *Korean Geography and Geographers*, Seoul: Hanul Publishing.

Lee, R.G. (1977) 'Alone with others: the paradox of privacy in the wilderness', *Leisure Services*, 1: 3–19.

Leiper, N. (1984) 'Tourism and leisure: the significance of tourism in the leisure spectrum', *Proceedings of the 12th New Zealand Geography Conference*, Christchurch: New Zealand Geographical Society.

— (1989) *Tourism and Tourism Systems*, Occasional Paper No. 1, Palmerston North: Department of Management Systems, Massey University.

— (1990) *Tourism Systems: An Interdisciplinary Perspective*, Occasional Paper No. 2, Palmerston North: Department of Management Systems, Massey University.

— (1999) 'A conceptual analysis of tourism-supported employment which reduces the incidence of exaggerated, misleading statistics about jobs', *Tourism Management*, 20: 605–13.

Lenček, L. and Bosker, G. (1999) *The Beach: The History of Paradise on Earth*, London: Pimlico.

Lennon, J. (ed.) (2003) *Tourism Statistics: International Perspectives and Current Issues*, London: Continuum.

Leopold, A. (1921) 'The wilderness and its place in forest recreational policy', *Journal of Forestry*, 19(7): 718–21.

— (1925) 'Wilderness as a form of land use', *Journal of Land and Public Utility Economics*, 1(4): 398–404.

Lesslie, R.G. (1991) 'Wilderness survey and evaluation in Australia', *Australian Geographer*, 22: 35–43.

Lesslie, R.G. and Maslen, M. (1995) *National Wilderness Inventory: Handbook of Principles, Procedures and Usage*, 2nd edn, Canberra: Australian Heritage Commission.

Lesslie, R.G. and Taylor, S.G. (1983) *Wilderness in South Australia*, Occasional Paper No. 1, Adelaide: Centre for Environmental Studies, University of Adelaide.

— (1985) 'The wilderness continuum concept and its implications for Australian wilderness preservation policy', *Biological Conservation*, 32: 309–33.

Lesslie, R.G, Abrahams, H. and Maslen, M. (1991a) *Wilderness Quality on Cape York Peninsula, National Wilderness Inventory: Stage III*, Canberra: Australian Heritage Commission.

Lesslie, R.G., Mackey, B.G. and Preece, K.M. (1987) *National Wilderness Inventory: A Computer Based Methodology for the Survey of Wilderness in Australia*, prepared for the Australian Heritage Commission, Canberra: Australian Heritage Commission.

— (1988a) 'A computer-based method for the evaluation of wilderness', *Environmental Conservation*, 15(3): 225–32.

Lesslie, R.G., Mackey, B.G. and Shulmeister, J. (1988b) *Wilderness Quality in Tasmania, National Wilderness Inventory: Stage II*, a report to the Australian Heritage Commission, Canberra: Australian Heritage Commission.

Lesslie, R., Taylor, D. and Maslen, M. (1993) *National Wilderness Inventory: Handbook of Principles, Procedures and Usage*, Canberra: Australian Heritage Commission.

Lesslie, R.G., Thackway, R. and Smith, J. (2010) *A National-level Vegetation Assets, States and Transitions (VAST) Dataset for Australia (Version 2.0)*, Canberra: Bureau of Rural Sciences.

Lesslie, R.G., Maslen, M., Canty, D., Goodwins, D. and Shields, R. (1991b) *Wilderness on Kangaroo Island, National Wilderness Inventory: South Australia*, Canberra: Australian Heritage Commission.

Lew, A.A. (1985) 'Bringing tourists to town', *Small Town*, 16: 4–10.

— (1987) 'A framework for tourist attraction research', *Annals of Tourism Research*, 14: 553–75.

— (1989) 'Authenticity and sense of place in the tourism development experience of older retail districts', *Journal of Travel Research*, 27(4): 15–22.

— (2001) 'Defining a geography of tourism', *Tourism Geographies*, 3: 105–14.

Lew, A. and McKercher, B. (2006) 'Modeling tourist movements: a local destination analysis', *Annals of Tourism Research*, 33: 403–23.

Lew, A.A. and van Otten, G.A. (eds) (1997) *Tourism on American Indian Lands*, New York: Cognizant Communication Corporation.

Lew, A.A. and Wu, L. (eds) (1995) *Tourism in China: Geographic, Political and Economic Perspectives*, Boulder, CO: Westview Press.

Lew, A.A., Hall, C.M. and Timothy, D.J. (2011) *World Regional Geography: Human Mobilities, Tourism Destinations, Sustainable Environments*, Dubuque, IA: Kendall Hunt.

Lew, A., Hall, C.M. and Williams, A. (eds) (2004) *A Companion to Tourism*, Oxford: Blackwell.

— (2014) *The Wiley-Blackwell Companion to Tourism*, Oxford: Wiley-Blackwell.

Ley, D. and Olds, K. (1988) 'Landscape as spectacle: World's Fairs and the culture of heroic consumption', *Environment and Planning D*, 6: 191–212.

Li, C., Su, Y.-P. and Hall, C.M. (2012) 'Critical issues of predicting extreme weather events: impacts on tourist flow', *Journal of Hospitality & Tourism*, 10(2): 45–65.

Li, S. and Jago, L. (2013) 'Evaluating economic impacts of major sports events – a meta analysis of the key trends', *Current Issues in Tourism*, 16: 591–611.

Li, Y. (2000) 'Geographical consciousness and tourism experience', *Annals of Tourism Research*, 27: 863–83.

Liddle, M. (1997) *Recreation Ecology*, London: Chapman and Hall.

Lillis, T. and Curry, M.J. (2010) *Academic Writing in a Global Context: The Politics and Practices of Publishing in English*, London: Routledge.

Lindberg, K. and McKercher, B. (1997) 'Ecotourism: a critical overview', *Pacific Tourism Review*, 1: 65–79.

Linebaugh, P. (2008) *The Magna Carta Manifesto*, Los Angeles: University of California Press.

Linton, D. (1968) 'The assessment of scenery as a recreation resource', *Scottish Geographical Magazine*, 84: 219–38.

Lipkina, O. and Hall, C.M. (2014) 'Russian second home owners in Eastern Finland: involvement in the local community', in M. Janoschka and H. Haas (eds) *Contested Spatialities of Lifestyle Migration*, London: Routledge.

Lipscombe, N. (2003) 'Demand', in J. Jenkins and J. Pigram (eds) *Encyclopedia of Leisure and Outdoor Recreation*, London: Routledge.

Liu, J. and Wang, R. (2010) 'Attractive model and marketing implications of Theme Shopping Tourism destination', *Chinese Geographical Science*, 20: 562–7.

Livingstone, D.N. (1992) *The Geographical Tradition: Episodes in the History of a Contested Enterprise*, Oxford: Blackwell.

Llewelyn-Davis Planning/Leisureworks (1987) *Tourism Development in London Docklands: Themes and Facts*, London: London Docklands Development Corporation.

Lloyd, M.G., Peel, D. and Duck, R.W. (2013) 'Towards a social–ecological resilience framework for coastal planning', *Land Use Policy*, 30: 925–33.

Lloyd, P. and Dicken, P. (1987) *Location in Space: A Theoretical Approach to Human Geography*, 2nd edn, London: Harper & Row.

Löfgren, O. (2002) *On Holiday: A History of Vacationing*, Berkeley: University of California Press.

Lohmann, G. and Dredge, D. (eds) (2012) *Tourism in Brazil*, London: Taylor & Francis.

London Borough of Newham (1993) *Newham's Unitary Development Plan: Written Statement Parts One and Two*, East Ham, London: London Borough of Newham.

— (2012) *Newham 2027 – Planning Newham – the Core Strategy*, Stratford, London: London Borough of Newham.

London Tourist Board (1987) *The Tourism Strategy for London*, London: London Tourist Board.

— (1988) *London Tourism Statistics*, London: London Tourist Board.

Long, J.A. (1984) 'Introduction – tourism and social change', in J. Long and R. Hecock (eds) *Leisure, Tourism and Social Change*, Dunfermline: Centre for Leisure Research, Dunfermline College of Physical Education.

— (1987) 'Continuity as a basis for change: leisure and male retirement', *Leisure Studies*, 6: 55–70.

— (2002) *Count Me In: The Dimensions of Social Inclusion through Culture, Media and Sport*, Leeds: Leeds Metropolitan University.

Long, P., Perdue, R. and Allen, L. (1990) 'Rural residents' perception and attitudes by community level of tourism', *Journal of Travel Research*, 29: 3–9.

López-i-Gelats, F., Tàbara, J.D. and Bartolomé, J. (2009) 'The rural in dispute: discourses of rurality in the Pyrenees', *Geoforum*, 40: 602–12.

Lösch, A. (1944) *Die räumliche Ordnung der Wirtschaft*, Jena: Gustav Fischer.

Lovingwood, P. and Mitchell, L. (1978) 'The structure of public and private recreational systems: Columbia, South Carolina', *Journal of Leisure Research*, 10: 21–36.

Lowenthal, D. (1975) 'Past time, present place: landscape and memory', *Geographical Review*, 65: 1–36.

— (1985) *The Past Is a Foreign Country*, Cambridge: Cambridge University Press.

Lozato, J. (1985) *Géographie du tourisme*, Paris: Masson.

Lucas, P. (1986) 'Fishy business', *Leisure Manager*, 4: 18–19.

Lucas, R. (1964) 'Wilderness perception and use: the example of the Boundary Waters Canoe Area', *Natural Resources Journal*, 3(1): 394–411.

Lück, M., Maher, P.T. and Stewart, E. (eds) (2010) *Cruise Tourism in Polar Regions: Promoting Environmental and Social Sustainability?*, London: Earthscan.

Lumsdon, L. and Page, S.J. (eds) (2004) *Tourism and Transport: Issues and Agendas for the New Millennium*, Oxford: Pergamon Press.

Lundgren, J.O. (1984) 'Geographic concepts and the development of tourism research in Canada', *GeoJournal*, 9: 17–25.

Lundmark, L. and Marjavaara, R. (2004) 'Second home localization in the Swedish mountain range', paper presented at the 13th Nordic Symposium on Tourism and Hospitality, Aalborg, November.

Lynch, K. (1960) *The Image of the City*, Cambridge, MA: MIT Press.

— (1984) 'Reconsidering the image of the city', in L. Rodwin and R. Hollister (eds) *Cities of the Mind*, New York: Plenum Press.

Lyon, D. (2007) *Surveillance Studies: An Overview*, London: Polity Press.

McArthur, S. (1996) 'Beyond the limits of acceptable change – developing a model to monitor and manage tourism in remote areas', in *Tourism Down Under: 1996 Tourism Conference Proceedings*, Dunedin: Centre for Tourism, University of Otago.

—— (2000a) 'Visitor management in action: an analysis of the development and implementation of visitor management models at Jenolan Caves and Kangaroo Island', unpublished PhD thesis, Belconnen: University of Canberra.

—— (2000b) 'Beyond carrying capacity: introducing a model to monitor and manage visitor activity in forests', in X. Font and J. Tribe (eds) *Forest Tourism and Recreation: Case Studies in Environmental Management*, Wallingford: CAB International.

McAvoy, L. (1977) 'Needs and the elderly: An overview', *Parks and Recreation*, 12(3): 31–5.

McAvoy, L. (2002) 'American Indians, place meanings and the old/new west', *Journal of Leisure Research*, 34: 383–96.

Macbeth, J., Selwood, J. and Veitch, S. (2012) 'Paradigm shift or a drop in the ocean? The America's Cup impact on Fremantle', *Tourism Geographies*, 14: 162–82.

McCabe, S., Minnaert, L. and Diekmann, A. (eds) (2011) *Social Tourism in Europe: Theory and Practice*, Bristol: Channel View.

MacCannell, D. (1973) 'Staged authenticity: arrangements of social space in tourist settings', *American Journal of Sociology*, 69: 578–603.

—— (1976) *The Tourist: A New Theory of the Leisure Class*, London: Macmillan.

McCarthy, J. (2007) 'Rural geography: globalizing the countryside', *Progress in Human Geography*, 32: 129–37.

McCool, S. (1978) 'Recreation use limits: issues for the tourism industry', *Journal of Travel Research*, 17(2): 2–7.

McCool, S. and Cole, D. (1997) *Proceedings – Limits of Acceptable Change and Related Planning Processes: Progress and Future Directions*, INT-GTR-371, Missoula: USDA, Forest Service, Rocky Mountain Research Station.

McDermott, D. and Horner, A. (1978) 'Aspects of rural renewal in Western Connemara', *Irish Geography*, 11: 176–9.

McDowell, A., Carter, R. and Pollard, J. (1990) 'The impact of man on the shoreline environment of the Costa del Sol, Southern Spain', in P. Wong (ed.) *Tourism vs Environment: The Case for Coastal Areas*, Dordrecht: Kluwer Academic.

McEwen, L., Hall, T., Hunt, J., Dempsey, M. and Harrison, M. (2002) 'Flood warning, warning response and planning control issues associated with caravan parks: the April 1998 floods on the lower Avon floodplain, Midlands region, UK', *Applied Geography*, 22(3): 271–305.

McGibbon, J. (2000) *The Business of Alpine Tourism in a Globalising World: An Anthropological Study of International Tourism in the Village of St. Anton am Arlberg in the Tirolean Alps*, Rosenheim: Vetterling Druck.

McGrath, F. (1989) 'Characteristics of pilgrims to Lough Derg', *Irish Geography*, 22: 44–7.

McInnis, K. and Page. S.J. (2009) 'Case study of tourist time budgets at an ecotourism lodge in South America', in S.J. Page and J. Connell, *Tourism: A Modern Synthesis*, 3rd edn, London: Cengage.

McIntosh, R.W. and Goeldner, C. (1990) *Tourism: Principles, Practices and Philosophies*, New York: Wiley.

McIntyre, N. (2003) 'Desire', in J. Jenkins and J. Pigram (eds) *Encyclopedia of Leisure and Outdoor Recreation*, London: Routledge.

McIntyre, N., Jenkins, J. and Booth, K. (2001) 'Global influences on access: the changing face of access to public conservation lands in New Zealand', *Journal of Sustainable Tourism*, 9: 434–50.

McIntyre, N., Williams, D.R. and McHugh, K.E. (2006) *Multiple Dwelling and Tourism: Negotiating Place, Home and Identity*, Wallingford: CAB International.

McKenry, K. (1972) *Value Analysis of Wilderness Areas*, Combined Universities Recreation Research Group, Monograph 2, Clayton: Monash University.

—— (1977) 'Value analysis of wilderness areas', in D. Mercer (ed.) *Leisure and Recreation in Australia*, Malvern: Sorrett Publishing.

McKercher, B. (1993a) 'Some fundamental truths about tourism: understanding tourism's social and environmental impacts', *Journal of Sustainable Tourism*, 1: 6–16.

— (1993b) 'The unrecognized threat to tourism: can tourism survive sustainability', *Tourism Management*, 14: 131–6.

— (1993c) 'Australian conservation organisations' perspectives on tourism in National Parks: a critique', *GeoJournal*, 29(3): 307–13.

— (1997) 'Benefits and costs of tourism in Victoria's Alpine National Park: comparing attitudes of tour operators, management staff and public interest group leaders', in C.M. Hall, J. Jenkins and G. Kearsley (eds) *Tourism Planning and Policy in Australia and New Zealand: Cases, Issues and Practice*, Sydney: Irwin Publishers.

— (1999) 'A chaos approach to tourism', *Tourism Management*, 20: 425–34.

— (2008) 'A citation analysis of tourism scholars', *Tourism Management*, 29(6): 1226–32.

— (2014) 'Tourist flows and spatial behavior', in A. Lew, C.M. Hall and A.M. Williams (eds) *The Wiley-Blackwell Companion to Tourism*, Oxford: Wiley-Blackwell.

McKercher, B. and Lau, G. (2008) 'Movement patterns of tourists within destinations', *Tourism Geographies*, 10: 353–74.

McKercher, B. and Lew, A.A. (2003) 'Distance decay and the impact of effective tourism exclusion zones on international travel flows', *Journal of Travel Research*, 42(2): 159–65.

McKercher, B., Chan, A. and Lam, C. (2008) 'The impact of distance on international tourist movements', *Journal of Travel Research*, 47: 208–24.

McKercher, B., Shoval, N., Ng, E. and Berenboim, A. (2012) 'First and repeat visitor behaviour: GPS tracking and GIS analysis in Hong Kong', *Tourism Geographies*, 14: 147–61.

MacLellan, L.R. (1999) 'An examination of wildlife tourism as a sustainable form of tourism development in North West Scotland', *International Journal of Tourism Research*, 1(5): 375–87.

McLennan, R., Inkson, K., Dakin, S., Dewe, P. and Elkin, G. (1987) *People and Enterprises: Human Behaviour in New Zealand Organisations*, Auckland: Rinehart Winston.

MacLeod, M., Silva, C. and Cooper, J. (2002) 'A comparative study of the perception and value of beaches in rural Ireland and Portugal: implications for coastal zone management', *Journal of Coastal Research*, 18(1): 14–24.

McMillan, S. (1997) 'Balancing the books: economic returns and corporate citizenship', paper presented at Business with Style: Adapting Heritage Buildings for Commercial Use, New South Wales Government, Heritage Office, Sydney.

McMorran, R., Price, M.F. and Warren, C.R. (2008) 'The call of different wilds: the importance of definition and perception in protecting and managing Scottish wild landscapes', *Journal of Environmental Planning and Management*, 51: 177–99.

McMurray, K.C. (1930) 'The use of land for recreation', *Annals of the Association of American Geographers*, 20: 7–20.

— (1954) 'Recreational geography', in P.E. James and C.F. Jones (eds) *American Geography: Inventory and Prospect*, Syracruse: Syracruse University Press.

McQuaid, J. and Dijst, M. (2012) 'Bringing emotions to time geography: the case of mobilities of poverty', *Journal of Transport Geography*, 23(1): 26–34.

McVey, M. (1986) 'International hotel chains in Europe: survey of expansion plans as Europe is rediscovered', *Travel and Tourism Analyst*, September: 3–23.

Madge, C. (1997) 'Public parks and the geography of fear', *Tijdschrift voor economische en sociale geografie*, 88: 237–50.

Madsen, H. (1992) 'Place-marketing in Liverpool: a review', *International Journal of Urban and Regional Research*, 16: 633–40.

Maguire, G.S., Miller, K.K., Weston, M.A. and Young, K. (2011) 'Being beside the seaside: beach use and preferences among coastal residents of south-eastern Australia', *Ocean & Coastal Management*, 54: 781–8.

Maitland, D. (1992) 'Space, vulnerability and dangers', *The Operational Geographer*, 9: 28–9.

Maitland, R. (2012) 'Capitalness is contingent: tourism and national capitals in a globalised world', *Current Issues in Tourism*, 15: 3–17.

Maitland, R. and Ritchie, B.W. (2007) 'Editorial: marketing national capital cities', *Journal of Travel & Tourism Marketing*, 22(3/4): 1–5.

Malamud, B. (1973) 'Gravity model calibration of tourist travel to Las Vegas', *Journal of Leisure Research*, 5(1): 13–33.

Malecki, E.J. (2004) 'Jockeying for position: what it means and why it matters to regional development policy when places compete', *Regional Studies*, 38: 1101–20.

Mandell, M.P. (1999) 'The impact of collaborative efforts: changing the face of public policy through networks and network structures', *Policy Studies Review*, 16(1): 4–17.

Manidis Roberts Consultants (1991) *National Estate NSW Wilderness Review*, Sydney: National Estate Grants Program, Department of Planning.

— (1996) *Tourism Optimisation Management Model for Kangaroo Island*, Adelaide: South Australian Tourism Commission.

Manning, R.E. (1984) 'Man and mountains meet: journal of the Appalachian Mountains Club, 1876–1984', *Journal of Forest History*, 28(1): 24–33.

— (1985) 'Crowding norms in backcountry settings: a review and synthesis', *Journal of Leisure Research*, 17(2): 75–89.

Manning, R., Valliere, W. and Hallo, J. (2010) 'Recreational carrying capacity of Lake Umbagog National Wildlife Refuge', *Journal of Fish and Wildlife Management*, 1(2): 175–82.

Mansfeld, Y. (1992) 'Industrial landscapes as positive settings for tourism development in declining industrial cities – the case of Haifa, Israel', *GeoJournal*, 28: 457–63.

Mansfield, N. (1969) 'Recreational trip generation', *Journal of Transport Economics and Public Policy*, 3(2): 152–64.

Mansvelt, J. (2005) 'Working at leisure: critical geographies of ageing', *Area*, 29: 289–98.

— (2010) 'Geographies of consumption: engaging with absent presences', *Progress in Human Geography*, 34: 224–33.

Marcouiller, D. and Prey, J. (2005) 'The tourism supply linkage: recreational sites and their related natural amenities', *Journal of Regional Analysis & Policy*, 35: 23–32.

Marcouiller, D., Lapping, M. and Furuseth, O. (eds) (2011) *Rural Housing, Exurbanization, and Amenity-Driven Development: Contrasting the Haves and the Have Nots*, Aldershot: Ashgate.

Marcouiller, D., Prey, J. and Scott, I. (2009) 'The regional supply of outdoor recreation resources: demonstrating the use of location quotients as a management tool', *Journal of Parks and Recreation Administration*, 27(4): 92–107.

Marcouiller, D., Green, G.P., Deller, S.C., Sumathi, N.R. and Erikkila, D.C. (1998) *Recreational Homes and Regional Development: A Case Study from the Upper Great Lakes States*, Madison: Cooperative Extension.

Mark, S. (1985) 'Wilderness inventory of Western Australia', *Environment W.A.*, 7(3): 30–2.

— (1991) 'Planning and development at Rim Village', in *Administrative History, Crater Lake National Park, Oregon*, Seattle: US Department of the Interior, National Park Service.

— (1996) 'Writing environmental and park histories', in C.M. Hall and S. McArthur (eds) *Heritage Management in Australia and New Zealand: The Human Dimension*, Melbourne: Oxford University Press.

Markusen, A. (1985) *Profit Cycles, Oligopoly and Regional Development*, Cambridge MA: MIT Press.

Marne, P. (2001) 'Whose public space is it anyway? Class, gender and ethnicity in the creation of the Sefton and Stanley Parks, Liverpool: 1858–72', *Social and Cultural Geography*, 2(4): 421–4.

Marrocu, E. and Paci, R. (2011) 'They arrive with new information: tourism flows and production efficiency in the European regions', *Tourism Management*, 32: 750–8.

— (2013) 'Different tourists to different destinations: evidence from spatial interaction models', *Tourism Management*, 39: 71–83.

Marsh, G.P. (1965 [1864]) *Man and Nature; Or, Physical Geography as Modified by Human Action*, ed. D. Lowenthal, Cambridge, MA: Belknap Press of Harvard University Press.

Marsh, J.G. (1983) 'Canada's parks and tourism: a problematic relationship', in P.E. Murphy (ed.) *Tourism in Canada: Selected Issues and Options*, Western Geographical Series, vol. 21, Victoria: Department of Geography, University of Victoria.

— (1985) 'The Rocky and Selkirk Mountains and the Swiss connection 1885–1914', *Annals of Tourism Research*, 12: 417–33.

Marsh, J.G. and Wall, G. (1982) 'Themes in the investigation of the evolution of outdoor recreation', in G. Wall and J. Marsh (eds) *Recreational Land Use, Perspectives on Its Evolution in Canada*, Ottawa: Carleton University Press.

Marshall, A. and Simpson, L. (2009) 'Population sustainability in rural communities: the case of two British national parks', *Applied Spatial Analysis and Policy*, 2: 107–27.

Marshall, R. (1930) 'The problem of the wilderness', *Scientific Monthly*, 30: 141–8.

Martin, R.L. (1999) 'The new "geographical turn" in economics: some critical reflections', *Cambridge Journal of Economics*, 23: 65–91.

— (2001) 'Geography and public policy: the case of the missing agenda', *Progress in Human Geography*, 25: 189–210.

— (2005) *Thinking about Regional Competitiveness: Critical Issues*, Background 'Think-Piece' Paper Commissioned by the East Midlands Development Agency.

Martin, W. and Mason, S. (1979) *Broad Patterns of Leisure Expenditure*, London: Sports Council and Social Science Research Council.

Maslow, A. (1954) *Motivation and Personality*, New York: Harper & Row.

Mason, P. (2003) *Tourism Impacts, Planning and Management*, Oxford: Butterworth Heinemann.

Masser, I. (1966–7) 'The use of outdoor recreational facilities', *Town Planning Review*, 37(1): 41–53.

Massey, D. and Allen, J. (eds) (1984) *Geography Matters! A Reader*, Cambridge: Cambridge University Press.

Mather, A. (2003) 'Access rights and rural sustainability in Britain', paper presented at the International Geographical Commission on Sustainable Rural Systems, Rio de Janeiro.

Mathieson, A. and Wall, G. (1982) *Tourism: Economic, Physical and Social Impacts*, London: Longman.

Matley, I.M. (1976) *The Geography of International Tourism*, Resource Paper No. 76–1, Washington, DC: Association of American Geographers.

Matson, J. (1892) 'The Australasian indigenous park', *New Zealand Country Journal*, 16(4): 356–60.

Matthews, H.G. (1983) 'Editor's page: on tourism and political science', *Annals of Tourism Research*, 10: 303–6.

Maude, A.J.S. and van Rest, D.J. (1985) 'The social and economic effects of farm tourism in the United Kingdom', *Agricultural Administration*, 20: 85–99.

Maver, I. (1998) 'Glasgow's public parks and the community 1850–1914', *Urban History*, 25(3): 323–47.

Mawani, R. (2004) 'From colonialism to multiculturalism? Totem poles, tourism and national identity in Vancouver's Stanley Park', *ARIEL: A Review of International English Literature*, 35(1–2), http://ariel.ucalgary.ca/ariel/index.php/ariel/article/view/3888.

Mawhinney, K.A. (1979) 'Recreation', in D.A. Gilmore (ed.) *Irish Resources and Land Use*, Dublin: Institute of Public Administration.

Mawhinney, K.A. and Bagnall, G. (1976) 'The integrated social economic and environmental planning of tourism', *Administration*, 24: 383–93.

May, V. (1993) 'Coastal tourism, geomorphology and geological conservation: the example of South Central England', in P. Wong (ed.) *Tourism vs Environment: The Case for Coastal Areas*, Dordrecht: Kluwer Academic.

Mazanec, J.A. (ed.) (1997) *International City Tourism: Analysis and Strategy*, London: Pinter.

Mazanec, J.A. and Wöber, K.W. (eds) (2010) *Analysing International City Tourism*, Vienna: Springer Vienna.

Medlik, S. (1993) *Dictionary of Travel, Tourism and Hospitality*, Oxford: Butterworth Heinemann.

Meinecke, E.P. (1929) *The Effect of Excessive Tourist Travel on California Redwood Parks*, Sacramento: California State Printing Office.

Meethan, K. (1996) 'Consuming (in) the civilised city', *Annals of Tourism Research*, 23(2): 322–40.

— (1997) 'York: managing the tourist city', *Cities: The International Journal of Urban Policy and Planning*, 14(6): 333–42.

— (2004) 'Transnational corporations, globalization and tourism', in A. Lew, C.M. Hall and A. Williams (eds) *A Companion to Tourism*, Oxford: Blackwell.

Mehta, V. (2011) 'Small business and the vitality of main street', *Journal of Architectural and Planning Research*, 28(4): 272–91.

Meleghy, T., Preglau, M. and Tafertsofer, A. (1985) 'Tourism development and value change', *Annals of Tourism Research*, 12: 201–19.

Mels, T. (1999) *Wild Landscapes: The Cultural Nature of Swedish National Parks*, Lund: Lund University Press.

— (2002) 'Nature, home, and scenery: the official spatialities of Swedish national parks', *Environment and Planning D: Society and Space*, 20: 135–54.

Mercer, D. (1970) 'The geography of leisure: a contemporary growth point', *Geography*, 55(3): 261–73.

— (1971a) 'Perception in outdoor recreation', in P. Lavery (ed.) *Recreational Geography*, Newton Abbot: David and Charles.

— (1971b) 'Discretionary travel behaviour and the urban mental map', *Australian Geographical Studies*, 9: 133–43.

— (1972) 'Beach usage in the Melbourne region', *Australian Geographer*, 12(2): 123–9.

— (1973) 'The concept of recreational need', *Journal of Leisure Research*, 5: 37–50.

— (1979a) 'Outdoor recreation: contemporary research and policy issues', in T. O'Riordan and R.D. Arge (eds) *Progress in Resource Management and Environmental Planning*, vol. 1, New York: Wiley.

— (1979b) 'Victoria's land conservation council and the alpine region', *Australian Geographical Studies*, 17(1): 107–30.

— (1994) 'Native peoples and tourism: conflict and compromise', in W.F. Theobald (ed.) *Global Tourism: The Next Decade*, Boston, MA: Butterworth Heinemann.

— (2000) *A Question of Balance: Natural Resources Conflict Issues in Australia*, 3rd edn, Leichardt: Federation Press.

— (2004) 'Tourism and resource management', in A. Lew, C.M. Hall and A. Williams (eds) *A Companion to Tourism*, Oxford: Blackwell.

Meyer-Arendt, K. (1990) 'Recreational Business Districts in Gulf of Mexico seaside resorts', *Journal of Cultural Geography*, 11: 39–55.

— (1993) 'Geomorphic impacts of resort evolution along the Gulf of Mexico coast: applicability of resort cycle models', in P.P. Wong (ed.) *Tourism vs Environment: The Case for Coastal Areas*, Dordrecht: Kluwer Academic.

— (2000) 'Commentary: tourism geography as the subject of North American Doctoral dissertations and Masters theses, 1951–98', *Tourism Geographies*, 2: 140–57.

Meyer-Arendt, K. and Lew, A. (1999) 'A decade of American RTS geography', *Tourism Geographies*, 1: 477–87.

Micallel, A. and Williams, A. (2002) 'Theoretical strategy considerations for beach management', *Ocean and Coastal Management*, 45: 261–75.

Michael, E. (2001) 'Public choice and tourism analysis', *Current Issues in Tourism*, 4: 308–30.

Michaud, J. (1983) *Le Tourisme face à l'environnement*, Paris: PUF.

— (ed.) (1992) *Tourismes: chance pour l'économie, risque pour les sociétés?*, Paris: PUF.

Middleton, V. (1988) *Marketing in Travel and Tourism*, Oxford: Butterworth Heinemann.

— (2012) 'The language of tourism, internationally, nationally and locally – making it fit for purpose', *Tourism* (London), 151: 12–13.

Mieczkowski, Z. (1985) 'The tourism climatic index: a method of evaluating world climates for tourism', *Canadian Geographer*, 29: 220–33.

Mihalic, T. (2002) 'The European Blue Flag campaign for beaches in Slovenia: a programme for raising environmental awareness', in R. Harris, T. Griffin and P. Williams (eds) *Sustainable Tourism: A Global Perspective*, Oxford: Butterworth Heinemann.

— (2003) 'Supply', in J. Jenkins and J. Pigram (eds) *Encyclopedia of Leisure and Outdoor Recreation*, London: Routledge.

Miller, G. and Kirk, E. (2002) 'The Disability Discrimination Act: time for the stick?', *Journal of Sustainable Tourism*, 10: 82–8.

Miller, G.A. and Ritchie, B.W. (2003) 'A farming crisis or a tourism disaster? An analysis of the Foot and Mouth disease in the UK', *Current Issues in Tourism*, 6: 150–71.

Miller, M. (1987) 'Tourism in Washington's coastal zone', *Annals of Tourism Research*, 14: 58–70.

— (1993) 'The rise of coastal and marine tourism', *Ocean and Coastal Management*, 21(1–3): 183–99.

Miller, M.L. and Auyong, J. (1991) 'Coastal zone tourism: a potent force affecting environment and society', *Marine Policy*, 15(2): 75–99.

Millward, H. (1993) 'Public access in the West European countryside: a comparative survey', *Journal of Rural Studies*, 9: 39–51.

— (1996) 'Countryside recreational access in the United States: a statistical comparison of rural districts', *Annals of the Association of American Geographers*, 86: 102–22.

— (2000) 'Countryside recreational access in west Europe and Anglo-America: a comparison of supply', *The Great Lakes Geographer*, 7(1): 38–52.

Millward, H. and Spinney, J. (2011) 'Time use, travel behavior, and the rural–urban continuum: results from the Halifax STAR project', *Journal of Transport Geography*, 19(1): 51–8.

Milman, A. and Short, A. (2008) 'Incorporating resilience into sustainability indicators: an example for the urban water sector', *Global Environmental Change*, 18: 758–67.

Milne, S. (1990) 'The impact of tourism development in small Pacific Island states', *New Zealand Journal of Geography*, 89: 16–21.

— (1998) 'Tourism and sustainable development: the global–local nexus', in C.M. Hall and A.A. Lew (eds) *Sustainable Tourism Development: Geographical Perspectives*, Harlow: Addison Wesley Longman.

Milward, H.B. (1996) 'Symposium on the hollow state: capacity, control and performance in interorganizational settings', *Journal of Public Administration Research and Theory*, 6(2): 193–5.

Minerbi, L. (1992) *Impacts of Tourism Development in Pacific Islands*, San Francisco, CA: Greenpeace Pacific Campaign.

Minhat, H. and Amin, R. (2012) 'Socio-demographic determinants of leisure participation among elderly in Malaysia', *Journal of Community Health*, 30: 840–7.

Ministry of Housing and Local Government (1955) *Green Belts*, Circular 42/55, London: HMSO.

Miossec, J.-M. (1977) 'Un Modèle de l'espace touristique', *Espace géographique*, 6(1): 41–8.

Mitchell, B. (1989) *Geography and Resource Analysis*, 2nd edn, Harlow: Longman.

Mitchell, C.J.A. (2004) 'Making sense of counterurbanization', *Journal of Rural Studies*, 20(1): 15–34.

Mitchell, L.S. (1969a) 'Recreational geography: evolution and research needs', *Professional Geographer*, 21(2): 117–19.

— (1969b) 'Towards a theory of public urban recreation', *Proceedings of the Association of American Geographers*, 1: 103–8.

— (1979) 'The geography of tourism: an introduction', *Annals of Tourism Research*, 9: 235–44.

— (1984) 'Tourism research in the United States: a geographical perspective', *GeoJournal*, 9: 5–15.

— (1991) *A Conceptual Matrix for the Study of Tourism*, Les Cahiers du Tourisme, Aix-en-Provence: Centre des Haute Etudes Touristiques.

— (1997) 'Rediscovering geography (i.e. RTS)', personal communication to Michael Hall, Friday, 13 June.

Mitchell, L.S. and Lovingwood, P. (1976) 'Public urban recreation: an investigation of spatial relationships', *Journal of Leisure Research*, 8: 6–20.

Mitchell, L.S. and Murphy, P.E. (1991) 'Geography and tourism', *Annals of Tourism Research*, 18: 57–70.

Mitchell, M. and Hall, D. (eds) (2005) *Rural Tourism and Sustainable Business*, Clevedon: Channel View.

Mitchell, R. and Hall, C.M. (2001) 'The winery consumer: a New Zealand perspective', *Tourism Recreation Research*, 26(2): 63–75.

— (2003) 'Consuming tourists: food tourism consumer behaviour', in C.M. Hall, E. Sharples, R. Mitchell, B. Cambourne and N. Macionis (eds) *Food Tourism around the World: Development, Management and Markets*, Oxford: Butterworth Heinemann.

Mittermeier, R.A., Mittermeier, C.G., Brooks, T.M., Pilgrim, J.D., Konstant, W.R., da Fonseca, G.A.B. and Kormos, C. (2003) 'Wilderness and biodiversity conservation', *Proceedings of the National Academy of Sciences*, 100(18): 10309–13.

Mohrman, K., Ma, W. and Baker, D. (2008) 'The research university in transition: the emerging global model', *Higher Education Policy*, 21: 5–27.

Molz, J.G. (2010) 'Performing global geographies: time, space, place and pace in narratives of round-the-world travel', *Tourism Geographies*, 12: 329–48.

Montanari, A. and Williams, A.M. (eds) (1995) *European Tourism: Regions, Spaces and Restructuring*, Chichester: Wiley.

Moore, K., Cushman, G. and Simmons, D. (1995) 'Behavioural conceptualisation of tourism and leisure', *Annals of Tourism Research*, 22: 67–85.

Moran, J. (2005) *Reading the Everyday*, London: Routledge.

— (2012) 'Imagining the street in post-war Britain', *Urban History*, 39: 166–86.

Moran, W. (1993) 'Rural space as intellectual property', *Political Geography*, 12: 263–77.

— (2001) 'Terroir – the human factor', *Australian and New Zealand Wine Industry Journal of Oenology, Viticulture, Finance and Marketing*, 16(2): 32–51.

Morgan, C. and King, J. (1966) *Introduction to Psychology*, New York: McGraw Hill.

Morgan, G. (1980) 'Wilderness areas in Queensland: the rakes approach', in R.W. Robertson, P. Helman and A. Davey (eds) *Wilderness Management in Australia, Proceedings of a Symposium Held at the Canberra College of Advanced Education, 19–23 July 1978*, Natural Resources, School of Applied Science, Canberra College of Advanced Education, Canberra.

— (1991) *A Strategic Approach to the Planning and Management of Parks and Open Space*, Reading: Institute of Leisure and Amenity Management.

Morgan, M., Elbe, J. and de Esteban Curiel, J. (2009) 'Has the experience economy arrived? The views of destination managers in three visitor-dependent areas', *International Journal of Tourism Research*, 11: 201–16.

Morgan, N.J. and Pritchard, A. (1999) *Power and Politics at the Seaside*, Exeter: University of Exeter Press.

Morgan, R. (1999) 'A novel, user-based rating system for tourist beaches', *Tourism Management*, 20: 393–410.

Morgan, R., Jones, T. and Williams, A. (1993) 'Opinions and perceptions of England and Wales Heritage Coast beach users: some management implications from the Glamorgan Heritage Coast, Wales', *Journal of Coastal Research*, 9: 1083–93.

Moreno, A. and Becken, S. (2009) 'A climate change vulnerability assessment methodology for coastal tourism', *Journal of Sustainable Tourism*, 17: 473–88.

Mormont, M. (1987) 'Tourism and rural change', in M. Bouquet and M. Winter (eds) *Who from Their Labours Rest? Conflict and Practice in Rural Tourism*, Aldershot: Avebury.

Morisset, L.K., Sarrasin, B. and Ethier, G. (2012) *Epistémologie des études touristiques*, Montreal: Presses de l'Université du Québec.

Morris, A. (1996) 'Environmental management in coastal Spain', in M. Barke, J. Towner and M. Newton (eds) *Tourism in Spain: Critical Issues*, Wallingford: CAB International.

Morrison, A. and Dickinson, G. (1987) 'Tourist development in Spain: growth versus conservation on the Costa Brava', *Geography*, 72: 16–25.

Moser, S. (2010) 'Creating citizens through play: the role of leisure in Indonesian nation-building', *Social & Cultural Geography*, 11: 53–73.

Moutinho, L. (1987) 'Consumer behaviour in tourism', *European Journal of Marketing*, 21(10): 3–44.

Mowbray, M. (2011) 'What became of the local state? Neo-liberalism, community development and local government', *Community Development Journal*, 46 (suppl. 1): 132–53.

Mowforth, M. and Munt, I. (1998) *Tourism and Sustainability: New Tourism in the Third World*, London: Routledge.

— (2003) *Tourism and Sustainability: New Tourism in the Third World*, 2nd edn, London: Routledge.

Mowl, G. and Turner, J. (1995) 'Women, gender, leisure and place: towards a more "humanistic" geography of women's leisure', *Leisure Studies*, 14: 102–16.

Mucciaroni, G. (1991) 'Unclogging the arteries: the defeat of client politics and the logic of collective action', *Policy Studies Journal*, 19: 474–94.

Mulford, C.L. and Rogers, D.L. (1982) 'Definitions and models', in D.L. Rogers and D.A. Whetten (eds) *Interorganizational Coordination: Theory, Research and Implementation*, Ames: Iowa State University Press.

Müller, D.K. (1999) *German Second Home Owners in the Swedish Countryside: On the Internationalization of the Leisure Space*, Umeå: Kulturgeografiska institutionen.

— (2002a) 'German second home development in Sweden', in C.M. Hall and A.M. Williams (eds) *Tourism and Migration: New Relationships between Production and Consumption*, Dordrecht: Kluwer.

— (2002b) 'Second home ownership and sustainable development in Northern Sweden', *Tourism and Hospitality Research*, 3: 343–55.

— (2002c) 'Reinventing the countryside: German second home owners in southern Sweden', *Current Issues in Tourism*, 5: 426–46.

— (2004) 'Tourism, mobility and second homes', in A.A. Lew, C.M. Hall and A.M. Williams (eds) *A Companion to Tourism*, Oxford: Blackwell.

— (2006) 'The attractiveness of second home areas in Sweden: a quantitative analysis', *Current Issues in Tourism*, 9: 335–50.

— (2007) 'Second homes in the Nordic countries: between common heritage and exclusive commodity', *Scandinavian Journal of Hospitality and Tourism*, 7(3): 193–201.

— (2011) 'Second homes in rural areas: reflections on a troubled history', *Norsk Geografisk Tidsskrift– Norwegian Journal of Geography*, 65(3): 137–43.

Müller, D.K. and Hall, C.M. (2003) 'Second homes and regional population distribution: on administrative practices and failures in Sweden', *Espace, populations, sociétés*, 2: 251–61.

Müller, D.K. and Jansson, B. (eds) (2006) *Tourism in Peripheries: Perspectives from the Far North and South*, Wallingford: CAB International.

Muller, S. (2003) 'Towards decolonisation of Australia's protected area management: the Nantawarrina Indigenous Protected Area experience', *Australian Geographical Studies*, 41: 29–43.

Mulligan, M., Ahmed, I., Shaw, J., Mercer, D. and Nadarajah, Y. (2012) 'Lessons for long-term social recovery following the 2004 tsunami: community, livelihoods, tourism and housing', *Environmental Hazards*, 11: 38–51.

Mullins, G. and Heywood, J. (1984) *Unobtrusive Observation: A Visitor Survey Technique*, Ohio Agricultural Research and Development Circular No. 20, Columbus, OH: Ohio Agricultural Research and Development Center.

Mullins, P. (1984) 'Hedonism and real estate: resort tourism and Gold Coast development', in P. Williams (ed.) *Conflict and Development*, Sydney: Allen & Unwin.

— (1990) 'Tourist cities as new cities: Australia's Gold Coast and Sunshine Coast', *Australian Planner*, 28(3): 37–41.

— (1991) 'Tourism urbanization', *International Journal of Urban and Regional Research*, 15: 326–43.

Murdoch, J. (1993) 'Sustainable rural development: towards a research agenda', *Geoforum*, 24: 225–41.

Murdock, J. (1997) 'Inhuman/nonhuman/human: actor-network theory and prospects for a non-dualistic and symmetrical perspective on nature and society', *Environment and Planning D: Society and Space*, 15: 731–56.

Murphy, A. (2004) 'Geography and a liberal education', *AAG Newsletter* 39(5): 3.

Murphy, L. and Le Heron, R. (1999) 'Encountering places, peoples and environments: introducing human geography', in R. Le Heron, L. Murphy, P. Forer and M. Goldstone (eds) *Explorations in Human Geography: Encountering Place*, Auckland: Oxford University Press.

Murphy, P.E. (1982) 'Tourism planning in London: an exercise in spatial and seasonal management', *Tourist Review*, 37: 19–23.

— (1985) *Tourism: A Community Approach*, New York: Methuen.

— (1988) 'Community driven tourism planning', *Tourism Management*, 9: 96–104.

— (1994) 'Tourism and sustainable development', in W. Theobold (ed.) *Global Tourism: The Next Decade*, Oxford: Butterworth Heinemann.

— (ed.) (1997) *Quality Management in Urban Tourism*, International Western Geographical Series, Chichester: Wiley.

Murphy, P.E. and Keller, C.P. (1990) 'Destination travel patterns: an examination and modelling of tourism patterns on Vancouver Island, British Columbia', *Leisure Sciences*, 12(1): 49–65.

Murphy, P.E. and Murphy, A.E. (2004) *Strategic Management for Tourism Communities: Bridging the Gaps*, Clevedon: Channel View.

Murphy, P.E. and Rosenblood, L. (1974) 'Tourism: an exercise in spatial search', *Canadian Geographer*, 18: 201–10.

Murphy, P.E. and Staples, W.A. (1979) 'A modernized family life cycle', *Journal of Consumer Research* 6(1): 12–22.

Murphy, R.E. (1963) 'Geography and outdoor recreation: an opportunity and an obligation', *Professional Geographer*, 15(5): 33–4.

Murphy, W. and Gardiner, J.J. (1983) 'Forest recreating economics', *Irish Forestry*, 40: 12–19.

Nahuelhual, L., Carmona, A., Lozada, P., Jaramillo, A. and Aguayo, M. (2013) 'Mapping recreation and ecotourism as a cultural ecosystem service: an application at the local level in Southern Chile', *Applied Geography*, 40: 71–82.

Naranjo, F. (2001) 'Relaciones entre formacion y dedicacion professional en la geografia espanola', *Documents d'Analisi Geografica*, 39: 37–56.

Nash, D. (1996) *The Anthropology of Tourism*, Oxford: Pergamon Press.

Nash, R. (1963) 'The American wilderness in historical perspective', *Journal of Forest History*, 6(4): 2–13.

—— (1967) *Wilderness and the American Mind*, New Haven, CT: Yale University Press.

—— (1982) *Wilderness and the American Mind*, 3rd edn, New Haven, CT: Yale University Press.

—— (1990) *The Rights of Nature: A History of Environmental Ethics*, Leichhardt: Primavera Press.

Nassauer, J., Cory, R. and Cruse, R.M. (2007) 'Alternative scanarios for future Iowa agricultural landscapes', in J. Nassauer, M. Santelmann and D. Scavia (eds) *Agricultural Landscapes. From the Corn Belt to the Gulf: Societal and Environmental Implications of Alternative Agricultural Futures*, Washington, DC: Resources for the Future.

National Capital Commission (NCC) (1991) *NCR Visitor Survey, Volume 1 – Analysis of Findings*, conducted for the National Capital Commission by Gallup Canada, Ottawa: NCC.

—— (1998) *A Capital in the Making*, Ottawa: NCC.

—— (1999) *Plan for Canada's Capital: A Second Century of Vision, Planning and Development*, Ottawa: NCC.

—— (2000a) *Summary of the Corporate Plan 2000–2001 to 2004–2005*, Ottawa: NCC.

—— (2000b) *Planning Canada's Capital Region*, Ottawa: NCC.

National Intelligence Council (NIC) (2012) *Global Trends 2030: Alternative Worlds*, Washington, DC: NIC.

National Oceanic and Atmospheric Administration (NOAA) (1997) *1998 Year of the Ocean – Coastal Tourism and Recreation*, discussion paper, http://www.yoto98.noaa.gov/yoto/meeting/tour_rec_316.html.

Naylon, J. (1967) 'Tourism – Spain's most important industry', *Geography*, 52: 23–40.

Needham, M.D. (2013) 'Encounters, norms, and crowding at six coastal and marine areas in Hawai'i', *Tourism in Marine Environments*, 9: 19–34.

Needham, M.D., Szuster, B.W. and Bell, C.M. (2011) 'Encounter norms, social carrying capacity indicators, and standards of quality at a marine protected area', *Ocean & Coastal Management*, 54: 633–41.

Nefedova, V. and Zemlianoi, O. (1997) 'Geographical forecast of recreation activity of development (the Moscow region case study)', *Vestnik-Moskovskogo-Universiteta-Seriya-Geografiya*, 4: 25–8.

Nelson, J.G. (ed.) (1970) *Canadian Parks in Perspective*, Montreal: Harvest House.

—— (1973) 'Canada's national parks – past, present and future', *Canadian Geographical Journal*, 86(3): 68–89.

—— (1982) 'Canada's national parks: past, present and future', in G. Wall and J.S. Marsh (eds) *Recreational Land Use: Perspectives on Its Evolution in Canada*, Carleton Library Series, Ottawa: Carleton University Press.

—— (1986) *An External Perspective on Parks Canada Strategies*, Occasional Paper No. 2, Waterloo: University of Waterloo Parks Canada Liaison Committee, University of Waterloo.

Nepal, S.K. (2009a) 'Traditions and trends: a review of geographical scholarship in tourism', *Tourism Geographies*, 11: 2–22.

— (2009b) 'Tourism geographies: a review of trends, challenges and opportunities', in T. Jamal and M. Robinson (eds) *The SAGE Handbook of Tourism Studies*, London: Sage.

Neulinger, J. (1981) *The Psychology of Leisure*, Springfield, IL: C. Thomas.

New Forest National Park Authority (NFNPA) (2007) *Tourism and Recreation: Facts and Figures*, Lymington: New Forest National Park Authority.

Newham Borough Council (1991a) *Newham's Policy for the Environment: A Consultation Document*, London: Borough of Newham.

— (1991b) *Shaped for Success: Leisure Development Strategy 1990–94*, London: Borough of Newham.

Newsome, D., Moore, S. and Dowling, R. (2012) *Natural Area Tourism: Ecology, Impacts and Management*, 2nd edn, Bristol: Channel View.

Ngubane, J.S. and Diab, R.D. (2005) 'Engaging the local community in tourism development planning: a case study in Maputaland', *South African Geographical Journal*, 87(2): 115–22.

Nicholls, S. (2001) 'Measuring the accessibility and equity of public parks: a case study using GIS', *Managing Leisure*, 6: 201–19.

Nichols, K. (1999) 'Coming to terms with integrated coastal management', *Professional Geographer*, 51: 388–99.

Nicholson, M.H. (1962) *Mountain Gloom and Mountain Glory*, New York: Norton.

Nicholson-Lord, D. (1994) 'Space for green reinvention', *Independent*, 4 April.

Nickels, S., Milne, S. and Wenzel, G. (1991) 'Inuit perceptions of tourism development: the case of Clyde River, Baffin Island, NWT', *Etudes/Inuit/Studies*, 15(1): 157–69.

Nicol, J.I. (1969) 'The National Parks movement in Canada', in J.G. Nelson and R.C. Scace (eds) *The Canadian National Parks: Today and Tomorrow*, vol. 1, Calgary: Department of Geography, University of Calgary.

Nielsen, N. (1990) 'Construction of a recreational beach using the original coastal morphology, Koege Bay, Denmark', in P. Fabbri (ed.) *Recreational Use of Coastal Areas*, Dordrecht: Kluwer.

Nordstrom, K., Lampe, R. and Vandemark, L. (2000) 'Reestablishing naturally functioning dunes on developed coasts', *Environmental Management*, 25: 37–51.

Norkunas, M.K. (1993) *The Politics of Memory: Tourism, History, and Ethnicity in Monterey, California*, Albany: State University of New York Press.

Norris, M. and Winston, N. (2010) 'Second-home owners: escaping, investing or retiring?', *Tourism Geographies*, 12: 546–67.

Nunn, P.D. (2013) 'The end of the Pacific? Effects of sea level rise on Pacific Island livelihoods', *Singapore Journal of Tropical Geography*, 34(2): 143–71.

O'Connor, A., Zerger, A. and Itami, B. (2005) 'Geo-temporal tracking and analysis of tourist movement', *Mathematics and Computers in Simulation*, 69 (1–2, special issue): 135–50.

O'Dell, A. (1935) 'European air services, June 1934', *Geography*, 19(4): 288–91.

O'Leary, J.T. (1976) 'Land use definition and the rural community: disruption of community leisure space', *Journal of Leisure Research*, 8: 263–74.

O'Malley, M.P., Lee-Brooks, K. and Medd, H.B. (2013) 'The global economic impact of Manta Ray watching tourism', *PloS one*, 8(5): e65051.

O'Riordan, T. (1971) *Perspectives on Resource Management*, London: Pion Press.

O'Riordan, T. and Paget, G. (1978) *Sharing Rivers and Canals*, Study 16, London: Sports Council.

O'Riordan, T. and Turner, R.K. (eds) (1984) *An Annotated Reader in Environmental Planning and Management*, Oxford: Pergamon Press.

Obrador, P. (2007) 'A haptic geography of the beach: naked bodies, vision and touch', *Social & Cultural Geography*, 8: 123–41.

Observer (1944) 'Britain can fight for her beaches: seaside slums must go', *Observer*, Sunday 11 June: 7.

Oelschlaeger, M. (1991) *The Idea of Wilderness: From Prehistory to the Age of Ecology*, New Haven, CT: Yale University Press.

Office for National Statistics (ONS) (2000) *Social Trends 30*, London: The Stationery Office.

— (2002) *Time Use Survey*, London: ONS.

— (2003) *Social Trends 33*, London: ONS.

— (2012) *The Geography of Tourism Employment*, London: ONS.

Office of the Deputy Prime Minister (ODPM) (2002) *Cleaner, Safer, Greener Public Space*, London: ODPM.

Office of Population Censuses and Surveys (OPCS) (1992) *1991 Census: Inner London*, London: OPCS.

Oh, C.O., Draper, J. and Dixon, A.W. (2010) 'Comparing resident and tourist preferences for public beach access and related amenities', *Ocean & Coastal Management*, 53(5): 245–51.

Ohmae, K. (1995) *The End of the Nation State: The Rise of Regional Economies*, New York: HarperCollins and The Free Press.

Oishi, Y. (2013) 'Toward the improvement of trail classification in national parks using the recreation opportunity spectrum approach', *Environmental Management*, 51: 1126–36.

Ólafsdóttir, R. and Runnström, M.C. (2011) 'How wild is Iceland? Wilderness quality with respect to nature-based tourism', *Tourism Geographies*, 13(2): 280–98.

Olds, K. (1998) 'Urban mega-events, evictions and housing rights: the Canadian case', *Current Issues in Tourism*, 1(1): 2–46.

Olkusnik, M. (2001) 'Countryside holidays as a cultural and social phenomenon in Warsaw at the end of the nineteenth century', *Kwartalnik Historii Kultury Materialnej*, 69(4): 367–86.

Ollenburg, C. and Buckley, R. (2007) 'Stated economic and social motivations of farm tourism operators', *Journal of Travel Research*, 45: 444–52.

Olszewska, A. (1989) 'Poland: the impact of the crisis on leisure patterns', in A. Olszewska and K. Roberts (eds) *Leisure and Lifestyle: A Comparative Analysis of Free Time*, London: Sage.

Olwig, K. and Olwig, K. (1979) 'Underdevelopment and the development of "natural" parks ideology', *Antipode*, 11(2): 16–25.

Okello, M., Kenana, L. and Kieti, D. (2012) 'Factors influencing domestic tourism for urban and semi-urban populations around Nairobi National Park, Kenya', *Tourism Analysis*, 17(1): 79–89.

Oosterman, J. (1992) 'Public consumption – rate culture', *Built Environment*, 18: 155–64.

Open Space Society (1992) *Making Space: Protecting and Creating Open Space for Local Communities*, Henley: Open Space Society.

Oppermann, M. (1992) 'International tourist flows in Malaysia', *Annals of Tourism Research*, 19: 482–500.

— (1993) 'German tourists in New Zealand', *The New Zealand Geographer*, 49(1): 31–4.

— (1994) 'Regional aspects of tourism in New Zealand', *Regional Studies*, 28: 155–67.

— (1995) 'Holidays on the farm: a case study of German hosts and guests', *Journal of Travel Research*, 33: 57–61.

— (1998a) 'What is new with the resort cycle?', *Tourism Management*, 19: 179–80.

— (1998b) 'Farm tourism in New Zealand', in R. Butler, C.M. Hall and J. Jenkins (eds) *Tourism and Recreation in Rural Areas*, Chichester: Wiley.

Oppermann, M. and Chon, K. (1997) *Tourism in Developing Countries*, London: International Thomson Business Publishing.

Orams, M. (1999) *Marine Tourism*, London: Routledge.

— (2002) 'Feeding wildlife as a tourism attraction: a review of issues and impacts', *Tourism Management*, 22: 281–93.

— (2005) 'Dolphins, whales and ecotourism in New Zealand: what are the impacts and how should the industry be managed?', in C.M. Hall and S. Boyd (eds) *Nature-based Tourism in Peripheral Areas: Development or Disaster*, Clevedon: Channel View.

Organisation for Economic Co-operation and Development (OECD) (1980) *The Impact of Tourism on the Environment*, Paris: OECD.

— (2008) *Tourism in OECD Countries: Trends and Policies*, Paris: OECD.

— (2012) *Food and the Tourism Experience*, Paris: OECD.

Ormond, M. (2011) 'Medical tourism, medical exile: responding to the cross-border pursuit of health-care in Malaysia', in C. Minca and T. Oakes (eds) *Real Tourism: Practice, Care and Politics in Contemporary Travel*, London: Routledge.

— (2012) 'Claiming "cultural competence": the promotion of multi-ethnic Malaysia as a medical tourism destination', in C.M. Hall (ed.) *Medical Tourism: The Ethics, Regulation, and Marketing of Health Mobility*, London: Routledge.

Orsi, F., Geneletti, D. and Borsdorf, A. (2013) 'Mapping wildness for protected area management: a methodological approach and application to the Dolomites UNESCO World Heritage Site (Italy)', *Landscape and Urban Planning*, 120: 1–15.

Outdoor Recreation Resources Review Commission (1962) *Outdoor Recreation for America*, Washington, DC: Government Printing Office.

Overton, J. (2010) 'The consumption of space: land, capital and place in the New Zealand wine industry', *Geoforum*, 41: 752–62.

Ovington, J.D. and Fox, A.M. (1980) 'Wilderness – a natural asset', *Parks*, 5(3): 1–4.

Owen, C. (1990) 'Tourism and urban regeneration', *Cities: The International Journal of Urban Policy and Planning*, August: 194–201.

Owen, J.G. (2003) 'The stadium game: cities versus teams', *Journal of Sports Economics*, 4: 183–202.

Owens, P. (1984) 'Rural leisure and recreation research: a retrospective evaluation', *Progress in Human Geography*, 8: 157–85.

Paasi, A. (2005) 'Globalisation, academic capitalism and the uneven geographies of international journal publishing spaces', *Environment and Planning A*, 37: 769–89.

Pacione, M.(1999a) 'Applied geography: in pursuit of useful knowledge', *Applied Geography*, 19: 1–12.

— (1999b) 'In pursuit of knowledge: the principles and practice of applied geography', in M. Pacione (ed.) *Applied Geography: Principles and Practice*, London: Routledge.

— (ed.) (1999c) *Applied Geography: Principles and Practice*, London: Routledge.

— (2001) *Urban Geography: A Global Perspective*, Routledge: London.

— (2004) 'Principles and practice', in A. Bailly and L.J. Gibson (eds) *Applied Geography: A World Perspective*, Paris: Economica.

Page, S.J. (1988) 'Poverty in Leicester 1881–1911: a geographical perspective', unpublished PhD thesis, Department of Geography, University of Leicester.

— (1989) 'Tourist development in London Docklands in the 1980s and 1990s', *GeoJournal*, 19(3): 291–5.

— (1992) 'Perspectives on the environmental impact of the Channel Tunnel on tourism', in C. Cooper and A. Lockwood (eds) *Progress in Tourism, Recreation and Hospitality Management*, vol. 4, London: Belhaven Press.

— (1994a) 'European bus and coach travel', *Travel and Tourism Analyst*, 1: 19–39.

— (1994b) *Transport for Tourism*, London: Routledge.

— (1994c) 'Perspectives on tourism and peripherality: a review of tourism in the Republic of Ireland', in C. Cooper and A. Lockwood (eds) *Progress in Tourism, Recreation and Hospitality Management*, vol. 5, Chichester: Wiley.

— (1995a) *Urban Tourism*, London: Routledge.

— (1995b) 'Waterfront revitalisation in London: market-led planning and tourism in London Docklands', in S. Craig-Smith and M. Fagence (eds) *Recreation and Tourism as a Catalyst for Urban Waterfront Development*, Westport, CT: Greenwood Publishing.

— (1997a) 'Urban tourism: analysing and evaluating the tourist experience', in C. Ryan (ed.) *The Tourist Experience. A New Introduction*, London: Cassell.

— (1997b) *The Cost of Accidents in the Adventure Tourism Industry*, Consultant's Report for the Tourism Policy Group, Ministry of Commerce, Wellington.

— (1998) 'Transport for recreation and tourism', in B. Hoyle and R. Knowles (eds) *Modern Transport Geography*, 2nd edn, Chichester: Wiley.

— (1999) *Transport and Tourism*, London: Addison Wesley Longman.

— (2000) 'Urban tourism', in C. Ryan and S.J. Page (eds) *Tourism Management: Towards the New Millennium*, Oxford: Pergamon Press.

— (2001) 'Hubs and gateways in South East Asia: implications for tourism', in P. Teo and T. Chang (eds) *Interconnected Worlds: South East Asian Tourism in the Twenty First Century*, Oxford: Pergamon Press.

— (2002) 'European rail travel – special length focus', *Travel and Tourism Analyst*, 2: 1–39.

— (2003a) *Tourism Management: Managing for Change*, Oxford: Butterworth Heinemann.

— (2003b) 'Evaluating research performance in tourism: the UK experience', *Tourism Management*, 24: 607–22.

— (2003c) 'European bus and coach travel', *Travel and Tourism Analyst*, 6: 1–32.

— (2005) *Transport and Tourism*, 2nd edn, Harlow: Pearson Education.

— (2009a) *Transport and Tourism: Global Perspectives*. Harlow: Pearson Education.

— (2009b) 'Current issue in tourism: the evolution of travel medicine research: a new research agenda for tourism?', *Tourism Management*, 30: 149–57.

— (2011) *Tourism Management: An Introduction*, 4th edn, Oxford: Elsevier.

Page, S.J. and Connell, J. (2006) *Tourism: A Modern Synthesis*, London: Thomson.

— (2010) *Leisure: An Introduction*. Harlow: Prentice Hall.

— (eds) (2012) *A Handbook of Events*, Abingdon: Routledge.

— (2014) *Tourism: A Modern Synthesis*, 4th edn, Andover: Cengage Learning.

Page, S.J. and Dowling, R. (2001) *Ecotourism*, Harlow: Pearson Education.

Page, S.J. and Durie, A. (2009) 'Tourism in wartime Britain 1914–18: adaptation, innovation and the role of Thomas Cook & Son', in J. Ateljevic and S.J. Page (eds) *Tourism and Entrepreneurship*, Oxford: Elsevier.

Page, S.J. and Getz, D. (eds) (1997) *The Business of Rural Tourism: International Perspectives*, London: International Thomson Business Press.

Page, S.J. and Hall, C.M. (2003) *Managing Urban Tourism*, Harlow: Pearson Education.

Page, S.J. and Hardyman, R. (1996) 'Place marketing and town centre management: a new tool for urban revitalisation', *Cities: The International Journal of Urban Policy and Planning*, 13(3): 153–64.

Page, S.J. and Lawton, G. (1997) 'The impact of urban tourism on destination communities: implications for community tourism planning in Auckland', in C.M. Hall, J. Jenkins and G. Kearsley (eds) *Tourism Planning and Policy in Australia and New Zealand: Cases, Issues and Practice*, Sydney: Irwin Publishers.

Page, S.J. and Meyer, D. (1996) 'Tourist accidents: an exploratory analysis', *Annals of Tourism Research*, 23(3): 666–90.

Page, S.J. and Sinclair, M.T. (1989) 'Tourism accommodation in London: alternative policies and the Docklands experience', *Built Environment*, 15(2): 125–37.

Page, S.J. and Thorn, K. (1997) 'Towards sustainable tourism planning in New Zealand: public sector planning responses', *Journal of Sustainable Tourism*, 5(1): 59–78.

— (1998) 'Sustainable tourism development and local government in New Zealand', in C.M. Hall and A. Lew (eds) *The Geography of Sustainable Tourism: Approaches, Issues and Experiences*, Harlow: Addison Wesley Longman.

— (2002) 'Towards sustainable tourism development and planning in New Zealand: the public sector response revisited', *Journal of Sustainable Tourism*, 10: 222–39.

Page, S.J., Bentley, T. and Walker, L. (2005) 'Scoping the nature and extent of adventure tourism operations in Scotland: how safe are they?', *Tourism Management*, 26: 381–97.

Page, S.J., Forer, P. and Lawton, G. (1999) 'Tourism and small business development: terra incognita', *Tourism Management*, 20: 435–59.

Page, S.J., Nielsen, K. and Goodenough, R. (1994) 'Managing urban parks: user perspectives and local leisure needs in the 1990s', *Service Industries Journal*, 14: 216–37.

Page, S.J, Song, H. and Wu, D. C. (2012) 'Assessing the impacts of the global economic crisis and swine flu on inbound tourism demand in the United Kingdom', *Journal of Travel Research*, 51: 142–53.

Page, S.J., Brunt, P., Busby, G. and Connell, J. (2001) *Tourism: A Modern Synthesis*, London: Thomson Learning.

Pahl, R.E. (1975) *Whose City? And Further Essays in Urban Society*, Harmondsworth: Penguin.

Pain, R. (1997) 'Social geographies of women's fear of crime', *Transactions of the Institute of British Geographers*, 22: 231–44.

Palm, R. and Brazel, A. (1992) 'Applications of geographic concepts and methods', in R. Abler, M. Marcus and J. Olsson (eds) *Geography's Inner Worlds*, New Brunswick, NJ: Rutgers University Press.

Panchuk, S. and Yudina, Y. (1977) 'Cottage settlements and garden cooperatives in the Moscow area', *Soviet Geography*, 18: 329–38.

Paniagua, A. (2012) 'The rural as a site of recreation: evidence and contradictions in Spain from a geographical perspective', *Journal of Tourism and Cultural Change*, 10: 264–75.

Papatheodorau, A. (2003) 'Corporate strategies of British tour operators in the Mediterranean region: an economic geography approach', *Tourism Geographies*, 5: 280–304.

Papson, S. (1981) 'Spuriousness and tourism: politics of two Canadian provincial governments', *Annals of Tourism Research*, 8: 220–35.

Parasuraman, A., Zeithmal, V. and Berry, L. (1985) 'A conceptual model of service quality and its implications for future research', *Journal of Marketing*, 49(4): 41–50.

Paris, C. (2009) 'Re-positioning second homes within housing studies: household investment, gentrification, multiple residence, mobility and hyper consumption', *Housing, Theory and Society*, 26: 292–310.

— (2010) *Affluence, Mobility and Second Home Ownership*, Abingdon: Routledge.

Park, K.S., Reisinger, Y. and Noh, E.H. (2010) 'Luxury shopping in tourism', *International Journal of Tourism Research*, 12: 164–78.

Park, R., Burgess, E. and McKenzie, R. (1925) *The City*, Chicago: University of Chicago Press.

Parker, A.J. (2010) 'A park of the people: the demotion of Platt National Park, Oklahoma', *Journal of Cultural Geography*, 27: 151–75.

Parker, S. (1999) *Leisure in Contemporary Society*, Wallingford: CAB International.

Parliamentary Commissioner for the Environment (1997) *Management of the Environmental Effects Associated with the Tourism Sector*, Wellington: Office of the Parliamentary Commissioner for the Environment.

Passmore, J. (1974) *Man's Responsibility for Nature*, London: Duckworth.

Pastor, I.O., Casermeiro Martínez, M.A., Canalejoa, A.E. and Mariño, P.E. (2007) 'Landscape evaluation: comparison of evaluation methods in a region of Spain', *Journal of Environmental Management*, 85: 204–14.

Paterson, S.K., O'Donnell, A. and Loomis, D.K. (2010) *The Social and Economic Effects of Shoreline Change: North Atlantic, South Atlantic, Gulf of Mexico, and Great Lakes Regional Overview*, Lexington, MA: Eastern Research Group.

Patmore, J.A. (1968) 'The spa towns of Britain', in R. Beckinsale and J. Houston (eds) *Urbanization and Its Problems*, Oxford: Blackwell.

— (1970) *Land and Leisure*, Newton Abbot: David and Charles.

— (1971) 'Routeways and recreation', in P. Lavery (ed.) *Recreational Geography*, Newton Abbot: David and Charles.

— (1973) 'Recreation', in J. Dawson and J. Doornkamp (eds) *Evaluating the Human Environment: Essays in Applied Geography*, London: Edward Arnold.

— (1977) 'Recreation and leisure', *Progress in Human Geography*, 1: 111–17.

— (1978) 'Recreation and leisure', *Progress in Human Geography*, 2: 142–7.

— (1979) 'Recreation and leisure', *Progress in Human Geography*, 3: 126–32.

— (1980) 'Recreation and leisure', *Progress in Human Geography*, 4: 91–8.

— (1983) *Recreation and Resources: Leisure Patterns and Leisure Places*, Oxford: Blackwell.

— (ed.) (1989) *Recreation and Conservation: Themes in Applied Geography*, Hull: School of Geography, University of Hull.

Patmore, J.A. and Collins, M. (1981) 'Recreation and leisure', *Progress in Human Geography*, 5: 87–92.

Patmore, J.A. and Rodgers, J. (eds) (1972) *Leisure in the North-West*, Salford: North-West Sports Council.

Paul, A.H. (1972) 'Weather and the daily use of outdoor recreation areas in Canada', in J.A. Taylor (ed.) *Weather Forecasting for Agriculture and Industry*, Newton Abbot: David and Charles.

Pawson, E. and Brooking, T. (eds) (2002) *Environmental Histories of New Zealand*, Melbourne: Oxford University Press.

Peak District National Park Authority (2013) State of the Park: Tourism, http://www.peakdistrict.

gov.uk/microsites/sopr/welcoming/tourism (accessed 25 September 2013).

Pearce, D.G. (1978) 'Form and function in French resorts', *Annals of Tourism Research*, 5: 142–56.

— (1979) 'Towards a geography of tourism', *Annals of Tourism Research*, 6: 245–72.

— (1981) *Tourist Development*, Harlow: Longman.

— (1986) 'The spatial structure of coastal tourism: a behavioural approach', paper presented at the International Geographical Union Commission on the Geography of Tourism and Leisure, Palma de Mallorca.

— (1987a) *Tourism Today: A Geographical Analysis*, Harlow: Longman.

— (1987b) 'Motel location and choice in Christchurch', *New Zealand Geographer*, 43(1): 10–17.

— (1988a) 'The spatial structure of coastal tourism: a behavioural approach', *Tourism Recreation Research*, 13(2): 11–14.

— (1988b) 'Tourist time-budgets', *Annals of Tourism Research*, 15: 106–21.

— (1988c) 'Tourism and regional development in the European Community', *Tourism Management*, 9: 11–22.

— (1989) *Tourist Development*, 2nd edn, Harlow: Longman.

— (1990) 'Tourism, the regions and restructuring in New Zealand', *Journal of Tourism Studies*, 1(2): 33–42.

— (1992a) 'Tourism and the European regional development fund: the first fourteen years', *Journal of Travel Research*, 30: 44–51.

— (1992b) *Tourist Organisations*, Harlow: Longman.

— (1993a) 'Comparative studies in tourism research', in D. Pearce and R. Butler (eds) *Tourism Research: Critiques and Challenges*, London: Routledge.

— (1993b) 'Domestic tourist travel patterns in New Zealand', *GeoJournal*, 29(3): 225–32.

— (1995a) *Tourism Today: A Geographical Analysis*, 2nd edn, Harlow: Longman.

— (1995b) 'Planning for tourism in the 90s: an integrated, dynamic, multi-scale approach', in R.W. Butler and D.G. Pearce (eds) *Change in Tourism: People, Places, Processes*, London: Routledge.

— (1998) 'Tourism development in Paris: public intervention', *Annals of Tourism Research*, 25: 457–76.

— (1999a) 'Towards a geography of the geography of tourism: issues and examples from New Zealand', *Tourism Geographies*, 1(4): 406–24.

— (1999b) 'Tourism districts in Paris: structure and functions', *Tourism Management*, 19(1): 49–65.

— (2007) 'Capital city tourism: perspectives from Wellington', *Journal of Travel & Tourism Marketing*, 22(3–4): 7–20.

Pearce, D.G. and Butler, R.W. (eds) (1993) *Tourism Research: Critiques and Challenges*, London: Routledge.

Pearce, D.G. and Kirk, D. (1986) 'Carrying capacities for coastal tourism', *Industry and Environment*, 9(1): 3–6.

Pearce, D.G. and Mings, R. (1984) 'Geography, tourism and recreation in the Antipodes', *GeoJournal*, 9(1): 91–5.

Pearce, J.A. (1980) 'Host community acceptance of foreign tourists: strategic considerations', *Annals of Tourism Research*, 7: 224–33.

Pearce, P.L. (1977) 'Mental souvenirs: a study of tourists and their city maps', *Australian Journal of Psychology*, 29: 203–10.

— (1981) 'Route maps: a study of travellers' perceptions of a section of countryside', *Journal of Environmental Psychology*, 1: 141–55.

— (1982) *The Social Psychology of Tourist Behaviour*, Oxford: Pergamon Press.

— (1993) 'The fundamentals of tourist motivation', in D. Pearce and R. Butler (eds) *Tourism Research: Critique and Challenges*, London: Routledge.

— (2005) *Tourist Behaviour: Themes and Conceptual Issues*, Clevedon: Channel View.

— (2011) *Tourist Behaviour and the Contemporary World*, Bristol: Channel View.

Pearson, R. (1968) 'Railways in relation to resort development in East Lincolnshire', *East Midland Geographer*, 4: 281–95.

Pedersen, K. and Viken, A. (1996) 'From Sami nomadism to global tourism', in M.F. Price (ed.) *People and Tourism in Fragile Environments*, Chichester: Wiley.

Peel, D. and Lloyd, G. (2010) 'Strategic regeneration: a policy coupling approach to managing a coastal resort in South Wales', *Environmental Hazards*, 9: 301–18.

Peet, R. (ed.) (1977a) *Radical Geography: Alternative Viewpoints on Contemporary Social Issues*, London: Methuen.

— (1977b) 'The development of radical geography in the United States', *Progress in Human Geography*, 1: 240–63.

— (1998) *Modern Geographical Thought*, Oxford: Blackwell.

— (2009) 'Radical geography', in R. Kitchin and N. Thrift (eds) *International Encyclopedia of Human Geography*, Oxford: Elsevier.

Peeters, P. (2013) 'Developing a long-term global tourism transport model using a behavioural approach: implications for sustainable tourism policy making', *Journal of Sustainable Tourism*, DOI: 10.1080/09669582.2013.828732.

Peeters, P. and Landré, M. (2011) 'The emerging global tourism geography—an environmental sustainability perspective', *Sustainability*, 4(1): 42–71.

Peeters, P., Gössling, S. and Becken, S. (2006) 'Innovation towards tourism sustainability: climate change and aviation', *International Journal of Innovation and Sustainable Development*, 1(3): 184–200.

Peeters, P., Szimba, E. and Duijnisveld, M. (2007) 'Major environmental impacts of European tourist transport', *Journal of Transport Geography*, 15: 83–93.

Pember-Reeves, M. (1979 [1913]) *Round a Pound a Week*, London: Virago.

Penning-Rowsell, E. (1973) *Alternative Approaches to Landscape Appraisal and Evaluation*, Planning Research Group, Report No. 11, Enfield: Middlesex Polytechnic.

— (1975) 'Constraints on the application of landscape evaluation', *Transactions of the Institute of British Geographers*, 66: 49–55.

Penning-Rowsell, E., Green, C., Thompson, P., Coker, A., Tunstall, S., Richards, C. and Parker, D. (1992) *The Economics of Coastal Management: A Manual of Benefit Assessment Techniques*, London: Belhaven Press.

Pentland, W., Harvey, A., Lawton, M. and McColl, M. (eds) (2002) *Time Use Research in the Social Sciences*, New York: Springer.

Pentz, D. (2002) *Towards an Open Space Strategy for the Papakura District*, Briefing Paper, Auckland: Papakura District Council.

People 1st (2010) *State of the Nation: Report 2010. An Analysis of Labour Market Trends, Skills, Education and Training within the UK Hospitality, Leisure, Travel and Tourism Industries*, Uxbridge: People 1st.

Pepper, D. (1984) *The Roots of Modern Environmentalism*, London: Croom Helm.

Perdue, R. (1985) 'The 1983 Nebraska Visitor Survey: achieving a high response rate', *Journal of Travel Research*, 24(2): 23–6.

Pereira, R.B. (2008) 'Leisure and ageing: the leisure experiences of older Italians in an Australian community', *Australian Occupational Therapy Journal*, 55: 218.

Perkins, H. (1993) 'Human geography, recreation and leisure', in H. Perkins and G. Cushman (eds) *Leisure, Recreation and Tourism*, Auckland: Longman Paul.

Perkins, H. and Thorns, D. (2001) 'A decade on: reflections on the Resource Management Act 1991 and the practice of urban planning in New Zealand', *Environment and Planning B*, 28: 639–54

Pettersson, R. (2004) *Sami Tourism in Northern Sweden: Supply, Demand and Interaction*, ETOUR European Tourism Research Institute 2004: 14, Umeå: Department of Social and Economic Geography, Umeå University.

Phaneuf, D.J. and Smith, V.K. (2005) 'Recreation demand models', in K.-G. Maler and J.R. Vincent (eds) *Handbook of Environmental Economics*, vol. 2, Oxford: Elsevier.

Phelps, N. (1992) 'External economies, agglomeration and flexible accumulation', *Transactions of the Institute of British Geographers*, 17: 35–46.

Phillips, M.R. and House, C. (2009) 'An evaluation of priorities for beach tourism: case studies from South Wales', *Tourism Management*, 30: 176–83.

Picton, R. (2010) 'Selling national urban renewal: the National Film Board, the National Capital Commission and post-war planning in Ottawa, Canada', *Urban History*, 37: 301–21.

Pierre, J. and Peters, B.G. (2000) *Governance, Politics and the State*, New York: St Martin's Press.

Pigram, J.J. (1977) 'Beach resort morphology', *Habitat International*, 2(5–6): 525–41.

— (1980) 'Environmental implications of tourism development', *Annals of Tourism Research*, 7: 554–83.

—— (1983) *Outdoor Recreation and Resource Management*, Beckenham: Croom Helm.

—— (1985) *Outdoor Recreation and Resource Management*, 2nd edn, London: Croom Helm.

—— (1987) *Tourism in Coffs Harbour: Attitudes, Perceptions and Implications*, Coffs Harbour: North Coast Regional Office, Department of Continuing Education, University of New England.

—— (1990) 'Sustainable tourism: policy considerations', *Journal of Tourism Studies*, 1(2): 2–9.

Pigram, J.J. and Jenkins, J. (1999) *Outdoor Recreation Management*, London: Routledge.

—— (2006) *Outdoor Recreation Management*, 2nd edn, London: Routledge.

Pike, S. (2008) *Destination Marketing Organisations*, Oxford: Elsevier.

Pine, J. and Gilmore, J. (1999) *The Experience Economy: Work Is Theatre & Every Business a Stage*, Boston, MA: Harvard Business School Press.

Piperoglou, J. (1966) 'Identification and definition of regions in Greek tourist planning', *Regional Science Association Papers*, 18: 169–76.

Pirie, G.H. (2009) 'Virtuous mobility: moralising vs measuring geographical mobility in Africa', *Afrika Focus*, 22(1): 21–35.

Pitkänen, K. (2011) 'Contested cottage landscapes: host perspective to the increase of foreign second home ownership in Finland 1990–2008', *Fennia*, 189(1): 43–59.

Piven, F. (1995) 'Is it global economics or neo-laissez-faire?', *New Left Review*, 213: 107–14.

Pizam, A. (1978) 'Tourism's impacts: the social costs to the destination community as perceived by its residents', *Journal of Travel Research*, 16(4): 8–12.

Place, S.E. (1998) 'How sustainable is ecotourism in Costa Rica?', in C.M. Hall and A.A. Lew (eds) *Sustainable Tourism Development: Geographical Perspectives*, Harlow: Addison Wesley Longman.

Plaza, B., Galvez-Galvez, C. and Gonzalez-Flores, A. (2011) 'Testing the employment impact of the Guggenheim Museum Bilbao via TSA', *Tourism Economics*, 17: 223–9.

Plog, S. (1974) 'Why destination areas rise and fall in popularity', *Cornell Hotel and Restaurant Administration Quarterly*, 15 (November): 13–16.

—— (1977) 'Why destination areas rise and fall in popularity', in E. Kelly (ed.) *Domestic and International Tourism*, Wellesey, MA: Institute of Certified Travel Agents.

—— (2001) 'Why destination areas rise and fall in popularity: an update of a Cornell Quarterly classic', *Cornell Hotel and Restaurant Administration Quarterly*, 42(3): 13–24.

Plummer, R. and Fennell, D.A. (2009) 'Managing protected areas for sustainable tourism: prospects for adaptive co-management', *Journal of Sustainable Tourism*, 17: 149–68.

Pocock, D. (1997) 'Some reflections on World Heritage', *Area*, 29(3): 260–8.

Pollard, J. (1995) 'Tourism and the environment', in P. Breathnach (ed.) *Irish Tourism Development*, Maynooth: Geographical Society of Ireland.

Poon, A. (1989) *Tourism, Technology and Competitive Strategies*, Wallingford: CAB International.

Poria, Y., Butler, R.W. and Airey, D. (2003) 'Revisiting Mieczkowski's conceptualisation of tourism', *Tourism Geographies*, 5: 26–38.

Porter, L., Jaconelli, M., Cheyne, J., Eby, D. and Wagenaar, H. (2009) 'Planning displacement: the real legacy of major sporting events; "just a person in a wee flat": being displaced by the Commonwealth Games in Glasgow's East End; Olympian masterplanning in London; closing ceremonies: how law, policy and the Winter Olympics are displacing an inconveniently located low-income community in Vancouver; commentary: recovering public ethos: critical analysis for policy and planning', *Planning Theory & Practice*, 10(3): 395–418.

Porter, M. (1980) *Competition in Global Industries*, Boston, MA: Harvard Business School Press.

Potier, F. and Cazes, G. (1996) *Le Tourisme urbain*, Paris: PUF.

—— (1998) *Le Tourisme et la ville: expériences européennes*, Paris: L'Harmattan.

Pouta, E., Sievänen, T. and Neuvonen, M. (2006) 'Recreational wild berry picking in Finland—reflection of a rural lifestyle', *Society and Natural Resources*, 19: 285–304.

Powell, J.M. (1978) *Mirrors of the New World: Images and Image – Makers in the Settlement Process*, Canberra: Australian National University Press.

— (1985) 'Geography, culture and liberal education', in R. Johnston (ed.) *The Future of Geography*, London: Methuen.

Pratt, A. (1998) 'The cultural industries production system: a case study of employment change in Britain, 1984–91', *Environment and Planning A*, 29: 1953–74.

Pred, A. (1977) 'The choreography of existence: comments on Hagerstrand's time-geography and its usefulness', *Economic Geography*, 53: 207–21.

— (1981) 'Production, family and free-time projects: a time-geographic perspective on the individual and societal changes in nineteenth century US cities', *Journal of Historical Geography*, 7: 3–86.

Preece, K.M. and Lesslie, R.G. (1987) *A Survey of Wilderness Quality in Victoria*, Melbourne/Canberra: Ministry for Planning and Environment (Vic) and Australian Heritage Commission.

Preston-Whyte, R.A. (2002) 'Construction of surfing space at Durban, South Africa', *Tourism Geographies*, 4: 307–28.

— (2004) 'The beach as liminal space', in A. Lew, C.M. Hall and A. Williams (eds) *A Companion to Tourism*, Oxford: Blackwell.

Priestley, G. and Mundet, L. (1998) 'The post-stagnation phase of the resort cycle', *Annals of Tourism Research*, 25: 85–111.

Prineas, P. (1976–7) 'The story of the park proposal', *National Parks Journal*, December/January: 9–11.

Prineas, P. and Gold, H. (1983) *Wild Places: Wilderness in Eastern New South Wales*, Chatswood, NSW: Kalianna Press.

Pritchard, A. and Morgan, N. (2000) 'Privileging the male gaze – gendered tourism landscapes', *Annals of Tourism Research*, 27: 884–905.

Pritchard, A., Morgan, N. and Sedgley, D. (2002) 'In search of lesbian space? The experience of Manchester's gay village', *Leisure Studies*, 21(2): 105–23.

Pritchard, R. (1976) *Housing and the Spatial Structure of the City*, Cambridge: Cambridge University Press.

Productivity Commission (2005) *Assistance to Tourism: Exploratory Estimates*, Canberra: Productivity Commission.

Pronovost, G. (1991) 'Western ethnocentricity in studies on leisure and cultural development', *World Leisure & Recreation*, 33(4): 19–21.

Prosser, G. (1986a) 'The limits of acceptable change: an introduction to a framework for natural area planning', *Australian Parks and Recreation* (autumn): 5–10.

— (1986b) 'Beyond carrying capacity: establishing limits of acceptable change for park planning', in *Developing Communities into the 21st Century: Proceedings from the 59th National Conference of the Royal Australian Institute of Parks and Recreation*, Melbourne: Royal Australian Institute of Parks and Recreation.

Qian, J., Lei, W. and Hong, Z. (2012) 'Consuming the tourist gaze: imaginative geographies and the reproduction of sexuality in Lugu Lake', *Geografiska Annaler B*, 94: 107–24.

Quah, E. (2002) 'Transboundary pollution in Southeast Asia: the Indonesian fires', *World Development*, 30: 429–41.

Queensland Department of Environment and Heritage (1993) *Green Island and Reef Management Plan*, Cairns: Department of Environment and Heritage.

Ram, Y., Nawijn, J. and Peeters, P.M. (2013) 'Happiness and limits to sustainable tourism mobility: a new conceptual model', *Journal of Sustainable Tourism*, DOI: 10.1080/09669582.2013.826233.

Rapoport, R.N. and Rapoport, R. (1975) *Leisure and the Family Life Cycle*, London: Routledge & Kegan Paul.

Ravenscroft, N. (1992) *Recreation Planning and Development*, Basingstoke: Macmillan.

Ravenscroft, N. and Markwell, S. (2000) 'Ethnicity and the integration and exclusion of young people through urban park and recreation provision', *Managing Leisure*, 5(3): 135–50.

Reeder, R.J. and Brown, D.M. (2005) *Recreation, Tourism, and Rural Well-being*, Washington, DC: US Department of Agriculture, Economic Research Service.

Reeves, N. (2000) 'The condition of public urban parks and greenspace in Britain', *Water and Environmental Management*, 14(3): 157–63.

Reid, D.G. (2003) *Tourism, Globalization and Development: Responsible Tourism Planning*, London: Pluto Press.

Reilly, W. (1931) *The Law of Retail Gravitation*, New York: Putnam Press.

Relph, E. (1976) *Place and Placelessness*, London: Pion Press.

— (1981) *Rational Landscapes and Humanistic Geography*, London: Croom Helm.

Rhodes, R.A.W. (1997) 'From marketisation to diplomacy: it's the mix that matters', *Australian Journal of Public Administration*, 56(2): 40–53.

Ribe, R.G. (1994) 'Scenic beauty perceptions along the ROS', *Journal of Environmental Management*, 42(3): 199–221.

Ribera-Fumaz, R. (2009) 'From urban political economy to cultural political economy: rethinking culture and economy in and beyond the urban', *Progress in Human Geography*, 33: 447–65.

Richards, G. (1995) 'Politics of national tourism policy in Britain', *Leisure Studies*, 14(3): 153–73.

— (1996) 'Production and consumption of European cultural tourism', *Annals of Tourism Research*, 23: 261–83.

Richards, G. and Wilson, J. (2006) 'Developing creativity in tourist experiences: a solution to the serial reproduction of culture?', *Tourism Management*, 27: 1209–23.

Rink, D.R. and Swan, J.E. (1979) 'Product life cycle research: literature review', *Journal of Business Research*, 78: 219–42.

Riordan, J. (1982) 'Leisure: the state and the individual in the USSR', *Leisure Studies*, 1(1): 65–80.

Ritchie, J.R.B. (1975) 'Some critical aspects of measurement theory and practice in travel research', in R. McIntosh and C. Goeldner, *Tourism Principles, Practices and Philosophies*, New York: Wiley.

— (1984) 'Assessing the impact of hallmark events: conceptual and research issues', *Journal of Travel Research*, 23(1): 2–11.

Ritchie, J.R.B. and Aitken, C. (1984) 'Assessing the impacts of the 1988 Olympic Winter Games: the research program and initial results', *Journal of Travel Research*, 22(3): 17–25.

Ritchie, J.R.B. and Beliveau, D. (1974) 'Hallmark events: an evaluation of a strategic response to seasonality in the travel market', *Journal of Travel Research*, 14 (fall): 14–20.

Ritchie, J.R.B. and Yangzhou, H. (1987) 'The role and impact of mega-events and attractions on national and regional tourism: a conceptual and methodological overview', 37th Annual Congress of the International Association of Scientific Experts in Tourism, Calgary: AIEST.

Ritzer, G. (1993) *The McDonaldization of Society*, Thousand Oaks, CA: Pine Forge.

Roberts, K. (1999) *Leisure in Contemporary Society*, Wallingford: CAB International.

— (2004) *The Leisure Industries*, Basingstoke: Palgrave.

— (2006) *Leisure in Contemporary Society*, 2nd edn, Wallingford: CAB International.

Roberts, K., Fagan, C., Bontenko, I. and Razlogou, K. (2001) 'Economic polarization, leisure practices and policies, and the quality of life: a study in post-communist Moscow', *Leisure Studies*, 20(3): 161–72.

Roberts, L. and Hall, D. (2004) 'Consuming the countryside: marketing for "rural tourism"', *Journal of Vacation Marketing*, 10: 253–63.

Roberts, R. (1971) *The Classic Slum: Salford Life in the First Quarter of the Century*, Harmondsworth: Penguin.

— (1976) *A Ragged Schooling: Growing Up in the Classic Slum*, London: Fontana.

Robinson, D. (1991) 'Living with peripherality', *Transport*, November/December: 177–85.

Robinson, G.M. (1990) *Conflict and Change in the Countryside*, London: Belhaven Press.

— (1999) 'Countryside recreation management', in M. Pacione (ed.) *Applied Geography: Principles and Practice*, London: Routledge.

Robinson, G.W. (1972) 'The recreational geography of South Asia', *Geographical Review*, 62: 561–73.

Robinson, H. (1976) *A Geography of Tourism*, Harlow: Longman.

Robinson, R. (1973) *The Drift of Things: An Autobiography 1914–52*, South Melbourne: Macmillan.

Robinson, W. (2009) *The Wild Garden*, expanded edition with new chapters and photography by Rick Darke, Portland, OR: Timber Press.

Robles Teigeiro, L. and Díaz, B. (2014) 'Estimation of multipliers for the activity of hotels and restaurants', *Tourism Management*, 40: 27–34.

Roca, E. and Villares, M. (2008) 'Public perceptions for evaluating beach quality in urban and semi-natural environments', *Ocean and Coastal Management*, 51: 314–29.

Roca, Z., Nazaré Roca, M. and Oliveira, J. (eds) (2013) *Second Homes in Europe: Lifestyle Issues to Policy Issues*, Aldershot: Ashgate.

Roche, F.W. and Murray, J.A. (1978) *Tourism and Archaeology: A Study of Wood Quay*, Dublin: McIver.

Roche, M. (1992) 'Mega-events and micro-modernisation: on the sociology of the new urban tourism', *British Journal of Sociology*, 43(4): 563–600.

— (2000) *Mega-Events and Modernity: Olympics and Expos in the Growth of Global Culture*, London: Routledge.

Rodgers, H. (1969) *British Pilot National Recreation Survey Report No. 1*, London: British Travel Association/University of Keele.

— (1973) 'The demand for recreation', *Geographical Journal*, 13(9): 467–73.

— (1977) 'The leisure future: problems of prediction', in J. Settle (ed.) *Leisure in the North-West: A Tool for Forecasting*, Sports Council Study No. 11, Manchester: Sports Council.

— (1993) 'Estimating local leisure demand in the context of a regional planning strategy', in S. Glyptis (ed.) *Leisure and the Environment: Essays in Honour of Professor J.A. Patmore*, London: Belhaven Press.

Rodgers, H. and Patmore, J.A. (eds) (1972) *Leisure in the North-West*, Manchester: North-West Sports Council.

Rodrigue, J.P. and Notteboom, T. (2013) 'The geography of cruises: itineraries, not destinations', *Applied Geography*, 38: 31–42.

Roe, M. and Benson, J. (2001) 'Planning for conflict resolution: jet-ski use on the Northumberland coast', *Coastal Management*, 29(1): 19–39.

Rogelj, J., Hare, W., Lowe, J., van Vuuren, D.P., Riahi, K., Matthews, B., Hanaoka, T., Jiang, K. and Meinshausen, M. (2011) 'Emission pathways consistent with 2°C global temperature limit', *Nature Climate Change*, 1: 413–18.

Rogers, G.F., Malde, H.E. and Turner, R.M. (1984) *Bibliography of Repeat Photography for Evaluating Landscape Change*, Salt Lake City: University of Utah Press.

Rogerson, C.M. (2013) 'Urban tourism, economic regeneration and inclusion: evidence from South Africa', *Local Economy*, 28: 188–202.

Rogerson, C.M. and Visser, G. (eds) (2004) *Tourism and Development Issues in Contemporary South Africa*, Arcadia: Africa Institute of South Africa.

— (2011) 'African tourism geographies: existing paths and new directions', *Tijdschrift voor economische en sociale geografie*, 102: 251–9.

Rolfe, J. and Gregg, D. (2012) 'Valuing beach recreation across a regional area: the Great Barrier Reef in Australia', *Ocean & Coastal Management*, 69: 282–90.

Roman, G.S., Dearden, P. and Rollins, R. (2007) 'Application of zoning and "Limits of Acceptable Change" to manage snorkelling tourism', *Environmental Management*, 39: 819–30.

Romeril, M. (1984) 'Coastal tourism – the experience of Great Britain', *Industry and Environment*, 7(1): 4–7.

— (1988) 'Coastal tourism and the Heritage Coast programme in England and Wales', *Tourism Recreation Research*, 13(2): 15–19.

Rose, M. (ed.) (1985) *The Poor and the City: The English Poor Law in Its Urban Context 1834–1914*, Leicester: Leicester University Press.

Rosemary, J. (1987) *Indigenous Enterprises in Kenya's Tourism Industry*, Geneva: UNESCO.

Rosenfried, S. (1997) 'Global sex slavery', *San Francisco Examiner*, 6 April.

Rothman, R.A. (1978) 'Residents and transients: community reaction to seasonal visitors', *Journal of Travel Research*, 16(3): 8–13.

Rothman, R.A., Donnelly, P.G. and Tower, J.K. (1979) 'Police departments in resort communities: organizational adjustments to population undulation', *Leisure Sciences*, 2: 105–18.

Rowntree, S. and Lavers, G. (1951) *English Life and Leisure: A Social Study*, London: Longmans, Green & Co.

Royer, L.E., McCool, S.F. and Hunt, J.D. (1974) 'The relative importance of tourism to state economies', *Journal of Travel Research*, 11(4): 13–16.

Rubio, F. (1998–9) 'La imagen geográfica del turismo en Espana (1962–1998): creónica breve de una gran expansión', *Boletín de la Real Sociedad Geográfica*, 134–5: 67–103.

Rudkin, B. and Hall, C.M. (1996) 'Unable to see the forest for the trees: ecotourism development in Solomon Islands', in R. Butler and T. Hinch (eds) *Tourism and Indigenous Peoples*, London: International Thomson Business Publishing.

Ruhanen, L. (2004) 'Strategic planning for local tourism destinations: an analysis of tourism plans', *Tourism and Hospitality Planning & Development*, 1: 239–53.

— (2010) 'Where's the strategy in tourism strategic planning? Implications for sustainable tourism destination planning', *Journal of Travel and Tourism Research*, 10(1/2): 58–76.

Runte, A. (1972) 'Yellowstone: it's useless, so why not a park', *National Parks and Conservation Magazine: The Environment Journal*, 46 (March): 4–7.

— (1973) '"Worthless" lands – our national parks: the enigmatic past and uncertain future of America's scenic wonderlands', *American West*, 10 (May): 4–11.

— (1977) 'The national park idea: origins and paradox of the American experience', *Journal of Forest History*, 21(2): 64–75.

— (1990) *Yosemite: The Embattled Wilderness*, Lincoln: University of Nebraska Press.

— (2002) 'Why national parks?', *The George Wright Forum*, 19(2): 67–71.

— (2010) *National Parks: The American Experience*, 4th edn, Lanham, MD: Taylor Trade Publishing.

Runyan, D. and Wu, C. (1979) 'Assessing tourism's more complex consequences', *Annals of Tourism Research*, 6: 448–63.

Rural Development Commission (1991) *Tourism in the Countryside: A Strategy for Rural England*, London: Rural Development Commission.

Russell, J.A., Matthews, J.H. and Jones, R. (1979) *Wilderness in Tasmania: A Report to the Australian Heritage Commission*, Occasional Paper 10, Hobart: Centre for Environmental Studies, University of Tasmania.

Rutin, J. (2010) 'Coastal tourism: a comparative study between Croatia and Tunisia', *Tourism Geographies*, 12: 264–77.

Ryan, C. (1991) *Recreational Tourism: A Social Science Perspective*, London: Routledge.

— (1995) *Researching Tourism Satisfaction: Issues, Concepts, Problems*, London: Routledge.

— (ed.) (1997) *The Tourist Experience: A New Introduction*, London: Cassell.

— (ed.) (2002) *The Tourist Experience*, 2nd edn, London: Continuum.

Ryan, C. and Hall, C.M. (2001) *Sex Tourism: Travels in Liminality*, London: Routledge.

Ryan, C. and Huyton, J. (2002) 'Tourists and aboriginal peoples', *Annals of Tourism Research*, 29: 631–47.

Saarinen, J. (1998) 'Cultural influence on response to wilderness encounters: a case study from Finland', *International Journal of Wilderness* 4(1): 28–32.

— (2001) 'The transformation of a tourist destination: theory and case studies on the production of local geographies in tourism in Finnish Lapland', *Nordia Geographical Publications* 30(1): 105.

— (2003) 'Tourism and recreation as subjects of research in Finnish geographical journals', *Tourism Geographies*, 5: 220–7.

— (2005) 'Tourism in the northern wildernesses: wilderness discourses and the development of nature-based tourism in northern Finland', in C.M. Hall and S. Boyd (eds) *Nature-based Tourism in Peripheral Regions: Development or Disaster*, Clevedon: Channel View.

— (2006) 'Traditions of sustainability in tourism studies', *Annals of Tourism Research*, 33: 1121–40.

Saarinen, J. and Hall, C.M. (eds) (2004) *Nature-Based Tourism Research in Finland: Local Contexts, Global Issues*, Finnish Forest Research Institute, Research Papers 916, Rovaniemi: Rovaniemi Research Station.

Saarinen, J., Rogerson, C. and Manwa, H. (2011) 'Tourism and Millennium Development Goals: tourism for global development?', *Current Issues in Tourism*, 14: 201–3.

Saarinen, J., Becker, F., Manwa, H. and Wilson, D. (eds) (2009) *Sustainable Tourism in Southern Africa: Perspectives on Local Communities and Natural Resources in Transition*, Bristol: Channel View.

Sacchi, C., Gera, G., Marcenaro, L. and Regazzoni, C. (2001) 'Advanced image-processing tools for counting people in tourist site-monitoring applications', *Signal Processing*, 81: 1017–40.

Sadd, D. (2009) 'Weymouth's once in a lifetime opportunity', in J. Ali-Knight, M. Robertson, A. Fyall and A. Ladkin (eds) *International Perspectives of Festivals and Events: Paradigms of Analysis*, Oxford: Elsevier.

Sæþórsdóttir, A.D. and Ólafsson, R. (2010a) 'Nature tourism assessment in the Icelandic Master Plan for geothermal and hydropower development. Part I: Rapid evaluation of nature tourism resources', *Journal of Heritage Tourism*, 5: 311–31.

— (2010b) 'Nature tourism assessment in the Icelandic Master Plan for geothermal and hydropower development. Part II: Assessing the impact of proposed power plants on tourism and recreation', *Journal of Heritage Tourism*, 5: 333–49.

Sæþórsdóttir, A.D., Hall, C.M. and Saarinen, J. (2011) 'Making wilderness: tourism and the history of the wilderness idea in Iceland', *Polar Geography*, 34, 249–73.

Saeter, J.A. (1998) 'The significance of tourism and economic development in rural areas: a Norwegian case study', in R. Butler, C.M. Hall and J. Jenkins (eds) *Tourism and Recreation in Rural Areas*, Chichester: Wiley.

Samdahl, D. and Jekubovich, N. (1997) 'A critique of leisure constraints: comparative analyses and understandings', *Journal of Leisure Research*, 29(4): 430–52.

Sant, M. (1982) *Applied Geography*, Harlow: Longman.

Sawicki, D. (1989) 'The festival marketplace as public policy', *Journal of the American Planning Association* (summer): 347–61.

Scarles, C. (2010) 'Where words fail, visuals ignite: opportunities for visual autoethnography in tourism research', *Annals of Tourism Research*, 37: 905–26.

Schaer, U. (1978) 'Traffic problems in holiday resorts', *Tourist Review*, 33: 9–15.

Schafer, A. (2000) 'Regularities in travel demand: an international perspective', *Journal of Transportation and Statistics*, 3(3): 1–31.

Schafer, A. and Victor, D. (2000) 'The future mobility of the world population', *Transportation Research A*, 34(3): 171–205.

Scheyvens, R. (2002) *Tourism for Development*, Harlow: Prentice-Hall.

Scheyvens, R. and Momsen, J. (2008a) 'Tourism and poverty reduction: issues for small island states', *Tourism Geographies*, 10: 22–41.

— (2008b) 'Tourism in small island states: from vulnerability to strengths', *Journal of Sustainable Tourism*, 16: 491–510.

Schilcher, D. (2007) 'Growth versus equity: the continuum of pro-poor tourism and neoliberal governance', *Current Issues in Tourism*, 10: 166–93.

Schilling, A., Coors, V. and Laakso, K. (2005) 'Dynamic 3D maps for mobile tourism applications', in L. Meng, A. Zipf and T. Reichenbacher (eds) *Map-based Mobile Services: Theories, Methods and Implementations*, New York: Springer.

Schmallegger, D., Carson, D. and Tremblay, P. (2010) 'The economic geography of remote tourism: the problem of connection seeking', *Tourism Analysis*, 15(1): 125–37.

Schofield, P. (1996) 'Cinematographic images of a city: alternative heritage tourism in Manchester', *Tourism Management*, 17: 333–40.

Schollmann, A., Perkins, H.C. and Moore, K. (2001) 'Rhetoric, claims making and conflict in touristic place promotion: the case of central Christchurch, New Zealand', *Tourism Geographies*, 3(3): 300–25.

Schreiner, A.S., Yamamoto, E. and Shiotani, H. (2005). Positive affect among nursing home residents with Alzheimer's dementia: The effect of recreational activity. *Aging and Mental Health*, 9(2), 129–134.

Schwanen, T. and Kwan, M. (2009) '"Doing" critical geographies with numbers', *Professional Geographer*, 61: 459–64.

Scott, A.J. (2001) *The Cultural Economy of Cities*, London: Sage.

Scott, D. (2011) 'Why sustainable tourism must address climate change', *Journal of Sustainable Tourism*, 19: 17–34.

Scott, D. and Lemieux, C. (2010) 'Weather and climate information for tourism', *Procedia Environmental Sciences*, 1: 146–83.

Scott, D., Gössling, S. and Hall, C.M. (2012) *Tourism and Climate Change: Impacts, Adaptation and Mitigation*, London: Routledge.

Scott, D., Peeters, P. and Gössling, S. (2010) 'Can tourism deliver on its aspirational greenhouse gas emission reduction targets?', *Journal of Sustainable Tourism*, 18: 393–408.

Scott, D., Amelung, B., Becken, S., Ceron, J.-P., Dubois, G., Gössling, S., Peeters, P. and Simpson, M. (2008) 'Technical report', in UNWTO, UNEP and WMO, *Climate Change and Tourism: Responding to Global Challenges*, Madrid: UNWTO; Paris: UNEP; Geneva: WMO.

Scott, N., Baggio, R. and Cooper, C. (2008) *Network Analysis and Tourism: From Theory to Practice*, Clevedon: Channel View.

Scott, N.R. (1974) 'Towards a psychology of the wilderness experience', *Natural Resource Journal*, 14: 231–7.

Scraton, S., Bramham, P. and Watson, B. (1998) 'Staying in and going out: elderly women, leisure and the postmodern city', in S. Scraton (ed.) *Leisure, Time and Space: Meanings and Values in People's Lives*, Eastbourne: Leisure Studies Association.

Seaton, A. and Bennett, M. (eds) (1996) *Marketing Tourism Products*, London: International Thomson Business Publishing.

Sedova, N.N. (2011) 'The leisure-time activity of citizens', *Russian Education & Society*, 53(5): 37–60.

Seeley, I. (1983) *Outdoor Recreation and the Urban Environment*, Basingstoke: Macmillan.

Seers, D. and Ostrom, K. (eds) (1982) *The Crisis of the European Regions*, New York: St Martin's Press.

Seers, D., Schaffer, B. and Kiljunen, M. (eds) (1979) *Underdeveloped Europe: Studies in Core–Periphery Relations*, Hassocks, Sussex: Harvester Press.

Seetaram, N., Page. S.J. and Song, H. (2012) 'Air Passenger Duty in the UK and outbound tourism', paper presented at the BEST XII Think Tank, Provence, France, June.

Segrelles-Serrano, J. (2002) 'Luces y sombras de la geografía aplicada', *Documents d'Analisi Geografica*, 40: 153–72.

Selin, S. (1993) 'Collaborative alliances: new interorganizational forms in tourism', *Journal of Travel and Tourism Marketing*, 2(2/3): 217–27.

Selke, A.C. (1936) 'Geographic aspects of the German tourist trade', *Economic Geography*, 12: 206–16.

Selwood, H.J. and Hall, C. (1986) 'The America's Cup: a hallmark tourist event', in J.S. Marsh (ed.) *Canadian Studies of Parks, Recreation and Tourism in Foreign Lands*, Occasional Paper 11, Peterborough: Department of Geography, Trent University.

Selwood, J. and May, A. (2001) 'Resolving contested notions of tourism sustainability on Western Australia's "Turquoise Coast": the squatter settlements', *Current Issues in Tourism*, 4: 381–91.

Sessa, A. (1993) *Elements of Tourism*, Rome: Catal.

Sewell, W.R.D. and Dearden, P. (1989) *Wilderness: Past, Present and Future*, special issue of *Natural Resources Journal*, 29: 1–222.

Shackelford, P. (1980) 'Keeping tabs on tourism: a manager's guide to tourism statistics', *International Journal of Tourism Management*, 1: 148–57.

Shackley, M. (ed.) (1998) *Visitor Management: Case Studies from World Heritage Sites*, Oxford: Butterworth Heinemann.

Shapin, S. (1998) 'Placing the view from nowhere: historical and sociological problems in the location of science', *Transactions of the Institute of British Geographers*, 23: 5–12.

Sharpley, R. (1993) *Tourism and Leisure in the Countryside*, Managing Tourism Series No. 5, Huntingdon: Elm Publications.

Sharpley, R. and Sharpley, J. (1997) *Rural Tourism*, London: International Thomson Business Publishing.

Sharpley, R. and Telfer, D. (eds) (2002) *Tourism and Development: Concepts and Issues*, Clevedon: Channel View.

Shaw, B.J. (1985) 'Fremantle and the America's Cup . . . the spectre of development?', *Urban Policy and Research*, 3: 38–40.

— (1986) *Fremantle W.A. and the America's Cup: The Impact of a Hallmark Event*, Working Paper No. 11, London: University of London, Australian Studies Centre.

Shaw, D.J. (1979) 'Recreation and the socialist city', in R. French and F. Hamilton (eds) *The Socialist City: Spatial Structure and Urban Policy*, Chichester: Wiley.

Shaw, G. and Williams, A.M. (1990) 'Tourism, economic development and the role of entrepreneurial activity', in C. Cooper (ed.) *Progress in Tourism, Recreation and Hospitality Management*, vol. 2, London: Belhaven Press.

— (1994) *Critical Issues in Tourism: A Geographical Perspective*, Oxford: Blackwell.

— (eds) (1997) *The Rise and Fall of British Coastal Resorts: Cultural and Economic Perspectives*, London: Mansell.

— (2002) *Critical Issues in Tourism: A Geographical Perspective*, 2nd edn, Oxford: Blackwell.

— (2004) *Tourism and Tourism Spaces*, Beverly Hills, CA: Sage.

— (2009) 'Knowledge transfer and management in tourism organisations: an emerging research agenda', *Tourism Management*, 30: 325–35.

Shaw, G., Agarwal, S. and Bull, P. (2000) 'Tourism consumption and tourist behaviour: a British perspective', *Tourism Geographies*, 2: 264–89.

Shaw, G., Bailey, A. and Williams, A.M. (2011) 'Aspects of service-dominant logic and its implications for tourism management: examples from the hotel industry', *Tourism Management*, 32: 207–14.

Shaw, S., Bonen, A. and McCabe, J. (1991) 'Do more constraints mean less leisure? Examining the relationship between constraints and participation', *Journal of Leisure Research*, 23: 286–300.

Shelby, B. and Heberlein, T.A. (1984) 'A conceptual framework for carrying capacity', *Leisure Sciences*, 6: 433–51.

— (1986) *Carrying Capacity in Recreation Settings*, Corvallis: Oregon State University Press.

Shelby, B., Bregenzer, N.S. and Johnston, R. (1988) 'Displacement and product shift: empirical evidence from Oregon Rivers', *Journal of Leisure Research*, 20: 274–88.

Shelby, B., Vaske, J.J. and Heberlein, T.A. (1989) 'Comparative analysis of crowding in multiple locations: results from fifteen years of research', *Leisure Sciences*, 11: 269–91.

Sheller, M. and Urry, J. (2006) 'The new mobilities paradigm', *Environment and Planning A*, 38, 207–26.

Shields, R. (1991) *Places on the Margin: Alternative Geographies of Modernity*, London: Routledge.

Shilling, F., Boggs, J. and Reed, S. (2012) 'Recreational system optimization to reduce conflict on public lands', *Environmental Management*, 50: 381–95.

Shinew, K. and Arnold, M. (1998) 'Gender equity in the leisure services field', *Journal of Leisure, Research*, 30(2): 177–94.

Shoard, M. (1976) 'Fields which planners should conquer', *Forma*, 4: 128–35.

Short, J.R. (1991) *Imagined Country: Society, Culture and Environment*, London: Routledge.

Shoval, N. (2008) 'Tracking technologies and urban analysis', *Cities*, 25. 21–8.

Shoval, N. and Isaacson, M. (2007) 'Tracking tourists in the digital age', *Annals of Tourism Research*, 34: 141–59.

— (2010) *Tourist Mobility and Advanced Tracking Technologies*, New York: Taylor & Francis.

Shucksmith, M. (1983) 'Second homes: a framework for policy', *Town Planning Review*, 54(2): 174–93.

Shurmer-Smith, P. and Hannam, K. (1994) *Worlds of Desire, Realms of Power: A Cultural Geography*, London: Arnold.

Sidaway, R. and Duffield, B. (1984) 'A new look at countryside recreation in the urban fringe', *Leisure Studies*, 3: 249–71.

Silberman, J.A. and Rees, P.W. (2010) 'Reinventing mountain settlements: a GIS model for identifying possible ski towns in the US Rocky Mountains', *Applied Geography*, 30: 36–49.

Silverman, N. (1992) 'Reading between the lines: textbooks as terrains of struggle over power and control', *Review of Education/Pedagogy/Cultural Studies*, 14: 203–13.

Simeon, R. (1976) 'Studying public policy', *Canadian Journal of Political Science*, 9: 558–80.

Simmons, I.G. (1974) *The Ecology of Natural Resources*, London: Edward Arnold.

— (1975) *Rural Recreation in the Industrial World*, London: Edward Arnold.

— (1993) *Environmental History: A Concise Introduction*. Cambridge: Blackwell.

Simmons, R., Davis, B.W., Chapman, R.J. and Sager, D.D. (1974) 'Policy flow analysis: a conceptual model for comparative public policy research', *Western Political Quarterly*, 27(3): 457–68.

Simpson Xavier Horwath (1990) *Irish Hotel Industry Review*, Dublin: Simpson Xavier Horwath.

Sinclair, M.T. (1991) 'The economics of tourism', in C. Cooper (ed.) *Progress in Tourism, Recreation and Hospitality Management*, vol. 3, London: Belhaven Press.

— (1998) 'Tourism and economic development: a survey', *Journal of Development Studies*, 34(5): 1–51.

Sinclair, M.T. and Stabler, M. (eds) (1992) *The Tourism Industry: An International Analysis*, Wallingford: CAB International.

Sinclair, M.T., Blake, A. and Sugiyarto, G. (2003) 'The economics of tourism', in C. Cooper (ed.) *Classic Reviews of Tourism*, Clevedon: Channel View.

Singh, S., Timothy, D. and Dowling, R. (eds) (2003) *Tourism in Destination Communities*, Wallingford: CAB International.

Slatyer, R. (1983) 'The origin and evolution of the World Heritage Convention', *Ambio*, 12(3–4): 138–45.

Slee, W. (1982) *An Evaluation of Country Park Policy*, Gloucestershire Papers in Local and Rural Planning No. 16, Cheltenham: GLOSCAT.

Sletten, M.A. (2010) 'Social costs of poverty: leisure time socializing and the subjective experience of social isolation among 13–16-year-old Norwegians', *Journal of Youth Studies*, 13: 291–315.

Smailes, P.J. (2002) 'From rural dilution to multifunctional countryside: some pointers to the future from South Australia', *Australian Geographer*, 33: 79–95.

Smallman, C. and Moore, K. (2010) 'Process studies of tourists' decision-making', *Annals of Tourism Research*, 37: 397–422.

Smith, A. and Hall, C.M. (2003) 'Restaurants and local food in New Zealand', in C.M. Hall, E. Sharples, R. Mitchell, B. Cambourne and N. Macionis (eds) *Food Tourism around the World: Development, Management and Markets*, Oxford: Butterworth Heinemann.

Smith, D.M. (1974) 'Who gets what *where*, and how: a welfare focus for human geography', Geography, 59: 289–97.

— (1977) *Human Geography: A Welfare Approach*, London: Edward Arnold.

Smith, K. (1990) 'Tourism and climate change', *Land Use Policy*, April: 176–80.

Smith, L., Waterton, E. and Watson, S. (eds) (2012) *The Cultural Moment in Tourism*, Abingdon: Routledge.

Smith, M. and Turner, L. (1973) 'Some aspects of the sociology of tourism', *Society and Leisure*, 3: 55–71.

Smith, M. and Richards, G. (eds) (2013) *The Routledge Handbook of Cultural Tourism*, Abingdon: Routledge.

Smith, P.E. (1977) 'A value analysis of wilderness', *Search*, 8(9): 311–17.

Smith, R.A. (1991) 'Beach resorts: a model of development evolution', *Landscape and Urban Planning*, 21: 189–210.

— (1992a) 'Beach resort evolution: implications for planning', *Annals of Tourism Research*, 19: 304–22.

— (1992b) 'Review of integrated beach resort development in South East Asia', *Land Use Policy*, 9: 211–17.

Smith, R.A., Henderson, J.C., Chong, V., Tay, C. and Jingwen, Y. (2011) 'The development and management of beach resorts: Boracay Island, the Philippines', *Asia Pacific Journal of Tourism Research*, 16: 229–45.

Smith, R.V. and Mitchell, L.S. (1990) 'Geography and tourism: a review of selected literature', in C. Cooper (ed.) *Progress in Tourism, Recreation and Hospitality Management*, vol. 2, London: Belhaven Press.

Smith, S.J. (1982) 'Reflections on the development of geographic recreation in recreation: hey, buddy, can you s'paradigm?', *Ontario Geography*, 19: 5–29.

— (1983a) *Recreational Geography*, Harlow: Longman.

— (1983b) 'Restaurants and dining out: geography of a tourism business', *Annals of Tourism Research*, 10: 515–49.

— (1987a) 'Fear of crime: beyond a geography of deviance', *Progress in Human Geography*, 11: 1–23.

— (1987b) 'Regional analysis of tourism resources', *Annals of Tourism Research*, 14: 253–73.

— (1989) *Tourism Analysis*, Harlow: Longman.

— (1990a) 'A test of Plog's allocentric/psychocentric model: evidence from seven nations', *Journal of Travel Research*, 28(4): 40–2.

— (1990b) 'Another look at the carpenter's tools: reply to Plog', *Journal of Travel Research*, 29(2): 50–1.

— (1994) 'The tourism product', *Annals of Tourism Research*, 21: 582–95.

— (1995) *Tourism Analysis*, 2nd edn, Harlow: Longman.

— (2000) 'New developments in measuring tourism as an area of economic activity', in W.C. Gartner and D.W. Lime (eds) *Trends in Outdoor Recreation, Leisure, and Tourism*, Oxford: CAB International.

— (2004) 'The measurement of global tourism: old debates, new consensus, and continuing challenges', in A.A. Lew, C.M. Hall and A.M. Williams (eds) *A Companion to Tourism*, Oxford: Blackwell.

— (2007) 'Duelling definitions: challenges and implications of conflicting international concepts of tourism', in D. Airey and J. Tribe (eds) *Progress in Tourism Research*, Oxford: Elsevier.

— (ed.) (2010) *The Discovery of Tourism*. Bingley: Emerald.

— (2011) 'Becoming a tourism scholar', *Tourism Geographies*, 13: 480–94.

Smith, S.L.J. and Brown, B.A. (1981) 'Directional bias in vacation travel', *Annals of Tourism Research*, 8: 257–70.

Smith, S.L.J. and Wilton, D. (1997) 'TSAs and the WTTC/WEFA methodology: different satellites or different planets?', *Tourism Economics*, 3: 249–64.

Smith, V.L. (ed.) (1977) *Hosts and Guests: The Anthropology of Tourism*, Philadelphia: University of Pennsylvania Press.

— (ed.) (1992) *Hosts and Guests: An Anthropology of Tourism*, 2nd edn, Philadelphia: University of Pennsylvania Press.

Smyth, H. (1994) *Marketing the City: The Role of Flagship Developments in Urban Regeneration*, London: E&FN Spon.

Snaith, T. and Haley, A. (1999) 'Resident opinions of tourism development in the historic city of York, England', *Tourism Management*, 20: 595–603.

Snepenger, D., Murphy, L., O'Connell, R. and Gregg, E. (2003) 'Tourists and residents use of a shopping space', *Annals of Tourism Research*, 30: 567–80.

Soja, E.W. (1989) *Postmodern Geographies: The Reassertion of Space in Critical Social Theory*, London: Verso.

Solecki, W. and Welch, J. (1995) 'Urban parks: green spaces or green walls?', *Landscape and Urban Planning*, 32: 93–106.

Song, H. (2012) *Tourism Supply Chain Management*, London: Routledge.

Song, H. and Li, G. (2008) 'Tourism demand modelling and forecasting: a review of recent research', *Tourism Management*, 29(2): 203–20.

Song, H., Dwyer, L., Li, G. and Cao, Z. (2012) 'Tourism economics research: a review and assessment', *Annals of Tourism Research*, 39: 1653–82.

Sopher, D. (1968) 'Pilgrim circulation in Gujurat', *Geographical Review*, 58: 392–425.

Sorokin, P. and Berger, C. (1939) *Time Budgets of Human Behaviour*, Cambridge, MA: Harvard University Press.

Soteriou, E.C. and Coccossis, H. (2010) 'Integrating sustainability into the strategic planning of national tourism organizations', *Journal of Travel Research*, 49(2): 191–205.

Spencer, J. and Thomas, W. (1948) 'The hill stations and summer resorts of the Orient', *Geographical Review*, 38: 637–51.

Spink, J. (1994) *Leisure and the Environment*, Oxford: Butterworth Heinemann.

Squire, S.J. (1993) 'Valuing countryside: reflections on Beatrix Potter tourism', *Area*, 25(1): 5–10.

— (1994) 'Accounting for cultural meanings: the interface between geography and tourism studies revisited', *Progress in Human Geography*, 18: 1–16.

Stabler, M. (1990) 'The concept of opportunity sets as a methodological framework for the analysis of selling tourism places: the industry view', in G.J. Ashworth and B. Goodall (eds) *Marketing Tourism Places*, London: Routledge.

Stamp, D. (1960) *Applied Geography*, London: Penguin.

Stankey, G.H. (1973) *Visitor Perception of Wilderness Carrying Capacity*, USDA, Forest Service Research Paper, INT–42, Ogden, UT: Intermountain Forest and Range Experiment Station.

— (1989) 'Beyond the campfire's light: historical roots of the wilderness concept', *Natural Resources Journal*, 29: 9–24.

Stankey, G.H. and McCool, S.F. (1984) 'Carrying capacity in recreational settings: evolution, appraisal, and application', *Leisure Sciences*, 6: 453–73.

Stankey, G.H. and Schreyer, R. (1987) 'Attitudes toward wilderness and factors affecting visitor behaviour: a state of knowledge review', in *Proceedings – National Wilderness Research Conference: Issues, State of Knowledge and Future Directions*, General Technical Report INT–220, Ogden, UT: Intermountain Research Station.

Stankey, G.H., Cole, D.N., Lucas, R.C., Petersen, M.E. and Frissell, S. (1985) *The Limits of Acceptable Change System for Wilderness Planning*, USDA, Forest Service Research Paper, INT–176, Ogden, UT: Intermountain Forest and Range Experiment Station.

Stansfield, C.A. and Rickert, J.E. (1970) 'The recreational business district', *Journal of Leisure Research*, 2(4): 213–25.

Stanton, J.P. and Morgan, M.G. (1977) *Project 'RAKES' – A Rapid Appraisal of Key and Endangered Sites, Report No. 1: The Queensland Case Study*, a report to the Department of Environment, Housing and Community Development, Armidale: School of Natural Resources, University of New England.

Stea, R. and Downs, R. (1970) 'From the outside looking in at the inside looking out', *Environment and Behaviour*, 2: 3–12.

Stebbins, R.A. (1979) *Amateurs: On the Margin between Work and Leisure*, Beverly Hills, CA: Sage Publications.

— (1982) 'Serious leisure: a conceptual statement', *Pacific Sociological Review*, 25: 251–72.

Steffen, R., deBarnardis, C. and Banos, A. (2003) 'Travel epidemiology – a global perspective', *International Journal of Antimicrobial Agents*, 21(2): 89–95.

Steiger, R. (2012) 'Scenarios for skiing tourism in Austria: integrating demographics with an analysis of climate change', *Journal of Sustainable Tourism*, 20: 867–82.

Stimson, R. and Haynes, K.E. (2012) 'Applied geography: relevance and approaches', in R. Stimson and K.E. Haynes (eds) *Studies in Applied Geography and Spatial Analysis: Addressing Real World Issues*, Cheltenham: Edward Elgar.

— (eds) (2013) *Studies in Applied Geography and Spatial Analysis*, Cheltenham: Edward Elgar.

Stockdale, J.E. (1985) *What Is Leisure? An Empirical Analysis of the Concept of Leisure and the Role of Leisure in People's Lives*, London: Sports Council.

Stoddart, D.R. (1981) 'Ideas and interpretation in the history of geography', in D.R. Stoddart (ed.) *Geography, Ideology and Social Concern*, Oxford: Blackwell.

Stodolska, M. (2000) 'Changes in leisure participation patterns after immigration', *Leisure Sciences*, 22(1): 39–63.

Stokowski, P. (2002) 'Languages of place and discourses of power: constructing new senses of place', *Journal of Leisure Research*, 34: 368–82.

Storchmann, K. (2010) 'The economic impact of the wine industry on hotels and restaurants: evidence from Washington State', *Journal of Wine Economics*, 5: 164–83.

Strachan, A. and Bowler, I. (1976) 'The development of public parks in the City of Leicester', *East Midland Geographer*, 6: 275–83.

Stradling, S. and Anable, J. (2008) 'Individual transport patterns', in R. Knowles, J. Shaw and I. Docherty (eds) *Transport Geographies: Mobilities, Flows and Spaces*, Oxford: Blackwell.

Stringer, P. (1984) 'Studies in the socio-environmental psychology of tourism', *Annals of Tourism Research*, 11: 147–66.

Stringer, P. and Pearce, P.L. (1984) 'Towards a symbiosis of social psychology and tourism studies', *Annals of Tourism Research*, 11: 5–18.

Stritthold, J.R. and Dellasala, D.A. (2001) 'Importance of roadless areas in biodiversity conservation in forested ecosystems: case study of the Klamath-Siskiyou ecoregion of the United States', *Conservation Biology*, 15: 1742–54.

Stumbo, N.J., Wang, Y. and Pegg, S. (2011) 'Issues of access: what matters to people with disabilities as they seek leisure experiences', *World Leisure Journal*, 53(2): 91–103.

Sullivan, P., Bonn, M.A., Bhardwaj, V. and DuPont, A. (2012) 'Mexican national cross-border shopping: exploration of retail tourism', *Journal of Retailing and Consumer Services*, 19: 596–604.

Sun, D. and Walsh, D. (1998) 'Review of studies on environmental impacts of recreation and tourism in Australia', *Journal of Environmental Management*, 53: 323–38.

Sun, Y., Wang, S. and Huang, K. (2012) 'Hygiene knowledge and practices of night market food vendors in Tainan City, Taiwan', *Food Control*, 23(1): 159–64.

Survey Research Associates (1991) *London Docklands Visitor Survey: Summary of Findings*, London: London Docklands Development Corporation.

Swaffield, S. and Fairweather, J. (1998) 'In search of arcadia: the persistence of the rural idyll in New Zealand rural sub-divisions', *Journal of Environmental Planning and Management*, 4(1): 111–27.

Szulczewska, B. and Kaliszuk, E. (2003) 'Challenges in the planning and management of "greenstructure" in Warsaw, Poland', *Built Environment*, 29: 144–56.

Taff, D., Newman, P., Pettebone, D., White, D.D., Lawson, S.R., Monz, C. and Vagias, W.M. (2013) 'Dimensions of alternative transportation experience in Yosemite and Rocky Mountain National Parks', *Journal of Transport Geography*, 30: 37–46.

Takeuchi, K. (1984) 'Some remarks on the geography of tourism in Japan', *GeoJournal*, 9(1): 85–90.

Talbot, M. (1979) *Women and Leisure*, London: Sports Council/Social Science Research Council Joint Panel on Leisure and Recreation Research.

Tanner, M. (1971) 'The planning and management of water recreation areas', in P. Lavery (ed.) *Recreational Geography*, Newton Abbot: David and Charles.

Tarrant, M. and Cordell, H. (1999) 'Environmental justice and the spatial distribution of outdoor recreation sites: an application of geographic information systems', *Journal of Leisure Research*, 31: 18–34.

Taylor, D. (1999) 'Central Park as a model for social control: urban parks, social class and leisure behaviour in nineteenth century America', *Journal of Leisure Research*, 31: 426–77.

Taylor, J., Legellé, J.G. and Andrew, C. (eds) (1993) *Capital Cities: International Perspectives/Les Capitales: perspectives internationales*, Ottawa: Carleton University Press.

Taylor, P.J. (1985) 'The value of a geographical perspective', in R.J. Johnston (ed.) *The Future of Geography*, London: Methuen.

Taylor, R., Shumaker, S. and Gottfredson, S. (1985) 'Neighbourhood-level links between physical features and local sentiments: deterioration, fear of crime and confidence', *Journal of Architectural and Planning Research*, 2: 261–75.

Taylor, S.G. (1990) 'Naturalness: the concept and its application to Australian ecosystems', *Proceedings of the Ecological Society of Australia*, 16: 411–18.

Taylor, Z. and Józefowicz, I. (2012) 'Intra-urban daily mobility of disabled people for recreational and leisure purposes', *Journal of Transport Geography*, 24: 155–72.

Tchistiakova, E. and Cabanne, C. (1997) 'Urban tourism and rural tourism in Russia', *Norois*, 176: 571–83.

Techera, E.J. and Klein, N. (2013) 'The role of law in shark-based eco-tourism: lessons from Australia', *Marine Policy*, 39: 21–8.

Telfer, D.J. (2000a) 'The Northeast Wine Route: wine tourism in Ontario, Canada and New York State', in C.M. Hall, E. Sharples, B. Cambourne and N. Macionis (eds) *Wine Tourism around the World: Development, Management and Markets*, Oxford: Butterworth Heinemann.

—— (2000b) 'Tastes of Niagara: building strategic alliances between tourism and agriculture',

International Journal of Hospitality & Tourism Administration, 1: 71–88.

— (2001) 'Strategic alliances along the Niagara Wine Route', *Tourism Management*, 22: 21–30.

Telfer, D.J. and Wall. G. (1996) 'Linkages between tourism and food production', *Annals of Tourism Research*, 23: 635–53.

Teo, P. (2009) 'Knowledge order in Asia', in T. Winter, P. Teo and T.C. Chang (eds) *Asia on Tour: Exploring the Rise of Asian Tourism*, Abingdon: Routledge.

Terkenli, T. (2002) 'Landscapes of tourism: towards a global cultural economy of space?', *Tourism Geographies*, 4(3): 227–54.

Tervo-Kankare, K., Hall, C.M. and Saarinen, J. (2013) 'Christmas tourists' perceptions of climate change in Rovaniemi, Finnish Lapland', *Tourism Geographies*, 15: 292–317.

Thackway, R. and Lesslie, R. (2006) 'Reporting vegetation condition using the Vegetation Assets, States, and Transitions (VAST) framework', *Ecological Management and Restoration*, 7: 53–62.

— (2008) 'Describing and mapping human-induced vegetation change in the Australian landscape', *Environmental Management*, 42: 572–90.

Therborn, G. (1996) *Monumental Europe: The National Years of the Iconography of European Capital Cities*, Gothenburg: University of Gothenburg.

Thomas, R. (ed.) (2003) *Tourism and Small Firms*, Oxford: Pergamon.

— (2011) 'Academics as policy-makers: (not) researching tourism and events policy formation from the inside', *Current Issues in Tourism*, 14: 493–506.

Thompson, P. (1985) 'Dunphy and Muir – two mountain men', *Habitat*, 13(2): 26–7.

— (1986) *Myles Dunphy: Selected Writings*, Sydney: Ballagirin.

Thoreau, H.D. (1968 [1854]) *Walden*, Everyman's Library, London: Dent.

Thorpe, H. (1970) 'A new deal for allotments: solutions to a pressing land use problem', *Area*, 3: 1–8.

Thorsell, J. and Sigaty, T. (2001) 'Human use in World Heritage natural sites: a global inventory', *Tourism Recreation Research*, 26(1): 85–101.

Thorsen, E.O. and Hall, C.M. (2001) 'What's on the wine list? Wine policies in the New Zealand restaurant industry', *International Journal of Wine Marketing*, 13(3): 94–102.

Thrift, N. (1977) *An Introduction to Time Geography*, Norwich: Catmog 13.

Thurot, J.M. and Thurot, G. (1983) 'The ideology of class and tourism confronting the discourse of advertising', *Annals of Tourism Research*, 10: 173–89.

Tietze, S. and Dick, P. (2013) 'The victorious English language: hegemonic practices in the management academy', *Journal of Management Inquiry*, 22: 122–34.

Tillman, A. (1974) *The Program Book for Recreation Professionals*, Palo Alto, CA: National Press Books.

Timothy, D.J. (2002) 'Tourism and community development issues', in R. Sharpley and D. Telfer (eds) *Tourism and Development: Concepts and Issues*, Clevedon: Channel View.

— (2004) 'Political boundaries and regional cooperation in tourism', in A. Lew, C.M. Hall and A. Williams (eds) *A Companion to Tourism*, Oxford: Blackwell.

— (2005) *Shopping Tourism: Retailing and Leisure*, Clevedon: Channel View.

— (2011) *Cultural Heritage and Tourism: An Introduction*, Bristol: Channel View.

Tiru, M., Kuusik, A., Lamp, M. and Ahas, R. (2010) 'LBS in marketing and tourism management: measuring destination loyalty with mobile positioning data', *Journal of Location Based Services*, 4: 120–40.

Tissot, L. (2000) *Naissance d'une industrie touristique: Les Anglais et la Suisse au XIXe siècle*, Lausanne: Editions Payot.

Torkildsen, G. (1983) *Leisure and Recreation Management*, London: E&FN Spon.

— (1992) *Leisure and Recreation Management*, 3rd edn, London: E&FN Spon.

Towner, J. (1985) 'The Grand Tour: a key phase in the history of tourism', *Annals of Tourism Research*, 12: 297–333.

— (1996) *An Historical Geography of Recreation and Tourism in the Western World 1540–1940*, Chichester: Wiley.

Townsend, A. (1991) 'Services and local economic development', *Area*, 23: 309–17.

Tóth, G. and Lóránt, D. (2010) 'Tourism and accessibility: an integrated approach', *Applied Geography*, 30: 666–77.

Treib, O., Bähr, H. and Falkner, G. (2007) 'Modes of governance: towards a conceptual clarification', *Journal of European Public Policy*, 14(1), 1–20.

Tress, G. (2002) 'Development of second-home tourism in Denmark', *Scandinavian Journal of Hospitality and Tourism*, 2: 109–22.

Tribe, J. (ed.) (2009) *Philosophical Issues in Tourism*, Bristol: Channel View.

— (2010) 'Tribes, territories and networks in the tourism academy', *Annals of Tourism Research*, 37: 7–33.

Truong, V.D. and Hall, C.M. (2013) 'Social marketing and tourism: what is the evidence?', *Social Marketing Quarterly*, 19(2): 110–35.

Tsai, C.T.L. (2010) 'A reflection on cultural conflicts in women's leisure', *Leisure Sciences*, 32: 386–90.

TSE Research (2013) *South Downs Visitor & Tourism Economic Impact Study: Technical Report on the Research Findings*, Eastleigh: TSE Research.

Tuan, Yi-Fu (1971) *Man and Nature*, Washington, DC: Commission on College Geography, Association of American Geographers.

— (1974) *Topophilia: A Study of Environmental Perception, Attitudes, and Values*, Englewood Cliffs, NJ: Prentice Hall.

— (1979) *Landscapes of Fear*, New York: Pantheon.

Tubridy, M. (ed.) (1987) *Heritage Zones: The Co-existence of Agriculture, Nature Conservation and Tourism: The Clonmacnoise Example*, Environmental Science Unit, Occasional Publication, Dublin: Trinity College.

Tudor, D.T. and Williams, A.T. (2006) 'A rationale for beach selection by the public on the coast of Wales, UK', *Area*, 38: 153–64.

Tufts, S. (2009) 'Hospitality unionism and labour market adjustment: toward Schumpeterian unionism?', *Geoforum*, 40: 980–90.

Tunbridge, J.E. (1998) 'Tourism management in Ottawa, Canada: nurturing in a fragile environment', in D. Tyler, Y. Guerrier and M. Robertson (eds) *Managing Tourism in Cities: Policy, Process and Practice*, London: Wiley.

— (2000) 'Heritage momentum or maelstrom? The case of Ottawa's Byward Market', *International Journal of Heritage Studies*, 6: 269–91.

Tunbridge, J.E. and Ashworth, G.J. (1996) *Dissonant Heritage: The Management of the Past as a Resource in Conflict*, Chichester: Wiley.

Tunstall, S. and Penning-Rowsell, E. (1998) 'The English beach: experience and values', *Geographical Journal*, 164: 319–32.

Turner, A. (2006) *An Introduction to Neogeography*, Sebastapol, CA: O'Reilly Media.

Turner, R., Lorenzon, I., Beaumont, N., Bateman, J., Langford, I. and McDonald, A. (1998) 'Coastal management for sustainable development: analysing environmental and socio-economic changes', *Geographical Journal*, 164: 269–81.

Twight, B. (1983) *Organizational Values and Political Power: The Forest Service versus the Olympic National Park*, University Park: Pennsylvania State University Press.

Tyler, D., Guerrier, Y. and Robertson, M. (eds) (1998) *Managing Tourism in Cities: Policy, Process and Practice*, Chichester: Wiley.

Tyler, N.J.C. (2010) 'Climate, snow, ice, crashes, and declines in populations of reindeer and caribou (*Rangifer tarandus* L.)', *Ecological Monographs*, 80: 197–219.

Ullman, E.L. (1954) 'Amenities as a factor in regional growth', *Geographical Review*, 54: 119–32.

Ullman, E.L. and Volk, D.J. (1961) 'An operational model for predicting reservoir attendance and benefits: implications of a location approach to water recreation', *Papers of the Michigan Academy of Science, Arts and Letters*, 47: 473–84.

United Nations (UN) (1994) *Recommendations on Tourism Statistics*, New York: United Nations.

United Nations and United Nations World Tourism Organization (UN and UNWTO) (2007) *International Recommendations on Tourism Statistics (IRTS)*.

Provisional Draft, New York and Madrid: UN and UNWTO.

United Nations Conference on Trade and Development (UNCTAD) (2008) *UNCTAD Handbook of Statistics 2008*, New York and Geneva: UN.

— (2012) *UNCTAD Handbook of Statistics 2012*, New York and Geneva: UN.

United Nations Educational, Scientific and Cultural Organization (UNESCO) (1976) 'The effects of tourism on socio-cultural values', *Annals of Tourism Research*, November/December: 74–105.

United Nations Environment Programme (UNEP) (2011) *Towards a Green Economy: Pathways to Sustainable Development and Poverty Eradication*, Geneva and Nairobi: UNEP.

United Nations Environment Programme/World Tourism Organization (UNEP/WTO) (1996) *Awards for Improving the Coastal Environment: The Example of the Blue Flag*, Paris: UNEP/WTO.

United Nations Framework Convention on Climate Change (UNFCCC) (2007) *Climate Change: Impacts, Vulnerabilities and Adaptation in Developing Countries*, Geneva: UNFCCC.

United Nations World Tourism Organization (UNWTO) (2005) *Tourism Market Trends: World Overview and Tourism Topics. 2004 Edition*, Madrid: WTO.

— (2006a) *International Tourist Arrivals, Tourism Market Trends, 2006 Edition – Annex*, Madrid: UNWTO.

— (2006b) *Tourism and Least Developed Countries: A Sustainable Opportunity to Reduce Poverty*. Madrid: UNWTO.

— (2007) *Tourism Will Contribute to Solutions for Global Climate Change and Poverty Challenge*s, press release, UNWTO Press and Communications Department, 8 March, Berlin and Madrid: UNWTO.

— (2008) *Emerging Tourism Markets – The Coming Economic Boom*, press release, 24 June. Madrid: UNWTO.

— (2009) *Handbook of Destination Branding*, Madrid: UNWTO.

— (2011a) *Tourism Towards 2030: Global Overview*, UNWTO General Assembly, 19th Session, Gyeongju, Republic of Korea, 10 October, Madrid: UNWTO.

— (2011b) *National Tourism Statistics 1995–2010*, CD Rom, Madrid: UNWTO.

— (2011c) *Policy and Practice for Global Tourism*, Madrid: UNWTO.

— (2011d) *Global Report on Women in Tourism 2010*, Madrid: UNWTO.

— (2012a) *UNWTO Tourism Highlights. 2012 Edition*, Madrid: UNWTO.

— (2012b) *Global Report on City Tourism*, Madrid: UNWTO.

— (2012c) *Report on Urban Tourism Development in China*, Madrid: UNWTO.

United Nations World Tourism Organization, United Nations Environment Programme and World Meterological Organization (UNWTO–UNEP–WMO) (2008) *Climate Change and Tourism: Responding to Global Challenges*, Madrid: UNWTO.

United States Department of the Interior (1978) *National Urban Recreation Study*, Washington, DC: United States Department of the Interior.

Unwin, K. (1976) 'The relationship of observer and landscape in landscape evaluation', *Transactions of the Institute of British Geographers*, 66: 130–4.

Urry, J. (1987) 'Some social and spatial aspects of services', *Society and Space*, 5: 5–26.

— (1988) 'Cultural change and contemporary holidaymaking', *Theory, Culture and Society*, 5: 35–55.

— (1990) *The Tourist Gaze: Leisure and Travel in Contemporary Societies*, London: Sage.

— (1991) 'The sociology of tourism', in C.P. Cooper (ed.) *Progress in Tourism, Recreation and Hospitality Management*, vol. 3, London: Belhaven Press.

— (1995) *Consuming Spaces*, London: Routledge.

— (2000) *Sociology Beyond Societies: Mobilities for the Twenty-First Century*, London: Routledge.

— (2004) 'Small worlds and the new "social physics"', *Global Networks*, 4(2): 109–30.

Uysal, M. (1998) 'The determinants of tourism demand: a theoretical perspective', in D. Ioannides and K. Debbage (eds) *The Economic Geography of the Tourist Industry: A Supply-side Analysis*, London: Routledge.

Uysal, M. and Crompton, J.L. (1985) 'An overview of approaches to forecasting tourist demand', *Journal of Travel Research*, 23(4): 7–15.

Uzzell, D. (1984) 'An alternative structuralist approach to the psychology of tourism marketing', *Annals of Tourism Research*, 11: 79–100.

— (1995) 'The myth of the indoor city', *Journal of Environmental Psychology*, 15: 299–310.

Valentine, G. (1989) 'The geography of woman's fear', *Area*, 21(4): 385–90.

— (1990) 'Women's fear and the design of public space', *Built Environment*, 16(4): 288–303.

Valentine, G., French, S. and Clifford, N. (eds) (2010) *Key Methods in Geography*, London: Sage.

Valentine, P. (1980) 'Tropical rainforest and the wilderness experience', in V. Martin (ed.) *Wilderness*, Findhorn, SC: Findhorn Press.

— (1984) 'Wildlife and tourism: some ideas on potential and conflict', in B. O'Rourke (ed.) *Contemporary Issues in Australian Tourism, 19th Institute of Australian Geographer's Conference and International Geographical Union Sub-Commission on Tourism in the South West Pacific*, Sydney: Department of Geography, University of Sydney.

— (1992) 'Review. Nature-based tourism', in B. Weiler and C.M. Hall (eds) *Special Interest Tourism*, London: Belhaven Press.

Van der Knaap, W. (1999) 'Research report: GIS-oriented analysis of tourist time–space patterns to support sustainable tourism development', *Tourism Geographies*, 1: 56–69.

Van Raaij, W.F. (1986) 'Consumer research on tourism: mental and behavioural constructs', *Annals of Tourism Research*, 13: 1–10.

Van Raaij, W.F. and Francken, D.A. (1984) 'Vacation decisions, activities, and satisfactions', *Annals of Tourism Research*, 11: 101–13.

Vargo, S.L. and Lusch, R.F. (2004) 'The four service marketing myths: remnants of a goods-based, manufacturing model', *Journal of Service Research*, 6: 324–35.

— (2008) 'From goods to service(s): divergences and convergences of logics', *Industrial Marketing Management*, 37: 254–9.

Vaske, J.J., Needham, M.D. and Cline, R.C. (2007) 'Clarifying interpersonal and social values conflict among recreationists', *Journal of Leisure Research*, 39: 182–95.

Vaughan, D.R. (1977) 'Opportunity cost and the assessment and development of regional tourism', in B.S. Duffield (ed.) *Tourism: A Tool for Regional Development*, Edinburgh: Tourism and Recreation Research Unit, University of Edinburgh.

Vaughan, D.R., Farr, H. and Slee, W. (2000) 'Estimating and interpreting the local economic benefits of visitor spending', *Leisure Studies*, 19(2): 95–118.

Veal, A.J. (1987) *Leisure and the Future*, London: Unwin Hyman.

— (1992) *Research Methods for Leisure and Tourism: A Practical Guide*, Harlow: Longman.

— (1994) *Leisure Policy and Planning*, London: Pitman.

— (2001) 'Using Sydney's parks', *Australian Parks and Leisure*, 4(3): 21–3.

— (2010) *Leisure, Sport and Tourism: Politics, Policy and Planning*, Wallingford: CAB International.

— (2011) 'Planning for leisure, sport, tourism and the arts: goals and rationales', *World Leisure Journal*, 53(2): 119–48.

Veal, A. and Travis, T. (1979) 'Local authority leisure services – the state of play', *Local Government Studies*, 5: 5–16.

Vendenin, Y. (1978) 'Evolution of the recreational functions of a territory', *Soviet Geography*, 19: 646–59.

Verghese, J., Lipton, R.B., Katz, M.J., Hall, C.B., Derby, C.A., Kuslansky, G., Ambrose, A., Silwinski, M. and Buschke, H. (2003) 'Leisure activities and the risk of dementia in the elderly', *New England Journal of Medicine*, 348(25): 2508–16.

Versichele, M., Neutens, T., Delafontaine, M. and Van de Weghe, N. (2012) 'The use of Bluetooth for analysing spatiotemporal dynamics of human movement at mass events: a case study of the Ghent Festivities', *Applied Geography*, 32, 208–20.

Vickerman, R. (1975) *The Economics of Leisure and Recreation*, London: Macmillan.

Vidal, J. (1994) 'Parks: who needs them?', *Guardian*, 21 July.

Virden, R. and Walker, G. (1999) 'Ethnic/racial and gender variations among meanings given to, and preferences for, the natural environment', *Leisure Sciences*, 21: 219–39.

Visser, G. (2004) 'Second homes and local development: issues arising from Cape Town's De Water-kant', *GeoJournal*, 60(3): 259–71.

— (2006) 'South Africa has second homes too! An exploration of the unexplored', *Current Issues in Tourism*, 9: 351–83.

Visser, G. and Rogerson, C. (eds) (2004) 'Tourism and development issues in South Africa', special issue, *GeoJournal*, 60(3).

Visser, N. and Njunga, S. (1992) 'Environmental impacts of tourism on the Kenya coast', *Industry and Environment*, 15(3/4): 42–52.

Vitterisø, G. (2007) 'Norwegian cabin life in transition', *Scandinavian Journal of Hospitality and Tourism*, 7: 266–80.

Vogeler, I. (1977) 'Farm and ranch vacationing', *Journal of Leisure Research*, 9: 291–300.

Wagar, J.A. (1964) *The Carrying Capacity of Wildlands for Recreation*, Forest Service Monograph No. 7, Washington, DC: Society of American Foresters.

Waitt, G. (1997) 'Selling paradise and adventure: representations of landscape in the tourist advertising of Australia', *Australian Geographical Studies*, 35(1): 47–60.

— (1999) 'Naturalizing the "primitive": a critique of marketing Australia's indigenous peoples as "hunter-gatherers"', *Tourism Geographies*, 1: 142–63.

Waitt, G. and Duffy, M. (2010) 'Listening and tourism studies', *Annals of Tourism Research*, 37: 457–77.

Waitt, G. and McGuirk, P.M. (1997) 'Marking time: tourism and heritage representation at Millers Point, Sydney', *Australian Geographer*, 27(1): 11–29.

Waitt, G. and Stapel, C. (2011) 'Fornicating on floats? The cultural politics of the Mardi Gras parade beyond the metropolis', *Leisure Studies*, 30(2): 197–216.

Waitt, G., Markwell, K. and Gorman-Murray, A. (2008) 'Challenging heteronormativity in tourism studies: locating progress', *Progress in Human Geography*, 32: 781–800.

Walker, L. and Page, S.J. (2003) 'Risk, rights and responsibilities in tourist well-being: who should manage visitor well-being at the destination?', in J. Wilks and S.J. Page (eds) *Managing Tourist Health and Safety in the New Millennium*, Oxford: Pergamon Press.

Walker, P.A., Greiner, R., McDonald, D. and Lyne, V. (1998) 'The tourism futures simulator: a systems thinking approach', *Environmental Modelling and Software*, 14(1): 59–67.

Wall, G. (1971) 'Car-owners and holiday activities', in P. Lavery (ed.) *Recreational Geography*, Newton Abbot: David and Charles.

— (1972) 'Socio-economic variations in pleasure trip patterns: the case of Hull car-owners', *Transactions of the Institute of British Geographers*, 57: 45–58.

— (1983a) 'Atlantic City tourism and social change', *Annals of Tourism Research*, 10: 555–6.

— (1983b) 'Cycles and capacity: a contradiction in terms?', *Annals of Tourism Research*, 10: 268–70.

— (ed.) (1989) *Outdoor Recreation in Canada*, Toronto: Wiley.

Wall, G. and Badke, C. (1994) 'Tourism and climate change: an international perspective', *Journal of Sustainable Tourism*, 2: 193–203.

Wall, G. and Marsh, J. (eds) (1982) *Recreational Land Use: Perspectives on Its Evolution in Canada*, Ottawa: Carleton University Press.

Wall, G. and Mathieson, A. (2006) *Tourism: Change, Impacts and Opportunities*, Harlow: Pearson.

Wall, G. and Wright, C. (1977) *The Environmental Impacts of Outdoor Recreation*, Publication Series No. 11, Waterloo: Department of Geography, University of Waterloo.

Wall, G., Dudycha, D. and Hutchinson, J. (1985) 'Point pattern analysis of accommodation in Toronto', *Annals of Tourism Research*, 12: 603–18.

Wall, G., Harrison, R., Kinnaird, V., McBoyle, G. and Quinlan, C. (1986) 'The implications of climatic change for camping in Ontario', *Recreation Research Review*, 13(1): 50–60.

Wall Reinius, S. (2004) 'Protected areas as tourist attractions', paper presented at Tourism Crossroads – Global Influences, Local Responses, 13th Nordic Symposium in Tourism and Hospitality Research, Aalborg, November.

— (2009) 'A ticket to national parks? Tourism, railways, and the establishment of national parks in Sweden', in W. Frost and C.M. Hall (eds) *Tourism and National Parks: International Perspectives on Development, Histories and Change*, London: Routledge.

— (2012) 'Wilderness and culture: tourist views and experiences in the Laponian World Heritage Area', *Society & Natural Resources*, 25: 621–32.

Walle, A. (1997) 'Quantitative versus qualitative tourism research', *Annals of Tourism Research*, 24: 524–36.

Walmsley, D.J. (2003) 'Rural tourism: a case of lifestyle-led opportunities', *Australian Geographer*, 34(1): 61–72.

Walmsley, D.J. and Jenkins, J. (1992) 'Tourism cognitive mapping of unfamiliar environments', *Annals of Tourism Research*, 19: 268–86.

— (1994) 'Evaluations of recreation opportunities: tourist impacts of the New South Wales North Coast', in D. Mercer (ed.) *New Viewpoints in Australian Outdoor Recreation Research and Planning*, Melbourne: Hepper Marriot & Associates.

Walmsley, D.J. and Lewis, G.J. (1993) *People and Environment: Behavioural Approaches in Human Geography*, 2nd edn, Harlow: Longman.

Walmsley, D.J., Boskovic, R.M. and Pigram, J.J. (1981) *Tourism and Crime*, Armidale: Department of Geography, University of New England.

— (1983) 'Tourism and crime: an Australian perspective', *Journal of Leisure Research*, 15: 136–55.

Walpole, M. and Goodwin, H. (2000) 'Local economic impacts of dragon tourism in Indonesia', *Annals of Tourism Research*, 27: 559–76.

Walsh, K. (1988) 'The consequences of competition', in J. Bennington and J. White (eds) *The Future of Leisure Services*, Harlow: Longman.

Walter, R.D. (1975) *The Impact of Tourism on the Environment*, ARRA Monograph 7, Melbourne: Australian Recreation Research Association.

Walton, J. (1983) *The English Seaside Resort: A Social History 1750–1914*, Leicester: Leicester University Press.

— (2000) 'The hospitality trades: a social history', in C. Lashley and A. Morrison (eds) *In Search of Hospitality: Theoretical Perspectives and Debates*, Oxford: Butterworth Heinemann.

— (2009) 'Prospects in tourism history: evolution, state of play and future developments', *Tourism Management*, 30: 783–93.

— (2012) '"The tourism labour conundrum" extended: historical perspectives on hospitality workers', *Hospitality & Society*, 2: 49–75.

— (2013) '"Social tourism" in Britain: history and prospects', *Journal of Policy Research in Tourism, Leisure and Events*, 5: 46–61.

Walton, J. and Smith, J. (1996) 'The first century of beach tourism in Spain: San Sebastian and the Playas del Norte from the 1830s to the 1930s', in M. Barke, J. Towner and M. Newton (eds) *Tourism in Spain: Critical Issues*, Wallingford: CAB International.

Ward, C. and Hardy, D. (1986) *Goodnight Campers: The History of the British Holiday Camp*, London: Mansell.

Ward, S. (2001) *Selling Places: The Marketing and Promotion of Towns and Cities 1850–2000*, London: E&FN Spon.

Warf, B. and Arias, S. (2009) 'Introduction: the reinsertion of space in the social sciences and humanities', in B. Warf and S. Arias (eds) *The Spatial Turn: Interdisciplinary Perspectives*, London: Routledge.

Warnes, A.M. (1992) 'Migration and the lifecourse', in A.G. Champion and A. Fielding (eds) *Migration Processes and Patterns*, vol. 1: *Research Progress and Prospects*, London: Belhaven.

Warnken, J. and Buckley, R. (2000) 'Monitoring diffuse impacts: Australian tourism developments', *Environmental Management*, 25: 453–61.

Warr, M. (1985) 'Fear of rape among urban women', *Social Problems*, 32: 238–50.

Watmore, S. (1998) 'Wild(er)ness: reconfiguring the geographies of wildlife', *Transactions, Institute of British Geographers*, NS23: 435–54.

— (2000) 'Elephants on the move: spatial formations of wildlife exchange', *Environment and Planning D: Society and Space*, 18: 185–203.

Watson, J.E., Fuller, R.A., Watson, A.W., Mackey, B.G., Wilson, K.A., Grantham, H.S., Turner, M.,

Klein, C.J., Carwardine, J., Joseph, L.N. and Possingham, H.P. (2009) 'Wilderness and future conservation priorities in Australia', *Diversity and Distributions*, 15: 1028–36.

Wayens, B. and Grimmeau, J.P. (2003) 'L'Influence du tourisme sur le géographie du commerce de détail en Belgique', *Belgeo*, 3: 289–302.

Weaver, D. (1998) *Ecotourism in the Less Developed World*, Wallingford: CAB International.

— (2000) 'A broad context model of destination development scenarios', *Tourism Management*, 21: 217–34.

— (ed.) (2001) *The Encyclopedia of Ecotourism*, Wallingford: CAB International.

— (2004) 'Tourism and the elusive paradigm of sustainable development', in A. Lew, C.M. Hall and A. Williams (eds) *A Companion to Tourism*, Oxford: Blackwell.

— (2006) *Sustainable Tourism: Theory and Practice*, Oxford: Butterworth Heinemann.

— (2010) 'Indigenous tourism stages and their implications for sustainability', *Journal of Sustainable Tourism*, 18: 43–60.

Weidenfeld, A. (2013) 'Tourism and cross border regional innovation systems', *Annals of Tourism Research*, 42: 191–213.

Weidenfeld, A. and Hall, C.M. (2014) 'Tourism in the development of regional and sectoral innovation systems', in A. Lew, C.M. Hall and A.M. Williams (eds) *The Wiley-Blackwell Companion to Tourism*, Oxford: Wiley-Blackwell.

Weiler, B. (ed.) (1991) *Ecotourism: Conference Proceedings*, Canberra: Bureau of Tourism Research.

Weiler, B. and Hall, C.M. (1991) 'Meeting the needs of the recreation and tourism partnership: a comparative study of tertiary education programmes in Australia and Canada', *Leisure Options: Australian Journal of Leisure and Recreation*, 1(2): 7–14.

— (eds) (1992) *Special Interest Tourism*, London: Belhaven Press.

Welch, D. (1991) *The Management of Urban Parks*, Harlow: Longman.

Wells, W.D. and Gubar, G. (1966) 'Life cycle concept in marketing research', *Journal of Marketing Research*, 3: 355–63.

Westover, T. (1985) 'Perceptions of crime and safety in three Midwestern parks', *Professional Geographer*, 37: 410–20.

Weyl, H. (2009) *Philosophy of Mathematics and Natural Science*, rev. edn, Princeton: Princeton University Press.

Whatmore, S. (1993) 'Sustainable rural geographies', *Progress in Human Geography*, 17: 538–47.

Whitbeck, R.H. (1920) 'The influence of Lake Michigan upon its opposite shores, with comments on the declining use of the lake as a waterway', *Annals of the Association of American Geographers*, 10: 41–55.

White, A., Barker, V. and Tantrigama, G. (1997) 'Using integrated coastal management and economics to conserve coastal tourism resources in Sri Lanka', *Ambio*, 26(6): 335–44.

White, D.D., Virden, R.J. and van Riper, C.J. (2008) 'Effects of place identity, place dependence, and experience-use history on perceptions of recreation impacts in a natural setting', *Environmental Management*, 42: 647–57.

White, G. (1972) 'Geography and public policy', *Professional Geographer*, 24: 101–4.

White, L., Jr (1967) 'The historical roots of our ecological crisis', *Science*, 155 (10 March): 1203–7.

Whyte, D. (1978) 'Have second homes gone into hibernation?', *New Society*, 45: 286–8.

Wiener, C.S., Needham, M.D. and Wilkinson, P.F. (2009) 'Hawaii's real life marine park: interpretation and impacts of commercial marine tourism in the Hawaiian Islands', *Current Issues in Tourism*, 12: 489–504.

Wight, P.A. (1993) 'Sustainable ecotourism: balancing economic, environmental and social goals within an ethical framework', *Journal of Tourism Studies*, 4(2): 54–66.

— (1995) 'Sustainable ecotourism: balancing economic, environmental and social goals within an ethical framework', *Tourism Recreation Research*, 20(1): 5–13.

— (1998) 'Tools for sustainability analysis in planning and managing tourism and recreation in the destination', in C.M. Hall and A.A. Lew (eds) *Sustainable Tourism Development: A Geographical Perspective*, Harlow: Addison Wesley Longman.

Wilks, J. and Page, S.J. (eds) (2003) *Managing Tourist Health and Safety in the New Millennium*, Oxford: Elsevier.

Williams, A. (2000) 'Consuming hospitality: learning from post-modernism?', in C. Lashley and A. Morrison (eds) *In Search of Hospitality: Theoretical Perspectives and Debates*, Oxford: Butterworth Heinemann.

Williams, A. and Zelinsky, W. (1970) 'On some patterns of international tourism flows', *Economic Geography*, 46(4): 549–67.

Williams, A., Alverinho-Dias, J., Garcia Novo, F., Garciá-Mora, M., Curr, R. and Pereira, A. (2001) 'Integrated coastal dune management: checklists', *Continental Shelf Research*, 21: 1937–60.

Williams, A.M. (2004) 'Toward a political economy of tourism', in A. Lew, C.M. Hall and A. Williams (eds) *A Companion to Tourism*, Oxford: Blackwell.

Williams, A.M. and Balaz, V. (2000) *Tourism in Transition: Economic Change in Central Europe*, London: I.B. Tauris.

Williams, A.M. and Hall, C.M. (2000) 'Tourism and migration: new relationships between production and consumption', *Tourism Geographies*, 2: 5–27.

— (2002) 'Tourism, migration, circulation and mobility: the contingencies of time and place', in C.M. Hall and A.M. Williams (eds) *Tourism and Migration*, Dordrecht: Kluwer.

Williams, A.M. and Morgan, R. (1995) 'Beach awards and rating systems', *Shore and Beach*, 63(4): 29–33.

Williams, A.M. and Shaw, G. (eds) (1988) *Tourism and Economic Development: Western European Experiences*, London: Belhaven Press.

— (eds) (1991) *Tourism and Economic Development: Western European Experiences*, 2nd edn, London: Belhaven.

— (1998) 'Tourism and the environment: sustainability and economic restructuring', in C.M. Hall and A.A. Lew (eds) *Sustainable Tourism Development: Geographical Perspectives*, Harlow: Addison Wesley Longman.

— (2011) 'Internationalization and innovation in tourism', *Annals of Tourism Research*, 38: 27–51.

Williams, A.M., King. R. and Warnes, A.M. (1997) 'A place in the sun: international retirement migration from Northern to Southern Europe', *European Urban and Regional Studies*, 4: 15–34.

Williams, D. and Kaltenborn, B. (1999) 'Leisure places and modernity: the use and meaning of recreational cottages in Norway and the USA', in D. Cronin (ed.) *Leisure/Tourism Geographies: Practices and Geographical Knowledge*, London: Routledge.

Williams, G.H. (1962) *Wilderness and Paradise in Christian Thought*, New York: Harper & Brothers.

Williams, P. (1978) 'Building societies and the inner city', *Transactions of the Institute of British Geographers*, 3(1): 23–49.

Williams, R. (1976) *Keywords*, London: Fontana.

Williams, S. (1995a) *Recreation in the Urban Environment*, London: Routledge.

— (1995b) 'On the street – public space for popular leisure', in D. Leslie (ed.) *Tourism and Leisure – Perspectives on Provision*, Brighton: Leisure Studies Association.

— (1998) *Tourism Geography*, London: Routledge.

Williamson, J., Rodger, K., Moore, S.A. and Warren, C. (2012) 'An exploratory study of community expectations regarding public forests in Western Australia', *Australian Forestry*, 75(2): 100–6.

Willis, A. (1992) *Women and Crime: Key Findings from the Report on Crime Prevention in the Leicester City Challenge Area*, Leicester: School of Social Work, Leicester University.

Wilson, J. (ed.) (2012) *The Routledge Handbook of Tourism Geographies*, London: Routledge.

Wilson, J. and Anton Clavé, S. (eds) (2013) *Geographies of Tourism: European Research Perspectives*, London: Emerald.

Wiltshier, P. and Cardow, A. (2008) 'Tourism, indigenous peoples and endogeneity in the Chatham Islands', *Journal of Enterprising Communities*, 2: 265–74.

Winsberg, M.P. (1966) 'Overseas travel by American civilians since World War II', *Journal of Geography*, 65: 73–9.

Winter, M. (1987) 'Farm-based tourism and conservation in the uplands', *Ecos: A Review of Conservation*, 5(3): 10–15.

Winter, T. (2007) *Post-conflict heritage, postcolonial tourism: culture, politics and development at Angkor*, Abingdon: Routledge.

— (2009) 'Asian tourism and the retreat of Anglo-Western centrism in tourism theory', *Current Issues in Tourism*, 12: 21–31.

Winter, T., Teo, P. and Chang, T.C. (eds) (2009) *Asia on Tour: Exploring the Rise of Asian Tourism*, London: Routledge.

Winterbottom, D. (1967) 'How much urban space do we need', *Journal of the Royal Town Planning Institute*, 53: 144–7.

Winters, P., Corral, L. and Mora, A.M. (2013) 'Assessing the role of tourism in poverty alleviation: a research agenda', *Development Policy Review*, 31(2): 177–202.

Wirth, L. (1938) 'Urbanism as a way of life', *American Journal of Sociology*, 44: 1–24.

Withington, W. (1961) 'Upland resorts and tourism in Indonesia: some recent trends', *Geographical Review*, 51: 418–23.

Withyman, W. (1985) 'The ins and outs of international travel and tourism data', *International Tourism Quarterly*, Special Report No. 55.

Witt, S. and Martin, C. (1989) 'Demand forecasting in tourism and recreation', in C.P. Cooper (ed.) *Progress in Tourism, Recreation and Hospitality Management*, vol. 1, London: Belhaven Press.

— (1992) *Modelling and Forecasting Demand in Tourism*, London: Academic Press.

Witt, S., Brooke, M. and Buckley, P. (1991) *The Management of International Tourism*, London: Routledge.

Wolfe, R.J. (1951) 'Summer cottages in Ontario', *Economic Geography*, 27(1): 10–32.

— (1952) 'Wasage Beach: the divorce from the geographic environment', *Canadian Geographer*, 1(2): 57–65.

— (1964) 'Perspectives on outdoor recreation: a bibliographical survey', *Geographical Review*, 54: 203–38.

— (1966) 'Recreational travel: the new migration', *Geographical Bulletin*, 9: 73–9.

— (1970) 'Discussion of vacation homes, environmental preferences and spatial behaviour', *Journal of Leisure Research*, 2(1): 85–7.

Women's Equality Unit (1993) *Women and Safety Project*, Leicester: Leicester City Council.

Wong, I.A. and Wan, Y. (2013) 'A systematic approach to scale development in tourist shopping satisfaction linking destination attributes and shopping experience', *Journal of Travel Research*, 52: 29–41.

Wong, J. and Law, R. (2003) 'Difference in shopping satisfaction levels: a study of tourists in Hong Kong', *Tourism Management*, 24: 401–10.

Wong, P.P. (1986) 'Tourism development and resorts on the east coast of Peninsular Malaysia', *Singapore Journal of Tropical Geography*, 7(2): 152–62.

— (1990) 'Recreation in the coastal areas of Singapore', in P. Fabbri (ed.) *Recreational Use of Coastal Areas*, Dordrecht: Kluwer.

— (1993a) 'Island tourism development in Peninsular Malaysia: environmental perspective', in P. Wong (ed.) *Tourism vs Environment: The Case for Coastal Areas*, Dordrecht: Kluwer Academic.

— (ed.) (1993b) *Tourism vs Environment: The Case for Coastal Areas*, Dordrecht: Kluwer Academic.

— (2003) 'Where have all the beaches gone? Coastal erosion in the tropics', *Singapore Journal of Tropical Geography*, 24(1): 111–32.

— (2004) 'Environmental impacts of tourism', in A. Lew, C.M. Hall and A. Williams (eds) *A Companion to Tourism*, Oxford: Blackwell.

Woo, Kyung-Sik (1996) 'Korean tourists' urban activity patterns in New Zealand', unpublished research report, Master of Business Studies, Massey University at Albany, Auckland, New Zealand.

Wood, R.E. (2000) 'Caribbean cruise tourism: globalization at sea', *Annals of Tourism Research*, 27: 345–70.

Woods, B. (2000) 'Beauty and the beast: preferences for animals in Australia', *Journal of Tourism Studies*, 11(2): 25–35.

Woods, M. (2011) 'The local politics of the global countryside: boosterism, aspirational ruralism and the contested reconstitution of Queenstown, New Zealand', *GeoJournal*, 76: 365–81.

Woolley, H. and Ul-Amin, N. (1999) 'Pakistani teenagers' use of public open space in Sheffield', *Managing Leisure*, 4(3): 156–67.

World Economic Forum (WEF) (2008) *The Travel and Tourism Competitiveness Report 2008: Balancing*

Economic Development and Environmental Sustainability, Geneva: WEF.

— (2009) *Towards a Low Carbon Travel & Tourism Sector*, Davos: WEF.

World Tourism Organization (WTO) (1981) *Guidelines for the Collection and Presentation of Domestic and International Tourism Statistics*, Madrid: WTO.

— (1983) *Definitions Concerning Tourism Statistics*, Madrid: WTO.

— (1991a) *Guidelines for the Collection and Presentation of Domestic and International Tourism Statistics*, Madrid: WTO.

— (1991b) *Resolutions of International Conference on Travel and Tourism, Ottawa, Canada*, Madrid: WTO.

— (1997) *Tourism 2020 Vision*, Madrid: WTO.

— (1998) *WTO Revises Forecasts for Asian Tourism*, Press Release, 27 January, Madrid: WTO.

— (1999) *Tourism Satellite Account: The Conceptual Framework*, Madrid: WTO.

— (2003) *Climate Change and Tourism*, Madrid: WTO.

World Travel and Tourism Council (WTTC) (2004) *The Caribbean: The Impact of Travel & Tourism on Jobs and the Economy*, London: WTTC.

— (2009) *Leading the Challenge*, London: WTTC.

Worster, D. (1977) *Nature's Economy: A History of Ecological Ideas*, Cambridge: Cambridge University Press.

— (ed.) (1988) *The Ends of the Earth: Perspectives on Modern Environmental History*, Cambridge: Cambridge University Press.

Wrathall, J.E. (1980) 'Farm-based holidays', *Town and Country Planning*, 49(6): 194–5.

Wray, K., Espiner, S., Perkins, H.C. (2010) 'Cultural clash: interpreting established use and new tourism activities in protected natural areas', *Scandinavian Journal of Hospitality and Tourism*, 10: 272–90.

Wright, D. (trans.) (1957) *Beowulf*, Harmondsworth: Penguin.

Wright, J. (1980) 'Wilderness, waste and history', *Habitat*, 8(1): 27–31.

Wright Wendel, H.E., Zarger, R.K. and Mihelcic, J.R. (2012) 'Accessibility and usability: green space preferences, perceptions, and barriers in a rapidly urbanizing city in Latin America', *Landscape and Urban Planning*, 107: 272–82.

Wrigley, G.M. (1919) 'Fairs of the Central Andes', *Geographical Review*, 2: 65–80.

Wu, C.-T. (1982) 'Issues of tourism and socioeconomic development', *Annals of Tourism Research*, 9: 317–30.

Wyly, E. (2009) 'Strategic positivism', *Professional Geographer*, 61: 310–22.

Xiaa, J.(C.), Zeephongsekul, P. and Packer, D. (2011) 'Spatial and temporal modelling of tourist movements using Semi-Markov processes', *Tourism Management*, 32(4): 844–51.

Xiao-Ting, H. and Bi-Hu, W. (2012) 'Intra-attraction: tourist spatial-temporal behaviour patterns', *Tourism Geographies*, 14: 625–45.

Xie, P.F., Chandra, V. and Gu, K. (2013) 'Morphological changes of coastal tourism: a case study of Denarau Island, Fiji', *Tourism Management Perspectives*, 5: 75–83.

Xu, Y. and McGehee, N.G. (2012) 'Shopping behavior of Chinese tourists visiting the United States: letting the shoppers do the talking', *Tourism Management*, 33: 427–30.

Yee, A.S. (2004) 'Cross-national concepts in supranational governance: state–society relations and EU-policy making', *Governance*, 17: 487–524.

Yeo, S., Hee, L. and Heng, K. (2012) 'Urban informality and everyday (night) life: a field study in Singapore', *International Development Planning Review*, 34: 369–90.

Young, G. (1973) *Tourism: Blessing or Blight*, Harmondsworth: Penguin.

Young, M. and Wilmott, P. (1973) *The Symmetrical Family*, London: Routledge & Kegan Paul.

Young, T. (1996) 'Modern urban parks', *Geographical Review*, 85: 535–51.

Yuksel, A. (2004) 'Shopping experience evaluation: a case of domestic and international visitors', *Tourism Management*, 25: 751–9.

Zacarias, D.A., Williams, A.T. and Newton, A. (2011) 'Recreation carrying capacity estimations to support beach management at Praia de Faro, Portugal', *Applied Geography*, 31: 1075–81.

Zampoukos, K. and Ioannides, D. (2011) 'The tourism labour conundrum: agenda for new research in the geography of hospitality workers', *Hospitality & Society*, 1: 25–45.

Zapata, M.J., Hall, C.M., Lindo, P. and Vanderschaeghen, M. (2011) 'Can community-based tourism contribute to development and poverty alleviation?', *Current Issues in Tourism*, 14: 725–49.

Zegre, S.J., Needham, M.D., Kruger, L.E. and Rosenberger, R.S. (2012) 'McDonaldization and commercial outdoor recreation and tourism in Alaska', *Managing Leisure*, 17: 333–48.

Zeppel, H. (2010) 'Sustainable tourism on Green Island, Great Barrier Reef National Park', in J. Carlsen and R. Butler (eds) *Island Tourism: A Sustainable Perspective*, Wallingford: CAB International.

Zetter, F. (1971) *The Evolution of Country Park Policy*, Cheltenham: Countryside Commission.

Zhang, H.Q., Chong, K. and Ap, J. (1999) 'An analysis of tourism policy development in modern China', *Tourism Management*, 20: 471–85.

Zimmermann, E.W. (1951) *World Resources and Industries: A Functional Appraisal of the Availability of Agricultural and Industrial Materials*, New York: Harper.

Zurick, D.N. (1992) 'Adventure travel and sustainable tourism in the peripheral economy of Nepal', *Annals of the Association of American Geographers*, 82: 608–28.

Zuzanek, J., Beckers, T. and Peters, P. (1998) 'The "harried leisure class" revisited: Dutch and Canadian trends in the use of time from the 1970s to the 1990s', *Leisure Studies*, 17(1): 1–20.

Index

Lightning Source UK Ltd.
Milton Keynes UK
UKOW04f1320051016

284516UK00009B/121/P

Holyoak and Torremans Intellectual Property Law

Eighth Edition

PAUL TORREMANS
Licentiaat in de Rechten (KU Leuven)
Licentiaat in het Notariaat (Examencommissie van de Staat, Leuven)
Geaggregeerde voor het HSO en het HOKT in de Rechten (KU Leuven)
LLM (Leicester)
PhD (Leicester)
Professor of Intellectual Property Law, University of Nottingham

OXFORD
UNIVERSITY PRESS

OXFORD
UNIVERSITY PRESS

Great Clarendon Street, Oxford, OX2 6DP,
United Kingdom

Oxford University Press is a department of the University of Oxford.
It furthers the University's objective of excellence in research, scholarship,
and education by publishing worldwide. Oxford is a registered trade mark of
Oxford University Press in the UK and in certain other countries

Fifth edition 2008
Sixth edition 2010
Seventh edition 2013

Impression: 2

Public sector information reproduced under Open Government Licence v3.0
(http://www.nationalarchives.gov.uk/doc/open-government-licence/open-government-licence.htm)

Published in the United States of America by Oxford University Press
198 Madison Avenue, New York, NY 10016, United States of America

British Library Cataloguing in Publication Data
Data available

Library of Congress Control Number: 2016942497

ISBN 978-0-19-873477-2

Printed in Great Britain by
Ashford Colour Press Ltd

HOLYOAK AND TORREMANS
INTELLECTUAL PROPERTY LAW

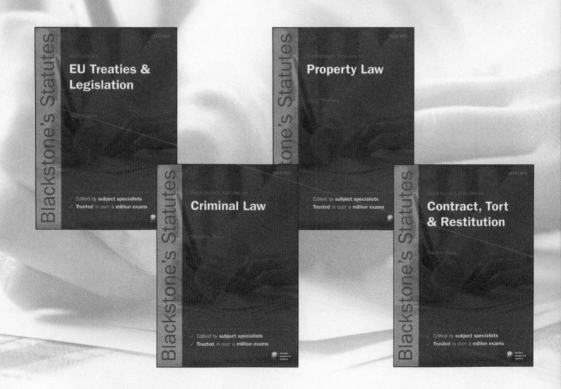

Outline contents

Section A Introduction

Section B Patents

Section C Copyright and Related Issues

Section D Designs

online resource centre
Franchising and intellectual property
Visit the Online Resource Centre at www.oxfordtextbooks.co.uk/orc/holyoak8e/
to access this chapter and other useful materials.

Detailed contents

Section A Introduction

Section B Patents

Section D Designs

Section F Issues in Intellectual Property

online resource centre
Franchising and intellectual property
Visit the Online Resource Centre at www.oxfordtextbooks.co.uk/orc/holyoak8e/
to access this chapter and other useful materials.

Preface to the eighth edition

Intellectual property has again seen rapid development over the last three years. Not only have there been new cases on existing points that take the debate further and the odd change in legislation at domestic and at European level, but in certain areas fundamental changes are taking place. In the trade mark field the recasting of the Directive and the Regulation is about to happen and the changes that are about to become a reality have been included in this edition. In the patent field the same has happened in relation to the unitary patent. These changes will come to fruition over the coming years, but that aspect will have to wait until the ninth edition.

There has also been the usual flood of CJEU cases in both the copyright and the trade mark area. European law in this area is rapidly taking shape. And national courts are doing a lot more than merely referring cases to the CJEU.

This eight edition benefitted greatly from the outstanding work of my team at Oxford University Press, including Carol Barber, Henry Cockburn, Robert Crossley, and Stephanie Hitch. My sincere thanks go to all of them.

I have attempted to state the law as it stands on 18 December 2015. It has nevertheless been possible to include some later materials at proof stage. Also, Regulation 2015/2424 did enter into force on 23rd March 2016. As a result, OHIM is now the EU Intellectual Property Office (EUIPO) and the Community Trade Mark is now the EU Trade Mark. The relevant chapters were written late in 2015 and they still use the old names.

Paul Torremans
18 December 2015

Table of legislation

Bold locators indicate text is quoted in part or in full

Statutory Instruments

Australia

Belgium

Table of cases

**Numerical listing of Patent
Decisions. These decisions are
also included in the preceding
alphabetical list**

Table of international agreements, conventions, and treaties

SECTION A
Introduction

1

Themes in intellectual property

Preliminary thoughts

This book is not only about ideas: it is about ideas skilfully expressed in writing, in music, or in a sculpture. It is about the bright idea for an invention, the details of which have been worked out and which takes the form of a product or a process that can be applied industrially. It is also about a logo or name applied to products in order to distinguish them from other products in the same category and to indicate their origin. It is also about clothes and exhaust pipes made to a new design. Intellectual property is more than a reward for inventors and creators on the basis of a bright idea.

We will investigate this further on all other pages of this book, but let us start with a down-to-earth overview of the plot of our story. The background is a concert given by a famous opera singer. His performance consists of songs taken from various operas. The lyrics and music of each of these songs can attract copyright protection for its author; the opera singer will have a right in his performance of them. A live recording is made and published on compact disc (CD), and the concert is beamed around the world as a satellite broadcast—two further occasions on which copyright interests arise. Copyright issues also arise when a clip of the concert is posted on the Internet on YouTube. Satellite technology involves various patented inventions both in relation to the missile technology and in relation to the transmission of broadcasts. The CD will bear the logo of the record company, which allows customers to distinguish the CD from that of another record company. It is most likely that the record company will have secured a trade mark for its logo to guarantee its exclusive right to use it. The CD's accompanying booklet raises copyright issues, because it contains a photograph in which the star is pictured standing next to a sculpture made by his wife. The photograph, the sculpture, and the text of the booklet can all be protected by copyright. T-shirts bearing the star's picture are of a different style, but allow him to merchandise his image and to benefit from his celebrity status.

By the time we have unravelled all of the intellectual property aspects of this concert—or at least the legal provisions underlying them—we will have reached the final page of our book. This example provides, however, a first impression of what intellectual property means in practice and alerts the reader to the intellectual property aspects of many elements of our everyday lives.

In a schematic way one could argue that within intellectual property six main rights can be distinguished, most of which surfaced in the concert example given.

Copyright protects literary and artistic works, such as writings, drawings, and music, by granting the right holder the exclusive right to reproduce the work and to communicate it to the public.

Related rights are essentially related to copyright, as they protect the performers, producers of phonograms, and broadcasters. Often these are rights in the performance of copyright works.

Patents cover technological inventions and grant an exclusive right in the making of the patented product or the use of the patented process.

Trade marks are essentially signs that are attached to products and services to distinguish them from identical goods or services from a different origin. Distinctiveness as to origin is a key concept for trade mark law, even if trade marks are also important marketing and advertising tools.

And finally one could add two types of designs to the example. Costumes for the performance are made to a specific design and some of the equipment used on stage has a functional design.

Registered designs play a role in protecting aesthetic designs by granting an exclusive right in them and (unregistered) design rights are available to protect functional designs.

Introduction

In recent years, intellectual property has attracted a lot of attention. Its importance for international trading relations was emphasized during the negotiations that led to the successful conclusion of the General Agreement on Tariffs and Trade (GATT)[1] Uruguay Round on the world trading system. The GATT Trade-Related Aspects of Intellectual Property Rights (TRIPS) initiative, which led eventually to the Agreement on Trade-Related Aspects of Intellectual Property Rights 1994 that was signed in Marrakesh,[2] was sparked off by a strong desire to eradicate international counterfeiting and piracy. It became clear at a very early stage, however, that the cure for the fake Gucci or Cartier watch, Lacoste shirt, or even counterfeited fire extinguishing system in a jet engine for a passenger plane[3]—or for what is often described as a plague threatening (among other things) the worldwide exploitation of intellectual property—also required a harmonization of national intellectual property laws.[4] It is much easier to eradicate counterfeits at source, with a common set of minimum protection rules, than afterwards, at a national border once they are in circulation.[5]

At European level, the realization of the single market gave rise to a series of initiatives in the intellectual property area. Harmonization directives—for example, that on the harmonization of the duration of the term of copyright protection[6] and the Trade

---

[1] The General Agreement on Tariffs and Trade—basically, the world free-trading system—which, as a structure and organization, was succeeded by the World Trade Organization (WTO) as a result of the Uruguay Round of trade negotiations.

[2] The final text of the TRIPS Agreement was published in (1994) 33 ILM 1197 and in (1994) 25 IIC 209. The agreement is administered by the WTO, which succeeded to GATT. See D. Gervais (2012) *The TRIPS Agreement: Drafting History and Analysis*, 4th edn, London: Sweet and Maxwell; C. Correa (2007) *Trade-Related Aspects of Intellectual Property Rights: A Commentary on the TRIPS Agreement*, Oxford: Oxford University Press. See <http://www.wto.org/english/docs_e/legal_e/legal_e.htm#TRIPs> and <http://www.wto.org/english/tratop_e/trips_e/trips_e.htm>.

[3] See M.-C. Piatti, 'Measures to Combat International Piracy' [1989] 7 EIPR 239, 239–40.

[4] See K. Thomas (2007) 'The Fight against Piracy: Working within the Administrative Enforcement System in China', in P. Torremans, H. Shan, and J. Erauw (eds.), *Intellectual Property and TRIPS Compliance in China: Chinese and European Perspectives*, Cheltenham/Northampton, MA: Edward Elgar, pp. 85–106.

[5] See the comments on the current debate between Europe and China in P. Torremans et al. (n. 4), esp.: G. Shoukang and Z. Xiaodong, 'Are Chinese Intellectual Property Laws Consistent with the TRIPS Agreement?', pp. 11–28; P. Torremans, 'Substantive Law Issues in Europe a Decade after TRIPS', pp. 29–61.

[6] Directive 93/98 harmonizing the term of protection of copyright and certain related rights (1993) OJ L 290/9, now codified as Directive 2006/116/EC of the European Parliament and of the Council of 12 December 2006 on the term of protection of copyright and certain related rights (codified version) [2006] OJ L 372/12.

Mark Directive[7]—were coupled with moves towards a set of truly European intellectual property rights[8] and Community responses to the computer industry's perceived need for adequate protection.[9] UK legislation was updated as a result of a number of these developments and we have also seen the further development of, for example, the tort of passing off, and the protection offered to the merchandising activities involving real and fictitious characters, to fill the gaps not covered internationally—for example, goodwill, characters, and information.

Due in part to these developments, the various intellectual property rights have become relatively well known, as we saw already when we started with some preliminary thoughts:

(a) trade marks;

(b) patents;

(c) copyright;

(d) rights in performances;

(e) registered designs;

(f) design rights.

Let us add some more examples to our concert example already discussed. Intellectual property addresses problems such as how the CD system, as a technological invention, is temporarily protected by patents, how the aesthetic appearance of a telephone in the shape of a golf caddy can be protected as a registered design, and whether the functional design of kitchen utensils can attract (unregistered) design protection. We could also use intellectual property laws to examine how the registration of the trade mark 'Sprite' by the Coca-Cola Company for its lemon-taste soft drink is linked to the fact that it allows consumers to identify the drink and to distinguish it from similar soft drinks; how such a trade mark is protected against imitation; how copyright grants and protects certain rights in literary, artistic, and musical creations; and which rights exist in performances. Other related areas that equally we will have to consider include the laws of confidence and passing off. These form an essential national addition to the types and level of protection provided on the basis of international conventions.

A brief historical overview—the origins

When we refer to 'intellectual property rights', we do not wish to make the distinction between industrial intellectual property rights—such as patents and trade marks—and artistic intellectual property rights—such as copyright. This distinction appears no longer to be valid, because copyright is now used in such a flexible way—for example, to

---

[7] Directive 89/104 on the approximation of the laws of Member States relating to trade marks (1989) OJ L40/1, now codified as Directive 2008/95/EC of the European Parliament and of the Council of 22 October 2008 to approximate the laws of the Member States relating to trade marks [2008] OJ L 299/25.

[8] E.g. the Community Trade Mark—see Council Regulation 40/94 on the Community Trade Mark (1994) OJ L11/1, (EC) 40/94 (1994) OJ L 11/1, now codified as Council Regulation (EC) 207/2009 of 26 February 2009 on the Community trade mark [2009] OJ L78/1—and the Community Design—see Council Regulation 6/2002 on Community Designs (2002) OJ L3/1.

[9] See e.g. Directive 91/250 on the legal protection of computer programs (1991) OJ L122/42, now codified as Directive 2009/24/EC of the European Parliament and of the Council of 23 April 2009 on the legal protection of computer programs [2009] OJ L 111/16, and Directive 96/9 on the legal protection of databases (1996) OJ L77/20.

protect computer programs—that it can no longer be called an exclusively artistic right. The same concepts underlie each type of intellectual property. A strong form of unity exists between all types of intellectual property and the common law concepts in use in this area. But this dichotomy between 'industrial' patents and 'artistic' copyright has been an essential element in the historical development of the protection of what we call 'intellectual property'. Before we try to define this term and to justify the continuing existence of intellectual property rights, let us have a brief look at the historical roots of our topic.

The origin and the evolution of the patent system

Patents can be traced back as far as the end of the Middle Ages.[10] Inventor privileges— which, in England, took the form of royal grants under the royal prerogative—were granted all over Europe. Although not altogether absent, the idea of the promotion of inventive activity through the grant of a market monopoly was strongly overshadowed by the idea that these privileges were the perfect tool with which to reward political creditors and to give them a trading monopoly granted by letters patent.

In England, Parliament reacted against this practice and, in 1624, the Statute of Monopolies was issued. It was primarily a response to the existing practice and the trading monopolies to which this practice gave rise, but it was also influenced by the idea that, in certain circumstances, a market monopoly would be necessary as an incentive to innovate. The result of this influence is found in s. 6 of the Statute of Monopolies: the *'true and first inventor'* was granted a patent monopoly for 14 years upon *'any manner of new manufacture'*.

Because England felt that France and Holland were further advanced in their technical development, any person who imported new technologies with a view to establishing an advanced domestic industry was equally considered to be an inventor. The flexibility on this point emphasizes that this new patent system should be seen as a deliberate act of economic policy.[11] By rewarding, eventually, both devisors and importers of new technologies, the development of industrial activity, growth, and employment emerges as the primary aim of the legislation; gratitude towards the inventor is only of secondary importance. The policy aspect is reinforced by the provision that manufactures that are *'contrary to the law or mischievous to the state, by raising prices of commodities at home, or hurt trade, or generally inconvenient'*[12] would not be protected. Only those manufactures that fit in with the policy would be protected, because the realization of the aims of the policy was the ultimate reason for the existence of the patents.

These early developments represent only the start of a long development process wherein the Industrial Revolution in Europe was the key element. The eighteenth century saw the development of the patent specification, first as a tool with which to define the content of the protected invention against infringers by means of a statement enrolled with the Court of Chancery and, later, in the modern sense, as a source of technical information provided by the patentee as consideration for the monopoly granted to him by the patent. The novelty concept, which corresponded previously to the fact that the invention

---

[10] See also R. Miller, G. Burkill, C. Birss, and D. Campbell (2011) *Terrell on the Law of Patents*, 17th edn, London: Sweet and Maxwell, pp. 3–10.

[11] See B. Dölemeyer, 'Einführungsprivilegien und Einführungspatente als historische Mittel des Technologietransfers' [1985] GRUR 735. This German article is the best source for this view.

[12] See Statute of Monopolies 1624, s. 6.

was not yet practised in the country, was enlarged to incorporate also the question of whether the trading community already knew of the invention through publication.

The Patent Law Amendment Act 1852 removed the inefficiencies and uncertainties in the procedures for securing a patent. The applicant could register his specification with the Commissioners of Patents, with an option to file a provisional application up to one year before the complete specification was worked out and filed. Patents were granted simply upon registration and at a reasonable fee. This led to an increase in the number of patents, some of which were of dubious value due to the absence of any examination of the applications.

The Patents, Designs and Trade Marks Act 1883 addressed the problems arising from the inadequacy of the patent litigation procedures. A single judge replaced the juries and patentees were obliged to delineate the scope of their monopoly in at least one of their claims; even more important, however, was the replacement of the Commissioners by the Patent Office, charged with the examination of the patent applications. In a first stage, the Office examined whether the formal requirements and the requirement that the patentee should provide a proper description of the patent had been observed. An examination of the novelty of the application, based on a search of previous British specifications, was added to the examination process from 1905 onwards.[13] This change clearly demonstrates how strongly the origins of intellectual property are linked with—and their evolution is a response to—commercial necessities.

All over Europe and in North America, specific patent legislation was introduced at national level in the course of the nineteenth century. As a similar evolution took place in all of these countries and because the technology that was being developed was not only to be used in the country in which it was developed, a need for international cooperation arose. In 1883, the Paris Convention for the Protection of Industrial Property was created as the basic instrument for international patent protection.[14] It provides minimal rules of protection, which have been translated into the national patent legislation. In addition, it contains a rule of national treatment that provides that foreign inventors shall be treated in the same way as their domestic counterparts and that their inventions shall be granted the same level of protection.[15]

The development of the first half of the twentieth century can be characterized as a consolidation effort at legal and organizational levels. The new phenomenon of the vast number of newly independent states created a crisis in the patent system in the early 1960s: a flood of patent applications had to be dealt with independently by an ever-growing number of national patent offices; international and regional cooperation was seen as the solution. There were attempts to arrive at regional patent systems,[16] and treaties providing assistance and combating the seemingly endless duplication of the examination procedures (such as the global Patent Co-operation Treaty)[17] were established during this period. Another problem that newly independent states faced—especially in the developing world—was the inappropriateness for their purposes of the existing patent legislation. The adoption of new patent laws in these countries and the reform of the international patent system to this new environment are processes that have not yet been concluded.[18]

---

[13] See Patents Act 1902.

[14] See F. K. Beier, 'The Significance of the Patent System for Technical, Economic and Social Progress' [1980] IIC 563, 570.

[15] Art. 2 of the Paris Convention.

[16] E.g. the Nordic Patent System and the European Patent Convention. [17] See Ch. 2.

[18] See, most recently, the Patent Law Treaty (Geneva, 2000) as an attempt to harmonize procedures before the national patent offices. The UK has signed the Treaty and, in relation to the UK, it entered into force on 22 March 2006. As yet, only a limited number of states have ratified it (33 at the time of writing).

The origin and evolution of trade marks

The use of marks that are added to goods to distinguish them from similar goods has a history of at least 2,000 years: the Romans embossed their pottery, or impressed it with a mark, and merchants have used marks ever since to distinguish their goods. Although the courts became involved in the actions against infringers,[19] no proper trade mark legislation was enacted and the system was, for a long time, based purely on common law principles. The main problem that traders faced was that, each time they brought an infringement action, they had to prove their title to the mark. This depended on the existence of an established reputation associated with the mark.

In France, this problem had been solved by the introduction of a registration system and a similar registration system was introduced in England, in 1875, under the Trade Marks Registration Act.[20] UK trade mark legislation was consolidated by the Patents, Designs and Trade Marks Act 1883—the same year in which the Paris Convention was signed. The principles contained in this Convention apply to trade marks as well as to patents.[21]

The next step in the consolidation process was the statutory definition of the term 'trade mark' in the Trade Marks Act 1905. This was followed, in the Trade Marks Act 1919, by the division of the register into Part A—within which stringent requirements were coupled with better protection in terms of remedies—and Part B. The Trade Marks Act 1938 was based on the same principles, but the drafting was more detailed. It was amended by the Trade Marks (Amendment) Act 1984 to also include service marks. Although the division of the register into two parts was abolished by the Trade Marks Act 1994, the UK system still retains an examination stage before the mark is registered.

The origin and the evolution of the copyright system

We have seen that, at international level, many of the principles applied to patents are equally applied to trade marks.[22] This is not always the case for copyright, however.

Copyright is historically linked to written literary works. Because handwritten copies were such a formidable investment of time and effort, few copies were made available and plagiarism was not a problem. All this changed when Gutenberg invented movable type and Caxton developed the printing press in the second half of the fifteenth century. The arrival of this technology made the printing of multiple copies possible, quickly and at relatively little expense.[23]

Stationers acquired the works from their authors, and organized the printing and the sale of these works. These entrepreneurs took the commercial risks involved in exploiting the works of the authors and they wanted exclusive rights in the publication of the works to protect them against copiers. They found an ally in the Crown, which wanted to control the importation and circulation of books. The stationers organized themselves

---

[19] See *Sykes v. Sykes* (1824) 3 B & C 541, a case that contains some basic principles: e.g. damages at common law, deceit.

[20] For a comprehensive overview of the historical development of the law of trade marks (and passing off), see C. Morcom, A. Roughton, and T. St. Quintin (2012) *The Modern Law of Trade Marks*, 4th edn, London: Lexis Nexis, Ch. 1.

[21] Paris Convention.   [22] Industrial designs are also found in this category.

[23] The history of copyright has been analysed in detail by R. Deazley (2004) *On the Origin of the Right to Copy: Charting the Movement of Copyright Law in Eighteenth-Century Britain (1695–1775)*, Oxford: Hart; R. Deazley (2006) *Re-Thinking Copyright: History, Theory, Language*, Cheltenham/Northampton, MA: Edward Elgar.

into a guild and the Crown granted the Stationers' Company a charter in 1556. Lawfully printed books were entered in the Company's register and, because the right to make an entry in the register was reserved for the stationers, this system effectively amounted to a licensing system and secured a printing monopoly for the Company members. On top of that, members were granted powers to act against infringing copies.

This system remained in place until the end of the seventeenth century, at which point there was a brief period of anarchy. This period was, however, followed by the first real copyright statute: the Statute of Anne 1709.[24] It gave the 'sole right and liberty of printing books' to authors and their assignees. There was, however, no shift from an entrepreneurial copyright to an author's right, with emphasis exclusively on literary creation and its creators: under the Statute of Anne, the emphasis remained focused on the commercial exploitation of books. Printers and booksellers were explicitly named among the author's assigns.[25] Their right started from first publication and lasted for 14 years, but it was only enforceable by seizure and penalties if the title of the book had been registered with the Stationers' Company before publication.[26] Before publication, the author could rely on certain common law rights of literary property to obtain protection against unauthorized copying[27] and, if the author was still alive on expiry of the term of protection of 14 years, the right was 'returned' to him for another 14 years.

At the end of the eighteenth and during the nineteenth centuries, the duration of the term of copyright protection was gradually increased; simultaneously, the scope of copyright was widened to include types of work other than literary works. Engravings, prints, lithographs, sculptures, and dramatic and musical works all received copyright protection during that period. But drama and music did not fit in well with the existing 'copy-right'—that is, the right to produce copies of the work and to prevent others from doing so—because their exploitation was more likely to involve performances, rather than the sale of printed copies. As a consequence, playwrights and composers sought a 'use' right, and a performing right for dramatic works was created in 1833[28] and extended to musical works in 1842.[29]

The British emphasis on the entrepreneurial exploitation aspect of copyright was not shared by those who saw copyright almost exclusively as the expression of reverence for the creating artist and his act of artistic creation. The latter tendency was particularly strong in France and Belgium, as illustrated by the use of the term droit d'auteur—that is, 'author's right'—rather than a 'copy' right. As a major exporter of copyright material, Britain had an important interest in a compromise that secured at least some form of copyright protection abroad. The approach taken bears strong similarities to the contemporary evolution regarding patents: the Convention for the Protection of Literary and Artistic Works was signed in Berne in 1886.[30] From that moment on, a personal connection between the author and a member state of the Berne Union, or first publication of the work in a member state of the Union, was sufficient for protection in all member states on a national treatment basis.

---

[24] See L. Bently, U. Suthersanen, and P. Torremans (eds.) (2010) Global Copyright: Three Hundred Years since the Statute of Anne, from 1709 to Cyberspace, Proceedings of the ALAI Congress London 2009, Cheltenham/Northampton MA: Edward Elgar, Chs. 1–5.

[25] See Statute of Anne 1709, s. 1.   [26] See Statute of Anne 1709, ss. 1 and 2.

[27] Donaldson v. Beckett (1774) 2 Bro P C 129, 4 Burr 2408.   [28] Dramatic Copyright Act 1833.

[29] Literary Copyright Act 1842, s. 20.

[30] For a full account of the history of the Berne Convention and the Berne Union, see S. Ricketson (1987) The Berne Convention for the Protection of Literary and Artistic Works: 1886–1986, London: Kluwer Law International, Ch. 1; S. Ricketson and J. C. Ginsburg (2006) International Copyright and Neighbouring Rights: The Berne Convention and Beyond, vol. I, Oxford: Oxford University Press, Ch. 1.

When the Convention was revised in 1908, it was felt that there was a need to agree on further minimal rules. Copyright protection was no longer to depend upon registration or any other formality, but upon the act of creation of the work, and the term of copyright protection would last for at least the author's life plus 50 years. When these changes were incorporated into the Copyright Act 1911, it signalled the end for the Stationers' Company. The 1911 Act also widened the scope of copyright further. The producers of sound recordings were granted the exclusive right to prevent unauthorized reproductions of their recordings.[31] Significantly, this right was not given to the performing artist, but to the entrepreneur involved. The right was also labelled 'copyright', but the *droit d'auteur* tradition would instead distinguish it as a neighbouring right, because it does not directly protect the original artistic creation of the author; the work protected is derived only from the author's original artistic creation.

This right in sound recordings was an important precedent. It indicated that copyright would be flexible enough to offer protection to all works in whose creation new technical possibilities for artistic expression had been used. The Copyright Act 1956 granted protection on a similar basis in cinematograph films, broadcasts, and the typographical format of published editions.

At international level, the developing countries advocated major changes to the Berne Convention during the 1960s. The Stockholm 1967 and Paris 1971 Revisions of the Berne Convention granted, in the end, only minimal concessions with a lot of strings attached: they allow only certain translations and publications of foreign works if these are not otherwise made available.[32] In a separate development, performing artists have been granted certain rights. The Convention on the Protection of Performers, Producers of Phonograms and Broadcasting Organizations was signed in Rome in 1961. Under the provisions of this Convention, performers have the right to prevent the fixation or the broadcasting of their live performances.[33] The makers of records can prevent the reproduction of their records,[34] and broadcasting organizations can control the rebroadcasting and the public performance for an entrance fee of their broadcasts.[35] The Rome Convention has, unfortunately, never reached the same level of adherence between nations as did the Berne Convention.[36] A second Phonograms Convention, which deals with mutual protection against the unauthorized commercial copying of sound recordings, was signed in 1971. In the UK, these international provisions have been translated into the Copyright, Designs and Patents Act 1988, mainly as Part II: Rights in Performances.[37]

---

[31] Copyright Act 1911, s. 19(1). The courts later held that the producers could also prevent public performances of their recordings: *Gramophone Co. v. Cawardine* [1934] Ch 450.

[32] For more details, see the appendix to the Berne Convention upon which agreement was reached at the Paris revision conference (1971). The text of this instrument can be found on the website of the World Intellectual Property Organisation (WIPO) at <http://www.wipo.int/treaties/en/ip/berne/trtdocs_wo001.html>.

[33] See Rome Convention, Arts. 7–9. The same right does not exist in relation to recorded performances.

[34] See Rome Convention, Arts. 10–12.

[35] See Rome Convention, Art. 13. They cannot, however, control the diffusion by wire or by cable of their broadcasts.

[36] Hopefully, the World Intellectual Property Organization (WIPO) Performances and Phonograms Treaty that was signed in Geneva in 1996, and entered into force in May 2002, will be more successful. The text of this Treaty is available at <http://www.wipo.int/treaties/en/ip/wppt/trtdocs_wo034.html>.

[37] Before the Copyright, Designs and Patents Act 1988 came into force, the Performers' Protection Acts 1958–72 offered some protection to performing artists, but the level and the type of that protection were unsatisfactory.

No absolute divide between patents and copyright

This brief historical overview of the development of patent and copyright law[38] clearly demonstrates that the divide between patents—as purely industrial rights—and copyright—as a purely artistic right—was never absolute in nature. Especially in the UK, copyright always had an entrepreneurial, almost industrial, orientation. Copyright was never an exclusively artistic right, as opposed to the other industrial property rights. In recent years, this tendency has been emphasized by the use of copyright to protect computer programs. It is, however, true that copyright is different from the other rights: patents protect the invention, while copyright protects not only the creation, but also grants some strong, additional, personal rights to the creator.

These moral rights have always been an essential aspect of the French *droit d'auteur* and, in the UK, they were incorporated in their own right for the first time in the Copyright, Designs and Patents Act 1988.[39] Each right is an intellectual property right, but each right has its own characteristics. Before examining each right in detail, we will try to define the term 'intellectual property' and we will also examine whether the continued existence of 'intellectual property rights' can be justified.

A definition and a justification of intellectual property

Intellectual property rights are, first, property rights[40]—but, secondly, they are property rights in something intangible; finally, they protect innovations and creations, and reward innovative and creative activity.[41]

We will look into each of these points in a bit more detail and this will lead on to the discussion of the justification of intellectual property. We will do so mainly from an economic perspective. Suffice it to add here that the property characterization is also reflected in the European Charter of Fundamental Rights, which protects property as a fundamental right in its Art. 17(1) and then goes on to protect intellectual property in its Art. 17(2).[42]

Property rights

The essential characteristic of property rights is that they are exclusionary rights through which third parties are prohibited from the use and exploitation of the subject precluded by these rights.[43] Through property rights, externalities can be

---

[38] More details can be found in K. Garnett, G. Davies, and G. Harbottle (2011) *Copinger and Skone James on Copyright*, 16th edn, London: Sweet and Maxwell, pp. 34–56.

[39] Copyright, Designs and Patents Act 1988, Pt I, Ch. 4, ss. 77–89.

[40] See in more detail U. Mattei and A. Pradi (2007) 'Property Rights: A Comparative Law and Economics Perspective in the Global Era', in D. Porrini and G. Ramello (eds.) *Property Rights Dynamics: A Law and Economics Perspective*, Routledge, pp. 40–53; and for a law and economics justification of intellectual property rights, see W. M. Landes and R. A. Posner (2003) *The Economic Structure of Intellectual Property Law*, Cambridge, Mass: Harvard University Press.

[41] US Council for International Business (1985) *A New MTN: Priorities for Intellectual Property*, p. 3.

[42] See P. Torremans (2014) 'Article 17(2)', in S. Peers, T. Hervey, J. Kenner, and A. Ward *The EU Charter of Fundamental Rights: A Commentary*, Oxford: Hart Publishing, pp 489–517.

[43] See M. Lehmann, 'The Theory of Property Rights and the Protection of Intellectual and Industrial Property' [1985] 16 IIC 525, 530.

internalized[44]—that is, the subject of the right is brought under the control of the owner of the property right. These rights will only develop when the cost of this internalization is smaller than the gains to which it leads.[45]

If we take a bicycle as an example of an item of tangible property, it is immediately clear that the owner of the bicycle has the exclusive right to use the bicycle, and that such a monopolistic right in real and personal property is conceded almost naturally. Property rights in items such as our bicycle developed because nobody would be prepared to invest time, materials, and skills in designing and producing bicycles[46] if he or she would have no right in the result of the process that would enable him or her to benefit from that work. The most obvious way in which to do so is to sell the bicycle—but few would wish to acquire the bicycle should they be unable to acquire the exclusive right to its use. The nature of the object gives this right a monopolistic character: if someone uses the bicycle, no one else can use it. The physical nature of the unique embodiment of certain limited resources in the bicycle automatically leads to a particular competitive[47] exclusionary effect.[48]

Intangible property rights

In this respect, intellectual property rights are fundamentally different from rights in tangible property. The nature of the property that is the subject of the right and which is protected does not necessarily lead to competitive exclusionary effects. Concurrent uses of inventions by a number of manufacturers, including the patentee, or simultaneous performances of a musical are possible.[49] The invention and the musical will not perish, nor will any use or performance lessen their value.

The subject matter of intellectual property rights—that is, inventions or creations—has a link with knowledge and ideas. In economic terms, this subject matter constitutes a public asset and its use is not, by its nature, individually appropriable.[50] In many cases, imitation is even cheaper than invention or creation.[51] The competitive exclusion only arises artificially when a legally binding intellectual 'property' right is created as an intangible property right. This gives the inventor or the creator—the owners of the intangible property right—the exclusive use of the invention or the creation.

---

[44] An externality is an economic situation in which an individual's pursuit of his or her self-interest has positive or negative spillover effects on the utility or welfare of others. It can be seen as a market failure and, in this context, a property right is a tool used to correct such a market failure: see R. Ekelund and R. Tollison (1986) *Economics*, Boston, MA: Little, Brown and Co., pp. 404–5.

[45] H. Demsetz, 'Toward a Theory of Property Rights' (1967) 57 American Economy Review 347, 350; for an overview of the property rights theory, see R. Cooter and T. Ulen (1988) *Law and Economics*, New York: HarperCollins, esp. Ch. 4, but also Ch. 5.

[46] At most, they would design and produce one bicycle to get from A to B themselves, but even that cannot be taken for granted in a situation in which no property rights exist.

[47] The difference is that between 'my bicycle' and 'bicycles as a concept'.

[48] Lehmann, 'The Theory of Property Rights and the Protection of Intellectual and Industrial Property' (n. 43) at 531.

[49] Lehmann, 'The Theory of Property Rights' (n. 43) at 531.

[50] H. Ullrich, 'The Importance of Industrial Property Law and other Legal Measures in the Promotion of Technological Innovation' [1989] 28 Industrial Property 102, 103.

[51] See E. Mansfield, M. Schwartz, and, S. Wagner, 'Imitation Costs and Patents: An Empirical Study' [1981] 91 Economic Journal 907.

An economic justification

Market failure and freeriders

So why are these intangible property rights created?[52] Economists argue that, if everyone were to be allowed to use the results of innovative and creative activity freely, the problem of the 'freerider'[53] would arise.[54] No one would invest in innovation or creation, except in a couple of cases in which no other solution were available,[55] because to do so would put them at a competitive disadvantage.[56] All competitors would simply wait until someone else made the investment, because they would then be able to use the results without having invested that money in innovation and creation, and without having taken the risk that the investment might not result in the innovative or creative breakthrough at which it aimed.[57] The cost of the distribution of the knowledge is relatively insignificant.[58]

As a result, it is argued, the economy would not function adequately, because innovation and creation are essential elements in a competitive free market economy. From this perspective, innovation and creation are required for economic growth and prosperity.[59] Property rights should be created if goods and services are to be produced, and used, as efficiently as possible in such an economy.[60] The knowledge that they will have a property right in the results of their investment will stimulate individuals and enterprises to invest in research and development,[61] and these property rights should be granted to those who will economically maximize profits.[62] It is assumed that the creator or inventor will have been motivated by the desire to maximize profits—either by exploiting the invention or

---

[52] We will approach the justification issue from the point of view of the developed countries. The international transfer of technology and the different level of development in developing countries present additional problems: see e.g. P. Braga 'The Economics of Intellectual Property Rights and the GATT: A View from the South' [1989] 22 Vand J Transnat'l L 243.

[53] See R. Benko (1987) *Protecting Intellectual Property Rights: Issues and Controversies*, Washington DC: American Enterprise Institute, p. 17.

[54] Inappropriability—the lack of the opportunity to become the proprietor of the results of innovative and creative activity—causes an under-allocation of resources to research activity, innovation, and creation: see K. Arrow (1962) 'Economic Welfare and the Allocation of Resources for Invention', in National Bureau for Economic Research, *The Rate and Direction of Inventive Activity: Economic and Social Factors*, Princeton, NJ: Princeton University Press, pp. 609–25.

[55] E.g. a case in which the existing technology is completely incapable of providing any form of solution to a new technical problem that has arisen.

[56] See Ullrich, 'The Importance of Industrial Property Law and other Legal Measures in the Promotion of Technological Innovation' (n. 50) at 103.

[57] One might advance the counterargument that inventions and creations will give the innovator an amount of lead time and that the fact that it will take imitators some time to catch up would allow the innovator to recuperate his or her investment during the interim period. In many cases, however, this amount of lead time will only be a short period—too short to allow the innovator to recuperate the investment in full and make a profit. See also Mansfield, Schwartz, and Wagner, 'Imitation Costs and Patents: An Empirical Study' (n. 51) at 915 *et seq*.

[58] See Benko *Protecting Intellectual Property Rights: Issues and Controversies* (n. 53) at 17.

[59] Benko *Protecting Intellectual Property Rights* (n. 53), Ch. 4, p. 15; US Council for International Business (1985), p. 3.

[60] See B. Pretnar, 'The Economic Impact of Patents in a Knowledge-Based Market Economy' (2003) 34 IIC 887; E. Mackaay (2007) 'The Economics of Intellectual Property Rights in Civil Law Systems', working paper received from the author.

[61] P. Lunn, 'The Roles of Property Rights and Market Power in Appropriating Innovative Output' [1985] 14 J Legal Stud 423, 425.

[62] M. Lehmann, 'Property and Intellectual Property: Property Rights as Restrictions on Competition in Furtherance of Competition' [1989] 16 IIC 1, 11.

creation him- or herself, or by having it exploited by a third party—so the creator or inventor is granted the rights.[63]

This argument applies as well to intangible property rights such as patents, which determine the value of an item in a direct way, as it does to rights such as trade marks, which do so only indirectly through their use as a means of communication.[64]

It is also worth mentioning that this is not a free-standing economic argument. From a fundamental moral perspective every human being has an equal right to freedom and well-being. New inventions and products, new literary and artistic works that add to culture and knowledge, etc are from this perspective capable of promoting that right to freedom and well-being.[65] That needs of course to work for both right holders and users in an intellectual property context and this leads us to the balance that needs to be struck between exclusive rights on the one hand and user rights on the other. Both the fundamental moral imperative that underpin the structures of our society and the legal rules that come with it need to safeguard and promote that equal right to freedom and well-being for each and every human being and the economic reasoning that requires intellectual property exclusive rights to deal with the risk of market failures lead us in the same direction. Exclusive rights can only be justified if they strike the right balance and achieve their fundamental aims. We now turn to the way in which such a balance can be determined and achieved.

Exclusivity and perfect competition

But how does such a legally created, monopolistic, exclusive property right fit in with the free market ideal of perfect competition? At first sight, every form of monopoly might seem to be incompatible with free competition, but we have already demonstrated that some form of property right is required to enhance economic development: competition can only play its role as market regulator if the products of human labour are protected by property rights.[66] In this respect, the exclusive monopolistic character of the property rights is coupled with the fact that these rights are transferable. These rights are marketable: they can, for example, be sold as an individual item. It is also necessary to distinguish between various levels of economic activity, as far as economic development and competition are concerned. The market mechanism is more sophisticated than the competition–monopoly dichotomy. Competitive restrictions at one level may be necessary to promote competition at another level.

Three levels can be distinguished: production, consumption, and innovation, as demonstrated in Figure 1.1. Property rights in goods enhance competition on the production level, but this form of ownership restricts competition on the consumption level. One has to acquire the ownership of the goods before one is allowed to consume them and goods owned by other economic players are not directly available for one's consumption. In turn, intellectual property imposes competitive restrictions on the production level: only the owner of the patent in an invention may use the invention and only the owner of the copyright in a literary work may produce additional copies of that work. These restrictions benefit competition on the innovative level. The availability of property rights on each level guarantees the development of competition on the next level.

---

[63] For an economic–philosophical approach, see also E. Mackaay (1991) 'Economic and Philosophical Aspects of Intellectual Property Rights', in M. Van Hoecke (ed.) *The Socio-Economic Role of Intellectual Property Rights, Brussels: Story-Scientia*, pp. 1–30.

[64] See Lehmann, 'The Theory of Property Rights and the Protection of Intellectual and Industrial Property' (n. 43) at 531.

[65] See S. Ang (2013) *The Moral Dimensions of Intellectual Property Rights*, Cheltenham: Edward Elgar Publishing.

[66] Lehmann, 'Property and Intellectual Property: Property Rights as Restrictions on Competition in Furtherance of Competition' (n. 62) at 12.

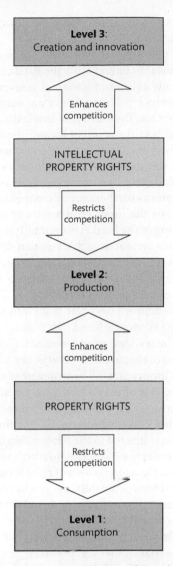

Figure 1.1 A justification of IP rights

Property rights are a prerequisite for the normal functioning of the market mechanism.[67] To take the example of patents: '*patents explicitly prevent the diffusion of new technology to guarantee the existence of technology to diffuse in the future*'.[68] Trade marks, meanwhile, distinguish identical goods or services of different sources. They therefore allow the consumer to distinguish between such products and services, and grant the right holder the exclusive right to apply the mark to the goods and services for which it has been registered. In doing so, trade marks enable competition between producers of identical goods or services. They therefore encourage the availability of a wider variety of

[67] Lehmann, 'The Theory of Property Rights and the Protection of Intellectual and Industrial Property' (n. 43) at 539.
[68] Benko, *Protecting Intellectual Property Rights: Issues and Controversies*, (n. 53), Ch. 4, p. 19.

goods and services between which the consumer can distinguish, by means of the trade mark, in terms of quality, price, etc.

This clearly demonstrates that it is not correct to see intellectual property rights as monopolies that are in permanent conflict with the fundamental rule of free competition. Free competition can only exist, and a market economy can only flourish, when certain restrictions in furtherance of competition are accepted. Intellectual property rights are necessary to achieve this. The main problem is that this only justifies the existence of exclusive property rights as the result of innovative activity. The particular form that intellectual property rights have taken in a particular national intellectual property statute—and, even more, the way in which these rights are used and exercised—are not automatically justified by this theory. The restrictions on competition are only justified in so far as they are restrictions in furtherance of competition on the next level, which is either the production level or the innovation level; any restriction that goes further hinders the optimal functioning of the market economy. It is the task of the provisions on competition law to regulate this system in such a way that this optimal level of functioning is achieved and maintained. This coexistence of intellectual property and the rules on free competition is a permanent balancing act, and one of the most challenging and interesting parts of the study of intellectual property.

If we focus on patents for a moment, in order to go into a bit more detail, we have to start from the premise that the economic justification does not give us ready-made rules on every aspect of patent law. Instead, we are confronted with a constant, built-in dialectic tension between the protection of the patented—that is, already realized—innovation and the promotion of subsequent innovation.[69] The strongest possible protection is therefore not only not a logical consequence of the economic justification, but would also unduly focus on one aspect of that tension. The promotion of subsequent innovation that builds on what has already been achieved would be harmed—and this would be all the more serious, because the tension is not restricted to the relationship between the patentee and its competitors. It does, indeed, influence the overall market's actual and potential competitive dynamics. What is needed, therefore, is a set of rules for a patent system that respects and enhances a rich dialectic interrelationship between the need to guarantee a differential return on activities and investments in research and development, on the one hand, and the need to safeguard the actual chance of third parties' subsequent innovation and the competitive fabric of the market as a whole, on the other. This balance will be struck in the rules on patentability—that is, that certain thresholds need to be passed before a patent is warranted—and in the scope of the patent and the limitations to the exclusive right, among others.[70]

An ideal patent system that can be fully justified will, therefore, not simply involve rewarding inventors in order to stimulate them to invent more, or stimulating them to achieve, in turn, inventive steps. The finer points of the system set out here require that such a patent system will more specifically reward:

> the innovation already developed in such a way that the reward granted to the current inventor stimulates both the inventor to continue and third parties to develop a subsequent innovation which might compete with the preceding one, thus also spurring on the first innovator, in a virtuous pro-innovation and pro-competition dynamic process.[71]

---

[69] See G. Ghidini (2006) *Intellectual Property and Competition Law: The Innovation Nexus*, Cheltenham/ Northampton, MA: Edward Elgar, p. 14.

[70] Ghidini, *Intellectual Property and Competition Law* (n. 69) at p. 14.

[71] Ghidini, *Intellectual Property and Competition Law* (n. 69) at p. 24.

Goods perish through use, while intangible property is—at least in theory—perpetual.[72] But the socio-economic value of these rights is not so important that a perpetual restriction on competition is necessary and justifiable to enhance competition on other levels. Innovative activity will be sufficiently enhanced, without restrictions of competition on the production level that are too far-reaching, when the intellectual property right is restricted in time. For patents, which grant the patentee extensive restrictive powers and whose protection is wide in scope, the term of protection is relatively short (20 years). From now on, literary works are to be protected under copyright for a period of the life of the author plus 70 years, but the protection granted is weaker than that offered under patents: only the particular expression of an idea is protected; the idea as such is left unprotected. This attempt to get the balance between restriction on, and freedom of, competition right through the use of a fixed term can be seen as lacking precision and potentially unjust, but introducing a sliding scale would require the determination of the term of protection on the basis of the merits of each individual invention or creation. This would create massive administrative costs that outweigh the benefits derived from the system and, on top of this, it would create an undesirable climate of legal uncertainty.[73]

A duty to exercise

Another way of getting the balance right is the duty to exercise and use, which is linked to patent and trade mark rights. Compulsory use and compulsory licences are an integral component of most intellectual property legislations. The idea behind this is, first of all, that use of the intellectual property right will provide an income to its owner and that this profit will encourage him to continue his innovative work. The only reason why a restriction of competition at the level of production is acceptable is the enhancement of competition on the innovative level, through the possibility for the owner of the right to realize a profit. This justification collapses if this right is not used, a defect that is remedied by the introduction of the duty to exercise and use.[74] The weaker protection accorded under copyright law renders this restriction superfluous in that area; neither does such a duty exist for real and personal property. This can be seen as an important difference between intangible industrial property, and real and personal property.

A second reason for the obligation to use is the feeling that the grant of an exclusive right should be counterbalanced by the fact that the previously unavailable subject matter of the right is made available to society. The obligation to use is necessary because, due to the exclusive right, the owner of the intellectual property right is the only one who makes it available. More specifically, for patents, there is the additional requirement to reveal the technical details and specifications of the invention, in order to bring them into the public domain. In exchange for the exclusive right, society has the right to share the development of technical knowledge, and, eventually, to use it for further research and further developments.

This represents an additional advantage of the patent system, because the alternative is to be found in the use of the secrecy system. Technological developments are, in the absence of a patent system,[75] kept secret. Society is unable to share this new knowledge

---

[72] It may, however, lose its economic value after a number of years: e.g. an inventive production process protected by a patent can be applied indefinitely, but will, after a number of years, be overtaken by new technological developments and so lose its economic value.

[73] For more details, see Lehmann, 'The Theory of Property Rights and the Protection of Intellectual and Industrial Property' (n. 43) at 535–6.

[74] Lehmann, 'The Theory of Property Rights' (n. 43) at 532–3.

[75] This technique can also be used as an alternative in a particular case for a patent application if the costs of revealing the technical detail of the invention and the other costs linked to such an application are perceived to be higher than the benefits of the stronger protection offered by the patent system. Potentially, the duration of the secrecy is endless, which is also an advantage over the patent system.

and the inventor can only use the invention in a way that does not reveal the technical functioning of it, because, once in the public domain, it can be used freely by all of the competitors. In that instance, the inventor is put in a very weak position. It has been demonstrated that a patent system that grants the inventor adequate property rights fulfils the task reserved for such a system in a market economy in a better way. The law of secrecy cannot replace the patent system fully; it can only be a useful addition to it.[76]

Copyright involves other factors too

To this point, we have mainly been concerned with patents and trade marks. Historically, copyright developed on a very different basis, with a lot of emphasis on the link between the author and his or her work. An attempt was made to make sure that it was the author, rather than someone else, who would secure the benefits resulting from the work and its exploitation.

Over the years, however, copyright has increasingly been used to protect the commercial exploitation of the work and new, more technologically orientated, types of work have been protected by copyright.[77] It is therefore submitted that the same economic justification theory can now be applied to copyright.[78] Protection against the copying of the work, for example, will restrict competition between the right holder and his or her exploitation of the work, on the one hand, and copyists, on the other. Such a restriction will encourage the right holder to create more works, thus enhancing competition at the higher, creative level, because there is now more of a prospect of securing a return. This is no doubt not the only motivation for authors, but it is clearly an important factor.

But one additional problem arises in relation to the economic analysis of copyright. Copyright has to strike a balance between providing the incentives for authors, on the one hand, and the right of access to information of the public, on the other. In the words of the famous study by Landes and Posner:

> Copyright protection—the right of the copyright's owner to prevent others from making copies—trades off the costs of limiting access to a work against the benefits of providing incentives to create the work in the first place. Striking the correct balance between access and incentives is the central problem in copyright law.[79]

Cooter and Ulen focus on the same issue when they argue: '*Put succinctly, the dilemma is that without a legal monopoly too little of the information will be produced but with the legal monopoly too little of the information will be used.*'[80]

Let us analyse the implications of these specificities of copyright in a little more detail. The innovation and creation level interacts with the production level; this is a given. In the copyright sphere, we are dealing with works that are the expression of ideas. Starting from these ideas, one has to recognize that they are, by their nature, public goods, and can therefore freely be accessed and used by anyone. The way in which these ideas enter the public domain is through their expression by an individual author, because such expression is required for the transmission of the idea. From an economic point of view, it is also important to keep in mind that such access is non-exhaustive in nature: the

---

[76] See Lunn, 'The Roles of Property Rights and Market Power in Appropriating Innovative Output' (n. 61) at 423.

[77] J. Reichman, 'Charting the Collapse of the Patent–Copyright Dichotomy: Premises for a Restructured International Intellectual Property System' (1995) 13 Cardozo Arts and Ent LJ 475.

[78] See R. Watt (2000) *Copyright and Economic Theory: Friends or Foes?*, Cheltenham/Northampton, MA: Edward Elgar.

[79] W. Landes and R. Posner, 'An Economic Analysis of Copyright Law' (1989) 18 J Legal Stud 325, 326.

[80] R. Cooter and T. Ulen (1988) *Law and Economics*, New York: HarperCollins, p. 145.

consumption of the expression does not necessarily make the expression and its material support unsuitable or unavailable for further consumption. It is also the case that, in the light of modern (digital) technological advances, the costs of reproduction and distribution of the expression of the idea have become marginal, and that such reproduction and distribution is easily achievable and can be done in a minimum amount of time. There is therefore plenty of room for free riders. The situation is therefore entirely in favour of competition at the production level; at the innovation and creation level, there is very little in terms of incentive to create. The creator may not be able to recoup the cost of production, because the cost of copying is lower and there is no tool to reap any substantial benefit from such creative activity. In economic terms, then, there is no efficient market of the authors' expression of ideas.[81]

Copyright, therefore, is the tool that is created to give authors a right in their expression of ideas, hence securing for them appropriate profits derived from their act of creation. Copyright will lead to the creation of an immaterial property right in the expression of an idea by the author, a right that the author can use to secure appropriate profit from that act of creation on the market.[82] This will enhance creation by providing an incentive, and therefore competition on the innovation and creation level will be stimulated, while any such right will inevitably limit competition at the production level, because competitors are no longer free to copy the copyright work. A restriction on competition is put in place in furtherance of competition.[83]

Copyright fulfils here the 'pro-competitive' regulating role filled by the property right when it comes to the consumption and the production level—but an important distinction must be drawn. Property rights are a legal recognition of a situation—that is, of the physical possession of and control over the goods—whereas copyright is not based on a de facto situation at all: it is rather an artificially created right, put in place by the legislator to regulate competition at the innovation and creation level, and to provide the much-needed incentive to create. This difference gives copyright a different standing. The legislator created it specifically as a tool through which to enhance competition.

Copyright plays therefore, *mutatis mutandis*, the same pro-competitive role in relation to literary and artistic works that patents play in relation to inventions. An important additional factor in the context of copyright, however, is the need to safeguard access to information and freedom of expression. This reflects itself in the basic rule that copyright will not protect ideas, but only their expression. The threshold for that expression to be protected will be the fact that it satisfies the originality expression that allows one to distinguish it from the mere idea. It has been said that copyright therefore protects '*independently achieved expressive results*',[84] which applies both in a *droit d'auteur* tradition, with its 'subjective' notion of originality, and in an Anglo-Saxon copyright environment. In the *droit d'auteur* tradition, the author's personal expression is therefore protected as a creative work, irrespective of the mediocrity or otherwise, of the expressive results; copyright systems focus instead on the concept of independent creation. Protection by means of copyright, therefore, depends on the objective attainment of a result—again, irrespective of its mediocrity or otherwise in terms of creative effort—that arises from a

[81] G. Ramello (2002) 'Copyright and Antitrust Issues', <http://www.serci.org/2002/ramello.pdf>, p. 8.

[82] K. Maskus (2000) *Intellectual Property Rights in the Global Economy*, Washington DC: Institute for International Economics, pp. 28–32.

[83] See Lehmann, 'Property and Intellectual Property: Property Rights as Restrictions on Competition in Furtherance of Competition' (n. 62) at 1–15.

[84] Ghidini, *Intellectual Property and Competition Law* (n. 69) at 54.

contribution that is neither copied from anyone else, nor reproduced using known standard models.[85]

Up until now, we have looked at 'traditional' copyright in literary and artistic works,
such as books and sculptures. It is however necessary to add that copyright has developed in two ways in recent years that may have influenced the position: on the one hand,
copyright has been expanded to protect the results of technological evolutions; on the
other, we have seen an increasing emphasis on the economic interests of those who
exploit copyright works, such as producers and publishers. It is important to note that,
as a result, copyright is increasingly used to protect information goods and the investment needed for the creation of these goods. It is clear that, in these circumstances, the
level of originality involved in the creation of such information goods is lower, and that
the link with the author and his or her creativity, which makes the work his or her own
individual creation, is weaker. This must also weaken the justification for strong copyright protection for these information works, because these elements were described as
the basis for the economic justification of copyright.[86] Another important element is the
fact that, by their nature, information goods have a poor substitutability.[87] This applies,
to some extent, to all copyright works: for example we are interested in a novel because
of the way in which the author has expressed the idea and therefore the novel cannot be
easily substituted by another novel in which another author expresses the same idea in
his or her different own way. This factor is, however, more strongly present in relation to
information goods.

A special type of monopoly

It may well be that some additional remarks on the type of monopoly that is granted by
intellectual property rights are appropriate. That monopoly is, in no way, absolute and it is
limited in time; it is also subject to competition with similar products, similar trade marks,
etc. Inventions compete with substitute technologies, so that the profits based on the exclusive use of the invention are rarely monopolistic rents.[88] The latter situation only arises in
those rare situations in which an invention is such a radical step forward that there is a
(temporary) absolute lack of substitutability.[89] In copyright, meanwhile, only one particular expression of an otherwise unprotected idea is granted copyright protection.

Intellectual property rights do not give their owners an automatic profit: they are
directly oriented towards demand. The reward that they provide for innovative activity
depends upon the competitive structure of the market concerned. Only when the market
appreciates the innovation on its merits will the owner be rewarded and make a profit:[90]
*'The ownership of intangibles in the sense of abstract property rights…is therefore limited
to a temporary, ephemeral competitive restriction.'*[91] Intellectual property rights confer

---

[85] Ghidini, *Intellectual Property and Competition Law* (n. 69).

[86] S. Lemarchand, O. Fréget, and F. Sardain, 'Biens informationnels: entre droits intellectuels et droit de
la concurrence' [2003] 6 Propriétés Intellectuelles 11, 18.

[87] Ramello, 'Copyright and Antitrust Issues' (n. 81) at 8.

[88] Ullrich, 'The Importance of Industrial Property Law and other Legal Measures in the Promotion of
Technological Innovation' (n. 50) at 105.

[89] Lehmann, 'The Theory of Property Rights and the Protection of Intellectual and Industrial Property'
(n. 43) at 537.

[90] See Ullrich, 'The Importance of Industrial Property Law and other Legal Measures in the Promotion
of Technological Innovation' (n. 50) at 112.

[91] Lehmann, 'The Theory of Property Rights and the Protection of Intellectual and Industrial Property'
(n. 43) at 537.

exclusive rights, but they hardly ever confer a real monopoly, in the sense that the monopolist can act in an arbitrary way without being influenced by his or her competitors.

Those in favour and those against

It has to be added that a number of economists have argued against the existence of intellectual property rights and especially against the existence of patents. In their view, patents do not promote technological innovation—or there are more effective ways in which to do so.[92] These critics are, however, unable to provide clear evidence that intellectual property rights do not fulfil a useful economical function and none of their alternatives has ever been tested successfully in practice.[93] All they can demonstrate is that some features of the existing patent system cannot be justified economically and that the existing system does not always achieve a perfect balance between the various levels of competition. This is undoubtedly true, but the solution is not the abolition of the whole system. What is required might rather be described as 'fine-tuning' of the system.[94]

There is also a substantial amount of empirical economic evidence that supports the economic justification for the existence of intellectual property rights. Most of these studies deal with patents, and the causal relationship between the availability of patent protection and investment in research and development and in innovation.[95]

Who gets the right?

Thus economic theory provides a justification for the existence of intellectual property rights. A related point is the issue of who gets these intellectual property rights. It has been suggested that the economic theory proves that it is valuable to have intellectual property rights, but is unable to guarantee that the enforcement of these rights will have valuable results in each individual case. The author and the inventor must obtain these rights to secure the best possible system—and this can only be accepted if one uses labour theory to justify the allocation of the property rights whose existence the economic theory justifies.[96]

Labour theory was formulated by John Locke[97] and is the combination of two concepts: the first is that everyone has a property right in the labour of his own body and brain; the second adds that the application of human labour to an unowned object gives you a property right in it. When applied to intellectual property rights,[98] this might

[92] See e.g. F. Machlup (1957) *An Economic Review of the Patent System*, Study No. 15 of the Senate Judiciary Subcommittee on Patents, Trademarks and Copyrights, Washington DC: US Congress; E. Penrose (1951) *The Economics of the International Patent System*, Baltimore, MD: Johns Hopkins University Press; see also F. Machlup and E. Penrose, 'The Patent Controversy in the Nineteenth Century' (1950) 10 J Econ Hist 1.

[93] This is admitted by Machlup, *An Economic Review of the Patent System* (n. 92) at the end of his study.

[94] See Beier, 'The Significance of the Patent System for Technical, Economic and Social Progress' (n. 14) at 572.

[95] E.g. C. T. Taylor and A. Silberston (1973) *The Economic Impact of the Patent System*, Cambridge: Cambridge University Press; the 1973–4 study of the Ifo-Institut für Wirtschaftsforschung in Munich concerning the relationship between the Patent System and Technical Progress, which is discussed in K. H. Oppenlander, 'Patent Policies and Technical Progress in the Federal Republic of Germany' [1977] IIC 97; A. Silberston (1987) *The Economic Importance of Patents*, Cambridge: Cambridge University Press. An overview of older studies can be found in J. Schmookler (1966) *Invention and Economic Growth*, Cambridge, MA: Harvard University Press; see also Lunn, 'The Roles of Property Rights and Market Power in Appropriating Innovative Output' (n. 61) at 423.

[96] H. Spector, 'An Outline of a Theory Justifying Intellectual and Industrial Property Rights' [1989] 8 EIPR 270, 272–3.

[97] J. Locke (1690) The Second Treatise of Government, Pt 27, reproduced in P. Laslett (ed.) (1970) *Two Treaties of Government*, Cambridge: Cambridge University Press.

[98] See R. Nozick (1974) *Anarchy, State and Utopia*, Oxford: Blackwell, pp. 181–2.

explain why it is the author who gets the copyright in the book and why it is the inventor who gets the patent in the invention.

The combination of the economic theory and the labour theory provides a full justification for the system of intellectual property rights.[99] This reference to the labour theory explicitly justifies the fact that it is the author or the inventor who should own the intellectual property right—but it is submitted here that this is already implicit in the economic theory. An intellectual property right, as a restriction on competition at production level (because not everyone can produce the goods protected by the right), will not stimulate competition on the innovation level if the right is not given to the innovator, whether an author or an inventor. One will only be stimulated to innovate when one gets the intellectual property rights in the innovation. This effect, which is the key element in the economic justification theory for intellectual property, disappears when someone else gets the intellectual property rights in the innovation. The actual exploitation of the right can be undertaken by the right holder or by a licensee—this does not affect the justification at all.

Other ways of justifying intellectual property

Thus economic analysis justifies the continued existence of intellectual property rights and economic history confirms the correctness of the analysis.[100] Our focus on the economic and utilitarian approach is also explained by the fact that over the last decades the EU and the construction of the single market has been the main source of developments in intellectual property. The same economic and utilitarian approach underpins both our justification for intellectual property and the single market. One nevertheless also finds a series of other elements of justification in an historical analysis and in a socio-economic analysis (reward theory).[101]

While these two theses, based on natural rights and rewards, are no longer fashionable as justifications for the existence of intellectual property rights,[102] the possibility to reward the inventor is still rightfully considered to be a positive side effect of the patent system.

A historical analysis

There seems to be a need for a system protecting innovation once a country starts to develop its industry. This becomes especially clear when one considers the example of patents. There is a correlation between industrialization and patent protection: patents are introduced when the process of industrialization starts and each increase in the level of patent protection corresponds to progress in the industrialization process. This evolution is visible in most European countries from the fifteenth century onwards, but it becomes very prominent in the nineteenth century, as a result of the Industrial Revolution.

It has to be added that this link between patents and industrialization is based on the idea that a country will not be able to benefit from the industrialization process in Europe if it does not introduce a system of patent protection—a conclusion that was reached as a

---

[99] Spector, 'An Outline of a Theory Justifying Intellectual and Industrial Property Rights' (n. 96) at 273.

[100] See Lehmann, 'Property and Intellectual Property: Property Rights as Restrictions on Competition in Furtherance of Competition' (n. 62) at 11.

[101] Beier, 'The Significance of the Patent System for Technical, Economic and Social Progress' (n. 14) at 563.

[102] Benko, *Protecting Intellectual Property Rights: Issues and Controversies*, (n. 53), Ch. 4, p. 17.

result of an active debate in which both the advantages and disadvantages of the introduction of a system of patent protection were fully taken into account.[103]

Apart from this historical correlation, we should turn our attention also to the evolution of economic output. The introduction of a system of patent protection in a country's legal system goes together with a clear increase in the industrial production of that country. We can refer here to the English example in the eighteenth century, but all other industrialized countries might equally serve as examples. Another striking feature is the high level of industrialization in all countries with a high level of patent protection. It might even be demonstrated that their level of industrialization is higher than the level reached by countries that refuse to grant patent protection or which only grant a weak form of patent protection. The successes of the Spanish and Italian pharmaceutical industries, and the Swiss chemical industry, at times when patent protection was not available do not prove the contrary: no new product emerged and success was based purely on imitation. This situation only improved with the introduction of a system of patent protection.[104] It is not, however, possible to establish a causal link between these two facts in a conclusive manner. Factors other than the patent system may be responsible for the higher level of industrialization.[105]

These historical elements provide additional arguments in favour of the patent system and a system of intellectual property rights in general, but, taken in isolation, they do not provide a complete and convincing justification for the existence of intellectual property rights. Other theses that have been suggested as justification for the existence of patents rely on natural rights, rewards for the inventor, and disclosure.[106] Immediately after the French Revolution, a tendency to explain and justify individual property rights as natural rights, on the basis of a series of moral and philosophical arguments, became fashionable and was extended to intangible property, such as patents and other intellectual property rights[107]—but this theory never found much support outside France.

The reward theory

Similar arguments are found in the reward theory, which sees patents as a reward owed by society to inventors in return for their creativity and their services to society[108]—that is, that society has a moral obligation to compensate and to reward the inventors.[109] But this argument cannot justify the existence of the patent system, even if one agrees that the inventor should be rewarded.

We demonstrated that a patent offers only a potential monopoly—that is, a potential reward to the inventor. Only those patents that are commercially attractive and the

---

[103] See Beier, 'The Significance of the Patent System for Technical, Economic and Social Progress' (n. 14) at 571–2.

[104] Beier, 'The Significance of the Patent System for Technical, Economic and Social Progress' (n. 14) at 573–4.

[105] Beier, 'The Significance of the Patent System for Technical, Economic and Social Progress' (n. 14) at 573–4.

[106] Beier, 'The Significance of the Patent System for Technical, Economic and Social Progress' (n. 14) at 16.

[107] This theory was endorsed by the French National Assembly and became part of the Preamble to the patent law of that period: see the quotation in Machlup and Penrose, 'The Patent Controversy in the Nineteenth Century' (n. 92) at 11.

[108] This theory applies also to the other intellectual property rights.

[109] Machlup and Penrose, 'The Patent Controversy in the Nineteenth Century' (n. 92) at 17, quoted, in this respect, J. S. Mill's statement: *'That he, the inventor, ought to be compensated and rewarded... will not be denied... it would be a gross immorality of the law to set everybody free to use a person's work without his consent, and without giving him an equivalent.'*

commercial exploitation of which is successful offer a reward to the inventor. Furthermore, this is an indirect reward. A direct reward—such as a lump sum, a decoration, or a title—would be a better idea if the aim of the measure is to reward the inventor.[110] The inventor would be assured of a reward and would be able to assess the nature or amount of the reward in advance.

Encouraging disclosure

A further thesis that is worth mentioning emphasizes the role that the patent system plays in encouraging inventors to disclose their secrets to society. Diffusion of technology, which is considered to be desirable for society, will only take place when inventors make the technical details of their inventions public. If, as already explained, there is no protection for the invention and everyone can use the technology freely, the inventor will rely on secrecy for protection, because imitation of the invention entails only minimal costs when compared to those of the inventor. The technical details of new inventions will not be disclosed in such a system and society will not benefit to the same extent.[111]

Although this theory is helpful and the disclosure of technical knowledge is a very positive aspect of the patent system, it has to be said that its value is, in part, undermined by two important details. The inventor without patent protection would have some lead time during which he or she would enjoy a kind of market monopoly and during which he or she could collect a reward for the work, because it would take the imitator some time before being ready to produce and to enter the market.[112] This is reinforced by the fact that the exploitation of a patent quite often requires a substantial amount of secret know-how, which the imitator will have to acquire if it is to exploit the invention successfully.[113] In many cases, however, that lead time may not be long enough for the inventor to recover all costs and to make a profit.[114]

The special position of copyright

The last paragraphs have focused extensively on patents. Many of the arguments can also be used for trade marks, but are there perhaps other additional elements that can justify the existence of copyright? Originally, copyright dealt with literary and artistic works. It could be argued that the author was given certain property rights in these works to reward his or her artistic performance, or that the author's claims were based on a natural or moral right. Specifically, in the *droit d'auteur* system, a lot of emphasis is placed on the fact that the work involves an expression of the personality of the author. Copyright is then also given certain aspects of a personality right (cf. moral rights) and does not

---

[110] See M. Blakeney (1989) *Legal Aspects of the Transfer of Technology to Developing Countries*, Oxford: ESC, pp. 51–3.

[111] See Blakeney, *Legal Aspects of the Transfer of Technology to Developing Countries* (n. 110) at 53; R. Benko (1987) *Protecting Intellectual Property Rights: Issues and Controversies* (n. 53), Ch. 4, pp. 16–17.

[112] See M. Braunstein, W. J. Baumol, and J. W. Mansfield (1980) 'The Economics of R&D', in B. V. Dean and J. C. Goldhar (eds.) *Management of Research and Innovation*, New York: John Wiley and Sons, pp. 19–32.

[113] See F. M. Scherer (1980) *Industrial Market Structure and Economic Performance*, Chicago, IL: University of Chicago Press, p. 447.

[114] Reichman, 'Charting the Collapse of the Patent–Copyright Dichotomy: Premises for a Restructured International Intellectual Property System' (n. 77), argues, in this respect, that patents and copyright should be restricted to the really desirable highly creative or innovative cases; anything else in between should be protected only by lead time. When necessary—because of the speed at which copying or reverse engineering takes place in the new digital environment—that lead time can be created artificially.

remain a pure property right. In general one could summarize matters by saying that there are four principles that justify the copyright system: just reward for labour, stimulus to creativity, natural law, and social requirements.

The strong emphasis on natural or moral right was perfectly acceptable for works, such as novels, songs, and poems, but it becomes increasingly difficult to justify copyright exclusively on this basis. Clearly, this theory does not suit computer programs and other highly technological works, which are now equally protected by copyright. As copyright has entered the technological field, it has becomes clear that its real justification is equally to be found in the economic justification theory.[115] Works protected by copyright are knowledge goods; they are concerned with creativity and innovation, and present, in this respect, the same characteristics as inventions. They too need to be protected as economic rights, if artistic, creative, and innovative activity in this area is to be promoted.

There is, however, one essential difference when it comes to inventions and trade marks. The right involved here is a copyright, the subject matter of which is the particular expression in a literary work, in a piece of music, in a sculpture, etc., by the author of an idea. There is no direct link between the copyright and the idea embodied in the work. One can distinguish between a book and the ideas expressed in it, whereas an invention and the novel idea involved are one and the same inseparable concept.[116] The ideas contained in a work protected under copyright are, on top of that, not necessarily novel. It would not be possible to justify the protection of these ideas under the economic justification theory. Fortunately, this is not necessary, because copyright only protects the expression by the author of a certain set of ideas. These ideas themselves are not protected by copyright.

But let us come back briefly to the link between the author and the work. This special aspect of copyright does not only refer to a personality right as we have seen, but also incorporates an important link with human rights. René Cassin, one of the architects of the current human rights framework, has emphasized the importance of the act of creation and the link with the creator in relation to rights that may flow from it. In his view, the ability and the desire to develop intellectual and creative activities from which copyright works may result is potentially found in all human beings. As such, it deserves respect and protection in the same way as do all other basic faculties that are common to all human beings. This would mean that creators can claim rights by the very fact of their creation.

This is a broad statement and it is by no means clear that such rights are, by definition, human rights, or that they must cover all creations and necessarily take the format of an exclusive right in such creations.[117] Further analysis is therefore warranted.

The first key provision in an international instrument that identifies copyright as a human right is found in Art. 27 of the Universal Declaration of Human Rights.[118]

---

[115] See, in M. Van Hoecke (ed.) (1991) *The Socio-Economic Role of Intellectual Property Rights*, Brussels: Story-Scientia; W. Grosheide, 'Economic Aspects of Intellectual Property Rights, Especially of Copyright', pp. 65–72; and A. Strowel, 'An Appraisal of the Economic Analysis of Copyright Law', pp. 103–35; R. Watt (2000) *Copyright and Economic Theory: Friends or Foes?*, Cheltenham/Northampton, MA: Edward Elgar.

[116] See R. Benko (1987) *Protecting Intellectual Property Rights: Issues and Controversies* (n. 53), Ch. 4, pp. 21 and 23.

[117] R. Cassin (1959) 'L'Intégration, parmi les droits fondamentaux de l'homme, des droits des créateurs des oeuvres de l'esprit', in M. Mélanges Plaisant, *Etudes sur la propriété industrielle, littéraire et artistique*, Paris: Sirey, p. 229; M. Vivant, 'Le Droit d'auteur: un droit de l'homme?' (1997) 174 RIDA 60, 87.

[118] Adopted and proclaimed by the United Nations in 1948 as General Assembly Resolution 217A(III) of 10 December 1948, specifically in relation to copyright: see J. A. L. Sterling (2008) *World Copyright Law*, 3rd edn, London: Sweet and Maxwell, pp. 47–50.

According to that Article, everyone has first of all '*the right to the protection of the moral and material interests resulting from scientific, literary or artistic production of which he is the author*'. But it is equally important to note another element stated in Art. 27(1): that '*everyone has the right freely to participate in the cultural life of the community, to enjoy the arts and to share in scientific advancement and its benefits*'. Copyright will therefore have to strike a balance somewhere in the middle.

The second key provision in an international instrument that identifies copyright as a human right is found in the International Covenant on Economic, Social, and Cultural Rights.[119] This Covenant can be seen as a follow-up action on the Universal Declaration of Human Rights—but it is important to note that this follow-up action took the form of a treaty and that, as such, it can impose legally binding obligations to implement its provisions on states that became contracting parties to it. Article 15 of the Covenant is very clear in this respect, and imposes a number of responsibilities and steps to be taken on contracting states in the following way:

> (2) The steps to be taken by the States Parties to the present Covenant to achieve the full realization of this right shall include those necessary for the conservation, development and the diffusion of science and culture.
>
> (3) The States Parties to the present Covenant undertake to respect the freedom indispensable for scientific research and creative activity.
>
> (4) The States Parties to the present Covenant recognize the benefits to be derived from the encouragement and development of international contacts and cooperation in the scientific and cultural fields.

These obligations apply to the substantive rights granted in Art. 15(1) of the Covenant, which is very much based on Art. 27 of the Universal Declaration of Human Rights, comprising the rights of everyone:

(a) to take part in cultural life;

(b) to enjoy the benefits of scientific progress and its applications;

(c) to benefit from the protection of the moral and the material interests resulting from any scientific, literary, or artistic production of which he is the author.

Once more, the need for copyright to strike a balance emerges, but the identification of copyright—or at least certain aspects of it—as a human right is an additional justification for the existence of copyright.[120] But it is not a complete justification, because it does not indicate where the balance lies, and, as such, it is not able to justify each and every aspect of the current shape of copyright law.

The current economic importance of intellectual property

Our historical overview demonstrated that intellectual property rights were introduced because they were thought to be essential for further industrial and economic development. We will now try to analyse the current economic importance of intellectual

---

[119] The International Covenant on Economic, Social, and Cultural Rights, 993 UNTS 3, GA Res 2200(XXI) 21 UN GAOR Supp (No. 16), 49, UN Doc A/6316 (1966), adopted on 16 December 1966.

[120] For a complete analysis on this point, see P. Torremans (2004) 'Copyright as a Human Right', in P. Torremans (ed.) *Copyright and Human Rights*, The Hague: Kluwer Law International, pp. 1–20 and P. Torremans (2008) 'Copyright (and Other Intellectual Property Rights) as a Human Right', in P. Torremans (ed.) *Intellectual Property and Human Rights, Enhanced Edition of Copyright and Human Rights*, Alphen aan den Rijn: Kluwer Law International, pp. 195–215.

property rights. It is submitted, on the basis of indirect evidence, that this importance is huge.

The GATT–World Trade Organization (WTO) agreement contained the TRIPS initiative on intellectual property. This initiative was a reaction by the governments that were concerned by the complaints of industry. Figures pointing to multimillion-dollar losses in royalties due to the counterfeiting of famous trade marks in countries that offered a low level of protection for intellectual property rights were published by industrial sources. One can understand and accept these figures on the basis that almost every product, and almost every service, now bears a trade mark. In 1974, the World Intellectual Property Organization (WIPO) estimated that 4 million trade marks were in use in the world[121] and there is every reason to believe that there are more trade marks in use now than there were in 1974. The GATT–WTO agreement attaches great importance to the strengthening of the protection for trade marks and the other intellectual property rights, which clearly emphasizes their tremendous economic value.

The evolution to an economic system based on high technological developments has resulted in the proliferation of patents. Many of these patents have an enormous commercial value.[122] Just think about the whole evolution in the field of genetic engineering: these disease-resistant plants, purified seeds, and drugs produced by genetically engineered bacteria—all protected by patents—are the products of the future and the patent holders are cashing in. It is clear that, if patent protection were not available, there would be no incentive to invest huge resources in high technology research and developments, because there would be no prospect of recuperating, and obtaining a fair return on, the investment—especially when one takes into account that not every research programme will lead to success.[123] One should also not forget the vast number of patents granted for relatively slight improvements upon the existing technology. They may not grab the headlines, but they have a tremendous importance in industry, because they allow the improver to appropriate the results of his or her work and gain a competitive edge over his or her competitors, who would otherwise, in a majority of cases, be able to reverse engineer the improvement at a fraction of the original cost.

What about the economic importance of copyright? Just imagine the range of products covered: books; CDs, movies, television broadcasts, computer programs, multimedia products, etc. Copyright has become very wide in scope and a number of the new technological developments protected under copyright are of enormous commercial importance. Add to that the business generated by the phenomenon of character merchandising, which allows goods featuring real and fictitious characters—such as pop stars, Popeye, or Mickey Mouse—to be marketed more easily by those who will earn more through this link than they do through their normal activities, and you will begin to perceive that the current economic importance of intellectual property is, indeed, huge.

Intellectual property is now involved in almost every aspect of our highly developed economic life, with its strong emphasis on technological progress and brand names. Intellectual property is pushed by market forces. The Marrakesh Agreement of the GATT, taken over by the WTO, led to many developing countries adopting stricter intellectual property protection regimes and saw an important expansion of the international

[121] This figure is quoted by Blakeney, *Legal Aspects of the Transfer of Technology to Developing Countries* (n. 110) at 113, with a reference to the United Nations Conference on Trade and Development (UNCTAD) 1981 report *The Role of Trade Marks in the Promotion of Exports from Developing Countries* (n. 108 above).

[122] See also G Parchomovsky and R Polk Wagner (2004) 'Patent Portfolios', Scholarship at Penn Law, Paper 51, <http://lsr.nellco.org/upenn_wps/51>.

[123] See Pretnar, 'The Economic Impact of Patents in a Knowledge-Based Market Economy' (n. 60).

intellectual property regime. Now, attention at WTO level is turning to a next step, in the direction of even stronger intellectual property protection, even if the economic impact of these current reforms is still the subject of a lively discussion.[124]

One might even argue that the original presumption in favour of free competition and the perception of intellectual property rights as exceptional rights, the grant of which was only appropriate in cases of exceptional, innovative, and creative activity, no longer exists. This point of view accepts that industry now presumes that intellectual property protection will be available for every new product and every new development, and sees full-scale free competition as the exception.[125] It is clear that such a reversal of attitude cannot be encouraged unconditionally. Indeed, serious consideration should be given to the questions of overlap between intellectual property rights, in the sense that recent expansion of rights has given rise, on many occasions, to several rights protecting the same thing.

This aspect of convergence of rights aggravates the existing inflation of rights. Innovators and creators are increasingly unable to go about their business without taking out a whole raft of licences in advance. Is this not an aberration? Has the time not come to start thinking about cutting back the, sometimes excessive, scope of intellectual property rights and about reducing the overlap between the various rights? Maybe the Doha Round of WTO negotiations and its demands to reduce, rather than expand on, the impact of TRIPS in certain areas is a sign that this is, indeed, the case, and that continued and almost unlimited expansion of intellectual property rights is not the way forward.[126] It is indeed clear, on the basis of the analysis in this chapter, that intellectual property rights should play a pro-competitive role if their existence is to be justified. Unduly wide and overlapping rights may well fail the test, and therefore endanger the survival of the whole system of intellectual property and the beneficial role it plays in our economy.

An overview

Intellectual property rights play an important role in economic life in this age of technological innovation. Their existence can be justified on an economic basis, with other factors offering further support. Intellectual property rights are also international in character and, in that respect, they fit in rather well with the economic reality of the global economy.

---

[124] See, in general, Maskus, *Intellectual Property Rights in the Global Economy* (n. 82 above) and, for a practical example in one particular country and industry, I. M. Azmi and R. Alavi, 'TRIPS, Patents, Technology Transfer, Foreign Direct Investment and the Pharmaceutical Industry in Malaysia' [2001] JWIP 947.

[125] R. Merges (1994) 'The Economic Impact of Intellectual Property Rights: An Overview and Guide', Paper delivered at the International Center for Art Economics (ICARE) international conference on The Economics of Intellectual Property Rights, 6–8 October, Venice; see also Reichman, 'Charting the Collapse of the Patent–Copyright Dichotomy: Premises for a Restructured International Intellectual Property System' (n. 77).

[126] See, already, in Reichman, 'Charting the Collapse of the Patent–Copyright Dichotomy' (n. 77). Now, even the judiciary is starting to make comments in that direction: see *MGM v. Grokster Ltd*, 380 F3d 1154 (9th Cir. 2004)—relating to copyright infringement in a US context—and *Lambretta Clothing Co. Ltd v. Teddy Smith (UK) Ltd and anor* [2005] RPC 6, per Jacob LJ at para. 101—relating to unregistered design right overlap in a UK context.

Further reading

BENTLY, L., SUTHERSANEN, U. and TORREMANS, P. (eds.) (2010) *Global Copyright: Three Hundred Years since the Statute of Anne, from 1709 to Cyberspace*, Proceedings of the ALAI Congress London 2009, Cheltenham/Northampton MA: Edward Elgar.

DEAZLEY, R. (2004) *On the Origin of the Right to Copy: Charting the Movement of Copyright Law in Eighteenth-Century Britain (1695–1775)*, Oxford: Hart.

DEAZLEY, R. (2006) *Re-Thinking Copyright: History, Theory, Language*, Cheltenham/Northampton, MA: Edward Elgar.

GHIDINI, G. (2006) *Intellectual Property and Competition Law: The Innovation Nexus*, Cheltenham/Northampton, MA: Edward Elgar.

LANDES, W. M. and POSNER, R. A. (2003) *The Economic Structure of Intellectual Property Law*, Harvard: Harvard University Press.

RICKETSON, S. and GINSBURG, J. C. (2006) *International Copyright and Neighbouring Rights: The Berne Convention and Beyond*, Oxford: Oxford University Press.

2

The international and European framework

Introduction

It has become clear, in the course of this introduction, that intellectual property is not necessarily exploited at a national level;[1] it is, in fact, exploited at a global level. DVDs and compact discs (CDs) containing materials protected by copyright are marketed in an increasing number of countries; patents in CD technology were exploited wherever a CD-pressing plant was built, until these rights recently expired; the 'Coca-Cola' trade mark is found on cans and bottles all over the world.

Inventors and creators would, under these circumstances, lose out if intellectual property regimes were to be completely different in each country. They would not get adequate protection and they would not be adequately rewarded for their work if intellectual property rights—based on the same principles, and equally applicable to inventions and creations made abroad—were not available in each country in which the patent, trade mark, or copyright is exploited. If this were the case, the whole economic justification theory would also collapse. A global economy, therefore, presupposes a global intellectual property system.

In this chapter we will therefore look at the international and European picture and at the treaties and other instruments that have been put in place to deal with the international aspects of intellectual property.

International intellectual property conventions

Two types of international cooperation can be distinguished in this respect. First, there are the treaties and conventions that lay down minimum uniform provisions and standards of protection.[2] These recognize that each country will have its own intellectual property laws, but they harmonize the minimum standards and the basis that underlies all these laws, and they also secure protection under these laws for works of foreign inventors and creators or for works created abroad. Anti-counterfeiting initiatives are also part of this category,[3] because they link in with global minimum standards of protection and their effective enforcement.

---

[1] All historical arguments refer to more than one country and the economic justification theory is not restricted to a particular national market.

[2] This is, of course, a second-best solution, but the best solution—uniform intellectual property laws—is clearly not available in practice.

[3] See e.g. the ill-fated ACTA (Anti-Counterfeiting Trade Agreement) that was rejected by the European Parliament, <http://ec.europa.eu/trade/tackling-unfair-trade/acta/>.

These treaties and conventions still require an inventor or creator to register in each country in which protection is sought; only copyright—which, as we shall see, does not have a registration requirement—is an exception to this rule. Thus the second category of treaties and conventions operates at this level. Many of these treaties and conventions involve a single application and examination procedure, or at least a certain level of cooperation between the national intellectual property authorities. The more advanced types of measure provide for uniform provisions in the various national intellectual property laws, or at least for a thorough harmonization of these provisions. Many of these more advanced measures are found in Europe.[4]

All of the conventions, treaties, agreements, and protocols that will be summarized shortly are administered by the World Intellectual Property Organization (WIPO), which has headquarters in Geneva.[5] Its international bureau deals with international registrations; the Universal Copyright Convention (UCC) is an exception to this system.

As part of the Uruguay Round of world trade negotiations, the states contracting to the General Agreement of Tariffs and Trade (GATT)—taken over by the World Trade Organization (WTO)—reached an agreement on the Trade-Related Aspects of Intellectual Property Rights (TRIPS) initiative. The aim of the initiative was to impose worldwide minimum terms for the protection of intellectual property. This system does not replace the existing conventions, but it works in addition to them. It obliges those countries that do not yet protect intellectual property to introduce that protection if they do not want to be excluded from the world free-trading system and from membership of WTO. In comparison, the old system had worked on an entirely voluntary basis; the standards of protection introduced by the TRIPS initiative are also slightly higher than the minimum standards under the old conventions, at which we will look now.

The various treaties, conventions, and other measures that are in place can be summarized as follows.[6]

Patents

In the area of patents, the minimum international rules are found in the Paris Convention for the Protection of Industrial Property, which was signed in 1883, but which has been updated by later Acts. The Convention has been implemented in the states adhering to it—of which there are now 176[7]— by means of national Patent Acts.

It is important to realize what the Paris Convention does and does not do: it *does* try to enable the protection abroad of inventions, but it *does not* create a proper international patent system. Article 1 of the Convention states that it deals with the protection of industrial property, which is said to include patents and is to be understood in the broadest

---

[4] It is also worth mentioning that there have been initiatives taken by a large group of South American countries—that is, by the Andean Group. It would, however, lead us too far to discuss these measures in this book, in which we are primarily concerned with UK and European law.

[5] We do not discuss plant variety rights in this book; for further information please see the International Convention for the Protection of New Varieties of Plants (the UPOV Convention), adopted in Paris in 1961; in the biotechnology area, the Budapest Treaty on the International Recognition of the Deposit of Micro-Organisms for the Purpose of Patent Procedure, in force since 1980, is also relevant.

[6] For the text of these instruments, see <http://www.wipo.int/treaties/en/>; <http://portal.unesco.org/en/ev.php-URL_ID=15381&URL_DO=DO_TOPIC&URL_SECTION=201.html>; <http://www.wto.org/english/tratop_e/trips_e/t_agm0_e.htm>; <http://ec.europa.eu/internal_market/copyright/acquis/index_en.htm>; and <http://portal.unesco.org/en/ev.php-URL_ID=15381&URL_DO=DO_TOPIC&URL_SECTION=201.html>.

[7] Figure correct as at 25 October 2015.

sense. But the closest that Art. 1 comes to a definition of a patent—let alone of any conditions for the grant of a patent—is at Art. 1(4):

> Patents shall include the various kinds of industrial patents recognized by the laws of the countries of the Union, such as patents of importation, patents of improvement, patents and certificates of addition, etc.

What the Paris Convention certainly does establish is a right to national treatment. Nationals of member states will, in all other member states, be treated as home applicants. At the time of drafting, this was an important step: it allowed inventors to apply for patent protection abroad. They would then be treated in the same way as would native applicants. It did mean, however, that one had to apply country by country and, in each country, the local law applied not only in terms of procedure, but also in terms of substantive requirements for patentability, etc. National treatment was also granted to whoever was domiciled, or had a real and effective business establishment, in a member state.[8]

The other core provision is Art. 4, which grants the priority right. National patent laws require, in one way or another, that an invention is new—but can it be 'new', when applying in a second member state, if it has already been revealed earlier in an application to a first member state? Any such revelation might also prompt a less scrupulous entrepreneur to apply in a second or third member state before the inventor has time to do so. It is these problems that the priority right addresses. Starting from the date of the first application, the applicant has a 12-month period during which that application will be taken, in all member states to which he or she applies, to have been filed on the date of the first application. Novelty is therefore preserved and the application will have priority over any other application that has been filed in that member state in the meantime.

Apart from these provisions, the Convention offers very little in terms of the harmonization of national patent laws. Additionally, it specifically states that national patents remain independent.[9] The refusal to grant or revocation in one country, for example, will therefore have no influence on parallel proceedings or on patents in another member state.

The impact of the Paris Convention was enlarged even further by the TRIPS Agreement.[10] Article 2 of that Agreement obliges all contracting states to comply with the main substantive provisions of the Paris Convention, even if they are not members of it. This guarantees a coverage that is virtually worldwide in scope, because very few countries will be able to afford staying outside the WTO-administered system, of which TRIPS forms part. On top of that, the Agreement contains, in Arts. 27–34, further and tighter substantive minimum rules in relation to patents. This is a key step. While national patent laws did already contain similar principles, important differences had remained. TRIPS introduces a first definition of the requirements for patentability—that is, novelty, inventive step, and industrial applicability. It also properly defines, in a broad sense, the types of invention that can be patentable and it obliges member states to grant patents in every field of technology.

Normally, an applicant files a separate patent application in each country in which he or she intends to work the invention or desires protection. This was felt to be a complicated procedure, because the details are different in each country, and a waste of time and effort. The Patent Cooperation Treaty (PCT), signed in Washington in 1970, provides for the filing of a single application and also provides a facility for a preliminary international search for the requirements for patentability. At present, 148 states[11] adhere to the PCT.

---

[8] Paris Convention, Arts. 2 and 3.   [9] Paris Convention, Art. 4bis.

[10] At the time of writing there are 161 WTO members bound by the agreement. See D. Gervais (2012) *The TRIPS Agreement: Drafting History and Analysis*, 4th edn, London: Sweet and Maxwell.

[11] Figure as at 25 October 2015.

In the end, however, the application is handed over to national patent offices and they grant the national patents.

Patents are also an important source of technological information. It might be argued that the most valuable aspect of the PCT is the central publication of the applications and, hence, an extremely valuable database to search for all involved. If the patent system is to fulfil this role adequately at an international level, a uniform system of classification is necessary. An invention must also be new if a patent is to be granted—and this can only be tested by means of a well-structured patent register. This classification system is contained in the Strasbourg Convention on the International Classification of Patents (IPC), signed in Strasbourg in 1971.[12]

Finally, an attempt has been made to streamline national patent procedures by means of the Patent Law Treaty, signed in Geneva in 2000, which entered into force in April 2005.[13]

Trade marks

The minimum rules for trade marks are also contained in the Paris Convention. Again, the main achievement has been national treatment in combination with a right of priority—of six months, in the UK. The rule on the independence of national rights also applies and, at a later stage, a rule on transborder protection for well-known marks was added as Art. 6bis. The TRIPS Agreement has added to that protection: most notably, by providing a definition of what can be registered as a trade mark, under which conditions, and with which rights resulting from registration,[14] as well as requiring all its contracting states to comply with the substantive provisions of the Paris Convention.

The international exploitation of a trade mark is facilitated by the Madrid Agreement concerning the International Registration of Marks, signed in Madrid in 1892. Registration in one state that is a signatory to the Madrid Agreement gives a person the right to file a single application for registration in any other signatory country designated in the application; a separate application in each state is no longer required. But some states including the UK—could not accept some of the provisions of the Madrid Agreement. They joined the system only through the Protocol to the Madrid Agreement, signed in Madrid in 1989.[15] There are a number of differences in substance between the Agreement and the Protocol,[16] but, again, the outcome is a series of national trade marks. A further attempt to harmonize the procedural aspects of a trade mark application is made in the Trade Mark Law Treaty, signed in Geneva in 1994[17] which has been added to by the Singapore Treaty on the Law of Trademarks (2006).[18] The latter takes precedence in case both states concerned have adhered to it.

---

[12] On 25 October 2015, 62 states had signed up to the Convention.

[13] At the time of writing there are 36 member states. In the UK, the Treaty entered into force on 22 March 2006.

[14] Arts. 15–21.

[15] On 14 December 2015, 97 states adhered to the Madrid system, 55 of them have ratified the Agreement, and 97 the Protocol. The EU and its Community trade mark system have now also adhered to the system.

[16] See Section E of this book; see also G. Kunze, 'The Protocol Relating to the Madrid Agreement Concerning the International Registration of Marks' [1992] 82 The Trademark Reporter 1; G. Kunze, 'The Madrid System for the International Registration of Marks as Applied under the Protocol' [1994] 6 EIPR 223–6.

[17] On 25 October 2015, 53 states adhered to this Agreement.

[18] On 25 October 2015, 38 states adhered to this Agreement.

A uniform classification system for trade marks—based on classes for goods and services, and lists of goods and services that fall into each of the classes—is provided by two agreements:

(i) the Nice Agreement concerning the International Classification of Goods and Services for the Purposes of the Registration of Marks, which was signed in Nice in 1861 and was last revised in Geneva in 1977;[19] and

(ii) the Vienna Agreement establishing an International Classification of the Figurative Elements of Marks, signed in Vienna in 1985.[20]

The latter also deals with device marks.

Design rights

This is the third area covered by the Paris Convention and the TRIPS Agreement, and in relation to this area, both play similar roles as they do in relation to patents and trade marks.

An industrial design can be deposited internationally and will attract protection in all member states of the 1925 Hague Agreement concerning the Deposit of Industrial Designs, to which 64 states now[21] adhere. The provisions of this Agreement have been updated by the 1999 Geneva Act of the Hague Agreement concerning the Deposit of Industrial Designs, which entered into force on 23 December 2003 and which is gradually being ratified by the member states. The European Union (EU) joined the system on 1 January 2008.[22]

An international uniform classification for industrial designs was established in the Locarno Agreement Establishing an International Classification for Industrial Designs, which has been in force since 1970.[23]

Copyright

The most important international convention in the copyright area is the 1886 Berne Convention for the Protection of Literary and Artistic Works (the latest Act of which is the Paris Act). This Convention is to copyright what the Paris Convention is to industrial property rights. As with the Paris Convention, the aim was not to create a supranational copyright system; the focus is once more on national treatment. Foreign authors—at least those with a link to member states—will get the same protection as national authors in any member state.

But, unlike the Paris Convention, the Berne Convention at least attempts to define the object of copyright protection—that is, literary and artistic works, and the list of examples in Art. 2. The focus is on a reproduction right that is given to right holders, but public performance rights and communication to the public eventually make their appearance. The most important point to note, however, is that there is a proper attempt to achieve at

---

[19] On 25 October 2015, 84 states adhered to this Agreement.

[20] On 25 October 2015, 32 states adhered to this Agreement.

[21] Figure as at 25 October 2015; the EU is counted as one state by WIPO on top of member states that ratified individually.

[22] See European Commission (2007) 'Industrial Property: EU Joins International Designs Treaty', Press release, 25 September, <europa.eu/rapid/pressReleasesAction.do?reference=IP/07/1388&format=HTML&aged= 0&language=EN&guiLanguage=fr> (EU states counted individually).

[23] On 25 October 2015, there were 54 member states.

least a minimalist harmonization of the protection and the rights that are granted. The Berne Convention establishes further provisions on limitations, term of protection, and moral rights, and 169 states are now members of the Berne Union.[24]

A competing Universal Copyright Convention (UCC), signed in Geneva in 1952 and revised at Paris in 1971, was promoted by the United Nations Educational, Scientific and Cultural Organization (UNESCO), but lost most of its importance when its most influential member state, the US, joined the Berne Convention. This effect is now reinforced by the fact that the TRIPS Agreement requires its contracting states to comply with most of the provisions of the Berne Convention.[25] Further substantive provisions are found in Arts. 9–14 of the TRIPS Agreement and yet further measures to take account of the new developments in copyright are found in the WIPO Copyright Treaty, signed in Geneva in 1996,[26] which is closely linked to the Berne Convention as a special treaty under Art. 20 of that Convention.

TRIPS plays a somewhat different role in relation to copyright than in relation to patents. The idea–expression dichotomy is spelled out *expressis verbis*, but otherwise there is modernization, rather than harmonization of basic principles of substantive law. Hence, we see provisions on computer programs and databases, and rental rights, before we return to Art. 13, and its limitations and exceptions (the famous three-step-test). The WIPO Copyright Treaty, meanwhile, continues that trend and might be seen as an Internet treaty.[27] The right of communication to the public is enshrined as the equivalent in the digital era of the right of reproduction and technical protection measures make their first appearance at international treaty level.

The Marrakesh Treaty to Facilitate Access to Published Works for Persons Who Are Blind, Visually Impaired or Otherwise Print Disabled was adopted on 27 June 2013 in Marrakesh. It has a clear humanitarian and social development dimension and its main goal is to create a set of mandatory limitations and exceptions for the benefit of the blind, visually impaired, and otherwise print disabled (VIPs). The treaty is still awaiting ratification at the time of writing.

The rights of performers, recorders, and broadcasting organizations required supplementary protection. In this respect, the most important convention is the 1961 Rome Convention for the Protection of Performers, Producers of Phonograms and Broadcasting Organizations.[28] The Rome Convention did not, however, achieve the number of ratifications that the Berne Convention did and proper international harmonization was never achieved. It did not come as a surprise, therefore, when Art. 14 of TRIPS started again from scratch, and introduced basic harmonized rules for the protection of performers, producers of phonograms, and broadcasting organizations.

The WIPO Performances and Phonograms Treaty, signed in Geneva in 1996,[29] provides major improvements in this area and entered into force on 20 May 2002. Broadcasting organizations were left out, however, and reaching a deal on this point proved to be extremely difficult.[30] After long negotiations the Beijing Treaty on Audiovisual

---

[24] Figure as at 30 January 2016.   [25] But not with those on moral rights: see Art. 9.

[26] This Treaty entered into force on 6 March 2002 and, as at 30 January 2016 it is in force between 94 states (now that the EU has adhered to it).

[27] See J. Ginsburg, 'The Author's Place in Copyright after TRIPs and the WIPO Treaties' (2008) 39(1) IIC 1.

[28] On 25 October 2015, 92 states had adhered to this Convention.

[29] On 25 October 2015, with the adhesion of the EU, the Treaty was in force between 94 states.

[30] See T. Rivers (2007) 'A Broadcasters' Treaty?', in P. Torremans (ed.) Handbook of Contemporary Copyright Research, Cheltenham: Edward Elgar, pp. 483–513.

Performances, which covers some of the issues on which there was no agreement in 1996, was signed on 26 June 2012 and is now awaiting ratification.

European initiatives

The creation of a single European market, based on the principle of free competition, required a further substantial harmonization of intellectual property provisions—what had previously been rather loose international cooperation on a standard basis of minimal rules was no longer sufficient.

Patents

In Europe, cooperation in the patent area was taken further than it was on an international level. The European Patent Convention (EPC), signed in Munich in 1973, provides a system comprising a single patent application and search. The EPC effectively contains a harmonized patent law for its member states, which covers the core elements such as patentability and patent infringements. The European Patent Office in Munich, which started working on 1 June 1978, carries out this search. At the end of the procedure, the applicant is granted a bundle of national patents: one for each member state indicated in the application. The EPC is not an initiative of the EU: it is adhered to by other European countries, such as Switzerland, Turkey, and Liechtenstein.[31]

The European Community wanted to go further and replace the bundle of national patents at the end of the granting procedure by a single Community patent. This was the aim of the Community Patent Convention signed at Luxemburg in 1975,[32] but the Convention never entered into force. Various attempts were made to revive the project as an EU regulation that would be administered by the European Patent Office, but eventually these came to nothing. The project continued as an enhanced cooperation initiative of 25 member states, with Italy and Spain refusing to participate, but late in 2012 agreement was finally secured on the creation of a unitary patent or a European patent with unitary effect. That will be coupled with a litigation agreement that will result in the creation of a single European Patent Court with seats in London, Paris, and Munich.[33]

Other initiatives of the Community relate to pharmaceutical inventions and inventions relating to plant protection products—for which the term of protection was extended by means of the introduction of supplementary protection certificates (SPCs) for pharmaceutical products[34] and for plant protection products[35]—and to biotechnological

---

[31] At the time of writing, there were 38 member states. A revised version of the EPC was agreed on 29 November 2000 and entered into force at the end of 2007.

[32] See Convention for the European Patent for the Common Market (Community Patent Convention) (1989) OJ L 401/10.

[33] See: <https://www.unified-patent-court.org/>; Regulation (EU) 1257/2012 of the European Parliament and of the Council implementing enhanced cooperation in the area of the creation of unitary patent protection [2012] OJL 361/1 and Council Regulation (EU) 1260/2012 implementing enhanced cooperation in the area of the creation of unitary patent protection with regard to the applicable translation arrangements [2012] OJ L 361/89.

[34] EC Council Regulation 1768/92 concerning the creation of a supplementary protection certificate for medicinal products (1992) OJ L 182/1, now codified as Regulation (EC) No. 469/2009 of the European Parliament and of the Council of 6 May 2009 concerning the supplementary protection certificate for medicinal products (Codified version) [2009] OJ L 152/1.

[35] EC Parliament and Council Regulation 1610/96 concerning the creation of a supplementary protection certificate for plant protection products (1996) OJ L 198/30.

inventions.[36] At the lower end of the innovation scale, some form of protection was planned for inventions that do not qualify for full patent protection. The utility model that was proposed some years ago should provide that protection, but progress in this area seems to have come to a halt.[37] The EU has also adopted a special registration system for plant varieties, which operates separately from the patent system and which is in line with the International Convention for the Protection of New Varieties of Plants (the UPOV Convention).[38]

Discussions relating to a directive on the patentability of computer-implemented inventions, however, eventually came to nothing.[39]

Trade marks

In relation to trade marks, the Community acted on two levels: the national trade mark laws of the member states have been harmonized by means of the First Council Directive to approximate the laws of the member states relating to trade marks[40] and a Community trade mark has been created by means of a Council Regulation on the Community Trade Mark.[41] This latter system has been in force since 1996, with far greater success than expected, and provides a single trade mark for the Community as a whole. The Community Trade Mark Office—which is officially called the Office for Harmonization in the Internal Market (trade marks and designs), or OHIM—is located in Alicante, Spain.

The Community has also joined the Madrid System.

Industrial designs

The Community undertook the same action in this area as that taken in relation to trade marks—that is, the harmonization of the national design laws by means of a directive and the creation of a single Community design right by means of a Regulation. The difficult issue of spare parts and a repair clause made negotiations very cumbersome, but, eventually, a directive on the legal protection of designs was agreed in October 1998.[42] Shortly afterwards, agreement on a Council regulation on community design[43] was reached and, in January 2003, the OHIM was able to extend its role from that relating only to Community trade marks to become a Community trade mark and design office.

The EU has also joined the Geneva Act of the Hague Agreement, with effect from 1 January 2008.

---

[36] After a first attempt to get a directive approved failed, the Commission made a second attempt, which led eventually to the adoption of the EC Parliament and Council Directive 98/44/EC on the legal protection of biotechnological inventions (1998) OJ L 213/13.

[37] See the Amended Proposal for a European Parliament and Council Directive approximating the legal arrangements for the protection of inventions by utility model (2000) OJ C 248/56, COM (99) 309 final.

[38] Council Regulation (EC) 2100/94 on Community plant variety rights (1994) OJ L 227/1, as amended.

[39] Proposal for a Directive of the European Parliament and of the Council on the patentability of computer-implemented inventions COM (2002) 92 final, dated 20 February 2002 (2002) OJ C 151/129.

[40] (1989) OJ L 40/1, now codified as Directive 2008/95/EC of the European Parliament and of the Council of 22 October 2008 to approximate the laws of the Member States relating to trade marks [2008] OJ L 299/25.

[41] (EC) 40/94 (1994) OJ L 11/1, now codified as Council Regulation (EC) 207/2009 of 26 February 2009 on the Community trade mark [2009] OJ L 78/1.

[42] EC Parliament and Council Directive 98/71/EC (1998) OJ L 289/28.

[43] Council Regulation 6/2002 (2002) OJ L 3/1.

Copyright

The Community has, up to now, refrained from making an attempt to harmonize copyright as a whole.[44] Only certain aspects of copyright—such as the term of copyright protection—have been harmonized.[45]

A number of areas have received special attention: computer programs;[46] rental rights and lending rights;[47] satellite broadcasting and cable retransmission;[48] databases.[49] Following on from this vertical approach a first horizontal Copyright Directive harmonized certain aspects of copyright and related rights in the information society.[50] The implementation of that Directive enabled the EU to accede to the WIPO Copyright Treaty and the WIPO Performances and Phonograms Treaty with effect from 14 March 2010. This was facilitated by an earlier undertaking from the member states to legislate in a timely way to meet the provisions on moral rights for performers that are not retained in the Directive.[51] Although not of the same importance and dealing with a small point in copyright law, agreement on the Directive to harmonize the provisions on *droit de suite* (meaning literally 'right to follow' and referring to a right granted to artists to receive a fee on the resale of their works of art) was only reached after heated debates.[52] Orphan works, i.e. works the owner of the copyright in which is unknown or cannot be traced, pose specific problems as there is no one to obtain a copyright licence from. A directive was agreed to allow publicly accessible libraries, educational establishments, and museums, as well as archives, film or audio heritage institutions, and public-service broadcasting organizations, established in the member states, to make orphan works in their collections available to the public, by acts of reproduction, for the purposes of digitization, making available, indexing, cataloguing, preservation, or restoration. These institutions can only do so in order to achieve aims related to their public interest missions, in particular the preservation and restoration of, and the provision of cultural and educational access to, works and phonograms contained in their collection. Once again this is a directive dealing with a narrow point.[53]

---

[44] For a private suggestion by the Wittem Group of academics see <http://www.copyrightcode.eu/>.

[45] EC Council Directive 93/98 harmonizing the terms of protection of copyright and certain related rights (1993) OJ L 290/9, now codified as Directive 2006/116/EC of the European Parliament and of the Council of 12 December 2006 on the term of protection of copyright and certain related rights (codified version) [2006] OJ L 372/12.

[46] EC Council Directive 91/250 on the legal protection of computer programs (1991) OJ L 122/42, now codified as Directive 2009/24/EC of the European Parliament and of the Council of 23 April 2009 on the legal protection of computer programs (Codified version) [2009] OJ L 111/16.

[47] EC Council Directive 92/100 on rental rights and lending rights related to copyright in the field of intellectual property (1992) OJ L 346/61, now codified as Directive 2006/115/EC of the European Parliament and of the Council of 12 December 2006 on rental right and lending right and on certain rights related to copyright in the field of intellectual property (codified version) [2006] OJ L 376/28.

[48] EC Council Directive 93/83 on the coordination of certain rules concerning copyright and rights related to copyright applicable to satellite broadcasting and cable retransmission (1993) OJ L 248/15.

[49] EC Parliament and Council Directive 96/9 on the legal protection of databases (1996) OJ L 77/20.

[50] EC Parliament and Council Directive 2001/29/EC on the harmonization of certain aspects of copyright and related rights in the information society (2001) OJ L 167/10.

[51] See COM (97) 193.

[52] EC Parliament and Council Directive 2001/84/EC on the resale right for the benefit of the author of an original work of art (2001)OJ L 272/32.

[53] Directive 2012/28/EU of the European Parliament and of the Council of 25 October 2012 on certain permitted uses of orphan works [2012] OJ L299/5. See P. Torremans et al. (2012) *Orphan Works: Compatibility of the Draft Directive with International Norms*, <http://www.nottingham.ac.uk/law/people/paul.torremans>.

Collective management is a necessity to make copyright function smoothly both for right holders and for users, but it has at the same time given rise to competition law concerns and its territorial nature tends to stand in the way of multi-territorial licences for the online use of musical works. This area has now been addressed by Directive 2014/26/EU on collective rights management and multi-territorial licensing of rights in musical works for online uses. The Directive aims at ensuring that right holders have a say in the management of their rights and envisages a better functioning of collective management organizations as a result of EU-wide standards. The new rules will also ease the multi-territorial licensing by collective management organizations of authors' rights in musical works for online use.[54]

Other European initiatives

The Intellectual Property (IP) Enforcement Directive[55] attempts to streamline the enforcement mechanisms of the member states and to achieve a common minimum standard. The Directive covers all intellectual property rights and has now been transposed into the national laws of the member states.[56]

The EU has also adopted measures in the areas of counterfeiting and customs enforcement of intellectual property,[57] topographies of semiconductor chips,[58] comparative advertising,[59] and electronic commerce.[60] A short directive dealing with the legal protection of conditional access services was also adopted on 20 November 1998.[61]

Trade secrets on the other hand was an area in which the Member States operated very different approaches and no harmonization had until recently been attempted. Now there

---

[54] Directive 2014/26/EU of the European Parliament and of the Council on collective management of copyright and related rights and multi-territorial licensing of rights in musical works for online use in the internal market [2014] OJ L 84/72. Member states have until 10 April 2016 to implement the Directive.

[55] EC Parliament and Council Directive 2004/48/EC on the enforcement of intellectual property rights (2004) OJ L 195/16.

[56] For a critical view of the original Commission proposal, see W. R. Cornish et al., 'Procedures and Remedies for Enforcing IPRS: The European Commission's Proposed Directive' [2003] EIPR 447 (supported by a large number of academics, including this author).

[57] Council Regulation 3842/86 laying down measures to prohibit the release for free circulation of counterfeit goods (1986) OJ L 357/1, first replaced by Council Regulation 3295/94 laying down measures to prohibit the release for free circulation, export, re-export or entry for a suspensive procedure of counterfeit and pirated goods (1994) OJ L 341/8, which in turn was replaced by Council Regulation (EC) 1383/2003 of 22 July 2003 concerning customs action against goods suspected of infringing certain intellectual property rights and the measures to be taken against goods found to have infringed such rights [2003] OJ L196/7. The final stage in this evolution is now Regulation (EU) 608/2013 of the European Parliament and of the Council concerning customs enforcement of intellectual property rights and repealing Council Regulation (EC) No 1383/2003 [2013] OJ L 181/15. See O. Vrins and M. M. Schneider (eds.) (2012) *Enforcement of Intellectual Property Rights through Border Measures*, 2nd edn, Oxford: Oxford University Press.

[58] EC Parliament and Council Directive 87/54 on the legal protection of topographies of semiconductor products (1987) OJ L 24/36.

[59] EC Parliament and Council Directive 97/55 amending Directive 84/450 on misleading advertising (1997) OJ L 290/18.

[60] EC Parliament and Council Directive 2000/31/EC on certain legal aspects of information society services, in particular electronic commerce, in the Internal Market (2000) OJ L 178/1.

[61] EC Parliament and Council Directive 98/84/EC on the legal protection of services based on, or consisting of, conditional access (1998) OJ L 320/54. Conditional access services are typically only available through the use of a decoder or upon payment of a fee. The number of these services that is available on the Internet is increasing rapidly.

is a draft to partially harmonize this area in the light of increasing evidence of industrial espionage.[62]

An overview

This chapter highlights the international context in which the UK intellectual property system operates. Starting from the founding treaties—that is, the Paris Convention and the Berne Convention—and their principle of national treatment, we have come a long way. Gradually, there has been a push to harmonize the substantive intellectual property law provisions; at the same time, application procedures and procedures in front of the national intellectual property offices have also been streamlined and harmonized. The TRIPS Agreement also greatly expanded the territorial scope of the intellectual property treaties, without overlooking its massive harmonization effort.

At a European level, we have seen even further integration in order to cope with the single market. A Community trade mark and a Community design right are now in place as single rights for the whole of the Community; parallel directives have harmonized national trade mark and design laws to a large extent. The unitary patent is finally about to leave the drawing board, and, in the meanwhile, the European Patent Convention allows the EPO to turn around several thousands of applications each year—and, at the end of the process, bundles of national patents are often granted. Copyright has seen a different evolution, but it is fair to say that the various directives have, in their own piecemeal way, achieved a fair degree of harmonization. It is interesting to see that the Court of Justice is now dealing with large numbers of copyright cases, as happened before in relation to trade marks, and this bring about a form of horizontal harmonization of key concepts whenever these are required to interpret the existing copyright directives.

All of this corresponds to the needs of international business that are ever increasing as intellectual property is increasingly exploited in a global market. No doubt this pressure will guarantee a further flood of initiatives and developments in this area.

Further reading

GERVAIS, D. (2012) *The TRIPS Agreement: Drafting History and Analysis*, 4th edn, London: Sweet and Maxwell.

RICKETSON, S. and GINSBURG, J. C. (2006) *International Copyright and Neighbouring Rights: The Berne Convention and Beyond*, Oxford: Oxford University Press.

<http://ec.europa.eu/internal_market/copyright/acquis/index_en.htm for EU copyright instruments>.

<http://ec.europa.eu/growth/industry/intellectual-property/index_en.htm> for EU instruments relating to industrial property.

<http://www.epo.org/law-practice/legal-texts/epc.html> for the text of the EPC.

<http://www.wipo.int/treaties/en> for the text of the treaties administered by WIPO.

---

[62] Proposal for a Directive of the European Parliament and of the Council on the protection of undisclosed know-how and business information (trade secrets) against their unlawful acquisition, use and disclosure COM/2013/0813 final.

SECTION B
Patents

3

Origin, background, and international aspects of the patent system

The longest-standing, best-known, and, arguably, economically most valuable form of protection of rights provided by the law of intellectual property comes in the form of the patent. A patent is, in essence, the grant of a monopoly to an inventor who has used his or her skill to invent something new. The monopoly is not absolute; patents are only granted for a limited period and are accompanied by public disclosure enabling others in the field to consider, and perhaps subsequently improve on, it. Each year, tens of thousands of patents are granted creating a monopoly right within the UK alone and they may cover a whole range of different types of subject matter, although it is fair to note that the level of patenting activity in the UK seems much greater than that in many major industrial nations.

Patents may cover entirely new products or, more often, enhancements to pre-existing products, or they may cover a new or improved process for performing an activity. A legal structure has been created to cover all of these variants that is elegant in its simplicity, but complex in its operation. Before we explore the detail of its ramifications, however, we must explore its origins and purpose, along with the background to, and sources of, the modern law of patents.

History

It will be seen shortly that patent law has a very distinct European dimension; consequently, it is appropriate to begin by considering the origins of patent law that are found in Europe. The German miners of the Alps seem to have been first to develop the notion of monopoly rights in their new processes as far back as the thirteenth century,[1] but the first more universal patent scheme evolved in Venice—which was then at the height of its international power—in a Decree of 1474, which rewarded inventors of new objects with a limited monopoly on condition that the invention was disclosed to the state. This is a model that, in its essentials, is still followed by the patent system five centuries later. It has been argued[2] that the earliest example of a patent being granted to an inventor in England was that granted by Queen Elizabeth I to one Acontius, an inventor from Italy

[1] H. Wegner (1993) *Patent Harmonization*, London: Sweet and Maxwell, pp. 2–3.
[2] J. Phillips, 'The English Patent as a Reward for Invention: The Importation of an Idea' (1982) 3 J Leg Hist 71.

who had been granted one of the earliest Venetian patents, but had fled to England for religious reasons.

Patents at this period were often not a reward for invention, but a reward for royal supporters, and patents were granted simply so as to reward loyalty with monopoly. Such abuses of power could not be countenanced by the courts, however, as was finally shown in the case of *Darcy v. Allin*.[3] In this case, a patent had been granted conferring a 14-year monopoly in the entire trade in playing cards and was not upheld on the grounds that it conferred an unreasonable monopoly. While it was accepted that patents could be granted for new trades and inventions, on the grounds that there was a public benefit in the form of whatever advantages the new development conferred,[4] there was no such benefit on the facts of this case.

Against the background of the changing roles of the monarch and legislature at this period in history, Parliament also decided to flex its muscles in relation to the grant of monopolies. It passed the Statute of Monopolies 1624, which, while seeking generally to stamp out monopolies, expressly allowed their retention in favour of inventors of new methods of manufacture, who were allowed a 14-year maximum period in which to exploit their creation, subject to certain protections for the public interest.

It may be that the essence of the modern patent can be traced back to this law, but this cannot be said of the system for gaining a patent. The grant remained an exercise of the royal prerogative and it was only as the number of patents sought increased against the background of the developing Industrial Revolution that clear rules and formalities very slowly began to make their appearance. It was in the eighteenth century, therefore, that the requirement of a written specification was established.

From the chaos of informality, the burgeoning bureaucracy and ever-greater demand for patents produced a different chaos—the chaos of sclerosis—and it became clear, eventually, that steps had to be taken to reform and regularize the system lest it threaten the dominance in world trade then enjoyed by Britain. The Patent Law Amendment Act 1852 greatly simplified the system—the existence of the Patent Office (now the UK Intellectual Property Office) dates from the appointment of Patent Commissioners at this time—but also liberalized the criteria for patentability and perhaps made obtaining a patent too easy. The next landmark, therefore, was the Patents, Designs and Trade Marks Act 1883, which established the Patent Office and empowered it to investigate applications in order both to weed out those that did not meet the official criteria and—after the Patents Act 1902—to investigate whether the subject matter of the patent was truly novel. Despite tinkering by Parliament over the years, the basic system then in place continued until the Patents Act 1977, which made significant changes to the system that reflected the growing internationalization of the world of patents—as will be noted later.

Purpose

The long history of patents and the remarkable consistency of common ideas and principles that has lain as a strand through that history, from the earliest times to the present day, suggests that strong forces led to the creation of the law and that those forces have remained in place ever since. What, then, are the factors that have shaped the law of patents? And what purposes does it fulfil?

---

[3] (1602) Noy 173, 74 ER 1131.   [4] (1602) Noy 173, 74 ER 1131 at 183 and 1139.

To answer these questions, it is best to consider the often competing interests of those involved with the patent system. Looked at, first, from the standpoint of the actual inventor, the traditional assumption is that a patent is the grant of a reward for all of the skill and hard work that has been put into the invention. There is much to be said for this perspective: undoubtedly, some inventors carry out their work with the future benefits that it will confer on them very much in mind; large firms can justify their research and development (R&D) staff to their accountants, and thus to their shareholders, by reference to the future rewards that will be gained.

This is, however, too simplistic a notion to be regarded as an acceptable universal solution. Some inventors receive no reward, because their invention is not a commercial success or because they do not have the resources to exploit it effectively. Little commercial benefit is likely to have flowed from the invention of jet engines for aeroplanes, for example, because years were to pass before aircraft construction technology caught up. Indeed, the number of successful applications for patents that give rise to a fully exploitable commercial product or process is believed to be a small fraction of the total amount, although this may be a consequence of the ethos and financial structure of the industrial sector generally rather than a criticism of the patent system as such. Does industry generally want to take what is inevitably a risk when failure might be at the expense of shareholders' dividends and—for a cynical perspective— directors' fees? The relationship between small-scale inventors, who cannot afford to exploit an invention themselves, and other larger firms, who may be rivals in the same trade or companies primarily interested in providing venture capital in the expectation of a return, is bound in either case to be fraught. Many inventors receive no reward, because they lose the race to patent their product. This is often the case in respect of pharmaceutical products, in which sector a new problem will be seized upon by all of the major firms, each of which will race to reach an answer—in the form of a new or improved drug on to the market—but in which race there will only be one winner. The quest for an effective viable drug to combat the HIV virus is a classic example.

The link between invention and reward has, in fact, always seemed tenuous. Arkwright's important 'Spinning Jenny' may have been a key ingredient in the Industrial Revolution, but it was refused a patent,[5] while Watt's steam engine needed special legislation before it was regarded as patentable. Other inventors are not even in the game to seek a reward. The public image of the typical inventor as a bumbling pseudoscientist working away in his potting shed in an attempt to create a perpetual-motion machine may be far from the reality of most companies' R&D divisions, but such individuals do exist and are clearly not in it for the money. Significant inventions—such as the 'cats' eyes', which enhance road safety by marking the middle of the road—are, from time to time, created by enthusiastic individuals rather than by businesses. It even appears that the ubiquitous 'Post-it' type of gummed message label was devised by a choir member who was exasperated at the way in which traditional bookmarks fell out of his hymn book. More significantly, much research is carried out by people motivated by a love of the subject, a quest for knowledge, and a desire to push back the proverbial frontiers: academics in universities, for example.

Perhaps a more appropriate refinement is to suggest that at least the patent system offers an incentive to invent. If reward is not guaranteed, at least there is a chance of it—even for the lone inventor and for the university professor too, if they choose to avail

---

[5] *R v. Arkwright* (1785) 1 Web Pat Cas 64.

themselves of it (as they usually will). But it may be best to regard that chance as, relatively speaking, not a great one: if the risk of unexploited or unexploitable inventions is added to the problems created by the limited time during which the reward can be enjoyed and the loss of secrecy when the patent application is made, the grant of a patent is a distinctly double-edged reward.

In looking at the patent system from other standpoints, the state, or society—as grantor of the patent—emerges as the other key player. The grant is not a generous act, in that the state is not giving up anything of its own; rather, it simply sacrifices the interests of other traders. In so doing, however, the state makes major gains. Clearly, society benefits from improvements in transport, industry, health care, or whatever other improvement is conferred by the patent and, more intangibly, by the increase in knowledge created by the inventive process. Sometimes, the state even benefits more directly: for example, by its ability to take over an invention and prevent its use by others.[6] In a capitalist society, the increase in trade and wealth generated by the advances of the patent system are also important justifications for that system. It may be queried—in the light of all of the developments of the Industrial Revolution, which occurred when patent protection was minimal, as the fates of Arkwright and Watt demonstrate—just how significant a role the patent system plays in the expansion of new industries, but this is perhaps a weaker argument now than then, given the need to provide legal protection for the huge investments many companies make in their R&D activity. All of the factors clearly justify the state's involvement in the patent system and go far towards explaining the presence of a system in all developed and developing countries.

Taken on their own, however, such factors would suggest a trend towards the over-generous grant of many patents, as in the UK after the 1852 legislation, which is not the norm in most patent systems today. The reason for this lies in the interests of other parties: parties who are not directly involved in the grant of a patent, but who are closely and directly affected by it, and whose interests require a more cautious approach to the patentability question. The two obvious groups concerned here are consumers and trade rivals. The interest of consumers as a class is, of course, served by the invention of new products and processes, but not if their inventor is able to take advantage of his or her monopoly position by its abuse in terms, for example, of restricting supply or inflating prices. We have already argued that such potential rewards are not always there for the enjoyment of the inventor, but the possibility clearly exists. Thus the monopoly is limited only to a set period and, should the inventor refuse to share the benefits thereof with society, the compulsory licensing system comes into play.[7]

Similar factors arise in relation to rival traders. Clearly, a permanent monopoly granted to an inventor would unduly distort the market; even a time-restricted monopoly distorts the market for the restriction period, but the harm that may be caused thereby is diminished by the disclosure requirement, giving the rival trader the chance to experiment and develop the original concept into a patentable improvement.

Clearly, therefore, no single interest group can shape the patent system. If there is a single justification or common purpose that underpins the system, it must be the attainment of a balance between the different interests involved. The consumer wants new products—so grants patents readily—but not at any price—so restricts the scope of the monopoly. A business wants the advantage of monopoly as a reward—but not at

---

[6] Patents Act 1977, ss. 22, 55–9. See Ch. 5.   [7] Patents Act 1977, s. 48. See Ch. 5.

any price—so insists on public disclosure as its price. Society wants increased trade and wealth—but not at any price—hence the various restrictions and limitations. In assessing the detail of the patent system, in due course, it will be useful to reflect on which interests are being harmed or promoted by different aspects of the law and their contemporary interpretation.

The international dimension

It is self-evident that trade between nations can be affected by the existence in each nation of differing intellectual property regimes. If I develop a new product in the UK and gain patent protection for it, at the very least it will be inconvenient if I cannot extend my business into France because someone else has succeeded in gaining a monopoly there. It will be equally awkward for my French counterpart, of course, if he or she seeks to expand into my market. The more international trade there is, the more of a problem this becomes—especially when that trade is taking place in what purports to be a common market, such as that created between the members of the European Union (EU), with free trade without any national interference as its core.

The Paris Convention

Inevitably, cries have long been heard clamouring for greater levels of harmonization in domestic patent law (and other aspects of the law relating to intellectual property) between trading nations. Such cries long predate the Treaty of Rome, but have tended to emanate from Europe.

The culmination of the first round of patent harmonization came with the agreement known as the Paris Convention for the Protection of Industrial Property 1883, the main feature of which was that each signatory state had to offer the same treatment to all within that jurisdiction irrespective of nationality. To revert to the earlier example, under this Convention, I might file my patent application in France knowing that the dispute between my French counterpart and me will be dealt with fairly on a footing of equal treatment. A common priority date—that is, the date from when protection runs—also applied as between all signatory states.

Slowly, the web of cooperation broadened: the US did not initially accept the 1883 Convention, not least because of different approaches to the priority date, but after the Convention was amended in 1890 in Brussels, the US became a signatory to it.[8] But while further conventions and revisions extended the scope of cooperation and the numbers of countries involved in the Paris Convention, it would be wrong to see it as a harmonizer of substantive law; rather, it is best seen as a way of facilitating procedural compatibility between the patent systems of signatory nations.

The Patent Cooperation Treaty

The next level of international agreement saw an attempt to ease the burden placed on a patentee by having to claim patent protection separately in each jurisdiction. This came to fruition in the form of the Washington Patent Cooperation Treaty 1970 (PCT), which sets up a system of international patent applications, overseen by the

---

[8] Wegner *Patent Harmonization* (n. 1) at p. 22.

World Intellectual Property Organization (WIPO), an international body. The system allows for a single application to be made that, if successful, will give patent protection in those signatory states in relation to which the applicant seeks protection. There is provision for either, or both, an international search of other patents and a preliminary examination of the claim made; there is not, however, an international definition of patentability, which remains a domestic matter in terms of whether an application meets the criteria of patentability. This scheme is not without its value and it facilitates thousands of applications each year, but its main problem—and the problem with much else in patent law—originates in the limited basis of both its accessibility and acceptability.

Over the last few years, the PCT system has seen a rapid expansion, both in terms of member states—numbering 148 at the last count in October 2015, compared to 111 in April 2001, for example—and in terms of applications. Now, more than half of the world's countries and territories participate in the scheme. Under the rules of the scheme, the applicant, first of all, files a single application. The treatment of that application can be subdivided into international and national phases.

In the international phase, the starting point is the filing of the application under the PCT rules with the national patent office of a member state or with the WIPO International Bureau in Geneva. The applicant designates in the application the member states that are of interest and in relation to which he or she would like to obtain a patent. In a second stage of the international phase, an international search is carried out by one of nine selected national patent offices. This search aims to throw up any relevant pre-existing materials. In a third step, the International Bureau will publish the application, and such international publication is one of the main advantages of the PCT system. It provides a single and complete source of information for any innovator, rather than the pre-existing multiple national patent registers, and this greatly enhances the effective dissemination of the technical knowledge contained in patent applications. In the light of the results of the international search, the applicant has to decide whether or not to request that the fourth step of the international phase be carried out: an international preliminary examination of the application by one of the nine selected patent offices. In practice, 80 per cent of all applicants take advantage of this option. It is important to stress, however, that this examination is preliminary and that no patent is granted at the end of the international phase. It is up to the applicant to decide whether he or she still wishes to pursue the application and to move on to the national phase. This national phase will take place in front of every national patent office in the countries that are still of interest to the applicant and it is only at the end of that national phase that each country involved will decide, according to its own rules, whether or not to grant a national patent.

This scheme is, therefore, nowhere near to a global patent system: not all countries participate in the system and there is no harmonization of substantive patent law; there is really only a streamlined application procedure. This may sound more damaging than it actually is, given that most major developed countries that are active in world trade and in innovation, and which have a developed patent system, are among the member states—but it raises the problem of whether worldwide patent law is ever likely to be feasible, given the different levels of development, innovatory capacity, and legal systems that are found around the world. What is appropriate for France or Germany, for example, may not play well in Burkina Faso or Papua New Guinea, or, in more significant cases, countries in the Far East—such as Thailand—which have, until recently, taken a distinctly relaxed view of their international obligations in respect of intellectual property rights.

The TRIPS Agreement

This lack of universality remains an important issue. Extensive discussion took place, as part of the Uruguay Round of General Agreement of Tariffs and Trade (GATT) negotiations, with a view to creating a broader international level of protection for patents and other intellectual property rights. This eventually led to the signing of the Trade-Related Aspects of Intellectual Property Rights (TRIPS) Agreement and the establishment of the World Trade Organization (WTO), the competence of which includes aspects of intellectual property.

But this trend towards broader protection for intellectual property has been a path paved with difficulty, especially for countries such as India, which have consciously developed patent law to reflect local, rather than Western, conditions and which have been faced with the need to return to a more mainstream approach to patent law as a result of the GATT negotiations. In some instances, this prospect has led to violent demonstrations in the streets—a rare case of public disorder being occasioned by patent law reform—justified by the alleged effect on India's burgeoning industrial sector.

The TRIPS Agreement imposes, for the first time, substantive minimum standards in patent law with which all WTO member states eventually have to comply. Apart from national treatment and a most-favoured-nation clause, there are substantive provisions covering points such as patentable subject matter, the rights that are conferred by a patent, exceptions, and the right to use the patent without the consent of the right holder. The latter points are dealt with in a very restrictive way and many conditions are imposed, while the concept of patentable subject matter is defined broadly on the basis that patents should be available for any inventions in any field of technology, as long as the invention is new, involves an inventive step, and is capable of industrial application.[9]

The European Patent Convention

In the light of all of this, it is perhaps unsurprising that the most successful and, in terms of its impact on domestic patent law, the most significant move towards the integration of patent law has been achieved among the relatively homogeneous nations of Europe.[10] It is significant to note at the outset that these developments fall outside the ambit of the EU, although they are closely associated with it, dating from the time at which the UK was a major trading country outside the Treaty of Rome.

The search for a common European concept of the patent led to the signing in Munich in 1973 of the European Patent Convention (EPC), which established the European Patent Office (EPO) that has, since 1978, effectively offered to applicants a European patent. This is achieved by signatory states agreeing to harmonize their own patent law with the definition in the European Patent Convention—hence the 1977 Patents Act in the UK—and the European Patent Office then awarding patents in all member states in relation to which the applicant has sought to acquire patent protection. The advantage of the system is that, on top of the harmonization of national patent laws, a single application now also leads to a single examination procedure. The downside of the system is that, at the end of the day, no single European patent is delivered: the applicant instead receives a bundle of national patents, one relating to each of the member states covered by the application.

---

[9] For more details, see Arts. 27–34.

[10] Although the homogeny can be exaggerated: e.g. the Netherlands had no patent system whatsoever between 1869 and 1912: Wegner (1993) *Patent Harmonization*, (n. 1) at 17.

This system has proved to be a considerable success. Applicants have shown a marked trend to seek the broader protection provided by the EPO to the extent that over 70 per cent of all applications seeking patent protection in the UK are now routed via the EPO in Munich, rather than through the UK Intellectual Property Office, graphically reflecting the international nature of both trade in general and innovation in particular. The system slowly extends its ambit; all of the EU member states are now within the scheme, along with other states such as Switzerland. A revised version of the EPC was agreed on 29 November 2000 and entered into force at the end of 2007.

The significance and far-reaching impact of the EPC system on the law of the UK is perhaps best shown by s. 130(7) of the Patents Act 1977. This declares that most key sections of the legislation are framed so as to have '*the same effect in the UK as the corresponding provisions of the European Patent Convention, the Community Patent Convention and the Patent Co-operation Treaty*'. In the light of this, it is clearly appropriate for the courts to consider not only those agreements but also their interpretations. In practice, this means that domestic litigation can, and does, make use of decisions of the EPO as to interpretation of key phrases that are common to the Convention and the 1977 legislation.

The Community patent/Unitary patent

There is, however, one further level of cooperation. Following the 1973 European Patent Convention, further discussion took place with a view to setting up a single European Community patent. This was separate from the EPO's harmonization work, because differences between member states at that time meant that it was easier to offer a measure of harmonization of the law between those countries prepared to proceed than to impose a single patent law on all member states. As far back as 1975, however, the Community Patent Convention[11] was agreed, although agreement on its implementation has never been reached.

After a long period of difficult additional negotiations, the Commission decided to revive the project in the form of an EU regulation[12] and the Council made it one of its priorities. It is understood that agreement was reached on most substantive points at the Council meeting in early December 2009, but a final agreement remained elusive. Spain and Italy could not agree to the final draft and eventually the project continued as an enhanced cooperation project of the 25 other member states. The EPO will still deal with the applications, with its language regime being applied, and the applicant will get the option to give unitary effect to the patent when it is granted.[13] This effectively turns it into a single patent for the territory of the participating member states[14] (Poland has signalled it will not continue the process, Croatia was not yet a member when the agreement was signed, and Italy and Spain did not participate in the enhanced cooperation. At the same time a Unified Patent Court is being set up. The Agreement on the Unified Patent Court[15] creates a specialized patent court ('Unified Patent Court', or UPC) with

[11] (1976) OJ L 17/1.

[12] See the Commission Proposal for a Council Regulation on the Community Patent (2000) OJ C 337/278, COM (00) 412 final.

[13] Regulation (EU) No 1257/2012 of the European Parliament and of the Council of 17 December 2012 implementing enhanced cooperation in the area of the creation of unitary patent protection [2012] OJ L-361/1. Council Regulation (EU) No 1260/2012 of 17 December 2012 implementing enhanced cooperation in the area of the creation of unitary patent protection with regard to the applicable translation arrangements [2012] OJ L-361/89.

[14] See J. Pila and C. Wadlow (2014) *The Unitary EU Patent System*, Oxford: Hart Publishing).

[15] [2013] OJ C-175/1. See <http://www.unified-patent-court.org/images/documents/upc-agreement.pdf>; see also <http://www.unified-patent-court.org/>.

exclusive jurisdiction for infringement and validity litigation relating to European patents (at least after a seven-year transition period during which the right holder can opt out) and European patents with unitary effect (unitary patents). The UPC will comprise a Court of First Instance, a Court of Appeal, and a Registry. The Court of First Instance will be composed of a central division (with seat in Paris and two sections in London and Munich) and by several local and regional divisions in the contracting member states to the agreement. The Court of Appeal will be located in Luxembourg. The same member states will participate in the UPC and Italy has recently rejoined at least the UPC.

At the time of writing the agreements are in the process of ratification and detailed rules of procedure are nearing completion. The system should become operational in 2017, according to the latest estimate.

The domestic system will remain and will provide domestic protection; the EPO's present system will remain if protection is sought either in a limited number of EU member states—with applicants selecting in relation to which countries they wish to have protection—and/or in relation to those states that are signatories to the Convention, but not EU members. The unitary patent will, eventually, automatically confer protection in all EU member states, minus Italy and Spain. For the sake of completeness, it should also be remembered that the WIPO procedures established under the Washington Patent Cooperation Treaty also remain, allowing an application for patents protection more widely again, beyond the frontiers of geographical or united Europe.

The Patent Law Treaty

Despite the existence of the Patent Cooperation Treaty and its current success, the lack of international harmonization in terms of the procedures operated by the various national patent offices still represents a major hurdle for patent applicants. WIPO member states have therefore negotiated the Patent Law Treaty (PLT), which was signed by 53 states on 1 July 2000 and which, in most cases, is currently still awaiting ratification. The UK has already ratified the PLT, which has been in force between the UK and the other countries that ratified it since 22 March 2006.[16]

The PLT does not deal with substantive law, but rather acts at procedural level and aims at harmonizing national patent formalities throughout the world. Even before ratification, however, this Treaty could be seen to be having an impact, because national patent offices and legislators were already using its provisions as a model for the updating of their own procedures.

Our discussion will be focused on the UK Patents Act 1977, but it will be appreciated that, due to the EPO's harmonization requirement that was the *raison d'être* for the legislation, the same principles govern the application for a domestic patent, an EPO patent, or the future unitary patent, and the same very broad principles will be significant features in an application made under the provisions of the Washington Treaty.

Obtaining a patent

This is not a book that is designed to give full instructions on the practicalities of applying for a patent. The substantive law and, in particular, some of the problems it poses for applicants are, however, shaped by the way in which the procedures operate, so it is

---

[16] 36 on 19 October 2015.

appropriate to begin our survey of the substantive law by providing an outline of the key steps to be taken in pursuit of a domestic patent.

The priority date

In relation to any patent application, the first vital point to establish is the priority date of the applicant's invention. The essence of a patent is that it is something new that has not previously existed and so it is vital to establish a priority date ahead of anyone else in the field—particularly in a typical patent race, in which rival firms are pursuing the same, or a similar, line of research.

The relevant date is the date of filing the application for a patent;[17] the only exception is if an earlier date is claimed, being a previous application within the past year that discloses matter in support of the subsequent application.[18] This priority date is important not only because it establishes priority over any rival applications from the date, but also because it sets the clock running for the period of validity of the patent itself.

The priority date works internationally. Under the provisions of the Paris Convention 1883, the applicant who files in one of the member states then has 12 months from the priority date to file in any other member state. During that period, the applicant will be able to benefit from the priority date of the original first application. For various, often procedural, reasons, not all of these applications are identical: it is therefore important to ascertain whether the document that is relied on in terms of priority covers the whole content of the application that claims the benefit of the earlier priority date. The Court of Appeal more recently held[19] that there should be sufficient detail and information in the priority document that is being relied on to give the 'skilled man' essentially the same information as that which formed the subject of the claim in the application for the benefit of which priority is claimed and which would enable him to work the invention in accordance with the claim. The priority document as a whole, therefore, must both disclose and enable the invention.

The filing of an application

Given that the priority date is the date on which the application is filed, the next issue to consider is what acts amount to a filing. This is defined in the UK Patents Act 1977, s. 15(1): the vital elements that are needed are the presentation to the UK Intellectual Property Office of documents that indicate that a patent is being sought, which identify the applicant for the patent, which contain a description of the invention, and which, naturally, are accompanied by the appropriate fee. In order to obtain an effective priority date, there has to be an enabling disclosure of the invention. The skilled person to whom the description of the invention is addressed must be able to reproduce it without engaging in inventive activity.[20] That issue is decided at the priority date, rather than at the time of the publication of the specification.[21]

These acts together create the filing date, but beg a vital question: when should an inventor time his or her filing date? On the one hand, if the inventor files at too early a stage

---

[17] Patents Act 1977, s. 5(1).   [18] Patents Act 1977, s. 5(2).

[19] In *Unilin Beheer BV v. Berry Floor NV and ors* [2004] All ER (D) 603; see also the decision of the Enlarged Board of Appeal of the EPO in Case G02/98, *In re Same Invention* [2001] OJ EPO 11, *sub nom. R v. X/Same invention* [2002] EPOR 167.

[20] See *Asahi Kasei Kogyo's Application* [1991] RPC 485.

[21] See *Biogen v. Medeva* [1997] RPC 1.

of development, there is a risk that, in subsequent examination by the UK Intellectual Property Office or later revocation proceedings instigated by a rival, the invention will be found not to fulfil the precise requirements of the law for patentability. On the other hand, the earlier that a claim is filed, the better placed the inventor is as against his or her rivals in a patent race, especially because the state of the art against which the novelty of the invention is judged is that pertaining at the date of filing the application.[22]

The law gives some assistance that helps to support a decision to apply earlier rather than later. The requirements of the Patents Act 1977, s. 15, are really very minimal and considerably understate the true amount of documentation that will be required by the UK Intellectual Property Office. Indeed, the section hints at this by stating that, after a period of 12 months,[23] the application will be deemed to have been withdrawn unless the claims and abstract have already been submitted.[24] This, in effect, gives the applicant a year's leeway to get from the minimalist position at the date of filing to finalizing the detail of the application before it is formally examined, during which period it is protected by having a priority date to use against other subsequent applications.

What, then, are these all-important 'claims' and 'abstracts' that must form part of the application? A starting point is s. 14 of the Act, which states that every application shall contain a request for a patent to be granted, a specification containing a description of the invention, a claim, and an abstract of it (although the position of other documents that still comply with s. 15(1) is reserved and these may also initiate an application). The vital elements are the specification and claim—the abstract simply being a help to later searchers through the files of the UK Intellectual Property Office—with the claim being supported by the description.

The reason why these documents are vital is that the specification and claim form the basis of the invention applied for and thus delimit its scope. The claim is part of the patent specification and will effectively delimit the scope of the monopoly. Precise drafting of the specification and claim is, therefore, important, because any subsequent litigation—whether in relation to patentability, infringement, or revocation –is bound to be very closely concerned with what is the true basis of the invention.

Statutory guidance is given as to the broad nature of these two crucial components in a patent application. Section 14(3) provides:

> The specification of an application shall disclose the invention in a manner which is clear enough and complete enough for the invention to be performed by a person skilled in the art.

Section 14(5), meanwhile, establishes that the claim must define the matter for which patent protection is sought, must be clear and concise, must be supported by the description, and must relate either to one invention, or to a related group of inventions.

In practice, the level of detail that goes into these documents—particularly the specification—is quite significant. The specification must, in effect, contain instructions by which someone other than the inventor—albeit someone who is skilled in the relevant art—might reproduce the invention and so the fullest information should be given for this purpose: if the specification were to be found to be unworkable, no patent would be granted. Likewise, the claims are so called because they delimit the extent of the monopoly that is being claimed, so it is essential to include as many different aspects of the new invention as possible. These documents are easier to read than to describe; extensive extracts appear in many reports of patent litigation. Two examples that have the added

---

[22] Patents Act 1977, s. 2(2). See Ch. 4. [23] Under r. 22 of The Patents Rules 2007, SI 2007/3291.
[24] Patents Act 1977, s. 15(10).

advantage of being in relation to ordinary—that is, non-scientific—subject matter are *Procter & Gamble Co. v. Peaudouce (UK) Ltd*[25] (relating to nappies) and *A. C. Edwards Ltd v. Acme Signs & Displays Ltd*[26] (relating to petrol price indicators).

Again, in this area, practical difficulties are quickly placed in the way of the applicant. It is apparent from the foregoing that, in terms of gaining and retaining patent protection, the fullest information possible should be provided for the specification and claims. For other reasons, however, it is tempting to provide as little information as possible. Remember that a key aspect of the patent system is public disclosure of the patent, so the more information provided to the UK Intellectual Property Office, the more information is also provided to trade rivals. Also, the longer the time spent in checking and testing that procedures work, or in adding additional claims, the greater the likelihood is that a trade rival may jump in first and claim patent protection for itself. In fairness, the latter point is somewhat tempered by the fact that amendments may be allowed during the application procedure, although not so as to extend the protection of the patent.[27] Typically, an amendment may consist either of a refinement of an aspect of the specification or claim within its terms as research work continues, or may be a withdrawal of some aspect of the protection sought, in the light, perhaps, of new evidence of the prior state of the art becoming available. It is even possible to seek an amendment of the patent after its grant,[28] which may be useful to pre-empt a threat of revocation by another. But it is important to note that such an amendment may never expand the claim to exclusivity of the patent;[29] only a reduction in scope is permissible.

The examination process

Returning to the steps necessary to be taken in order to gain a patent, on receipt of all of the information furnished by the applicant, the UK Intellectual Property Office will conduct a search among other patents—records of all patents are held—with a particular view to a provisional assessment of the application's novelty and obviousness, which are two vital factors in deciding whether it is patentable. After this takes place and assuming, of course, that the applicant has not been deterred by the experience, publication of the application then takes place no more than 18 months after the priority date.

This is another important juncture in the tactics of patent application and opposition. From the time of publication, the information in the application is obviously in the public domain, which is good for the applicant in that he or she will now be able to establish clearly that he or she has won any race to patent the invention and can claim damages for infringement from this time onwards, but bad news in that rivals are now able to find out about the invention and so can, variously, seek to develop it further, consider issues of revocation and/or infringement, or, most immediately, decide to register an objection to the grant of a patent. Interested parties have a right under the Patents Act, s. 21, to submit observations as to patentability during the next stage of the patent procedure.

The UK Intellectual Property Office will now proceed to a full examination of all aspects of the patent application, offering ample opportunity for the applicant to contribute his or her own observations to the process. Obviously, the time that this will take can vary enormously from case to case, depending on the problems that arise and including possible s. 21 representations by third parties. The UK Act does, however, stipulate a

---

[25] [1989] FSR 180.   [26] [1992] RPC 131.   [27] Patents Act 1977, ss. 19 and 76(2)(b).
[28] Patents Act 1977, s. 27; see also s. 75.
[29] See *Baker Hughes Inc. v. Halliburton Energy Services Inc.* (2003) 26(1) IPD 26003.

maximum period of four and a half years from the filing date (or any earlier appropriate priority date).[30] It may seem harsh that, if the application has not been completed by that time, it will be deemed to have been refused unless an appeal is pending,[31] but, because an appeal may be lodged against the deemed refusal itself,[32] that hardship is mitigated.

After that time—and the UK Intellectual Property Office claims that most applications take between two and three years—a patent can be granted by the UK Intellectual Property Office. This has the effect of creating a proprietary right in the patentee,[33] one that exists for 20 years, subject to the payment of a fee for renewal after the first five years have passed.[34] It is significant to note that the 20-year period is calculated not from the grant of the patent itself, but from the date on which the application is filed, which we have just seen can be up to four and a half years earlier—and this represents around a 20 per cent loss of usable exploitation time for the patent. The trend has, however, been towards lengthening the term of patent protection. The 1883 Act offered only 14 years from the date of filing, while the 1939 Act stretched this to 16 years; the current period stems from the EPC and the 1977 legislation. It is also true that, during the period between filing and grant, much preparatory work can be done to get the patent ready for the market and that there is protection against exploitation by others during this period.

There may, however, be some substance to complaints from industries such as the pharmaceutical trade who can point to the fact that, even after the grant of a patent, more time will be lost not only by the usual final preparations for marketing the launch of a new product that are common to all industries, but also the further delays that result from the need to comply with the rigorous testing requirements that have to be undergone by new products in such specific industries. It seems unlikely that the 20-year period will be extended any further for now, except in relation to specific areas such as pharmaceuticals, for which the EPC was amended in 1991 to permit such extensions, following the lead already set by the US and Japan, and subject to the ratification of the amendment by EPC signatories. It may, however, be doubted whether this ratification will occur in the near future[35] and, besides, this problem has, to an extent, been alleviated by the idea of the supplementary protection certificate (SPC), which can, in limited circumstances, extend the period of protection for medical products and which is considered separately in Chapter 7. This point is, of course, relevant to the discussions in Chapter 1 about the incentive to invent that is provided by the patent system: until the argument of the drug firms was accepted, it might be argued that the battle to gain a monopoly would have borne a result for only a little over a decade, which suggests that general profits from sales, rather than the extra profits from monopoly sales, may be just as much of an inducement.

Whether it is actually a valuable asset or not, the volume of litigation arising from the process of awarding a patent suggests that it is seen to be such and the way in which the law has created such a thorough system—some may even call it an ordeal—through which applicants must pass before a patent is granted tends to support such a perception. The fact that a proprietary right is being created is perhaps some justification for the elaborate procedures involved, but it hardly reflects the relative ease with which trade marks and copyright can be acquired. Perhaps a better justification is that the criteria issued by the law in deciding the issue of patentability are not easy to use, reflecting the difficulty encountered in translating an abstract concept, such as an invention, into

---

[30] Patents Act 1977, s. 20; Patents Rules 2007, r. 30.   [31] Patents Act 1977, s. 20(1).

[32] Patents Act 1977, s. 97.   [33] Patents Act 1977, s. 30.   [34] Patents Act 1977, s. 25.

[35] J. N. Adams, 'Supplementary Protection Certificates: The Challenge to EC Regulation 1768/92' [1994] 8 EIPR 323, 326.

black-and-white legal principles. These are, however, issues that need to be considered in the light of the substantive rules that the following chapters will consider and the whole area can be overviewed in Chapter 8. The next chapter, then, will consider the criteria used in the patentability assessment.

An overview

The patent system originated as a system of privileges that were granted to attract foreign technologies to the country. Gradually, it became a system with set benchmarks and criteria under which any inventor could apply, which is very much in line with its main purpose to reward the inventor in order to encourage R&D and innovation. Newer and better products and processes are seen to be desirable, and the patent system offers incentives in this respect.

At the international level, the Paris Convention set out the basic principle of national treatment. Further harmonization and cooperation was achieved by means of the Patent Cooperation Treaty, the Patent Law Treaty, and the TRIPS Agreement. In Europe, the European Patent Convention even provided an integrated patent system of sorts.

In order to obtain a patent in the UK, an application needs to be filed. The priority date is vital in this respect because we are dealing with a 'first to file' system. The claims and specification are also extremely important, but the application can be completed after the initial filing of a skeleton application. The Patent Office then examines the claim and, usually between two and three years after the initial filing, a patent will be granted in appropriate cases.

Further reading

DENT, CH. 'An Exploration of the Principles, Precepts and Purposes that Provide Structure to the Patent System' (2008) 4 IPQ 456.

NUYTS, A. (ed.) (2008) *International Litigation in Intellectual Property*, London: Kluwer Law International.

PHILLIPS, J. 'The English Patent as a Reward for Invention: The Importation of an Idea' (1982) 3 J Leg Hist 71.

WEGNER, H. (1993) *Patent Harmonization*, London: Sweet and Maxwell.

4

Patentability

In this chapter we look at the conditions that need to be met for a patent to be granted and for the invention to be patentable.

Few things appear simpler in patent law than the basic definition of patentability. According to s. 1(1) of the UK Patents Act 1977, which is based on Art. 52 of the European Patent Convention (EPC):

> A patent may be granted only for an invention in respect of which the following conditions are satisfied, that is to say—
>
> (a) the invention is new;
> (b) it involves an inventive step;
> (c) it is capable of industrial application;
> (d) the grant of a patent for it is not excluded by subsections (2) and (3) below;
>
> and references in this Act to a patentable invention shall be construed accordingly.

Figure 4.1 schematically illustrates this. Section 1(2) goes on to make clear that discoveries, scientific theories, and mathematical methods cannot be regarded as inventions and are thus not patentable; likewise barred from this status are works properly found within copyright, schemes for performing a mental act, playing a game or doing business, and computer programs, and also the presentation of information. Section 1(3) also limits the role of patents by denying their protection to offensive, immoral, or antisocial inventions. So the discovery in a tropical jungle of a new curative drug, or the development of a new, but unlawful, relaxant cannot be patented even if all of the s. 1(1) requirements are met.

All of these different points will require clarification and elucidation; many have been the subject of extensive litigation and resultant case law. Our methodology will be simply to examine each aspect in turn so as to build up an overall picture of what the law will regard as matter appropriate for a successful patent application—what, in other words, will come within the legal definition of the concept of an invention. As will be seen later, the meaning of 'invention' itself has to be given some consideration, but, initially, we will approach the issue of patentability through the elements declared by s. 1(1). Note, however, that these key concepts tend to overlap in practice and that discussion in many leading cases covers more than one closely related aspect.

Traditionally, a distinction is made between patents for inventions that relate to new products—that is, product patents—and patents for inventions that relate to new processes—that is, process patents. Some discussion has arisen in relation to patents containing a claim to products produced by a process. In some decisions, the European Patent Office (EPO) seems to suggest that the limitation of a claim to such products produced by a process could not impart novelty on the claim.[1] The Court of Appeal rejected

---

[1] Decision T150/82 *International Flavors & Fragrances Inc./Claim Categories* [1984] OJ EPO 309.

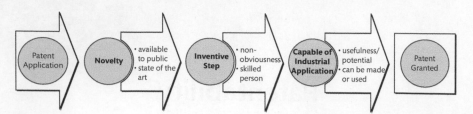

Figure 4.1 Requirements for patentability

that approach under UK law, only for the House of Lords to align itself with the EPO.[2] Any categorization of patents is without legal meaning on this point and one should instead focus on whether the application—and, in particular, the claims (to exclusivity)— meet the requirements for patentability to which we will now turn.

Novelty

Most laymen would understand that an invention is something new and the law reflects this. The way in which s. 2(1) of the 1977 Act expresses this is that '*an invention shall be new if it does not form part of the state of the art*', so the reward (if such it be) of a patent goes to those who have gone beyond pre-existing knowledge, whether by creating a new product that was not previously available on the market or by developing a process not hitherto available. (The Act, for the most part, does not distinguish between patents for products and those for processes.)

The basic definition of novelty obviously begs the question of what matter is regarded as forming part of the 'state of the art'. Section 2(2) helps:

The state of the art in the case of an invention shall be taken to comprise all matter (whether a product, a process, information about either, or anything else) which has at any time before the priority date of that invention been made available to the public (whether in the United Kingdom or elsewhere) by written or oral description, by use or in any other way.

The state of the art

Clearly, the 'state of the art' is broadly defined and represents a major hurdle for the patent applicant.[3] Several points need to be emphasized in considering what information forms part of the state of the art and what effect it has on the later patent application. An obvious point is that the key date is the priority date and applications made after that date cannot form part of the state of the art by definition, because they do not anticipate the claimant's application. Particular problems arise, however, in relation to patents for which applications were received on an earlier date, but which have not yet been published. It may seem harsh for something that is inherently not yet available to the public to be regarded as part of the state of the art, but to allow the later applicant to proceed would lead to a very high risk of 'double patenting'—that is, of two people having exclusive patent rights in respect of the same thing, which is, of course, a complete contradiction in terms. Accordingly, s. 2(3) establishes that, for the purpose of assessing the

---

[2] *Kirin-Amgen Inc. v. Transkaryotic Therapies Inc.* [2003] RPC 31 (CA), [2005] 1 All ER 667 (HL).
[3] For a good example, see *Smithkline Beecham plc v. Apotex Europe Ltd* [2005] FSR 23.

state of the art for an invention, material in subsequently published patent applications is included, as long as the priority date of that application is earlier than the priority date of the invention in question—and this is so even if the actual material in the subsequently published specification was not filed until after the priority date of the invention in question. In applying this rule, the EPO will only consider those applications that have been made in respect of the same states.[4] So while it is a harsh rule, perhaps, it is a clear rule that promotes certainty and, in a patent race, a rule that is an inducement to make an application sooner rather than later. The only potential dent in the rule comes from *Asahi Kasei Kogyo KK's Application*,[5] which will be considered later in this chapter.

Normally the priority date is the date on which the application has been made, but an invention can claim to be entitled to priority from an earlier application. In such a case the application should be supported by matter disclosed in the earlier application, i.e. the earlier application has to clearly and unambiguously disclose the invention claimed in the later application along the lines of the criterion set out in s. 5(2) Patents Act 1977.[6] Its equivalent in the EPC, Art. 87(1), speaks about both covering the same invention. One does of course accept that the language used in both documents is different, as long as it means the same thing to the skilled person.[7] In *Medimmune v. Novartis*,[8] the Court of Appeal argued that the requirement falls apart in three points:

- it needs to be the same invention. The skilled person can derive the subject matter directly and unambiguously (using common general knowledge) from the priority document;
- the approach is not formulaic, but a matter of technical disclosure; and
- the document as a whole is enabling and gives the skilled person what is in the claim.[9]

Available to the public

The widening of the relevant prior information that makes up the state of the art to include any material available to the public anywhere creates the next problem. Availability to the public is not too difficult an issue, at least in the sense that a clear line can usually be drawn between public and private circulation of information: an internal company document is clearly private, but publication of a research paper in a learned journal—even one of some obscurity—clearly places its contents into the public domain. This is particularly so in respect of any publication in the UK, copies of which must be sent to the British Library and normally to the other five so-called 'copyright libraries', in Oxford, Cambridge, Edinburgh, Aberystwyth, and Dublin.[10]

Borderline cases on the public–private divide have been the subject of some litigation. It is clear that internal documentation may become public by its subsequent use, as in *Monsanto Co. (Brignac's) Application*,[11] in which a patent was being sought for a process for colouring nylon. This was successfully opposed on the grounds that around 30 or 40 copies of a brochure giving information about the process had been given out to salesmen employed by the patentees and that it was expected that these, in turn, would

---

[4] EPC, Art. 54.   [5] [1991] RPC 485.

[6] *Intervet UK Ltd v. Merial* [2010] EWHC 294 (Pat), *Medimmune Ltd v. Novartis Pharmaceuticals UK Ltd and Medical Research Council* [2011] EWHC 1669 (Pat), and *Generics (UK) Ltd (t/a Mylan) v. Yeda Research and Development Co. Ltd and Teva Industries Ltd* [2012] EWHC 1848 (Pat).

[7] *Unilin v. Berry Floor* [2005] FSR 6, at para. 39.   [8] [2013] RPC 27, at paras. 151–4.

[9] See also *Unwired Planet International Ltd v. Huawei and Samsung* [2015] EWHC 3366 (Pat), per Birss J.

[10] Legal Deposit Libraries Act 2003, ss. 1 and 14.   [11] [1971] RPC 153.

be passed on to potential customers. This, then, amounted to prior publication. This decision may seem to make advance publicity and prior contact with potential customers a risky business, and it is clearly safer to wait until after the priority date. But this is not essential, as was shown in the case of *Pall Corp. v. Commercial Hydraulics (Bedford) Ltd*,[12] in which a new membrane could be patented in spite of an earlier demonstration to a potential customer and others. That demonstration had been undertaken at a private gathering, under what all present understood to be circumstances of confidentiality, and also was such that vital information about the nature of the new product was not disclosed and could not be deduced. Not only was it not a disclosure to the public, neither was it an enabling disclosure: it did not allow any witnesses to gain enough information to make a similar membrane themselves. Thus it was not relevant. This concept of the 'enabling disclosure' is important and will be considered later in this chapter.

Greater problems arise not so much with the 'public' aspect of public availability, but in considering what is meant by 'availability'. Copyright libraries may resolve the problem domestically, but, on the face of it, a literal interpretation of s. 2(2) means that anything anywhere in the public domain will form part of the state of the art. Revelations made in Mongolia's press, for example, while unknown to anyone in the West, might render an invention unpatentable and liable to revocation when uncovered. This may seem unlikely, but major and growing trading nations pose similar problems of accessibility of information: Japan, China, or Thailand are all obvious examples. One argument would be to give the word 'available' a broad interpretation, in the spirit of the European origin of this part of patent law,[13] and exclude matters in the Thai technical press as not being de facto available to the public, because, in practice, the public would have no access to it. Indeed, it is a fair point that searches by the UK Intellectual Property Office are also unlikely to discover such obscure items of information, whether at the domestic, EPO, or Washington Patent Cooperation Treaty level of search. But this approach might lead back to the menace of double patenting and it is suggested that the better view is that, as a bar to patentability, the existence of material publicly available anywhere—even if available only after the most extensive searches—best reflects the interests of the international trading community. This has the support of the decision in *Woven Plastic Products Ltd v. British Ropes Ltd*,[14] which is to be considered later in this chapter.

The six-month grace period

One type of information that is available to the public is expressly excluded from any consideration when the state of the art is being assessed: any information that has been disclosed from six months prior to the filing date onwards, which is information that has been obtained either unlawfully or in breach of confidence, or, alternatively, if it has been divulged in breach of confidence. The protection also extends to disclosure resulting from the display of the invention at an international exhibition,[15] this being a limited category of events such as world fairs and international 'expos'. This subsection will often confer a double benefit on the inventor who, in an appropriate case, can not only exclude the revealed information from the state of the art, but also, in appropriate cases, bring an action against the confider for breach of confidence. This is a most useful reminder that actions for breach of confidence often arise from situations in which patents are being

---

[12] [1990] FSR 329. See also *Strix Ltd v. Otter Controls Ltd* [1995] RPC 607.
[13] See Ch. 6 for discussion on interpretation after the *Catnic* case.   [14] [1970] FSR 47.
[15] Patents Act 1977, s. 2(4).

discussed and developed, and form a useful supplement to the remedies of the patentee even if—or especially if—no patent is awarded (as seen in Chapter 29).

Anticipation

So far, we have concentrated on what information forms part of the state of the art. Now we must investigate more carefully the nature of that information and, in particular, whether it actually does anticipate the patent for which an application is subsequently received. 'Anticipation' is the word commonly used to assess the impact of the prior state of the art on the later invention and the question is whether the operation of the prior product or process forestalls the later patent.[16]

A first example can be found in *Van der Lely (C) NV v. Bamfords*,[17] in which a photograph of a hayrake machine, the rake-wheels of which were turned by contact with the ground rather than by an engine, anticipated the patent application for a hayrake machine with the same feature. It was no longer new once the courts had accepted that the photograph was sufficiently clear to reveal the intention of the photographed object to an informed person.

An equally simple example is provided by *Windsurfing International Inc. v. Tabur Marine (Great Britain) Ltd.*[18] In this case, a patent had been granted in 1968 to the plaintiffs for the invention of the windsurfing board and other related forms of propulsion. On finding that the defendants were also selling such equipment, they sought to take action for infringement of their patent. The defendants, in turn, objected to the initial validity of the patent and sought to have it revoked. It should be noted that this is a very common method of raising the patentability question as a counterclaim to an allegation of infringement. The acts that were put forward as evidence of anticipation were those of a boy aged 12 back in 1958, who, while on holiday at Hayling Island in Hampshire, made and used a primitive sailboard for his own amusement. The temporary, personal, and little-known character of the user were all regarded as irrelevant,[19] and, although the patented device had a more sophisticated control mechanism than that of the boy's, this apparatus was irrelevant for the purposes of anticipation given that the same basic control principles were used. (Whether the improvements were obvious is reviewed later in this chapter.) Likewise, the existence of an article featuring the excitement of the new sport of 'sailboarding', which appeared in 1966, also anticipated the patent by demonstrating something similar to the patented boards, again adopting the same basic principles of construction. Prior use can destroy novelty if it releases information in the same way that a publication would do—that is, a skilled worker must be able to discover and reproduce the invention through observation and analysis of the use.[20]

It is clear from the case law that relatively minor acts are sufficient to anticipate, but more may be needed because the anticipation has to be of the invention itself. *Fomento Industrial SA Biro Swan Ltd v. Mentmore Manufacturing Co.*[21] illustrates both points. The plaintiffs had a 1945 patent for the manufacture of a particular type of improved ballpoint pen and its revocation was sought on the basis of prior use, in the form of the limited availability of pilot models of the new pen in the 1944–5 period. There was enough non-private use that these events could, and did, amount to anticipation, but now we must consider if what was revealed by these events was the subsequently patented

[16] *General Tire & Rubber Co. v. Firestone Tyre & Rubber Co.* [1972] RPC 457, per Sachs LJ at 485.
[17] [1963] RPC 61.   [18] [1985] RPC 59.   [19] [1985] RPC 59 at 77–8, per Oliver LJ.
[20] See *Stahlwerk Becker's Patent* (1919) 36 RPC 13.   [21] [1956] RPC 87.

invention. Mere use of a biro may well not disclose anything about its workings—the patent was specifically for a method of producing the more regular flow of ink—but of greater significance was an earlier patent application by a group related to the plaintiffs for a broadly similar pen. This, however, did not amount to anticipation, because the best that could be said for it was that it 'might well' achieve the result of the later patent, whereas the effect of the later patent was effectively to ensure that the desired result *was* achieved. Thus the prior use, but not the prior patent application, was a ground for revocation.

Since 1977, public availability has been the sole test and it would therefore have to be asked whether the use of the pen disclosed the inventive concept. This will be a question of fact: in *Windsurfing*—although also under the pre-1977 law—there was a clear visible relationship between the anticipating use and the later patent, but in a case such as *Fomento*, it is less obvious that mere use will reveal the inventive concept of the improved operation of the ball point, which is almost always firmly encased in plastic, and it may be unlikely that there would be any anticipation on the facts of *Fomento* today.

Here too, though, further refinements are needed before the law can be fully appreciated. One interesting problem is that provided by the facts that underlie the decision in *Merrell Dow Pharmaceuticals Inc. v. H. N. Norton & Co. Ltd*.[22] The fundamental issue in relation to this case is whether the availability of a product to the public necessarily carries with it all of the relevant knowledge and information that lies behind that product. In *Merrell Dow*, litigation arose in relation to an antihistamine drug including the ingredient terfenadine. The problem was that it was 'available to the public', in the sense that it was known to exist under a patent from 1972 onwards, but that research, including clinical trials, continued into how precisely it worked for some years thereafter, until fuller understanding was reached as to its workings. As a result of this research, the vital by-product that resulted from its use—the acid metabolite—was identified and itself patented in 1980. So, did the use of terfenadine, inevitably producing the acid metabolite, after 1992 infringe Merrell Dow's earlier patent or did the company's rights survive until 2000?[23] The House of Lords took the view that the earlier patent, which—albeit unknowingly—produced the acid metabolite, was the relevant patent; accordingly, rivals were free to use this drug from 1992 onwards. Anticipation had occurred by disclosure and the creation of the acid metabolite had been occurring since 1972 as an inevitable consequence of following the specification of the oldest patent; the specific 1980 patent for the acid metabolite was therefore revocable.

Lest the complexities of antihistamine drugs are less than clear, Lord Hoffmann, in the sole speech in the case,[24] uses an example that is perhaps clearer. For centuries, Amazonian Indians have used a powdered tree bark to treat malaria. In 1820, it was discovered by French scientists that the active ingredient within the particular bark in question was quinine and, by 1944, its precise chemical composition had been worked out, meaning that it could be made synthetically. Lord Hoffmann argued cogently that the centuries of past history would anticipate any post-1944 attempt to patent the creation of quinine:

> The Amazonian Indian who treats himself with powdered bark for fever is using quinine, even if he thinks that the reason why the treatment is effective is that the tree is favoured by the

---

[22] [1996] RPC 76.   [23] In each case, 20 years from the original patent's priority date.
[24] [1996] RPC 76 at 88.

Gods. The teachings of his traditional medicine contain enough information to enable him to do exactly what a scientist in the forest would have done if he wanted to treat a fever but had no supplies of quinine sulphate.[25]

So even ignorant use may anticipate, with the result in this case—which is one with wide implications—that the years of subsequent research into the precise working of terfenadine would be pointless in terms of patentability,[26] at least for the purposes for which the drug was used.[27]

This issue has been further considered in *Chiron Corp. v. Evans Medical Ltd.*[28] Applying *Merrell Dow*, it was found that, for the purposes of anticipation, there was no need to know that a product was being created by a process, but that anticipation would occur if there was a conscious decision to engage in a process rather than if the product was created unintentionally and, perhaps, unexpectedly.

The notional 'skilled reader'

The notion of ignorant use of a product or process begs a further question: we need to know whose use is under consideration. To revert to the *Fomento* example, we all pick up ballpoint pens continually without (until now) considering how they work; to a ballpoint expert, however, much would be clear very quickly even from mere use, let alone a quick examination. We therefore need to consider the issue of whose eyes should be used in assessing whether the anticipatory event reveals the actual inventive concept or, to put it another way, whether the prior disclosure is an 'enabling disclosure'.

Clear guidance on this issue is provided by *General Tire & Rubber Co. v. Firestone Tyre & Rubber Co.*[29] The plaintiffs had a patent for making tyres from a mixture of synthetic rubber, oil, and carbon black. The defendants attacked it on various grounds, including anticipation of the patent by three earlier specifications for similar products and an article in the journal *Rubber Age*. The Court of Appeal approached the issue by comparing the patentee's claim and the earlier documents, and construing them at the respective relevant dates by a reader skilled in the art to which they relate having regard to the state of knowledge in such art at the relevant date.[30] This creates the idea of the court placing itself in the position of the 'notional skilled reader', an upmarket version of tort law's 'reasonable man', blessed with reasonable knowledge, but not, in this case, universal knowledge appropriate to the area in which the patent applies. Further, the notional skilled reader should, in an area of high technology, be replaced by a team of readers whose collective skills would be those employed in making the comparison. It was also established that it is the result of the alleged anticipatory process or product that is vital, not the expression or intention of the author, thus enabling anticipation to occur by virtue of the inadvertent qualities of the earlier activity.[31] It was found by the Court of Appeal that use of none of the alleged anticipations would have been likely to achieve the particular benefits of General Tire's new method of manufacture.

Union Carbide Corp. v. BP Chemicals[32] provides a different slant on this by noting, appropriately, that doing something that, although recognized in the prior art, was regarded as something that should not be done was clearly novel, because it would go against the perceptions of the normal skilled man.

---

[25] [1996] RPC 76 at 91.   [26] See I. Karet, 'A Question of Epistemology' (1996) 2 EIPR 97.
[27] Per Lord Hoffmann in *Merrell Dow* [1996] RPC 76 at 91.   [28] [1998] RPC 517.
[29] [1972] RPC 457.   [30] [1972] RPC 457, per Sachs LJ at 485.
[31] E.g. *Molins v. Industrial Machinery Co. Ltd* (1937) 55 RPC 31.   [32] [1998] RPC 1.

Anticipation requires an enabling disclosure

A useful application of the 'enabling disclosure' approach is to be found in *Quantel Ltd v. Spaceward Microsystems Ltd*.[33] This concerned computer-based videographic systems, the plaintiffs owning the patents of their 'Paintbox' system for producing graphics, which was a popular system, numbering the UK's British Broadcasting Corporation (BBC) and the US National Broadcasting Company (NBC) among its users. In considering whether four other earlier videographic systems anticipated the plaintiffs' system, it was emphasized by Falconer J,[34] following *General Tire*, that the prior publication had to provide clear and unmistakable directions to its addressee before it would count as an enabling disclosure.

The use of stored data in the graphics of the plaintiffs' system was not present in those of the first rival, Levoy, so that did not anticipate. Those of the second, Paint, had many similarities, but again did not go as far as the plaintiffs' in that they did not have processing means and variants of it also did not anticipate. Two systems devised at the New York Institute of Technology (NYIT) were not seen as being properly regarded as video image creation systems. Finally, the demonstration by the plaintiffs of a prototype of their system did not anticipate, because key features had not, at that stage, been invented and a demonstration that allowed use, but provided no inspection or explanation of the equipment used, was not to be regarded as an enabling disclosure.

This area has now been considered at the highest level in *Asahi Kasei Kogyo KK's Application*,[35] in which a patent was sought for a genetically engineered polypeptide, a product useful for treating tumours. The problem was that an earlier application had claimed the existence of the polypeptide, but had not gone so far as to describe how it may be produced. The House of Lords held that this did not count as an anticipation: the indication of the existence of the polypeptide did not itself show how it could be produced, nor was it so self-evident how it may be produced that it would be regarded as an enabling disclosure. For there to be anticipation, the common general knowledge in this industry—which can be added to the material contained in the allegedly anticipating disclosure—should have allowed the skilled person to select or secure the starting material, or to make intermediate products.

The problem with the case is that, by interpreting s. 2(3) of the 1977 Act as only applying to enabling disclosures in earlier applications, it dents the force of that subsection by creating cases in which there is a risk of double patenting of the same invention. In this case, different patents could exist for the polypeptide and for its use, which seems unproductive. This issue was recognized by the House of Lords, but was thought to be something that would only happen rarely,[36] and, in any event, appeared to accord with the approach of both the 1977 Act and Art. 54 of the EPC.

The norm in *Synthon*: disclosure and enablement

This case[37] suggested an alternative approach when anticipation was claimed on the back of an application with an earlier priority date that had not yet been published when the allegedly anticipated second application was filed. The judge had suggested that the better approach in such a case was to ask whether the two inventors had, in substance, reached the same invention. If so, the application with the earlier priority date would anticipate

---

[33] [1990] RPC 83.   [34] [1990] RPC 83 at 112.

[35] [1991] RPC 485, approved in *Biogen Inc. v. Medeva plc* [1997] RPC 1.

[36] [1991] RPC 485 at 542.

[37] *Synthon BV v. Smithkline Beecham plc* [2005] All ER (D) 235, [2006] RPC 10 (HL).

the other application. The Court of Appeal explicitly overruled that decision,[38] however, and reiterated the test laid down in *General Tire* and *Asahi*. The *Synthon* case eventually went all the way to the House of Lords and provided a seminal judgment on what are the requirements for an enabling disclosure that leads to anticipation. The House of Lords reversed the judgment of the Court of Appeal and held that, in the context of s. 2 of the 1977 Act, 'disclosure' and 'enablement' are distinct concepts, each of which has to be satisfied for there to be anticipation.

The House defined the concept of disclosure along the following lines: the matter relied upon as prior art must disclose subject matter that, if performed, would necessarily result in an infringement of the patent. That may be because the prior art disclosed the same invention, but patent infringement does not require that one should be aware that one is infringing. From this, it follows that—whether or not it would be apparent to anyone at the time—whenever subject matter described in the prior disclosure is capable of being performed and is such that, if performed, it must result in the patent being infringed, the disclosure requirement is satisfied. This is so even if a person who reads the patent and sets out to make what is described in the application thinks that he or she is making something different because of an error in the application, as long as a skilled person would inevitably produce that which is described.

The second concept that is required in the context of s. 2—the enablement concept—was defined as follows. In *Synthon*, the applicant's application disclosed the use of a solvent that, in fact, proved to be unsuitable for crystallization, but the trial judge was correct in his view that the skilled man would have sought to try some other solvent that either was mentioned in the application or which formed part of his general knowledge. It is therefore not necessary that the disclosure enabled the invention to be performed for the first time without any trial and error on the part of the skilled person or team; enablement requires only that the skilled man or team is able to perform the disclosed invention by using the disclosure and common general knowledge.

Summing up

In essence, this judgment reformulates the *General Tire* test somewhat by stressing the presence of two requirements of disclosure and enablement,[39] but it does not significantly change it. Anticipation can therefore be summed up as follows when the claims in the patent are for a process or a method of use.

Anything that is to anticipate the patent and remove its novelty is to give clear and unmistakable directions to what the patentee claims to have invented[40]—that is, anticipation will only occur and the novelty of the application in respect of an invention will only be destroyed if the anticipating information made the invention available to the public, which means that it must have contained clear and unmistakable directions to make the invention (making allowances for the general knowledge of the skilled person).[41] One is in this respect always evaluating a single piece of potentially anticipating information. If the claims in the patent refer to a product, the anticipating item must enable the skilled reader to perceive the discovery at once, and to understand and be able to apply it

---

[38] *Synthon BV v. Smithkline Beecham plc (No. 2)* [2003] RPC 43 (CA), overruling *Synthon BV v. Smithkline Beecham plc* [2003] RPC 6.

[39] *Synthon BV v. Smithkline Beecham plc* (HL) (n. 37).

[40] *Chiron Corp. v. Evans Medical Ltd* [1998] RPC 517 at 560–1, with reference to *Flour Oxidising v. Carr* (1908) 25 RPC 428, per Parker J at 457; see also *Beecham Group's (Amoxycillin) Application* [1980] RPC 261 and *General Tire & Rubber Co. v. Firestone* (n. 16).

[41] *Synthon BV v. Smithkline Beecham plc (No. 2)* (CA) (n. 38).

practically without the necessity for further experiments.[42] Nevertheless, the anticipating information must not be so detailed that it could support a valid patent.[43]

Selection patents

It should be noted that the jurisprudence on the nature of the addressee in patent cases is more extensive and more developed in the context of obviousness, but care must be taken in applying that law here, because there are clear differences in the law relating, for example, to the mosaicking—that is, the combining of potentially anticipating documents that is only possible if they cross-refer to one another—of two separate aspects of the state of the art. In any event, a different question is being asked: the novelty of an invention is easier to assess than its obviousness and, arguably, it is for this reason that the law in the latter areas has had no option but to become more developed.

The areas in which the characteristics of the notional addressee of the patent claim and the anticipatory material are particularly important is when the patent claim is, as is quite usual, not a bolt from an otherwise clear blue sky, but rather a development of some pre-existing product or process. In this case, it is easy for an objector to say that the pre-existing product in its claims or by its working was an anticipation—*Quantel* is perhaps a good example. The problem is heightened in cases in which all that is being sought in the subsequent patent is a new method of using pre-existing matter.

Sometimes, it is easy to see that there is novelty even in such a case. This problem can particularly arise in selection patents—that is, in patents that select one particular category from a more general group that is already known. A good example of this is *Beecham Group's (Amoxycillin) Application*,[44] in which Beechams had been granted a patent for a large class of various penicillins for use as antibiotics and had then, in a further patent, singled out nine of them as being especially effective. At issue was a further application for a patent for one type of one of those nine penicillins that was especially amenable to absorption into the blood, the question being whether the naming of this sort of penicillin in the earlier patent was an anticipation. The Court of Appeal denied that it was such: the earlier patent simply showed that this sort of penicillin appeared to be effective in mice, whereas the patent in suit was for a developed, tested, and workable application of one type of that particular penicillin. It could not be anticipated by an earlier patent that gave no hint of whether or how its subject matter might be used for human consumption, even to its skilled addressees.

The essence of this type of case is to emphasize the advantage and/or difference that the selection makes so as to create a clear gap between the earlier and later matters. In *Re Shell Refining & Marketing Co. Ltd's Patent*,[45] therefore, Esso had made a 1940 patent application relating to improved fuel consumption, which referred to the use of a particular chemical additive to fuel as being of benefit to combat corrosion in fuel tanks; Shell had subsequently obtained a patent for the use of several additives, including a small proportion of that used by Esso, for various purposes including the prevention of engine knock, of the fouling of spark plugs, and of exhaust valve corrosion. It was held that Esso's application did not anticipate the final version of Shell's patent, amended to emphasize the small amount of additive and its effectiveness in dealing with the problems that Shell

---

[42] *Van der Lely (L) NV v. Bamfords* [1963] RPC 61 at 71, with reference to *Hill v. Evans* (1862) 4 De G F & J 288, per Lord Westbury at 300.

[43] *Ransburg v. Aerostyle* [1968] RPC 287 at 299, with reference to *King Brown v. Anglo American Brush* (1892) 9 RPC 313, per Lord Watson at 320.

[44] [1980] RPC 261.   [45] [1960] RPC 35.

sought to counteract. A more broadly drafted claim that did not emphasize the precise amount of the additive to be used by Shell was, however, anticipated—because it was, after all, the same additive in the same fuel.

The *Shell* case is also useful in giving more general guidelines on the correct approach to selection patents. Lord Evershed MR starts with the obvious basic proposition that a man who merely picks out a number of items from an already disclosed group or series has not 'invented' anything,[46] but argues that this would not be the case should later research reveal *'that certain items in the group or series possess qualities or characteristics peculiar to themselves and hitherto unknown'*.[47] He adopts the approach of Maugham J to selection patents in an earlier case,[48] identifying them as being grantable if there is a substantial advantage associated with the selected group, if that advantage is common to all of the selected group, and if that advantage is peculiar to that group.

This approach has the approval of the House of Lords in two cases: *Beecham Group Ltd v. Bristol Laboratories International SA*[49] and *E. I. Du Pont de Nemours & Co. (Witsiepe's) Application*.[50] In *Du Pont*, Lord Wilberforce points to the need to protect the original inventor, while encouraging others to improve and enhance that invention by the discovery of fresh advantages in the selected class. On the facts, this was reflected by the finding that a previous disclosure by ICI that the use of nine glycols would produce a particular result in no way anticipated the discovery by Du Pont, after extensive research, that one of the glycols had particular benefits in a different field; this was clearly the fresh advantage of the selected class.

In a sense, these patents are not best served by being described as 'selection' patents; what signifies them and justifies their patentability is not the mere fact of selection, but the uniqueness of what is selected and the development or advantage that the selection represents. As such, their recognition is entirely justified as a reward for the work that will go into making the selection, as both *Beecham* and *Shell* demonstrate, and in recognizing them the law reflects the commercial reality of the nature of much of the inventive work that goes on in the pharmaceutical and other chemical industries.

The (first) medical use exception

In one respect, the 1977 Act makes specific provisions for particular patents of this type: medical use. In the original version s. 2(6) expressly permitted the patenting of a substance used in medical treatment, even if the substance itself was already part of the state of the art, as long as the use of the substance in medical treatment was not part thereof. It is clear that this only applied to first use as a medicine, and not to second and subsequent medical uses, even if these are completely distinct.

This exception arises from the interpretation of s. 2(6) by the court in *John Wyeth & Brother Ltd's Application; Schering AG's Application*,[51] in which two appeals were heard together: Wyeth found that compounds called guanidines used to lower blood pressure were also valuable in combating diarrhoea, while Schering sought a patent for its research finding that substances used for the treatment of breast cancer could also be used against prostatic hyperlasia. The Patent Court *en banc* interpreted s. 2(6) as described earlier on the grounds that the precise wording of the legislation is that medical use of a known substance is allowed as long as its use *'in any such method does not form part of the state of the art'* and a prior medical use would be *'any such method'*. But the matter did

---

[46] [1960] RPC 35 at 53.   [47] [1960] RPC 35 at 55.

[48] *Re I. G. Farbenindustrie AG's Patent* (1930) 47 RPC 289 at 322–3.   [49] [1970] RPC 521 at 579.

[50] [1982] FSR 303 at 310.   [51] [1985] RPC 545.

not end there: amended claims were also considered that sought a patent for the use of a known subject in the manufacture of a new drug, thus emphasizing not the use of, for example, the guanidines as a treatment for diarrhoea, but their use in a new drug (which by coincidence, of course, would be used in the treatment of diarrhoea). Claims in this form had been allowed by the EPO on the grounds that the use in manufacture of the new drug could provide the necessary element of novelty.[52] Because judicial notice has to be taken of appellate decisions within the EPO under s. 91(1) of the 1977 Act, the court was obliged to follow this lead and allowed the subtly amended claims.

As a result of the decision of the EPO's Enlarged Board of Appeal in *Eisai*,[53] claims in a patent application that are directed to the use of a product for the manufacture of a medicament for a specified new therapeutic use do not lack novelty.[54] On that basis, a new, second, pharmaceutical use for compounds that have previously been recognized as having a different pharmaceutical use can be patented. This type of claim is called a 'Swiss-type' claim. The Court of Appeal recently had the opportunity to consider such claims.[55] The outcome of that analysis is that, apart from being inventive, the new therapeutic application also has to be new. There must be use for a new and completely different purpose, and novelty must lie in the therapeutic purpose for which the substance was used, rather than in the method of use.[56] The compounds—the second medical use of which is patented[57]—must also be effective to achieve the new treatment; it must be suitable for that purpose.[58]

As this meant that there are now effectively two exceptions, the Patents Act 2004 did away with s. 2(6) in the 1977 Act and replaced it with paragraphs 3 and 4 of the new s. 4A which codifies these exceptions as follows:

Methods of treatment or diagnosis …

(3) In the case of an invention consisting of a substance or composition for use in any such method, the fact that the substance or composition forms part of the state of the art shall not prevent the invention from being taken to be new if the use of the substance or composition in any such method does not form part of the state of the art.

(4) In the case of an invention consisting of a substance or composition for a specific use in any such method, the fact that the substance or composition forms part of the state of the art shall not prevent the invention from being taken to be new if that specific use does not form part of the state of the art.

This amendment to the Act also reflects the changes contained in the 2000 revision of the EPC that do away for the future with Swiss claims. Instead, claims for the use of compound X for treatment of disease Y are now allowed. English courts have held that the term 'for' should be read as 'suitable and intended for'.[59]

---

[52] *Re Eisai Co. Ltd*, Decision Gr 05/83 (1985) OJ EPO 64.   [53] *Re Eisai Co. Ltd* (n. 52).

[54] In the same decision, it was held that, on the other hand, claims for the use of a product for the treatment of an illness are not patentable, because they come under the exclusion for methods of treatment of the human or animal body.

[55] *Bristol-Myers Squibb Corp. v. Baker Norton Pharmaceuticals Inc.* [2001] RPC 1 (CA) and *Actavis UK Ltd v. Merck & Co. Inc.* [2008] RPC 26, [2008] 1 All ER 196, [2009] 1 WLR 1186 (CA).

[56] *Bristol-Myers Squibb* (n. 55) at 25–7. See also *American Home Products Co. v. Novartis Pharmaceuticals UK Ltd* [2001] RPC 159.

[57] Such a patent is to be treated as a process patent: see *Monsanto & Co. v. Merck & Co. Inc.* [2000] RPC 77.

[58] See also *Pfizer Ltd's Patent* [2001] FSR 16 at 219–20. If more than one compound is used in a combination, each of them is used for the treatment.

[59] *Hospira UK Ltd v. Genentech Inc* [2014] EWHC 1094 (Pat) at para. [58] per Birss J, cited with approval by the Court of Appeal in *Warner-Lambert Company v. Actavis Group, Actavis UK and Caduceus Pharma* [2015] EWCA Civ 556.

A constructive approach

In making this point on a narrow issue, a broader point also becomes relevant and is an appropriate note on which to end this section. The proper approach to issues of patentability in general, and of novelty in particular, is a constructive one; the proper question is not 'Is this patentable?', but rather 'What parts of this are patentable?' Given that the courts are prepared to allow quite fine adjustments as being patentable, as in *Quantel*, it will often be possible to find some part of the product or process that is novel, even if other aspects are not. This care in identifying the true novelty must then be matched by equal care in drafting the application for a patent, particularly in emphasizing those elements that have been identified as being novel. *Wyeth & Schering* stands as a monument to careful drafting, even in the post-1977 era of broader attitudes to the interpretation of patents.

Overall, with the courts taking a fairly positive attitude both to what information is in the public domain and whether that information, as properly understood, does amount to an enabling disclosure, this is an area of law that appears to be working with reasonable effectiveness.[60] The obstacle presented by novelty will be resolved, either way, at an early stage of most applications, although the interpretation of s. 2(2) may occasionally lead to disruption when a patent's revocation is sought on the grounds of the discovery of a long-standing, but previously unknown, article in the trade press in Japan, for example. A more typical problem—that of prior use—has been resolved by the 1977 Act and the fact that such use now has to be an enabling disclosure revealing its inventive concept should minimize the kind of problem epitomized by the *Fomento* decision. *Merrell Dow*, however, while probably correct in its conclusion, does create an additional doubt in cases in which ignorant prior use has taken place and will therefore stop a later patent application in its tracks—but at least this might stop the disagreeable habit of some multinationals of acquiring sundry secrets of indigenous peoples and then gaining their own monopoly by patenting them.[61] Overall, then, the sensible attitude of the law towards selection patents better exemplifies the general workability of this aspect of patent law, and shows that a reasonable balance is maintained between patentees and their rivals in trade.

Inventive step

The principle

Not everything that is new is patentable. The next requirement imposed by the law is that the invention contains an inventive step, a leap forward by the inventor that puts him or her ahead of the pack and, it may be said, justifies the reward of a patent. Section 3 of the 1977 Act states:

> An invention shall be taken to involve an inventive step if it is not obvious to a person skilled in the art, having regard to any matter which forms part of the state of the art by virtue only of section 2(2) above (and disregarding section 2(3) above).

So that which is obvious does not gain patent protection; only that which is inventive. Note also that, by excluding s. 2(3) from the definition of state of the art for the purposes

---

[60] For a good example, see *Smithkline Beecham plc v. Apotex Europe Ltd* (n. 3).
[61] On this see, inter alia, M. Blakeney, 'Bioprospecting and the Protection of Traditional Medical Knowledge of Indigenous Peoples: An Australian Perspective' (1997) 6 EIPR 298.

of this section, the discussion of obviousness ignores patent applications that have already been filed, but which are yet to be published. Apart from that the examination for inventive step is carried out at the priority date.[62]

A good example of the concepts of inventiveness and obviousness in operation is provided, once again, by *Windsurfing International Inc. v. Tabur Marine (Great Britain) Ltd.*[63] We have already seen, in the context of the discussion of novelty, that the plaintiffs' 1968 patent for windsurfing equipment had been anticipated a decade previously by a boy on holiday. The two boards were, however, by no means identical: the boy used a simple straight boom with which to hold the sail taut and provide a handhold for the rider, while the patented boom was a more sophisticated arc-shaped model, which helped the sail to assume an aerofoil shape and thus attain greater speed. This difference was held to be insignificant; the use of the boom was common and the arc-shaped design was an obvious improvement on the boy's design, because, when in use, even his boom began to assume an arc shape. Thus the admitted improvement carried out by the patentee was not sufficient to gain the protection of a patent, because there was no inventive step in making an improvement that was regarded as obvious.

In discussing what is, or is not, obvious, great care needs to be taken. What is an obvious improvement to all in an ordinary common-sense situation such as that in the *Windsurfing* case may be much less clear in a high-technology field. In particular, in such a case, what may seem to the ordinary citizen to be a dazzling miracle of invention may be routine or commonplace to the person who is expert in that particular field. It is thus necessary to take care in formulating an approach to the obviousness question that is appropriate to all cases. It is also important to note, from the start, the significance of the obviousness question. Even where, as in the *Windsurfing* case, an advance is said to be obvious and thus non-patentable, it is still likely that the disappointed applicant will have put a significant amount of work into the development and perfection of the product. If patents are intended to reward the efforts of inventors, or if, more generally, intellectual property rights are expected to match up with activity of value in the commercial sector, the failure to protect such activity by the grant of the patent is a significant failing in the system. Obviously, the more often that the law depicts an advance as being obvious, the greater that this failing will be, and any willingness to expand the notion of obviousness will clearly go against the interests of new inventors and favour the interests of those already in the game, whose activities will already form part of the state of the art.

The starting point when s. 3 is put into practice can be described as follows:

> The question of obviousness must be considered on the facts of each case. The court must consider the weight to be attached to any particular factor in the light of all the relevant circumstances. These may include such matters as the motive to find a solution to the problem the patent addresses, the number and extent of the possible avenues of research, the effort involved in pursuing them and the expectation of success.[64]

---

[62] The time needed to perform tests or put knowledge that is part of the state of the art into practice is ignored and cannot save an application filed shortly after the information became part of the state of the art. *Teva UK Ltd v. Merck & Co. Inc.* [2011] EWCA Civ 382.

[63] [1985] RPC 59.

[64] *Generics (UK) Ltd v. H Lundbeck A/S* [2007] RPC 32 at para. 72, per Kitchin J, approved by the House of Lords in *Conor Medsystems Inc. v. Angiotech Pharmaceuticals Inc.* [2008] UKHL 49, [2008] RPC 28 (HL) at para 42, per Lord Hoffmann.

The *Windsurfing* test, rearranged by *Pozzoli*

How then is obviousness approached? The starting point is clearly that, in an objective test and without taking account of the views of the inventor, the invention is to be compared to the existing state of the art. The basic test was clearly outlined by Oliver LJ in the *Windsurfing* case[65] as a fourfold approach. More recently the Court of Appeal rearranged the four steps of the test,[66] effectively making the second question in the *Windsurfing* version the first question in the *Pozzoli* version and vice versa. But because obviousness has always been considered something of a jury-type issue,[67] all that is really provided is a procedure and a vague, qualitative yardstick. The Court of Appeal added, in *Dyson Appliances Ltd v. Hoover Ltd*,[68] that it was useful, but not essential, to use the four-step approach when assessing obviousness. The ultimate criterion is, indeed, still the statutory provision itself.

In the *Pozzoli* order of things the first point is that the court has to assume the mantle of the normally skilled but unimaginative addressee in the art at the priority date and to impute to him what was, at that date, common general knowledge in the art in question.[69]

This first stage is vital and will be considered in detail shortly.

Secondly, it is necessary to '*identify the inventive concept embodied in the patent in suit*'.[70] This is the problem that fell to be considered in *Biogen Inc. v. Medeva plc*,[71] in which it was made clear that the inventive concept was neither the identification of the problem, nor the general approach to be taken to it, but rather the problem and its precise resolution. To adopt an analogy employed by Lord Hoffmann,[72] people ruminated for centuries on the problem of flying machines, so this could not be, on its own, an inventive concept; later, more precise thought was given to matters such as wing shape and engine type, but, again, mere thought is not enough. It was only when the Wright brothers succeeded in making a machine that was actually capable of powered flight that it could be said that the 'inventive concept' had come into existence. In *Biogen*, the House of Lords assumed, without deciding, that the genetic engineering techniques employed to resolve a known problem in a new way were not obvious.

In assessing the inventive concept as the problem and its precise solution, care needs to be taken to avoid an overly analytical approach. Often several events or elements are involved and these are often related. One needs to look at the combination of these events and elements, and they should not necessarily be seen as unrelated events and elements.[73] It is also important to keep in mind that the test for inventive step is to be applied for each single inventive concept. What seems to be one invention may, indeed, be a juxtaposition of more than one invention and one needs to decide whether there is one or more inventions before applying the test for inventiveness under s. 3. This is, in a sense, a preliminary point.[74]

---

[65] *Windsurfing International Inc.* (n. 63) at 73–4. This approach is confirmed by *Mölnlycke AB v. Procter & Gamble Ltd (No. 5)* [1994] RPC 49, per Sir Donald Nicholls VC at 115, and—more significantly, but not uncritically—by Lord Hoffmann in *Biogen Inc. v. Medeva plc* (n. 35).

[66] *Pozzoli v. BDMD* [2007] FSR 37 (CA).

[67] See e.g. *Johns-Manville's Patent* [1967] RPC 479 at 491.   [68] [2002] RPC 465.

[69] *Windsurfing International Inc.* (n. 63), per Oliver LJ at 73.

[70] *Windsurfing International Inc.* (n. 63), per Oliver LJ at 73.   [71] [1997] RPC 1.

[72] *Biogen v. Medeva* (n. 35) at 43.

[73] *Rockwater Ltd v. Technip France SA (formerly Coflexip SA) & Technip Offshore UK Ltd (formerly Coflexip Stena Offshore Ltd)*, judgment of the Court of Appeal of 1 April 2004, unreported.

[74] *SABAF v. Menghetti* [2005] RPC 10, (2004) 148 SJLB 1217 (HL).

The third stage is to identify the differences that exist between the generally known matter and the subject matter of the patent for which the application is being made, after which:

> the court has to ask itself whether, viewed without any knowledge of the alleged invention, those differences constitute steps which would have been obvious to the skilled man or whether they require any degree of invention.[75]

In *Dyson Appliances Ltd v. Hoover Ltd*, this fourth step was held to require a technical comparison of the technical differences between the claims and the prior art. Proof of commercial obviousness was neither here nor there.

On the facts of the *Windsurfing* case, as we have seen, the development was obvious.[76] The essential inventive concept in the patent was the free-sail concept, as opposed to the rigid masts of rigging of conventional yachts—but the state of the art included the 1966 article describing sailboarding and that revealed the essence of the later invention to an audience who were, given the specialist nature of the publication, almost by definition going to be knowledgeable in the art. The only differences were in the shape of the boom and the shape of sail used, and these differences would be obvious, in the view of the Court of Appeal, to the informed reader who would use his or her own knowledge to make the same adjustments him- or herself, thus depriving the holders of the patent from legitimately claiming that they had made an inventive step. Often, the informed reader will combine general common knowledge in a particular field—for example, information contained in standard texts—with a specific document—such as the 1966 article in this case—to make a decision on the obviousness point.

In applying the *Windsurfing/Pozzoli* test, then, it is of vital importance to avoid hindsight. The court is confronted with the question at a later stage, but the question needs to be answered as at the time at which the application was examined. Later scientific and technical evolutions should neither be taken into account, nor influence a decision on obviousness.[77]

The addressee of the test

It is apparent that it is at the first stage of this process that the key feature arises, because, in deciding through whose eyes the question of the inventive step should be viewed, the law is able to set the level at which the dividing line between obviousness and inventiveness is to be drawn. The classic formulation of this test is provided by Lord Reid in *Technograph Printed Circuits Ltd v. Mills & Rockley (Electronics) Ltd*,[78] when, in discussing obviousness, he described the notional addressee in the following terms:

> It is not disputed that the hypothetical addressee is a skilled technician who is well acquainted with workshop technique and has carefully read the relevant literature. He is supposed to have an unlimited capacity to assimilate the contents of, it may be, scores of specifications but to be incapable of a scintilla of invention.[79]

---

[75] *SABAF v. Menghetti* (n. 74) at 73–4. The Court of Appeal recently argued that there is no conflict with the EPO's problem/solution approach, as the fourth step of the *Pozzoli* test implements this very problem/solution approach; *Generics v. Daiichi* [2009] RPC 23 (CA).

[76] For two good examples based on rather straightforward facts, see *Rocky Mountain Traders Ltd v. Hewlett Packard GmbH, Westcoast Ltd & Fellowes Manufacturing (UK) Ltd* [2000] FSR 411 (confirmed on appeal, 12 December 2000, unreported) and *Minnesota Mining & Manufacturing Co. v. ATI Atlas Ltd & North American Science Associates Inc.* [2001] FSR 31.

[77] *Ferag AG v. Muller Martini Ltd* (2007) 151 SJLB 163 (CA).   [78] [1972] RPC 346.

[79] [1972] RPC 346 at 355.

On the facts, the House of Lords found that the jump from a pre-existing US electrostatic shield to the patentee's printed circuits was an inventive one, in the light of expert evidence that the necessary adaptations and the alterations were far from obvious. It is clear that such expert evidence will often be of the utmost value in deciding the obviousness question.

This particular variant of the reasonable man is not, however, without its critics. His character would seem to be unrealistic: like a sponge, he apparently soaks up all known facts from, since 1977, all over the world. Yet, although he understands all this—which demonstrates a brain with a great power of understanding—he has no idea what to do with it and sits, bloated with facts but bereft of ideas, incapable of developing ideas from all that he knows. (Leading comedy actors must yearn to play his part.) The courts themselves have expressed occasional concern as to whether such characters hinder, rather than help, the law's development. In the *Windsurfing* case, Oliver LJ notes that such figures must not be permitted to obscure the basic statutory terminology in the objective quest as to whether an invention is obvious or not, and that the temptation to add various human qualities to this non-existent entity may well lead to confusion in the view of the judge.[80] Hoffmann LJ has also been critical of the way in which this distended version of the reasonable man has come to be utilized, noting that what may be '*a folksy way of explaining the law to a jury*' is no substitute for an analysis of the actual statutory language.[81]

It has become quite clear now that no real character is involved.[82] If there is more than one route to the desired goal, the notional person will, by definition, see all of them, whereas a real person might, out of personal experience, focus on one route and might not even see some of the others. The notional skilled person never misses the obvious, but also never sees the inventive. Evidence from real persons working in the field is, therefore, not necessarily conclusive and has to be assessed in that light by the court. But also, the fact that alternative routes are available is, therefore, not evidence of the fact that the invention is not obvious; rather, whether something was obvious depends, to a large extent, on balancing the expected rewards in the case of a successful attempt against the risks of failure.[83] In making such an evaluation, the notional skilled person will take any piece of prior art and put it in the context of the common general knowledge.[84] That will allow the notional skilled person to give each piece of prior art its proper value and meaning and in turn those elements will be determinative when the notional skilled person decides whether what is found in the patent application is obvious or not. The concept of common general knowledge can be defined as follows:

> The common general knowledge is the technical background to the notional man in the art against which the prior art must be considered. This is not limited to material he has memorised and has at the front of his mind. It includes all that material in the field he is working in which he knows exists, which he would refer to as a matter of course if he cannot remember it and which he understands is generally regarded as sufficiently reliable to use as a foundation for further work or to help understand the pleaded prior art. This does not mean that everything on the shelf which is capable of being referred to without difficulty is common general knowledge nor does it mean that every word in a common text book is either. In

---

[80] [1985] RPC 59 at 71.

[81] *Société Technique de Pulvérisation Step v. Emson Europe Ltd* [1993] RPC 513 at 519.

[82] See e.g. *Pfizer Ltd's Patent* (n. 58).

[83] Laddie J, in *Pfizer Ltd's Patent* (n. 58), refers in this respect to Decision T379/96 of the EPO's Technical Board of Appeal in *Minnesota Mining/Aerosol Propellants*.

[84] For a good example, see *Burnden Group plc v. Ultraframe (UK) Ltd* (2005) EWCA Civ 867.

the case of standard textbooks, it is likely that all or most of the main text will be common general knowledge. In many cases common general knowledge will include or be reflected in readily available trade literature which a man in the art would be expected to have at his elbow and regard as basic reliable information. In this case, for example, the general technical discussion of conductive polymers in the Cabot technical report was common general knowledge well before the priority date. So too would be the general teaching in the leading articles and textbooks on the subject.[85]

The Court of Appeal emphasized the importance of the concept of common general knowledge that the notional addressee brings to the test in *Angiotech v. Conor*.[86] It is a broad concept and includes, for example, all steps that a skilled person would try without additional external intervention on the basis of his or her knowledge of the area concerned. It also includes any prior art described in documents, even if the approach described is subjected to technical prejudice. The latter will not remove the conclusion of obviousness.[87] But there are nevertheless limitations to the very broad concept of common general knowledge, as was shown by the Court of Appeal on the basis of a passage from *Beloit v. Valmet*[88] which was quoted with approval:

> It has never been easy to differentiate between common general knowledge and that which is known by some. It has become particularly difficult with the modern ability to circulate and retrieve information. Employees of some companies, with the use of libraries and patent departments, will become aware of information soon after it is published in a whole variety of documents; whereas others, without such advantages, may never do so until that information is accepted generally and put into practice. The notional skilled addressee is the ordinary man who may not have the advantages that some employees of large companies may have. The information in a patent specification is addressed to such a man and must contain sufficient details for him to understand and apply the invention. It will only lack an inventive step if it is obvious to such a man.

It follows that evidence that a fact is known or even well known to a witness does not establish that that fact forms part of the common general knowledge. Neither does it follow that it will form part of the common general knowledge if it is recorded in a document. As stated by the Court of Appeal in *General Tire & Rubber Co. v. Firestone Tyre & Rubber Co. Ltd*:[89]

> The two classes of documents which call for consideration in relation to *common general* knowledge in the instant case were individual patent specifications and widely read publications. As to the former, it is clear that individual patent specifications and their contents do not normally form part of the relevant *common general* knowledge, though there may be specifications which are so well known amongst those versed in the art that upon evidence of that state of affairs they form part of such knowledge, and also there may occasionally be particular industries (such as that of colour photography) in which the evidence may show that all specifications form part of the relevant knowledge.

As regards scientific papers generally, it was said by Luxmoore J in *British Acoustic Films*:[90]

---

[85] *Raychem Corporation's Patent* [1998] RPC 31 at 40, per Laddie J, approved on appeal at [1999] RPC 497 at 503.

[86] [2007] RPC 20 (CA).

[87] Case T-882/03, *Du Pont Teijin Films/Polyester Film*, Technical Board of Appeal of the EPO [2006] EPOR 48.

[88] *Beloit Technologies Inc. v. Valmet Paper Machinery Inc.* [1997] RPC 489 at 494–5.

[89] [1972] RPC 457 at 482, line 33.   [90] 53 RPC 221 at 250.

In my judgment it is not sufficient to prove common general knowledge that a particular disclosure is made in an article, or series of articles, in a scientific journal, no matter how wide the circulation of that journal may be, in the absence of any evidence that the disclosure is accepted generally by those who are engaged in the art to which the disclosure relates. A piece of particular knowledge as disclosed in a scientific paper does not become common general knowledge merely because it is widely read, and still less because it is widely circulated. Such a piece of knowledge only becomes general knowledge when it is generally known and accepted without question by the bulk of those who are engaged in the particular art; in other words, when it becomes part of their common stock of knowledge relating to the art.[91]

In other words, the piece must be generally regarded as a good basis for further action, even if that may depend on the circumstances. This does not means that the piece must generally be seen as correct.[92] It is also arguable to state that there is a territorial aspect to common knowledge. For European and UK patents a piece of information must therefore be common knowledge in the UK, rather than merely in other parts of the world.[93]

In contrast with the position on mosaicking in relation to novelty, in relation to the inventive step, the notional skilled person may supplement any information by consulting other readily accessible public information and sources,[94] as long as it is obvious to someone with an uninventive mind to do so.[95] In addition, when, in a particular context, it would be obvious to call in special expertise, the notional skilled person is supposed to have done so.[96] Equally, in areas in which inventive work is now regularly based on teamwork, the notional skilled team replaces the notional skilled person.[97]

Streamlining the approach

Conor made it eventually to the House of Lords[98] and it gave the House the opportunity to clarify details of the way in which the test for inventive step will be operated by the skilled person. This was a case about a stent impregnated with taxol. When the stent was unfolded in an artery, which inevitably bruised the wall of the artery a bit and gave rise to the risk of restinosis whereby muscle tissue would grow out of proportion and block the unblocked artery again, the taxol stopped the growth of the muscle cells. The main issue was that the patent only mentioned that it was worth trying taxol for this purpose. Was that sufficient to meet the inventive step requirement?

The House held that the inventive step requirement should be applied to the invention as it has been specified in the claims. The sufficiency requirement whereby the application for a patent should contain enough information for the examiner in the UK Intellectual Property Office or skilled person to perform or reproduce it is a separate requirement and has no role to play at this stage. In the *Conor* case the claims described the invention as a stent impregnated with taxol. This was a new product, but the question was whether it involved an inventive step. Any potential inventive step was not to be

[91] See also *Generics v. Daiichi* [2009] RPC 23 (CA) at 838–9.

[92] *Novartis AG v. Focus Pharmaceuticals Ltd* [2015] EWHC 1068 (Pat) at paras 91–92; *KCI Licensing Inc v. Smith & Nephew plc* [2010] EWHC 1487 (Pat) (approved on appeal [2010] EWCA Civ 1260).

[93] *Generics (UK) Ltd trading as Mylan v. Warner-Lambert Company LLC, Actavis Group v. Warner-Lambert* [2015] EWHC 2548 (Pat), para. 124.

[94] *Pfizer Ltd's Patent* (n. 58) at 16.

[95] It may, therefore, still be inventive to put information from unrelated sources together.

[96] *NI Industries/Filler Mass* [1992] OJ EPO 725; and see also *Richardson-Vick's Patent* [1997] RPC 888.

[97] *Boehringer Mannheim v. Genzyme* [1993] FSR 716 at 727.

[98] *Conor Medsystems Inc. v. Angiotech Pharmaceuticals Inc.* (n. 64).

found in its (routine) production process, but in the product's capability of remedying restinosis. Focusing on the description in the claim the skilled person was therefore answering the question whether the use of a stent impregnated with taxol for this purpose was an obvious thing to do when looking at the state of the art.

It is important, according to the House, to keep in mind that the inventive-step requirement does not demand that the patent specification explains how the product works or that the product is effective. In *Conor* the applicant had expressed the view that the use of taxol and the impregnation approach presented advantages in the fight against restinosis (i.e. the question was whether it was obvious that the stent coated with taxol would prevent or treat restinosis, rather than whether taxol might have that effect as in the latter case there is no invention). The House of Lords was satisfied that this was sufficient, as the specification supported this hypothesis and the hypothesis was therefore more than mere speculation. Mere speculation would indeed not have been sufficient, as there would in such a case be no indication what the inventive step was.

The House of Lords argued that in practice there would only not have been an inventive step in *Conor* if the skilled person had taken the view that he or she had, on the basis of the state of the art, an expectation of success that was sufficient to induce him or her to incorporate taxol in the stent. On the facts of the case the skilled person would not have taken that view. The real value of the case is that it strips the exercise down to the bare essentials and rules out those factors that may come and cloud the test for inventive step.[99]

Let us come back for a second to the separate requirement of sufficiency that was also raised in the case. The standard here is different from the expectation of success that one finds in relation to obviousness. Sufficiency merely requires that that invention is plausible. This means that the skilled person considers it to be credible, i.e. that there is a reason to believe it is true. It should not be merely speculative.[100]

Taking it all together,[101] the structured approach in *Pozzoli* is often a helpful way of approaching the question. The fourth question remains the vital one. Or in the words of Kitchin LJ:

> 89. It is step (4) which is key and requires the court to consider whether the claimed invention was obvious to the skilled but unimaginative addressee at the priority date. He is equipped with the common general knowledge; he is deemed to have read or listened to the prior disclosure properly and in that sense with interest; he has the prejudices, preferences and attitudes of those in the field; and he has no knowledge of the invention.
>
> 90. One of the matters which it may be appropriate to take into account is whether it was obvious to try a particular route to an improved product or process. There may be no certainty of success but the skilled person might nevertheless assess the prospects of success as being sufficient to warrant a trial. In some circumstances this may be sufficient to render an invention obvious. On the other hand, there are areas of technology such as pharmaceuticals and biotechnology which are heavily dependent on research, and where workers are faced with many possible avenues to explore but have little idea if any one of them will prove fruitful. Nevertheless they do pursue them in the hope that they will find new and useful products. They plainly would not carry out this work if the prospects of success were so low

---

[99] Confirmed in the context of the 'obvious to try' argument in *MedImmune v. Novartis* [2012] EWCA Civ 1234; and *Novartis v. Genetics (trading as Mylan)* [2012] EWCA Civ 1623.

[100] *Actavis v. Eli Lilly and Company* [2015] EWHC 3294 (Pat).

[101] See *Teva UK Ltd and Teva Pharmaceutical Industries Ltd v. Leo Pharma A/S and Leo Laboratories Ltd* [2015] EWCA Civ 779, paras 4–7.

as not to make them worthwhile. But denial of patent protection in all such cases would act as a significant deterrent to research.

91. For these reasons, the judgments of the courts in England and Wales and of the Boards of Appeal of the EPO often reveal an enquiry by the tribunal into whether it was obvious to pursue a particular approach with a reasonable or fair expectation of success as opposed to a hope to succeed. Whether a route has a reasonable or fair prospect of success will depend upon all the circumstances including an ability rationally to predict a successful outcome, how long the project may take, the extent to which the field is unexplored, the complexity or otherwise of any necessary experiments, whether such experiments can be performed by routine means and whether the skilled person will have to make a series of correct decisions along the way. Lord Hoffmann summarised the position in this way in Conor [*Conor Medsystems Inc v. Angiotech Pharmaceuticals Inc [2008] UKHL 49; [2008] RPC 28*] at [42]:

'In the Court of Appeal, Jacob LJ dealt comprehensively with the question of when an invention could be considered obvious on the ground that it was obvious to try. He correctly summarised the authorities, starting with the judgment of Diplock LJ in *Johns-Manville Corporation's Patent [1967] RPC 479*, by saying that the notion of something being obvious to try was useful only in a case where there was a fair expectation of success. How much of an expectation would be needed depended on the particular facts of the case.'

92. Moreover, whether a route is obvious to try is only one of many considerations which it may be appropriate for the court to take into account. In *Generics (UK) Ltd v. H Lundbeck, [2008] EWCA Civ 311, [2008] RPC 19* , at [24] and in *Conor [2008] UKHL 49, [2008] RPC 28* at [42], Lord Hoffmann approved this statement of principle which I made at first instance in *Lundbeck* :

'The question of obviousness must be considered on the facts of each case. The court must consider the weight to be attached to any particular factor in the light of all the relevant circumstances. These may include such matters as the motive to find a solution to the problem the patent addresses, the number and extent of the possible avenues of research, the effort involved in pursuing them and the expectation of success.'

93. Ultimately the court has to evaluate all the relevant circumstances in order to answer a single and relatively simple question of fact: was it obvious to the skilled but unimaginative addressee to make a product or carry out a process falling within the claim. As Aldous LJ said in Norton Healthcare v Beecham Group Plc (unreported, 19 June 1997):

'Each case depends upon the invention and the surrounding facts. No formula can be substituted for the words of the statute. In every case the Court has to weigh up the evidence and decide whether the invention was obvious. This is the statutory task.'[102]

On top of *Pozzoli* the courts see the EPO's problem-solution approach, whereby a problem that could not be solved before and its detailed solution are identified, as helpful,[103] and they emphasize that the question of obviousness needs to considered on the facts of each case.[104] The approach that there is no inventive step if the approach was obvious to try is also helpful in certain cases, but it can only be applied if there was a fair expectation of success.[105]

Finally, it remains clear that the judgement that the test asks the skilled person to make still does not require inventiveness, but there is a clear judgement to be made and

---

[102] *MedImmune Ltd v. Novartis Pharmaceuticals UK Ltd* (n. 99) at paras 89–93.
[103] *Actavis v. Novartis* [2010] EWCA Civ 82.
[104] *Generics v. Lundbeck* (n. 64) at para. 72, per Kitchin J.
[105] *Conor Medsystems Inc. v. Angiotech Pharmaceuticals Inc.* (n. 64) at para. 42 per Lord Hoffmann.

this move away from a mechanical exercise brings us closer to the approach in other European countries. German law allows a form of imagination[106] and that idea seemed also present in one important UK case. It is to this decision that we will now turn.

The *Genentech* case

The case of *Genentech Inc.'s Patent*[107] is of great significance. It is also of great length—the report extends to 140 pages—and complexity. Nevertheless, careful analysis of the case and its implications is essential.

The case arose in relation to the area of genetic engineering. A patent had been granted to Genentech, in respect of various claims relating to the production of human plasminogen activator by the use of recombinant DNA technology in workable quantities. The relevant technology had been used previously in synthesizing a number of other substances, but this was the first time that it had been employed to synthesize a particular activator known as t-PA, which was of great value in combating blood clotting and thus of importance in treating thrombosis. The production of quantities of t-PA was clearly of great medical and commercial value; it was also the result of much work. Genentech took over a year to achieve the production of enough t-PA and many skilled scientists were involved. At the same time, other teams elsewhere were racing towards the same approach, but lost the race to Genentech.

In effect, Genentech were then the holders of a patent for a new application of pre-existing technology and the nub of the dispute—when others in the field sought a revocation of the Genentech patent—was whether what had been achieved by Genentech was a breakthrough permitting the synthesis of the valuable t-PA for the first time and thus deserving of patent protection, or whether the discovery was simply part of the ordinary process of development of the pre-existing recombinant DNA technology, and thus did not amount to an inventive step.

The Court of Appeal found that the patent had been wrongly granted and ordered that it should be revoked. A key issue was how the hypothetical addressee concept could cope with an area of such intellectual complexity as this and the court recognized that the traditional model was unworkable in these exceptional circumstances. As Purchas LJ recognized in relation to this type of situation:

> the artisan has receded into the role of the laboratory assistant and the others have become segregated into groups of highly qualified specialists in their own spheres of all whom must possess a degree of inventiveness.[108]

In other words, because there is no one working in the field who is incapable of invention, the 'person skilled in the art' must have inventive capacity.

Mustill LJ noted that it was wrong to assume that the person skilled in the art for the purposes of s. 3 was the same person as that envisaged in considering the information in the specification and its use by the person skilled in the art envisaged by s. 14(3).[109] The latter character could be realistically seen as non-inventive in the context of having merely to read and understand a specification, but for the purposes of s. 3:

---

[106] E. Pakuscher, 'Examination for Non-Obviousness: A Response' (1981) 12 IIC 816. See also J. Schmidt-Szalewski, 'Non-Obviousness as a Requirement of Patentability in French Law' (1992) IIC 725 for the position in France, where the average person skilled in the art is the test. Presumably, such a person has an average amount of imagination.

[107] [1989] RPC 147.   [108] [1989] RPC 147 at 214.   [109] [1989] RPC 147 at 279.

where one is looking at the research team one cannot treat them as dull plodders, for such people would not be members of the team at all, except as laboratory assistants.[110]

Later, he comments that, in a case of this type, *'some substantial measure of ingenuity is an essential qualification for being engaged in the enterprise'.*[111]

In the light of these views—which were not, apparently, shared by the third member of the Court, Dillon LJ[112]—it became clear that Genentech should not be allowed any patent protection. The problems faced by the firm were the problems to be expected out at the cutting edge of genetic engineering and, as such, were capable of being surmounted by others skilled in the art, with their inevitable high intellectual and inventive qualities. As Mustill LJ expresses it:

> it is inventiveness which counts, and I cannot find it here in any degree which exceeds the amount of resource expected of a group mustering the skills, remarkable as they seem to the layman, ordinarily to be expected of persons skilled in this most difficult array of arts.[113]

Purchas LJ, however, found that some of the steps taken along the way were inventive steps even by the high standards expected in this field, but found against Genentech on other grounds. Dillon LJ found it relevant, in the establishing of obviousness, that the other participants in the patent race were following the same track as Genentech, confirming his view that the steps being taken were obvious to those skilled in the art.[114]

There is much more to *Genentech*, but this is an appropriate moment to make some comments on this core part of the decision. It is unfortunate that such a range of judicial opinion exists on the obviousness point and this merely adds to the problems of the complex subject matter—but the confusion should not mask the result. In this case, the company spent substantial amounts of time and money, using its resources and those represented by its highly qualified staff (almost all of whom had a PhD), in devising a workable method of making a pharmaceutical product of great potential benefit to society. This sounds exactly the sort of scenario in which, on a traditional analysis of the rationale of the patent system, the endeavour and beneficial result to society should be rewarded by the grant of a patent; yet the patent was revoked. So no incentive or reward for the patentee exists, other than in the form of short-term, market-leading profits. Of course, society and consumers benefit in the short term from the freer availability of this type of treatment, as do the rival firms, which are freely able to market their rival treatments. In the longer term, however, Genentech gets no high-yield return on its investment in the absence of a patent and may, as a result, not be able to work towards the next step forward in the—far from cheap—advance in scientific technique. In the absence of reward or incentive, it may also simply determine it to be unwise to devote resources to research and development (R&D) in situations in which the chance of a patentable result being reached has been substantially diminished by this decision. Thus society and the customers may, in the future, be less likely to gain any benefit from future advances in genetic engineering technology.

The effect of the *Genentech* decision is not, of course, confined to that one particular field. It would seem logical to assume that it will apply to any field of scientific activity in which the players in the field are all working at a high doctoral or post-doctoral level. This is the norm in most major industries—such as electronics or telecommunications, for example—and means that the impact of *Genentech* is of great significance in reducing the availability of patents by raising the standard of inventiveness in a potentially significant

---

[110] [1989] RPC 147.   [111] [1989] RPC 147 at 280.
[112] [1989] RPC 147 at 241.   [113] [1989] RPC 147 at 286–7.
[114] [1989] RPC 147 at 243.

range of commercially important activities. On the other hand, *Genentech* was not widely used in the decade since the decision, and even less later on, and it may increasingly come to be regarded as a decision made very much on its own facts—which is, of course, the common lawyer's classic method of marginalizing, or even ignoring, unhelpful decisions.

Either way, it should be made clear that the problem raised by *Genentech* exists only in a small minority of patent applications in relation to which protection is sought for an advance in an area of high technology. At lower levels, the traditional approach to obviousness still makes sense: for example, in a typical patent application for a relatively routine development or extension of a previous patent, such as a minor but new improvement in the way in which the ink flows in the operation of a ballpoint pen. In such a case, invention and obviousness are genuine alternatives, but, unfortunately, *Genentech* reveals that this cannot always be the case.

So why has this come about? The key problem is alluded to in the judgment of Mustill LJ,[115] and is simply that the definition in s. 3 of the 1977 Act and in EPC, Art. 56, does not make universal sense. It makes the assumption that 'inventiveness' and 'obviousness' are but two sides of the same coin, but the facts of a case such as *Genentech* explode that assumption with a violent blast. Simply, in high-tech areas—such as genetic engineering, with its teams of highly qualified and experienced scientists—the process of invention is the norm; invention is an obvious thing for its skilled proponents to undertake. To deny invention its legal protection and economic reward in relation to the very kinds of activities for which inventiveness is most common and from which, arguably, society gains some of the greatest rewards is regrettable, to say the least. To have standards of inventiveness that vary so greatly from industry to industry also, arguably, runs contrary to the traditional idea that the enquiry into inventiveness was to be an objective one. By changing the nature of the hypothetical addressee to one who, in certain cases, is possessed with the facility of invention, the decision also changes the availability of patents for the worse. If nothing else, the case shows the vital importance of determining the true character of the hypothetical addressee and warns of the immense significance of changes to those characteristics—a lesson that should be borne in mind if the superficially more attractive Continental models are ever to be adopted.

This is not necessarily a criticism of the judgments in the case; rather, it suggests that the legal definition of inventiveness needs to be reconsidered fundamentally in the light of the high-tech times in which we live. The fact that Purchas LJ was able to find some inventive steps, even on the basis that the hypothetical addressee had some inventive capacity, also gives some ground for hope: perhaps we should now be looking for a new category of 'super-inventiveness' in businesses such as genetic engineering, or else still finding that there is inventiveness on quite narrow grounds in such a context.[116]

Equally, there are many points raised in the judgments that go some way to resolving arguments from the past. It is clear that the focus of the obviousness question should be asked in the context not of each individual, but by looking at the overall team, with all of the varying specialities that would be typical in such cases,[117] and with all of the appropriate time and equipment at its disposal.

There was particular discussion of some factors that have, from time to time, been found significant in determining the obviousness question. The fact that Genentech had

---

[115] [1989] RPC 147 at 274.

[116] E.g. *Chiron Corp. v. Murex Diagnostics Ltd & Organon Teknika Ltd* [1996] RPC 535, per Aldous J at 574; cf. Morritt LJ at 608.

[117] *Genentech Inc.'s Patent* [1989] RPC 147, 203, per Dillon LJ at 247, and per Mustill LJ at 278.

won a patent race did not help that company, but neither did the fact that there was such a race in the first place. Dillon LJ was quite clear that the fact that the competing research teams were all following the same path tended to show that their activities were obvious and that the position may very well have been different if Genentech were out on its own pursuing a novel idea to a successful conclusion,[118] while Mustill LJ commented to similar effect[119] and also, in the context, made the telling remark that '*first to the post is the test of novelty, but novelty is not enough*'.[120]

Also canvassed was the idea that an inventive step is one that will often be signified by the heavy expenditure of time, skill, money, and energy. Again, the words of Mustill LJ summarize the position: '[I]*t may be that (diligent and skilled) labour and the resulting success deserve a prize, but the law, as I read it, calls for something more.*'[121] This must be right: the time and energy may be being expended because of the inefficiency or stupidity of the workers involved, who are perhaps engaged in no more than honest plodding, although Purchas LJ takes a contrary view, suggesting that the time taken on the project suggested that there was something non-obvious present.[122]

Maybe there is a clearer way forward from *Genentech* if one puts the focus on the outcome of the case. *Genentech* was special in terms of its facts: the substance that was to be made was known and occurred in the human body; the relevant procedures of recombinant DNA technology that were to be used to produce it outside the body in larger amounts were also known. Hence, both the starting point and the outcome were known, as was the route to get there. Actually doing it involved working through the relevant procedures, solving specific problems arising from their application to this substance, and a lot of hard labour by specialists in the field. Winning that race down the established track to a known goal may not involve any inventive activity and anything involved, even if it remained a long and difficult exercise, may therefore be seen as obvious. This depended, in part, on the special nature of the area involved, in which major breakthroughs are followed by periods of consolidation during which small steps are taken to apply the newly acquired insight to all kinds of subject matter. The latter steps may involve a lot of work, but the outcome and the way to get there are known, rendering the process obvious.

What remains, however, is that this approach to obviousness, although in line with the traditional approach, is very harsh in its effects on industries in which research is carried out in circumstances similar to the biotechnology example in *Genentech*. The criticisms raised remain applicable—especially in the light of the terms of the judgment—but, in recent cases, the courts seem to have backed away somewhat from the radical view that *Genentech* might be seen as putting forward. In those cases in which there was nothing to highlight the particular line of research actually pursued by the patentee as the first thing to try to reach the (known) goal and in which the notional research group (or person) would not immediately be led to that line of research as a first thing to try, the courts have been willing to accept that an inventive step might well be involved.[123] Lord Hoffmann has also argued, in *Biogen v. Medeva*,[124] that an inventive step can be present when the patentee attempts something that a person who is somewhat less skilled in the art might regard as obvious, if the real expert in that particular field would have argued that it was not even worth trying as a result of the many formidable obstacles involved.

[118] *Genentech Inc.* (n. 117) at 243.   [119] *Genentech Inc.* (n. 117) at 277.
[120] *Genentech Inc.* (n. 117) at 278.   [121] *Genentech Inc.* (n. 117) at 280.
[122] *Genentech Inc.* (n. 117) at 221.
[123] See *Brugger v. Medic-Aid* [1996] RPC 635 and *Hoechst Celanese v. BP Chemicals* [1997] FSR 547.
[124] [1997] RPC 1.

It may be, therefore, that *Genentech* is nothing more than a reflection of the problems that are associated with the traditional approach to obviousness. The EPO instructs its examiners to consider whether the skilled person 'would' use the approach suggested in the patent application, rather than 'could' use such an approach: only in the former scenario is the approach obvious.[125] In those cases in which the skilled person 'would' use the approach, the use of the approach is dictated by the expectation of achieving a good result. This is to be distinguished from the scenario in which the skilled person 'could' use the approach, because he or she acknowledges that there is a hope of success: that, on its own, is not sufficient to demonstrate obviousness.[126] This is an approach that predates the biotech era. Its use in an era of, and in relation to, technologies that move forward with small steps, on the basis that the art has a well-defined problem, and with most elements of a possible solution in mind, can lead to an increasing number of cases in which obviousness is established. That is a problem that comes on top of the traditional problem that, while the approach works particularly well in cases in which the art has a particular problem in mind, there are also other cases in which the art has no problem in mind, but in relation to which a certain solution is nevertheless obvious. Despite these problems, the approach may be helpful in a large number of cases when applying the inventive step, or obviousness, test set out in the Act.

Commercial success

One further factor in dealing with inventiveness may conveniently be dealt with here, although it does not arise in *Genentech*. A further argument that has been said to favour a finding of inventiveness is the subsequent commercial success of the invention. The argument appears to be based on the idea that the popularity and utility of a new device indicates that it fills, for the first time, a long-standing want, and that this commercial success shows that there must have been an inventive step in the process of thinking up something new that users have greeted with such acclaim.[127] This is evidently nonsense. All manner of factors go towards explaining the success of a new product, with the marketing effort being often of as much significance as the qualities of the product itself; the award of a patent—unless solely seen as the conferral of a reward by grateful society—can hardly be denied to a product that is only of use in a small number of, perhaps highly technical, situations.

The view of Mummery J expressed in *Mölnlycke AB v. Procter & Gamble Ltd (No. 3)*,[128] that obviousness is a technical question and not a commercial one, is therefore to be preferred. This view was followed by Jacob J, in *Beloit Technologies Inc. v. Valmet Paper Machinery Inc.*,[129] in which commercial success was no more than a matter of some evidential value in considering the issue of obviousness. Laddie J goes further in *Brugger v. Medic-Aid Ltd*,[130] suggesting that commercial factors may disguise the issue of the obviousness of, for example, a development that, though obvious, has not occurred for purely commercial, rather than technical, reasons. This is further confirmed by the judgment of Laddie J in *Raychem Corp.'s Patent*,[131] in which, again, novelty alone is not enough. In

---

[125] *Japan Styrene/Foam Articles* [1994] OJ EPO 154.

[126] *Lilly Icos v. Pfizer* [2002] FSR 809 (CA); see also *Pharmacia v. Merck* [2002] RPC 775 (CA).

[127] The classic formulation is by Tomlin J in *Samuel Parkes & Co. Ltd v. Cocker Brothers Ltd* (1929) 46 RPC 241 at 248. A more recent example of this approach is *Fichera v. Flogates Ltd* [1983] FSR 198.

[128] [1990] RPC 498 at 503.   [129] [1995] RPC 705.   [130] [1996] RPC 635.

[131] [1998] RPC 31 at 66.

Biogen Inc. v. Medeva plc,[132] Lord Hoffmann also took the view that commercial factors were irrelevant, in so far as a commercially motivated decision to research in the area did not stop the research strategy and its consequences from being an inventive step.

There is therefore no role for commercial success as primary evidence as to obviousness, but there may well be cases where it can assist in making a judgement by way of secondary evidence, i.e. where the primary evidence is strengthened by it and where there is no other explanation for the commercial success.[133]

The inventiveness of further developments

Just as is the case with the issue of novelty, problems arise in relation to the inventive step when a patent is being sought not for some entirely new product or process, but for something that is only a relatively minor advance on what has gone before. It therefore becomes very important to consider whether the step forward that has been made is an inventive one.

This was a problem in the *Genentech* case: at the beginning of its research, DNA technology existed and, at least in theory, could be adapted to produce t-PA, because it already had been to produce growth hormones, insulin, and other valuable products of a broadly similar nature. The production of t-PA was a natural challenge, in view of the known value of the substance. In the light of these factors, and bearing in mind the high level of the hypothetical addressee's knowledge and inventiveness, it was obvious to try to match the DNA technology to the challenge of t-PA production.[134] Dillon LJ adopted the notion that it was an obvious development for which the materials were '*lying in the road*' and available for the research worker to pick up.[135]

What *Genentech* is less clear on is what type of work is necessary to allow the steps being taken to transcend into inventive ones. We have already seen that hard work alone does not confer inventiveness and there is also discussion about the type of work. Mere trial-and-error experimentation is not sufficient, because such work is an obvious way for the uninventive to proceed, according to Mustill LJ.[136] In the view of Dillon LJ, however, '*empirical research industriously pursued may lead to a patentable invention*';[137] he cites House of Lords' *dicta* in support of the view.[138] It is suggested that this latter approach is incorrect in so far as it begs the question of why the industrious work was being carried out and whether the decision to embark on the work was obvious or not; it is also necessary to consider the inventiveness, or obviousness, issue at each stage of the research programme.[139] In so doing, the focus should be on the process and materials employed, and their obviousness (or otherwise), rather than on their use and its consequence.[140]

The quest for inventiveness at the beginning, and at each stage, of the development of the product or process is obviously important to the writer of the specification, enabling him or her to focus on those aspects in which inventiveness is most clearly to be found. It is also a helpful way of approaching the question of whether a minor step forward from what has gone before is inventive or obvious. A good example is the idea of mosaicking, which refers to the practice of taking two or more pre-existing products or processes and combining

[132] [1997] RPC 1.

[133] *Schlumberger Holdings Ltd v. Electromagnetic Geoservices AS* [2010] EWCA Civ 819.

[134] [1989] RPC 147, per Dillon LJ at 243 and per Mustill LJ at 276.   [135] [1989] RPC 147 at 243.

[136] [1989] RPC 147 at 274.   [137] [1989] RPC 147 at 241.

[138] Lord Simonds in *May & Baker Ltd v. Boots Pure Drug Co.* (1950) 67 RPC 23 at 34.

[139] See Mustill LJ in *Genentech* (n. 117) at 275–6.

[140] Per Laddie J in *Raychem Corp's Patents* (n. 85) at 41–2.

them together. Whether this combination is then able to gain patent protection will depend on whether the decision to combine is one that is inventive. The classic example is *Williams v. Nye*,[141] in which a patent was obtained for a combination of the previously separate mincing and filling machines used in the manufacture of sausages into one machine that was able to perform both functions. The Court of Appeal ruled that the patent was invalid, because the only step taken by the patentee was an obvious one; it was not inventive to combine two machines performing closely related functions into one, with no real alteration to the operation of either of the two machines. A more recent case[142] concerned the combination in one pill of two known therapeutic substances: neither interaction between the substances, nor any heightened effect due to the substances being taken together could be shown, which led to the logical conclusion that there was no inventive step.

It would be easy, however, to think of slight changes to the facts whereby it would be possible to claim inventiveness: for example, in the *Williams v. Nye* scenario, if one machine were to originate in a completely unrelated field of activity in relation to recognizing the transferability of which the patentee would have made an inventive step, or if the combined machine were to offer enormous savings in time or cost that it was not obvious to seek. In cases in which the two previously separate objects are, as is likely, in some way related to a common field, however, it is likely that the courts will expect the hypothetical addressee to make the obvious connection between them.[143]

Similar issues arise in cases in which the patent is sought for a new use of a pre-existing product or process. On the one hand, if the pre-existing item is unchanged, then the same objection as that in *Williams v. Nye* will be appropriate; if, on the other hand, some adaptation of the earlier item is necessary, the patent application should focus on this and the question will be whether inventiveness was present in the decision to make the adaptation and/or during its exercise. It is the combination of the inventive idea and the inventive method of putting it into operation that seems to give the best chance of securing patent protection.[144] This approach is also applicable to selection patents: if the selection and development of one from a larger class is obvious, that will be fatal to any patent claim; it must be shown that the decision to make the selection was itself an inventive step.[145]

Selection patents

On top of the issues concerning anticipation that were highlighted previously, selection patents also present problems in terms of obviousness. If the broader class is already known, where is the inventive step to be found when a selection is made and a patent is applied for in that respect? What is required (to go beyond the mere step of novelty and anticipation) is a technical contribution. It is that specific technical contribution of the selection that may establish inventiveness. It is the hitherto unknown technical effect that must justify the selection. Arbitrary selections are clearly not sufficient. In addition, the technical effect which justifies the selection of the claimed group must be one which can fairly be assumed to be produced by substantially all the selected members.[146] In

---

[141] (1890) 7 RPC 62.

[142] *Ancare NZ v. Fort Dodge* [2003] RPC 8, [2002] UKPC 8. See also *SABAF v. Menghetti* (n. 74).

[143] See e.g. *Allamanna Svenska Elekriska A/B v. Burntisland Shipping Co. Ltd* (1951) 69 RPC 63.

[144] *Burrough's Application* [1974] RPC 147 at 158.

[145] *Du Pont de Nemours & Co. (Witsiepe) Application* [1982] FSR 303. See also *Hallen Co. v. Brabantia (UK) Ltd* [1991] RPC 195, in which a combination of known technologies—self-pulling corkscrew and friction-reducing coating material—was obvious and not patentable even as a selection patent; but cf. *Mölnlycke AB v. Procter & Gamble Ltd (No. 5)* [1994] RPC 49.

[146] Case T-939/92, *AGREVO/Triazoles* 6 OJEPO 309, EOP Board of Appeal and *Dr Reddy's Laboratories (UK) Ltd v. Eli Lilly & Co. Ltd* [2009] EWCA Civ 1362, [2010] RPC 9.

other words, when a selection is claimed the *Pozzoli* test should apply to each element of the selection, i.e. the non-obvious technical results or effects must be shared by everything falling within the claim. It must at least be plausible that the (whole) selection has the technical significance claimed for it.[147]

Obviousness for lack of technical contribution in general

Lack of technical contribution can be an alternative for obviousness in the light of prior art. An invention can also be obvious because it lacks a technical contribution. Arnold J summarized the law on this point as follows:

> What these cases show is that the principles to be applied in determining whether a claimed invention is obvious are the same regardless of the field of the invention, but that the application of those principles can vary according to the circumstances of the case, including the field of the invention. An arbitrary selection from the prior art is not inventive, regardless of the field. Nevertheless this is a problem which is more likely to arise with claims to classes of chemical compounds for the reasons explained by the Board of Appeal in Agrevo. Where it is suggested that a claimed invention is obvious as being an arbitrary selection, the key question is whether the specification 'passes the threshold test of disclosing enough to make the invention plausible' as Lord Hoffmann put it in *Conor v. Angiotech*, that is to say, to make it plausible that the selection has the technical significance claimed for it.[148]

Limitless knowledge—how broad is the art?

In all of the discussion of the hypothetical addressee, one important factor has, until now, been avoided: the question of how much he knows—that is, of how limitless is his limitless capacity for knowledge. The theory is clear that in the area of inventiveness, as in relation to that of novelty, the state of the art encompasses all material that is available to the public at any time, anywhere (the definition provided by s. 2(2) of the 1977 Act appears equally applicable here). A clear illustration of this point is provided in the context of both novelty and obviousness by *Woven Plastic Products Ltd v. British Ropes Ltd*.[149] With evident regret, the Court of Appeal found that apparently unworked patent applications made some years earlier in Japan, not unreasonably in Japanese, had to be regarded as part of the state of the art, thus rendering the patent being worked by the plaintiffs as being invalid on the grounds that the use of polyvinyl chloride as the basis of a floor covering was not novel, and that the difference between the Japanese proposal and the English product was too minor to be regarded as anything other than an obvious variation.

A more difficult problem is in identifying the relevant art: the hypothetical addressee in, for example, a medical case will be expected to know all that there is to know about matters medical and, possibly—after *Genentech*—may even have to think about these matters. But what happens if there is a development in a very different field that may, in fact, be relevant to him, but of which, in practice, he is likely to know nothing? A possible

---

[147] *Generics UK Ltd v. Yeda Research & Development Co Ltd* [2013] EWCA Civ 925, *Sandvik Intellectual Property AB v. Kennametal Uk Ltd* [2011] EWHC 3311 (Pat), *Idenix v. Gilead Sciences and others* [2014] EWHC 3916 (Pat).

[148] *Sandvik Intellectual Property AB* (n. 147) at para. 185 and *Generics [UK] Limited (t/a Mylan) v. Yeda Research and Development Co. Ltd and Teva Pharmaceutical Industries Ltd* [2012] EWHC 1848 (Pat), at para. 336. See also T 939/92, *Agrevo/Triazoles* [1996] EPOR 171; *Abbott Laboratories Ltd v. Evysio Medical Devices ULC* [2008] EWHC 800 (Ch), [2008] RPC 23; *Conor Medsystems Ltd v. Angiotech Pharmaceuticals Inc.* (n. 64); and *Dr Reddy's Laboratories (UK) Ltd v. Eli Lilly & Co. Ltd* [2009] EWCA Civ 1362, [2010] RPC 9.

[149] [1970] FSR 47.

example might be developments in metallurgy, which produce a new and lighter alloy. Once our hypothetical medical addressee learns of this, it may well be obvious to consider using it in the making of artificial limbs, but it being a development in a very different art, he may never learn of it.

Guidance in relation to this problem is provided by *Johns-Manville Corp.'s Patent*.[150] The patent in this case had been granted for the use of a flocculating agent—that is, an agent that causes particles of solutions to adhere to one another, thus assisting the separation of the solids from the liquids in a solution—in the manufacture of shaped asbestos cement articles, which are made from a slurry-like solution. In seeking revocation of the patent, it was argued that all that the patentee had done was obvious in the light of two previously published documents relating to the use of such flocculating agents in two other industries: mining and paper manufacture. Both of these industries, although very different from that of the patentee, can readily be imagined to find flocculating agents valuable. The Court of Appeal agreed to revoke the patent; the common factor of flocculation was sufficient for the court to say that the patentee's knowledge should extend to what were effectively applications of the same art in different circumstances. This finding was easy to reach in the light of evidence that one of the patentee's employees had investigated (and rejected) the use of the agent in question some time previously, on hearing of its use in other industries. A similar decision was reached in the case of *Buhler AG v. Satake Ltd*,[151] in which the use of a milling machine for milling grain when a machine had been used in a similar way in the paint and chocolate industries was held to be obvious to the skilled expert in the construction of machines of that type, even though it was accepted that the particular use was novel.

It appears from these cases that the courts will interpret the 'art' in question broadly, to include related matters in other areas of activity. The transplanting of ideas from those related areas to that of the patentee will be regarded as obvious—but the corollary of this would appear to be that it is not obvious for the patentee to have considered apparently unrelated fields that do not form part of the state of his art and that, to do so, will represent an inventive step. It has also been held[152] that a team member whose expertise was in the field of obtaining regulatory approval for a new drug was not the notional addressee in question, because his expertise lay in the regulation of drugs rather than in the drug's creation.

A difficult key step

The quest for the inventive step is, perhaps, the most difficult aspect of the patent application procedure. It involves the UK Intellectual Property Office, on application, or the court, in subsequent revocation proceedings, in forming a qualitative judgement about the work of the patentee. Difficulties abound at every stage in relation to what was known originally, what is the patent's role in relation to the original matter, and what not the patentee himself but the hypothetical addressee in his place would have known and deduced from that knowledge. The value judgement is then made as to whether the deduction of that hypothetical addressee—often in a highly technical field—was one that was obvious and thus not worthy of patent protection, or one that can be described by the magic word 'inventive' and thus secure the coveted reward.

---

[150] [1967] RPC 479.   [151] [1997] RPC 232.
[152] *Richardson-Vicks Inc.'s Patent* [1997] RPC 888.

This has always been an onerous burden on the applicant, but the *Genentech* decision has made it harder in raising the standard of inventiveness to be expected from the hypothetical addressee in certain industries employing the highest levels of modern technology, so that some developments that are accepted as being an inventive step are nonetheless damned by obviousness. The realization stemming from *Genentech* that there is such a concept as the 'obvious invention' reveals a fatal flaw in the approach of the law, because s. 3 declares obviousness and inventiveness to be incompatible opposites. Until this paradox is resolved, the inventive step cannot be lauded as an effective legislative approach and a resolution of the problem. Either *Genentech* must be accepted, with its common ground with some European jurisdictions that some inventions may be obvious and its serious adverse implications for inventors in high-tech industries—and, subsequently, for the broader interests of society—or inventiveness will have to be redefined in new terms, perhaps by demoting obviousness to being merely a factor to be considered, and/or by equating inventiveness with that which the reasonable exponent of the art in question would regard as an inventive step worthy of patent protection. The only alternative is for a court to cast around to find something that is inventive, even in the post-*Genentech* era, as in the *Chiron* case at first instance,[153] while at the same time interpreting *Genentech* in a restrictive way.

Certainly, the difficulty of defining—let alone proving the existence of—the inventive step must be the largest single contributor to the time and expense involved in making a patent application, whether successful in the end or (disastrously in economic terms) ultimately unsuccessful. It may be that the whole area needs to be reconsidered,[154] but that time has yet to come and the current patchwork is the only picture that we presently have.

Industrial application

The third key requirement of the 1977 Patents Act is that, in order to be patented, an invention must be capable of 'industrial application'. This phrase is new to the 1977 Act—previously, the invention had had to represent '*a new manner of manufacture*'[155]—and this clearly shows that a broader approach, more favourable to patentees, is now being taken and also that previous case law is not now of great assistance. This part of the law casts a useful shaft of light on the aims and purposes of the patent system: only that which is usable—or, to be precise, capable of industrial use—is regarded as deserving of the protection afforded by the grant of a patent. It also poses an important practical barrier to a patentee deciding at what stage of the inventive process an application for a patent should be sought; clearly, if the invention is still at a theoretical stage, no matter how advanced, it will be premature to make an application if its potential industrial applicability is yet to be demonstrated.

Section 4(1) of the 1977 Act is of little assistance in explaining the new terminology, simply informing the reader that '*an invention shall be capable of industrial application if it can be made or used in any kind of industry, including agriculture*'. This broad approach does seem to signify that it will be no ground for objection to a patent that it is found to work in a different field of industry from that which the inventor originally had in mind.

---

[153] [1998] RPC 517.
[154] See P. Cole, 'Inventive Step: Meaning of the EPO Problem and Solution Approach and Implications for the United Kingdom' [1998] EIPR 214 and 267.
[155] Patents Act 1949, s. 101(1).

Potential or capability are the norm, but the application needs to give an indication of the function of the invention. Some practical application, some profitable use, at least in terms of a potential, needs to be disclosed. The use of the word 'industry' and the hint at profitable use should not be seen though as requiring use in trade for financial benefit. Other forms of profit such as solving a technical problem or offering a cure for a rare disease can also be envisaged. In essence the description needs to disclose some form of potential practical application. This became clear in *Eli Lilly v. Human Genome Sciences*,[156] where capability of industrial application was denied on these grounds by the judge at first instance and by the Court of Appeal. All the patentee had done was to determine by means of a computer program the nucleotide and amino acid sequence of a novel member of the anti-tumour ligand superfamily. The application did not disclose what could be done with the material, even if it was clear that at some stage a (useful) use would be discovered and that the identification itself of the sequence was a great scientific achievement. On its own though the identification did not meet the requirement of being capable of industrial application. This approach fits also in with what Lord Hoffmann said in *Conor Medsystems v. Angiotech Pharmaceuticals*[157] in an inventive step context. Patents will not be granted for an idea which is mere speculation and product claims which have no evident utility, provide no technical contribution, or solve no technical problem are obvious. Patents have a focus on usable matter, which will eventually either take the form of a new product or of a new process.

When the case went up to the Supreme Court the decision was, however, overruled. The Supreme Court held that the judge and the Court of Appeal had applied a standard that was too exacting and preferred to bring the UK in line with the EPO approach.[158] The latter was summarized along the following guidelines.

1. General requirements:
    (i)   The patent had to disclose 'a practical application' and 'some profitable use' for the claimed substance, so that the ensuing monopoly 'can be expected [to lead to] some … commercial benefit';
    (ii) A 'concrete benefit', namely the invention's 'use … in industrial practice' had to be 'derivable directly from the description', coupled with common general knowledge;
    (iii) A merely 'speculative' use would not be sufficient, so a vague and speculative indication of possible objectives that might or might not be achievable would not do;
    (iv) The patent and common general knowledge had to enable the skilled person 'to reproduce' or 'exploit' the claimed invention without 'undue burden', or having to carry out 'a research programme'.
2. Where a patent disclosed a new protein and its encoding gene:
    (v)   The patent, when taken with common general knowledge, had to demonstrate 'a real as opposed to a purely theoretical possibility of exploitation';
    (vi)   Merely identifying the structure of the protein, without attributing to it a 'clear role', or 'suggesting' any 'practical use' for it, or suggesting 'a vague and speculative indication of possible objectives that might be achieved', was not enough;
    (vii) The absence of experimental or wet lab evidence of activity of the claimed protein was not fatal;
    (viii) A 'plausible' or 'reasonably credible' claimed use, or an 'educated guess', could suffice;

---

[156] *Eli Lilly v. Human Genome Sciences* [2008] RPC 29 confirmed on appeal [2010] EWCA CSU 33; see also *Laboratorios Almirall SA v. Boehringer Ingelheim International GmbH* [2009] FSR 12.
[157] *Conor Medsystems v. Angiotech Pharmaceuticals* (n. 64).
[158] The Supreme Court referred to cases T 0870/04, *Max-Planck/BDP1 Phosphatase* [2006] EPOR 14, EPO Technical Board of Appeal; T 0898/05, *Zymogenetics/Hematopoietic Cytokine receptor*, 7 July 2006, EPO

(ix) Such plausibility could be assisted by being confirmed by 'later evidence', although later evidence on its own would not do;

(x) The requirements of a plausible and specific possibility of exploitation could be at the biochemical, the cellular or the biological level.

3. Where the protein is said to be a family or superfamily member:

(xi) If all known members had a 'role in the proliferation, differentiation and/or activation of immune cells' or 'function in controlling physiology, development and differentiation of mammalian cells', assigning a similar role to the protein may suffice;

(xii) So 'the problem to be solved' in such a case could be 'isolating a further member of the [family]';

(xiii) If the disclosure was 'important to the pharmaceutical industry', the disclosure of the sequences of the protein and its gene may suffice, even though its role had not 'been clearly defined';

(xiv) The position may be different if there was evidence, either in the patent or elsewhere, which called the claimed role or membership of the family into question;

(xv) The position may also be different if the known members had different activities, although they need not always be 'precisely interchangeable in terms of their biological action', and it may be acceptable if 'most' of them had a common role.[159]

When they looked at the evidence in the case on the basis of these guidelines the Supreme Court judges decided that they had been satisfied and that the patent passed the hurdle of being capable of industrial application.

All this does not detract from the conclusion though that in the average case the requirement that patents must be capable of industrial application adds little to the general picture, although it also represents bad news for the ever-optimistic designers of perpetual motion machines.

Methods of treatment and pharmaceutical products

In the original version of s. 4 Patents Act 1977, s. 4(1) was followed by a provision on methods of treatment which were excluded from patentability, and pharmaceutical products which were held to be patentable. The exclusion is, in essence, a policy exclusion[160] and the link with industrial application was an artificial one. The legislator took that into account eventually and the Patents Act 2004 deleted these provisions from s. 4 and inserted[161] a new free-standing s. 4A into the Act:

4A Methods of treatment or diagnosis

(1) A patent shall not be granted for the invention of—

(a) a method of treatment of the human or animal body by surgery or therapy, or

(b) a method of diagnosis practised on the human or animal body.

Technical Board of Appeal; T 0604/04, *Genentech Inc./Human PF4A receptors*, 16 March 2006, EPO Technical Board of Appeal; T 1452/06, *Bayer HealthCare AG/Human epithin-like serine protease*, EPO Technical Board of Appeal, 10 May 2007; T 1165/06, *Schering/IL-17 related polypeptide*, 19 July 2007, EPO Technical Board of Appeal; and T 1329/04, *Johns Hopkins University School of Medicine/Growth differentiation factor-9* [2006] EPOR 8, EPO Technical Board of Appeal.

[159] *Human Genome Sciences, Inc. v. Eli Lilly & Co.* [2011] UKSC 5, [2012] 1 All ER 1154, [2012] RPC 6 (SC).

[160] See E. D. Ventose, 'In the Footsteps of the Framers of the European Patent Convention: Examining the Travaux Préparatoires' (2009) 31(7) EIPR 353.

[161] Section 1 of the Patents Act 2004 has this effect.

(2) Subsection (1) above does not apply to an invention consisting of a substance or composition for use in any such method.

(3) In the case of an invention consisting of a substance or composition for use in any such method, the fact that the substance or composition forms part of the state of the art shall not prevent the invention from being taken to be new if the use of the substance or composition in any such method does not form part of the state of the art.

(4) In the case of an invention consisting of a substance or composition for a specific use in any such method, the fact that the substance or composition forms part of the state of the art shall not prevent the invention from being taken to be new if that specific use does not form part of the state of the art.

Subsections (1) and (2) are the key provisions for our current purposes. The basic effect of these two subsections is clear. Section 4A(1) disallows the creation of a patent monopoly on a method of treatment. This is best explained on policy grounds: it is not in society's interests for one doctor to be able to rely on a monopoly to deny the use of a method of treatment to other doctors and, of course, to their patients. The benefits of a new treatment should be available to all.[162]

Section 4A(2), however, takes the opposite approach to pharmaceutical products, which, in many cases, will form a vital part of the treatment method and it is seen as entirely appropriate to permit a monopoly over the supply of drugs for the lifetime of the patent. This might be thought by cynics to be a reflection of the respective lobbying strengths of the medical profession and the drugs industry, but it can be justified to an extent. Precise methods of treatment will vary from surgeon to surgeon and would be hard to define accurately for the purposes of a patent specification; it is also fair to note that doctors have duties towards their profession that have no parallel in the case of a researcher employed by a pharmaceutical company. The Court of Appeal has held[163] that a patent containing a claim that a (known) product called taxol could be used with sufficient medication to prevent severe anaphylactic reactions for the purposes of producing a medicament fell foul of what now is s. 4A(1), because, as a result of the use of premedication and the selection by the doctor of the amount of taxol in each case, the real medicament was produced in the patient out of these two ingredients. The patent therefore did not explain how to manufacture the medicament, but instead explained how to treat the patient—hence the court's conclusion that the invention was not capable of industrial application.[164] Similarly, a claim to a particular regime for the administration of a drug to treat osteoporosis was rejected on the grounds that it was, in reality, a method of treatment.[165]

This discussion must be seen alongside subsections (3) and (4) of s. 4A, which were already discussed earlier in this chapter as they deal with novelty. The fact that they are now part of the same section, though, highlights the fact that they are linked. It will be recalled that this allows the patenting of a pre-existing product only for the first occasion on which it is found to have a medical or related use. In extending the definition of novelty, this provides further assistance to an applicant for a patent in the area of pharmaceutical products, and the circumvention of the ban on patents for a second or subsequent medical use[166]—by focusing on the manufacturing process used for that drug with

---

[162] See Ventose, 'In the Footsteps of the Framers of the European Patent Convention: Examining the Travaux Préparatoires' (n. 160).

[163] *Bristol-Myers Squibb Co. v. Baker Norton* (n. 55).   [164] *Bristol-Myers Squibb Co.* (n. 55) at 21.

[165] *Teva Pharmaceutical Industries Ltd v. Instituto Gentili SpA and ors* [2004] FSR 330 (CA).

[166] *John Wyeth & Brother Ltd's Application; Schering AG's Application* [1985] RPC 545. For a case that shows the limitations of these widening attempts, see *Teva Pharmaceutical Industries Ltd* (n. 165).

a view to that use, which is now explicitly part of the Act[167]—only confirms that there is ample scope for patenting the drugs used in treatment and confirms the contrast in the approach to the two aspects of medical care. The latter is in line with the EPO's approach that allowed so-called 'Swiss' claims—that is, claims to the use of a substance for making it up into a medicament for pharmaceutical administration in pursuit of a subsequently discovered use.[168] The 2000 revision of the EPC did away for the future with Swiss claims, but instead, claims for the use of compound X for treatment of disease Y are now allowed and this change is now also reflected in s. 4.

This area creates problems: the intelligent applicant will make use of this area of the law to seek backdoor protection by patent of the inherently unpatentable. Careful drafting of a patent claim can give a monopoly on the drugs used in a method of treatment and thus confers a de facto monopoly on the treatment itself. An extreme example of this arose under the admittedly different provisions of US law, when a child was born with leukaemia and its placenta was preserved for use in future medical treatment. When the time for treatment arose, it could not occur without payment of a substantial royalty to the owner of the patent in respect of that kind of treatment.[169] This sad tale explains why s. 4A(1) is so important, but equally demonstrates the potentially alarming consequences of its circumvention.

The main area of concern in this part of the law has traditionally been with the establishment of the boundaries of the medical treatment exception. The proper approach to be taken is spelt out in *Unilever Ltd (Davis's) Application*.[170] In this case, a patent was sought for a method of immunizing poultry against the disease coccidiosis by using certain microorganisms as food additives. Such immunization has the effect not of curing the animals of disease, but rather of preventing them from catching the disease in the first place. The question arose whether this was a therapy for the purposes of what now is s. 4A(1). After extensive consideration of both general and medical dictionaries, Falconer J found that therapy had a broader meaning than that only of curing diseases and covered any form of medical treatment of disease;[171] this broad interpretation, albeit the result of classic common lawyers' pedantry, appears to fit well with the new era of purposive construction of the patent legislation.

Still, however, the frontiers of the s. 4A(1) exception have to be delimited. The connection with disease seems to be an important feature of the exception in the *Unilever* case and this is reflected in *Stafford-Miller's Applications*,[172] in which patents were sought for a method of chemical treatment of head lice. Whitford J refused to throw out the application on what are now s. 4A(1) grounds: regarding the case as '*on the absolute frontier*',[173] he held that it was arguable that an infestation of head lice, while an undoubted irritant, may very well not be regarded as disease and thus its treatment is potentially patentable. Likewise, the view has been taken by the EPO that medical tests that may be carried out in order to see whether a disease is present do not fall within this exception and that thus, in an appropriate case, patent protection may be secured.[174]

Particular problems have been generated by contraception, which, in the form of birth-control pills, involves the use of chemicals on the body. In a decision on the then common law-based exception, which appears to be equally applicable in the current statutory regime, it was held, in *Schering AG's Application*,[175] that it was acceptable to

---

[167] See also *Actavis UK Ltd v. Merck & Co. Inc.* (n. 55).   [168] *Eisai's & other Applications* (n. 52).
[169] BBC 2 *Newsnight*, 22 July 1998.   [170] [1983] RPC 219.   [171] [1983] RPC 219 at 228.
[172] [1984] FSR 258.   [173] [1984] FSR 258 at 261.
[174] *Bruker's Application* [1988] OJ EPO 308.   [175] [1971] RPC 337.

patent contraceptives. This decision is, again, consistent with the need for there to be some connection with a disease for the s. 4A(1) exception to be applicable and represents a significant advance on the previous refusal to grant patents for contraception.[176] An alternative method of securing patent protection for contraception without getting entangled with the medical treatment exception is illustrated by *Organon Laboratories Ltd's Application*,[177] in which a patent was permitted for a pack containing two different types of contraceptive pill, with clear indications of the dates on which each should be taken and with the pills presented in an appropriate order. Taken together, these elements amounted to what was then a new and more effective method of contraception—but it seems that the novelty of the combination of the pills was of the essence in this case; merely making an improvement in the packaging or presentation of a product to improve its use is not sufficient to gain a patent, according to *Ciba-Geigy AB (Durr's Application)*.[178]

Non-patentable matter

Even if the requirements of novelty, inventive step, and industrial application are satisfied by an applicant for a patent, there is one further group of hurdles placed in his or her way—namely, the deliberate exclusion of various matters from the ambit of patentability by s. 1(2) and (3) of the 1977 Act.

It will be recalled that the excluded matter under s. 1(2) is:

(a) a discovery, scientific theory or mathematical method;
(b) a literary, dramatic, musical or artistic work or any other aesthetic creation whatsoever;
(c) a scheme, rule or method for performing a mental act, playing a game or doing business, or a program for a computer;
(d) the presentation of information.

Non-patentable matter, but only 'as such'

It is vital at the outset to establish one important restriction on the ban in s. 1(2): it is only applicable to the prohibited matter '*as such*' and the effect of these two vital words is that, while it is not possible to patent, for example, a discovery on its own, it is quite appropriate to patent some process embodying the discovery, or a product in which the discovery has been transformed into a product of practical value. This means that, in this area too, the drafting of the specification and the claims is of vital significance. A scientist may discover a new source of energy, but it is highly likely that much work will need to be done to harness and control the new energy source, and to create the necessary technology that will embody it—and it is all of this kind of work that should be the focus of the application for the grant of a patent.

The classic example of this is provided by *Otto v. Linford*,[179] in which patent protection was sought for an internal combustion engine at the very early stages of the development of the motor car—the engine introducing, for the first time, air into the combustion process to enhance its effectiveness. The claim was found to be valid not as a discovery of the role of air, which, as a discovery would not be patentable, but as a machine that embodied and gave practical effect to that discovery. A more recent example is provided by *Rhodes'*

---

[176] *Riddlesbarger's Application* (1936) 53 RPC 57.
[177] [1970] RPC 574.   [178] [1977] RPC 83.   [179] (1882) 46 LT 35.

Application,[180] in which a patent was successfully sought for a new speedometer that informed the driver both of his or her road speed and of the square of that figure, which represented kinetic energy and thus, as it was termed, the 'impact speed' of the car. The application did not founder on the rock of being merely a presentation of information, because there was, in the then statutory phrase, *'a manner of new manufacture'*[181] in the form of a working machine that combined the idea of providing a driver with an indication of his or her impact speed with a workable method of so doing. Today, this remains more than only a presentation of information 'as such'.

The precise relationship between non-patentable matter, such as a discovery, and an attempt to gain patent protection for a product or process closely connected with it was subject to further review in *Genentech*.[182] Remember that this case concerned the use of known DNA technology to produce quantities of a potentially valuable activator, t-PA, for use against blood clots. Purchas LJ expressed the view that *'a claim to a method embracing a discovery which may well be an invention … is patentable'*,[183] rejecting the view previously expressed in *Merrill Lynch Inc.'s Application*[184] that the method of using the discovery must be novel, over and beyond the novelty of the discovery. In *Genentech*,[185] Dillon LJ made clear his view that a patent could be sought even though, once the discovery is made, the way forward to the application of it is an obvious one. The additional albeit obvious work to harness the discovery provides the additional element that means that the patent is not just for a discovery 'as such'.[186] It was clear that Mustill LJ was unhappy with the reasoning at this point, although not with the ultimate conclusion reached.[187] This did not avail Genentech, however, because the court found that some of its claims were for pure discoveries and were non-patentable, and, as we have seen, the steps that it had taken to isolate the t-PA were obvious to people of its team's expertise.

To an extent, it is appropriate to share the doubts expressed by Mustill LJ: a combination of a non-patentable discovery with its obvious application does not seem to provide the strongest of bases for the grant of a patent. The wording of s. 2 appears, however, to lead inexorably to that result, with a very fine line emerging between the non-patentable discovery of something without more, which is not patentable even if inventive, and the inventive discovery of something that is then obvious in its application, which is. The user of the discovery is protected, while the discoverer is not, which might again be said to reflect a function of patent law as the conferral of a reward on the inventor of something useful that benefits society. Also, given earlier criticisms of other aspects of *Genentech*, it may seem churlish to object to what appears to be one of its more generous aspects. The approach has been confirmed by the Court of Appeal in *Chiron Corp. v. Murex Diagnostics Ltd & Organon Teknika Ltd*,[188] in which it was held that the patent claim was for the polypeptide that resulted from the genetic sequence that had been discovered.

There is also a broader aspect to this part of *Genentech*. Mustill LJ points out the importance of identifying that there is an invention in the first place, before proceeding to consider the three legal elements that make it patentable.[189] He is fortified in this view by EPO Guidelines,[190] which make clear that this is a question that is separate and distinct from the other elements. Actions that may fall foul of s. 1(2) as being non-patentable are

---

180 [1973] RPC 243.   181 Patents Act 1949, s. 101.
182 [1989] RPC 147.   183 [1989] RPC 147 at 208.
184 [1988] RPC 1 (but see [1989] RPC 561 on appeal).   185 [1989] RPC 147 at 240.
186 [1989] RPC 147.   187 [1989] RPC 147 at 269–70.
188 [1996] RPC 535, per Morritt LJ at 605–6.   189 [1989] RPC 147 at 263–4.
190 Guidelines for Examination in the EPO, Ch. 4, paras 1.1 and 2.2.

in some cases, he argues, not going to pass the first test of there being an invention in any event. Purchas LJ took the same view.[191]

This argument has, however, been somewhat dented by the approach adopted by Lord Hoffmann in *Biogen Inc. v. Medeva plc*.[192] He doubts whether the question of whether there is an invention or not is one of any practical importance, on the basis that the requirements in the legislation for patentability have the effect of restricting claims within the general category of 'inventions'. Lord Hoffmann claims that the drafters of the EPC and the Patents Act 1977, and even the learned counsel in *Biogen*, were unable to think of any examples of something that would be unpatentable purely because it was not an invention. So while it is, to an extent, useful to check that there is an invention, the check is unlikely to add anything to the consideration of patentability.

From these matters relevant to the whole of s. 1(2), we can now move on to consider the specific exclusions.

Section 1(2)(a)

The first exclusions in s. 1(2)(a) are self-evident in their character, but what may be less clear is the rationale for their exclusion, especially because, for example, the development of scientific theory is much more likely to be as a result of years of effort than the product of a shriek of 'Eureka!' while idling in the bathtub. The explanation is, however, that what these exclusions have in common is that they do not advance progress in the sense of creating something new, but merely reveal the existence of something that has always been there, but is only now revealed. The application of science is thus much better rewarded than its pure form; research is not enough—there must also be development.[193]

Section 1(2)(b)

The second group of exclusions—that of matter more at home in the field of copyright—is easier to explain, in so far as it is clearly convenient to have a clear dividing line between the law of patents and that relating to copyright. Section 1(2)(b) appears to achieve this: a new method of painting may be the subject of a patent, but the painting itself will only qualify for copyright. It may be, however, that the electronic creation of music, or the making of technical and similar drawings, may push the intended division closer to the limit, as would a novel work of art capable of an industrial application. In this case, the approach of s. 1(2) in allowing patents for excluded matter not used 'as such' would seem to give rise to a potential clash with both patent and copyright protection being secured, contrary to the assumed intention that lies behind paragraph (b).

Section 1(2)(c) and (d)

The next category—those in s. 1(2)(c) and (d)—gives rise to the usual need for careful reading of the patent application to see whether it covers the excluded material 'as such': if it goes beyond the excluded material, it will be able to get a patent, but it would be prudent to emphasize the matter over and beyond, for example, the presentation of information at the drafting stage.

A useful set of facts with which to illustrate this simply is that of *ITS Rubber Ltd's Application*,[194] in which a patent application was made for a squash ball coloured blue in order that its location could be detected more readily by players. At the time, it was found by Whitford J to be potentially patentable as a manner of new manufacture,[195] but now it would appear likely to fall within paragraphs (c) or (d) as being the presentation

---

[191] [1989] RPC 147 at 224.   [192] [1997] RPC 1.   [193] [1989] RPC 147 at 228.
[194] [1979] RPC 318.   [195] [1979] RPC 318 at 325.

of information as to the location of the ball. Because this would make no change to the method of playing squash, it would seem to be claimed 'as such' and thus non-patentable, whereas the dual speedometer noted in the *Rhodes* case was incorporated into something new and would still be awarded a patent, if drafted appropriately. The concept of presentation of information was held to include providing information. It is indeed difficult to see what sense the provision would still have if this were not the case, but the decision assists in focusing on the meaning of presentation of information.[196]

A case that illustrates the key distinction at issue well is *Lux Traffic Controls Ltd v. Pike Signals & Faronwise Ltd*.[197] The patents in this case were for traffic light control systems, one of which extended the green period by an additional period if it detected a vehicle crossing, thus ensuring that opposing traffic was held by a red light, and the other of which gave a pause on each change of lights during which no one had a green light for a time. Aldous J found that a method of regulating traffic as such would not be patentable, because it was not an invention, but rather merely an abstract plan, which at best presented information, following the EPO's decision in the *Christian Franceries* case.[198] The patent claimed was, however, for the device that, by detecting both the movement and non-movement of traffic in a novel way, created a new form of technological contribution to traffic management; it is the technical character of the improvement made that is vital[199] and that was found to be present in the first patent. Likewise, in the second patent, a known type of traffic regulation was in consideration, so, on the face of it, both non-patentability and anticipation applied; again, however, what was, in fact, being created was a new device to control this type of traffic regulation centrally, with the maximum ease, and that was sufficient to justify the grant of a patent in that instance too.

The decision in *Raytheon Co.'s Application*[200] provides a contrast with this. It was concerned with a system for improving ship recognition by creating a digital record of known ships that could then be compared with the digital silhouette of an unknown ship. This was seen as non-patentable: its two sole features were that it was a system for performing a mental act and non-patentable as such, and its other feature was a computer program and also non-patentable. There was nothing that amounted to a technical advantage here; it was the obvious mosaicking of two non-patentable items.

What emerges is that the exclusion 'as such' of a mental act from patentability is a narrow one. Its purpose is to make sure that patent claims could not be performed by purely mental means and this is achieved by making sure there is no patentability for such claims. The logic behind a narrow interpretation is therefore that it would prevent patents being granted which could be infringed by a purely mental process. But once one goes beyond that very narrow scope there is something else for which there may be a place in patent law and a mere exclusion from patentability is no longer warranted.[201] The same logic applies to the exclusion of computer programs 'as such'.[202]

More detail on the computer element that is intrinsic to *Raytheon* is to be found in Chapter 30;[203] it is appropriate to note briefly here a particular point that arises in relation to computer programs, but which also casts light on the preceding area. In *Merrill*

---

[196] *In the Matter of Patent Application No. GB0301172.3, sub nom Stephen Townsend* [2004] EWHC 482.
[197] [1993] RPC 107.
[198] [1993] RPC 107 at 138; *Christian Franceries/Traffic Regulation*, T16/83, 1998 EPOR 65, 69 (Technical Bd. App. 1985).
[199] Guidelines for Examination in the EPO, Ch. 4, para. 1.2(ii).   [200] [1993] RPC 427.
[201] *Halliburton Energy Services Inc.'s Patent Applications* [2011] EWHC 2508 (Pat), [2012] RPC 12.
[202] *Protecting Kids the World Over (PKTWO) Ltd* [2011] EWHC 2720 (Pat).
[203] See also R. B. Bakels, 'Software Patentability: What Are the Right Questions?' (2009) 31(10) EIPR 514.

Lynch's Application,[204] the Court of Appeal was faced with the issue of patentability of a program drawn up by the applicants for a data processing system for making a trading market in securities. In the post-*Genentech* world, it was clear that the applicants were under an obligation to prove that what they had done was to create something more than a computer program 'as such', so they pointed to the programming of the computer by the program as being the necessary extra element.

This was rejected by Fox LJ:

> it cannot be permissible to patent an item excluded under section 1(2) under the guise of an article which contains that item—that is to say in the case of a computer program, the patenting of a conventional computer containing that program.[205]

There must once again be a technical advance in the form of a new result and this was a requirement that had not been satisfied in *Merrill Lynch*. This was a standard computer program and thus non-patentable, and its application was to do no more than create a method of doing business, which is also non-patentable.

A similar decision was also reached in *Gale's Application*,[206] in which an inventor created a program on a disc that gave an easier method of calculating the square roots of numbers. No patent was allowed: all that the computer did was to generate a program; placing it on the disc was, as in *Merrill Lynch*, not a technical advance and, in any event, it was only a discovery of a mathematical method and thus fell foul of s. 1(2) (a) as well. The fact that the retired plaintiff appeared in person probably explains why this matter had to go up as far as the Court of Appeal for its ultimate, and obvious, disposition.

A contested approach

The Court of Appeal reviewed this area of the law in the *Aerotel* case.[207] The court found the current situation to be unsatisfactory, because different approaches emerge from the case law of the UK courts and that of the EPO. The court suggested that the EPO should convene an Enlarged Board of Appeal to clarify the law; in the meantime, it found itself bound by the cases that require there to be a technical effect to bring the subject matter outside the scope of s. 1(2). Nevertheless, the court suggested a new four-stage approach to apply s. 1(2) and to bring the technical effect requirement into practice:

1. It is necessary properly to construe the claim: what exactly is claimed?

2. The contribution made by the invention is identified.

3. It is then asked whether that contribution falls solely within the excluded subject matter.

4. Finally, it is checked whether the contribution is technical in nature.

Biotechnology

Two distinct types of matter that are of fundamental importance as biotechnology[208] develops apace were excluded by the original text of s. 1(3) of the 1977 Act, which stated:

---

[204] [1989] RPC 561.   [205] [1989] RPC 561 at 569.   [206] [1991] RPC 305.

[207] *Aerotel Ltd v. Tesco Holdings Ltd; Macrossan's Patent Application* [2007] RPC 7.

[208] See, generally, M. Llewelyn, 'The Legal Protection of Biotechnical Inventions: An Alternative Approach' (1997) 3 EIPR 115.

A patent shall not be granted—

(a) for an invention the publication or exploitation of which would be generally expected to encourage offensive, immoral or anti-social behaviour;

(b) for any variety of animal or plant or any essentially biological process for the production of animals or plants, not being a micro-biological process or the product of such a process.

These matters were, and are, not exclusive to issues of biotechnology, but impact more in this area than any other. Likewise, in considering this topic, regard should, of course, be had to important cases considered elsewhere, such as *Biogen*, *Chiron*, and *Genentech*.[209]

The wording of s. 1(3) has now been amended[210] and brought into line with that used in the Trade-Related Aspects of Intellectual Property Rights (TRIPS) Agreement 1994, but no change in the substantive law was envisaged. The new text stipulates: '*A patent shall not be granted for an invention the commercial exploitation of which would be contrary to public policy or morality.*' Section 1(4) adds:

For the purposes of subsection (3) above exploitation shall not be regarded as contrary to public policy or morality only because it is prohibited by any law in force in the United Kingdom or any part of it.

It is appropriate, though, before we look at the detailed implications of the morality clause, to have a closer look at the relationship between biotechnology and patent law in order to understand how certain issues arise, and why the situation is somewhat different from that relating, for example, to mechanical engineering.

Biotechnology and biotechnological techniques

In essence, biotechnology is concerned with the application of scientific techniques to living organisms. These living organisms are manipulated in one way or another—such as through the insertion of another gene, for example. According to the EPO Guidelines, biotechnological inventions are inventions that '*concern a product consisting of or containing biological material or a process by means of which biological material is produced, processed or used*' and biological material is '*any material containing genetic information and capable of reproducing itself or being reproduced in a biological system*'.[211]

There have been significant developments in biotechnology over the last decades, and the area is now seen as an important potential source of new medical treatments and drugs, and plants that are disease-resistant. This explains the massive investments in the area and hence also the attempts to patent the outcome of the research to secure a return on the huge investments made.

There are several techniques that are frequently used in the field of biotechnology. We will briefly describe them here, because a minimal insight is required to understand the specific aspects of patent applications that flow from the use or development of these techniques. The first of these is tissue and cell culture technology, which essentially involves the production of cell lines. This is a vital research tool, because these cell lines are self-replicating samples of cells that are grown outside the original host, and, in principle, these lines are immortal and constitute a constant supply of the relevant cells. The original host might be a bacterium or a plant, but might also be an animal, or even a

---

[209] See N. Jones and I. Britton, 'Biotech Patents: the Trend Reversed Again' (1996) 3 EIPR 171.

[210] The Patents Regulations 2000, SI 2000/2037, r. 2.

[211] EPO Guidelines, Pt C, Ch. IV, para. 2a.

human being. The most advanced cell lines are arguably those involving human embryonic stem cells.[212]

The use of human material, in particular, can make this technique controversial. The most important aspect of cell lines is their uniformity: all of the cells share identical characteristics and genetic make-up. Accurate comparative tests therefore become possible, for example, in relation to the effect of drugs on living matter or the study of biological processes.

'Hybridoma' technology deals with the human immune response and involves two of its key players: white blood cells and antibodies. At its most basic, antibody-producing white blood cells are fused with tumour cells, which have the advantage that they produce indefinitely, and when such a hybridized cell is injected into an antigen—that is, a foreign body that will provoke an antibody response—an indefinite supply of antibodies is produced. This technique is invaluable for the research into the operation of the immune system, and has been used in the production of diagnostic and other testing kits.[213]

In silico techniques, meanwhile, search and compare databases of gene sequences using a combination of genetic and bioinformatic knowledge. The aim is to attribute a function to gene sequences on the basis of matches with already-known proteins that have a similar function.

Genetic engineering is probably the most well-known, or at least well-publicized, technique. Its full name is 'recombinant DNA technology' and it involves the manipulation of matter at a sub-cellular level. DNA strings are contained in the nucleus of almost all living cells; it is DNA that is being manipulated. DNA stands for 'deoxyribonucleic acid'. It appears in strings and dictates the function of the cell in which it exists through genes, which are essentially sequences of DNA that activate the production of proteins (also known as polypeptides). They do this by bringing together different combinations of amino acids, which will, in turn, produce the proteins. Scientists talk about coding for proteins and the different proteins make cells function in different ways. By interfering with the DNA—for example, by removing fragments or inserting bits that are alien to the cell—one can influence the production of proteins and the function that is fulfilled by the cell.

Biotechnology patent applications

All of these techniques have developed rapidly over the last decades and some of these developments have been the object of patent applications. The knowledge, modified cells, gene sequences, and proteins, etc. that have resulted from the use of these techniques have also been the object of patent applications. A first idea of the problems that arise in this area can be gained from the basic proposition that a large part of what is being done involves unravelling the biological and genetic structure of living material. That living material was, naturally, already in existence and, apart from the morality issue, one might also question whether an inventive activity is involved when a gene is isolated and its function is discovered, for example.

---

[212] A. Plomer and P. Torremans (eds.) (2009), *Embryonic Stem Cell Patents: European Law and Ethics*, Oxford: Oxford University Press; A. Plomer et al. (2006) *Stem Cell Patents: European Patent Law and Ethics Report*, Report for the European Commission, <http://www.nottingham.ac.uk/law/StemCellProject/project.report.pdf>. See also S. Crespi, 'The Human Embryo and Patent Law: A Major Challenge Ahead?' (2006) 28(11) EIPR 569–75.

[213] See G. van Overwalle (ed.) (2007) *Gene Patents and Public Health*, Brussels: Bruylant.

Discoveries and inventions

This brings us back to the discussion of the relationship between a 'discovery' and an 'invention'. As we have seen before, patent law sees an invention as an inventive concept that brings about a technical solution for a pre-existing problem that had not yet been solved. A patentable invention involves, therefore, the application of knowledge; a mere discovery does not have that added aspect of the application of knowledge in a problem-solving context.

From a legal point of view, the conclusion is therefore, at least in theory, rather simple. The mere discovery of a gene sequence is not patentable, but locating a previously unknown gene, determining its function, and making it accessible for further exploitation brings about the required application of knowledge: the problem of the inaccessibility of the genetic problem has been solved. Patent law only excludes a mere discovery 'as such' as we have seen earlier in this chapter. The fact that the invention involves also biological or genetic material does not, therefore, stand in the way of patentability. On that basis, patents have been granted for DNA sequences, protein molecules, and recombinant DNA molecules that are used as research tools, as well as for purified forms of bacteria, vitamins, and viruses.

Novelty and inventive step

But there remains a need to look at the requirements for patentability, even if one assumes that we are in the presence of an invention. The earlier discussion of the *Genentech* case[214] allowed us to focus on the problems raised in this area in terms of inventive step; here, we would like to touch briefly on the question of novelty. In this respect, the argument that most of what is applied for in biotechnology patent applications already exists in nature is often raised. But, especially if we keep in mind the discussion about the techniques involved and the fact that we are not dealing with mere discoveries, it becomes clear that what is applied for is 'as such' not available to the public—and that is, after all, the key test for novelty. Knowing that something exists in nature is not enough to anticipate the invention: if human beings cannot access the existing material, it is not available to the public. One simply needs to recall the facts in the House of Lord decision in *Asahi*.[215] The fact that the protein was known could not anticipate a patent for the genetically engineered version of the protein—that is, a patent involving how to make the product.

Patents also often claim artificially manufactured versions of the product. Protection is even more widely available, especially if one takes into account Art. 5(2) of the Directive on the protection of biotechnological inventions,[216] in which one finds the confirmation that patents are available for:

> elements that are isolated from the human body or otherwise produced by means of a technical process, including the sequence or partial sequence of a gene, even if the structure of that element is identical to that of a natural element.

The restriction in Art. 5(1) of the Directive, that patents are not available for '*the human body or its parts in their natural state or for the simple discovery of one of its elements*', is,

[214] *Genentech Inc.'s Patent* (n. 117).

[215] *Asahi Kasei Kogyo KK's Application* [1991] RPC 485 (HL); see also *Kirin-Amgen Inc. v. Transkaryotic Therapies Inc.* [2003] RPC 31 (CA), [2005] 1 All ER 667 (HL).

[216] European Parliament and Council Directive 98/44/EC on the legal protection of biotechnological inventions (1998) OJ L 213/13.

in that respect, little more than a restatement of an obvious conclusion that only marginally reduces the scope for patentability in this area.

Overall, therefore, there is plenty of scope for patentability in this area.

The current situation

One of the perceived problems has been that a huge number of patents have been granted in the field of biotechnology, many of which have been for fundamental research tools that are needed for most forms of future research or for small incremental improvements only. The latter type of patent is due to the nature of the research in the area. Further research is therefore necessarily happening in a sea of patents, which is a complicating factor, and licensing strategies and policies are therefore becoming vital,[217] as is the control—by means of competition law, for example—of any abusive practices.

Morality and *ordre public*

The historical first group of exclusions that has now been retained in the new version of s. 1(3) is the UK's response to the requirement under Art. 53(a) of the EPC that no patent should be granted if so to do would be contrary to 'ordre public *or morality*'.[218] There is little jurisprudence on this section, but the key issue would appear to be whether the UK Intellectual Property Office and the courts are prepared to recognize personal views—which are genuinely held, but controversial—as a reason for invoking s. 1(3) of the 1977 Act. A patent that, in some way, made abortion easier would be deeply repugnant to many people, but greatly welcomed by many others; given that, as has been seen, patents are granted for methods of contraception to which significant minority groups in society are opposed, it would seem unlikely that the section would be invoked in such a case.

The legislation refers to matters 'generally' regarded as objectionable and this, it is suggested, appropriately reflects the universal, rather than personal, ideals that make up the notion of *ordre public*. So a patent that is designed to assist in some action that is universally regarded as wrong—such as safe-blowing—would be unlikely to secure patent protection; this is so, it is suggested, notwithstanding s. 1(4), which ordains that the mere fact that an act is contrary to the law does not, of itself, translate that act into one within the ban on patent protection within s. 1(3). Thus a patent for something that enables cars to travel at speeds above the current statutory limits may be patentable if it is felt that the attainment of such speeds is not contrary to the *ordre public*. A harder case that might fall either side of the boundary would be weapons or explosives, the existence of which may benefit a state's military power, but the use of which in the wrong hands may be against the public interest: an undetectable explosive, such as Semtex, is a case in point.

A real-life example of a finely balanced decision would be the objections to the patenting of the genetically engineered 'OncoMouse', which offered potential benefits to cancer victims. These objections were made under Art. 53(a) of the EPC and were ultimately rejected, on the basis that the suffering of the animal, which was intended to develop cancers, nonetheless conferred benefits on humanity and was unavoidable at this stage of our scientific development.

---

[217] See G. van Overwalle (n. 213).

[218] See P. Ford, 'The Morality of Biotech Patents: Differing Legal Obligations in Europe?' (1997) 6 EIPR 315.

Plant and animal varieties

The other exclusion in the old s. 1(3)(b) meant that a patent could not be granted for animal or plant varieties, or for a biological process for the production of animals or plants; microbiological processes were, however, patentable. It is submitted that this is still the case and that the change in wording has no impact on the substantive law—but the reasons for excluding animals and plants are, in many ways, very different.

Plant varieties are appropriately excluded from the realm of patent law, because there is a separate intellectual property regime in their respect. This is now provided in the form of the Plant Varieties Act 1997,[219] which develops the pre-existing law[220] by incorporating into domestic law an implementation of the 1991 revisions of the International Convention for the Protection of New Varieties of Plants (the UPOV Convention), and also fulfils the obligations created by European regulations[221] and the TRIPS Agreement.[222] The basic principles remain, however—namely, that the plant variety must be distinct, uniform, stable,[223] and new[224] in order to secure patent-style protection.[225] Unlike patents, however, the protection extends not only to the plant breeder, but also to anyone who discovers the new variety. It should be noted that entirely new plants appear to fall within the traditional patent sector.[226]

The period of protection varies: for example new types of roses acquire a 15-year term of right,[227] while developments in rhubarb gain a 20-year period[228] and potatoes enjoy a 30-year period of protection.[229]

The ban on patents for animal varieties creates more problems, because there is no separate system for granting intellectual property rights in their respect. The basis for the exclusion of animal varieties seems to be based on moral grounds, the law viewing with disfavour Frankenstein-like experiments on living things. This is now covered by the general provision in s. 1(3). The problem is nevertheless that such a model is quite inappropriate in modern times: the law clearly allows patents to be granted in respect of living matter through its recognition of microbiological processes, and the distinction between a biological, and thus non-patentable, process and one that is patentable as a microbiological process is very fine, and even rather artificial. The circumstances under which a new animal may be created are, in reality, likely to involve highly controlled laboratory conditions with the purpose being an advance in medical science and thus a benefit to society. Whether patents are seen as a reward for the conferring of benefits on society or whether they are seen as a recompense for hard work and energy is immaterial here: both factors separately suggest that the refusal of the law to give patent protection to animals is now anomalous. In any case, the exclusion is limited to animal varieties and does not affect individual animals.

This was once thought to be an entirely academic issue—but it is no longer so. Experimentation has created the famous 'Dolly', a cloned sheep, and a substantial number of mice have also been created in the same way. Meanwhile, Europe has been

---

[219] See also The Plant Breeders' Rights Regulations 1998, SI 1998/1027. The Act came into force on 8 May 1998 (SI 1998/1028).

[220] Plant Varieties and Seeds Act 1964.   [221] Regulation (EC) 2100/94.

[222] See P. Torremans (2001) 'Plant Varieties in the TRIPS Agreement: Time for Reform?' in J. McMahon (ed.) *Trade and Agriculture: Negotiating a New Agreement?*, London: Cameron May, pp. 381–402.

[223] Plant Varieties Act 1997, Sch. 2, Pt 1.   [224] Plant Varieties Act 1997, Sch. 2, Pt 1, paras. 4–7.

[225] Plant Varieties Act 1997, s. 6 expands the scope of protection.

[226] See T. Roberts 'Patenting Plants around the World' (1996) 10 EIPR 531.

[227] Plant Breeders' Rights (Roses) Scheme 1965/725.

[228] Plant Breeders' Rights (Rhubarb) Scheme 1966/644.

[229] Plant Breeders' Rights (Potatoes) (Variation) Scheme 1992/454.

struggling to find an acceptable answer to the problem of legal control of biotechnology, as will be seen.

There are several ways in which rights in new or cloned animals may be considered. The issue might be considered as an issue of *ordre public* or it might be argued that a separate *sui generis* right should be created,[230] by analogy with plants. The law has already had to consider the moral issues involved in the famous OncoMouse litigation. Following the lead from the US, the EPO has granted a patent for the so-called OncoMouse, which is a live mouse genetically adapted to develop cancers as part of a new approach to the treatment of cancer and which, as such, clearly is deserving of some form of legal protection. But such a conclusion can only be reached via a very narrow interpretation of Art. 53 of the EPC, which is the counterpart to the UK's Patent Act 1977, s. 1(3). The decision distinguishes new animal varieties, which are not patentable, from new animals which, as a result of their not being expressly mentioned in the relevant Article, can be granted patent protection. The OncoMouse was merely a variation on a pre-existing species and could be the subject matter of a patent.

This is an area that now calls for reform to allow the patentability of animals without recourse to artificially and atypically narrow interpretations of the law, and the EPO is in the process of reviewing its policy in this regard. After all, the more general ban on the patenting of that which is generally offensive remains and would be appropriate to control undesirable animal experimentation; whether it is more appropriate to allow patent protection for the creation of new animals or whether it is better to create a new animal variety right by analogy with the law relating to plant patents is debatable. Certainly, an independent right would need an *ordre public* provision to protect society from undesirable or dangerous attempts at genetic manipulation, but it now looks increasingly unlikely that a *sui generis* approach will be developed. Patent law seems bound to become the general tool in this area. Thus moves are being taken, but—inevitably in this legal, moral, and scientific minefield—they are being taken slowly and cautiously.

The Biotechnology Directive

Years of discussion have finally led to advance on the European front in the form of a directive on the legal protection of biotechnological inventions.[231] On the one hand, this provides for the protection of such biotechnological inventions through the patent law of member states,[232] but does not extend to plant or animal varieties, or to essentially biological processes for their creation. On the other:

> Biological material which is isolated from its natural environment or produced by means of a technical process may be the subject of an invention even if it previously occurred in nature.[233]

The scope of protection is rather wide, as Art. 9 states:

> The protection conferred by a patent on a product containing or consisting of genetic information shall extend to all material ... in which the product is incorporated and in which the genetic information is contained and performs its function.

But in a case concerning patented genetic material originating in soy plants found in soy meal deriving from the plants, the Court of Justice held that Art. 9 was not conferring

---

[230] See N. Peace and A. Christie, 'Intellectual Property Protection for the Products of Animal Breeding' (1996) 4 EIPR 213.

[231] European Parliament and Council Directive 98/44/EC on the legal protection of biotechnological inventions (1998) OJ L 213/13.

[232] Biotechnology Directive, Arts. 1 and 3(1).   [233] Biotechnology Directive, Art. 3(2).

patent right protection in circumstances such as those of the case in the main proceedings, in which the patented product is contained in the soy meal, where it does not perform the function for which it was patented, but did perform that function previously in the soy plant, of which the meal is a processed product, or would possibly again be able to perform that function after it had been extracted from the soy meal and inserted into the cell of a living organism.[234]

There is also a specific exclusion within a general *ordre public* exception that prevents the registration of processes for human cloning and related activities, including the use of human embryos for industrial or commercial purposes.[235] The human body, unlike genes isolated from it, cannot constitute a patentable invention;[236] likewise excluded is the genetic modification of animals that causes suffering and which is not conferring any substantial medical benefit.[237] Thus the OncoMouse would still be patentable, but more experimental variation would not be. There are also further detailed provisions on the scope of protection to be awarded to biotechnological inventions and provisions concerning the deposit of biotechnological material.[238]

It is clear that the European art of compromise was instrumental in securing the safe passage of the Directive, but the consequence of this is that it fails to address the most pressing concerns in this controversial area: science presses ahead, while the law lags behind. The creation of new animals and the cloning of pre-existing animals—including, in theory, humans—is taking place and the law must, therefore, have a response. The Directive is not the full answer to the problems that remain in this ethical minefield; it merely confirms that biotechnological inventions are patentable. The positive side of it is that it clarifies the law on this point, but, on the negative side, one can only conclude that the Directive did not really cover a lot of new ground. The UK has implemented the Directive by means of the Patents Regulations 2000,[239] as a result of which a series of minor changes were made to the Patents Act 1977.[240]

Recently, a debate has been sparked by inventions that involve (potentially) human embryonic stem cells: are they patentable under the terms of the Directive or do they fall foul of the morality clause? Could it be that they are necessarily caught by Art. 6 of the Directive—that is, the specific exclusion relating to the registration of processes for human cloning and related activities? National patent offices have expressed different views and, in society, there is a clear split of opinion—but some questions can no longer be avoided. What is meant by 'morality' under Art. 53 of the EPC? There is no indication as to how a common concept of morality is to be identified or created. Are we to refer back to the national situation in each member state in the absence of a common approach? What exactly is the link between Arts. 5 and 6 of the Biotech Directive? Article 5 talks in broad terms about the human body and what is patentable; Art. 6 then talks about morality and gives examples of what is not patentable: is Art. 5 the principle and Art. 6 the exception? Or does Art. 6 reduce the scope of Art. 5? And how broadly or narrowly do we need to define the unpatentable examples in Art. 6 of the Directive:

(a) processes for cloning human beings;
(b) processes for modifying the germ line genetic identity of human beings;

---

[234] Case C-428/08, *Monsanto Technology LLC v. Cefetra BV, Cefetra Feed Service BV, Cefetra Futures BV, Alfred C. Toepfer International GmbH* [2011] All ER (EC) 209, [2012] 3 CMLR 7, [2011] FSR 6.

[235] Biotechnology Directive, Art. 6.   [236] Biotechnology Directive, Art. 5.

[237] Biotechnology Directive, Art. 6.

[238] Biotechnology Directive, Arts. 8–12 and 13–14, respectively.   [239] SI 2000/2037.

[240] See also Patents (Amendment) Rules 2001, SI 2001/1412.

(c) uses of human embryos for industrial or commercial purposes;

(d) processes for modifying the genetic identity of animals which are likely to cause them suffering without any substantial medical benefit to man or animal, and also animals resulting from such processes.

These are fundamental questions and a careful answer is needed. The EPO considered these in the reference to the Enlarged Board of Appeal in the *WARF/Stem Cells* case.[241] It came to the conclusion that any patent at the roots of which is an embryonic stem cell extracted from a human embryo offended against the EPO rules and was therefore not patentable. The decision was narrowly worded though and its motivation was rather narrow. The German courts referred the issue to the Court of Justice under the parallel provisions in the Directive. The Court adopted a similar approach and decided that Art. 6(2)(c) of the Directive must be interpreted as meaning that:

any human ovum after fertilisation, any non-fertilised human ovum into which the cell nucleus from a mature human cell has been transplanted, and any non-fertilised human ovum whose division and further development have been stimulated by parthenogenesis constitute a 'human embryo'[242]

and that on that basis that Article:

excludes an invention from patentability where the technical teaching which is the subject-matter of the patent application requires the prior destruction of human embryos or their use as base material, whatever the stage at which that takes place and even if the description of the technical teaching claimed does not refer to the use of human embryos.[243]

The High Court took the view that the CJEU had misunderstood the parthenogenesis technique in the sense that current scientific knowledge tells us that an ovum whose division has been stimulated by parthenogenesis does not have the capacity to develop into a human being and asked the CJEU to reconsider that part of its judgment in *Brüstle*. The CJEU then excluded the ovum whose division has been stimulated by parthenogenesis from the scope of the definition of a human embryo for the purposes of Art. 6(2)(c) of the Directive.[244]

An overview

It is appropriate to step back at this juncture and assess the way in which the law has approached the overall question of patentability. The obstacles placed in the way of an applicant are quite considerable, particularly when viewed in the light of the result achieved: a monopoly right only over the matters directly claimed for a de jure 20-year

---

[241] For the referral, see Case T-1374/04, *WARF/Stem Cells* [2006] EPOR 31. The decision is reported at [2009] EPOR 15 (Case G2/06, *WARF/Stem Cells*). An academic study has already examined this area: A. Plomer et al. (2006) *Stem Cell Patents: European Patent Law and Ethics Report*, Report for the European Commission, <http://www.nottingham.ac.uk/law/StemCellProject/project.report.pdf>; and A. Plomer and P. Torremans (eds.) (2009) *Embryonic Stem Cell Patents: European Law and Ethics*, Oxford: Oxford University Press. See also S. Crespi, 'The Human Embryo and Patent Law: A Major Challenge Ahead?' (2006) 28(11) EIPR, and A. Warren-Jones, 'Identifying European Moral Consensus: Why Are the Patent Courts Reticent to Accept Empirical Evidence in Resolving Biotechnological Cases?' (2006) 28(1) EIPR 26–37.

[242] Case C-34/10, *Oliver Brüstle v. Greenpeace eV* [2012] All ER (EC) 809, [2012] 1 CMLR 41.

[243] *Oliver Brüstle* (n. 242).

[244] Case C-364/13, *International Stem Cell Corporation v. Comptroller General of Patents, Designs and Trade Marks* [2015] 2 CMLR 26, [2015] All ER (EC) 362; [2015] CEC 895, [2015] RPC 19.

period that will, in actual fact, only allow commercial exploitation for a lesser period, while all the time rivals are free to experiment on producing a better product at any time, or a rival imitation as soon as the 20 years are over.

There are essentially three requirements for patentability. Novelty requires the invention to be new—that is, that the prior art must not anticipate the invention. Anticipation requires there to be an enabling disclosure, which means that the requirements of both disclosure and enablement must be satisfied. The 'new' invention must also involve an inventive step: 'inventiveness' is defined as non-obviousness by the Act. Finally the invention must be capable of industrial application.

In order to win this somewhat less-than-glittering prize, novelty is a reasonable requirement for the applicant to have to satisfy, but this cannot always be said in relation to inventive steps, in relation to which the convolutions of the judges in the Court of Appeal in the *Genentech* saga stand as a pointer to the fact that it may not, in all cases, be sensible to define an inventive step as one that it is not obvious to take. More generally, the case indicates the difficulties that will inevitably attend any tribunal that seeks to locate itself as a notional, highly knowledgeable, but profoundly uninventive, reasonable man and then attempts to make the qualitative judgement of whether an inventive step made was, at that time, obvious or not. It is a question asked by the ill-equipped, which is close to unanswerable.

Reviewing what a court will regard as non-patentable matter also shows that this area is not without its problems. Section 1(2) of the Patents Act 1977 excludes much that may be the subject of prolonged research work, although careful drafting and the generosity of the courts in allowing inventive non-patentable matter to provide the element of inventiveness in a broader patent both go some way to limiting the difficulty for patentees. The law also seems reluctant to invoke s. 1(3) to stop patents being granted even in cases in which, as in the case of the OncoMouse, to do so would, on the face of it, be contrary to the words of the legislation.

If a patent is a reward, it is one that is not readily gained. The need for the applicant to satisfy the various requirements, coupled with the years that the process will take, suggest that the law regards the grant of a monopoly as a matter of the utmost seriousness and gravity. Whether the consequences of being granted a patent are so wondrous as to justify the application of so much seriousness and gravity is more questionable, especially when evidence indicates that many patents are granted for inventions that do not lead to commercially successful exploitation and when the 'cutting edge' of biotechnology is not well protected by the patent system. It may be that a lifetime obligation of confidentiality *inter partes* may increasingly be seen to be a better answer in a number of cases.

Further reading

BRENNAN, D., '*Biogen* Sufficiency Reconsidered' (2009) 4 IPQ 476.

COOK, W. and LEES, G., 'Test Clarified for UK Software and Business Method Patents: But What about the EPO?' (2007) 29(3) EIPR 115–88.

CRESPI, S., 'The Human Embryo and Patent Law: A Major Challenge Ahead?' (2006) 28(11) EIPR 569–75.

FREELAND, R., 'Disclosure and Enablement: The House of Lords Clarifies the Law on Novelty' (2006) 1(3) JIPLP 163–5.

GRANT, G. and GIBBINS, D., '"Inventive Concept": Is It a Good Idea?' (2007) 27(5) EIPR 170–5.

PLOMER, A. and TORREMANS, P. (eds.) (2009) *Embryonic Stem Cell Patents: European Law and Ethics*, Oxford: OUP.

PLOMER, A et al. (2006) *Stem Cell Patents: European Patent Law and Ethics Report*, Report for the European Commission, <http://www.nottingham.ac.uk/law/StemCellProject/project.report.pdf>.

SHARPLES, A., 'Industrial Applicability, Patents and the Supreme Court: Human Genome Sciences *Inc v Eli Lilly and Co*' (2012) 34(4) EIPR 284–6.

SHARPLES, A. and CURLEY, D., 'Experimental Novelty: *Synthon v. Smithkline Beecham*' (2006) 28(5) EIPR 308–11.

SIMS, A., 'The Case against Patenting Methods of Medical Treatment' (2007) 29(2) EIPR 43–51.

VENTOSE, E., 'Patenting Surgical Methods in Europe after MEDI-PHYSICS' (2011) 6 JIPLP 108–19.

WARREN-JONES, A., 'Identifying European Moral Consensus: Why Are the Patent Courts Reticent to Accept Empirical Evidence in Resolving Biotechnological Cases?' (2006) 28(1) EIPR 26–37.

5

Use and grant in the UK and Europe

A patentable invention aims to be put into practice. But once we have determined that the invention is patentable the question arises who is entitled to the patent and who will own it. These questions play an important role in the exploitation of the patent and we will therefore address them first, before turning to the commercial exploitation of the patent.

Whose patent is it anyway?[1]

Entitlement

We have so far referred generally to applicants for patents without examining who is, in fact, entitled to be granted a patent. Section 7 of the 1977 Act is the starting point for this enquiry. Under s. 7(1), any person may make an application either alone or jointly; under s. 13(2), however, the applicant must include in the application a statement of who the inventor is, in case the inventor him- or herself is not applying, and, if others are involved, an indication of what right the applicant has to be granted the patent, so that there is no danger of a patent being granted to a usurper.

This is borne out by s. 7(2) of the 1977 Act, which states that a patent may be granted:

(a) primarily to the inventor or joint inventors;
(b) in preference to the foregoing, to any person or persons who, by virtue of any enactment or rule of law, or any foreign law or treaty or international convention, or by virtue of an enforceable term of any agreement entered into with the inventor before the making of the invention, was or were at the time of the making of the invention entitled to the whole of the property in it (other than equitable interests) in the United Kingdom;[2]
(c) in any event, to the successor or successors in title of any person or persons mentioned in paragraph (a) or (b) above or any person so mentioned and the successor or successors in title of another person so mentioned; and to no other person.

The words 'primarily' and 'in preference' simply indicate that the inventor is, first and foremost, the normal patentee, but will sometimes have lost that right: for example, to

---

[1] With apologies to television star and patent expert Clive Anderson, as in The Patent Office's Laser Disc Patent Training Package (Patent Office, 1992). It was held, in *IDA Ltd v. University of Southampton* [2005] RPC 11, that the inventor is the person who came up with the inventive concept and that other contributions do not count.

[2] Section 7(2)(b) Patents Act 1977 makes it possible not just to assign the beneficial interest in the invention before it was made, but also the legal title to the invention: *KCI Licensing Inc. v. Smith & Nephew plc* [2010] EWHC 1487 (Pat), [2010] FSR 31; not overturned on appeal on this point by *KCI Licensing Inc. v. Smith & Nephew plc* [2010] EWCA Civ 1260, [2011] FSR 8.

an employer under a contract of employment, as will be seen later in the chapter. Under s. 7(3), an inventor is simply defined as '*the actual deviser of the invention*'.

The House of Lords dealt with the issue of entitlement and clarified s. 7 in *Yeda v. Rhone-Poulenc*.[3] It was held that s. 7(2) and the definition in s. 7(3) form an exhaustive code for determining who is entitled to the grant of a patent. Primarily, we are talking about the inventor, but legal or treaty provisions, as well as agreements, can also give someone else that entitlement. A successor in title can also be entitled to a patent. There is no need to cross-refer to other provisions in the Act, or to prove entitlement by virtue of a contract or a breach of confidence, as the Court of Appeal had held in *Markem*.[4] Section 7(3) then adds a definition of the inventor and s. 7(4) deals with the burden of proof of the person who wants to be added as joint inventor. That person needs to prove that he or she contributed to the inventive concept, bringing him or her within the scope of the definition in s. 7(3).

Another key decision in this area dealing with the key point of that definition was the appeal in *University of Southampton's Applications*,[5] which the court allowed. The judgment clearly establishes that, in entitlement proceedings, the court had to identify who, in substance, had made the invention—that is, who had been responsible for the inventive concept—and who had contributed what (in terms of input or information and rights, if any, in such information). The court had to look for the 'heart' of the invention. The House of Lords confirmed this in *Yeda v. Rhone-Poulenc*, in which it was held that s. 7(3) defined the inventor as the '*actual deviser of the invention*' and that the word 'actual' needed to be contrasted with the deemed, or pretended, deviser of the invention: hence the emphasis on the person that came up with the inventive concept. A mere contribution to the claims is not sufficient, because these may include non-patentable integers derived from prior art.[6] This point had also been made in *Markem*.[7]

The case at issue in *University of Southampton* dealt with insect traps, and there was an exact parallel between the application at issue and a patent filed in 1994. In the 1994 patent the exposure of the insect was '*to particles carrying an electrostatic charge*', while in the patent in suit the exposure was '*to a composition comprising particles containing or consisting of at least one magnetic material*'. The change from electrostatic particles to magnetic particles was the only new and inventive element; it was the sole key to the information in the patent in suit, and that key had been provided solely by the appellant and not by the University or its staff. The appellant did not know whether the idea would work and the University's staff did all of the testing work—but the latter was, in essence, only a matter of simple and routine experimentation, and was mere verification. All that the University staff added was the common general knowledge of those in the art. The appellant therefore provided the 'heart' of the invention and was entitled to the patent.

In cases in which a patent is awarded jointly to more than one inventor, it is important to establish the respective entitlements of the holders. Section 36 of the 1977 Act does this by establishing that each joint patentee is entitled to an equal undivided share of the patent, although this may be varied by agreement between the joint patentees. The obvious analogy is with the position of tenants in common of real property. Joint patentees have the right to do anything with the invention without having to consult their

---

[3] *Yeda Research & Development Co. Ltd v. Rhone-Poulenc Rorer International Holdings Inc. and ors* [2008] RPC 1, [2008] 1 All ER 425 (HL).

[4] *Markem Corp. v. Zipher Ltd* [2005] RPC 31 (CA), overruled in *Yeda Research* (n. 3), despite the fact that the House of Lords agreed that the case had been correctly decided, but because the House disapproved of some of its reasoning.

[5] [2006] RPC 21. [6] *Yeda Research* (n. 3). [7] *Markem Corp. v. Zipher Ltd* (n. 4).

fellow patentees, with some exceptions: most significantly, that the consent of the others is required to any licensing or assignment of the patent.[8] Thus one joint patentee could exploit the invention on his or her own and pocket the proceeds without any obligation to account in any way to his or her fellow patentees in the absence of any agreement to the contrary.

Disposal of the patent can give rise to problems, especially if the need for disposal arises from a dispute between the joint patentees—if, for example, one is opposed to, and thus blocks, a proposed licensing arrangement. In *Florey's Patent,*[9] the Patent Office was faced with a dispute between a group of medical researchers who had jointly secured a patent for a new form of penicillin. All but one then wished to assign the patent to the National Research Development Council for further development and ultimate exploitation; the objector, while not opposing the assignment as such, held out for a half-share of the proceeds to which he felt entitled. Under what is now the power granted to the Patent Office to determine disputes between joint patentees under s. 37(1)(b) of the 1977 Act, the Office ordered that the assignment proceed with an equal distribution of the proceeds being made as is the normal route when, as in this case, no contrary agreement could be proven. The Court of Appeal has also held that s. 37 and the power contained therein for the Comptroller to determine the transfer of rights in the patent does include the power for the Comptroller to order the grant of a licence against the will of one of the owners of the patent in a case in which exploitation of the patent has effectively been blocked.[10]

Section 37(5) of the Patents Act 1977 allows orders to be made in relation to entitlement. *Rhone-Poulenc Rorer International Holdings Inc. v. Yeda Research & Development Co. Ltd*[11] is an interesting case in this respect. The grant of the patent in suit was mentioned in the European Patent Bulletin on 27 March 2002 and, on 26 March 2004, the respondent filed a reference under s. 37 claiming joint entitlement to the patent. On 29 June 2005, the respondent filed an amended statement of case, in which it claimed sole ownership of the patent. If the latter statement were a new claim, the limitation period contained in s. 37(5) would potentially apply and, in this case, only the first claim would have been made validly. The clear intention of the legislator was to avoid entitlement claims being made a long period into the life of the patent. At such a late stage, third parties—such as licensees—may already have acquired rights and a change in ownership could then complicate things unduly. Alternatively, one could hold that, as long as a claim was brought within the two-year period, s. 37 allowed the Comptroller to decide who was entitled to the patent, irrespective almost of the exact content of the claim.

Lewison J emphatically rejected the latter interpretation, as did the Court of Appeal, but the House of Lords overturned their decisions. It was held that the claim needs to be made within the two-year period by submitting the form stipulated in the Patent Rules.[12] Once that has been done, it is up to the Comptroller to make a decision. In the course of that process, the requesting party is free to file evidence and amended statements. The limitation period only applies to bringing the case in front of the Comptroller in the first place.[13]

Employee inventions

The main area in which disputes arise over entitlement to the grant of a patent is between employers and employees. Many inventions will be made by employees, such as

---

[8] Patents Act 1977, s. 36(2) and (3).   [9] [1962] RPC 186.
[10] *Derek Hughes v. Neil Paxman* [2007] RPC 2.   [11] [2006] RPC 24.
[12] The Patents Rules 1995, SI 1995/2093.   [13] *Yeda Research* (n. 3).

university professors or research and development (R&D) staff in private industry; in making their inventions, these people will, in all probability, be using the facilities and resources of their employer, and this has led the law to declare—in s. 39 of the 1977 Act—that, in many instances, the employer, rather than the employee, will be the person entitled to the grant of a patent. Although the current appearance of the law dates from the 1977 Act, there were earlier common law rules covering the same ground and decisions from those cases are said to offer guidance in the interpretation of the statutory rules.[14] Unusually, this is purely domestic law; there is no equivalent provision in the European Patent Convention (EPC).

There are two categories of situations in which the Act envisages that a grant to the employer is appropriate. First, s. 39(1)(a) of the Act provides that the employer gains the patent if the employee is in the course of his or her duties and if the circumstances are such that an invention might reasonably be expected to result. Put simply, if an employee is paid to research, he or she gains a reward in the form of his or her salary cheque and the employer gains the patent as a reward for its foresight in hiring the researcher in the first place.

The second situation in which the employer is entitled to the patent is that in which the invention is made in the course of duties by an employee who has a *special obligation to further the interests of the employer's undertaking*[15] by virtue of his or her duties and responsibilities. So, for example, the head of a company's R&D division would fit within this category; indeed, such a person may fall into both situations. The test in s. 39 is an objective one, but it has to be applied to the circumstances of the particular case and this includes the specific job that the employee was asked to do and the fact that it was this specific employee carrying them out. The question was therefore held to be whether *'an invention might reasonably be expected to result from the carrying out of his* [the appellant's] *duties'*.[16]

The first situation is well illustrated by the pre-1977 Act case of *Electrolux Ltd v. Hudson*.[17] The defendant was employed as a storeman by the plaintiffs, who were manufacturers of electrical goods. In the evenings, at home, the defendant and his wife amused themselves by considering possible inventions and, one night, devised a new kind of adaptor to facilitate more easily the connection of the dust bag to a vacuum cleaner. The plaintiffs claimed that they were entitled to this invention by reference to a very broad term in their contract of employment, which appeared to permit the employer to reap the benefits of all inventive activity. In striking down this clause as being too broad and thus in restraint of trade, Whitford J pointed out that Hudson earned a low salary (£1,302 per annum in 1971) and commented: *'It is not the sort of salary that is paid to a research worker. He was not employed to do research or to make inventions.'*[18] It would seem sensible, in the light of this, for employers in an appropriate case to stipulate that research and invention is part of the duties of a particular employee.

More problems have arisen in deciding just who comes into the other category of employees with a special obligation to the company. Clearly, directors and other senior managers who owe a fiduciary duty to the company must come within this category,[19] but precisely where the line is to be drawn is not an easy question. The courts have provided some guidance in *Harris' Patent*.[20] Harris was an employee of a company selling valves under licence from a Swiss firm. He was the manager of the sales department,

[14] *Harris' Patent* [1985] RPC 19, per Falconer J at 28.   [15] Patents Act 1977, s. 39(1)(b).
[16] *LIFFE Administration & Management v. Pavel Pinkava* [2007] RPC 30 (CA).
[17] [1977] FSR 312.   [18] [1977] FSR 312 at 323.
[19] *Worthington Pumping Engine Co. v. Moore* (1903) 20 RPC 41.   [20] [1985] RPC 19.

which involved advising potential customers and also providing after-sales service. After learning that he was to be made redundant in five months' time, Harris designed a new valve, which was an improvement on the valves sold by his firm, and sought the grant of a patent for it. His employer claimed ownership of the patent, but was unsuccessful in this argument. Falconer J found that Harris' normal duties did not include invention, but were concerned with sales and after-sales service, thus putting the case outside s. 39(1)(a). He had to be highly knowledgeable about valves and their use, but that is not the same as saying that he was under a duty to invent. An alternative argument based on his position within the company also failed: his title as a manager was not enough in itself, and examination of his powers and status in the firm—and especially the lack of discretion that he could exercise—showed that he did not owe a special obligation to the firm, and thus could retain the patent for his own benefit. This leaves open the question of where, above Harris' position as manager and below board level, the line will be drawn; the presence of a broad duty to the company over and above the day-to-day performance of the duties assigned to an employee seems necessary as an implication of *Harris*.

Harris was also referred to in the more recent case of *Staeng Ltd's Patents*,[21] in which an employee, whose primary role was in the field of marketing, was nevertheless expected to generate new ideas for new products as part of his job. This is sensible: marketing and product development are very closely related concepts and it is clear that a senior marketing executive will be expected to participate in product development activity. The senior status of the employee was also seen as relevant: as a senior executive, it was held that he had an obligation towards his employer's business and its development within the terms of s. 39(1)(b) of the Patents Act 1977.

The relationship between ordinary work and innovation remains less clear. In *Greater Glasgow Health Board's Application*,[22] a doctor employed by the Health Board had created a new type of ophthalmoscope on his own initiative and in his own time. The view was taken that the doctor's duty was to treat patients and, although the device in question would improve treatment and diagnosis, it was not part of his duties as an employee to invent such a device.

Compensation

If this appears to be harsh on employees whose vital inventions are promptly taken over by their employers, some relief is at hand in the form of the provisions that were new to the law in 1977, and which can be found in ss. 40 and 41 of the Patents Act. These entitle an employee to apply for an award of compensation by the employer if:

> having regard among other things to the size and nature of the employer's undertaking, the invention or the patent for it (or the combination of both) is of outstanding benefit[23] to the employer ... [24]

A similar provision applies in cases in which the employee has formally assigned the invention or the patent for it (or both)[25] to the employer for an inadequate sum,[26] although these rights do not exist if a collective agreement provides for the payment of compensation to employees,[27] as is quite common.

---

[21] [1996] RPC 183.   [22] [1996] RPC 207.
[23] A new s. 43(5A) has been added by s. 10(7) of the Patents Act 2004, which limits the benefit by excluding any benefit derived from the invention after the patent has expired, been surrendered, or been revoked.
[24] Patents Act 1977, s. 40(1)(b).   [25] Patents Act 2004, s. 10(2).
[26] Patents Act 1977, s. 40(2).   [27] Patents Act 1977, s. 40(3).

Under s. 41, the compensation payable by the employer should represent a fair share of the benefit to the employer of the invention, the patent, or an assignment thereof.[28] The fairness of the share will depend on various factors established by s. 41(4) as including the nature of the employee's duties, pay, the effort and skill used, and the contribution of the employer and of other employees to the invention. It should also be noted that no contract term may diminish these rights[29] and that, for obvious reasons, they only apply to employees mainly employed in the UK.[30]

Before employees emboldened by these provisions rush out to buy a new Daimler or two, however, it is clear that this legislation is not designed to produce a bonanza of payments. Outstanding benefits to the employer are one of many obstacles placed in the way of an applicant and case law confirms that it will be an uphill struggle to take advantage of these provisions. Until recently the reported cases on this area have resulted in failure by the claimant. In *GEC Avionics Ltd's Patent*,[31] the inventor of a new method of displaying information to the pilots of aircraft made a claim. This invention resulted in sales valued at US$72m, as well as other related contracts and the chance of further future sales. This was not regarded as outstanding in the context of the real profit being around US$10m and of that profit being part of the turnover of a major international firm regularly making multimillion-dollar deals. This also shows up the problem of assessing fair compensation: what is fair to the inventor, in relation to his or her salary, and to the employer, in relation to its (perhaps vast) turnover, will always be very different.

In *British Steel plc's Patent*,[32] the decision against the inventor is perhaps more understandable. The claim was made by the inventor of a new type of valve that would be of great value in controlling the flow of molten steel. The benefit was regarded as marginal: partly because the valve was only used in one steelworks; partly because the company had to spend much time and money perfecting the invention into a working product; partly because the size of British Steel meant that the proven benefits of the invention represented only 0.01 per cent of turnover and 0.08 per cent of profits. It was emphasized that the word 'outstanding' is a superlative and hard to prove, especially in the case of an application for payment that was made only seven months after the grant of the patent.

Both of these decisions were Patent Office hearings; a similar tale is told by the first case to reach the courts: *Memco-Med Ltd's Patent*.[33] The patent in this case was for a new door detector unit for passenger lifts and the applicant was a director of the company at the time of the invention. Aldous J found that the employee had the onus of proof in making the application; in this case, it was unclear even that there was a benefit created by the patent, because sales of the patented product were all to the Otis Co., with whom Memco-Med had a long-standing record of sales. Although the patented product was, in some years, responsible for 80 per cent of the sales of the company, there was no proof of the profitability of those sales and thus it was impossible to say that it was an outstanding benefit.

In themselves, these decisions are not too surprising. The claim in *Memco-Med* really came to grief for evidential reasons; in *British Steel*, the benefits of the invention appeared limited, and, in any event, the applicant had received an *ex gratia* payment at the time and had also been appointed a Member of the British Empire (MBE). But *GEC* is a reminder that almost anyone working in a large firm, in which it is reasonable to assume that the bulk of R&D work goes on, is going to find it next to impossible to make

---

[28] As amended by Patents Act 2004, s. 10(3).   [29] Patents Act 1977, s. 42.
[30] Patents Act 1977, s. 43.   [31] [1992] RPC 107.   [32] [1992] RPC 107 at 117.
[33] [1992] RPC 403.

a successful claim under s. 40. This suggests, therefore, that the section was the product of the politics of gesture, rather than of substance.

Case law shows, however, that in a limited number of cases the compensation provisions will be applied by the courts. Although the amounts awarded were small and definitively much smaller than what had been claimed, compensation was awarded in *Kelly v. GE Healthcare*.[34] The court made it clear that only the actual devisor of the invention can claim under s. 40 and that the 'outstanding benefit' requirement remains a formidable hurdle. 'Outstanding' was held to mean something special or out of the ordinary. It means more than substantial, significant, or good. In turn the 'benefit' had to go well beyond what could normally be expected as a result of the employee's work and could be ascertained by comparing the employer's position with the benefit of the patent to that where the patent would not have been granted.[35] It is also clear that one has to show that the patent caused the benefit. Once these hurdles have been overcome, as was the case here, the amount of the compensation was to be determined on the basis of the evidence, so as to secure a fair and just reward. Such a reward is not limited to compensation for loss or damage, but it does not go as far as what would have been earned by the employee as an external patentee or licensor. The calculation of the benefit may also become difficult if the patent is assigned to a company that is connected to the employer, as normal market conditions will not apply. The Court of Appeal rejected the idea that the benefit should be looked at in a situation where the connected company was replaced by a fully independent hypothetical third party. The court instead insisted that one should look at the actual assignee with its actual attributes.[36] This of course puts a significant limitation on the outcome of the calculation under s. 41(2).

Grant and dealing

Let us assume that the requirements of patentability have been met and an appropriate patentee is in place. The Comptroller of Patents waves a magic wand and a patent comes into existence for a period of 20 years, normally from the date of filing the application.[37] The principal implication of this is that the patent—as well the related application—is deemed to be an item of personal property[38] and, subject to what follows, can be dealt with by its owner just like any other item of personal property.

In at least one respect, it is a somewhat odd example of personal property, because it may change its form: there is a process for the amendment of the specification even after grant[39] and this may be a useful way of pre-empting an attack on the validity of the patent. The owner of the patent may wish to deal with the valuable commodity that is his or her patent in various ways. He or she may wish to assign it to another—perhaps to someone better able than him- or herself to exploit it commercially—and this is allowed by the 1977 Act, as long as the assignment is in writing and is signed by the parties to the transaction.[40] The drafting of such an assignment contract is of vital importance, especially when it comes to determining the ownership of future improvements to the

---

[34] *Kelly v. GE Healthcare* [2009] RPC 12.

[35] See also *Ian Alexander Shanks v. Unilever plc, Unilever NV, Unilever UK Central Resources Limited* [2014] EWHC 1647 (Pat); an appeal was outstanding at the time of writing.

[36] *Shanks v. Unilever* [2010] EWCA Civ 1283, [2011] RPC 12, overruling *Shanks v. Unilever* [2009] EWHC 3164 (Ch).

[37] Patents Act 1977, s. 25(1).   [38] Patents Act 1977, s. 30(1).   [39] Patents Act 1977, s. 27.

[40] Patents Act 1977, s. 30(3) and (6). Arguably, the latter sets out the conditions that the assignment needs to meet in an exhaustive way and consideration is then not required. This position gained support in *Wright Hassall LLP v. George Shortland Horton Jr and Jane Cowles Horton* [2015] EWHC 3716 (QB).

invention and any rights in them.[41] Similarly, the owner of the patent may wish to use it as part of a mortgage transaction, perhaps to raise funds with which to develop the patent into a commercial success in his or her own right; this is permitted subject to the same conditions.[42]

All such transactions can, and should, be registered with the UK Intellectual Property Office, because registered transactions in relation to patents take priority over those that have not been registered.[43]

Licensing in UK law

The most likely form of dealing by the patentee is that he or she will seek to license out the patent by a formal agreement that allows another party to work the patent without fear of an infringement action. The virtue of this method of exploiting a patent is the flexibility that it allows: the patentee may not wish, or be able, to develop his or her invention into a perfected commercial product, for example, but by licensing it out to someone else, this can happen without the patentee losing control as would be the case in an assignment of the patent. The patent licensing agreement determines the precise extent of control retained. These agreements are documents that merit careful drafting, and are often extremely long and complex.

Another common reason for licensing is that it is easier, when developing the market for a product in another jurisdiction, to use a local firm—with its plant, distribution network, customers, and contacts—rather than to seek to create the entire necessary infrastructure to one's own account. Licensing of the product or process to a local firm is a sensible way of proceeding.

Another possible reason for using a licence is as part of a collaboration between two firms working in the same field, who may cross-license each other's patents.

The alert reader may already have picked up on some of the major potential problems with licensing: cross-licensing between collaborators immediately evokes a picture of monopoly, while the creation of subsidiaries of other licensees in other jurisdictions reveals that this is an issue that may have international implications. Add to this the fact that many licences are exclusive licences—in other words, A only licenses B to work the patent in a given area—and it becomes clear that the creation of exclusive monopolies in an international setting is bound to attract the wrath of the European Union (EU), which is devoted to the pursuit of free trade and free competition throughout its member states.

It is this aspect that will form the major part of this section, but we will proceed by first looking at some of the different types of licence that exist.

Licences as of right

Section 46 of the Patents Act 1977 provides that the patentee may apply to the UK Intellectual Property Office to enter into the register of patents a statement that licences for a patent are available 'as of right'. But why should a patentee declare 'open house', and allow anyone to come in and work the patent? A typical reason would be if the patentee him- or herself is unable to work up the invention into a viable product or process in the commercial marketplace, but is keen nonetheless that the patent should be exploited. Of course, the real likelihood of this occurring if the patent is truly of value is low, because,

---

[41] *Buchanan v. Alba Diagnostics Ltd* [2004] RPC 681 (HL).
[42] For an example, see *Buchanan* (n. 41)   [43] Patents Act 1977, s. 33.

in such a case, an assignment or licensing agreement would already be likely to have been made. Thus those licences that are as of right are rarely of the highest value.

A minor incentive to use the process is that patent renewal fees are halved if a licence as of right exists. The only other incentive is that the licensee has to agree terms—or have them imposed by the Comptroller in the event of a failure to agree—and this will give the patentee an opportunity to secure an appropriate fee or royalty for the licence; this will, in reality, only reflect the dubious value of a patent that is subject to this procedure.

Compulsory licences

Whereas the patentee initiates the demand for the licence as of right, it is the UK Intellectual Property Office itself that imposes the availability of compulsory licences. This seems totally contrary to the picture of the patentee's ownership of a piece of personal property: it is up to the owner to decide whether to use a bicycle or not—surely the same should apply to a patent? That this is not the case in relation to a patent relates to the interests of society, which, in this part of the law, are deemed to take priority over those of the patentee in certain limited circumstances.

Some examples of potential problems that can be resolved by compulsory licensing will be helpful before looking at the detailed legislation. If a monopoly represents power, and all power can be abused, while a company that has produced a new drug of great value is entitled to due reward, it might also seek artificially to push up the price by closely limiting the amount of the drug that is put on the market. Alternatively, the inadequacies of the patentee may mean that, having revealed the existence of a new process through the application process, he or she is unable to develop it properly him- or herself and hence frustrates those of greater ability and/or resources. A new product might even be withheld from the market to protect pre-existing trade: the existence of, for example, a reusable condom or a light bulb of infinite duration might be concealed from the public by an established manufacturer who, having invented it, realizes that it will drastically restrict trade. (Of course, a sensible manufacturer would recognize the problem at an early stage and would not apply for the patent.) The legislation thus has to balance the interests of society and inventor.

Overall, a cautious approach is taken. After three years of a patent's life, application can be made for an individual licence, or a licence as of right, on various grounds.[44] At first, the 1977 Act stated that, if the patent is capable of being commercially worked in the UK, but is not, or is not fully, so worked, that could ground an application, as could the failure to meet the demand for a product on reasonable terms or by domestic production as opposed to imports. The failure to work an invention domestically and the use of imports instead is a further ground to the application, under the UK legislation, as is the refusal to grant a licence on reasonable terms, which refusal acts to the detriment of the export or domestic market, or the working of another related invention. The imposition of unreasonable conditions attached to licences is a final ground for objection. From 29 July 1999 onwards,[45] the relevant original text of s. 48 relating to these grounds for the grant of a compulsory licence became s. 48B and now applies only to those patents the proprietor of which is not a World Trade Organization (WTO) proprietor—that is, a proprietor who is not a national of, or domiciled in, a country that is a WTO member

---

[44] Patents Act 1977, s. 48(1) and (3). See the full analysis of this area in *Therma-Tru Corp's Patent* [1997] RPC 777.

[45] Patents and Trade Marks (World Trade Organization) Regulations 1999, SI 1999/1899, reg. 3.

state, or who has no real and effective industrial or commercial establishment in such a country.[46]

This group of non-WTO proprietors is becoming increasingly narrow. In relation to patents the owner of which is a WTO proprietor, different grounds for the grant of a compulsory licence apply from 29 July 1999 onwards. A first ground is that, in the case of a product patent, the demand for the product in the UK has not been met on reasonable terms (in any way). Another ground is the refusal to grant a licence on reasonable terms as a result of which another important and valuable patent cannot be exploited, or which leads to the establishment and development of commercial or industrial activities being unfairly prejudiced. Finally, a compulsory licence can be granted if the patentee imposes conditions on the grant of a licence that are such that a form of unfair prejudice results.[47]

Even in the presence of any of these grounds, further restrictions apply to the grant of a compulsory licence. These restrictions reflect the provisions of the TRIPS Agreement on this point.[48] Prior to any grant, the applicant must, first, have made unsuccessful attempts to secure a normal licence on reasonable commercial terms and conditions. Second, any compulsory licence that is granted must be non-exclusive in nature, must be predominantly for the supply of the local UK market, must be limited in scope and duration to the purpose for which it was granted, and must be subject to the payment of an adequate remuneration to the patentee in the light of the economic value of the licence. A compulsory licence can also only be assigned in combination with the part of the business of the licensee that enjoys the use of the patent or in combination with the goodwill that relates to that part of the business.[49]

The grounds appear fairly wide and, as such, may be thought to permit frequent intervention against the interests of the inventor—but this impression would be misleading. The decision to grant a compulsory licence is entirely discretionary and s. 50 of the 1977 Act guides the exercise of that discretion. In relation to patents, the proprietor of which is a non-WTO proprietor, consideration must be given to the need to work inventions as much as possible, but only in so far as it is reasonably practicable to do so and also reflecting the need for the inventor to receive reasonable remuneration. In relation to all patents, regard should be had to the nature of the invention—some may take years to perfect in the light of their complexity—and to the abilities and resources of the proposed licensee seeking to work the unworked invention.

The reality is that few people who go to all of the time and effort of obtaining a patent will then ignore it. Even if they do so, because of their own ignorance or lack of resources, the patent, if of value, is likely to be the subject of an assignment or licensing deal. If the difficulties of working a patent are genuine, it is not likely that an applicant can clearly show that his or her ability and resources will crack problems in relation to which the patentee has failed. Such relatively few cases that arise in the first place, in which someone might want to seek a compulsory licence, will then have to be decided against the broad discretion imposed by the law.

It may be thought that some aspects of this part of the law have a somewhat protectionist tone, but s. 53(5) of the 1977 Act makes clear that no order may be made contrary to international obligations, thus including the Treaty of Rome and the European Patent Convention. It was argued, in *Extrude Hone Corp.'s Patent*,[50] that to impose a compulsory licence in the UK was wrong, because demand was being met by imports from

[46] Patents Act 1977, s. 48(5).   [47] Patents Act 1977, s. 48A(1).

[48] TRIPS Agreement, Art. 31.   [49] Patents Act 1977, s. 48A(2)–(6).   [50] [1982] RPC 361.

Ireland—but this argument was rejected on the grounds that the licence had not imposed a restriction on imports, but had, on the contrary, promoted free competition. Hoffmann J took a different view in *Research Corp.'s (Carboplatin) Patent*.[51] In this case, a licence of right had arisen under transitional provisions connected with the extension of the patent period from 16 to 20 years in the 1977 Act[52] and the licence was drafted in terms of preventing importation of carboplatin from outside the Community. Hoffmann J pointed out that it would not be possible to prevent imports from within the Community.[53] This does not, as such, contradict *Extrude Hone*, but it is a reminder of the single market in which we live.

Confirmation of this in the context of compulsory licences now comes from the European Court of Justice. In *Re Compulsory Patent Licences, EC Commission v. UK & Italy*,[54] the Commission objected to the original version of the text of s. 48 of the 1977 Act as permitting compulsory licences to be granted in the UK where provision of the product was taking place by importation from elsewhere in the EC, this being contrary to Art. 28 of the Treaty of Rome (now Art. 34 on the Treaty on the Functioning of the European Union). The Court rejected the UK's arguments and found that s. 48 of the 1977 Act did run contrary to that Article. The threat of a compulsory licence was capable of hindering intra-Community trade by persuading the patentee to make its product in the UK, rather than in other member states;[55] the reduction in imports that would be consequent upon a licence being granted further contravened Art. 28[56] and thus the Court contradicted the *Extrude Hone* decision. It was therefore clear that any compulsory licence issued, in situations under which demand is met by imports from the EU, would be ineffective and, as was argued in a previous edition of this book, s. 48 of the 1977 Act should be amended to take this into account. Exercise of an invention anywhere in the EU, and not only domestically, was to be the test. The 1999 reforms do not refer to the EU, but all of its member states are also members of the WTO. The relevant section is, therefore, now s. 48A of the Patents Act 1977, and any reference to importation and local exploitation has disappeared from that section. The new section meets the requirements set out by the European Court of Justice.

A final point to note is that the terms of the compulsory licence will include appropriate compensation for the patentee, even if only the new s. 48A explicitly refers to this point; this will normally be on a royalty basis.[57] By way of general summary, then, it is clear that compulsory patent licensing is not the threat to the interests of patentees that it may at first appear to be: such licences are rarely sought, more rarely granted, and, in the future, will be even more rarely available after the decision of the European Court of Justice.

Crown rights

In one further respect, the patentee may find him- or herself forced to share the benefits of the patent with another. Although it is not technically licensing, this is a convenient moment at which to consider the extent to which the Crown can intervene and exploit the patent itself. The fact that the Crown has any such rights is a useful reminder that the grant of a patent is—and has been since its earliest days—an act of the Crown; this area

---

[51] [1990] RPC 663.   [52] Patents Act 1977, Sch. 1, paras. 3 and 4.

[53] [1990] RPC 663 at 694.

[54] [1993] RPC 283. If the importation is prohibited from outside the EU, there is no such restriction: see *Generics (UK) Ltd v. Smith Kline & French Laboratories (UK) Ltd* [1993] RPC 333.

[55] [1993] RPC 283 at 328.   [56] [1993] RPC 283 at 329.

[57] *Smith Kline & French Laboratories Ltd's (Cimetidine) Patent* [1990] RPC 203, per Lloyd LJ at 245.

of the law is also significant in showing a very direct way in which the state, and thus society, can gain an undoubted advantage from inventive activity.

It is s. 55 of the 1977 Act that establishes the basic rights of the Crown in respect of patents. It empowers any government department, or person authorized thereby, to do various acts in relation to a patent without the consent of the owner, if acting for the services of the Crown. This latter aspect is interpreted broadly and includes the activities of health authorities.[58]

The acts that are authorized by the section include use or sale of either a product or a process, or the offer to another of an essential element of the invention with a view to putting the invention into effect. All of the actions listed by the section would normally count as infringements of the patent, but do not so count as a result of that section.

In so far as these provisions may be seen as draconian in their potential impact on patentees, this impression may be tempered by the obligation of the Crown to pay compensation to the patentee on either agreed, or court-imposed, terms in most instances.[59] This obligation does not arise in the cases of any invention tried or recorded by the Crown before the priority date of the invention and not as a result of information provided by the inventor. So if a private inventor and the Army are simultaneously working on the same invention, the private inventor could be forced to allow the Army to go ahead using the invention without the payment of any compensation. This is, however, clearly a narrow exception and, in the normal run of events, the inventor will receive compensation. Indeed, it is easy to envisage a situation in which the inventor will be happy for the Crown to intervene, because it will in effect guarantee that there is a market for the invention, thus removing many of the risks inherent in the decision to exploit an invention.

The provisions of s. 57 emphasize the priority enjoyed by the Crown and override third-party rights already created in respect of the patent, such as licences in favour of the Crown, although there is, again, provision for the payment of compensation to those affected.[60] During an official state of emergency, the powers of the Crown are increased by s. 59 of the 1977 Act and this allows the Crown to exercise its powers to use an invention for a range of reasons, from the efficient prosecution of a war, to the promotion of industrial productivity.

The Crown enjoys further privileges by virtue of s. 22 of the 1977 Act, under which any information in a patent application that may be prejudicial to the defence of the realm or to the safety of the public may be prohibited from publication, or be restricted in terms of circulation. The practical effect of this is that any information in a patent application that is, for example, of military significance can be withheld from the documentation that is available to the public, but can still be disseminated to relevant official bodies.

The powers of the Crown in relation to patents are far-reaching, particularly when compared with the less draconian powers in most other jurisdictions. While it is true that due compensation is, in most cases, payable, this does not wholly meet the objection that the interests of the patentee are given short shrift across the many areas of activity in which the Crown may have an interest in the exploitation of an invention.

Exclusive licences

In many cases, the licensing of a patent will be on a basis of exclusivity. This is of benefit to the licensor, who will thus only have to make one agreement and deal with one partner, and it is of particular benefit to the licensee, who thus acquires the monopoly

---

[58] *Dory v. Sheffield Health Authority* [1991] FSR 221.   [59] Patents Act 1977, s. 55(4).

[60] Patents Act 1977, s. 57A (added by the Copyright, Designs and Patents Act 1988, Sch. 5, para. 16(1)).

power inherent in the grant of a patent. The law reflects this reality by giving to the holder of an exclusive patent licence the same rights as the original patentee in relation to the bringing of infringement proceedings.[61] The obligation to register the exclusive licence on the other hand serves the interests of the public. They are made aware of the fact that an exclusive licence has been granted and of the identity of the exclusive licensee to whom they should turn.[62] The exact content of the licence is less important in this context.[63]

As a consequence of the evident power that resides in an exclusive licence, controls have been placed on the contents of all licensing agreements, originally by s. 44 of the 1977 Act. These controls meant that any agreement tying further terms to the licence that obliged the licensee to acquire other things from the licensor, or which prevented the licensee from using the technology of others, would be void in respect of such terms. Any agreement of this type, which gave the licensee an alternative without such a tie and which was terminable on three months' written notice, was, however, acceptable.[64] That section was repealed by the Competition Act 1998—but instead of weakening the control exercised by competition law, this Act reinforced these controls and modelled them on the existing EU competition law framework.[65] Any EU block exemption, for example, will also be deemed to be applicable locally at the UK level.[66]

Indeed, the principal implication of the widespread use of exclusive licences is that their monopoly implications trigger off the interest of the EU. This is, therefore, an appropriate time to consider the range of issues that this invokes, not only in patent licences, but also across the board of intellectual property law, because its propensity towards monopoly clashes with basic principles of EU law.

Commercial exploitation in European law

We can see in the text of the chapters of this book that European intellectual property law has a great influence on the substantial provisions of that of the UK. This does not give us the complete picture, however, because the free movement and competition law provisions of the Treaty of Rome also exert influence[67]—and it is to this influence that we now turn.

The founding fathers of the EU clearly did not believe that intellectual property was very relevant for their purposes when they negotiated the Treaty of Rome. They therefore did not find it necessary to include a chapter on intellectual property in the Treaty of Rome and, during its first ten years, virtually no problem related to intellectual property arose. Indeed, the most important obstacles to the creation of the European Economic Community and, gradually, that of a single market were the existence of internal custom tariffs and quantitative restrictions on importations from other member

[61] Patents Act 1977, s. 67.

[62] Patents Act 1977, s. 33, with s. 68 providing sanctions in terms of available remedies in case of non-respect of the registration obligation.

[63] *Schütz (UK) Ltd v. Werit UK Ltd* [2011] EWCA Civ 927.   [64] Patents Act 1977, s. 44(4).

[65] See Competition Act 1998, Pt I, Chs. I and II.

[66] The rest of our analysis will focus on the relevant provisions of EU law. These now have mirroring provisions under the Competition Act 1998, but a full discussion of the latter would be duplication and is therefore not proposed.

[67] See, in general, A. Jones and B. Sufrin (2001) *EC Competition Law: Text, Cases and Materials*, Oxford: Oxford University Press, Ch. 10; R. Whish and D. Bailey (2012) *Competition Law*, 7th edn, Oxford: Oxford University Press, Ch. 19.

states. The Treaty dutifully set out to remove these obstacles and it was only when a certain level of success had been achieved in this area that intellectual property became a problem.

In the absence of European intellectual property provisions, it was left to the member states to legislate in this area and to grant intellectual property rights on a national basis. But when they were no longer protected by custom tariffs or quantitative restrictions placed on foreign imports, certain competitors turned to intellectual property rights to protect their market share or the higher price that they could charge in the absence of competition. They tried to invoke infringement of their national intellectual property rights by the importation of the goods, or to use their intellectual property right to prevent competition. Infringement of a patent for a pharmaceutical product in member state A was, for example, invoked to prevent importation of the same drug from member state B—or one company might apply for parallel patents in all member states and use its one patent per member state to grant one exclusive licence for each, and to exclude all competition as a result. The Community felt that it had to react, to prevent the use of intellectual property rights to partition the market and to exclude competition. The European Court of Justice summarized the situation in *Parke, Davis v. Centrafarm*,[68] when it stated:

> The national rules relating to the protection of industrial property have not yet been unified within the Community. In the absence of such unification, the national character of the protection of industrial property and the variations between the different legislative systems on this subject are capable of creating obstacles both to the free movement of the patented products and to the competition within the Common Market.[69]

This absence of Community intellectual property provisions does not mean, however, that intellectual property law is not subject to the general provisions of the Treaty of Rome. The provisions on free movement and competition law apply to all areas, and, therefore, one has to start from the presumption that they also apply to intellectual property rights. Each of these provisions requires specific comments and we will consequently discuss them separately. For each, a patent-specific section will follow a general introduction—and it is self-evident that we will come back to these issues when discussing trade marks, copyright, and design.

Free movement of goods

The Treaty provisions

The general rule on the free movement of goods is found in Art. 34 of the Treaty on the Functioning of the European Union, which sets out to eliminate all quantitative restrictions that hinder the free movement of goods by stating that '*Quantitative restrictions on imports and all measures having equivalent effect shall be prohibited between member states.*' This provision is qualified by the first sentence of Art. 36 of the Treaty on the Functioning of the European Union (formerly Art. 30 of the Treaty of Rome), which contains certain exceptions:

> The provisions of Articles 34 and 35 shall not preclude prohibitions or restrictions on imports, exports or goods in transit justified on the grounds of ... the protection of industrial and commercial property.

---

[68] Case 24/67, *Parke, Davis & Co. v. Probel, Reese, Beintema-Interpharm & Centrafarm* [1968] ECR 55.
[69] *Parke, Davis & Co.* (n. 68) at 71.

At first sight, this would render Art. 34 inapplicable in relation to intellectual property—but this cannot be a correct conclusion, because the second sentence of Art. 36 limits the exception to the rule in Art. 34: '*Such prohibitions or restrictions shall not, however, constitute a means of arbitrary discrimination or a disguised restriction on trade between member states.*'

There must therefore be cases in which Art. 34 applies to intellectual property. Before we attempt to clarify this situation, two details need to be mentioned. First, European law should not be interpreted in the same way as an English statute is interpreted.

A teleological or purposive interpretation, rather than a purely literal interpretation, should be given to the provisions of the Treaty and it should therefore be specifically kept in mind that the free movement provisions had as their purpose the creation of a single market within the Community. On the issue of interpretation, it is also important to note that exceptions such as those contained in Art. 36 should be interpreted restrictively.[70]

Secondly, it has been suggested that Art. 345 of the Treaty of the Functioning of the European Union (formerly Art. 295 of the Treaty of Rome) plays, or should play, an important role in relation to intellectual property: '*This Treaty shall in no way prejudice the rules in member states governing the system of property ownership.*' If this really means that the Treaty does not interfere with intellectual property rights,[71] we can stop struggling with Arts. 34 and 36—but this is clearly not the case. Article 34 would not provide for a partial exception for intellectual property rights if the Treaty were not applicable to them in the first place; additionally, Art. 345 is a final provision, rather than a principle, of the Treaty. The Treaty principles are contained in Arts. 1–17 and have to be interpreted broadly, and the Articles implementing them—such as Art. 34—also have to be interpreted broadly. The final provisions in Arts. 335–56, however, do not override the principles: that much is clear from their place in the structure of the Treaty and from their heading. Most importantly, Art. 345 has a very different purpose from that of Arts. 34 and 36: it was derived from Art. 83 of the European Coal and Steel Community Treaty and both Articles have no purpose other than to emphasize the freedom of the member states to allow companies to be privately or publicly owned.[72] This detail was particularly important, because many governments wanted to preserve the possibility of nationalizing certain companies, even in a free-competition European environment. It is thus impossible to interpret Art. 345 teleologically and we arrive at the conclusion that it has no role whatsoever in relation to intellectual property, leaving Arts. 30 and 36 as the only relevant provisions of the Treaty.

Article 34 lays down the rule that quantitative restrictions are not acceptable. These are defined by the Court as '*measures which amount to a total or partial restraint of, according to the circumstances, imports, exports or goods in transit*',[73] but the text of Art. 34 makes it clear that this does not necessarily have to be the aim of the measure. Measures that simply have the same effect are also struck down.

The effect of Art. 35 is to add a further requirement for measures relating to intellectual property and to raise the threshold in Art. 34 by requiring that the measure should

---

[70] See D. Pollard and M. Ross (1994) *European Community Law: Text and Materials*, London: Butterworths, pp. 218–19.

[71] Supported wrongly by C. Miller, '*Magill*: Time to Abandon the "Specific Subject-Matter" Concept' [1994] 10 EIPR 415, 421.

[72] See C. Tritton, 'Articles 30 to 36 and Intellectual Property: Is the Jurisprudence of the ECJ now of an Ideal Standard?' (1994) 10 EIPR 422, 423; and T. Vinje, '*Magill*: Its Impact on the Information Technology Industry' (1992) 11 EIPR 397, 398.

[73] Case 2/73 *Geddo v. Ente* [1974] ECR 865, [1974] 1 CMLR 13.

amount to a means of arbitrary discrimination or a disguised restriction on trade between member states. Only measures that amount to a total or partial restraint of imports, exports, or goods in transit, and which also constitute a means of arbitrary discrimination or a disguised restriction of trade, will fall foul of the Treaty obligations. One should thus distinguish between intellectual property measures that are legitimate under the provisions of the Treaty and those measures that go too far, and fall foul of the threshold of Arts. 34 and 36.

Further evaluation

This system provided by the Treaty is logical. The Treaty set out to create a single market based on free competition and, as we discussed in Section A of this book, intellectual property rights are justified as restrictions on competition in furtherance of competition in such a system, because competition takes place at more than one level and intellectual property rights, while restricting competition on one level, enhance competition on another level. Intellectual property rights have, as a result, a place in a European free single market, but only in so far as they fulfil this task. When they are abused to do more than that, they will lead to arbitrary discrimination or to disguised restrictions on trade between member states, and will fall foul of Arts. 34 and 36.

It is clear therefore that, in such a system, the existence of intellectual property rights is a positive element,[74] but that the use that is made of them—that is, the way in which they are exercised—can either be lawful or can constitute an abuse. The European Court of Justice has summarized the position as follows:

> whilst the Treaty does not affect the existence of rights recognised by the legislation of a member state in matters of industrial and commercial property, yet the exercise of those rights may nevertheless, depending on the circumstances, be restricted by the prohibitions in the Treaty. Inasmuch as it provides an exception to one of the fundamental principles of the Common Market, Article [30] in fact admits exceptions to the free movement of goods only to the extent to which such exceptions are justified for the purposes of safeguarding the rights which constitute the specific subject-matter of that property.[75]

In the last sentence of this quotation, the Court hints at the tool that will be used to distinguish legitimate forms of exercising intellectual property rights from those that are abusive. We will have to define what is required for each intellectual property right in order for it to fulfil its task in a system of free competition: the Court calls this the 'specific subject-matter' of an intellectual property right. Once that is done, it will be possible to hold that any other use of an intellectual property right that goes further is an abuse, falling foul of Arts. 34 and 36, because restrictions on competition through the use of intellectual property rights are only acceptable in so far as they are necessary to maintain an optimal level of competition within the various levels at which competition takes place.

Logically speaking, and subject to the analysis that will follow, such a specific subject matter will necessarily include the exclusive right to use, or exploit, the intellectual property right and to oppose infringements. To hold otherwise would render the existence

---

[74] The Court explicitly stated that Arts. 28 and 30 of the Treaty of Rome do not affect the existence of intellectual property rights, and leaves the determination of the existence of these rights to the member states in the absence of Community harmonization. See Case 35/87, *Thetford Corp. v. Fiamma SpA* [1990] Ch 339, [1989] 2 All ER 801.

[75] Case 119/75, *Terrapin (Overseas) Ltd v. Terranova Industria CA Kapferer* [1976] ECR 1039, [1976] 2 CMLR 482 at 1061 and 505.

of intellectual property rights meaningless: a theoretical right that cannot be exercised would, indeed, be absurd. The exploitation of the right must allow the inventor or creator to be rewarded for his or her work and must stimulate him or her to go on inventing or creating. This is, however, only one essential element of the economic justification theory that is applicable to intellectual property in a free competition environment; the other essential element is the beneficial effect on society of making the invention or creation available. The European Court of Justice strikes the balance between the two elements by including, in the specific subject matter of each intellectual property right, that the right will be exhausted through first use by, or with, the consent of the right holder. This is often referred to as the 'exhaustion' doctrine.[76]

The Court also includes the 'essential function' of the intellectual property right in the definition of its specific subject matter,[77] because, from the point of view of the economic justification theory, the exercise of intellectual property rights is only tolerated in a free-competition economic model to perform a specific function. In turn, the performance of that function is required to maintain an optimal level of competition in the various levels at which competition takes place. To use the patent law example, the essential function is to reward the inventor, because that is necessary to stimulate further inventions, and to create an adequate level of competition on the level of invention and innovation. The economic model on which the justification of patents is based would be distorted and the free competition market would no longer operate adequately if the essential function of patents were not to be fulfilled. We will further clarify these principles when applying them to patents.

A last general point relates, once more, to the teleological interpretation of the relevant Treaty provisions. The interpretation given here is only valid if the provisions are seen as a tool with which to reach the ultimate goal of the creation of the single market;[78] the Court may not interpret the same provisions in the same way in a context in which the goal of the creation of a single market is absent. This has its practical importance, because the literal text of Arts. 34 and 36 is often included in treaties that the EU concludes with third-party countries. This situation arose in *Polydor v. Harlequin*[79] and, on that occasion, the Court did indeed refuse to interpret these provisions in the way it would have interpreted them in an intra-Community case. Particular caution has to be exercised in relation to the European Economic Area (EEA) Agreement,[80] because this includes the aim of the creation of a single market and, to a large extent, the interpretation that the Court gave to the relevant provision in intra-Community cases.[81]

It is submitted that the principle laid down in the *Polydor* case does not apply in relation to the EEA countries,[82] which appears now to have been confirmed by both Advocate-General Jacobs and the European Court of Justice in *Silhouette v. Harlauer*.[83] The EEA Agreement has effectively made the full exhaustion doctrine applicable to the whole of the EEA.

---

[76] See e.g. Case 15/74, *Centrafarm BV v. Sterling Drug Inc.* [1974] ECR 1147 at 1162.

[77] See e.g. *Centrafarm BV* (n. 76).

[78] Case 270/80, *Polydor Ltd v. Harlequin Record Shops* [1982] ECR 329 at 349.

[79] *Polydor* (n. 78).

[80] (1994) OJ L 1/3, in force since 1 January 1994 (1 May 1995 for Liechtenstein).

[81] See S. Von Lewinski, 'Copyright within the External Relations of the European Union and the EFTA Countries' (1994) 10 EIPR 429, 433.

[82] The European Economic Area is comprised of the EU, Iceland, Liechtenstein and Norway.

[83] Opinion of Advocate-General Jacobs in Case C-355/96, *Silhouette International Schmied GmbH & Co. KG v. Hartlauer Handelsgesellschaft mbH* [1998] 2 CMLR 953 at paras. 2 and 3.

Free movement of goods and patents

The starting point

Many of these criteria were laid down and applied in relation to patents in the *Centrafarm v. Sterling Drug* case.[84] This case involved a drug used for the treatment of urinary infections, for which Sterling Drug held parallel patents in the UK and the Netherlands. Due to the tight regulation of drug prices in the UK, the drug was sold there at approximately half the price at which it was sold in the Netherlands. Centrafarm specialized in the parallel import of drugs, and bought a large quantity of the drug in the UK and imported it into the Netherlands for resale purposes. Sterling Drug brought a case alleging infringement of its Dutch patent by the importation of the drug.

The European Court of Justice ruled that the essential function of a patent was '*to reward the creative effort of the inventor*'.[85] Although it can be argued that the patent system has many other functions—such as making the technological information available to the public—this must, indeed, be the essential one. Without reward, many inventors will, or will have to, stop their activity and their creative efforts must necessarily precede anything else, because without creation, there is no technological information to be passed on. With that essential function in mind, it was necessary to define the specific subject matter in such a way that that function was fulfilled by the patent system and an adequate level of competition was created on the innovation level, while not unduly compromising the adequate levels of competition on the other levels at which competition takes place.

The Court defined the specific subject matter of a patent as follows:

> the guarantee that the patentee, to reward the creative effort of the inventor, has the exclusive right to use an invention with a view to manufacturing industrial products and putting them into circulation for the first time, either directly or by the grant of licences to third parties as well as the right to oppose infringements.[86]

The patentee has the exclusive right to use the invention to manufacture industrial products and, obviously, he or she also has the right to oppose infringement. This is the hard core of the patent. If the function of it all is to reward the inventor, this has to be achieved through the commercial exploitation of the monopoly created by the exclusive right—that is, by allowing the patentee the exclusive right to put the product on the single market for the first time, because that will bring in the profit. But it was felt that this was sufficient to fulfil the function of rewarding the inventor and that allowing the inventor to control further transactions concerning the industrial product would unduly distort competition at other levels.

Sterling Drug had been rewarded when it got its profit when putting the drugs on the market in the UK; it was the only company that was allowed to use the patent to produce the drug and it could act against any infringing use of the patent. If it was allowed to interfere with the further commercial life of the drug, that would unduly distort competition. It would then be able to partition the single market by relying on its relevant national parallel patent in the importing country each time the drug was imported in another member state, '*where no such restriction was necessary to guarantee the essence of the exclusive rights flowing from the parallel patents*'.[87] Not only was this not necessary to reward the inventor; it went straight against the major aim of the Community. The Court

---

[84] Case 15/74, *Centrafarm BV v. Sterling Drug Inc.* [1974] ECR 1147, [1974] 2 CMLR 480.
[85] *Centrafarm BV* (n. 84) at 1162.   [86] *Centrafarm BV* (n. 84).
[87] *Centrafarm BV* (n. 84) at 1163.

therefore limited the exploitation right that forms part of the specific subject matter to the first marketing of the drug and held that, by putting the drug on the single market for the first time, all rights under all parallel patents would be exhausted. By putting the drug on the single market through marketing it in the UK, Sterling had exhausted all of its rights under the parallel patents and could no longer use any right under its Dutch parallel patent to oppose the subsequent importation into the Netherlands of the drugs it had put on the market in the UK. It is also important to note that the essential function is an integral part of the specific subject matter, which stresses the fact that the specific subject matter is defined in such a way that the essential function will be fulfilled.

An important point is that the patentee can undertake the first exploitation him- or herself or can grant a licence to a third party to undertake the first exploitation. The crucial element is that the first exploitation needs to be undertaken with the consent of the patentee.[88] The first exploitation will only lead to the exhaustion of the rights under all parallel patents if the patentee has consented to the first exploitation. This means, in practical terms, that a patentee will still be able to block the importation of goods by relying on the patent if these goods have been manufactured by a third party without the consent of the patentee. In such a situation, the third party is legally and economically independent, and owns the patent in the member states in which its manufacturing activities are based.

It is also important to clarify what are 'parallel patents'. As long as national patent legislation is not fully harmonized, it may lead to slightly different patents, because the claims are worded differently, for example. The European Court of Justice therefore adopted the only workable approach. All patents that protect the same invention are held to be parallel patents.[89]

On the basis of this analysis, the conclusion on the facts of *Centrafarm v. Sterling Drug* was that:

> the exercise, by a patentee, of the right which he enjoys under the legislation of a member state to prohibit the sale, in that State, of a product protected by the patent which has been marketed in another member state by the patentee or with his consent is incompatible with the rules of the EEC Treaty concerning the free movement of goods within the Common Market.[90]

Only those ways of exercising the patent right that stay within the specific subject matter of the right are compatible with the Treaty. Because the Treaty has an overriding effect on national law, the national provisions that allow more extensive use of the patent right can no longer be applied in a Community context.

Essential function and consent developed further

The Court had to analyse the essential function and consent ideas further in *Merck & Co. Inc. v. Stephar*.[91] This case again involved a patent for a drug, which, this time, was used to treat high blood pressure. Merck held patents relating to the drug in the Netherlands, while Stephar was importing the drug into the Netherlands from Italy. The interesting aspect of the case was the fact that, at the time, there was no patent protection for pharmaceutical products under Italian law. Merck had put the drug on the market in Italy, but argued that to hold that it had thereby exhausted its rights and could no longer rely on its Dutch patent would go against the essential function of the patent, because, due to

---

[88] *Centrafarm BV* (n. 84) at 1162–3.   [89] *Centrafarm BV* (n. 84) at 1163.
[90] *Centrafarm BV* (n. 84) at 1163.
[91] Case 187/80, *Merck & Co. Inc. v Stephar BV* [1981] ECR 2063 [1901] 3 CMLR 463.

the impossibility of patenting the drug in Italy, the sale there had not taken place under monopolistic conditions, and thus the lower price and profit had not fully rewarded its creative efforts.

The Court rejected this interpretation. First, no specific reward is guaranteed, because the exact amount of the reward depends, in all cases, on the market conditions. Second, if, in these circumstances, a choice to put the product on the market without the benefit of a patent is made, the inventor accepts the reward that the market will offer. This means that the essential function is fulfilled and that the specific subject matter will indicate the limit of the exercise of the patent rights. In other words, by marketing the drug in Italy, Merck had exhausted all rights under the existing parallel patents within the Community and the fact that no patent could exist in Italy did not influence that conclusion. It is up to the patentee to decide whether or not to market the product in a market within which a weaker form of protection, or no protection at all, is available. Needless to say, the conclusion would have been the same had Merck decided not to market the drug in Italy itself, but to have it marketed there with its consent by a third party.

The Court expressed the conclusion as follows:

> That the right of first placing a product on the market enables the inventor, by allowing him a monopoly in exploiting his product, to obtain the reward for his creative effort without, however, guaranteeing that he will obtain such a reward in all circumstances. It is for the proprietor of the patent to decide, in the light of all the circumstances, under what conditions he will market his product, including the possibility of marketing it in a member state where the law does not provide patent protection for the product in question. If he decides to do so he must accept the consequences of his choice as regards the free movement of the product within the Common Market, which is a fundamental principle forming part of the legal and economic circumstances which must be taken into account by the proprietor of the patent in determining the manner in which his exclusive right will be exercised.[92]

Merck had been rewarded for its creative activity and the patent rights had been exhausted by the marketing of the drug in Italy. It could not block the importation of the drug into the Netherlands by Stephar, because that exercise of the patent rights would go beyond the specific subject matter of the patent.

The Court was subsequently given an opportunity to overturn its *Merck v. Stephar* ruling in a case relating to the parallel importation of drugs from Spain and Portugal. Its judgment in *Merck v. Primecrown*[93] makes it clear, though, that *Merck v. Stephar* remains good law. The Court specifically rejected the argument that the manufacturers of a drug were under a moral obligation to market their products even in countries in relation to which no patent protection was available and any suggestion that this took away the free consent of the manufacturers to the marketing of the drugs was rejected.

Consent and elements of compulsion

The consent idea also needs to be applied to compulsory licence cases. The issue is, then, whether the exploitation and first marketing by the licensee amount to putting the

---

[92] *Centrafarm BV* (n. 84) at 2081–2.

[93] Joined Cases C-267/95 and 268/95, *Merck & Co. Inc., Merck Sharp & Dohme Ltd, Merck Sharp & Dohme International Services BV v. Primecrown Ltd, Ketan Himatlal Mehta, Necessity Supplies Ltd; Beecham Group plc v. Europharm of Worthing Ltd* [1996] ECR I-6285, (1997) 1 CMLR 83; see P. Torremans and I. Stamatoudi, '*Merck v. Stephar* Survives the Test' (1997) 22 EL Rev 248; P. Torremans and I. Stamatoudi, '*Merck* is Back to Stay: The Court of Justice's Judgment in *Merck v. Primecrown*' (1997) 9 EIPR 545.

product on the market for the first time with the consent of the patentee, and therefore exhaust the rights under all parallel patents.

This situation arose in *Pharmon BV v. Hoechst*.[94] Hoechst owned parallel patents in a drug in the UK, Germany, and the Netherlands, and a compulsory licence had been granted to a third party in the UK. The Court held that '*such a (compulsory licence) measure deprives the patent proprietor of his right to determine freely the conditions under which he markets his products*'.[95] As a result, the product was not put on the market with the consent of the patentee in case this was done on the basis of a compulsory licence and the rights under all parallel patents were not exhausted. Hoechst could rely on the Dutch parallel patent to prevent importation into the Netherlands by Pharmon of the drugs it had bought in the UK from the licensee who had produced these under a compulsory licence.

Similarly, there was no consent in a case in which the patent holder took six weeks before bringing an infringement action after having been served with an *ex parte* injunction that the defendant's product did not infringe. The six weeks' delay did not demonstrate consent.[96]

In *Merck v. Primecrown*,[97] the Court clarified the consent issue further by ruling that there is also no consent if the holder of a patent is under a genuine, existing legal obligation to market its product, or to allow marketing by a third party under a compulsory licence. It is clear from the reasoning of the Court that such a legal obligation is highly unlikely to exist and that it will be difficult to prove. The presence of a legal obligation to market distinguishes the rule in *Pharmon v. Hoechst*[98] from that in *Merck v. Stephar*.[99] The two rules do not contradict each other.[100]

Articles 30 and 36 were subsequently raised on a couple of occasions in relation to compulsory licences and licences of right. Section 46 of the UK Patents Act 1977 allowed for licences of right as licences available upon application. As such, this does not create a problem, but the law clearly envisaged production only in the UK under such a licence of right. In case the holder of a licence of right imported the product from another member state, rather than produced it in the UK, an injunction could still be granted. This was exactly what Allen and Hanbury's were asking for when Generics intended to import the products for which it had obtained a licence of right from Italy, rather than produce them itself in the UK.[101] In that case, the European Court of Justice held that this was a restriction on the free movement of goods in the Community, because it blocked certain forms of importation from a member state and encouraged local production, rather than importation from within the single market. If all countries were to adopt this measure, national markets would, in the cases concerned, once again replace the single market. This measure amounted to an arbitrary discrimination under Art. 36 and could therefore no longer be applied within the Community. Similarly, the provision in s. 48 of the Patents Act 1977 that allows for the grant of a compulsory licence if the patent is exploited by importing the products from another member state, rather than by producing the products in the

---

[94] Case 19/84, *Pharmon BV v. Hoechst AG* [1985] ECR 2281. [95] *Pharmon BV* (n. 94) at 2298.

[96] See the English case *Sandvik Aktiebolag v. K. R. Pfiffner (UK) Ltd* [2000] FSR 17.

[97] Joined Cases C-267/95 and 268/95, *Merck & Co. Inc., Merck Sharp & Dohme Ltd, Merck Sharp & Dohme International Services BV v. Primecrown Ltd, Ketan Himatlal Mehta, Necessity Supplies Ltd; Beecham Group plc v. Europharm of Worthing Ltd* (n. 93).

[98] *Pharmon* (n. 94). [99] *Merck & Co. Inc. v. Stephar* (n. 91).

[100] See Joined Cases C-267/95 and 268/95, *Merck & Co. Inc., Merck Sharp & Dohme Ltd, Merck Sharp & Dohme International Services BV v. Primecrown Ltd, Ketan Himatlal Mehta, Necessity Supplies Ltd; Beecham Group plc v. Europharm of Worthing Ltd* (n. 93) at paras. 40 and 41.

[101] Case 434/85, *Allen & Hanbury's Ltd v. Generics (UK) Ltd* [1988] ECR 1245, [1988] 1 CMLR 701.

UK, fell foul of Arts. 24 and 36 because it is an arbitrary discrimination.[102] It encouraged local production, rather than importation from within the single market, and therefore hindered the free movement of goods.[103] In neither of these cases were these provisions necessary to safeguard the specific subject matter of the patent.

It has also been argued that Art. 34 stands in the way of the requirement that local patent protection depends on the filing of a translation of the patent in the local language if the patent was originally filed and granted—for example, by the European Patent Office—in a foreign language. The European Court of Justice rejected this argument and upheld the provisions of national law that require the filing of a translation on sanction of the patent being declared void *ab initio*. The Court held that, even if, in certain circumstances, the translation requirement may have restrictive effects on the free movement of goods, these effects were too uncertain and too indirect to be considered an obstacle as referred to in Art. 34.[104]

Patents and competition law

Articles 101 and 102 of the Treaty on the Functioning of the European Union (formerly Arts. 81 and 82 of the Treaty of Rome) deal with competition law, and neither of these Articles contains an exception for a specific area. Intellectual property must thus be subject to the EU rules on competition. We will first discuss the impact of Art. 101 on intellectual property and we will then turn our attention to Art. 102.

Article 101

Article 101 of the Treaty consists of three paragraphs:

(1) The following shall be prohibited as incompatible with the Common Market: all agreements between undertakings, decisions by associations of undertakings and concerted practices which may affect trade between member states and which have as their object or effect the prevention, restriction or distortion of competition within the Common Market, and in particular those which:
  (a) directly or indirectly fix purchase or selling prices or any other trading conditions;
  (b) limit or control production, markets, technical development, or investment;
  (c) share markets or sources of supply;
  (d) apply dissimilar conditions to equivalent transactions with other trading parties, thereby placing them at a competitive disadvantage;
  (e) make the conclusion of contracts subject to acceptance by the other parties of supplementary obligations which, by their nature or according to commercial usage, have no connection with the subject of such contracts.

(2) Any agreements or decisions prohibited pursuant to this Article shall be automatically void.

(3) The provisions of paragraph 1 may, however, be declared inapplicable in the case of:
  (a) any agreement or category of agreements between undertakings;
  (b) any decision or category of decisions by associations of undertakings;
  (c) any concerted practice or category of concerted practices;

---

[102] Joined Cases C-30/90 and C-235/89, *EC Commission v. UK; EC Commission v. Italy* [1992] ECR I-829, [1992] 2 CMLR 709.

[103] The provision can still be used if the patent is not exploited by local production and if the goods are instead imported from a non-member state, because, in these cases, the creation of a single market is not affected: see Case C-191/90, *Generics (UK) Ltd v. Smith Kline & French Laboratories Ltd* [1993] RPC 333.

[104] Case C-44/98, *BASF AG v. Präsident des Deutschen Patentamts* [1999] ECR I-6269.

which contributes to improving the production or distribution of goods or to promoting technical or economic progress, while allowing consumers a fair share of the resulting benefit, and which does not:

(a) impose on the undertakings concerned restrictions which are not indispensable to the attainment of these objectives;

(b) afford such undertakings the possibility of eliminating competition in respect of a substantial part of the products in question.

We shall start by analysing this provision briefly.[105] Article 101(1) outlaws a number of deals because they are anti competitive, while Art. 101(2) sanctions that by declaring them void; Art. 101(3) contains an exception clause. When a number of requirements are met, a deal that would normally fall foul of Art. 101(1) will be exempted and neither that paragraph, nor Art. 101(2), will be applied to it.

So with which deals is Art. 101(1) concerned? The obvious category consists of the agreements concluded between undertakings. These will be affected if they have as their object, or simply as their effect, the prevention of competition, the restriction of competition, or the distortion of competition within the Common Market. This provision might easily be circumvented, however, if it were to stand on its own by avoiding a formal agreement. Competition could nevertheless be affected if the parties were to coordinate their actions and replace competition by coordination. The same effect might also be reached by replacing an agreement with a decision of an association of undertakings. The drafters of the Treaty avoided this risk, however, by including both concerted practices and decisions of associations of undertakings as separate categories that are covered by Art. 101. A last additional requirement is that trade between member states must be affected for Art. 101 to operate. Small deals that do not affect trade between member states are not important enough, because they will not have a substantial influence on competition at Community level. National competition authorities may nevertheless decide to pick up these deals and scrutinize them under national competition law.

When a deal is caught by Art. 101(1), the sanction provided by Art. 101(2) is that it is automatically void. No declaratory decision by a court or competition authority is necessary and, in law, we act as if the deal never existed. The deal will not bind anyone and no one will be able to rely upon it.

Exemptions that effectively place the deal outside the scope of Art. 101(1) can be granted under the authority of Art. 101(3) if four conditions—two that are positive and two that are negative—are met. These conditions are applied cumulatively—that is, all four need to be met at any one time. The anti competitive deal must:

- provide a contribution to the improvement of the production or distribution of goods, or to promoting technical or economic progress;

- allow consumers a fair share of the resulting benefit;

- impose no restrictions that are not indispensable to the attainment of these objectives;

- allow no possibility of eliminating competition in respect of a substantial part of the products in question.

---

[105] For a full analysis from a competition law perspective, see R. Whish and D. Bailey (2012) *Competition Law*, 7th edn, Oxford: Oxford University Press, Chs. 3 and 4. For a more recent application, see Case T-168/01, *GlaxoSmithKline Services v. EC Commission*, judgment of 27 September 2006 (the appeal to the European Court of Justice as Case C-501/06P was rejected on 6 October 2009).

If these four requirements are met, an individual exemption can be granted. In practice, this is done by submitting the deal to the Commission, which implements and polices the Community's competition law, as an application for an individual exemption. This individual process is fairly lengthy and it causes a lack of legal certainty, because the parties to a deal do not know in advance which restrictive clauses will be acceptable to the Commission. In order to solve these problems and to avoid being unable to cope with a flood of applications, the Commission issues block exemptions, in the form of a regulation containing lists of acceptable and non-acceptable clauses. Agreements that stay within the limits set out by the block exemption are automatically exempted and no further application or other procedure is required.

The next issue to address now that we know what Art. 101 is all about is whether agreements concerning intellectual property are caught by it. On the one hand, licence contracts, or eventually assignments, can restrict competition between the licensor and the licensee, or between licensees, to a considerable extent. Exclusive licences are prime examples of this. On the other hand, there is no provision in the Treaty that provides an exception for the intellectual property area. The conclusion must accordingly be that Art. 101 applies unreservedly to intellectual property agreements.[106]

Patent licences—general comments and individual exemptions

The Commission has applied Art. 101 to patent licence contracts on several occasions, and important guidance can also be derived from the *Windsurfing* case[107] and, on the point of exclusivity, from the *Maize Seeds* case.[108] Before we look at some clauses, some preliminary points need to be made. Article 101 does not apply to agreements of minor importance. The problem with this provision is that it is difficult to predict the success of certain licences and certain products, and so a licence agreement that is originally not covered may become such a success that it becomes important enough to be considered under that Article[109]—and this may have very undesirable consequences. Article 101 will also not apply if trade between member states is not affected.[110]

A normal exercise of the patent will not infringe Art. 101(1). Accordingly, the licensor may charge royalties[111] and may try to ensure that his or her licensee exploits the patent adequately. The latter element implies that minimum royalty clauses,[112] under which the licensee is obliged to pay a minimum amount in royalties, even if the frequency of its use of the patented technology does not mathematically justify this, and clauses that require a licensee to produce minimum quantities of the patented product or to carry out a minimum number of operations using the patented process are acceptable, and do not restrict competition.[113] Clauses that go further than that, however, may restrict competition and have been held to infringe Art. 101(1): for example, clauses that require the licensee to pay royalties for non-patented products[114] and clauses that require the licensee to continue paying royalties after the patent has expired.[115] It is not, however, an infringement to require the licensee to keep paying royalties for know-how that the

---

[106] See Cases 56 and 58/64, *Consten & Grundig v. EC Commission* [1966] ECR 299, [1966] CMLR 418; Case 24/67, *Parke, Davis & Co. Ltd* (n. 68).

[107] Case 193/83, *Windsurfing International Inc. v. EC Commission* [1986] ECR 611, [1986] 3 CMLR 489.

[108] Case 258/78, *LC Nungesser KG v. EC Commission* [1982] ECR 2015, [1983] 1 CMLR 278.

[109] *Burroughs/Deplanque* (1972) OJ L 13/50 and *Burroughs/Geha-Werke* (1972) OJ L 13/53.

[110] *Raymond/Nagoya* (1972) OJ L 143/39.

[111] Fourth Annual Report on Competition Policy, s. 20.

[112] See *AOIP/Beyrard* (1976) OJ L 6/8, in which such a clause was not condemned.

[113] See the old Patent Licence Block Exemption (1984) OJ L 219/15, Art. 2(1)(2).

[114] See *AOIP/Beyrard* (n. 112).   [115] *AOIP/Beyrard* (n. 112).

licensee continues to use after the patent has expired if that know-how is still secret and has not yet fallen in the public domain.[116]

The term of the licence agreement may be shorter than the remaining life of the patent,[117] but tie-up clauses,[118] which bind the licensee to the licensor once the patent has expired by obliging him or her to take out further licences for other technology, do infringe Art. 101(1). A licensor may also want to restrict the use that the licensee can make of the licensed technology to a certain field of application, particularly if the technology can be used in very different areas—such as, for example, a drug that can be used both in human and in veterinary medicine. These 'field of use' restrictions will fall outside Art. 101(1) if they restrict the use of the licensee to one or more specific and identifiable fields of application,[119] in line with the Commission's view that a clause prohibiting the licensee to compete with the licensor or with any connected undertakings in respect of research and development—that is, the so-called 'no competition' clause[120]—or a 'no challenge' clause,[121] which prevents the licensee—who is, in this respect, particularly well placed as user of the technology—from challenging the validity of the patent are, generally speaking,[122] bound to infringe Art. 101(1).

Clauses that equally infringe Art. 101(1) are exclusive grant-back clauses,[123] which oblige the licensee to grant an exclusive licence to the licensor in relation to all improvements of the technology, or to all new and related technology that it may develop, or, even worse, to assign these improvements or this technology outright to the licensor. This would deprive the licensee of any incentive to develop its own technology, which it will need to compete on the market and give the licensor an unwarranted permanent technological advantage. Only exclusive licences are banned; non-exclusive grant-back clauses are acceptable.[124]

The licensor has a legitimate interest in the protection of its brand image and the quality of the products. As a result, clauses requiring the licensee to promote the product, to label the product—but not non-patented items as well[125]—in a particular way and to comply with certain quality standards fall outside the scope of Art. 101(1).[126] A difficult borderline case is presented by a clause obliging a licensee to use the patentee's trade mark and get-up. This type of clause will make it difficult for the licensee to be identified as a separate entity and may make competition unworkable. It is only acceptable if it is combined with a right for the licensee to identify itself while using the patentee's trade mark and get-up.[127] The Commission's approach is that the latter clause may be caught, but may qualify for an exemption.

Tie-in clauses that, for example, oblige the licensee to buy raw materials from the licensor will only avoid being caught by Art. 101(1) if they are really indispensable for the

---

[116] *Kabel- und Metallwerke/Etablissements Luchaire SA* (1975) OJ L 222/34.

[117] Fourth Annual Report on Competition Policy, s. 29.

[118] See *AOIP/Beyrard* (n. 112); and *Velcro/Aplix* [1989] 4 CMLR 157, (1985) OJ L 233/22.

[119] Fourth Annual Report on Competition Policy, s. 28.   [120] See *AOIP/ Beyrard* (n. 115).

[121] *Windsurfing International* (1983) OJ L 229/1 and on appeal from the Commission decision, Case 193/83, *Windsurfing International Inc. v. EC Commission* [1986] ECR 611, [1986] 3 CMLR 489.

[122] The conclusion may be different in exceptional circumstances: see Case 65/86, *Bayer AG & Maschinenfabriek Hennecke GmbH v. Sullhöfer* [1988] ECR 5249, [1990] 4 CMLR 182.

[123] See *Kabel- und Metallwerke/Etablissements Luchaire SA* (1975) OJ L 222/34; *AOIP/Beyrard* (n. 112); *Velcro/Aplix* [1989] 4 CMLR 157, OJ L 233/22; *Roses* (1985) OJ L 369/9.

[124] *Re Davidson Rubber Co. Agreements* [1972] CMLR D52, OJ L 143/31.

[125] Case 193/83, *Windsurfing International Inc. v. EC Commission* [1986] ECR 611, [1986] 3 CMLR 489.

[126] See the old Patent Licence Block Exemption (1984) OJ L 219/15, Art. 2(6) and 2(9).

[127] Old Patent Licence Block Exemption (1984) OJ L 219/15, Art. 1(1)(7).

successful exploitation of the patent.[128] Any other tie-in clause will not even be granted an exemption, because this is a perfect tool with which to control the price at which the licensee can sell and thus restrict competition.[129] Customer allocation clauses,[130] export bans,[131] vertical price fixing,[132] and obligations only to sell the patented product as part of a package[133] will also be caught by Art. 101(1).

A number of other clauses are, on the other hand, considered to fall outside the scope of Art. 101(1). Examples of these clauses are obligations of secrecy,[134] 'most-favoured licensee' clauses,[135] obligations to prevent infringement of the patent,[136] and restrictions on the assignment and the sub-licensing by the licensee.[137]

Exclusivity is the most difficult issue, because it can be used easily to stop intra-brand competition between the licensor and the licensee, and between the various licensees; it can also lead to a compartmentalization of the market. The bottom line of the debate is that the European Commission and the CJEU will never tolerate absolute closed exclusivity, which would oblige the licensor and the licensee not to compete, through an active or even through a passive sales policy, in each other's area and this in combination with a similar obligation between licensees, coupled with an obligation not to deal with parallel importers.[138]

All other forms of exclusivity also fall within the scope of Art. 101(1), but may be exempted.[139] The EU is particularly keen to keep the parallel import option open, and normally requires the licensee to be free to have a passive sales policy in the territories of the licensor and other licensees. The latter means, in practice, that the licensee, while based in its own territory, can respond to unsolicited orders from these territories. In circumstances under which the licensee would not have been prepared to take the risk of taking out a licence and incurring expense in producing the patented goods if it were not given some protection against intra-brand competition at the production level in the allocated territory, an open exclusive licence exceptionally does not infringe Art. 101(1).[140] In practice, this means that no one else will be allowed to work the patent in the allocated territory, while leaving unaffected the parallel import route, whereby an importer buys the patented goods from the licensor or another licensee to import them into the allocated territory.[141] The Commission has, however, interpreted this exception restrictively.[142]

---

[128] Old Patent Licence Block Exemption (1984) OJ L 219/15, Art. 2(1)(1).

[129] See *Vaessen/Moris* (1979) OJ L19/32.

[130] See the old Patent Licence Block Exemption (1984) OJ L 219/15, Art. 3(7).

[131] *AOIP/Beyrard* (n. 112); *Velcro/Aplix* [1989] 4 CMLR 157, OJ L 233/22.

[132] See the old Patent Licence Block Exemption (1984) OJ L 219/15, Art. 3(6).

[133] See Case 193/83 *Windsurfing International Inc. v. EC Commission* [1986] ECR 611, [1986] 3 CMLR 489, in which the Court upheld the Commission's objections against the obligation to sell the patented rig only as part of a complete sailboard.

[134] See the Old Patent Licence Block Exemption (1984) OJ L 219/15, Art. 2(1)(7).

[135] Old Patent Licence Block Exemption (1984) OJ L 219/15, Art. 2(1)(11).

[136] Old Patent Licence Block Exemption (1984) OJ L 219/15, Art. 2(1)(8).

[137] Old Patent Licence Block Exemption (1984) OJ L 219/15, Art. 2(1)(5).

[138] Case 258/78, *LC Nungesser KG v. EC Commission* [1982] ECR 2015, [1983] 1 CMLR 278.

[139] See *AOIP/Beyrard* (n. 112).   [140] *LC Nungesser KG v. EC Commission* (n. 138).

[141] See D. Hoffmann and O. O'Farrell, 'The "Open Exclusive Licence": Scope and Consequences' (1984) 4 EIPR 104.

[142] See *Velcro/Aplix* [1989] 4 CMLR 157, OJ L 233/22; *Tetra Pak I* (1988) OJ L 272/27 (upheld on appeal: Case T-51/89, *Tetra Pak Rausing SA v. Commission* [1990] ECR II-309, [1991] 4 CMLR 334); *Delta Chemie/DDD* [1989] 4 CMLR 157, OJ L 309/34; but see also Case 27/87, *Erauw-Jacquery SPrl v. La Hesbignonne Société* [1988] ECR 1919, [1988] 4 CMLR 576.

The patent licence block exemption

As we discussed earlier, the Commission has not restricted itself to granting individual exemptions; it has also drafted block exemptions. The patent licence block exemption was issued in 1984,[143] entered into force in 1985, and was bound to expire on 31 December 1994, but its life was extended until 30 June 1995.[144] It applied to patent licences, and to combined patent and know-how licences, as long as only two undertakings were parties to such an agreement.[145] Patent pool agreements and, to a more limited extent after the 1993 amendments, licence agreements between partners in a joint venture were excluded from its scope, as were reciprocal licence agreements.[146]

The block exemption introduced a standard format. Article 1 contained a list of clauses that did not come within the scope of Art. 101(1) of the Treaty of Rome altogether, while exemption Art. 2 contained a list of clauses that were exempted in case they came within the scope of Treaty Art. 101(1). These permitted clauses were called the 'white list'. Finally, Art. 3 of the patent licence block exemption contained a list of clauses that were not exempted and the presence of one of these clauses in a licence agreement meant that it could not benefit from the block exemption.

The know-how block exemption

The know-how block exemption was issued in 1988,[147] came into force in 1989, and would normally have been in force until the very end of the century.[148] In both form and substance, it was clearly modelled on the patent licence block exemption and we will therefore only highlight some differences.

The exemption covered know-how agreements and mixed know-how patent agreements, and thus a choice between two block exemptions was offered for the latter category.[149] It required 'know-how' to be a body of technical information that is secret, substantial, and identified in any appropriate form.[150] The most obvious example is the know-how that goes with the patent: all that is explained in the patent application is the invention itself. There is, of course, a most appropriate way to exploit the invention and the patent holder often keeps that knowledge secret. That body of technical information is quite substantial, and can be identified and separated from other general knowledge.

The general impression was that the know-how block exemption was slightly more flexible and that it was more advantageous to the licensor.

The first technology transfer block exemption

Rather than replace the old patent licence block exemption with a new one, the Commission preferred, at the time, to repeal the know-how licence block exemption and to replace both block exemptions at the same time.[151] The technology transfer block

---

[143] Commission Regulation 2349/84 of 23 July 1984 on the application of Art. 85(3) of the Treaty to certain categories of patent licensing agreements (1984) OJ L 219/15, as amended by (1985) OJ L 113/34 and (1993) OJ L 21/8; see V. Korah (1985) *Patent Licensing and EEC Competition Rules: Regulation 2349/84 ESC*, Oxford: ESC.

[144] Art. 14. [145] Art. 1(1). [146] Art. 5.

[147] Commission Regulation 556/89 of 30 November 1988 on the application of Art. 85(3) of the Treaty to certain categories of know-how licensing agreements (1989) OJ L 61/1, as amended by (1993) OJ L 21/8; see Korah, *Patent Licensing and EEC Competition Rules: Regulation 2349/84 ESC* (n. 143).

[148] Art. 12. [149] Art. 1(1). [150] Art. 7(1)–(4).

[151] Commission Regulation (EEC) 240/96 on the application of Art. 85(3) to certain categories of technology transfer agreements (1996) OJ L 31/2.

exemption[152] that took over covered all patent licences, know-how licences, and mixed patent and know-how licences to which there are only two parties.[153] As with its predecessors, the block exemption did not cover reciprocal licences, patent or know-how pools, and most licences between competing undertakings in the context of a joint venture.[154] In case other intellectual property rights were involved, the block exemption would only operate as long as these other intellectual property rights were ancillary.[155]

The technology transfer block exemption entered into force on 1 April 1996 and was to remain in force for a period of 10 years.[156]

The second and third technology transfer block exemptions

Five years into the life of the first technology transfer block exemption, the Commission published an evaluation report and the public debate that followed resulted in the early withdrawal of the first technology transfer block exemption. It was replaced, from 1 May 2004 onwards, by a new technology transfer block exemption.[157] That block exemption adopted a radically different format and moved away from the lists of permitted or non-permitted clauses, towards a more economics-based approach. It should also be noted that the individual exemption no longer has a place in the scheme. It had already been withdrawn one year earlier in the Modernization Regulation.[158] Having exhausted its 10-year term, the second technology transfer block exemption was replaced by the third technology block exemption on 1 May 2014.[159] The approach did, however, remain the same and there are only modest changes.

The third block exemption applies to technology transfer agreements, but the term 'agreement' is defined widely and includes decisions of an association of undertakings, along with concerted practices.[160] The concept of a technology transfer agreement that is used is also wider than ever before: the Regulation covers know-how, as well as IP rights such as patents, design rights, utility models, supplementary protection certificates, topographies of semiconductor products, software copyright, and plant breeders' certificates, either on their own or in combination with one another. Even assignments of patents, know-how, software copyright, or any of the other rights, or a combination thereof are included in the scope of application of the block exemption, in so far as a part of the risk of the economic exploitation of the technology remains with the assignor. This is, for example, the case when part of the sum payable to the assignor in consideration of the assignment is dependent on the turnover achieved by the assignee in exploiting the technology.[161]

Article 2 of the block exemption contains its main principle. Transfer of technology agreements are, in application of Treaty Art. 101(3), exempted from the application of Treaty Art. 101(1) in so far as any of their provisions fall within the scope of the latter Article. Clauses that relate to the purchase by the licensee of products are also exempted. One restriction is to be noted immediately: the exemption will only apply for as long as the intellectual property right in the licensed technology has not expired, lapsed, or been declared invalid. In the case of know-how, the exemption only applies for as long as the know-how remains secret,

---

[152] See A. Robertson, 'Technology Transfer Agreements: An Overview of How Regulation 240/96 Changes the Law' (1996) 3 ECLR 157; C. Kerse, 'Block Exemptions under Article 85(3): The Technology Transfer Regulation—Procedural Issues' (1996) 6 ECLR 331.

[153] Art. 1(1).   [154] Art. 5(1).   [155] Art. 5(1)(4).   [156] Art. 13.

[157] Commission Regulation (EC) 772/2004 on the application of Art. 81(3) to certain categories of technology transfer agreements (2004) OJ L 123/11.

[158] Regulation 1/2003 [2003] OJ L1/1. Undertakings are to conduct their own assessments.

[159] Commission Regulation (EU) 316/2014 on the application of Article 101(3) of the Treaty on the Functioning of the European Union to categories of technology transfer agreements [2014] OJ L93/17.

[160] Regulation 316/2014, Art. 1(1)(a).   [161] Regulation 316/2014, Art. 1(1)(b) and (c).

but the exemption will continue to apply for the duration of the agreement if the know-how becomes known as a result of an action by the licensee. The now-superseded second block exemption only exempted agreements between two undertakings—agreements between more than two undertakings fell outside the scope of the block exemption. This is no longer a restriction and the new block exemption also covers patent pools and similar agreements.

One of the main innovations that was retained in the new block exemption is the fact that the exemption provided for in its Art. 2 is linked to market share thresholds.[162] In this respect, a distinction needs to be made between competing and non-competing undertakings. Competing undertakings are undertakings that, in relation to the relevant technology or on the relevant product market, license out competing technologies that are regarded as interchangeable with, or substitutable for, the licensed technology by the licensees, or that are active on the relevant product and geographic markets in which the contract products are sold (or which might, realistically, be expected to undertake the necessary investment to enter that market). The relevant product market includes products that are regarded as interchangeable with, or substitutable for, the contract products by buyers.[163]

In case the undertakings that are party to the agreement are competing undertakings, the exemption will only apply on condition that their combined market share on the affected relevant technology and product market does not exceed 20 per cent.[164] In case the undertakings that are party to the agreement are *not* competing undertakings, the exemption will only apply on condition that the market share of each of the parties does not exceed 30 per cent in relation to the affected relevant technology and product market.[165]

The main problems with market shares are, on the one hand, the way in which they are to be calculated and, on the other, the fact that they vary—that is, that companies may meet the requirements set out in Art. 3 of the exemption at the conclusion of their agreement, but they may exceed the permitted market share levels at a later date.

The block exemption deals with these problems in Art. 8. The basis for the calculation of market shares will be market sales value data and only if these are not available can estimates based on other reliable market information be used. The data used will refer to the preceding calendar year. In case the market share goes above the 20 per cent threshold, the exemption will continue to apply for another two calendar years following that in which the 20 per cent threshold was first exceeded. In relation to the 30 per cent threshold, that extension will last for three calendar years.[166]

It is, however, self-evident that the market share mechanism is not sufficient to weed out any agreement that may seriously harm levels of competition. The block exemption therefore rules out its own application to agreements that have certain undesirable objects. Once more, a distinction is made between agreements between competing undertakings and agreements between non-competing undertakings.[167]

Let us deal with agreements between competing undertakings first. The exemption does not apply to agreements between competing undertakings that have either directly, or indirectly, in isolation from, or in combination with, other factors under the control of the parties, one of the following four goals as their object:

(a) the restriction of a party's ability to determine its prices when selling products to third parties;
(b) the limitation of output, except limitations on the output of contract products imposed on the licensee in a non-reciprocal agreement or imposed on only one of the licensees in a reciprocal agreement;

---

[162] Regulation 316/2014, Art. 2. [163] Regulation 316/2014, Art. 1(1)(n).
[164] Regulation 316/2014, Art. 3(1). [165] Regulation 3162014, Art. 3(2).
[166] Regulation 316/2014, Art. 8. [167] Regulation 316/2014, Art. 4.

(c) the allocation of markets or customers except:
  (i) the obligation on the licensor and/or the licensee, in a non-reciprocal agreement, not to produce with the licensed technology rights within the exclusive territory reserved for the other party and/or not to sell actively and/or passively into the exclusive territory or to the exclusive customer group reserved for the other party,
  (ii) the restriction, in a non-reciprocal agreement, of active sales by the licensee into the exclusive territory or to the exclusive customer group allocated by the licensor to another licensee provided the latter was not a competing undertaking of the licensor at the time of the conclusion of its own licence,
  (iii) the obligation on the licensee to produce the contract products only for its own use provided that the licensee is not restricted in selling the contract products actively and passively as spare parts for its own products,
  (iv) the obligation on the licensee, in a non-reciprocal agreement, to produce the contract products only for a particular customer, where the licence was granted in order to create an alternative source of supply for that customer;
(d) the restriction of the licensee's ability to exploit its own technology rights or the restriction of the ability of any of the parties to the agreement to carry out research and development, unless such latter restriction is indispensable to prevent the disclosure of the licensed know-how to third parties.[168]

We now turn to agreements between non-competing parties. The exemption does not apply to agreements between non-competing undertakings that have either directly, or indirectly, in isolation from, or in combination with, other factors under the control of the parties one of the following three goals as their object:[169]

(a) the restriction of a party's ability to determine its prices when selling products to third parties, without prejudice to the possibility of imposing a maximum sale price or recommending a sale price, provided that it does not amount to a fixed or minimum sale price as a result of pressure from, or incentives offered by, any of the parties;
(b) the restriction of the territory into which, or of the customers to whom, the licensee may passively sell the contract products, except:
  (i) the restriction of passive sales into an exclusive territory or to an exclusive customer group reserved for the licensor,
  (ii) the obligation to produce the contract products only for its own use provided that the licensee is not restricted in selling the contract products actively and passively as spare parts for its own products,
  (iii) the obligation to produce the contract products only for a particular customer, where the licence was granted in order to create an alternative source of supply for that customer,
  (iv) the restriction of sales to end-users by a licensee operating at the wholesale level of trade,
  (v) the restriction of sales to unauthorised distributors by the members of a selective distribution system;
(c) the restriction of active or passive sales to end-users by a licensee which is a member of a selective distribution system and which operates at the retail level, without prejudice to the possibility of prohibiting a member of the system from operating out of an unauthorised place of establishment.[170]

---

[168] Regulation 316/2014, Art. 4(1).   [169] Regulation 772/2004, Art. 4(2).
[170] Regulation 316/2014, Art. 4(2).

Finally, the rules for non-competing undertakings will continue to apply on this point for the life of the agreement if those undertakings become competing undertakings at a later stage, unless the agreement is amended in any material aspect.[171]

Up to now, we have dealt with restrictions that exclude an agreement altogether from the scope of the block exemption. Now we turn to restrictions that are, themselves, not covered by the exemption, but the presence of which does not take the whole agreement outside the scope of the block exemption. According to Art. 5 of the exemption, it does not apply to the following obligations in technology transfer agreements:

(a) any direct or indirect obligation on the licensee to grant an exclusive licence to the licensor or to a third party designated by the licensor in respect of its own severable improvements to or its own new applications of the licensed technology;

(b) any direct or indirect obligation on the licensee not to challenge the validity of intellectual property rights which the licensor holds in the Common Market, without prejudice to the possibility of providing for termination of the technology transfer agreement in the event that the licensee challenges the validity of one or more of the licensed intellectual property rights.[172]

In addition:

Where the undertakings party to the agreement are not competing undertakings, the exemption provided for in Article 2 shall not apply to any direct or indirect obligation limiting the licensee's ability to exploit its own technology or limiting the ability of any of the parties to the agreement to carry out research and development, unless such latter restriction is indispensable to prevent the disclosure of the licensed know-how to third parties.[173]

The block exemption contains two emergency measures to balance the increased flexibility it offers to undertakings. Indeed, the Commission, first, reserves for itself the right to withdraw any exemption granted under the terms of the block exemption if it thinks that an agreement nevertheless has, or has started to have, certain effects that are incompatible with the requirements of Art. 101(3) of the Treaty.[174] National competition authorities can do the same in respect of a member state, if the effects are limited to the market of that member state.[175]

The block exemption gives two examples of circumstances that may prompt a withdrawal of its benefit. These circumstances will arise if access of third parties' technologies to the market is restricted or if access of potential licensees to the market is restricted.[176]

Secondly, the Commission may declare, by regulation, that the block exemption does not apply to certain agreements if parallel networks of similar technology transfer agreements cover more than 50 per cent of a relevant market. Such a regulation will, at the earliest, come into force six months after being adopted.[177]

The second transfer of technology block exemption inaugurated this rather different approach, through which the Commission has attempted to address the concerns raised by those involved in the licensing business, while at the same time addressing its competition concerns. The fact that the third transfer of technology block exemption adopts the same approach and even brings in modest elements of further flexibility demonstrates that the approach is working in practice to the satisfaction of all parties concerned.

---

[171] Regulation 316/2014, Art. 4(3).   [172] Regulation 316/2014, Art. 5(1).
[173] Regulation 316/2014, Art. 5(2).   [174] Regulation 316/2014, Art. 6(1).
[175] Regulation 316/2014, Art. 6(2).   [176] Regulation 316/2014, Art. 6(1).
[177] Regulation 316/2014, Art. 7.

Article 102

Article 102 of the Treaty on the Functioning of the European Union (formerly Article 82 of the Treaty of Rome) prohibits the abuse of a dominant position. We will first examine what constitutes a dominant position for the purposes of the Treaty, but it would lead us too far to discuss all of the issues related to the technical application of Art. 102 in detail and we will need to restrict our comments to a couple of essential points.[178]

'Dominance', then, should not exist in an abstract way, but in the context of a market, and three aspects are important: a position needs to be dominant in the relevant product market, it needs to be dominant in the relevant geographical market, and the market is also restricted in time when considering the issue of dominance. The determination of the relevant product market raises issues such as the interchangeability and substitutability of products, while, in many cases, the relevant geographical and temporal markets are more obvious to determine. Once a dominant position has been established, Art. 102 requires that that dominant position be held in a substantial part of the Common Market.[179]

But dominance, as such, is not sufficient for the purposes of Art. 102, because there also needs to be an abuse of that dominant position. Article 102 does not contain an exhaustive list of what would amount to an 'abuse', but it offers as obvious examples the charging of unfair prices, the limiting of production, and discrimination. We will have to discuss the case law in detail to discover what may amount to an abuse of a dominant position in the context of intellectual property: while it is clear that monopoly rights, such as intellectual property rights, can lead to a dominant position, an abuse of a dominant position involves a certain action and a certain use of rights. It is therefore correct to assume that, as in relation to the free movement of goods, the existence of intellectual property rights as such cannot amount to an abuse of a dominant position[180] and neither can certain uses of these rights. We will have to focus our attention on what constitutes an abusive use or exercise of an intellectual property right.

As with the free movement of goods, the existence and the normal use of intellectual property rights will not be affected, because only the abusive use of intellectual property rights for a purpose that is unrelated to intellectual property—namely, the distortion of competition and the distortion of the free movement of goods—will be targeted by the Treaty provisions. In fact, many of these elements transpire already from one of the earliest intellectual property judgments of the European Court of Justice.

The Court indicated, for the first time, that Art. 102 could interfere with intellectual property rights in its *Parke, Davis* judgment of 1968,[181] when it ruled that the existence of the intellectual property rights granted by a member state is not affected by the prohibition contained in Art. 102 of the EC Treaty and that, in the absence of any abuse of a dominant position, the exercise of such rights cannot of itself fall under that Article:

> Although a patent confers on its holder a special protection within the framework of a State, it does not follow that the exercise of the rights so conferred implies the existence of the three elements mentioned (the existence of a dominant position on the single market or on a substantial part thereof, abuse of that dominant position and a negative effect on trade between

---

[178] For more details, see Whish and Bailey, *Competition Law* (n. 105) Ch. 5.

[179] Whish and Bailey, *Competition Law* (n. 105) Ch. 5.

[180] See Case 238/87, *Volvo (AB) v. Erik Veng (UK) Ltd* [1988] ECR 6211, [1989] 4 CMLR 122 at para. 8.

[181] Case 24/67, *Parke, Davis & Co.* (n. 68).

member states). It could only do so if the utilisation of the patent could degenerate into an improper exploitation of the protection.[182]

In this first case, the Court found that a higher sale price for the patented product, as compared with that of the unpatented product coming from another member state, does not necessarily constitute an abuse of a dominant position. The possibility of asking a higher price for the product as a result of the patent protection was seen as being the normal result of the existence of that patent protection and, even if—in this first case— no abuse of a dominant position was found, it opened the way for a series of other cases.

A last important preliminary point in relation to Art. 102 is that it will only apply if there is an effect on interstate trade.[183] The Court has held that this requirement will be satisfied if conduct brought about an alteration in the structure of competition in the Common Market.[184]

Article 102 applied to patents

So far, only one case[185]—and a rather peculiar case, at that—has arisen at the European level, when Tetra Pak, which occupies a dominant position in the market for cartons and machines for packaging milk, took over Liquipak. Liquipak had previously obtained an exclusive licence for technology that related to a new method of sterilizing cartons that were suitable for long-life milk and Tetra Pak gained access to that technology by taking over Liquipak. The Commission held that it was an abuse for Tetra Pak to take over this company and the exclusive licence. The Commission had particular difficulties in accepting that Tetra Pak held onto the licence and did not attempt to turn it into a non-exclusive licence.

On appeal, the decision was upheld by the Court of First Instance.[186] The abuse in this case seems to be situated in the reinforcement of an already dominant position and on the basis of the acquisition of an exclusive licence. It is submitted that a non-exclusive licence would not have had the same effect. It must also be remembered that this was a very extreme case, because Tetra Pak's position was an extremely dominant one and the supplementary exclusive licence concerning a new technology would prevent every new competitor from getting into the market. It would almost eliminate any competition on the relevant market. These extreme factors were clearly important for the Commission and the Court of First Instance in reaching their decision and judgment, respectively.[187]

As a result of the European Court of Justice's decision in the *Magill* case,[188] in relation to the area of copyright, a few English cases have been brought in which an attempt was made to apply the reasoning in *Magill* to the area of patent law.[189] It has been argued

---

[182] *Parke, Davis & Co.* (n. 68) at [1968] ECR 72; in relation to copyright, see Case 78/70, *Deutsche Grammophon GmbH v. Metro-SB-Grossmarkte GmbH & Co. KG* [1971] ECR 487, [1971] CMLR 631; in relation to trade marks, see Case 51/75, *EMI Records Ltd v. CBS United Kingdom Ltd* [1976] ECR 811, [1976] 2 CMLR 235.

[183] See Whish and Bailey, *Competition Law*, (n. 105) Chs. 3 and 4.

[184] Cases 6/73 and 7/73, *Instituto Chemioterapica Italiano SpA & Commercial Solvents Corp. v. EC Commission* [1974] ECR 223, [1974] 1 CMLR 309.

[185] *Tetra Pak I (BTG Licence) Decision* [1990] 4 CMLR 47, OJ L 272/27.

[186] Case T-51/89, *Tetra Pak Rausing v. EC Commission* [1990] ECR II-309, [1991] 4 CMLR 334.

[187] See now also the Commission's decision in Case COMP/A.37.507/F3, *Astra Zeneca* [2006] OJ L 332/24.

[188] Joined Cases C-241/91 P and C-242/91, *P Radio Telefis Éireann & Independent Television Publications Ltd v. EC Commission* [1995] ECR I-743, [1995] All ER (EC) 416; see Ch. 18 for a full analysis.

[189] *Philips Electronics NV v. Ingman Ltd & the Video Duplicating Co. Ltd* [1999] FSR 112; *Sandvik Aktiebolag v. K. R. Pfiffner (UK) Ltd* [2000] FSR 17.

in these cases that the exercise of a patent can amount to an abuse of a dominant position. The courts made it clear that *Magill* was an exceptional case and that exceptional features, such as those in *Magill*, will have to be demonstrated before the courts will be willing to refuse to assist in the enforcement of a patent on grounds of an abuse of dominant position.[190] The courts will therefore only in very exceptional circumstances—such as the abuse of the patent to reserve a secondary market for the patentee or to refuse to supply (certain) independent repairers—depart from the basic position that the patent, as such, does not amount to an abuse of a dominant position and that neither does the exercise by the patentee of his or her basic right to grant, or to refuse to grant, a licence.[191] Objectively, unreasonably high royalties, for example, did not amount to an abuse in this respect, because they were the mere equivalent of the exercise of the right to refuse to grant a licence.[192] And even in those cases in which an abuse was found, there needed to be a nexus between the alleged unlawfulness under Art. 102 and the relief that was claimed: for example, the grant of a compulsory licence in the case of an arbitrary refusal to supply repairers with spare parts.[193]

A special scenario arises when a patent gets adopted as a standard. A typical example is easily found in the mobile phone sector. All equipment needs to be 4G compatible, i.e. all involved will need to use the 4G-related patents that have become part of the 4G standard. Becoming part of a standard does make it highly likely that the owner of the patent will occupy a dominant position. Any potential licensee on the other hand now experiences a need to use the patented technology. Typically such a right holder will undertake to grant licences on a FRAND basis, i.e. on fair, reasonable, and non-discriminatory terms. Can a right holder still enforce the patent by way of injunctive relief if no licence is taken or would that in the circumstances amount to an abuse of a dominant position?

This conflict between, on the one hand, the right holder who needs access to injunctive relief to enforce his exclusive right and, on the other hand, the potential licensee and user of the technology who needs access to the technology came before the CJEU in the *Huawei* case. Huawei undertook to grant FRAND licences and ZTE used the patented technology. When licence negotiations led nowhere Huawei wanted to apply for an injunction. In this conclusion,[194] Advocate-General Wathelet tried to reconcile the various points of view in a creative way. On the one hand, he sees a weakened position of the patent owner due to the FRAND licence obligation. It is in his view therefore essential that the right holder retains in principle the right to seek injunctive relief and to exercise its fundamental right to have access to a court.[195] The potential licensee on the other hand needs to use the patent to be able to compete. It can therefore in the Advocate-General's view make a start with the use of the patent and only later on seek a licence.[196] The speed and complexity of the telecoms market reinforce that point in this particular case. It is then up to the right holder to alert the potential licensee to the alleged infringement (unless it is clear that the potential infringer is fully aware of the patent and of the

[190] In a UK context, see *Sandisk v. Philips Electronics* [2007] I L Pr 22.

[191] See also Case 238/87, *AB Volvo v. Erik Veng* (n. 221); Case 53/87, *Consorzio Italiano della Componentistica di Ricambio per Autoveicoli & Maxicar v. Régie nationale des Usines Renault* [1988] ECR 6039, [1990] 4 CMLR 265.

[192] *Philips Electronics NV v. Ingman Ltd & the Video Duplicating Co. Ltd* [1999] FSR 112; see also Case 238/87, *AB Volvo v. Erik Veng* (n. 180).

[193] *Sandvik Aktiebolag v. K R Pfiffner (UK) Ltd* [2000] FSR 17, applying *Philips Electronics NV v. Ingman Ltd & the Video Duplicating Co. Ltd* [1999] FSR 112.

[194] Conclusion of Advocate-General Wathelet in Case C-170/13, *Huawei v. ZTE*, EU:C:2014:2391.

[195] A-G Wathelet in *Huawei v. ZTE* (n. 194) at para. 77.

[196] A-G Wathelet in *Huawei v. ZTE* (n. 194) at para. 82.

fact that its activity is infringing) and to make an offer to take a licence. That offer has to include all conditions of the proposed licence.[197] The potential licensee is not obliged to accept the proposal, but it is under an obligation to reply to it in a detailed and serious way and to make a counterproposal. Only a reply that is merely aimed at delaying matters and that is not serious would avoid the conclusion that at this stage the seeking of injunctive relief amounts to an abuse of a dominant position.[198]

If no negotiations are started or if they are not completed successfully, the potential licensee can ask the court or an arbitral tribunal to establish FRAND conditions, but the right holder can then ask for a bank warrantee to cover the ongoing alleged infringement.[199] The potential licensee also retains the right to apply for the invalidity of the patent at a later stage or to argue later that the patent is not essential for the standard.[200] The right holder on the other hand can seek access to the books of the potential licensee without abusing its dominant position.[201] And it can institute a claim for damages with regard to infringing activities that have already been carried out, once again without this amounting to an abuse of its dominant position.[202]

What emerges is an approach that attempts to facilitate the conclusion of a FRAND licence and that reserves the right to seek injunctive relief in those cases where the infringement is blatant, i.e. the alleged infringer is aware of the matter and makes no attempt to seek a licence, or where no serious attempt has been made to agree a FRAND licence.[203] Determining when the latter situation has arisen may well prove to be the Achilles heel of this approach. Be that as it may the CJEU's judgment is less detailed than the conclusion of its Advocate-General, although the Court endorses the approach.[204]

An overview

Patent law operates a 'first to file' system and the presumption is that the person filing the application is entitled to the patent. Section 7 of the UK Patents Act 1977 nevertheless brings the inventor into the picture as the person who is logically entitled to the patent. There is also room for contractual transactions in this area.

A key problem is the ownership issue between employer and employee. Section 39 determines when inventions made in the course of duty will belong to the employer. This can depend on the inventive activity falling with the normal duties of, or duties specifically assigned to, the employee or on the employee having a special duty to further the interest of the employer's undertaking. In practice, this section gives rise to complex evaluations. Employees may also be granted compensation for inventions owned by the employer in exceptional circumstances.

The importance of that section goes far beyond the specific issue of the grant of, and dealing in, patents. That there is an inherent contradiction between the EU's ideals of free

---

[197] A-G Wathelet in *Huawei v. ZTE* (n. 194) at paras. 84–85.
[198] A-G Wathelet in *Huawei v. ZTE* (n. 194) at para. 88.
[199] A-G Wathelet in *Huawei v. ZTE* (n. 194) at paras. 93 and 98.
[200] A-G Wathelet in *Huawei v. ZTE* (n. 194) at paras. 94 and 96.
[201] A-G Wathelet in *Huawei v. ZTE* (n. 194) at para. 101.
[202] A-G Wathelet in *Huawei v. ZTE* (n. 194) at para 102.
[203] A-G Wathelet in *Huawei v. ZTE* (n. 194) at para. 103. The approach relies, in the view of the A-G, more on the *Volvo v. Veng* (n. 180) and *Renault v. Maxicar* (n. 191) cases than on the *Magill* case (n. 188). The latter is based on a somewhat different factual scenario in his view.
[204] Case C-170/13, *Huawei Technologies Co Ltd v. ZTE Corp and ZTE Deutschland GmbH*, judgment of 16 July 2015, <http://curia.europa.eu>.

trade and free competition, and intellectual property law's blasé creation of monopoly rights is self-evident, but much of the potential force of the clash between these two fundamental principles is tempered by the (inevitable) compromise position adopted. Legitimate use of property rights for their true purpose is condoned and appropriate exemptions are given to reflect this.

The general approach is well embodied in this area of patent law, whereby a patent will be upheld unless its use is for unjustifiable purposes, as shown by such cases as *Centrafarm*. Equally, its exclusive licensing—potentially likely to fall foul of anti-trust rules—will be permitted by the sensibly pragmatic block exemption approach.

If nothing else, all of this shows that, in the context of what is intended to be a free, single market, the fact that such concessions are made in favour of intellectual property rights confirms that they are of fundamental economic importance to the effective functioning of a modern capitalist economy.

Further reading

ANDERMAN, S. (1998) *EC Competition Law and Intellectual Property Rights: The Regulation of Innovation*, Oxford: Oxford University Press.

GHIDINI, G. (2006) *Intellectual Property and Competition Law: The Innovation Nexus*, Cheltenham/Northampton, MA: Edward Elgar.

MILLER, R. et al. (eds.) (2011) *Terrell on the Law of Patents*, 17th edn, London: Sweet and Maxwell, Chs. 16–17.

MORRIS, P. S., 'Patent Licensing and No-Challenge Clauses: A Thin Line between Article 81 EC Treaty and the New Technology Transfer Block Exemption Regulation' (2009) 2 IPQ 217.

PILA, J., '"Sewing the Fly Buttons on the Statute": Employee Inventions and the Employment Context' (2012) 32 OJL 265.

TORREMANS, P. and STAMATOUDI, I., '*Merck* is Back to Stay: The Court of Justice's Judgment in *Merck v. Primecrown*' (1997) 9 EIPR 545.

TORREMANS, P. and STAMATOUDI, I., '*Merck v. Stephar* Survives the Test' (1997) 22 EL Rev 248.

6

Infringement and revocation

In the context of the use of the patent the exclusive right granted by the patent becomes a tool to stop others from making the patented product, and so on. Enforcing the right means stopping alleged infringement.

As will already have been apparent from discussion of many of the leading cases on patentability, the topics of infringement and revocation are inextricably interlinked. The standard counter-attack of an alleged infringer is to question the validity of the patent itself and to seek its revocation, while the initiation of a revocation claim may well be an attempt to clear an inconvenient patent out of the way, thus avoiding any threat of claims of infringement. In either event, the action will focus sharply on what has been actually claimed for the invention by the patentee in his or her specification and claims. It will be recalled that the specification must, under s. 14(3) of the UK Patents Act 1977, disclose the invention sufficiently that it enables the person skilled in the art to make the invention him- or herself, while s. 14(5) insists that the claims clearly and concisely define the subject matter of the patent. Consideration of these documents lies at the heart of all infringement and revocation disputes. It is logical to proceed first to consider revocation, because, if no patent exists, it makes little sense to discuss an infringement of it.

Revocation

The grounds on which a patent may be revoked are clearly established by s. 72 of the 1977 Act. Any person may bring an application for the revocation of a patent; his or her motives and whether or not he or she is bringing the application at the instigation of another are irrelevant.[1] No additional requirements are imposed on this point by the Act.

The only grounds for revocation now permitted are:

(a) the invention is not a patentable invention;

(b) that the patent was granted to a person who was not entitled to be granted that patent;

(c) the specification of the patent does not disclose the invention clearly enough and completely enough for it to be performed by a person skilled in the art;

(d) the matter disclosed in the specification of the patent extends beyond that disclosed in the application for the patent, as filed, or, if the patent was granted on a new application filed under ss 8(3), 12, or 37(4) above or as mentioned in s 15(9) above, in the earlier application, as filed;

(e) the protection conferred by the patent has been extended by an amendment which should not have been allowed.[2]

---

[1] *In the Matter of an Application by Edward Evans Barker for Revocation of UK Patent No. 2314392 in the Name of Oystertec plc; sub nom. Oystertec plc v. Edward Evans Barker* [2003] RPC 559.

[2] Patents Act 1977, s. 72(1).

This is a shorter list than in earlier legislation; former objections on grounds of inutility, inadequate description, failure to claim clearly, falsity, or illegality, which were permitted grounds for revocation under the 1949 Act,[3] are no longer so, at least as such.

Patentability and entitlement

These first two of the grounds for revocation under the 1977 Act are straightforward; many of the cases that we have already considered on patentability[4] and on patent rights have arisen in the context of revocation. One of the problems that may arise if it is argued that a patent is invalid and should be revoked for reasons of obviousness is that this happens at a later date and that in the meanwhile post-dated evidence may have become available. Such post-dated evidence may not be relied upon to contradict a technical effect that was made plausible by the specification or to establish a technical effect that was not made plausible by the specification. Post-date evidence can only be relied upon to confirm that the disclosure in the patent either does or does not make it plausible that the invention solves a technical problem. The plausibility question as such remains focused at the grant stage.[5]

Insufficiency

The third ground, however, raises issues that relate directly to the wording of the specification itself and to s. 14(3) of the Act, and poses a further burden on the patent applicant trying to resolve the perpetual dilemma of how much or how little to disclose in the application. Under s. 72(1)(c), there is now the added risk that, if insufficient disclosure occurs, the threat of revocation will loom.[6] Note that it is only the specification and its shortcomings that give rise to this threat; there is no comparable provision to ensure the clarity of the claims made for an invention. Insufficiency is therefore a serious risk to a patent applicant who is naturally inclined to disclose as little as possible, making the issue of sufficiency a key issue in many patent cases, especially as a counter-attack argument in many infringement cases.[7]

This requirement begs several questions, not least what degree of detail is, in fact, going to be necessary. Obviously, this will ultimately depend on the facts of each case, but some guidance is given by *No-Fume Ltd v. Frank Pitchford & Co. Ltd*.[8] The subject of this dispute was an ashtray designed to retain the smoke inside itself. Romer LJ, in the Court of Appeal, upheld the validity of the patent, even though the application—in describing the various features of the ashtray—failed to indicate the size and relative proportions of the various parts of the ashtray. He stated that it was not necessary that the specification had all the detail in it that might be expected in the detailed specification

---

[3] Patents Act 1949, s. 32(1).

[4] E.g. patents were revoked on grounds of obviousness in *Rocky Mountain Traders Ltd v. Hewlett Packard GmbH, Westcoast Ltd & Fellowes Manufacturing (UK) Ltd* [2000] FSR 411 (confirmed on appeal on 20 December 2000, unreported); *Minnesota Mining & Manufacturing Co. v. ATI Atlas Ltd & North American Science Associates Inc.* [2001] FSR 31; *Pfizer Ltd's Patent* [2001] FSR 202.

[5] *Generics (UK) Ltd (t/a Mylan) v. Yeda Research & Development Co. Ltd and Teva Pharmaceutical Industries Ltd* [2012] EWHC 1848 (Pat).

[6] For a useful summary of the law, see *Sandvik Intellectual Property AB v. Kennametal UK Ltd* [2011] EWHC 3311 (Pat), [2012] RPC 23, per Arnold J.

[7] See e.g. *Kirin-Amgen Inc. v. Transkaryotic Therapies Inc.* [2003] RPC 31 (CA), [2005] 1 All ER 667, [2005] RPC 9 (HL).

[8] (1935) 52 RPC 231.

given to a workman in order to make such an item; rather it was sufficient if the workman could reach the desired result through a combination of the information in the specification and the common knowledge of his or her trade, using trial and error if necessary to achieve the desired result.[9] The disclosure has therefore (only) to be sufficiently clear for the invention to be carried out by the skilled person over the whole area claimed without undue burden and without needing inventive skill. In essence the question is: 'can you make it?'[10]

The next question to be faced is that of the character of the notional person skilled in the art. Once again, the law has to try and put some flesh on the dry bones of this artificial character. The leading case in this context is *Valensi v. British Radio Corp.*,[11] a case concerned with the invention of colour television. On the one hand, the Court of Appeal summarized the character of the hypothetical addressee as '*not a person of exceptional skill and knowledge ... not to be expected to exercise any invention nor any prolonged research, inquiry or experiment*'.[12] On the other hand, that person must:

> be prepared to display a reasonable degree of skill and common knowledge in making trials and to correct *obvious* errors in the specification if a means of correcting them can readily be found.[13]

Applying these principles to the case, the problem was that the difficulties faced by the pioneers of colour television were highly technical and it was accepted that an ordinary shop-floor workman was not the appropriate model to consider. Equally, however, the specialist researchers in the field, who the trial judge had used as his model, were also inappropriate. Rather, between the two models were the skilled technicians, who were knowledgeable in their own right, but who would equally be reliant on the guidance provided by the specification, and they were the best model to use in considering the question of insufficiency of the information in the specification.

That the *Valensi* test remains good law under the 1977 Act is not in doubt: this has been confirmed by *Mentor Corp. v. Hollister Inc.*,[14] a decision of the Court of Appeal concerning a patent for a male incontinence device. The Court took note of the European Patent Convention (EPC) Rules,[15] which, by r. 27, state that the description '*shall disclose the invention, as claimed, in such terms that the technical problem ... and its solution can be understood*'. Lloyd LJ considered that it was reasonable to expect the addressee to perform routine trials in using the specification to follow and perform the invention, and, in the light of that, the specification disclosed sufficiently the manner of manufacture and should not therefore be revoked.[16]

Put simply, the specification should be looked at to see what it teaches the *Valensi* type of reasonable man, who can be expected to carry out at the very least routine trials of this character. In doing so, the specification should be looked at as of the date of the patent application to avoid any risk of hindsight and it should be kept in mind that the skilled man is seeking success, rather than failure. The skilled man with a positive mind is also concerned with practicalities, rather than with any legal puzzles thrown up by

---

[9] (1935) 52 RPC 231 at 243 and 245.
[10] *Novartis v. Johnson & Johnson* [2010] EWCA Civ 1039 at para. 74 and *Eli Lilly v. Human Genome Sciences* [2012] EWCA Civ 1185.
[11] [1972] FSR 273, [1973] RPC 337.
[12] [1972] FSR 273 at 311. Confirmed by the Court of Appeal in *Mentor Corp. v. Hollister Inc.* [1993] RPC 7.
[13] [1973] RPC 337 at 377.   [14] [1993] RPC 7.
[15] See <http://www.european-patent-office.org/legal/epc/e/r27.html>.
[16] [1993] RPC 7 at 14. See also *Mölnlycke AB v. Procter & Gamble Ltd (No. 5)* [1992] FSR 549 at 594–602.

lawyers.[17] As the Technical Board of Appeal of the European Patent Office (EPO) put it, the requirements of sufficiency of disclosure will be satisfied only if the invention can be performed by a person skilled in the art using common general knowledge and having regard to further information given in the patent.[18]

While the skilled person can put in some work on the back of his or her common knowledge, and engage in trial-and-error experimentation, the amount of work to be put in cannot be unreasonable in the circumstances. The skilled person will try to make the invention work. Insufficiency will therefore not follow if, for example, the skilled person realizes that one method would work and another would fail if the claim is broad enough to include both methods;[19] he cannot, however, engage in inventive activity to fill gaps in the common general knowledge that he possesses, augmented by the information given in the patent.[20] Despite all of this, the question of whether or not the specification was sufficient remains highly sensitive to the nature of the invention. It is therefore important to identify the invention in a first stage and to decide what it claims to enable the skilled man to do. That simplifies the further question of whether the specification enables the skilled man to do that.[21]

One helpful aspect of the current law is that the applicant does not have to put in his or her specification the best possible method of carrying out the invention. This was necessary prior to the 1977 Act; the removal of this requirement aids the inventor by enabling him or her to keep secret the best method and thus retain an additional advantage over rivals, unless and until, of course, they derive the best method themselves, in which case the tables of advantage are turned.

Up to this point the discussion has been concerned with what could be called classical insufficiency, i.e. a failure to enable the invention to be performed without undue burden, in its most common format based on a lack of information. In *Kirin-Amgen* the House of Lords made it clear that there is a second form of classical insufficiency that is based on ambiguity. Such ambiguity goes beyond a mere lack of clarity and makes it impossible for the skilled person to perform the invention as one cannot determine what falls inside the claim or not. Lord Hoffmann explained it as follows:

> The claim appeared to assume that all uEPOs had effectively the same molecular weight, irrespective of source and method of isolation. This had been shown not to be the case. So which uEPO did the claim require to be used for the test? Simply to use the first uEPO which came to hand would turn the claim into a lottery. On the other hand, it would be burdensome to have to work one's way through several specimens of uEPO (which were, as I mentioned at the beginning of my speech, extremely hard to come by) and even then the result would be inconclusive because *non constat* that some untried specimen did not have a different molecular weight.
>
> The judge decided that the lack of clarity made the specification insufficient. It did not merely throw up the possibility of doubtful cases but made it impossible to determine in any case whether the product fell within the claim. The invention was not disclosed 'clearly enough and completely enough for it to be performed by a person skilled in the art': s. 72(1)(c).
>
> ... If the claim says that you must use an acid, and there is nothing in the specification or context to tell you which acid, and the invention will work with some acids but not with others but finding out which ones work will need extensive experiments, then that in my

[17] *Kirin-Amgen Inc. v. Transkaryotic Therapies Inc.* (n. 7), applying *British Thomson-Houston Co. Ltd v. Corona Lamp Works Ltd* (1922) 39 RPC 49 (HL).

[18] Case T-1121/03, *Union Carbide/Indicator Ligands* [2006] EPOR 49.

[19] *Kirin-Amgen Inc. v. Transkaryotic Therapies Inc.* [2005] 1 All ER 667, [2005] RPC 9 (HL).

[20] *Halliburton Energy Services Inc. v. Smith International (North Sea) Ltd* (2007) 30 (2) IPD 30009 (CA).

[21] *Biogen v. Medeva* [1997] RPC 1 (HL).

opinion is not merely lack of clarity; it is insufficiency. The lack of clarity does not merely create a fuzzy boundary between that which will work and that which will not. It makes it impossible to work the invention at all until one has found out what ingredient is needed.[22]

The courts now regularly use the following summary of the relevant principles:

The specification must disclose the invention clearly and completely enough for it to be performed by a person skilled in the art. The key elements of this requirement which bear on the present case are these:

(i)   the first step is to identify the invention and that is to be done by reading and construing the claims;

(ii) in the case of a product claim that means making or otherwise obtaining the product;

(iii) in the case of a process claim, it means working the process;

(iv) sufficiency of the disclosure must be assessed on the basis of the specification as a whole including the description and the claims;

(v)   the disclosure is aimed at the skilled person who may use his common general knowledge to supplement the information contained in the specification;

(vi) the specification must be sufficient to allow the invention to be performed over the whole scope of the claim;

(vii) the specification must be sufficient to allow the invention to be so performed without undue burden.[23]

The specification must enable the invention to be performed and this requirement covers not just a single embodiment. *Biogen v. Medeva*[24] teaches that the specification must enable the invention to be performed to the full extent of the monopoly claimed.[25] This is a second form of insufficiency, often called Biogen insufficiency or excessive claim breadth. In this sense, there is a complete parallelism between s. 14(3), which requires the specification of an application to disclose the invention in a manner that is clear and complete enough for the invention to be performed by the skilled man, and the requirements for sufficiency in s. 72(1)(c). But that parallelism does not extend to the requirement in s. 14(5) that the claims be clear and concise, and supported by the description. The latter requirements are no ground for a finding of insufficiency or for revocation on any other basis. In practice, then, it might be hard to establish infringement of unclear claims, but there is no link with revocation. Returning to *Biogen*, it is clear that this case deals with a different version of insufficiency from classical insufficiency.[26] Insufficiency can also be based on excessive claim breadth. Arnold J recently offered the following summary of the position in *Biogen*:

(i)   A claim will be invalid for insufficiency if the breadth of the claim exceeds the technical contribution to the art made by the invention. It follows that it is not necessarily enough to disclose one way of performing the invention in the specification.

(ii) The breadth of the claim will exceed the technical contribution if the claim covers ways of achieving the desired result which owe nothing to the patent or any principle it discloses. Two classes of this are where the patent claims results which it does

---

[22] *Kirin-Amgen Inc. v. Hoechst Marion Roussel Ltd* [2004] UKHL 46, [2005] RPC 9, 536–7 at paras. 124–6.

[23] *Eli Lilly v. Human Genome System* [2008] EWHC 1903 (Pat) (quoted with approval on appeal); see *Idenix v. Gilead and others* [2014] EWHC 3916 (Pat), at 463 and *Generics (trading as Mylan) v. Warner-Lambert and Actavis Group v. Warner-Lambert* [2015] EWHC 2548 (Pat) at 339.

[24] [1997] RPC 1 (HL), per Lord Hoffmann.

[25] For a clear example of a case concerning extended wear contact lenses where insufficiency turned out to be an issue, see *Novartis and Cibavision v. Johnson & Johnson Medical and Johnson & Johnson Vision Care* [2009] EWHC 1671 (Ch, 10 July 2009).

[26] See *MedImmune Ltd v. Novartis Pharmaceuticals UK Ltd* [2011] EWHC 1669 (Pat) at paras. 459–84.

not enable, such as making a wider class of products when it enables only one and discloses no principle to enable the others to be made, and where the patent claims every way of achieving a result when it enables only one way and it is possible to en-visage other ways of achieving that result which make no use of the invention.

(iii) The patent in *Biogen v. Medeva* was invalid because it was an example of the second class of objectionable claim.[27]

The scope of such an approach is potentially very wide and may catch many claims. Particularly claims to principles of general application may run into difficulty. Lord Hoffmann clarified the approach to these principles of general application in *Kirin-Amgen*:

In my opinion there is nothing difficult or mysterious about [the notion of a principle of gen-eral application]. It simply means an element of the claim which is stated in general terms. Such a claim is sufficiently enabled if one can reasonably expect the invention to work with anything which falls within the general term. For example, in Genentech I/Polypeptide ex-pression (T 292/85) [1989] O.J. EPO 275, the patentee claimed in general terms a plasmid suitable for transforming a bacterial host which included an expression control sequence to enable the expression of exogenous DNA as a recoverable polypeptide. The patentee had obviously not tried the invention on every plasmid, every bacterial host or every sequence of exogenous DNA. But the Technical Board of Appeal found that the invention was fully enabled because it could reasonably be expected to work with any of them.

This is an example of an invention of striking breadth and originality. But the notion of a 'principle of general application' applies to any element of the claim, however humble, which is stated in general terms. A reference to a requirement of 'connecting means' is enabled if the invention can reasonably be expected to work with any means of connection. The patentee does not have to have experimented with all of them.[28]

Generics v. Lundbeck offered an opportunity to clarify the approach for cases where the facts are somewhat different.[29] Arnold J summarized the House of Lord's additional teaching in that case as follows:

(i) The House agreed with Lord Hoffmann in *Biogen v Medeva* ...

(ii) The House considered that the instant case was to be distinguished from *Biogen v Medeva* because it was concerned with a claim to a single chemical compound whereas *Biogen v Medeva* concerned a product-byprocess claim of broad scope.

(iii) It was a mistake to equate the technical contribution of the claim with its inventive con-cept. In the instant case, the technical contribution made by claims 1 and 3 was the product, and not the process by which it was made, even though the inventive step lay in finding a way to make the product. It followed that the breadth of the claim did not exceed the technical contribution which the invention made to the art.[30]

And from a practical point of view this means:

100. It must therefore be possible to make a reasonable prediction the invention will work with substantially everything falling within the scope of the claim or, put another way, the assertion that the invention will work across the scope of the claim must be plausible or credible. The products and methods within the claim are then tied together by a unifying characteristic or a common principle. If it is possible to make such a prediction then it cannot

---

[27] *Sandvik Intellectual Property AB v. Kennametal UK Ltd* (n. 6) at para. 122.

[28] *Kirin-Amgen Inc. v. Hoechst Marion Roussel Ltd* (n. 22) at paras. 112–13. See *Regeneron Pharmaceuticals Inc. and Bayer Pharma AG v. Genentech Inc.* [2012] EWHC 657 (Pat) at para. 155.

[29] *Generics (UK) Ltd v. H. Lundbeck A/S* [2009] UKHL 12, [2009] RPC 13.

[30] *Sandvik Intellectual Property AB v. Kennametal UK Ltd* (n. 6) at para. 124.

be said the claim is insufficient simply because the patentee has not demonstrated the invention works in every case.

101. On the other hand, if it is not possible to make such a prediction or if it is shown the prediction is wrong and the invention does not work with substantially all the products or methods falling within the scope of the claim then the scope of the monopoly will exceed the technical contribution the patentee has made to the art and the claim will be insufficient. It may also be invalid for obviousness, there being no invention in simply providing a class of products or methods which have no technically useful properties or purpose.[31]

Grounds for invalidity that relate to the EPC and the role of the EPO

The final two grounds for revocation in s. 72 can be dealt with speedily and were new to the law in 1977, corresponding as they do to EPC provisions.[32] They ensure that no new matter is unfairly added to broaden the scope of the patent, as is forbidden by s. 76 of the 1977 Act, by allowing revocation if such addition has occurred. This upholds the importance of the application date as the starting point of all rights in relation to patents.

Section 76, taken on its own, establishes the broad principle that amendments should not include added matter. 'Added matter' is to be understood as matter extending beyond the matter disclosed in the original application or the original patent. One might, for example, extract a feature that was not remarked upon in the specification and which was not of significance to the person skilled in the art of one of the preferred embodiments of the invention, and insert it in a claim by way of amendment.[33] But to do so will fall foul of s. 76—especially if one then also ignores the other features of the embodiment.[34] Added matter is not necessarily added in bad faith. It often occurs unintentionally when claims are rewritten during the examination process, i.e. after the filing of the application but before the granting of the patent. Care is needed to avoid this risk, as the sanction is particularly severe.[35]

The EPO has set a standard for added matter. A patent may only be amended within the limits of what a skilled person would derive directly and unambiguously, using common general knowledge and seen objectively and relative to the date of filing, from the whole of the documents as filed.[36] That led the English courts to set out the following test for added matter:

> 'I think the test for added matter is whether a skilled man would, upon looking at the amended specification, learn anything about the invention which he could not learn from the unamended specification.'[37]

---

[31] *Regeneron Pharmaceuticals Inc v. Genentech Inc* [2013] EWCA Civ 93, per LJ Kitchin; see *Idenix v. Gilead* (n. 23) at 466 and *Generics (trading as Mylan) v. Warner-Lambert* (n. 23) at 341.

[32] EPC, Arts. 100(c) and 138(1)(c).

[33] Even when amending by means of a disclaimer that excludes certain areas one needs to be careful. If subject matter remains that was not explicitly or implicitly disclosed in the application as filed, added matter will remain and revocation will follow. G 2/10 EPO Enlarged Board of Appeal, <http://www.epo.org/law-practice/case-law-appeals/recent/g100002ex1.html>.

[34] *L. G. Philips LCD Co. Ltd v. Tatung (UK) Ltd* [2007] RPC 21; *Palmaz v. Boston Scientific BV* [1999] RPC 47.

[35] For an example, see *Wagner International AG v. Eralex Ltd* [2012] EWHC 984 (Pat).

[36] G 2/10 EPO Enlarged Board of Appeal, <http://www.epo.org/law-practice/case-law-appeals/recent/g100002ex1.html>, approved in *Wagner International AG* (n. 35) at para. 32, with further reference to *Abbott Laboratories Limited v. Medinol Limited* [2010] EWHC 2865 (Pat) at paras. 251–3.

[37] *Richardson-Vicks' Patent* [1995] RPC 568, at 576; see also *Nokia v. IPCom* [2012] EWCA Civ 567 and *Teva UK Ltd and TEVA Pharmaceutical Industries Ltd v. Leo Pharma A/S and Leo Laboratories Ltd* [2015] EWCA Civ 779.

A European patent is, in the nine months after its grant, also subject to opposition proceedings in the EPO. This affects the European patent for each member state in relation to which it was granted and, if the opposition is successful, the outcome is similar to the revocation of the European patent. After grant, national proceedings can be brought, because, in each country in relation to which it was granted, the European patent becomes the equivalent of a national patent. It is therefore possible that national infringement or invalidity proceedings may be brought while the opposition proceedings are still pending.

This is what happened in *Unilin Beheer BV v. Berry Floor NV and ors*.[38] The English courts had held the patent to be valid and infringed; at the same time, the opposition proceedings were still pending in the EPO. The English court then held that it could not award a stay in the proceedings concerning damages until the opposition proceedings were completed, because the matter was *res judicata* and the defendants would be estopped from challenging the claimant's entitlement if the patent were to be revoked by the EPO.

Infringement

Patents Act 1977, s. 60—the principle

We now turn to the heart of the matter in considering the grounds for, and the general approach to, the issue of infringement. Section 60 of the 1977 Act is the key provision and unusually makes separate, although not dissimilar, provisions for patents that are for products and those that are for processes.

Section 60(1) states that the following actions are infringements if they occur without the permission of the patentee:

(a) where the invention is a product, he makes, disposes of, offers to dispose of, uses or imports the product or keeps it whether for disposal or otherwise;

(b) where the invention is a process, he uses the process or he offers it for use in the United Kingdom when he knows, or it is obvious to a reasonable person in the circumstances, that its use there without the consent of the proprietor would be an infringement of the patent;

(c) where the invention is a process, he disposes of, offers to dispose of, uses or imports any product obtained directly by means of that process or keeps any such product whether for disposal or otherwise.

Under s. 60(2), it is also an infringement if unauthorized disclosure takes place of an essential element of the invention such that the recipient of that disclosure will be able to put the invention into effect. This applies to all inventions, whether products or processes, but does not apply to the supply of a staple commercial product unless it is supplied with a view to inducing an infringement under the section.[39] These provisions relate to what is commonly described as 'indirect infringement'—that is, when the act of infringement consists of enabling another to infringe. Section 60(2) therefore stipulates that:

a person ... also infringes a patent for an invention if ... he supplies or offers to supply[40] in the United Kingdom a person other than a licensee or other person entitled to work the invention with any of the means, relating to an essential element of the invention, for putting

---

[38] [2007] FSR 25 (CA).   [39] Patents Act 1977, s. 60(3).

[40] The offer must be made in the UK, to supply in the UK. *Fabio Perini SpA v. LPC Group plc and ors* [2009] EWHC 1929 (Pat). See also *Fabio Perini SpA v. LPC Group plc and ors* [2012] EWHC 911(Ch) at para. 20.

the invention into effect when he knows, or it is obvious to a reasonable person in the circumstances, that those means are suitable for putting, and are intended to put, the invention into effect in the United Kingdom.

It is clear that s. 60 covers a very wide range of activities in relation to a patented product or process. Activity before, during, or after the unauthorized manufacture of a patented item can count as infringement, and actions as diverse as importing and disposing of an item will both fall within the definition. The most significant gap in the law is that it only applies to actions within the UK and thus a sale that takes place abroad of an infringing item does not fall within the provisions—and even an offer made within the jurisdiction to dispose of an item outside of it does not fall within s. 60.[41]

An action will lie under what are likely to be similar rules in that other jurisdiction, of course, because the subsections under consideration equate to EPC, Arts. 29 and 30. But the impact of the provision becomes clear in a case in which the product is made lawfully abroad and title to the goods is transferred abroad. The manufacturer does not, in that case, infringe the patent even if it arranges the contract of carriage on behalf of the buyer: that does not amount to importation into the jurisdiction.[42] In more general terms, s. 60(2) is concerned with the means to implement the invention in the UK, such as the apparatus needed to put the invention into effect in the UK. In *Menashe Business Mercantile Ltd v. William Hill Organisation Ltd*,[43] the Court of Appeal held that a patent for a gaming system was therefore infringed through the use of a computer program supplied by the defendant on CD-ROM, which turned its customers' computers into terminals in the defendant's system despite the fact that the host computer in the latter system was located outside the UK. The input and output of the host computer was essential, but the supply of the CD-ROM and of access in the UK amounted to use in the UK.

A further, and sensible, gap in liability arises from a decision that is of assistance to those who find themselves at risk of liability under these broad provisions while acting in all innocence. In *Smith Kline and French Laboratories Ltd v. R. D. Harbottle (Mercantile) Ltd*,[44] the first defendants sought to export the drug cimetidine from Italy to Nigeria. The consignment was routed via London and, while it was in storage in a British Airways cargo warehouse, became the subject of a patent infringement claim by the plaintiffs, to which the airline were joined as 'keepers' of the offending consignment. Oliver J found in favour of the airline.[45] In his view, it was appropriate to consider Art. 29 of the Community Patent Convention, which speaks of '*making, offering, putting on the market, or using*' a product, and, in the light of that, it was clearly some form of positive action that was envisaged as amounting to an infringement; the passive warehousing or transporting of an item does not count as positive action in relation to the item. Clearly, the commercial implications of any other decision would have been significant and adverse.

Section 60(1)(c) gives rise to problems in terms of proof. How does one demonstrate that where the invention is a process the product that one encounters is obtained by means of that process, rather than by an alternative process? Section 100 provides a solution and introduces a rebuttable presumption that such a new product produced by a person other than the patentee or its licensee shall be taken to have been obtained by the process. For a product to be new for the purpose of s. 100 it is sufficient to demonstrate

[41] *Kalman v. PCL Packaging* [1982] FSR 406.

[42] *Sabaf SpA v. MFI Furniture Centres Ltd* [2003] RPC 14 (CA), (2004) 148 SJLB 1217 (HL).

[43] [2003] 1 All ER 279, [2003] 1 WLR 1462, affirming the first-instance decision reported at [2002] RPC 950 on different grounds.

[44] [1980] RPC 363.   [45] [1980] RPC 363 at 373.

that it is novel in the sense that is has not been made available to the public before. It would go too far to require that the new product could have been the subject of a product claim in the patent.[46]

Section 60(2)

Section 60(2) creates a statutory tort. Its main features are that the tort is actionable (1) even though what was supplied was capable of perfectly lawful, non-infringing use; (2) even though what was supplied never had been and might never in fact be used in a way directly infringing the patent in suit; (3) without any damage being suffered by the patentee; and (4) at the moment of supply, irrespective of anything that might or might not occur afterwards. Direct infringement does not actually need to take place for s. 60(2) to apply. Offering to sell an essential means is therefore an infringement even if at the time of the offer one does not have any particular end user in mind. Even though a patented machine worked with rubber rollers, the supply of a machine with steel rollers constituted the 'means, relating to an essential element of the invention, for putting the invention into effect' and amounted to infringement under s. 60(2). There is no limitation to parts of a machine only. The machine with steel rollers was designed and indeed promoted to enable the steel rollers to be changed for rubber rollers. It was therefore plainly the supply of the means by which that could be achieved, and was the supply of a means essential for that purpose. The fact that a steel-rollered machine, so long as it remains steel-rollered, did not infringe and was capable of lawful use as a complete machine in that state was irrelevant. Section 60(2) is intended to apply to, among other things, products which were perfectly capable of being used in a manner which would not constitute a direct infringement within s. 60(1).[47]

Section 60(2) therefore has a very wide potential scope and the requirements as to suitability and knowledge of intended use are brought in to limit the scope of the statutory provision. In terms of knowledge the supplier needs to know that the means are intended to put the invention into effect. That intention needs to be present in the head of the person who is being supplied with the means. But it can be someone who is only indirectly supplied with the means, i.e. the person at the end of the supply chain. It is not necessary for there to be an actual, already formed, intention in the user. It is sufficient for a finding of infringement if the supplier knows (or it is obvious in the circumstances) at the time of the offer to supply or supply that some ultimate users (disregarding freak use) will intend to use, adapt, or alter the 'means essential' so as to infringe. It is sufficient if it is shown that the invention will be put into effect by some users. That has to be established on a balance of probabilities. It is more accurate to state the test in terms of what probably will be intended and what probably will be the use to which the means will be put. In the light of the publicity accompanying the steel-rollered machine it was established that some end users would replace the steel rollers by rubber rollers.[48]

The knowledge and intention requirements of s. 60(2) are satisfied if, at the time of supply or offer of supply, the supplier knows, or it is obvious in the circumstances, that ultimate users will intend to put the invention into effect. Mere suitability of the means for putting the intention into effect is not enough, but the requirements are likely to be

---

[46] *Magnesium Elektron Ltd v. Molycorp Chemicals & Oxides (Europe) Ltd and Zibo Jia Hua Advanced Materials Co Ltd* [2015] EWHC 3596 (Pat) at para.31.

[47] *Grimme Landmaschinenfabrik GmbH & Co. KG v. Scott (t/a Scotts Potato Machinery)* [2010] EWCA Civ 1110, [2011] FSR 7.

[48] *Grimme Landmaschinenfabrik* (n. 47).

established where the supplier proposes or recommends or even indicates the possibility of such use in his promotional material, as in the steel/rubber-rollers case.[49]

This interpretation of s. 60(2) stays very wide and the Court of Appeal applied it even to a case where a medical pump was supplied without the clamping system of the patented original. The court argued that some users would use a clamping device with the alternative pump and that the manufacturer ought to have been aware of the fact that this was likely to happen.[50]

Defences

The courts generally seem to take a generous view of legitimate activity, even though there is no general defence of innocence. A useful pre-Act case, which would appear to be consistent with the statutory approach, is *Solar Thomson Engineering Co. Ltd v. Barton*.[51] In this case, the plaintiffs sold a conveyor system, the pulleys of which were the subjects of a patent. After some years of use, the pulleys began to wear out and the defendants repaired them by replacing a vital part with one of their own manufacture—although, of course, because it was part of a broader system, it had to be identical to the design of the plaintiffs. It was held by the Court of Appeal that it was quite in order to carry out repairs to an item without this infringing any relevant patents, as long as the work of repair could not be said to amount to the manufacture of a new item.

The House of Lords has now confirmed this approach in *United Wire v. Screen Repair Services*,[52] in which it was held that the notions of repair and of making are mutually exclusive for the purposes of the 1977 Act. Repair can therefore not amount to an infringement, because s. 60 requires the making of the patented item. There is also no need to confer an implied licence on the repairer, because he or she is free to do whatever is not covered by the concept of making the product. Whether or not one makes the product is a matter of judgement, fact, and degree according to the Supreme Court.[53]

The provisions relating to indirect infringement are not, however, without their problems. The essential concept of 'essential element' goes undefined and is bound, at some stage, to give rise to difficulties in litigation. The exception for the supply of a staple commercial product is also shrouded in uncertainty, at least to UK and European lawyers, but appears to protect the innocent seller of a common product that has obvious non-infringing uses. If A supplies water to B, for example, this may enable B to infringe C's water-powered invention, but it would clearly be unfair to burden A with any liability in the absence of any knowledge of the offending use.

There are also statutory defences provided by the 1977 Act in s. 60(5), under which acts that would otherwise count as infringements do not do so if they are done privately for non-commercial purposes. This points to the patent as an item of industrial property: it is only protected in the field of commercial exploitation. Also outside the scope of the infringement provisions are acts done by others for experimental purposes relating to the

---

[49] *Grimme Landmaschinenfabrik* (n. 47).

[50] *KCI Licensing Inc. v. Smith & Nephew plc* [2010] EWCA Civ 1260, [2011] FSR 8.

[51] [1977] RPC 537.

[52] *United Wire Ltd v. Screen Repair Services (Scotland) Ltd* [2001] RPC 439, [2001] FSR 24, [2000] 4 All ER 353.

[53] The Court of Appeal also excluded an additional 'whole invention concept' test (i.e. no infringement as long as the whole inventive concept is left untouched even if product is made) in *Schütz (UK) Ltd v. Werit UK Ltd* [2011] EWCA Civ 303, [2011] FSR 19, 515 at para. 69, but was overruled by the Supreme Court in *Schütz (UK) Ltd v. Werit (UK) Ltd* [2013] UKSC 16 at para. 78.

invention.[54] This is also significant in giving others trading in the same field the right to carry out experiments using the public information made available via the Patent Office as a result of the application procedure, thus ensuring the high likelihood of a further patent race hotting up as the patentee's 20-year period of protection draws to a close.

One case in particular has had to consider the experimental purposes defence. In *Monsanto Co. v. Stauffer Chemical Co.*,[55] the plaintiffs owned the patent for a herbicide and claimed infringement by the defendants, who had carried out some trials of their allegedly infringing product with a view to obtaining official product safety clearances. It was held by the Court of Appeal that experiments permitted by the Act were only those carried out for scientific purposes: for example, to test a hypothesis or to discover something unknown about the subject matter of the invention.[56] The tests in question, however, were of a very different kind and tests that were carried out for commercial, rather than scientific, purposes would not be exempt from the threat of an infringement action.

Section 60(5) contains in its paragraph (i) a narrow Bolar exemption for the testing of generic medicines alongside the experimental use exemption. The Legislative Reform (Patents) Order 2014[57] introduced a broad Bolar exemption in the following terms:

> For the purposes of subsection (5)(b), anything done in or for the purposes of a medicinal product assessment which would otherwise constitute an infringement of a patent for an invention is to be regarded as done for experimental purposes relating to the subject-matter of the invention.

But rather remarkably, it did not attach that to paragraph (i), but to the experimental use exemption in paragraph (b).

Other defences also arise from s. 60(5) and can be recorded briefly. The extemporaneous preparation in a pharmacy of a medicine under the terms of a prescription is outside s. 60; this is again directed to what, in fact, would be likely to be an innocent infringement. Also outside s. 60 are various uses of patented equipment in ships, aircraft, and even hovercraft, temporarily or accidentally in UK waters or airspace. The Court of Appeal held that, in those cases, the term 'temporarily' should be construed as 'transient', or 'for a limited period of time'.[58] The frequency with which such vessels or aircraft entered UK territorial waters or airspace was not relevant in this respect; neither was the regular and repeated nature of such presence. For example, an Irish registered ferry that made three to four trips a day and spent about three to four hours in UK territorial waters on each trip was only entering these territorial waters 'temporarily'.[59]

A more significant exception relates to prior use—that is, to use of a product or process without patent protection by A and the impact upon it of a grant of a patent for such a product or process to B. It may seem harsh to penalize A in this example by making his or her acts into infringements of B's later patent if he or she continues with his preexisting use. Section 64 of the 1977 Act deals with this type of situation by allowing the prior user to continue that use after the grant of a patent to another without it being an infringement, as long as the user is in good faith. The problem will only arise in cases in which the prior use was secret; if it were not, the later actions would not be novel and thus not patentable. The relatively rare instances in which the section is thus likely to be

---

[54] See T. Cook, 'Responding to Concerns about the Scope of the Defence from Patent Infringement for Acts Done for Experimental Purposes Relating to the Subject Matter of the Invention' (2006) 3 IPQ 193–222.

[55] [1985] RPC 515.   [56] [1985] RPC 515, per Dillon LJ at 542.   [57] SI 2014/1997.

[58] *Stena Rederi AB v. Irish Ferries Ltd* [2003] RPC 37 (CA) at 676.

[59] *Stena Rederi AB* (n. 58) at 676.

invoked mean that it may be some time before the courts have an opportunity to sort out the obvious problem that it creates—namely, whether the later act, to be permitted to continue, has to be exactly, or merely substantially, identical to the prior user. Given the steady evolution likely to occur in the history of the development of a product or process, to permit only exact replication would deprive s. 64 of much of its already limited value.

Procedural elements

The right to take action against an infringer is, under s. 66, conferred on any one among a group of joint proprietors, although the others must be joined to the action. As has been seen already, s. 67 gives exclusive licensees (but no other licensee) the right to take action against infringers, thus contributing to the popularity of this type of licence.

The legislation also sets out the remedies available to anyone who has rights against an infringer. Section 61 confers an exciting choice of any, or all, of an injunction, an order to deliver up infringing items, damages, an account of profits (these two are alternatives), and a declaration. It should be noted that both account of profits and delivery up are equitable remedies, and thus, by definition, discretionary in their approach.

The choice between account of profits and damages, meanwhile, is not easy. It is clearly good news for the claimant that he or she is entitled to ask for an account of all the profits and not only that proportion which is due to infringement,[60] but, equally, it is a laborious process to prove the profit actually engendered by one product that may be among many produced by a large firm.[61] Seeking damages seems simpler, but, in a competitive trading environment, precise assessment of the loss caused to the claimant by the infringement, rather than by any other of a myriad of factors, may also prove troublesome. By s. 62, damages and account of profits are not available as against an infringer who can prove that they were, and should have been, unaware of the existence of the relevant patent at the time of the infringing act. Damages in these cases are generally on a royalty basis: the question is what royalties or licensing fees would have been earned by a lawful licensing of the patent? Patent infringement actions have a reputation for being long and costly, and the breadth of the different activities that can amount to an infringement means that trade in a product even threatened with an infringement action is likely to be suspended for the often considerable period of time that lapses while the litigation takes its course. In a legitimate case, this is acceptable, but a more cynical trader may recognize the disruptive effect of launching an infringement action against a rival and do so simply to achieve that effect. Section 70 of the 1977 Act does, however, provide protection against this possibility. The section creates a right for anyone aggrieved to take to court anyone who threatens an action against either the applicant or anyone else for infringement of a patent. Letters claiming infringement and demanding payment under threat of legal proceedings sent to the alleged infringer, as well as letters sent to potential customers of the latter, are covered, but a letter to a customer informing him or her that proceedings in another jurisdiction have effectively been brought does not equal a threat.[62] A declaration, injunction, or damages may be granted unless the defendant can establish that the threats are justifiable. This protection does not, however, extend to a threat of bringing proceedings for an infringement in the form of making or importing a product for

---

[60] *Peter Pan Manufacturing Corp. v. Corsets Silhouette Ltd* [1963] 3 All ER 402, [1964] 1 WLR 96 (a breach of confidence case).

[61] See *Gerber Garment Technology Inc. v. Lectra Systems Ltd* [1997] RPC 443, noted by S. Moss and D. Rogers, 'Damages for Loss of Profits in Intellectual Property Litigation' (1997) 8 EIPR 425.

[62] *Cintec International Ltd v. Parkes and anor* (2004) 27(2) IPD 27011.

disposal or of using a process.[63] This is a valuable provision and it is prudent for the claimant in an infringement action to bear it in mind before proceeding too far. The law has recognized the adverse effect of even the threat of an infringement action on a wide range of business dealings.

Procedural difficulties can also arise if the allegedly infringed patent is a process patent. All the right holder may have access to is the product that results from the use of the process. Proving the use of the process is then not easy. The legislator comes to the rescue in s. 100(1) of the Patents Act 1977:

> If the invention for which a patent is granted is a process for obtaining a new product, the same product produced by a person other than the proprietor of the patent or a licensee of his shall, unless the contrary is proved, be taken in any proceedings to have been obtained by that process.

What is a new product though? One should not require the product to pass the novelty test for patentability, as that would make the provision largely inapplicable in most cases. It is sufficient that the product that results from the process has not been made available to the public before. That makes it logical to think that the same product produced by a third party must have involved use of the new and patented process. It is then acceptable to shift the burden of proof, i.e. that a different process has been used, to the alleged infringer.[64]

Overall, the statutory provisions on infringement appear, for the most part, to be straightforward and workable, which may make somewhat surprising the assertion that such proceedings may well be long and complex. The problem is that the statute somehow seems to assume that it will be easy to look at the patent and see what it covers, and then place that alongside the allegedly infringing act and make a comparison. Section 125 of the 1977 Act makes clear that the definition of the invention is that which is:

> specified in a claim of the specification or the application, as the case may be, as interpreted by the description and any drawings contained in that specification, and the extent of the protection conferred by a patent or application of a patent shall be construed accordingly.

It tells us, then, in a moderately clear way, what the court should be looking at in deciding what the invention is for the purpose of an infringement action; it still does not tell us, though, *how* it should be looked at—and here a clash arises between the scientist and the lawyer. The scientist may be caricatured as a bluff, commonsensical character, who is skilled in his trade and who will use his expertise to discern the inventive notion. The lawyer, however, may be caricatured as a wordsmith, rather than a blacksmith, who will use his interpretative skills—or pedantic ones, if preferred—to understand the words that define the inventive notion. Whether the specification should be read with the scientist's purposive outlook or the lawyer's literal one has been the subject of a major battle in recent years, which the scientists have won with, as will be seen, more than a little assistance from their European friends.

The Court of Appeal has summarized the position by arguing that the invention of a patent is to be taken to be that specified in the claims.[65] These claims have to be interpreted with the aid of the description and, in doing so, the court should adopt a middle way between literal construction and taking the claims as mere guidelines.

---

[63] Patents Act 1977, s. 70(4). See *Bowden Controls Ltd v. Acco Cable Controls Ltd* [1990] RPC 427.

[64] *Magnesium Elektron Ltd* (n. 46) at paras. 30–31.

[65] *BASF AG v. Smithkline Beecham plc* [2003] All ER (D) 327, [2003] RPC 49 (CA).

Interpretation of specifications and claims

The historical background

It should be made clear at the outset that the first part of this section describes the law as what it was and not as it is now. It is, however, valuable, for the purposes of contrasting the old and new positions, to start with the earlier approach and a good starting point is *C. Van der Lely NV v. Bamfords Ltd.*[66]

In this case, the House of Lords was faced with a claim against the patentee of a hay rake seeking revocation of that patent, with a cross-claim by the patentee alleging infringement by the claimant. The key part of the litigation centred on a claim that one of the rows of wheels on which the patented hay rake was driven could be removed for different aspects of the haymaker's art. The claim specifically referred to the removal of the hindmost wheels, while the allegedly infringing device for the same reason removed wheels, but removed the front ones instead. At this time, courts claimed to study the 'pith and marrow' of the invention to see what the true inventive step was, but the decision of the House of Lords shows the ambiguity of this phrase. It may be thought to involve a purposive type of enquiry, but this was not so. Speaking as one of the majority of the Law Lords who found that there was no infringement, Lord Jenkins stated that the patentee had deliberately claimed only the hindmost wheels and that this left it open for the rivals to arrange their wheels in any other way, even though the two machines were both achieving the same result by using the same principle.[67] Viscount Radcliffe, too, said that the words used delimit what the applicant has claimed.[68] Lord Reid dissented on the issue, however, taking the view that the precise wheels involved were not essential integers of the invention and that there was therefore no infringement.[69]

Then, in *Rodi & Wienenberger AG v. Henri Showell Ltd,*[70] the issue returned to the House of Lords. This time, the issue related to expandable watch straps and, in particular, the connections between the bands in them. The patented straps were linked together by U-shaped connecting bows; the allegedly infringing straps used C-shaped bows instead. Notwithstanding the obvious point that a 'U' shape and a 'C' shape are not exactly dissimilar, the House of Lords found, once again, that there was no infringement here. Even adopting the essential integers approach, the majority found that those were defined in the terms of the words of the specification and claim, and that therefore the 'U' shape defined itself, in effect, as an essential integer. Lord Reid, this time, was joined by Lord Pearce in dissent, seeking to look at the self-evidently similar way in which the two shapes functioned.[71]

Inexorably, at the pace of a constipated tortoise, the House of Lords inched away from the hardest of hard-line literal approaches to patent specifications. In *Beecham Group Ltd v. Bristol Laboratories Ltd,*[72] Beechams had patent rights in a type of penicillin called ampicillin, while Bristol was importing into the UK hetacillin, which was similar, but not identical to ampicillin. It was derived from it and, once in the bloodstream, it reacted with water and became ampicillin, and thus worked as an antibiotic in precisely the same way. The House of Lords found that this was an infringement by applying the 'pith and marrow' test in the broader way that we have suggested the phrase properly implies. Lord Diplock accepted that, on the most literal approach, the two products were different, but that, in their actual use, they worked in precisely the same way. The variation, he said, was '*evanescent and reversible*' and the actual use in hetacillin was a use of ampicillin.[73]

---

[66] [1963] RPC 61.   [67] [1963] RPC 61 at 80.   [68] [1963] RPC 61 at 78.
[69] [1963] RPC 61 at 71.   [70] [1969] RPC 367, [1968] FSR 100.
[71] [1968] FSR 100 at 102 and 115, respectively   [72] [1978] RPC 153.
[73] [1978] RPC 153 at 202.

The EPC and the Protocol on the interpretation of Article 69

This welcome outbreak of common sense is perhaps better seen as a surrender to the inevitable, because, while the *Beecham* case was being argued in the Lords, Parliament was considering the new Patents Act—and that legislation, with its tie-in to the EPC, betokened a very different approach. The way in which this arises is as follows.

We have already seen that s. 125 of the 1977 Act provides that the documents at the heart of the application procedure define the invention and that s. 125(3) goes on to say that the Protocol on the Interpretation of Article 69 of the EPC should apply to the interpretation of that section of the domestic legislation. Turning, then, to Art. 69 itself, we find that it says simply that the extent of protection given by a European patent shall be determined by '*the claims*'.[74] This seems to advance us little until we find that the Protocol to it states as follows:

> Article 69 should not be interpreted in the sense that the extent of the protection conferred by a European patent is to be understood as that defined by the strict, literal meaning of the wording used in the claims, the description and drawings being employed only for the purpose of resolving an ambiguity found in the claims. Neither should it be interpreted in the sense that the claims serve only as guideline and that the actual protection conferred may extend to what, from a consideration of the description and drawings by a person skilled in the art, the patentee has contemplated. On the contrary, it is to be interpreted as defining a position between these extremes which combines a fair protection for the patentee with a reasonable degree of certainty for third parties.[75]

The background to the Protocol merits some explanation. In harmonizing any law—let alone an area of law as complex as that of patent law—compromises have to be reached and the Protocol is that compromise. It sets out two extremes of interpretation—the mindless literalism, typified by cases such as *Rodi & Wienenberger*, and the 'broad guideline' approach, which could be taken to typify the practice at this time in Germany and elsewhere—and requires a court to eschew them both, and instead to seek a compromise that balances protection for the patentee's interest in preserving a broad monopoly and regard for the need for others—subsequent inventors, users, and other infringers—to know where they stand in a way that, for all its other faults, the literal approach does allow them.

It is important to emphasize the significance of this change. The old UK literal approach gave a narrow protection to the patentee, particularly if he or she was cautious in his or her claims (a caution encouraged by the need to ensure that all of the claims made for a patent are justified during the application procedure). By moving, as we clearly are, towards a looser approach with broader methods of interpretation in use, we are moving towards greater protection for the patentee. Equally, more risk of infringement is placed on others who are now to be offered only a 'reasonable degree of certainty', as opposed to the utter—if, at times, unpalatable—certainty of the former literal approach.

Catnic—the principle of purposive interpretation in the UK

The problem with all of this, however, is that the Protocol is keener to tell us what *not* to do than what *to* do in interpreting patents. Thus it fell to the House of Lords to consider, yet again, the appropriate approach to interpretation in the new era of patent law and

---

[74] This is the wording put in place by the revised version of the EPC (dated 29 November 2000), whereas the original version used the words '*by the terms of the claims*'. No substantive change was intended and the change was seen simply as a matter of clarifying the language used even further.

[75] Art. 1 of the Protocol.

the opportunity to do so arose in *Catnic Components Ltd v. Hill & Smith Ltd.*[76] It must be emphasized that this was a case under the 1949 Act and that no express mention is made of the 1977 Act, the EPC, or of the Protocol. But it would be naive to see the developments in *Catnic* as solely the continuing evolution of the UK approach to the issue.[77] The *Catnic* approach represents the first UK answer to the conundrum posed by the Protocol to Art. 69 and it provides an answer that, it is suggested, is entirely compatible with European approaches.

The facts of *Catnic* were simple enough. The plaintiffs had a patent for a type of steel lintel (a load-bearing beam), which specified in its wording that the rear side of the lintel should be vertical. The defendants produced a similar lintel, but—presumably in the hope of avoiding an infringement action—made the rear side of their lintel at an angle of 6° from the vertical, which reduced its load-bearing powers by 0.6 per cent. Did this minor variation avoid the infringement danger?

Lord Diplock gave the sole substantive judgment.[78] He found that there was an infringement on the facts. The key passage makes clear that it is the purposive approach of the scientists and Europeans that should take precedence over the old approach of the common lawyers, because the patent specification is aimed at other workers in the field:

> My Lords, a patent specification is a unilateral statement by the patentee, in words of his own choosing, addressed to those likely to have a practical interest in the subject matter of his invention (ie 'skilled in the art'), by which he informs them of what he claims to be the essential features of the new product or process for which the letters patent grant him a monopoly. It is those novel features only that he claims to be essential that constitute the so-called 'pith and marrow' of the claim. A patent specification should be given a purposive construction rather than a purely literal one derived from applying to it the kind of meticulous verbal analysis in which lawyers are too often tempted by their training to indulge. The question in each case is: whether persons with practical knowledge and experience of the kind of work in which the invention was intended to be used, would understand that strict compliance with a particular descriptive word or phrase appearing in a claim was intended by the patentee to be an essential requirement of the invention so that any variant would fall outside the monopoly claimed, even though it could have no material effect upon the way the invention worked.[79]

This being the test, it then becomes very easy to conclude that no lintel manufacturer could be imagined to have thought that the vertical rear side was, in literal terms, essential, because this would enable anyone else to use the idea of the patent, but, by varying it by a degree or two, avoid an infringement action with impunity. Why bother with a patent if that were so? Of course, such arguments will depend very much on the facts of each case. It is easy to imagine a patent in which the description of something as being vertical is of great importance: for example, in some form of new guillotine, in relation to which a much cleaner cut would be best achieved by a precisely vertical drop.

It is important to put the new purposive test of interpretation derived from *Catnic* in its context. Although new to patent infringement in the UK, purposive methods of interpretation are becoming more and more important; this is because the European influence of the law is also becoming more and more important, both in patents and

---

[76] [1982] RPC 183.

[77] W. R. Cornish and M. Vitoria, 'Catnic in the House of Lords: A New Approach to Infringement' [1981] JBL 136. Cf. Jacob J, 'The Herchel Smith Lecture 1993' (1993) 9 EIPR 312.

[78] *Catnic Components Ltd v. Hill & Smith Ltd* [1982] RPC 183 at 239.

[79] [1982] RPC 183 at 244. See also *Improver Corp. v. Remington Consumer Products Ltd* [1990] FSR 181, per Hoffmann J at 190.

elsewhere. To a Continental lawyer, purposive or teleological approaches to interpretation are the norm. Within the context of the EU, the European Court of Justice takes such a course in its approach to the legal rules of the Union, prefaced as they are by extensive preambles spelling out the purposes for which the legislation is being passed.[80]

Of course, we do not suggest that the *Catnic* test is, of itself, perfect: it will still leave some inevitable uncertainty. The volume of litigation and the different approaches taken by the courts in the years since *Catnic* speak eloquently about the difficulties facing common lawyers let loose on Continental approaches to statutory interpretation. These cases will be considered shortly, but, if we look at *Catnic* in its own terms, significant changes clearly have occurred to pre-existing case law. *Rodi & Wienenberger* would surely now be decided the other way, in accordance with the approach of the dissenting minority, but *Van der Lely* poses a problem. On the one hand, the removal of either set of wheels served the same purpose and this factor suggests a different decision post-*Catnic*; on the other hand, however, it is surely going further than *Catnic* to move from saying 'vertical equals almost vertical' to saying 'back means front'. The logic of *Catnic* does, however, suggest that, in cases in which, in terms of purpose, it is immaterial whether it is the back or front wheels that are removable, 'back' means nothing at all and might thus be ignored.

The struggle to put *Catnic* into practice

Further discussion of the impact and importance of *Catnic* is best postponed, to be resumed in the light of the development and application of the law since that decision. A key moment in its acceptance and use came quickly in *Codex Corp. v. Racal-Milgo Ltd*.[81] In this case, the Court of Appeal was faced with a patent relating to a method of high-speed data transmission through a modem. The alleged infringement was by a system of broadly the same type, but which was much faster and more complex in its operation. The court adopted the *Catnic* approach without reservation and consigned previous case law to the outer darkness. It was at pains to point out, however, that the *Catnic* approach was not as radical a change as some had argued, emphasizing that the investigation is not of the principle of the patent itself, but of the purposive construction of the relevant documents.[82] This must be right: Art. 69, it will be recalled, talks of the 'terms of the claim'.

In the light of this, the Court of Appeal was able to identify three key features in the patented system—namely, that it took in a particular sequence of signals, identified that sequence, and signalled that information onwards. Although each of these aspects was carried out in subtly different ways in the other system, the same key features were present, carrying out the same sort of functions, and thus there was an infringement.

It is not our intention to look at every case decided on the subject—but the acceptance of the *Catnic* approach meant that, as one would expect, minor variations were now no longer enough to save a later product or process from being an infringing one. So an improved method of loading skips into lorries was still an infringement, because it used the same basic idea as the earlier patent,[83] while a dental pin made out of two parts that were put together for use, but which could be separated with difficulty, infringed an

---

[80] See, inter alia, L. Neville Brown and T. Kennedy (1994) *The Court of Justice of the European Communities*, 4th edn, London: Sweet and Maxwell, Ch. 14, esp. pp. 311–14 and cases cited therein.

[81] [1983] RPC 369.   [82] [1983] RPC 369 at 381.

[83] *Société Nouvelle des Bennes Saphem v. Edbro Ltd* [1983] RPC 345.

earlier patent for a dental pin made in one piece, given that both pins operated in exactly the same way.[84]

Two important post-*Catnic* cases show that the law could function well, finding that there was an infringement where the old law would not. In *A. C. Edwards Ltd v. Acme Signs & Displays Ltd*,[85] the Court of Appeal had to consider the familiar digital price display panels that are typically found outside petrol stations, which work by providing seven lines that make up a rectangular figure eight, but which, by masking one or more of the lines, can make up any figure, as prices fluctuate. It is obviously important that the masked lines stay masked, and this is where conflict arose between the plaintiffs' patented product and the defendants' allegedly infringing one. The plaintiffs used springs to hold the lines in their required position, while the defendants employed a flexible piece of plastic for the same task. It was held that this did infringe: the essential idea of the use of a flexible piece of apparatus to hold lines in place was the same in both products and whether this was done by a spring, as in the patent specification, or by a piece of the plastic that, though not a spring, acted in the same way as one was immaterial. The use of the word 'spring' by the plaintiff was not a use of any particular significance.

In *Minnesota Mining & Manufacturing Co. v. Rennicks (UK) Ltd*,[86] the dispute was in connection with reflective sheeting of the kind used in road signs. The patented product was stated to have particularly effective adhesion between its different layers of plastic materials by reason of the layers having undergone a process of curing. The allegedly infringing product also claimed increased adhesion and achieved this by a different method of curing. Again, this was found to amount to an infringement, because the different methods of curing did not disguise the fact that the essential elements of the two methods were the same.[87]

The cases so far considered exemplify well what the *Catnic* approach is intended to achieve. The more flexible approach that it embodies and which is demanded by the EPC means that it will be easier for patentees to secure protection against later infringers, thus increasing the value of their patents; the infringer, in turn, will not be able to rely on purely literal interpretations of the specification and claims to disguise the fact that he or she has stolen the essential idea at the heart of the patented invention. The two cases just described show precisely this pattern—but, unfortunately, they do not represent an invariable approach and some more restrictive decisions need to be considered. It is therefore important to consider a second group of such cases, to see whether the courts are using *Catnic* properly or whether they are slipping back into older, and more literal, methods of construction.

In *Harrison v. Project & Design Co. (Redcar) Ltd*,[88] the dispute was between a private individual who devised a chair lift to enable his invalid wife to get upstairs, which he subsequently patented, and the defendants, a commercial firm that, after dealings with Harrison, began to make its own chair lifts. The case ultimately hinged on whether earlier proceedings were *res judicata*, but there was discussion of infringement too. The main difference between the two lifts was that the plaintiff used a weight to balance the progress of the chair lift and ensure the smooth running of the chain mechanism, while the defendants had abandoned this approach at an early stage and used an additional length of chain in place of the weight primarily as a safety device. The Court of Appeal found that this did not infringe: this was a different method of achieving the same overall purpose and, given that the plaintiff had specified the use of a weight and the defendants'

---

[84] *Fairfax (Dental Equipment) Ltd v. S. J. Filhol Ltd* [1986] RPC 499.   [85] [1992] RPC 131.
[86] [1992] RPC 331.   [87] [1992] RPC 331, per Aldous J at 346.   [88] [1987] RPC 151.

chain did not operate as a weight, there was no clash between them. This seems sensible: in purely functional or purposive terms, there was a significant difference and no problem arises from the case.

Improver and what became the Protocol questions

More problematic, perhaps, is the decision of Hoffmann J in *Improver Corp. v. Remington Consumer Products Ltd.*[89] The plaintiffs had a European patent for an electronic hair-removing device known as the 'Epilady'. The defendants had placed on the market a similar device called 'Smooth & Silky'. The principal difference between them was that the plaintiffs' device plucked hairs from the skin by capturing the hairs in a high-speed rotating arc-shaped spring, while that of the defendants employed a high-speed rotating arc-shaped synthetic rubber rod with slits cut in it to capture the hairs.

Hoffmann J summarized the *Catnic* approach in clear terms:[90]

> The proper approach to the interpretation of English patents registered under the Patents Act 1949 was explained by Lord Diplock in *Catnic Components Ltd v. Hill & Smith Ltd*. The language should be given a 'purposive' and not necessarily a literal construction. If the issue was whether a feature embodied in an alleged infringement which fell outside the primary, literal or a contextual meaning of a descriptive word or phrase in the claim ('a variant') was nevertheless within its language as properly interpreted, the court should ask itself the following three questions:
>
> (1) Does the variant have a material effect upon the way the invention works? If yes, the variant is outside the claim.[91] If no—
> (2) Would this (i.e. that the variant had no material effect) have been obvious at the date of publication of the patent to a reader skilled in the art. If no, the variant is outside the claim. If yes—
> (3) Would the reader skilled in the art nevertheless have understood from the language of the claim that the patentee intended that strict compliance with the primary meaning was an essential requirement of the invention. If yes, the variant is outside the claim.

> On the other hand, a negative answer to the last question would lead to the conclusion that the patentee was intending the word or phrase to have not a literal but a figurative meaning (the figure being a form of synecdoche or metonymy) denoting a class of things which included the variant and the literal meaning, the latter being perhaps the most perfect, best-known or striking example of the class.

Applying these criteria, the judge found that the variant had no material effect on the way in which the invention worked and that to adopt a rubber rod was obvious to the notional skilled man.[92] On the vital third question, however, he found that the claim, in specifically referring to a helical spring, could not be interpreted so broadly as to extend to a rubber rod, which presented many different problems and on which the plaintiff had done no work.[93]

Certainly, this promotes the actual words of the patent to a high level. The fact that the patent only used the helical spring, with no alternatives, was also regarded as significant in adding to the impression that the skilled reader would not think of going beyond it. Given that both products employed a high-speed rotating arc-shaped object with gaps in the outer edge, it may be thought that the defendants had hijacked the basic inventive

[89] [1990] FSR 181.   [90] [1990] FSR 181 at 189.
[91] For an example, see *Rohm & Haas Co. v. Collag Ltd* [2001] FSR 28.
[92] [1990] FSR 181 at 192.   [93] [1990] FSR 181 at 197.

concept and that the demand of the Protocol to Art. 69 for a balance to be achieved between fair protection for the patentee and reasonable certainty for third parties had not been met, with undue respect still being paid to the form of the words used.

What is more worrying is that parallel litigation in Germany came to the opposite conclusion. Hoffmann J described and referred to this in his judgment,[94] and took consolation from the fact that, at an earlier stage of the litigation there, a view similar to his own had been taken. This is frankly shoddy: in this case, we see a European patent that is designed to provide Europe-wide protection and yet two courts in different states come to opposite conclusions. The German court found no reason to ask the third question asked by Hoffmann J, because the way in which the device functioned was clear and its implications obvious in suggesting that any kind of arc-shaped slitted part would achieve the same result.

The question is, then, do we need to ask the third question? It is tentatively suggested that the outcome of the *Improver* case suggests that we should not. The defendants' 'Smooth & Silky' was designed by an engineer whose wife claimed that her 'Epilady' hurt her, and he directly adapted the 'Epilady' design to give fewer slits and thus less pain. He thus altered one minor aspect of the 'Epilady' in such a way that would make it unlikely that he could gain patent protection for himself, it being an obvious variation. Yet, by focusing on the words used by the patentee, the *Improver* decision allows an admitted adoption of the patented product with an obvious variant to go unpunished. If this is the effect of the third question, it is suggested it is a bad effect—and thus a bad question.

Catnic as the *via media* and a structured approach

So where did all this lead? The final phase in this historical evolution was the confirmation that *Catnic* and its purposive interpretation approach was the *via media*. The Court of Appeal confirmed this in *Wheatley v. Drillsafe*[95] and *American Home Products v. Novartis Pharmaceuticals*.[96] We will now consider these cases in more detail, while adding some further cases, in order to clarify the current position under UK law.

Wheatley v. Drillsafe confirms that the test set out in *Catnic* and reformulated in *Improver* remained the standard test for infringement. The three questions were rebaptized '*the Protocol questions*', because, in the view of the court, they aimed simply at assisting in arriving at the proper purposive construction and contextual interpretation—and they were no more than aids for doing so.[97] One should, however, keep in mind that a purposive construction is only possible if the inventive purpose of the patent is clear. This requires that the meaning of the patent and the claims, in particular, should be discernible from the face of the patent documents.[98] A proper, and somewhat wider, scope of protection presupposes, therefore, the proper drafting of the patent and its claims.

The first 'Protocol question' envisages that the claim has an ambit wider than the literal meaning of the words, so as to give fair protection to the patentee. This is achieved by including all variants that do not have a material effect on how the invention works within the scope of the claim and hence potentially within the exclusive right of the patentee. The effect of this question became very clear in *American Home Products v. Novartis Pharmaceuticals*,[99] which was concerned with a claim for the '*use of rapamycin for*

[94] [1990] FSR 181 at 197–8. See also Jacob J, 'The Herchel Smith Lecture 1993' (1993) 9 EIPR 312, 313.

[95] *Wheatley (Davina) v. Drillsafe Ltd* [2001] RPC 133.

[96] *American Home Products Corp. v. Novartis Pharmaceuticals UK Ltd* [2001] RPC 159.

[97] *Wheatley (Davina)* (n. 95) at 134–5.

[98] *Rohm & Haas Co. v. Collag Ltd (No. 1)* [2002] FSR 28 (CA).

[99] *American Home Products Corp.* (n. 96).

the preparation of a medicament for inhibiting organ or tissue transplant rejection in a mammal in need thereof. The alleged infringement was a derivative of rapamycin with a slightly different peripheral chemical structure, known as 'SDZ RAD'. The Court of Appeal ruled, first, that the variant for the purposes of this question was either SDZ RAD or all potential derivates of rapamycin. It did so after concluding that the reference to any derivatives in the title of the patent was not backed up by a reference to anything other than rapamycin, as a single molecule, in the claims. The claim therefore had to be construed as excluding any derivatives, especially because the specification did not identify a single derivative that had been shown to work. The patent only taught something about rapamycin itself.

The court then went on to hold that there was no evidence that the use of the variant SDZ RAD would materially affect the way in which the invention worked. This negative answer to the first Protocol question went, therefore, in favour of the patentee and left open the possibility that the variant would infringe. At a more general level, it is worth keeping in mind that the issue of whether a variant has a material effect on the way in which the invention works depends upon the level of generality that is used to describe how the invention works.[100] The wider the description is, the easier it also is to fit the variant within the description. The correct approach to construing the way in which the invention works is therefore to describe its working at the level of generality with which it was described in the claim of the patent. This is the best way to secure a reasonable amount of certainty and predictability for third parties, which is one of the aims built into the first Protocol question.

One should also not exclude any differences between the invention and variant from consideration by defining the way in which the invention worked unduly broadly. For example, a variant was concerned with an endogenous DNA sequence that needed the introduction of a construct in order to be activated and be able to express erythropoietin, while the patent claimed an exogenous DNA sequence that was suitable to express erythropoietin when introduced to a host cell. The need for activation in case of the variant, especially, led to the conclusion that it was different and that it had a material effect on the way in which the invention worked.[101]

The second Protocol question builds in a safeguard and takes into account the interests of third parties, as different from those of the patentee. It does so by excluding any variants from the scope of the exclusive right that is enjoyed by the patentee unless the third parties should have realized that they were immaterial. Reasonable certainty on this point is achieved by excluding only those variants that are obviously or clearly immaterial. In the circumstances of *American Home Products v. Novartis Pharmaceuticals*, all that could be said was that it was likely that some derivatives of rapamycin might work, while it was impossible to predict whether a particular variant would work. It was therefore not obvious at the relevant time that SDZ RAD would obviously or clearly have no material effect. That meant, in this case, that the variant did not infringe. The Court of Appeal interprets the second Protocol question as asking whether an inventive step was involved in reaching the variant, given the teaching disclosed in the patent that it allegedly infringes. If that is, indeed, the case and if the skilled person would have concluded so at the time of publication of the patent, then the variant does not infringe the patent.[102]

[100] *Kirin-Amgen Inc. v. Transkaryotic Therapies Inc.* [2003] RPC 31. In the House of Lords, the approach of asking whether the variant solves the underlying problem by means that have the same technical effect was preferred: [2005] 1 All ER 667, [2005] RPC 9 (HL).

[101] *Kirin-Amgen* (n. 100).

[102] *Kirin-Amgen* (n. 100); *American Home Products Corp.* (n. 96).

The Court of Appeal nevertheless went on to consider the third Protocol question. The court decided that the third question should have received a positive answer, because the word 'rapamycin' was clearly used throughout the specification to indicate a single molecule, rapamycin itself.[103] A distinction can be made in relation to the third question between the situation in which the limitations expressed in the exact wording of the claim have a technical justification and the situation in which the limitations appear to be arbitrary to the skilled man. The latter can be the case, for example, when the claim refers to a circular rod, in line with the example given in the specifications, whereas, from a technical point of view such limitation was not required and other shapes of rod were also suitable. In such a situation, the skilled man is entitled to arrive at the conclusion that such an arbitrary limitation is intended by the patentee and that, as a result, in our example, protection is limited to circular rods, and other shapes of rod will therefore not infringe the patent.[104]

Returning to *American Home Products v. Novartis Pharmaceuticals*, the exclusive right was therefore limited to rapamycin, because the court held that the skilled person would have to engage in proper research, going beyond the level of his skill and application to perform the invention, when finding out whether a particular variant had certain properties. In relation to the latter point, the specification and the claims were insufficient, and would therefore, in any case, have been invalid.[105]

As if all this were not yet complex enough, we need to add one more layer of complications. One should indeed keep in mind that the Protocol questions are nothing more than a test in order to facilitate the implementation under UK patent law of EPC, Art. 69, and the Protocol to that Article; in other words, it is ultimately the Protocol that takes precedence. This is not to say that the Protocol questions have become useless and can be set aside easily—they remain a useful indicator in the vast majority of cases—but there will be a small number of cases in which the judge will find it impossible to apply them and to come to a logical conclusion on their basis. The Court of Appeal has recognized that, in those cases, the Protocol questions can be set aside and that direct reference can be made to the Protocol in order to resolve the case, and to strike a fair balance between the interests of the patentee, who is entitled to certainty and fairness in relation to the degree of protection, and the interest of third parties, so as not to stifle competition and to allow for a healthy degree of competition.[106] Purposive interpretation and the Protocol questions, as the key tool when equivalents become involved, therefore emerged clearly as the cornerstones of the law in this area, but, in the light of all of the complications that went before, some uncertainty remained. When given the welcome opportunity to do so in the *Kirin-Amgen* case, the House of Lords seized the opportunity to restate the position with authority.

The House of Lords provides a summary

One might summarize the UK position,[107] when the courts had to construe a patent and interpret the claims, as follows. When confronted with claims that have a plain meaning

---

[103] *American Home Products Corp.* (n. 118).

[104] *Russell Finex Ltd v. Telesonic AG* [2004] RPC 744, applying *Société Technique de Pulvérisation Step v. Emson Europe Ltd* [1993] RPC 513 (CA), per Hoffmann LJ at 522.

[105] *American Home Products Corp.* (n. 118).

[106] *Pharmacia Corp. v. Merck & Co. Inc.* [2002] RPC 775, approved by the House of Lords in *Kirin-Amgen v. Transkaryotic Therapies* [2005] 1 All ER 667, [2005] RPC 9 (HL), which also approved the approach to equivalents that we have suggested.

[107] As did the House of Lords in *Kirin-Amgen* (n. 129).

in themselves, the courts will not have recourse to the body of the patent or the specification to make the claims mean something different. The context only needs to be looked at if the language of the claim is ambiguous and capable of more than one meaning. One needs to keep in mind, however, that the author of the patent is using language to make a communication for a practical purpose: the meaning that the language has for the person for whom it was intended needs to be taken into account. In patent cases, this must include the person skilled in the art.

Hence we arrive at purposive interpretation. This does not involve extending or going beyond the definition of the technical matters for which the patentee sought protection in the claims; the question was, instead, what a person skilled in the art would have understood the patentee to mean by the language used. The choice of language is therefore of critical importance. One should recognize, however, that the patentee was describing something new and for which there might not yet be a generally accepted definition. There are, therefore, rare situations in which it is obvious to the skilled person that the patentee has departed from the conventional use of language or that non-essential elements have been included. That purposive approach is found in the Protocol to Art. 69 and it is also the approach set out in *Catnic*. It gives the patentee the full extent—but no more than that—of the monopoly that a reasonable person skilled in the art would think the patentee was claiming when he read the claims in their context.

The main problem in the context of this purposive approach is how to deal with equivalents. They clearly do not correspond to the exact language of the claim, but they fulfil an equivalent purpose, which makes it difficult to determine whether or not they fall within the scope of the claims. While it is important to distinguish between the core *Catnic* principle of purposive interpretation—which implements the Protocol—on the one hand, and guidance on the application of that very principle to equivalents, on the other, this is where the Protocol questions come in. They allow the court to apply the principle of purposive interpretation to equivalents—but, as such, they are only guidance and there will be cases in which they will not be useful. In those cases, one has to fall back on the Protocol and the principle of purposive interpretation itself.

The *Kirin-Amgen* facts show an example. There was, indeed, no suggestion that the term '*an exogenous DNA sequence coding for erythropoietin*' could have a loose meaning including '*an endogenous DNA sequence coding for erythropoietin*'. In this context, there is a clear equivalent, but the Protocol questions make no sense. Instead, the essential question was whether the person skilled in the art would have understood the invention to operate at such a level of generality that it was irrelevant whether the DNA that coded for erythropoietin was exogenous or not. The answer depends entirely on what that person thinks the invention is and, once that answer is in place, the rest follows automatically.

The leading authority on claim construction is clearly the House of Lords' decision in *Kirin-Amgen v. Hoechst Marrion Roussel*,[108] with *Catnic* and the decisions of the Court of Appeal providing additional guidance. The late Pumfrey J (as he then was) summarized the position as follows in *Halliburton v. Smith*:[109]

(a) The first, overarching principle, is that contained in Art. 69 itself. Sometimes I wonder whether people spend more time on the gloss to Art. 69, the Protocol, than to the Article itself, even though it is the Article which is the main governing provision.

---

[108] *Kirin-Amgen v. Hoechst Marrion Roussel* [2005] RPC 169 (HL).
[109] *Halliburton v. Smith* [2006] RPC 2.

(b) Art. 69 says that the extent of protection is determined by the terms of the claims. It goes on to say that the description and drawings shall be used to interpret the claims. In short the claims are to be construed in context.

(c) It follows that the claims are to be construed purposively—the inventor's purpose being ascertained from the description and drawings.

(d) It further follows that the claims must not be construed as if they stood alone—the drawings and description only being used to resolve any ambiguity. The Protocol expressly eschews such a method of construction but to my mind that would be so without the Protocol. Purpose is vital to the construction of claims.

(e) When ascertaining the inventor's purpose, it must be remembered that he may have several purposes depending on the level of generality of his invention. Typically, for instance, an inventor may have one, generally more than one, specific embodiment as well as a generalised concept. But there is no presumption that the patentee necessarily intended the widest possible meaning consistent with his purpose be given to the words that he used: purpose and meaning are different.

(f) Thus purpose is not the be-all and end-all. One is still at the end of the day concerned with the meaning of the language used. Hence the other extreme of the Protocol—a mere guideline—is also ruled out by Art. 69 itself. It is the terms of the claims which delineate the patentee's territory.

(g) It follows that if the patentee has included what is obviously a deliberate limitation in his claims, it must have a meaning. One cannot disregard obviously intentional elements. Hoffmann LJ put it this way in *STEP v. Emson* [1993] RPC at 522:

'The well known principle that patent claims are given a purposive construction does not mean that an integer can be treated as struck out if it does not appear to make any difference to the inventive concept. It may have some other purpose buried in the prior art and even if this is not discernible, the patentee may have had some reason of his own for introducing it.'

(h) It also follows that where a patentee has used a word or phrase which, acontextually, might have a particular meaning (narrow or wide) it does not necessarily have that meaning in context. A good example of this is the *Catnic* case itself—'vertical' in context did not mean 'geometrically vertical', it meant 'vertical enough to do the job' (of supporting the upper horizontal plate). The so-called 'Protocol questions' (those formulated by Hoffmann J in *Improver v. Remington* [1990] FSR 181 at p.189) are of particular value when considering the difference of meaning between a word or phrase out of context and that word or phrase in context. At that point the first two Protocol questions come into play. But once one focuses on the word in context, the Protocol question approach does not resolve the ultimate question—what does the word or phrase actually mean, when construed purposively? That can only be done on the language used, read in context.

(i) It further follows that there is no general 'doctrine of equivalents.' Any student of patent law knows that various legal systems allow for such a concept, but that none of them can agree what it is or should be. Here is not the place to set forth the myriad versions of such a doctrine. For my part I do not think that Art. 69 itself allows for such a concept—it says the extent of protection shall be determined by the terms of the claims. And so far as I can understand, the French and German versions mean the same thing. Nor can I see how the Protocol can create any such doctrine.

(j) On the other hand purposive construction can lead to the conclusion that a technically trivial or minor difference between an element of a claim and the corresponding element of the alleged infringement nonetheless falls within the meaning of the element when read purposively. This is not because there is a doctrine of equivalents: it is because that is the fair way to read the claim in context.

(k) Finally purposive construction leads one to eschew what Lord Diplock in *Catnic* called (at p. 243):

'the kind of meticulous verbal analysis which lawyers are too often tempted by their training to indulge.'

Pedantry and patents are incompatible. In *Catnic* the rejected 'meticulous verbal analysis' was the argument that because the word 'horizontal' was qualified by 'substantially' whereas 'vertical' was not, the latter must mean 'geometrically vertical'.[110]

The current state of affairs

To determine the extent of protection conferred by a patent one needs to ask nothing more than what a person skilled in the art would have understood the patentee to have been using the language of the claim to mean.[111] That was the conclusion which the House of Lords in *Kirin-Amgen* drew from the whole evolution described here. The Court of Appeal further summarized the guidelines to apply this approach in *Virgin Atlantic Airways*.[112] The combination of the *Kirin-Amgen* rule and the *Virgin Atlantic* guidelines is now the standard approach of the English courts.[113] This approach takes the historical evolution that was described earlier in this chapter fully on board, but it looks at a wider range of factors to fully implement Art. 69 EPC in all possible circumstances. The guidelines read as follows:

> One might have thought there was nothing more to say on this topic after *Kirin-Amgen Inc v Hoechst Marion Roussel Ltd* [2005] R.P.C. 9. The judge accurately set out the position, save that he used the old language of Art. 69 EPC rather than that of the EPC 2000, a Convention now in force. The new language omits the terms of from Art. 69. No one suggested the amendment changes the meaning. We set out what the judge said, but using the language of the EPC 2000:

> The task for the court is to determine what the person skilled in the art would have understood the patentee to have been using the language of the claim to mean. The principles were summarised by Jacob L.J. in *Mayne Pharma Pty Ltd v Pharmacia Italia SpA* [2005] EWCA Civ 137 and refined by Pumfrey J. in *Halliburton Energy Services Inc v Smith International (North Sea) Ltd* [2005] EWHC 1623 (Pat) following their general approval by the House of Lords in *Kirin-Amgen Inc v Hoechst Marion Roussel Ltd* [2005] R.P.C. 9. An abbreviated version of them is as follows:

> (i) The first overarching principle is that contained in Art.69 of the European Patent Convention.

> (ii) Art.69 says that the extent of protection is determined by the claims. It goes on to say that the description and drawings shall be used to interpret the claims. In short the claims are to be construed in context.

---

[110] *Halliburton* (n. 109) at para. 68.

[111] E.g. a patent for a wound dressing based on a cellulose derivative had not been infringed, as, on a purposive interpretation, the patent called for a mixture of two classes of gel-forming fibre and the defendant's product contained modified cellulose only. *Convatec Ltd v. Smith & Nephew Healthcare Ltd* [2011] EWHC 2039 (Pat). The focus on the claims and the language used in them is also emphasized by the decision of the Court of Appeal in *Rovi Guides Inc v. Virgin Media Ltd and others* [2015] EWCA Civ 1214, which stresses that language used in expert evidence cannot be substituted for the actual words in the claim. The skilled person will merely look at what the latter mean to him or her.

[112] *Virgin Atlantic Airways Ltd v. Premium Aircraft Interiors Group* [2009] EWCA Civ 1062, [2010] RPC 8.

[113] See e.g. *Convatec Ltd, Convatec Technologies Inc. and Convatec Inc. v. Smith & Nephew Healthcare Ltd, Smith & Nephew plc and Speciality Fibres & Materials Ltd* [2012] EWCA Civ 520; *Molnlycke Health Care AB and Molnlycke Health Care Ltd v. BSN Medical Ltd and BSN Medical GmbH* [2012] EWHC 3157 (Pat); and *Generics (UK) Ltd (t/a Mylan) v. Yeda Research & Development Co. Ltd and Teva Pharmaceutical Industries Ltd* [2012] EWHC 1848 (Pat).

(iii)   It follows that the claims are to be construed purposively—the inventor's purpose being ascertained from the description and drawings.

(iv)   It further follows that the claims must not be construed as if they stood alone—the drawings and description only being used to resolve any ambiguity. Purpose is vital to the construction of claims.

(v)   When ascertaining the inventor's purpose, it must be remembered that he may have several purposes depending on the level of generality of his invention. Typically, for instance, an inventor may have one, generally more than one, specific embodiment as well as a generalised concept. But there is no presumption that the patentee necessarily intended the widest possible meaning consistent with his purpose be given to the words that he used: purpose and meaning are different.

(vi)   Thus purpose is not the be-all and end-all. One is still at the end of the day concerned with the meaning of the language used. Hence the other extreme of the Protocol—a mere guideline—is also ruled out by Art.69 itself. It is the terms of the claims which delineate the patentee's territory.

(vii)   It follows that if the patentee has included what is obviously a deliberate limitation in his claims, it must have a meaning. One cannot disregard obviously intentional elements.

(viii)   It also follows that where a patentee has used a word or phrase which, contextually, might have a particular meaning (narrow or wide) it does not necessarily have that meaning in context.

(ix)   It further follows that there is no general "doctrine of equivalents."

(x)   On the other hand purposive construction can lead to the conclusion that a technically trivial or minor difference between an element of a claim and the corresponding element of the alleged infringement nonetheless falls within the meaning of the element when read purposively. This is not because there is a doctrine of equivalents it is because that is the fair way to read the claim in context.

(xi)   Finally purposive construction leads one to eschew the kind of meticulous verbal analysis which lawyers are too often tempted by their training to indulge.[114]

An overview

Infringement is, perhaps, the area of patent law that has been most radically transformed by the 1977 legislation. A statutory framework replaced the old common law rules and this appears to have worked well. The case law in relation to that framework suggests, however, that there remain a few problems, with the potential differences of language between the UK legislation and the European patent approach being at the heart of the difficulty.

The all-important issue is how the courts will approach the interpretation of specifications and claims. *Catnic* clearly represents the dawning of a new era, in which the patentee is treated more generously and his or her rivals are more likely to be ensnared in the web of infringement. In so far as it is appropriate to rely on the tip of reported cases that are part of the iceberg of litigation, it seems that, for the most part, the courts have understood the import of what was intended in *Catnic*.

The *Improver* litigation is, however, a sorry tale and suggests that the UK courts are yet to fully embrace a Continental approach to interpretation, being held back by the third

---

[114] *Virgin Atlantic Airways Ltd v. Premium Aircraft Interiors Group* [2009] EWCA Civ 1062, [2010] RPC 8 at para. 5.

of the three questions that now have to be asked—namely, whether the skilled reader, having seen that a variant was obvious, would then still consider that the words of the specification required strict compliance. Thus expressed, the bizarre nature of the question becomes clear: it requires the skilled reader consciously to ignore that which is obvious to him—which is quite a mental feat. Imposing this bizarre question then leads to the unacceptable situation in which, in a case such as *Improver*, a European patent has differing effects in different member states, quite contrary to the whole rationale and purpose of international patent cooperation. The *Improver* saga and the *PLG* case seem now to represent a low-water mark, however, with the *Catnic* approach restored—however uncertainly—to its central position.

It could be concluded from this that *Catnic* did not intend to go as far as is required by the EPC, which, as has been noted, was not, on the face of it, in the minds of the Law Lords at the time. The better view is that, like children on new bicycles, judges asked to give purposive interpretations to specifications and claims will be inevitably cautious at first, may make the odd mistake or two, but will, as time passes and the unfamiliar becomes the familiar, grow in confidence and eventually banish those mistakes. With more and more European legislation coming to the courts to be considered, it seems likely that the necessary confidence and accuracy will evolve sooner, rather than later, and that judges, deprived as they now are of what has been described by Professor Cornish as the rigid 'fenceposts' of literally interpreted patents,[115] will be equally able to gain as much assistance from the guidance of the 'signposts' that represent the results of the new purposive approach.

This evolution simply has to occur: if it does not, there is an obvious danger that UK patent law will start to become isolated from the mainstream international approach. Luckily, there is increasing evidence that can be derived from the judgments of the Court of Appeal that we are getting there. The House of Lords seems to have finalized developments in this area in *Kirin-Amgen*; purposive interpretation is the norm, and that puts us in line with the EPC and the Protocol to Art. 69. And when it comes to equivalents, the Protocol questions offer guidance as to how to apply the principle of purposive interpretation.

Virgin Atlantic offers the final version of the guidelines and for now the courts seem to be continuing to put it all into practice ... *Stretchline Intellectual Properties v. H & M Hennes and Mauritz UK Ltd*[116] provides a good example of the new approach in a not unduly technical or scientific area. In the words of Carr J:

> 9. The Patent is concerned, in particular, with tubular fabric used to encase underwires in garments such as brassieres. The Description states that there was a known problem with such fabric tubing at the priority date (page 1 lines 12-19):
> 'A considerable problem with known fabric tubing for underwires is that the ends of the underwires can penetrate the tubing, either during the course of garment manufacture or in use by a wearer.
> At present, a significant proportion of brassiere (bra) manufacturers (sic) products are returned because of protrusion of the underwire through the fabric tubing.'
> 10. The Patent proposes to solve this problem by inclusion of a fusible yarn which, on melting, strengthens the tubular fabric.
> 11. Claim 1 of the Patent is a process claim which provides for:

---

[115] See W. R. Cornish and D. Llewelyn (2003) *Intellectual Property*, 5th edn, London: Sweet and Maxwell, Ch. 6, p. 236.
[116] [2015] EWHC 3298 (Pat).

'a method for making a tubular fabric comprising providing a support yarn and an elasto-meric yarn; characterised in that a fusible yarn is also provided and in that the yarns are formed into a tubular fabric whereby the fusible yarn is arranged within the fabric tube so that it is capable of forming a penetration barrier.'

12. The dispute between the parties concerns the correct interpretation of the final words of the claim and in particular whether the garments allegedly sold in breach of the Settlement Agreement contain 'a penetration barrier'.

13. In summary, Stretchline contends that a penetration barrier is created by incorporating (in particular by weaving) a fusible yarn into the tubular fabric and heating it. A fusible yarn acts, in effect, as an adhesive. When heated during the fabric dyeing process, the adhesive melts and the fusible yarn ceases to exist. The adhesive spreads itself over the surrounding fibres in the fabric to form points of adhesion or bonding between those fibres. Stretchline submits that this is what is meant by "a penetration barrier". The Patent is claiming a structure that, by reason of bonding of the fibres, is better able to resist penetration (for example by wire) than would be the case if the fusible yarn had not been used.

14. H&M contends that the Patent requires that the fusible yarn must an identifiable, layer-like barrier or lining. On this basis, points of adhesion are not sufficient. H&M argues that the Patent describes and claims fusible yarn which, on melting, forms a substantially continuous liner which provides the required penetration barrier. It denies that it is possible to equate increased resistance to penetration with the presence of a barrier.

Asking himself what a person skilled in the art would have understood the patentee to have been using the language of the claim to mean the judge preferred Stretchline's interpretation. The skilled person would have understood that when heated the fusible yarn would melt and that as a glue it would stick the surrounding fibres together. The result is a stronger structure that acts as a barrier to penetration by the (sharp) ends of the metal underwire, but fusible yarn no longer forms a separate line or structure on its own (i.e. the penetration barrier is not meant to be a separate line created solely by the fusible yarn).

Further reading

BRINKHOF, J., 'Is there a European Doctrine of Equivalence?' (2002) 33 IIC 911.

COLE, P., 'Purposive Construction under English Law' (1994) 16(10) EIPR 455.

COOK, T., 'Responding to Concerns about the Scope of the Defence from Patent Infringement for Acts Done for Experimental Purposes Relating to the Subject Matter of the Invention' (2006) 3 IPQ 193–222.

CURLEY, D. and SHERATON, H., 'The Lords Rule in *Amgen v. TKT*' (2005) 27(4) EIPR 154–8.

PEARCE, D. and MOORE, S., 'The Court of Appeal Gives Indirect Infringement of Patents a Broad Interpretation', (2011) 33(2) EIPR 122–5.

THORLEY, S. et al. (eds.) (2006) *Terrell on the Law of Patents*, 16th edn, London: Sweet and Maxwell, Chs. 6, 7, and 8.

7

Supplementary protection certificates and the unitary patent

In this chapter, we are concerned with certain aspects of the involvement of the European Union (EU) with patent law. These aspects all represent add-ons to a traditional patent system that is based on national patents. The first—supplementary protection certificates (SPCs)—is already in place; the other—the unitary patent—is still on the drawing board, but finally seems close to becoming a reality now that political agreement has apparently been reached.

Supplementary protection certificates

Background

Pharmaceutical products can attract patent protection just as any other product that satisfies the requirements for patentability. The complicating factor, however, is that new pharmaceutical products need testing and government authorization before they can be marketed. All of this generally takes place after the patent application has been filed and the whole process may take years, rather than months or weeks. Because the term of a patent is calculated on the basis of the filing date, patent protection for research and development-based products[1] is, in practice, eroded. The period between the first marketing of the drug and the expiry of the patent was shortened, and there have been cases in which the patent had expired before marketing authorization was obtained. Because the copying of drugs is, in addition, rather easy—especially when compared with the independent development process—this phenomenon was seriously damaging the pharmaceutical industry.[2]

The situation became particularly pressing when the US and Japan introduced measures to restore the term of patent protection for pharmaceutical products.[3] When France and Italy started introducing national measures aiming to produce a similar effect, the European Community took over the initiative and introduced supplementary protection certificates (SPCs) as a *sui generis* intellectual property right for medicinal products.[4]

---

[1] Generic drugs are not faced with the same problem, because they do not need the extensive testing, etc., and rely, to a great extent, on the work done in respect of the original drug of which they are a copy.

[2] J. N. Adams, 'Supplementary Protection Certificates: The Challenge to EC Regulation 1768/92' (1994) 8 EIPR 323; D. Delcourt, 'Public Health and the Preservation of Economic Competitiveness: The European Supplementary Protection Certificate for Medicinal Products' (2009) 4(6) JIPLP 439.

[3] Two Japanese laws—one dated 1980 and the other dated 1987—address the problem and the US introduced the Drug Price Competition and Patent Term Restoration Act of 1984 (informally known as the Hatch-Waxman Act).

[4] Regulation 1768/92 concerning the creation of a supplementary protection certificate for medicinal products [1992] OJ L 182/1, now codified as Regulation (EC) 469/2009 of the European Parliament and of the Council concerning the supplementary protection certificate for medicinal products [2009] OJ L 152/1.

EC Regulation 1768/92, now EC Regulation 469/2009

In Europe, an extension of the patent term required the amendment of Art. 63 of the European Patent Convention (EPC). Because a number of the contracting parties have a pharmaceutical industry that is almost exclusively based on generics, it was felt that the required unanimous vote was out of reach.[5] The Convention does allow for the introduction by the contracting states of other *sui generis* rights, although only in so far as they grant new and different kinds of industrial property protection. Because the extension of the patent term was not an option, the Community took the route of the *sui generis* right and called it the 'supplementary protection certificate'.[6]

The Regulation provides that any product that is protected by a patent in a member state and which is as a medicinal product subject to an authorization procedure can be the subject of a certificate.[7] A 'product' is defined widely as the active ingredient, or the combination of active ingredients, of a medicinal product and the latter category comprises substances or combinations of substances that are used to prevent, diagnose, or treat a disease, or to restore, correct, or modify physiological functions in humans or in animals.[8] This wide definition does, however, have its limitations. Only active ingredients are covered as products and a combination of active ingredients does not include a combination of one active ingredient and another ingredient that is simply there to make a certain pharmaceutical form possible.[9] For the purposes of the definition of the concept of a 'product' in Art. 1 of the Regulation, the intended use is not decisive, but, in any case, a second medical use of an active ingredient is not part of that concept.[10] Protection is only granted for the product covered by the original authorization or by any subsequent authorization that takes place before the expiry of the patent.[11] This is particularly important in cases in which the scope of the patent is wider than that of the authorization. The various ways in which the active ingredient can be formulated are, arguably, all covered.[12] It has, indeed, now been held that the product, as a medicinal product, for the purposes of Art. 3 of the Regulation, includes all forms of it that enjoy protection under the basic patent[13]—but no supplementary protection certificate will be available for products that are not protected by the basic patent in force.[14] For example, no certificate can be granted for the combination of an anti-ulcer agent with two specific

---

[5] An amendment to Art. 63, EPC, which would allow the term of protection for pharmaceutical products to be extended awaits ratification, but which is not likely to be ratified and come into force in the near future.

[6] H. P. Kunz-Hallstein, 'The Compatibility of a Community "Certificate for the Restoration of Protection" with the European Patent Convention' (1990) 6 EIPR 209.

[7] Art. 2. The first authorization to place on the market in the Community has to be a marketing authorization issued in compliance with Directive 65/65. See Case C-127/00, *Hassle AB v. Ratiopharm GmbH* [2003] ECR I-14781; see also *Generics (UK) Ltd v. Synaptech Inc.* [2009] EWHC 659 (Ch, 20 May 2009).

[8] Art. 1.

[9] Case C-431/04, *Massachusetts Institute of Technology* [2006] ECR I-4089. See N. Klix and B. Hermann, 'Bitter Pill for the Pharmaceutical Industry' (2006) 1(10) JIPLP 639–42.

[10] Case C-202/05, *Yissum Research & Development Co. of the Hebrew University of Jerusalem v. Comptroller-General of Patents* [2007] OJ C 96/19 (ECJ).

[11] Art. 4.

[12] This is logical for anyone familiar with chemistry and the pharmaceutical industry. The *travaux préparatoires* of the Regulation seem to spell this out by referring to salts and esters of acids as coming under one product definition. See R. Whaite and N. Jones, 'Pharmaceutical Patent Term Restoration: The European Commission's Regulation' (1992) 9 EIPR 324, 325.

[13] Case C-392/97, *Farmitalia Carlo Erba Srl* [1999] ECR I-5553, [2000] 2 CMLR 253.

[14] See also *Generics (UK) Ltd v. Daiichi Pharmaceutical Co. Ltd* [2009] RPC 4.

antibiotics if the patent only refers to the anti-ulcer agent.[15] Also, a supplementary protection certificate will not be granted for active ingredients which are not identified in the wording of the claims of the basic patent relied on in support of the application for such a certificate and, even if such an active ingredient is identified in the wording of the claims as an active ingredient forming part of a combination in conjunction with another active ingredient, there will not be a supplementary protection certificate for such an active ingredient if it is not the subject of any claim relating to that active ingredient alone.[16] But on the other hand, a supplementary protection certificate can be granted for an active ingredient specified in the wording of the claims of the basic patent relied on, where the medicinal product for which the marketing authorization is submitted in support of the supplementary protection certificate application contains not only that active ingredient but also other active ingredients.[17]

Despite all these attempts at clarification by the Court of Justice the concept of a product protected by a basic patent in force remains highly problematical.[18] In *Actavis Group PTC EHF and anor v. Sanofi Pharma Bristol-Myers Squibb SNC*[19] Arnold J therefore (again) referred the issue to the Court of Justice and also asked whether in a situation in which multiple products are protected by a basic patent in force a certificate for each of the products protected can be granted. The CJEU gave a negative answer to the latter question and ruled that no second SPC can be obtained for a product combining the active ingredient and another substance that is also claimed in the patent if a first SPC was granted for the active ingredient that was claimed in the patent (on its own).[20]

Only the patentee of the original patent[21] or any successor in title can file an application for a certificate.[22] Licensees are excluded from this procedure, which has to take place at the national patent office that granted the patent. The whole granting procedure takes place at national level.[23] Two statutory instruments translate this into UK intellectual property law and allow the UK Intellectual Property Office to issue the certificate: the Patents (Compulsory Licensing and Supplementary Protection Certificates) Regulations 2007 and the Patents Rules 2007.[24]

An application for a certificate must be filed within six months of the date on which the marketing authorization for the medicinal product was granted. The one exception

---

[15] *Takeda Chemical Industries Ltd's Applications (No. 3)* [2004] RPC 37.

[16] Similarly, if a patent claims that a product is composed of two active ingredients, but no claims are made to the active ingredients individually, no supplementary protection certificate can be granted for one of the active ingredients in isolation. See Cases C-322/10, *Medeva*, C-630/10, *University of Queensland* and *CSL*, C-518/10, *Yeda Research and Development Company and Aventis Holdings* and C-6/11, *Daiichi Sankyo*, <http://curia.europa.eu>.

[17] Cases C-422/10, *Georgetown University and ors* and C-322/10, *Medeva*, <http://curia.europa.eu>.

[18] See e.g. *Novartis Pharmaceuticals UK Ltd v. Medimmune Ltd and Medical Research Council* [2012] EWHC 181 (Pat).

[19] *Actavis Group PTC EHF and anor v. Sanofi Pharma Bristol-Myers Squibb SNC* [2012] EWHC 2545 (Pat).

[20] Cases C-443/12 *Actavis Group PTC EHF and anor v. Sanofi Pharma Bristol-Myers Squibb SNC*; and C577/13 *Actavis Group PTC EHF and Actavis UK Ltd v. Boehringer IngelheimPharma GmbH & Co KG*, <http://curia.europa.eu>.

[21] A product may be covered by more than one patent. In such a case, a supplementary protection certificate can be granted for each basic patent (one basic patent and certificate per holder). For further details on this point, and on the problems that arise when patents and marketing authorization are owned by different companies, see Case C-181/95, *Biogen Inc. v. Smithkline Biologicals SA* [1996] ECR I-717, [1997] 1 CMLR 704.

[22] Art. 6.   [23] Art. 9.

[24] SI 2007/3293, which inserts a new s. 128B and a Sch. 4A in the Patents Act 1977, and SI 2007/3291, which deals with the procedural and formal issues in reg. 116, respectively.

to this rule is the situation in which the authorization is granted before the patent is granted. In that case, the application for the certificate must be lodged with the national patent office within six months of the date of the grant of the patent.[25]

If at the date of the application the patent covering the medicinal product[26] is in force and the marketing authorization is valid, a single certificate[27] can be granted for the medicinal product.[28] It should be noted that the Regulation refers to the first marketing authorization—whether that is a medicinal product for human use or a medicinal product for veterinary use[29]—in relation to the application for, and the grant of, the certificate,[30] but that any therapeutic use that is authorized before the expiry of the certificate comes within the scope of the protection offered by the certificate.[31] A certificate confers the same rights as the basic patent[32] and is subject to the same limitations.[33] These are granted for a period that runs from the end of the patent term and the length of that period is calculated in relation to the period for which protection was lost due to the authorization process. The starting point is the period that lapsed between the date on which the patent application was lodged and that on which the marketing authorization was granted; this period is reduced by five years. A final restriction is that the resulting term of protection offered by the certificate cannot exceed five years.[34]

Once granted, the continued existence of the certificate is subject to the payment of an annual fee[35] and the certificate will also expire if the marketing authorization for that medicinal product is withdrawn.[36] A certificate becomes invalid if the basic patent is revoked or limited to the extent that the product for which the certificate was granted would no longer be protected by the claims of the basic patent. Once the basic patent has expired, the certificate becomes invalid and anyone has the right to submit an application or to bring an action in this respect if grounds exist that would have justified the revocation or limitation of the patent.[37]

---

[25] Art. 7.

[26] The aim of Art. 3(c) is to preclude the grant of successive certificates for one and the same product, and hence the strong link with the patent. But different patents protecting the same product can be in different hands and, then, the grant of a supplementary protection certificate for a product to a holder of a basic patent before an application was lodged, in relation to the same product by a different holder of a different patent on the basis of a common marketing authorization, does not provide a ground for rejecting the latter application: *Chiron Corp's & Novo Nordisk A/S's Application* [2005] RPC 24 (Patent Office).

[27] No second certificate covering the same member state can be granted according to Art. 3(c).

[28] Art. 3.

[29] Case C-31/03, *Pharmacia Italia SpA, formerly Pharmacia & Upjohn SpA* [2004] ECR I-10001. A later authorization for human use can be taken into account, despite an earlier authorization for veterinary use: Case C-130/11, *Neurim Pharmaceuticals (1991) Ltd v. Comptroller-General of Patents*, <http://curia.europa.eu>.

[30] *Pharmacia Italia SpA* (n. 29).

[31] Art. 4, subject to the general limitation of the protection to anything coming within the scope of the basic patent. See also Whaite and Jones, 'Pharmaceutical Patent Term Restoration' (n. 12) at 325.

[32] See the order in case C-442/11, *Novartis*, <http://curia.europa.eu>.

[33] Art. 5. Interesting and outstanding questions are whether, and to what extent, certificates and patents will be treated in an identical way under national law, and how certificates will relate to Art. 101 of the Treaty on the Functioning of the European Union and to the block exemptions: see Whaite and Jones, 'Pharmaceutical Patent Term Restoration' (n. 12) at 236. The High Court decided, some time ago, that the limitations to which both the patent and the certificate are subject must include compulsory licences and licences of right under the Patents Act 1977. (The case is reported as *In the matter of an application by Faulding Pharmaceuticals plc to settle the terms of a licence of right under Supplementary Protection Certificate SPC/GB93/032, in the name of Research Corporation Technologies Inc.* [1995] 1 EIPR D-16 and 17.)

[34] Art. 13.   [35] Arts. 12 and 14.   [36] Art. 14(d).   [37] Art. 15.

Clearly, the certificate is very closely linked to the patent covering the medicinal product that is the subject of the certificate. One might even argue that it is, in reality, more than an extension of the patent term for pharmaceutical products. There are, however, differences[38]—although one has to admit that the *sui generis* right was moulded along the lines of the patent model. The certificate is only available for products that are subject to an authorization procedure and there is no link to any disclosure. The scope of protection is in no way determined by the patent claims; the patent is only the precondition for the grant of the certificate and it is the authorization that defines the real scope of the certificate. It is submitted that the certificate constitutes a genuine *sui generis* right.[39] But the argument that it is different from the patent system only because it protects successful inventions[40] cannot be endorsed: a patented invention is successful in the sense that it fulfils the requirements for patentability and the pharmaceutical industry often finds very lucrative exploitation opportunities even for those patented products that are not granted a marketing authorization as medicinal products. The real tests for success are the sales figures for the drugs and these will only be known after the deadline for the filing of an application for a certificate— that is, in general, six months after the first authorization to market the product was obtained.

The original Regulation came into force on 2 January 1993. All products that were, at that date, covered by a patent and for which the first marketing authorization within the Community was granted after 1 January 1985, qualified for a certificate. The codified Regulation specifies that the Regulation shall also apply to supplementary protection certificates granted in accordance with national legislation in the Czech Republic, Estonia, Cyprus, Latvia, Lithuania, Malta, Poland, Slovenia, and Slovakia before 1 May 2004 and in Romania before 1 January 2007.[41]

The extension of the system

Industry has lobbied hard to see the system of supplementary protection certificates extended to other products. The argument is that the system should be applied to all products that are subject to a marketing authorization. The Commission has now recognized this argument and has extended the system of supplementary protection certificates to plant protection products.[42] These products are subject to an authorization procedure under Directive 91/414[43] and first marketing of these products can only take place once the marketing authorization has been obtained.

The new Regulation defines plant protection products as '*active substances and preparations containing one or more active substances, put up in the form in which they are supplied to the user*',[44] which have a number of intended uses: first, they can '*protect plants or plant products against all harmful organisms or prevent the action of such*

---

[38] Kunz-Hallstein, 'The Compatibility of a Community "Certificate for the Restoration of Protection" with the European Patent Convention' (n. 6) at 209.

[39] Kunz-Hallstein, 'The Compatibility of a Community "Certificate"' (n. 6); see also CLIP report, *Supplementary Protection Certificates* (1991), pp. 16 *et seq.*

[40] CLIP report, *Supplementary Protection Certificates* (n. 39), pp. 16 *et seq.*

[41] Arts. 21 and 23.

[42] European Parliament and Council Regulation 1610/96 concerning the creation of a supplementary protection certificate for plant protection products [1996] OJ L 198/30.

[43] [1991] OJ L 230/1, as amended by Directive 95/36 [1995] OJ L 172/8.

[44] Art. 1 of the Regulation.

organisms;[45] secondly, they can be used to influence the life processes of plants, in so far as they do not do that as a nutrient. They can also be used to preserve plant products, to destroy undesirable plants, to destroy parts of plants, or to check or prevent undesirable growth of plants.[46] This is followed, in Art. 1 of the Regulation, by further definitions of 'substances', 'preparations', 'plants', and 'plant products'. The rest of the provisions of the Regulation are almost exact copies of the provisions in the Regulation on pharmaceutical products: the same rules apply as if one were simply to replace the words 'pharmaceutical product' with 'plant protection product'. But it is important to emphasize that the existence of a patent for the product is, once again, a prerequisite[47] and that only the first marketing authorization for the product—to be taken in the sense of its active ingredient—counts.[48] If more than one patent exists for one product, only one certificate shall be granted in case the same holder owns the patents. More than one certificate can only be granted in respect of the same product if there are multiple patents owned by different holders, who each apply separately for the certificates.[49]

The Regulation entered into force on 9 January 1997,[50] but it only applies from 2 January 1998 onwards for those member states whose national law did not provide for the patentability of plant protection products on 1 January 1990.[51] The Patents (Supplementary Protection Certificates) Rules 1997[52] provide the procedure under which these certificates will be granted in the UK.

The challenge to the Regulation

Spain has a pharmaceutical industry that relies heavily on generic drugs and which is affected negatively by the Regulation. It brought an action in the European Court of Justice to annul Regulation 1768/92.[53] The main argument that Spain used was that the Regulation is *ultra vires*, in that the Community did not have the competence to create the certificate.[54] This argument was based on Arts. 30 and 295 of the EC Treaty (now respectively Arts. 36 and 345 of the Treaty on the Functioning of the European Union). Specifically, Art. 295 provided (as Art. 345 now provides) that the Treaty shall not interfere with the system of property ownership,[55] while Art. 30 could be said to deal only with the exercise of existing rights and the extent to which such exercise is acceptable. The arguments come down to the point that these provisions reserve the power to regulate substantive intellectual property law for the member states and exclude Community action in this area.

The Court flatly rejected this argument.[56] It repeated its ruling that Art. 295:

cannot be interpreted as reserving to the national legislature, in relation to industrial and commercial property, the power to adopt measures which would adversely affect the principle of free movement of goods within the common market.[57]

---

[45] Art. 1 of the Regulation.   [46] Art. 1 of the Regulation.   [47] Art. 3(1).
[48] A subsequent authorization for the active ingredient produced by a patented improved manufacturing process cannot be the basis for the grant of a supplementary protection certificate: see *BASF AG's SPC Application* [2000] RPC 1.
[49] Art. 3(2).   [50] Art. 21.   [51] Art. 20.   [52] SI 1997/64.
[53] Case C-350/92, *Spain v. EU Council* [1995] ECR I-1985, [1996] 1 CMLR 415.
[54] See also Adams, 'Supplementary Protection Certificates' (n. 2) at 323.
[55] This argument attacks the validity of almost all intellectual property initiatives taken by the EU.
[56] Case C-350/92, *Spain v. EU Council* [1995] ECR I-1985 at 2009–12.
[57] *Spain v. EU Council* (n. 56) at 2010–11.

It can be derived from this ruling that the argument that rules concerning the very existence of industrial property rights fall within the sole jurisdiction of the national legislature cannot be endorsed;[58] the rules of the Treaty must be allowed to interfere in appropriate cases. In relation to Art. 30, the Court referred to its judgment in *Simmenthal SpA v. Italian Minister for Finance*[59] and repeated the part of that judgment within which it ruled that '*Article* [30] *is not designed to reserve certain matters to the exclusive jurisdiction of member states*'.[60]

Having rejected Spain's main argument, the Court turned to Spain's second argument, which concerned the legal basis for the Regulation. The Council had used Art. 95 of the EC Treaty (now Art. 114 of the Treaty on the Functioning of the European Union) as a legal basis for the Regulation. This meant that the Regulation must pursue the objective of the creation of the single market, as set out in Art. 18 of the EC Treaty (now Art. 21 of the Treaty on the Functioning of the European Union). It might be argued that the Regulation does not pursue that objective, because:

> as far as the free movement of goods is concerned, the certificate, by its very nature, tends to extend the compartmentalization of the market beyond the duration of the basic patent, and thus adds to the exceptions provided for in Article 30 of the Treaty, without the extension of the scope of that provision being justified by the Community objective.[61]

Thus, Spain concluded that the introduction of the certificate would create obstacles to the free movement of goods: because the creation of a single market with a free flow of goods was one of the principal aims of the Treaty, such a measure must be *ultra vires*.

This argument cannot, however, be accepted and it was also rejected by the Court.[62] The Court first stated that Art. 18 allowed the Community to take harmonization measures to achieve its objective. Such harmonization measures may be necessary to deal with disparities between the laws of the member states if, and in so far as, these are hindering the free movement of goods. In this particular case, Italy and France had already been creating their own national certificates, and so the only way to avoid the partitioning of the market was the creation of a measure at Community level. Indeed, differences in protection given to one and the same medicine would fragment the Common Market. The situation in which a product would still be protected in some national markets, but not in others, would give rise to different market conditions in different parts of the Common Market. The Court thus agreed with the drafters of the Regulation, who argued, in the sixth Recital:

> The regulation thus aims to prevent the heterogeneous development of national laws leading to further disparities which would be likely to create obstacles to the free movement of medicinal products within the Community and thus directly affect the establishment and the functioning of the internal market.[63]

In conclusion, the Court rejected all arguments that had been put forward by Spain and its challenge to the Regulation failed.

Another approach that leads to the same conclusion is that taken by Jean-François Verstrynghe:

> The Court has already given some hint of its thinking in its recent judgment in the Article [226] infringement procedure as applied to compulsory licenses for non-use of patents in the UK. In this judgment of 18 February 1992, it declared a particular feature of the British law to be illegal

---

58 *Spain v. EU Council* (n. 56) at 2011.   59 Case 35/76 [1976] ECR 1871, [1977] 2 CMLR 1.
60 *Spain v. EU Council* (n 56) at 2011.   61 *Spain v. EU Council* (n. 56) at 2013.
62 *Spain v. EU Council* (n. 56) at 2012–16.   63 *Spain v. EU Council* (n. 56) at 2014–15.

under Article [28].[64] If this is so, it must then also be accepted that this feature concerning the scope and conditions of patent protection in the UK might affect the establishment and functioning of the internal market under Article [95], and that therefore the European Community could have harmonised this detail of patent protection—and by implication many other details of national IPR laws [and thus also the certificate]—which affect the establishment and functioning of the internal market.[65]

The importance of this case is not limited to the issue of supplementary protection certificates. It gives clear guidance in relation to the way in which the EU can operate in the area of intellectual property rights. As we have demonstrated in previous chapters, EU law will interfere with the exercise of intellectual property rights whenever that exercise conflicts with the EU's principles of free movement and free competition. But the role of the EU is not a purely negative one based on Arts. 34–36 and 101–102 of the Treaty on the Functioning of the European Union. This case shows clearly that Art. 21 allows the EU to create new rights and harmonize the existing national provisions, in so far as this is necessary for the creation of the single market; Art. 114 will provide a legal basis for such measures. Further measures—such as the creation of new supranational rights that are superimposed on national rights[66]—which fall outside the scope of Arts. 21 and 114, can be based on Arts. 115 and 352 of the Treaty (formerly Arts. 94 and 308, respectively, of the Treaty of Rome).[67]

In the case at issue, the measure did, indeed, have as its object the establishment and the functioning of the internal market, because it was introduced as a measure to replace national measures that would have partitioned the internal market. The use of Art. 114 is particularly helpful in such circumstances, because it only requires a qualified majority; Arts. 115 and 352 require unanimity. One can easily see the political background to the Spanish challenge on these grounds. If its arguments had succeeded, the Council would have been obliged to use Arts. 115 and 352 as a legal basis, and Spain would have been able to veto any supplementary protection certificate scheme that it, and its generics-based pharmaceutical industry, did not like.

The unitary patent

It will be remembered here that the main aim of the establishment of a Community patent was to build upon the achievements of the EPC by adding the grant of a unitary patent for the whole of the Community to the single application and single examination system. As far back as 1975, the Community Patent Convention was agreed,[68] although agreement on its implementation was never reached. What followed was a long period of difficult negotiations without real progress, until the Commission decided to revive the project in the form of an EU Regulation[69] and the Council made it one of its priorities. It is understood that agreement was reached on most substantive points, but

---

[64] Case C-30/90, *Commission of the European Communities v. UK* [1992] ECR I-829, [1992] 2 CMLR 709.

[65] J.-F. Verstrynghe, 'The Spring 1993 Horace S Manges Lecture: The European Commission's Direction on Copyright and Neighbouring Rights—Towards the Regime of the Twenty-first Century' (1993) 17 Colum-VLA JL & Arts. 187 and 194.

[66] E.g. the Community trade mark: see Regulation 40/94 [1994] OJ L 11/1.

[67] See also Opinion 1/94 [1994] ECR I-5267 (concerning the Community's competence to sign the TRIPS Agreement).

[68] (1976) OJ L 17/1.

[69] See the Commission Proposal for a Council Regulation on the Community Patent (2000) OJ C 337/278, COM (00) 412 final. The latest full text version is available as Council document 8539/03, dated 16 April

the language regime and some other details remained controversial. In an Opinion the Court of Justice also rejected the proposal on the basis that it was not consistent with EU law.[70] Eventually, the negotiations stalled, primarily over the language issue and Spain and Italy left the project that continued on the basis of enhanced cooperation between 25 member states. The negotiations then yielded agreement on a substantive patent law regulation that will create a unitary patent for the 25 member states.[71] This will effectively be a European Patent to which unitary effect will be given in those 25 member states. The language regime will be English, French, and German and the EPO will administer the scheme. With the language issue out of the way attention focused on the idea of creating a single court system, the Unified Patent Court.[72]

Problems had indeed also arisen in the past in relation to the suggestion to set up a single European patent court system that would deal with infringement and validity issues that arise in relation to unitary patents. This time though an Agreement was eventually reached.[73] The Unified Patent Court will deal with issues relating to both unitary patents and European Patents. The specialized single patent court will have exclusive jurisdiction to deal with infringement and validity issues, as well as with revocation issues. There will be a central main chamber and an appeal level, all staffed with experienced patent judges from all over the EU. Larger member states and groupings of member states that have a minimum volume of cases will be able to ask for the creation of local regional divisions. The language in which the patent was granted will define the language of the procedure in the central division, whereas local and regional divisions will in principle use the language of the host member state. And the idea that raising a validity question can derail an infringement question and force a hand over to the exclusive jurisdiction of the courts of the country that granted the right seems to have been abandoned too. This is obviously important for the unitary patent, but it is important too for the European patents that will continue to exist and to which the system will also apply. The EPO will also continue in its role as the central patent office, not only for European patents, but also for unitary patents. In the end an agreement was reached to have the seat of the unitary court's central division in Paris, with two separate thematic clusters in Munich and London.[74] The objections raised by the Court of Justice in its Opinion seem to have been overcome by assurances that the Unitary Patent Court will respect and apply EU law in collaboration with the Court of Justice, with contracting member states being responsible for any infringements of EU law.

There was a fear though that too much involvement of the Court of Justice could result in unduly long delays if cases from the Unitary Patent Court's Appeal Court could be appealed to the Court of Justice. The European Parliament on the other hand wanted the Court of Justice to remain involved. This led to a final compromise that sees Arts. 6–8 that deal with restricted acts, limitations, and exceptions, and that could be the basis for an appeal to the Court of Justice, being removed from the Unitary Patent Regulation

2003, online at <http://ec.europa.eu/growth/industry/intellectual-property/patents/unitary-patent/index_en.htm>, where further progress can be monitored.

[70] Opinion 1/09, <http://curia.europa.eu>.

[71] Regulation (EU) No 1257/2012 of the European Parliament and of the Council of 17 December 2012 implementing enhanced cooperation in the area of the creation of unitary patent protection [2012] OJ L-361/1. Council Regulation (EU) No 1260/2012 of 17 December 2012 implementing enhanced cooperation in the area of the creation of unitary patent protection with regard to the applicable translation arrangements [2012] OJ L-361/89.

[72] See J. Pila and C. Wadlow (eds) (2014) *The Unitary EU Patent System*, Oxford: Hart Publishing.

[73] [2013] OJ C-175/1. See <http://www.unified-patent-court.org/images/documents/upc-agreement.pdf>; see also <http://www.unified-patent-court.org/>.

[74] See <http://www.consilium.europa.eu/uedocs/cms_data/docs/pressdata/en/ec/131388.pdf>.

and moved to the Unitary Court Agreement. The latter will be a separate treaty, not part of the Community system as it also covers European patents, and as such there is less option to appeal to the Court of Justice on points of substantive patent law. Whilst the Regulation can enter into force straight away, the Unitary Patent Court deal will need to be ratified by at least 13 member states first. And the Court is needed before the Unitary Patent system can become operational. And until all ratify (and Spain and Italy eventually get on board one way or another) the 'unitary' patent risks being anything but unitary. For now, Spain is clearly outside the system, but Italy has joined the Unitary Patent Court Agreement (but not the unitary patent as such), whilst Poland seems to have no intention to ratify the UPC Agreement (and will therefore stay out altogether). The next edition of this book will hopefully finally be able to set out the exact details of a scheme that is now optimistically forecast to enter into force some time in 2017.

An overview

This chapter went beyond the traditional boundaries of patent law in the UK. The first transgression is caused by the fact that certain inventions, such as pharmaceutical products, also need marketing authorization before they can be marketed; a patent on its own is not sufficient. This may involve a shortening of the period during which commercial exploitation can take place under conditions of exclusivity put in place by the patent. Supplementary protection certificates have therefore been established in relation to these specific categories of invention. They are strongly linked to the patent and, in a sense, extend the protection for the invention. The loss of exclusivity for reasons that are not linked to the patent system is undone.

The second transgression is not mentioned in this chapter, because it is not of the same nature, but one could consider that the Biotech Directive is the second transgression even if it purportedly only clarifies the application of patent law in the area of biotechnology. The final transgression is the saga of the unitary patent. It goes beyond the UK, in the sense that it would create a single unitary patent for the 25 member states involved. Decades of negotiations have yielded draft after draft and a deal has finally been done.

Further reading

ADAMS, J. N., 'Supplementary Protection Certificates: The Challenge to EC Regulation 1768/92' (1994) 8 EIPR 323.

DELCOURT, D., 'Public Health and the Preservation of Economic Competitiveness: The European Supplementary Protection Certificate for Medicinal Products' (2009) 4(6) JIPLP 439–44.

KLIX, N. and HERMANN, B., 'Bitter Pill for the Pharmaceutical Industry' (2006) 1(10) JIPLP 639–42.

MILLER, R. et al. (eds.) (2011) *Terrell on the Law of Patents*, 17th edn, London: Sweet and Maxwell, Ch. 6.

TILMANN, W., 'Community Patent and European Patent Agreement' (2005) 27(5) EIPR 65–7.

ULLRICH, H. (2006) 'National, European and Community Patent Protection: Time for Reconsideration', Law Working Paper No. 2006/41, Florence: European University Institute, <http://cadmus.iue.it/dspace/bitstream/1814/6421/1/LAW-%202006–41.pdf>.

8

Patents—an overview

Critics of the patent system have ample ammunition at their disposal. To get a patent, much time and energy have to be expended in pursuit of an uncertain outcome—particularly if others are active in the field—that is, at best, a limited-period monopoly. Within the law itself are some real horror stories, such as the exposure in *Genentech*[1] of the falsity of the obviousness–inventiveness dichotomy and the inherent uncertainty of the purposive approach to patents being compounded by the additional uncertainty created by common law judges having to learn Continental approaches to issues of interpretation. Add to this the uncertainty that attends the basic question of the proper purpose of the patent system, and the practical problem of how much and when to claim in an application for a patent, and despair may seem an appropriate response.

Yet thousands of patents are granted annually. This fact alone may be thought to suggest that all is not lost in the patent system. Much of the law functions well and the time taken to grant a patent is a result of painstaking examination to ensure that the invention fits in with the legal criteria. Remember, too, what the thousands of applicants get from the time and effort of application. It is the triumph of the patent system that the nebulous concept of invention is translated by the law into an item of personal property that can be assigned or licensed to others and used to prevent others from infringing the monopoly it confers. Requiring change to mend some damaged parts of the law does not, in any way, prevent the conclusion that the patent system works well, on both national and international levels, balancing as it does, in different ways at different times, the competing interests of all of those affected by the law in this area: inventors, their rivals, consumers, and society itself.

In so far as the patent system may be criticized, it is clearly having trouble getting to grips with 'cutting edge' issues, such as biotechnology, nanotechnology, and synthetic biology. The extent to which the numbers of successfully worked patents does not match the number of patents granted also suggests that there are imperfections in the system. But the bottom line must be that the—albeit imperfect—patent system is a high-quality system involving detailed claims and their full examination. Critics of the time and cost involved in a patent application forget that these problems arise from the quality of the system: the system is neither fast nor cheap, but it generally succeeds in its aims. It would be equally churlish to criticize a Rolls-Royce motor car for being large and expensive: how else could its qualities thrive, uncompromised? It is significant that a government that was especially keen to promote business efficiency and to remove restrictions on commerce failed signally, at the height of its power in the mid-1980s, to implement

---

[1] *Genentech Inc.'s Patent* [1989] RPC 147.

proposals made for lower levels of patent protection[2] so as to suit business interests. Since then the trend has been inverted.

Further reading

GHIDINI, G. (2006) *Intellectual Property and Competition Law: The Innovation Nexus*, Cheltenham/Northampton, MA: Edward Elgar, Ch. 2.

---

[2] Cmnd 9117, 1983, esp. paras. 4.7–4.13.

SECTION C
Copyright and Related Issues

9
An introduction to copyright

The roots of copyright

Copyright has two types of root. On the one hand, it started as an exclusive right to make copies—that is, to reproduce the work of an author. This entrepreneurial side of copyright is linked in tightly with the invention of the printing press, which made it much easier to copy a literary work and, for the first time, permitted the entrepreneur to make multiple identical copies. On the other hand, it became vital to protect the author now that his or her work could be copied much more easily and in much higher numbers. It was felt that the author should share in the profits of this new exploitation of the work, although this feeling was much stronger in Continental Europe than it was in the UK.

Before the arrival of the printing press, many original literary or musical works were commissioned. One copy was written and the commissioner paid the author for that copy. The printing technology resulted in the production of multiple copies and it was almost naturally felt that the author should be paid for each copy that was made. Because the technique also reduced the possibility of the author controlling the format and contents of the various copies, and because the entrepreneur now undertook the reproduction work, it became necessary to think about minimum guarantees for the author in this area. This resulted in the creation of certain so-called 'moral rights', which protected the author against unfair use of his or her work. This double set of roots is still reflected in modern copyright law.

Ever since it was created, copyright was directed towards the protection of a reproduction of the work. It was, first of all, a right in the production of printed copies of the work, which means that it is exclusively concerned with the material expression of the ideas on which the work is based. Copyright is not about ideas, but about the way in which they are expressed.

Copyright has nonetheless proven to be a valuable and flexible tool. It could be used to protect various works, because it was merely a reproduction right that could be applied to very different forms of expression of ideas. At various moments in time, literary works, musical works, artistic works—such as sculptures and paintings—works of architecture, computer programs, etc. all started to attract copyright protection. A similar expansion of copyright can be seen in relation to the carriers of the various works, as sound recordings, tapes, broadcasts, films, video, etc. all entered the copyright arena.

It is, however, to the essential elements of copyright that we will turn first.

Essential elements

The Copyright, Designs and Patents Act 1988 characterizes copyright as a property right. As we saw in Chapter 1, there are many types of copyright. First of all, we will have to distinguish them, and find out which requirements should be fulfilled by the various works and materials to attract copyright protection.

In the next stage, we will have to consider who becomes the owner of the property right, what will be the duration of the right, and what constitutes infringement of this intangible property right.

A copyright work

Does a work attract copyright? This will depend upon the nature of the material involved, produced through intellectual or entrepreneurial activity, and upon the qualification issue. The latter element is more international in scope.

The copyright and related rights conventions[1] contain minimum provisions that are translated and implemented by the national copyright Acts. The provisions also require that authors and works linked in a certain way to one of the adherents to the conventions will be treated by national copyright legislation in the same way as will national authors and works. On the one hand, this link or qualification issue constitutes a separate hurdle and only those works that pass it will attract copyright protection; on the other, no formalities—such as registration—are required to secure copyright protection.[2]

In relation to the material involved, the Berne Convention defines this broadly as literary and artistic works and the CJEU increasingly focuses in this respect on the originality criterion.[3] There needs to be a degree of creative freedom that is then used by the author to create his or her own expression of the unprotected underlying idea. That original expression then constitutes a work in as far as it falls into the broad category of literary and artistic works. That gives rise to the (open) question whether national laws can operate a (narrower) closed system of categories of works, as is the case in the CDPA 1988.

The idea–expression dichotomy

A further key preliminary point is that ideas are not protected—that is, only the particular expression of an idea is protected. The dichotomy between 'idea' and 'expression' is a key element in copyright law, but its real meaning, as well as its application in practice, raises difficult issues.

Lord Hoffmann offered the following explanation in *Designers Guild v. Russell Williams Textiles Ltd*:[4]

My Lords, if one examines the cases in which the distinction between ideas and the expression of ideas has been given effect, I think it will be found that they support two quite distinct propositions. The first is that a copyright work may express certain ideas which are not protected because they have no connection with the literary, dramatic, musical or artistic nature of the work. It is on this ground that, for example, a literary work which

[1] Such as the Berne Convention for the Protection of Literary and Artistic Works 1886 and the Rome Convention for the Protection of Performers, Producers of Phonograms and Broadcasting Organisations 1961.

[2] The familiar copyright notice—that is, '© name of the copyright owner and year of first publication'—is a formality required not by the Berne Convention, but by the Universal Copyright Convention (UCC); it is required if a published work is to attract copyright in a country that adheres only to the UCC.

[3] Case C-5/08, *Infopaq International A/S v. Danske Dagblades Forening* [2009] ECDR 16.

[4] [2000] 1 WLR 2416.

describes a system or invention does not entitle the author to claim protection for his or her system or invention as such. The same is true of an inventive concept expressed in an artistic work. However striking or original it may be, others are (in the absence of patent protection) free to express it in works of their own: see *Kleeneze Ltd v. DRG (UK) Ltd* [1984] FSR 399. The other proposition is that certain ideas expressed by a copyright work may not be protected because, although they are ideas of a literary, dramatic or artistic nature, they are not original, or so commonplace as not to form a substantial part of the work. *Kenrick & Co. v. Lawrence & Co.* (1890) 25 QBD 99 is a well-known example. It is on this ground that the mere notion of combining stripes and flowers would not have amounted to a substantial part of the plaintiff's work. At that level of abstraction, the idea, though expressed in the design, would not have represented sufficient of the author's skill and labour as to attract copyright protection.[5]

As is clear from this quote, the author needs to invest a minimum amount of skill and labour in his or her work. That makes it an expression of an idea and it can therefore be protected by copyright. Copyright therefore protects works that are the author's own expression of the underlying idea. These works are then the author's own intellectual creation. Limiting the protection offered by copyright to the author's own expression of the idea leaves the idea unprotected and part of the common heritage of mankind. It is free to be used by others to create their own expressions when they exercise their freedom of expression, with which copyright is carefully balanced.[6]

In those cases, the expression will be original. Originality is therefore linked to the idea–expression dichotomy. Copyright uses the concepts of idea–expression and originality to determine what can be appropriated through the grant of copyright; anything else will be in the public domain and will not be subject to an exclusive right. Through these concepts, copyright really regulates the balance and tension that was set out in Chapter 1. Striking a correct balance is essential to justify copyright as an exclusive right.[7] There remains a level of discretion on this point for national legislators, as the Berne Convention does not define originality. The *travaux préparatoires* give the clear hint that literary and artistic works are by their nature original, but in the past that concept has been filled in differently in common law countries such as the UK, where minimum amounts of skill and labour were the norm, and in civil law countries, where the imprint of the author's personality was the norm. European instruments tend to go for the concept of the author's own intellectual creation. Recently the Court of Justice argued that that criterion now applies across the board in copyright in the EU.[8] That may not be such a straightforward conclusion, but on the other hand one could argue that the House of Lords has effectively endorsed that line when it defined what is to be understood by skill and labour and how idea and expression are to be distinguished.[9] In other words, the different wording may refer to an almost identical concept.

---

[5] [2000] 1 WLR 2416 at 2423.

[6] See P. Torremans (ed.) (2008) *Intellectual Property and Human Rights*, Vol. 18, Information Law Series, The Hague: Kluwer Law International, now in its third edition: P. Torremans (ed.) (2015) *Intellectual Property and Human Rights*, Vol. 34, Information Law Series, The Hague: Kluwer Law International.

[7] See T. Dreier (2001) 'Balancing Proprietary and Public Domain Interests: Inside or Outside of Proprietary Rights', in R. Dreyfuss, D. Zimmerman, and H. First (eds.) *Expanding the Boundaries of Intellectual Property: Innovation Policy for the Knowledge Society*, Oxford: Oxford University Press, p. 303.

[8] *Infopaq* (n. 3).

[9] *Newspaper Licensing Agency Ltd v. Marks & Spencer plc* [2001] 3 WLR 290 at para. 19, per Lord Hoffmann.

Fixation

It flows from the need for an expression of an idea that all subject matter, i.e. all works, needs to exist in some permanent form before it can attract copyright. This goes beyond the limited literal function requirement in the Act. Instead it is linked to the idea that there needs to be work, the author's work. And in order to move from a mere idea to the author's personal expression of such an idea one needs a minimal degree of permanency. Works can be erased and be of a temporary nature, but expression requires that they take a perceivable format, an expression that can be identified as the personal imprint of the author. In practice, this issue gives rise to interesting interpretation problems in the sphere of artistic activity: for example, is a face make-up that is used repeatedly permanent enough in nature,[10] and what about a device used to make sand pictures that contained sand and glycerine?[11] In both cases, the answer was negative. In the latter case, the user of the device turned it over and made the pictures. It would have been problematical to hold that all of these were the work of the marker of the device.

For many works, however, this does not create a problem, because the creation and fixation of the work take place at the same time. For example, the idea in a painting is only expressed—and can, as a consequence, only attract protection—when the work is executed and fixation takes place automatically. But we will have to come back to this issue, because its application to certain other works is more problematical.

An overview

Copyright has come a long way from its roots as a right to copy in the sphere of literary and artistic works. It has proven itself to be a very flexible tool that can also cope with various new technological developments and very different types of work.

Copyright is based on a couple of key concepts. First, it protects works and, if these meet the requirements, they become copyright works. But ideas are not protected by copyright, only expressions of ideas are covered—and, in making that distinction, the originality requirement as a precondition to copyright protection plays a vital role. Additionally, works have to be fixated if they are to attract copyright protection.

Further reading

DREIER, T. (2001) 'Balancing Proprietary and Public Domain Interests: Inside or Outside of Proprietary Rights', in R. Dreyfuss, D. Zimmerman, and H. First (eds.) *Expanding the Boundaries of Intellectual Property: Innovation Policy for the Knowledge Society*, Oxford: Oxford University Press, pp. 295–316.

GENDREAU, Y. 'The Criterion of Fixation in Copyright Law' (1994) 159 RIDA 110.

KARNELL, G. (1998) 'European Originality: A Copyright Chimera', in J. Kabel et al. (eds.) *Intellectual Property and Information Law*, The Hague: Kluwer, pp. 201–9.

---

[10] *Merchandising Corp. of America Inc. v. Harpbond Inc.* [1983] FSR 32 (the *Adam Ant* case).
[11] *Komesaroff v. Mickle* [1988] RPC 204.

10

The various types of copyright and the quality issue

Copyright protects literary and artistic works, according to the Berne Convention. These two broad categories of works are subdivided into several types of works and copyright protection also seems to be linked to a minimum level of originality. This chapter therefore essentially looks at the conditions a work needs to meet in order for it to attract copyright.

Section 1(1) of the Copyright, Designs and Patents Act (CDPA) 1988 lists the various types of copyright, which are further defined in the following sections. The case law is also a helpful source of information in this respect. In reality, various types of work are defined. Every work that can be classified as one of these types of work will attract copyright, if all of the other requirements are met. By defining various types of work[1] the Act is trying to cover the spectrum of literary and artistic works set out in the Berne Convention.

This classification of works is an important aspect of our copyright system: a work that does not come within the definition of any of the types of work will not be protected by copyright. It might also be argued that each work must be classified in one category: a work would not be able to get copyright protection under two different classifications at the same time. Indeed, slight differences may exist between the various regimes of copyright protection for each of the types of work and this could give rise to problems. A product may include more than one work for copyright purposes, but each of these works will be classified and protected as a single type of work. This point was summarized as follows by Laddie J:[2]

> although different copyrights can protect simultaneously a particular product and an author can produce more than one copyright work during the course of a single episode of creative effort, for example a competent musician may write the words and the music for a song at the same time, it is quite another thing to say that a single piece of work by an author gives rise to two or more copyrights in respect of the same creative effort.[3]

This point has now been addressed further by the Court of Appeal, however, and it is submitted that the view of Laddie J now needs to be confined to those copyrights that are listed in s. 1(1)(a) of the 1988 Act. This seems to flow logically from the decision of the Court of Appeal in *Norowzian v. Arks*,[4] in which the court held that a film could

---

[1] The concept of a work is as such, though, not defined and this results in a certain amount of uncertainty. See Ch. Handig, 'The Copyright Term "Work": European Harmonisation at an Unknown Level' (2009) 40(6) IIC 665–85.

[2] *Electronic Techniques (Anglia) Ltd v. Critchley Components Ltd* [1997] FSR 401, per Laddie J; see also *Anacon Corp. Ltd v. Environmental Research Technology Ltd* [1994] FSR 659.

[3] *Electronic Techniques (Anglia) Ltd v. Critchley Components Ltd* (n. 2) per Laddie J at 41?

[4] *Norowzian v. Arks Ltd (No. 2)* [2000] FSR 363.

also constitute a dramatic work, as long as the criteria for both categories were met. This means that a work can, at the same time, be protected as an original work in one of the categories listed in s. 1(1)(a) of the 1988 Act and as sound recording, film, or broadcast under s. 1(1)(b) of that Act.

There is no harmonized EU rule that either prohibits or imposes the classification approach as it is found in the UK. It is nevertheless interesting to note that the CJEU placed a lot of emphasis on the originality criterion in *Infopaq* and did not require a specific provision in a directive to do so.[5] One could arguably derive from this decision that originality is the sole criterion. That would effectively mean that the combination of originality and expression, i.e. any original expression, would result in a copyright work. The classification system that requires as a first step a work that falls within a category would then no longer be required and even be in breach of EU law. For the time being there is no final decision on this point, but the debate also demonstrates a trend that puts originality at its heart and goes from there to the definition of a work rather than to start with the concept of a work and only then to look for originality.

Original literary, dramatic, musical, and artistic works

The first groups of categories are literary, dramatic, musical, or artistic works respectively. In order for it to come within the scope of one of these categories a work has to satisfy first of all the originality requirement. Only 'original' works will attract copyright.

The originality requirement

All works in this first category have in common the originality requirement. Originality should not, however, be taken in the normal sense: neither novelty nor innovation is required; the starting point is that the work is not copied and originates from the author.[6] The author must produce his or her own expression of the idea, but the test to establish whether the work originates from the author is in origin only a minimum-effort standard. It is not required that the idea is new, because the *idea* is not covered by copyright at all. A radically new and different expression of the idea of the passionate love story between two people with irreconcilable cultural backgrounds set in outer space is equally not required; the author's own expression of the classic *Romeo and Juliet* tale will suffice. The author must only have expended 'skill, judgement and labour', or 'selection, judgment and experience', or 'labour, skill and capital' in creating the work.[7]

In reality, two cumulative requirements are involved: first, the work must originate from the author; secondly, there must have been a minimum investment by the author of skill, judgement, and labour. Both requirements have to be met. The investment of skill, judgement, and labour merely in the process of copying someone else's work cannot confer originality.[8] But even if that threshold is low,

---

[5] Case C-5/08, *Infopaq International A/S v. Danske Dagblades Forening* [2009] ECDR 16.

[6] *Ladbroke (Football) Ltd v. William Hill (Football) Ltd* [1964] 1 All ER 465, [1964] 1 WLR 273, per Lord Pearce at 479 and 291; *University of London Press Ltd v. University Tutorial Press Ltd* [1916] 2 Ch 601, per Peterson J at 609.

[7] *Ladbroke (Football)* (n. 6), per Lord Pearce at 479 and 291; and *University of London Press* (n. 6), per Peterson J at 609.

[8] This was reconfirmed by the Court of Appeal in *Biotrading & Financing OY v. Biohit Ltd* [1998] FSR 109 at 116; see also Lord Oliver's opinion in *Interlego AG v. Tyco Industries Inc.* [1989] AC 217 at 258.

works that do not meet this minimum standard will not attract copyright protection: a copy that incorporates some minor alterations of a work which is no longer protected under copyright, for example, will not attract copyright.[9] Even if the content of a work may be nothing more than a compilation of existing elements, some skill and labour must have been invested in the way in which those elements are organized and expressed.[10] On the one hand, that skill and labour must not be so trivial that it could be characterized as a purely mechanical exercise; on the other, creativity, as such, is not required either.[11] Football pool coupon lists, for example, can be protected, but only if it can be shown that the presentation of the material is special: it must be shown that the author has invested skill and labour in the way in which the table is organized. There must be *a relation of creation between the work and the author whatever this act of creation (sometimes only presentation) means*.[12] But what amounts to a sufficient amount of independent skill, labour, and judgement is not capable of definition in advance; it has to be determined on the facts of each case.[13]

Most other European countries have in origin a slightly higher originality threshold. They define an original work as a work that constitutes the expression of the personality of its author and a work should be the author's own intellectual creation.[14] This version of originality is found in the European Community Copyright Directives,[15] which introduced a very partial harmonization of copyright in the Community.[16]

We will have to come back to this issue when we discuss the relevant types of work in detail. Suffice it to say here that this higher originality requirement has now been included in the Copyright, Designs and Patents Act 1988,[17] in relation to copyright in databases, as a result of the implementation of the Database Directive.[18] It is interesting to note though that recent House of Lords decisions seem to depart from a strict interpretation of the 'mere skill and labour' test and the Court of Justice has recently hinted that the harmonized European concept of originality may apply across the board. Harmonization may therefore be further advanced than one would have thought, which is possible in the absence of a statutory definition of 'originality'. One can indeed see a tendency for English courts to use the concept of the author's own intellectual creation as the standard for originality.[19] Let us now move away from the historical cases and look in more detail at the recent evolution.

---

[9] See *Interlego AG* (n. 8).

[10] See *Cramp (GA) & Sons Ltd v. Smythson* [1944] AC 329, [1944] 2 All ER 92.

[11] See the decision of the Supreme Court of Canada in *The Law Society of Upper Canada v. CCH Canadian Ltd, Thomson Canada Ltd & Canada Law Book Inc.* [2004] SCC 13.

[12] A. Dietz, 'The Artist's Right of Integrity under Copyright Law: A Comparative Approach' (1994) 25 IIC 177, at 182.

[13] *Biotrading & Financing* (n. 8) at 116.

[14] For a recent example, see *Bettina Rheims v. M. Jakob Gautel and others*, decision of the 1st Civil Division of the French Cour de Cassation (Supreme Court) of 13 November 2008, 40 (2009) 4 IIC 485.

[15] See e.g. Art. 1(3) of the Council Directive of 14 May 1991 on the legal protection of computer programs (1991) OJ L 122/42, now Art. 1(3) of the codified Directive 2009/24/EC of the European Parliament and of the Council of 23 April 2009 on the legal protection of computer programs [2009] OJ L 111/16.

[16] See also the amended draft Directive (1998) OJ L 289/28 and Regulation (2001) OJ C 120/12 on industrial design.

[17] As s. 3A.

[18] European Parliament and Council Directive 96/9/EC (1996) OJ L 77/20 and the Copyright and Rights in Databases Regulations 1997.

[19] See e.g. *SAS Institute Inc v. World Programming Ltd* [2013] EWCA Civ 1482.

An attempt at clarification in *Hyperion*

The exact meaning of the concept of originality in English law has never been absolutely clear, but a recent case allowed the Court of Appeal to shed some more light on it. In *Hyperion Records v. Lionel Sawkins*,[20] the question arose of whether originality could be found in a restored musical work. The original musical work by Lalande was out of copyright, but Dr Lionel Sawkins had restored the work by making performing editions that allowed the work to be played again. In doing so, Sawkins had made additions and corrections, but he had done so with the aim of restoring the work in its original format— that is, as Lalande would have composed it.

A lot has been made in relation to this case of the public policy issue that granting copyright in a restored, out-of-copyright work would hinder access to the work itself. The underlying argument seems to be that the real originality and the real work is that which is out of copyright, and, in that line of thought, granting a new copyright would clash with public policy. The *Hyperion* case offered a unique opportunity to dispel that myth. Copyright only protects a particular expression of a certain idea and not the idea itself. Copyright in a restored or reconstituted version of an out-of-copyright work will protect only the expression of the restored or reconstituted version; everyone remains free to use the out-of-copyright material itself. To use the specific facts of *Hyperion*: granting Lionel Sawkins copyright in his performing editions will not protect anyone from copying Lalande's music or from making their own performing editions. All they cannot do is use the shortcut offered by the existence of Sawkins' performing editions by copying these without his consent.

This last point is the most basic expression of the public policy of copyright—namely, to prevent the unauthorized copying of certain material forms of expression. One should therefore be very careful in using the public policy argument in this type of case.

The broad perspective restated

The key point is, however, found in the fact that only certain material forms of expression are, from a public policy point of view, worth protecting by copyright. Only original forms of expression are to be protected.

Let us look at this from a broad perspective. Remember that originality should not be taken in the normal (dictionary) sense here: neither novelty nor innovation is required; the starting point is that the work is not copied and originates from the author, as the House of Lords made clear in *Ladbroke v. William Hill*.[21] The author must produce his or her own expression of the idea, but the test to establish whether the work indeed originates from the author is only a minimum-effort standard. It is not required that the idea is new, because the idea is not covered by copyright at all. The author must only have expended 'skill, judgement and labour', or 'selection, judgement and experience', or 'labour, skill and capital' in creating the work, in relation to which two cumulative requirements are involved: that the work must originate from the author and that there must have been a minimum investment by the author of skill, judgement, and labour. The investment of skill, judgement and labour merely in the process of copying someone else's work cannot confer originality, as was confirmed by the Court of Appeal in *Biotrading v. Biohit*,[22] with reference to Lord Oliver's famous dictum in *Interlego v. Tyco*.[23]

But even if the threshold is low, works that do not meet this minimum standard will not attract copyright protection. The question of whether an item that is similar to a

---

[20] [2005] 3 All ER 636, [2005] 1 WLR 3281 (CA).

[21] *Ladbroke (Football)* (n. 6), per Lord Pearce at 479 and 291; *University of London Press Ltd* (n. 6), per Peterson J at 609.

[22] *Biotrading & Financing OY* (n. 8) at 116.

[23] *Interlego AG* (n. 8) at 258.

copyright work is, in its own right, an original copyright work is a difficult question, in relation to which the Court of Appeal provided some guidance in *Guild v. Eskander Ltd.*[24] A piecemeal approach should be guarded against; the question was, instead, whether all—and not just any one or more—of the additional features gave rise to the requisite quality of originality. The need to look at the work as a whole is crucial and the Court of Appeal also emphasizes this in *Hyperion*. Despite that, some consideration of individual features would be unavoidable in answering that question.

A copy that incorporates some minor alterations of a work that is no longer protected under copyright will not attract copyright.[25] The principle is clearly stated in the *Interlego* case and is widely accepted. Its exact coverage, however, and the answer to the question of whether it can be reconciled with the judgment of the House of Lords in *Walter v. Lane*,[26] is less clear. The *Hyperion* case obliged the Court of Appeal to rule on these points and we will return to that ruling shortly, but here we will mention only that copyright infringement in a performing edition of a fourth work was ruled out, because there had been only a very limited editorial input by Dr Sawkins.

Even if the content of a work may be nothing other than a compilation of existing elements, some skill and labour must have been invested in the way in which they are organized and expressed.[27] That skill and labour must not be so trivial that it could be characterized as a purely mechanical exercise, but creativity as such is not required either, as can be seen from the decision of the Supreme Court of Canada in *The Law Society of Upper Canada v. CCH Canadian Ltd, Thomson Canada Ltd & Canada Law Book Inc.*[28]

There is no better way to conclude this overview of the general approach to originality in English law than to quote Dr Dietz, who wrote that there must be '*a relation of creation between the work and the author whatever this act of creation (sometimes only presentation) means*'.[29] With hindsight, these wise words almost sound prophetic in a *Hyperion* context. What amounts to a sufficient amount of independent 'skill, labour and judgement' is not capable of definition in advance, it has to be determined on the facts of each case.[30]

How does Hyperion *apply in practice?*

It is now time to return to the somewhat narrower perspective of the *Hyperion* case and to apply these principles in detail. Mummery LJ looks at this from the following angle:

> The first question is whether the performing editions are incapable of being regarded as 'original' works because Lalande composed the music and Dr Sawkins made his editions of that music with the intention that they should be as close as possible to the Lalande originals.[31]

The Court of Appeal answers that question by relying very strongly on the dictum of the House of Lords of over century ago in *Walter v. Lane*.[32] The Court of Appeal suggests that that decision is still good law as a result of the confirmation it received in *Express Newspapers plc v. News (UK) Ltd.*[33]

---

[24] *Guild v. Eskander Ltd* [2003] FSR 23.   [25] See *Interlego AG* (n. 8).

[26] *Walter v. Lane* [1900] AC 539 (HL).   [27] See *Cramp (GA) & Sons* (n. 10).

[28] The *Law Society of Upper Canada v. CCH Canadian Ltd, Thomson Canada Ltd & Canada Law Book Inc.* [2004] SCC 13.

[29] Dietz, 'The Artist's Right of Integrity under Copyright Law: A Comparative Approach' (n. 12) at 182.

[30] *Biotrading & Financing OY v. Biohit Ltd* (n. 8) at 116.

[31] *Hyperion Records v. Lionel Sawkins* [2005] 3 All ER 636, [2005] 1 WLR 3281 (CA) at para. 32 of the judgment.

[32] *Walter v. Lane* (n. 26), a decision on the Copyright Act 1842 that used a different kind of wording when compared to the CDPA 1988.

[33] *Express Newspapers plc v. News (UK) Ltd* [1990] FSR 359 at 365–6.

In *Walter v. Lane*, the House of Lords held that copyright subsisted in shorthand writers' reports of public speeches as 'original literary' works. The Earl of Rosebery had made the speeches in public, with the reporters present. The reporters had made notes in shorthand; they had later transcribed them, corrected, revised, and punctuated them, and they had published them in newspapers as verbatim reports of the speeches. From the copyright point of view adopted by the House of Lords, a speech and a *report* of a speech are two different things. Lord Rosebery was the author of his speeches; the shorthand writers were the authors of their reports of his speeches. They spent effort, skill, and time in writing up their reports of speeches that they themselves had not written. For our current purposes, it is very important to note that the reports were held to be 'original' literary works, even though the intention of the reporters was to produce as accurate a report as possible of a work of which they were not the authors.

This analysis led Mummery LJ to the following conclusion in the *Hyperion* case:[34]

> In my judgment, on the application of *Walter v. Lane* to this case, the effort, skill and time which the judge found Dr Sawkins spent in making the 3 performing editions were sufficient to satisfy the requirement that they should be 'original' works in the copyright sense. This is so even though (a) Dr Sawkins worked on the scores of existing musical works composed by another person (Lalande); (b) Lalande's works are out of copyright; and (c) Dr Sawkins had no intention of adding any new notes of music of his own.

This reliance on *Walter v. Lane* cannot be accepted, however, without considering the dictum in the *Interlego* case with which it seems at odds. One has, indeed, in the past derived a *de minimis* rule from the words of Lord Oliver in that case[35]—that is, that a copy incorporating some minor alterations of a work that is no longer protected under copyright will not attract copyright. But the question must be asked whether the impact of the following words does not go further:

> Take the simplest case of artistic copyright, a painting or photograph. It takes great skill, judgment and labour to produce a good copy by painting or to produce an enlarged photograph from a positive print, but no one would reasonably contend that the copy painting or enlargement was an 'original' artistic work in which the copier is entitled to claim copyright. Skill, labour or judgment merely in the process of copying cannot confer originality.[36]

In other words, does this dictum in any way reverse what was said in *Walter v. Lane* in the context of a somewhat differently worded statutory provision?

It is submitted that the two provisions are not incompatible and that the dictum in *Interlego* needs to be interpreted restrictively. The court was, after all, dealing with drawings for plastic toy blocks that had barely been touched and the attempt of the producer of the blocks effectively to prolong the term of their protection was all too obvious. Jacob LJ makes this point very clearly in the second (concurring) judgment in *Hyperion*.[37] Like him, I would like to refer to the authors of the *Modern Law of Copyright*,[38] who interpret the dictum in *Interlego* as follows:

> However, whilst the remarks made in *Interlego* may be valid if confined to the subject matter then before the Privy Council, they are stated too widely. The Privy Council was

---

[34] *Hyperion Records* (n. 31) at para. 36 of the judgment.
[35] See e.g. the fourth edition of this book, p. 175.   [36] *Interlego* (n. 8) per Lord Oliver at 371.
[37] At paras. 79–82 of the judgment.
[38] H. Laddie, P. Prescott, and M. Vitoria (1995) *The Modern Law of Copyright and Designs* 2nd edn, London: Butterworths.

there considering fairly simple technical drawings. This is a rather special subject-matter. While the drawing of such a work is more laborious than it looks, it is a fact that any competent draftsman (perhaps, any conscientious amateur) who sets out to reproduce it exactly will almost certainly succeed in the end, because of the mathematical precision of the lines and measurements. This should be contrasted with, e.g. a painting by Vermeer, where it will be obvious that very few persons, if any, are capable of making an exact replica. Now, assume a number of persons do set out to copy such a painting, each according to his own personal skill. Most will only succeed in making something which all too obviously differs from the original—some of them embarrassingly so. They will get a copyright seeing that in each instance the end result does not differ from the original yet it took a measure of skill and labour to produce. If, however, one of these renders the original with all the skill and precision of a Salvador Dali, is he to be denied a copyright where a mere dauber is not? The difference between the two cases (technical drawing and old master painting) is that in the latter there is room for individual interpretation even where faithful replication is sought to be attempted while in the former there is not. Further, a photographer who carefully took a photograph of an original painting might get a copyright and, if this is so, it is rather hard to see why a copy of the same degree of fidelity, if rendered by an artist of the calibre aforementioned, would not be copyright. These considerations suggest that the proposition under discussion is suspect. It is therefore submitted that, for example, a picture restorer may get a copyright for the result of his efforts. Be that as it may, it is submitted that the *Interlego* proposition is anyway distinguishable where the replicator succeeds in preserving for posterity an original to which access is difficult.[39]

To quote Jane Ginsburg:[40]

Reproductions requiring great talent and technical skill may qualify as protectable works of authorship, even if they are *copies* of pre-existing works. This would be the case for photographic and other high quality replicas of works of art.

In conclusion, the two dicta are not incompatible: *Walter v. Lane* sets out the rule, but presupposes some creative input; *Interlego* deals with the other end of the spectrum, at which there is only mere copying.

In the words of Jacob LJ:[41]

I think the true position is that one has to consider the extent to which the 'copyist' is a mere copyist—merely performing an easy mechanical function. The more that is so the less is his contribution likely to be taken as 'original'.

One should not underestimate the importance for English copyright law of the fact that the Court of Appeal has now, in *Hyperion*, clarified the approach that is to be taken to originality by reconfirming the dictum in *Walter v. Lane* and by ruling out any conflict with *Interlego*, which is confined to its particular mere copying scenario.

A new general rule in *Infopaq*?

The Court of Justice dealt with the originality issue in the *Infopaq* case.[42] The Court was asked essentially to look at copyright infringement and exceptions and limitations, but it accepted that in copyright one needs to know what the work is and whether it attracts

---

[39] At para. 4.39.

[40] J. Ginsburg, 'The Concept of Authorship in Comparative Copyright Law' (2003) 52 DePaul L Rev 1063.

[41] *Hyperion Records v. Lionel Sawkins* (n. 31), at para. 82 of the judgment.

[42] *Infopaq International A/S* (n. 5).

copyright before one can deal with infringement and limitations. One cannot infringe what is not protected in the first place and exceptions and limitations necessarily apply to the copyright protection of the work. From that perspective the Information Society Directive[43] dealt necessarily with the concept of (copyright) works when it harmonized limitations and exceptions for all categories of copyright works. The Directive is not limited in scope to certain categories of copyright works. It does not, on the other hand, contain a definition of a work, let alone of originality. Nevertheless one needs a definition in order to be able to address the questions on infringement and limitations and exceptions before the court. Under EU rules of interpretation these undefined concepts are then given an autonomous interpretation, i.e. one does not refer back to the law of the member states.[44] The court then finds that in EU law reference is made to the Software and Database Directives, as this is also the case in the Information Society Directive, and in those two Directives the only indication that is found is that of the originality as the work being 'the author's own intellectual creation'. In the absence of conflicting elements of a common definition the court therefore accepted that across the EU the Directive now imposes that concept of originality for all categories of works.[45]

One can see this as harmonization via the back door or as the imposition of a higher originality criterion on countries such as the United Kingdom or one can see it as the correct application of the rules of interpretation to the provisions of the Information Society Directive to which all member states agreed. Be that as it may, one needs to ask the question whether this decision changes a lot in UK copyright law. Arguably it does not change a lot in relation to original literary, dramatic, musical, or artistic works. More recent decisions, such as *Hyperion*,[46] had paid lip service to the skill and labour idea, but they had emphasized the point that the author must produce his or her own expression of the idea. In doing so the author surely does not copy, and invests his or her own skill and judgement. The question then arises how one ascertains that the author produces his or her own expression of the idea. Where does the originality lie? What is the original contribution of the author? The cases clearly show that a mere copy is not what one is looking for and that the author's own individual interpretation is needed as a minimum requirement. That is not the same as requiring creativity or artistic value, but it is a particular kind of skill and labour and not mere sweat of the brow. The House of Lords made this specifically clear when it argued that one needs to look at the reason why a work is given copyright protection.[47] For each category of works there is a specific 'original' contribution that is required. For literary works it is literary originality and for artistic works it is artistic originality and so on. That approach cannot be reconciled with a definition of originality as mere sweat of the brow. A specific kind of skill and labour is required and it is necessarily put in by the author. Without going into the issue of (literary or artistic) merit, that clearly links originality to the input into the expression of the idea by the author. In choosing that expression the author will necessarily use his or her intellect and it therefore becomes 'the author's own intellectual creation'.

The House of Lords may have come to this position from a (specific) skill and labour angle, but the outcome differs little from the outcome reached by the French Supreme Court that

---

[43] Directive 2001/29/EU of the European Parliament and of the Council of 22 May 2001 on the harmonization of certain aspects of copyright and related rights in the information society [2001] OJ L 167/10.

[44] *Infopaq International A/S* (n. 5) at para. 27.   [45] *Infopaq International A/S* (n. 5) at para. 37.

[46] *Hyperion Records* (n. 31).

[47] *Newspaper Licensing Agency Ltd v. Marks & Spencer plc* [2001] 3 WLR 290 at para. 19 (HL).

started from an expression of the author's personality angle. The French Supreme Court[48] recently held that the inscription of the word 'Paradis'[49] in gilded letters with a special effect and graphic form on an old door with a lock in the shape of a cross, embedded in a dilapidated wall with peeling paint, is a combination that involves aesthetic choices that reflect the author's personality. That led the court to the conclusion that the artist's conceptual approach, which consists of placing a word in a specific place and changing its usual meaning, constitutes an original material creation that enjoys copyright protection. One sees an emphasis on concepts of personality and creativity that one would not find in a House of Lords or Supreme Court judgment, but that use of wording cannot hide that one can also decide the case by using the UK wording that the artist invested his specific skill, labour, and judgement and applied it to the work to come to a copyright work as the expression of the author's own intellectual creation. The actual difference may therefore be very small or non-existent, without even taking into account the *Infopaq* harmonization. *Infopaq* may therefore be a mere confirmation of a somewhat higher level of originality being required. This does, of course, mean that certain works will no longer attract copyright protection in the UK and that copyright can no longer be used as a stop-gap solution to protect these works in the absence of a tort of unfair competition.

What may surprise in the French judgment, as well as in the *Infopaq* decision is that small amounts of words, i.e. one and eleven respectively, are seen as potentially constituting a copyright work. *Infopaq* confirms specifically that the originality test applies to parts of the work as well as to the whole work.[50] The question whether a part of a work attracts copyright protection is therefore dependent on whether the part is original and involves therefore an element of the author's own intellectual creation (and this is not necessarily a low hurdle that can be passed easily). That excludes non-original and copied parts, but it also means that parts of the work can attract protection and that using or copying them can amount to an infringement. It is arguable that the old UK system offered less protection in this area and that *Infopaq* therefore broadens the scope of copyright. That conflicts with the idea that UK copyright traditionally combines this weaker form of protection with a restrictive approach to limitations and permitted exceptions.[51] Our limitations and exceptions may now become too narrow and copyright owners may get an unduly broad protection (to the detriment of the user) if protection is also available to parts of the work. What is clear though is that the English courts are now adopting the approach set out in *Infopaq*[52] and there is a clear trend towards the use the concept of the author's own intellectual creation as the standard for originality.[53] The *Infopaq* standard was used to decide that certain newspaper headlines could attract copyright protection in the *Meltwater* case[54] and that decision was confirmed on appeal.[55] The case is also a good example of how small parts of a work can attract their own copyright by meeting the *Infopaq* standard.

Recorded expression

Another essential rule is that copyright does not protect ideas; only a particular expression of an idea is protected. This does not create a specific problem for artistic works, but,

---

[48] *Bettina Rheims v. M. Jakob Gautel and ors*, decision of the 1st Civil Division of the French Cour de Cassation (Supreme Court) of 13 November 2008, 40 (2009) 4 IIC 485.

[49] Meaning 'paradise'.   [50] *Infopaq International A/S* (n. 5) at para. 39.   [51] See Ch. 16.

[52] See also *Temple Island Collections Ltd v. New English Teas Ltd and Nicholas John Houghton* [2012] EWPCC 1.

[53] See e.g. *SAS Institute Inc* (n. 19).

[54] *Newspaper Licensing Agency Ltd v. Meltwater Holding BV* [2010] EWHC 3099 (Ch), [2011] RPC 7.

[55] [2011] EWCA Civ 890, [2012] RPC 1.

if one is not to protect the idea in a literary, dramatic, or musical work, the expression should be recorded in a permanent form. This can be in writing or in any other form and all new technological recording or fixation methods are automatically included.

One could see an impromptu speech and a tune devised while playing the guitar, which are not recorded, as the perfect illustration of this problem. The author can record the work him- or herself, but this is not required; the requirement only mentions recording—in relation to which, not even the permission of the author is required.[56] This means that the recording requirement will be met as soon as *someone* records the work.

Apart from the permanent fixation aspect, the rule that copyright protects expression, but not ideas, has an even more fundamental aspect to it. Two situations arise in this context. In the first, a copyright work may express ideas that are not protected, because they lack any connection with the literary, dramatic, musical, or artistic nature of the work.[57] This could be the case, for example, if a literary work expresses the idea of a technical innovation.[58] In the second situation, certain ideas protected by a copyright work may themselves be denied protection, because they are not original or because they are commonplace,[59] despite the fact that they are ideas of a literary, dramatic, musical, or artistic nature.[60]

Literary works

A definition and some examples

The Act characterizes literary works as '*any work, other than a dramatic or musical work, which is written, spoken or sung*'.[61] This category should not be restricted to works of literature. As Peterson J put it, this category contains every '*work which is expressed in print or writing, irrespective of the question whether the quality or style is high*'.[62]

The case law supplements high-quality works with all kinds of compilations and tables.[63] Trade catalogues,[64] street directories,[65] timetable indexes,[66] examination papers,[67] football fixtures lists,[68] a listing of programmes to be broadcast,[69] a racing information service,[70] business letters,[71] and consignment notes[72] have all been held to be literary works protected by copyright. Lyrics for songs and computer programs are also protected.

An exception is presented by compilations of (only) artistic works. Compilations are protected as literary works, but only if they are written. Most artistic works are not written and such compilations of artistic works will therefore not attract copyright

---

[56] Copyright, Designs and Patents Act 1988, s. 3(3).

[57] See e.g. *Kleeneze Ltd v. DRG (UK) Ltd* [1984] FSR 399.

[58] *Designer Guild Ltd v. Russell Williams Textiles Ltd* [2000] 1 WLR 2416, per Lord Hoffmann at 2423; *Ultra Marketing (UK) Ltd & Thomas Alexander Scott v. Universal Components Ltd*, judgment of 12 March 2004, Ch D, unreported.

[59] See e.g. *Kenrick & Co. v. Lawrence & Co.* (1890) 25 QBD 99.

[60] *Designer Guild Ltd v. Russell Williams (Textiles) Ltd* [2000] 1 WLR 2416, per Lord Hoffmann.

[61] CDPA 1988, s. 3(1).   [62] *University of London Press Ltd* (n. 6) at 608.

[63] See also CDPA 1988, s. 3(1)(a).

[64] *Collis v. Cater* (1898) 78 LT 613; *Purefoy Engineering Co. Ltd v. Sykes Boxall* (1955) 72 RPC 89.

[65] *Kelly v. Morris* (1866) LR 1 Eq 697.   [66] *Blacklock (H) & Co. Ltd v. Pearson* [1915] 2 Ch 376.

[67] *University of London Press* (n. 6).

[68] *Football League v. Littlewoods* [1959] Ch 637, [1959] 2 All ER 546; *Ladbroke (Football)* (n. 6).

[69] *Independent Television Publications v. Time Out Ltd* [1984] FSR 64; a subsequent competition law initiative made the copyright owners grant licences and made the listings available to other publishers.

[70] *Portway Press v. Hague* [1957] RPC 426.

[71] *British Oxygen Co. Ltd v. Liquid Air Ltd* [1925] Ch 383.

[72] *Van Oppen & Co. Ltd v. Van Oppen* (1903) 20 RPC 617.

protection.[73] The addition of a substantial quantity of written work will solve this problem, because the originality requirement will be met in these cases.

Originality as a *de minimis* rule

In practice, the historical UK originality requirement requires such a low amount of skill, labour, and judgement to be invested in a literary work that it operates as a *de minimis* rule. Only works that are not substantial enough do not attract copyright protection. A first group of works falls in this category because the amount of skill and labour invested in them is almost non-existent: case law examples include a card containing spaces and directions for eliciting statutory information,[74] and an advertisement consisting of four commonplace sentences.[75] In the mid-90s, it was held that a formula for calculating racing forecasts was not an original literary work; nor were the forecasts produced by using the formula. The calculation was held to be a routine repetitive task that involved feeding the relevant information into a computer and that task did not involve sufficient skill, labour, or judgement to produce an original literary work each time the formula was used.[76] This remains the case at present. These works do not attract copyright protection as they do not pass the (current) originality requirement test.

A second group of works falls into this category because the volume of these works is not substantial enough. There is not enough space to distinguish between ideas and expression, if there is an underlying idea at all, and copyright should not be used to monopolize words. Obvious examples in this category are trade marks[77] and most titles of books, plays, films, etc.[78] Cases such as *Infopaq*[79] suggest that very short works can attract copyright, but one needs to keep in mind that this will only be possible if they pass the originality test—i.e. it needs to be possible to identify the author's own intellectual creation and this will by definition only be possible if one can distinguish between that expression and the generic idea underlying the work. In practice this will remain the exception rather than the rule. The *Meltwater* case shows an example of such an exception, when the Court of Appeal confirmed the decision that some particularly well-crafted newspaper headlines can attract copyright as literary works.[80]

A literary work based on existing sources can be seen as a different expression of the same idea if no substantial amount of copying is involved, and if skill and labour has been invested in the new work. Because the idea is not protected, no infringement problem arises and the new work can attract copyright protection as a literary work. Translations,[81] compilations,[82] selection and abridgment,[83] critical annotation and

---

[73] A. Monotti, 'The Extent of Copyright Protection for Compilations of Artistic Works' (1993) 5 EIPR 156, at 160–1.

[74] *Libraco v. Shaw* (1913) 30 TLR 22.   [75] *Kirk v. Fleming Macg Cap Cas* (1928) 44.

[76] *Bookmakers' Afternoon Greyhound Services Ltd v. Wilf Gilbert (Staffordshire) Ltd* [1994] FSR 723.

[77] *Exxon Corp. v. Exxon Insurance Consultants International Ltd* [1982] Ch 119; aff'd [1981] 3 All ER 241; copyright should not be used to expand the protection granted by a trade mark to a well-known brand name to an entirely different category of products or services.

[78] See *Ladbroke (Football)* (n. 6), per Lord Hodson at 476 and 286; *Francis Day & Hunter Ltd v. Twentieth Century Fox Corp. Ltd* [1940] AC 112, per Lord Wright at 123.

[79] *Infopaq International* (n. 5).

[80] *Newspaper Licensing Agency Ltd v. Meltwater Holding BV* [2011] EWCA Civ 890, [2012] RPC 1.

[81] *Byrne v. Statist Co.* [1914] 1 KB 622; *Cummins v. Bond* [1927] 1 Ch 167.

[82] *Portway Press v. Hague* [1957] RPC 426; *Football League v. Littlewoods* [1959] Ch 637, [1959] 2 All ER 546; *Ladbroke (Football) Ltd* (n. 6).

[83] *Macmillan v. Cooper* (1923) 93 LJPC 113; condensation of a single text may not be sufficient, but collecting an anthology of verse is likely to be sufficient: *Sweet v. Benning* (1855) 16 CB 459.

explanation,[84] and editorial work that involves amendments[85] all come under the head of literary works and qualify for protection irrespective of whether the material taken from existing sources is in, or out, of copyright. As for all literary works, the *de minimis* principle applies. On this basis, copyright protection for the times of local trains, extracted from a general timetable,[86] and for a collection of existing tables made for the front of a pocket diary[87] was refused.

It may, at first, seem contradictory, but certain similar works do not fall foul of the *de minimis* rule. These works involve a sufficient amount of skill and labour in the selection and use of the existing elements on the basis of a commercial judgement. Skill and labour are not restricted to literary selection, expression, and presentation, as became clear in *Ladbroke v. William Hill*.[88] Copyright protection was granted to a fixed-odds football pool that consisted of a compilation of 16 known forms of bet, when the commercial judgement and skill used in the selection of these forms of bet was taken into account and reference was not solely made to the presentation on the pool form.[89]

Works that derive, in some way, from an earlier source—such as a selection of poetry or a selection of letters written by a celebrity—attract copyright if more than a minimal amount of skill and labour is invested in the choice and presentation of the material.[90] The poems or letters that are reproduced by a substantial amount may still attract copyright, which will coexist with the copyright in the new work. It is obvious that the permission of all owners of a copyright is required to reproduce their work or to deal with the copyright in any other way; each copyright creates an independent exclusive right in this respect. All of this follows logically from the restrictive definition that is given to the originality requirement.

Works can also derive from an earlier source in another way. Many literary works go through many drafts before they are eventually published: each one of these (unpublished) drafts will attract its own copyright as a literary work, as long as a minimum amount of skill and labour has been invested in adapting the previous draft. Correcting obvious incorrect typing errors will not suffice for that purpose, but any alterations to the work itself almost inevitably will.[91]

At a more fundamental level, one needs to identify what exactly one is looking for as a work. In a book, each chapter, page, or maybe even each sentence can be said to amount to a (separate) literary work, but when each of them is incorporated into a larger work—that is, the book—one looks at the larger work or book in which it existed.[92] For copyright purposes, one looks primarily at the format in which the work is released

---

[84] The notes appended to a condensed text showed sufficient literary skill, taste, and judgment in *Macmillan v. Cooper* (n. 83).

[85] *Warwick Film Productions Ltd v. Eisinger* [1969] 1 Ch 508, [1967] 3 All ER 367 was concerned with an edited version of a trial transcript.

[86] *Leslie v. Young* [1894] AC 335; see also *Blacklock v. Pearson* [1915] 2 Ch 376.

[87] *Cramp v. Smythson* [1944] AC 329; see also *Rose v. Information Services* [1987] FSR 254.

[88] [1964] 1 All ER 465, [1964] 1 WLR 273.

[89] For another example that attracted copyright (a random choice game in a newspaper with grids of letters printed on cards as the only literary material), see *Express Newspapers v. Liverpool Daily Post* [1985] 3 All ER 680, [1985] 1 WLR 1089; see also *Mirror Newspapers Ltd v. Queensland Newspapers Pty* [1982] Qd R 305; *Kalamazoo (Aust) Pty Ltd v. Compact Business Systems Pty Ltd* (1985) 5 IPR 213.

[90] See the comparison in *Ladbroke (Football) Ltd* (n. 6).

[91] *Sweeney v. Macmillan Publishers Ltd* [2002] RPC 35 at 651. See also *LA Gear Inc. v. Hi-Tec Sports* [1992] FSR 121, per Nourse LJ at 136; *Robin Ray v. Classic FM Ltd* [1998] FSR 622.

[92] *Sweeney v. Macmillan Publishers Ltd* (n. 91) at 651.

onto the market. That does of course not mean that each part of a work can no longer attract copyright when looked at in isolation. As was explained, each part that passes the originality requirement attracts copyright. Purely functional works, e.g. instructions for use of a certain product, can in this model also attract copyright protection as long as they pass the originality test. Business competitors are therefore obliged to express their own identical message (in terms of content) in a different format (in terms of expression). One might argue that copyright should leave this field to unfair competition rules, but under the current rules in Europe most of these functional works pass the originality test, unless they are purely factual (see the example given previously).

The exclusion of dramatic and musical works

Let us return briefly to the definition that the 1988 Act gives of a 'literary work'.[93] A literary work is defined widely as any work that is written, spoken, or sung, and that is not a dramatic or musical work. The exclusion of any work that comes within the definition of a musical or a dramatic work from the category of literary works implements the basic principle that every original work can only fall within a single category of original types of work. This exclusion slightly narrows the category of literary works, but it remains rather wide.

The last point is demonstrated by the fact that a literary work need not be expressed in words or any particular notation: any kind of notation can turn a work into a work that is written.[94] As a result of this, a software program that is written in any kind of computer programming language will fall within the category of literary works.

Computer programs, tables, and compilations as literary works

That brings us to the types of work that are explicitly included in the definition of a 'literary work'. Section 3(1) of the 1988 Act mentions specifically that a computer program and the preparatory design material for a computer program are literary works. The same goes for tables and compilations. A table consists of a series of facts or numbers that have been arranged in a systematic way; a compilation is mainly a body of materials that have been brought together. There is no need to distinguish whether a particular work is a table or a compilation, because the Act treats them in exactly the same way.

It is important to note that the Act does not require that the author of the table or compilation is also the person from whom the materials, numbers, or facts that are included in these works originate. Copyright in a table or compilation consists in protecting the skill and labour employed in selecting, collecting, or arranging the materials, numbers, or facts. The materials, numbers, or facts, as such and on their own, are not protected by the copyright in the table or compilation, but they may, or may not be protected by copyright in their own right: for example, five short stories in a compilation may be protected by copyright as five separate literary works. Any copyright in the compilation comes on top of existing separate copyrights in the contents of the compilation and leaves the latter unchanged.

Finally, databases are also defined as literary works for copyright purposes.

---

[93] CDPA 1988, s. 3(1).
[94] See H. Laddie, P. Prescott, and M. Vitoria (2000) *The Modern Law of Copyright and Designs*, 3rd edn, London: Butterworths, p. 64.

Databases

Databases have a lot in common with compilations. Most databases could be described as a kind of compilation. The Act makes it clear, however, that no overlap between the two types of literary work can exist for copyright purposes, by defining compilations as *'compilations, other than a database'*.[95] A database such as the Westlaw legal information system would be a good example: legal materials from a range of sources are collated by the publisher into a database, which is used skilfully by the subscriber.

Section 3A of the 1988 Act defines a database. The starting point is that a database is a collection of works, data, or other materials. First, these works, data, or other materials that form the components of, or items of content comprised in, the collection need to be independent from one another. A collection of titles and names of authors of all books published in English in the nineteenth century might be a good example. Each title or name of an author would be able to stand on its own; this independence would not be destroyed were a search facility to allow the user of the database to retrieve several of these data from the database at the same time. Each title or name of an author would remain independent when jointly listed on the screen as the search result, for example, of a search for all titles of books that were published in 1830. But such independence does not exist, for example, in relation to a film. A cinematographic film is composed of a succession of still frames. Each frame can stand on its own as a photograph, but, in the context of the film, the frames are dependent on other frames. The essence of the film is the moving image and that moving image can only be produced by a combination of frames. That means that the individual frames cannot be considered to be independent from one another.

Second, a collection will only be a database if the independent works, data, or other materials that form the collection are arranged in a systematic or methodical way.[96] In relation to our earlier example of titles and names of authors of books published in English during the nineteenth century, this means that the data must, for example, be organized by year of publication, or alphabetically by name of author, or on the basis of all books published by a certain author in that period. A random collection of names of authors and titles from the nineteenth century will not do. It is, however, sufficient that the data has been given a systematic code in the database and can be retrieved—for example, on the screen of the terminal in relation to an electronic database—in a systematic way. The precise way or order in which they are technically stored in any electronic storage medium is irrelevant for this purpose.

Third, the works, data, or other materials need to be individually accessible.[97] Access to each individual and independent work needs to be possible. In our example, this means that it must be possible to retrieve the data about a specific name of an author or a specific title of a book from the database. Such access can be by electronic or other means, which provision makes it clear that electronic databases are not the only ones that are protected. Hard-copy databases—for example, in card or book format—also come under the definition.

An additional hurdle remains, even if a collection meets these three requirements: such a collection will only be a database if it is original. Originality is defined in a specific way for the purposes of a database.[98] A slightly higher criterion than the normal UK originality criterion is used. The database must constitute the author's own intellectual

---

[95] One could wonder, however, whether, in the light of the wide definition that is given to the concept of a database, there are de facto any compilations left.

[96] CDPA 1988, s. 3A(1)(a).　　　[97] CDPA 1988, s. 3A(1)(b).　　　[98] CDPA 1988, s. 3A(2).

creation, by reason of the selection or arrangement of the contents of the database, with the emphasis firmly placed on the selection or the arrangement of the contents of the database. Copyright in a database is not concerned with the contents of the database as such. The selection and arrangement criterion, and the way in which they take place, must be the author's own intellectual creation: he or she must have devised them and they cannot, therefore, be commonplace. For example, a standard alphabetical arrangement by name in a telephone directory, comprising all people with a telephone connection in a certain area, must be commonplace and that arrangement cannot be seen as the author's own intellectual creation.

Any collection that does not meet these three requirements and the special originality requirement will not be a database for the purposes of the Act. It may nevertheless attract copyright protection as a compilation, for example, if it only meets the lower standard originality criterion. Those collections that meet the three requirements and the originality criterion will attract copyright protection as a database—but that protection does not cover the contents of the database though. What is protected is the structure of the database, because that is the expression of the author's original selection and arrangement of the contents of the database. Other aspects of a database may be protected by a *sui generis* right.[99]

The introduction of a new originality criterion for databases in s. 3A(2) of the 1988 Act creates problems in relation to computer programs. Both databases and computer programs are the subject matter of two EC directives.[100] Both contain the same originality criterion of *'author's own intellectual creation'*,[101] but this criterion has only been transposed into the 1988 Act in relation to databases. After the Software Directive, it could be argued that the Act did not define originality and that we, therefore, did not have to copy the Directive's originality criterion. In the absence of a definition in the Act, we could simply interpret the level of originality required for computer programs in the light of the Directive and apply our old originality criterion to all other works. Alternatively, one might unconvincingly argue that, in practice, there was no difference between the Directive's originality criterion, and the skill and labour approach in the first place. If either of these explanations were true, there was no need to include the 'author's' own intellectual creation' originality criterion in the 1988 Act in relation to databases.

The only logical conclusion must be that the new originality criterion that is specifically defined for databases departs from the originality criterion that applies to other works. That means that we have failed to implement the Software Directive correctly.[102] The 'author's own intellectual creation' originality criterion should at least apply to databases and computer programs. Be that as it may, the practical importance of the matter may have become almost non-existent now because the current UK interpretation of the originality requirement is almost if not completely identical to that of the Directive.[103]

---

[99] See Ch. 30.

[100] European Parliament and Council Directive 96/9/EC on the legal protection of databases (1996) OJ L 77/20 and Council Directive 91/250/EEC on the legal protection of computer programs (1991) OJ L 122/42 (the Software Directive), now codified as Directive 2009/24/EC of the European Parliament and of the Council of 23 April 2009 on the legal protection of computer programs [2009] OJ L 111/16.

[101] Arts. 3(1) and 1(3) respectively.

[102] See, in this context, the broader discussion in Laddie, Prescott, and Vitoria, *The Modern Law of Copyright and Designs* (n. 94), Preface and Ch. 3.

[103] See *Newspaper Licensing Agency Ltd v. Marks & Spencer plc* (n. 47) at para. 19 (HL) and *Infopaq International* (n. 5).

Dramatic works

The category of 'dramatic works' shares the same set of general rules with the literary works category from which it is excluded by s. 3(1) of the Act. The obvious example is a synopsis or script for a play or for a film,[104] but dance and mime are also included in this category.[105] An interesting issue is raised by certain contributions to scripts made by other writers. It is clear that someone who suggests a series of ideas and key storylines for a work written by others will not share in the copyright protection in the work.[106] All that he or she contributes are ideas, which are expressed by the writer, and only the expression is protected by copyright. This would seem to require a contribution to the precise expression of the ideas, such as the full text of a scene or a number of lines for a synopsis, script, or play. Another relevant rule is the recording requirement: no copyright can be granted if those lines are not recorded and this same conclusion was reached in a case that was concerned with an elaborated visual skit for a music hall sketch involving the use of fireworks.[107]

Titles are excluded from protection on the basis of the originality requirement, which applies to this category as well and results in a *de minimis* rule. This rule also covers the names of characters and the typical way in which they behave,[108] unless the link and the characteristics are so strong that they become an independent and recognizable entity.[109] All this is of course subject to the exception that items for which the expression can be distinguished from the mere idea and where that expression passes the originality test and includes the author's own intellectual creation, will attract copyright. But the protection granted to scripts for plays and movies does not extend to costumes and scenic effects, which will only attract copyright if they are artistic works. Characters and the merchandising rights involved can be protected under passing off, but only in the cases in which they benefit from an established trading reputation.[110]

What has become clear from the examples is that dramatic works involve action and movement. This is also reflected in the comment by Lord Bridge that a dramatic work must be capable of performance.[111] It is submitted that a dramatic work can be best defined as '*a work created in order to be communicated in motion, that is, through a sequence of actions, movements, irrespective of the technique by which this movement is retrieved or expressed*'.[112]

The communication in motion must be required for the proper representation of the work if the work is to be classified as a dramatic work. Any work can be performed before an audience—for example, a literary work can be read—but communication in motion is not required for the proper representation of a literary work. The Court of Appeal has now gone down the same path in holding that a dramatic work is any work of action, with or without words or music, that is capable of being performed before an audience.[113]

---

[104] The film itself attracts a separate copyright.   [105] CDPA 1988, s. 3(1).

[106] *Tate v. Thomas* [1921] 1 Ch 503; see also *Wiseman v. Weidenfeld & Nicolson Ltd* [1985] FSR 525; *Ashmore v. Douglas-Home* [1987] FSR 553.

[107] *Tate v. Fullbrook* [1908] 1 KB 821.

[108] See *Kelly v. Cinema Houses Macg Cap Cas* (1932) 362, per Maugham J at 368.

[109] *Exxon Corp. v. Exxon Insurance Consultants International Ltd* [1982] Ch 119, [1981] 2 All ER 495, which refers to Lewis Carroll's *Jabberwocky* as an example.

[110] See Ch. 31 on character merchandising.

[111] *Green v. Broadcasting Corp. of New Zealand* [1989] 2 All ER 1056, [1989] RPC 700.

[112] P. Kamina, 'Authorship of Films and Implementation of the Term Directive: The Dramatic Tale of Two Copyrights' (1994) 8 EIPR 319, 320; cf. J. Phillips, R. Durie, and I. Karet (1993) *Whale on Copyright*, 4th edn, London: Sweet and Maxwell, p. 27.

[113] *Norowzian v. Arks Ltd (No. 2)* (n. 4).

This definition implies that a cinematographic or audiovisual work will be a dramatic work, because it clearly meets the requirement of a work created to be communicated in motion. This dramatic work is distinct from the script: various other aspects—such as music, dance, etc.—have been added, making the cinematographic or audiovisual work more than a performance of the script. Although based on the script, it will constitute a new (derivative) dramatic work.[114] The Court of Appeal formally adopted this line of argument in the *Norowzian* case,[115] in which it was held that a film could also be a dramatic work, apart from being eventually the recording of another dramatic work. The Court argued that a film would often, although not always, be a work of action that was capable of being performed before an audience.

A proper distinction does, however, need to be drawn between a dramatic work and a performance. Copyright in a dramatic work will only cover the work as such—that is, what can be printed and published[116]—and not the interpretation that is given to it by the person who performs it in motion.

Musical works

A first definition

Lyrics are protected as literary works, so what remains of a song is the music. Every overlap is excluded, because a musical work is defined as a work consisting of music, exclusive of any words or action intended to be sung, spoken, or performed with it.[117] For copyright purposes, music and lyrics are distinct works. They can be owned by different persons and can expire at different times, etc. A musical work is, then, *'intended to be performed by the production of a combination of sounds to be appreciated by the ear'*.[118]

Originality

The general rules governing the two previous categories apply to musical works as well. There is no subjective quality requirement: what is a beautiful piece of music to one person is nothing more than an awful cacophony and noise to another person, and a couple of notes and chords will be sufficient to attract copyright.[119] Secondary musical works based on an existing musical work may attract their own copyright. In this category, we find, for example, arrangements or transcriptions for another type of orchestra.[120] These will attract their own copyright if the minimum amount of skill and labour requested by the originality requirement is invested in them, but this does not rule out the possibility of infringement of the copyright in the earlier musical work if, for example, the arrangement is made without the permission of the owner of the copyright in the earlier work.

The situation in relation to arrangements must be distinguished from that in relation to the mere interpretation in a performance of a work. In the latter case, there will be no separate copyright in a (new) musical work, but a right in the performance may arise.

---

[114] P. Kamina, 'Authorship of Films and Implementation of the Term Directive: The Dramatic Tale of Two Copyrights' (1994) 8 EIPR 319, 320–1.

[115] *Norowzian v. Arks Ltd (No. 2)* (n. 4).   [116] See *Tate v. Fullbrook* (n. 107).

[117] CDPA 1988, ss. 1(1)(a) and 3(1).

[118] Laddie, Prescott, and Vitoria, *The Modern Law of Copyright and Designs*, (n. 94) at 79.

[119] See *Lawson v. Dundas* (1985) *The Times*, 13 June, copyright in the then Channel 4 television logo music.

[120] *Metzler & Co. (1920) Ltd v. Curwen* (1928–1935) MacG Cap Cas 127; *Wood v. Boosey* (1868) LR 3 QB 223; *Redwood Music v. Chappell* [1982] RPC 109.

Exploring the boundaries

The 1988 Act does not offer a definition of a musical work. In many cases, one recognizes a musical work if one sees (or hears) one, but, on the borderlines, problems were bound to arise, as happened in the *Hyperion* case,[121] which gave the Court of Appeal the opportunity to clarify the concept of a musical work. It will be recalled that Dr Lionel Sawkins had restored out-of-copyright musical works by Lalande, with the aim of recreating the works as Lalande would originally have created them. The question arose whether such a restoration effort that led to new performing editions of the works involved the creation of musical works. Hyperion did not want to pay royalties to Sawkins for the use of the performing editions when it recorded its CD and had argued that no new musical work had been created. In its view, the performing edition has no impact on the sound that is produced and perceived by the audience. That sound is essentially the result of Lalande's musical work and has nothing to do with Sawkins' work. The fact that Sawkins wanted to stay as close as possible to Lalande's original work provides a further argument for denying the existence of a new copyright work.

The court summarized that argument as follows:[122]

> The effect of the editorial interventions of Dr Sawkins was, as he asserted was his intention, only to produce more faithful and better copies of Lalande's original music and to make it playable, rather than to create new music of his own. The kind of effort and skill expended by Dr Sawkins was not appropriate or relevant to the creation of a fresh musical copyright, such as might be achieved by changes to the melody and harmony of the underlying work.

At first instance, Patten J had summarized Hyperion's position on subsistence as follows:[123]

> [U]nless the edition includes the composition of new music in the form of the notes on the score (and not merely the correction of wrong or unsatisfactory notes in the scores used) then no copyright would exist in the edition as a musical work.

Both Patten J and the Court of Appeal refused to follow this unduly narrow approach. It seems, indeed, that there is more to music than notes on a score. Any plain language definition will, for example, also refer to sound and rhythm, and the impact on the ear in general. By focusing narrowly on notes only, Hyperion's argument is also inconsistent with the approach of assessing the work as a whole that the House of Lords laid down in *Ladbroke v. William Hill*.[124]

The Court of Appeal summarized these two points as follows, on the basis of which it rejected Hyperion's argument and held the performing editions to amount to a musical work:[125]

> In my judgment, the fallacies in Hyperion's arguments are that (a) they only treat the actual notes in the score as music and (b) they approach the issue of subsistence from the wrong direction by dividing the whole of the performing edition into separate segments and by then discarding particular segments on the basis that they are not music and not therefore covered by copyright. That is contrary to the correct approach to subsistence of copyright

[121] *Hyperion Records* (n. 31).   [122] *Hyperion Records* (n. 31) at para. 41 of the judgment.

[123] At para. 50 of his judgment, which the Court of Appeal praised unanimously and which is reported at [2004] 4 All ER 418. See also V. Jones, 'Musical Works: Out with the Old and In with the New' (2005) 16 Ent LR 89; P. Groves, 'Better than it Sounds: Originality of Musical Works' (2005) 16 Ent LR 20; V. Jones, 'What Constitutes a Copyright Work: Does it really Matter?' (2005) 16 Ent LR 129.

[124] *Ladbroke (Football)* (n. 6) at 277–91 (HL).

[125] *Hyperion Records* (n. 31) at para. 49 of the judgment.

laid down by the House of Lords in *Ladbroke (Football) Ltd v. William Hill (Football) Ltd...* The subsistence of copyright involves an assessment of the whole work in which copyright is claimed. It is wrong to make that assessment by dissecting the whole into separate parts and then submitting that there is no copyright in the parts. Hyperion's arguments ignore the fact that the totality of the sounds produced by the musicians are affected, or potentially affected, by the information inserted in the performing editions produced by Dr Sawkins. The sound on the CD is not just that of the musicians playing music composed by Lalande. In order to produce the sounds the musicians played from Dr Sawkins' scores of his edition. Without them Ex Cathedra would not have produced the combination of sounds of *Te Deum, La Grande Piece Royale* or *Venite Exultemus* for recording on the CD.

There is indeed no reason for restricting the coverage of musical copyright to the actual notes of the music only; after all, a dramatic work is not limited to the words that are to be spoken by the actors either. It is thus common sense that a recording of a person's spontaneous singing or any form of improvization also amounts to music for copyright purposes.

Sawkins' work was required for the musician to play Lalande's work in the way that they did and, more importantly, it produced aural effects—that is, it changed what people heard. From a subsistence point of view, a separate musical work had therefore been created. Music is therefore more than notes on a score: what the audience hears also counts. The court did not arrive at a definition in statutory language, but the concept of a musical work has at least been clarified somewhat.

Artistic works

This category of original works is wide in scope and can be subdivided into three parts.[126] There are works that are protected irrespective of artistic quality, which are followed by the intermediate group of works of architecture; after this, there are works of artistic craftsmanship. In relation to the last of these works, artistic quality might play a role. This represents a clear departure from the previous categories of work, for which the possession of artistic quality was irrelevant.

Artistic works irrespective of their artistic quality

The various types of works

Graphic works, photographs, sculptures, or collages are protected as artistic works irrespective of their artistic quality.[127] 'Graphic works' include any painting, drawing, diagram, map, chart, plan, engraving, etching, lithograph, woodcut, or similar work.[128] This means that works ranging from a painting by Salvador Dali, to an engineer's plans and drawings for an electromagnetic train, are protected in the same way: no distinction is made between aesthetic, functional, and utilitarian works.

Casts, moulds, or models made for a sculpture are treated as a sculpture.[129] The word 'sculpture' should, however, be given its normal plain English meaning. In that sense, for a work to be a sculpture in the first place, it must be a three-dimensional work made by an artist's hand. It follows therefore that not every mould is an artistic work. A mould will not be an artistic work if nothing:

suggests that the manufacturers of [this] mould considered themselves, or were considered by anybody else, to be artists when they designed the [mould] or that they were concerned

---

[126] CDPA 1988, ss. 1(1)(a) and 4(1)(a)–(c).   [127] CDPA 1988, s, 4(1)(a).
[128] CDPA 1988, s. 4(2).   [129] CDPA 1988, s. 4(2)

in any way with the shape or appearance of what they were making, save for the purpose of achieving a precise functional effect.[130]

An attempt was also made to keep pace with future technological developments: a photograph was defined as '*a recording of light or other radiation on any medium on which an image is produced or from which an image may by any means be produced, and which is not part of a film*'.[131] Any conflict with films, which may be seen as a succession of a huge number of photographs, is thus ruled out.

Technological developments are nonetheless bound to raise questions. Computer and video games involves a succession of frames, and the question of whether they are to be considered artistic works has arisen. The individual frames might be seen as graphic works—but the question was also asked whether the series of frames as an entity could also be considered to be a graphic work, as part of the wider category of artistic works. In *Nova Productions*,[132] the Court of Appeal held that an artistic work was defined in the Act as including the types of things listed in s. 4, all of which shared the characteristic of being static—that is, non-moving. A series of drawings or frames is therefore a series of graphic works and not a single graphic work or artistic work in itself. Individual frames are graphic works, however, and, as such, they come within the category of artistic works. Section 4 therefore also covers images that are generated on a screen and bitmap files.

The originality requirement for this first group of artistic works is the same as that for all previous types of work. The work should not be copied, should originate from the author, and its creation should involve the minimal amount of skill and labour.[133] That originality relates to artistic matters, rather than, for example, to technical matters in relation to the content of the drawing. The term 'artistic' should be defined here as anything that is visually significant.[134] That minimal amount of skill and labour is clearly present when a photographer makes a photograph from a picture[135] or any other single static object.[136] This is shown by the choice of the angle under which the picture is taken, the exposure time, the degree of focus, the positioning of the object, etc.[137] The decisive element in relation to whether the photograph is the author's own intellectual creation are these arrangements selected by the photographer him- or herself.[138] Often the skill, and therefore the originality, of the photographer is found in reproducing faithfully what is in front of the lens. And the visually significant aspect of the work is found not in the

[130] *Metix (UK) Ltd v. GH Maughlan (Plastics) Ltd* [1997] FSR 718, per Laddie J.

[131] CDPA 1988, s. 4(2).

[132] *Nova Productions Ltd v. Mazooma Games Ltd and ors; Nova Productions Ltd v. Bell Fruit Games Ltd* [2007] RPC 25 (CA).

[133] On that basis the work becomes the author's own intellectual creation.

[134] *Interlego AG* (n. 8), per Lord Oliver at 266; *Ultra Marketing (UK) Ltd & Thomas Alexander Scott v. Universal Components Ltd*, judgment of 12 March 2004, Ch D, unreported.

[135] *Graves' Case* (1869) LR 4 QB 715. For a detailed analysis of copyright in relation to photographs, see Y. Gendreau, A. Nordemann, and R. Oesch (1999) *Copyright and Photographs*, London: Kluwer Law International.

[136] *Antiquesportfolio.com plc v. Rodney Fitch & Co. Ltd* [2001] FSR 23. There may also be cases in which the person who arranges the scene that is to be photographed specifically for a picture to be taken is the joint author of the photograph. That will, however, not be the case of any later pictures taken of the same scene without authorization: see *Creation Records v. News Group* [1997] EMLR 444.

[137] *Antiquesportfolio.com plc v. Rodney Fitch & Co. Ltd* (n. 136); see K. Garnett, G. Davies, and G. Harbottle (2005) *Copinger and Skone James on Copyright*, 15th edn, London: Sweet and Maxwell, pp. 128–9; K. Garnett, 'Copyright in Photographs' (2000) 22 EIPR 229.

[138] E.g. placing a red London doubledecker bus centrally in a grey background of famous London landmark buildings: *Temple Island Collections Ltd v. New English Teas Ltd and Nicholas John Houghton* [2012] EWPCC 1.

scene or object before the lens, but in the image of it, which is produced on the photograph. The details of the arrangements made by the photographer are then particularly important.[139] Other good examples are a woodcut made from a drawing[140] and the label design for a sweet tin.[141]

But the skill and labour does not necessarily need to be artistic: a plan for a technical device containing three concentric circles was protected, because technical judgement was involved in drawing them to precise measurements, which allowed the technical device to work.[142] Meanwhile, a plan containing a design for toy bricks that was only different from an earlier plan because minor variations were mentioned in words and figures, which are not themselves artistic works, fell foul of the originality requirement and was not awarded distinct copyright.[143]

A definition of 'a sculpture'

One of the characteristics of the statutory provision on artistic works is that it does not define the concept of an artistic work or the concept of any of the works it gives as examples of artistic works. The Court of Appeal has now attempted to define the concept of a 'sculpture' in *Lucasfilm v. Ainsworth*.[144] In doing so the Court relied heavily on the first-instance decision[145] and the Supreme Court[146] upheld the decision on this point. Mr Ainsworth has produced the helmet worn by the Stormtroopers in the first three Star Wars film produced by Lucasfilm. He did so on the basis of a painting and a clay model that were supplied to him. Thirty years on he started to sell these helmets as memorabilia and Lucasfilm sued for copyright infringement. In the course of the litigation the question arose whether the helmet was a sculpture. In the absence of a statutory definition the courts start their analysis with the ordinary meaning of the word.[147] Both Mann J at first instance and the Court of Appeal drew a firm line between the concept of a sculpture as an artistic work on the one hand and the concept of a design on the other hand. This is done primarily on the basis of the intention with which the work has been created. Sculptures as artistic works are created for their visual aspect. This has nothing to do with artistic value or merit, but it permits to distinguish them from designs that are created primarily for their utilitarian value, i.e. they are functional objects. Sculptures may also have a utilitarian function and value, but they are sculptures in as far as they were primarily created with the visual aspect in mind, i.e. they were created to attract attention to their visual aspect. Designs on the other hand are created to have a utilitarian function even if that does not stop them from also being appreciated for their visual aspect. One could think in the latter case of little statues of soldiers, i.e. lead soldiers, that are designed as toys for kids to play with, but that may also be visually attractive. Statues sold in a gallery and created for their visual aspect remain sculptures on the other hand despite the fact that the buyer later uses them in a utilitarian way as functional objects,

---

[139] *Temple Island Collections Ltd* (n. 138).

[140] Or a coin engraved in three dimensions from a drawing: *Martin v. Polyplas Manufacturers Ltd* [1969] NZLR 1046; see also *Wham-O Manufacturing Co. v. Lincoln Industries Ltd* [1985] RPC 127, the New Zealand frisbee case in which wooden models from which moulds for the plastic frisbees were made were protected as sculptures, while the moulds themselves were protected as engravings.

[141] *Tavener Rutledge v. Specters* [1959] RPC 355.

[142] *Solar Thomson Engineering Co. Ltd v. Barton* [1977] RPC 537 at 558.

[143] *Interlego AG* (n. 8).

[144] *Lucasfilm Ltd, Star Wars Productions Ltd, Lucasfilm Entertainment Company Ltd v. Andrew Ainsworth, Shepperton Design Studios Ltd*, [2010] Ch 503, [2009] EWCA Civ 1328 (CA).

[145] [2009] FSR 103.   [146] [2011] UKSC 39, [2012] 1 AC 208.

[147] [2011] UKSC 39, [2012] 1 AC 208 at para. 44.

e.g. a bookstand. In the case at issue it was held that the helmets were primarily created as functional objects to form part of the costume of the Stormtroopers and to express an aspect of their character, rather than for their visual aspect. They therefore failed to come within the scope of the definition of a sculpture as an artistic work. Or as the Court of Appeal put it (borrowing from the wording used by Mann J):

> First, the original Stormtrooper helmet. This has, as its genesis, the McQuarrie paintings. The purpose of the helmet was that it was to be worn as an item of costume in a film, to identify a character, but in addition to portray something about that character—its allegiance, force, menace, purpose and, to some extent, probably its anonymity. It was a mixture of costume and prop. But its primary function is utilitarian. While it was intended to express something, that was for utilitarian purposes. While it has an interest as an object, and while it was intended to express an idea, it was not conceived, or created, with the intention that it should do so other than as part of character portrayal in the film. That, in my view, does not give it the necessary quality of artistic creation inherent in the test suggested by Laddie J. Not everything which has design appeal is necessarily a sculpture. I think that the ordinary perception of what is a sculpture would be over-stretched by including this helmet within it, and when rationalised the reasons are those just given. It is not that it lacks artistic merit; it lacks artistic purpose. I therefore find that the Stormtrooper helmet is not a sculpture.
>
> The same reasoning applies to the armour, and to the other helmets. They all shared the same sort of original purpose.

He took the same view about the toy Stormtroopers:

> Next, it is necessary to consider the toy Stormtroopers, and other characters, which are taken as being reproductions of the armour and helmets for the purposes of section 52. These are, as already described, articulated models which are sold as toys and which are intended for the purposes of play. Play is their primary, if not sole, purpose. While their appearance is obviously highly important (if they did not look like the original, the child would not be so interested) they are not made for the purposes of their visual appearance as such. While there is no accounting for taste, it is highly unlikely that they would be placed on display and periodically admired as such. The child is intended to use them in a (literally) hands-on way, in a form of delegated role play, and that is doubtless how they are actually used. That means, in my view, they are not sculptures. They can be distinguished from the model in Britain which apparently had a significant element of being admirable for its own visual sake. That does not apply to the Stormtrooper, whose only real purpose is play. In reaching this conclusion I am not saying that the Britain model is better at what it portrays than the Stormtrooper model. That would be to make judgments about artistic quality, which the statute understandably forbids. It is making a judgment about whether there is anything in the model which has an artistic essence, in the sense identified above. I conclude that there is not.[148]

This approach does of course fall short of the aim to provide a precise definition of a sculpture. Based on the general rule that the visual aspect and the aim with which the work was created are important factors, the Court of Appeal approves the approach taken by Mann J and lists a number of considerations that can assist the court in deciding whether or not it finds itself in the presence of a sculpture:

(i)   the normal use of the word sculpture had to be considered;
(ii) the concept could extend beyond what would normally be understood as a sculpture in the sense of a work in an art gallery;

---

[148] *Lucasfilm Ltd* (n. 144) at paras. 51 and 52 of the judgment.

(iii)   it would be inappropriate to stray too far from normal considerations of what is a sculpture;

(iv)   no judgment may be made about artistic merits;

(v)   not every three dimensional representation of a concept is a sculpture;

(vi)   a sculpture has visual appeal as part of its purpose;

(vii) an object having an additional use may also qualify as a sculpture but it must still have a visual appeal to qualify;

(viii) the purpose for which the object was created should be considered;

(ix)   the process of fabrication is relevant but not determinative.[149]

The aim with which the work was created is an important factor, but all these important considerations are to be taken into account and none overrides the other.

Works of architecture

A second group of artistic works comprises works of architecture.[150] Buildings or models for a building, which are commonly used to attract potential investors, fall into this group, but the architect's plans are protected as a graphic work and fall into the previous group. A model made of a building also falls outside of this group.

Section 4(1)(b) does not contain the rule that works in this group are protected irrespective of their artistic quality. This omission means that we have to consider the originality requirement carefully. It is submitted that artistic quality is not required: the inclusion of the additional line in s. 4(1)(a) was necessary to avoid all arguments about the artistic quality of such items as a sculpture that consists only of a rectangular piece of metal. Such arguments do not normally arise concerning buildings and it was not necessary to specify once more that the originality requirement is not an artistic quality test.[151]

Works of artistic craftsmanship

Works of artistic craftsmanship comprise the last—but, admittedly, the most difficult—part of the category of artistic works. Many items or artefacts might be called works of craftsmanship.[152] Jewellery made to a special design, furniture, clothing, or cutlery can all be called works of craftsmanship. Arguably we are dealing here with works of applied art. The Act offers no definition of this term, but, through the inclusion of the word 'artistic', makes it clear that some artistic quality is required if a work of craftsmanship is to attract copyright protection.

Hensher v. Restawhile

The House of Lords was given the opportunity to consider the issues raised by works of artistic craftsmanship in *George Hensher Ltd v. Restawhile Upholstery (Lancs) Ltd.*[153] This case was concerned with a prototype for a suite of furniture, the boat shape of which was said, by the House, to have given it a particular low-brow appeal. The first important issue is whether artistic quality is required and what level must be attempted or reached. The House of Lords disagreed with the lower court, which had held that the work qualified for copyright, and the judgment makes it clear that some artistic quality is required. The fact that the work is a work of craftsmanship that is not purely utilitarian is not sufficient;

---

[149]   A full explanation of the nine factors is found at para. 54 of the judgment.

[150]   CDPA 1988, s. 4(1)(b).

[151]   Along the same lines, see Laddie, Prescott, and Vitoria, *The Modern Law of Copyright and Designs* (n. 94) 194–5; cf. W. Cornish (1999) *Intellectual Property: Patents, Copyright, Trade Marks and Allied Rights*, 4th edn, London: Sweet and Maxwell, p. 390.

[152]   CDPA 1988, s. 4(1)(c).   [153]   [1976] AC 64; aff'd [1974] 2 All ER 420.

artistry and craftsmanship are both required. This is the real significance of the judgment, because this is the only point on which their Lordships agreed. Lord Reid and Lord Morris seem to think that a prototype can never satisfy the artistry requirement, because it is, by definition, not intended to have any value or permanence.[154] It is submitted that the intention of the craftsman is more relevant to a second and separate issue.

Should one look at the craftsman's intention to create something artistic or should one focus on the public's perception of artistic quality? The Court of Appeal had suggested that one should ask whether the public would purchase the thing for its aesthetic appeal, rather than for its functional utility,[155] but this approach was rejected by the House of Lords. Lord Simon of Glaisdale suggested that the Court of Appeal's approach was wrong, because aesthetic appeal was derived from functional utility and vice versa in the English aesthetical tradition.[156] But the speeches do not offer a clear-cut alternative approach. Lord Morris and Viscount Dilhorne suggest that an objective approach on the basis of a detached judgment of the work, without giving priority to the craftsman's intention or the perception by the public, is the better approach.[157] Lord Kilbrandon[158] and Lord Simon[159] attach more importance to the intention of the craftsman, although Lord Simon would also look at the work. And Lord Reid suggested that a work of craftsmanship could only be artistic if a substantial part of the public valued it positively for its appearance.[160]

Some further guidance is provided by *Merlet v. Mothercare*.[161] The criterion suggested by Walton J is whether the craftsman had the conscious purpose of creating a work of art.[162] In his view, the work must be a work of art and he considered this to be the common ground in the speeches in the House of Lords in the *Hensher* case. This leads to the conclusion that the intention of the creator prevails. This case was concerned with a prototype of a cape for babies, called 'Raincosy', and provides helpful guidance by making it clear that only the work itself should be submitted to the test; the use of the work should not be taken into account. In this case, this meant that the cape should be considered without a baby in it and one should clearly not look at the combination of a mother wearing the baby in a baby sling, with the baby protected by the 'Raincosy'.

A last interesting point is that the judge can rely on expert witnesses to determine whether the work meets the relevant standards. Their Lordships did not adopt a common position in this respect in the *Hensher* case, but it is clear that they all refer to expert evidence as a determining factor.

Uncertainty remains

All of this leaves us with a considerable amount of uncertainty. It is not clear what level of artistic quality is required, and no proper and comprehensive test is available. In practice, no problems arise for handcrafted jewellery and similar items, but the position for machine-made objects is problematic. In *Hensher*, Lord Simon seems to suggest that this

---

[154] [1976] AC 64 at 77, 80; aff'd [1974] 2 All ER 420 at 423 and 425.

[155] [1976] AC 64 at 71, [1973] 3 All ER 414 at 419.

[156] [1976] AC 64 at 90–2; aff'd [1974] 2 All ER 420 at 433–5.

[157] [1976] AC 64 at 81, 86; aff'd [1974] 2 All ER 420 at 433–5 at 426 and 430.

[158] [1976] AC 64 at 97; aff'd [1974] 2 All ER 420 at 439.

[159] [1976] AC 64 at 95; aff'd [1974] 2 All ER 420 at 437.

[160] [1976] AC 64 at 78; aff'd [1974] 2 All ER 420 at 424; see also *Cuisenaire v. Reed* [1963] VR 719 for a similar approach.

[161] *Merlet v. Mothercare plc* [1986] RPC 115. The case went up to the Court of Appeal, but only the point of infringement of the drawing was considered.

[162] [1984] FSR 358.

should not disqualify an object and that copyright protection would still be possible,[163] but Lord Reid seems to disagree.[164] The problem is potentially aggravated if the object is utilitarian in nature and is produced in mass. This is especially the case, because a lot of money is invested in the development of these objects. This situation is particularly regrettable, because this category of works is becoming more and more important now that a proper industrial design right has been created. This will create more intellectual property activity in this area, and requires a clear delimitation of the copyright and design areas, respectively—all of which is hampered by the absence of a clear definition of what constitutes a work of artistic craftsmanship.

No clear solution is available either for the situation in which one person supplies the craftsmanship, but another supplies the idea for the work of artistic craftsmanship. An old precedent[165] suggests that no copyright is available in such a case, but it is submitted that this approach is wrong as long as the craftsman's contribution gives the required level of artistic quality to the work.[166] A more recent case goes even further, and allows the craftsman and the artist to be two separate persons.[167]

This situation of 30 years' legal uncertainty is undesirable and unacceptable. The scope of copyright protection is, in general, extremely wide, which allows it to be used to prevent unfair competition. The stricter requirements for works of artistic craftsmanship are an exception to this rule. But even if, as submitted, one would prefer a narrower scope of copyright protection coupled with a proper unfair competition tort, it is hard to justify why works of artistic craftsmanship should be treated differently. This is clearly an area in which statutory clarification would be desirable.

Towards a way forward

What we have described is the generally accepted position. We think, however, that the case law allows for an alternative interpretation that may clarify things on a number of points.

This interpretation starts from Lord Simon's speech in the *Hensher* case: what is protected is a work of artistic craftsmanship, not an artistic work of craftsmanship.[168] A glazier, a plumber, and others are all craftsmen,[169] although it is clear that the legislator did not seek to protect all of their professional activities, because craftsmanship requires only that one is able to make something in a skilful way—that is, that one knows one's trade properly.[170] The purpose was to protect a certain type of craftsmanship and the legislator attempted to distinguish that activity by calling it 'artistic craftsmanship'.[171] The glazier who makes stained-glass windows, for example, engages in artistic craftsmanship.[172] In making the distinction, the judge can rely on the evidence provided by expert witnesses.[173]

---

[163] [1976] AC 64 at 90–2; aff'd [1974] 2 All ER 420 at 433–5.

[164] [1976] AC 64 at 77; aff'd [1974] 2 All ER 420 at 423.

[165] *Burke & Margot Burke v. Spicers Dress Designs* [1936] Ch 400.

[166] Some decisions expressed disagreement with the case: see *Radley Gowns Ltd v. C. Spyrou* [1975] FSR 455, per Oliver J; *Bernstein v. Sydney Murray* [1981] RPC 303, per Fox J; *Merlet v. Mothercare plc* (n. 161), per Walton J at 123–4.

[167] *Vermaat & Powell v. Boncrest Ltd* [2001] FSR 43.

[168] *George Hensher Ltd v. Restawhile Upholstery (Lancs) Ltd* [1976] AC 64 at 94; aff'd [1974] 2 All ER 420, per Lord Simon at 437.

[169] *George Hensher Ltd* (n. 168) at 94; aff'd per Lord Simon at 91 and 434.

[170] See *Vermaat & Powell* (n. 167).

[171] *George Hensher Ltd* (n 168), per Lord Simon at 89–91 and 432–4.

[172] *George Hensher Ltd* (n. 168), per Lord Simon at 91 and 434.

[173] *George Hensher Ltd* (n. 168), per Lord Simon at 94 and 437.

It follows from this starting point that it is not required that each individual work produced is a work of art, as long as it is the result of an activity that is considered, by the relevant circles, to be an activity of artistic craftsmanship as opposed to ordinary craftsmanship. The distinction is also easier to make if one accepts that the originality that is required is that the work of artistic craftsmanship is the author's own intellectual creation.[174] This brings this type of work in line with the rest of the copyright works, for which no artistic value of the individual work is required, and leads to the application of the normal originality requirement to the individual work.

Or does it?

In deciding whether artistic craftsmanship is involved, the expert evidence will be directed towards the fact that '*artists have vocationally an aim and impact which differ from those of the ordinary run of humankind*'.[175] This covers both the intention of the creator and the result of his or her activity.[176] So the work that is produced is taken into account in deciding whether the activity is artistic in nature.[177] But this refers to the work of the author and the relevant kind of activity in general in requiring some artistic level, and has the advantage of not referring to the individual piece of work under consideration for the purpose of copyright. Artistic craftsmanship thus involves a type of work with material that requires manual dexterity, which leads to the creation of an object that certain members of the public wish to acquire and retain for its visual appearance, rather than for its functional purpose. This is also in line with the idea that artistic craftsmanship is concerned with works of applied art. In this test, the artistic element applies to the type of work carried out by the craftsman and not to the issue of whether each individual work is a piece of art. When the issue arose in first instance in the *Lucasfilm* case Mann J adopted this approach and he quoted with approval the decision of Tipping J in the High Court of New Zealand[178] who had held that:

> ...[F]or a work to be regarded as one of artistic craftsmanship it must be possible fairly to say that the author was both a craftsman and an artist. A craftsman is a person who makes something in a skilful way and takes justified pride in their workmanship. An artist is a person with creative ability who produces something which has aesthetic appeal.[179]

It is submitted that this approach could remove some of the doubts present in the speeches in the House of Lords and that it would provide us with a workable solution. It would not affect the outcome of the *Hensher* and *Merlet* cases, because both types of activity would be held not to be artistic craftsmanship.

This approach is also reflected in an Australian decision. In *Burge v. Swarbrick*,[180] the High Court of Australia held that, while an exhaustive definition should not be attempted, it could be said that the determination of whether a work was a work of artistic craftsmanship '*does not turn on assessing the beauty or aesthetic appeal of the work or on assessing any harmony between its visual appeal and its utility*'.[181] What is vital is the extent to which the particular work's artistic expression, in its form, is unconstrained

---

[174] See P. Masiyakurima, 'Copyright in Works of Artistic Craftsmanship: An Analysis', [2016] OJLS 1, at 15.

[175] *George Hensher Ltd* (n. 168), per Lord Simon at 94 and 437.

[176] *George Hensher Ltd* (n. 168), per Lord Simon at 94 and 437.

[177] Cf. *Vermaat & Powell* (n. 167).

[178] *Lucasfilm Ltd, Star Wars Productions Ltd, Lucasfilm Entertainment Company Ltd v. Andrew Ainsworth, Shepperton Design Studios Ltd* [2009] FSR 2, 103 at 158.

[179] *Bonz Group (Pty) Ltd v. Cooke* [1994] 3 NZLR 216. Also repeated by the High Court in London in *Vermaat & Powell v. Boncrest* [2001] FSR 5.

[180] *Burge v. Swarbrick* [2007] FSR 27 (High Court of Australia).   [181] *Burge* (n. 180) at 708.

by functional considerations: if the expression is fully constrained by functional considerations, there may well be a work of craftsmanship, but it will not amount to a work of artistic craftsmanship. The latter requires creative expression outside the constraints of functional considerations and, as such, it is not incompatible with machine and mass production. There is no antithesis between utility and beauty, or between function and creativity. A work of artistic craftsmanship requires both.

Entrepreneurial rights

Section 1 of the 1988 Act also grants copyright protection to sound recordings, films, broadcasts, and typographical arrangements of published editions. These are, in most cases, derivative rights that protect the entrepreneur and the commercial exploitation of copyright. A sound recording of a pop song is a typical example. Original copyrights exist in the lyrics and the music of the song, and are, at least in the first stage, owned by their respective authors. An additional copyright is granted to the sound recording and this copyright is derivative. These rights were introduced to give the entrepreneur his or her own protection. This protection is particularly important, because, often, the financial cost of copyright exploitation is high. Many of the derivative works incorporate a series of original works protected by copyright. A film may incorporate lyrics, music, and a script, which is a dramatic work. In case of infringement, it is extremely helpful that the owner of the copyright in the film can sue. This avoids a series of parallel lawsuits by the owners of the original rights, which may each face the problem of demonstrating that his or her copyright was infringed. The absence of a derivative right would, in practice, greatly facilitate film piracy.

In fact, all of these derivative copyrights are neighbouring rights when compared to the original copyrights. They need, in general, an original copyright work as their basis. A sound recording of a musical work is a good example and so is the script as the dramatic work that is a basis for a film. In a sense, they involve a first exploitation of the original work. This distinction is reflected in many provisions of the Act[182] and is not just of theoretical importance. Unfortunately, the Act does not adopt this terminology and calls all of these rights 'copyrights', although it is clear that they are, in many respects, different from the original copyrights.

These works need not be based on works protected by copyright. If we go back to the example of the sound recording and replace the pop song by the noise of the sea unleashing its forces on the Cornish coast, the conclusion is that the recording is still a sound recording for the purposes of the Act and will attract copyright. Whether the derivative work is based on works protected by copyright or not, the originality requirement for original works will not apply to it.

Sound recordings

The Act defines the term 'sound recording' in s. 5A(1) as:

> a recording of sounds, from which the sounds may be reproduced, or...a recording of the whole or any part of a literary, dramatic or musical work, from which sounds reproducing the work or part may be produced, regardless of the medium on which the recording is made or the method by which the sounds are reproduced or produced.

---

[182] See e.g. CDPA 1988, s. 9(2).

It is important to stress that the Act deliberately uses the word 'sound' and not the word 'music'. Not only does this eliminate the discussion on the quality issue, but it also means that speech and other noises are included. In brief, all non-musical works are also included.

The 'recording' part of the definition is equally wide in scope. All that is required is the recording of the sound and the possibility of reproducing it; the medium on which the recording is made and the method by which the sound is produced or reproduced is irrelevant.[183] This means that all existing formats—such as CD, magnetic tape, and digital audio tape (DAT)—are included and that all new formats that may be developed in the years to come will automatically be included. It is obvious that the sound that is recorded may include the whole, or part of, a literary, musical, or dramatic work, but copyright will not exist in a sound recording that is, or to the extent that it is, taken from a previous sound recording.[184] In the music industry—or, perhaps more appropriately, the sound industry—this means that copyright will subsist in the master copy of the recording. This master copy is used to produce the copies on sale to the public. The CDs and cassettes do not attract their own copyright, but are protected indirectly through the copyright in the master copy.[185] This technique does not reduce the level of copyright protection, but eliminates the possibility that, in the absence of an originality requirement, each new and identical copy would attract copyright and extend the duration of copyright protection.

Each recording made independently will, however, attract copyright. If we take the Cornish example, and many persons make their own recording of the noise of the sea at the same time and place, each of these recordings will attract its own copyright and the person making his or her recording will be able to sue for infringement if someone makes, without permission, a copy of his or her recording. Such a copy will not only infringe, but it will also not attract copyright in its own right.[186]

Films

The Act defines a film in s. 5B(1) as *'a recording on any medium from which a moving image may by any means be reproduced'*. The essential element here is the recording from which a moving image may be reproduced; the technique used to make the recording, the medium on which it is made, and the means of reproduction are irrelevant.[187] All existing formats—such as celluloid film, video, and laser disc—are included and all new formats will also be included, the provision being drafted in such a way that it will not be outdated by technological developments.

Another important point is that only images are referred to: the soundtrack will attract its own separate copyright as a sound recording. Nevertheless, the term 'film' should be taken to include the soundtrack accompanying the moving images, because s. 5B(2) makes it clear that the soundtrack shall be treated as part of the film. This solution is unfortunate in so far as it represents a departure from the basic rule that one work should only be classified and protected as a single type of work, but the solution does reflect the way in which soundtracks are exploited. They are nowadays, on the one hand, an integral part of a film and it might be argued that they deserve protection as such; on the other hand, they are also exploited as separate sound recordings and people buy them

---

[183] CDPA 1988, s. 5A(1).   [184] CDPA 1988, 5A(2).

[185] For more details on the indirect infringement issue, see Ch. 15 on infringement.

[186] *Metix (UK) Ltd v. GH Maughlan (Plastics) Ltd* [1997] FSR 718, per Laddie J.

[187] CDPA 1988, s. 5B(1).

separately on CDs or as downloads. Neither is there therefore any reason to take away the protection of a soundtrack as a sound recording simply because it is also used in a film.

Only the master copy of a film will attract copyright protection; this rule applies to films in exactly the same way as it applies to sound recordings. Copyright will not subsist in a film that is, or to the extent that it is, a copy of a previous film.[188] On the one hand, indirect protection for authorized copies is eventually available, because copying them means indirectly copying the original master version; on the other, an unauthorized copy will not only not attract copyright, but will also infringe the copyright in the master copy.

It has to be emphasized that this form of copyright in a film is independent from, and does not influence, the copyright as a dramatic work in the cinematographic or audiovisual work that will, in many cases, be recorded in the film. That copyright as a dramatic work may arise if the director adds significantly to the scenario or script of an acted film, or even in the absence of a pre-existing dramatic work if the film or cinematographic work is a work of action that is capable of being performed before an audience.[189]

The breadth of the references to a recording on any medium and to the reproduction of moving images in the definition of a film do not only allow the wording of the Act to cope with further technological developments in terms of recording medium; it also allows for the classification as films of certain works that would not necessarily be described as films in the plain English sense of the word. For example, many multimedia products that are produced in a digital format seem to fall within the Act's definition of a film. Digital recording media do not create a problem and the requirement that a moving image can be reproduced from the recording is also met. Most of these products do, indeed, include moving images, in addition to texts, photographs, sound recordings, and computer programs. These additional elements, as well as the potential for interactivity, cannot reverse the reality that all elements of the definition of a film are met. Once again, the copyright as a film in the multimedia work comes on top of, and is independent from, the copyright that may exist in any of the works that are included in it. For example, if a photograph is included in a multimedia work, the film copyright in the multimedia work does not affect the copyright in the photograph as an artistic work. The maker of the multimedia work will require a licence to use the photograph if he or she does not own the copyright in it.

Broadcasts

Terrestrial broadcasts

The Copyright, Designs and Patents Act 1988 grants copyright protection to broadcasts.[190] Originally, a distinction was made between wireless transmissions, which were protected as broadcasts, and transmissions by wire, which were protected as cable programmes. That distinction has now been swept away and the category of broadcasts has been widened.[191]

---

[188] CDPA 1988, 5B(4).

[189] *Norowzian v. Arks Ltd (No. 2)* (n. 4). In this sense, this recreates the distinction between the work and the recording, and the protection as a dramatic work may be necessary to meet our obligations under the Berne Convention to protect cinematographic works: per Buxton LJ. It is also interesting to see the parallelism with the dual-track approach to musical works and sound recordings. This case does away with the idea that the Act proposed a one-track approach in relation to films.

[190] CDPA 1988, s. 6.

[191] The Copyright and Related Rights Regulations 2003, regs. 4 and 5. Among other things, CDPA 1988, s. 7, which dealt with cable programmes, has been abolished.

The Act, as amended, defines a broadcast as:

an electronic transmission of visual images, sounds or other information which—

(a) is transmitted for simultaneous reception by members of the public and is capable of being lawfully received by them, or

(b) is transmitted at a time determined solely by the person making the transmission for presentation to members of the public.[192]

The concept of transmission includes both cable transmissions and wireless broadcasts; all that is required is that the transmission is electronic.

This is a clear attempt to make the definition technology-neutral in order to cover any future developments. The definition is even wider, because it includes the transmission of information, any kind of information, on top of sounds and visual images. It is also important to keep in mind that the law attempts here to protect the investment in transmitting the signal and the provision of the service, and not anything fixed on a certain support of the works included in the transmission. The transmission can either be made for simultaneous reception by members of the public—that is, the traditional radio and television broadcasts—or at a time that is determined solely by the person making the transmission—that is, by the radio or television station. If we analyse the definition even further, we see that broadcasts that cannot be lawfully received by members of the public—such as certain military broadcasts—do not attract copyright. An interesting problem arises when broadcasts are encrypted. This means that the sound and image are emitted in a way that will result in a distorted image and sound being produced on a normal television set. Commercial satellite broadcasters, who charge fees to viewers, often do this. One needs to subscribe to the service, and one then receives a decoder to recreate the normal sound and image. These broadcasts are regarded as capable of being lawfully received if—and only if—decoding equipment has been made available to members of the public by, or with the authority of, the person making the transmission. The person providing the contents of the transmission can replace the latter.[193]

What is meant by transmission for presentation to members of the public? This becomes clear if we contemplate the example of a giant rock concert, in Hyde Park, for example. Not all fans can attend, and giant screens may be placed in halls in Edinburgh and Manchester where fans who pay an entrance fee can attend to watch the concert on a large screen. The transmission from Hyde Park to Manchester and Edinburgh is a transmission of sound and images for presentation to members of the public, and will attract copyright as a broadcast. Reception of a broadcast may be by means of a telecommunications system,[194] and copyright does not subsist in a broadcast that infringes, or to the extent that it infringes, the copyright in another broadcast.[195] Broadcasts are also often relayed. Section 6(5A) of the Act now stipulates that the relaying of a broadcast by reception and immediate retransmission is to be regarded as a separate act of broadcasting from the making of the broadcast which is being retransmitted.[196]

In principle, there is one major exception from the wide definition of a broadcast: any Internet transmission is not a broadcast, unless the transmission takes place simultaneously on the Internet and by other means, unless it is a concurrent transmission of a live event, or unless it is a transmission of recorded moving images or sounds that form part of a programme service that is offered by the person making the transmission.[197] In the

---

[192] CDPA 1988, s. 6(1).   [193] CDPA 1988, 6(2).   [194] CDPA 1988, 6(5).
[195] CDPA 1988, 6(6).
[196] CDPA 1988, s. 6(5A), inserted by Copyright and Related Rights Regulations 2003, reg. 4(d).
[197] CDPA 1988, s. 6(1A), inserted by Copyright and Related Rights Regulations 2003, reg. 4(a).

latter circumstances, the service concerned must be a service in which programmes are transmitted at scheduled times that are determined by the person making the transmission. These three exceptions, which will bring Internet transmissions within the scope of the definition of a broadcast, are explained easily: in each of the circumstances, the Internet is used as a medium for what amounts effectively to a traditional broadcast. The medium used may be different, but the transmission, as such, is not. It is therefore logical to treat these kinds of transmissions as broadcasts for copyright purposes. This means that an Internet transmission has, as a key element, the fact that it is the recipient—that is, the user—who chooses to receive the transmission at a place and time chosen by him or her and, on top of that, these transmissions tend to be interactive. Near on-demand services will, however, still be broadcasts, because they come within the third exception.

Satellite broadcasts

Satellite broadcasting is a form of broadcasting that raises additional problems.[198] The signal is transmitted to the satellite (the 'up-leg') from where it is retransmitted towards the earth (the 'down-leg'). Many countries are covered by the foot of the satellite and the question can be raised which copyright law will be applicable to the broadcasts. The choice is restricted by the fact that the Berne Convention for the Protection of Literary and Artistic Works 1886 speaks about broadcasting in terms of communication to the public.[199] This could lead to the conclusion that both emission and reception are essential elements, and that the copyright law of the emission country and the copyright laws of the countries inside the foot of the satellite should be applied cumulatively.[200]

The Copyright, Designs and Patents Act 1988[201] and the EC Council Directive on Satellite Broadcasting[202] reject this approach, focusing instead on the 'up-leg' and applying only the copyright law of the country of emission.[203] Communication to the public occurs, from the perspective of those instruments, solely in the country from which the signal is emitted (to the satellite). This approach carries with it the risk that satellite broadcasters will locate their uplink stations in countries with weak copyright laws to evade paying royalties to the largest possible extent. The Directive provides, therefore, for an exception in case the emission takes place in a non-member state that does not provide a sufficient level of copyright protection.[204] That exception has now been implemented by the UK as s. 6A of the 1988 Act and its scope has been extended to include the states adhering to the European Economic Area (EEA) as well as the EU member states.

Regulation 5 of the Copyright and Related Rights Regulations 2003[205] makes it clear, in line with the widening of the definition of a broadcast, that we are here concerned uniquely with wireless transmission and wireless broadcasting, because no wires or cables are used to carry the signal. If the signal is emitted to the satellite from the territory of a

---

[198] See A. Dietz, 'Copyright and Satellite Broadcasts' (1989) 20 IIC 135–50.

[199] Berne Convention, Art. 11bis.

[200] This theory is called the 'Bogsch theory': see M. Ficsor, 'Direct Broadcasting by Satellite and the "Bogsch Theory"' (1990) 18 IBL 258. Dr Arpad Bogsch is the former Director General of the World Intellectual Property Organization (WIPO).

[201] CDPA 1988, s. 6(4).

[202] EC Council Directive 93/83/EEC of 27 September 1993 on the coordination of certain rules concerning copyright and rights related to copyright applicable to satellite broadcasting and cable retransmission (1993) OJ L 248/15 at Art. 1(2)(b); see also P. Kern, 'The EC "Common Position" on Copyright Applicable to Satellite Broadcasting and Cable Retransmission' (1993) 8 EIPR 276.

[203] On the emission theory, see G. Karnell, 'A Refutation of the Bogsch Theory on Direct Satellite Broadcasting Rights' (1990) 18 IBL 263; this theory provides, in practice, a more workable solution.

[204] CDPA 1988, s. 5A(2).   [205] SI 2003/2498.

member state of the EEA, the copyright laws of that member state will apply[206] and the person operating the uplink station will be treated as the person making the broadcast.[207] In all member states, the level of copyright protection will be at a harmonized level. If the signal is emitted from the territory of a non-member state and that country does not provide a minimum level of protection, the exceptional rule comes into operation. The minimum level of protection is defined as equivalent rights for authors of literary, dramatic, musical, and artistic works; films; and broadcasts to those given to them by s. 20 of the 1988 Act in relation to the broadcasting of their works, plus the requirement that the consent of the performer be obtained before a performance is broadcast live, and a right for authors of sound recordings and performers to share in a single equitable remuneration in respect of the broadcasting of sound recordings.[208] The exceptional rule states that, if the emission has been commissioned by a person or a broadcasting organization established in a member state, then the laws of the member state in which that person or the broadcasting organization has its principal establishment will apply.[209]

The copyright protection for satellite broadcasts is not dependent on the type of satellite used, as long as the signals can be lawfully received by members of the public. As a result, only point-to-point communication is excluded if it is exclusively meant for reception and retransmission by a local broadcaster.[210]

Typographical arrangements

This category of works is concerned with the typographical arrangements of published editions. The type and size of the letters used, the number of words on a page, and the place of illustrations in relation to the text, are all examples of typographical arrangements. Typographical arrangements have been described as '*graphical images pertaining or relating to printing by which literary, dramatic or musical works may be conveyed to the reader*'.[211]

The typographical arrangement copyright arises in relation to published editions of the whole, or any part, of one or more literary, dramatic, or musical works.[212] The copyright exists, however, only in relation to the published edition as a whole as it is published by the publisher, irrespective of how its content is composed.[213] For example, in relation to a newspaper, the copyright existed in relation to the newspaper, as published, rather than in relation to the arrangement of individual articles within the newspaper.[214]

The typographical arrangement copyright does not arise in relation to artistic works and does not subsist in the typographical arrangement of a published edition if, or to the extent that, it simply reproduces the typographical arrangement of a previous edition.[215]

An overview

Copyright will only exist if a work comes within the scope of a category of works that has been defined in the Copyright, Designs and Patents Act 1988. A first set of categories

---

[206] See Art. 1(2)(d) of the Directive.   [207] See CDPA 1988, s. 6A(2).

[208] CDPA 1988, s. 6A(2).   [209] CDPA 1988, s. 6A(1).   [210] See Art. 1(1) of the Directive.

[211] Laddie, Prescott, and Vitoria, *The Modern Law of Copyright and Designs* (n. 94) at 435.

[212] CDPA 1988, s. 8(1).

[213] *Newspaper Licensing Agency Ltd v. Marks & Spencer plc* [2001] Ch 257, [2000] All ER 239, [2001] Ch 281, per Mance LJ.

[214] *Newspaper Licensing Agency Ltd* (n. 213), per Mance LJ.   [215] CDPA 1988, s. 8(2).

requires some level of originality. It comprises literary, dramatic, musical, and artistic works. The precise definition of each of these types of work has given rise to a considerable amount of case law, because the Act does not always offer a definition. Sometimes, a list of works is given instead of a definition, but even then problems remain.

Original works do not, however, require artistic quality, even if the concept of originality is not always very specific and seems to be influenced by the type of work under consideration. All of these definitional problems unite to make the case of works of artistic craftsmanship into a very colourful example in point.

A second set could be said to involve mainly entrepreneurial rights. Originality as such is not required; often, these are derivative rights. In this category, we find films, sound recordings, broadcasts, and typographical arrangements of published editions.

Further reading

GENDREAU, Y., NORDEMANN, A., and OESCH, R. (eds.) (1999) *Copyright and Photographs: An International Survey*, London: Kluwer Law International.

HINTON, C., 'Can I Protect My TV Format?' (2006) 17 Ent LR 3, 91.

JONES, V., 'What Constitutes a Copyright Work: Does It Really Matter?' (2005) 16 Ent LR 5, 129.

MASIYAKURIMA, P., 'Copyright in Works of Artistic Craftsmanship: An Analysis' (2016) 36 OJLS 1.

PILA, J., 'An Intentional View of the Copyright Work' (2008) 71(4) MLR 535–8.

PILA, J., 'Copyright and Internet Browsing' (2012) 128 LQR 204–8.

RAHMATIAN, A., 'Music and Creativity as Perceived by Copyright Law' [2005] IPQ 267.

TORREMANS, P. (2007) 'Legal Issues Pertaining to the Restoration and Reconstitution of Manuscripts, Sheet Music, Paintings and Films for Marketing Purposes', in P. Torremans, *Copyright Law: A Handbook of Contemporary Research*, Cheltenham/Northampton, MA: Edward Elgar, pp. 28–48.

11

Qualification

Works that come under one of the categories described in the previous chapter have to pass one more hurdle to secure copyright protection—namely, the qualification requirement. This requirement is linked to the principle of national treatment contained in the Berne Convention for the Protection of Literary and Artistic Works 1886, in the Universal Copyright Convention, and now also in the TRIPS Agreement.[1] Authors connected with another member state are to be treated in the same way as a member state's own authors and should receive the same copyright. That connection with a member state might be provided in two ways: the author may have a personal relationship with the member state or the work may be first published in that member state.[2] The latter option is not available as long as a work remains unpublished.

This principle is implemented in the UK through a two-stage process:

1. The criteria used to establish a connection with the UK[3]—whether through the author or through publication—are laid down.

2. The system is applied to works connected with other member states of both Conventions. Such application is effected by an Order in Council.[4]

Things become further complicated because countries adhere to one, or both, Conventions at different dates. This creates problems for works published before the date on which the country adheres to the Conventions. Unfortunately, the provisions dealing with this issue are not identical in both Conventions. On the one hand, the Berne Convention works, in part, retroactively. If a work is still in copyright under its own national copyright legislation when a country adheres to the Convention, the work will attract copyright protection in the UK for the remaining part of the term of copyright. On the other hand, the Universal Copyright Convention does not work retroactively and a work published before a country, which is not a member of the Berne Convention, adheres to the Universal Copyright Convention will not be granted copyright in the UK.

Qualification by means of the personal status of the author

The issue here is whether the author of the work, being the creator of the work,[5] is a qualifying person. This will be the case if the author is a British national,[6] is domiciled or

---

[1] Berne Convention, Art. 3; Universal Copyright Convention, Art. 2; TRIPS Agreement, Art. 3.

[2] See also, for the implementation of this Convention rule, CDPA 1988, s. 153.

[3] And with dependent territories to which the CDPA 1988 is extended—the Isle of Man, the Channel Islands, etc.—see CDPA 1988, s. 157 and the relevant Orders in Council taken on the basis of that section.

[4] CDPA 1988, s. 159.   [5] Defined more precisely in Ch. 13.

[6] British dependent territories citizens, British nationals (overseas), British overseas citizens, British subjects, and British protected persons within the meaning of the British Nationality Act 1981 are added to this category: CDPA 1988, see s. 154(1)(a).

resident in the UK, or is a body incorporated under the laws of the UK. Application to a foreign work depends on the question of whether the author is a citizen, subject, domiciliary, or resident of a Convention country listed in an Order in Council, or a company incorporated in such country.[7]

Because all of these connecting factors can change over time, the connection has to exist at the material time—that is, at the date on which the work is made for unpublished literary, dramatic, musical, and artistic works. If the work is published, reference is made to the date of first publication and the author's status at that date, or to the date on which the author died if that occurs before the work is published.[8] There is only one rule for works that do not come within the scope of the 'original' category: the date on which a sound recording or film is made is the material time for these works. For broadcasts, the date of transmission is the material time, and for typographical arrangements, this is the time of first publication.[9]

Once qualification has been achieved, subsequent events cannot take it away.[10]

Qualification by means of first publication

The country of first publication is also a separate connecting factor. A work that is first published in the UK will qualify for copyright protection and so will a work first published in another Convention country.[11] The country of transmission is the connecting factor for broadcasts.[12]

Really simultaneous publication does not create a problem if one of the countries in which the work is published is the UK or another contracting state, but a problem may be created if the country in which publication takes place a couple of days before publication in other countries is not a contracting state to one of the copyright conventions. This would normally jeopardize the option of qualification for copyright protection through first publication in a contracting state, but a period of grace of 30 days has been built in. Publication in that period in the UK or another contracting state will be treated as really simultaneous publication and will secure qualification for copyright protection.[13]

But what amounts to publication? The definition of the term 'publication' is, first of all, relevant for the qualification issue, but, in many cases, it is also of importance for the term of copyright protection, as we will discuss in the next chapter. For copyright purposes, 'publication' means issuing copies of the work to the public in sufficient quantities with the intention of satisfying public demand.[14] Copies are issued to the public if they are put into circulation by sale, gift, or hire[15] and this takes place if the publisher invites the public to acquire the copies.[16] The intention of the publisher is an important element, because he or she must be prepared to meet public demand.[17]

For literary, dramatic, musical, and artistic works, copies can also be issued to the public through the inclusion of the work in an electronic retrieval system that makes the

---

[7] CDPA 1988, s. 154.   [8] CDPA 1988, s. 154(4).   [9] CDPA 1988, s. 154(5).
[10] CDPA 1988, s. 153(3).   [11] CDPA 1988, s. 155(1) and (2).   [12] CDPA 1988, s. 156.
[13] CDPA 1988, s. 155(3).   [14] CDPA 1988, s. 175(1)(a).
[15] See *British Northrop v. Texteam Blackburn Ltd* [1974] RPC 57, per Megarry J at 67.
[16] *British Northrop* (n. 15), per Megarry J at 67. It would not be workable to take into account the place where the public receives the copies, because this would make the country of first publication dependent on where shipments of the work were received first.
[17] Cf. *Copex v. Flegon* (1967) *The Times*, 18 August.

work available to the public.[18] The number of copies issued is of secondary importance,[19] as shown by the Court of Appeal's decision to accept that the release for sale of six copies of a song that was not (yet) known amounted to publication.[20]

Copies are not issued to the public by the performance of a literary, dramatic, or musical work. The same goes for broadcasting, exhibiting an artistic work, and issuing graphic works or photographs of sculptures, works of architecture, or works of artistic craftsmanship.[21]

The concept of copies is to be construed along the lines of s. 17 of the Copyright, Designs and Patents Act (CDPA) 1988. The main outstanding question is how exact the copies should be in order to constitute publication of the original work. The infringement criterion of a substantial part of the work is not suitable in this context; the whole work should be contained in the copies. There should be no difference in material respects between the copies and the original work, even if minor variations can be accepted.[22]

Unauthorized acts are not taken into account when it is established whether a work has been published or not.[23] A related, but fairly specific and exceptional, problem is raised by an adaptation—by the author, or with his or her consent—of an unpublished work. Does the translation into English of an unpublished African Swahili literary tale, or the conversion of an unpublished novel into a play, have the effect of publishing the original if copies of the adaptation are issued to the public? The Act provides no clear guidance, but it seems reasonable to assume that, if the adaptation is 'original' enough to attract its own copyright, it is distinct enough from the original to conclude that it does not constitute publication of the original work, which is clearly distinct from the adaptation. If, however, the adaptation merely reproduces the older unpublished work, publication of the adaptation will probably have the effect of publication of the older work. An example of the latter case would be a three-dimensional embodiment of a two-dimensional drawing.[24] As we will see later in Chapter 15 on infringement, this latter example is very similar to cases of copyright infringement.

The Berne Convention has a built-in preference for qualification by means of the country of first publication over qualification by means of the personal status of the owner.[25]

The latter option will only be taken into account once it has been established that first publication did not take place in a contracting state. This preference is not found in the 1988 Act: the Act treats both methods of qualification as equal.

An overview

The UK copyright system is based on a series of international conventions, which have been implemented into national law. The main principle of the international copyright system is that foreign authors and their works will, in each member state be given

---

[18] CDPA 1988, s. 175(1)(b).

[19] Mere colourable publication, which is not intended to satisfy public demand, is not taken into account: CDPA 1988, s. 175(5).

[20] *Francis Day & Hunter v. Feldman* [1914] 2 Ch 728; see also *Bodley Head Ltd v. Flegon* [1972] 1 WLR 680, [1972] RPC 587.

[21] CDPA 1988, s. 175(4).   [22] See *Sweeney v. Macmillan Publishers Ltd* [2002] RPC 35 at 651.

[23] CDPA 1988, s. 175(6).   [24] *Merchant Adventurers v. Grew* [1973] RPC 1 at 10.

[25] Berne Convention, Art. 5(4). Under the Convention, this is the normal way to determine the country of origin of a work. First publication is, relatively speaking, easier to determine for any third party and is relatively easily proved in comparison with any aspect of the personal status of the author.

national treatment. In practice, this requires a tool with which to determine whether an author or a work qualifies for this national treatment and therefore for copyright protection in the UK. The qualification rules deal with this matter. Authors and works that pass the test will have access to the copyright system in the UK; authors and works that do not qualify will not benefit from copyright protection. Qualification can be achieved by means of the personal status of the author or by means of first publication of the work.

Further reading

GARNETT, K., DAVIES, G., and HARBOTTLE, G. (2010) *Copinger and Skone James on Copyright*, 16th edn, London: Sweet and Maxwell, paras. 3–154 *et seq.*

RICKETSON, S. and GINSBURG, J. (2006) *International Copyright and Neighbouring Rights: The Berne Convention and Beyond*, Oxford: Oxford University Press, pp. 239–78.

STERLING, J. A. L. (2003) *World Copyright Law*, 2nd edn, London: Sweet and Maxwell, pp. 604–7.

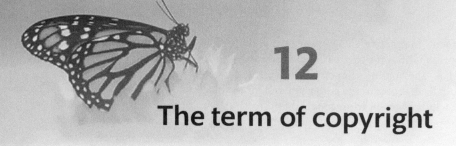

12

The term of copyright

General principles

A harmonized term of protection

We have now established which works attract copyright, but what is the duration of copyright? We will mainly have to distinguish between 'original' works and films, on the one hand,[1] and all other works, on the other.

The term of copyright in 'original' works used to be 50 years in the UK.[2] In other member states of the European Union (EU), longer terms of protection were in force—such as 70 years in Germany and 60–80 years in Spain. This was possible because the Berne Convention for the Protection of Literary and Artistic Works 1886 only imposes a minimum term of protection upon its members,[3] but it could impede the free movement of goods within the EU and was therefore held to be undesirable.

A directive was adopted with the aim of harmonizing the term of copyright protection in the EU, broadly speaking, at the 70-year level.[4] It brought radical change to the relevant sections of the Copyright, Designs and Patents Act (CDPA) 1988 when it was eventually implemented by the Duration of Copyright and Rights in Performances Regulations 1995.[5] In the UK, the changes took effect on 1 January 1996.

Comparison of term

A preliminary point that affects the transition from a 50-year term to a 70-year term is the issue of the comparison of term. This technique is introduced—or perhaps one should say 'tolerated'—by Art. 7(8) of the Berne Convention. It means that works in relation to which the country of origin has a shorter term of copyright protection will not attract copyright protection in a country with a longer term of protection once the term of protection in the country of origin has expired. In practical terms, this means, for example, that a Canadian work with a Canadian term of protection would not attract 20 extra years of copyright protection in Germany; the Germans are allowed to discriminate and apply the 70-year term only to works in relation to which the country of origin

---

[1] Art. 1 of the Directive refers to works within the meaning of Art. 2 of the Berne Convention.

[2] CDPA 1988, s. 12, as it stood before the amended version that was contained in the Duration of Copyright and Rights in Performances Regulations 1995, SI 1995/3297, regs. 4 and 5(1), took effect on 1 January 1996.

[3] Berne Convention, Art. 7(6). The minimum term is 50 years.

[4] EC Council Directive 93/98/EEC of 29 October 1993 on the harmonizing of the term of copyright and certain related rights (1993) OJ L 290, now codified as Directive 2006/116/EC of the European Parliament and of the Council of 12 December 2006 on the term of protection of copyright and certain related rights (codified version) [2006] OJ L 372/12 (the 'Term Directive').

[5] SI 1995/3297.

is Germany or any other country that allows a minimum term of protection of 70 years for German works. Article 7 of the Directive makes the application of the comparison of term rule mandatory for all member states. Works originating in third countries that do not offer at least a 70-year copyright term will not benefit from the longer protection in the EU, the obvious aim of which is to convince third countries also to adopt a 70-year term of copyright.

The UK has implemented Art. 7 by inserting into the 1988 Act a provision that stipulates that a work that has a state that is not part of the European Economic Area (EEA) as its country of origin and the author of which is not a national of a EEA state will only be protected in the UK for the term for which it is granted protection in its country of origin.[6] On top of that, the provision stipulates that under no circumstances will a term that is longer than the new UK term of protection be granted. This means, for example, that the UK will only grant a 50-year term of protection to a novel published in Toronto by a Canadian national. Should Canada put in place a copyright system that grants protection for an 80-year term, the UK will still only protect the work for its own 70-year term.

The new UK provision applies to all types of copyright work.[7] The country of origin is defined as follows for the purposes of the 1988 Act: if the work is first published in a contracting state to the Berne Convention, that country of first publication will be the country of origin of the work;[8] for unpublished works and works that are first published in a country that is not a Berne Convention country, the country of which the author of the work is a national will normally be the country of origin of the work.[9] Special rules that depart from this latter rule exist for films, works of architecture, and artistic works that are incorporated in a building. The country in which the maker of the film has either its headquarters, its domicile, or its residence will be the country of origin of the film if that country is a contracting state to the Berne Convention.[10] The Berne Convention country in which the work of architecture is constructed, or in which the building or structure in which the artistic work is incorporated is situated, will be the country of origin of the work of architecture or the artistic work, respectively.[11]

Non-discrimination in the EU

The provision in Art. 7(8) of the Berne Convention has strange implications in relation to the Term Directive, due to the transition from a 50-year term to a 70-year term in the majority of member states. Indeed, Art. 18 of the Treaty on the Functioning of the European Union (formerly Art. 12 of the Treaty of Rome) rules out any discrimination on the basis of nationality and this rule applies also to copyright issues. Thus Germany was not entitled to use its comparison-of-term rule in relation to works of nationals of another member state:[12] these works should have enjoyed a 70-year term of protection in Germany all along.

---

[6] CDPA 1988, ss. 12(6), 13A(4), 13B(7), and 14(3).

[7] CDPA 1988, ss. 12(6), 13A(4), 13B(7), and 14(3). The comparison-of-term rule is dropped in relation to sound recordings and broadcasts in those cases in which its application would be at variance with the UK's international obligations as they stood on 29 October 1993: CDPA 1988, ss. 13A(5) and 14(4).

[8] CDPA 1988, s. 15A(2). Special provisions for cases of simultaneous publication are found in s. 15A(3) and (4).

[9] CDPA 1988, s. 15A(5)(c).   [10] CDPA 1988, s. 15A(5)(a).   [11] CDPA 1988, s. 15A(5)(b).

[12] Cases C-92 and 326/92, *Phil Collins v. Imtrat Handelsgesellschaft GmbH* [1993] ECR I-5145, [1993] 3 CMLR 773.

When the Directive came into force, the area in which these works enjoy protection became the whole territory of the EU. As a strange consequence, all works that were still protected in Germany did benefit from the 70-year term in the whole of the EU, even if some of these works were out of copyright and in the public domain in a number of member states, eventually including the member state of origin, which used to have a 50-year term. An English literary work, written by an English author who died in 1943 and first published in the UK, no longer attracted copyright protection in the UK under the old provisions of the 1988 Act when the Directive came into force, its term of protection having expired at the end of 1993—but it did still attract copyright in Germany until the end of 2013. The work came back into copyright through the implementation of the Directive and its term of copyright protection expired at the end of the year 2013 in the whole of the EU, including the UK. Additionally, the fact that a work never enjoyed copyright protection in a member state will not stop it from benefiting from the extension of term even in that member state in as far as the work still enjoyed copyright protection in at least one member state.[13]

All of this is the inevitable result of the combined application of Art. 18 of the Treaty on the Functioning of the European Union (formerly Art. 6 of the EC Treaty), as applied in the *Phil Collins*[14] case, and Art. 7 of the Term Directive.[15]

Transition issues

In practical terms, all of those works to which a new longer term would now apply if they were created after the date on which the Directive was implemented saw their term of protection increased to the new longer period. For example, the first edition of this book was written in 1995; the old 50-year term applied to it at first, but, from 1 January 1996 onwards, its term of protection in the UK was increased under the new 70-year rule. If the copyright had already lapsed under the old rules, but the new longer period had not yet expired, the copyright would have been revived for the remaining period of the new longer term.

For example, the works of an author such as D. H. Lawrence, who died in 1930, went out of copyright at the end of 1980, but their copyright was revived under the new rules for the period between 1 January 1996 and the end of the year 2000. While this may have been good news for right holders and those who held copyrights before they lapsed under the old rules, it created an odd situation for those who had exploited the works, for example, by publishing a complete collection of the works of D. H. Lawrence in 1990, on the understanding that they were out of copyright.

This situation has been addressed by the implementing statutory instrument[16] and transition measures have been put in place.[17] Anything done before the UK's implementation date of 1 January 1996 cannot amount to infringement and copies that were made

---

[13] Art. 10(2) of the Directive, as interpreted by the Court of Justice in case C-240/07, *Sony Music Entertainment (Germany) GmbH v. Falcon Neue Medien Vertrieb GmbH* [2009] ECDR 12.

[14] *Phil Collins* (n. 12).

[15] G. Dworkin and J. A. L. Sterling, '*Phil Collins* and the Term Directive' (1994) 5 EIPR 187.

[16] See reg. 23.

[17] Bizarre situations remain, however, especially because the 1988 Act also contained transitional measures in relation to works created under previous UK Copyright Acts. The combination of the various transition measures can give rise to odd results: see J. N. Adams and M. Edenborough, 'The Duration of Copyright in the UK after the 1995 Regulations' (1996) 11 EIPR 590; and see also P. Torremans and C. Otero García-Castrillón, 'Revisionary Copyright: A Ghost of the Past or a Current Trap to Assignments of Copyright?' (2012) 2 IPQ 77.

before the Directive's implementation date of 1 July 1995 can be issued to the public without giving rise to copyright infringement, even if that effectively takes place once the new system is in force. This means that no royalties will be payable for the collection of the works of D. H. Lawrence that was published in 1990 in our example and that its publishers can continue to sell existing copies of the collection. On top of that, any allegedly infringing acts for which arrangements were made before 1 January 1995 and which are subsequently implemented in relation to works that were out of copyright at that time will not amount to copyright infringement.

Original works

The term of copyright protection is calculated from the end of the year in which the author dies and runs for 70 years.[18] As a result, copyright in original literary, dramatic, musical, and artistic works expires 70 years after the end of the year in which the author of the work died. The term of protection for computer-generated works, which have no human author who can die, continues to run for 50 years and the death of the author is replaced by the date on which the work was made.[19]

Computer-generated works are virtually unknown outside the UK. Their introduction in the 1988 Act was not followed by similar moves in other European countries. The Term Directive does not affect these works and the UK opted to keep its term of protection at 50 years. All terms are, for reasons of simplicity, calculated from 1 January of the year following the event that gives rise to them.[20] In the case of joint authorship, the 70-year term of protection for the work is calculated from the end of the year in which the last surviving author dies.[21]

Anonymous or pseudonymous works create a problem for the application of these rules. For these works, the term of protection runs for 70 years from the lawful publication[22] of the work. That lawful publication needs to occur within a period of 70 years from the end of the calendar year in which the work was made. If no lawful publication takes place within that period, the copyright expires at the end of the 70 years after the work was made.[23] These rules apply unless the author discloses his or her identity during the 70-year period, or if his or her identity becomes known during that period. In this situation, the normal rule for non-anonymous and non-pseudonymous works will apply.[24]

Films

Cinematographic and audiovisual works present a different case. The Directive does not simply lay down a term of protection, but also stipulates that the principal director of such a work shall be considered as its author or as one of its authors. Member states are, in addition, given the freedom to designate other co-authors for these works. The latter provision can be seen as a compromise between the Continental tendency to give directors rights in a film and the UK's tradition to give the same rights to producers.

---

[18] CDPA 1988, s. 12(2).   [19] CDPA 1988, s. 12(7).
[20] Art. 8 of the Directive confirms this existing principle in UK copyright law.
[21] CDPA 1988, s. 12(8).   [22] As defined in CDPA 1988, s. 12(5).
[23] CDPA 1988, s. 12(3).   [24] CDPA 1988, s. 12(4).

It also becomes clear from these provisions that films, to use the UK term, are increasingly associated with, or considered as, original works, rather than entrepreneurial recording rights. Historically, films were very much part of the latter category, which was illustrated by the fact that the original version of the 1988 Act dealt with the duration of sound recordings and films in a single section. Originality is still not required for films, but the fact that the 'artistic' creators of a film are now seen as its authors—with the emphasis shifting somewhat away from the 'entrepreneurial' producers—explains why films are now given a duration regime that resembles, above all, the regime for original works.

From 1 January 1996 onwards, the following regime has applied. The term of copyright protection for a film will expire 70 years after the end of the year in which the last of the following persons dies:

- the principal director;
- the author of the screenplay;
- the author of the dialogue;
- the composer of the music specifically created for use in the film.[25]

If the identity of one or more of the persons concerned is not known, these persons can be deleted from the list and the death of the last known person will trigger the start of the 70-year term.[26] If the identity of all of the persons concerned is unknown, the film will be protected for 70 years from the end of the calendar year in which it was made. This period is extended to 70 years from the end of the calendar year in which the film was made available to the public if the film is made available before the 70-year period after making expires.[27] A film is made available to the public when it is first shown in public or broadcast, unless it is the consequence of an unauthorized act.[28] If the identity of at least one of the persons concerned becomes known before the 70-year period for anonymous films expires, the normal rules that rely on the death of the author or of the last of the co-authors as the triggering event replace the rules for anonymous films in determining the term of protection for the film.[29] An author's identity shall not be assumed to be unknown simply because the person who wants to find out whether a film is still in copyright does not know it; the criterion is rather that it is not possible to ascertain the identity by reasonable enquiry.[30]

Regrettably, the UK took a minimalist approach when implementing the Directive. This means that the list of people that are referred to in relation to the term of copyright in a film does not correspond with that used in relation to the authorship of a film. On the latter point, the UK was obliged to include the director in addition to the producer, who was traditionally included under UK law, but it declined to use the option to add other people. There seemed to be an unwritten rule that the rules on the term of copyright referred to the authors of the work; this rule has now been set aside in relation to films, and the 1988 Act no longer displays a clear and systematic approach to this matter. Such a political compromise, or a bending of the rules in favour of one group of lobbyists, does not enhance the transparency and the inherent logic of the copyright system in the UK, and is therefore to be regretted. This also represents a missed chance to achieve harmonized rules for films that are, after all, exploited across Europe and not only in the UK.

---

[25] CDPA 1988, s. 13B(2).   [26] CDPA 1988, s. 13B(3).   [27] CDPA 1988, s. 13B(4).
[28] CDPA 1988, s. 13B(6).   [29] CDPA 1988, s. 13B(5).   [30] CDPA 1988, s. 13B(10).

It is submitted that the better solution would have involved the creation of a new heading in the 1988 Act, which would cover cinematographic and audiovisual works. These would then be expressly excluded from the scope of the dramatic works provision.[31] This approach would lead to two separate rights: one for, eventually among others, the director in the cinematographic or audiovisual work, and a second right for the producer in the film as the recording of the cinematographic or audiovisual work.[32] This is also the approach taken in the Belgian Copyright Act of 1994, which was adopted after the Directive had been adopted.[33] Such an approach would underscore the fact that films are increasingly seen as original works. A separate recording right, or right in the first fixation, would then exist on top of the original right. But maybe such a coherent and systematic approach has too much of a Continental flavour to it for the pragmatic UK copyright lawyer.

The current state of confusion is shown by two contrasting developments. On the one hand, there is the implementation in the UK of the Term Directive, which clearly treats films as a single category, including both the fixation and the cinematographic work. Arguably, this is a breach of the provisions of the Directive, because, in taking the fixation on board, the UK also extended the term for moral rights protection in films, which is something for which the Directive did not provide a mandate.[34] On the other hand, there is the Court of Appeal's decision in *Norowzian*.[35] While it was not open to the court to create a separate copyright category of cinematographic works, the court did offer a form of dual protection, by arguing that some works can be protected as films and as dramatic works at the same time.

Other entrepreneurial works

Sound recordings are the first 'other' type of work. Sound recordings are protected for 50 years from the end of the calendar year in which the sound recording was made. This period is extended to 50 years from publication[36] if the recording is published before the 50-year period after making expires.[37] In the absence of publication, a recording can still be made available to the public during the 50-year period after the recording was made. Publication can take the form of the recording being played in public or communicated to the public and the term of protection will then expire at the end of a 50-year term that starts running from the end of the calendar year in which the recording is made available. In determining whether a sound recording has been published, played in public, or communicated to the public, no account is to be taken

---

[31] Cf. P. Kamina, 'Authorship of Films and Implementation of the Term Directive: The Dramatic Tale of Two Copyrights' (1994) 8 EIPR 319.

[32] The provisions on employer ownership of the copyright in the work and assignment of copyright could still grant the producer most of the rights. Contractual provisions will continue to play an important role in this area.

[33] Wet betreffende het auteursrecht en de naburige rechten—Loi relative au droit d'auteur et aux droits voisins of 30 June 1994 [1994] Belgisch Staatsblad—Moniteur Belge, 27 July, pp. 19297 *et seq.*; see Arts. 2, 14, and 39, now Book XI, title 5 in the Code of Economic Law; see Art. XI 179 by way of example.

[34] See H. Laddie, P. Prescott, and M. Vitoria (2000) *The Modern Law of Copyright and Designs*, 3rd edn, London: Butterworths, p. 19.

[35] *Norowzian v. Arks Ltd (No. 2)* [2000] FSR 363.

[36] Starting at the end of the calendar year during which publication took place.

[37] CDPA 1988, s. 13A(2), as amended by Copyright and Related Rights Regulations 2003, reg. 29.

of an unauthorized act.[38] The European Commission's proposal to extend the term of protection met with a lot of opposition.[39] What emerged in the end is an extension for performances that have been fixated in a phonogram. From 1 November 2013 onwards member states are to bring in provisions that offer 70 years of protection if the fixation of the performance in a phonogram is lawfully published or lawfully communicated to the public within 50 years after the date of the performance. The 70-year term shall run from the earlier date of first publication or first communication to the public. Performances that are fixated otherwise than in a phonogram will (still) only be entitled to 50 years of protection.[40]

The term of protection for broadcasts is 50 years from first transmission.[41] A broadcast that is a repeat of a broadcast previously made is not able to prolong the term of copyright in the broadcast or to attract a new copyright after the original term has expired. The copyright in the repeat broadcast will expire at the same time as the copyright in the original broadcast.[42] For typographical arrangements, the term of copyright protection is only 25 years from first publication.[43]

All of these terms start to run from the end of the year in which the triggering event takes place.

An overview

The basic rule is simple: the term of copyright has been harmonized at life of the author plus 70 years in the EU. One can ask plenty of questions about the justification for this move, but, because the US followed suit, it is unlikely to be reversed in the near future. The basic rule applies to the original category of works—that is, literary, dramatic, musical, and artistic works—and to films.

Entrepreneurial works, such as sound recordings and broadcasts, benefit from 50 years of copyright protection. Performances fixated in a phonogram will in future be protected for 70 years.

The term of protection for typographical arrangements is 25 years.

Further reading

ADAMS, J. N. and EDENBOROUGH, M., 'The Duration of Copyright in the UK after the 1995 Regulations' (1996) 11 EIPR 590.

EMILIANIDES, A. C., 'The Author Revived: Harmonisation without Justification' (2004) 26(12) EIPR 538.

GARNETT, K., DAVIES, G., and HARBOTTLE, G. (2010) *Copinger and Skone James on Copyright*, 16th edn, London: Sweet and Maxwell, Ch. 6.

---

[38] Regulation 29.

[39] See R. M. Hilty et al., 'Comment by the Max-Planck Institute on the Commission's Proposal for a Directive to Amend Directive 2006/116 Concerning the Term of Protection for Copyright and Related Rights' (2009) 31(2) EIPR 59–72.

[40] Directive 2011/77/EU of the European Parliament and of the Council of 27 September 2011 amending Directive 2006/116/EC on the term of protection and certain related rights [2011] OJ L265/1.

[41] CDPA 1988, s. 14(2).   [42] CDPA 1988, s. 14(5) and (6).   [43] CDPA 1988, s. 15.

HILTY, R. M. et al., 'Comment by the Max-Planck Institute on the Commission's Proposal for a Directive to Amend Directive 2006/116 Concerning the Term of Protection for Copyright and Related Rights' (2009) 31(2) EIPR 59–72.

LADDIE, H., PRESCOTT, P., and VITORIA, M. (2000) *The Modern Law of Copyright and Designs*, 3rd edn, London: Butterworths, Ch. 10.

PARKER, N., 'A Raw Deal for Performers: Part 1—Term of Copyright' (2006) 17 Ent LR 6, 161.

13

Authorship and ownership of copyright

Authorship

The creator as author

The person who creates the work is the author of the work.[1] This hardly creates problems for the original literary, dramatic, musical, and artistic works. Thus the writer of a literary work, such as a novel, will be its author; the composer will be the author of a musical work;[2] the sculptor will be the author of a sculpture; the photographer will be the author of a photograph. For derivative works, however, the application of this principle is not as easy: who creates a sound recording?

The Copyright, Designs and Patents Act (CDPA) 1988 provides further guidance on this point in s. 9(2). The original rule in the UK in 1988 was that the person who creates a sound recording and becomes its author is the person who makes the necessary arrangements for the making of the recording. The same solution was adopted for films. In practice, this meant that the producer becomes the author of a film, because he or she makes the arrangements for making the film. But most other European countries adopted a different approach: from their point of view, the director of a film was the creator of the work, even if he or she was not always the sole creator of the work. In an attempt to harmonize these provisions, the Community introduced the obligation to consider the principal director of a film as its author and left it to the member states to designate other co-authors if they so wished.[3] In the UK, the 1988 Act was amended in the light of the Directive by the Copyright and Related Rights Regulations 1996.[4] The original rule in relation to sound recordings and films disappeared entirely. For films, it was replaced by a rule that designates the director and the producer as the co-authors of a film,[5] and the Act now expressly states that the producer is the author of a sound recording.[6]

---

[1] CDPA 1988, s. 9(1).

[2] For an interesting example, see *Hyperion Records Ltd v. Lionel Sawkins* [2005] 3 All ER 636, [2005] 1 WLR 3281 (CA).

[3] EC Council Directive 93/98/EEC of 29 October 1993 harmonizing the term of protection of copyright and certain related rights (1993) OJ L 290/9, Art. 2(1), now codified as Directive 2006/116/EC of the European Parliament and of the Council of 12 December 2006 on the term of protection of copyright and certain related rights (codified version) [2006] OJ L 372/12.

[4] SI 1996/2967, regs. 4 and 18(1).

[5] CDPA 1988, s. 9(2)(ab). It follows that the director has an intellectual property right and that that right covers all elements of the exclusive right in copyright. See Case C-277/10, *Martin Luksan v. Petrus van der Let*, 9 February 2012 at para. 48, <http://curia.europa.eu>.

[6] CDPA 1988, s. 9(2)(aa).

But who creates a computer-generated literary, dramatic, musical, or artistic work? The obvious answer would be the computer—but then the computer becomes the author of the work and it would be absurd to have a machine as a player in a system that grants property rights. The 1988 Act solves this problem by adopting an approach that is identical to that originally taken in relation to sound recordings and films: the person who makes the necessary arrangements for the creation of the work becomes the author of the work.[7]

In relation to broadcasts, the person making the broadcast is its creator, unless it relays another broadcast by reception and immediate retransmission. In the latter case, the person making that other broadcast will be the creator and author.[8] This avoids the unhealthy situation of two equal authors for one work, which one of them created and transmitted, and which the other one only retransmits. In relation to a typographical arrangement, meanwhile, the publisher of the edition is its author.[9]

It is recognized that the identity of the author is not always known: obvious examples of such a situation are presented by anonymous works. A work is of unknown authorship[10] if a person cannot identify the identity of the author by reasonable enquiry.[11] It is not clear, however, which person undertakes this reasonable enquiry. A logical solution would be to make this a subjective test, to be performed by the person who wishes to deal with the work and therefore needs to trace the origin of the work, starting with its author, if he or she wants to obtain the permission to deal with the work.[12] An author who has not yet claimed authorship always retains the opportunity to make such a claim. There is no time limit for it, as was demonstrated in *Fisher v. Brooker* where the claim was made after 38 years.[13]

Multiple authors—joint authorship

An increasing number of works are produced as a result of collaboration between two or more authors. In this case, the rules outlined apply to each of the authors, as long as it is possible to distinguish and identify the individual contribution of each of them to the work. Each will be treated as the creator and author of his or her own individual contribution to the work. A good example is the organ solo which Matthew Fisher created for the Procol Harum song 'A Whiter Shade of Pale', with the rest of the song written by Gary Brooker. They are both co-authors in the sense that each of them is the author of his part of the song.[14]

This approach does not work, however, when a group of jazz musicians records its own impromptu jazz session. It is impossible to distinguish afterwards between the contribution of one musician and that of another musician. The Act calls this a work of 'joint authorship'[15]— but in order to be a joint author, a person must establish a significant and original contribution to the creation of the work, albeit not necessarily equal to that of the other joint authors. This will apply even if the performance of an existing work involves an improvization.[16]

---

[7] CDPA 1988, s. 9(3).   [8] CDPA 1988, s. 9(2)(b).   [9] CDPA 1988, s. 9(2)(d).

[10] If the identity of the author is, or becomes, known at one stage, the work can no longer fall in this category: CDPA 1988, s. 9(5).

[11] CDPA 1988, s. 9(4) and (5).

[12] See R. Merkin (1989) *Copyright, Designs and Patents: The New Law*, Harlow: Longman, p. 50; the alternative option of relying on the concept of the ubiquitous reasonable man is less attractive.

[13] *Fisher v. Brooker* [2009] FSR 25 (HL).   [14] *Fisher* (n. 13).   [15] CDPA 1988, s. 10(1).

[16] *Hadley v. Kemp* [1999] EMLR 589 (the *Spandau Ballet* case). A common intention to produce a joint work is not required; collaboration in the execution, the creation of the work is the essence: see *Beckingham v. Hodgens* [2003] EMLR 18 (CA).

Joint authorship requires in other words a contribution,[17] collaboration,[18] and the inability to identify distinct contributions.[19]

The contribution must be to the work, rather than to its performance. For example, a director of a play who made a contribution to the script in the course of the rehearsals, even before the first performance, did not become the joint author of the play. She was only carrying out her task as a director in relation to the performance of the work.[20] Similarly, a university that cooperated with a company to design new software was not a joint author either, because its contribution was limited to providing background information about the existing software, assistance in the compilation of the technical specifications, and vetting of the suggestions of third parties.[21] In this case, there was no contribution to the creation of the new work itself. This can be contrasted with the case of the lyrics for a rap song, in relation to which one person had been responsible for a draft that was then amended by a second person. Some of the language had been changed, Jamaican English had been introduced to match word rhythm to music, and exclamations had been added. In this case, both persons were joint authors, because they had collaborated on the final work and it was no longer possible to separate their contributions in the final work.[22]

In the case of a work of joint authorship, all authors are referred to as the author of the work for the purposes of the 1988 Act.[23] Rather than become the author of a part of the work, each of them becomes (joint) author of the whole work. This has important consequences for the ownership of the copyright in the work that we will discuss in the next section of this chapter.

Section 10(1A) of the 1988 Act clarifies the relationship between the director and the producer as co-authors of a film. They are to be treated as joint authors and the film is to be treated as a work of joint authorship, unless the producer and the principal director are the same person. Section 10(2) deals with joint authorship in broadcasts. The person making the broadcast is the person transmitting the programme, if he or she has responsibility to any extent for its content, and any person providing the programme who makes, along with the person transmitting it, the arrangements necessary for its transmission.[24] In many cases, this results in more than one person making the broadcast and joint authorship for these persons.

It is of course understood that one is thinking here of authors working together at the same time. In the digital environment there are also a lot of so-called derivative works. To take an easy example, one takes the music from a Gangnam-style music video and produces new lyrics and images to add one more to the thousands of version on YouTube. One then becomes the author of what one adds, but there is no joint authorship with the composer of the music. Instead, one may need copyright permission to use the music. We will come back to that in an infringement/exemption context.

Creators and fixators

The rule that the creator of the work is the author of it has to be combined with the necessity of recording, or fixating, original literary, musical, and dramatic works. Remember

---

[17] *Pamela Dallas Brighton & Dubbeljoint Co. Ltd v. Marie Jones* [2005] FSR 16, [2004] EMLR 26.

[18] *Beckingham v. Hodgens* (n. 16).   [19] *Beckingham v. Hodgens* [2003] ECDR 6.

[20] *Pamela Dallas Brighton & Dubbeljoint Co. Ltd v. Marie Jones* [2005] FSR 16, 288.

[21] *Cyprotex Discovery Ltd v. University of Sheffield* [2004] RPC 4, aff'd in other grounds [2004] RPC 44 (CA).

[22] *Brown v. Mcasso Music* [2005] FSR 40.   [23] CDPA 1988, s. 10(3).

[24] CDPA 1988, s. 6(3).

that ideas are not protected,[25] while their expression is protected only when it is recorded or fixated. This creates problems in a situation such as that which arose in *Walter v. Lane*.[26] Reporters from *The Times* recorded speeches by Lord Rosebery in writing. As we have seen, the speeches attract copyright as a literary work once they are recorded and it is not necessary that the speaker records them himself—so who is the author of the literary work so created? In this case, it was held that the reporters were the creators of the work and, as such, the authors.

This case was decided before the introduction of the originality requirement.[27] It is submitted that a verbatim report[28] of the complete speech would not now pass this originality requirement. The report would not be an original literary work and would not attract copyright, but, because they are now recorded, the speeches themselves would attract copyright and the speaker would be the author. This situation corresponds to that of a secretary writing down dictation. For the purposes of copyright, the person dictating will be the author of the work. The secretary who does the writing can, at best, be said to be acting as an agent. If the reporters had edited the work by selecting parts of the speech and had added their own comments—for example, on the venue at which the speech was delivered—the situation would have been different. The report would have been an original literary work and would have attracted its own copyright, because the reporters would have applied skill, labour, and judgement in drafting the report.

Corporate bodies

A final issue in relation to authorship of copyright is the question of whether a corporate body can be the author of a work. This is particularly relevant in the film and music industries, within which many arrangements for the making of a sound recording or movie[29] are made by large production companies that may de facto become the producers of the works.

It is submitted that this question receives a positive answer under copyright law. Works of a body incorporated under the laws of the UK qualify for copyright protection according to s. 154(1)(c) of the 1988 Act. There would be no reason to deal with this qualification issue if corporate bodies could not create works that attract copyright.[30] In theory, there could be a problem in relation to sound recordings and film, because an author (company) that never dies could give rise to a never-ending copyright. This problem is avoided, in practice, because the duration of copyright in a sound recording is not dependent on the concept of the author and because the duration of copyright in

---

[25] As shown by the case in which a journalist supplied the idea for an article written by his editor. His idea did not attract copyright—he was not the creator of the literary work—but his editor's expression of the idea attracted copyright. The editor was the creator of the expression of the idea and thus as creator of a literary work its author: *Springfield v. Thame* (1903) 19 TLR 650.

[26] [1900] AC 539.   [27] The originality requirement was introduced by the Copyright Act 1911.

[28] The case refers to the corrections and revisions made by the reporters. This should be seen as correcting the spelling and other small mistakes, while taking down in a hurry the words of the speaker and checking that the report is, indeed, a full and correct account or written version of the speech.

[29] Even in the new regime for films, the question of whether or not they will be co-authors remains.

[30] The position that companies can be authors receives support in *Mad Hat Music Ltd v. Pulse 8 Records Ltd* [1993] EMLR 172; *Adventure Film Productions SA v. Tully* [1993] EMLR 376; *Century Communications Ltd v. Mayfair Entertainment UK Ltd* [1993] EMLR 335. See also H. Laddie, P. Prescott, and M. Vitoria (2000) *The Modern Law of Copyright and Designs*, 3rd edn, London: Butterworths, p. 355.

a film is now calculated according to s. 13B(2) of the 1988 Act, on the basis of a list of persons that does not include the producer (which can be a company).

Ownership

The starting point–the author as first owner

The general principle of ownership is that the author is the first owner of the copyright.[31] A sculptor will be the first owner of his or her sculpture and I will be the first owner of the copyright in the poems I write for my own enjoyment. But contracts of employment undermine this general principle. The first owner of the copyright in a literary, dramatic, musical, or artistic work, or in a film,[32] created by an employee in the course of his or her employment, will be the employer. Agreements to the contrary are, however, possible.[33]

This provision creates some difficulties:[34] who is an employee? What are the characteristics of the employer–employee relationship? And what is the meaning of this in the course of his or her employment?

Let us start with some obvious examples. On the one hand, a cleaner who writes poetry in her own time will be the first owner of the copyright in her poems.[35] The poems are clearly not written in the course of that employment and that individual is not in employment as a poet. If, on the other hand, a purchasing manager of an engineering company writes, for the board of directors of the company and during normal working hours, a report on the options open for his or her company to find an alternative supplier of cylinder valves, this work will obviously have been made in the course of that employment and the employer will be the first owner of the work. The contract of employment and the job description contained in it are important elements in this respect. They can facilitate the application of the test of whether the skill, labour, and judgement invested by the employee in the creation of the work are part of the employee's normal duties—which can be either express or implied in the contract—or come within the special duties that the employer has assigned to the employee, because they reveal the intentions of the parties. If the answer is affirmative, the work will have been created in the course of employment and the employer will be the first owner of the copyright in it.

This approach is supported by *Stephenson Jordan & Harrison Ltd v. MacDonald*.[36] An accountant was employed to advise clients. He started giving lectures and, eventually, he published them. He owned the copyright in the book, because giving lectures was not part of his normal duties and he had not been instructed by his employers to give the lectures or produce the book—but two elements complicate this case. First, his employer had provided secretarial help, which he had used for his project: the court held

[31] CDPA 1988, s. 11(1).

[32] This addition to CDPA 1988, s. 11(2), was made by the Copyright and Related Rights Regulations 1996, SI 1996/2967, regs. 4 and 18(3). Once more, copyright in a film was treated as copyright in an original work, rather than in an entrepreneurial work, although the roots of copyright in a film are found in the latter category.

[33] CDPA 1988, s. 11(2). But s. 11 offers a complete solution on first ownership. Later provisions such as s. 91 deal with assignments, but not with first ownership. See *PRS Ltd v. B4U Network (Europe) Ltd* [2012] EWHC 3010 (Ch).

[34] For a good, but somewhat complex, example, see *Cyprotex Discovery Ltd v. University of Sheffield* [2004] RPC 44, (2004) 148 SJLB 421 (CA).

[35] For a somewhat more complex example, see *Ultra Marketing (UK) Ltd & Thomas Scott v. Universal Components Ltd* [2002] EWHC 2285.

[36] (1952) 69 RPC 10.

that the use of the employer's facilities or assistance is not relevant to this copyright test.[37] Second, the accountant had used a report that he had written for a client of his employer in the book: the copyright in this part of the book was owned by his employer.

It is in the interest of both employer and employee that there is no doubt about the ownership of copyright. A clear and detailed job description is required and, if the content of a job changes, a new description of the employee's duties should be drafted. This does not rule out that a job description can be wide in scope. When someone is employed as a research and development (R&D) engineer, this description makes it clear that the copyright in every work that is useful to his or her employer will be owned by the employer. But this system depends on the classification of the author of the work as employee, which itself depends on the existence of a contract of service or apprenticeship between the author and the alleged employer claiming the ownership of the copyright in the work.[38]

The establishment of such a relationship is not obvious if the author is a freelance worker or a consultant.

It is submitted that these consultants and freelancers have a contract to do a certain job or a certain amount of work, but are not directly subject to the instructions of the employer. For example, a management consultant will be asked to produce a report on the management of a company, but he or she will decide how to produce that report. The consultant's only obligation is to submit a report that meets the standards laid down in the contract by the date agreed in the contract. Employees, on the contrary, are subject to the instructions of their employer. For them, there is a mutuality of agreement, in the sense that they are subject to an obligation to accept and perform some minimum—or at least reasonable—amount of work for their alleged employer.[39] The freelance worker and the consultant will own the copyright in their work, because they do not come within the definition of an employee.

The employer may allow the employee to become the first owner of the copyright in the work created in the course of employment. This option is left open by s. 11(2) of the 1988 Act. For normal transfers of ownership of copyright, the Act requires the transfer to be in writing and signed by, or on behalf of, the copyright owner,[40] but this requirement does not apply here. In this situation, there is no transfer of copyright ownership—that is, no one owning the copyright before the first owner of the copyright in the work. This case should be contrasted with the case of a work produced by a consultant or a freelancer. Because they are not employees, s. 11(1) will apply and the freelancer or consultant will be the first owner of the copyright. Any subsequent transfer of the copyright will have to be in writing and will have to be signed by the owner or on his behalf.[41]

A clause in the contract concluded with the freelancer or consultant stipulating that the ownership of the work produced will be transferred is more than advisable. Otherwise, one has to rely on the concept of the implied licence. Someone ordering a report from a consultant will have necessarily included in the contract a right to use

---

[37] But it may well have its relevance for other aspects of the employer–employee relationship—e.g. breach of the contract of employment.

[38] CDPA 1988, s. 178.

[39] See *Nethermere (St Neots) Ltd v. Taverna* [1984] IRLR 240, per Kerr LJ.   [40] CDPA 1988, s. 90(3).

[41] The use of the concept of beneficial ownership was suggested in *Warner v. Gestetner Ltd* [1988] EIPR D-89. It is submitted that this approach cannot be accepted, because it includes a partial assignment of the ownership of copyright that does not satisfy the requirements laid down in CDPA 1988, s. 90(3). See *R. Griggs Group Ltd v. Evans (No. 1)* [2005] FSR 31, [2005] ECDR 30 (CA).

the result of the consultant's activity. Someone who requests a plan for a house to be built on a certain plot of land from an architect implies, in the contract with the architect, a clause giving him or her the right to build the house on that plot, because the contract is necessarily for a plan that is to be used to build a house. The architect keeps the ownership of the copyright in the plans, but grants an (implied) licence to use them to build the house.[42]

Away from any employment issue there are those works that are created by more than one author without being work of joint authorship. Co-authorship then translates itself in each of them owning the copyright in their contribution (i.e. in a part of the work they created together). Going back to the Procol Harum example mentioned previously, Matthew Fisher owned the copyright in the organ solo and Gary Brooker owned the copyright in the rest of the song. Exploitation of the song as a single item therefore requires the permission of both copyright owners.[43]

Joint owners

It is possible that there are two or more joint owners of the copyright in a work if it is a work of joint authorship. The latter possibility was previously raised; we will now discuss its implications on the issue of ownership.

These owners will own the copyright in the work as tenants in common[44] and will each have their own individual rights in the work that they can assign individually. They can also act individually against infringement. But, because they will never own the whole copyright individually, they will not be able to license someone to exploit the work without the consent of their co-owners;[45] otherwise, they would be able to transfer rights that they do not fully own. The co-owner of the copyright in a book will be able to assign his or her right to one of his or her creditors, which will allow that creditor to recuperate—through the royalties—the debt owed, but the creditor does not deal with the copyright.

The same co-owner will not be able to allow a film director to make a movie based on the book without the consent of the co-owners.

Anonymous works

Until now, we have examined the ownership issue, assuming that the author with whom the ownership chain starts is known. An anonymous work would, in this system, lead to an unknown owner of the copyright. This system would endanger the commercial exploitation of the work and would be undesirable. Therefore, the 1988 Act contains a presumption that the publisher of an anonymous work is the owner of the copyright in it at the time of publication.[46] This presumption can, however, be rebutted.[47]

---

[42] See *Blair v. Osborne & Tomkins* [1971] 2 QB 78, [1971] 1 All ER 468, per Lord Denning MR at 470 and 507.

[43] *Fisher v. Brooker* [2009] FSR 25 (HL).

[44] Not as joint tenants—see *Lauri v. Renad* [1892] 3 Ch 402—because this would deny them individual rights and oblige them to act together on each occasion.

[45] *Cescinsky v. George Routledge & Sons Ltd* [1916] 2 KB 325. The opposite is true in patent law: see Patents Act 1977, s. 36.

[46] CDPA 1988, s. 104(4).

[47] For an example of an unsuccessful attempt to rebut the presumption, see *Warwick Film Productions Ltd v. Eisinger* [1969] 1 Ch 508, [1967] 3 All ER 367.

A caveat–moral rights

The issue of ownership touches upon the commercial exploitation of copyright. We will come back to this issue later, but it is worth noting here that not all aspects of copyright are directed to commercial exploitation. Copyright is, to a certain extent, also an author's right. This will become clear in the next chapter, through the analysis of the new, separate, but closely related, moral rights that the 1988 Act grants to authors, and which protect them and their works against certain aspects of abusive commercial exploitation.

An overview

The concept of authorship is approached in a very pragmatic way. The creator of a work will, in principle, be its author. There can be more than one creator for a work and therefore also more than one author. Joint authorship, and the specific rules that go with it, arises when more than one creator is involved in the creation of the work and the contribution of each creator can no longer be separated out in the final result.

From authorship, the law moves on to ownership. Copyright is a property right and, as such, it needs an owner. The general principle is that the author will be the first owner of the copyright in his or her work. Works created by employees complicate life somewhat in this area. There is a legal presumption that the employer, rather than the employee-creator, will be the first owner of the copyright in the work that is created in the course of employment, but agreements to the contrary are possible. This rule has nothing to do with high principle. In a business context, it simply makes sense to have the employer own the rights, and a systematic need for a contractual transfer of rights would be somewhat cumbersome.

Further reading

BAINES, R., 'Copyright in Commissioned Works: A Cause for Uncertainty' (2005) 27(3) EIPR 122.

CHRISTY, L., 'Joint Authorship and Infringement by "Altered Copying": Some Lessons from the *Stones in his Pockets* Case' (2004) 26(10) EIPR 472.

GRIFFIN, J., 'The Changing Nature of Authorship: Why Copyright Law Must Focus on the Increased Role of Technology' (2005) 2 IPQ 135.

LAUTERBACH, T., 'Joint Authorship in a Copyright Work Revisited' (2005) 27(3) EIPR 119.

ZEMER, L., 'Contributions and Collaboration in Joint Authorship: Too Many Misconceptions' (2006) 1(4) JIPLP 283.

14

Moral rights

In the previous chapters we looked at copyright as an intellectual property right in an economic context. Due to its strong nexus with the person of the author as the creator of the work copyright has another side to it though. Apart from the economic side there are moral rights that are given to the author to reflect that strong nexus between work and creator. This chapter looks at these rights that only appear in a copyright context.

General principles

Copyright in Continental Europe is, in the first place, an author's right. Much attention is paid to the rights of the creator.[1] Because copyright law is based on international conventions, a compromise with the UK's more entrepreneurial approach was reached in the Berne Convention for the Protection of Literary and Artistic Works 1886. This led eventually to the formal inclusion of moral rights in UK in the Copyright, Designs and Patents Act (CDPA) 1988.[2] Previous Acts did not explicitly acknowledge these moral rights, although some protection was offered through, for example, the torts of defamation[3] or passing off.[4]

We submit that the compromise should go much further. The focal points of both approaches work in a complementary manner: everything starts with the author, who has to create works; if there are no works, there is nothing for the entrepreneur to exploit. But if one offers an extremely strong protection to the author-creator, this may make the work of the entrepreneur impossible. If the author has all of the rights and the entrepreneur is left with no flexibility or bargaining power based on legal rights, the exploitation of the work becomes impossible, or at least economically unsound. This could seriously affect the incentive of the author to create works, because it would reduce the chances of making a living as an author. It is clear that the volume of the works created would be seriously affected: what is needed in a perfect copyright system is a sound balance between the rights of the author-creator and those of the entrepreneur who exploits the work. We submit that the Continental approach has much to contribute to such a perfect system in relation to the rights of the author, while the UK's traditional approach would be the dominant contributor in relation to the rights given to the entrepreneur.

---

[1] See N. Walravens, 'La Protection de l'oeuvre d'art et le droit moral de l'artiste' (2003) 197 RIDA 2; A. Lucas, H.-J. Lucas, and A. Lucas-Schloetter (2012) *Traité de la propriété littéraire et artistique*, 4th edn, Paris: Litec. See also E. Adeney (2006) *The Moral Rights of Authors and Performers: An International and Comparative Analysis*, Oxford: Oxford University Press.

[2] See, in general, I. Stamatoudi, 'Moral Rights of Authors in England: The Missing Emphasis on the Role of Creators' [1997] IPQ 478.

[3] See *Humphreys v. Thomson* (1908) Mac CC 148.

[4] See *Samuelson v. Producers Distributing* [1932] 1 Ch 201.

Such a perfect copyright system is not just an ideal. European integration and harmonization of the provisions dealing with copyright means that, inevitably, a compromise has to be reached each time, between both approaches, in an attempt to make copyright in the European Union (EU) resemble the perfect model.[5] But how does this relate to the issue of moral rights?

It is submitted that the author-creator should not merely become the first owner of the work and then, by implication, lose control over the work almost immediately afterwards when the exploitation of the work gets underway. On the one hand, the possibility of unfair use of the work can deter the author from creating works and so he or she should be protected against that possibility; on the other, a good exploitation of the work requires as much freedom for the entrepreneur as possible. Moral rights reconcile these two aims. They give minimum long-lasting rights against manifestly unfair use of the work to the author-creator, while allowing maximum flexibility for the entrepreneur, because only manifestly unfair forms of exploitation will be affected. In this approach, moral rights are an essential component of the bundle of rights that is given by copyright—and it is for this reason that we discuss them here, rather than at the end of the chapters on copyright. All the authors of original works and directors of films[6] are given moral rights, while the owners of the entrepreneurial neighbouring rights are not granted any moral rights.[7] This clearly vindicates our approach. The real copyrights are the original ones and moral rights are an essential component of the rights granted by copyright. Neighbouring rights often rely on copyright works and are secondary rights, such as the recording of an original musical work. They are linked to the entrepreneurial exploitation of copyright and therefore moral rights are not needed in relation to such secondary rights. And there is another argument that we may wish to consider: the Berne Convention—which is the international basis of the UK's copyright regime—deals with moral rights in Art. 6bis. It is situated right in the middle of the Articles that deal with the substance of copyright, suggesting that moral rights are an essential element of copyright, rather than an addendum to it.

Four moral rights are included in the UK's 1988 Act:

- the right to be identified as the author or director of a work—that is, the 'paternity right';[8]

- the right of the author or a director of a work to object to derogatory treatment of that work—that is, the 'integrity right';[9]

- the right for everyone not to have a work falsely attributed to him;[10] and

- the commissioner's right of privacy in respect of a photograph or film made for private and domestic purposes.[11]

Only the first two rights are full moral rights, while the latter two are hybrid in nature, because they do not confer special rights on the creator of the work.

All of these rights aim to restore the balance between the interests of the commercial exploitation of the work and the interests of the creator of the work. This cannot be done through contractual negotiations, in which the author or director quite often occupies a

---

[5] See J. F. Verstrynghe, 'The Spring 1993 Horace S Manges Lecture: The European Commission's Directive on Copyright and Neighbouring Rights—Toward the Regime of the Twenty-first Century' (1993) 17 Colum-VLA JL & Arts 187, 206–9.

[6] Note that films are treated, once more, in the same way as original works.

[7] CDPA 1988, ss. 77, 80, and 84.   [8] CDPA 1988, ss. 77–9.   [9] CDPA 1988, ss. 80–3.

[10] CDPA 1988, s. 84.   [11] CDPA 1988, s. 85.

weak bargaining position. To protect the author or director as the weaker party, moral rights are inalienable to others—but they are transmissible on death.[12] Because they are coupled to the commercial rights granted by copyright, the term of moral rights is coupled to that of copyright in the work to which they relate.[13] The one exception to the latter rule is the right to object to false attribution, which expires 20 years after a person's death.[14]

The paternity right

The right to be identified

The creator of a work has the right to be identified as its author; this is the basic concept behind the paternity right. Because this right has to restore the balance with the commercial exploitation of the work that attracts copyright protection, it is also restricted to those works that attract copyright. The scope of the right is further restricted to literary, dramatic, musical, or artistic works, and films, and identification should only take place in certain cases.[15] These cases are different for the various categories of work, and the categories themselves are different from those used in relation to the existence of copyright. In particular, lyrics for songs are not treated as literary works, but as musical works, and films are the only category of non-'original' works to be included.

The author of a literary work that is not intended to be spoken or sung with music and the author of a dramatic work both have the right to be identified whenever the work is published commercially, performed in public, or broadcast, or whenever copies of a film or sound recording of the work are issued to the public.[16] Non-commercial exploitation—such as the private performance of a play—does not give rise to the obligation to identify the author. This fits in with the logic that this moral right only restores the balance with the commercial exploitation of the work. Another interesting point is the meaning given to 'issuing copies of the work'. It cannot be restricted to the narrow meaning it has in s. 18(2) of the Act: every commercial publication and every public performance requires the identification of the author, and not only the first publication or first performance. Issuing copies is mentioned together with publication and performance, and should mean making copies available, not only making them available in the UK for the first time. Only this interpretation conforms to the logical sense of the system.

Musical works and lyrics are subjected to the same regime.[17] Their commercial publication and the issuing of copies of a sound recording of the work to the public give rise to the obligation to identify the author.[18] Performance of the work—which was included in relation to literary and dramatic works—is not included here, because it would not be practicable to require that, for example, a disc jockey identify the author of every song before or after playing it. If a film, the soundtrack of which includes the work, is shown in public or copies of the film are issued to the public, however, the author of the musical works and their lyrics should be identified. This provision fits in with the rules for films. Indeed, the director of a film has the right to be identified each time that the film is shown in public or broadcast, and when copies of the film are issued to the public.[19] The director of the film gets preference over the producer in relation to moral rights. The

---

[12] CDPA 1988, ss. 94 and 95.   [13] CDPA 1988, s. 86(1).   [14] CDPA 1988, s. 86(2).
[15] CDPA 1988, s. 77(1).   [16] CDPA 1988, s. 77(2).
[17] See *Hyperion Records Ltd v. Leonard Sawkins* [2005] 3 All ER 636, [2005] 1 WLR 3281 (CA).
[18] CDPA 1988, s. 77(3).   [19] CDPA 1988, s. 77(6).

creative activity is the director's contribution, which deserves the special moral rights protection, while the entrepreneurial contribution of the producer does not deserve that. The provisions for artistic works are similar, but include also public exhibition of the work.[20]

Identification should take place in a clear and prominent way—for example, in or on each copy of the work[21]—or in any other way that brings the identity of the author or director to the attention of the person who acquires a copy of the work.[22] The author or director also has the right to be identified in relation to an adaptation of the work. When a textbook on public international law written by an English professor is translated into Russian, the English author has the right to be identified in the Russian translation. If we assume that it is not the whole work that is translated, but only a couple of chapters, the right to be identified will still apply, because it applies in relation to the whole work or to a substantial part of it.[23] The test to determine whether or not a part is substantial is probably the same as that used in relation to copyright infringement.[24]

Preconditions and exceptions

This leaves us with one major precondition and some exceptions to the right to be identified. The paternity right is not granted automatically: the author or director who seeks its benefit has to assert it.[25] Such an assertion can be general in nature or can be in relation only to specified acts. This can be done in the form of a statement that is included in an instrument assigning copyright in the work. Such a document has to be in writing and has to be signed by, or on behalf of, the author.[26] This method of asserting the paternity right has to be recommended, because it will not only bind the assignee, but also anyone claiming through him—such as the person to whom the assignee assigns part of his or her rights—even if those other persons did not receive notice of the assertion.[27] The assertion can also be made by another written instrument signed by the author or director, but this assertion will only bind those with notice of it.[28] The paternity right can be asserted at any time during the life of the author, but it is not retrospective in nature—that is, the right only arises once it has been asserted.[29] The assertion does not cover past use of the work. Any delay in asserting the right can only work to the detriment of the author or director, because it should be taken into account in determining whether an injunction should be granted, and in the determination of damages and other relief.[30]

There is also a long list of exceptions to the paternity right contained in s. 79 of the 1988 Act. Some of them are particularly important.[31] No paternity right exists in relation to computer programs, computer-generated works, and typefaces,[32] and publications in newspapers, periodicals, encyclopaedias, and dictionaries are excluded.[33] The first category is clearly too much linked to technical and technological elements, and too far away from the moral rights idea of the artist-creator who should be identified; in the second category, identification of the author of each article or contribution would

---

[20] CDPA 1988, s. 77(4); see also s. 77(5) on works of architecture.

[21] The obvious technique for e.g. books.

[22] E.g. when a play is performed, the programme can contain the name of the author of the play.

[23] CPDA 1988, s. 89(1). [24] See Ch. 15 on copyright infringement.

[25] CPDA 1988, s. 78(1). [26] CPDA 1988, s. 78(2). [27] CPDA 1988, s. 78(4).

[28] CPDA 1988, s. 78(2) and (4). [29] CPDA 1988, s. 78(1). [30] CPDA 1988, s. 78(5).

[31] For a more detailed critical analysis, see K. Garnett and G. Davies (eds.) (2010) *Moral Rights*, London: Sweet & Maxwell, p. 155 *et seq.*

[32] CPDA 1988, s. 79(2). [33] CPDA 1988, s. 79(6).

overload the works and would be impractical, because editors edit and each edition of a newspaper may change dramatically. All of these identifications could effectively take up a substantial percentage of the whole work.

Additionally, the employer or first owner of the copyright in a work created in the course of employment, or anyone acting with his or her authority, is not obliged to identify the creator-employee.[34] This avoids the considerable problem that would have been created had an employee-engineer—or later, eventually, an ex-employee-engineer—been allowed to interfere with the exploitation of the drawings he made for a series of products through the exercise of his moral rights. The paternity right will, under certain circumstances, not be infringed by acts done in relation to the reporting of current events or by incidental inclusion of the work.[35]

Performers

The paternity right, as it existed at the time that the 1988 Act was passed, applied only to literary, dramatic, musical, or artistic works and to films, but Art. 5 of the World Intellectual Property Organization (WIPO) Performances and Phonograms Treaty 1996 introduced a right of paternity for performers. The UK has implemented this Treaty obligation by means of the Performances (Moral Rights, etc.) Regulations 2006.[36] This has resulted in the performer being given a right of paternity in his or her live aural performances and his or her performances fixed in phonograms. The performer has the right to be identified as such when he or she performs live, when the performance is broadcast, or when a recording of the performance is communicated to the public, or when copies of it are issued to the public.[37] That identification needs to take place in such a way that it is likely to be noticed by the audience.[38] No identification is required when it is not reasonably practical or when the performance is given for reasons relating to advertising or news reporting.[39]

Unfortunately, the provisions do not offer guidance on what is meant by 'not reasonably practical'. Does this, for example, include a failure to name all musicians performing on a recording when it is played as part of a radio show?

The moral right to be identified is not infringed unless the performer has first asserted his or her moral right in writing.[40] The approach that has been taken is therefore similar to that taken in relation to the moral rights of authors. It therefore comes as no surprise that the duration of the moral rights of performers are also linked to the duration of the (economic) rights in the performance.[41]

The integrity right

The nature of the right to object to derogatory treatment

The beneficiaries of this moral right—the integrity right—are the same as those of the paternity right: authors of literary, dramatic, musical, and artistic works, and directors

---

[34] CPDA 1988, s. 79(3)(a).
[35] The fair dealing and incidental inclusion concepts will be analysed fully in Ch. 15 on copyright infringement, in which they find their roots; see CDPA 1988, s. 79(4).
[36] SI 2006/18, in force since 1 February 2006.   [37] CDPA 1988, s. 205C.
[38] CDPA 1988, s. 205C.   [39] CDPA 1988, s. 205E.   [40] CDPA 1988, s. 205D.
[41] CDPA 1988, s. 205I.

of films. The integrity right applies only to the extent that works are, and remain, in copyright.[42] Derogatory treatment of the work involves addition,[43] deletion, alteration, or adaptation that amounts to distortion or mutilation of the work, or which is otherwise prejudicial to the honour or reputation of the author or the director.[44] This would be the case, for example, if a tale for young children written by a reputed children's author were to be turned into a pornographic story through addition and alteration.

Criticism of a work, however, is in no way complicated by this integrity right. Criticism does not involve distortion or mutilation and does not affect the honour or reputation of the author. It takes place at a different level and derogatory criticism should not be called criticism, but should be called instead by its true name: derogatory treatment. The focus on the treatment should not hide the fact that there is a second cumulative require-ment that involves proof of honour or reputation, as well as evidence of prejudice to that honour or reputation.[45]

The essential issue is when does an act amount to distortion[46] or mutilation of the work, or when is it otherwise prejudicial to the honour or reputation of the author or the director? The integrity right can clearly not be exercised at the discretion of the author or the director.[47] It has to be proven '*that the distortion or other mutilation of* [the] *work really prejudices* [the author's] *lawful intellectual or personal interests in the work*'.[48] This involves the balancing of all of the relevant interests involved.

In this process, the nature and the purpose of the work to which the allegedly infrin-ging act is done is an important factor. It is submitted that, for example, an act done to a drawing containing technical details and a draft plan for an industrial product will less easily infringe the integrity right of the author than will a similar act done to a work of fine art, such as a painting. The author of the drawing knows that his or her work is just the starting point for a long process of development and change involving many other people. The painter who delivers the painting to an art dealer, however, readily assumes that the painting will not be changed at all. A first criterion in the balancing test is thus whether the work is, relatively speaking, more utilitarian or more artistic in nature.[49]

In one case, it was, indeed, held that the integrity right of the author of a cut-away drawing for a tourist brochure had not been infringed by little changes that were so trivial that they could only be detected upon close inspection:[50]

Additional criteria could be, for example, the nature and the extent of the alteration of the work and also how far the latter is reversible or irreversible; the number of people or the size of the public addressed by the user of the work in altered form; the fact whether the author created the work in an employment relationship or as a self-employed author, or else whether a com-missioning party did not have a decisive influence on the final result of the creation...[A]lso the possible consequences for the professional life of the author and, of course, for his or her reputation have to be taken into consideration.[51]

---

[42] CDPA 1988, s. 80(1).

[43] E.g. the addition of a rap line to the recording of a piece of music: see *Confetti Records, Fundamental Records & Andrew Alcee v. Warner Music UK Ltd (t/a East West Records)* [2003] ECDR 336.

[44] CDPA 1988, s. 80(1) and (2).   [45] See *Confetti Records* (n. 43).

[46] See *Emma Delves-Broughton v. House of Harlot Ltd* [2012] EWPCC 29.

[47] See the decision of the Supreme Court of Canada in *Galérie d'Art du Petit Champlain Inc., Galérie d'Art Yves Laroche Inc., Editions Multi-Graph Itée, Galérie d'Art Laroche, Denis Inc. & Serge Rosa v. Claude Théberge* [2002] SCC 34.

[48] A. Dietz, 'The Artist's Right of Integrity under Copyright Law: A Comparative Approach' (1994) 25 IIC 177, 183.

[49] Dietz, 'The Artist's Right of Integrity under Copyright Law' (n. 48) at 184–5.

[50] *Pasterfield v. Denham* [1999] FSR 168 (a decision of the Plymouth County Court).

[51] *Pasterfield* (n. 50) at 185.

Because the integrity right and other moral rights very strongly involve the issue of fundamental fairness between the author and the user of the work, one might add the purpose and the character of the use of the work as another relevant criterion. Finally, certain well-established customs and traditions in certain parts of industry may also be taken into account.[52]

All of these elements point towards a rather objective test. It is submitted that the determination of whether the author's, or the director's, honour or reputation has been prejudiced by the treatment of the work by a third party is to be effected by answering the question of whether right-thinking members of the public would think less of him or her as a result of the treatment.[53] This test bears similarities to that which is applied in cases of defamation and the view that a *'certain subjective element or judgment on the part of the author so long as it is reasonably arrived at'*[54] is involved needs to be rejected. The latter view would push the integrity right beyond its role as a fundamental right that preserves the balance of rights between the author or director and those exploiting the work. It is encouraging to note, in this respect, that, in another case,[55] it has indeed been held that the fact that the author was aggrieved by what had occurred was not sufficient to hold that the author's honour and reputation had been affected.

The courts in the UK have not yet decided any major case on moral rights since the introduction of the 1988 Act.[56] German and Swiss courts, however, have used the balancing test on the basis of similar provisions.[57] The Swiss Federal Supreme Court used it to rule that the proposed alterations to a school building—which involved, among other things, the replacement of the original flat roof by a saddleback roof—did not amount to a mutilation of the architectural work and did not infringe the integrity right of the architect.[58]

Authors and directors can invoke this right to object to derogatory treatment of their work if it occurs when copies of the work are published commercially, when copies of a sound recording or film are made available to the public, when the work is performed, played, or shown in public,[59] and when it is broadcast.[60] The right also applies to parts of works that were previously adapted or translated by someone else. When a French translation of a novel by J. K Rowling is subjected to derogatory treatment, she will still be able to object to the infringement of her integrity right.[61]

Exceptions

The wide scope of the right is, however, subject to a series of exceptions.[62] The integrity right is not infringed if the treatment of the work does not go further than the translation of a literary or dramatic work, or the arrangement or transcription of a musical work

---

[52] *Pasterfield* (n. 50) at 185–7.

[53] See *Tidy v. Trustees of the Natural History Museum* [1996] 3 EIPR D-81.

[54] *Snow v. Eaton Centre* (1982) 70 CPR 105 (2d) (a decision of the Canadian High Court).

[55] *Pasterfield* (n. 50).

[56] For a first timid attempt, see *Pasterfield* (n. 50) and *Tidy* (n. 53). See also *Confetti Records* (n. 43).

[57] German Supreme Court Decision of 31 May 1974 [1974] GRUR 675; see also German Supreme Court Decision of 2 October 1981 [1982] GRUR 107; both cases cited in Dietz, 'The Artist's Right of Integrity under Copyright Law: A Comparative Approach' (n. 48) at 188.

[58] Swiss Federal Supreme Court Decision of 24 September 1991.

[59] For a French example, see *Lindon v. Boussagol*, judgment of the Tribunal de Grande Instance de Paris, 3rd Chamber, 15 October 1992, 155 (1993) RIDA Chronique de Jurisprudence.

[60] CDPA 1988, s. 80(3)–(6).   [61] CDPA 1988, s. 80(7).

[62] For a more detailed critical analysis, see Garnett and Davies (eds.) *Moral Rights* (n. 31) at 275 *et seq.*

involving no more than a change of key or register.[63] Furthermore, the integrity right does not apply to computer programs and computer-generated works; nor does it apply in relation to publication in a newspaper, periodical, encyclopaedia, or yearbook and any subsequent unmodified republication thereof. Should the author or director of a work made in the course of employment that is altered be identified, the right is restricted to a sufficient disclaimer of association with the altered work.[64] The impact of the right is further compromised by the introduction of a special remedy for this moral right. By means of an injunction, the court may allow the act complained of to continue once a disclaimer dissociating the author or director from the altered work is made.[65] A clear example of this is that an architect's integrity right is restricted to him being allowed to request the removal of his identification from the building.[66]

A broadcasting authority may, in certain circumstances, wish to censor certain works, and to make excisions and alterations, because its broadcasts should not incite crime, offend good taste and decency, lead to disorder, or be offensive to public feeling. Because this could eventually amount to derogatory treatment of the works concerned, the Act explicitly allows the BBC—but, oddly, not the commercial channels—to censor the works by stipulating that this will not infringe the integrity right in the work.[67]

The scope of the right and its effectiveness are, however, widened by the fact that the right is also infringed by possessing, in the course of a business, or dealing with an infringing item if such a person knows, or has reason to believe, that there is a false attribution.[68] It may be easier to find someone in possession of, or dealing with, the infringing item than to find the person responsible for the alterations. An action for infringement is now more readily available, which makes it easier to enforce the integrity right.

Performers

The integrity right, as it existed at the time that the 1988 Act was passed, applied only to literary, dramatic, musical, or artistic works and to films, but Art. 5 of the WIPO Performances and Phonograms Treaty 1996 introduced a right of integrity for performers. The UK has implemented this Treaty obligation by means of the Performances (Moral Rights, etc.) Regulations 2006.[69] The integrity right will be infringed if the performance is broadcast live, or if it is played in public or communicated to the public by means of a sound recording, with any distortion, mutilation, or other modification that is prejudicial to the reputation of the performer.[70]

Exceptions to the right of integrity include modifications that are consistent with normal editorial practice and performances that are given for reasons related to advertising or news reporting.[71] No guidance is provided as to the interpretation of the concept of normal editorial practice. Possessing infringing copies of the work in the course of business or dealing in them is also an infringement of the integrity right.[72] The approach that has been taken is therefore similar to that taken in relation to the moral rights of authors. It therefore comes as no surprise that the duration of the moral rights of performers is also linked to the duration of the (economic) rights in the performance.[73]

---

[63] CDPA 1988, s. 80(2)(a).   [64] CDPA 1988, ss. 81 and 82.   [65] CDPA 1988, s. 103(2).

[66] CDPA 1988, s. 80(5).   [67] CDPA 1988, s. 81(5)(c).

[68] See Ch. 15 on copyright infringement for a proper definition of the concepts of possessing or dealing with an infringing copy; CDPA 1988, s. 81.

[69] SI 2006/18, in force since 1 February 2006.   [70] CDPA 1988, s. 205F.

[71] CDPA 1988, s. 205G.   [72] CDPA 1988, s. 205H.   [73] CDPA 1988, s. 205I.

The right against false attribution of the work

The author or director of the work has the right to be identified as such; he or she should also have a right only to be identified if he or she really is the creator of the work. This right is laid down by the 1988 Act as the right to oppose '*false attribution of the work*'.[74] It applies to literary, dramatic, musical, and artistic works, and to films. Any person to whom such a work is attributed falsely and who is not its creator may object to it.[75] This right would be useful, for example, if someone were to plagiarize the style of a famous novelist, such as Stephen King, in producing a mediocre work in which he or she advocates the imposition of Mafia-style taxes—that is, extortion—to generate funds for a political party and prints Stephen King's name on the cover page. We may assume that the famous novelist would like to object to the attribution of this work to him.

The opportunity to object arises when copies of the work containing the false attribution are issued to the public; when an artistic work or a copy of it in or on which there is a false attribution is exhibited in public; when a literary, dramatic, or musical work is performed in public, or broadcast as being the work of the claimant; and when a film is shown in public, or broadcast as being directed by the claimant.[76] The claimant is also given a right of action against anyone possessing a copy of the work in the course of business or dealing with a copy of the work if such a person knows, or has reason to believe, that there is a false attribution.[77] A special problem arises in relation to an artistic work that is left in the possession of a dealer before it is altered. When such a work is dealt with afterwards as the unaltered work of the author, he or she will have the right to object to this as being a false attribution.[78]

The right also applies to adaptations that are falsely being presented as adaptations of the work of a person. In the case of an artistic work, this means a copy of a work that is falsely presented as being a copy made by the author of the artistic work.[79]

The right expires 20 years after the death of the person to whom the work is attributed falsely.[80] In this sense, it comprises an exception to the rule that the term of moral rights and commercial copyright are the same. This rule cannot be applied in this case, because there is no equivalent copyright for the person to whom a work is attributed falsely.

The right to object to false attribution is particularly relevant in relation to certain forms of parody. By definition, a parody has to resemble the original work closely enough that people can make the link between the two works. It is easy to see how the impression can be created that the parody is the work of the author of the original work in this context. A good example of such a situation is found in *Clark v. Associated Newspapers Ltd*.[81] Alan Clark famously published his diaries some years ago; the defendants published a parody of the diaries as a column in *The Evening Standard*. A Mr Peter Bradshaw wrote the newspaper columns, and they carried the headings 'Alan Clark's secret Election' and 'Alan Clark's political diary'. A photograph of Mr Clark accompanied the headings and Mr Bradshaw's name, albeit in capital letters, appeared only in the introductory paragraph. That paragraph mentioned the fact that the column was, in fact, all about how Mr Bradshaw imagined Mr Clark might record certain events. Mr Clark brought a case in passing off and he relied also on s. 84 of the 1988 Act. In relation to the latter point, he argued that the readers of *The Evening Standard*—or, at least, a large number of

---

[74] CDPA 1988, s. 84.   [75] CDPA 1988, s. 84(1).   [76] CDPA 1988, s. 84(2)–(4).
[77] CDPA 1988, s. 84(5).   [78] CDPA 1988, s. 84(6).   [79] CDPA 1988, s. 84(8).
[80] CDPA 1988, s. 86(2).   [81] [1998] 1 All ER 959, [1998] 1 WLR 1558.

them—would assume that he was the author of the column. In his view, confusion as to who is the author was sufficient for the purposes of s. 84.

The court started its analysis of s. 84 by stating:

> Two distinctive features of the statutory tort are: (a) that it is unnecessary that the plaintiff be a professional author and accordingly that he has any goodwill or reputation as an author to protect or which may be damaged by false attribution; and (b) consequently the tort is actionable per se without proof of damage. In short s 84 confers a personal or civic right on everyone not to have authorship of any literary work falsely attributed to him.[82]

It is, however, up to the claimant to establish that the work contains what is a false attribution of authorship. It is not sufficient that a few, or more, people may understand it to be a false attribution.[83] On this basis, the court ruled that '[t]*he proper approach ... is to determine what is the single meaning which the literary work conveys to the notional reasonable reader*'.[84] On the basis of the facts of this case, the court concluded that the articles contained, in their title and through the addition of a photograph, a clear and unequivocal false statement attributing their authorship to Mr Clark. The court accepted that such a statement could, in certain cases, be neutralized by an express contradiction—but such a contradiction had to be as bold, precise, and compelling as the false statement, and this requirement had not been met in this case.

Similarly, s. 84 could also be used to object to the attribution to an interviewee of the comments made in an interview in circumstances in which the interviewer added or made up 90 per cent of the comments.[85]

The right to privacy in relation to commissioned photographs

When someone commissions a photograph, the photographer gets the ownership of the copyright as creator of the work. He or she can use the negatives for all kinds of purposes and does not need the consent of the commissioner.[86] This can be undesirable if the photograph is commissioned for private and domestic purposes: for example, one would not want to see one's own wedding pictures as part of a billboard advertising campaign for life insurance policies or on the front page of the tabloids next to a story headed 'How many husbands are unfaithful right from the start?'

The right to privacy grants the commissioner some protection in this respect. The commissioner has the right not to have copies of the photograph issued to the public, not to have them exhibited in public, and not to have the photograph included in a broadcast. Anyone who does, or who authorizes, these acts infringes the right to privacy—but two further requirements have to be met: the photograph has to have been commissioned for private and domestic purposes, and needs to attract copyright. An identical right exists in relation to films commissioned for private and domestic purposes.[87] There are no

---

[82] [1998] 1 WLR 1558 at 1564.

[83] Support for the single meaning view can be found in *Moore v. News of the World Ltd* (1972) 1 QB 441, [1972] 1 All ER 915 at 451–2 and 921–2.

[84] [1998] 1 WLR 1558 at 1568.

[85] See *Moore v. News of the World Ltd* (n. 83); see also *Noah v. Shuba* [1991] FSR 14.

[86] See Y. Gendreau, 'Copyright Ownership of Photographs in Anglo-American Law' (1993) 6 EIPR 207, 211–13. See also Ch. 31 on character merchandising.

[87] CDPA 1988, s. 85(1).

other requirements for the existence of the right: it is, for example, immaterial whether the commissioner hired a professional photographer at an enormous price or an unpaid friend or relative.

The term of the right is equal to that of the copyright in the photograph or film[88] and the right is given independently to each joint co-commissioner.[89] It applies to the whole work or to a substantial part of it.[90]

There are some minor exceptions to the right.[91] The most important is that the right to privacy is not infringed in case of the incidental inclusion in an artistic work, film, or broadcast.[92] This right compensates, in this particular area, the lack of a general right to privacy, even if the adoption of the Human Rights Act 1998 alleviated the problem somewhat. And, of course, this measure became necessary because the 1988 Act no longer gives the commissioner any ownership of the copyright in the commissioned work.

An interesting case, in this respect, was decided before the 1988 Act came into force. In *Mail Newspapers plc v. Express Newspapers plc*,[93] wedding pictures were at the centre of the debate. The wife had suffered a brain haemorrhage and was kept alive artificially to give birth. The husband had sold the exclusive right in the pictures to one newspaper and the other newspaper tried to obtain copies from the photographer. Under the new provision, the husband could have stopped the photographer from giving copies of the picture to the newspaper. This case is also interesting, because it illustrates that the right is not only a negative right: in practice, it will often be used to secure exclusivity and gain a higher price for the use of the photographs or films. In the example, it is clear that the husband could stop the photographer without having to rely on the consent of his wife. The interesting point is whether the photographer-owner of the copyright can interfere with the exclusivity contract. It is submitted that the commissioner has an implied licence to use the photographs and the privacy right does not play any special role.

Interestingly, the right is given to the commissioner rather than to the person in the photograph or film, while, in most cases, it is the latter's privacy that is at issue. The problem obviously only arises when the commissioner is not the person in the photograph or film. But the rule can be justified on the basis that it is much easier to identify and contact the commissioner, whose name and address will be known to the photographer or the maker of the film. There may also be a single commissioner, but many people may figure in the photograph or film. The owners of the copyright in the work may also not necessarily have known names and addresses of the latter parties.

Consent and waiver

It could be accepted that the moral rights of a person who consented to an act being done are not infringed.[94] When the author consents to the publication of his or her novel without being identified, he or she cannot complain about the infringement of his or her paternity right immediately afterwards. But the Act goes further and allows moral rights to be waived. The person entitled to any of the four moral rights can surrender them in a written and signed instrument.[95] Contractual consideration is not required.

[88] CDPA 1988, s. 86(1).
[89] CDPA 1988, s. 88(6). This must mean that the right does not disappear when the commissioner dies, but is transmissible on death.
[90] CDPA 1988, s. 89(1).   [91] CDPA 1988, s. 85(2).   [92] CDPA 1988, s. 85(2)(a).
[93] [1987] FSR 90.   [94] CDPA 1988, s. 87(1).
[95] CDPA 1988, s. 87(2). But the passing of equitable title in the copyright or the grant of an implied licence to use the copyright work are not sufficient: see *Pasterfield* (n. 50).

This can be done even before an issue arises. Such a waiver may relate to one or more specific rights, or to all moral rights; it may relate to one specific work, to a class of works, to all works, and even to future works. The waiver can be conditional or unconditional, and can also be expressed to be subject to revocation.[96] This possibility for the author to waive his or her moral rights substantially weakens the impact and value of the moral rights. An author or director quite often occupies a weak bargaining position in negotiating the conditions for the creation and the commercial exploitation of the work, and can be leaned upon to waive all moral rights. It is submitted that the possibility of waiving moral rights contradicts the essence of the concept of moral rights as essential safeguards for the author or director as the weaker party. Nevertheless, a similar waiver provision has also been introduced in relation to the moral rights of performers.[97]

Even worse in its weakening impact is the possibility of an informal waiver under the general principles of contract or estoppel.[98] The enforcement of the paternity right may become impossible if conduct of the author or director leads another person to believe that he or she will not insist upon identification.

The introduction of moral rights in the Act was clearly a step in the right direction: the protection of the weaker party cannot be left entirely to the contractual freedom of the parties. But the flexible waiver facility undermines the whole system. It is clear, then, that the concept of moral rights is not yet fully integrated in the UK's entrepreneurial style copyright system.[99]

An overview

Moral rights emphasize the strong link between the work and its author. Whatever form the commercial exploitation of the work takes, that link survives. Moral rights are therefore inalienable and stay with the author.

There are two core moral rights. First, there is the right to be identified, or the paternity right. This applies traditionally to literary, dramatic, musical, or artistic works, but it has been expanded to include films and performances. While important for the author, the paternity right also has its importance for the user of copyright works. Many copyright works are bought or consumed because of the fame of the author and because the buyer or consumer sees, in the name of the author, a guarantee of quality.

Second, there is the right of integrity, or the right to object to derogatory treatment of the work. This protects the reputation of the author, which again also has its value for users of the work.

Both of these rights are minimal rights that protect fundamental aspects of the link between the author, the work, and the public. It is clearly not envisaged that moral rights will constantly interfere with the normal exploitation of the work; they are essentially there to stop abuses. From that perspective, the relatively important scope of certain exceptions to these rights, and, specifically, the fact that they can be waived or need to be asserted before they come into force, is to be regretted. They do not correspond with the goal of moral rights and hinder their proper functioning within our copyright system.

---

[96] CDPA 1988, s. 87(3).   [97] CDPA 1988, s. 205J.   [98] CDPA 1988, s. 87(4).
[99] See Stamatoudi, 'Moral Rights of Authors in England: The Missing Emphasis on the Role of Creators' (n. 2) at 478.

The legislature has also used the chapter on moral rights to deal with the right to object to false attribution, which can be seen as the other side of the paternity-right coin, and the right to privacy in relation to commissioned photographs.

Further reading

ADENEY, E. (2006) *The Moral Rights of Authors and Performers: An International and Comparative Analysis*, Oxford: Oxford University Press.

GARNETT, K. and DAVIES, G. (eds.) (2010) *Moral Rights*, London: Sweet & Maxwell.

MASIYAKURIMA, P., 'The Trouble with Moral Rights' (2005) 68(3) MLR 411.

MCBRIDE NEWMAN, S. T., 'Human Rights and Copyrights: A Look at Practical Jurisprudence with Reference to Authors' Rights' (2009) 31(2) EIPR 88–92.

NOCELLA, L., 'Copyright and Moral Rights Versus Author's Right and Droit Moral: Convergence or Divergence?' (2008) 19(7) Ent LR 151–7.

RIGAMONTI, C., 'Deconstructing Moral Rights' (2006) 47(2) Harv Int LJ 353.

SIMON, I., 'The Introduction of Performers' Moral Rights: Part I' (2006) 28(11) EIPR 552.

SIMON, I., 'The Introduction of Performers' Moral Rights: Part II' (2006) 28(12) EIPR 600.

15

Copyright infringement

The owner of the copyright in a work is given a property right according to s. 1 of the Copyright, Designs and Patents Act (CDPA) 1988—but what is the content of this property right? The owner is given the exclusive right to perform certain acts in relation to the work, but in relation to an intangible right it is easier to approach things from an infringement perspective. Anyone who performs an act that has been reserved exclusively for the copyright owner will infringe the copyright in the work if he or she has not, in advance, obtained the permission of the copyright owner to perform that act. This chapter will therefore be concerned with the various acts that can infringe copyright and the content of the property right of the copyright owner will be defined in this indirect way.

Essentially, copyright is a right to make copies; copyright infringement can therefore be seen as making unauthorized copies of a work. At least, this was the historical starting point: now, much refinement has taken place, and a distinction is made between primary and secondary infringement.

Primary infringement

In one way or another, all forms of primary infringement involve copying, whether through reproduction or through performance of the work. According to s. 16(1) of the 1988 Act, the rights of the copyright owner are infringed if:

- the work is copied;
- copies of the work are issued to the public;
- the work is lent or rented to the public;
- the work is performed, shown, or played in public;
- the work is communicated to the public; or
- an adaptation is made of the work or any of the above is done in relation to an adaptation.[1]

It is an infringement to do these acts, but also to authorize someone else to do them.[2] These acts are called 'restricted acts' and only the owner of the copyright, or someone with his or her consent, can do them.

Normally, infringing acts are carried out by one party, or by several parties, each of which carries out separate infringing acts. There are, however, cases in which the alleged infringers really act together in carrying out a single infringing act. Such copyright infringement cases in which the alleged infringers are sued jointly as joint

---

[1] Inserted by Copyright and Related Rights Regulations 2003, reg. 6(2).   [2] CDPA 1988, s. 16(2).

tortfeasors require proof of an intended, procured, and shared common design for such infringement.[3]

Copyright infringement is the infringement of an intangible right in the expression of an idea. The idea is not protected and copying the idea is not an infringement of copyright.[4] The work should also be dissociated from its physical, tangible carrier: when you buy a wooden sculpture, you buy the piece of wood; the ownership of the copyright is not transferred.[5]

Infringement requires misappropriation

The causal link

Appropriation of the expression of the copyright work is an essential element of copyright infringement. Because only the particular expression of an idea is protected by copyright, a work expressing the same idea is not necessarily an infringement. This will be the case and no infringement will arise if the result is reached independently[6] or if a common source is relied upon.[7] This will, for example, be the case if two authors describe the Venice Marathon race in a very similar way, while sitting at opposite sides of the Rialto Bridge over the Canal Grande: they will reach the similar result independently. A common source may be found in two very different tables of matches on football pools coupons, each of which has to rely on the list of matches provided by the Football Association. It is necessary to demonstrate that the alleged infringement is linked to the original work and that part of its expression has been taken.

Case law provides a straightforward example in relation to a film.[8] The plaintiff had shown the defendant an advertising film. The defendant had declined the offer to utilize the film, but he had afterwards taken the idea that was contained in it to make his own film. It was held that copyright in the original film is not infringed when the defendant does not make an exact copy of the film itself, but makes another film in a way that is designed to, and which does, closely resemble and imitate the film in which copyright subsists.[9] This is to be contrasted with the case where the defendant tried to independently develop his own version of the concept of a red London doubledecker bus in the centre of a picture against a grey background of landmark London buildings. The judge held in this case that there had been access to the original picture, that a causal link had been established, and that part of the expression had been taken, despite the best intentions of the defendant. Or to put it in the judge's words:

> In this case it is not a coincidence that both images show Big Ben and the Houses of Parliament in black and white and a bright red bus driving from right to left and a blank white sky. The reason the defendants' image is like that is obviously because Mr Houghton saw the claimant's work. The differences do not negative copying, on the facts of this case they have a bearing on whether a substantial part is taken.[10]

---

[3] *MCA Records Inc. v. Charly Records Ltd* [2002] FSR 401, [2002] EMLR 1 (CA).

[4] *IPC Media Ltd v. Highbury-Leisure Publishing Ltd (No. 2)* [2005] FSR 20.

[5] This does not exclude a separate transfer of copyright.

[6] See *Francis Day & Hunter Ltd v. Bron* [1963] Ch 587, [1963] 2 All ER 16.

[7] E.g. factual, scientific, and historical data, which is readily available and forms the basis of a number of works: see *Harman Pictures NV v. Osborne* [1967] 2 All ER 324, [1967] 1 WLR 723 at 328 and 728.

[8] *Norowzian v. Arks Ltd* [1998] FSR 394.

[9] The fact that the work was a film explains certain peculiarities of the case.

[10] *Temple Island Collections Ltd v. New English Teas Ltd and Nicholas John Houghton* [2012] EWPCC 1, [2012] FSR 9 at para. 56, per Judge Birss QC.

The burden of proof

The owner who alleges infringement of his or her copyright bears the burden of proving that the similarity between his or her work and the alleged infringement is explained by this causal connection. Part of the evidence required is that the claimant's work was created *before* the alleged infringement, which rules out the possibility that it borrowed subject matter from the alleged infringement. An infringement case therefore failed when it emerged that the articles with the allegedly infringing design had been imported prior to the creation of the claimant's allegedly infringed drawings, despite the obvious similarity between them.[11]

In practice, it is extremely difficult to demonstrate the causal link fully. In most cases, all that the claimant can do is demonstrate strong similarities between the earlier work and the allegedly infringing work, which are of evidential value, but not conclusive; these are then coupled with evidence that the defendant had the opportunity to know the claimant's work. If the defendant does not provide another convincing explanation for the similarities, most judges will accept that the claimant has discharged the burden of proof and will find copying proved.

Lord Millett summarized it as follows in *Designers Guild Ltd v. Russell Williams Textiles Ltd:*[12]

> The first step in an action for infringement of artistic copyright is to identify those features of the defendant's design which the plaintiff alleges have been copied from the copyright work. The court undertakes a visual comparison of the two designs, noting the similarities and the differences. The purpose of the examination is not to see whether the overall appearance of the two designs is similar, but to judge whether the particular similarities relied on are sufficiently close, numerous or extensive to be more likely to be the result of copying than of coincidence. It is at this stage that similarities may be disregarded because they are commonplace, unoriginal, or consist of general ideas. If the plaintiff demonstrates sufficient similarity, not in the works as a whole but in the features which he alleges have been copied, and establishes that the defendant had prior access to the copyright work, the burden passes to the defendant to satisfy the judge that, despite the similarities, they did not result from copying. Even at this stage, therefore, the inquiry is directed to the similarities rather than the differences. This is not to say that the differences are unimportant. They may indicate an independent source and so rebut any inference of copying, but differences in the overall appearance of the two works due to the presence of features of the defendant's work about which no complaint is made are not material.[13]

The nexus that needs to be shown between the original work and the alleged copy should be one in terms of expression. A nexus at a high level of abstraction at which only the ideas are linked is not sufficient, because copyright protection does not operate at that level.[14]

It should be kept in mind, however, that the underlying rule requires proof of borrowing and a causal connection. In the absence of proof of actual knowledge of the original work, it was therefore held that infringement was not established in a case in which a designer created a pattern for a carpet on the basis of instructions that led to

---

[11] *T&A Textiles and Hosiery Ltd v. Hala Textile UK Ltd, Abdul Hadi Shehezad and Irfan Ahmad* [2015] EWHC 2888 (IPEC), para. 59.

[12] [2000] 1 WLR 2413, [2001] FSR 113 at 2425 and 124.

[13] See also *Ultra Marketing (UK) Ltd & Thomas Alexander Scott v. Universal Components Ltd* [2004] EWHC 468; *Nouveau Fabrics Ltd v. Voyage Decoration Ltd & Dunelm Soft Furnishings Ltd* [2004] EWHC 895.

[14] *IPC Media Ltd v. Highbury-Leisure Publishing Ltd (No. 2)* [2005] FSR 20.

strong similarities with the original design.[15] The alleged infringer did not have to be able to explain in full detail how he came up independently with the similar aspects of the design. In these circumstances, the claimant copyright owner can only succeed on the issue of copying by demonstrating similarities between the works that could not be coincidental.[16] The presence in both the original work and the alleged copy of a host of small, unimportant details is often an indication of copying.[17] Similarly, a particular feature—especially in a technical drawing, for example, of a design feature that solves a technical problem—may also be so ingenious and unique that any subsequent appearance of it must be the result of borrowing, because it is unrealistic to assume that someone could independently have arrived at exactly the same solution.[18] In the latter case, a lot will obviously depend upon the extreme nature of the facts of the case.

The intention of the infringer and subconscious copying

The intention of the defendant is not relevant. The fact that he or she believed that, for whatever reason, he or she was allowed to reproduce or perform the work does not influence the finding of infringement. Even an intention to independently create another work based on the same idea cannot exclude a finding of infringement.[19] The defendant may not realize that he or she is infringing copyright; one also finds situations in which the defendant does not realize that he or she is copying. We all frequently come into contact with copyright works. Some of them leave untraceable impressions in our memory. Unconsciously, we may copy these works or parts of them when creating our own work. This will also constitute infringement, because copying does not need to happen consciously.[20] The obvious example is that of a composer who listens to hundreds of melodies and, when composing his own music, unconsciously copies fragments of the melodies that he heard.[21]

Full proof of a causal link will be even more difficult in cases of unconscious copying. Judges will consider:

> the degree of familiarity (if proved at all, or properly inferred) with the plaintiff's work, the character of the work, particularly its qualities of impressing the mind and memory, the objective similarity of the defendant's work, the inherent probability that such similarities as found could be due to coincidence, the existence of other influences on the defendant...the quality of the defendant's...own evidence on the presence in his mind of the plaintiff's work.[22]

Indirect copying

The causal relationship can be turned into a causal chain: a copy of a copy indirectly copies the original work and constitutes an infringement.[23] Drawings are often made

---

[15] *Stoddard International plc v. William Lomas Carpets Ltd* [2001] FSR 848.

[16] *Stephan Malmstedt v. EMI Records Ltd & Per Gessle* [2003] ECDR 162.

[17] *Nova Productions Ltd v. Mazooma Games Ltd and ors; Nova Productions Ltd v. Bell Fruit Games Ltd* [2007] RPC 25, [2007] EMLR 14 (CA).

[18] *George Jones v. Tower Hamlets London Borough Council & Samuel Lewis Housing Association* [2001] RPC 407.

[19] *Temple Island Collections Ltd* (n. 10).

[20] See *Rees v. Melville* (1911–16) Macq Cop Cas 168; *Ricordi v. Clayton & Waller* (1928–30) Macq Cop Cas 154; *Francis Day & Hunter Ltd* (n. 6); *Industrial Furnaces v. Reaves* [1970] RPC 605 at 623.

[21] See *Stephan Malmstedt* (n. 16).

[22] *Francis Day & Hunter Ltd* (n. 6), per Willmer LJ at 614, adopting the words of Wilberforce J at first instance.

[23] CDPA 1988, s. 16(3); this provision is based on the case law of e.g. *King Features Syndicate v. Kleeman* [1941] AC 417, [1941] 2 All ER 403 and *British Leyland Motor Corp. v. Armstrong Patents Co. Ltd* [1986] RPC 279.

before a three-dimensional object is made; if someone makes his or her own drawing after having seen the object, but without having seen the original drawing, the copyright in that drawing will nevertheless be infringed.[24]

This chain can be long, but it must be uninterrupted and run in the same direction. The final infringing copy must be linked to the original work, the copyright in which it is infringing—but it is not required that all intermediate acts produce works that can attract copyright.[25] To go back to our example, it is not required that the three-dimensional object attracts copyright. A case law example concerned parts of cartridges for laser printers and photocopiers.[26] The copying by the defendant of parts of the plaintiff's cartridges constituted an indirect reproduction of the plaintiff's drawings, in which artistic copyright existed. The fact that the cartridges were functional three-dimensional objects was irrelevant.

The provision cannot be used, however, if two similar objects are created and drawings of each of these objects are made. In that situation, there is no indirect infringement of the drawing of the first object, because the objects are the starting point in the chain, not the drawing.[27]

Substantial copying

Two separate requirements

Copying is all about reproducing. This means, traditionally, that new copies of the work are produced in material form. This new copy, or these new copies, can now also be produced in digital form, but there still needs to be at least one 'new' copy. This was held not to be the case, for example, when an art gallery used a special technique to transfer the ink by which an authorized reproduction of a painter's work had been made on a poster to a canvas. No ink was left on the original poster and hence no 'new' copy of the work had been made.[28]

It remains equally true that not every act of copying is actionable: the defendant must have copied either the whole work or a substantial part of it.[29] This is the issue of 'substantiality', which comes on top of that of copying as such. It should be stressed that copying and taking a substantial part are two separate things: both are required and it is not correct to say that, when copying is found, it will follow that a substantial part has been taken.[30] But it is also the case that as *Infopaq*[31] acknowledges that originality can be found in (small) parts of a larger work, making these parts copyright works in their own right, it has become easier to establish that the part of such a smaller work that has been copied amounts to a substantial part.[32]

---

[24] See *LB (Plastics) v. Swish Products Ltd* [1979] RPC 551. [25] CDPA 1988, s. 16(3).

[26] *Canon Kabushiki Kaisha v. Green Cartridge Co. (Hong Kong) Ltd* [1997] 3 WLR 13, [1997] FSR 817 (PC).

[27] *Purefoy Engineering Co. Ltd v. Sykes Boxall* (1954) 71 RPC 227 at 232. Cf. the Court of Appeal's approach in the same case, which is differently worded: (1955) 72 RPC 89 at 99.

[28] See the decision of the Supreme Court of Canada in *Galérie d'Art du Petit Champlain Inc., Galérie d'Art Yves Laroche Inc., Editions Multi-Graph Itée, Galérie d'Art Laroche, Denis Inc. & Serge Rosa v. Claude Théberge* [2002] SCC 34.

[29] CDPA 1988, s. 16(3)(a).

[30] *Nova Productions Ltd v. Mazooma Games Ltd and ors; Nova Productions Ltd v. Bell Fruit Games Ltd* [2007] RPC 25, [2007] EMLR 14 (CA).

[31] Case C-5/08, *Infopaq International A/S v. Danske Dagblades Forening* [2009] ECDR 16.

[32] *Newspaper Licensing Agency Ltd v. Meltwater Holding BV* [2010] EWHC 3099 (Ch), [2011] RPC 7, confirmed on appeal [2011] EWCA Civ 890 [2012] RPC 1.

A qualitative approach

Cases in which the whole work has been copied are not problematic, but what is a 'substantial part' of a work? It is not determined on a quantitative basis: it is not possible to derive, from the 1988 Act and the case law, a rule that the copying of X per cent of a work will not be substantial copying, while the copying of Y per cent of the work will be such. Although, obviously, the quantity taken from the original work plays a certain role, it is much more a qualitative approach that is taken to determine whether the copying was substantial.[33]

Substantial taking also needs to be demonstrated in relation to each copyright work individually. If elements of more than one copyright work have been taken, the taking of a substantial part has to be demonstrated for each work.[34] This is linked to the fact that copyright is used in the UK as a tool against unfair competition. Copying will be allowed only in so far as it does not lead to unfair competition. A qualitative approach fits this purpose much more easily. Another relevant factor is the principle that ideas are not protected. A substantial part of the expression of the idea can be copied, but it is not possible to translate that into a percentage of the work, because one does not know the balance between idea and expression in the work.

Whether or not a substantial part of the work has been copied will have to be determined on a case-by-case basis. It is a matter of fact and degree, and will depend on the circumstances of the case.[35] Lord Hoffmann summarized the basic position as follows:

> The House of Lords decided in *Ladbroke (Football) Ltd v. William Hill (Football) Ltd* [1964] 1 All ER 465, [1964] 1 WLR 273 that the question of substantiality is a matter of quality rather than quantity. The relevant passages are too well known to require citation... But what quality is one looking for? That question, as it seems to me, must be answered by reference to the reason why the work is given copyright protection. In literary copyright, for example, copyright is conferred (irrespective of literary merit) upon an original literary work. It follows that the quality relevant for the purposes of substantiality is the literary originality of that which has been copied. In the case of an artistic work, it is the artistic originality of that which has been copied. So, in the recent case of *Designer Guild Ltd v. Russell Williams (Textiles) Ltd* [2001] 1 All ER 700, [2000] 1 WLR 2416, the House decided that although not the smallest part of a fabric had been reproduced with anything approaching photographic fidelity, the copying of certain of the ideas expressed in that design which, in their conjoined expression, had involved original artistic skill and labour, constituted the copying of a substantial part of the artistic work.[36]

This passage clearly hints at the fact that the quality one is looking for to decide whether qualitatively speaking a substantial part of the work has been copied corresponds essentially to the quality of originality that made the work gain copyright protection in the first place. That specific originality is at the heart of the copyright work and if that has been copied to a large extent, the essence of the work has been taken and there will have been substantial taking, leading to a finding of infringement. *Infopaq* as well puts the focus squarely on originality. There will be infringement if the originality of the work

---

[33] *Ladbroke (Football) Ltd v. William Hill (Football) Ltd* [1964] 1 All ER 465, [1964] 1 WLR 273, per Lord Reid at 469 and 276; see also Lord Pearce's speech at 481 and 293.

[34] *IPC Media Ltd v. Highbury-Leisure Publishing Ltd (No. 2)* [2005] FSR 20.

[35] E.g. in *Hawkes & Sons (London) Ltd v. Paramount Film Service Ltd* [1934] Ch 593, it was held that the inclusion of a 20-second portion of the main melody of the march 'Colonel Bogey', which lasts for four minutes, in a newsreel amounted to substantial copying.

[36] *Newspaper Licensing Agency Ltd v. Marks & Spencer plc* [2001] UKHL 38, [2001] 3 WLR 290 at para. 19.

has been taken, i.e. in those cases the taking will be substantial.[37] The *Temple Island Collections* case provides a good example. Both pictures contained a bright-red London double-decker bus in a central position and Big Ben and the Houses of Parliament in black and white in the background against a clear sky, whilst there were differences such as the absence of the structure of the bridge and of the river in the allegedly infringing picture. Nevertheless, the court held:

> The elements which have been reproduced are a substantial part of the claimant's work because despite the absence of some important compositional elements, they still include the key combination of what I have called the visual contrast features with the basic composition of the scene itself. It is that combination which makes Mr Fielder's image visually interesting. It is not just another photograph of clichéd London icons.[38]

Further guidance

Some further general guidance can, however, be given. The court will have to concentrate on the similarities between the part of the work that has allegedly been copied and the equivalent part in the alleged copy. Differences between the two can only be used to ascertain the similarities.[39] The qualitative approach to determining whether a substantial part of the work has been copied means that particular weight will be given to the copying of the most important and interesting parts of the original work.[40] In a case that was concerned with cacao crop reports, the copying of the pod count summary from the much longer report was held to constitute the copying of a substantial part of the work for this very reason.[41] In another case, a few lines had been taken from a manuscript authored by James Joyce.[42] The earlier edition of the work did not contain these lines, because they had been omitted at the typescript stage; they had been reinstated in the allegedly infringing edition. Even though only a few lines of text were at issue, they were held to amount to a substantial part of the work, because they were particularly important. Their reinstatement gave the public access to the complete original manuscript. If parts of more than one work—for example, a series of articles—are copied in the allegedly infringing work, each of the original works must be considered separately for the purposes of determining whether a substantial part of it has been copied.[43]

Once the court is convinced that unfair competition is taking place,[44] it will be hard to convince it that the alterations made are so substantial that the part of the original work that is copied is no longer substantial.[45] Indeed, the mere presence of additional new material is, as such, not diminishing the substantial copying.[46] In those cases the

---

[37] *Infopaq* (n. 31)   [38] *Temple Island Collections Ltd* (n. 10) at para. 63, per Judge Birss QC.

[39] *Biotrading & Financing OY v. Biohit Ltd* [1998] FSR 109 at 121.

[40] Care needs to be taken, though, that these do not include underlying ideas and concepts, because these are not protected by copyright. See *Baigent and anor v. Random House Group Ltd* [2007] FSR 24 (CA) (the *Da Vinci Code* case).

[41] *PCR Ltd v. Dow Jones Telerate Ltd* [1998] FSR 170.

[42] *Sweeney v. Macmillan Publishers Ltd* [2002] RPC 35 at 651. The judgment gives the impression that the lines also amount to a substantial part of the work, because they make the allegedly infringing edition special and distinct. It is respectfully submitted that this argument is not acceptable, because it refers to the allegedly infringing work, whereas the real issue is whether a substantial part—in a qualitative sense—of the copyright work has been copied.

[43] *PCR Ltd v. Dow Jones Telerate Ltd* [1998] FSR 170.

[44] Especially if the judges adhere to the hard-line approach suggested by Peterson J that '*what is worth copying is prima facie worth protecting*': *University of London Press v. Universal Tutorial Press* [1916] 2 Ch 601 at 610 (quoted in *Ladbroke (Football) Ltd v. William Hill (Football) Ltd* (n. 33) at 279).

[45] An excellent example is found in *Elanco Products v. Mandops (Agrochemical Specialists) Ltd* [1980] RPC 213.

[46] *Hyperion Records Ltd v. Lionel Sawkins* [2005] 1 WLR 3281 (CA).

originality of the work has been taken, namely, the essence of what is protected by copyright. This should also be seen against the background of the vague dividing line between idea and expression. Judges in the type of case described often take the view that the idea is restricted to the thought underlying the work, such as a joke underlying a cartoon.[47] The only way in which the defendant can avoid copying the expression is by drawing a different cartoon starting from the same joke, but not based on the completed original cartoon.[48] This extremely wide interpretation of what is expression facilitates, of course, the finding that a substantial part of it has been copied. The case law contains various examples of this approach in relation to scripts for plays or films based on plots found in a play or a novel.[49] The actual words were often not copied; only the plot, as such, was taken and eventually slightly adapted.[50] The courts decided that substantial copying had, nevertheless, taken place. In their view, the idea was confined to the thought that was the starting point for the development of the plot, such as making a play about the homecoming of a husband who was presumed dead.[51]

It is submitted that this approach should be confined to cases in which there is a very strong sense of unfair competition or in which the starting point is the essential element of the work that determines its economic value. The economic value of a plot, and that of the play or film based on it, is often determined on the basis of the value of the initial starting point. This is less so for a novel, in relation to which literary style is also extremely important, or for an artistic work, in relation to which visual appeal is the other extremely important factor.[52]

Alterations while copying

In all other circumstances, the idea is wider in scope. Under these circumstances, other elements become prominent in determining whether substantial copying has taken place. One obvious element is the unaltered copying of a key element of the original work, such as the refrain of a song.[53] This amounts, qualitatively speaking, to substantial copying, even if the amount taken is not large in comparison to the whole work.[54]

A smart copier alters and reworks the part that he or she has copied: does this still amount to substantial copying? The test is whether a substantial part of the original work survives in the new work.[55] It has been suggested that this means that no substantial and actionable copying will occur if the copier has invested enough skill and labour in the alteration of the copied parts[56] for the result to attract its own

---

[47] *McCrum v. Eisner* (1917) 87 LJ Ch 99, 117 LT 536.

[48] *McCrum* (n. 47); see also *Krisarts SA v. Briarfine Ltd* [1977] FSR 557 (defendant painting independently a scene that the plaintiff painted at an earlier time, resulting in a similar process of creation, while only the idea was borrowed).

[49] *Corelli v. Gray* (1913) 30 TLR 116 and *Vane v. Famous Players* (1928–35) Macq Cop Cas 394 are good examples of this approach.

[50] *Kelly v. Cinema Houses Ltd* (1928–35) Macq Cop Cas 362; *Dagnall v. British & Dominion Film Corp.* (1928–1935) Macq Cop Cas 391; *Fernald v. Jay Lewis* [1975] FSR 499 (case decided in 1953).

[51] An example given in *Vane v. Famous Players* (n. 49), per Scrutton LJ.

[52] See *Bauman v. Fussell* [1978] RPC 485, per Somervell LJ at 487.

[53] Cf. *Hawkes & Sons (London) Ltd v. Paramount Film Service Ltd* (n. 35).

[54] But one line taken from the refrain of a popular song did not amount to substantial copying in *Joy Music Ltd v. Sunday Pictorial Newspapers (1920) Ltd* [1960] 2 QB 60; see later.

[55] *Schweppes Ltd v. Wellington Ltd* [1984] FSR 210; *Redwood Music v. Chappell & Co. Ltd* [1982] RPC 109.

[56] It is essential that the copied work does not rely exclusively on information gathered by the claimant, using his or her skill and judgement: see *Elanco Products v. Mandops (Agrochemical Specialists) Ltd* (n. 45). It must be remembered, however, that this was a case in which there were strong indications of unfair competition, because the first version of the instruction leaflet for a weed killer was an exact copy of

copyright.[57] This is, however, not the real test, and it should be emphasized that the skill and labour approach should, in any case, be restricted to the parts based on the copying. Other parts of the allegedly infringing work, and the skill and labour invested in them, should not be taken into account when discussing the infringement issue. It is therefore possible to determine whether the production of an altered copy constitutes a copyright infringement by asking whether the infringer has incorporated a substantial part of the independent skill and labour contributed by the original author in creating the copyright work.[58]

Two excellent examples of circumstances in which alterations lead to difficulties in this respect are satirical versions of works and summaries of works. The satirical version has to stay close enough to the original for people to recognize the link and, for reasons of accuracy, a summary has to contain the essential elements of the original work. A song, the lyrics of which had been altered and parodied in pursuit of Prince Philip, was held not to be an infringing copy, because only one repeated phrase had been taken from the original lyrics.[59] Selection of the essential elements of the work,[60] condensation, and revision must amount to enough skill and labour to attract copyright for a summary to escape the infringement sanction.[61]

The originality of what is copied

The work that has been copied may also contain unoriginal parts. This leads to special problems if the part that was copied included the unoriginal parts. It was held that, if an unoriginal part was taken, and that part was used in a similar context and way as in the original copyright work, the latter aspect meant that also part of the work of the author that provided originality was taken.[62] It is likely that, in these circumstances, the amount taken would be likely to amount to a substantial part of the work.[63]

Industrial drawings are a good example in this context. They often consist of unoriginal shapes, which are copied from earlier drawings, in combination with new original shapes. When such an industrial drawing is copied, the copying of the unoriginal shape may not amount to the copying of a substantial part, but substantial copying may be involved when the amount copied includes the context in which the shape was portrayed. The latter conclusion is reached because the copier has also taken much of the work of the author in deciding how, and in what way, the unoriginal shape should be combined with the original shape. The inclusion of the unoriginal shape in what is copied has little relevance in deciding whether or not a substantial part has been copied.[64]

the plaintiff's leaflet and the second version was only revised to such extent as to give the same information in other words; the judgment can be criticized, because it gives the plaintiffs—authors of a trivial work—an almost absolute monopoly in the only possible way to express these instructions efficiently, concisely, and accurately.

[57] *Joy Music Ltd v. Sunday Pictorial Newspapers (1920) Ltd* [1960] 2 QB 60, [1960] 1 All ER 703; *Glyn v. Weston Feature Film Co.* [1916] 1 Ch 261.

[58] *Designers Guild Ltd v. Russell Williams Textiles Ltd* [2001] FSR 113, per Lord Scott at 131, with reference to H. Laddie, P. Prescott, and M. Vitoria (2000) *The Modern Law of Copyright*, 3rd edn, London: Butterworths, pp. 92–3. See also *Nouveau Fabrics Ltd v. Voyage Decoration Ltd & Dunelm Soft Furnishings Ltd* [2004] EWHC 895.

[59] *Joy Music Ltd v. Sunday Pictorial Newspapers (1920) Ltd* (n. 57).

[60] This aspect is essential, because the Court of Appeal held, in *Elanco Products* (n. 45), that the defendant could not rely exclusively on the plaintiff's effort and judgement in selecting the information.

[61] See *Sweet v. Benning* (1855) 16 CB 459, per Jervis CJ at 483.

[62] *Biotrading & Financing OY v. Biohit Ltd* [1998] FSR 109 at 121.

[63] *Biotrading & Financing OY* (n. 62) at 121.   [64] *Biotrading & Financing OY* (n. 62) at 122.

It cannot be the aim of copyright to give the claimant a wide-ranging monopoly. This could happen if works involving substantial copying of a part of a work that itself involves only the minimum amount of skill and labour to attract copyright are held to be infringements. This would be an undesirable consequence of the low requirements for a work to attract copyright and judges have fortunately responded to it by taking the extent of the effort invested by the claimant into account when deciding whether substantial copying has occurred. The answer will only be affirmative if an exact copy of the work, which itself involved an extremely low level of creativity, is produced.[65]

A particular problem arises when a work that is itself an edited version, or which consists of selected and compiled material, is allegedly copied to a substantial extent. This might occur in relation to a collection of selected poems, of which some poems are copied, together with some of the annotation. It occurs also in cases concerning tables, in relation to which the commercial judgement in selecting the material secures copyright and in which that selection is copied. Copyright arises in the whole work, but it is obvious that the real skill and labour expended by the claimant are located in the areas of selection, editing, and annotation. This is taken into account when determining whether the material copied amounts to a substantial part of the work.[66] The infringement of the claimant's contribution must be substantial as well.

Copying the various types of work

As a general rule, the idea of copying can be said to involve two elements:

> first, there must be sufficient objective similarity between the infringing work and the copyright work, or a substantial part thereof, for the former to be properly described, not necessarily as identical with, but as a reproduction or adaptation of the latter; secondly, the copyright work must be the source from which the infringing work is derived.[67]

The technical definition of copying depends on the type of work. But once such a case arises, the principles laid down here apply to it.

Original literary, artistic, dramatic, and musical works

An original work is copied through reproduction in any material form.[68] This includes storing the work in any medium by electronic means, such as storing the content of a book on a CD-ROM; it also includes materialization on a television monitor.[69] A special option arises for artistic works.[70] A two-dimensional copy can be made of a three-dimensional work, or a three-dimensional copy can be made of a two-dimensional work. The work is also reproduced in a material way in these cases. Such a case arises, for example, when a cartoon is enacted.[71]

---

[65] *Kenrick v. Lawrence & Co.* (1890) 25 QBD 99 (a drawing of a hand, showing voters where to cast their vote).

[66] *Warwick Film Productions Ltd v. Eisinger* [1969] 1 Ch 508, [1967] 3 All ER 367.

[67] *Francis Day & Hunter Ltd* (n. 6), per Diplock LJ at 583.

[68] CDPA 1988, s. 17(2). See *HRH Prince of Wales v. Associated Newspapers Ltd* [2006] ECDR, confirmed on appeal [2007] 3 WLR 222.

[69] *Bookmakers' Afternoon Greyhound Services Ltd v. Wilf Gilbert (Staffordshire) Ltd* [1994] FSR 723.

[70] CDPA 1988, s. 17(3).

[71] *Bradbury, Agnew & Co. v. Day* [1916] WN 114. The dimensional shift rule only applies to artistic works; it does not apply when e.g. a literary work is involved: see *Brigid Foley Ltd v. Eliott* [1982] RPC 433.

Films and television broadcasts

Films and television broadcasts are copied when they are reproduced.[72] This can take place when a film is made of a film or a broadcast; it also takes place when a photograph of the whole, or of any substantial part, of an image that forms part of the film or broadcast is made.[73] The courts held that making a photograph of a single frame of a *Starsky and Hutch* film was an infringement.[74] This situation also covers the case in which a photograph of a television screen, on which the work is momentarily displayed, is made.

Typographical arrangements of published editions

Copying a typographical arrangement involves making a facsimile copy of that arrangement.[75] That copy can be enlarged or reduced in scale,[76] which means that infringement often takes place by means of a photocopy or a fax.

All works

Copying of any kind of work also includes making copies that are transient or incidental to some other use of the work.[77] The prime example in this case would be making a series of photographs while copying a film.

Issuing copies to the public

Copying is not the only restricted act: copyright is also infringed when copies of a work are issued to the public. In the language of EU copyright the right holder has a distribution right in relation to the work. This applies to all works; no distinction is made between the various categories. Copies are issued to the public when they are put into circulation for the first time. It is essential that copies of the work were not previously available and that they are now put into circulation.[78] But it is not essential that the alleged infringer physically operates locally in issuing the copies. A combination of advertising directed at local members of the public in combination with the creation and making available of a specific delivery and payment method, which allow those members of the public to receive copies of the copyright work, namely, to have the copies issued to them, is sufficient.[79] And in *Dimensione Direct Sales*,[80] the CJEU went even further and ruled that the distribution right had been infringed by an offer for sale or a targeted advertisement of the original or a copy of the work, despite the absence of evidence of actual purchases. This obviously gives a very wide sense to the somewhat restrictive wording of s. 18 CDPA 1988.

A distinction is made between putting copies into circulation in the UK or in any other member state of the European Economic Area (EEA), on the one hand, and putting copies into circulation outside the EEA member states, on the other. Copies are issued to the public by putting them into circulation in the territory of the EEA if these copies have not previously been put into circulation in that territory by, or with the consent of, the copyright owner. Copies are also issued to the public when they are put into circulation outside

---

[72] CDPA 1988, s. 17(4).

[73] On a conceptual basis, copying needs to be distinguished from making another film in a way that is designed to, and which does, closely resemble and imitate the film in which copyright subsists, if no exact copy is made in the latter case: see *Norowzian v. Arks Ltd* [1998] FSR 394.

[74] *Spelling Goldberg Productions Inc. v. BPC Publishing Ltd* [1981] RPC 283.

[75] CDPA 1988, s. 17(5).   [76] CDPA 1988, s. 17(8).   [77] CDPA 1988, s. 17(6).

[78] See *HRH Prince of Wales v. Associated Newspapers Ltd* (n. 68).

[79] Case C-5/11, *Titus Alexander Jochen Donner* [2015] ECDR 22.

[80] Case C-516/13, *Dimensione Direct Sales and Michela Labianca v. Knoll International SpA* 13 May 2015, <http://curia.europa.eu>.

the territory of the EEA if they have not previously been put into circulation in that territory or elsewhere. All of this reflects also in the fact that subsequent dealings with a copy that is put into circulation do not constitute the restricted act of issuing copies to the public. When a book that has not been published is put into circulation, this will be an infringement of the copyright in the book, but subsequent importation of copies of the book and the loan of these copies will not constitute issuing copies to the public.[81] Rental and lending are, however, subject to special provisions, and it is to these provisions that we now turn.

Rental and lending of the work to the public

Rental and lending of a work[82] mean that a copy of the work is made available for use, on terms that it will, or may, be returned. Hire purchase-type deals are therefore also included. In the case of rental, the work is made available for direct or indirect commercial or economic advantage. The activities of video shops come to mind as an obvious example. Lending covers all cases in which no direct or indirect commercial or economic advantage is involved[83] and the copy of the work is made available through an establishment that is accessible to the public, such as a library.[84] Unauthorized rental or lending of copies of certain types of work to the public will constitute an infringement of the copyright in the work. The types of work involved are literary, dramatic, and musical works; films; and sound recordings. Artistic works are only involved in so far as they are not a work of architecture in the form of a building or a model for a building, or a work of applied art.[85]

The right to object to unauthorized rental and lending does not apply to a limited number of cases, because they have been excluded from the scope of the definition of rental and lending. These exclusions cover making a copy of the work available for the purpose of public performance, playing, or showing in public, broadcasting, and making a copy available for the purpose of exhibition in public, as well as making the copy available for on-the-spot reference use.[86] The latter excludes, for example, all use of a work inside a library without taking it out.

Rental and lending are based on the European Copyright (Rental and Lending) Directive,[87] which contains a minimum principle of equitable remuneration to which the right holder is entitled despite any potential contractual provisions by means of which he or she may have renounced his or her rights. The European Court of Justice has now expressed its views on the interpretation of that concept of equitable remuneration. The equitable remuneration for performing artists and phonogram producers was the point of discussion in *SENA v. NOS*.[88] The Court held that the member states are free to establish their own criteria within the boundaries set by the Directive and by Community law. It then applied that test to the Dutch criteria and found that the Dutch model passes the test, in so far as it relies on a combination of fixed and variable factors:

- the number of hours of phonograms broadcast;
- the viewing and listening densities achieved by the radio and television broadcasters represented by the broadcast organization;

[81] CDPA 1988, s. 18.   [82] CDPA 1988, 18A(2).

[83] This does not exclude the payment of an amount to cover the *operating* costs of the establishment: CDPA 1988, s. 18A(5).

[84] Interlibrary transactions are excluded from the scope of lending: CDPA 1988, s. 18A(4).

[85] CDPA 1988, s. 18A(1).   [86] CDPA 1988, s. 18A(3).

[87] Council Directive 92/100/EEC on rental and lending right and on certain rights related to copyright in the field of intellectual property (1992) OJ L 346/61.

[88] [2003] ECR I-1251.

- the tariffs fixed by agreement in the field of performance rights and broadcast rights in respect of musical works protected by copyright;

- the tariffs set by the public broadcast organizations in the member states bordering the Netherlands; and

- the amounts paid by commercial stations.

This conclusion was reached in the understanding that the model is such that it will enable a proper balance to be achieved between the interests of performing artists and producers in obtaining remuneration for the broadcast of a particular phonogram, and the interests of third parties in being able to broadcast the phonogram on terms that are reasonable. While this is perhaps not a turnkey solution offered by the Court, it is nevertheless some kind of a workable tool for those concerned.

Public performance of the work and showing or playing the work in public

In this category of restricted acts, public performances apply to literary, dramatic, and musical works only. The copyright in these works is infringed by the public performance of the work. This includes any visual or acoustic presentation of the work, even if the presentation is done by means of sound recordings, films, or broadcasts. Lectures, speeches, and addresses obviously come within this category.[89]

It is also an infringement of copyright to play or show a sound recording, film, or broadcast in public.[90] This kind of infringement arises, for example, when background music is played in a shop or restaurant.[91] The application of this provision is not, however, without problems: how do we define 'in public'? It is clear that this is not a reference to the public at large: showing the work to a group of 10 members of the public can be an infringement,[92] but private showings, even if to a larger number of people than 10, are not caught. To avoid infringement, then, the audience has to be of a domestic nature: copyright will not be infringed when a parent plays a CD and the rest of the family is listening in the lounge of the family home. This distinction is not, however, always clear: is the showing of a film in a hotel equipped with a central DVD player and a television set in every room private or public?[93] People will watch the film in the private atmosphere of their room, but the work will be available to a large group of people. Judges seem to attach a lot of importance to the question of whether the economic interests of the copyright owner are harmed.[94] If the answer is positive, the showing or playing will be public and will infringe. This will often be the case if everyone can gain access to the place at which the showing or playing takes place, with or without payment.

When a work is performed, played, or shown by means of apparatus receiving visual images or sounds that are conveyed by electronic means, the infringer will

---

[89] CDPA 1988, s. 19(1) and (2).   [90] CDPA 1988, s. 19(3).

[91] Blanket licences are available from collecting societies: see Ch. 18.

[92] Cf. Art. 3(1) of the Directive 2001/29/EC of the European Parliament and the Council on the harmonization of certain aspects of copyright and related rights in the information society [2001] OJ L 167/10.

[93] The European Court of Justice has held that Art. 1 of the Cable and Satellite Directive (Directive 93/83 on the coordination of certain rules concerning copyright and rights related to copyright applicable to satellite broadcasting and cable retransmission [1993] OJ L 248/15) did not define whether this amounted to communication to the public and that this was a matter for national law: Case C-293/98 *EGEDA v. Hosteleria Asturiana SA* [2000] ECR 231.

[94] See *Duck v. Bates* (1884) 13 QBD 843; *Ernest Turner Electrical Instruments Ltd v. Performing Right Society Ltd* [1943] Ch 167, [1943] 1 All ER 413; see also *Performing Right Society Ltd v. Harlequin Record Shops* [1979] FSR 233.

not be the person who sends the sounds or images (and the performer, in case of a performance),[95] but the person who makes the arrangements for the infringing act to take place.

Communication to the public

In implementing the Information Society Directive,[96] the new, broader concept of broadcast has now also been reflected in the new s. 20 of the 1988 Act.[97] Infringement by broadcasting or inclusion in a cable programme service has been replaced by infringement by communication to the public. That communication to the public of the work is now an act restricted by the copyright in a literary, dramatic, musical, or artistic work, a sound recording or film, or a broadcast, and any reference to 'communication to the public' is to communication to the public by electronic transmission. In relation to a work, this includes the broadcasting of the work and the making available to the public of the work by electronic transmission in such a way that members of the public may access it from a place, and at a time, individually chosen by them.

Whereas s. 19 is concerned with public performance in cases in which the public is present, s. 20 is solely concerned with communication to the public in cases in which the public is not present at the place of communication:[98] for example, in relation to the place at which the act of broadcasting takes place.[99] Communication is, by definition, also concerned only with the electronic transmission of the work[100]—but all forms of electronic transmission are covered, which includes on-demand services. Internet transmissions are also included, because they are electronic transmissions through which members of the public may access the work from a place, and at a time, that they individually choose. They come therefore within the definition of communication to the public.[101] The fact that the public may be composed of a single person (sitting in front of a computer) is not an issue. There are, after all, potentially many such persons at any one time and the communication is aimed at an indeterminate and large number of potential recipients (there is therefore a public in the sense of EU law).[102] It was therefore arguable that a website that allowed users to watch broadcasts they missed was communicating these broadcasts to the public and in doing so infringing the copyright in them.[103] Similarly, making photographs included in a back issue of a newspaper available on the newspaper's website, where the original licence granted by the photographer only included publication

---

[95] CDPA 1988, s. 19(4).

[96] Directive 2001/29/EC of the European Parliament and the Council on the harmonization of certain aspects of copyright and related rights in the information society [2001] OJ L 167/10.

[97] Inserted by Copyright and Related Rights Regulations 2003, reg. 6.

[98] See Recital 23 to the Directive. Case C-283/10, *Circul Globus Bucuresti v. Uniunea Compozitorilor si Muzicologilor din România - Asociatia pentru Drepturi de Autor* [2011] ECR I-12031.

[99] Broadcasting, and therefore communication to the public, will take place in both the country in which the principal audience and the seat of the organization is located, and in the country in which the transmitter is located in a scenario within which the latter is, for technical reasons, located on the other side of the border: Case C-192/04, *Lagardère Active Broadcast v. SPRE & GVL* [2005] ECR I-07199 (ECJ).

[100] A hotel that makes available television sets in individual bedrooms is communicating television programmes as copyright works to the public. Liability under copyright arises despite the fact that each guest watches in the privacy of his or her room; that does not mean that no communication to the public is involved. Case C-306/05, *SGAE v. Rafael Hoteles SA* [2006] ECR I-11519 (ECJ).

[101] See, under the original text of the CDPA 1988, *Shetland Times v. Wills* [1997] FSR 604.

[102] Case C-607/11, *ITV v. TV Catchup* [2013] 3 CMLR 1

[103] *ITV Broadcasting Ltd v. TV Catchup Ltd* [2010] EWHC 3063 (Ch), [2011] FSR 16. This view was confirmed by the Court of Justice of the EU in *ITV v. TV Catchup* (n. 102).

in the (hard copy) newspaper, also amounted to (an authorized) communication to the public of the photographs.[104]

The Court of Justice has also been asked on a number of occasions to define the concept of communication to the public, and as the European instruments talk about 'any communication', the Court has construed the concept broadly. The starting point was a case where hotels made television programmes available to customers via individual television sets in each bedroom. That was held to be a (new) communication to the public, as it makes it possible to the customers to enjoy the broadcast.[105] The Court then held that the proprietor of a public house who uses a satellite dish to receive a broadcast and then transmits it to its clients present in the public house via a television screen and speakers infringes the copyright in the broadcast as this amounts to a communication to the public of the broadcast without the authorization of the right holder. The Court did specify that such an infringing communication to the public required transmission of the copyright work to a new public. The concept of a new public means for the Court that the work is transmitted to a public that was not taken into account by the authors of the protected works when they authorized their communication to the original public.[106] Both the customers of the hotel and the clients in the public house form such a new public. They were not the envisaged public when the broadcaster was granted the right to communicate the copyright work by broadcasting it. Or in the words of the Court:

> When those authors authorise a broadcast of their works, they consider, in principle, only the owners of television sets who, either personally or within their own private or family circles, receive the signal and follow the broadcasts. Where a broadcast work is transmitted, in a place accessible to the public, for an additional public which is permitted by the owner of the television set to hear or see the work, an intentional intervention of that kind must be regarded as an act by which the work in question is communicated to a new public.[107]

Having confirmed its concept of communication to the public and of a new public in the *Airfield* case,[108] the Court was asked to determine whether a dentist playing phonograms in his waiting room[109] on the one hand and a hotel that was providing DVDs and a DVD player in each room on the other hand were communicating copyright works to the public.[110] One might accept that in both cases there is a new public. But arguably there is no communication to the public by merely providing the hardware. The Court rejected that argument and widened the concept of communication to the public to include this scenario. The Court seems to do so because in fact this technique is the equivalent of rebroadcasting on demand to each room in the hotel. The intervention of the hotel and

[104] *Grisbrook v. MGN Ltd* [2010] EWCA Civ 1399, [2011] Bus LR 599.

[105] Case C-306/05, *SGAE v. Rafael Hoteles SA* [2006] ECR I-11519. See also Case C-351/12, *OSA-Ochranny svaz autorsky pro prava k dilum hudebnim o.s. v. Leecebne lazne Marianske Lazne a.s.*, 27 February 2014, <http://curia.europa.eu>.

[106] Joined Cases C-403/08 and C-429/08, *Football Association Premier League Ltd, Netmed Hellas SA, Multichoice Hellas SA v. QC Leisure, David Richardson, AV Station plc, Malcolm Chamberlain, Michael Madden, Sr Leisure Ltd, Philip George Charles Houghton, Derek Owen* (C-403/08) and *Karen Murphy v. Media Protection Services Ltd* (C-429/08) [2012] 1 CMLR 29, [2012] FSR 1 at para. 198. See also *Football Association Premier League Ltd v. QC Leisure* [2012] EWHC 108 (Ch), [2012] FSR 12.

[107] Joined Cases C-403/08 and C-429/08 (n. 106) at para. 198.

[108] Joined Cases C-431/09 and C-432/09, *Airfield NV and Canal Digitaal BV v. SABAM* and *Airfield NV v. Agicoa Belgium BVBA* [2012] ECDR 3 (rebroadcasting by satellite of TV broadcasts that include copyright work is a new communication to the public).

[109] Case C-135/10, *SCF v. Marco Del Corso* [2012] ECDR 16.

[110] Case C-162/10, *Phonographic Performance (Ireland) Ltd v. Ireland and A-G* [2012] 2 CMLR 29, [2012] ECDR 15.

the fact that without it the works would not have been available to the clients seem to be important factors. Nevertheless, this case stretches the definition of communication to the public significantly and almost beyond the borderline with the distribution of hard copies.[111] On the other hand one sees the same Chamber of the Court impose restrictions in the other case decided on the very same day. The Court decided indeed that the dentist was not communicating the work to the public. The Court argued that the decisive element was that playing music is not part of the business of the dentist. It does not bring in more clients and clients do not go to the dentist to enjoy music. The new public is also insignificant in terms of numbers and there is no extra income for the dentist.[112] One can indeed argue that in the hotel cases and in the public house cases the communication to the public aims to attract customers and is charged for. But the music in the waiting room is also part of the package offered by the dentist and for which he is paid. The difference between the cases is therefore only a matter of degree and one can either eagerly await the next decisions to see how the Court will draw the borderline or argue that the two cases are not to be reconciled. One could of course point out that the dentist case highlights additional relevant factors, such as the absence of a commercial aim and the *de minimis* nature of the communication to the public, and that it merely involved related rights where only a right to compensation is involved, rather than copyright as such where the right holder has a stronger right, a right to prevent certain actions from being carried out. The Court seems to rely on these elements to argue that the approach is consistent, but it is open to debate whether it really allows the cases to be reconciled with one another.

This leaves us with the situation that from the perspective of the CJEU there is a new communication to the public either if there is a new public or if use is made of a specific technical method of communication that is different from that of the original communication.[113] The CJEU argues that the concept of 'communication to the public' includes two cumulative criteria, namely, an 'act of communication' of a work and the communication of that work to a 'public'. An 'act of communication' refers to any transmission of the protected works, irrespective of the technical means or process used.[114] In terms of exclusive right it follows that every transmission or retransmission of a work which uses a specific technical means must, as a rule, be individually authorized by the author of the work in question.[115] The term 'public', on the other hand, refers to an indeterminate number of recipients, potential viewers, and implies, moreover, a fairly large number of persons that form a chosen or targeted audience.[116] It follows that a broadcasting organization does not carry out an act of communication to the public when it transmits its programme-carrying signals exclusively to signal distributors without those signals being accessible to the public during, and as a result of that transmission, those distributors then sending those signals to their respective subscribers so that they may watch those programmes because, whilst there is a communication in such a scenario, there will be no public. That would change if the intervention of the distributors in question is just a technical means, as the final public would then become the public of the original broadcaster.[117]

---

[111] *Phonographic Performance (Ireland) Ltd* (n. 110 above).

[112] Case C-135/10, *SCF v. Marco Del Corso* [2012] ECDR 16.   [113] *ITV v. TV Catchup* (n. 102).

[114] Joined Cases C-403/08 and C-429/08 (n. 106) at para. 193.

[115] *ITV v. TV Catchup* (n. 102) at para. 24.

[116] *ITV v. TV Catchup* (n. 102) at para. 32 and Case C-306/05, *SGAE v. Rafael Hoteles SA* [2006] ECR I-11519, paras. 37 and 38.

[117] Case C-325/14, *SBS Belgium NV v. Belgische Vereniging van Auteurs, Componisten en Uitgevers (SABAM)*, 19 November 2015, <http://curia.europa.eu>.

Finally, the question arose where the communication to the public takes place. This might become relevant in circumstances such as cloud computing where the act of re-sending the data and their reception do not happen in the same jurisdiction. Copyright is, in other words, forced to define its concept much more clearly. The Court of Justice ruled that the communication to the public also takes place where the user receives the data. Despite the fact that this case involved databases and the re-utilization right, the concepts are identical and the suggestion that communication to the public only takes place where the data are sent or where the work is rebroadcast was clearly rejected by the Court. Communication to the public takes place, at least, in the sender's and the receiver or user's place.[118]

In an Internet context the question arises whether a hypertext link through which one website provides access to material on another website amounts to the communication to the public of the material contained on that other website. A positive answer to this question would involve a severe restriction on the Internet, as each hypertext link would require a licence form the right holder concerned. In the *Svensson* case, the CJEU held that the provision of a clickable link, which encompasses hypertext links, to works that are freely available on another website does not constitute an act of communication to the public. One should emphasize that the material should be freely available. If that is the case, the public of the first communication is the whole Internet community and there is then no new public left for the communication through the hypertext link (which also uses the same technological means). The opposite is true if material is not freely available because it is protected by technical protection measures or if material is no longer freely available. Hyperlinks to that kind of material will involve a communication to the public and will amount to an infringement if no authorization is obtained from the right holder.[119] The CJEU later held that the *Svensson* approach also applied to framing.[120] On the other hand, the right of communication to the public requires in an Internet context that the work is made available to the public by electronic transmission in such a way that members of the public may access it from a place, and at a time, individually chosen by them. Providing a clickable link that unlocks access to the live broadcast of a sporting event does therefore not involve a communication to the public as the members of the public cannot choose the time.[121] Member states can, however, extend protection on this point. Similarly, the Court of Appeal referred the question whether a pure streaming service could amount to a communication to the public and whether s. 73 CDPA could in that case offer a valid defence to the CJEU.[122]

Making an adaptation

Making an adaptation of a literary, dramatic, or musical work is also a restricted act.[123] Adaptations of artistic works are excluded. The adaptation is made when it is recorded,

---

[118] Even if for the latter a form of targeting that jurisdiction may be required. Case C-173/11, *Football Dataco Ltd, Scottish Premier League Ltd, Scottish Football league and PA Sport UK Ltd v. Sportradar GmbH and Sportradar AG*, 18 October 2012, <http://curia.europa.eu>. The country-of-emission approach had been suggested by *Football Dataco Ltd v. Sportradar GmbH* [2010] EWHC 2911 (Ch).

[119] Case C-466/12, *Svensson v. Retriever Sverige AB* [2014] 3 CMLR 4, [2015] CEC 17; [2014] ECDR 9.

[120] Order of the Court of 21 October 2014 in Case C-348/13, *BestWater International GmbH v. Michael Mebes and Stefan Potsch*, <http://curia.europa.eu>.

[121] Case C-279/13, *C More Entertainment AB v. Linus Sandberg*, 26 March 2015, <http://curia.europa.eu>.

[122] *ITV Broadcasting and others v. TV Catchup and others* [2015] EWCA Civ 204.

[123] CDPA 1988, s. 21(1).

in writing or otherwise. Examples are the translation of a literary work into a foreign language, adapting a novel into a play, or making an arrangement of a musical work. The making of an adaptation of an adaptation or doing any other restricted act to an adaptation—for example, including it in a broadcast—is also an act restricted by the copyright in the work and will constitute an infringement.[124]

Authorization

It is not merely an infringement to do any of the restricted acts; it is also an infringement to authorize someone else to do them.[125] This issue came to the front in cases related to peer-to-peer filesharing websites when the question was asked whether the website operators were liable for infringement. The courts held the Pirate Bay website operators liable for authorizing infringement by their users, because the website facilitated the infringement and its hostile views on copyright encouraged users to infringe. Arnold J approved and applied the definition of authorization[126] given in the earlier *Newzbin* case by Kitchin J:

> In my judgment it is clear from this passage that 'authorise' means the grant or purported grant of the right to do the act complained of. It does not extend to mere enablement, assistance or even encouragement. The grant or purported grant to do the relevant act may be express or implied from all the relevant circumstances. In a case which involves an allegation of authorisation by supply, these circumstances may include the nature of the relationship between the alleged authoriser and the primary infringer, whether the equipment or other material supplied constitutes the means used to infringe, whether it is inevitable it will be used to infringe, the degree of control which the supplier retains and whether he has taken any steps to prevent infringement. These are matters to be taken into account and may or may not be determinative depending upon all the other circumstances.[127]

Secondary infringement

Copyright can also be infringed by dealing commercially with copies of works that attract copyright.[128] This is known as 'secondary infringement', because in all forms of primary infringement an infringing copy of the work is made, while in this type of infringement case these copies are only exploited commercially. The other main difference between primary and secondary infringement is found in the psychological element relating to the infringer: the intention to infringe, or the fact that one is infringing copyright knowingly, is irrelevant for primary infringement—it is also possible to infringe copyright unconsciously. In cases of secondary infringement, however, the alleged infringer must have had knowledge or reason to believe that his or her activity would be a secondary infringement of copyright.[129] This requirement is approached objectively. It should have been obvious to the defendant that his or her activity would infringe copyright.[130] Obviousness may be

---

[124] CDPA 1988, s. 21(2).   [125] CDPA 1988, s. 16(2).

[126] *Dramatico Entertainment Ltd and others v. British Sky Broadcasting Ltd and ors* [2012] EWHC 268 (Ch), [2012] 3 CMLR 14.

[127] *Twentieth Century Fox v. Newzbin* [2010] ECDR 8 at para. 90.   [128] CDPA 1988, ss. 22–6.

[129] CDPA 1988, ss. 22–6, each section *in fine*.

[130] It has been held that a failure of the claimant to provide details of the alleged infringement may mean that the defendant has no reason to believe that his or her activities infringe the claimant's copyright: see *Vermaat (t/a Cotton Productions) v. Boncrest Ltd (No. 2)* [2002] FSR 21.

tested by taking the 'reasonable man' approach:[131] would it have been obvious to a reasonable man that the activity would infringe?

Knowledge of infringement proceedings is not sufficient to establish that the alleged infringer must have had knowledge or a reasonable belief that the activities would be an infringement. Setting aside money for a fighting fund does not change that. On the one hand, this is a logical conclusion, because, in certain cases, the reasonable man might expect the alleged infringer to win the case;[132] on the other, the alleged infringer must make the reasonable man assessment in all of the circumstances and cannot escape liability for secondary infringement simply by relying on a representation, to the extent that no infringement is involved, made by a business partner who has a self-interest in the case. In one case, it was indeed held that a distributor of records could not rely on a representation that everything was in order, made by the recording company involved, to escape secondary infringement liability.[133] Newspaper stories and an interlocutory injunction in a foreign court should have led any reasonable man to the obvious belief that the activity would infringe.

Despite all of this, it is fair to say that the precise meaning of having 'reason to believe' is not entirely clear. What seems clear, however, is that there has to be more than mere knowledge of certain facts, because the facts need to lead to a belief. In the words of Morritt J:[134]

> Nevertheless, it seems to me that 'reason to believe' must involve the concept of knowledge of facts from which a reasonable man would arrive at the relevant belief. Facts from which a reasonable man might suspect the relevant conclusion cannot be enough. Moreover, as it seems to me, the phrase does connote the allowance of a period of time to enable the reasonable man to evaluate those facts so as to convert the facts into a reasonable belief.

Facts giving rise to a 'reason to suspect' are therefore not enough. The defendant must also evaluate all factors known to him or her, without accepting the claimant's assertions at face value, but also without ignoring them. The grounds for suspicion have to harden into grounds for belief, which has to be assessed on an objective basis—that is, by taking the reasonable man's beliefs into account, rather than the actual beliefs of the defendant. The defendant's evaluation will often involve him or her in making enquiries and the answers received will help to determine whether the defendant acquired 'reason to believe'. A defendant who fails to carry out sensible enquiries, having received assertions of infringement and who had 'reason to suspect', is, however, capable of becoming a person with 'reason to believe'.[135]

Various types of secondary infringement in the exploitation of copies of a work are listed in the 1988 Act. All apply in relation to any kind of work that attracts copyright and the list includes the following:

- importing into the UK an infringing copy of the work, if this copy is not imported for the importer's private and domestic use[136] (if we assume that a novel is translated without the consent of the copyright owner, you can import an infringing copy to read it at home, but you cannot import 10 copies to sell them as exclusive pieces in your book shop without infringing copyright);

[131] See *Infabrics Ltd v. Jaytex Shirt Co.* [1978] FSR 451, per Whitford J at 464–5 (a case interpreting the similar provisions of the previous Copyright Act). This approach, adopted by the courts before the introduction of the new criteria in the 1988 Act, will be continued: see also *LA Gear Inc. v. Hi-Tech Sports plc* [1992] FSR 121.

[132] *Metix (UK) Ltd v. GH Maughan (Plastics) Ltd* [1997] FSR 718; see also *Hutchison Personal Communications Ltd v. Hook Advertising Ltd* [1995] FSR 365.

[133] *ZYX Music GmbH v. King* [1997] 2 All ER 129, [1997] EMLR 319.

[134] *LA Gear Inc. v. Hi-Tec Sports plc* [1992] FSR 121 at 129.

[135] *Nouveau Fabrics Ltd v. Voyage Decoration Ltd & Dunelm Soft Furnishings Ltd* [2004] EWHC 895.

[136] CDPA 1988, s. 22.

- possessing an infringing copy in the course of a business, selling it, letting it for hire, offering or exposing it for sale or hire, exhibiting it in public in the course of a business or otherwise, to such an extent that it affects the copyright owner prejudicially;[137]

- providing the medium with which to make infringing copies of the work, which medium—such as machines—must be designed specifically for this purpose[138] (the double cassette or video recorder, for example, is not specifically designed for the purpose of copying films from one cassette to the other, because it can also be used to record legally something that is not protected by copyright, the length of which exceeds the maximum recording time of one cassette);[139]

- transmission of the work by means of a telecommunications system when it is likely that infringing copies of the work will be made due to the reception of the transmission (broadcasting the work will not constitute transmission of the work for the purposes of this provision);[140]

- permitting the use of a place of public entertainment for an infringing performance of the work (the person permitting the use of such a place will escape liability if he or she believed, on reasonable grounds, that the performance would not infringe copyright);[141]

- the provision of material or equipment required for the infringing performance, if the person providing the material or equipment knows, or has reason to believe, that it will be used for an infringing performance.[142]

These provisions all refer to the concept of an infringing copy of the work. This concept is defined in s. 27 of the Act. An item, the making of which constituted an infringement of copyright, is an infringing copy; items, the making of which would have constituted an infringement of copyright had they been made in the UK, or a breach of an exclusive licence agreement, and which have been, or will be, imported into the UK are also infringing copies, as are copies that are infringing copies by virtue of several provisions relating to the acts permitted in relation to copyright.[143] The latter are defences to copyright infringement and will be analysed in the next chapter.

Technical measures

Increasingly, copyright holders use technical devices to prevent the unauthorized copying of their works. This development will now get legal support to protect it, primarily against the persistent attempt by hackers and others to circumvent any such device or measure. The Information Society Directive describes a technological measure as *'any technology, device, or component that, in the normal course of its operation, is designed to prevent or restrict acts, which are not authorized by the rightholder of any copyright'*.[144] Member states are required to provide:

adequate legal protection against the circumvention of any effective technological measure, which the person concerned carries out in the knowledge, or with reasonable grounds to believe that he or she is pursuing that objective.[145]

---

[137] CDPA 1988, s. 23.　　[138] CDPA 1988, s. 24(1).
[139] *CBS Songs Ltd v. Amstrad Consumer Electronics plc* [1988] AC 1013, [1988] 2 All ER 484.
[140] CDPA 1988, s. 24(2).　　[141] CDPA 1988, s. 25.　　[142] CDPA 1988, s. 26.
[143] CDPA 1988, s. 27.　　[144] Information Society Directive, Art. 6(3).
[145] Information Society Directive, Art. 6(1).

The additional requirement that the measure must be effective is defined as the situation in which:

> the use of the protected work or other subject-matter is controlled by the right holders through application of an access control or protection process, such as encryption, scrambling or other transformation of the work or other subject-matter or a copy control mechanism, which achieves the protection objective.[146]

The implementation in the UK of the Directive, by means of the Copyright and Related Rights Regulations 2003, is a classical example of highly complex and detailed legislation. In essence, a distinction is made between the circumvention of technical devices applied to computer programs and technical devices applied to other copyright works. Technical devices applied to a computer program are defined as '*any device intended to prevent or restrict acts that are not authorized by the copyright owner of that program and are restricted by copyright*'.[147] When such a device has been applied to a computer program, the copyright owner and certain other persons are given the same rights that the copyright owner has in relation to copyright infringement. These rights are given if a person knowing, or having reason to believe, that it will be used to make infringing copies either manufactures for sale or hire, imports, distributes, sells, or lets for hire, offers or exposes for sale or hire, advertises for sale or hire, or has in his or her possession for commercial purposes any medium, the sole intended purpose of which is to facilitate the unauthorized removal or circumvention of the technical device, or if such a person publishes information that is intended to enable or assist persons to remove or circumvent the technical device.[148] A similar right of action and entitlement to a remedy is provided when effective technological measures have been applied to a copyright work that is not a computer program and a person does anything that circumvents those measures, while knowing, or having reasonable grounds to know, that he or she is pursuing that objective.[149]

This affects the act of circumvention itself, but there is an additional provision that deals directly with the devices, components, or services that are used to achieve circumvention. Member states are required to provide adequate legal protection against the manufacture, import, distribution, sale, rental, advertisement for sale or rental, or possession for commercial purposes of devices, products, or components, or the provision of services that are promoted, advertised, or marketed for the purpose of circumvention of any effective technological measure, or which have only a limited commercially significant purpose or use other than circumvention, or which are primarily designed, produced, adapted, or performed for the purpose of enabling or facilitating the circumvention of effective technological measures.[150] As the new s. 296ZB of the 1988 Act puts it:

> (1) A person commits an offence if he—
>   (a) manufactures for sale or hire, or
>   (b) imports otherwise than for his private and domestic use, or
>   (c) in the course of a business—
>   (i) sells or lets for hire, or
>   (ii) offers or exposes for sale or hire, or
>   (iii) advertises for sale or hire, or

---

[146] Information Society Directive, Art. 6(3).
[147] CDPA 1988, s. 296(6), inserted by Copyright and Related Rights Regulations 2003, reg. 24.
[148] CDPA 1988, s. 296(1) and (2), inserted by Copyright and Related Rights Regulations 2003, reg. 24.
[149] CDPA 1988, s. 296ZA(1), inserted by Copyright and Related Rights Regulations 2003, reg. 24.
[150] Art. 6(2) of the Directive.

        (iv) possesses, or

        (v) distributes, or

   (d) distributes otherwise than in the course of a business to such an extent as to affect prejudicially the copyright owner, any device, product or component which is primarily designed, produced, or adapted for the purpose of enabling or facilitating the circumvention of effective technological measures.

(2) A person commits an offence if he provides, promotes, advertises or markets—

   (a) in the course of a business, or

   (b) otherwise than in the course of a business to such an extent as to affect prejudicially the copyright owner, a service the purpose of which is to enable or facilitate the circumvention of effective technological measures.[151]

An important limitation applies though. Section 296ZF limits the measures affecting activity and devices to the circumvention of measures designed to prevent or restrict infringement. These are measures that deny a person access to a copyright work or that limit that person's capability to make copies once access has been gained. Measures that were designed to prevent pirate games on a console fall outside the scope of these provisions as they only prevent access once the infringement (the making of the pirate games) has already taken place. They do not prevent access to a copyright work and neither do they limit the making of copies of a copyright work.[152]

Apart from technological measures, right holders often add electronic rights management information to copies of the work, in order to be able to trace copies of the work, for example. The Directive defines such information as any information provided by right holders that identifies the work, the author, or any other right holder, or information about the terms and conditions of use of the work, and any numbers or codes that represent such information.[153] Member states are required to provide adequate legal protection against any person who knowingly and without authorization removes or alters any electronic rights management information, or who distributes, imports for distribution, broadcasts, communicates, or makes available to the public works from which electronic rights management information has been removed or altered without authority, if such a person knows, or had reasonable grounds to know, that by so doing he or she is inducing, enabling, facilitating, or concealing an infringement of any copyright.[154] In terms of UK copyright infringement in the new s. 296ZG of the 1988 Act:

(1) This section applies where a person (D), knowingly and without authority, removes or alters electronic rights management information which—

   (a) is associated with a copy of a copyright work, or

   (b) appears in connection with the communication to the public of a copyright work, and

   where D knows, or has reason to believe, that by so doing he is inducing, enabling, facilitating or concealing an infringement of copyright.

(2) This section also applies where a person (E), knowingly and without authority, distributes, imports for distribution or communicates to the public copies of a copyright work from which electronic rights management information—

   (a) associated with the copies, or

   (b) appearing in connection with the communication to the public of the work,

---

[151] Inserted by Copyright and Related Rights Regulations 2003, reg. 24. See *R v. Christopher Paul Gilham* [2010] ECDR 5 (CA).

[152] *R v. Higgs (Neil Stanley)* [2009] 1 WLR 73, [2008] FSR 34 (CA). See also *Stevens v. Sony* [2005] HCA 58.

[153] See CDPA 1988, s. 296ZG(7)(b), inserted by Copyright and Related Rights Regulations 2003, reg. 25.

[154] Art. 7 of the Directive.

has been removed or altered without authority and where E knows, or has reason to believe, that by so doing he is inducing, enabling, facilitating or concealing an infringement of copyright.[155]

The artists' resale right

A Directive has been adopted that puts in place a resale right for authors of an original work of art.[156] These works are mainly exploited through the sale of the original, or of a few copies of the work, and this is to be contrasted with the exploitation by means of multiple copies or uses of other copyright works. Some member states felt that this disadvantaged authors of original rights, whose works are often resold at a later stage for a much higher price. These member states had, therefore, introduced a resale right—or *droit de suite*—and the Artists' Resale Right Directive 2001 is an attempt to harmonize the existing rules on this point. The Directive was highly controversial, and the Council and the Parliament adopted very different positions.[157] Finally, a reconciliation procedure produced a compromise to which all parties could agree. The member states had to implement the Directive by 1 January 2006.[158]

Despite being strongly opposed to the introduction of an artists' resale right during the negotiations, the UK transposed the Directive into national law on 14 February 2006 by means of the Artist's Resale Right Regulations 2006.[159] The author of an original work of art shall be given an additional exclusive right as part of his or her copyright. This right is inalienable[160] and cannot be waived,[161] even in advance, but it can be transmitted on death[162] or transferred to a charity.[163] While the aim behind the creation of the resale right is clearly economic, these latter aspects emerge from its strong link with the person of the author and are reminiscent of certain key aspects of moral rights.

The right will entitle the author to a royalty, based on the price at which the work of art is sold on any occasion after the initial sale,[164] until the end of the copyright term,[165] as long as a professional market professional is involved in one way or another.[166] Sales between private individuals are exempted, because such a right could not be enforced for such transactions. The works that are covered by the right are any work of graphic or plastic art, such as a picture, a collage, a painting, a drawing, an engraving, a print, a lithograph, a sculpture, a tapestry, a ceramic, an item of glassware, or a photograph, according to reg. 4. In essence, originals are covered, but copies that are made by the artist or under his or her authority will also be considered to be original works of art if they

---

[155] Inserted by Copyright and Related Rights Regulations 2003, reg. 25.

[156] European Parliament and Council Directive 2001/84/EC on the resale right for the benefit of the author of an original work of art (2001) OJ L 272/32.

[157] See, in general, P. Torremans (2000) 'The Proposed *droit de suite*: A Critique and a Euro–Polish Comparison', in P. Torremans (ed.) *Legal Convergence in the Enlarged Europe of the New Millennium*, London: Kluwer Law International, p. 71.

[158] Art. 12 of the Directive.   [159] SI 2006/346.   [160] No assignments are possible: reg. 7(1).

[161] Artist's Resale Right Regulations 2006, reg. 8(1).

[162] Artist's Resale Right Regulations 2006, reg. 9. Unlike the UK some member states exclude transmission on death by means of a will. The Directive has no binding rule on this point and it is therefore under private international law left to the law applicable to the succession. Case C-518/08, *Fundación Gala-Salvador Dalí v. VEGAP* [2010] ECDR 13, [2011] FSR 4.

[163] Artist's Resale Right Regulations 2006, reg. 7(3)–(5).

[164] A resale after the first transfer of ownership of the work of art by the author is required: reg. 12.

[165] Artist's Resale Right Regulations 2006, reg. 3.

[166] Artist's Resale Right Regulations 2006, reg. 12(2)–(3).

have been made in limited numbers.[167] This will, for example, be the case for a limited series of numbered prints, or for any other copies that have (normally) been numbered, signed, or otherwise been duly authorized by the artist.

The royalty is calculated according to a decreasing scale in relation to the resale price:[168]

From €0–50,000	4%
From €50,000.01–200,000	3%
From €200,000.01–350,000	1%
From €350,000.01–500.000	0.5%
Exceeding €500,000	0.25%

In any case, however, the total amount of royalty payable on the sale shall not exceed €12,500.[169] Sales of less than €1,000 are not subject to the resale right as well as sales of up to € 10,000, on condition that the seller previously acquired the work directly from the author less than three years before the sale.[170]

The exercise of the resale right and the collection of the royalty can only take place through a collecting society. The artist is free to choose a collecting society, but, in the absence of choice, the task shall be carried out by the collecting society that manages copyright on behalf of artists: for example, the Design and Artists Copyright Society (DACS).[171] Those liable to pay the resale right are the seller and, if acting in the course of a business of dealing in works of art, the seller's agent, the buyer's agent (if there is no seller's agent), and the buyer (if there are no such agents). Liability is joint and several, and arises upon completion of the sale.[172] Those liable remain free to agree contractually with a third party, i.e. the buyer, that that party will bear the cost, but such a contractual arrangement does not affect any obligation or liability vis-à-vis the author.[173]

Third-country nationals will only be able to benefit from the right if their own national legislation offers a similar right to EU authors.[174] This should be seen as a way of encouraging other countries to adopt a resale right, which Art. 14 of the Berne Convention for the Protection of Literary and Artistic Works 1886 still describes as an optional right that contracting states are not bound to implement.

Finally, the right holder will have a three-year period, following every sale, during which any information necessary to secure the payment of the royalty can be requested from any art market professional involved with such a sale.[175]

An overview

In the aftermath of the implementation of the Information Society Directive, copyright provides essentially for three main rights, which are also available in a digital online

---

[167] Artist's Resale Right Regulations 2006, reg. 4(2).

[168] Which, according to reg. 3(4), is defined as *'the price obtained for the sale, net of the tax payable on the sale, and converted into euro at the European Central Bank reference rate prevailing at the contract date'*.

[169] Sch. 1 to the Regulations.   [170] Artist's Resale Right Regulations 2006, reg. 12.

[171] Artist's Resale Right Regulations 2006, reg. 14.

[172] Artist's Resale Right Regulations 2006, reg. 13.

[173] Case C-41/14, *Christie's France SNC v. Syndicat national des antiquaires*, 26 February 2015, <http://curia.europa.eu>.

[174] Regulation 10 and Sch. 2 to the Regulations.

[175] Artist's Resale Right Regulations 2006, reg. 15.

environment: the reproduction right, the right of communication to the public and of making available to the public, and the distribution right.

In relation to the reproduction right, authors have the exclusive right to authorize or to prohibit direct or indirect, temporary or permanent reproduction of their work by any means, and in any form, in whole or in part. Copying and borrowing remain infringements, irrespective of the analogue or digital environment in which they may take place. Similarly, a reproduction right is given to producers of films in respect of the original and copies of their films, and to broadcasting organizations in respect of their broadcasts, irrespective of whether these broadcasts are transmitted by wire or over the air (including cable and satellite broadcasting). The crucial element in this case is that it is accepted as a starting point that temporary reproduction, as well as permanent reproduction, amounts to an infringement of copyright if it is done without the prior authorization of the right holder. Such temporary reproductions are made on numerous occasions in a digital online environment.[176]

In a digital online environment, many works are no longer dealt with in hard copy, but they are instead delivered online. Right holders are therefore given a right to authorize or to prohibit the communication of their works to the public by wire or by wireless means. The most important aspect of this right is that it also applies to on-demand services, in relation to which the work is made available to the public in such a way that members of the public may access the work from a place and time that they have chosen. This removes the doubt that still existed on this point under the old existing legislation.

Producers of the first fixations of films receive an exclusive right to authorize or to prohibit the making available to the public, by wire or by wireless means, of the original or of copies of their films. Again, this right is explicitly held to apply also to on-demand systems and a similar right is given to broadcasting organizations in relation to fixations of their broadcasts. This right is independent of the way in which the broadcast was transmitted: transmission by wire, over the air, by cable, or by satellite are all included.[177]

The third right is the distribution right, which mainly affects hard copies of the work. The right applies to originals or copies of works that are distributed to the public through sale or otherwise.[178]

In addition copyright owners are also protected through the provisions on indirect infringement, but in relation to this type of infringement they will have to prove knowledge or reason to believe on the part of the alleged infringer.

Further reading

CONNOR, I., 'IPC Media Ltd v. Highbury-SPL Publishing Ltd' (2005) 27 EIPR 9, 338.

GARNETT, K., DAVIES, G., and HARBOTTLE, G. (2011) Copinger and Skone James on Copyright, 16th edn, London: Sweet and Maxwell, Chs. 7 and 8.

HAYS, T., 'The Evolution and Decentralisation of Secondary Liability for Infringements of Copyright-Protected Works' (2006) 28(12) EIPR 617.

HAYS, T., 'Secondary Liability for Infringements of Copyright-Protected Works' (2007) 29(1) EIPR 15.

KLEMENT, U., 'Copyright Protection of Unauthorised Sequels under the Copyright, Designs and Patents Act 1988' (2007) 18(1) Ent LR 13.

---

[176] Art. 2 of the Directive.   [177] Art. 3 of the Directive.   [178] Art. 4 of the Directive.

16

Defences to copyright infringement

Certain acts that constitute infringements of copyright on the basis of the provisions analysed in the previous chapter are permitted acts. In certain circumstances copyright will not be infringed because a defence is available making the allegedly infringing act a permitted act. These defences exist in order to restore the balance between the rights of the owner of copyright and the rights of society at large. They restrict the exclusive rights granted by copyright in cases in which it is felt that they go too far. This is particularly useful, because copyright is extremely wide in scope and its term of protection is long.

But before we start our analysis of the permitted acts or the exceptions to copyright infringement, it has to be emphasized that these exceptions are exceptions to copyright infringement only.[1] If a case also involves a breach of confidence, the exception will not apply to the breach of confidence.

The first two defences are of a general nature and are not listed in Ch. III of the Copyright, Designs and Patents Act (CDPA) 1988 as permitted acts.

Authorization or consent of the owner

Copyright in a work is not infringed if the owner of the copyright in the work authorized or consented to the allegedly infringing act.[2] No formal contractual licence to do these acts is required: informal, or even implied,[3] licences are acceptable. An amateur musician does not infringe the copyright in a musical work when he or she makes a copy of it with the authorization of the composer of the musical work who owns the copyright in it. In cases of joint ownership of copyright, a licence from all of the joint owners is required.[4]

Public interest

The concept

If the allegedly infringing act is in the public interest, this will provide a valid defence against the alleged infringement, despite the fact that the 1988 Act did not give the court any general power to enable an infringer to use another's copyright in the public interest. Instead, the public interest defence is based on the court's inherent jurisdiction to refuse

---

[1] CDPA 1988, s. 28(1).

[2] CDPA 1988, s. 16(2). See *Confetti Records, Fundamental Records & Andrew Alcee v. Warner Music UK Ltd (t/a East West Records)* [2003] ECDR 336 and *JHP Ltd v. BBC Worldwide Ltd* [2008] FSR 29.

[3] Although the use of an implied licence may lead to problems: see *Warner v. Gestetner Ltd* [1988] EIPR D-89; *Blair v. Osborne & Tomkins* [1971] 2 QB 78, [1971] 1 All ER 468.

[4] CDPA 1988, s. 173.

an action for infringement of copyright in cases in which the enforcement of copyright would offend against the policy of the law. This inherent power has been preserved by s. 171(3) of the 1988 Act.[5] This defence also applies to the law of confidence, but in that respect, it is based on different grounds.[6]

It remains difficult to determine precisely what is in the public interest in a theoretical way. What *is* clear is that the circumstances in which the court could invoke its inherent jurisdiction depend on the work at issue, rather than on the issue of the ownership of the work.[7] These circumstances include those in which the work was immoral, scandalous, or contrary to family life,[8] or in which the work is injurious to public life, public health and safety, or the administration of justice. Also included are circumstances in which the work would encourage others to act in a way that would cause such injury.[9]

The Court of Appeal's judgment in *Ashdown v. Telegraph Group Ltd*[10] makes it clear, however, that the public interest defence cannot be restricted solely to these circumstances—that is, to circumstances in which where there had been serious wrong-doing on the part of the claimant. The court held that the circumstances in which the public interest could override copyright were not capable of precise categorization or definition. This is in line with the public policy role of the public interest defence, which is to refuse an action for infringement of copyright if the enforcement of copyright would offend against the policy of the law. Like all such broad emergency brakes, it is not capable of precise definition.

Let us turn to the practical implications of all of this by way of the facts of the *Hyde Park Residence* case.[11] Photographs that had been taken from a security video recording of a brief visit paid by the late Diana, Princess of Wales, and Dodi Fayed to a villa in France were an infringement of copyright, and the publication of these pictures in *The Sun* more than one year after their tragic deaths could not be justified by means of the public interest defence—even if they showed that statements made by Mr Fayed's father were anything but accurate. The latter point could be made without there being a need for copyright infringement and therefore no circumstances remained that made it necessary to breach copyright in the public interest. All that could be said was that these pictures remained of interest to the public, but that is something rather different altogether.[12]

In general, in the copyright context, the defence is often used to justify publication of information in breach of copyright and confidence in the information,[13] because—especially when that information is embarrassing for someone—an attempt to use copyright to stop the publication of the information will be launched.

Freedom of expression

The interaction between copyright and human rights has been at the centre of attention in recent times.[14] The Human Rights Act 1998 incorporated into UK law the European

---

[5] *Hyde Park Residence Ltd v. Yelland* [2000] 3 WLR 215, [2001] Ch 143, per Aldous LJ at 160. See A. Sims, 'The Denial of Copyright Protection on Public Policy Grounds' (2008) 30(5) EIPR 189–98.

[6] *Hyde Park Residence Ltd* (n. 5) at 167.   [7] *Hyde Park Residence Ltd* (n. 5) at 168.

[8] See also *A v. B* [2000] EMLR 1007.

[9] *Hyde Park Residence Ltd* (n. 5), per Aldous LJ at 168.

[10] *Ashdown v. Telegraph Group Ltd* [2001] 4 All ER 666, [2002] RPC 235.

[11] *Hyde Park Residence Ltd* (n. 5).   [12] *Hyde Park Residence Ltd* (n. 5) at 168.

[13] See *Beloff v. Pressdram Ltd* [1973] 1 All ER 241 at 259.

[14] See C. J. Angelopoulos, 'Freedom of Expression and Copyright: The Double Balancing Act' (2008) 3 IPQ 328–53.

Convention on Human Rights and, with it, the Art. 10 right to freedom of expression. It is easy to see how a right to freedom of expression may clash with copyright, which creates an exclusive right in certain expressions—but that exclusive right takes the form of a property right and the latter is also protected by Art. 1 of the Convention.[15] These conflicting interests have been reconciled in the 1988 Act and that reconciliation has mainly been achieved by the following tools:

- the idea–expression dichotomy—that is, the fact that ideas are not protected and that freedom of expression is guaranteed by the option to express the same idea differently;
- the fair dealing defence, as will be seen later; and
- the public interest defence—that is, the denial of copyright enforcement in cases in which the inappropriate use of copyright would crush freedom of expression.

This is the argument that there are internal safeguards in copyright to deal with the issue. In most cases, these internal safeguards will indeed suffice, but there are cases in which that will not be the case and in which the application of copyright law will not suffice to solve the external conflict between copyright and human rights.[16]

The Court of Appeal recognized this in *Ashdown v. Telegraph Group Ltd.*[17] The newspaper had used substantial quotes from a (confidential) memo of a meeting between Paddy Ashdown and the Prime Minister. Mr Ashdown had dictated the memo and claimed copyright infringement. The newspaper defended itself by relying on the fair dealing exception, the public interest defence, and freedom of expression.[18] The newspaper mainly criticized the actions of those involved in the meeting, which made it harder to rely on fair dealing. The court therefore turned to the question of whether the right of freedom of expression could justify the verbatim publication of the copyright work at issue. It ruled that, in principle, the use of the exact words used by the author is not justifiable by the right to freedom of expression and the public interest defence, and that the alleged infringer could express the matter in a different way.

The court also recognized, however, that there may be exceptional circumstances in which the exact words and format were of interest to the public—that is, circumstances in which the point cannot be made without copying the exact words and or format used by the author. In this case, there was a need to use the exact words of the memo to convince the public that the newspaper had a copy of the memo and was able to give an authentic account of events—but such a reason justified only a short quotation and the real motivation for the large quotes had been commercially motivated in order to appeal to readers, rather than being necessary for journalistic reasons. Only those necessary quotes could be defended by invoking freedom of expression and, even then, the use of the work is not free. In other words, the freedom of expression argument may serve to avoid an injunction against use, but not to avoid a claim for indemnification.[19]

---

[15] The right of every person to peaceful enjoyment of his possessions in this Article has been understood in such a way that possession can include copyright.

[16] See M. Birnhack, 'Acknowledging the Conflict between Copyright Law and Freedom of Expression under the Human Rights Act' [2003] Ent LR 24.

[17] [2001] 4 All ER 666, [2002] RPC 235.

[18] See P. Masuyakurima (2004) 'Fair Dealing and Freedom of Expression', in P. Torremans (ed.) *Copyright and Human Rights*, London: Kluwer Law International.

[19] *Ashdown v. Telegraph Group Ltd* (n. 10).

Allowing an injunction to enforce copyright would be against the public interest in such a case.

Copyright not enforced in the public interest

The public interest defence can be used to punish anyone who acts against the public interest and who has a copyright interest that results from that act. The public interest concept will allow the courts in such a case not to enforce that copyright and infringers will no longer be liable for copyright infringement.

The concept was applied in this way in the *Spycatcher* case.[20] The House of Lords held that the book's author, Peter Wright, had acted against the public interest in revealing details about the operations of the secret service, because it is in the public interest that the operations of the nation's secret service are kept secret. His conduct could harm national security. The courts in this country would, as a result—or perhaps as a punishment—not enforce the copyright in his book *Spycatcher*.[21] In terms of the facts of the case, everyone was free to publish substantial extracts from the book without being liable for copyright infringement.

The rule can be phrased in a slightly wider way. The public interest can also be used to back positive action, rather than purely negative non-enforcement. It can be said that it is against the public interest that a convicted criminal should benefit from his or her crime and that he or she should therefore not be allowed to receive, or retain, profit directly derived from the commission of the crime. Copyright royalties for the publication of a book in which the crime is described should therefore not be paid to the offender and the courts are authorized to use the public interest principle to grant an injunction to that extent (upon the application of the Attorney-General).[22]

Alleged infringement is not relevant

Alleged infringement of copyright by the claimant does not, however, warrant the operation of the public interest principle. In this case, the private interest of a copyright holder is at stake, rather than the public interest. The (alleged) infringement of the copyright of a third party by the claimant, when he or she made the adaptation of the original work, is therefore not a public interest defence to the infringement of the claimant's copyright by the defendant's arrangement of a further adaptation of that first adaptation.[23] If the concept of originality is satisfied, the author of the first adaptation will receive copyright in it, notwithstanding the fact that he or she may, at the same time, have infringed the copyright in the original work.[24] Any damages for copyright infringement that the claimant recovers from the author of the second adaptation will have to be shared with the author of the original work.[25]

The concept of public interest needs, therefore, to be described narrowly.

---

[20] *A-G v. Guardian Newspapers Ltd (No. 2)* [1990] 1 AC 109, [1988] 3 All ER 545; see also *A-G v. Times Newspapers Ltd* [1992] 1 AC 191, [1991] 2 All ER 398.

[21] *A-G v. Guardian Newspapers Ltd (No. 2)* (n. 20).

[22] See *A-G v. Chaudry* [1971] 3 All ER 938, [1971] 1 WLR 1614; *A-G v. Blake (Jonathan Cape Ltd, third party)* [1998] Ch 439, [1998] 1 All ER 833.

[23] *ZYX Music GmbH v. King* [1995] 3 All ER 1.

[24] See also *Redwood Music Ltd v. Chappell & Co. Ltd* [1982] RPC 109 at 120.

[25] *ZYX Music GmbH v. King* (n. 23).

The Copyright (Visually Impaired Persons) Act 2002

New legislation has been put in place in the form of the Copyright (Visually Impaired Persons) Act 2002 to address the specific problems that are faced by visually impaired persons. This instrument allows the copying in large fonts—or in any other way that is necessary to make the work accessible—of copyright material to assist visually impaired people on the basis of a lawfully obtained copy of the work. This will no longer infringe copyright. The exception applies to literary, dramatic, musical, or artistic works, or to a published edition, in so far as the copyright owner has not made accessible formats of the work available on a commercial basis. On each occasion, a statement that the exception is used is a sufficient acknowledgement. Third persons can only make such copies for a visually impaired person if the amount that they charge for that service does not exceed the cost of making and supplying the copy.

The Act allows for the making of single copies for personal use,[26] as well as for the making of multiple copies by approved bodies.[27] In the latter case, commercial publication of the work copied is a precondition and the exception can also be replaced by a licensing scheme.[28]

The exemption was extended to other disabilities by the Copyright and Rights in Performances (Disability) Regulations 2014.[29] The beneficiary is now defined as a person who has a physical or mental impairment which prevents him or her from enjoying the copyright work to the same degree as a person who does not have that impairment. Leaving to one side the element of cross-border exchanges, this exemption also complies with the minimum requirements of the Marrakesh Treaty to Facilitate Access to Published Works for Persons Who Are Blind, Visually Impaired or Otherwise Print Disabled (2013).

The making of temporary copies

The implementation of the Information Society Directive[30] by the Copyright and Related Rights Regulations 2003, and the changes to the 1988 Act that resulted from it, have removed any remaining doubts about the fact that even temporary copies infringe copyright. Modern digital technology, such as computers accessing the Internet, makes frequent use of such temporary copies to access works, and declaring any such use an infringement was therefore an unduly blunt tool. The solution was the creation of a new s. 28A[31] of the 1988 Act, in which an exemption for temporary reproduction is contained. According to its wording, copyright in a literary work—other than a computer program or a database—or in a dramatic, musical, or artistic work, the typographical arrangement of a published edition, a sound recording, or a film, is not infringed by the making of a temporary copy that is transient or incidental; that is an integral and essential part of a technological process, and the sole purpose of which is to enable a transmission of the work in a network

---

[26] CDPA 1988, s. 31A, inserted by Copyright (Visually Impaired Persons) Act 2002, s. 1.
[27] CDPA 1988, s. 31B, inserted by Copyright (Visually Impaired Persons) Act 2002, s. 2.
[28] CDPA 1988, s. 31D, inserted by Copyright (Visually Impaired Persons) Act 2002, s. 4.
[29] SI 2014/1384.
[30] European Parliament and Council Directive 2001/29/EC on the harmonization of certain aspects of copyright and related rights in the information society [2001] OJ L 167/10.
[31] Inserted by Copyright and Related Rights Regulations 2003, reg. 8.

between third parties by an intermediary; or a lawful use of the work, and which has no independent economic significance. Only those temporary copies that meet all of these requirements will benefit from the exemption.

This means that transient and temporary acts of reproduction, such as those performed by a media-monitoring firm that scans newspapers for search terms and reproduces the term and the five words that come before and after it, can only be covered by the exception if it fulfils the five conditions set out in the provision: that is, the act is temporary (1); transient, or incidental (2); it is an integral and essential part of a technological process (3); the sole purpose of that process is to enable a transmission in a network between third parties by an intermediary or a lawful use of a work or protected subject matter (4); and the act has no independent economic significance (5). These conditions are cumulative. Any voluntary human process or intervention brings the activity outside the scope of the exemption.[32] In addition, the duration of the existence of the copies is limited to what is necessary for the proper completion of the technological process in question, it being understood that that process must be automated so that it deletes that act automatically, without human intervention, once its function of enabling the completion of such a process has come to an end. In *Infopaq* the data capture, storing, and printing exercise went well beyond this, especially as the decision to delete the copies was not automatic, but manual.[33] On the other hand the defence succeeded in the *Murphy* case in relation to the copies in the decoder and on the screen when satellite dishes are used to watch broadcasts in a private circle. The latter is not an infringement under copyright and the ephemeral acts of reproduction that enable the broadcast to be received have as their sole purpose to enable the 'lawful use' of the works. More specifically the Court of Justice held that the temporary acts of reproduction, carried out within the memory of the satellite decoder and on the television screen, formed an inseparable and non-autonomous part of the process of reception of the broadcasts transmitted containing the works in question and were performed without influence on, or even awareness of, the persons thereby having access to the protected works. Consequently they were, according to the Court, not capable of generating additional economic advantage going beyond the advantage derived from mere reception of the broadcasts at issue and as such could not be regarded as having independent economic significance and hence all the requirements for the exemption to apply had been met.[34]

This exception is of particular benefit to Internet service providers though, which will escape liability for activities such as caching.

Fair dealing

The Act allows 'fair dealing' with the work that attracts copyright. This means, roughly, that there will be no copyright infringement if the use made of the work is fair. The defence only becomes relevant when the part taken from the work is substantial; otherwise no copying arises in the first place and any defence is without purpose.[35]

---

[32] *Newspaper Licensing Agency Ltd v. Meltwater Holding BV* [2011] EWCA Civ 890, [2012] RPC 1. Case C-360/13, *Public Relations Consultants Association Ltd v. Newspaper Licensing Agency Ltd and Others*, 5 June 2014, <http://curia.europa.eu>.

[33] Case C-5/08, *Infopaq International A/S v. Danske Dagblades Forening* [2009] ECDR 16.

[34] Joined Cases C-403/08 and C-429/08, *Football Association Premier League Ltd and others v. QC Leisure and others (No. 2)* and *Murphy v. Media Protection Services* [2012] 1 CMLR 29, [2012] FSR 1 at paras. 176–8.

[35] Contra, but with respect, arguably wrong. '*Indeed once the conclusion is reached that the whole or a substantial part of the copyright work has been taken, a defence under (the fair dealing provisions) is unlikely*

The fairness issue will have to be determined by the judge, taking into account all circumstances of the case. The Act provides no definition, but restricts the defence to fair use for a number of purposes. In *Hubbard v. Vosper*,[36] a case on fair dealing for the purposes of review and criticism, Lord Denning described the scope of the fair dealing defence and how a judge should assess it when he said:

> You must first consider the number and the extent of the quotations...Then you must consider the use made of them. If they are used as a basis of comment, criticism or review, that may be fair dealing. If they are used to convey the same information as the author, for a rival purpose, they may be unfair. Next you must consider the proportions. To take long extracts and attach short comments may be unfair. But short extracts and long comments may be fair. Other considerations may come to mind also. But...it must be a matter of impression.[37]

There is no reason to restrict the scope of this quote to one particular type of fair dealing; it applies to fair dealing in general.

A number of factors are extremely important in the assessment:

- For which purpose was a substantial part of the work copied? The degree to which the challenged use competes with the exploitation of the copyright by its owner will be an important consideration.[38]

- What is the proportion of the copied part in relation to the whole work? The relevance of this extent of use will, however, depend very much on the particular circumstances of the case.[39]

- What motive led to the copying? If the motive was to compete with the original work, this is likely to make the dealing with the work unfair and the defence unavailable.[40]

- And finally, what is the status of the work from which a substantial part is copied? If that work is not published or confidential, the defence is unlikely to succeed;[41] the same conclusion is reached in case of a 'leak'.[42]

Although a number of quantitative elements are taken into account, the final assessment will be qualitative in nature. In practice, this means that, depending upon the circumstances of the case, the fair dealing defence may be unavailable for someone who copies only marginally more than the minimal substantial part of a work, or may be available, in the other extreme case, to someone who copies almost the whole work.

---

to succeed': Independent Television Publications Ltd v. Time Out Ltd [1984] FSR 64, per Whitford J at 75. In this view, the defence would justify only insubstantial copying, but insubstantial copying is no infringement. It cannot be accepted that Parliament included a useless and unneeded defence in the 1988 Act.

[36] [1972] 2 QB 84, [1972] 1 All ER 1023.

[37] [1972] 2 QB 84, [1972] 1 All ER 1023, per Lord Denning MR at 94.

[38] *Pro Sieben Media AG v. Carlton UK Television Ltd* [1999] 1 WLR 605, [1999] FSR 610, per Robert Walker LJ at 619.

[39] *Pro Sieben Media AG* (n. 38), per Robert Walker LJ at 619.

[40] *Newspaper Licensing Agency Ltd v. Meltwater Holding BV* [2011] EWCA Civ 890 and *England and Wales Cricket Board Ltd and Sky UK Ltd v. Tixdaq Ltd and Fanatix Ltd* [2016] EWHC 575 (Ch).

[41] *Hyde Park Residence Ltd* (n. 5), per Aldous LJ at 158. Art. 5(3)(d) of the Information Society Directive even makes the fact that the work must already have been made available lawfully to the public a prerequisite for the existence of the defence.

[42] *British Oxygen Co. Ltd v. Liquid Air Ltd* [1925] Ch 383; *Beloff v. Pressdram Ltd* [1973] 1 All ER 241, [1973] FSR 33.

In the end, then, *'the court must judge the fairness by the objective standard of whether a fair-minded and honest person would have dealt with the copyright, in the manner that* [the alleged infringer] *did'*.[43]

Research and private study

Fair dealing with a work may be for the purposes of research and private study.[44] This defence applies, first of all, to substantial copying in relation to literary, dramatic, musical, and artistic works.[45] It will allow me to copy a passage of a book on the history of Crete by hand, but a problem may arise if I use a photocopier to make the copy, because the typographical arrangement will be copied as well. Therefore, the defence applies also to typographical arrangements. This becomes particularly relevant in cases in which the work as such is out of copyright, but the typographical arrangement is not. There will be no infringement through the fair dealing with the published edition, indirectly affecting the copyright in the typographical arrangement, nor will there be infringement through fair dealing with the typographical arrangement itself.[46]

At present the exception does not apply to films, broadcasts, and sound recordings, but the government has issued a consultation on a proposed amendment that would bring these works too within the scope of the exception.[47]

Research

The 1988 Act distinguishes between fair use for the purposes of research, on the one hand, and fair dealing for the purposes of private study, on the other. Fair dealing with a literary, dramatic, musical, or artistic work for the purposes of research for a non-commercial purpose does not infringe any copyright in the work, provided that it is accompanied by a sufficient acknowledgement.[48] The key points to note are the exclusion of research for a commercial purpose and the need for an acknowledgement—but no acknowledgement is required in connection with fair dealing for the purposes of research if this would be impossible for reasons of practicality or otherwise.

The exclusion of research for commercial purposes is not entirely straightforward either. There is, of course, the obvious problem of defining research. Research may be said to be scientific by definition, and to involve a diligent and systematic enquiry or investigation of a particular subject, but the Act does not contain a precise definition. In addition, there is the problem that non-commercial academic research may, sooner or later, feed directly or indirectly into a commercial (scientific) publication. Would that make the original research commercial in nature? Or does the commercial nature of the research depend, to a large extent, on the environment in which it is carried out? Research by commercial entities such as companies would then, by definition, be commercial in nature, while academic research would be non-commercial (except, perhaps, for contract research). Sooner or later, the courts will have to provide clarification on this point.

---

[43] *Hyde Park Residence Ltd* (n. 5), per Aldous LJ at 158. In an EU context, see also Case C-117/13, *Technische Universität Darmstadt v. Eugen Ulmer KG*, 14 September 2014, <http://curia.europa.eu>.

[44] CDPA 1988, s. 29.

[45] CDPA 1988, s. 29(1) and (1C), inserted by Copyright and Related Rights Regulations 2003, reg. 9.

[46] CDPA 1988, s. 29(2).

[47] See <http://www.legislation.gov.uk/ukia/2014/154/pdfs/ukia_20140154_en.pdf>.

[48] CDPA 1988, s. 29(1), inserted by Copyright and Related Rights Regulations 2003, reg. 9.

In summary, the fair dealing exception for the purposes of research is subject to four conditions:

- there must be fair use;
- the use must be for the purposes of research;
- the research must be non-commercial; and
- there must be a sufficient acknowledgement of the source of the material that has been used.

Private study

Fair dealing with a literary, dramatic, musical, or artistic work for the purposes of private study does not infringe any copyright in the work either.[49] In relation to private study, there appear to be only two conditions—that is, fair use and use for the purposes of private study—but, in fact, there are three. Private study was always deemed to be non-commercial and this has now been made explicit in s. 178 of the 1988 Act, where the definition of private study excludes any form of study that is either directly or indirectly undertaken for a commercial purpose. There is, however, no need for an acknowledgement.

The publication in breach of copyright of a student textbook was held not to be fair dealing for the purposes of research and private study.[50] This book involved substantial copying to facilitate someone else's research and private study, the defendant itself not being involved in research or private study. This does not mean that the researcher or student has to make his or her own copies, but the person who makes the copies should not know, or have reason to believe, that the copying will result in copies of substantially the same material being provided to more than one person at substantially the same time and for substantially the same purpose.[51]

How much can be taken?

It is submitted that even the copying of a fairly large part of a work can amount to fair dealing with the work for the purposes of research and private study. Very large parts of books and, eventually, whole articles may be copied if the number of them needed for one's research and private study, in combination with the limited direct use of the information contained in them for the purposes of that research and private study, makes it impracticable to buy all of the books and to subscribe to all of the periodicals containing these articles. The situation will be entirely different when one book is used and a photocopy is made even though it would still be possible to buy a copy of the book (at a slightly higher price). In the latter case, the dealing with the book would be unfair.

The defence clearly aims to facilitate research and private study. Copyright should not become a financial and practical factor obstructing research and private study. There needs to be a balance between the interests of copyright owners and society in the good functioning of the copyright system, and the interest of society in the development, by means of the research and private study, of its members.

Computer programs

The observation, study, or testing of the functioning of a computer in order to determine the ideas and principles underlying the program will not amount to fair dealing. This exclusion is a logical one, because s. 50BA of the 1988 Act deals with this specific issue.[52]

---

[49] CDPA 1988, s. 29(1C), inserted by Copyright and Related Rights Regulations 2003, reg. 9.
[50] *Sillitoe v. McGraw-Hill Book Co. (UK) Ltd* [1983] FSR 545.   [51] CDPA 1988, s. 29(3).
[52] CDPA 1988, s. 29(4A), inserted by Copyright and Related Rights Regulations 2003, reg. 9.

Review, quotation, and criticism

The starting point

Fair dealing, for the purpose of review and criticism ('quotation' was added recently to the provisions by the legislator), applies to any form of work or to a performance of a work.[53] Copyright will not be infringed if a sufficient acknowledgement[54]—comprising the title, or another description, of the work and the identification of the author—is given[55], unless this would be impossible for reasons of practicality or otherwise.[56] The identification has to be to the audience and any wording or other indication that would make the reasonably alert member of the audience realize that the person that is identified is the author of the work will be sufficient.[57] The presence of the logo of the television company on the screen when borrowed images were shown was sufficient in this respect, because the majority of viewers would be able to identify the author in this way.[58]

The bottom line seems therefore to be that there needs to be sufficient acknowledgement, even if it does not amount to express identification.[59] It is fair to deal with one work in order to criticize another work or a performance of the work. There is no requirement that parts of only the work that is reviewed or criticized should be used; this book can be reviewed or criticized using parts and quotes from other textbooks on intellectual property. There is, however, a requirement that the dealing with a work should be for the purposes of review and criticism, whether of the subject matter of the work or of its style. Criticism of the work may extend to the ideas found in the work, but the defence does not cover those cases in which only ideas, doctrine, philosophy, and events are criticized.

Pro Sieben

Laddie J repeated this in the *Pro Sieben* case[60] when he ruled:

> The Act does not provide a general defence to the effect that it is permissible to fairly deal in any copyright work for the purpose of criticizing or reviewing that work or anything else[;] the defence is limited to criticizing or reviewing that or another work or a performance of a work.[61]

In *Pro Sieben*, the plaintiffs, Pro Sieben, had conducted an interview with Mandy Allwood and her boyfriend about Ms Allwood's decision to carry on with her pregnancy after it had been revealed that she was carrying eight live embryos, and a television programme had resulted from this. The defendants copied parts of the German programme and included it in one of their own programmes. It was held, in the High Court, that the defendants could not rely on the fair dealing defence to justify their copying, because

---

[53] CDPA 1988, s. 30(1). The issue of ownership of the work is entirely irrelevant: see *Hyde Park Residence Ltd* (n. 5), per Aldous LJ at 158.

[54] See *Sillitoe v. McGraw-Hill Book Co.* (n. 50).

[55] *Sillitoe* (n. 50); see also CDPA 1988, s. 178. There is no need to include the name of the author if the work is published anonymously (see *PCR Ltd v. Dow Jones Telerate Ltd* [1998] FSR 170) or if the name of the author cannot be ascertained by reasonable enquiry.

[56] As added by reg. 3(3) of The Copyright and Rights in Performances (Quotation and Parody) Regulations 2014, SI 2014/2356.

[57] *Pro Sieben Media AG v. Carlton UK Television Ltd* [1998] FSR 43.

[58] *Pro Sieben Media AG v. Carlton UK Television Ltd* [1999] 1 WLR 605, [1999] FSR 610, per Robert Walker LJ at 625.

[59] It all comes down to a matter of fact: *Fraser-Woodward v. BBC* [2005] EMLR 22, [2005] FSR 35.

[60] *Pro Sieben Media AG v. Carlton UK Television Ltd* [1999] 1 WLR 605, [1999] FSR 610.

[61] *Pro Sieben Media AG* (n. 60), per Robert Walker LJ at 625.

their programme did not criticize or review the Pro Sieben programme, but rather Pro Sieben's decision to pay for an interview.

The Court of Appeal later overturned that decision and held that the Carlton programme was criticizing various works representing the fruits of chequebook journalism, of which the allegedly copied work was only one example. In that context, there was reason to allow the application of the fair dealing defence. Indeed, fair dealing refers to the true purpose of the allegedly infringing activity in the sense of its good faith, intention, and genuineness. The court held that, in this case, the programme incorporating the infringing material was a genuine piece of criticism or review, rather than an attempt to dress ordinary copyright infringement up as criticism; in the latter case, the defence should not apply. One should be careful, however, not to rely solely on the intentions and motives of the alleged infringer. The notion that all that is required is for the alleged infringer to have the sincere belief, however misguided, that he or she is criticizing a work should not be encouraged. It is therefore better to construe the phrase for the purposes of review and criticism as a whole, and to treat it as the equivalent of making use of the work in the context of review and criticism.[62]

Once it has been established that proper criticism is at stake, that criticism should not be limited to criticism of style. The ideas that are found in the work and its social or moral implications can also be criticized. Carlton could therefore use the extracts of the Pro Sieben programme to criticize chequebook journalism and its consequences.[63] In finding that Carlton's actions were covered by the fair dealing doctrine, the Court of Appeal also attached importance to the fact there was no unfair competition with the copied work.[64]

Fraser-Woodward

The unauthorized use of photographs of David and Victoria Beckham, and their family, in a British Broadcasting Corporation (BBC) programme about celebrity journalism, and the links between the press and celebrities, provided an interesting factual background for a further analysis of the exemption for fair dealing for the purposes of review and criticism in *Fraser-Woodward Ltd v. BBC*.[65]

The court dealt, first of all, with the concepts of review and criticism. 'Criticism or review' was held to be an expression of wide and indefinite scope that was to be interpreted liberally. It is therefore not possible to define the boundaries of the expression precisely, and it is therefore not helpful to attempt to draw a distinction between bare comment and something that went further into criticism.[66] More importantly, criticism or review of the photographs could also extend to the philosophy or ideas underlying them, including the ideas or philosophy underlying a certain style of journalism, as manifested in the works themselves. But one should not confine the notion of ideas and philosophy narrowly, or see it in a strictly scientific sense: ideas and philosophy are merely a formulation of the extent to which criticism might extend. That review or criticism can be concerned with another work: in this case, the works of celebrity journalism.

In relation to the facts in *Fraser-Woodward*, this meant that the programme contained frequent shots of newspapers, their mastheads and stories, as well as pictures showing the public presentation of the Beckhams. All of the material was there to demonstrate a

---

[62] *Pro Sieben Media AG* (n. 60), per Robert Walker LJ at 620.
[63] *Pro Sieben Media AG* (n. 60), per Robert Walker LJ at 620.
[64] *Pro Sieben Media AG* (n. 60), per Robert Walker LJ at 624.
[65] *Fraser-Woodward v. BBC* [2005] EMLR 22, [2005] FSR 35.
[66] *Fraser-Woodward* (n. 65); see also *IPC Media Ltd v. News Group Newspapers Ltd* [2005] EMLR 23.

certain style of journalism—namely, the coverage of celebrity—and to comment on that style as manifested in the relevant publications. Various points were made about the fact that certain celebrity items were covered at all on the grounds of newsworthiness, the manipulation by the Beckhams of media interest in their lives, the extent of coverage, and the extent to which rival publications covered or disdained celebrity stories. Most photographs were used in that critical context and in order to illustrate the themes of the programme. Accordingly, these photographs were deployed in the context, and for the purpose, of criticism or review of other works—namely, the tabloid press and magazines. As such, the defence was deployed successfully.

Banier

Many of these factors were missing in another case[67] and therefore, when *The Sun* newspaper copied and published a photograph of Princess Caroline of Monaco without having obtained the prior authorization of the photographer, Mr Banier, it could not successfully invoke the defence. The photograph was not used to illustrate any review or criticism of the copyright work—that is, the photograph itself; it was plain copying and competing use, with an attempt to disguise it as review and criticism.

Factors to be taken into account

The aim of the defence is to give a critic or a reviewer a reasonable freedom of quotation or copying for the purpose of criticism or review. This means, as indicated, that one has to take into account the state of the reviewer or critic's mind at the time of the alleged infringement, but that one should also consider the likely impact on the audience.[68] The dealing with the work must also be fair, even in those cases in which the reviewer or critic had the right state of mind, in that he or she intended to deal with the work for the purposes of review or criticism. This does not mean that the judge should decide whether the criticism or the review is fair, but it does mean that the extent of the copying must be fair, in all of the circumstances, to support or illustrate the criticisms or the review.

The dealing or copying must be directed at supporting or illustrating the review or criticism; the defence cannot justify any other dealing with the work or any dealing with the work that goes further. Copying with the main aim of advancing one's own competing purposes therefore falls outside the scope of the defence,[69] even if it is accompanied by some review or criticism.[70] The examination of this point should not, however, involve a requirement for the defendant to demonstrate that no alternative way of reviewing or criticizing the work was available.[71] There is no requirement of necessity and it is irrelevant that the criticism or review might have been achieved without use of the copyright work as long as the requirement of fair dealing is met.[72]

Thus this defence will not apply in cases of copying in which there is neither review nor criticism, or in which there is only review and criticism to a minimal extent. It is not fair dealing with the correspondence between the Duke and Duchess of Windsor when extracts are published without review or criticism.[73] The defence covers any type of

---

[67] *Banier v. News Group Newspapers Ltd* [1997] FSR 812.

[68] *Pro Sieben Media AG* (n. 60), per Robert Walker LJ at 622.

[69] *Newspaper Licensing Agency Ltd v. Meltwater Holding BV* [2011] EWCA Civ 890, [2012] RPC 1.

[70] *IPC Media Ltd v. News Group Newspapers Ltd* [2005] FSR 35, [2005] EMLR 23.

[71] *Pro Sieben Media AG v. Carlton UK Television Ltd* [1998] FSR 43.

[72] *Fraser-Woodward* (n. 65).

[73] *Associated Newspapers Group plc v. News Group Newspapers Ltd* [1986] RPC 515.

review or criticism, from the most polite and laudatory forms, to the most scathing—or, in the words of Robert Walker LJ:[74]

> If the fair dealing is for the purpose of criticism that criticism may be strongly expressed and unbalanced without forfeiting the fair dealing defence; an author's remedy for malicious and unjustified criticism lies (if it lies anywhere) in the law of defamation, not copyright.

How much can be taken?

If the defence is to have any proper value, it has to apply to cases in which the review and criticism involve a substantial part of a work. In *Hubbard v. Vosper*,[75] substantial parts of confidential, as well as non-confidential, works—such as books and letters—written by the plaintiff were used in a book written by the defendant who was an ex-member of the Church of Scientology. The book was highly critical of the movement, and reviewed and criticized its views. The defence of fair use for the purpose of review and criticism was raised successfully against the alleged copyright infringement. The proportion of the work that can be taken may be large, but review and criticism do not require such large amounts of the work to be taken as what is possible for the purpose of research and private study.[76]

Further clarification on this point was provided by *Time Warner v. Channel 4*.[77] Channel 4 wished to use fragments from Stanley Kubrick's notorious film *A Clockwork Orange* in an arts documentary. Time Warner had withdrawn the film from British cinemas 20 years previously at the request of the director himself and was not prepared to give Channel 4 a licence to show the fragments. When Channel 4 proceeded without a licence, Time Warner obtained an injunction, which was lifted by the Court of Appeal, which accepted that Channel 4 was engaging in fair dealing for the purpose of the review and criticism defence.

In this case, the fragments shown by Channel 4 amounted to almost 10 per cent of the film. It is submitted that this high percentage of allowed copying under the defence was reached because of the very large amount, and high quality, of review and criticism equally included in the programme, and the fact that a documentary is particularly suited for review and criticism. But it gives an impression of how far-reaching the defence can potentially be.

A work that is available to the public

Fair dealing for the purposes of review and criticism is, however, limited in one important way:[78] the work that is used must previously have been made available to the public. Any infringement for criticism, review, and news reporting will therefore only be exempted if the work used has previously been made available to the public.[79]

A work has been made available to the public if it has been made available by any means, including the issue of copies to the public; an electronic retrieval system; the rental or lending of copies of the work to the public; the performance, exhibition, playing, or showing of the work in public; and the communication to the public of the work. In

---

[74] *Pro Sieben Media AG* (n. 60) at 619.   [75] [1972] 2 QB 84, [1972] 1 All ER 1023.

[76] See *Hubbard v. Vosper* [1972] 2 QB 84, [1972] 1 All ER 1023; *Walter v. Steinkopff* [1892] 3 Ch 489.

[77] *Time Warner Entertainments Co. v. Channel 4 Television plc* (1993) The Independent, 23 October, [1994] EMLR 1 (CA).

[78] CDPA 1988, s. 30, as amended by Copyright and Related Rights Regulations 2003, reg. 10.

[79] Because the diaries of the Prince of Wales had not previously been made available to the public, the defence failed in *HRH Prince of Wales v. Associated Newspapers Ltd* [2006] ECDR 20, upheld on appeal [2007] 3 WLR 222.

determining generally whether a work has been made available to the public, no account shall be taken of any unauthorized act.[80]

Quotation

Until recently there was no explicit exception for quotation. The Copyright and Rights in Performances (Quotation and Parody) Regulations 2014 remedied this and inserted a fair dealing exception for quotation in the exception for review and criticism. The quotation does not necessarily have to be for the purposes of review or criticism though. There are merely four requirements:

- (a) the work has been made available to the public,
- (b) the use of the quotation is fair dealing with the work,
- (c) the extent of the quotation is no more than is required by the specific purpose for which it is used, and
- (d) the quotation is accompanied by a sufficient acknowledgement (unless this would be impossible for reasons of practicality or otherwise).[81]

This quotation exception cannot be departed from by contract.[82]

A summary of conditions

In summary, four conditions need to be met for the exception of fair dealing for the purpose of review and criticism to apply:

1. The use has to be fair.
2. The use must be for the purposes of review and criticism or for the purposes of quotation.
3. There must be a sufficient acknowledgement.
4. The work must have been made available to the public.

The concept of fairness is itself linked to certain requirements that were set out by Mann J in *Fraser-Woodward*:

1. Regard should be had to the motives of the user.
2. Fair dealing is a matter of impression.
3. The amount of the work used is relevant and excessive use could render the use of the work unfair.
4. The court can have regard to the purpose of the use to determine whether it is a genuine piece of review or criticism or something else.[83]

Finally, the three-step test found in the international treaties and the Information Society Directive comes into play. Indeed, irrespective of the factors mentioned, the use should not unreasonably prejudice the legitimate interests of the author or conflict with the author's normal exploitation of the work. It follows that risk to the commercial value of the copyright of the work involved might go towards demonstrating unfairness, even if no damage or risk makes any use of the material unfair.[84] The three-step test is not a separate requirement, but it is clearly part of any determination of fairness.

---

[80] CDPA 1988, s. 30(1A).   [81] CDPA 1988, s. 30(1ZA), inserted by reg. 3(4), SI 2014/2356,
[82] Inserted by reg. 3(6), SI 2014/2356,   [83] *Fraser-Woodward* (n. 65).
[84] *Fraser-Woodward* (n. 65); see also *IPC Media Ltd v. News Group Newspapers Ltd* [2005] EMLR 23, in which it was held that the issue of whether the work was commercially competing with the exploitation of the copyright work was the most important factor in assessing fair dealing.

Reporting current events

The defence includes fair dealing with a work in order to report current events. Copyright will not be infringed unless the work is a photograph. Newspapers quite often copy stories that were published 24 hours earlier by another newspaper. The defence covers this, but, without copyright permission, they will not be able to copy the photograph accompanying the story. A sufficient acknowledgement is required.[85] Due to practical problems and the speed at which these media work, an acknowledgement is not required in connection with the reporting of current events by means of a sound recording, film, or broadcast, if this would be impossible for reasons of practicality or otherwise.[86]

It is hard to understand why the special treatment accorded to photographs should not be applied to broadcasts and films. The definition of the concept of 'current events' is an important issue in this respect. That concept must include all matters of current interest or concern,[87] as opposed to matters of historical interest or concern. On top of that, the concept should be construed liberally and the fair use of copyright material cannot be restricted, for example, to the reporting of news events that are less than 24 hours old.[88]

In a case in which the defendant copied substantial parts of the plaintiff's reports of the current status of cacao crops around the world,[89] the defendant could argue that the following points came within the concept of current events:

- the fact that the reports had been published;
- the broad substance of the reports;
- the impact of the reports on the market.

The defendant could copy parts of the reports to report these issues, but, once more, the nature and the extent of the copying should not go beyond what is reasonable and appropriate to report these current events.[90]

This last decision is ultimately one of impression. In the *Cacoa Reports* case, it was held that the copying of the full pod-count report went beyond what is fair dealing to report the current events as described. In this case, the concept of fair dealing involved a balancing of the interests of the owner of the copyright and those of the news reporter.[91]

Caricature, parody, or pastiche

The Copyright and Rights in Performances (Quotation and Parody) Regulations 2014 introduced an explicit exception for caricature, parody, or pastiche into the CDPA 1988 in the form of a new fair dealing s. 30A.[92] In the original version of the Act there was no such exception and other fair dealing exceptions had to be relied on, but these have their obvious limitations. The new exception does not attempt to define caricature, parody, or pastiche or to distinguish between them. It merely states that 'fair dealing with a work for the purposes of caricature, parody or pastiche does not infringe copyright in the

---

[85] CDPA 1988, s. 30(2).

[86] CDPA 1988, s. 30(3), as amended by Copyright and Related Rights Regulations 2003, reg. 10; see also *BBC v. British Satellite Broadcasting Ltd* [1992] Ch 141, [1991] 3 All ER 833.

[87] See *Pro Sieben Media AG* (n. 60), per Robert Walker LJ at 625.

[88] *Pro Sieben Media AG v. Carlton UK Television Ltd* [1998] FSR 43 and *England and Wales Cricket Board Ltd and Sky UK Ltd v. Tixdaq Ltd and Fanatix Ltd* [2016] EWHC 575 (Ch).

[89] *PCR Ltd v. Dow Jones Telerate Ltd* [1998] FSR 170.   [90] See *Hyde Park Residence Ltd* (n. 5).

[91] CDPA 1988, s. 36A.   [92] Inserted by reg. 5, SI 2014/2356.

work'. But this is, according to s. 30A(2), another exception that cannot be overruled contractually.

The legislature left it, in other words, to the courts to define the concepts of caricature, parody, and pastiche. The CJEU beat the UK courts to that task in the *Deckmyn* case.[93] The Court ruled that the concept of a parody comprises two essential characteristics. First, the parody has to evoke the existing work that is being parodied, while being noticeably different. One could argue that this means that the public should by no means confuse the parody with the original work. Second the parody has to constitute an expression of humour or mockery. It is suggested that the term humour should be interpreted broadly to include any form of review, comment, or criticism. The Court specifically rejected any other criteria such as the originality of the parody or the need to demonstrate that one needed to borrow as much as one did, that it can be attributed to another author, or that it should relate to the parodied work or mention the source of the parodied work. The only additional guidance provided by the Court refers to the need to strike a fair balance between the rights of the right holder, on the one hand, and the interests of the user of the exception, on the other hand. That includes the nondiscrimination principle and respect for fundamental rights and in a UK context the element of fairness should allow the courts to achieve such a balance with the contours of the exception.

Incidental inclusion

When a foreign tourist visits London and takes some photographs, it is almost inevitable that at least one of the photographs will include a work protected by copyright, such as a building, an artistic work, or simply the front page of a newspaper. The same applies when a television news crew films a demonstration in the city and the report is broadcast. It is not feasible to require that, on each of these occasions, copyright permission is obtained in advance or it would be impossible to make these photographs, films, and broadcasts. The 1988 Act gets around this problem by introducing a rule that copyright in a work that is accidentally included in an artistic work, a sound recording, a film, or a broadcast will not be infringed.[94]

Subsequent dealings with the work in which another work was accidentally included are also exempted.[95] Copies can be issued to the public, the work can be shown or played, or it can be broadcast. The film made in the city can be broadcast without infringing indirectly the copyright in the works accidentally included in it. But the inclusion must be accidental: this defence will not be available if a work is included deliberately. If we go back to our news crew, they may decide to add some background music to the soundtrack of the film. The background music will not be included accidentally and, if the copying through the inclusion is substantial, copyright in the musical work will be infringed if no advance copyright permission was obtained.

This rule applies to all musical works, lyrics, and all works embodying them.[96] In *Hawkes & Sons (London) Ltd v. Paramount Film Service Ltd*,[97] copyright infringement took place and the accidental inclusion defence did not apply, because the 28 bars of the march 'Colonel Bogey' were included deliberately in the newsreel as background music. The outcome of the case would have been different if the newsreel's

[93] Case C-201/13, *Deckmyn v. Vandersteen* [2014] ECDR 21.   [94] CDPA 1988, s. 31(1).
[95] CDPA 1988, s. 31(2).   [96] CDPA 1988, s. 31(3).   [97] [1934] Ch 593.

topic had been a parade by a band playing the march. Then, the inclusion of part of the march—recorded live during the parade together with the images—would have been accidental.

The Court of Appeal handed down a major judgment interpreting the scope of this defence to copyright infringement in *Football Association Premier League Ltd v. Panini UK Ltd.*[98] Panini had reproduced, without the permission of the claimant, photographs of football players. These included the logos of the football clubs and of the Premier League, in which the claimants claimed copyright. Panini argued that the logos had been included incidentally. A first important point mentioned by the Court of Appeal is that incidental inclusion does not rule out that the work is included in its entirety and is therefore not limited to partial inclusion. More importantly, though, the Court of Appeal ruled that one must look at all of the circumstances in which the derivative work has been created and the reasons why, in that context, the copyright work has been included. This evaluation can include aesthetic, as well as commercial, motives, but the incidental inclusion can hardly be defended on aesthetic grounds if the decision to include the work was based on commercial motives. In the case at issue, commercial motives had prevailed, because players pictured in their club outfits would probably enhance sales. The conclusion was, therefore, that the inclusion was, from this point of view, essential to success from an economic point of view and could therefore not be characterized as incidental.[99]

Educational use

Instruction and examination

Copyright will not be infringed if a literary, dramatic, artistic, or musical work, or a substantial part of any of them, is copied in the course of instruction or while preparing instruction if four preconditions are met.[100] The first two preconditions are that the person giving instruction or the person receiving instruction must do the copying and that it may not be done by means of a reprographic process.[101] When a student writes down a substantial part of a legal article in his or her essay in support of his or her own point of view, for example, copyright in the article as a literary work will not be infringed. Neither will it be infringed when a lecturer writes down the same quote on his or her whiteboard, for discussion with the students during a tutorial.

The two further preconditions are that the instruction must be carried out for a non-commercial purpose and that, where practicable, an acknowledgement of the source is required. On top of that, the copying of any literary, dramatic, artistic, or musical work that has previously been made available to the public must also meet the fair dealing requirements.[102]

In the same circumstances, copies of a sound recording, a film, or a broadcast can be made in making a film or soundtrack for the purpose of instruction, without infringing copyright.[103]

---

[98] [2003] 4 All ER 1290, [2004] FSR 1.   [99] See also *Fraser-Woodward* (n. 65).

[100] See Copyright (Educational Establishments) (No. 2) Order 1989.   [101] CDPA 1988, s. 32(1).

[102] CDPA 1988, s. 32(1). These extra requirements have been inserted by the Copyright and Related Rights Regulations 2003, reg. 11.

[103] CDPA 1988, s. 32(2), as amended by Copyright and Related Rights Regulations 2003, reg. 11. Obviously, the condition that no reprographic means can be used does not apply here.

In an exam situation, copyright will not be infringed by anything done in setting the questions, communicating them to the students, or answering them. But, even in an examination context, an acknowledgement is required.[104] The question can thus contain a large quote taken from a literary work before asking students to analyse it and comment on it. The only exception to this rule is the making of reprographical copies of a musical work that is to be performed by the students during the examination.[105] In this case, copyright permission is required.

This educational exception does not cover any subsequent dealings in the copies made for educational use. Copyright will be infringed when they are sold, let for hire, or offered or exposed for sale or hire.[106] A poem may be copied for the purpose of setting an exam question, but the subsequent sale of the exam paper containing the poem will infringe the copyright in the poem.

Anthologies

Short passages of published literary and dramatic works may be included in a book that consists of a collection of passages, mainly taken from works that are not, or no longer, protected by copyright. The book—known as an anthology—has to be clearly intended for educational use.[107]

Performing, playing, or showing a work

Literary, dramatic, and musical works can be shown, played, or performed at an educational establishment without infringing copyright. This can either be done by the students and teachers, in the course of the activities of the educational establishment, or by a third person, in the course of instruction. Students, teachers, and other persons directly connected with the activities of the establishment may form part of the audience,[108] but parents and any other persons that are only connected indirectly to the activities of the educational establishment may not.[109] School plays to which parents are invited will require copyright permission to perform the work.

Neither will copyright be infringed if a sound recording, film, or broadcast is played or shown before a similar audience, as long as the event takes place at the educational institution for the purposes of instruction.[110]

Recording, reprographic copying,[111] and lending

An educational establishment[112] may record, for educational purposes and for its own use, broadcasts.[113] Under the same preconditions, it can copy reprographically—in

---

[104] CDPA 1988, s. 32(3).   [105] CDPA 1988, s. 32(4).   [106] CDPA 1988, s. 32(5).
[107] CDPA 1988, s. 33(1).   [108] CDPA 1988, s. 34(1).   [109] CDPA 1988, s. 34(3).
[110] CDPA 1988, s. 34(2).

[111] See Copyright (Certification of Licensing Scheme for Educational Recording of Broadcast and Cable Programmes) (Educational Recording Agency Limited) Order 1990, SI 1990/879; Copyright (Certification of Licensing Scheme for Educational Recording of Broadcast and Cable Programmes) (Educational Recording Agency Limited) (Amendment) Order 1993, SI 1993/193; Copyright (Certification of Licensing Scheme for Educational Recording of Broadcasts) (Open University Educational Enterprises Limited) Order 1993, SI 1993/2755; Copyright (Certification of Licensing Scheme for Educational Recording of Broadcast and Cable Programmes) (Educational Recording Agency Limited) (Amendment) Order 1994, SI 1994/247.

[112] As defined in CDPA 1988, s. 174.   [113] CDPA 1988, s. 35(1).

practice, with a photocopier—passages of published works. The latter copying is restricted to one per cent of each work per term.[114]

If the educational institution stays within the framework of these two exceptions, copyright in the recorded or copied works will not be infringed. But these two exceptions have two further aspects in common. Copyright will be infringed if the authorized recordings and copies are subsequently dealt with, and both exceptions can, in practice, be superseded by a licensing scheme allowing the educational institutions to make recordings and reprographic copies subject to certain conditions.[115]

There is also a special exception to the lending right of copyright owners. Lending of copies of the work by an educational establishment[116] will not infringe the copyright in the work. As a result of the implementation of the Information Society Directive, ss. 35 and 36[117] of the 1988 Act—that is, the sections with which we are concerned in relation to this area—have seen the introduction of the requirements that instruction and education for commercial purposes falls outside the scope of the exemptions, and that, wherever practicable, an acknowledgement is required. The broadcast that has been recorded can now also explicitly be communicated to the public, albeit strictly within the borders of the educational establishment concerned. The government issued a consultation document early in 2010 in which it proposes to delete the latter requirement to take account of the needs for distance learning and to replace it with a best efforts clause that would cover the putting in place of technical measures to restrict access to persons linked to the educational establishment. One can in this respect think, for example, of a secure intranet.

Libraries, archives, and public administration

Further exceptions to copyright infringement are provided for the benefit of libraries, archives, and public administration.[118] We will only refer generally to a couple of these detailed exceptions; none of the acts specified in the following will give rise to copyright infringement.

The exceptions for libraries and archives only apply to those libraries and archives that are prescribed by statutory instrument.[119] A librarian can make one copy of an article in a periodical for a person who requires it for the purposes of non-commercial research and private study. It is essential that no person is supplied with more than one copy of the article at the same time[120] and that not more than one article from the same issue of the periodical is supplied.[121] Under the same conditions, librarians can copy part of a published edition of a literary, dramatic, or musical work.[122] The person supplied with the copies must pay the costs. The readers of this book will all be familiar with the system of interlibrary loans, and will recognize the legal basis for this system and the particular format of the copyright declaration accompanying them. The librarian or archivist may rely on the contents of that declaration: if the declaration is false, the person making the declaration will have infringed the copyright in the work

---

[114] CDPA 1988, s. 36(1) and (2).   [115] CDPA 1988, ss. 35 and 36.   [116] CDPA 1988, ss. 35 and 36.

[117] As amended by Copyright and Related Rights Regulations 2003, regs. 12 and 13.

[118] CDPA 1988, ss. 37–50.

[119] See Copyright (Librarian Archivists) (Copying of Copyright Material) Regulations 1989, SI 1989/1212.

[120] Multiple copies are banned by the Act.   [121] CDPA 1988, s. 38.   [122] CDPA 1988, s. 39.

of which he or she obtained copies, as if he or she made them him- or herself, and the copies will be infringing copies.

The lending of copies of a work by libraries or archives is also subject to a special regime.[123] The copyright in any work is not infringed by the lending of a book that is within the public lending right scheme if the lending takes place through a public library; neither is copyright in a work infringed through the lending of copies of the work by a prescribed library or archive[124] if that lending is not conducted for profit.

Librarians can also supply each other with copies of articles in periodicals or, if the identity of the person who can authorize the copying is unknown and cannot be ascertained by reasonable enquiry, the whole or part of a published edition of a literary, dramatic, or musical work.[125] Copies can also be made to replace copies of works that have been lost, destroyed, or damaged, or to preserve the original.[126] The latter will only be possible if it is not reasonably practicable to buy another copy of the work.[127]

Acts done for the purposes of public administration will not infringe copyright. In copyright infringement cases, copies of the respective works can be made in the course of the proceedings, judicial proceedings can be reported,[128] entries in the Register of Trade Marks can be copied, and copies of works can be made for the purposes of judicial proceedings,[129] etc.

Miscellaneous

Copyright infringement does not occur if buildings, sculptures, works of artistic craftsmanship, or models for buildings that are permanently situated in a public place or premises open to the public are photographed. One may also make a graphic work of them—that is, a drawing or painting—film them, and include a visual image of them in a broadcast.[130] The reconstruction of a building will not involve an infringement of the copyright that exists in the building or in the plans for the building.[131]

When artistic works are put up for sale, copies made for advertising purposes will not infringe the copyright in the artistic work. This will occur only if the copies are subsequently dealt with for other purposes[132]—that is, if they are sold themselves.

Video recorders, DVD recorders, and other recording devices are quite useful if you want to watch a broadcast that is emitted when you have something else to do or when you are not at home. You let the recording device do its work and you can watch it any time you want. There is only one small problem: you have recorded the broadcast and your activity may infringe copyright. The Act solves this problem by allowing anyone to record a broadcast for private and domestic use if this recording is made for the purpose of time shifting[133]—that is, the recording may only be made if it is made in order to view

---

[123] CDPA 1988, s. 40A.   [124] Other than a public library.   [125] CDPA 1988, s. 41.

[126] Which may be particularly valuable or fragile. The government consultation that was under way at the time of writing also proposes an expansion of the options open to libraries and archives in order to preserve rare and fragile works.

[127] CDPA 1988, s. 42.

[128] Obviously, this does not cover the copying of published reports of judicial proceedings.

[129] *A v. B* [2000] EMLR 1007, in which copies of confidential diaries had been made for use by the other partner in divorce proceedings.

[130] CDPA 1988, s. 62; copies may also be issued to the public.   [131] CDPA 1988, s. 65.

[132] CDPA 1988, s. 63.   [133] CDPA 1988, s. 70.

the broadcast at a (more) convenient time. Only in these particular circumstances is the recording exempted.

Sony Music Entertainment (UK) and ors v. Easyinternetcafé Ltd[134] was concerned with the scope of the time-shifting defence to copyright infringement. The defendant allowed clients to download material from the Internet and to store the files on a private part of the server used by it. Its employees did not have access to that part of the server, but offered a CD-burning service. Confronted with a claim of illegal copying of music files, the defendant ran the defence of time shifting. The court held that it had not been proven that the copies were made for time-shifting purposes and that, in any case, such copies were supposed to be made privately by the person concerned and not by a third party, such as the Internet café that was involved in the business for commercial purposes.

The Copyright and Related Rights Regulations 2003[135] have now further tightened up the conditions for the application of the time-shifting exemption. The exemption will now apply only if the act of copying takes place '*in domestic premises*', and if a copy that would otherwise be an infringing copy is made in accordance with the regulation but is subsequently dealt with, it shall be treated as an infringing copy for the purposes of that dealing; if that dealing infringes copyright, it shall be treated as an infringing copy for all subsequent purposes. The exemption in s. 71 of the 1988 Act for photographs taken of television broadcasts has been the object of similar changes.[136]

A club or society that was not established for profit and the main objectives of which are charitable can play sound recordings in the course of its activities without infringing copyright, if the proceeds of such activity are applied solely for the purposes of the organization concerned.[137] The Copyright and Related Rights Regulations have also tightened the requirements for this exception. Additional requirements have been added,[138] according to which it is required that the sound recording is played by a person who is acting primarily and directly for the benefit of the organization, and who is not acting with a view to gain, that the proceeds of any charge for admission to the place at which the recording is to be heard are applied solely for the purposes of the organization, and that the proceeds from any goods or services sold by, or on behalf of, the organization in the place at which the sound recording is heard and on the occasion when the sound recording is played are applied solely for the purposes of the organization. A local council that organized aerobics classes was held not to qualify for this exemption.[139] The status of the organization, rather than the activity, is of primary importance in this respect.

If anything done to an adaptation is exempted on the basis of the provisions analysed here, the copyright in the original work will not be infringed.[140]

Having been excluded from the scope of fair dealing, a new exception covering the acts of observing, studying, and testing of computer programs was in order. According to the new s. 50BA[141] of the 1988 Act, it is not an infringement of copyright for a lawful user of a copy of a computer program to observe, study, or test the functioning of the program in order to determine the ideas and principles that underlie any element if he or she does so while performing any of the acts of loading, displaying, running, transmitting,

[134] *Sony Music Entertainment (UK) and ors v. Easyinternetcafé Ltd* [2003] FSR 48.
[135] SI 2003/2498, reg. 19.   [136] See reg. 20.
[137] *Phonographic Performance Ltd v. South Tyneside Metropolitan Borough Council* [2001] 1 WLR 400; see also CDPA 1988, s. 67.
[138] See reg. 18.   [139] CDPA 1988, s. 76.
[140] European Parliament and Council Directive 2001/29/EC on the harmonization of certain aspects of copyright and related rights in the information society [2001] OJ L 167/10.
[141] Inserted by Copyright and Related Rights Regulations 2003, SI 2003/2498, reg. 15.

or storing the program that he or she is entitled to do. And if an act is permitted under this section, it is irrelevant whether or not there exists any term or condition in an agreement that purports to prohibit or restrict the act.

Once more, the Information Society Directive

In the subject matter covered in this chapter, the implementation of the Information Society Directive has been the source of quite a few changes; one additional important point is to be retained. Article 5(5) of the Directive formally adopts the three-step test of the Berne Convention for the Protection of Literary and Artistic Works 1886 to any exception. Exceptions can therefore only be introduced and applied if they refer to certain special cases, if these cases do not conflict with the normal exploitation of the work, and if the exception does not unreasonably prejudice the legitimate interests of the right holder.[142]

The inclusion of this overarching principle into EU law represents an important step, also enabling the use of the three-step test in interpreting the exact scope that is to be given to each of the exceptions under EU and national law.[143] It is arguable though that the test was essentially addressed to legislators and that the Directive should not be implemented in the sense that national courts will also apply the test a second time when applying an exception that has already passed the test at the legislative stage to the facts of an individual case. Such a doubling-up exercise risks restricting unduly the application of valid limitations and exceptions. It is therefore regrettable that the Court of Justice seems to suggest this approach in *Infopaq* as being the correct one.[144]

Orphan works

Orphan works, namely works protected by copyright but whose right holder is unknown or cannot be traced, create specific problems. Users may wish to apply for a licence, but they have no one to turn to and going ahead with their use of the work will lead to copyright infringement and liability. A new EU Directive[145] deals with a number of instances where this problem arises and it does so by creating what looks like an exemption. Hence its appearance in this chapter.

An orphan work is defined in Art. 2 as:

1. A work or a phonogram shall be considered an orphan work if none of the rightholders in that work or phonogram is identified or, even if one or more of them is identified, none is located despite a diligent search for the rightholders having been carried out and recorded in accordance with Article 3.

2. Where there is more than one rightholder in a work or phonogram, and not all of them have been identified or, even if identified, located after a diligent search has

---

[142] See C. Geiger, J. Griffiths, and R. M. Hilty, 'Declaration on a Balanced Interpretation of the "Three-Step Test" in Copyright Law' (2008) 39(6) IIC 707–13. Also published as C. Geiger, J. Griffiths and R. M. Hilty, 'Towards a Balanced Interpretation of the "Three-Step Test" in Copyright Law' (2008) 30(12) EIPR 489–96.

[143] See M. Senftleben (2004) *Copyright, Limitations and the Three-Step Test: An Analysis of the Three-Step Test in International and EC Copyright Law*, London: Kluwer Law International.

[144] Case C-5/08, *Infopaq International A/S v. Danske Dagblades Forening* [2009] ECDR 16.

[145] Directive 2012/28/EU of the European Parliament and of the Council of 25 October 2012 on certain permitted uses of orphan works [2012] OJ L299/5.

been carried out and recorded in accordance with Article 3, the work or phonogram may be used in accordance with this Directive provided that the rightholders that have been identified and located have, in relation to the rights they hold, authorised the organisations referred to in Article 1(1) to carry out the acts of reproduction and making available to the public covered respectively by Articles 2 and 3 of Directive 2001/29/EC.

Article 1(2) provides:

The Directive applies to:

(a) works published in the form of books, journals, newspapers, magazines or other writings contained in the collections of publicly accessible libraries, educational establishments or museums as well as in the collections of archives or of film or audio heritage institutions;

(b) cinematographic or audiovisual works and phonograms contained in the collections of publicly accessible libraries, educational establishments or museums as well as in the collections of archives or of film or audio heritage institutions; and

(c) cinematographic or audiovisual works and phonograms produced by public-service broadcasting organisations up to and including 31 December 2002 and contained in their archives;

which are protected by copyright or related rights and which are first published in a Member State or, in the absence of publication, first broadcast in a Member State.[146]

The Directive also applies to such works and phonograms which have never been published or broadcast but which have been made publicly accessible by the organizations referred to in paragraph 1 with the consent of the right holders, provided that it is reasonable to assume that the right holders would not oppose the use.[147] In addition the Directive shall also apply to works and other protected subject matter that are embedded or incorporated in, or constitute an integral part of, the works or phonograms. This means for example that whilst photographs as such are not covered by the Directive, they will be covered when they appear as illustrations in a written work.

The exemption created by the Directive will only benefit publicly accessible libraries, educational establishments, and museums as well as archives, film or audio heritage institutions, and public-service broadcasting organizations, established in the member states. And they will only be allowed to make certain uses of the orphan work in order to achieve aims related to their public interest missions.[148] But before any use is allowed one has to establish that the work is an orphan work. This is done through a diligent search carried out in good faith by consulting the appropriate sources for the category of works and other protected subject matter in question. Article 3 provides guidance on the format of the diligent search:

2. The sources that are appropriate for each category of works or phonogram in question shall be determined by each Member State, in consultation with rightholders and users, and shall include at least the relevant sources listed in the Annex.

3. A diligent search shall be carried out in the Member State of first publication or, in the absence of publication, first broadcast, except in the case of cinematographic or audiovisual works the producer of which has his headquarters or habitual residence in a Member State, in which case the diligent search shall be carried out in the Member State of his headquarters or habitual residence.

---

[146] Orphan Works Directive, Art. 1(2).   [147] Orphan Works Directive, Art. 1.
[148] Orphan Works Directive, Art. 1.

4. In the case referred to in Art. 1(3), the diligent search shall be carried out in the member state where the organization that made the work or phonogram publicly accessible with the consent of the right holder is established.

5. If there is evidence to suggest that relevant information on rightholders is to be found in other countries, sources of information available in those other countries shall also be consulted.

Once the diligent search has been carried out and the orphan status of the work has been established, that outcome shall be mutually recognized in the other member states and a central register shall be kept, making it unnecessary to repeat the exercise elsewhere.[149] But the right holder retains the right to make itself known at any stage and to end the orphan status of the work.[150]

The real crux of the matter is of course what is exempted in these circumstances and within these confines. The exemption will cover the right of reproduction and the right of communication to the public and is specifically aimed at allowing the orphan work to be made available to the public. The orphan work can also be reproduced for the purposes of digitization, making available, indexing, cataloguing, preservation, or restoration. Any use of the orphan work will have to be in order to achieve aims related to the public interest missions, in particular the preservation of, the restoration of, and the provision of cultural and educational access to, works and phonograms contained in the collection of the institutions concerned. The organizations may on the other hand generate revenues in the course of such uses, for the exclusive purpose of covering their costs of digitizing orphan works and making them available to the public. And any use requires the indication of the name of identified authors and other right holders and a fair compensation is due to right holders that put an end to the orphan work status of their works or other protected subject matter for the use that has been made by the organizations of such works and other protected subject matter.[151]

Member states had been given until 29 October 2014 to bring their national copyright laws in line with the Directive.[152] At the time of writing there is no indication yet how the UK intends to proceed in this respect.

An overview

Once we have ascertained that copyright does subsist in the work, we examine the allegedly infringing act:

- Is it a restricted act, such as copying?
- Has the act been done to a substantial part of the work?

Only if these two questions are answered affirmatively can there potentially be infringement.

There will nevertheless be no infringement if any of the next stages of our examination receives a positive answer:

- Did the owner of the copyright in the work authorize the act or consent to it, whether expressly or impliedly?
- Is the copyright infringement in the public interest?
- Is the act covered by any of the permitted acts?

---

[149] Orphan Works Directive, Art. 4.   [150] Orphan Works Directive, Art. 5.
[151] Orphan Works Directive, Art. 6.   [152] Orphan Works Directive, Art. 9.

Only a negative answer to these three further questions will allow us to conclude that the copyright in the work has been infringed.

Further reading

DE ZWART, M., 'A Historical Analysis of the Birth of Fair Dealing and Fair Use: Lessons for the Digital Age' (2007) 1 IPQ 60.

GARNETT, K., DAVIES, G., and HARBOTTLE, G. (2011) *Copinger and Skone James on Copyright*, 16th edn, London: Sweet and Maxwell, Ch. 9.

GEIGER, C., GRIFFITHS, J., and HILTY, R. M., 'Declaration on a Balanced Interpretation of the "Three-Step Test" in Copyright Law' (2008) 39(6) IIC 707–13. Also published as GEIGER, C., GRIFFITHS, J. and HILTY R. M.,'Towards a Balanced Interpretation of the "Three-Step Test" in Copyright Law' (2008) 30(12) EIPR 489–96.

MASUYAKURIMA, P. (2004) 'Fair Dealing and Freedom of Expression', in P. Torremans (ed.) *Copyright and Human Rights*, London: Kluwer Law International.

MITCHELL, P. and BOURN, S., '*HRH The Prince of Wales v. Associated Newspapers Ltd*: Copyright Versus the Public Interest' (2006) 17(7) Ent LR 210.

SENFTLEBEN, M. (2004) *Copyright, Limitations and the Three-Step Test: An Analysis of the Three-Step Test in International and EC Copyright Law*, London: Kluwer Law International.

SIMS, A., 'The Public Interest Defence in Copyright Law: Myth or Reality?' (2006) 28(6) EIPR 335.

SIMS, A., 'The Denial of Copyright Protection on Public Policy Grounds' (2008) 30(5) EIPR 189–98.

THEOBALD, T., 'Copyright Infringement or Is it Just Fair Dealing?' (2005) 16(6) Ent LR 153.

17

Rights in performances

The problem

Luciano Pavarotti adored live performances in front of mass audiences.[1] Imagine him performing, live at Wembley, a series of songs taken from Gaetano Donizetti's famous opera *Lucia di Lammermoor*. Someone in the audience makes a bootleg recording of Pavarotti's performance and sells it to a record company other than Decca, with whom Pavarotti had a recording contract. There is very little that can be done on the basis of the copyright rules that we have described in earlier chapters: Donizetti died in 1848, the copyright in the music and the libretto have long expired. The Decca recording is not copied or dealt with; the bootleg recording is an entirely separate and independent recording. No copyright infringement can be found, and both Pavarotti as the performer and Decca as the recording company are left unprotected.

This was felt to be undesirable, because both performers and recording companies[2] make a substantial contribution, and would be less inclined to do so if they were unable to secure a proper return for their contribution. Apart from the financial implications, the performer contributes to the artistic value of the work in bringing it to life and the recording company's entrepreneurial investment is considerable. To remedy the absence of protection for these groups under traditional copyright rules, the Convention for the Protection of Performers, Producers of Phonograms and Broadcasting Organizations was concluded in Rome in 1961.

Before the Copyright, Designs and Patents Act (CDPA) 1988 entered into force, the old rules[3] in the UK tried to offer some protection. The performers were given a right to civil remedies on top of the statutory criminal penalties in *Rickless v. United Artists Corp.*[4] The defendant took clips and discarded excerpts from old *Pink Panther* films starring the late Peter Sellers to make a new film without obtaining the permission of the actor's executors. The Court of Appeal argued that the statutory provision of criminal penalties created an obligation or prohibition for the benefit of the performers. Any aggrieved performer thus had a cause of action. The same Court of Appeal felt obliged, however, to deny similar civil remedies to a recording company that wished to act against the making of a bootleg recording.[5] Effective protection is only achievable when the interested parties

---

[1] Luciano Pavarotti passed away in 2007, but that does not affect the example. As we will see, rights remain in place for 50 years and rights given to the performer are transmissible *ex mortem*, by testamentary disposition or otherwise.

[2] See G. Boytha, 'The Intellectual Property Status of Sound Recordings' (1993) 24 IIC 295–306.

[3] See the Dramatic and Musical Performer's Protection Act 1925, the Dramatic and Musical Performer's Protection Act 1958, the Performer's Protection Act 1963, and the Performer's Protection Act 1972; criminal penalties were made available.

[4] *Rickless v. United Artists Corp.* [1988] QB 40, [1987] 1 All ER 679.

[5] *RCA Corp. v. Pollard* [1983] Ch 135, [1982] 3 All ER 771.

can enforce their rights themselves and have access to civil remedies. The old system could not provide that in all cases and was replaced by Pt II of the 1988 Act.[6]

Subsistence of rights

Rights in performances are given to the performers and to the person who has recording rights in relation to the performance. A performance, in this context, means a live performance by one person or a group of persons. It can be a musical performance, such as Pavarotti's performance in our example, a dramatic performance, a dance, or a mime. It can also be the reading or recitation of a literary work, a performance of a variety act, or a similar presentation.[7] This definition is extremely wide in scope. The consent of the performer(s) is required for any exploitation of such a performance.[8]

No film or sound recording can be made of a performance without the consent of the performer or the person having recording rights in relation to the performance. The latter will have an exclusive recording contract, such as that which Pavarotti had with Decca, under which he alone has the right to make the recording. The Act covers recordings made directly from the live performance, recordings made from a broadcast of the performance, as well as any recording made, directly or indirectly, from another recording of the performance.[9] Once again, this is a definition that is very wide in scope.

Term of protection

These rights in performances come on top of the rights conferred by copyright and they are independent rights[10] that expire after a 50-year term. The rights in the performance normally expire 50 years after the end of the calendar year in which the performance to which they relate took place. But if a recording of the performance is lawfully released during this normal 50-year period, the rule changes and the rights shall only expire 50 years after the end of the calendar year in which the first release of the recording of the performance took place.[11] The concept of 'release' includes the first publication, showing, or playing in public, broadcasting, or inclusion in a cable programme service of a recording.[12] Unauthorized acts cannot be taken into account to determine whether or not a recording has been released or to determine the date of release.[13]

---

[6] For a detailed analysis, see R. Arnold (2008) *Performer's Rights*, 4th edn, London: Sweet and Maxwell.
[7] CDPA 1988, s. 180(2).   [8] CDPA 1988, s. 180(1).
[9] CDPA 1988, ss. 180(1), (2), and 185(1).   [10] CDPA 1988, s. 180(4).
[11] CDPA 1988, s. 191(2).
[12] The Term Directive did not distinguish between publication and communication to the public, and such a distinction is therefore also not found in the current provisions of the 1988 Act. In order to avoid uncertainty over the term of a right if publication and communication to the public both took place, but on different dates, the Term Directive gave preference to the earlier date. The combination of two dates could, however, give rise to problems—especially because the date of communication to the public is not always easy to ascertain. The Information Society Directive (European Parliament and Council Directive 2001/29/EC on the harmonization of certain aspects of copyright and related rights in the information society [2001] OJ L 167/10) has, therefore, changed the system and gives preference to the publication of the phonogram to determine the duration of the right of its producer. Only in cases in which no publication occurs in the relevant period will the lawful communication to the public be taken into account as a starting point for the calculation of the term of the right: Art. 11(2).
[13] CDPA 1988, s. 191(3).

These rules are different from those that are normal in copyright, which refer to the life of the author: in this case, no reference is made to the life of the performer. The restriction of the term of protection to that offered in the country of which the performer is a national for performers who are not nationals of a European Economic Area (EEA) state, meanwhile, shows strong similarities with the copyright comparison of term regime.[14]

If we go back to Pavarotti's Wembley performance, his performer's right will expire 50 years after the end of the year in which the concert takes place. The situation changes when Decca makes a lawful recording of the concert. This constitutes a fixation of the performance and, assuming that no other communication to the public takes place, Pavarotti's performer's right will expire 50 years after the end of the year in which the recording was released. Decca's recording right expires 50 years after the end of the year in which the recording of the performance is released, assuming that the recording will be released before the expiry of the period of 50 years from the end of the year in which the recorded performance took place. The European Commission had launched a proposal to expand the duration of the term of protection for sound recordings.[15] The proposal met with a lot of opposition.[16] What emerged in the end is an extension for performances that have been fixated in a phonogram. From 1 November 2013 onwards member states have been bringing in provisions that offer 70 years of protection if the fixation of the performance in a phonogram is lawfully published or lawfully communicated to the public within 50 years after the date of the performance. The 70-year term shall run from the earlier date of first publication or first communication to the public. Performances that are fixated otherwise than in a phonogram will (still) only be entitled to 50 years of protection.[17]

The qualification requirement

The qualification requirement also exists for rights in performances.[18] The performance must be a qualifying performance—that is, a performance given in a qualifying country, or by a person who is a citizen or a subject of such a qualifying country. A country qualifies if it offers reciprocal protection.[19] The UK, the other member states of the European Union (EU), and some other countries designated by Order in Council are qualifying countries, but the complete list is much shorter because the Rome Convention has only been adhered to by approximately one-third of the states that adhere to the Berne Convention for the Protection of Literary and Artistic Works 1886. This weakens the international protection for rights in relation to performances, performers, and recorders. Progress has been made though through the inclusion of the basic principles in this area in the TRIPs Agreement.[20]

---

[14] The new term can only be shorter than that put in place by s. 191(2) of the 1988 Act; see CDPA 1988, s. 191(4).

[15] Proposal for a European Parliament and Council Directive amending Directive 2006/116/EC of the European Parliament and of the Council on the term of protection of copyright and related rights {SEC(2008) 2287} {SEC(2008) 2288} /* COM/2008/0464 final - COD 2008/0157 */, <http://eur-lex.europa.eu/LexUriServ/LexUriServ.do?uri=COM:2008:0464:FIN:EN:HTML>.

[16] See R. M. Hilty et al., 'Comment by the Max-Planck Institute on the Commission's proposal for a Directive to amend Directive 2006/116 concerning the term of protection for copyright and related rights' (2009) 31(2) EIPR 59–72.

[17] Directive 2011/77/EU of the European Parliament and of the Council of 27 September 2011 amending Directive 2006/116/EC on the term of protection and certain related rights [2011] OJ L265/1.

[18] CDPA 1988, s. 181.   [19] CDPA 1988, ss. 206–8.

[20] See now the Copyright and Performances (Application to Other Countries) Order 2008/677, which entered into force on 6 April 2008 and contains the revised longer list of countries.

Content and infringement

The content of the intangible right in a performance is best examined by means of the list of those acts that will constitute an infringement of the right. In general, the rights in performances are infringed whenever a performance is exploited without the consent of the performer, or whenever the performance is recorded without the consent of the person who owns the exclusive recording right. The consent of the owners of the rights in the performance is essential.[21] Helpfully, consent given in respect of one particular use does not mean that no consent is given for any other use unless there are special indications that further consent was required.[22]

The performer's right is infringed when certain acts are done to the whole, or a substantial part, of the performance. Within the scope of these acts fall:

- making a recording of the live performance,[23] which is not exclusively for private and domestic use;[24]

- broadcasting the performance live or including it live in a cable programme service;[25]

- making, otherwise than for private and domestic use, either directly or indirectly,[26] a copy of a recording of the performance[27]—that is, the reproduction right[28] (the making of a copy of a recording includes the making of a copy that is transient or incidental to another use of the original recording);[29]

- issuing copies or the original[30] of a recording of the performance to the public[31]— that is, the distribution right;[32]

- renting or lending copies of a recording of the performance[33] to the public;[34]

- making a recording of the performance directly from a broadcast of the live performance;[35]

- showing a recording of the performance in public, broadcasting it;[36]

- importing into the UK an illicit recording of the performance if the person importing it knows, or has reason to believe, that it is an infringing copy;[37]

- possessing, in the course of business, selling or letting for sale, offering or exposing for sale or hire, or distributing an illicit recording of the performance

---

[21] CDPA 1988, see s. 197.

[22] See *Grower v. British Broadcasting Corp.* [1990] FSR 595: consent given for the broadcasting of a recording of a performance in a radio programme does not exclude consent for other use of the recording in the absence of special indications to the contrary.

[23] CDPA 1988, s. 182(1)(a).   [24] CDPA 1988, s. 182(2).   [25] CDPA 1988, s. 182(1)(b).

[26] CDPA 1988, s. 182A(2).   [27] CDPA 1988, s. 182A(1).   [28] CDPA 1988, s. 182A(3).

[29] CDPA 1988, s. 182A(1A), inserted by Copyright and Related Rights Regulations 2003, reg. 8(3).

[30] CDPA 1988, s. 182B(4).

[31] CDPA 1988, s. 182B(1). Issuing to the public is defined in s. 182B(2) and (3) as including exclusively *'the act of putting into circulation in the EEA copies not previously put into circulation in the EEA by or with the consent of the performer'* or *'the act of putting into circulation outside the EEA copies not previously put into circulation in the EEA or elsewhere'.*

[32] CDPA 1988, s. 182B(5).

[33] See T. Dreier and B. Hugenholtz (eds.) (2006) *Concise European Copyright Law*, London: Kluwer Law International, pp. 245–58.

[34] CDPA 1988, s. 182C, in which 'rental' and 'lending' are defined.

[35] CDPA 1988, s. 182(1)(c).   [36] CDPA 1988, s. 183.   [37] CDPA 1988, s. 184(1)(a).

if the person importing it knows, or has reason to believe, that it is an infringing copy.[38]

Broadly speaking, these rights might be described as the reproduction and the distribution right. The Information Society Directive[39] and the Copyright and Related Rights Regulations 2003[40] that implemented it under UK law have added a third major right: that of making available a recording. Section 182CA of the 1988 Act now stipulates that a performer's rights are infringed by a person who, without that performer's consent, makes available to the public a recording of the whole, or any substantial part, of a qualifying performance by electronic transmission in such a way that members of the public may access the recording from a place and at a time individually chosen by them. The inclusion in this definition of a 'making available' right for performers, which can be seen as the equivalent of the right of communication to the public for copyright owners of on-demand services, is of vital importance in the digital age.

The performer is also given a right to equitable remuneration for the exploitation of a sound recording of the whole, or a substantial part of, the performance, but the right only applies to cases in which the sound recording is communicated to the public otherwise than by being made available to the public.[41] This remuneration is to be paid by the owner of the copyright in the commercially published sound recording when it is played in public or when it is included in a broadcast. The determination of the exact amount payable is to be determined in negotiations between the parties and, in default of agreement, the amount will be determined by the Copyright Tribunal. The right to equitable remuneration cannot be assigned, except to a collecting society that will enforce the right on behalf of the right holder.[42]

The rights of a person who has the exclusive recording right of a performance are infringed when the same acts are done to the whole, or a substantial part of, the performance, but the person having recording rights is not given the rights of reproduction, distribution, rental, and lending.[43] There is one further exception to this rule that the rights of such a person are similar to those of the performer: the recording rights are not infringed by a live broadcast of the performance or by the live inclusion of the performance in a cable programme service.[44] One might argue that this does not involve the recording of the performance, nor any dealings with illicit copies.

These lists contain forms of primary and secondary infringement, and bear similarities to the regime for normal copyright infringement.

Defences against alleged infringements

The defences available are very similar to those available in cases of alleged copyright infringement. They are contained in Sch. 2 to the 1988 Act: review and criticism, reporting

---

[38] CDPA 1988, s. 184(1)(b).

[39] European Parliament and Council Directive 2001/29/EC on the harmonization of certain aspects of copyright and related rights in the information society [2001] OJ L 167/10.

[40] Regulation 7.

[41] CDPA 1988, s. 182D, as modified by Copyright and Related Rights Regulations 2003, reg. 7(2).

[42] Regulation 7(2).

[43] These will nevertheless exist in relation to the copyright in the sound recording (or film) that results from the exercise of the recording right. In practice, the owners of these various rights will often be the same persons.

[44] CDPA 1988, ss. 185–8.

current events,[45] educational use (although it is slightly less extensive in this context), incidental inclusion, public administration, etc. It has to be noted that there is no exception for research and private study. The Copyright and Rights in Performances (Quotation and Parody) Regulations 2014 added a quotation defence, as well as a caricature, parody, or pastiche exception, to Sch. 2 and stipulated that these exceptions cannot be overruled by contract.[46]

The nature of the performer's rights and their transfer

Two types of right are given to the performer: some rights are property rights and others are non-property rights. The reproduction right, the distribution right, and the rental and lending right fall into the first category. They are the performer's property rights.[47] These property rights can be assigned and they are transmissible, just as any other item of personal or moveable property. Just as can any other assignment, this type of assignment can be partial, and needs to be in writing and signed by, or on behalf of, the assignor.[48] Normally, such an assignment cannot be presumed—but the Act contains an exception to this rule. This exception operates in cases in which an agreement relating to film production is concluded between a performer and a film producer. To avoid a situation in which too many persons—each of whom has made a small contribution to the film—need to give their approval for the exploitation of the film, the performer shall be presumed to have transferred to the producer any rental right in relation to the film. That rental right would arise due to the inclusion of the recording of the performer's performance in the film. The presumption is overturned in case the agreement provides to the contrary.[49] In any event, the performer retains always a right to equitable remuneration when he or she has transferred his or her rental rights concerning a sound recording or a film to the producer of the latter works.[50]

The performer is also given certain non-property rights,[51] which include the rights granted by ss. 182–4 of the 1988 Act. This list comprises all rights that are not specifically listed as property rights. The non-property rights in performances are normally not assignable or transmissible[52]—but the right given to the performer is transmissible *ex mortem*, by testamentary disposition or otherwise, and the exclusive recording licence, as the benefit of the rights in the performance, can be assigned, for example, from one recording company to another.[53]

Moral rights

At the international level, the Rome Convention, on which the rights in performances are based, never attracted the level of support that is enjoyed by the Berne Convention in the copyright area. The TRIPS Agreement only managed to provide a basic framework in 1994. The World Intellectual Property Organization (WIPO) tried to remedy this lack of international recognition for rights in performances and build on the minimum

---

[45] These three defences do not seem to require a sufficient acknowledgement, at least in cases in which it is not required by copyright itself.

[46] SI 2014/ 2356, regs. 4 and 5(2).   [47] CDPA 1988, s. 191A.   [48] CDPA 1988, s. 191B.

[49] CDPA 1988, s. 191F.   [50] CDPA 1988, s. 191G.   [51] CDPA 1988, s. 192A.

[52] CDPA 1988, ss. 192A and 192B.

[53] CDPA 1988, ss. 192A(2), 192B(2), and 185(2)(b) and (3)(b).

framework that had been achieved. That attempt resulted, on 20 December 1996, in the signing of the WIPO Performances and Phonograms Treaty (WPPT). This Treaty offers enhanced levels of international protection, and it is hoped that its link with the Berne Convention will convince the vast majority of countries to sign up to it and ratify it. It entered into force on 20 May 2002 and has rapidly been attracting ratifications ever since. One of its main achievements is that it gives the performer inalienable moral rights[54] and this is a significant step forward.

The UK has implemented its Treaty obligation by means of the Performances (Moral Rights, etc.) Regulations 2006.[55] Performers have been given a paternity right and an integrity right. The performer has the right to be identified as such when he or she performs live, when the performance is broadcast, when a recording of the performance is communicated to the public, or when copies of it are issued to the public.[56] That identification needs to take place in such a way that it is likely to be noticed by the audience.[57] No identification is required when it is not reasonably practical or when the performance is given for reasons relating to advertising or news reporting.[58] Unfortunately, the provisions do not offer guidance on what is meant by 'not reasonably practical': does this, for example, include a failure to name all musicians performing on a recording when it is played as part of a radio show? The moral right to be identified is not infringed unless the performer has first asserted his or her moral right in writing.[59]

The integrity right will be infringed if the performance is broadcast live, or if it is played in public or communicated to the public by means of a sound recording, with any distortion, mutilation, or other modification that is prejudicial to the reputation of the performer.[60] The performer therefore faces a high burden of proof. There is also a series of exceptions to the right of integrity. These include modifications that are consistent with normal editorial practice and performances that are given for reasons related to advertising or news reporting.[61] No guidance is provided as to the interpretation of the concept of 'normal editorial practice'. Possessing infringing copies of the work in the course of business or dealing in them is also an infringement of the integrity right.[62]

The overall approach that has been taken is therefore similar to that in relation to the moral rights of authors. It therefore comes as no surprise that the duration of the moral rights of performers is also linked to the duration of the (economic) rights in the performance.[63] The grant of moral rights to performers is clearly a positive development, and their similarity to the moral rights for authors underlines the increasing recognition for the creative efforts of performers and the role that they play.

An overview

Performers play an important role in bringing copyright works to a wider audience; recordings of their performances also make a vast contribution. The interests of those that are involved with performances are, nevertheless, not necessarily the same as those of copyright owners. Copyright on its own was therefore not sufficient to protect the contribution of those involved with performances.

---

[54] WIPO Performances and Phonograms Treaty, Art. 5.
[55] SI 2006/18, in force since 1 February 2006.   [56] CDPA 1988, s. 205C.
[57] CDPA 1988, s. 205C.   [58] CDPA 1988, s. 205E.   [59] CDPA 1988, s. 205D.
[60] CDPA 1988, s. 205F.   [61] CDPA 1988, s. 205G.   [62] CDPA 1988, s. 205H.
[63] CDPA 1988, s. 205I.

A separate set of rights in performances has consequently been created, which covers all aspects of the making of a recording of a performance and its subsequent exploitation.

The rights follow the commercial needs on this point. They involve a reproduction right, a distribution right, and a rental and lending right, but, recently, moral rights have been added, in the form of a paternity and an integrity right.

At the international level the protection for performers was further strengthened by the adoption of the Beijing Treaty on Audiovisual Performances on 24 June 2012. The Treaty offers copyright-style protection in the context of audiovisual fixations for performers, who are defined as actors, singers, musicians, dancers, and other persons who act, sing, deliver, declaim, play in, interpret, or otherwise perform literary or artistic works or expressions of folklore. It includes a paternity and integrity right and a 50-year term of protection. It will now have to be ratified and it can then filter through to the national level.

Further reading

Arnold, R. (2008) *Performer's Rights*, 4th edn, London: Sweet and Maxwell.

Bently, L. et al., 'Creativity Stifled? A Joint Academic Statement on the Proposed Term Extension for Sound Recordings' (2008) 30(9) EIPR 341–7.

Boytha, G., 'The Intellectual Property Status of Sound Recordings' (1993) 24 IIC 295.

Dreier, T. and Hugenholtz, B. (eds.) (2006) *Concise European Copyright Law*, London: Kluwer Law International, pp. 245–58.

Garnett, K., Davies, G., and Harbottle, G. (2011) *Copinger and Skone James on Copyright*, 16th edn, London: Sweet and Maxwell, Ch. 12.

Geiger, Ch., 'The Extension of the Term of Copyright and Certain Neighbouring Rights: A Never-ending Story?' (2009) 40(1) IIC 78–82.

Laddie, H., Prescott, P., and Vitoria, M. (2011) *The Modern Law of Copyright and Designs*, 4th edn, London: Butterworths, Ch. 12.

18

Dealing in copyright

In this chapter we look essentially at the commercial exploitation of copyright, both in a domestic and in a European context. In that context the existence of Crown copyright in the UK plays a role too. And commercial exploitation of copyright almost inevitably causes friction with the free movement and competition law aspects of the single market.

Crown copyright

It is clear, in principle, that works made by Her Majesty or by officers or servants of the Crown will attract copyright if they come within the normal copyright rules already described. But the Copyright, Designs and Patents Act (CDPA) 1988 contains a few special provisions in relation to Crown copyright. These rules apply to works made by Her Majesty and, if the works are made in the course of his or her duties, works made by an officer or servant of the Crown.[1]

It is clear that the Crown will own the copyright in these works.[2] If no special rules exist, the normal copyright rules apply. A first rule affects literary, dramatic, musical, and artistic works. The term of copyright protection for such a work is 125 years from the end of the calendar year in which they were made if the work is not published commercially.[3] The term of copyright protection is, however, reduced to the more standard 50-year term if the work is published commercially during the first 75 years of the 125-year term. This reduced 50-year term—which the UK may, in due course, decide to harmonize with the new standard term of 70 years—starts running from the end of the calendar year in which first commercial publication took place.[4] As we know, 'commercial publication' is defined by the 1988 Act as:

> issuing copies to the public at a time when copies made in advance of the receipt of orders are generally available to the public [or] making the work available by means of an electronic retrieval system.[5]

Most works that are protected by Crown copyright will be published as soon as they are created. In practice, the 50-year term therefore seems to be the rule rather than that of 125 years.

Acts of Parliament and Measures of the General Synod of the Church of England present us with another copyright particularity. They will attract copyright protection, owned by Her Majesty, for a 50-year term, which will start running from the end of the calendar year in which they received royal assent.[6] Parliamentary copyright is copyright in works that are made by, or under the direction or control of, the House of Commons or the House of Lords. The House will own the copyright in the works so produced. In

---

[1] CDPA 1988, s. 163. [2] CDPA 1988, s. 163(1)(b). [3] CDPA 1988, s. 163(3)(a).
[4] CDPA 1988, s. 163(3)(b). [5] CDPA 1988, s. 175(2). [6] CDPA 1988, s. 164.

general, these works are subject to the normal copyright rules, but the term of protection for literary, dramatic, musical, or artistic works is 50 years from the end of the calendar year in which the work was made.[7] In these categories, we find works such as reports of select committees; only parliamentary bills are catered for separately. Copyright in bills will expire when they receive royal assent,[8] or when they are rejected or withdrawn at the end of the session.[9]

While retaining the principle of Crown copyright,[10] the 1999 White Paper on the *Future Management of Crown Copyright*[11] introduced the idea of a waiver of Crown copyright in respect of, among other works, primary and secondary legislation, such as Acts of Parliament and statutory instruments, and their typographical arrangements.[12] The retention of the right guarantees the possibility of controlling the integrity of the works, while the waiver in respect of any enforcement enables their unrestricted use and wide dissemination. The dominating idea in this area is the government's idea of open government and the reuse of public sector information. Crown copyright should not stand in the way of the implementation of that idea, but it can be useful as a regulation tool. Copyright held by third parties is respected when it comes to the reuse of public sector information, but it is fair to say that copyright remains a thorny issue in this context.[13]

Commercial exploitation of copyright in the UK

Copyright, as a form of intellectual property, has the same kind of commercial value as any other property right. Its contractual exploitation can take various forms, such as a sale or a more restricted right to do something in relation to the subject matter of the right. Authors can exploit their works themselves, but they may not be interested in doing so. Often they do not have the financial, material, and organizational means to exploit their works, or at least to do so efficiently. They can then leave the exploitation to a third party. This normally involves the transfer of some, or all, of the rights in the work to that third party.[14]

Some aspects of copyright are, however, slightly peculiar: first, exploitation of copyright takes place through a material item in which the work is recorded. This implies that, if one acquires that material item, one does not normally acquire the intellectual property right as well. If I buy a book, as a recording of a literary work, for example, I buy the paper and the ink, but not the copyright in the book or any right in relation to the copyright, such as the right to reproduce the work. This separation between the copyright and the right in the carrier is a special characteristic of intellectual property rights.

Second, copyright works are normally still created by an individual author or by a couple of individuals. These individuals will normally rely on a third party to exploit their work and that third party is often a corporate body. This results in the fact that the

---

[7] CDPA 1988, s. 165.   [8] The copyright in the Act commences at this point.

[9] CDPA 1988, s. 166.

[10] See S. Saxby, 'Crown Copyright Regulation in the UK: Is the Debate Still Alive?' (2005) 13(3) Int JL & IT 299.

[11] Cm 4300, 1999, <www.opsi.gov.uk/advice/crown-copyright/future-management-of-crown-copyright. pdf>.

[12] Cm 4300, 1999, Ch. 5.

[13] Directive 2003/98/EC of the European Parliament and of the Council of 17 November 2003 on the reuse of public sector information [2003] OJ L345/90 and see <http://data.gov.uk/>.

[14] On the economic importance of the exploitation of copyright, see H. Cohen-Jehoram, 'Critical Reflections on the Economic Importance of Copyright' (1989) 20 IIC 485–97.

balance of bargaining and negotiating powers tilts almost necessarily in favour of the party exploiting the work, while the author is left behind as the weaker party.

Third, copyright offers only a weak form of protection, because only the reproduction of expression is protected. This leaves the idea of the work unprotected and leaves the author powerless to act against various things that can be done to his or her work, such as the production of a satirical work that clearly, through the borrowing of the idea, refers to the author's work. This reinforces the view that the author is in a weak position.

In the UK, we have historically not been too bothered about this: we have seen copyright as an entrepreneurial right that primarily protects the interests of the person who exploits the work. In contrast, Continental copyright emphasized the role of the artist—that is, the creator of the copyright work. The focus on moral rights is a good example of this emphasis on the artist. Now, we have seen the introduction of moral rights in the 1988 Act in the UK and we see the European Union (EU) developing initiatives in the copyright area: have we therefore arrived at a compromise? It is submitted that the use of the word 'compromise' would be misleading in this context, because it implies that concessions have been made on both sides; instead, what has happened is that the UK has moved towards a better and more complete set of copyright rules.

It is logical to start with the author. If the author does not create copyright works, there will be nothing to exploit and performing artists will have no works to perform. We may encounter the odd artist who keeps all of his or her works to themselves, but the vast majority of creators of copyright works want to see their works exploited. This can be explained by the desire to disseminate their work and the ideas behind it, or simply through the need for remuneration to allow them to keep creating works. The role of the person who exploits the copyright work is therefore in no way secondary in importance to the role of the author.

If we go back to the author who comes first, he or she becomes the first owner of the copyright in the work. The author is also given certain moral rights to compensate for the weak position in which he or she finds him- or herself and which we have described. These moral rights are minimal rights and, as such, they do not in any way obstruct the normal exploitation of the work, because they only allow the author to act against forms of abusive exploitation of the work. It is therefore extremely important—also taking the weak position of the author into account—that these moral rights are inalienable. It is submitted that the possibility for the author to waive the moral rights has no place in this system.[15]

The person who exploits the rights should also have an exclusive right. There should be a transfer of all economic rights if each of these rights has been contracted against an equitable remuneration. A producer who has acquired exploitation rights from authors or performers has to possess all of the exclusive rights that are required for an efficient exploitation in the interest of all right holders. Clearly, a right to act independently against infringers should form part of these exclusive rights. This should be the starting point of the legislation and it should be left to the contractual freedom of the parties to add to this set of rules or to derogate from it.[16]

The essential feature of this system is that neither party gains total control over each other: both are given parallel exclusive rights and this should incite them to cooperate, which is in the best interests of both parties and in the best interest of copyright.[17] It is

[15] See J.-F. Verstrynghe, 'The Spring 1993 Horace S. Manges Lecture: The European Commission's Direction on Copyright and Neighbouring Rights: Toward the Regime of the Twenty-first Century' (1993) 17 Colum-VLA JL & Arts 187, 206–8.

[16] Verstrynghe, 'The Spring 1993 Horace S. Manges Lecture' (n. 15) at 206–7.

[17] Verstrynghe, 'The Spring 1993 Horace S. Manges Lecture' (n. 15) at 206–7.

probably also the only system that will be able to cope with the challenge of the digital exploitation of copyright, which will make worldwide, high-speed exploitation of copyright in various formats possible, and which offers the opportunity to play around with an original work and to amend it efficiently, speedily, and, in practice, on a worrying number of occasions.[18]

Assignment of copyright and copyright licences

Assignment of copyright and copyright licences are the two forms of contract involved in the exploitation of a copyright work by a third party.[19] Each has its own distinct characteristics.

Assignment

An assignment involves the disposal of the copyright: the author (the assignor) assigns the copyright to another person (the assignee). The 1988 Act requires that an assignment is in writing[20] and is signed by, or on behalf of, the assignor.[21] The standard type of assignment involves the transfer of the complete copyright, but this need not be the case.[22] Two forms of partial assignment are possible: it is possible to assign only certain aspects of the copyright or certain rights, and not the whole copyright, and it is also possible to restrict the assignment to a certain period.[23] This makes it possible to assign, for example, the copyright in the novel, to assign only the public performance right or the translation right, or to assign all or any of these rights only for a period of 10 years. The assignor will normally receive a lump sum in return for the assignment of the copyright in the work. It is also possible to provide for an automatic reverter of the rights to the assignor in a (partial) assignment when a future event, such as an unremedied material breach of contract by the assignee, takes place.[24]

An assignment can also take place in relation to a work that has yet to be created. The Act calls this the assignment of 'future copyright'—that is, of copyright that will come into existence once the potential author decides to create the work and the work is effectively created. The author will then become the first owner of the copyright and the assignment will take effect immediately.[25]

A difficult point is presented by the assignment of copyright in equity. The courts have, on a couple of occasions, accepted that an assignment can take place even if the formal requirements of s. 90 of the 1988 Act are not met. In *Warner v. Gestetner*,[26] the court held that there had been an assignment of copyright in equity only.[27] Warner had produced

[18] T. Dreier 'Copyright Digitized: Philosophical Impacts and Practical Implications for Information Exchanges in Digital Networks', in *WIPO Worldwide Symposium on the Impact of Digital Technology on Copyright and Neighbouring Rights*, Harvard University, Geneva: WIPO (1993).

[19] CDPA 1988, s. 90(1).

[20] But secondary evidence can be admitted in later proceedings if the written original can no longer be traced: see the decision of the Court of Appeal in *Masquerade Music Ltd v. Bruce Springsteen* [2001] EMLR 25.

[21] CDPA 1988, s. 90(3).

[22] See *Peer International Corp., Southern Music Publishing Co. Inc. & Peermusic (UK) Ltd v. Termidor Music Publishers Ltd, Termidor Musikverlag GmbH & Co. KG & Editora Musical de Cuba* [2004] RPC 455, which also raises interesting points of private international law.

[23] CDPA 1988, s. 90(2).

[24] *Crosstown Music Co 1 LLC v. Rive Droite Music Ltd* [2010] EWCA Civ 1222.

[25] CDPA 1988, s. 91(1) and (2). See *PRS Ltd v. B4U Network (Europe) Ltd* [2012] EWHC 3010 (Ch).

[26] [1988] EIPR D-89.

[27] See also the unreported decision of the Court of Appeal of 26 November 1999 in *Lakeview Computers plc v. Steadman*.

drawings of cats for Gestetner. These drawings were to be used to produce a new product at a fair and Warner would remain the owner of the copyright in the drawings. Gestetner later used them in promotional literature. The court decided that Gestetner was entitled to use the drawings and implied a clause assigning beneficial ownership of the copyright to Gestetner. In this construction, there is a legal owner of the copyright and an owner at equity who is free to use the work. It seems to be the case, however, that an equitable owner of copyright cannot bring an infringement case without the assistance of the legal owner of the copyright in the work.[28]

An implied assignment may also potentially arise if there is a written contract, but it does not contain an explicit assignment. One could think of a recording contract that grants all rights to exploit the recording to the record company. The question can then arise whether such contract includes also an implied assignment of copyright. The House of Lords has imposed a heavy burden of proof on whoever invokes the existence of such an implied assignment. One has to show that at the time of the assignment it was clear to the person assigning the rights that all his rights were transferred and that the commercial relationship between the parties could not logically have continued to function without such an assignment. There will also not be an implied assignment if the behaviour of the parties afterwards can be explained on the basis of a less radical transaction than an assignment.[29]

Licences

A licence does not involve a transfer of the copyright in the work: the owner of the copyright (the licensor) simply grants permission to a third party (the licensee) to do certain acts in relation to the copyright work that would otherwise constitute an infringement. An obvious example is a licence to perform a play: without the licence being granted, the performance would have constituted an infringement of the copyright in the play. A licence can be granted in return for the payment of a lump sum or royalties, which involve the payment of a fixed sum or a percentage of the return each time that the act allowed by the licence takes place.

In the same way as an assignment, the licence can be restricted in relation to its scope—that is, in relation to the acts that are allowed or in relation to its term.[30] It is indeed quite common to grant various licences—eventually in combination with a partial assignment—to various persons in relation to the exploitation of a work. Let us consider a novel as an example: the owner of the copyright in the novel can assign the publication rights in the UK to a publisher, can license the performing rights, can license another publisher to produce a translation in French, can license a German producer to make a sound recording, and can assign the film rights to MGM in the US, etc.

A licence can be exclusive or non-exclusive. An exclusive licence[31] is subject to certain additional provisions. It is the only type of licence for which the 1988 Act requires a written format, which has to be signed by, or on behalf of, the copyright owner-licensor.[32] It allows the exclusive licensee to exercise certain rights in relation to the copyright work on an exclusive basis. This means that all other persons, including the licensor, will be excluded from exercising that right. The exclusive licensee can also bring an independent infringement action after joining the owner or by leave of the court; a non-exclusive

---

[28] *Performing Right Society Ltd v. London Theatre of Varieties Ltd* [1924] AC 1.

[29] *Fisher v. Brooker* [2009] FSR 25 (HL). See also *Meridian International Services Ltd v. Richardson* (2008) 152 (23) SJLB 28 (CA).

[30] CDPA 1988, s. 90(2).   [31] For an example, see *JHP Ltd v. BBC Worldwide Ltd* [2008] FSR 29.

[32] CDPA 1988, s. 92(1).

licensee needs the assistance of the licensor to do so, because, in that case only the owner can sue. The exclusive licensee also has the same rights against a successor in title who is bound by the licence as he or she has against the original licensor.[33]

This brings us to the question of who is bound by a licence. In principle, the licence binds every successor in title to the licensor and there is only one exception to this rule. A purchaser in good faith and for valuable consideration, or someone deriving his or her title from such a purchaser, is not bound by the terms of the licence if he or she had no actual or constructive notice of the licence.[34] These requirements are extremely difficult to meet in practice, because, once exploitation has taken place, it is almost impossible for a purchaser to prove that he or she did not even have constructive notice of the licence. Nevertheless, this rule is one of the reasons why publishers prefer an assignment of copyright to an exclusive licence.

A prospective owner can license future copyright, in the same way as it can be assigned.[35] In this case again, however, the purchaser in good faith is granted protection.[36]

It is clear that it is extremely difficult to distinguish certain copyright licences from certain assignments of copyright: it is a matter of construction and the actual words used by the parties are not conclusive.[37] The payment of royalties points towards a licence and the difference regarding the right to sue independently is also an important factor in this respect.

Collecting societies

The normal way of exploiting copyright by way of licences involves the grant of a licence for every use that is made of the copyright work. In cases in which the work is a recording, to do so would involve the creation of a licence every time that the recording is played. It is probably not very convenient for the copyright owner to collect a minimum fee on every occasion. The overhead costs would be tremendous; it would take up all of his or her time and he or she would, in practice, only be able to collect a fraction of royalties owed to him or her. The user of these records is in a similar position. If a restaurant owner wants to play background music in the restaurant, to so do requires a separate licence for every work that is played: how is the restaurant owner going to find all of the right owners in the first place?

This problem is addressed by the creation of collecting societies, such as the Performing Right Society (PRS) or Phonographic Performance Ltd (PPL).[38] There is normally one collecting society per type of work and per country. Owners of the copyright become members of this body, which will license the use of their works and collect the royalties for them. The PRS takes an assignment of the copyright in the performance and broadcasting of musical works[39], grants licences, collects royalties, and distributes these among its members after the deduction of administration costs. This presents a tremendous advantage to copyright owners, but it is also advantageous for the users of the works. They now have to deal only with one body and they will be able to get a blanket licence that will allow them to use any work that is among the repertoire of the society.[40]

---

[33] CDPA 1988, s. 92(2).   [34] CDPA 1988, s. 90(4).   [35] CDPA 1988, s. 91(3).
[36] CDPA 1988, s. 91(3).

[37] *Jonathan Cape Ltd v. Consolidated Press Ltd* [1954] 3 All ER 253, [1954] 1 WLR 1313.

[38] See P. Torremans (2010) 'Collective Management in the United Kingdom (and Ireland)', in D. Gervais (ed.), *Collective Management of Copyright and Related Rights*, (2nd edn), London: Kluwer Law International, pp. 251–82.

[39] See *PRS Ltd v. B4U Network (Europe) Ltd* [2012] EWHC 3010 (Ch).

[40] See D. Gervais (2006) 'The Changing Role of Copyright Collectives', in D. Gervais (ed.), *Collective Management of Copyright and Related Rights* (n. 38) at 3–36.

Certain members of the collecting society may also bring infringement proceedings against those who do not have a licence or who are in breach of its terms if they are, for example, exclusive licensees of the copyright in various sound recordings. Despite not having actual authority from the members of the collective society, it is accepted that they can sue as a representative claimant in a representative capacity if they, and the other members, have a common interest and a common grievance, and if the relief sought would, in its nature, be beneficial to the relevant members of the collecting society.[41]

But the fact that a society has a double monopoly creates some problems. Copyright owners are obliged to deal with the one existing society if they want to exploit their works effectively. This situation can give rise to discrimination by the society against certain of its members by imposing different membership rules, for example, for foreign owners of copyright, or by the adoption of discriminatory royalty distribution rules for certain types of work or certain classes of members. The society is also an unavoidable partner for the users of copyright works, and abuse could consist in this area, for example, in charging exorbitant royalties. The 1988 Act took this into account and gave the Copyright Tribunal jurisdiction to deal with such cases.[42]

Collective management has as a major advantage for users that they have access to any work via a single collective management organization. This presupposes that all right holders bring their works under the scheme run by the collective management organization. That does not necessarily happen and this is where extended collective licensing or ECL comes in. ECL occurs where a collecting society is granted permission to license specific kinds of copyright works across an entire sector, thereby representing the interests of non-member right holders in addition to those of their own members. In essence, instead of engaging in time-consuming rights clearance, users will be able to obtain mass, non-exclusive licences directly from collecting societies to cover a range of uses, and right holders will be assured of remuneration for their works. The UK introduced such a scheme in 2014 by means of the Copyright and Rights in Performances (Extended Collective Licensing) Regulations 2014.[43] Collecting societies can apply to operate an Extended Collective Licensing Scheme. Permission will only be granted subject to safeguards. The collecting society making the application must be able to demonstrate 'significant' representation for the particular type of work that is to be licensed and it must obtain consent from their members. There can also be no obligation to join the scheme and have one's works dealt with under it. This means that non-member right holders of the copyright works involved must be provided with the option of opt-out from the scheme, either for some or all of their works. Existing collecting societies that wish to apply for permission to engage in ECL will be expected to review their codes of practice: to ensure clear governance, improve transparency, and provide clear and concise information to users, members, and non-members alike. They must also provide sufficient publicity about the ECL scheme, and create mechanisms for the distribution of licence fees to non-member right holders.[44] Any permission will be granted for a five-year period.

---

[41] *Independiente Ltd and ors v. Music Trading OnLine (HK) Ltd and ors* [2003] EWHC 470 (Ch).

[42] See also *Association of Independent Radio Companies Ltd v. Phonographic Performance Ltd* [1994] RPC 143.

[43] SI 2014/2588.

[44] Copyright and Rights in Performances (Extended Collective Licensing) Regulations 2014, regs. 4 and 5.

Licensing schemes

The owner of the copyright in a work may be willing to set standard conditions on which licences to do certain acts are available. This is, for example, the case in relation to the photocopying of literary works. Every owner knows that this is happening and that it is unrealistic to expect every person who engages in the photocopying of the work to apply for a separate licence for each work of which he or she wishes to copy a part. It is also unrealistic to assume that the copyright owner could act effectively against this form of infringement in cases in which no licence is applied for. The solution is to pool resources and to arrive at standard conditions on which licences are available, and to do so with a large group of copyright owners. More copiers will be prepared to take a licence and the body administering the licence will be more effective in acting against infringement. The Act also sees this from another perspective: by giving the Copyright Tribunal jurisdiction over these schemes, it can prevent the abuse of monopoly powers by the copyright owners.

A licensing scheme is defined as:

> a scheme setting out the classes of case in which the operator of the scheme, or the person on whose behalf he acts, is willing to grant copyright licences, and the terms on which licences would be granted in those classes of case.[45]

A licensing body, meanwhile, means:

> a society or other organisation which has as its main object, or one of its main objects, the negotiation or granting, either as owner or prospective owner of copyright or as agent for him, of copyright licences, and whose objects include the granting of licences covering works of more than one author.[46]

The Copyright Tribunal

The Copyright Tribunal has a wide jurisdiction. The following types of case can be referred to it:

- the determination of the royalty or other remuneration to be paid with respect to the retransmission of a broadcast that includes the work;

- an application to determine the amount of the equitable remuneration that remains payable in those cases in which the author has transferred his or her rental rights, relating to a sound recording or film, to the producer;

- disputes about the terms or the operation of a proposed or existing licensing scheme,[47] which is operated by a licensing body and which covers works of more than one author (such an action can, for example, be brought by an organization that represents persons who require licences that are covered by the scheme)—the licences must cover[48] the copying of the work, the rental or lending of copies of the work, the performing, showing, or playing of the work in public, or the broadcasting of the work;

- an application in relation to entitlement under such a licensing scheme—that is, if someone is refused a licence;

---

[45] CDPA 1988, s. 116(1); see *Universities UK Ltd v. Copyright Licensing Agency Ltd* [2002] RPC 693.
[46] CDPA 1988, s. 116(2); see *Universities UK Ltd v. Copyright Licensing Agency Ltd* (n. 45).
[47] CDPA 1988, ss. 118 and 119; see *Universities UK Ltd v. Copyright Licensing Agency Ltd* (n. 45).
[48] CDPA 1988, s. 117.

- a reference in relation to licensing by a licensing body (for example, a case relating to the terms of a licence)—the licences must cover the same acts as those listed in relation to licensing schemes;[49]
- an application or reference in relation to the use as of right of sound recordings in broadcasts;[50]
- an appeal against the coverage of a licensing scheme or a licence;
- an application to settle the royalties for the rental of sound recordings, films, or computer programs in cases in which the Secretary of State uses the exceptional powers contained in s. 66 of the 1988 Act;
- an application to settle the terms of a copyright licence that has become available as of right.[51]

Appeals on a point of law from the decisions of the Copyright Tribunal can be made to the High Court, or, in Scotland, to the Court of Session.[52]

The rental and the lending right

If we consider video cassettes or DVDs containing a copy of a film as an example, it is easy to understand that exploitation through rental of a film has become one of the leading ways of exploiting a film. Rental and lending of copyright works have, indeed, acquired an important status in the field of copyright exploitation and, because they have replaced, in a number of cases, the acquisition of a copy of the work and the royalty payment that goes with it, it was felt that the authors of the works that are exploited in this way were entitled to some form of remuneration. Section 66 of the 1988 Act provides for the payment of a reasonable royalty in rental cases—but this provision is, in fact, a last remedy against abuse by the owners of copyright in sound recordings, films, and computer programs of their copyright, and it is unlikely that the Secretary of State will ever use his power under this section to grant licences and ask the Copyright Tribunal to determine the reasonable royalty in default of agreement. In the absence of any substantial rental or lending provisions in many of its member states, the EU took the initiative to introduce these rights in a harmonized way and this resulted in a Council Directive.[53]

The implementation of the Directive[54] in the UK added the rental and lending of the work or of copies of it to the list of restricted acts.[55] The fact that these acts are now restricted to the owner of the copyright in the work enables the copyright owner to charge royalties for the rental and lending of the work, and to receive payment for this way of exploiting his or her work. The general structure of the relevant provisions has been discussed and need not be repeated here.[56] We also discussed the introduction of rental and

---

[49] CDPA 1988, s. 124.

[50] CDPA 1988, ss. 135D and 135E; see *Phonographic Performance Ltd v. Virgin Retail Ltd* [2001] EMLR 139.

[51] CDPA 1988, s. 149.   [52] CDPA 1988, s. 152.

[53] Council Directive 92/100 on rental right and lending right and on certain rights related to copyright in the field of intellectual property (1992) OJ L 346/61.

[54] A challenge against the Directive, in which its validity was questioned, was rejected by the European Court of Justice on 28 April 1998 in Case C-200/96, *Metronome Musik GmbH v. Music Point Hokamp GmbH* [1998] ECR I-1953, [1998] 3 CMLR 919.

[55] CDPA 1988, s. 16(1)(ba).

[56] See Ch. 15; see also Case C-245/00, *SENA v. NOS* [2003] ECR I-1251 on the point of equitable remuneration.

lending rights as part of the rights in performances. We therefore turn our attention to a few special aspects of the rental and lending rights regime.

As the credits that appear on the screen at the end of the showing of a film demonstrate, a long list of people are generally involved in the making of a film. The list of those people that will possess rental rights is significantly shorter, but can nevertheless still be rather long. Once the film is made, each of them will normally go his or her own way; it might therefore be rather impractical to impose a system whereby the film can only be exploited through rental if the authorization of each contributor has been obtained. Some of the contributors may be hard to trace, or even a single one might hold the whole project to ransom. The Directive and the 1988 Act therefore provide the possibility of concentrating the rental rights in a single pair of hands. The Act contains a presumption[57] that, unless the agreement provides to the contrary, the conclusion of an agreement concerning the production of a film between the producer and an author of a literary, musical, dramatic, or artistic work[58] is presumed to include a transfer to the producer of any rental right in relation to the film arising by virtue of the inclusion of a copy of the author's work in the film. As we saw in the last chapter, an identical provision exists in relation to performers.[59] Due to the higher level of bargaining power of the producer, such a presumption might be to the detriment of authors or performers, who would hardly be able to secure a proper remuneration for the transfer of their rental rights in the production agreement. The Act tries to overcome this problem by introducing a rule that the authors or performers remain entitled to an equitable remuneration for the rental, even after the transfer of their right.[60]

The producer may be the only person who can authorize the rental of the work, but he or she has to provide an equitable remuneration for those whose rights have been transferred. That right of equitable remuneration cannot be assigned, except to a collecting society that will enforce the right on behalf of the right holder.[61] For the purposes of this rule, the category of authors also includes the principal director of the film, in addition to the author of a literary, dramatic, musical, or artistic work.[62]

The amount payable by way of equitable remuneration is to be agreed between the author and performers, on the one hand, and the producers or his or her successor in title as assignee of the rental rights in the film, on the other.[63] In default of an agreement, the Copyright Tribunal will determine the amount upon application.[64]

These provisions successfully overcome the problems that arise when too many persons potentially get rental rights in relation to a single work. The general conclusion must therefore be that the system of rental rights enhances the copyright position of the people involved, and constitutes an appropriate and necessary response to the change in the way in which certain copyright works are exploited commercially. The position of the performers is especially enhanced by this change, because their protection was, until now, rather weak.

---

[57] CDPA 1988, s. 93A.

[58] Screenplays, dialogues, or music that are specifically created for, and used in, a film are excluded according to CDPA 1988, s. 93A(3).

[59] CDPA 1988, s. 191F.   [60] CDPA 1988, s. 93B(1).

[61] CDPA 1988, s. 93B(2). The non-transferable nature of the right to equitable remuneration was also confirmed by the Court of Justice in case C-277/10, *Martin Luksan v. Petrus van der Let*, 9 February 2012, <http://curia.europa.eu>.

[62] CDPA 1988, s. 93B(1).   [63] CDPA 1988, s. 93B(4); see Ch. 15; see also *SENA v. NOS* 9 (n. 56).

[64] CDPA 1988, ss. 93C and 191G.

The exploitation of copyright works through hard copy has further been eroded through the rise of the Internet. Many works are now available online and their use online reduces the use of hard copies. The existing provisions of copyright—including those concerning rental and lending—are, perhaps, not entirely capable of successfully tackling the problems that arise. The World Intellectual Property Organization (WIPO) Copyright Treaty 1996 and the WIPO Performances and Phonograms Treaty 1996 are attempts, at an international level, to update copyright in this respect. The EU has translated these international commitments into the Information Society Directive.[65] The UK has implemented the Directive through the Copyright and Related Rights Regulations 2003.[66] The provisions of the Directive—especially the enhanced bundle of rights consisting of the reproduction right, the distribution right, and the right to communicate the work to the public and to make it available to the public—have already been discussed. Suffice it to mention here that the Directive fully preserves the existing rental and lending rights.[67]

Apart from the Internet, there are other forms of exploitation of copyright works in this area in addition to online services, which include pay-per-view television, video or music on demand, and electronic publishing. These can be called 'conditional access' services. Authors can only be paid properly in this context if unauthorized (pirate) access without payment to these services is prohibited and prevented. The EU harmonized the law on conditional access services and their protection through the adoption of a Directive.[68] The purpose of the Directive was to create a uniform legal environment for the protection of these conditional access services—that is, services offered to the public in relation to which access is subject to payment of subscriptions, such as pay-per-view television and interactive online services. The Directive required member states to prohibit, and provide suitable sanctions against, the manufacture and commercial dealing in illegal decoders, smart cards, and software, etc. In the UK, this resulted in the insertion of s. 297A into the 1988 Act, which does exactly that.[69]

Copyright exploitation and free competition

The position in the UK under domestic law in relation to the conflict between copyright exploitation and free competition is clear, in that it gives priority to copyright exploitation. Section 66 of the 1988 Act could lead to compulsory licences in a restricted area, but, as discussed, the provision will probably never be used. This leaves us with the licences of right as the only effective tool with which to act against an abuse during the exploitation of the rights granted by copyright law. A report of the Competition Commission[70] may lead to the creation of licences of right, which means essentially that

---

[65] Directive 2001/29/EC on the harmonization of certain aspects of copyright and related rights in the information society [2001] OJ L 167/10.

[66] SI 2003/2498.   [67] Information Society Directive, Art. 1(2)(b).

[68] European Parliament and Council Directive 98/84/EC on the legal protection of services based on, or consisting of, conditional access (1998) OJ L 320/54.

[69] Inserted by Conditional Access (Unauthorized Decoders) Regulations 2000, SI 2000/1175, reg. 2. The question of whether a card for a satellite receiver which was bought in another EU member state can be an 'illicit device' for these purposes arose in *Football Association Premier League Ltd v. QC Leisure* [2008] FSR 32, [2009] 1 WLR 1603 and *Murphy v. Media Protection Services Ltd* [2008] FSR 33 and was referred to the Court of Justice. The Court eventually held that it was not; see Joined Cases C-403/08, *Football Association Premier League Ltd v. QC Leisure* and C-429/08, *Murphy v. Media Protection Services Ltd* [2012] FSR 1, [2012] 1 CMLR 29.

[70] CDPA 1988, s. 144.

licences become available to anyone who applies for them. What is required for the creation of such licences is that the public interest is, or has been, or may be, prejudiced. This can be on the basis of conditions in licences restricting the use of the work or the right of the owner to grant other licences, or on the basis of a refusal of the copyright owner to grant licences on reasonable terms.[71] The UK's improved general competition provisions, contained in the Competition Act 1998, are based on the example found in the Treaty of Rome. The latter provisions have shown to be of real practical importance and it is to these that we now turn.

Exploitation under European law—copyright and the free movement of goods

Article 30 of the Treaty of Rome (Article 36 TFEU) refers to 'industrial and commercial property', and this clearly includes patents and trade marks—but does it also include copyright? Does it really mean the same as 'intellectual property'? The European Court of Justice has now given a positive answer to these questions,[72] and all of the general principles that we outlined in Chapter 5 on patents can now be applied to copyright, subject to what follows.

Copyright is a difficult area, because its scope is so extremely wide and because it protects, as a result, very different types of work. This makes it extremely difficult to define the specific subject matter of copyright and the European Court of Justice has not yet made an attempt to do so. It is submitted that, for these purposes, there are two types of copyright, which probably have a different specific subject matter: the first category comprises all non-performance copyrights, such as those in books, paintings, and sound recordings; the second comprises all performance copyrights. The latter category includes live performances, but also all performances of films. We will discuss both categories separately.

The Treaty obviously deals with matters at EU level, but questions can remain as to what member states can do at a purely international level. The Court was asked, in *Laserdisken ApS v. Kulturministeriet*,[73] whether the rule on exhaustion was, in relation to copyright, limited to exhaustion within the European Economic Area (EEA) or whether the member states remained free to apply the principle of international exhaustion. This case concerned the right of distribution. The Court declined to open the door for international exhaustion and clarified that, in the area of copyright, exhaustion is also limited to the EEA level.[74]

Non-performance copyrights

Deutsche Grammophon

Non-performance copyrights are treated very similarly to patents. In fact, the oldest case in which the exhaustion doctrine was applied was a case relating to records. In *Deutsche Grammophon v. Metro*,[75] the Court was faced with the following issue. Deutsche

---

[71] CDPA 1988, s. 144.

[72] Cases 55 and 57/80, *Musik-Vertrieb Membran GmbH & K-tel International v. GEMA* [1981] ECR 147, [1981] 2 CMLR 44.

[73] Case C-479/04, *Laserdisken ApS v. Kulturministeriet* [2006] ECDR 30.

[74] See Ch. 27 for a broader discussion in the context of trade marks.

[75] Case 78/70, *Deutsche Grammophon GmbH v. Metro-SB-Grossmarkte GmbH & Co. KG* [1971] ECR 487, [1971] CMLR 631.

Grammophon sold the same records in Germany and in France, but its French subsidiary, Polydor, could only charge a lower price due to market conditions. Metro bought the records in France for resale in Germany at a price below the price that Deutsche Grammophon charged. Deutsche Grammophon invoked its copyright[76] in the records to stop this practice. The Court ruled that Deutsche Grammophon had exhausted its copyright in the records by putting them on the market in France with its consent and could not oppose the importation of the records by Metro.[77]

This approach was confirmed in *Musik-Vertrieb Membran v. GEMA*.[78] Once more, records and cassettes were being imported into Germany after they had been put on the market in another member state with the consent of the copyright owner. The German collecting society, GEMA (*die Gesellschaft für musikalische Aufführungs-und mechanische Vervielfältigungsrechte*) tried to rely on the German copyright in the works to levy the difference between the low royalty that had been paid abroad and the higher German royalty. The Court reiterated that, by putting the records and cassettes on the market with its consent, the owner of the copyright had exhausted all copyright in them. It could, as a result, not rely on any copyright to prevent the importation, nor could it rely on that copyright to charge an additional royalty. In the Court's view, the copyright owner who markets its works in member states in which the royalties are low has to abide by that decision and accept its consequences.

The approach sounds identical to that taken in the patent case of *Merck v. Stephar*[79] and the case law of the Court has now also been reflected in the Information Society Directive, Art. 4(2) of which stipulates that:

> the distribution right shall not be exhausted within the Community in respect of the original or copies of the work, except where the first sale or other transfer of ownership in the Community of that object is made by the right holder or with his consent.

Warner Bros.

In *Warner Bros. v. Christiansen*,[80] a difficult problem arose. Video cassettes, which were put on the market in both the UK and Denmark, were being imported from the UK into Denmark. It is clear that the plaintiff could not rely on its Danish copyright to stop the importation of the video cassettes, because this only requires a normal application of the dictum in the two previous cases. The problem arose because Danish law granted a rental right to the author or the producer, while such a right did not exist in the UK and Christiansen had imported the cassettes to hire them out afterwards. Christiansen argued that the rights in the cassettes had been exhausted, because they had been marketed in the UK with the consent of the owner, but the Court rejected this argument. Indeed, the rental right has to be treated as a separate right and, because it did not exist in the UK, it could not have been exhausted.[81] Warner Bros. could invoke the Danish rental right to stop Christiansen hiring out the video cassettes.[82]

---

[76] For the purposes of our discussion of the case, we can assume that the German exclusive distribution right is akin to copyright.

[77] Case 78/70, *Deutsche Grammophon GmbH v. Metro-SB-Grossmarkte GmbH & Co. KG* [1971] ECR 487 at 500.

[78] Joined Cases 55 and 57/80, *Musik-Vertrieb Membran v. GEMA* [1981] ECR 147, [1981] 2 CMLR 44; see also Case 58/80, *Dansk Supermarked A/S v. Imerco A/S* [1981] ECR 181, [1981] 3 CMLR 590.

[79] Case 187/80, *Merck & Co. Inc. v. Stephar BV* [1981] ECR 2063, discussed in Ch. 5.

[80] Case 158/86, *Warner Bros. Inc. v. Christiansen* [1988] ECR 2605.

[81] See M. Henry, 'Rental and Duration Directives: Issues Arising from Current EC Reforms' (1993) 12 EIPR 437, 439.

[82] Henry, 'Rental and Duration Directives: Issues Arising from Current EC Reforms' (n. 81).

It is easier to understand why the rental right should be treated as a separate right by looking at the consequences of not doing so: that would effectively have rendered the rental right worthless, because it would have been exhausted by sale in a member state in which the right is not known. As we discussed in relation to patents in Chapter 5, Arts. 34 and 36 of the Treaty on the Functioning of the European Union are construed in such a way that they must leave the existence of the right and a certain exercise untouched, because any other interpretation would render them senseless. The approach taken by the Court must therefore be correct.

It may be tempting to argue that this case presented similar features to those of *Merck v. Stephar*[83] in relation to patents and that, as a result, the Court should have ruled that Warner Bros. could not rely on the Danish rental right, because it should accept the consequences of its decision to market the video cassettes in a country where no rental right was available. It is submitted that this approach is wrong. In *Merck*, Italy had a patent law, but excluded pharmaceuticals from its scope. The Court argued that Merck should accept the consequences of a weaker or absent patent protection in Italy and could not invoke its Dutch patent. Only one right was involved. In the *Warner* case, however, two rights were involved. The copyright had been exhausted, but was not relied upon, because only the Danish rental right was used—and it is this that allows us to distinguish the cases.

EMI Electrola

A problem relating to the term of copyright arose in *EMI Electrola GmbH v. Patricia*,[84] because the term of copyright protection for records in Denmark was shorter than that available in Germany. Patricia bought Cliff Richard sound recordings in Denmark once they were out of copyright and imported them into Germany, where EMI Electrola tried to stop it by relying on the German copyright in the recordings that had not yet expired. The European Court of Justice held that the German copyright had not been exhausted, because the marketing in Denmark had not occurred with the consent of the copyright owner, but was due to the fact that the term of copyright had expired.

This case can now be described as legal history, because the term of copyright has now been harmonized in the Community and because the *Phil Collins* judgment[85] would now result in the work in a similar case remaining in copyright in the whole of the EU, as discussed in relation to the term of copyright. The problem will therefore not reoccur.

Usedsoft

It had been generally accepted that the exhaustion of the distribution right was limited to hard copies. On the other side of the barrier one found things like the showing of movies, which rather resemble the provision of a service. But increasingly we no longer buy software on CDs or any other tangible support. Instead we download it over the Internet. That download then takes the place of the hard copy we buy. The question was therefore raised whether the sale of unused but still valid software licences in cases where the user downloads the software from the Internet gives, just like the sale of a hard copy, rise to exhaustion of the distribution right. The Court of Justice was asked the question in the *Usedsoft* case[86] and in its judgment the Court ruled that the principle of exhaustion of

[83] Case 187/80 *Merck & Co. Inc. v. Stephar BV* [1981] ECR 2063, discussed in Ch. 5.

[84] Case 341/87, *EMI Electrola GmbH v. Patricia Im- und Export* [1989] ECR 79, [1989] 2 CMLR 413.

[85] Case C-92/92, *Phil Collins v. Imtrat Handelsgesellschaft MbH* [1993] 3 CMLR 773, in which the parallel case Case 362/92, *Patricia v. EMI Electrola*, concerning Cliff Richard's work, is also reported; see also G. Dworkin and J. A. L. Sterling 'Phil Collins and the Term Directive' (1994) 5 EIPR 187.

[86] Case C-128/11, *Usedsoft Gmbh v. Oracle International Corp.*, 3 July 2012, <http://curia.europa.eu>.

the distribution right applies not only where the copyright holder markets copies of his software on a material medium (CD-ROM or DVD) but also where he distributes them by means of downloads from his website.

Where the copyright holder makes available to his customer a copy—tangible or intangible—and at the same time concludes, in return for payment of a fee, a licence agreement granting the customer the right to use that copy for an unlimited period, that right holder sells the copy to the customer and thus exhausts his exclusive distribution right. Such a transaction involves a transfer of the right of ownership of the copy. Therefore, even if the licence agreement prohibits a further transfer, the right holder can no longer oppose the resale of that copy. The first sale gives the right holder its adequate remuneration and any additional restriction of the resale of copies of computer programs downloaded from the Internet would go beyond what is necessary to safeguard the specific subject matter of the intellectual property concerned.

Moreover, the exhaustion of the distribution right extends to the copy of the computer program sold as corrected and updated by the copyright holder. The Court points out, however, that if the licence acquired by the first acquirer relates to a greater number of users than he needs, that acquirer is not authorized by the effect of the exhaustion of the distribution right to divide the licence and resell only part of it. The exhaustion necessarily relates to what is bought, i.e. to the whole licence. And at the time of resale the reseller needs to delete its original copy. After all, in contrast to the exclusive right of distribution, the exclusive right of reproduction is not exhausted by the first sale. However, the Software Directive[87] authorizes any reproduction that is necessary for the use of the computer program by the lawful acquirer in accordance with its intended purpose. Such reproduction may not be prohibited by contract. In this context, the Court's answer is that any subsequent acquirer of a copy for which the copyright holder's distribution right is exhausted constitutes such a lawful acquirer. He can therefore download onto his computer the copy sold to him by the first acquirer. Such a download must be regarded as a reproduction of a computer program that is necessary to enable the new acquirer to use the program in accordance with its intended purpose.

The latter point makes it clear that the judgment specifically relies on the provisions of the Software Directive. The Court was after all asked to explain the meaning of these provisions. The fact that the Court therefore logically refers to the specific provisions of the Directive should however not lead one to conclude that its exhaustion decision is limited to software and the Software Directive. It is striking to see that the Court's starting point is that any transaction that in the online era takes the place of the sale of a hard copy will be subject to the exhaustion rule. The Court argues specifically that in those cases a copy of the software is effectively sold. The principle established in this case may therefore also apply if I buy other things, such as music, online, even if the Software Directive and its specific provisions do not apply. The fact that I buy a track from an online store and effectively download the track on my digital device may in the eyes of the Court also be (the equivalent) of a sale of the copy. Exhaustion may therefore apply and the Court may argue in future that that principle justifies whatever it takes to get the (second-hand) copy onto the device of the acquirer.

It is on the other hand also clear that the Court does not have the intention to apply the exhaustion rule to just any case. There has to be the equivalent of a sale of a hard copy. In other words, music streaming services such as Spotify and cloud computing business

---

[87] Directive 2009/24/EC of the European Parliament and of the Council of 23 April 2009 on the legal protection of computer programs [2009] OJ L 111/16.

models whereby I use software stored 'in the Cloud' without downloading a copy on my computer or portable device remain unaffected. In those cases the equivalent is not the sale of a copy, but rather something along the lines of the provision of a service.

One could of course argue that the Court's judgment will not lead far.[88] The easy way to get out of it would be to take away the right to use the software for an unlimited period on which the Court seems to rely. In other words, contracts that allow the download but that are limited in time would allow the software industry to avoid the consequences of this judgment. And for copyright purists one would get rid of the unwanted extension by the Court of the exhaustion of the distribution right beyond hard copies. That may well be wishful thinking though. The Court seems to have established the principle that exhaustion applies whenever the business model effectively provides a substitute for the sale of a hard copy. The fact that the user gets a copy with which he or she can work freely may be the bottom line. All the other elements may be related to the facts of the case and once the copy is provided, the Court may object to any contractual attempt by the software industry to get rid of the exhaustion rule.

Art and Allposters International

The facts of this recent case involve a return to the analogue world. Art and Allposters markets posters and other reproductions depicting the work of famous painters. In the Netherlands, the collective management organization that represents the interests of the painters is Stichting Pictoright. The litigation arose regarding the process of canvas transfer that was applied by Art and Allposters to arrive at a 'painting' on canvas on the basis of a poster. Stichting Pictoright objected to the application of this technique, which the CJEU described as follows:

> Among other products, Allposters offers its clients reproductions in the form of posters, framed posters, posters on wood and images on canvases. In order to produce an image on canvas, a synthetic coating (laminate) is first applied to a paper poster depicting the chosen work. Next, the image on the poster is transferred from the paper to a canvas by means of a chemical process. Finally, that canvas is stretched over a wooden frame. The image of the work disappears from the paper backing during the process. Allposters refers to both it and its result as 'canvas transfer'.[89]

The CJEU has no problem in accepting that the first sale of the poster of the painting took place with the consent of the right holder and that exhaustion flowed from that first sale of the poster as an object in which the intangible work is contained. But exhaustion applies only to the object and to the object as it was first sold. Trade mark law and in particular Art. 7.2 of the Trade Mark Directive shows very clearly that alterations are dangerous and that altered goods are no longer benefiting from the exhaustion rule. In this case there is an alteration of the medium and the resale of the poster takes place in a new format, i.e. the canvas. The altered medium is not covered by the exhaustion of the poster format. And the first sale of the canvas does not occur with the consent of the right holder. But most importantly, the Court goes back to its arguments concerning the need for equitable remuneration and rules that exhaustion would in this case deprive the right holder of the possibility to enforce its copyright effectively and to require an appropriate reward for the commercial exploitation of the work. The new format on canvas would indeed allow the right holder to claim a higher reward on the market.

---

[88] See A. Lucas' commentary on the case [2012] 44 Propriétés Intellectuelles 333–7.

[89] Case C-419/13, *Art & Allposters International BV v. Stichting Pictoright*, 22 January 2015, <http://curia.europa.eu>, at para. 15.

The new format is clearly by no means ancillary and in the absence of consent to the market of the canvas format and the absence of an appropriate reward, with on top of everything damage to the essential function of the copyright in the painting, there is no room for exhaustion in this case.

The difficulty of defining the essential function of copyright

The essential function of copyright was first described by the Court of First Instance in the *Magill* cases,[90] which are concerned with competition law, as being '*to protect the moral rights in the work and to ensure a reward for the creative effort, while respecting the aims of, in particular, Article [82]*'. This definition is not precise enough, although it rightly indicates the two essential elements of copyright—moral rights and economic rights—that are granted to the author. The reference to creativity must be understood against the background of the low originality requirement in copyright. This definition should, therefore, be treated with caution.

The *Warner Bros.* case[91] shows clearly that there are many facets to the essential function of copyright and, especially, to the specific subject matter of copyright. The rental right point was clearly a separate aspect within the latter. This should not come as a surprise: copyright is a broad right that protects a wide variety of products. It may, in each case and broadly speaking, be the aim to protect the author and the subsequent right holders, because it is felt that their creative efforts deserve encouragement and protection, but the exact way in which this is put into practice by including different aspects within the specific subject matter of copyright is not always as easy to determine as it is with the narrower patent right.

While it can be understood that rental, as a separate way in which the work is exploited, may have been entitled to be promoted to a separate aspect of the specific subject matter, one should not construe the latter too broadly either. The *Dior* case[92] illustrates this point. Dior had exhausted all copyrights in the box in which it sold its perfume bottles by putting the perfumes, in the box, on the market for the first time. This is normal copyright exhaustion and the reward for the copyright in the design of the boxes is seen as being included in the sales price of the perfume. Any further use of the copyright in the design of the boxes would therefore go beyond the specific subject matter of copyright in this case. A problem arose because the parallel importer wanted to reproduce the design of the boxes in its publicity. Printing a photograph of the boxes to advertise the fact that the perfume is now available at a lower price from certain outlets certainly involves copying: could Dior stop this on the basis of its copyright?

The European Court of Justice ruled that it could not. The exhaustion of the copyright by putting the product on the market exhausted all rights. Reprinting for publicity purposes is clearly not a separate aspect of the specific subject matter of the right; it is part of the main aspect of copyright. It could rather be argued that the parallel importer, who has the right to import the perfume bottles that Dior put on the market in another member state, must also have the right to advertise these products. Otherwise, the consumer will not be informed and, in the absence of real sales, the whole system of parallel import will de facto collapse. Any use of copyright to stop the advertising of the products would therefore be a use to block parallel imports of legitimately acquired products. This

[90] Cases T-69/89, *Radio Telefis Éireann v. Commission* [1991] ECR II-485, [1991] 4 CMLR 586; T-70/89, *BBC v. EC Commission* [1991] ECR II-535, [1991] 4 CMLR 669; T-76/89, *Independent Television Productions v. EC Commission* [1991] ECR II-575, [1991] 4 CMLR 745.

[91] Case 158/86, *Warner Bros. v. Christiansen* [1988] ECR 2605, [1990] 3 CMLR 684.

[92] Case C-337/95, *Parfums Christian Dior SA v. Evora BV* [1998] RPC 166.

cannot be part of the essential function of copyright; it must be an abusive use of the right. It must therefore be treated as falling outside the specific subject matter of the right and the right must be treated as having been exhausted for this purpose.[93]

Performance copyrights

The category of performance copyrights is concerned with plays and films, and their performance. The exploitation of these works takes place through public exhibitions, which can be repeated an indefinite number of times. It is like rendering a service and the whole area has more links with the free movement of services provided for in Art. 56 of the Treaty on the Functioning of the European Union (formerly Art. 49 of the Treaty of Rome) than with the free movement of goods. This implies that this category of rights should be treated differently.

The European Court of Justice was confronted with this problem in the *Coditel* case.[94] This case made the French film *Le Boucher*—the copyright in which was owned by the French company Les Films la Boétie—famous. A seven-year exclusive licence to exhibit the film in Belgium had been given to Ciné Vog. One of the clauses of the licence stipulated that Ciné Vog could only allow the film to be broadcast on Belgian television 40 months after its first cinema showing. A different exclusive licensee was appointed for Germany and that licence contract did not restrict the showing of the film on television. The film was shown on German television before it could have been shown on Belgian television, and the Belgian cable company Coditel picked up the German signal and retransmitted it on its cable network. This required the authorization of the Belgian licensee under Belgian copyright law, because it was held to be a communication to the public. Because no authorization had been applied for and because it feared loss of revenue, because the Belgian television stations would be less interested in acquiring the right to broadcast a film that many of their viewers had already seen in the German version, Ciné Vog sued Coditel for infringement of copyright. Coditel based its defence, inter alia, on the freedom to provide services and argued that, because the film had been shown with the consent of the owner of the copyright, all copyright in it had been exhausted.

The problem with the free movement of services provision of the Treaty, however, is that it does not provide for an exception for intellectual property. This did not prevent Advocate-General Warner suggesting that Art. 30 applied by analogy in this context. The Court must have agreed with this suggestion because it ruled:

> Whilst Article 49 of the Treaty prohibits restrictions upon the freedom to provide services, it does not hereby encompass limits upon the exercise of certain economic activities which have their origin in the application of national legislation for the protection of intellectual property, save where such application constitutes a means of arbitrary discrimination or a disguised restriction on trade between member states. Such would be the case if that application enabled parties to create artificial barriers to trade between member states.[95]

In a next step, the specific subject matter of the performing right in a film was defined as the right of authorities to forbid each and every performance of the film, including the right of it being televised. Because the retransmission of the film by Coditel amounted to

---

[93] See also I. Stamatoudi, 'From Drugs to Spirits and from Boxes to Publicity: Decided and Undecided Issues in Relation to Trade Mark and Copyright Exhaustion' [1999] IPQ 95.
[94] Case 62/79, *Coditel SA v. Ciné Vog Films SA* [1980] ECR 881, [1981] 2 CMLR 362.
[95] *Coditel SA v. Ciné Vog Films SA* (n. 94) at 903.

a new performance, the performing right in the film had not been exhausted and Ciné Vog could rely on it. The restriction on the showing of the film that Ciné Vog claimed was necessary in order to guarantee it the benefit of the essence of the exclusive performing right. The remaining issue was whether the practice of having one exclusive licensee per member state was an example of the artificial barriers to trade to which the Court objected. But the Court did not see it as such and accepted that such an approach was objectively justifiable, because, at that time, all television services were organized on the national basis of a legal broadcasting monopoly.[96] Its conclusion was that:

> the provisions of the Treaty relating to the freedom to provide services did not preclude an assignee of the performing right in a cinematographic film in a member state from relying upon his right to prohibit the exhibition of that film in that State, without its authority, by means of cable diffusion if the film so exhibited is picked up and transmitted after being broadcast in another member state by a third party with the consent of the original owner of the right.[97]

In a digital online environment, similar situations arise. Works are, for example, delivered online whenever the user needs them, such as through access to a database. Concepts such as communication to the public and making the work available to the public carry with them an element of services, rather than a material copy of the work, being provided to the user. The Information Society Directive takes this into account and stipulates, in its Art. 3(3), that the communication to the public right and the making available to the public right will *'not be exhausted by any act of communication to the public or making available to the public as set out in this Article'*.

Recently questions have been raised, however, about the continued application of the *Coditel* approach and about potential limitations on its scope. These questions arose particularly in the context of the live broadcasts of sporting events by satellite. The Premier League supplies images of football matches to single licensees in each member state on an exclusive territorial basis. Each licensee sells cards for decoders and subscriptions in its own member state. But cards bought (at a lower price) in one member state are used in another member state and when infringement claims are brought the question arises whether exhaustion can provide a defence. A strict application of *Coditel* would not allow such a defence, but arguably one can distinguish *Coditel* in these cases. *Coditel* was based on a rebroadcasting scenario, with normal exploitation based on repeat showings of the film. In the Premier League business model there is no rebroadcasting, only a single live broadcast and there is no repeat exploitation. The later sale of DVDs cannot change that and is not affected anyway. There is also, contrary to the *Coditel* scenario, no freeriding. A subscription has been taken out (abroad). The Court of Justice emphasized the fact that in the country of origin the broadcast happened with the authorization of the right holder and that the right holder is therefore able to factor in actual and potential audiences in other member states. There is therefore appropriate remuneration, which copyright guarantees (instead of the highest possible remuneration) and the premium that can be charged by separating territories completely is not part of such an appropriate remuneration. Instead it is irreconcilable with the fundamental aim of the

---

[96] Arguably, this is no longer the case now that Directive 93/83 on copyright and neighbouring rights relating to satellite broadcasting and cable retransmission (1993) OJ L 248/15 has been adopted; e.g. Art. 7(3) of that Directive, on co-production agreements, shows that licences may have to be granted on a Community scale, thereby excluding territorial licensing. See P. Kern, 'The EC "Common Position" on Copyright Applicable to Satellite Broadcasting and Cable Retransmission' (1993) 8 EIPR 276, 280.

[97] Case 62/79, *Coditel SA v. Ciné Vog Films SA* (n. 94) at 904.

Common Market. The Court therefore departed from *Coditel (No. 1)* in these circumstances and held that national provisions blocking the importation of decoder cards are irreconcilable with the aim of Art. 56 of the Treaty on the Functioning of the European Union. The fact that the decoder card had been obtained by giving a false identity and/ or address with the intention of circumventing certain provisions was unable to change that conclusion. Intellectual property in general and copyright in particular can after all only justify a restriction on the fundamental freedoms of the Treaty if it serves the public interest and does not go beyond what is necessary in that context. This leads the Court to accept respect for copyright and a normal exploitation within the specific subject matter of copyright. That includes appropriate remuneration, but not the right to demand the highest possible remuneration.[98]

Exploitation under European law—copyright and competition law

Article 101

Agreements related to copyright may restrict competition and thus may fall within the scope of Art. 101 of the Treaty on the Functioning of the European Union (formerly Art. 81 of the EC Treaty). Such infringing agreements will involve an improper or abusive exercise of copyright, as confirmed by the European Court of Justice in the *Coditel (No. 2)* case.[99] The key question is how to distinguish between infringing and non-infringing agreements. The decoder cases[100] raised interesting questions in this respect on the basis that the agreement by which the Premier League grants exclusive and strictly territorially limited licences for its copyright-protected satellite broadcasts of football matches may be a good example of a copyright agreement that is in breach of Art. 101 of the Treaty. Or as the Court of Justice put it:

> As regards licence agreements in respect of intellectual property rights, it is apparent from the Court's case-law that the mere fact that the right holder has granted to a sole licensee the exclusive right to broadcast protected subject-matter from a Member State, and consequently to prohibit its transmission by others, during a specified period is not sufficient to justify the finding that such an agreement has an anti-competitive object.[101]
>
> That being so, and in accordance with Article 1(2)(b) of the Satellite Broadcasting Directive, a right holder may in principle grant to a sole licensee the exclusive right to broadcast protected subject-matter by satellite, during a specified period, from a single Member State of broadcast or from a number of Member States.
>
> None the less, regarding the territorial limitations upon exercise of such a right, it is to be pointed out that, in accordance with the Court's case-law, an agreement which might tend to restore the divisions between national markets is liable to frustrate the Treaty's objective of achieving the integration of those markets through the establishment of a single market. Thus, agreements which are aimed at partitioning national markets according to national borders or make the interpenetration of national markets more difficult must be

---

[98] Joined Cases C-403/08, *Football Association Premier League Ltd v. QC Leisure* and C-429/08, *Murphy v. Media Protection Services Ltd* [2012] FSR 1, [2012] 1 CMLR 29 at paras. 85–133.

[99] Case 262/81, *Coditel SA v. Ciné Vog Films SA ('Coditel No. 2')* [1982] ECR 3381, [1983] 1 CMLR 49.

[100] *Football Association Premier League Ltd v. QC Leisure* [2008] FSR 32, [2009] 1 WLR 1603 and *Murphy v. Media Protection Services Ltd* [2008] FSR 33.

[101] See, to this effect, *Coditel and ors ('Coditel No. 2')* (n. 99) at para. 15.

regarded, in principle, as agreements whose object is to restrict competition within the meaning of Article 101(1) TFEU.[102] Since that case-law is fully applicable to the field of the cross-border provision of broadcasting services, as follows inter alia from paragraphs 118 to 121 of the present judgment, it must be held that, where a licence agreement is designed to prohibit or limit the cross-border provision of broadcasting services, it is deemed to have as its object the restriction of competition, unless other circumstances falling within its economic and legal context justify the finding that such an agreement is not liable to impair competition.

In the main proceedings, the actual grant of exclusive licences for the broadcasting of Premier League matches is not called into question. Those proceedings concern only the additional obligations designed to ensure compliance with the territorial limita-tions upon exploitation of those licences that are contained in the clauses of the cont-racts concluded between the right holders and the broadcasters concerned, namely the obligation on the broadcasters not to supply decoding devices enabling access to the protected subject-matter with a view to their use outside the territory covered by the licence agreement.

Such clauses prohibit the broadcasters from effecting any cross-border provision of ser-vices that relates to those matches, which enables each broadcaster to be granted absolute territorial exclusivity in the area covered by its licence and, thus, all competition between broadcasters in the field of those services to be eliminated.

...

In light of the foregoing, the answer to the questions referred is that the clauses of an ex-clusive licence agreement concluded between a holder of intellectual property rights and a broadcaster constitute a restriction on competition prohibited by Article 101 TFEU where they oblige the broadcaster not to supply decoding devices enabling access to that right holder's protected subject-matter with a view to their use outside the territory covered by that licence agreement.[103]

Territorial licences remain therefore possible,[104] but they should allow at least for passive cross-border trade. Stopping a licensee from supplying decoder devices to customers at their demand in scenarios where use outside the licensed territory is envisaged in order to stop any cross-border trade and provide absolute exclusivity and the freedom to charge very different prices that comes with it is clearly a bridge too far and will bring the agreement in conflict with Art. 101.

Apart from this it cannot be said that many cases have arisen in this area, but the practice of the Commission shows that its approach is similar to its approach in patent licence cases. For example, 'no challenge' clauses, royalty clauses that were extended to non-protected goods or works, non-competition clauses that were to continue after the expiry date of the agreement, an exclusive grant-back clause,[105] export bans,[106] and at-tempts to guarantee absolute exclusivity[107] were disputed by the Commission and the

---

[102] See, by analogy, in the field of medicinal products, Joined Cases C-468/06 to C-478/06, *Sot. Lélos kai Sia and ors* [2008] ECR I-7139, para. 65, and *GlaxoSmithKline Services and ors v. Commission and ors*, paras. 59 and 61.

[103] Joined Cases C-403/08, *Football Association Premier League Ltd v. QC Leisure* and C-429/08, *Murphy v. Media Protection Services Ltd* [2012] FSR 1, [2012] 1 CMLR 29 at paras. 137–46.

[104] *Coditel No. 2* stands in this respect, *Coditel and ors ('Coditel No. 2')* (n. 99) 3381.

[105] *Neilsen-Hordell/Reichmark*, reported in EC Commission (1982) *Twelfth Annual Report on Competition Policy*, points 88–9.

[106] *Re Ernest Benn Ltd*, reported in EC Commission (1979) Ninth Annual Report on Competition Policy.

[107] *Knoll/Hille-Form*, reported in EC Commission (1983) Thirteenth Annual Report on Competition Policy, points 142–6.

relevant agreements were modified at the Commission's request so that no formal decisions were issued.

In recent years the reciprocal representation agreements concluded by collecting societies and under which they grant each other the right to license their repertoires in their respective territories[108] have also come under intense scrutiny. In a first stage the Commission raised objections on the basis of Art. 81, but was prepared to grant exemptions;[109] later, however, the tone hardened. In relation to Internet, satellite transmission, or cable retransmission the Commission increasingly objects to territorial restrictions. It wants to impose a one-stop-shop solution whereby users can buy a single licence covering the whole of the EU instead of the current country-by-country licences and it wants the collecting societies to compete with each other in this respect. The collecting societies see this as an attack on their very business model and fear that price competition will only result in lower royalties for their members, the artists, and performers. The Commission's *CISAC* decision[110] is therefore heavily contested and the matter is likely to end up before the Court of Justice. And the Commission is preparing a directive on collective management to help the societies address certain of these issues.[111]

Article 102—collecting societies

The largest number of cases in which Art. 102 of the Treaty on the Functioning of the European Union (formerly Art. 82 of the EC Treaty) has been applied to copyright relates to those involving collecting societies. The European Court of Justice has indicated that there is nothing intrinsically objectionable about the establishment of collecting societies, which may be necessary in order that individual artists can obtain a reasonable return for their endeavour[112]—but, usually, these collecting societies occupy a dominant position, because they operate as a de facto monopoly in the member states—that is, in relation to a substantial part of the Common Market. Trade between member states is affected by the fact that the creation of a single market for copyright services is prevented. So the way in which these collecting societies exploit their dominant position will be closely examined and improper exploitation will be an infringement of Art. 102.[113]

The early cases

The internal rules of the collecting societies have to take account of all of the relevant interests and the result must be a balance between '*the requirement of maximum freedom for authors, composers, and publishers to dispose of their works and that of the effective management of their rights*'.[114] Every exaggeration towards one side can imply an abuse

---

[108] I.e. the collecting society in country X allows the society in country Y to license the repertoire of society X to users in country Y and vice versa. The use is of course only licensed for that country.

[109] See Decision 2003/300, *IFPI 'Simulcasting'* [2003] OJ L107/58.

[110] Case COMP/C2/38.698, *Re CISAC Agreement* [2009] 4 CMLR 12. See Ch. Stothers, 'Copyright and the EC Treaty: Music, Films and Football' (2009) 31(5) EIPR 272–82.

[111] See the Proposal for a Directive of the European Parliament and of the Council on collective management of copyright and related rights and multi-territorial licensing of rights in musical works for online uses in the internal market, COM (2012) 372 final.

[112] Case 127/73, *Belgische Radio en Televisie & Société Belge des Auteurs, Compositeurs et Editeurs v. SV SABAM & NV Fonior* [1974] ECR 313, [1974] 2 CMLR 238.

[113] See J.-F. Bellis (1989) 'Collecting Societies and EEC Law', in D. Peeperhorn and C. van Rij (eds.) *Collecting Societies in the Music Business,* Reports presented at the meeting of the International Association of Entertainment Lawyers, MIDEM, Cannes, Apeldoorn: Maklu, p. 78; B. Cawthra (1973) *Industrial Property Rights in the EEC*, Farnborough: Gower Press, pp. 70–1.

[114] *Belgische Radio en Televisie & Société Belge des Auteurs, Compositeurs et Editeurs* (n. 112).

of dominant position. This abuse takes the form of discrimination against nationals of other member states and among members, or the binding of members with excessive obligations.[115]

There is no doubt that any discrimination on grounds of nationality is an abuse of dominant position. The Commission made that clear in its *GEMA* decision.[116] Membership cannot be made dependent on the establishment of a tax domicile in the member state in which the collecting society operates and special forms of membership, or membership of the organs of the society, cannot be denied to persons or companies that have the nationality of a different member state from that of the collecting society. Account should also be taken of income received from other collecting societies in order to determine if a member qualifies for a special form of membership.[117] GEMA did not appeal to the European Court of Justice, but the Court approved of the Commission's point of view by giving judgment against GVL (another collecting society) when it refused to represent anyone not resident in Germany, because secondary exploitation rights in other member states were generally less comprehensive and more difficult to assert.[118]

Discrimination among members in relation to the distribution of income is also an abuse. Every classification procedure has to be cost-justified and, without cost justification, an undertaking in a dominant position cannot pay loyalty bonuses[119]—especially not to certain members with funds coming from all members. The Commission found that GEMA was infringing these principles.[120] But if royalty income from all sources is taken into account, a collecting society is still permitted to set a reasonable level of royalty income as a condition of membership.[121] It was stated:[122]

> The abuse also lies in the fact that GEMA binds its members by obligations which are not objectively justified and which, in particular, unfairly complicate the movement of its members to another society.

It cannot be accepted that members are required to assign their rights for all categories of works and for the entire world to the collecting society, especially not if the assignment period and the waiting period for the acquisition of certain benefits are excessive and if future works also have to be assigned. The two latter points are already abuses when considered on their own.[123] The Commission held that members should be free to assign all, or part, of their rights for the countries in which the collecting society does not operate directly to other societies, and that they should be equally free to assign only certain categories of rights to the collecting society and to withdraw from it the administration of certain categories at the end of a three-year period.[124]

---

[115] Bellis, 'Collecting Societies and EEC Law' (n. 113) at 78. [116] (1971) OJ L 134/15.

[117] (1971) OJ L 134/15.

[118] Case 7/82, *Gesellschaft zur Verwertung von Leistungsschutzrechten mbH (GVL) v. EC Commission* [1983] ECR 483, [1983] 3 CMLR 645.

[119] See Case 85/76, *Hoffmann-La Roche & Co. AG v. EC Commission* [1979] ECR 461, [1979] 3 CMLR 211.

[120] *GEMA decision* (1971) OJ L 134/15.

[121] Bellis, 'Collecting Societies and EEC Law' (n. 113) at 79.

[122] *GEMA decision* (n. 120). [123] *GEMA decision* (n. 120).

[124] The original period was one year and seven categories were defined. This option is still open: *GEMA decision* (n. 120). The Commission's decision of 6 July 1972—(1972) OJ L 166 22—offered the alternative of a three-year period compensated by these narrower categories: the general performance right; the radio broadcasting right; the public performing right of broadcast works; the right to transmit by television; the public performing right of televised works; the motion picture performance right; the right of mechanical reproduction and distribution; the public performing right of mechanically reproduced works; the motion picture production right; the right to produce, reproduce, and distribute on videotape; the public performing right of works reproduced on videotape; the utilization rights arising in the future as a result of technical development or a change in legislation.

Members must have the opportunity to choose another collecting society to represent them outside the Community. An abuse that relates only to performance outside the Community stays an infringement of Art. 102 if parties within the jurisdiction of one of the member states concluded the contract in the Community.[125]

A couple of final details can be added, such as the rule that the right of judicial recourse may not be excluded by an undertaking occupying a dominant position[126] and that, if they are essential to strengthen the position of the collecting society in negotiations with powerful large customers such as national radio and television stations, restrictions imposed on members can be accepted.[127]

The relationship between collecting societies and third parties can also be problematic, and raises certain issues in relation to Art. 102. The first abuses to be found in this area were the imposition of a higher royalty on imported tape and video recorders than that levied on equipment produced in the member state in which the collecting society is established and the contractual extension of royalty payments to works that are no longer protected.[128]

The more recent cases provide more details

A series of more recent cases allowed the European Court of Justice to work out a more detailed point of view. In the *Basset v. SACEM* case,[129] the Court ruled that it is no abuse, in the sense of Art. 102, if a collecting society charges a royalty called a 'supplementary mechanical reproduction fee', in addition to a performance royalty, on the public performance of sound recordings. This only amounted to a normal copyright exploitation and no act of arbitrary discrimination, nor a disguised restriction on trade between member states, could be seen in it because the fee was charged for all sound recordings, regardless of their origin. The fact that such a fee did not exist in the member state in which the sound recordings were lawfully placed on the market did not influence this conclusion.

Even more important in that case was the following obiter dictum: '*It is not impossible, however, that the amount of the royalty, or of the combined royalties, charged by the copyright-management society may be such that Article [82] applies.*'[130] The Court elaborated this obiter dictum further by laying the burden of proving that an appreciably higher scale of royalty fees is justified by a better copyright protection on the collecting society. If such proof is not brought, the imposition of the higher fees forms an abuse of dominant position.[131]

In the subsequent *Lucazeau* cases,[132] the Court ruled:

> When an undertaking holding a dominant position imposes scales of fees for its services which are appreciably higher than those charged in other member states and where a

---

[125] Case 22/79, *Greenwich Film Production, Paris v. SACEM* [1979] ECR 3275, [1980] 1 CMLR 629.

[126] *GEMA decision* (n. 120).

[127] *Belgische Radio en Televisie & Société Belge des Auteurs, Compositeurs et Editeurs* (n. 112).

[128] *GEMA decision* (n. 120), but collecting societies have the right to round off the playing time to the nearest minute.

[129] Case 402/85, *G. Basset v. Société des Auteurs, Compositeurs et Editeurs de Musique (SACEM)* [1987] ECR 1747, [1987] 3 CMLR 173.

[130] *G. Basset v. Société des Auteurs, Compositeurs et Editeurs de Musique (SACEM)* (n. 129) at 1769. This dictum fell outside the scope of the prejudicial question referred to the Court by the French judge.

[131] See also Case C-351/12, *OSA – Ochranny svaz autorsky pro prava k dilum hudebnim o.s. v. Leecebne lazne Marianske Lazne a.s.*, 27 February 2014, <http://curia.europa.eu>.

[132] Cases 110/88, 241/88, and 242/88, *François Lucazeau v. Société des Auteurs, Compositeurs et Editeurs de Musique (SACEM)* [1989] ECR 2811.

comparison of the fee levels has been made on a consistent basis, that difference must be regarded as indicative of an abuse of a dominant position. In such a case it is for the undertaking in question to justify the difference with reference to objective dissimilarities between the situation in the member state concerned and the situation prevailing in all the other member states.[133]

The Court had reached the same conclusion some weeks earlier in the *Tournier* case.[134] But in *Tournier*, the Court ruled also that a collecting society that refuses to grant the users of recorded music access only to its foreign repertoire does not abuse its dominant position, in the sense of Art. 102:

> unless access to a part of the protected repertoire could entirely safeguard the interests of the authors, composers and publishers of music without thereby increasing the costs of managing contracts and monitoring the use of protected musical works.[135]

The main issues with a Community interest in relation to collecting societies have now been addressed. *BEMIM*[136] and *Tremblay*[137] showed that the outstanding issues lack a Community interest and therefore fall under the jurisdiction of the national courts. This may suit the EU well, because it becomes clear that it will need the cooperation of the collecting societies if these are to be increasingly involved in collecting royalties for the exploitation of copyright works in the information society.[138] These developments do not, however, involve a change in policy as far as the points of substantive law are involved.

This approach has been continued in the recent *Kanal 5* case.[139] The Swedish collecting society STIM had applied to the commercial television channel Kanal 5 a remuneration model that calculated the royalty that was to be paid for the use of musical works partly on the basis of the (advertising) revenues of the channel. Kanal 5's objections were refuted by the Court of Justice in as far as that part is proportionate overall to the quantity of musical works protected by copyright actually broadcast or likely to be broadcast. That decision accepts this idea of a blanket licence only on the basis though that there is no other method that enables the use of those works and the audience to be identified more precisely without, however, resulting in a disproportionate increase in the costs incurred for the management of contracts and the supervision of the use of those works. If a more precise method exists and does not result in a disproportionate increase in costs, it should be applied. The fact that STIM used different models to calculate royalties for commercial and public service broadcasters on the other hand was held to result in all likelihood in an abuse of its dominant position, if STIM applied with respect to the commercial broadcasters dissimilar conditions to equivalent services and if it placed them as a result at a competitive disadvantage. The only way to avoid that conclusion was if such a practice can be objectively justified. This case provides not only an interesting

---

133 *François Lucazeau* (n. 132) at 2831.

134 Case 395/87, *Ministère Public v. Jean-Louis Tournier* [1989] ECR 2521, [1991] 4 CMLR 248.

135 *Ministère Public v. Jean-Louis Tournier* (n. 134) at 2580.

136 Case T-114/92, *Bureau Européen des Médias de l'industrie Musicale (BEMIM) v. EC Commission* [1995] ECR II-147, [1996] 4 CMLR 305.

137 Case T-5/93, *Roger Tremblay v. EC Commission (Syndicat des Exploitants de Lieux de Loisirs (SELL), intervening)* [1995] ECR II-185, [1996] 4 CMLR 305; Case C-91/95P, *Roger Tremblay v. EC Commission* [1996] ECR I-5547, [1997] 4 CMLR 211.

138 See P. Torremans and I. Stamatoudi, 'Collecting Societies: Sorry, the Community Is No Longer Interested!' (1997) 22 EL Rev 352; see also I. Stamatoudi, 'The European Court's Share–State Relationship with Collecting Societies' (1997) 6 EIPR 289–97.

139 Case C-52/07, *Kanal 5 Ltd v. Föreningen Svedska Tonsättares Internationella Musikbyrå (STIM) UPA* [2009] 5 CMLR 18, [2009] ECDR 5.

application of the *Lucazeau/Tournier* approach 20 years after the original cases; it also seems to hint at a much more accommodating line taken by the Court in relation to collecting societies than the one the Commission is taking in relation to Art. 81.

Article 102—does dominance force an undertaking to grant a licence?

The central issue involved in relation to the question of whether dominance forces an undertaking to grant a licence is whether an undertaking in a dominant position can itself be forced to grant a 'licence' of an intellectual property right that it holds and if a refusal to do so implies an abuse of its dominant position. In recent years, this issue has arisen on several occasions in the areas of design and copyright. We discuss these design and copyright cases here together, because they strongly draw upon each other.

Volvo and *Renault*

The issue arose for the first time in two cases that were concerned with designs for spare parts for cars: *Maxicar v. Renault*[140] and *Volvo v. Veng*.[141] Maxicar and Veng were involved in car repairs and maintenance, and wanted to obtain a licence to produce spare parts themselves. When unsuccessful in obtaining these licences, they argued that Volvo and Renault occupied a dominant position in the relevant market and that, by refusing to grant licences, they abused their dominant position. They wanted to see Volvo and Renault obliged to grant the licences, and submitted that the European Court of Justice should interpret Art. 102 accordingly.

The Court started its analysis by ruling out the possibility that the existence of the fact that an intellectual property right was obtained could be an abuse of a dominant position. The Court held that the existence and the issue of obtaining an intellectual property right is a matter for the national rules of the member states, which rules determine the nature and extent of the protection.[142] In the *Maxicar* case, the Court stated that '*the mere fact of obtaining protective rights...does not constitute an abuse of a dominant position within the meaning of Article [82]*'.[143]

The obligation for a dominant undertaking to grant a licence[144] was ruled out in the *Veng* case:

> the right of the proprietor of a protected design to prevent third parties from manufacturing and selling or importing, without its consent, products incorporating the design constitutes the very subject-matter of his exclusive right. It follows that an obligation imposed upon the proprietor of a protected design to grant to third parties, even in return for a reasonable royalty, a licence for the supply of products incorporating the design would lead to the proprietor thereof being deprived of the substance of his exclusive right, and that a refusal to grant such a licence cannot in itself constitute an abuse of a dominant position.[145]

---

[140] Case 53/87, *Consorzio Italiano della Componentistica di Ricambio per Autoveicoli & Maxicar v. Régie nationale des usines Renault* [1988] ECR 6039, [1990] 4 CMLR 265.

[141] Case 238/87, *AB Volvo v. Erik Veng (UK) Ltd* [1988] ECR 6211, [1989] 4 CMLR 122.

[142] *AB Volvo* (n. 141), with reference to Case 144/81, *Keurkoop BV v. Nancy Kean Gifts BV* [1982] ECR 2853, [1983] 2 CMLR 47.

[143] Case 53/87, *Consorzio Italiano della Componentistica di Ricambio per Autoveicoli & Maxicar v. Régie nationale des usines Renault* [1988] ECR 6039, [1990] 4 CMLR 265 at 6073.

[144] See V. Korah, 'No Duty to License Independent Repairers to Make Spare Parts: The *Renault*, *Volvo* and *Bayer* Cases' (1988) 12 EIPR 381.

[145] Case 238/87, *AB Volvo v. Erik Veng (UK) Ltd* [1988] ECR 6211, [1989] 4 CMLR 122 at 6235.

The situation may, however, be different if the owner of the right refuses to supply spare parts, fixes prices at an unfair level,[146] or discontinues production. Provided that such conduct is liable to affect trade between member states, such exercise of the intellectual property right is prohibited by Art. 102 and, in this situation, the grant of a 'compulsory' licence becomes possible.[147] But it is clear from the cases that more than the existence of the right creating a dominant position and the simple refusal to grant a licence is required if an abuse is to be proved. The starting point must be that the power to decide whether or not to grant licences is an essential component of the right with which Art. 102 does not interfere. *Volvo v. Veng* dealt with designs, but the Court's ruling in *Maxicar v. Renault* does not permit any different conclusion when patents are concerned.[148]

Magill

Facts and early stages of the Magill litigation

In the *Magill* cases,[149] the problem arose when Magill wished to publish the listings of programmes of the British Broadcasting Corporation (BBC), Independent Television (ITV), and Radio Telefís Éireann (RTE) in a single weekly publication. The three companies refused to supply those listings and invoked their copyright in the listings to do so. It should be noted that they published their own guides, which thus enjoyed a form of monopoly, and supplied, free of charge, the weekly listings to foreign publications; they also supplied daily listings to the press. The Commission[150] ruled that the three companies abused their dominant position in exercising their copyright in such a way and required that advance information be supplied to Magill.

The Court of First Instance upheld the decision on this point.[151] The judgment of the Court of First Instance reads:

> conduct of that type (the exercise of the copyright in the way described above)...clearly goes beyond what is necessary to fulfil the essential function of the copyright as permitted in Community law.[152]

---

[146] Products protected by an intellectual property right may be sold at a higher price than similar unprotected products if the price difference forms a reasonable return of the investments made: see Case 24/67, *Parke, Davis & Co. v. Probel, Reese, Beintema-Interfarm & Centrafarm* [1968] ECR 55, [1968] CMLR 47, confirmed in Case 53/87, *Maxicar v. Régie nationale des usines Renault* [1988] ECR 6039, [1990] 4 CMLR 265.

[147] Case 238/87, *AB Volvo v. Erik Veng (UK) Ltd* [1988] ECR 6211, [1989] 4 CMLR 122; Case 53/87, *Maxicar v. Régie nationale des usines Renault* [1988] ECR 6039, [1990] 4 CMLR 265.

[148] *AB Volvo* and *Maxicar* (n. 147); see C. Bellamy and G. Child (1991) *Common Market Law of Competition*, 1st Supp. to 3rd edn, London: Sweet and Maxwell, p. 86. The Patents Court in London dealt with an application to patents in *Philips Electronics NV v. Ingman Ltd & the Video Duplicating Co. Ltd* [1999] FSR 112.

[149] Case T-69/89, *Radio Telefís Éireann v. EC Commission (Magill TV Guide Ltd intervening)* [1991] ECR II-485, [1991] 4 CMLR 586; Case T-70/89, *British Broadcasting Corp. & BBC Enterprises Ltd v. EC Commission (Magill TV Guide Ltd intervening)* [1991] ECR II-535, [1991] 4 CMLR 669; Case T-76/89, *Independent Television Publications Ltd v. EC Commission (Magill TV Guide Ltd intervening)* [1991] ECR II-575, [1991] 4 CMLR 745.

[150] *Magill TV Guide/ITP, BBC & RTE decision* (1989) OJ L 78/43, [1989] 4 CMLR 757.

[151] Case T-69/89, *Radio Telefís Éireann v. EC Commission (Magill TV Guide Ltd intervening)* [1991] ECR II-485, [1991] 4 CMLR 586; Case T-70/89, *BBC & BBC Enterprises Ltd v. EC Commission (Magill TV Guide Ltd intervening)* [1991] ECR II-535, [1991] 4 CMLR 669; Case T-76/89, *Independent Television Publications Ltd v. EC Commission (Magill TV Guide Ltd intervening)* [1991] ECR II-575, [1991] 4 CMLR 745.

[152] Case T-69/89, *Radio Telefís Éireann v. EC Commission (Magill TV Guide Ltd intervening)* [1991] 4 CMLR 586 at 618.

After failing to find an objective and specific justification for this conduct, the Court of First Instance continued:

> the aim and effect of the applicant's exclusive reproduction of its programme listings was to exclude any potential competition…in order to maintain the monopoly enjoyed…by the applicant on that market. From the point of view of outside undertakings interested in publishing a television magazine, the applicant's refusal to authorise, on request and on a non-discriminatory basis, any third party to publish its programme listings is therefore comparable…to an arbitrary refusal by a car manufacturer to supply spare parts…to an independent repairer…[153]

The Court of First Instance applied the *Volvo v. Veng* doctrine to copyright. This situation falls under the exception in the doctrine in relation to which the grant of a 'compulsory' licence is possible, because the intellectual property right is exercised in a way that is prohibited by Art. 102.[154]

The Court of First Instance also stressed that it is enough, in order for Art. 102 to be applicable, that the abusive conduct is capable of affecting trade between member states; no present and real effect on such trade is required.[155]

Magill *before the Court of Justice—a turning point*

The *Magill* cases went on to be appealed before the European Court of Justice.[156] The main problem with the approach taken by the Commission and the Court of First Instance is that it could suggest that, once an undertaking occupies a dominant position, the simple refusal to grant a licence could constitute an abuse of that dominant position.[157] This cannot be a correct interpretation of Art. 102. As suggested in *Volvo* and *Renault*, the interpretation of Art. 102 develops along the lines of the interpretation of Arts. 34 and 36. This is the approach that we advocated in relation to the free movement of goods and it was also the approach taken by Advocate-General Gulmann in his conclusion, which was delivered in June 1994.[158]

In a controversial judgment, the wording of which strongly resembles the *Commercial Solvents*[159] line of thought, the Court declined to overrule the Court of First Instance. The reasons given and the implications of the judgment do, however, require some careful examination.[160] The main principle is that a refusal to license intellectual property

---

[153] *Radio Telefís Éireann* (n. 152); similar rulings are found in the other *Magill* cases.

[154] Cf. R. Whish (1993) *Competition Law*, 3rd edn, London: Butterworths, p. 648; C. Bellamy and G. Child (1991) *Common Market Law of Competition*, 1st Supp. to 3rd edn, London: Sweet and Maxwell, p. 87 could not reconcile the Commission's decision with the *Volvo v. Veng* doctrine.

[155] Case T-69/89, *Radio Telefís Éireann v. EC Commission (Magill TV Guide Ltd intervening)* [1991] ECR II-485, [1991] 4 CMLR 586; Case T-70/89, *BBC & BBC Enterprises Ltd v. EC Commission (Magill TV Guide Ltd intervening)* [1991] ECR II-535, [1991] 4 CMLR 669; Case T-76/89, *Independent Television Publications Ltd v. EC Commission (Magill TV Guide Ltd intervening)* [1991] ECR II-575, [1991] 4 CMLR 745.

[156] Joined Cases C-241/91 P and C-242/91 P, *Radio Telefís Éireann & Independent Television Publications Ltd v. EC Commission* [1995] ECR I-743, [1995] 4 CMLR 718.

[157] See S. Haines, 'Copyright Takes the Dominant Position: The Advocate-General's Opinion in *Magill*' (1994) 9 EIPR 401, 401.

[158] See Haines, 'Copyright Takes the Dominant Position' (n. 157).

[159] See Case 6, 7/73, *ICI & Commercial Solvents v. EC Commission* [1974] ECR 223, [1974] 1 CMLR 309. This was a straight case of an unlawful refusal to supply by an undertaking in a dominant position. No exclusive rights, let alone intellectual property rights, were involved.

[160] See I. Stamatoudi, 'The Hidden Agenda in *Magill* and its Impact on New Technologies' (1998) 1 JWIP 153.

rights can contravene Art. 102 in 'exceptional circumstances'. In those cases, compulsory licensing is an available remedy.[161]

When it established that the broadcasters occupied a dominant position, the Court indicated, first of all, that it accepted that the relevant product and geographical market should be defined as the market in comprehensive television listings guides in Ireland and Northern Ireland. The Court went on to confirm that the mere ownership of an intellectual property right—in this case, the copyright in the programme listings—does not confer a dominant position.[162] That dominant position did, however, exist in the particular circumstances of the case. This was derived from the fact that the broadcasters were the only source of the basic programming information, that they had a de facto monopoly over the raw material that the programming information constituted,[163] and that they could therefore prevent effective competition in the secondary market of weekly television magazines.[164]

Even so, the question remained whether the refusal to license amounted to an abuse of that dominant position. The existing case law pointed towards the fact that the mere existence of the intellectual property right and a use that stays within the specific subject matter of the right cannot amount to an abuse. If the possession of the immaterial right is to have any value, its owner must be free to decide under which circumstances and under which financial conditions he or she is prepared to grant a licence. A right to refuse to grant a licence must be part of such a system and must therefore come within the specific subject matter of the right. In normal circumstances, such a refusal can therefore not be in breach of Art. 102. There may, however, be circumstances in which the intellectual property right is used improperly, to serve purposes that have nothing to do with the real purpose and essential function of the right. If the right is abused, the refusal to grant a licence is no longer used to implement the essential function of the right and, just as anything else in relation to an exclusive or monopoly intellectual property right, exposes itself to the sanction of Art. 102.

This approach is endorsed by the Court's judgment. The Court argued that a refusal might, in exceptional circumstances, constitute an abuse.[165] These exceptional circumstances involved the following in this case: the broadcaster's main activity is broadcasting; the television guides market is only a secondary market for the broadcaster. By refusing to provide the basic programme listing information, of which they were the only source, the broadcasters prevented the appearance of new products that they did not offer and for which there was a consumer demand. The refusal could not be justified by virtue of their normal activities and, by denying access to the basic information that was required to make the new product, the broadcasters were effectively reserving the secondary market for weekly television guides to themselves. The use of copyright to block the appearance of a new product for which the copyright information is essential, and to reserve a secondary market to oneself, is an abuse and cannot be said to be necessary to fulfil the essential function—that is, the reward and encouragement of the author—of copyright. This is especially so if one is the only source of the copyright information or material, and especially the latter element is of vital importance. It may not be part of the abuse, but the availability of other sources for the material would take away the element of dominance. Without dominance, there can simply be no abuse of a dominant position.

---

[161] Joined Cases C-241/91 P and C-242/91 P *Radio Telefis Éireann & Independent Television Publications Ltd v. EC Commission* [1995] ECR I-743, [1995] All ER (EC) 4161.

[162] *Radio Telefis Éireann* (n. 161) at para. 46.   [163] *Radio Telefis Éireann* (n. 161) at para. 53.

[164] *Radio Telefis Éireann* (n. 161) at para. 47.

[165] *Radio Telefis Éireann* (n. 161) at paras. 54 and 57.

Looking at it this way, the Court has allayed the fears that had arisen on the basis of the problematically worded judgment of the Court of First Instance. It is also clear that the judgment of the European Court of Justice in *Magill* is by no means a departure from its existing case law; it is rather an application of that case law in an extreme set of circumstances. All intellectual property rights still have their role in a free market economy, but, as we explained earlier, that role is restricted to their capacity to enhance overall levels of competition. This means that intellectual property rights can only be used to fulfil their essential function. This point has been overlooked on too many occasions and the specific subject matter of a right has too often been seen as a list, set in stone, of things that the right holder is allowed to do. Refusing a licence had to be on that list. But *Magill* has shown that the list is by no means so set and that the listed items are only included in so far as they fulfil the essential pro-competitive function of the intellectual property right involved. They will be caught by the operation of competition law if they are (ab)used for other purposes. This will be the case in what the Court described as 'exceptional circumstances' and the essential-facilities doctrine, which is so prominently present in the judgment, provides just one—albeit a poignant—example of exceptional circumstances in which the use of an intellectual property right falls outside of what is required for the fulfilment of the essential function of the intellectual property right concerned.

One can find, between the lines of the *Magill* case, criticism of the fact that the UK and Ireland grant copyright to basic programme information listings that have such a low level of originality. But this point will have to be addressed by the member states concerned or by means of a Parliament and Council directive. The Court has no power to interfere with issues such as what is original enough to attract copyright or, in trade marks terms, with the determination of whether there is de facto confusion between two trade marks. The Court made this clear in *Deutsche Renault v. Audi*.[166] These issues of substantive law are part of the sovereign powers of the member states in the absence of Community harmonization measures on the points concerned.

It must be obvious that these exceptional circumstances will rarely be found and that the operation of the rule in *Magill* will be restricted to unusual and special cases, but the essential function is by no means a narrow concept. *Magill* must also be seen against the background of the fact that a weak copyright was involved. Most other member states would not even have given copyright in the basic programme information concerned. Basic information is more easily an indispensable raw material for new products than the more traditional highly creative personal expressions of certain ideas by authors. This means that the *Magill* rule will more easily bite in the former cases. The more original the work is, the more creative the expression that has gone into a particular expression of an idea, the more unlikely it is that a refusal to licence will be an abuse. The refusal to grant a licence for the television listings became abusive, among other things, because, without the licence, Magill could not publish any guide: the whole market and the emergence of a new product were blocked. A refusal to grant a licence to turn a novel into a movie is clearly not in the same league: plenty of other films can be made and the monopolization of any secondary market is simply not present.

Ladbroke

The conclusion that *Magill* needs to be confined to a small number of extreme cases is also supported by the judgment of the Court of First Instance in one of the many

---

[166] Case C-317/91, *Deutsche Renault v. Audi* [1993] ECR I-6227, [1995] 1 CMLR 461.

Ladbroke cases.[167] This case was concerned with the question of whether a refusal by the French copyright owners to license sound and pictures of French horse races to a Belgian betting agency amounted to a *Magill*-style abuse of a dominant position.[168]

The emphasis in this case lies squarely on the issue of abuse. That abuse must be found on the relevant geographical market and any activity or decision outside that market is irrelevant. The Court of First Instance ruled that no *Magill*-style abuse could be found. It reached this conclusion for a couple of reasons.[169] First, Ladbroke was not prevented from entering another market by the refusal to license. It was already an important player in the market concerned and it could not be argued that the French horse racing organizations reserved that betting market for themselves, especially because they were not even present in it. The pictures were not essential for the exercise of the activity in question.

Secondly, the emergence of a new product was not blocked and, in any case, the sound and pictures were not the essential ingredient of such a product; Ladbroke rather wanted to offer an additional service to its clients for its main betting activity. Only a refusal to license that concerned either a new product, the introduction of which might be prevented, despite specific, constant, and regular potential consumer demand, or a product of service that was essential, due to the absence of a real or potential substitute for the activity concerned, would fall foul of Art. 102.

Ladbroke was also not excluded from a market in which the French horse racing organizations were operating by the refusal to license and neither was it discriminated against on the Belgian market.[170]

IMS Health

Facts and issues

It has become clear from this discussion that it is at least arguable that *Magill* had left open several issues.[171] These issues were primarily open to argument, because it was not clear whether the decision on that point in *Magill* depended entirely on the facts of the case—that is, on whether other facts could receive a different treatment—or whether they were a necessary element from a legal point of view. One of the issues left open is the question of whether a finding of exceptional circumstances required, cumulatively, the facts that the intellectual property right was linked to essential inputs for secondary markets, on the one hand, and that a new product had to be introduced in that market for which there was significant and unmet demand, on the other. Do the conditions in *Magill* apply cumulatively—as was the case in *Magill* on its facts—or are they alternative conditions? The latter option would see the essential-facilities doctrine apply to many more cases, because there would be more exceptional circumstances. *Magill* also stresses the need for monopolization of a secondary market—but

---

[167] Case T-504/93, *Tiercé Ladbroke SA v. EC Commission (Société d'Encouragement et des Steeple-Chases de France intervening)* [1997] ECR II-923, [1997] 5 CMLR 309. The same conclusion was also strongly emphasized in the UK courts in *Philips Electronics NV v. Ingman Ltd & the Video Duplicating Co. Ltd* [1999] FSR 112. See also Case C-7/97, *Oscar Bronner GmbH & Co. KG v. Mediaprint Zeitungs- und Zeitschriftenverlag GmbH & Co. KG* [1998] ECR I-7791, [1999] 4 CMLR 112.

[168] See D. Fitzgerald, '*Magill* Revisited: *Tiecé Ladbroke SA v. The Commission*' [1998] EIPR 154.

[169] See Case T-504/93, *Tiercé Ladbroke SA v. EC Commission (Société d'Encouragement et des Steeple-Chases de France intervening)* [1997] ECR II-923, [1997] 5 CMLR 309 at paras. 129–131.

[170] *Tiercé Ladbroke SA* (n. 169) at paras. 124–128 and 133.

[171] See the discussion in paras. 88–105 and the conclusion in para. 106 that there is 'a very serious dispute' concerning these in the Order of the President of the Court of First Instance of 26 October 2001 in Case T-184/01 R [2001] ECR II-3193. This Order was upheld by the Order of the President of the Court of Justice of 11 April 2002 in Case C-481/01 P(R) [2002] 5 CMLR 44. See also *Intel Corp. v. Via Technologies Inc.* [2003] FSR 574 (CA).

how secondary should that market be? Is it simply a separate or derivative market? And could the essential-facilities doctrine apply if the competitor that was refused a licence wanted to compete on the right holder's main market? In other words, how close to the core business of the right holder can one come?

The *IMS Health* saga provided an opportunity to answer some of these questions. *IMS Health* was developing along two parallel tracks on the basis of the following facts. IMS Health is a major supplier of marketing data to pharmaceutical and other health-care companies. In the German market, it has established a structure of local geographic segments—1,860 in total—called 'bricks', each containing a comparable number of pharmacies, in order to collect standardized data without violating data protection laws, which do not allow for the identification of individual pharmacies' data. That structure is protected by copyright under German copyright law. That point as such is not in dispute, but there is more to it than pure copyright.

From the user or consumer perspective, there is a high demand for the data collected through use of the brick structure, which has become an impressive success on the market. The brick structure has de facto become the industry standard and its competitors asked for it to be licensed to them in order for them to be able to compete. The user is, indeed, only interested in data that is presented in a comparable fashion. When IMS Health's competitors, NDC Health and AzyX Deutschland GmbH Geopharma Information Services, applied for a licence covering the brick structure at various stages during the complex timeline and developments of the case, the details of which are not necessary for our present purposes, the grant of such a licence was refused by IMS Health and that resulted, in the end, in a complaint by NDC and AzyX to the European Commission for abuse of dominant position. In due course, the Commission issued its decision, in which it went against IMS in a first stage, but without reaching a final conclusion. Interim measures were imposed. That Commission decision was appealed and, as a result, two Orders of the President of the Court of First Instance[172] and one Order from the President of the European Court of Justice,[173] which suspended those interim measures, followed. In the light of that suspension and of the sceptical attitude that the Presidents of the two courts took towards the Commission's approach, the Commission withdrew its interim measures decision.[174]

At the same time, however, IMS Health's competitors had decided to make use of the brick structure anyway, without waiting for the grant of the licence. IMS Health therefore brought copyright proceedings against them in the German courts. In the course of these copyright proceedings, the German court referred the case to the European Court of Justice for a preliminary ruling.[175]

The Commission's approach

We will start by analysing the Commission's decision first. In this way, the approach the Commission takes to the wider issue of the essential-facilities doctrine in relation to intellectual property rights will become clear. Afterwards, we will move on to consider the

---

[172] Order of the President of the Court of First Instance of 10 August 2001 in Case T-184/01 R [2001] ECR II-2349; Order of the President of the Court of First Instance of 26 October 2001 in Case T-184/01 R [2001] ECR II-3193.

[173] Order of the President of the Court of Justice of 11 April 2002 in Case C-481/01 P(R) [2002] 5 CMLR 44.

[174] Commission Decision of 13 August 2003 (2003) OJ L 268/59, based on the fact that urgent measures were no longer needed.

[175] Case C-418/01, *IMS Health v. NDC Health* [2004] 4 CMLR 1543.

decision of the European Court of Justice. Let us therefore now, first of all, have a look at the process followed by the Commission in giving its decision,[176] in order to find out how it interpreted and applied the essential-facilities doctrine in this case.

Following the standard provisions for any case in which the abuse of a dominant position is alleged, the Commission first of all identified the relevant geographical market. In its view, that relevant geographical market is Germany,[177] whereas the relevant product market is the regional sales data services.[178]

In relation to the position of dominance, IMS Health is found to be dominant after examining several factors, but the Commission primarily refers to the fact that IMS Health holds a high market share not only in Germany, but also in Europe.[179] Because Germany is the country that has *'the largest market for regional sales data services in Europe'*,[180] it may therefore be regarded as a *'substantial part of the common market'* in this respect.[181]

Let us now return to the relevant market for German regional sales data services. In order to understand the background to the case, we need to know what these services are in this case and why they are needed. Pharmaceutical companies need the brick system and, in particular, the system put in place by IMS, because this system enables them to gather data in which they can record sales of a particular drug, comparing the sales figures for each of their products with those for the products of their competitors; it also offers them a tool to measure the performance of their sales representatives.[182] In the brick structure, this data is collected in each brick for a small number of pharmacies in a local area. This allows the pharmaceutical companies to obtain a detailed picture showing possible local differences, without, at the same time, infringing German data protection laws, under which the use of data relating to individual doctors or pharmacies would cause problems.

The Commission adopts the conclusion that IMS Health occupies a position of quasi-monopoly,[183] and this is, according to the Commission, due to the fact that IMS Health owns the copyright in a unique structure for recording sales data for pharmaceutical products and services and that, in the relevant market, there was simply no competition before the arrival on the market of NDC and AzyX. The Commission argues that IMS obtained this quasi-monopoly position through a close collaboration with the German pharmaceutical industry, which led to the creation of a 1,860-brick structure[184] that is segmenting the German market in several sectors in which many data are collected, including those of names of sales representatives, customers, and doctors. The exact shape of the brick structure is therefore, to a large part, the outcome of that collaborative effort. That involvement of the primary customer in the establishment of the structure also helps to explain why this structure seems to be indispensable for other competitors, which made enormous investments to enter into that market and yet found it impossible

---

[176] Commission Decision 2001/165/EC of 3 July 2001 in Case COMP D3/38.044—*NDC Health/IMS Health*: Interim Measures [2002] OJ L 59/18.

[177] Commission Decision 2001/165/EC at para. 55.

[178] Commission Decision 2001/165/EC at para. 51.

[179] Commission Decision 2001/165/EC at para. 59, where the Commission refers on this point to the Court of Justice's judgment in Case C-62/86, *AKZO Chemie BV v. Commission* [1991] ECR I-3359.

[180] Commission Decision 2001/165/EC at para. 60.

[181] Commission Decision 2001/165/EC at para. 60.

[182] Commission Decision 2001/165/EC at para. 93.

[183] Commission Decision 2001/165/EC at para. 58.

[184] See the first sentence of para. 83 and the first sentence of para. 86 of Commission Decision 2001/165/EC; see also para. 87 of the Decision and the opinion expressed by some pharmaceutical companies; see also para. 185 of the Decision.

to build a new structure due primarily to the unwillingness[185] of the pharmaceutical industry to switch to another structure—a process in which the industry would incur important additional costs.[186]

The Commission is further sustaining that the IMS brick structure is becoming a de facto industry standard or a 'common language', as defined by the Commission,[187] in the sense that the common language of that structure is well known and commonly used. For the Commission, the '1860 brick structure is becoming a common language for communicating the information'[188] and all of the pharmaceutical companies that assisted with its creation are, in the end, effectively 'locked in' in relation to that structure—even if one needs to add that they are locked in on a voluntarily basis. Everything turns around that structure[189] and the situation in Germany does not offer so much space for a substitution. The 1,860-brick structure is especially a large and unique source of information[190]—and it is in this respect that the Commission sees parallels with the *Magill* case, in which the information concerned was contained in the television listings on the basis of which the broadcasters had, indeed, a unique source of information.[191]

The possibility of changing the system for the collection of data exists, but, despite the fact that competing companies tried it,[192] this did not lead to a structure very different from that put in place by IMS Health. Changing that structure will also mean changing other data[193] linked to that structure, and this will therefore increase the costs and work as a deterrent for any such change. Also, the relationship of the companies using the (new) structure with their sales representatives will be harmed, because this relationship has also been shaped around the 1,860-brick structure.[194] The Commission's analysis— despite the fact that, in its defence, IMS Health accuses the Commission on more than one occasion of not being precise enough[195]—has shown that IMS Health's brick structure became indispensable and the overall standard.

---

[185] See final sentence of para. 86 of Commission Decision 2001/165/EC.

[186] Especially, it has been argued by the competitors of IMS that a change to the brick structure involves a change in working conditions under German labour law, and that the additional costs therefore include the fact that the contract of service of the sales representatives has to be renegotiated using the German system of codetermination, and that any such change to the brick structure used will therefore mean a long and costly procedure due to the involving the workers' council in the renegotiation procedure: see para. 115 of Commission Decision 2001/165/EC.

[187] In para. 123 of Commission Decision 2001/165/EC and in paras. 86 and 89 in response to the defence of IMS Health (in para. 88) regarding the legal requirements for something to be considered an industry standard.

[188] Commission Decision 2001/165/EC at para. 89.

[189] Also marketing campaigns and market research are organized according to the data in this structure.

[190] Commission Decision 2001/165/EC at paras. 102–104. Also data companies, as well as software companies, make use of the brick structure and deliver their products in it. All of the other data effectively follows the 1,860-brick structure.

[191] The crucial fact in *Magill* is that the monopoly was a monopoly over information and that information happened to be the raw material required by a third party. Therefore *Magill* is now no longer the only case to be remembered for its unusual facts: the unusual protection of copyright of factual information.

[192] See the comments in paras. 124 and 128 of Commission Decision 2001/165/EC.

[193] Commission Decision 2001/165/EC at para. 100.

[194] Commission Decision 2001/165/EC at paras. 107 and 108. Pharmacia also stated that '*each restructuring of sales force destroys customers' relationships with our reps, which means that we would lose significant numbers of sales at the end of the day*': Commission Decision 2001/165/EC at para. 107. See also Commission Decision 2001/165/EC at para. 114, where the loss of the special relationship between doctors and sales representatives in case of a change of the brick structure is highlighted.

[195] Commission Decision 2001/165/EC at para. 122.

Moreover, there are *'technical and legal constraints'*[196] that make it even more difficult and, in the Commission's view, even impossible for other companies to create a new structure for regional sales data in Germany that is able to compete with the 1,860-brick structure. The Commission concluded, therefore, that IMS Health should grant all of its competitors a licence upon payment of a reasonable royalty for the use of its copyright work. The Commission justifies its conclusion as follows: there is an abuse that is due to the dominant position occupied by IMS Health and, moreover, IMS Health owns an essential facility that is impossible to substitute.

In its decision, the Commission refers repeatedly to the essential facility doctrine—especially in the sense in which it was set out by the European Court of Justice in the *Oscar Bronner* case.[197] *Bronner* was not a case concerned with intellectual property rights, but it may nonetheless be important, because it is clearly a case about essential facilities. *Bronner* could therefore shed light on the correct interpretation of the essential-facilities doctrine in European competition law.

Bronner dealt with a system for the house-to-house distribution of newspapers in Austria, set up by the major national newspaper. A smaller competitor argued that it should be allowed to make use of the system in order to be able to compete. In its view, the system had become an essential facility. The Court followed the suggestion of its Advocate-General Francis Jacobs in interpreting the essential-facilities doctrine restrictively and then ruled that it did not apply here. Important for our current purposes is the establishment of a test that a firm violates Art. 102 if:

- the refusal of access to the facility is likely to eliminate all competition in the relevant market;
- such refusal is not capable of being objectively justified; and
- the facility itself is indispensable to carry on business, inasmuch as there is no actual or potential substitute in existence for that facility.[198]

The Commission forgets to mention, however, that *Bronner* is a case that can only show how the essential-facilities doctrine can be applied in a European competition law context in general, being a case of pure competition rules application. It is indeed vital to recall that, in a normal situation, competition rules are the only set of rules used to regulate market behaviour; this is the case in *Bronner*.

The presence of copyright does, however, complicate things. Because copyright confers an exclusive right, there is, almost by definition, also a possibility that such an exclusive right will be used in one way or another to restrict competition. There may therefore be a conflict between competition law, on the one hand, and copyright law, on the other, in a given situation.[199] But in order to understand the nature of such a potential conflict better, one needs to see how both regulatory systems—that is, copyright and competition law—operate.

Copyright operates at a structural level. It puts in place a rewards and incentives structure that applies to all relevant cases, and which aims to enhance competition at creation and innovation level by granting an exclusive right in the copyright work that

---

[196] Commission Decision 2001/165/EC at para. 124.

[197] Case C-7/97, *Oscar Bronner GmbH and Co. KG v. Mediaprint Zeitungs- und Zeitschriftenverlag GmbH & Co. KG* [1998] ECR I-7791, [1999] 4 CMLR 112.

[198] *Oscar Bronner GmbH and Co. KG* (n. 197).

[199] See M. Furse (2002) *Competition Law of the UK and the EC*, 3rd edn, Oxford: Oxford University Press, pp. 205 and 214.

restricts, to some extent, competition at the production level. In so doing, copyright defines (intellectual) property rights. Competition law, meanwhile, operates in an entirely different way. It operates at the behavioural level and it does so almost on a case-by-case basis. It is therefore not the case that there is a conflict between two sets of rules that operate in the same way and at the same level.[200] Copyright and competition law share the same objective, but they have different ways of achieving it and they operate at a different level.[201]

Competition law does not operate at the structural level and, as such, it does not interfere with the structure created by copyright to enhance creation and innovation competition at that stage. What is true, however, is that it may interfere, at a later stage, with some of the behaviour that flows from the grant of copyright. In more down-to-earth terms, copyright may be used or exercised in an improper way, and such behaviour is then regulated and addressed by means of competition law. The factor that complicates matters is that it is, to a fair extent, the incentives and exclusive rights created at the structural level by copyright that facilitate, or at least make possible, the emergence of inefficient behaviour that might infringe competition law rules. What can be derived at this early stage is that a system that is designed to regulate behaviour should not operate in a way that undoes the structure put in place by a system such as copyright. The legislator has made a policy decision to put a structure such as copyright in place to enhance, and reward, creativity and innovation, and that decision should be respected. In other words, competition law should restrict itself to its proper role, which is to address anticompetitive behaviour—such as any use of copyright that is not pro-competitive—as was envisaged when the structural system was set up.[202] This conclusion should not surprise anyone, because it should be kept in mind that it is competition law itself that allows for the grant of exclusive rights if, on the one hand, they are necessary and unavoidable to obtain the benefits that the right holder brings about for the consumer, and if, on the other hand, they do not lead to a complete elimination of competition.[203]

As we have demonstrated, in intellectual property cases in general—and particularly in copyright cases—there is not only one set of rules that affects the market behaviour regulation point: both intellectual property and copyright rules, on the one hand, and competition rules, on the other, set out to regulate competition conditions, and to steer certain forms of behaviour, in the market. The presence of such a second set of rules must have an impact on the test that is used, otherwise its vital role is completely ignored. It is therefore submitted that it is not possible to transfer the test set out in the *Bronner* case to intellectual property and copyright-related cases without modifying it.[204]

This must mean that any strict reliance by the Commission on the *Bronner* case in its *IMS Health* decision must be misguided. The decision cannot be based solely and straightforwardly on the Court's judgment in *Bronner*.

---

[200] G. Ramello (2002) 'Copyright and Antitrust Issues', SERCI research paper, <www.serci.org/2002/ramello.pdf>, p. 28.

[201] S. Lemarchand, O. Fréget, and F. Sardain, 'Biens informationnels: entre droits intellectuels et droit de la concurrence' [2003] Propriétés Intellectuelles 11, 17–19.

[202] See the introductory comments in R. Whish (2001) *Competition Law*, 4th edn, London: Butterworths, p. 676.

[203] S. Lemarchand, O. Fréget, and F. Sardain (n. 201) at 11, 19.

[204] For a complete analysis of the case, see P. Treacy, 'Essential Facilities: Is the Tide Turning?' [1999] IPQ 501; C. Stothers, 'Refusal to Supply as Abuse of a Dominant Position: Essential Facilities in the European Union' [2001] 22 Eur Competition LR 256.

To be fair to the Commission, it also argues that its decision follows from the judgments in *Magill*[205] and *Ladbroke*.[206] The exceptional circumstances referred to by the Court in relation to the broadcasters' refusal to license the programme listings in *Magill* come down to two elements. By refusing to make programme listings available to Magill under licence, the broadcasters prevented the appearance of a new product that they did not offer, but for which there was a clear demand from the side of the consumer. It is important to add, in relation to this first element, that, as a result of their exclusive copyright in the listings, the broadcasters were the only source for any such information, which is vital for anyone wishing to publish a weekly television guide.

The second element is that, by denying access to that vital material without which the new product could not see the light of day, the broadcasters were effectively reserving the secondary market for weekly television guides to themselves. The Court clearly emphasizes the secondary market point by indicating that the broadcasters' main activity is broadcasting and that the prohibited activity therefore did not affect that primary activity, but only the guides market that is only a secondary market for the broadcasters. The refusal therefore could not be justified by virtue of the broadcasters' normal activities.

At this stage, one clearly sees the appearance of the essential-facilities doctrine. Because the broadcasters are the only source of the necessary copyright material and because that material is essential—that is, the television guide cannot be produced without it—the copyright-protected information concerning programme listings has become an essential facility for any company that wishes to operate in the relevant market. *Magill* can therefore be seen as an application of the essential-facilities doctrine in a copyright case, whereas *Bronner* applies the same doctrine to a 'normal', non-intellectual-property-related case, as discussed.[207] It is also important to highlight the fact that the Court emphasized that there was a clear and unmet demand on the consumers' side. Like all essential facilities cases in the US, *Magill* also links the essential-facilities doctrine to the benefit that arises for the consumer from its application.[208]

When the Commission refers to the Court's judgment in *Magill*, it summarizes the position adopted by the Court as follows:

> The Court therefore recognised that in exceptional circumstances the exercise of an exclusive right deriving from an intellectual copyright may be abusive even in the absence of additional abusive conduct when, *inter alia*, it prevents the appearance of a new product.[209]

This summary is causing problems in so far as the use of the term 'inter alia' is possibly a misrepresentation of the Court's judgment in *Magill*. Indeed, the Commission seems to suggest that the appearance of a new product is not a necessary element and that other elements might replace it. In the Commission's view, the appearance of a new product is only one of the exceptional circumstances to which the Court refers.

---

[205] Case T-69/89, *Radio Telefis Éireann v. Commission (Magill TV Guide Ltd intervening)* [1991] 4 CMLR 586; Case T-70/89, *British Broadcasting Corp. & BBC Enterprises Ltd v. Commission (Magill TV Guide Ltd intervening)* [1991] 4 CMLR 669; Case T-76/89, *Independent Television Publications Ltd v. Commission (Magill TV Guide Ltd intervening)* [1991] ECR II-575, [1991] 4 CMLR 745.

[206] Case T-504/93, *Tiercé Ladbroke SA v. Commission (Société d'Encouragement et des Steeple-Chases de France intervening)* [1997] ECR II-923, [1997] 5 CMLR 309.

[207] See F. Woolridge, 'The Essential Facilities Doctrine and *Magill II*: The Decision of the ECJ in *Oscar Bronner*' [1999] IPQ 256; P. Treacy, 'Essential Facilities' (n. 204); C. Stothers, 'Refusal to Supply as Abuse of a Dominant Position: Essential Facilities in the European Union' (n. 204).

[208] See P. Areeda, 'Essential Facilities: An Epithet in Need of Limiting Principles' (1989) 58 ATLJ 84.

[209] Commission Decision 2001/165/EC at para. 67.

It is submitted that it is wrong to use the term 'inter alia' in this way and to give this interpretation to the judgment of the Court. Instead, it is submitted that the 'inter alia' type of exceptional circumstances that the Court saw in *Magill* amounts to the fact that the information concerned had become an essential facility for the publishers of television guides. The judgment in *Magill* supports the point of view that the application of the essential-facilities doctrine in relation to intellectual property—that is, for there to be an abuse of the dominant position, the possession of which is not an abuse per se—requires the presence of all elements set out here. The prevention of the emergence of a new product is therefore a necessary component and not only an optional element, as suggested by the Commission.

The Commission also argues that its point of view is supported by the judgment of the Court of First Instance in *Ladbroke*.[210] That Court came to the conclusion that the facts of the *Ladbroke* case did not warrant the application of the rules set out in *Magill*. One could argue that the main reason behind the Court not examining the point of the emergence of a new product is the fact that, if one condition had not been met, the case was bound to fail, because the conditions apply cumulatively. But one might go further, as the Commission seems to be doing in its *IMS Health* decision, and highlight the statement of the Court of First Instance that:

> [the] refusal to supply the applicant could not fall within the prohibition laid down by Article [82] unless it concerned a product or service which was either essential for the exercise of the activity in question, in that there was no real or potential substitute, OR was a new product whose introduction might be prevented, despite specific, constant and regular potential demand on the part of the consumer.[211]

Taken on its own, this quote might suggest that there is no need to establish that the abuse takes place on a downstream market before *Magill* can be applied and, even more importantly, that the conditions found in *Magill* might be alternatives, which excludes the need for their cumulative application.

It is submitted that this is not a correct approach. The whole approach hinges on the literal interpretation, out of context of the single word 'or'; if one adds that context, that interpretation becomes difficult. The Court of First Instance felt hardly any need to investigate the second point.[212] It dismissed the case on the first ground. Anything that it said about the second point is therefore obiter. If it had seen the requirements as real alternatives, as the Commission suggests, it would have needed to deal with the second point in much more depth, even if the truth is probably that the emergence of a new product was not blocked and that, in any case, the sound and pictures were not the essential ingredient of any such product.

The Commission's interpretation, which dismisses the new product requirement that seemed so prominent in *Magill*, is therefore based on flimsy grounds and reliance on the passage from the judgment of the lower European court in *Ladbroke* to achieve this is precarious.[213] This is even more so because it disregards the economic analysis previously set out. The approach may well work in a non-intellectual property context. The *Bronner*

---

[210] Case T-504/93, *Tiercé Ladbroke SA v. European Commission (Société d'Encouragement et des Steeple-Chases de France intervening)* [1997] 5 CMLR 309. For a complete overview of the case, see D. Fitzgerald, '*Magill* Revisited: *Tiecé Ladbroke SA v. The Commission*' [1998] EIPR 154.

[211] Commission Decision 2001/165/EC at para. 68.

[212] D. Hull, J. Atwood, and J. Perrine, 'Intellectual Property: Compulsory Licensing' [2002] European Antitrust Review 36, 37 (a global competition review special report).

[213] Hull, Atwood, and Perrine, 'Intellectual Property: Compulsory Licensing' (n. 212).

case showed how the essential-facilities doctrine could work in this context; similarly, the *Commercial Solvents*[214] judgment leads one to the conclusion that there is an abuse of a dominant position on the sole ground of the monopolization of a secondary market. In non-intellectual property cases, that is an abuse as such even if a new product is not prevented from appearing on the market; in this case, the requirements do not need to be applied cumulatively. But we have already explained that the presence of intellectual property rights and their competition-regulating function change the picture dramatically. It is therefore submitted that the Commission is misguided in its reliance on *Ladbroke* for its views in the *IMS Health* decision.[215]

IMS *in the European Court of Justice*

The scepticism towards the broad interpretation of the essential-facilities doctrine proposed by the Commission that has been expressed in the foregoing analysis was also reflected in the Orders of the President of the Court of First Instance and the President of the Court of Justice. It is therefore welcome to see that the European Court of Justice adopted a much more careful and sensible approach in its judgment in *IMS Health v. NDC Health*.[216]

The Court, first of all, turned its attention to the vital question of when, in a copyright context, a facility has become an essential facility. The Court held that, in order to determine whether a product or service is indispensable for the purposes of enabling an undertaking to carry on business in a particular market, it must be determined whether there are products or services that constitute alternative solutions. It does not matter in that respect that these alternative solutions are less advantageous, or whether there are technical, legal, or economic obstacles capable of making it impossible—or at least unreasonably difficult—for any undertaking seeking to operate in the market to create—possibly in cooperation with other operators—the alternative products or services. The existence of economic obstacles will only be able to rule out an alternative solution if it is established, at the very least, that the creation of those products or services is not economically viable for production on a scale that is comparable to that of the undertaking in control of the existing product or service. This is a very strict interpretation of the essential facility point and, because the existence of an essential facility is a prerequisite that must be met before even the issue of abuse can be addressed, this will severely limit the number of cases in which the exercise of copyright will be interfered with.

In the *IMS* case, the Court advised the German court that, in applying the test, account must be taken of the fact that a high level of participation by the pharmaceutical laboratories in the improvement of the 1,860-brick structure protected by copyright has created a dependency by users in relation to that structure, particularly at a technical level. The Court went on to say:

> In such circumstances, it is likely that those laboratories would have to make exceptional organisational and financial efforts in order to acquire the studies on regional sales of pharmaceutical products presented on the basis of a structure other than that protected by copyright. The supplier of that alternative structure might therefore be obliged to offer terms which are such as to rule out any economic viability of business on a scale comparable to that of the undertaking which controls the protected structure.[217]

---

[214] See *ICI & Commercial Solvents v. Commission* [1974] ECR 223.

[215] D. Hull, J. Atwood, and J. Perrine, 'Intellectual Property: Compulsory Licensing' (n. 212) at 37.

[216] Case C-418/01 [2004] 4 CMLR 1543.　　　[217] Case C-418/01 [2004] 4 CMLR 1543 at 1577.

The strong suggestion to the German court is therefore no doubt that these additional circumstances have turned the block structure into an essential facility.

Once it has been established that the facility—in this case, the block structure, as protected by copyright—is an essential facility, the second step—that is, the issue of whether there has been an abuse of a dominant position, in this case, by refusing to license the block structure—can be addressed. The Court ruled on this point that three conditions have to be met cumulatively for there to be an abuse:

- the refusal is preventing the emergence of a new product for which there is a potential consumer demand;
- there is no objective justification for this refusal;
- the refusal is such as to exclude any competition on a secondary market.[218]

In this way, the Court clearly adopts a very restrictive interpretation of its earlier dicta in *Magill* and *Bronner*. The Commission's suggestions that the criteria could be applied alternatively, rather than cumulatively, and, in particular, that the existence of separate markets was not required has been straightforwardly rejected. The point is now clear: all three requirements apply cumulatively if there is to be a finding of abuse.

The Court then went on to clarify each of the three requirements and their application to the *IMS Health* case. The third condition—relating to the likelihood of excluding all competition on a secondary market—requires that it is possible to distinguish an upstream market, constituted by the product or service that forms the essential facility (for example, in *Bronner*, the market for home delivery of daily newspapers, and in *IMS Health*, the market for brick structures) and a (secondary) downstream market, on which the product or service in question—that is, the essential facility—is used for the production of another product or the supply of another service (for example, in *Bronner*, the market for daily newspapers themselves, and in *IMS Health*, the market for the supply of sales data).[219] The fact that the essential facility is not marketed separately is not regarded as precluding, from the outset, the possibility of identifying a separate market. It is indeed sufficient that a potential market, or even a hypothetical market, can be identified.[220] One of the positive aspects of this approach is that an abuse can also be found in those circumstances in which the right holder's behaviour does not simply hinder competition, but acts to exclude competition completely to such an extent that, in reality, no downstream market exists.

Second, it is now clear that a secondary market does not have to be of secondary importance to the right holder, as was the case on the facts in *Magill*. All that is required is the existence of two markets—or in the words of the Court:

> Accordingly, it is determinative that two different stages of production may be identified and that they are interconnected, the upstream product is indispensable inasmuch as for supply of the downstream product.[221]

It is therefore possible that the applicant for the licence that is refused wanted to compete head on with the right holder on the same market.

In practical business terms, it will be relatively easy to determine the markets involved in those cases in which there is a real existing market for the goods or services that

[218] Case C-418/01 [2004] 4 CMLR 1543 at 1579.
[219] Case C-418/01 [2004] 4 CMLR 1543 at 1580.
[220] See V.-L. Bénabou, 'Chroniques: transversales' [2004] Propriétés Intellectuelles 807, 825.
[221] Case C-418/01 *IMS Health v. NDC Health* [2004] 4 CMLR 1543 at 1580.

allegedly amount to an essential facility, but things get more difficult when one is looking at the potential or hypothetical markets that the Court mentions and which are likely to represent the majority of cases. Indeed, the abuse complained of prevents the existence of a real market in business terms. The Court's approach is to argue that there is a potential or a hypothetical market if two conditions are met:

- the products or services must indispensable in order to carry on a particular business;
- there is an actual demand for them on the part of undertakings, which seek to carry on the business for which they are indispensable.

In terms of the *IMS Health* case, this means asking whether the 1,860-brick structure constitutes, upstream, an indispensable factor in the downstream supply of German regional sales data for pharmaceutical products, coupled with the demand on the part of the competitors of IMS.[222]

The approach adopted by the Court refers back to the criteria used to determine whether or not a facility is indeed an essential facility. One could allege that it is therefore a circular reasoning. More importantly, however, this may well be a workable solution. Admittedly, copyright itself is narrowly associated with its exploitation: for example, IMS only created the brick structure in order to be able to supply the sales data, and the brick structure and the copyright in it have little, or no, value outside the sales data business. The distinction between two markets for the creation of the copyright work, and the right and the work, on the one hand, and for the exploitation of the work on the sales data market, on the other, may therefore seem artificial. But this is a peculiarity of copyright and one should resist the temptation to argue that the creation of two, somewhat artificial, markets in this way opens the door for the application of the essential-facilities doctrine in a vast number of cases to the detriment of copyright.[223] It should indeed be remembered that two additional requirements must to be met before the essential-facilities doctrine can be applied.

It is to these two other requirements that we now turn. The first condition relates to the emergence of a new product. The Court clarified, in this respect, that, in the balancing of the interest in protection of copyright and the economic freedom of its owner against the interest in protection of free competition, the latter interest can only prevail over the copyright interest if refusal to grant a licence prevents the development of the secondary market to the detriment of consumers. There is therefore a need for the applicant for a licence to offer a new and different product, and to show consumer demand for such a product. The consumer interest point is therefore of vital importance. Copyright is indeed not granted to stop the emergence of new and different products for which there is a demand; any use of copyright to that end must amount to an abuse of right.

The final requirement is that the refusal to license must be unjustified. This means simply that the court is to examine whether the refusal of the request for a licence is justified by objective considerations.

In conclusion, a lot of points have been clarified in relation to the essential-facilities doctrine and its application in relation to copyright (and intellectual property rights in general).[224] It is submitted that the Court's restrictive approach is to be

---

[222] *IMS Health* (n. 221) at 1580.

[223] See V.-L. Bénabou, 'Chroniques: transversales' (n. 220) at 825.

[224] For a UK application of the *Magill–IMS* case law, see *Attheraces Ltd v. British Horse Racing Board Ltd* [2006] FSR 20, rev'd on appeal [2007] ECC 7.

applauded, because it does justice to the pro-competitive role of copyright (and other intellectual property rights), on the one hand, and because it allows, on the other, competition law to stop any abuse for undue purposes of copyright (or other intellectual property rights). Those cases in which copyright (or intellectual property rights in general) will be interfered with will be limited to a small number and this may well be rightly so. The Court may not have ruled out all difficulties in applying the test in practice and further difficult cases will no doubt arise, but it did at least did get the balance right in theory.

An overview

The exclusive rights granted by copyright come to life through their commercial exploitation. Assignment and licence contracts take centre stage in this context. There are, of course, plenty of contractual dealings between right holders and individual users, and these may concern one or more works, and single or multiple uses of works. All of this is left to the contractual freedom of the parties. To facilitate the exploitation of rights—both from the point of view of the right holders and from the point of view of the users—multiple contracts for use of many works and contracts with a low monetary value are often replaced by a system of collective licensing.

As an exclusive right, copyright can contribute to the creation of a dominant position. Owing to the fact that there is often one collecting society per country, collecting societies find themselves, almost by nature, in a dominant position in relation both to their members (the right holders) and in relation to their users. Certain items that are protected by copyright may also become an essential facility. These aspects of the commercial exploitation have come under intense scrutiny of the competition authorities. The bottom line is, however, that copyright establishes a structure that has a pro-competitive orientation. Copyright and its use are, as such, therefore not leading to a breach of competition law. But like many instruments, copyright can also be used for the wrong purposes: one can speak of a possible abuse of right. Such abuse takes place at behavioural level and it is at this level that competition law intervenes to stop the abuse. Rather than a straight fight for dominance, then, the interaction between copyright and competition law turned out to be all about complementary actors.

Exhaustion and the rules on free movement also intervene with the exploitation of copyright in the EU. In this respect, an important distinction appears between non-performance copyrights, on the one hand, in relation to which one is typically concerned with the physical distribution of copyright goods, and performance copyright, on the other, in relation to which one is typically concerned with broadcasting and communication to the public of copyright works.

Further reading

DREXL, J. (2007) 'Competition in the Field of Collective Management: Preferring "Creative Competition" to Allocative Efficiency in European Copyright Law', in P. Torremans (ed.) *Copyright Law: A Handbook of Contemporary Research*, Cheltenham/Northampton, MA: Edward Elgar, pp. 255–82.

FRABBONI, M. M., 'From Copyright Collectives to Exclusive "Clubs": The Changing Faces of Music Rights Administration in Europe' (2008) 19(5) Ent LR 100–5.

GERVAIS, D. (2006) 'The Changing Role of Copyright Collectives', in D. Gervais (ed.) *Collective Management of Copyright and Related Rights*, London: Kluwer Law International, pp. 3–36.

RICOLFI, M. (2007) 'Individual and Collective Management of Copyright in a Digital Environment', in P. Torremans (ed.) *Copyright Law: A Handbook of Contemporary Research*, Cheltenham/Northampton, MA: Edward Elgar, pp. 283–314.

STOTHERS, CH., 'Copyright and the EC Treaty: Music, Films and Football' (2009) 31(5) EIPR 272–82.

TORREMANS, P. (2010) 'Collective Management in the United Kingdom (and Ireland)', in D. Gervais (ed.) *Collective Management of Copyright and Related Rights*, 2nd edn, London: Kluwer Law International, pp. 251–82.

TORREMANS, P. (2007) 'The Ongoing Copyright as an Essential Facility Saga', in G. Ramello and D. Porrini (eds.) *Property Rights Dynamics: A Law and Economics Perspective*, London: Routledge-Taylor and Francis, pp. 157–76.

19

Copyright—an overview

Copyright is a right of diversity. We started our analysis by referring to the dual roots of the right and this element proved to be omnipresent in the rest of our analysis. Copyright is a constant balancing act between the author and his or her rights, and the entrepreneur (who exploits copyright works) and his or her rights. This is inevitable, because the two parties are heavily interdependent.

We discussed the wide variety of, sometimes very different, types of work that attract copyright protection. The one point that they have in common is that they form the original expression of an idea, or that, if they are derivative works, they are a technical format that allows the exploitation of that expression. The essence of the copyright in a work is the exclusive right to make copies of the work. This right is often transferred to the entrepreneur who undertakes the commercial exploitation of the work. The author then maintains his or her moral rights to prohibit any abusive form of exploitation of the work and the transfer of rights normally also involves a form of remuneration for the author.

The constant evolution in the way in which copyright works are exploited resulted in rights for performers and producers of phonograms, on the one hand—now even including moral rights—and in things such as rental and lending rights, on the other hand. The exploitation of copyright is also linked very strongly to the evolution of the reproduction technology.

Because copyright is a rather weak right that only protects the expression and not the idea, it offers, as a form of compensation, a rather long term of protection. In general, this term is now 70 years from the death of the author, although some 50-year terms still exist.

Copyright has, over the years, proved to be a flexible and extremely useful tool; it also plays an important economic role. New technical developments in the area of computing are, however, stretching it to the limit. We will discuss some of these developments in Chapter 30 on computers and intellectual property rights—but suffice it to say here that it is essential that copyright sticks to the core elements of the right that we have described, because bending these too strongly would turn a flexible right into a hollow right. We have to preserve the common core that is formed by the essential copyright requirements.

Further reading

TORREMANS, P. (2007) *Copyright Law: A Handbook of Contemporary Research*, Cheltenham/ Northampton, MA: Edward Elgar.

SECTION D
Designs

20

Design and copyright

Introduction

Various definitions of what is a design might be given. Design law sees design as features of shape or configuration, which can be either of an aesthetic or a functional nature. For each of these, there is now a separate design right: aesthetic designs are protected under the provisions of the Registered Designs Act 1949, while functional designs are governed by the provisions of the Copyright, Designs and Patents Act (CDPA) 1988. This has always been an area of substantial complexity, due in part to the influence of copyright.

The wall between design and copyright

There seems to be a natural overlap between design law and copyright, because, in the majority of cases, designs are laid down in drawings, plans, or blueprints that attract copyright protection. A copy of an item incorporating the design involves making a three-dimensional copy of the drawing, plan, or blueprint, and infringes its copyright.

And whilst one can be critical of the case, the CJEU's decision in *Flos*[1] sanctions cumulative copyright and design protection. One will therefore have to deal with the overlap, as it cannot be eliminated.

The overlap problem

The problems involved became very clear in the famous case of *British Leyland Motor Corp. Ltd v. Armstrong Patents Co. Ltd*,[2] which deals with functional designs. British Leyland owned the copyright in the drawings for exhaust pipes for its vehicles, which were built to a functional design. Armstrong reverse engineered the exhaust pipes—that is, it made its own exhaust pipes by taking the original apart and using the information acquired to make identical copies. Armstrong wanted to sell these pipes as spare parts for British Leyland cars.

On the basis of our analysis, British Leyland could successfully bring a case for copyright infringement—but this would lead to the undesirable situation that a manufacturer has a de facto monopoly in the supply of spare parts for the life of the author plus (then) 50 years and could eventually abuse that monopoly. The House of Lords attempted to get around the problem by applying the land law principle of non-derogation from grant to soften the exaggerated strength of copyright protection for

[1] Case C-168/09, *Flos SpA v. Semeraro Casa e Famiglia SpA* [2011] ECR I-181.
[2] [1986] AC 577, [1986] 1 All ER 850.

functional designs. By selling cars, British Leyland had impliedly promised to make spare parts available during the life of the car to facilitate its maintenance. It was clear that law reform was needed.

The solution in the Copyright, Designs and Patents Act 1988

The 1988 Act tried to remove the overlap between copyright and designs once and for always. Section 51 is the provision that is supposed to take care of that. Section 51(1) reads:

> it is not an infringement of any copyright in a design document or model recording or embodying a design for anything other than an artistic work or a typeface to make an article to the design or to copy an article made to the design.

The section goes back to the old method of protecting a design through the copyright in the design drawings. It does not abolish copyright in these drawings, or in any other design document, but it provides an exception in relation to copyright infringement. It is no longer an (indirect) infringement of the copyright in the design document, or in a model recording or embodying the design, to make an item to that design or to copy an item made to that design. This means that a photocopy of the design document will still infringe the copyright in the design document, but that an item made on the basis of that design document will no longer infringe the copyright in the design document as a three-dimensional copy of a two-dimensional work. Instead, the infringement action will now have to be brought under the new design right provisions.

In a case such as *British Leyland*, the copyright in the two-dimensional drawing of the three-dimensional product would not be infringed. An action for infringement of the design right in the copied design is the only available option.

Section 51 explained

A couple of points in this system need clarification and a number of details need to be added.

A 'design document' includes any record of a design. This can, for example, take the format of a literary work, a set of computer data, a model, or a photograph, apart from the obvious drawing.[3] It has to be a design document or model that records or embodies the design; this clearly refers to a document or model made for that purpose. Taken on its own, a drawing of Mickey Mouse made for a comic strip is not made for the production of items, such as toy figures, to that design. It is submitted that such drawings are therefore not design documents for the purposes of s. 51. Otherwise, all kinds of drawings and photographs would lose a substantial part of their copyright protection, especially the possibility of infringement by making a three-dimensional copy of the two-dimensional original, just because someone may, at one stage, want to use them for design purposes.

More importantly, s. 51 excludes design documents or models for artistic works or typefaces from its scope. Copyright in these will still be infringed if an item is made to their design or if an item made to that design is copied. The exclusion of artistic works evidently applied in a case in which an attempt was made to apply s. 51 to drawings made by a freelance graphic designer and that were to be applied to the surface of a set of badges.[4] As designs for artistic works, these clearly fell outside the scope of s. 51. The exclusion of artistic works from the scope of s. 51 also took centre stage in *Lucasfilm*

---

[3] CDPA 1988, s. 51(1) and (3).

[4] *Flashing Badge Co. Ltd v. Brian David Groves (t/a Flashing Badges by Virgo & Virgo Distribution)* [2007] ECDR 17, [2007] FSR 36.

v. Ainsworth,[5] where the case turned on the decision whether or not the helmet of the Stormtroopers in the *Star Wars* movies was an artistic work or not. Having decided that the helmets were not sculptures and therefore not artistic works, Ainsworth was allowed to rely on s. 51 as a defence against copyright infringement.[6]

Another good example may be found in the production of furniture.[7] It will not be an infringement to make furniture to someone else's design without having obtained permission to do so unless the furniture, as such, is an artistic work. Furniture can indeed qualify for copyright protection as an artistic work, whether as a sculpture or a work of artistic craftsmanship, and, if this is the case, the exclusion clause in s. 51 will apply and copyright will still be infringed.[8] In everyday life, most cases of furniture production rely on mass industrial production and artistic copyright protection is unlikely to exist in these cases. Nonetheless, one should not underestimate the impact of the exclusion of artistic works from the scope of s. 51. It has been held that the design of rubber mats for cars that were made by using a metal plate as a mould involved artistic works, both in the shape of the drawing and the shape of the metal plate.[9] Both the metal plates and the impression made on the mats in the mould amounted to engraving, and were therefore artistic works.

One should, however, keep in mind that the exception covers a design 'for' an artistic work or typeface. This means, as we have seen, that s. 51 will not exclude copyright infringement if the (design) document is made for the purpose of making an engraving, sculpture, or etching as an artistic work. But if the design is for something that, in itself, is not an artistic work, such as a design for dolls, the exception for artistic works will not apply and even the fact that a three-dimensional model is made as an intermediate stage towards final production will not exclude the application of s. 51.[10]

The definition of a design

The definition of a 'design' in s. 51(3) is also important. Apart from any aspect of shape, the design can also consist of any aspect of the configuration of the whole, or part, of an item. The concept of configuration is a broad one and includes the relative arrangement of the parts or elements of an item. It cannot be limited to the physical geometry of the item concerned.[11]

But the definition excludes surface decoration. An example of this was found when a graphic design was applied to badges with a shape that followed the contours of the graphic design: that graphic design provided the surface decoration of the badges and was therefore excluded from the scope of the definition of a design under s. 51(3).[12] The existence, in s. 51(3), of a separate definition of a design has important consequences. Section 51 does not require the existence of a design right to operate; as long as the

---

[5] *Lucasfilm Ltd, Star Wars Productions Ltd and Lucasfilm Entertainment Company Ltd v. Andrew Ainsworth and Shepperton Design Studios Ltd* [2009] EWCA 1328, [2010] Ch 503, [2010] FSR 10.

[6] As confirmed by the Supreme Court: *Lucasfilm v. Ainsworth* [2011] UKSC 39, [2011] FSR 41.

[7] CDPA 1988, s. 51(1).

[8] See H. MacQueen, 'A Scottish Case on Unregistered Designs' (1994) 2 EIPR 86, on *Squirewood Ltd v. Morris & Co. Ltd* at 87. The case was not reported, but is available on Lexis.

[9] *Hi Tech Autoparts Ltd v. Towergate Two Ltd (No. 2)* [2002] FSR 270.

[10] *BBC Worldwide Ltd v. Pally Screen Printing Ltd* [1998] FSR 665.

[11] *Mackie Designs Inc. v. Behringer Specialised Studio Equipment (UK) Ltd* [1999] RPC 717. The correctness of this view has been disputed, because it could lead to an unduly broad right: see H. Laddie, P. Prescott, and M. Vitoria (2000) *The Modern Law of Copyright and Designs*, 3rd edn, London: Butterworths, pp. 2171–3.

[12] *Flashing Badge Co. Ltd* (n. 4).

design meets the requirements of the definition of a design (and a design document) contained in s. 51(3), the exclusion rule in s. 51 will operate and copyright infringement cannot be relied upon. For example, if the design of a tracksuit top involving a colour pattern applied to the shape of the garment did not meet the requirements for design right protection, this did not mean that s. 51 did not apply and that copyright could be relied upon.[13] The only thing that mattered was the question of whether the design met the criteria contained in the definition in s. 51(3). Because the answer to that question was positive, the exclusion of copyright infringement applied, irrespective of the issue of design right protection. The majority in the Court of Appeal disregarded this, but it should be kept in mind that s. 51(3) refers *expressis verbis* to the design of any aspect of the shape or configuration of an item. One might therefore argue that, as long as one only copies surface decoration and colour patterns, that does not involve the shape and configuration of the item, and s. 51 should therefore not apply.[14] The majority clearly felt this to be an unduly fine distinction.

Items made to the design

Section 51 covers items made to the design and copies of such items made to the design. Here, too, a wide definition is in order and no additional requirements relating to the result of the copying can be imposed. Lists of components, circuit diagrams, and boards that resulted from the analysis of an existing mixing desk for use in recording studios carried out by a competitor with the aim of gathering knowledge for the construction of its own mixing desk were therefore covered by the definition and, by implication, by s. 51.[15] Items that are not infringing copyright can also be issued to the public or included in films or broadcasts, without infringing copyright.[16] This completes the copyright exception, which would otherwise have little practical economic importance.

The scope of s. 51

If s. 51 is to be really effective in reducing the overlap and the confusion, it should cover both the overlap between copyright and unregistered-functional design, and the overlap between registered aesthetic design and copyright. There is no doubt that it covers the overlap with unregistered designs, because cases such as *British Leyland* arose in relation to functional designs, and we will see that the definition of an unregistered design is identical to that found in s. 51.

Although it is submitted that that definition is, at first glance, wide enough in scope to encompass the definition of registered designs,[17] there are a number of elements that complicate things. First, most design documents that are copied in aesthetic designs will be artistic works and this category of copyright works is excluded from the scope of s. 51. Secondly, surface decoration is also excluded from the scope of s. 51, while it may come inside the scope of the definition of a registered design, in relation to which no similar exclusion is found.

It is not necessary to go into the detail of the various definitions right now before we discuss the two design rights in substance. It is indeed clear that, in practice, s. 51 is almost exclusively restricted to cases of unregistered design. This creates the impression that the overlap between copyright and registered design is left untouched, and may still create problems, but this impression is not correct.

---

[13] *Lambretta Clothing Co. Ltd v. Teddy Smith (UK) and anor* [2005] RPC 6 (CA).

[14] See the dissenting opinion of Mance LJ in *Lambretta Clothing Co. Ltd* (n. 13) at para. 80.

[15] *Lambretta Clothing Co. Ltd* (n. 13) at para. 80; *BBC Worldwide Ltd v. Pally Screen Printing Ltd* (n. 10).

[16] CDPA 1988, s. 51(2).   [17] Registered Designs Act 1949, s. 1; see Ch. 21.

Section 52

Indeed, for purposes of completeness, a brief reference should be made to s. 52 of the 1988 Act. This section refers to authorized use of an artistic work and restricts the term of copyright protection in these works to 25 years if copies of the work are made by an industrial process or if such copies are marketed.[18] Items can be made to the description of the artistic work without infringing copyright, starting 25 years after the end of the calendar year in which the first marketing of the items authorized by the owner of the artistic copyright took place.[19] This effectively reduces the duration of copyright to that of the registered design right, as we will see. The two rights coexist, but no substantial problems arise, because the two forms of protection have the same coverage and will disappear together.

Parliament decided in principle to repeal s. 52. This decision is contained in s. 74 of the Enterprise and Regulatory Reform Act 2013, which left it to the Government to determine the date on which the provision would come into force. After a consultation the Government picked the date of 6 April 2020 and set out savings provisions for the period up to that date.[20] When a judicial review was launched the Government revoked its commencement order[21] and at the time of writing there is no new commencement order on the horizon and s. 74 Enterprise and Regulatory Reform Act 2013 remains in limbo and s. 52 CDPA remains in force.

Does the *British Leyland* defence survive?

But what was the influence of the law reform on the defence created in the *British Leyland* case? The provisions of the 1988 Act and especially ss. 51 and 52—effectively replaced the existing law in this area. One of the reasons why Parliament introduced new legislation in this area was that the old law was not satisfactory. It is submitted that, in practice, the *British Leyland* defence no longer exists under the regime of the 1988 Act. Section 171(3) keeps the defence alive only in theory, because it stipulates that the provisions of the 1988 Act do not affect any rule of law that prevents or restricts the enforcement of copyright. The *British Leyland* defence clearly had that effect. But for the defence to operate, there must, first of all, be a case of copyright infringement and the effect of s. 51 is exactly that this will no longer be possible in design-related cases. The copyright in the design document will not be infringed, so, in practice, there is no use for a rule restricting the enforcement of copyright. Making items, such as the infamous exhaust pipes, to the design contained in the design document, such as the drawing of the exhaust pipe, will not infringe the copyright in the design document.[22] The alleged copyright infringer does not infringe and the production can go ahead. There is no need for the *British Leyland* defence against copyright infringement to arrive at this conclusion.

---

[18] In the UK or elsewhere: CDPA 1988, s. 52(1)(b).   [19] CDPA 1988, s. 52.

[20] Enterprise and Regulatory Reform Act 2013 (Commencement No. 8 and Saving Provisions) Order 2015, SI 2015/641.

[21] Enterprise and Regulatory Reform Act 2013 (Commencement No. 8 and Saving Provisions) (Revocation) Order 2015, SI 2015/1558.

[22] Contra, *Flogates Ltd, USX Corp. & USX Engineers & Consultants Inc. v. Refco Ltd & Graham Peter Briggs* [1996] FSR 935. The comments by Jacob J were obiter, because the case was concerned with the transitional provisions of the 1988 Act. (CDPA 1988, Sch. 1, para. 19(9) keeps the defence alive for cases that come under the transitional provisions.)

Nevertheless, the Act has not abolished the *British Leyland* defence. Maybe the defence can still play a role, when defined properly—which proper definition was provided by the Privy Council in the *Canon* case.[23] The Privy Council ruled that the *British Leyland* spare-parts exception must be seen as a proper exception from copyright infringement. It is the expression of the public policy rule that will prevent manufacturers using their copyright to control the aftermarket in spare parts. That public policy rule will operate if two requirements are met: first, there must be a manifest unfairness to the consumer, who is using the original product for which the spare part is intended; secondly, the monopoly must plainly be anticompetitive in nature. The Privy Council added that the jurisprudential and economic basis for the doctrine of the exception becomes very fragile if these requirements are not met.

The *Canon* case applied this to a situation in which replacement ink cartridges for photocopiers and laser printers infringed the copyright in the drawings of the original Canon cartridges. It was held that the defence did not apply, because the replacement of a cartridge was not a repair that an ordinary purchaser would assume he or she could carry out him- or herself in order to have the continuing enjoyment of the product purchased. The manufacture of the cartridges was an infringement of the copyright in the drawings and the defence could not change that position (the provisions of the 1988 Act did not apply in this case), because the purchaser accepted that he or she would, every so often, need to buy a replacement cartridge. The interests of the consumer were not affected unfairly and the practices of Canon were not anticompetitive.[24]

It is submitted that the decision to found the *British Leyland* spare-parts exception—also called the common law spare-parts exception—on grounds of public policy needs to be applauded.[25] It must, indeed, be the case that, even in a purely domestic context, intellectual property rights need to be fitted in with the overall principle of the enhancement of free competition. Public policy rules should be able to stop the operation of intellectual property whenever these rights are put to improper use, whenever they are abused, and whenever they are used for an anticompetitive goal for which they were not intended. Although narrowly focused on the spare-parts issue, the decision of the Privy Council could open the door for a wider application of this exceptional public policy safeguard in other cases of abuse. It could eventually be developed into a rule that fulfils the same role in domestic competition law as that fulfilled by the essential function-specific subject matter doctrine in the *Magill* case[26] at European level in relation to intellectual property rights.

The next chapter will, however, look at the substantive provisions on registered designs.

An overview

Overlaps in protection between intellectual property rights with different aims and rationales are never desirable. Attempts have therefore been made to avoid an overlap between copyright and design rights. The courts struggled on this point, but, in *British*

---

[23] *Canon Kabushiki Kaisha v. Green Cartridge Co. (Hong Kong) Ltd* [1997] AC 728, [1997] 3 WLR 13.

[24] *Canon Kabushiki Kaisha* (n. 23).

[25] See *Mars UK Ltd v. Teknowledge Ltd (No. 1)* [2000] FSR 138; cf. *Hyde Park Residence Ltd v. Yelland* [2000] RPC 604.

[26] Joined Cases C-241/91 P and C-242/91 P, *Radio Telefís Éireann & Independent Television Publications Ltd v. EC Commission* [1995] ECR I-743, [1995] 4 CMLR 718.

Leyland, a solution was found, albeit on the basis of principles that are alien to intellectual property.

The legislature then intervened and s. 51 of the 1988 Act was an attempt at a comprehensive solution. According to its terms:

> it is not an infringement of any copyright in a design document or model recording or embodying a design for anything other than an artistic work or a typeface to make an article to the design or to copy an article made to the design.

As it turned out, the solution was more problematic, and less clear and comprehensive than envisaged. Section 51(1) excludes designs for artistic works or typefaces; the definition of a design in s. 51(3) excludes surface decoration. The exact circumscription of these exclusions and their impact on the overall solution to the problem has been causing problems. Gradually, a picture of a workable, but not watertight, separation between copyright and designs is emerging—but it is clear that there is also still a place for the *British Leyland* defence. Or as the Supreme Court put it in the *Lucasfilm* case, a graduated way of protecting three-dimensional objects without too much of mere overlap is emerging:

> It is possible to recognise an emerging legislative purpose (though the process has been slow and laborious) of protecting three-dimensional objects in a graduated way, quite unlike the protection afforded by the indiscriminate protection of literary copyright. Different periods of protection are accorded to different classes of work. Artistic works of art (sculpture and works of artistic craftsmanship) have the fullest protection; then come works with 'eye appeal' (AMP Inc v Utilux Pty Ltd [1971] FSR 572); and under Part III of the 1988 Act a modest level of protection has been extended to purely functional objects (the exhaust system of a motor car being the familiar example). Although the periods of protection accorded to the less privileged types have been progressively extended, copyright protection has always been much more generous. There are good policy reasons for the differences in the periods of protection, and the court should not, in our view, encourage the boundaries of full copyright protection to creep outwards.[27]

Further reading

DERCLAYE, E., 'Flashing Badge Co Ltd v. Groves: A Step Forward in the Clarification of the Copyright/Design Interface' (2008) 30(6) EIPR 251–4.

MACQUEEN, H., 'A Scottish Case on Unregistered Designs' [1994] 2 EIPR 86.

SCANLAN, G., 'The Future of the Design Right: Putting s. 51 Copyright, Designs and Patents Act 1988 in its Place' (2005) 26(3) Stat LR 146.

---

[27] *Lucasfilm* (n. 6) at para. 48.

21

Registered designs

In the UK there are two types of designs, registered and unregistered designs. This chapter deals with the former. When design law was harmonized in Europe it was done at this level, even if the Community design has an unregistered component too. This chapter will therefore also look at the Community design right.

Starting points

One could be forgiven for thinking that a design is a plan or blueprint that shows how an item is to be constructed or how the elements of the item are arranged. Intellectual property law, however, has never accepted that simple definition. For our purposes, a design is concerned with aspects of an item or with features applied to it, and is never concerned with the item itself. To complicate things further, two types of designs exist in the UK: registered designs—based on the Registered Designs Act (RDA) 1949, as amended—and (unregistered) designs—based on the Copyright, Designs and Patents Act (CDPA) 1988.

Design law has now been harmonized in Europe, by means of the Design Directive.[1] For the UK, this has resulted in the original Registered Designs Act 1949 virtually being emptied of its original content. The new provisions that have been inserted by the Registered Design Regulations 2001[2] and the Registered Design Regulations 2003[3] are entirely based on the provisions of the Directive.[4] In this book, we will deal exclusively with these new provisions.[5]

On top of these (harmonized) national design laws, a Community registered design has been put in place by the Community Designs Regulation.[6] Under this additional system, a single registered design right is granted for the whole of the European Union (EU). The right has in other words a unitary character. That system is administered by the Office for the Harmonization of the Internal Market (OHIM), which is based in Alicante, Spain, and which also administers the Community trade mark.[7] In this chapter, we will examine the registered designs system and look at the Regulation. The UK system of unregistered designs—also referred to as 'design rights'—will be analysed in Chapter 22.

Registered designs were, in origin under English law, aesthetic designs that were intended to appeal to the eye. Decorative features or items such as a beautifully decorated

---

[1] European Parliament and Council Directive 98/71/EC on the legal protection of designs [1998] OJ L 289/28.

[2] SI 2001/3949.   [3] SI 2003/550.

[4] See also M. Howe (ed.) (2010) *Russell-Clarke and Howe on Industrial Design*, 8th edn, London: Sweet and Maxwell.

[5] The old provisions were discussed at length in Ch. 20 of the third edition of this book (2001).

[6] Council Regulation (EC) 6/2002 of 12 December 2001 on community designs [2002] OJ L 3/1.

[7] Art. 2 of the Regulation.

crystal vase, or patterns applied to household porcelain, would attract registered design protection. But registered designs may also be functional in nature. Exhaust pipes for cars are the prime example,[8] but there are plenty of other examples, such as kitchen utensils that fall within the scope of the (unregistered) design right. Oversimplification led to the rule that aesthetic designs were covered by the registered design, while the (unregistered) design right covered functional designs. In reality, there was—and still is—a considerable overlap. Many aesthetic designs are also functional and may meet the requirements of the (unregistered) design right, such as food containers of a particular shape made to distinguish the product of one manufacturer from the identical product of a competitor, while some primarily functional designs may also have eye appeal and may also be covered by the new system of registered designs.

Requirements for the grant of a registered design

The system put in place by the Design Directive is still relatively new and little exists in the form of case law to clarify its provisions, even if a series of clarifying judgments is building up. It should also be kept in mind that, as with any European Directive, it will eventually be up to the European Court of Justice to rule on its interpretation.

Whereas the old system required the registration of a design for each product separately, the essence of the new system is that it protects a design for a product. The emphasis is on the design, even if it has to be a design for a product. This gives the protection potentially a very wide scope indeed and it is therefore of capital importance to consider carefully how the concepts involved are defined.

A design

The concept of a 'design' is now defined as '*the appearance of the whole or a part of a product resulting from the features of, in particular, the lines, contours, colours, shape, texture of materials of the product or its ornamentation*'.[9] A design is therefore an element of appearance in products.

This definition is much wider than that under the old law and the requirement of 'eye appeal' that characterized the old system no longer exists. The Directive emphasizes this by indicating, in its Recital 14, that no aesthetic quality is required, meaning that arbitrary, but non-appealing, features can now be covered by the definition. What comes in its place, however, is a reference in Recital 11 to '*features which are shown visibly*'. This has to be combined with the use of the word 'appearance' in the definition of a design and, as such, the definition clearly points primarily to aesthetic elements and to an aesthetic impression being created in the mind of the consumer on seeing the design. We are primarily concerned, in this respect, with the 'look and feel'[10] of the product. The design should primarily have been adopted for aesthetic or associative reasons, rather than for technical reasons. We will return to this point in more detail at a later stage. It is, however, worth pointing out that this wide design definition clearly covers the appearance of some trade marks. This will therefore create an overlap in protection, also referred to as the 'convergence' of intellectual property rights.

---

[8] Spare parts occupy a special position in design law: see *British Leyland Motor Corp. Ltd v. Armstrong Patents Co. Ltd* [1986] AC 577, [1986] 1 All ER 850.

[9] RDA 1949, s. 1(2).

[10] See *Apple Computer Inc. v. Design Registry* [2002] ECDR 191, per Jacob J.

A design for a product

What is protected is a 'design for a product'. That concept of a 'product' is defined, in turn, and is said to mean '*any industrial or handicraft item other than a computer program; and, in particular, includes packaging, get-up, graphic symbols and typographical typefaces and parts intended to be assembled into a complex product*', while a complex product is, in turn, defined as '*a product which is composed of at least two replaceable components permitting disassembly and re-assembly of the product*'.[11] In reality, in relation to the latter, the legislator had primarily costly, complex, and long-lasting products—such as cars or computers—in mind.

The only restrictive element in this definition is the exclusion of computer programs[12]—but this is a logical exclusion, because a special regime of protection has already been established for computer programs. Apart from that, the definition is very wide and does away with the restrictions that had surfaced in the UK in relation to what amounts to an item. There is no longer a need for the design to be applied to a product by an industrial process, as is evidenced by the inclusion of handicrafts in the definition. Another consequence of this wide definition will be a substantial weakening of the link between the design and the item or product to which it is applied. The inclusion of 'get-up' in the definition will increasingly make it possible to register the design almost as such, or at least to see its scope of protection against infringement widened in practice. In general, there is no longer a need to register the design in respect of every specific item or group of items. The use of the word 'item' in the definition leads to a degree of uncertainty. The word 'item' seems to suggest some physical form, which is easy to understand in relation to packaging and get-up, because bottle shapes and distinctive labels come to mind, but what is meant by items that consist of graphic symbols or typefaces?

It is likely that the legislator wanted to indicate that the design could be on any kind of surface. Things printed on paper, stamps, and posters are therefore, for example, also covered, as are the more traditional designs for curtains and wallpapers. This clearly expands the traditional scope of design law and some even argue that the carrying medium or product does not need to be permanent.[13] It could therefore even include things such as computer screen icons.[14] Designs can also be for a part of an item; there is no longer a need for the product to which the design refers to be sold separately.

Requirements for protection

That brings us to the main requirements for protection It is worth setting out these *expressis verbis*:

1. A design shall be protected by a Community design to the extent that it is new and has individual character.
2. A design applied to or incorporated in a product which constitutes a component part of a complex product shall only be considered to be new and to have individual character:
   (a) if the component part, once it has been incorporated into the complex product, remains visible during normal use of the latter; and

---

[11] RDA 1949, s. 1(3).   [12] RDA 1949, s. 1(3).

[13] See A. Kur, 'Protection of Graphical User Interfaces under European Design Legislation' (2003) 34 IIC 50.

[14] *Apple Computer Inc. v. Design Registry* [2002] ECDR 191, per Jacob J.

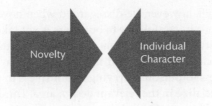

Figure 21.1 Key requirements for registered designs

(b) to the extent that those visible features of the component part fulfil in themselves the requirements as to novelty and individual character.
3. 'Normal use' within the meaning of paragraph (2)(a) shall mean use by the end user, excluding maintenance, servicing or repair work.[15]

The latter part of the Article repeats the requirement that the design must remain visible, which we already referred to above as having been highlighted in the recitals of the Directive.

This starting point is followed up by two provisions dealing explicitly with the requirements of novelty and individual character respectively. Will discuss these in detail first, and they are set out in Figure 21.1, before returning to the special situation for complex products.

Novelty

In order to be registrable, a design must also be new.[16] Novelty is defined in a far less strict way than in patent law: '*a design is new if no identical design or no design whose features differ only in immaterial details has been made available to the public before the relevant date*'.[17]

The first point in this definition of novelty that needs to be clarified is the concept of the 'relevant date'. Normally, this will be the date on which the application for protection is filed. In international cases, however, the applicant may be able to take advantage of the rule in the Paris Convention for the Protection of Industrial Property 1883 that allows an applicant to rely on the date of his or her first application in a contracting state during a six-month period whenever an application in another contracting state is filed within that period and to claim priority on that basis.[18]

On that relevant date, the test that should be applied is whether the same design—or one with a similar character—is already available to the public through publication, whether following registration or otherwise, through exhibition, through use in trade, or through any other form of disclosure. Any design that is already available to the public in this way will no longer be new and cannot be registered, because it is part of the prior art.[19] That prior art is composed of designs. In other words, only designs, as defined in s. 1(2) of the 1949 Act, are to be taken into account. Even if that is now a wide definition, which will include many artistic works of copyright and general designs for any kind of item, there are still limitations: for example, human beings are excluded even if they have become icons and are used as such in publicity campaigns.[20]

---

[15] Art. 4 of the Regulation.   [16] RDA 1949, s. 1B(1).   [17] RDA 1949, s. 1B(2).
[18] RDA 1949, ss. 1B(7) and 14(2).
[19] See case T-450/08, *Coverpla v. OHIM - Heinz-Glas*, <http://curia.europa.eu>.
[20] See *Spice Girls' Application* [2000] ECDR 148.

Certain disclosures will, however, be disregarded when novelty is examined.[21] First, any disclosure that is made in confidence to outsiders is not taken into account. Second, in a certain sense, novelty—unlike in patent law—is limited to novelty within Europe, by disregarding any disclosures that could not reasonably have become known in the normal course of business to persons carrying out business in the European Economic Area (EEA) and who specialize in the relevant design area. Thirdly, there is a set of exclusions that are based on the same 12-month grace-period principle. On the basis of this principle, disclosures made in that period by the designer or a successor in title, disclosures made by the recipient of information from the designer or such a successor, or disclosures made by anyone in abuse of a relation with the designer or such a successor are to be disregarded. This latter limitation may be an advantage, as well as a disadvantage. On the positive side, it allows a designer to show—that is, disclose—the design at a trade exhibition to assess its success before filing an application for protection. This will only trigger the start of the grace period and the designer will still be able to claim novelty during that grace period. The negative consequences—that is, the destruction of the novelty of the design—will surface if another designer picks up the design at the exhibition, copies it, and brings the product on the market within the EEA before the designer files its application. Such behaviour is, on top of anything else, not at all uncommon in the relevant trade circles.

Not only an identical design, but also a design that differs only in immaterial details can destroy novelty. A good example is an application for a design for a bottle carrier. An existing design for a bottle carrier had many features in common with the new design, but the two differed in that:

- they had a different ratio between width and height;
- the handle part in the design applied for encompassed its top half, while that in the existing design comprised only its top third;
- the hole in the handle was circular in shape in the design applied for, while it was oval in the existing design; and
- the body part in the design applied for encompassed its bottom half, while in the existing design it encompassed its bottom two-thirds.[22]

These were held by the OHIM's Invalidity Division to be more than immaterial differences and the design that was applied for satisfied the novelty requirement. One should also keep in mind that in assessing novelty (and for that purpose individual character) one cannot exclude from the comparison a prior design just because the design was for a product used for a different purpose from the one the subject of the registration.[23]

A design for a heater radiator that shared the same pattern of arrangement of features, shapes, and contours with an existing design for radiators was, however, held not to be new, despite the fact that the ratio between width and height had been changed from 1:2.5 to 1:2. In this case, these differences were held to be immaterial details.[24] All other aspects of the design were the same.

A design that is nothing more than a combination of models that were already available to the public and in relation to which an indication was given that they were destined

---

[21] RDA 1949, s. 1B(6).

[22] *Built NY Inc. v. I-Feng Kao*, decision of 8 May 2006, OHIM Invalidity Division.

[23] *Gimex International Groupe Import Export v. The Chill Bag Company Ltd, Kiki's Import & Export Ltd, David Samuel Turner, Colin David Brand and David Frederick Brand* [2012] EWPCC 31 at para. 41.

[24] *Pitacs Ltd v. Kamil Korhan Karagülle*, decision of 26 April 2006, OHIM Invalidity Division.

to work together, e.g. as parts of shower drain, cannot be taken to possess the required degree of novelty.[25] Novelty is assessed through the eyes of the informed user. We will discuss this in detail in the section on individual character. Suffice it to say here that one is dealing with a user of the product that incorporates the design, who is particularly observant, pays attention, compares the features directly, and who has knowledge of the design corpus and the features used.[26]

Individual character

In addition to being new, the new registered design system requires the design to have 'individual character', which is defined as follows:

> A design has individual character if the overall impression it produces on the informed user differs from the overall impression produced on such a user by any design which has been made available to the public before the relevant date.[27]

The background against which this criterion will be evaluated is that of a design that has at an earlier date been made available to the public, i.e. a single specific design.[28] The latter concept is the same as the one used in relation to novelty and that means in the first place that the earlier design has been published following registration or otherwise,[29] but a design can also be made available to the public by being exhibited, used in trade, or by being otherwise disclosed. In other words, the concept is much broader than publication as a registered design by the competent office. This was demonstrated clearly by the General Court in a case involving the Puma bounding feline trade mark. The General Court saw no problem in the fact that Puma never registered its bounding feline sign as a design. Registration as a trade mark was held to be sufficient to make it available to the public and it could be used to demonstrate that the later design did not have an individual character[30] No particular standard of proof is imposed when it comes to showing prior availability to the public.[31]

Whereas novelty essentially looks at whether the design is, save for immaterial details, identical to a pre-existing design, the requirement of individual character is much more in the eye of the particular beholder. The question that is asked is whether the overall impression that the design produces on the informed user differs from the overall impression that a prior design produced on that person. The emphasis is on the overall impression, so bringing together existing features that exist in different products may suffice. And it is the informed user who decides on the issue of the individual character of a design.[32] There should be no feeling of 'déjà vu'. Small differences that do not alter the overall impression should be disregarded, even if they are by no means insignificant details.[33]

---

[25] Case T-15/13, *Group Nivelles v. OHIM*, 13 May 2015, <http://curia.europa.eu> (an appeal is pending), para. 78.

[26] See *Whitby Specialist Vehicles Ltd v. Yorkshire Specialist Vehicles Ltd and others* [2014] EWHC 4242 (Pat).

[27] RDA 1949, s. 1B(3).

[28] *Whitby Specialist Vehicles Ltd v. Yorkshire Specialist Vehicles Ltd and others* (n. 26)

[29] See the decision of the OHIM's third Board of Appeal on 15 April 2013 in case 442/2011-3 *Profile Vox Sp z.o.o. Spolka Komandytowa v. Cezar Przedsiebiorstwo Produkcyjne Dariusz Bogdan Niewinski.*

[30] Case T-666/11, *Danuta Budziewska v. OHIM (Puma SE intervening)*, 7 November 2013, <http://curia.europa.eu>.

[31] See Case T-450/08, *Coverpla v. OHIM - Heinz-Glas*, <http://curia.europa.eu>.

[32] Case T-246/10, *Industrias Francisco Ivars v. OHIM*, <http://curia.europa.eu> See also *PMS International Group plc v. Magmatic Ltd* [2016] UKSC 12.

[33] *Danuta Budziewska v. OHIM (Puma SE intervening)* (n. 30); and Case T-153/08, *Shenzen Taiden v. OHIM (Bosch Security Systems)* [2010] ECR II-2517.

One should look out for differences that are sufficiently pronounced so that they alter the overall impression.[34] The exercise is one with a synthetic nature. Merely listing differences and similarities is not sufficient. The comparison is also limited to the aspects that are protected or will be protected by the registered design. And it is carried out on the basis of the design. The products to which the design will be applied in trade can only be taken into account by way of illustration.[35] But the overall impression which the design produces must be compared with and must be different from the one produced by an individual earlier design. It is not permissible to combine features taken from a range of earlier designs for this purpose.[36]

This should not obscure the fact, however, that this is a tough test. In many cases, a design will show differences when compared with prior designs, but that by no means guarantees that the informed user will judge that a different overall impression is created. The new law offers no definition of the concept of the 'informed user'. But the fact that the words 'user' and 'informed' are combined suggests that we are dealing with someone who has a certain level of knowledge of the design area concerned, either as a professional working in that field, or as a consumer. That, yet again, makes the test harder, because such users will be particularly well aware of the design features that already exist in the field. The CJEU was given the opportunity to define the concept of the informed user in the *Pepsico v. Grupo Promer* case. It held that the concept must be understood as lying somewhere between that of the average consumer, applicable in trade mark matters, who need not have any specific knowledge and who, as a rule, makes no direct comparison between the trade marks at issue, and the sectoral expert, who is an expert with detailed technical expertise.[37] In a case dealing with a design for an armchair it was therefore held that the informed user was a person who habitually bought armchairs and put them to their intended use and who had informed himself on the subject through catalogues etc.[38] It is also important to retain the point that the article to which the design has been applied will be looked at by the informed user both in rest and in use.[39]

The 'informed user' refers therefore, not to a user of average attention, but to a particularly observant one, either because of his personal experience or his extensive knowledge of the sector in question.[40] The informed user compares the proposed design with what is already available in the field and according to the Court he or she does that with a particular level of attention:

> [A]s regards the informed user's level of attention, it should be noted that, although the informed user is not the well-informed and reasonably observant and circumspect average

---

[34] *Danuta Budziewska v. OHIM (Puma SE intervening)* (n. 30); and Case T-513/09, *Baena Grupo v. OHIM (Neuman and Galdeano del Sel)*, 16 December 2010.

[35] Case C-281/10 P, *Pepsico Inc. v. Grupo Promer Mon Graphic SA and OHIM* [2011] ECR I-10153, [2012] FSR 5 at para. 73.

[36] Case C-345/13, *Karen Millen Fashions Ltd v. Dunnes Stores and Dunnes Stores (Limerick) Ltd* [2014] Bus LR 756 at para. 35.

[37] See Case T-337/12, *El Hogar del Siglo XXI v. OHIM (Wenf International Advisers Ltd, intervening)* [2014] ECDR 1; and Case T-15/13, *Group Nivelles v. OHIM*, 13 May 2015, <http://curia.europa.eu> (an appeal is pending), para. 127.

[38] Case T-339/12, *Gandia Blasco SA v. OHIM* [2014] ECDR 15.

[39] Case T-337/12, *El Hogar del Siglo XXI v. OHIM (Wenf International Advisers Ltd, intervening)* [2014] ECDR 1.

[40] *Pepsico Inc. v. Grupo Promer Mon Graphic SA* (n. 35) at para. 53 and Joined Cases C-101/11 P and C-102/11 P, *Herbert Neuman and Andoni Galdeano de Sel v. OHIM and José Manuel Baena Grupo SA* [2013] ECDR 76, at para. 53.

consumer who normally perceives a design as a whole and does not proceed to analyse its various details (see, by analogy, *Lloyd Schuhfabrik Meyer & Co GmbH v. Klijsen
Handel BV* (C-342/97) [1999] E.C.R. I-3819; [1999] 2 C.M.L.R. 1343; [2000] F.S.R. 77 at [25]
and [26]), he is also not an expert or specialist capable of observing in detail the minimal differences that may exist between the designs in conflict. *Thus, the qualifier 'informed' suggests that, without being a designer or a technical expert, the user knows the
various designs which exist in the sector concerned, possesses a certain degree of knowledge with regard to the features which those designs normally include, and, as a result of
his interest in the products concerned, shows a relatively high degree of attention when he
uses them.*[41]

The concept of the observant user who is not a technical expert reinforces the idea that
designs that do not present significant differences produce the same overall impression on such an informed user and will therefore not lead to a finding of individual
character.[42]

The comparison is normally a direct comparison, i.e. with both designs being present
in front of the informed user. That may however be impracticable or uncommon in certain sectors and then an indirect comparison is acceptable. In the latter case, the Court
accepts that the informed user may have an imperfect recollection of the overall impression produced by both designs. But those features for which the designer had more
design freedom and where there were no or fewer technical constraints are more likely
to be remembered.[43]

The only flexibility that has been built into the system is the sensible approach by
which the degree of freedom that was available to the author of the design in creating it
should be taken into account when assessing individual character.[44] Indeed, if there is
little room for manoeuvre, maybe for technical reasons (but maybe also because there
are economic restrictions or because certain common features need to be included[45]),
small differences between a new design and existing designs may be particularly telling, and may therefore confer individual character.[46] On this point the nature of the
product to which the design is applied or in which it is incorporated, as well as the industrial sector concerned, should be taken into account,[47] as they have an impact on the
design freedom. In cases where there is a lot of freedom the informed user is entitled to
expect more by way of individual character (and if that is the case, more protection and
a stronger design right will flow from it[48]), whereas a limited amount of design freedom
will moderate what is expected by way of individual character (and weaker protection for
the design will flow from it[49]).[50]

A first good example concerned designs for bicycle wheels.[51] The individual character
of an application was challenged on the basis of a 2002 international patent application

---

[41] *Pepsico Inc. v. Grupo Promer Mon Graphic SA* (n. 35) at para. 59, emphasis added.

[42] Case T-11/08 *Kwang Yang Motor v. OHIM (Honda Giken Kogyo)* <http://curia.europa.eu>, at para. 33;
and *Danuta Budziewska v. OHIM (Puma SE intervening)* (n. 30) at para. 32.

[43] *Herbert Neuman* (n. 40) at paras. 56–7; and *Pepsico Inc. v. Grupo Promer Mon Graphic SA* (n. 35) at para. 57.

[44] RDA 1949, s. 1B(4). Case T-9/07, *Grupo Promer Mon Graphic SA v. OHIM* [2010] ECDR 7, confirmed
on appeal *Pepsico Inc. v. Grupo Promer Mon Graphic SA* (n. 35).

[45] *Whitby Specialist Vehicles Ltd v. Yorkshire Specialist Vehicles Ltd and others* (n. 26).

[46] See Case T-22/13, *Senz Technologies BV v. OHIM* [2015] ECDR 19.

[47] See Case T-41/14, *Argo Development and Manufacturing Ltd v. OHIM* [2015] ECDR 21.

[48] *Whitby Specialist Vehicles Ltd v. Yorkshire Specialist Vehicles Ltd and others* (n. 26).

[49] *Whitby Specialist Vehicles Ltd v. Yorkshire Specialist Vehicles Ltd and others* (n. 26).

[50] Case T-525, *H&M Hennes & Mauritz BV & Co KG v. OHIM* [2015] ECDR 20.

[51] *Rodi Comercial SA v. Vuelta International SpA*, decision of 20 December 2005, OHIM Invalidity
Division.

that contained a bicycle wheel. The informed user was obviously aware of the functional requirements of such wheels and of the prior art known to those who specialize in this area. The informed user would also be aware of the fact that design freedom was limited by the need to lace the wheel with spokes between the hub and the rim. That would focus attention on areas in relation to which design freedom remained, such as the pattern of distribution of spokes around the hub. In this case, the number of spokes was the same, and the same symmetrical, orderly arrangement and pattern had been used. This consequently produced the same overall impression on the user and the design failed the individual character test.

Another example concerned dolls.[52] The dolls in question were very similar, but the addition of features such as the shape of the nose or belly button, which made the dolls appear more human, made the design pass the novelty test. Despite that finding, however, the dolls still produced the same overall impression on the informed user and they therefore failed the individual character test.

The General Court did derive from all this that the question whether or not a design possesses individual character is best approached in four stages. In stage one, one identifies the sector of the goods to which the design is to be applied. In stage two, one puts in place the theoretical concept of the informed user of such goods, and with it the level of attention that will be paid by the informed user during the (direct) comparison. In a third stage, one considers the design freedom that was available to the creator of the design under consideration. And in stage four, the comparison is made and one decides whether the design possesses individual character. Before embarking on this test one obviously has to establish the existence and the anteriority of any design with which the design, the individual character is examined, is to be compared, i.e. which designs are already out there that may deny the design applied for its individual character.[53]

Component parts of complex products

Additionally, novelty and individual character are said to require that a design that is applied to a component part of a complex product remains visible during the normal use of the complex product, and the novelty and individual character requirements obviously have to be met by the visual features of the component part.[54] This additional rule applies to separate removable parts of a product, rather than to the inside surface of the product. Consumables, such as staples in a staple gun, are also not component parts of the product—that is, the staple gun.

Normal use is defined as use by the end user,[55] with the exclusion of maintenance, servicing, or repair work in relation to the product. The requirement that the design must remain visible in normal use applies therefore in relation to use by the user, rather than by a maintenance technician. Components of an engine that are only visible when the latter is carrying out maintenance work on the engine of a car, for example, are therefore excluded.

---

[52] *Aktiebolaget Design Rubens Sweden v. Marie Ekman Bäcklund*, decision of 20 December 2005, OHIM Invalidity Division.

[53] *Danuta Budziewska v. OHIM (Puma SE intervening)* (n. 30) at para. 21.

[54] RDA 1949, s. 1B(8).   [55] RDA 1949, s. 1B(9).

Grounds for refusal of registration

Technical function

As we have already indicated, registered designs are not available to grant rights in technical effects; they are rather oriented towards aesthetic designs. While this works well as a starting point, its implementation, in practice, is not entirely straightforward. The legislator has decided that no registered design right shall subsist in features of the appearance of a product that are solely dictated by the product's technical function.[56] Much will depend on the interpretation of this provision. A narrow interpretation will exclude virtually nothing and might allow a designer to monopolize the product by registering a few designs for all of the practical ways of giving effect to a clever technical idea, while a wide interpretation may limit design registrations unduly.

What seems relatively clear from the wording of the provision is that the exclusion will only operate if the features concerned are solely dictated by the product's technical function. This must mean that the main idea is to cover those cases in which the designer had no choice, owing to technical constraints linked to the technical function of the product. The exclusion will not apply if the designer can show that there is sufficient design freedom for the product at issue to enable others to create a product that performs the same technical function, while being designed differently. It may be that the exact line separating both options might be drawn up along the line of which features are essential to obtain a technical result—that is, to allow the product to fulfil its technical function up to the same standard; those features that are not essential in this sense can be the subject of design registration, while essential features, in the sense that they are dictated by technical necessity, cannot.[57]

It is important, however, to add that the exception does not directly exclude designs. All that it excludes are features of appearance that are solely dictated by the product's technical function; all features that are not solely dictated by the product's technical function remain open for design protection. A design for the appearance of a product is therefore still possible if there are enough non-technical features left to meet the criteria for design registration. It is not the case that the presence of one or more technical features excludes the whole appearance of the product from design registration. This makes a lot of business sense, because competitors need those technical features in order to compete, but there is no need for them to copy the non-technical features.

Overall, this interpretation of the provision does, it is submitted, strike a correct competition-friendly balance between adequate design protection and the risk of competition excluding technical designs.[58]

Matters were neatly summarized by the OHIM's third Board of Appeal:

It follows from the above that art. 8(1) CDR denies protection to those features of a product's appearance that were chosen exclusively for the purpose of designing a product that performs its function, as opposed to features that were chosen, at least to some degree, for the purpose of enhancing the product's visual appearance. It goes without saying that these matters must be assessed objectively: it is not necessary to determine what actually

---

[56] RDA 1949, s. 1C(1).

[57] Cf. the decision of the European Court of Justice on trade marks for shapes that are necessary to obtain a technical result in Case C-299/99, *Koninklijke Philips v. Remington* [2002] ECR I-5475, [2003] RPC 14.

[58] Cf., under the old law, *Cow (PB) & Co. Ltd v. Cannon Rubber Manufacturers Ltd* [1959] RPC 240; the slightly different approach adopted by the House of Lords in *Amp Inc. v. Utilux Pty Ltd* [1972] RPC 103.

went on in the designer's mind when the design was being developed. The matter must be assessed from the standpoint of a reasonable observer who looks at the design and asks himself whether anything other than purely functional considerations could have been relevant when a specific feature was chosen.[59]

The 'must fit' exception

The other important exception for non-aesthetical features from the scope of registered designs is the 'must fit' exception, which deals with a type of functional design features. Section 1C(2) defines the scope of the exception in the following way:

> A right in a registered design shall not subsist in features of appearance of a product which must necessarily be reproduced in their exact form and dimensions so as to permit the product in which the design is incorporated or to which it is applied to be mechanically connected to, or placed in, around or against, another product so that either product may perform its function…[60]

Clear examples in practice are electrical plugs and sockets, connectors for lamps to fit into sockets, and batteries to fit into watches. In all of these cases, there is a need for the features of appearance to be reproduced in their exact form and dimensions, and this necessity for exact reproduction is therefore the key element in the exception.

This exception is clearly very similar to the technical function exception and there could arguably be an overlap. In fairness to the drafters of the legislation, it can be said that the technical function exception primarily deals with a product that works on its own and in relation to which the design features are dictated by the technical function of that product, whereas the 'must fit' exception deals with two products that need to be connected, etc., in order for them to work. Rather than a technical, this is more a functional exception. But it is clear that the exception is vital to make sure that no single designer or trader monopolizes a connector system owing to the fact that interoperability of products is a vital element to enhance competition. The technical function exception on its own may not have been able to achieve this result, because the shape of the connector is not dictated solely by the product's technical function. Indeed, as the electrical plug and socket example shows, for example, different plugs and sockets can be devised, and are in use in the UK and in Continental Europe. A narrowly defined technical function exception would therefore not cover this example, because the design features of one system are not essential for any product to carry out its technical function.

There is one exception to the 'must fit' exception: designs that serve *'the purpose of allowing multiple assembly or connection of mutually interchangeable products within a modular system'*[61] will still be registrable. Lego toy bricks or stackable chairs come to mind by way of examples. This exception is not based on any particular logic or argument, but is the result of effective lobbying by the toy industry.

Public policy and morality

Designs that are contrary to public policy or to accepted principles of morality will not be registered.[62] Morality can only be invoked, however, if the design would offend against

---

[59] Case R 690/2007-3, *Lindner Recyclingtech GmbH v. Franssons Verkstäder AB* [2010] ECRD 1, approved by *Dyson v. Vax* [2010] FSR 39, per Arnold J and *Samsung Electronics (UK) Ltd v. Apple Inc.* [2012] EWHC 1882 (Pat), per HH Judge Birss QC.

[60] RDA 1949, s. 1C(2).   [61] RDA 1949, s. 1C(3).   [62] RDA 1949, s. 1D.

the moral principles of right-thinking members of society; the fact that some people might find the design distasteful is not sufficient.[63]

This is a standard prohibition. The theoretical reason for its existence is clear, but its application, in practice, is often problematic, because public policy and public morality are hard to define.

General exception

There is, of course, also a provision that excludes from registrability anything that does not come within the definition of a design in s. 1(2) of the 1949 Act—and neither will a design that does not meet the requirements of novelty and individual character be registered.[64]

Ownership of a registered design

The author of a design—as the person who creates the design[65]—will be the first owner of the registered design.[66] There are only two exceptions to this rule: the employer of the employee who creates a design will be the first owner of the registered design if the design is created in the course of employment;[67] the person who commissions a design will be the first owner of the registered design if the design was commissioned for money, or for money's worth.[68] A specific problem arises when a design is computer-generated. The computer is not a person and cannot become the first owner of the registered design, but there is no human author. In such a case, the ownership of the registered design is then attributed to the nearest person involved in its creation—that is, to the person who made the arrangements necessary for the creation of the design.[69]

Ownership, of course, presupposes the registration of the design. The provisions governing such registration can be found in ss. 3 and 3A–3D of the Act. It should be kept in mind that a registration is effective against the use of the design on any item in so far as no different overall impression is created. The design will nevertheless have to be registered for a specific product on which it is to be used. This will be done on the basis of an international classification,[70] which facilitates searches of the register by interested parties. Registration in multiple categories is possible.

The ownership of a registered design right or the right to apply the design to any item can be transferred. This can be done by an assignment or any other form of transmission.[71] The transferee can either become the full owner of the right, or he or she can become joint owner of the right together with the assignor.[72] Licences can also be granted.[73] Partial transfers, such as of the right to apply the design to one specific item, and transfers to more than one party resulting in joint ownership, are possible. But all assignments of a registered design right must be registered. This means that, in practice, it is advisable that assignments and licences are in writing, although this is, in theory, not an express requirement.[74]

---

[63] *Re Masterman's Design* [1991] RPC 89 (a design for a Scottish doll with a kilt, which exposed male genitalia when lifted), but note that a design that shows directly representations of genitalia may still infringe morality.

[64] RDA 1949, s. 1A(1).   [65] RDA 1949, s. 2(3).   [66] RDA 1949, s. 2(1).

[67] RDA 1949, s. 2(1B).   [68] RDA 1949, s. 2(1A).   [69] RDA 1949, s. 2(4).

[70] See the Locarno Agreement 1968.   [71] RDA 1949, s. 2(2).   [72] RDA 1949, s. 2(2).

[73] RDA 1949, s. 19(4).   [74] RDA 1949, s. 19.

These are purely national rules, as the Directive does not deal specifically with the matter. The Regulation on the other hand contains detailed rules on these points. According to Art. 14, 'the right to the Community design shall vest in the designer or his successor in title'. The starting point is therefore that the author of a design, i.e. the designer, as the person who creates the design, will be entitled to the Community design.[75] The logical consequence is then of course that joint developers of a design will jointly be entitled to the Community design. But the provision also mentions an eventual successor in title. This might not merely mean the heir of a deceased designer; the Regulation clearly envisages that the entitlement to the Community design can be transferred in advance by contract, e.g. to the person commissioning the design. The latter will then be entitled to register the Community design directly in its name. There is only one exception to this rule. The employer of the employee who creates a design will be the first owner of the registered design if the design is created in the course of employment, unless the parties (or the applicable national law) agree otherwise.[76] There is, however, no presumptive transfer of ownership to the commissioner of the design.[77] But the designer shall in any case retain the right to be cited as such in the register.[78] It is of course possible that the Community design has either been applied for or registered in the name of a person who it not entitled to it. Article 15 gives in those circumstances the person entitled to the Community design a claim to become recognized as the legitimate owner of the Community design.

Ownership of a registered Community design can change and the right can be transferred. Article 27 clearly envisages that, but put forward the principle that the Community design shall be dealt with in its entirety and for the whole of the Community. Licences, as well as assignments, can therefore be envisaged. Any transfer can at the request of one of the parties to it be registered and will then be published. Until the transfer has been entered into the register it cannot be invoked against third parties, which means that the successor in title cannot invoke the rights that arise from the registration of the Community design.[79] This means that, in practice, it is advisable that assignments and licences are in writing, although this is, in theory, not an express requirement.

Rights of the owner and infringement

The Design Directive led to changes in UK law in the areas of the rights of the owner and infringement. In terms of the rights that are granted by a registered design, the basic principles are found in Art. 12 of the Directive, which provides:

> The registration of a design shall confer on its holder the exclusive right to use it and to prevent any third party not having its consent from using it. The aforementioned use shall cover, in particular, the making, offering, putting on the market, importing, exporting or using of a product in which the design is incorporated or to which it is applied, or stocking such a product for those purposes.

It seems easy enough to understand the traditional intellectual property approach. An exclusive right is granted and the design cannot be used without the consent of its

---

[75] See the *Bolero* case, German Bundesgerichtshof I ZR 23/12 [2014] IIC 239.

[76] Art. 14(3) of the Regulation.

[77] See Case C-32/08, *Fundación Española para la Innovación de la Artesanía (FEIA) v. Cul de Sac Espacio Creativo SL and Acierta Product & Position SA* [2009] ECDR 19.

[78] Art. 18 of the Regulation.   [79] Art. 28 of the Regulation.

owner. And that is coupled with a list of examples of activities that amount to use, such as the making, offering, putting on the market, importing, exporting, or using of a product in which the design is incorporated or to which it is applied, or stocking such a product for those purposes. The answer thus provided to the question which rights are granted is, however, only easy if one assumes that any alleged infringer makes an exact copy of the design and uses that for similar or identical products. That is a of course not necessarily the case. A slightly different and merely similar design may be used and then the question arises how one defines use of 'the design'. How broadly or how narrowly does one construe this question and therefore also the scope of protection for the right holder? The Directive provides guidance on this point in a separate article, Art. 9. Under the heading 'scope of protection' this article provides that:

(1) The scope of the protection conferred by a design right shall include any design which does not produce on the informed user a different overall impression.
(2) In assessing the scope of the protection, the degree of freedom of the designer in developing his design shall be taken into consideration.

One does in other words go back to the question and standard of individual character. A similar design that provides a different overall impression will not infringe…and may be entitled to registration in its own right. This creates a neat line between entitlement to protection and infringement. And it gives the right owner a fair degree of protection, i.e. any design that is not different enough to be entitled to its own protection will lead to a finding of infringement. So maybe the better way to put it is that a similar design that provides a different overall impression will not infringe, because it may be entitled to registration in its own right. And logically the design freedom of the creator of the design shall also play a role in shaping the scope of protection. The influence this factor has in terms of individual character and therefore on what can amount to a design obviously translates itself in a parallel way to the scope of the right once it is protected.

Section 7 of the 1949 Act puts this into practice under UK law by granting the owner of the design the exclusive right to use the design, as well as any design that does not produce a different overall impression on the informed user.[80] The concept of 'use' is wider than that used previously and includes making, offering, putting on the market, exporting, or using a product in which the design is incorporated, or to which it has been applied, or stocking such a product for any of these purposes.[81]

Infringement, then, logically occurs if, without the consent of the owner of the design right, a person does anything that, by virtue of s. 7, is the exclusive right of the owner of the registered design right.[82] The key test on this point is whether a different overall impression is created on the informed user by the allegedly infringing design; there will only be an infringement if no different overall impression is created. In assessing this issue of different overall impression, the degree of freedom of the author in creating the design is to be taken into account.[83] Article 9(2) is, in this respect, a limiting provision.

But this does not solve our main problem: how does one deal with the relationship between the design, on the one hand, and the item, on the other? The design will still be registered for a product, or a class of products, and any infringement case is almost bound to compare design as applied to products, rather than design in isolation, but infringement is in the new law no longer confined to use on the product for which the design is registered. The design may be infringed if no different overall impression is

---

[80] RDA 1949, s. 7(1).   [81] RDA 1949, s. 7(2).   [82] RDA 1949, s. 7A(1).
[83] RDA 1949, s. 7A(3).

created, irrespective of the type of product to which it is applied. The design may also only affect a part of a product. This may make it rather difficult to apply the negative test of not creating a different impression to the design. How, in practice, is one going to make abstraction of the product to assess the overall impression created by the allegedly infringing design? On top of that, the negative formulation of the test does nothing to alleviate the problem (which is fairly inevitable in relation to designs). Does 'different' mean that the design must not create the same identical impression or will some (strong) form of similarity infringe in practice? It will be up to the courts—and, eventually, the European Court of Justice—to determine the exact boundaries in this respect.

The Court of Appeal made a start in *Procter & Gamble v. Reckitt Benckiser.*[84] This case was concerned with a design applied to sprayers for air-freshener products. The canister for the defendant's 'Air-Wick' product was inspired by the claimant's design for its 'Febreze' canister. The question arose whether there was more than inspiration and whether an infringement had occurred.[85]

The Court of Appeal, first of all, turned its attention to the concept of the 'informed user'. Similar characters in both patent and trade mark law were held not to be of assistance. What we are dealing with here is a user who is aware of the existing design corpus in the area.[86] Such a user has experience of other similar items and designs, and will therefore be reasonably discriminatory. He or she will be able to appreciate enough detail to decide whether a design creates an allegedly infringing design or produces a different overall impression. In doing so, there is no decisive role for the idea that the user must have an imperfect recollection. He or she would view things carefully and, as such, remember more details. What matters in making the decision is what strikes the mind of the informed user when the designs are viewed carefully. The informed user therefore has more extensive knowledge than an average consumer in possession of average information, awareness, and understanding. In particular, the informed user is open to design issues and is fairly familiar with them.[87] This includes the knowledge of the fact that, by reason of function, shapes can be, to a certain extent, required to conform to a certain standard.

The Court then turned its attention to the concept of 'a different overall impression'. A difference that allows the informed user to discriminate between the two designs is required, but it is not required that the allegedly infringing design 'clearly differs' from the registered design. What one has in mind is the question of whether or not the designs are substantially different. The Court offered the following guidelines for the application of the test:

i)   ...the test is 'different' not 'clearly different.'

ii)   The notional informed user is 'fairly familiar' with design issues...

iii) Next [it] is not a proposition of law but a statement about the way people (and thus the notional informed user) perceive things. It is simply that if a new design is markedly different from anything that has gone before, it is likely to have a greater overall visual impact than if it is 'surrounded by kindred prior art.'... It follows that the 'overall

[84] *Procter & Gamble Co. v. Reckitt Benckiser (UK) Ltd* [2008] ECDR 3, [2008] FSR 8.

[85] For a good example of a case where only the idea and inspiration had been taken, see *Rolawn Ltd and Rolawn (Turf growers) Ltd v. Turfmech Machinery Ltd* [2008] RPC 27, [2008] ECDR 13.

[86] See *J. Choo (Jersey) Ltd v. Towerstone Ltd* [2008] FSR 19, [2009] ECDR 2.

[87] The Court of Appeal in *Procter & Gamble Co. v. Reckitt Benckiser (UK) Ltd* (n. 92) cited, with approval, the conclusion reached in a case between the same parties by the Higher Provisional Court in Vienna 4Ob 239/04g: *Procter & Gamble Co. v. Reckitt Benckiser (UK) Ltd* [2007] EWCA Civ 936, at para. 26; see also *Woodhouse v. Architectural Lighting* [2006] RPC 1.

impression' created by such a design will be more significant and the room for differences which do not create a substantially different overall impression is greater. So protection for a striking novel product will be correspondingly greater than for a product which is incrementally different from the prior art, though different enough to have its own individual character and thus be validly registered.

iv) On the other hand it does not follow, in a case of markedly new design (or indeed any design) that it is sufficient to ask 'is the alleged infringement closer to the registered design or to the prior art', if the former infringement, if the latter not. The test remains 'is the overall impression different?'

v) It is legitimate to compare the registered design and the alleged infringement with a reasonable degree of care. The court must 'don the spectacles of the informed user' to adapt the hackneyed but convenient metaphor of patent law. The possibility of imperfect recollection has a limited part to play in this exercise.

vi) The court must identify the 'overall impression' of the registered design with care. True it is that it is difficult to put into language, and it is helpful to use pictures as part of the identification, but the exercise must be done.

vii) In this exercise the level of generality to which the court must descend is important. Here, for instance, it would be too general to say that the overall impression of the registered design is 'a canister fitted with a trigger spray device on the top.' The appropriate level of generality is that which would be taken by the notional informed user.

viii) The court should then do the same exercise for the alleged infringement.

ix) Finally the court should ask whether the overall impression of each is different. This is almost the equivalent to asking whether they are the same—the difference is nuanced, probably, involving a question of onus and no more.[88]

When the court applied these guidelines to the case at issue, it again agreed with the Austrian court's decision:

In reality, even though the same features are found in both, there are clear differences between the two sprayers resulting from the different mode of their execution: the Febreze sprayer is smaller, has a slightly larger diameter and so looks more compact. The head of this sprayer is shallower but also broader, so that the Febreze sprayer fits the hand differently than the Airwick sprayer (with the Airwick sprayer, which has the considerably narrower head, there is a feeling that it could slip out of the user's hand). In contrast to the Airwick sprayer, the metal can of the Febreze sprayer tapers upwards, so that the waist begins lower down than in the Airwick sprayer. The 'train' goes down much further in the Febreze sprayer, so that the lower boundary of the plastic part echoes the angle of the head part far more markedly than in the Airwick sprayer. The shape of head too is different: while the head of the Febreze sprayer—to draw a comparison from the animal kingdom—is reminiscent of a snake's head, the shape of the Airwick sprayer head is like a lizard's head.[89]

The similarities are clearly only found at a general level and it was therefore held that a different overall impression was produced on the informed user. On that basis, the infringement case failed.[90]

One should also keep in mind that this is a visual exercise. What counts is what the court can see with its own eyes.[91] So when Apple sued Samsung arguing that the design of Samsung's tablet computer infringed the design of Apple's iPad the court put the emphasis on the fact that one design was markedly thinner and that the back of the devices

---

[88] *Procter & Gamble Co. v. Reckitt Benckiser (UK) Ltd* (n. 87) at para. 35.
[89] *Procter & Gamble Co.* (n. 87) at para. 61.   [90] *Procter & Gamble Co.* (n. 87) at paras. 62–63.
[91] *Dyson v. Vax* [2012] FSR 4 at paras. 8 and 9.

was very different. The similarities of the screen and the front of the tablets were less important as it was down to functionality and offered very little design freedom. On that basis the court held that a different overall impression was created and the infringement case failed.[92]

A defendant who has received a cease and desist letter may of course try to register its own design before being sued for infringement, but the fact that the defendant has its own design registered has no influence on the infringement assessment. There is no need to invalidate the later design before an infringement case can be brought.[93]

Exclusion from protection—defences to infringement

The exclusive rights of the right holder are subject to certain limitations and exclusions. For an alleged infringer, these turn into a series of defences.

1. Acts done privately and for non-commercial purposes will not constitute an infringement.[94]

2. Acts done for experimental purposes are exempted.[95]

3. Acts of reproduction for the purposes of making citations or of teaching are also exempted provided that the act of reproduction is compatible with fair trade practices and does not unduly prejudice the normal exploitation of the design, on the one hand, and that the source is mentioned, on the other.[96]

4. There are specific exceptions in relation to foreign registered ships and aircraft, which are temporarily in the UK, the repairing of these, and the importation of spare parts for that purpose.[97]

These limitations and defences are subject to the condition that such acts are compatible with fair trade practice, do not unduly prejudice the normal exploitation of the design, and that mention is made of the source.[98]

The exhaustion rule will also apply at EEA level.[99] The usual rule applies in this respect. Accordingly, s. 7A(4) of the 1949 Act stipulates:

> The right in a registered design is not infringed by an act which relates to a product in which any design protected by the registration is incorporated or to which it is applied if the product has been put on the market in the European Economic Area by the registered proprietor or with his consent.

The Crown has the right to use a registered design for the services of the Crown or to authorize such use, normally against compensation.[100] This is not an exclusion from protection in the purest sense, but it does limit the exclusive right of the right holder to some extent.

---

[92] *Samsung Electronics (UK) Ltd v. Apple Inc.* [2012] EWHC 1882 (Pat), confirmed on appeal *Samsung Electronics (UK) Ltd v. Apple Inc.* [2012] EWCA Civ 1339. See also *Dyson v. Vax* [2010] EWHC 1923 (Pat), [2010] FSR 39, confirmed on appeal *Dyson v. Vax* [2011] EWCA Civ 1206, [2012] FSR 4.

[93] Case C-488/10, *Celaya Emparanza y Galdos Internacional SA (Cegasa) v. Proyectos Integrales de Balizamiento SL* [2012] ECDR 17.

[94] RDA 1949, s. 7A(2)(a).　　[95] RDA 1949, s. 7A(2)(b).　　[96] RDA 1949, s. 7A(2)(c).

[97] RDA 1949, s. 7A(2)(d)–(f).　　[98] RDA 1949, s. 7A(3).

[99] See already Case 144/81, *Keurkoop BV v. Nancy Kean Gifts BV* [1982] ECR 2853, [1983] 2 CMLR 47.

[100] RDA 1949, s. 12.

Invalidity

A design may be declared invalid on the basis of four grounds of invalidity. The first ground of invalidity is that the design does not meet the requirements set out in s. 1A of the Act.[101] The second ground is that the registered proprietor is not the real proprietor of the design and that the real proprietor objects to the existing registration.[102] These two grounds refer to deficiencies in the registration.

The first and obvious grounds for invalidity therefore arise where the design does not meet the definition of a design or the requirements of novelty and individual character[103], or where there are problems with disclosure, morality, or public policy.

A person who is entitled to the design may also apply for its invalidity if the applicant or holder is not entitled to it. The Regulation requires a prior court decision on the latter point.

The other two grounds focus on clashes with other rights. A design registration can also be declared invalid if it incorporates a registered or unregistered trade mark;[104] the final ground of invalidity is that the registered design constitutes the unauthorized use of a copyright work.[105] In both of these cases, the right holder in the mark or copyright needs to object to the design registration.

A design can therefore also be declared invalid if a distinctive sign is used in a subsequent design, and Community law or the law of the member state governing that sign confers on the right holder of the sign the right to prohibit such use.[106] It is also a ground for invalidity of a design if the design constitutes an unauthorized use of a work protected under the copyright law of a member state.[107]

Duration of the registered design right

If the design is registered and published[108] after the examination of the application by the Designs Registry, a branch of the UK Intellectual Property Office, that registration will initially be valid for a period of five years[109] from the date of registration.[110] The registration of the design can be renewed four times, bringing the maximum term of protection to 25 years.[111]

The Directive contains a similar 25-year maximum term of protection, but, according to Art. 10, the term is to be calculated from the date of filing of the application.

---

[101] RDA 1949, s. 11ZA(1). See Cases T-10/08, *Kwang Yang Motor Co. Ltd v. OHIM* [2012] ECDR 2; T-68/10, *Sphere Time v. OHIM* [2011] ECDR 20; and T-153/08, *Shenzhen Taiden v. OHIM*, <http://curia.europa.eu>.

[102] RDA 1949, s. 11ZA(2).

[103] See *Danuta Budziewska v. OHIM (Puma SE intervening)* (n. 30); Case T-10/08, *Kwang Yang Motor Co. Ltd v. OHIM* [2012] ECDR 2; T-68/10, *Sphere Time v. OHIM* [2011] ECDR 20; and T-153/08, *Shenzhen Taiden v. OHIM*, <http://curia.europa.eu>.

[104] RDA 1949, s. 11ZA(3). See Case T-148/08, *Beifa Group Co. Ltd v. OHIM* [2010] ETMR 42.

[105] RDA 1949, s. 11ZA(4).

[106] See Case T-148/08, *Beifa Group Co. Ltd v. OHIM* [2010] ETMR 42.

[107] See Cases T-566/11 and T-567/11, *Viejo Valle SA v. OHIM (Etablissements Coquet intervening)*, 23 October 2013, <http://curia.europa.eu>.

[108] But see RDA 1949, s. 5, which contains exceptional rules.   [109] RDA 1949, s. 8(1).

[110] Earlier applications will have a priority right that can be claimed for up to six months.

[111] RDA 1949, s. 8(2).

Section 3C(1) of the 1949 Act now overcomes this difference by stipulating that a design shall be registered as of the date of application, which means that the two approaches will now overlap. In practice, the commercial life of an aesthetic design will often be shorter than 25 years and it can be expected that many registered designs will be allowed to lapse, because their owners request no further renewal. Fashions do indeed exist in eye-appealing designs. Many features of appearance that were very popular around 2000 are no longer popular, so there is no need to renew the design registration. In doing so, one would incur a cost that could no longer be recuperated by profits through sales of items made to the design.

The application for renewal of the registered design right must be addressed to the Registrar during the last six months of the previous five-year period; in the absence of such an application, the right will cease to exist upon expiry of the previous five-year period.[112] The owner of the right is, however, given an additional six-month period during which he or she can renew the right,[113] although a restoration fee will be payable on top of the normal renewal fee. If the right is restored, it shall be treated as if it had never expired.[114]

Spare parts

Spare parts have been a stumbling block in relation to design law for several years. The idea that manufacturers of consumer products would be able to monopolize the spare-part market by means of design registrations has proved to be at least controversial, if not straightforwardly unacceptable. It is indeed true that many parts take distinctive shapes; some of these shapes reflect the design features of the larger part in which they are inserted. One might think, for example, of doors for a certain make of car. Others may have a functional shape and, in this respect, one might think, for example, of exhaust pipes for a certain make of car. All of these, when bought as spare parts, will, in most cases, need to take the same shape if they are to be suitable for repair or replacement purposes. The consumer will therefore have no choice of supplier if a design registration allows the manufacturer of the original product to be the only parts supplier. The risk of monopoly pricing and other abuses, such as failure to supply parts for older products, is then not simply a remote prospect.

As a result, many legislators and courts have acted by providing a special regime for design rights in spare parts. When the EU agreed the Directive (and the Regulation), no agreement could be reached on this point. In relation to spare parts and registered designs, the member states have therefore, in the end, retained the right to maintain their existing national provisions. They can, however, only introduce changes to these provisions if the changes have the effect of liberalizing the market for spare parts.[115] The Commission was to draft a report by the end of 2004, on the basis of which a new attempt to solve the outstanding spare-parts issue is being undertaken.[116] Looking back at the controversy surrounding this area, it is hard to see how this will be achieved in the short term.

---

[112] RDA 1949, s. 8(3).

[113] This is not an automatic right; the Registrar has a discretion: see RDA 1949, s. 8A.

[114] RDA 1949, s. 8(4).   [115] Design Directive, Art. 14.

[116] Design Directive, Art. 18. The Commission accordingly produced its Proposal for a Directive of the European Parliament and of the Council amending Directive 98/71/EC on the legal protection of designs, SEC (2004) 1097, COM/2004/0582 final, <eur-lex.europa.eu/smartapi/cgi/sga_doc?smartapi!celexapi!prod !CELEXnumdoc&lg=en&model=guicheti&numdoc=52004PC0582>.

In the UK Act, the spare-parts issue is now addressed in s. 7A(5). A registered design right in a component part that may be used for the purpose of the repair of a complex product so as to restore its original appearance is not infringed by the use for that purpose of any design protected by the registration.[117] Spare parts can therefore be manufactured without infringing the registered design,[118] but it is important to note that the provision does not take the design right away altogether; it will simply not be infringed if the part involving the design is used to restore the original appearance of a complex product. The latter is also an important limitation that is placed on the exception. Any use that goes beyond restoring the original appearance of the complex product will still amount to an infringement of the registered design.

It is also important to note that the current solution is rather more consumer-friendly than it looks at first sight. Indeed, complex products are those in relation to which the spare parts issue arises most frequently. The existence of design requires that a design that is applied to a component part of a complex product remains visible during the normal use of the complex product, and also that the component itself is new and has individual character. Because complex products have been defined in a loose way, this will reduce the number of possible design registrations for spare parts.

International commercial exploitation

International exploitation of registered designs is facilitated by the fact that the Paris Convention, to which the UK is a party, covers this area. A design application in one of the contracting states will result in a priority right, the term of which is six months, in relation to applications made in other contracting states.[119] But substantial problems relating to the international exploitation of a registered design are created by the tremendous international disparity in design protection systems. So, contrary to the UK system, many foreign systems do not provide for a search, but operate a deposit system, which means that designs are entered into the register upon application, with a possibility for all interested parties to object to the validity of the design and to request its removal from the register. The latter option was also taken by the contracting parties to the Hague Agreement 1925,[120] which aimed at creating a unified registration system for designs, but this system never managed to attract much international support (and, obviously, the UK never adhered to it).

Many Commonwealth countries copied the principles of the UK's registered design system. A large group among them extends protection to UK registered designs without requiring local registration.[121] These countries even request that local applicants

---

[117] RDA 1949, s. 7A(5).

[118] We are concerned here with replacement car parts, such as body panels, bumpers, and windows. Replica alloy wheels are not covered. See *BMW AG v. Round & Metal Ltd* [2012] EWHC 2099 (Pat), [2012] ECC 28.

[119] RDA 1949, s. 14. A resident of the UK can only make a second application six weeks after the application in the UK was made: s. 5.

[120] Which had attracted 56 contracting states as of February 2010. The 1999 Act of the Agreement entered into force on 23 December 2003. Despite the UK not being a contracting party the Agreement is of importance in the UK as the EU has adhered to it in the context of the Community Design Right.

[121] Antigua, Bermuda, Botswana, Cyprus, Fiji, Ghana, Gibraltar, Hong Kong, Kenya, Malaysia, Sierra Leone, Singapore, and Uganda are all included in this group.

register their designs in the UK. Some other countries and territories[122] require local re-registration before they extend protection to the design.

The Community design

We have indicated that the EU approach to registered designs has been based on two tracks. The first track consisted of the Directive, aimed at harmonizing national registered design laws. In the UK, this resulted in the substantial revision of the Registered Designs Act 1949, the provisions of which we have analysed in depth.

The second track consists of the Regulation,[123] which puts in place a system under which a single Community (registered) design will be granted as a result of a central single application with the Community Design Office, which is located in Alicante as part of the existing OHIM structure. Once granted, the Community design will apply in the whole of the Community.

The Community design is separate from any national design rights.

Procedural issues

In procedural terms, the OHIM deals with the registration of Community designs.[124] It examines whether the formal requirements and the definition of a design have been met. Novelty and individual character are not examined, but third parties can bring invalidity proceedings before the Office if they consider that the design should not be registered validly, because of lack of such.[125]

Appeals against a decision made by the OHIM—such as a decision to refuse registration—can be brought before the OHIM Boards of Appeal. A further appeal can then be brought before the European Court of Justice, via the General Court and, ultimately, before the Court of Justice itself.[126] Invalidity can also be raised as a counterclaim before the national courts, which will also deal with infringement cases. Each member state has selected, for this purpose, a limited number of Community design courts among its national courts, both at first instance and on appeal.[127]

Substantive provisions

The substantive provisions of the Regulation are supposed to mirror those of the Directive. We will therefore not repeat here what has already been said, but one important point of difference can be found in the provisions on initial ownership of the Community design. The Directive had left that matter to the national laws of the member states and no harmonization had taken place; this solution was unworkable in relation to a single Community design. The Regulation therefore provides that '*the design shall vest in the designer or his successor in title*' and that the employer is presumptively the person who becomes the first owner of a design made by the employee in the course of employment.[128] There is, however, no presumptive transfer of ownership to

---

[122] E.g. the Channel Islands, Malta, and Tanzania.
[123] Council Regulation (EC) 6/2002 on community designs [2002] OJ L 3/1.
[124] Title IV of the Regulation.   [125] Arts. 24 and 25 of the Regulation.
[126] Title VII of the Regulation.   [127] Arts. 80 and 81 of the Regulation.
[128] Art. 14 of the Regulation.

the commissioner of the design.[129] This is an important departure from the traditional UK approach. It may nevertheless be possible for the courts to read an implied licence transferring ownership to the commissioner into the contract between the designer and the commissioner in cases in which all of the circumstances suggest it.[130] This will, of course, not apply to all cases and it does therefore not solve the problem as such.

A few points were not covered at Community level. These lacunae have been filled at national level by the Community Design Regulations 2005.[131] Regulation 2 provides for an action against groundless threats.

A somewhat peculiar situation in this respect arose in *Quads 4 Kids v. Campbell*.[132] The defendant had applied to register a number of Community design rights, but had requested the deferment of the publication of that registration. When the claimant sold children's bikes made to an allegedly similar design on eBay, the defendant used eBay's own verified rights owner (VERO) programme, but made it clear that no further action would be taken. eBay uses the VERO system to allow intellectual property right holders to report infringements of their rights. eBay then removes the allegedly infringing listings, without any investigation. The seller whose listings are removed is simply informed of their removal. The sole purpose of the system is to make sure that eBay cannot be liable for infringement.

The normal test in groundless threat cases is whether the reasonable person in the position of the threatened would have understood that he or she might have been subject to infringement proceedings at some point in the future. This was not the case in *Quads*, because the defendant had made it clear that no further action would be taken. Nevertheless, the claimant was no longer able to trade on the basis of allegations that had not been proven. This was exactly the situation that the groundless threat provision was supposed to address. Pumfrey J proposed, therefore, a new test for this type of case.[133] This involved determining whether eBay would have understood that it could be subject to future infringement proceedings, had it not adopted the policy, via the VERO system, of removing any items alleged to infringe. In this case, the answer was affirmative and the claimant was therefore successful in securing the injunction for which it had applied.

The Community unregistered design right

The Regulation also created a Community *unregistered* design right, which complements the registered right. We will discuss it here because of that link and because, as such, it provides a link with the next chapter.

The need for an unregistered right had become apparent in those industries in which fashion changes every couple of months and for which the registration process will simply last too long. There are also many cases in which registration will be costly and in relation to which the applicant would rather test the market for the design first before deciding on registration.[134]

---

[129] See Case C-32/08, *Fundación Española para la Innovación de la Artesanía (FEIA) v. Cul de Sac Espacio Creativo SL and Acierta Product & Position SA* [2009] ECDR 19.

[130] See *Blair v. Osborne & Tomkins* [1971] 2 QB 78 (CA).   [131] SI 2005/2339.

[132] *Quads 4 Kids v. Campbell* [2006] EWHC 2482, [2006] All ER (D) 162.

[133] *Quads 4 Kids* (n. 132) at para. 30.

[134] See V. Saez, 'The Unregistered Community Design' (2002) 144 EIPR 585.

The Community unregistered design right addresses these concerns by providing for a three-year term of protection without registration or other formalities. In order to be protected, the design will need to meet the same requirements as its registered counterpart. In terms of novelty this means that no identical design must have been made available to the public before the date on which the (unregistered) design for which protection is claimed has first been made available to the public.[135] And the same date is also determinative for the examination of the individual character of the (unregistered) design and the overall impression made on the informed user.[136] The three-year term starts to run on the date on which the design was first made available to the public by publication, exhibition, use in trade, or any other way of disclosing the design if it could be reasonably known in specialized Community circles.[137] The latter should not be restricted to designers in the relevant field and can include mere traders or retailers in the field.[138] In this respect, again, there are important similarities with its registered counterpart. And when it comes to using the concept of availability to the public for the purposes of disclosure in the context of Art. 7 (novelty and individual character) all will depend on the factual circumstances, but the CJEU was not prepared to rule out the conclusion that a design has not become available to the public as a result of a single demonstration of the design in the showroom of a manufacturer outside the EU (or on the basis of a mere registration in a design register in a country outside the EU), even when coupled with the delivery of a single copy of an article made to the design to a company in the EU.[139] Returning to Art. 11, one should also note that there is no presumption of proprietorship of the unregistered design to the benefit of the person who made the design available to the public. The normal rule applies and the designer will be entitled to the unregistered design.[140]

Infringement of the Community unregistered design right occurs in the same way as infringement of the registered right, apart from the fact that, in the absence of registration, the claimant must also prove that the defendant copied the protected design. There will be no infringement if there has been independent creation by the alleged infringer if the latter may reasonably be thought not to have been familiar with the unregistered design that was disclosed to the public by its holder.[141] It is up to the holder of the unregistered design to prove that the contested use results from copying that design. However, if a Community design court finds that the fact of requiring that holder to prove that the contested use results from copying that design is likely to make it impossible or excessively difficult for such evidence to be produced, that court is required to use all procedures available to it under national law to counter that difficulty.[142]

When proceedings are brought for the infringement or the threatened infringement of an unregistered Community design, the Community design court shall presume that the unregistered design right is valid if the holder produces proof that the conditions of Art. 11 have been met and indicates what is the individual character of the design. It is up to the defendant to contest the validity by plea or counterclaim for a declaration of invalidity.[143] The right holder is, however, not required to prove that the

---

[135] Art. 5(1)(a) of the Regulation.   [136] Art. 6(1)(a) of the Regulation.

[137] Art. 11 of the Regulation.

[138] Case C-479/12, *H. Gautzsch Großhandel GmbH & Co. KG v. Münchener Boulevard Möbel Joseph Duna GmbH* [2014] ECDR 14, at para. 30.

[139] *H. Gautzsch Großhandel GmbH & Co. KG v. Münchener Boulevard Möbel* (n. 138) at para. 36.

[140] See the *Bolero* case in Germany, German Bundesgerichtshof (n. 75).

[141] Art. 19(2) of the Regulation.

[142] *H. Gautzsch Großhandel GmbH & Co. KG v. Münchener Boulevard Möbel* (n. 138) at para. 44.

[143] Art. 85(2) of the Regulation.

design has individual character within the meaning of Art. 6. A mere indication of what in its view are the elements of the design that give it its individual character will be sufficient.[144]

In terms of invalidity the standard rules of the Regulation apply to the unregistered Community design right if a problem with its validity arises. The Regulation merely adds that such a design shall be declared invalid by a Community design court on application to such a court on the basis of a counterclaim in infringement proceedings.[145]

The seamless connection with the registered right is assured by the provision that allows a one-year grace period between the publication and the application for the registered right.[146] Novelty will, in other words, not be lost by publication giving right to a Community unregistered design right. This allows the designer to test the market before deciding on an application, as long as that application for a registered design is launched before the end of the one-year grace period.

An overview

This is an area of the law of intellectual property that is undergoing important and radical changes at present. Much of the 1949 Act had become outdated and the courts had struggled to maintain a workable system. The Design Directive and its implementation, in the form of the recent radical shake-up of the 1949 Act, puts in place a harmonized and more modern approach to registered designs. That approach is rather radically different on a number of key points and this will inevitably bring with it some uncertainty in its initial implementation. It will eventually be up to the courts, both at national and at EU levels, to provide the necessary clarifications.

What remains true, however, and what drives this whole overhaul of the system is the fact that designs can be of tremendous commercial value. They do not amount to an invention and are not necessarily a trade mark; neither does copyright protect the idea behind the design. So there is a very real need to register the design as a registered design. It is the only way in which to prevent competitors from cashing in on a good and valuable design by using one that is substantially identical.

The new system should be far better equipped to allow designers to secure adequate protection for their valuable designs.

Further reading

CARBONI, A., 'Design Validity and Infringement: Feel the Difference' (2008) 30(3) EIPR 111–17.

DREXL, J., HILTY, R., and KUR, A. 'Design Protection for Spare Parts and the Commission's Proposal for a Repairs Clause' (2005) 36 IIC 448.

HOWE, M. (ed.) (2010) *Russell-Clarke and Howe on Industrial Design*, 8th edn, London: Sweet and Maxwell.

IZQUIERDO PERIS, J. J. 'Registered Community Design: First Two-Year Balance from an Insider's Perspective' (2006) 30(2) EIPR 146.

---

[144] Case C-345/13, *Karen Millen Fashions Ltd v. Dunnes Stores and Dunnes Stores (Limerick) Ltd* [2014] Bus LR 756 at para. 47.

[145] Art. 24(3) of the Regulation.   [146] Art. 7(2) of the Regulation.

IZQUIERDO PERIS, J. J. 'OHIM Practice in the Field of Invalidity of Registered Community Designs' (2008) 30(2) EIPR 56–65.

SAEZ, V. 'The Unregistered Community Design' (2002) 144 EIPR 585.

SCANLAN, G. and GALE, S. 'Industrial Design and the Design Directive: Continuing and Future Problems in Design Rights' [2005] JBL 91.

SYKES, J. (2005) *Intellectual Property in Designs*, London: Butterworths Lexis-Nexis.

22

Unregistered designs

The UK also has a second kind of design, often called the design right. It does not involve registration and it is primarily concerned with functional designs. Historically these designs were not covered necessarily by the Registered Designs Act 1949 and hence the decision to provide a specific regime of design protection for them.

Introduction

The unregistered design right was introduced by the Copyright, Designs and Patents Act (CDPA) 1988 in an attempt to overcome various problems. Before that time, functional, non-aesthetic designs—such as those for exhaust pipes for cars—did not qualify for registered design protection and neither were they covered by a special intellectual property right. But there was an overlap with copyright, because, in the majority of cases, functional designs are laid down in drawings, plans, or blueprints that attract copyright protection. A copy of an item incorporating the design involves making a three-dimensional copy of the drawing, plan, or blueprint and infringes their copyright. This system provided indirect protection for the majority of functional designs, but it is hard to see why a certain category of designs—those that are aesthetic—deserve the creation of a special intellectual property right, while the other designs—that are purely functional in nature—should only be protected indirectly through copyright.

This argument becomes even more forceful if one considers that, in theory, all design rights—both aesthetical and functional—benefit potentially from the overlap with copyright. In practice, designs that met all of the requirements for registration were often not registered, because the non-bureaucratic and fee-free copyright system offered long-term protection. Parliament tried to remedy this by means of a series of arbitrary measures: in the Copyright Act 1956, copyright protection was denied to designs that could have been registered; in the Design Copyright Act 1968, copyright was once again permitted, but the term of copyright protection in such cases was restricted to the term of the registered design right.[1]

This created absurd situations such as that in *Dorling v. Honnor Marine*.[2] This case was concerned with a sailing dinghy. The design for the dinghy met the requirements for registration, but had not been registered. Before their relationship turned sour, the defendant built the dinghies—both in complete and in kit forms—under a licence granted by the plaintiff. The case arose when the defendant went on to assign his licence to a limited company that he had formed; the company became the co-defendant in the case. Drawings of the dinghy and of all its parts existed, and, theoretically speaking, the copyright in them was infringed by making three-dimensional copies. In practice, the Copyright Act 1956

---

[1] At that stage, 15 years; now extended to 25 years, as discussed in the previous chapter.
[2] *Dorling v. Honnor Marine Ltd* [1965] Ch 1, [1964] 1 All ER 241.

had removed copyright protection for designs that could have been registered, so no intellectual property right had been infringed in building the dinghies. But kits of parts were also made: the design of each of the included parts was purely functional and could not be registered. As a result, the provisions of the Copyright Act 1956 did not exclude copyright protection in the drawings for the kit parts and the production of the parts formed an indirect infringement of the copyright in the drawings by making three-dimensional copies of these two-dimensional drawings. The functional design of the parts enjoyed protection for the life of the author plus 50 years, while no protection was available for the aesthetical design of the complete dinghy.[3] This discrepancy in protection for the two types of design could not be justified.

But it is not only the discrepancy that caused problems: copyright protection for functional designs also proved to be an inadequate solution. This became clear in the famous *British Leyland Motor Corp. Ltd v. Armstrong Patents Co. Ltd*,[4] which we discussed in Chapter 20. The case most strongly indicated the need for design law reform and action needed to be undertaken on two points. A specific intellectual property right needed to be created for functional designs, meaning that the whole design area would be covered by two specific design rights: aesthetical designs would still be protected by the registered design right and the non-aesthetical functional designs would be covered by the new design right.

The second point that needed to be addressed is the overlap with copyright: a clear delimitation of both the copyright and the design area was required. The reform of the 1988 Act attempted to reach that conclusion and created the (unregistered) design right, which is officially called the design right—but, in order to distinguish it from the registered design and because there is no registration requirement, we will describe it as the (unregistered) design.

Subsistence of the (unregistered) design right

A design

The technical definition of a 'design' that was given in the original version of the CDPA 1988 was that it is *'the design of any aspect of the shape or configuration (whether internal or external) of the whole or part of an article'*.[5] The Intellectual Property Act 2014 deleted the words *'any aspect of'* from this provision. We will come back to that shortly. The concept of 'shape' is understood relatively easily, but that of 'configuration' is somewhat more vague. In relation to the former, suffice it to say that there is no reason why a simple geometric shape could not be a protectable design for an item.[6] In relation to the latter, however, the Court of Appeal has indicated that 'configuration' refers to the relative arrangement of three-dimensional elements.[7] These elements need to be configured and the mere choice of colourways of a standard track top was therefore not an aspect of the shape or configuration of an item or of a part of an item.[8] The addition of the term 'aspect' to the notions of shape and configuration refers to something discernible or recognizable.[9]

---

[3] Even if the design had been registered, the term of protection would have been much shorter.
[4] [1986] AC 577, [1986] 1 All ER 850. [5] CDPA 1988, s. 213(2).
[6] *Sales v. Stromberg* [2006] FSR 7.
[7] *Lambretta Clothing Co. Ltd v. Teddy Smith (UK) Ltd & anor* [2005] RPC 6 (CA).
[8] *Lambretta Clothing Co. Ltd* (n. 7).
[9] *A. Fulton Co. Ltd v. Totes Isotoner (UK) Ltd* [2004] RPC 301 (CA), at 311.

This definition and approach means that various aspects of the shape or configuration of an item can be the subjects of different design rights, and that a design does not necessarily relate to the whole item. A design right can be asserted in only certain aspects of a larger article. It is, however, quite possible that both the individual parts and the machine as a whole come within the definition of a design.[10] This was, for example, the case for a slurry machine as a whole, on the one hand, and its various components, on the other.[11]

The case law also offers another example in a case concerning pig fenders for use in pig arks, which provide shelter for a single sow and her piglets. A two-inch tube protected the teats of the sow; this two-inch tube was held to be an aspect of the shape or configuration of a part of the fender—that is, the tube element constituted a design.[12] A clear distinction must, however, be made between the design and the item to which it is applied: the design is protected, while the item is not; the right protects the design itself and not the item on which it has been recorded or to which it has been applied.[13] The right in the design is not a right in the item itself.[14]

Aspects of the internal shape or configuration of the whole, or part, of an item can also be taken into account. This marks a clear difference from the 'eye appeal' requirement for registered designs. (Unregistered) designs are intended to offer protection for functional designs; eye appeal is not required. The worth and ingenuity of such a design might be found in its detailed relative dimensions. A design might even exist (and be different and new) if the eye is not able to distinguish the shape (in relation to other designs).[15] Larger, and more clearly visible, shapes are obviously also possible and remain eligible for protection.

The deletion of the words 'any aspect of' has provided more clarity. One is in essence concerned with the shape or the configuration of the article, as these are described by (a combination of) features and these features must specifically be embodied in all or part of the claimant's article.[16] The design can no longer be described with a very high level of abstraction. The maximum level of abstraction is now that exhibited by the actual article (or part of the article) which embodies the design. This results from the now clear link between shape and configuration on the one hand and the article on the other hand.[17] The dilutive element 'any aspect of' no longer weakens that link.

An original design

The design right will only subsist in designs that are original. This clearly means that the design should not be copied and that it should be the result of its creator's own work. The design should be the independent work of the designer and should not be copied from

---

[10] *A. Fulton Co. Ltd* (n. 9) at 307–11; *Albert Packaging Ltd v. Nampak Cartons & Healthcare Ltd* [2011] EWPCC 15, [2011] FSR 32.

[11] *Farmers Build Ltd (in liq.) v. Carier Bulk Materials Handling Ltd* [1999] RPC 461.

[12] *C & H Engineering v. Klucznik & Sons Ltd* [1992] FSR 421, per Aldous J at 428; see J. Turner, 'A True Design Right: *C & H Engineering v. Klucznik and Sons*' (1993) 1 EIPR 24.

[13] *Electronic Techniques (Anglia) Ltd v. Critchley Components Ltd* [1997] FSR 401; *Scholes Windows Ltd v. Magnet Ltd (No. 1)* [2002] FSR 172 (CA) at 180.

[14] *Scholes Windows Ltd v. Magnet Ltd (No. 1)* (n. 13) at 180.

[15] *Ocular Sciences Ltd & another v. Aspect Vision Care Ltd; Geoffrey Harrison Galley v. Ocular Sciences Ltd* [1997] RPC 289 at 423.

[16] *DKH Retail Ltd v. H. Young (Operations) Ltd* [2014] EWHC 4034 (IPEC).

[17] *Whitby Specialist Vehicles Ltd v. Yorkshire Specialist Vehicles Ltd and others* [2014] EWHC 4242 (Pat), at paras. 40–5.

previous designs. Time, labour, and skill should have been invested to such an extent that copyright protection could have been attracted.[18] Recent cases argue that the new higher criterion of the author's own intellectual creation should also apply here.[19] When examining originality, one should ask whether all of the additional features added by the designer give rise to the requisite quality of originality. One should not focus exclusively on one or more features or adopt a piecemeal approach, even if individual features will unavoidably require some attention and consideration.[20] If design rights are asserted (only) in certain aspects of a larger article, the issue of originality needs to be considered separately for each aspect.[21] But that is not all: s. 213(4) of the 1988 Act specifies that '*a design is not "original" if it is commonplace in the design field in question at the time of its creation*'.

The concept of 'commonplace'

Laddie J has defined as 'commonplace' any design that is '*trite, trivial, common or garden, hackneyed or of the type which would excite no particular attention in those in the relevant art*'.[22] For example, in a case that was concerned with designs for leather cases for individual models of mobile phones, it was held that those aspects of the design that were found in industry standard cases were commonplace;[23] they were therefore excluded from the design right. It is possible, however, to arrive at a design that is not commonplace through the combination of commonplace and trite ingredients. The test applies to the design: if the design is a combination of ingredients, that combination itself must not be commonplace.[24] It should be kept in mind, however, that no design right is conferred on the item; the right is conferred on aspects of shape of configuration of the item. One should therefore not derive any conclusion from the fact that the item itself is commonplace: its shape and configuration may still not be commonplace.[25]

The provision that is contained in s. 213(4) of the 1988 Act makes the originality requirement for designs clearly more stringent than that for copyright. Indeed, it introduces an objective component akin to the novelty consideration in patents.[26] Some form of objective assessment is required.[27] A design that is already known and is, in reality, nothing more than a copy of an existing design will not be original;[28] neither will mere changes in scale produce a different or new design.[29] It is submitted that the design must be innovative, although the fact that it is new does not carry with it any qualitative judgement. The design must not be good or better than all existing designs, nor should it present a technical advantage. But this does not imply that one should simply use the novelty requirement as applied in patent law,[30] nor is it possible to import concepts such

---

[18] *Farmers Build Ltd (in liq.)* (n. 11), per Mummery LJ at 475; *C & H Engineering v. F Klucznik & Sons Ltd* [1992] FSR 421.

[19] *Whitby Specialist Vehicles Ltd* (n. 17).   [20] *Guild v. Eskander Ltd* [2003] FSR 23 (CA) at 39.

[21] *Albert Packaging Ltd v. Nampak Cartons & Healthcare Ltd* [2011] EWPCC 15, [2011] FSR 32 at para. 14.

[22] *Ocular Sciences Ltd* (n. 15) at 429, in which there was a reference to semiconductor products and the design right in them. The definition was repeated in *Mayfair Brassware v. Aqualine International Ltd* [1998] FSR 135, in a context that refers to design rights.

[23] *Philip Parker v. Stephen Tidball* [1997] FSR 680.

[24] *Farmers Build Ltd (in liq.)* (n. 11), per Mummery LJ at 476.

[25] *Farmers Build Ltd (in liq.)* (n. 11), per Mummery LJ at 483.

[26] *Philip Parker v. Stephen Tidball* (n. 23).

[27] *Farmers Build Ltd (in liq.)* (n. 11), per Mummery LJ at 476.

[28] The fact that a design becomes well known does not mean it loses its design right, but further variations may become commonplace: see *Dyson Ltd v. Qualtex (UK) Ltd* [2006] RPC 31 (CA).

[29] *Ocular Sciences* (n. 15) at 423.   [30] See *Dyson Ltd v. Qualtex (UK) Ltd* [2005] RPC 19.

as 'novelty' and 'variants commonly used in trade' from the law on registered designs.[31] The 1988 Act itself restricts the scope of the provision to the design field in question and nothing outside that specific design field will influence the decision regarding the originality of the design. A design that is known in another unrelated design field will still be original. (Patent anticipation is clearly much wider in scope.)

In a case that was concerned with design rights in a slurry separator for use in the agricultural industries, it was held that the relevant design field was that of slurry separators, rather than any wider agricultural field. Evidence relating to agricultural machines or engineering outside this narrow field was irrelevant for the determination whether the designs for the slurry separators were commonplace.[32]

The design field

Such a determination of the relevant design field remains, however, one of fact and degree for each case.[33] The court is quite entitled to take the views of the customer, rather than the view of a design expert, into account when determining how broad the relevant field should be. For example, the customer would compare all types of window, whether made of aluminium, uPVC, or wood, rather than restrict him- or herself to uPVC windows, as might an expert.[34] In addition, by pointing out that the design should not be commonplace, the Act clearly does not deprive of the required level of originality any design that has been circulated to a limited extent. Showing a limited number of items incorporating the new design at a trade fair, or consulting colleagues or potential customers on the qualities of the new design by showing them a drawing of it, will not necessarily make the design commonplace.

Further, the relevant moment in time is the creation of the design rather than the filing date of the application used in patent law. This is, of course, a consequence of the fact that there is no registration requirement for this design right. Arguably, this originality requirement comes close to the novelty requirement for registered designs, although there is a clear difference in relation to anticipation by publication for certain purposes in restricted circles.

When looking at the design field in question, no attention should be paid to when other designs in a certain field with which comparison was made were first produced, or to whether they were still in use or had fallen into disuse at the time at which the new design appeared. Old designs could not be excluded from the design field, because they could still form part of the design field in question, because, for example, designers and members of the public can still see them.[35]

A narrow approach

All of these elements are mere signposts in the direction of a commonplace test. What is clear is that the concept of 'commonplace' is to be given a narrow interpretation, because the design right itself should cover designs of functional items. A broad definition would—in combination with the shorter life of the right and the narrower protection against copying—effectively remove protection for the majority of such designs for functional items.[36]

---

[31] *Farmers Build Ltd (in liq.)* (n. 11), per Mummery LJ at 481.

[32] *Farmers Build Ltd (in liq.)* (n. 11), per Mummery LJ at 476.

[33] See *Ultraframe (UK) Ltd v. Eurocell Building Plastics Ltd* [2005] RPC 36 (CA).

[34] See *Scholes Windows Ltd v. Magnet Ltd (No. 1)* [2002] FSR 172 (CA) at 182.

[35] *Scholes Windows Ltd* (n. 34) at 181–2.

[36] *Farmers Build Ltd (in liq.)* (n. 11), per Mummery LJ at 481.

A test was outlined by Mummery LJ in *Farmers Build Ltd (in liq.) v. Carier Bulk Materials Handling Ltd.*[37] It can be summarized in the following four steps.

1. In a first stage, the court needs to ascertain how similar the design under consideration is to the design of similar items in the same design field that are made by third parties.

2. That comparative exercise needs to be carried out objectively in the light of expert evidence that highlights the similarities and differences between the various designs, and which explains their respective significance. The final decision whether a design is commonplace rests with the court, and it involves a judgement of fact and degree that reflects the evidence of the particular case.

3. Designs are more likely to be commonplace if, in the absence of copying, they are close to one another. The closer the designs are, the more likely it becomes that they are commonplace, because this may be evidence of the fact that only one—commonplace—way of designing the item exists.

4. A design is not commonplace if it contains various aspects that are not found in any other design in the relevant design field, even if these aspects are found in the alleged infringer's design.[38]

The tangible form requirement

No registration is required before a design can attract design protection, but one cannot protect something if the content—and thus the precise subject of protection—is not known. A design therefore has to have a tangible form if it is to attract design protection.[39] This requirement can be met in two ways: the design can be recorded in a design document, as previously defined, or an item can be made to the design. The design right will subsist from the moment of recording or from the moment of incorporation onwards.[40] And it is clear that the recording does not need to be made by the designer for this requirement to be met.[41]

In the case of registered designs, the tangible form is evidently required for the purposes of registration. One cannot, materially speaking, put together an application if the design does not exist, in the application, in a tangible form. In the registration system, the date of registration is the starting point for the term of protection. Because that element is not available in a system without registration, the date of recording is substituted for the date of registration.

The commencement date for the new design regime was 1 August 1989. Designs that were recorded in a design document or which were applied to an item before that date will not attract design right protection.[42]

Exceptions to the design right

Design rights will not subsist in a number of items. These are listed in s. 213(3) of the 1988 Act, as follows.

---

[37] *Farmers Build Ltd (in liq.)* (n. 11) at 481.

[38] *Farmers Build Ltd (in liq.)* (n. 11), per Mummery LJ at 482. See also *A. Fulton Co. Ltd v. Grant Barnett & Co. Ltd* [2001] RPC 257.

[39] CDPA 1988, s. 213(6).   [40] CDPA 1988, s. 213(6).

[41] *C & H Engineering v. Klucznik & Sons Ltd* [1992] FSR 421, per Aldous J at 428.

[42] CDPA 1988, s. 213(7).

Methods or principles of construction

The first items on the list are 'methods or principles of construction'.[43] This is an obvious exception, which also exists in relation to registered designs.[44] Particular features of shape or configuration—as applied to an item or a part of it—are protected, but not general, theoretical, and eventually underlying principles. This exception is similar in nature to the scientific theories and mathematical methods exceptions that relate to patentable subject matter.[45]

An interesting example of the operation of s. 213(3)(a) is provided by a case that was concerned with a design of a polyvinyl alcohol (PVA), warp-knitted, ladder-resistant, micromesh bait bag for anglers. The court held that the basic appearance of the design was generated by the Atlas warp-stitch method that had been used and that it therefore was nothing more than a method or principle of construction. As such, the design was excluded from protection as an unregistered design. Similarly, the layering of items in a combined urinary catheter removal and insertion pack was excluded.[46]

The arrangement of zippers and piping for the expansion section of a suitcase design, meanwhile, was held not to be a principle or method of construction.[47] Indeed, the exception does not aim to preclude a design from protection merely because it has a functional purpose and other designers can still use the construction features in quite distinct designs. The exception aims rather to avoid monopolization of the entire principle method of construction and such monopolization did not occur in this case. Since design right does not protect ideas per se but only their actual physical manifestation, even if ideas may have been important in arriving at a certain design, s. 213(3)(a) operates to limit the level of generality permitted in defining a design. The more abstract the definition, the more likely it is that it will fail to pass the hurdle of s. 213(3)(a).[48]

Surface decoration

Also on the list is 'surface decoration',[49] which does not come within the category of functional, rather than aesthetic, design that the 1988 Act set out to protect. Surface decoration includes two things: first, it includes decoration lying on the surface of the item; second, it includes decorative features of the surface itself. Surface decoration cannot be confined to features that are essentially two-dimensional and it also includes, potentially, those features that serve a functional purpose.[50] Accordingly, the painted finish, cockbeading, and V-grooves that were all aspects of the external appearance of a single wall unit in a range of kitchens were excluded from the scope of the design protection that was held to exist in the unit.[51] And as a case involving dying the fabric used for a standard track top and the colourways used for that purpose demonstrates, the concept of surface decoration not only involves cases in which the surface was covered with a thin layer, but also cases in which the decoration ran right through the item.[52]

---

[43] CDPA 1988, s. 213(3)(a).   [44] See Registered Designs Act 1949, s. 1(1)(a).

[45] Patents Act 1977, s. 1(2)(a).

[46] *Bailey (t/a Elite Angling Products) v. Haynes (t/a Rags)* [2007] FSR 10; and *Clinisupplies Ltd v. Karen Park, Richardson Healthcare Ltd and Mayur Patel* [2012] EWHC 3453 (Ch) respectively.

[47] *Landor & Hawa International Ltd v. Azure Designs Ltd* [2006] ECDR 31, [2007] FSR 9 (CA).

[48] *Landor & Hawa International Ltd* (n. 47); *Rolawn Ltd v. Turfmech Machinery Ltd* [2008] RPC 27; and *Albert Packaging Ltd v. Nampak Cartons & Healthcare Ltd* [2011] EWPCC 15, [2011] FSR 32 at paras. 18–22.

[49] CDPA 1988, s. 213(3)(c).

[50] A visor-stiffening effect of the double-scalloping feature of a firefighter's helmet does not bring it outside the scope of the exception for surface decoration: see *Helmut Integrated Systems Ltd v. Tunnard* [2006] FSR 41.

[51] *Mark Wilkinson Furniture Ltd v. Woodcraft Designs (Radcliffe) Ltd* [1998] FSR 63.

[52] *Lambretta Clothing Co. Ltd* (n. 7).

The exclusion of certain aspects of the design as surface decoration does not mean, for example, that the rest of the aspects of the shape of the kitchen unit could not attract an (unregistered) design right.[53]

'Must fit'

One of the most important exceptions on the list is the 'must fit'[54] exception, which excludes '*features of shape or configuration which enable the article to be connected to, placed in, around or against another article so that either article may perform its function*'[55] from the scope of the design right. The exception—which is also referred to as the 'interface provision'—is confined to those situations in which two items, produced by one or two producers, are linked and certain features of shape or configuration enable either item to perform its function. It also applies to the interface features of two interfitting items that are later assembled together to form the whole, or part, of another, larger, item.[56] The exception is confined strictly to those features that play this enabling role and which must be of a certain precise shape or configuration to be able to play it; other features of shape or configuration of the same item may well attract design protection.

No feature of shape or configuration will escape from the scope of the exception because it also performed some other purpose: for example, because it was also attractive.[57] In certain cases, two or more different designs would enable the items to be fitted together in a way that allowed one or all of them to perform their function. In such cases, all of these designs fall within the exclusion and no (unregistered) design right will exist in them. This indicates the wide scope of the exception, which has, as its purpose, the prevention of '*the designer of a piece of equipment from using design right to prevent others from making parts which fitted his equipment*'.[58] That purpose will only be met if the drafting, in wide terms of the exception, is given its proper wide and extensive interpretation. The word 'article'—that is, item—can therefore be applied to living and formerly living things, as well as to inanimate things. This means that, in a case concerning contact lenses, the back radius, the diameter, and the parallel peripheral carrier of the contact lens were all excluded from the design right, because they were features that enabled the lens to fit against the eyeball so as to allow the lens to perform its function of correcting the focusing ability of the eye and to remain in a stable position in the eye.[59] Another example is found in an electrical currency adaptor that allows the use of equipment built for 110V on the UK's 220V system and which has many peculiar functional features of shape, but also rods that fit into a wall socket. This example may well result in design rights for the various features of shape, but no design right will subsist in the shape of the rods, because this shape will be dependent upon the shape of the socket, enabling the adaptor to be connected to the socket and the electricity network, and allowing the socket and the adaptor to perform their functions. Those features of the shape of leather cases for individual mobile phones that enable the cases to be placed around the phones, so that either the phones or the cases may perform their function, are yet another example of design features that fall foul of the exception.[60]

Many of these aspects of the 'must fit' exception have now been reviewed by the Court of Appeal in *Dyson v. Qualtex*.[61] This case concerned spare parts for Dyson vacuum

---

[53] *Mark Wilkinson Furniture Ltd* (n. 51).   [54] CDPA 1988, s. 213(3)(b)(i).
[55] CDPA 1988, s. 213(3)(b)(i).
[56] *Electronic Techniques (Anglia) Ltd v. Critchley Components Ltd* [1997] FSR 401.
[57] *Ocular Sciences* (n. 15) at 424.   [58] *Ocular Sciences* (n. 15), per Laddie J.
[59] *Ocular Sciences* (n. 15) at 425–8.   [60] *Philip Parker v. Stephen Tidball* (n. 23).
[61] *Dyson Ltd v. Qualtex (UK) Ltd* [2005] RPC 19, affirmed [2006] RPC 31 (CA).

cleaners. Dyson claimed design protection, while Qualtex relied on the exception. The court determined that once a handle is shaped in a certain way, for example, the catch must necessarily adopt a certain shape to fit with the handle. That latter shape is therefore covered by the exception. The words of the exception should not be interpreted particularly narrowly or widely. It does not matter that there are two ways of achieving the necessary fit or connection between the item and the item to which it fits. If the design chosen by the design right holder is a way of achieving that fit or interface, then it does not attract design right, no matter how many alternative ways of achieving the same fit or interface might be available. It is also not necessary for the items to touch each other for the exception to apply.[62]

This exception has an equivalent in s. 1(1)(b)(i) of the Registered Designs Act 1949, but the latter refers to the 'purpose solely dictated by function' and is therefore wider in scope.

'Must match'

The second of the most important exceptions is the '*must match*'[63] exception, which covers all features of shape or configuration that '*are dependent upon the appearance of another article of which the article is intended by the designer to form an integral part*';[64] the classic example of which would be the doors of a car. The design of the doors is determined by the appearance of the bodywork of the car. If I were to buy a door as a spare part for my car, it would be rather essential that it fits in the gap left in the body. When considering the 'must match' exception, the court will have to consider whether there is a dependency of the kind, or to the extent, that it would make the overall item in question radically different in appearance if the first item were not shaped as at present. Ultimately, this is a matter of fact, degree, and impression.[65]

Of course, the exception— like the 'must fit' exception—does not extend to other features of the same item; it does not apply if one item was not intended to form an integral part of another. For example, the features of a kitchen unit were not caught by the exclusion, because the complete kitchen unit was a series of matching items, none of which formed an integral part of another.[66] The fact that one item could incidentally be made to form an integral part of another is not relevant. This makes it also clear that things made in sets—such as plates and glasses—are not covered by the exception. In these cases, one design will be applied to the whole set.

The example concerning the design of the doors of a car that already indicates that spare parts occupy a special position in relation to the design right—but not only do they cover a very substantial part of the whole design activity, the exceptions also seem to exclude them almost entirely from design protection. This meets the need for competition in this area. The legislature found it unacceptable that the producer of an item could, through copyright (at one time) and design protection regimes, monopolize the spare-parts market. This market is opened up for competition by means of the 'must fit' and 'must match' exceptions to the design right. But the fact that other features are not covered by the exception can create some difficulty: on the one hand, the alternative producer of spare parts should be careful not to infringe the design right in these features, should it exist; on the other, the fact can be seen as a tool through which the original producer is enabled to distinguish its spare parts from those of alternative producers.

---

[62] *Dyson Ltd* (n. 61).   [63] CDPA 1988, s. 213(3)(b)(ii).   [64] CDPA 1988, s. 213(3)(b)(ii).
[65] *Dyson Ltd* (n. 61).   [66] *Mark Wilkinson Furniture Ltd* (n. 51).

Qualification

Designs that meet all previous requirements will only be protected if they meet one additional requirement: the design should also qualify for protection. This requirement is very similar to the qualification requirement in copyright, and forms an inherent part of any intellectual property right that is not subject to a registration requirement and which is, after all, granted on a national basis. The qualification requirement is met if the designer,[67] the commissioner of the design[68] (if the design is commissioned for money or money's worth),[69] or the employer of the designer[70] (for designs created in the course of employment) is a qualifying person. The position of the designer is only relevant if the design is neither created in the course of employment, nor in pursuance of a commission.[71]

The system starts with the definition of what is a 'qualifying country'.[72] This is defined as the UK and the other member states of the European Union (EU), eventually supplemented by other countries by an Order in Council.[73] A qualifying individual is a citizen of, or an individual habitually resident in, such a qualifying country. Together with any corporate body or any body having legal personality that is formed under the law of a qualifying country or which has at least a place of business at which substantial business activity[74] is carried out in a qualifying country, these qualifying individuals comprise the category of the qualifying persons.[75]

The qualification requirement can also be met by reference to the country and person of first marketing of items made to the design if the designer, and, eventually, the commissioner or employer do not qualify.[76] This is the case if the first marketing takes place by a qualifying person in a qualifying country. On top of that, the qualifying person must be exclusively authorized by the person who would have been the first owner of the design right, if it came into existence, to put the items made to the design on the market in the UK and that exclusivity must be enforceable by legal proceedings in the UK. For qualification purposes, the place at which the design was created is utterly irrelevant.

The substance of the design right

The design right is a property right[77] that grants to its owner the exclusive right to reproduce the design for commercial purposes. The obvious way to do so is by making items to the design, but the owner can also make a design document in which the design is recorded and which enables such items to be made by a third party.[78] An item is reproduced for 'commercial purposes' if the reproduction is undertaken with a view to its being sold or hired in the course of business.[79]

The person behind the design

The preceding analysis refers often to the 'person behind the design'; it is now time to fill in that notion. The designer is the person who creates the design.[80] Should this rule lead

---

[67] CDPA 1988, s. 218(2).   [68] CDPA 1988, s. 219(1).   [69] CDPA 1988, s. 263(1).
[70] CDPA 1988, s. 219(1).   [71] CDPA 1988, s. 218(1).   [72] CDPA 1988, s. 217(3).
[73] See Design Right (Reciprocal Protection) (No. 2) Order 1989, SI 1989/1294.
[74] '*Dealings in goods which are at all material times outside the country*' shall not be taken into account: CDPA 1988, s. 217(5).
[75] CDPA 1988, s. 217(1).   [76] CDPA 1988, s. 220.   [77] CDPA 1988, s. 213(1).
[78] CDPA 1988, s. 226(1).   [79] CDPA 1988, s. 263(3).   [80] CDPA 1988, s. 214(1).

us to a computer, the person that undertakes the necessary arrangements for the creation of the design by the computer will be regarded as the designer.[81] Creation should be interpreted as having the idea for the design; it does not necessarily include the recording of the design.[82]

This leads us to the issue of who will be the first owner of the design. If the design is neither commissioned, nor created in the course of employment, the designer will be the first owner of the design right.[83] The commissioner and the employer are the first owners of the design right in a design created in pursuance of a commission or in the course of employment, respectively.[84] A particular problem arises, in practice, when a design is created by a 100 per cent shareholder of a company through which he or she carries on business: is such a person employed by the company or did the company commission the design?

The Court of Appeal has shed some light on the matter by holding that a contract of employment—even if it can be concluded entirely orally—requires the presence of three elements, as follows:[85]

1. The alleged employee must have agreed that, in consideration for a wage or any other form of consideration, he or she would provide skill and labour in the performance of some service for his or her employer.

2. Expressly or impliedly, the alleged employee must have accepted that, in the performance of that service, he or she would be subject to the control of the employer to such an extent that the employer can be described as his or her 'master'.

3. The other provisions of the contract must be consistent with it being a contract of employment.[86]

The idea of commissioning a work involved, in the eyes of the Court of Appeal, a contract involving mutual obligations prior to the production of the relevant design.[87] If neither of these situations occur, but if the 100 per cent shareholder acts for the company and created the design through the company, the shareholder will hold the design and any rights in it in trust for the company.[88]

These rules apply in all circumstances except in those of s. 220 of the 1988 Act: if the design qualifies through first marketing only, the first owner of the design right will be the person that markets the items made to the design.[89]

Joint creation—which will arise when the contribution of two or more designers is not distinct and cannot be distinguished—and joint ownership are also possible, and do not create specific problems. It is worth pointing out, however, that in cases in which not all of the persons involved are qualifying persons, only those that are will be entitled to the design right;[90] the design, meanwhile, will meet the qualifying requirement as soon as any of the persons involved is a qualifying person.[91] A design jointly created by eight designers, for example, will qualify for design protection as long as one of the designers

---

[81] CDPA 1988, s. 214(2).

[82] *C & H Engineering v. Klucznik & Sons Ltd* [1992] FSR 421, per Aldous J at 428.

[83] CDPA 1988, s. 215(1).

[84] CDPA 1988, s. 215(2) and (3). The person asserting a commission will need to prove it, see *Bruhn Newtech Ltd v. Datanetex Ltd* [2012] EWPCC 17.

[85] *Ultraframe UK Ltd v. Fielding* [2004] RPC 479 (CA).

[86] *Ultraframe UK Ltd* (n. 85); *Ready Mixed Concrete (South East) Ltd v. Minister of Pensions & National Insurance* [1968] 2 QB 497.

[87] *Ultraframe UK Ltd* (n. 85); *Ready Mixed Concrete* (n. 86); *Apple Corps Ltd v. Cooper* [1993] FSR 286.

[88] *Ultraframe UK Ltd* (n. 85).   [89] CDPA 1988, s. 215(4).

[90] CDPA 1988, ss. 218(4) and 219(3).   [91] CDPA 1988, s. 218(3) and 219(2).

is a qualifying person. In that case, that one (qualifying) person alone will be entitled to the design right. Should four of the designers qualify, the four of them will be jointly entitled to the design right. In any case, designers that are not qualifying persons will not be entitled to the design right.

The term of (unregistered) design protection

We have already discussed the fact that the design right comes into existence at the moment at which it is either recorded in a design document or when an item is made to the design. As with most terms in copyright, the duration of the design right is then linked to the end of the calendar year in which such recording or production takes place. We will call this important point the 'end of the creation year'.

Most designs will be exploited before the end of a five-year period, which starts running from the end of the creation year. If such exploitation takes the form of items made to the design being made available for sale or hire, the term of (unregistered) design protection is ten years. This term starts running at the end of the calendar year during which the exploitation first occurred.[92] The exploitation can take place anywhere in the world, as long as it is done by the owner of the design right or with its licence.[93]

The absence of exploitation, as already defined, within the first five years does not, however, lead to an unlimited design right protection. In that case, the term of (unregistered) design protection expires 15 years after the end of the creation year.[94]

These terms of protection are substantially shorter than those used in copyright and are much more in line with those used in patent law. This is probably a recognition of the fact that functional designs are, in general, an industrial property right and that a fair return on the investment they require can be obtained in a relatively short period. As we have seen in Chapter 1 of this book, the term of protection should indeed be linked to the determination of the correct balance between the innovation (creation of new designs) and production levels (items produced to the design). Approximately ten years of design exclusivity will allow for the ongoing creation of new designs and will not unduly restrict the free use of the design.

Infringement and remedies

Primary infringement

Because the owner of the design right has the exclusive right to reproduce the design for commercial purposes, the design right will, first of all, be infringed by anyone making an item to the design without the licence of the owner of the design right and by anyone making a design document that records the design for the purpose of enabling someone to make items to it, once again, if this is done without the licence of the design right owner. One can immediately add to this the case in which someone authorizes someone else to do one of these two things.

Design right infringement is subject to the same principles as copyright infringement.[95] This means, first, that an objective similarity between the allegedly infringing

---

[92] CDPA 1988, s. 216(1)(b).   [93] CDPA 1988, s. 216(2).   [94] CDPA 1988, s. 216(1)(a).
[95] *Mark Wilkinson Furniture Ltd* (n. 51).

item and the design must exist. All features that are covered by an exclusion—such as the interface exclusion—should be disregarded for this purpose. Secondly, a causal connection between the design and the allegedly infringing item needs to be established.[96]

Making items to the design

The act of making items to the design is circumscribed more precisely: the design has to be copied in such a way that items exactly or substantially similar to the design are produced. Mere similarity is not sufficient. This latter element involves an objective test that should be decided through the eyes of the person to whom the design is directed[97]—that is, the person who will use the items made to the design. In a case that was concerned with design rights in the features of shape of a kitchen unit, the design was held to be directed to the person interested in buying a fitted kitchen.[98]

That person should look at the similarities and differences between the two designs. Infringement will arise if the allegedly infringing item is simply made to the claimant's design or if it is made substantially to that design. The latter situation will definitely cover all occasions on which all of the elements linked to the functional role of the design have been copied and the differences are not relevant for that role. It is submitted that the approach should bear important similarities to that adopted in relation to patent law in the *Catnic* case,[99] but only the case law can shed some more light on this issue in a decisive way over the next few years. In addition, it should be emphasized that the objective test through the eyes of the person to whom the design is directed may involve the item being dismantled to allow that person to compare the designs if they apply to an internal part of the item, because design rights can exist in features of shape or configuration of an internal part of the item. Despite the fact that design right infringement shares some of its principles with copyright infringement, it is important to stress that, on this point, there clearly are differences and that similarities with patent law also creep in. As the Court of Appeal put it, there is a difference between an enquiry into whether the item copied forms a substantial part of a copyright work and an enquiry into whether the whole design containing the element that had been copied was substantially the same design as that which enjoyed design right protection.[100]

In practice one does essentially look for evidence of copying. Once copying has been established, it normally follows that the items that are exactly or substantially similar to the design have been produced. In examining copying one looks for what has been copied by comparing the allegedly infringing article to the document or article incorporating the design. One looks at the similarities and the differences, even if at this stage the similarities are more important. It is the role of the expert witnesses to point out these similarities and differences to the court, as well as their importance, but the decision on copying remains a decision of the court and the witnesses should not draw a conclusion on this point in their evidence.[101] One should also be wary of the similarities that are not the result of copying but of the functional nature of the design. Shared functional

---

[96] As in the equivalent copyright cases, it is not required that the infringer has the protected design in front of him or her when the allegedly infringing item is made: see *Philip Parker v. Stephen Tidball* (n. 23).

[97] *C & H Engineering v. Klucznik & Sons Ltd* [1992] FSR 421, per Aldous J at 428.

[98] *Mark Wilkinson Furniture Ltd* (n. 51).

[99] *Catnic Components Ltd and anor v. Hill & Smith Ltd* [1982] RPC 183.

[100] *L. Woolley Jewellers Ltd v. A and A Jewellery Ltd* [2003] FSR 255 (CA).

[101] *Virgin Atlantic Airways v. Premium Aircraft Interiors Group* [2009] ECDR 11 (an appeal followed, but this concerned only the patent issues).

requirements can indeed also be an explanation for certain similarities. Mummery LJ expressed this warning as follows:

> Substantial similarity of design might well give rise to a suspicion and an allegation of copy-ing in cases where substantial similarity was often not the result of copying but an inevitable consequence of the functional nature of the design... Copying may be inferred from proof of access to the protected work, coupled with substantial similarity. This may lead to unfounded infringement claims in the case of functional works, which are usually bound to be substan-tially similar to one another.
>
> ... [The court] must not forget that, in the field of designs of functional articles, one design may be very similar to, or even identical with, another design and yet not be a copy: it may be an original and independent shape and configuration coincidentally the same or similar.[102]

Finally, when looking at substantiality one should steer clear of the somewhat simplistic approach along the lines of the *University of London Press v. University Tutorial Press* (what is worth copying is prima facie worth protection).[103] In relation to designs the copied elements can be swamped by additional elements and features. The (new) article will then no longer substantially be made to the design.[104]

An objective test

It is extremely important, however, to see what is being compared in the objective test and it is respectfully submitted that the approach taken obiter[105] in the *Klucznik* case[106] is not detailed enough.[107] Infringement is situated in the fact of making items to the design without having obtained a licence to do so—but the design right covers features of shape or configuration of the whole, or part, of the item and the test is directed to see whether the design right has been infringed. It is submitted that s. 226(2) of the 1988 Act directs us to look at the similarities and differences between the designs, rather than between the items. If the design right covers features of shape or configuration of the whole item, the result will not necessarily vary, but the importance of the nuance is found in the fact that the design right can also cover features of shape or configuration of a part of the item. Making reference to the whole item would, in such a case, reduce the number of cases in which infringements would be found substantially and weaken the design right as such. It would also be absurd to take into account additional non-protected features and, eventually, features that form the subject of another design right, and which are applied to another part of the same item in deciding whether a design right has been infringed. The test should only take into consideration those parts of the item to which the design refers, although this can eventually be the whole item;[108] otherwise, there could almost

---

[102] *Farmers Build Ltd (in liq.)* (n. 11), per Mummery LJ at 481–2. See also *Albert Packaging Ltd v. Nampak Cartons & Healthcare Ltd* [2011] EWPCC 15, [2011] FSR 32, and *Kohler Mira Ltd v. Bristan Group Ltd* [2013] EWPCC 2.

[103] [1916] 2 Ch 601, at 610.

[104] *DKH Retail Ltd v. H. Young (Operations) Ltd* [2014] EWHC 4034 (IPEC).

[105] Klucznik's claim to the design right failed because Aldous J was unable to reach the conclusion that it was the owner of the design (had Klucznik thought of it or had C & H Engineering thought of it?), thus the infringement action accordingly also failed. Aldous J nevertheless considered the infringement issue, but that part of the judgment is thus obiter.

[106] *C & H Engineering v. Klucznik & Sons Ltd* [1992] FSR 421.

[107] *C & H Engineering* (n. 106), per Aldous J at 428, but the approach received nevertheless support from a differently constituted Court of Appeal in *L. Woolley Jewellers Ltd v. A and A Jewellery Ltd* [2003] FSR 255 (CA).

[108] Cf. J. Turner, 'A True Design Right: *C & H Engineering v. Klucznik and Sons*' (1993) 1 EIPR 24, 25.

never be an infringement when only the design for part of an item is reproduced. But the emphasis on the design does not change the fact that the observer is forced to compare the original design to the item in which allegedly a substantial part of the design has been copied. One should '*ask oneself what by way of comparative design would be suggested to the interested observer*'[109] and this should be done in the light of the entirety of the allegedly infringing item.

This issue arose in part because whereas in the definition of a design, reference is made to aspects of shape or configuration of the whole or part of an article, that reference to a part of the article is not found in the context of infringement in s. 226(3). There the reference is only to the article as a whole. The High Court has now clarified that in terms of reproduction the infringement can also refer to a part only of the article—that is to say, Parliament did not intend that the approach in terms of infringement would be more restrictive than when defining the design.[110]

In the *Klucznik* case, the test was indeed described as an objective one, having the pig farmer—as the person to whom the design is directed—look at the similarities and differences between the two pig fenders. The conclusion reached was that the designs were not substantially the same, but it is submitted that this conclusion could be wrong, because it relies on an additional feature of the allegedly infringing fender. This feature was not part of the design right that was allegedly infringed and the features of shape covered by the design right—that is, the two-inch tube—were only features of the shape of a part of the fender. Attention should, in this case, primarily be directed to that part of the fender and other additional features should be left aside. One should only turn to the whole of the allegedly infringing item in a second stage to determine whether its overall features allow for a conclusion that the overall impression of the observer is not that the allegedly infringing item has been made to the original design; this should only be the case if the other features have become its essential features. In that case, the item is no longer produced to the original design, even if the two have certain aspects in common. This slightly more complicated test follows from the fact that design infringement is not completely similar to copyright infringement and that additional emphasis is put on the point that the copying must lead to the production of an item exactly, or substantially, to the design. That judgment, in relation to the allegedly infringing item, comes on top of the copyright-style substantial copying test (from one design to another, or to the relevant part of the allegedly infringing item).

An enabling recording

The enabling recording of a design document as an infringing activity bears strong similarities to its equivalent in copyright, but it is slightly harder to prove the design version. The recording should be made for the purpose of enabling someone to make items to the design. The only purpose one needs to establish for its copyright infringement alternative is the purpose to copy;[111] the design intention should be present at the time at which the recording was made, otherwise the recording was not made for that purpose. It is, indeed, not sufficient that the recording can eventually later be used to enable someone to make items to the design.

---

[109] *Philip Parker v. Stephen Tidball* (n. 23).

[110] *Virgin Atlantic Airways v. Premium Aircraft Interiors Group* [2009] ECDR 11 (an appeal followed, but this concerned only the patent issues).

[111] H. MacQueen, 'A Scottish Case on Unregistered Designs' (1994) 2 EIPR 86, 87.

Direct or indirect reproduction

The reproduction of the design may be direct or indirect. Indirect reproduction will still infringe, even if the intervening acts do not infringe the design right themselves.[112] This has important consequences in relation to the reverse engineering of designs. One can easily take apart an item made to the design, analyse the design, and copy the non-protected elements; eventually, this can lead to the creation of a new original design. But if reverse engineering simply precedes reproduction, making an item to the design will still infringe.

Innocent infringement

Innocent infringement is possible. This clarification is made indirectly in s. 233 of the 1988 Act. If, at the time of the infringement, the defendant was unaware and had no reason to believe that design right subsisted in the design, the claimant will not be entitled to damages against the defendant. Other remedies do, however, remain available.[113] This provision offers a limited amount of protection to the reasonable bona fide user of the design who thought that there was no design right he or she could be infringing. This is bound to happen on a number of occasions, such as when a user cannot check in any register of designs in order to pre-empt this situation.

Secondary infringement

The design right will also be infringed if a person does any of the following acts in relation to an infringing item without the licence of the owner of the design right:

- imports the item into the UK for commercial purposes;[114]
- has the item in his or her possession for commercial purposes;[115]
- sells, hires, or offers or exposes for sale or hire, the item in the course of a business.[116]

First of all, what is an infringing item? An item is an infringing item if the making of the item to the design constituted an infringement of the design right in the design.[117] Items that have been imported into the UK, or which are proposed to be imported into it, and the making of which would have constituted an infringement of the design right (or a breach of an exclusive licence agreement) had the items been made in the UK are also infringing items.[118] In addition, an action for secondary design infringement can only be successful if it is proven that the defendant knew, or had reason to believe, that the item was infringing.[119] This additional knowledge requirement is identical to that found in copyright and does not exist for registered designs.[120]

This knowledge requirement, taken in combination with the fact that only designs created after the commencement date of the design provisions of the 1988 Act attract design protection, could create a problem for the claimant in proving that the item was made at a time when the right subsisted and is thus an infringing item. The Act therefore introduced a presumption in favour of the claimant. The item made to the design is presumed to have been made at a time when the design right in the design subsisted, unless the contrary can be proven.[121] This is even more favourable for the claimant, because he or she will quite often be the only person able to prove when the design right first arose.

---

[112] CDPA 1988, s. 226(4).   [113] CDPA 1988, s. 233(1).   [114] CDPA 1988, s. 227(1)(a).
[115] CDPA 1988, s. 227(1)(b).   [116] CDPA 1988, s. 227(1)(c).   [117] CDPA 1988, s. 228(2).
[118] CDPA 1988, s. 228(3).   [119] CDPA 1988, s. 227(1).   [120] See Chs. 15 and 21.
[121] CDPA 1988, s. 228(4).

If the defendant in an action for secondary infringement is able to show that he or she, or a predecessor in title, acquired the infringing item innocently, this will not imply that the action is bound to fail; rather, it only restricts the remedies available to damages of up to what would be a reasonable amount of royalties in respect of the complained-of act.[122]

Defences

A defendant in a design right infringement action can try to argue that the design right has expired, or that it was not valid in the first place, because one of the requirements was not met and that the design right thus never came into existence. Apart from these arguments, it is obvious that the defendant will try to argue that the requirements for primary and secondary infringement to take place are not met. A last defence could, in relevant cases, be based on s. 236 of the 1988 Act.

These relevant cases are those in which copyright exists in a work that consists of, or includes, a design in which a design right subsists. Anything that is an infringement of the copyright in the work will not be an infringement of the design right.[123] This provision clearly aims to complete the separation between copyright and design right. It applies to design right infringement cases, whereas s. 51 applies to the copyright infringement cases.

Commercial exploitation

Assignment and licences

As is the case with most other intellectual property rights, an (unregistered) design right can be exploited commercially in various ways. Owners of the design right can exploit the right themselves by making an item to the design, but can also leave the exploitation or part of it to a third party. In such cases, the design right can be assigned or a licence can be granted. An assignment can be compared to a sale and is particularly appropriate if the owners of the design right do not want to exploit the design themselves. Granting a licence is more like hiring out the right to use the design. If the licence is not exclusive, it allows the owners to exploit the design themselves too and the exclusive licence may ultimately even expire, at which point the exploitation right will return to the owners.

This is, of course, only a rough description of assignments and licences. They can be moulded to perform special functions through the insertion of special clauses in the contract. A future design right—that is, one that will, or may, come into being—can be the subject of an assignment or of a licence. The same rules apply to the exploitation of both the existing design right and the future design right.[124]

Assignments

When the design right is assigned, this must be done in writing and the assignment must be signed by, or on behalf of, the owner-assignor.[125] An assignment effectively transfers the design right to the assignee, but it can be partial in two ways:[126]

- The assignment can be limited in terms of its duration. This implies that the design right returns to the assignor after the expiry of the term agreed in the assignment contract.

---

[122] CDPA 1988, s. 233(2). See *Badge Sales v. PSM International* [2006] FSR 1.
[123] CDPA 1988, s. 236.   [124] CDPA 1988, s. 223.   [125] CDPA 1988, s. 222(3).
[126] CDPA 1988, s. 222(2).

- It can also be limited in scope, in the sense that not all of the exclusive rights of the owner are assigned to the assignee.

In relation to the rights assigned to him or her, the assignee has exactly the same rights as those that the owner-assignor had before the assignment and would have had if the assignment had not taken place.

Apart from by assignment, the design right can also be transferred by testamentary disposition or by the operation of law,[127] such as in the case of a liquidation of a company that owned a design right.

Licences

The alternative to an assignment is a licence, which authorizes the licensee to do certain things in relation to the design right. The owner can grant an exclusive licence or a non-exclusive licence: an exclusive licence gives the licensee the exclusive right to exploit the design right in a certain area and/or the exclusive right to exploit the design right in a certain way. All other persons—including the owner-licensor—are excluded from exploiting the design right in the area and/or form of exploitation covered by the exclusive licence. Such a licence has to be in writing and signed by, or on behalf of, the owner-licensor of the design right,[128] and it gives the exclusive licensee the same rights and remedies as an assignment. But there is one exception to the latter point: the rights and remedies are not the same in relation to the owner-licensor. The exclusive licensee can, as can the assignee, act independently against infringers[129]—but because the licensor retains certain rights in relation to the design right, there will be cases in which the two parties have a right of action. The Act calls this a 'concurrent right of action' and requires that the other party is either joined as a claimant or added as a defendant before the action proceeds.[130]

One or more non-exclusive licences can also be granted and these may give the licensee the non-exclusive right to exploit the design right in a certain area and/or the non-exclusive right to exploit the design right in a certain way. The licensor will remain free to exploit the design right him- or herself and may also appoint other licensees. There are no requirements regarding the format of a non-exclusive licence and the licensor will have to rely on the contract in infringement cases. No rights to act independently are transferred; the licensee will have to request the licensor to take action against the infringer. A licence granted by the owner of the design right shall normally bind him or her and every successor in title. It will not bind a purchaser of the design right who purchases in good faith, for valuable consideration, and who has no actual or constructive notice of the licence.[131] An assignor who meets the additional requirements could be such a purchaser. This clearly puts the licensee in a weaker position than the licensor and makes an assignment theoretically more attractive than a licence. It remains to be seen, however, whether an assignment is available in practice and, even if that is the case, the higher price linked to it may well outweigh the advantage.

Licences of right

Licences of right are available during the last five years of the term of protection offered by the design right. This weakens the value of the design right, but opens another opportunity for the exploitation of the design right. The Comptroller-General of Patents,

---

[127] CDPA 1988, s. 222(1).   [128] CDPA 1988, s. 225(1).   [129] CDPA 1988, s. 234.
[130] CDPA 1988, s. 235(1).   [131] CDPA 1988, s. 222(4).

Designs and Trade Marks will settle the terms of the licence if the parties fail to agree upon it.[132] It will not always be easy for the potential licensee to find out when these licences of right become available, because, in cases in which the design is recorded some time before it is exploited, the owner of the design right is often the only person to know the real date on which the design right came into existence.

One design, two design rights

Some designs meet the requirements of the Registered Designs Act 1949 as well as those for the (unregistered) design right. If they are registered, they will attract double design protection. An example may be a teapot, the spout or handle of which is both aesthetically pleasing and also fulfils a functional role. This could create problems when only one right is assigned or licensed and commercial exploitation of the design takes place. This could constitute an infringement of the other design. The Act therefore provides that, if the owners of both design rights are the same persons, an assignment of the registered design will include an assignment of the (unregistered) design right unless an intention to the contrary appears from the transaction or its circumstances.[133] The opposite situation is covered by s. 19(3B) of the Registered Designs Act 1949, which provides that, if the owners of both design rights are the same persons, an assignment of the (unregistered) design right will include an assignment of the registered design unless an intention to the contrary appears.

This is, of course, only a partial solution. The presumption may be rebutted and the rights may become separated, should different persons own them. The latter risk is reduced by the fact that the Registrar is not supposed to register a registered design if the person who claims to be the owner of the design right does not make the application.[134] The legislature clearly attempts to keep the ownership of both design rights in the same hands, while leaving it up to the parties to negotiate the terms of the licences, which are just a temporary right to use. It can indeed be accepted that no one would agree to a licence for one of the rights if the use of that right would infringe the second design right and that, even if that were the case, the courts might imply a licence for the second design right.

Crown use

The 1988 Act also contains provisions on Crown use of design rights. It refers to the use by the Crown without a licence, but with a form of remuneration of designs protected by design rights, for purposes such as health and other needs of the services of the Crown. There are also provisions on the supply of items made to the design for foreign defence purposes.[135]

Competition law

Agreements on the exploitation of design rights may infringe competition law. In relation to UK competition law, the 1988 Act allows action to be taken in such cases,[136] but the most relevant provisions are to be found in the EC Treaty. Licence agreements in relation to design rights may infringe Art. 101 of the Treaty on the Functioning of the

---

[132] CDPA 1988, s. 237.   [133] CDPA 1988, s. 224.   [134] Registered Designs Act 1949, s. 3.
[135] CDPA 1988, see ss. 240–4.   [136] CDPA 1988, s. 238.

European Union. We may refer here to our discussion of this Treaty provision in Chapter 18, because it applies in the same way to all intellectual property rights. Suffice it to say that no block exemption covers design rights. In theory, there is also no reason why Art. 102 of the Treaty on the abuse of a dominant position could not apply in relation to a design right, although it is not too likely that such a case will often arise in practice.

The European Court of Justice was invited to rule on the relationship between design rights and the free movement provisions of the EC Treaty in *Keurkoop v. Nancy Kean Gifts*.[137] The judgment makes it clear that designs form an intellectual property right for the purposes of these provisions and that the exhaustion doctrine applies to them. The Court did not find it necessary, however, to define the specific subject matter of designs, because it could reach its conclusion without doing so. It said that, in the absence of Community harmonization, it is left to the member states to decide which system of design rights they have, and to decide accordingly on the terms and conditions under which protection is granted. The existing disparity did not influence the applicability of the free movement provisions to design rights. This means that there is nothing special about design rights in this context and that the principles that we have discussed in relation to other intellectual property rights apply equally to them.

An overview

Unregistered designs are essentially functional, non-aesthetic designs. The 1988 Act defines them as the design of any aspect of the shape or configuration (whether internal or external) of the whole, or part, of an item. In order to attract protection, such a design must be original, in the sense that it should not be commonplace in the design field in question at the time of its creation.

Certain items are excluded from design protection, essentially because a design right in them would confer upon the right holder an unduly broad exclusive right. There is clearly an underlying logic that other designers should be able to come up with another design that has the same functional effectiveness. Granting designs rights for methods or principles of construction, or for designs that must fit or must match, would undermine that logic. Surface decoration is also excluded, because its functional credentials are weaker.

Unregistered design rights roughly offer 15 years of protection during which the right holder has the exclusive right to reproduce the design for commercial purposes. Infringement will therefore consist in anyone making an item to the design without authorization and in the making of a design document that records the design for the purposes of enabling someone else to make items to it, again without authorization. Authorizing someone else to do either of these two things will also constitute an infringement. Just as in copyright, there are also provisions on secondary infringement that cover dealing with infringing items.

Further reading

CLARK, S., 'Design Rights All Wrapped Up: A Case Comment on Albert Packaging Ltd v Nampak Cartons & Healthcare Ltd' (2012) 34 EIPR 343–6.

---

[137] Case 144/81, *Keurkoop BV v. Nancy Kean Gifts BV* [1982] ECR 2853, [1983] 2 CMLR 47.

FITZGERALD, J., '"Innocent Infringement" and the Community Unregistered Design Right: The Position in the UK and Ireland' (2008) 3(4) JIPLP 236–45.

GARNETT, K., DAVIES, G., and HARBOTTLE, G. (2011) *Copinger and Skone James on Copyright*, 16th edn, London: Sweet and Maxwell, Ch. 13.

MALLINSON, R. and YOUNG, C., 'Industrial Plagiarism and the "Gap" in Design Protection' (2005) 27(2) EIPR 68.

MICHAELS, A., 'The End of the Road for "Pattern Spare" Parts? *Dyson Ltd v. Qualtex (UK) Ltd*' (2006) 28(7) EIPR 396.

SYKES, J., 'The Unregistered Design Right: Interpretation and Practical Application of the Must-Match Exemption' (2006) 1 JIPLP 442.

WILKINSON, D., 'Case Closed: Functional Designs Protected By Design Right' (2007) 29(3) EIPR 118.

23

Designs—an overview

Registered design is like the 'little brother' of patents and trade marks, but that does not mean that design rights are not valuable for industry; on the contrary, enormous amounts of money are spent on designs. Registration alone is simply not the best way of protecting designs and it would be wrong to disregard anything smaller than patents and trade marks as not important.

The old UK system was based on a strict separation between registered and unregistered design, and between aesthetical and functional designs. Aesthetical designs were protected as registered designs and functional designs were protected by means of an unregistered right. The problems that aesthetical designs often change rapidly, and that the delays and costs involved in a registered designs system represent major hurdles in a substantial number of cases, were not addressed under this two-part system. The two types of design had been separated on, allegedly, the wrong basis. We had therefore already concluded, in the third edition of this book, that having one design right that could serve both aesthetic and functional designs would eliminate much confusion—this suggestion was made before the EU reforms were implemented.

It is submitted that the situation now is worse. The Design Directive, as implemented in the revised version of the Registered Designs Act 1949, has put in place a modern system of registered design protection. That system does away with the aesthetical requirements of the old 1949 Act and the new concept of a design only attempts to exclude technical matters that should, in principle, be dealt with by patent rather than design law. Design law should not become a second-best option for failed patent applications. Such a system can cover the whole design spectrum at national level, and the Community design, as introduced by the Community Designs Regulation, duplicates that at Community level. The Regulation also complements the registered rights system with an unregistered design right that is strictly limited in time, so as not to compete with the registered right, while at the same time offering an effective and fast protection at no cost for designs for which the registered system is too slow and costly.

It is submitted that maintaining in force, on top of all of this, a domestic unregistered design right that was supposed to fit in seamlessly with a system of registered rights that no longer exists is itself no longer necessary. The overlap of protection creates confusion and an undue duplication of rights. The fact that some designs will get protection under a UK unregistered right while failing to be protected—or worse, while expressly being excluded from protection—under its European counterpart or by the European registered design is clearly an absurd and unjustifiable consequence of a historical legal maze. Especially hard to justify is the fact that the UK keeps in force an unregistered right that has a much longer term than that of its Community counterpart.

The only reason why the UK unregistered right may justifiably survive is the fact that, unlike the Community right, it does not exclude purely technical designs, apart from those covered by its 'must fit' exemption. This justification disappears, however, if the EU technical exemption is defined sensibly and not too widely, as suggested in Chapter 21.

As demonstrated earlier, the technical exemption would then only eliminate a limited number of cases and all of these would be cases in which there are good competition-related reasons to deny any form of protection whatsoever.

Maybe the time has therefore come to reconsider the existence of a UK unregistered design right on the basis of the Copyright, Designs and Patents Act 1988.[1] Especially at a time of increasing duplication of protection and overprotection, any opportunity to reduce these problems should be looked at seriously. After all, there will still be a wide design right, as well as a potential overlap at the fringes with copyright, trade marks, and—to a lesser extent—patents.[2]

Further reading

DERCLAYE, E., 'The British Unregistered Design Right: Will It Survive its New Community Counterpart to Influence Future European Case Law?' (2004) 10 Colum J Eur L 265.

DERCLAYE, E. and LEISTNER, M. (2011) *Intellectual Property Overlaps: A European Perspective*, Oxford: Hart Publishing.

---

[1] See also the obiter comment by Jacob LJ in *Lambretta Clothing Co. Ltd v. Teddy Smith (UK) Ltd and anor* [2005] RPC 6 at [41].

[2] See Recital 31 of Council Regulation (EC) 6/2002 on Community Design [2002] OJ L 3/1.

SECTION E

Trade Marks and other Image Rights

24

Trade marks—an introduction

Today, the trade mark industry is such a vital component of the whole structure of advertising and marketing that is a key feature of the commercial scene. Logos, catchphrases, and images all fall within the ambit of the trade mark and form a valuable part of the goodwill of the business with which they are associated. In law, however, trade marks have in recent years been the subject of increasing controversy; this has culminated in an entirely new legislative framework, in the form of the Trade Marks Act 1994.[1]

Trade marks—development

The earliest form of trade mark is both the most obvious and the type that is still at the heart of the law of trade marks today. Even in Roman times, pottery was made (and has survived) bearing the name of the potter responsible for it. Then, as now, the trade mark was an important badge of origin for the product; the origin, of course, also being indicative of the quality of the product associated. Many major brand names are the names of the founder of the brand: Ford for cars or Kelloggs for breakfast cereals are obvious examples. Exceptionally, the name may even become synonymous with the product itself: people will often refer to any brand of vacuum cleaner as a 'Hoover', for example.

But throughout history, with only a couple of minor exceptions, trade marks were essentially a part of the private sector, attracting legal protection by use, rather than by formal grant by the state.[2] This was unacceptable in a society that was rapidly changing and industrializing, and it became clear both that a more formal system was required and that the central authority of the state should form a central feature of that system. In 1862, a Trade Marks Bill was considered, but did not go ahead for various reasons. There were doubts about whether a formal and transferable legal right was appropriate to reflect the personal nature of the typical trade mark, and the common law of passing off was, as will be seen later, already in the process of development. Deliberate counterfeiting was seen to be more of a problem abroad than at home and this called into question the effectiveness of the proposed new law. Nonetheless, pressure continued to mount in favour of a statutory system of trade marks and that demand was ultimately fulfilled, in the first instance, by the Trade Marks Act 1875.

The 1875 Act created a central Trade Marks Registry (now subsumed within the UK Intellectual Property Office), which could award a proprietary right in the form of a trade

---

[1] See, in general, J. Mellor et al. (2011) *Kerly's Law of Trade Marks and Trade Names*, 15th edn, London: Sweet and Maxwell; C. Morcom, A. Roughton, and T. St Quintin (2012) *The Modern Law of Trade Marks*, 4th edn, London: Lexis-Nexis.

[2] See N. Dawson, 'English Trade Mark Law in the Eighteenth Century: The Fate of Thomas Hill' (2009) 30(1) J Leg Hist 71–9, discussing *Blanchard v. Hill* (1742) 2 Atkyns 484.

mark, and also register its existence and ownership for the benefit and guidance of future prospective applicants. Then, as now, at the heart of the notion of the trade mark lay the idea that it should be distinctive, thus going far beyond the notion of the mark as being a badge of origin. From 1875, then, the essence of the modern system of trade mark law and practice was in place, but the law was never likely to stay in a settled form for too long. New Acts extended the law in 1883, 1905, and 1919, the last of which split the Register into two sections; the keynote Act was, until recently, the Trade Marks Act (TMA) of 1938. But the 1938 Act did not survive unadorned, with some of the recommendations of the Mathys Committee of 1974[3] being enacted by the Trade Marks (Amendment) Act 1984, which created, among other things, a mark for services as well as for goods.

But even more change was considered necessary.

The need for reform

Reform was canvassed in a government White Paper titled *Reform of Trade Marks Law*[4] in 1990. The Paper recognized that many of the recommendations of the Mathys Committee had never been taken up, but that there were other factors that tended to suggest that more fundamental reform was needed. First and foremost among these factors was the 'Europeanization' of yet another area of intellectual property.

The influence of the European Union (EU) on trade mark law takes two separate, but related, forms. First, a Directive was passed as far back as 1988[5] that sought to harmonize the national laws relating to trade marks so as to remove potential barriers to freer trade. The terms of the Directive required compliance with its terms by the end of 1991 (later extended by a year)—a deadline that was well missed by the UK, although the 1994 Act appears now to fulfil this requirement in almost all respects.

The second aspect of EU activity that has had a significant impact on the reform process is the establishment of a Community-wide trade mark, distinct from the individual national marks. After interminable discussion and the traditional haggling, the Regulation approving the creation of such a mark was finalized in 1994.[6] The Community Trade Marks Office is sited in Alicante in Spain and it has been confronted with an (unexpected) flood of applications ever since it opened its doors to the public. This new mark is, of course, not subject to amendment by domestic legislation, but, conversely, has represented a sensible opportunity to try to match the domestic and European procedures so as to minimize any conflict or duplication between the two systems.[7]

A third international factor also at play in the formulation of the 1994 legislation was that trade—and thus trade marks—takes on an increasingly international dimension all the time and that, thus, the international protectability of trade mark rights takes on an even greater importance. For over a century, an international register of trade marks has been maintained under the provisions of the Madrid Agreement[8] with an International

---

[3] Cmnd 5601, 1974.   [4] Cm 1203, 1990.

[5] Council Directive 89/104 EEC to approximate the laws of the member states relating to trade marks (1989) OJ L 40/1.

[6] Council Regulation (EC) 40/94 on the Community trade mark (1994) OJ L 11/1.

[7] See A. Von Muhlendahl, 'Community Trade Mark Riddles: Territoriality and Unitary Character' [2008] EIPR 66. In 2011 a study on way to reform and improve the system was completed. See Max Planck Institute for Intellectual Property Law and Competition Law, *Study on the Overall Functioning of the European Trade Mark System*, <http://www.ip.mpg.de/de/pub/aktuelles/trade_mark_study.cfm> or <http://ec.europa.eu/internal_market/indprop/docs/tm/20110308_allensbach-study_en.pdf>.

[8] Madrid Agreement Concerning the International Registration of Marks of 14 April 1891.

Register maintained by the World Intellectual Property Organization (WIPO) in Geneva. This system was not entirely successful, because it reflected Continental rather than common law approaches to the topic, but the era of harmonization meant that change was not only appropriate, but also necessary. In consequence, a protocol[9] was added to the Madrid Agreement enabling the UK and many other countries to fall within its scope, and the 1994 Act had the further task of adapting domestic law to this new international agreement.[10] Finally, further implementation of the Paris Convention for the Protection of Intellectual Property of 1883 is facilitated by the new legislation.

Other, domestic, factors also shaped the new law of trade marks. There is no doubt that the old law was in a messy state. The 1938 Act—which was far from clear in certain aspects even from day one—had been changed by successive amendments in 1984, 1986, and 1988, and divining the precise text of the legislation on service marks, in particular, was not an easy task. This alone suggested that an urgent clarification of the law was required, but broader political forces were also at play. The government was consistently in favour of the promotion of the interests of business groups and this, in its own right—coupled with the related drive towards deregulation—meant that a simpler, clearer, and more market-focused system of trade marks law was deemed to be a necessity.[11] An efficient and less costly system has consequently emerged from the 1994 reforms.

As part of this process of simplification, there were mysteries created by the law that it was opportune to resolve. The fact, for example, that the shape of a container such as a Coca-Cola bottle could not be registered[12] may or may not be objectionable, but it is difficult to justify such a view when the entire surface of a two-coloured pill could be registered.[13] Such narrow distinctions may have been the stuff of life to medieval philosophers, but were less familiar to provincial solicitors.

Equally arcane distinctions between the different types of trade mark—the Part A and the Part B marks—were also found to pose problems. The need in a Part A mark was to establish its distinctiveness by considering whether it was 'adapted to distinguish' the goods of its proprietors from those of others.[14] This was to be done with reference to its inherent adaptability to distinguish and the extent to which its use, in fact, adapted it to distinguish. For a Part B trade mark, the test of distinctiveness was whether the mark was capable of distinguishing the goods from others,[15] but this was done with reference to inherent capability and factual capability. The difference between 'adapted' and 'capable' was at once vital and obscure. Any thoughts that a Part B mark could be identified by the presence of 100 per cent factual distinctiveness was scotched by the House of Lords in *York Trailers Holdings v. Registrar of Trade Marks*,[16] in which the fact that the applicant was the only manufacturer of trailers in York, Canada (or indeed, it seems, any other York), did not justify the grant of a trade mark on the grounds that it would create too great a monopoly were the claim by one manufacturer to use as a trade mark the

---

[9] Protocol Relating to the Madrid Agreement Concerning the International Registration of Marks of 28 June 1989.

[10] The UK became a party to the Protocol to the Madrid Agreement on 1 December 1995: see the Trade Marks (International Registration) Order 1996, SI 1996/714. The Protocol itself became operational on 1 April 1996. The UK is still not a party to the Madrid Agreement. The EU (the Community Trade Mark) adhered to the Madrid Protocol on 1 October 2004.

[11] Cm 1203 (n. 4) at 2.

[12] *Re Coca-Cola Co's Applications* [1986] 2 All ER 274, *sub nom. In re Coca-Cola Co.* [1986] 1 WLR 695.

[13] *Smith, Kline & French Laboratories v. Sterling-Winthrop Group* [1975] 2 All ER 578, [1975] 1 WLR 914.

[14] TMA 1938, s. 9(3)(b).   [15] TMA 1938, s. 10(2).

[16] [1982] 1 All ER 257, *sub nom. In re Coca-Cola Co.* [1982] 1 WLR 195.

name of a substantial chunk of territory to be allowed. Thus additional rules of law were created to complicate further an already tangled web.

A third example can be given from the world of infringement. It is obvious that it is wrong to claim the trade mark of another for your own use on rival goods or services, but the old law also treated as an infringement the situation in which the use of another's mark in some way connoted that the use of the mark was with the proprietor's permission or otherwise—in the words of s. 4(1)(b) of the 1938 Act—that the use *'imported a reference to some person having the right as proprietor to use the trade mark'*.

A good example of the perhaps surprising consequences of this is offered in the comparative advertising case of *News Group Ltd v. Mirror Group Ltd*.[17] In this case, the publishers of the *Daily Mirror* decided to exploit the unpopularity of the Conservative government and its then leader, and the slavish support that was nevertheless afforded to it by most other newspapers, by launching an advertising campaign. One poster featured, under the words 'Yes, Prime Minister', the masthead logos of all of the pro-Conservative papers, including the claimant's organ, *The Sun*. Another poster, under the words 'No, Prime Minister', featured, in solitary splendour, the masthead logo of the *Daily Mirror*. In spite of the context in which *The Sun* was appearing to be criticized for its editorial stance, it was still found that its trade-marked logo had been infringed as a result of the route of 'importing a reference'.

But all of this is now part of history, as cases arising from the old law and the various transitional provisions have worked their weary way through the system. The Trade Marks Act 1994 summarily repeals the 1938 legislation in its entirety and replaces it with a new code. It is also clearly the case that the myriad complexities of the case law arising from earlier legislation are now of little value, because the new law is based on different principles. Therefore reliance will not, for the most part, be placed on the old law as such, although, of course, there will be ample occasions to cite past cases as examples of areas of difficulty that may—or may not—have been resolved by the new law.

From Community trade mark to European Union trade mark

A further step in the reform process was initiated by a study by the Max Planck Institute on the functioning of the European trade mark system that formed the basis of proposals to reform the current legal framework.[18] The Commission, the Parliament, and the Council reached a provisional agreement on a reform package on 21 April 2015 and the final package and the new pieces of legislation were published in late December 2015.[19]

---

[17] [1989] FSR 126.

[18] Max Planck Institute for Intellectual Property Law and Competition Law, *Study on the Overall Functioning of the European Trade Mark System*, <http://www.ip.mpg.de/de/pub/aktuelles/trade_mark_study.cfm>.

[19] Directive (EU) 2015/2436 of the European Parliament and of the Council of 16 December 2015 to approximate the laws of the Member States relating to trade marks (Recast) [2015] OJ L 336/1 and Regulation (EU) 2015/2424 of the European Parliament and of the Council of 16 December 2015 amending Council Regulation (EC) No 207/2009 on the Community trade mark and Commission Regulation (EC) No 2868/95 implementing Council Regulation (EC) No 40/94 on the Community trade mark, and repealing Commission Regulation (EC) No 2869/95 on the fees payable to the Office for Harmonization in the Internal Market (Trade Marks and Designs) [2015] OJ L 341/21.See also the original proposals: Proposal for a Directive of the European Parliament and of the Council to approximate the laws of the Member States relating to trade marks (Recast) COM/2013/0162 final - 2013/0089 (COD), <http://eur-lex.europa.

A key element in the package is the fact that the requirement that marks should be capable of being represented graphically is to be dropped. Rights and limitations will be clarified and procedures will be streamlined. There will also be new measures to deal with counterfeits and particularly with goods in transit. The Community trade mark will become the European Union trade mark and the OHIM in Alicante will become the European Union Intellectual Property Office. The changes will take effect in early 2019.

Why trade marks?

Before examining the detail of the new law, it is appropriate to investigate the rationale of a system of trade marks. It is clear that trade mark law has to achieve a balance between various potentially competing interests: the trader seeks to protect the image and reputation of his or her goods, but the rival trader—in a society based on free competition—has every reason to wish to compete on level terms within the same market and will, at the very least, hope that the monopoly conferred by the grant of a trade mark is confined to reasonable limits so as not to inhibit legitimate competition. The consumer also has an interest: he or she associates the product or service and its quality with its associated brand name or logo, and will not wish to be confused by similar names or logos placed on different—particularly inferior—products.

As has been seen, the trade mark originally evolved in the private sector at the behest of the traders themselves and this has generally been the principal interest given protection by the trade marks system. The protection afforded has centred on the origin of the goods and, while this has also been of benefit to consumer interests, this has been, first and foremost, in the interests of the proprietor of the trade mark. In indicating origin, the mark, being distinctive, differentiates that product from another and by doing so, in turn, guides the consumer in the exercise of choice. This, it is suggested, may now be seen as the 'core' function of trade marks and it will be pertinent to bear this view in mind, particularly when considering the direction taken by the new law of trade marks.[20]

There can be no doubt as to the commercial significance of trade marks in modern society. Brand names or product identities, such as that of Guinness or Coca-Cola, are hugely valuable assets to their owners and are vigorously protected by them. It may be confidently predicted that the advent of a new and more flexible law of trade marks will continue to give rise to a flood of new registrations of previously unregistrable marks, thus adding further to the value of this sector.

An overview

The historical roots of trade marks go back a very long time. There is also something fashionable about trade marks: they are very commercial in nature. Over the last decades, trade mark law has been harmonized in Europe and, in the UK; the 1994 Act saw a

---

eu/legal-content/EN/ALL/?uri=CELEX:52013PC0162> and Proposal for a Regulation of the European Parliament and of the Council amending Council Regulation (EC) No 207/2009 on the Community trade mark COM/2013/0161 final - 2013/0088 (COD), http://eur-lex.europa.eu/legal-content/EN/ALL/?uri=CELEX:52013PC0161.

[20] See F. Schechter, 'The Rational Basis for Trade Mark Protection' (1926–7) 40 Harvard LR 813–3 and W. Landes and R. Posner, 'Trademark Law: An Economic Perspective' (1987) 30(2) Journal of Law and Economics 265–309.

sea change in the law of trade marks. An abundant flow of cases followed and they have gone a long way in clarifying the new system, as we will see in the next chapters.

Trade marks are essentially pro-competitive, because they allow the origin of goods to be distinguished. A producer of goods can therefore distinguish his or her goods from those of other producers of the same goods. That allows each to set itself apart and to compete with one another. At least in theory, each can always pick another trade mark. Exclusive rights in one or other mark therefore do not restrict the opportunity for competitors to pick their own mark and compete.

A mark therefore allows one to create goodwill in a brand; that goodwill necessarily exists in the relationship with the consumer. The mark allows the consumer to get information about the goods or services and the consumer should be able to rely on that information. Trade marks operate in the relationship between right holder and consumers, and the interests of both sides to the relationship are necessarily reflected in trade mark law.

Further reading

DAWSON, N., 'English Trade Mark Law in the Eighteenth Century: The Fate of Thomas Hill' (2009) 30(1) J Leg Hist 71–9.

LANDES, W. and POSNER, R., 'Trademark Law: An Economic Perspective' (1987) 30(2) Journal of Law and Economics 265–309.

MAX PLANCK INSTITUTE FOR INTELLECTUAL PROPERTY LAW AND COMPETITION LAW, *Study on the Overall Functioning of the European Trade Mark System*, <http://www.ip.mpg.de/de/pub/aktuelles/trade_mark_study.cfm>.

MELLOR, J. et al. (2011) *Kerly's Law of Trade Marks and Trade Names*, 15th edn, London: Sweet and Maxwell.

MORCOM, C., ROUGHTON, A., and ST. QUENTIN, T. (2012) *The Modern Law of Trade Marks*, 4th edn, London: Lexis-Nexis.

SCHECHTER, F., 'The Rational Basis for Trade Mark Protection' (1926–7) 40 Harvard LR 813–33.

VON MUHLENDAHL, A., 'Community Trade Mark Riddles: Territoriality and Unitary Character' [2008] EIPR 66.

25

Trade marks—registrability and use

In this chapter we will look at the requirements that need to be met before a sign can be registered as a trade mark. In the original version of the Directive and therefore also in the version of the Trade Marks Act 1994 in force at the time of writing (December 2015) there are three standard requirements for this purpose, but there are also absolute grounds and relative grounds on the basis of which registration can be refused. A major overhaul of the EU's trade mark system is under way and a political agreement had been reached between the Council and the Parliament at the time of writing.[1] We will refer to the changes it contains wherever possible on the basis of the Recast Directive, even if the latter will only fully replace the current Directive early in 2019. There is no draft yet for the changes to the Trade Marks Act 1994. At the end of the chapter we will also briefly look at the use of the trade mark, by licensing it or assigning it.

Trade mark recognition—the UK framework

In the UK the trade mark system is administered by the Trade Mark Registry at the UK Intellectual Property Office (UK IPO). Applications for UK trade marks are made to it in respect of specific goods or services. The Register of Trade Marks is a public document that can be consulted by interested parties. Joining it—and thus gaining access to the alleged prosperity that will then ensue—is a matter of formal application and examination before a registration is awarded. The applicant must provide, by virtue of s. 32 of the Trade Marks Act (TMA) 1994:

- a request for registration of the mark;
- a statement of the goods or services in relation to which the mark is sought;
- a representation of the mark;
- a statement that the mark is used or is intended to be used, whether by the applicant him- or herself or with his or her consent, in connection with those goods or services.

Non-use of a mark will prevent its registration. On receipt of all bar the last of these items, the application receives an official filing date, which may be of importance in deciding which of two rival marks has priority—a problem that we have already encountered in the system for the registration of patents. It is important to add that the statement of the goods or services for which the trade mark is sought does not have to use the class headings in the Nice classification. It may specify certain goods or services only. What

---

[1] Directive (EU) 2015/2436 of the European Parliament and of the Council of 16 December 2015 to approximate the laws of the Member States relating to trade marks (Recast) [2015] OJ L 336/1.

is important is that there is a sufficient degree of clarity and precision for the authorities and other traders to be able to determine the extent of protection. If the general indications of the class headings are used, there is no problem as far as it results in a clear and precise identification of the goods or services concerned and any limitation must also be expressed clearly.[2]

The Registrar of Trade Marks then examines the application to see that the proposed mark fulfils the formal legal requirements in addition, from 2008 onwards, only the question whether it avoids any of the absolute grounds for refusal of registration. Conflicts with earlier registered marks are no longer examined by the Registry.[3] The Registrar must ask for further details from the applicant if not satisfied[4] and must publish the application[5] so that other interested parties can oppose or make comments on the proposed mark. It is now indeed up to the owner of earlier trade marks to oppose the registration on the basis of earlier rights they have, essentially on the basis of earlier registered or unregistered trade marks. They have three months to do so.[6] The oppositions are dealt with by the Registrar, with appeals being open to the Appointed Person and to the courts. If the necessary criteria have been met, the Registrar *'shall accept the application'*,[7] but only *'if it appears to the Registrar'* that the criteria have been fulfilled. This suggests that some discretionary powers remain with the Registrar and it would seem that registration is not automatic, because it is for the Registrar to determine, in his own opinion, whether the, at times vague, requirements for registration have been met before permitting it to take place. If and when it occurs, the registered trade mark is deemed (by s. 2 of the Act) to be a property right. Registration is granted for a period of 10 years, but it can be renewed an indefinite number of times.[8]

A trade mark is granted not for all purposes, but only for those classes of goods and services for which an application has been made,[9] although one of the advantages of the 1994 Act is to make multiple applications easier by allowing one application to be made for more than one class, unlike in the old law. The classification of goods and services is carried out in accordance with the Nice Classification[10] (sixth edition), an international agreement that splits goods and services into, respectively, 34 and 8 classes. These are incorporated into domestic law by reference to the *'prescribed system of classification'* in s. 34 of the 1994 Act, but new rules have had to be promulgated to incorporate the classification into the law, there formerly having been a schedule to the old Trade Marks Act.[11] Internationally, there is also the 1985 Vienna Agreement Establishing an International Classification of the Figurative Elements of Marks; this, however, does not form part of the domestic law.

The Nice Classification is designed to be comprehensive and, by definition, covers the whole range of manufacturing and service industry. Thus, as a random example, Class 12 of the classification comprises all vehicles, while firearms, ammunition, explosives, and

---

[2] Case C-307/10, *Chartered Institute of Patent Attorneys v. Registrar of Trade Marks* [2012] ETMR 42.

[3] TMA 1994, s. 37(1).   [4] TMA 1994, s. 37(3).   [5] TMA 1994, s. 38.

[6] TMA 1994, s. 38, Trade Marks (Relative Grounds) Order 2007, SI 2007/1976, and Trade Marks (Amendment) Rules 2007, SI 2007/2076.

[7] TMA 1994, s. 37(5).   [8] TMA 1994, s. 42.

[9] The final decision on classification is a matter of administrative convenience and rests with the Registrar, rather than with the applicant: *Altecnic Ltd v. Reliance Water Controls Ltd*, judgment of 12 December 2000, unreported.

[10] Under the World Intellectual Property Organization (WIPO) Nice Agreement concerning the International Classification of Goods and Services for the Purposes of the Registration of Marks of 1957, <www.wipo.int/treaties/en/classification/nice/index.html>.

[11] By Sch. 4 of the Trade Marks Rules 1994, SI 1994/2583.

fireworks comprise Class 13. Inevitably, there are anomalies: beers and soft drinks form Class 32, while all alcoholic drinks other than beers form Class 33.

One can also apply for a Community trade mark, either directly with the OHIM (the European trade mark registry) or indirectly through UK IPO. The Recast Directive re-baptizes the Community Trade Mark as the EU Trade Mark.[12] Again there will only be a check regarding absolute grounds for refusal and other parties will have three months to enter an opposition after publication. The OHIM itself deals with these oppositions, as well as an appeal to one of its Boards of Appeal. Further appeals can be brought before the General Court and finally before the Court of Justice.

Clearly, the requirements for registration lie at the heart of this process and it is to these and, first and foremost, to the key question of what is a trade mark that we now turn.

Trade marks defined

The basic definition of a 'trade mark', as illustrated by Figure 25.1, is given by s. 1(1) of the 1994 Act and appears alarmingly straightforward. The Act states that a 'trade mark' is *any sign capable of being represented graphically which is capable of distinguishing goods or services of one undertaking from those of another*'. (It should immediately be stated that certain marks that fall within this broad definition are nevertheless refused registration in accordance with ss. 3, 4, and 5 of the 1994 Act, considered subsequently.)

The Recast Directive sheds light on the matter, emphasizing the key requirement of distinctiveness, in its Art. 3:

> A trade mark may consist of *any signs*, in particular words, including personal names, or designs, letters, numerals, colours, the shape of goods or of the packaging of goods, or sounds, provided that such signs are capable of:
>
> (a) *distinguishing the goods or services of one undertaking from those of other undertakings*; and
>
> (b) *being represented on the register in a manner which enables* the competent authorities and the public to determine the clear and precise subject matter of the protection afforded to its proprietor. (emphasis added)

A sign

On its own, s. 1(1) contains three elements. The graphical representation point and the distinctiveness point will be discussed in more detail later on, but it is important to mention the third element at this stage: a trade mark is described as 'any sign'. This term is very wide in scope and should be taken to mean 'anything which can convey information'.[13] There are nevertheless limits to what can be a sign. Dyson attempted to register two trade marks consisting of a transparent bin or collection chamber forming part of the external surface of a vacuum cleaner. It tried to register the marks as a concept, which could then be applied in a specific way to each of its vacuum cleaners. The European Court of Justice refused to allow the registration, because, in the Court's view, the requirement that there needs first to be a sign was not fulfilled. Abstract concepts are not signs; the latter need to

---

[12] As the Recast Directive had not come into force at the time of writing the reader will continue to find the term 'Community Trade Mark' on the pages of this edition of the book.

[13] *Philips Electronics BV v. Remington Consumer Products* [1998] RPC 283, per Jacob J.

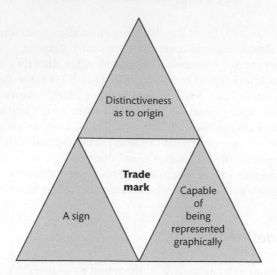

Figure 25.1 Requirements for trade mark registration

take a specific format.[14] That decision needs to be balanced with the *Apple*[15] decision of the Court where it was held that design of the layout of a retail store (here the Apple concept store) that does not indicate the size or the proportions can be a registrable sign. The emphasis in that decision is on the single concept and the single trade dress. For the Court that is sufficient to constitute a specific format. And the consumer may also perceive it as such. The case does, however, not mean such trade dress concepts can be registered in all cases. The CJEU points starkly at the need for them to be distinctive and that may be a significant hurdle in such cases.

Once it is decided that a mark may fall within s. 1(1), it is necessary to consider whether it will fall foul of the inherent bars to registration, in ss. 3 and 4 of the 1994 Act, and then to see whether there are problems relating to the existence of other marks that may also present a difficulty in the way of registration, as per s. 5 of the Act. Meanwhile, the initial section of the Act continues: '*A trade mark may, in particular, consist of words (including personal names), designs, letters, numerals or the shape of goods or their packaging.*' These provisions closely follow—and clearly equate to—the words of Art. 2 of the Harmonization Directive.[16]

These definitions need to be examined closely, but their import is clear. To be registrable, a mark can consist of anything, with the items in the second paragraph of s. 1(1) clearly being no more than illustrations. It is clear, however, that no mark can be registered unless it satisfies the two vital, but related, factors of being capable of being represented graphically and also capable of distinguishing one trader's products from those of others.

---

[14] Case C-321/03, *Dyson Ltd v. Registrar of Trade Marks* [2007] ECR I-687, [2007] 2 CMLR 14, [2007] RPC 27. The Court clearly gave consent to the concept of 'a sign' in order to avoid an unduly broad trade mark being granted, which would have damaged the unfair competition avoidance function of the trade mark system. See also *JW Spear & Sons Ltd, Mattel Inc. and Mattel UK Ltd v. Zynga Inc.* [2012] EWHC 3345 (Ch).

[15] Case C-421/13 *Apple Inc v. Deutsches Patent- und Markenamt* [2015] CEC 120, [2014] ETMR 48, [2015] RPC 14.

[16] Council Directive 89/104 EEC to approximate the laws of the member states relating to trade marks (1989) OJ L 40/1.

Capable of being represented graphically

The concept of distinctiveness will, in due course, warrant further examination, but the requirement of capability of graphical representation may, in certain cases, create more of a problem than was first thought. Swizzels Matlow's trade mark application for a chewy sweet on a stick[17] illustrates that point clearly. The application was rejected, because it was not possible to understand the mark precisely without reference to samples of the goods. This meant that the mark, in all of its aspects, was not capable of being represented graphically. But the focus of the provision is much broader than the single idea of it being able to fit on the register. The text of Art. 3 of the Recast Directive is particularly clear in this respect when it states that the sign must be capable of 'being represented on the register in a manner which enables the competent authorities and the public to determine the clear and precise subject matter of the protection afforded to its proprietor'. Both the registrar and the public (including potential competitors who may wish to register a similar non-infringing mark) need to be perfectly clear what the mark is and what its scope is. This wording replaces the somewhat arcane requirement that the sign must be capable of being represented graphically, but the legislator makes it clear that the criteria which the CJEU put in place in its *Sieckmann* line of cases to which we will turn shortly remain applicable, albeit with the caveat that if new technological methods can achieve the aim set out in the new wording, registration can in future go ahead. A degree of flexibility, enabled by technological change, is therefore built in.

In recent years, the issue of graphical representation has become the focus of attention in relation to olfactory (smell), sound, and colour marks.

Olfactory marks

A first question mark arises from the fact that all of the examples of registrable signs that are listed in s. 1(1) of the 1994 Act are, in themselves, capable of being perceived visually, whereas an olfactory sign is not and relies on an indirect route in this respect. But when confronted with this question for the first time in *Ralf Sieckmann v. Deutsches Patent- und Markenamt*,[18] the European Court of Justice brushed the suggestion aside, confirming that there is no fourth requirement in this respect and that the list should be considered as containing nothing more than random examples. In the words of the Court:

> The Directive must be interpreted as meaning that a trade mark may consist of a sign which is not in itself capable of being perceived visually, provided that it can be represented graphically.[19]

This quotation draws attention to what has become the major issue—that is, is the olfactory mark capable of being represented graphically? Looking back at olfactory marks that were granted at an early stage, it cannot be denied, on the one hand, that the Sumitomo mark (the smell of roses for tyres and wheels) and marks such as 'the smell of freshly cut grass' are not defined very precisely. Both roses and freshly cut grass can mean many different things in different circumstances and to different persons. On the other hand, any third party should be able to find out exactly what the trade mark is from consulting the register, not only to avoid infringement, but also to find out whether another mark can still be registered. The Registrar of Trade Marks must also know exactly what the mark is in order to carry out its examination and publication role. And all of this must be done on the basis of the register—that is, the graphic representation only—because that is

---

[17] [1998] RPC 244.   [18] Case 273/00 [2002] ECR I-11737, [2003] Ch 487, [2003] RPC 685.
[19] Case 273/00 [2002] ECR I-11737, [2003] Ch 487, [2003] RPC 685; [2003] Ch 487 at 509.

the material that is in the public domain and therefore accessible to third parties. In the *Sieckmann* case, the Court drew from this the following conclusion:

> If the users of that register are to be able to determine the precise nature of a mark on the basis of its registration, its graphic representation in the register must be self-contained, easily accessible and intelligible.
>
> Furthermore, in order to fulfil its role as a registered trade mark a sign must always be perceived unambiguously and in the same way so that the mark is guaranteed as an indication of origin. In the light of the duration of a mark's registration and the fact that, as the Directive provides, it can be renewed for varying periods, the representation must be durable.
>
> Finally, the object of the representation is specifically to avoid any element of subjectivity in the process of identifying and perceiving the sign. Consequently, the means of graphic representation must be unequivocal and objective.
>
> In the light of the foregoing observations, the answer to the first question must be that...the Directive must be interpreted as meaning that a trade mark may consist of a sign which is not in itself capable of being perceived visually, provided that it can be represented graphically, particularly by means of images, lines or characters, and that the representation is clear, precise, self-contained, easily accessible, intelligible, durable and objective.[20]

But what did that mean in practice? Mr Sieckmann had described, and represented graphically, the olfactory trade mark he applied for as follows:

> Trade mark protection is sought for the olfactory mark deposited with the Deutsches Patent-und Markenamt of the pure chemical substance methyl cinnamate (= cinnamic acid methyl ester), whose structural formula is set out below. Samples of this olfactory mark can also be obtained via local laboratories listed in the Gelbe Seiten (Yellow Pages) of Deutsche Telekom AG or, for example, via the firm E. Merck in Darmstadt.
>
> $C_6H_5\text{-}CH = CHCOOCH_3$.

Mr Sieckmann also submitted, with his application, an odour sample of the sign in a container and stated that the scent was usually described as '*balsamically fruity with a slight hint of cinnamon*'.

The question was therefore whether, in relation to an olfactory mark, a chemical formula, a description in words, the deposit of an odour sample, or any combination of these elements could satisfy the requirements concerning the mark's capability of being represented graphically, as set out by the Court. The Court came to the conclusion that it could not and gave the following reasons for reaching that conclusion:

> As regards a chemical formula...few people would recognise in such a formula the odour in question. Such a formula is not sufficiently intelligible. In addition...a chemical formula does not represent the odour of a substance, but the substance as such, and nor is it sufficiently clear and precise. It is therefore not a representation for the purposes of...the Directive.
>
> In respect of the description of an odour, although it is graphic, it is not sufficiently clear, precise and objective.
>
> As to the deposit of an odour sample, it does not constitute a graphic representation for the purposes of...the Directive. Moreover, an odour sample is not sufficiently stable or durable...
>
> In the light of the foregoing considerations, the answer to the second question must be that, in respect of an olfactory sign, the requirements of graphic representability are not satisfied by a chemical formula, by a description in written words, by the deposit of an odour sample or by a combination of those elements.[21]

---

[20] Case 273/00 [2002] ECR I-11737, [2003] Ch 487, [2003] RPC 685; [2003] Ch 487 at 509.
[21] Case 273/00 [2002] ECR I-11737, [2003] Ch 487, [2003] RPC 685; [2003] Ch 487 at 511.

This seems to leave very little room indeed for olfactory marks and most of the marks already granted do not meet these stringent requirements.

Sound marks

Let us now move on to sound marks, as did the European Court of Justice 11 months after the *Sieckmann* case, when it delivered its judgment in *Shield Mark BV v. Joost Kist hodn Memex*.[22] Shield Mark had registered various signature tunes or jingles as sound trade marks with the Benelux Trade Marks Office. Let us consider the following Shield Mark marks as an example:

> Four of those trade marks consist of a musical stave with the first nine notes of the musical composition *Für Elise*, by Ludwig von Beethoven. Two of them also state: Sound mark. The trade mark consists of the representation of the melody formed by the notes (graphically) transcribed on the stave, plus, in one case, played on a piano…
>
> Three further marks consist of the sequence of musical notes E, D#, E, D#, E, B, D, C, A. Two of them also state: Sound mark. The trade mark consists of the reproduction of the melody formed by the sequence of notes as described, plus, in one case, played on a piano.
>
> Two of the trade marks registered by Shield Mark consist of the denomination Kukelekuuuuu (an onomatopoeia suggesting, in Dutch, a cockcrow). One of them states: Sound mark, the trade mark consists of an onomatopoeia imitating a cockcrow.

As a preliminary matter, the issue was raised whether sound marks could, by their nature, be distinctive. Having disposed of that issue by ruling that sound signs are not, by nature, incapable of distinguishing the goods or services of one undertaking from those of other undertakings, the Court returned to the key issue of graphical representation and applied its *Sieckmann* approach to sound marks. The written description of a sound, the onomatopoeia, and the musical notes all failed to pass the *Sieckmann* test: they were neither clear, nor precise, nor objective enough.

But whereas the Court did not have a suggestion as to how olfactory marks could pass the test, it did come up with a solution for sound marks:

> a stave divided into bars and showing, in particular, a clef (a treble clef, bass clef or alto or tenor clef), musical notes and rests whose form (for the notes: semibreve, minim, crotchet, quaver, semiquaver, etc.; for the rests: semibreve rest, minim rest, crotchet rest, quaver rest, etc.) indicates the relative value and, where appropriate, accidentals (sharp, flat, natural)—all of this notation determining the pitch and duration of the sounds—may constitute a faithful representation of the sequence of sounds forming the melody in respect of which registration is sought. This mode of graphical representation of the sounds meets the requirements of the case-law of the Court that such representation must be clear, precise, self-contained, easily accessible, intelligible, durable and objective.
>
> Even if such a representation is not immediately intelligible, the fact remains that it may be easily intelligible, thus allowing the competent authorities and the public, in particular traders, to know precisely the sign whose registration as a trade mark is sought.[23]

Colour marks

That leaves us with the question of whether the door also remains open—even if not wide open—for the registration of a single colour as a trade mark. This extreme scenario was put before the European Court of Justice in May 2003 in *Libertel Groep BV v. Benelux-Merkenbureau*.[24] Libertel had applied for the registration of the colour orange, per se,

---

[22] Case C-283/01 [2003] ECR I-14313, [2004] Ch 97, [2004] RPC 315.
[23] Case C-283/01 [2003] ECR I-14313, [2004] Ch 97, [2004] RPC 315; [2004] Ch 97 at 118.
[24] Case C-104/01 [2003] ECR I-3793, [2004] FSR 65.

and, in the box for reproducing the trade mark, the application form contained an orange rectangle and in the space for describing the mark it contained the word 'orange' without reference to any colour code. The Court once more put the focus on graphical representation and the need for it to be clear, precise, self-contained, easily accessible, intelligible, durable, and objective, along the lines of the approach set out in the *Sieckmann* case.

The Court held that a mere sample of a colour is not durable enough, because it may fade; it may also change slightly depending on the background on which it is printed or against which it is put. The mere sample therefore fails the *Sieckmann* test, but, in the view of the Court, a verbal description of a colour could pass the test, depending on the circumstances of the case, as may the combination of a sample and a verbal description. The Court also deemed an internationally recognized colour identification code to be precise and stable enough to pass the test. Libertel therefore failed—but the addition of a colour code to the sample and the (maybe somewhat fuller) verbal description might have seen the colour orange being registered successfully.

But even in those cases, the mark will still have to pass the distinctiveness test.[25] Without wishing to anticipate the discussion of this requirement that is to follow, it is important to note that in *Libertel* itself the Court admitted that this will be a difficult hurdle for a colour mark to pass, as colours possess little inherent capacity for communicating specific information. But as the Court went on to say:

> that factual finding would not justify the conclusion that colours per se cannot, as a matter of principle, be considered to be capable of distinguishing the goods or services of one undertaking from those of other undertakings. The possibility that a colour per se may in some circumstances serve as a badge of origin…cannot be ruled out.[26]

What is clear though is that the Court will systematically apply the *Sieckmann* test to check whether a sign is capable of being represented graphically.

At European level the discussion has remained restricted to applications where the applicant registers a single colour as such and puts that colour, with or without a colour code in the box. A further complication could arise if the applicant wants to register the 'predominant' colour applied to the whole visible surface of the packaging of the goods, leaving it free to add features and vary the amount of surface covered by the colour. The Court of Appeal ruled in the *Cadbury* case[27] that this did not satisfy the requirement of a sign being capable of being represented graphically, as set out in *Sieckmann* and *Libertel*. The Court argued that mark lacked the required clarity, precision, self-containment, durability, and objectivity to qualify for registration. Obiter one of the members of the Court suggested that a formula such as 'covering more than 50%' would on the other hand pass the test. Whether the CJEU and other national courts will agree with this approach remains to be seen. The debate surrounding colour trade marks has clearly not yet been exhausted.

Distinctiveness in trade

In order for a sign to be registered as a trade mark it has to be capable of distinguishing the goods or services of one undertaking from those of other undertakings. This is a fundamental requirement, but it is defined in much more detail through the application of the absolute grounds for refusal of registration. Several other issues need to be addressed

---

[25] See Case T-173/00, *KWS Saat v. OHIM* [2002] ECR II-3843.
[26] Case C-104/01, *Libertel Groep BV v. Benelux-Merkenbureau* [2003] ECR I-3793, [2004] FSR 65 at para. 41.
[27] *Société des Produits Nestlé SA v. Cadbury UK Ltd* [2013] EWCA Civ 1174, reversing [2012] EWHC 2637.

further in the context of what a mark can be, but it is first appropriate to consider the significance of the use of the word 'mark', especially if such a mark has to be capable of distinguishing. Gradually this analysis will shed light on what is meant by the 'distinctiveness' requirement.

Names and signatures as marks

From its very concept it is clear that distinctiveness operates in a commercial or trade context. That raises the issue whether certain signs are by definition not capable of being registered as a trade mark on that basis.

People's signatures may quite appropriately be regarded as their 'mark', but although a person's signature is both graphic and distinctive,[28] it is at least potentially not a trade mark, because no trade is normally likely to be involved. That is not, however, to say that it could never be: the Trade Marks Act 1938 expressly permitted registration of a signature of the proprietor of a mark or his or her predecessor in business[29]—but it is this last word that is the clue: personal marks are not registrable and only those that are used in business—that is, trade—are. Under s. 103(1) of the 1994 Act, 'trade' is unhelpfully stated to '*include any profession or business*', but this nevertheless gives some indication that this whole area is once again concerned solely with the commercial exploitation of the relevant intellectual property rights.

Ex-footballer Paul Gascoigne, like many others with a similar name, has the nickname 'Gazza'—this, as such, is not registrable; once this particular 'Gazza' attains fame or notoriety and can enter trade—for example, in the character merchandising industry—then the name or signature can be registered as a *trade* mark (as long as all other criteria are satisfied). Thus there has to be trade, but—unlike in the old law[30]—there does not appear to be any need for the trade in question to be for valuable consideration. Use in announcements, advertising, and on badges by a non-profit-making association was after all held to be use of the trade mark and therefore use in trade.[31] This is not to say, however, that the registration of a name or a signature as a trade mark is now a straightforward issue. The distinctiveness requirement can still create major problems if the mark is not adapted to distinguish the goods of the applicant from those of other traders.

The *Elvis Presley* case[32] graphically illustrates these problems. In that case, a cursive rendition of the singer's name was held not to be distinctive. Laddie J ruled that the public bought memorabilia carrying the Elvis name, because it referred to the singer; the public did not assume that these goods came from one source that was linked to the singer. The proposed mark was therefore not capable of distinguishing memorabilia marketed by the applicant from those marketed by other traders. A famous name refers to the person and, as such, it does not necessarily possess the distinctiveness required to distinguish goods from one source from those of another.[33]

---

[28] Laddie J's judgment in *Re Elvis Presley Trade Marks* [1997] RPC 543 correctly qualifies this basic starting point and argues that signatures, although prima facie distinctive, are not inevitably distinctive. Only those signatures that are stylistically unique are really distinctive. In practice, the latter are often a highly distorted way of writing a name and can be seen as a private graphic tied to one person.

[29] TMA 1938, s. 9(1)(b).   [30] See *Re Dee Corp. plc's Application* [1990] RPC 159.

[31] Case C-442/07, *Verein Radetzky-Orden v. Bundesvereinigung Kameradschaft, Feldmarschall Radetzky'* [2009] ETMR 14.

[32] *Re Elvis Presley Trade Marks* (n. 28).

[33] *Re Elvis Presley Trade Marks* (n. 28). The test for name trade marks is not different from that for any other trade, however, and s. 11 (2) has no influence: see Case C-404/02, *Nichols plc v. Registrar of Trade Marks* [2004] ECR I-8499, [2005] 1 WLR 1418.

Overall, the distinctiveness requirement means that the main purpose of a trade mark is to convey a message about the source of, and responsibility for, quality of the goods or services that are labelled with the mark.[34] This does not exclude the option that the goods are made for the trade mark owner by a third party using the trade mark owner's specification or that the services are provided by a third party according to the trade mark owner's specification, but the trade mark owner must adopt the goods or services as his or her own in those cases after having checked that they match his or her specification.[35]

This approach has now been confirmed by the European Court of Justice. The question of whether a common surname could be a trade mark arose in *Nichols plc v. Registrar of Trade Marks.*[36] The Court held that the distinctive character of such a mark needed to be assessed in the same way as that of any other mark. No special criteria applied and such an assessment should therefore focus, first, on the products or services in respect of which registration is applied for and, second, on the perception of the relevant consumers. In other words, one needs to determine whether, in relation to the relevant product or service, the relevant consumers would see the name as a mark distinguishing the goods or services of one source from the goods or services of another, or whether they would see it as nothing more than a surname.

A general rule

Nichols was a case about names, but in dealing with the matter the Court of Justice made it clear that in analysing distinctiveness any kind of mark is subject to exactly the same rule. No special criteria should be applied and the analysis should therefore simply focus, first, on the products or services in respect of which registration is applied for and, second, on the perception of the relevant consumers. These are the consumers to which the product is directed. In other words, one needs to determine whether, in relation to the relevant product or service, the relevant consumers would see the name as a mark distinguishing the goods or services of one source from the goods or services of another.[37]

The average consumer, who is deemed to be reasonably well informed and reasonably observant and circumspect, and who also appears in an infringement context, is a legal construct. The consumer is the one who uses the relevant products or services and whose level of attention varies in relation to the importance attached to the goods or services. The concept of the 'average' consumer is a legal construct in the sense that it is a theoretical attribution by the CJEU. The court considers the market concerned and who lives there and then puts itself in the position of the average consumer of these goods and services on that market. The mark must allow such an average consumer to retrace the origin of the goods or services. Recognition of the mark and a mere link to the producer is not enough, at least for the English courts. A significant proportion of the relevant class of persons must be seen to rely upon the mark (rather than other signs also present on the goods or services) as indicating the origin of the goods or services.[38]

---

[34] *Glaxo Group v. Dowelhurst Ltd* [2000] FSR 529. For an example of a mark that failed to clear this hurdle at the time of the application for registration, see '*800-Flowers*' *Trade Mark* [2001] FSR 191 (CA).

[35] *Primark Stores Ltd & Primark Holdings v. Lollypop Clothing Ltd* [2001] ETMR 30.

[36] Case C-404/02, *Nichols plc v. Registrar of Trade Marks* (n. 33).

[37] Case C-144/06 P, *Henkel v. OHIM* [2007] ECT I-8109 at para. 34; Case C-304/06 P, *Eurohypo v. OHIM* [2008] ECR I-3291 at para. 66; Joined Cases C-473/01 P and C-474/01 P, *Procter & Gamble v. OHIM* [2004] ECR I-5173 at para. 51; and Case C-64/02 P, *OHIM v. Erpo Möbelwerk* [2004] ECR I-10031 at para. 36.

[38] *Enterprise Holdings Inc v. Europcar Group UK Ltd and Europcar International SASU* [2015] EWHC 17 (Ch), paras. 130–50.

Kinds of mark

From this, then, we can return to the issue of the kinds of marks that will attract registration, as even if the rule is the same, its application to some kinds of marks warrants closer attention. The 1938 Act, by virtue of s. 68(1), gave a list of things that could count as marks and most of these have been retained within the similarly non-inclusive list in s. 1(1) of the new law. (Those that have not, such as devices or headings, are not incapable of trade mark registration, but must simply satisfy the general requirements of the first paragraph of s. 1(1).) It must be emphasized, however, that even the types of mark listed must also satisfy these requirements. It is not every word or numeral that can now be registered as a trade mark; only those that can be both graphically represented and are product-distinctive, the latter point often giving difficulty.

It is important to point out, at this stage, that the list of potential marks does expressly include an important new area. By clarifying that 'the shape of goods or their packaging' can be registrable in appropriate circumstances, the 1994 Act at once removes not only such awkward cases as *Re Coca-Cola*,[39] thus allowing registration of a suitably distinct bottle and other containers (a picture of the container will count as a graphic representation), but also appears to go even further back to overrule cases such as *James v. Soulby*,[40] which prevented the registration of the distinctive shape of the thing itself. Registration of the shape, if distinctive, is now permissible under the 1994 Act.

It is appropriate to consider some of the problems that dogged the old law here and to use some examples from the previous case law to illustrate those problems. The use of a name, per se, may well not be distinctive, if the name is relatively common. The old law, by s. 9(1)(a) of the 1938 Act, insisted that a name could only be registered if in a special or particular manner, as demonstrated by *Re Standard Cameras Ltd's Application*.[41] In this case, the name 'Robin Hood' was used for a camera and registration was allowed, because the first letter was shaped as an archer similar to the well-known historical figure and the last letter in the name portrayed as a target. Under the new regime, the answer would appear to be the same—but by the simpler route of the clear factual distinctiveness that such a mark would appear to enjoy.

The category of words has given rise to various problems, because the courts were constrained by the 1938 Act[42] to allow only invented words or words that conveyed no connection with the object itself and which were neither a geographical name nor a surname. The goal for trade mark proprietors was to sail as close to the wind as possible, so as to try to associate the goods as directly as possible with the name chosen. Thus in *De Cordova v. Vick Chemical Co.*,[43] a chest rub was named 'Vaporub'. The claim that was made was that this was an invented word and thus registrable. In a narrow sense, the word was not to be found in any dictionary, but it was too obvious in its origins to be regarded as invented and thus registrable. In *Re Hallgarten*,[44] however, a whisky-based liqueur marketed as 'Whisquer' was seen as sufficient of a variant from the new word's origins that it was to be regarded as invented and thus could be registered. Now, under s. 1(1) of the 1994 Act, the test is whether the names distinguish their product from others and it would seem likely that the presence of other products of that type on the market would mean that 'Vaporub' would remain unregistrable, while 'Whisquer' might

---

[39] *Re Coca-Cola Co's Applications* [1986] 2 All ER 274, *sub nom. In re Coca-Cola Co.* [1986] 1 WLR 695, discussed in the previous chapter.

[40] (1886) 33 Ch D 392.   [41] (1952) 69 RPC 125.

[42] Trade Marks Act 1938, s. 9(1)(c) and (d).   [43] (1951) 68 RPC 103.

[44] (1948) 66 RPC 105.

survive in the absence—as far as is known—of any similar product name or description in the marketplace.

The law has taken and, it seems likely, will continue to take cognizance of the problem of phonetic equivalence. This is shown by the case of *Re Exxate Trade Mark*,[45] in which the use of Exxate on petrochemical products was allowed not as an invented word, the origin being too obvious, but as a mark that was nevertheless distinctive, bearing no obvious relation to the goods. This would seem still to represent the conclusion that the law is likely to reach even after its rewriting.

This argument is reinforced by the decision of the Appointed Person in the *Froot Loops Trade Mark* case.[46] Trade mark registration for 'Froot Loops' in relation to cereals and cereal preparations was refused, because it was the phonetic equivalent of 'fruit loops'. As such, the mark lost its distinctiveness and became a description of the goods involved.

The old law's concern to restrict the use of laudatory epithets, lest an over-extensive monopoly be created, is perhaps harder to retain under the new law. In *Re Joseph Crosfield & Sons Ltd*,[47] the name 'Perfection' was denied trade mark registration for a soap as being too broad a monopoly and as being, in the future, potentially misleading. It seems difficult to argue today that such a general word could be distinctive even within a particular category of goods, although, of course, distinctiveness will ultimately be a question of fact. In the first case to raise this issue under the 1994 Act, Jacob J denied trade mark protection to the laudatory epithet 'Treat', which was used in relation to dessert sauces and syrups.[48]

The Court of Justice dealt on a number of occasions with laudatory epithets and advertising slogans that applicants wanted to register as a trade mark.[49] The starting point is that one applies the general rule for distinctiveness. The fact that the mark can also be seen as and used as a laudatory epithet or as an advertising slogan (or indications of quality or incitements to purchase) does not therefore exclude the marks from registration.[50] Use as a mark and other use can go together and does not warrant the application of a stricter rule on distinctiveness (such as e.g. that the advertising slogan should be imaginative).[51] However, when applying the general rule one needs to take into account that the relevant public's perception is not necessarily the same for each kind of mark and each use. It could therefore be more difficult to establish distinctiveness in relation to certain kinds of marks.[52] All that is required, though, is that apart from being seen by the relevant public as a laudatory epithet, an advertising slogan etc., the mark is also seen[53] by the relevant public as an indication of the commercial origin of the goods or services.[54] On this basis registration of Audi's slogan 'Vorsprung durch Technik'[55] as a trade mark was ultimately allowed by the Court of Justice for cars and other goods, as the public would also see it as distinctive for goods coming from Audi,[56] but the term 'Real People, Real Solutions' was refused registration as a trade mark for technical support services in the computer industry,[57] as the relevant public would only see it as a promotional message, without a hint of distinctiveness as to commercial origin.

---

[45] [1986] RPC 567.   [46] [1998] RPC 240.

[47] [1910] 1 Ch 118, HC; on appeal [1910] 1 Ch 130 at 142–3, CA.

[48] *British Sugar plc v. James Robertson & Sons Ltd* [1996] RPC 281.

[49] *Erpo Möbelwerk* (n. 37); and Case C-517/99, *Merz & Krell* [2001] ECR I-6959 at para. 40.

[50] *Merz & Krell* (n. 50) at para. 40.   [51] *Erpo Möbelwerk* (n. 37).

[52] *Erpo Möbelwek* (n. 37).

[53] 'Also' means here 'as well' and not 'immediately' or 'in the first place'.

[54] *Erpo Möbelwerk* (n. 37).   [55] 'Advance or advantage through technology'.

[56] Case C-398/08 P, *Audi v. OHIM*, judgment of 21 January 2010, nyr, <http://curia.europa.eu>.

[57] Case T-130/01, *Sykes Enterprises Inc v. OHIM* [2002] ECR II-5179.

Disclaimers

Some trade marks may be created from more than one image: for example, a distinctive name written in a distinctive manner, such as the way in which 'Coca-Cola' is written on its tins. The question that arises is whether a problem is created if one of the elements is not distinctive and thus, in itself, not able to gain trade mark protection. This problem is dealt with, at least in part, by the system of disclaimers under which an applicant can disclaim parts of his or her trade mark by denying any claim to the exclusive use of that element.[58] The classic illustration of this is the old case of *Re Diamond T Trade Mark*,[59] in which a mark had three distinct elements—namely, the word 'diamond', the shape of a diamond, and the letter 'T'. None of these were, in themselves, distinctive and each of the individual items was thus the subject of a disclaimer, but a trade mark was held to subsist in what was left—namely, the (distinctive) combination of the three items.

The 1994 Act varies from its predecessor in one vital way in relation to cases in which the use of disclaimers is concerned. Formerly, the Registrar could impose disclaimers, but this is now a voluntary matter for the applicant. There is a clear incentive for the applicant to avail him- or herself of this facility: there is always a risk that the failure so to do will often be counterproductive, because, as will be seen, a mark may be refused or may subsequently be struck down at the instigation of a rival trader if, for example, it is thought to be likely to cause confusion with other similar marks or other similar goods. Clearly, the incorporation of non-distinctive matter will readily raise such potential confusion.

That said, the use of the disclaimer enables trade marks to incorporate, albeit under the disclaimer, much valuable descriptive matter. The proprietor of 'Torremans' Fresh Orange Juice' cannot monopolize the description of the product—but if the name is printed in distinctive purple spiky lettering, a trade mark can be obtained in the overall mark and it may then be that, as a matter of fact, the public associates the general product description with the particular trade-marked product.

It is important to note, however, that the effect of a disclaimer is not limited to the grant of a trade mark: it also has an effect when it comes to infringement and opposition. So if the only point of similarity with a registered trade mark is the disclaimed element, that disclaimed element can also no longer be relied on in opposition or infringement proceedings.[60]

Unregistrable marks

Fulfilling the basic requirements of trade mark registration does not guarantee that a trade mark will be obtained. The 1994 Act makes clear that certain marks are either never registrable or are unregistrable in the light of market conditions. It is the first category that we now examine.

Absolute grounds for refusal of registration

Section 3 of the 1994 Act establishes the principal rules relating to absolute unregistrability. It lists a range of different grounds and, by s. 3(1), states that the following marks shall not be registered:

(a) signs which do not satisfy the requirements of section 1(1),
(b) trade marks which are devoid of any distinctive character,

---

[58] TMA 1994, s. 13.   [59] (1921) 38 RPC 373.
[60] *General Cigar Co. Ltd v. Partagas y Cia SA* [2005] FSR 45.

(c) trade marks which consist exclusively of signs or indications which may serve, in trade, to designate the kind, quality, quantity, intended purpose, value, geographical origin, the time of production of goods or of rendering of services, or other characteristics of goods or services,

(d) trade marks which consist exclusively of signs or indications which have become customary in the current language or in the bona fide and established practices of the trade;

provided that a trade mark shall not be refused registration by virtue of paragraph (b), (c) or (d) above if, before the date of application for registration, it has in fact acquired a distinctive character as a result of the use made of it.

These complex provisions go to the heart of the issue of distinctiveness already flagged up as crucial by s. 1 of the Act. They help to define the requirement of distinctiveness and each of them reflects (different) public policy considerations.[61] The four paragraphs of s. 3(1) are by no means mutually exclusive and may apply in combination in any given case.[62] Nevertheless, each of the grounds and paragraphs is independent from the others and calls for a separate examination.[63] Overcoming one of the grounds does therefore also not guarantee the same result for the other grounds.[64]

Section 3(1)(a)

This section restates the principle that signs that are not capable of being represented graphically and that are not distinctive as to commercial origin cannot be registered as a trade mark and that this is an absolute ground for refusal of registration. The Recast Directive spells that out by defining the signs concerned in its Art. 4(1)(a) as 'signs which cannot constitute a trade mark'. From that perspective the first paragraph of s. 3 is self-evident—but the Court of Appeal's judgment in *Bach & Bach Flower Remedies Trade Marks*,[65] which dealt with this point, had the potential to create confusion and could be seen as irreconcilable with the decision of the European Court of Justice in *Philips Electronics NV v. Remington Consumer Products Ltd.*[66] The Court of Appeal sought to clarify the matter in *West (t/a Eastenders) v. Fuller Smith & Turner plc*[67] and held that the rule was that the second half of the definition of a trade mark in s. 1(1) of the 1994 Act does not impose any requirement of distinctiveness separate from that imposed by s. 3(1)(b)–(d), and that there was no requirement that a mark be both 'capable of distinguishing' and 'not devoid of distinctive character'. There is therefore, as the Court of Justice said in *Philips*, no category of marks that are not excluded under paragraphs (b)–(d) that then goes on to be excluded under paragraph (a).[68] One cannot reverse that statement though. Even if a sign is in general capable of constituting a trade mark, it may still face problems under paragraphs (b)–(d).[69]

Taken on its own though, the effect of paragraph (a) seems to be limited. The Court of Justice used it to hold that there is no reason to find that the mark 'Postkantoor'

---

[61] Case C-104/01, *Libertel Groep BV* [2003] ECR I-3793 at para. 50 and Cases C-456/01 P and C-457/01 P, *Henkel v. OHIM* [2004] ECR I-5089 at para. 46.

[62] *Bach & Bach Flower Remedies Trade Marks* [2000] RPC 512, CA.

[63] Case C-53/01, *Linde AG* [2003] ECR I-3161 at para. 67.

[64] Case C-363/99, *Koninklijke KPN Nederland NV* [2004] ECR I-1619 at para. 70.

[65] [2000] RPC 513.   [66] Case C-299/99 [2002] ECR I-5475, [2003] Ch 159, [2003] RPC 14.

[67] [2003] FSR 816.

[68] Case C-299/99, *Philips Electronics NV v. Remington Consumer Products Ltd* [2002] ECR I-5475 at paras. 37 and 38.

[69] *Henkel* (n. 61).

is not capable of fulfilling the essential function of a trade mark for certain goods.[70] As such, paragraph (a) was therefore not a problem in that case. That was more the case when the distinctiveness of a colour was at issue. The Court of Justice doubted whether a colour would, in most circumstances, have the distinctive character that is required:

> Save in exceptional case, colours do not initially have a distinctive character, but may be capable of acquiring such character as a result of the use made of them in relation to the goods or services claimed.
>
> Subject to the above, it must be accepted that…colours and combinations of colours, designated in the abstract and without contours, may be capable of distinguishing the goods or services from one undertaking from those of other undertakings.[71]

Section 3(1)(b)

Section 3(1)(b) denies trade mark registration to trade marks that are devoid of any distinctive character. A trade mark must, at the very least, be able to serve as a guarantee of trade origin—that is, it must be capable of distinguishing the goods that originate with one trader from similar goods that originate with another.[72] A mark that is devoid of any distinctive character can never convey the message 'these are the goods of a particular trader';[73] that conclusion is reached by considering the mark on its own, taking into account no use, but looking at it with reference to the goods or services for which it is registered as well as the relevant public. So, when Grundig Multimedia tried to register the wordmark 'Pianissimo' as a Community trade mark for electrical engines the application failed, because one of the meanings of the Italian word pianissimo is 'extremely silent'. In relation to electrical engines that can for the relevant public, which includes Italian consumers, never mean electrical engines made by Grundig.[74] It was also, for example, held that the word 'treat' was devoid of any distinctive character, when looked at on its own.[75] The same applied to the PREPARE mark, which, as such, was unable to distinguish the teaching aids of one trader from those of another trader and only referred to the word 'prepare'.[76] 'Eurolamb',[77] as an abbreviation of European lamb;[78] 'Froot Loops',[79] as the phonetic equivalent of fruit loops (cereals); and 'CREATE SPACE', as a mark for use in relation to the provision of storage space[80] were also held not to be distinctive and therefore excluded from registration through the operation of s. 3(1)(b). And when Philips tried to register its three-headed rotary shaver as a trade mark, it was held that the shaver as a *'sign can never only denote shavers made by Philips and no one else because it primarily says "here is a three-headed rotary shaver"'* and that the sign *'is not "capable" of*

---

[70] *Koninklijke KPN Nederland NV* (n. 64).

[71] Case C-49/02, *Heidelberger Bauchemie GmbH* [2004] ECR I-6129 at paras. 39 and 40.

[72] *Philips Electronics BV v. Remington Consumer Products Ltd* (n. 13). The case went on to the Court of Appeal, which made a reference for a preliminary ruling to the European Court of Justice: [1999] RPC 809; see *Philips Electronics NV v. Remington Consumer Products Ltd* (n. 68).

[73] Joined Cases C-468/01 P to C-472/01 P, *Procter & Gamble v. OHIM* [2004] ECR I-5141 at para. 32; *OHIM v. Erpo Möbelwerk* (n. 37) at para. 42; and Case C-304/06 P, *Eurohypo v. OHIM* [2008] ECR I-3297.

[74] Case T-11/14, *Grundig Multimedia AG v. OHIM*, 21 January 2015, <http://curia.europa.eu>

[75] *British Sugar plc* (n. 48).   [76] [1997] RPC 884.

[77] *Eurolamb Trade Mark* [1997] RPC 279.

[78] The Court of First Instance also held that two generic words that describe the range of products of a manufacturer cannot be registered as a trade mark, because they lack distinctive character, even if the two words are stuck together: see Case T-19/99, *DKV v. OHIM (Companyline)* [2000] ECR II-1.

[79] *Froot Loops Trade Mark* [1998] RPC 240.

[80] *Easistore Ltd's Trade Mark Application*, 21 September 2010, Appointed Person, nyr.

denoting only Philips goods'.[81] The mark was therefore invalid. It is important to note that the Philips sign did not include the name 'Philips' and that any other three-headed rotary shaver design would have infringed the mark if it had been granted. It was also irrelevant that no other manufacturer had hitherto made such shavers.

The European Court of Justice confirmed these finding in the *Philips* case.[82] The Court agreed that the shape of a three-headed rotary shaver as such could not be a trade mark, because it only conveyed the message that the item was a three-headed rotary shaver and could therefore not distinguish one such shaver from one manufacturer from another such shaver from another manufacturer.

Similarly, Lego was denied trade mark registration for its toy plastic bricks when it tried to register them without the name 'Lego' stamped on them.[83] This does not mean that trade mark protection for shapes of goods is to be ruled out altogether: the distinctive Coca-Cola bottle is probably a good example of a successful case. In relation to word marks, the meaning of a word can depend on its usage, and it is permissible and necessary to determine the meaning of a word as used at the time of the application for registration. 'Usage' means usage by those engaged in the relevant trade and includes the average consumer, as well as manufacturers, wholesalers, and retailers. Through usage, a word could acquire—but also lose—a distinctive character. It was therefore necessary to determine the meaning of the word on the basis of the usage before deciding whether, under s. 3(1)(b), the mark was, or had become, devoid of distinctive character, or whether instead distinctive character had been acquired.[84]

West (t/a Eastenders) v. Fuller Smith & Turner plc[85] raised interesting questions concerning s. 3(1) of the 1994 Act. The trade mark concerned was 'E.S.B.', an acronym of Extra Strong Bitter, and its revocation was sought on the basis that it was devoid of distinctive character and that is was merely descriptive. In the Court of Appeal, it was held that if, at the date of registration, the mark served as a trade mark to the interested public (as the judge had held it did in fact), it could not be regarded as being devoid of distinctive character. The mark would offend against s. 3(1)(b) only if the average consumer knew that the sign 'E.S.B.' was used exclusively as an indication or the kind or quality of the goods or was in common use. The word 'devoid' had to be construed strictly and the concession that the mark possessed distinctiveness *in vacuo* was fatal to the objection under this subsection. The Court followed the guidance of the European Court of Justice in *Procter & Gamble v. OHIM*[86] on this point.

Acronyms and abbreviations can also be used in conjunction with the descriptive terms they stand for in an attempt to take away the merely descriptive nature of the latter. Attempts were made, for example, to register 'Multi Market Fund MMF' and 'NAI - Der Natur-Aktien-Index'. The Court of Justice held that these signs were still caught by s. 3(1)(b) if the public understand the abbreviation as another way to describe the descriptive content.[87]

---

[81] *Philips Electronics NV v. Remington Consumer Products Ltd* (n. 13), per Jacob J. Similarly, the Court of First Instance held that the rectangular shape of washing powder tablets in two colours could not be registered as a trade mark, because it indicated the product, and did not allow the consumer to distinguish between the product and another tablet from another manufacturer, because the shape was used commonly: see Case T-335/99, *Henkel v. OHIM* [2001] ECR II-2581. The cylindrical shape of a torch was not registrable, because it referred to the product rather than to a specific manufacturer; again, the distinctive character of the mark was lacking: see Case T-88/00, *Mag Instrument v. OHIM* [2002] ECR II-467.

[82] *Philips Electronics NV v. Remington Consumer Products Ltd* (n. 68).

[83] *Interlego AG's Trade Mark Application* [1998] RPC 69 (a case under the 1938 Act).

[84] *Bach & Bach Flower Remedies Trade Marks* (n. 62).   [85] [2003] FSR 816.

[86] Case C-383/99 P [2001] ECR I-6251.

[87] Joined Cases C-90/11 and C-91/11, *Alfred Strigl v. Deutsches Patent- und Markenamt* and *Securvita Gesellschaft zur Entwicklung alternativer Versicherungskonzepte mbH v. Öko-Invest Verlagsgesellschaft mbH*, <http://curia.europa.eu>.

Section 3(1)(b) is therefore particularly concerned with those marks that, from the point of view of the relevant public, are commonly used, in trade, for the presentation of the goods or services concerned, or in connection with which there exists, at the very least, concrete evidence justifying the conclusion that they are capable of being used in that manner.[88] Moreover, these marks are incapable of performing the essential function of a trade mark—namely, that of identifying the origin of the goods or services—thus enabling the consumer who acquired them to repeat or avoid the experience on a subsequent occasion.[89] The emphasis is placed on the fact that they are completely devoid of distinctive character and incapable to distinguish as to commercial origin.[90] Another example that makes this clear is the refusal of the Court of First Instance (now called the General Court) to register an exclamation mark (!) in a standard font as a trade mark in its own right. Despite the fact that for years it had successfully been used in the combination mark 'JOOP!', the exclamation mark as such remained devoid of distinctive character.[91]

It is important to note that, for the purposes of s. 3(1)(b), no distinction should be made between different categories of mark. It is therefore not appropriate to apply more stringent criteria when assessing the distinctiveness of three-dimensional marks comprising the shape of the goods themselves or the shape of the packaging of those goods than in the case of other categories of mark, even if, in practice, fewer three-dimensional marks will pass the test.[92] But nonetheless one needs to keep in mind, when applying those criteria in each case,[93] that the relevant public perception is not necessarily the same in the case of a three-dimensional mark that consists of the appearance of a product itself as it is in case of word or figurative marks that consist of signs that are unrelated to the appearance of the product. Consumers are simply not used to making assumptions about the origin of products on the basis of their shape, or of the shape of their packaging, without reference to any word or graphic element. It must therefore be more difficult to establish distinctiveness for three-dimensional marks.[94] The practical outcome is therefore that only a mark that departs significantly from the norm of the sector can fulfil its essential function of indicating origin and can therefore potentially escape being devoid of distinctive character.[95] But even in those cases, the fact that they now fulfil the essential function of indicating origin on their own is not a foregone conclusion and needs to be demonstrated.[96] Lindt's application for a three-dimensional sign

---

[88] Case T-305/02, *Nestlé Waters France v. OHIM* [2004] ETMR 566 at para. 28; Joined Cases T-79/01 and T-86/01, *Bosch v. OHIM (Kit Pro & Kit Super Pro)* [2002] ECR I1–4881 at para. 19.

[89] Case T-79/00, *Rewe Zentral v. OHIM (LITE)* [2002] ECR I1–705 at para. 26; Case T-305/02, *Nestlé Waters France v. OHIM* (n. 88) at para. 28.

[90] See Case C-398/08 P, *Audi v. OHIM* [2010] FSR 24.

[91] Case T-75/08, *JOOP! GmbH v. OHIM*, 30 September 2009, nyr, <http:curia.europa.eu>.

[92] Joined Cases C-53/01 and C-55/01, *Linde AG and ors v. Deutsches Patent- und Markenamt* [2003] ECR I-3161 at para. 49. See also Case T-88/00, *Mag Instrument v. OHIM* [2002] ECR II-467 at para. 32; *Nestlé Waters France v. OHIM* (n. 88) at para. 35. The same applies to laudatory epithets and advertising slogans, see *OHIM v. Erpo Möbelwerk* (n. 37); Case C-398/08 P, *Audi v. OHIM* [2010] FSR 24 and Case C-311/11 P, *Smart Technologies ULC v. OHIM* (refusal to register 'WIR MACHEN DAS BESONDERE EINFACH' for computerized systems) [2012] ETMR 49.

[93] One needs to examine each case on its facts, and types of marks such as single letters cannot be excluded as such on the basis of s. 3(1)(b); see Case C-265/09 P, *OHIM v. BORCO-Marken-Import-Matthiesen* [2011] ETMR 4 (the sign α).

[94] See recently Case C-96/11 P, *August Storck KG v. OHIM*, 6 September 2012, <http://curia.europa.eu>.

[95] Case C-24/05, *Storck KG v. OHIM* [2006] ECR I-5677; Case C-173/04, *Deutsche SiSi-Werke GmbH & Co. Betriebs KG v. OHIM* [2006] ECR I-551, [2006] ETMR 41 at para. 31.

[96] *Bongrain SA's Trade Mark Application* [2005] RPC 14 (CA). A six-lobed shape for cheese, unusual as it may be, was held not to be distinctive.

consisting of the shape of a chocolate rabbit with a red ribbon and golden wrapping paper is a good example of an application that failed to pass this hurdle, as the shape, the ribbon and the golden wrapping paper were in use by plenty of other manufacturers and failed to refer the consumer exclusively to Lindt.[97]

A minimum degree of distinctive character is, on the other hand, sufficient to render inapplicable the ground for refusal set out in s. 3(1)(b). In a case involving bottles for mineral water,[98] the sign claimed consisted of the shape of the packaging of the product, rather than the product itself, because beverages, such as mineral waters, cannot be sold without packaging. That three-dimensional mark was composed of commonly used elements, but they were combined in a particular way that made the combination stand out. The mark therefore had the minimum degree of distinctiveness required.

Language issues can also arise: is a descriptive word in one language necessarily devoid of distinctiveness when it is used as a trade mark in another language area? In *Matratzen Concord AG v. Hulka SA*,[99] the mark concerned was 'Matratzen'—'mattresses' in German. The mark was, however, registered and used in Spain. In Spanish, the word has no meaning and the European Court of Justice ruled therefore that it could be distinctive for mattresses, unless the relevant parties in the member state in relation to which registration was sought were capable of identifying the meaning of the term. Unless the latter situation arises, the mark is not caught by s. 3(1).

Specific problems arise in relation to compound signs, namely signs that are composed of several elements. In assessing distinctiveness it is unavoidable that one looks at each of the parts separately, but the final decision needs to be taken on the basis of the whole compound sign. When SAT.2 was applied for in relation to satellite broadcasts it was clear that on its own the element SAT was a mere abbreviation of satellite and that was exactly what it meant to the relevant public (merely descriptive), whilst the element 2 was equally devoid of distinctive character. The Court of Justice[100] decided nevertheless that the same conclusion did not apply to the compound mark. SAT.2 is not merely descriptive and can distinguish, as consumers could identify the channel on the basis of it. As such it was not devoid of distinctive character. Or to quote the Court of Justice:

> Finally, as regards a trade mark comprising words or a word and a digit, such as that which forms the subject-matter of the dispute, the distinctiveness of each of those terms or elements, taken separately, may be assessed, in part, but must, in any event, depend on an appraisal of the whole which they comprise. Indeed, the mere fact that each of those elements, considered separately, is devoid of distinctive character does not mean that their combination cannot present a distinctive character.[101]

On the other hand, BioID® as a trade mark for the computer-aided identification and/or verification of live organisms based on one or more specific biometric characteristics was held to be devoid of distinctive character as it was merely descriptive and unable to be distinctive as to commercial origin.[102] Similarly, a series mark using the word 'simply', using for some words in the series italics or adding [...], for a range of basic products sold by Lidl failed as the word is descriptive and the addition of common

[97] Case C-98/11 P, *Chocoladefabriken Lindt & Sprüngli AG v. OHIM*, 24 May 2012, <http://curia.europa.eu>.
[98] *Nestlé Waters France v. OHIM* (n. 88).
[99] Case C-421/04, *Matratzen Concord AG v. Hulka SA* [2006] ECR I-2303, [2006] ETMR 48.
[100] Case C-329/02 P, *SAT.1 Satellitenfernsehen GmbH v. Office for Harmonization of the Internal Market* [2004] ECR I-8317.
[101] *SAT.1 Satellitenfernsehen GmbH* (n. 100) at para. 28.
[102] Case C-37/03 P, *BioID AG v. OHIM* [2005] ECR I-7975.

elements such as the use of italics and the addition of [...] cannot create a different impression. The overall impression made by the mark cannot acquire distinctiveness as a result.[103]

Finally, it should be noted that the European Court of Justice has held that the distinctiveness of a trade mark must be assessed by reference to, first, the goods or services in respect of which registration is sought and, second, the perception of the relevant persons—namely, the consumers of the goods or services. According to the Court, that means the presumed expectations of an average consumer of the category of goods or services in question, who is reasonably well informed, and reasonably observant and circumspect.[104]

Section 3(1)(d)

A similar approach applies to s. 3(1)(d) of the 1994 Act.[105] The starting point for subsection (d) is that, for it to apply, the mark must consist exclusively of signs or indications that have become customary in the current language or in the established practices of the trade in the products or services in respect of which the mark is to be registered. This should not be taken to mean, however, that the signs or indications must have become a direct description of the goods or services concerned and that they describe their essential elements or characteristics; it is sufficient that the signs or indications bring the goods or services to mind to the average consumer.[106] Whether or not the sign describes the properties or characteristics of the goods or services is irrelevant. Subsection (d) does not exclude signs on the basis that they are descriptive, but on the basis that they have become customary as a term for the goods or services, for example as a result of persistent advertising.[107]

Section 3(1)(c)

Section 3(1)(c) is designed to deny trade mark registration to descriptive marks that, as such, are likely not to be distinctive. Once more, the *Treat* case[108] can serve as an example: 'Treat' was held to be a sign that designated exclusively the kind, quality, and intended purpose of the product. Similarly, Philips' shaver head fell foul of this provision in so far as the public took it as a picture of the goods[109] and not as a trade mark.[110] It is important to note that the bar on registration applies only if the mark is exclusively composed of these types of descriptive matter and marks can be registered that, among other elements, include matters of this sort, whether the subject of a disclaimer or not. A trade mark can therefore include descriptive matter, as long as it does so in combination with other matter that adds a distinctive character to the combination. For a mark to be caught there must be a direct and specific relationship with the goods or services in question to enable the public to immediately perceive, without further thought, a description of the category of goods and services or one of their characteristics.

[103] Case O-382-15, *Lidl Stiftung (Simply)*, Appointed Person, 3 August 2015.

[104] Case C-210/96, *Gut Springenheide & Tusky* [1998] ECR I-4657 at para. 31; Joined Cases C-53/01 and C-55/01, *Linde AG and ors v. Deutsches Patent- und Markenamt* [2003] ECR I-3161 at para. 41.

[105] *Gut Springenheide & Tusky* and *Linde AG and ors* (n. 105).

[106] Conclusion of Advocate-General Damaso Ruiz-Jarabo Colomer in Case C-517/99, *Merz & Krell & Co.*, delivered on 18 January 2001, [2001] ETMR 48.

[107] *Merz & Krell & Co.* (n. 50).   [108] *British Sugar plc* (n. 48).

[109] See also *Froot Loops Trade Mark* (n. 79) (the trade mark is understood as fruit loops and, as such, describes the cereals involved); *Eurolamb Trade Mark* (n. 77) (the trade mark means European lamb and that is a description of the product).

[110] *Philips Electronics NV v. Remington Consumer Products Ltd* (n. 13).

West (t/a Eastenders) v. Fuller Smith & Turner plc[111] raised interesting questions concerning s. 3(1) of the 1994 Act. The trade mark concerned was 'E.S.B.' (an acronym of Extra Strong Bitter) and its revocation was sought on the basis that it was devoid of distinctive character and that it was merely descriptive. In relation to the descriptiveness argument, the Court of Appeal held that s. 3(1)(c) of the Act did not present a high hurdle to an applicant. The principles summarized by the judge in the following four propositions were held to be correct:

(1) s. 3(1)(b), (c), and (d) were not designed to exclude from registration marks that merely possessed an indirect descriptive connotation—the words 'devoid of any' in subsection (b) and 'exclusively' in (c) were to be given effect to;

(2) the fact that some mental activity was necessary to discern a reference to the quality, or characteristic, of the goods could assist in its registrability;

(3) uncertainty as to the precise nature of the reference to the quality or character of the goods would also be of assistance; and

(4) marks that could only refer to the quality or character of the goods had to be refused registration, because such a mark did not *'differ from the usual way of designating the goods or their characteristics'* and because it might serve in normal usage, from a customer's point of view, to designate the relevant goods either directly or indirectly, or by reference to one of their essential characteristics.[112]

But an application to register the sign TDI for cars and their engines failed as in the car world it is generally known that the sign consists merely of the first letters of the words contained in the expressions 'turbo direct injection' or 'turbo diesel injection'.[113] Point (4) of the propositions seems to apply and the consumer will not see TDI as referring to a single brand of cars.

Common words

The distinctive character of trade marks that consist of common words has also taken up a lot the time in the courts. The European Court of Justice held, in *Procter v. Gamble Co. v. OHIM* (the *Baby-Dry* case),[114] that the combination of the words 'baby' and 'dry' was not simply descriptive, and that the distinctive character of the mark could be established. In order to do so, the Court held that the descriptive character does not solely relate to the individual words, but also to the sign of which they form part. The distinctive character can, in other words, be shown by any difference in use and expression between the combination of words and the normal terminology, and the normal use of the words in everyday language. In the *Baby-Dry* case, the distinctive character was derived from the fact that the words 'baby' and 'dry' are not normally used in that particular combination in relation to nappies. Such a difference should be in relation to important aspects of form or meaning of the sign. It is submitted that the key element in the *Baby-Dry* case was, indeed, the fact that, while common words were used, they were used in a weird combination that, on its own, is not a common word and that is not part of normal everyday language.

The debate surrounding trade marks that consist of common words continued though and came to a climax in the *Doublemint* case.[115] Wrigley wanted to register 'Doublemint'

---

[111] [2003] FSR 816.

[112] [2003] FSR 816 at 829. See also Case T-426/11 *Maharishi Foundation v. OHIM*, 6 February 2013, <http://curia.europa.eu>.

[113] Case T-318/09, *Audi and Volkswagen v. OHIM* [2011] ETMR 61.

[114] Case C-383/99 P [2001] ECR I-6251, [2002] Ch 82.

[115] Case C-191/01 P, *OHIM v. Wm Wrigley Jr Co.* [2004] RPC 327, [2004] ETMR 121.

as a trade mark for mint-flavoured chewing gum. The European Court of Justice was eventually called upon to sort out the *Doublemint* saga. The key question was whether the absolute ground for refusal of marks that are descriptive under s. 3(1)(c) of the 1994 Act applies only if the mark is exclusively descriptive. The Court of First Instance had held that the word 'Doublemint' was not exclusively descriptive in this case.[116] It found that the adjective 'double' was unusual when compared with other English words, such as 'much', 'strong', 'extra', 'best', or 'finest', and that, when combined with the word 'mint', it had two distinct meanings for the potential consumer: twice the usual amount of mint or flavoured with two varieties of mint. Furthermore, it found that mint is a generic term that includes spearmint, peppermint, and other culinary herbs, and that there are several possible ways of combining two sorts of mint and, in addition, various strengths of flavour are possible in the case of each combination. The registration had therefore been allowed.

On appeal, the Court of Justice overturned that decision.[117] According to the Court, s. 3(1)(c) pursues an aim that is in the public interest—namely, that descriptive signs or indications relating to the characteristics of goods or services in respect of which registration is sought may be freely used by all. That provision accordingly prevents such signs and indications from being reserved to one undertaking alone, because they have been registered as trade marks. In order for the registration to be refused, it is therefore not necessary that the signs and indications composing the mark that are referred to in that section actually be in use at the time of the application for registration in a way that is descriptive of goods or services such as those in relation to which the application is filed, or of characteristics of those goods or services. It is sufficient, as the wording of that provisions itself indicates, that such signs and indications could be used for such purposes.[118] The rule that has been established is therefore clearly that a sign must be refused registration under that provision if at least one of its possible meanings designates a characteristic of the goods or services concerned. Because, at least in one sense, 'Doublemint' was descriptive, its registration as a trade mark therefore had to be refused.[119] It is also not required that the sign is the most common or usual way to describe the goods or services.[120]

Slightly different issues arise, as we saw earlier in relation to distinctiveness, when a descriptive word from another language is used as a mark. In *Matratzen Concord AG v. Hulka SA*,[121] the mark concerned was 'Matratzen', which means 'mattresses' in German. The mark was, however, registered and used in Spain. In Spanish, the word has no meaning and the European Court of Justice ruled therefore that it could be distinctive for mattresses, unless the relevant parties in the member state in relation to which registration was sought were capable of identifying the meaning of the term. Unless the latter situation arises, the mark is not caught by s. 3(1); if, however, the word is descriptive and understood as such by the public, any particular representation of the word will remain caught by the exclusion.[122]

---

[116] Case T-193/99, *Wm Wrigley Jr Co. v. OHIM* [2001] ECR II-417.

[117] *Wm Wrigley Jr Co.* (n. 116).

[118] *Wm Wrigley Jr Co.* (n. 116) and Case C-51/10 P, *Agencja Wydawnicza Technopol v. OHIM* [2011] ETMR 34 at para. 38. See also *Starbucks (HK) Ltd, PCCW Media Ltd and UK Broadband Ltd v. British Sky Broadcasting Group Plc, British Sky Broadcasting Ltd and Sky IP International Ltd* [2012] EWHC 3074 (Ch).

[119] *Wm Wrigley Jr Co.* (n. 116 above).

[120] *Agencja Wydawnicza Technopol v. OHIM* (n. 118).

[121] *Matratzen Concord AG v. Hulka SA* (n. 99).

[122] *Hormel Foods Corp. v. Antilles Landscape Investments NV* [2005] RPC 28.

Arnold J had such a case in front of him with the 'Now' trade mark. Six fine lines arranged in a star or sun shape emanating from the central letter 'o' had been added. But in relation to telecommunication services and broadcasting over the Internet the word 'now' could be held to describe the instantaneous nature of the goods and services. The additions could not change that conclusion. Or in the words of Arnold J:

> Taking all of the evidence into account, I conclude that the CTM is precluded from registration by [section 3(1)(c)] in relation to the services in issue because NOW would be understood by the average consumer as a description of a characteristic of the service, namely the instant, immediate nature of the service. The figurative elements of the CTM do not affect this conclusion.[123]

There is also an obvious overlap between s. 3(1)(b) and (c). A sign that fails to clear one hurdle also often stumbles at the other hurdle. Or as the Court of Justice put it:

> [I]t should be noted, first of all, that, although each of the grounds for refusal to register listed in Article 3(1) of the directive is independent of the others and calls for separate examination, there is none the less a clear overlap between the scope of each of the grounds for refusal set out in Article 3(1)(b) and (c)…
>
> Thus, a sign which, in relation to the goods or services in respect of which its registration as a mark is applied for, has descriptive character for the purposes of Article 3(1)(c) of the directive is therefore necessarily devoid of any distinctive character as regards those goods or services, within the meaning of Article 3(1)(b) of that directive.[124]

A need to look at all of the circumstances

The same approach was used by Advocate-General Ruiz-Jarabo Colomer in his conclusions in *Campina Melkunie BV v. Benelux-Merkenbureau* (the *Biomild* case)[125] and in *Koninklijke KPN Nederland NV v. Benelux-Merkenbureau* (the *Postkantoor* case).[126] He added that, in examining whether a sign is suitable for registration as a trade mark, the trade mark office should not limit its analysis to the sign as it appears in the application; attention should also be paid to all other relevant circumstances and these include the acquisition of distinctive character through use that has been made of the sign, as well as the danger that the average consumer will be confused or misled by the use of the mark for the goods or services in relation of which registration is sought.

The European Court of Justice confirmed the approach in the *KPN Postkantoor* case in the following terms:

> Article 3(1)(c) of Directive 89/104 must be interpreted as meaning that a mark consisting of a word composed of elements, each of which is descriptive of characteristics of the goods or services in respect of which registration is sought, is itself descriptive of the characteristics of those goods or services for the purposes of that provision, unless there is a perceptible difference between the word and the mere sum of its parts: that assumes either that because of the unusual nature of the combination in relation to the goods or services the word creates an impression which is sufficiently far removed from that produced by

---

[123] *Starbucks (HK) Ltd, PCCW Media Ltd and UK Broadband Ltd v. British Sky Broadcasting Group plc, British Sky Broadcasting Ltd and Sky IP International Ltd* [2012] EWHC 3074 (Ch) at para. 116.

[124] Joined Cases C-90/11 and C-91/11, *Alfred Strigl v. Deutsches Patent- und Markenamt* and *Securvita Gesellschaft zur Entwicklung alternativer Versicherungskonzepte mbH v. Öko-Invest Verlagsgesellschaft mbH*, <http://curia.europa.eu> at paras. 20–1. See *Koninklijke KPN Nederland* (n. 65) at paras. 85 and 86; and *Agencja Wydawnicza Technopol v. OHIM* (n. 119) at para. 33.

[125] Case C-265/00, *Campina Melkunie BV v. Benelux-Merkenbureau* [2004] ETMR 821.

[126] *Koninklijke KPN Nederland NV v. Benelux-Merkenbureau* (n. 64).

the mere combination of meanings lent by the elements of which it is composed, with the result that the word is more than the sum of its parts, or that the word has become part of everyday language and has acquired its own meaning, with the result that it is now independent of its components. In the latter case, it is necessary to ascertain whether a word which has acquired its own meaning is not itself descriptive for the purposes of the same provision.

For the purposes of determining whether Art.3(1)(c) of Directive 89/104 applies to such a mark, it is irrelevant whether or not there are synonyms capable of designating the same characteristics of the goods or services mentioned in the application for registration or that the characteristics of the goods or services which may be the subject of the description are commercially essential or merely ancillary.[127]

Three-dimensional marks

It has also been argued that s. 3(1)(c) of the 1994 Act has no relevance for three-dimensional shape of product trade marks. The European Court of Justice has rejected that argument and has added:

> When examining the ground for refusing registration in Article 3(1)(c) of the Directive in a concrete case, regard must be had to the public interest underlying that provision, which is that all three-dimensional shape of product trade marks which consist exclusively of signs or indications which may serve to designate the characteristics of the goods or service within the meaning of that provision should be freely available to all and, subject always to Article 3(3) of the Directive, cannot be registered.[128]

This policy consideration is of crucial importance in relation to the application of s. 3(1)(c) in practice and applies across the board.

The proviso

Obviously, certain—but not all—marks can become distinctive and capable of distinguishing through use,[129] and through educating the public that the sign is a trade mark.[130] If there is evidence that this has happened before an application is made to register the marks, then there is no problem. Indeed, in such a case, the position of the applicant is further enhanced by the proviso to s. 3(1)(b)–(d), which provides that, in such a case, registration of the trade mark shall not be refused.[131]

The European Court of Justice has held that this proviso constitutes a major exception to the rules laid down in s. 3(1)(b)–(d).[132] The distinctive character that can be obtained through use must therefore '*serve to identify the product…as originating from a particular undertaking and thus to distinguish that product from goods of another undertaking*'.[133] Only then will the geographical indication—or any of the other items listed in s. 3(1)(c)—have gained a new significance and will its connotation, which is no longer purely descriptive, justify its registration as a trade mark. In making the assessment of

---

[127] *Koninklijke KPN Nederland NV v. Benelux-Merkenbureau* (n. 64). See also *Campina Melkunie BV v. Benelux-Merkenbureau* (n. 125).

[128] Joined Cases C-53/01 and C-55/01, *Linde AG and ors v. Deutsches Patent- und Markenamt* [2003] ECR I-3161 at paras. 76–77.

[129] The Coca-Cola bottle may be seen as an example. The shape of the bottle clearly became a sign that refers uniquely to the Coca-Cola Company.

[130] See Jacob J's comments concerning the 'Treat' mark in *British Sugar plc* (n. 48).

[131] For an application, see *Waterford Wedgwood plc v. David Nagli Ltd* [1998] FSR 92.

[132] Cases C-108/97, *Windsurfing Chiemsee Produktions und Vertriebs GmbH v. Boots- und Segelzubehör Walter Huber*; C-109/97, *Windsurfing Chiemsee Produktions und Vertriebs GmbH v. Attenberger* [1999] ECR I-2779.

[133] *Windsurfing Chiemsee Produktions* cases (n. 132).

whether the mark has acquired such a distinctive character, the court may take account of points such as the market share held by the mark; how intensive, geographically wide-spread, and long-standing the use of the mark has been; the amount that the applicant has invested in promoting the mark; the proportion of the relevant class of persons who identify the goods as originating from a particular undertaking as a result of the use of the mark; and statements from trade and professional associations. The final test in this respect is that at least a significant part of the relevant class of persons must identify goods as originating from a particular undertaking because they are labelled with the mark.[134] Or, as the CJEU put it recently:

> the trade mark applicant must prove that the relevant class of persons perceive the goods or services designated exclusively by the mark applied for, as opposed to any other mark which might also be present, as originating from a particular company.[135]

This is the pure origin function of the trade mark. The fact that a significant proportion of people recognize the mark is not sufficient. The mark must be relied on to refer to origin, irrespective of other marks that may also be present.[136]

If this is the case, the distinctive character will have been acquired. *Windsurfing* was of course a case where a real location was used as a trade mark. It is therefore not re-quired that the goods are also manufactured in the desired location. In cases in which a real link between the location and the goods or services is absent, nothing stands, in principle, in the way of registering a geographical location as a trade mark for those goods or services, as long as that location does not evoke any connotation in the mind of the consumer.[137]

A somewhat complex set of facts arose in *Bovemij v. Benelux-Merkenbureau*,[138] in which the mark involved was 'Europolis'. In Dutch (one of the languages spoken in the Benelux), this is a contraction of 'euro' and 'polis', the latter word meaning policy, as in insurance policy. The mark was indeed to be used in relation to insurance. At first glance, the mark therefore failed the test in s. 3(1). The Court ruled that the proviso could only save the application if the sign has acquired distinctive character throughout the member state concerned. For the Benelux, this means the part of the territory for which the ground of refusal exists. When the ground for refusal is based on the use of a language in a part of a member state or in the Benelux, evidence of acquired distinctiveness in that part of the member state or the Benelux will suffice.

As such, there is nothing special about the judgment: it is a logical application of the provision concerned. It is, however, interesting to contrast the decision with another decision of the European Court of Justice on s. 3(1) in *Matratzen Concord AG v. Hulka SA*.[139] It is important to see, though, that the second decision is not concerned with the proviso, but with s. 3(1)(b) and (c) itself. The mark concerned was 'Matratzen', and as that German word is not understood in Spain it is not caught by s. 3(1) in the first place and there is therefore no need to turn to the proviso. On that basis the mark could be distinctive for mattresses.

---

[134] Case T-399/02, *Eurocermex v. OHIM (Shape of a beer bottle)* [2004] ECR II-1391 at para. 42; and Case T-262/04, *BIC v. OHIM (Shape of a lighter)* [2005] ECR II-5959 at para. 61.

[135] Case C-215/14, *Société des Produits Nestlé SA v. Cadbury UK Ltd* [2015] ETMR 50, at para. 67.

[136] See *Société des Produits Nestlé SA v. Cadbury UK Ltd* [2016] EWHC 50 (Ch), implementing *Société des Produits Nestlé SA v. Cadbury UK Ltd* (n. 135) and holding the KitKat shape not to be distinctive.

[137] Cases C-108/97, *Windsurfing Chiemsee Produktions und Vertriebs GmbH v. Boots- und Segelzubehör Walter Huber*; *Windsurfing* (n. 132).

[138] Case C-108/05, *Bovemij v. Benelux-Merkenbureau* [2006] ECR I-7605.

[139] *Matratzen Concord AG v. Hulka SA* (n. 99).

The use that is required to acquire distinctiveness through use may be the result of the use of the mark in conjunction with, or as part of, another registered trade mark. The Court of Justice so held in *Nestlé v. Mars UK*.[140] The case turned around Nestlé's attempt to register 'Have a Break' as a trade mark, while they already had trade marks in the name KIT KAT and in the slogan 'Have a break...have a KIT KAT'.

The proviso to s. 3(1)(b)–(d) of the 1994 Act fits in with its emphasis on factual distinctiveness as being the test for trade mark protection and irrevocably overturns the *York Trailers*[141] decision that had occasioned so much controversy. Thus, whether the mark in question is not distinctive, is exclusively descriptive, or has become a common or generic name will not be a bar to registration if it can be proven that, at that time, the mark was already 100 per cent factually distinctive. This meets head-on one of the strongest objections to the old law of trade marks. But if the mark is registered while still not being distinctive, the registration can normally be declared invalid. The proviso to s. 47(1), however, allows for the mark to stay on the register and for it not to be declared invalid in those cases in which the mark has, after registration, acquired a distinctive character in relation to the goods or services for which it is registered. But it must be added that, in the case of descriptive or laudatory words, the burden of proof will be very high. Evidence of the fact that 60 per cent of the public would recognize the word 'Treat' as a British Sugar Silver Spoon trade mark was held to be insufficient in this respect.[142]

Section 3(2)

Section 3(2) creates further instances of unregistrability arising directly from the extension of trade mark protection to shapes of items. Article 4(e) of the Recast Directive updates the provision slightly and broadens its scope by adding the words 'or another characteristic' to the term 'shape'. The provision will now read as follows:

(e) signs which consist exclusively of:
   (i)   the shape, or another characteristic, which results from the nature of the goods themselves,
   (ii) the shape, or another characteristic, of goods which is necessary to obtain a technical result,
   (iii) the shape, or another characteristic, which gives substantial value to the goods.

There are three grounds that may prevent the mark from being registered. It follows that if one of the grounds is satisfied, the sign cannot be registered as a trade mark. It is irrelevant whether the sign can be denied registration on a number of grounds, as long as one of the grounds is fully applicable to the sign concerned.[143]

Shapes resulting from the nature of the goods and shapes necessary to achieve a technical result

Clearly, there is a risk of overlap between trade marks and other intellectual property rights, and this is addressed by the provision that shapes (in each case exclusively) resulting from the nature of the goods themselves[144] and shapes necessary to achieve a technical result[145] shall not be registered. But how does one determine whether a sign consists exclusively of a shape that results from the nature of the goods themselves? The definition that is

---

[140] Case C-353/03, *Societe des Produits Nestlé SA v. Mars UK Ltd* [2005] ECR I-6135, [2005] 3 CMLR 12.
[141] [1982] 1 All ER 257.
[142] *British Sugar plc* (n. 48), but Jacob J was happy to accept that 90 per cent would clearly do.
[143] *Société des Produits Nestlé SA v. Cadbury UK Ltd* (n. 135) at para. 47.
[144] TMA 1994, s. 3(2)(a).   [145] TMA 1994, s. 3(2)(b).

given to the concept of the goods themselves is vital in this respect. If the goods are defined narrowly—for example, as three-headed rotary shavers in the *Philips* case—any shape mark would be rendered invalid. It could, of course, be argued that the goods should be taken to mean the specification of goods for which the mark is intended to be registered.

Jacob J rejected that argument in the *Philips* case and called the whole issue '*a practical business matter*'.[146] He arrived at his ruling that the goods in the case at issue were electric shavers on the basis of the criterion that this was how things were in practice, as articles of commerce.

The CJEU turned its attention to this particular absolute ground for refusal in *Hauck GmbH & Co. KG v. Stokke A/S*.[147] This case was concerned with the well-known Tripp Trapp chair for children. The functional design features of the chair had been incorporated in the shape mark. The question that arose was whether the ground for refusal of registration may apply only to a sign which consists exclusively of the shape which is indispensable to the function of the product in question or whether it may also apply to a sign which consists exclusively of a shape with one or more characteristics which are essential to the function of that product and which consumers may be looking for in the products of competitors; i.e. are functional features which consumers like to see in any such product, also those of other manufacturers, part of a shape that results from the nature of the goods? The CJEU based its analysis on the single policy consideration underlying Art. 3(1)(e), which is to prevent trade mark protection from granting its proprietor a monopoly on technical solutions or functional characteristics of a product which a user is likely to seek in the products of competitors. Consequently, in order to apply the first indent of Art. 3(1)(e) of the Trade Marks Directive correctly, it is necessary to identify the essential characteristics—that is, the most important elements—of the sign concerned on a case-by-case basis, that assessment being based either on the overall impression produced by the sign or on an examination of each the components of that sign in turn.

The Court emphasized that the ground for refusal of registration set out in the first indent of Art. 3(1)(e) cannot be applicable where the trade mark application relates to a shape of goods in which another element, such as a decorative or imaginative element, which is not inherent to the generic function of the goods, plays an important or essential role. The condition of a shape consisting 'exclusively' of a shape resulting from the nature of the goods would then not be satisfied.

But, an interpretation whereby the provision is to apply only to signs which consist exclusively of shapes which are indispensable to the function of the goods in question, leaving the producer of those goods no leeway to make a personal essential contribution, would not allow the objective of the ground for refusal set out therein to be fully realized. Indeed, an interpretation to that effect would result in limiting the products to which that ground for refusal could apply to (i) 'natural' products (which have no substitute) and (ii) 'regulated' products (the shape of which is prescribed by legal standards), even though signs consisting of the shapes formed by such products could not be registered in any event because of their lack of distinctive character. Account should be taken of the fact that the concept of a 'shape which results from the nature of the goods themselves' means that shapes with essential characteristics which are inherent to the generic function or functions of such goods must, in principle, also be denied registration. These characteristics cannot and should not be reserved to one operator.

---

[146] *Philips Electronics BV v. Remington Consumer Products Ltd* (n. 13) at 305.
[147] Case C 205/13, *Hauck GmbH & Co. KG v. Stokke A/S, Stokke Nederland BV, Peter Opsvik, Peter Opsvik A/S* [2015] CEC 634, [2014] ETMR 60.

As a result, the ground for refusal of registration may apply to a sign which consists exclusively of the shape of a product with one or more essential characteristics which are inherent to the generic function or functions of that product and which consumers may be looking for in the products of competitors.

Alternatively, the problem under s. 3(2) may lie in the fact that the shape of the goods is necessary to achieve a technical result. This was held not to mean that there was no other route to that result;[148] rather it means that, in substance, the shape is motivated by function. The test was established as whether, in substance, the shape solely achieves a technical result.[149] The Philips three-headed rotary shaver shape was held to have been chosen to achieve a technical result and it therefore fell foul of s. 3(2)(b),[150] which approach has now been confirmed by the European Court of Justice. The Court additionally explained in the *Philips* case, that the exclusion from trade mark registrability of a shape that is necessary to achieve a technical result still applies if other shapes could allow the same or a similar result to be reached, as long as the essential features of the shape were chosen to achieve the result.[151]

When Lego attempted to register the shape of their toy bricks as a trade mark and took the case all the way up to the Grand Chamber, the Court of Justice was given the opportunity to restate the law on this absolute ground for refusal. Building on the *Philips* case, the Court started its analysis by stating that this absolute ground for refusal to register must be interpreted in the light of the public interest underlying it, which is to prevent trade mark law granting an undertaking a monopoly on technical solutions or functional characteristics of a product.[152] The rule balances two elements, both of which are likely to help establish a healthy and fair system of competition. On the one hand the prohibition on registration as a trade mark of any sign consisting of the shape of goods which is necessary to obtain a technical result ensures that undertakings may not use trade mark law in order to perpetuate, indefinitely, exclusive rights relating to technical solutions. On the other hand, there is the recognition that any shape of goods is to an extent functional and that it would therefore be inappropriate to refuse to register a shape of goods as a trade mark solely on the ground that it has functional characteristics. That explains the appearance of the terms 'exclusively' and 'necessary' to ensure that solely shapes of goods which only incorporate a technical solution, and whose registration as a trade mark would therefore actually impede the use of that technical solution by other undertakings, are not to be registered. Putting that into practice it was held that the ground for refusal precludes registration of any shape consisting exclusively, in its essential characteristics, of the shape of the goods which is technically causal of, and sufficient to obtain, the intended technical result, even if that result can be achieved by other shapes using the same or another technical solution. One starts by looking at the essential characteristic of the shape, here for example the two rows of studs to connect the toy bricks, and these are excluded from registration if they only incorporate a technical solution in the sense that all essential characteristics

---

[148] Conclusion of Advocate-General Damaso Ruiz-Jarabo Colomer in Case C-299/99, *Philips Electronics BV v. Remington Consumer Products Ltd*, delivered on 23 January 2001, [2001] ETMR 48.

[149] Advocate-General Damaso Ruiz-Jarabo Colomer (n. 148); *Philips Electronics BV v. Remington Consumer Products Ltd* (n. 13).

[150] *Philips Electronics BV v. Remington Consumer Products Ltd* (n. 13).

[151] *Philips Electronics NV v. Remington Consumer Products Ltd* (n. 68).

[152] See Case C-173/04 P, *Deutsche SiSi-Werke v. OHIM* [2006] ECR I-551 at para. 59; *Philips Electronics NV v. Remington Consumer Products Ltd* (n. 68) at para. 78; and Joined Cases C-53/01 to C-55/01, *Linde and ors* [2003] ECR I-3161 at para. 72.

of the shape perform a technical function. It is irrelevant that the result can also be achieved by another shape and that non-essential characteristics of the shape perform other non-technical functions.[153] On that basis the shape of the toy bricks could not be registered.

In *Nestlé v. Cadbury* the question arose whether the scope of the exclusion applies only to the manner in which the goods at issue function, or whether it also includes the manner in which the goods are manufactured. The CJEU opted for a narrow interpretation as the use of the term technical result refers to the outcome only of a particular method of manufacturing the shape in question. The manner of manufacturing is therefore not included in the scope of the exclusion.[154]

Patent and design law may offer alternative routes to intellectual property protection in appropriate cases that are excluded from trade mark law through the operation of s. 3(2). This is also the clear steer given by the CJEU in the *Tripp Trapp* case.[155]

Shapes that give substantial value to the goods

More difficulty is provided by the third exclusion in this group—namely, the exclusion under s. 3(2)(c) of a shape '*which (exclusively) gives substantial value to the goods*'. This is an entirely new provision in the law and has its origins in the trade marks law of the Benelux countries. Taken at face value, it appears to exclude a significant range of products from trade mark protection, because those involved in marketing will obviously seek to attract customers to a product by, among other things, its distinctive shape and, if this ploy succeeds, they will have enhanced the value of the product.

Examples are manifold. The success of the film *Jurassic Park* caused many manufacturers of such foodstuffs as fish fingers and burgers to shape their products so as to resemble dinosaurs. It would be reasonable to assume that this helped the sales of the products and thus the shape gave added value (although there is a query as to whether it gave substantial added value) to the product. Many items of designer clothing or jewellery also seem to fall within this exception, and significant litigation has occurred in the Benelux countries from which this new provision is derived. The guidance provided by Benelux decisions may not be followed in the UK; the 1994 Act does not require reference to be made to it. Nevertheless, it would seem sensible to see what issues this provision can raise. The need for the value conferred by the shape to be substantial has been emphasized,[156] and it must be the shape itself, rather than the overall image of the product, that must be responsible for the extra value.[157]

The section was invoked in the *Philips* case and this gave an English court the opportunity to express itself on the matter for the first time. It was held that the provision excluded '*shapes which exclusively add some sort of value (design or functional appearance or perhaps something else...) to the goods* disregarding *any value attributable to the trade mark* [that is, source identification] *function*'.[158] In the case at issue, the shaving head had an engineering function that rendered it very effective and this was seen as adding substantial value to the product, especially because it had already been held that the shape was not distinctive and could therefore not have a source identification function.

---

[153] Case C-48/09 P, *Lego Juris v. OHIM* [2010] ECR I-8403. See also Case T-164/11, *Reddig GmbH v. OHIM - Morleys Ltd*, 19 September 2012, <http://curia.europa.eu>.
[154] *Société des Produits Nestlé SA v. Cadbury UK Ltd* (n. 135) at paras. 54 and 57.
[155] *Hauck GmbH & Co. KG v. Stokke A/S, Stokke Nederland BV, Peter Opsvik, Peter Opsvik A/S* (n. 147).
[156] *Adidas v. De Laet*, Benelux Court, 23 December 1985, [1985] Jun 38.
[157] *Superconfex v. Burberrys*, Benelux Court, 14 April 1989, [1989] Jun 19.
[158] *Philips Electronics BV v. Remington Consumer Products Ltd* (n. 13), per Jacob J.

The exception is logical in so far as it targets the trade mark protection of the sign when it does not fulfil the traditional trade mark function of source identification. The *Philips* case is an extreme example of such a case, because the sign was held not to be distinctive and capable of identifying a source at all.

A case in which the shape does allow source identification, but nevertheless gives substantive value to the goods presents more of a dilemma. Trade mark protection will necessarily apply to both aspects, comprised in a single shape, and not just to the trade mark function. One needs to keep in mind that the Court of Justice's emphasis on the public interest underlying the ground for refusal, as set out in the *Lego Juris* case in relation to technical effect,[159] applies to this absolute ground for refusal too. In other words, one refuses to grant a trade mark in a shape that gives substantial value to the goods in order to prevent trade mark law granting an undertaking a monopoly on functional characteristics of a product.[160] On top of anything, such a monopoly in a shape that gives substantial value to the product would potentially be of unlimited duration. Other traders have a legitimate right to use the same shape for their competing products. The rule balances two elements, both of which are likely to help establish a healthy and fair system of competition. On the one hand the prohibition on registration as a trade mark of any sign consisting of the shape of goods which gives substantial value to the goods ensures that undertakings may not use trade mark law in order to perpetuate, indefinitely, exclusive rights that go beyond the essential distinctiveness function of a trade mark. On the other hand, there is the recognition that any shape of goods is to an extent functional and that it would therefore be inappropriate to refuse to register a shape of goods as a trade mark solely on the ground that it has functional characteristics. That explains the appearance of the term 'exclusively'. The General Court therefore held in the *Bang & Olufsen* case[161] that all essential elements of the shape of a rather peculiar design of loudspeaker had been chosen merely in function of the peculiar design, as the latter would give additional and substantive value to the product. The consumer would buy the loudspeaker for its design and would be prepared to pay a substantially higher price for it. The shape therefore added substantive value to the goods and registration was denied. The General Court added that the fact that there were other characteristics of the goods, such as the sound quality it produced, that also give substantial value to them was irrelevant.[162] This case is a good example of a shape that gives substantial value to the goods, but it is important to recognize that this case comes at the end of a long story. In an earlier decision the General Court had held that the shape was not devoid of distinctive character. In other words, contrary to what happened in the *Philips* case,[163] the shape was distinctive. Distinctiveness does not seem to stop the application of this absolute ground for refusal to register the shape as a trade mark, but it is important to note that the shape in all its essential characteristics has primarily been chosen for the value it adds to the product and that its distinctiveness is merely a side effect. That seems to be the effect of the insertion in the legislation of the term 'exclusively'. The same logic seems to underpin the Court of Justice's decision in the *G-Star* case. This case dealt with an application for the registration of sloping stitching, contrasting colour bands, seams,

---

159 Case C-48/09 P, *Lego Juris v. OHIM* [2010] ECR I-8403.

160 See Case C-173/04 P, *Deutsche SiSi-Werke v. OHIM* [2006] ECR I-551 at para. 59; *Philips Electronics NV v. Remington Consumer Products Ltd* (n. 69) at para. 78; and Joined Cases C-53/01 to C-55/01, *Linde and ors* [2003] ECR I-3161 at para. 72.

161 Case T-508/08, *Bang & Olufsen A/S v. OHIM* [2012] ETMR 10.

162 *Bang & Olufsen A/S* (n. 161).

163 *Philips Electronics NV v. Remington Consumer Products Ltd* (n. 68).

and further stitching for trousers (G-Star trousers).[164] The national court had accepted that such a sign added substantial value to the goods: the shape of the trousers that resulted from it had indeed become the example par excellence of a style or fashion. That added substantial value, but also made it necessary, from a policy point of view, that other traders could compete with goods of the same style or fashion. The Court of Justice accepted that the emphasis on the stitching had given that particular shape substantial added value. It had become a style wanted by consumers and other traders should be able to offer goods in that style too. But important for our purposes is also that all courts involved seem to accept that the shape was distinctive, as consumers recognize the products of the brand on the basis of it.

Section 3(3)

The next part of the Act, s. 3(3), adds further restrictions. No mark may be registered if, first, it is contrary to public policy or accepted principles of morality or, second, if it would have the effect of deceiving the public.

Morality

The first category will, of course, be one that will be hard to predict given the inherent changeability of such issues as public policy and morality. On the one hand, the Registrar has taken the view that the religious connotations of the word 'Hallelujah' meant that it was inappropriate to allow it as a trade mark for women's clothing,[165] and presumably there would be similar protection granted to, for example, symbols of significance to Muslims or Buddhists. On the other hand, claims that the use of the mark 'Oomphies' for footwear should be refused, because of its connotations of sex appeal and even its potential encouragement for foot fetishists, were ignored and registration allowed in *Re La Marquise Footwear's Application*.[166]

The logic behind these cases seems to be that one needs to look at the intrinsic qualities of the mark. These intrinsic qualities need to contravene generally accepted moral principles for the prohibition to apply.[167] It is not sufficient that the mark is seen as distasteful. Morality demands a stronger reaction and an application to offend against morality is more likely to be one that was calculated to cause outrage amongst a large part of the population.[168] The test applies with the public at large in mind, rather than the specific professional community at which the mark is targeted.[169] Common ground on morality is of course notoriously difficult to find in our modern pluralist and multicultural society. Marks that need to be used in a certain context to become objectionable are not covered by the prohibition. An example of the latter scenario was the mark 'FCUK', which was capable of being seen as a swear word, but whether and to what extent this would be the case depended on the circumstances of its use.[170] It escaped the prohibition. An example of the former scenario was the mark 'Jesus' for clothing. Any commercial use or appropriation of that name would be anathema to Christians.[171] The General Court also refused to register the verbal sign 'PAKI', on an application from a German transport

---

[164] Case C-371/06, *Benetton Group SpA v. G-Star International BV* [2008] ETMR 5.
[165] *Re Hallelujah Trade Mark* [1976] RPC 605.   [166] (1946) 64 RPC 27.
[167] Case T-140/02, *Sportwetten GmbH Gera v. OHIM* [2005] ECR II-3247.
[168] See *Ghazilian's Trade Mark Application* [2002] ETMR 56.
[169] Case T-526/09, *Paki Logistics GmbH v. OHIM*, 5 October 2011, <http://curia.europa.eu> at para. 18.
[170] *Woodman v. French Connection Ltd* [2007] RPC 1.
[171] *Basic Trademark SA's Trade Mark Application* [2005] RPC 25, but religious significance on its own is not sufficient.

company, as an English-speaking audience would necessarily interpret that as a derogatory term for people of Pakistani descent.[172]

Deceiving the public

The second category of prohibited marks in s. 3(3) of the 1994 Act has given rise—in its earlier, but similar, formulations—to more extensive discussion. The subsection itself points out, inter alia, that the deception may arise in connection with the nature of the goods or services, their quality, or their geographical origin. In *Re Royal Worcester Corset Co.'s Application*,[173] trade mark registration was refused for the use of the company's name as a trade mark on corsets, because the application did not distinguish between corsets made by the company in Worcester, Massachusetts, and other corsets, and, in any event, no royal patronage had been conferred on the goods.[174] Thus the proposed mark was doubly deceptive. Likewise, the word 'Orlwoola' could not be registered for use on goods that were not all wool;[175] here the phonetic equivalence gave rise to the deception. More fortunate was the proprietor of the *Queen Diana Trade Mark*[176] used on Scotch whisky. The typical consumer may have assumed that there had been royal patronage of a drink named after the then likely future designation of Diana Princess of Wales, but it was held that there was no deception because—by what, at the time, must have seemed to the proprietor a remarkable stroke of good fortune—the name had been in use since 1971 and this honest use, during which time a reputation had been gained, was sufficient to deny any allegation of deception.

Elizabeth Florence Emanuel v. Continental Shelf 128 Ltd[177] provided the European Court of Justice with an opportunity to explain the underlying provision in the Directive on which s. 3(3)(b) is based. Ms Emanuel is a well-known designer of wedding wear. She registered the trade mark 'Elizabeth Emanuel' for her company. Later, the business, goodwill, and the registered trade mark were assigned to Frostprint Ltd, which immediately changed its name to Elizabeth Emanuel International. Soon afterwards, Ms Emanuel left the business. After another assignment, the new company, with which Ms Emanuel has no links, applied to register another trade mark, 'ELIZABETH EMANUEL'. Ms Emanuel filed a notice of opposition to that application and, in September 1999, she lodged an application to revoke the registered trade mark 'ELIZABETH EMANUEL'. In her view, the registration of her name by a company with which she had no links was likely to deceive the public that still associated her name with wedding gear, but she had no involvement whatsoever in that company's wedding gear.

The Court refused to establish the narrow link between the use of a name and deception, simply because the person whose name is used is no longer involved. In the view of the Court:

(i) A trade mark corresponding to the name of the designer and first manufacturer of the goods bearing that mark may not, by reason of that particular feature alone, be refused registration on the ground that it would deceive the public, ... in particular where the goodwill associated with that trade mark, previously registered in a different graphic form, has been assigned together with the business making the goods to which the mark relates.

---

[172] *Paki Logistics GmbH* (n. 169).   [173] (1909) 26 RPC 185.
[174] See also *Waterford Wedgwood plc v. David Nagli Ltd* [1998] FSR 92 (a case decided under the 1994 Act).
[175] (1909) 26 RPC 185.   [176] [1991] RPC 395.
[177] Case C-259/04, *Elizabeth Florence Emanuel v. Continental Shelf 128 Ltd* [2006] ECR I-3089, [2006] ETMR 56.

(ii) A trade mark corresponding to the name of the designer and first manufacturer of the goods bearing that mark is not, by reason of that particular feature alone, liable to revocation on the ground that that mark would mislead the public,...in particular where the goodwill associated with that mark has been assigned together with the business making the goods to which the mark relates.[178]

The applicant is therefore required to prove actual deception. In the absence of that proof, the right holder that has acquired the trade mark in a bona fide way as a tradable commodity in its own right can continue to use it. Or, having obtained the business, nothing will stand in the way of additional trade mark registrations.

Clearly, s. 3(3) represents a sensible and necessary set of controls.

Section 3(4)

It is not possible to register any mark use of which is forbidden by other laws, according to s. 3(4). The best example of this is the provision preventing the use of red crosses or red crescents for any purpose apart from the humanitarian activities of the Red Cross and related organizations.[179]

Section 3(5)

Section 3(5) prevents registration of specially protected emblems. This is a reference to s. 4, which establishes that the use of a wide range of royal arms and insignia is only allowed with the permission of royalty, and also makes clear[180] that a representation of either the Union Jack or of the national flags of the component countries of the UK shall not be registered if that use would be either misleading or grossly offensive.

There is analogous protection, conferred by s. 4(3), for national emblems and other such insignia of all signatory states to the Paris Convention,[181] and of international agencies of which any Paris Convention state is a member.[182] When the maple leaf symbol that appears in the Canadian flag became the subject of a trade mark application the Court of Justice seized the opportunity to clarify the meaning of this exclusion. State emblems are protected irrespective of whether there is in the mind of the consumer a connection between the mark that is applied for and the emblem. And the protection extends to cases where the emblem was not the whole mark, but only an element of the trade mark applied for. Exact copies of emblems as well as imitations are protected. It is, however, required that the reproduction or imitation do not refer to the image as such (i.e. any maple leaf), but to its heraldic expression. The public had to perceive the mark as an imitation of the heraldic expression of the emblem.[183]

Thus the unauthorized use of a wide range of insignia is controlled as a matter of law, rather than as one of discretion. In this and other ways, the 1994 Act has fulfilled the government's aim of reducing the (inherently unpredictable) discretionary powers of the Registrar.

Section 3(6)

Having said that, however, the final part of s. 3 appears to lead in an entirely opposite direction. Under s. 3(6), a trade mark shall not be registered if the application is made in bad

---

[178] *Elizabeth Florence Emanuel* (n. 177) at paras. 51 and 53.

[179] Geneva Conventions Act 1957, s. 6; *Harrison v. Teton Valley Trading Co. Ltd* [2004] 1 WLR 2577 (CA).

[180] TMA 1994, s. 4(2).   [181] TMA 1994, s. 57.   [182] TMA 1994, s. 58.

[183] Joined Cases C-202/08 P and C-208/08 P, *American Clothing Associates SA v. OHIM, OHIM v. American Clothing Associates SA* [2010] ETMR 3.

faith. The Court of Appeal dealt with the concept of registration in bad faith in *Harrison v. Teton Valley Trading Co. Ltd*.[184] The Court held that, when determining whether an application to register was made in bad faith within s. 3(6) of the 1994 Act, the court was required to consider the applicant's mental state and all of the relevant circumstances of the particular case. And, because registration of a trade mark was designed to enable bona fide proprietors to protect their proprietary rights without having to prove unfair trading, the dishonest person or the person with low standards could not be permitted to obtain such a registration in circumstances under which a person abiding by a reasonable standard would not proceed with the registration. The test, in this respect, is a combined objective and subjective test, and the proper standard is that of acceptable commercial behaviour as observed by reasonable and experienced persons in the particular commercial area being examined—which excludes behaviour that might have become prevalent, but which, on examination, would not be deemed acceptable.

In the case at issue, the applicant had applied to trade mark the name of a drink ('Chinawhite'), the recipe of which he had received from the bar manager of the bar with the same name, which had developed the recipe and made its staff sign an agreement of confidentiality. In the circumstances, a person in the applicant's position, adopting proper standards and despite believing what the bar manager had told him—that is, that he was not bound by such an agreement—would not have applied for a monopoly that would enable him to prevent opponents carrying on their business of selling Chinawhite cocktails and drinks under that name as they presently were. Accordingly, the application to register was made in bad faith.

The Court of Justice went down a very similar path when it was confronted with the bad faith issue in *Lindt & Sprüngli*. In this case a number of competing undertakings had for years been selling chocolate Easter bunnies in similar shapes and presentations. One of them then registered its version and tried to use it to stop the other from making the Easter bunnies with a similar shape and presentation. The question arose whether the application for the trade mark had been made in bad faith. The Court argued that an overall assessment that takes account of all the relevant factors to a specific case needs to be made at the time of the application. Bad faith requires that an intention is shown and that intention needs to be demonstrated on the basis of objective elements arising from the facts of the case. In this case the commercial reality was such that the applicant must have known about the use of the shape by its competitors. That knowledge alone, though, does not prove an intention of bad faith. That element is rather found in the intention to stop others from making the products in that shape. Long undisturbed use by the competitors also points toward the idea that registration is sought to gain an unfair advantage. The fact that technical and commercial constraints limit the competitors' freedom to choose another shape also points in the direction of bad faith. Other factors such as the reputation earned by the sign may, however, point in the opposite direction and they need to be taken into account too. On the facts of the case, though, there were strong indications of bad faith.[185]

Section 3(6) of the 1994 Act was also raised in *Mickey Dees (Nightclub) Trade Mark*,[186] a case that came before the Register of Trade Marks and which, to a certain degree, involved both examples. MD—known as 'Mickey Dee'—had applied for a trade mark in the name 'Mickey Dees' in respect of '*provision of nightclub services; presentation of live*

[184] *Harrison v. Teton Valley Trading Co. Ltd* (n. 179).

[185] Case C-529/07, *Chocoladefabriken Lindt & Sprüngli AG v. Franz Hauswirth GmbH* [2009] ETMR 56.

[186] [1998] RPC 359.

music performances'. He only provided the latter of the range of services listed in the application, however, and, at the same time, he was employed as manager of a nightclub that his employer had baptized Mickey Dees. It was held that he acted in bad faith when he applied for the mark in respect of the provision of nightclub services;[187] his application resulted in his employer being unable to register the trade mark.

A similar result was reached when a sole distributor for the UK registered the 'Travelpro' trade mark in the UK for goods that were very similar to those that he distributed under the contract and in respect of which his US partner had obtained a trade mark registration in the US. The distributor's application was held to have been made in bad faith.[188]

Section 3(6) presents a clear overlap with the earlier provisions of the section: an application that is clearly deceptive, or which implies, without permission, some royal connection, will also be an application not made in good faith. It also overlaps with the protection conferred by s. 5 on owners of previous marks, because clearly a later attempt to register an already registered name is likely to be one made in bad faith. Thus the 'bad faith' exception has potential for considerable use; it may best be regarded as a general catch-all provision.

Relative grounds for refusal of registration

It is now necessary to turn to the second group of unregistrable marks—namely, those that cannot be registered not because of their own inherent problems, but because of the pre-existing presence in the market of other similar or identical marks on other similar or identical goods or services. Section 5 of the 1994 Act and its related provisions provide the relevant rules.[189]

An earlier mark

The first thing to establish is that, in looking at the pre-existing marks that may affect the registrability of a new mark, it is necessary to cast the net widely and look beyond merely what trade marks have been registered in the UK. Section 5 refers to an 'earlier trade mark' and this key phrase is explained by the following section as including all UK marks, the Community trade mark, and trade marks registered through the provisions of the Madrid Protocol, and also applications for trade marks[190] in each case in which that mark has, in effect, an earlier priority date. Even marks that have lapsed are protected for a year after their expiry unless they have not been used in the two years prior to their expiry, according to s. 6(3) of the Act.

That phrase, by virtue of s. 6(1)(c) of the 1994 Act, also covers well-known trade marks—that is, those marks explained by s. 56 of the Act as being well known for the purposes of the Paris Convention—namely, a mark of a person or business from any signatory country who, although not in business or even in possession of business goodwill in the UK, nevertheless has a mark that is well known. It is not clear from the wording of the legislation whether the mark in question has to be well known in the UK or merely in one or more other signatory states. If the latter is the case, then an example of such a mark may be the logo of a major airline, but one that does not fly into the UK; if the former is the case,[191] the airline, in order to benefit from this protection, would have to

---

    [187] [1998] RPC 359.   [188] *Travelpro Trade Mark* [1997] RPC 867.
    [189] See *Wild Child Trade Mark* [1998] RPC 455.   [190] TMA 1994, s. 6(2).
    [191] As suggested by R. Annand and H. Norman (1994) *Blackstone's Guide to the Trade Marks Act 1994*, Oxford: Blackstone Press, p. 31. See also M. Blakeney '"Well-Known" Marks' (1994) 11 EIPR 481.

show that its mark was well known in the UK, which is difficult to disassociate from the presence of goodwill. If the airline is, in fact, used by many UK travellers, this will suggest that it has goodwill in the UK and is also well known, but if it confines itself primarily to flying citizens of its own state, it seems that it will neither be well known in the UK, nor have goodwill here, and thus will not be protected by these provisions.

If there is goodwill in the UK, which will therefore be protected separately by the tort of passing off, a further route exists to protect that goodwill against the possibility of the subsequent registration of an overlapping trade mark. Section 5(4) of the 1994 Act makes clear that registration of a later trade mark will be denied if its use will be prevented by any prior legal right, including by a specific reference the tort of passing off (and also copyright and design law).[192] Thus the holder of a non-proprietary right in goodwill is also regarded as the holder of a relevant 'earlier right', although not an 'earlier trade mark', and this will give rights not under the rest of s. 5, but, for example, in s. 7.

The relative grounds

Having ascertained what is an 'earlier trade mark', it is now necessary to consider the ways in which such a mark will intervene so as to prevent a subsequent registration. The Act offers a three-tier system of protection. This system is, in essence, the same as that used for infringement cases. We therefore refer the reader to the next chapter for a more in-depth analysis.

Section 5(1)

First, and most simply, no trade mark can ever be registered if it is identical to an earlier mark and is used on identical goods or services,[193] this being perhaps a relatively unlikely scenario. The more likely situation is that in which either, or both, the mark, or the goods or services are not identical, but merely similar.

Section 5(2)

So, secondly, a mark must also not be registered if it is *either* identical to an earlier mark and to be used on similar goods and services, *or* similar to an earlier mark and to be used on identical *or* similar goods and services.[194] This is, however, subject to a proviso—namely, that the overlap must cause confusion on the part of the public. So the essential question to ask is whether the similarities in question are likely to confuse. Obviously there is a likelihood that any such proposed mark may already have hit trouble under s. 3 as being either a deceptive mark or one sought in bad faith.

What will be regarded as 'similar' for the purpose of s. 5(2) is unclear, but the courts have experience of considering this type of issue under s. 12 of the 1938 Act. It is clear from the old case law, which still appears to be relevant here, that the question of similarity cannot really be untangled from the necessary presence of confusion. So, in *Re Revue Trade Mark*,[195] 'Revue' had been registered for a range of photographic equipment—including cameras, light meters, exposure meters, binoculars, and other apparatus—and the applicants for a mark in 'Revuetronic' sought to remove it from the register on the grounds of non-use. There was, however, clear use—at the least in relation to binoculars and exposure meters—and this was regarded as evidence of use in the photographic

---

[192] See *Wild Child Trade Mark* (n. 189).   [193] TMA 1994, s. 5(1).

[194] TMA 1994, s. 5(2). For a recent example, see Case T-424/10, *Dosenbach-Ochsner AG Schuhe und Sport v. OHIM - Sisma SpA*, 7 February 2012 and Case T-64/11, *Run2Day Franchise BV v. OHIM - Runners Point Warenhandels GmbH*, 7 February 2012, both available at <http://curia.europa.eu>.

[195] [1979] RPC 27.

trade. The Registrar pointed out that exposure meters were the same type of goods as cameras, flashguns, and other items used in the actual process of photography, but that goods such as projectors and enlargers used in the process of developing the film were in a separate category. Clearly, there may be some confusion between the various items used to take a photograph, but not between those items and the physically quite separate items used to develop the film, elsewhere, later, and often by someone else.

Another illustration of this is the splendid case of *Re Seahorse Trade Mark*.[196] 'Seahorse' was already registered for marine engines, but its proprietor was in the business of making outboard motors for dinghies and suchlike with a horsepower ranging from 1 to 115. A new application was made to register 'Seahorse', again for marine engines, but this time the engines were huge engines designed to power large seagoing ships of over 5,000 horsepower. The registration was allowed, because the different character of the products ensured that there would be no confusion.

Re Hack's Application[197] provides a final instance in which the similarity of the goods was the subject of discussion. The mark 'Black Magic' had already been registered for what remains a widely recognized box of chocolates and the proprietors of that mark objected to the proposed use of the same words on a new brand of laxatives. Evidence that some laxatives were sold with a chocolate flavouring, and further evidence that many shops sold both chocolates and laxatives, combined to enable Morton J to find that there was a clear risk of confusion and thus that the application in respect of laxatives should not be registered.

From cases concerned with the similarity of goods, we can now turn to cases that consider similarities between marks. Again, this will be a question of fact and relevant factors may include not only the mark itself, but also the surrounding circumstances of its use. Clearly, the marks 'Lancia' and 'Lancer' are, in themselves, very similar and, if the products in question were sold in a crowded market or a busy pub, registration of one would not be appropriate if there was a prior registration of the other. In *Re Lancer Trade Mark*,[198] however, the products in question were two types of car. Cars are bought with care, and with the likelihood of inspections, detailed brochures, and guidance (or persuasion) by attentive sales staff. In those circumstances, both could be registered, because all of the circumstances indicated that confusion would not be caused.

Section 5(3)

There is a third level of protection. In certain circumstances, prior use of a mark, whether similar or identical, will prevent a subsequent registration even for totally dissimilar goods or services. This arises in cases in which the earlier mark has gained a reputation and the subsequent use of the same mark in a different context would either take unfair advantage of, or be detrimental to, the distinctive character or repute of the earlier trade mark.[199] This is an entirely new provision in the UK trade mark law[200] and its effect is therefore not entirely clear. It seems to revolve around the mark having developed a reputation such that people associate the mark with that proprietor. It is less clear what form the subsequent use might take. Clearly, if a subsequent trade mark applicant were to seek to use a renowned mark such as, for example, the masthead logo of *The Independent* newspaper as a trade mark on a range of violent videos, clear detriment

---

[196] [1980] RPC 250.   [197] (1940) 58 RPC 91.   [198] [1987] RPC 303.

[199] TMA 1994, s. 5(3). For a recent example, see case T-301/09, *IG Communications Ltd v. OHIM – Citigroup Inc and Citibank NA*, 26 September 2012, <http://curia.europa.eu>.

[200] Although cf. the passing-off case of *Lego System A/S v. Lego M Lemelstrich* [1983] FSR 155, discussed in Ch. 28.

would be caused to the newspaper proprietors—but the phrase 'unfair advantage' appears to go much further.[201] Arguably, any use of a renowned trade mark by another is making an unwarranted and unfair use of the mark to the repute of which the later applicant has done nothing to contribute. It has nevertheless been held that dilution and detriment need to be demonstrated, and cannot simply be assumed to exist.[202] An interesting question arose when a reputation in one member state was invoked to stop the registration of a later trade mark in another member state. The CJEU held that as long as the reputation existed in a substantial part of the EU it did not need to exist in the member state of application. It was sufficient that the risk existed that a commercially significant part of the public knew the mark and would make the connection with the mark applied for. That gave rise to a risk of injury and damage to the trade mark. The registration could then be stopped on the basis of the reputation of the prior mark, in the case in issue a Community trade mark, in another member state.[203]

Thus identical marks used on identical goods lead to immediate unregistrability. In cases in which similarities are involved, it is the presence of confusion that leads to unregistrability. And in those in which identical or similar marks are used on dissimilar goods and services, it is the presence of harm to the reputation of the earlier mark that will prevent registration of the later mark.

In all cases, the consent of the proprietor of the earlier mark negates the operation of the section.[204]

Section 7

This clear framework, designed to ensure that there is no damaging duplication of trade marks, has, however, one clear and surprising exception. This is created by s. 7 of the 1994 Act. This provides that the Registrar can still register a trade mark even when there is already an earlier trade mark as designated by s. 5(1), (2), or (3), or an earlier right, as defined by subsection (4). This possibility arises in cases in which there has been '*honest concurrent use*'[205] of the two marks and this phrase is stated to have the same meaning as in s. 12(2) of the 1938 Act.[206]

In deciding whether the honest concurrent use should be allowed, the principles laid down by Lord Tomlin in *Re Alex Pirie & Sons Ltd's Application*[207] remain relevant. The extent of confusion, the honesty of the parties, the length of the use, and the size of the applicant's trade are all factors to be brought into the equation. Longer use and larger trade will both help the honest applicant.

Problems are caused by this provision. First, the very fact that honest concurrent use may be permitted means that the risk of confusion to the consumer remains a clear possibility, and this clearly undermines and devalues the entire concept of the trade mark as a clear badge of origin, and as a valuable trading asset. Second, the effect of the section is limited in that the presence of earlier rights of all kinds in respect of which there has been honest concurrent use, although no bar to a registration as such, is stated[208] to confer on the proprietor of those earlier rights a right to object to the later registration. The Registrar, in the first place, will then have to decide whether confusion or harm to reputation will ensue from the prospective dual registration. So considerable additional uncertainty will arise from the operation of the section.

---

[201] See H. Carty, 'Do Marks with a Reputation Merit Special Protection?' [1997] 12 EIPR 684.
[202] *Intel Corp. Inc. v. CPM United Kingdom Ltd* [2007] RPC 35.
[203] Case C-125/14, *Iron & Smith kft v. Unilever NV* [2015] ETMR 45.   [204] TMA 1994, s. 5(5).
[205] TMA 1994, s. 7(1).   [206] TMA 1994, s. 7(3).   [207] (1933) 50 RPC 147 at 159–60.
[208] TMA 1994, s. 7(2).

The third problem is, however, more fundamental: there is no provision whatsoever in the Harmonization Directive for an exception of this type. Indeed, the position is quite the opposite under Art. 4, which is the basis of s. 5 of the 1994 Act. Article 4 states clearly that a mark shall not be registered in the cases to which s. 5 of the 1994 Act applies, while s. 7 of the 1994 Act specifically applies as an exception to cases in relation to which s. 5 of the Act would otherwise apply. It is hard to see any reason why the proprietor of an earlier mark whose interests are harmed by a subsequent registration based on the honest concurrent use exception should not jump on the first plane to Luxembourg and require that the European Court of Justice (assuming that no domestic tribunal is so willing) strike out s. 7 of the 1994 Act as being wholly incompatible with both the Directive that it ostensibly seeks to implement and, for good measure, with the Community trade marks system as well.

The examination system

When the 1994 Act was first passed, the Registrar would examine the application on the point of relative grounds and eventually decide whether or not to grant the trade mark. Many other European countries already at that stage had an opposition system instead. An opposition system leaves it to the existing right holders to defend their rights by raising an opposition against a new application that could fall foul of s. 5 of the UK's 1994 Act.

The Act allowed for the eventual introduction of such a system in the UK and this has now happened as of 1 October 2007. The Registrar will still search the relevant registers and send the results to the applicant; if, in the view of the examiner, there are existing marks that conflict with the mark applied for, the applicant is given a choice of whether to continue with the application, to amend it by reducing the list of goods or services, or to withdraw it. If the application is not withdrawn, the Registrar will notify all existing right holders: holders of UK trade marks are notified automatically; EU trade mark owners need to opt in and pay a fee. It is then up to the existing right holders to oppose the registration and launch the opposition procedure.[209]

The final word

Much of the new law on unregistrable marks is nothing but sensible, for the most part building on previous good practice—but the new law provides, in places, for great potential uncertainty, for example in denying registration for shapes that add value to a product and in creating the bad faith exception.

Special marks

So far, we have been concerned entirely with registration by a proprietor of the trade mark that he or she uses him- or herself on his or her own goods. There are now, however, two quite distinct ways in which groups of traders, rather than individuals, can seek a form of joint trade mark that protects their joint, rather than individual, reputation. The

---

[209] The Trade Marks (Relative Grounds) Order 2007, SI 2007/1976 and The Trade Marks (Amendment) Rules 2007, SI 2007/2076. The power to make these changes was conferred on the Secretary of State by TMA 1994, s. 8.

1994 Act retains the pre-existing category of certification marks, but adds the new concept of the collective mark.

Certification marks

Certification marks are unique in that, until 1994, they were the only way in which a group of traders could obtain trade mark protection as a group and also unique in that, then and now, they are the only form of trade mark under which the quality of the product is testified to by the existence of the trade marks. Of course, many trade marks, in reality, make a link in the consumer's mind between the mark and the quality of the goods or services provided, but a mark can equally be created in respect of poor quality goods or services, other than in this field.

The principal provision of the 1994 Act in respect of these marks is s. 50. This defines a certification mark as an indication that the goods or services in question are, by the mark, *'certified by the proprietor of the mark in respect of origin, material, mode of manufacture of goods or performance of services, quality, accuracy or other characteristics'*. Note that this is a mark rather than a trade mark; there appears to be no requirement that the mark is used in the course of trading activity under the 1994 Act.[210] Indeed no such mark can be granted if the proprietors of the certification mark are in the business of supplying goods or services of the kind certified.[211] It will thus normally be a trade association who will seek this type of mark.

Detailed regulations adapting the general trade mark regime to the needs of this different type of mark are found in Sch. 2 to the 1994 Act, but the general principles remain applicable. The main change of any significance is that the geographical origin of goods or services—normally unregistrable unless prior factual distinctiveness can be shown[212]—can be appropriately—indeed, typically—registered as a certification mark, because the origin of goods or services is often the hallmark of their quality. Champagne, from that region of France, would be an excellent example.

Problems of geographical origin arose in one of the few reported cases on these marks. In *Re Stilton Trade Mark*,[213] a certification trade mark was sought by an association of manufacturers of Stilton cheese, a business long associated with the area around the Leicestershire town of Melton Mowbray. The problem arose, however, that Stilton is itself a village some 50 miles away. The court was, however, satisfied that no cheese of any kind had been made in the village for many years, and that there was ample evidence of the connection between the cheese and the Melton Mowbray area so as to justify the award of a certification trade mark.

Unfortunately, the other grounds for refusal of registration in s. 3(1)(c) of the 1994 Act have not been waived and apply equally to certification marks. Thus a certification mark certifying the quality of the goods—as did the mark in the *Stilton* case, for example—which is a criterion in s. 50 of the Act for the grant of such a mark will fall foul of s. 3(1)(c), which excludes quality if a trade mark exclusively consists of a mark indicating the quality of the goods unless prior factual distinctiveness can be shown. Thus the need to show either such distinctiveness or to include other material in the mark, which may not fall within the rules on certification marks, will pose further problems that will, in all likelihood, further restrict the already limited use made of certification marks.

---

[210] Cf. *'Sea Island Cotton' Certification Trade Mark* [1989] RPC 87.
[211] TMA 1994, Sch. 2, para. 4.   [212] TMA 1994, s. 3(1)(c).   [213] [1967] RPC 173.

Collective marks

This is, then, an appropriate moment to introduce the new collective mark. This is introduced into UK law (the concept having long been familiar in Europe and the US) by s. 49 of the 1994 Act. This states that a collective mark is one that '*distinguishes the goods or services of members of the association which is the proprietor of the mark from those of other undertakings*'. Thus the only lawful proprietor of this type of mark will be a trade association.

Again there are detailed rules applying to such marks, found in Sch. 1 to the 1994 Act, but, again, these adapt the mainstream rules to this type of mark. As with certification marks, an indication of geographical origin—but no other matter excluded by s. 3(1) (c)—can be registered as a collective mark, but this does not entitle the proprietor to prohibit others from using such indications themselves, as long as that use is '*in accordance with honest practices in industrial or commercial matters*'.[214] No definition of this phrase is provided.

Such marks, being easier to obtain, may well replace the certification mark over a period of time. In any event, it is easy to envisage situations in which a group of small traders decides to pool their energies and resources, and seek to obtain a collective mark in relation to which it would be beyond them to gain individual trade mark registration, either through lack of resources or, if all in a common trade, because of potential problems with lack of distinctiveness. The 1994 Act has sought to ease the burden placed on the applicant for a trade mark. To a great extent, the criteria for registration have been eased in favour of the applicant and against the exercise of discretion by the Registrar. It is, however, clear from this area of the law in particular that fuller thought could, and should, have been given to the precise drafting of the 1994 Act.

Uses of trade marks

If a trade mark is registered in accordance with the foregoing rules, it confers on the proprietor of the mark exclusive rights in the mark and the right to bring actions for infringement of the mark;[215] the mark becomes an item of personal property.[216] The effect of the registration is to confer these exclusive rights for a period of ten years, which is renewable for further periods of ten years[217]—an extension of the seven-year period provided by the law prior to 1994 and bringing UK law into harmony with that of most other countries.

Given that a trade mark is an item of property, naturally, proprietors of trade marks will wish to trade with them and the 1994 Act understands that this is the case. Clear provisions exist permitting (relatively) unrestricted dealing with trade marks.

Assignment

The first major provision is found in s. 24 of the 1994 Act, which permits assignment or other disposition of a trade mark in just the same way as is the case with any other items of personal property. This right to assign is expressly stated to exist irrespective of whether business goodwill is assigned at the same time or not, and is also capable of being exercised

---

[214] TMA 1994, Sch. 1, para. 3.   [215] TMA 1994, s. 9.   [216] TMA 1994, s. 72.
[217] TMA 1994, s. 42.

in part, rather than wholly: for example, in respect of particular uses of the mark or its application to particular goods. Assignments must be made in writing or, in case of an English company, by the affixing of the company's seal.

Although clearly a sensible provision and one that reflects commercial reality, the ease by which assignment is permitted clearly goes far towards breaking down the traditional link between the mark and its proprietor. This is echoed by s. 32(3) of the 1994 Act, which, as has been seen, insists that the proposed use of the mark has to be declared as part of the registration procedure, but that use does not have to be by the applicant him- or herself and may merely be with his or her consent. Thus use by an assignee will count as use for these purposes, as will use by a licensee.

Licensing

Licensing of trade marks is permitted by s. 28 of the 1994 Act and the sections that follow it. The restriction under the old s. 28 of the 1938 Act on the registration of a mark if the purpose of that registration was to facilitate trafficking or dealing in the mark has been completely swept away,[218] again reflecting the commercial need to use a trade mark as a tradable asset. A licence may be granted in whole, or in part, but, in any event, there is a requirement that, to be valid, the licence must be put in writing by its grantor.[219] A licensee of a trade mark is entitled, subject to any agreement to the contrary, to require the proprietor of the mark to take infringement proceedings if his or her interests are threatened and, in the case of inaction by the proprietor, after two months, the licensee is granted the right to take proceedings in his or her own name.[220] This approach fits in with the fact that a trade mark licence is traditionally seen as a right to use the trade mark, which remains owned by the licensor. Any goodwill created through the use of the trade mark accrues in the mark and is owned by the right holder-licensor.[221]

In many cases, the parties will wish to restrict the number of licences so that the licensee gains the monopoly benefits normally enjoyed by the proprietor of a mark. This can be done in the form of an exclusive licence, under which the licensee has the sole right to use a trade mark, excluding even exploitation by the proprietor of the mark him- or herself.[222] An exclusive licensee has his or her own right to bring infringement proceedings that is not contingent on any action by the proprietor and is, in effect, in the same position as an assignee of the trade mark,[223] subject again to the terms of the agreement.

There is, of course, a problem that arises in relation to exclusive licences. Any such licence has the effect of moving the monopoly right from the originator of the trade mark, who may, in broad terms, be regarded as having deserved such a privilege, to another. Such extensions of monopoly rights have naturally attracted the interest of the EU, but in this area, there are no block exemptions, making the likely interest of EU competition law all the stronger at first glance.

---

[218] For criticism of this provision, see *Re American Greeting Corp's Application* [1984] 1 All ER 426, [1984] 1 WLR 189.

[219] TMA 1994, s. 28(2).   [220] TMA 1994, s. 30(2) and (3).

[221] The latter point seems to have been doubted in *Scandecor Development AB v. Scandecor Marketing AB* [1998] FSR 500, HC and [1999] FSR 26, CA (23 July 1998, unreported). It is submitted, however, that this case must be seen as a special case, due to the fact that the rights in the mark were at first owned by one company and that the licence deal formed part of the splitting-up process of that original company. In general, there is an absolute lack of cases in this area relating to licence contracts.

[222] TMA 1994, s. 29(1).   [223] TMA 1994, s. 31(1).

Registering the transaction

The fact that both assignees and licensees may enjoy rights of action means that care needs to be taken to alert others to the existence of their interests. This is achieved by s. 25 of the 1994 Act, which insists that various transactions relating to trade marks can be registered alongside the mark itself. The process is voluntary in that it is up to, for example, an assignee or licensee to seek registration of the transaction in question, but there is, to put it mildly, an incentive to register the transaction, because, by virtue of s. 25(3), rights against persons claiming a conflicting interest in the mark in ignorance of any such transaction and all the rights of licensees are ineffective in the absence of an application to register the relevant transaction. So, in reality, all affected transactions are likely to be formally registered.

An overview

That the old law needed reform was undoubted: its convolutions and complexities were considerable, and became worse as amendment after amendment was made. Its failure to slot in with internationally recognized approaches was equally regrettable—but does the Trade Marks Act 1994 meet the objective of redressing these difficulties?

The answer must be that, in broad measure, it does. The new law creates a simpler, clearer, and better internationally coordinated approach and this is obviously to be welcomed. There is a pleasing symmetry, too, to the interrelationship and overlap between the principal provisions on registrability, infringement, and revocation, and it reflects an understanding of reality in terms of the need to assign or license trade marks.

That there turned out to be gremlins in the drafting of the new law was inevitable and that there has been, and will have to be, considerable litigation to mark the boundaries of the new law in relation to new types of mark, such as shape and, in particular, tastes and smells, is unavoidable. Less justifiable perhaps are some of the inherently vague items of terminology that, for the most part, are, unsurprisingly, inherited from the Directive. Clearly, it takes time before a clear picture emerges as to what, for example, is a shape that gives value to a product or in what circumstances registration will be refused on the grounds of bad faith. Some clarifications have already been provided, but we are not yet there entirely. The retention of honest concurrent use as a defence seems particularly unfortunate, because it is flying in the face of the words of the Directive itself.

In terms of requirements for registration, the 1994 Act represents a move away from the role of trade mark law as a method of consumer protection and does not have the traditional assurance provided by the mark as a badge of quality. It offers registration to those trade marks that function (as a minimum) as a badge of origin, protecting a business against predatory rivals often engaged in cynical counterfeiting activity. Indeed, in this respect, the best litmus test of the new law—both in its pure domestic context and in its promotion of international accord—is whether it is successful in going at least some way to stemming the tidal wave of blatantly counterfeit goods that form a major blot on our trading landscape.

Further reading

CLARK, J., 'Adorning Shavers with Clover Leaves: *Koninklijke Philips Electronics NV v. Remington Consumer Products Ltd*' (2006) 28(6) EIPR 352.

GIOLA, F., 'Alicante and the Harmonisation of Intellectual Property Law in Europe: Trade Marks and Beyond' (2004) 41(4) CML Rev 975.

HANDLER, M., 'The Distinctive Problem of European Trade Mark Law' (2005) 27(9) EIPR 306.

KITCHIN, D. et al. (2005) *Kerly's Law of Trade Marks and Trade Names*, 14th edn, London: Sweet and Maxwell, Chs. 8 and 9.

MANIATIS, S. and BOTIS, D. (2010) *Trade Marks in Europe: A Practical Jurisprudence*, 2nd edn, London: Sweet and Maxwell, Ch. 4.

MOSCONA, R., 'Bad Faith as Ground for Invalidation under the Community Trade Mark Regulation: The ECJ Decision in Chocoladefabriken Lindt & Sprüngli AG v. Franz Hauswirth GmbH' (2010) 32(1) EIPR 48–50.

THOMPSON, C. and LADAS, B., 'How Green is my Trade Mark? *Woolworths v. BP*' (2007) 29(1) EIPR 29.

26

Trade marks—infringement and revocation

In trade mark law, just as in patent law, the issues of infringement and revocation, although separate, are inevitably interlocked in many examples of litigation. It is typical for a claim that a trade mark has been infringed to be countered by the argument that the trade mark has been wrongly registered in the first place; similarly, a revocation claim may be met by the counter-threat of an infringement allegation. The Trade Marks Act (TMA) 1994 recognizes this symbiosis and the two separate concepts are the subject of well-coordinated legislation. It can be added that, in defining what will amount to an infringement, the Act also indirectly defines the scope of the rights that are given to the trade mark owner.

Infringement

Section 10 of the 1994 Act establishes the basic criteria for an infringement action. It is written to accord with the provisions of s. 5 of the Act, which, as has been seen, is designed to prevent the concurrent use of duplicate or similar marks. If a mark is already on the Trade Marks Register, it is an infringement to use the same mark for the same goods or services.[1] If either, or both, of the two marks and the product in question are similar rather than identical, there will be an infringement if the later use of the earlier mark will be likely to cause confusion to the public.[2] Finally, unauthorized use of an identical or a similar mark, even on totally different goods, will also be an infringement if the repute of the original mark would be harmed by such a use.[3]

This crucial section is worded as follows:

10 Infringement of registered trade mark

(1) A person infringes a registered trade mark if he uses in the course of trade a sign which is identical with the trade mark in relation to goods or services which are identical with those for which it is registered.

(2) A person infringes a registered trade mark if he uses in the course of trade a sign where because—

(a) the sign is identical with the trade mark and is used in relation to goods or services similar to those for which the trade mark is registered, or

(b) the sign is similar to the trade mark and is used in relation to goods or services identical with or similar to those for which the trade mark is registered,

there exists a likelihood of confusion on the part of the public which includes the likelihood of association with the trade mark.

---

[1] TMA 1994, s. 10(1).   [2] TMA 1994, s. 10(2).   [3] TMA 1994, s. 10(3).

(3) A person infringes a registered trade mark if he uses in the course of trade a sign which—

    (a) is identical with or similar to the trade mark, and

    [(b) is used in relation to goods or services which are not similar to those for which the trade mark is registered,][[4]] no longer in force

where the trade mark has a reputation in the United Kingdom and the use of the sign, being without due cause, takes unfair advantage of, or is detrimental to, the distinctive character or the repute of the trade mark.

The Recast Directive contains in its Art. 10 a cleaned-up version of this key provision:

Article 10 Rights conferred by a trade mark

1. The registration of a trade mark shall confer on the proprietor exclusive rights therein.

2. Without prejudice to the rights of proprietors acquired before the filing date or the priority date of the registered trade mark, the proprietor of that registered trade mark shall be entitled to prevent all third parties not having his consent from using in the course of trade, in relation to goods or services, any sign where:

    (a) the sign is identical with the trade mark and is used in relation to goods or services which are identical with those for which the trade mark is registered;

    (b) the sign is identical with, or similar to, the trade mark and is used in relation to goods or services which are identical with or similar to the goods or services for which the trade mark is registered, if there exists a likelihood of confusion on the part of the public; the likelihood of confusion includes the likelihood of association between the sign and the trade mark;

    (c) the sign is identical with, or similar to, the trade mark irrespective of whether it is used in relation to goods or services which are identical with, similar to, or not similar to those for which the trade mark is registered, where the latter has a reputation in the Member State and where use of that sign without due cause takes unfair advantage of, or is detrimental to, the distinctive character or the repute of the trade mark.[5]

Whilst this hopefully clarifies the starting point, we will continue to use the provision of the Trade Marks Act 1994 for our further analysis.

The application of each of these three subsections involves an assessment that is carried out through the eyes of the 'average consumer', who is deemed to be reasonably well informed and reasonably observant and circumspect.[6] The 'average consumer' is a legal construct rather than a real member of the public.[7] In practice this means that the judge can often put him- or herself in the position of average consumer.[8]

Even so, the application of each of the three subsections gives rise to a number of issues. Before turning to these issues, however, one preliminary matter is worth highlighting: a trade mark is often used as a shorthand term to describe the goods—but

---

[4] TMA 1994, s. 10(3)(b) has now been deleted in the aftermath of the *Adidas* case (see later in this chapter), by means of the Trade Marks (Proof of Use, etc.) Regulations 2004, SI 2004/946.

[5] Directive (EU) 2015/2436 of the European Parliament and of the Council of 16 December 2015 to approximate the laws of the Member States relating to trade marks (Recast) [2015] OJ L 336/1.

[6] Case C-342/97, *Lloyd Schuhfabrik Meyer & Co. GmbH v. Klijsen Handel BV* [1999] ECR I-3819 at para. 26.

[7] *Bach and Bach Flower Remedies Trade Marks* [2000] RPC 513.

[8] Case C-201/96, *Gut Springerheide GmbH v. Oberkreisdirektor des Kreises Steinfurt–Amt für Lebensmitterüberwachung* [1998] ECR I-4657; *Dalgety Spillers Foods v. Food Brokers Ltd* [1994] FSR 504; *esure Insurance Ltd v. Direct Line Insurance plc* [2008] EWCA Civ. 842, [2009] Bus LR 438; and *Marks & Spencer Plc v. Interflora Inc and Interflora British Unit* [2012] EWCA Civ 1501. The latter case also deals with the use of surveys on this point.

might this be an infringement of the mark? In other words, exactly how far do the rights of the trade mark owner under s. 10(1) and (2) of the 1994 Act go to stop use in the course of trade?

The judgment of the European Court of Justice in *Holterhoff v. Freiesleben*[9] sheds some light on this. Mr Freiesleben had registered the marks 'Spirit Sun' and 'Context Cut' in relation to diamonds and precious stones. Both marks correspond to a particular cut of precious stone and Mr Holterhoff had used the names to describe the kind of cut to his clients. Did this amount to trade mark infringement? The Court held that it did not, on the basis that the proprietor of a trade mark cannot rely on his or her exclusive right if a third party, in the course of commercial negotiations, reveals the origin of goods that he or she has produced him- or herself and uses the sign in question solely to denote the particular characteristics of the goods on offer for sale, in such a way that there can be no question of the trade mark used being perceived as a sign indicative of the undertaking of origin.

Trade mark infringement requires the 'use in the course of trade' of the goods labelled with the trade mark.[10] It is generally accepted that 'use' includes importation, even if the territorial scope of the 1994 Act is limited to the UK. So what exactly is the meaning of the concepts of 'use' and 'importation'? This is what the judgment of the European Court of Justice in *Class International BV v. Colgate-Palmolive Co. and ors*[11] addressed.

In this case, the goods—branded toothpaste—were lawfully under the external transit procedure or the customs warehousing procedure. There was no evidence that a purchaser had already been found. The Court had to define what was meant by the concept of 'importation' and whether it also covered the external transit procedure or the customs warehousing procedure. The Court held that interference with the exclusive right of the right holder needed to be shown. That exclusive right is necessarily limited to the member state concerned, or to the Community, in the case of a Community trade mark. The interference that may be pleaded consists, in the Court's view, either in the release for free circulation of the goods or an offering or sale of those goods that necessarily entails putting them on the market in the Community. In the absence of such interference, the goods have not been imported and the right holder cannot invoke infringement of its trade mark. In this case, such interference had not been shown, because only warehousing under the customs procedure and the use of the external transit procedure had been demonstrated. The infringement claim was therefore bound to fail.[12]

We now turn to the three main subsections on infringement, s. 10(1), (2), and (3), which each deal with a different form of trade mark infringement.

Section 10(1)

Here we are concerned with the use of a sign that is identical to the trade mark in relation to identical good or services.

---

[9] Case C-2/00, *Holterhoff v. Freiesleben* [2002] ECR I-4187.

[10] Filling cans that carry an infringing sign is therefore not use of the mark if the cans were delivered with the marks on them by the company awarding the contract to fill the cans. Case C-119/10, *Frisdranken Industrie Winters BV v. Red Bull GmbH* [2012] ETMR 16.

[11] Case C-405/03, *Class International BV v. Colgate-Palmolive Co. and ors* [2006] 1 CMLR 14, [2006] 2 WLR 507.

[12] See also *Mastercigars Direct Ltd v. Hunters & Frankau Ltd* [2006] RPC 32.

A sign used in the course of trade

Section 10(1) of the 1994 Act refers to a 'sign' that is allegedly infringing and that is used by the alleged infringer. It is, first of all, necessary to define what is a 'sign' in any particular case.

In the *British Sugar* case,[13] Jacob J took the sign to be the word 'Treat'. The defendant, Robertson, had also used the phrase 'Robertson's Toffee Treat', but the two first words were regarded as added matter that described the goods. 'Treat' was the sign, or label, that was used to distinguish the goods. Additionally, s. 10(1) requires that the sign is used in the course of trade. That does not mean, however, that the sign should be used in a trade mark sense—that is, as a distinctive sign. In the *British Sugar* case, Jacob J gave the example of the phrase '*give your child a treat, give it Robertson's marmalade*'.[14] He argued that the use of the word 'treat' in that sentence, while clearly not used in a trade mark sense, could still come within the provisions of s. 10.[15] On the other hand, the use of the sign 'Crate & barrel', which was identical to the 'Crate & Barrel' mark registered in the UK, on the website of a shop in the Irish capital Dublin was not used in the course of trade in the UK, because the advertisement was merely intended to address a local Irish clientele to the shop premises and because no trade was taking place on the Internet through the website.[16]

One should not be carried away too easily by this 'use in the course of trade' argument, however, and one should, in any case, not rush too easily to the conclusion that there was no use in the course of trade—as the *Arsenal v. Reed* saga demonstrates clearly. Arsenal had registered a series of trade marks in relation to memorabilia. Reed sold Arsenal memorabilia bearing these or similar marks without having obtained a licence from Arsenal Football Club. When sued for trade mark infringement, Reed ran as a defence the argument that there was no use in the course of trade, because he was only using the marks to express loyalty towards the club. In the High Court,[17] Laddie J had accepted Reed's defence, and ruled that such use to express loyalty was not use in the course of trade and did therefore not amount to infringement. Nevertheless, he referred the matter to the European Court of Justice for a preliminary opinion.

That Court[18] disagreed with Laddie J's view and ruled that, in cases such as this, there would be infringement and that it is immaterial that, in the context of the use of the mark, the sign is perceived as a badge of support for, or loyalty or affiliation to, the trade mark proprietor. Laddie J, in his second judgment,[19] argued that, in coming to this conclusion, the European Court of Justice had reached a different conclusion on the facts and had therefore gone beyond its powers. He felt not bound by the judgment and ruled again in favour of Matthew Reed.

On appeal, the Court of Appeal[20] rejected Laddie J's approach to the interpretation and application of the European Court of Justice's opinion. The Court of Appeal's judgment highlights a couple of important points. First, the reference to the European Court of Justice started from the point of view that any decision on infringement hinged on

---

[13] *British Sugar plc v. James Robertson & Sons Ltd* [1996] RPC 281.   [14] *British Sugar plc* (n. 13).

[15] It had been accepted in the Scottish case *Bravado Merchandising Services Ltd v. Mainstream Publishing (Edinburgh) Ltd* [1996] FSR 205—the *Wet Wet Wet* case—that s. 10(1) required use in a trade mark sense. While applauding the outcome of the case, Jacob J disagreed with that view.

[16] *Euromarket Designs Inc. v. Peters* [2001] FSR 20.

[17] *Arsenal v. Reed* [2001] 2 CMLR 481, [2001] RPC 922.

[18] Case C-206/01, *Arsenal v. Reed* [2002] ECR I-7945, [2003] Ch 454.

[19] *Arsenal v. Reed* [2003] 1 All ER 137, [2003] 1 CMLR 382.

[20] *Arsenal v. Reed* [2003] RPC 696, [2003] 2 CMLR 800.

whether or not the use of the mark was use in the course of trade—that is, on trade mark use and an indication of origin. That issue was a separate point and a prerequisite for s. 10(1); if the prerequisite was not met, there was no need to continue the infringement examination under s. 10(1). The Court of Appeal, as well as the European Court of Justice, disagreed. In its view, one has to consider the mark as a property right and the question that needs to be asked is whether the use of the sign causes damage to the trade mark as a property right. In other words, would there be damage to the essential function of the trade mark as a badge of origin? There is therefore no prerequisite, but rather one substantial test that includes the trade issue. There is an inextricable link between the property-essential function issues and the use in the course of trade issue.

In this case, once Mr Reed's memorabilia left his stand, no one was able to determine any more whether they originated from him or from Arsenal. The origin function of the mark was therefore affected. That confusion element is vital in this context. This case is also remarkable because, in this way, it represents the first application of the after-sale confusion doctrine in English trade mark law: the confusion only arose when the consumers and the goods had left Mr Reed's stand.

The comparison

The main point in s. 10(1), and the test for infringement, is the comparison that needs to be made between the use of the claimant's trade mark in a normal and fair manner in relation to the goods for which it has been registered, and the way in which the defendant actually used its allegedly infringing sign, discounting added or surrounding[21] matter or circumstances.[22] For example, the use by the defendant of the surrounding words 'independent' and 'specialist' in combination with the claimant's 'Volvo' trade mark in a style that was similar to that of the registered trade mark had to be discounted.[23] The defendant still used an identical word in the course of trade and that constituted prima facie infringement under s. 10(1).

This brings us back to the test in relation to s. 10(1).

Identical signs

First, this test will have to determine whether the sign and the trade mark can be considered to be identical. *LTJ Diffusion SA v. Sadas Vertbaudet SA*[24] clarifies the application in relation to this issue. When confronted with the question of whether the sign ARTHUR ET FÉLICIE was identical to the mark ARTHUR (mark and sign written in the same way, but in the sign, additional material has been added), the European Court of Justice ruled that a sign is identical with the trade mark if it reproduces, without any modification or addition, all of the elements constituting the trade mark or if, viewed as a whole, it contains differences so insignificant that they may go unnoticed by an average consumer.[25] In that sense, both aural and visual identity may be required. Additions and modification bring the case outside the scope of s. 10(1), which seems to be restricted merely to cases of blatant piracy. In the same way that ARTHUR ET FÉLICIE was not identical

---

[21] See *United Biscuits (UK) Ltd v. Asda Stores Ltd* [1997] RPC 513.

[22] *Origins Natural Resources Inc. v. Origin Clothing Ltd* [1995] FSR 280, repeated obiter in *British Sugar plc* (n. 13).

[23] *Aktiebolaget Volvo v. Heritage (Leicester) Ltd* [2000] FSR 253. The fact that the defendant had, until recently, been an approved Volvo dealer was also a factor in this case; cf. Case C-63/97, *BMW AG v. Ronald Deenik* [1999] ECR I-905, [1999] All ER (EC) 235.

[24] Case C-291/00, *LTJ Diffusion SA v. Sadas Vertbaudet SA* [2003] ECR I-2799.

[25] *Reed Executive plc v. Reed Business Information Ltd* [2004] RPC 767 (CA).

to ARTHUR, COMPASS LOGISTICS was held not to be identical to COMPASS.[26] The criterion of identity is therefore a very strict one, even if the use of the average consumer somewhat blurs the test.[27]

Use in relation to identical goods or services

Second, because the section requires use of the sign in relation to goods or services that are identical to those for which the mark has been registered, one must also determine whether the goods or services in relation to which the allegedly infringing sign is used fall within the specification contained in the trade mark registration.[28]

In the *Treat* case,[29] that meant answering the question of whether Robertson's product was a dessert sauce or a syrup. Jacob J adopted a pragmatic approach on this point. He argued that the words in a trade mark specification should be construed in a practical manner, taking into account how the product is regarded for the purposes of trade. A trade mark specification was, after all, concerned with use in trade. Robertson's spread would hardly be used on desserts; despite the comments on the label, it was marketed in a jam jar and supermarkets regarded it as a spread. The pragmatic conclusion had indeed to be that, for the purposes of trade, it was neither a dessert sauce nor a syrup. Isolated and rare use of the product as a dessert sauce could not change that conclusion. The product was not identical to the goods in relation to which the trade mark was registered and the infringement claim based on s. 10(1) failed.

The CJEU considers that goods will be identical if all goods in relation to which the allegedly infringing mark is used are included in a larger category for which the original trade mark is used. The comparison is also carried out on the basis of the description of the goods for which the trade mark is registered, rather than the description of the goods for which the trade mark is used in practice.[30]

An example

Section 10(1) can have consequences that may surprise at first glance. The trade mark badge is also reproduced faithfully when one produces a scale model of a car. In *Adam Opel AG v. Autec AG*,[31] Opel had also registered its trade mark for toys. When Autec affixed the mark to the scale model, it was held to be a straightforward infringement under s. 10(1). AdWords, on the other hand, proved to be less straightforward.

AdWords

AdWords are a service provided by Internet service providers, such as Google, whereby a trader buys a term as an AdWord, which means in practice that the website of the trader and his little advert will show up on the screen as a promotional link whenever the user searches for that particular term. For the purposes of trade mark infringements matters become interesting when the term that is bought is the trade mark of a competitor. Will the use of the AdWord amount to trade mark infringement? The Court of Justice addressed this question for the first time in *Google v. Louis Vuitton*.[32] Vuitton's trade marks

---

[26] *Compass Publishing BV v. Compass Logistics Ltd* [2004] RPC 809.

[27] *Reed Executive plc* (n. 25).

[28] *Reed Executive plc* (n. 25); see also *Avnet Inc. v. Isoact Ltd* [1998] FSR 16.

[29] *British Sugar plc* (n. 13).

[30] Case T-257/14, *Novomatic AG v. OHIM*, 6 March 2015, <http://curia.europa.eu>.

[31] Case C-48/05, *Adam Opel AG v. Autec AG* [2007] ETMR 33.

[32] Case C-236/08, *Google France Sarl v. Louis Vuitton Malletier SA* [2011] All ER (EC) 411, [2010] ETMR 30, [2010] RPC 19 at para. 121.

had been used as AdWords by third parties and the goods advertised had not necessarily been used as genuine goods. The Court held as a matter of principle that s. 10(1) must be interpreted as meaning that:

> the proprietor of a trade mark is entitled to prohibit an advertiser from advertising, on the basis of a keyword identical with that trade mark which that advertiser has, without the consent of the proprietor, selected in connection with an internet referencing service, goods or services identical with those for which that mark is registered, in the case where that advertisement does not enable an average internet user, or enables that user only with difficulty, to ascertain whether the goods or services referred to therein originate from the proprietor of the trade mark or an undertaking economically connected to it or, on the contrary, originate from a third party.[33]

A typical example of a s. 10(1) scenario is the one where a company selling erotic products owns the trade mark 'Bananabay' and finds out that a competitor has bought 'Bananabay' as an AdWord to advertise its own sales of erotic products. A sign that is identical to the trade mark is then used for identical goods.[34] And there is use in the course of trade even if the sign selected as an AdWord does not appear in the advertisement itself.[35]

The fundamental point behind this which is made by the Court is that in this situation the use of the AdWord amounts to an infringement because the origin function of the trade mark is affected.[36] The trade mark's investment function may also be adversely affected if there is a substantial interference with the owner's use of its trade mark to acquire or preserve a reputation that is capable of attracting consumers and retaining their loyalty.[37] On the other hand, the use of an identical sign by way of AdWord does not have an adverse effect on the advertising function of the trade mark.[38] It is therefore clear that the Court once more starts its infringement analysis from the point of view that the functions of the trade mark must be affected negatively and that that starting point is also the key element in this context. It is to be regretted that the Court fails to take account at this central stage of the balance between the functions of the trade mark, representing the interests of the right holder, on the one hand and countervailing interests, such as those of the consumer, on the other hand. This balance is considered by many to be at the very heart of trade mark law. The Court, however, seems to stick to the functions of the trade mark and then afterwards in the implementation of the rule there is some bending going on to accommodate elements of the balance in order to achieve the desired result.

But by focusing on the functions of the trade mark it does not come as a surprise that the Court held that the origin function is affected and that there is infringement of the trade mark if the packaging of the goods has been removed and if the consequence of the removal is that essential information, such as the information relating to the identity of the manufacturer or the person responsible for the marketing of the product, is missing.

---

[33] *Google France Sarl* (n. 32) at para. 121. See also Case C-558/08, *Portakabin Ltd v. Primakabin* [2010] ETMR 52 and Case C-278/08, *Die BergSpechte Outdoor Reisen und Alpinschule Edi Koblmuller GmbH v. Guni* [2010] ETMR 33.

[34] Case C-91/09, *Eis.de GmbH v. BBY Vertriebsgesellschaft mbH*, order dated 26 March 2010, <http://curia.europa.eu>.

[35] *Eis.de GmbH* (n. 34) at para. 18; and Case C-278/08, *Die BergSpechte Outdoor Reisen und Alpinschule Edi Koblmuller GmbH v. Guni* [2010] ETMR 33 at para. 19.

[36] *Google France Sarl* (n. 32) at paras. 81–4.

[37] Case C-323/09, *Interflora Inc. v. Marks & Spencer Plc* [2012] CEC 755, [2012] ETMR 1, [2012] FSR 3.

[38] *Interflora Inc.* (n. 37) and Case C-236/08 *Google France Sarl* (n. 32) at para. 98.

That means that in certain circumstances one can sue the advertiser who buys the AdWords from Google, but on the other hand Google itself cannot be sued for its automated service. According to the Court 'an internet referencing service provider which stores, as a keyword, a sign identical with trade mark and organizes the display of advertisements on the basis of that keyword does not use that sign' within the meaning of s. 10.[39] The same conclusion applies to the operator of an online marketplace when marks appear in offers for sale displayed on its site.[40] That changes radically when the online market place operator, such as eBay, buys on behalf of the traders using its service AdWords on Google to advertise. eBay's liability was then based on the negative impact on the origin function on the condition that:

> the advertising does not enable reasonably well-informed and reasonably observant internet users, or enables them only with difficulty, to ascertain whether the goods concerned originate from the proprietor of the trade mark or from an undertaking economically linked to that proprietor or, on the contrary, originate from a third party.[41]

And the safe haven provision of the E-Commerce Directive will not provide shelter if the operator of the website provides assistance, in particular, in optimizing the presentation of the offers for sale or their promotion.[42]

The *eBay* case also clarifies that use of the trade mark in advertisements on an online marketplace that are targeted at an audience in a country where the trade mark is protected will as such amount to infringing use in the course of trade of the trade mark, even if the goods are located in a third state when the advertising takes place.[43]

It is remarkable that the Court of Justice is not prepared to transpose its strict approach to signs being (absolutely) identical to the mark to its approach to the question whether the goods or services are identical. On the latter point a much more flexible approach is taken. The *eBay* case was after all decided on the basis of the equivalent in the Directive of s. 10(1). eBay's liability is therefore based on the finding that advertising cosmetics sold by other parties and reserving AdWords is using the trade mark for identical goods or services, despite the fact that it is not eBay but the vendors using its platform that use the trade mark in relation to the cosmetics and their sale. One could argue that this is improper use of s. 10(1) that empties s. 10(2) and its need to prove similarity and confusion from its scope in this context, but one has to agree that in practice the outcome is convenient.[44]

The summary

For a right holder to succeed under s. 10(1), according to the case law, six conditions need to be met:

1. There must have been use of a sign by a third party.

2. That use must have been in the course of trade.

3. The use was without the consent of the trade mark owner.

---

[39] *Google France Sarl* (n. 32).

[40] Case C-324/09, *L'Oréal SA v. eBay International AG* [2012] All ER (EC) 501, [2011] ETMR 52, [2011] RPC 27.

[41] *L'Oréal SA v. eBay* (n. 40).

[42] *L'Oréal SA v. eBay* (n. 40) and Art. 14(1) of Directive 2000/31/EC of the European Parliament and of the Council of 8 June 2000 on certain legal aspects of information society services, in particular electronic commerce, in the Internal Market ('Directive on electronic commerce') [2000] OJ L 178/1.

[43] *L'Oréal SA v. eBay* (n. 40 above).   [44] *L'Oréal SA v. eBay* (n. 40 above).

4. The sign was identical to the trade mark.

5. The use was in relation to goods or services that are identical to those for which the trade mark was registered.

6. The use affected or was liable to affect the functions of the trade mark, in particular its essential function of guaranteeing the origin of the goods or services to consumers.[45]

The use is normally in relation to a third party's goods, but that is not required. The use can also be infringing if the third party uses the sign in relation to the right holder's goods, for example in an advertising context, as long as the functions of the trade mark are affected.[46]

Section 10(2)

Section 10(2) of the 1994 Act resembles s. 10(1). The term 'sign' and the concept of 'use in the course of trade' are used in the same way here as they were in relation to s. 10(1); once more, the comparison that needs to be made is between the use of the claimant's trade mark in a normal and fair manner in relation to the goods for which it has been registered, and the way in which the defendant actually used its allegedly infringing sign,[47] discounting added or surrounding[48] matter or circumstances.[49] The essential difference is that s. 10(2) deals either with a similar, rather than identical, sign that is used in relation to identical or similar goods or services, or with an identical sign, but this time in relation to similar, rather than identical, goods or services. And the use of the allegedly infringing sign must give rise to a likelihood of confusion, because of the similarity.

If we restrict the analysis to s. 10(2)(a) in a first stage, it might be said that the section involves a three-point test (as seen in Figure 26.1):[50]

- Is the sign used in the course of trade?
- Are the goods or services for which the sign is used similar to those in relation to which the trade mark has been registered?
- Is there a likelihood of confusion because of that similarity?

Similarity

The first point of the test requires no further comment; the question of similarity, however, needs some further analysis. That question is wholly independent of the particular mark or of the defendant's sign and similarity constitutes a separate issue that needs to be established independently before one considers the third point of likelihood of confusion. The category of similar goods needs to be defined narrowly, because the trade mark owner should, as a starting point, be encouraged to register the mark for all classes of

---

[45] *L'Oreal SA v. eBay International AG* [2009] RPC 21, [2009] ETMR 53.

[46] Case C-48/05, *Adam Opel AG v. Autec AG* [2007] ETMR 33; and Case C-533/06, *O2 Holdings Ltd v. Hutchinson 3G UK Ltd* [2008] ECR I-4231.

[47] *O2 Holdings Ltd v. Hutchison 3G UK Ltd* (n. 46); and *Och-Ziff Management Europe Ltd and Oz Management LP v. Och Capital LLP, Union Investment Management Ltd and Ochocki* [2010] EWHC 2599 (Ch), [2011] ETMR 1.

[48] See *United Biscuits (UK) Ltd v. Asda Stores Ltd* [1997] RPC 513.

[49] *Origin Natural Resources Inc. v. Origin Clothing Ltd* [1995] FSR 280, repeated obiter in *British Sugar plc* (n. 13).

[50] *British Sugar plc* (n. 13).

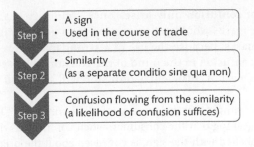

Figure 26.1 Trade mark infringement: similarity and confusion

goods for which he or she wants to use the mark. A comparison of the use, users, and physical nature of the claimant's and the defendant's goods or services, the way in which they were sold or offered, and the extent to which they were competitive were the relevant factors in considering similarity.

When applying these criteria in the *Treat* case,[51] Jacob J arrived at the conclusion that Robertson's spread was not similar to dessert sauces and syrups, because it was different in physical nature (hardly pourable and in need of spooning out, as opposed to pourable), because market research put it in a different sector, and because it was sold in another location in the supermarket. In another case, it was held that television programmes with an adult content were not similar to videotapes and video discs, which were the products in relation to which the claimant had registered his trade mark.[52] In that case, the products were distributed in a different way.

Overall, in assessing similarity, account must be taken of all of the relevant factors that characterize the relationship between the goods or services. Among these factors, one finds the nature, intended purpose, method of use of the goods or services, and whether they are in competition with each other or whether instead they are complementary.[53]

One should not forget, however, that, as a minimum, similarity between the goods or services must be established. Absence of similarity cannot be overcome for the purposes of s. 10(2),[54] not even if the mark is virtually identical to a mark that is distinctive to a very high level.[55] Glassware and wine were held not to be similar, and that meant that there could not be infringement, even if the mark 'Waterford' was used for both.[56]

Confusion

The third point of confusion has created grave difficulties; what is clear is that it can only been treated separately from similarity and once the latter has been established.[57] There is no threshold of similarity, there either is similarity or there isn't.

---

[51] *British Sugar plc* (n. 13).

[52] *Baywatch Production Co. Inc. v. The Home Video Channel* [1997] FSR 22.

[53] Case C-39/97, *Canon Kabushiki Kaisha v. Metro-Goldwyn-Mayer Inc.* [1998] ECR I-5507 at para. 23; Case T-169/03, *Sergio Rossi v. OHIM – Sissi Rossi* [2005] ECR II-685 at para. 54.

[54] *J. W. Spear & Sons Ltd, Mattel Inc and Mattel UK ltd v. Zynga Inc* [2015] EWCA Civ 290, at para. 60.

[55] The similarity requirement applies cumulatively, both between sign and mark on the one hand and between goods and services on the other hand. *Canon Kabushiki Kaisha v. Metro-Goldwyn-Mayer Inc.* (n. 53); Case C-106/03 P *Vedial SA v. OHIM* [2004] RPC I-9573 at para. 51. See also *Daimler AG v. Sany Group Co. Ltd* [2009] ETMR 58.

[56] Case T-105/05, *Assembled Investments (Proprietary) Ltd v. OHIM – Waterford Wedgwood plc*, judgment of the Court of First Instance of 12 June 2007, nyr, <http://curia.europa.eu>.

[57] See *Baywatch Production Co. Inc. v. The Home Video Channel* [1997] FSR 22.

And the question of confusion only arises once similarity has been established.[58] Otherwise, stronger marks would get protection for a greater range of goods or services than weaker marks, because the use of a strong mark in relation to dissimilar goods might create confusion in the mind of the consumer. It is equally clear though that similarity as such is not sufficient. Confusion will also need to be demonstrated (separately).[59]

'Confusion' requires simply that the consumer will be confused.[60] Traditionally, this has been interpreted as meaning that the consumer, when confronted with the similar goods or services that are labelled with the sign, is confused about the origin of these goods or services and thinks that they originate from the trade mark owner. The major problem that arises in relation to this traditional link between confusion and origin is created by the Benelux law-based addition in the 1994 Act that confusion must now include the likelihood of association with the trade mark. Laddie J ruled, in *Wagamama*,[61] that the traditional approach could remain unchanged and that the addition did not change anything in English trade mark law.

That conclusion must now be doubted, however, even though the practical outcome in the *Wagamama* case must be correct. The reason for the doubt is found in the European Court of Justice's decision on the confusion–association point in *Sabel v. Puma*.[62] That case concerned two bounding feline trade marks and the German *Bundesgerichtshof* (Supreme Court) asked the European Court of Justice to explain the relevant provisions of the Trade Mark Directive.[63]

Sabel v. Puma

A careful analysis of the *Sabel* case is required in an attempt to clarify the situation (and the marks are shown in Figure 26.2).

The new concept of confusion

Two views were put to the Court. First, the Benelux countries argued that their concept of association had been incorporated into the wording of the Directive and should be followed.[64] That meant that, in an extreme case, the likelihood of association may arise *'where the public considers the sign to be similar to the mark and perception of the sign calls to mind the memory of the mark, although the two are not confused'*.[65] For example, the 'Sabel' mark would infringe if, when confronted with that mark, the public would associate it with the 'Puma' mark in the sense that the Puma mark would come to mind, without leading the public to confuse the two marks and think that it saw the Puma mark.

Sabel, the Commission, and the UK strongly opposed this view. They argued that the wording of the Directive excluded this interpretation. The Court agreed and argued that:

---

[58] *J. W. Spear & Sons Ltd* (n. 54) at para. 60.

[59] *O2 Holdings Ltd v. Hutchinson 3G UK Ltd* (n. 46).

[60] The 'average consumer', that is. Trade mark confusion is therefore different from that required in passing off. The passing-off idea that a substantial part of the public is confused does not apply to trade mark cases. *Marks & Spencer Plc v. Interflora Inc and Interflora British Unit* (n. 8).

[61] *Wagamama Ltd v. City Centre Restaurants* [1995] FSR 713.

[62] See further P. Torremans, 'The Likelihood of Association of Trade Marks: An Assessment in the Light of the Recent Case Law of the Court of Justice' [1998] IPQ 295–310.

[63] Council Directive 89/104 EEC to approximate the laws of the member states relating to trade marks (1989) OJ L 40/1.

[64] Case 251/95, *Sabel BV v. Puma AG* [1997] ECR I-6191, [1998] 1 CMLR 445 at paras. 14 and 15.

[65] *Sabel BV* (n. 64) at para. 16.

it follows from th[e] wording[66] that the concept of likelihood of association is not an alternative to that of likelihood of confusion, but serves to define its scope[; t]he terms of the provision itself exclude its application where there is no likelihood of confusion on the part of the public.[67]

The Directive only uses the concept of 'association' to define the scope of the concept of 'confusion'. For the purposes of the Directive, there can be no likelihood of association if there is not at least a certain form of confusion.[68] Likelihood of association is not an alternative to, but a way to define the meaning of, likelihood of confusion.[69]

The Court backs its view up with a reference to the '*tenth recital in the preamble of the Directive, according to which "the likelihood of confusion... constitutes the specific condition for such protection"*'.[70] But two types of likelihood of confusion need to be distinguished.[71] First, the straightforward type of direct consumer confusion—that is, confusion as to origin—arises in the situation in which the public sees the sign, and links the goods labelled with it to the trade mark and its owner. In the *Sabel v. Puma* example, such a situation would arise if the public was confronted with the Sabel mark, thought that it saw the Puma mark, and assumed that the Sabel goods originated from Puma.

Figure 26.2 The marks involved

<hr />

[66] Of TMA 1994, s. 10(2)—that is, '*there exists a likelihood of confusion on the part of the public, which includes the likelihood of association with the earlier trade mark*'.

[67] *Sabel BV* (n. 64) at para. 18.

[68] Even the Benelux Court now recognizes that its previous views that were strictly based on association no longer apply under the Directive's regime. Consequently, on the one hand, the owner of a trade mark can oppose the use of a sign that resembles his or her own if the public is likely to be confused (in one way or the other); on the other hand, the possibility that the public may simply associate the two marks because they are worded similarly is, in itself, not enough for there to be infringement: *Val-Valvert*, Benelux Court, judgment of 2 October 2000 [2000] Ing-Cons 361.

[69] Case C-425/98, *Marca Mode CV v. Adidas AG* [2000] All ER (EC) 694, [2000] 2 CMLR 1061; *Canon Kabushiki Kaisha v. Metro-Goldwyn-Mayer Inc.* (n. 53).

[70] *Marca Mode CV* (n. 69) at para. 19.   [71] *Marca Mode CV* (n. 69) at paras. 16 and 17.

The second type of likelihood of confusion is somewhat more sophisticated. In this situation, the public is not directly confused, but it makes a connection between the proprietors of the sign and those of the mark, and confuses them. This type of confusion can be described as indirect confusion or association, and it is here that the inclusion of the concept of association in the concept of confusion plays its widening role. An example would be the situation in which the public connects the Sabel mark with the Puma mark due to the similarity between the two marks and assumes that there is a link between the two trade mark owners. The public might unjustifiably suspect the existence of a licence or any other kind of business link between the two companies involved.[72]

A likelihood of confusion needs, however, to be demonstrated[73] and that assessment needs to be made at global level.[74] There is no ground for presuming the existence of confusion merely because a likelihood of pure association existed, even for highly distinctive marks. Neither is the mere fact that a risk or possibility that an association may give rise to confusion could not be excluded sufficient.[75]

It is submitted that both types of confusion are now covered by the Directive and the 1994 Act, because, whereas the prerequisite of the likelihood of confusion needs to be adhered to, the limitation of the concept of confusion to confusion in relation to the origin of the product or service can no longer be sustained; to do so would be to empty the concept of association of its content. The argument that European trade mark law must now include a finding of infringement in cases in which there is, strictly speaking, no confusion in relation to origin and therefore offers an increased level of protection to the trade mark owner is supported by a number of factors. First, at no point does the Court's judgment refer to the notion of confusion in relation to origin, even if the Advocate-General had made such a reference in his conclusion. Second, in a couple of more recent cases,[76] the Court has given the trade mark owner a right under the trade mark to oppose shoddy advertising of his or her product or shoddy repackaging of it, even if no doubt is created in relation to origin. That must mean that trade mark law must protect more than the original function of the trade mark and that the quality guarantee function of the trade mark is now also protected. In turn, that means that the trade mark must be infringed by confusing associations that affect that guarantee of a certain level of quality.

Assessing the likelihood of confusion

A number of elements can be taken into account when determining whether or not there exists a likelihood of confusion. In *Sabel v. Puma*, the European Court of Justice elaborated on this point.[77] The Court lists, in a non-exhaustive way, a number of factors that are to be taken into account by the national courts in arriving at their decision on the point of likelihood of confusion, but adds that account must be taken of all factors that are relevant in the circumstances of each individual case. The degree of recognition of the trade mark on the market,[78] the degree of similarity between the sign and the trade mark, and between the goods and services that are labelled, as well as the possibilities to make associations with the registered trade mark are factors that the Court borrows

---

[72] *Canon Kabushiki Kaisha v. Metro-Goldwyn-Mayer Inc.* (n. 53).
[73] Mere aural similarity between marks ('Lloyd' and 'Loint's'), for example, can create a likelihood of confusion: *Lloyd Schuhfabrik Meyer & Co. GmbH v. Klijsen Handel BV* (n. 6).
[74] *Reed Executive plc* (n. 25).   [75] *Marca Mode CV* (n. 69).
[76] Cases C-427/93, C-429/93, and C-436/93, *Bristol Myers Squibb v. Paranova* [1996] ECR I-3457, [1997] 1 CMLR 1151; Case C-337/95, *Parfums Christian Dior v. Evora* [1997] ECR I-6013, [1998] 1 CMLR 737.
[77] *Sabel BV* (n. 64) at paras. 22–25 of the judgment.
[78] See also *Canon Kabushiki Kaisha v. Metro-Goldwyn-Mayer Inc.* (n. 53).

from the Preamble to the Directive. Likelihood of confusion is to be assessed globally, taking into account all factors relevant to the circumstances of the case:[79]

> The assessment is carried out through the eyes of the average consumer: For the purposes of that global appreciation, the average consumer of the category of products concerned is deemed to be reasonably well-informed and reasonably observant and circumspect. However, account should be taken of the fact that the average consumer only rarely has the chance to make a direct comparison between the different marks but must place his trust in an imperfect picture of them that he has kept in his mind. It should also be borne in mind that the average consumer's level of attention is likely to vary according to the category of goods or services in question.[80]

It is important to note that the assessment needs to take place at the moment at which the allegedly infringing sign starts to be used. The perception of the public at that stage, as a group of reasonably circumspect individuals, is the starting point.[81] What is assessed is whether there is a likelihood of confusion in that the public might believe that the goods or services originate from the same undertaking or from economically linked undertakings. That assessment must be undertaken in a comprehensive way, by reference to the perception of the relevant public of the goods or services and taking into account all relevant factors of the case that arise from the contact of the public with the sign, the mark, and the goods or services. Particular attention needs to be paid to the interdependence between the similarity of the sign and the mark, and that of the goods or services.[82] Accordingly, a lesser degree of similarity between the goods or services may be offset by a greater degree of similarity between the sign and the mark.[83] Or, to put it in the words of the Court:

> A global assessment of the likelihood of confusion implies some interdependence between the relevant factors, and in particular a similarity between the trade marks and between these goods or services. Accordingly, a lesser degree of similarity between these goods or services may be offset by a greater degree of similarity between the marks, and vice versa. The interdependence of these factors is expressly mentioned in the tenth recital of the preamble to the Directive, which states that it is indispensable to give an interpretation of the concept of similarity in relation to the likelihood of confusion, the appreciation of which depends, in particular, on the recognition of the trade mark on the market and the degree of similarity between the mark and the sign and between the goods or services identified.[84]

One must also take into account the distinctive character of the earlier mark. In particular, its reputation must be taken into account when determining whether there is a likelihood of confusion.[85] The more distinctive the earlier mark, the higher will be the likelihood of confusion.[86] Therefore, highly distinctive marks enjoy broader protection. A good example is a case in which both the sign and the mark involved a cowhide and were used for milk goods.[87] There were, of course, conceptual similarities between the sign and the mark, but there were also strong visual differences. The goods were, of course, entirely similar. It was held that the cow-related nature of the sign and the mark

---

[79] *Sabel BV* (n. 64) at para. 22.
[80] *Lloyd Schuhfabrik Meyer & Co. GmbH v. Klijsen Handel BV* (n. 6) at para. 26.
[81] Case C-145/05, *Levi Strauss & Co. v. Casucci SpA* [2006] ECR I-3703.
[82] Case T-162/01, *Laboratorios RTB v. OHIM – Giorgio Beverly Hills* [2003] ECR II-2821 at paras. 29–33.
[83] Case C-171/06 P, *T.I.M.E. Art Uluslararasi Saat Ticareti ve dis Ticaret AS* [2007] ETMR 38 at para. 13.
[84] *Canon Kabushiki Kaisha* (n. 53) at para. 17.   [85] *Canon Kabushiki Kaisha* (n. 53) at para. 24.
[86] *Lloyd Schuhfabrik Meyer & Co. GmbH v. Klijsen Handel BV* (n. 6) at para. 20.
[87] Case T-153/03, *Inex SA v. OHIM* [2006] ECR II-1677.

made the similarity not very distinctive—that is, that the consumer expects something of that nature in that line of business. The mark was, however, not particularly distinctive. This led to the conclusion that there was no likelihood of confusion.

Another interesting scenario arises when a mark is combined by a third party with its company name in practice: for example, 'Life' and 'Thomson Life', respectively. If the mark still plays an independent distinctive role in the composite mark, and if the goods and services are identical, there can be a likelihood of confusion, even if the mark only has normal distinctiveness.[88]

It is indeed the case in this respect that the more similar the goods or services covered and the more distinctive the earlier mark, the greater will be the likelihood of confusion. And in determining the distinctive character of a mark and, accordingly, in assessing whether it is highly distinctive, it is necessary to make a global assessment of the greater or lesser capacity of the mark to identify the goods or services for which it has been registered as coming from a particular undertaking, and thus to distinguish those goods or services from those of other undertakings. In making that assessment, account is to be taken of all relevant factors and, in particular, of the inherent characteristics of the mark, including the fact that it does or does not contain an element that is descriptive of the goods or services for which it has been registered.[89] It is indeed recognized that, in the case of a largely descriptive mark, small differences may suffice to avoid confusion, because the consumer realizes that other traders are likely to rely on the same descriptive content.[90] The Court added in *Sabel* that the national court is to adopt the perspective of the average reasonably circumspect consumer and that the mark must be considered as a whole. It is clear that, in this perspective, a more distinctive mark will more easily give rise to a likelihood of confusion.[91] The Court specifically cited the German *Bundesgerichtshof* with approval on the point that the overall impression of a mark as a whole, while giving proper weight to special distinctive characteristics, must be the starting point of the analysis.

It is arguable that confusion also covers 'initial interest confusion' whereby the consumer is initially confused, despite the fact that that confusion is resolved by the time the transaction or purchase goes through.[92] And the concept of a family of marks has also been recognized in the context of confusion. A family of marks consists of a series of similar marks registered by the same owner, for example Citibank has registered 'Citi', 'Citicorp', 'Citigold', 'Citicard', 'Citibank', etc. Confusion can then arise when another sign is associated with the family of marks by the average consumer, who may believe the sign is part of the family. That can then result, for example, in confusion as to origin, but only if the earlier trade marks in the family are effectively present on the market.[93]

Section 10(2)(b)

That brings us back to s. 10(2) of the 1994 Act and, in particular, to s. 10(2)(b). Only the second point of the test changes here: the similarity test now applies to the sign and eventually also to the goods or services. Similarity in relation to the sign (when compared to

---

[88] Case C-120/04, *Medion AG v. Thomson Multimedia Sales Germany & Austria GmbH* [2005] ECR I-8551.

[89] *Lloyd Schuhfabrik Meyer & Co. GmbH v. Klijsen Handel BV* (n. 6).

[90] *Reed Executive plc* (n. 25).   [91] *Canon Kabushiki Kaisha* (n. 53).

[92] *Och-Ziff Management Europe Ltd and Oz Management LP v. Och Capital LLP, Union Investment Management Ltd and Ochocki* [2010] EWHC 2599 (Ch), [2011] ETMR 1, with reference to Case C-278/08, *Die BergSpechte Outdoor Reisen under Alpinschule Edi Koblmüller GmbH v. Guni* [2010] ETMR 33 and Case C-558/08, *Portakabin Ltd v. Primakabin BV* [2010] ETMR 52.

[93] Cases C-553/11, *Bernhard Rintisch v. Klaus Eder* [2013] CEC 845, [2013] ETMR 5 and T-301/09, *IG Communications Ltd v. OHIM - Citigroup Inc and Citibank NA* [2013] ETMR 17.

the trade mark) was held to be a question of degree; a degree of similarity is tolerable, provided that the mark and the sign were not confusingly similar.[94] The mark and the sign will be similar when, from the point of view of the relevant public, they are at least partially identical as regards one or more relevant aspects.[95] Once more, all surrounding matter needs to be disregarded, both in relation to the mark and to the sign.[96] The assessment of similarity is to be carried out on a global basis, with reference to the degree of similarity between the mark and the sign. The specific nature of the mark and the sign and of their similarity is relevant on this point.[97] For example, the fact that the mark is the shape of the product itself, without the addition of a fanciful element is relevant.[98] That brings one down to a rule that a sign and a mark are similar when in the eyes of the relevant public there is between them at least a partial identity in relation to one or more essential aspects of the sign.[99] It is therefore clear that a sign that is composed of the mark, with the addition of another word, is likely to be similar to the earlier mark.[100]

There may also be cases in which the mark and the sign are visually different, but phonetically similar.[101] The aural effect of the mark is particularly relevant to the comparison in those cases, but nevertheless the claimant cannot rely on such an aural effect to disregard those distinctive features of its mark that could be seen, but not heard.[102] The assessment of the visual, aural, or conceptual similarity between the sign and the mark is to be based on the overall impression that is made by them on the average consumer.[103] In making that assessment, the distinctive and dominant component of the sign and the mark should be kept in mind.[104] On this basis Red Bull's 'Bullit' trade mark was held to have been infringed by the use by the defendant of the confusingly similar mark 'Bullet'.[105] But Gutter-Clear and Gutterclear UK (in a striking green-black-blue-grey colour scheme) were held to be far less similar than the aural element leads one to believe, as the distinctive colour scheme became the dominant distinctive element of the mark.[106]

One also needs to remember that the consumer only rarely has the chance to make a direct comparison with both the sign and the mark in front of him or her.[107] Instead, the consumer relies on an imperfect recollection of them, and the reality is then that the dominant and distinctive features are most easily remembered.[108] In assessing the overall

---

[94] See the guidance given in *Conran v. Mean Fiddler Holdings Ltd* [1997] FSR 856.

[95] E.g. a naive representation of an elephant, even if it is a single elephant in one case and multiple elephants in a frame in the other. Case T-424/10, *Dosenbach-Ochsner AG Schuhe und Sport v. OHIM – Sisma SpA*, 7 February 2012, <http://curia.europa.eu>: and see also Case T-6/01, *Matratzen Concord v. OHIM – Hukla Germany* [2002] ECR II-4335 at para. 30; and Case T-257/14 *Novomatic AG v. OHIM*, 6 March 2015, <http://curia.europa.eu>, at para. 28..

[96] *United Biscuits (UK) Ltd v. Asda Stores Ltd* [1997] RPC 513 (the supermarket lookalike brands case).

[97] Case C-252/07, *Intel Corp. Inc v. CPM United Kingdom Ltd* [2008] ECR I-8823.

[98] *Whirlpool Corp. v. Kenwood Ltd* [2010] ETMR 7 (CA).

[99] *Matratzen Concord v. OHIM – Hukla Germany* (n. 95) at para. 30; Case T-363/04, *Koipe v. OHIM – Aceites del Sur* [2007] ECR II-3355 at para. 98; and Case T-273/08, *X-Technology R&D Swiss GmbH v. OHIM – Ipko-Amcor BV*, 28 October 2009, nyr, <http://curia.europa.eu>, at para. 29.

[100] Case T-22/04, *Reemark v. OHIM* [2005] ECR II-1559 at para. 40.

[101] See *Conran v. Mean Fiddler Holdings Ltd* [1997] FSR 856 (zinc and the chemical symbol Zn).

[102] *European Ltd v. Economist Newspaper Ltd* [1998] FSR 283.

[103] *Specsavers International Healthcare Ltd v. Asda Stores Ltd* [2012] EWCA Civ 24, [2012] FSR 19 and *Red Bull GMBH v. Sun Mark Limited, Sea Air & Land Forwarding Limited* [2012] EWHC 1929 (Ch).

[104] Case T-292/01, *Phillips-Van Heusen v. OHIM–Pash Textilvertrieb und Einzelhandel (BASS)* [2003] ECR II-4335 at para. 47.

[105] *Red Bull GMBH v. Sun Mark Limited, Sea Air & Land Forwarding Limited* [2012] EWHC 1929 (Ch).

[106] *Envirotecnic v. Gutterclear UK Ltd* [2015] EWHC 3450 (Ch).

[107] Case C-342/97, *Lloyd Schufabrik Meyer* [1999] ECR I-3819 at para. 26.

[108] Case T-104/01, *Oberhauser v. OHIM–Petit Libero (Fifties)* [2002] ECR II-4359 at paras. 47 and 48,

impression, one is therefore not barred from assessing each of its components in order to identify the dominant features. That has led the European courts to decide, for example, that, in principle, there will be similarity between a sign and a mark if one consists of a word that has no conceptual meaning to the public and the second copies that word in combination with another word, which again has no conceptual meaning either alone or in combination, as long as the word found in both is identical, both visually and aurally.[109] But conceptual differences between sign and mark can be such as to counteract, to a large extent, the visual and aural similarities between them.[110]

AdWords

The Court of Justice's case law on AdWords which we discussed in relation to section 10(1) also applies to section 10(2) cases.[111] Once more the starting point will be that the functions of the trade mark must be affected by use of the trade mark in the course of trade. How the typical 10(2) scenario with similarity and confusion, and in the appropriate cases the suggestion that there is an economic link, works out was explained as follows by the Court of Justice:

> In respect of the function of indicating origin, the Court held that the question whether that function is adversely affected when internet users are shown, on the basis of a keyword identical with a mark, a third party's ad depends in particular on the manner in which that ad is presented. The function of indicating the origin of the mark is adversely affected if the ad does not enable normally informed and reasonably attentive internet users, or enables them only with difficulty, to ascertain whether the goods or services referred to by the ad originate from the proprietor of the trade mark or an undertaking economically connected to it or, on the contrary, originate from a third party.
>
> On that point the Court also stated that, in the case where a third party's ad suggests that there is an economic link between that third party and the proprietor of the trade mark, the conclusion must be that there is an adverse effect on the function of indicating origin. Similarly, in the case where the ad, while not suggesting the existence of an economic link, is vague to such an extent on the origin of the goods or services at issue that normally informed and reasonably attentive internet users are unable to determine, on the basis of the advertising link and the commercial message attached thereto, whether the advertiser is a third party vis-à-vis the proprietor of the trade mark or, on the contrary, economically linked to that proprietor, the conclusion must also be that there is an adverse effect on that function of the trade mark.[112]

An attempt at summarizing

The courts have attempted to summarize the approach to s. 10(2) as follows:

(a) The likelihood of confusion must be appreciated globally, taking account of all relevant factors.

---

[109] Case C-120/04, *Medion AG v. Thomson Multimedia Sales Germany & Austria GmbH* [2005] ECR I-8551; Case T-286/02, *Oriental Kitchen v. OHIM–Mou Dybfrost (KIAP MOU)* [2003] ECR II-4953 at para. 39; Case T-22/04, *Reemark Gesellschaft für Markenkooperation mbH v. OHIM–Bluenet Ltd (Westlife)* [2005] II-1559 at para. 37. Use of similar Internet domain names can also amount to an infringement: see *Tesco Stores Ltd v. Elogicom Ltd and anor* [2006] ETMR 91.

[110] Case C-171/06 P, *T.I.M.E. Art Uluslararasi Saat Ticareti ve dis Ticaret AS* [2007] ETMR 38 at para. 13, approving of the Court of First Instance decision in the case and copying the reference to Case T-292/01, *Phillips-Van Heusen v. OHIM – Pash Textilvertrieb und Einzelhandel (BASS)* [2003] ECR II-4335 at para. 54.

[111] Case C-278/08, *Die BergSpechte Outdoor Reisen und Alpinschule Edi Koblmuller GmbH v. Guni* [2010] ETMR 33 and Case C-558/08, *Portakabin Ltd v. Primakabin* [2010] ETMR 52.

[112] Case C-278/08, *Die BergSpechte Outdoor Reisen und Alpinschule Edi Koblmuller GmbH v. Guni* [2010] ETMR 33 at paras. 35–6.

(b) The matter must be judged through the eyes of the average consumer of the goods or services in question, who is deemed to be reasonably well informed and reasonably circumspect and observant, but who rarely has the chance to make direct comparisons between marks and must instead rely upon the imperfect picture of them he has kept in his mind, and whose attention varies according to the category of goods or services in question.

(c) The average consumer normally perceives a mark as a whole and does not proceed to analyse its various details.

(d) The visual, aural and conceptual similarities of the marks must normally be assessed by reference to the overall impressions created by the marks bearing in mind their distinctive and dominant components, but it is only when all other components of a complex mark are negligible that it is permissible to make the comparison solely on the basis of the dominant elements.

(e) Nevertheless, the overall impression conveyed to the public by a composite trade mark may, in certain circumstances, be dominated by one or more of its components.

(f) Beyond the usual case, where the overall impression created by a mark depends heavily on the dominant features of the mark, it is quite possible that in a particular case an element corresponding to an earlier trade mark may retain an independent distinctive role in a composite mark, without necessarily constituting a dominant element of that mark.

(g) A lesser degree of similarity between the goods or services may be offset by a greater degree of similarity between the marks, and vice versa.

(h) There is a greater likelihood of confusion where the earlier mark has a highly distinctive character, either per se or because of the use that has been made of it.

(i) Mere association, in the strict sense that the later mark brings the earlier mark to mind, is not sufficient.

(j) The reputation of a mark does not give grounds for presuming a likelihood of confusion simply because of a likelihood of association in the strict sense.

(k) If the association between the marks causes the public to wrongly believe that the respective goods [or services] come from the same or economically linked undertakings, there is a likelihood of confusion.[113]

Section 10(3)

Finally, we turn to s. 10(3) of the 1994 Act, which deals with infringement of trade marks with a reputation. The original version of the section also required use in relation to dissimilar goods or services, but as will be seen this is no longer the case. There are a number of requirements that need to be met for there to be infringement of the trade mark under this section.[114]

Requirements

First, the sign that is used in relation to the other goods or services must at least be similar to the trade mark. Obviously, the use of an identical sign will also be covered. It can be argued that the similarity of the mark must give rise to a likelihood of confusion

[113] *WHG (International) Ltd, WHG Trading Ltd and William Hill plc v. 32ed plc* [2012] EWCA Civ 19, [2012] RPC 19 at para. 79 and *Och-Ziff Management Europe Ltd and Oz Management LP v. Och Capital LLP, Union Investment Management Ltd and Ochocki* [2010] EWHC 2599 (Ch), [2011] ETMR 1 at para. 73.

[114] See Case T-131/12, *Spa Monopole, compagnie fermière de Spa SA/NV v. OHIM*, 5 May 2015, <http://curia.europa.eu>, for a recent application of the four requirement test.

on the part of the public; otherwise, the arguably illogical result that greater protection was granted in relation to dissimilar goods or services would be reached if, in comparison to s. 10(2), the confusion requirement were dropped.[115] But the requirement that likelihood of confusion is required was doubted by the Court of Appeal in the *One-in-a-Million* case[116] and has now effectively been ruled out by the European Court of Justice.[117]

Second, the mark must also have a reputation in the UK, meaning that not all marks can benefit under this section. The mark must be a strong mark—and this may also explain why likelihood of confusion is not required and why that is not that illogical after all. Strong or famous marks may be entitled to a stronger protective regime. In order to enjoy this stronger protection extending to non-similar goods or services, the European Court of Justice has imposed the requirement that the registered mark must be known to a significant part of the public concerned by the products or services covered by the mark.[118] That significant part of the public can obviously be a significant part of the public in the country concerned, but it can also be a significant part of the public in a substantial part of the country concerned if the goods or services bearing the mark are specifically marketed (only) in that part of the country.[119] Apart from that exceptional scenario, though, there is an expectation that the reputation applies throughout the country concerned. A strictly local reputation in a town and the surrounding area was explicitly rejected.[120] In relation to the Community trade mark the standard case will be that of a reputation throughout the European Union (EU) but, depending on the strength of the reputation, one that exists only in a certain member state can also be acceptable. The minimum requirement is that the reputation must exist in a substantial part of the EU.[121] There are also situations in which a registered mark is effectively used in combination with another mark, e.g. the wordmark SPA for mineral water was used in practice as part of a combination figurative mark that also included a Pierrot device. When the question of the reputation of the SPA mark arose the General Court held that the right holder could rely on evidence of use in a different form in the combination mark and on the reputation of the combination mark provided that the relevant public continued to perceive the goods at issue as originating from the same undertaking when the word mark was used on its own. In those circumstances reliance can be placed on the reputation of another (more complex) mark.[122]

Third, the use of the sign must be without due cause. An example of use that is not without due cause might be found in the car repair business. An independent repairer may be entitled to use a sign that corresponds to the trade mark of a car manufacturer to indicate to the public that he or she specializes in repair work in relation to cars of

---

[115] *Baywatch Production Co. Inc. v. Home Video Channel* [1997] FSR 22.

[116] *British Telecommunications plc v. One In A Million Ltd* [1998] 4 All ER 476, [1999] 1 WLR 903. Aldous LJ was prepared to accept that confusion is required for the purposes of this case.

[117] Case C-408/01, *Adidas-Salomon & Adidas Benelux BV v. Fitnessworld Trading Ltd* [2004] Ch 120, [2004] FSR 401, [2004] 1 CMLR 448.

[118] Case C-375/97, *General Motors Corp. v. Yplon SA* [1999] ECR I-5421, [2000] RPC 572, applied by the third Board of Appeal of OHIM in Case R 551/1999-3, *Hollywood Partners* (unreported).

[119] Case C-375/97, *General Motors Corp. v. Yplon SA* [1999] ECR I-5421, [2000] RPC 572.

[120] Case C-328/06, *Alfredo Nieto Nuño v. Leonci Monlleó Franquet (Fincas Tarragona)* [2007] ECR I-40093.

[121] Case C-301/07, *PAGO International GmbH v. Tirolmilch registrierte Genossenschaft mbH* [2010] ETMR 5.

[122] *Spa Monopole* (n. 114).

that particular make. He or she may, for example, wish to describe him- or herself as an 'independent Mercedes specialist'.[123]

Fourth, that use of the sign must take advantage of, or must be detrimental to, the distinctive character or the repute of the mark.[124] This requirement effectively adds to the similarity requirement and can be seen as a more flexible alternative to the likelihood of confusion requirement. On the one hand, a negative example by means of which unfair advantage might be demonstrated arose when Daimler Chrysler sued a clothing retailer who used the name 'Merc' for his cloths.[125] The court acknowledged that the mark 'Merc' was commonly used as an abbreviation of the mark 'Mercedes', which had been registered by the claimant, but, in the light of the defendant's long-standing use of the mark and the claimant's recent entry in the clothing market, no unfair advantage or damage to reputation could be established. On the other hand, by way of a positive example, it was held, when cyberpirates registered domain names comprising the trade marks of well-known companies, that this use of a similar sign—for example, 'sainsburys.com'—did come under s. 10(3) and the use was held to be detrimental to the marks by damaging the claimant's exclusivity.[126] It was accepted that the domain names were registered to take advantage of the distinctive character and reputation of the mark, and that this was unfair and detrimental.[127] It was also held, in that case, that use in the course of trade meant use in the course of business, without requiring use of a trade mark. The use of a trade mark in the course of a business of a professional dealer for the purposes of making domain names more valuable through registration and extracting money from the trade mark owner before handing over the registration was clearly use in the course of trade.[128] Let us therefore summarize the requirements in Figure 26.3 on the next page.

A wide approach in the courts

Another example of a case that would fit in well under s. 10(3) is the controversial Benelux case *Claeryn/Klarein*.[129] Because of their phonetic similarity in Dutch, these were similar signs and they were used in relation to gin and a toilet cleaner, respectively. That means that there was use in relation to dissimilar products. The finding of infringement in the

---

[123] Case C-63/97, *Bayerische Motorenwerke AG & BMW Nederland BV v. Ronald Karel Deenik* [1999] ECR I-905, [1999] All ER (EC) 235; see also the Opinion of Advocate-General Jacobs in this case of 2 April 1998 (unreported).

[124] *Baywatch Production Co. Inc. v. Home Video Channel* [1997] FSR 22; see also Jacob J's obiter comments in relation to s 10(3) in *British Sugar plc* (n. 13).

[125] *Daimler Chrysler AG v. Alavi (t/a Merc)* [2001] RPC 813.

[126] *Tesco Stores Ltd v. Elogicom Ltd and anor* [2006] ETMR 91.

[127] The territorial nature of trade marks and the global scope of domain names often lead to clashes between trade marks and domain names. The World Intellectual Property Organization (WIPO) has established guidelines in this respect, and its Arbitration and Mediation Centre is very active in resolving these conflicts. The following two cases are examples in which actress Nicole Kidman and the city council of the city of Barcelona (Spain) were able to reclaim domain names that included their marks on the basis of the trade marks that they had registered in their respective names. The fact that the defendant attempted to take unfair advantage of famous names was an important factor in these cases: Case D2000–1415, *Nicole Kidman v. John Zuccarini, d/b/a Cupcake Party*; Case D2000–0505, *Excellentisimo Ayuntamiento de Barcelona v. Barcelona.com Inc.* (both available online at <http://www.wipo.int>).

[128] *British Telecommunications plc v. One In A Million Ltd* [1998] 4 All ER 476, [1999] 1 WLR 903 (CA), in which the first-instance decision was approved: *Marks & Spencer plc v. One In A Million, Ladbrokes plc v. One In A Million, J Sainsbury plc v. One In A Million, Virgin Enterprises Ltd v. One In A Million, British Telecommunications plc v. One In A Million* [1998] FSR 265.

[129] Benelux Court of Justice, 1 March 1975, [1975] NJ 472; see also P. Torremans, 'The Likelihood of Association of Trade Marks: An Assessment in the Light of the Recent Case Law of the Court of Justice' [1998] IPQ 295–310 and the comment made by Jacob J in *British Sugar plc* (n. 13).

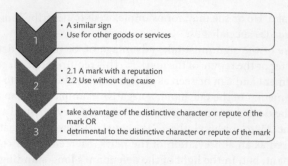

Figure 26.3 The requirements

case was primarily based on the fact that the strong mark was diluted and suffered detriment, because a sign once exclusively associated with gin would now also be associated with a toilet cleaner. Also, no due cause for the use of the sign could be established in this case.

The European Court of Justice has rendered a series of wide-ranging and remarkable judgments in this area. In order to understand these, as well as the new interpretation of the law in this area, a brief return to basics is warranted. Section 10(3) of the 1994 Act, based on Art. 5(2) of the Directive, contains an additional ground for infringement and member states were left to decide whether or not to implement this ground. Trade marks that have a reputation will get additional protection and they will also be infringed through the use of an identical or similar sign in relation to goods or services that are not similar to those in respect of which the mark has been registered. That additional protection is conditional upon the use of the sign being without due cause and taking unfair advantage of, or being detrimental to, the distinctive character or repute of the trade mark.

When the Directive was implemented in the Trade Marks Act 1994, it seemed clear that this was not an overall third layer of rights, but a special rule that dealt with an exceptional situation. First of all, it did not apply to all trade marks, but only to those trade marks with a reputation. The approach seemed to have a lot of similarities with the approach to famous trade marks in the historical Paris Convention for the Protection of Industrial Property 1883: it seemed to represent an equally narrow category. Additionally, there needed to be use of the similar or identical sign without due cause and that use needed to be detrimental to the distinctive character or repute of the trade mark, or it needed to take unfair advantage of that distinctive character or repute, which could be described as the dilution scenario. And, most importantly, the additional protection would only apply when the sign was used in relation to goods or services that were not similar to those for which the trade mark had been registered.

Or would it?

There is, of course, also the argument that the fact that a trade mark has a reputation—that is, that it is not your ordinary trade mark—entitles it to stronger protection. Its reputation gives it a special kind of goodwill, which is both important for the trade mark owner and for the public. Trade mark law should therefore not allow that goodwill to be diluted without due cause as a result of the use of an identical or similar sign over which the trade mark owner has no control. After all, the third party using the sign is free to pick another sign and does not necessarily lose out. Section 10(3) and Art. 5(2), respectively, seem to support this argument. If that is the case, then, why should there be a distinction between use in relation to goods or services that are not similar to those for which the trade mark has been registered, on the one hand, and goods or services that are identical or similar, on the other? The negative impact of dilution is indeed even more likely to be felt, or to be felt more strongly, as a result of use of the sign in relation to identical or similar goods.

Davidoff

The potential problem could, of course, be defused or would not even exist if the concept of taking unfair advantage of, or of being detrimental to, the distinctive character of the repute of the trade mark were to be, in fact, based on the public being confused. The latter would then cover the use in relation to identical or similar goods or services, and s. 10(3) and Art. 5(2), respectively, would simply expand that same kind of protection for marks with a reputation to use in relation to goods or services that are not similar.

The European Court of Justice was confronted with this issue for the first time when it rendered its judgment in *Davidoff & Cie SA & Zino Davidoff SA v. Gofkid Ltd*.[130] Davidoff objected to the use of the sign 'Durffee' by Gofkid for goods that were similar. It alleged that the use of the similar sign, while not causing confusion, caused its 'Davidoff' mark to be diluted, without there being a good cause for Gofkid to use that sign.

The Court made it clear, first of all, that Art. 5(2)—and thus also s. 10(3) of the 1994 Act—is not based on the concept of confusion, but on a wider concept. In the words of the Court:

> where there is no likelihood of confusion, Article 5(1)(b) of the Directive could not be relied upon by the proprietor of a mark with a reputation to protect himself against impairment of the distinctive character or repute of the mark.[131]

But to the surprise of many, the Court went on to hold:

> In those circumstances,…Articles 4(4)(a) and 5(2) of the Directive are to be interpreted as entitling the Member States to provide specific protection for registered trade marks with a reputation in cases where a later mark or sign, which is identical with or similar to the registered mark, is intended to be used for goods or services identical with or similar to those covered by the registered mark.[132]

The Court accepted therefore that marks with a reputation deserve wider protection and that that logic exists not only in a case of use of the identical or similar sign in relation to goods or services that are not similar, but also in relation to similar or identical goods or services.

In *Davidoff & Cie SA & Zino Davidoff SA v. Gofkid Ltd*,[133] however, the Court seemed only to say member states are entitled to provide such a protection. Some of the points were barely spelled out and the exact width of the judgment was not clear, especially because questions could be asked about how this freedom for member states that seemed to go against the specific wording used in Art. 5(2)—'not similar' can hardly be said to mean 'identical, similar of not similar'—could be reconciled with the idea that the Directive would provide a complete harmonization on certain points such as this.

Adidas v. Fitnessworld

Of course, that sparked a lot of debate and there were far more questions than answers in terms of how far the Court really wanted to go—but the debate was fairly short-lived.

---

[130] Case C-292/00, *Davidoff & Cie SA & Zino Davidoff SA v. Gofkid Ltd* [2003] ECR I-389, [2003] 1 WLR 1734.
[131] *Davidoff* (n. 130) at 1735.   [132] *Davidoff* (n. 130) at 1735.   [133] *Davidoff* (n. 130) at 1735.

Nine months after starting the debate in *Davidoff*, the Court handed down a much more robust judgment in *Adidas-Salomon & Adidas Benelux BV v. Fitnessworld Trading Ltd.*[134] The case dealt with the use by Fitnessworld of a motif composed of two parallel stripes of equal width that contrast with the main colour of the item of clothing and which is applied to the side seams of the clothing. The clothing was sold under the name 'Perfetto'. Adidas considered this to amount to the use of a sign that was similar to its trade mark, which consisted of three, very striking, vertical stripes of equal width that run parallel to each other. In the presence of a mark with a reputation and in the absence of confusion in the sense of s. 10(2), this was another case about the use of s. 10(3) in relation to similar goods or services.

Use in relation to identical, similar or non-similar goods or services

First of all, the Court made it clear that, as a result of its decision in *Davidoff*, s. 10(3) could be used to offer anti-dilution-style protection in cases in which the goods or services were identical or similar, not merely in cases in which the goods or services were not similar. It went on to add that:

> where the sign is used for identical or similar goods or services, a mark with a reputation must enjoy protection which is at least as extensive as where a sign is used for non-similar goods or services.[135]

It then concluded:

> In the light of those findings, the Member State, if it transposes Article 5(2) of the Directive, must therefore grant protection which is at least as extensive for identical or similar goods or services as for non-similar goods or services. The Member State's option thus relates to the principle itself of granting greater protection to marks with a reputation, but not to the situations covered by that protection when the Member State grants it.[136]

In other words, the Court opts for a full purposive interpretation of Art. 5(2) and s. 10(3), respectively, even if it goes against the explicit language of the provision. In the Court's view, the logic of the overall scheme of trade mark protection prevails: what had seemed to be an option nine months earlier had now become an obligation for the member states.

Dilution instead of confusion

Once the principle was established, the Court went on to clarify some of the concepts used—which was, indeed, much needed, because a lot of questions had remained unanswered in the aftermath of *Davidoff*.

First, the idea that confusion might be involved as a requirement was buried once and for all when the Court ruled that:

> it must be noted at the outset that, unlike Article 5(1)(b) of the Directive, which is designed to apply only if there exists a likelihood of confusion on the part of the public, Article 5(2) of the Directive establishes, for the benefit of trade marks with a reputation, a form of protection whose implementation does not require the existence of such a likelihood. Article 5(2) applies to situations in which the specific condition of the protection consists of a use of the

---

[134] Case C-408/01, *Adidas-Salomon & Adidas Benelux BV v. Fitnessworld Trading Ltd* [2003] ECR I-12537, [2004] Ch 120, [2004] FSR 401, [2004] 1 CMLR 448.

[135] *Adidas* (n. 134) at 138.   [136] *Adidas* (n. 134) at 138.

sign in question without due cause which takes unfair advantage of, or is detrimental to, the distinctive character or the repute of the trade mark.[137]

A key point of difference with confusion is that the risk that the use without due cause of the mark will take unfair advantage of the distinctive character or the repute of the trade mark continues to exist when the consumer, without necessarily confusing the commercial origin of the product or service, is attracted by the mark for itself and will buy the product or service on the ground that it bears the mark, which is identical or similar to an earlier mark with a reputation.[138] There must, however, be an unfair advantage or detriment to the distinctive character or the repute of the trade mark; that is the essence of the dilution.

The owner of the earlier trade mark, meanwhile, is not required to demonstrate actual or present harm to his or her mark: all that needs to be shown is prima facie evidence of a future risk, which is not hypothetical, of unfair advantage or detriment.[139] The European Court of Justice has left it to the national court to determine whether or not an unfair advantage or detriment will exist, but the burden does not seem to be unduly high, because it was not ruled out that detriment could arise through the use of a trade mark for cars on scale models of those cars.[140]

A link

The crucial concept is, of course, that of 'dilution' and the interpretation that 'dilution' is to be given to the final section of Art. 5(2) and s. 10(3), respectively.

This is the definition put forward by the Court:

> The infringements referred to in Article 5(2) of the Directive, where they occur, are the consequence of a certain degree of similarity between the mark and the sign, by virtue of which the relevant section of the public makes a connection between the sign and the mark, that is to say, establishes a link between them even though it does not confuse them. The existence of such a link must, just like a likelihood of confusion in the context of Article 5(1)(b) of the Directive, be appreciated globally, taking into account all factors relevant to the circumstances of the case.[141]

One needs to be slightly careful with this typical association–dilution requirement in terms of there being a link. One needs to prove that the public makes the link between the sign and the trade mark, and while, until that point, the case seemed to be going Adidas' way, this proved to be its difficulty, because there was evidence that the public saw the Fitnessworld motif as an embellishment rather than as a mark, and did not make the link with the Adidas trade mark. Or, as the Court put it:

> The fact that a sign is viewed as an embellishment by the relevant section of the public is not, in itself, an obstacle to the protection conferred by Article 5(2) of the Directive where the degree of similarity is none the less such that the relevant section of the public establishes a link between the sign and the mark.
>
> By contrast, where, according to a finding of fact by the national court, the relevant section of the public views the sign purely as an embellishment, it necessarily does not establish any

---

[137] *Adidas* (n. 134) at 139.

[138] Case T-215/03, *Sigla SA v. OHIM* [2007] ETMR 79, [2007] Bus LR D 53 at para. 42.

[139] Case T-67/04, *Spa Monopole v. OHIM & Spa-Finders Travel Arrangements* [2005] ECR II-1825, [2005] ETMR 9. See also *Sigla SA* (n. 138) at para. 46.

[140] Case C-48/05, *Adam Opel AG v. Autec AG* [2007] ETMR 33 at para. 36.

[141] Case C-408/01 *Adidas-Salomon & Adidas Benelux BV v. Fitnessworld Trading Ltd* [2004] Ch 120 at 139.

link with a registered mark. That therefore means that the degree of similarity between the sign and the mark is not sufficient for such a link to be established.[142]

The establishment of such a link with the trade mark[143] will then make the unfair advantage or the detriment possible.[144]

Due cause

The one point that the Court did not address was the concept of 'due cause'. Even if all of the other requirements are met, Art. 5(2) will only lead to a finding of infringement if the use of the sign was without due cause. There was clearly no due cause in *Adidas v. Fitnessworld*, but it is not always such a clear-cut case. In other words, it is important to know how strictly the requirement needs to be interpreted. It is submitted that the concept of 'due cause' should be used as a balancing tool to avoid unduly strong protection for marks with a reputation. Arguably there will be a 'due cause' whenever a market operator needs to use the trade mark to communicate effectively with the market, for example to indicate the product for which there is not yet a commonly accepted name, such as the Sedgway, or to indicate a specific expertise in relation to goods made by a the manufacturer whose trade mark is used. One can of course then argue that the word can be used, but not the surrounding matter, such as, for instance, a colour scheme. But 'due cause' defined in such a way goes beyond a mere necessity to use the mark. The CJEU has, for example, held that the earlier use, i.e. before the registration of the trade mark, of a similar sign (The Bulldog, Red Bull being the trade mark) for the same class of goods amounts to use with due cause if the earlier sign is used for identical goods (within the class of registration) in good faith.[145]

This is all the more important as a result of the relative ease with which a link can be demonstrated, which may bring rather a lot of cases within the scope of s. 10(3) when coupled with the low threshold for marks with a reputation that was set out by the Court in the *BMW* case.[146] The fact that the mark must be known to a significant part of the public concerned with the product or service to which the mark is applied is not going to be a major hurdle; the future will tell us whether this broad interpretation of s. 10(3) will effectively do away, in practice, with the careful approach and the restrictions that seemed to have been put in place in relation to association under s. 10(2). It will also make clear whether s. 10(3) will set the norm or whether the courts will tighten up the requirements for reputation, while widening the scope of the due cause exception.

Intel

After *Adidas v. Fitnessworld* the question remained open whether the presence of the link will automatically result in dilution and damage. And the establishment of a link seemed relatively easy as long as the link proved to be a link with the mark. Such a wide approach

---

[142] *Adidas* (n. 141) at 140.

[143] The existence of a family of trade marks is a factor to be taken into account, but nothing more, in this respect if the trade mark is part of a family of trade marks. Case T-301/09, *IG Communications Ltd v. OHIM–Citigroup Inc and Citibank NA*, 26 September 2012, <http://curia.europa.eu>.

[144] *Specsavers International Healthcare Ltd v. Asda Stores Ltd* [2012] EWCA Civ 24, [2012] FSR 19 (straplines providing the link) and *Red Bull GMBH v. Sun Mark Limited, Sea Air & Land Forwarding Limited* [2012] EWHC 1929 (Ch).

[145] Case C-65/12, *Leidseplein Beheer BV and Hendrikus de Vries v. Red Bull GmbH and Red Bull Nederland BV* [2014] ETMR 24.

[146] Case C-63/97, *Bayerische Motorenwerke AG & BMW Nederland BV v. Ronald Karel Deenik* [1999] ECR I-905.

risked making s. 10(3) the norm and to limit s. 10(2) to a small number of cases, whereas in origin the opposite scenario seemed to be the reasonable expectation of almost everyone. The *Intel* case offered the Court of Justice the opportunity to clarify whether this scenario would indeed unfold.[147] Intel is of course the world-famous chip maker and it objected on the basis of its Intel trade mark against the use of 'INTELMARK' for marketing and telemarketing services. The fact that the Intel trade mark has a reputation was beyond doubt.

Turning to the link, one could summarize the Intel argument by saying that the term INTELMARK called to mind the mark Intel. That was allegedly obvious and beyond doubt due to the massive reputation enjoyed by the Intel mark. The Court of Justice rejected that argument. A link between sign and the mark could not be implied and has to be demonstrated.[148] That should be done on the basis of a global assessment that takes account of the similarity between the mark and the sign, the nature of the goods and services for which the mark is registered (including how similar or dissimilar the respective good or services concerned are and the relevant section of the public), the strength of the earlier mark's reputation, the degree of the earlier mark's distinctive character, and the likelihood of confusion on the part of the public. A link was held to be likely to exist if the sign called the mark to mind for the average reasonably well-informed, observant, and circumspect consumer. Nevertheless, a huge reputation for certain types of goods or services was not enough to imply a link.[149]

Such a huge reputation was not enough to imply that the sign would take unfair advantage of or be detrimental to the mark. Focusing on detriment, the Court argued that harm, or at least a serious likelihood of it,[150] should be proven.[151] The existence of a link will not automatically mean the requirement of detriment has been met. Again a global assessment that takes account of all relevant factors is being called for. The bottom line is, though, that the trade mark owner must demonstrate actual harm in the sense that there is a change in the economic behaviour of the average consumer or a serious likelihood that such a change will occur in the future.[152]

When we return to the facts of the case it becomes clear that Intel failed on this point. There was no evidence whatsoever that consumers would buy fewer Intel chips (or computers containing them) as a result of the use of the sign INTELMARK for marketing and telemarketing services. *Intel* puts therefore important limits to the potentially broad application of the link doctrine and of s. 10(3). The link needs to be demonstrated and most importantly detriment needs to be proven through positive evidence of a change in the economic behavior of the consumer.[153]

---

[147] Case C-252/07, *Intel Corp Inc v. CPM United Kingdom Ltd* [2008] ECR I-8823, [2009] RPC 15.

[148] *Intel* (n. 147); the link requirement was again emphasized in Case C-320/07 P, *Antartica Srl v. OHIM* [2009] ETMR 47; see also *Whirlpool Corp. v. Kenwood Ltd* [2010] ETMR 7 (CA). The Court of First Instance held in case T-438/07, *SPA MONOPOLE v. OHM* that the similarity between 'Spago' for alcoholic drinks and 'SPA' for mineral water was not sufficient for a link to be demonstrated in practice. See <http://curia.eu>.

[149] *Intel* (n. 47).

[150] See also Case C-197/07 P, *Aktieselskabet af 21 November 2001 v. OHIM* [2009] ETMR 36.

[151] *Intel* (n. 47). There must be a serious risk that the injury will occur in the future. Case C-100/11 P, *Helena Rubinstein SNC and L'Oréal SA v. OHIM–Allergan Inc*, 10th May 2012, <http://curia.europa.eu>, at para. 93.

[152] *Intel* (n. 147).

[153] *Intel* (n. 47), For another case where lack of detriment was the main issue, see *G-Star International BV v. Pepsico Inc* (Arrondissementsrechtbank The Hague) [2009] ETMR 18.

L'Oréal

Whilst *Intel* provided a lot of clarification, it left at least one point rather vague. The emphasis on the need to prove detriment makes one wonder how all this applies to situations where unfair advantage is being taken. Surely one cannot insist on proof of detriment in those cases. *L'Oréal* was all about unfair advantage and it allowed the Court the opportunity to express itself on that point.[154] In this case the defendant made and sold imitation perfumes. The smells, names, and packaging of the perfumes were similar to the originals made by L'Oréal. It also produced a table of comparison which included both the original perfumes and the imitation perfumes.

The Court held that there was no requirement that there be detriment to the distinctive character of the mark. Taking advantage of the reputation of the mark was sufficient. And in the view of the Court there was an unfair advantage where the third party sought to ride on the coat-tails of the mark with a reputation in order to benefit from its power of attraction, its reputation, and its prestige and to exploit, without paying any financial compensation, the marketing effort expanded by the right holder.[155]

That allowed the Court of Appeal later on to argue that no unfair advantage had been taken and that a s. 10(3) action failed where Kenwood entered the market for kitchen robots with a model that resembled the iconic KitchenAid kitchen robot that is protected by a shape trade mark. Kenwood had after all established its own goodwill in kitchen appliances and it did not ride on the coat-tails of the right holder. In order to compete in a niche market where the right holder and its shape had had a monopoly for years it needed to offer the same basic shape though. That was due to the commercial circumstances and the case was in that sense very different from *L'Oréal*.[156]

Perhaps more controversially, *L'Oréal* confirms also the line started in *Arsenal* which signals at least for marks with a reputation a move away from pure distinctiveness. It has long been said that trade mark law only protected the distinctiveness function of the mark. The Court of Justice now clearly goes beyond it and states that as a property right the mark is also offering the right holder protection for the advertising, investment, and communication functions of the mark. The list is not exhaustive and further case law will have to show how far the Court is prepared to go down this path.[157]

AdWords

The Court of Justice was also asked if and how the use of AdWords could have a detrimental effect on trade marks with a reputation. As expected, the outcome was that there could indeed be a detrimental effect on the functions of such a trade mark, for example by riding on the coat-tail, and that as a result:

> the proprietor of a trade mark with a reputation is entitled to prevent a competitor from advertising on the basis of a keyword corresponding to that trade mark, which the competitor has, without the proprietor's consent, selected in an internet referencing service, where the competitor thereby takes unfair advantage of the distinctive character or repute of the trade mark (free-riding) or where the advertising is detrimental to that distinctive character (dilution) or to that repute (tarnishment).

[154] Case C-487/07, *L'Oréal SA v. Bellure NV* [2009] ETMR 55.   [155] *L'Oréal* (n. 154).

[156] *Whirlpool Corp. v. Kenwood Ltd.* [2010] ETMR 7 (CA).

[157] Case C-487/07, *L'Oréal SA v. Bellure NV* [2009] ETMR 55. An automated adword service created by Google did not, however, constitute an infringement under s. 10(3). See Case C-236, *Google v. Louis Vuitton*, ECJ 23 March 2010, NYZ.

Advertising on the basis of such a keyword is detrimental to the distinctive character of a trade mark with a reputation (dilution) if, for example, it contributes to turning that trade mark into a generic term.

By contrast, the proprietor of a trade mark with a reputation is not entitled to prevent, inter alia, advertisements displayed by competitors on the basis of keywords corresponding to that trade mark, which put forward—without offering a mere imitation of the goods or services of the proprietor of that trade mark, without causing dilution or tarnishment and without, moreover, adversely affecting the functions of the trade mark with a reputation—an alternative to the goods or services of the proprietor of that mark.[158]

Further examples and an extension of infringement rules

The 1994 Act goes on to give examples (non-inclusively) of the kind of acts that may equate to an infringement. The use of a sign on goods or on their packaging and the offer or sale of goods under the sign in question will both amount to an infringement; so too, potentially, will the import or export of goods under the sign and the use of the sign on any business papers or in advertising.[159] The provision of s. 10(2), whereby the use of a mark can still be capable of being an infringement even if the use is other than by a graphical representation, plugs a previous loophole and means that, unlike under the previous law, it will be an infringement to speak the name of a trade mark registered in its written form perhaps, as an example, in a radio advert criticizing a rival product.

It is clear from the careful matching of the phraseology of ss. 5 and 10 that the definitions of confusion, through similar marks or goods, and of reputation, in the case of dissimilar products, should be the same and the discussion of these points in the context of s. 5 need not be repeated here.

An extension to the normal infringement rules arises under s. 10(5). This extends the protection of the trade mark proprietor to include a right to act against anyone who applies a trade mark to labels or packages of goods, business papers, or advertising material if that person knew, or had reason to believe, that the use of the mark was not authorized by its proprietor. Accordingly, it is now not only the person who makes the decision to infringe who will be liable: as an example, the printer who fails to act on his or her suspicions as to the unauthorized use of a trade mark will also be at risk of infringement litigation.

The Recast Regulation introduces a further extension in the context of goods in transit. In the past, goods that were merely in transit and not released for free circulation and that bore the trade mark without permission were very hard to deal with for the right holder. The new provisions will allow the right holder to sue for infringement even if the goods are merely in transit if the mark is identical or cannot be distinguished in its essential parts from the original trade mark. The customs procedure that is the subject of further discussion in the final chapter of this book in the context of enforcement will then kick in. The party in possession of the goods will then have the burden of proof to demonstrate that the proprietor of the registered trade mark is not entitled to prohibit the placing of the goods on the market in the country of final destination. Only then will the infringement proceedings be brought to a close.[160]

---

[158] Case C-323/09, *Interflora Inc v. Marks & Spencer Plc* [2012] CEC 755, [2012] ETMR 1, [2012] FSR 3.

[159] TMA 1994, s. 10(4). On the latter point, see also *Cheetah Trade Mark* [1993] FSR 263.

[160] Recast Directive, Art. 10(4).

Comparative advertising

A final element of the law in this area is significant in that it offers liberalization of the approach to comparative advertising—that is, the practice of promoting one's own product with reference to its rivals and the alleged lack of quality in their goods.[161] As has been seen, the convoluted approach of the old law, as exemplified by *News Group Ltd v. Mirror Group Ltd*,[162] meant that the use of other marks in seemingly harmless comparative advertising activity could give rise to infringement actions.

Section 10(6)

Now, however, s. 10(6) specifically addresses this issue. Its primary objective is to allow comparative advertising:[163] it allows the use of a mark by anyone to take place without there being an infringement if the use is to identify any goods or services as being those of the proprietor of the mark.[164] So the use, as in the *News Group* case, of a rival paper's logo so as to emphasize the difference between the papers would now seem, as such, to be legitimate.[165] But the subsection has a proviso: such use will continue to be an infringement if it is not '*in accordance with honest practices in industrial or commercial matters*' and also if it takes unfair advantage of, or is detrimental to, the reputation of the mark.

To start with that proviso—because it is in this area that the problems are found—the owner of the registered trade mark has been given the onus to show that the factors indicated in it exist.[166] But as long as the use of the mark is honest, there is nothing wrong in telling the public of the relative merits of competing services and using trade marks to identify these competing services. Advanta was, in this sense, entitled to use Barclays Bank's Barclaycard trade mark to identify it as a competing service in a publicity leaflet in which a table comparing the features, and advantages and disadvantages, of the various credit cards—including the Barclaycard and its own card—were detailed.[167] There will therefore be no trade mark infringement unless the use of the registered trade mark is not in accordance with honest practices.[168]

The test that is applied in this respect is an objective one: would a reasonable man be likely to say, upon being given the full facts, that the advertisement is not honest?[169] Or would a reasonable trader have made the statement contained in the advertising based on the information he or she had at the time?[170] Obviously, a person who knowingly put forward a false claim is not honest and his or her activity is not in accordance with honest practice.[171] A comparative advertisement is also not in accordance with honest practices if it is objectively misleading to a substantial proportion of the reasonable audience.[172] Statutory or industry codes of conduct, however, are not helpful in deciding whether or not the advertisement is honest.

---

[161] See B. Mills, 'Comparative Advertising: Should it Be Allowed?' (1995) 9 EIPR 417.
[162] [1989] FSR 126. See Ch. 24.   [163] *Barclays Bank plc v. RBS Advanta* [1996] RPC 307 at 315.
[164] See *Wolters Kluwer (UK) Ltd v. Reed Elsevier (UK) Ltd* [2006] FSR 28.
[165] See *MacMillan Magazines Ltd v. RCN Publishing Co. Ltd* [1998] FSR 9.
[166] *Barclays Bank plc v. RBS Advanta* [1996] RPC 307 at 315; see also *Vodafone Group plc v. Orange Personal Communications Services Ltd* [1997] FSR 34.
[167] *Barclays Bank plc v. RBS Advanta* [1996] RPC 307.   [168] *Barclays* (n. 167) at 315.
[169] *Barclays* (n. 167) at 315; see also *Vodafone Group plc v. Orange Personal Communications Services Ltd* [1997] FSR 34; *British Airways plc v. Ryanair Ltd* [2001] FSR 32.
[170] *Cable & Wireless plc v. British Telecommunications plc* [1998] FSR 383.
[171] *Cable & Wireless plc* (n. 170).
[172] *Vodafone Group plc v. Orange Personal Communications Services Ltd* [1997] FSR 34. The 'one meaning rule' that is found in the law of malicious falsehood is not applicable in trade mark cases.

Honesty also has to be gauged against the reasonable expectations of the relevant public in relation to advertisements for the particular type of goods or services.[173] These expectations of the public form the benchmarks in this area. It should be borne in mind, in this context, that the general public is well used to the ways of advertisers and that the public consequently expects to see hyperbole.[174] This leads, nevertheless, to the inevitable conclusion that an advertisement that is significantly misleading is not honest for the purposes of s. 10(6).[175] But in examining an advertisement, it should also be borne in mind that the public will not normally engage in a minute textual examination[176] and the advertisement must be considered as a whole.[177]

The second half of the proviso to s. 10(6) seems to introduce the additional requirement that the use of the trade mark in a comparative advertisement without due cause must take unfair advantage of, or must be detrimental to, the distinctive character or repute of the mark. It has been held that, in most cases, this adds nothing of significance to the first half of the proviso.[178] Any form of misleading comparative advertising and any dishonest use of the trade mark in this context must, almost by definition, be seen as detrimental to, or as taking unfair advantage of, the distinctive character or repute of the trade mark.

The *Advanta* case was concerned with comparative advertising practices in relation to credit cards, but most other more recent cases deal with the battle for market shares in the telecommunications market. *Vodafone v. Orange*,[179] for example, was concerned with a campaign in which Orange claimed that its users saved, on average, £20 per month in comparison with someone that used the equivalent Vodafone tariffs. Obviously, in practice, not every user saved £20 per month and transfer costs to Orange had not fully been taken into account. Vodafone's claim for dishonest use of its trade mark was nevertheless rejected, because the ordinary man would expect some hyperbole in this type of market. He would have interpreted the slogan at face value and not literally; he would not have assumed that the saving would apply to every single customer, but only to an average customer. Looked at in that way, the claim of falsity and dishonesty had not been made out.

The Directive

The EU has now also taken an interest in the issue of comparative advertising. A specialist EU Directive[180] also accepts the principle that comparative advertising should be allowed in principle. It defines comparative advertising as '*any advertising which explicitly or by implication identifies a competitor or goods or services offered by a competitor*'.[181]

---

[173] *Barclays* (n. 167) at 316.

[174] *Barclays* (n. 167) at 315; see also *Vodafone Group plc v. Orange Personal Communications Services Ltd* [1997] FSR 34.

[175] *Barclays* (n. 167) at 316; see also *Vodafone* (n. 174).

[176] *British Telecommunications plc v. AT & T Communications (UK) Ltd* (18 December 1996, unreported), High Court.

[177] *Barclays Bank plc v. RBS Advanta* [1996] RPC 307 at 316–18.

[178] *Vodafone Group plc v. Orange Personal Communications Services Ltd* [1997] FSR 34.

[179] *Vodafone* (n. 178).

[180] In origin there were a couple of directives: Parliament and Council Directive 97/55/EC amending Directive 84/450/EEC concerning misleading advertising so as to include comparative advertising (1997) OJ L 290/18. This area has now been codified: Directive 2006/114/EC of the European Parliament and of the Council concerning misleading and comparative advertising (codified version) [2006] OJ L 376/21.

[181] Directive 2006/114/EC of the European Parliament and of the Council concerning misleading and comparative advertising (codified version) [2006] OJ L 376/21, Art. 2(c).

As this definition already indicates, the European approach is wider in scope than only the use of a competitor's trade mark: for example, the use of an equipment manufacturer's identification numbers by a producer of alternative toner cartridges for the manufacturer's equipment in a catalogue of products can be a form of comparative advertising that objectively compares one or more material, relevant, verifiable, and representative features of the goods, and can thus be a permissible form of comparative advertising under the Directive's rules.[182] And in terms of the potential to take unfair advantage, the Court added that:

> where product numbers...of an equipment manufacturer are, as such, distinguishing marks...their use in the catalogues of a competing supplier enables him to take unfair advantage of the reputation attached to those marks only if the effect of the reference to them is to create, in the mind of the persons at whom the advertising is directed, an association between the manufacturer whose products are identified and the competing supplier, in that those persons associate the reputation of the manufacturer's products with the products of the competing supplier. In order to determine whether that condition is satisfied, account should be taken of the overall presentation of the advertising at issue and the type of persons for whom the advertising is intended.[183]

The provisions of the Directive are, in general, also more detailed in nature and their implementation will probably require the introduction of additional legislation in the UK, even if the operation of s. 10(6) TMA has not been qualified.[184]

The interaction between the Directives concerning trade marks and comparative advertising is not straightforward, especially because, in the UK, part of the Directive on comparative advertising has been implemented in the Trade Marks Act 1994. The Court of Appeal has held that advertising that complies with the Comparative Advertising Directive must be covered by the exception in s. 11(2) of the 1994 Act and must meet the standard of 'honest practices' set out in that section.[185] What is not clear, however, is whether use of the mark must be indispensable: must there be a necessity of using the mark?[186] And if one uses the mark, does that also cover use of the mark not exactly as registered? For example, could one use the 'O2' trade mark of static images in a modified form as a background for a television advert for a competitor?

That was the question in the *O2* case,[187] in which all of these questions were referred to the European Court of Justice. The Court of Justice focused on the interaction between the two Directives and the cornerstone of its analysis is that both operate a concept of confusion and that that must be the same concept of confusion.[188] That leads the Court to start its analysis with Art. 3(a)(1) of the Comparative Advertising Directive. That Article only permits comparative advertising if it is not misleading, does not create confusion between the advertiser's trade mark and those of competitors, does not take unfair advantage of the reputation of the trade mark, and does not present the goods or services as imitations or replicas of the goods or services bearing a protected trade mark.[189] In

---

[182] Case C-112/99, *Toshiba Europe GmbH v. Katun Germany GmbH* [2001] ECR I-7945. See also Case C-44/01, *Pippig Augenoptik GmbH & Co. KG v. Hartlauer Handelsgesellschaft mbH & Verlassenschaft Nach Dem Verstorbenen Franz Josef Hartlauer* [2003] ECR I-3095.

[183] *Toshiba* (n. 182) at para. 60.   [184] *British Airways plc v. Ryanair Ltd* [2001] FSR 32.

[185] *O2 Holding Ltd v. Hutchinson 3G Ltd* [2007] ETMR 19 (CA).

[186] Case C-112/99, *Toshiba Europe GmbH v. Katun Germany GmbH* [2001] ECR I-7945 does not seem to require necessity.

[187] *O2 Holding Ltd v. Hutchinson 3G Ltd* [2007] ETMR 19 (CA).

[188] Case C-533/06, *O2 Holdings Ltd v. Hutchinson 3G UK Ltd* [2008] ECR I-4231, [2008] 3 CMLR 14.

[189] The latter two requirements were not respected by the use of the comparative perfume table in case C-487/07, *L'Oréal SA v. Bellure NV* [2009] ETMR 55.

order to let this provision play its role, trade mark law should not overrule it by holding the comparative advertising use of a mark to be an infringement in those cases where the requirements of Art. 3(a)(1) Comparative Advertising Directive have been met.[190] That is not such a strange approach after all, as confusion is then ruled out and that is a fundamental requirement in trade mark infringement cases. Confusion is the key and needs to be looked at in the exact circumstances of the advertising use, but the emphasis on confusion must also mean there is no obligation to use an identical mark. A sign that is similar to the mark must also be allowed under these circumstances (in as far as it meets the definition of a comparative advertisement). There is also no need to prove that the use is indispensable. On the other hand, the Court of Justice found it not necessary to provide a definition of honest practices.

The Court of Appeal asked that question again in the *L'Oréal* case. The Court of Justice responded by ruling that the right holder could rely on damage not just to the distinctiveness function of the trade mark, but also on damage to other functions of the trademark such as the advertising, communication, and investment function in those cases where the requirements of Art. 3(a)(1) Comparative Advertising Directive had not been met. The comparison lists in that case constituted comparative advertising and did do damage to these functions. The right holder could therefore successfully rely on its trade mark, even if there still was no general definition of honest practices.[191] The Recast Directive now proposes to codify this approach by adding 'using the sign in comparative advertising in a manner that is contrary to Directive 2006/114/EC' to the list of examples of ways in which a trade mark can be infringed.[192]

The Court of Justice added in *O2* that trade mark infringement rules will also not be of any use to stop comparative advertisements that do not meet the standards of the Comparative Advertising Directive in circumstances such as O2 where the domestic court had found that there was no confusion.[193] That may sound like an awkward conclusion, but it is logical and it says more about the need for enforcement of the comparative advertising standards than about trade mark law.[194]

Exceptions to infringement

There are, of course, some exceptions to the foregoing in respect of which what would otherwise be an infringement is exempted. Section 11(1) of the 1994 Act refuses an infringement action to the owner of a mark if it is directed against use of another registered trade mark (in relation to goods or services for which the latter user registered). Obviously, in a properly functioning system of examination of trade marks, this situation should never arise; it is a second proprietor who will be in difficulty facing the prospect of revocation of his or her mark. However, a later registered Community trade mark does not have to be declared invalid before the owner of an earlier registered Community trade mark is allowed to bring an infringement action.[195]

---

[190] Case C-533/06, *O2 Holdings Ltd v. Hutchinson 3G UK Ltd* [2008] ECR I-4231, [2008] 3 CMLR 14.

[191] Case C-487/07, *L'Oréal SA v. Bellure NV* [2009] ETMR 55.

[192] Recast Directive, Art. 10(3)(f).

[193] Case C-533/06, *O2 Holdings Ltd v. Hutchinson 3G UK Ltd* [2008] ECR I-4231, [2008] 3 CMLR 14.

[194] Cf. C. Howell, 'O2 v Hutchinson 3G Comparative Advertising: European Trade Mark Law Beyond Compare?' (2008) 13 Comms Law 155–8.

[195] TMA 1994, s. 47(2), and Case C-51/11 *FCI v. FCIPPR*, 21 February 2013, <http://curia.europa.eu> respectively.

Section 11(2) of the 1994 Act also removes the threat of an infringement action from a range of different situations, in each case subject to a proviso that the use that would otherwise be an infringement is a use that is, once again, '*in accordance with honest practices in industrial or commercial matters*'.[196] The test for honesty is to be judged by an objective standard.[197] This fits in well with s. 3(6), which, as has been seen, may prevent an application for a mark from succeeding if made in bad faith—although this would not prevent the possibility of a mark being registered in good faith and then being used in bad faith, in which case, infringement actions will still be available.

Section 11(2)(a)

The activities exempted by s. 11(2) include, first, the use by a person of his or her own name or address. English courts have held that this includes the use by a company of its own registered name.[198] A company's trading name is also potentially covered, but only if it is an established trade name and used in accordance with honest practices avoiding any form of unfair competition.[199] The exception also covers trade mark use of the name.[200] As the referral case was settled, the CJEU did not get the opportunity to rule on the matter. It is, however, interesting to note that Art. 14(1)(a) of the Recast Directive restricts the own name defence to the name or address of natural persons.

Although this seems obvious and only fair, the use in trade of a sign including name and address is not an essential feature of many trades and may well therefore not be honest. If a Mr Ronald McDonald of Leicester were to want to open a burger bar, there are many burger-related names that would be more appropriate than his own name and the only reason for using it would be the less-than-honest desire to steal trade from his better-known namesake; if a Mr Herbert Smith of Leicester wants to set up a solicitor's firm, this may be honest, given that a solicitor normally trades under his or her own name if a sole practitioner.

According to the European Court of Justice, the condition of 'honest practices' to which s. 11(2) is subject constitutes, in substance, the expression of a duty to act fairly in relation to the legitimate interests of the trade mark owner.[201] There must also be some degree of coexistence and some degree of confusion must therefore be tolerated. The extent of confusion that is to be tolerated is a matter of degree and infringement is only to be found if, objectively, the use of his or her name or address by the person concerned amounted to unfair competition. No doubt the Court will, in future, be called upon again to clarify this test further.[202] The domestic courts have held that the own name defence could not be

---

[196] See *Philips Electronics NV v. Remington Consumer Products Ltd* [1998] RPC 283, per Jacob J.

[197] *Aktiebolaget Volvo v. Heritage (Leicester) Ltd* [2000] FSR 253; see also *Cable & Wireless plc v. British Telecommunications plc* [1998] FSR 383.

[198] *Scandecor Developments AB v. Scandecor Marketing AB* [2001] 2 CMLR 30. The House of Lords nevertheless decided that this was not *acte clair*, and referred the issue for a preliminary ruling and further clarification to the European Court of Justice. The case has, however, been settled and withdrawn from the Register. See *Fields v. Klaus Kobec Ltd* [2006] EWHC 350, judgment of 2 March 2006; see also *Euromarket Designs Inc. v. Peters* [2001] FSR 20.

[199] *Hotel Cipriani SRL and ors v. Cipriani (Grosvenor Street) Ltd and ors* [2009] RPC 9, as clarified by the Court of Appeal [2010] EWCA Civ 110, [2010] RPC 16. See also *Asprey & Garrard Ltd v. WRA (Guns) Ltd (t/a William R Asprey Esquire)* [2001] EWCA Civ 1499, [2002] ETMR 47 and *Redd Solicitors LLP v. Red Legal Ltd and Martin Crighton* [2012] EWPCC 54.

[200] *Premier Luggage & Bags Ltd v. Premier Co. (UK) Ltd* [2003] FSR 69 (CA); Case C-100/02, *Gerolsteiner Brunnen GmbH & Co. v. Putsch GmbH* [2004] RPC 761.

[201] *Gerolsteiner Brunnen* (n. 200) at para. 24.

[202] *Reed Executive plc* (n. 25). See also Case C-63/97, *BMW AG v. Ronald Deenik* [1999] ECR I-905; *Gerolsteiner Brunnen* (n. 200).

invoked in a case where the defendant knew in advance that someone else operated under the same name in exactly the same field. That ruled out that the defendant's behaviour was in compliance with honest practices in the field.[203]

Second, the subsection allows the honest use of all the descriptive matter that cannot be registered under s. 3(1), unless entirely factually distinctive prior to registration. Thus a trade mark granted on the basis of distinctive, but descriptive, words cannot be protected when the distinctiveness is lost by subsequent usage, as long as that use was honest.

Section 11(2)(b)

It is the purpose of s. 11(2)(b) of the 1994 Act to permit the fair use of the claimant's mark to indicate the characteristics of goods or services of the user of the sign.[204] That purpose does not extend to performing the dual function of indicating both the characteristics and the trade origin of the goods.[205] Use of a sign as a trade mark can, indeed, never constitute descriptive use that is authorized under s. 10(2)(b).[206] In *Philips v. Remington*,[207] Jacob J held that the use by Remington of the shaver mark was use as an indication of the kind, quality, etc. of the goods. Remington could therefore rely on the exception in s. 10(2)(b).

A somewhat exceptional set of facts arose in *Adam Opel AG v. Autec AG*.[208] This case deals with a trade mark, 'Opel', that had been registered both for motor vehicles and for toys. The question then arose whether the use of the trade mark on scale reproductions of these motor vehicles constituted trade mark infringement. The European Court of Justice held that if a trade mark is registered, inter alia, in respect of motor vehicles, the affixing by a third party of a sign identical to that mark to scale models of that make of vehicle, without the authorization of the proprietor of the trade mark, in order faithfully to reproduce those vehicles and the marketing of those scale models does not constitute use of an indication concerning a characteristic of those scale models, within the meaning of s. 11(2)(b).

Section 11(2)(c)

The third exception relates to the use of a mark to indicate the purpose of goods or services: for example, as spare parts or accessories. Thus if I am free to make spare parts for Ford cars, it will not be an infringement to use—as ever, honestly—the name, or even the mark, of Ford to indicate the suitability of my parts for Ford cars.

The European Court of Justice dealt with the lawfulness of use of the trade mark by a third party in *The Gillette Company & Gillette Group Finland Oy v. LA-Laboratories Ltd Oy*.[209] In this case, the defendant made replacement shaving knives that were compatible with Gillette's originals. The Court held that, in these circumstances, the legitimacy of the use of the trade mark depended on whether that use was necessary to indicate the intended purpose of the product. This is the case, for example, if such use is the only means of providing the public with comprehensible and complete information on that intended purpose in order to preserve the undistorted system of competition in the market for that product; any other conclusion would lead to the use of the trade mark for anticompetitive purposes. The fact that the product involved is not a spare part of accessory, but could be

---

[203] *Ukulele Orchestra of Great Britain v. Clausen* [2015] EWHC 1772 (IPEC), at paras. 76–8.

[204] See *D. Green & Co. (Stoke Newington) & Plastico Ltd v. Regalzone Ltd* [2002] ETMR 241 (CA).

[205] *European Ltd v. Economist Newspaper Ltd* [1998] FSR 283, per Millett LJ.

[206] *British Sugar plc* (n. 13).

[207] *Philips Electronics NV v. Remington Consumer Products Ltd* [1998] RPC 283, per Jacob J.

[208] Case C-48/05, *Adam Opel AG v. Autec AG* [2007] ETMR 33.

[209] Case C-228/03, *The Gillette Company & Gillette Group Finland Oy v. LA-Laboratories Ltd Oy* [2005] ECR I-2337, [2005] 2 CMLR 62.

described as the product itself—or, at the very least, the essential part of it—does not affect these findings. The use by the third party must, however, be honest use. The third party is therefore obliged to act fairly in relation to the legitimate interests of the trade mark owner. One should therefore not use the mark in such a way as to suggest a connection between the third party and the trade mark owner, or present one's own product as an imitation or replica of the original product. Neither should one discredit or denigrate the mark, or affect its value by taking unfair advantage of its distinctive character or repute.

Section 11(3)

A further area covered by these provisions that permit what would otherwise be infringements is created by s. 11(3) of the 1994 Act. This is a somewhat odd provision that protects the use in a particular locality of an earlier right applicable only in that locality. Such a right must be enjoyed continuously prior to the first use of the registration of the mark by its user. No assistance is given as to the definition of a 'locality' and, once again, the use of this provision should be infrequent, given that the earlier local mark should, in an effective system of examination, be unearthed and thus deprive the later mark of the necessary distinctiveness. Because of this, it is far from easy to think of an example of the operation of the provision, but a possible example may be if a trade mark is granted in respect of a Scotch named after an island and it is then discovered that a small local firm on the island has been brewing whisky for the locals using the island's name as part of the brand name.

Exhaustion

Section 12 of the 1994 Act creates an important and different restriction of the right to bring infringement actions. It brings into this area of the law the 'exhaustion of rights' principle that is familiar from other areas of intellectual property. In brief, this is the principle whereby goods that bear, in this case, a trade mark go beyond the control of the proprietor of the mark once they are put on the market—his or her rights in them are exhausted once the goods are in circulation and he or she cannot object to any use of them. This has a particular relevance in the European context, where the principle of the single market has obliged Community law to assert that the circulation of goods in any one member state equates to their circulation in all such states,[210] unless any of the standard objections to free movement principles apply, as exemplified by the *Hag II* case.[211]

The problem arises primarily in the context of parallel imports, in which case a company makes goods bearing a mark in both the UK, for example, and, more cheaply, through a subsidiary in Portugal. Ideally, such a company would prevent goods from Portugal being imported cheaply into the UK, thus undermining its home market, but the two principles of exhaustion and single market now combine to make this impossible.

This situation is given effect in UK law by s. 12. This removes the right to bring an infringement action in relation to goods put on to the market anywhere in the European Economic Area (EEA) by the proprietor with his or her consent. But s. 12(2) goes on to remove this if the proprietor has legitimate reasons to oppose further dealings, such as a change in the conditions of the product, again reflecting the jurisprudence of the

---

[210] See e.g. Case 78/70, *Deutsche Grammophon GmbH v. Metro-SB-Grossmärkte GmbH & Co. KG* [1971] ECR 487, [1971] CMLR 631.

[211] Case C-10/89, *CNL-Sucal NV SA v. HAG GF AG* [1990] ECR I-3711, [1990] 3 CMLR 571.

European Court of Justice.[212] Clearly, however, UK trade mark law can still be used to stop parallel imports from countries elsewhere in the world. This confirms the approach taken under the former law, as exemplified by *Colgate-Palmolive Ltd v. Markwell Finance Ltd*.[213] In that case, the US Colgate company operated through subsidiaries in both the UK and Brazil. Toothpaste from Brazil of an inferior quality was imported into the UK under the Colgate name, causing complaint and confusion, and both trade mark law and passing off combined to defeat the importer's appeal.

Consequences of trade mark infringement

The consequences of there being a trade mark infringement are far-reaching. The proprietor of the mark is entitled to bring infringement proceedings,[214] as is the exclusive licensee or, in certain cases, a non-exclusive licensee.[215] The only specific rule to note is that, in trade mark cases in which the infringement is innocent, damages can be awarded, but no account of profits may be ordered.[216] In addition to the usual remedies in the form of damages, injunctions, and accounts of profits, which are available in the usual manner, specific additional remedies are made available to the victim of trade mark infringement.

Under s. 15 of the 1994 Act, the court is given a discretionary power to order that the infringing sign be erased, removed, or obliterated from the offending goods. Naturally, this will not always be possible; if this is the case, the court can go to the next stage and order that the goods in question be destroyed. In the alternative, s. 16 enables the proprietor to request the court to order any person to deliver to him or her the infringing material, although this right is then lost if six years have elapsed since the infringing act took place—a period that may be extended if there has been concealed fraud or other such disability.[217] If goods are thus delivered up, then an order must be made by the court under the provisions of s. 19 of the Act. This may be for the destruction or forfeiture of those goods, or, alternatively, no order may be made, in which event the property will be returned to its source.

Regard must be had to the availability of other remedies in making such orders. This remedy appears to apply irrespective of the guilt or otherwise of the recipient of the order for delivery up, thus potentially affecting, for example, an innocent shopkeeper who was unaware that goods he or she obtained from a manufacturer infringe a trade mark. There seems to be no provision for the proprietor to take possession of the infringing goods himself.[218]

So what goods are infringing goods? Section 17 of the Act makes clear that goods, material, or items can all infringe and all are referred to in all of the remedies provisions. The section provides full definitions in this respect. Under s. 17(2), infringing goods must bear a sign that is identical or similar to the mark and must be either an infringement or be about to be imported, which would mean that they would then (subject to EU rules) infringe; finally, they may infringe in any other way—although it is far from clear what is achieved by this last part of the provision. Infringing material may include the labelling or packaging of goods, or the use of the mark on business paper or in adverts; infringing items are those that are specifically designed or adapted for making copies of the mark or something similar to it, in relation to which the person in possession, custody, or control is, or should be, aware of its use in the process of infringement.

---

[212] Case C-3/78, *Centrafarm BV v. American Home Products Corp.* [1978] ECR 1823, [1979] 1 CMLR 326.
[213] [1989] RPC 497.   [214] TMA 1994, s. 14.   [215] See Ch. 25.
[216] *Gillette UK Ltd v. Edenwest Ltd* [1994] RPC 279.   [217] TMA 1994, s. 18.
[218] TMA 1994, ss. 16(3), 19(1), and (5).

A new range of criminal offences concerning the unauthorized use of trade marks has also been created by s. 92 of the 1994 Act and other offences about false claims about registration are created by ss. 94 and 95. Also, goods, material, or items that may come into the possession of anyone in connection with the investigation or prosecution of these and related offences may be the subject of forfeiture if it appears to the court that such offences have been created.

Why are these extra remedies necessary in trade mark law? The answer is simple: the production of counterfeit goods has proceeded apace both in the UK and elsewhere. The value of the trade mark is under general threat from a tidal wave of counterfeit goods that, in order to succeed on the market, are very likely to infringe the trade marks on 'real' products. Wide-ranging measures, including those directed against importation and illicit manufacture, are thus necessary to protect the very real economic interests of the proprietors of trade marks.

The draconian nature of infringement proceedings means, however, that they represent a real threat to anyone innocently accused and thus also give a real motive to rivals to make groundless threats of infringement proceedings. Thus, for the first time, the 1994 Act makes provision for remedies for the victim of such groundless threats in relation to trade marks[219] as has been the case for some time in patent law.[220] This right is given only to what may be described as 'secondary infringers'—that is, not the person who actually applies the mark to the goods, or imports them, or supplies the infringing service, but rather those in the wholesale network, such as shop owners and distributors. Such claimants may seek redress in the form of a declaration, injunction, and/or damages, and the onus is on the defendant to show that the claim of infringement is justified. This is useful, if limited, protection for innocent parties.

The draconian nature of the remedies for trade mark infringement is particularly evident in the context of a Community trade mark with a reputation. Things are made worse by the decision of the Court of Justice to accept the existence of a reputation, even if it can only be demonstrated in a single member state.[221] But there seems to be a countervailing rule. According to it, the territorial scope of the remedy, for instance a prohibition that is imposed, may, in certain circumstances, be restricted. The Court argues that the exclusive right is only granted to enable the trade mark to fulfil its functions and that the exercise of that right must therefore be reserved to cases in which a third party's use of the sign affects or is liable to affect the functions of the trade mark. In other words, if the functions of the trade mark are not affected, no remedy should be granted. The acts or future acts of a defendant (i.e. the person whose use of the Community trade mark is complained of) which do not affect the functions of the Community trade mark, cannot be prohibited.[222]

Revocation and invalidity

The grant of a trade mark lasts initially for ten years from the date of its registration[223] and this may be renewed for a seemingly indefinite number of further periods of ten

---

[219] TMA 1994, s. 21; see *Prince plc v. Prince Sports Group Inc.* [1998] FSR 21.

[220] Patents Act 1977, s. 70.

[221] Case C-301/07, *PAGO International GmbH v. Tirolmilch Registrierte Genossenschaft mbH* [2009] ECR I-9429, [2010] ETMR 5.

[222] Joined Cases C-236/08 to C-238/08, *Google France and Google* [2011] All ER (EC) 411, [2010] ETMR 30, [2010] RPC 19 at para. 75; Case C-235/09, *DHL Express France SAS, formerly DHL International SA v. Chronopost SA* [2011] ETMR 33, [2011] FSR 38 at paras. 46–7.

[223] TMA 1994, s. 42(1).

years thereafter on payment of the appropriate fee[224]—currently £200 for a renewal in one class and £50 in any extra classes in relation to which the renewal of the registration is sought.[225] These are small prices to pay for the maintenance of a famous trade mark on the Register and thus the retention of a commercially valuable monopoly.

As ever, however, there is a problem: such rights may be lost in two ways—either by way of a successful application for the revocation of the trade mark or, alternatively, by way of a claim that the initial registration was invalid. Either of these routes will, if pursued successfully, lead to the sudden end of the trade mark and the rights therein. The increasing use of opposition proceedings during which some of the grounds for revocation may have been raised brings about the question of estoppel for the purposes of the revocation proceedings. The Court of Appeal has held, however, that unsuccessfully raising an issue in the course of opposition proceedings does not mean that one is estopped from raising it again in the course of revocation proceedings, because the Act clearly created two different and parallel sets of provisions.[226]

Revocation

There are four grounds listed in s. 46(1) of the 1994 Act as being reasons for revocation. First, five years' lack of genuine use of the mark in the UK[227] without cause can lead to revocation of the registration and it is for the proprietor to prove that there has been use.[228] It is not clear, however, whether the courts can revoke the trade mark in respect of part of the goods or services for which it has been registered on grounds of non-use in respect of that part of the registration. That matter has been referred to the European Court of Justice for a preliminary ruling, but it appears that the case has been settled and that no answer will therefore be forthcoming from the Court. National courts seem, however, to go ahead with partial revocations.[229] The Recast Directive explicitly backs the idea of partial revocations in its Art. 21, so this issue will be resolved soon.

Secondly, a suspension for the same period (after initial use) is a ground for revocation. A third ground is that, whether due to the acts or the inactivity of the proprietor, the mark has become the common name for the product in question in the trade. The main difficulty here is to determine the scope of the trade—that is, of the relevant circles in which the mark is now used as a common name for the product. This is a particularly difficult issue in those cases in which the product is not directly sold to the end user, but in which intermediaries are also involved. The European Court of Justice has provided the following guidance on that point:

> in cases where intermediaries participate in the distribution to the consumer or the end user of a product which is the subject of a registered trade mark, the relevant circles whose views fall to be taken into account in determining whether that trade mark has become the common name in the trade for the product in question comprise all consumers and end users and, depending on the features of the market concerned, all those in the trade who deal with that product commercially.[230]

---

[224] TMA 1994, s. 42(2) and s. 43.   [225] Trade Marks (Fees) Rules 2000, SI 2000/137.

[226] *Special Effects Ltd v. L'Oréal SA* [2007] RPC 15 (CA).

[227] See *United Biscuits (UK) Ltd v. Asda Stores Ltd* [1997] RPC 513.   [228] TMA 1994, s. 100.

[229] *Daimler Chrysler AG v. Alavi (t/a Merc)* [2001] RPC 813; see also *Decon Laboratories v. Fred Baker Scientific & Veltek Associates Ltd* [2001] RPC 293 and *Stichting BDO and others v. BDO Unibank Inc and others* [2013] EWHC 418 (Ch).

[230] Case C-371/02, *Björnekulla Fruktindustrier AB v. Procordia Food AB* [2004] ETMR 977 at para. 26.

Finally, revocation of a mark is also appropriate if it has been used in a misleading manner, especially as to the nature, quality, or origin of the goods or services in question. In effect, the first two grounds penalize non-use, while the latter two grounds are aimed at confusing use of a mark.

Genuine use

'Use' seems to be generously defined by the new law. Use by someone other than the proprietor—although with his or her consent—will suffice, which is an obvious corollary of the more relaxed approach to the licensing of trade marks. The grant of a trade mark licence on its own, however, was held not to be sufficient evidence of use of the trade mark; real genuine use by the licensee was also required.[231] Similarly use of a mark that is not identical, but equally not different, in its essential character (i.e. as long as the distinctive character is not altered)[232] will count as use of the mark, as will the use of it in the UK solely for export purposes.[233]

A good example from the old law of the first type of revocation is provided by the facts of *Imperial Group Ltd v. Philip Morris & Co. Ltd*,[234] in which the word 'Nerit' was registered for cigarettes by the defendants, who were hoping in due course to launch the 'Merit' brand of cigarettes, which was, of course, unregistrable as a laudatory epithet, but the use of which by others could be blocked by the 'Nerit' mark. A tiny number of cigarettes were sold under the name, but the Court of Appeal saw through the subterfuge.[235] There was no genuine use of the mark and it was accordingly expunged from the Register. This case would appear to be one that would be decided similarly under the new law. But there will be genuine use of the mark if another (registered) mark is used if the differences between the marks, for example 'Proti' and 'Protiplus' or 'Proti Power' respectively, do not alter the distinctive character of the trade mark. Use of the distinctive aspect 'Proti' as a component of the two other marks was sufficient to demonstrate genuine use of the mark 'Proti', even if the registration could be considered to be a defensive one.[236] This line of argument also allowed the Court of Appeal to hold that Specsavers had made genuine use of their wordless logo mark. The evidence showed abundant use of the shaded logo mark that as it were includes the shape of the wordless mark and that use had not changed the distinctive character of the wordless logo mark. The latter was also seen by the public as a trade mark and not merely as background. In these somewhat exceptional circumstances use of the shaded logo mark (shown in Figure 26.4) constituted use of the wordless logo mark.[237]

The question of what amounts to genuine use of the trade mark in this context was examined by the European Court of Justice in *Ansul v. Ajax*.[238] The Court ruled that there is 'genuine use' of a trade mark if the mark is used in accordance with its essential function—that is, to guarantee the identity of the origin of the goods or services for which it is registered—in order to create or preserve an outlet for those goods or services. The use has to be sufficient to maintain or to create market share for the goods or services

---

[231] *Philosophy Inc. v. Ferretti Studio Srl* [2003] RPC 288 (CA) (the '*Philosophy di Alberta Ferretti*' *Trade Mark* case).

[232] *Thomas Pink Ltd v. Victoria's Secret UK Ltd* [2014] EWHC 2631 (Ch).

[233] TMA 1994, s. 46(2).   [234] [1982] FSR 72.

[235] See also *Bud & Budweiser Budbräu Trade Marks* [2003] RPC 477.

[236] Case C-553/11, *Bernhard Rintisch v. Klaus Eder*, 25 October 2012, <http://curia.europa.eu>.

[237] *Specsavers International Healthcare Ltd, Specsavers BV, Specsavers Optical Group Ltd and Specsavers Optical SuperstoresLtd v. Asda Stores Ltd* [2014] EWCA Civ 1294, at para. 34.

[238] Case C-40/01, *Ansul v. Ajax* [2003] ECR I-2349; see also *Laboratoires Goemar SA v. La Mer Technology Inc.* [2006] FSR 5.

Figure 26.4 The shaded logo mark (the wordless mark shows only the two elliptic and overlapping shapes

Source: Specsavers Int'l Healthcare v. Asda Stores [2012] EWCA Civ 24, [2012] FSR (19) 555

covered by the mark.[239] Genuine use does not include token use for the sole purpose of preserving the rights conferred by the mark. When assessing whether use of the trade mark is genuine, regard must be had to all of the facts and circumstances that are relevant to establishing whether the commercial exploitation of the mark is real, particularly whether such use is viewed as warranted in the economic sector concerned to maintain or create a share in the market for the goods or services protected by the mark, the nature of the goods or services at issue, the characteristics of the market, and the scale and frequency of use of the mark. Genuine use will normally be use across borders, but market conditions may limit such use to a single member state. There is no *de minimis* rule.[240] The fact that a mark that is not used for goods that are newly available on the market, but for goods that were sold in the past, does not mean that its use is not genuine if the proprietor makes actual use of the same mark for component parts that are integral to the make-up or structure of such goods, or for goods or services directly connected with the goods previously sold and intended to meet the needs of customers of those goods.

Genuine use does not have to be use for profit. In the words of the Court of Justice:

> a trade mark is put to genuine use where a non-profit-making association uses the trade mark, in its relations with the public, in announcements of forthcoming events, on business papers and on advertising material and where the association's members wear badges featuring that trade mark when collecting and distributing donations.[241]

Use only on promotional items that are handed out for free as a reward to purchasers of other goods or to encourage the sale of these other goods did not, on the other hand, amount to genuine use.[242]

---

[239] Conclusion of Advocate General Sharpston in case C-149/11, *Leno Merken BV v. Hagelkruis Beheer BV*, 5 July 2012, <http://curia.europa.eu>.

[240] In a set of objective circumstances to be considered it can even be enough to put the product on the market, even if there are not real final consumers and just sales of stocks to a retailer. See *Laboratoires Goemar SA v. La Mer Technology Inc.* [2006] FSR 5. For use in a single member state see Case C-149/11 *Leno Merken BV v. Hagelkruis Beheer BV*, 19 December 2012, <http://curia.europa.eu>.

[241] Case C-442/07, *Verein Radetzky-Orden v. Bundesvereinigung Kameradschaft, Feldmarschall Radetzky* [2009] ETMR 14 at para. 24.

[242] Case C-495/07, *Silberquelle GmbH v. Maselli-Strickmode mbH* [2009] ETMR 28.

In the absence of genuine use, revocation can only be averted if there is a proper reason for the non-use. A proper reason must arise independently of the will of the trade mark owner, because any inference from the owner would enter into conflict with the basic premise that a trade mark registration carries with it a desire to exploit, rather than to block, opportunities for other competitors. The hurdle must also have a direct relationship with the mark. The potential to use the mark must depend on the hurdle being overcome successfully. Hurdles that are only indirectly related to the mark, but that, for example, make exploitation of the mark less profitable or more cumbersome than foreseen in the initial business plan will not be sufficient. On top of that, a hurdle that simply makes it more difficult to use the mark is not sufficient: the use must have become impossible or at least unreasonable. The appropriate use of the mark must have been jeopardized seriously. For example, a trade mark owner cannot seriously be required to sell its goods in the outlets of its competitors. In such a case, the use of the mark is not impossible, but it has become unreasonable. Or as the European Court of Justice summarized it:

> only obstacles having a sufficiently direct relationship with a trade mark making its use im-possible or unreasonable, and which arise independently of the will of the proprietor of that mark, may be described as 'proper reasons for non-use' of that mark.[243]

Confusing use

The 'confusing use' grounds for revocation pose separate issues. The fact that the acts, in particular, of a proprietor lead to his or her trade mark becoming a household or generic name may be thought to be grounds for acclaim, rather than for the revoca-tion of the mark. But the fact that this ground for revocation only arises from the acts or omissions of the proprietor is the explanation for the provision, the scope of which is quite narrow, and justifies its presence. If the public habitually refers to all vacuum cleaners as 'Hoovers', no ground for revocation arises; it is only if the proprietors cause the confusion—perhaps by failing to make clear that their use of 'Hoover' is as a trade mark—that this ground arises.

Misleading use is the most obvious ground for revocation, given that, if the intention was present at the time of registration, such a mark would never be allowed in the first place. Inactivity when a mark turns into a common name is also a risk: the mark 'spam-buster', for example, turned into a common name for computer programming services to prevent or combat spam. The right holder's inactivity then exposed it to the possibility of revocation on the basis of s. 46(1)(c) of the 1994 Act.[244]

The case *Backaldrin Österreich The Kornspitz Company GmbH v. Pfahnl Backmittel GmbH* provides a typical example.[245] Backaldrin has an Austrian trade mark for the word KORNSPITZ and it supplies a breadmix to bakeries. The latter then bake typical breads and Backaldrin allows them to sell these under the name KORNSPITZ. The bakeries are aware of the trade mark, but end users and consumers see the term as a descriptive term for the bakery product (irrespective of the source of the breadmix). Bakeries do not draw the atten-tion of their customers to the fact that Kornspitz is a registered trade mark. And Backaldrin does not oblige the bakeries to use the trade mark when selling products made on the basis of the breadmix. The CJEU drew harsh consequences on this basis. The Court ruled that the fact that the proprietor of a trade mark does not encourage sellers to make more use

---

[243] Case C-246/05, *Armin Häupl v. Lidl Stiftung & Co. KG* [2007] ETMR 61 at para. 54.
[244] *Hormel Foods Corp. v. Antilles Landscape Investments NV* [2005] RPC 28.
[245] Case C-409/12, *Backaldrin Österreich The Kornspitz Company GmbH v. Pfahnl Backmittel GmbH* [2014] ETMR 30.

of that mark in marketing a product in respect of which the mark is registered amounts to 'inactivity' in the sense of the revocation provision and that revocation will follow and that a trade mark is liable to revocation in respect of a product for which it is registered if, in consequence of acts or inactivity of the proprietor, that trade mark has become the common name for that product from the point of view solely of end users of the product.

The issue of whether use of a mark under a bare licence can render the mark deceptive and susceptible to revocation under s. 46(1)(d) remains an open and complex question. The Act clearly sees a mark as a sign that certain goods or services come from a single business source or undertaking[246] and it was therefore arguable that that function was still fulfilled as long as the goods came from one (or more) licensee(s)—but doubts are bound to arise if the licence involved is a bare licence that does not involve any cooperation or quality control.[247] As a matter of fact, it was even more likely that the public would be misled if, after the termination of a licence, two unrelated undertakings were allowed to continue the use of the same trade mark. The mark would then no longer be able to fulfil its function to distinguish and it would therefore fall to be revoked under s. 46(1)(d).[248]

Anyone can apply

Generally, the 1994 Act allows anyone to apply for revocation,[249] although the burden of proof is placed on the objector to overcome the presumption that the registration is valid.[250] The only restriction on this appears to be that five years of acquiescence in the use of a trade mark by the holder of an earlier right will debar such a person from objecting to the validity of the trade mark.

Section 46(1) of the 1994 Act provides that a trade mark may be revoked in any of the circumstances listed, but the wording of Art. 12(2) of the Directive that the section implements is not clear on the point of whether revocation is mandatory or whether it involves a discretion for the court.[251]

Invalidity

Turning to removal of a trade mark from the Register on the grounds of its invalidity, it is s. 47 of the 1994 Act that provides the relevant rules. It is important to note that the key distinction between 'revocation' and 'invalidity' is that, in the latter case, the registration is deemed to have never been made and thus amounts to a complete legal nullity, except in relation to transactions that are past and closed.[252]

The grounds for claiming invalidity are straightforward and refer back to the rules on unregistrable marks created by ss. 3 and 5 of the Act.[253] Any mark gained in contradiction

---

[246] See e.g. *Glaxo Group v. Dowelhurst Ltd* [2000] FSR 529.

[247] *Scandecor Developments AB v. Scandecor Marketing AB* [2001] 2 CMLR 30 (HL).

[248] *Scandecor* (n. 247). For another example on this point, see *Zakritoe Aktsionernoe Obchtechestvo 'Torgovy Dom Potomkov Postavechtchika Dvora Ego Imperatorskago Velitschestva Pa Smirnova' v. Diageo North America Inc.*, Ch D, judgment of 7 April 2003, [2003] EWHC 970.

[249] TMA 1994, s. 46(4).

[250] TMA 1994, s. 72.

[251] *Scandecor Developments AB v. Scandecor Marketing AB* [2001] 2 CMLR 30.

[252] TMA 1994, s. 47(6) and (7).

[253] A good example where both the registrability and the invalidity were considered was the '32Red' trade mark that could be read as describing a particular result in roulette, but that does not designate a characteristic of the game of roulette (let alone a characteristic of the whole range of goods or services provided by an online casino) and as such escaped being held invalid. *WHG (International) Ltd, WHG Trading Ltd and William Hill Plc v. 32ed plc* [2012] EWCA Civ. 19, [2012] RPC 19.

to those provisions is an invalid mark. The sole exception to this is in relation to marks that should not have been registered on the grounds of non-distinctiveness, descriptiveness, or customary or generic use.[254] These will not lose their validity if, after registration, they acquire by their use the necessary distinctive character that, had it been present at the time of registration, would have, in any event, justified their valid registration at that time. Any person may once again object to the validity of a mark and, if registration has been obtained in bad faith,[255] the Registrar may himself initiate the application for a declaration of invalidity. Partial invalidity is an option in the relevant cases, as Art. 7 of the Recast Directive clarifies.

A case dealing with chocolate Easter bunnies which both parties had produced in a similar shape for a number of years before one of them registered the shape as a trade mark gave the Court of Justice the chance to look at the issue of bad faith. The Court ruled that in order to determine whether an applicant was acting in bad faith one has to consider whether, at the time of filing the application for registration, (a) the applicant knew or must have known that the third party was using an identical or similar sign for an identical or similar product capable of being confused with the sign for which registration was sought; (b) the applicant intended to prevent that third party from continuing to use such a sign; and (c) the third party's and the applicant's signs enjoyed a degree of legal protection.[256]

In general, it is clear that the symbiotic relationship of infringement and revocation arguments has been well understood by the authors of the new trade mark legislation. The same basic ideas stemming from the basic notion of trade mark registrability run through both infringement and revocation provisions. This makes for a generally cogent piece of legislation, especially by contrast with its (much-amended) predecessor.

One should not wait too long if one wants to rely on an earlier trade mark[257] in support of an invalidation action. Acquiescence for a five-year period will take away the right to rely on the earlier mark. This takes away prolonged uncertainty and increases the degree of legal certainty. However, the proprietor of an earlier trade mark cannot be held to have acquiesced in the long and well-established honest use, of which he has long been aware, by a third party of a later trade mark which is identical with that of the proprietor if that proprietor was not in any position to oppose that use, for example because both parties have been authorized by the court to register the mark 'Budweiser'. The five-year limitation period will start to run from the registration of the later mark.[258]

An overview

That the old law needed reform was undoubted: its convolutions and complexities were considerable, and became worse as amendment after amendment was made.

Radical changes were introduced in relation to trade mark infringement and the scope of trade mark protection. In these areas, the legal system now extends its protection

---

[254] TMA 1994, s. 3(1).

[255] *Hotel Cipriani SRL and ors v. Cipriani (Grosvenor Street) Ltd and ors* [2010] EWCA Civ 110, [2010] RPC 16.

[256] Case C-529/07, *Chocoladefabriken Lindt & Sprungli AG v. Franz Hauswirth GmbH* [2009] ECR I-4893, [2009] ETMR 56.

[257] Or another right, such as the right to a name, see Art. 52 CTMR and Case C-263/09 P, *Edwin Co Ltd v. OHIM- Elio Fiorucci* [2011] ETMR 45.

[258] Case C-482/09, *Budějovický Budvar, národní podnik v. Anheuser-Busch Inc.* [2012] RPC 11. See also *Budějovický Budvar, národní podnik v. Anheuser-Busch Inc.* [2012] EWCA Civ 880, [2012] 3 All ER 1405.

beyond the origin function of the trade mark, even if the latter is still its primary function. This evolution is clearly based on the influence of the Directive; it is not always reflected clearly in the 1994 Act and initially the courts in this country did not necessarily readily accept it. Nevertheless, it clearly emerges from the case law of the European Court of Justice. *Sabel v. Puma*[259] provided a first indication in this respect and this has now been followed up by a ruling that confusion can exist if the public perceives the goods or services as being produced in different places and by economically linked undertakings, rather than necessarily by the same undertaking.[260] This clearly goes beyond the protection of the function of origin.[261] The trade mark owner also gets protection for some of the non-origin uses of its trade mark.

At one stage, one had the impression that things would stop there and that s. 10(3) of the 1994 Act would really remain reserved for exceptional cases. That has now all changed, and it seems easy for a mark to acquire a reputation and bring itself under the scope of that subsection. On top of that, the requirements contained in the subsection have been interpreted liberally and the impression was created that s. 10(3) would become the norm, and that s. 10(2) and its stricter norms would only apply to a limited number of cases. Such a move could not be welcomed unreservedly and would have represented a massive expansion of the rights of the owners of trade marks. With *Intel* the tide seems to have turned and proper limitations are being put in place such as the need to actually prove detriment or the taking of unfair advantage.

Clearly, the legal debate has not yet reached a final conclusion in this area. But whatever the final outcome will turn out to be, the changes in this area will have been far more revolutionary than the initial cases tried to make us believe.

Further reading

Carboni, A., 'Two Stripes and You're Out! Added Protection for Trade Marks with a Reputation' (2004) 26(5) EIPR 229.

Cheung, A. S. Y. and Pun, K. K. H., 'Comparative Study on the Liability for Trade Mark Infringement of Online Auction Providers' (2009) 31(11) EIPR 559–67.

Davis, J., 'The European Court of Justice Considers Trade Mark Dilution' (2009) 68(2) Cambridge Law Journal 290–2.

Mellor, J. et al. (2011) *Kerly's Law of Trade Marks and Trade Names*, 15th edn, London: Sweet and Maxwell, Ch. 14.

Morcom, Ch., 'L'Oréal v. Bellure: Who Has Won?' (2009) 31(12) EIPR 627–35.

Morcom, Ch., 'Trade Marks and the Internet: Where Are We Now?' (2012) 34(1) EIPR 40–53.

Simon, I., 'Embellishment: Trade Mark Use Triumph or Decorative Disaster' (2006) 28(6) EIPR 321.

Würtenberger, G., 'Community Trade Mark Law Astray or Back to the Roots!' (2006) 28(11) EIPR 549.

---

[259] *Sabel BV* (n. 64).   [260] *Canon Kabushiki Kaisha v. Metro-Goldwyn-Mayer Inc.* (n. 53).
[261] P. Torremans 'The Likelihood of Association of Trade Marks: An Assessment in the Light of the Recent Case Law of the Court of Justice' [1998] IPQ 295–310.

27

Trade marks—European and international aspects

International aspects—introduction

We have already noted that one of the reasons for a new law of trade marks in 1994 was the need for the UK to bring its system into accord with its various international and European obligations. It is Part II of the Trade Marks Act 1994 that seeks to do this by, in turn, making provision with regard to the European Union (EU) Community trade mark, the new Protocol to the 1891 Madrid Agreement concerning the International Registration of Marks, and the provisions of the Paris Convention for the Protection of Industrial Property 1883. The latter two are long-standing examples of the traditional incompatibility of aspects of the common lawyer's approach to trade marks with the general international approach.

Later on in the chapter we will look at the interaction between trade mark law and EU law.

The Community trade mark

The 1994 Act itself deals with each of these matters in an apparently cursory manner. Under s. 52 of that Act, the Secretary of State is simply given the power to make such regulations that he feels are appropriate in connection with the operation of the Community Trade Mark Regulation.[1] In particular, applying for a Community mark through the Patent Office, the interrelationship of domestic and Community marks and jurisdictional issues are flagged up as particular issues in respect of which UK regulations may need to be made.[2] The Trade Mark Regulation will be updated in a substantial manner early in 2016.[3]

But this low-key legislative approach should not be allowed to disguise the significance of the developments taking place under this heading: the Regulation establishing the new Community trade mark is, of course, binding in itself and this creates an entirely new trade mark system in parallel to that which operates in the UK, but the new system is not to be seen as a rival; rather, proprietors have a choice. If they are active across Europe, the Community trade mark will provide valuable comprehensive and consistent

---

[1] Regulation 40/94 (1994) OJ L 11/1.

[2] Community Trade Mark Regulations 1996, SI 1996/1908.

[3] See the draft for a Regulation (EU) 2015/…of the European Parliament and of the Council amending Council Regulation (EC) No 207/2009 on the Community trade mark and Commission Regulation (EC) No 2868/95 implementing Council Regulation (EC) No 40/94 on the Community trade mark, and repealing Commission Regulation (EC) No 2869/95 on the fees payable to the Office for Harmonization in the Internal Market (Trade Marks and Designs), as approved by the European Parliament on 14 December 2015.

coverage from a single application. But for many applicants, only a domestic registration will be needed and this will be the (presumably) cheaper way forward that will be preferred by many.

The language of the Regulation is almost identical to that of the Harmonization Directive that, in turn, the 1994 Act implements, and the basic structure of the system and its key definitions are the same across the Regulation, the Directive, and the Act. It is not therefore proposed to go through the Regulation Article by Article, because to do so would simply be to repeat much of what has been said. It is, however, useful to refer to the overall structure of the Regulation for the sake of reference.

Article 1 of the Regulation[4] establishes that the mark shall have a unitary character—that is, that it will be equally effective and be equally treated throughout the Community: a single mark in a single market. Article 4 gives the basic definition of a mark, which must be a sign that is capable of being represented graphically and of distinguishing goods or services from those of other traders. Article 7 provides the absolute grounds for non-registration, closely similar to those in s. 3 of the 1994 Act, while Art. 8 provides the so-called 'relative grounds for refusal of a mark', this approximating to s. 5 of the UK legislation. Article 29 creates a priority date system, and there is a full examination and search procedure.[5] The mark lasts for 10 years and is renewable for further 10-year periods thereafter.[6]

There are, of course, some points of distinction between the Regulation and other trade mark legislation. The unitary nature of the Community trade mark is reinforced by the provision[7] that the grounds for absolute unregistrability apply across the whole Community even if they are applicable in only a part of the Community. So, if a UK company uses a mark that happens, in Greek, to be a word regarded as being against public morality, no Community mark can be granted and resort would thus have to be had to individual national registrations of the mark. Protection is given for prior rights even in unregistered marks, but only if they are 'of more than mere local significance'.[8]

There is, unlike in the UK system, no need to file a declaration of use or bona fide intention to use the mark. Perhaps of more significance is that all of the relative grounds for not registering a mark apply only when they are raised in opposition proceedings.[9] The Office itself conducts a more limited official search: in essence, only formalities and absolute grounds for refusal are checked. A list of possibly conflicting marks and applications is also drawn up, and sent to the applicant and the right holders that are potentially affected by the application are informed of it. It is then up to them to follow the matter up via opposition proceedings. The number of opposition proceedings and of potential appeal to the European General Court and, eventually, to the Court of Justice, is therefore rather high. There is a Community collective mark, but there is no provision for a Community certification mark. Once granted, a Community trade mark can only be dealt with as an entity—that is, it can only be assigned as a whole etc.[10] Infringement proceedings are brought before national courts, but each member state has had to designate a small number of specialized Community trade mark courts, at both first instance and appeal levels.[11]

As soon as the new Community trade mark system came into being, the sceptics were proved to be wrong. The system has, in its first few years in operation, been highly

---

[4] Council Regulation (EC) No. 207/2009 of 26 February 2009 on the Community trade mark (codified version) [2009] OJ L78/1, Art. 1(2).

[5] Regulation No. 207/2009, Arts. 36–39.   [6] Regulation No. 207/2009, Arts. 46–47.

[7] Regulation No. 207/2009, Art. 7(2).   [8] Regulation No. 207/2009, Art. 8(4).

[9] Regulation No. 207/2009, Art. 8(1); cf. TMA 1994, s. 8.   [10] Regulation No. 207/2009, Art. 16.

[11] Regulation No. 207/2009, Arts. 91–2. These courts have exclusive jurisdiction to deal with infringement proceedings, actions for a declaration of non-infringement, actions for compensation for acts done during the application period, and counterclaims for revocation or for declarations of invalidity.

successful. It has attracted more registrations than expected and it clearly has taken away business from the national trade mark registries. Its procedures are complex, but this is mainly due to the international nature of the whole operation and its fees are not unduly high, especially when compared to the fees of the European Patent Office in Munich as the other transnational intellectual property office. The Community Trade Mark Office will not make searches itself, but will depend on rivals to initiate opposition proceedings, thus alleviating the examination process and reducing it to purely administrative checks.

But the functioning of a system that has to consider the meaning and significance of words in all of the languages of an expanded Community is bound to be difficult; the fact that enforcement of rights conferred by Community trade marks is, to a large extent, left to national courts will surely hinder, rather than help, the creation of a unitary system. In any event, national registrations will continue and may well still have the effect of distorting the single market. More significantly, there is an alternative method of obtaining international registrations and it is to this that we now turn.

The international registration of marks

The second part of the 1994 Act with international repercussions concerns the international registration of marks. Once again, the legislation itself adopts a minimalist approach, s. 54 of the Act allowing the Secretary of State to make *'such provisions as he thinks fit'* for giving domestic effect to the provisions of the Madrid Protocol. Again, however, the significance of this is far-reaching.

There has long been an International Register of Trade Marks, maintained by the World Intellectual Property Organization (WIPO) and established under the Madrid Agreement. An international registration lasts for a period of 20 years, with provision for recurrent renewals for another period of the same duration. Only one application needs to be made nominating the signatory countries in relation to which the applicant wishes to be granted registration. If an international registration is secured, the national trade mark offices in the nominated countries must recognize it unless it falls foul of a domestic provision that would prevent a domestic registration. The effect is that a single application leads to a collection of domestic marks.

The Madrid Protocol of 1989 is designed to create a similar parallel system that enables many more countries to join the international system. The basis of an international registration may, under the Protocol, be a domestic application and not only, as hitherto, a domestic registration, and the periods of registration and renewal are reduced to 10 years. The overall picture, however, is the same as that under the Agreement, in that a single international application should confer a collection of national trade marks.[12]

When provision was made under s. 54 of the 1994 Act,[13] two things were provided for: first, a UK application or registration was allowed to be directed onto the international level by establishing appropriate rules; second, provision was made for the recognition by the UK of an international registration that has originated in another jurisdiction—which will be known as an 'international trade mark (UK)'.[14]

---

[12] For an excellent full account of the workings of the Madrid Protocol, see G. Kunze, 'The Madrid System for the International Registration of Marks as Applied under the Protocol' (1994) 6 EIPR 223.

[13] The Trade Marks (International Registration) Order 1996, SI 1996/714. (The UK became a party to the Protocol to the Madrid Agreement on 1 December 1995 and the Protocol itself became operational on 1 April 1996. The UK is still not a party to the Madrid Agreement.)

[14] TMA 1994, s. 53.

The Madrid system and the Community trade mark

It is tempting to view the Madrid Protocol system and the Community trade mark as being rivals to each other, and this is indeed so for a business trading in a limited number of European countries, for example France and the Benelux states. For a truly multinational company, however, it seems likely that both systems may be employed, with a Community application being made and this then forming the basis of an international registration (the Community trade mark will be recognized for this purpose) that allows a registration to be secured for non-EU states such as Switzerland and Norway. The only real advantage that the Madrid system enjoys is that, by establishing registration on a national, rather than an international, level, it avoids the problem that the unacceptability of a mark in one particular state would entirely prevent the registration of a Community trade mark and that it would simply allow registration to occur in all other states under the Madrid system.

The Paris Convention

The third and final area of the international aspects of trade mark law dealt with by the 1994 legislation concerns the changes made to the law in order to bring the UK into line with provisions of the Paris Convention 1883. The 1994 Act extends the protection of the law, as has been seen, to cover well-known trade marks held by nationals of, or businesses domiciled in, signatory countries, irrespective of whether there is business activity or goodwill in the UK.[15] This is the principal change, and has significant implications for both trade mark law and also for the tort of passing off, considered in the next chapter.

Additional provisions in the 1994 Act also clearly fulfil Paris Convention obligations: s. 57 protects flags and other state insignia of a signatory country, which shall not be registered without appropriate permission; similar protection is granted to any international organization of which one or more Paris signatories are members. Such emblems cannot be used as, or as a part of, trade marks if the use suggests a misleading connection between the organization and the trade mark. Thus entrepreneurs will not be able to sell WIPO sweatshirts, but WIPO apparently can.

A final Paris-related provision is found in s. 60 of the 1994 Act, which allows the holder of an overseas mark to render invalid a mark registered in respect of it in the UK by an agent or representative who has acted without the appropriate authority. An example of this under similar provisions of the old law is provided by *K. Sabatier Trade Mark*,[16] in which a distributor had registered the mark of a French manufacturer of knives; this was expunged from the Register.

There is an obligation under the Paris Convention[17] to provide protection against unfair competition. Clearly, much of trade mark law and the tort of passing off has this effect, but the absence of any action for unfair competition as such is bound to raise a potential clash that may arise in the future.

Internationalization of both trade mark law and trade

The internationalization of the trade mark scene is an inevitable reflection of multinational companies and multinational trade. Clearly, such interests need protection as a reflection of their commercial value—but there must be a slight note of caution. The

---

[15] TMA 1994, ss. 56, 6(1)(c).   [16] [1993] RPC 97.   [17] Paris Convention, Art. 10bis.

promotion of image through trade marks is not an abstract exercise, but one that inter-acts with the citizen, who is being persuaded to buy a product or use a service. Individual perceptions vary from state to state and are nurtured in different ways by different lan-guages. International cooperation may be essential, but international conformity is not and may even be unwise. The permissive Madrid approach may be thought to reflect this more satisfactorily than the single Community trade mark, but more and more compan-ies do business across the EU and treat it as a single market in which they market their goods or services under a single trade mark. For them, the Community trade mark may be the ideal tool and they may use the Madrid system only to expand protection to cer-tain non-EU member states.

Trade marks and the free movement of goods

We discussed, in relation to patents, how the provisions on free movement and competi-tion law in the Treaty of Rome apply to intellectual property rights. The principles we set out there obviously also apply to trade marks[18] and this section will only be concerned with the specific application of these principles.

Towards a definition of the specific subject matter and the essential function

Centrafarm v. Winthrop

The first case decided by the European Court of Justice is a parallel case to that of *Centrafarm v. Sterling Drug*[19] in relation to patents and is, in relation to trade marks, *Centrafarm v. Winthrop*.[20] As in the patent case, Centrafarm was buying drugs in the UK and importing them into the Netherlands for resale. In both countries, the drug was marketed under the trade mark 'Negram'. Winthrop, the Dutch subsidiary of Sterling, owned the trade mark in the Netherlands, and tried to exercise its rights under that right to block the importation into, and resale operation in, the Netherlands. Unfortunately, the Court did not spell out fully the essential function of a trade mark in this case, al-though it is fair to say that the approach taken is identical to that taken in relation to patents, because the Court went on to define the specific subject matter, which included a reference to the exhaustion doctrine.

The specific subject matter of a trade mark is:

> the guarantee that the owner of the trade mark has the exclusive right to use that mark, for the purpose of putting products protected by the trade mark into circulation for the first time, and is therefore intended to protect him against competitors wishing to take advantage of the status and reputation of the trade mark by selling products illegally bearing that mark.[21]

---

[18] And along the same lines to geographical indications, appellations of origin, and designations for food-stuffs. The European Court of Justice held, for example, that '*Article 30 of the Treaty (now, after amendment, Article 28 EC) precludes a member state from applying to products imported from another member state, where they are lawfully produced and marketed, a national rule prohibiting the marketing of a cheese without rind under the designation "Emmenthal" in that member state*.' The Court argued that consumers were not effectively being misled and that, even if they were, the measure would have been disproportionate; a bit of information added to the designation would have been sufficient: Case C-448/98, *Jean-Pierre Guimont* [2001] ETMR 14.

[19] Case 15/74, *Centrafarm BV v. Sterling Drug Inc.* [1974] ECR 1147, [1974] 2 CMLR 480.

[20] Case 16/74, *Centrafarm BV v. Winthrop BV* [1974] ECR 1183, [1974] 2 CMLR 480.

[21] *Centrafarm BV v. Winthrop BV* (n. 20) at 1194 and 5080.

The owner of the trade mark has the exclusive right to use the trade mark for commercial purposes and can oppose infringement. He or she can exercise the right by putting products (or services) labelled with the trade mark on the market for the first time, but, afterwards, his or her rights are exhausted.

These are all rights available under parallel trade marks in the Community. The comments that we made in Chapter 4 in relation to the similar specific subject matter of a patent apply here as well. Any exercise of the trade mark that goes further will fall foul of Arts. 34 and 36 of the Treaty on the Functioning of the European Union. Obviously, the trade mark owner can put the products on the market him- or herself, or he or she can allow a third party to exploit the trade mark with his or her consent. The option taken does not influence the application of the exhaustion doctrine: Winthrop could thus not be allowed to exercise its Dutch trade mark rights to block the importation and resale operation that Centrafarm was setting up for Negram, because the marketing in the UK had been done by the Sterling group, meeting the consent requirement, and had exhausted all rights under parallel trade marks in the Community. Such exercise of its trade mark rights by Winthrop would go beyond the specific subject matter of a trade mark, and it therefore falls foul of Arts. 34 and 36. In the words of the Court:

> the exercise, by the owner of a trade mark, of the right which he enjoys under the legislation of a Member State to prohibit the sale, in that State, of a product which has been marketed under the trade mark in another Member State by the trade mark owner or with his consent is incompatible with the rules of the EEC Treaty concerning the free movement of goods within the Common Market.[22]

The fact that the product has been manufactured outside the EU, before it was put on the market inside the EU, is irrelevant as long as the product was put into circulation in the EU by, or with the consent of, the trade mark owner.[23]

The consent for the marketing within the EU is the crucial element. In its decision in *Peak Holding*,[24] the European Court of Justice clarified the concept of putting the goods on the market with the consent of the proprietor. In this case, the proprietor had imported the goods into the EEA and had offered them for sale in its own shops, but it had not actually sold them. The Court held that the goods had not been put on the market with the consent of the proprietor of the mark in the absence of a first sale of the goods; such a first sale would take place were the goods to be sold to another operator in the EEA even if the contract were to prohibit resale in the EEA. The onus to prove the consent—whether express or implied[25]—of the proprietor of the trade mark lies with the parallel importer, but the standard of proof is the usual one in civil litigation—that is, the balance of probabilities. The Court has used the term 'unequivocal consent' simply to indicate that the consent must be clear and that proven acts that can be consistent with consent, but also with its absence, are not sufficient to demonstrate consent. That does not change the standard of proof.[26] The parallel importer can, however, demonstrate that the goods were put on the EEA market by a third party which has no economic link with the right holder with the implied consent of the latter. In that case the consent must be inferred

---

[22] *Centrafarm BV v. Winthrop BV* (n. 20) at 1195 and 510.

[23] Case C-352/95, *Phytheron International SA v. Jean Bourdon* [1997] ECR I-1729.

[24] Case C-16/03, *Peak Holding AB v. Axolin-Elinor AB* [2005] ECR I-11313, [2005] Ch 261, [2005] 2 WLR 650.

[25] Case C-127/09, *Coty Prestige Lancaster Group GmbH v. Simex Trading AG* [2010] FSR 48, [2010] ETMR 41 and *Peak Holding AB* (n. 24).

[26] *Mastercigars Direct Ltd v. Hunters & Frankau Ltd* [2007] RPC 24, [2007] ETMR 44 (CA).

from facts and circumstances prior to, simultaneous with, or subsequent to the placing on the market of the goods, but they must unequivocally demonstrate that the proprietor has renounced his exclusive rights. This is a tall order.[27]

Whereas consent is the key component, one should also not forget the requirement that the goods must have been put on the market. The Court of Justice has held that that requirement is not satisfied when the goods that are parallel imported started life as 'testers', 'demonstrators', or 'samples' (e.g. for perfumes) which the right holder/manufacturer puts at the disposal of shops inside its distribution chain and that are clearly labelled as such. These have not been put on the market and the trade mark can therefore not be exhausted in relation to them.[28] The Court of Appeal in Brussels applied that same approach to toner cartridges sold by Xerox whilst retaining the title in the cartridge and obliging the customer to return the empty cartridge after use as part of a service contract. The price was the same as the one used in a straightforward sale. The court argued that the retention of title meant the goods had not been put on the market with the consent of the right holder.[29] This may take us too far though. Xerox received the real economic value of the cartridge and it is arguable that is the equivalent of putting the cartridge on the market with consent. The CJEU did after all look beyond the 'licence' logo and held the transaction to amount to the equivalent of a sale in *UsedSoft GmbH v. Oracle International Corp.*[30] Maybe the same logic would lead the court here to conclude that consent was present and that these cases can be distinguished from the tester cases.

Hoffmann-La Roche v. Centrafarm

The essential function of the trade mark was spelled out in the next trade mark case to reach the European Court of Justice. In *Hoffmann-La Roche v. Centrafarm*,[31] the Court said that the essential function of a trade mark was:

> to guarantee the identity of the trade marked product to the consumer or ultimate user, by enabling him without any possibility of confusion to distinguish that product from products which have another origin.[32]

This has to be read in conjunction with the partial statement on the subject in *Centrafarm v. Winthrop*,[33] in which the protection of the goodwill of the owner of the trade mark was emphasized—but why this seemingly odd combination?

It is submitted that, in relation to trade marks, it is impossible to say that one function is more essential than the other as was the case in relation to patents. Goodwill is an essential element of a trade mark for its owner, but it will only exist if the consumer distinguishes the product or service labelled with the trade mark from other products or services. The guarantee for consumers or users that the product or service labelled with the trade mark is of a standard quality is essential in order for the goodwill—whether negative or positive—to be created. The combination of these two elements forms the essential function of a trade mark, which is fulfilled by the exercise of the rights within its specific subject matter.

---

[27] Case C-324/08, *Makro Zelfbedieningsgroothandel CV, Metro Cash & Carry BV and Remo Zaandam BV v. Diesel SpA* [2010] ETMR 2.

[28] *Coty Prestige* (n. 25); Case C-324/09, *L'Oréal v. eBay* [2011] ETMR 52, [2011] RPC 27.

[29] *Xerox Corp. v. Impro Europe Bvba*, case 2013/AR/2763, 8th Division Civ. Court of Appeal Brussels, 20 October 2015.

[30] Case C-128/11, *UsedSoft GmbH v. Oracle International Corp* [2012] 3 CMLR 44, [2012] ECDR 19, [2013] RPC 6.

[31] Case 102/77, *Hoffmann-La Roche & Co. AG v. Centrafarm* [1978] ECR 1139, [1978] 3 CMLR 217.

[32] *Hoffmann-La Roche* (n. 31) at 1164 and 241.   [33] *Centrafarm BV v. Winthrop BV* (n. 20).

It should also be remembered that this whole area of law is concerned with putting goods on the single market. The right holder can, in respect of lawfully manufactured goods, only act if the goods are to be put on the market. Lawfully manufactured goods that are in transit in order to be placed on a market outside the EU cannot be stopped and detained by customs authorities without infringing Art. 34 of the Treaty.[34] Things are different though if goods that were originally T1 goods in customs terms under the customs suspension arrangement for external transit are released for free circulation, but then put in a warehouse under a duty suspension arrangement. That means that during such storage the duty is not yet payable and that there is no yet a link with the (end) consumer. The CJEU held that the trade mark on the goods is then nevertheless used in the course of trade and that the right holder can oppose such use of the trade mark.[35] These goods have then entered the single market. This approach puts an end to certain abuses of the customs regime that were taking place and that made it difficult for right holders to enforce their rights effectively.

The repackaging and relabelling saga

The starting point—repackaging in *Hoffmann-La Roche*

Further complications arose when certain trade-marked drugs were sold in different packing formats in various member states. In the *Hoffmann-La Roche* case, the drug Valium was sold in packs containing a different number of pills in the UK and in Germany. Centrafarm bought the drugs in the UK, removed the outer packing and repacked the drug for the German market in packs containing the number of pills that was normal on the German market. It applied the Valium trade mark, which Hoffmann-La Roche owned all over Europe, to the packs destined for the German market. Hoffmann-La Roche wanted to rely on its German Valium trade mark to stop Centrafarm. It argued that it had not exhausted its rights in the trade mark, because it had not applied it to the repacked goods.

The European Court of Justice rejected the argument. Hoffmann-La Roche had marketed the drugs in the UK under the Valium trade mark and thereby exhausted its rights in all parallel trade marks. The way in which Hoffmann-La Roche wanted to use its trade mark went beyond its specific subject matter and fell foul of Arts. 34 and 36. The interesting element in this case relates to the essential function of trade marks, because this needs to be fulfilled by the exercise of the rights under the specific subject matter of the trade mark. The goodwill of Hoffmann-La Roche and the interest of the consumers had therefore to be protected. This is the reason why the Court laid down additional requirements. It specified that there needs to be a guarantee that the repacking has no adverse effect on the original condition of the goods, because tampering with the goods would affect the goodwill of the owner of the trade mark and undermine the identity guarantee to which the consumer is entitled. The fact that the goods have been repacked means that the identity of the repacker should also figure on the repacked goods for the information of the consumer;[36] the owner of the trade mark should be informed of the intention to

---

[34] Case C-115/02, *Administration des Douanes et Droits Indirects v. Rioglass SA & Transremar SL* [2004] ETMR 519.

[35] Case C-379/14, *TOP Logistics BV, Van Caem International BV v. Baccardi & Company Ltd and Bacardi International Ltd* [2015] ETMR 43.

[36] The key element in mentioning the name of the entity repacking the goods is that of liability. It is therefore acceptable to mention merely the name of the entity assuming responsibility and liability for the operation, even if the actual act of repackaging is carried out by another entity in the same group of

repack the goods so that it can keep an eye on the market to safeguard its goodwill and act when that is threatened. If these conditions are met, the essential function of the trade mark is fulfilled and every exercise that goes beyond the specific subject matter of the trade mark will fall foul of Arts. 34 and 36.[37]

The Court confirmed this approach in *Pfizer Inc. v. Eurim-Pharm GmbH*.[38]

The starting point—relabelling in *American Home Products*

It is not only repackaging that caused problems: a company could also use different trade marks for one product in different member states. This can, of course, be done for legitimate reasons, because it may not be possible to register the same trade mark in certain member states if a similar mark already exists or if the trade mark has a negative connotation in the language of that member state. The trade mark owner can, however, have less legitimate reasons. One trade mark per member state effectively partitions the single market: the owner of the trade marks can operate freely in each of the national markets from a dominant position. A challenger should be entitled to use the trade mark that the owner uses in that market in order to mount an effective challenge, and the owner will try to prevent this by relying on the trade mark and by alleging infringement.

This is what happened in *Centrafarm BV v. American Home Products Corp.*[39] American Home Products marketed the same drug in the UK under the trade mark 'Serenid', while using the trade mark 'Seresta' in the Benelux countries and Germany. Centrafarm bought the drug in the UK and sold it in the Netherlands, after changing the trade mark to Seresta, because Dutch consumers were familiar with this trade mark. American Home Products objected to this practice and argued that it infringed its Dutch Seresta trade mark. In this case, there was no legitimate reason to use a different trade mark in the Netherlands.[40] The goodwill of American Home Products was not affected and the interests of the consumers were unharmed, safeguarding the essential function of the trade mark. The rights conferred by the trade mark were exercised to serve one function—that is, to restrict the free movement of goods and to partition the single market. Therefore this exercise of the trade marks should fall foul of Arts. 34 and 36, because it constitutes a disguised restriction of trade, and this was indeed what the Court decided.[41] To be precise, the specific subject matter of the trade mark as a description of what is allowed was preserved, because the trade mark owner still put all products concerned on the market for the first time.

This case has been criticized, because it introduces a subjective criterion by relying on the intent of the owner of the trade marks.[42] Subsequent developments in the case law of the European Court of Justice have shown that it never intended to introduce a subjective element: the parallel importer does not have to prove that the right holder set out to partition the market deliberately.

---

companies or by a third party. Joined Cases C-400/09, *Orifarm A/S v. Merck, Sharp & Dohme Corp* and C-207/10, *Paranova Denmark A/S and Paranova Pack A/S v. Merck, Sharp & Dohme Corp* [2012] 1 CMLR 10, [2011] ETMR 59.

[37] Case 102/77, *Hoffmann-La Roche & Co. AG v. Centrafarm* [1978] ECR 1139, [1978] 3 CMLR 217.

[38] Case 1/81, *Pfizer Inc. v. Eurim-Pharm GmbH* [1981] ECR 2913, [1982] 1 CMLR 406.

[39] Case 3/78, *Centrafarm BV v. American Home Products Corp.* [1978] ECR 1823, [1978] 1 CMLR 326.

[40] For an example of a case in which there was such a legitimate reason, see Case C-313/94, *Fratelli Graffione SNC v. Ditta Fransa* [1996] ECR I-6039, [1997] 1 CMLR 925.

[41] Case 3/78, *Centrafarm BV v. American Home Products Corp.* (n. 39).

[42] C. H. Baden Fuller, 'Economic Issues Relating to Property Rights in Trade Marks' (1981) 6 Eur LR 162.

We now turn to the detailed analysis of these subsequent developments, which have clarified a number of points.

Article 7 of the Directive: mere codification?

This, then, was the position before the harmonization of national trade mark laws. The Court's case law dealt with the apparent clash between the national trade mark laws of the member states, and Arts. 34 and 36 of the Treaty. The First Harmonization Directive changed that picture.[43] It deals with exhaustion in its Art. 7 and, on the basis of that Article, the pharmaceutical industry challenged the validity of the Court's case law.[44] The issue of whether *Hoffmann-La Roche v. Centrafarm*[45] was still good law was brought before the Court as a preliminary question on the interpretation of Art. 7 of the Directive after a series of cases had been brought in the national courts by pharmaceutical companies that objected to the repackaging activity of parallel importers.[46]

The Directive grants the trade mark owner the exclusive right to affix the trade mark to the product or its packaging,[47] subject to the impact of the exhaustion principle. That principle is said, in Art. 7(1), not to '*entitle the proprietor to prohibit* [the trade mark's] *use in relation to goods which have been put on the market within the Community under that trade mark by the proprietor or with his consent*'. Article 7(2) adds that Art. 7(1) will not stop the trade mark owner from opposing the continued marketing of the goods if he or she does so on reasonable grounds. Obvious examples of such grounds are cases in which the goods have been impaired or altered after having been put on the market by the trade mark owner, or with his or her consent.

The pharmaceutical companies argued that Art. 7(1) should be interpreted in such a way that the goods are the goods in the format and the unit in which they have been put on the market. This would mean, for example, 20 tablets of the pharmaceutical product in a box with certain dimensions, colours, etc. The parallel importer would be free to buy these boxes in another member state and resell them as they are, but any repackaging and reaffixing of the trade mark would constitute an infringement of the trade mark. Article 7(2) would only operate, for example, to allow the trade mark owner to stop the marketing of damaged products. The same result is achieved if one admits that Art. 7(1)

---

[43] Council Directive 89/104/EEC to approximate the laws of the member states relating to trade marks (1989) OJ L 40/1.

[44] The real reason why parallel imports of pharmaceutical products are such a problem in the Community—and especially in the eyes of the main pharmaceutical companies—is the difference in prices between the different member states. This would not be such a problem if the different prices were determined entirely freely by the pharmaceutical companies that produce the drugs, but, in practice, there is also a lot of government regulation in the area. The circumvention of the absence of a harmonization in the national rules regulating the prices of pharmaceutical products and the perceived lack of political will to achieve it by breaching the rules on free movement is not, however, allowed. National trade mark law cannot be allowed to disregard Community law in this area: the purpose of trade marks is not to remedy the market distortions caused by the national price-regulating regimes; what needs to be done is harmonizing those different national regimes.

[45] Case 102/77 [1978] ECR 1139, [1978] 3 CMLR 217.

[46] Cases C-427, 429, and 436/93, *Bristol-Meyers Squibb, CH Boehringer Sohn, Boehringer Ingelheim KG, Boehringer Ingelheim A/S & Bayer AG, Bayer Danmark A/S v. Paranova A/S* [1996] ECR I-3457, [1997] 1 CMLR 1151; Cases C-71, 72, and 73/94, *Eurim-Pharm Arzneimittel GmbH v. Beiersdorf AG; Boehringer Ingelheim KG & Farmitalia Carlo Erba GmbH* [1996] ECR I-3603, [1997] 1 CMLR 1222; Case C-232/94, *MPA Pharma GmbH v. Rhone-Poulenc Pharma GmbH* [1996] ECR I-3671; see also P. Torremans, 'New Repackaging under the Trade Mark Directive of Well-Established Exhaustion Principles' (1997) 11 EIPR 664.

[47] Art. 5(3)(a) of the Directive.

results in the exhaustion of the trade mark as soon as the trade-marked product has been put on the market in any form, while giving a broad interpretation to Art. 7(2) by including any change of the brand presentation—that is, any form of repackaging and/or reaffixing of the trade mark—as a reasonable ground on which to exclude the operation of the exhaustion principle in Art. 7(1).[48]

This would, of course, involve a radical change in the definition of the exhaustion principle and it would reverse the Court's case law. Can the Directive be interpreted in this way? Or should one stick to the interpretation that Art. 7(1) results in the exhaustion of the trade mark as soon as the trade-marked product has been put on the market in any form, while the only reasonable ground on the basis of which the trade mark owner can object involves a change to the product that is actually consumed—that is, the tablets in our earlier example?

Article 7 of the Directive: a return to basics

Before jumping to any conclusion, one should start with the basics. The starting point of all Community law in this area is Arts. 34 and 36 of the Treaty on the Functioning of the European Union. Any secondary Community legislation can only apply and not change the Treaty, and should therefore be interpreted in a way that is in line and compatible with its provisions.[49] The provisions of the Directive must thus be interpreted in the light of Arts. 34 and 36 of the Treaty. What is not under discussion is that Art. 36 only provides for a partial exemption of trade mark rights from the application of Art. 34 and its free movement rule; what is exempted is the specific subject matter of the trade mark. The trade mark can play its competition-enhancing role[50] in the economy, but any other use is caught by Art. 34.

What, then, is the essence of a trade mark? A trade mark is essentially an indication of origin. The trade mark guarantees the consumer that a certain product has been manufactured by, or under the control of, a certain company that bears responsibility for the fact that the product meets certain standards or expectations of quality. The trade mark is the means by which the product is identified. That identification by customers leads to the establishment of goodwill for the company that is able to bind the customers to itself.[51]

The next question that needs to be answered therefore is the origin of what is indicated by the trade mark. The obvious answer is that of the goods that are labelled with the trade mark—but this does not solve our problem if one considers that marketing experts might suggest that the whole trade dress of a carefully marketed product forms part of the goods. A return to the basic principles of trade mark law provides the solution to this problem: a trade mark is a sign to distinguish goods that is registered in relation to a certain category or certain categories of goods. This means that a trade mark is,

---

[48] See K. Dyekjaer-Hansen, 'The Trade Mark Directive and the Protection of Brands and Branding' (1996) 1 EIPR 62, 63.

[49] See Case C-47/90, *Etablissements Delhaize Frères v. Promalvin* [1992] ECR I-3669 at para. 26; Case C-315/92, *Verband Sozialer Wettbewerb* [1994] ECR I-317 at para. 12, referred to in Joined Cases C-427, 429, and 436/93, *Bristol-Meyers Squibb v. Paranova A/S* [1996] ECR I-3457 at para. 27.

[50] The Court explicitly recognized that trade mark rights (within the constraints of their specific subject matter) form an essential element of the system of free competition on the Common Market that the Treaty set out to establish: Joined Cases C-427, 429, and 436/93, *Bristol-Meyers Squibb v. Paranova A/S* [1996] ECR I-3457 at para. 43.

[51] *Bristol-Meyers Squibb* (n. 50) at para. 43, with reference to Case C-10/89, *CNL-SUCAL NV SA v. HAG GF AG (Hag II)* [1990] ECR I-3711 at para. 13 and Case C-9/93, *IHT Internationaler Heiztechnik GmbH & Danziger v. Ideal Standard GmbH* [1994] ECR I-2789 at paras. 37 and 45.

for example, registered in relation to pharmaceutical products; no one will pretend that anything other than the product that is actually used for medicinal purposes is covered by this category.

The trade dress, meanwhile, is not part of the goods. The goods or products are, for example, the tablets, but they do not include the box in which they are packed by the manufacturer. This is the maximum coverage of trade mark law before the Treaty provisions interfere with it, which interference can only reduce the level of protection and the options offered to the trade mark owner due to the fact that Art. 34 rules out restrictions to the free movement and Art. 36 only partially alleviates that ban. The outcome of the process can therefore not be that trade dress is now included in the definition of the goods to which a trade mark is applied and in relation to which it creates certain exclusive rights.

Let us now turn to the Directive: it must be clear that the Directive, or any other piece of secondary Community legislation, cannot introduce quantitative restrictions if it can only apply the provisions of the Treaty. Any other conclusion would involve a violation of Arts. 34 and 36[52]—and only a new Treaty can change these Articles.

The final step brings us to the national trade mark laws. These must obviously be interpreted along the lines of the Directive. Because the Directive was supposed to harmonize the trade mark laws of the member states and the protection of trade marks as allowed in the context of Art. 36, one should, first of all, turn to the Directive when the compatibility of a provision of national trade mark law with Community law is at issue.[53] The Directive is supposed to offer more detailed rules and guidance, which is fully in line with the provisions of the Treaty.

Article 7 of the Directive: practical implications

Where does all of this theory lead us in practical terms? The question of whether or not national trade mark law can allow a trade mark owner to oppose the repackaging of pharmaceutical products and/or the reaffixing of the trade mark needs to be answered on the basis of the provisions of the Directive.[54]

Article 7 deals with the exhaustion issue in a complete way. The trade mark owner can oppose the activities of the parallel importer if that Article does not exhaust his or her right to object to these activities. On the basis of the text of Art. 7(1), it could be suggested that the term 'goods' can be said to include the goods as packed. It has been shown, however, that this would involve an unjustifiable expansion of trade mark protection and that such an interpretation of the Directive would not be in line with the Treaty provisions—which leaves us with the question of whether a change of packaging can be a reasonable ground under Art. 7(2) of the Directive. If so, no exhaustion would take place. Once more, the text of the Directive does not provide a conclusive answer. We have to turn to the provisions of the Treaty[55] and analyse whether such a wide interpretation of the reasonable ground concept is required to guarantee that the trade mark can fulfil its essential role.

It is submitted that the European Court of Justice rightly decided that this was not the case. The trade mark should function as an indication of origin. For the consumer, this

---

[52] See Case C-51/93, *Meyhui NV v. Schott Zwiesel Glaswerke AG* [1994] ECR I-3879 at para. 11, referred to in *Bristol-Meyers Squibb* (n. 50) at para. 35.

[53] See Case 5/77, *Tedeschi v. Denkavit Commerciale srl* [1977] ECR 1555 at para. 35; Case 227/82, *Van Bennekom* [1983] ECR 3883 at para. 35; Case C-37/92, *Vanacker & Lesage* [1993] ECR I-4947 at para. 9; Case C-323/93, *Société Civile Agricole du Centre d'insémination de la Crespelle* [1994] ECR I-5077 at para. 31; referred to in *Bristol-Meyers Squibb* (n. 50) at para. 25.

[54] *Bristol-Meyers Squibb* (n. 50) at para. 26.   [55] See *Bristol-Meyers Squibb* (n. 50) at para. 40.

means that he or she needs to be sure that, when buying the trade-marked product, he or she is buying the original pharmaceutical product—for example, the tablets—produced by the trade mark owner or under his or her control. No other products should be marketed under the trade mark to achieve this aim. In the cases under discussion, there was no evidence that the pharmaceutical products had been tampered with or that any product was passed off as the product of the trade mark owner. Indeed, in the one instance in which a vaporizer was added by the parallel importer,[56] that item did not bear the trade mark and it was made clear that the item had been added by, and under the sole responsibility of, the parallel importer.

The consumer should also be able to rely on the trade mark to be sure that the pharmaceutical product he or she buys is of a certain quality, which requirement is met as long as the original product is not tampered with. The trade mark owner should also be allowed to preserve the goodwill created by the trade mark. The indication of origin points indeed towards certain goods, of a certain quality, coming from one source, or at least with one party—the trade mark owner—controlling the system. This requirement is met as long as no other goods are labelled with the trade mark and as long as the goods are not tampered with.[57]

To guarantee this, further additional rules have been added. The packaging should clearly indicate who produced the goods, so as not to create the impression that the parallel importer or any third party has any right to the trade mark.[58] The parallel importer responsible for the repackaging needs also to be identified clearly on the packaging, in order to show that the third party, and not the trade mark owner, is responsible for the packaging. The straightforward way to do so is to print on the new packaging in a prominent way a message that 'X' manufactured the product, while 'Y', the parallel importer, imported and repacked the product.[59] Even so, the packaging should not be of a low standard, because that association with materials of a low quality would damage the high quality standard that is associated with pharmaceutical products.[60] The key element in mentioning the name of the entity repacking the goods is that of liability. It is therefore acceptable to mention merely the name of the entity assuming responsibility and liability for the operation, even if the actual act of repackaging is carried out by another entity in the same group of companies or by a third party.[61]

The trade mark owner should also be allowed to control the use of the trade mark and to prevent any damage to the goodwill associated with the trade mark that any inappropriate use of the trade mark could cause. This means that the trade mark owner should be advised in advance of any repackaging activity and should be given the opportunity to request a sample copy of the repacked product for inspection.[62] It is the responsibility of the parallel importer to give that notice and the right holder should at least be given 15 days in which to object.[63]

---

[56] *Bristol-Meyers Squibb* (n. 50) at para. 61.   [57] *Bristol-Meyers Squibb* (n. 50) at para. 59–64.

[58] Joined Cases C-71, 72, and 73/94, *Eurim-Pharm v. Beiersdorf* [1996] ECR I-3603 at para. 64, with reference to Case 1/81, *Pfizer v. Eurim-Pharm* [1981] ECR 2913 at para. 11.

[59] Joined Cases C-427, 429, and 436/93, *Bristol-Meyers Squibb 9* (n. 50) at para. 70.

[60] *Bristol-Meyers Squibb* (n. 50) at paras. 65–6 and 75–6. See also Case C-348/04, *Boehringer Ingelheim KG and ors v. Swingward Ltd and ors (No. 2)* [2007] 2 CMLR 52.

[61] Joined Cases C-400/09, *Orifarm A/S v. Merck, Sharp & Dohme Corp.* and C-207/10, *Paranova Denmark A/S and Paranova Pack A/S v. Merck, Sharp & Dohme Corp.* [2012] 1 CMLR 10, [2011] ETMR 59.

[62] Joined Cases C-427, 429, and 436/93, *Bristol-Meyers Squibb v. Paranova A/S* [1996] ECR I-3457 at para. 78.

[63] Case C-143/00, *Boehringer Ingelheim AG v. Swingward Ltd* [2002] ECR I-3759.

Under these conditions, the trade mark can fulfil its role as an indication of origin. Any further requirement goes beyond that role and would therefore be out of line with Art. 36 of the EC Treaty. A requirement, for example, that the fact that the repackaging took place without the consent of the trade mark owner should be mentioned explicitly on the packaging would create the impression that there might be something wrong with the product.[64]

Article 7 of the Directive: a mere codification!

Article 7(2) of the Directive is really only a way of restating the rule contained in Art. 36 of the Treaty on the Functioning of the European Union.[65] The interpretation that the Court had previously given to that Article in a repackaging context remains good law; all that these new cases have added to it is the fact that the Court seized the opportunity to clarify the rule and to provide the national court with more detailed guidance.

The parallel importer of pharmaceutical products is not free to repack them in any circumstances. Repackaging only becomes an option if the product is de facto marketed in different quantities in different member states. The right of the trade mark owner to oppose repackaging is only exhausted if the repackaging is necessary for the product to be marketable in the country of importation,[66] for example because health insurance legislation prescribes a standard size.[67] This can be seen as a prerequisite for any repackaging and reaffixing of trade mark operation. Any consent to put the goods on the market needs, however, to have been given by the party that is trying to prevent importation if exhaustion is to flow from it.[68]

There is, however, no need for the parallel importer to prove that the trade mark owner set out to partition the market deliberately by marketing the product in different quantities in different member states. It was therefore also held in a relabelling case that one has to assess whether all of the circumstances at the time of the marketing in the import state made it objectively necessary to use another mark to make marketing possible. In the absence of such objective necessity, there will be no artificial partitioning of the market, which is required to allow relabelling. By requiring an artificial partitioning of the market to be demonstrated before allowing the repackaging of products, the Court left open only the option of opposing the marketing of parallel imported products by the trade mark owner in those cases in which this is necessary to preserve the specific subject matter of the trade mark. A de facto use of different packaging sizes is all that the parallel importer needs to demonstrate initially to justify its activity.[69]

Necessity

This set of cases could create the false impression that the parallel importer has an almost absolute freedom to repack and relabel the products. The analysis has shown that this is

---

[64] Joined Cases C-427, 429, and 436/93, *Bristol-Meyers Squibb v. Paranova A/S* [1996] ECR I-3457 at para. 72.

[65] *Bristol-Meyers Squibb* (n. 50) at para. 40. For an application of Art. 7(2) in the context of AdWords, see Case C-558/08, *Portakabin Ltd v. Primakabin* [2010] ETMR 52.

[66] The fact that the product is, apart from the size in which it is bought by the parallel importer, also available in the country of exportation in the size in which it is repacked does not alter this conclusion: see *Bristol-Meyers Squibb* (n. 50) at para. 54.

[67] See *Bristol-Meyers Squibb* (n. 50) at paras. 53–56.

[68] See *Flynn Pharma Ltd v. DrugrusLtd and Tenolol Ltd* [2015] EWHC 2759 (Ch).

[69] See *Bristol-Meyers Squibb* (n. 50) at para. 57; Case C-379/97, *Pharmacia & Upjohn SA v. Paranova A/S* [2000] 1 CMLR 51.

not the case, and that the parallel importer's activity is restricted to what is required and necessary to allow parallel imports.

The necessity point has become a vital one. The European Court of Justice summarized it as follows:

> a trade mark proprietor may rely on its trade mark rights in order to prevent a parallel importer from repackaging pharmaceutical products unless the exercise of those rights contributes to artificial partitioning of the markets between Member States[70]

It continued, vitally, to state that:

> replacement packaging of pharmaceutical products is objectively necessary within the meaning of the Court's case-law if, without such repackaging, effective access to the market concerned, or to a substantial part of that market, must be considered to be hindered as the result of strong resistance from a significant proportion of consumers to relabelled pharmaceutical products.[71]

It is therefore clear that the necessity test applies to the act of repackaging[72], but the question of whether it also applies to the presentation of the repackaged product—that is, should the parallel importer also show that it had done nothing more than what was necessary in the terms of the manner of repackaging?—needed to be answered. How broad exactly is the concept of necessity?

The Court clarified the point by holding that the condition that the repackaging of the pharmaceutical product—either by reboxing the product and reapplying the trade mark, or by applying a label to the packaging containing the product—be necessary for its further commercialization in the importing member state is directed solely at the fact of repackaging, and not at the manner and style of the repackaging. There is therefore no need to show that a particular manner and style of repackaging or relabelling were required.[73] The style of repackaging and the exact presentation that results from it are therefore not to be assessed against the condition of necessity and a minimum-change-only requirement is to be ruled out, but the condition that the presentation should not be liable to damage the reputation of the trade mark or its proprietor remains applicable.[74]

The *Ballantines* case[75] also illustrates the necessity point. The parallel importer was given a certain freedom to bring the labelling of the bottles of whisky in line with the requirements of each member state and to identify itself, but the Court did not approve of the removal of the identification numbers from the bottles.[76] The latter was not required to allow parallel import to take place. Obviously, the presence of these numbers would also allow the producer of the whisky to trace the suppliers of the parallel importer. The Court argued that competition law would provide a remedy in case the producer decided

---

[70] Case C-143/00, *Boehringer Ingelheim AG v. Swingward Ltd* [2002] ECR I-3759.

[71] Case C-443/99, *Merck, Sharp & Dohme GmbH v. Paranova Pharmazeutika Handels GmbH* [2003] Ch 327, [2002] ETMR 923; *Boehringer Ingelheim* (n. 70).

[72] For examples of national cases that deal with the necessity to rebrand in order to gain effective market access, see *Speciality European Pharma Ltd v. Doncaster Pharmaceuticals Group Ltd and Madaus GmbH* [2015] EWCA Civ 54 and *Flynn Pharma Ltd v. DrugrusLtd and Tenolol Ltd* (n. 68).

[73] Case C-348/04, *Boehringer Ingelheim KG and ors v. Swingward Ltd and ors (No. 2)* [2007] 2 CMLR 52 and Case C-276/05, *Wellcome Foundation Ltd v. Paranova Pharmazeutika Handels GmbH* [2009] ETMR 20.

[74] *Wellcome Foundation Ltd* (n. 73).

[75] Case C-349/95, *Frits Loendersloot v. George Ballantine & Son Ltd* [1997] ECR I-6227, [1998] 1 CMLR 1015.

[76] It has been held, along the same lines, by Belgian courts that trade mark law allowed the trade mark owner to oppose acts of the parallel importer such as the deletion of bar codes, the deletion of the mention that the product can only be sold through recommended distributors, and the cutting of the seal on the

to take action against the supplier of the parallel importer in an attempt to stop the parallel importation.[77] This is, however, not necessarily a straightforward conclusion and the decision of the Court of First Instance to annul a Commission decision on this point is a stark reminder of the difficulties of applying competition law successfully on this point.[78]

Marketing authorization

It should also not be forgotten that the marketing of pharmaceutical products is subject to a marketing authorization and that the parallel import licence of the parallel importer makes reference to the marketing authorization of the original product.[79] Deliberately revoking the marketing authorization for the original product when bringing a newer version of the product on the market might therefore be a means for the producer to block parallel imports of the original product. The European Court of Justice held therefore that Arts. 28 and 30 of the EC Treaty (now Arts. 34 and 36 of the Treaty on the Functioning of the European Union) preclude national legislation under which the withdrawal, at the request of its holder, of the marketing authorization of reference automatically entails the withdrawal of the parallel import licence granted for the medicinal product in question. Restrictions on parallel imports of products are only allowed in such cases if there is, in fact, a risk to the health of humans as a result of the continued existence of that medicinal product on the market of the importing member state.[80]

Article 7 and licence agreements

A somewhat peculiar set of facts arises when the trade mark proprietor enters into an agreement with a seller that includes a clause stipulating that the latter shall not sell to discount stores with the consent of the proprietor. What happens if the seller nevertheless does so? Can the third party rely on exhaustion? The Court of Justice argued that the seller who breaches the agreement must be held to have acted without the consent of the proprietor. The breach must refer to the essential clauses and aspects of the trade mark that are found in Art. 8(2) of the Directive. The Court accepted that in the case of luxury goods that quality did not only result from the material characteristics of the goods, but also from the allure and the prestigious image conferred by the aura of luxury. The outlets in which they were sold were part of this picture. And in cases where the seller must be considered to have sold to the discount stores with consent the proprietor may

---

boxes of a perfume. It was held that these measures were not necessary to allow parallel import and that less invasive measures that did not affect the goodwill of the trade mark owner (such as mention on the shop window or shelves that, despite the impression created by the products, the parallel importer is not a recommended distributor) would have been sufficient. The cutting of the seals specifically could create the impression or the suspicion that the bottle in the box had been tampered with or had been replaced and this could seriously affect the goodwill of the trade mark owner: *Delhaize v. Dior*, Court of Appeal Liège, 13 April 1995, [1995] Ing-Cons 379; *SA Parfums Nina Ricci v. SA Best Sellers Belgium*, Commercial Court Liège, 18 October 1999, [2000] TBH 386.

[77] For further details see I. Stamatoudi, 'From Drugs to Spirits and from Boxes to Publicity: Decided and Undecided Issues in Relation to Trade Mark and Copyright Exhaustion' [1999] IPQ 95.

[78] Case T-41/96, *Bayer AG and EFPIA v. Commission & Bundesverband der Arneimittel-Importeure eV* [2000] ECR II-3383, [2001] All ER (EC) 1, [2001] 4 CMLR 4. Upheld by the Court of Justice on appeal (Cases C-2/01 P and C-3/01P) [2004] 4 CMLR 13.

[79] See also *Aventis Pharma Deutschland GmbH v. Kohlpharma GmbH & MTK Pharma Vertriebs-GmbH* [2002] 3 CMLR 659.

[80] Cases C-15/01, *Paranova v. Läkemedelsverket* [2003] 2 CMLR 856; C-175/00, *Ferring Arzneimittel GmbH v. Eurim-Pharm Arzneimittel GmbH* [2002] ECR I-6891.

nevertheless rely on Art. 7(2) to avoid exhaustion on the condition that the sale damages the reputation of the trade mark. The Court accepted in this case that impairing the aura of luxury effectively affected the actual quality of the goods. Hence the need to be able to rely on Art. 7 to stop exhaustion. This is a far-reaching interpretation, though, which uses Art. 7 in a wide sense.[81]

A summary

The second *Boehringer Ingelheim v. Swingward* case[82] gave the European Court of Justice the opportunity to summarize the position on parallel imports of trade-marked goods. The Court highlighted the following key points. The trade mark owner may legitimately oppose further commercialization of a pharmaceutical product imported from another member state in its original internal and external packaging with an additional external label applied by the importer, unless:

- it is established that reliance on trade mark rights by the proprietor in order to oppose the marketing of the overstickered product under that trade mark would contribute to the artificial partitioning of the markets between member states;
- the repackaging of the pharmaceutical product—either by reboxing the product and reapplying the trade mark, or by applying a label to the packaging containing the product—is necessary for its further commercialization in the importing member state, albeit that this condition is directed solely at the fact of repackaging, and not at the manner and style of the repackaging;
- it is shown that the new label cannot affect the original condition of the product inside the packaging;
- the packaging clearly states who overstickered the product and the name of the manufacturer;
- the presentation of the overstickered product is not likely to damage the reputation of the trade mark and of its proprietor—that is, the label must not be defective, of poor quality, or untidy;
- the importer gives notice to the trade mark proprietor before the overstickered product is put on sale and, on demand, supplies the proprietor with a specimen of that product;
- the presentation of the pharmaceutical product after repackaging or relabelling is not such as to be liable to damage the reputation of the trade mark and of its proprietor. This condition is not limited to cases in which the repackaging is defective, of poor quality, or untidy. The standard usually applied in the trade is to be adhered to.

The question of whether the fact that a parallel importer responsible for any of the following is likely to damage the trade mark's reputation is a question of fact for the national court to decide in the light of the circumstances of each case:

- failure to affix the trade mark to the new exterior carton—that is, 'de-branding';
- application of either his or her own logo, house style, get-up, or a get-up used for a number of different products—that is, 'co-branding';

---

81 Case C-59/08, *Copad SA v. Christian Dior Couture SA* [2009] FSR 22, [2009] ETMR 40.
82 Case C-348/04, *Boehringer Ingelheim KG and ors v. Swingward Ltd and ors (No. 2)* [2007] 2 CMLR 52.

- positioning of the additional label so as wholly or partially to obscure the proprietor's trade mark;
- failure to state on the additional label that the trade mark in question belongs to the proprietor;
- printing of the name of the parallel importer in capital letters.

In terms of burden of proof, it is for the parallel importer to prove the existence of the conditions that:

- reliance on trade mark rights by the proprietor in order to oppose the marketing of repackaged products under that trade mark would contribute to the artificial partitioning of the markets between member states;
- the repackaging cannot affect the original condition of the product inside the packaging;
- the new packaging clearly states who repackaged the product and the name of the manufacturer;
- the presentation of the repackaged product is not such as to be liable to damage the reputation of the trade mark and of its proprietor;
- he or she has given notice to the trade mark proprietor before the repackaged product is put on sale and, on demand, supplied him or her with a specimen of the repackaged product. If a parallel importer has failed to give prior notice to the trade mark proprietor concerning a repackaged pharmaceutical product, he or she infringes that proprietor's rights on the occasion of any subsequent importation of that product, as long as he or she has not given the proprietor such notice.

As regards the condition that it must be shown that the repackaging cannot affect the original condition of the product inside the packaging, it is sufficient, however, that the parallel importer furnishes evidence that leads to the reasonable presumption that the condition has been fulfilled. This applies *a fortiori* also to the condition that the presentation of the repackaged product must not be such as to be liable to damage the reputation of the trade mark and of its proprietor. If the importer furnishes such initial evidence that the latter condition has been fulfilled, it will then be for the proprietor of the trade mark, who is best placed to assess whether the repackaging is liable to damage his or her reputation and that of the trade mark, to prove that they have been so damaged.[83]

Exhaustion without parallel import

Most exhaustion cases involve an element of parallel importation, but that is not necessarily the case. Article 7(1) of the Directive does not require parallel importation. A good example is found in the *Viking Gas* case. Bottled gas was put on the market in design bottles, rather than in the standard ones. These design bottles were later refilled by an independent trader. The bottles were unchanged and sported still the original trade mark and the refilling company added its own identification as refiller by means of a large sticker. The Court of Justice held that the refiller was not liable for trade mark infringement, as the first sale of the design bottle had exhausted the trade mark. The Court rejected the argument that the bottle was mere packaging and that as a result exhaustion only applied

---

[83] *Boehringer Ingelheim KG and ors* (n. 82). For a recent application of the exhaustion rules in the UK, see *Oracle America Inc. v. M-Tech Data Ltd* [2012] UKSC 27.

to the resale of the original bottle filled with the original gas. The design bottle had its own economic value, reflected in a higher price than the standard one, which had been realized when it was first sold. The refilling operation did not therefore in the circumstances fall foul of Art. 7(2) of the Directive either. The bottle still carried the original trade mark and was in its original condition, whilst the refiller clearly identified itself as such and took responsibility for the new gas in the bottle and for the refilling activity. Exhaustion therefore applied.[84]

Exhaustion covers publicity

Parallel importation can only work in practice if the parallel importer can sell the goods successfully. This requires that he or she can advertise the fact that the original product is now also available through his or her outlets and that his or her prices are lower. Can the parallel importer reproduce the trade mark for the purposes of this advertising?

The answer to this question can only be affirmative if the exhaustion of the trade mark by putting it on the market in the member state from which it was imported by the parallel importer also covered the trade mark's reproduction for advertising purposes. This should indeed be the case, because normal advertising practices will not damage the goodwill of the trade mark owner, if they only inform the public about the availability of the product. The consumer is not misled either, because the original product is advertised, rather than any similar product. The advertising does not normally create the impression that the parallel importer manufactures the product; on the contrary, the importer will try to emphasize that he or she is selling the 'real thing'—that is, the original product, from the original producer—but only at a lower price. That is his or her best strategy by which to maximize sales. This means that the essential function of the trade mark is fulfilled and that there is no need to allow the trade mark owner to use his or her trade mark to stop the advertising, because the goods concerned have been marketed with his or her consent.

The European Court of Justice approved this approach in the *Dior* case,[85] when it stopped Dior from relying on its trade marks to stop the parallel importer from advertising its goods by reproducing in its publicity the boxes in which the perfumes were sold. These boxes obviously carried the trade marks. The advertising took place in the format that was normally used by the parallel importer and others in the same type of trade. Dior argued that the form of advertising did not meet its high standards and could therefore affect the reputation of its trade marks in a negative way. The Court ruled that any form of advertising in the way and quality in which the parallel importer normally advertised its goods could not damage the goodwill of Dior.

The Court expressed this ruling as follows:

> The proprietor of a trade mark may not rely on Article 7(2) of Directive 89/104 to oppose the use of the trade mark, by a reseller who habitually markets articles of the same kind, but not necessarily of the same quality, as the trade-marked goods, in ways customary in the reseller's sector of trade, for the purpose of bringing to the public's attention the further commercialisation of those goods, unless it is established that, given the specific circumstances of the case, the use of the trade mark for this purpose seriously damages the reputation of the trade mark.[86]

---

[84] Case C-46/10, *Viking Gas A/S v. Kosan Gas A/S* [2011] ETMR 58.
[85] Case C-337/95, *Parfums Christian Dior SA & Parfums Christian Dior BV v. Evora BV* [1998] RPC 166.
[86] *Parfums Christian Dior* (n. 85); see Stamatoudi, 'From Drugs to Spirits and from Boxes to Publicity' (n. 77).

The only reason why Dior could stop the use of its trade marks was the fact that its goodwill would be affected. This had to be demonstrated on the basis of the facts of the case. Advertising of a very low and sloppy quality, far below the normal standards of the type of business concerned, could be an example of such an exceptional case. In that case, the essential function of the trade mark could no longer be fulfilled, which justifies the use of the trade mark to stop such a practice.

International exhaustion

The concept of international exhaustion

The Agreement on the European Economic Area expanded the area in which exhaustion applies to the whole of the EEA, which means that, apart from the EU, it applies to Iceland, Liechtenstein, and Norway.[87] Until recently, however, it was unclear whether the EU would opt for the principle of international exhaustion or not.

In very simple terms, 'international exhaustion' means that all trade mark rights are exhausted once the product labelled with the trade mark has been put on the market anywhere in the world by, or with the consent of, the trade mark owner. Trade mark owners in the EU would no longer be able to stop parallel importation of their products from outside the EEA by relying on their parallel trade marks in the member states if the principle of international exhaustion were to apply.

Traditionally, certain member states—such as Austria—had incorporated the principle of international exhaustion into their domestic trade mark system, but, recently, the majority of the member states and the Commission seemed to have abandoned the principle of international exhaustion. One could take a cynical view and argue that this was a symptom of the 'Fortress Europe' mentality and that they only wanted to protect themselves from cheap imports. The crucial issue was whether the Trade Mark Directive[88] had decided the issue or not.

Article 7 of the Directive deals with the issue of exhaustion and refers to goods that have been put on the market in the EEA. It is clear that this provision does not oblige the member states to operate an international exhaustion rule. In so far as it imposes a system of exhaustion, the provision restricts its scope to the EEA. Two conclusions seemed possible on this basis: first, it could be left to the member states to decide whether or not they wanted to adopt an international exhaustion rule, which argument sees Art. 7 as the minimum, but a minimum to which additions can be made; second, one could argue that Art. 7 is a restriction on the rights of trade mark owners and that the Directive does not allow the member states to add the further restrictions that an international exhaustion rule would necessarily carry with it.

Silhouette

The *Silhouette* case[89] gave the European Court of Justice the opportunity to decide the issue. Silhouette had sold a large number of its spectacle frames in Bulgaria and these had been reimported into the EEA by Hartlauer, a parallel importer, for sale in the latter's outlets in Austria. Silhouette sued for infringement of its Austrian trade mark and the Austrian court asked the Court whether it could still operate an international exhaustion rule.

---

[87] [1994] OJ L 1/3.   [88] [1989] OJ L 40/1.

[89] Case C-355/96, *Silhouette International Schmied GmbH & Co. KG v. Hartlauer Handelsgesellschaft mbH* [1998] All ER (EC) 769, [1998] 2 CMLR 953.

The Court argued that the Trade Mark Directive set out to harmonize fully all of those elements of trade mark law that may distort competition within, and the functioning in general of, the Common Market. The Court derives, from this starting point, the rule that 'Article 5 to 7 of the Directive must be construed as embodying a complete harmonization of the rules relating to the rights conferred by a trade mark'[90] and that member states can add only those rules that are included as optional provisions in this Article. Any other additions would destroy the aim of the Directive. Member states are therefore no longer free to operate a rule of international exhaustion, because such a rule was not included in the Directive as an option. The Court effectively declared international exhaustion dead under the existing legislation.[91]

Evaluation

This decision is, however, highly political and regrettable. There is nothing in the essential function of a trade mark that can justify the fact that exhaustion needs to stop at the borders of the EEA; on the contrary, the logic of the system is that the system of exhaustion should operate on all occasions when the original product is concerned and when that product has been marketed by, or with the consent of, the trade mark owner, irrespective of the place of first marketing. Exhaustion should only be put aside in exceptional cases, for example if the product has been tampered with or if the quality of the parallel imported product is inferior to the product marketed under the same name by the original producer in the area into which parallel importation takes place. In those examples, the operation of the exhaustion rule would impinge on the goodwill of the producer and the interests of the consumers would be harmed. The essential function of the trade mark would be affected in these exceptional cases.

It is submitted that neither does the Directive rule out this radically different conclusion: the full harmonization in Art. 7 could be restricted to the operation of an EEA-wide exhaustion rule. All points that have not been decided by what is, after all, called a 'First' Harmonization Directive should be left to the discretion of the member states. Any such state would then be free to introduce an international exhaustion rule—and, arguably, any use of a trade mark to block parallel importation under the laws of a member state that had opted against international exhaustion would amount to an abusive use of the rights granted by a trade mark, because it would obstruct the operation of the Common Market.

Alternatively, the free circulation of the parallel imported goods that were first marketed outside the EEA could be restricted to the member state under the international exhaustion rule of which their importation took place, because they were not put on the market in the EEA by, or with the consent of, the trade mark owner. In either case, this solution would have fitted in much better with the current climate of worldwide free trade and the expectation for the latter that was created by the World Trade Organization (WTO) agreement signed in Marrakesh.

Davidoff to no avail

The European Court of Justice was yet again given an opportunity to reconsider its approach to the issue of international exhaustion when requests for a preliminary ruling were forwarded to the Court by the courts in the UK. Laddie J had ruled, in the *Davidoff*

---

[90] *Silhouette* (n. 89) at para. 25.

[91] See also the confirmation of the approach in Case C-173/98, *Sebago & Maison Dubois* [1999] ECR I-4103.

case,[92] that contract law had a role to play in this area and that, as a result, goods that had been put on the market outside the EEA with the consent of the trade mark owner could be parallel-imported into the EEA if the trade mark owner had not used his or her right to include a reservation of title in the contract and to prohibit certain forms of re-exportation. In the absence of effective constraints, UK contract law allowed the conclusion that the trade mark owner had impliedly consented to the goods being re-exported and parallel imported into the EEA. It was argued that this approach could be adopted in parallel with the Court's ruling in *Silhouette* and that the latter remained unaffected.

The Court rejected this approach and ruled that the consent of a trade mark proprietor to the marketing within the EEA of products bearing that mark that have previously been placed on the market outside the EEA by that proprietor, or with his or her consent, may be implied—if that implied consent follows from facts and circumstances prior to, simultaneous with, or subsequent to the placing of the goods on the market outside the EEA that, in the view of the national court, unequivocally demonstrates that the proprietor has renounced his or her right to oppose placing of the goods on the market within the EEA.[93]

The need to demonstrate unequivocally that the right holder renounces his or her right to oppose marketing of the goods in the EEA had already slammed the brakes on Laddie J's approach, but the Court went on to really shut the door almost entirely when it added:

Implied consent cannot be inferred:

- from the fact that the proprietor of the trade mark has not communicated to all subsequent purchasers of the goods placed on the market outside the European Economic Area his opposition to marketing within the European Economic Area;
from the fact that the goods carry no warning of a prohibition of their being placed on the market within the European Economic Area;
- from the fact that the trade mark proprietor has transferred the ownership of the products bearing the trade mark without imposing any contractual reservations and that, according to the law governing the contract, the property right transferred includes, in the absence of such reservations, an unlimited right of resale or, at the very least, a right to market the goods subsequently within the European Economic Area.[94]

Ignorance on the side of the importer or failure by authorized retailers to reimpose the restrictions imposed originally by the right holder have also been excluded as grounds that could allow the parallel importation. The Court held in this respect that:

With regard to exhaustion of the trade mark proprietor's exclusive right, it is not relevant:

- that the importer of goods bearing the trade mark is not aware that the proprietor objects to their being placed on the market in the European Economic Area or sold there by traders other than authorised retailers;
- or that the authorized retailers and wholesalers have not imposed on their own purchasers contractual reservations setting out such opposition, even though they have been informed of it by the trade mark proprietor.[95]

---

[92] *Zino Davidoff SA v. A&G Imports Ltd (No. 1)* [2000] Ch 127, [1999] 3 All ER 711. The Scottish courts adopted a slightly different approach: see *Zino Davidoff SA v. M&S Toiletries Ltd (No. 1)* [2000] 2 CMLR 735, 2000 SLT 683. See also P. Torremans and I. Stamatoudi, 'International Exhaustion in the European Union in the Light of *Zino Davidoff*: Contract v. Trade Mark Law?' (2000) 2 IIC 123.

[93] Joined Cases C-414/99, *Zino Davidoff SA v. A&G Imports Ltd*; C-415/99, *Levi Strauss & Co. v. Tesco plc*; and C-416/99, *Levi Strauss & Co. v. Costco Wholesale UK Ltd* [2001] ECR I-1891, [2002] RPC 403 at 414.

[94] *Davidoff, Strauss* (n. 93) at 416.

[95] *Davidoff, Strauss* (n. 93) at 417.

This amounts to a very stringent approach that effectively blocks the door to parallel importation based on international exhaustion. The Court has squarely put the ball back in the camp of the legislator, but the latter is, at present, unable to reach any kind of agreement on this point.

The only slight comfort for the parallel importer in this context is to be derived from the fact that, where they would normally have to prove that they acquired the goods from a source that allows them to rely on Community exhaustion, they can argue that revealing their sources would bring with it a real risk of partitioning of the market. This would, for example, be the case if the right holder were to use an exclusive distribution system. The burden of proof then shifts to the right holder, who should demonstrate that the goods were originally marketed outside the EU. Proof of that point would require the parallel importer to prove the consent of the right holder to subsequent marketing of the goods in the EEA. Small as it may be, this is a welcome concession to the parallel importer, because revealing its sources may well get it off the hook, but it would, at the same time, make sure that the sources dried up quickly afterwards.[96]

The real context

Although the impression might be created that the interference of the Court and of European law in relation to trade marks is enormous, this is not correct and the whole issue must be seen in its real context. Generally, the grant of trade marks and the right to take action against infringement are national (harmonized) competences. The Court will only interfere when these provisions are applied in a discriminatory manner.[97]

This was emphasized in the *Audi* case,[98] in which the Court verified whether the German requirements for trade mark protection were equally applied to trade marks of national and foreign origin, while leaving it to the German courts to decide whether, under German trade mark law, the use of the name 'Quadra' by Renault created confusion with Audi's 'Quattro' trade mark.[99] The Court merely focuses on the abusive exercise of trade mark rights.

The doctrine of common origin

The European Court of Justice set out the doctrine of common origin in the *Hag I* case,[100] which was a rather peculiar case. A German company, Hag AG, owned the trade mark 'Hag' in Germany, Belgium, and Luxembourg, but, after the war, its Belgian and Luxembourg property was sequestrated, and the trade mark was assigned to the Van Zuylen Frères company. Both companies produced coffee under the 'Hag' trade mark and a problem arose when Van Zuylen tried to rely on its Belgian trade mark to prevent

---

[96] Case C-244/00, *Van Doren+Q. GmbH v. Lifestyle sports + sportswear Handelsgesellschaft mbH & Michael Orth* [2003] ECR I-3051.

[97] See G. Würtenberger, 'Determination of Risk of Confusion in Trade Mark Infringement Proceedings in the European Union: The *Quattro* Decision' (1994) 7 EIPR 302, 304.

[98] Case C-317/91, *AG Deutsche Renault v. Audi AG* [1993] ECR I-6227, [1995] 1 CMLR 461.

[99] See Würtenberger, 'Determination of Risk of Confusion in Trade Mark Infringement Proceedings in the European Union' (n. 97); see also N. Reich, 'The "November Revolution" of the European Court of Justice: *Keck, Meng and Audi* Revisited' (1994) 31 CMLR 459, 463.

[100] Case 192/73, *Van Zuylen Frères v. Hag AG* [1974] ECR 731, [1974] 2 CMLR 127 (*Hag I*).

Hag AG from importing coffee into Belgium. The argument was that Van Zuylen had not consented to the use of its trade mark, and had thus not exhausted its rights and could stop Hag AG from using the 'Hag' trade mark in Belgium.

This would have been the logical conclusion under the free movement rules as we have discussed them, but the Court arrived at a different conclusion by focusing on the common origin of the trade mark in the period before the war. The Court held that:

> one cannot allow the holder of a trade mark to rely upon the exclusiveness of a trade mark right—which may have the consequence of a territorial limitation of national markets—with a view to prohibiting the marketing in a member state of goods legally produced in another member state under an identical mark having the same origin.[101]

If the trade marks have a common origin, one cannot rely on the trade mark to prevent the other party from using it in the member state in which one owns the trade mark. Van Zuylen could not exercise any right under its 'Hag' trade mark to prevent its use in Belgium by Hag AG. The Court feared the partitioning of the single market—but this approach did not make sense, because it endangered the essential functions of the trade mark by putting both the goodwill of the trade mark owner and the interests of the consumers at risk: confusion would inevitably arise when two coffee producers started marketing their coffee 'Hag' in the same market.

The Court never used the doctrine in any other decisions until the *Hag II* case made its way to it. More than 15 years after the *Hag I* case had been decided, Van Zuylen had been acquired by Jacobs-Suchard and it intended to market the Belgian 'Hag' coffee in Germany. Under the doctrine of common origin, Hag AG could not object to this, because the trade marks had a common origin. The Court used the *Hag II* case[102] to admit that it had made a mistake in *Hag I* and repealed the doctrine of common origin. Hag AG was consequently allowed to rely on its German trade mark, which had not been exhausted, to stop the importation into Germany of the Belgian coffee 'Hag'.

The Court expressed its decision as follows:

> Articles [28 and 30] of the EEC Treaty do not preclude national legislation from allowing an undertaking which is the holder of a trade mark in a member state from opposing the importation from another member state of similar products lawfully bearing an identical trade mark in the latter state or liable to confusion with the protected mark even though the mark under which the contested products are imported originally belonged to a subsidiary of the undertaking which opposes the importation and was acquired by a third undertaking as a result of the expropriation of that subsidiary.[103]

This created some doubt as to whether the doctrine of common origin had really been repealed or whether it might still apply in a case in which there was a common origin of the trade mark, followed by a voluntary assignment, rather than by a forced expropriation. This issue was solved in the *Ideal Standard* case,[104] in which the Court applied its dictum in *Hag II* to a case involving the voluntary assignment of a trade mark.

The doctrine of common origin is now legal history, because the dictum in *Hag I* has now been repealed fully by the combined effect of the *Hag II* and the *Ideal Standard* decisions.

---

[101] *Hag I* (n. 100) at 744 and 143–4 (different translations to the same effect).
[102] Case C-10/89, *CNL-Sucal NV SA v. HAG GF AG* [1990] ECR I-3711, [1990] 3 CMLR 571 (*Hag II*).
[103] *Hag II* (n. 102) at paras. 22 and 609 (different translations to same effect).
[104] Case C-9/93, *IHT International Heiztechnik GmbH v. Ideal Standard GmbH* [1995] FSR 59.

Trade marks and competition law

Article 101 (formerly Article 81)

Trade mark licence agreements can restrict competition and are, in that respect, not different from patent licence agreements. The Commission will use its powers to enforce Art. 101 of the Treaty on the Functioning of the European Union if an agreement has, as its effect or as its object, the restriction of competition and the partitioning of the single market.

The Commission's prime target is so-called 'absolute territorial protection'. It is based on the grant of a single exclusive trade mark licence per member state, coupled with an obligation for each exclusive licensee (and for the licensor) not to pursue any active or passive sales policy outside its licensed territory. Its aim is to produce full exclusivity, resulting in the product being available from a single source in each part of the single market, which is covered by an exclusive licence and which licence fully excludes parallel imports.

The Commission was not prepared to grant an exemption for this type of trade mark licence and, on two occasions, an appeal to the European Court of Justice on this point failed: in *Consten & Grundig v. Commission*[105] and in *Tepea BV v. Commission*.[106] The Commission was, however, prepared to grant an exemption if at least parallel imports remained possible even if the licence was exclusive, and licensees were prohibited from pursuing an active sales policy outside their territory.[107] An exemption was also possible if the agreement had a positive effect on intra-brand competition and widened the consumer's choice.[108]

Article 102 (formerly Article 82)

Certain ways of using a trade mark can amount to an abuse of a dominant position, but, in practice, few, if any, problems have arisen in this area up to now.[109]

An overview

Going beyond our national borders, trade mark law is based on the Paris Convention and the TRIPS Agreement, with the Madrid system offering an international registration system. Inside the EU, one can also register a single trade mark for the whole of the Community by means of the Community Trade Mark Regulation. The substantive provisions of the Regulation run parallel to those of the Directive that harmonized national trade mark laws.

---

[105] Joined Cases 56 and 58/64, *Establissements Consten & Grundig v. EC Commission* [1966] ECR 299, [1966] CMLR 418. For a recent UK case in which the point arose, see *Oracle America Inc. v. M-Tech Data Ltd* [2012] UKSC 27, at paras. 30–32.

[106] Case 28/77, *Tepea BV v. EC Commission* [1978] ECR 1391, [1978] 3 CMLR 392.

[107] *Re Davide Campari-Milano SpA Agreement* [1978] 2 CMLR 397, OJ L 70/69.

[108] *Moosehead/Whitbread* [1991] 4 CMLR 391, (1990) OJ L 100/32, which was a combined trade mark/know-how case in which the trade mark aspect was clearly dominant.

[109] See *Chiquita/Fyffes plc*, Commission press release, 4 June 1992. The Commission invoked both Arts. 81 and 82, although it seems this was more an Art. 81 case dealing with an agreement between the parties, whereby one of them would restrict the use of its trade mark in Continental Europe.

Trade mark law also has a substantial interaction with the Treaty provisions on the free movement of goods. Parallel importation has given rise to a constant supply of challenging cases and heated debate. That debate focuses essentially on the relabelling and repackaging of parallel-traded goods. In *Boehringer Ingelheim v. Swingward*,[110] the European Court of Justice summarized the main points as follows.

The trade mark owner may legitimately oppose further commercialization of a pharmaceutical product imported from another member state in its original internal and external packaging with an additional external label applied by the importer, unless:

- it is established that reliance on trade mark rights by the proprietor in order to oppose the marketing of the overstickered product under that trade mark would contribute to the artificial partitioning of the markets between member states;

- the repackaging of the pharmaceutical product, either by reboxing the product and reapplying the trade mark or by applying a label to the packaging containing the product, is necessary for its further commercialization in the importing member state, albeit that this condition is directed solely at the fact of repackaging and not at the manner and style of the repackaging;

- it is shown that the new label cannot affect the original condition of the product inside the packaging;

- the packaging clearly states who overstickered the product and the name of the manufacturer;

- the presentation of the overstickered product is not such as to be liable to damage the reputation of the trade mark and of its proprietor; thus, the label must not be defective, of poor quality, or untidy;

- the importer gives notice to the trade mark proprietor before the overstickered product is put on sale, and, on demand, supplies him with a specimen of that product;

- the presentation of the pharmaceutical product after repackaging or relabelling cannot be such as to be liable to damage the reputation of the trade mark and of its proprietor. This condition is not limited to cases where the repackaging is defective, of poor quality, or untidy. The standard usually applied in the trade is to be adhered to.

The Community does, however, limit exhaustion to the EEA sphere and international exhaustion has been ruled out. At one stage, a doctrine of common origin was also applied, but this has now been put to rest.

Competition law issues arise rather sparingly in relation to trade marks.

Further reading

DYRBERG, P., 'For EEA Exhaustion to Apply, Who Has to Prove the Marketing of the Trade Marked Goods: The Trade Mark Owner or the Defendant?' (2004) 26 EIPR 81.

MURPHY, G., 'Who's Wearing the Sunglasses Now?' (2000) 21 Eur Comp LR 1.

---

[110] Case C-348/04, *Boehringer Ingelheim KG and anor v. Swingward Ltd* [2007] 2 CMLR 1445 at 1488–90.

Stamatoudi, I., 'From Drugs to Spirits and from Boxes to Publicity: Decided and Undecided Issues in Relation to Trade Mark and Copyright Exhaustion' [1999] IPQ 95.

Stamatoudi, I. and Torremans, P., 'International Exhaustion in the European Union in the Light of *Zino Davidoff*: Contract Versus Trade Mark Law?' (2000) 31 IIC 123.

Stothers, C., 'Political Exhaustion: the EU Commission's Working Paper on Possible Abuses of Trade Mark Rights within the EU in the Context of Community Exhaustion' (2003) 25 EIPR 457.

28

Tortious protection of intellectual property rights

Now we move away from the creation of formal rights in intellectual property to consider the various ways in which the common law, in the form of the law of tort, creates rights of action, as opposed to proprietary rights, which have the effect of protecting activity in the area of intellectual property. Passing off and malicious falsehood will be the principal torts considered, although attention will also be paid to the ways in which defamation can assist. It must be emphasized that these rights are supplementary, and complementary, to the statutory formal rights. In particular, trade mark law and passing off closely overlap, although s. 2(2) of the Trade Marks Act (TMA) 1994 preserves passing off as a separate cause of action. That said, the extensions to the range of protection afforded by the trade mark regime by the 1994 Act inevitably diminish the role of these tortious rights, especially in the absence of proprietary rights arising from them.[1]

Let us briefly look, in a little more detail, at the suggestion in the 1994 Act that the Act does not interfere with the law of passing off. Things are not as easy as this initial statement suggests, as became clear in *Inter Lotto (UK) Ltd v. Camelot Group plc*.[2] The claimant used the name 'Hotpick' as the unregistered mark for a lottery game sold in bars and pubs from 28 November 2001 onwards. The defendant filed an application for the registration of the name 'Hotpicks' for lottery games on 17 October 2001 and started using the mark in July 2002. The Court of Appeal was confronted with the question of which of the two marks took preference.

According to the claimant, s. 2(2) of the 1994 Act means that it has no impact on the tort of passing off and, in passing off, the relevant date on which to assess the goodwill of the claimant is the day of first use of the mark—that is, the moment of the first misrepresentation. At that moment, the claimant had developed goodwill in the name.

According to the defendant, reliance is instead to be placed on s. 5(4), which means that the relevant date for priority is the application date for the trade mark. Section 5(4) then deals with rights acquired under passing off before that date. Of course, in this scenario, the defendant wins.

In its judgment, the Court of Appeal recognized that the interaction between trade marks and passing off is far more complex than was suggested at first, but, in this case, it gave preference to s. 2(2). The court argued that this section establishes the principle and that a specific rule, such as that in s. 5(4) on relative grounds for refusal, cannot deviate from that principle and can deal only with an additional point. Section 5(4) will therefore only apply once the question of passing off has been dealt with on its own terms in application of s. 2(2).

---

[1] See M. Ni Shuilleabhain, 'Common Law Protection of Trade Marks: The Continuing Relevance of the Law of Passing Off' (2003) 34 IIC 722.

[2] [2003] 4 All ER 575, [2003] RPC 186.

Passing off

As will be clear to any student of patent law, some areas of the law of intellectual property appear, on the surface, to be deceptive in their simplicity; the tort of passing off, however, stands at the opposite end of the spectrum. Much heat and noise has been generated in the quest for definitions of the tort—but it is useful to assert at the outset that the essence of the tort is the protection of both consumers and other traders from the effect of confusion on their goodwill in trade. That confusion is generated by the activity of a trader in causing his or her goods or services and/or their presentation to become confused with those of the claimant, and that protection is afforded by the grant of a right of action to the trader whose economic interests and trading goodwill are harmed by the confusion.[3]

Historical development

The 'informal' protection of rights by the tort of passing off closely parallels the formal rights created by trade mark law. It is significant, however, that the tortious right came into existence long before the establishment of a trade mark system. It appears that the law first began to address the problem of trade confusion in the late sixteenth century: reference is made in *Southern v. How*[4] to a case arising in the 1580s, in which an action was successfully maintained by a cloth manufacturer whose distinguishing mark was used by a rival trader on his greatly inferior cloth. The use of the term 'passing off' can be traced back to *Perry v. Truefitt*,[5] an unedifying dispute between two hair oil manufacturers, both selling their brands of 'Medicated Mexican Balm', in relation to which the claimant was refused an injunction, but not denied a legal right to protect his original use of the trade name in question.

A key point in the development of the tort appeared early in the twentieth century: *Spalding & Bros. v. A. W. Gamage*[6] was a consideration by the House of Lords of a dispute between rival football sellers, the claimant manufacturer objecting to the sale of its balls by the defendant at a greatly reduced price in adverts that failed to disclose that the balls under offer were of an older and inferior design in comparison with the claimant's current model. Lord Parker emphasized, in finding for the claimant, that the essence of a passing off action was the protection of rights in the business and its goodwill, which may be harmed by the defendant's conduct. It was equally clear, however, that this right in goodwill was not a property right as such, but rather a right to seek a remedy during such period of time as the goodwill continues to exist. From this, the tort of passing off comes to exist in its modern form.

'Passing off' defined

Attempts to define 'passing off' have been, at times, confusing, particularly after the decision of the House of Lords in *Erven Warnink v. J. Townend & Sons (Hull) Ltd*[7] offered two separate definitions.

---

[3] See, in general, C. Wadlow (2011) *The Law of Passing-Off: Unfair Competition by Misrepresentation*, 4th edn, London: Sweet and Maxwell.

[4] (1618) Poph 143 at 144, 79 ER 1243.   [5] (1842) 6 Beav 66, 49 ER 749.

[6] (1915) 32 RPC 273.

[7] [1979] AC 731, [1979] 2 All ER 927.

That case is worth a moment's pause: the claimants produced Advocaat, a blend of spirit and eggs, while the defendants entered the market with 'Keeling's Old English Advocaat', a concoction of Cyprus sherry and egg powder. This attracted a lower rate of duty, being wine-based rather than spirit-based. It was found that this was a case of passing off, because, in so far as common ground could be found between the leading judgments, damage could be caused to the claimant's goodwill by the confusion engendered by the activities of the defendants. This analysis explains, if not defines, the essence of the action.

Various attempts were made to apply this case,[8] but a definitive answer has now been provided by the famous *Jif Lemon* case—*Reckitt & Colman Products Ltd v. Borden Inc.*[9]—aspects of which will be considered later in this chapter. In this case, Lord Oliver offered a clear and concise definition of the three elements that, in his view, were the essential ingredients of the tort:

> First, he must establish a goodwill or reputation attached to the goods or services which he supplies in the mind of the purchasing public by association with the identifying 'get-up' (whether it consists simply of a brand name or a trade description, or the individual features of labelling or packaging) under which his particular goods are offered to the public, such that the get-up is recognised by the public as distinctive specifically of the claimant's goods or services. Second, he must demonstrate a misrepresentation (whether or not intentional) leading or likely to lead the public to believe that goods or services offered by him are the goods or services of the claimant. Whether the public is aware of the claimant's identity as the manufacturer or supplier of the goods and services is immaterial, as long as they are identified with a particular source which is in fact the claimant. For example if the public is accustomed to rely upon a particular brand name in purchasing goods of a particular description, it matters not at all that there is little or no public awareness of the identity of the proprietor of the brand name. Third, he must demonstrate that he suffers or, in a *quia timet* action, that he is likely to suffer damage by reason of the erroneous belief engendered by the defendant's misrepresentation that the source of the defendant's goods or services is the same as the source of those offered by the claimant.[10]

The three requirements of goodwill, misrepresentation, and damage are the key test. But we have moved a long way from the oldest cases in which the tort was defined as a defendant passing his or her goods off as those of the claimant. The Court of Appeal even went as far as to argue obiter that the tort is perhaps now best referred to as unfair competition.[11]

What is really at the heart of the tort is the fact that goodwill will be protected whenever someone engages in unfair competition or takes unfair advantage of the goodwill by making a misrepresentation. The latter is often nothing more than a false association that is created, even involuntarily, in the minds of part of the public. The modern approach is illustrated well by the example Cross J gave more than three decades ago:

> A man who does not know where Champagne comes from can have not the slightest reason for thinking that a bottle labelled 'Spanish Champagne' contains a wine produced in France. But what he may very well think is that he is buying the genuine article—real Champagne—and that, I have no doubt, was the sort of deception which the judge had in

---

[8] See e.g. *Anheuser-Busch Inc. v. Budejovicky Budvar Narodni Podnick* [1984] FSR 413 (and on this *Budweiser* litigation also *Re Bud Trade Mark* [1988] RPC 535); *Consorzio del Prosciutto di Parma v. Marks & Spencer plc* [1991] RPC 351, esp. at 386.

[9] [1990] 1 All ER 873, [1990] 1 WLR 491.   [10] *Jif Lemon* (n. 9) at 880 and 499.

[11] *Arsenal Football Club plc v. Reed* [2003] 3 All ER 865, [2003] RPC 696 (CA).

mind. He thought, as I read his judgment, that if people were allowed to call sparkling wine not produced in Champagne 'Champagne,' even though preceded by an adjective denoting the country of origin, the distinction between genuine Champagne and 'champagne type wines produced elsewhere would become blurred; that the word 'Champagne' would come gradually to mean no more than 'sparkling wine;' and that the part of the plaintiff's goodwill which consisted in the name would be diluted and gradually destroyed. If I may say so without impertinence I agree entirely with the decision in the Spanish Champagne case—but as I see it uncovered a piece of common law or equity which had till then escaped notice—for in such a case there is not, in any ordinary sense, any representation that the goods of the defendant are the goods of the plaintiffs, and evidence that no-one has been confused or deceived in that way is quite beside the mark. In truth the decision went beyond the well-trodden paths of passing-off into the unmapped area of 'unfair trading' or 'unlawful competition'.[12]

This is the starting point of the law as it stands now, which we will now analyse in further detail. Obviously, in so doing, reference will often be made to the case law developed in the area over the last century, not least because it shows the flexibility of the passing off action.[13]

Goodwill

The leading case of *Spalding & Bros. v. A. W. Gamage*[14] identifies, as has been seen, the element of goodwill as being at the heart of an action in the tort of passing off. On its facts, it was clear that the footballs made by the claimant under the brand name 'Orb' had been on the market from 1910 and that goodwill in the name was well established by August 1912, at which time the defendant began to market 'Orb' balls that were, in fact, discarded stock rejected by the claimant, and far below the standard (and price) of the improved balls that were now being produced by the claimant still under the 'Orb' name. This is a clear and straightforward case of passing off, but the question of goodwill is not always so easy to answer and will always ultimately hinge on factual considerations. The importance of the existence of goodwill should not be underestimated: in the absence of goodwill, no passing off can be established, even if the public is confused in relation to the source of the product.[15]

The Court of Appeal recommended Lord MacNaghten's definition of goodwill as the best one available in relation to passing off.[16] Accordingly, goodwill can be said to be:

the benefit and advantage of the good name, reputation, and connection of a business. It is the attractive force that brings in custom. It is the one thing which distinguishes an old-established from a new business at its first start. The goodwill of a business must emanate from a particular centre or source. However widely or extended or diffused its

---

[12] *Vine Products Ltd v. Mackenzie & Co. Ltd* [1969] RPC 1 at 23, referring to the decision in *Bollinger J v. Costa Brava Wine Coy Ltd* [1960] RPC 16 and [1961] RPC 116, and cited with approval by Aldous LJ in *Arsenal Football Club plc v. Reed* (n. 11) at 715–16.

[13] Historically, the five-stage test that was put forward by Lord Diplock in the *Advocaat* case (n. 7) has also been important. The test involved (1) a misrepresentation (2) made by a trader in the course of trade (3) to prospective customers of his, or ultimate consumers of goods or services supplied by him, (4) which is calculated to injure the goodwill of another trader, and (5) which causes actual damage to a business or goodwill of the trader by whom the action is brought. It is submitted that this test is not substantially different from the three-stage *Jif Lemon* test and that the latter summarizes it in a more convenient way.

[14] (1915) 32 RPC 273.   [15] *HFC Bank v. Midland Bank* [2000] FSR 176 at 182–3.

[16] *Scandecor Development AB v. Scandecor Marketing AB* [1999] FSR 26 at 41.

influence may be, goodwill is worth nothing unless it has power of attraction sufficient to bring customers home to the source from which it emanates. Goodwill is composed of a variety of elements. It differs in its composition in different trades and in different trades in the same trade. One element may preponderate here and another element there.[17]

One of the key elements in this definition refers back to the point made previously that goodwill is the necessary starting point for any passing off action. As such, the goodwill must also be linked to the next elements and play an active role. In practice, the goodwill must be the reason why the consumer gives custom to the business. Customers must not be using the business for random reasons, but they must be giving it their custom as a result of the reputation that has been developed by the business.[18] But while goodwill must obviously be proven to exist, the requirements for it to exist are not unduly stringent and the Court of Appeal has held that the goodwill test is less demanding than that for distinctiveness in relation to trade marks.[19]

Duration of goodwill

When a business is started, as a question of fact, it is clear that it may take time to establish its goodwill. The courts appear reasonably generous in providing support for relatively new traders against their predatory rivals. This is shown by two contrasting cases in 1967. First, in *Stannard v. Reay*,[20] both parties independently decided to establish a mobile fish-and-chip shop business in the Isle of Wight. Both hit upon the name 'Mr Chippy' as being appropriate for the venture, but the claimants had a head start of about five weeks. Once the rival operation began, the claimants sought an injunction and this was granted on an interlocutory basis by Buckley J, in the light of the fact that the evidence showed that the claimants had built up a substantial trade very quickly and could thus be said to have developed goodwill in the use of the name.

By contrast, in *Compatibility Research Ltd v. Computer Psyche Co. Ltd*,[21] two companies independently set up the then new business of running a computer dating agency. The claimants began one month earlier than the defendants and, with both companies using the biological male and female symbols in their publicity, the claimants sought to establish that their one-month head start had been sufficient to confer upon them goodwill in that pair of symbols. Their claim was rejected by Stamp J, who took the view that '*where a trader seeks to say that the name descriptive of his trade has become distinctive of his trade and no other, he assumes a heavy burden*'.[22]

It is clear, however, that, in deciding against the claimants, much emphasis was placed on their use of a commonplace and partly descriptive symbol that would make it much harder to develop goodwill than if they had thought up their own original logo that was then copied by a subsequent rival. It was not so much the short time for which they had traded, but the lack of a distinctive image that flawed their claim. The key element that emerges is that goodwill and reputation have to be demonstrated to exist at the time at which the defendant began the activities complained of; the protection of future goodwill, even if it can protect the logical and legitimate expansion of a growing business, does not come within the scope of passing off.[23]

---

[17] *IRC v. Muller & Co.'s Margarine* [1901] AC 217 at 224.
[18] *HFC Bank v. Midland Bank* (n. 15) at 183.
[19] *Phones 4U Ltd and anor v. Phone4u.co.uk Internet Ltd and ors* [2007] RPC 5 (CA).
[20] [1967] RPC 589.   [21] [1967] RPC 201.   [22] 1967] RPC 201 at 207.
[23] *Cadbury Schweppes v. Pub Squash* [1981] RPC 429; *Teleworks Ltd v. Telework Group plc* [2002] RPC 535.

That these cases hinge on factual issues is well shown by the contrast between the *Compatibility* case and that of *BBC v. Talbot Motor Co. Ltd.*[24] The heavy launch publicity in the media arranged by Compatibility Research did not avail it in its goodwill argument, yet, in the *BBC* case, goodwill was found to exist for the 'Carfax' service of radio traffic information broadcasts from television and specialist press coverage, even though the service had not—and still has not—come into being. The BBC was thus held to be entitled to prevent the defendants from using the same name for their spare car part sales operation. The publicity has to lead to goodwill though. In *Starbucks (HK) Ltd v. SkyB Ltd* the Supreme Court left open the question whether heavy pre-launch publicity coupled with a stated intent to launch the product or service imminently can exceptionally be sufficient for a passing off action, even in the absence of goodwill.[25]

Clearly, in cases in which neither the project nor its preliminaries are under way, there is no chance that a passing off action can succeed. In *Marcus Publishing plc v. Hutton-Wild Communications Ltd,*[26] the two parties were rushing to be first into the market with identically named journals, but neither had yet reached the newsstands or, indeed, had gone beyond the stage of producing a pilot edition for advertisers. The Court of Appeal found that neither party had done enough to establish any goodwill, even for the purposes of an interlocutory injunction, although both parties had been planning their projects for the best part of a year.

Similar problems arise at the end of a business' life in assessing the time at which goodwill finally dissipates. In this respect, *Ad-lib Club Ltd v. Glanville*[27] is instructive. The Ad-Lib Club was a trendy London nightspot that operated from 1964 to early 1966, at which time it was closed due to complaints about noise and no substitute premises could be found. Late in 1970, the defendant proposed to open his own Ad-Lib Club and, in spite of the five-year gap, the claimants were held entitled to object to this. The issue was not the lapse of time, but rather whether the claimant's goodwill had lapsed. The fact that the press confused the two operations in stories concerning the 'reopening' of the famous club and the strong suspicion that the defendant's choice of name was quite deliberate were helpful factors in the claimant's case, but, ultimately, it was the retention of goodwill in its name and its right to exploit that, while it still lasted, was crucial to the success of the claim, even though it had no precise plans for reopening. Of course, the presence of such plans would always be helpful to a claimant, as evidenced by *Levey v. Henderson-Kenton (Holdings) Ltd,*[28] in which trade by the claimant under the name 'Kentons' was held to retain goodwill during a temporary closure caused by two fires and a compulsory purchase.

It is clear that goodwill cannot only survive the closing down of a business,[29] but that it can also survive the death of a person. For example, the death of the composer who had released various recordings with his orchestra and toured the UK did not extinguish the goodwill held in his name.[30] Whether another person can benefit from that goodwill is another matter, however: inherited goodwill is not easy to prove and, in that case, the fact that the son of the composer had continued the business did not automatically mean that he had inherited the goodwill from his father; neither did the prolonged absence of the orchestra from the UK after the latest tour led by the composer himself help matters.

---

[24] [1981] FSR 228.   [25] [2015] UKSC 31.   [26] [1990] RPC 576.   [27] [1972] RPC 673.
[28] [1974] RPC 617.
[29] For an example where goodwill in relation to the 1966 World Cup was held to have survived, see *Jules Rimet Cup Ltd v. Football Association Ltd* [2008] FSR 10.
[30] *Riddle v. United Service Organisation Ltd*, Ch D, judgment of 26 April 2004, [2004] EWHC 1263, (2004) 27(7) IPD 27079.

Geographical extent of goodwill

In relation to the question of the geographical area over which goodwill may be regarded as extending, the *Levey* case provides a simple example. The claimant's shop was well known in Newcastle only, while the defendants were successfully trading under the same name, but primarily in the Midlands, with no store within 120 miles of Newcastle until the proposed opening of a store in Newcastle triggered off the claimant's action. The interlocutory injunction only extended to Newcastle and, if the claimant had sought to trade in the defendants' heartland in the Midlands, the claim would inevitably have been inverted.

This case may, however, be the exception rather than the rule in terms of how clear-cut is the geographical separation. A more complex—and perhaps more typical—set of facts arose in *Chelsea Man Menswear Ltd v. Chelsea Girl Ltd*.[31] The claimants sold clothes under the 'Chelsea Man' label in their shops in Leicester, Coventry, and London; the defendants proposed to extend their business from women's clothing to that for men and, naturally, also wanted to use 'Chelsea Man' in this venture. The defendants argued that any injunction against them should be confined to the areas of the claimants' pre-existing business, but this was rejected by the Court of Appeal, which allowed an injunction covering all of England and Wales, regard being paid to the fact that both people and goods move around the country, and also to the desire of the claimants themselves to extend their business in the future (although no specific plans appear to have been made). Nourse LJ noted[32] that the *Levey* case was the only reported case to have imposed a geographical limit and at only a pretrial stage. The desire of businesses to expand legitimately in the future may well make the *Chelsea Man* case the model for the future.

But there may still be circumstances in which local goodwill exists and in which a geographically limited injunction is appropriate. The *Daily Mail* relied successfully on its goodwill in London and the south-east of England to stop the publication of a London evening newspaper under the name *London Evening Mail*.[33]

International goodwill

Goodwill can, it seems, also transcend international boundaries. Many companies—such as, for example, the international oil companies—trade in dozens of countries and clearly have international goodwill. This area of the law needs to be considered in two different ways: first, the approach taken by the case law in recent years will be considered; second, it will be necessary to review the impact of the new protection of internationally well-known marks introduced into UK law for the first time by the 1994 Act.

The problem that has arisen in litigation is whether, in the absence of trade, goodwill can nevertheless be established within the jurisdiction. The case law suggests that this is possible, at least in some cases. The principal support for such a proposition comes from *Maxim's Ltd v. Dye*,[34] in which the owners of one of Paris' grandest and most prestigious restaurants succeeded in preventing the use of the name 'Maxim's' for a bistro in Norwich. Graham J refused to follow an earlier High Court decision[35] in which the owners of Paris' 'Crazy Horse Saloon' nightclub failed to stop the use of the same name on London premises, because, he insisted, goodwill could transcend frontiers and, indeed, was more likely so to do in an era of international integration, particularly within the

---

[31] [1987] RPC 189.   [32] [1987] RPC 189 at 208.
[33] *Associated Newspapers, Daily Mail & General Trust v. Express Newspapers* [2003] FSR 51.
[34] [1977] FSR 364.   [35] *Alain Bernardin et Cie v. Pavilion Properties Ltd* [1967] RPC 581.

Common Market.[36] In this case, there was ample evidence that the Paris restaurant was known in the UK, was patronized by its citizens, and—although no weight seems to have been attached to this factor—was owned by a UK-registered company. The judge also considered that to fail to protect the goodwill enjoyed by a French company in the UK was discriminatory under the Treaty of Rome as being a disguised restriction on trade, a distortion of level competition, and a restriction on the free supply of services within the European Union (EU).[37] It seems that the goodwill of a company trading elsewhere within the EU will be treated henceforth on equal terms with that of a domestic business, with the factors already noted being relevant to the scope of the injunction awarded geographically.

But it is equally clear that *Maxim's* is not a door left wide open through which any foreign business can mount a passing off action in the UK: *Athletes Foot Marketing Associates Inc. v. Cobra Sports Ltd*[38] demonstrates this well. The claimants are a leading US business franchising a chain of sports shoe shops under the brand name 'The Athlete's Foot'—presumably the foot infection of that name bears a different appellation across the Atlantic. Beyond abortive discussions, no steps had been taken to develop the chain in England, so the defendants filled the gap by christening their London store 'Athlete's Foot Bargain Basement', a name apparently coined while watching a rugby match from the bar at Twickenham Rugby Stadium. After a full survey of the authorities, Walton J concluded that passing off does not confine its protection to those currently carrying on a business within the jurisdiction, as long as they have a reputation from which goodwill can arise. On these facts, however, the claimants did not even have a reputation, having provided no evidence of any transactions with UK citizens. It was consequently impossible to say that there was the necessary goodwill within the jurisdiction and this is a significant point of distinction from the *Maxim's* case.

A further twist is provided by *My Kinda Bones Ltd v. Dr Pepper's Stove Co. Ltd.*[39] This, on the face of it, looks like the *Athlete's Foot* case, with a US firm intending to open, for the first time, one of its now successful 'Chicago Rib Shack' restaurants in London, only to find, to its irritation, that the defendants were also proposing to operate a 'Rib Shack'. The claimants sued and the defendants sought to strike out the claim as giving no grounds for action, in the light of the *Athlete's Foot* case. Slade J refused to strike out the claim—which, of course, is not to say that he confirmed that it would succeed at trial. He simply felt that the lack of customers in the UK for the claimants' business could not be the sole test, because there was evidence that the claimants had begun to promote their new venture not least in their pre-existing chain of pizzerias. In the light of this, there was at least a triable issue under the principle established in *BBC v. Talbot*[40] that they had carried out enough preparation and interested enough people in their forthcoming product that goodwill had been created; it is hard to disagree with Slade J[41] that the claimants' prospects of success were, however, slender. And the higher courts have recently put the bar even higher. The Court of Appeal has ruled that goodwill must have been created and that such goodwill must exist in the jurisdiction.[42] And the Supreme Court has added that goodwill in the jurisdiction involves customers in the jurisdiction for the products or services concerned.[43] If one defines the latter somewhat broadly, *My Kinda Bones*

---

[36] [1977] FSR 364 at 368.

[37] EC Treaty, Arts. 30 and 49 respectively (now Arts. 36 and 56 of the Treaty on the Functioning of the European Union).

[38] [1980] RPC 343.   [39] [1984] FSR 289.   [40] [1981] FSR 228.

[41] [1984] FSR 289 at 303.   [42] *Starbucks (HK) Ltd v. BSkyB Group plc* [2013] EWCA 1465.

[43] *Starbucks (HK) Ltd v. BSkyB Group plc* [2015] UKSC 31.

had a fighting chance, as they had goodwill in the jurisdiction in the food and beverage sector, albeit not as 'Rib Shack'. *BBC v. Talbot* may no longer be good law, unless one accepts that the BBC had goodwill already in relation to traffic information.

In summary, it seems clear that the starting point of the court in considering passing off will be to give protection across the whole of the relevant jurisdiction to anyone with a reputation within that jurisdiction. Such a reputation is most easily established by evidence of customers within that jurisdiction, so going a long way to show goodwill there. But other acts such as self-promotion or work done preparatory to the product launch may also be helpful to showing goodwill within the jurisdiction. In the absence of any real business conducted in the UK one can go as far as saying that customers in the UK are required. In the absence of customers in the UK any slender chance of success based on promotion activities or preparations for a product launch seems to require an existing activity in the UK that has a reputation. In *My Kinda Bones Ltd* the claimants used their existing chain of pizzerias in the UK as a launch pad for their proposed new activity and in the *BBC* case the BBC had a lot of activities and a sizeable reputation in the UK.[44]

The position at common law has, however, now been altered by s. 56 of the 1994 Act. This section brings into UK law, for the first time, the protection given by Art. 6bis of the Paris Convention for the Protection of Intellectual Property 1883. This creates an obligation on signatory states to protect well-known marks belonging to any national of any Convention state. This allows such a person to act within this jurisdiction by obtaining an injunction against the use in the UK of a trade mark (or an essential part thereof) that is *'identical or similar to his mark, in relation to identical or similar goods or services, where the use is likely to cause confusion'.*[45] This right arises irrespective of whether the claimant has any business, or even any goodwill, in the UK, although the mark must be 'well known'.

The implications of this are far from clear. The key case to reconsider is *Athlete's Foot*. The claim there failed through lack of goodwill on the part of the claimants; this, in itself, would no longer bar them from opposing the use by their UK counterpart of the same name as a trade mark. But it seems that it would still be necessary to establish that theirs was a 'well-known' mark and it is not clear whether it is necessary to show that the mark is well known in the applicant's country or in the UK. Clearly, there is no problem in the former event, but if the latter is the case,[46] it will be an unusual mark indeed that has no goodwill but is nonetheless well known. It seems that s. 56 is therefore unlikely to make any great difference.

Goodwill in trading

In terms of the activities in respect of which goodwill may arise or be protected, just as in trade mark law, protection is not given universally, but rather only for the class, or classes, of activity in which trade is carried out. A parallel restriction therefore applies in passing off—but, first, a further parallel needs exploring: while in trade mark law there must be trade before any protection is conferred, so too, in a passing off action, there must be a recognizable trading activity.[47]

---

[44] *Plentyoffish Media Inc. v. Plenty More LLP* [2011] EWHC 2568 (Ch), [2012] RPC 5.

[45] TMA 1994, s. 56(2).

[46] R. Annand and H. Norman (1994) *Blackstone's Guide to the Trade Marks Act 1994*, Oxford: Blackstone, p. 31.

[47] *Erven Warnink v. J. Townend & Sons (Hull) Ltd* [1979] AC 731, [1979] 2 All ER 927, per Lord Diplock at 742 and 932.

Professional bodies[48] and political parties are consequently unlikely to succeed in a passing off claim: it will not be easy for them to show that they are engaged in sufficient commercial activity. Charities, non-profit organizations, and certain unincorporated associations—such as, for example, the Countryside Alliance—may, however, find it easier to prove that they trade and that, as a result, they have acquired goodwill. They do not trade in a narrow sense, because they do not buy or sell goods or services, but, in achieving their aim of the promotion of the well-being of a section of the community, they engage in some commercial activity, even if it is only of secondary importance and aimed solely at raising funds. The concept of trade involved has to be interpreted in a wide sense.[49]

From here, it is appropriate to return to the question of what activities by a company or individual admittedly in trade are protected by the passing off action. To take an example, Oxford University Press—through its name and logo—has a reputation for, and consequent goodwill in, the production of leading legal tomes and could accordingly use the tort of passing off to prevent a newcomer to the field from using the name and logo, or anything close thereto. But if a new dairy products business were to decide to use the Oxford name, it would be far from clear that any harm would be done, because confusion is unlikely to arise, the publishers not being engaged in, and therefore enjoying no goodwill in, the dairy business. The way in which this has traditionally been considered is in the form of the need for a representation by the defendant to the customers of the claimant. If the customers are different, or are in entirely distinct areas of activity, then no goodwill is harmed and there will be no action in passing off; it is a common field of activity that is traditionally necessary.

A common field of activity

An easy example of this is shown by *Granada Group Ltd v. Ford Motor Co. Ltd.*[50] The claimants had a solid reputation in the television and cinema industry, and became concerned when they found out that the defendants were intending to christen their new luxury car the Ford 'Granada'. The claimants argued that the use of this well-known name would cause boundless confusion, but the defendants replied that the name had been chosen with regard to its Europe-wide effectiveness and that their business was in so different a field of activity that no impact on Granada's goodwill would be discernible. Graham J found for the defendants, refusing even an interlocutory injunction. No confusion would arise in the public mind between the very different companies and their very different products. Some of their customers may be the same, but there was no common field of activity to cause confusion even to those common customers.

Likewise, in *Wombles Ltd v. Wombles Skips Ltd,*[51] the claimants had the rights in the Wombles, fictitious furry creatures who, inter alia, were devoted to cleansing Wimbledon Common of litter and whose popularity meant that the claimants enjoyed the fruits of a successful merchandising programme. The defendants were a new company providing domestic rubbish skips and chose their name precisely because of both its popularity and its connotations of cleanliness. Walton J was clear that no injunction should be awarded, because there was no common field of activity and thus no common customers to be

---

[48] *British Association of Aesthetic Plastic Surgeons v. Cambright* [1987] RPC 549. Cf. *Society of Incorporated Accountants v. Vincent* (1954) 71 RPC 325.

[49] *Burge & Armstrong v. Haycock* [2002] RPC 553 (CA). Cf. *Kean v. McGivan* [1982] FSR 119, which must now effectively have been overturned by the decision of the Court of Appeal.

[50] [1973] RPC 49.   [51] [1977] RPC 99.

confused, as between toys and other merchandising items, on the one hand, and rubbish removal, on the other.

In considering whether there is a common field of activity and therefore a representation by the defendant to the customers of the claimant, some tenuous connections are sometimes made to assist the claimant's cause of action. In *BBC v. Talbot Motor Co. Ltd*,[52] the differences between the claimants' proposed 'Carfax' radio traffic information services and the defendants' 'Carfax' car parts appear to be obvious, yet Megarry V-C found the dangers of confusion to be real, because both operations were concerned with motor vehicles and confusion could particularly affect car radio purchases (although Talbot had offered in court to exclude car radios from its parts service).

In *Annabel's (Berkeley Square) Ltd v. Schock*,[53] the claimants were (and are) a top London nightspot frequented by the social elite. The defendant operated a business under the name 'Annabel's Escort Agency', providing young ladies to escort clients to dinner, dances, etc. The Court of Appeal, fortified by evidence of men ringing the nightclub in search of escorts and women arriving there seeking an escort job, found that there was a common field of activity in the field of night entertainment, that confusion could arise and had arisen, and that the public image of escort agencies was such that harm may be caused to the nightclub, and so an injunction was obtained in favour of the defendants.[54]

The courts have seemed more willing to uphold this type of case when the whiff of fraud is in the air: *Eastman Photographic Materials Co. Ltd v. John Griffiths Cycle Co. Ltd*[55] is such a case. Eastman made Kodak cameras while the defendants sought to sell a new brand of bicycle, the Kodak cycle. In the light of the fact that the claimants sold special 'Cycle Kodak' cameras specially adapted for use on bicycles and the deliberate conduct of the defendants, an injunction was awarded. Similarly, in *Harrods Ltd v. R. Harrod Ltd*,[56] the claimant department store succeeded in preventing the defendants from using its name for a money-lending business. The claimants did have a small banking section, but did not lend money; nonetheless, the Court of Appeal awarded an injunction, partly because of the closeness of the two businesses, partly because of evidence of customer confusion, and partly because of the fact that there was no legitimate reason for the defendants to use that name, no one called Harrod being in any way involved with the business.

Another *Harrods* case[57] was concerned with the use of the name 'Harrodian School' for a school that was unrelated to Harrods, but which was established in the buildings of the former 'Harrodian Club', membership of which had, at one stage, been restricted to employees of Harrods. Harrods alleged passing off, but, unlike the first case, this action failed. In relation to the common field of activity, it was held by the Court of Appeal that there was no requirement that the claimant should be carrying on a business that competed with that of the claimant or which would compete with any natural extension of the claimant's business. It was added, however, that the absence of a common field of activity was an important and highly relevant consideration in deciding whether there was a likelihood of confusion. Passing off will only protect goodwill against damage resulting from misrepresentations if there is a likelihood of confusion that makes damage to goodwill plausible. In this case, there was no common field of activity between the defendant, who was running a school, and the claimant, who was running a department store. The only question was whether there was a real risk that members of the public would be deceived into thinking that a school called 'Harrodian School' was owned or managed by

---

[52] [1981] FSR 228.   [53] [1972] RPC 838.
[54] For a similar decision, on less interesting facts, see *Walter v. Ashton* [1902] 2 Ch 282.
[55] (1898) 15 RPC 105.   [56] (1923) 41 RPC 74.
[57] *Harrods Ltd v. Harrodian School Ltd* [1996] RPC 697.

Harrods or under Harrods' supervision or control. Did the public believe that the goods or services offered by the defendant were the goods or services of the claimant? Only if this was established could the claimant's reputation for excellence potentially suffer damage. This was a matter of fact and, in this case, no likelihood of confusion had been established.

Beyond the common field of activity

In summary, reasonably clear guidelines have been established to set the boundaries of goodwill created by trade. First, there must be trade; second, there must be trade by both parties to the same customers and in the same, or at least broadly similar, fields of activity, with the level of broad similarity required being the area of greatest uncertainty or, if preferred, discretion.

But one significant decision appears to erode the clarity of the picture as far as the need for a common field of activity is concerned. In *Lego Systems Aktieselskab v. Lego M Lemelstrich Ltd*,[58] the claimants—well-known manufacturers of toy plastic bricks—took action against the sale by the defendants of 'Lego' brand water sprinklers and other such items of gardening irrigation equipment. Falconer J allowed an injunction to be granted. He rejected the argument that the common field of activity was essential here by pointing to the great fame of the 'Lego' name and the assumption that would be made by customers of Lego sprinklers that they were buying products made by the Danish toy brick firm. In other words, Lego's goodwill is so great that it extends beyond its sole trading field into both related and, as here, unrelated areas of activity. People would be misled into thinking that any defect in the sprinklers was the fault of the toy firm and Lego would be prevented from using the goodwill in its name to diversify in the future into the garden sprinkler trade.

This is a bold decision that surely stretches the notion of goodwill in trade close to its breaking point. It goes far beyond cases in which there has been protection afforded by passing off for an active intention on the part of the claimant to diversify into related areas,[59] let alone those cases in which the courts have refused relief because the activities, although obviously related in a broad sense, have not amounted to a common field of activity: for example, ice lollies and bubble gum.[60] And yet it does not seem unacceptable: the phrase 'common field of activity' has never been part of the mainstream of the vocabulary of passing off,[61] and the approach now seems entirely compatible, in principle, with the language and approach of s. 5(3) of the 1994 Act.[62] The area in which the *Lego* decision still has a role, arguably, is when the threat of damage to the claimant's reputation is as vague (or illusory) as in the case itself, as opposed to the statute's requirement of detriment to the mark or its reputation, or, of course, if the claimant does not have trade mark protection.

The courts have now finally put to rest any remaining doubts concerning the requirement of a common field of activity in relation to passing off. Laddie J held, in *Irvine v. Talksport Ltd*,[63] that it was the purpose of the law of passing off to vindicate the claimant's exclusive right to his goodwill and to protect it against damage. The law would therefore not allow others to use that goodwill so as to reduce, blur, or diminish its exclusivity. It followed from this that it was not necessary to show that the claimant and

---

[58] [1983] FSR 155.   [59] E.g. *LRC International Ltd v. Lilla Edets Sales Co. Ltd* [1973] RPC 560.

[60] *Lyons Maid Ltd v. Trebor Ltd* [1967] RPC 222.

[61] *McCulloch v. Lewis A. May Ltd* [1947] 2 All ER 845. See J. Phillips and A. Coleman, 'Passing-Off and the "Common Field of Activity"' (1985) 101 LQR 242.

[62] See Ch. 25.   [63] *Irvine v. Talksport Ltd* [2002] FSR 943, confirmed on appeal [2003] FSR 619.

the defendant shared a common field of activity, or that the sales of products or services would be diminished either substantially or directly, at least in the short term. Instead, the essential point was to show a misrepresentation, because that element was required to enable the defendant to take advantage of the defendant's reputation. The unauthorized manipulation of a photograph of Mr Irvine, by means of which a Talksport Radio was put in his hand, and its subsequent use for publicity purposes amounted to such a mis-representation, because it created the impression that Mr Irvine was endorsing Talksport Radio. This could affect Mr Irvine's goodwill and reputation, and the requirements for passing off were therefore met. The Court of Appeal upheld the decision on this point, while raising the amount of damages awarded to Mr Irvine.[64]

Meanwhile, some of the earlier case law may need rethinking: are not Granada and were not Wombles equally the possessors of the widest amount of goodwill? The first *Harrods* decision would now seem unduly cautious and narrow. Clearly, in the light of *Lego*, there is the potential for well-known brand names to establish broader goodwill than in the past if no longer confined to any type of common field of activity in bring-ing claims of passing off. But any *Lego*-based approach must be subject to one restric-tion: there must be a likelihood of confusion or deception and, in this respect, any indi-cation of a common field of activity may still be a very relevant factor.[65]

Goodwill in real names

We have just seen in the *Harrods* decision that the unnecessary use of the name by an-other business amounted to passing off—but what would have happened if the proprietor of the rival business was indeed a 'Mr Harrod'? Clearly, just as much confusion and thus harm to goodwill may arise, but it may seem harsh to restrict the fictitious Mr Harrod from proudly using his own name for his business.

The courts do, however, seem prepared to so order. In *Baume & Co. Ltd v. A. H. Moore Ltd*,[66] the claimants sold watches under the trade mark 'Baume' and had done so for well over a century. The defendants began to import Swiss watches made by Baume and Mercier Ltd of Geneva, a fact marked both on the watches and their boxes. This was held to amount to passing off, although the use of the name was genuine in every respect (there had previously been a family connection between the two firms). The use of a real name could be actionable if it is used in such a way as to cause confusion with another's business and *'the defence of innocent and honest use of the manufacturers' name on the watches which the defendants have sold will not avail them as a defence if the other ingre-dients of passing off are established'.*[67] Confusion was likely given the similarity of both the name and the type of product.

If this seems harsh, it is worth reflecting that the importers of Baume and Mercier watches had taken no deliberate steps to distinguish them from the watches already on the market. This explains the opposite conclusion reached by Hoffmann J in *Anderson & Lembke Ltd v. Anderson & Lembke Inc.*[68] A specialist advertising agency in Sweden set up, and then sold off, international subsidiaries, including the parties to this litigation, based respectively in London and Connecticut. The US firm gained contracts in Europe and decided to open an office in London. The claimants' complaint was rejected; the de-fendants had taken steps to change the name under which they traded to 'A & L Europe'

---

[64] *Irvine* (n. 63).

[65] *Nice & Safe Attitude Ltd v. Piers Flook (t/a 'Slaam! Clothing Company')* [1997] FSR 14; *Harrods Ltd v. Harrodian School Ltd* [1996] RPC 697.

[66] [1958] Ch 907, [1958] 2 All ER 113.   [67] *Baume* (n. 66), per Romer LJ at 917 and 117.

[68] [1989] RPC 124.

and then to 'Business Advertising Europe', and while there was reference in some documents to the connection with the US parent firm, this was regarded as inevitable and appropriate, and did not amount to passing off. It seems that honesty, although not a formal defence, is not unhelpful to a defendant's cause.

Another possible way of getting round *Baume* is to emphasize that the other ingredients of passing off need to be satisfied and it is far from clear that the defendants in that case had made any misrepresentation; they were, after all, selling watches made by Baume and Mercier, and it is customary for watches to bear the name of their manufacturer. It seems that the courts are more generous in allowing the honest use of a name for a business than for its products,[69] in relation to which greater care must be taken to distinguish one item from another.

In summary, if your name is McDonald and you want to open a burger bar, the tort of passing off will be reluctant to prevent the use of your name for your business—but if you invite McDonald to join your business just so as to be able to use his name, this is unlikely to be regarded as bona fide, after *Harrods*; in any event, it may be prudent to make your business as distinct as possible from that of your namesake, to avoid the problems of *Baume*. Likewise, use of the name or variants thereof on products rather than for the business at large is less likely to escape legal objection. In passing, use of the 'Mc' prefix seems to be regarded as a popular marketing weapon in the fast food trade; it would seem difficult, without more, for McDonalds to prevent this, unless other steps were taken to confuse customers.

The Court of Appeal repeated recently that there can be goodwill in one's own name and that, after the name and the business have been sold, one can, in principle, use one's own name in connection with a competing business. But there is a risk: if the public perceives your activity as passing off the new business as that which you have sold—that is, if the three conditions for passing off have been met—the fact that you are using your own name will not be a valid defence.[70]

An unusual case in this area is the case of *Alan Clark v. Associated Newspapers*,[71] in which the distinguished—if controversial—politician succeeded in a complaint against the *Evening Standard* for a spoof column based on his diary-style of writing and using his name (although the columns were attributed to the journalist who wrote them). It was held that the prominent use of Alan Clark's name would be seen by the public as associating him with the articles and thus would amount to passing off.

Similar considerations are also found in the *Irvine* case,[72] in which a photograph of Mr Irvine was at the heart of the matter, rather than his name, as such.

Goodwill in real words

Similar risks of granting an overgenerous monopoly arise in respect of the use of real words—especially those that are descriptive of a product. Clearly, the first person to make ice cream should not have a monopoly on those words that are descriptive of his or her product and this is reflected by the legal position.

County Sound plc v. Ocean Sound plc[73] is a good contemporary example. The parties are both local radio stations in southern England, broadcasting to adjacent, but overlapping, catchment areas. The claimants decided to launch a new service, broadcasting old records on their MW/AM frequency, which they christened 'The Gold AM'. Six months

---

[69] *Marengo v. Daily Sketch & Sunday Graphic Ltd* (1948) 65 RPC 242, esp. per Lord Simonds at 251.
[70] *I. N. Newman Ltd v. Adlem* [2006] FSR 16 (CA).   [71] [1998] RPC 261. See also Ch. 31.
[72] *Irvine v. Talksport Ltd* [2002] FSR 943, confirmed on appeal [2003] FSR 619.
[73] [1991] FSR 367.

later, the defendants began to broadcast a similar service and used the same name. The Court of Appeal refused to grant an injunction against the defendants on the grounds that, although the claimants had had time to develop the necessary goodwill, no goodwill could develop around 'The Gold AM' because 'Gold' was, in the view of Nourse LJ,[74] a word *'descriptive of popular hits of the 1950s, 1960s, and 1970s and AM was simply the description of the frequency on which the service could be found'*. Descriptive words could only develop goodwill by the use of that name and no other for goods over a substantial period of time, as authority for which the old case of *Reddaway v. Banham*[75] was cited, in which more than a decade's usage of 'Camel Hair Belting' was held sufficient to generate the necessary goodwill. But this is clearly the exception, rather than the rule, and here, too, the question must arise as to whether there is anything in the nature of a misrepresentation in a subsequent use by another of purely descriptive wording.

The name 'Farm Fluids', a description of an agrichemical product has likewise been held to be unable to be used by a rival producer, because the name was known in the relevant market as synonymous with the claimant's business.[76]

Collective goodwill

In most of the cases so far examined, the claimant trader has generated, by his or her trading endeavours, his or her own goodwill and will therefore be its owner. This is not, however, a requirement of the tort of passing off; it is equally possible for the necessary goodwill to be generated by a group of traders collectively, as the group of cases colloquially known as the *Alcohol* cases clearly shows.

The first of these cases is *Bollinger v. Costa Brava Wine Co.*, heard first[77] on preliminary points of law and subsequently[78] as a full trial. The claimants were a group of French producers of champagne from that region of France and they were seeking to prevent the defendants from marketing their sparkling wine from Spain as 'Spanish champagne'. Obviously, no single producer has any sort of exclusive right to the word 'champagne', but the argument was that, together, the French manufacturers of the drink had developed a collective goodwill and reputation in the name. This then novel argument was successful. Danckwerts J[79] felt that the nature and purpose of passing off was to prevent unfair trading, and to control unfair competition, and that the necessary goodwill could just as easily be developed by, as here, a group of persons producing particular goods in a particular locality—although each of the claimants is separately entitled to bring his or her own legal action in respect of harm to his or her own share of the goodwill.[80] The decision represented both a substantial advance for the tort of passing off and a growing recognition of the potential that the tort has as a tool for regulating unfair trading—which latter aspect will be considered later in this chapter.

The lead given in *Bollinger* was followed in *Vine Products Ltd v. Mackenzie & Co. Ltd.*[81] This time, the drink in question was sherry—or, to be precise, British sherry—and the action was brought by a group of manufacturers seeking to establish their right to use the name 'sherry' against the objections of Spanish producers of the drink from the Jerez region from which traditional sherry originates. Cross J upheld the objections to a limited extent,

[74] *County Sound* (n. 73) at 373.
[75] [1896] AC 199. This approach is now reflected in the proviso to TMA 1994, s. 3(1)(c).
[76] *Antec International Ltd v. South Western Chicks (Warren) Ltd* [1998] FSR 738.
[77] [1960] Ch 262, [1959] 3 All ER 800.
[78] *Bollinger v. Costa Brava Wine Co. Ltd (No. 2)* [1961] 1 All ER 561, [1961] 1 WLR 277.
[79] [1960] Ch 262, [1959] 3 All ER 800 at 284 and 811.
[80] [1961] 1 All ER 561, [1961] 1 WLR 277 at 563 and 281.   [81] [1969] RPC 1.

in so far as the word 'sherry' itself was not to be used on its own on any drink other than that from Jerez; the long usage of 'British sherry' and other non-Spanish varieties, such as sherry from South Africa and Cyprus, was permitted to continue. In effect, then, 'British sherry is good' would be a permitted form of advert, but 'British sherry is good sherry' would not. Cross J[82] appeared to regard *Bollinger* as creating a new tort of unfair competition, rather than as passing off, because the normal requirements of representation and confusion were absent. This appears to be an odd remark, because the drinks described as 'champagne' and 'sherry' were not from the relevant geographical areas, and this surely may amount to a misrepresentation and thus may cause confusion. Nonetheless, these remarks were expressly adopted by Foster J in the third case in this group, *John Walker & Sons Ltd v. Henry Ost & Co. Ltd*.[83] In this case, the claimants were a group of Scotch whisky producers who were held able to prevent the name of Scotch whisky from being besmirched by its use on a blend of whiskey and cane spirit that was available in Ecuador.

The *Advocaat* case, however, restores the cases to the fold of passing off, albeit '*in an extended form*'[84] and also bearing in mind that the larger a group claiming collective goodwill, the harder it will be to show the public recognition of distinctiveness that a word such as 'champagne' had attracted.[85] (One manufacturer only brought the action, so these comments are presumably obiter.)

The continuing relevance of this area of case law, and its continuing existence within the tort of passing off, is confirmed by a more recent case—one that is still concerned with alcohol. Once again, the highly litigious champagne industry came to the courts, this time to restrain the use of 'its' word in a non-alcoholic product made from elderflowers known as 'Elderflower champagne'. In *Taittinger v. Allbev Ltd*,[86] the Court of Appeal held that the industry could so restrain the use of 'champagne'. After consideration of mainstream passing-off case law, the view was taken that there was a clear threat to the collective goodwill of the champagne industry if this cheap, non-alcoholic drink could continue to bear the hallowed name.

The claimants also sought and gained an injunction on the alternative ground that the defendants were in breach of EC Regulation 823/87 laying down special provisions relating to quality wines produced in specified regions.[87] These regulations insist on correct wine labelling, of which there was a clear breach in this respect, and so an injunction was appropriate in view of the fact that the purpose of the Regulation was to avoid the very confusion that the use by the defendants of the word 'champagne' had caused. Collective goodwill thus remains a valid method of satisfying the first requirement of the tort of passing off, but *Vine Products* reminds us that it may only receive limited protection by a restrictively drawn injunction, while the *Advocaat* case suggests that use of collective goodwill may not be widely available except in the clearest of cases.

The most recent example of this type of claim is the successful action by Swiss chocolatiers to prevent the UK-based Cadbury from using the name and image of Swiss chocolate in promoting what is doubtless a fine product—but which was made in Birmingham—through the use of the 'Chocosuisse' name.[88] This case illustrates the

---

[82] *Vine Products* (n. 81) at 23 and 28.   [83] [1970] 2 All ER 106, [1970] 1 WLR 917.

[84] [1979] AC 731 at 739, [1979] 2 All ER 927, per Lord Diplock at 929.

[85] [1979] AC 731 at 744, [1979] 2 All ER 927, per Lord Diplock at 934.

[86] [1994] 4 All ER 75, [1993] 2 CMLR 741.

[87] Incorporated into UK law by the Common Agricultural Policy (Wine) Regulations 1992, SI 1992/672, now, in the latest form, the Wine Regulations 2011, SI 2011/2936.

[88] *Chocosuisse Union des Fabricants Suisse de Chocolat v. Cadbury Ltd* [1998] RPC 117. See now also *Fage UK Ltd and anor v. Chobani UK Ltd and anor* [2014] EWCA Civ 5, where the Court of Appeal recognized

difficulties that surround the use of descriptive words as names in which collective goodwill is claimed to exist. The case makes it clear that a passing off action can only get off the ground if these descriptive words—here, the reference to Swiss chocolate—are taken by a significant part of the public to be used in relation to, and indicating a particular group of, products having a discrete reputation as a group. The requirement does not go as far as demanding that the goods which fall into the group and which are protected by the name must be distinguishable, in fact, from all competing goods. In the case at issue, the public clearly identified Swiss chocolate as a group of products with a separate reputation, despite the fact that it is not possible to point towards a particular recipe that is used for all Swiss chocolate and which is used nowhere else in the world.

The new collective trade mark, created by s. 49 of the 1994 Act, will, of course, meet many of these problems, but only if the claimants are part of a formal association of traders, rather than simply a group of rivals with, nonetheless, a common interest in seeing off outside competition. In many of these cases, the issue of who owns the goodwill and is therefore entitled to sue consequently arises. It may be difficult to argue that an unincorporated trade association that does not manufacture or sell any particular product can establish goodwill of its own, but its unincorporated status does not impede it from owning goodwill through its members if it does trade in one way or another, for example by putting on trade exhibitions. In the latter case, a member of the association acting in a representative capacity could commence an action in passing off on the basis of that goodwill in trading.[89]

Range of goodwill protected

In most of the cases considered so far, the attack on the claimant's goodwill has been straightforwardly aimed at some feature at the heart of the claimant's business, such as brand name, company name, or distinctive product description. The question arises, however, of how broadly the notion of goodwill can extend towards more peripheral parts of the claimant's trading activity.

A notable extension of the range of goodwill protected by the tort of passing off has been provided by the Privy Council in *Cadbury Schweppes Pty Ltd v. Pub Squash Co. Pty Ltd*.[90] This litigation arose when the claimants and, subsequently, the defendants both entered the Australian drinks market with lemon-flavoured soft drinks. There was no doubt that the defendants were seeking to exploit the large market that the claimants' product, called 'Solo', had shown existed for this type of product, but the defendants chose a very different name, 'Pub Squash', for their product. The problem arose in the two firms' respective marketing campaigns: both used a broadly similar strategy; both tried to associate their drink with two separate themes—heroic masculine endeavour and nostalgia for tasty drinks in the past; both products were sold in a yellow can. The issue then was plain: would the tort of passing off extend to more general imagery associated with the product?

The answer given by Lord Scarman was clearly that passing off could so extend. The tort may have originated with the name and description of the product itself, but it was

---

that a large part of the public understood the term Greek yoghurt as yoghurt coming from Greece, leading to goodwill on which Fage as a Greek producer could rely. Calling yoghurt made elsewhere to the same recipe Greek yoghurt then amounted to a misrepresentation.

[89] *Chocosuisse* (n. 88); *Artistic Upholstery Ltd v. Art Forma (Furniture) Ltd* [1999] 4 All ER 277, [2000] FSR 311; see also *Consorzio del Prosciutto di Parma v. Marks & Spencer plc* [1991] RPC 351.

[90] [1981] 1 All ER 213, [1981] 1 WLR 193.

not in any way constrained to remain there. Rather, it was now capable of conferring protection on goodwill created by many other types of descriptive material:

> such as slogans or visual images, which radio, television or newspaper advertising campaigns can lead the market to associate with a claimant's product, provided that such material has become part of the goodwill of the product. And the test is whether the product has derived from the advertising a distinctive character which the market recognises.[91]

So, in allowing the protection of passing off to be thus extended, Lord Scarman is being doubly cautious. Not all advertising and other such imagery will be protected—only that which is part of the company's goodwill. So a standard advert of a contented family group or a sunny tropical isle will never attract the necessary goodwill, but an innovative advert or campaign in which unlikely concepts—such as rugged masculine endeavour—are linked with the product—here, lemonade—may do so. They also appear to fulfil Lord Scarman's second constraint—namely, that of distinctiveness. Only those brands are thus advertised and there is no inherent reason why they should be: creativity has been employed so as to establish distinctiveness.

After this, a successful conclusion to the claimants' claim may have been anticipated—but they were unable to restrain Pub Squash's use of their marketing material. As a matter of policy, Lord Scarman expressed concern that to allow the claim would be to blur the line between fair and unfair methods of competition: '*a defendant, however, does no wrong by entering a market created by another and there competing with its creator*'.[92] Passing off was not to be confused with a wider tort of unfair competition and, here, the defendants—although consciously trying to grab part of the claimants' market share—were not trying to make the public think that their product was that of the claimants: there was thus no deception, no misrepresentation, and no infringement of the rights of the claimants.

In spite of its outcome, *Cadbury Schweppes* is clearly a decision of potentially great significance. Its broadening out of the range of goodwill protected is a major advance on the previous position; its practical effect may well, however, be limited. After the initial expansion, Lord Scarman is cautious to dampen down expectations by emphasizing that only that material which is both distinctive and becomes part of goodwill is protected, and the need for fair competition to be preserved clearly also reduces the chance of claiming successfully. Indeed, arguments based on this expansion of goodwill have been notable only by their absence in ensuing years. A likely explanation of this is that goodwill in such cases is generated so far away from the product itself that no misrepresentation is likely.[93] The basic differences—for example, in the product name—far outweigh the broad similarities found in the marketing campaign.

Notwithstanding this, it is still appropriate to conclude the entire section on goodwill with such a case because it typifies, in its own way, the continuing development and expansion of the notion of goodwill that has been a common feature of many of the areas discussed. Granted that findings of fact can diminish their overall impact, it remains significant that the concept of goodwill has expanded in many areas. In some areas it is still expanding, or has at least the potential to do so. By contrast, the concept has contracted in only a few areas.

---

[91] [1981] 1 All ER 213, [1981] 1 WLR 193 at 218 and 200.

[92] [1981] 1 All ER 213, [1981] 1 WLR 193 at 218 and 200.

[93] Some authors have argued that a strict approach is the only correct approach and that the three traditional requirements should be adhered to strictly. Passing off should remain a misrepresentation tort. See e.g. H. Carty, 'Passing Off at the Crossroads' (1996) 11 EIPR 629.

Misrepresentation

The next vital element in any passing off action is that the defendant must represent his or her goods or services to be those of the claimant. The representation must create a false belief of connection between the two products in the mind of the consumer and, accordingly, it is appropriate to refer to it as a *mis*representation. The creation of an association is sufficient for there to be a misrepresentation:[94] to sell orange-flavoured cakes as 'Jaffa cakes' does not amount to passing off, because that is no more than a description of the product and does not create any form of confusion in the mind of the consumer—but to market the cakes in packs of similar design to that of the market leader may be actionable in passing off, because, by using that design, customers may be likely to confuse the two products. It may therefore be a misrepresentation so to do.[95] In other words, the defendant must make a statement that leads to confusion. Mere confusion as to origin, irrespective of any statement made by the defendant, is not sufficient. And the misrepresentation and confusion cannot be merely transitory. There is no longer a problem if the misunderstanding is dispelled before action is taken.[96] The confusion resulting from the misrepresentation must not affect every single member of the public, a substantial number of members of the public is sufficient in this respect.[97] In that respect the judge is asked to make a quantitative and qualitative assessment taking account of the market and the product or service concerned, which leaves the judge with a lot of discretion and flexibility.[98]

In recent years, supermarket lookalike products have tried to resemble the original, but supermarkets have at least claimed[99] that they made every effort to avoid giving rise to confusion by making a misrepresentation. To put it another way, a true representation of a product, quite apart from being unlikely to attract goodwill, will not cause any confusion and will not therefore be actionable. The hallmark of the misrepresentation is that confusion is its result. Of course, not all confusion in trading is necessarily the result of a misrepresentation; confusion is inevitable whenever a monopoly is first broken. There must be a representation that the newcomer's goods are, or are connected with, those of the original seller.[100] A simple belief, for example, that the claimant had sponsored or given financial support to the defendant would not ordinarily give the public the impression that the claimant had made himself responsible for the quality of the defendant's goods or services.[101] Such a connection would not constitute a misrepresentation, because there has to be deception; mere confusion or likelihood of confusion is not sufficient.[102] A full misrepresentation must take place and such a misrepresentation is a necessary ingredient of a cause of action of passing off.[103]

---

[94] *Sir Robert McAlpine Ltd v. Alfred McAlpine plc* [2004] RPC 711.

[95] See *United Biscuits (UK) Ltd v. Burton Biscuits Ltd* [1992] FSR 14.

[96] *Woolley and anor v. Ultimate Products Ltd and anor* [2012] EWCA Civ 1038.

[97] Passing off requires a substantial proportion of the population to be confused. This approach to confusion is different from the one in relation to trade mark infringement, where the legal construct of the 'average consumer' is used as a test for confusion (and it has been held that members of the public cannot stand proxy for it). *Marks & Spencer plc v. Interflora Inc. and Interflora British Unit* [2012] EWCA Civ 1501.

[98] *Neutrogena Corpn v. Golden Ltd* [1996] RPC 473.

[99] Asda did not succeed in this respect, although in *United Biscuits (UK) Ltd v. Asda Stores Ltd* [1997] RPC 513, it was held to have passed off its lookalike 'Puffin' biscuits as United Biscuits' 'Penguin' biscuits.

[100] *My Kinda Town Ltd v. Soll & Grunts Investments* [1983] RPC 407.

[101] *Harrods Ltd v. Harrodian School Ltd* [1996] RPC 697.

[102] *Phones 4u Ltd v. Phone4u.co.uk Ltd* [2007] RPC 5 (CA).

[103] *Barnsley Brewery Co. Ltd v. RBNB* [1997] FSR 462.

A recent case involving the singer Rihanna presents a good example.[104] Topshop had produced a T-shirt sporting her picture in a professional pose. This had been done without her permission and came in the context of previous highly publicized visits to Topshop outlets by the singer, who is seen by her followers as a fashion icon. The T-shirt was an icon of fashion, but it did not carry the Rihanna logo and was not presented as a memorabilia. Despite all these factors, both the High Court and the Court of Appeal held that the representation made to the public by Topshop through the picture on the T-shirt amounted to a misrepresentation, as on balance part of the public saw this as an endorsement by Rihanna of the T-shirt, whilst this was not the case. And her followers may have bought the T-shirt as a result of this confusion.

The range of misrepresentations is very broad. They may relate to the nature of the product itself, as the cases on champagne already noted exemplify well. In many other cases, the get-up of the product—that is, its packaging and presentation—may be the source of confusion. It may be more remote: the *Cadbury Schweppes* case considered previously shows that goodwill may extend to cover general aspects of the marketing campaign and thus misrepresentations may exist in that context too.

Misrepresentation by get-up

The most common category appears to be cases concerning the get-up of a product. The courts do not seem to object to essential similarities in appearance dictated, for example, by the function that a product has to perform. In *J. B. Williams Co. v. H. Bronnley Co. Ltd*,[105] the separate brands of shaving stick were sold in similar containers. The Court of Appeal found that the claimants' container was not distinctive; all of its features were either dictated by the shape of the stick or were common to many other types of container in everyday use.

William Edge & Sons Ltd v. William Niccolls & Sons Ltd,[106] meanwhile, was a case in which the similarity was not necessary and therefore did amount to a misrepresentation. The claimant had long sold laundry blue, a type of dye, in bags with a wooden stick attached, to enable it to be lowered into a sink of washing without the hands of the user coming into contact with the water and dye. The defendants then began to sell a similar product of almost identical appearance. The House of Lords found that this amounted to passing off, because there was nothing essential about the size and shape of the stick— any stick would perform the same useful function—and so there was no justification for the defendants to have used the same type of get-up.

Jif Lemon

The principal case of this type is now *Reckitt & Colman Products Ltd v. Borden Inc.*[107] This concerns the sale of 'Jif Lemon' juice in lemon-shaped containers, which had been going on successfully and profitably for over 30 years. The defendants then decided to market their lemon juice in similar, although not identical, containers, different models of container being of a different size from that of Jif, or with a different coloured cap and/ or label. None of these refinements detracted from the essential lemon shape and colour that was at the base of Borden's marketing strategy. Lord Oliver emphasized[108] that the key questions in a passing off action were always those of fact and the vital finding of

---

[104] *Robyn Rihanna Fenty and others v. Arcadia Group Brands Ltd and another* [2013] EWHC 2310 (Ch), and on appeal [2015] EWCA Civ 3.

[105] (1909) 26 RPC 765; see also *Scott v. Nice-Pak Products* [1989] FSR 100.   [106] [1911] AC 693.

[107] [1990] 1 All ER 873, [1990] 1 WLR 491.

[108] [1990] 1 All ER 873, [1990] 1 WLR 491 at 880 and 499.

fact made by the trial judge, Walton J, was that there was a likelihood of confusion in the marketplace if both firms sold their juice in similar containers. This conclusion was reached with regard to the way in which this particular product was purchased by a busy shopper rushing around a busy supermarket, making an occasional low-price purchase of an ordinary item; in such circumstances, no great care can be expected to be taken and confusion can readily ensue.

Several points arise from the significant *Jif* case. First, it shows the tort of passing off to be in good health, offering protection beyond that given by the trade mark registration that, at that time, did not extend to goods and/or containers following *Re Coca-Cola Co.'s Application*.[109] Second, it stands out as a rare instance of the House of Lords, in recent times, extending the scope of monopoly. Lord Oliver addressed this issue by asserting '*the principle that no man is entitled to steal another's trade by deceit is one of at least equal importance to the alleged need to curtail monopolies*'.[110] Lord Bridge, however, clearly regretted that the judge's findings of fact left him with no option but to grant an injunction in the case.[111]

Jif is also notable for its confirmation that the identity of likely customers is an element in the equation. Were great care taken habitually by lemon juice purchasers, no confusion would arise and no action would have succeeded, but Walton J confirms that, in practice, care is not taken in such a minor and routine transaction (incidentally, enabling Jif to be sold at a far higher unit price than bottled lemon juice). But if the differences are so great that the reasonable man will be able to discern them, the fact that a few still may get confused is not sufficient to ground an action. This was well illustrated by Foster J in *Morning Star Co-operative Society Ltd v. Express Newspapers Ltd*,[112] when he observed that the differences between the austere broadsheet *Morning Star* and the racy tabloid *Daily Star* were such that '*only a moron in a hurry would be misled*',[113] and thus no passing off had occurred. The knowledge—actual or imputed—of the customers is also relevant; separate firms trading as 'JSB Motor Policies at Lloyds' and 'BJS Motor Syndicate at Lloyds' did not generate any confusion, because the defendants only traded with insurance brokers whose expertise included knowledge of the separate nature of the two operations.[114]

The *Jif* case also highlights a most important practical point in passing off litigation—namely, how to obtain the all-important evidence that confusion has been, or is likely to be, engendered. This is particularly difficult in a case in which the offending new project is yet to be launched, so no members of the public have, as yet, been confused. The vital evidence in *Jif* itself came from tests carried out by the claimants, involving stopping shoppers in the street, offering them one of the defendants' lemons, holding interviews with shoppers, and displaying the defendants' lemon in a supermarket on Shrove Tuesday, when much lemon juice is sold for use on pancakes; each of these tests showed a great degree of confusion, with shoppers believing that the defendants' lemon was, in fact, a Jif lemon.

Evidence

Such unequivocal evidence is, however, rare: too often, survey evidence is not found to be convincing by the courts, because of flaws in the survey itself. Useful guidelines were

---

[109] [1986] 2 All ER 274, *sub nom. In re Coca Cola Co.* [1986] 1 WLR 695; cf. TMA 1994, s. 1(1). See Ch. 24.
[110] [1990] 1 All ER 873, [1990] 1 WLR 491 at 889 and 509.
[111] [1990] 1 All ER 873, [1990] 1 WLR 491 at 877 and 495.   [112] [1979] FSR 113.
[113] At 117.
[114] *John Hayter Motor Underwriting Agencies Ltd v. RBHS Agencies Ltd* [1977] FSR 285. The lack of confusion at the point of sale prevented a passing off claim in *Bostick Ltd v. Sellotape GB Ltd* [1994] RPC 556.

set out by Whitford J in *Imperial Group plc v. Philip Morris Ltd*.[115] He insisted that, in order to be of any value in court, a survey should be of an adequately large size and be fairly conducted. Full details of results and methods should be made available to the defence. Care should be taken about the use of questions that lead, or otherwise direct, their target.

A good example of survey evidence failing this test is provided by *United Biscuits (UK) Ltd v. Burtons Biscuits Ltd*.[116] This was a dispute between rival brands of Jaffa cakes. A straw poll questionnaire and a survey were regarded as worthless by Vinelott J, as being ill-defined and capable of misinterpretation, while a tachistoscope test, which tests the operator's recognition of a brand by quickly flashing an image of it, was also of no help, because the false recognition of the defendants' package as that of the claimants could be equally explained by the fact that the claimants were the clear brand leader.

Clearly, care needs to be taken by the parties in the collection of survey evidence and caution will be the hallmark of the courts in their use of it;[117] its dramatic impact in the *Jif* case shows, however, that, in an appropriate case, it will have great value. Equally, the courts are also unwilling to hear evidence from marketing 'experts' if the issue relates to potential confusion among the public at large.[118]

Other examples

A few other examples of passing off by confusing get-up may be helpful. In *Rizla Ltd v. Bryant & May Ltd*,[119] the claimants' long-standing business of selling packs of cigarette papers faced a serious threat of competition from the defendants. They proposed to market three different types of paper, as did the claimants, and were proposing to use the same colour as their rivals for each type of paper. There, however, the similarity ceased with the defendants' 'Swan' brand name being prominently displayed, preventing any confusion with the Rizla papers arising.

Likewise, the inclusion of a pink paper section for business news in the tabloid evening newspaper the *Evening Standard* was not thought likely to cause any confusion with the broadsheet morning pink paper newspaper the *Financial Times*.[120]

Nor too could the proprietor of the magazine *Gourmet* restrain the introduction of a new journal *BBC Gourmet Good Food* when its get-up was different and it would be typically purchased from a rack on the basis of that get-up, rather than orally purchased from behind the newsagent's counter.[121]

Low-cost airline Easyjet was, however, able to stop an unrelated defendant from trading as Easyrealestate. Passing off could be established in this case, despite the fact that Easyjet could not appropriate the word 'Easy', because the defendant had copied the four distinctive features of Easyjet's get-up on its website.[122]

Misrepresentation by name

In other cases, it is not the get-up of the goods, but the name being used that is the source of potential confusion. In *Newsweek Inc. v. BBC*,[123] the publishers of the international news magazine sought to prevent the use of *Newsweek* as the title of a current affairs

---

[115] [1984] RPC 293 at 302.   [116] [1992] FSR 14.

[117] See C. Morcom, 'Survey Evidence in Trade Mark Proceedings' (1984) 1 EIPR 6.

[118] *Dalgety Spillers Foods Ltd v. Food Brokers Ltd* [1994] FSR 504.   [119] [1986] RPC 389.

[120] *Financial Times Ltd v. Evening Standard Co. Ltd* [1991] FSR 7.

[121] *Advance Magazine Publishing Inc. v. Redwood Publishing Ltd* [1993] FSR 449.

[122] *Easyjet Airline Co. v. Tim Dainty (t/a Easyrealestate)* [2002] FSR 111.

[123] [1979] RPC 441.

television programme. The Court of Appeal rejected the claim, because the BBC would broadcast the programme with its usual logos etc., and there would be no risk of confusing it with the claimants' magazine. The mere use of a name used by another trader does not necessarily create the impression that the businesses are in some way connected, it seems.

But the use of the same name in a related field of activity is more likely to be restrained. In this respect, *Island Trading Co. v. Anchor Brewing Co.*[124] is instructive. The claimants sold 'Newquay Real Steam Bitter', with a steam theme used as part of its promotion. The defendants then began to import from California, for the first time, their 'Anchor Steam Beer' and the claimants feared that confusion would arise. Knox J found that the Newquay brand was often referred to by customers as 'Steam Beer', and he awarded an injunction against the sale of Anchor Steam Beer in kegs, but allowed it in bottles. The reasoning was that kegs of beer in pubs might well cause confusion when a drinker asks for a 'pint of Steam', but bottled beer sold from the shelves of off-licences would not give rise to such confusion, the bottles being very different in appearance, the customer being more likely to be sober, the sales staff being less under pressure, and the noise level being likely to be lower.

The famous luxury goods company Asprey and Garrard successfully brought a claim in passing off relying on the goodwill in its 'Asprey' name against another trader in luxury goods in the London area that wanted to include the word 'Asprey' in its trading name, William R. Asprey Esquire. It was held that any use of the word 'Asprey' in such a context was likely to confuse, and was especially likely to confuse the high proportion of potential foreign customers of Asprey and Garrard.[125]

Much will, however, depend on the facts: in another case, the use of the words 'Arsenal' and 'Gunners', or other signs related to Arsenal football club, in relation to unlicensed memorabilia was not enough to establish passing off, because, in this case, the specific habit of marking licensed merchandise as 'original' meant that, in the absence of this mention on the merchandise at issue, the public would not be confused into thinking that they were offered 'official' Arsenal merchandise.[126]

A particular problem arises when the same name is used on two similar products in cases in which a real name is being used: can the use of your own name amount to a misrepresentation, given that goodwill may attach, as we have seen, to a person's name? Well-known families appear to be particularly susceptible to this kind of dispute. In *Tussaud v. Tussaud*,[127] the claimants ran the famous Madame Tussaud waxworks in London; this had been a family business, but had just been sold to an outsider. Young Louis Tussaud had worked in the family business, but was now intending to open his own rival waxworks as Louis Tussaud Ltd. An injunction was awarded to the claimants stopping the defendant from registering a company of that name, because of the confusion that would arise and also because Louis Tussaud was not in the process of incorporating a pre-existing business.

Similar decisions have been reached in other cases. *Parker-Knoll Ltd v. Knoll International Ltd*[128] saw a clash between the claimants, manufacturers of traditional furniture, and the defendants, who made more modern designs primarily for industrial use.

---

[124] [1989] RPC 287.

[125] *Asprey & Garrard Ltd v. WRA (Guns) Ltd (t/a William R Asprey Esquire)* [2002] FSR 477, upheld on appeal [2002] FSR 487.

[126] *Arsenal Football Club plc v. Matthew Reed* [2001] 2 CMLR 23, [2001] RPC 922.

[127] (1890) 44 Ch D 678.

[128] [1962] RPC 265.

The proprietor of the defendants was the wife of the nephew of the original Knoll who lent his name to the claimant firm. The House of Lords found, by a majority, that the defendants could be prevented by injunction from using their name because of the likelihood that they would be referred to as 'Knoll' and the confusion that would arise thereby. More recently, the Gucci family have also resorted to litigation. In *Guccio Gucci SpA v. Paolo Gucci*,[129] the defendant was also prevented from trading under his own name, because the evidence was that the buyers of designer label clothes might be confused by the use of the Gucci name by anyone other than the claimants. These decisions may appear harsh on defendants legitimately using their own name, but they are a reminder that the first in the field has the opportunity to develop a reputation and thus acquire goodwill, and that this inevitably confers on him an advantage over later entrants into the market who, after all, do not have to use their own name in their trading activities and only do so because of the cachet that their (well-known) name may confer.

The Court of Appeal recently held that, after the name and the business have been sold, one can, in principle, use one's own name in connection with a competing business—but there is a risk: if the public perceives your activity as passing off the new business as that which you have sold—for example, because you make comments indicating that you are the 'real' one or even because you do not correct a self-induced misapprehension by the public[130]—this will amount to a misrepresentation for the purposes of passing off.[131]

Cybersquatting

The development of the Internet has, in recent years, given rise to a new type of case in which misrepresentation by name takes place. 'Cyberpirates' have tried to register the names of famous companies as domain names in order to be able to sell them to the companies involved for a profit. Some would call it extortion, but actions in passing off have proved useful to stop this practice. The goodwill of the famous companies is not in doubt and it was held that the registration of the names by cyberpirates amounted to a misrepresentation. The least that could be said was that the registration amounted to the creation of an instrument of deception.[132]

This flexible approach to misrepresentation is, however, linked to one condition: what is complained of must inherently tell a lie in order for it to be an instrument of deception.[133]

Misrepresentation of the product itself

Another form of misrepresentation may arise when the product itself appears to be that of the claimants. This can particularly arise in cases of parallel imports, in relation to which goods made elsewhere by a multinational firm are imported and compete with their home-grown product, at a lower price, because of the cheaper manufacturing costs elsewhere.

---

129 [1991] FSR 89.

130 *British Sky Broadcasting Group plc & ors v. Sky Home Services Ltd and ors* [2007] FSR 14.

131 *I. N. Newman Ltd v. Adlem* [2006] FSR 16 (CA).

132 *Marks & Spencer plc v. One in A Million Ltd, Ladbroke's plc v. One in A Million Ltd; J Sainsbury plc v. One in A Million Ltd, Virgin Enterprises Ltd v. One in A Million Ltd; British Telecommunications plc v. One in A Million Ltd* [1998] FSR 265 at 271, confirmed on appeal *British Telecommunications plc v. One in A Million Ltd* [1998] 4 All ER 476. See also *Phones 4U Ltd and anor v. Phone4u.co.uk Internet Ltd and ors* [2007] RPC 5 (CA). Other cases are concerned with the registration of company names in bad faith: *Glaxo plc v. Glaxowellcome Ltd* [1996] FSR 388; *Direct Line Group Ltd v. Direct Line Estate Agency Ltd* [1997] FSR 374.

133 *L'Oréal SA, Lancôme Parfums et Beauté & Cie & Laboratoire Garnier & Cie v. Bellure NV, Malaika Investments (t/a Honeypot Cosmetic & Perfumery Sales) & Starion International Ltd* [2008] RPC 9 (CA).

In *Colgate-Palmolive Ltd v. Markwell Finance Ltd*,[134] the claimants made and sold toothpaste in the UK as a subsidiary of its US parent company. There was also a Brazilian subsidiary, which made toothpaste of poorer quality; it was not intended to compete in the markets of other members of the Colgate group, but the defendants succeeded in circumventing the restrictions that had been placed on the trading activity of the Brazilian firm. It was clear that confusion was caused—complaints were made to the claimants about what was, in fact, toothpaste from Brazil. The Court of Appeal found that this amounted to passing off, even though both types of Colgate product derived from a common origin: it was not the origin, but the quality, of the goods that was at issue and the use by the defendants of products bearing the 'Colgate' name amounted to a misrepresentation to their customers of the quality to be expected from those goods. A similar decision was reached much earlier in *Gillette Safety Razor Co. v. Franks*,[135] in which the defendant was prevented from selling second-hand imported Gillette razor blades in Gillette packaging as new blades.

Imitation products—such as perfumes with similar-sounding names, in similar-looking bottles, and with a similar smell—are another interesting case. The original perfumes may be well known and possess a lot of goodwill; the mere fact that someone is seeking to emulate them does not amount to a misrepresentation. This remains true as long as the public does not see the imitation as the genuine goods originating from the original producer and that also explains why the conclusion in *L'Oréal*[136] was different from that in *Colgate-Palmolive*.

Developments in misrepresentation

It is evident that the law is willing to recognize a variety of different ways in which trading activity can amount to a misrepresentation. In areas in which there is such flexibility, it is always open to litigants to try to exploit that flexibility by seeking gradually to extend the frontiers of liability. There is evidence, from two decisions, of this happening in respect of misrepresentations in passing off cases.

Bristol Conservatories Ltd v. Conservatories Custom Built Ltd[137] was a case of what may be described as reverse passing off. Usually, the representor seeks to establish that his or her goods are the goods of the claimant, but here the opposite was the case and the claim was that the goods of the claimant were, in fact, his. This arose in relation to the erection of ornamental conservatories as extensions to buildings. The claimants were engaged in this business when an employee left and joined the defendants' newly formed business. He then touted for business, showing prospective customers pictures of conservatories erected by the claimants, conveying the impression that they had been the work of the defendants.

The Court of Appeal ruled on a preliminary point that these facts disclosed a good cause of action. The basis of the decision is, in essence, that any confusion—however caused and even if indirect in origin—will be enough to ground a misrepresentation claim and, clearly, here customers would become confused as to the true origin of the conservatories. In fact, the defendants' salesman had been silent as to the basis of the pictures, so inferences drawn from a silence can also amount to a misrepresentation, which is a long way from traditional definitions of misrepresentation. Ralph Gibson LJ

---

[134] [1989] RPC 497.   [135] (1924) 41 RPC 499.

[136] *L'Oréal SA, Lancôme Parfums et Beauté & Cie & Laboratoire Garnier & Cie v. Bellure NV, Malaika Investments (t/a Honeypot Cosmetic & Perfumery Sales) & Starion International Ltd* [2008] RPC 9 (CA).

[137] [1989] RPC 455, noted J. Holyoak 'Reverse Passing Off: A New Liability' (1990) 106 LQR 564.

specifically endorsed[138] the view that the common law should seek to parallel the legislative trend towards ever higher standards of commercial integrity and this invitation, if taken up, will only strengthen the expansionist tone adopted in recent times by the tort of passing off.

More recently, the existence of this type of claim has been confirmed by the sale of 'Welsh Whiskey', which was, in fact, based on a blend of Scotch whisky and herbs. This was found to be an abuse of the name and reputation of Scotch whisky by dressing it up as being Welsh.[139]

The other case that, again, shows a broad approach to misrepresentation is that of *Associated Newspapers plc v. Insert Media Ltd.*[140] The claimants, newspaper proprietors, sought to prevent the unauthorized insertion of advertising material into copies of their newspapers. Just as in *Bristol Conservatories*, the problem was that, in one sense, there was no misrepresentation, because nothing was said to the readers to indicate that the inserts were not by, or with the permission of, the proprietors.

The Court of Appeal found for the claimants. While accepting that the mere act of inserting copy into the papers may not, in itself, amount to a misrepresentation, it would do so if all of the surrounding circumstances suggested that the inserts were there with the permission of the proprietor and, in particular, if, as a result, the public is likely to be confused because of what has been done. On these facts, the defendant had himself, in his publicity, pointed to the link that would be made by people associating the insert and the product it promoted with the quality newspaper that accompanied it; thus confusion would be generated, with members of the public thinking that the publishers of the paper were responsible for the insertion. This was sufficient to lead to a finding that the conduct of the defendants amounted to a misrepresentation—and one that could cause harm to the reputation of the claimants in appropriate circumstances.

Unintentional misrepresentation

Throughout the entire discussion of misrepresentation in the tort of passing off, there is one common element that may be emphasized: in common law actions for misrepresentation, much depends on the state of the defendant's mind in making the statement, but that is not the case in passing off claims; rather it is merely necessary, as Lord Diplock put it in the *Advocaat* case,[141] that the misrepresentation is '*calculated to injure*' the goodwill of the other trader.

But even this formulation is prone to mislead, because 'calculating' is normally thought to involve some element of deliberate conduct, which is not the case here. The view has long been taken that all that is needed is to show that the misrepresentation is likely to harm the claimant's interests, and that this may be the case even if the defendant is innocent and does not intend to cause harm.[142] In a case in which the defendant becomes aware of a self-induced misapprehension on behalf of the public—that is, in which he or she played no active part—but if he or she then fails to react to eliminate the misapprehension, a finding that this amounts to a misrepresentation will be inevitable.[143]

The only exception to this clear rule arises when the misrepresentation occurs through the actions of a third party on facts such as those of *Bovril Ltd v. Bodega Co. Ltd.*[144] In this

---

[138]　[1989] RPC 455 at 466.
[139]　*Matthew Gloag & Sons Ltd v. Welsh Distillers Ltd* [1998] FSR 718.
[140]　[1991] 3 All ER 535, [1991] 1 WLR 571.
[141]　[1979] AC 731, [1979] 2 All ER 927 at 742 and 933.
[142]　See e.g. *Baume & Co. v. A. H. Moore Ltd* [1958] Ch 907, [1958] 2 All ER 113 at 916 and 116.
[143]　*British Sky Broadcasting Group plc and ors v. Sky Home Services Ltd and ors* [2007] FSR 14.
[144]　(1916) 33 RPC 153.

case, the defendant had served Oxo in response to requests for Bovril; clearly, in such a case, the innocence of the manufacturers of Oxo would count in their favour, although their goods were, in fact, being passed off as the goods of another. Perhaps the simplest way of explaining such a case is that Oxo made no representation at all. The innocent passer off may be at a slight advantage when remedies are considered; any account of profits may be limited to the time after which the defendant becomes aware of the situation and continues with the misrepresentation,[145] but there seems to be no ground for differentiating between innocent and other defendants in relation to the award of damages. This has been an area of controversy in the past,[146] but this view is now confirmed by the decision of Blackburne J in *Gillette UK Ltd v. Edenwest Ltd*.[147]

The failure to require any intention on the part of the defendant can lead to ironic results. On the one hand, the defendants in the *Cadbury Schweppes* case intentionally copied the marketing ideas of the claimants, but were not liable, because no one was deceived. On the other hand, in the *Jif* case, clear attempts were made to differentiate the products (although admittedly without abandoning the basic lemon shape), yet their failure to avoid confusion led to the defendants being found liable. The failure to provide a defence of innocence adds to the force of the tort of passing off, and shows that traders must be continually on their guard not to generate confusion between their product and that of another trader.

Damage

All of the various proffered definitions of the elements of the tort of passing off include the necessity of damage being incurred by the claimant or, in a case in which injunctive relief is sought, the likelihood of damage. Passing off is therefore not actionable per se and harm to goodwill resulting from the misrepresentation has to be proven.

Or does it?[148]

Isolated instances of case law show that the courts may be prepared to assume the existence of damage. In *Draper v. Trist & Tristbestos Brake Linings Ltd*,[149] the trial judge was only prepared to award nominal damages in the absence of proof that the passing off caused any specific damage. The Court of Appeal, however, substituted an award of £2,000. Sir Wilfrid Greene MR noted that:

> [the] right which is infringed in a passing-off case is one which was regarded at law as one the mere violation of which led to damage...it was not regarded at law as a case in which damage was of the gist of the action.[150]

Goddard LJ, meanwhile, commented that the law 'assumes...that if the goodwill of a man's business has been interfered with by the passing-off of goods, damage results therefrom'.[151] Although the claimant could not show direct loss of trade from the passing off, he was able to show that this was a 'real business possibility'[152] and thus succeeded.

This case was followed in *Procea Products Ltd v. Evans & Sons Ltd*,[153] in which the defendants were selling a type of loaf known as 'process bread', which the claimants

---

[145] *Spalding & Bros. v. A. W. Gamage Ltd* (1915) 32 RPC 273 per Lord Parker at 283.

[146] See e.g. *Marengo v. Daily Sketch & Sunday Graphic Ltd* (1948) 65 RPC 242.

[147] [1994] RPC 279.

[148] It is at least not clear whether the claimant must identify some specific head of pecuniary loss in order to succeed: see *Law Society of England & Wales v. Society of Lawyers* [1996] FSR 739.

[149] (1939) 56 RPC 429.   [150] (1939) 56 RPC 429 at 435.   [151] (1939) 56 RPC 429 at 442.

[152] (1939) 56 RPC 429, per Sir Wilfrid Greene MR at 440.

[153] (1951) 68 RPC 210.

thought would engender confusion with their product name. There was no evidence of actual loss of trade and only nominal damages were being sought. Roxburgh J followed the *Draper* decision and awarded £1 in damages. (This was an innocent misrepresentation and the judge was clearly troubled by the same doubt as already noted as to whether anything more than nominal damages should be awarded in a case of innocence—as has been seen, this has been resolved and full damages may now be awarded.)

The status of these two cases is somewhat hazy. They have not been the subject of attack or criticism, but may appear inconsistent with the demands that damage be proven. It is suggested that they can be reconciled. Clearly, a claimant has to show damage has occurred,[154] but the exact loss of trade is very often difficult to pinpoint. If a firm's business declines, a whole range of factors quite apart from passing off by rivals—poor product, high price, etc.—as well as legitimate, as opposed to illegitimate, forms of competition may be to blame. As a result of this, in a case such as *Draper*, the court is requiring proof of likely losses rather than actual losses and the assumption being made is not that any passing off always causes damage, but that the particular circumstances are such that damage of some kind is likely to occur.

A case such as *Procea* is different again: if no damage has (yet) been shown to occur, although some may be likely to result, nominal damages is clearly all that can be awarded (as well as the injunction that was granted). In deciding whether the facts show the likelihood of damage, the scope of the goodwill of the claimant and the way in which confusion may arise will be of importance to the court in deciding whether there is liability by inferring the risk of damage from those elements.[155] What is clear, though, is that the concept of damage cannot be restricted to loss of sales or directly provable losses and that the loss of goodwill can almost be presumed to lead to damage.[156]

A useful case demonstrating this process and showing that damage remains of importance is *Stringfellow v. McCain Foods (GB) Ltd*.[157] The claimant owned a top London nightclub, while the defendant named its new brand of long, thin, oven chip 'Stringfellows' and advertised it on television with a disco scene set in a domestic kitchen. Clearly, the claimant was possessed of goodwill, and it may be thought that the name and imagery suggested that the chips were, in some way, connected with the nightclub. The Court of Appeal rejected the claim. This was, in part, due to its view that there was no misrepresentation in the use of the name, but also because, even after the television adverts, which may have amounted to a misrepresentation, there was no actual evidence of goodwill being damaged. Although the claimant feared loss of goodwill, that was not enough: there was no evidence of trade declining and the argument that his future merchandising activity may be compromised was short-circuited by Stringfellow's admission that it was only this action that had alerted him to the possibility of merchandising. No damage was therefore found likely to occur and the claim was, as a result, found not to succeed.

The damage requirement also proved to be problematical when the tort was used to combat the practices of cyberpirates. The Court of Appeal was prepared to accept that the registration of a domain name that included the famous name would amount to an erosion of the exclusive goodwill in the name and it was assumed that damage was likely to result from the registration as such. Use of the registered name would definitely lead

---

[154] *Reckitt & Colman Products Ltd v. Borden Inc.* [1990] 1 All ER 873, [1990] 1 WLR 491, per Lord Oliver at 880 and 499.

[155] See e.g. *Annabel's (Berkeley Square) Ltd v. Schock* [1972] RPC 838. Cf. *Miss World (Jersey) Ltd v. James Street Productions Ltd* [1981] FSR 309.

[156] *Sir Robert McAlpine Ltd v. Alfred McAlpine plc* [2004] RPC 711.   [157] [1984] RPC 501.

to damage and the court was prepared to grant interlocutory relief to stop damage from occurring. Aldous LJ ruled:

> In my view there be discerned from the case a jurisdiction to grant injunctive relief where a defendant is equipped with or is intending to equip another with an instrument of fraud. Whether any name is an instrument of fraud will depend upon all the circumstances. A name which will, by reason of its similarity to the name of another, inherently lead to passing-off is such an instrument. If it would not inherently lead to passing-off, it does not follow that it is not an instrument of fraud. The Court should consider the similarity of the names, the intention of the defendant, the type of trade and all the surrounding circumstances. If it be the intention of the defendant to appropriate the goodwill of another or enable others to do so, I can see no reason why the Court should not infer that it will happen, even if there is a possibility that such an appropriation would not take place. If, taking all the circumstances into account the Court should conclude that the name was produced to enable passing-off, is adapted to be used for passing-off and, if used, is likely to be fraudulently used, an injunction will be appropriate.[158]

When can an action be brought?

The ruling of the Court of Appeal is also helpful in another respect: it shows clearly in which different situations the passing off action can be used. Aldous LJ summarized it as follows:

> It follows that the Court will intervene by way of injunction in passing-off cases in three types of case. First, where there is passing-off established or it is threatened. Second, where the defendant is a joint tortfeasor with another in passing-off, either actual or threatened. Third, where the defendant has equipped himself with or intends to equip another with an instrument of fraud. This third type is probably a mere quia timet action.[159]

It should be added, however, that merely providing assistance is not sufficient to become a joint tortfeasor.[160]

Remedies

There is little that needs to be said specifically about remedies in the context of passing off. Injunctive relief is often sought, particularly to prevent the alleged passing off from ever occurring given the speculative nature of the damage in fact caused by the passing off, as has just been noted. Alternatively, but unusually, the claimant may seek a declaration instead: for example, in cases in which the defendant has already ceased his or her wrongful trading.[161]

As far as monetary compensation is concerned, the claimant is faced with a choice of a claim for damages or an account of profits. The latter is, of course, discretionary and, as has been seen previously, not available in respect of innocent passing off. That said, if available to a claimant, it is clearly advantageous, because the account will be for profits from all sales of the offending product even if the passing off does not contribute to the sales in question.[162]

Damages are awarded on standard tortious principles to reflect the harm caused to the goodwill of the claimant with all of the attendant difficulties of deciding what

---

[158] *British Telecommunications plc v. One in A Million Ltd* [1998] 4 All ER 476.
[159] *British Telecommunications* (n. 158).
[160] See *Crédit Lyonnais Bank Nederland NV v. Export Credit Guarantee Department* [1998] 1 Lloyd's Rep 19.
[161] E.g. *Treasure Cot Co. Ltd v. Hamleys Bros. Ltd* (1950) 67 RPC 89.
[162] *Lever v. Goodwin* (1887) 36 Ch D 1.

harm is attributable to the conduct of the defendant. Perhaps as a response to that, an alternative approach has been canvassed in the case of *Dormeuil Frères SA v. Feraglow Ltd*,[163] in which the defendants had been quite extensively engaged in the manufacture of cloth that contained, and thus infringed, the trade mark of the claimants. The difficulty of assessing the losses of the claimant led to the argument that damages should be awarded on a royalty basis, as in patent cases, and that relevant licensing agreements could be examined to come up with an appropriate figure. Knox J reviewed the law in detail and concluded that it was possible, but not certain, that a royalty-based claim could be made and, because this was a preliminary hearing, it was not appropriate at this stage to create a new royalty-based approach. The key question is whether the analogy suggested with patent cases is appropriate; there, of course, it is the claimant's proprietary right that is being usurped by the defendant, whereas the rights created by the tort of passing off are not proprietary in character. It would therefore be something of a jump to allow passing off damages to be calculated in this manner and would enhance the protection of the claimant's goodwill considerably. This may be too big a leap for the tort to take, although equally it has not recently been noted for its timidity.

Passing off—an overview

In reviewing the contemporary role of this tort, several issues arise:

- Why has it expanded in so many ways in recent years?
- Will it still have a role in the light of the Trade Marks Act 1994?
- Does it have the effect of being a tort of unfair competition?

The first question can easily be answered with reference to two factors. The most obvious is the shortcomings of the, at times, ill-thought-out trade marks legislation at the time of the key developments in the tort's recent development. Most of the expansion of the tort has been in response to these difficulties; an analogy might be made with the way in which the tort of negligence, in its expansionist period, rushed in to fill some of the holes in contract law and public law.

The second factor to bear strongly in mind is that goodwill, although not a proprietary interest as such, is nevertheless a real and tradeable commodity. If, for example, I decide to sell my cruise ship, that will cost the buyer £X; if I decide to make available to the new owner of the ship the business that it has been operating, I would expect a further £Y to reflect the goodwill of that business. It is suggested that only passing off can protect that goodwill interest.

This all leads logically to our second question. Clearly, the broader scope of the new legislative approach reduces the role of the tort. As we have seen, several problems that were previously the exclusive province of passing off are now broadly, although not precisely, covered by the 1994 Act. Examples would include the *Bollinger* type of case (under s. 49) and the *Lego* type of case (under s. 5(3)).

But both of these examples have gaps, and a provisional list of instances in relation to which the law of tort still has a role to play might be:

- cases of attack on general goodwill rather than on the mark itself, especially if no mark has been registered, in that area (as in *Lego*) or at all;

---

[163] [1990] RPC 449.

- cases of attack on general image, which is not capable of being protected by a trade mark, of which *Cadbury Schweppes* is the classic example;
- cases like *Bristol Conservatories*, in which it is not clear that the odd facts can be resolved in any way other than through the tort of passing off, unless a trade mark had been, on those facts, registered in the pictures of the conservatories, which seems unlikely.

We may add to this list the likelihood that a claim in passing off will continue to be co-pleaded with a trade mark action due to a combination of the uncertainties still attaching to the 1994 Act and the understandable conservatism in these matters of the legal professions.

In relation to the tort of unfair competition, the claims that there may be one in the alcohol cases have been soundly and authoritatively refuted in *Cadbury Schweppes*. The absence of such an immediate remedy distinguishes the UK jurisdiction from that of many others, such as, for example, the broad approach of Australia's Trade Practices Act 1974. So, as so often in the common law, the question has to be whether the sundry elements of the law provide adequate protection for the parties. In *Arsenal v. Reed*,[164] there has been an obiter comment that passing off has effectively been turned into a tort of unfair competition; whatever may be in a name, the Court of Appeal has subsequently refused to invent a separate tort of unfair competition. The requirements for passing off remain the hurdles that a case must clear in order for there to be a legal remedy.[165]

Meanwhile, passing off clearly still has a role. As we have seen, it has a role—albeit a diminished one—in filling the gaps in trade mark law; it also stands out in the world of tort law as a protector of economic interests, directly, those of traders and, indirectly, those of consumers too. Also, as a tort created by the courts and developed by them, it has an inherent flexibility that is not a quality normally associated with statutory provisions. This tort will therefore not fade away.

Defamation and malicious falsehood

The law of defamation—that is, of libel and slander[166]—provides protection for the reputation of an individual, while malicious falsehood—which is also sometimes referred to as 'injurious falsehood' or 'slander of goods'—provides a parallel protection for the reputations of businesses. It is thus convenient to consider them in the same section.

Defamation

It is clear that, in its protection of an individual's reputation, the tort of defamation will extend its coverage to the professional or business aspects of that individual's life. The classic instance of this is provided by *Tolley v. J. S. Fry Ltd*,[167] in which the claimant, a (genuinely) amateur golfer, was appalled to discover that a likeness of him was appearing in the newspaper adverts for the defendants' chocolate bars, accompanied by a banal limerick comparing the excellence of Tolley's golf with that of the defendants' product.

---

[164] *Arsenal Football Club plc v. Reed (No. 2)* [2003] 3 All ER 865, [2003] RPC 696 (CA).
[165] *L'Oréal SA, Lancôme Parfums et Beauté & Cie & Laboratoire Garnier & Cie v. Bellure NV, Malaika Investments (t/a Honeypot Cosmetic & Perfumery Sales) & Starion International Ltd* [2008] RPC 9 (CA).
[166] See P. Milmo et al. (2008) *Gatley on Libel and Slander*, 11th edn, London: Sweet and Maxwell.
[167] [1931] AC 333.

Tolley complained not on grounds of taste or with regard to the as-yet-unconceived notion of character merchandising, but because he felt that his status as an amateur would be hopelessly compromised in the minds of readers, because they would assume that, contrary to the then rules, he must have been paid to lend his name to the adverts. The House of Lords found that that was an appropriate conclusion for them to reach, and thus the adverts amounted to defamation by innuendo and were thus actionable.

But the role of defamation in this field goes further than that.[168] There is also clear authority that a business can sue in defamation when its reputation is falsely impugned and this amounts to a back-door method of protecting a trading reputation against false allegations. Cases of this nature have been few and far between, and have not always been accompanied by success, but it seems reasonably clear that such a cause of action exists.[169] In *South Hetton Coal Co. v. North-Eastern News Association Ltd*,[170] criticism was published of the insanitary state of the housing provided by the coal company for its employees. Lord Esher MR[171] was quite clear that the laws of libel gave a company the same rights as an ordinary person, but that this was not an actionable libel as being legitimate fair comment on a matter of public interest.

In *Lewis v. Daily Telegraph Ltd*,[172] a company and its chairman brought an action in libel against the defendants for a news story reporting that the police had raided the company's premises in a fraud enquiry. The House of Lords seemed to accept that a company could sue in libel without demur, but ruled that the stories were not libellous, because they only referred to the investigation of possible crimes and did not state or imply that actual crimes had been committed. The House of Lords also denied the availability of libel to a local authority,[173] but this was on the particular ground of the public interest in democratic free speech; cases in the *South Hetton* line of authority were approved, and it is difficult to see how public interest would act so compellingly to prevent any claim in libel by a company.[174]

Malicious falsehood

It is evident that the role of defamation in this field is peripheral and that most cases are more likely to be brought by companies within the more appropriate, but also more restrictive, tort of malicious falsehood. This is a classic example of an action on the case that evolved and developed a long way from its initial roots to the role that it now plays. It began to deal with wrongful allegations of unlawful claims to proprietary rights in land,[175] but now extends to cover the trading reputation of a business and its product. It is only in the latter part of the nineteenth century that the tort came to fulfil this type of need.

Two significant cases in its development at this time were *The Western Counties Manure Co. v. Lawes Chemical Manure Co.*[176] and *Riding v. Smith*.[177] In the *Manure* case, the defendants wrongly impugned the quality of the claimants' product and this attack on the goods was found to give a novel cause of action to the claimants; in *Riding*, it was the business itself that was the subject of criticism. In this enchanting case, the defendant alleged that the claimant's wife (who helped in his shop) had committed adultery in the shop with

---

[168] See e.g. *McKenna v. MGN Ltd* (2006) 103 (33) LSG 23.
[169] See e.g. *Berkoff v. Burchill* [1996] 4 All ER 1008, CA.   [170] [1894] 1 QB 133.
[171] [1894] 1 QB 133 at 138.   [172] [1964] AC 234, [1963] 2 All ER 151.
[173] *Derbyshire County Council v. Times Newspapers Ltd* [1993] AC 534, [1993] 1 All ER 1011.
[174] Cf. F. Patfield, 'Defamation, Freedom of Speech and Corporations' [1993] Jur Rev 294.
[175] *Gerard v. Dickenson* (1590) 4 Co Rep 18a, 76 ER 903.   [176] (1874) LR 9 Exch 218.
[177] (1876) 1 Ex D 91.

the new vicar. Whereas today the tabloids would encourage flocks of their readers to visit the shop, in those stern times there was evidence of a falling off in the trade of the claimant following the allegations and this too was held to represent a good cause of action.

The strands of this emergent tort were pulled together in *Ratcliffe v. Evans*,[178] in which the defendant falsely alleged that the claimant's business had ceased to exist. This was clearly harmful to the interests of the claimant, but was inaccurate, rather than defamatory. In spite of this, Bowen LJ found the statements to be actionable, stating that:

> an action will lie for written or oral falsehoods, not actionable *per se* nor even defamatory, where they are maliciously published, where they are calculated in the ordinary course of things to produce, and where they do produce, actual damage.[179]

The House of Lords confirmed that this was so in *White v. Mellin*,[180] but added that it was necessary for the claimant to establish that special damage had been suffered and, for this reason—and also for the reason that the facts did not reveal the necessary denigration of the claimant's goods (White sold Mellin's baby food, but put on the wrappers a notice stating that another brand in which he had an interest was more nutritious)—no action was judged to exist on the facts as then found.

In the light of these cases, it can be established that several elements go to make up this tort and that all need to be established if a claim is to succeed. It is necessary to show that the defendant has made a false statement that is derogatory of the claimant's goods or business, that the statement has been made with malice, and that it has resulted in damage to the claimant.

It is also worth noting that, in recent years, an action in defamation in an intellectual property case has been brought in combination with an action for trade mark infringement.[181] A pattern similar to that in relation to passing off and trade marks is being established—but the wisdom of such an approach can be questioned and malicious falsehood is difficult to prove.[182]

Falsity

The requirement of falsity in relation to malicious falsehood is simple: as in relation to defamation, the statement must not be true. If the claimant cannot prove falsity, he or she will not succeed.[183] The action brought by British Airways against the Ryanair advertisements 'Expensive BA——DS' and 'Expensive BA' failed to clear this first hurdle, because the price comparisons contained in them were not false and apparently did not mislead the public. As a result, BA's action, as a whole, failed spectacularly.[184]

This contrasts with the position in mainstream defamation cases, in which it is for the defence to justify the truth of statements made. In determining the falsity of a statement, the 'one meaning rule' applies, meaning that the single natural and ordinary meaning of the words used must be determined.[185]

Denigration

For this tort, it is not sufficient that the statement be false; it must go further and damage the reputation of the goods or business by denigrating it—that is, by making derogatory

---

[178] [1892] 2 QB 524.   [179] [1892] 2 QB 524 at 527.   [180] [1895] AC 154.

[181] See *Vodafone Group plc v. Orange Personal Communications Services Ltd* [1997] FSR 34; *Macmillan Magazines Ltd v. RCN Publishing Co. Ltd* [1998] FSR 9; *WebSphere Trade Mark* [2004] FSR 39.

[182] *British Airways plc v. Ryanair Ltd* [2001] FSR 32; *WebSphere* (n. 181).

[183] *Anderson v. Liebig's Extract of Meat Co. Ltd* (1881) 45 LT 757.

[184] *British Airways plc v. Ryanair Ltd* [2001] FSR 32.

[185] *Vodafone Group plc v. Orange Personal Communications Services Ltd* [1997] FSR 34. See also *Ajinomoto Sweeteners Europe SAS v. Asda Stores Ltd* [2009] FSR 16.

statements that harm the reputation of the goods or business. As we have just seen, this was a problem in *White v. Mellin*, in which there was no derogatory comment about the claimant's product, but rather only a suggestion that that of the defendant was superior. It would have been different if it had been stated that White's product was in some way harmful to children.

The context in which the statement is made will be an important factor in deciding whether it is derogatory or not. *De Beers Abrasive Products Ltd v. International General Electric Co. of New York Ltd*[186] demonstrates this well. The defendants circulated to the trade results of tests that purported to demonstrate, in a highly technical manner that would only be comprehensible to people within the trade, that the defendants' synthetic diamond abrasive (used for cutting concrete) was of a superior quality to the natural diamond abrasive of the claimants. Walton J found that the defendants would be liable if the facts, as assumed at that stage of the proceedings, were proven and, in so doing, emphasized that the offending statements were not mere puffs, but detailed technical information aimed solely at people expert in the field who would understand it and its significance, and who would clearly see the alleged inferiority of the claimants' goods.

Statements that, on the face of it, are innocuous may come to be regarded as denigratory once placed in context. In *Lyne v. Nicholls*,[187] the defendant stated falsely that his newspaper's circulation was 20 times that of any local rival. This was found to denigrate rivals in potentially causing advertisers to switch away from other papers to that of the defendant. An odd case, however, is *Serville v. Constance*.[188] In this case, the claimant was the official welterweight boxing champion of Trinidad who, on arrival in London, discovered that the defendant was claiming that title. Harman J found that, had malice been proven, that would amount to a malicious falsehood against the claimant, presumably in suggesting that his claims to the title were false and that he was therefore a liar. Other more obvious examples of the tort are claims that a claimant had departed from the address used for his business[189] and claims by the defendant that the goods of the claimant were infringing a trade mark.[190]

A significant case showing how the denigration can arise indirectly and/or by conduct is *Kaye v. Robertson*.[191] The claimant, a well-known actor, suffered life-threatening head injuries in an accident during a gale, which blew a plank through the windscreen of his car. While lying in hospital, still very ill, representatives of the *Sunday Sport* newspaper broke in, took photographs of the actor, and recorded his delirious utterances, with a view to running a major feature in its next edition. An injunction was sought and granted to prevent publication. The Court of Appeal thought that the publication, with the implication that Kaye had consented to its tasteless content, would amount to defamation, but felt constrained from injuncting it on this basis, following a long line of authority restricting the use of injunctions in libel cases.[192] No such caution attended Kaye's alternative claim in malicious falsehood: by implying his consent, the proposed feature amounted to denigration of Kaye's trade as a celebrity.[193] He may have wished to publish his story of the incident himself and in a more salubrious forum, and this expectation was harmed by the conduct of the defendants. The case both shows the inherent flexibility of the tort and also the great ease with which injunctions can be obtained.

---

[186] [1975] 2 All ER 599, [1975] 1 WLR 972.   [187] (1906) 23 TLR 86.
[188] [1954] 1 All ER 662, [1954] 1 WLR 487.   [189] *Joyce v. Motor Services Ltd* [1948] Ch 252.
[190] *Greers Ltd v. Pearman & Corder* (1922) 39 RPC 406.   [191] [1991] FSR 62.
[192] From *William Coulson & Sons v. James Coulson & Co.* (1887) 3 TLR 846 onwards.
[193] See Ch. 31 on this aspect of the case.

Malice

The element of malice is at the core of this tort and, in insisting that the claimant proves this element, it greatly reduces the impact of the tort, because, in many cases, a defendant will be able to claim accidental mistake rather than deliberate malice as the reason for the false statement. This element also makes this tort stand out from its neighbours, passing off and defamation, in relation to each of which it is not a necessary element of the cause of action.[194]

Given the importance of malice, it is perhaps surprising that the courts have, over the years, had some difficulty in deciding how precisely to define it. In *Shapiro v. La Morta*,[195] the claimant musician lost her claim against the defendants, who had claimed wrongly that she would be performing at their music hall, because she could not prove malice, defined by Atkin LJ[196] as being an intentionally or recklessly made statement. Earlier, in one of the leading cases, *Royal Baking Powder Co. v. Wright, Crossley & Co.*,[197] Lord Bankes had defined 'malice' as meaning the absence of any 'just cause or excuse'[198]—clearly a much less rigorous definition, but one that seems not now to be followed,[199] thus adding to the burden placed on the claimant.

One case to touch on this area is that of *McDonald's Hamburgers Ltd v. Burgerking (UK) Ltd.*[200] As we have already seen in the *De Beers* case,[201] this tort has great potential in cases of comparative advertising. In *McDonald's*, the defendants advertised their Whopper burger under the slogan 'It's Not Just Big, Mac' and went on to claim that their product was 100 per cent beef 'unlike some burgers'. The claimants saw this as an attack on their Big Mac burger, described memorably by Whitford J as the '*flagship of the McDonald's range, though not, I apprehend, with reference to the ease with which it can be sunk*'.[202] The claimants' claim in passing off was successful, because readers may have deduced from the overall appearance of the advert that Big Macs could be purchased from Burgerking outlets, but their claim in malicious falsehood that Big Macs were wrongly imputed to be less than 100 per cent beef did not succeed, partly because it required a sophisticated analysis of a kind not normally reserved for adverts in Underground trains to reach this conclusion and so was probably not denigratory, and also because there was no evidence of malice, which Whitford J regarded as, at the least, a reckless indifference as to whether harm may be caused to the interests of the claimant.[203]

The courts have now accepted that malice can be defined in four ways.

1. Malice will exist if one makes a false statement that one knows to be false.

2. It will also exist if one makes a false statement when one does not care whether it is true or false.

3. It will exist if one makes a false statement that one believes to be true, but when one makes the statement to give vent to one's personal spite or ill will.

4. Malice will also exist if one makes a statement the purpose of which is to injure.

In each of these situations the requirement of malice will be satisfied.[204]

---

[194] Many defamation cases fail because the claimant cannot prove the element of malice in a convincing way: see *Vodafone Group plc v. Orange Personal Communications Services Ltd* [1997] FSR 34.

[195] (1923) 40 TLR 201.   [196] (1923) 40 TLR 201 at 203.   [197] (1900) 18 RPC 95.

[198] (1900) 18 RPC 95 at 99.   [199] See e.g. *Balden v. Shorter* [1933] Ch 427.

[200] [1986] FSR 45; rev'd [1987] FSR 112 (on another point).

[201] *De Beers Abrasive Products Ltd v. International General Electric Co. of New York Ltd* [1975] 2 All ER 599, [1975] 1 WLR 972.

[202] *McDonald's Hamburgers Ltd v. Burgerking (UK) Ltd* [1986] FSR 45 at 47.

[203] *McDonald's* (n. 202) at 61.

[204] *WebSphere Trade Mark* [2004] FSR 39; *Horrocks v. Lowe* [1975] AC 139 (HL), per Lord Diplock at 149; *Spring v. Guardian Assurance plc* [1993] 2 All ER 273 (CA, overruled by the House of Lords on another point).

Damage

Traditionally, there has been the need for the claimant in actions based on this tort to have to prove special damage—that is, to bring distinct evidence of harm to their business. This requirement is, however, no longer present in most cases, following the Defamation Act 1952, s. 3(1). This section establishes, in respect of this tort, that special damage is not necessary if the words used are '*calculated to cause pecuniary damage to the* [claimant] *and are published in writing or other permanent form*' or alternatively are '*calculated to cause pecuniary damage to the* [claimant] *in respect of any office, profession, calling, trade or business*'. Given the requirement of malice and the way in which it is interpreted by the courts, it is most likely that cases of malicious falsehood will fall within this exception. The word 'calculated' should be interpreted as meaning 'likely' or 'probable' in an objective way; the simple fact that damage is possible, without further proof being added, is not sufficient.[205]

Guidance on quantum in such cases was provided in *Fielding v. Variety Inc.*,[206] in which the *Variety* newspaper singled out a musical promoted by the claimant as being a disastrous flop. This was not the case: it was, and continued to be, a great success. It was difficult to see what loss the claimant had suffered as a result of the falsehood and a nominal figure of £100 was awarded in respect of the malicious falsehood.

An overview

The impact of malicious falsehood on intellectual property law is limited, to a great degree, by the requirement of malice. It is, however, a notable recognition that businesses and products have reputations too, which the tort will, in its terms, protect, just as do the proprietors of businesses, whose personal reputation falls within the ambit of the tort of defamation. Clearly, however, the notion of a business' reputation overlaps extensively with the notion of its goodwill and much more effective protection is afforded by the tort of passing off, most significantly because of its focus on the likely consequences of words and acts, rather than on the intention of those making them. Trade mark law will also deal with most cases if the case is brought as one involving trade mark infringement. The question needs therefore to be asked whether a falsehood claim can really still add anything in most cases.[207]

It is true, however, that passing off requires there to be the all-important confusion between the goods or services of the parties, while malicious falsehood goes wider, to cover any attack on the quality of those goods or services. It may therefore remain that, together, the torts provide vital back-up to the proprietary intellectual property rights in covering the vague, but vital, areas of goodwill and repute.

Further reading

CARTY, H., 'Advertising, Publicity Rights and English Law' (2004) 3 IPQ 209.

MIDDLEMISS, S. and WARNER, S., 'Is There Still a Hole in this Bucket? Confusion and Misrepresentation in Passing Off' (2006) 1(2) JIPLP 131.

---

[205] *WebSphere* (n. 204 above).   [206] [1967] 2 QB 841.
[207] See *Cable & Wireless v. BT* [1998] FSR 383, per Jacob J at 385; *British Airways v. Ryanair* [2001] FSR 541, per Jacob J at 545–6.

MOSCONA, R., 'The Sale of Business Goodwill and the Seller's Right to Use his Own Name' (2006) 28(2) EIPR 106.

NI SHUILLEABHAIN, M., 'Common Law Protection of Trade Marks: The Continuing Relevance of the Law of Passing Off' (2003) 34 IIC 722.

WADLOW, C. (2011) *The Law of Passing Off: Unfair Competition by Misrepresentation*, 4th edn, London: Sweet and Maxwell.

SECTION F
Issues in Intellectual Property

This section merits a brief explanation. So far, we have been concerned with identifying the nature and scope of the individual rights that make up intellectual property law. In this section, however, we are concerned with some broader issues in intellectual property law and practice that can only be understood with reference to a wide range of different rights that, collectively, provide—or at least go some way towards providing—a resolution of these important issues.

29

Confidentiality and trade secrets

The laws protecting the confidentiality of information arise in a broad range of decided cases. It is inevitable that discussion of the current state of the law will reflect this fact, but it is important to assert at the outset that the remit of this chapter is to consider the use of actions for breach of confidence as a means of protecting intellectual and industrial property rights. The ramifications of the case law for personal privacy and governmental secrecy are matters on the periphery of the scope of this work, and will only receive passing attention. It is fair to say, though, that there have been significant developments in relation to personal privacy in recent years and that a somewhat different approach has been developed in that area. As that approach can interact with the approach taken to commercial secrecy this aspect will need to be addressed.

It is also important from the outset to establish why this action is relevant, indeed vital, to an understanding of intellectual property law. A right of action for breach of confidence underpins and, in many cases, predates a more formed intellectual property right. As an example, it is obvious that I have no copyright protection in my idea for a new film until the idea is translated into concrete form; if, however, I discuss the idea with you secretly and then discover subsequently that you have created a film using the same idea, then, in principle, an action for breach of confidence may arise. Equally, this area of law may protect the idea for a new invention long before I achieve a working, and thus patentable, model. In trade mark law too, discussions about marks prior to their registration, rough drafts, etc., may all give rise to an obligation on the part of anyone privy to such discussions.

A final preliminary point is important: in all of these actions, the claimant is seeking to restrict the propagation of information that is true. Clearly, the law has an interest in protecting both an individual victim and society more generally from falsity, and, for example, the various torts such as passing off and injurious falsehood exist to achieve this purpose. Where truth is concerned, however, the interest of the individual and that of society may part company. On the one hand, the individual will wish to keep information close to his or her chest, whether for commercial or personal reasons; society, on the other, may be thought to have an interest in the free availability of all true information.

Historical development and conceptual basis

The law of breach of confidence took its modern form in the middle of the nineteenth century.[1] Perhaps the leading case from this period is *Prince Albert v. Strange*.[2] This

---

[1] For a fuller discussion, see F. Gurry (1984) *Breach of Confidence*, Oxford: Clarendon Press and T. Aplin et al. (2012) *Gurry on Breach of Confidence: The Protection of Confidential Information*, 2nd edn, Oxford: Oxford University Press.

[2] (1849) 2 De G & SM 652; aff'd (1849) 41 ER 1171.

action—oddly foreshadowing the excesses of modern tabloid journalism—was an action brought by the husband of the reigning monarch, Queen Victoria. It appeared that the royal couple had been in the habit of, privately, making drawings and etchings. Some of these works were sent away to be printed professionally and it seemed that this printer (Strange) made unauthorized copies, which he then intended to display for gain in a public exhibition. Strange claimed that such an event would add to the reputation of the royal couple by showing their 'eminent artistic talent'. The outcome of such a case was inevitably a finding in favour of the claimant, but the reasoning of the court is important too.

Clearly, the action against Strange was not an action based on any contract, for reasons of privity. The House of Lords, in the speech of Lord Cottenham LC,[3] seemed to take the view that the action arose as an aspect of the claimant's proprietary rights in the draw-ings, but he was keen to point out that the action was equally sustainable on grounds of equity, confidence, and (presumably as against the printer only) contract law. It should be noted that there have been attempts subsequently to use contract as the basis of breach of confidence actions[4] and, clearly, confidentiality will often arise, whether expressly or impliedly, as a term of a contract—but the leading *Spycatcher* case[5] has made clear that the obligation may arise independently of any contractual relationship.[6]

The nature of an action for breach of confidence was further considered in another of the pioneer cases—namely, *Morison v. Moat*.[7] The parties and families had jointly been involved in the development of a commercial medicine rejoicing in the name of 'Morison's Universal Medicine'. Subsequently, the partnership arrangements ended and the defendant continued to make the medicine. The claimant claimed that this was im-properly using information gained during the period of the partnership and sought an injunction. This was granted, with the court accepting that the basis of the action was far from certain, but may well be based on trust or confidence creating an obligation on the defendant's conscience not to breach that confidence—a distinctly equitable tinge to the obligation. An important point was also made in this case: faced with the claim that to allow the claimants' claim would give him patent-style protection for non-patentable subject matter, it was made clear that the key distinction was that Morison was protected only against Moat and not against the world at large.

Returning to the precise basis of the obligation, *Robb v. Green*[8] is also instructive. In this case, the defendant secretly copied a customer list from his employer. The Court of Appeal found that this conduct was in breach of an implied contractual term, but the basis of that term was the good faith that must exist between employer and employee. Kay LJ[9] made clear that it was immaterial whether the action was founded on breach of trust or on breach of contract, because, in either event, an injunction should be granted.

The *Spycatcher* case[10] confirms this approach. In the words of Lord Keith: '[The obli-gation] *may exist independently of any contract on the basis of an independent equitable principle of confidence.*'[11] The equitable nature of the action appears to be an important part of its foundation,[12] with obvious consequences for anyone seeking to bring an action who has him- or herself behaved in an unconscionable manner. There is on the other

---

[3] (1849) 1 Mac & G 25 at 44, 41 ER 1171 at 1178.   [4] E.g. *Vokes v. Heather* (1945) 62 RPC 135.
[5] *A-G v. Guardian Newspapers (No. 2)* [1990] 1 AC 109, [1988] 3 All ER 545.
[6] Per Lord Keith at 255 and 639.   [7] (1851) 9 Hare 241, 68 ER 492.   [8] [1895] 2 QB 315.
[9] [1895] 2 QB 315 at 319.   [10] *A-G v. Guardian Newspapers (No. 2)* (n. 5).
[11] Per Lord Keith at 255 and 639.
[12] See also *Moorgate Tobacco Ltd v. Philip Morris Ltd* [1985] RPC 219 (High Court of Australia) and *Cadbury Schweppes Inc v. FBI Foods Ltd* [2000] FSR 491 (Supreme Court of Canada).

hand no property right in confidential information, despite the frequent use of property style approaches and language. Arnold J repeated this recently in *Force India Formula One Team v. 1 Malaysian Racing Team*:

> Confidential information is not property, however, even though businessmen often deal with confidential information as if it were property and judges often use the language of property when discussing breach of confidence...It follows that the user principle is not directly applicable to claims for breach of confidence. Although proprietary remedies have sometimes been granted in breach of confidence cases, these have been based not purely upon breach of confidence, but upon breach of a fiduciary duty, as for example in *Boardman v. Phipps*.[13]

Elements of the action

The leading modern case that formulated the ingredients of a successful action for breach of confidence is *Coco v. A. N. Clark (Engineers) Ltd*.[14] In this case, once again, what began as a cooperative venture between the parties, in respect of a new moped engine, ended in tears when the parties went their separate ways, the defendant allegedly then making use of confidential information acquired during the period of cooperation. In the High Court, Megarry J pointed to the absence of any formal contractual relationship and concluded that he was dealing with '*the pure equitable doctrine of confidence unaffected by contract*'.[15] He went on to state that there were three essential elements necessary in a claim for breach of confidence.[16]

1. The information must be, in itself, of a confidential character.

2. The imparting of the information must occur in circumstances or on an occasion of confidence.

3. The information must be used in an unauthorized way and so as to cause detriment to the claimant.

Clearly, the same principles will be applicable in a contractual context, subject, of course, to any contrary express terms of the contract.

Each of these elements will be considered in turn, but the *Coco* saga should first be concluded: Megarry J held that the claim should not succeed. Although the information was passed on an 'occasion of confidence', it was not clear that the nature of the (rather vague) information was confidential, nor could the claimant establish clear misuse of the information.

When is information confidential?

It is clear that a very wide range of different items of information may be regarded as confidential in character. Examples include items of considerable commercial significance, such as sales lists,[17] or information of a personal and private character.[18] What these, and many other, examples have in common is that people would generally recognize that such information was not intended for the public domain and that fact alone is sufficient

---

[13] *Force India Formula One Team v. 1 Malaysian Racing Team* [2012] EWHC 616 (Ch) at para. 376.
[14] [1969] RPC 41.   [15] [1969] RPC 41 at 46.   [16] [1969] RPC 41 at 47.
[17] As in *Robb v. Green* [1895] 2 QB 315.
[18] E.g. *Argyll v. Argyll* [1967] Ch 302, [1965] 1 All ER 611.

to give the information in question the cachet of confidentiality.[19] In other words, the necessary quality of confidence can be defined by its antithesis, namely, it is not something which is public property and public knowledge.[20]

It is best regarded as an objective test, dependent upon the expectations of ordinary or reasonable men[21] who will, with an unerring instinct, be aware that commercially valuable lists of customers or the secrets of the boardroom should not be spread beyond those persons who have to know of the facts in question. An example is provided by the case in which the operator of a gossip website was held to be in breach of confidence when it gave more prominence to a third-party posting of the draft advice of counsel to a celebrity. It was held that the nature of the material would have made any reasonable man realize that it was confidential in nature.[22]

The cachet of confidentiality may, however, be bestowed upon the most trivial bit of information if it is not yet in the public domain. In such cases, it is sufficient that the reasonable man realizes (or is told about) the confidential character of the information.[23] In relation to information about the private life of a person, a duty of confidence will arise if the person subject to the duty is in a situation in which he or she knows, or ought to know, that the other person concerned can reasonably expect that privacy to be protected.[24]

A more subjective element is, however, imported into the equation by the decision of Megarry V-C in *Thomas Marshall (Exports) Ltd v. Guinle*.[25] In this case, a company's managing director set up rival operations in a similar field. Unsurprisingly, the company gained an injunction; it was observed that information in this type of case becomes confidential when the owner of the information believes that its release would be harmful to him or her and when he or she believes that it remains outside the public domain, in each case that belief being reasonable, with regard to the relevant area of activity and its practices. This simply suggests that the decision as to whether information is confidential or not will include the beliefs of the owner of that information, but the requirement that only reasonably held beliefs are considered means that it is not likely that the subjective views of the owner of the information are likely to contradict the objective view of the reasonable man.

The private or restricted nature of the information

It is clear that the private—or at least restricted—nature of information is an essential element if it is to become confidential. In *Woodward v. Hutchins*,[26] lurid revelations by a former employee of the management company of a group of pop stars under such headlines as 'Tom Jones, Superstud' could not be the subject of an injunction, because several of the incidents described took place in public: for example, on board an airliner.

Information may, however, go beyond its initial source to other people, while still remaining confidential, an example of which is provided by *Stephens v. Avery*.[27] In this

---

[19] For a negative example in which the confidential nature of the information was rejected, see *Cray Valley Ltd v. Deltech Europe Ltd, John Scanlan & Christopher Riley* [2003] EWHC 728.

[20] *Saltman Engineering Co. Ltd v. Campbell Engineering Co. Ltd* (1948) 65 RPC 203, per Lord Greene MR at 215.

[21] For an application in an employment context, see *Ocular Sciences Ltd v. Aspect Vision Care Ltd, Geoffrey Harrison Galley v. Ocular Sciences Ltd* [1997] RPC 289.

[22] *Elton John v. Countess Joulebine* [2001] Masons CLR 91.

[23] See *PCR Ltd v. Dow Jones Telerate Ltd* [1998] FSR 170. Arguably, the claim based on breach of confidence also failed in this case, because the information had not been passed on during an occasion of confidence.

[24] *Campbell v. MGN Ltd* [2004] 2 All ER 995 (HL); see also *A v. B plc* [2002] EMLR 21.

[25] [1979] Ch 227, [1978] 3 All ER 193.   [26] [1977] 2 All ER 751, [1977] 1 WLR 760.

[27] [1988] Ch 449, [1988] 2 All ER 477.

case, the claimant sued in relation to a newspaper story telling of her lesbian relationship with the wife of a notorious criminal. She had revealed this to a friend, who unhelpfully passed on the information to the press. It was argued that, by telling her friend, she had removed the label of confidentiality, but this claim did not succeed. The High Court held that information could retain its secret character even while being passed on. In the words of Sir Nicolas Browne-Wilkinson V-C:

> the mere fact that two people know a secret does not mean that it is not confidential. If in fact information is secret, then in my judgment it is capable of being kept secret by the imposition of a duty of confidence on any person to whom it is communicated. Information only ceases to be capable of protection as confidential when it is in fact known to a substantial number of people.[28]

Further litigation has to be awaited to find out how 'substantial' this group must be.

The springboard doctrine

One group of cases, now clarified by and large, appears to suggest that an action for breach of confidence may lie in respect of information that is in the public domain. This apparently contradictory notion first arose in *Terrapin Ltd v. Builders Supply Co. (Hayes) Ltd*.[29] The defendants made portable buildings designed by the claimants and, in due course, began to sell their own buildings made to a markedly similar design. The problem for a breach of confidence action was that these buildings were widely available and could be inspected by anyone who so desired. Nonetheless, at first instance, Roxburgh J found in Terrapin's favour. He stated that:

> the essence of this branch of the law is that a person who has obtained information in confidence is not allowed to use it as a spring-board for activities detrimental to the person who made the confidential communication.[30]

In this respect, the technical information disclosed while the parties were in collaboration would assist the defendants materially in making their own design of portable building. The Court of Appeal consequently upheld the trial judge's judgment.

Likewise, in *Cranleigh Precision Engineering Ltd v. Bryant*,[31] the defendant was the managing director of the claimant company, which made and sold a unique type of swimming pool, who set up his own business selling similar pools. These pools were made under an assigned Swiss patent that had been known to Bryant (but not his employer) for some years and which incorporated features of Cranleigh's pools. In spite of this information being, albeit obscurely, in the public domain, an injunction was awarded, because Bryant had gained his knowledge of the Swiss patent in his capacity as managing director of Cranleigh and thus it should be regarded as confidential information. In effect, Bryant had gained a springboard that put him in a uniquely advantageous position when he set up his own business.

Speed Seal Products Ltd v. Paddington[32] provides a further example. The defendant had been employed by the claimants on the design of oil pipe couplings and had then set up his own company in the same trade. Paddington ran the defence that the information he had used was not confidential, in that it appeared in his publicity brochures and in a patent application that he had filed, and was thus known to the world. This did not

---

[28] [1988] Ch 449, [1988] 2 All ER 477 at 454 and 481.
[29] [1967] RPC 375 (HC), [1960] RPC 128 (CA).   [30] [1967] RPC 375 at 391.
[31] [1964] 3 All ER 289, [1965] 1 WLR 1263.   [32] [1986] 1 All ER 91, [1985] 1 WLR 1327.

succeed; the first disclosure was by the defendant and this could not prevent the claimants from taking action, with *Cranleigh* expressly followed.

This surprising trio of cases has now happily been reviewed by the House of Lords in the *Spycatcher* case.[33] Because it will be mentioned so often, it is appropriate here to recall the basic facts of *Spycatcher*. A former British spy, Wright, produced a book detailing clearly confidential information gleaned during his career. The British government, in this action, sought to prevent newspapers from printing extracts from it, but failed—basically, because the book was widely available in other jurisdictions and the information contained in the book had lost its confidential character as a result of its widespread availability. The defendant newspapers offered, as one of their defences, the fact that the information was no longer confidential, because it was widely available: for example, in the many countries in which the *Spycatcher* book was freely available in open sale.

Lord Goff of Chieveley addressed the issue directly.[34] He considered the *Cranleigh* decision to be merely an example of the 'springboard' principle derived from the earlier *Terrapin* decision. He refused to allow the case to stand as a general principle and denied that there was any rule that disclosure by a third party released the confidant from his or her obligations. It then followed that *Speed Seal*, based as it was on *Cranleigh*, could not stand either. So it seems that, after all, information must remain private and outside the public domain if it is to be subject to the obligation of confidence. Lord Goff discussed at length whether this is tantamount to allowing the holder of confidential information to rid himself of the obligation of confidence by disclosure, but pointed to the existence of other remedies, such as copyright and criminal law. He reserved his position on the question left unanswered by his analysis of *Cranleigh*—namely, what is the scope of any 'springboard' type of obligation imposed on a confider who benefits from his or her destruction of a confidence.

This, added to the obiter character of Lord Goff's views and the failure of the other Law Lords to address the issue in detail given that they were of the view that the obligation of confidentiality was ongoing, means that a conclusive view of the law in this area cannot yet be reached.[35] The understandable reluctance of the courts to allow a confidant to benefit by breaching his or her confidence stands in the way of a clear unequivocal statement by the law that, as would seem sensible, information that is confidential cannot be public. The point that information that is supposed to be confidential cannot be public was, however, emphasized by Laddie J in a case in which the element of reluctance was almost absent due to the vexatious nature of the proceedings brought by the claimant and the oppressive way in which these proceedings had been conducted by the claimant.[36]

A conclusive view was, however, offered in the *Vestergaard* case by Arnold J.[37] That view is based on the fact that at best cases such as *Terrapin* point to information that has a limited degree of confidentiality even if one could gain access to the information by compiling it from public domain sources or by reverse engineering it (e.g. in *Terrapin* through a thorough analysis of the buildings in the public domain). The springboard doctrine protects that limited degree of confidentiality if the defendant gained access by breaching confidentiality rather than by compiling the information themselves or

---

[33] *A-G v. Guardian Newspapers (No. 2)* (n. 5).   [34] At 285–6 and 661–2.

[35] See the Law Commission's view, Cmnd 8388, 1981, para. 4.30. See also F. M. Patfield, 'Attorney-General v. The Observer Ltd; Attorney-General v. The Times Newspapers Ltd: The Decision of the House of Lords in the *Spycatcher* Litigation' (1989) 11 EIPR 27.

[36] *Ocular Sciences* (n. 21) at 368 and 373–5.

[37] *Vestergaard Frandsen A/S, Vestergaard Frandsen SA and Disease Control Textiles SA v. Bestnet Europe and ors* [2010] FSR 2.

by reverse engineering it. The doctrine would stop the defendant from gaining an illegitimate head start. That means that an injunction can be granted, but only for a limited period. The duration of the injunction would be determined on the basis of the time needed to reverse engineer the confidential information starting from the public domain.[38] But the Court of Appeal refused to apply the doctrine to a defendant that could have had access to the information, but was not actually using the information and had never done so. The defendant had in practice no knowledge about the confidential information and the court refused to imply a concept of strict liability. The defendant's active involvement in the competing company could not change that outcome. The key element is therefore the use, even subconsciously, of the confidential information.[39] Secondary liability in turn presupposes knowledge of the abuse of the confidential information by its recipient.[40]

There is on the other hand no legal basis for the sweeping proposition that an injunction can be granted to restrain continued misuse of confidential information once the information was no longer confidential. Publication of the information brings the obligation of confidence to an end, as was clearly seen in *A-G v. Times Newspapers Ltd*[41] and *A-G v. Observer Ltd*.[42] It was in that respect irrelevant who brought the obligation of confidence to an end. As the House of Lords indicated in the *Spycatcher* case though, the lack of an injunction based on breach of confidence does not mean that there will be no other sanction for whoever brings the confidentiality of the information to an end in an illegitimate matter. Damages and other sanctions, for example for copyright infringement, for that act as such remain a possibility.[43]

Past misuse of confidential information is normally addressed by means of a financial remedy, such as the award of damages. The only argument in favour of an injunction is that it can serve to stop the defendant from benefiting from past misuse of such confidential information. But as the information can be freely obtained by anyone at that stage, considerable caution must be exercised in order not to penalize the defendant unduly. The claimant should also not gain a better position than the one it would have been in in the absence of misuse. The law is not clear on this point, but in any case an injunction should not be granted for a longer term than the one during which the defendant's illegitimate advantage is expected to continue. Despite the fact that the defendant no longer uses the confidential information itself, it may still find itself in a better position than the competitor who reverse engineered from public domain sources and in some circumstances a limited injunction might then be a more effective remedy than damages that may be hard to quantify.[44]

Arguably in this way all the pieces of the jigsaw fit together. But the courts will without doubt be invited again at a later stage to revisit this delicate and complex point of law.

Encrypted information

Encrypted information presents an interesting problem: does encrypted information that is only in the public domain in its encrypted form possess the necessary quality of being confidential information? Jacob J was confronted with this issue in a case

---

[38] *Vestergaard Frandsen* (n. 37). See also *First Conferences Services Ltd v. Bracchi* [2009] EWHC 2176 (ch).
[39] *Vestergaard Frandsen S/A (MVF3 APS) v. Bestnet Europe Ltd* [2011] EWCA Civ 424. Confirmed on appeal by the Supreme Court *Vestergaard Frandsen S/A (MVF3 APS) v. Bestnet Europe Ltd* [2013] UKSC 31. See also Aplin et al. (2012) *Gurry on Breach of Confidence* (n. 1) at p. 676.
[40] *Vestergaard Frandsen S/A (MVF3 APS) v. Bestnet Europe Ltd* [2013] UKSC 31.
[41] *A-G v. Times Newspapers Ltd* [2001] 1 WLR 885 (CA).
[42] *A-G v. Observer Ltd* [1990] 1 AC 109 (HL).   [43] *Vestergaard Frandsen* (n. 37).
[44] *Vestergaard Frandsen* (n. 37).

concerning discriminators for coin-receiving and coin-changing machines, and ruled that the information could not be confidential, because anyone with the necessary skill to decrypt had the possibility to have access to the information. The defendant, who had reverse engineered the piece of equipment in that way, was therefore not in breach of confidence.[45]

What is not—or is no longer—confidential information

One clear example does exist whereby confidential information ceases so to be—that is, when the confider himself discloses the information—and this arose in the 1928 case of *Mustad & Son v. Allcock & Co. Ltd & Dosen*.[46] In this case, an employer was held unable to sue an employee for breach of confidence once they had themselves applied for a patent, thus disclosing the relevant information.

It should in this context be kept in mind that confidentiality is a relative concept. It may apply differently to different categories of information. In many cases a lot will depend on the generality of the information. If technical information can, for example, readily be ascertained from an article that is publicly acceptable or sold, the information will not be confidential. But detailed information recorded in drawings that cannot be ascertained from inspection and that requires a process of reverse engineering will be confidential, even if the reverse engineering activity is possible.[47]

Equally, it seems clear that lapse of time may cause there to be an erosion of the obligation of confidentiality, as in *A-G v. Jonathan Cape Ltd*,[48] a case arising from the publication of the diaries of the late Richard Crossman, written when he was a Cabinet minister a decade previously. The information contained in them was held to have lost its confidentiality simply because of the years that had passed, although with due regard also paid to the nature of the information and its likely effect. Crossman's chronicling of political gossip had long lost the chance of causing any serious harm.

There is also a simple rule that information that has entered the public domain is no longer confidential. For this very reason the BBC's breach of confidence case against the publishers of a book that revealed the identity of the Stig in the *Top Gear* programme was thrown out when it became clear that the information was in the public domain through newspaper coverage. The fact that not everyone was aware of it or that there was a (potential) breach of contract by the author of the book could not change that outcome.[49]

Finally, in looking at what is not confidential information, it is worth recording the comment of Megarry J in *Coco v. Clark*[50] that it is not appropriate for protection to be given to 'trivial tittle-tattle': such matters of little consequence do not deserve the mighty protection of equity.[51] Whether this should raise a question about the role of confidence in cases involving lesbian relationships with prisoners' wives[52] or the active sex life of an arms dealer's wife[53] is not, it seems, the point, because, in these cases, no such objection has been taken. In any event, information that is of commercial significance is hardly likely to fall within the category of 'tittle-tattle'.

---

[45] *Mars v. Teknowledge* [2000] FSR 138.   [46] [1963] 3 All ER 416, [1964] 1 WLR 109 NOTE.

[47] *Force India Formula One Team Ltd* (n. 13) at paras. 218–22.

[48] [1976] QB 752, [1975] 3 All ER 484.

[49] *BBC v. HarperCollins Publishers Ltd* [2010] EWHC 2424 (Ch), [2011] EMLR 6.

[50] [1969] RPC 41 at 48.   [51] See also *Force India Formula One Team Ltd* (n. 13) at para. 223.

[52] See *Stephens v. Avery* [1988] 2 All ER 477. Sir Nicolas Browne-Wilkinson V-C said that the question could only arise at the trial and not at the interlocutory injunction stage.

[53] See *Khashoggi v. Smith* (1980) 124 Sol Jo 149.

The public interest exception

A major gap—but one that is justifiable—is opened up in the law's protection of confidential information by the exception created to allow the dissemination of information in cases in which that dissemination is seen as being in the public interest. Thus the truth will come out in an appropriate case. One of the earliest cases to use this approach was *Gartside v. Outram*,[54] in which a firm of wool-brokers sought to prevent their former sales clerk from using customer information gained by him during his period of employment, while he, in turn, alleged that their business was conducted in a fraudulent manner. It was held that, if proven, these allegations would wipe out any obligation of confidence, because *'there is no confidence in the disclosure of an iniquity'*.[55]

What is covered by the exception?

Over the years, a wide range of differing instances have been found to fall within this exception. Sometimes, the exception is used if upholding confidence would have the effect of concealing evidence of wrongdoing. A classic example is provided by *Lion Laboratories Ltd v. Evans*.[56] The claimants in this case were the manufacturers of the intoximeter device used by the police for measuring alcohol consumption by road users. The defendants were ex-employees of the firm, who revealed to the press documents obtained while they were employees, which indicated that the devices were erratic and unreliable. An action against them for breach of confidence failed, on the grounds that the faulty intoximeters represented a serious threat to the fair administration of justice and that it was essential to ventilate public disquiet about the accuracy of the evidence provided by the machines.

W v. Egdell[57] also illustrates this area well. W was a mental patient who had been convicted of multiple manslaughter and who had been examined by the defendant. His concern at W's condition was such that he sent a copy of his report to the Home Secretary. W sued, alleging breach of confidence, the doctor–patient relationship clearly being one in which an obligation of confidence can normally be expected to arise. But the Court of Appeal found that, exceptionally, the interests of the public outweighed the interests of the patient and the doctor was justified in disclosing the report, so as to minimize the chances of W being freed and thus the public being put at risk of further attacks.[58]

This case followed on from *X v. Y*,[59] although in this case a different answer was reached. In this case, two doctors were revealed in the press as suffering from AIDS, the story being based on internal health authority documents. The paper's argument that the public had an interest in knowing of these facts was not enough to overturn the vital confidentiality of patient records and an injunction was granted to restrain the information from being published. The same vital confidentiality exists in the relationship between the police and the accused in relation to statements made by the accused under caution to the police. The information contained in those statements could only be used for the purposes for which it was provided and not for extraneous

---

[54] (1856) 26 LJ Ch 113.   [55] (1856) 26 LJ Ch 113, per Wood V-C at 114.

[56] [1985] QB 526, [1984] 2 All ER 417.   [57] [1990] Ch 359, [1989] 1 All ER 1089.

[58] This approach was confirmed in *R v. Chief Constable of the North Wales Police, ex p. AB* [1998] 3 All ER 310, [1998] 3 WLR 57, in which the Court of Appeal accepted that confidential police information concerning paedophiles who had served their sentences could be released to the owner of a campsite in order to allow him to take precautionary measures to safeguard the children that were to arrive on the campsite over the Easter holidays. Once more, the interests of the public prevailed over the obligation of confidence.

[59] [1988] 2 All ER 648.

purposes.[60] It is likely therefore that *W v. Egdell* and its extreme facts will be the exception, rather than the rule.

In other cases, the harm cited to justify the breach of confidence may be less tangible. In *Hubbard v. Vosper*,[61] the defendant left the Scientology movement and subsequently wrote a book denouncing it, which drew heavily on material issued by the movement itself. The Court of Appeal found that the disclosures were justified as revealing what Lord Denning MR described as '*medical quackeries of a sort which may be dangerous if practised behind closed doors*',[62] while Megaw LJ highlighted evidence that the movement was prepared to use violence against those who had criticized it.[63]

An attractive, if simplistic, argument that has the effect of widening the likely scope of this exception was proposed in *Woodward v. Hutchins*.[64] An ex-employee was selling stories about the private lives of rock stars, clearly in prima facie breach of his obligations of confidence. Nevertheless, the Court of Appeal found that no injunction should be granted, because of the fact that the stars were keen to manage and manipulate their own images so as to appear in the best possible light, and therefore they could not object if what were presumed to be true, but less flattering, tales about them were released. In the words of Lord Denning MR, just as there should be '*truth in advertising*', so there should be '*truth in publicity*';[65] Bridge LJ sternly warned:

> it seems to me that those who seek and welcome publicity of every kind bearing on their private lives so long as it shows them in a favourable light are in no position to complain of an invasion of their privacy by publicity which shows them in an unfavourable light.[66]

While not normally sympathetic to people such as the claimants in this case, it may be thought harsh to offer less protection against breaches of confidence to those who are most likely to be the subject of such breaches.

There seems to be no reason, in principle, why this argument should not also be used to justify breaches of confidence about heavily advertised goods or services, although it is fair to note that the approach in *Woodward* has not been expressly adopted in subsequent cases. On the contrary, the courts have taken away some of the sharper edges and the potential for a broad application. It has, for example, been held that public figures who have been tolerant of, or welcoming to publicity, on other occasions have no less a right to complain of unwanted intrusion in relation to events that they wanted to keep private.[67] The court contrasted this with the situation in which the claimant has fostered an image that is not true[68] or has behaved in a way that is contrary to the image that he or she portrays publicly.[69] In that latter case, there is still a prevailing public interest in correcting the fostered and portrayed information that is out of line with reality.

---

[60] *Bunn v. BBC* [1998] 3 All ER 552, but the action for breach of confidence failed in this case and no injunctive relief was granted, because the information had been read out in open court and it had also been published in a book, of which 2,000 copies had already been distributed. These facts had brought the obligation of confidence to an end.

[61] [1972] 2 QB 84, [1972] 1 All ER 1023.

[62] [1972] 2 QB 84, [1972] 1 All ER 1023 at 96 and 1029.

[63] [1972] 2 QB 84, [1972] 1 All ER 1023 at 100–1 and 103.

[64] [1977] 2 All ER 751, [1977] 1 WLR 760; see also *Lennon v. News Group Newspapers Ltd* [1978] FSR 573.

[65] [1977] 2 All ER 751, [1977] 1 WLR 760 at 754 and 764.

[66] [1977] 2 All ER 751, [1977] 1 WLR 760 at 755 and 765.

[67] *Douglas v. Hello! Ltd (No. 5)* [2003] 3 All ER 996.

[68] See *Campbell v. MGN Ltd* (n. 24), even if restrictions were imposed on what could be done in the public interest.

[69] *Woodward v. Hutchins* [1977] 2 All ER 751, [1977] 1 WLR 760, referred to in *Douglas v. Hello! Ltd (No. 5)* (n. 67).

Limits of the public interest exception

Just as the breach of confidence action does not extend to protect lightweight gossip, so also the public interest exception is curtailed. In *Beloff v. Pressdram Ltd*,[70] the claimant was a senior journalist who had sent a memo to her colleagues concerning a senior government minister and allegations of possible misconduct. This memo subsequently was reprinted in the satirical magazine *Private Eye*. The action was framed in breach of copyright, but the principle of public interest applies there too. Ungoed-Thomas J found that the exception did not apply. This was not a case involving grave misdeeds, but was rather only the retelling of current political gossip and, as such, did not attract the public interest exception.

Naturally, as time goes by, so do public perceptions of conduct change. This reflects itself when a court has to decide what amounts to 'iniquity'. In *Stephens v. Avery*,[71] the court was faced with an attempt to use confidence to protect a story of a lesbian relationship. Sir Nicolas Browne-Wilkinson V-C took the view that there was no widespread view within society that sexual activity, even homosexual acts, between consenting adults was grossly immoral and thus appears to suggest that only universally deplored activity—on grounds of it being immoral, scandalous, or contrary to family life[72]—would count as being iniquitous for the purposes of the public interest exception.

Ironically, perhaps, *Stephens* suggests that the heart of the public interest exception—namely, claims of iniquity—is diminishing in importance just as the broader exception seems to expand into an ever-increasing range of different instances. The courts seem willing to subordinate confidentiality to the public interest in a wide range of cases, with perhaps *W v. Egdell*[73] the clearest indication that the rights of the public can take priority over one of the longest-established relationships of confidence: that between doctor and patient. The inherent flexibility of the public interest immunity is an obvious asset in aiding its sensible and flexible use. The purpose for which the confidential information may be used will be relevant: in *Lion Laboratories*,[74] for example, the defendants were motivated by a sense of civic responsibility and the decision may well have been different had they simply been seeking to sell the information for a personal profit.

A clash between different interests

The clash between the interests of the owner of the information in keeping it confidential and the interests of society in making it accessible in the interests of the general public may be seen as a clash between private and public interests. A case such as *W v. Egdell*, however, adopts the view that both of the conflicting interests are public: the interest of W in keeping his medical record to himself and his doctor is part of the general public interest in knowing that private information is able to retain its confidentiality. The decision in the case merely reflected that one aspect of public interest in the freedom from threats of attack by W was so important that it should take priority over the confidentiality of the relationship.

All cases in which this exception comes into play have in them this inherent clash. The facts of the *Spycatcher*[75] case illustrate it well. As a society, it may be argued that we have an interest in having a secret service that is just that, so we can argue that its workings

---

[70] [1973] 1 All ER 241.   [71] [1988] Ch 449, [1988] 2 All ER 477.

[72] See *A v. B* [2000] EMLR 1007, in which the content of pages of a wife's diary were held not to come within any of these categories, which would have justified the refusal to enforce the confidence in them.

[73] [1990] Ch 359, [1989] 1 All ER 1089.

[74] *Lion Laboratories Ltd v. Evans* [1985] QB 526, [1984] 2 All ER 417.

[75] *A-G v. Guardian Newspapers (No. 2)* (n. 5).

should be protected by confidentiality, but, equally, in a democratic society, we want openness so that we can learn and act upon information that the intelligence community is acting (or threatening to act) against the elected government of the country. In resolving this difficult choice, the House of Lords made one important pro-disclosure point in following the High Court of Australia in *Commonwealth of Australia v. John Fairfax & Sons Ltd*[76] by ruling that a government must prove that any disclosure is harmful to the public interest. The force of this is, however, reduced by the assertions—particularly of Lord Keith[77]—that wholesale disclosure of information about the workings of the secret service was obviously against the public interest and far more significant than that small part of the book that suggested that there had been improprieties.

Perhaps the most pointed of clashes comes when use is sought to be made in legal proceedings of information that the law would normally regard as being confidential in character. The leading case on this is now *R v. Licensing Authority, ex p. Smith, Kline & French Laboratories Ltd.*[78] The statutory function of the authority is to award product licences for drugs that have been appropriately tested and proven to be safe. Smith, Kline & French had secured a licence for the drug Cimetidine and, in the course of its application, had revealed various items of confidential information to the authority. It was concerned that rival firms were now seeking product licences for generic versions of the same drug and that the authority would make use of, and thus possibly reveal, the information provided earlier, and so it brought an action against the authority.

The claim did not succeed. The House of Lords held that the statutory duty of the authority should take priority, and that it had both the right and the duty to make whatever use it saw fit of all information that was available to it. This was, it must be said, not a particularly meritorious claim by Smith, Kline & French, which, by making objections to the grant of licences for generic counterparts of its drug, was effectively seeking to extend the lifespan of its own patent monopoly. That the interests of justice and the merits of the claim thus came together to defeat the company's claims is a pleasing coincidence.

The use of confidential information in court proceedings

The use of confidential information in court proceedings themselves has been at the heart of two interesting cases. In *Marcel v. Metropolitan Police Comr*,[79] the police had obtained documents from the claimants under the powers of the Police and Criminal Evidence Act 1984. The claimants then found that the defendants in a civil fraud case in which they were also claimants subpoenaed the police to give evidence from the documents in question. The Court of Appeal held that the claimants could not succeed in an action claiming that the documents contained confidential information and that they therefore should not be used. While accepting that an obligation of confidentiality was imposed on the police in respect of evidence obtained pretrial,[80] except in so far as disclosure was intended to occur for the purpose of the statute, that obligation was overcome by the subpoena issued to the police and which, equally, could have been issued against the claimants if still in possession of the documents themselves. In *Hoechst UK Ltd v. Chemiculture Ltd*,[81] these principles were applied when information supplied to

---

[76] (1980) 147 CLR 39.   [77] [1990] 1 AC 109, [1988] 3 All ER 545 at 259 and 642.

[78] [1990] 1 AC 64, *sub nom Smith Kline & French Laboratories Ltd v. Licensing Authority* [1989] 1 All ER 578.

[79] [1992] Ch 225, [1992] 1 All ER 72.

[80] For the position in relation to statements made to the police during an interview under caution, see *Bunn v. BBC* (n. 60).

[81] [1993] FSR 270.

the Health & Safety Executive was given to Hoechst, who promptly used it as the basis of an Anton Piller order (now the search order) in trade mark and passing off litigation against the defendants. Morritt J found that disclosure of this information, which related to use of an unauthorized pesticide, was not in breach of confidence as being within the purposes envisaged by the relevant legislation: the Food and Environment Protection Act 1985.

Thus disclosure of information that is otherwise confidential is quite likely to occur in legal and related proceedings. The statute may authorize disclosure for all or, more likely, limited purposes; the duty of the court or other agency may be to make the fullest use of all information before it and, finally, a subpoena will take priority.

Generally, the public interest exception is vital to the health of the action for breach of confidence. It recognizes that simple assertions of secrecy or privacy do not do enough to resolve the inexorable contradiction between one person's right to confidentiality and one person's right to knowledge.

Privacy

The issue of the confidential character of the information has in recent years seen a different development when it comes to private and personal information, rather than commercial information. The requirement of confidentiality seems to have been relaxed when it comes to such personal and private information. This is no doubt due in part to the entry into force of the Human Rights Act 1998. That fact has shifted the focus in relation to privacy to Art. 8 of the European Convention on Human Rights, which gives individuals a right of respect for their private and family life. That right is in turn subject to the limitation that rights and freedoms of others are also protected. An example of such freedoms in this area is found in Art. 10 which guarantees freedom of expression (and which is subject to a similar limitation). The Convention does therefore call for a careful balancing of interests and rights.

The courts have made it clear that, in their view, English law still has no right of privacy and that to create one would be a matter for Parliament—but they have accepted that an action for breach of confidence can have a person's right to protect his or her privacy at its heart. In other words, while there is no special right of privacy with a specific action linked to it, breach of confidence will cover the area and it is hence appropriate for us to deal with the matter here.[82] With the Human Rights Act 1998 in mind we will have to determine what influence Arts. 8 and 10 of the Convention have. Let us first look at the two major cases that developed in this area.

Douglas v. Hello!

The important legal developments in this area after the Human Rights Act 1998 were put in motion by the litigation brought by Michael Douglas and Catherine Zeta-Jones against *Hello!* magazine to stop the publication of unauthorized photographs of their wedding. While accepting the principle of a right of privacy for citizens as a result of Art. 8 of the Convention, the Court of Appeal discharged the injunction prohibiting publication of the pictures. It was held that the wedding was by no means a fully private affair and that the right of privacy had to be balanced with the right of freedom of expression. The limited amount of privacy left could, at the trial stage, be compensated by the award of damages.[83] At the full trial, the court built upon this limited first step.

---

[82] *Campbell v. MGN Ltd* (n. 24) (HL).
[83] *Douglas v. Hello! Ltd* [2001] QB 967, [2001] 2 All ER 289, [2001] 2 WLR 992 (CA).

The case then moved on to the House of Lords, which allowed the appeal in *Douglas v. Hello!*[84] Although information about the wedding generally was information that anyone was free to communicate, the photographic images of the wedding were not publicly available and were therefore confidential information. From that starting point, the majority in the House of Lords derived that there was no conceptual reason why the obligation of confidence should not be imposed only in respect of the photographs if the third claimants were willing to pay for the right to be the only source of that particular form of information and that it did not mind that others were free to communicate other information about the wedding. The photographs of the wedding constituted information of commercial value over which the claimants had sufficient control to enable them to impose an obligation of confidence and there was no public policy reason why the law of confidence should not protect that obligation. The journal, having bought the benefit of the obligation of confidence imposed by the claimants on those present at the wedding, was entitled to protect the right to that benefit against any third party who intentionally destroyed it. The duty of confidence imposed was binding upon the unauthorized photographer and, by reason of the circumstances in which the defendant had acquired the photographs, the duty of confidentiality had also been binding upon it. Publication of the authorized photographs before the defendants had published the unauthorized photographs did not necessarily mean that the photographic images were by then in the public domain so that they could no longer be the subject of confidence; whether information was in the public domain and whether there was still any point in enforcing the obligation of confidence thereafter depended on the nature of the information and the facts of the case. Breach of confidence had therefore been established.

Turning to the issue of the right of freedom of expression, the series of judgments in this case demonstrates that, as such, the right of freedom of expression cannot justify such an intrusion. It is indeed necessary to strike a balance between Arts. 8 and 10 of the European Convention on Human Rights. In a sense, that balance is already found in Art. 10 itself: the right to freedom of expression in Art. 10(1) is made subject in Art. 10(2) to the right to respect for private and family life contained in Art. 8, but it is also made subject to rights recognized by the law as to confidence even outside the rights contained in the Convention.[85]

What remains outstanding, however, is the influence of the test in *Coco v. Clark* on the issue of relief. The first limb of the test in *Coco v. Clark* deals only with the issue of whether the information is already public property and public knowledge; the issue of whether the information is private, in the sense that its disclosure would be significantly harmful, does not arise at that stage. The degree of offensiveness and its propensity to injure only comes into play once all requirements under the test have been met and the issue of relief is addressed. Substantive relief is not a foregone conclusion. Confidence in an inequity would not be protected, for example, and, at this stage, the balance between confidentiality and freedom of expression should be taken into account.[86]

Campbell v. MGN

This approach involving the balancing of rights, but offering protection for a person's privacy by means of an action for breach of confidence, has now been approved by the House of Lords in the *Naomi Campbell* case.[87] *The Mirror* newspaper published two

[84] *Douglas and ors v. Hello! Ltd and ors (No. 3)* [2007] 2 WLR 920, [2007] EMLR 12 (HL).

[85] *Douglas* (n. 84); see also *Venables v. News Group Newspapers Ltd* [2001] EMLR 10; *A v. B plc* [2002] EMLR 21.

[86] *Douglas v. Hello! Ltd (No. 5)* (n. 67); see also *A-G v. Guardian Newspapers Ltd (No. 2)* (n. 5).

[87] *Campbell v. MGN Ltd* (n. 24).

articles revealing that, contrary to her previous false assertions, Naomi Campbell, the internationally known fashion model and celebrity, was a drug addict and that she was attending meetings of Narcotics Anonymous (NA) in order to overcome her addiction. The articles were accompanied by covertly taken photographs of Naomi Campbell leaving a meeting of NA. The newspaper had been tipped off about the fact that the claimant was attending NA meetings by an unknown source.

Naomi Campbell brought proceedings seeking damages for breach of confidence. She accepted that, because of her previous false statements, *The Mirror* was entitled to publish the fact of her addiction and the fact that she was seeking treatment for it, but she contended that the fact that she was receiving treatment at NA, the details of the treatment, and her appearance leaving a meeting were private and confidential matters, and that there was no overriding public interest justifying their publication. *The Mirror* argued that it was entitled to publish the articles in the exercise of its right to freedom of expression.

The House of Lords[88] ruled, with a three-to-two majority, that a duty of confidence arises whenever the person subject to the duty is in a situation in which he or she knew, or ought to know, that the other person could reasonably expect his or her privacy to be protected. In considering whether there is a reasonable expectation that privacy would be protected, it is important to bear in mind that, if the information in question was obviously private, there would normally be no need to ask whether it would be highly offensive for it to be published.[89] The details of Naomi Campbell's attendance at the NA meetings were, according to the House of Lords, to be considered as private information that imported a duty of confidence and the private nature of the meetings encouraged addicts to attend in the belief that they could do so anonymously. The assurance of privacy was an essential part of the exercise. The therapy was at risk of being damaged if the duty of confidence that participants owed to each other was breached by making details of the therapy public. Accordingly, those details were obviously private.

The right to privacy interest had, on the other hand, to be balanced with the interest of *The Mirror* in the right of freedom of information and expression. The House of Lords argued that the conclusion that the details of the claimant's treatment were private meant that the protection of the claimant's right to respect for her private life was sufficiently important to justify limiting the right to freedom of expression of the press, provided that the limitation was rational, fair, and not arbitrary, and did not impair the right more than necessary. It was, in this respect, important to note that the right of the public to receive information about the details of Naomi Campbell's treatment was of a much lower order than its undoubted right to know that she was misleading the public when she said that she did not take drugs. And it should be taken into account by the court that publication of the details of the treatment had the potential to cause harm to Naomi Campbell.[90]

On the basis of the facts of the case, the House of Lords concluded therefore that the reasonable person of ordinary sensibilities would regard publication of the photographs, and the way in which they were linked to the text, as adding greatly to the intrusion that the article as a whole made into Naomi Campbell's private life. The taking of photographs in a public street should be taken as one of the incidents of living in a free community, but the real question was whether publicizing the content of the photographs

---

[88] *Campbell v. MGN Ltd* (n. 24).

[89] In other cases, the correct test was to ask whether publication of the information would be highly offensive to a reasonable person of ordinary sensibilities if he or she were in the same position as the claimant.

[90] *Campbell v. MGN Ltd* (n. 24).

was offensive. Naomi Campbell could therefore not have complained if the photographs had been taken to show the scene in the street by a passer-by and later published as street scenes—but the photographs published by *The Mirror* had been taken deliberately, in secret, and with a view to their publication in conjunction with the articles. The argument that the photographs added credibility to the story had little weight, because they were not self-explanatory and neither the place nor the person was instantly recognizable.

In conclusion, the publication of the fact that Naomi Campbell was receiving treatment at NA, the details of the treatment, and her appearance leaving a meeting as part of the articles was an infringement of her right to privacy that could not be justified.[91] This endorsement at the highest level of the approach developed in relation to privacy and of the role of the action for breach of confidence in this respect is a welcome development. It greatly enhances the protection available to a private person against unwanted intrusions of his or her privacy, while at the same time safeguarding the interests of the right of freedom of expression.

Privacy—a brief summary

The Human Rights Act 1998 has brought significant changes to the action for breach of confidence in relation to personal or private information, as we have just seen. When the conflict between privacy and freedom of expression is played out, the requirement of a relation of confidence seems to disappear and the emphasis shifts towards the private, rather than the confidential, nature of the information.[92]

It is indeed fair to say that the first limb of the test in *Coco v. Clark* has, for cases relating to private or personal information, been replaced by the question whether the claimant has 'a reasonable expectation of privacy' in respect of the facts that were disclosed.[93] A good example is that of a picture taken in the street of the young son of the author J. K. Rowling. The child himself is by no means a public figure and whilst on a private walk with his mother pushing the pram had a reasonable expectation of privacy.[94] At this stage Art. 8 has a strong influence. In determining whether or not a reasonable expectation exists the courts will have to examine in detail all the circumstances of the case. In *Murray* it was held that the relevant factors include:

> ...the attributes of the claimant, the nature of the activity in which the claimant was engaged, the place at which it was happening, the nature and purpose of the intrusion, the absence of consent and whether it was known or could be inferred, the effect on the claimant and the circumstances in which and the purposes for which the information came into the hands of the publisher.[95]

The Court of Appeal provided another good example when it held that the children of a well-known UK musician had a reasonable expectation of privacy during a family shopping outing in California.[96] Paparazzi pictures taken of them during that shopping outing went against that reasonable expectation as they had not consented to the pictures being taken and the fact that the daughter had dabbled in modelling at an earlier stage did not

---

[91] *Campbell v. MGN Ltd* (n. 24).

[92] See T. Aplin, 'The Development of the Action for Breach of Confidence in a Post-HRA Era' [2007] IPQ 19.

[93] *Campbell v. MGN Ltd* (n. 24). See also *Lord Browne of Madingley v. Associated Newspapers Ltd* [2007] 3 WLR 289 (CA); *McKennitt v. Ash* [2007] 3 WLR 194, [2007] EMLR 4 (CA); and *HRH Prince of Wales v. Associated Newspapers Ltd* [2007] 3 WLR 222, [2007] 2 All ER 139 (CA).

[94] *Murray v. Express Newspapers plc* [2008] EWCA Civ 446, [2008] ECDR 12.

[95] *Murray* (n. 94) at para. 36, per Sir Anthony Clarke MR.

[96] *Weller and others v. Associated Newspapers Ltd* [2015] EWCA Civ 1176.

change that conclusion and neither did the fact that taking the pictures was lawful under the law of the place where they were taken. The first step is therefore to ask whether there is a reasonable expectation of privacy. The action will fail in case the answer is negative. The decision of the European Court of Human Rights in *Von Hannover* will also play a role in this context.[97] The Court ruled in that case that although a very public figure, Princess Caroline of Monaco had the right not be photographed whilst going around on private business, such a horse-riding, holidaying, or on shopping trips. She did at that stage not exercise any official function and these elements were not of interest to the public, apart from satisfying the readers' curiosity. The public had in these circumstances no right to know about the activities of the Princess, even if these took place in a public place. This is a far-reaching decision that broadens the scope of Art. 8.

It is clear, though, that this is not the end of the matter. Article 10 still has a role to play, especially if the information reported concerns a topic of general interest or if the celebrity has already put elements of their private life in the public domain.[98] The second step will therefore involve a balancing exercise.[99] So in order to fully understand these developments it is necessary to look at the second and third limb of the *Coco v. Clark* test as well in the context of personal and private information.

The second limb requires that the imparting of the information must occur in circumstances or on an occasion of confidence. The House of Lords has swept this step aside when it comes to personal and private information. It argued that this limb is no longer relevant when the defendant knows of the reasonable expectation of privacy.[100]

The third limb normally requires that the information must be used in an unauthorized way and so as to cause detriment to the claimant. For personal and private information this has been replaced by the balancing act between Arts. 8 and 10. The balancing act between privacy and freedom of expression can briefly be summarized as follows. In cases about the wrongful publication of private information, the court has to decide, first, whether the information was private in the sense of Art. 8 of the Convention. If that is the case, the court then has to decide whether, in all of the circumstances, the interests of the owner of the private information has to yield to the right of freedom of expression in the sense of Art. 10 of the Convention.[101] In *Weller*, the expectation of privacy of the children of a musician in relation to pictures taken during a family shopping outing was said to outweigh the publisher's right to freedom of expression to publish these paparazzi pictures.[102] In applying this notoriously opaque test of proportionality, the nature of the relationship that gave rise to the duty of confidentiality might be important.[103]

When it comes to damages for the misuse of confidential private information the courts have awarded damages for the distress caused[104] and in the phone-hacking cases it has been accepted that substantial damage can be awarded for the infringement of privacy itself.[105]

---

[97] *Von Hannover v. Germany* (2005) 40 EHHR 1.

[98] For two cases where Art. 10 eventually prevailed, see *Axel Springer v. Germany* (2012) 55 EHRR 6, [2012] EMLR 15 and *Von Hannover v. Germany* (2012) 55 EHRR 15, [2012] EMLR 16.

[99] *Weller and others v. Associated Newspapers Ltd* (n. 96) at para. 15.

[100] *Campbell v. MGN Ltd* (n. 24) at 480, per Lord Hope.

[101] *McKennitt v. Ash* (n. 93). See also *Edward Rocknroll v. News Group Newspaper Ltd* [2013] EWCH 24 (Ch).

[102] *Weller and others v. Associated Newspapers Ltd* (n. 96) at para. 72 *et seq.*

[103] *HRH Prince of Wales v. Associated Newspapers Ltd* (n. 93).

[104] *Mosley v. News Group Newspapers* [2008] EWHC 1777 (QB).

[105] *Gulati v. MGN Ltd* [2015] EWHC 1482 (Ch).

Moving away from private persons

Let us end this discussion with a reminder that these points about privacy are not solely relevant in relation to private persons: equally, this area is important in reminding commercial interests that their private activity may have public interest implications. Firms, such as drug or food companies, may wish to keep their manufacturing problems secret, but the public may need to know about those problems—and any attempt to conceal the problems behind a cloak of confidentiality may, in turn, be overcome by an allegation of iniquity, as the *Lion Intoximeters* case has vividly shown.

It is also possible for information to be private and commercial at the same time. This was, for example, the case with the wedding photographs of Catherine Zeta Jones and Michael Douglas. Both aspects will then be considered according to their own criteria in a breach of confidence context.[106]

The obligation of confidence

The second element in the action, as defined by Megarry J in *Coco v. Clark*,[107] is the issue of what circumstances give rise to an obligation of confidentiality. This question focuses not on the nature of the information itself, but on the relationship between the parties and, in particular, whether the relationship is one that should give rise to the obligation of confidentiality.[108] Megarry J makes it quite clear that the test is an objective one, with the ever-popular judicial device of the reasonable man being employed to encapsulate the appropriate tests:

> it seems to me that if the circumstances are such that any reasonable man standing in the shoes of the recipient of the information would have realised that upon reasonable grounds the information was being given to him in confidence, then this should suffice to impose upon him the equitable obligation of confidence.[109]

The judge also emphasizes the independence of this element from the confidentiality of the information itself:

> However secret and confidential the information, there can be no binding obligation of confidence if that information is blurted out in public or is communicated in other circumstances which negative any duty of holding it confidential.[110]

Equally, if the circumstances do support the existence of a duty of confidentiality, it will be hard for the recipient of information to deny the existence of the obligation; the type of case in this category envisaged by Megarry J is that in which information is of commercial value and is passed on in a business context, such as a joint venture.[111]

Many different types of relationship may give rise to the obligation of confidence. On the one hand, as has just been noted, business dealings will often create obligations of confidentiality even when no contract is ultimately concluded, as in *Coco v. Clark* itself.[112] On the other hand, private and personal relationships such as marriage may also create an obligation not to divulge confidences, as in *Argyll v. Argyll*,[113] in which the claimant Duchess was able to prevent her ex-husband from revealing personal matters in the tabloid press, doubtless to the regret of millions.

---

[106] *Douglas v. Hello! Ltd* [2008] 1 AC 1 (HL).   [107] [1969] RPC 41.
[108] For a negative example, see *Cray Valley Ltd* (n. 19).   [109] [1969] RPC 41 at 48.
[110] [1969] RPC 41 at 47–8.   [111] [1969] RPC 41 at 48.   [112] [1969] RPC 41 at 48.
[113] [1967] Ch 302, [1965] 1 All ER 611.

In relation to privacy, the House of Lords has held that a duty of confidence will arise whenever the person subject to the duty was in a situation in which he or she knew, or ought to have known, that the other person would reasonably expect his or her privacy to be respected. That reasonable expectation would normally be determined on the basis of a test asking whether publication of the information would be highly offensive to a reasonable person of ordinary sensibilities if he or she were to be in the same position as the claimant. That test should not, however, be applied if the information was obviously private. In those cases, the reasonable expectation can be presumed.[114]

It is obviously not sensible to list every possible relationship in which the reasonable man may decree that an obligation of confidence is created, but certain types of case have given rise to frequent litigation and it is therefore appropriate to proceed by giving detailed consideration to cases arising from fiduciary relationships, contractual relationships (especially in the context of employment), and third-party relationships in which parties outside the initial bond of confidence are nonetheless caught up in its obligations.

Fiduciary relationships

The essence of a fiduciary relationship is that equity imposes a strong obligation on the trustee to act not in his or her own interests, but in those of the beneficiary. The close relationship between the parties is inevitably one in which information will pass between the parties and this information is likely to be regarded as confidential. The obligation can arise in a range of different cases: company directors and top managers owe a fiduciary duty to their companies;[115] professionals, such as accountants and lawyers, may owe fiduciary duties to their clients. A useful example is provided by *Jarman & Platt Ltd v. I. Barget Ltd*,[116] in which the claimant company, engaged in the reproduction furniture trade, commissioned a report on its somewhat parlous financial condition. One of the defendants, Hutchins, then the sales manager of the claimants, appears to have taken the report from someone's desk in the company and then circulated it to other sales representatives of the company, seemingly so as to lure them to a rival firm that Hutchins was intending to join. This was held to be a clear breach of confidence by a senior employee and was accordingly held to be actionable.

Not every fiduciary duty necessarily gives rise to liability for breach of confidence. A simple example of this is *Baker v. Gibbons*,[117] in which a director of a cavity wall insulation firm set up a rival operation and solicited some of the company's agents in the hope of persuading them to transfer their allegiance to him. This was clearly contrary to his fiduciary obligations towards the company, but the action did not succeed for the simple reason that the name and addresses of the agents concerned were in the public domain, and thus did not represent confidential information.

Contractual relationships

Parties to contracts are naturally free to make whatever provision is felt to be appropriate in relation to information passing as a result of the contractual nexus.[118] It is common to stipulate expressly that information is not to be passed beyond the parameters of the contract; *Exchange Telegraph Co. v. Gregory & Co.*[119] provides a good example of the potential effect of this. The claimants operated a news agency service providing up-to-date share price information to its subscribers. The defendants were originally subscribers,

---

[114] *Campbell v. MGN Ltd* (n. 24).

[115] See *Breitenfeld UK Ltd v. Harrison* [2015] EWHC 399 (Ch).   [116] [1977] FSR 260.

[117] [1972] 2 All ER 759, [1972] 1 WLR 693.

[118] *Force India Formula One Team Ltd* (n. 13) at para. 224.   [119] [1896] 1 QB 147.

but the claimants did not renew the contract, because the London Stock Exchange—the source of the information—did not want the service offered to parties such as the defendants who were 'outside brokers', not subject to its rules. In pique, the defendants arranged to obtain the information service from another subscriber and then sold it on to their own subscribers. The terms of the claimants' subscription contract included a provision that information was not to be passed on to non-subscribers. Clearly, had they been identified, the subscriber who was prepared to allow the defendants access to the service would have been liable directly for breach of contract; the defendants, as past subscribers, knew of the terms of the agreement and so knew of the confidentiality obligation—and, accordingly, were held to be liable for infringing the claimants' rights of confidentiality.

In many other cases, it will be an implied term rather than an express one that is relied upon, because many contracts will only be workable if information passed under their arrangements remains confidential: for example, as between doctor and patient, or between the manufacturer of a new product and its advertising agency. A clear illustration is provided by *Tournier v. National Provincial & Union Bank of England*,[120] in which the claimant banked with the defendants and was overdrawn. The bank kept a careful eye on Tournier's affairs and noted that he had endorsed a cheque payable to his account over to someone else's account, this party being a bookmaker. The bank accordingly rang his employer and revealed this nugget of information, resulting in his dismissal. The Court of Appeal found for Tournier; it was an implied term in the banker–customer relationship that the bank should not disclose information derived from that contract, unless the law compels such a disclosure.

Just as a contract can create an obligation of confidence, so, of course, it can deny that obligation, as the claimant in *Fraser v. Evans*[121] discovered. He wrote a report for the Greek government (then a military junta) on its public relations. A copy of the report found its way back to Britain, and the *Sunday Times* proposed to write an article featuring the report and making criticisms of Fraser, who objected that it was a confidential report. On examination of the contract under the terms of which the report had been written, the Court of Appeal found that, while Fraser was expressly bound by an obligation of confidentiality, there was no such obligation placed on the government of Greece. In effect, it had bought the information from Fraser and was free to use it as it saw fit; if the disclosure had been unauthorized, then the Greek government would be able to restrain publication, but it had taken no steps to do so.

The employment relationship

Particular problems arise in relation to the inevitably large amount of information of a confidential character that passes between employer and employee—information about working methods, manufacturing processes, etc. Express terms, either in the employment contract or in a separate contract,[122] may frequently be used,[123] but it is clear that the courts, in any event, regard the employee as being under a duty of fidelity towards his or her employer and will use this to enforce the obligation of confidentiality.

The basic duty of fidelity arises throughout the course of the employment relationship and can be far-reaching in its effect. The leading case is *Hivac Ltd v. Park Royal Scientific Instruments Ltd*.[124] The claimants employed Mr and Mrs Davis as production engineer

---

[120] [1924] 1 KB 461.   [121] [1969] 1 QB 349, [1969] 1 All ER 8.
[122] *Caterpillar Logistics Services (UK) Ltd v. Huesca de Crean* [2012] EWCA Civ 156, [2012] 3 All ER 129. The separate contract does not necessarily have to include a time limit on the obligation of confidence.
[123] E.g. *Bents Brewery v. Hogan* [1945] 2 All ER 570.   [124] [1946] Ch 169, [1946] 1 All ER 350.

and forewoman, respectively, at their plant, which made the midget valves that were in great demand during the war. The defendants started a business nearby, also making midget valves, and the evidence was clear that Mr Davis had been involved in the foundation of the business, albeit only in his spare time, and that Mrs Davis, who had left Hivac on health grounds, was soon well enough to work for Park Royal. They also encouraged several of their colleagues to join them in their 'moonlighting'. Hivac sought an injunction to prevent the Davis couple from working for the rival firm.

The trial judge found as a fact, perhaps surprisingly, that no confidential information had been used in setting up and operating Park Royal, although it was clear that there was an ongoing risk that this would happen: for example, if Hivac were to improve its process, there would be an obvious temptation for that improvement also to be made at Park Royal. In the light of this, the Court of Appeal was prepared to award an interlocutory injunction, having additional regard to several other factors. The duty of fidelity owed by an employee was said to be variable depending on the status of the employee, with Morton LJ noting that these were skilled employees;[125] it was also relevant that their activities—even without (yet) breaking confidences—were clearly harmful to their employers, putting at risk the lucrative monopoly that they had enjoyed, and the fact that those activities were carried out in a highly secretive manner was a further factor militating against the defendants.

This important decision is ultimately resolved with close reference to the specific facts of the case—but it does seem to imply that any employee who discloses confidential information is in breach of his or her obligations, given that an injunction was awarded with reference to what was merely a risk of future disclosure, albeit a significant risk. This is illustrated too by *Printers & Finishers Ltd v. Holloway*,[126] in which the defendant was dismissed for inviting an employee of a rival firm to inspect a testing room; indeed, that employee was also the subject of an injunction preventing him from using any confidential information that he may have gleaned while there.

Clearly, the more senior the employee, the greater and more onerous the duty that is imposed upon him or her; indeed, at the more senior end of the scale, the duty is probably best regarded as fiduciary in character.[127] More lowly employees are less likely to be affected, as illustrated by *Nova Plastics v. Froggatt*,[128] in which an 'odd-job man' was allowed to work for a rival in his spare time, given that there was no evidence of any harm to his main employer having occurred or even being likely. More questionable is the decision in *Laughton v. Bapp Industrial Supplies Ltd*,[129] in which a warehouse manager and a driver used their knowledge of the company's suppliers to write to them requesting price lists and other information, with a view to setting up their own competing business. It was held that their dismissals were unfair, in circumstances under which they had acted in their own time and not that of the firm, and under which there was no clear evidence of their present or future breach of confidence. This seems a generous decision in the light of the status of the warehouse manager within the firm and in the light of the fate of the employees in *Hivac*.

But it is clear that subsequent cases are prepared to make use of the *Laughton* decision, albeit on rather different facts. In *Balston Ltd v. Headline Filters Ltd*,[130] an employee-director gave notice in March 1986 that he would leave in that July. He had already agreed to lease his own premises. In fact, he resigned as director and ceased work in April

---

[125] [1946] Ch 169, [1946] 1 All ER 350 at 181 and 356.
[126] [1964] 3 All ER 731, [1965] 1 WLR 1.
[127] *Boardman v. Phipps* [1967] 2 AC 46, [1966] 3 All ER 721.   [128] [1982] IRLR 146.
[129] [1986] ICR 634.   [130] [1990] FSR 385.

1986, and then moved quickly, making contact with his former employer's customers and workforce with a view to establishing a rival business. Falconer J held that there was no breach of his duties as both director and employee in respect of the minimal acts carried out prior to his resignation as a director, but that he was in breach of his employee's duty of fidelity in actively competing with the claimants while still on their payroll, even though not actually working for them. *Laughton* was used as the basis of this decision and also that of *Marshall v. Industrial Systems & Control Ltd*,[131] in which a managing director, while still in his post, made active plans to set up a rival business, and contacted employees and customers of his firm to that end. His status and his actions were both the opposite of the facts of *Laughton*, which was duly distinguished, and Marshall was held to be fairly dismissed. This decision is in line with the earlier case of *Sanders v. Parry*,[132] in which an assistant solicitor negotiated a deal with one of the law firm's main clients, whereby he was to set up on his own and handle all of the client's legal work in his own right. By doing this while still employed by the firm, he was held to be clearly in breach of his implied duties of good faith and fidelity.

Taken together, these cases show an awareness that the company's whole business—its plans, its customers, its employees—is given clear protection by the law. An action for breach of confidence or the broader *Hivac*-type action for breach of fidelity duty almost has the effect of protecting the current trading activity of the business in the same way as the tort of passing off protects its business goodwill, and it will be interesting to see whether there grows a clearer conception of what is 'protectable trading activity', the use of which is improper, and what is 'just fair competition' as in *Laughton* itself. Meanwhile, the courts provide further support for the protection of trading activity by restricting the use that can be made by former employees of information gained during the period of employment.

In general, it is arguable that a duty of confidence that has been assumed expressly under a contract carries more weight, when balanced, for example, against the right of freedom of expression, than a duty of confidentiality that was not buttressed by an express agreement. While this starting point has an obvious impact on the position in relation to former employees, it is not clear what the effect of a wrongful repudiation of the contract will be on such an obligation of confidentiality agreed by contract.[133]

The former employee's obligations

Once an employee has left, his or her duties in relation to confidential information diminish, but do not disappear. It may well be that the contract itself has laid down stipulations as to future conduct, perhaps restricting the nature and location of subsequent work to avoid the risk of prejudicial competition, or limiting the use that may be made of information learnt during the period of employment. In imposing such terms, however, great care needs to be taken by the employer, because there is a clear risk that a court will strike them down as being void for restraint of trade.

This is a complex issue of contract law, but, in short, the courts will uphold clauses that are seen as being legitimately necessary to protect the employer's interests, while seeking to preserve, as far as possible, free and fair competition. Two examples illustrate the point. In *International Consulting Services UK Ltd v. Hart*,[134] the court upheld a restrictive covenant that prevented the former employee from canvassing existing and potential clients of his former employers for a period of 12 months from the termination

---

[131] [1992] IRLR 294.   [132] [1967] 2 All ER 803, [1967] 1 WLR 753.
[133] *Campbell v. Frisbee* [2003] EMLR 3 (CA).   [134] [2000] IRLR 227.

of his employment, because this looked reasonable in the circumstances. But in *Barry Allsuch & Co. v. Jonathan Harris*,[135] a covenant that restricted the former employee from working in a defined area for two years was rejected as unreasonably long in terms of its duration, especially because there seemed to be very little confidential information worth protecting involved in the case. There is also no prerequisite that the (separate) contract must contain a time limit. The absence of one does not make the contract null and void per se.[136]

Quite irrespective of any contractual stipulations, however, the law of confidence may also be prepared to intervene; the leading case in this area is now *Faccenda Chicken Ltd v. Fowler*.[137] Fowler was the company's sales manager and established a surprisingly successful aspect of the company's operation, running a fleet of vans around the streets selling fresh chickens. On leaving the firm—he resigned after being charged with stealing company property, of which he was later acquitted—he set up his own business, which also was to sell fresh chickens from vans in the same area. Clearly, Fowler was aided by his prior knowledge of the identity and requirements of regular chicken customers, and he also recruited his staff from among Faccenda's employees.

At first instance,[138] Goulding J categorized information that an employee may acquire into three types:

1. Some information will not be regarded as confidential at all, given its easy accessibility from the public domain, and the employee is always free to disclose this—the logos used by the company would be a good example.

2. Some information is confidential during the period of employment, but not after the employment has ceased, when the ex-employee is entitled to use it as part of the package of skills that he or she brings to the workplace—examples include the basic manufacturing processes used, or customer information remembered, by the ex-employee after he or she has finished employment (although this does not extend to lists deliberately copied during employment).[139]

3. Some information is best described as a 'trade secret'—such as secret manufacturing processes—and this information remains confidential even after employment has ceased.

Both Goulding J and, subsequently, the Court of Appeal ruled that Fowler had only used information in the second category and, no longer being in Faccenda's employment, was therefore at liberty to make use of it, there being no express stipulation in his contract of employment.

The Court of Appeal provided some useful guidance as to what should be regarded as a trade secret. Consideration should be given, according to Neill LJ,[140] to the nature of the employment—habitual handling of confidential information giving rise to a higher burden on the employee, because its importance is more likely to be realized—the nature of the information and the aura of secrecy (or otherwise) that surrounds it, whether the employer has stressed the secret nature of the information, and whether the information is separate or whether it forms an inevitable part of the employee's package of skills that he or she is entitled to take to a new post. On this latter matter, the Court of Appeal left

---

[135] QBD, judgment of 4 May 2001, unreported (2001 WC 720358).
[136] *Caterpillar Logistics Services (UK) Ltd v. Huesca de Crean* (n. 122).
[137] [1987] Ch 117, [1986] 1 All ER 617.
[138] [1984] ICR 589. The rule also applies to consultants. See *Vestagaard Frandsen* (n. 37).
[139] *Robb v. Green* [1895] 2 QB 315.   [140] [1987] Ch 117, [1986] 1 All ER 617 at 137–8 and 626–7.

open the question of whether the answer would be different had Fowler not been legitimately using his skills, but simply selling the customer information to another for profit.

It is clear from *Faccenda* that the number of instances in which an obligation of confidence will survive will be significantly limited and this represents a stark contrast with the wide-ranging character of the duty of fidelity while the course of the employment continues. Or in the words of Neill LJ:

> The implied term which imposes an obligation on the employee as to his conduct after the determination of the employment is more restricted in its scope than that which imposes a general duty of good faith. It is clear that the obligation not to use or disclose information may cover secret processes of manufacture such as chemical formulae (*Amber Size and Chemical Co. Ltd v Menzel* [1913] 2 Ch 239), or designs or special methods of construction (*Reid & Sigrist Ltd v Moss and Mechanism Ltd* (1932) 49 RPC 461), and other information which is of a sufficiently high degree of confidentiality as to amount to a trade secret. The obligation does not extend, however, to cover all information which is given to or acquired by the employee while in his employment, and in particular may not cover information which is only 'confidential' in the sense that an unauthorised disclosure of such information to a third party while the employment subsisted would be a clear breach of the duty of good faith. This distinction is clearly set out in the judgment of Cross J in *Printers & Finishers Ltd v Holloway* [1965] 1 WLR 1, [1965] RPC 239.[141]

Subsequent case law indicates that the courts appear to be reluctant to characterize information as being in the trade secret category. In *Roger Bullivant Ltd v. Ellis*,[142] a company's managing director left and set up in competition using a copy of the firm's customer card index. This was regarded as being confidential only during employment, but this was when he had misappropriated it, so it might be expected that an injunction would be awarded against him. The trial judge did so award, and the Court of Appeal agreed that this was right and rejected Ellis' argument that much of the information in the index was also in his memory. The injunction was, however, discharged solely on the grounds that the benefit of the information was short-lived, providing no more than a quick bounce on the springboard.

This type of case makes the important point that trade secrets are not restricted to secret formulae, but might also include highly confidential information of a non-technical nature, such as lists of names of customers that, if disclosed to a competitor, could cause real and significant harm.[143] In *Berkeley Administration Inc. v. McClelland*,[144] use by former employees of figures in a company's business plan was not grounds for an injunction; the information was really little more than assumptions made in the plan, and the figures were not accurate figures of turnover and profitability, and did not attain any level of protection. Some figures were in the public domain; others represented the kind of guess that anyone in the relevant trade—that is, a currency exchange bureau—would know as part of his or her ordinary experience of that trade. Similarly, in a case concerning contact lenses,[145] it was held that the use by the former employees-defendants of formulations within the ranges of the target figures of the claimant's master formulae was not a breach of confidence. This was so because every skilled man in the area would have spent a significant part of his working life working with the specific class of polymers concerned and would know how to adjust the mix of reagents in order to make the various polymers differing in their water-absorbing qualities. These things could

---

[141] [1987] Ch 177 at 135G–138H.   [142] [1987] FSR 172.
[143] *Intelsec Systems Ltd v. Grech Cini* [1999] 4 All ER 11, [2000] 1 WLR 1190.
[144] [1990] FSR 505.   [145] *Ocular Sciences* (n. 21) at 385–6.

easily be worked out on the basis of details that were in the public domain. In *Mainmet Holdings v. Austin*[146] too, the information used by the defendant, documenting defects in his former employer's products, was not even confidential information.

In reviewing these cases, two things are clear. First, the courts seem to be reluctant to hold that information is in the second category of confidentiality during the period of employment, let alone that it amounts to being a trade secret and is thus protectable beyond the period of employment. This is good news for ex-employees, who will often be free to transfer their skills, knowledge, and experience to other firms without fear of legal redress, and thus good news for those enthused by free competition. The law, however, does not provide any great protection for the original employer unless he or she goes out of his or her way expressly to declare matters to be confidential in nature, thus helping them to become trade secrets. The second point is very different: several of the cases in this area of the law are notable for the length of the hearings involved, which may suggest that the courts are finding this area difficult to apply, perhaps because of the evidential difficulties of deciding in what category each item of information belongs and in seeing what advantage, if any, has been gained by its use.

In determining whether a certain piece of information should be classified as a trade secret, the courts seem to use a variant of the objective test that is generally used in relation to breach of confidence. The notional reasonable man reappears, to assess what forms the part of the employee's acquired general skill and knowledge that he is free to use, and to distinguish that part of the information that is a trade secret. The test is whether:

> the information in question can fairly be regarded as a separate part of the employee's stock of knowledge which a man of ordinary honesty and intelligence would recognise to be the property of his employer, and not his own to do as he likes with.[147]

Restricted as the idea of the trade secret has become, it is still important to assert its value in what may be described as its 'core' area—namely, that in which the employer has gone out of his or her way to establish that secrecy of work is vital. A classic example of this is during the development work predating a patent application. Key employees will know of the vital need for secrecy even without any added reminders from the management. The employee who leaves with information that is vital to the proposed patent and who prevents its registration by giving or, worse, selling such information to a rival, thus disclosing it, is an obvious example in relation to which the use of trade secrets will be grounds for an injunction. Equally, the example shows the vital importance of trade secret law in protecting the steps taken prior to the application for a patent.

Third-party relationships

If I tell you some information in confidence, you will be bound by that confidence—but what if you tell someone else? Can the obligation of confidentiality extend onwards to third parties?

The short answer to this question is 'Yes' and the leading case is *Saltman v. Campbell*.[148] This was a 1948 decision[149] in which the claimants were the owners of drawings of a type of tool used for making leather punches. They instructed another linked company,

---

[146] [1991] FSR 538.

[147] *Ocular Sciences* (n. 21) at 371; applying *Printers & Finishers Ltd v. Holloway* [1965] 1 WLR 1, [1965] RPC 239.

[148] [1963] 3 All ER 413 (Note), (1948) 65 RPC 203.

[149] Contemporaneously reported at (1948) 65 RPC 203.

Monarch, to arrange with the defendants to manufacture tools from the drawings and the defendants did this, but also retained the drawings for their own use. In finding that there had been a breach of confidence, the Court of Appeal ruled that it made no difference that the parties had not been in a direct contractual nexus, because the confidentiality of the drawings and the rights of Saltman in their respect were obvious to the defendants.

Cases involving disclosure to newspapers also illustrate the proposition. In *Argyll v. Argyll*,[150] what the Duchess told the Duke, the Duke was now telling to the Sunday papers, but, clearly, the papers were aware from the nature of the information that it was of a private and confidential character, and thus they too were restrained by the confidentiality. The *Spycatcher* case[151] can be analysed in similar terms, although, of course, the element of confidentiality had been lost by the time of the hearing: were this the first disclosure of such information, its nature would have been such as to render it obviously confidential in character.

It must be emphasized that the third party only enters the liability picture when the information is not only known, but is also known to be of a confidential nature. *Fraser v. Thames Television Ltd*[152] shows this well: the claimants had the idea for a television drama series concerning the exploits of an all-female rock group and this was discussed confidentially with a scriptwriter, who discussed it with a producer, and Thames itself was fully aware of these discussions. The project did not proceed, but, shortly afterwards, the producer, scriptwriter, and Thames collaborated on a series called *Rock Follies*, which closely resembled the claimants' original proposal. All were held liable for breach of confidence, because, at every stage, both the identity of the originators of the proposal and the need for confidentiality were clearly known, and therefore all of the defendants were aware of those matters and thus in breach of their obligations. The case is also a useful reminder of a point made at the outset of this chapter: no final scripts were ever produced by the claimants, being still at the ideas stage, so no copyright protection could exist; the ideas stage was protectable by an action for breach of confidence.

Particular difficulty is caused by unauthorized acquisition of confidential information by a third party: the two main cases involve information gained by the use of unauthorized telephone tapping and do not appear to tell a consistent tale, so consideration must be given to both *Malone v. Metropolitan Police Comr*[153] and *Francome v. Mirror Group Newspapers*.[154]

In *Malone*, the prosecution in a handling stolen goods case made use of authorized phone taps by the police and the claimant applied to the courts for a declaration that use of the taps was unlawful. Megarry V-C refused to give this: in discussing whether a breach of confidence had occurred, he stated that, in any situation, a speaker recognizes that there is a risk of an unknown person overhearing the conversation and that, in the case of telephone calls, there is always the risk of being overheard by a crossed line or by a deliberate tapping of the telephone.[155] In such cases, the speaker takes the risk that any confidences that he or she divulges may be intercepted and no obligation of confidence is created on that third party. In any event, in such a case as *Malone*, it may well be that the public interest in the revelation of iniquity would, in any event, overcome the obligation of confidentiality.

---

[150] [1967] Ch 302, [1965] 1 All ER 611.   [151] *A-G v. Guardian Newspapers (No. 2)* (n. 5).

[152] [1984] QB 44, [1983] 2 All ER 101.

[153] [1979] Ch 344, *sub nom Malone v. Metropolitan Police Comr (No. 2)* [1979] 2 All ER 620.

[154] [1984] 2 All ER 408, [1984] 1 WLR 892.

[155] [1979] Ch 344, [1979] 2 All ER 620 at 376 and 633–4. There are significant differences between the two reports.

In *Francome*, the facts were rather different. The claimant was a well-known jockey, whose phone was tapped by an unknown party. The tap appeared to reveal evidence that Francome was breaching various rules of the racing business and the recordings were made available to the *Daily Mirror*, with a view to its making their contents public. This time, an interlocutory injunction was granted, restraining publication of the recordings on the grounds that there appeared to be a breach of confidence and any suggestion that the public interest defence was relevant could be dealt with at a subsequent full trial.

It is possible to reconcile these two decisions, either by pointing to *Francome* as being purely an interlocutory proceeding and thus easy to distinguish, or to *Malone* as hinging on a remedies point (as discussed later in this chapter), or, more satisfactorily, by emphasizing, as it was in *Francome*, the words of Megarry V-C in *Malone*[156] that he was only seeking to lay down principles to govern the use of authorized police phone taps in criminal proceedings and did not purport to be dealing with other categories of cases.

This is a convenient let-out, but it is surely not satisfactory. The basis of *Malone* is clearly flawed. While it is acceptable to argue that there is a risk of any conversation being overheard, it does not, in any way, follow logically from this that any hearer should be freed automatically from an obligation to help the information gleaned stay confidential. The basic approach in cases of third parties, from *Saltman v. Campbell*[157] onwards, is that a third party is bound if he or she receives confidential information in circumstances under which he is aware of that confidentiality. If you overhear my counsellor and me discussing my private sexual problems, you will realize that this is confidential information and will become enveloped in the web of confidence that already binds my counsellor and me. It surely makes matters worse, not better, for the third party if the information is gained not by an inadvertent overhearing, but by a deliberate telephone tap. And this is not a charter for criminals: if my statements include confessions of criminal behaviour, it is clear that the defence of iniquity will act to justify the breach of confidence, as shown by the practice of reputable film developers of disclosing to the police photographs that they develop that appear to show evidence of illegal conduct. *Malone* does not sit within the general principles of third-party confidentiality, provides a quite unnecessary breach in the web of confidence that protects individuals, and should thus be regarded as incorrectly decided.

When an occasion is one of confidence, an obligation is created. Overall, the law has developed clear guidelines to deal with the principal examples of such an occasion and the attempts to balance free access to, and use of, information that have clearly been made by the law have generally reached an acceptable compromise. But it should always be borne in mind that these are merely examples of the general principle and that the judicial cypher of the reasonable man is always at hand to vary the balance, particularly in novel situations.

Unauthorized use of confidential information

Use of the information

Several elements come together at this stage of the definition. First, and obviously, there has to be use of the information,[158] but it is clear that not every use will be sufficient.

---

[156] [1979] Ch 344, [1979] 2 All ER 620 at 384 and 651.

[157] [1963] 3 All ER 413 (Note), (1948) 65 RPC 203.

[158] E.g. the unauthorized copying of a substantial part of a confidential list of a forensic services company by a police officer in *Forensic Telecommunications Services Ltd v. Chief Constable of West Yorkshire* [2011] EWHC 2893 (Ch), [2012] FSR 15.

In *Amber Size & Chemical Co. Ltd v. Menzel*,[159] the defendant was an ex-employee who had been misusing a trade secret in his subsequent employment. The trade secret in question was a scientific process involving various materials, the proportions between them, the density of the ensuing mixture, and the timing of the operation. Menzel knew which materials were involved, but did not know the proportions and density precisely. He knew, however, that the claimants used a particular type of hydrometer in the process and this, coupled with his knowledge of the materials and the timing, was brought to bear in his new employment. The High Court found that this was enough to ground a breach of confidence action: Menzel had been aware of the principal features of the process, and he and his new employers were expecting him to be able to recreate the process from his stolen knowledge, even though not all the details were known to him.

It seems to follow from this that use of a minor or unimportant part of the information may not ground a breach of confidence action, but that might seem to dent the protection afforded by the law to confidentiality. A better view may be to assume that the approach in *Amber Size* was calculated to consider merely whether it was usable information that the claimant had acquired. On this basis, too, *Fraser v. Thames Television Ltd*[160] is also explicable: the mere idea of a drama series about a female rock group may not have been usable as such, but considerable plot and character development had taken place, and this was directly used in the subsequent unauthorized (by the claimants) programme.

Deliberate and innocent use

Next, it is important to note that the law does not seek to concern itself with the way in which the information is used and, in particular, with the state of mind of the person using, or rather *mis*using, the information. In other words, the law will intervene to protect not only deliberate, but also innocent, uses of confidential information. This is important because, often, it will be tempting for the user to claim that the use of information is subconscious or coincidental. To adapt the facts of *Fraser v. Thames*, it would be easy for someone in the position of the defendants to say, 'Yes, now you mention it I do recall a conversation about a female rock group series; it must have been lurking at the back of my mind all this time', but the law will still act to control such apparently innocent uses of confidential information.

The clearest example of this is provided by the decision of the Court of Appeal in *Seager v. Copydex Ltd (No. 1)*,[161] when scandal and intrigue rocked the world of stair-carpet grip manufacture. Seager designed a new type of stair-carpet grip, and he and the defendants discussed its possible manufacture to no avail. Soon after this, the defendant company produced a new type of stair-carpet grip, which embodied the key design features of Seager's grip, although not so far as to infringe Seager's patent. The name used, 'Invisigrip', had also been suggested by Seager; the company claimed that it was all its own work. The court took the view that this was subconscious copying and so found in Seager's favour, awarding him damages.

The latter aspect is not entirely compatible with the case of *Nichrotherm Electrical Company Ltd v. Percy*.[162] This was a dispute about a machine for artificially rearing pigs. It was a notably unsuccessful machine, but this was no bar to—it may even have been the cause of—litigation. The defendant was found to have misused the claimants' confidential

[159] [1913] 2 Ch 239.   [160] [1984] QB 44, [1983] 2 All ER 101.
[161] [1967] 2 All ER 415, [1967] 1 WLR 923.
[162] [1956] RPC 272 (HC), aff'd [1957] RPC 207 (CA).

information in making his own rival, and equally unsuccessful, pig-rearing machine, but the problem arose that the second defendants gave Percy the claimants' plans for the machine, apparently in innocence, having received them from the claimants, with a view to their involvement in the manufacture of the devices. In the view of Harman J at first instance, the second defendants were liable in breach of confidence, but their innocence should mean that they were not obliged to pay damages, thus presumably suggesting that an innocent breach of confidence is only remediable by an injunction if appropriate.[163] Because only Percy appealed, the Court of Appeal gave no consideration to the position of the second defendant.

Nichrotherm was not considered in *Seager* and the latter case bears the stamp of the Court of Appeal's authority. It may also be suggested that *Nichrotherm* is not entirely compatible with the provisions in Lord Cairns' Act 1858, which allows a court to award damages in its equitable jurisdiction '*in lieu of or in addition to*' an injunction; at best Harman J was not willing to exercise this discretion. In any event, the fact that Harman J nevertheless ordered an enquiry into damages against both defendants suggests that there was some confusion present and it is suggested that *Seager* is the more reliable authority, at least in relation to cases in which there has been a change of position following the innocent use of the confidential information.

Authorization

Sometimes, an issue arises as to whether the use of the confidential material is unauthorized. This happens particularly if the confidential information is the result of a joint effort and one or more members of the team that put in the joint effort commit(s) the alleged breach of confidence. Typically, the claimant is a member of the team that did not authorize the use that was made of the information.

Murray v. Yorkshire Fund Managers Ltd[164] was such a case. Mr Murray had contributed a vital section on marketing to a business plan that was drafted by a team of people seeking to take over a company. At a later stage, Mr Murray had been excluded from the team. Nevertheless, the takeover went ahead on the basis of the business plan and Mr Murray sued for breach of confidence. He argued that his section on marketing was protected by an obligation of confidence and that unauthorized use had been made of the information. The action failed in the Court of Appeal, because the court ruled that there had been no unauthorized use of the information. Nourse LJ relied on a dictum of Kekewich J in *Heyl-Dia v. Edmunds*[165] when he considered that, when a team of people had collaborated in the production of confidential information, they were co-owners of it and, in the absence of any contractual restraint, each co-owner was free to deal with the information.[166] In this case, this meant that Mr Murray's former partners were free to use all of the confidential information when they took over the company, because they were the co-owners of the property right in the information.

This outcome is perfectly acceptable in the sense that a single person should not be given a veto over the use of the confidential information in such a situation; that would be an abusive use of the law of confidence. Such a person should rather pursue an action in restitution for the value of his contribution. But the outcome does raise some questions concerning the nature of the action for breach of confidence. The Court of Appeal treated information as property, and drew parallels with co-ownership cases concerning

---

[163] Such an injunction was awarded by Cross J in *National Broach & Machine Co. v. Churchill Gear Machines Ltd* [1965] RPC 61.

[164] [1998] 2 All ER 1015.   [165] (1899) 81 LT 579 at 580.

[166] *Murray v. Yorkshire Fund Managers Ltd* [1998] 2 All ER 1015.

patents and the proprietary aspects of the latter. This may have provided a neat solution in this case, but, clearly, one cannot simply ignore the equitable nature of the action for breach of confidence. It is hard to see how, on this point, *Murray v. Yorkshire Fund Managers Ltd* could have provided the final and conclusive answer.

Detriment

The final element that makes up this head of the law of confidentiality is the question of whether the claimant has to suffer a detriment as a result of the breach of confidence. Clearly, the presence of such detriment is of great assistance in a case in which damages are sought and its presence will strengthen the case for an injunction— but is it essential? Certainly, in *Coco v. A. N. Clark Engineers Ltd*,[167] Megarry J referred to detriment as being part of the definition of the breach of confidence action, although he accepted that there may be arguments for a broader approach to the action without the requirement of detriment and the issue has been discussed in two significant cases.

In *X v. Y*,[168] discussion on the point was obiter, because the doctors who were the subjects of the newspaper story about doctors with AIDS did suffer detriment, in the form of distress caused by the unwarranted intrusion into their lives of reporters in hot pursuit of the story. Nonetheless, Rose J addressed the issue and concluded that detriment in the use of the information was unnecessary, and that an injunction, at least, could be awarded if there was no actual or likely detriment. He emphasized that the cause of action related to the initial disclosure and not the subsequent publication, which was the effective cause of the distress suffered.[169]

In *Spycatcher*[170] too, the issue is considered, but a less-than-clear picture emerges. The failure of the government to restrain the publication of extracts from the book could be seen as reflecting the lack of detriment, due to the pre-existing wide knowledge of the book and its contents. But this factor simultaneously removed the confidentiality of the information itself and it is not therefore clear evidence for the essential role of detriment. Lord Keith[171] took the view that the disclosure of that which was intended to be kept a secret was itself a detriment, so there would thus always be a detriment present and neatly sidestepping the question, although he adds that, in a case brought by the government, harm to the public interest must be demonstrated anyway. Lord Griffiths adopted[172] the *Coco* test as his basic definition and thus appeared to embrace detriment as being essential, agreeing with Lord Keith on the special position in claims by government. Lord Goff, meanwhile, felt that it was still an open question.[173]

In attempting to resolve this conundrum, the first thing to reiterate is the value of detriment in strengthening a claim, whether for damages or for an injunction. Beyond this, it is tempting to follow Rose J and deny the vital nature of detriment in a breach of confidence action. This would help in cases in which confidential information about two people is to be leaked, in which it would disclose negative information about one, who may therefore be reluctant to take the public action of litigation, but which would still permit the other to take action. If a police document is about to be leaked, revealing that A and B have been questioned about a murder, and that A's answers were satisfactory and B's were not, A suffers no detriment by its disclosure, yet clearly still ought to have a right of action.

---

[167] [1969] RPC 41 at 48.   [168] [1988] 2 All ER 648.   [169] [1988] 2 All ER 648 at 658.
[170] *A-G v. Guardian Newspapers (No. 2)* (n. 5).   [171] At 256 and 640.
[172] At 269–70 and 650–1.   [173] At 282 and 659.

The same conclusion can, of course, be reached courtesy of Lord Keith's intellectual acrobatics and the tentative conclusion is offered that no detriment beyond that created by the fact of disclosure per se is necessary to be proven in bringing a breach of confidence action and that, in particular, this should justify injunctive relief with substantial damages available if greater harm ensues.

Remedies for breach of confidence

Injunctions

Little needs to be said here about injunctive relief; the law and practice in relation to breach of confidence is, in most ways, no different from that in other areas of intellectual property and the general coverage of remedies in Chapter 32 is fully relevant here. In *Coco v. Clark*,[174] however, Megarry J laid down some guidelines as to factors that may be relevant in exercising the discretion whether or not to issue an injunction in actions of this type and suggests that damages alone may suffice in a case of subconscious copying (as in *Seager*, two years earlier). He also suggests that the use made by the defendant in reliance on the information may make an injunction to restore the status quo difficult (if not impossible) to award. Clearly, in business-related cases, it may be relatively easier to award damages rather than an injunction, because the damage may be readily quantifiable if, for example, business has been lost, as opposed to cases involving personally confidential matter, in which the distress caused by the disclosure will be far harder to quantify and injunctive relief thus more appropriate. Nevertheless, injunctive relief may still be an appropriate remedy in commercial cases, especially if pre-empting the defendants (often former employees in this case) from disclosing the confidential information is the vital aim of the case.[175]

Therefore, where the claimant has established that the defendant has acted in breach of confidence and that there is a sufficient risk of repetition, the claimant will generally be entitled to an injunction. In exceptional circumstances this will not be the case and there may exist specific discretionary reasons not to grant an injunction.[176] These exceptional circumstances are to be evaluated according to the guidance set out in *Shelfer v. City of London Electric Lighting Co.* by Smith LJ:

> …he is *prima facie* entitled to an injunction.
>
> There are, however, cases in which this rule may be relaxed, and in which damages may be awarded in substitution for an injunction as authorized by this section.
>
> In any instance in which a case for an injunction has been made out, if the plaintiff by his acts or laches has disentitled himself to an injunction the Court may award damages in its place. So again, whether the case be for a mandatory injunction or to restrain a continuing nuisance, the appropriate remedy may be damages in lieu of an injunction, assuming a case for an injunction to be made out.
>
> In my opinion, it may be stated as a good working rule that—
> If the injury to the plaintiff's legal rights is small,
> And is one which is capable of being estimated in money,
> And is one which can be adequately compensated by a small money payment,
> And the case is one in which it would be oppressive to the defendant to grant an injunction:—

---

[174] [1969] RPC 41 at 49 and 50. [175] See *Ocular Sciences* 9 (n. 21) at 409.
[176] *Vestergaard Frandsen* (n. 37).

then damages in substitution for an injunction may be given.

...

It is impossible to lay down any rule as to what, under the differing circumstances of each case, constitutes either a small injury, or one that can be estimated in money, or what is a small money payment, or an adequate compensation, or what would be oppressive to the defendant. This must be left to the good sense of the tribunal which deals with each case as it comes up for adjudication.[177]

Damages

In considering the award of damages in an action for breach of confidence, the first question to consider is what is the precise nature of the action. If the breach of confidence is also a breach of an express or implied term of a contract, an award of damages is appropriate and should be based on the standard contractual principles on which those damages are assessed, as in *Nichrotherm Electrical Company Ltd v. Percy*.[178] If the action is not based on contract, but on the more general equitable principle of confidence, it is clear that damages may also be awarded under the modern successor to Lord Cairns' Act, s. 50 of the Senior Courts Act 1981. This permits the court to award damages '*in addition to, or in substitution for, an injunction*' in any cases in which the court has the '*jurisdiction to entertain an application for an injunction*' and leaves no doubt that damages can be awarded in any case: there is no need for any injunction claim to succeed; it must merely fall within the jurisdiction of the court.[179]

This then raises the question of the way in which these non-contractual damages will be awarded. An answer is provided by a return to the torrid world of stair-carpet grip manufacture in *Seager v. Copydex (No. 2)*.[180] This hearing followed the first case in which it was held that damages should be paid for unconscious copying, because the parties could not agree on an appropriate measure. Lord Denning MR[181] drew an analogy with damages for conversion, under which damages are paid reflecting the value of the goods stolen. Here, too, information has effectively been stolen and so the court has to place a value on it. This can be done in one of two alternative ways: if the information is ordinary confidential information that might be obtained by the use of the services of an expert consultant, then the measure of damages should be the cost of using such a consultant, because that is, in effect, the cost of the information; if, however, the information has a special character and was so inventive or otherwise unusual that no consultant would be likely to be able to provide such information, its value is what it would receive if sold on the open market between a willing seller and a willing buyer,[182] or, perhaps, might be based on what royalties may be gained by exploitation of the information, although this would have the side effect of legitimizing the acquisition of the information by the defendant.

This approach is not without its problems. While claiming to be tortious in approach, the focus seems to be not so much on the claimant's loss, as is usual in tort, but on the defendant's gain, making the claim more quasi-contractual in character.[183] The de jure approval of the defendant's de facto acquisition of the information may

---

[177] *Shelfer v. City of London Electric Lighting Co. (No. 1)* (1895) 1 Ch 287 (CA), per Smith LJ at 322–3.

[178] [1957] RPC 207.

[179] Megarry V-C in *Malone v. Metropolitan Police Comr* [1979] Ch 344 at 360, *sub nom Malone v. Metropolitan Police Comr (No. 2)* [1979] 2 All ER 620 at 633.

[180] [1969] 2 All ER 718, [1969] 1 WLR 809.

[181] [1969] 2 All ER 718, [1969] 1 WLR 809 at 719 and 813.

[182] See *Gorne v. Scales* [2006] EWCA Civ 311.

[183] See N. Jones, 'Restitution of Benefits Obtained in Breach of Another's Confidence' (1970) 86 LQR 463.

also be harsh on a claimant who may still want to exploit the information him- or herself. The fact that the Court of Appeal remitted the application of these principles back to the court of first instance is not helpful to understanding their precise operation.

A particular problem in assessing damages in breach of confidence actions arises in cases in which it is not clear what proportion of the defendant's subsequent trade is due to the misuse of the information and what is due to other factors, such as his or her own efforts, contract, reputation, etc. This was the problem in *Universal Thermosensors Ltd v. Hibben*.[184] The defendants left their employment with the claimants to set up a rival business. They took customer information and other documents away with them. This was clearly in breach of their obligations of confidentiality, but because there was no contractual bar on their setting up a rival business, because they were not using any trade secrets, and given that they were free to use contacts and other information within their own memories, the rest of their activity was legal. The claimants argued, however, that all of the business of the defendants was irrebuttably presumed to be due to the misuse of the confidential information.

Sir Donald Nicholls V-C did not accept this: each item of business was to be looked at separately to see whether the profits were gained by use of the information. The use of common sense might suggest that it was more likely that contacts were made through use of a list of customers deliberately stolen for that purpose than through memory— why else steal the list?—and, generally, doubts would tend to be resolved in the claimant's favour. But applying these principles to the facts, the judge found that only one minor contract was due to misuse of the secret information and the claimant's claim for over £36,000 in damages was reduced finally to £18,610—scant reward for five weeks in court, and a reflection of the fact that the claimant had to show both that the defendants had made contracts using the claimant's information *and* that they would not otherwise have gained the contracts themselves.[185]

Other equitable remedies

The equitable character of the breach of confidence action means that the range of equitable remedies is also available to the claimant. Most significant among these is the action for an account of profits, whereby the claimants can simply demand that the profits made by the defendant after the acquisition of the confidential information are handed over. This is the essence of the claim in *Peter Pan Manufacturing Corp. v. Corsets Silhouette Ltd*.[186] Peter Pan licensed Silhouette to make, on its behalf, a then new design of women's brassieres. After a while, Silhouette used diagrams and examples provided under the licensing agreement to make similar garments to its own account. The obvious problem is, again, to what extent did the breach of confidence contribute to the profits made by Silhouette? Pennycuick J accepted the principle that the account should only be of that proportion of the profits attributable to the breach of confidence, but, on the facts of the case, he found that the manufacture of the garments by Silhouette would have been entirely impossible without the information, reflecting presumably the quantum leap forward that Peter Pan had taken with this new

---

[184] [1992] 3 All ER 257, [1992] 1 WLR 840.

[185] The defendants successfully counterclaimed for £20,000 for losses they had suffered due to the excessive breadth of the interlocutory injunction awarded to the claimants and the consequent harm to their business.

[186] [1963] 3 All ER 402, [1964] 1 WLR 96.

type of garment, and that, in the light of this, the entire profits made on the products in question should be passed to Peter Pan.

In *Spycatcher*,[187] an account of profits was allowed by the House of Lords in favour of the government, as owner of the information, against the *Sunday Times*, which ran extracts from the offending book—but this award begs the kind of questions just raised. Fearing an injunction, no prior publicity was given to the fact that the extracts were to be published; indeed, the first edition did not include them, in case an injunction was promptly obtained. It is far from easy to calculate what proportion, if any at all, of the profits of that edition—which, of course, carried hundreds of articles and advertisements—was due to the unlawful publication of the confidential information.

The House of Lords has now added that an account of profits is only to be awarded as a remedy in those exceptional cases in which the normal remedies, such as damages and injunctions, are inadequate compensation for the breach of the contractual obligation of confidence. The profits of an autobiography that a spy wrote in breach of his obligation of confidence therefore had to be paid to the Attorney-General, because this was the only effective way of stopping the former secret agent from benefiting from his breach of confidence and of securing the proper functioning of the secret service. An injunction that simply froze the payment of royalties to the author until he returned to stand trial, which was an unrealistic prospect, was not an effective remedy and had no basis in law, because it de facto amounted to a confiscatory order.[188]

It is worthwhile noting that other possible remedies that may be available include orders for delivery up and/or destruction of goods that have been made by virtue of unauthorized confidential information.[189] Such orders were appropriately made in the *Peter Pan* case, but, again, this must hinge on the fact that no such manufacture could possibly have taken place but for the misuse of the claimant's confidential information.[190]

The *Norwich Pharmacal* order

A breach of confidence may also happen when confidential information is posted on a website. It may not always be possible for the person affected by the breach to determine who posted the information on the website and is therefore responsible for the breach. The courts have therefore deployed the tool of the *Norwich Pharmacal* order[191] which obliges the owner of the website to reveal the identity of the person posting the message and thereby committing the breach of confidence. A first action is therefore directed against the website owner, in the case at issue the Wikimedia Foundation, and when the order has been issued and the identity of the breach of confidence defendant, who posted the confidential information on Wikipedia, has been revealed a second action, this time for breach of confidence, is brought against the latter defendant.[192]

---

[187] *A-G v. Guardian Newspapers (No. 2)* (n. 5).

[188] *A-G v. Blake (Jonathan Cape Ltd third party)* [2001] 1 AC 268, [2000] 4 All ER 385.

[189] *Ocular Sciences* (n. 21) at 410.

[190] *Ocular Sciences* (n. 21) at 410. But that case also illustrates the point that all legitimate interests of all parties will need to be balanced carefully before these remedies are awarded in all cases in which the defendant's activity is not, in every single detail, based on misuse of the confidential information.

[191] See Ch. 32.

[192] *G and G v. Wikimedia Foundation Inc.* [2009] EWHC 3148 (QB) (2 December 2009, nyr.)

Information—the international dimension

This whole area of confidential information has been regarded as very much the creation of the common law or, rather, of equity. But in this respect, too, the internationalization of the law of intellectual property is now having its impact. Two separate developments need to be noted. First, the problems of patent licensing in EU law, discussed earlier, spill over to information, which is not in itself patentable, but which may be essential to the operation of the patented product or process, or for the most economical manner for using a patented process. Examples might be the instructions for the best possible use of a patented machine. A block exemption on such know-how was created, alongside the block exemption on patent licensing[193] and these have now been fused together into the technology transfer block exemption discussed previously.[194] It is important to note that 'know-how'-type information and the patented product or process are inherently distinct legal notions—but, that said, the controls on their use and dissemination are now the same.

The second development that needs noting is that the TRIPS agreement also extends to cover 'trade secrets',[195] this phrase not equating to the same words in the UK law, but rather relating to the know-how type of information. Signatory states have to ensure that such information is given an appropriate level of legal protection.

Further problems arise due to the fact that confidential information is protected in different national ways in each country: no international level of protection exists. Nonetheless, the use of international communication networks, such as the Internet, has substantially facilitated and increased the international and cross-border flow of (confidential) information. Which court will have jurisdiction to deal with actions concerning breach of confidence or any equivalent action, and which law will be applied by that court? These formidable questions of private international law remain to be answered and a solution is urgently needed.[196]

The Paris Convention and the TRIPS Agreement

Let us come back to the international foundations of this area of law in a bit more detail. Article 10bis of the Paris Convention obliges the member states to provide effective protection and unfair competition. The appropriation of trade secrets without permission is probably one of the clearest examples of acts of unfair competition and, as was seen above, Article 10bis and the reliance on principles of unfair competition is reflected in the national laws of many member states. Section 7 of the TRIPS Agreement then builds on this starting point and Art. 39 of the TRIPS Agreement deals explicitly with the protection of undisclosed information. As all EU member states are bound by the TRIPS Agreement and in the absence of an EU instrument dealing with trade secrets,

---

[193] Regulation 2349/84 on the application of Art. 85(3) of the Treaty to certain categories of patent licensing agreements (1984) OJ 219/15, as amended; Regulation 556/89 on the application of Art. 85(3) of the Treaty to certain categories of know-how licensing agreements (1989) OJ L 61/1, as amended.

[194] Commission Regulation (EEC) 240/96 on the application of Art. 85(3) to certain categories of technology transfer agreements (1996) OJ L 31/2; see Ch. 5. For the most recent version, see Commission Regulation (EU) 316/2014 on the application of Article 101(3) of the Treaty on the Functioning of the European Union to categories of technology transfer agreements [2014] OJ L/93, 17–23.

[195] Part II, Ch. 7, Art. 39 of the TRIPS Agreement [1994] 25 11C 209–37 at 224.

[196] See further J. J. Fawcett and P. Torremans (2nd edn, 2011) *Intellectual Property and Private International Law*, Oxford: Oxford University Press.

the following provision is the common core of the national approaches to trade secret protection:

SECTION 7: PROTECTION OF UNDISCLOSED INFORMATION

Article 39

1. In the course of ensuring effective protection against unfair competition as provided in Article 10*bis* of the Paris Convention (1967), Members shall protect undisclosed information in accordance with paragraph 2 and data submitted to governments or governmental agencies in accordance with paragraph 3.

2. Natural and legal persons shall have the possibility of preventing information lawfully within their control from being disclosed to, acquired by, or used by others without their consent in a manner contrary to honest commercial practices so long as such information:

   (a) is secret in the sense that it is not, as a body or in the precise configuration and assembly of its components, generally known among or readily accessible to persons within the circles that normally deal with the kind of information in question;

   (b) has commercial value because it is secret; and

   (c) has been subject to reasonable steps under the circumstances, by the person lawfully in control of the information, to keep it secret.

3. Members, when requiring, as a condition of approving the marketing of pharmaceutical or of agricultural chemical products which utilize new chemical entities, the submission of undisclosed test or other data, the origination of which involves a considerable effort, shall protect such data against unfair commercial use. In addition, Members shall protect such data against disclosure, except where necessary to protect the public, or unless steps are taken to ensure that the data are protected against unfair commercial use.

Note: For the purpose of this provision, 'a manner contrary to honest commercial practices' shall mean at least practices such as breach of contract, breach of confidence and inducement to breach, and includes the acquisition of undisclosed information by third parties who knew, or were grossly negligent in failing to know, that such practices were involved in the acquisition.

A first important point in this Article is the definition that is offered of the concept of undisclosed information. That definition falls apart into three requirements. First of all, protection is, or should be, available if the information is secret. That is in turn defined as information that is not generally known among or readily accessible to persons within the circles that normally deal with the kind of information in question. Availability of the information in the public domain seems to be the bottom line here. Second, on top of that, the aspect of secrecy must give or add commercial value to the information. And third, the person lawfully in control of the information must take reasonable steps to keep it secret. This is summarized in Figure 29.1:

The importance of this definition is, for example, also shown by the fact that the Italian intellectual property code has copied it quasi-verbatim when defining its trade secret right.

Whilst the focus is clearly on secrecy and the confidential nature of the information, there is virtually no restriction, apart from the element of 'commercial value', on the kind of information that can be protected. In practice, a diverse range of information is covered. Technical knowledge, often referred to in this context as know-how, is the obvious example, but all kinds of commercial data such as information on customers and suppliers, business plans, market strategies, and market research are also included in the range of information that can be protected as a trade secret.

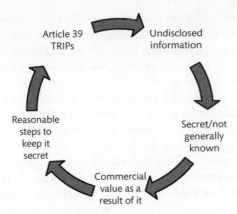

Figure 29.1 Undisclosed information as a cornerstone

A second important point is the indication that is given as to what kind of dealings with trade secrets will entitle their holder to a remedy. Or, if one wants to put it this way, what will amount to an act of unfair competition or when will a tort be committed in relation to a trade secret? On this point Art. 39 of the TRIPS Agreement places the emphasis on the unauthorized disclosure by, acquisition of, or use by others without the consent of the holder of the undisclosed information in a manner contrary to honest commercial practices. The concepts of disclosure, acquisition, or use without the consent of the holder of the undisclosed information are rather straightforward and do not require additional clarification. The qualification that these things need to happen in a manner contrary to honest commercial practices is interesting though and goes beyond a mere reference to unfair competition. The note to Art. 39 explains that for the purpose of that provision, 'a manner contrary to honest commercial practices' shall mean at least practices such as breach of contract, breach of confidence, and inducement to breach, and includes the acquisition of undisclosed information by third parties who knew, or were grossly negligent in failing to know, that such practices were involved in the acquisition. In particular, the reference to third parties who know or who were grossly negligent in failing to know brings in a subjective element. There is, on the other hand, a strong tendency to keep this element to an objective test. Obliging the claimant to prove a subjective element in the mind of the defendant makes effective trade secret protection more burdensome and harder to achieve. There may not be a right in the information that forms the trade secret, but applying merely an objective test makes obtaining protection easier and seems to be more aligned to the practice in relation to intellectual property rights. We will return to this debate later on in this chapter in the context of the proposed EU Directive. Suffice it to say here that the Commission proposal included a subjective element, clearly based in the wording of Art. 39 of the TRIPS Agreement and the note to it, whilst the Council prefers an objective test.

The draft EU Directive

A minimalist approach is proposed

Pushed to an extent by allegations of large-scale espionage by the US, the European Commission proposed a 'Directive on the protection of undisclosed know-how and business information (trade secrets) against their unlawful acquisition, use and disclosure' in

November 2013.[197] The Council has now issued its Opinion (19 May 2014)[198] on the draft Directive, but the European Parliament is still debating the draft. There is therefore not yet a European instrument in this area, let alone one that has been implemented by the member states, but the EU is clearly edging towards a degree of harmonization when it comes to the protection of trade secrets.

Whilst it is true that cybercrime and industrial espionage are challenges that companies in the EU are faced with every day, protecting the strategic assets of EU companies adequately against theft and misuse is only part of the background to the draft Directive. Small and medium-size companies often find the patent system unduly complicated and expensive and they lack the in-house expertise to use it successfully and efficiently. They therefore often rely on the law of trade secrets. A single approach to the threat of the theft of trade secrets will not only simplify matters, it will also boost the confidence of businesses, creators, researchers, and innovators in collaborative innovation across the internal market. What will remain unchanged, however, is that the protection of trade secrets themselves, i.e. the foundation of the alternative to the patent system and of the additional protection that is available for trade secrets, will remain governed by 28 different national laws. These approaches are very different indeed and wholesale harmonization would have been extremely complex and hard to achieve. It is also not clear that there is a real need for such wholesale harmonization in the area of trade secrets. The idea behind the initiative is that the draft will cover the most urgent matters in detail and that in doing so confidence in trade secrets as a tool will increase and that the whole system, whilst still relying on 28 national laws, will become more effective.

The aim is therefore not to put in place a comprehensive EU regime for the protection of trade secrets. There will only be a partial harmonization of the national laws of the member states, focusing on the unlawful acquisition, disclosure, and use of trade secrets, and that harmonization will be of a minimalist nature in the sense that member states may provide, in compliance with the provisions of the Treaty, for more far-reaching protection against the unlawful acquisition, use, or disclosure of trade secrets than that required in the Directive. The Council thought it wise to add that *expressis verbis* to Art. 1 of the draft Directive. Whilst businesses will be able to rely on a minimal level of protection for the their trade secrets in every member state, they will still have to contend with 28 (slightly) different national laws routed in different areas of law. The benefits of this harmonization will therefore be much more limited that the benefits in other areas of intellectual property law, such as trade marks, design, and even copyright.

Definitions

The Directive does of course need a definition of a trade secret. In this respect the draft sticks closely to Art. 39 of the TRIPS Agreement. This is the version of Art. 2 of the draft Directive:

> For the purposes of this Directive, the following definitions shall apply:
>
> (1) 'trade secret' means information which meets all of the following requirements:
>
>   (a) is secret in the sense that it is not, as a body or in the precise configuration and assembly of its components, generally known among or readily accessible to persons within the circles that normally deal with the kind of information in question;

[197] See <http://ec.europa.eu/internal_market/iprenforcement/docs/trade-secrets/131128_proposal_en.pdf>.

[198] See <http://register.consilium.europa.eu/doc/srv?l=EN&f=ST%209870%202014%20INIT>.

   (b) has commercial value because it is secret;

   (c) has been subject to reasonable steps under the circumstances, by the person lawfully in control of the information, to keep it secret;

(2) 'trade secret holder' means any natural or legal person lawfully controlling a trade secret;

(3) 'infringer' means any natural or legal person who has unlawfully acquired, used or disclosed trade secrets;

(4) 'infringing goods' means goods whose design, quality, functioning, manufacturing process or marketing significantly benefits from trade secrets unlawfully acquired, used or disclosed.

Whilst it is the generally accepted definition, it should not be forgotten that this definition is very wide in scope and covers an immense variety of technical and commercial information.

The scope of unlawful acquisition, use, and disclosure

Article 3 then turns to the crux of the matter and defines the scope of violation of a trade secret. Redress is provided for the unlawful acquisition, use, or disclosure of a trade secret. The key concept here is that the relevant activity must be unlawful. In the Commission's proposal proving unlawfulness involved passing a threshold of intention or (at least) gross negligence. This subjective element might raise the burden of proof and is out of line with the traditional approach towards primary infringement of intellectual property. The Council therefore proposed to replace it with a more objective approach that holds that any acquisition, use, or disclosure which is, under the circumstances, considered contrary to honest commercial practices will be unlawful. This is also a return to the text of Art. 39 of the TRIPS Agreement, whereas the Commission had taken over the language of the final sentence of the note to that article. Knowledge as a factor is then restricted to forms of violation that can be characterized as indirect or secondary. In the Council's version this results in the following provision:

[...] 2. The acquisition of a trade secret without the consent of the trade secret holder shall be considered unlawful, whenever carried out by [...] unauthorised access to, copying or appropriation of any documents, objects, materials, substances or electronic files, lawfully under the control of the trade secret holder, containing the trade secret or from which the trade secret can be deduced [or] any other conduct which, under the circumstances, is considered contrary to honest commercial practices.

3. The use or disclosure of a trade secret shall be considered unlawful whenever carried out, without the consent of the trade secret holder by a person who is found to meet any of the following conditions:

   (a) have acquired the trade secret unlawfully;

   (b) be in breach of a confidentiality agreement or any other duty to not disclose the trade secret;

   (c) be in breach of a contractual or any other duty to limit the use of the trade secret.

4. The acquisition, use or disclosure of a trade secret shall also be considered unlawful whenever a person, at the time of acquisition, use or disclosure, knew or should, under the circumstances, have known that the trade secret was obtained directly or indirectly from another person who was using or disclosing the trade secret unlawfully within the meaning of paragraph 3.

5. The production, offering or placing on the market of infringing goods, or import, export or storage of infringing goods for those purposes, shall also be considered an unlawful use of a trade secret when the person carrying out such activities knew, or should,

under the circumstances, have known that the trade secret was used unlawfully within the meaning of paragraph 3.

This provision gives the protection of trade secrets an extremely wide scope. And in certain circumstances such a wide scope of protection will not be appropriate and could trample on other rights. Article 4 tries to address that problem by putting in place a number of limitations. In a first step the article holds the acquisition of trade secrets to be lawful if it is achieved by independent discovery or creation; through observation, study, disassembly, or test of a product or object that has been made available to the public or that it is lawfully in the possession of the acquirer of the information who is free from any legally valid duty to limit the acquisition of the trade secret; or any other practice which, under the circumstances, is in conformity with honest commercial practices. In all these circumstances there is no real obligation of secrecy and definitively no breach of any such obligation. There is, in other words, no clash or conflict with the protection of the trade secret. In a second step, the Article has, however, to deal with those circumstances where there is a real clash with other rights or interests. One thinks here of the freedom of expression of investigative journalists, whistleblowers, workers representatives, etc. The Council has made this distinction very clear by adding a sentence that inserts the principle that any acquisition, use, or disclosure of a trade secret will be lawful to the extent that it is required or allowed, not merely by EU law, but also by the national law of the member state concerned. The reference to national law should not simply be seen as a sign of weak harmonization. National law still governs major issues in our society where trade secrets could potentially interfere with other rights and interests, e.g. in relation to criminal justice, press regulation, or certain elements of labour law and the representation of workers in companies. It is therefore important to state clearly that the Directive will not overrule those other legal provisions. The final paragraph of Art. 4 illustrates that principle by ruling out any remedy for any alleged acquisition, use or disclosure of a trade secret that was carried out:

(a) for making legitimate use of the right to freedom of expression and information;
(b) for the purpose of revealing a misconduct, wrongdoing or illegal activity, provided that the alleged acquisition, use or disclosure of the trade secret was necessary for such revelation and that the respondent acted in the public interest;
the trade secret was disclosed by workers to their representatives as part of the legitimate exercise of their representative functions, provided that such disclosure was necessary for that exercise; [...]
(e) for the purpose of protecting a legitimate interest recognised by Union or national law.

One should not underestimate the importance of Art. 4. There was a clear need to protect other rights and interests, not all of which are in areas of (exclusive) EU competence. The version of the Article suggested by the Council goes a long way in getting the balance between the interest of the holder of the trade secret, on the one hand, and the various other rights and interests that count in our society, on the other, right. The remainder of the effort lies with the member states and the courts when they will implement and apply the Directive.

Redress

The draft Directive provides various form of redress, but the Commission's draft and, even more explicitly through the insertion of the word 'civil' in Art. 5, the Council's draft make it very clear that the draft Directive is only concerned with civil redress. Criminal law is not affected, which, in combination with the minimalist approach of the draft Directive, also means that those national laws that do have criminal sanctions, e.g. for the violation of manufacturing trade secrets, will be allowed to retain these or to introduce additional criminal sanctions. The measures, procedures, and remedies that the member states put in place by way of civil redress need to meet the general standards of fairness, equitableness, effectiveness, and dissuasiveness and need not be unnecessarily complicated or costly, nor entail unreasonable time limits or unwarranted delays. This approach has been copied from the TRIPS Agreement and the Enforcement Directive. Similarly, any application of such measures, procedures and remedies needs to be proportionate and provide safeguards against their abuse. There will also be a limitation period for claims based on the Directive's provisions, but whereas the Commission wants to work with a very short period of one to two years after the holder of the trade secret becomes aware of the breach, the Council prefers to leave this to the member states and to impose merely a maximum limitation period of six years. Both approaches reflect the perceived need to deal quickly with these matters and to remove any uncertainty in the interest of all parties involved.

Legal proceedings concerning a trade secret and its allegedly illegal acquisition, use, or disclosure are of course in themselves a risk for the disclosure of a trade secret. It is therefore important that those involved in the proceedings can be given an obligation not to disclose the trade secret. That is what the Commission's draft did in its Art. 8. The Council's draft takes a more cautious approach and requires a reasoned application by the interested party to install a secrecy regime in relation to information that the competent authorities have identified as confidential. However one deals with it, confidentiality of trade secrets in the course of proceedings is in certain cases necessary and a vital ingredient of any regime dealing with trade secrets.

Just as with many other intellectual property rights, time is often of the essence. Secrecy is something that cannot be restored once it has been broken, making fast measures to prevent the acquisition, use, or disclosure of a trade secret vital. Once a violation has occurred it is vital to stem the breach and to avoid that the consequences of the violation of the trade secret cause irreparable or large-scale damage. The draft Directive addresses these concerns in its Art. 9 by putting in place a system of interim and precautionary measures. The holder of a trade secret can apply to the court for an interim injunction that prohibits or orders the cessation of the use or the disclosure of the trade secret on an interim basis. The holder can also apply for interim measures that deal with allegedly infringing goods. These measures can take the format of an order prohibiting the production, offering, or placing on the market of the allegedly infringing goods, their importation, exportation, or storage for these purposes. Allegedly infringing goods can also be seized or their delivery up can be ordered to prevent their entry into the market or their circulation within the market.

Once a decision on the merits has been reached and the acquisition, use, or disclosure of the trade secret has been held to be unlawful the Draft Directive provides a range of possible measures in its Art. 11. At the top of the list of measures one finds injunctions, essentially to order the cessation or prohibition of the use of the disclosure of the trade secret. A prohibition to produce, offer, place on the market, or use infringing goods that have benefited from the trade secret in any way, or import, export, or store such infringing goods for those purposes may also be granted by the court by way of injunctive relief. On top of that the draft Directive proposes corrective measures with regard to the infringing goods. These infringing goods can be recalled from the market[199] or

---

[199] The holder of the trade secret can also request that the infringing goods are delivered up to it or to charitable organizations.

their infringing quality can be removed. The court can also order the destruction of the infringing goods or the destruction of all or part of any document, object, material, substance or electronic file containing or implementing the trade secret or, where appropriate, the delivery up to the applicant of all or part of those documents, objects, materials, substances, and electronic files.

In addition damages can be awarded, either damages that are commensurate to the actual prejudice suffered or damages as a lump sum (e.g. on the basis of an estimate of royalties that could have become payable for the lawful use of the trade secret). The courts can also order the publication of the judgment.

An overview

Information is not property,[200] at least for the purposes of the criminal law. Nonetheless, the law of breach of confidence has, as it has developed, gone forward to construct a network of rights and duties that protects information and its owners. Once the information crosses the threshold of confidentiality and is transmitted on what we have described as an occasion of confidence, that protection is attained. In defining what is confidential, the law is defining the boundaries of truth that is protected from revelation, and, in drawing this line, it is setting out the balance between the right of the individual or firm to keep a secret and the right of the public at large. Whether this balance is correctly drawn is, ultimately, a matter for the individual reader, but the existence and importance of the public interest defence is of significance in relation to the public's right to know, which is vital in an open and democratic society. If information does not fall within this exception, then it has almost tangible form in the range of rights and remedies open to its owner against those who abuse its confidential character.

The employment cases create variants on this information right. Trade secrets are the subject of strong protection and increasingly appear to be part of a company's property, but cases such as *Hivac Ltd v. Park Royal Scientific Instruments*[201] show a broader legal recognition and protection of a wider range of trading activity. In non-trade-secret cases, meanwhile, it seems that it is the employee who is allowed to transfer skills and knowledge from one job to the next as part of his or her repertoire, and his or her former employer cannot restrain him or her from doing so. So the employee, too, gains new intangible rights from the developing law of breach of confidence and all of these rights have the potential to grow into more tangible forms in years to come, if that is the way in which the law wishes to progress.

Legal history shows that such rights can develop slowly, but inexorably, if there is a perceived need for them so to do. As more and more information becomes available, through the evolution of time and the revolution of technology, it may be that such a need will be perceived—which is not a prediction so much as an awareness of future potential of what may lie at the end of the information superhighway down which we presently inexorably surf.

It may be that trade secrets and confidentiality law will evolve into some form of 'right in information'.[202] The practical circumstances will push it in this direction because a

---

[200] *Oxford v. Moss* (1978) 68 Cr App Rep 183. And see *Force India Formula One Team* (n. 13) at para. 376, per Arnold J.

[201] [1946] Ch 169, [1946] 1 All ER 350.

[202] See J. Reichman, 'Legal Hybrids between the Patent and Copyright Paradigms' (1994) 94 Col LR 2432; see also critiques thereof (1994) 94 Col LR 2559 *et seq.*

common law action can arise without the need to resort to expensive, yet limited term, patent, or trade mark protection, and it nevertheless can protect the essential secrets underlying those property rights. It seems an obvious area for the potential development of a yet stronger new right in due course.

Meanwhile, actions for breach of confidence can already be clearly seen to be filling the gaps between long-standing rights. Copyright could not protect the idea for *Rock Follies*, but confidence could. Patent law could not protect Nichrotherm's hopeless pig-rearing machine, but confidence could. In these and many other cases, it is at the difficult early stages of a project—when a formal intellectual property right is a target, but one that has yet to be achieved—that rights in confidential information may have their most valuable role to play.

Further reading

APLIN, T. et al. (2012) *Gurry on Breach of Confidence: The Protection of Confidential Information*, 2nd edn, Oxford: Oxford University Press.

APLIN, T., 'The Development of the Action for Breach of Confidence in a Post-HRA Era' [2007] IPQ 19.

APLIN, T., 'A Right of Privacy for Corporations?', in P. Torremans (ed.) (2008), *Intellectual Property and Human Rights*, Alphen aan den Rijn: Kluwer Law International, 475–505.

CONAGLEN, M., 'Thinking about Proprietary Remedies for Breach of Confidence' [2008] IPQ 82–109.

SCHREIBER, A., 'Confidence Crisis, Privacy Phobia: Why Invasion of Privacy Should Be Independently Recognised in English Law' [2006] IPQ 160.

SIMS, A., '"A Shift in the Centre of Gravity": The Dangers of Protecting Privacy through Breach of Confidence' [2005] IPQ 27.

30

Computer technology and intellectual property

The relationship between computer technology and intellectual property is a complicated issue, and a huge number of theoretical and practical problems arise in relation to it. It is not our intention to go into much detail here.[1] Our analysis will focus on the headlines and we will accordingly discuss five issues:

- the availability of patent protection for computer hardware and for computer software (computer programs);
- copyright[2] in computer software;
- databases and the *sui generis* right;
- the Internet; and
- semiconductor chip protection.

It should be emphasized that the protection for databases also involves copyright. That aspect has already been referred to in the chapters on copyright and not all of the details will be restated here. Most databases are, nowadays, in electronic form—hence our decision to discuss them in the computer technology chapter—but the regime of protection for databases also extends to non-electronic databases—that is, those based on paper supports.

Patent protection for computer technology

Hardware

It is obvious, but nevertheless important to note, that the normal requirements of patent law will apply in relation to computer technology. In other words, any piece of computer equipment must be new, must involve an inventive step, and must be capable of industrial application if it is to attract patent protection. This does not create specific problems, although the number of patents granted is, in relative terms, rather low, because most developments in computer hardware are constant minor improvements of existing technology, which, although new, do not involve an inventive step and are obvious.

---

[1] We refer the reader to the specialized works on computer law and information technology law.

[2] Other technology-related aspects of copyright infringement, e.g. technical protection measures, are discussed in Ch. 15.

Software

More difficulties arise when one attempts to determine whether a computer program can attract patent protection.[3] The starting point seems rather easy, because s. 1(2)(c) of the Patents Act 1977 explicitly excludes computer programs—but it is not entirely correct to conclude that a computer program will never be patentable, because the exclusion is restricted to a computer program 'as such'.[4] This means that patents cannot be granted for the computer program alone and this rule applies irrespective of the content of the program. For patentability purposes, the invention must comprise something other than the computer program: it must be a computer-related invention.[5]

Various attempts were made to patent software incorporated in a ROM chip,[6] as a piece of hardware, or recorded on any other carrier, such as a floppy disk. All were unsuccessful on the grounds that the applications involved nothing other than the computer program as such: '*The disc or ROM is no more than an established type of artefact in which the instructions are physically embedded. It is merely the vehicle used for carrying them.*'[7]

It would indeed make no sense at all to exclude a computer program from the scope of patent law and allow it back in the form of a CD-ROM containing the very same program.[8] The same conclusion is normally reached when a computer program is loaded into a computer, because it would deprive the computer software exclusion of any practical sense if a non-patentable program, the only conceivable use of which is to run it on a computer, would become patentable if the claims made reference to conventional hardware elements.[9]

Computer-related inventions are not excluded from the scope of patentability.[10] This category is extremely wide in scope, because more and more new inventions involve the use of some software that is incorporated in the device. For example, production-line robots are instructed through the use of a computer program, and all kinds of engines— from that in your car, to those that move the lens and the film in your camera—are controlled by computer software. As long as a technical effect is produced and a technical problem is solved, the exclusion of a computer program as such no longer applies and the invention might be patentable. An example of this approach is found in the *Vicom* case,[11] in which the patent application was concerned with a method and apparatus for improving the quality of pictures and speeding up their processing. A computer program

---

[3] For a detailed analysis, see I. Lloyd (2014) *Information Technology Law*, 7th edn, Oxford: Oxford University Press, Chs. 16 and 17; G. Dworkin (1993) 'The Patentability of Computer Software', in C. Reed (ed.) *Computer Law*, 2nd edn, Oxford: Blackstone, Ch. 5. See also C. Reed (ed.) (2011) *Computer Law*, 7th edn, Oxford: Oxford University Press; D. Booton, 'The Patentability of Computer-Implemented Inventions in Europe' (2007) 1 IPQ 92.

[4] The narrowness of the exception was stressed once more in *Kapur's Patent Application (No. GB05319365.1)* [2008] Bus LR D77.

[5] See *Research in Motion UK Ltd v. Visto Corp.* [2008] Bus LR D89.

[6] *Gale's Application* [1991] RPC 305.   [7] Per Nicholls LJ at 325.

[8] See *Genentech Inc.'s Patent* [1989] RPC 147, per Dillon LJ.

[9] See *IBM/Documents abstracting and retrieving* (T-22/85) [1990] EPOR 98; *IBM/Text processing* (T-65/86) [1990] EPOR 181.

[10] The EU tried to agree a Directive on the patentability of computer-implemented inventions in an attempt to harmonize the different national approaches, but the Council and the Parliament disagreed fundamentally, and, in the end, the project was shelved. See EC Commission (2002) *Proposal for a Directive of the European Parliament and of the Council on the Patentability of Computer-Implemented Inventions*, COM (2002) 92 final, <http://www.europarl.europa.eu/sides/getDoc.do?type=REPORT&reference=A5-2003-238&language=EN>.

[11] *Vicom Systems Inc's Application* (T 208/84) [1987] 2 EPOR 74.

guided all of this, but the technical invention produced a technical effect on the pictures and was thus patentable. One should look at the invention as a whole[12] in assessing whether a technical effect occurs, and it is the question of whether the whole invention as a combination between a computer program and all other elements is patentable that is at issue. It is also not relevant when the technical effect occurs and there is no need to balance the technical features of the invention against its non-technical features. If these requirements are met, a software-related invention may be patentable if it meets the other standard requirements for patentability.[13] The focus of all attention is therefore placed on what the claimed invention achieves, rather than on the manner in which it achieves it.

It must be emphasized, however, that the courts seem to apply the exclusion test twice. The exclusion also applies if a technical effect is produced, but only if that effect or result is itself caught by the exclusion. This means that what is produced is a prohibited item under s. 1(2) of the 1977 Act. A clear illustration is found in Merrill Lynch's application for a patent for a business system and, specifically, for an improved data processing system for implementing an automated trading market for securities. It was said that:

> whatever the technical advance may be, is simply the production of a trading system. It is a data processing system for doing a specific business, that is to say making a trading market in securities. The end result, therefore, is simply 'a method…of doing business', and is excluded by section 1(2)(c)…A data processing system operating to produce a novel technical result would normally be patentable. But it cannot, it seems to me, be patentable if the result itself is a prohibited item under s 1(2). In the present case it is such a prohibited item.[14]

Merrill Lynch's application failed on the second application of the test, even though there was a technical effect.

The position on the issue of patents for software was subsequently summarized neatly in the case of *Fujitsu's Application*.[15] The patent application concerned crystal structures that could be depicted and manipulated on a computer screen by chemists through the use of virtual reality, replacing the use of three-dimensional lattices. The application was turned down for lack of a technical effect. Laddie J summarized the general position as follows at first instance:

1. The types of subject matter referred to in s. 1(2) are excluded from patentability as a matter of policy. This is so whether the matter is technical or not.
2. The exclusion from patentability is a matter of substance, not form. Therefore the exclusion under s. 1(2) extends to any form of passive carrier or recording of excluded subject matter. Thus, merely because a piece of paper is in principle patentable (save to the extent that it lacks novelty), it is not permissible, for example, to record a literary work (s. 1(2)(b)) or a computer program (s. 1(2)(c)) on a piece of paper and then seek patent monopoly for the paper bearing the recorded work. Similarly, it is not permissible, without more, to seek protection for a computer program when it is stored on a magnetic medium or when merely loaded into a computer.
3. Prima facie a computer running under the control of one program is a different piece of apparatus from the same computer when running under the control of another program. It follows that a claim to a computer when controlled by a program or to a method of controlling a computer by a program or to a method of carrying out a process by use of a computer so controlled can be the subject of patent protection.

[12] *Koch & Sterzel/X-ray apparatus* (T-26/86) [1988] EPOR 72; *Merrill Lynch's Application* [1988] RPC 1.
[13] See G. Kolle, 'Patentability of Software-Related Inventions' (1991) 22 IIC 660.
[14] *Merrill Lynch's Application* [1989] RPC 561 at 569.
[15] [1996] RPC 511 (HC), confirmed on appeal [1997] RPC 608 (CA).

However, because the court is concerned with substance, not form, it is not enough for the designer of a new program to seek protection for his creation merely by framing it in one of these terms. The court or patent office has to direct its intention not to the fact that the program is controlling the computer, but to what the computer, so controlled, is doing.

4. Therefore, a data processing system operating to produce a novel result would not be deprived of protection on the ground that it was a program as such. On the other hand, even if the effect of the program is to make the computer perform in a novel way, it is still necessary to look at precisely what a computer is doing, i.e. at the nature of the process being carried out. If all that is being done, as a matter of substance, is the performance of one of the activities defined under s. 1(2) as unprotectable, then it is still unprotectable.[16]

The approach set out in *Fujitsu*[17] was subsequently confirmed in *Crawford's Application*.[18] The patent application at issue described a display system for buses, which could be used to indicate in which of two modes the bus was operating. If the bus were operating in boarding mode, then it would both pick up and drop off passengers; if it were operating only in exit mode, then it would only drop off passengers. The object of the invention was to provide a means of preventing 'bus bunching'—that is, the phenomenon whereby buses arrive in groups rather than at regular intervals. This object was achieved by allowing the bus at the front of a queue to switch into exit mode when it was considered necessary to increase the separation between it and the following buses. When sufficient separation had been achieved, the front bus reverted to a normal mode of operation and the display was switched accordingly. The application for what would effectively have been a business model patent was turned down, because it was the mere presentation of information or a method of doing business. The absence of a technical effect meant it fell under the exclusion from patentability.

The English courts are therefore bound to check whether the invention as defined in the claims made a technical contribution to the known art.[19] If it does not, the exclusion in s. 1(2) of the 1977 Act or its equivalent in Art. 52(2) of the European Patent Convention (EPC) applies. Different approaches have been around though and the approach of the European Patent Office (EPO) has not been consistent. The Court of Appeal identified the different approaches in *Aerotel v. Telco & Marcossan's Application*[20] and suggested that the EPO convene an Enlarged Board of Appeal to arrive at a uniform approach.[21]

The Court described the different approaches as follows:[22]

(1) *The contribution approach*
Ask whether the inventive step resides only in the contribution of excluded matter—if yes, Art. 52(2) applies. This approach was supported by Falconer J. in *Merrill Lynch*[23] but expressly rejected by this Court.

(2) *The technical effect approach*
Ask whether the invention as defined in the claim makes a technical contribution to the known art—if no, Art. 52(2) applies. A possible clarification (at least by way of exclusion) of this approach is to add the rider that novel or inventive purely excluded matter does

---

[16] [1996] RPC 511 (HC) at 530.   [17] *Fujitsu's Application* [1997] RPC 608 (CA).
[18] *Crawford's Application* [2006] RPC 11.
[19] *Aerotel v. Telco & Marcossan's Application* [2007] 1 All ER 225, [2007] RPC 7 (CA) at para. 38.
[20] *Aerotel* (n. 19) at para. 38.
[21] *Aerotel* (n. 19) at para. 75. After a bit of a delay the review did get under way, see President's Reference/ Computer program exclusion (G3/08) [2009] EPOR 9.
[22] *Aerotel* (n. 19), per Jacob LJ at para. 26.   [23] *Merrill Lynch's Application* [1988] RPC 1.

not count as a 'technical contribution'. This is the approach (with the rider) adopted by this Court in *Merrill Lynch*.[24] It has been followed in the subsequent decisions of this Court, *Gale*[25] and *Fujitsu*.[26] The approach (without the rider as an express caution) was that first adopted by the EPO Boards of Appeal, see *Vicom*,[27] *IBM/Text processing*[28] and *IBM/Data processor network*.[29]

(3) *The 'any hardware' approach*

Ask whether the claim involves the use of or is to a piece of physical hardware, however mundane (whether a computer or a pencil and paper). If yes, Art. 52(2) does not apply. This approach was adopted in three cases, *Pension Benefits*,[30] *Hitachi*[31] and *Microsoft/ Data transfer*[32] (the 'trio'). It was specifically rejected by this Court in *Gale*.[33]

However there are variants of the 'any hardware' approach:

(i) Where a claim is to a method which consists of an excluded category, it is excluded by Art. 52(2) even if hardware is used to carry out the method. But a claim to the apparatus itself, being 'concrete' is not so excluded. The apparatus claim is nonetheless bad for obviousness because the notional skilled man must be taken to know about the improved, excluded, method. This is the *Pension Benefits* approach.

(ii) A claim to hardware necessarily is not caught by Art. 52(2). A claim to a method of using that hardware is likewise not excluded even if that method as such is excluded matter. Either type of claim is nonetheless bad for obviousness for the same reason as above. This is *Hitachi*, expressly disagreeing with *Pensions Benefits* about method claims.

(iii) Simply ask whether there is a claim to something 'concrete', e.g. an apparatus. If yes, Art. 52(2) does not apply. Then examine for patentability on conventional grounds— do not treat the notional skilled man as knowing about any improved excluded method. This is *Microsoft/Data Transfer*.

Because in the view of the court there was no immediate prospect of the EPO arriving at a uniform approach, the court suggested that the courts, in applying the UK test, should apply the following structured approach when looking for a technical effect:

(1) properly construe the claim;

(2) identify the actual contribution;

(3) ask whether it falls solely within the excluded subject matter;

(4) check whether the actual or alleged contribution is actually technical in nature.[34]

This approach has since been adopted in a number of cases.[35] At the EPO level the President's reference was held to be inadmissible. The decision of the Enlarged Board[36] also denies that there are contradictory decisions. Instead the Board sees a logical

---

[24] *Merrill Lynch's Application* [1989] RPC 561 (CA).
[25] *Gale's Application* [1991] RPC 305 (CA).   [26] *Fujitsu's Application* [1997] RPC 608 (CA).
[27] *Vicom Systems Inc's Application* (T-208/84) [1987] 2 EPOR 74.
[28] *IBM/ Text processing* (T-65/86) [1990] EPOR 181.
[29] *IBM/Data Processor Network* (T-6/83) [1990] EPOR 91.
[30] *Pension Benefits* (T-931/95) [2002] EPOR 52.   [31] *Hitachi* (T-258/03) [2004] EPOR 55.
[32] *Microsoft/Data Transfer* (T-424/05) [2006] EPOR 52.   [33] *Gale's Application* (n. 25).
[34] *Aerotel* (n. 19) at paras. 48–49.
[35] See e.g. *Symbian Ltd v. Comptroller General of Patents, Designs and Trademarks* [2009] RPC 1 (CA); *Astron Clinica Ltd v. Comptroller General of Patents, Designs and Trademarks* [2008] 2 All ER 742; and *Research in Motion UK Ltd v. Visto Corp.* [2008] Bus LR D89.
[36] <http://www.epo.org/law-practice/case-law-appeals/pdf/g080003ex1.pdf>.

evolution in the EPO's approach. In its view technical effect remains the criterion and whether that technical effect was on a physical entity in the real world is irrelevant.[37]

Copyright protection for computer software

Preliminary issues

The drafters of the Copyright, Designs and Patents Act (CDPA) 1988 included computer programs in the category of literary works.[38] We outlined the provisions of the 1988 Act that apply to literary works in Chapter 10 and we do not intend to repeat them here. These normal copyright rules apply simply to computer programs; we will highlight only specific provisions and the troublesome application of some copyright provisions in relation to computer programs.

The 1988 Act does not define computer programs. This allows for the necessary amount of flexibility in a fast-developing area, in which technological evolutions outdate definitions rapidly. In general terms, it can be said that a computer program is a series of coded instructions that are intended to bring about a particular result when used in a computer.[39] Most computer programs are first written in high-level programming languages, such as COBOL, which bear a fair amount of similarity with normal languages, before they are compiled into machine code in order to allow the computer to run them. This machine code is in binary form—the well-known collection of '0's and '1's.

The 1988 Act protects computer programs; it does not protect, as such, individual files or parts of a program, in the same way as it protects, for example, a novel as a literary work rather than each individual chapter of the novel. It is submitted that the distinction is vital in infringement cases in order to determine whether or not substantial copying has taken place. The program must be taken as a whole when analysing whether infringement has taken place. This seems logical in relation to a novel, for which the test is whether there has been 'substantial' copying of the novel, rather than copying of a paragraph or sentence. This applies *mutatis mutandis* to computer programs. Separate programs can, of course, afterwards be combined in one program, which would, in copyright terms, be treated as a compilation.[40]

A number of authors and practitioners have relied heavily, in this area, on US case law. We do not intend to follow that approach, because there is an important difference between US copyright law and UK copyright law in that the US courts have systematically excluded functional works from the scope of copyright. This has had a profound influence on the case law in relation to computer programs and we will therefore not take this case law as the starting point of our analysis. Although we may have to come back to some of the US cases, we agree with Jacob J that the provisions of the 1988 Act must be the starting point of the analysis.[41]

---

[37] Clearly the UK judiciary and the EPO had a different definition of the word 'technical' in mind. It remains to be seen whether they can now agree on a common or at least compatible approach.

[38] CDPA 1988, ss. 1(1)(a) and 3(1)(b); preparatory design materials for a computer program are also protected as literary work: CDPA 1988, s. 3(1)(c).

[39] See entry 'computer program' in the Britannica Concise Encyclopedia, *Britannica.com*. See also F. Maddix and G. Morgan, *Systems Software: An Introduction to Language Processors and Operating Systems*, Chichester and New York: Halstead Press (1989).

[40] It is not clear from the report in FSR whether this distinction was really made in *Ibcos Computers Ltd v. Barclays Mercantile Highland Finance Ltd* [1994] FSR 275.

[41] *Ibcos* (n. 40) at 302.

Computer programs as literary works in copyright

Originality

Only original literary works attract copyright protection and a computer program must thus be original if it is to attract copyright. The 1988 Act does not, however, define originality. In the UK, we have traditionally used the minimalist definition of originality, which required only that the work was not copied and that a sufficient amount of skill, judgement, and labour had been invested in it. In the copyright chapters, we drew the reader's attention to the marginally higher threshold in the European Copyright Directives and, because the computer program is one of the areas in which the provisions inserted in the 1988 Act find their origin and *raison d'être* in the Computer Software Directive,[42] it is crucial to interpret the originality requirement for computer programs in a European sense, which requires the program to be the author's own intellectual creation. The lack of a definition of the concept of originality in the 1988 Act enables us to adopt the European approach for computer programs and we are bound to accept it, because otherwise we would be in breach of our duty to implement the Directive.

A major part of the originality of traditional literary works such as novels or plays is found in the plot. The issue is more complex when software is concerned, but it can be argued that the alternative for the plot is in such a case the algorithms or the operational sequences and that the required originality is to be found there, as well as potentially in the architecture of the program if a lot of work and expertise had gone into creating the latter.[43]

Idea and expression

Copyright only protects expression and does not protect ideas. This statement, which was qualified in the copyright chapter, must now be applied to computer programs: so what is an idea? Clearly, the starting point and the reason for which a computer program is written come within this category. In the famous US *Whelan* case,[44] a program was written to manage a dentistry laboratory. This was clearly part of the idea, as was the list of functions that the program should be able to perform and the targets it should meet; how all of this was to be achieved in practice forms part of the expression of that idea and this not only includes the code lines of the program, but also its structure. The latter refers to the way in which the various parts and files are organized.[45] But the precise borderline between idea and expression cannot be drawn in theory. As Judge Learned Hand said, already more than half a century ago: '*Nobody has ever been able to fix that boundary and nobody ever can.*'[46] It has to be fixed in each individual case on the basis of the facts of that case.

In a case that was concerned with computer games, the Court of Appeal held that the mere 'idea' as to what the program should do was not protected by copyright, because it had nothing to do with the nature of the work. The nature of the work was instead

---

[42] EC Council Directive on the legal protection of computer programs (1991) OJ L 122/42; the modifications were introduced in the CDPA 1988 by the Copyright (Computer Programs) Regulations 1992, SI 1992/3233. The Directive has now been codified as Directive 2009/24/EC of the European Parliament and of the Council on the legal protection of computer programs (codified version) [2009] OJ L 111/16.

[43] *Cantor Fitzgerald International v. Tradition (UK) Ltd* [2000] RPC 95.

[44] *Whelan Associates Inc. v. Jaslow Dental Laboratory Inc.* [1987] FSR 1.

[45] Jacob J rejects the idea–expression dichotomy in *Ibcos Computers Ltd v. Barclays Mercantile Highland Finance Ltd* (n. 40) at 291, but reintroduces it as the general–detailed idea dichotomy. It is submitted that there is no difference in substance between his concept and ours.

[46] *Nichols v. Universal Pictures Corp.* 45 F 2d 119 (1930).

a computer program that had all of the necessary coding to function. That expression would be a copyright work. The general idea was only faintly related to that.[47] Similarly, it was held in a case concerning booking software for airlines that, while the computer program as such could be protected, it would be an unjustifiable extension of copyright to include the protection of mere ideas if copyright were to be granted to the business logic of the program on its own.[48]

Fixation

The obvious way that comes to mind of recording a computer program is the written draft version of the source code of a program. It is indeed reasonable to expect that many software developers would write the source code down, and develop flow charts and other similar things, when developing a new computer program. In this scenario, the machine code version of the program could be seen to be an adaptation of the work. But it is possible that the program never existed in such form and this does not deny it copyright protection. Section 3(2) of the 1988 Act allows the work to be recorded 'in writing or otherwise' and what is really required is a fixation of the work with a certain degree of permanency. Fixation on the hard disk or on a floppy disk clearly meets this requirement.

A program can also be permanently hard wired in a microprocessor in the form of 'microcode' or 'microprograms'.[49] The RAM memory of a computer constitutes a difficult problem. A program that exists only in the RAM memory of the computer exists only in the form of electrical currency and, when the power supply is interrupted, the program disappears. At first sight, this does not involve the required degree of permanency, but the conclusion may be different if such a program lives in the RAM or a similar memory of a computer network[50] and if it is quite unreasonable to expect the network to be shut down in the foreseeable future.[51] The example of software made available via the various bulletin boards of the Internet comes to mind.

So what is really protected?

In a computer program, the expression is protected. We hold this to include the code lines and the structure of the program. But this expression is only protected in so far as it meets the originality requirement: it must be the author's own intellectual creation. This implies that there is more than one way to express the idea, otherwise the one possible way of doing so cannot be the author's own intellectual creation or his or her particular way of expressing the idea. This leads us to the conclusion that those parts of the computer program that can only be expressed in one way if a certain result is to be achieved, due to technical restrictions, are not original and do not attract copyright.[52] These parts of the program can be copied freely; to hold otherwise would bring the development of new software and the whole software industry to a standstill.

---

[47] *Nova Productions Ltd v. Mazooma Games Ltd, Nova Productions Ltd v. Bell Fruit Games Ltd* [2007] RPC 25, [2007] ECC 21 (CA).

[48] *Navitaire Inc. v. Easyjet Airline Co. Ltd* [2005] ECDR 17, [2006] RPC 3.

[49] Programs stored in the ROM (read-only memory) of the computer are still literary works in the copyright sense, because the mode of storage does not affect the nature of the program: see the US case *NEC Corp. v. Intel Corp.*, 645 F Supp 1485 (D Minn 1985).

[50] See *TriadSystems Corp. v. Southeastern Express Co.*, US District Court for the Northern District of California 31 USPQ 2D 1239; *Mai Systems Corp. v. Peak Computer Inc., Vincent Chiechi & Eric Francis*, US Court of Appeals for the ninth Circuit 991 F 2d 511, 26 USPQ 2D 1458.

[51] Especially because other electromagnetic ways of storing works—such as audio cassettes—will also only last for a number of years.

[52] *Total Information Processing Systems v. Daman* [1992] FSR 171.

It can be seen here why the European interpretation of the originality requirement is vital in this context. It fulfils an essential role in the system set up by the Directive and implemented in UK law. It also allows the UK to avoid the need to rely on the US case law[53] and its principle that functional works do not attract protection for which there is no legal basis at all in UK copyright law.

Directive 91/250 protects all forms of expression of a computer program and the preparatory design work capable of leading, respectively, to the reproduction or the subsequent creation of such a program. That led the Court of Justice first of all to the conclusion that the source code and the object code of a computer program were forms of expression which were entitled to copyright protection as computer programs, by virtue of Art. 1(2) of the Directive.[54] However, neither the functionality of a computer program,[55] nor the programming language and the format of data files used in a program to exploit certain of its functions, constituted a form of expression of that program for the purposes of Art. 1(2) of the Directive. To accept that the functionality of a program could be protected by copyright would after all amount to making it possible to monopolize ideas and only the individual expression of such work is capable of protection.[56] On the same basis, a computer program's graphical user interface is excluded from protection as a computer program, as it does not constitute a form of expression of a computer program. That does, however, not exclude it from (potential) copyright protection as a normal copyright work.[57]

Infringement

Infringement can take various forms, but the most obvious is copying. It is important to keep in mind that, in relation to copying, a three-stage test has to be applied:

1. Does the work attract copyright protection?
2. Has there been copying of the elements protected by copyright?
3. Was the copying substantial?[58]

If copying took place, the next issue to consider is whether a defence was available, but let us first turn to infringement and, more specifically, to the various forms of copying.

Literal copying

The literal copying of a computer program, in which parts of code lines are copied and both programs are written in the same programming language, was discussed at length by Jacob J in *Ibcos Computers v. Barclays Mercantile Highland Finance.*[59] Having established that copyright existed in the program that was allegedly copied,

---

[53] *Whelan Associates Inc. v. Jaslow Dental Laboratory Inc.* [1987] FSR 1 uses the phrase that the task dictates the form, while *Computer Associates v. Altai*, 982 F 2d 693 (1992) (2nd Cir) refers to elements dictated by efficiency.

[54] Case C-393/09, *Bezpecnostni Softwarova Asociace - Svaz Softwarove Ochrany v. Ministerstvo Kultury* [2011] ECDR 3.

[55] See also *SAS Institute Inc v. World Programming Ltd* [2013] EWCA Civ 1482, [2014] RPC 8.

[56] Case C-406/10, *SAS Institute Inc. v. World Programming Ltd* [2012] 3 CMLR 4.

[57] Case C-393/09, *Bezpecnostni Softwarova Asociace - Svaz Softwarove Ochrany v. Ministerstvo Kultury* (n. 54)

[58] Cf. *Ibcos Computers* (n. 40).

[59] *Ibcos Computers* (n. 40); see also *Cantor Fitzgerald International v. Tradition (UK) Ltd* [2000] RPC 95.

the judge turned his attention to the question of whether there had been copying. He stated:

> For infringement there must be copying. Whether there was or not is a question of fact. To prove copying the plaintiff can normally do no more than point to bits of his work and the claimant's work which are the same and prove an opportunity of access to his work. If the resemblance is sufficiently great then the court will draw an inference of copying. It may then be possible for the claimant to rebut the inference—to explain the similarities in some other way. For instance he may be able to show both parties derived similar bits from some third party or material in the public domain. Or he may be able to show that the similarities arise out of a functional necessity—that anyone doing this particular job would be likely to come up with similar bits.[60]

He went on to clarify that '*at this stage... both the important and the unimportant bits of the works being compared count*'.[61]

In the case before him, Jacob J found that there was plenty of evidence of copying. There were common spelling mistakes, similar headings, redundant and unexplained bits of code that appeared in both programs, and the allegedly infringing program contained a part of the original program in its source code even though it did not use this part.[62] All of these items are good examples of the kind of evidence for which the claimant is looking and with which the defendant will have great difficulties if he or she is to explain away the similarities.

The next issue is whether that copying amounts to the copying of a substantial part of the copyright-protected work. It should be remembered that a purely quantitative approach is not appropriate here and that qualitative issues are predominant. Jacob J suggested that it comes down to:

> a question of degree where a good guide is the notion of overborrowing of the skill, labour and judgment which went into the copyright work.... In the end the matter must be left to the value judgment of the court.[63]

He agreed with the statement of Ferris J in the *John Richardson* case[64] that '[c]onsideration is not restricted to the text of the code',[65] while adding:

> That must be right: most literary copyright works involve both literal matter (the exact words of a novel or computer program) and varying levels of abstraction (plot, more or less detailed of a novel, general structure of a computer program). I therefore think it right to have regard in this case not only to... 'literal similarities' but also to... 'program features' and 'design features'.[66]

In the *Ibcos Computers* case, substantial copying had clearly taken place. Reference was, in this respect, made to the program structure, to an extremely long list of individual parts of the program, and to the file transfer programs.[67]

Non-literal copying

It flows from our discussion of what is the expression that is protected by copyright in the context of computer programs that non-literal copying can also infringe the copyright in a computer program. Examples are the copying of the structure of the program and the copying of parts of the program, while translating it in another programming language.

[60] *Ibcos Computers* (n. 40) at 296–7.   [61] *Ibcos Computers* (n. 40) at 297.
[62] *Ibcos Computers* (n. 40) at 297–301.   [63] *Ibcos Computers* (n. 40) at 302.
[64] *John Richardson Computers Ltd v. Flanders* [1993] FSR 497.
[65] *John Richardson Computers* (n. 64) at 526.   [66] *Ibcos Computers* (n. 40) per Jacob J at 302.
[67] *Ibcos Computers* (n. 40) at 304–14.

The test we described in the previous section also applies to cases of indirect copying, but it will, in practice, be more difficult to determine what exactly has been copied and whether that copying is substantial.

Ferris J was confronted with a case of indirect copying in the *John Richardson* case.[68] In this case, the original program was written in BASIC, for use on a Tandy computer, and aimed to assist pharmacists in controlling their stock and in producing labels for prescriptions. A former employee produced the allegedly infringing version, which was written in QuickBasic, for use on an IBM personal computer. Owing to the use of different programming languages, the judge found no literal copying, but, when looking at the structure and the sequence of the programs, the input and output routines, the formats, the menus, the options, and facilities of the programs, he found 17 objective similarities that could not readily be justified by the defendant.

Ferris J then considered and applied the test established by the US case of *Computer Associates v. Altai*.[69] He stated:

> In the test propounded in *Computer Associates* the discovery of a program's abstraction is the first step. The second step is to filter these abstractions in order to discover a 'core of protectable material'. In the process of filtration there are to be excluded from consideration (a) elements dictated by efficiency; (b) elements dictated by external factors and (c) elements taken from the public domain.[70]

We agree with Jacob J's comment in *Ibcos Computers* that this approach is neither appropriate nor helpful.[71] In any case, Ferris J found it difficult to apply the test to the facts of the case that he had in front of him and his application was criticized for not carrying out the second stage of the test.

We submit that a proper application of the originality criterion, as explained, will result in the elements that the *Computer Associates* test sets out to eliminate to arrive at the core of protectable elements not being protected by copyright in the first place. At the infringement stage, it is then only necessary to consider those parts that are protected by copyright, and to determine which of them have been copied and whether that copying is substantial. This is also the core of the approach taken by Jacob J in *Ibcos Computers*. Although that was a case involving literal copying, he seemed to suggest that his approach was also valid in non-literal copying cases.[72]

That focus on what is protected by copyright and on whether a substantial part of the protected work has been copied is also found in *Nova v. Mazooma*.[73] The Court of Appeal in that case also helpfully restated the principle that not every non-literal similarity means that there is infringement and, indeed, that merely making a program that emulated another program without copying any of the code or graphics is legitimate, and does not amount to an infringement.[74]

Navitaire Inc. v. Easyjet Airline Co. & Bulletproof Technologies Inc.[75] dealt with copyright in software and while it is, in essence, an infringement case, it also neatly

---

[68] *John Richardson Computers Ltd v. Flanders* (n. 64).

[69] *American Computer Associates v. Altai* 982 F 2d 693 (1992).

[70] *American Computer Associates* (n. 69) at 526. [71] *Ibcos Computers* (n. 40) at 302.

[72] *Ibcos Computers* (n. 40) at 302; see L. Jacobs, 'Demystifying Copyright Infringement of Computer Software: *Ibcos Computers v. Barclays Mercantile*' [1994] 5 EIPR 206, 208–9.

[73] *Nova Productions Ltd v. Mazooma Games Ltd, Nova Productions Ltd v. Bell Fruit Games Ltd* [2007] RPC 25, [2007] ECC 21 (CA).

[74] In the process, the Court of Appeal referred to *Navitaire Inc. v. Easyjet Airline Co. & Bulletproof Technologies Inc* [2005] ECDR 17, [2006] RPC 3 with approval.

[75] *Navitaire* (n. 74).

summarizes a couple of other points concerning the scope of copyright in relation to software. Navitaire brought an infringement action against easyJet and BulletProof software developers. In the past, easyJet had taken a licence from Navitaire's predecessor in title for an airline booking system, OpenRes, for use in so-called 'ticketless' flight reservation transactions. Under the licence agreement, Navitaire also supplied easyJet with a program, TakeFlight, that provided an interface to OpenRes that enabled it to be used on the Internet. Subsequently, easyJet used another web interface. BulletProof, in consultation with easyJet's information technology department, wrote the code for a booking system, eRes, which allegedly breached the terms of the licence and infringed Navitaire's copyright in various works that contributed to the source code of OpenRes.

Navitaire maintained that the 'business logic' of the OpenRes system had been appropriated by easyJet's new system, which possessed a user interface that was substantially indistinguishable from the OpenRes system. Navitaire claimed that the copyright in OpenRes had been infringed by, among other things, 'non-textual copying'. It is important to note that the parties agreed that none of the underlying software in any way resembled that of the other. The similarity was limited to the fact that the software acted upon identical, or very similar, inputs and that it produced very similar results. The non-textual copying allegations focused on command names and screen displays.

Navitaire submitted, among other things, that:

(i)   each individual computer command name was a copyright work in its own right or that each complex group of commands was a work in its own right;

(ii) the collection of commands as a whole was entitled to copyright protection as an original literary work in that it was a 'compilation'; and

(iii) the template of certain of the screen displays was a copyright work in respect of each display derived from it.

Pumfrey J held that neither individual command names nor collections of complex commands had the necessary qualities of a literary work for them to be regarded as being protectable by copyright. The source code of Navitaire's program recorded the complex commands, in the sense that it was possible to analyse the code to ascertain that a computer, operating according to that code, would recognize the command. The 'syntax' of commands was, however, recorded without being stated and, although a computer program controlled a machine, the result of that control might not appear from the program at all. A defined user command interface did, in fact, amount to an ad hoc computer language and the Software Directive[76] made it clear that computer languages were not protected.

Screen displays comprised of characters were properly to be viewed as 'tables' under s. 3 of the 1988 Act. They were therefore literary works for the purposes of copyright protection. They provided a static framework for the display of dynamic data that it was the task of the software to produce. But when the court turned to the facts of the case, it ruled that, on consideration of display aspects of OpenRes and eRes, there had been no infringement of the character-based screen displays. Navitaire's action accordingly failed in this respect.[77]

Screen layouts comprised of material other than characters may, in the view of the court, be protected under copyright as artistic works. Although Navitaire's visual screen displays were recorded as such only in the complex code that displayed them, this form of

---

[76] EC Council Directive on the legal protection of computer programs (1991) OJ L 122/42, Recitals 13–15.
[77] *Navitaire* (n. 74).

recording was strictly analogous to simpler digital representations of graphic works and, in that respect, sufficient skill and labour had been utilized. There had been infringement of that copyright and Navitaire's action therefore succeeded in respect of those screens.[78]

The court also found that a sufficient degree of skill and labour had gone into the drawings of icons appearing in Navitaire's software for them to be protected by copyright, and that these had been copied exactly by easyJet and BulletProof. There had therefore been copyright infringement in this respect.[79]

Adaptations

Copyright can also be infringed by making an adaptation of a protected work; this also applies to computer programs.[80] In this context, an adaptation of a computer program is made whenever the source code, which is written in a high-level programming language, is compiled into machine code (also referred to as 'object code') in binary. An adaptation is also made when the binary machine code is disassembled into a low-level assembly language. This process is used to reveal the ideas and the techniques that are contained in the program, and which are not identifiable in an endless binary sequence. The reverse process is called assembling and also involves, obviously, an adaptation of the program.

Defences

Copyright contains a long list of defences against alleged copyright infringement. We will refer here only to defences that are available only in relation to computer programs.

Reverse engineering

It is a common practice in the software industry to reverse engineer a computer program. This means that the object code version of the program is converted into a more readily understandable version, such as the source code. This allows the programmer to discover how the program works and this knowledge will then be used to develop a new program. This new program can eventually be a competing program, although, in most cases, the main objective of the process of reverse engineering is to discover the interfaces of the program, which are to be copied in the new program if it is to be compatible with the existing one. The latter technique is known as decompilation for interoperability purposes and the European Software Directive[81] has introduced it into copyright as a defence against the copying that necessarily forms part of the technique. It has to be emphasized that copyright only allows the reverse engineering decompilation technique to be used for the purposes of achieving interoperability.

The decompilation right makes it lawful to convert a computer program that is expressed in a low-level language into a version in a higher-level language[82] and to copy the program incidentally in the course of converting it.[83] A number of conditions apply to this decompilation right. First, it must be necessary to decompile the program to obtain the information necessary to create an independent program that can be operated with the program decompiled or with another program.[84] Second, the information that is obtained is not to be used for any purpose other than the objective that is outlined in the first condition.[85] The decompilation right does not exist if the potential decompiler has ready access to the information that he or she needs to obtain interoperability.[86] This will

---

[78] *Navitaire* (n. 74).   [79] *Navitaire* (n. 74).   [80] See CDPA 1988, s. 21(3) and (4).
[81] (1991) OJ L 122/42, Art. 6.   [82] CDPA 1988, s. 50B(1)(a).   [83] CDPA 1988, s. 50B(1)(b).
[84] CDPA 1988, s. 50B(2)(a).   [85] CDPA 1988, s. 50B(2)(b).   [86] CDPA 1988, s. 50B(3)(a).

obviously be the case if, for example, the interfaces are described in the user manual or are available from the producer of the program upon simple request. The right also no longer exempts any infringement if the information obtained is communicated to third persons when this is not necessary to achieve interoperability,[87] or when the information obtained is used to create a program that is similar in its expression.[88] Other acts that are restricted by copyright cannot be defended by invoking the decompilation defence, which means that the decompiler's activity is restricted to those acts that are necessary to get access to the information concerning the interfaces.[89]

The defence will make it possible to gain access to the technical details of, for example, an operating program such as Microsoft Windows, should Microsoft not make that information available itself. Because it is vital for independent producers of application software that their program can be run under Windows—the world's most popular operating program—in order to make their potential market as large as possible, they need to know these interfaces and incorporate them into their program. The defence thus plays an important role in the software industry and enhances competition, while not permitting the outright copying of other parts of a computer program. To make sure that it fulfils this role adequately, it cannot be restricted or prohibited by contract.[90]

Having excluded the matter from the scope of the fair dealing provisions, the Copyright and Related Rights Regulations 2003 have added a s. 50BA to the 1988 Act.[91] According to that new section:

(1) It is not an infringement of copyright for a lawful user of a copy of a computer program to observe, study or test the functioning of the program in order to determine the ideas and principles which underlie any element of the program if he does so while performing any of the acts of loading, displaying, running, transmitting or storing the program which he is entitled to do.

(2) Where an act is permitted under this section, it is irrelevant whether or not there exists any term or condition in an agreement which purports to prohibit or restrict the act.

That provision is based on Art. 5(3) of the Directive and this exception to observe, study, or test the functioning of the programme without authorization cannot be overruled or restricted by contract. A licensee is therefore not restricted to what is allowed in the licence (e.g. the purpose for which the program can be tested could purportedly be restricted in the licence) and can rely on the full breadth of the exception.[92]

An important restrictive condition that applies to the decompilation right, as well as to any of the other computer software specific defences that we will discuss in the next two sections, is that the defences can only be invoked by a person described in the 1988 Act as a 'lawful user'.[93] This is a person who has the right to use the computer program and who has obtained this right under a licence or otherwise. Licensees and persons who act for them, such as their employees, are clearly lawful users, but it is submitted that the category also includes independent consultants and agents working for the licensee, and all persons who need to use and eventually copy the program if they are to exercise their legal duties, such as receivers, auditors, or solicitors executing a search order.[94] It also includes persons who obtained a copy of the program through rental or loan.

---

[87] CDPA 1988, s. 50B(3)(c).   [88] CDPA 1988, s. 50B(3)(d).   [89] CDPA 1988, s. 50B(3)(b).

[90] CDPA 1988, s. 50B(4).

[91] Regulations 9 and 15, respectively. And see *SAS Institute Inc. v. World Programming Ltd* [2013] EWHC 69 (Ch).

[92] Case C-406/10, *SAS Institute Inc. v. World Programming Ltd* [2012] 3 CMLR 4.

[93] CDPA 1988, s. 50A(2).   [94] See Ch. 32 on remedies for more details.

Backup copies, adapting a program, and error correction

The lawful user of a computer program is allowed to make a back-up copy of the computer program if he or she needs to have such a copy for the lawful use of the program[95] and this right cannot be restricted or prohibited by contract.[96] The lawful user can also adapt the program or copy it if this is necessary for the lawful use of the program—for example, to adapt the standard program slightly to meet the specific needs of the lawful user—but this facility can be prohibited by the terms of the contract under which the lawful user is using the computer program.[97]

The lawful user always has the right to correct errors in the program;[98] to hold otherwise would deprive the lawful user of the full use of the program and of some of his or her contractual rights, because it must be an implied term of each contract by which a computer program and the lawful right to use it is acquired that the program is supplied for error-free use.

Databases

The UK has implemented the EU Database Directive[99] and the discussion that follows is therefore primarily based on the Copyright and Rights in Databases Regulations 1997.[100] The regime[101] came into force on 1 January 1998.

A database

The term 'database' has been defined as a collection of independent works, data, or other materials, which are arranged in a systematic or methodical way, and are individually accessible by electronic or other means.[102] This definition can be summarized by means of a number of points, as follows:

1. A database has to be a collection of independent material. In practice, this means that separate items that do not interact with each other are stored in a database. The non-interaction rule excludes items such as a film, in which the script, music, etc. interact to form the final work.

   This requirement raises the question how small an item of independent material can be. The CJEU uses in this respect the criterion that the piece of information concerned must after extraction or when seen as such on its own retain sufficient value for a third party to be interested in it. In the case at issue[103] Freistaat Bayern published topographic maps. These are essentially composed of data describing the nature of each specific point on the surface of the territory concerned (e.g. hill, tree, or building) in terms of the feature and its coordinates. The defendant had

---

[95] CDPA 1988, s. 50A(1).   [96] CDPA 1988, s. 50A(3).   [97] CDPA 1988, s. 50C(1).

[98] CDPA 1988, s. 50C(2).

[99] European Parliament and Council Directive on the protection of databases [1996] OJ L 77/20.

[100] SI 1997/3032.

[101] See J. N. Adams, '"Small Earthquake in Venezuela": the Database Regulations 1997' [1998] EIPR 129.

[102] CDPA 1988, s. 3A(1); the European Court of Justice ruled that a database is 'any collection of works, data, or other materials, separable from one another without the value of their contents being affected, including a method or system ... for the retrieval of each of its constituent material' in Case C-444/02, Fixtures Marketing v. OPAP [2004] ECR I-10549.

[103] Case C-490/14 Freistaat Bayern v. Verlag Esterbauer GmbH, 29 October 2015, nyr, see <http://curia.europa.eu>.

extracted some of these data through scanning to make its own specific maps. The question arose whether the original maps were databases and this hinged on the answer to the question whether each bit of geographical data that was extracted amounted to independent material for the purposes of the Directive. The CJEU held that it did, because the material kept its informative value for the defendant, even if most of its informative value was lost when the extraction took it out of the context of the overall map. This approach is very wide in scope and brings many items within the definition of a database, be it in analogue or in digital form.

2. The works in a database can be works that are protected by copyright, as well as non-copyrightable data or any other materials. Copyright protection for these items, as such, is not required and a database can contain a mixture of different items: for example, a combination of copyright works and other data.

3. The items in a database must be accessible on an individual basis—that is, one must be able to retrieve them individually. This excludes numerous multimedia works in which the user necessarily gets access to a combination of works in different media at any one time during the use of the work.

4. Both electronic and non-electronic collections or databases are included in the scope of the definition.

5. The independent works, etc., must be arranged in a systematic or methodical way. Putting random information and items in a box will therefore not create a database—but it can be argued that a newspaper is a database, because the articles in it (which are independent and individually accessible works) are arranged in a systematical way (grouped by home news pages, overseas news pages, etc.).

This final requirement creates specific problems in relation to electronic databases. Often, the information is fed into the system in a random way, while the software of the database[104] organizes the information afterwards. The physical storage of the information in the memory of the computer (or on floppy disk, CD-ROM, etc.) is not even necessarily in the same or another systematic way.

It is submitted that these collections nevertheless meet the arrangement criterion. A systematic or methodical arrangement exists and it is provided by an element of the database itself. The technical way in which this is achieved is irrelevant in this context. The conclusion must be different when the arrangement is provided by an element outside the database itself. A clear example is the Internet, which forms a collection of independent and individually accessible materials. A systematic arrangement is missing, however, and the presence of search engines[105] cannot change that. These search engines are external to the collection of materials and so is the arrangement of the materials that they provide. A collection such as the Internet is therefore not a database.

Copyright protection for a database

A database is a complex product or work, in relation to which copyright can be involved at many stages. A first distinction needs to be drawn between the computer program,[106] which allows the database to be set up and which organizes the data, and provides the search facilities, etc. and the contents of the database. The special regime of protection

---

[104] Which forms part of the database as a product and is sold, or made available, as an integral part of it.
[105] These pieces of software can be protected by copyright as computer programs.
[106] See Art. 1(3) of the Directive.

for the database does not affect either of these. The computer program will potentially be protected by copyright as a computer program, under the provisions that implement the Software Directive, if it meets the standard requirements for computer programs. Those items that are included in a database and which were works protected by copyright will continue to benefit from the protection afforded to them in that way. The rights of the owner of the copyright in these works will not change and neither will the ownership of that copyright. Unprotected works, data, and other materials will not attract copyright through their inclusion in a database.

Second, the contents and the computer programs, and the copyright in them, need to be distinguished from the database and any potential copyright in the database. Any copyright in a database will have to be independent from the rights in the contents etc. and will come on top of the existing rights; it may also be awarded to different owners. What is left apart from the contents etc. resembles a compilation. Prior to the implementation of the Database Directive, many databases could indeed be protected and the new regime makes it clear that the category of compilations now excludes any work that is a database.[107]

Copyright in a database is thus confined to the selection and arrangement or structure of the materials that are contained in it. As a work, a database has been categorized as a form of literary work.[108] The originality criterion that applies to databases is the slightly higher originality criterion that is found in all European Directives:

> a literary work consisting of a database is original if, and only if, by reason of the selection or arrangement of the contents of the database the database constitutes the author's own intellectual creation.[109]

This 'author's own intellectual creation' criterion has now been copied *expressis verbis* into UK legislation in relation to databases. In so far as this implies that it only applies to databases, the UK is flagrantly in breach of the Software Directive, because, as we have seen, the slightly higher criterion should apply there too. The new originality criterion means that some intellectual judgement that is the author's own must have gone into the selection of the materials or into the method of their arrangement.[110] This approach will deny copyright protection to most modern databases: for example, because they aim at a complete coverage of a certain topic, rather than at selecting material, or because they arrange their materials in an alphabetical or other standard way, rather than in an original way. This approach must be applauded, because the alternative would have involved the grant of multiple copyrights in standard and commonplace structures, and such a multitude of exclusive rights could have stifled competition in this area.

The limited scope of copyright protection on this point became even clearer when the Court of Justice ruled that the Directive's emphasis on the fact that the selection or arrangement of the data amounts to an original expression of the creative freedom of the author implies that any intellectual effort located not in the selection or arrangement of the data but in their creation is irrelevant and cannot lead to copyright protection for the database. The focus on the originality in terms of selection and arrangement of the data also means that it is irrelevant whether or not that selection or arrangement includes the addition of important significance to the data and on its own the investment

---

[107] CDPA 1988, s. 3(1).   [108] CDPA 1988, s. 3(1).   [109] CDPA 1988, s. 3A(2).

[110] Cf. the US approach in *Feist Publications v. Rural Telephone* 499 US 330 (1991) (Supreme Court). In the UK case *Waterlow Directories Ltd v. Reed Information Services Ltd* [1992] FSR 409, the opportunity to address this issue was missed.

of significant amounts of skill and labour in setting up the database is neither here nor there too.[111]

As a form of literary work, a database is subject to the normal copyright regime. For example, copying the selection of the materials or the structure of the database, or a substantial part of them, will be an infringement of the copyright in the database. A few special provisions do, however, exist. Making an adaptation or doing a restricted act in relation to an adaptation of a database will still be an infringement of the copyright in the database, but the term 'adaptation' has been redefined to mean an *'arrangement or altered version of the database or a translation of it'* in relation to a database and a database has been excluded from the list of works to which the normal definition of an adaptation applies.[112] The fair dealing for the purposes of research and private study defence does not apply to databases in its normal form either. The special rule stipulates that *'fair dealing with a database for the purposes of research or private study does not infringe any copyright in the database provided that the source is indicated'* and it has been added that *'doing anything... for the purposes of research for a commercial purpose is not fair dealing with the database'.*[113] Additionally, a legitimate user of a database is allowed to do anything that is necessary for the purposes of gaining access to the database and for the use of the contents of the database. That latter right cannot be restricted by agreement.[114]

The database right

A new *sui generis* right to protect databases has been created and that right operates irrespective of whether the database, or any of its contents, attracts copyright protection.[115] The creation of this right was necessary because copyright was not the appropriate instrument to protect non-original databases, which are nevertheless valuable and have required a substantial investment. Electronic databases especially are, in such a situation, extremely vulnerable and it was felt that some form of protection was needed to protect the valuable investment in these databases.

The new right

The new database right has been defined as a property right and it is granted *'if there has been a substantial investment in obtaining, verifying or presenting the contents of the database'.*[116] Once again, this right does not interfere with any of the existing materials and the rights in them. As a right in the database, it comes on top of any existing rights and its existence rewards, and is conditional on, a substantial or sizeable investment either in collecting, in verifying, or in presenting the contents of the database. For example, the substantial investment requirement will not be met by simply putting different works together on a single support; such a collection will not be protected by the database right.[117]

The European Court of Justice held that 'obtaining' must be interpreted as referring to the resources used to seek out existing independent materials and to collect them in the database. The resources used for the creation of materials that make up the contents of the database are not covered. 'Verification', however, refers to the resources used with a view to ensuring the reliability of the information contained in the database, to monitor

---

[111] Case C-604/10, *Football Dataco and ors v. Yahoo! UK Ltd and ors* [2012] 2 CMLR 24, [2012] ECDR 10.
[112] CDPA 1988, s. 21(3).   [113] CDPA 1988, s. 29(1A) and (5).   [114] CDPA 1988, s. 50D.
[115] Copyright and Rights in Databases Regulations 1997, reg. 13(2).
[116] Copyright and Rights in Databases Regulations 1997, reg. 13(1).
[117] See E. Derclaye, 'Database *Sui Generis* Right: What Is a Substantial Investment? A Tentative Definition' (2005) 36(1) Int Rev IP & Comp L 2.

the accuracy of the material originally collected, as well as later on. Resources used to verify materials that are created for the database are not covered.[118] It follows that investment in common data will not trigger the *sui generis* right. Databases that consist of created data, such as television listings or dates of sports fixtures, will thus remain unprotected.[119]

The *British Horseracing* case[120] offers the example of lists of riders and runners that were intending to run in a certain race. Without further verification as to who would actually be running etc. there could not be a database right in simply listing existing independent material.

The first owner of the database right has been identified as the maker of the database.[121] The maker of the database is, in turn, '*the person who takes the initiative in obtaining, verifying, or presenting the contents of the database and assumes the risk of investing in that obtaining, verification or presentation*'.[122] Making a database may involve more than one person. If several people act together in relation to the activities that have to be undertaken by the maker, they will be the joint makers of the database and the joint first owners of the right.[123] A database made by an employee in the course of his or her employment will be considered to have been made by the employer, subject to any agreement to the contrary.[124]

The database right exists for a 15-year term. That term starts running from the end of the calendar year in which the database was completed, but that rule is displaced if the database is made available to the public before the end of that period. In that case, the right expires 15 years from the end of the calendar year in which the database was first made available to the public.[125] A substantial change to the contents of the database that can be considered to be a substantial new investment will lead to the grant of a new 15-year term of protection. Such a change may be the result of the '*accumulation of successive additions, deletions or alterations*' to the database.[126] Any sustained effort and investment to keep the database up to date will therefore automatically lead to permanent protection through the ever-renewed database right in the latest version of the database. This is the case because the concept of 'substantial change' to the contents of a database, which qualifies the database for its own term of protection, entails that the resulting database must be considered to be a new, separate database.[127]

Infringement of the right

The owner of the database right is granted the right to object to the extraction or reutilization of all, or a substantial part, of the contents of the database. The right in the

---

[118] Case C-203/02, *The British Horseracing Board Ltd and ors v. William Hill Organisation Ltd* [2004] ECR I-10425, [2005] 1 CMLR 15, [2005] RPC 13.

[119] See E. Derclaye, 'The Court of Justice Interprets the Database *Sui Generis* Right for the First Time' (2005) 30(3) Eur LR 420.

[120] *British Horseracing Board Limited and ors v. William Hill Organisation Ltd* [2005] RPC 35, [2005] ECDR 28.

[121] Copyright and Rights in Databases Regulations 1997, reg. 15.

[122] Copyright and Rights in Databases Regulations 1997, reg. 14(1).

[123] Copyright and Rights in Databases Regulations 1997, reg. 14(5).

[124] Copyright and Rights in Databases Regulations 1997, reg. 14(2); provisions on Crown rights are contained in reg. 14(3) and (4).

[125] Copyright and Rights in Databases Regulations 1997, reg. 17(1) and (2).

[126] Copyright and Rights in Databases Regulations 1997, reg. 17(3).

[127] Opinion of Advocate-General Stix-Hackl in Case C-203/02, *The British Horseracing Board Ltd and ors v. William Hill Organisation Ltd* [2005] RPC 13.

investment clearly covers the use of the contents of the database. The right will be infringed by the unauthorized extraction or reutilization of all, or a substantial part, of the contents of the database.[128] The threshold of a substantial part of the contents of the database can be passed through the repeated and systematic extraction or reutilization of insubstantial parts of these contents.[129] A typical example of an infringement would consist of the taking out of a substantial part of the contents of the database and their reorganization by computer into a prima facie different database.[130]

In the first case to arise before an English court on this issue, Laddie J had to deal with an issue involving information related to horseracing, which was originally contained in the British Horseracing Board's database, emerging on the website of the Internet betting service of William Hill Organisation.[131] The judgment was appealed and the Court of Appeal decided to request a preliminary opinion from the European Court of Justice. That Court rendered its judgment on 9 November 2004, but we will also need to look at the very complete opinion of the Advocate-General.[132] The domestic proceedings were then finalized in the Court of Appeal.[133]

In this case, the information had been supplied to the claimant by an intermediary, but it was virtually certain that it had been derived from the claimant's website. The first essential point that arose was whether extraction and/or reutilization of a substantial part of the database had taken place. The judge rightfully pointed out that, while a systematic and methodical organization of the information was required for a database right to exist, extraction and reutilization as forms of infringement of such a database right were not linked to the arrangement of the database being used by the alleged infringer. Extraction and/or reutilization of the data as such was sufficient for there to be infringement of the database right.[134]

The European Court of Justice ruled that the terms 'extraction' and 'reutilization' must be interpreted as referring to an unauthorized act of appropriation and distribution to the public of the whole, or part, of the contents of a database. In the view of the Court, direct access to the database is not implied in this definition; the fact that the contents of the database were made accessible to the public by the maker of the database or with its consent has no impact on the right of the maker of the database to prevent acts of extraction and/or reutilization of the whole, or a substantial part, of the contents of its database.[135] It is therefore fairly certain that the question of whether the works, data, or other materials derived from the database have the same systematic or methodical arrangement and individual accessibility as in the original database is not relevant to the interpretation of the expressions *'a substantial part…of the contents of that database'* or *'insubstantial parts of the contents of the database'.*[136] Extraction of data from a database did *not*, according to Laddie J (and the Advocate-General), need to involve data being taken away from the database. Mere copying of data and its transfer

---

[128] Copyright and Rights in Databases Regulations 1997, reg. 16(1).

[129] Copyright and Rights in Databases Regulations 1997, reg. 16(2).

[130] Such a case could have been problematical under a 100 per cent copyright system.

[131] *British Horseracing Board Limited and ors v. William Hill Organisation Ltd* [2001] 2 CMLR 12.

[132] Opinion of Advocate-General Stix-Hackl in Case C-203/02, *The British Horseracing Board Ltd and ors v. William Hill Organisation Ltd* [2005] RPC 13.

[133] *British Horseracing Board Limited and ors v. William Hill Organisation Ltd* [2005] RPC 35, [2005] ECDR 28.

[134] *British Horseracing Board Limited and ors v. William Hill Organisation Ltd* [2001] 2 CMLR 12 at 232–5.

[135] Case C-203/02, *The British Horseracing Board Ltd and ors v. William Hill Organisation Ltd* [2004] ECR I-10425, [2005] 1 CMLR 15, [2005] RPC 13.

[136] *British Horseracing Board* (n. 133).

to a new medium were sufficient,[137] in so far as a substantial part of the database had been extracted.

The latter question depends, in essence, on a comparison between what has been taken (or used) with what was left in the claimant's database, but the importance of the data that had been extracted to the claimant also had to be taken into account. Additionally, account has to be taken of the protection that the Directive affords for the investment made by the database owner in obtaining, verifying, and presenting the contents of the database. A substantial part can therefore be extracted and/or reutilized if the claimant relies upon, and takes advantage of, the completeness and accuracy of the information in the database. Qualitative considerations are therefore also to be taken into account.[138]

The Court of Justice has since followed up this analysis in a couple more cases and it has consistently taken the line that the concept of extraction is to be interpreted broadly. It involves any unauthorized act of appropriation of the whole or part of the contents of a database, irrespective of the nature and the form of the process used. It also covers both a permanent and a temporary transfer and there is extraction as soon as material is taken and copied (stored) somewhere else. The distinction between permanent and temporary depends simply on the length of storage on the other medium.[139]

One could argue that a selection process taking place when poems were taken from a database resulted in there no longer being extraction. The Court adamantly rejected this and held that critical assessment of the material that was transferred was irrelevant, as was in general the objective pursued by the transfer of the material.[140] In the same vein subsequent changes to the material that is transferred and differences in structure between the database from which material is taken and the newly created database are irrelevant in deciding whether extraction took place. Similarities between both databases may, however, point in the direction of infringement.[141] And with that we return to *British Horseracing*. In the view of the European Court of Justice, the term 'substantial part' refers to the volume of data extracted from the database and/or reutilized. It must be assessed in relation to the total volume of the contents of the database. The scale of the investment in obtaining, verifying, and presenting of the content of the subject of the act of extraction and/or reutilization is to be taken into consideration as an important factor, irrespective of whether that subject represents a quantitatively substantial part of the contents of the database. An 'insubstantial part' of the database is simply defined by the Court as any part that does not fulfil the definition of a substantial part, evaluated both quantitatively and qualitatively.[142]

Having concluded that a substantial part of the database had been extracted along the lines of his analysis, Laddie J moved on to consider the reutilization point. He ruled that any use by the defendant of a database through which the extracted data was transmitted or made available to the public amounted to reutilization, and that this included loading the information concerned onto the defendant's computers for the purpose of making it available on its website. The fact that some of the information was also available from another source was entirely irrelevant in this respect.[143] The issue of

---

[137] *British Horseracing Board Limited and ors v. William Hill Organisation Ltd* (n. 134) at 236–8.

[138] *British Horseracing Board* (n. 135) at 235–6.

[139] Case C-545/07, *Apis-Hristovich EOOD v. Lakorda AD* [2009] 3 CMLR 3, [2009] ECDR 13.

[140] Case C-304/07, *Directmedia Publishing GmbH v. Albert-Ludwigs-Universität Freiburg* [2008] ECR I-7565.

[141] Case C-545/07, *Apis-Hristovich EOOD v. Lakorda AD* (n. 139).

[142] Opinion of Advocate-General Stix-Hackl in Case C-203/02, *The British Horseracing Board Ltd and ors v. William Hill Organisation Ltd* [2005] RPC 13.

[143] *British Horseracing Board Limited and ors v. William Hill Organisation Ltd* [2001] 2 CMLR 12 at 238–9.

the localization of the act of reutilization was subsequently addressed by the Court of Justice in the *Football Dataco* case.[144] The defendants were providing information about football matches that found its origins in the claimant's database to betting websites and via these ultimately to the consumer. The hardware used was located in different countries and the question arose where the act of reutilization took place. The Court was not satisfied by the argument that the consumer can access the website anywhere, namely, that is not enough for there to be reutilization in any of these places. The act also had to target persons in a certain territory for there to be reutilization in that territory. In the *Dataco* case there was reutilization in the United Kingdom, as the data related to English and Scottish football matches that would therefore be of interest to the public there. The use of the English language, namely, the language of the target market rather than the language of the defendant was also relevant, as was the fact that the contract between the defendant and the betting companies was tailored to the UK market. The Court concluded that an act of reutilization 'is located in the territory of the Member State of the location of the user to whose computer the data in question is transmitted at his request, for the purposes of storage and display on screen'.[145] The Court does hereby not exclude that the act of reutilization also takes place upstream in the chain of communication and it specifically rejects the suggestion that the act of reutilization exclusively takes place in the territory of the member state in which the webserver from which the data is sent is located. Any application of the emission theory is therefore turned down by the Court.

Returning to the *British Horseracing Board* case, the second essential point that arose was whether the defendant had engaged in repeated and systematic extraction or reutilization of the contents of the database. The defendant's database was in constant evolution and was updated on a day-to-day basis. The defendant took information from it on a daily basis and this prejudiced the legitimate interests of the claimant, and amounted to repeated and systematic extraction or reutilization of the contents of the database.[146]

It should be remembered, too, that the threshold of a substantial part of the contents of the database can be passed through the repeated and systematic extraction or reutilization of insubstantial parts of these contents. In this respect, the Court held that the prohibition contained in Art. 7(5) of the Database Directive refers to unauthorized acts of extraction or reutilization that have, as their cumulative effect, the reconstitution or the making available to the public of the whole or a substantial part of the contents of the database, in the absence of any prior authorization by the maker of the database. In being made available in this way, they seriously prejudice the investment of the maker of the database.[147]

Exceptions to the right

The exceptions to the database right are not numerous and they are also narrower in scope than those of their copyright counterparts. Some form of fair dealing exception

---

[144] Case C-173/11, *Football Dataco Ltd, Scottish Premier League Ltd, Scottish Football League and PA Sport UK Ltd v. Sportradar GmbH and Sportradar AG*, [2013] 1 CMLR 29; [2013] FSR 4.

[145] *Football Dataco* (n. 144) at para. 43.

[146] *British Horseracing Board Limited and ors v. William Hill Organisation Ltd* (n. 143) at 239–43. There are also indications in other member states that deep-linking on the Internet to another website containing a database and thereby skipping the front page of the latter, giving the user the impression that both databases are one and the same amounts to reutilizing a substantial part of a database: see A. Bennett, 'Euro Copyright Law Used to Block Link to Web Site' Yahoo News, 22 January 2001, <http://news.yahoo.com>.

[147] Case C-203/02, *The British Horseracing Board Ltd and ors v. William Hill Organisation Ltd* [2004] ECR I-10425, [2005] 1 CMLR 15, [2005] RPC 13.

exists, but not for the purpose of criticism, review, or news reporting, and the library exceptions are also missing. Regulation 20 of the Copyright and Rights in Databases Regulations 1997 contains the narrow exception that:

(1) Database right in a database which has been made available to the public in any manner is not infringed by fair dealing with a substantial part of its content if—
   (a) that part is extracted from the database by a person who is apart from this paragraph a lawful user of the database,
   (b) it is extracted for the purpose of illustration for teaching or research and not for any commercial purpose, and
   (c) the source is indicated.
(2) The provisions of Schedule 1 specify other acts which may be done in relation to a database notwithstanding the existence of database right.

Qualification

There is also a qualification requirement that has to be met before the database right can be granted. The main principle of this is that an attempt has been made to require reciprocity in the sense that non-European Economic Area (EEA) persons will only be granted the right if their country offers a similar level of protection to that of the European makers of databases. Qualification is made dependent on the fact that at least one of the makers of the database was, at the material time at which the database was made:

(a) an individual who was a national of an EEA State or habitually resident within the EEA,
(b) a body which was incorporated under the law of an EEA state and which, at that time, satisfied one of the conditions in paragraph (2), or
(c) a partnership or other unincorporated body which was formed under the law of an EEA state and which, at that time, satisfied the condition in paragraph (2)(a).[148]

These conditions are:

(a) that the body has its central administration or principal place of business within the EEA, or
(b) that the body has its registered office within the EEA and the body's operations are linked on an ongoing basis with the economy of an EEA State.[149]

Outstanding questions and the risk of abuse

These rather vague provisions will undoubtedly give rise to a whole series of disputes before the courts.

The database right presents the inherent danger that it will grant a monopoly right over major sources of (statistical or other) information and that this right will be owned by a single right holder (either the producer of the information or the holder of the sources). Any abuse of the database right will be restrained through the use of Art. 102 TFEU, but there are no special provisions available to counter this threat, apart from the *Magill*[150] style action against the abuse of a dominant position.

---

[148] Copyright and Rights in Databases Regulations 1997, reg. 18(1).
[149] Copyright and Rights in Databases Regulations 1997, reg. 18(2).
[150] See Case C-241/91 P, *Radio Telefís Éireann v. Commission of the European Communities* [1995] ECR I-743.

The Internet

It would lead too far to discuss all intellectual property-related aspects of the Internet in this chapter; we will consequently restrict our comments to some copyright-related issues.[151] Three major questions will be addressed:

1. Is material found on the Internet protected by copyright and, if so, how?

2. What amounts to copyright infringement in an Internet context?

3. How do the defences to copyright infringement apply to alleged infringement on the Internet?

Two preliminary points also need to be addressed. The first of these is that the Internet and the use of works on it do not change copyright: works that are protected, as such, do not lose this status when they appear on the Internet. The situation in this respect is identical to that we described in relation to copyright in databases. Equally, copyright applies to Internet-related issues. Up to now, there has been no change to the provisions of copyright: we simply need to apply the existing rules to the Internet—but our comment will highlight some of the problems that arise through that application.

The second preliminary point flows naturally from the borderless and international nature of the Internet. Works cross borders on the Internet as a way of life. The contrast with the national nature of the UK copyright legislation gives rise to numerous issues of private international law. Examples are in plentiful supply, but the most obvious relates to the copying of a work: where does the copying take place? Does it take place on the server on which the work is stored, on the foreign terminal on which the user views the work and from which he or she prints a copy of it, or in any of the countries through which the work passes on its way from the server to the user's computer? Which national court will have jurisdiction to decide the issue? And under which law will the issue be decided? Similar definitional problems arise in relation to communication to the public, and even more so in a cloud computing context. These issues come on top of the discussion that follows and in which we will describe the UK's substantial provisions. The private international law issues are highly complex and we refer the reader to Fawcett and Torremans (2nd edn, 2011) for further details.

Existence of copyright and classification

A lot of websites contain text, music, and artistic works, such as photographs and drawings. These works will be protected as literary, musical, or artistic works as long as they meet the normal copyright requirements. Copyright in the works that are specifically created by the creator of the website for that purpose will be owned by that creator, subject to the employer–employee rule. Collaborative efforts may give rise to joint authorship and joint ownership. Sound recordings, films, and broadcasts also maintain their copyright status when they are put on the Internet.

But can a website, as such, be classified as a work that attracts copyright protection? The arrangement of a website can be protected by means of the copyright that is available in a typographical arrangement. This conclusion is reached through the interpretation of

---

[151] See H. MacQueen (1997) 'Copyright and the Internet', in C. Waelde and L. Evans (eds.), *Law and the Internet: Regulating Cyberspace*, Oxford: Hart, p. 67.

the concept of 'publication'. The website is published, because copies are made available to the public by means of an electronic retrieval system.[152] The Internet fits in with that requirement, which means that the author of the arrangement of a website has a typographical arrangement copyright in that arrangement.

The Scottish *Shetland Times* case[153] suggested that a website was a cable programme service or a cable programme, as these were defined in the original text of the 1988 Act. A cable programme was any item that was included in a cable programme service under the original text of that Act. Such a service was defined as:

> a service which consists wholly or mainly in sending visual images, sounds or other information by means of a telecommunication system, otherwise than by wireless telegraphy, for reception at two or more places [whether or not simultaneously], or for presentation to members of the public.[154]

Two-way or interactive communication systems were excluded.[155]

Lord Hamilton came to the conclusion that a website came within this definition by rejecting the argument that the public accessed information, rather than being sent information, and the argument that a website was an interactive system. One could indeed argue that the information is sent by the owner of the website when the request of the user arrives, or at least that the Act allows for the word 'sending' to include the concept of enabling the information to be sent. The interactivity exists because the user can send email messages to the operator of the website and is even invited to do so, but for the exclusion to apply, the interactivity—or the potential for interactivity—must be an essential feature of the service. The definition that is given to the word 'essential' is clearly the crucial point. Sites that are mainly there to provide information in a passive way—such as the websites of a newspaper—may well have escaped the exclusion, but it was hard to see how a website that was accessed for the purposes of interactivity—such as the catalogues of mail order shops or the Internet ticket reservation sites of airlines—could escape the exclusion.

Clearly, the *Shetland Times* case did not provide the definitive answer; it merely got the discussion started. The category of cable programs has now been included in the broad category of broadcasts, but most websites have been excluded specifically by the new s. 6(1A) of the 1988 Act, which states:

> Excepted from the definition of 'broadcast' is any internet transmission unless it is—
>
> (a) a transmission taking place simultaneously on the internet and by other means,
> (b) a concurrent transmission of a live event, or
> (c) a transmission of recorded moving images or sounds forming part of a programme service offered by the person responsible for making the transmission, being a service in which programmes are transmitted at scheduled times determined by that person.

Those websites that are excluded from the category of broadcasts may still attract protection, however—for example, as databases, literary works, or artistic works—but a single categorization is no longer possible. One should also not forget that the issue of the protection of the website as such as a copyright work does not affect the fact that copyright may subsist in the various works contained in the website.

---

[152] CDPA 1988, s. 175(1).

[153] *Shetland Times v. Wills* 1997 SLT 669, 1997 SCLR 160; see also *British Telecommunications plc v. One in a Million* [1998] 4 All ER 476, [1999] 1 WLR 903.

[154] CDPA 1988, s. 7(1).　　　[155] CDPA 1988, s. 7(2).

Infringement issues

Reproduction

Browsing the Internet involves storing material in the RAM memory of the computer: does this amount to copying? Copying is defined as *'reproducing the work in any material form'* in as far as literary, dramatic, musical, and artistic works are concerned.[156] Such a reproduction may be made through the storage of the work in any medium by electronic means;[157] transient or incidental copies are also included.[158] Loading software or the contents of a page of a website into the RAM memory of a computer must thus involve an act of copying. Laddie J indeed held that it did and that the fact that the material was only present for a limited time was irrelevant.[159]

But as the technical operation of a computer, especially when browsing on the Internet, involves necessarily a degree of copying, Art. 5(1) of the Information Society Directive[160] provides an exemption for those temporary acts of reproduction that are transient or incidental, that are an essential and integral part of the technological process and whose sole purpose is to enable a transmission in a network or lawful use of the work concerned. These acts should also have no independent economic value. The CJEU later held that this provision applies to copies on the user's computer screen and to copies in the Internet cache of the computer's hard disk that are made by an end user in the course of viewing a website.[161] These activities, whilst technically infringing the reproduction right, are exempted.

When material is downloaded, things become even clearer. Printouts and copies on the hard disk or on a USB stick are clearly copies. The typographical arrangement copyright in the site is also copied on each occasion.[162] As with software, there may also be a case of non-literal copying when (only) the design and the structure of the website are copied.[163]

Public performance and communication to the public

The copyright in literary, dramatic, or musical works can also be infringed through their public performance, showing, or playing.[164] That might easily be accomplished by displaying them on a computer screen or by playing them over the computer's audio system. The only problematical point is the fact that the performance etc. needs to take place in public.

The latter concept no longer requires that there be a group of paying people forming an audience for whom the work is performed; neither is there a need for a gathering of people in one place. 'In public' rather seems to mean that there must be an audience,

---

[156] CDPA 1988, s. 17(2).   [157] CDPA 1988, s. 17(2).

[158] CDPA 1988, s. 17(6). See also European Parliament and Council Directive 2001/29/EC on the harmonization of certain aspects of copyright and related rights in the information society [2001] OJ L 167/10, Art. 2.

[159] *Kabushiki Kaisha Sony Computer Entertainment Inc. (also t/a Sony Computer Entertainment Inc.), Sony Computer Entertainment Europe Ltd & Sony Computer Entertainment UK Ltd v. Gaynor David Ball and ors* [2004] ECDR 323.

[160] European Parliament and Council Directive 2001/29/EC on the harmonization of certain aspects of copyright and related rights in the information society [2001] OJ L 167/10, Art. 5(1). This provision was transposed into UK law as CDPA 1988, s. 28A.

[161] Case C-360/13, *Public Relations Consultants Association Ltd v. Newspaper Licensing Agency and Others* [2014] ECDR 22.

[162] CDPA 1988, s. 17(5).   [163] See MacQueen, 'Copyright and the Internet' (n. 151) at 81.

[164] CDPA 1988, s. 19.

from whom the author is entitled to expect remuneration for the enjoyment of his or her work. Some foreign decisions have shown that such an audience exists in cases in which several people listen at different times to recorded music when their call is put on hold when they use their mobile phones[165] or when several people watch non-simultaneous television and video broadcasts in individual hotel rooms.[166]

The European Court of Justice has now also confirmed the latter point.[167] As a result of the implementation of the Information Society Directive[168] the point has now been re-solved definitively, and the right of communication to the public and the right of making available to the public will also apply to situations in which members of the public may gain access from a place and time individually chosen by them. The incorporation of copyright works, without owning the rights in them or without authorization, into a website for it to be accessed by Internet users will infringe the copyright in these works, because it amounts to communicating the work to the public. Disseminating live broad-casts of Champions League football matches via a website was therefore also an infringe-ment as an unauthorized communication to the public.[169]

Hypertext links

Hypertext links to other websites or other copyright works could be seen as making the work available and therefore they could be seen as amounting to an infringement under s. 20 of the 1988 Act. Indeed, through the link, the work becomes available to differ-ent audiences. But, arguably, most hypertext links are more akin to endnotes, bibliog-raphies, or hints for further reading: they make it easier to locate and access works that are already available to the public. They refer to the other sites, but they do not include the sites themselves in the site of the alleged infringer. It is therefore submitted that the better view is that hyperlinks do not amount to infringement through reproduction or communication to the public.

It is submitted, however, that such a conclusion is no longer valid if the alleged in-fringer organizes the links in such a way that the other sites will be shown inside the frame of the alleged infringer's site. Such a link is stronger and should be seen as inclu-sion, especially because the alleged infringer sets out to derive an economic benefit from the contents of the other site.[170] Traffic is directed away from the original site, which may suffer a loss of earnings (publicity etc.) as a result.

The CJEU was confronted with the hypertext link issue in the *Svensson* case.[171] The court argued that a hyperlink to a website to which access is freely available and that is not protected by technical protection measures (TPMs) does not make that website available to a new public, as it was already available to the whole Internet community. That means that there is no communication to the public involved in the provision of the hypertext link and that there is therefore no infringement. That conclusion changes if the website to which one links is not freely accessible or is protected by TPMs or if it is no longer freely accessible. The Court did not feel the need to distinguish between various

---

[165] *Australasian Performing Right Association Ltd v. Telstra Corp. Ltd* [1997] IIC 136 (Federal Court of Australia, 23 August 1995).

[166] *SGAE v. Hotel Blanco Don J SA* [1997] 1 EIPR D-21 Supreme Court of Spain, 11 March 1996.

[167] Case C-306/05, *SGAE v. Rafael Hoteles SA* [2007] ECDR 2.

[168] Art. 3. This applies to all kinds of original copyright works, as well as to performances, phonograms, films, and broadcasts: see the new CDPA 1988, s. 20(2). Performers have a similar right to object to their works being made available to the public without their prior consent: see CDPA 1988, s. 182CA.

[169] *Union des Associations Européennes de Football v. Briscomb* (2006) 150 SJLB 670.

[170] Cf. MacQueen, 'Copyright and the Internet' (n. 151) at 84.

[171] Case C-466/12, *Svensson and others v. Retriever Sverige AB* [2014] 3 CMLR 4; [2014] ECDR 9.

types of hypertext links and in a later decision clarified that its approach also applied to framing.[172] This lack of distinction is regrettable in the light of the comments we made above and one can even ask whether the *Svensson* approach is compatible with the international copyright treaties.[173]

A newspaper clipping service that sent its clients the titles of the articles selected on the basis of their search term in the form of a hypertext link, accompanied by a couple of words of the relevant article to demonstrate its relevance, needed a copyright licence for its own activities and its users needed also their own licence. The reason for this conclusion was, on the on the one hand, that titles may attract copyright protection and, on the other hand, that upon clicking on the title the article was reproduced on the computer of the user. The copies made were therefore likely to amount to a substantial part of the work.[174] And these were not temporary and technically necessary copies in the browsing process. It is clear though that this case went beyond the mere provision of a hypertext link.

Authorization

Copyright infringement by authorizing someone else to commit certain acts[175] is less of a problem in relation to the Internet. It is true that those who provide end users with access to the Internet—for example, universities or cybercafés that make networked terminals available—provide these users with the means to copy etc. But all of that equipment can also be used for the lawful use of the Internet and that is sufficient to counter the threat of infringement liability as a result of providing equipment.[176]

Service providers that participate in the infringing activities of the users—for example, by providing road maps to items that can be downloaded—may not escape liability, but temporary acts of reproduction that are transient or incidental and an integral part of a technical process, and the sole purpose of which is to enable a transmission in a network between parties or a lawful use of a work have been exempted specifically from the right of reproduction, if the copies made have no independent economic significance.[177] This provision is vital for the functioning of the Internet. Secondary infringement by assisting the user who is engaging in activities that amount to primary infringement is a different matter and it is to that issue that we now turn.

Peer-to-peer

Peer-to-peer file sharing over the Internet gives rise to a whole range of issues. There is no doubt about the fact that the actual act of sharing involves, at the very least, reproducing the material. The individuals involved are therefore infringing copyright if the material shared is protected by copyright. Innocence or ignorance is not a defence, and simply connecting a computer containing the material and making it available to download will

---

[172] Order of the Court in Case C-348/13, *Bestwater International GmbH v. Michael Mebes and Stefan Potsch*, 21 October 2014, see <http://curia.europa.eu>.

[173] See the opinions of ALAI: Opinion Proposed to the Executive Committee and adopted at its meeting, 17 September 2014 on the criterion 'New Public', developed by the Court of Justice of the European Union (CJEU), put in the context of making available and communication to the public, <http://www.alai.org/en/assets/files/resolutions/2014-opinion-new-public.pdf>; and ALAI Report and Opinion on a Berne-compatible reconciliation of hyperlinking and the communication to the public right on the internet, <http://www.alai.org/en/assets/files/resolutions/201503-hyperlinking-report-and-opinion-2.pdf>.

[174] *Newspaper Licensing Agency Ltd v. Meltwater Holding BV* [2011] EWCA Civ 890, [2012] RPC 1.

[175] CDPA 1988, s. 16(2).

[176] See *CBS Inc. v. Ames Records & Tapes Ltd* [1982] Ch 91, [1981] 2 All ER 812; *CBS Songs Ltd v. Amstrad Consumer Electronics plc* [1988] AC 1013, [1988] 2 All ER 484.

[177] CDPA 1988, s. 28A, which implements Art. 5(1) of the Information Society Directive into UK law.

be sufficient.[178] It might, however, be rather impractical for the copyright holder to sue all of the individual users of peer-to-peer software. But might it be argued that the Internet service providers (ISPs), and the designers and suppliers of the software, also commit an infringement?

Service providers do not normally engage in making the copy and they escape liability unless they can be seen to authorize the making of the copy. If they do nothing more than offer the Internet service, however, it is hard to see how that can be fitted into the concept of authorizing the user to copy: authorization requires more than mere enabling. Peer-to-peer software suppliers that operated a central server, such as the old Napster, were much easier targets. At least under US copyright law, they could be seen to contribute to copyright infringement. The old Napster had, at least, knowledge of what was going on on its server and could act by cutting off copyright infringers.[179] Newer peer-to-peer software is more sophisticated and works without a central server. The software is supplied to individual users and the suppliers have no further control over its use. Importantly, from a US copyright law point of view, there is an opportunity for substantial non-infringing use to be made of the software and it was at least arguable that, in those circumstances, contributory liability presupposes that the defendant had reasonable knowledge of specific infringing files and had failed to act on that knowledge to prevent infringement.

In the *Grokster* case,[180] that debate went all the way up to the Supreme Court. The final ruling held that the providers of software that is designed to enable the file sharing of copyright works may be held liable for copyright infringement that takes place through use of the software by users. In the Court's words:

> one who distributes a device with the object of promoting its use to infringe copyright, as shown by clear expression or other affirmative steps to foster infringement, is liable for the resulting acts of infringement by third parties.[181]

The only peer-to-peer software that escapes this ruling is that which has genuine dual non-infringing use and does not promote infringement or take affirmative steps to foster it.[182]

Recently right holders have started to use s. 97A CDPA to apply for an injunction obliging service providers to block or at least seriously impede access to peer-to-peer file-sharing websites once the latter have been found liable.[183] This has now become a routine for the court and a standard practice.[184] The condition in s. 97A that the service providers have knowledge of clients using their service to infringe copyright is then

---

[178] *Polydor Ltd v. Brown* [2005] EWHC 3191, (2006) 29(3) IPD 29021.   [179] 239 F 3d at 1027.

[180] *MGM v. Grokster*, 545 US 913 (2005), Supreme Court, 27 June 2005, overruling *MGM and ors v. Grokster & Streamcast*, US Court of Appeals for the Ninth Circuit, judgment of 19 August 2004.

[181] *MGM v. Grokster* (n. 180) at 10–24.

[182] For a case where this argument failed and the website was held liable and shut down, see *Twentieth Century Fox Film Corp. v. Newzbin Ltd* [2010] EWHC 608 (Ch).

[183] See *Twentieth Century Fox v. Newzbin* (n. 182).

[184] *Twentieth Century Fox Film Corp. v. British Telecommunications Plc* [2011] EWHC 1981 (Ch), [2011] RPC 28, [2012] 1 All ER 806; *Dramatico Entertainment Ltd and ors v. British Sky Broadcasting Ltd and ors* [2012] EWHC 268 (Ch); *EMI Records Ltd v. British Sky Broadcasting Ltd* [2013] EWHC 379 (Ch); *Football Association Premier League Ltd v. British Sky Broadcasting Ltd* [2013] EWHC 2058 (Ch); *Paramount Home Entertainment International Ltd v. British Sky Broadcasting Ltd* [2013] EWHC 3479 (Ch); *1967 Limited, Dramatico Entertainment Ltd and others v. British Sky Broadcasting Ltd and others* [2014] EWHC 3444 (Ch); and *Paramount Home Entertainment International Ltd v. British Sky Broadcasting Ltd* [2014] EWHC 937 (Ch). A similar approach was applied to a case involving trade marks: *Cartier International AG v. British Sky Broadcasting Ltd* [2014] EWHC 3554 (Ch).

met and, having found that both the website operators and the individual clients in-fringe copyright, the courts have been willing to grant such injunctions.[185] These deci-sions are fully in line with Art. 8(3) of the Copyright Directive[186] and the third sentence of Art. 11 of the Enforcement Directive,[187] which when read together authorize holders of intellectual property rights to apply for an injunction against intermediaries, such as ISPs, whose services are being used by a third party to infringe their rights. National courts could order those intermediaries to take measures aimed not only at bringing to an end infringements already committed against intellectual property rights using their information-society services, but also at preventing further infringements.[188] The Court of Justice added, however, that national rules had, in particular, to respect Art. 15(1) of the E-Commerce Directive,[189] which prohibited national authorities from adopting measures which would require an ISP to carry out general monitoring of the information that it transmitted on its network. Those overly broad injunctions can therefore not be ordered on the basis of s. 97A.[190]

An enforcement role for ISPs

ISPs are increasingly called upon to assist with the enforcement of copyright, as bring-ing actions against individual users that infringe copyright is impractical and costly. The Digital Economy Act put in place a mechanism that facilitates the involvement of ISPs. It inserted new ss. 124A–N into the Communications Act 2003 as a response to the growing problem of subscribers to Internet services uploading and accessing material online in breach of copyright. These new provisions impose 'initial obligations' on ISPs to notify subscribers of copyright infringement reports received from copyright owners, and to provide copyright infringement lists to copyright owners, if an 'initial obliga-tions code' is in force. The provisions also allow for the approval or making of an initial obligations code and as to the content of such a code, and they empower the Secretary of State to specify provisions that must be included in the code about payment of con-tributions towards costs incurred. The draft Costs Order is to be made in the exercise of that power. The idea behind this system is that ISPs know the identity of the client using an Internet connection, whereas the right holder does not. The ISP is therefore ideally placed to pass on notices about infringing activity to the user with the idea that they change their behaviour and they are also ideally placed to inform the right holder of the identity of the alleged infringer in case legal action needs to be taken. Internet service providers brought legal action to test the legality of these new provisions, but they were upheld by the Court of Appeal.[191] The scheme may, however, never really be put into practice as right holders and internet service providers (ISPs) have voluntarily agreed on

[185] *Twentieth Century Fox Film Corp. v. British Telecommunications Plc* [2011] EWHC 1981 (Ch), [2011] RPC 28, [2012] 1 All ER 806; *Dramatico Entertainment Ltd and ors v. British Sky Broadcasting Ltd and ors* [2012] EWHC 268 (Ch).

[186] Directive 2001/29/EC of the European Parliament and of the Council of 22 May 2001 on the har-monization of certain aspects of copyright and related rights in the information society [2001] OJ L167/10.

[187] Directive 2004/48/EC of the European Parliament and of the Council of 29 April 2004 on the enforce-ment of intellectual property rights [2004] OJ L195/16.

[188] Case C-324/09, *L'Oréal SA v. eBay International AG* [2012] Bus LR 1369.

[189] Directive 2000/31/EC of the European Parliament and of the Council of 8 June 2000 on certain legal aspects of information society services, in particular electronic commerce, in the Internal Market (Directive on electronic commerce) [2000] OJ L178/1.

[190] Case C-70/10, *Scarlet Extended SA v. Sabam* [2012] ECDR 4; Case C-360/10 *Sabam v. Netlog NV* [2012] 2 CMLR 18.

[191] *R. on the application of British Telecommunications plc and TalkTalk Telecom Group plc v. Secretary of State for Culture, Olympics, Media and Sport and ors* [2012] EWCA Civ 232, [2012] 2 CMLR 23.

an alternative framework for educating alleged infringers about the harm of piracy. This has effectively put the scheme contained in ss. 124 A–N on hold.

Defences that may come to the rescue

Consent

There is no doubt a whole host of reasons that motivate people to set up their own website and home pages, and to make material available on them. One of these reasons must be that other users may access their material and that they feel they have something to say or to offer to these other users. The whole concept of an Internet, or any other network, is that a connection will be made with other people, with whom content will be shared.

From a legal point of view, this must mean that whoever makes material available on the Internet consents to the fact that others will access that material: there must be some kind of implied licence to do certain acts that are necessary to access the material. Such a licence must be non-exclusive in nature, because it is given on equal terms to all potential accessors of the material. Copyright law finds no problem with such a non-exclusive implied licence, because there is no ban on them and no written instrument is required for this type of licence. The licence can be implied from the way in which the dealings between the parties have been set up. In this respect, the whole set-up of the Internet points towards the conclusion that an implied licence must exist.[192]

The remaining problem is that it is not necessarily clear what can be done under such an implied licence. The starting point seems uncontroversial: it must be a licence for any Internet user to access the material on the site and to perform all acts of copying that are necessary to gain access. Any intermediary provider of services must be allowed to transmit the material and to make transient copies, in so far as this is required from a technical point of view. It is less clear whether the user can download the accessed material onto any hard disk, CD, etc., whether he or she can print it, and whether he or she can make any further use of the material. It is submitted that this depends on the type of material that is accessed and the type of site on which it is found.

The starting point must be that the Internet medium does not change the basic rules of copyright. Any material that qualifies for copyright protection will still be protected when it is made available on the Internet. Users are licensed to access the site on which the material is contained in the same way as they are licensed to read a book, or to play a CD or videotape. Copying or any other restricted act requires a further licence. That further licence can only be implied if it is clear, from the type of material or from the type of site, that further use is intended, or at least authorized. That can be derived from the fact that the material on the site has no use through access only and that further potentially infringing acts are required for its use. For example, pieces of software are clearly not intended to be read on a computer screen, and must therefore come with an implied licence to download and to use, while poetry or other texts can be read on the screen and need not be downloaded before proper access to them can be gained. Sites that are labelled 'shareware' clearly come with an implied licence to copy the material on them and to make further use of the material. The only limitation on such further use may be that the product can only be used as such and in its entirety under the implied licence: maybe it is only a licence to share the original product with other interested users, even if that sharing can be undertaken on a commercial basis.[193]

---

[192] Cf. MacQueen, 'Copyright and the Internet' (n. 151) at 89–90.
[193] See the Australian case *Trumpet Software Pty Ltd v. OzEmail Pty Ltd* [1996] 12 EIPR 69.

Notices

It is submitted that notices on sites can obviously change the pattern. The site owner can license any other users to make use of the material in a particular way and that may even take the form of a blanket licence to do anything with the material. Obviously, a site owner can only waive rights through such a licence in so far as he or she possesses these rights him- or herself. For example, he or she cannot waive copyright in material on a site in which he or she does not own the copyright, unless he or she is authorized by the right owner to do so. Alternatively, certain, or all, types of use may explicitly be prohibited or made subject to a further authorization. A clear notice that certain materials or certain rights in them are for sale, or the presentation of the site as a commercial trade catalogue must be seen as an example of the latter reservation of rights. Certainly, the use of notices on sites would provide a far greater degree of transparency and clarity than that which is currently available on the Internet.

Addresses and search engines

The copying of site addresses and the use of search engines raises further issues. Sites are created in order for access to them to be gained: this must mean that an implied licence is given to any user to copy the address of the site onto the hard disk of his or her computer, in order to gain easy access to that site on a future occasion. Copying undertaken by search engines must also be allowed under an implied licence, in so far as it is necessary to facilitate access to the site. The access aim of the creator of the site can only be realized through the use of search engines, due to the untransparent technical structure of the Internet.

All the aspects of the implied licence that have been described in this paragraph apply only to addresses and titles, in so far as the latter are protected by copyright in the first place for obvious reasons.[194]

Fair dealing

The fair dealing defence to copyright infringement[195] may also be used in an Internet context. It may be fair dealing for the purposes of research or private study to make hard or electronic copies of a certain part of the material that the user accesses on the Internet, but the constraints of the defence apply here, as in any other copyright context. It must, for example, be the user's own research or private study that is facilitated, and it may be difficult to justify the copying of whole works. Copying materials from other websites to put them on your own site is clearly something that is not exempted by this defence.

Fair dealing for the purposes of review and criticism can also be used as a defence, but, in this respect, a fair level of review and criticism is required. The amount of copying must be justifiable in comparison with the amount of commentary.

Time shifting

The 1988 Act also allows a broadcast to be viewed at a time that is more convenient to the viewer.[196] This 'time shifting' exception might be pleaded by the users of a website who copied its contents, but only in those now very limited cases in which the site comes within the definition of a broadcast.

---

[194] See e.g. *Exxon Corp. v. Exxon Insurance Consultants International* [1982] Ch 119, aff'd [1982] RPC 81.
[195] CDPA 1988, ss. 29 and 30.   [196] CDPA 1988, s. 70.

Technical protection measures (TPMs)

The Information Society Directive also put in place new measures concerning technical measures and rights management information,[197] which are intended to reinforce copyright and related rights protection in the electronic and digital environment. The implementation of these measures into English law has already been discussed in the chapters on copyright and related rights, and will not be repeated here.[198]

Semiconductor chip protection

Introduction

Semiconductor chips are integrated circuits, usually made out of layers of materials that are conductive to a different extent. In most cases, some layers are not conductive at all, while other layers are made out of semiconductive materials, such as silicon. The production of these chips involves an etching process, whereby photographically made masks are used; these masks determine the final wiring of the chip.

It was not immediately clear which intellectual property right should be used for the protection of semiconductor chips and what exactly would be the subject of protection. The latter issue was solved when it was decided to protect the topography of the integrated circuit, rather than the chip itself. Because it was dissatisfied with the protection offered by the conventional intellectual property rights and after intense lobbying by the chip industry, the US became the first country to enact a statute that provides a *sui generis* intellectual property right that covers semiconductor chips.[199] The European Community followed suit and a directive[200] obliged the member states to introduce protection for topographies of integrated circuits. Most member states created a *sui generis* right, while the UK decided to offer protection via the design right.

The Design Right (Semiconductor) Regulations 1989

The Design Right (Semiconductor) Regulations 1989[201] rely upon the provisions in the 1988 Act for the design right and add a number of special provisions to them to protect semiconductor topographies. A design is further defined as:

(a) the pattern fixed, or intended to be fixed, in or upon—
   (i) a layer of a semiconductor product, or
   (ii) a layer of material in the course of and for the purpose of the manufacture of a semiconductor product, or
(b) the arrangement of the patterns fixed, or intended to be fixed, in or upon the layers of a semiconductor product in relation to one another.[202]

---

[197] Arts. 6 and 7 of the Information Society Directive.

[198] See also *Kabushiki Kaisha Sony Computer Entertainment Inc. (also t/a Sony Computer Entertainment Inc.), Sony Computer Entertainment Europe Ltd & Sony Computer Entertainment UK Ltd v. Gaynor David Ball & ors* [2004] ECDR 323.

[199] Semiconductor Chip Protection Act of 1984, Pub L No 98–620, Title III, Stat 3347 (codified at 17 USC 901–914, Supp II 1984).

[200] EC Council Directive on the legal protection of topographies of semiconductor products (1987) OJ L 24/36.

[201] The Design Right (Semiconductor) Regulations 1989, SI 1989/1100.

[202] Design Right (Semiconductor) Regulations, 1989 reg. 2(1).

A semiconductor product is, in turn, defined as:

> an article the purpose, or one of the purposes, of which is the performance of an electronic function and which consists of two or more layers, at least one of which is composed of semi-conducting material and in or upon one or more of which is fixed a pattern appertaining to that or another function.[203]

A semiconductor topography that forms such a design is only protected if it is original and, as is usual for designs, it will not be original if it is commonplace in the relevant design field at the time of its creation. There is also a qualification requirement.[204] Its only noticeable difference from that for designs is that any sale or hire, or any offer or exposure for sale or hire, that is subject to an obligation of confidence[205] is to be taken into account when qualification through first marketing is examined.

A semiconductor topography design that satisfies these requirements is owned in the same way as any other design right, apart from the fact that commissioners and employers do not have to be qualifying persons.[206] The term of protection normally expires ten years after the end of the year in which the design was first commercially exploited anywhere in the world. Exceptionally, the design right expires 15 years from the time at which the topography was first recorded in a design document or from the time at which an item was made to the design, whichever is the earlier. This rule will apply in cases in which the design is not exploited within 15 years of the creation of the topography.[207]

In general, the provisions on primary and secondary infringement are similar to those that generally apply to design rights, but the Regulations introduce some particular provisions. Anyone can freely reproduce the design privately for non-commercial purposes[208] and '*the reproduction of a design for the purpose of analysing or evaluating the design or analysing, evaluating or teaching the concepts, processes, systems or techniques embodied in it*'[209] will not infringe the design right in the topography. But the most interesting departure from the traditional design rules is the introduction of a provision that allows for the reverse engineering of a semiconductor design right. Regulation 8(4) states that it is not an infringement of the semiconductor design right to create another original topography on the basis of the outcome of the reverse analysis and evaluation of an existing semiconductor design. This exception even includes the making of a copy of that existing semiconductor design.[210] This exception is, however, narrow in scope, because it will only apply if the new design meets the originality requirement.

Two minor provisions should also be mentioned here. The exhaustion doctrine is applicable in relation to semiconductor designs,[211] while licences of right, which are normally available during the last five years of the term of design protection, are not available in relation to semiconductor designs.[212]

These provisions are too narrowly linked to an increasingly outdated production process for semiconductors. Their application has therefore remained limited in scope.

---

[203] Design Right (Semiconductor) Regulations 1989, reg. 2(1).
[204] Design Right (Semiconductor) Regulations 1989, reg. 4.
[205] Design Right (Semiconductor) Regulations 1989, reg. 7.
[206] Design Right (Semiconductor) Regulations 1989, regs. 4 and 5.
[207] Design Right (Semiconductor) Regulations 1989, reg. 6.
[208] Design Right (Semiconductor) Regulations 1989, reg. 8(1).
[209] Design Right (Semiconductor) Regulations 1989, reg. 8(1).
[210] Design Right (Semiconductor) Regulations 1989, reg. 8(4).
[211] Design Right (Semiconductor) Regulations 1989, reg. 8(2).
[212] Design Right (Semiconductor) Regulations 1989, reg. 9.

An overview

The presence of several pages dealing with the issue of how computer technology can be brought under the intellectual property umbrella can be explained in two ways. The first, easy explanation is that computer technology is not easy to understand and that it is appropriate to give more detail in relation to how it fits in with intellectual property. A difficult example simply needs more explanation.

The second explanation is that computer technology does not fit into any of the existing intellectual property rights and that all attempts to make it fit distort the existing categories of intellectual property rules. From this point of view, *sui generis* regimes need to be created for the various aspects of computer technology if the long-term effectiveness and viability of intellectual property is not to be undermined.

The relatively smooth interaction between copyright and software seems to support the first explanation, while the *sui generis* approach taken in relation to databases and semiconductor chips seems to support the second. It is, indeed, not possible to regard the semiconductor design right as a 100 per cent normal design right. It is submitted that it is, at present, not possible to choose between both explanations. But it is clear that computer technology raises a series of complex and challenging questions in relation to intellectual property.

Further reading

BAKELS, R. B., 'Software Patentability: What Are the Right Questions?' (2009) 31(10) EIPR 514–22.

BOOTON, D., 'The Patentability of Computer-Implemented Inventions in Europe' (2007) 1 IPQ 92.

DE MAUNAY, Ch., 'Court of Appeal Clarifies Patenting of Computer Programs' (2009) 31(3) EIPR 147–51.

DERCLAYE, E., 'Database *sui generis* Right: What Is a Substantial Investment? A Tentative Definition' (2005) 36(1) Int Rev IP & Comp L 2.

DERCLAYE, E., 'The Court of Justice Interprets the Database *Sui Generis* Right for the First Time' (2005) 30(3) Eur LR 420.

FAWCETT, J. and TORREMANS, P. (2011) *Intellectual Property and Private International Law*, 2nd edn., Oxford: Clarendon Press.

FLINT, D., 'Computers and Internet: Making the News' (2007) 28(2) Bus LR 34.

GEIGER, Ch., 'The Answer to the Machine Should Not Be the Machine: Safeguarding the Private Copy Exception in the Digital Environment' (2008) 30(4) EIPR 121–9.

KLEIN, S., 'Search Engines and Copyright: An Analysis of the Belgian Copiepresse Decision in Consideration of British and German Copyright Law' (2008) 39(4) IIC 451–83.

LLOYD, I. (2014) *Information Technology Law*, 7th edn, Oxford: Oxford University Press.

REED, C. (ed.) (2011) *Computer Law*, 7th edn, Oxford: Oxford University Press.

31

Character merchandising

The topic of character merchandising is one of great commercial significance, but one that, as yet, has received only limited legal recognition in the UK.[1] We are concerned with rights in 'character'—another vague concept that the law has to struggle to turn into something tangible[2]—and such rights can take two forms. A right in character might be seen as the private right of an individual to develop and protect his or her own character, which is really an issue that falls within the ambit of any tortious protection of privacy, a topic on which tort lawyers wail endlessly and, so far, fruitlessly. It falls outside the ambit of a work such as this, unlike the other forms of character right, which relate to the commercial exploitation of a character and its attributes.

The commercial exploitation of character is the antithesis of privacy. Far from wishing to keep quiet about one's character, the character merchandising industry is devoted to its, at times, ruthless exposure. No self-respecting rock star would nowadays dream of giving a concert without ensuring the supply at the venue of T-shirts and other souvenirs; a celebrity can command fees for showing his or her home to the excited readers of *Hello!* magazine or for telling amusing tales of past antics to a talk show host. The entire Disney industry shows the value of successful character merchandising activity.

As a broad generalization, it may be argued that the whole development of intellectual property law has been as a response to commercially important activity that has merited legal protection. Thus patent law grew as a response to growing industrialization, while copyright's expansion has reflected the growing importance of, and differing forms of, mass media. As yet, however, character merchandising does not have much in the way of specific recognition in UK law in spite of the eloquent arguments of Frazer[3] that there should be a statutory tort giving a right of protection to a victim of the unlawful appropriation for commercial purposes of aspects of character, such as name, image, or voice. Indeed, the recent review of the law on trade marks, faced with the opportunity of creating a form of character right, declined so to do, claiming that so to do would create '*legal or administrative difficulties disproportionate to any problems that it would obviate*'.[4]

Faced with this refusal to address their concerns directly, the character merchandising industry—because it is an industry—has to seek legal protection in the form of the adaptation of other intellectual property rights and their application to the merchandising field. It may be that statutory protection would be a simpler approach, but, equally,

[1] See T. Frazer, 'Appropriation of Personality: A New Tort?' (1983) 99 LQR 281; J. Holyoak, 'UK Character Rights and Merchandising Rights Today' [1993] JBL 444; H. Carty, 'Character Merchandising and the Limits of Passing Off' (1993) 13 LS 289.

[2] See J. Adams (2007) *Merchandising Intellectual Property*, 3rd edn, Haywards Heath: Tottel; H. Ruijsenaars (2003) *Character Merchandising in Europe*, New York: Aspen.

[3] (1983) 99 LQR 281.   [4] Cm 1203, 1990, para. 4.43.

it will be seen that, taken overall, a fair range of protection is provided and we are now at a stage where the number of worthy cases that will slip between the gaps between the various intellectual property rights that may be relevant to a character merchandising situation will be few indeed.

In assessing the way in which copyright, trade mark law, and various torts combine to confer legal protection on character merchandising, it is important at the outset to point to an important distinction between two types of character. Merchandising may take place in relation to either a real character (or characters)—Madonna or Take That, for example—or in relation to a fictitious character—such as Noddy, Elsa from *Frozen*, or Superman—but the key distinction is that copyright is only relevant to the latter category. It is thus sensible to look at ways in which the law can protect *any* type of character merchandising before returning to the specific issue of fictitious characters.

Trade mark law

Clearly, many characters will be associated with an image and this, if distinctive, may very well form part of the character merchandising activity. If de facto distinctive, then, of course, that image will be able to attract the protection of registration as a trade mark under the Trade Marks Act (TMA) 1994. Pictures of celebrities, their real names or nicknames, their caricatures, or representations of objects associated with them—such as Dame Edna Everage's spectacles—could all be protected in this way.

Hurdles of the past

In the past, however, relatively little use was made of trade marks in this way. The likely reason for this was the prohibition, by s. 28(6) of the Trade Marks Act 1938, of trafficking in trade marks by disallowing the registration of any mark used for trafficking. This was considered by the House of Lords in *Re Hollie Hobby Trade Mark*,[5] in which the image of a winsome small girl, originally in use on greeting cards, was the subject of considerable licensing activity with other traders so that goods, such as toys and toiletries, could be made featuring the girl's image. Unfortunately, this perfectly legitimate commercial activity could not be protected by trade mark law. The House of Lords was clear that, to its regret, this was trafficking, described by Lord Brightman as:

> dealing in a trade mark primarily as a commodity in its own right and not primarily for the purpose of identifying or promoting merchandise in which the proprietor of the mark is interested.[6]

Most characters do not want to get their hands dirty in making the merchandise themselves, and it is normal and sensible for the exploitation to be carried out by others under licence. The *Hollie Hobby* case denied the protection of trade mark registration to this typical example of valuable commercial activity. This was unacceptable, so the White Paper on *Trade Mark Reform* that presaged the 1994 Act recommended that s. 28(6) should be repealed. The 1994 Act contains no reference to the problem of trafficking and a simplified licensing system now applies to trade marks.[7]

---

[5] [1984] RPC 329.   [6] [1984] RPC 329 at 356.   [7] TMA 1994, ss. 28–31.

A bright future?

The future of the trade mark approach to character merchandising thus looks promising, at least from the viewpoint of the celebrity who is actively engaging in merchandising activity. The emphasis in the 1994 Act on distinctiveness accords with the desire of the marketing expert to accentuate the distinctive. It seems likely that many other celebrities will follow—for example, Paul 'Gazza' Gascoigne obtained trade mark registration, in that case for his nickname, to help with lucrative merchandising activity. Others who may seek to register the character as a mark will be likely to fall foul of the provisions in s. 3(3) and (6) preventing deceptive marks and marks sought in bad faith from being registered.

But such non-authorized use may prevent the character him- or herself from registering a descriptive type of mark as being not distinctive enough for the purposes of the proviso to s. 3(1)(c) of the 1994 Act, if personal origin is regarded as within that subsection. Geographical origin is seen as descriptive as are 'other characteristics' and it must at least be arguable that personal origin is a factor belonging in this subsection. This could mean that earlier unauthorized use could prevent the registration of a trade mark in legitimate character merchandising activity.

Hurdles of the future

The requirement of distinctiveness could prove to be the major hurdle. This was already clear in the *Elvis Presley* case,[8] even though that case was still decided under the 1938 Act. Laddie J emphasized that distinctiveness means that the trade mark must enable the consumer to distinguish the goods of one trader from the similar goods of another trader. In his view, the use of the names 'Elvis' and 'Elvis Presley' did not provide the consumer with an indication concerning the origin of the product; the name of the celebrity was rather the subject matter of the goods. Laddie J did not accept that the consumer would expect that a product bearing either of the marks originated from Elvis Presley Enterprises Inc., the company that had applied to register the marks. Most people would buy the product because it had the name of the celebrity on it and would not bother about the origin of the product. That conclusion was reinforced by the fact that other manufacturers did de facto manufacture and sell Elvis Presley memorabilia, without there being any indication that the consumer believed that these products originated from Elvis Presley Enterprises. The judgment indicates that similar problems would arise in relation to the registration of the Elvis Presley signature as a trade mark. It is also clear from the emphasis on distinctiveness that the approach taken in this case will also apply under the 1994 Act.

The judgment in the *Elvis Presley* case can be criticized for its refusal to accept that the public is aware of these merchandising activities. One could, indeed, argue that the public may, in certain circumstances, believe that a product that is labelled with the name of a celebrity originates from a producer that has been approved by the celebrity.[9] The celebrity's name could then distinguish these products from similar products (not featuring the name) made by other traders. In those cases, the application to register the celebrity's name as a trade mark may be able to pass the distinctiveness hurdle, but the facts of the *Elvis Presley* case make it clear that the situation was quite different in that case.

---

[8] *Re Elvis Presley Trade Mark* [1997] RPC 543, aff'd on appeal *Elvis Presley Enterprises Inc. v. Sid Shaw Elvisly Yours* [1999] RPC 567.

[9] See, indirectly, *Re Anne Frank Trade Mark* [1998] RPC 379 (a Trade Mark Registry case).

Laddie J did accept that someone might be able to build up a reputation and goodwill in a celebrity name in the course of trade. But that will not be easy: a very famous name—such as Diana, Princess of Wales, or Jane Austen—was held to trigger such a strong reference to the celebrity involved that it would, in normal circumstances, outweigh any acquired distinctiveness in relation to merchandise sold under that name. Any trade mark registration will therefore depend on evidence being provided that the name now (also) fulfils the function, in the eyes of the public, of guaranteeing that items bearing it had originated under the control of a single undertaking responsible for their quality; otherwise, any use of the name to endorse a product would not be a trade mark use.[10] Or as Simon Brown LJ put it in the *Elvis Presley* case:

> there should be no a priori assumption that only a celebrity of his successors may ever market (or licence the marketing of) his own character. Monopolies should not be so readily created.[11]

Evidence that the character works as a proper trade mark in terms of distinctiveness as to origin will need to be provided, including proof that the celebrity aspect does not take the upper hand. In any case, a name of a character cannot be registered if the goods are seen to be 'mere image carriers'. What is being sold then is, in essence, the name or the character and any trade mark would then not be a mark, but would instead refer to the goods themselves in a descriptive way. It must therefore fail by lack of distinctiveness.[12] It should on the other hand be emphasized that the criterion of distinctiveness applies to names in the same way it applies to any other mark and that the test is exactly the same.[13]

Even if a trade mark is eventually secured, the celebrity aspect may still pose a risk. The European Court of Justice argued, in the *Picasso* case,[14] that, because the name Picasso was so famous, the public would recognize it immediately—but they would also immediately notice the difference with a slightly different sign, here 'Picaro'. The Picasso trade mark could therefore not oppose the registration of the Picaro mark. The more well known the name is, therefore, the narrower the scope of the trade mark protection will be as against similar marks. This comes on top of the already lower distinguishing capacity in relation to the goods for which it is registered in those circumstances.

Assigning trade marks that consist of the names of well-known individuals is, however, well accepted. The public does not expect the famous person to be involved with any aspect of the business or to stay involved indefinitely. The mark can be assigned with the business to a third party without there necessarily being a risk of revocation, because the public is being misled even in those circumstances in which the celebrity whose name is used as a trade mark (for example, a fashion designer) is no longer involved.[15]

The fact that most of the issues lie with the use as marks of real names should not make us forget that fictitious characters, represented by their names and drawings primarily, can now readily be registered as trade marks. Distinctiveness, even after *Elvis Presley*, is a hurdle that can be overcome. This was shown in the *Jules Rimet* case where it was

---

[10] *Diana, Princess of Wales Trade Mark* [2001] ETMR 25; *Jane Austen Trade Mark* [2000] RPC 879 (two Trade Mark Registry cases).

[11] *Elvis Presley Enterprises Inc. v. Sid Shaw Elvisly Yours* [1999] RPC 567 at 597.

[12] See also *Linkin Park LLC's Application* [2005] ETMR 17 and *Linkin Park LLC's Application* [2006] ETMR 74.

[13] Case C-404/02, *Nichols plc v. Registrar of Trade Marks* [2004] ECR I-8499, [2005] 1 WLR 1418.

[14] Case C361/04 P, *Ruiz-Picasso v. OHIM* [2006] ECR I-643, [2006] ETMR 29.

[15] Case C259/04, *Elizabeth Emanuel v. Continental Shelf 128 Ltd* [2006] ECR I-3089, [2006] ETMR 56.

accepted that the lion device used in relation to the World Cup Football in 1966 could be registered as a trade mark in combination with the words 'World Cup Willie' (on top of a registration simply for the words), despite the fact that in that case the registration had been applied for in bad faith.[16] Another example is found in the case in which Hearst Holdings successfully sued for the infringement of their trade marks for the cartoon character Betty Boop when unauthorized Betty Boop merchandise appeared on the market.[17]

Design law

In some cases, the two design rights may be appropriately used to protect character merchandising. Under the Registered Designs Act (RDA) 1949, a design can be registered for the appearance of the whole, or a part, of a product resulting from the features of, in particular, the lines, contours, colours, shape, texture, or materials of the product, or its ornamentation.[18] The production of a coffee mug shaped so as to depict the facial feature of a well-known personality would fit easily within this definition. Similarly, such an object could fall within the newer unregistered design right created by s. 213 of the Copyright, Designs and Patents Act (CDPA) 1988—but this expressly excludes surface decoration, so a mug bearing only a picture of a celebrity would not qualify for this right, although it would appear to be within the registered design right. A mug shaped in the form of the face of a celebrity could also be the subject of an unregistered design right. In each case, it is an item, or features thereof, that are the subject of the right and this obviously limits the use of these rights to a small proportion of merchandising activities.

Tort

Passing off

Prior to the passage of the new trade marks legislation, it was the tort of passing off that did most to protect the commercial exploitation of character by merchandising. It seems likely that this tort will continue to function in this area, although, in the future, it will be overshadowed more by trade mark law. It is nonetheless only relatively recently that the tort of passing off has come to play a role in this field, having been held back for some time.

The common field of activity hurdle

The problem previously was that it was generally thought that, for liability to exist, the parties must be working in a common field of activity. So an action would be between two rival clothing manufacturers, but not between a celebrity and a clothing manufacturer, even if the celebrity wanted to engage in merchandising activity involving clothing.

This was used to prevent a claim from succeeding in respect of authorized character merchandising as long ago as 1947. In *McCulloch v. Lewis A. May (Produce Distributors)*,[19] the claimant was a well-known children's broadcaster, known as 'Uncle Mac'. As a BBC

---

[16] *Jules Rimet Cup Ltd v. The Football Association Ltd* [2008] FR 10.
[17] *Hearst Holdings Inc v. AVELA Inc* [2014] EWHC 439 (Ch), [2014] FSR 36.
[18] RDA 1949, s. 1.   [19] [1947] 2 All ER 845.

employee at that time, involvement with anything so sordid as commerce was out of the question, so he was doubly appalled when the defendant began selling 'Uncle Mac's Puffed Wheat' without permission. The breakfast cereal was advertised in such a way as to associate closely the product and the celebrity. Wynn-Parry J found against the claimant: he was a broadcaster, not a cereal manufacturer, and there was thus no common field of activity and no passing off claim.

This approach was resolutely adhered to by the UK courts. In *Lyngstad v. Anabas Products*,[20] an attempt to prevent the sale of unauthorized Abba merchandise was unsuccessful on this ground, in spite of the fact that Abba had developed a sizeable merchandising trade alongside their musical activities. Similarly, in *Tavener Rutledge Ltd v. Trexapalm Ltd*,[21] the supposed lack of common field of activity was enough to defeat an attempt to prevent the sale of 'Kojakpops' lollipops designed to evoke the image of Kojak, a popular, lollipop-sucking, television detective. This was especially ironic, because, by being first in the field, the unauthorized trader was able to prevent a properly licensed manufacturer from putting 'Kojak lollies' on the market. Law and commercial reality were not working hand in hand at this stage of the law's development.

A way forward emerges

The Australian courts soon showed the way forward. In *Henderson v. Radio Corp. Pty Ltd*,[22] the High Court of New South Wales rejected the *McCulloch* approach and allowed two well-known dancers to prevent the unauthorized use of their picture on the cover of a record of dance music. Particularly instructive is *Children's Television Workshop Inc. v. Woolworths (NSW) Ltd*.[23] In this case, the claimants had rights in the characters from *The Muppet Show* and they were able to prevent the sale by the defendants of unauthorized Muppet memorabilia by demonstrating that they had their own merchandising operation, and that, although it was conducted on a licensed basis, they continued to exercise close quality control over it. It was also relevant that the public were aware of the merchandising link and, in particular, of the existence of quality control.

Slowly, then, the UK courts have come to grips with the phenomenon of character merchandising. An important first stage was recognition of the practice and, with it, recognition of public awareness. This came in *IPC Magazines Ltd v. Black & White Music Corp. Ltd*,[24] in which the proprietors of a magazine featuring the exploits of Judge Dredd sought protection against the release of a pop record featuring the fabled jurist. Although no injunction was awarded (damages at full trial being thought to be an adequate remedy), Goulding J was prepared to recognize that the public would assume that the claimants had, in some way, authorized the record. In other words, once it is realized that character merchandising does go on and that the public have realized that, for example, not every Abba sweatshirt was personally knitted by one or other of the Swedish superstars, but that Abba are nevertheless trading in sweatshirts as well as songs, the celebrity has goodwill that the tort of passing off can protect in not only songs and records, but also in sweatshirts. This reflects the modern reality that many films, shows, or items are nowadays launched as a package in which the revenue from merchandising activity is as important as that derived from the entertainment performances. There is no point launching, for example, a new pop group into the world to great acclaim if you have no souvenirs to sell to their excited fans and, in practice, these will be already in the warehouse.

[20] [1977] FSR 62.   [21] [1977] RPC 275.   [22] [1969] RPC 218.
[23] [1981] RPC 187.   [24] [1983] FSR 348.

Recognition of a role for passing off

The recognition of broader ideas of goodwill in these claims and the more general renewed emphasis on goodwill in the *Jif Lemon* case[25] all help the use of the tort of passing off in character merchandising situations, but formal recognition of its role at last transpired in *Mirage Studios v. Counter Feat Clothing Co.*,[26] in which the use of images of the Teenage Mutant Ninja Turtles on clothing was at issue. The launch of the Turtles was a classic example of the development of an overall product in relation to which sales of merchandise were as significant as sales of the television programmes. It was thus clear that the claimants enjoyed goodwill in the clothing trade, as well as in the entertainment business. The knowledge of the buying public that properly licensed merchandising activity is common meant that there was a misrepresentation in the form of the unauthorized sales and that obvious damage could be envisaged to the trade of the claimants. Thus the elements of passing off were satisfied and an injunction granted. The earlier Australian cases were approved and the earlier English cases distinguished as being inappropriate to cases in which the claimant has copyright in the character and is already in the business of merchandising. In reality, it is unlikely that the 'no common field of activity' argument has any life in it.

Meanwhile, the Federal Court of Australia has gone yet further in the protection of character merchandising in *Pacific Dunlop Ltd v. Hogan*.[27] Paul Hogan, actor, comedian, and star of the film *Crocodile Dundee*, successfully brought an action against an advert for shoes that mimicked one particular scene in the film; the Hogan character in the advert wore similar clothes to those worn by Hogan in the film. It was held that Hogan, who himself appeared in many adverts and always in the role of 'a good-natured larrikin'[28] had a right to be protected against the unauthorized use of his character, because it would harm his own marketing opportunities. Hogan was trading not only as an actor and comedian, but as a general all-round celebrity and thus any activity deriving from his fame would be protected by the tort of passing off.

One further development in passing off is also relevant and perhaps accords with the *Hogan* case. As we have seen in an earlier chapter, the case of *Lego System Aktieselkab v. Lego M Lemelstrich Ltd*[29] allowed Lego to use the tort of passing off against another, but totally unrelated, user of the Lego name on the basis that the fame of Lego is such that anyone seeing the name would automatically assume, whatever the context, that it was the name of the renowned Danish toy brick manufacturer and any defects would be assumed to be its fault, thus risking harm to its reputation. This fits well into the character merchandising field. For example, an unauthorized dealer sells a David Cameron pen that often leaks; the public knows of the practice of character merchandising and thus blames David Cameron for the leaks. This would harm his current merchandising activity, if there were any, but, after *Lego*, the possible harm to any future merchandising activity will also be enough to sustain an action in passing off.

We have argued earlier that this is a tort bursting with vigour in recent years. Its application to character merchandising shows this well, if perhaps belatedly. The flexibility and adaptability of the common law afforded protection comparable to that which legislation might be expected to provide. However, fresh doubt was cast over the fact that the public is now aware of the practice of character merchandising—but, at the same time, Laddie J seemed to recognize in the *Elvis Presley trade mark* case[30] that it must be

---

[25] *Reckitt & Colman Products Ltd v. Border Inc.* [1990] 1 All ER 873, [1990] 1 WLR 491.
[26] [1991] FSR 145.   [27] (1989) 14 IPR 398.   [28] (1989) 14 IPR 398 at 400.
[29] [1983] FSR 155   [30] *Re Elvis Presley Trade Marks* [1997] RPC 543.

possible to use the name of a celebrity to market a product, and to build up a reputation and goodwill in that name in the course of trade.

This point receives additional support from the judgment in the *Alan Clark* case.[31] It was readily accepted in the latter case that Mr Clark had goodwill in his name, and that the passing off of the spoof diaries in the *Evening Standard* newspaper through the false attribution of authorship could lead to substantial damage to his reputation (and earnings) as a columnist and diarist. But Mr Clark had the advantage of a reputation as a writer and not only as a celebrity: it is no doubt still easier to succeed in an action in passing off if the goodwill relates specifically to the merchandising activity or to any other commercial activity, rather than only to the general reputation and goodwill that one acquires as a celebrity.

But the latter is also possible following the *Eddie Irvine* case,[32] in which Laddie J held that it was the purpose of the law of passing off to vindicate the claimant's exclusive right to his goodwill and to protect it against damage. The law would therefore not allow others to use that goodwill so as to reduce, blur, or diminish its exclusivity. It followed from this that it was not necessary to show that the claimant and the defendant shared a common field of activity, or that the sales of products or services would be diminished either substantially or directly, at least in the short term. Instead, the essential point was to show a misrepresentation, because that element was required to enable the defendant to take advantage of the defendant's reputation. The unauthorized manipulation of a photograph of Mr Irvine, by means of which a Talksport Radio was put in his hand, and its subsequent use for publicity purposes amounted to such a misrepresentation, because it created the impression that Mr Irvine was endorsing Talksport Radio. This could affect Mr Irvine's goodwill and reputation, and the requirements for passing off were therefore met.

The Court of Appeal followed a similar approach when it held that Topshop was liable for passing off when it sold, without the pop-start's consent, T-shirts bearing the image of Rihanna. The application of the photo to the T-shirt resulted in Topshop telling a lie and created the impression of approval or authorization. This was even more so because Topshop emphasized the star's visits to their shops and Rihanna clearly has a reputation as a fashionista. As a result the star's followers were confused by the misrepresentation and would want to buy the T-shirt they understood was endorsed by Rihanna.[33]

It should also be noted that fictitious characters create far fewer issues in this respect and that their protection by means of passing off has become rather straightforward.[34]

Defamation

We have, elsewhere in this book, noted the decision in *Tolley v. J. S. Fry Ltd*[35] that an amateur golfer could sue in defamation for the unauthorized use of his character in an advert that carried the implication that he had compromised his amateur status. This is clearly applicable to protect character merchandising activity, but its use is limited to those cases in which reputation is lowered. So it would be defamatory to create a false quote from the dean of the law faculty of a prestigious university apparently endorsing a pornographic magazine, but it was not appropriate for David Frost to use defamation

---

[31] *Clark v. Associated Newspapers Ltd* [1998] 1 All ER 959.

[32] *Irvine v. Talksport Ltd* [2002] FSR 943, upheld (while raising the amount of the damages) by the Court of Appeal [2003] 2 All ER 881.

[33] *Fenty v. Arcadia Group Brands (t/a Topshop)* [2015] EWCA Civ 3, [2015] FSR 14.

[34] *Jules Rimet Cup Ltd v. The Football Association Ltd* [2008] FR 10.   [35] [1931] AC 333.

law against a hotel that falsely claimed his endorsement, because no harm was done to his reputation thereby.[36]

Malicious falsehood

If character merchandising activity is already under way, it is easy to see how the unauthorized merchandising of poor-quality goods could be seen by customers as being an attack on that activity by implication and, if false and denigratory, thus actionable in the tort of malicious falsehood. The use of this tort has, however, been considerably enhanced in the context of character merchandising by the notable decision in *Kaye v. Robertson*,[37] in which an injured actor was able to use the tort to prevent the publication of a true story about his condition in hospital after a serious accident. The basis of the decision was that publication would imply that the actor had consented; the tawdry context of the publication would be harmful to his image as a celebrity, but, more particularly, it would harm his own right to sell his story on his own terms for his own gain on his recovery. This loss then forms the necessary damage to complete the grounds for a claim.

The easier availability of injunctive relief was a key to Kaye's success in malicious falsehood rather than defamation. Another reason for preferring to use malicious falsehood was that, unlike in defamation, it was possible to obtain legal aid for it, a point highlighted in *Joyce v. Sengupta*.[38] This is now no longer the case though. A newspaper alleged that the claimant, Princess Anne's maid, had stolen embarrassing royal correspondence, but this was false. She was allowed to frame her claim in malicious falsehood in view of the obvious harm to her trade as royal servant caused by the inaccurate story.

These two cases show that malicious falsehood can be used against any falsity that may have the effect of harming the victim's trade and that, after *Kaye*, if the victim is a celebrity, it will be assumed that he or she is trading not only as, in that case, an actor, but also as a celebrity. This notion neatly parallels that in the *Crocodile Dundee* case. There remain, however, limits on the use of this tort. A celebrity who does not trade as such may have difficulty establishing that there is damage; the exception to this requirement, under s. 3 of the Defamation Act 1952, in cases of words calculated to cause pecuniary damage is also of no assistance to a claimant who is not using his or her celebrity status as the base of merchandising activity.

More seriously, there is a need to prove malice and this may be difficult if a trader honestly, but without authorization, puts good-quality character merchandise on the market. In *Kaye*, however, it was asserted by Glidewell LJ that:

> malice will be inferred if it be proved that the words were calculated to cause damage and that the defendant knew when he published the words that they were false or were reckless as to whether they were false or not.[39]

False words may be equated to the act of merchandising goods falsely, attributing them as being authorized by the character in question, and, on this basis, it would seem that malice will be found to be present at least if the claimant is him- or herself engaged in merchandising activity.

---

[36] Example cited in R. Wacks (1980) *The Protection of Privacy*, London: Butterworths, p. 167.

[37] [1991] FSR 62. [38] [1993] 1 All ER 897, [1993] 1 WLR 337.

[39] [1991] FSR 62 at 67. Cf. P. Milmo et al. (2005) *Gatley on Libel and Slander*, 10th edn, London: Sweet and Maxwell, pp. 303 and 323. See also P. Milmo et al. (2008) *Gatley on Libel and Slander*, 11th edn, London: Sweet and Maxwell.

Copyright

Can traditional copyright concepts apply?

If we now confine our attention to fictitious characters, it is evident that copyright protection for artistic or literary works will be available. An unauthorized drawing of Donald Duck on a T-shirt will soon be met with a writ from the Disney organization; the creation of a character in the words of a book is the result of much literary effort, whether in putting together the stunts and wit that are Ian Fleming's James Bond, or the more refined characteristics that make up Agatha Christie's Miss Marple. The principal authority in this field is the decision of the House of Lords in *King Features Syndicate Inc. v. Kleeman*,[40] in which unauthorized merchandise was being sold exploiting the popular newspaper cartoon figure of Popeye. This merchandise was held to infringe the copyright in the Popeye character.

The case is particularly significant in so far as the drawings of Popeye were made by the defendant and were not direct copies of any of the claimants' drawings. Of course, they used the distinctive features of Popeye to ensure the necessary recognition essential for sales. The problems of using copyright in cases of imprecise copying were referred to in *Mirage Studios v. Counter Feat Clothing Ltd*,[41] in which the drawings of humanoid turtles were again not directly copied by the defendants. Although an interlocutory injunction was granted, it was by no means clear that, at trial, there would be no problem in saying that drawings of the concept of a humanoid turtle infringed copyright in the claimant's specific drawings. This is a classic example of the problems posed by the way in which copyright law will protect the expression of ideas, but not the ideas themselves.[42]

Further problems arise in cases relating to the use of a fictitious name. Copyright is only granted to those who have exercised some degree of creative energy. Thus in *Exxon Corp. v. Exxon Insurance Consultants International Ltd*,[43] the invented name 'Exxon' was not capable of copyright protection as being a highly artificial word that was not the product of creative endeavour, but it was conceded by Graham J at first instance[44] that a title could be registered for copyright if it has qualities or characteristics in itself. Lewis Carroll's 'Jabberwocky' is cited as an example in relation to which the name, coupled with the literary work in which it appears and the images evoked by it, is enough to justify the grant of copyright protection. In *Mirage Studios*, however, the name 'Ninja Turtles' alone was held not to be capable of copyright protection, so doubt remains as to the precise boundary of copyright protection of names. The general rule remains that there will be no copyright in a name as such, or in a signature.[45]

The image of a celebrity is also probably not capable of protection by copyright. The pop star Adam Ant used to wear distinctive face make-up, but this was not regarded as an artistic work for copyright purposes in *Merchandising Corp. of America Inc.*

---

[40] [1941] AC 417.   [41] [1991] FSR 145.

[42] *Jules Rimet Cup Ltd v. The Football Association Ltd* (n. 34). Section 52 CDPA 1988 may also provide a defence in certain cases. For a similar case decision under German copyright law, see *Re Pippi Longstocking character (infringement of a copyright user's rights)* I ZR 52/12, Bundesgerichtshof, [2014] ECC 27.

[43] [1982] Ch 119, aff'd [1981] 3 All ER 241.

[44] [1982] Ch 119 at 131, [1981] 2 All ER 495 at 504. The decision was upheld by the Court of Appeal and nothing said there contradicts the approach of Graham J at first instance.

[45] *Re Anne Frank Trade Mark* [1998] RPC 379 (a Trade Mark Registry case); see also *Re Elvis Presley Trade Marks* [1997] RPC 543.

v. Harpbond.[46] Maybe a more permanent form of decoration would provide a different decision and it is clear, in general, that copyright provides a useful protection against the unauthorized merchandising of fictitious characters, particularly given the length of protection afforded.

False attribution

The moral right to object to the false attribution of authorship[47] may also assist celebrities, albeit in a defensive way. It can be used to stop the unauthorized use of the celebrity's name to suggest that he or she is the author of work with which no such link exists in reality. The successful use of this right by Alan Clark to stop the attribution to him—or at least that belief in the eyes of a substantial number of readers—of the spoof diaries that appeared without his authorization in the London *Evening Standard* newspaper demonstrates this point clearly.[48] The right cannot, however, be used positively to protect any form of merchandising activity.

An overview

Although no specific character protection right has been developed in the UK, this does not of itself dent the initial suggestion in this chapter that intellectual property rights develop in response to the need to protect commercially significant activity. As when Frazer argued[49] that a new character right was needed, such an argument had more force than it does now. Since then, the law of trade marks has been amended to remove a key block to character merchandising activity's protection in law, while passing off has learnt to recognize the existence and importance of such activity in the *IPC* and *Mirage Studios* cases that, when coupled with the broad sweep of the *Lego* decision, give a far broader degree of protection than seemed likely a decade or so ago. Meanwhile, the recognition that one can trade as a celebrity, in *Kaye*, gives further protection to the famous.

It may be argued that this patchwork of remedies is fine for the famous, but does not protect ordinary citizens from exploitation. The answer to this, once again, is the law's reflection of commercially important activity and the fact that there is no such commercial need for legal intervention. There is no need to protect Holyoak and Torremans from the unauthorized use of their names on T-shirts, because such a use has no commercial value (yet). There may be reasons related to personal privacy to extend protection, but these we leave to civil libertarians to debate. From our commercial standpoint, we would assert the need to take care in the formulation of any new law. It would be absurd if, for example, everyone on board a crowded paddle steamer had any right to prevent the sale, or demand a royalty from, a postcard showing the vessel heading into port.

It may be that a simple statutory move to create a character right would be beneficial in terms of simplicity and legal elegance—but the developments of the last two decades show that the law has become seized of the legal and commercial importance of character merchandising activity, and has moved to protect it in an entirely adequate manner.

---

[46] [1983] FSR 32.   [47] CDPA 1988, s. 84.   [48] *Clark v. Associated Newspapers Ltd* (n. 31).
[49] T. Frazer, 'Appropriation of Personality: A New Tort?' (1983) 99 LQR 281.

Further reading

ADAMS, J. (2007) *Merchandising Intellectual Property*, 3rd edn, Haywards Heath: Tottel.

BEVERLEY-SMITH, H. (2002) *The Commercial Appropriation of Personality*, Cambridge: Cambridge University Press.

BEVERLEY-SMITH, H., OHLY, A., and LUCAS-SCHLOETTER, A. (2005) *Privacy, Property and Personality: Civil Law Perspectives on Commercial Appropriation*, Cambridge: Cambridge University Press.

BLACK, G. (2011) *Publicity Right and Image Exploitation and Legal Control*, Oxford: Hart Publishing.

HOFMANN, F., 'The Right to Publicity in German and English Law' (2010) 3 IPQ 325.

MACLEOD, C. and WOOD, A., 'The *Picasso* Case, Famous Names and Branding Celebrity' (2006) 17(1) Ent LR 44.

RUIJSENAARS, H. (2003) *Character Merchandising in Europe*, New York: Aspen.

32

Remedies in intellectual property litigation

Throughout this book, we have been pointing out the ways in which the various legal remedies can be used in relation to the various different intellectual property rights. In this chapter, we will give a relatively brief overview of the enforcement procedures that are used in relation to intellectual property rights, of the civil remedies that apply, and of some issues that arise in relation to the gathering of evidence in intellectual property cases.

Intellectual property rights are often applied for in many countries. In such cases, many of these rights may be involved in a single infringement action or similar infringing acts may have been committed in the various jurisdictions. Intellectual property rights are also increasingly exploited internationally; that exploitation may also give rise to transnational litigation. The interaction between intellectual property and private international law gives rise to complex issues, both at the jurisdictional level (which court will decide the case) and at the choice-of-law level (which law will that court apply). A full discussion of these issues would lead too far and we refer the reader to the full discussion of these issues that can be found in *Fawcett and Torremans* (2nd edn, 2011). At international level, principles have now also been drafted to assist parties, judges and legislators dealing with these complex issues.[1]

Enforcement issues

Intellectual property rights can be enforced in four ways: civil actions are used most commonly); criminal proceedings: administrative proceedings; and measures of self-help complete the picture.

Civil actions

Despite a slight reservation for breach of confidence, most intellectual property rights can be characterized as property rights. The way in which that property right is affected in cases of infringement can consequently be described as tortious in nature. Essentially, what we are dealing with are torts committed against property. On top of that come the actions between assignors and assignees, and between licensors and licensees, some of which are contractual in nature, because the claim is not based on the infringement of

---

[1] For Europe, see European Max Planck Group on Conflict of Laws in Intellectual Property (2013) *Conflict of Laws in Intellectual Property: The CLIP Principles and Commentary*, Oxford: Oxford University Press. See also <http://www.cl-ip.eu/_www/cn/pub/home.html>.

the intellectual property right involved, but on a breach of the contractual provisions that had been agreed. This can lead to actions for breach of contract.

Infringing acts may also give reason for concern to licensees of intellectual property. But while it is obvious that the owner of the right is entitled to bring an action against the alleged infringer, the same cannot be said about the licensee. The starting point is that a licensee cannot sue for infringement and must rely on the owner of the intellectual property right to bring the action. Exceptionally, an exclusive licensee can bring the action. This possibility is subject to a number of restrictions.

1. It has only been made possible in relation to exclusive patent,[2] trade mark,[3] copyright,[4] and unregistered design[5] licences. Registered design licences and know-how licences, etc. are not covered by it.

2. The exclusive licence must be fully exclusive, in the sense that even the licensor cannot exploit the right in the area that has been allocated to the licensee.[6]

3. The licensor has to be joined as a party to the proceedings, normally as a claimant, or alternatively as a defendant.[7]

On the defendant's side one finds the alleged infringer: this is normally the person who performed the restricted act. Anyone who collaborates with that person in common design can be sued as joint tortfeasor.[8] An employer, but not someone who commissions a work, is vicariously liable for the infringement of intellectual property that an employee committed in the course of his or her employment, just as this is the case for any other tort. Such an employer is quite often a company, but also the real person behind the company, such as a company director, can be personally liable for torts committed on behalf of the company if he or she has ordered or procured their commission.[9]

All of these civil actions are normally brought before the Chancery Division of the High Court of England and Wales,[10] or before the Outer House of the Court of Session in Scotland. Actions that involve lower amounts of money can also be brought in the county court and there is now, in London, also a specialized patents county court.

This is primarily an area of domestic law—but the TRIPS Agreement imposes minimum standards on all contracting states and, now, the European Union (EU) has decided to harmonize this area of intellectual property law by means of an Enforcement Directive.[11] This move has been criticized,[12] but when the scope of the Directive was reduced, the changes to domestic law turned out to be minimal.[13]

Later on in the chapter we will look in more detail at crucial aspects, such as the gathering of evidence and sanction. Each of these will then also be placed in the context of the Enforcement Directive. Apart from these core aspects the Directive also recognizes that there are circumstances in which the public and the trade need to be

---

[2] Patents Act 1977, s. 67.   [3] TMA 1994, s. 31.   [4] CDPA 1988, s. 101.

[5] CDPA 1988, s. 234.

[6] And it must exist when the claim form is issued: *Procter & Gamble v. Peaudouce* [1989] FSR 180.

[7] See e.g. CDPA 1988, ss. 102 and 235.

[8] See *Mölnlycke AB v. Procter & Gamble Ltd* [1992] RPC 21 at 29; *Unilever plc v. Gillette (UK) Ltd* [1989] RPC 583 at 608.

[9] *MCA Records v. Charly Records* [2002] FSR 401, [2002] EMLR 1 (CA).

[10] Within the Chancery Division of the High Court, the Patents Court deals with patent matters.

[11] European Parliament and Council Directive 2004/48/EC on the enforcement of intellectual property rights [2004] OJ L 195/16.

[12] W. R. Cornish et al.,'Procedures and Remedies for Enforcing IPRS: The European Commission's Proposed Directive' (2003) 25 EIPR 447.

[13] The Intellectual Property (Enforcement, etc.) Regulations 2006, SI 2006/1027.

alerted. Its Art. 15 allows therefore the judicial authorities to order appropriate measures for the dissemination of information concerning their decision. This is done at the request of the applicant and at the expense of the infringer and may include the publication or display of the judgment, for example in national newspapers or specialist magazines.

Criminal proceedings

Criminal proceedings do not play an important role in the area of intellectual property. Some offences do, however, exist and these types of proceedings are specifically concerned with cases of infringement that are seen as particularly serious from a public policy point of view. Obvious examples are actions against copyright or trade mark pirates.

The commission of the kind of acts that amount to secondary infringement of copyright now also leads to criminal liability in the circumstances that are described in s. 107 of the Copyright, Designs and Patents Act (CDPA) 1988.[14] The Act also makes provision for orders for delivery up[15] and for search orders[16] in this context. Infringing goods can be disposed of[17] and can be forfeited.[18]

In those cases in which both criminal and civil proceedings can be brought, the court cannot express a preference or make a choice. The right owner makes his or her choice when bringing the case either via civil or via criminal proceedings.[19] These offences can, in serious instances, be prosecuted summarily or on indictment.[20]

Counterfeiting of registered trade marks can also give rise to criminal liability. This will, for example, be the case if the trade mark, or a similar and confusing mark, is applied to goods or their packaging, if such goods are sold or offered for sale, or if such a sign is applied to packaging or labelling material.[21] A defendant manning a market stall and found in possession of counterfeit clothing which he was offering for sale received on this basis a sentence of six months' imprisonment, suspended for two years,[22] whereas an offender that had been involved in the planning and organization of such an enterprise was given a sentence of two years' imprisonment.[23] The goods to which the mark is applied can obviously be goods within the class for which the mark has been registered, but other goods are also covered in cases of improper dilution.[24]

---

[14] For an example concerning a provision of German law on the basis of which a transporter was held liable for aiding and abetting the unlawful distribution of a work protected by copyright law (but not protected in the country where it was manufactured), see Case C-5/11, *Donner*, 21 June 2012, <http://curia.europa.eu>.

[15] CDPA 1988, s. 108.

[16] CDPA 1988, s. 109, as amended by Copyright, etc. and Trade Marks (Offences and Enforcement) Act 2002, s. 2. The latter Act also expanded the search order system to unauthorized decoders by inserting s. 297B into the CDPA 1988.

[17] CDPA 1988, ss. 114 and 204 in relation to illicit recordings.

[18] CDPA 1988, ss. 114A (infringing copies), 204A (illicit recordings), and 297C (unauthorized decoders) inserted by Copyright etc. and Trade Marks (Offences and Enforcement) Act 2002, ss. 3–5.

[19] *Thames & Hudson Ltd v. Designs & Artists Copyright Society Ltd* [1995] FSR 153.

[20] CDPA 1988, ss. 107–110.

[21] TMA 1994, ss. 92 and 93. The system of search warrants has also been added here as s. 92A by Copyright etc. and Trade Marks (Offences and Enforcement) Act 2002, s. 6. Section 92 does, however, require use of the mark as a trade mark; descriptive use is not covered: see *R v. Johnstone* [2003] FSR 748, [2003] 3 All ER 884 (HL).

[22] *R v. Singh (Harpreet)* [2012] EWCA Crim 1855.

[23] *R v. Brayford (Richard Frederick)* [2010] EWCA Crim 2329.   [24] TMA 1994, s. 92(4).

Other offences exist in relation to intellectual property registers. It is an offence to make, or cause to be made, false entries in the Trade Marks Register;[25] another offence covers the act of falsely representing a trade mark as registered.[26] Both of these types of offence also exist in relation to patents[27] and registered designs.[28]

In more general terms, the crime of conspiracy to defraud can also be committed in relation to intellectual property. This could, for example, be the case for those agreeing to try to bribe cinema employees into handing over copies of films that would subsequently be copied and released on video in an unauthorized way, because the conspirers seek to obtain a pecuniary advantage and they try to make others act contrary to their duties.[29] The crime also applies to cases in which the conspirers are proposing to acquire property, which could include intellectual property, dishonestly. The outcome of the attempt to obtain an advantage, or to make others act against their duties, or to acquire property is not particularly relevant, because it is the conspiracy element that counts, and neither is the fact that the infringement of the right amounts to an offence as such.

These criminal offences are hard to prove: the defendant must be shown to be guilty 'beyond reasonable doubt', rather than 'on the balance of probabilities' as is the case in most civil cases, and the type of *mens rea* must be that the defendant knew, or had reason to believe, that he or she was committing an infringing act or another offence.

Administrative procedures

Customs officers, trading standards authorities, advertising standards authorities, and Ofcom (the office of communications that assumed the duties of the Radio Authority and the Independent Television Commission in this area at the end of 2003) play an ancillary role in the enforcement of intellectual property rights. Only the role played by customs officers is really of great significance in relation to the main intellectual property rights.

At the request of the right holder, customs officers may arrest infringing imports at their point of entry. These infringing imports must either be infringing copies of literary, dramatic, or musical works, of sound recordings or of films,[30] or, in the case of trade marks, goods in relation to which the use of the trade mark would amount to an infringement.[31] These measures operate together with an EU regulation to stop the release into free circulation of counterfeit goods.[32]

The EU Regulation sets up a set of rules that are aimed at facilitating the cooperation between right holders and the customs authorities. The public policy aim is to stop counterfeit and pirated goods from entering the single market and prevent their marketing. In that sense the Regulation also implements Arts. 51–60 of the TRIPS Agreement 1994. All of the procedures are based on an application by the owner of the right—that is,

---

[25] TMA 1994, s. 94.   [26] TMA 1994, s. 95.
[27] Patents Act 1977, ss. 109 and 110; see also s. 111.
[28] Registered Designs Act 1949, ss. 34 and 35.
[29] See *Scott v. Metropolitan Police Comr* [1975] AC 819.   [30] CDPA 1988, ss. 111 and 112.
[31] TMA 1994, ss. 89–91.

[32] Regulation (EU) No. 608/2013 of the European Parliament and of the Council concerning customs enforcement of intellectual property rights and repealing Council Regulation (EC) No 1383/2003 [2013] OJ L 181/15. Previously: Council Regulation (EC) No. 1383/2003 concerning customs action against goods suspected of infringing certain intellectual property rights and the measures to be taken against goods found to have infringed such rights [2003] OJ L 196/7. See also the Goods Infringing Intellectual Property Rights (Customs) Regulations 2004, SI 2004/1473, as most recently amended by the Goods Infringing Intellectual Property Rights (Customs) (Amendment) Regulations 2010, SI 2010/324 (dealing with goods abandoned for destruction).

a 'tip-off', including a description of the goods—but customs authorities can also act on their own initiatives, for instance by means of random checks. The system in the Regulation falls apart in a phase where specific attention is being paid and preparatory measures are being taken on the one hand and a phase that is characterized by the actual intervention of the customs authorities on the other hand.

The first phase can of course be activated on the basis of information about a suspect shipment that is passed on to customs by the right holder or one of its affiliates. Each member state designates a customs department to which these applications can be sent and the Commission provides a standard application form that contains details about the applicant, the intellectual property right concerned, and information about the alleged infringement.[33] In addition it is wise to give customs as much information as possible, for example to point out the differences between the authentic goods and counterfeit items that have been found or that are suspected to be in the shipment or information about the value and routing of the goods. There is no fee involved.[34] The customs department will reach a decision on the application within 30 days.[35] The parties agree to exchange updated information and the applicant enters into an undertaking to pay damages if the third parties affected are found not to be dealing in infringing goods. Once the application is granted the customs authorities will look out for the allegedly infringing goods and if they are identified, their release is suspended or they are detained. The applicant is then notified of the action that has been taken[36] and an opportunity to inspect or sample the goods follows.[37] The right holder can also benefit from the provisions of the Regulation in case the goods have been bought on an online platform outside the EU, even in the absence of advertising in the EU. The Regulation will then apply upon the goods entering the EU.[38]

The holder of the goods can agree to the destruction of the goods,[39] but if that is not the case the applicant shall bring legal proceedings to determine whether an intellectual property right has been infringed within 10 working days of the notification of the suspension or detention.[40] In case of perishable goods a three-working-day period applies. Failure to bring proceedings will end the retention of the goods and, subject to a right of appeal, customs can *ex officio* take the initiative in these circumstances to release the goods.[41] The right holder can also request the names and addresses of the consignee, the consignor, the declarant of the holder of the goods, and the origin of the goods.[42]

But often smaller and medium-size companies do not have the means to gather the kind of information that allows them to make an application. Article 18 therefore

---

[33] Arts. 5 and 6 of Regulation (EU) No. 608/2013 of the European Parliament and of the Council concerning customs enforcement of intellectual property rights and repealing Council Regulation (EC) No 1383/2003 [2013] OJ L 181/15.

[34] Regulation (EU) No. 608/2013, Art. 8.   [35] Regulation (EU) No. 608/2013, Art. 9.

[36] Regulation (EU) No. 608/2013, Art. 17.   [37] Regulation (EU) No. 608/2013, Art. 19.

[38] Case C-98/13 *Martin Blomqvist v. Rolex SA and Manufacture des Montres Rolex SA* [2014] ETMR 25, [2014] ECDR 10.

[39] See Case C-93/08, *Schenker SIA v. Valsts Ienemumu Dienests* [2009] ETMR 35.

[40] Art. 23 of Regulation (EU) No. 608/2013 of the European Parliament and of the Council concerning customs enforcement of intellectual property rights and repealing Council Regulation (EC) No 1383/2003 [2013] OJ L 181/15.

[41] Case C-583/12, *Sintax Trading OÜ v. Maksu-ja TolliametS'* [2014] ECDR 11.

[42] Art. 17(4) of Regulation (EU) No. 608/2013 of the European Parliament and of the Council concerning customs enforcement of intellectual property rights and repealing Council Regulation (EC) No 1383/2003 [2013] OJ L 181/15.

provides a mechanism for the customs authorities to take action *ex officio*. This also gives them an option to act before the grant of an application, so one does not exclude the other. This mechanism is triggered when during an action the customs authorities come to believe that there are sufficient grounds to suspect that goods they discover in the course of such action are infringing intellectual property rights. The mechanism then provides for the suspension of the release or the retention by the customs authorities of these goods and the immediate notification of both the holder of the goods and the owner of the intellectual property right that may be infringed. It is then up to the right holders to file an application and that application will then follow its normal course.[43]

In this whole system definitions of concepts are essential. These are contained in Art. 2:

For the purposes of this Regulation:

(1) 'intellectual property right' means:
  (a) a trade mark;
  (b) a design;
  (c) a copyright or any related right as provided for by national or Union law;
  (d) a geographical indication;
  (e) a patent as provided for by national or Union law;
  (f) a supplementary protection certificate for medicinal products as provided for in Regulation (EC) No 469/2009 of the European Parliament and of the Council of 6 May 2009 concerning the supplementary protection certificate for medicinal products ([11]);
  (g) a supplementary protection certificate for plant protection products as provided for in Regulation (EC) No 1610/96 of the European Parliament and of the Council of 23 July 1996 concerning the creation of a supplementary protection certificate for plant protection products ([12]);
  (h) a Community plant variety right as provided for in Council Regulation (EC) No 2100/94 of 27 July 1994 on Community plant variety rights ([13]);
  (i) a plant variety right as provided for by national law;
  (j) a topography of semiconductor product as provided for by national or Union law;
  (k) a utility model in so far as it is protected as an intellectual property right by national or Union law;
  (l) a trade name in so far as it is protected as an exclusive intellectual property right by national or Union law;
(2) 'trade mark' means:
  (a) a Community trade mark as provided for in Council Regulation (EC) No 207/2009 of 26 February 2009 on the Community trade mark ([14]);
  (b) a trade mark registered in a Member State, or, in the case of Belgium, Luxembourg or the Netherlands, at the Benelux Office for Intellectual Property;
  (c) a trade mark registered under international arrangements which has effect in a Member State or in the Union;
(3) 'design' means:
  (a) a Community design as provided for in Council Regulation (EC) No 6/2002 of 12 December 2001 on Community designs ([15]);
  (b) a design registered in a Member State, or, in the case of Belgium, Luxembourg or the Netherlands, at the Benelux Office for Intellectual Property;
  (c) a design registered under international arrangements which has effect in a Member State or in the Union;

---

[43] Regulation (EU) No. 608/2013, Art. 18.

(4) 'geographical indication' means:

  (a) a geographical indication or designation of origin protected for agricultural products and foodstuff as provided for in Regulation (EU) No 1151/2012 of the European Parliament and of the Council of 21 November 2012 on quality schemes for agricultural products and foodstuffs ([16]);

  (b) a designation of origin or geographical indication for wine as provided for in Council Regulation (EC) No 1234/2007 of 22 October 2007 establishing a common organisation of agricultural markets and on specific provisions for certain agricultural products (Single CMO Regulation) ([17]);

  (c) a geographical designation for aromatised drinks based on wine products as provided for in Council Regulation (EEC) No 1601/91 of 10 June 1991 laying down general rules on the definition, description and presentation of aromatized wines, aromatized wine-based drinks and aromatized wine-product cocktails ([18]);

  (d) a geographical indication of spirit drinks as provided for in Regulation (EC) No 110/2008 of the European Parliament and of the Council of 15 January 2008 on the definition, description, presentation, labelling and the protection of geographical indications of spirit drinks ([19]);

  (e) a geographical indication for products not falling under points (a) to (d) in so far as it is established as an exclusive intellectual property right by national or Union law;

  (f) a geographical indication as provided for in Agreements between the Union and third countries and as such listed in those Agreements;

(5) 'counterfeit goods' means:

  (a) goods which are the subject of an act infringing a trade mark in the Member State where they are found and bear without authorisation a sign which is identical to the trade mark validly registered in respect of the same type of goods, or which cannot be distinguished in its essential aspects from such a trade mark;

  (b) goods which are the subject of an act infringing a geographical indication in the Member State where they are found and, bear or are described by, a name or term protected in respect of that geographical indication;

  (c) any packaging, label, sticker, brochure, operating instructions, warranty document or other similar item, even if presented separately, which is the subject of an act infringing a trade mark or a geographical indication, which includes a sign, name or term which is identical to a validly registered trade mark or protected geographical indication, or which cannot be distinguished in its essential aspects from such a trade mark or geographical indication, and which can be used for the same type of goods as that for which the trade mark or geographical indication has been registered;

(6) 'pirated goods' means goods which are the subject of an act infringing a copyright or related right or a design in the Member State where the goods are found and which are, or contain copies, made without the consent of the holder of a copyright or related right or a design, or of a person authorised by that holder in the country of production;

(7) 'goods suspected of infringing an intellectual property right' means goods with regard to which there are reasonable indications that, in the Member State where those goods are found, they are prima facie:

  (a) goods which are the subject of an act infringing an intellectual property right in that Member State;

  (b) devices, products or components which are primarily designed, produced or adapted for the purpose of enabling or facilitating the circumvention of any technology, device or component that, in the normal course of its operation, prevents or restricts acts in respect of works which are not authorised by the holder of any copyright or any right related to copyright and which relate to an act infringing those rights in that Member State;

(c) any mould or matrix which is specifically designed or adapted for the manufacture of goods infringing an intellectual property right, if such moulds or matrices relate to an act infringing an intellectual property right in that Member State;

(8) 'right-holder' means the holder of an intellectual property right;

(9) 'application' means a request made to the competent customs department for customs authorities to take action with respect to goods suspected of infringing an intellectual property right;

(10) 'national application' means an application requesting the customs authorities of a Member State to take action in that Member State;

(11) 'Union application' means an application submitted in one Member State and requesting the customs authorities of that Member State and of one or more other Member States to take action in their respective Member States;

(12) 'applicant' means the person or entity in whose name an application is submitted;

(13) 'holder of the decision' means the holder of a decision granting an application;

(14) 'holder of the goods' means the person who is the owner of the goods suspected of infringing an intellectual property right or who has a similar right of disposal, or physical control, over such goods;

(15) 'declarant' means the declarant as defined in point (18) of Article 4 of Regulation (EEC) No 2913/92;

(16) 'destruction' means the physical destruction, recycling or disposal of goods outside commercial channels, in such a way as to preclude damage to the holder of the decision;

(17) 'customs territory of the Union' means the customs territory of the Community as defined in Article 3 of Regulation (EEC) No 2913/92;

(18) 'release of the goods' means the release of the goods as defined in point (20) of Article 4 of Regulation (EEC) No 2913/92;

(19) 'small consignment' means a postal or express courier consignment, which:

(a) contains three units or less;

or

(b) has a gross weight of less than two kilograms.For the purpose of point (a), 'units' means goods as classified under the Combined Nomenclature in accordance with Annex I to Council Regulation (EEC) No 2658/87 of 23 July 1987 on the tariff and statistical nomenclature and on the Common Customs Tariff ([20]) if unpackaged, or the package of such goods intended for retail sale to the ultimate consumer.

For the purpose of this definition, separate goods falling in the same Combined Nomenclature code shall be considered as different units and goods presented as sets classified in one Combined Nomenclature code shall be considered as one unit;

(20) 'perishable goods' means goods considered by customs authorities to deteriorate by being kept for up to 20 days from the date of their suspension of release or detention;

(21) 'exclusive licence' means a licence (whether general or limited) authorising the licensee to the exclusion of all other persons, including the person granting the licence, to use an intellectual property right in the manner authorised by the licence.

This shows also the limitation of the system. Problems do arise when goods are in customs terms subject to a suspensive procedure such as customs warehousing or external transit. Those goods are goods in transit and have not been put on the market and, as they are technically not in the country, cannot infringe a national intellectual property right.[44] They are therefore not 'counterfeit goods'. This will change if the goods in transit

---

[44] *Eli Lilly & Co. v. 8PM Chemist Ltd* [2008] FSR 12 (CA).

are subject to an act of a third party that necessarily entailed their being put on the market.[45] And the goods would also become counterfeit goods if it is proven that they were intended to be put on sale in the EU, such proof being provided, inter alia, where it turned out that the goods had been sold, offered for sale, or advertised to a customer in the EU or where it was apparent from documents or correspondence concerning the goods that their diversion to EU consumers was envisaged.[46] A mere risk of diversion is not sufficient for the right holder to discharge this burden of proof. On this basis Nokia was unable to stop a consignment of mobile phones bearing its trade mark in transit in the UK as they were destined for another country outside the EU and never entered the UK (where Nokia could have relied on its trade mark).[47]

In turn, the customs authority to which an application for action was made had, as soon as there were indications before it giving grounds for suspecting that such an infringement existed, to suspend the release of or detain the goods. Those indications could include, inter alia, the fact that the destination of the goods was not declared whereas the suspensive procedure requested required such a declaration, the lack of precise or reliable information as to the identity or address of the manufacturer or consignor of the goods, a lack of cooperation with the customs authorities, or the discovery of documents or correspondence concerning the goods in question suggesting that there was liable to be a diversion of those goods to EU consumers.[48]

Self-help

The 1988 Act gives the copyright owner an additional right that can be used as a self-help remedy. This is the only example of self-help in the intellectual property area and no equivalent to the general right of recaption for those that are entitled to the possession of chattels (tangible property) exists.

Section 100 of the 1988 Act enables the copyright owner or his agent to seize and detain infringing copies. A series of restraints quite rightly applies to this far-reaching right.

1. The infringing copy must be exposed, or otherwise immediately available, for sale or hire.[49]

2. No force may be used, and advance notice of the time and place of the proposed seizure must be given to a local police station.[50]

3. In any event, nothing may be seized from what appears to be a regular place of business and only premises to which the public[51] has access may be entered in the exercise of this right. While it may appear clear that stalls outside pop concerts are not regular places of business, it will depend on the circumstances whether market stalls are permanent, or at least regular, places of business.[52] It should also be emphasized that the term 'premises' is given a wide definition and includes vehicles, vessels, aircraft, and hovercraft, apart from land, buildings, and moveable structures.[53]

---

[45] Case C-281/05, *Montex Holdings Ltd v. Diesel SpA* [2006] ECR I-10881.

[46] Joined Cases C-446/09 and C-495/09, *Philips and Nokia* [2012] ETMR 13.

[47] *Nokia Corporation v. Revenue & Customs Commissioners* [2010] FSR 5.

[48] Joined Cases C-446/09 and C-495/09, *Philips and Nokia* [2012] ETMR 13.

[49] CDPA 1988, s. 100(1).   [50] CDPA 1988, s. 100(2) and (3).   [51] CDPA 1988, s. 100(3).

[52] See J. Phillips, R. Durie, and I. Karet (1993) *Whale on Copyright*, 4th edn, London: Sweet & Maxwell, p. 89.

[53] CDPA 1988, s. 100(5).

4. A notice in a form prescribed by the Copyright and Rights in Performances (Notice of Seizure) Order[54] must be left behind when anything is seized. This notice should mention the grounds on which the seizure took place and the identity of the copyright owner.[55]

The seizure is normally followed by an application for an order for forfeiture or destruction of the infringing goods.[56]

The remainder of this chapter will be concerned with civil actions, and the remedies and evidence issues that relate to them.[57]

Civil remedies

Injunctions

The right holder's first concern in cases of infringement is that the infringement of his or her right stops: the sooner this happens, the easier it will be to limit the damage to his or her trade, rights, and reputation. As an order of the court that directs a party—here, the alleged infringer—to do an act or to refrain from doing an act, the injunction is an excellent tool and remedy for that purpose, hence its frequent use in intellectual property cases. The injunction will almost necessarily be prohibitory and will either stop the threatened commission[58] of infringing acts or the continuation of infringing activities. The order is normally highly effective, partly because wilful non-compliance will amount to contempt of court and contempt is punishable by fine, imprisonment, or sequestration of assets.[59]

Interlocutory injunctions

If you discover that a rival trader is seeking to attack your market share by flooding the shops with counterfeit clothing, bootleg records, or stair-carpet grips made in breach of confidence, there is no time to waste.[60] Allowing this trade to develop will obviously be harmful to you, yet the losses will be difficult to calculate precisely in a competitive capitalist society. So immediate action is necessary and the obvious legal route to take is to seek an injunction to prevent the allegedly illegal trade that is about to develop. In this respect, the usual delays of the civil justice system are not helpful and it is therefore necessary to expedite matters with the use of an interlocutory injunction in a quest to freeze the situation before damage can start to occur, pending a subsequent trial on the merits. Of course, the reality, in many cases, is that proceedings are subsequently abandoned or settled and thus the interlocutory stage is the only formal litigation that is ever recorded. This means that the basis of such proceedings must be examined closely.

---

[54] Copyright and Rights in Performances (Notice of Seizure) Order 1989, SI 1989/1006.

[55] CDPA 1988, s. 100(4).   [56] CDPA 1988, s. 114.

[57] Note that the action for breach of confidence forms a special case. The comments underneath apply in general terms to all other intellectual property rights. Monetary awards are readily made for breach of confidence, whether they take the form of an award in damages or an account of profits. Whether proprietary remedies are also possible is far less clear. See M. Conaglen, 'Thinking about Proprietary Remedies for Breach of Confidence' [2008] IPQ 82–109.

[58] The *quia timet* injunction.

[59] See *A-G v. Newspaper Publishing plc* [1988] Ch 333, [1987] 3 All ER 276; *Director General of Fair Trading v. Smith's Concrete* [1991] 4 All ER 150.

[60] Civil Procedure Rules, r. 25.1(a); see also Art. 9 of the Enforcement Directive.

The Enforcement Directive places a lot of importance on provisional and precautionary measures. In the UK these will come in most cases as interlocutory injunctions. The demands imposed by the Directive read as follows:

Article 9
Provisional and precautionary measures

1. Member States shall ensure that the judicial authorities may, at the request of the applicant:
   (a) issue against the alleged infringer an interlocutory injunction intended to prevent any imminent infringement of an intellectual property right, or to forbid, on a provisional basis and subject, where appropriate, to a recurring penalty payment where provided for by national law, the continuation of the alleged infringements of that right, or to make such continuation subject to the lodging of guarantees intended to ensure the compensation of the rightholder; an interlocutory injunction may also be issued, under the same conditions, against an intermediary whose services are being used by a third party to infringe an intellectual property right; injunctions against intermediaries whose services are used by a third party to infringe a copyright or a related right are covered by Directive 2001/29/EC;
   (b) order the seizure or delivery up of the goods suspected of infringing an intellectual property right so as to prevent their entry into or movement within the channels of commerce.
2. In the case of an infringement committed on a commercial scale, the Member States shall ensure that, if the injured party demonstrates circumstances likely to endanger the recovery of damages, the judicial authorities may order the precautionary seizure of the movable and immovable property of the alleged infringer, including the blocking of his/her bank accounts and other assets. To that end, the competent authorities may order the communication of bank, financial or commercial documents, or appropriate access to the relevant information.
3. The judicial authorities shall, in respect of the measures referred to in paragraphs 1 and 2, have the authority to require the applicant to provide any reasonably available evidence in order to satisfy themselves with a sufficient degree of certainty that the applicant is the rightholder and that the applicant's right is being infringed, or that such infringement is imminent.
4. Member States shall ensure that the provisional measures referred to in paragraphs 1 and 2 may, in appropriate cases, be taken without the defendant having been heard, in particular where any delay would cause irreparable harm to the rightholder. In that event, the parties shall be so informed without delay after the execution of the measures at the latest.

   A review, including a right to be heard, shall take place upon request of the defendant with a view to deciding, within a reasonable time after notification of the measures, whether those measures shall be modified, revoked or confirmed.
5. Member States shall ensure that the provisional measures referred to in paragraphs 1 and 2 are revoked or otherwise cease to have effect, upon request of the defendant, if the applicant does not institute, within a reasonable period, proceedings leading to a decision on the merits of the case before the competent judicial authority, the period to be determined by the judicial authority ordering the measures where the law of a Member State so permits or, in the absence of such determination, within a period not exceeding 20 working days or 31 calendar days, whichever is the longer.
6. The competent judicial authorities may make the provisional measures referred to in paragraphs 1 and 2 subject to the lodging by the applicant of adequate security or an

equivalent assurance intended to ensure compensation for any prejudice suffered by the defendant as provided for in paragraph 7.

7. Where the provisional measures are revoked or where they lapse due to any act or omission by the applicant, or where it is subsequently found that there has been no infringement or threat of infringement of an intellectual property right, the judicial authorities shall have the authority to order the applicant, upon request of the defendant, to provide the defendant appropriate compensation for any injury caused by those measures.

Let us now look at the position in the UK in more detail.

Two basic points in the UK

In order to obtain any injunction, two basic points need to be established:

1. It must be clear that damages will not be an adequate remedy,[61] although this, as just explained, should not be too frequent a problem in an intellectual property case. The matter must be urgent or the granting of an injunction must otherwise be desirable in the interests of justice.[62]

2. It is important to remember that an injunction is an equitable right and is thus subject to equity's ever-present requirement of conscionability.[63]

American Cyanamid

The leading case on interlocutory injunctions remains the decision of the House of Lords in *American Cyanamid Co. v. Ethicon Ltd.*[64] In this case, the claimants were the holders of a patent for absorbable surgical sutures and they were displeased to discover that the defendants were proposing to put on to the market a similar, and allegedly infringing, product. The House of Lords agreed with the judgment of the court of first instance and allowed the claimants an interlocutory injunction preventing Ethicon from proceeding with its plans.

The House of Lords, in the sole speech of Lord Diplock, took the opportunity to clarify the general approach to interlocutory injunctions.[65] Lord Diplock pointed out that the general practice was to require the claimant to undertake to compensate the defendants for any losses incurred by them if the claimant failed to prove the case at full trial.[66] This appeared to justify a generous approach to the award of interlocutory injunctions. It was necessary merely to show that there was a 'serious question to be tried'[67] and that the balance of convenience as between the parties, having regard to the utility or otherwise of an award of damages to the claimant or an indemnity by the

---

[61] *London & Blackwall Rly v. Cross* (1886) 31 Ch D 354, per Lindley LJ at 369.

[62] Civil Procedure Rules, r. 25.2(2)(b).

[63] See e.g. *Leather Cloth Co. Ltd v. American Leather Cloth Co. Ltd* (1863) 4 De G J & Sm 137, aff'd 11 HL Cas 523.

[64] [1975] AC 396, [1975] 1 All ER 504.

[65] This approach was again confirmed by the Court of Appeal in *Dyrlund A/S v. Turberville Smith Ltd* [1998] FSR 774.

[66] *American Cyanamid* (n. 64) at 406 and 509. This principle was applied in a case between a patentee and a generics manufacturer when the patent that formed the basis for the injunction was eventually declared invalid in the UK. The generic drug was manufactured in Canada and there the relevant patent was held to be valid. The payment of compensation was opposed on grounds of illegality, as the manufacture of the drug in Canada to supply the UK market would remain an infringement. The Supreme Court rejected that argument and refused to re-open the compensation debate, see *Les Laboratoires Servier v. Apotex Inc.* [2014] UKSC 55.

[67] *American Cyanamid* (n. 64) at 407 and 510.

claimant, should then be considered.[68] Both of these factors were found to be favourable to the claimants.

It should be noted therefore that there is not really, in most cases, an enquiry into the merits of a dispute, but rather simply a finding that there is a genuine issue at stake. This therefore carries a vitally important implication that has been alluded to frequently, but which needs to be spelled out clearly at this juncture. The decision to award an interlocutory injunction in, for example, a case of alleged passing off does not mean that a right has been infringed, but merely that one might have been; there is a serious issue to be tried, in theory, at a future date. So, on the one hand, the court is answering 'maybe', rather than 'yes', to the question of whether a right exists. On the other hand, a refusal to award an interlocutory injunction is really rather damning: not only is an injunction refused, but the basis of the claimant's entire argument is regarded as quite unsustainable.

It is, however, more appropriate to examine the merits of the claims more closely in cases in which, as in those typical of passing off or trade mark infringement, the interlocutory stage is likely, in fact, to be the only stage of the proceedings. The evident strength of the claimant's claim may assist in gaining injunctive relief[69] and this is a justifiable consideration if it is the only stage in the proceedings; the courts are prepared to make a preliminary assessment of the evidence in deciding whether the grant of an injunction is justified or not.[70] There should, however, by no means be a mini-trial on the merits of the claim at this stage.[71]

Applications

Plenty of examples can be found of courts endeavouring to apply these general principles. In *BBC v. Precord Ltd*,[72] the defendants proposed to make a rap record featuring illicitly obtained extracts from an unbroadcast interview in which the then Opposition leader had famously lost his temper. This was an appropriate case for interlocutory relief. Although a delay to the record might harm its sales at the peak Christmas season and there were arguable defences, the key point was that a clear property right had been infringed and this was the fundamental issue that merited protection.

In *Mothercare UK Ltd v. Penguin Books Ltd*,[73] meanwhile, the complete lack of likely confusion meant that no interlocutory relief was permitted in the passing off claim and that the defendants were allowed to continue publishing a serious sociological study entitled *Mother Care/Other Care*. Likewise, the small and quantifiable harm to an established claimant, as compared with the very disruptive effects of an interlocutory injunction on a new magazine with a similar title that was just in the process of being launched, meant that no injunction was awarded in *Emap Pursuit Publishing v. Clive (t/a Matchday)*.[74] On the other hand, an interlocutory injunction was granted to prevent an online children's game company from promoting an animated character known as 'Lady Goo Goo' and its song on the YouTube website and from making it available on iTunes as there was a real risk of confusion between the character and the music artist Lady Gaga. Her associated trade mark would be tarnished and the substantial damage would be hard to quantify. The clear risk of confusion and substantial damages that are hard to quantify shift the balance in favour of the award of an injunction in this case.[75]

---

[68] *American Cyanamid* (n. 64) at 408 and 511.

[69] *Quaker Oats Co. v. Alltrades Distributors Ltd* [1981] FSR 9.

[70] See e.g. *Rizla Ltd v. Bryant & May Ltd* [1986] RPC 389.

[71] *Epoch Co Ltd v. Character Options Ltd* [2015] EWHC 3436 (IPEC).   [72] [1992] 3 EIPR D-52.

[73] [1988] RPC 113. Cf. *Games Workshop Ltd v. Transworld Publishers Ltd* [1993] 9 EIPR D-221.

[74] [1993] 2 EIPR D-40.

[75] *Ate My Hearth Inc. v. Mind Candy Ltd and Moshi Music Ltd* [2011] EWHC 2741 (Ch).

The courts do indeed seem prepared to look very carefully at where the balance of convenience lies and should *'take whichever course appears to carry the lower risk of injustice if it should turn out to have been "wrong"'.*[76] Thus in *Neutrogena Corp. & Neutrogena (UK) Ltd v. Golden Ltd & L'Oréal (UK) Ltd,*[77] a dispute concerning possible passing off of the claimants' product 'Neutrogena' by the defendants' new 'Neutralia', Ferris J considered that an injunction would cause loss to the defendant through loss of sales, wasted preliminary expenditure, loss through having to compensate others, loss of opportunity to enter the market, and general disruption, and so, in the light of these factors, refused interlocutory relief. This case and the *Emap* case both show that the time of the actual launch of a rival product may well be too late to gain injunctive relief, given the commitments entered into by the defendant and the resultant shift in the balance of convenience. *Cowshed Products*[78] is another case that shows the mechanism clearly. Here the grant of an injunction would effectively destroy the defendant's business as they would be unable to enter the market as planned, whereas a refusal of an injunction would only see the claimant suffer modest damage in the period leading up to a speedy trial that would take place within months. But one should also not forget the need to show that the matter is urgent and that damages are no alternative. In *Thane Direct*[79] the court refused to grant an injunction enjoining the sale of an allegedly infringing five-function steam mop because the defendant had undertaken to stop selling the product within a couple of weeks and the damage was largely quantifiable.

Overall, the post-*Cyanamid* approach to the award of interlocutory injunctions[80] shows the courts able to invoke a range of potentially contradictory factors in a generally sensible way. In any event, the more cautious approach to their use in cases in which they may well be the final solution rather than a mere preliminary,[81] which will be the case in many intellectual property examples, goes some way to cushion the impact of *Cyanamid* in this particular area. They will thus remain a significant way of resolving intellectual property disputes.

An attempt to summarize matters

A lot of factors need to be considered and an attempt was made in *Series 5 Software Ltd v. Clarke*[82] to summarize the matters that the court should take into account when considering whether or not to grant an interim injunction:[83]

- the grant of an interim injunction is a matter of discretion and depends on all the facts of the case;

- there are no fixed rules as to when an injunction should or should not be granted—the relief must be kept flexible;

---

[76] *Films Rover International Ltd v. Cannon Film Sales Ltd* [1986] 3 All ER 772, [1987] 1 WLR 670, per Hoffmann J at 781 and 680; see also *Dalgety Spillers Foods Ltd v. Food Brokers Ltd* [1994] FSR 504.

[77] [1994] 6 EIPR D-157; see also *Vollers The Corset Company Ltd v. Cook and ors* [2004] ECDR 288.

[78] *Cowshed Products Ltd v. Island Origins Ltd* [2010] EWHC 3357 (Ch).

[79] *Thane Direct Co v. Pitch World Ltd* Chancery Division, 27 February 2012, unreported (available on Westlaw).

[80] The court now also has to take certain human rights aspects into account and, in cases in which the injunction may have an effect on the right to freedom of expression, no relief that restrains publication prior to trial is to be granted *'unless the court is satisfied that the applicant is likely to establish that publication should not be allowed'*: Human Rights Act 1998, s. 12(3).

[81] E.g. an injunction cannot be used as protection against irrecoverable losses, or to avoid damages that would be too remote, if suffered: see *Peaudouce SA v. Kimberly-Clark Ltd* [1996] FSR 680.

[82] *Series 5 Software v. Clarke* [1996] 1 All ER 853, [1996] FSR 273.

[83] See J. Adams (2007) *Merchandising Intellectual Property*, 3rd edn, Haywards Heath: Tottel, pp. 205–6.

- because of the practice adopted on the hearing of applications for interlocutory injunctions, the court should rarely attempt to resolve complex issues of disputed fact or law.

Major factors that the court can bear in mind are:

- the extent to which damages are likely to be an adequate remedy for each party and the ability of the other party to pay;
- the balance of convenience;
- the maintenance of the status quo; and
- any clear view that the court may reach as to the relevant strength of the parties' cases.

Helpful as it may be, it should, of course, be kept in mind that this summary stems from a first-instance decision that is yet to be affirmed by a higher court.

Final injunctions

A final injunction can be granted as a remedy after a trial in which the infringement of the claimant's right was established.[84] The injunction is, at that stage, granted to protect the proprietary right or interest of the claimant, but the court retains its discretion. An injunction is readily[85] granted against the proven infringement of patents, designs, trade marks, and copyright. Otherwise the claimant would be unable to stop the continuation of the infringement and would be compelled to grant a de facto licence. The court will exercise its discretion in favour of granting an injunction if it is necessary and appropriate to do so if there is a threat that the defendant will infringe again or if the infringement has not ceased entirely.[86] This will readily be the case.[87]

The Enforcement Directive approaches the issue as follows:

Article 11

Injunctions

Member States shall ensure that, where a judicial decision is taken finding an infringement of an intellectual property right, the judicial authorities may issue against the infringer an injunction aimed at prohibiting the continuation of the infringement. Where provided for by national law, non-compliance with an injunction shall, where appropriate, be subject to a recurring penalty payment, with a view to ensuring compliance. Member States shall also ensure that rightholders are in a position to apply for an injunction against intermediaries whose services are used by a third party to infringe an intellectual property right, without prejudice to Article 8(3) of Directive 2001/29/EC.

In practice a lot of factors need to be taken into account in the exercise of the court's discretion. The court provided a summary of how this will work, emphasizing that the

---

[84] See also Art. 11 of the Enforcement Directive.

[85] Unless the claimant comes with unclean hands or if any repetition of the infringement is not likely. Other special circumstances may also change the situation and the claimant can obviously decline to seek an injunction.

[86] *Stretchline Intellectual Property Ltd v. H&M Hennes & Mauritz (UK) Ltd*, nyr, Ch Division 21 January 2016; and *Coflexip SA v. Stolt Comex Seaway MS Ltd* [2001] 1 All ER 952 (Note).

[87] But in case the parties have reached a settlement, reliance will need to be placed on contractual remedies if a party argues that the settlement has been breached (breach of contract). *Stretchline Intellectual Property Ltd v. H&M Hennes & Mauritz (UK) Ltd* (n. 86) and *Cantor Gaming Ltd v. GameAccount Global Ltd* [2007] EWHC 1914 (Ch).

complex mechanism will not stand in the way of the grant of injunctions in many intellectual property cases, in *Cantor Gaming Ltd v. GameAccount Global Ltd*:

> I therefore summarise the applicable principles as follows. First, an injunction may be granted pursuant to s. 37(1) of the Supreme Court Act 1981, whenever it is just and convenient to do so. Secondly, the grant of an injunction involves the exercise of the court's discretion, and the court should, in so doing, take account of all of the circumstances, one factor of which is the importance or triviality of the breach. Thirdly, there are certain kinds of case, of which intellectual property cases are examples, in which an injunction will normally be granted if a claimant has established infringement of its rights and there is a threat to continue (or at least no clear and unequivocal undertaking not to continue). Fourthly, where there is no threat to continue acts which have been held to be unlawful, because the defendant has clearly and unequivocally agreed not to do them before the action was brought, it is not right in principle to grant an injunction. Fifthly, there may, however, be situations where, even though a defendant may have agreed not to undertake the acts in question, an injunction may be just and convenient, having regard to all the circumstances. This may be, for example, because of the greater incentive for respect of a claimant's rights that an injunction would provide, and which, in particular cases, it may appear just to grant. Sixthly, the court may, in appropriate cases, take proportionality into account in granting or refusing injunctive relief.[88]

An injunction remains a flexible remedy. Its terms can be amended at a later stage if the circumstances change, for example because the right that was infringed has since been invalidated by the court.[89]

Recently there have been several attempts to get an injunction against Internet service providers (ISPs) that would oblige them to monitor the information that is transmitted over their networks and to install a filtering system that would catch files that infringe copyright and particularly those that originate from peer-to-peer file sharing. The Court of Justice has, however, ruled that such a general obligation to monitor and filter all transmissions over a network goes beyond the scope of Art. 11 of the Directive and is therefore illegal.[90] Article 11 is therefore limited to specific measures that prevent further infringement.[91]

Delivery up

An injunction may stop any further infringement, but the defendant may consequently be left with a supply of infringing goods. The pile of illegally copied tapes or the T-shirts illegally labelled with a famous trade mark may still be sitting in a warehouse. An order for delivery up of all infringing items is the ideal tool with which to solve this problem. Under a 'delivery up' order, the defendant is ordered to hand over all infringing items or documents and these will normally be destroyed. For example, in a case where the parallel importation of a pharmaceutical product infringed a patent it was held to be appropriate to order the delivery up of the imported products.[92] Exceptionally, the defendant

---

[88] *Cantor Gaming Ltd v. GameAccount Global Ltd* (n. 87).

[89] *Adobe Systems Inc v. Netcom Online.co.uk Ltd and anor* [2012] EWHC 446 (Ch), [2012] 2 CMLR 41 at para. 39.

[90] Case C-70/10, *Scarlet Extended v. Sabam* [2012] ECDR 4; Case C-360/10, *Sabam v. Netlog* [2012] 2 CMLR 18.

[91] Case C-324/09, *L'Oréal and ors v. eBay* [2011] ETMR 52, [2012] EMLR 6, [2011] RPC 27.

[92] *Merck Canada Inc. v. Sigma Pharmaceuticals plc (Form of Order)* [2012] EWPCC 21.

can also be authorized to destroy them under oath or the erasure of the trade mark can be ordered.

All of these measures will effectively remove the infringing goods or documents—or at least their infringing element—from circulation.[93] In relation to trade marks, this power for the court to make an order for delivery up has now been incorporated in the Trade Marks Act (TMA) 1994.[94] The CDPA 1988 adds to this general power of the courts through special provisions in relation to copyright and (unregistered) designs. Orders for delivery up for destruction are still possible under these special provisions, but the infringing copies, items, and apparatus may, at the discretion of the court, be forfeited to the right holder in order to compensate him or her for the loss suffered as a result of the infringement.[95]

Damages

Damages are awarded with the aim of undoing the effects of the defendant's breach of contract or commission of a tort.[96] The claimant is compensated for the harm that is caused by the tort or the breach of contract, but losses that are unforeseeably remote are excluded. Exemplary damages that exceed the amount needed for the compensation of the harm suffered may only be awarded in exceptional cases in which the defendant's conduct was calculated to make a profit that would exceed the damages that would have to be paid to the claimant.[97]

Article 13 of the Enforcement Directive sets out the basics:

1. Member States shall ensure that the competent judicial authorities, on application of the injured party, order the infringer who knowingly, or with reasonable grounds to know, engaged in an infringing activity, to pay the rightholder damages appropriate to the actual prejudice suffered by him/her as a result of the infringement. When the judicial authorities set the damages:

    (a) they shall take into account all appropriate aspects, such as the negative economic consequences, including lost profits, which the injured party has suffered, any unfair profits made by the infringer and, in appropriate cases, elements other than economic factors, such as the moral prejudice caused to the rightholder by the infringement; or

    (b) as an alternative to (a), they may, in appropriate cases, set the damages as a lump sum on the basis of elements such as at least the amount of royalties or fees which would have been due if the infringer had requested authorisation to use the intellectual property right in question.

2. Where the infringer did not knowingly, or with reasonable grounds know, engage in infringing activity, Member States may lay down that the judicial authorities may order the recovery of profits or the payment of damages, which may be pre-established.

Contrary to an injunction, damages are completely *res judicata* once the judgment has been granted and the defendant is estopped from raising the issue again. That means that the damages will stand and remain payable even if the right that was infringed has since been declared invalid by the court, unless the inquiry as to damages is still ongoing.[98]

---

[93] See e.g. *Peter Pan Manufacturing Corp. v. Corsets Silhouette Ltd* [1963] 3 All ER 402, [1964] 1 WLR 96.
[94] TMA 1994, ss. 15–19.   [95] CDPA 1988, ss. 99 and 230.
[96] See also Art. 13 of the Enforcement Directive.
[97] See *Rookes v. Barnard* [1964] AC 1129 at 1220–31.
[98] *Virgin Atlantic v. Zodiac Seats* [2013] UKSC 46. In such an inquiry a right holder that has been successful at trial can raise further alleged infringements, see *Unilin* [2007] EWCA Civ 364 and *AP Racing Ltd v. Alcon Components Ltd*, Ch D, 4 March 2016 (nyr).

The assessment of damages

There is no standard rule for the assessment of damages in intellectual property cases. In a first scenario, the claimant and the defendant may be competitors. If the claimant would have been willing to grant a licence if only the defendant had applied for one, the amount of damages will normally be calculated on the basis of the royalties and other costs that would have been payable under the licence.[99] If the claimant would not have been willing to grant a licence, the amount of damages is normally calculated on the basis of the losses suffered by the claimant through the defendant's competition. Lost profits, lost opportunities, and competitive position acquired by the defendant may all be taken into account.[100] Article 13 of the Directive also allows for moral prejudice to be compensated, even if the royalty basis is used (and fn 100bis: Case C-99/15 *Liffers v. Mandarina and Mediaset*, 17 March 2016, <http://curia.europa.eu>).

In a second scenario, the parties do not find themselves in a competitive relationship. Damages are then calculated on the basis of a reasonable royalty for a licence for non-competing use. If neither of these scenarios suggests itself as the most appropriate way forward, the claimant is left the choice between damages calculated on the basis of lost profits or damages calculated on a royalty basis. Even a combination of both can be envisaged in appropriate cases.[101]

The grounds on which damages need to be assessed have now been set out in the course of the implementation of the Enforcement Directive in reg. 3 of the Intellectual Property (Enforcement, etc.) Regulations 2006,[102] in which it is stipulated:

(1) Where in an action for infringement of an intellectual property right the defendant knew, or had reasonable grounds to know, that he engaged in infringing activity, the damages awarded to the claimant shall be appropriate to the actual prejudice he suffered as a result of the infringement.

(2) When awarding such damages—
    (a) all appropriate aspects shall be taken into account, including in particular—
        (i) the negative economic consequences, including any lost profits, which the claimant has suffered, and any unfair profits made by the defendant; and
        (ii) elements other than economic factors, including the moral prejudice caused to the claimant by the infringement; or
    (b) where appropriate, they may be awarded on the basis of the royalties or fees which would have been due had the defendant obtained a licence.

It is important to keep in mind, though, that the burden of establishing that the loss claimed is caused by the infringement is on the claimant. Let us turn to a couple of examples to see how this works in practice. If we take a patent infringement case as an example, this means in practice that since the object of a patent is to confer a monopoly of profit and advantage, any infringement is likely to cause some loss or damage through loss of actual sales or chance of sales, or through the appropriation of something of value. So in a case where the patent belonged to a manufacturer who exploited the invention by selling products at a profit, the legal burden would be discharged by the inference that the effect of the infringement was to divert sales to the infringer.[103] In those cases where the infringer is able to adduce evidence that shows that the usual inference is not to be drawn, the claimed loss is to be decided on the proved facts and inferences properly

---

[99] *General Tire & Rubber Co. v. Firestone Tyre & Rubber Co.* [1976] RPC 197 at 212.

[100] See *Gerber Garment Technology Inc. v. Lectra Systems Ltd* [1995] RPC 383.

[101] *Gerber Garment Technology Inc. v. Lectra Systems Ltd* [1997] RPC 443 at 486, CA.

[102] SI 2006/1027.

[103] *Fabio Perini SPA v. LPC Group plc, Paper Converting Machine Co Italia, Paper Converting Machine Co. Ltd and LPC (UK) Ltd* [2012] EWHC 911 (Ch).

drawn from those facts, using commercial common sense, taking account of all relevant factors, particularly the fact that the patent owner has a right to a monopoly in respect of the invention and that the infringer has destroyed that monopoly.[104] The focus of any enquiry is then on whether the patent owner would or might have secured the infringer's contract themselves. In a copyright case where a newspaper without a licence issued a free CD containing songs of a concert in London by the Jimi Hendrix Experience in 1969 the claimants proved that the infringement had delayed the launch of their film of that concert by a year. Their damage was assessed on the basis of that loss and they were compensated accordingly.[105]

Innocent infringement

Damages are also payable for the innocent infringement of a trade mark,[106] but the same rule does not apply to copyright, registered designs,[107] designs, and patents. In these cases, Parliament felt that it would have been rather harsh to oblige an innocent infringer to pay damages. The concept of 'innocence' is defined in a narrow way and the alleged infringer must show that he or she made reasonable enquiries to check whether his or her activities would infringe any existing rights. The defendant will only be innocent if he or she did not know, and had no reason to believe, that the rights that he or she infringed existed.[108]

Additional damages

The Copyright, Designs and Patents Act 1988 introduced the concept of additional damages for the infringement of copyright and (unregistered) design rights. These additional damages come on top of the normal damages[109] and are awarded in flagrant cases of infringement. The court will determine the amount on the basis that justice must be done in each case, and will take the flagrancy of the infringement and the benefit accruing to the defendant by reason of the infringement into account when deciding whether or not to award additional damages.[110]

Account of profits

The claimant is entitled to reclaim the amount earned by the defendant by way of unjust enrichment through the infringement of the claimant's intellectual property right. To achieve this, the claimant can use the remedy of an account of profits, which is restitutionary and equitable[111] in nature. Rather than be compensated by damages, the claimant may opt to investigate the actual accounts of the defendant

---

[104] *Coflexip SA v. Stolt Offshore MS Ltd (formerly Stolt Comex Seaway MS Ltd) (No.2)* [2003] EWCA Civ 296, [2003] FSR 41

[105] *Experience Hendrix LLC v. Times Newspapers Ltd* [2010] EWHC 1986 (Ch).

[106] *Gillette (UK) Ltd v. Edenwest Ltd* [1994] RPC 279.

[107] There is an unfortunate discrepancy though between UK design law and the Community Design system in relation to innocent infringement: see *J. Choo (Jersey) Ltd v. Towerstone Ltd* [2008] FSR 19.

[108] Registered Designs Act 1949, s. 9(1); Patents Act 1977, s. 62(1); CDPA 1988, ss. 97(1) and 233.

[109] They can only be awarded if damages are the other remedy that is awarded: *Redrow Homes Ltd v. Bett Bros. plc* [1998] 1 All ER 385, [1998] 2 WLR 198, overruling *Cala Homes (South) Ltd v. Alfred McAlpine Homes East Ltd (No. 2)* [1996] FSR 36.

[110] CDPA 1988, ss. 97(2) and 229(3). See the application of these rules in *Nottinghamshire Healthcare National Health Service Trust v. News Group Newspapers Ltd* [2002] RPC 49.

[111] The court therefore has a discretion whether or not to grant this remedy: see *Sir Terence Conran v. Mean Fiddlers Holding* [1997] FSR 856, in which an account of profits was refused in relation to a case in which the trade mark infringement was innocent, and in which the causal link between the profits and the infringement was hard to establish.

and to require that any profit that was made as a result of the infringement be handed over.[112] That profit may be the profit on each item that is sold and in which the protected subject matter is included,[113] or the increase in the defendant's profit made through the use, other than by inclusion in the defendant's products, of the protected subject matter.[114]

It is clear that the exercise is to ascertain the net profits realized by the defendant on the basis of the infringing activity. The defendant is allowed to deduct from any profit only the overheads that are directly associated with the infringing activity. Taking into account (a proportion of) general overheads is not allowed. The claimant, on the other hand, cannot bring the amount of damage it suffered into the equation, when it opted for an account of profits rather than the award of damages.[115]

In practice, it is often difficult to calculate the profit that is caused by the infringement, because the latter is often not the single cause of the profit. Often, only a part of a product is an infringement and, in all of these cases, the courts face the difficult task of determining what part of the profit has been caused by the infringing acts.[116] This remedy is therefore not used often, because it involves a lot of work and an expensive accounting procedure. The decision by the House of Lords that additional damages cannot be awarded in copyright or unregistered design cases in which the claimant opted for an account of profits is bound to make it an even less popular remedy.[117] Nevertheless, the claimant could be well advised to consider the use of this remedy in those cases in which he or she could never have made the profits that were made by the defendant, because it may enable the claimant to obtain a higher amount by way of compensation.

The gathering of evidence

The gathering of evidence is often a crucial issue in intellectual property cases. In this part of the chapter, we will highlight the instruments that are used most often; an overview of all of the relevant aspects of the law of civil procedure is not envisaged. The Enforcement Directive also addresses the issues surrounding evidence.[118] The starting point is set out in Art. 6 of the Directive:

Evidence

1. Member States shall ensure that, on application by a party which has presented reasonably available evidence sufficient to support its claims, and has, in substantiating those claims, specified evidence which lies in the control of the opposing party, the competent judicial authorities may order that such evidence be presented by the opposing party, subject to the protection of confidential information. For the purposes of this paragraph, Member States may provide that a reasonable sample of a substantial number of copies of a work or any other protected object be considered by the competent judicial authorities to constitute reasonable evidence.

---

[112] See Patents Act 1977, s. 61(2); CDPA 1988, s. 96(2).

[113] *Peter Pan Manufacturing Corp. v. Corsets Silhouette Ltd* [1963] 3 All ER 402.

[114] *United Horse Shoe v. Stewart* (1888) 13 App 401, 3 RPC 139 at 266–7.

[115] *Hollister Inc. v. Medik Ostomy Supplies Ltd* [2012] EWCA Civ 1419.

[116] See *Celanese International v. BP Chemicals* [1999] RPC 203.

[117] *Redrow Homes Ltd v. Bett Bros plc & Nail Co.* [1999] 1 AC 197, [1998] 1 All ER 385, overruling *Cala Homes (South) Ltd v. Alfred McAlpine Homes East Ltd (No. 2)* [1996] FSR 36.

[118] Arts. 6 and 7 of the Enforcement Directive.

2. Under the same conditions, in the case of an infringement committed on a commercial scale Member States shall take such measures as are necessary to enable the competent judicial authorities to order, where appropriate, on application by a party, the communication of banking, financial or commercial documents under the control of the opposing party, subject to the protection of confidential information.

In a UK court setting most of these principles are readily implemented in our procedural rules. One thinks particularly of the rules on disclosure in an intellectual property context, as it is of such a vital importance.

Search orders

This is then followed up in Art. 7 by rules on measures to preserve the evidence. In the UK system this refers to what is now known as the search order. Article 7 expresses it as follows:

1. Member States shall ensure that, even before the commencement of proceedings on the merits of the case, the competent judicial authorities may, on application by a party who has presented reasonably available evidence to support his/her claims that his/her intellectual property right has been infringed or is about to be infringed, order prompt and effective provisional measures to preserve relevant evidence in respect of the alleged infringement, subject to the protection of confidential information. Such measures may include the detailed description, with or without the taking of samples, or the physical seizure of the infringing goods, and, in appropriate cases, the materials and implements used in the production and/or distribution of these goods and the documents relating thereto. Those measures shall be taken, if necessary without the other party having been heard, in particular where any delay is likely to cause irreparable harm to the rightholder or where there is a demonstrable risk of evidence being destroyed.

   Where measures to preserve evidence are adopted without the other party having been heard, the parties affected shall be given notice, without delay after the execution of the measures at the latest. A review, including a right to be heard, shall take place upon request of the parties affected with a view to deciding, within a reasonable period after the notification of the measures, whether the measures shall be modified, revoked or confirmed.

2. Member States shall ensure that the measures to preserve evidence may be subject to the lodging by the applicant of adequate security or an equivalent assurance intended to ensure compensation for any prejudice suffered by the defendant as provided for in paragraph 4.

3. Member States shall ensure that the measures to preserve evidence are revoked or otherwise cease to have effect, upon request of the defendant, without prejudice to the damages which may be claimed, if the applicant does not institute, within a reasonable period, proceedings leading to a decision on the merits of the case before the competent judicial authority, the period to be determined by the judicial authority ordering the measures where the law of a Member State so permits or, in the absence of such determination, within a period not exceeding 20 working days or 31 calendar days, whichever is the longer.

4. Where the measures to preserve evidence are revoked, or where they lapse due to any act or omission by the applicant, or where it is subsequently found that there has been no infringement or threat of infringement of an intellectual property right, the judicial authorities shall have the authority to order the applicant, upon request of the defendant, to provide the defendant appropriate compensation for any injury caused by those measures.

5. Member States may take measures to protect witnesses' identity.

The origin of the order in the UK

The success of infringement actions and the effectiveness of remedies depend on the availability at the trial stage of evidence relating to the alleged infringement. It is vital that the claimant is given the opportunity to discover this evidence. It is relatively easy for a mala-fide defendant to alter or to destroy incriminating documents, to move goods, or to hide machinery and raw materials, once he or she has been served with a writ. The production of infringing copies of audio cassettes provides a good example: all that is needed is a number of cassette players and tapes, plus some labels; all of this can be moved within a few hours and it can be hidden in any spare room or shed.

What is required, then, is a tool that would allow the claimant to discover the evidence without any advance warning being given to the defendant. This tool would involve an *ex parte* application to the court, which would then authorize the claimant and his or her solicitors to enter the defendant's premises, so as to discover the evidence and to seize or copy any relevant information. It would be a kind of civil search warrant.

Such a tool was introduced by the Court of Appeal[119] in *Anton Piller KG v. Manufacturing Processes Ltd*[120] and consequently became known as the 'Anton Piller order'. Changes in the wake of the Civil Procedure Act 1997 led to that order being renamed the 'search order'.[121]

Lord Denning MR has described the order as follows:

> Let me say at once that no court in this land has any power to issue a search warrant to enter a man's house so as to see if there are papers or documents there which are of an incriminating nature. But the order sought in this case is not a search warrant. It does not authorise the claimant's solicitors or anyone else to enter the defendants' premises against their will. It only authorises entry and inspection by the permission of the defendants. It does more, it actually orders them to give permission—with, I suppose, the result that if they do not give permission they are guilty of contempt of court.[122]

Applications for a search order are to be made *ex parte* to a patents judge in the High Court or to the patents county court. They can eventually also be made to a Chancery judge.[123]

The order and its expansion

The essential prerequisites for making such an order were set out by Ormerod LJ:

> First, there must be an extremely strong prima facie case. Second, the damage, potential or actual, must be very serious for the applicant. Third, there must be clear evidence that the defendants have in their possession incriminating documents or things, and that there is a real possibility that they may destroy such material before any application inter partes can be made.[124]

The claimant's solicitor will be authorized to carry out the order as an officer of the court and the defendant is obliged to permit the inspection, otherwise he or she will face proceedings for contempt of court.[125] This does not, however, deprive the defendant

---

[119] On the basis of a limited previous practice in the Chancery Division: see *EMI v. Pandit* [1975] 1 All ER 418, [1975] 1 WLR 302.

[120] [1976] Ch 55, [1976] 1 All ER 779.

[121] Section 7; Civil Procedure Rules, r. 25; Practice Direction, para. 25.

[122] *Anton Piller KG v. Manufacturing Processes Ltd* [1976] Ch 55 at 58.

[123] Civil Procedure Rules, r. 25A; Practice Direction, para. 8.5.

[124] *Anton Piller KG v. Manufacturing Processes Ltd* (n. 122) at 62; see also *Thermax Ltd v. Schott Industrial Glass Ltd* [1981] FSR 289; *Columbia Picture Industries v. Robinson* [1987] Ch 38, [1986] 3 All ER 338.

[125] On the issue of failure to comply, see *Wardle Fabrics v. Myristis* [1984] FSR 263.

completely of the possibility to refuse to permit the inspection, but this option becomes very risky and needs to be combined with a swift application for discharge of the order. The applicant has a duty of full and frank disclosure of all relevant elements to the court, and the granting of the order is subject to the applicant making a cross-undertaking in damages.

It is the basis of the search order to preserve evidence that may otherwise be destroyed by the defendant. The real need meant that the order became an instant success, rather than the exceptional measure it was supposed to be. One of the first cases to extend the order slightly was *EMI Ltd v. Sarwar & Haidar,*[126] in which the defendants were also ordered:

> to disclose to the person serving the order, the names and addresses of the persons or companies responsible for supplying the defendants and to place into custody all invoices, books of sale, order books, and all other documents in their possession, power, custody or control relating to the acquisition, disposal or distribution of the infringing tape recordings.[127]

This will enable the defendant to obtain full evidence regarding anyone involved in an infringement network on the basis of a single search order and it increases the value of the order substantially. It also became possible to obtain an order against a represented class of persons if there is a sufficient amount of identity of interest among the members of such a class. This extension allowed EMI Records to act against all persons dealing in a certain type of pirated audio cassettes with one search order, because they all had an interest in preventing EMI from tracing the source of these pirated cassettes.

The expansion of the search order and its growing effectiveness came under threat when the House of Lords decided that orders requiring the defendant to make a disclosure that could be self-incriminating were contrary to the principle of privilege against self-incrimination.[128] The possibility for the defendant to withhold information on the basis that he or she would otherwise be incriminating themselves reduces the potential and value of the order substantially. This conclusion, which had been reached by a reluctant House of Lords, was reversed by s. 72 of the Supreme Court Act 1981 when the legislature stepped in to preserve the order. The self-incrimination defence will now no longer be available against the implementation of a search order,[129] although the statements or admissions made at that stage will not be admissible as evidence in relation to any related offence.

Abuse of the order and its redress

Abuse

Not only did search orders become a frequently used tool, they also gave rise to abuses,[130] of which two forms can be identified. First, the courts became too flexible in granting the order[131] and it became fashionable to use them to go on a 'fishing expedition'. An order was, in such cases, granted on the basis of a mere suspicion of infringement, rather than on the basis of a very strong prima facie case, and was used simply to establish whether

---

[126] [1977] FSR 146.   [127] [1977] FSR 146 at 147.

[128] *Rank Film Distributors Ltd v. Video Information Centre* [1982] AC 380, aff'd [1981] 2 All ER 76.

[129] See *Universal City Studios Inc. v. Hubbard* [1984] Ch 225, [1984] 1 All ER 661.

[130] See e.g. *TRP v. Thorley* [1993] Court of Appeal, unreported, Lexis transcript available; *Lock International plc v. Beswick* [1989] 3 All ER 373, [1989] 1 WLR 1268, per Hoffmann J.

[131] See the remarks in this sense by Whitford J in *Systematica Ltd v. London Computer Centre Ltd* [1983] FSR 313.

the infringement took place.[132] Often, the applicant also obtained very valuable commercial information on a competitor.

Second, the execution of the order was not always impeccable. The limits and restrictions imposed in the order were often exceeded, documents disappeared,[133] etc., and the orders were also used to harass the defendant and to drive him or her out of business.[134] Orders were executed at impossible times[135] or with a great deal of publicity. So much material was taken that the defendant could no longer operate properly and meet his or her contractual obligations[136] or improper publicity surrounding the order scared customers away from further dealings with the defendant.[137]

Towards a solution

The urgent need to weed out these abuses, while at the same time preserving the search order as an extremely useful tool in certain circumstances, became clear and Sir Donald Nicholls V-C suggested a way to achieve this double goal in *Universal Thermosensors v. Hibben*.[138] Most points of his advice were then incorporated in a new Practice Direction[139] and further refinement followed in the wake of the Civil Procedure Act 1997.

Search orders will now only be given if the matter is urgent or if the order is otherwise desirable in the interest of justice.[140] Search orders should also only be executed on working days in office hours and not during weekends, or early in the morning, or late at night.[141] This implies that the defendant should be in a position to use effectively his or her right to consult a solicitor and to obtain legal advice at the very moment that he or she is presented with an order before complying with it, without running the risk of being in contempt of court by delaying the execution of the order.[142] A woman should also be present when the order is to be executed by a male solicitor at premises that are likely to be occupied by an unaccompanied woman.[143] Additionally, when the nature of the items that are removed makes this necessary, the applicant should insure them.[144]

The Practice Direction contains a further range of provisions and also allows the judge more time to consider the application more in depth,[145] but by far the most important change is that the claimant's solicitor should now no longer execute a search order. The role of the claimant's solicitor is reduced to securing the grant of the order and, afterwards, the execution is entrusted to a solicitor who does not act for the applicant.[146] This *'supervising solicitor should be an experienced solicitor, having some familiarity with the operation of* [search] *orders, who is not a member or employee of the firm acting for the applicant'*.[147] The supervising solicitor must also explain the terms

---

[132] *Systematica* (n. 131).

[133] *Universal Thermosensors v. Hibben* [1992] 1 WLR 840, [1992] FSR 361.

[134] *Columbia Picture Industries v. Robinson* [1987] Ch 38, [1986] 3 All ER 338.

[135] *Universal Thermosensors* (n. 131).   [136] *Columbia Picture Industries* (n. 134).

[137] *BUPA v. First Choice Health Care* [1993] 4 EIPR 87.

[138] *Universal Thermosensors Ltd v. Hibben* (n. 133) at 860–1.

[139] Practice Direction [1994] 4 All ER 52, [1994] RPC 617.

[140] Civil Procedure Rules, r. 25.2(2)(b).

[141] Practice Direction [1994] 4 All ER 52 at 54, Annex 1; *Universal Thermosensors Ltd v. Hibben* (n. 133), per Sir Donald Nicholls V-C at 860.

[142] *Universal Thermosensors Ltd v. Hibben* (n. 133), per Sir Donald Nicholls V-C at 860.

[143] Practice Direction [1994] 4 All ER 52 at 53; CDPA 1988, s. 3B(2); *Universal Thermosensors* (n. 133), per Sir Donald Nicholls V-C at 860. See now Civil Procedure Rules, r. 25A; Practice Direction, para. 7.4(5).

[144] Practice Direction [1994] 4 All ER 52 at 53; CDPA 1988, s, 3B(3).

[145] Practice Direction [1994] 4 All ER 52 at 53; CDPA 1988, ss. 3A(1) and 3B(5).

[146] See also *Universal Thermosensors Ltd v. Hibben* (n. 133), per Sir Donald Nicholls V-C at 861.

[147] Practice Direction [1994] 4 All ER 52 at 53; CDPA 1988, s. 3B(1)(a).

of the search order to the respondents in plain English and he or she must advise them of their rights.[148]

In the old situation, the claimant's solicitor was torn between the interests of his or her client, who was also footing the bill, and his or her neutral role as an officer of the court. This will now no longer be the case, although the risk of bias remains at the application stage due to the *ex parte* nature of the proceedings.[149] The Practice Direction and the Civil Procedure Rules are also unsuccessful in solving the difficult problem of who may consent to entry to the premises, to the searching of these premises, and to seizure. In the absence of the obvious defendant, the Practice Direction gives this power to '*a responsible employee of the defendant*' as well as to the more established category of '*person(s) appearing to be in charge of the premises*'.[150] The precise definition of these categories is bound to cause confusion, which may lead to incidents when a search order is executed under these circumstances.[151]

It is nevertheless submitted that the Practice Direction and the new Civil Procedure Rules will be successful in eliminating the abuse, and in securing the survival, of the search order. In the new system, claimants who:

> wish to take advantage of this truly draconian type of order…must be prepared to pay for the safeguards experience has shown are necessary if the interests of defendants are fairly to be protected.[152]

Freezing orders

Derived from the name of one of the parties in the oldest case in this area, *Mareva Cia Naviera SA v. International Bulk Carriers SA*,[153] the so-called 'Mareva injunction' was often called a 'freezing injunction', because this *ex parte* injunction freezes the assets of a party by restraining that party from removing them from the jurisdiction. In the wake of the Civil Procedure Act 1997, the order has now been renamed the 'freezing order'.

Lord Denning MR laid down the following guidelines in *Third Chandris Shipping Corp. v. Unimarine SA*.[154]

1. The claimant must make full and frank disclosure of all relevant information and materials.

2. He or she must set out his or her claim and the grounds for it, as well as the arguments raised against this claim by the defendant. He must also give indications that the defendant has assets within the jurisdiction and that there is a risk that the assets will be removed from the jurisdiction.

3. The claimant must give an undertaking in damages.

These guidelines were later supplemented by two further guidelines.[155]

4. The claimant must show that his or her case has a certain strength.

5. That strength needs to be balanced against all other relevant factors before the judge uses the discretion to grant a freezing order.

---

[148] Civil Procedure Rules, r. 25A; Practice Direction, para. 7.4.

[149] M. Davies, 'Anton Pillers after the Practice Direction' (1996) 15 CJQ 17.

[150] Practice Direction [1994] 4 All ER 52 at 54–5, Annex 1.

[151] Davies, 'Anton Pillers after the Practice Direction' (n. 149).

[152] *Universal Thermosensors Ltd v. Hibben* (n. 133), per Sir Donald Nicholls V-C at 861.

[153] [1980] 1 All ER 213, [1975] 2 Lloyd's Rep 509.

[154] *Third Chandris Shipping Corp. v. Unimarine SA* [1979] QB 645, *sub nom Third Chandris v. Unimarine* [1979] 2 All ER 972.

[155] *Ninemia Maritime Corp. v. Trane Schiffarhtsgesellschaft mbH und Co. KG (The Niedersachsen)* [1984] 1 All ER 398.

Banks and other third parties can be bound by a freezing order,[156] which therefore becomes another useful tool in the war against untrustworthy defendants in intellectual property infringement cases.[157] Quite often, a search order is combined with a freezing order[158] and, while this offers a great deal of relief to the claimant, it must be clear that this can also be used quite effectively to put a defendant out of business.[159] This risk is especially present in cases brought by commercially powerful claimants against small innovative competitors, because the latter may go out of business before the case is fully argued in court. It can even be said that, on certain occasions, that has been the purpose of the claimants, because it has been quite clear, on these occasions, that no infringement would eventually be found, and yet an application for a search order and a freezing order was nevertheless brought.

The *Norwich Pharmacal* order

Infringement actions often start when the owner of an intellectual property right finds an infringing product at the end of the distribution chain; the goods may alternatively be in transit. It is vital for the right owner that he or she is able to trace the source of the infringing product in order to be able to stop the infringement at its roots, because the person in whose hands the product is found may not even know that the product is a copy or an infringing product and may not be infringing him- or herself. The person may also be unaware of the fact that others must have infringed any intellectual property right. The only way for the right owner to proceed successfully in such a case is to get hold of the names and addresses of any consignors or consignees, and to track the infringing product all the way up to its manufacturers.

The *Norwich Pharmacal* order has the same aim and such an order obliges the party against whom it is made to reveal these names and addresses.[160] In the original case,[161] from which the name of this disclosure order is derived, the Commissioner of Customs and Excise was obliged to reveal the names of the importers of a patented drug. Later cases obliged telephone operators, for example, to reveal the names of mobile phone users that were allegedly involved in passing off.[162]

The order is discretionary in nature and as a starting point requires frank disclosure on the part of the applicant.[163] The order will normally only be granted if it is the only way in which the claimant can get hold of the information, which in essence imposes a

---

[156] See *Z Ltd v. A-Z & AA-LL* [1982] QB 558, [1982] 1 All ER 556.

[157] Third parties, such as banks, may be liable for contempt of court if the order is not implemented correctly, but they do not own a duty of care towards the third party that obtained the order: *Customs & Excise Comrs v. Barclays Bank plc* [2007] 1 AC 181 (HL).

[158] Civil Procedure Rules, r. 25(f); see e.g. *McDonald v. Graham* [1994] RPC 407.

[159] See *CBS United Kingdom Ltd v. Lambert* [1983] Ch 37, [1982] 3 All ER 237.

[160] Civil Procedure Rules, r. 31.

[161] *Norwich Pharmacal v. Comr of Customs & Excise* [1974] AC 133, rev'd [1974] RPC 101; see also *British Steel Corp. v. Granada Television Ltd* [1981] AC 1096, [1981] 1 All ER 417, a case that shows the potential of the order in a wider context.

[162] *Coca-Cola Co. v. British Telecommunications* [1999] FSR 518.

[163] E.g. withholding information about a revenue sharing agreement between the right holder and a third party will be held against the applicant, as will the indiscriminate practice of sending out threatening letters demanding £700 from persons whose Internet connection was used in a file-sharing activity, without properly pointing out the options available to these persons. See *Golden Eye (International) Ltd v. Telefonica UK Ltd* [2012] EWHC 723. But the presence of a revenue-sharing agreement did not disentitle a category of right holders to be granted a *Norwich Pharmacal* order. See *Golden Eye (International) Ltd v. Telefonica UK Ltd* [2012] EWCA Civ 1740.

condition of necessity, and if it is demonstrated that the person against whom it is made is (unwittingly) facilitating the infringement or any other wrongful act. There is also a requirement of proportionality.[164] The order will only go as far as is necessary to allow the rights to be asserted. On the other hand, the order may be extended to cover also a prohibition to remove the infringing goods.

The *Norwich Pharmacal* order is often applied in tort—that is, infringement—cases, but it is not confined to tort. It can, for example, also arise in the context of breach of contract, such as breach of a licence contract, and in the context of breach of confidence.[165] If it is applied in an infringement context, bringing proper infringement proceedings in a court is not a prerequisite for the order being granted.[166]

In practice, the *Norwich Pharmacal* order deals with what Art. 8 of the Enforcement Directive specifies as follows:

Right of information

1. Member States shall ensure that, in the context of proceedings concerning an infringement of an intellectual property right and in response to a justified and proportionate request of the claimant, the competent judicial authorities may order that information on the origin and distribution networks of the goods or services which infringe an intellectual property right be provided by the infringer and/or any other person who:
   (a) was found in possession of the infringing goods on a commercial scale;
   (b) was found to be using the infringing services on a commercial scale;
   (c) was found to be providing on a commercial scale services used in infringing activities; or
   (d) was indicated by the person referred to in point (a), (b) or (c) as being involved in the production, manufacture or distribution of the goods or the provision of the services.

2. The information referred to in paragraph 1 shall, as appropriate, comprise:
   (a) the names and addresses of the producers, manufacturers, distributors, suppliers and other previous holders of the goods or services, as well as the intended wholesalers and retailers;
   (b) information on the quantities produced, manufactured, delivered, received or ordered, as well as the price obtained for the goods or services in question.

3. Paragraphs 1 and 2 shall apply without prejudice to other statutory provisions which:
   (a) grant the rightholder rights to receive fuller information;
   (b) govern the use in civil or criminal proceedings of the information communicated pursuant to this Article;
   (c) govern responsibility for misuse of the right of information; or
   (d) afford an opportunity for refusing to provide information which would force the person referred to in paragraph 1 to admit to his/her own participation or that of his/her close relatives in an infringement of an intellectual property right; or
   (e) govern the protection of confidentiality of information sources or the processing of personal data.

In *Coty Germany v. Stadtsparkasse Magdeburg*,[167] the question arose whether the right holder who bought infringing articles of its own branded goods on the Internet could

---

[164] *Golden Eye (International) Ltd v. Telefonica UK Ltd* [2012] EWHC 723 at paras. 83 and 117; *Rugby Football Union v. Viagogo Ltd* [2011] EWCA Civ 1585.

[165] *Ashworth Hospital Authority v. MGN Ltd* [2003] FSR 311 (HL); see also *Interbrew v. Financial Times* [2002] EMLR 446.

[166] See *Golden Eye (International) Ltd v. Telefonica UK Ltd* (n. 174) at para. 53; *British Steel Corp v. Granada Television Ltd* [1981] AC 1096.

[167] Case C-580/13, *Coty Germany v. Stadtsparkasse Magdeburg* [2015] 1 WLR 4283, [2015] ETMR 39.

use Art. 8 to oblige a bank to reveal the identity of the account into which the purchase price had been paid. German banking secrecy laws seemed to allow the bank to turn down such a request, but the CJEU did not accept this argument, as there was no leeway in German law. The Court argued that the right of information and Art. 8 need in such a situation to be balanced with the right of privacy and data protection. A solution that uniquely protects one side of the balance is not acceptable. Article 8 protects the fundamental right of IP and its enforcement, as recognized as part of the fundamental right of property in Art. 17(2) of the European Charter of Fundamental Rights, and which needs to be balanced with other fundamental rights.

Arguably the order goes further than what is strictly required by Art. 8 of the Enforcement Directive. A national rule obliging ISPs to release personal information concerning clients that committed copyright infringement online was held by the Court of Justice not to be imposed by European law. That is effectively what the result of a *Norwich Pharmacal* order would be though. But it did not breach European law either, according to the Court.[168] UK courts too have held that the order complies with Art. 8 of the Human Rights Act (the right to private life) and with the rules on data protection. This is another aspect of the requirement of proportionality. The court will not hold back from granting the order, but a proper balance with data protection rules and fundamental rights will be struck.[169]

Bringing all these elements together Arnold J set out the following test in *Golden Eye*:

> In my judgment the correct approach to considering proportionality can be summarised in the following propositions. First, the Claimants' copyrights are property rights protected by Article 1 of the First Protocol to the ECHR and intellectual property rights within Article 17(2) of the Charter. Secondly, the right to privacy under Article 8(1) ECHR/Article 7 of the Charter and the right to the protection of personal data under Article 8 of the Charter are engaged by the present claim. Thirdly, the Claimants' copyrights are 'rights of others' within Article 8(2) ECHR/Article 52(1) of the Charter. Fourthly, the approach laid down by Lord Steyn where both Article 8 and Article 10 ECHR rights are involved in In re S [2004] UKHL 47, [2005] 1 AC 593 para 17 is also applicable where a balance falls to be struck between Article 1 of the First Protocol/Article 17(2) of the Charter on the one hand and Article 8 ECHR/Article 7 of the Charter and Article 8 of the Charter on the other hand. That approach is as follows: (i) neither Article as such has precedence over the other; (ii) where the values under the two Articles are in conflict, an intense focus on the comparative importance of the specific rights being claimed in the individual case is necessary; (iii) the justifications for interfering with or restricting each right must be taken into account; (iv) finally, the proportionality test—or 'ultimate balancing test'—must be applied to each.[170]

This test was subsequently endorsed by the Supreme Court, which added some refinement.[171] The Supreme Court held that a *Norwich Pharmacal* order could be issued to oblige the operator of a website on which Twickenham tickets had been resold anonymously for

---

[168] Case C-275/06, *Productores de Musica de España (Promusicae) v. Telefonica de España SAU* [2008] ECR I-271.

[169] *Golden Eye (International) Ltd v. Telefonica UK Ltd* (n. 174) at para. 117 and at European level Case C-461/10, *Bonnier, Earbooks, Norstedts Förlagsgrupp, Piratförlaget and Storyside v. Perfect Communication Sweden* [2012] 2 CMLR 42.

[170] *Golden Eye (International) Ltd v. Telefonica UK Ltd* (n. 169) at para. 117.

[171] *Rugby Football Union v. Consolidated Information Services Ltd (Formerly Viagogo Ltd) (In Liquidation)* [2012] UKSC 55 at paras. 44 and 45.

highly inflated prices against the RFU's policy to reveal the identity of those involved. The Supreme Court argued that:

> [a]n 'intense focus' on the rights being claimed in individual cases does not lead to the conclusion that the individuals who will be affected by the grant of the order will have been unfairly or oppressively treated,[172]

but that suggesting that it would generally be proportionate:

> to make an order where it had been shown that there was arguable wrongdoing and there was no other means of discovering the identity of the arguable wrongdoers,

would go too far.[173]

According to the Supreme Court,

> [t]he particular circumstances affecting the individual whose personal data will be revealed on foot of a Norwich Pharmacal order will always call for close consideration and these may, in some limited instances, displace the interests of the applicant for the disclosure of the information even where there is no immediately feasible alternative way in which the necessary information can be obtained.[174]

Abuse of enforcement proceedings

Enforcement proceedings can also be abused. Such proceedings can, for example, be threatened in cases where on substance there is clearly no case to answer. Particularly in patent cases that are notoriously long and expensive such a tactic when applied by a party with deep pockets against a smaller less well-funded opponent can be particularly damaging. It comes therefore as no surprise that Art. 41.1 of the TRIPS Agreement and Art. 3(2) of the Enforcement Directive demand that states take appropriate measures against the abuse of enforcement proceedings.[175]

In the Patents Act 1977 this demand is met by s. 70 which deals specifically with groundless threats:

(1) Where a person (whether or not the proprietor of, or entitled to any right in, a patent) by circulars, advertisements or otherwise threatens another person with proceedings for any infringement of a patent, a person aggrieved by the threats (whether or not he is the person to whom the threats are made) may, subject to subsection (4) below, bring proceedings in the court against the person making the threats, claiming any relief mentioned in subsection (3) below.

(2) In any such proceedings the claimant or pursuer shall, subject to subsection (2A) below, be entitled to the relief claimed if he proves that the threats were so made and satisfies the court that he is a person aggrieved by them.

...

(3) The said relief is—
   (a) a declaration or declarator to the effect that the threats are unjustifiable;
   (b) an injunction or interdict against the continuance of the threats; and
   (c) damages in respect of any loss which the claimant or pursuer has sustained by the threats.

---

[172] *Rugby Football Union* (n. 171) at para. 45.   [173] *Rugby Football Union* (n. 171) at para. 46.

[174] *Rugby Football Union* (n. 171) at para. 46.

[175] See C. Heath, 'Wrongful Patent Enforcement: Threats and Post-Infringement Invalidity in Comparative Perspective' (2008) 39(3) IIC 307–22.

(4) Proceedings may not be brought under this section for–

    (a) a threat to bring proceedings for an infringement alleged to consist of making or importing a product for disposal or of using a process, or

    (b) a threat, made to a person who has made or imported a product for disposal or used a process, to bring proceedings for an infringement alleged to consist of doing anything else in relation to that product or process.

Those threatened with groundless proceedings get therefore their own action for relief. It does not apply though to those that make or import the product (even if they also distribute or sell), but those parties can bring an action for a negative declaration (i.e. that they do not infringe) in case the patentee fails to follow the threats up with a claim form. When is there a threat, though? The approach taken by the courts involves putting an ordinary reasonable person in the position of the actual recipient and asking whether such a person, with his knowledge of the circumstances on the date of the communication, would see the whole of the communication as a sign that the writer of the letter intended to convey an intention to enforce his rights by bringing legal proceedings.[176] Such a communication may be veiled, covert, or conditional[177] and a general warning not to infringe is only excluded if it is understood not to refer to products of a specific manufacturer, importer, or vendor.

Another problem that seems to create injustice arises when a successful infringement action (leading to the award of substantial damages) is followed by a decision by the European Patent Office to invalidate the patent on which the action was based. Surely it cannot be just to award damages for the infringement of a patent that was not valid in the first place. Typically, though, the problem of invalidity arises once the infringement decision has become *res judicata*. English courts have in those cases bluntly refused to offer a remedy, arguing that it would be fundamentally wrong to tinker with the principle of *res judicata* leading to estoppel.[178] The decision to award damages can no longer be reopened. Other legal systems offer a more constructive approach and hopefully the UK will be able to follow their example in the future.[179] Injunctions present a different picture though, and can be modified or lifted.

An overview

Three elements are really important in the relationship between intellectual property rights and remedies. First, there are the traditional remedies headed by damages that are normally granted at the trial and which we discussed in the various chapters concerned with each of the substantive intellectual property rights. Second, intellectual property infringement often requires immediate action or a pre-emptive strike. This is the area in which interlocutory injunctions play an important role. Finally, gathering evidence that is vital for the full trial is not always easy, but it would not be just to allow infringers to 'get away with it' simply because the right owner did not have the means of discovering the evidence needed in an infringement case. Search orders address this problem.

---

[176] *Best Buy v. Worldwide Sales Corporation España* [2011] EWCA Civ 618.

[177] *L'Oréal UK Ltd v. Johnson & Johnson* [200] FSR686; *Generics (UK) (trading as Mylan) v. Warner-Lambert, Actavis v. Warner-Lambert* [2015] EWHC 2548 (Pat) at para. 963.

[178] *Unilin Beheer v. Berry Floor and ors* [2007] FSR 25.

[179] Heath, 'Wrongful Patent Enforcement: Threats and Post-Infringement Invalidity in Comparative Perspective' (n. 175).

Further reading

CONAGLEN, M., 'Thinking about Proprietary Remedies for Breach of Confidence' [2008] IPQ 82–109.

CORNISH, W. R. et al., 'Procedures and Remedies for Enforcing IPRS: The European Commission's Proposed Directive' (2003) 25 EIPR 447.

FAWCETT, J. and TORREMANS, P. (2010) *Intellectual Property and Private International Law*, 2nd edn, Oxford: Oxford University Press.

GARNETT, K., DAVIES, G., and HARBOTTLE, G. (2011) *Copinger and Skone James on Copyright*, 16th edn, London: Sweet and Maxwell, Ch. 21.

HEATH, Ch., 'Wrongful Patent Enforcement: Threats and Post-Infringement Invalidity in Comparative Perspective' (2008) 39(3) IIC 307–22.

HUNIAR, K., 'The Enforcement Directive: Its Effects on UK Law' (2006) 28 EIPR 92.

MELLOR J. et al. (2011) *Kerly's Law of Trade Marks and Trade Names*, 15th edn, London: Sweet and Maxwell, Ch. 20.

MILLER, R. et al. (eds.) (2011) *Terrell on the Law of Patents*, 17th edn, London: Sweet and Maxwell, Ch. 19.

TREACY, P. and WRAY, A., 'IP Crimes: The Prospect for EU-Wide Criminal Sanctions—A Long Road Ahead?' (2006) 28 EIPR 1.

Index